Cassell's Concise
French–English
English–French
Dictionary

Cassell's Concise
French–English
English–French
Dictionary

COMPILED BY

J. H. DOUGLAS

B.A.(Lond.), Chevalier dans l'Ordre des Palmes Académiques,
Headmaster, Caldew School, Dalston, Cumbria

DENIS GIRARD

Agrégé de l'Université
Inspecteur de l'Académie de Paris

W. THOMPSON

M.A.(Edin.), Deputy Headmaster,
The White House Grammar School, Brampton, Cumbria

CASSELL LTD.   MACMILLAN PUBLISHING CO., INC.
London   New York

Cassell Ltd.
35 Red Lion Square, London, WC1R 4SG
and at Sydney, Toronto,
Johannesburg, Auckland
an affiliate of
Macmillan Publishing Co., Inc.,
866 Third Avenue, New York, N.Y. 10022

CASSELL'S COMPACT FRENCH–ENGLISH ENGLISH–FRENCH
DICTIONARY
First Edition 1968
2nd Impression 1968
3rd Impression 1968
4th Impression 1969
5th Impression 1972
6th Impression 1974
7th Impression 1975
8th Impression 1976
9th Impression (title changed to CASSELL'S CONCISE FRENCH–
ENGLISH ENGLISH–FRENCH DICTIONARY) 1977
10th Impression 1979
I.S.B.N. 0 304 52267 8

Library of Congress Cataloging in Publication Data
        Main entry under title:
    Cassell's concise French dictionary.
Reprint of the ed. published by Funk & Wagnalls, New York
under title:
Cassell's new compact French–English, English–French dictionary.
        1. French language – Dictionaries – English.
        2. English language – Dictionaries – French.
I. Douglas, John Henry.
II. Girard, Denis.
III. Thompson, W., M.A.
IV. Title: Concise French dictionary.
    PC2640.C28 1977   443'.21   77–7667

Macmillan I.S.B.N. 0 02 522670 3

First Macmillan Edition 1977

Printed in Spain by Grijelmo, S.A., Bilbao

Contents

Preface   vii

Advice to the User   viii

Avis au Lecteur   ix

Key to Pronunciation   xii

List of Abbreviations   xiv

French–English Dictionary   1

English–French Dictionary   333

French Verbs   636

English Verbs   652

Preface

This new edition of a work which appeared for the first time in 1904 represents a departure from tradition in that it is not a revised version of its immediate predecessor, but an entirely new work based on 'Cassell's New French Dictionary' compiled by Denis Girard and first published in 1962.

The availability of such a recent publication, and one moreover which has been widely accepted as a reliable work, has made the editors' task much easier than it could ever have been otherwise. The dead wood had already been cut away and many new words had been introduced, but it will come as no surprise that there are entries in the 'Concise' which do not appear in the 'New', e.g. 'escalate', and that others which were included in the 'New' for the first time in 1962 have already been discarded as obsolete, e.g. 'teddy boy'.

It is, of course, the question of selection which poses the greatest problem for anyone concerned with the compilation of a dictionary of limited size. Many uncommon words inevitably fail to find a place, as do the less frequent uses of some which have been included. We have tried wherever possible to illustrate by examples, but we have not attempted to incorporate information which properly belongs to a grammar book rather than a dictionary. It is assumed that the user will have a knowledge not only of parts of speech but also of the essential basic grammar of both languages. Although personal preference may have played a part, we have always tried to regard suitability for this type of dictionary as the primary consideration for or against the inclusion of a word, and we hope that we have, if anything, erred on the safe side.

Several features in the general layout of the 'New French Dictionary' have been incorporated for the first time in the 'Concise'. These include the use of the symbols of the International Phonetic Association throughout, the detailed information given in the 'Advice to the User' and the tables of English and French verbs. Completely new features are the notes at the head of the verb tables and the increased use of French in the explanatory parentheses in the English–French section.

J. H. D.

Advice to the User

Grouping of Words
In both sections of the dictionary alphabetical order has been strictly observed for all entries, including proper nouns.

Numbering of Identical Words
Words which are spelt alike but which differ in origin or pronunciation are numbered separately.

Punctuation
When several translations are given for one word it can generally be assumed that those which are separated by commas have much the same meaning; semi-colons are used where there is a clear difference in meaning or usage.

Words or meanings marked with an asterisk (*) are obsolete.

Pronunciation
The phonetic transcription is given in square brackets immediately after the key-word and alternative pronunciations have been given where necessary. The mark (ˈ) precedes the syllable which carries the stress.

The symbols of the International Phonetic Association have been used throughout the dictionary, and the user who is unfamiliar with these should refer to the Key to Pronunciation.

Daniel Jones' *English Pronouncing Dictionary* has usually been followed in the English–French section.

Grammatical Information
It is assumed that the user will have a reasonable knowledge of the basic grammar of the two languages. For example, when a noun merely adds -s for the plural or an adjective -e for the feminine, it has not been considered necessary to show this. Parts of speech are indicated by an abbreviation in italics (*a.*, *n.m.*, *v.t.*, *adv.* etc.) except in the case of proper nouns where in English no indication has been given and in French only the gender. For the meanings of the abbreviations the user is referred to the list on page xiv.

Nouns and Adjectives

In the French–English section French nouns are classed as *n.m.* for the masculine, *n.f.* for the feminine or *n.* for a noun which may be masculine or feminine according to context. In the English–French section the gender of French nouns is shown by the abbreviations *m.* or *f.*; where a noun, without change of form, may be masculine or feminine both genders are given. In a list of nouns the gender is not given after each one and the user should therefore read on to the next gender mentioned, e.g. under **damage** he will find 'dommage; tort,

Groupement des Mots

Dans les deux parties du dictionnaire l'ordre alphabétique a été strictement suivi pour tous les articles, y compris les noms propres.

Numérotage de Mots Identiques

Les mots qui ont la même orthographe sont numérotés séparément lorsqu'ils ont une racine ou une prononciation différente.

Ponctuation

Quand plusieurs traductions sont données pour un même mot, celles qui ne sont séparées que par des virgules ont en règle générale des sens à peu près identiques; le point-virgule est utilisé pour indiquer des différences très nettes de sens ou d'emploi.

Les mots précédés d'un astérisque (*) sont désuets.

Prononciation

La transcription phonétique est donnée entre crochets immédiatement après le mot principal. Lorsqu'il y a d'autres prononciations possibles, elles sont également indiquées. L'accent (') précède la syllabe qui porte l'accent tonique.

Les signes de l'Association Internationale de Phonétique sont utilisés dans les deux parties du dictionnaire et le lecteur qui n'est pas familiarisé avec ces signes devra consulter la Table de Prononciation.

Pour la section Anglais–Français, on a généralement suivi le dictionnaire de M. Daniel Jones, *An English Pronouncing Dictionary*.

Indications Grammaticales

Le lecteur est considéré comme ayant une connaissance suffisante de la grammaire de base des deux langues. Par exemple, quand un nom français forme son pluriel en **-s** et quand un adjectif forme son féminin en **-e**, il n'a pas paru nécessaire de l'indiquer. La nature des mots est indiquée par une abréviation en italique (*a.*, *n.m.*, *v.t.*, *adv.* etc.) excepté dans le cas des noms propres pour lesquels aucune indication n'a été donnée dans la partie Anglais–Français et seulement le genre dans la partie Français–Anglais. On trouvera la signification des abréviations à la page xiv.

Noms et adjectifs

Dans la partie Français–Anglais, les noms français sont classés en *n.m.* pour les noms masculins, en *n.f.* pour les noms féminins et *n.* pour ceux qui se modifient selon le contexte. Dans la partie Anglais–Français, le genre des noms français est indiqué par les abréviations *m.* ou *f.*; lorsqu'un nom peut, sans changer de forme, être soit du masculin soit du féminin, les deux genres sont donnés. Dans une dégât; (*fig.*) préjudice, détriment, *m.*' and he will know from this that all these five nouns are masculine. In the English–French section the feminine forms of French adjectives and nouns (where applicable) are not normally given. The user should consult the relevant French word in the French–English section.

Where plurals or feminines of nouns or adjectives are given, abbreviated forms are used. For example the entry **cheval** (pl. **-aux**) means that the full plural word is **chevaux**. Similarly, **acteur** (*fem.* **-trice**) indicates that the feminine form is **actrice**.

Verbs

All Verbs, other than reflexive verbs, form their compound tenses with **avoir** unless there is an indication with the entry that they take **être**. For all further information on verb entries please consult notes on Verb Tables below.

Verb Tables

1. French verbs have been listed in the tables as follows:

   a. A pattern verb for each of the three regular conjugations.
   b. Pattern verbs which may best be described as 'anomalous', i.e. verbs which are basically regular but which, for one reason or another, show slight variations from the normal forms.
   c. An alphabetical list of irregular verbs, some of which are used as a reference for other verbs which show similar irregularities.

Full conjugations have been given for the regular verbs but elsewhere only where it is considered necessary or desirable.

2. An alphabetical list of all irregular English verbs included in this dictionary is given. The user is referred to the Verb Tables for a note on the following:

   a. Verbs ending in **-y** preceded by one or more consonants.
   b. Certain verbs ending in a consonant preceded by a vowel.

3. The following explanation of verb entries in the dictionary may be helpful:

   a. *irr.* See the verb in question in the list of irregular verbs.
   b. *irr.* (*conjug. like* . . . . . .) See the pattern verb in the list of irregular verbs.
   c. (*see Verb Tables*) See the verb in question in the list of anomalous verbs.
   d. (*conjug. like* . . . . . .) See the pattern verb in the list of anomalous verbs.

liste de noms, le genre n'est pas donné après chacun d'eux et le lecteur doit alors se référer au premier genre indiqué, e.g. pour **damage** il trouvera 'dommage; tort, dégât; (*fig.*) préjudice, détriment, *m.*' et il en déduira que ces cinq noms sont du masculin. Dans la partie Anglais–Français, le féminin des mots français, lorsqu'il existe, n'est en principe pas indiqué; on le trouvera dans la partie Français–Anglais.

Lorsque le pluriel ou le féminin des noms ou des adjectifs est indiqué, il est donné en abrégé. Par exemple, **cheval** (*pl.* **-aux**) signifie que la forme de ce mot au pluriel est **chevaux**. De même, **acteur** (*fem.* **-trice**) signifie que la forme du féminin est **actrice**.

Verbes
Tous les verbes, autres que les verbes réfléchis, forment leurs temps composés avec l'auxiliaire **avoir**, à moins qu'il soit indiqué qu'ils se conjuguent avec **être**. On trouvera ci-dessous des renseignements complémentaires sur les verbes.

Tables des Verbes
1. Les verbes français sont présentés de la façon suivante:
   a. un verbe-type pour chacune des trois conjugaisons régulières.
   b. des verbes-types 'anomaux', c'est-à-dire, des verbes qui sont fondamentalement réguliers mais qui comportent de légères variations par rapport aux formes normales.
   c. une liste alphabétique des verbes irréguliers dont certains servent de références à d'autres verbes présentant des irrégularités analogues.

La conjugaison des verbes réguliers a été donnée en entier, mais pour les autres verbes elle ne figure que lorsque cela paraît nécessaire.

2. On trouvera une liste alphabétique de tous les verbes irréguliers anglais qui sont donnés dans ce dictionnaire, précédée par des renseignements sur les groupes suivants:
   a. Verbes qui se terminent en **-y** précédé d'une ou plus d'une consonne.
   b. Certains verbes qui se terminent en une consonne précédée d'une voyelle.

3. Les renseignements suivants concernant la présentation des verbes dans le dictionnaire pourront s'avérer utiles:
   a. *irr.* Se reporter à la liste des verbes irréguliers.
   b. *irr.* (*conjug. like* . . . . . .) Voir le verbe-type dans la liste des verbes irréguliers.
   c. (*see Verb Tables*) Voir ce verbe dans la liste des verbes anomaux.
   d. (*conjug. like* . . . . . .) Voir le verbe-type dans la liste des verbes anomaux.

Key to Pronunciation

VOWELS

French (i)

i	as in	cri [kri], difficile [difi'sil]
i:	,, ,,	écrire [e'kri:r], finir [fi'ni:r]
e	,, ,,	thé [te], mélodie [melə'di]
ɛ	,, ,,	réel [re'ɛl], aile [ɛl]
ɛ:	,, ,,	bête [bɛ:t], dentaire [dã'tɛ:r]
a	,, ,,	patte [pat], apparat [apa'ra]
a:	,, ,,	tard [ta:r], barbare [bar'ba:r]
ɑ	,, ,,	pas [pɑ], tailler [tɑ'je]
ɑ:	,, ,,	gaz [gɑ:z], pâte [pɑ:t]
ɔ	,, ,,	coter [kɔ'te], voler [vɔ'le]
ɔ:	,, ,,	confort [kɔ̃'fɔ:r], porc [pɔ:r]
o	,, ,,	côté [ko'te], gros [gro], tôt [to]
o:	,, ,,	dôme [do:m], rôle [ro:l]
u	,, ,,	coup [ku], tourner [tur'ne]
u:	,, ,,	bourre [bu:r], cour [ku:r]
y	,, ,,	cru [kry], salut [sa'ly]
y:	,, ,,	littérature [litera'ty:r]
ø	,, ,,	neveu [nə'vø], rocheux [rɔ'ʃø]
ø:	,, ,,	mitrailleuse [mitra'jø:z]
œ	,, ,,	feuillet [fœ'jɛ]
œ:	,, ,,	faveur [fa'vœ:r]
ə	,, ,,	le [lə], refaire [rə'fɛ:r]

English (i)

i:	as in	seat [si:t]
i	,, ,,	finish ['finiʃ], physics ['fiziks]
e	,, ,,	neck [nek], bread [bred]
æ	,, ,,	man [mæn], malefactor ['mælifæktə]
ɑ:	,, ,,	father ['fɑ:ðə], task [tɑ:sk]
ɔ	,, ,,	block [blɔk], waddle [wɔdl]
ɔ:	,, ,,	shawl [ʃɔ:l], tortoise ['tɔ:təs]
o	,, ,,	domain [do'mein]
u	,, ,,	good [gud], July [dʒu'lai]
u:	,, ,,	moon [mu:n], tooth [tu:θ]
ʌ	,, ,,	cut [kʌt], somewhere ['sʌmwɛə]
ə:	,, ,,	search [sə:tʃ], surgeon ['sə:dʒən]
ə	,, ,,	cathedral [kə'θi:drəl], never ['nevə]

Nasal Vowels

ɛ̃	as in	faim [fɛ̃], vingt [vɛ̃]
ɛ̃:	,, ,,	feindre [fɛ̃:dr], poindre [pwɛ̃:dr]
ã	,, ,,	ensemencement [ãsmãs'mã]
ã:	,, ,,	défendre [de'fã:dr]
õ	,, ,,	son [sõ], fonder [fõ'de]
õ:	,, ,,	contre [kõ:tr], trompe [trõ:p]
œ̃	,, ,,	défunt [de'fœ̃], un [œ̃]
œ̃:	,, .	humble [œ̃:bl]

Diphthongs

ei	as in	great [greit]
ou	,, ,,	show [ʃou]
ai	,, ,,	high [hai]
au	,, ,,	crowd [kraud]
ɔi	,, ,,	boy [bɔi]
iə	,, ,,	steer [stiə]
ɛə	,, ,,	hair [hɛə]
uə	,, ,,	moor [muə]

CONSONANTS

FRENCH (I)

p   as in peine [pɛn], papier [pa'pje]
b   ,, ,, bon [bɔ̃]
t   ,, ,, tâter [tɑ'te], thé [te]
d   ,, ,, dinde [dɛ̃:d]
k   ,, ,, coquelicot [kɔkli'ko]
g   ,, ,, gare [ga:r]
m   ,, ,, maman [ma'mɑ̃], même [mɛ:m]
n   ,, ,, nonne [nɔn]

ɲ   ,, ,, agneau [a'ɲo], soigner [swa'ɲe]
f   ,, ,, fier [fjɛ:r]
v   ,, ,, vivre [vi:vr]

s   ,, ,, sucre [sykr]
z   ,, ,, raser [rɑ'ze]
l   ,, ,, lettre [lɛtr], valise [va'li:z]
ʃ   ,, ,, charme [ʃarm]
ʒ   ,, ,, ronger [rɔ̃'ʒe], joue [ʒu]
r   ,, ,, arrière [a'rjɛ:r]

ENGLISH (I)

p   as in paper ['peipə]
b   ,, ,, ball [bɔ:l]
t   ,, ,, tea [ti:], till [til]
d   ,, ,, deed [di:d]
k   ,, ,, cake [keik]
g   ,, ,, game [geim]
m   ,, ,, mammoth ['mæməθ]
n   ,, ,, nose [nouz], nun [nʌn]
ŋ   ,, ,, bring [briŋ], finger ['fiŋgə]

f   ,, ,, fair [fɛə], far [fɑ:]
v   ,, ,, vine [vain]
θ   ,, ,, thin [θin], bath [bɑ:θ]
ð   ,, ,, this [ðis], bathe [beið]
s   ,, ,, since [sins]
z   ,, ,, busy ['bizi]
l   ,, ,, land [lænd], hill [hil]
ʃ   ,, ,, shield [ʃi:ld], sugar ['ʃugə]
ʒ   ,, ,, visionary ['viʒənəri]
r   ,, ,, rut [rʌt], brain [brein]
h   ,, ,, here [hiə], horse [hɔ:s]
x   ,, ,, loch [lɔx]

SEMI-CONSONANTS

j   as in rien [rjɛ̃]
w   ,, ,, ouate [wat], oui [wi]
ɥ   ,, ,, huile [ɥil]

j   as in yellow ['jelou], yes [jes]
w   ,, ,, wall [wɔ:l]

When the same symbol is used in both English and French it often represents a different sound in each language.

'   denotes that the stress is on the following syllable.
:   denotes that the preceding vowel is long.
~   placed over a vowel-symbol shows that the vowel has a nasal sound.

List of Abbreviations

a.	adjective	*foll.*	the following	*pers.*	person, personal
abbr.	abbreviation	*Fort.*	Fortification	*Pharm.*	Pharmacy
Adm.	Administration	*Fr.*	French	*Phil.*	Philosophy
adv.	adverb	*Ftb.*	Assoc. Football	*Philol.*	Philology
adv. phr.	adverbial phrase	*fut.*	future	*Phon.*	Phonetics
affirm.	affirmative	*Gard.*	Gardening	*Phot.*	Photography
Agric.	Agriculture	*Geog.*	Geography	*phr.*	phrase
Alg.	Algebra	*Geol.*	Geology	*Phys.*	Physics
Am.	American	*Geom.*	Geometry	*Physiol.*	Physiology
Anat.	Anatomy	*Gr.*	Greek	*pl.*	plural
Ant.	Antiquities	*Gram.*	Grammar	*poet.*	poetical
Arch.	Architecture	*Gym.*	Gymnastics	*Polit.*	Politics
Archaeol.	Archaeology	*Her.*	Heraldry	*pop.*	popular
Arith.	Arithmetic	*Hist.*	History	*poss.*	possessive
art.	article	*Horol.*	Horology	*p.p.*	past participle
Artill.	Artillery	*Hort.*	Horticulture	*prec.*	the preceding
Astron.	Astronomy	*Hunt.*	Hunting	*pref.*	prefix
aux.	auxiliary	*Hydr.*	Hydrostatics	*prep.*	preposition
Av.	Aviation	*i.*	intransitive	*pres.*	present
Bibl.	Bible, Biblical	*Ichth.*	Ichthyology	*pres. p.*	present participle
Biol.	Biology	*imp.*	imperfect	*Print.*	Printing
Bookb.	Bookbinding	*impers.*	impersonal	*pron.*	pronoun
Bot.	Botany	*Ind.*	Industry	*prop.*	proper, properly
Box.	Boxing	*indec.*	indecent	*Pros.*	Prosody
Build.	Building	*indef.*	indefinite	*Psych.*	Psychology
(*C*)	Canadian usage	*indic.*	indicative	*Pyro.*	Pyrotechnics
Carp.	Carpentry	*inf.*	infinitive	*r.*	reflexive; recipro-
Ch.	Church	*int.*	interjection		cal
Chem.	Chemistry	*inter.*	interrogative	*Rad.*	Radio
Cine.	Cinema	*inv.*	invariable	*Rail.*	Railway
Civ. Eng.	Civil Engineering	*iron.*	ironical	*R.C.*	Roman Catholic
Coin.	Coinage	*irr.*	irregular (see	*reg.*	registered
collect.	collective		table of Irregular	*rel.*	relative
colloq.	colloquially		Verbs, pp. 636–	*Relig.*	Religion
comb.	combination		58)	*rhet.*	rhetoric
comb. form	combining form	*It.*	Italian	*Rom.*	Roman
Comm.	Commerce	*Jew.*	Jewish	*Row.*	Rowing
comp.	comparative	*Journ.*	Journalism	*Sc.*	Scottish
Conch.	Conchology	*L.*	Latin	*Sch.*	Schools
cond.	conditional	*Lit.*	Literature	*Sci.*	Science
conj.	conjunction	*Log.*	Logic	*Sculp.*	Sculpture
conjug.	conjugated	*m.*	masculine	*sing.*	singular
contr.	contraction	*Mach.*	Machinery	*s.o.'s*	someone's
Cook.	Cookery	*Manuf.*	Manufacturing	*Spt.*	Sport
Cost.	Costume	*masc.*	masculine	*St. Exch.*	Stock Exchange
Cycl.	Cycling	*Math.*	Mathematics	*subj.*	subjunctive
dat.	dative	*Mech.*	Mechanics	*superl.*	superlative
def.	definite	*Med.*	Medicine	*Surg.*	Surgery
dem.	demonstrative	*Metal.*	Metallurgy	*Surv.*	Surveying
Dent.	Dentistry	*Meteor.*	Meteorology	*Swim.*	Swimming
dial.	dialect	*Mil.*	Military	*t.*	transitive
dim.	diminutive	*Min.*	Mineralogy	*Tech.*	Technical
Dress.	Dressmaking	*Motor.*	Motoring	*Tel.*	Television
Eccles.	Ecclesiastical	*Mount.*	Mountaineering	*Teleg.*	Telegraphy
Econ.	Economics	*Mus.*	Music	*Teleph.*	Telephone
Elec.	Electricity	*Myth.*	Mythology	*Ten.*	Tennis
ellipt.	elliptic	*n.*	noun	*Tex.*	Textiles
emphat.	emphatic	*Nat.*	Natural	*Theat.*	Theatrical
Eng.	Engineering	*Naut.*	Nautical	*Theol.*	Theological
Engl.	English	*neg.*	negative	*Trig.*	Trigonometry
Engr.	Engraving	*obj.*	object	*Univ.*	University
Ent.	Entomology	*obs.*	obsolete	*U.S.*	United States
esp.	especially	*Opt.*	Optics	*usu.*	usually
Exam.	Examination	*Orn.*	Ornithology	*v.*	verb
f.	feminine	*Paint.*	Painting	*Vet.*	Veterinary
fam.	familiarly	*Parl.*	Parliamentary	*v.i.*	intransitive verb
facet.	facetiously	*part.*	participle, par-	*v.r.*	reflexive *or* reci-
fem.	feminine		ticipial		procal verb
Fenc.	Fencing	*Path.*	Pathology	*v.t.*	transitive verb
Feud.	Feudal	*pej.*	pejorative	*vulg.*	vulgar
fig.	figuratively	*perf.*	perfect	*Zool.*	Zoology
Fin.	Financial				

xiv

A, a [a], *n.m.* in French *a* has two sounds: (1) as in *part*, shown in this dictionary by 'a'; (2) as in *pas*, shown by 'ɑ'.

à [a], *prep.* [*see also* AU, AUX] to, at, in, into, on, by, for, from, with.

abaisse [a'bɛːs], *n.f.* undercrust of pastry.

abaissement [abɛs'mɑ̃], *n.m.* lowering, falling, abatement, depression; humiliation, abasement.

abaisser [abɛ'se], *v.t.* to let down, to let fall, to lower; to diminish, to reduce; (*fig.*) to bring low, to humble, to depress; to roll out (*paste*). **s'abaisser**, *v.r.* to sink, to subside, to decrease, to abate, to decline; to humble oneself, to stoop, to cringe.

abajoue [aba'ʒu], *n.f.* (*Zool.*) cheek pouch.

abalourdir [abalur'diːr], *v.t.* to make dull *or* stupid.

abalourdissement [abalurdis'mɑ̃], *n.m.* dullness, stupidity.

abandon [abɑ̃'dɔ̃], *n.m.* relinquishment, surrender, cession; abandonment, forlornness, destitution; lack of restraint; *à l'abandon,* at random, in confusion, at sixes and sevens; (*Naut.*) adrift.

abandonné [abɑ̃dɔ'ne], *a.* abandoned, forsaken; lost to decency, shameless, profligate.

abandonnement [abɑ̃dɔn'mɑ̃], *n.m.* abandonment; desertion; (*fig.*) dissoluteness, profligacy.

abandonnément [abɑ̃dɔne'mɑ̃], *adv.* freely, unreservedly.

abandonner [abɑ̃dɔ'ne], *v.t.* to give up, to hand over, to surrender; to renounce; to forsake, to desert, to abandon; to leave, to quit; to neglect. **s'abandonner**, *v.r.* to give oneself up, to give way (*à*); to indulge (*à*); to neglect oneself.

abaque [a'bak], *n.m.* (*Arch.*) abacus; (*Arith.*) abacus.

abasourdir [abazur'diːr], *v.t.* to stun, to dumbfound; (*fig.*) to astound.

abasourdissant [abazurdi'sɑ̃], *a.* astounding, overwhelming.

abasourdissement [abazurdis'mɑ̃], *n.m.* stupefaction, bewilderment.

*****abat** [a'ba], *n.m.* killing, knocking down; heavy shower.

abâtardi [abɑtar'di], *a.* degenerate, corrupt, debased.

abâtardir [abɑtar'diːr], *v.t.* to render degenerate; to debase, to corrupt. **s'abâtardir**, *v.r.* to degenerate.

abâtardissement [abɑtardis'mɑ̃], *n.m.* degeneracy.

abatée *or* **abattée** [aba'te], *n.f.* swoop (*of plane*).

abat-jour [aba'ʒuːr], *n.m. inv.* sky-light; lamp shade; shade for the eyes.

abat-son [aba'sɔ̃], *n.m.* (*pl. unchanged or* **abat-sons**) a series of sloping louvres in the window of a bell tower for directing the sound downwards.

abattage [aba'taːʒ], *n.m.* cutting down, felling (*of trees*); slaughtering (*of animals*).

abattant [aba'tɑ̃], *n.m.* flap (*of a counter etc.*).

abattée [ABATÉE].

abattement [abat'mɑ̃], *n.m.* weakening; prostration; dejection, despondency, low spirits.

abatteur [aba'tœːr], *n.m.* one who fells (*trees etc.*); slaughterer.

abattis [aba'ti], *n.m.* things *or* materials brought down (*such as houses, walls, trees*); slaughtered animals, game etc.; killing of game; giblets (*of poultry*).

abattoir [aba'twaːr], *n.m.* slaughter-house.

abattre [a'batr], *v.t.* (*conjug. like* BATTRE) to throw *or* hurl down; to knock, beat *or* batter down; to pull down; to fell; to kill, to slaughter; to overthrow, to demolish; to dishearten, to discourage, to depress. **s'abattre**, *v.r.* to throw oneself down, to fall, to tumble down; to crash (down); to abate; to be cast down *or* dejected; to pounce upon; **le vent s'abat,** the wind is dropping.

abattu [aba'ty], *a.* cast down, depressed, dejected; humbled, crestfallen.

abat-vent [aba'vɑ̃], *n.m. inv.* louvre-boards (*of a window*); wind-cowl (*of a chimney*).

abat-voix [aba'vwa], *n.m. inv.* sounding board (*of a pulpit*).

abbaye [abe'ji], *n.f.* monastery, abbey.

abbé [a'be], *n.m.* abbot, abbé; *l'abbé Martin,* Father Martin.

abbesse [a'bɛs], *n.f.* abbess.

A.B.C. [abe'se], *n.m.* alphabet; primer, spelling-book.

abcéder [apse'de], *v.i.* (*conjug. like* CÉDER) to turn into an abscess, to gather.

abcès [ap'sɛ], *n.m.* abscess, gathering; *abcès aux gencives,* gumboil.

abdication [abdika'sjɔ̃], *n.f.* abdication; renunciation (*of property etc.*); surrender (*of authority*).

abdiquer [abdi'ke], *v.t.* to abdicate, to resign, to renounce.

abdomen [abdɔ'mɛn], *n.m.* abdomen.

abdominal [abdɔmi'nal], *a.* abdominal.

abducteur [abdyk'tœːr], *a.* (*Anat.*) abducent. —*n.m.* (*Anat.*) abductor.

abduction [abdyk'sjɔ̃], *n.f.* abduction.

abécédaire [abese'dɛːr], *a.* alphabetical; *ordre abécédaire,* alphabetical order.— *n.m.* spelling book; elementary reading book; primer.

abecquer [abɛ'ke], *v.t.* to feed (*a bird*).

abeille [a'bɛːj], *n.f.* bee; *abeille mère,* queen bee.

aberration [abɛra'sjɔ̃], *n.f.* deviation from the normal *or* the correct course; (*Astron., Opt. etc.*) aberration.

abêtir [abɛ'tiːr], *v.t.* to render stupid; to dull, to blunt.—*v.i.* to become dull *or* stupid. **s'abêtir**, *v.r.* to grow stupid.

abêtissement [abɛtis'mɑ̃], *n.m.* stultification.

abhorrer [abɔ're], v.t. to abhor, to hate, to loathe.

abîme [a'bi:m], n.m. abyss, the deep, chasm; hell.

abîmé [abi'me], a. swallowed up, engulfed; ruined; damaged.

abîmer [abi'me], v.t. *to engulf, to swallow up; to ruin; to damage. **s'abîmer**, v.r. to fall into ruin; to be spoiled.

abject [ab'ʒɛkt], a. abject, base.

abjectement [abʒɛktə'mɑ̃], adv. abjectly.

abjection [abʒɛk'sjɔ̃], n.f. abasement, humiliation; vileness.

abjuration [abʒyra'sjɔ̃], n.f. solemn renunciation, abjuration.

abjurer [abʒy're], v.t. to abjure, to renounce; to foreswear.

ablatif [abla'tif], a. (fem. **-tive**) ablative. —n.m. (Gram.) ablative (case).

ablation [abla'sjɔ̃], n.f. (Surg.) removal (of a part).

able [abl], n.m. any small freshwater fish of the bleak family [ABLETTE].

ablette [a'blɛt], n.f. bleak [ABLE].

ablution [ably'sjɔ̃], n.f. ablution, washing, purification.

abnégation [abnega'sjɔ̃], n.f. abnegation, renunciation, sacrifice, self-denial.

aboi [a'bwa], n.m. (dog's) bark, barking, baying; (fig.) desperate condition; **aux abois**, at bay.

aboiement [abwa'mɑ̃], n.m. barking, baying.

abolir [abɔ'li:r], v.t. to abolish, to repeal, to annul, to suppress.

abolissement [abɔlis'mɑ̃], n.m. abolition.

abolition [abɔli'sjɔ̃], n.f. abolition, repeal.

abominable [abɔmi'nabl], a. abominable, execrable; heinous.

abominablement [abɔminablə'mɑ̃], adv. abominably.

abomination [abɔmina'sjɔ̃], n.f. abomination, detestation, horror.

abominer [abɔmi'ne], v.t. to abominate, to detest.

abondamment [abɔ̃da'mɑ̃], adv. abundantly.

abondance [abɔ̃'dɑ̃:s], n.f. a great quantity, abundance, plenty; affluence.

abondant [abɔ̃'dɑ̃], a. abundant, plentiful, copious; exuberant, effusive.

abonder [abɔ̃'de], v.i. to abound, to be plentiful, to be in great quantity; **abonder dans le sens de quelqu'un**, to support somebody's views strongly.

abonné [abɔ'ne], n.m. (fem. **-ée**) subscriber (to periodicals etc.); season ticket holder.

abonnement [abɔn'mɑ̃], n.m. subscription (to periodicals, theatres etc.); agreement; season ticket; **carte d'abonnement**, season ticket.

abonner (s') [sabɔ'ne], v.r. to become a subscriber.

abonnir [abɔ'ni:r], v.t. to mend, to improve (wine).—v.i. to become good. **s'abonnir**, v.r. to mend, to grow better.

abonnissement [abɔnis'mɑ̃], n.m. improvement.

abord [a'bɔ:r], n.m. landing; arrival; access, approach, meeting; onset, attack; (pl.) approaches, surroundings; **d'abord**, at first.

abordable [abɔr'dabl], a. accessible, easily approached, affable.

abordage [abɔr'da:ʒ], n.m. (Naut.) boarding; fouling, colliding.

abordée [abɔr'de], n.f. the act of meeting, accosting or beginning.

aborder [abɔr'de], v.t. to arrive at; to approach, to accost; to enter upon (a subject etc.); to grapple (a vessel); to run foul of (a ship).—v.i. to arrive; to land. **s'aborder**, v.r. to accost each other; to run foul of each other.

aborigène [abɔri'ʒɛ:n], a. native, original.— n.m. aboriginal, aborigine.

aborner [abɔr'ne], v.t. to mark out, to delimit.

abortif [abɔr'tif], a. (fem. **-tive**) abortive.

abouchement [abuʃ'mɑ̃], n.m. interview, conference.

aboucher [abu'ʃe], v.t. to bring (things or persons) together. **s'aboucher**, v.r. to have an interview, to confer (with); to get in touch (with).

aboutement [abut'mɑ̃], n.m. abutment; placing or fitting end to end.

abouter [abu'te], v.t. to join end to end.

aboutir [abu'ti:r], v.i. to end at or in, to result (à); (Surg.) to come to a head (with aux. ÊTRE or AVOIR).

aboutissant [abuti'sɑ̃], a. bordering upon, abutting on, ending in.

aboutissement [abutis'mɑ̃], n.m. result, issue.

aboyer [abwa'je], v.i. (conjug. like EMPLOYER) to bark, to bay, to yelp.

abracadabra [abrakada'bra], n.m. abracadabra (magic word).

abracadabrant [abrakada'brɑ̃], a. stupendous, amazing, stunning.

abrasif [abra'zif], n.m. abrasive.

abrégé [abre'ʒe], a. short, summary.—n.m. abridgment, résumé, précis, abstract, summary.

abrégement [abreʒ'mɑ̃], n.m. abridging, abridgment.

abréger [abre'ʒe], v.t. (conjug. like ASSIÉGER) to abridge, to shorten; to abbreviate.

abreuvage [abrœ'va:ʒ], **abreuvement** [a brœv'mɑ̃], n.m. watering, soaking, steaming.

abreuver [abrœ've], v.t. to water (animals); to water (the ground etc.). **s'abreuver**, v.r. to drink, to be watered (of animals).

abreuvoir [abrœ'vwa:r], n.m. watering place, horse pond; drinking trough.

abréviation [abrevja'sjɔ̃], n.f. abbreviation, shortening.

abri [a'bri], n.m. shelter, cover, refuge, dugout.

abricot [abri'ko], n.m. apricot.

abricotier [abrikɔ'tje], n.m. apricot tree.

abriter [abri'te], v.t. to shelter, to shade, to protect. **s'abriter**, v.r. to take refuge.

abrogation [abrɔga'sjɔ̃], n.f. abrogation, repeal, annulment.

abroger [abrɔ'ʒe], v.t. (conjug. like MANGER) to abrogate, to repeal, to annul. **s'abroger**, v.r. to fall into disuse.

abrupt [a'brypt], a. abrupt, steep, sheer; (fig.) blunt, rugged, rough (of style etc.).

abruptement [abryptə'mɑ̃], adv. abruptly.

abruti [abry'ti], a. and n.m. (fem. **-e**) brutalized, stupid (person).

abrutir [abry'ti:r], v.t. to stupefy, to brutalize. **s'abrutir**, v.r. to become brutalized or stupid.

abrutissant [abryti'sɑ̃], a. brutalizing, stupefying.

abrutissement [abrytis'mɑ̃], n.m. the act of brutalizing; brutishness, degradation.

absence [ap'sɑ̃:s], n.f. absence; want, lack; **absence d'esprit**, absence of mind.

absent [ap'sɑ̃], a. absent, away from home; wandering, woolgathering.—n.m. (fem. -e) absentee.

absentéisme [apsɑ̃te'ism], n.m. absenteeism.

absenter (s') [apsɑ̃'te], v.r. to absent oneself, to be away; to play truant.

abside [ap'si:d], n.f. apse.

absinthe [ap'sɛ̃:t], n.f. absinth; wormwood.

absolu [apsɔ'ly], a. absolute; despotic, arbitrary; unrestricted; peremptory; positive.

absolument [apsɔly'mɑ̃], adv. absolutely; arbitrarily.

absolution [apsɔly'sjɔ̃], n.f. absolution, acquittal.

absolutisme [apsɔly'tism], n.m. absolutism.

absorbant [apsɔr'bɑ̃], a. absorptive, absorbent; engrossing.—n.m. absorbent.

absorber [apsɔr'be], v.t. to absorb, to imbibe; to eat or drink; (fig.) to engross. **s'absorber**, v.r. to be absorbed; (fig.) to be entirely taken up with (**dans**).

absorption [apsɔrp'sjɔ̃], n.f. absorption.

absoudre [ap'sudr], v.t. irr. to absolve, to acquit; to exonerate, to forgive.

abstenir (s') [apstə'ni:r], v.r. irr. (conjug. like TENIR) to abstain (from voting); to refrain, to forbear, to forgo.

abstention [apstɑ̃'sjɔ̃], n.f. abstention.

abstinence [apsti'nɑ̃:s], n.f. abstinence; temperance, sobriety; (pl.) fasts, fasting.

abstinent [apsti'nɑ̃], a. abstemious, sober.

abstraction [apstrak'sjɔ̃], n.f. abstraction, abstract question or idea.

abstraire [aps'trɛ:r], v.t. irr. (conjug. like TRAIRE) to abstract; to separate, to isolate.

abstrait [aps'trɛ], a. abstract, abstruse; absent-minded.

abstraitement [apstrɛt'mɑ̃], adv. abstractedly; separately; in the abstract.

abstrus [aps'try], a. abstruse; obscure.

absurde [ap'syrd], a. absurd, nonsensical, stupid, silly, preposterous.

absurdement [apsyrdə'mɑ̃], adv. absurdly, nonsensically.

absurdité [apsyrdi'te], n.f. absurdity, nonsense.

abus [a'by], n.m. abuse; grievance; misuse.

abuser [aby'ze], v.t. to deceive, to lead astray, to delude.—v.i. to misuse, to make ill use (de); to take advantage (de). **s'abuser**, v.r. to be mistaken, to deceive oneself.

abusif [aby'zif], a. (fem. -sive) irregular, improper.

abusivement [abyziv'mɑ̃], adv. irregularly, improperly.

abyssal [abi'sal], a. unfathomable.

abysse [a'bis], n.m. abyss, unfathomable gulf or depth.

Abyssinie [abisi'ni], l', f. Abyssiñia.

abyssinien [abisi'njɛ̃] (fem. -enne), **abyssin** [abi'sɛ̃], a. Abyssinian.—n.m. (**Abyssinien**, fem. -enne) Abyssinian (person).

acabit [aka'bi], n.m. quality (of fruits, vegetables); character, nature, stamp (of persons).

acacia [aka'sja], n.m. (Bot.) acacia.

académicien [akademi'sjɛ̃], n.m. academician.

académie [akade'mi], n.f. academy, society of learned men, esp. the Académie Française; school (of dancing, fencing, riding etc.).

académique [akade'mik], a. proper, appropriate or belonging to an academy, academic(al).

acagnarder [akaɲar'de], v.t. to make lazy. **s'acagnarder**, v.r. to drift into an idle, slothful life.

acajou [aka'ʒu], n.m. mahogany.

acanthe [a'kɑ̃:t], n.f. acanthus.

acariâtre [aka'rjɑ:tr], a. contrary, crabbed, cross-grained, quarrelsome, shrewish.

acariâtreté [akarjɑtrə'te], n.f. crabbedness, peevishness, shrewishness.

accablant [aka'blɑ̃], a. oppressive, overwhelming, crushing.

accablement [akɑblə'mɑ̃], n.m. prostration, oppression, extreme discouragement or dejection.

accabler [aka'ble], v.t. to crush, to overpower, to overcome; (fig.) to weigh down, to overload, to overwhelm.

accalmie [akal'mi], n.f. (Naut.) lull.

accaparant [akapa'rɑ̃], a. engrossing.

accaparement [akapar'mɑ̃], n.m. monopoly, monopolizing.

accaparer [akapa're], v.t. to monopolize, to hoard, to engross.

accapareur [akapa'rœ:r], n.m. (fem. -euse) monopolist, monopolizer, hoarder.

accéder [akse'de], v.i. (conjug. like CÉDER) to arrive, to reach, to have access; to accede, to comply with.

accélérateur [akselera'tœ:r], a. (fem. -trice) accelerative, with increasing speed.—n.m. (Elec., Mech., Phot. etc.) accelerator; (fam.) **appuyer sur l'accélérateur**, to step on the gas.

accélération [akselera'sjɔ̃], n.f. acceleration.

accéléré [aksele're], a. accelerated.

accélérer [aksele're], v.t. (conjug. like CÉDER) to accelerate, to quicken, to hasten, to press, to dispatch.

accent [ak'sɑ̃], n.m. pitch, accent, stress, tone; pronunciation; expression (of the voice).

accentuation [aksɑ̃tɥa'sjɔ̃], n.f. accentuation, stressing.

accentuer [aksɑ̃'tɥe], v.t. to accent, to accentuate, to stress.

acceptable [aksɛp'tabl], a. acceptable, worth accepting.

acceptation [aksɛpta'sjɔ̃], n.f. acceptance; acceptation.

accepter [aksɛp'te], v.t. to accept, to agree to, to welcome (what is offered or proposed).

acception [aksɛp'sjɔ̃], n.f. respect, regard, sense, meaning, acceptation.

accès [ak'sɛ], n.m. access, opportunity of approach, admittance; attack, fit, paroxysm.

accessibilité [aksɛsibili'te], n.f. accessibility.

accessible [aksɛ'sibl], a. accessible, approachable; within reach.

accession [aksɛ'sjɔ̃], n.f. accession; adhesion, union (of a country, province etc. to another).

accessit [aksɛ'sit], n.m. award of merit, honorable mention; 'proxime accessit'.

accessoire [aksɛ'swa:r], a. accessory, additional, subordinate.—n.m. an accessory; (pl.) (Theat.) properties.

accessoiriste [aksɛswa'rist], n.m. props man.

accident [aksi′dɑ̃], *n.m.* accident, fortuitous incident; casualty, mishap, mischance; unevenness, irregularity (*in the ground*).

accidenté [aksidɑ̃′te], *a.* varied, unequal (*of style etc.*); rough, uneven, broken, hilly (*of ground*); chequered (*of life, career etc.*).—*n.m.* (*fem.* **-ée**) one injured by an accident.

accidentel [aksidɑ̃′tel], *a.* (*fem.* **-elle**) accidental, adventitious, fortuitous, unexpected; *signe accidentel*, (*Mus.*) accidental.

accidentellement [aksidɑ̃tel′mɑ̃], *adv.* accidentally, casually, by chance.

accidenter [aksidɑ̃′te], *v.t.* to make irregular *or* uneven; to diversify, to chequer, to make picturesque.

accise [ak′si:z], *n.f.* (*Law*) inland duty, excise; *préposé à l'accise*, exciseman.

acclamation [aklamɑ′sjɔ̃], *n.f.* acclamation, cheering.

acclamer [akla′me], *v.t.* to acclaim, to applaud, to cheer.

acclimatable [aklima′tabl], *a.* that may be acclimatized.

acclimatation [aklimata′sjɔ̃], *n.f.* acclimatization.

acclimater [aklima′te], *v.t.* to acclimatize. **s'acclimater**, *v.r.* to become acclimatized.

accointance [akwɛ̃′tɑ̃:s], *n.f.* (*used generally in pl. and in a bad sense*) intimacy, familiarity; *avoir des accointances* (*avec*), to have dealings (*with*).

accointer [akwɛ̃′te], *v.t.* to make acquainted.

accolade [ako′lad], *n.f.* embrace; kiss; accolade (*in knighting*).

accolader (**s'**) [sakola′de], *v.r.* to embrace mutually.

accolage [ako′la:ʒ], *n.m.* tying up, training (*branches etc.*).

accolement [akol′mɑ̃], *n.m.* joining, uniting.

accoler [ako′le], *v.t.* to embrace; to tie up, to fasten, to place against; (*fig.*) to couple, to join together, to bracket.

accommodable [akomo′dabl], *a.* that may be arranged; adjustable.

accommodage [akomo′da:ʒ], *n.m.* preparation *or* dressing (*of meat*).

accommodant [akomo′dɑ̃], *a.* accommodating, easy-going, courteous.

accommodation [akomoda′sjɔ̃], *n.f.* accommodation.

accommodement [akomod′mɑ̃], *n.m.* accommodation, arrangement, composition; settlement, reconciliation, compromise.

accommoder [akomo′de], *v.t.* to adapt, to accommodate, to fit, to adjust; to reconcile; to conciliate; to dress, to trim; to cook, to do up; to suit, to be convenient. **s'accommoder**, *v.r.* to agree, to come to terms; to accommodate oneself, to adapt oneself (*à*); to put up with (*de*).

accompagnateur [akɔ̃paɲa′tœ:r], *n.m.* (*fem.* **-trice**) accompanist (*with instrument or voice*); conductor (*of a tour*).

accompagnement [akɔ̃paɲ′mɑ̃], *n.m.* accompanying; attendance, retinue; an accompaniment, an accessory; (*Mus.*) accompaniment.

accompagner [akɔ̃pa′ɲe], *v.t.* to accompany, to attend on; to go with, to escort; (*Mus.*) to accompany.

accompli [akɔ̃′pli], *a.* accomplished, performed, fulfilled; complete, faultless perfect, out and out.

accomplir [akɔ̃′pli:r], *v.t.* to fulfil, to effect, to perform; to realize, to carry out.

accomplissement [akɔ̃plis′mɑ̃], *n.m.* accomplishment, fulfilment, realization.

accon, acconier [ACON etc.].

accord [a′kɔ:r], *n.m.* accord, concurrence, unanimity, harmony; agreement, bargain; convention, settlement; (*Mus.*) chord; *être d'accord*, to agree; *d'accord*, granted, agreed.

accordable [akɔr′dabl], *a.* that may be accorded; reconcilable; (*Mus.*) tunable.

accordage [akɔr′da:ʒ], **accordement** [akɔrdə′mɑ̃], *n.m.* tuning (*of a musical instrument*).

accordailles [akɔr′dɑ:j], *n.f.* (*used only in pl.*) betrothal.

accordant [akɔr′dɑ̃], *a.* accordant, harmonious.

accordé [akɔr′de], *n.m.* (*fem.* **-ée**) fiancé, fiancée; *les accordés*, the bride and bridegroom.

accordéon [akɔrde′ɔ̃], *n.m.* accordion.

accordéoniste [akɔrdeɔ′nist], *n.* accordionist.

accorder [akɔr′de], *v.t.* to bring into harmony *or* accord, to make agree, to reconcile; to concede, to grant; to admit, to avow; (*Mus.*) to tune, to harmonize; to bestow (*hand in marriage*). **s'accorder**, *v.r.* to agree, to concur; to correspond; to suit, to be suited.

accordeur [akɔr′dœ:r], *n.m.* tuner (*of musical instruments*).

accordoir [akɔr′dwa:r], *n.m.* tuning hammer, key *or* cone.

accore [a′kɔ:r], *a.* abrupt, sheer, vertical (*of a coast*).

accort [a′kɔ:r], *a.* gracious, courteous.

accostable [akɔs′tabl], *a.* easy of access, approachable.

accostage [akɔs′ta:ʒ], *n.m.* the act of accosting, approaching *or* drawing alongside.

accoster [akɔs′te], *v.t.* to accost, to go up to; (*Naut.*) to come alongside.

accotement [akɔt′mɑ̃], *n.m.* (*Civ. Eng.*) roadside; footpath.

accoter [akɔ′te], *v.t.* to prop up, to support, to stay. **s'accoter**, *v.r.* to lean (*contre*).

accotoir [akɔ′twa:r], *n.m.* prop, support, leaning post.

accouardir [akwar′di:r], *v.t.* to make a coward. **s'accouardir**, *v.r.* to turn coward.

accouchée [aku′ʃe], *n.f.* woman in childbirth, woman who has just had a child.

accouchement [akuʃ′mɑ̃], *n.m.* childbirth, delivery, confinement; *centre d'accouchement*, maternity home.

accoucher [aku′ʃe], *v.t.* to deliver (*a woman*). —*v.i.* to lie in, to be brought to bed, to be delivered.

accoucheur [aku′ʃœ:r], *n.m.* male midwife, accoucheur.

accoucheuse [aku′ʃø:z], *n.f.* midwife.

accoudement [akud′mɑ̃], *n.m.* the act of leaning (*on*).

accouder (**s'**) [saku′de], *v.r.* to lean on one's elbow.

accoudoir [aku′dwa:r], *n.m.* elbow rest; (*Arch.*) rail, balustrade.

4

accouple [a'kupl], *n.f.* leash (*for tying dogs in couples*).

accouplement [akuplə'mã], *n.m.* coupling; pairing.

accoupler [aku'ple], *v.t.* to couple; to join together in pairs; (*Elec.*) to connect, to group (*batteries etc.*).

accourci [akur'si], *n.m.* abridgement (*of a book*).

accourcir [akur'si:r], *v.t.* to shorten, to abridge, to curtail. **s'accourcir**, *v.r.* to become shorter, to decrease.

accourcissement [akursis'mã], *n.m.* shortening, diminution.

accourir [aku'ri:r], *v.i.* irr. (*conjug. like* COURIR) to run up to, to hasten, to flock.

accoutrement [akutrə'mã], *n.m.* garb, dress, *esp.* as an object of ridicule.

accoutrer [aku'tre], *v.t.* to rig out, to dress. **s'accoutrer**, *v.r.* to dress absurdly, to rig oneself out.

accoutumance [akuty'mã:s], *n.f.* habit, custom, wont, usage.

accoutumé [akuty'me], *a.* ordinary, accustomed, habitual.

accoutumer [akuty'me], *v.t.* to accustom, to habituate, to inure.—*v.i.* (*only in compound tenses*) to use, to be wont. **s'accoutumer**, *v.r.* to be accustomed, to be used (*à*).

accouvage [aku'va:ʒ], *n.m.* hatching (*esp. by artificial means*), incubation.

accouver [aku've], *v.t.* to set (*a hen etc.*).—*v.i.* to sit, to hatch.

accréditation [akredita'sjɔ̃], *n.f.* accreditation, accrediting (*of an ambassador*).

accréditer [akredi'te], *v.t.* to give credit, standing *or* sanction to; to authorize; to accredit (*an ambassador etc.*); to confirm, to spread (*rumors etc.*). **s'accréditer**, *v.r.* to gain credit *or* reputation; to ingratiate oneself; to spread (*of rumors etc.*).

accréditeur [akredi'tœ:r], *n.m.* guarantor, surety.

accroc [a'kro], *n.m.* impediment, hitch; hindrance; rent, tear.

accrochage [akro'ʃa:ʒ], *n.m.* hanging, hooking, hitching; catching, retarding, stopping; grazing (*vehicles*).

accroche-cœur [akroʃ'kœ:r], *n.m. inv.* spit curl.

accrochement [akroʃ'mã], *n.m.* hooking, catching (*in something*).

accrocher [akro'ʃe], *v.t.* to hang upon a hook; to hook, to catch, to hitch, to catch and tear; to get hold of; to pick up (*a radio station*). **s'accrocher**, *v.r.* to catch in, to be caught *or* hooked (*par*); to lay hold of, to cling (*à*).

accroire [a'krwa:r], *v.t.* irr. (*used only in the infinitive after* **faire**) to believe.

accroissement [akrwas'mã], *n.m.* increase, growth, enlargement, extension.

accroître [a'krwa:tr], *v.t.* irr. (*conjug. like* CROÎTRE *except for p.p.* accru) to increase, to augment, to enlarge, to amplify. **s'accroître**, *v.r.* to increase, to grow.

accroupi [akru'pi], *a.* crouched, crouching, cowering, squatting.

accroupir (s') [sakru'pi:r], *v.r.* to sit down on the hams *or* heels, to squat, to crouch.

accroupissement [akrupis'mã], *n.m.* cowering, squatting, crouching.

accru [a'kry], *n.m.* (*Gard.*) sucker, scion.

accrue [a'kry], *n.f.* increase of land through the retreat of waters; encroachment of a forest on adjoining land.

accu [a'ky], *n.m. abbr.* [ACCUMULATEUR].

accueil [a'kœ:j], *n.m.* reception, welcome, greeting.

accueillir [akœ'ji:r], *v.t.* irr. (*conjug. like* CUEILLIR) to receive (*well or ill*); to receive graciously, to welcome.

acculer [aky'le], *v.t.* to drive into a corner; to bring to a standstill. **s'acculer**, *v.r.* to set one's back against something.

accumulateur [akymyla'tœ:r], *a.* (*fem.* **-trice**) storing, heaping up, hoarding up.—*n.m.* accumulator (*person or thing*); (*Elec.*) storage cell *or* battery.

accumulation [akymyla'sjɔ̃], *n.f.* accumulation; mass, pile.

accumuler [akymy'le], *v.t.* to accumulate, to pile up, to amass. **s'accumuler**, *v.r.* to accumulate, to increase.

accusable [aky'zabl], *a.* accusable, chargeable.

accusateur [akyza'tœ:r], *a.* (*fem.* **-trice**) accusing, accusatory.—*n.m.* (*fem.* **-trice**) accuser, denouncer.

accusatif [akyza'tif], *a.* (*fem.* **-tive**) and *n.m.* (*Gram.*) accusative (*case*); **à l'accusatif**, in the accusative.

accusation [akyza'sjɔ̃], *n.f.* accusation, indictment, charge; (*fig.*) prosecution; **mise en accusation**, arraignment.

accusatoire [akyza'twa:r], *a.* accusatory.

accusé [aky'ze], *n.m.* (*fem.* **-ée**) the accused, prisoner, defendant; **accusé de réception**, acknowledgment of a letter, receipt.

accuser [aky'ze], *v.t.* to impute, to charge with; to reproach, to blame; to indict, to impeach, to prosecute. **s'accuser**, *v.r.* to admit, to avow, to confess.

acéphale [ase'fal], *a.* acephalous, headless.

acérain [ase'rɛ̃], *a.* like *or* pertaining to steel, steely.

acerbe [a'sɛrb], *a.* sour, harsh, sharp, astringent; (*fig.*) bitter, acrimonious.

acerbité [asɛrbi'te], *n.f.* acerbity, harshness; (*fig.*) bitterness, severity.

acéré [ase're], *a.* steely, steeled; sharp, keen; (*fig.*) mordant, trenchant, acute.

acérer [ase're], *v.t.* (*conjug. like* CÉDER) to steel; to sharpen, to render biting, incisive *or* mordant.

acétate [ase'tat], *n.m.* (*Chem.*) acetate.

acéteux [ase'tø], *a.* (*fem.* **-euse**) acetous, sour, tasting like vinegar.

acétique [ase'tik], *a.* acetic.

acétone [ase'tɔn], *n.m.* acetone.

acétoselle [aseto'sɛl], *n.f.* wood-sorrel.

acétylène [aseti'lɛ:n], *n.m.* acetylene.

achalandage [aʃalã'da:ʒ], *n.m.* custom, customers; goodwill (*of a shop*).

achalandé [aʃalã'de], *a.* having plenty of custom; **boutique bien achalandée**, a well-frequented shop.

achalander [aʃalã'de], *v.t.* to get custom, to attract customers, to draw trade.

acharné [aʃar'ne], *a.* fleshed, fierce, tenacious, implacable; stubborn, obstinate, intense.

acharnement [aʃarna'mã], *n.m.* tenacity; rancor, animosity, fury; stubbornness, obstinacy, desperation.

5

acharner [aʃar'ne], *v.t.* to flesh; to set on; to excite, to madden; to embitter, to envenom. **s'acharner,** *v.r.* to be intent, bent *or* obstinately set upon; to set one's heart upon, to persist in; to be infuriated *or* implacable.

achat [a'ʃa], *n.m.* purchasing, buying; purchase; *faire des achats,* to go shopping; *pouvoir d'achat,* purchasing power.

acheminement [aʃmin'mã], *n.m.* progress, advance, conveying.

acheminer [aʃmi'ne], *v.t.* to send on (*towards a place* or *object*); to train (*a horse*). **s'acheminer,** *v.r.* to set out (*pour*), to make one's way towards.

achetable [aʃ'tabl], *a.* purchasable.

acheter [aʃ'te], *v.t.* (*conjug. like* AMENER) to buy, to purchase; (*fig.*) to bribe. **s'acheter,** *v.r.* to be bought; to be for sale, to be venal.

acheteur [aʃ'tœːr], *n.m.* (*fem.* **-euse**) buyer, purchaser.

achevage [aʃ'vaːʒ], *n.m.* completion, finishing; finish (*of a work of art*).

achevé [aʃ've], *a.* finished, accomplished, perfect, exquisite; absolute, downright, consummate, arrant.

achèvement [aʃɛv'mã], *n.m.* completion, conclusion.

achever [aʃ've], *v.t.* (*conjug. like* AMENER) to finish, to terminate; to put the finishing touch to; to complete, to achieve; to consummate, to perfect; (*fig.*) to do for completely, to ruin, to kill.

Achille [a'ʃil], *m.* Achilles.

achoppement [aʃɔp'mã], *n.m.* obstacle, impediment; unforeseen difficulty, embarrassment; *pierre d'achoppement,* stumbling block.

achopper [aʃɔ'pe], *v.i.* and **s'achopper,** *v.r.* to stumble, to knock against something; (*fig.*) to come to grief; to fail.

achromatopsie [akrɔmatɔp'si], *n.f.* achromatopsy, color blindness.

acide [a'sid], *a.* acid, sour, tart, sharp.—*n.m.* acid.

acidifier [asidi'fje], *v.t.* to acidify. **s'acidifier,** *v.r.* to become acidified.

acidité [asidi'te], *n.f.* acidity, sourness, sharpness, tartness.

acidule [asi'dyl], *a.* subacid, acidulous.

acidulé [asidy'le], *a.* acidulated; *bonbons acidulés,* acid drops, sour balls.

aciduler [asidy'le], *v.t.* to acidulate.

acier [a'sje], *n.m.* steel; *acier chromé,* chrome steel; *acier coulé* or *fondu,* cast steel; *acier doux,* mild steel; *acier inoxydable,* stainless steel.

aciération [asjera'sjõ], *n.f.* steeling, plating with steel.

aciérer [asje're], *v.t.* (*conjug. like* CÉDER) to convert into steel, to cover with steel; to acierate. **s'aciérer,** *v.r.* to steel oneself.

aciéreux [asje'rø], *a.* (*fem.* **-euse**) steely, like steel.

aciérie [asje'ri], *n.f.* steel factory, steelworks.

acné [ak'ne], *n.f.* (*Med.*) acne.

acolyte [akɔ'lit], *n.m.* (*Eccles.*) acolyte; (*fig.*) assistant, confederate, associate, accomplice.

acompte [a'kõːt], *n.m.* instalment, partial payment.

acon or **accon** [a'kõ], *n.m.* small lighter, punt.

aconier or **acconier** [akɔ'nje], *n.m.* lighterman.

aconit [akɔ'nit], *n.m.* aconite.

acoquinant [akɔki'nã], *a.* alluring, engaging, captivating.

acoquiner [akɔki'ne], *v.t.* to make fond, to allure, to bewitch, to captivate. **s'acoquiner,** *v.r.* (*fam.*) to be bewitched, to be greatly attached to.

Açores [a'sɔːr], **les,** *f.pl.* the Azores.

à-côté [akɔ'te], *n.m.* aside; (*pl.*) little extras.

à-coup [a'ku], *n.m.* jerk, jolt; sudden stop.

acousticien [akusti'sjɛ̃], *n.m.* (*fem.* **-enne**) acoustician.

acoustique [akus'tik], *a.* acoustic.—*n.f.* acoustics.

acquéreur [ake'rœːr], *n.m.* (*fem.* **-euse**) buyer, purchaser.

acquérir [ake'riːr], *v.t. irr.* to purchase, to buy, to get; to earn, to win, to gain; to acquire, to obtain. **s'acquérir,** *v.r.* to get *or* win for oneself; to be acquired, obtained *or* purchased.

acquiescement [akjɛs'mã], *n.m.* acquiescence, compliance, consent, willingness.

acquiescer [akjɛ'se], *v.i.* (*conjug. like* COMMENCER) to acquiesce, to agree, to assent, to yield, to comply.

acquis [a'ki], *a.* acquired, secured.—*n.m.* acquirements, attainments, experience.

acquisitif [akizi'tif], *a.* (*fem.* **-tive**) acquisitive.

acquisition [akizi'sjõ], *n.f.* acquisition, acquiring, attaining, acquirement, attainment; purchase, conquest.

acquisivité [akizivi'te], *n.f.* acquisitiveness.

acquit [a'ki], *n.m.* receipt, discharge, release, acquittance; (*Billiards*) break (*i.e. start*).

acquittement [akit'mã], *n.m.* payment, quittance; (*Law*) acquittal.

acquitter [aki'te], *v.t.* to pay; to discharge, to pay off (*a dependant*); to acquit. **s'acquitter,** *v.r.* to fulfil, to perform; to pay off one's debts, to be quits (*in gambling*); to acquit oneself (*well* or *ill*).

acre [akr], *n.f.* acre.

âcre [aːkr], *a.* sour, sharp, tart, acrid; (*fig.*) bitter, pungent, caustic.

âcrement [ɑːkrə'mã], *adv.* tartly, sourly.

âcreté [ɑːkrə'te], *n.f.* sourness, acridity, sharpness, tartness, acrimony.

acrimonie [akrimɔ'ni], *n.f.* bitterness, sharpness, keenness, acrimony.

acrimonieux [akrimɔ'njø], *a.* (*fem.* **-euse**) pungent, acrimonious, ill-natured, sharp.

acrobate [akrɔ'bat], *n.* acrobat, rope-dancer.

acrobatie [akrɔba'si], *n.f.* acrobatics; (*Av.*) stunt.

acrobatique [akrɔba'tik], *a.* acrobatic.

acrobatisme [akrɔba'tism], *n.m.* acrobatics.

acrocéphale [akrɔse'fal], *a.* having a pointed head, acrocephalic, acrocephalous.—*n.* a person with a pointed head.

acropole [akrɔ'pɔl], *n.f.* acropolis.

acrostiche [akrɔs'tiʃ], *a.* and *n.m.* acrostic.

acrotère [akrɔ'tɛːr], *n.m.* (*Arch.*) acroterium, ornamental summit (*of a pediment*).

acte [akt], *n.m.* action, deed; (*Law*) deed, indenture; instrument; document, charter; (*Theat.*) act; (*pl.*) records, public registers, rolls, transactions, proceedings; *acte de naissance,* birth certificate.

acteur [ak'tœːr], *n.m.* (*fem.* **-trice**) actor; actress; player.

administrer

actif [ak'tif], *a.* (*fem.* **-tive**) active, busy, energetic, assiduous; nimble, brisk, agile; (*Gram. etc.*) active.—*n.m.* (*Gram.*) active voice; assets, credit balance.

action [ak'sjɔ̃], *n.f.* action, operation, work; activity, motion; deed, feat, performance; fight, engagement, battle; (*Law*) action, law-suit; (*Theat.*) gesture; (*Lit.*) subject, action, plot; (*Comm.*) share, stock.

actionnaire [aksjɔ'nɛːr], *n.* shareholder.

actionnariat [aksjɔna'rja], *n.m.* shareholding; **actionnariat ouvrier**, industrial co-partnership.

actionner [aksjɔ'ne], *v.t.* to bring an action against, to sue at law; to bestir, to rouse up, to set going; to operate, to run, to drive. **s'actionner**, *v.r.* to bestir oneself.

activement [aktiv'mã], *adv.* actively, vigorously.

activer [akti've], *v.t.* to press, to accelerate, to forward, to expedite, to stir up (*a fire, people*).

activisme [akti'vism], *n.m.* (*Polit.*) militancy, activism.

activiste [akti'vist], *n.m.* activist.

activité [aktivi'te], *n.f.* activity, full swing; nimbleness, alacrity, promptitude, dispatch.

actrice [ak'tris], [ACTEUR].

actuaire [ak'tɥɛːr], *n.m.* actuary.

actualisation [aktɥaliza'sjɔ̃], *n.f.* actualization; realization.

actualiser [aktɥali'ze], *v.t.* to bring up to date. **s'actualiser**, *v.r.* to become real.

actualité [aktɥali'te], *n.f.* actuality; event of the moment, present interest; (*Cine.*) **les actualités**, the newsreel.

actuel [ak'tɥɛl], *a.* (*fem.* **-elle**) present, of the present time.

actuellement [aktɥɛl'mã], *adv.* now, at the present time.

acuité [akɥi'te], *n.f.* sharpness, acuteness, keenness.

acutangle [aky'tãːgl], **acutangulaire** [a kytãgy'lɛːr], *a.* acute-angled (*of triangles etc.*).

acutesse [aky'tɛs], *n.f.* acuteness, sharpness.

adage [a'daːʒ], *n.m.* adage, proverb, saying.

Adam [a'dã], *m.* Adam.

adamantin [adamã'tɛ̃], *a.* adamantine.

adaptable [adap'tabl], *a.* adaptable.

adaptateur [adapta'tœːr], *n.m.* adapter, converter.

adaptation [adapta'sjɔ̃], *n.f.* adaptation.

adapter [adap'te], *v.t.* to adapt, to adjust, to apply (*à*); to fit, to make suitable. **s'adapter**, *v.r.* to fit, to suit, to adapt oneself (*to*).

addition [adi'sjɔ̃], *n.f.* adding up, addition; an addition; bill, reckoning; check.

additionnel [adisjɔ'nɛl], *a.* (*fem.* **-elle**) additional.

additionner [adisjɔ'ne], *v.t.* to add up.

Adélaïde [adela'id], *f.* Adelaide.

Adèle [a'dɛl], *f.* Adela.

adénite [ade'nit], *n.f.* adenitis, inflammation of the glands.

adénoïde [adenɔ'id], *a.* adenoid; **végétations adénoïdes**, adenoids.

adent [a'dã], *n.m.* dovetail, tenon.

adenter [adã'te], *v.t.* to dovetail, to join with mortise and tenon.

adepte [a'dɛpt], *n.m.* adept, initiate, follower.

adéquat [ade'kwa], *a.* adequate; (*Phil.*) equal in content; appropriate.

adhérence [ade'rãːs], *n.f.* adhesion, adherence; (*fig.*) attachment.

adhérent [ade'rã], *a.* adherent.—*n.m.* (*fem.* **-e**) adherent, follower, partisan.

adhérer [ade're], *v.i.* (*conjug. like* CÉDER) to adhere, to cling; (*fig.*) to hold (*à*), to cleave (*to a sect etc.*).

adhésif [ade'zif], *a.* (*fem.* **-sive**) adhesive.—*n.m.* (*Phot.*) dry-mounting tissue.

adhésion [ade'zjɔ̃], *n.f.* adhesion, adherence, union; compliance; joining (*a party*).

adhésivité [adezivi'te], *n.f.* adhesiveness.

adieu [a'djø], *int.* adieu, good-bye, farewell. —*n.m.* (*pl.* **-eux**) farewell, parting, leave; **faire ses adieux à**, to take leave of, to say good-bye to.

adipeux [adi'pø], *a.* (*fem.* **-euse**) adipose, fat.

adiposité [adipozi'te], *n.f.* adipose *or* fatty condition.

adjacence [adʒa'sãːs], *n.f.* adjacency.

adjacent [adʒa'sã], *a.* adjacent, bordering upon, contiguous.

adjectif [adʒɛk'tif], *a.* (*fem.* **-tive**) (*Gram.*) adjectival.—*n.m.* adjective.

adjectivement [adʒɛktiv'mã], *adv.* adjectivally.

adjoindre [ad'ʒwɛ̃ːdr], *v.t. irr.* (*conjug. like* CRAINDRE) to adjoin, to associate, to add as an assistant. **s'adjoindre**, *v.r.* to join as a partner *or* associate; to take on.

adjoint [ad'ʒwɛ̃], *a.* adjunct, associate.—*n.m.* (*fem.* **-e**) associate, assistant, deputy; **adjoint au maire**, deputy mayor.

adjonction [adʒɔ̃k'sjɔ̃], *n.f.* adjunction.

adjudant [adʒy'dã], *n.m.* company sergeant-major; warrant officer; **adjudant-major**, adjutant.

adjudicataire [adʒydika'tɛːr], *a.* and *n.* contracting party; successful tenderer, highest bidder.

adjudicateur [adʒydika'tœːr], *n.m.* (*fem.* **-trice**) adjudicator, awarder; auctioneer.

adjudication [adʒydika'sjɔ̃], *n.f.* auction; knocking down; adjudication.

adjuger [adʒy'ʒe], *v.t.* (*conjug. like* MANGER) to adjudge, to adjudicate, to knock down (*to the highest bidder*); to award; **adjugé !** (*at auctions*) gone!

adjuration [adʒyra'sjɔ̃], *n.f.* adjuration, imprecation.

adjurer [adʒy're], *v.t.* to adjure, to conjure; to call upon, to beseech.

admettre [ad'mɛtr], *v.t. irr.* (*conjug. like* METTRE) to admit, to let in; to concede, to allow, to acknowledge.

administrateur [administra'tœːr], *n.m.* (*fem.* **-trice**) manager, director; administrator, administratrix, trustee (*of an estate*).

administratif [administra'tif], *a.* (*fem.* **-tive**) administrative.

administration [administra'sjɔ̃], *n.f.* administration, management, direction, government; (*collect.*) the management, the administration.

administré [adminis'tre], *n.m.* (*fem.* **-ée**) person under one's administration *or* jurisdiction.

administrer [adminis'tre], *v.t.* to manage, to govern, to direct; to administer, to dispense.

7

admirable

admirable [admi'rabl], *a.* admirable; wonderful.

admirablement [admirablə'mã], *adv.* admirably; wonderfully.

admirateur [admira'tœːr], *n.m.* (*fem.* **-trice**) admirer, praiser.

admiratif [admira'tif], *a.* (*fem.* **-tive**) admiring, wondering.

admiration [admira'sjõ], *n.f.* admiration.

admirer [admi're], *v.t.* to admire.

admissibilité [admisibili'te], *n.f.* admissibility.

admissible [admi'sibl], *a.* admittable, admissible.

admission [admi'sjõ], *n.f.* admission, admittance; *soupape d'admission*, inlet valve.

admonestation [admɔnɛsta'sjõ], *n.f.* admonishment, admonition.

admonester [admɔnɛs'te], *v.t.* to reprimand, to admonish.

admoniteur [admɔni'tœːr], *n.m.* (*fem.* **-trice**) admonisher.

admonitif [admɔni'tif], *a.* (*fem.* **-tive**) admonitory.

admonition [admɔni'sjõ], *n.f.* (*chiefly R.-C. Ch.*) admonition, advice, reprimand.

adolescence [adɔlɛ'sãːs], *n.f.* adolescence.

adolescent [adɔlɛ'sã], *a.* adolescent.—*n.m.* (*fem.* **-e**) adolescent, youth, teenager.

Adonis [adɔ'niːs], *n.m.* Adonis, beau.

adonné [adɔ'ne], *a.* given to, addicted, devoted. **s'adonner**, *v.r.* to give, devote *or* addict oneself (*à*).

adopté [adɔp'te], *a.* adopted *or* adoptive (*child*).

adopter [adɔp'te], *v.t.* to adopt; to embrace, to espouse; to pass, to carry (*a bill*).

adoptif [adɔp'tif], *a.* (*fem.* **-tive**) adoptive, by adoption.

adoption [adɔp'sjõ], *n.f.* adoption.

adorable [adɔ'rabl], *a.* adorable, charming, delightful, exquisite.

adorablement [adɔrablə'mã], *adv.* adorably, delightfully.

adorateur [adɔra'tœːr], *n.m.* (*fem.* **-trice**) adorer, worshipper.

adoration [adɔra'sjõ], *n.f.* adoration, worship; admiration, respect, reverence.

adorer [adɔ're], *v.t.* to adore, to worship.

adossé [adɔ'se], *a.* with one's back against.

adosser [adɔ'se], *v.t.* to set *or* lean with the back against; to put back to back. **s'adosser**, *v.r.* to lean one's back (*à*, *contre*).

adoucir [adu'siːr], *v.t.* to soften, to sweeten; to mitigate, to alleviate, to smooth. **s'adoucir**, *v.r.* to grow mild *or* soft; to get milder (*of weather*).

adoucissement [adusis'mã], *n.m.* softening, sweetening; assuaging, appeasing; ease, mitigation, alleviation; consolation.

adrénaline [adrena'lin], *n.f.* adrenalin.

adresse [a'drɛs], *n.f.* address; memorial, a document addressed to an assembly *or* person in authority; skill, dexterity, cleverness.

adresser [adrɛ'se], *v.t.* to direct, to address; to turn, to direct (*one's steps etc.*). **s'adresser**, *v.r.* to be directed; to speak, to address oneself, to make application, to appeal (*à*); *s'adresser ici*, apply within.

Adriatique [adria'tik], **l'**, *f.* the Adriatic.

adroit [a'drwa], *a.* ingenious, clever, skilful; artful.

adroitement [adrwat'mã], *adv.* skilfully, artfully, cleverly.

adulateur [adyla'tœːr], *a.* (*fem.* **-trice**) flattering, adulatory.—*n.m.* (*fem.* **-trice**) adulator, flatterer, sycophant.

adulatif [adyla'tif], *a.* (*fem.* **-tive**) flattering, adulatory.

adulation [adyla'sjõ], *n.*,. adulation, flattery, sycophancy.

aduler [ady'le], *v.t.* to flatter, to fawn upon.

adulte [a'dylt], *a.* adult, grown-up.—*n.* adult.

adultère [adyl'tɛːr], *a.* adulterous; *femme adultère*, adulteress.—*n.m.* adultery.—*n.* adulterer, ɐdulteress.

adultérer [adylte're], *v.t.* (*conjug. like* CÉDER) (*Pharm.*) to adulterate; (*Law*) to falsify (*money*); (*fig.*) to corrupt, to pervert, to falsify.

adultérin [adylte'rɛ̃], *a.* adulterine.

advenir [advə'niːr], *v.i. irr.* (*used only in inf. and 3rd pers.*) to occur, to happen, to befall.

adventice [advã'tis], *a.* adventitious.

adventif [advã'tif], *a.* (*fem.* **-tive**) (*Bot.*) adventitious, casual.

adverbe [ad'vɛrb], *n.m.* adverb.

adverbial [advɛr'bjal], *a.* adverbial.

adverbialement [advɛrbjal'mã], *adv.* adverbially.

adversaire [advɛr'sɛːr], *n.* adversary, opponent.

adverse [ad'vɛrs], *a.* adverse, opposite, contrary; calamitous.

adversité [advɛrsi'te], *n.f.* adversity, misfortune.

aérage [ae'raːʒ], *n.m.* ventilation, airing.

aérateur [aera'tœːr], *n.m.* ventilator.

aération [aera'sjõ], *n.f.* ventilation, airing.

aéré [ae're], *p.p.* ventilated.—*a.* airy.

aérer [ae're], *v.t.* (*conjug. like* CÉDER) to ventilate, to air, to renew the air of; (*Chem.*) to aerate.

aérien [ae'rjɛ̃], *a.* (*fem.* **-enne**) aerial; living *or* occurring in the air, celestial; (*fig.*) light, airy; *base aérienne*, air base; *fil aérien*, overhead wire; *ligne aérienne*, airline; *pont aérien*, airlift; *raid aérien*, air raid.

aérifère [aeri'fɛːr], *a.* air-conducting.

aérification [aerifika'sjõ], *n.f.* gasification.

aérifier [aeri'fje], *v.t.* to gasify.

aéro-club [aero'klœb], *n.m.* (*pl.* **aéro-clubs**) flying club.

aérodrome [aero'droːm], *n.m.* aerodrome, airfield.

aérodynamique [aerodina'mik], *a.* aerodynamic, streamlined.—*n.f.* aerodynamics.

aérogare [aero'gaːr], *n.f.* air terminal.

aérographe [aero'graf], *n.m.* aerograph.

aérographie [aerogra'fi], *n.f.* aerography.

aérolithe [aero'lit], *n.m.* aerolite.

aérolithique [aeroli'tik], *a.* aerolitic.

aérologie [aerolɔ'ʒi], *n.f.* aerology.

aéromètre [aero'mɛtr], *n.m.* aerometer, air-poise.

aéronaute [aero'noːt], *n.* aeronaut.

aéronautique [aerono'tik], *a.* aeronautic.—*n.f.* aeronautics, aerial navigation.

aéronef [aero'nɛf], *n.m.* airship.

aéroplane [aero'plan], *n.m.* airplane.

aéroport [aero'pɔːr], *n.m.* airport.

aéroporté [aeropɔr'te], *a.* airborne (*troops*).

8

aérosphère [aerɔ'sfɛːr], *n.f.* the mass of air surrounding the globe, atmosphere.

aérostat [aerɔs'ta], *n.m.* aerostat, air-balloon.

aérostation [aerɔsta'sjɔ̃], *n.f.* aerostation, air navigation.

aérostatique [aerɔsta'tik], *a.* aerostatic.— *n.f.* aerostatics.

aérostier [aerɔs'tje], *n.m.* aeronaut, one directing an aerostat.

aérothérapie [aerɔtera'pi], *n.f.* aerotherapy.

affabilité [afabili'te], *n.f.* affability, kindness, courtesy.

affable [a'fabl], *a.* affable, courteous.

affadir [afa'diːr], *v.t.* to make unsavory or insipid; (*fig.*) to make flat or dull. **s'affadir**, *v.r.* to become insipid.

affadissement [afadis'mɑ̃], *n.m.* insipidity, nausea, sickliness.

affaiblir [afɛ'bliːr], *v.t.* to enfeeble, to weaken; to lessen. **s'affaiblir**, *v.r.* to grow weak; to abate.

affaiblissement [afɛblis'mɑ̃], *n.m.* weakening; allaying, abatement.

affaire [a'fɛːr], *n.f.* affair, business, concern, matter; trouble, scrape; lawsuit; transaction, bargain; *c'est mon affaire*, it is my own concern; *mêlez-vous de vos affaires!*, mind your own business!; *être dans les affaires*, to be in business; *homme d'affaires*, business man, legal adviser.

affairé [afɛ're], *a.* busy.

affairement [afɛr'mɑ̃], *n.m.* hurry, bustle, ado.

affaissement [afɛs'mɑ̃], *n.m.* depression, subsidence, giving way, collapse.

affaisser [afɛ'se], *v.t.* to cause to sink, to weigh down, to press down; to bear down, to overwhelm. **s'affaisser**, *v.r.* to sink, to subside; to give way; to be bent down (*by age*); to collapse.

affamé [afa'me], *a.* famished, hungry, starving; greedy, craving; *être affamé de*, to be greedy or eager for.

affamer [afa'me], *v.t.* to starve, to famish, to deprive of food.

affectation [afɛkta'sjɔ̃], *n.f.* appropriation, destination or attribution (*to a certain object*); simulation, show, pretence, affectation; preference; distinction; (*Mil.*) *recevoir une affectation*, to be posted.

affecté [afɛk'te], *a.* affected, assumed, simulated, put on; attributed, destined (*to a certain object*); (*Path.*) affected (*by a disease etc.*); (*Mil.*) posted to.

affecter [afɛk'te], *v.t.* to affect, to make frequent or habitual use of, to have a predilection for; to assume (*a certain shape etc.*); to feign, to pretend; to set apart, to earmark, to destine, to appropriate (*to a certain object*); to move, to touch, to impress emotionally. **s'affecter**, *v.r.* to be affected.

affection [afɛk'sjɔ̃], *n.f.* affection, love, attachment; (*Med.*) affection, ailment.

affectionné [afɛksjɔ'ne], *a.* affectionate, loving, attached, loved, liked.

affectionner [afɛksjɔ'ne], *v.t.* to love, to be fond of, to like.

affectueusement [afɛktɥøz'mɑ̃], *adv.* affectionately, fondly.

affectueux [afɛk'tɥø], *a.* (*fem.* **-euse**) affectionate, tender, warm-hearted.

afférent [afe'rɑ̃], *a.* reverting; relating to; assignable to; accruing to.

affermage [afɛr'maːʒ], *n.m.* farming, renting.

affermataire [afɛrma'tɛːr], *n.m.* tenant farmer.

affermateur [afɛrma'tœːr], *n.m.* (*fem.* **-trice**) lessor.

affermer [afɛr'me], *v.t.* to farm or let out by lease; to take a lease of, to rent.

affermir [afɛr'miːr], *v.t.* to strengthen, to make firm; to confirm, to establish, to consolidate. **s'affermir**, *v.r.* to become strong, firm, or fast; to become established.

affermissement [afɛrmis'mɑ̃], *n.m.* strengthening, consolidation, establishment; support, prop, stay.

affété [afe'te], *a.* affected, prim, finical; canting, mincing, pretty-pretty.

afféterie [afe'tri], *n.f.* affectation, mannerisms, primness.

affichage [afi'ʃaːʒ], *n.m.* bill-posting; placarding.

affiche [a'fiʃ], *n.f.* placard, bill, poster; *homme affiche*, sandwichman; *affiche électorale*, election poster.

afficher [afi'ʃe], *v.t.* to post up; to publish, to divulge, to proclaim; to make a show of, to parade; *défense d'afficher*, post no bills; billposting prohibited. **s'afficher**, *v.r.* to set up (*for*); to attract public notice.

afficheur [afi'ʃœːr], *n.m.* bill-poster.

affidavit [afida'vit], *n.m.* affidavit.

affidé [afi'de], *a.* trusty, trustworthy; in the know.—*n.m.* (*fem.* **-ée**) confederate, confidential agent; spy.

affilage [afi'laːʒ], **affilement** [afil'mɑ̃], *n.m.* whetting, sharpening, setting.

affilé [afi'le], *a.* sharp; nimble, glib (*of the tongue*).

affilée (d') [dafi'le], *adv. phr.* at a stretch; *trois heures d'affilée*, three hours at a stretch.

affiler [afi'le], *v.t.* to sharpen, to set, to put an edge on.

affiliation [afilja'sjɔ̃], *n.f.* affiliation (*to a society, company, plot etc.*).

affilié [afi'lje], *a.* affiliated, admitted a member or associate.—*n.m.* (*fem.* **-ée**) affiliated member, associate, confederate.

affilier [afi'lje], *v.t.* to admit, to affiliate, to receive. **s'affilier**, *v.r.* to become admitted or affiliated, to join.

affiloir [afi'lwaːr], *n.m.* hone, oilstone, steel, strop.

affinage [afi'naːʒ], **affinement** [afin'mɑ̃], *n.m.* refining, fining (*of metals, sugar etc.*); heckling (*of hemp*), maturing (*of a wine*), ripening (*of a cheese*).

affiner [afi'ne], *v.t.* to fine, to refine. **s'affiner**, *v.r.* to be refined, to be fined; to become finer, wittier etc. (*of the mind*).

affinerie [afin'ri], *n.f.* metal refinery.

affineur [afi'nœːr], *n.m.* metal refiner.

affinité [afini'te], *n.f.* affinity, relationship.

affinoir [afi'nwaːr], *n.m.* carding brush.

affiquet [afi'kɛ], *n.m.* knitting sheath; (*pl.*) gewgaws, trinkets.

affirmatif [afirma'tif], *a.* (*fem.* **-tive**) affirmative, asserting.—*n.f.* (**-tive**) affirmative statement, answer etc.; asseveration; *répondre par l'affirmative*, to answer in the affirmative.

affirmation [afirma'sjɔ̃], *n.f.* affirmation, assertion.

affirmativement [afirmativ′mɑ̃], *adv.* affirmatively.

affirmer [afir′me], *v.t.* to affirm, to assert, to vouch, to declare; to confirm by *or* on oath. **s'affirmer,** *v.r.* to grow stronger, to assert oneself.

affixe [a′fiks], *n.m.* affix.

affleurement [aflœr′mɑ̃], *n.m.* levelling, making flush; (*Mining*) outcrop.

affleurer [aflœ′re], *v.t.* to make even, to level; (*Arch.*) to make flush.—*v.i.* to be level, to be flush (*with*); (*Mining*) to crop out.

affliction [aflik′sjɔ̃], *n.f.* affliction, trouble, distress; trial, vexation.

affligé [afli′ʒe], *a.* afflicted, grieved, distressed.

affliger [afli′ʒe], *v.t.* (*conjug. like* MANGER) to afflict, to trouble, to distress, to grieve, to vex, to torment; to mortify, to chasten. **s'affliger,** *v.r.* to grieve, to be afflicted, troubled *or* cast down; to take something to heart.

afflouage [aflu′a:ʒ], *n.m.* (*Naut.*) refloating (*of a ship*).

afflouer [aflu′e], *v.t.* to refloat.

affluence [afly′ɑ̃:s], *n.f.* affluence, abundance; concourse, crowd; *heures d'affluence*, rush hour.

affluent [afly′ɑ̃], *a.* falling into, running into (*of rivers*).—*n.m.* tributary.

affluer [afly′e], *v.i.* to fall, run *or* flow into (*as a tributary*) (*dans*); to abound; to come in great quantity (*à, vers*).

affolant [afɔ′lɑ̃], *a.* distracting.

affolé [afɔ′le], *a.* distracted, panic-stricken; (*Mech.*) disconnected, defective.

affolement [afɔl′mɑ̃], *n.m.* distraction, panic.

affoler [afɔ′le], *v.t.* to distract; to infatuate; to bewitch; to madden, to drive crazy. **s'affoler,** *v.r.* to fall into a panic, to stampede.

afforestage [afɔrɛs′ta:ʒ], *n.m.* right of cutting firewood, estovers.

afforestation [afɔrɛsta′sjɔ̃], *n.f.* afforestation.

affouillable [afu′jabl], *a.* subject *or* liable to undermining.

affouillement [afuj′mɑ̃], *n.m.* undermining, washing away.

affouiller [afu′je], *v.t.* to undermine, to wash away.

affouragement *or* **affourragement** [afuraʒ′mɑ̃], *n.m.* foraging, foddering.

affourager *or* **affourrager** [afura′ʒe], *v.t.* (*conjug. like* MANGER) to fodder, to give fodder to.

affourcher [afur′ʃe], *v.t.* to seat astride; (*Carp.*) to join a tongue and groove.

affranchi [afrɑ̃′ʃi], *a.* set free, freed.—*n.m.* (*fem.* -e) freedman; freedwoman.

affranchir [afrɑ̃′ʃi:r], *v.t.* to free, to set free, to enfranchise; to absolve, to exempt; to frank (*a letter*), to stamp. **s'affranchir,** *v.r.* to free oneself; to rid oneself of (*de*), to shake off, to break away from.

affranchissement [afrɑ̃ʃis′mɑ̃], *n.m.* enfranchisement; exemption; discharge; deliverance; payment of postage (*of a letter*).

affranchisseur [afrɑ̃ʃi′sœ:r], *n.m.* emancipator, liberator.

affres [a:fr], *n.f.* (*used only in pl.*) dread, horror, agony; *les affres de la mort*, the pangs of death, death throes.

affrètement [afrɛt′mɑ̃], *n.m.* chartering, freighting.

affréter [afre′te], *v.t.* (*conjug. like* CÉDER) (*Naut.*) to charter, to freight (*a vessel*).

affréteur [afre′tœ:r], *n.m.* charterer, freighter.

affreusement [afrøz′mɑ̃], *adv.* frightfully, horribly, dreadfully.

affreux [a′frø], *a.* (*fem.* -euse) frightful, hideous, shocking, horrible, ghastly.

affriander [afriɑ̃′de], *v.t.* to allure, to entice to tempt.

affricher [afri′ʃe], *v.t.* to leave fallow.

affrioler [afriɔ′le], *v.t.* to allure, to entice.

affront [a′frɔ̃], *n.m.* affront, insult; disgrace.

affronter [afrɔ̃′te], *v.t.* to face, to confront, to brave; to attack boldly.

affruiter [afrɥi′te], *v.t.* to plant with fruit-trees.—*v.i.* to bear *or* supply fruit. **s'affruiter,** *v.r.* to come into fruit.

affublement [afyblə′mɑ̃], *n.m.* grotesque make-up *or* rig-out (*of dress*).

affubler [afy′ble], *v.t.* to dress up, to rig out (*grotesquely*). **s'affubler,** *v.r.* to dress up ridiculously.

affût [a′fy], *n.m.* stand *or* place for lying in wait, watch; gun carriage; *être à l'affût*, to lie in wait.

affûtage [afy′ta:ʒ], *n.m.* setting *or* sharpening (*of tools*).

affûter [afy′te], *v.t.* to grind, to sharpen.

affûteur [afy′tœ:r], *n.m.* sharpener, setter, grinder; stalker.—*n.f.* (-euse) sharpening machine.

afghan [af′gɑ̃], *a.* Afghan.—*n.m.* (**Afghan,** *fem.* -ane) Afghan (*person*).

Afghanistan [afganis′tɑ̃], l', *m.* Afghanistan.

afin [a′fɛ̃], *conj.* **afin de** (*with inf.*) to, in order to, so as to; **afin que** (*with subj.*) to, in order that, so that.

africain [afri′kɛ̃], *a.* African.—*n.m.* (**Africain** *fem.* -aine) African (*person*).

Afrique [a′frik], l', *f.* Africa.

agaçant [aga′sɑ̃], *a.* irritating, worrying; provoking, provocative; alluring, enticing.

agace *or* **agasse** [a′gas], *n.f.* magpie.

agacement [agas′mɑ̃], *n.m.* irritation, setting on edge.

agacer [aga′se], *v.t.* (*conjug. like* COMMENCER) to worry, to irritate, to set on edge; to excite, to provoke; to entice, to allure.

agacerie [aga′sri], *n.f.* allurement, coquetry, enticement.

agaillardir [agajar′di:r], *v.t.* to cheer up.

agate [a′gat], *n.f.* agate.

Agathe [a′gat], *f.* Agatha.

âge [ɑ:ʒ], *n.m.* age, years; period, epoch, era, (*pl.*) the ages, time; *Moyen Âge*, Middle Ages; *d'un certain âge*, elderly; *entre deux âges*, of uncertain age.

âgé [ɑ′ʒe], *a.* aged (*so many years*); old, elderly; *âgé de vingt ans*, twenty years old.

agence [a′ʒɑ̃:s], *n.f.* agency, bureau, branch office.

agencement [aʒɑ̃s′mɑ̃], *n.m.* arrangement, grouping, ordering; (*Arch.*) composition, layout.

agencer [aʒɑ̃′se], *v.t.* (*conjug. like* COMMENCER) to arrange, to dispose.

agenda [aʒɛ̃′da], *n.m.* notebook; diary; engagement book.

agenouiller (s') [saʒnu'je], *v.r.* to kneel down, to fall on one's knees; (*fig.*) to bow down (*devant*).

agenouilloir [aʒnuj'waːr], *n.m.* hassock.

agent [a'ʒɑ̃], *n.m.* agent; deputy; middleman; broker; **agent de change**, stockbroker; **agent électoral**, canvasser; **agent de liaison**, liaison officer; **agent de police**, policeman.

agglomération [aglɔmerɑ'sjɔ̃], *n.f.* agglomeration, built-up area.

aggloméré [aglɔme're], *n.m.* compressed fuel, briquette.

agglomérer [aglɔme're], *v.t.* (*conjug. like* CÉDER) to agglomerate, to mass together, to pile up, to assemble.

agglutinant [aglyti'nɑ̃], *a.* adhesive.

agglutiner [aglyti'ne], *v.t.* to bind, to cake. **s'agglutiner**, *v.r.* to unite, to cohere; to heal over (*wound*).

aggravant [agra'vɑ̃], *a.* (*Law*) aggravating, making more heinous.

aggravation [agrava'sjɔ̃], *n.f.* aggravation, additional penalty; **aggravation de peine**, increase of punishment.

aggraver [agra've], *v.t.* to aggravate, to make worse. **s'aggraver**, *v.r.* to worsen (*illness, situation*).

agile [a'ʒil], *a.* agile, nimble.

agilement [aʒil'mɑ̃], *adv.* nimbly, with agility.

agilité [aʒili'te], *n.f.* agility, nimbleness, lightness.

agio [a'ʒjo], *n.m.* stock-jobbing, speculation.

agiotage [aʒjɔ'taːʒ], *n.m.* stockjobbing; **faire l'agiotage**, to deal in stocks.

agioter [aʒjɔ'te], *v.i.* to speculate, to job.

agioteur [aʒjɔ'tœːr], *n.m.* speculator, jobber.

agir [a'ʒiːr], *v.i.* to act, to do; to operate; to have an effect (*sur*); to negotiate, to manage a business; to sue, to prosecute, to proceed (*contre*); to behave. **s'agir**, *v.r.* (*impers.*) to be in question, to be the matter; **de quoi s'agit-il?** what is it about? **il s'agit de votre vie**, your life is at stake.

agissant [aʒi'sɑ̃], *a.* active, busy; efficacious, effective.

agitateur [aʒita'tœːr], *n.m.* (*fem* **-trice**) agitator.—*n.m.* stirring rod.

agitation [aʒita'sjɔ̃], *n.f.* agitation; disturbance, tossing, shaking, tumult; trouble, emotion, uneasiness, restlessness.

agité [aʒi'te], *a.* restless (*sleep*); rough (*sea*); fretful (*child*).

agiter [aʒi'te], *v.t.* to agitate, to put in motion, to shake, to stir; to disturb, to trouble; to excite, to perturb; to debate, to discuss. **s'agiter**, *v.r.* to be agitated or in movement; to get rough; to be restless, disturbed or uneasy; to toss, to wave, to flutter; to be debated.

agneau [a'ɲo], *n.m.* (*fem.* **-elle**, *pl.* **-eaux**) lamb.

agnelage [aɲə'laːʒ], **agnèlement** [aɲɛl'mɑ̃], *n.m.* lambing; lambing time.

agneler [aɲə'le], *v.i.* (*conjug. like* AMENER) to lamb, to yean.

Agnès [a'nɛːs], *f.* Agnes.

agnès [a'nɛːs], *n.f.* raw young girl.

agnosticisme [agnɔsti'sism], *n.m.* agnosticism.

agnosticiste [agnɔsti'sist], **agnostique** [agnɔs'tik], *a.* and *n.* agnostic.

agonie [agɔ'ni], *n.f.* agony, death pangs;

(*fig.*) trouble, anguish, torture; **être à l'agonie**, to be at the point of death.

agonir [agɔ'niːr], *v.t.* to insult grossly.

agonisant [agɔni'zɑ̃], *a.* dying, in a dying condition.—*n.m.* (*fem.* **-e**) dying person.

agoniser [agɔni'ze], *v.i.* to be at the point of death.

agoraphobie [agɔrafɔ'bi], *n.f.* agoraphobia.

agrafe [a'graf], *n.f.* fastener, clasp, clip, staple (*for papers*); **agrafe et porte**, hook and eye.

agrafer [agra'fe], *v.t.* to hook, to clasp, to fasten with a clasp; to staple.

agrafeuse [agra'føːz], *n.f.* stapler.

agraire [a'grɛːr], *a.* agrarian.

agrandir [agrɑ̃'diːr], *v.t.* to make greater, to enlarge, to augment; to widen; to exaggerate; to promote, to advance; (*fig.*) to elevate. **s'agrandir**, *v.r.* to become greater or larger.

agrandissement [agrɑ̃dis'mɑ̃], *n.m.* enlargement, increase; aggrandizement, elevation.

agrandisseur [agrɑ̃di'sœːr], *n.m.* (*Phot.*) enlarger.

agréable [agre'abl], *a.* agreeable, pleasing, pleasant, acceptable.

agréablement [agreablə'mɑ̃], *adv.* agreeably, pleasantly.

agréé [agre'e], *n.m.* solicitor; attorney.

agréer [agre'e], *v.t.* to accept, to approve, to allow, to receive kindly.—*v.i.* to please, to be agreeable; **veuillez agréer mes salutations**, yours truly.

agrégat [agre'ga], *n.m.* aggregate, composite mass.

agrégation [agregɑ'sjɔ̃], *n.f.* (*Phys.*) aggregation, aggregate; (=**concours d'agrégation**) competitive examination for admission on the teaching staff of State secondary schools or of faculties of law, medicine, pharmacy.

agrégé [agre'ʒe], *a.* and *n.m.* **professeur agrégé**, one who has passed the **agrégation**.

agréger [agre'ʒe], *v.t.* (*conjug. like* ASSIÉGER) to admit into a society, to incorporate; (*Phys.*) to aggregate.

agrément [agre'mɑ̃], *n.m.* consent, approbation; pleasure, charm, gracefulness; amenity; (*pl.*) ornaments, embellishments, amenities (*of life*); **arts d'agrément**, accomplishments.

agrémenter [agremɑ̃'te], *v.t.* to set off, to ornament, to adorn.

agrès [a'grɛ], *n.m.* (*used only in pl.*) rigging (*of a ship etc.*); apparatus, gear (*of a gymnasium etc.*).

agresseur [agre'sœːr], *n.m.* aggressor.

agressif [agre'sif], *a.* (*fem.* **-ive**) aggressive.

agression [agre'sjɔ̃], *n.f.* aggression.

agressivité [agresivi'te], *n.f.* aggressiveness.

agreste [a'grɛst], *a.* rustic; countrified (*manners*).

agrestement [agrɛstə'mɑ̃], *adv.* rustically.

agricole [agri'kɔl], *a.* agricultural.

agriculteur [agrikyl'tœːr], *n.m.* agriculturist, husbandman, farmer.

agriculture [agrikyl'tyːr], *n.f.* agriculture, husbandry, tillage.

agriffer [agri'fe], *v.t.* to claw; to clutch, to grip. **s'agriffer**, *v.r.* to cling (*at*).

agrion [agri'ɔ̃], *n.m.* dragonfly.

agripper [agri'pe], *v.t.* to grip, to snatch. **s'agripper**, *v.r.* to cling (*to*).

agronome [agrɔ'nɔm], *n.m.* agriculturist.
aguerri [agɛ'ri], *a.* inured to war; disciplined.
aguerrir [agɛ'riːr], *v.t.* to train *or* inure to the hardships of war; to accustom, to inure (*to hardships etc.*). **s'aguerrir**, *v.r.* to inure *or* accustom oneself (*to hardships, abstinence etc.*), to be inured.
aguerrissement [agɛris'mã], *n.m.* inuring to war, hardening.
aguets [a'gɛ], *n.m.* (*used only in pl.*) watch, lookout; **être aux aguets**, to be on the watch.
aheurter (s') [saœr'te], *v.r.* to persist (*in*).
ahuri [ay'ri], *a.* bewildered, perplexed, flurried.
ahurir [ay'riːr], *v.t.* to bewilder, to flurry, to stupefy.
ahurissant [ayri'sã], *a.* bewildering.
ahurissement [ayris'mã], *n.m.* bewilderment, confusion, perplexity.
aï [a'i], *n.m.* (*Zool.*) sloth.
aide [ɛːd], *n.f.* help, relief, assistance; succor, support, protection, rescue; relief (*of the poor etc.*); helper, female assistant, help; **à l'aide de**, with the help of.—*n.m.* a male assistant; **aide de camp** (*pl.* **aides de camp**), aide-de-camp.
aide-mémoire [edme'mwaːr], *n.m.* *inv.* précis; memorandum.
aider [ɛ'de], *v.t.* to aid, to help, to relieve, to assist, to succor; to abet; to conduce to, to further.—*v.i.* to be helpful, to be of assistance (*à*). **s'aider**, *v.r.* to make use (*de*); to avail oneself.
aïe! [aj], *int.* oh! oh dear!
aïeul [a'jœl], *n.m.* (*fem.* **aïeule**, *pl.* **aïeuls**, **aïeules**) grandfather, grandsire; grandmother, grandam; (*pl.* **aïeux**) forebears, ancestors.
aigle [ɛːgl], *n.* eagle; (*fig.*) clever *or* brilliant person, genius.—*n.m.* reading desk, lectern (*with effigy of an eagle*).
aiglefin [ɛglə'fɛ̃], **aigrefin** (1) [ɛgrə'fɛ̃], *n.m.* haddock.
aiglon [ɛ'glɔ̃], *n.m.* (*fem.* **-onne**) eaglet.
aigre [ɛgr], *a.* sour, tart; (*fig.*) harsh, bitter, shrill.—*n.m.* sourness, mustiness.
aigre-doux [ɛgrə'du], *a.* (*fem.* **-douce**) sourish, bitter-sweet.
aigrefin (2) [ɛgrə'fɛ̃], *n.m.* sharper, swindler; adventurer; [AIGLEFIN].
aigrelet [ɛgrə'lɛ], *a.* (*fem.* **-ette**) sourish.
aigrement [ɛgrə'mã], *adv.* acrimoniously, sourly, bitterly; roughly, harshly.
aigret [ɛ'grɛ], *a.* (*fem.* **-ette** (1)) sourish.
aigrette (2) [ɛ'grɛt], *n.f.* aigrette, tuft, cluster *or* plume (*of feathers, diamonds etc.*); horn (*of an owl*); crest (*of a peacock*); egret, tufted heron.
aigreur [ɛ'grœːr], *n.f.* sourness, sharpness, tartness; (*fig.*) harshness, bitterness, surliness, animosity, spite.
aigrir [ɛ'griːr], *v.t.* to make sour *or* sharp, to sour; (*fig.*) to irritate, to embitter, to make worse, to incense, to make ill-humoured. **s'aigrir**, *v.r.* to turn sour; (*fig.*) to grow worse, to be exasperated, to be irritated.
aigrissement [ɛgris'mã], *n.m.* souring, embittering.
aigu [ɛ'gy], *a.* (*fem.* **aiguë**) pointed, sharp, keen, acute; (*fig.*) shrill, piercing; **accent aigu**, acute accent.

aiguë [AIGU].
aigue-marine [ɛgma'rin], *n.f.* (*pl.* **aigues-marines**) aquamarine.
aiguière [ɛ'gjɛːr], *n.f.* ewer.
aiguillage [egɥi'jaːʒ], *n.m.* (*Rail.*) shunting, switch.
aiguillat [egɥi'ja], *n.m.* dogfish.
aiguille [ɛ'gɥiːj], *n.f.* needle; index, pointer, hand (*of a dial, watch etc.*); spire (*steeple*); point (*of an obelisk, peak etc.*); rock pinnacle *or* needle-shaped peak; **trou d'une aiguille**, eye of a needle; (*pl., Rail.*) switch.
aiguiller [egɥi'je], *v.t.* (*Rail.*) to shunt.
aiguillette [egɥi'jɛt], *n.f.* aglet, point; (*Mil.*) ornamental shoulder-knot.
aiguilleur [egɥi'jœːr], *n.m.* (*Rail.*) switchman, shunter.
aiguillier [egɥi'je], *n.m.* (*fem.* **-ière**) needlemaker.
aiguillon [egɥi'jɔ̃], *n.m.* goad, sting; (*fig.*) spur, incentive; (*Bot.*) prickle.
aiguillonner [egɥijɔ'ne], *v.t.* to goad, to prick; (*fig.*) to incite, to spur on; to stimulate.
aiguisage [egi'zaːʒ], **aiguisement** [egiz'mã], *n.m.* whetting, sharpening.
aiguisé [egi'ze], *a.* whetted, sharpened.
aiguiser [egi'ze], *v.t.* to whet, to sharpen, to set an edge on; to point; (*fig.*) to make keen, acid, piquant etc.; to excite, to stimulate.
aiguiseur [egi'zœːr], *n.m.* knife-grinder, sharpener.
aiguisoir [egi'zwaːr], *n.m.* sharpening-tool, whetstone.
ail [a:j], *n.m.* (*pl.* (*Cook.*) **aulx** [o:], (*Bot.*) **ails**) garlic.
aile [ɛl], *n.f.* wing; brim (*of a hat*); flipper (*of a penguin*); blade (*of a propeller*); vane, sail (*of a windmill*); flank *or* wing (*of an army, building etc.*); fender, mudguard (*of a car*).
ailé [ɛ'le], *a.* winged.
aileron [ɛl'rɔ̃], *n.m.* pinion (*of a bird*); aileron, balancing flap (*of an aircraft*); fin (*of some fish*).
ailette [ɛ'lɛt], *n.f.* small wing; vane (*of a torpedo etc.*); (*Motor.*) rib, fin, flange.
ailier [ɛ'lje], *n.m.* (*Ftb.*) wing forward, wing three-quarter.
ailleurs [a'jœːr], *adv.* elsewhere, somewhere else; **d'ailleurs**, besides, moreover, in other respects.
aimable [ɛ'mabl], *a.* kind, amiable, obliging.
aimablement [ɛmablə'mã], *adv.* amiably, kindly.
aimant [ɛ'mã], *a.* loving, affectionate.—*n.m.* magnet; (*fig.*) attractiveness.
aimantation [ɛmãta'sjɔ̃], *n.f.* magnetization.
aimanter [ɛmã'te], *v.t.* to magnetize.
Aimée [ɛ'me], *f.* Amy.
aimer [ɛ'me], *v.t.* to love, to be fond of, to be in love with; to like; **aimer mieux**, to prefer. **s'aimer**, *v.r.* to love oneself, to be vain; to love each other.
aine (1) [ɛːn], *n.f.* groin.
aine (2) [ɛːn], *n.f.* herring-stick; leather band on organ bellows.
aîné [ɛ'ne], *a.* (*fem.* **-ée**) eldest, elder, senior.—*n.m.* (*fem.* **-ée**) eldest son *or* daughter.
aînesse [ɛ'nɛs], *n.f.* seniority, priority by age, primogeniture; **droit d'aînesse**, birthright.

ainsi [ɛ̃'si], *adv.* thus, so, in this *or* that manner; **ainsi de suite,** and so on and so forth; **ainsi soit-il,** so be it, amen; *pour ainsi dire,* so to speak, as it were; **ainsi que,** in the same way (*as*).

air (1) [ɛːr], *n.m.* air; wind; (*Chem. etc.*) gas; (*pl.*) atmosphere; *chambre à air,* inner tube; *courant d'air,* draught; *en plein air,* in the open air.

air (2) [ɛːr], *n.m.* mien, look, expression, air, manner, appearance.

air (3) [ɛːr], *n.m.* (*Mus.*) tune.

airain [ɛ'rɛ̃], *n.m.* bronze; (*Poet.*) cannon, bell.

aire [ɛːr], *n.f.* area, space; threshing floor; eyrie; *aire d'atterrissage,* (*Av.*) landing area, apron.

airelle [ɛ'rɛl], *n.f.* whortleberry, bilberry.

ais [ɛ], *n.m.* board, plank; stave (*of a barrel*).

aisance [ɛ'zɑ̃ːs], *n.f.* ease, facility; easiness, affluence; competency; (*Mach.*) play; freedom; the comforts *or* conveniences of life; *cabinet* (or *lieu*) *d'aisances,* public convenience.

aisceau [AISSETTE].

aise [ɛːz], *a.* glad, well pleased; *je suis bien aise de vous voir,* I am very glad to see you.—*n.f.* ease, comfort, convenience; (*pl.*) comforts, comfortable circumstances; *à l'aise,* at ease, comfortable; *être à son aise,* to be well off.

aisé [ɛ'ze], *a.* easy; convenient, comfortable; in easy circumstances.

aisément [ɛze'mɑ̃], *adv.* easily, readily, freely; comfortably.

aisseau [ɛ'so], *n.m.* (*pl.* **-eaux**), **aissante** [ɛ'sɑ̃ːt], *n.f.* (*Carp.*) shingle, wooden tile.

aisselier [ɛsə'lje], *n.m.* (*Carp.*) tie beam, brace, strut.

aisselle [ɛ'sɛl], *n.f.* armpit; (*Bot.*) axil.

aissette [ɛ'sɛt], *n.f.*, **aisceau** [ɛ'so] (*pl.* **-eaux**), *n.m.* adze (*of a cooper*); hooked hammer (*of a tiler*).

Aix-la-Chapelle [ɛkslaʃa'pɛl], *f.* Aachen.

ajointer [aʒwɛ̃'te], *v.t.* to join on to, to fit.

ajonc [a'ʒɔ̃], *n.m.* furze, gorse.

ajournement [aʒurnə'mɑ̃], *n.m.* adjournment, postponement; (*Law*) summons.

ajourner [aʒur'ne], *v.t.* to adjourn; to defer; (*Law*) to summon (*for a specified day*).

ajouter [aʒu'te], *v.t.* to add, to join, to subjoin, to interpolate. **s'ajouter,** *v.r.* to be joined, to attach oneself.

ajusté [aʒys'te], *a.* close-fitting (*clothes*).

ajustement [aʒystə'mɑ̃], *n.m.* adjustment, arranging, fitting, settlement; laying out; attire, apparel.

ajuster [aʒys'te], *v.t.* to adjust, to regulate, to square, to fit, to adapt (*one thing to another*); to take aim at; to set in order; (*Mus.*) to tune; to bedeck; to settle *or* arrange (*a dispute*). **s'ajuster,** *v.r.* to accommodate oneself, to be adapted; to dress, to deck oneself out.

ajusteur [aʒys'tœːr], *n.m.* fitter; weigher (*at the mint*).

alacrité [alakri'te], *n.f.* alacrity, cheerful briskness.

Aladin [ala'dɛ̃], *m.* Aladdin.

Alain [a'lɛ̃], *m.* Alan.

alaise [a'lɛːz], *n.f.* rubber sheet for pram *or* cot.

alambic [alɑ̃'bik], *n.m.* alembic, still.

alambiquer [alɑ̃bi'ke], *v.t.* to distil, to refine.

alangui [alɑ̃'gi], *a.* languid, downcast.

alanguir [alɑ̃'giːr], *v.t.* to enfeeble, to make languid. **s'alanguir,** *v.r.* to languish, to flag, to become languid.

alanguissement [alɑ̃gis'mɑ̃], *n.m.* languor.

alarmant [alar'mɑ̃], *a.* alarming, startling.

alarme [a'larm], *n.f.* alarm, affright, sudden fear, uneasiness.

alarmer [alar'me], *v.t.* to alarm; to startle, to render anxious *or* frightened. **s'alarmer,** *v.r.* to take alarm, to be alarmed.

alarmiste [alar'mist], *a.* and *n.* alarmist.

albanais [alba'nɛ], *a.* Albanian.—*n.m.* Albanian (*language*); (**Albanais,** *fem.* **-aise**) Albanian (*person*).

Albanie [alba'ni:], **l'**, *f.* Albania.

albâtre [al'bɑːtr], *n.m.* alabaster; (*fig.*) whiteness.

albatros [alba'trɔs], *n.m.* albatross.

albinisme [albi'nism], *n.m.* albinism.

albinos [albi'nos], *a.* and *n.* albino.

album [al'bom], *n.m.* album, scrapbook, sketch book.

albumine [alby'min], *n.f.* albumen.

alcaïque [alka'ik], *a.* alcaic (*verse*).

alcali [alka'li], *n.m.* alkali.

alcalin [alka'lɛ̃], *a.* alkaline.

alcalinité [alkalini'te], *n.f.* alkalinity.

alcaliser [alkali'ze], **alcaliniser** [alkalini'ze], *v.t.* to alkalify.

alchimie [alʃi'mi], *n.f.* alchemy.

alchimique [alʃi'mik], *a.* alchemical.

alchimiste [alʃi'mist], *n.m.* alchemist.

alcool [al'kɔl], *n.m.* alcohol; spirit(s); *alcool à brûler,* **alcool dénaturé,** methylated spirit.

alcoolique [alkɔ'lik], *a.* alcoholic.

alcoolisme [alkɔ'lism], *n.m.* alcoholism.

Alcoran [alkɔ'rɑ̃], [CORAN].

alcôve [al'koːv], *n.f.* alcove, recess.

alcyon [al'sjɔ̃], *n.m.* halcyon; (*Orn.*) kingfisher.

alcyonien [alsjɔ'njɛ̃], *a.* (*fem.* **-enne**) halcyon, peaceful.

aléa [ale'a], *n.m.* chance, hazard.

aléatoire [alea'twaːr], *a.* hazardous, uncertain.

alène [a'lɛn], *n.f.* awl.

alentour or **à l'entour** [alɑ̃'tuːr], *adv.* about, around, round about.

alentours [alɑ̃'tuːr], *n.m.* (*used only in pl.*) environs, neighborhood.

Aléoutiennes [aleu'sjɛn], **les**, *f.pl.* the Aleutian Islands.

alerte [a'lɛrt], *a.* alert, vigilant; active, lively, agile.—*n.f.* alarm, warning; *alerte aérienne,* air-raid warning.

alerter [alɛr'te], *v.t.* to give the alarm to, to warn.

alésage [ale'zaːʒ], *n.m.* boring, drilling; bore (*of cylinder*).

aléser [ale'ze], *v.t.* (*conjug. like* CÉDER) to smooth *or* enlarge the bore of (*a tube, gun etc*); *aléser un canon,* to bore a cannon.

aléseuse [ale'zøːz], *n.f.* boring machine.

alésoir [ale'zwaːr], *n.m.* borer, boring tool.

alester [alɛs'te], **alestir** [alɛs'tiːr], *v.t.* (*Naut.*) to lighten *or* disencumber (*a vessel*).

alésure [ale'zyːr], *n.f.* metal turnings *or* filings.

alevin [al'vɛ̃], *n.m.* fry, young fish.

aleviner [alvi'ne], *v.t.* to stock with fry.

alevinier [alvi'nje], *n.m.* breeding pond.
Alexandre [alɛk'sɑːdr], *m.* Alexander.
Alexandrie [alɛksɑ'dri], *f.* Alexandria.
alexandrin [alɛksɑ'drɛ̃], *a.* and *n.m.* (*Pros.*) Alexandrine.
alezan [al'zɑ̃], *a.* and *n.m.* chestnut (horse).
alèze or **alèse** [a'lɛːz], [ALAISE].
alfa [al'fa], *n.m.* esparto grass.
algarade [alga'rad], *n.f.* insult, affront; rating.
algèbre [al'ʒɛbr], *n.f.* algebra.
algébrique [alʒe'brik], *a.* algebraical.
algébriquement [alʒebrik'mɑ̃], *adv.* algebraically.
Alger [al'ʒe], *m.* Algiers.
Algérie [alʒe'ri], **l'**, *f.* Algeria.
algérien [alʒe'rjɛ̃], *a.* (*fem.* **-enne**) Algerian.—*n.m.* (**Algérien**, *fem.* **-enne**) Algerian (*person*).
algie [al'ʒi:], *n.f.* ache.
algue [alg], *n.f.* seaweed, alga.
alibi [ali'bi], *n.m.* (*Law*) alibi.
aliboron [alibɔ'rɔ̃], *n.m.* jackass, stupid *or* self-conceited fellow.
aliénable [alje'nabl], *a.* alienable, transferable.
aliénation [aljena'sjɔ̃], *n.f.* (*Law*) conveyance of property to another; (*fig.*) alienation, mental derangement; estrangement, aversion.
aliéné [alje'ne], *a.* lunatic, mad.—*n.m.* (*fem.* **-ée**) lunatic.
aliéner [alje'ne], *v.t.* (*conjug. like* CÉDER) to alienate, to give away (*property*), to transfer, to make over; to estrange, to make hostile; to derange (*the mind*). **s'aliéner**, *v.r.* to become estranged (*from*).
aliéniste [alje'nist], *n.m.* alienist.
alignée [ali'ne], *n.f.* line, row.
alignement [aliɲə'mɑ̃], *n.m.* alignment; laying out in line; (*Mil.*) dressing; (*Print.*) ranging.
aligner [ali'ne], *v.t.* to align, to lay out in line; to put in a straight line; (*Mil.*) to dress; (*Print.*) to range. **s'aligner**, *v.r.* (*Mil.*) to dress.
aliment [ali'mɑ̃], *n.m.* aliment, food, nourishment, nutriment; (*Law, pl.*) alimony, maintenance.
alimentaire [alimɑ̃'tɛːr], *a.* alimental, alimentary; (*Mech.*) **pompe alimentaire**, feed pump, donkey engine.
alimentateur [alimɑ̃ta'tœːr], *a.* (*fem.* **-trice**) alimentary.
alimentation [alimɑ̃ta'sjɔ̃], *n.f.* alimentation; nourishment, feeding; **rayon d'alimentation**, food department.
alimenter [alimɑ̃'te], *v.t.* to feed, to nourish; to maintain; to supply, to provision; to fuel, to keep up.
alimenteux [alimɑ̃'tø], *a.* (*fem.* **-euse**) nutritive.
alinéa [aline'a], *n.m.* indented line; new paragraph.
alisé [ALIZÉ].
aliter [ali'te], *v.t.* to confine to bed; **être alité**, to be bedridden. **s'aliter**, *v.r.* to take to one's bed.
alizé or **alisé** [ali'ze], *a.* soft (*said of the trade winds*); **vents alizés**, trade winds.—*n.m.* trade wind.
alkali etc. [ALCALI].
Alkoran [alkɔ'rɑ̃], [CORAN].

Allah [a'la], *m.* Allah.
allaitement [alɛt'mɑ̃], *n.m.* lactation, nursing, suckling; **allaitement artificiel**, bottle feeding.
allaiter [alɛ'te], *v.t.* to suckle, to nurse.
alléchant [ale'ʃɑ̃], *a.* alluring, seductive.
allèchement [alɛʃ'mɑ̃], *n.m.* allurement, enticement, seduction, attraction.
allécher [ale'ʃe], *v.t.* (*conjug. like* CÉDER) to allure, to entice, to attract.
allée [a'le], *n.f.* passage, drive, alley, avenue, walk; (*pl.*) goings.
allégation [alega'sjɔ̃], *n.f.* allegation, assertion.
allège [a'lɛːʒ], *n.f.* lighter, hopper; (*Arch.*) window basement, sill of window.
allégeance [ale'ʒɑ̃:s], *n.f.* alleviation, relief; allegiance.
allégement [aleʒ'mɑ̃], *n.m.* alleviation, relief; reduction.
alléger [ale'ʒe], *v.t.* (*conjug. like* ASSIÉGER) to ease, to unburden, to lighten; to unload (*a boat*); to alleviate, to relieve, to assuage (*pain* or *grief*).
allégorie [alego'ri], *n.f.* allegory.
allégorique [alego'rik], *a.* allegorical.
allégoriquement [alegorik'mɑ̃], *adv.* allegorically.
allégoriser [alegori'ze], *v.t.* to allegorize.
allégoriste [alego'rist], *n.m.* allegorist.
allègre [al'lɛgr], *a.* lively, nimble, sprightly; jolly, cheerful.
allègrement [allɛgrə'mɑ̃], *adv.* briskly; joyfully, merrily, joyously.
allégresse [alle'grɛs], *n.f.* gaiety, joy, mirth, cheerfulness; sprightliness.
alléguer [alle'ge], *v.t.* (*conjug. like* CÉDER) to allege, to advance, to urge; (*Law*) to quote, to adduce, to cite, to plead.
alléluia [allely'ja], *n.m.* and *int.* hallelujah.
Allemagne [al'maɲ], **l'**, *f.* Germany.
allemand [al'mɑ̃], *a.* German.—*n.m.* German (*language*), (**Allemand**, *fem.* **-ande**) German (*person*).
aller [a'le], *v.i. irr.* (*with aux.* ÊTRE) to go, to go on, to proceed, to progress (*well, ill etc.*); to be (*in good* or *ill health*); to act (*in a certain way*); to suit, to fit (*well* or *ill*); to be going to; **aller au pas**, to go at a walking pace; **aller et venir**, to go up and down; **je ne ferai qu'aller et venir**, I won't be a minute; **cela va tout seul**, it is plain sailing; **cet enfant ira loin**, this child will go far; **comment allez-vous?** how are you? **je vais bien**, I am well; (*fam.*) **ça va!** all right! **cet habit vous va mal**, this coat does not fit you; **allons!** come on! **allons donc!** surely not! **cela va sans dire**, it stands to reason; **il y va de sa vie**, his life is at stake; **se laisser aller**, to yield, to give way, to abandon oneself to a thing. **s'en aller**, *v.r.* to go away, to run away; to vanish, to disappear; to die, to wear out; **va-t'en! allez-vous-en!** go away! be off with you!—*n.m.* going, course, run; outward voyage, trip, journey; **billet d'aller et retour**, return ticket.
allergie [alɛr'ʒi], *n.f.* allergy.
allergique [alɛr'ʒik], *a.* allergic.
alliage [a'lja:ʒ], *n.m.* alloy, mixture; (*fig.*) impure mixture *or* combination.

alliance [a'ljã:s], *n.f.* alliance; marriage; union, league, coalition, confederacy; compact, covenant; mixture, blending; wedding ring.

allié [a'lje], *a.* allied; related (*by marriage*); akin, kindred.—*n.m.* (*fem.* **-ée**) ally; connection (*by marriage*).

allier [a'lje], *v.t.* to mix; to combine; to join, to unite, to ally, to marry; to reconcile; to match. **s'allier**, *v.r.* to be incorporated *or* mixed; to become allied, to join forces (*avec*); to combine (*of metals*).

alligator [aliga'tɔːr], *n.m.* alligator.

allitération [alitera'sjɔ̃], *n.f.* alliteration.

allo! [a'lo], *int.* (*Teleph.*) hello!

allocataire [alɔka'tɛːr], *n.* recipient of an allowance.

allocation [alɔka'sjɔ̃], *n.f.* allocation, allowance; *allocation de chômage*, unemployment benefit; *allocations familiales*, family allowances.

allocution [alɔky'sjɔ̃], *n.f.* allocution, short address, speech.

allonge [a'lɔ̃:ʒ], *n.f.* leaf (*of a table*); flyleaf, addendum; rider (*of a document*); reach (*in boxing*); *allonge de boucher*, meat hook.

allongé [alɔ̃'ʒe], *a.* lengthened, elongated, out-stretched; downcast, long (*of face*).

allongement [alɔ̃ʒ'mã], *n.m.* lengthening, elongation, protraction.

allonger [alɔ̃'ʒe], *v.t.* (*conjug. like* MANGER) to lengthen, to elongate, to eke out; to stretch; to drag out, to protract. **s'allonger**, *v.r.* to stretch out, to grow longer; to stretch, to lie down at full length.

allouer [a'lwe], *v.t.* to allow, to grant, to accord; to allocate.

alluchon [aly'ʃɔ̃], *n.m.* cog, tooth (*of a wheel*).

allumage [aly'ma:ʒ], *n.m.* lighting, kindling; ignition; *un raté d'allumage*, misfire; *mettre l'allumage*, to switch on; *couper l'allumage*, to switch off.

allumé [aly'me], *a.* lighted, ignited; (*colloq.*) excited; drunk, lit-up.

allume-feu [alym'fø], *n.m. inv.* firewood, firelighter, kindling.

allume-gaz [alym'ga:z], *n.m. inv.* gas lighter.

allumer [aly'me], *v.t.* to light; to kindle, to set on fire; (*fig.*) to inflame, to incite, to stir up. **s'allumer**, *v.r.* to light, to take *or* catch fire; to blaze, to sparkle, to glare; to flare up, to break out.

allumette [aly'mɛt], *n.f.* match.

allumeur [aly'mœ:r], *n.m.* (*fem.* **-euse**) lighter.

allure [a'ly:r], *n.f.* carriage, gait, pace, way of walking; demeanor; aspect, look; speed; (*pl.*) ways (*of a person*); *à toute allure*, at full speed.

allusion [aly'zjɔ̃], *n.f.* allusion, hint, innuendo.

alluvial [aly'vjal], *a.* (*m. pl.* **-aux**) alluvial.

alluvion [aly'vjɔ̃], *n.f.* alluvium.

almanach [alma'na], *n.m.* almanac, calendar.

aloès [alɔ'ɛːs], *n.m.* aloe; aloes.

aloi [a'lwa], *n.m.* the statutory degree of purity of gold and silver; (*fig.*) standard (*good* or *bad*), quality, kind (*of persons etc.*).

alors [a'lɔːr], *adv.* then, that time; in that case; *d'alors*, of that time; *alors que*, while, whereas; *jusqu'alors*, up to then, till that moment; *alors même que*, even though.

alose [a'lo:z], *n.f.* shad.

alouette [a'lwɛt], *n.f.* (*Orn.*) lark.

alourdir [alur'di:r], *v.t.* to make heavy, dull *or* stupid. **s'alourdir**, *v.r.* to grow heavy *or* dull.

alourdissant [alurdi'sã], *a.* oppressive, burdensome.

alourdissement [alurdis'mã], *n.m.* heaviness, dullness.

aloyau [alwa'jo], *n.m.* (*pl.* **-aux**) sirloin.

alpaca [alpa'ka], **alpaga** [alpa'ga], *n.m.* alpaca.

alpenstock [alpɛn'stɔk], *n.m.* alpenstock.

Alpes [alp], **les**, *f.pl.* the Alps.

alpestre [al'pɛstr], *a.* Alpine (*scenery, flora*).

alpha [al'fa], *n.m.* alpha; (*fig.*) beginning.

alphabet [alfa'bɛ], *n.m.* alphabet.

alphabétique [alfabe'tik], *a.* alphabetical.

alphabétiquement [alfabetik'mã], *adv.* alphabetically.

alpin [al'pɛ̃], *a.* Alpine (*club etc.*).

alpinisme [alpi'nism], *n.m.* mountaineering.

alpiniste [alpi'nist], *n.m.* Alpinist, mountaineer.

Alsace [al'zas], **l'**, *f.* Alsace.

alsacien [alza'sjɛ̃], *a.* (*fem.* **-enne**) Alsatian. —*n.m.* (**Alsacien**, *fem.* **-enne**) inhabitant of Alsace.

altérable [alte'rabl], *a.* alterable, corruptible, adulterable.

altérant [alte'rã], *a.* causing thirst.

altération [altera'sjɔ̃], *n.f.* deterioration; falsification, adulteration, debasing (*of money etc.*); weakening, impairing.

altercation [altɛrka'sjɔ̃], *n.f.* altercation, wrangle, dispute, quarrel.

altérer [alte're], *v.t.* (*conjug. like* CÉDER) to alter for the worse; to impair, to adulterate, to corrupt, to pervert, to debase, to falsify; to disturb, to trouble, to upset; to make thirsty. **s'altérer**, *v.r.* to be impaired, to degenerate.

alternance [altɛr'nã:s], *n.f.* alternation, rotation.

alternant [altɛr'nã], *a.* alternating, rotating (*as crops*).

alternat [altɛr'na], *n.m.* rotation (*of crops etc*).

alternatif [altɛrna'tif], *a.* (*fem.* **-tive**) alternate, alternating, alternative.—*n.f.* (**-tive**) alternation; alternative, choice, option (*between two possible actions*).

alternativement [altɛrnativ'mã], *adv.* alternately, by turns.

alterne [al'tɛrn], *a.* (*Geom.*) alternate (*of angles*); (*Bot.*) alternate.

alterner [altɛr'ne], *v.t.* to grow (*crops*) in rotation.—*v.i.* to alternate, to succeed each other alternately.

Altesse [al'tɛs], *n.f.* Highness.

altier [al'tje], *a.* (*fem.* **-ière**) haughty, proud, arrogant, lordly, lofty.

altimètre [alti'mɛtr], *n.m.* altimeter.

altitude [alti'tyd], *n.f.* altitude.

alto [al'to], *n.m.* alto; tenor violin; tenor saxhorn.

altruisme [altry'ism], *n.m.* altruism.

altruiste [altry'ist], *a.* altruistic.—*n.* altruist.

alumine [aly'min], *n.f.* alumina, oxide of aluminum.

aluminer [alymi′ne], *v.t.* to aluminate, to aluminize.

aluminium [alymi′njɔm], *n.m.* aluminum.

alun [a′lœ̃], *n.m.* alum.

alunage [aly′na:ʒ], *n.m.* (*Dyeing*) steeping in alum; (*Phot.*) hardening (*negatives etc.*) in an alum bath.

aluner [aly′ne], *v.t.* (*Dyeing*) to steep in alum water; (*Phot.*) to harden in an alum bath.

alunière [aly′njɛ:r], *n.f.* alum pit *or* mine, alum-works.

alunir [aly′ni:r], *v.i.* to land on the moon.

alvéole [alve′ɔl], *n.m.* alveolus, cell (*in a honey-comb*); socket (*of a tooth*).

amabilité [amabili′te], *n.f.* amiability, affability, kindness.

amadou [ama′du], *n.m.* amadou, (German) tinder; touchwood.

amadouer [ama′dwe], *v.t.* to coax, to wheedle, to cajole.

amaigrir [amɛ′gri:r], *v.t.* to make lean, meager *or* thin, to emaciate; to reduce, to lessen (*in bulk etc.*); to impoverish; to exhaust (*soil etc.*).—*v.i.* to fall away, to grow lean *or* thin. **s'amaigrir**, *v.r.* to grow thin, to fall away.

amaigrissant [amɛgri′sɑ̃], *a.* causing emaciation; *régime amaigrissant*, slimming diet.

amaigrissement [amɛgris′mɑ̃], *n.m.* emaciation, wasting away.

amalgamation [amalgama′sjɔ̃], *n.f.* amalgamation.

amalgame [amal′gam], *n.m.* amalgam; (*fig.*) medley, heterogeneous mixture.

amalgamer [amalga′me], *v.t.* to amalgamate, to blend, to combine. **s'amalgamer**, *v.r.* to amalgamate, to blend, to combine.

amande [a′mɑ̃:d], *n.f.* almond; kernel; *amandes lissées*, sugar-plums.

amandier [amɑ̃′dje], *n.m.* almond tree.

amant [a′mɑ̃], *n.m.* (*fem.* **-e**) lover, suitor; sweetheart, mistress; gallant, paramour; passionate admirer.

amarante [ama′rɑ̃:t], *n.f.* amaranth.

amareilleur *or* **amareyeur** [amarɛ′jœ:r], *n.m.* worker on an oyster bed.

amarinage [amari′na:ʒ], *n.m.* (*Naut.*) manning (*a prize*).

amariner [amari′ne], *v.t.* to man (*a prize*); to inure (*a crew etc.*) to sea. **s'amariner**, *v.r.* to become used to the sea.

amarrage [ama′ra:ʒ], *n.m.* (*Naut.*) mooring; anchorage; lashing.

amarre [a′ma:r], *n.f.* (*Naut.*) cable, rope, hawser.

amarrer [ama′re], *v.t.* to moor, to belay, to make fast.

amaryllis [amari′lis], *n.f.* amaryllis.

amas [a′mɑ], *n.m.* mass, heap, pile, accumulation.

amasser [amɑ′se], *v.t.* to accumulate, to heap up, to amass; to hoard; to collect, to get together. **s'amasser**, *v.r.* to gather, to get together, to accumulate, to be collected, to crowd, to assemble.

amassette [amɑ′sɛt], *n.f.* small palette knife.

amasseur [amɑ′sœ:r], *n.m.* (*fem.* **-euse**) hoarder.

amateur [ama′tœ:r], *n.m.* amateur; devotee; connoisseur.

amazone [ama′zo:n], *n.f.* Amazon, female warrior; horse-woman; riding habit; *habit d'amazone*, riding habit; *monter en amazone*, to ride side-saddle.

ambages [ɑ̃′ba:ʒ], *n.f.* (*pl.*) circumlocution; *sans ambages*, straight out.

ambassade [ɑ̃ba′sad], *n.f.* embassy, ambassador's staff.

ambassadeur [ɑ̃basa′dœ:r], *n.m.* ambassador; (*fig.*) envoy, messenger.

ambassadrice [ɑ̃basa′dris], *n.f.* ambassadress.

ambiance [ɑ̃′bjɑ̃:s], *n.f.* surroundings, environment; atmosphere.

ambiant [ɑ̃′bjɑ̃], *a.* ambient, surrounding.

ambidextre [ɑ̃bi′dɛkstr], *a.* ambidextrous.— *n.* ambidexter.

ambigu [ɑ̃bi′gy], *a.* (*fem.* **-guë**) ambiguous, equivocal.—*n.m.* heterogeneous mixture, medley.

ambiguïté [ɑ̃bigɥi′te], *n.f.* ambiguity.

ambigument [ɑ̃bigy′mɑ̃], *adv.* ambiguously.

ambitieusement [ɑ̃bisjøz′mɑ̃], *adv.* ambitiously.

ambitieux [ɑ̃bi′sjø], *a.* (*fem.* **-euse**) ambitious.—*n.m.* (*-euse*) ambitious person.

ambition [ɑ̃bi′sjɔ̃], *n.f.* ambition.

ambitionner [ɑ̃bisjɔ′ne], *v.t.* to desire earnestly; to be ambitious of, to aspire to.

ambivalence [ɑ̃biva′lɑ̃:s], *n.f.* ambivalence.

ambivalent [ɑ̃biva′lɑ̃], *a.* ambivalent.

amble [ɑ̃:bl], *n.m.* amble.

ambler [ɑ̃′ble], *v.i.* to amble.

ambleur [ɑ̃′blœ:r], *a.* (*fem.* **-euse**) ambling.

amblyope [ɑ̃′bljɔp], *a.* amblyopic, weak-sighted.—*n.* weak-sighted person.

ambre [ɑ̃:br], *n.m.* amber; *ambre gris*, ambergris.

ambré [ɑ̃′bre], *a.* amber-colored.

ambrer [ɑ̃′bre], *v.t.* to perfume with amber.

ambrette [ɑ̃′brɛt], *n.f.* amber seed; musk seed.

ambroisie [ɑ̃brwa′zi], *n.f.* ambrosia.

ambulance [ɑ̃by′lɑ̃:s], *n.f.* ambulance; field hospital; peripatetic clerkship; *chirurgien d'ambulance*, field surgeon.

ambulancier [ɑ̃bylɑ̃′sje], *n.m.* (*fem.* **-ière**) ambulance man, stretcher-bearer, nurse.

ambulant [ɑ̃by′lɑ̃], *a.* ambulant, ambulatory, itinerant, peripatetic; travelling (*of a railway post office*); strolling (*players*).

ambulatoire [ɑ̃byla′twa:r], *a.* ambulatory; (*Law*) movable.

âme (1) [ɑ:m], *n.f.* soul, spirit; sentiment, sensibility; (*fig.*) inhabitant, person (*on a lost ship etc.*); core, pith, heart (*of a thing etc.*); *rendre l'âme*, to give up the ghost.

âme (2) [ɑ:m], *n.f.* sounding board (*of a violin etc.*); bore (*of gun*).

amélioration [ameljɔra′sjɔ̃], *n.f.* amelioration, improvement; (*pl.*) repairs, decorations (*of a house etc.*).

améliorer [ameljɔ′re], *v.t.* to ameliorate, to improve, to better. **s'améliorer**, *v.r.* to get better, to mend, to improve.

amen [a′mɛn], *int.* and *n.m.* amen.

aménagement [amenaʒ′mɑ̃], *n.m.* arrangement; disposition (*of a house etc.*); management (*of a forest*).

aménager [amena'ʒe], *v.t.* (*conjug. like* MANGER) to dispose, to arrange, to lay out; to regulate the felling of (*a wood* or *forest*).

amendable [amã'dabl], *a.* improvable, mendable.

amende [a'mã:d], *n.f.* fine, penalty, forfeit, compensation, reparation; *faire amende honorable*, to make a full apology; *mettre* or *condamner à l'amende*, to fine.

amendement [amãd'mã], *n.m.* amendment; improvement; manuring (*of land*).

amender [amã'de], *v.t.* to amend, to better; to manure (*land*). **s'amender**, *v.r.* to mend, to grow better.

amène [a'mɛ:n], *a.* agreeable, pleasant (*site*).

amener [am'ne], *v.t.* (*see Verb Tables*) to lead (*hither*); to bring; to induce, prevail upon; to introduce; to bring about; to occasion, to lead to; (*Naut.*) to lower, to strike (*colors, sails etc.*); *mandat d'amener*, warrant.

aménité [ameni'te], *n.f.* amenity, pleasantness, affability; grace, urbanity.

amenuiser [amənɥi'ze], *v.t.* to make thinner *or* smaller. **s'amenuiser**, *v.r.* to grow thinner *or* smaller.

amer (1) [a'mɛ:r], *a.* (*fem.* **amère**) bitter, harsh, painful, grievous; biting, galling.—*n.m.* something bitter; gall; bitterness; (*pl.*) bitters.

amer (2) [a'mɛ:r], *n.m.* (*Naut.*) any landmark *or* leading mark.

amèrement [amɛr'mã], *adv.* bitterly, grievously.

américain [ameri'kɛ̃], *a.* American.—*n.m.* (**Américain**, *fem.* **-aine**) American (*person*).

américanisme [amerika'nism], *n.m.* Americanism.

Amérique [ame'rik], l', *f.* America.

amérir *or* **amerrir** [ame'ri:r], *v.i.* (*Av.*) to alight on the water.

amerrissage [ameri'sa:ʒ], *n.m.* alighting (*on the water*).

amertume [amɛr'tym], *n.f.* bitterness, grief; gall, venom.

améthyste [ame'tist], *n.f.* amethyst.

ameublement [amœblə'mã], *n.m.* furniture, suite of furniture.

ameublir [amœ'bli:r], *v.t.* (*Agric.*) to make (*soil*) more broken up *or* lighter.

ameublissement [amœblis'mã], *n.m.* (*Agric.*) loosening, mellowing.

ameulonner [amølɔ'ne], *v.t.* to stack (*hay, corn etc.*).

ameuter [amø'te], *v.t.* to train dogs as a pack; (*fig.*) to stir up, to rouse, to excite.

ami [a'mi], *n.m.* (*fem.* **amie**) friend; well-wisher, partisan; lover; *chambre d'ami*, spare room.—*a.* friendly; sympathetic, favorable, kindly-disposed; kind, propitious.

amiable [a'mjabl], *a.* friendly, courteous; amicable, conciliatory; *vente à l'amiable*, sale by private contract.

amiablement [amjablə'mã], *adv.* amicably.

amiante [a'mjã:t], *n.m.* asbestos.

amibe [a'mib], *n.f.* amoeba.

amical [ami'kal], *a.* (*m. pl.* **-aux**) amicable, friendly

amicalement [amikal'mã], *adv.* amicably, in a friendly manner.

amidon [ami'dõ], *n.m.* starch.

amidonner [amidɔ'ne], *v.t.* to starch.

amincir [amɛ̃'si:r], *v.t.* to make thinner. **s'amincir**, *v.r.* to become thinner.

amincissement [amɛ̃sis'mã], *n.m.* thinning.

amiral [ami'ral], *n.m.* (*pl.* **-aux**) admiral; *contre-amiral*, rear admiral; *grand amiral*, high admiral; *vice-amiral*, vice admiral; *vaisseau amiral*, flagship.

Amirauté [amiro'te], **Îles de l'**, *f.* Admiralty Islands.

amirauté [amiro'te], *n.f.* admiralship; admiralty.

amitié [ami'tje], *n.f.* friendship, affection; favor, kindness; (*pl.*) kind regards, compliments; *mes amitiés à tout le monde*, love to all; *par amitié*, out of friendship.

ammoniac [amɔ'njak], *a.* (*fem.* **-iaque**) ammoniac; *sel ammoniac*, sal ammoniac. —*n.f.* (**-iaque**) ammonia.

ammonite [amɔ'nit], *n.f.* ammonite.

amnésie [amne'zi], *n.f.* amnesia.

amnistie [amnis'ti], *n.f.* amnesty, pardon.

amnistier [amnis'tje], *v.t.* to pardon by amnesty.

amoindrir [amwɛ̃'dri:r], *v.t.* to lessen, to decrease, to diminish. **s'amoindrir**, *v.r.* to grow less.

amoindrissement [amwɛ̃dris'mã], *n.m.* lessening, decrease.

amollir [amɔ'li:r], *v.t.* to soften; (*fig.*) to mollify. **s'amollir**, *v.r.* to soften, to grow soft; to grow effeminate *or* weak.

amollissant [amɔli'sã], *a.* softening; enervating.

amollissement [amɔlis'mã], *n.m.* softening, enervation, effeminacy.

amonceler [amõs'le], *v.t.* (*conjug. like* APPELER) to heap up, to lay in a heap; (*fig.*) to accumulate. **s'amonceler**, *v.r.* to gather; to accumulate, to drift together.

amoncellement [amõsɛl'mã], *n.m.* accumulation; heap.

amont [a'mõ], *n.m.* upstream water (*used chiefly in en amont*, up-stream, up-river).

amoral [amɔ'ral], *a.* (*m. pl.* **-aux**) amoral.

amorçage [amɔr'sa:ʒ], *n.m.* priming (*of pumps, motors, guns etc.*); baiting (*of hook*).

amorce [a'mɔrs], *n.f.* bait; (*fig.*) allurement, charm; priming, percussion cap (*of guns etc.*); priming (*for a pump*).

amorcer [amɔr'se], *v.t.* (*conjug. like* COMMENCER) to bait; (*fig.*) to allure, to entice, to decoy; (*Hydraulics*) to prime; (*Artill.*) to cap (*a shell*).

amorphe [a'mɔrf], *a.* amorphous.

amortir [amɔr'ti:r], *v.t.* to deaden, to allay, to moderate; to weaken, to break (*a fall, shock etc.*); to redeem, to pay off; to cool (*passions*).

amortissable [amɔrti'sabl], *a.* redeemable.

amortissement [amɔrtis'mã], *n.m.* redemption, buying up; liquidation; deadening (*of a blow etc.*); *fonds d'amortissement*, sinking fund.

amortisseur [amɔrti'sœ:r], *n.m.* shock absorber.

amour [a'mu:r], *n.m.* (*usu. fem. in pl.*) love, affection, passion; the object of love, flame, fancy; *l'Amour*, (*Myth.*) Eros, Cupid.

amouracher (s') [samura'ʃe], *v.r.* to be smitten with, to become enamored (*de*).

amourette [amu'rɛt], *n.f.* passing amour, love affair.

amoureusement [amurøz′mã], *adv.* amorously, lovingly; tenderly.

amoureux [amu′rø], *a.* (*fem.* **-euse**) loving, in love, smitten, enamored (*de*); amorous. —*n.m.* (*fem.* **-euse**) lover, sweetheart; fiancé *or* fiancée.

amour-propre [amur′prɔpr], *n.m.* self-respect; vanity, conceit.

amovibilité [amɔvibili′te], *n.f.* removability, liability to removal; precariousness of tenure.

amovible [amɔ′vibl], *a.* removable, revocable.

ampère [ã′pɛːr], *n.m.* (*Elec.*) ampere.

amphibie [ãfi′bi], *a.* amphibious.—*n.m.* amphibian.

amphibiens [ãfi′bjɛ̃], *n.m. pl.* (*Zool.*) Amphibia.

amphigouri [ãfigu′ri], *n.m.* rigmarole, gibberish.

amphithéâtre [ãfite′a:tr], *n.m.* amphitheatre, the whole body of occupants of this; the gallery in a theatre rising above the boxes and facing the stage; lecture·room; **en amphithéâtre**, in semi-circular tiers.

Amphitryon [ãfitri′ɔ̃], *n.m.* Amphitryon; host, entertainer.

amphore [ã′fɔːr], *n.f.* amphora.

ample [ã:pl], *a.* ample, full; large, vast, spacious; copious.

amplement [ãplə′mã], *adv.* amply, fully; largely, plentifully.

ampleur [ã′plœːr], *n.f.* width, fullness (*of clothes*); abundance; profusion; dignity (*of style etc.*); volume (*of voice*).

amplifiant [ãpli′fjã], *a.* magnifying (*of a lens etc.*); amplifying.

amplificateur [ãplifika′tœːr], *a.* (*fem.* **-trice**) magnifying; amplifying.—*n.m.* (*Phot.*) enlarger.

amplification [ãplifika′sjɔ̃], *n.f.* amplification; magnification, enlargement; (*fig.*) exaggeration.

amplifier [ãpli′fje], *v.t.* to amplify, to develop, to enlarge.

amplitude [ãpli′tyd], *n.f.* extent, amplitude.

ampoule [ã′pul], *n.f.* blister, swelling; (*Elec.*) bulb; (*Med.*) ampoule.

ampoulé [ãpu′le], *a.* bombastic, turgid.

amputation [ãpyta′sjɔ̃], *n.f.* amputation; (*fig.*) curtailment.

amputer [ãpy′te], *v.t.* to amputate, to cut off.

amulette [amy′lɛt], *n.f.* amulet, charm.

amusant [amy′zã], *a.* amusing, diverting, entertaining.

amusement [amyz′mã], *n.m.* amusement, entertainment, diversion; fooling, trifling.

amuser [amy′ze], *v.t.* to amuse, to divert, to entertain; to fool, to beguile, to dupe; to detain, to delay. **s'amuser**, *v.r.* to amuse oneself, to divert oneself; to trifle; to have a good time; **s'amuser de quelqu'un**, to make fun of someone; **amusez-vous bien!** enjoy yourselves, have a good time.

amusette [amy′zɛt], *n.f.* petty amusement.

amuseur [amy′zœːr], *n.m.* (*fem.* **-euse**) amuser, entertainer.

amygdale [ami′dal], *n.f.* (*Anat.*) tonsil.

an [ã], *n.m.* year; (*pl.*) years, time, age; **elle a quinze ans**, she is fifteen; **le jour de l'an**, New Year's Day.

anacarde [ana′kard], *n.m.* cashew nut.

anachorète [anakɔ′rɛt], *n.* anchorite, hermit.

anachronisme [anakrɔ′nism], *n.m.* anachronism.

anaéroïde [ANÉROÏDE].

anagramme [ana′gram], *n.f.* anagram.

analgésie [analʒe′zi], **analgie** [anal′ʒi], *n.f.* (*Med.*) analgesia.

analgésique [analʒe′zik], **analgique** [anal′ʒik], *a.* and *n.m.* analgesic.

analogie [analɔ′ʒi], *n.f.* analogy.

analogique [analɔ′ʒik], *a.* analogous, analogical.

analogue [ana′lɔg], *a.* analogous, similar.

analyse [ana′liːʒ], *n.f.* analysis; outline, précis, abstract (*of a book etc.*); (*Gram.*) parsing, analysis.

analyser [anali′ze], *v.t.* to analyze.

analyste [ana′list], *n.m.* analyst.

analytique [anali′tik], *a.* analytic, analytical.

analytiquement [analitik′mã], *adv.* analytically.

ananas [ana′na], *n.m.* pineapple.

anarchie [anar′ʃi], *n.f.* anarchy; (*fig.*) disorder, confusion.

anarchique [anar′ʃik], *a.* anarchical.

anarchiste [anar′ʃist], *n.* anarchist.

anathème [ana′tɛːm], *n.m.* anathema; sentence of reprobation *or* excommunication, ban, curse.

anatomie [anatɔ′mi], *n.f.* anatomy; dissection; (*fam.*) body, figure.

anatomique [anatɔ′mik], *a.* anatomical.

anatomiquement [anatɔmik′mã], *adv.* anatomically.

anatomiser [anatɔmi′ze], *v.t.* to anatomize, to dissect.

anatomiste [anatɔ′mist], *n.* anatomist.

ancêtre [ã′sɛ:tr], *n.* ancestor, ancestress.—*n.m. pl.* ancestors, forefathers.

anchois [ã′ʃwa], *n.m.* anchovy.

ancien [ã′sjɛ̃], *a.* (*fem.* **-ienne**) ancient, old; former, late, ex-; antique; **un ancien élève**, an old boy.—*n.m.* (*fem.* **-ienne**) senior; ancient; (*Eccles.*) elder; (*Mil.*) veteran; (*pl.*) the ancients; our forefathers.

anciennement [ãsjɛn′mã], *adv.* formerly; *of yore; in former times.

ancienneté [ãsjɛn′te], *n.f.* antiquity; seniority.

ancillaire [ãsil′lɛ:r], *a.* ancillary.

ancrage [ã′kra:ʒ], *n.m.* anchorage.

ancre [ã:kr], *n.f.* anchor; **ancre de miséricorde** (*or* **de salut**), sheet anchor; (*fig.*) last resource; cramp iron, tie plate (*of a wall*).

ancrer [ã′kre], *v.t.* to anchor; (*fig.*) to fix or establish firmly.—*v.i.* to anchor. **s'ancrer**, *v.r.* to establish oneself, to get a footing (*in a place*), to take deep root (*in*).

Andalousie [ãdalu′zi], l', *f.* Andalusia.

Andes [ã:d], **les**, *f. pl.* the Andes.

Andorre [ã′dɔːr], l', *m.* Andorra.

andouille [ã′duːj], *n.f.* pork sausage (*made of chitterlings*); (*pop.*) imbecile, duffer.

andouiller [ãdu′je], *n.m.* tine (*of antler*).

André [ã′dre], *m.* Andrew.

Andromède [ãdrɔ′mɛd], *f.* Andromeda.

âne [ɑːn], *n.m.* ass, donkey; blockhead, stupid, ignorant *or* foolish pe son, idiot.

anéantir [aneã′tiːr], *v.t.* to annihilate, to destroy utterly; to abolish; (*fig.*) to overwhelm.

anéantissement [aneãtis'mã], *n.m.* annihilation; destruction, ruin, overthrow; humiliation, prostration.

anecdote [anɛg'dɔt], *n.f.* anecdote.

anecdotique [anɛgdɔ'tik], *a.* anecdotic.

anémie [ane'mi], *n.f.* anaemia.

anémique [ane'mik], *a.* anaemic.

anémone [ane'mɔn], *n.f.* anemone, windflower.

ânerie [ɑn'ri], *n.f.* stupidity; gross ignorance; gross blunder.

anéroïde [anerɔ'id], **anaéroïde** [anaerɔ'id], *a.* aneroid.—*n.m.* aneroid barometer.

ânesse [ɑ'nɛs], *n.f.* she-ass.

anesthésie [anɛste'zi], *n.f.* (*Med.*) anaesthesia.

anesthésier [anɛste'zje], *v.t.* to anaesthetize.

anesthésique [anɛste'zik], *a.* and *n.m.* anaesthetic.

anesthésiste [anɛste'zist], *n.m.* anaesthetist.

anévrisme [ane'vrism], *n.m.* aneurism.

anfractueux [ãfrak'tɥø], *a.* (*fem.* **-euse**) anfractuous, winding, sinuous, craggy.

anfractuosité [ãfraktɥozi'te], *n.f.* anfractuosity, cragginess, twist, jagged *or* rugged outlines.

ange [ã:ʒ], *n.m.* angel; (*fig.*) an adorable *or* beloved person.

Angèle [ã'ʒɛl], *f.* Angela.

angélique [ãʒe'lik], *a.* angelic, angelical.

angélus [ãʒe'ly:s], *n.m.* angelus.

angevin [ãʒə'vɛ̃], *a.* of Anjou.—*n.m.* (**Angevin**, *fem.* **-ine**) native of Anjou.

angine [ã'ʒin], *n.f.* angina, quinsy, sore throat.

anglais [ã'glɛ], *a.* English; British.—*n.m.* English (*language*); (**Anglais**, *fem.* **-aise**) Englishman, English girl *or* woman; (*pl.*) the English.

angle [ã:gl], *n.m.* angle, corner; (*Arch.*) quoin; *angle aigu*, acute angle; *angle droit*, right angle.

Angleterre [ãglə'tɛ:r], **l'**, *f.* England.

anglican [ãgli'kã], *a.* and *n.m.* (*fem.* **-e**) Anglican.

angliciser [ãglisi'ze], *v.t.* to Anglicize. **s'angliciser**, *v.r.* to become Anglicized *or* English.

anglicisme [ãgli'sism], *n.m.* Anglicism.

anglomanie [ãglɔma'ni], *n.f.* Anglomania.

anglo-normand [ãglɔnɔr'mã], *a.* and *n.m.* (*fem.* **-e**) Anglo-Norman; *les Îles anglo-normandes*, the Channel Islands.

anglophile [ãglɔ'fil], *a.* and *n.m.* Anglophil.

anglo-saxon [ãglɔsak'sɔ̃], *a.* and *n.m.* (*fem.* **-saxonne**) Anglo-Saxon.

angoisse [ã'gwas], *n.f.* anguish, agony, great distress; (*Med.*) angor, anguish.

angora [ãgɔ'ra], *a.* Angora.—*n.m.* Angora cat.

anguille [ã'gi:j], *n.f.* eel; (*pl.*, *Naut.*) launching ways, slips; *il y a anguille sous roche*, I smell a rat.

angulaire [ãgy'lɛ:r], *a.* angular.

angusture [ãgys'ty:r], *n.f.* (*Pharm.*) angostura.

anhélation [anelɑ'sjɔ̃], *n.f.* panting.

anhéler [ane'le], *v.i.* (*conjug. like* CÉDER) to pant.

anhydre [a'nidr], *a.* (*Chem.*) anhydrous.

anhydride [ani'drid], *n.m.* anhydride; *anhydride carbonique*, carbon dioxide.

anicroche [ani'krɔʃ], *n.f.* slight obstacle.

animadversion [animadvɛr'sjɔ̃], *n.f.* animadversion, reproof, reprimand, censure.

animal [ani'mal], *n.m.* (*pl.* **-aux**) animal; beast, brute; *société protectrice des animaux*, Society for the Prevention of Cruelty to Animals.—*a.* (*m.pl.* **-aux**) animal; sensual, carnal.

animateur [anima'tœ:r], *a.* (*fem.* **-trice**) animating.

animation [animɑ'sjɔ̃], *n.f.* animation, vitality, life; liveliness; excitement; irritation.

animé [ani'me], *a.* animated; spirited, gay, sprightly; *rue animée*, busy street.

animer [ani'me], *v.t.* to animate, to give life to; to arouse, to excite, to urge on; to enliven, to give force to (*style etc.*). **s'animer**, *v.r.* to become animated *or* lively; to cheer up; to become angry.

animosité [animozi'te], *n.f.* animosity, ill will, spite, rancor.

anis [a'ni], *n.m.* anise, aniseed.

aniser [ani'ze], *v.t.* to flavor with aniseed.

anisette [ani'zɛt], *n.f.* aniseed cordial.

ankylose [ãki'lo:z], *n.f.* (*Path.*) anchylosis, stiffness in the joints.

annales [a'nal], *n.f.* (*used only in pl.*) annals, public records.

annaliste [ana'list], *n.m.* annalist.

anneau [a'no], *n.m.* (*pl.* **anneaux**) ring; link (*of a chain*); ringlet (*of hair*).

année [a'ne], *n.f.* year, period of twelve months; *année bissextile*, leap year; *souhaiter la bonne année*, to wish a happy New Year.

année-lumière [anely'mjɛ:r], *n.f.* (*pl.* **années-lumière**) light-year.

annelé [an'le], *a.* having *or* arranged in rings, ringed; (*Zool.*) annulated.

annelet [an'lɛ], *n.m.* ringlet, small ring.

annexe [a'nɛks], *n.f.* annex; appendage; appendix, schedule, rider; chapel of ease.

annexer [anɛk'se], *v.t.* to annex, to attach.

annexion [anɛk'sjɔ̃], *n.f.* annexation.

annihilation [aniilɑ'sjɔ̃], *n.f.* annihilation; (*Law*) annulment.

annihiler [anii'le], *v.t.* to annihilate, to destroy; (*Law*) to annul.

anniversaire [anivɛr'sɛ:r], *a.* and *n.m.* anniversary, birthday.

annonce [a'nɔ̃:s], *n.f.* announcement, notification; indication, sign, mark; advertisement; *annonce de mariage*, banns of marriage.

annoncer [anɔ̃'se], *v.t.* (*conjug. like* COMMENCER) to announce, to give notice of; to advertise; to announce (*a visitor*), to usher *or* show in; to proclaim; to foretell, **s'annoncer**, *v.r.* to present oneself; to manifest itself.

Annonciation [anɔ̃sjɑ'sjɔ̃], *n.f.* Annunciation; Lady Day (March 25).

annoncier [anɔ̃'sje], *n.m.* publicity manager.

annotateur [anɔta'tœ:r], *n.m.* (*fem.* **-trice**) annotator (*of a book etc.*).

annotation [anɔta'sjɔ̃], *n.f.* annotation.

annoter [anɔ'te], *v.t.* to annotate, to make notes on (*a text etc.*).

annuaire [a'nɥɛ:r], *n.m.* annual, year-book; *l'Annuaire des Téléphones*, the telephone directory.

annuel [a'nɥɛl], *a.* (*fem.* **-elle**) annual, yearly.

annuellement [anɥɛl'mã], *adv.* annually, yearly.

annuité [anɥi'te], *n.f.* annuity.
annulable [any'labl], *a.* revocable.
annulaire [any'lɛːr], *a.* annular, ring-shaped. —*n m.* ring finger, third finger.
annulation [anyla'sjɔ̃], *n.f.* annulment, cancellation, repeal, abolition.
annuler [any'le], *v.t.* to annul, to rescind, to cancel, to abolish, to set aside, to make void.
anobli [anɔ'bli], *a.* ennobled.—*n.m.* newly created nobleman.
anoblir [anɔ'bliːr], *v.t.* to ennoble, to raise to the rank of the nobility.
anoblissement [anɔblis'mã], *n.m.* ennoblement.
anode [a'nɔd], *n.f.* (*Elec.*) anode, positive pole.
anodin [anɔ'dɛ̃], *a.* (*Med.*) anodyne, soothing; (*fig.*) harmless, mild, inoffensive, insignificant.
anomal [anɔ'mal], *a.* (*m. pl.* **-aux**) (*Gram.*) anomalous, irregular.
anomalie [anɔma'li], *n.f.* anomaly, irregularity.
ânon [ɑ'nɔ̃], *n.m.* ass's foal, young ass; (*fig.*) a little fool.
ânonnement [anɔn'mã], *n.m.* faltering, mumbling way of reading a text.
ânonner [anɔ'ne], *v.t.* to mumble and blunder through (*a lesson etc.*).—*v.i.* to read in a faltering way.
anonymat [anɔni'ma], *n.m.* anonymity.
anonyme [anɔ'nim], *a.* anonymous, nameless; **société anonyme**, joint-stock company. —*n.* anonymous person.
anonymement [anɔnim'mã], *adv.* anonymously.
anorak [anɔ'rak], *n.m.* (*reg. trade mark*) anorak.
anormal [anɔr'mal], *a.* (*m. pl.* **-aux**) abnormal, irregular, mentally deficient.
anormalement [anɔrmal'mã], *adv.* abnormally.
anse [ɑ̃ːs], *n.f.* handle (*of a pot, basket etc.*); bay, cove.
antagonique [ãtagɔ'nik], *a.* antagonistic.
antagonisme [ãtagɔ'nism], *n.m.* antagonism.
antagoniste [ãtagɔ'nist], *a.* antagonistic.—*n.m.* antagonist, adversary, opponent; competitor, rival.
*****antan** [ã'tã], *n.m.* yesteryear; **les neiges d'antan**, the snows of yesteryear.
antarctique [ãtark'tik], *a.* Antarctic.
antécédent [ãtese'dã], *a.* antecedent, preceding, foregoing, previous.—*n.m.* precedent; (*Gram.*) antecedent.
antéchrist [ãte'krist], *n.m.* Antichrist.
antédiluvien [ãtedily'vjɛ̃], *a.* (*fem.* **-ienne**) antediluvian.
antenne [ã'tɛn], *n.f.* (*Rad., Tel.*) aerial; (*Ent.*) antenna, (*pl.*) antennae.
antépénultième [ãtepenyl'tjɛm], *a.* antepenultimate.
antérieur [ãte'rjœːr], *a.* anterior, earlier, antecedent, previous, former.
antérieurement [ãterjœr'mã], *adv.* previously, before.
antériorité [ãterjori'te], *n.f.* anteriority, priority, precedence.
anthologie [ãtɔlɔ'ʒi], *n.f.* anthology.
anthracite [ãtra'sit], *n.m.* anthracite.
anthrax [ã'traks], *n.m.* (*Med.*) anthrax.
anthropoïde [ãtrɔpɔ'id], *a.* and *n.m.* (*Zool.*) anthropoid.

anthropologie [ãtrɔpɔlɔ'ʒi], *n.f.* anthropology.
anthropologiste [ãtrɔpɔlɔ'ʒist], **anthropologue** [ãtrɔpɔ'lɔg], *n.* anthropologist.
anthropophage [ãtrɔpɔ'faːʒ], *n.* cannibal.
anti-aérien [ãtiae'rjɛ̃], *a.* (*fem.* **-enne**) antiaircraft.
antibiotique [ãtibiɔ'tik], *a.* and *n.m.* antibiotic.
anti-brouillard [ãtibru'jaːr], *n.m.* (*Motor.*) fog light.
anti-buée [ãti'bye], *a.* (*Motor.*) demisting.—*n.m.* demister.
antichambre [ãti'ʃãːbr], *n.f.* (*formerly m.*) antechamber, anteroom.
anti-char [ãti'ʃaːr], *a.* anti-tank.
antichrétien [ãtikre'tjɛ̃], *a.* and *n.m.* (*fem.* **-ienne**) antichristian.
anticipation [ãtisipa'sjɔ̃], *n.f.* anticipation; encroachment, trespass; **par anticipation**, in advance, beforehand.
anticipé [ãtisi'pe], *a.* done *or* occurring in advance.
anticiper [ãtisi'pe], *v.t.* to anticipate, to forestall.—*v.i.* to encroach *or* trespass (**sur**).
anticlimax [ãtikli'maks], *n.m.* anticlimax.
anticommunisme [ãtikɔmy'nism], *n.m.* anti-communism.
anticonstitutionnellement [ãtikɔ̃stity sjɔnɛl'mã], *adv.* (*the longest French word*) anticonstitutionally.
anticorps [ãti'kɔːr], *n.m.* (*Med.*) antibody.
anticyclone [ãtisi'klɔn], *n.m.* (*Meteor.*) anticyclone.
antidate [ãti'dat], *n.f.* antedate.
antidater [ãtida'te], *v.t.* to antedate.
antidérapant [ãtidera'pã], *a.* non-skidding; **pneu antidérapant**, non-skid tire.
antidote [ãti'dɔt], *n.m.* antidote, antitoxin; (*fig.*) cure.
anti-éblouissant [ãtieblui'sã], *a.* (*Motor.*) antidazzle.
antienne [ã'tjɛn], *n.f.* antiphon; anthem.
antigel [ãti'ʒɛl], *n.m. inv.* anti-freeze.
antillais [ãti'jɛ], *a.* West Indian.—*n.m.* (**Antillais,** *fem.* **-aise**) West Indian (*person*).
Antilles [ã'tiːj], **les,** *f.pl.* the West Indies; **la mer des Antilles**, the Caribbean Sea.
antilope [ãti'lɔp], *n.f.* antelope.
anti-mite [ãti'mit], *a.* moth-proof.
antimoine [ãti'mwan], *n.m.* antimony.
Antioche [ã'tjɔʃ], *f.* Antioch.
antiparasite [ãtipara'zit], *n.m.* suppressor.
antiparlementaire [ãtiparləmã'tɛːr], *a.* unparliamentary.
antipathie [ãtipa'ti], *n.f.* antipathy, aversion.
antipathique [ãtipa'tik], *a.* antipathetic, repugnant.
antiphonaire [ãtifɔ'nɛːr], *n.m.* antiphonal.
antipode [ãti'pɔd], *n.m.* the region of the globe diametrically opposite; (*pl.*) antipodes.
antiputride [ãtipy'trid], *a.* and *n.m.* antiseptic.
antiquaire [ãti'kɛːr], *n.m.* antiquary, antiquarian, antique dealer.
antique [ã'tik], *a.* antique, ancient; oldfashioned.—*n.f.* antique, ancient work of art.
antiquité [ãtiki'te], *n.f.* antiquity; old times; (*pl.*) antiquities; **magasin d'antiquités**, old curiosity shop.
antirouille [ãti'ruːj], *n.m.* rust preventive.

antirrhine [ɑ̃ti'rin], *n.f.* (*Bot.*) antirrhinum, snapdragon.
antisémite [ɑ̃tise'mit], *n.* anti-Semite.
antisémitique [ɑ̃tisemi'tik], *a.* anti-Semitic.
antisemitisme [ɑ̃tisemi'tism], *n.m.* anti-Semitism.
antiseptique [ɑ̃tisɛp'tik], *a.* and *n.m.* (*Med.*) antiseptic.
antisocial [ɑ̃tisɔ'sjal], *a.* (*m. pl.* **-aux**) antisocial.
antisportif [ɑ̃tispɔr'tif], *a.* (*fem.* **-ive**) unsportsmanlike; opposed to sports.
antithèse [ɑ̃ti'tɛːz], *n.f.* antithesis.
antitoxine [ɑ̃titɔk'sin], *n.f.* (*Med.*) antitoxin.
anti-vol [ɑ̃ti'vɔl], *a. inv.* anti-theft.—*n.m.* burglar-proof device.
antivivisection [ɑ̃tivivisɛk'sjɔ̃], *n.f.* antivivisection.
Antoine [ɑ̃'twan], *m.* Anthony.
antre [ɑ̃ːtr], *n.m.* den, lair; cavern.
anuiter (s') [sanɥi'te], *v.r.* to be benighted.
anus [a'nyːs], *n.m.* anus.
Anvers [ɑ̃'vɛr], *m.* Antwerp.
anxiété [ɑ̃ksje'te], *n.f.* anxiety; uneasiness; (*Med.*) pain in the heart.
anxieusement [ɑ̃ksjøz'mɑ̃], *adv.* anxiously.
anxieux [ɑ̃k'sjø], *a.* (*fem.* **-euse**) anxious, uneasy, restless.
aorte [a'ɔrt], *n.f.* (*Anat.*) aorta.
août [u(t)], *n.m.* August; (*fig.*) harvest; *la mi-août*, the middle of August.
aoûté [u'te], *a.* ripened by the heat of August.
aoûter (s') [su'te], *v.r.* to ripen (*in August*).
apache [a'paʃ], *n.m.* ruffian of the Paris streets, hooligan.
apaisement [apɛz'mɑ̃], *n.m.* appeasement; abatement, lull.
apaiser [apɛ'ze], *v.t.* to pacify, to calm, to appease; to quiet; to mitigate, to alleviate (*pain, sorrow etc.*); to stay (*hunger*); to quench (*thirst*). **s'apaiser**, *v.r.* to be appeased; to sober down; to grow quiet; to abate, to subside.
Apalaches [apa'laʃ], *m.pl.* Appalachians.
(C) **apalachien** [apala'ʃjɛ̃], *a.* (*fem.* **-chienne**) Appalachian.
apanage [apa'naːʒ], *n.m.* apanage; (*fig.*) lot.
apanager [apana'ʒe], *v.t.* (*conjug. like* MANGER) to endow.
aparté [apar'te], *n.m.* aside.
apathie [apa'ti], *n.f.* apathy, indolence, listlessness.
apathique [apa'tik], *a.* apathetic, listless.
apatride [apa'trid], *a.* and *n.* stateless (person).
Apennins [apɛ'nɛ̃], **les**, *m.pl.* the Apennines.
apepsie [apɛp'si], *n.f.* (*Path.*) apepsy, indigestion.
apeptique [apɛp'tik], *a.* dyspeptic.
apercevable [apɛrsə'vabl], *a.* perceivable, perceptible.
apercevoir [apɛrsə'vwaːr], *v.t.* (*conjug. like* RECEVOIR) to catch sight of, to notice; to perceive, to understand, to comprehend. **s'apercevoir**, *v.r.* (*de quelque chose*) to remark, to notice, to be aware of; to find out, to discover; to be visible.
aperçu [apɛr'sy], *n.m.* rapid view, glance or survey; rough estimate or summary; judgment, idea.
apéritif [aperi'tif], *a.* (*fem.* **-ive**) aperient, appetizing.—*n.m.* (*Med.*) aperient, laxative; appetizer, aperitif (*e.g. vermouth, bitters*).

à peu près [apø'prɛ], *n.m.* approximation, approach; a word roughly standing for another.—*adv.* nearly, about.
apeuré [apø're], *a.* frightened, scared.
apex [a'pɛks], *n.m.* apex.
aphélie [afe'li], *n.m.* (*Astron.*) aphelion.
aphide [afi'de], **aphidien** [afi'djɛ̃], *n.m.* (*Ent.*) aphis, greenfly.
aphone [a'fɔn], *a.* voiceless.
aphonie [afɔ'ni], *n.f.* aphony, loss of voice.
aphorisme [afɔ'rism], *n.m.* aphorism.
à-pic [a'pik], *n.m.* steep hill, cliff.
apiculteur [apikyl'tœːr], *n.m.* bee-keeper.
apiculture [apikyl'tyːr], *n.f.* apiculture, beekeeping.
apitoiement [apitwa'mɑ̃], *n.m.* pity, compassion.
apitoyant [apitwa'jɑ̃], *a.* piteous.
apitoyer [apitwa'je], *v.t.* (*conjug. like* EMPLOYER) to move to pity, to soften. **s'apitoyer**, *v.r.* to pity.
aplanir [apla'niːr], *v.t.* to smooth, to level, to make even; (*fig.*) to level down or remove (*obstacles, difficulties etc.*). **s'aplanir**, *v.r.* to grow easy, smooth etc.
aplanissement [aplanis'mɑ̃], *n.m.* smoothing, levelling, making even; smoothness, evenness.
aplat [a'pla], *n.m.* flat tint.
aplatir [apla'tiːr], *v.t.* to flatten, to beat flat; (*fig.*) to vanquish, to silence, to floor. **s'aplatir**, *v.r.* to become flat, to be flattened; (*fig.*) to crouch, to cringe.
aplatissement [aplatis'mɑ̃], **aplatissage** [aplati'saːʒ], *n.m.* flattening, flatness; (*fig.*) humiliation.
aplomb [a'plɔ̃], *n.m.* perpendicularity; equilibrium; (*fig.*) assurance, self-possession, steadiness, coolness; impudence, cheek; *d'aplomb*, perpendicularly, upright.
apocalypse [apɔka'lips], *n.f.* Apocalypse, the Book of Revelation.
apocalyptique [apɔkalip'tik], *a.* apocalyptic, obscure.
apocryphe [apɔ'krif], *a.* apocryphal, spurious.
apode [a'pɔd], *a.* (*Zool.*) apodal, footless.
apogée [apɔ'ʒe], *n.m.* apogee; (*fig.*) acme, height, zenith.
apologétique [apɔlɔʒe'tik], *a.* by way of apology, apologetic.
apologie [apɔlɔ'ʒi], *n.f.* apology, vindication, justification.
apologue [apɔ'lɔg], *n.m.* apologue, fable.
apoplectique [apɔplɛk'tik], *a.* and *n.* apoplectic.
apoplexie [apɔplɛk'si], *n.f.* apoplexy.
apostasie [apɔsta'zi], *n.f.* apostasy.
apostat [apɔs'ta], *a.* and *n.m.* (*fem.* **-e**) apostate.
aposter [apɔs'te], *v.t.* to place in ambush, to station.
apostille [apɔs'tiːj], *n.f.* marginal note, postscript, footnote.
apostiller [apɔsti'je], *v.t.* to add a postscript or marginal recommendation.
apostolat [apɔstɔ'la], *n.m.* apostleship.
apostolique [apɔstɔ'lik], *a.* apostolic; papal.
apostrophe [apɔs'trɔf], *n.f.* (*Rhet. and Gram.*) apostrophe; address; (*fig.*) reprimand, attack.

apostropher [apɔstrɔ'fe], *v.t.* to apostrophize, to address; (*fig.*) to reprimand.

apothéose [apɔte'o:z], *n.f.* apotheosis.

apothicaire [apɔti'kɛ:r], *n.m.* apothecary.

apôtre [a'po:tr], *n.m.* apostle; (*fig.*) leader of a cause.

apparaître [apa'rɛ:tr], *v.i. irr.* (*conjug. like* CONNAÎTRE) to appear, to become visible; to be evident.

apparat [apa'ra], *n.m.* pomp, show, ostentation, parade.

apparaux [apa'ro], *n.m.* (*used only in pl.*) (*Naut.*) gear, tackle, outfit etc.

appareil [apa'rɛ:j], *n.m.* formal preparation; pomp, display; appearance, show; apparatus, appliances, machinery, paraphernalia; (*Surg.*) dressing; *appareil (photographique)*, camera; *qui est à l'appareil?* who is speaking?

appareillage [apaɛ'ja:ʒ], *n.m.* installation; (*Naut.*) act of getting under sail, weighing.

appareillement [apaɛj'mã], *n.m.* coupling, yoking; pairing (*for breeding*).

appareiller [apaɛ'je], *v.t.* to install equipment; to match; to pair (*animals*).—*v.i.* to get under way, to weigh anchor. **s'appareiller,** *v.r.* to pair (*of birds*).

appareilleur [apaɛ'jœ:r], *n.m.* (*Building*) stone dresser; *appareilleur à gaz*, gas fitter.

apparemment [apara'mã], *adv.* apparently.

apparence [apa'rã:s], *n.f.* appearance, look, semblance, likelihood, probability; *en apparence*, seemingly, apparently.

apparent [apa'rã], *a.* visible, prominent.

apparenté [aparã'te], *a.* related; *bien apparenté*, well connected.

apparentement [aparãt'mã], *n.m.* political alliance.

apparenter [aparã'te], *v.t.* to ally, to connect by marriage. **s'apparenter,** *v.r.* to ally oneself (*by marriage*).

appariement or **appariment** [apari'mã], *n.m.* pairing, matching; coupling, mating; *appariement d'écoles*, school consolidation.

apparier [apa'rje], *v.t.* to assort by pairs, to pair (*birds etc.*), to match (*horses, gloves etc.*).

apparition [apari'sjɔ̃], *n.f.* apparition, sudden appearance; phantom, ghost; *apparition d'anges*, vision of angels.

appartement [aparta'mã], *n.m.* apartment.

appartenances [apartə'nã:s], *n.f.* (*used in pl.*) appurtenances.

appartenant [apartə'nã], *a.* belonging, appertaining.

appartenir [apartə'ni:r], *v.i. irr.* (*conjug. like* TENIR) to belong, to appertain; to relate, to pertain, to concern; to behoove, to be the right, privilege, duty etc. of (*à*); *il appartient,* (*v. impers.*) it is meet or fit; it behooves, concerns. **s'appartenir,** *v.r.* to be master of one's own actions, to be free.

appas [a'pα], *n.m. pl.* feminine charms, attractions.

appât [a'pα], *n.m.* bait; lure, allurement, enticement.

appâter [apa'te] *v.t.* to attract with a bait, to allure; to fatten (*fowls etc.*).

appauvrir [apo'vri:r], *v.t.* to impoverish. **s'appauvrir,** *v.r.* to grow poor, to become impoverished.

appauvrissement [apovris'mã], *n.m.* impoverishment.

appel [a'pɛl], *n.m.* appeal, call, summons; (*Mil.*) roll call, muster; summoning of conscripts to the colors; (*Law*) appeal to a higher court; *battre* or *sonner l'appel*, (*Mil.*) to sound the fall-in.

appelé [ap'le], *a.* called up.—*n.m.* soldier called up for service.

appeler [ap'le], *v.t.* (*see Verb Tables*) to call, to send for; to call over; to call up, to call together; to summon, to cite, to invoke, to call upon, to invite; to name, to term; to challenge.—*v.i.* to appeal (*to a higher court*). **s'appeler,** *v.r.* to be called, to call oneself.

appellation [apɛla'sjɔ̃], *n.f.* calling; appellation; trade name; *appellation contrôlée*, registered trade name.

appendice [apã'dis], *n.m.* appendix, appendage, addition.

appendicite [apãdi'sit], *n.f.* (*Path.*) appendicitis.

appendre [a'pã:dr], *v.t.* to hang up, to suspend; to attach.

appentis [apã'ti], *n.m.* shed, lean-to.

appesantir [apəzã'ti:r], *v.t.* to make heavy, to weigh down; (*fig.*) to make dull. **s'appesantir,** *v.r.* to grow heavy and dull, to be weighed down; to dwell on, to expatiate (*sur*).

appesantissement [apəzãtis'mã], *n.m.* heaviness, dullness.

appétissant [apeti'sã], *a.* desirable, appetizing, tempting; dainty, delicious.

appétit [ape'ti], *n.m.* appetite, relish; desire, sensuous craving (*usu. in pl.*); appetite (*for food*); (*fig.*) inclination, taste, stomach.

applaudir [aplo'di:r], *v.t., v.i.* to clap the hands, to applaud; to praise, to commend, to approve. **s'applaudir,** *v.r.* to boast, to glory (*in a thing*); to congratulate oneself (*de*); to rejoice (*de*).

applaudissement [aplodis'mã], *n.m.* (*usually pl.*) applause, public praise; cheering.

applicabilité [aplikabili'te], *n.f.* applicability, appositeness.

applicable [apli'kabl], *a.* applicable, apposite, relevant, suitable.

application [aplika'sjɔ̃], *n.f.* application, applying; employment (*of a sum of money*); infliction (*of a penalty*); attention, care, diligence; applied lace.

applique [a'plik], *n.f.* ornamental accessories, candelabrum or bracket fixed to a wall.

appliqué [apli'ke], *a.* studious; *sciences appliquées*, applied sciences.

appliquer [apli'ke], *v.t.* to apply (*à*), to stick; to apply (*one's mind*); to adapt, to employ; to inflict, to impose (*a penalty etc.*). **s'appliquer,** *v.r.* to apply oneself, to work hard.

appoint [a'pwɛ̃], *n.m.* money paying off an account, balance; change; contribution; *faire l'appoint,* to pay the exact sum.

appointé [apwɛ'te], *a.* receiving a salary.

appointement [apwɛt'mã], *n.m.* (*pl.*) salary (*of employee*); emoluments; (*Eccles.*) stipend.

appointer (1) [apwɛ'te], *v.t.* to give a salary to.

appointer (2) [apwɛ'te], *v.t.* to sharpen to a point, to point.

appontement [apɔ̃t'mã], *n.m.* (*Naut.*) bridgelike structure for loading vessels; (*wooden*) wharf *or* pier.

apport [a'pɔːr], *n.m.* property brought by a husband or wife into the common stock; a shareholder's contribution to the assets of a company.

apporter [apɔr'te], *v.t.* to bring; to furnish, to supply; to bring to bear, to employ (*trouble, pains etc.*); to cause, to produce, to bring about.

apposer [apo'ze], *v.t.* to set, to put, to affix; to insert (*a clause etc.*).

apposition [apozi'sjɔ̃], *n.f.* setting, putting, affixing; (*Gram.*) apposition.

appréciable [apre'sjabl], *a.* appreciable, perceptible.

appréciateur [apresja'tœːr], *n.m.* (*fem.* **-trice**) valuer.

appréciatif [apresja'tif], *a.* (*fem.* **-ive**) denoting the value of; *état* or *devis appréciatif*, estimate.

appréciation [apresja'sjɔ̃], *n.f.* appreciation, valuation, estimation; rise in value.

apprécier [apre'sje], *v.t.* to value, to estimate, to appraise, to judge; to appreciate, to esteem.

appréhender [apreɑ̃'de], *v.t.* to arrest, to apprehend; to be apprehensive of, to fear, to dread.

appréhensible [apreɑ̃'sibl], *a.* apprehensible, comprehensible.

appréhensif [apreɑ̃'sif], *a.* (*fem.* **-ive**) apprehensive, timid.

appréhension [apreɑ̃'sjɔ̃], *n.f.* apprehension, fear, dread.

apprendre [a'prɑ̃ːdr], *v.t. irr.* (*conjug. like* PRENDRE) to learn; to hear of, to be informed of; to acquire (*a habit etc.*); to tell, to inform; to teach, to impart knowledge of (*a subject*).

apprenti [aprɑ̃'ti], *a.* apprenticed, articled.— *n.m.* (*fem.* **-e**) apprentice; (*fig.*) novice.

apprentissage [aprɑ̃ti'saːʒ], *n.m.* apprenticeship; trial, experiment.

apprêt [a'prɛ], *n.m.* preparation; cooking, dressing (*of food*); manner of preparing cloth, silk, lace etc.; the substance used in this process; (*pl.*) preparations.

apprêtage [aprɛ'taːʒ], *n.m.* dressing, application of the preliminary preparation to cloth, silk etc.

apprêté [aprɛ'te], *a.* studied, affected, stiff.

apprêter [aprɛ'te], *v.t.* to prepare, to get ready; to dress, to cook; to apply the *apprêts* [*q.v.*] to. **s'apprêter**, *v.r.* to prepare oneself, to get ready (*à*).

apprêteur [aprɛ'tœːr], *a.* and *n.m.* (*fem.* **-euse**) dresser, finisher.—*n.f.* (**-euse**) hat trimmer.

apprivoisé [aprivwa'ze], *a.* tame.

apprivoisement [aprivwaz'mɑ̃], *n.m.* taming.

apprivoiser [aprivwa'ze], *v.t.* to tame (*animals*); to win (*people*) over, to make sociable or tractable.

apprivoiseur [aprivwa'zœːr], *n.m.* (*fem.* **-euse**) tamer.

approbateur [aprɔba'tœːr], *a.* (*fem.* **-trice**) approving.

approbatif [aprɔba'tif], *a.* (*fem.* **-tive**) approbatory; *geste approbatif*, nod of approbation or approval.

approbation [aprɔba'sjɔ̃], *n.f.* approbation, consent, approval.

approbativement [aprɔbativ'mɑ̃], *adv.* approvingly.

approchable [aprɔ'ʃabl], *a.* approachable, easy of access.

approchant [aprɔ'ʃɑ̃], *a.* like, much the same, something like, approximate, bordering on.

approche [a'prɔʃ], *n.f.* approach, coming, advance, nearness; (*pl.*) approaches, access.

approcher [aprɔ'ʃe], *v.t.* to bring, put or draw near or nearer; to come near or nearer; to approach.—*v.i.* to approach, to draw near, to come near; to be something like, to be nearly. **s'approcher**, *v.r.* to approach, to advance.

approfondir [aprɔfɔ̃'diːr], *v.t.* to deepen, to make deeper; to examine thoroughly, to investigate. **s'approfondir**, *v.r.* to become deeper.

approfondissement [aprɔfɔ̃dis'mɑ̃], *n.m.* deepening; fathoming; thorough investigation.

appropriation [aprɔpria'sjɔ̃], *n.f.* adaptation, assimilation; appropriation.

approprier [aprɔpri'e], *v.t.* to make appropriate, to accommodate, to adapt; to clean, to tidy etc.; to suit, to fit, (*style to subject etc.*). **s'approprier**, *v.r.* to appropriate a thing to oneself; to conform, to adapt oneself.

approuver [apru've], *v.t.* to sanction, to consent to, to ratify, to authorize; to approve, to approve of; to pass (*accounts*).

approvisionnement [aprɔvizjɔn'mɑ̃], *n.m.* victualling, supply, stock.

approvisionner [aprɔvizjɔ'ne], *v.t.* to supply with necessaries, to victual, to stock. **s'approvisionner**, *v.r.* to supply oneself; to lay in supplies.

approvisionneur [aprɔvizjɔ'nœːr], *n.m.* (*fem.* **-euse**) caterer, purveyor.

approximatif [aprɔksima'tif], *a.* (*fem.* **-tive**) approximate.

approximation [aprɔksima'sjɔ̃], *n.f.* approximation, rough estimate.

approximativement [aprɔksimativ'mɑ̃], *adv.* approximately.

appui [a'pɥi], *n.m.* support, prop, stay; any kind of mechanical support, *as* buttress, rail, handrail, sill (*of windows*); (*Mech.*) fulcrum; (*fig.*) corroboration; (*Gram.*) stress.

appui-main [apɥi'mɛ̃], *n.m.* (*pl.* **appuis-main**) painter's maulstick *or* hand rest.

appuyer [apɥi'je], *v.t.* (*conjug. like* EMPLOYER) to prop up, to support; to lean (*something against a wall etc.*); (*fig.*) to second, to back up, to uphold, to stand by, to reinforce.— *v.i.* to weigh upon, to lay stress (*sur*); (*fig.*) to insist; *appuyer à droite*, to bear to the right. **s'appuyer**, *v.r.* to lean, to rest (*sur*); to rely upon, to depend (*sur*); to lay stress or a stress on, to dwell (*sur*).

âpre [ɑːpr], *a.* hard, rough, harsh, rugged; sharp, tart, sour; bitter, biting, bleak raw; grating (*of sound*); (*fig.*) austere; crabbed; violent, eager (*in pursuit of something*); *âpre à la curée*, out for the kill (*of animals*); (*fig.*) on the make (*of persons*).

âprement [ɑːprə'mɑ̃], *adv.* harshly, roughly; peevishly, crabbedly; violently, eagerly.

après

après [a′prɛ], *prep.* after, behind (*in time, order etc.*); next to; in pursuit of; *d'après*, after, according to.—*adv.* afterwards, later; *et après?* (*ellipt.*) what next? what then? so what?—*conj.* **après que**, after, when.

après-demain [aprɛd′mɛ̃], *adv.* the day after tomorrow.

après-midi [apremi′di], *n.m.* or *f. inv.* afternoon.

âpreté [ɑprə′te], *n.f.* harshness, tartness, sharpness; roughness, ruggedness; (*fig.*) acrimony, asperity; eagerness; keenness; greediness.

à-propos [aprɔ′po], *n.m.* aptness, suitability.

apside [ap′sid], *n.f.* (*Astron.*) apsis.

apte [apt]. *a.* apt, fit, proper, suitable.

aptitude [apti′tyd], *n.f.* aptitude, natural disposition *or* capacity (*for*).

apurement [apyr′mɑ̃], *n.m.* verification *or* audit (*of accounts*).

apurer [apy′re], *v.t.* to verify, to audit.

aquaplane [akwa′plan], *n.f.* surf-board; *faire de l'aquaplane*, to go surf-riding.

aquarelle [akwa′rɛl], *n.f.* painting in water-colors, aquarelle.

aquarelliste [akwarɛ′list], *n.m.* painter in water-colors.

aquarium [akwa′rjɔm], *n.m.* aquarium.

aquatique [akwa′tik], *a.* aquatic.

aqueduc [akø′dyk], *n.m.* aqueduct, conduit; (*Anat.*) duct.

aqueux [a′kø], *a.* (*fem.* -euse) aqueous, watery.

aquilin [aki′lɛ̃], *a.* aquiline, curved, hooked, Roman (*of noses etc.*).

aquilon [aki′lɔ̃], *n.m.* north wind, cold blast.

ara [a′ra], *n.m.* (*Orn.*) ara, macaw.

arabe [a′rab], *a.* Arabic, Arabian.—*n.m.* Arabic (*language*).—*n.* (**Arabe**) Arab, Arabian.

arabesque [ara′bɛsk], *n.f.* arabesque.

Arabie [ara′bi], **l'**, *f.* Arabia; *Arabie Séoudite*, Saudi Arabia.

arabique [ara′bik], *a.* Arabic, Arabian; *gomme arabique*, gum arabic.

arable [a′rabl], *a.* arable, tillable.

arachide [ara′ʃid], *n.f.* pea-nut, ground-nut.

araignée [arɛ′ɲe], *n.f.* spider; a spider-like implement etc.; (*Mil.*) a series of branching galleries in a mine; (*Naut.*) crowfoot; *toile d'araignée*, cobweb.

arasement [araz′mɑ̃], *n.m.* levelling, making even.

araser [ara′ze], *v.t.* to level (*a wall, a building etc.*).

aratoire [ara′twa:r], *a.* pertaining to farming.

arbalète [arba′lɛt], *n.f.* arbalest, cross-bow.

arbalétrier [arbale′trje], *n.m.* cross-bowman; (*Carp.*) principal rafters of a roof; strut (*of plane*); (*Orn.*) (black) swift.

arbitrage [arbi′tra:ʒ], *n.m.* arbitration; (*Banking*) arbitrage.

arbitraire [arbi′trɛ:r], *a.* arbitrary; absolute, despotic.

arbitrairement [arbitrɛr′mɑ̃], *adv.* arbitrarily; despotically.

arbitral [arbi′tral], *a.* (*m. pl.* -aux) by arbitration; composed of arbitrators (*of a tribunal etc.*).

arbitralement [arbitral′mɑ̃], *adv.* by arbitration.

arbitre [ar′bitr], *n.m.* arbitrator, umpire, referee; arbiter, disposer; will.

arbitrer [arbi′tre], *v.t.* to arbitrate, to judge, to settle (*a dispute etc.*), to referee *or* umpire (*a match*).

arborer [arbɔ′re], *v.t.* to put up, to hoist, to unfurl (*a flag or as a flag*); (*fig.*) to put on.

arbre [arbr], *n.m.* tree; (*fig.*) anything resembling this (*e.g. a genealogical tree*); (*Mach.*) arbor, shaft, spindle, axle-tree; (*Naut.*) mast; (*Motor.*) **arbre moteur**, mainshaft; **arbre coudé**, crankshaft.

arbrisseau [arbri′so], *n.m.* (*pl.* -eaux) shrubby tree.

arbuste [ar′byst], *n.m.* bush, shrub.

arc [ark], *n.m.* bow, long-bow; (*Arch.*) arch; (*Geom., Phys. etc.*) arc.

arcade [ar′kad], *n.f.* arch-shaped opening; (*pl.*) arcade.

arcanes [ar′kan], *n.m. pl.* secrets, mysteries.

arc-boutant [arkbu′tɑ̃], *n.m.* (*pl.* **arcs-boutants**) (*fig.*) buttress, arched flying buttress; supporter, pillar.

arc-bouter [arkbu′te], *v.t.* to strengthen by a flying buttress; (*fig.*) to support, to buttress.

arceau [ar′so], *n.m.* (*pl.* -eaux) curved part of a vault *or* arch; anything shaped like an arch; (*croquet*) hoop.

arc-en-ciel [arkɑ̃′sjɛl], *n.m.* (*pl.* **arcs-en-ciel**) rainbow.

archaïque [arka′ik], *a.* archaic.

archaïsme [arka′ism], *n.m.* archaism, obsolete word etc.

archange [ar′kɑ̃:ʒ], *n.m.* archangel.

arche (1) [arʃ], *n.f.* arch (*of a bridge*).

arche (2) [arʃ], *n.f.* ark; *l'arche de Noé*, Noah's ark.

archéologie [arkeɔlɔ′ʒi], *n.f.* archaeology.

archéologique [arkeɔlɔ′ʒik], *a.* archaeological.

archéologue [arkeɔ′lɔg], *n.m.* archaeologist.

archer [ar′ʃe], *n.m.* archer, bowman.

archet [ar′ʃɛ], *n.m.* (*Mus.*) bow, fiddle-stick.

archevêché [arʃəve′ʃe], *n.m.* archbishopric; archiepiscopal diocese; archbishop's residence.

archevêque [arʃə′vɛk], *n.m.* archbishop.

archi- [ar′ʃi *or* ar′ki], *pref.* arch-, archi-, chief; extremely *as in* **archiriche** etc.

archidiacre [arʃi′djakr], *n.m.* archdeacon.

archiduc [arʃi′dyk], *n.m.* archduke.

archiduché [arʃidy′ʃe], *n.m.* archdukedom, archduchy.

archiduchesse [arʃidy′ʃes], *n.f.* archduchess.

archiépiscopal [arkiepiskɔ′pal], *a.* (*m. pl.* -aux) archiepiscopal.

archière [ar′ʃjɛ:r], *n.f.* loophole.

Archimède [arʃi′mɛd], *m.* Archimedes.

archipel [arʃi′pɛl], *n.m.* archipelago.

archiprêtre [arʃi′prɛ:tr], *n.m.* arch-priest, high priest.

architecte [arʃi′tɛkt], *n.m.* architect; *architecte paysagiste*, landscape gardener.

architectural [arʃitɛkty′ral], *a.* (*m.pl.* -aux) architectural.

architecture [arʃitɛk′ty:r], *n.f.* architecture.

architrave [arʃi′tra:v], *n.f.* (*Arch.*) architrave.

archives [ar′ʃi:v], *n.f.* (*used only in pl.*) archives; state, civic *or* family records; record office, muniment room.

archiviste [arʃi′vist], *n.m.* archivist, keeper of records, registrar; filing clerk.

arçon [ar'sõ], *n.m.* saddle-bow; bow-shaped tool used by hat makers etc.

arcot [ar'ko], *n.m.* dross, slag.

arctique [ark'tik], *a.* Arctic.

ardemment [arda'mã], *adv.* ardently.

ardent [ar'dã], *a.* burning, hot, fiery, scorching; (*fig.*) violent, intense; ardent, vehement, fervent, earnest, energetic, active; red, reddish (*of hair*); *charbons ardents*, live coals; *buisson ardent*, the burning bush.

ardeur [ar'dœ:r], *n.f.* intense heat; ardor, intense activity, fervor, earnestness; fire, spirit, mettle.

ardoise [ar'dwa:z], *n.f.* slate; (*colloq.*) score, account.

ardoisé [ardwa'ze], *a.* slate-colored.

ardoiser [ardwa'ze], *v.t.* to cover (*a roof*) with slates.

ardoisier [ardwa'zje], *n.m.* owner of *or* workman in a slate quarry.

ardoisière [ardwa'zjɛ:r], *n.f.* slate quarry.

ardu [ar'dy], *a.* steep, abrupt; (*fig.*) arduous, difficult.

are [a:r], *n.m.* 100 sq. metres (*approx.* 120 *sq. yds.*).

arène [a'rɛ:n], *n.f.* (*poet.*) sand; arena; (*fig.*) cock-pit, battle ground, theatre, scene; (*pl.*) the ancient Roman amphitheatres.

arénière [are'njɛ:r], *n.f.* sand pit.

aréomètre [areo'mɛtr], *n.m.* areometer, hydrometer.

aréopage [areo'pa:ʒ], *n.m.* areopagus.

arête [a'rɛ:t], *n.f.* fish-bone; awn *or* beard of wheat etc.; (*Geog. etc.*) ridge; *arête du nez*, bridge of the nose.

argent [ar'ʒã], *n.m.* silver; silver money; money, cash; (*fig.*) wealth, riches; (*Her.*) argent; *argent doré*, silver-gilt; *vif-argent*, quicksilver; *argent comptant*, ready money.

argentage [ARGENTURE].

argenté [arʒã'te], *a.* plated, silvered over; silvery.

argenter [arʒã'te], *v.t.* to silver over, to plate; to give the appearance of silver to.

argenterie [arʒã'tri], *n.f.* plate, silver plate.

argentin [arʒã'tɛ̃], *a.* silvery, argentine (*tint*); silver-toned (*ringing*); Argentinian, Argentine.—*n.m.* (**Argentin**, *fem.* **-ine** (1)) Argentinian (*person*).

Argentine (2) [arʒã'tin], l', *f.* Argentina, the Argentine.

argenture [arʒã'ty:r], *n.f.*, **argentage** [arʒã'ta:ʒ], *n.m.* silvering, silver-plating.

argile [ar'ʒil], *n.f.* clay, potter's clay, argil; *argile à porcelaine*, china clay; *argile réfractaire*, fire clay.

argileux [arʒi'lø], *a.* (*fem.* **-euse**) clayey, clayish.

argilière [arʒi'ljɛ:r], *n.f.* clay pit.

argon [ar'gõ], *n.m.* (*Chem.*) argon.

argonaute [argo'no:t], *n.m.* argonaut, nautilus.

argot [ar'go], *n.m.* slang, cant.

arguer [ar'gɥe], *v.t.* to infer, to deduce, to argue (j'arguë, nous arguions)

argument [argy'mã], *n.m.* argument, reasoning; proof, evidence; summary; theme, subject.

argumentateur [argymãta'tœ:r], *n.m.* (*fem.* **-trice**) habitual arguer *or* disputer.

argumentation, [argymãta'sjõ], *n.f.* argumentation, reasoning.

argumenter [argymã'te], *v.i.* to argue; to quibble.

argutie [argy'si], *n.f.* quibble, hair-splitting, cavil.

aria [a'rja], *n.m.* (*Mus.*) aria; (*pop.*) nuisance; fuss, bother.

arianisme [arja'nism], *n.m.* Arianism.

aride [a'rid], *a.* arid, dry; sterile.

aridité [aridi'te], *n.f.* aridity, dryness, barrenness, sterility.

arien [a'rjɛ̃] *a.* (*fem.* **arienne**) Arian.—*n.m.* (**Arien**, *fem.* **Arienne**) Arian (*person*).

aristocrate [aristo'krat], *a.* aristocratic.—*n.* aristocrat.

aristocratie [aristokra'si], *n.f.* aristocracy.

aristocratique [aristokra'tik], *a.* aristocratic.

aristocratiquement [aristokratik'mã], *adv.* aristocratically.

Aristote [aris'tot], *m.* Aristotle.

arithmétique [aritme'tik], *n.f.* arithmetic.—*a.* arithmetical.

arithmétiquement [aritmetik'mã], *adv.* arithmetically.

arlequin [arlə'kɛ̃], *n.m.* harlequin; (*fig.*) turn-coat; weathercock; *habit d'arlequin*, patchwork, motley.

arlequinade [arləki'nad], *n.f.* harlequinade.

armagnac [arma'nak], *n.m.* brandy (*made in Armagnac, S. of France*).

armateur [arma'tœ:r], *n.m.* shipowner; captain of a privateer; privateer.

armature [arma'ty:r], *n.f.* armature, iron braces, stays, casing, gear etc.

arme [arm], *n.f.* arm, weapon; branch *or* arm (*of the service*); (*Her.*) armorial bearings; *arme blanche*, cold steel; *aux armes!* to arms! *un maître d'armes*, a fencing master.

armé [ar'me], *a.* armed, equipped; (*Her.*) armed (*with claws, horns, teeth etc.*); *béton armé*, reinforced concrete.

armée [ar'me], *n.f.* army; forces, troops, host; (*fig.*) body (*of officials etc.*); *l'Armée du Salut*, the Salvation Army.

armement [armə'mã], *n.m.* arming, raising of forces, warlike preparations; armament, equipment; (*Am.*) ordnance.

Arménie [arme'ni], l', *f.* Armenia.

arménien [arme'njɛ̃], *a.* (*fem.* **-enne**) Armenian.—*n.m.* Armenian (*language*); (**Arménien**, *fem.* **-enne**) Armenian (*person*).

armer [ar'me], *v.t.* to equip, to arm; (*Artill.*) to load, to mount (*guns etc.*); to cock (*a gun etc.*); (*fig.*) to fortify; to strengthen; (*Naut.*) to fit out. **s'armer**, *v.r.* to arm oneself, to take up arms; to protect oneself (*against something*).

armistice [armis'tis], *n.m.* armistice.

armoire [ar'mwa:r], *n.f.* closet, cupboard; clothes-press, wardrobe.

armoiries [armwa'ri], *n.f.* (*used only in pl.*) arms, armorial bearings.

armorial [armo'rjal], *a.* (*m. pl.* **-aux**) armorial, pertaining to heraldry.—*n.m.* armorial, book of heraldry.

armoricain [armori'kɛ̃], *a.* Armorican (*of Brittany*).

armorier [armo'rje], *v.t.* to put *or* paint a coat of arms upon, to blazon.

Armorique [armɔ'rik], **l'**, *f.* Armorica.
armoriste [armɔ'rist], *n.m.* armorist, heraldic engraver.
armure [ar'my:r], *n.f.* armor, arms and armor; casing, wrapper; armature (*of a magnet, dynamo etc.*); (*Agric.*) tree-guard; (*Naut.*) fish (*of a mast, yard etc.*); (*fig.*) defence, protection.
armurerie [armyrə'ri], *n.f.* armory; manufacture of arms; arms factory.
armurier [army'rje], *n.m.* armorer, gunsmith.
arnica [arni'ka], *n.m.* (*Bot.*) arnica.
aromatique [arɔma'tik], *a.* aromatic, fragrant, spicy.
aromatiser [arɔmati'ze], *v.t.* to aromatize, to perfume, to flavor.
arome [a'ro:m], *n.m.* aroma, perfume, scent.
aronde [a'rɔ̃:d], *n.f.* (*Carp.*) dovetail, tenon.
arpège [ar'pɛ:ʒ], *n.m.* arpeggio.
arpéger [arpe'ʒe], *v.i.* (*conjug. like* ASSIÉGER) to play arpeggios.
arpent [ar'pɑ̃], *n.m.* acre (*French; about one and a half English or American acres*).
arpentage [arpɑ̃'ta:ʒ], *n.m.* land measurement; survey, measurement.
arpenter [arpɑ̃'te], *v.t.* to survey, to measure (*land*); (*fig.*) to stride up and down.
arpenteur [arpɑ̃'tœ:r], *n.m.* land surveyor.
arpon [ar'pɔ̃], *n.m.* ripsaw, crosscut saw.
arqué [ar'ke], *a.* bent, curved, arched (*of horses*).
arquebuse [arkə'by:z], *n.f.* arquebus.
arquebusier [arkəby'zje], *n.m.* arquebusier; gunsmith, armorer.
arquer [ar'ke], *v.t., v.i.* to bend, to curve, to arch.
arraché [ara'ʃe], *a.* uprooted.
arrachement [araʃ'mɑ̃], *n.m.* tearing up or away, pulling or rooting up or out; drawing, extraction.
arrache-pied (d') [daraʃ'pje], *adv. phr.* without interruption; **travailler d'arrache-pied**, to work with a will.
arracher [ara'ʃe], *v.t.* to pull or tear away, up or out; to extract, to uproot, to grub up; (*fig.*) to extort. **s'arracher**, *v.r.* to tear oneself away, to get away; to break away or off.
arraisonner [arɛzɔ'ne], *v.t.* (*Naut.*) to hail (*a ship*); to stop and examine (*a ship*).
arrangeant [arɑ̃'ʒɑ̃], *a.* accommodating, easy to deal with or get on with.
arrangement [arɑ̃ʒ'mɑ̃], *n.m.* arrangement, disposition, adjustment, setting in order; order, plan, method; agreement, settlement; (*pl.*) terms; measures; (*Math.*) permutations.
arranger [arɑ̃'ʒe], *v.t.* (*conjug. like* MANGER) to arrange, to put in order; to settle, to compromise, to compose (*a difference etc.*); to manage, to regulate; to make suitable; to fit up (*a house*); to trim up; *cela m'arrange*, that suits me; *comme vous voilà arrangé!* what a sight you look! **s'arranger**, *v.r.* to prepare oneself, to make arrangements (*pour*); to come to an agreement; to be satisfied (*de*); *arrangez-vous*, that is your lookout.
arrérages [are'ra:ʒ], *n.m.* (*used only in pl.*) arrears.

arrestation [arɛsta'sjɔ̃], *n.f.* arrest, apprehension; custody.
arrêt [a'rɛ], *n.m.* stoppage, stop, check, pause, halt; suspension, cessation; (*Law*) award, judgment; arrest, apprehension; (*fig.*) decree; (*pl.*) imprisonment; **arrêt fixe**, regular (bus) stop; **arrêt facultatif**, request stop; **arrêt de mort**, sentence of death; **chien d'arrêt**, setter, pointer; **robinet d'arrêt**, stopcock.
arrêté (1) [arɛ'te], *a.* stopped; decreed, agreed upon, resolved; arrested; fastened.
arrêté (2) [arɛ'te], *n.m.* departmental minute, order, decree, decision; **arrêté ministériel**, order in council.
arrêter [arɛ'te], *v.t.* to check, to stop the movement of, to throw out of gear; to delay, to detain, to hinder, to impede, to hold up; to arrest; to decide, to resolve; to settle (*an account*). **s'arrêter**, *v.r.* to stop, to pause, to hesitate; to remain, to loiter; to lag; to leave off; to be concluded, determined or resolved (*of bargains etc.*); to resolve upon; to dwell (*upon*), to insist (*sur*).
arrhes [ar], *n.f. pl.* earnest (*money*), deposit.
arrière [a'rjɛːr], *adv.* behind (*of time and place*); backward; (*Naut.*) aft, abaft; *en arrière*, backward; behindhand, in arrears; at the back, at the rear (*of a train*); *en arrière de*, behind.—*int.* away!—*n.m.* back part, rear; (*Naut.*) stern (*of a vessel*); (*Ftb.*) back.
arriéré [arje're], *a.* in arrears; behindhand, backward, poorly developed.—*n.m.* arrears.

[In *pl.* of all the following compounds *arrière* is *inv.* The *n.* has its normal *pl.*]

arrière-boutique [arjɛrbu'tik], *n.f.* room at the back of a shop.
arrière-cour [arjɛr'ku:r], *n.f.* back yard.
arrière-cousin [arjɛrku'zɛ̃], *n.m.* (*fem.* **cousine**) distant cousin, cousin several times removed.
arrière-cuisine [arjɛrkɥi'zin], *n.f.* back kitchen, scullery.
arrière-garde [arjɛr'gard], *n.f.* rear guard.
arrière-goût [arjɛr'gu], *n.m.* after-taste.
arrière-grand-mère [arjɛrgrɑ̃'mɛːr], *n.f.* (*pl.* **-grand-mères**) great-grandmother.
arrière-grand-père [arjɛrgrɑ̃'pɛːr], *n.m.* (*pl.* **-grands-pères**) great-grandfather.
arrière-main [arjɛr'mɛ̃], *n.f.* back of the hand; (*Ten.*) backhand (stroke).—*n.m.* hindquarters (*of a horse*).
arrière-neveu [arjɛrnə'vø], *n.m.* (*pl.* **-eux**) grand-nephew.
arrière-nièce [arjɛr'njɛs], *n.f.* grand-niece.
arrière-pays [arjɛr'pei], *n.m. inv.* hinterland.
arrière-pensée [arjɛrpɑ̃'se], *n.f.* mental reservation, hidden motive, underlying design.
arrière-petite-fille [arjɛrpətit'fi:j], *n.f.* (*pl.* **-petites-filles**) great-granddaughter.
arrière-petit-fils [arjɛrpəti'fis], *n.m.* (*pl.* **-petits-fils**) great-grandson.
arrière-petits-enfants [arjɛrpətizɑ̃'fɑ̃], *n.m. pl.* great-grandchildren.
arrière-plan [arjɛr'plɑ̃], *n.m.* (*Paint., Cine.*) background.
arrière-point [arjɛr'pwɛ̃], *n.m.* back-stitch.
arrière-port [arjɛr'pɔ:r], *n.m.* inner harbor.

arriérer [arje're], *v.t.* (*conjug. like* CÉDER) to defer, to put off; to leave in arrears. **s'arriérer**, *v.r.* to stay behind; to be in arrears.

arrière-saison [arjɛrsɛ'zɔ̃], *n.f.* end of autumn.

arrière-train [arjɛr'trɛ̃], *n.m.* hindquarters (*of an animal*).

arrimage [ari'ma:ʒ], *n.m.* (*Naut.*) stowage.

arrimer [ari'me], *v.t.* (*Naut.*) to stow (*cargo etc.*).

arrimeur [ari'mœːr], *n.m.* stower, stevedore.

arrivée [ari've], *n.f.* arrival, moment of landing, coming etc., advent.

arriver [ari've], *v.i.* (*conjug. with* ÊTRE) to arrive, to come; to arrive at, to attain, to get to, to reach (*à*); to make one's way, to succeed; to happen, to occur, to take place; to veer; *quoi qu'il arrive*, come what may.

arrivisme [ari'vism], *n.m.* push, unscrupulous ambition.

arriviste [ari'vist], *n.m.* an unscrupulously ambitious person.

arrogamment [arɔga'mã], *adv.* arrogantly, haughtily; insolently.

arrogance [arɔ'gɑ̃:s], *n.f.* arrogance, haughtiness, superciliousness.

arrogant [arɔ'gã], *a.* arrogant, haughty, supercilious, overbearing.

arroger (s') [sarɔ'ʒe], *v.r.* (*conjug. like* MANGER) to assume *or* claim presumptuously.

arrondi [arɔ̃'di], *a.* rounded.—*n.m.* curve (*of shoulder, face etc.*).

arrondir [arɔ̃'diːr], *v.t.* to make round; to give a curved shape to, to round off; (*fig.*) to enlarge, to extend. **s'arrondir**, *v.r.* to grow *or* become round; to increase one's estate.

arrondissement [arɔ̃dis'mã], *n.m.* rounding, making round; roundness; division of a (*French*) department; (*in Paris*) one of the 20 wards.

arrosage [aro'za:ʒ], **arrosement** [aroz'mã], *n.m.* watering, sprinkling; irrigation.

arroser [aro'ze], *v.t.* to water, to wet, to sprinkle; to irrigate (*land*); to soak, to moisten; to flow through (*of a river*); to bathe (*with tears*).

arrosoir [aro'zwaːr], *n.m.* watering can.

arsenal [arsə'nal], *n.m.* arsenal; *arsenal maritime*, naval dockyard.

arsenic [arsə'nik], *n.m.* arsenic.

arsenical [arsəni'kal], *a.* (*m.pl.* -**aux**) arsenical. —*n.m. pl.* (-**aux**) arsenical compounds.

art [aːr], *n.m.* art; skill, dexterity, artifice; *arts d'agrément*, accomplishments; *les beaux-arts*, the fine arts.

artère [ar'tɛ:r], *n.f.* artery; (*fig.*) thoroughfare (*in a town*).

artériel [arte'rjɛl], *a.* (*fem.* -**elle**) arterial; *tension artérielle*, blood pressure.

artériole [arte'rjɔl], *n.f.* small artery.

artésien [arte'zjɛ̃], *a.* (*fem.* -**enne**) artesian; *puits artésien*, artesian well.—*n.m.* (**Artésien**, *fem.* -**enne**) inhabitant *or* native of Artois.

arthrite [ar'trit], *n.f.* arthritis.

arthritique [artri'tik], *a.* arthritic.

artichaut [arti'ʃo], *n.m.* globe artichoke.

article [ar'tikl], *n.m.* article (*in all English senses*); clause, provision (*of a treaty etc.*); item; commodity; (*pl.*) goods; *article de fond*, leading article, éditorial.

articulaire [artiky'lɛ:r], *a.* articular.

articulation [artikyla'sjɔ̃], *n.f.* articulation, pronunciation; (*Bot., Anat.*) joint, articulation; (*Law*) enumeration of facts.

articulé [artiky'le], *a.* articulate, clear, distinct; jointed, articulated.

articuler [artiky'le], *v.t.* to articulate, to put together by the joints; to pronounce distinctly; (*Law*) to enumerate. **s'articuler**, *v.r.* to be connected by joints.

artifice [arti'fis], *n.m.* artifice, contrivance, expedient; dodge, trick, stratagem; craft, ruse; *un feu d'artifice*, fireworks.

artificiel [artifi'sjɛl], *a.* (*fem.* -**elle**) artificial; fictitious, spurious.

artificiellement [artifisjɛl'mã], *adv.* artificially.

artificieusement [artifisjøz'mã], *adv.* cunningly, craftily, artfully, slyly.

artificieux [artifi'sjø], *a.* (*fem* -**euse**) artful, cunning.

artillerie [artij'ri], *n.f.* artillery, ordnance.

artilleur [arti'jœ:r], *n.m.* artilleryman, gunner.

artimon [arti'mɔ̃], *n.m.* mizen-mast *or* -sail.

artisan [arti'zã], *n.m.* artisan, operative, mechanic; (*fig.*) author, architect, contriver, maker.

artiste [ar'tist], *a.* artistic (*of persons*).—*n.* artist; player, performer.

artistement [artistə'mã], *adv.* in an artistic manner; skilfully, artistically.

artistique [artis'tik], *a.* artistic, pertaining to art.

as [ɑ:s], *n.m.* ace (*at cards, dice*); as (*Roman coin and weight*).

asbeste [az'bɛst], *n.m.* asbestos.

ascendance [asã'dã:s], *n.f.* ascent; ancestry.

ascendant [asã'dã], *n.m.* ascendant; ascendency, influence; (*pl.*) ancestors.—*a.* ascending, ascendant; going upward, rising.

ascenseur [asã'sœ:r], *n.m.* lift, (*Am.*) elevator.

ascension [asã'sjɔ̃], *n.f.* ascent, climbing, rising; upstroke (*of machinery*); (*Jour de*) *l'Ascension*, Ascension Day.

ascète [a'sɛt], *n.* ascetic.

ascétique [ase'tik], *a.* ascetic, rigid, severe.

ascétisme [ase'tism], *n.m.* asceticism.

asepsie [asɛp'si], *n.f.* (*Med.*) asepsis.

aseptique [asɛp'tik], *a.* and *n.m.* aseptic.

aseptiser [asɛpti'ze], *v.t.* to render aseptic.

asexué [asɛk'sɥe], **asexuel** [asɛk'sɥɛl] (*fem.* -**elle**), *a.* asexual.

asiatique [azja'tik], *a.* Asiatic; *grippe asiatique*, Asian flu.—*n.* (**Asiatique**) native of Asia.

Asie [a'zi], *f.* Asia; *Asie Mineure*, Asia Minor.

asile [a'zil], *n.m.* asylum, place of refuge, sanctuary, retreat, home (*for the aged etc.*); (*fig.*) protection, refuge; *asile d'aliénés*, mental hospital.

asine [a'zin], *a.* asinine.

aspect [as'pɛ], *n.m.* aspect, view, look; countenance; phase, bearing; point of view.

asperge [as'pɛrʒ], *n.f.* asparagus (*head of*).

aspergement [aspɛrʒə'mã], *n.m.* sprinkling.

asperger [aspɛr'ʒe], *v.t.* (*conjug. like* MANGER) to sprinkle.

aspergerie [aspɛrʒə'ri], **aspergière** [aspɛr'ʒjɛ:r], *n.f.* asparagus bed.

27

aspérité [asperi'te], *n.f.* roughness, harshness; unevenness, ruggedness; (*fig.*) asperity.

aspersion [aspεr'sjɔ̃], *n.f.* aspersion, sprinkling.

aspersoir [aspεr'swa:r], *n.m.* holy water sprinkler; rose (*of a watering can*).

asphaltage [asfal'ta:ʒ], *n.m.* asphalting.

asphalte [as'falt], *n.m.* bitumen, asphalt.

asphalter [asfal'te], *v.t.* to asphalt.

asphodèle [asfo'dεl], *n.m.* asphodel.

asphyxiant [asfik'sjɑ̃], *a.* asphyxiating, suffocating; **gaz asphyxiant**, poison gas.

asphyxie [asfik'si], *n.f.* (*Med.*) asphyxia, suffocation.

asphyxié [asfik'sje], *a.* asphyxiated.—*n.m.* (*fem.* **-ée**) person in a state of asphyxia.

asphyxier [asfik'sje], *v.t.* to asphyxiate, to suffocate. **s'asphyxier**, *v.r.* to commit suicide by suffocation.

aspic [as'pik], *n.m.* asp, viper; (*Bot.*) spike lavender; (*Cook.*) cold meat *or* fish, in jelly.

aspidistra [aspidis'tra], *n.m.* aspidistra.

aspirail [aspi'ra:j], *n.m.* (*pl.* **-aux**) airhole (*in a stove, oven etc.*).

aspirant (1) [aspi'rɑ̃], *a.* suction, sucking (*of pumps*).

aspirant (2) [aspi'rɑ̃], *n.m.* aspirant, candidate; suitor; officer-cadet; midshipman.

aspirateur [aspira'tœ:r], *n.m.* ventilator; suction pump; vacuum cleaner.

aspiration [aspira'sjɔ̃], *n.f.* aspiration (*of the letter* h *etc.*); inhaling, inspiration; (*of pumps*) exhaustion, suction; (*fig.*) yearning, aspiration; (*Motor.*) suction, intake.

aspirer [aspi're], *v.t.* to inspire, to inhale; to draw in, to suck in; (*Gram.*) to aspirate. —*v.i.* to aspire, to aim at.

aspirine [aspi'rin], *n.f.* aspirin.

assagir [asa'ʒi:r], *v.t.* to make wiser, to impart wisdom to. **s'assagir**, *v.r.* to become wiser; to settle down.

assaillant [asa'jɑ̃], *a.* attacking, aggressive.— *n.m.* (*fem.* **-e**) aggressor, assailant, besieger.

assaillir [asa'ji:r], *v.t. irr.* to assault, to assail; to worry, to molest, to beset.

assainir [asε'ni:r], *v.t.* to render healthy; (*fig.*) to cleanse, to purify morally etc. **s'assainir**, *v.r.* to become healthy.

assainissement [asεnis'mɑ̃], *n.m.* purification, sanitation salubrity; drainage.

assaisonnement [asεzɔn'mɑ̃], *n.m.* condiment, seasoning, dressing.

assaisonner [asεzɔ'ne], *v.t.* to season, to dress, to give a relish to.

assassin [asa'sε̃], *a.* killing, murderous.— *n.m.* (*fem.* **-e**) assassin, murderer; ruffian.

assassinat [asasi'na], *n.m.* assassination, wilful murder, homicide.

assassiner [asasi'ne], *v.t.* to assassinate, to murder; (*fig.*) to bore; to tease, to importune.

assaut [a'so], *n.m.* assault, onset, attack.

assèchement [asεʃ'mɑ̃], *n.m.* drying up, drainage.

assécher [ase'ʃe], *v.t.* (*conjug. like* CÉDER) to drain (*a mine, pond etc.*).—*v.i.* to become dry, to be drained.

assemblage [asɑ̃'bla:ʒ], *n.m.* assemblage, collection, union, combination; (*Print.*) gathering; (*Carp.*) joint, scarf; **chaîne d'assemblage**, assembly line.

assemblée [asɑ̃'ble], *n.f.* assembly, meeting, company, party; convocation, congregation (*of churches*); meet (*of hunters*).

assembler [asɑ̃'ble], *v.t.* to assemble, to call together; to collect, to gather; to bring together; (*Print.*) to gather; (*Carp.*) to trim, to scarf. **s'assembler**, *v.r.* to assemble, to meet, to congregate.

asséner [ase'ne], *v.t.* (*conjug. like* CÉDER) to strike *or* deal (*a blow*).

assentiment [asɑ̃ti'mɑ̃], *n.m.* assent, agreement.

asseoir [a'swa:r], *v.t. irr.* to seat, to put on a seat, to set, to place, to fix, to establish; to pitch (*a camp etc.*). **s'asseoir**, *v.r.* to sit, to sit down, to take a seat, to settle, to perch.

assermenté [asεrmɑ̃'te], *a.* sworn in, attested.

assermenter [asεrmɑ̃'te], *v.t.* to swear in.

assertif [asεr'tif], *a.* (*fem.* **-tive**) assertive.

assertion [asεr'sjɔ̃], *n.f.* assertion, affirmation.

asservir [asεr'vi:r], *v.t.* to enslave, to reduce to servitude; to subdue, to conquer. **s'asservir**, *v.r.* to obey, to submit (*à*).

asservissant [asεrvi'sɑ̃], *a.* enslaving, subjecting, coercive.

asservissement [asεrvis'mɑ̃], *n.m.* bondage, servitude, slavery, subjection.

assez [a'se], *adv.* enough, sufficiently; tolerably, passably, rather.

assidu [asi'dy], *a.* assiduous, diligent, attentive; punctual; regular, constant.

assiduité [asidɥi'te], *n.f.* assiduity, application, diligence, attention.

assidûment [asidy'mɑ̃], *adv.* assiduously, diligently, constantly; punctually.

assiéger [asje'ʒe], *v.t.* (*see Verb Tables*) to besiege; to lay siege to; to surround; to importune.

assiette [a'sjεt], *n.f.* plate; plateful; attitude *or* posture (*in sitting etc.*), pose, situation, bearing, basis; seat (*in the saddle*); position, site; tone, state, disposition (*of the mind etc.*).

assiettée [asjε'te], *n.f.* plateful.

assignation [asiɲa'sjɔ̃], *n.f.* order to pay, transfer; (*Law*) summons, subpoena, writ; appointment, rendezvous, assignation.

assigner [asi'ɲe], *v.t.* to assign (*property in payment of a debt etc.*); to cite, to summon, to subpoena; to appoint, to make (*a rendezvous etc.*).

assimilation [asimila'sjɔ̃], *n.f.* assimilation.

assimiler [asimi'le], *v.t.* to make like; to liken, to compare, to assimilate.

assis [a'si], *a.* seated, sitting, situated; established.

assise [a'si:z], *n.f.* course (*of stones etc.*), foundation, basis; (*Geol.*) stratum; (*Mining*) measure (*of coal*); (*pl.*) assizes; **cour d'assises**, assize court.

assistance [asis'tɑ̃:s], *n.f.* audience, company, bystanders; congregation (*in a church*); assistance, help, aid; relief.

assistant [asis'tɑ̃], *n.m.* (*fem.* **-ante**) assistant (*priest, teacher etc.*); person present, bystander, witness etc.; **assistant(e) social(e)**, social welfare worker.

assisté [asis'te], *a.* receiving public assistance. —*n.m.* (*fem.* **-ée**) person in receipt of relief.

assister [asis'te], *v.t.* to assist, to help, to succor.— *v.i.* to be at, to be present (**à**), to look on, to be a witness (**à**).

association [asɔsja'sjɔ̃], *n.f.* association; union; partnership, fellowship, society, order.

associé [asɔ'sje], *a.* associated, admitted (*as a member*).—*n.m.* (*fem.* **-ée**) associate, fellow, member, partner.

associer [asɔ'sje], *v.t.* to associate, to take into partnership etc.; to divide *or* share something with someone; to link together, to connect (*ideas etc.*). **s'associer**, *v.r.* to enter into partnership, to associate oneself, to combine (*with*).

assoiffé [aswa'fe], *a.* thirsty; eager (*for*).

assolement [asɔl'mã], *n.m.* (*Agric.*) rotation (*of crops*).

assoler [asɔ'le], *v.t.* to vary *or* rotate (*crops*).

assombrir [asɔ̃'briːr], *v.t.* to darken, to throw a gloom over, to cloud. **s'assombrir**, *v.r.* to become dark *or* gloomy; to darken (*of the brow*).

assombrissement [asɔ̃bris'mã], *n.m.* darkening, gloom.

assommant [asɔ'mã], *a.* wearisome, tiresome, boring.

assommer [asɔ'me], *v.t.* to beat to death, to knock on the head; to overpower; to overwhelm, to stun; (*fig.*) to bore, to importune, to oppress.

assommeur [asɔ'mœːr], *n.m.* (*fem.* **-euse**) slaughterer (*of oxen etc.*).

assommoir [asɔ'mwaːr], *n.m.* poleaxe; bludgeon.

Assomption [asɔ̃p'sjɔ̃], *n.f.* (*Eccles.*) Assumption of the Blessed Virgin (August 15).

assomption [asɔ̃p'sjɔ̃], *n.f.* assumption.

assonance [asɔ'nãːs], *n.f.* assonance.

assonant [asɔ'nã], *a.* assonant.

assorti [asɔr'ti], *a.* assorted, matched, paired.

assortiment [asɔrti'mã], *n.m.* suitability, match; assortment, set.

assortir [asɔr'tiːr], *v.t.* to assort, to match, to pair; to stock, to furnish (*with things that go together or match*).—*v.i.* to match, to suit, to go well together. **s'assortir**, *v.r.* to match, to agree, to go well together.

assortissant [asɔrti'sã], *a.* suitable, matching, going well (*with something else*).

assoupi [asu'pi], *a.* dozing; dormant (*volcano*).

assoupir [asu'piːr], *v.t.* to make drowsy, sleepy, heavy *or* dull; (*fig.*) to assuage, to allay, to deaden. **s'assoupir**, *v.r.* to grow drowsy, sleepy, dull *or* heavy; to doze; (*fig.*) to be assuaged, to be appeased, to be stilled.

assoupissant [asupi'sã], *a.* making drowsy *or* sleepy, soporific.

assoupissement [asupis'mã], *n.m.* drowsiness, sleepiness, heaviness; (*fig.*) carelessness, sloth; (*Med.*) coma.

assouplir [asu'pliːr], *v.t.* to make supple, flexible *or* tractable; to break in (*a horse*). **s'assouplir**, *v.r.* to become supple, tractable *or* manageable.

assouplissement [asuplis'mã], *n.m.* suppleness, tractability, docility.

assourdir [asur'diːr], *v.t.* to deafen, to stun; to muffle.

assourdissant [asurdi'sã], *a.* deafening.

assourdissement [asurdis'mã], *n.m.* deafening, muffling, deadening; deafening noise; temporary deafness.

assouvir [asu'viːr], *v.t.* to glut, to satiate, to surfeit; to gratify; to cloy. **s'assouvir**. *v.r,* to be satiated, gratified *or* cloyed.

assouvissement [asuvis'mã], *n.m.* glutting, satiating.

assujettir [asyʒe'tiːr], *v.t.* to subdue, to subjugate; to compel; to fix, to fasten. **s'assujettir**, *v.r.* to subject oneself, to submit.

assujettissant [asyʒeti'sã], *a.* binding, constraining, fettering, restrictive.

assujettissement [asyʒetis'mã], *n.m.* subjection, subjugation; obligation, fixing.

assumer [asy'me], *v.t.* to take upon oneself, to assume.

assurance [asy'rãːs], *n.f.* confidence, security, assurance; certainty, conviction; warrant, pledge; insurance, underwriting; (*fig.*) boldness; (**les**) **assurances sociales**, the French equivalent of social security.

assuré [asy're], *a.* assured, confident; sure, secure, positive, certain; trusty; insured.— *n.m.* (*fem.* **-ée**) insured person.

assurément [asyre'mã], *adv.* assuredly, confidently; surely, undoubtedly; certainly.

assurer [asy're], *v.t.* to fix securely, to fasten, to steady; (*Naut.* and *Mount.*) to belay; to assure, to guarantee; to insure; to underwrite; to assert, to affirm. **s'assurer**, *v.r.* to make sure of, to ascertain.

assureur [asy'rœːr], *n.m.* underwriter, insurer, assurer.

Assyrie [asi'ri], *f.* Assyria.

assyrien [asi'rjɛ̃], *a.* (*fem.* **-enne**) Assyrian.— *n.m.* (**Assyrien**, *fem.* **-enne**) Assyrian (*person*).

aster [as'tɛːr], *n.m.* (*Bot.*) aster.

astérie [aste'ri], *n.f.* starfish.

astérisque [aste'risk], *n.m.* asterisk.

astéroïde [astero'id], *n.m.* asteroid.

asthmatique [asma'tik], *a.* asthmatic.

asthme [asm], *n.m.* asthma.

asticot [asti'ko], *n.m.* gentle (*bait for fishing*); maggot.

asticoter [astiko'te], *v.t.* (*colloq.*) to tease, to worry.

astigmate [astig'mat], *a.* astigmatic.

astigmatisme [astigma'tism], *n.m.* astigmatism.

astiquer [asti'ke], *v.t.* to polish, to furbish, to glaze.

astracan *or* **astrakan** [astra'kã], *n.m.* astrakhan, Persian lamb (*fur*).

astral [as'tral], *a.* (*m. pl.* **-aux**) astral.

astre [astr], *n.m.* star; (*fig.*) celebrity.

astreindre [as'trɛ̃:dr], *v.t. irr.* (*conjug. like* CRAINDRE) to oblige, to compel, to subject. **s'astreindre**, *v.r.* to confine oneself, to tie oneself down (**à**).

astreinte [as'trɛ̃:t], *n.f.* (*Law*) compulsion; fine for delay in the performance of a contract.

astringence [astrɛ̃'ʒã], *n.f.* astringency.

astringent [astrɛ̃'ʒã], *a.* and *n.m.* astringent.

astroïde [astro'id], *a.* star-shaped.

astrologie [astrolɔ'ʒi], *n.f.* astrology.

astrologique [astrolɔ'ʒik], *a.* astrological.

astrologue [astro'lɔg], *n.m.* astrologer.

astronaute [astro'noːt], *n.m.* astronaut.

astronautique [astrono'tik], *n.f.* astronautics.

astronome [astro'nɔm], *n.m.* astronomer.

astronomie [astrɔnɔ'mi], *n.f.* astronomy.
astronomique [astrɔnɔ'mik], *a.* astronomical, astronomic.
astrophysique [astrɔfi'zik], *a.* astrophysical. —*n.f.* astrophysics.
astuce [as'tys], *n.f.* craft, guile; cunning.
astucieusement [astysjøz'mã], *adv.* craftily, cunningly.
astucieux [asty'sjø], *a.* (*fem.* **-euse**) crafty, wily.
Asturies [asty'ri], **les,** *f. pl.* the Asturias.
asymétrie [asime'tri], *n.f.* asymmetry.
asymétrique [asime'trik], *a.* asymmetrical.
atelier [atə'lje], *n.m.* workshop, studio, atelier; (*collect.*) gang of workmen etc.; (*Freemasonry*) lodge, lodge meeting.
atermoyer [atɛrmwa'je], *v.t.* (*conjug. like* EMPLOYER) to put off, to delay (*a payment*). —*v.i.* (*fig.*) to put off, to make shifts. **s'atermoyer,** *v.r.* to compound with one's creditors.
athée [a'te], *a.* atheistic.—*n.* atheist.
athéisme [ate'ism], *n.m.* atheism.
Athènes [a'tɛːn], *f.* Athens.
athénien [ate'njɛ̃], *a.* (*fem.* **-enne**) Athenian. —*n.m.* (**Athénien,** *fem.* **-enne**) Athenian (*person*).
athlète [a'tlɛt], *n.m.* athlete.
athlétique [atle'tik], *a.* athletic.
athlétisme [atle'tism], *n.m.* athleticism; athletics.
Atlantide [atlã'tid], *f.* Atlantis.
atlantique [atlã'tik], *a.* Atlantic.—*n.m.* (**L'Atlantique**) the Atlantic (Ocean).
atlas [a'tlɑːs], *n.m.* atlas.
atmosphère [atmɔs'fɛːr], *n.f.* atmosphere.
atmosphérique [atmɔsfe'rik], *a.* atmospheric; **pression atmosphérique,** atmospheric pressure.
atoll [a'tɔl], *n.m.* atoll.
atome [a'toːm], *n.m.* atom; corpuscle.
atomicité [atɔmisi'te], *n.f.* (*Chem.*) atomicity, valency.
atomique [atɔ'mik], *a.* atomic(al); **commissariat à l'énergie atomique,** atomic energy authority.
atomiser [atɔmi'ze], *v.t.* to pulverize.
atomiste [atɔ'mist], *n.m.* atomist.
atomistique [atɔmis'tik], *a.* atomic(al).
atone [a'tɔn], *a.* atonic, debilitated, dull; lacklustre, expressionless (*of eyes*); (*Gram.*) atonic, unaccentuated.
atonie [atɔ'ni], *n.f.* atony, debility.
atonique [atɔ'nik], *a.* atonic.
atours [a'tuːr], *n.m.* (*used only in pl.*) woman's attire, dress, ornament.
atout [a'tu], *n.m.* trump; trump card.
atoxique [atɔk'sik], *a.* non-poisonous.
atrabilaire [atrabi'lɛːr], *a.* morose, peevish.
âtre [ɑːtr], *n.m.* hearth; fireplace.
atroce [a'trɔs], *a.* atrocious, cruel, excruciating; heinous, odious, dreadful.
atrocement [atrɔs'mã], *adv.* atrociously, cruelly, outrageously.
atrocité [atrɔsi'te], *n.f.* atrociousness, heinousness; atrocity, cruelty.
atrophie [atrɔ'fi], *n.f.* (*Path.*) atrophy.
atrophié [atrɔ'fje], *a.* atrophied, wasted, withered, stunted.
atrophier [atrɔ'fje], *v.t.* to cause to waste *or* wither. **s'atrophier,** *v.r.* to waste away, to atrophy.

atrophique [atrɔ'fik], *a.* atrophic.
attablé [ata'ble], *a.* seated at table.
attabler (s') [ata'ble], *v.r.* to sit down to *or* take one's place at table.
attachant [ata'ʃã], *a.* engaging, winning, attractive.
attache [a'taʃ], *n.f.* bond, cord, leash, strap; (*fig.*) attachment, affection for.
attaché [ata'ʃe], *n.m.* attaché (*of an embassy*).
attachement [ataʃ'mã], *n.m.* attachment; affection, liaison; eagerness, zeal.
attacher [ata'ʃe], *v.t.* to fasten, to tie, to attach, to fix; (*fig.*) to apply, to addict; to connect, to associate; to engage, to endear.— **s'attacher,** *v.r.* to take hold, to attach *or* fasten oneself; to cling, to adhere; to have an affection for; to apply oneself to.
attaquable [ata'kabl], *a.* assailable; of doubtful validity.
attaquant [ata'kã], *n.m.* assailant.
attaque [a'tak], *n.f.* attack, assault, aggression; fit, stroke.
attaquer [ata'ke], *v.t.* to attack, to assail, to assault; to seize suddenly (*of illness etc.*); to criticize; **attaquer en justice,** to sue for. **s'attaquer,** *v.r.* to make *or* conduct an attack (*à*), to set upon.
attaqueur [ata'kœːr], *n.m.* assailant.
attardé [atar'de], *a.* late, behindhand; mentally retarded (*child*).
attarder [atar'de], *v.t.* to make late, to delay. **s'attarder,** *v.r.* to be belated; to loiter, to linger.
atteindre [a'tɛ̃ːdr], *v.t. irr.* (*conjug. like* CRAINDRE) to reach, to hit, to attain; to arrive at; to overtake, to come up to.—*v.i.* to reach with difficulty, to attain (*à*); **atteindre à la perfection,** to attain to perfection.
atteint [a'tɛ̃], *a.* hit, struck; attacked, seized, affected; reached.
atteinte [a'tɛ̃ːt], *n.f.* reach, blow, stroke, touch; attack, fit, seizure (*of disease*); injury, damage, harm, wrong.
attelage [at'laːʒ], *n.m.* harnessing, yoking; team, yoke, set, pair; carriage, horses; (*Rail.*) coupling.
atteler [at'le], *v.t.* (*conjug. like* APPELER) to put horses etc. (*to*); to harness, to yoke; (*fig.*) to subjugate. **s'atteler,** *v.r.* to settle down to (*à*); (*fig.*) to apply oneself to, to hitch one's wagon to.
attelle [a'tɛl], *n.f.* hame; (*Surg.*) splint.
attenant [at'nã], *a.* contiguous, adjoining, next door to, close by (*à*).
attendre [a'tãːdr], *v.t.* to await, to wait for, to stay for; to look forward to, to expect; to look for, to count upon. **s'attendre,** *v.r.* to rely upon, to count upon, to trust (*à*); to expect, to look forward (*à*).
attendrir [atã'driːr], *v.t.* to make tender, to soften; to touch, to move. **s'attendrir,** *v.r.* to grow tender; to be moved, to melt, to pity, to relent.
attendrissant [atãdri'sã], *a.* moving, touching.
attendrissement [atãdris'mã], *n.m.* compassion, pity; tears, sensibility; tenderness.
attendu [atã'dy], *prep.* considering, on account of, in consideration of.—*conj.* **attendu que,** seeing that, as, whereas, since.
attenir [at'niːr], *v.i. irr.* (*conjug. like* TENIR) to adjoin, to be contiguous (*à*); to be related.

attentat [atɑ̃'ta], *n.m.* attempt at crime; crime, attempt; outrage, violation.

attente [a'tɑ̃:t], *n.f.* waiting, expectation; hope; *salle d'attente*, waiting-room.

attenter [atɑ̃'te], *v.i.* to make a criminal attempt.

attentif [atɑ̃'tif], *a.* (*fem.* **-tive**) attentive, heedful; considerate.

attention [atɑ̃'sjɔ̃], *n.f.* attention, notice; heed, care, vigilance; regard, respect, consideration; *attention!* look out! stand by!

attentionné [atɑ̃sjɔ'ne], *a.* attentive, considerate.

attentivement [atɑ̃tiv'mɑ̃], *adv.* attentively, carefully.

atténuant [ate'nɥɑ̃], *a.* mitigating; (*Law*) extenuating.

atténuation [atenɥɑ'sjɔ̃], *n.f.* attenuation, extenuation, mitigation.

atténué [ate'nɥe], *a.* attenuated, wasted, emaciated.

atténuer [ate'nɥe], *v.t.* to make smaller, thinner, feebler etc.; to attenuate; to extenuate, to mitigate.

atterrant [atɛ'rɑ̃], *a.* astounding, startling, overwhelming.

atterrement [atɛr'mɑ̃], *n.m.* overthrow; prostration, amazement.

atterré [atɛ're], *a.* horror-stricken, dumbfounded.

atterrer [atɛ're], *v.t.* to overwhelm; to astound.

atterrir [atɛ'ri:r], *v.i.* to land, to make land.

atterrissage [atɛri'sa:ʒ], *n.m.* landing; *terrain d'atterrissage*, landing-ground.

atterrissement [atɛris'mɑ̃], *n.m.* alluvion, accretion, alluvium.

attestation [atɛstɑ'sjɔ̃], *n.f.* attestation, evidence; certificate, voucher, testimonial; *attestation sous serment*, affidavit.

attester [atɛs'te], *v.t.* to attest, to certify, to avouch, to witness, to testify.

attiédir [atje'di:r], *v.t.* to cool, to make lukewarm; to take the chill off. **s'attiédir**, *v.r.* to grow cool *or* lukewarm; to cool off.

attiédissement [atjedis'mɑ̃], *n.m.* lukewarmness, coolness; abatement.

attifage [ati'fa:ʒ], **attifement** [atif'mɑ̃], *n.m.* get-up, rig-out.

attifer [ati'fe] (*always in a bad sense*), *v.t.* to dress up. **s'attifer**, *v.r.* to dress up, to rig oneself out.

attique [a'tik], *a.* Attic; (*fig.*) witty, urbane.—*n.m.* (*Arch.*) attic.

attirail [ati'ra:j], *n.m.* (*collect.*) apparatus, implements, utensils, gear, tackle; baggage, paraphernalia; show, pomp.

attirance [ati'rɑ̃:s], *n.f.* attraction (*vers*).

attirant [ati'rɑ̃], *a.* attractive, alluring, enticing, engaging.

attirer [ati're], *v.t.* to attract, to draw; to win *or* gain over, to lure, to wheedle, to entice; to occasion. **s'attirer**, *v.r.* to draw to *or* down upon one, to bring upon one; to incur, to win.

attisage [ati'za:ʒ], **attisement** [atiz'mɑ̃], *n.m.* the act of stirring up, poking (*a fire*), fanning (*flame*).

(**C**) **attisée** [ati'ze], *n.f.* a good fire; armful (*of stove wood*).

attiser [ati'ze], *v.t.* to make *or* stir up (*a fire*); to poke; (*fig.*) to incense, to stir up.

attisoir [ati'zwa:r], **attisonnoir** [atizɔ'nwa:r], *n.m.* poker (*especially in foundries*), fire rake.

attitré [ati'tre], *a.* recognized, appointed, regular, ordinary; hired.

attitude [ati'tyd], *n.f.* attitude; (*Paint.*) posture; (*fig.*) attitude of mind etc.

attouchement [atuʃ'mɑ̃], *n.m.* touch, contact.

attracteur [atrak'tœ:r], *a.* (*fem.* **-trice**) attractile.

attractif [atrak'tif], *a.* (*fem.* **-tive**) attractive.

attraction [atrak'sjɔ̃], *n.f.* attraction; (*pl.*) cabaret show.

attractivement [atraktiv'mɑ̃], *adv.* attractively.

attrait [a'trɛ], *n.m.* allurement, attraction, charm; inclination, bent; (*pl.*) attractions, charms; bait.

attrape [a'trap], *n.f.* trap, gin; (*fig.*) trick, take-in, sell, hoax; (*Naut.*) hawser.

attrape-mouche or **attrape-mouches** [atrap'muʃ], *n.m. inv.* flycatcher.

attrape-nigaud [atrapni'go], *n.m.* (*pl.* **attrape-nigauds**) booby trap.

attraper [atra'pe], *v.t.* to catch; to entrap, to ensnare; to take in, to trick, to bamboozle; to imitate; (*fam.*) to scold; to hit; to overtake, to catch up; to get accidentally (*a cold etc.*); *attrape!* take that! **s'attraper**, *v.r.* to hit (*against*); to be caught (*in*); to get hold of; to seize, to stick (*à*).

attrapeur [atra'pœ:r], *n.m.* (*fem.* **-euse**) deceiver, cheat, trickster.

attrayant [atrɛ'jɑ̃], *a.* attractive, winning, engaging, charming.

attribuable [atri'bɥabl], *a.* attributable, due to.

attribuer [atri'bɥe], *v.t.* to assign, to confer; to attribute, to ascribe, to impute (*a thing to someone*). **s'attribuer**, *v.r.* to assume, to take upon oneself, to claim.

attribut [atri'by], *n.m.* attribute, prerogative; special symbol *or* emblem; (*Gram.*) predicate.

attributif [atriby'tif], *a.* (*fem.* **-tive**) (*Gram.*) attributive; predicative; (*Law*) conferring a right.

attribution [atriby'sjɔ̃], *n.f.* attribution, conferment, awarding (*of a grant*); (*usu. in pl.*) privilege, prerogative (*of a person*); province, department, jurisdiction.

attristant [atris'tɑ̃], *a.* saddening, sorrowful, melancholy, grievous.

attrister [atris'te], *v.t.* to grieve, to sadden, to trouble. **s'attrister**, *v.r.* to be sad, to become sorrowful.

attrition [atri'sjɔ̃], *n.f.* attrition, friction.

attroupement [atrup'mɑ̃], *n.m.* riotous assemblage, mob, crowd, gathering of people.

attrouper [atru'pe], *v.t.* to assemble, to gather together in troops *or* a mob. **s'attrouper**, *v.r.* to flock together, to gather in crowds.

au [o], (*contraction of* À LE) to the.

aubade [o'bad], *n.f.* aubade, dawn song; (*iron.*) hot reception.

aubaine [o'bɛn], *n.f.* (*Law*) escheat; windfall, piece of good luck.

aube [o:b], *n.f.* the dawn; alb (*priest's vestment*).

31

aubépine [obe'pin], *n.f.* hawthorn, white-thorn, may.

aubère [o'bɛːr], *a.* red roan (*horse*).

auberge [o'bɛrʒ], *n.f.* inn, public-house, tavern; *auberge de (la) jeunesse*, youth hostel.

aubergine [obɛr'ʒin], *n.f.* aubergine, egg-plant.

aubergiste [obɛr'ʒist], *n.* innkeeper, publican, landlord, host.

aubour [o'buːr], *n.m.* laburnum; guelder-rose.

aucun [o'kœ̃], *a.* and *pron.* none, no one, not one; not any; anyone; any.

aucunement [okyn'mɑ̃], *adv.* in no wise, not at all, not in the least; at all.

audace [o'das], *n.f.* audacity, daring, bold-ness; impudence, insolence; *payer d'audace*, to brazen it out.

audacieusement [odasjøz'mɑ̃], *adv.* audaci-ously, daringly, boldly; rashly; impudently.

audacieux [oda'sjø], *a.* (*fem.* **-euse**) audaci-ous, bold, daring; impudent, presumptuous.

au deçà, au dedans, au dehors, au delà [DEÇÀ, DEDANS, DEHORS, DELÀ].

au-dessous [od'su], *prep.* below.

au-dessus [od'sy], *prep.* above.

au-devant [od'vɑ̃], *prep.* towards; *aller au-devant d'un danger*, to anticipate danger.

audibilité [odibili'te], *n.f.* audibility.

audible [o'dibl], *a.* audible.

audience [o'djɑ̃ːs], *n.f.* audience, hearing; reception; sitting, session, court, tribunal.

audiomètre [odjo'mɛtr], **audimètre** [odi'mɛtr], *n.m.* audiometer.

audiophone [odjo'fɔn], **audiphone** [odi'fɔn], *n.m.* audiphone.

audio-visuel [odjovi'zɥɛl], *a.* (*fem.* **-elle**) audio-visual; *moyens audio-visuels*, audio-visual aids.

auditeur [odi'tœːr], *n.m.* (*fem.* **-trice**) hearer, listener.

auditif [odi'tif], *a.* (*fem.* **-tive**) auditory.

audition [odi'sjɔ̃], *n.f.* hearing; (*Law*) hearing (*of a case etc.*); audition (*of a singer etc.*).

auditionner [odisjo'ne], *v.t.* to audition.

auditoire [odi'twaːr], *n.m.* auditory; congre-gation (*in church*), audience (*theatre etc.*).

auditrice [odi'tris], [AUDITEUR].

auge [oːʒ], *n.f.* trough (*for drinking etc.*); (*plasterer's*) hod; (*Elec.*) cell.

auget [o'ʒɛ], *n.m.* small trough; seed box.

augmentation [ɔgmɑ̃ta'sjɔ̃], *n.f.* augmenta-tion, increase, addition, rise (*in salary*).

augmenter [ɔgmɑ̃'te], *v.t.* to augment, to increase; to enlarge; to raise the salary of.—*v.i.* to augment, to increase, to grow, to rise (*in price*), to multiply. **s'augmenter**, *v.r.* to increase, to enlarge, to improve.

augural [ogy'ral], *a.* (*m. pl.* **-aux**) augural.

augure [o'gyːr], *n.m.* augur, soothsayer; augury, omen, sign; *de mauvais augure*, ominous, portentous.

augurer [ogy're], *v.t.* to augur; (*fig.*) to con-jecture, to surmise.

Auguste [o'gyst], *m.* Augustus.

auguste [o'gyst], *a.* august, majestic.

augustin [ogys'tɛ̃], *n.m.* (*fem.* **-ine**) Augustin-ian *or* Austin friar *or* (*f.*) nun.

aujourd'hui [oʒur'dɥi], *adv.* today, during this day; nowadays, now, at present.

aulnaie [AUNAIE].

aulne [AUNE].

aulx [oː], [AIL].

aumône [o'moːn], *n.f.* alms, alms-giving; (*fig.*) charity, favor.

aumônerie [omon'ri], *n.f.* chaplaincy.

aumônier [omo'nje], *n.m.* (*Eccles.*) almoner, chaplain; *aumônier militaire*, army chap-lain, padre.

aunaie *or* **aulnaie** [o'nɛ], *n.f.* grove of alders.

aune (1) *or* **aulne** [oːn], *n.m.* alder tree.

aune (2) [oːn], *n.f.* ell; (*fig.*) measure, standard.

aunée [o'ne], *n.f.* length of an ell.

auparavant [opara'vɑ̃], *adv.* before, formerly previously.

auprès [o'prɛ], *adv.* near, by, close by.—*prep.* **auprès de**, near to, close to; in com-parison with; in the service of; in the opinion of.

auquel [o'kɛl], *contraction* of À LEQUEL (*fem.* **à laquelle**, *pl.* **auxquels, auxquelles**) to whom, to which.

auréole [ore'ɔl], *n.f.* aureole, halo, nimbus; (*fig.*) glory, prestige.

auréoler [oreo'le], *v.t.* to crown with a halo.

auriculaire [oriky'lɛːr], *a.* auricular.—*n.m.* the little finger.

auricule [ori'kyl], *n.f.* lower lobe of the ear, auricle; (*Bot.*) auricula.

auriculiste [oriky'list], *n.m.* ear specialist.

aurifère [ori'fɛːr], *a.* auriferous.

auriste [o'rist], *n.m.* ear specialist.

aurore [o'rɔːr], *n.f.* dawn, morn, daybreak; (*fig.*) promise, beginning, the East; (*Astron.*) aurora.

auscultation [oskyltɑ'sjɔ̃], *n.f.* (*Med.*) auscul-tation.

ausculter [oskyl'te], *v.t.* to sound a patient.

auspice [os'pis], *n.m.* auspice, omen, presage; (*pl.*) protection, patronage.

aussi [o'si], *adv.* also, likewise, too, besides; as; so.—*conj.* and so, accordingly, therefore, consequently; but then.

aussière [o'sjɛːr], *n.f.* (*Naut.*) hawser.

aussitôt [osi'to], *adv.* immediately, forthwith. —*conj.* **aussitôt que**, as soon as.

austère [os'tɛːr], *a.* austere, severe, stern.

austèrement [ostɛr'mɑ̃], *adv.* austerely.

austérité [osteri'te], *n.f.* austerity; severity; strictness.

austral [os'tral], *a.* (*m. pl.* **-als** *or* **-aux**) austral, southern.

Australasie [ostrala'zi], **l'**, *f.* Australasia.

australasien [ostrala'zjɛ̃], *a.* (*fem.* **-enne**) Australasian.

Australie [ostra'li], **l'**, *f.* Australia.

australien [ostra'ljɛ̃], *a.* (*fem.* **-enne**) Austra-lian.—*n.m.* (**Australien**, *fem.* **-enne**) Aus-tralian (*person*).

autant [o'tɑ̃], *adv.* as much, so much, as many, so many; *autant de têtes, autant d'avis*, there are as many opinions as there are men; *autant que*, as much as, as many as, as far as, in the same way as; *d'autant*, in the same proportion; *d'autant mieux* or *d'autant plus*, the more, so much the more.—*conj. d'autant que*, seeing that, since, more especially as.

autel [o'tel], *n.m.* altar; (*fig.*) ministry, Church, religious life.

auteur [oʹtœːr], *n.m.* author, creator, maker; writer (*of a book etc.*); perpetrator; achiever, contriver, framer; composer, sculptor; informant, authority; *droit d'auteur*, royalty.

authenticité [otɑtisiʹte], *n.f.* authenticity, genuineness.

authentique [otɑʹtik], *a.* authenticated, genuine, incontestable, positive.

authentiquement [otɑtikʹmɑ̃], *adv.* authentically.

authentiquer [otɑtiʹke], *v.t.* to authenticate; (*Law*) to make legal and binding.

auto [oʹto], *n.f. abbr.* [AUTOMOBILE].

auto-allumage [otoalyʹmaːʒ], *n.m.* knocking (*of a car*).

autobiographe [otɔbjɔʹgraf], *n.m.* autobiographer.

autobiographie [otɔbjɔgraʹfi], *n.f.* autobiography.

autobiographique [otɔbjɔgraʹfik], *a.* autobiographical.

autobus [otoʹbys], *n.m.* bus.

autocar [otoʹkaːr], *n.m.* motor coach.

autochenille [otoʹʃniːj], *n.f.* caterpillar tractor; half-track vehicle.

autoclave [otoʹklaːv], *a.* and *n.m.* vacuum pan, sterilizer; *marmite autoclave*, autoclave, digester; pressure cooker.

autocopie [otɔkɔʹpi], *n.f.* cyclostyling.

autocopier [otɔkɔʹpje], *v.t.* to cyclostyle.

autocopiste [otɔkɔʹpist], *n.m.* duplicator, cyclostyle.

autocrate [otɔʹkrat], *n.m.* autocrat.

autocratie [otɔkraʹsi], *n.f.* autocracy.

autocratique [otɔkraʹtik], *a.* autocratic.

autocratiquement [otɔkratikʹmɑ̃], *adv.* autocratically.

autocritique [otokriʹtik], *n.f.* self-criticism.

auto-cuiseur [otokɥiʹzœːr], *n.m.* pressure cooker.

autodidacte [otɔdiʹdakt], *n.* self-taught person.

autodrome [otɔʹdroːm], *n.m.* race-track for motor cars.

auto-école [otoeʹkɔl], *n.f.* school of motoring.

autogare [otɔʹgaːr], *n.f.* bus or coach station.

autographe [otɔʹgraf], *a.* autographic.—*n.m.* autograph.

autographie [otɔgraʹfi], *n.f.* autography.

autographier [otɔgraʹfje], *v.t.* to autograph.

autogyre [otɔʹʒiːr], *n.m.* autogyro.

automate [otɔʹmat], *n.m.* automaton, robot.

automation [otɔmaʹsjɔ̃], *n.f.* automation.

automatique [otɔmaʹtik], *a.* automatic; *distributeur automatique*, (penny-in-the-) slot machine; *machine à vente automatique*, vending machine.—*n.m.* *l'Automatique*, automatic telephone.

automatiquement [otɔmatikʹmɑ̃], *adv.* automatically.

automatisme [otɔmaʹtism], *n.m.* automatism, purely mechanical movement.

automitrailleuse [otomitraʹjøːz], *n.f.* light armored car.

automnal [otɔʹnal], *a.* (*m. pl.* **-aux**) autumnal.

automne [oʹtɔn], *n.m.* or *f.* autumn.

automobile [otɔmɔʹbil], *a.* self-moving, self-propelling; *canot automobile*, motor-boat.—*n.f.* motor car; *salon de l'automobile*, motor show.

automobilisme [otɔmɔbiʹlism], *n.m.* automobilism, motoring.

automobiliste [otɔmɔbiʹlist], *n.* motorist.

automoteur [otɔmɔʹtœːr], *a.* (*fem.* **-trice**) self-acting, self-moving, self-propelling. (*C*) **auto-neige** [otoʹnɛːʒ], *n.f.* snowmobile.

autonome [otɔʹnɔm], *a.* autonomous.

autonomie [otɔnɔʹmi], *n.f.* autonomy, self-government; cruising range.

autonomiste [otɔnɔʹmist], *n.m.* autonomist.

autoplastie [otɔplasʹti], *n.f.* (*Surg.*) plastic surgery.

auto-portrait [otɔpɔrʹtrɛ], *n.m.* self-portrait.

auto-propulsé [otɔpropylʹse], *a.* self-propelled.

auto-propulsion [otɔpropylʹsjɔ̃], *n.f.* self-propulsion.

autopsie [otɔpʹsi], *n.f.* autopsy; post-mortem examination.

autorail [otɔʹraːj], *n.m.* rail car.

autorisation [otɔrizaʹsjɔ̃], *n.f.* authorization; authority, warrant; written consent or permission, license (*of a preacher*).

autoriser [otɔriʹze], *v.t.* to authorize, to empower, to commission; to license, to warrant, to permit, to sanction. **s'autoriser**, *v.r.* to have, get or assume authority; to act on the authority (*of*), to be warranted by (*de*).

autoritaire [otɔriʹtɛːr], *a.* and *n.* authoritative, commanding, arbitrary (person).

autoritairement [otɔritɛrʹmɑ̃], *adv.* authoritatively.

autorité [otɔriʹte], *n.f.* authority, legal or legitimate power; an authority; (*fig.*) control.

autoroute [otɔʹrut], *n.f.* motorway; (*Am.*) speedway.

auto-stop [otɔʹstɔp], *n.m.* hitch-hiking; *faire de l'auto-stop*, to hitch-hike.

autostrade [otɔʹstrad], *n.f.* special road for motor cars, motorway.

autosuggestion [otɔsygʒɛsʹtjɔ̃], *n.f.* auto-suggestion.

autour (1) [oʹtuːr], *adv.* about, round about.— *prep. phr.* **autour de**, about, round, around.

autour (2) [oʹtuːr], *n.m.* (*Orn.*) goshawk.

autre [oːtr], *a.* other; second; another different, distinct (*but of the same kind*).— *pron. indef.* another person, someone else; (*pl.*) the others, the rest.

autrefois [otrəʹfwa], *adv.* formerly, in former times; of old; *d'autrefois*, former, bygone; *des mœurs d'autrefois*, bygone customs.

autrement [otrəʹmɑ̃], *adv.* otherwise, after another manner; else; or else; *autrement dit*, in other words.

Autriche [oʹtriʃ], **l'**, *f.* Austria.

autrichien [otriʹʃjɛ̃], *a.* (*fem.* **-enne**) Austrian. —*n.m.* (**Autrichien**, *fem.* **-enne**) Austrian (*person*).

autruche [oʹtryʃ], *n.f.* ostrich.

autrucherie [otryʃʹri], *n.f.* ostrich farm.

autrui [oʹtrɥi], *pron. indef. inv.* others, other people, one's or our neighbors.

auvent [oʹvɑ̃], *n.m.* weather-board, porch roof; *auvent de capot*, hood louver.

aux [o], *pl.* [AU].

auxiliaire [oksiʹljɛːr], *a.* auxiliary, aiding, subsidiary.—*n.* auxiliary; helper, assistant.

auxquels [oʹkɛl], *pl.* (*fem.* **-elles**) [AUQUEL].

avachi [avaʹʃi], *a.* out of shape, worn out; (*fam.*) flabby, floppy, downcast (*of a person*).

avachir

avachir (s') [savaʃiːr], *v.r.* to flag; to grow fat and flabby; to get out of shape *or* down at heel.

avachissement [avaʃisˈmɑ̃], *n.m.* flabbiness; lack of energy.

aval (1) [aˈval], *n.m.* (*pl.* **avals**) guarantee, endorsement.

aval (2) [aˈval], *n.m.* down stream; **en aval de,** below.

avalaison [avalɛˈzɔ̃], **avalasse** [avaˈlas], *n.f.* sudden flood, spate; (*Naut.*) a long-continued wind from the sea.

avalanche [avaˈlɑ̃ːʃ], *n.f.* avalanche.

avalasse [AVALAISON].

avalement [avalˈmɑ̃], *n.m.* descent, lowering, letting down; swallowing.

avaler [avaˈle], *v.t.* to swallow, to swallow down; to drink, to gulp down; to let down, to lower (*things into a cellar*); (*fig.*) to endure, to pocket (*an affront*); to believe.— *v.i.* to go down (*a river etc. with the stream*).

avaliser [avaliˈze], *v.t.* to guarantee, to endorse [AVAL (1)].

avance [aˈvɑ̃ːs], *n.f.* part of a building etc. projecting forwards; advance; start, distance in advance; payment of money in advance; (*fig., pl.*) attentions, first steps in an acquaintanceship.

avancé [avɑ̃ˈse], *a.* advanced, forward, early; late (*of the hour*); over-ripe, tainted, high; liberal, progressive (*of opinions etc.*); paid in advance; put forward, enunciated.

avancement [avɑ̃sˈmɑ̃], *n.m.* projection; progress, advancement; preferment, promotion, rise.

avancer [avɑ̃ˈse], *v.t.* (*conjug. like* COMMENCER) to move, bring, put *or* hold forward, to advance; to pay beforehand *or* in advance; to assert, to bring forward, to urge; to promote, to give promotion to; to advantage, to profit; (*fig.*) to bring nearer, to hasten, to forward; to put on (*a clock*).—*v.i.* to advance, to proceed, to keep on; to project, to jut out; to make progress, to thrive, to get on, to gain ground; to go too fast; **l'horloge avance,** the clock is fast. **s'avancer,** *v.r.* to advance, to go on, to move forward; to get on, to improve; to get promoted, to be successful; to grow old; to project.

avanie [avaˈni], *n.f.* insult, affront; snub.

avant [aˈvɑ̃], *prep.* before, in advance of (*of time and order*); **avant J.-C.,** B.C.—*adv.* before, previously; forward, in front; farther in advance.—*conj.* **avant que,** before; **en avant!** forward!—*n.m.* front; prow, head, bow (*of a ship*); (*Ftb.*) forward.

avantage [avɑ̃ˈtaːʒ], *n.m.* advantage, benefit, profit, superiority, whip-hand; (*Ten.*) advantage, vantage.

avantager [avɑ̃taˈʒe], *v.t.* (*conjug. like* MANGER) to advantage, to give an advantage to; to favor. **s'avantager,** *v.r.* to take advantage.

avantageusement [avɑ̃taʒøzˈmɑ̃], *adv.* advantageously, to advantage; usefully, favorably.

avantageux [avɑ̃taˈʒø], *a.* (*fem.* **-euse**) advantageous, profitable, favorable; conceited, presumptuous; (*of dress*) becoming.

[In *pl.* of the following compounds *avant* is *inv.* The *n.* has its normal *pl.*]

avant-bassin [avɑ̃baˈsɛ̃], *n.m.* outer dock.

avant-bras [avɑ̃ˈbra], *n.m. inv.* forearm.

avant-centre [avɑ̃ˈsɑ̃ːtr], *n.m.* (*Ftb.*) centre-forward.

avant-corps [avɑ̃ˈkɔːr], *n.m. inv.* (*Arch.*) forepart (*of a building*).

avant-cour [avɑ̃ˈkuːr], *n.f.* fore-court.

avant-coureur [avɑ̃kuˈrœːr], *a.* going in front, preceding, presaging.—*n.m.* forerunner, precursor, harbinger.

avant-courrier [avɑ̃kuˈrje], *n.m.* (*fem.* **-ière**) (*fig.*) herald, forerunner, harbinger.

avant-dernier [avɑ̃dɛrˈnje], *a.* and *n.m.* (*fem.* **-ière**) the last but one.

avant-garde [avɑ̃ˈgard], *n.f.* vanguard, van.

avant-goût [avɑ̃ˈgu], *n.m.* foretaste; earnest; anticipation.

avant-guerre [avɑ̃ˈgɛːr], *n.m.* the pre-war period.

avant-hier [avɑ̃ˈtjeːr], *adv.* and *n.m.* the day before yesterday.

avant-main [avɑ̃ˈmɛ̃], *n.m.* flat of the hand; forehand (*of a horse*); (*Ten.*) forehand (stroke); (*Cards*) lead.

avant-port [avɑ̃ˈpɔːr], *n.m.* outer harbor, tide dock.

avant-poste [avɑ̃ˈpɔst], *n.m.* (*Mil.*) advanced post, outpost; (*fig.*) outer defence.

avant-première [avɑ̃prəˈmjɛːr], *n.f.* dress rehearsal; (*Cine.*) preview.

avant-projet [avɑ̃prɔˈʒɛ], *n.m.* rough draft.

avant-propos [avɑ̃prɔˈpo], *n.m. inv.* preface, preamble, introduction, foreword.

avant-scène [avɑ̃ˈsɛːn], *n.f.* front of the stage (*between curtain and orchestra*), proscenium.

avant-toit [avɑ̃ˈtwa], *n.m.* eaves.

avant-train [avɑ̃ˈtrɛ̃], *n.m.* fore-carriage, limber.

avant-veille [avɑ̃ˈvɛːj], *n.f.* two days before.

avare [aˈvaːr], *a.* avaricious, miserly, covetous, stingy, close-fisted.—*n.m.* miser, niggard.

avarement [avarˈmɑ̃], *adv.* stingily.

avariable [avaˈrjabl], *a.* perishable, damageable.

avarice [avaˈris], *n.f.* avarice, greed, covetousness; niggardliness, stinginess.

avaricieusement [avarisjøzˈmɑ̃], *adv.* avariciously.

avaricieux [avariˈsjø], *a.* (*fem.* **-euse**) avaricious, covetous, stingy.

avarie [avaˈri], *n.f.* damage (*to a ship or cargo*); deterioration.

avarié [avaˈrje], *a.* damaged, spoiled, deteriorated.

avarier [avaˈrje], *v.t.* to damage, to spoil. **s'avarier,** *v.r.* to become damaged.

avec [aˈvɛk], *prep.* with, at the same time as, along *or* together with; by means of, by; regarding; against, in spite of; **avec ça!** (*colloq.*) nonsense!

aveline [aˈvlin], *n.f.* filbert, Kentish cob.

avelinier [avliˈnje], *n.m.* filbert tree, hazel tree.

aven [aˈvɛ̃], *n.m.* pothole, swallow, chasm (*in mountain limestone*).

avenant [avˈnɑ̃], *a.* personable, prepossessing, comely, pleasing, taking.—*adv. phr.* **à l'avenant,** in keeping, in the same proportions, of a piece.—*n.m.* additional clause (*to an insurance policy*); rider (*to a verdict*); codicil (*to a treaty*).

34

avènement [avɛn'mã], *n.m.* coming, advent; accession, succession (*to a throne etc.*).

avenir [av'ni:r], *n.m.* future, future ages; posterity; (*fig.*) prospects; *à l'avenir*, in future, henceforth.

Avent [a'vã], *n.m.* (*Ch.*) Advent.

aventure [avã'ty:r], *n.f.* surprising *or* unexpected event *or* experience, chance, accident, luck; adventure, daring enterprise, hazardous exploit; love affair *or* intrigue; *à l'aventure*, at random; *d'aventure* or *par aventure*, by chance, perchance.

aventurer [avãty're], *v.t.* to venture, to hazard, to risk. **s'aventurer**, *v.r.* to venture, to take one's chance, to take risks.

aventureux [avãty'rø], *a.* (*fem.* **-euse**) venturesome, adventurous; left to chance.

aventurier [avãty'rje], *n.m.* (*fem.* **-ière**) adventurer, adventuress.

avenue [av'ny], *n.f.* approach; avenue.

avéré [ave're], *a.* authenticated, established by evidence.

avérer [ave're], *v.t.* (*conjug. like* CÉDER) to verify, to confirm, to establish. **s'avérer**, *v.r.* (*used only in inf. and p.p.*) to appear, to be distinctly, to turn out to be, to prove.

avers [a'vɛ:r], *n.m.* obverse (*of coins etc.*).

averse [a'vɛrs], *n.f.* sudden and heavy shower of rain, downpour; (*fig.*) flood (*of talk etc.*).

aversion [avɛr'sjõ], *n.f.* aversion, dislike, detestation.

averti [avɛr'ti], *a.* warned, informed; wide awake; well-informed, experienced.

avertir [avɛr'ti:r], *v.t.* to inform, to acquaint with, to give notice, to warn, to admonish (*de*).

avertissement [avɛrtis'mã], *n.m.* information, notification, advice, warning, caution; *avertissement au lecteur*, foreword (*of a book*).

avertisseur [avɛrti'sœ:r], *n.m.* look-out man; (*Theat.*) callboy; call bell, hooter; *avertisseur d'incendie*, fire-alarm.

aveu [a'vø], *n.m.* (*pl.* **-eux**) admission, avowal, confession; approbation, consent; *homme sans aveu*, vagrant, vagabond.

aveuglant [avœ'glã], *a.* blinding, dazzling; (*fig.*) distracting, misleading.

aveugle [a'vœgl], *a.* blind, sightless; blinded by passion etc., deluded.—*n.* blind person.

aveuglement [avœglə'mã], *n.m.* blindness; (*fig.*) infatuation, delusion.

aveuglément [avœgle'mã], *adv.* blindly, rashly; implicitly.

aveugle-né [avœglə'ne], *a.* and *n.m.* (*fem.* **-née**, *pl.* **aveugles-nés**) blind from birth.

aveugler [avœ'gle], *v.t.* to blind, to make blind; (*fig.*) to dazzle; to delude. **s'aveugler**, *v.r.* to shut one's eyes (*to*); (*fig.*) to be blinded, to be infatuated.

aveuglette [avœ'glɛt], *n.f.* (*only used in*) *à l'aveuglette*, blindly; *aller à l'aveuglette*, to go groping along, to go blindly *or* rashly; (*Av.*) *voler à l'aveuglette*, to fly blind.

aveulir [avœ'li:r], *v.t.* to render weak, to enfeeble, to enervate. **s'aveulir**, *v.r.* to sink into sloth.

aveulissant [avœli'sã], *a.* enfeebling, enervating.

aveulissement [avœlis'mã], *n.m.* enfeeblement, enervation.

aviateur [avja'tœ:r], *n.m.* (*fem.* **-trice**) aviator; air-man, air-woman; flyer.

aviation [avja'sjõ], *n.f.* aviation; *terrain d'aviation*, flying ground, airfield.

aviculteur [avikyl'tœ:r], *n.m.* one who raises birds *or* poultry; bird fancier.

aviculture [avikyl'ty:r], *n.f.* bird raising; poultry farming.

avide [a'vid], *a.* greedy, voracious, rapacious; eager for, grasping.

avidement [avid'mã], *adv.* greedily, voraciously; eagerly.

avidité [avidi'te], *n.f.* avidity, greediness; eagerness.

avilir [avi'li:r], *v.t.* to debase, to depreciate, to disparage; to lower; to degrade, to disgrace. **s'avilir**, *v.r.* to degrade oneself, to stoop to (*doing something*).

avilissant [avili'sã], *a.* debasing, degrading, humiliating.

avilissement [avilis'mã], *n.m.* debasement, degradation; depreciation, disparagement.

avilisseur [avili'sœ:r], *a.* (*fem.* **-euse**) debasing, degrading.—*n.m.* (*fem.* **-euse**) one who debases, disparages *or* degrades.

aviné [avi'ne], *a.* drunk, unsteady (*from drink*); wine-soaked (*of a cask*).

aviner [avi'ne], *v.t.* to soak *or* fill with wine. **s'aviner**, *v.r.* to get drunk.

avion [a'vjõ], *n.m.* airplane, aircraft; *avion de bombardement*, bomber; *avion de chasse*, fighter; *avion de ligne*, airliner; *avion à réaction*, jet-plane; *avion-fusée*, rocket-plane; *avion-taxi*, charter-plane; *par avion*, by air, by air mail.

aviron [avi'rõ], *n.m.* oar; (*Spt.*) rowing.

avis [a'vi], *n.m.* opinion, way of thinking, judgment; vote, motion; advice, counsel; information, notice, warning, caution, intelligence; *à mon avis*, in my opinion; *j'ai changé d'avis*, I have changed my mind; *avis au public*, notice.

avisé [avi'ze], *a.* shrewd, clear-sighted, wary, circumspect, prudent.

aviser [avi'ze], *v.t.* to perceive, to espy; to inform, to apprise; (*Comm.*) to advise by letter.—*v.i.* to consider, to think (*about*), to look (*to*). **s'aviser**, *v.r.* to think (*of*), to be minded (*to*); to venture to do.

avivage [avi'va:ʒ], *n.m.* brightening, reviving (*of colors*).

aviver [avi've], *v.t.* to revive, to brighten; to sharpen the edges of, to polish, to burnish; to irritate, to exacerbate (*a wound, resentment etc.*). **s'aviver**, *v.r.* to revive.

avocat (1) [avɔ'ka], *n.m.* (*fem.* **-e**) barrister, advocate, counsel; (*fig.*) pleader, intercessor, champion.

avocat (2) [avɔ'ka], *n.m.* avocado, alligator pear.

avoine [a'vwan], *n.f.* oats.

avoir [a'vwa:r], *v.t. irr.* to have; to possess; to experience, to feel (*pain, hunger etc.*); to obtain, to get, to buy etc.; to be aged (*so many years*); to have on, to wear; to ail; *avoir à*, to have to, to be under obligation to (*do etc.*); *y avoir* (*impers.*), to be; *avoir faim*, to be hungry; *combien y a-t-il de Paris à Londres?* how far is it from Paris to London? *il a quarante ans*, he is forty; *il n'y a pas de quoi*, don't mention it, no offence taken; *il y a deux mois que je* *suis ici*, I have been here two months; *il est arrivé il y a trois semaines*, he arrived three weeks ago; *j'ai à vous parler*, I have something to tell you; *qu'avez-vous donc?* what's the matter? *quel âge avez-vous?* how old are you? *qu'est-ce que vous avez?* what is the matter with you? *la pièce a cinq mètres de large*, the room is fifteen feet wide.—*n.m.* possessions, property, what one is worth.

avoisinant [avwazi'nã], *a.* neighboring, adjoining, close by.

avoisiner [avwazi'ne], *v.t.* to border upon, to be contiguous to.

avortement [avɔrtə'mã], *n.m.* abortion, miscarriage; failure.

avorter [avɔr'te], *v.i.* to miscarry, to have a miscarriage; to fail to develop, ripen etc. (*of plants, fruit etc.*); to prove abortive, to fail.

avorton [avɔr'tɔ̃], *n.m.* abortion; abortive child; (*fig.*) a paltry *or* miserable person *or* thing, a miserable specimen.

avoué [a'vwe], *n.m.* attorney, solicitor; *une étude d'avoué*, a solicitor's office.

avouer [a'vwe], *v.t.* to own, to acknowledge, to confess; to approve; to recognize as one's own, to avow.

avril [a'vril], *n.m.* April.

avunculaire [avõky'lɛːr], *a.* avuncular.

axe [aks], *n.m.* axis; axle, axle-tree, spindle, trunnion; (*Bot., Geol., Anat. etc.*) axis; (*fig.*) central support *or* main axis of a system of ideas etc.; (*Polit.*) the Nazi-Fascist Axis.

axiomatique [aksjɔma'tik], *a.* axiomatic.

axiome [ak'sjoːm], *n.m.* axiom; (*fig.*) an accepted proposition, truism.

ayant [ɛ'jã], *pres. p.* [AVOIR].

ayant cause [ɛjã'koːz], *n.m.* (*pl.* **ayants cause**) (*Law*) trustee, executor, assign.

ayant droit [ɛjã'drwa], *n.m.* (*pl.* **ayants droit**) beneficiary, rightful claimant.

azalée [aza'le], *n.f.* azalea.

azotate [azɔ'tat], *n.m.* nitrate.

azote [a'zɔt], *a.* nitric.—*n.m.* nitrogen.

azoté [azɔ'te], *a.* nitrogenized.

azoter [azɔ'te], *v.t.* to charge with nitrogen; to azotize.

azoteux [azɔ'tø], *a.* (*fem.* **-euse**) nitrous.

azotique [azɔ'tik], *a.* nitric.

azur [a'zyːr], *n.m.* azure, blue, sky-color; washing blue; *la Côte d'Azur*, the French Riviera.

azuré [azy're], *a.* azure, sky-colored; *la voûte azurée*, the azure skies.

azyme [a'zim], *a.* azymous, unleavened (*bread*).—*n.m.* azyme, unleavened bread; *fête des azymes*, feast of unleavened bread.

B

B, b [be], *n.m.* the second letter of the alphabet.

baba [ba'ba], *n.m.* a sponge cake, with sultanas, steeped in rum and syrup.

Babel [ba'bɛl], *n.f.* Babel; (*fig.*) uproar, disorder.

babeurre [ba'bœːr], *n.m.* buttermilk.

babil [ba'bi], *n.m.* babble, prattle; chit-chat, tattle; chattering, babbling.

babillage [babi'jaːʒ], **babillement** [babij'mã], *n.m.* prattle, babbling, twaddle; tittle-tattle.

babillard [babi'jaːr], *a.* babbling, prattling, talkative, garrulous; gossiping, tell-tale.—*n.m.* (*fem.* **-e**) chatterer, babbler; tattler, blabber, gossip, tell-tale.

babillement [BABILLAGE].

babiller [babi'je], *v.i.* to babble, to prattle, to chat; to gossip, to chatter; (*fig.*) to blab, to backbite.

babine [ba'bin], **babouine** [ba'bwin], *n.f.* the pendulous lip (*of certain animals*); (*colloq.*) chops.

babiole [ba'bjɔl], *n.f.* bauble, trinket, toy; (*fig.*) trifle, trumpery affair.

bâbord [ba'bɔːr], *n.m.* (*Naut.*) port (*side*).

babouche [ba'buʃ], *n.f.* Turkish heelless slipper, babouche.

babouin [ba'bwɛ̃], *n.m.* baboon, monkey.

Babylone [babi'lɔn], *f.* Babylon.

babylonien [babilɔ'njɛ̃], *a.* (*fem.* **-enne**) Babylonian.—*n.m.* (**Babylonien**, *fem.* **-enne**) Babylonian (*person*).

bac [bak], *n.m.* ferry, ferry-boat; vat; (*Elec.*) *bac d'accumulateurs*, accumulator-car.

baccalauréat [bakalɔre'a], *n.m.* baccalaureate, bachelorship (*of arts, science etc.*), school-leaving certificate.

bacchanal [baka'nal], *n.m.* (*colloq.*) racket, uproar.

bacchante [ba'kãːt], *n.f.* bacchante, lewd woman.

bâche [baːʃ], *n.f.* cart tilt; awning; tank, cistern; *bâche (goudronnée)*, tarpaulin.

bachelier [baʃə'lje], *n.m.* (*fem.* **-ière**) Bachelor (*ès Lettres, ès Sciences, of Arts, Science*).

bachique [ba'ʃik], *a.* bacchic, jovial, convivial; *chant bachique*, drinking song.

bachot [ba'ʃo], *n.m.* wherry, small ferry-boat; (*Univ. slang*) baccalaureate.

bachoteur [baʃɔ'tœːr], *n.m.* ferryman.

bacille [ba'sil], *n.m.* (*Biol.*) bacillus; *porteur de bacilles*, germ carrier.

bacillose [basi'loːz], [TUBERCULOSE].

bâclage [ba'klaːʒ], *n.m.* closing of a port by means of chains, booms etc.; line of boats (*in a port*) for the discharge *or* loading of cargo; (*fig.*) hasty, scamped work.

bâcle [baːkl], *n.f.* bar (*for door or gate*).

bâcler [ba'kle], *v.t.* to bar, fasten *or* secure (*a door, window etc.*); to stop, obstruct *or* interrupt (*traffic, navigation etc.*); (*fig.*) to do hastily, to polish off, to scamp (*work*); to bungle.

bactérie [bakte'ri], *n.f.* bacterium, microbe.

bactérien [bakte'rjɛ̃], *a.* (*fem.* **-enne**) bacterial.

bactériologie [bakterjɔlɔ'ʒi], *n.f.* bacteriology.

bactériologique [bakterjɔlɔ'ʒik], *a.* bacteriological; *guerre bactériologique*, germ warfare.

bactériologiste [bakterjɔlɔ'ʒist], *n.m.* bacteriologist.

bactériothérapie [bakterjɔtera'pi], *n.f.* medical treatment by means of bacteria.

badaud [ba'do], *n.m.* (*fem.* **-e**) ninny, booby, star-gazer; lounger, idler, rubber-neck.

badaudage [bado'da:ʒ], *n.m.* star-gazing, lounging, loitering, idling.

badauder [bado'de], *v.i.* to go gaping about; to lounge, to saunter, to loiter.

badauderie [bado'dri], *n.f.* star-gazing, silliness; lounging, idling, sauntering.

Bade [bad], *f.* Baden.

badigeon [badi'ʒɔ̃], *n.m.* badigeon, filling paste; whitewash; calcimine.

badigeonnage [badiʒɔ'na:ʒ], *n.m.* filling up with badigeon, making up; daubing; whitewashing.

badigeonner [badiʒɔ'ne], *v.t.* to fill up (*stonework*, *sculpture etc.*) with badigeon; to whitewash; (*fig.*) to disguise defects with varnish, rouge etc.; (*Med.*) to anoint.

badigeonneur [badiʒɔ'nœ:r], *n.m.* whitewasher; (*pej.*) dauber.

badin [ba'dɛ̃], *a.* waggish, jocular, roguish, droll.—*n.m.* (*fem.* **-e** (1)) wag, joker; buffoon.

badinage [badi'na:ʒ], *n.m.* badinage, raillery, banter; playfulness, jocularity (*of style*); mere child's-play.

badine (2) [ba'din], *n.f.* switch, light cane, wand; (*pl.*) small tongs.

badiner [badi'ne], *v.i.* to trifle, to dally, to toy; to speak *or* write banteringly *or* playfully.

badinerie [badin'ri], *n.f.* jesting, foolery, trifling; silliness, childishness.

(C) **bâdrant** [ba'drɑ̃], *a.* bothersome.

(C) **bâdrer** [ba'dre], *v.t.* to annoy, to bother.

bafouer [ba'fwe], *v.t.* to scoff at, to make game of.

bafouillage [bafu'ja:ʒ], *n.f.* gibberish, rigmarole; spluttering; bad running (*of engine*).

bafouiller [bafu'je], *v.i.* (*colloq.*) to stammer; to splutter; to miss, to chatter (*of engine*).

bafouilleur [bafu'jœ:r], *n.m.* (*fem.* **-euse**) stammerer.

bagages [ba'ga:ʒ], *n.m. pl.* luggage; *bagages enregistrés*, checked luggage.

bagarre [ba'ga:r], *n.f.* riot; uproar; crush, squabble, scuffle.

bagatelle [baga'tɛl], *n.f.* bauble, trinket, trifle, anything frivolous; trifling sum, mere nothing.

bagne [baɲ], *n.m.* penitentiary; penal servitude.

bagnole [ba'nɔl], *n.f.* (*fam.*) (old) motor car.

bague [bag], *n.f.* ring; ring band (*for birds*).

bague-agrafe [baga'graf], *n.f.* (*d'un stylo*) (fountain-pen) clip.

baguer [ba'ge], *v.t.* to baste, to tack, to stitch; to decorate *or* hang with rings; (*Hort.*) to ring (*trees*); to ring (*a bird*).

baguette [ba'gɛt], *n.f.* switch, rod, wand; pointer; clock (*of stockings*); glove-stretcher; long roll (*French bread*).

baguier [ba'gje], *n.m.* casket for rings, jewels etc., jewel box, ring stand.

bah! [ba], *int.* pooh! pshaw! nonsense! fudge!

bahut [ba'y], *n.m.* cabinet, trunk, chest; press, cupboard; (*Sch. slang*) grammar school.

bahutier [bay'tje], *n.m.* maker of trunks, chests, cabinets, etc.

bai [bɛ], *a.* bay; *une jument baie*, a bay mare.

baie (1) [bɛ], *n.f.* bay, gulf; (*Arch.*) bay, opening.

baie (2) [bɛ], *n.f.* berry.

baignade [bɛ'ɲad], *n.f.* bathing; bathing place.

baigner [bɛ'ɲe], *v.t.* to bathe, to give a bath to, to dip; (*fig.*) to wash, to water (*a coast etc.*); to wet, to suffuse.—*v.i.* to be plunged into; to welter (*in blood etc.*). **se baigner**, *v.r.* to bathe, to wash.

baigneur [bɛ'ɲœ:r], *n.m.* (*fem.* **-euse**) bather; bathkeeper *or* attendant, bathing attendant.

baignoire [bɛ'ɲwa:r], *n.f.* bathtub, bath; (*Theat.*) ground-floor box.

bail [ba:j], *n.m.* (*pl.* **baux** [bo]) lease.

bâillement [baj'mɑ̃], *n.m.* yawning, yawn.

bâiller [ba'je], *v.i.* to yawn, to gape; to open (*of fissures etc.*); to be ajar (*of doors*).

bailleur [ba'jœ:r], *n.m.* (*fem.* **-eresse**) one who leases, lessor.

bâilleur [ba'jœ:r], *n.m.* (*fem.* **-euse**) yawner; gaper.

bailli [ba'ji], *n.m.* (*Fr. Hist.*) bailiff.

bâillon [ba'jɔ̃], *n.m.* gag, muzzle.

bâillonnement [bajɔn'mɑ̃], *n.m.* gagging.

bâillonner [bajɔ'ne], *v.t.* to stop the mouth of, to gag, to muzzle; (*fig.*) to silence.

bain [bɛ̃], *n.m.* bath; bathing tub; (*pl.*) baths, bathing establishment, watering place, spa; *la salle de bain(s)*, the bathroom.

bain-douche [bɛ'duʃ], *n.m.* shower bath.

bain-marie [bɛma'ri], *n.m.* (*pl.* **bains-marie**) (*Cook.*) double saucepan for foods that burn easily; boiler (*in a kitchen range etc.*).

baïonnette [bajɔ'nɛt], *n.f.* bayonet.

baiser [bɛ'ze], *v.t.* (*of strictly literary use, no longer decent in conversation, practically replaced by* **embrasser**) to kiss.—*n.m.* kiss, kissing; salute.

baisse [bɛ:s], *n.f.* fall, abatement, decline; reduction *or* fall (*of prices etc.*); falling off (*of credit etc.*).

baisser [bɛ'se], *v.t.* to let down, to lower; to reduce the height of; to strike (*a flag etc.*); to bow (*the head etc.*).—*v.i.* (*with aux.* ÊTRE *or* AVOIR) to go down; to ebb; to be on the decline *or* the wane; to flag, to droop; to fail, to diminish. **se baisser**, *v.r.* to stoop; to bow down; to be lowered.

bajoue [ba'ʒu], *n.f.* jowl, chap (*of pigs etc.*); full and pendulous cheek.

bakélite [bake'lit], *n.f.* bakelite (*trade mark*).

bal [bal], *n.m.* ball, dance; *bal costumé*, fancy-dress ball.

baladeuse [bala'dø:z], *n.f.* street vendor's barrow; portable lamp; trailer (*for cycle or tram*).

baladin [bala'dɛ̃], *n.m.* (*fem.* **-e**) mountebank; buffoon.

balafre [ba'la:fr], *n.f.* gash, slash, cut; scar.

balafrer [bala'fre], *v.t.* to gash, to slash.

balai (1) [ba'lɛ], *n.m.* broom, besom; (*Elec.*) brush.

(C) **balai** (2) [ba'lɛ], *n.m.* cedar.

balalaïka [balalai'ka], *n.f.* balalaika.

balance [ba'lɑ̃:s], *n.f.* balance, scales, pair of scales; (*Comm.*) balance (*of an account*), balance sheet.

balancement [balɑ̃s'mɑ̃], *n.m.* balancing, poising; rocking, see-saw; (*fig.*) fluctuation, wavering, hesitation.

37

balancer [balɑ̃'se], v.t. (conjug. like COM-
MENCER) to balance, to poise, to hold in
equilibrium; to swing to and fro, to rock;
(fig.) to weigh, to consider; to square (accounts); to counterbalance.—v.i. to hesitate,
to be in suspense, to waver; to fluctuate, to
oscillate, to remain undecided. **se balancer**
v.r. to swing, to rock.

balancier [balɑ̃'sje], n.m. maker of weights
and scales; pendulum, balance; balancing-
pole.

balançoire [balɑ̃'swaːr], n.f. see-saw; swing.

balandre [ba'lɑ̃ːdr], n.f. flat canal boat.

balayage [balɛ'jaːʒ], **balayement** [balɛ
'mɑ̃], n.m. sweeping; (Tel.) scanning.

balayer [balɛ'je], v.t. (conjug. like PAYER) to
sweep, to clean with a broom; (Tel.) to scan.

balayette [balɛ'jɛt], n.f. small broom, whisk.

balayeur [balɛ'jœːr], n.m. (fem. -euse)
sweeper, scavenger.—n.f. (-euse) sweeping-
machine.

balayures [balɛ'jyːr], n.f. (used only in pl.)
sweepings.

balbutier [balby'sje], v.t. to pronounce
indistinctly.—v.i. to stammer, to stutter;
to mumble.

balbutieur [balby'sjœːr], n.m. (fem. -euse)
stutterer, stammerer.

balcon [bal'kɔ̃], n.m. balcony; (Theat.) dress
circle.

baldaquin [balda'kɛ̃], n.m. baldachin,
canopy; tester (of bed).

Bâle [baːl], f. Basel, Basle.

Baléares [bale'aːr], les, f. pl. the Balearic
Isles.

baleine [ba'lɛːn], n.f. whale; whalebone; rib
of an umbrella.

baleiné [balɛ'ne], a. stiffened with whalebone.

baleineau [balɛ'no], n.m. (pl. -eaux) young
whale.

baleinier [balɛ'nje], n.m. (fem. -ière) whaler.
—n.f. (-ière) whaleboat.

balisage [bali'zaːʒ], n.m. (Naut.) buoying,
signalling; (Av.) ground lights.

balise [ba'liːz], n.f. sea mark, buoy, beacon;
(Av.) ground light.

baliser [bali'ze], v.t. to buoy; to mark with
beacons or ground lights.

balistique [balis'tik], a. ballistic.—n.f. bal-
listics.

balivage [bali'vaːʒ], n.m. *staddling.

baliveau [bali'vo], n.m. (pl. -eaux) *staddle;
sapling.

baliverne [bali'vɛrn], n.f. nonsense, humbug.

baliverner [balivɛr'ne], v.i. to talk idly, to
talk twaddle.

balkanique [balka'nik], a. Balkan.

ballade [ba'lad], n.f. ballade; ballad.

ballant [ba'lɑ̃], a. waving, swinging, dangling.

ballast [ba'last], n.m. (Rail.) ballast.

balle [bal], n.f. ball; bullet, shot; bale, pack.

ballerine [bal'rin], n.f. ballerina.

ballet [ba'lɛ], n.m. ballet.

ballon [ba'lɔ̃], n.m. hand-ball; football; balloon; air balloon (child's).

ballonné [balɔ'ne], a. distended, swollen.

ballonnier [balɔ'nje], n.m. maker or vendor of
toy balloons.

ballon-sonde [balɔ̃'sɔ̃ːd], n.m. sounding
balloon.

ballot [ba'lo], n.m. small pack (of wares for
sale).

ballottement [balɔt'mɑ̃], n.m. tossing,
shaking.

ballotter [balɔ'te], v.t. to toss, to toss about;
to bandy; to keep in suspense.—v.i. to
shake, to rattle.

balnéaire [balne'ɛːr], a. pertaining to baths
etc.; **station balnéaire**, watering place;
seaside resort.

balourd [ba'luːr], a. dull, heavy, thick-
headed.—n.m. (fem. -e) stupid or dull person,
numskull, dunce.

balourdise [balur'diːz], n.f. gross blunder;
stupidity.

balsamier [balza'mje], **baumier** [bo'mje],
n.m. balsam tree.

balsamine [balza'min], n.f. balsamine.

Baltique [bal'tik], **la**, f. the Baltic (Sea).

balustrade [balys'trad], n.f. balustrade; low
railing etc.

balustre [ba'lystr], n.m. baluster, hand rail.

balustrer [balys'tre], v.t. to rail in, to surround.

balzane [bal'zan], n.f. white stocking (of a
horse).

bambin [bɑ̃'bɛ̃], n.m. (fem. -e) (colloq.) urchin,
brat, tiny tot.

bambou [bɑ̃'bu], n.m. bamboo (cane).

ban [bɑ̃], n.m. ban, announcement, public
order, edict or proclamation; banishment,
proscription; (pl.) banns (of matrimony).

banal [ba'nal], a. (m. pl. -aux) common,
commonplace, trite.

banalité [banali'te], n.f. vulgarity; banality,
commonplace, trite expression.

banane [ba'nan], n.f. banana.

bananier [bana'nje], n.m. banana tree;
banana boat.

banc [bɑ̃], n.m. bench, settle, form; reef,
sand bank; shoal (of fish); (Geol.) layer, bed;
dock, bar; **banc d'essai**, (Motor.) test
bench; (C) **banc de neige**, heap of snow;
banc d'huîtres, oyster bed.

bancal [bɑ̃'kal], a. (m. pl. -als) bandy-
legged.—n.m. (fem. -e) bandy-legged person.

bandage [bɑ̃'daːʒ], n.m. application of
bandages; bandage; belt; truss; tire (of
wheels).

bande (1) [bɑ̃ːd], n.f. band, belt, strip; ribbon;
bandage; **bande de papier**, slip of paper,
wrapper.

bande (2) [bɑ̃ːd], n.f. band, troop, company;
gang, crew, set (of brigands etc.); flock,
pack.

bandé [bɑ̃'de], a. bandaged, taut, stretched.

bandeau [bɑ̃'do], n.m. (pl. -eaux) headband,
bandage (for the eyes).

bandelette [bɑ̃'dlɛt], n.f. little band, string
fillet.

bander [bɑ̃'de], v.t. to bind or tie up; to
bandage; to tighten, to bend (a bow etc.)—
v.i. to be stretched, to be taut or too tight.

banderole [bɑ̃'drɔl], n.f. banderole, streamer.

bandit [bɑ̃'di], n.m. brigand, bandit; ruffian,
blackguard; scamp.

bandoulière [bɑ̃du'ljɛːr], n.f. shoulder strap,
bandolier; **en bandoulière**, slung across
the back.

banjo [bɑ̃'ʒo], n.m. banjo.

banlieue [bɑ̃'ljø], n.f. suburbs, outskirts (of
a town).

banne [ban], n.f. hamper; awning; tilt,
tarpaulin.

banni [ba'ni], *a.* banished, outlawed; (*fig.*) banned, forbidden.—*n.m.* (*fem.* **-e**) exile, outlaw.

bannière [ba'njɛ:r], *n.f.* banner, standard, flag.

bannir [ba'ni:r], *v.t.* to banish; (*fig.*) to expel, to dismiss.

bannissement [banis'mã], *n.m.* banishment.

banque [bã:k], *n.f.* bank, banking.

banqueroute [bã'krut], *n.f.* bankruptcy; (*fig.*) failure, collapse.

banqueroutier [bãkru'tje], *n.m.* (*fem.* **-ière**) bankrupt.

banquet [bã'kɛ], *n.m.* banquet, feast.

banquette [bã'kɛt], *n.f.* bench; towing path; (*Fort.*) banquette.

banquier [bã'kje], *n.m.* banker.

banquise [bã'ki:z], *n.f.* ice floe, ice pack.

bantam [bã'tam], *n.m.* bantam.

baptême [ba'tɛ:m], *n.m.* baptism, christening; *nom de baptême*, Christian name.

baptiser [bati'ze], *v.t.* to baptize; (*fig.*) to christen, to give a name *or* nickname to.

baptismal [batiz'mal], *a.* (*m. pl.* **-aux**) baptismal.

baptistaire [batis'tɛ:r], *a.* of baptism; *registre baptistaire*, parish register.

Baptiste [ba'tist], *n.m.* Baptist.

baquet [ba'kɛ], *n.m.* tub; (*Av.*) cockpit.

bar (1) [ba:r], *n.m.* (*Ichth.*) bass.

bar (2) [ba:r], *n.m.* bar (*of a public-house etc.*).

baragouin [bara'gwɛ̃], *n.m.* gibberish, jargon, lingo.

baragouinage [baragwi'na:ʒ], *n.m.* talking, gibberish, jargon etc.

baragouiner [baragwi'ne], *v.t.* to sputter out (*words*).—*v.i.* to talk gibberish; to gabble.

baraque [ba'rak], *n.f.* hut, shed, shanty; (*fam.*) hovel; booth (*at a fair*).

baraquement [barak'mã], *n.m.* (*Mil.*) hutting.

barattage [bara'ta:ʒ], *n.m.* churning.

baratte [ba'rat], *n.f.* churn.

baratter [bara'te], *v.t.* to churn.

barbacane [barba'kan], *n.f.* (*Fort.*) barbican.

Barbade [bar'bad], *f.* Barbados.

barbare [bar'ba:r], *a.* barbarous, barbarian; cruel, inhuman; (*fig.*) uncouth, rude; incorrect, ungrammatical.—*n.m.* (*usu. in pl.*) barbarians.

barbarement [barbar'mã], *adv.* barbarously.

barbaresque [barba'rɛsk], *a.* of *or* pertaining to Barbary.

Barbarie [barba'ri], **la**, *f.* Barbary.

barbarie [barba'ri], *n.f.* barbarity, rudeness; (*fig.*) cruelty.

barbarisme [barba'rism], *n.m.* (*Gram.*) barbarism.

barbe (1) [barb], *n.f.* beard; whiskers (*of cats, dogs etc.*); beard (*of grain*); wattles (*of fowls*).

barbe (2) [barb], *n.m.* barb, barbary horse.

barbeau [bar'bo], *n.m.* (*pl.* **-eaux**) barbel; (*Bot.*) bluebottle, cornflower.

barbelé [barba'le], *a.* barbed, spiked; *(fil de fer) barbelé*, barbed wire.

barbiche [bar'biʃ], **barbichette** [barbi'ʃɛt], *n.f.* beard growing only on the chin, goatee.

barbier [bar'bje], *n.m.* barber.

barbiturate [barbity'rat], **barbiturique** [barbity'rik], *n.m.* (*Chem.*) barbiturate.

barboter [barbɔ'te], *v.i.* to dabble about in mud *or* water (*with the beak, like a duck*); to paddle, to flounder about in the mud; (*fig.*) to mumble.

barboteuse [barbɔ'tø:z], *n.f.* rompers.

barbotière [barbɔ'tjɛ:r], *n.f.* duck pond; trough.

barbouillage [barbu'ja:ʒ], *n.m.* daubing; daub; scrawl; (*fig.*) twaddle.

barbouiller [barbu'je], *v.t.* to soil, to dirty, to blot; to daub, to besmear; to scrawl, to scribble; to splutter out, to mumble; to bungle.

barbouilleur [barbu'jœ:r], *n.m.* (*fem.* **-euse**) dauber, scribbler; mumbler.

barbu [bar'by], *a.* bearded.

barbue [bar'by], *n.f.* brill.

barcarolle [barka'rɔl], *n.f.* (*Mus.*) barcarolle.

Barcelone [barsə'lɔn], *f.* Barcelona.

bardane [bar'dan], *n.f.* burr, burdock.

barde (1) [bard], *n.m.* bard.

barde (2) [bard], *n.f.* bard (*iron armor for horses*); thin rasher of bacon used for larding poultry etc.

bardé [bar'de], *a.* barded; larded.

barder [bar'de], *v.t.* to bard a horse; to cover with thin slices of bacon, to lard; (*slang*) *ça barde* or *ça va barder*, things are beginning to hum.

bardot or **bardeau** (*pl.* **-eaux**) [bar'do], *n.m.* hinny; pack mule.

barème [ba'rɛ:m], *n.m.* ready-reckoner.

barguignage [bargi'na:ʒ], *n.m.* (*colloq.*) hesitation, wavering, dilly-dallying.

barguigner [bargi'ne], *v.i.* to be irresolute, to waver, to shilly-shally.

barguigneur [bargi'nœ:r], *n.m.* (*fem.* **-euse**) waverer, haggler.

baril [ba'ri], *n.m.* small barrel, cask, keg.

bariolage [barjɔ'la:ʒ], *n.m.* variegation, odd medley of colors, motley.

bariolé [barjɔ'le], *a.* gaudy, motley, many-colored.

barioler [barjɔ'le], *v.t.* to streak with several colors, to variegate.

barnache [BERNACLE].

baromètre [barɔ'mɛtr], *n.m.* barometer.

barométrique [barɔme'trik], *a.* barometrical.

baron [ba'rõ], *n.m.* (*fem.* **-onne**) baron, baroness.

baronnet [barɔ'nɛ], *n.m.* baronet.

baronnial [barɔ'njal], *a.* (*m. pl.* **-aux**) baronial.

baronnie [barɔ'ni], *n.f.* barony.

baroque [ba'rɔk], *a.* irregular, grotesque, odd; baroque.

barque [bark], *n.f.* bark, boat, small craft.

barquerolle [barka'rɔl], *n.f.* small mastless barge.

barquette [bar'kɛt], *n.f.* small craft; light puff-biscuit.

barrage [ba'ra:ʒ], *n.m.* barrier; toll bar; dam, weir, barrage.

barre [ba:r], *n.f.* bar (*of metal, wood etc.*); dash, cross, stroke (*of the pen etc.*); bar (*in courts*) of justice; (*Naut.*) helm, tiller, bar; (*Mus.*) bar; bore (*of river*).

barreau [ba'ro], *n.m.* (*pl.* **-eaux**) small bar (*of wood, metal etc.*); bench reserved for barristers; (*fig.*) lawyers, barristers; rung (*of a ladder*); *être reçu* or *admis au barreau*, to be admitted to the bar.

barrer

barrer [ba're], *v.t.* to bar up, to fence off; to obstruct, to thwart; to cross off, to erase.

barrette (1) or **barette** [ba'rɛt], *n.f.* square flat cap, biretta; cardinal's hat.

barrette (2) [ba'rɛt], *n.m.* axle, pin, bolt, etc. (*in watches, jewelry etc.*); bar (*of medal*).

barreur [ba'rœːr], *n.m.* helmsman, coxswain.

barricade [bari'kad], *n.f.* barricade.

barricader [barika'de], *v.t.* to barricade, to obstruct.

barrière [ba'rjɛːr], *n.f.* railing, barrier; gateway; farm gate.

barrique [ba'rik], *n.f.* large barrel *or* cask, hogshead.

baryton [bari'tɔ̃], *n.m.* baritone.

baryum [ba'rjɔm], *n.m.* barium.

bas (1) [ba], *a.* (*fem.* **basse** (1)) low; in a low situation; inferior; (*fig.*) vile, base, sordid; mean; subdued (*of sounds*); decadent; *la marée est basse*, it is low tide; *les Pays-Bas*, the Netherlands.—*adv.* low, down; in a subdued voice, tone, etc.; *ici bas*, here below; *là-bas*, over there, yonder.—*n.m.* the lower part, bottom *or* foot (*of something*); *en bas*, below, downstairs; *le bas de l'escalier*, the foot of the stairs.

bas (2) [ba], *n.m. inv.* stocking.

basalte [ba'zalt], *n.m.* basalt.

basane [ba'zan], *n.f.* sheepskin.

basané [baza'ne], *a.* sunburnt, bronzed, swarthy, tawny.

bascule [bas'kyl], *n.f.* see-saw; weighing machine.

basculer [basky'le], *v.i.* to see-saw; to rock, to swing.

base [baːz], *n.f.* base, foundation; lower part, bottom; basis.

base-ball [bes'bɔl], *n.m.* baseball.

baser [ba'ze], *v.t.* to found, to base, to ground. **se baser**, *v.r.* to be grounded; to depend, to rely.

bas-fond [ba'fɔ̃], *n.m.* (*pl.* **bas-fonds**) low-lying ground, hollow, bottom; shallow, shallow water; (*fig., pl.*) underworld.

basilic [bazi'lik], *n.m.* (*Bot.*) basil, sweet basil; (*Myth.*) basilisk, cockatrice.

basilique [bazi'lik], *n.f.* basilica.

basket-ball [baskɛt'bɔl], *n.m.* basketball.

basketteur [baskɛ'tœːr], *n.m.* (*fem.* **-euse**) basketball player.

basque (1) [bask], *n.f.* flap, skirt, tail (*of a garment*).

basque (2) [bask], *a.* Basque.—*n.m.* Basque (*language*).—*n.* (**Basque**) Basque (*person*).

bas-relief [barə'ljɛf], *n.m.* (*pl.* **bas-reliefs**) bas-relief.

basse (1) [baːs], [BAS (1)].

basse (2) [baːs], *n.f.* bass; violoncello; saxhorn.

basse (3) [baːs], *n.f.* shallow, reef.

basse-contre [bas'kɔ̃ːtr], *n.f.* (*pl.* **basses-contre**) (*Mus.*) contra-bass, lower tenor.

basse-cour [bas'kuːr], *n.f.* (*pl.* **basses-cours**) farmyard, poultry yard.

bassement [bas'mɑ̃], *adv.* basely, meanly, vilely.

bassesse [ba'sɛs], *n.f.* baseness; lowness (*of station etc.*); meanness, vileness; mean *or* sordid action.

basset [ba'sɛ], *n.m.* basset hound; *basset allemand*, dachshund.

basse-taille [bas'taːj], *n.f.* (*pl.* **basses-tailles**) (*Mus.*) baritone; (*Sculp.*) bas-relief.

bassin [ba'sɛ̃], *n.m.* basin; pond; dock; (*Anat.*) pelvis.

bassine [ba'sin], *n.f.* deep, wide pan.

bassiner [basi'ne], *v.t.* to warm (*a bed etc.*); to bathe (*with warm lotions*), to foment, to steep; to water, to sprinkle (*crops etc.*).

bassinet [basi'nɛ], *n.m.* small basin, pan, bowl.

bassinoire [basi'nwaːr], *n.f.* warming pan; (*pop.*) bore.

bassiste [ba'sist], *n.m.* saxhorn player; 'cellist.

basson [ba'sɔ̃], *n.m.* bassoon; bassoonist.

bastide [bas'tid], *n.f.* (*Provence*) country cottage, villa.

bastille [bas'tiːj], *n.f.* bastille, fort.

bastion [bas'tjɔ̃], *n.m.* bastion.

bastionner [bastjɔ'ne], *v.t.* to bastion, to fortify with bastions.

bastonnade [bastɔ'nad], *n.f.* bastinado; caning.

bastringue [bas'trɛ̃ːg], *n.m.* (*pop.*) dance hall; (*slang*) noise.

bas-ventre [ba'vɑ̃ːtr], *n.m.* (*pl.* **bas-ventres**) lower part of the belly.

bât [ba], *n.m.* pack-saddle.

bataclan [bata'klɑ̃], *n.m.* (*fam.*) paraphernalia.

bataille [ba'taːj], *n.f.* battle, fight, engagement.

batailler [bata'je], *v.i.* to give battle; to be at war, to fight; to struggle hard, to strive.

batailleur [bata'jœːr], *a.* (*fem.* **-euse**) combative, pugnacious, quarrelsome; disputatious.

bataillon [bata'jɔ̃], *n.m.* battalion; (*fig.*) host; (*pl.*) troops.

bâtard [ba'taːr], *a.* and *n.m.* (*fem.* **-e**) bastard, illegitimate *or* natural (child).

bâté [ba'te], *a.* saddled with a pack; *c'est un âne bâté*, he is an ignorant lout.

bateau [ba'to], *n.m.* (*pl.* **-eaux**) boat; *bateau mouche*, pleasure steamer (*Paris and Lyons*).

batelage [ba'tlaːʒ], *n.m.* juggling, legerdemain; lighterage charges.

bateleur [ba'tlœːr], *n.m.* (*fem.* **-euse**) juggler, buffoon, mountebank.

batelier [batə'lje], *n.m.* (*fem.* **-ière**) boatman, boatwoman, ferryman, ferrywoman.

bâter [ba'te], *v.t.* to load with a pack-saddle.

bathyscaphe [batis'kaf], *n.m.* bathyscaphe.

bâti [ba'ti], *n.m.* framing, structure; basting, tacking (*of a garment*).

batifolage [batifɔ'laːʒ], *n.m.* romping; fondling.

batifoler [batifɔ'le], *v.i.* to play, to romp; to fondle.

bâtiment [bati'mɑ̃], *n.m.* building, structure, edifice; building trade; ship, vessel.

bâtir [ba'tiːr], *v.t.* to build, to erect, to construct; *faire bâtir*, to have built, to build; *terrain à bâtir*, building site.

bâtisse [ba'tis], *n.f.* masonry, ramshackle building.

batiste [ba'tist], *n.f.* cambric.

bâton [ba'tɔ̃], *n.m.* stick, staff, cudgel, cane.

bâtonner [batɔ'ne], *v.t.* to cudgel, to cane.

batracien [batra'sjɛ̃], *n.m.* (*Zool.*) batrachian.

battant (1) [ba'tɑ̃], *n.m.* clapper (*of a bell*); leaf (*of a table or door*); fly (*of a flag*); *porte à deux battants*, double door.

battant (2) [ba'tɑ̃], *a.* beating, pelting, falling heavily (*of rain etc.*); *mener tambour battant*, to hurry on (*a business*).
batte [bat], *n.f.* long wooden staff *or* beater; *batte de blanchisseuse*, washing board; *batte* (*de cricket*), (cricket) bat.
battée [ba'te], *n.f.* jamb of door *or* window.
battement [bat'mɑ̃], *n.m.* beating; clapping (*of hands*), stamping (*of feet*), flapping (*of wings*); beating (*of the heart*); shuffling (*of cards*).
batterie [ba'tri], *n.f.* (*Artill., Elec., Cook. etc.*) battery; *batterie de cuisine*, complete set of kitchen utensils.
batteur [ba'tœːr], *n.m.* (*fem.* **-euse**) beater; (*cricket etc.*) batsman; (*jazz*) drummer.—*n.f.* (**-euse**) threshing machine.
battre [batr], *v.t.* (*see Verb Tables*) to strike upon, against etc.; to beat, to thrash, to whip (*a horse etc.*); to beat up, to mix; to defeat; to shuffle (*cards*); *battre des mains*, to clap; *la fête battait son plein*, the party was in full swing.—*v.i.* to beat, to knock; to pant, to throb. **se battre**, *v.r.* to fight, to combat; to hit oneself (*contre etc.*).
battu [ba'ty], *a.* beaten (*of a path, road etc.*); frequented; (*fig.*) trite, commonplace.
battue [ba'ty], *n.f.* (*Shooting*) wholesale slaughter, battue.
baudet [bo'dɛ], *n.m.* ass; (*fig.*) dolt, donkey; sawyer's trestle.
bauge [boːʒ], *n.f.* lair of a wild boar; squirrel's nest; (*fig.*) a dirty hovel.
baume [boːm], *n.m.* balm; balsam; (*fig.*) consolation.
baumier [BALSAMIER].
baux [BAIL].
bauxite [bo'sit], *n.f.* bauxite.
bavard [ba'vaːr], *a.* prating, talkative, loquacious.—*n.m.* (*fem.* **-e**) prater, babbler, chatterer.
bavardage [bavar'daʒ], *n.m.* babbling, prattling, (*fig.*) twaddle, nonsense.
bavarder [bavar'de], *v.i.* to babble, to prattle.
bavarois [bava'rwa], *a.* Bavarian.—*n.m.* (**Bavarois, -oise**) Bavarian (*person*).
bave [baːv], *n.f.* slaver, dribble; foam; (*fig.*) slime.
baver [ba've], *v.i.* to slobber, to dribble.
bavette [ba'vɛt], *n.f.* bib.
baveux [ba'vø], *a.* (*fem.* **-euse**) dribbling, slobbering.
Bavière [ba'vjɛːr], **la**, *f.* Bavaria.
bavure [ba'vyːr], *n.f.* seam (*left by a mold*); smudge (*of a pen*).
bazar [ba'zaːr], *n.m.* bazaar; ill-kept, untidy house; (*fam.*) *mettre tout son bazar dans une malle*, to put all one's belongings in a trunk.
bazooka [bazu'ka], *n.m.* (*Artill.*) bazooka.
béant [be'ɑ̃], *a.* gaping, yawning, wide open.
béat [be'a], *a.* blessed; devout; sanctimonious.
béatement [beat'mɑ̃], *adv.* sanctimoniously.
béatification [beatifika'sjɔ̃], *n.f.* beatification.
béatifier [beati'fje], *v.t.* to beatify.
béatifique [beati'fik], *a.* beatific, blissful.
béatitude [beati'tyd], *n.f.* beatitude, blessedness.
beau [bo], **bel** [bɛl] (*before nouns singular beginning with a vowel or h mute*), *a.* (*fem.* **belle**, *pl.* **beaux, belles**) beautiful, fine, handsome, fair; smart, spruce; glorious; lofty, noble;

seemly, becoming; (*iron.*) nice, precious; *au beau milieu*, in the very middle; *il fait beau*, it is a fine day; *il l'a échappé belle*, he has had a narrow escape.—*adv.* finely, promisingly; in vain; *avoir beau dire*, to speak in vain; *de plus belle*, with renewed ardor, worse than ever; *tout beau*, gently, not so fast.—*n.m.* that which is beautiful, fine, excellent etc.; beauty; beau.—*n.f.* (**belle**) belle; *la Belle et la Bête*, Beauty and the Beast.
beaucoup [bo'ku], *adv.* many, much; a great many, a great deal; *avoir beaucoup d'argent*, to have plenty of money.
beau-fils [bo'fis], *n.m.* (*pl.* **beaux-fils**) stepson.
beau-frère [bo'frɛːr], *n.m.* (*pl.* **beaux-frères**) brother-in-law.
beau-père [bo'pɛːr], *n.m.* (*pl.* **beaux-pères**) father-in-law; step-father.
beaupré [bo'pre], *n.m.* (*Naut.*) bowsprit.
beauté [bo'te], *n.f.* beauty; fineness, loveliness, comeliness, elegance, agreeableness.
beaux-arts [bo'zaːr], *n.m. pl.* fine arts.
beaux-parents [bopa'rɑ̃], *n.m. pl.* father-in-law and mother-in-law.
bébé [be'be], *n.m.* baby; baby doll.
bec [bɛk], *n.m.* beak, bill; (*fig.*) mouth; snout (*of some fishes*); lip (*of a jug*), spout (*of a kettle etc.*); gas jet, burner; mouthpiece (*of musical instrument*); nib (*pen*); *avoir bon bec*, to have the gift of the gab.
bécane [be'kan], *n.f.* (*pop.*) bike.
bécarre [be'kaːr], *a. and n.m.* (*Mus.*) natural.
bécasse [be'kas], *n.f.* woodcock; (*fam.*) stupid woman.
bécassine [beka'sin], *n.f.* snipe.
bec-de-lièvre [bɛkdə'ljɛːvr], *n.m.* (*pl.* **becs-de-lièvre**) harelip; harelipped person.
bec-fin [bɛk'fɛ̃], *n.m.* (*pl.* **becs-fins**) warbler; pipit.
béchamel [beʃa'mɛl], *n.f.* cream sauce, béchamel sauce.
bêche [bɛːʃ], *n.f.* spade.
bêcher [be'ʃe], *v.t.* to dig.
becquée [be'ke], **béquée** [be'ke], *n.f.* billful; *donner la becquée*, to feed.
becqueter [bɛk'te], **béqueter** [bek'te], *v.t.* (*conjug. like* AMENER) to peck; (*colloq.*) to eat. **se becqueter, se béqueter**, *v.r.* to peck one another.
bedaine [bə'dɛn], *n.f.* (*colloq.*) paunch.
bedeau [bə'do], *n.m.* (*pl.* **-eaux**) beadle, verger.
bedonnant [bədɔ'nɑ̃], *a.* stout, pot-bellied.
bedonner [bədɔ'ne], *v.i.* to get *or* grow stout.
bédouin [be'dwɛ̃], *a.* Bedouin.—*n.m.* (**Bédouin**, *fem.* **-e**) Bedouin.
bée [be], *a.* only used in *bouche bée*, gaping, open-mouthed.
beffroi [bɛ'frwa], *n.m.* belfry.
bégaiement [begɛ'mɑ̃], *n.m.*, **bégayant** [begɛ'jɑ̃], *a.* stammering, faltering.
bégayer [begɛ'je], *v.t.* (*conjug. like* PAYER) to stammer out, to stutter, to lisp.—*v.i.* to stammer.
bégayeur [begɛ'jœːr], *n.m.* (*fem.* **-euse**) stammerer, stutterer.
bégonia [begɔ'nja], *n.m.* begonia.
bègue [bɛg], *a.* stammering, stuttering.—*n.* stammerer, stutterer.
bégueule [be'gœl], *a.* prudish, squeamish; straitlaced.—*n.f.* (*fam.*) prude.

41

bégueulerie [begœl'ri], *n.f.* prudery, prudish airs, squeamishness.

béguin [be'gɛ̃], *n.m.* hood, child's cap; *avoir un béguin pour*, to be sweet on; *c'est mon béguin*, he *or* she is my darling.

béguine [be'gin], *n.f.* beguine (*Flemish nun*); nun; bigoted person.

bégum [be'gɔm], *n.f.* begum.

beige [bɛ:ʒ], *a.* natural, undyed (*of wool*); beige.—*n.f.* unbleached serge.

beignet [bɛ'ɲɛ], *n.m.* fritter.

béjaune [be'ʒo:n], *n.m.* (*Falconry*) eyas, unfledged hawk; (*fig.*) ninny, novice; blunder, silliness, mistake.

bel [BEAU].

bêlant [bɛ'lɑ̃], *a.* bleating.

bêlement [bɛl'mɑ̃], *n.m.* bleating (*of sheep*).

bêler [bɛ'le], *v.i.* to bleat.

belette [bə'lɛt], *n.f.* weasel.

belge [bɛlʒ], *a.* Belgian.—*n.* (**Belge**) Belgian (*person*).

Belgique [bɛl'ʒik], **la**, *f.* Belgium.

bélier [be'lje], *n.m.* ram; battering-ram; Aries.

bélière [be'ljɛ:r], *n.f.* sheep bell; clapper ring (*of a bell*); watch ring; sword sling.

bélître [be'litr], *n.m.* rascal, cad.

belladone [bɛla'dɔn], *n.f.* belladonna, deadly nightshade.

bellâtre [bɛ lɑ:tr], *a.* having insipid beauty; foppish.—*n.m.* insipid beauty; fop, coxcomb.

belle-fille [bɛl'fi:j], *n.f.* (*pl.* **belles-filles**) daughter-in-law; stepdaughter.

belle-maman [bɛlma'mɑ̃], (*colloq.*) [BELLE-MÈRE].

bellement [bɛl'mɑ̃], *adv.* prettily, charmingly, softly, gently.

belle-mère [bɛl'mɛ:r], *n.f.* (*pl.* **belles-mères**) mother-in-law; stepmother.

belles-lettres [bɛl'lɛtr], *n.f. pl.* polite literature, belles-lettres.

belle-sœur [bɛl'sœ:r], *n.f.* (*pl.* **belles-sœurs**) sister-in-law; stepsister.

belligérance [bɛliʒe'rɑ̃:s], *n.f.* belligerence, belligerency.

belligérant [bɛliʒe'rɑ̃], *a.* and *n.m.* (*fem.* **-e**) belligerent.

belliqueux [bɛli'kø], *a.* (*fem.* **-euse**) warlike, martial; bellicose, quarrelsome.

belvédère [bɛlve'dɛ:r], *n.m.* turret, terrace, belvedere, gazebo.

bémol [be'mɔl], *a.* and *n.m.* (*Mus.*) flat.

bémoliser [bemɔli'ze], *v.t.* (*Mus.*) to mark flat *or* with a flat.

bénédicité [benedisi'te], *n.m.* grace (*before meals*).

bénédictin [benedik'tɛ̃], *a.* and *n.m.* (*fem.* **-e**) Benedictine.

bénédiction [benedik'sjɔ̃], *n.f.* benediction, blessing, consecration; (*fig.*) expression of thanks.

bénéfice [bene'fis], *n.m.* benefit, gain, profit; privilege, advantage; (*Eccles.*) benefice, living.

bénéficiaire [benefi'sjɛ:r], *a.* receiving a benefit *or* benefice.—*n.* beneficiary, recipient.

bénéficial [benefi'sjal], *n.m.* beneficiary (*of ecclesiastical livings*).

bénéficier [benefi'sje], *v.i.* to gain, to profit.—*n.m.* beneficed clergyman, incumbent.

benêt [bə'nɛ], *a.* silly, foolish, simple.—*n.m* booby, fool, simpleton.

bénévole [bene'vɔl], *a.* well-disposed, kindly; unpaid.

bénévolement [benevɔl'mɑ̃], *adv.* out of good will; voluntarily, spontaneously.

Bengale [bɛ̃'gal], **le**, *m.* Bengal.

bengali [bɛ̃ga'li], *a.* Bengali.—*n.m.* Bengali (*language*).—*n.* (**Bengali**) Bengali (*person*).

Béni-oui-oui [beniwi'wi], *n.m.* *invl* (*fam.*) yes-man.

bénignement [beniɲ'mɑ̃], *adv.* benignly, kindly, graciously.

bénignité [beniɲi'te], *n.f.* benignity, kindness; mildness (*of a disease*).

bénin [be'nɛ̃], *a.* (*fem.* **bénigne**) benign, good-natured, indulgent; mild (*of attacks of disease, remedies etc.*).

bénir [be'ni:r], *v.t.* to bless, to hallow, to consecrate; to call down blessings on; to thank; to praise.

bénit [be'ni], *a.* hallowed, consecrated.

bénitier [beni'tje], *n.m.* holy-water basin; font.

benjamin [bɛ̃ʒa'mɛ̃], *n.m.* favorite (*especially the youngest child*).

benjoin [bɛ̃'ʒwɛ̃], *n.m.* benjamin, benzoin.

benne [bɛn], *n.f.* hamper, basket; (*Mining*) hopper, bucket.

benzine [bɛ̃'zin], *n.f.* benzine.

benzol [bɛ̃'zɔl], *n.m.* benzol.

béquillard [beki'ja:r], *a.* (*pop.*) crippled, going on crutches.—*n.m.* (*fem.* **-e**) cripple.

béquille [be'ki:j], *n.f.* crutch; (*Av.*) tail-skid.

béquiller [beki'je], *v.i.* to walk on crutches.

berbère [bɛr'bɛ:r], *a.* Berber.—*n.* (**Berbère**) Berber (*person*).

berbéris [bɛrbe'ris], *n.m.* (*Bot.*) barberry, berberis.

bercail [bɛr'ka:j], *n.m.* (*used only in sing.*) sheepfold, fold.

berce [bɛrs], *n.f.* cow-parsnip.

berceau [bɛr'so], *n.m.* (*pl.* **-eaux**) cradle; (*fig.*) infancy; origin, source; (*Hort.*) arbor, bower.

bercement [bɛrsə'mɑ̃], *n.m.* rocking; lulling.

bercer [bɛr'se], *v.t.* (*conjug. like* COMMENCER) to rock, to lull asleep; to lull, to soothe; (*fig.*) to delude *or* flatter with vain hopes. **se bercer**, *v.r.* to rock; (*fig.*) to delude oneself (*de*).

berceuse [bɛr'sø:z], *n.f.* woman who rocks an infant; rocking chair; cradle that rocks; (*Mus.*) lullaby.

béret [be'rɛ], *n.m.* beret, tam-o'-shanter (*worn by the French Alpine regiments*).

berge [bɛrʒ], *n.f.* steep bank (*of a river*); side (*of a canal, ditch, roadway etc.*).

berger [bɛr'ʒe], *n.m.* (*fem.* **-ère** (1)) shepherd, shepherdess; (*poet.*) swain; (*fig.*) pastor, guardian (*of the people etc.*); (*Chess*) *le coup du berger*, fool's mate.

bergère (2) [bɛr'ʒɛ:r], *n.f.* large and deep armchair.

bergerie [bɛrʒə'ri], *n.f.* sheepfold, pen; (*Lit.*) (*chiefly used in the plural*) pastoral.

bergeronnette [bɛrʒərɔ'nɛt], *n.f.* (*Orn.*) wagtail.

berlue [bɛr'ly], *n.f.* dimness of sight.

Bermudes [bɛr'myd], **les**, *f. pl.* the Bermudas.

bernacle [bɛr'nakl], **bernache** [bɛr'naʃ], **barnache** [bar'naʃ], *n.f.* barnacle goose; barnacle (*shell-fish*).
bernard-l'ermite [bɛrnarlɛr'mit], *n.m.* hermit crab.
berne (1) [bɛrn], *n.f.* tossing in a blanket.
berne (2) [bɛrn], *n.f.* (*Naut.*) *mettre le pavillon en berne*, to fly the flag at half-mast.
berner [bɛr'ne], *v.t.* to toss in a blanket; (*fig.*) to ridicule, to make a fool of, to deride; to deceive, to hoax.
bernique [bɛr'nik], *int.* (*pop.*) no use; not a bit of it, no go.
berthon [bɛr'tɔ̃], *n.m.* a small collapsible boat.
béryl or **béril** [be'ril], *n.m.* beryl.
besace [bə'zas], *n.f.* beggar's wallet, scrip.
bésigue [be'zig], *n.m.* bezique (*card game*).
besogne [bə'zɔɲ], *n.f.* work, business, labor; job, piece of work.
besogner [bəzɔ'ɲe], *v.i.* to work, to labor.
besogneux [bəzɔ'ɲø], *a.* and *n.m.* (*fem.* **-euse**) necessitous, needy (person).
besoin [bə'zwɛ̃], *n.m.* need, want; necessity; poverty, distress, emergency; *au besoin*, at a pinch, if need be.
Bessarabie [bɛsara'bi], **la**, *f.* Bessarabia.
bestial [bɛs'tjal], *a.* (*m. pl.* **-aux** (1)) bestial, brutish.
bestialement [bɛstjal'mɑ̃], *adv.* bestially, brutally, like a beast.
bestialité [bɛstjali'te], *n.f.* bestiality.
bestiaux [BESTIAL].
bestiole [bɛs'tjɔl], *n.f.* little animal.
bêta [be'ta], *n.m.* (*fem.* **-asse**) a bit of a blockhead, rather a simpleton.
bétail [be'ta:j], *n.m.* (*pl.* **bestiaux** (2) [bɛs'tjo]) cattle, livestock; *gros bétail*, oxen etc.; *menu bétail*, sheep, goats etc.
bêtasse [be'ta:s], [BÊTA].
bête [bɛ:t], *a.* silly, stupid, nonsensical.—*n.f.* animal, beast, brute; fool, blockhead, stupid creature; *bête noire*, pet aversion; *bête sauvage*, wild animal.
bêtement [bɛt'mɑ̃], *adv.* like a fool, foolishly, stupidly.
Bethléem [betle'ɛm], *f.* Bethlehem.
bêtise [be'ti:z], *n.f.* silliness, stupidity; tomfoolery, foolish act, suggestion etc., silly thing, absurdity.
béton [be'tɔ̃], *n.m.* (*Masonry*) beton (*a kind of concrete*); *béton armé*, reinforced concrete.
bétonnière [betɔ'njɛ:r], **bétonneuse** [betɔ'nø:z], *n.f.* concrete mixer.
bette [bɛt], **blette** (2) [blɛt], *n.f.* beet.
betterave [bɛ'tra:v], *n.f.* beets; *betterave à sucre*, sugar beet; *betterave fourragère*, mangel-wurzel.
beuglement [bøglə'mɑ̃], *n.m.* bellowing, lowing (*of cattle*).
beugler [bø'gle], *v.i.* to bellow, to low.
beurre [bœ:r], *n.m.* butter.
beurrée [bœ're], *n.f.* slice of bread and butter.
beurrer [bœ're], *v.t.* to butter (*bread etc.*).
beurrerie [bœr'ri], *n.f.* butter factory.
beurrier [bœ'rje], *n.m.* butter dish.
bévue [be'vy], *n.f.* blunder, oversight, mistake; (*colloq.*) howler.
bey [bɛ], *n.m.* bey.
biais [bjɛ], *a.* slanting, sloping, askew; oblique.—*n.m.* bias, obliquity, slope; (*fig.*) shift, subterfuge.

biaisement [bjɛz'mɑ̃], *n.m.* sloping, slanting, shift, evasion.
biaiser [bjɛ'ze], *v.i.* to be oblique, to go obliquely, to slope, to slant, to lean on one side; to use shifts *or* evasions.
bibelot [bi'blo], *n.m.* trinket, knick-knack.
biberon (1) [bi'brɔ̃], *n.m.* (*Med.*) feeding cup; feeding bottle (*for infants*).
biberon (2) [bi'brɔ̃], *n.m.* (*fem.* **-onne**) tippler, toper.
Bible [bibl], *n.f.* Bible.
bibliographe [biblio'graf], *n.m.* bibliographer.
bibliographie [bibliogra'fi], *n.f.* bibliography.
bibliographique [bibliogra'fik], *a.* bibliographical.
bibliomane [biblio'man], *n.m.* book collector.
bibliomanie [biblioma'ni], *n.f.* bibliomania.
bibliophile [biblio'fil], *n.m.* book lover.
bibliothécaire [bibliote'kɛ:r], *n.m.* librarian.
bibliothèque [biblio'tɛk], *n.f.* library; bookcase.
biblique [bi'blik], *a.* Biblical.
bicarbonate [bikarbo'nat], *n.m.* (*Chem.*) bicarbonate.
biceps [bi'sɛps], *n.m.* biceps.
biche [biʃ], *n.f.* hind, doe.
bichon [bi'ʃɔ̃], *n.m.* (*fem.* **-onne**) lap dog with long, silky hair.
bichonner [biʃɔ'ne], *v.t.* to curl; (*fig.*) to caress. **se bichonner**, *v.r.* to curl one's hair; to make oneself smart.
biconcave [bikɔ̃'ka:v], *a.* bi-concave.
biconvexe [bikɔ̃'vɛks], *a.* bi-convex.
bicoque [bi'kɔk], *n.f.* (*colloq.*) ramshackle house, shanty.
bicorne [bi'kɔrn], *a.* and *n.m.* cocked (hat).
bicyclette [bisi'klɛt], *n.f.* bicycle.
bidet [bi'dɛ], *n.m.* pony, small nag; bidet (*bath*).
bidon [bi'dɔ̃], *n.m.* tin, can (*esp. gas can*); camp kettle; soldier's water bottle.
bidonville [bidɔ̃'vil], *n.m.* shanty town.
bielle [bjɛl], *n.f.* (*Mach.*) connecting rod.
Biélorussie [bjelory'si], **la**, *f.* Byelorussia, White Russia.
bien [bjɛ̃], *n.m.* good; that which is pleasant, useful *or* advantageous; benefit, welfare, well-being, blessing; wealth, estate, property; gift, boon, mercy; (*pl.*) goods, chattels; fruits (*of the soil etc.*); *biens de consommation*, consumer goods; *biens immobiliers*, real estate.—*adv.* well; rightly, finely; much, very, far, entirely, completely; about, well-nigh; favorably, successfully; well off; on good terms, in favor; certainly, truly, indeed; formally, clearly, expressly; *aussi bien*, anyhow, in any case; *bien de*, plenty of, many; *bien mieux*, far better; *bien plus*, besides, moreover; *bien que*, although; *c'est bien*, that's right; *cette femme est bien*, that woman is good-looking; *eh bien!* well! *or* well? *je vous l'avais bien dit*, I told you so; *ou bien*, or else; *si bien que*, so that; *tant bien que mal*, so-so.—*int.* (*sometimes pronounced colloq.* [bɛ̃]) well!
bien-aimé [bjɛ̃ɛ'me], *a.* beloved, well-beloved.—*n.m.* (*fem.* **-ée**) darling, dear.
bien-dire [bjɛ̃'di:r], *n.m.* (*no pl.*) fine speaking.

bien-être

bien-être [bjɛ̃'nɛːtr], *n.m.* (*no pl.*) well-being, welfare, comfort.
bienfaisance [bjɛ̃fə'zɑ̃ːs], *n.f.* beneficence, charity, munificence.
bienfaisant [bjɛ̃fə'zɑ̃], *a.* charitable, beneficent, kind, gracious; beneficial, salutary.
bienfait [bjɛ̃'fɛ], *n.m.* good turn, kindness, benefit, favor, courtesy.
bienfaiteur [bjɛ̃fɛ'tœːr], *n.m.* (*fem.* **-trice**) benefactor, benefactress, patron.
bien-fonds [bjɛ̃'fɔ̃], *n.m.* (*pl.* **biens-fonds**) real estate.
bienheureux [bjɛ̃nœ'rø], *a.* (*fem.* **-euse**) happy, fortunate; (*Eccles.*) blessed.
biennal [biɛ'nal], *a.* (*m. pl.* **-aux**) biennial.
bienséance [bjɛ̃se'ɑ̃ːs], *n.f.* propriety decency, decorum, seemliness.
bienséant [bjɛ̃se'ɑ̃], *a.* decent, becoming, seemly, decorous, fit.
bientôt [bjɛ̃'to], *adv.* soon, before long, shortly; *à bientôt!* see you soon!
bienveillance [bjɛ̃vɛ'jɑ̃ːs], *n.f.* benevolence, goodwill, favor, kindness.
bienveillant [bjɛ̃vɛ'jɑ̃], *a.* benevolent, kind, friendly, favorable.
bienvenu [bjɛ̃v'ny], *a.* welcome; *soyez le bienvenu,* it's nice to have you with us.
bienvenue [bjɛ̃v'ny], *n.f.* welcome; *souhaiter la bienvenue à quelqu'un,* to greet *or* welcome someone.
bière (1) [bjɛːr], *n.f.* beer.
bière (2) [bjɛːr], *n.f.* coffin.
biffer [bi'fe], *v.t.* to cancel, to blot out, to erase.
biflore [bi'flɔːr], *a.* (*Bot.*) biflorate.
bifocal [bifɔ'kal], *a.* (*m. pl.* **-aux**) bifocal.
bifolié [bifɔ'lje], *a.* (*Bot.*) bifoliate.
bifteck [bif'tɛk], *n.m.* beefsteak.
bifurcation [bifyrka'sjɔ̃], *n.f.* bifurcation, fork (*of a road*).
bigame [bi'gam], *a.* bigamous.—*n.* bigamist.
bigamie [biga'mi], *n.f.* bigamy.
bigarré [biga're], *a.* parti-colored, streaked.
bigarrer [biga're], *v.t.* to chequer, to streak, to variegate.
bigarrure [biga'ryːr], *n.f.* medley, mixture, motley, variegation.
bigot [bi'go], *a.* bigoted.—*n.m.* (*fem.* **-e**) bigot.
bigoterie [bigɔ'tri], *n.f.*, **bigotisme** [bigɔ'tism], *n.m.* bigotry.
bigoudi [bigu'di], *n.m.* curling pin *or* curler (*for the hair*).
bijou [bi'ʒu], *n.m.* (*pl.* **-oux**) jewel, gem; (*fig.*) darling.
bijouterie [biʒu'tri], *n.f.* jewelry.
bijoutier [biʒu'tje], *n.m.* (*fem.* **-ière**) jeweler.
bilan [bi'lɑ̃], *n.m.* balance sheet.
bilatéral [bilate'ral], *a.* (*m. pl.* **-aux**) bilateral.
bilboquet [bilbɔ'kɛ], *n.m.* cup-and-ball (*toy*); small weighted figure that balances itself.
bile [bil], *n.f.* bile, spleen, gall; (*fig.*) anger.
bilieux [bi'ljø], *a.* (*fem.* **-euse**) bilious; (*fig.*) choleric, passionate.
bilingue [bi'lɛ̃ːg], *a.* bilingual.
billard [bi'jaːr], *n.m.* billiards; billiard table; billiard room.
bille [biːj], *n.f.* billiard ball; marble, taw; log, unworked piece of timber; *roulement à billes,* ball bearings.
billet [bi'jɛ], *n.m.* note, missive, bill, hand-bill; ticket, lottery ticket; promissory note;

billet (*for quartering soldiers*); *billet de banque,* bank note; *billet d'aller et retour,* return ticket; *billet doux,* love-letter.
billevesée [bilvə'ze], *n.f.* idle story, stuff, nonsense, bunkum.
billion [bi'ljɔ̃], *n.m.* (*since* 1948 = 1 *followed by* 12 *ciphers*), billion, one million million(s); (*Am.*) trillion.
billot [bi'jo], *n.m.* block; executioner's block.
bimbelot [bɛ̃'blo], *n.m.* plaything, toy, bauble.
bimensuel [bimɑ̃'sɥɛl], *a.* (*fem.* **-elle**) twice monthly, fortnightly.
bimoteur [bimɔ'tœːr], *a.* and *n.m.* twin-engined (plane).
binaire [bi'nɛːr], *a.* binary.
biner [bi'ne], *v.t.* (*Agric.*) to dig again; to hoe.
binette [bi'nɛt], *n.f.* hoe; (*colloq.*) face.
biniou [bi'nju], *n.m.* Breton bagpipe.
binôme [bi'noːm], *n.m.* (*Alg.*) binomial.
biochimie [biɔʃi'mi], *n.f.* biochemistry.
biographe [biɔ'graf], *n.m.* biographer.
biographie [biɔgra'fi], *n.f.* biography.
biographique [biɔgra'fik], *a.* biographical.
biologie [biɔlɔ'ʒi], *n.f.* biology.
biologique [biɔlɔ'ʒik], *a.* biological.
biologiste [biɔlɔ'ʒist], **biologue** [biɔ'lɔg], *n.m.* biologist.
bion [bjɔ̃], *n.m.* sucker, shoot.
bioxyde [biɔk'sid], *n.m.* dioxide.
biparti [bipar'ti], **bipartite** [bipar'tit], *a.* bipartite.
bipède [bi'pɛd], *a.* and *n.* (*Zool.*) biped.
biplan [bi'plɑ̃], *n.m.* biplane.
bipolaire [bipɔ'lɛːr], *a.* bipolar.
bique [bik], *n.f.* nanny goat.
biréacteur [bireak'tœːr], *n.m.* twin-engined jet plane.
birloir [bir'lwaːr], *n.m.* window catch.
birman [bir'mɑ̃], *a.* Burmese.—*n.m.* (**Birman**, *fem.* **-ane**) Burmese (*person*).
Birmanie [birma'ni], **la**, *f.* Burma.
bis (1) [bi], *a.* brown; tawny, swarthy; *du pain bis,* brown bread.
bis (2) [biːs], *adv.* twice.—*int.* encore!
bisaïeul [biza'jœl], *n.m.* great-grandfather.
bisaïeule [biza'jœl], *n.f.* great-grandmother.
bisannuel [biza'nɥɛl], *a.* (*fem.* **-elle**) (*Bot.*) biennial.
bisbille [biz'biːj], *n.f.* (*fam.*) petty quarrel, tiff, bickering.
biscornu [biskɔr'ny], *a.* irregular, misshapen; (*fig.*) outlandish, odd, queer.
biscotte [bis'kɔt], *n.f.* rusk.
biscuit [bis'kɥi], *n.m.* biscuit; pastry made with flour, eggs, and sugar; (*Am.*) cracker; unglazed porcelain.
bise [biːz], *n.f.* dry and cold north wind; (*colloq.*) kiss.
biseau [bi'zo], *n.m.* (*pl.* **-eaux**) bevel, chamfer; bevelling tool.
biseauter [bizo'te], *v.t.* to bevel.
bismuth [biz'myt], *n.m.* bismuth.
bison [bi'zɔ̃], *n.m.* bison, buffalo.
bisque [bisk], *n.f.* soup made of crayfish, chicken *or* game, fish etc.; (*colloq.*) ill-humor, spite.
bisquer [bis'ke], *v.i.* (*colloq.*) to be vexed *or* riled.
bissac [bi'sak], *n.m.* double wallet, sack *or* bag, haversack.
bissecter [bisɛk'te], *v.t.* to bisect.

bisser [bi′se], *v.t.* to encore.
bissextile [bisɛk′til], *a.* **année bissextile**, leap year.
bissexué [bisɛk′sɥe], **bissexuel** [-sɥɛl] (*fem.* **-elle**), *a.* (*Bot.*) bisexual.
bistouri [bistu′ri], *n.m.* bistoury, lancet.
bistourner [bistur′ne], *v.t.* to twist, to distort; to castrate.
bistre [bistr], *n.m.* bistre, sepia.
bistro or **bistrot** [bis′tro], *n.m.* (*slang*) pub.
bitume [bi′tym], *n.m.* bitumen.
bituminer [bitymi′ne], *v.t.* to asphalt.
bitumineux [bitymi′nø], **bitumeux** [bity′mø], *a.* (*fem.* **-euse**) bituminous.
bivalent [biva′lɑ̃], *a.* divalent, bivalent.
bivalve [bi′valv], *a.* bivalvular.—*n.m.* bivalve.
bivouac [bi′vwak], *n.m.* bivouac.
bivouaquer [bivwa′ke], *v.i.* to bivouac.
bizarre [bi′za:r], *a.* queer, strange, whimsical, bizarre.
bizarrement [bizar′mɑ̃], *adv.* oddly, queerly, whimsically.
bizarrerie [bizar′ri], *n.f.* singularity, oddness; caprice, whim.
black-out [blak′aut], *n.m.* black-out.
blafard [bla′fa:r], *a.* pale, wan; livid.
blague [blag], *n.f.* tobacco pouch; (*slang*) chaff, humbug, hoax, fib; trick, practical joke; *sans blague!* you don't say!
blaguer [bla′ge], *v.i.* to chaff, to hoax, to humbug.
blagueur [bla′gœ:r], *n.m.* (*fem.* **-euse**) wag, hoaxer, humbug.
blaireau [blɛ′ro], *n.m.* (*pl.* **-eaux**) badger; shaving brush; badger-hair brush.
blâmable [blɑ′mabl], *a.* blameworthy.
blâme [blɑ:m], *n.m.* blame; reproach, reprimand.
blâmer [blɑ′me], *v.t.* to blame, to criticize; to censure, to reprimand.
blanc [blɑ̃], *a.* (*fem.* **blanche** (1) [blɑ̃:ʃ]) white; hoar, hoary; clean; blank; *gelée blanche*, hoar frost; *passer une nuit blanche*, to have a sleepless night; *vers blancs*, blank verse.—*n.m.* white; blank; target, mark; *blanc de chaux*, whitewash; *de but en blanc*, point-blank; *en blanc*, left blank.
blanc-bec [blɑ̃′bɛk], *n.m.* (*pl.* **blancs-becs**) beardless youth, youngster; greenhorn; sucker.
blanchaille [blɑ̃′ʃa:j], *n.f.* whitebait.
blanchâtre [blɑ̃′ʃa:tr], *a.* whitish.
blanche (1) [BLANC].
blanche (2) [blɑ̃:ʃ], *n.f.* (*Mus.*) minim.
blancheur [blɑ̃′ʃœ:r], *n.f.* whiteness; cleanliness; light; (*fig.*) purity, innocence.
blanchiment [blɑ̃ʃi′mɑ̃], *n.m.* whitening, bleaching; blanching.
blanchir [blɑ̃′ʃi:r], *v.t.* to whiten; to whitewash; to wash, to bleach, to clean; to blanch.—*v.i.* to whiten.
blanchissage [blɑ̃ʃi′sa:ʒ], *n.m.* washing; refining (*of sugar etc.*).
blanchissant [blɑ̃ʃi′sɑ̃], *a.* that whitens *or* grows white; foaming.
blanchisserie [blɑ̃ʃis′ri], *n.f.* laundry, washhouse.
blanchisseuse [blɑ̃ʃi′sø:z], *n.f.* washerwoman; laundress.
blanc-manger [blɑ̃mɑ̃′ʒe], *n.m.* (*pl.* **blancs-mangers**) blancmange.

blaser [blɑ′ze], *v.t.* to blunt, to cloy, to sicken, to surfeit.
blason [blɑ′zɔ̃], *n.m.* coat of arms; blazon; heraldry, blazonry.
blasonner [blazɔ′ne], *v.t.* to blazon; to interpret (*coats of arms*).
blasphémateur [blasfema′tœ:r], *n.m.* (*fem.* **-trice**) blasphemer.
blasphématoire [blasfema′twa:r], *a.* blasphemous.
blasphème [blas′fɛ:m], *n.m.* blasphemy.
blasphémer [blasfe′me], *v.t.*, *v.i.* (*conjug. like* CÉDER) to blaspheme, to curse.
blatte [blat], *n.f.* cockroach, black beetle.
blé [ble], *n.m.* corn, wheat; *halle au blé*, corn exchange; *manger son blé en herbe*, to spend one's money before one has it.
blême [blɛ:m], *a.* sallow, pale, wan; ghastly.
blêmir [blɛ′mi:r], *v.i.* to turn *or* grow pale.
blèsement [blɛz′mɑ̃], *n.m.* lisping.
bléser [ble′ze], *v.i.* (*conjug. like* CÉDER) to lisp.
blessant [blɛ′sɑ̃], *a.* wounding; (*fig.*) offensive, mortifying.
blessé [blɛ′se], *a.* wounded; (*fig.*) offended.—*n.m.* (*fem.* **-ée**) (*Mil.*) casualty.
blesser [blɛ′se], *v.t.* to wound, to hurt; to offend, to injure; to shock. **se blesser**, *v.r.* to hurt oneself; (*fig.*) to take offence.
blessure [blɛ′sy:r], *n.f.* wound, hurt, injury; offence; *coups et blessures*, assault and battery.
blet [blɛ], *a.* (*fem.* **-ette** (1)) over-ripe, sleepy (*of fruit*).
blette (2) [BETTE].
bleu [blø], *a.* blue, black and blue (*as a bruise*); (*fig.*) amazed; *cordon bleu*, first-rate cook.—*n.m.* blue, bluness; blueprint; greenhorn, novice; (*C*) Conservative, Tory.
bleuâtre [blø′a:tr], *a.* bluish.
bleuet [BLUET].
bleuir [blø′i:r], *v.t.* to make blue, to blue (*in washing*).—*v.i.* to become blue.
blindage [blɛ̃′da:ʒ], *n.m.* iron-plating, armor-plating.
blindé [blɛ̃′de], *a.* armored, armor-plated; screened; (*slang*) drunk.
blinder [blɛ̃′de], *v.t.* to armor-plate (*a ship, fort etc.*).
bloc [blɔk], *n.m.* block, lump, the whole lot.
blocage (1) [blɔ′ka:ʒ], *n.m.* blockading; blocking; block (*of traffic*); obstruction; (*Fin.*) freezing.
blocage (2) [blɔ′ka:ʒ], *n.m.* rubble.
blockhaus [blɔ′ko:s], *n.m. inv.* blockhouse.
bloc-note(s) [blɔk′nɔt], *n.m.* writing pad.
blocus [blɔ′ky:s], *n.m. inv.* blockade.
blond [blɔ̃], *a.* blond, fair; light (*ale*); *blond ardent*, auburn; *blond cendré*, ash-blond.—*n.f.* (**-e**) (*C*) sweetheart.
blondin [blɔ̃′dɛ̃], *a.* fair-haired.—*n.m.* (*fem.* **-e**) fair-haired child.—*n.m.* spark, beau.
blondir [blɔ̃′di:r], *v.i.* to grow blond *or* fair.
blondissant [blɔ̃di′sɑ̃], *a.* growing yellow *or* golden (*of corn etc.*).
bloquer [blɔ′ke], *v.t.* to block up, to fill up (*cavities in walls*) with mortar; (*Mil.*) to blockade; (*Fin.*) to freeze; to jam on (*brakes*).
blottir (se) [səblɔ′ti:r], *v.r.* to curl up, to snuggle, to huddle; to cower, to crouch.
blouse [blu:z], *n.f.* smock; tunic; blouse; pinafore; overall.

blouser [blu'ze], *v.t.* to mislead, to cheat. **se blouser**, *v.r.* (*Billiards*) to pocket one's own ball; (*fig.*) to blunder; to bark up the wrong tree.

blouson [blu'zɔ̃], *n.m.* lumber-jacket, windcheater.

bluet [bly'ɛ], **bleuet** [blœ'ɛ], *n.m.* bluebottle, corn-flower; (*C*) blueberry.

bluette [bly'ɛt], *n.f.* spark; (*fig.*) literary trifle, novelette.

bluff [blœf], *n.m.* bluff.

bluffer [blœ'fe], *v.t.* to bluff.

blutage [bly'ta:ʒ], *n.m.* bolting, sifting (*of flour*).

bluter [bly'te], *v.t.* to bolt, to sift (*flour etc.*).

boa [bɔ'a], *n.m.* boa (*snake*); boa (*of feathers*).

bobèche [bɔ'bɛʃ], *n.f.* socket (*of a candlestick*); sconce.

bobine [bɔ'bin], *n.f.* bobbin, spool, reel; (*Cine.*) reel; **bobine d'induction**, induction coil.

bobiner [bɔbi'ne], *v.t.* to wind on a bobbin, to spool.

bobineuse [bɔbi'nø:z], *n.f.* winder, winding machine.

bobo [bɔ'bo], *n.m.* (*Childish*) hurt, sore, bump; **avoir bobo** or **du bobo**, to have a slight pain, sore etc.; **faire bobo**, to hurt.

bocage [bɔ'ka:ʒ], *n.m.* copse, grove.

bocager [bɔka'ʒe], *a.* (*fem.* **-ère**) of groves or woodlands; shady.

bocal [bɔ'kal], *n.m.* (*pl.* **-aux**) druggist's short-necked bottle; carboy; glass jar, fishbowl.

boche [bɔʃ] (*aphæresis of* **Alboche**), *n.* (*pej.*) German, Jerry.

bock [bɔk], *n.m.* bock or glass (*beer*).

bœuf [bœf], *n.m.* (*pl.* **bœufs** [bø]) ox; beef.

Bohême [bɔ'ɛ:m], **la**, *f.* Bohemia.

bohème [bɔ'ɛ:m], *a.* Bohemian.—*n.* Bohemian, person of careless, unconventional habits.

bohémien [bɔe'mjɛ̃], *a.* and *n.m.* (*fem.* **-enne**) Bohemian; gipsy.

boire [bwa:r], *v.t. irr.* to drink; to consume or waste on drink; to absorb; to swallow (*an insult etc.*).—*v.i.* to drink (*to someone's health*); to tipple; to blot (*of paper*).—*n.m.* drink; drinking.

bois [bwa], *n.m.* wood, forest; wood, timber; wooden part or object; horns (*of a deer etc.*).

boisage [bwa'za:ʒ], *n.m.* wood-work; timbering (*of mines etc.*); wainscotting.

(*C*) **bois-brûlé** [bwabry'le], *n.m.* half-breed.

(*C*) **bois-debout** [bwad'bu], *n.m.* standing timber.

boisé [bwa'ze], *a.* wooded, well-timbered.

boisement [bwaz'mɑ̃], *n.m.* planting land with trees.

boiser [bwa'ze], *v.t.* to put woodwork to; to timber (*a mine etc.*); to wainscot; to plant with woods.

boiserie [bwaz'ri], *n.f.* wainscot, wainscotting.

boisseau [bwa'so], *n.m.* (*pl.* **-eaux**) bushel.

boisson [bwa'sɔ̃], *n.f.* drink; beverage; (*fig.*) drinking, drunkenness; (*C*) hard liquor; **boisson forte**, strong drink, (*Am.*) liquor.

boîte [bwat], *n.f.* box; casket, caddy, chest; case (*of a watch, rudder etc.*); (*pop.*) mouth; **boîte à feu**, stoke-hole; (*Motor.*) **boîte de vitesses**, gear box; **boîte de nuit**, night club; (*pop.*) **ta boîte !** shut your big mouth!

boitement [bwat'mɑ̃], *n.m.* halting, limping.

boiter [bwa'te], *v.i.* to limp; to be lame.

boiteux [bwa'tø], *a.* (*fem.* **-euse**) lame, halt, limping; rickety (*furniture*).—*n.m.* (*fem.* **-euse**) lame man or woman.

boîtier [bwa'tje], *n.m.* surgeon's case of instruments; case (*of a watch, an electric torch*).

bol [bɔl], *n.m.* bowl, basin.

bolchevik [bɔlʃə'vik], *n.m.* Bolshevik.

bolchevisme [bɔlʃə'vism], *n.m.* Bolshevism.

bolée [bɔ'le], *n.f.* bowlful.

boléro [bɔle'ro], *n.m.* bolero (*dance and garment*).

Bolivie [bɔli'vi], **la**, *f.* Bolivia.

bolivien [bɔli'vjɛ̃], *a.* (*fem.* **-enne**) Bolivian.—*n.m.* (**Bolivien**, *fem.* **-enne**) Bolivian (*person*).

bombance [bɔ̃'bɑ̃:s], *n.f.* feasting, junketing.

bombardement [bɔ̃bardə'mɑ̃], *n.m.* bombardment, shelling; **bombardement en piqué**, dive-bombing.

bombarder [bɔ̃bar'de], *v.t.* to bombard, to bomb; **quartier bombardé**, bombed site.

bombardier [bɔ̃bar'dje], *n.m.* bombardier.

bombe [bɔ̃:b], *n.f.* bomb; spray flask; **bombe atomique**, atom bomb; **bombe à hydrogène**, H-bomb; **bombe incendiaire**, incendiary bomb; (*colloq.*) **faire la bombe**, to be on a binge.

bombé [bɔ̃'be], *a.* convex, arched.

bombement [bɔ̃bə'mɑ̃], *n.m.* convexity, swelling, bulge.

bomber [bɔ̃'be], *v.t.* to cause (*something*) to bulge, jut, swell out, arch, curve or barrel.—*v.i.* to bulge, to jut out.

bombyx [bɔ̃'biks], *n.m.* (*Ent.*) bombyx; silkworm.

bon (1) [bɔ̃], *a.* (*fem.* **bonne** (1)) good; kind, favorable; fine, convenient, advantageous, profitable, proper; well-executed, cleverly done etc.; easy, good-natured; (*iron.*) simple, credulous; **à quoi bon tant de peine?** what is the good of so much trouble? **il fait bon dans cette pièce**, this room is nice and warm; **pour de bon**, for good and all.—*n.m.* that which is good; the best.—*adv.* well, right, properly; **tout de bon**, seriously, truly.

bon (2) [bɔ̃], *n.m.* bond, coupon, voucher; **bon du trésor**, treasury bond; **bon d'essence**, gasoline coupon.

bonasse [bɔ'nas], *a.* simple-minded, credulous; soft.

bon-bec [bɔ̃'bɛk], *n.m.* (*pl.* **bons-becs**) chatterbox, gossip.

bonbon [bɔ̃'bɔ̃], *n.m.* sweet, (*Am.*) candy.

bond [bɔ̃], *n.m.* bound, leap, jump, caper; **faire faux bond**, to give (*someone*) the slip.

bonde [bɔ̃:d], *n.f.* bung-hole; bung; sluice, flood-gate.

bondé [bɔ̃'de], *a.* chock-full, packed, crammed.

bondir [bɔ̃'di:r], *v.i.* to bound, to leap, to bounce, to caper, to frisk.

bondissant [bɔ̃di'sɑ̃], *a.* bounding, skipping.

bondissement [bɔ̃dis'mɑ̃], *n.m.* bounding, skipping, frisking.

bonheur [bɔ'nœ:r], *n.m.* happiness, prosperity, welfare; good fortune, good luck, success.

bouclé

bonhomie [bɔnɔ′mi], *n.f.* good nature; simplicity, credulity.
bonhomme [bɔ′nɔm], *n.m.* (*pl.* **bonshommes** [bɔ̃′zɔm]) simple, good-natured man; foolish *or* credulous person; (*fig.*) rough drawing *or* effigy of a man; *bonhomme de neige*, snowman.
boni [bɔ′ni], *n.m.* bonus.
boniface [bɔni′fas], *a.* and *n.* (*pop.*) simple, artless (person).
bonification [bɔnifika′sjɔ̃], *n.f.* amelioration, improvement (*of land*); (*Fin.*) bonus, discount.
bonifier [bɔni′fje], *v.t.* to better, to improve; (*Fin.*) to pay, to transfer.
boniment [bɔni′mɑ̃], *n.m.* quack's show; (*fig.*) humbug.
bonjour [bɔ̃′ʒuːr], *n.m.* and *int.* good morning, good afternoon, good day.
bonne (1) [BON (1)].
bonne (2) [bɔn], *n.f.* servant-maid; housemaid; *bonne d'enfants*, nursery-maid; *bonne à tout faire*, general maid.
bonnement [bɔn′mɑ̃], *adv.* plainly, simply, honestly; *tout bonnement*, quite frankly.
bonnet [bɔ′nɛ], *n.m.* cap; *c'est bonnet blanc et blanc bonnet*, it is six of one and half a dozen of the other.
bonneterie [bɔn′tri], *n.f.* hosiery business; hosiery.
bonnetier [bɔn′tje], *n.m.* (*fem.* **-ière**) hosier.
bon-prime [bɔ̃′prim], *n.m.* (*Comm.*) free-gift coupon.
bonsoir [bɔ̃′swaːr], *n.m.* and *int.* good evening, good night.
bonté [bɔ̃′te], *n.f.* goodness, kindness.
boom [bum], *n.m.* (*Fin.*) boom.
borax [bɔ′raks], *n.m.* borax.
bord [bɔːr], *n.m.* edge, margin, brink, brim, border, rim; shore, bank, side; *au bord de la mer*, at the seaside; *à bord*, on board; *par-dessus bord*, overboard.
bordage [bɔr′daːʒ], *n.m.* bordering, hemming etc.; (*Naut.*) planking, bulwarks.
bordé [bɔr′de], *n.m.* hem, edging, bordering (*of a garment*); (*Naut.*) planking.
bordeaux [bɔr′do], *n.m.* Bordeaux wine; *bordeaux rouge*, claret.
bordée [bɔr′de], *n.f.* (*Naut.*) broadside; volley, salvo; (*C*) *une bordée de neige*, a snow-fall.
bordelais [bɔrdə′lɛ:], *a.* of Bordeaux.—*n.m.* (**Bordelais**, *fem.* **-aise**) native of Bordeaux.
border [bɔr′de], *v.t.* to border, to edge, to hem, to skirt; to bind; to tuck in (*bedclothes*); (*Naut.*) to haul (*the sheets*).
bordereau [bɔrdə′ro], *n.m.* (*pl.* **-eaux**) memorandum, note, schedule, account.
bordure [bɔr′dyːr], *n.f.* frame, edge, edging; margin, border, curb; rim.
boréal [bɔre′al], *a.* (*m. pl.* **-aux**) boreal, northern.
borée [bɔ′re], *n.m.* Boreas, north wind (*poet.*).
borgne [bɔrɲ], *a.* one-eyed; *rue borgne*, blind alley.—*n.* one-eyed person.
borique [bɔ′rik], *a.* boric.
borne [bɔrn], *n.f.* landmark; boundary, limit, confine; milestone; (*Elec.*) terminal; *borne kilométrique*, milestone.
borné [bɔr′ne], *a.* bounded, limited, confined; narrow, mean, hide-bound.

borne-fontaine [bɔrnfɔ̃′tɛːn], *n.f.* (*pl.* **bornes-fontaines**) street fountain (*like a boundary post*).
borner [bɔr′ne], *v.t.* to set landmarks to; to bound, to limit, to confine.
Bosphore [bɔs′fɔːr], **le**, *m.* the Bosphorus.
bosquet [bɔs′kɛ], *n.m.* grove, thicket, arbor.
bosse [bɔs], *n.f.* hump, hunch; bump, bruise; knob, protuberance, lump, boss; (*Arch.*) embossment; (*Sculp.*) relief.
bosselage [bɔs′la:ʒ], *n.m.* embossing.
bosseler [bɔs′le], *v.t.* (*conjug. like* APPELER) to dent; to emboss.
bossu [bɔ′sy], *a.* hunch-backed; deformed, crooked; pigeon-breasted.—*n.m.* (*fem.* **-e**) hunch-back; *rire comme un bossu*, to split one's sides with laughter.
bossuer [bɔ′sɥe], *v.t.* (*Fenc.*) pass, thrust
boston [bɔs′tɔ̃], *n.m.* boston (*card game, dance*).
bot [bo], *a.* *pied bot*, club foot; club-footed.
botanique [bɔta′nik], *a.* botanical.—*n.f.* botany.
botaniser [bɔtani′ze], *v.i.* to botanize.
botaniste [bɔta′nist], *n.* botanist.
botte (1) [bɔt], *n.f.* wellington boot, jack-boot.
botte (2) [bɔt], *n.f.* bunch, truss, bale.
botte (3) [bɔt], *n.f.* (*Fenc.*) pass, thrust
bottelage [bɔ′tla:ʒ], *n.m.* tying up in bundles.
botteler [bɔ′tle], *v.t.* (*conjug. like* APPELER) to put up in bundles, to truss.
botteloir [bɔt′lwa:r], *n.m.*, **botteleuse** [bɔ′tlø:z], *n.f.* sheaf-binding machine, binder.
botter [bɔ′te], *v.t.* to put boots on (*a person*).
bottier [bɔ′tje], *n.m.* bootmaker.
bottin [bɔ′tɛ̃], *n.m.* a directory published by the firm of Didot Bottin.
bottine [bɔ′tin], *n.f.* (ankle) boot.
bouc [buk], *n.m.* billy goat; *bouc émissaire* scapegoat.
boucanage [buka′na:ʒ], *n.m.* smoke-drying.
boucaner [buka′ne], *v.t.* to smoke (*meat, hides etc.*).
boucanier [buka′nje], *n.m.* buccaneer; freebooter.
(*C*) **boucanière** [buka′nɛ:r], *n.f.* smokehouse (*for fish*).
bouchage [bu′ʃa:ʒ], *n.m.* stopping, corking.
bouche [buʃ], *n.f.* mouth; lips; tongue; voice; victuals; muzzle (*of a cannon*); *bouche d'eau*, hydrant.
bouchée [bu′ʃe], *n.f.* mouthful.
boucher (1) [bu′ʃe], *v.t.* to stop, to choke.
boucher (2) [bu′ʃe], *n.m.* butcher.
bouchère [bu′ʃɛ:r], *n.f.* butcher's wife; woman keeping a butcher's shop.
boucherie [buʃ′ri], *n.f.* butcher's shop; butchery, slaughter.
bouche-trou [buʃ′tru], *n.m.* (*pl.* **bouche-trous**) stopgap.
bouchon [bu′ʃɔ̃], *n.m.* stopper, cork; wisp (*of straw etc.*).
bouchonner [buʃɔ′ne], *v.t.* to rub down (*a horse*).
bouchonnier [buʃɔ′nje], *n.m.* one who cuts *or* sells corks.
boucle [bukl], *n.f.* buckle; curl, lock (*of hair*); loop (*of a river etc.*).
bouclé [bu′kle], *a.* buckled, curled.

boucler [bu′kle], *v.t.* to buckle; to put a ring to; to curl (*hair*); **boucler la boucle**, to loop the loop. **se boucler**, *v.r.* to curl one's hair.

bouclier [bu′klje], *n.m.* buckler, shield; (*fig.*) defense.

Bouddha [bu′da], *m.* Buddha.

bouddhisme [bu′dism], *n.m.* Buddhism.

bouddhiste [bu′dist], *n.* Buddhist.

bouder [bu′de], *v.i.* to sulk, to be sullen, to pout. **se bouder**, *v.r.* to be cool towards each other.

bouderie [bu′dri], *n.f.* pouting, sulkiness.

boudeur [bu′dœːr], *a.* (*fem.* **-euse**) sulky, sullen.

boudin [bu′dɛ̃], *n.m.* blood sausage; spring (*of a coach*).

boudoir [bu′dwaːr], *n.m.* boudoir, lady's private room.

boue [bu], *n.f.* mud, mire, dirt, filth.

bouée [bu′e], *n.f.* buoy.

boueux [bu′ø], *a.* (*fem.* **-euse**) muddy, dirty, miry; foul.—*n.m.* scavenger; garbage man.

bouffant [bu′fɑ̃], *a.* puffed (*sleeve*), baggy (*trousers*).

bouffe [buf], *a.* comic.—*n.m. pl.* **Les Bouffes**, the Italian opera (*in Paris*).

bouffée [bu′fe], *n.f.* puff, gust, blast, whiff.

bouffette [bu′fɛt], *n.f.* bow of ribbon; tassel.

bouffi [bu′fi], *a.* puffed up, swollen, inflated.

bouffir [bu′fiːr], *v.t.* to puff up, to swell, to bloat.—*v.i.* to swell.

bouffissure [bufi′syːr], *n.f.* swelling, puffing up.

bouffon [bu′fɔ̃], *a.* (*fem.* **-onne**) jocose, facetious, comical.—*n.m.* buffoon, clown, jester.

bouffonner [bufɔ′ne], *v.i.* to play the buffoon; to be jocose *or* full of jests.

bouffonnerie [bufɔn′ri], *n.f.* buffoonery, drollery, jesting.

bougainvillée [bugɛvi′le], *n.f.*, **bougainvillier** [bugɛvi′lje], *n.m.* bougainvillea.

bouge [buːʒ], *n.m.* den, dirty hole, hovel.

bougeoir [bu′ʒwaːr], *n.m.* flat candlestick.

bouger [bu′ʒe], *v.i.* (*conjug. like* MANGER) to stir, to budge, to fidget.

bougie [bu′ʒi], *n.f.* wax candle; (*Elec.*) candlepower; **bougie d'allumage**, (*Motor.*) spark plug.

bougran [bu′grɑ̃], *n.m.* buckram.

bouillabaisse [buja′bɛs], *n.f.* Provençal fish soup with saffron etc.

bouillant [bu′jɑ̃], *a.* boiling, hot, scalding.

bouilleur [bu′jœːr], *n.m.* brandy distiller; boiler tube (*of an engine*).

bouilli [bu′ji], *n.m.* boiled beef.

bouillie [bu′ji], *n.f.* pap (*for infants*), porridge; pulp.

bouillir [bu′jiːr], *v.t. irr.* to boil (*milk etc.*). —*v.i.* to boil.

bouilloire [buj′waːr], *n.f.* kettle.

bouillon [bu′jɔ̃], *n.m.* broth, beef tea; bubble; ebullition.

bouillonnement [bujɔn′mɑ̃], *n.m.* bubbling up, spouting, gushing.

bouillonner [bujɔ′ne], *v.i.* to bubble, to boil; (*fig.*) to be in a state of excitement.

bouillotte [bu′jɔt], *n.f.* foot warmer; hot-water bottle; small kettle.

boulanger [bulɑ̃′ʒe], *n.m.* (*fem.* **-ère**) baker, baker's wife.—*v.t.* (*conjug. like* MANGER) to make, knead *or* bake (*bread*).

boulangerie [bulɑ̃′ʒri], *n.f.* baking, baker's business; baker's shop.

boule [bul], *n.f.* ball; bowl; (*pop.*) face, pate, head.

bouleau [bu′lo], *n.m.* (*pl.* **-eaux**) birch, birch tree.

bouledogue [bul′dɔg], *n.m.* bulldog.

boulet [bu′lɛ], *n.m.* cannon *or* musket ball.

boulette [bu′lɛt], *n.f.* pellet; forcemeat ball.

boulevard [bul′vaːr], *n.m.* rampart; boulevard.

bouleversement [bulvɛrsə′mɑ̃], *n.m.* overthrow; commotion, confusion; destruction, ruin.

bouleverser [bulvɛr′se], *v.t.* to overthrow, to throw down; to subvert; (*fig.*) to agitate, to upset.

boulier [bu′lje], *n.m.* (*Fishing*) bag net; scoring board (*at billiards*).

bouline [bu′lin], *n.f.* (*Naut.*) bowline.

boulon [bu′lɔ̃], *n.m.* bolt, large iron pin.

boulonner [bulɔ′ne], *v.t.* to fasten with iron pins, to bolt.

boulot [bu′lo], *a.* (*fem.* **-otte**) fat, dumpy, squat.

bouquet [bu′kɛ], *n.m.* bunch (*of flowers*), nosegay, bouquet; aroma (*of wine*), perfume.

bouquetier [buk′tje], *n.f.* flower vase.

bouquetière [buk′tjɛːr], *n.f.* flower girl.

bouquetin [buk′tɛ̃], *n.m.* ibex.

bouquin (1) [bu′kɛ̃], *n.m.* (*Zool.*) old billy goat; old hare.

bouquin (2) [bu′kɛ̃], *n.m.* old book; second-hand book; (*colloq.*) book.

bouquiner [buki′ne], *v.i.* to hunt after old books; (*colloq.*) to read.

bouquineur [buki′nœːr], *n.m.* (*colloq.*) lover of old books, book fancier.

bouquiniste [buki′nist], *n.m.* dealer in second-hand books.

bourbe [burb], *n.f.* mud, mire, slush.

bourbeux [bur′bø], *a.* (*fem.* **-euse**) miry, muddy, sloshy.

bourbier [bur′bje], *n.m.* slough, puddle, mire.

bourdaine [bur′dɛn], **bourgène** [bur′ʒɛn], *n.f.* black alder.

bourdon (1) [bur′dɔ̃], *n.m.* pilgrim's staff.

bourdon (2) [bur′dɔ̃], *n.m.* bumblebee; great bell; (*Organ*) drone.

bourdonnant [burdɔ′nɑ̃], *a.* humming, buzzing.

bourdonnement [burdɔn′mɑ̃], *n.m.* buzz, buzzing; humming.

bourdonner [burdɔ′ne], *v.t.* to hum.—*v.i.* to buzz, to hum; to murmur.

bourdonneur [burdɔ′nœːr], *a.* humming.—*n.m.* hummingbird, colibri.

bourg [buːr], *n.m.* borough, market-town.

bourgade [bur′gad], *n.f.* small market-town.

bourgène [BOURDAINE].

bourgeois [bur′ʒwa], *a.* middle-class; plain, common, ordinary.—*n.m.* (*fem.* **-e**) citizen, townsman, townswoman; commoner; middle-class person, bourgeois.

bourgeoisie [burʒwa′zi], *n.f.* bourgeoisie, middle class.

bourgeon [bur′ʒɔ̃], *n.m.* (*Bot.*) bud, shoot; pimple.

bourgeonnement [burʒɔn′mɑ̃], *n.m.* budding.

bourgeonner [burʒɔ'ne], *v.i.* to bud; to break out in pimples.
bourgeron [burʒə'rɔ̃], *n.m.* workman's blouse, smock frock.
bourgmestre [burg'mɛstr], *n.m.* burgomaster.
Bourgogne [bur'gɔɲ], **la**, *f.* Burgundy.
bourguignon [burgi'ɲɔ̃], *a.* (*fem.* **-onne**) Burgundian, of Burgundy.—*n.m.* (**Bourguignon**, *fem.* **-onne**) native or inhabitant of Burgundy.
bourrade [bu'rad], *n.f.* blow, thrust, buffet.
bourrasque [bu'rask], *n.f.* squall, gust; fit of anger.
bourre [bu:r], *n.f.* hair, fluff (*of animals*); flock (*of wool*); floss (*of silk*); (*fig.*) stuff, trash.
bourreau [bu'ro], *n.m.* (*pl.* **-eaux**) hangman, executioner; tyrant.
bourrée [bu're], *n.f.* brushwood, faggot; an Auvergne dance.
bourreler [bur'le], *v.t.* (*conjug. like* APPELER) to torment, to rack.
bourrelet [bur'lɛ], *n.m.* pad, cushion.
bourrelier [burə'lje], *n.m.* harness maker.
bourrellerie [burɛl'ri], *n.f.* harness maker's shop.
bourrer [bu're], *v.t.* to tamp; to stuff, to cram; (*fig.*) to ill-treat, to thrash. **se bourrer**, *v.r.* to cram oneself; to thrash each other.
bourriche [bu'riʃ], *n.f.* game basket, basket of game.
bourrique [bu'rik], *n.f.* she-ass; (*fig.*) stupid person, dolt.
bourriquet [buri'kɛ], *n.m.* ass's colt or small ass; hand barrow.
bourru [bu'ry], *a.* cross, peevish, moody, surly.
Bourse [burs], *n.f.* Stock Exchange; *Bourse du travail*, labor exchange.
bourse [burs], *n.f.* purse, bag; scholarship, grant, bursary; rabbit net.
boursier [bur'sje], *a.* (*fem.* **-ière**) pertaining to the Stock Exchange.—*n.m.* (*fem.* **-ière**) speculator on the Stock Exchange, exchange broker; purse maker; scholarship holder.
boursouflage [bursu'fla:ʒ], *n.m.* bombast.
boursouflé [bursu'fle], *a.* bloated; bombastic, swollen.
boursouflement [bursuflə'mɑ̃], *n.m.* bloatedness, puffiness; blister (*of paint*).
boursoufler [bursu'fle], *v.t.* to bloat, to puff up.
boursouflure [bursu'fly:r], *n.f.* bloatedness (*of face etc.*); (*fig.*) turgidity (*of style*).
bousculade [busky'lad], *n.m.* jostling, hustling; scrimmage.
bousculer [busky'le], *v.t.* to throw into disorder; to jostle, to hustle. **se bousculer**, *v.r.* to jostle each other.
boussole [bu'sɔl], *n.f.* compass.
bout [bu], *n.m.* end, tip, top, point; fragment, bit; *venir à bout de*, to succeed, to get through (*something*).
boutade [bu'tad], *n.f.* whim, fit, start, caprice; witticism.
boute-en-train [butɑ̃'trɛ̃], *n.m. inv.* one who promotes gaiety in others, merry-maker; *être le boute-en-train*, to be the life and soul of the party.
boutefeu [but'fø], *n.m.* (*pl.* **-eux**) (*fig.*) incendiary, fire-brand.

bouteille [bu'tɛ:j], *n.f.* bottle; bottleful.
bouteillerie [butɛj'ri], *n.f.* bottle-works.
boutique [bu'tik], *n.f.* shop; work-shop; (*collect.*) tools, implements.
boutiquier [buti'kje], *n.m.* (*fem.* **-ière**) shopkeeper.—*a.* (*fem.* **-ière**) shopkeeping.
bouton [bu'tɔ̃], *n.m.* bud; pimple; button, stud, knob; (*Elec. etc.*) switch.
bouton d'or [butɔ̃'dɔ:r], *n.m.* (*pl.* **boutons d'or**) (*Bot.*) buttercup.
boutonné [butɔ'ne], *a.* buttoned; pimpled.
boutonner [butɔ'ne], *v.t.* to button; (*Fenc.*) to touch.—*v.i.* to bud; to button up. **se boutonner**, *v.r.* to button one's coat.
boutonnière [butɔ'njɛ:r], *n.f.* buttonhole.
bouture [bu'ty:r], *n.f.* slip, cutting.
bouveau [bu'vo] (*pl.* **-eaux**), **bouvelet** [buv'lɛ], *n.m.* young ox.
bouverie [bu'vri], *n.f.* cattle shed, byre.
bouvet [bu'vɛ], *n.m.* joiner's grooving-plane.
bouvetage [buv'ta:ʒ], *n.m.* grooving and tonguing.
bouveter [buv'te], *v.t.* (*conjug. like* APPELER) to groove and tongue.
bouvier [bu'vje], *n.m.* (*fem.* **-ière**) cow-herd, ox-drover.
bouvillon [buvi'jɔ̃], *n.m.* young bullock, steer.
bouvreuil [bu'vrœ:j], *n.m.* bullfinch.
bovin [bɔ'vɛ̃], *a.* bovine.
box [bɔks], *n.m.* (*pl.* **boxes**) horse box, loose box; lock-up garage; *le box des accusés*, the dock.
boxe [bɔks], *n.f.* boxing.
boxer [bɔk'se], *v.i.* to box, to spar.
boxeur [bɔk'sœ:r], *n.m.* boxer, prize-fighter.
boy [bɔj], *n.m.* groom; native servant.
boyau [bwa'jo], *n.m.* (*pl* **-aux**) bowel, gut; catgut; hose-pipe; (*Cycl.*) racing tire.
brabançon [brabɑ̃'sɔ̃], *a.* (*fem.* **-onne**) Brabantine, Belgian.—*n.m.* (**Brabançon**, *fem.* **-onne**) Brabantine, Belgian (*person*).
bracelet [bras'lɛ], *n.m.* bracelet, armlet, bangle.
bracelet-montre [braslɛ'mɔ̃:tr], *n.m.* (*pl.* **bracelets-montres**) wrist watch.
braconnage [brakɔ'na:ʒ], *n.m.* poaching.
braconner [brakɔ'ne], *v.i.* to poach, to steal game.
braconnier [brakɔ'nje], *n.m.* (*fem.* **-ière**) poacher.—*a.* (*fem.* **-ière**) poaching; pertaining to poaching.
braguette [bra'gɛt], *n.f.* fly (*of trousers*).
brahmane [bra'man], **brahme** [bram], *n.m.* Brahmin.
brahmanisme [brama'nism], *n.m.* Brahminism.
brahme [BRAHMANE].
brai [brɛ], *n.m.* resin, rosin, pitch.
braillard [bra'ja:r], *a.* brawling, squalling; obstreperous.—*n.m.* (*fem.* **-e**) brawler, squaller.—*n.m.* small speaking-trumpet.
braille [braj], *n.m.* braille.
braillement [braj'mɑ̃], *n.m.* squalling.
brailler [bra'je], *v.i.* to bawl, to shout, to be noisy.
brailleur [bra'jœ:r], *a.* and *n.m.* (*fem.* **-euse** [BRAILLARD].
braiment [brɛ'mɑ̃], *n.m.* braying (*of an ass*).
braire [brɛ:r], *v.i. irr.* to bray; (*fig.*) to cry, to whine.
braise [brɛ:z], *n.f.* wood embers, live coals.

braiser [brɛˈze], *v.t.* to braise.
braisier [brɛˈzje], *n.m.* brazier.
braisière [brɛˈzjɛːr], *n.f.* braising pan.
bramer [braˈme], *v.i.* to bell (*of deer*).
brancard [brɑ̃ˈkaːr], *n.m.* stretcher, litter; hand barrow; shaft (*of a cart*).
brancardier [brɑ̃karˈdje], *n.m.* stretcher bearer, ambulance man.
branchage [brɑ̃ˈʃaːʒ], *n.m.* (*collect.*) branches, boughs.
branche [brɑ̃ːʃ], *n.f.* branch, bough; part, division.
brancher [brɑ̃ˈʃe], *v.t.* to divide into branches; (*Elec.*) to connect, to plug in; to tap (*a gas or water pipe*).—*v.i.* to branch off.
branchu [brɑ̃ˈʃy], *a.* forked, bifurcated, ramifying.
brande [brɑ̃ːd], *n.f.* heather; heath.
Brandebourg [brɑ̃dˈbuːr], *m.* Brandenburg.
brandebourgs [brɑ̃dˈbuːr], *n.m. pl.* braid; frogs and loops (*on a uniform*).
brandillement [brɑ̃dijˈmɑ̃], *n.m.* tossing; swinging.
brandiller [brɑ̃diˈje], *v.t.* to swing, to shake to and fro.—*v.i.* to swing, to move to and fro. **se brandiller**, *v.r.* to swing.
brandir [brɑ̃ˈdiːr], *v.t.* to brandish, to flourish.
brandissement [brɑ̃disˈmɑ̃], *n.m.* brandishing, flourishing.
brandon [brɑ̃ˈdɔ̃], *n.m.* torch, fire-brand.
branlant [brɑ̃ˈlɑ̃], *a.* shaking, loose, tottering.
branle [brɑ̃ːl], *n.m.* oscillation, shaking *or* tossing motion; jog; an old-fashioned dance.
branle-bas [brɑ̃lˈba], *n.m. inv.* (*Naut.*) clearing for action; (*fig.*) commotion, disturbance.
branlement [brɑ̃lˈmɑ̃], *n.m.* oscillation, shaking, swing.
branler [brɑ̃ˈle], *v.t.* to shake, to wag.—*v.i.* to shake, to stagger, to rock; to move; to waver.
braquage [braˈkaːʒ], *n.m.* aiming; steering, lock (*of a car*).
braque (1) [brak], *n.m.* French pointer.
braque (2) [brak], *a.* madcap, hare-brained.
braquer [braˈke], *v.t.* to aim, to level, to point.
bras [bra], *n.m.* arm; bracket; branch (*of a stream etc.*); (*fig.*) power, action, assistance.
braser [braˈze], *v.t.* to braze.
brasier [braˈzje], *n.m.* quick clear fire; brazier, furnace.
brasiller [braziˈje], *v.t.* to grill, to broil.—*v.i.* to glitter, to shine (*of the sea*).
brassage [braˈsaːʒ], *n.m.* mashing, brewing.
brassard [braˈsaːr], *n.m.* brace (*armor*); armlet.
brasse [bras], *n.f.* fathom, six feet; armful; stroke (*in swimming*).
brassée [braˈse], *n.f.* armful; stroke (*in swimming*).
brassement [brasˈmɑ̃], *n.m.* brewing; mixing.
brasser [braˈse], *v.t.* to mix; to brew, to mash; to stir up.
brasserie [brasˈri], *n.f.* brewery; brewing; drinking-saloon, 'pub'.
brasseur [braˈsœːr], *n.m.* brewer.
brassière [braˈsjɛːr], *n.f.* shoulder strap (*of a knapsack etc.*); infant's undershirt.
brassin [braˈsɛ̃], *n.m.* brewing tub; mash tub; a boiling (*quantity boiled or brewed*).

bravache [braˈvaʃ], *n.m.* bully, swaggerer, blusterer.—*a.* blustering, bullying.
bravade [braˈvad], *n.f.* bravado, boast, bluster.
brave [braːv], *a.* brave, courageous, gallant; worthy, honest, good.—*n.m.* brave *or* courageous man; good fellow.
bravement [bravˈmɑ̃], *adv.* bravely, stoutly, valiantly; skilfully, finely.
braver [braˈve], *v.t.* to defy, to dare; to brave, to beard.
bravo [braˈvo], *n.m.* (*pl.* **bravos**) and *int.* bravo; hear, hear!
bravoure [braˈvuːr], *n.f.* bravery, courage, gallantry; (*pl.*) exploits.
break [brɛk], *n.m.* break (*carriage*).
brebis [brəˈbi], *n.f.* ewe; (*fig.*) sheep; (*pl.*) flock.
brèche [brɛʃ], *n.f.* breach, flaw; notch, gap.
bréchet [breˈʃɛ], *n.m.* (*Orn.*) breast-bone.
bredouillage [brəduˈjaːʒ], **bredouillement** [brədujˈmɑ̃], *n.m.* stammering, stuttering, sputtering.
bredouille [brəˈduːj], *n.f.*(*backgammon*)lurch. *a. inv.* empty-handed; **revenir bredouille**, to return with an empty bag (*of sportsmen*).
bredouillement [BREDOUILLAGE].
bredouiller [brəduˈje], *v.t., v.i.* to stammer, to stutter.
bredouilleur [brəduˈjœːr], *a.* (*fem.* **-euse**) stammering, stuttering.—*n.m.* (*fem.* **-euse**) stammerer, stutterer.
bref [brɛf], *a.* (*fem.* **brève** (1)) short, brief, concise; brusque.—*adv.* in short, in fine, in a word.
brelan [brəˈlɑ̃], *n.m.* brelan (*card game*); gaming house.
brêler *or* **breller** [brɛˈle], *v.t.* to lash.
breller [BRÊLER].
breloque [brəˈlɔk], *n.f.* trinket, gewgaw, charm.
Brême [brɛːm], *m.* Bremen.
brème [brɛːm], *n.f.* bream.
Brésil [breˈzil], **le**, *m.* Brazil.
brésil [breˈzil], *n.m.* Brazil-wood (*for dyeing*).
brésilien [breziˈljɛ̃], *a.* (*fem.* **-enne**) Brazilian.—*n.m.* (**Brésilien**, *fem.* **-enne**) Brazilian (*person*).
Bretagne [brəˈtaɲ], **la**, *f.* Brittany; **la Grande-Bretagne**, Great Britain; **la Nouvelle-Bretagne**, New Britain.
bretelle [brəˈtɛl], *n.f.* strap; brace; (*pl.*) pair of braces; (*Rail.*) switch; (*rifle*) sling.
breton [brəˈtɔ̃], *a.* (*fem.* **-onne**) Breton.—*n.m.* Breton (*language*); (**Breton**, *fem.* **-onne**) Breton (*person*).
bretteur [brɛˈtœːr], *n.m.* swashbuckler, duellist.
bretzel [brɛtˈsɛl], *n.m.* pretzel.
breuil [brœːj], *n.m.* enclosed coppice, covert.
breuvage [brœˈvaːʒ], *n.m.* beverage, drink, liquor.
brève (1) [brɛːv], [BREF].
brève (2) [brɛːv], *n.f.* short syllable; (*Mus.*) breve.
brevet [brəˈvɛ], *n.m.* warrant, brevet, certificate (*school etc.*); diploma, license (*of printers*); patent; badge (*of boy scouts*); (*Mil.*) commission.
breveté [brəvˈte], *a.* patented; (*Mil.*) certificated—*n.m.* (*fem.* **-ée**) patentee.

breveter [brəv'te], *v.t.* (*conjug. like* APPELER) to patent; to license; to certificate.

bréviaire [bre'vjɛ:r], *n.m.* breviary.

brévité [brevi'te], *n.f.* shortness (*of syllables*).

bribes [brib], *n.f. pl.* scraps, bits; odds and ends.

bric-à-brac [brika'brak], *n.m. inv.* curios, bric-a-brac; curiosity shop.

brick [brik], *n.m.* brig.

bricolage [briko'la:ʒ], *n.m.* puttering.

bricoler [briko'le], *v.i.* to putter, to do odds and ends.

bricoleur [briko'lœ:r], *n.m.* (*fem.* **-euse**) odd job man, handyman *or* woman.

bride [brid], *n.f.* bridle, bridle rein; check, curb; string (*of a woman's cap, bonnet etc.*).

brider [bri'de], *v.t.* to bridle; to restrain, to curb; to truss (*a fowl*); to tie; to check.

bridge [bridʒ], *n.m.* bridge (*card game*); bridge (*in dentistry*).

bridger [bri'dʒe], *v.i.* to play bridge.

bridgeur [bri'dʒœ:r], *n.m.* (*fem.* **-euse**) bridge player.

bridon [bri'dɔ̃], *n.m.* snaffle bridle.

brie [bri], *n.m.* Brie cheese.

brièvement [briɛv'mã], *adv.* briefly, succinctly, in short.

brièveté [briɛv'te], *n.f.* brevity, briefness, conciseness.

brigade [bri'gad], *n.f.* brigade; (*fig.*) troop, gang, body.

brigadier [briga'dje], *n.m.* corporal (*in cavalry, artillery*); sergeant (*of police*).

brigand [bri'gã], *n.m.* brigand; (*fig.*) robber, thief.

brigandage [brigã'da:ʒ], *n.m.* brigandage, plunder.

brigander [brigã'de], *v.i.* to rob, to plunder.

brigantin [brigã'tɛ̃], *n.m.* brigantine.

brigantine [brigã'tin], *n.f.* (*Naut.*) spanker; small vessel.

brigue [brig], *n.f.* intrigue, cabal, faction.

briguer [bri'ge], *v.t.* to canvass for, to solicit, to court.

brigueur [bri'gœ:r], *n.m.* (*fem.* **-euse**) intriguer, canvasser.

brillamment [brija'mã], *adv.* brilliantly, in a brilliant manner.

brillance [bri'jã:s], *n.f.* (*Opt.*) brilliancy.

brillant [bri'jã], *a.* brilliant, sparkling, glittering; radiant.—*n.m.* brilliance, splendor; brilliant (*diamond*).

brillanter [brijã'te], *v.t.* to cut into a brilliant.

brillantine [brijã'tin], *n.f.* brilliantine (*hair-oil*); glossy cotton cloth.

briller [bri'je], *v.i.* to shine, to glitter, to sparkle; (*fig.*) to distinguish oneself, to stand out.

brimade [bri'mad], *n.f.* ragging; vexation, persecution.

brimborion [brɛ̃bɔ'rjɔ̃], *n.m.* knick-knack, bauble.

brimer [bri'me], *v.t.* to rag, to bully.

brin [brɛ̃], *n.m.* blade, slender stalk, shoot (*of corn etc.*); (*fig.*) bit, jot.

brindille [brɛ̃'di:j], *n.f.* sprig, twig.

brio [bri'o] [*It.*], *n.m.* (*Mus. etc.*) dash, spirit, go.

brioche [bri'ɔʃ], *n.f.* brioche, bun; (*fig.*) blunder.

brique [brik], *n.f.* brick; *brique anglaise*, Bath brick.

briquet [bri'kɛ], *n.m.* tinder box; (cigarette) lighter.

briquetage [brik'ta:ʒ], *n.m.* brick work; imitation brick work.

briqueter [brik'te], *v.t.* (*conjug. like* APPELER) to brick, to pave with bricks.

briqueterie [brik'tri], *n.f.* brick field, brick making; brickworks.

briqueteur [brik'tœ:r], *n.m.* bricklayer.

briquetier [brik'tje], *n.m.* brick maker.

briquette [bri'kɛt], *n.f.* briquette; compressed slack.

brisant [bri'zã], *n.m.* sand bank, reef, shoal; (*pl.*) breakers.

brise [bri:z], *n.f.* breeze; strong wind.

brisé [bri'ze], *a.* broken to pieces; (*fig.*) harassed.

brise-bise [briz'bi:z], *n.m. inv.* draft excluder; sash curtain.

brisées [bri'ze], *n.f.* (*used only in pl.*) footsteps, wake; *aller or marcher sur les brisées de quelqu'un*, to poach on someone's preserves.

brise-glace [briz'glas], *n.m.* (*pl.* **brise-glace** *or* **-glaces**) ice-breaker (*ship*).

brise-jet [briz'ʒɛ], *n.m. inv.* anti-splash tap nozzle.

brise-lames [briz'lam], *n.m. inv.* breakwater.

brisement [briz'mã], *n.m.* breaking, dashing (*of waves*); (*fig.*) trouble, contrition.

briser [bri'ze], *v.t.* to break to pieces, to smash, to break, to shatter; to burst; to crack; to destroy.—*v.i.* to break; to dash (*of waves*).

brise-tout [briz'tu], *n.m. inv.* person who breaks everything; rough, clumsy fellow.

briseur [bri'zœ:r], *n.m.* (*fem.* **-euse**) one who breaks *or* likes to break anything; iconoclast.

brise-vent [briz'vã], *n.m.* (*pl.* **brise-vent** *or* **brise-vents**) wind-screen (*for protecting plants*).

brisque [brisk], *n.f.* a card game; (*Mil.*) stripe; war service chevron.

brisure [bri'zy:r], *n.f.* break; folding-point in a piece of joiner's work; small fragment.

britannique [brita'nik], *a.* British, Britannic; *Les Îles Britanniques*, the British Isles.

broc [bro], *n.m.* large jug *or* quart pot.

brocantage [brokã'ta:ʒ], *n.m.* dealing in second-hand goods, broker's business; bartering.

brocante [brɔ'kã:t], *n.f.* second-hand trade; article of trifling value.

brocanter [brokã'te], *v.i.* to deal in second-hand goods; to exchange, to barter.

brocanteur [brokã'tœ:r], *n.m.* (*fem.* **-euse**) dealer in second-hand goods, junk-shop owner.

brocard [brɔ'ka:r], *n.m.* taunt, jeer; lampoon.

brocarder [brokar'de], *v.t.* to taunt, to ridicule.

brocardeur [brokar'dœ:r], *n.m.* (*fem.* **-euse**) scoffer, jeerer.

brocart *or* **broquart** [brɔ'ka:r], *n.m.* brocade.

brochage [brɔ'ʃa:ʒ], *n.m.* stitching (*of books*).

broche [brɔʃ], *n.f.* spit; spindle; skewer; spigot; knitting needle; brooch; (*pl.*) tusks (*of wild boars*); (*Elec.*) *fiche à deux broches*, two-pin plug.

broché

broché [brɔ'ʃe], *a.* embossed (*of linen*); brocaded, figured (*of other materials*); *livre broché*, paper-bound book.
brocher [brɔ'ʃe], *v.t.* to stitch (*a book etc.*); to figure (*materials*); to emboss (*linen*).
brochet [brɔ'ʃɛ], *n.m.* pike (*fish*).
brocheter [brɔʃ'te], *v.t.* (*conjug. like* APPELER) to skewer.
brochette [brɔ'ʃɛt], *n.f.* (*Cook.*) small spit.
brocheur [brɔ'ʃœːr], *n.m.* (*fem.* **-euse**) stitcher, esp. book-stitcher.
brochure [brɔ'ʃyːr], *n.f.* stitching; booklet, brochure, pamphlet, tract; embroidery.
brocoli [brɔkɔ'li], *n.m.* broccoli.
brodequin [brɔd'kɛ̃], *n.m.* buskin, half-boot.
broder [brɔ'de], *v.t.* to embroider; to adorn, to embellish (*a story etc.*).—*v.i.* to romance.
broderie [brɔd'ri], *n.f.* embroidery; (*fig.*) embellishment.
brodeur [brɔ'dœːr], *n.m.* (*fem.* **-euse**) embroiderer.
broiement or **broîment** [brwa'mã], **broyage** [brwa'jaːʒ], *n.m.* grinding, powdering.
bromure [brɔ'myːr], *n.m.* bromide.
bronche [brɔ̃ːʃ], *n.f.* (*pl.*) (*Anat.*) bronchial tubes.
bronchement [brɔ̃ʃ'mã], *n.m.* stumbling; flinching.
broncher [brɔ̃'ʃe], *v.i.* to stumble, to trip, to reel; to falter.
bronchial [brɔ̃'ʃjal], *a.* (*m. pl.* **-aux**) (*Anat.*) bronchial.
bronchique [brɔ̃'ʃik], *a.* bronchial.
bronchite [brɔ̃'ʃit], *n.f.* (*Path.*) bronchitis.
broncho-pneumonie [brɔ̃kɔpnømɔ'ni], *n.f.* broncho-pneumonia.
bronze [brɔ̃ːz], *n.m.* bronze; bronze statue *or* medal.
bronzer [brɔ̃'ze], *v.t.* to bronze; to tan (*the face etc.*).
broquart [BROCART].
broquette [brɔ'kɛt], *n.f.* tack, carpet nail.
brosse [brɔs], *n.f.* brush; painter's brush *or* pencil; *cheveux en brosse*, crew-cut hair.
brosser [brɔ'se], *v.t.* to brush. **se brosser**, *v.r.* to brush oneself.
brosserie [brɔs'ri], *n.f.* brushmaking business; brush factory.
brou [bru], *n.m.* husk *or* peel (*of nuts, esp. walnuts*); *brou de noix*, walnut stain, walnut liquor.
brouet [bru'ɛ], *n.m.* thin broth.
brouette [bru'ɛt], *n.f.* wheelbarrow.
brouettée [bruɛ'te], *n.f.* barrow load.
brouetter [bruɛ'te], *v.t.* to wheel in a barrow.
brouetteur [bruɛ'tœːr], **brouettier** [bruɛ'tje], *n.m.* barrowman.
brouhaha [brua'a], *n.m.* hubbub, uproar, hurly-burly.
brouillage [bru'jaːʒ], *n.m.* (*Rad.*) atmospherics, jamming.
brouillard [bru'jaːr], *n.m.* fog, mist, haze; (*Comm.*) daybook.
brouillasse [bru'jas], *n.f.* drizzle, Scotch mist.
brouillasser [bruja'se], *v.impers.* to drizzle.
brouille [bru:j], **brouillerie** [bruj'ri], *n.f.* quarrel, falling-out.
brouillé [bru'je], *a.* scrambled (*eggs*); blurred; on bad terms.
brouillement [bruj'mã], *n.m.* mixing together, jumbling.

brouiller [bru'je], *v.t.* to mix together, to jumble up, to shuffle; to embroil, to confuse; (*Rad.*) to jam. **se brouiller**, *v.r.* to fall out (*with someone*).
brouillerie [BROUILLE].
brouillon [bru'jɔ̃], *a.* (*fem.* **-onne**) mischief-making; blundering.—*n.m.* rough draft, rough copy; blunderer, bungler.
brouillonner [brujɔ'ne], *v.t.* to write in a blundering *or* confused way, to botch.
brouir [bru'iːr], *v.t.* to blight, to nip, to parch.
brouissure [brui'syːr], *n.f.* blight, scorching.
broussailles [bru'saːj], *n.f.* (*usu. in pl.*) bushes, brushwood, undergrowth.
broussailleux [brusa'jø], *a.* (*fem.* **-euse**) bushy, covered with bushes.
brousse [brus], *n.f.* brushwood, bush (*Australia etc.*).
brouter [bru'te], *v.t., v.i.* to browse, to graze.
broutilles [bru'ti:j], *n.f. pl.* sprigs; (*fig.*) trifles.
brownien [bro'njɛ̃], *a. mouvements browniens,* molecular motion.
browning [bro'niŋ], *n.m.* automatic pistol.
broyage [brwa'jaːʒ], *n.m.* crushing (*of ore*), grinding (*of colors*).
broyer [brwa'je], *v.t.* (*conjug. like* EMPLOYER) to grind, to pound, to pulverize.
broyeur [brwa'jœːr], *a.* (*fem.* **-euse**) grinding.—*n.m.* (*fem.* **-euse**) grinding; grinder, pounder.
bru [bry], *n.f.* daughter-in-law.
brucelles [bry'sɛl], *n.f. pl.* tweezers.
brugnon [bry'ɲɔ̃], *n.m.* nectarine.
bruine [bryin], *n.f.* light drizzling rain.
bruiner [bryi'ne], *v.impers.* to drizzle.
bruineux [bryi'nø], *a.* (*fem.* **-euse**) drizzly, drizzling.
bruire [bryiːr], *v.t. irr.* to make a noise; to rustle, to rattle; to roar, to sough (*of the wind*).
bruissant [bryi'sã], *a.* rustling, rattling; roaring.
bruissement [bryis'mã], *n.m.* rustling noise, rattling, roaring.
bruit [bryi], *n.m.* noise, din, uproar, clamor; fame, renown; report, talk, rumor.
bruitage [bryi'taːʒ], *n.m.* sound effects.
bruiter [bryi'te], *v.i.* to make sound effects.
bruiteur [bryi'tœːr], *n.m.* sound-effects specialist.
brûlage [bry'laːʒ], *n.m.* burning (*of rubbish*); singeing (*of hair*); roasting (*of coffee*).
brûlant [bry'lã], *a.* burning, scorching, hot, torrid; (*fig.*) eager, ardent.
brûlé [bry'le], *n.m.* smell of burning; (*C*) burnt-out area *or* field.
brûle-gueule [bryl gœl], *n.m. inv.* (*colloq.*) short pipe, cutty.
brûle-pourpoint, à [abrylpur'pwɛ̃], *adv.* point-blank (*of shooting*).
brûler [bry'le], *v.t.* to burn; to cauterize; to scorch, to parch; to singe (*hair*).—*v.i.* to burn, to be on fire; (*fig.*) to be eager. **se brûler**, *v.r.* to burn oneself, to be burnt.
brûleur [bry'lœːr], *n.m.* (*fem.* **-euse**) burner; incendiary; *brûleur à gaz*, gas-ring, gas jet.
brûlis [bry'li], *n.m.* burnt part of a wood *or* field.
brûloir [bry'lwaːr], *n.m.* coffee burner *or* roaster.

52

brûlot [bry'lo], *n.m.* fire ship; (*fig.*) firebrand, incendiary; (C) kind of gnat *or* midge.

brûlure [bry'ly:r], *n.f.* burn, frost nip, scald.

brumaire [bry'mɛ:r], *n.m.* Brumaire (*second month of the calendar of the first French Republic, from Oct. 22nd to Nov. 20th*).

brume [brym], *n.f.* haze, mist.

brumeux [bry'mø], *a.* (*fem.* **-euse**) hazy, misty; (*fig.*) sombre.

brun [brœ], *a.* brown, dark, dusky.—*n.m.* brown (*color*); (*fem.* **-e** (1)) dark-complexioned person.

brunâtre [bry'nɑ:tr], *a.* brownish.

brune (2) [bryn], *n.f.* dusk (*of the evening*); dark woman, dark girl, brunette.

brunet [bry'nɛ], *a.* (*fem.* **-ette**) brownish.— *n.f.* (**-ette**) dark woman, dark girl.

brunir [bry'ni:r], *v.t.* to make brown; to burnish.—*v.i.* to turn brown. **se brunir**, *v.r.* to turn dark *or* brown.

brunissage [bryni'sa:ʒ], *n.m.* burnishing.

brunisseur [bryni'sœ:r], *n.m.* (*fem.* **-euse**) burnisher.

brunissoir [bryni'swa:r], *n.m.* burnisher (*tool*).

brunissure [bryni'sy:r], *n.f.* burnishing; polish.

brusque [brysk], *a.* blunt, abrupt, rough; unexpected.

brusquement [bryskə'mɑ̃], *adv.* bluntly, abruptly; uncivilly.

brusquer [brys'ke], *v.t.* to be sharp with (*someone*); to offend; (*fig.*) to precipitate.

brusquerie [bryskə'ri], *n.f.* abruptness, bluntness; hastiness.

brut [bryt], *a.* rough, raw, unhewn; uncultured.—*adv.* (*Comm.*) gross (*as opposed to* net).

brutal [bry'tal], *a.* (*m.pl.* **-aux**) brutal; surly, churlish.—*n.m.* (*fem.* **-e**) brute, brutal person.

brutalement [brytal'mɑ̃], *adv.* brutally.

brutaliser [brytali'ze], *v.t.* to bully; to brutalize.

brutalité [brytali'te], *n.f.* brutality, brutishness.

brute [bryt], *n.f.* brute, brutal person; boor.

Bruxelles [bry'sɛl], *f.* Brussels.

bruyamment [bryja'mɑ̃], *adv.* noisily.

bruyère [bry'jɛ:r], *n.f.* heath, heather.

buanderie [bɥɑ̃'dri], *n.f.* wash house, laundry.

buandier [bɥɑ̃'dje], *n.m.* (*fem.* **-ière**) bleacher; washerman, washerwoman.

bube [byb], *n.f.* pimple.

bubonique [bybɔ'nik], *a.* bubonic.

Bucarest [byka'rest], *m.* Bucharest.

buccin [byk'sɛ̃], *n.m.* (*Mus. Ant.*) long trumpet; (*Conch.*) whelk.

bûche [byʃ], *n.f.* log; (*fig.*) blockhead, dolt.

bûcher (1) [by'ʃe], *n.m.* wood house; funeral pile, pyre; stake.

bûcher (2) [by'ʃe], *v.t.* to roughhew. —*v.i.* to cram, to bone.

bûcheron [byʃ'rɔ̃], *n.m.* (*fem.* **-onne**) wood cutter.

bûchette [by'ʃɛt], *n.f.* stick of dry wood.

bucolique [bykɔ'lik], *a.* bucolic.

budget [byd'ʒɛ], *n.m.* budget.

budgétaire [bydʒe'tɛ:r], *a.* budgetary.

buée [bɥe], *n.f.* steam (*on window panes*).

buffet [by'fɛ], *n.m.* sideboard; buffet; refreshment room.

buffetier [byf'tje], *n.m.* (*fem.* **-ière**) refreshment room manager.

buffle [byfl], *n.m.* buffalo; buffalo hide; buff leather.

buffleterie [byflə'tri], *n.f.* buff belts, straps etc. (*of a soldier*).

bugle [bygl], *n.m.* key bugle.

buis [bɥi], *n.m.* box; box tree, boxwood.

buissaie [bɥi'sɛ], **buissière** [bɥi'sjɛ:r], *n.f.* box grove.

buisson [bɥi'sɔ̃], *n.m.* bush; thicket.

buissoner [bɥisɔ'ne], *v.i.* to grow into a bush.

buissonnet [bɥisɔ'nɛ], *n.m.* little bush.

buissonneux [bɥisɔ'nø], *a.* (*fem.* **-euse**) bushy.

buissonnier [bɥisɔ'nje], *a.* (*fem.* **-ière**) retiring into the bushes; *faire l'école buissonnière*, to play truant; *lapins buissonniers*, thicket-rabbits.—*n.m.* shrubbery.

bulbe [bylb], *n.m.* bulb.

bulbeux [byl'bø], *a.* (*fem.* **-euse**) bulbous.

bulgare [byl'ga:r], *a.* Bulgarian.—*n.m.* Bulgarian (*language*).—*n.* (**Bulgare**) Bulgarian (*person*).

Bulgarie [bylga'ri], **la**, *f.* Bulgaria.

bulle [byl], *n.f.* bubble; blister; a papal bull.

bullé [by'le], *a.* authenticated with a seal; by papal bull.

bulletin [byl'tɛ̃], *n.m.* bulletin, official report (*school etc.*); certificate, receipt; ballot; ticket; *bulletin d'information* news bulletin; *bulletin météorologique*, weather forecast.

bulleux [by'lø], *a.* (*fem.* **-euse**) bubbly, blistery.

buraliste [byra'list], *n.* receiver of taxes; tobacco dealer.

bure [by:r], *n.f.* drugget; fustian, baize.

bureau [by'ro], *n.m.* (*pl.* **-eaux**) writing table, desk; office; board; committee; *Deuxième Bureau*, Intelligence Service, M.I.5.

bureaucrate [byrɔ'krat], *n.m.* (*pej.*) bureaucrat.

bureaucratie [byrɔkra'si], *n.f.* bureaucracy; (*fig.*) red tape.

bureaucratique [byrɔkra'tik], *a.* bureaucratic; formal.

burette [by'rɛt], *n.f.* cruet; oil-can; (*Chem.*) burette.

burin [by'rɛ̃], *n.m.* graver, graving tool; (*fig.*) pen.

buriner [byri'ne], *v.t.* to engrave; to drill (*a tooth*).

burineur [byri'nœ:r], *n.m.* engraver.

burlesque [byr'lesk], *a.* burlesque, ludicrous. —*n.m.* burlesque.

burnous [byr'nus], *n.m.* burnous, hooded Arab cloak.

busard [by'za:r], *n.m.* buzzard.

buse (1) [by:z], *n.f.* buzzard; (*fig.*) blockhead.

buse (2) [by:z], *n.f.* channel, pipe; nozzle; (*Mining*) air shaft.

busqué [bys'ke], *a.* aquiline (*nose*).

buste [byst], *n.m.* bust, head and shoulders.

but [by(t)], *n.m.* mark; object, end; purpose, design, goal, objective; *de but en blanc* bluntly; (*Ftb.*) *marquer un but*, to score.

buté [by'te], *a.* stubborn, (*fam.*) dead set on.

buter *or* **butter** (1) [by'te], *v.t.* to support, to prop.—*v.i.* to rest *or* abut (*contre*); to stumble *or* hit (*contre*). **se buter**, *v.r.* to be bent on, to stick (*à*).

butin [by'tɛ̃], *n.m.* booty, spoils, prize, plunder.
butiner [byti'ne], *v.t.*, *v.i.* to pillage, to plunder.
butoir [by'twa:r], *n.m.* buffer, buffer-stop (*on railway*); tappet.
butor [by'tɔ:r], *n.m.* bittern; (*fig.*) churl, lout, booby.
butte [byt], *n.f.* rising ground; knoll, mound.
butter (1) [BUTER].
butter (2) [by'te], *v.t.* to earth up.
butteur [BUTTOIR].
buttoir [by'twa:r], **butteur** [by'tœ:r], *n.m.* ridging plough.
buvable [by'vabl], *a.* drinkable, fit to drink.
buvard [by'va:r], *a. papier buvard,* blotting paper.—*n.m.* blotting pad, blotter.
buvetier [byv'tje], *n.m.* (*fem.* **-ière**) innkeeper, publican.
buvette [by'vɛt], *n.f.* refreshment room (*railway station*); pump room (*at spa*).
buveur [by'vœ:r], *n.m.* (*fem.* **-euse**) drinker; toper; *buveur d'eau,* teetotaller.
buvoter [byvɔ'te], *v.i.* to sip, to tipple.
Byzance [bi'zɑ̃:s], *f.* Byzantium.
byzantin [bizɑ̃'tɛ̃], *a.* Byzantine.—*n.m.* (**Byzantin,** *fem.* **-ine**) Byzantine (*person*).

C

C, c [se], *n.m.* the third letter of the alphabet.
ça [sa], *pron.* [*contraction of* **cela**] that; *comme ci comme ça,* only so-so; *donnez-moi ça,* give me that.
çà [sa], *adv.* here; *çà et là,* here and there. —*int.* now; *çà alors!* well, I never!
cabale [ka'bal], *n.f.* cabal, faction.
cabaler [kaba'le], *v.i.* to cabal, to plot.
cabaleur [kaba'lœ:r], *n.m.* (*fem.* **-euse**) caballer, intriguer.
caban [ka'bɑ̃], *n.m.* hooded cloak, oilskins.
cabane [ka'ban], *n.f.* hut, shed, cabin, shanty; central part (*of an airplane*).
cabanon [kaba'nɔ̃], *n.m.* small hut; prison cell; padded room.
cabaret [kaba'rɛ], *n.m.* inferior kind of wine shop, tavern; night club.
cabaretier [kabar'tje], *n.m.* (*fem.* **-ière**) publican, tavern keeper.
cabas [ka'ba], *n.m.* flat two-handled basket.
cabeliau [CABILLAUD].
cabestan [kabes'tɑ̃], *n.m.* capstan, windlass.
cabillaud [kabi'jo], **cabeliau** [kab'ljo] (*pl.* **-aux**), *n.m.* fresh cod.
cabine [ka'bin], *n.f.* cabin; (*Av.*) *cabine de pilotage,* cockpit; *cabine téléphonique,* telephone booth.
cabinet [kabi'nɛ], *n.m.* closet, study; practice (*of a professional man*); office (*of a lawyer, barrister etc.*); (*Polit.*) Cabinet; *cabinet d'aisances* or *les cabinets,* lavatory.
câblage [kɑ'bla:ʒ], *n.m.* (*Elec.*) wiring.
câble [kɑ:bl], *n.m.* cable.
câbler [kɑ'ble], *v.t.* to twist into a cord; to telegraph by cable.

câblogramme [kɑblɔ'gram], *n.m.* cablegram.
cabochon [kabɔ'ʃɔ̃], *n.m.* fancy brass nail; (*Cycl.*) *cabochon rouge,* red reflector.
cabosse [ka'bɔs], *n.f.* (*pop.*) bruise, bump.
cabosser [kabɔ'se], *v.t.* to bump, to bruise; to dent.
cabotage [kabɔ'ta:ʒ], *n.m.* coasting, coasting trade.
caboter [kabɔ'te], *v.i.* to coast.
caboteur [kabɔ'tœ:r], **cabotier** [kabɔ'tje], *n.m.* coasting vessel; coaster.
cabotin [kabɔ'tɛ̃], *n.m.* strolling player; bad actor, mummer.
cabotiner [kabɔti'ne], *v.i.* to act badly; (*fig.*) to strut.
cabré [kɑ'bre], *a.* rearing (*of a horse*); bucking (*of a plane*).
cabrer [kɑ'bre], *v.t.* to make (*a horse, a plane*) rear. **se cabrer,** *v.r.* to prance, to rear; (*fig.*) to revolt, to fly into a passion.
cabri [ka'bri], *n.m.* kid.
cabriole [kabri'ɔl], *n.f.* caper, leap.
cabrioler [kabriɔ'le], *v.i.* to caper, to cut capers.
cabriolet [kabriɔ'lɛ], *n.m.* cabriolet, cab.
cacahouète [kaka'wɛt], **cacahuète** [kaka'ɥɛt], *n.f.* peanut, monkey nut.
cacao [kaka'o], *n.m.* cacao, chocolate nut.
cacaoyer [kakaɔ'je], **cacaotier** [kakaɔ'tje], *n.m.* cacao tree.
cacaoyère [kakaɔ'jɛ:r], **cacaotière** [kakaɔ'tjɛ:r], *n.f.* cacao plantation.
cacatois [kaka'twa], **cacatoès** [kakatɔ'ɛ:s], *n.m.* cockatoo.
cachalot [kaʃa'lo], *n.m.* sperm whale.
cachalotier [kaʃalɔ'tje], *n.m.* whaler.
cache [kaʃ], *n.f.* hiding place.
cache-cache [kaʃ'kaʃ], *n.m.* hide-and-seek.
cachemire [kaʃ'mi:r], *n.m.* cashmere.
cache-nez [kaʃ'ne], *n.m.* muffler, comforter.
cacher [ka'ʃe], *v.t.* to hide, to conceal; to mask. **se cacher,** *v.r.* to hide, to lurk.
cache-sexe [kaʃ'sɛks], *n.m.* trunks; panties; (*colloq.*) G-string.
cachet [ka'ʃe], *n.m.* seal, stamp; signet ring; ticket; tablet (*of aspirin*); (*fig.*) character, stamp, mark.
cacheter [kaʃ'te], *v.t.* (*conjug. like* APPELER) to seal.
cachette [ka'ʃɛt], *n.f.* hiding place.
cachot [ka'ʃo], *n.m.* dungeon, prison.
cachotter [kaʃɔ'te], *v.t.* to make a mystery of, to conceal.
cachotterie [kaʃɔ'tri], *n.f.* mysterious ways; underhand work.
cachottier [kaʃɔ'tje], *a.* (*fem.* **-ière**) mysterious, sly.—*n.m.* (*fem.* **-ière**) one who makes a mystery of things.
cachou [ka'ʃu], *n.m.* cachou.
cacophonie [kakɔfɔ'ni], *n.f.* cacophony.
cacophonique [kakɔfɔ'nik], *a.* cacophonous.
cactier [kak'tje], **cactus** [kak'ty:s], *n.m.* cactus.
cadastral [kadas'tral], *a.* (*m. pl.* **-aux**) cadastral, referring to the register of lands.
cadastre [ka'dastr], *n.m.* cadastre, register of the survey of lands.
cadastrer [kadas'tre], *v.t.* to survey.
cadavéreux [kadave'rø], *a.* (*fem.* **-euse**) cadaverous, corpse-like, ghastly.
cadavérique [kadave'rik], *a.* of *or* pertaining to a corpse.

cadavre [ka'dɑ:vr], *n.m.* corpse, dead body.
cadeau [ka'do], *n.m.* (*pl.* **-eaux**) present, gift.
cadenas [kad'nɑ], *n.m.* padlock; clasp.
cadenasser [kadna'se], *v.t.* to padlock; to snap, clasp.
cadence [ka'dɑ̃:s], *n.f.* cadence, rhythm, time (*in dancing*).
cadencer [kadɑ̃'se], *v.t.* (*conjug. like* COMMENCER) to cadence, to harmonize.
cadène [ka'dɛ:n], *n.f.* chain (*for convicts*); chain gang.
cadenette [kad'nɛt], *n.f.* tress (*of hair*).
cadet [ka'dɛ], *a.* and *n.m.* (*fem.* **-ette**) younger, junior (*of two*).
Cadix [ka'diks], *f.* Cadiz.
cadmium [kad'mjɔm], *n.m.* cadmium.
cadrage [ka'dra:ʒ], *n.m.* (*Phot., Cine.*) centering.
cadran [ka'drɑ̃], *n.m.* dial plate, dial; *cadran solaire*, sundial.
cadre [kɑ:dr], *n.m.* frame, framework; (*Mil.*) the staff; (*pl.*) the higher staff (*of an administration or a firm*).
cadrer [kɑ'dre], *v.t.* (*Phot., Cine.*) to center.— *v.i.* to agree, to tally, to square (*à or avec*).
caduc [ka'dyk], *a.* (*fem.* **-uque**) decrepit, decayed; frail, tumble-down; lapsed, null, void (*of legacies*); (*Bot.*) deciduous.
caducité [kadysi'te], *n.f.* caducity, decrepitude.
cafard [ka'fa:r], *a.* hypocritical, sanctimonious.— *n.m.* (*fem.* **-e**) hypocrite, sanctimonious person; humbug; (*Sch.*) sneak.— *n.m.* cockroach.
cafarder [kafar'de], *v.i.* (*fam.*) to sneak, to tell tales (*at school*).
cafarderie [kafar'dri], *n.f.* cant, hypocrisy, sanctimoniousness.
café [ka'fe], *n.m.* coffee; café, coffee house; coffee berry.
caféière [kafe'jɛ:r], *n.f.* coffee plantation.
caféine [kafe'i:n], *n.f.* caffeine.
cafetan or **caftan** [kaf'tɑ̃], *n.m.* caftan.
cafetier [kaf'tje], *n.m.* (*fem.* **cafetière** (1)) coffee-house keeper.
cafetière (2) [kaf'tje:r], *n.f.* coffee pot, percolator.
cafouillage [kafu'ja:ʒ], *n.m.* floundering.
cafre [kɑ:fr], *a.* and *n.* (**Cafre**) Kaffir, Bantu.
caftan [CAFETAN].
cage [ka:ʒ], *n.f.* cage; coop.
cageot [ka'ʒo], *n.m.* little cage, hamper, crate.
cagibi [kaʒi'bi], *n.m.* small hut or room.
cagneux [ka'nø], *a.* (*fem.* **-euse**) knock-kneed, pigeon-toed.
cagnotte [ka'nɔt], *n.f.* kitty, pool, jackpot.
cagot [ka'go], *a.* (*fem.* **-otte**) bigoted, hypocritical.— *n.m.* (*fem.* **-otte**) bigot, hypocrite.
cagoterie [kago'tri], *n.f.* an act or word of hypocrisy or bigotry.
cagotisme [kago'tism], *n.m.* hypocrisy, bigotry.
cagoule [ka'gul], *n.f.* monk's cloak; penitent's cowl; hood.
cahier [ka'je], *n.m.* stitched paper-book; exercise book; quarter of a quire of paper.
cahot [ka'o], *n.m.* jerk, jolt.
cahotage [kao'ta:ʒ], **cahotement** [kaot'mɑ̃], *n.m.* jolting, jerking.
cahotant [kao'tɑ̃], *a.* rough, jolting.
cahoter [kao'te], *v.i.* to jolt, to be jerked about.

cahute [ka'yt], *n.f.* hut, hovel.
cïad [ka'id], *n.m.* Arab chief or judge.
caïeu or **cayeu** [ka'jø], *n.m.* (*pl.* **-eux**) (*Hort.*) offshoot of a bulb, clove.
caillage [kɑ'ja:ʒ], *n.m.* curdling, congealing.
caille [kɑ:j], *n.f.* quail.—(*C*) *a.* piebald.
caillé [kɑ'je], *n.m.* curdled milk, curds.—*a.* curdled.
caillebottage [kɑjbɔ'ta:ʒ], *n.m.* curdling.
caillebotte [kɑj'bɔt], *n.f.* curds.
caillebotter (se) [səkɑjbɔ'te], *v.r.* to curdle.
caille-lait [kɑj'lɛ], *n.m. inv.* rennet.
caillement [kɑj'mɑ̃], *n.m.* curdling, coagulating.
cailler [kɑ'je], *v.t.* to curdle, to clot. **se cailler**, *v.r.* to coagulate, to turn to curds.
cailleteau [kɑj'to], *n.m..* (*pl.* **-eaux**) young quail.
caillette (1) [kɑ'jɛt], *n.f.* rennet.
caillette (2) [kɑ'jɛt], *n.f.* (*Orn.*) petrel; flirt.
caillot [kɑ'jo], *n.m.* clot of blood, coagulum.
caillou [kɑ'ju], *n.m.* (*pl.* **-oux**) pebble, small stone, flint, flint stone.
cailloutage [kaju'ta:ʒ], *n.m.* gravelling; ballasting; rough-cast, pebble-work.
caillouter [kaju'te], *v.t.* to gravel, to ballast.
caillouteux [kaju'tø], *a.* (*fem.* **-euse**) pebbly, flinty.
cailloutis [kaju'ti], *n.m.* broken stones, gravel; road metal.
caïman [kai'mɑ̃], *n.m.* American crocodile, cayman.
Caïn [ka'ɛ̃], *m.* Cain.
caïque or **caïc** [ka'ik], *n.m.* (*Naut.*) caique.
Caire [kɛ:r], **Le**, *m.* Cairo.
caisse [kɛ:s], *n.f.* chest, case, box, trunk; till; cash; cashier's office, pay desk; *la grosse caisse*, the (big) drum; *caisse d'épargne*, savings bank.
caissette [kɛ'sɛt], *n.f.* small box.
caissier [kɛ'sje], *n.m.* (*fem.* **-ière**) treasurer, cashier.
caisson [kɛ'sɔ̃], *n.m.* ammunition wagon; (*Naut.*) locker.
cajoler [kaʒɔ'le], *v.t.* to cajole, to coax.
cajolerie [kaʒɔl'ri], *n.f.* cajolery, coaxing.
cajoleur [kaʒɔ'lœr], *n.m.* (*fem.* **-euse**) cajoler, coaxer.—*a.* cajoling, coaxing.
cal [kal], *n.m.* callosity, callus.
Calabre [ka'lɑ:br], **la**, *f.* Calabria.
calage [ka'la:ʒ], *n.m.* lowering (*of sails etc.*) propping, wedging (*of furniture*).
calaison [kalɛ'zɔ̃], *n.f.* load line, sea gauge.
calaminage [kalami'na:ʒ], *n.m.* (*Motor.*) carbonizing.
calamine [kala'min], *n.f.* carbon (*on plugs of a car etc.*).
calamité [kalami'te], *n.f.* calamity, misfortune.
calamiteusement [kalamitøz'mɑ̃], *adv.* calamitously.
calamiteux [kalami'tø], *a.* (*fem.* **-euse**) calamitous.
calandrage [kalɑ̃'dra:ʒ], *n.m.* calendering, hot-pressing.
calandre [ka'lɑ̃:dr], *n.f.* mangle, calender; (*Motor.*) radiator grill.
calandrer [kalɑ̃'dre], *v.t.* to calender, to press, to smooth.
calandrette [kalɑ̃'drɛt], *n.f.* song-thrush.
calcaire [kal'kɛ:r], *a.* calcareous.—*n.m.* limestone.
calcéolaire [kalseɔ'lɛ:r], *n.f.* calceolaria.

calcination [kalsinɑ'sjɔ̃], *n.f.* calcination.
calciner [kalsi'ne], *v.t.* to calcine, to burn. **se calciner**, *v.r.* to calcine.
calcium [kal'sjɔm], *n.m.* calcium.
calcul [kal'kyl], *n.m.* calculation; arithmetic; reckoning, counting; (*Math.*) calculus; (*fig.*) design, selfish motive; (*Med.*) calculus (*stone*).
calculable [kalky'labl], *a.* computable, calculable.
calculateur [kalkyla'tœːr], *a.* (*fem.* **-trice**) calculating, scheming.—*n.m.* (*fem.* **-trice**) calculator, reckoner; schemer.—*n.f.* (**-trice**) computer.
calculer [kalky'le], *v.t.* to calculate, to compute, to estimate; *machine à calculer*, computer.
cale (1) [kal], *n.f.* hold (*of a ship*); stocks, slip; ducking, keel-hauling (*punishment*); *cale sèche*, dry dock.
cale (2) [kal], *n.f.* wedge, block; prop, strut.
calebasse [kal'bas], *n.f.* calabash, gourd.
calèche [ka'lɛʃ], *n.f.* calash; barouche, open carriage.
caleçon [kal'sɔ̃], *n.m.* (*men's*) drawers, pants; *caleçon de bain*, bathing trunks.
Calédonie [kaledɔ'ni], **la**, *f.* Caledonia.
calédonien [kaledɔ'njɛ̃], *a.* (*fem.* **-enne**) Caledonian.—*n.m.* (**Calédonien**, *fem.* **-enne**) Caledonian (*person*).
caléfaction [kalefak'sjɔ̃], *n.f.* heating, calefaction.
calembour [kalɑ̃'buːr], *n.m.* pun.
calembourdiste [kalɑ̃bur'dist], *n.m.* punster.
calembredaine [kalɑ̃brə'dɛn], *n.f.* quibble, subterfuge, nonsense.
calendes [ka'lɑ̃ːd], *n.f. pl.* (*Ant.*) calends; convocation of the clergy of a diocese.
calendrier [kalɑ̃dri'e], *n.m.* calendar, almanac.
calendule [kalɑ̃'dyl], *n.f.* calendula.
cale-pied [kal'pje], *n.m.* toe clip.
calepin [kal'pɛ̃], *n.m.* notebook, memorandum book.
caler (1) [ka'le], *v.t.* (*Naut.*) to lower, to strike; to draw, to have a draft of.
caler (2) [ka'le], *v.t.* to prop up, to wedge; to steady; to jam; (*Motor.*) to stall.—*v.i.* (*Motor.*) to stall.
calfeutrage [kalfø'traːʒ], **calfeutrement** [kalføtr'mɑ̃], *n.m.* stopping of chinks.
calfeutrer [kalfø'tre], *v.t.* to stop up the chinks of, to make air-tight. **se calfeutrer**, *v.r.* to shut oneself up.
calibre [ka'libr], *n.m.* calibre, bore (*of a gun*); size (*of a bullet*); (*fig.*) kind, sort.
calibrer [kali'bre], *v.t.* to calibrate; to give the proper calibre to (*bullets etc.*).
calice (1) [ka'lis], *n.m.* chalice, communion cup; (*fig.*) grief, sacrifice.
calice (2) [ka'lis], *n.m.* (*Bot.*) calyx, flower, cup.
calicot [kali'ko], *n.m.* unbleached muslin; (*slang*) dry-goods store clerk.
calicule [kali'kyl], *n.m.* calicle, caliculus.
califat [kali'fa], *n.m.* caliphate.
calife [ka'lif] *n.m.* caliph.
Californie [kalifɔr'ni], **la**, *f.* California.
califourchon [kalifur'ʃɔ̃], *n.m.* **à califourchon**, astride.
câlin [ka'lɛ̃], *a.* wheedling, winning, coaxing. —*n.m.* (*fem.* **-e**) wheedler, cajoler.

câliner [kɑ:li'ne], *v.t.* to cajole, to wheedle. **se câliner**, *v.r.* to coddle oneself, to take one's ease.
câlinerie [kɑ:lin'ri], *n.f.* wheedling, cajolery, caressing.
calleux [ka'lø], *a.* (*fem.* **-euse**) callous, horny.
calligraphe [kali'graf], *n.m.* calligrapher, good penman.
calligraphie [kaligra'fi], *n.f.* calligraphy, penmanship.
callisthénie [kaliste'ni], *n.f.* callisthenics.
callosité [kalozi'te], *n.f.* callosity.
calmant [kal'mɑ̃], *a.* calming, soothing, sedative.—*n.m.* (*Med.*) anodyne, sedative.
calme [kalm], *a.* tranquil, quiet, serene, calm; composed, dispassionate.—*n.m.* calm, stillness, quiet; composure.
calmer [kal'me], *v.t.* to calm, to still, to quiet, to allay, to soothe.—*v.i.* (*Naut.*) to lull, to become calm. **se calmer**, *v.r.* to become calm, to compose oneself; to blow over.
calomel [kalɔ'mɛl], *n.m.* calomel.
calomniateur [kalɔmnja'tœːr], *a.* (*fem.* **-trice**) slanderous.—*n.m.* (*fem.* **-trice**) calumniator, slanderer.
calomnie [kalɔm'ni], *n.f.* calumny, slander.
calomnier [kalɔm'nje], *v.t.* to calumniate, to slander.
calomnieusement [kalɔmnjøz'mɑ̃], *adv.* calumniously, slanderously.
calomnieux [kalɔm'njø], *a.* (*fem.* **-euse**) calumnious, slanderous.
calorie [kalɔ'ri], *n.f.* calorie, unit of heat.
calorifère [kalɔri'fɛːr], *n.m.* hot-air stove *or* pipe; central heating.—*a.* heat-conveying.
calorifique [kalɔri'fik], *a.* calorific.
calorifuger [kalɔrify'ʒe], *v.t.* (*conjug. like* MANGER) to insulate, to lag (*pipes*).
calorique [kalɔ'rik], *a.* and *n.m.* caloric, heat.
calotte [ka'lɔt], *n.f.* skullcap (*esp. that worn by priests*); small dome; box on the ears.
calotter [kalɔ'te], *v.t.* to box the ears of.
calque [kalk], *n.m.* tracing; close copy.—*a.* *papier calque*, tracing paper.
calquer [kal'ke], *v.t.* to trace; to copy, to imitate closely. **se calquer**, *v.r.* (**sur**) to model oneself (*on*).
calumet [kaly'mɛ], *n.m.* pipe, calumet.
calvados [kalva'dɔs], *n.m.* apple brandy, calvados.
calvaire [kal'vɛːr], *n.m.* calvary; (*fig.*) torture, suffering, tribulation.
calvinisme [kalvi'nism], *n.m.* Calvinism.
calviniste [kalvi'nist], *a.* Calvinistic.—*n.* (**Calviniste**) Calvinist.
calvitie [kalvi'si], *n.f.* baldness.
camaïeu [kama'jø], *n.m.* (*pl.* **-eux**) cameo (*brooch etc.*).
camail [ka'maːj], *n.m.* (*pl.* **-ails**) hood, capuchin; hackles (*of poultry*).
camarade [kama'rad], *n.* comrade, fellow, mate, chum, playmate.
camaraderie [kamara'dri], *n.f.* comradeship, intimacy.
camard [ka'maːr], *a.* snub-nosed, flat.—*n.m.* (*fem.* **-e**) snub-nosed person.
Cambodge [kɑ̃'bɔdʒ], **le**, *m.* Cambodia.
cambodgien [kɑ̃bɔ'dʒjɛ̃], *a.* (*fem.* **-enne**) Cambodian.—*n.m.* (**Cambodgien**, *fem.* **-enne**) Cambodian (*person*).
cambouis [kɑ̃'bwi], *n.m.* dirty cart-grease, dirty lubricating oil.

cambrage [kã'bra:ʒ], *n.m.* cambering, bending.

cambrai [kã'brɛ], *n.m.* machine-made lace; cambric.

cambré [kã'bre], *a.* bent, cambered.

cambrement [kãbrə'mã], *n.m.* arching, curving.

cambrer [kã'bre], *v.t.* to arch, to bend, to curve. **se cambrer**, *v.r.* to be cambered; to warp; to draw oneself up.

cambriolage [kãbriɔ'la:ʒ], *n.m.* housebreaking, burglary.

cambrioler [kãbriɔ'le], *v.t.* to break into (*a house*), to burgle.

cambrioleur [kãbriɔ'lœːr], *n.m.* housebreaker, burglar.

cambrure [kã'bry:r], *n.f.* bend, curvature, arch; the arched part in a shoe.

cambuse [kã'by:z], *n.f.* (*Naut.*) storeroom, canteen.

came [kam], *n.f.* cam, wiper; *arbre à cames* camshaft.

camée [ka'me], *n.m.* cameo.

caméléon [kamele'õ], *n.m.* chameleon.

camélia [kame'lja], *n.m.* camellia.

camelot [kam'lo], *n.m.* camlet; cheap-jack, pedlar, hawker.

camelote [kam'lɔt], *n.f.* inferior merchandise, shoddy; (*fig.*) trash.

caméra [kame'ra], *n.f.* ciné camera.

camérier [kame'rje], *n.m.* chamberlain (*of the Pope etc.*).

Cameroun [kamə'run], **le**, *m.* Cameroon.

camion [ka'mjõ], *n.m.* dray, low wagon,truck.

camionnage [kamjɔ'na:ʒ], *n.m.* carting, carriage.

camionner [kamjɔ'ne], *v.t.* to convey on a dray, lorry, truck etc.

camionnette [kamjɔ'nɛt], *n.f.* light motor lorry; van.

camionneur [kamjɔ'nœːr], *n.m.* drayman; vanman; haulage contractor, trucker.

camisole [kami'zɔl], *n.f.* woman's morning jacket; *camisole de force*, strait jacket.

camomille [kamo'mi:j], *n.f.* camomile.

camouflage [kamu'fla:ʒ], **camouflement** [kamuflə'mã], *n.m.* disguise; camouflage.

camoufler [kamu'fle], *v.t.* to disguise; to camouflage. **se camoufler**, *v.r.* to disguise *or* camouflage oneself.

camouflet [kamu'flɛ], *n.m.* whiff of smoke (*in the face*); (*fig.*) affront, snub.

camp [kã], *n.m.* camp; (*fig.*) army; party; (C) country cottage.

campagnard [kãpa'naːr], *a.* rustic, countrified, rural.—*n.m.* (*fem.* -e) countryman *or* countrywoman, peasant; clodhopper.

campagne [kã'pan], *n.f.* the country, the fields, plain; seat, estate, country house; campaign; (*Naut.*) cruise.

campagnol [kãpa'nɔl], *n.m.* vole, field mouse.

campanile [kãpa'nil], *n.m.* campanile, bell tower.

campanule [kãpa'nyl], *n.f.* campanula, bellflower, bluebell.

campé [kã'pe], *a.* established, firmly planted, well set up.

campement [kãp'mã], *n.m.* encamping; encampment; camp party, billeting party.

camper [kã'pe], *v.t.* to encamp (*troops etc.*); to place, to seat, to clap down.—*v.i.* to live in camp, to encamp. **se camper**, *v.r.* to encamp; to plant oneself.

campeur [kã'pœːr], *n.m.* (*fem.* -euse) camper.

camphre [kã:fr], *n.m.* camphor.

camphré [kã'fre], *a.* camphorated.

camphrier [kãfri'e], *n.f.* camphor tree.

camus [ka'my], *a.* flat-nosed, snub-nosed.

Canada [kana'da], **le**, *m.* Canada.

canadien [kana'djɛ̃], *a.* (*fem.* -enne) Canadian.—*n.m.* (**Canadien**, *fem.* -enne) Canadian (*person*).

canaille [ka'na:j], *n.f.* rabble, riffraff, mob.

canaillerie [kanaːj'ri], *n.f.* blackguardism; vulgarity.

canal [ka'nal] *n.m.* (*pl.* -aux) canal; conduit, drain; pipe, tube, spout; water-course.

canalisation [kanaliza'sjõ], *n.f.* canalization; mains; *canalisation de gaz*, gas mains.

canaliser [kanali'ze], *v.t.* to canalize;to install pipes (*for gas etc.*).

canamelle [kana'mɛl], *n.f.* sugar cane.

canapé [kana'pe], *n.m.* sofa, couch.

canapé-lit [kanape'li], *n.m.* divan-bed.

canard [ka'naːr], *n.m.* duck; drake; (*fig.*) hoax.

canardeau [kanar'do], *n.m.* (*pl.* -eaux) young duck.

canarder [kanar'de], *v.t.* to shoot from behind a shelter; to snipe.—*v.i.* (*Naut.*) to pitch heavily.

canardière [kanar'djɛ:r], *n.f.* duck pond; duck gun.

canari [kana'ri], *n.m.* canary (*bird*).

Canaries [kana'ri], **les Iles**, *f. pl.* the Canary Islands.

canasta [kanas'ta], *n.f.* canasta.

cancan [kã'kã], *n.m.* tittle-tattle, scandal; French cancan.

cancaner [kãka'ne], *v.i.* to tattle, to invent stories.

cancanier [kãka'nje], *a.* (*fem.* -ière) addicted to gossip.—*n.m.* (*fem.* -ière) scandal-monger.

cancer [kã'sɛːr], *n.m.* (*Astron., Geol., Med.*) cancer.

cancéreux [kãse'rø], *a.* (*fem.* -euse) cancerous.

cancre [kã:kr], *n.m.* crab; (*fig.*) dunce (*at school*).

cancrelat or **cancrelas** [kãkrə'la], *n.m.* cockroach.

candélabre [kãde'la:br], *n.m.* candelabrum, sconce.

candeur [kã'dœːr], *n.f.* artlessness, guilelessness, ingenuousness.

candi [kã'di], *a.m.* candied; *fruits candis*, crystallized fruits.—*n.m.* sugar candy.

candidat [kãdi'da], *n.m.* candidate.

candidature [kãdida'ty:r], *n.f.* candidature.

candide [kã'did], *a.* ingenuous, artless.

candidement [kãdid'mã], *adv.* ingenuously.

candir [kã'di:r], *v.i.* or **se candir**, *v.r.* to candy, to crystallize.

cane [kan], *n.f.* (*female*) duck.

canebière [CANNEBIÈRE].

canepetière [kanpə'tjɛ:r], *n.f.* lesser bustard.

caneton [kan'tõ], *n.m.* duckling.

canette (1) or **cannette** (1) [ka'nɛt], *n.f.* small duck, duckling; teal.

canette (2) or **cannette** (2) [ka'nɛt], *n.f.* measure for beer; spool (*inside shuttle*).

canevas [kan'va], *n.m.* canvas; sailcloth; outline sketch, rough draft.

caniche [ka'niʃ], *n.m.* poodle.

canichon [kani'ʃɔ̃], *n.m.* small poodle; duckling.

caniculaire [kaniky'lɛːr], *a.* canicular.

canicule [kani'kyl], *n.f.* dog-days; (*Astron.*) Dog Star.

canif [ka'nif], *n.m.* penknife.

canin [ka'nɛ̃], *a.* canine.—*n.f.* (*dent*) *canine*, canine (tooth).

canitie [kani'si], *n.f.* whiteness of the hair.

caniveau [kani'vo], *n.m.* (*pl.* **-eaux**) (*Arch.*) channel stone, gutter.

cannage [ka'naːʒ], *n.m.* cane work (*in chairs etc.*).

cannaie [ka'nɛ], *n.f.* cane plantation, cane field.

canne [kan], *n.f.* cane, reed; walking stick; glass-blower's pipe.

canneberge [kan'bɛrʒ], *n.f.* cranberry.

cannebière or **canebière** [kan'bjɛːr], *n.f.* (*S.-E. France*) [CHÈNEVIÈRE].

cannelé [kan'le], *a.* fluted (*column*); grooved (*tire*).—*n.m.* ribbed silk.

canneler [kan'le], *v.t.* (*conjug. like* APPELER) to flute, to channel, to groove.

cannelier [kanə'lje], *n.m.* cinnamon tree.

cannelle (1) [ka'nɛl], *n.f.* cinnamon bark, cinnamon.

cannelle (2) [ka'nɛl], **cannette** (3) [ka'nɛt], *n.f.* spigot, tap.

cannelure [kan'lyːr], *n.f.* fluting, channelling.

cannette (1) [CANETTE (1).]

cannette (2) [CANETTE (2).]

cannette (3) [CANNELLE (2).]

cannibale [kani'bal], *n.m.* cannibal.

cannibalisme [kaniba'lism], *n.m.* cannibalism; (*fig.*) ferocity.

canon (1) [ka'nɔ̃], *n.m.* cannon, gun; barrel (*of a gun*); cylinder, pipe, tube (*of lock*).

canon (2) [ka'nɔ̃], *n.m.* (*Eccles.*) canon; (*Mus.*) round, canon.

cañon [ka'ɲɔ̃], *n.m.* canyon.

canonial [kanɔ'njal], *a.* (*m.pl.* **-aux**) canonical.

canonicat [kanɔni'ka], *n.m.* canonry; (*fig.*) sinecure.

canonicité [kanɔnisi'te], *n.f.* canonicity.

canonique [kanɔ'nik], *a.* canonical.

canonisation [kanɔniza'sjɔ̃], *n.f.* canonization.

canoniser [kanɔni'ze], *v.t.* to canonize.

canonnade [kanɔ'nad], *n.f.* cannonading, cannonade.

canonner [kanɔ'ne], *v.t.* to attack with heavy artillery, to cannonade.

canonnier [kanɔ'nje], *n.m.* gunner.

canonnière [kanɔ'njɛːr], *n.f.* pop-gun; gunboat.

canot [ka'no], *n.m.* small open boat, dinghy; (*C*) Canadian canoe; *canot automobile*, motor-boat; *canot de sauvetage*, lifeboat.

canotage [kanɔ'taːʒ], *n.m.* boating, rowing.

cantate [kã'tat], *n.f.* (*Mus.*) cantata.

cantatrice [kãta'tris], *n.f.* cantatrice, (*classical*) singer.

cantharide [kãta'rid], *n.f.* (*Ent.*) cantharis, Spanish fly.

cantilène [kãti'lɛːn], *n.f.* cantilena, ballad, popular song.

cantine [kã'tin], *n.f.* canteen; kit-case.

cantique [kã'tik], *n.m.* canticle, hymn.

canton [kã'tɔ̃], *n.m.* canton (*district*); (*C*) township.

cantonade [kãtɔ'nad], *n.f.* (*Theat.*) either of the wings; *parler à la cantonade*, to speak to an actor off the stage.

cantonnement [kãtɔn'mã], *n.m.* (*Mil.*) cantonment, billet, quarters.

cantonner [kãtɔ'ne], *v.t.* (*Mil.*) to billet (*troops*). **se cantonner**, *v.r.* to take up a position, quarters *or* abode; to fortify oneself.

cantonnier [kãtɔ'nje], *n.m.* roadman; (*Rail.*) platelayer.

cantonnière [kãtɔ'njɛːr], *n.f.* valance.

canule [ka'nyl], *n.f.* clyster pipe, injection tube, douche tube.

caoutchouc [kau'tʃu], *n.m.* (India-)rubber mackintosh; (*pl.*) galoshes.

cap [kap], *n.m.* head; bow (*of a ship*); cape, headland, promontory.

capable [ka'pabl], *a.* able, fit, capable; apt; competent.

capacité [kapasi'te], *n.f.* extent, size; ability.

caparaçon [kapara'sɔ̃], *n.m.* caparison, trappings.

caparaçonner [kaparasɔ'ne], *v.t.* to caparison (*a horse*).

cape [kap], *n.f.* cape, mantle *or* cloak with a hood.

capharnaüm [kafarna'ɔm], *n.m.* lumberroom, storeroom for odds and ends.

capillaire [kapi'lɛːr], *a.* capillary.—*n.m.* capillary; maidenhair fern.

capilotade [kapilɔ'tad], *n.f.* hash, ragoût; (*fig.*) thrashing.

capitaine [kapi'tɛn], *n.m.* captain; (*fig.*) eminent commander.

capital [kapi'tal], *a.* (*m.pl.* **-aux**) capital, main, chief, principal.—*n.m.* capital, principal; property stock.

capitale [kapi'tal], *n.f.* capital, chief city; capital letter.

capitaliser [kapitali'ze], *v.t.* to put at compound interest; to add to the capital; to realize, to capitalize.—*v.i.* to save, to lay by.

capitaliste [kapita'list], *n.* capitalist, moneyed man *or* woman.

capitan [kapi'tã], *n.m.* braggadocio, swaggerer.

capitation [kapita'sjɔ̃], *n.f.* capitation, poll tax.

capiteux [kapi'tø], *a.* (*fem.* **-euse**) heady, strong.

Capitole [kapi'tɔl], *n.m.* Capitol (*of Rome etc.*).

capitonner [kapitɔ'ne], *v.t.* to stuff, to pad.

capitulaire [kapity'lɛːr], *a.* and *n.m.* capitulary.

capitulation [kapityla'sjɔ̃], *n.f.* capitulation; compromise.

capituler [kapity'le], *v.i.* to capitulate; to compound, to compromise.

capoc [ka'pɔk], *n.m.* kapok.

capon [ka'pɔ̃], *a.*(*fem.* **-onne**) cowardly.—*n.m.* (*fem.* **-onne**) mean fellow, sneak; coward.

caponner [kapɔ'ne], *v.i.* to cheat; to be cowardly; to rat.

caporal [kapɔ'ral], *n.m.* (*pl.* **-aux**) corporal; sort of 'shag' (*tobacco*).

capot (1) [ka'po], *n.m.* (*Motor.*) bonnet, (*Am.*) hood.

capot (2) [ka'po], *a. inv.* capot (*at piquet etc.*); flabbergasted.

capote [ka'pɔt], *n.f.* capote, large cloak with a hood; (*soldier's*) overcoat; baby's bonnet.

capoter [kapɔ'te], *v.i.* (*Naut. etc.*) to capsize; to turn turtle.

câpre [kɑːpr], *n.f.* (*Bot.*) caper.

caprice [ka'pris], *n.m.* caprice, whim, humor; flight, sally.

capricieusement [kaprisjøz'mã], *adv.* capriciously, whimsically.

capricieux [kapri'sjø], *a.* (*fem.* **-euse**) capricious, whimsical, fickle.

capricorne [kapri'kɔrn], *n.m.* (*Astron.*) Capricorn.

capsule [kap'syl], *n.f.* capsule; pod; percussion cap (*of firearms*).

captation [kapta'sjõ], *n.f.* captation, inveigling; intercepting.

captatoire [kapta'twaːr], *a.* inveigling.

capter [kap'te], *v.t.* to obtain by underhand methods; to win by bribery etc.

captieusement [kapsjøz'mã], *adv.* insidiously, cunningly, deceitfully.

captieux [kap'sjø], *a.* (*fem.* **-euse**) insidious, cunning, specious.

captif [kap'tif], *a.* and *n.m.* (*fem.* **-tive**) captive.

captivant [kapti'vã], *a.* captivating; enthralling.

captiver [kapti've], *v.t.* to captivate, to charm.

captivité [kaptivi'te], *n.f.* captivity, bondage.

capture [kap'tyːr], *n.f.* capture, prize, booty.

capturer [kapty're], *v.t.* to capture; to arrest.

capuchon [kapy'ʃõ], *n.m.* hood, cowl.

capuchonné [kapyʃɔ'ne], *a.* cowled; hooded.

capucin [kapy'sɛ̃], *n.m.* (*fem.* **capucine** (1) [kapy'sin]) Capuchin friar *or* nun.

capucine (1) [CAPUCIN].

capucine (2) [kapy'sin], *n.f.* nasturtium.

caque [kak], *n.f.* keg, barrel.

caquet [ka'kɛ], *n.m.* cackle (*of geese etc.*); tittle-tattle, gossip, scandal.

caquetage [kak'taːʒ], *n.m.*, **caqueterie** [kak(ə)'tri], *n.f.* babbling, prattling; tattling, gossiping.

caqueter [kak'te], *v.i.* (*conjug. like* APPELER) to cackle, to chatter; to gossip.

car (1) [kaːr], *conj.* for, because.

car (2) [kaːr], *n.m.* (*fam.*) coach, long-distance bus.

carabin [kara'bɛ̃], *n.m.* (*colloq.*) saw-bones, medical student.

carabine [kara'bin], *n.f.* carbine, rifle.

carabiné [karabi'ne], *a.* rifled; (*colloq.*) strong, violent.

carabiner [karabi'ne], *v.t.* to rifle (*a gun barrel*).

carabinier [karabi'nje], *n.m.* carabinier, rifleman.

caractère [karak'tɛːr], *n.m.* character, letter; handwriting; nature, disposition; temper, spirit; stamp; quality.

caractériser [karakteri'ze], *v.t.* to characterize, to describe.

caractéristique [karakteris'tik], *a.* and *n.f.* characteristic.

carafe [ka'raf], *n.f.* carafe, decanter, water-bottle.

carafon [kara'fõ], *n.m.* small carafe *or* decanter.

Caraïbes [kara'ib], **les**, *f.pl.* the Caribbean Isles.

carambolage [karãbɔ'laːʒ], *n.m.* (*Billiards*) carom; (*pop.*) affray, shindy; (*fig.*) rebound (*against*).

caramboler [karãbɔ'le], *v.i.* (*Billiards*) to carom.

caramel [kara'mɛl], *n.m.* caramel.

carapace [kara'pas], *n.f.* (*Zool.*) carapace, shell.

carat [ka'ra], *n.m.* (*Gold*) carat.

caravane [kara'van], *n.f.* caravan, convoy; trailer (*car*).

carbonate [karbɔ'nat], *n.m.* (*Chem.*) carbonate.

carbone [kar'bɔn], *n.m.* carbon.

carboné [karbɔ'ne], *a.* carbonated, carbonized.

carbonique [karbɔ'nik], *a.* carbonic.

carboniser [karbɔni'ze], *v.t.* to carbonize.

carburant [karby'rã], *a.* and *n.m.* motor fuel.

carburateur [karbyra'tœːr], *n.m.* carburetor.

carbure [kar'byːr], *n.m.* (*Chem.*) carbide.

carburé [karby're], *a.* carburetted.

carcasse [kar'kas], *n.f.* carcass, skeleton.

cardage [kar'daːʒ], *n.m.* carding.

cardan [kar'dã], *n.m.* (*Mech.*) universal joint.

carde [kard], *n.f.* (*Bot.*) cardoon.

carder [kar'de], *v.t.* to card, to comb.

cardialgie [kardjal'ʒi], *n.f.* cardialgy, heartburn.

cardiaque [kar'djak], *a.* and *n.* cardiac (case).

cardinal [kardi'nal], *a.* (*m. pl.* **-aux**) cardinal, chief, principal.—*n.m.* (*pl.* **-aux**) (*Eccles.*) cardinal.

cardinalat [kardina'la], *n.m.* cardinalate, cardinalship.

cardiogramme [kardio'gram], *n.m.* cardiogram.

cardiographe [kardio'graf], *n.m.* cardiograph.

cardon [kar'dõ], *n.m.* (*Bot.*) cardoon.

carême [ka'rɛːm], *n.m.* Lent; Lent sermons.

carénage [kare'naːʒ], *n.m.* careening.

carence [ka'rãːs], *n.f.* (*Law*) insolvency.

carène [ka'rɛːn], *n.f.* (*Naut.*) bottom (*keel and sides up to water-mark*).

caréné [kare'ne], *a.* (*Bot.*) carinate; keeled; (*Motor.*) streamlined.

caréner [kare'ne], *v.t.* (*conjug. like* CÉDER) to careen; to streamline.

caressant [karɛ'sã], *a.* caressing, endearing; tender.

caresse [ka'rɛs], *n.f.* caress, endearment.

caresser [karɛ'se], *v.t.* to caress, to fondle, to stroke.

caret (1) [ka'rɛ], *n.m.* rope-maker's reel.

caret (2) [ka'rɛ], *n.m.* turtle.

cargaison [kargɛ'zõ], *n.f.* cargo, freight.

cargo [kar'go], *n.m.* (*Naut.*) tramp, cargo boat.

carguer [kar'ge], *v.t.* to reef (*sails*).

cargueur [kar'gœːr], *n.m.* (*Naut.*) reefer.

cari [ka'ri], *n.m.* curry powder.

cariatide [karja'tid], *n.f.* caryatid.

caribou [kari'bu], *n.m.* cariboo.

caricature [karika'tyːr], *n.f.* caricature; (*fam.*) fright (*person*).

caricaturer [karikaty're], *v.t.* to caricature.

caricaturiste [karikaty'rist], *n.* caricaturist.

carie [ka'ri], *n.f.* (*Path.*) caries, decay; (*Bot.*) brown rust; rot (*of timber*).

carier [ka'rje], *v.t.* to make carious, to rot.

carillon [kari'jõ], *n.m.* carillon; chime, peal.

carillonnement [karijɔn'mã], *n.m.* chiming, jingling.

carillonner [karijɔ'ne], *v.i.* to chime; to ring the changes; to jingle.

carillonneur [karijɔ'nœ:r], *n.m.* bell ringer.

carlin [kar'lɛ̃], *a.* pug; turned-up (*nose*).

carlingue [kar'lɛ̃:g], *n.f.* (*Av.*) cockpit.

carmagnole [karma'ɲɔl], *n.f.* Piedmontese jacket; carmagnole.

carme [karm], *n.m.* Carmelite friar, White friar.

carmélite [karme'lit], *n.f.* Carmelite nun.— *a.* light brown.

carmin [kar'mɛ̃], *a.* and *n.m.* carmine.

carnage [kar'na:ʒ], *n.m.* carnage, slaughter.

carnassier [karna'sje], *a.* (*fem.* **-ière**) carnivorous, flesh-eating.—*n.m.* feline animal; flesh-eater.—*n.f.* (**-ière**) game bag.

carnation [karna'sjɔ̃], *n.f.* complexion; flesh color.

carnaval [karna'val], *n.m.* carnival; masquerade, festival; good fellow.

carné [kar'ne], *a.* flesh-colored; composed of meat.

carnet [kar'nɛ], *n.m.* notebook, log book.

carnier [kar'nje], *n.m.* game bag.

carnivore [karni'vɔ:r], *a.* carnivorous.—*n.* carnivore.

carogne [ka'rɔɲ], *n.f.* hag, jade, impudent slut.

carotide [karɔ'tid], *a.* and *n.f.* carotid.

carotte [ka'rɔt], *n.f.* carrot; (*slang*) fake, ruse, hoax; sign outside a tobacconist's shop.—*a.* (*inv.*) ginger (*hair*).

carotter [karɔ'te], *v.t.* to cheat.

carotteur [karɔ'tœ:r], **carottier** [karɔ'tje], *n.m.* (*fem.* **-euse, -ière**) cheat, trickster; wangler.

carpe (1) [karp], *n.f.* (*Ichth.*) carp.

carpe (2) [karp], *n.m.* (*Anat.*) wrist.

carquois [kar'kwa], *n.m.* quiver.

carrare [ka'ra:r], *n.m.* Carrara marble.

carré [ka're], *a.* square; well-set; plain, straightforward.—*n.m.* square; landing, floor; (*Hort.*) plot.

carreau [ka'ro], *n.m.* (*pl.* **-eaux**) small square; square tile *or* brick, small flagstone; pane (*of glass*); diamond (*at cards*).

carrefour [kar'fu:r], *n.m.* crossroads.

carrelage [kar'la:ʒ], *n.m.* tile flooring, paving squares.

carreler [kar'le], *v.t.* (*conjug. like* APPELER) to pave (*a floor*) with square tiles, bricks, stones etc.; to cobble (*shoes etc.*).

carrelet [kar'lɛ], *n.m.* plaice.

carrelette [kar'lɛt], *n.f.* flat file.

carreleur [kar'lœ:r], *n.m.* floor tiler.

carrément [kare'mɑ̃], *adv.* squarely; (*fig.*) bluntly, plainly.

carrer [ka're], *v.t.* to square. **se carrer**, *v.r.* to strut, to pose.

carrier [ka'rje], *n.m.* quarryman.

carrière (1) [ka'rjɛ:r], *n.f.* career, course; scope, play, vent; profession, vocation; *la Carrière*, the diplomatic service.

carrière (2) [ka'rjɛ:r], *n.f.* quarry.

carriole [ka'rjɔl], *n.f.* light covered cart.

carrossable [karɔ'sabl], *a.* practicable for vehicles (*of roads*).

carrosse [ka'rɔs], *n.m.* state-coach, four-wheeled carriage.

carrosserie [karɔ'sri], *n.f.* coach-building; body (*of motors*).

carrossier [karɔ'sje], *n.m.* coach maker, carriage builder.

carrousel [karu'zɛl], *n.m.* merry-go-round; tournament.

carrure [ka'ry:r], *n.f.* breadth of shoulders.

cartable [kar'tabl], *n.m.* school satchel.

carte [kart], *n.f.* pasteboard; card, playing card, postcard; ticket; bill of fare; map, chart; *avoir carte blanche*, to have full power; *carte d'abonnement*, season ticket; *carte d'alimentation*, ration card, ration book; *un jeu de cartes*, a pack of cards.

cartel [kar'tɛl], *n.m.* challenge; cartel; dial case; wall clock; frieze panel.

carte-lettre [kartə'lɛtr], *n.f.* (*pl.* **cartes-lettres**) letter-card.

carter [kar'tɛr], *n.m.* gearcase (*of bicycle*); crankcase (*of car*).

cartésianisme [kartezja'nism], *n.m.* Cartesian philosophy.

cartésien [karte'zjɛ̃], *a.* and *n.m.* (*fem.* **-ienne**) Cartesian.

cartilage [karti'la:ʒ], *n.m.* cartilage, gristle.

cartilagineux [kartilaʒi'nø], *a.* (*fem.* **-euse**) cartilaginous, gristly.

cartographe [kartɔ'graf], *n.m.* cartographer.

cartographie [kartɔgra'fi], *n.f.* cartography.

carton [kar'tɔ̃], *n.m.* cardboard, pasteboard; cardboard box, hatbox; (*Paint.*) cartoon; (*Phot.*) mount.

cartonnage [kartɔ'na:ʒ], *n.m.* (*Bookb.*) boarding.

cartonneur [kartɔ'nœ:r], *n.m.* (*fem.* **-euse**) binder (*of books*).

carton-pâte [kartɔ̃'pɑ:t], *n.m.* millboard; papier mâché.

carton-pierre [kartɔ̃'pjɛ:r], *n.m.* pasteboard for making ornaments.

cartothèque [kartɔ'tɛk], *n.f.* card index.

cartouche (1) [kar'tuʃ], *n.m.* escutcheon, scroll.

cartouche (2) [kar'tuʃ], *n.f.* cartridge.

cartouchier [kartu'ʃje], *n.m.*, **cartouchière** [kartu'ʃjɛ:r], *n.f.* cartridge pouch or box.

cas [kɑ], *n.m.* case; instance, circumstance, state of things, conjuncture; (*Law*) cause; *c'est le cas ou jamais*, it is now or never; *en tout cas*, at all events.

casanier [kaza'nje], *a.* (*fem.* **-ière**) domestic, stay-at-home, home-loving.

cascade [kas'kad], *n.f.* cascade, waterfall.

case [kɑ:z], *n.f.* cabin, hut, small house; division, compartment; box (*for animals*); pigeonhole; square (*of chess-* or *draught-board*); (*Naut.*) berth.

casemate [kaz'mat], *n.f.* (*Fort.*) casemate.

caser [kɑ'ze], *v.t.* to put in order, to file (*documents*), (*fam.*) to provide for; to marry off.—*v.i.* (*backgammon*) to make a point. **se caser**, *v.r.* to take up one's abode, to settle.

caserne [ka'zɛrn], *n.f.* barracks.

caserner [kazɛr'ne], *v.t.* to quarter in barracks.—*v.i.* to be in barracks.

casier [kɑ'zje], *n.m.* rack, card *or* music stand, set of pigeonholes; *casier judiciaire*, police record.

casilleux [kazi'jø], *a.* (*fem.* **-euse**) brittle.

casino [kazi'no], *n.m.* casino, club.

casque [kask], *n.m.* helmet, headpiece; (*Nat. Hist.*) crest; headphone (*radio*).

casquette [kas'kɛt], n.f. cap.
cassable [kɑ'sabl], a. breakable.
cassage [kɑ'saːʒ], n.m. breakage.
cassant [kɑ'sɑ̃], a. brittle; crisp; breakable; (fig.) abrupt, gruff.
cassation [kasɑ'sjɔ̃], n.f. (Law) cassation, annulment, repeal; cour de cassation, the highest court of appeal in France.
casse (1) [kɑːs], n.f. breakage(s); damage, losses.
casse (2) [kɑːs], n.f. (Print.) case; bas de casse, lower case.
casse-cou [kas'ku], n.m. inv. death trap; roughrider; daredevil.
casse-croûte [kas'krut], n.m. inv. quick meal, snack.
casse-noisette [kɑsnwɑ'zɛt], n.m. (pl. casse-noisettes) nutcracker; (Orn.) nuthatch.
casse-noix [kɑs'nwɑ], n.m. inv. nutcrackers.
casse-pipes [kɑs'pip], n.m. inv. shooting gallery; (pop.) war.
casser [kɑ'se], v.t. to break, to smash; to cashier (an officer), to reduce to the ranks; to dissolve (Parliament etc.); to annul, to rescind. se casser, v.r. to break, to snap; to break down.
casserole [kas'rɔl], n.f. saucepan, stewpan.
casse-tête [kɑs'tɛːt], n.m. inv. cudgel, club; (fig.) din; conundrum.
cassette [ka'sɛt], n.f. casket; cash box.
casseur [kɑ'sœːr], n.m. (fem. -euse) breaker, smasher.
cassis [kɑ'sis], n.m. black currant.
casson [kɑ'sɔ̃], n.m. piece of broken glass or pottery; rough lump (of sugar).
cassonade [kasɔ'nad], n.f. moist brown sugar.
cassoulet [kasu'le], n.m. stew of beans with mutton and pork.
cassure [kɑ'syːr], n.f. break, crack, fracture; broken piece.
castagnette [kasta'ɲɛt], n.f. castanet.
caste [kast], n.f. caste.
castillan [kasti'jɑ̃], a. Castilian.—n.m. Castilian (speech); (Castillan, fem. -ane) Castilian (person).
castine [kas'tin], n.f. (Metal.) flux.
castor [kas'tɔːr], n.m. beaver.
casuel [ka'zɥɛl], a. (fem. -uelle) casual, fortuitous, accidental.—n.m. perquisites, fees.
casuiste [ka'zɥist], n.m. casuist.
cataclysme [kata'klism], n.m. cataclysm; (fig.) disaster.
catacombes [kata'kɔ̃ːb], n.f. pl. catacombs.
catafalque [kata'falk], n.m. catafalque.
cataire [ka'tɛːr], n.f. (Bot.) catmint.
catalan [kata'lɑ̃], a. Catalan.—n.m. Catalan (language); (Catalan, fem. -ane) Catalan (person).
catalepsie [katalɛp'si], n.f. catalepsy.
catalogue [kata'lɔg], n.m. list, catalogue.
cataloguer [katalɔ'ge], v.t. to catalogue.
catalyse [kata'liːz], n.f. (Chem.) catalysis.
catalyseur [katali'zœːr], n.m. catalyst.
catalytique [katali'tik], a. catalytic.
cataphote [kata'fɔt], n.m. cat's eye (reflector).
cataplasme [kata'plasm], n.m. cataplasm, poultice.
cataracte [kata'rakt], n.f. cataract, waterfall; (Path.) cataract.
catarrhal [kata'ral], a. (m.pl. -aux) catarrhal.
catarrhe [kata'ːr], n.m. catarrh.

catastrophe [katas'trɔf], n.f. catastrophe, calamity.
catastrophique [katastrɔ'fik], a. catastrophic.
catéchiser [kateʃi'ze], v.t. to catechize; (fig.) to reason with; to lecture.
catéchisme [kate'ʃism], n.m. catechism.
catégorie [katego'ri], n.f. category.
catégorique [katego'rik], a. categorical, explicit.
catégoriquement [kategorik'mɑ̃], adv. categorically.
catharsis [katar'sis], n.f. (Med.) catharsis.
cathédral [kate'dral], a. (m.pl. -aux) cathedral.
cathédrale [kate'dral], n.f. cathedral.
cathode [ka'tɔd], n.f. cathode.
cathodique [katɔ'dik], a. cathode.
catholicisme [katɔli'sism], n.m. Catholicism.
catholique [katɔ'lik], a. catholic; moral, orthodox.—n. Catholic (person).
cati [ka'ti], n.m. gloss, luster.
catir [ka'tiːr], v.t. to give a gloss to.
catissage [kati'saːʒ], n.m. glossing, pressing.
catisseur [kati'sœːr], a. and n.m. (fem. -euse) presser.
Caucase [ko'kɑːz], le, m. the Caucasus.
caucasien [koka'zjɛ̃], a. (fem. -enne) Caucasian.—n.m. (Caucasien, fem. -enne) Caucasian (person).
cauchemar [koʃ'maːr], n.m. nightmare.
caudataire [koda'tɛːr], n.m. train-bearer.
cauri, cauris or coris [ko'ri], n.m. cowrie.
causal [ko'zal], a. causal.
causant [ko'zɑ̃], a. chatty, talkative.
causatif [koza'tif], a. (fem. -tive) (Gram.) causative, causal.
cause [koːz], n.f. cause; grounds, motive; interest; case, trial, suit, action; à cause de, because of; mettre en cause, to sue.
causer (1) [ko'ze], v.t. to cause, to be the cause of.
causer (2) [ko'ze], v.i. to chat, to talk; to prate.
causerie [koz'ri], n.f. talk, chat, gossip; chatty essay, review etc.
causette [ko'zɛt], n.f. chit-chat, small talk.
causeur [ko'zœːr], a. (fem. -euse) talkative, chatty.—n.m. (fem. -euse) talker.—n.f. (-euse) small sofa, settee for two.
causticité [kostisi'te], n.f. causticity.
caustique [kos'tik], a. caustic, biting, cutting. —n.m. caustic.
caustiquement [kostik'mɑ̃], adv. caustically.
cauteleusement [kotløz'mɑ̃], adv. craftily, slyly.
cauteleux [kot'lø], a. (fem. -euse) cunning, crafty.
cautère [ko'tɛːr], n.m. (Med.) cautery; issue.
cautérisation [koteriza'sjɔ̃], n.f. cauterization.
cautériser [koteri'ze], v.t. to cauterize.
caution [ko'sjɔ̃], n.f. security, bail, surety; (fig.) pledge, guarantee; verser une caution, to pay a deposit.
cautionnement [kosjɔn'mɑ̃], n.m. bail; security.
cautionner [kosjɔ'ne], v.t. to stand bail for someone.
cavage [ka'vaːʒ], n.m. cellarage.
cavalcade [kaval'kad], n.f. procession; cavalcade.
cavale [ka'val], n.f. mare.
cavalerie [kaval'ri], n.f. cavalry.

cavalier [kava'lje], *n.m.* horseman, rider, trooper; (*Dancing*) partner; (*C*) lover, sweetheart; (*Chess*) knight.—*a.* (*fem.* **-ière**) cavalier, unceremonious (*of manners etc.*); off-hand, flippant.

cavalièrement [kavaljɛr'mā], *adv.* cavalierly, bluntly.

cave (1) [ka:v], *a.* hollow.

cave (2) [ka:v], *n.f.* (*wine*) cellar, vault; cellarage.

caveau [ka'vo], *n.m.* (*pl.* **-eaux**) small cellar; burial vault.

caver [ka've], *v.t.* to hollow, to scoop out, to dig under; to undermine; (*Fenc.*) to lunge. **se caver**, *v.r.* to become hollow *or* sunken.

caverne [ka'vɛrn], *n.f.* cavern, cave, hollow; (*fig.*) retreat, lair.

caverneux [kavɛr'nø], *a.* (*fem.* **-euse**) cavernous, hollow.

caviar [ka'vja:r], *n.m.* caviare.

cavillation [kavila'sjɔ̃], *n.f.* sophistry, cavil.

cavité [kavi'te], *n.f.* cavity, hollow.

ce (1) [sə], *dem. a.* (*before vowels* **cet**, *fem.* **cette**, *pl.* **ces**) this, that, (*pl.*) these, those.

ce (2) [sə], *dem. pron. inv.* it, that (*sometimes* = he, she, *or*, *with plural verb*, they); **c'en est fait**, it is all over, it is done; **c'est-à-dire**, that is to say; **c'est que**, the fact is that; **pour ce qui est de . . .**, as for . . . .

*****céans** [se'ā], *adv.* within, here within, in this house, at home.

ceci [sə'si], *dem. pron.* this, this thing.

cécité [sesi'te], *n.f.* blindness.

cédant [se'dā], *a.* that grants; (*Law*) that assigns, transfers.—*n.m.* (*fem.* **-e**) (*Law*) grantor, assignor, transferrer.

céder [se'de], *v.t.* (*see Verb Tables*) to give up, to yield, to surrender, to cede; to transfer, to make over.—*v.i.* to give way; to submit.

cédille [se'di:j], *n.f.* cedilla.

cédrat [se'dra], *n.m.* citron tree; citron.

cèdre [se:dr], *n.m.* cedar.

cédule [se'dyl], *n.f.* schedule, memorandum; notice; (*Law*) notification.

cégétiste [seʒe'tist], *n.m.* a member of the C.G.T. (Confédération Générale du Travail.)

ceindre [sɛ̃:dr], *v.t. irr.* (*conjug. like* CRAINDRE) to gird, to encircle, to encompass, to surround; to bind *or* gird on. **se ceindre**, *v.r.* to bind round one, to put on (*a scarf etc.*).

ceinture [sɛ̃'ty:r], *n.f.* sash, girdle, belt, waistband; waist; enclosure, circle; **ceinture de sauvetage**, life belt.

ceinturer [sɛ̃ty're], *v.t.* to girdle, to surround.

ceinturon [sɛ̃ty'rɔ̃], *n.m.* belt, sword belt.

cela [sə'la, sla], *dem. pron.* that, that thing (*in opposition to this, of which we are speaking*); **c'est cela**, that's it. *In popular speech* **cela** *becomes* **ça**; **pas de ça**, none of that; **comme ci comme ça**, middling.

céladon [sela'dɔ̃], *a.* and *n.m.* sea-green (*color*).

célébrant [sele'brā], *n.m.* celebrant.

célébration [selebra'sjɔ̃], *n.f.* solemn performance, celebration.

célèbre [se'lɛbr], *a.* celebrated, famous, renowned.

célébrer [sele'bre], *v.t.* (*conjug. like* CÉDER) to celebrate, to praise, to extol; to solemnize.

célébrité [selebri'te], *n.f.* celebrity.

*****celer** [sə'le], *v.t.* (*conjug. like* AMENER) to conceal, to keep secret. *****se celer**, *v.r.* to conceal oneself, to hide.

céleri [sel'ri], *n.m.* celery; **un pied de céleri**, a stick of celery.

célerin [sel'rɛ̃], *n.m.* (*Ichth.*) pilchard.

célérité [seleri'te], *n.f.* celerity, rapidity.

céleste [se'lɛst], *a.* celestial, heavenly, divine.

célibat [seli'ba], *n.m.* celibacy, single life.

célibataire [seliba'tɛ:r], *a.* single.—*n.m.* bachelor.—*n.f.* spinster.

celle [sɛl], [CELUI].

cellérier [sele'rje], *n.m.* (*fem.* **-ière**) cellarer.

cellier [sɛ'lje], *n.m.* cellar, storeroom.

cellophane [sɛlɔ'fan], *n.f.* cellophane.

cellulaire [sɛly'lɛ:r], *a.* cellular.

cellule [se'lyl], *n.f.* cell; **cellule photoélectrique**, electric eye.

celluleux [sɛly'lø], *a.* (*fem.* **-euse**) cellular.

celluloïd *or* **celluloïde** [sɛlylo'id], *n.m.* celluloid.

cellulose [sɛly'lo:z], *n.f.* cellulose.

Celte [sɛlt], *n.* Celt.

celtique [sɛl'tik], *a.* Celtic.—*n.m.* Celtic (*language*).

celui [sə'lɥi], *dem. pron. m.* (*fem.* **celle**, *pl.* **ceux, celles**) the one, that, those (*sometimes* = he *or* she). *Followed by* **-ci** *or* **-là** = this one; that one etc., *or* the latter *and* the former.

cément [se'mā], *n.m.* (*Metal.*) cement.

cémentation [semāta'sjɔ̃], *n.f.* (*Metal.*) cementation.

cémenter [semā'te], *v.t.* (*Metal.*) to cement.

cénacle [se'nakl], *n.m.* (*Ant.*) guest chamber; (*fig.*) literary society *or* coterie.

cendre [sā:dr], *n.f.* ashes, embers, cinders; dust, ashes (*of the dead*).

cendré [sā'dre], *a.* ashy, ashen.

cendrée [sā'dre], *n.f.* small shot; cinders (*for track*); **piste en cendrée**, dirt track, cinder track.

cendrer [sā'dre], *v.t.* to paint ash-grey; to mix *or* cover with ashes.

cendreux [sā'drø], *a.* (*fem.* **-euse**) ashy.

cendrier [sādri'e], *n.m.* ash pan, ash pit; ash tray.

cendrière [sādri'ɛ:r], *n.f.* peat.

Cendrillon [sādri'jɔ̃], *n.f.* Cinderella, drudge.

Cène [sɛ:n], *n.f.* The Lord's Supper, Holy Communion.

cenelle [sə'nɛl], *n.f.* haw.

cénobite [seno'bit], *n.m.* coenobite.

cénotaphe [seno'taf], *n.m.* cenotaph.

cens [sā:s], *n.m.* census; rating.

censé [sā'se], *a.* accounted, reputed, supposed.

censeur [sā'sœ:r], *n.m.* censor; critic; proctor (*of Engl. Univ.*); assistant headmaster (*in French Lycée*).

censure [sā'sy:r], *n.f.* censorship; criticism, censure; audit (*of accounts*).

censurer [sāsy're], *v.t.* to find fault with, to criticize; to censure.

cent [sā], *a.* one hundred; **faire les cent pas**, to walk up and down.—*n.m.* a hundred; **cinq pour cent**, five per cent.

centaine [sā'tɛn], *n.f.* a hundred; a hundred or so.

centaure [sā'tɔ:r], *n.m.* centaur.

centenaire [sāt'nɛ:r], *a.* a hundred years old.—*n.* centenarian.—*n.m.* centenary.

centième [sɑ̃'tjɛm], *a.* hundredth.—*n.m.* hundredth part.

centigrade [sɑ̃ti'grad], *a.* centigrade.

centigramme [sɑ̃ti'gram], *n.m.* centigram, the hundredth part of a gram (.15 43 grain).

centilitre [sɑ̃ti'litr], *n.m.* centiliter, hundredth part of a liter (.61028 cubic in.).

centime [sɑ̃'tim], *n.m.* centime, hundredth part of a franc.

centimètre [sɑ̃ti'mɛtr], *n.m.* centimeter, hundredth part of a meter (.39371 in.).

centipède [sɑ̃ti'pɛd], *n.m.* centipede.

central [sɑ̃'tral], *a.* (*m. pl.* **-aux**) central; chief, principal, head.—*n.m.* **central téléphonique**, telephone exchange.—*n.f.* **centrale électrique**, electric power station.

centralement [sɑ̃tral'mɑ̃], *adv.* centrally.

centralisateur [sɑ̃traliza'tœːr], *a.* (*fem.* **-trice**) centralizing.

centralisation [sɑ̃traliza'sjɔ̃], *n.f.* centralization.

centraliser [sɑ̃trali'ze], *v.t.* to centralize.

centre [sɑ̃ːtr], *n.m.* center, middle.

centrer [sɑ̃'tre], *v.t.* to center.

centrifuge [sɑ̃tri'fyːʒ], *a.* centrifugal.

centripète [sɑ̃tri'pɛt], *a.* centripetal.

centuple [sɑ̃'typl], *a.* and *n.m.* centuple, hundredfold.

centupler [sɑ̃ty'ple], *v.t.* to multiply a hundredfold.

centurion [sɑ̃ty'rjɔ̃], *n.m.* centurion.

cep [sɛp], *n.m.* vine stock.

cépage [se'paːʒ], *n.m.* vine plant.

cépée [se'pe], *n.f.* (*Agric.*) tuft of shoots from a pollarded stump; copse of one or two years' growth.

cependant [spɑ̃'dɑ̃], *adv.* in the meantime, meanwhile.—*conj.* yet, still, however, nevertheless.

céramique [sera'mik], *a.* ceramic.—*n.f.* ceramics.

Cerbère [sɛr'bɛːr], *m.* (*Myth.*) Cerberus.

cerceau [sɛr'so], *n.m.* (*pl.* **-eaux**) hoop, ring; hoop net.

cerclage [sɛr'klaːʒ], *n.m.* hooping (*of casks*).

cercle [sɛrkl], *n.m.* circle, ring; circumference; club, club-house.

cercler [sɛr'kle], *v.t.* to bind with hoops, to hoop.

cercueil [sɛr'kœːj], *n.m.* coffin; (*fig.*) the tomb.

céréale [sere'al], *n.f.* cereal, corn, grain.

cérébral [sere'bral], *a.* (*m. pl.* **-aux**) cerebral.

cérémonial [seremɔ'njal], *a.* (*m. pl.* **-aux**) ceremonial.—*n.m.* (*no pl.*) ceremonial, pomp.

cérémonie [seremɔ'ni], *n.f.* ceremony; pomp; fuss, ado.

cérémonieux [seremɔ'njø], *a.* (*fem.* **-euse**) ceremonious, formal.

cerf [sɛːr], *n.m.* stag, hart, deer.

cerfeuil [sɛr'fœːj], *n.m.* chervil.

cerf-volant [sɛrvɔ'lɑ̃], *n.m.* (*pl.* **cerfs-volants**) stag beetle; kite, paper kite.

cerisaie [sri'ze], *n.f.* cherry orchard.

cerise [sə'riːz], *n.f.* cherry.—*n.m.* cherry-color, cerise.—*a.* cherry-colored, cerise.

cerisier [sri'zje], *n.m.* cherry tree, cherry wood.

cerner [sɛr'ne], *v.t.* to cut *or* dig round (*a tree*), to ring (*a tree*); to surround, to encompass, to hem in.

certain [sɛr'tɛ̃], *a.* certain, sure, positive; fixed, determined; *d'un certain âge*, not so young.—*n.m.* certainty; a sure thing.

certainement [sɛrtɛn'mɑ̃], *adv.* certainly.

certes [sɛrt], *adv.* indeed, most certainly.

certificat [sɛrtifi'ka], *n.m.* certificate; testimonial; diploma.

certification [sɛrtifika'sjɔ̃], *n.f.* certification.

certifier [sɛrti'fje], *v.t.* to certify, to testify, to vouch for.

certitude [sɛrti'tyd], *n.f.* certitude, certainty.

cerveau [sɛr'vo], *n.m.* (*pl.* **-eaux**) brain; mind, intellect, intelligence.

cervelas [sɛrvə'la], *n.m.* saveloy.

cervelle [sɛr'vɛl], *n.f.* brains; mind, intelligence.

cervin [sɛr'vɛ̃], *a.* cervine; *le* (*Mont*) *Cervin*, the Matterhorn.

César [se'zaːr], *m.* Caesar.—*n.m.* Caesar, emperor.

césarien [seza'rjɛ̃], *a.* (*fem.* **-ienne**) Caesarean.—*n.f.* (**-ienne**) Caesarean operation.

cessant [sɛ'sɑ̃], *a.* ceasing, suspended.

cessation [sɛsa'sjɔ̃], *n.f.* cessation, suspension, stoppage.

cesse [sɛs], *n.f.* ceasing, intermission, respite.

cesser [sɛ'se], *v.t.* to leave off, to break off, to stop.—*v.i.* to cease, to leave off, to stop.

cession [sɛ'sjɔ̃], *n.f.* transfer, assignment (*of property*).

cessionnaire [sɛsjɔ'nɛːr], *n.m.* grantee, assignee.

césure [se'zyːr], *n.f.* caesura.

cet, cette [sɛt], [CE].

cétacé [seta'se], *a.* cetaceous.—*n.m.* cetacean.

ceux [sø:], [CELUI].

Ceylan [sɛ'lɑ̃], **le**, *m.* Ceylon.

chablis (1) [ʃa'bli], *n.m.* deadwood.

chablis (2) [ʃa'bli], *n.m.* Chablis (*white wine*).

chacal [ʃa'kal], *n.m.* jackal.

chacun [ʃa'kœ̃], *pron. indef. sing.* each, each one, every one.

chafouin [ʃa'fwɛ̃], *a.* weasel-faced, mean-looking.

chagrin (1), [ʃa'grɛ̃], *n.m.* grief, chagrin; sorrow.—*a.* gloomy, melancholy, sad.

chagrin (2) [ʃa'grɛ̃], *n.m.* shagreen.

chagrinant [ʃagri'nɑ̃], *a.* distressing, sad.

chagriner [ʃagri'ne], *v.t.* to grieve, to afflict; to cross, to vex. **se chagriner**, *v.r.* to fret, to grieve.

chahut [ʃa'y], *n.m.* row, shindy.

chahuter [ʃay'te], *v.i.* to make a row, to kick up a shindy.

chaîne [ʃɛːn], *n.f.* chain; shackle, fetters; bonds, bondage; (*Naut.*) cable; (*fig.*) series, range; (*Ind.*) **chaîne de montage**, assembly line.

chaîner [ʃɛ'ne], *v.t.* (*Surveying*) to measure (*land*) with the chain.

chaînette [ʃɛ'nɛt], *n.f.* little chain; (*Arch.*) catenary arch.

chaînon [ʃɛ'nɔ̃], *n.m.* link.

chaintre [ʃɛ̃:tr], *n.m.* (*Agric.*) balk, headland.

chair [ʃɛːr], *n.f.* flesh; meat; (*fig.*) the human body, the flesh; (*Paint., pl.*) naked flesh.

chaire [ʃɛːr], *n.f.* pulpit; professorship; bishop's throne.

chaise [ʃɛːz], *n.f.* chair, seat; post chaise.

chaland (1) [ʃa'lɑ̃], *n.m.* lighter, barge.

chaland (2) [ʃa'lɑ̃], *n.m.* (*fem.* **-e**) customer, client.

chalandeau [ʃalɑ̃'do], *n.m.* (*pl.* **-eaux**) lighterman, bargeman.

chalcographe [kalkɔ'graf], *n.m.* chalcographer, engraver on metal.

chalcographie [kalkɔgra'fi], *n.f.* chalcography; engraving establishment.

chaldaïque [kalda'ik], *a.* Chaldaic.

Chaldée [kal'de], *f.* Chaldea.

chaldéen [kalde'ɛ̃], *a.* (*fem.* **-éenne**) Chaldean. —*n.m.* (**Chaldéen,** *fem.* **-éenne**) Chaldean (*person*).

châle [ʃɑ:l], *n.m.* shawl.

chalet [ʃa'lɛ], *n.m.* chalet, Swiss cottage.

chaleur [ʃa'lœːr], *n.f.* heat; warmth, warm weather; (*fig.*) glow; zeal, ardor; *'craint la chaleur'*, 'store in a cool place'.

chaleureusement [ʃalœrøz'mɑ̃], *adv.* cordially, warmly.

chaleureux [ʃalœ'rø], *a.* (*fem.* **-euse**) warm, cordial.

chalicose [ʃali'ko:z], *n.f.* silicosis.

châlit [ʃɑ'li], *n.m.* bedstead.

chaloupe [ʃa'lup], *n.f.* ship's boat, launch.

chalumeau [ʃaly'mo], *n.m.* (*pl.* **-eaux**) stalk of wheat; drinking-straw; flute, pipe.

chalut [ʃa'ly], *n.m.* dragnet, trawl.

chalutier [ʃaly'tje], *n.m.* trawler.

chamaillard [ʃama'jaːr], *a.* squabbling, quarrelsome.

chamailler [ʃama'je], *v.i.* to bicker, to squabble. **se chamailler,** *v.r.* to squabble, to wrangle.

chamaillis [ʃama'ji], *n.m.* fray; squabble; uproar.

chamarrer [ʃama're], *v.t.* to bedizen, to bedeck.

chambellan [ʃɑ̃bɛ'lɑ̃], *n.m.* chamberlain.

chambranle [ʃɑ̃'brɑ̃:l], *n.m.* door frame, window frame.

chambre [ʃɑ̃:br], *n.f.* chamber, room; apartment; House (*of Parliament*); court (*of justice*); *chambre à air,* inner tube (*bicycle etc.*); *chambre à un (deux) lit(s),* single (double) room; *chambre d'ami,* spare bedroom; *chambre d'écluse,* lock; *chambre noire,* camera obscura.

chambrée [ʃɑ̃'bre], *n.f.* barrack room; roomful; (*Theat. etc.*) house.

chambrer [ʃɑ̃'bre], *v.t.* to keep (*someone*) confined; to bring wine to room temperature.—*v.i.* to lodge (*together*). **se chambrer,** *v.r.* to become pitted.

chambrette [ʃɑ̃'brɛt], *n.f.* little room.

chameau [ʃa'mo], *n.m.* (*pl.* **-eaux**) camel; (*pop.*) nasty, evil-minded person.

chamelier [ʃamə'lje], *n.m.* camel driver.

chamelle [ʃa'mɛl], *n.f.* female camel.

chamelon [ʃam'lɔ̃], *n.m.* young camel.

chamois [ʃa'mwa], *n.m.* chamois; chamois leather.—*a.* chamois-colored; buff.

chamoiseur [ʃamwa'zœːr], *n.m.* chamois or leather dresser.

champ [ʃɑ̃], *n.m.* field, piece of ground; scope, range; (*poet.*) land; (*fig.*) space; *sur-le-champ,* at once, immediately.

champagne [ʃɑ̃'paɲ], *n.m.* champagne; *champagne frappé,* iced champagne; *champagne mousseux,* sparkling champagne; *fine champagne,* liqueur brandy.

champenois [ʃɑ̃pə'nwa], *a.* of Champagne. —*n.m.* (**Champenois,** *fem.* **-oise**) inhabitant of Champagne.

champêtre [ʃɑ̃'pɛːtr], *a.* rural, rustic; *garde champêtre,* village policeman.

champignon [ʃɑ̃pi'ɲɔ̃], *n.m.* mushroom, fungus.

champion [ʃɑ̃'pjɔ̃], *n.m.* (*fem.* **-onne**) champion.

championnat [ʃɑ̃pjɔ'na], *n.m.* championship.

chançard [ʃɑ̃'saːr], *a.* and *n.m.* (*fem.* **-e**) (*fam.*) lucky (*person*).

chance [ʃɑ̃:s], *n.f.* chance; luck, good luck, good fortune; (*pl.*) chances, (*fam.*) odds.

chancelant [ʃɑ̃s'lɑ̃], *a.* staggering, tottering.

chanceler [ʃɑ̃s'le], *v.i.* (*conjug. like* APPELER) to stagger, to totter; to reel.

chancelier [ʃɑ̃sə'lje], *n.m.* chancellor.

chancellement [ʃɑ̃sɛl'mɑ̃], *n.m.* tottering, staggering.

chancellerie [ʃɑ̃sɛl'ri], *n.f.* chancellery.

chanceux [ʃɑ̃'sø], *a.* (*fem.* **-euse**) lucky, fortunate; risky, doubtful (*of things*).

chanci [ʃɑ̃'si], *a.* moldy.

chancir [ʃɑ̃'siːr], *v.i.* to grow musty or moldy.

chancissure [ʃɑ̃si'syːr], *n.f.* mustiness, moldiness.

chancre [ʃɑ̃:kr], *n.m.* ulcer, tumor; canker.

chancreux [ʃɑ̃'krø], *a.* (*fem.* **-euse**) ulcerous; cankered.

chandail [ʃɑ̃'daːj], *n.m.* jersey, sweater.

Chandeleur [ʃɑ̃'dlœːr], *n.f.* Candlemas.

chandelier [ʃɑ̃də'lje], *n.m.* candlestick.

chandelle [ʃɑ̃'dɛl], *n.f.* (*tallow*) candle; (*fig.*) light; (*Tennis*) lob.

change [ʃɑ̃:ʒ], *n.m.* exchange; exchange of money; exchange office; agio; (*Hunt.*) wrong scent; *agent de change,* stockbroker; *cours du change,* rate of exchange.

changeant [ʃɑ̃'ʒɑ̃], *a.* changeable, fickle; unstable; unsettled (*of the weather*).

changement [ʃɑ̃ʒ'mɑ̃], *n.m.* change, alteration; (*Law*) amendment.

changer [ʃɑ̃'ʒe], *v.t., v.i.* (*conjug. like* MANGER) to change, to exchange; to alter.

changeur [ʃɑ̃'ʒœːr], *n.m.* (*fem.* **-euse**) money-changer.

chanoine [ʃa'nwan], *n.m.* canon.

chanson [ʃɑ̃'sɔ̃], *n.f.* song, ballad; (*fig.*) idle story, stuff, trash; *chansons que tout cela!* humbug!

chansonner [ʃɑ̃sɔ'ne], *v.t.* to lampoon.

chansonnette [ʃɑ̃sɔ'nɛt], *n.f.* little song, ditty.

chansonneur [ʃɑ̃sɔ'nœːr], *n.m.* lampooner.

chansonnier [ʃɑ̃sɔ'nje], *n.m.* (*fem.* **-ière**) song-writer, ballad writer; singer of satirical songs.

chant [ʃɑ̃], *n.m.* singing; song; air, tune; poem; canto; chant, hymn.

chantable [ʃɑ̃'tabl], *a.* fit to be sung, worth singing.

chantage [ʃɑ̃'taːʒ], *n.m.* extortion of hush money, blackmail.

chantant [ʃɑ̃'tɑ̃], *a.* easily sung; tuneful, harmonious.

chanteau [ʃɑ̃'to], *n.m.* (*pl.* **-eaux**) hunk (*of bread*), bit (*of material etc.*), remnant; (*Dress.*) gore.

chantepleure [ʃɑ̃t'plœːr], *n.f.* funnel pierced with holes; strainer.

chanter [ʃɑ̃'te], *v.t.* to extol, to praise, to celebrate; to sing.—*v.i.* to sing; to chirp, to warble, to crow; *cela vous chante-t-il?* how do you like the idea? **se chanter,** *v.r.* to be sung.

chanterelle [ʃɑ̃'trɛl], *n.f.* first string of a violin etc.; decoy bird.

chanteur [ʃɑ̃'tœːr], *a.* (*fem.* **-euse**) singing.— *n.m.* (*fem.* **-euse**) singer, vocalist.

chantier [ʃɑ̃'tje], *n.m.* timber-yard, wood-yard; stone-yard; dockyard; site; (*C*) shanty, lumber camp.

chantonner [ʃɑ̃tɔ'ne], *v.t., v.i.* to hum.

chantourner [ʃɑ̃tur'ne], *v.t.* to cut in profile; *scie à chantourner,* bow saw.

chantre [ʃɑ̃ːtr], *n.m.* singer, *esp.* a chorister; precentor, lay clerk; (*fig.*) songster (*of birds*).

chanvre [ʃɑ̃ːvr], *n.m.* hemp.

chanvreux [ʃɑ̃'vrø], *a.* (*fem.* **-euse**) hempen.

chaos [ka'o], *n.m.* chaos; (*fig.*) confusion, disorder.

chaotique [kaɔ'tik], *a.* chaotic.

chaparder [ʃapar'de], *v.t.* (*slang*) to steal, to scrounge.

chape [ʃap], *n.f.* cope (*ecclesiastical vestment*); tread (*of a tire*).

chapeau [ʃa'po], *n.m.* (*pl.* **-eaux**) hat; (*Mech. etc.*) cap; *un coup de chapeau,* a bow.

chapelain [ʃa'plɛ̃], *n.m.* chaplain.

chapelet [ʃa'plɛ], *n.m.* rosary, beads; (*Arch. etc.*) chaplet; *chapelet de bombes,* stick of bombs; *chapelet d'oignons,* string of onions.

chapelier [ʃapə'lje], *n.m.* (*fem.* **-ière**) hatter.

chapelle [ʃa'pɛl], *n.f.* chapel; coterie, school (*of literature etc.*); church plate; living.

chapellenie [ʃapɛl'ni], *n.f.* chaplaincy.

chapellerie [ʃapɛl'ri], *n.f.* hat-making; hat trade, shop *or* business.

chapelure [ʃa'plyːr], *n.f.* grated bread-crumbs.

chaperon [ʃa'prɔ̃], *n.m.* hood; (*fig.*) chaperon; *Le Petit Chaperon Rouge,* Little Red Riding Hood.

chaperonner [ʃaprɔ'ne], *v.t.* to cope (*a wall*); (*fig.*) to chaperon.

chapiteau [ʃapi'to], *n.m.* (*pl.* **-eaux**) capital (*of column etc.*); cornice (*of a wardrobe etc.*); big top (*circus*).

chapitre [ʃa'pitr], *n.m.* chapter (*of a book, of knights, of a cathedral*); subject matter of discourse.

chapitrer [ʃapi'tre], *v.t.* to reprimand, to rebuke.

chapon [ʃa'pɔ̃], *n.m.* capon; sop in broth.

chaponner [ʃapɔ'ne], *v.t.* to caponize.

chaque [ʃak], *a.* each, every.

char [ʃaːr], *n.m.* chariot, carriage, vehicle; *char d'assaut,* (*Mil.*) tank.

charabia [ʃara'bja], *n.m.* gibberish.

charade [ʃa'rad], *n.f.* charade.

charançon [ʃarɑ̃'sɔ̃], *n.m.* weevil.

charbon [ʃar'bɔ̃], *n.m.* coal, charcoal; (*pl.*) embers; (*Path.*) anthrax; (*Chem.*) carbon.

charbonnée [ʃarbɔ'ne], *n.f.* piece of grilled meat; charcoal drawing.

charbonner [ʃarbɔ'ne], *v.t.* to char; to black with coal. **se charbonner,** *v.r.* to be charred, to burn black.

charbonnerie [ʃarbɔn'ri], *n.f.* coal depot.

charbonneux [ʃarbɔ'nø], *a.* (*fem.* **-euse**) coaly; affected *or* infected with anthrax.

charbonnier [ʃarbɔ'nje], *n.m.* (*fem.* **-ière**) charcoal burner; coal man.—*n.m.* coal heaver; coal hole; (*Naut.*) collier.—*n.f.* (**-ière**) charcoal kiln; coal scuttle; (*Orn.*) great tit.

charcuter [ʃarky'te], *v.t.* to hack and hew (*meat*); to hack, to butcher (*of a surgeon*).

charcuterie [ʃarky'tri], *n.f.* pork-butcher's meat; pork-butcher's business *or* shop.

charcutier [ʃarky'tje], *n.m.* (*fem.* **-ière**) pork-butcher; (*colloq.*) sawbones.

chardon [ʃar'dɔ̃], *n.m.* thistle; spikes (*on a wall* or *railing*).

chardonneret [ʃardɔn'rɛ], *n.m.* goldfinch.

charge [ʃarʒ], *n.f.* pack; load; expense, cost; accusation; post, employment; care, custody; charge, onset; *à charge de revanche,* provided that I may return the favor.

chargé [ʃar'ʒe], *a.* loaded, burdened.

chargement [ʃarʒə'mɑ̃], *n.m.* cargo, freight; bill of lading; load; charging (*of a battery*).

charger [ʃar'ʒe], *v.t.* (*conjug. like* MANGER) to load, to charge; to burden; to charge with; to register (*a letter*). **se charger,** *v.r.* to take upon oneself, to saddle oneself with (*de*).

chargeur [ʃar'ʒœːr], *n.m.* loader, shipper; stoker; (*Phot., Cine.*) cassette.

chariot [ʃa'rjo], *n.m.* wagon, go-cart; (*Mach.*) truck, trolley.

charitable [ʃari'tabl], *a.* charitable.

charitablement [ʃaritablə'mɑ̃], *adv.* charitably.

charité [ʃari'te], *n.f.* charity; benevolence, alms.

charivari [ʃariva'ri], *n.m.* rough music; hubbub, clatter.

charlatan [ʃarla'tɑ̃], *n.m.* charlatan, mountebank, quack.

charlatanisme [ʃarlata'nism], *n.m.* quackery, charlatanism.

charlot [ʃar'lo], *n.m.* (*Orn.*) curlew.

charmant [ʃar'mɑ̃], *a.* charming, delightful.

charme (1) [ʃarm], *n.m.* charm; spell, enchantment.

charme (2) [ʃarm], *n.m.* (*Bot.*) hornbeam.

charmer [ʃar'me], *v.t.* to charm, to enchant, to bewitch, to fascinate, to captivate, to delight.

charmeur [ʃar'mœːr], *n.m.* (*fem.* **-euse**) charmer, enchanter; bewitching woman, enchantress.

charmille [ʃar'miːj], *n.f.* hedge of young hornbeam; bower, arbor.

charnel [ʃar'nɛl], *a.* (*fem.* **-elle**) carnal; sensual (*person*).

charnellement [ʃarnɛl'mɑ̃], *adv.* carnally.

charnier [ʃar'nje], *n.m.* charnel house.

charnière [ʃar'njɛːr], *n.f.* hinge; joint, articulation.

charnu [ʃar'ny], *a.* fleshy, plump; pulpy (*of fruits*).

charogne [ʃa'rɔɲ], *n.f.* carrion; (*pop.*) blackguard; slut.

charpente [ʃar'pɑ̃ːt], *n.f.* frame, framework.

charpenter [ʃarpɑ̃'te], *v.t.* to square (*timber*); (*fig.*) to frame, to construct.

charpenterie [ʃarpɑ̃'tri], *n.f.* carpentry, carpenter's work *or* trade.

charpentier [ʃarpɑ̃'tje], *n.m.* carpenter.
charpie [ʃar'pi], *n.f.* lint.
charretée [ʃar'te], *n.f.* cartload.
charretier [ʃar'tje], *n.m.* (*fem.* **-ière**) carter, wagoner. —*a.* passable for carts etc.
charrette [ʃa'rɛt], *n.f.* cart; *charrette à bras*, hand cart.
charriage [ʃa'ria:ʒ], *n.m.* cartage; haulage.
charrier [ʃa'rje], *v.t.* to cart.—*v.i.* to drift (*of ice*).
charroi [ʃa'rwɑ], *n.m.* cartage.
charron [ʃa'rɔ̃], *n.m.* wheelwright.
charroyer [ʃarwa'je], *v.t.* (*conjug. like* EM-PLOYER) to cart (*heavy things*).
charrue [ʃa'ry], *n.f.* plow.
charte [ʃart], *n.f.* charter.
chartreuse [ʃar'trø:z], *n.f.* Carthusian monastery *or* convent; Carthusian nun; isolated country house; chartreuse (*liqueur*).
chartreux [ʃar'trø], *n.m.* Carthusian friar; cat of a bluish-grey color.
chartrier [ʃartri'e], *n.m.* keeper of charters; archives; muniment room.
Charybde [ka'ribd], *n.m.* Charybdis.
chas [ʃɑ], *n.m.* eye (*of a needle*).
chasme [kasm], *n.m.* chasm.
châsse [ʃɑ:s], *n.f.* reliquary, shrine; frame.
chasse [ʃas], *n.f.* hunting, shooting, fowling; the hunt, the chase; game preserve; play (*of machinery etc.*); flush (*of lavatory*).
chassé [ʃa'se], *n.m.* chassé (*a step in dancing*).
chassé-croisé [ʃasekrwa'ze], *n.m.* (*pl.* **chassés-croisés**) (*Dancing*) a dance step; (*fig.*) *faire un chassé-croisé*, to exchange places.
chasselas [ʃas'la], *n.m.* table grapes.

[In the following compounds **chasse** is *inv.*]

chasse-marée [ʃasma're], *n.m.* fish cart.
chasse-mouches [ʃas'muʃ], *n.m.* a form of fan; fly swatter.
chasse-neige [ʃas'nɛ:ʒ], *n.m.* snow plow.
chasse-pierre(s) [ʃas'pjɛ:r], *n.m.* (*Rail.*) guard-iron, cow-catcher.
chasser [ʃa'se], *v.t.* to hunt; to chase, to pursue; to drive in (*a nail etc.*); to expel, to turn out, to discharge; to propel.—*v.i.* to go shooting *or* hunting; to glide along; (*Motor.*) to skid.
chasseresse [ʃas'rɛs], *n.f.* huntress.
chasseur [ʃa'sœ:r], *n.m.* (*fem.* **-euse**) hunter *or* huntress, sportsman *or* sportswoman.— *n.m.* page boy; light infantry soldier; (*Av.*) fighter.
chassie [ʃa'si], *n.f.* gum on the edge of the eyelids.
chassieux [ʃa'sjø], *a.* (*fem.* **-euse**) blear-eyed.
châssis [ʃɑ'si], *n.m.* case, frame; window sash; garden frame; printer's chase; (*Motor.*) chassis; (*Theat.*) flat for scenery.
chaste [ʃast], *a.* chaste; pure, virtuous.
chastement [ʃastə'mɑ̃], *adv.* chastely, purely, virtuously.
chasteté [ʃastə'te], *n.f.* chastity, purity.
chasuble [ʃa'zybl], *n.f.* chasuble.
chat [ʃa], *n.m.* (*fem.* **chatte**) cat; darling, dear little thing; *à bon chat bon rat*, set a thief to catch a thief; (C) *chat sauvage*, raccoon; *Le Chat Botté*, Puss in Boots.
châtaigne [ʃɑ'tɛɲ], *n.f.* chestnut.
châtaignier [ʃɑtɛ'ɲje], *n.m.* chestnut tree.

châtain [ʃa'tɛ̃], *a. inv.* chestnut, nut-brown, auburn.
chat-cervier [ʃasɛr'vje], *n.m.* (*pl.* **chats-cerviers**) lynx.
château [ʃɑ'to], *n.m.* (*pl.* **-eaux**) castle, fortress; country seat, mansion, hall, palace.
châteaubriant [ʃatobri'ɑ̃], *n.m.* large grilled rump steak.
châtelain [ʃɑ'tlɛ̃], *n.m.* (*fem.* **-aine**) lord *or* lady of a manor, squire *or* squire's wife.
chat-huant [ʃa'ɥɑ̃], *n.m.* (*pl.* **chats-huants**) tawny owl.
châtiable [ʃɑ'tjabl], *a.* chastisable, punishable.
châtier [ʃɑ'tje], *v.t.* to chastise, to punish; (*fig.*) to correct.
chatière [ʃa'tjɛ:r], *n.f.* cat's hole (*in door etc.*).
châtiment [ʃɑti'mɑ̃], *n.m.* chastisement, punishment.
chatoiement *or* **chatoîment** [ʃatwa'mɑ̃], *n.m.* play of colors, changing luster (*as of shot silk, opals etc.*).
chaton (1) [ʃa'tɔ̃], *n.m.* kitten; catkin.
chaton (2) [ʃa'tɔ̃], *n.m.* setting of a gem; stone in a setting.
chatouillant [ʃatu'jɑ̃], *a.* tickling.
chatouillement [ʃatuj'mɑ̃], *n.m.* tickling, titillation.
chatouiller [ʃatu'je], *v.t.* to tickle, to titillate; (*fig.*) to please, to gratify, to flatter.
chatouilleux [ʃatu'jø], *a.* (*fem.* **-euse**) ticklish; (*fig.*) delicate, touchy.
chatoyant [ʃatwa'jɑ̃], *a.* shot, glistening (*of colors etc.*).
chatoyer [ʃatwa'je], *v.i.* (*conjug. like* EM-PLOYER) to shimmer, to glisten.
châtrer [ʃa'tre], *v.t.* to castrate, to geld; (*Hort.*) to lop, to prune; (*fig.*) to expurgate.
chattée [ʃa'te], *n.f.* litter of kittens.
chatte [ʃat], [CHAT].
chatterie [ʃat'ri], *n.f.* playfulness, pretty *or* coaxing way; wheedling caress; (*pl.*) titbits.
chatterton [ʃatɛr'tɔn], *n.m.* insulating tape.
chaud [ʃo], *a.* hot, warm, burning, glowing.— *n.m.* heat, warmth; *il fait chaud*, it is hot. —*adv.* hot, warm.
chaudeau [ʃo'do], *n.m.* (*pl.* **-eaux**) egg flip.
chaudement [ʃod'mɑ̃], *adv.* warmly; (*fig.*) quickly, eagerly, fiercely, hotly.
chaud-froid [ʃo'frwa], *n.m.* cold jellied chicken *or* game with mayonnaise.
chaudière [ʃo'djɛ:r], *n.f.* copper; boiler (*of a steam engine etc.*); (C) pail.
chaudron [ʃo'drɔ̃], *n.m.* cauldron.
chaudronnerie [ʃodrɔn'ri], *n.f.* boiler works.
chaudronnier [ʃodro'nje], *n.m.* brazier, coppersmith, tinker.
chauffage [ʃo'fa:ʒ], *n.m.* heating, warming; stoking; fuel, firewood; *chauffage central*, central heating.
chauffard [ʃo'fa:r], *n.m.* (*pop.*) road hog.
chauffe [ʃo:f], *n.f.* furnace.
chauffe-bain [ʃof'bɛ̃], *n.m.* (*pl.* **chauffe-bains**) geyser.
chauffe-eau [ʃof'o], *n.m. inv.* water heater.
chauffelinge [ʃof'lɛ:ʒ], *n.m. inv.* clothes-horse, airing cupboard.
chauffer [ʃo'fe], *v.t.* to heat, to warm; (*fig.*) to excite.—*v.i.* to grow hot; to be brewing; (*fig.*) to be urgent *or* pressing. **se chauffer**, *v.r.* to warm oneself.
chaufferette [ʃo'frɛt], *n.f.* foot warmer.

chauffeur [ʃoˈfœːr], *n.m.* fireman; (*fem.* **-euse**)(*Motor.*)driver, chauffeur, chauffeuse.
chaufour [ʃoˈfuːr], *n.m.* lime kiln.
chaulage [ʃoˈlaːʒ], *n.m.* (*Agric.*) liming.
chauler [ʃoˈle], *v.t.* to lime (*soil*).
chaume [ʃoːm], *n.m.* stubble; stubble field; thatch.
chaumer [ʃoˈme], *v.t.*, *v.i.* (*Agric.*) to cut stubble.
chaumière [ʃoˈmjɛːr], *n.f.* thatched house, cottage.
chausse [ʃoːs], *n.f.* shoulder band (*worn in universities etc.*); *(*pl.*) hose (*covering the body from waist to foot*).
chaussée [ʃoˈse], *n.f.* embankment, dike; causeway; roadway, (*Am.*) pavement; **le rez-de-chaussée**, the ground floor.
chausse-pied [ʃosˈpje], *n.m.* (*pl.* **chausse-pieds**) shoe-horn.
chausser [ʃoˈse], *v.t.* to put on (*footwear*); to shoe, to make (*the shoes etc.*) for; (*colloq.*) to fit, to suit.—*v.i.* **chausser du 40**, to take a 7 (*in shoes*). **se chausser**, *v.r.* to put on one's shoes etc.
chausse-trape [ʃosˈtrap], *n.f.* (*pl.* **chausse-trapes**) snare, trap.
chaussette [ʃoˈsɛt], *n.f.* sock.
chausseur [ʃoˈsœːr], *n.m.* footwear dealer.
chausson [ʃoˈsɔ̃], *n.m.* slipper; gym shoe; bootee (*for infants*).
chaussure [ʃoˈsyːr], *n.f.* footwear.
chauve [ʃoːv], *a.* bald.
chauve-souris [ʃovsuˈri], *n.f.* (*pl.* **chauves-souris**) bat, flittermouse.
chauvin [ʃoˈvɛ̃], *n.m.* fanatical patriot.—*a.* chauvinistic, jingoistic.
chaux [ʃo], *n.f.* lime; limestone.
chavirage [ʃaviˈraːʒ], **chavirement** [ʃavirˈmã], *n.m.* capsizing, upsetting.
chavirer [ʃaviˈre], *v.t.*, *v.i.* to capsize, to upset.
chef [ʃɛf], *n.m.* chief, commander, conductor, master, principal, ringleader; chef.
chef-d'œuvre [ʃɛˈdœːvr], *n.m.* (*pl.* **chefs-d'œuvre**) chef-d'œuvre, masterpiece.
chef-lieu [ʃɛfˈljø], *n.m.* (*pl.* **chefs-lieux**) chief town, county seat.
cheik [SCHEIK].
chelem or **schelem** [ʃlɛm], *n.m. inv.* slam (*at cards*).
chemin [ʃəˈmɛ̃], *n.m.* way, road, path, track; (*fig.*) means; course; **chemin de fer**, railway, (*Am.*) railroad.
chemineau [ʃəmiˈno], *n.m.* (*pl.* **-eaux**) tramp.
cheminée [ʃəmiˈne], *n.f.* chimney; funnel; fire-place; mantelpiece; nipple (*of a percussion gun*).
cheminer [ʃəmiˈne], *v.i.* to walk, to tramp; to proceed.
cheminot [ʃəmiˈno], *n.m.* railwayman; rail layer.
chemise [ʃəˈmiːz], *n.f.* shirt; wrapper, cover.
chemiserie [ʃəmiˈzri], *n.f.* shirt factory; shirt making.
chemisette [ʃəmiˈzɛt], *n.f.* short-sleeved shirt (*men*).
chemisier [ʃəmiˈzje], *n.m.* (*fem.* **-ière**) shirt maker *or* seller.
chênaie [ʃɛˈnɛ], *n.f.* oak plantation.
chenal [ʃəˈnal], *n.m.* channel, fairway.
chenapan [ʃənaˈpã], *n.m.* vagabond, good-for-nothing, scamp.

chêne [ʃɛːn], *n.m.* oak.
chêneau [ʃeˈno], *n.m.* (*pl.* **-eaux**) young oak.
chéneau [ʃeˈno] *n.m.*(*pl.* **-eaux**)(eaves) gutter.
chenet [ʃəˈnɛ], *n.m.* fire-dog.
chènevière [ʃɛnˈvjɛːr], *n.f.* hemp-field.
chènevis [ʃɛnˈvi], *n.m.* hemp-seed.
chènevotte [ʃɛnˈvɔt], *n.f.* stalk (*of hemp*).
chenil [ʃəˈnil], *n.m.* dog-kennel; kennels; dirty hovel.
chenille [ʃəˈniːj], *n.f.* caterpillar; kind of silk cord, chenille; **tracteur à chenille**, caterpillar tractor.
chenillère [ʃəniˈjɛːr], *n.f.* nest of caterpillars.
chenillette [ʃəniˈjɛt], *n.f.* (*Mil.*) caterpillar.
chenu [ʃəˈny], *a.* hoary, grey-headed; snow-capped.
cheptel [ʃəˈtɛl, ʃɛpˈtɛl], *n.m.* live-stock (*of a country*).
chèque [ʃɛk], *n.m.* cheque, (*Am.*) check.
chéquier [ʃeˈkje], *n.m.* cheque-book.
cher [ʃɛːr], *a.* (*fem.* **chère** (1)) dear, beloved; precious; expensive.—*adv.* dear, dearly, expensively.
chercher [ʃɛrˈʃe], *v.t.* to seek, to look for, to search for; to endeavour, to try, to attempt; **aller chercher**, to go for; to fetch.
chercheur [ʃɛrˈʃœːr], *n.m.* (*fem.* **-euse**) seeker, searcher; research worker.
chère (1) [ʃɛːr], [CHER].
chère (2) [ʃɛːr], *n.f.* entertainment, fare; **bonne chère**, good cheer, good living.
chèrement [ʃɛrˈmã], *adv.* dearly, tenderly; dear, at a high price.
chéri [ʃeˈri], *a.* beloved; cherished.—*n.m.* (*fem.* **-e**) darling, dearest.
chérif [ʃeˈrif], *n.m.* shereef (*Arabian prince*).
chérir [ʃeˈriːr], *v.t.* to love dearly, to cherish.
cherté [ʃɛrˈte], *n.f.* dearness, high price.
chérubin [ʃeryˈbɛ̃], *n.m.* cherub.
chérubique [ʃeryˈbik], *a.* cherubic.
chester [ʃɛsˈtɛr], *n.m.* Cheshire cheese.
chétif [ʃeˈtif], *a.* (*fem.* **-tive**) puny, pitiful; worthless.
chétivement [ʃetivˈmã], *adv.* meanly, pitifully, poorly, feebly.
chétiveté [ʃetivˈte], *n.f.* puniness, paltriness.
cheval [ʃəˈval], *n.m.* (*pl.* **-aux**) horse; nag, steed; **aller à cheval**, to ride; **cheval d'arçons**, **cheval de bois**, (*Gym.*) vaulting horse; **cheval à bascule**, rocking-horse; **chevaux de bois**, merry-go-round; **cheval marin**, sea horse; walrus.
chevaleresque [ʃəvalˈrɛsk], *a.* chivalrous, knightly.
chevaleresquement [ʃəvalrɛskˈmã], *adv.* chivalrously.
chevalerie [ʃəvalˈri], *n.f.* knighthood, chivalry.
chevalet [ʃəvaˈlɛ], *n.m.* easel; bridge (*of a stringed instrument*); sawing-trestle; buttress, prop; clothes-horse.
chevalier (1) [ʃəvaˈlje], *n.m.* knight.
chevalier (2) [ʃəvaˈlje], *n.m.* (*Orn.*) sand-piper; redshank.
chevalière [ʃəvaˈljɛːr], *n.f.* knight's lady; signet-ring.
chevalin [ʃəvaˈlɛ̃], *a.* equine; **boucherie chevaline**, horse butcher's shop.
cheval-vapeur [ʃəvalvaˈpœːr], *n.m.* (*pl.* **chevaux-vapeur**) horsepower.
chevauchant [ʃəvoˈʃã], *a.* overlapping.
chevauchée [ʃəvoˈʃe], *n.f.* ride, excursion on horseback; cavalcade.

chevauchement [ʃəvoʃ'mã], *n.m.* overlap *or* crossing (*tiles, wires*).
chevaucher [ʃəvo'ʃe], *v.i.* to ride on horseback; to be astride; to overlap.
chevaucheur [ʃəvo'ʃœ:r], *n.m.* rider, horseman.
chevauchure [ʃəvo'ʃy:r], *n.f.* overlapping.
chevelu [ʃə'vly], *a.* hairy, long-haired; (*Bot.*) fibrous.
chevelure [ʃə'vly:r], *n.f.* hair, head of hair.
chevesne [ʃə'vɛn], *n.m.* (*Ichth.*) chub.
chevet [ʃə'vɛ], *n.m.* head (*of a bed*); bolster; pillow; bedside.
cheveu [ʃə'vø], *n.m.* (*pl.* **-eux**) a single hair; *pl.* the hair (*of the head*).
chevillage [ʃəvi'ja:ʒ], *n.m.* fastening, bolting, dowelling.
cheville [ʃə'vi:j], *n.f.* ankle; peg, pin, dowel, bolt; plug.
cheviller [ʃəvi'je], *v.t.* to dowel, to peg, to bolt.
cheviotte [ʃə'vjɔt], *n.f.* cheviot (*tweed*).
chèvre [ʃɛ:vr], *n.f.* goat, nanny goat.
chevreau [ʃə'vro], *n.m.* (*pl.* **-eaux**) kid (*animal or skin*).
chèvrefeuille [ʃɛvrə'fœ:j], *n.m.* honeysuckle.
chèvrerie [ʃɛvrə'ri], *n.f.* goat pen.
chevrette [ʃə'vrɛt], *n.f.* small goat; young roe.
chevreuil [ʃə'vrœ:j], *n.m.* roe, roe deer.
chevrier [ʃəvri'e], *n.m.* (*fem.* **-ière**) goatherd.
chevron [ʃə'vrɔ̃], *n.m.* rafter; chevron, stripe.
chevronnage [ʃəvrɔ'na:ʒ], *n.m.* rafters, raftering.
chevronné [ʃəvrɔ'ne], *a.* (*fam.*) experienced
chevrotain *or* chevrotin [ʃəvrɔ'tɛ̃], *n.m.* chevrotain, musk deer.
chevrotant [ʃəvrɔ'tɑ̃], *a.* quavering, tremulous.
chevrotement [ʃəvrɔt'mɑ̃], *n.m.* tremulous motion, trembling (*of the voice etc.*).
chevroter [ʃəvrɔ'te], *v.i.* to sing *or* speak in a tremulous voice.
chevrotin (1) [CHEVROTAIN].
chevrotin (2) [ʃəvrɔ'tɛ̃], *n.m.* fawn of roe deer; kid (*leather*).
chevrotine [ʃəvrɔ'tin], *n.f.* buckshot.
chez [ʃe], *prep.* at, to, in (*the house, family or country of*); in, with, among; in the works of, (*on letters*) care of.
chiasse [ʃjas], *n.f.* dross, scum.
chibouque *or* chibouk [ʃi'buk], *n.f.* chibouk (*Turkish pipe*).
chic [ʃik], *n.m.* style, chic; aplomb, ease and elegance.—*a. inv.* stylish, smart.
chicane [ʃi'kan], *n.f.* cavil, evasion, quibble; chicanery.
chicaner [ʃika'ne], *v.t.* to quarrel *or* wrangle with.—*v.i.* to cavil, to quibble.
chicanerie [ʃikan'ri], *n.f.* chicanery, quibbling, cavilling.
chicaneur [ʃika'nœ:r], *n.m.* (*fem.* **-euse**) *or* chicanier [ʃika'nje], *n.m.* (*fem.* **-ière**) caviller, pettifogger.—*a.* litigious, cavilling, wrangling.
chiche (1) [ʃiʃ], *a.* niggardly, stingy.
chiche (2) [ʃiʃ], *a.* **pois chiches**, chickpeas.
chichement [ʃiʃ'mã], *adv.* stingily.
chicorée [ʃikɔ're], *n.f.* endive; chicory.
chicot [ʃi'ko], *n.m.* stub *or* stump (*of tree or tooth*).

chicotin [ʃikɔ'tɛ̃], *n.m.* bitter juice of aloes.
chien [ʃjɛ̃], *n.m.* (*fem.* **chienne**) dog; hammer, cock (*of a gun or pistol*); **chien de mer**, dogfish.
chiendent [ʃjɛ̃'dɑ̃], *n.m.* couch grass.
chiennée [ʃjɛ'ne], *n.f.* litter of pups.
chiffe [ʃif], *n.f.* poor stuff, rag; (*fig.*) weakling; spineless person.
chiffon [ʃi'fɔ̃], *n.m.* rag, scrap, bit; frippery.
chiffonnage [ʃifɔ'na:ʒ], *n.m.* rumpled drapery, rumpling, crumpling.
chiffonner [ʃifɔ'ne], *v.t.* to rumple, to crumple; (*colloq.*) to ruffle, to tease, to vex.—*v.i.* to be a rag collector.
chiffonnier [ʃifɔ'nje], *n.m.* (*fem.* **-ière**) ragpicker; chiffonnier.
chiffrage [ʃi'fra:ʒ], **chiffrement** [ʃifr'mã], *n.m.* figuring, figures; calculation; writing in cipher, coding.
chiffre [ʃifr], *n.m.* figure, number; total amount; cipher; monogram.
chiffrer [ʃi'fre], *v.t.* to calculate, to tot up; to code.—*v.i.* to cipher.
chiffreur [ʃi'frœ:r], *n.m.* (*fem.* **-euse**) reckoner, cipherer.
chignole [ʃi'nɔl], *n.f.* ratchet drill.
chignon [ʃi'nɔ̃], *n.m.* chignon, coil of hair.
Chili [ʃi'li], **le**, *m.* Chile.
chilien [ʃi'ljɛ̃], *a.* (*fem.* **-enne**) Chilean.—*n.m.* (**Chilien**, *fem.* **-enne**) Chilean (*person*).
chimère [ʃi'mɛ:r], *n.f.* chimera; myth, idle fancy.
chimérique [ʃime'rik], *a.* chimerical, visionary.
chimériquement [ʃimerik'mã], *adv.* chimerically.
chimie [ʃi'mi], *n.f.* chemistry.
chimique [ʃi'mik], *a.* chemical.
chimiquement [ʃimik'mã], *adv.* chemically.
chimiste [ʃi'mist], *n.m.* chemist (*not pharmaceutical chemist*).
chimpanzé [ʃɛ̃pɑ̃'ze], *n.m.* chimpanzee.
chinchilla [ʃɛ̃ʃil'la], *n.m.* chinchilla.
Chine [ʃin], **la**, *f.* China.
chiner [ʃi'ne], *v.t.* to color differently; to figure (*stuffs*).
chinois [ʃi'nwa], *a.* Chinese.—*n.m.* Chinese (*language*); **un chinois**, a small green orange preserved in brandy; (**Chinois**, *fem.* **-oise**) Chinese (*person*).
chinoiserie [ʃinwa'zri], *n.f.* Chinese thing, curio; (*fig.*) trick; red tape.
chiot [ʃjo], *n.m.* puppy.
chiourme [ʃjurm], *n.f.* convict gang.
chipolata [ʃipɔla'ta], *n.f.* onion stew; small sausage.
chipotage [ʃipɔ'ta:ʒ], *n.m.* dawdling; haggling.
chipoter [ʃipɔ'te], *v.i.* to dally, to dawdle; to haggle; to peck at a dish.
chipotier [ʃipɔ'tje], *n.m.* (*fem.* **-ière**) trifler, dallier, shuffler.
chique [ʃik], *n.f.* quid of tobacco.
chiquement [ʃik'mã], *adv.* smartly.
chiquenaude [ʃik'no:d], *n.f.* flick.
chiquenauder [ʃikno'de], *v.t.* to flick.
chiquer [ʃi'ke], *v.i.* to chew tobacco.
chiquet [ʃi'kɛ], *n.m.*, **chiquette** [ʃi'kɛt], *n.f.* driblet, bit, shred.
chiqueur [ʃi'kœ:r], *n.m.* chewer of tobacco; pretender.

chiromancie [kiromɑ̃'si], *n.f.* chiromancy, palmistry.
chiromancien [kiromɑ̃'sjɛ̃], *n.m.* (*fem.* **-ienne**) chiromancer, palmist.
chirurgical [ʃiryrʒi'kal], *a.* (*m. pl.* **-aux**) surgical.
chirurgicalement [ʃiryrʒikal'mɑ̃], *adv.* surgically.
chirurgie [ʃiryr'ʒi], *n.f.* surgery.
chirurgien [[ʃiryr'ʒjɛ̃], *n.m.* surgeon.
chirurgique [ʃiryr'ʒik], *a.* surgical.
chiure [ʃjy:r], *n.f.* flyspeck.
chlorate [klɔ'rat], *n.m.* chlorate.
chlore [klɔ:r], *n.m.* (*Chem.*) chlorine.
chloré [klɔ're], *a.* containing chlorine.
chlorhydrate [klɔri'drat], *n.m.* (*Chem.*) hydrochlorate.
chlorhydrique [klɔri'drik], *a.* hydrochloric.
chloroforme [klɔrɔ'fɔrm], *n.m.* chloroform.
chloroformer [klɔrɔfɔr'me], *v.t.* to chloroform.
chlorure [klɔ'ry:r], *n.m.* (*Chem.*) chloride.
choc [ʃɔk], *n.m.* shock; impact; clash, encounter.
chocolat [ʃɔkɔ'la], *n.m.* chocolate.—*a.* chocolate-colored.
chocolaterie [ʃɔkɔla'tri], *n.f.* chocolate-making; chocolate factory.
chocolatier [ʃɔkɔla'tje], *n.m.* (*fem.* **-ière**) chocolate maker *or* seller.—*n.f.* (**-ière**) chocolate pot.
chœur [kœ:r], *n.m.* choir; chancel; (*Ant. and fig.*) chorus.
choir [ʃwa:r], *v.i. irr.* to fall, to drop.
choisir [ʃwa'zi:r], *v.t.* to choose, to single out, to select.
choix [ʃwa], *n.m.* choice, alternative; selection; distinction.
choléra [kɔle'ra], *n.m.* cholera.
cholérique [kɔle'rik], *a.* choleraic.—*n.* person affected with cholera.
chômable [ʃo'mabl], *a.* (*of days, fêtes etc.*) to be kept as a holiday.
chômage [ʃo'ma:ʒ], *n.m.* unemployment, enforced idleness; stoppage; *allocation de chômage*, unemployment benefit, 'dole'.
chômer [ʃo'me], *v.i.* to be doing nothing; to be unemployed.
chômeur [ʃo'mœ:r], *n.m.* (*fem.* **-euse**) idle *or* unemployed person.
chope [ʃɔp], *n.f.* large beer glass; mug of beer.
chopper [ʃɔ'pe], *v.i.* to stumble, to trip (*contre*).
choquant [ʃɔ'kɑ̃], *a.* offensive, unpleasant, improper.
choquer [ʃɔ'ke], *v.t.* to shock, to strike *or* dash against; to displease, to offend.—*v.i.* to clink glasses; to be offensive, to be shocking. **se choquer**, *v.r.* to take offence; to come into collision with each other.
choral [kɔ'ral], *a.* choral.—*n.m.* (*pl.* **-als**) choral(e).—*n.f.* (**chorale**) choir, choral society.
chorée [kɔ're], *n.f.* chorea, St. Vitus's dance.
chorégraphe [kɔre'graf], *n.m.* choreographer.
chorégraphie [kɔregra'fi], *n.f.* choreography.
choriste [kɔ'rist], *n.m.* chorister; (*Theat.*) member of the chorus.
chorus [kɔ'ry:s], *n.m.* chorus.

chose [ʃo:z], *n.f.* thing; matter, business, affair; (*Law*) chattel, property.
chou [ʃu], *n.m.* (*pl.* **choux**) cabbage, kale; (*colloq.*) puff paste; darling, dear; bow, rosette; *choux de Bruxelles*, Brussels sprouts.
chouan [ʃwã], *n.m.* Chouan, Breton royalist insurgent (*during the French Revolution*).
choucas [ʃu'ka], *n.m.*, **chouchette** [ʃu'ʃɛt] *n.f.* jackdaw.
choucroute [ʃu'krut], *n.f.* sauerkraut.
chouette (1) [ʃwɛt], *n.f.* owl.
chouette (2) [ʃwɛt], *int.* (*pop.*) fine, marvellous.—*a.* nice, fine, good of its kind.
chou-fleur [ʃu'flœ:r], *n.m.* (*pl.* **choux-fleurs**) cauliflower.
chou-rave [ʃu'ra:v], *n.m.* (*pl.* **choux-raves**) kohl rabi, turnip-cabbage.
choyer [ʃwa'je], *v.t.* (*conjug. like* EMPLOYER) to take great care of, to be fond of, to pamper, to pet. **se choyer**, *v.r.* to pamper oneself.
chrême [krɛ:m], *n.m.* chrism, holy oil.
chrémeau [kre'mo], *n.m.* (*pl.* **-eaux**) chrism cloth.
chrétien [kre'tjɛ̃], *a.* and *n.m.* (*fem.* **-enne**) Christian.
chrétiennement [kretjɛn'mɑ̃], *adv.* like a Christian.
chrétienté [kretjɛ̃'te], *n.f.* Christendom.
christ [krist], *n.m.* crucifix; representation of Christ crucified; *le Christ*, Jesus Christ.
christianisme [kristja'nism], *n.m.* Christianity.
Christophe [kris'tɔf], *m.* Christopher.
chromage [kro'ma:ʒ], *n.m.* chromium plating.
chromate [krɔ'mat] *n.m.* (*Chem.*) chromate.
chromatique [krɔma'tik], *a.* (*Chem., Mus.*) chromatic.—*n.f.* (*Mus., Paint.*) chromatics.
chrome [kro:m], *n.m.* chromium, chrome.
chromé [kro'me], *a.* chromium-plated.
chromer [kro'me], *v.t.* to chrome.
chromique [kro'mik], *a.* chromic.
chromosome [kromo'zo:m], *n.m.* chromosome.
chronique (1) [krɔ'nik], *n.f.* chronicle, history; news summary.
chronique (2) [krɔ'nik], *a.* (*Med.*) chronic.
chroniqueur [krɔni'kœ:r], *n.m.* (*fem.* **-euse**) chronicler; newswriter, columnist.
chronologie [krɔnɔlɔ'ʒi], *n.f.* chronology.
chronologique [krɔnɔlɔ'ʒik], *a.* chronological.
chronomètre [krɔnɔ'mɛ:tr], *n.m.* chronometer.
chronométrer [krɔnɔme'tre], *v.t.* (*conjug. like* CÉDER) to time.
chronométreur [krɔnɔme'trœ:r], *n.m.* timekeeper.
chrysalide [kriza'lid], *n.f.* chrysalis.
chrysanthème [krizɑ̃'tɛ:m], *n.m.* chrysanthemum.
chuchotement [ʃyʃɔt'mɑ̃], *n.m.* whispering, whisper, rustling.
chuchoter [ʃyʃɔ'te], *v.t., v.i.* to whisper.
chuchoterie [ʃyʃɔ'tri], *n.f.* whispering.
chuchoteur [ʃyʃɔ'tœ:r], *n.m.* (*fem.* **-euse**) whisperer.
chuinter [ʃɥɛ̃'te], *v.i.* to hoot (*of owls*); to hiss (*of gas*).
chut [ʃ:t], *int.* and *n.m.* hush!

69

chute [ʃyt], *n.f.* fall, tumble; collapse, ruin, downfall; disaster.

chuter [ʃy'te], *v.i.* (*fam.*) to fall, to fail.

Chypre [ʃipr], *f.* Cyprus.

ci [si], *adv.* here.

cible [sibl], *n.f.* target, mark; (*fig.*) purpose.

ciboire [si'bwa:r], *n.m.* sacred vase, pyx.

ciboule [si'bul], *n.f.* Welsh onion, scallion.

ciboulette [sibu'lɛt], *n.f.* chive.

cicatrice [sika'tris], *n.f.* scar, seam, mark.

cicatrisant [sikatri'zã], *a.* cicatrizing.

cicatrisation [sikatriza'sjõ], *n.f.* cicatrization.

cicatriser [sikatri'ze], *v.t.* to cicatrize; to close, to heal up. **se cicatriser**, *v.r.* to skin over, to heal up.

Cicéron [sise'rõ], *m.* Cicero.

cicérone [sise'ron], *n.m.* cicerone, guide.

cicéronien [sisero'njɛ̃], *a.* (*fem.* **-enne**) Ciceronian.

cidre [sidr], *n.m.* cider.

cidrerie [sidrə'ri], *n.f.* cider making; cider factory.

ciel [sjɛl], *n.m.* (*pl.* **cieux**) the heavens, the firmament, the sky; heaven.

cierge [sjɛrʒ], *n.m.* taper, church candle.

cigale [si'gal], *n.f.* cicada.

cigare [si'ga:r], *n.m.* cigar.

cigarette [siga'rɛt], *n.f.* cigarette.

cigogne [si'gɔɲ], *n.f.* stork.

cigogneau [sigɔ'ɲo], *n.m.* (*pl.* **-eaux**) young stork.

ciguë [si'gy], *n.f.* hemlock (*plant* or *poison*).

cil [sil], *n.m.* eyelash.

cilice [si'lis], *n.m.* cilice, hair shirt.

cillement [sij'mã], *n.m.* blink, winking.

ciller [si'je], *v.t.*, *v.i.* to wink, to blink (*the eyes*).

cimaise or **cymaise** [si'mɛ:z], *n.f.* cyma, ogee; dado rail, picture rail.

cime [sim], *n.f.* top, summit, peak.

ciment [si'mã], *n.m.* cement.

cimenter [simã'te], *v.t.* to cement; to strengthen, to consolidate.

cimentier [simã'tje], *n.m.* cement maker.

cimeterre [sim'tɛ:r], *n.m.* scimitar.

cimetière [sim'tjɛ:r], *n.m.* cemetery, churchyard.

cimier [si'mje], *n.m.* crest (*of a helmet*); rump (*of beef*).

cinéaste [sine'ast], *n.m.* film producer.

cinéma [sine'ma], *n.m.* cinema.

cinémascope [sinemas'kɔp], *n.m.* cinemascope.

cinémathèque [sinema'tɛk], *n.f.* film library.

cinématographier [sinematɔgra'fje], *v.t.* to film.

cinérama [sinera'ma], *n.m.* cinerama.

cinétique [sine'tik], *n.f.* kinetics.—*a.* kinetic, motive (*energy*).

cinétiquement [sinetik'mã], *adv.* kinetically.

cingalais [sɛ̃ga'lɛ], *a.* Sin(g)halese or Cingalese.—*n.m.* Sin(g)halese or Cingalese (*language*); (**Cingalais**, *fem.* **-aise**) Sin(g)halese or Cingalese (*person*).

cinglage [sɛ̃'gla:ʒ], *n.m.* sailing, ship's course, run of a ship in twenty-four hours.

cinglement [sɛ̃gl'mã], *n.m.* lashing, slashing.

cingler (1) [sɛ̃'gle], *v.i.* to sail before the wind.

cingler (2) [sɛ̃'gle], *v.t.* to lash; (*fig.*) to chastize.

cinname [si'nam], **cinnamome** [sina'mɔm], *n.m.* cinnamon.

cinq [sɛ̃:k], *a.* five.—*n.m.* five.

cinquantaine [sɛ̃kã'tɛn], *n.f.* about fifty.

cinquante [sɛ̃'kã:t], *a.* fifty.

cinquantenaire [sɛ̃kãt'nɛ:r], *a.* and *n.* quinquagenarian.—*n.m.* fiftieth anniversary, jubilee.

cinquantième [sɛ̃kã'tjɛm], *a.* fiftieth.—*n.m.* fiftieth part.

cinquième [sɛ̃'kjɛm], *a.* fifth.—*n.m.* fifth part; fifth floor.

cintrage [sɛ̃'tra:ʒ], *n.m.* arching, curving (*of arches etc.*).

cintre [sɛ̃:tr] *n.m.* curve of an arch; coathanger.

cintrer [sɛ̃'tre], *v.t.* to arch, to curve.

cipaye [si'pa:j], **cipahi** [si'pai], *n.m.* sepoy.

cipolin [sipɔ'lɛ̃], *n.m.* cipollino, cipolin marble.

cippe [sip], *n.m.* cippus (*half-column*).

cirage [si'ra:ʒ], *n.m.* waxing; blacking (*composition* or *process*); shoe polish.

circoncire [sirkõ'si:r], *v.t. irr.* (*conjug. like* CONFIRE *except for p.p.* **circoncis**) to circumcise.

circoncis [sirkõ'si], *a.* circumcised.—*n.m.* one who is circumcised.

circoncision [sirkõsi'zjõ], *n.f.* circumcision.

circonférence [sirkõfe'rã:s], *n.f.* circumference.

circonflexe [sirkõ'flɛks], *a.* and *n.m.* circumflex.

circonlocution [sirkõlɔky'sjõ], *n.f.* circumlocution.

circonscription [sirkõskrip'sjõ], *n.f.* circumscription; district; constituency.

circonscrire [sirkõs'kri:r], *v.t. irr.* (*conjug. like* ÉCRIRE) to circumscribe, to encircle; to limit.

circonspect [sirkõs'pɛkt, -spɛ], *a.* circumspect, wary, discreet, reserved.

circonspection [sirkõspɛk'sjõ], *n.f.* circumspection, wariness, caution.

circonstance [sirkõs'tã:s], *n.f.* circumstance; occurrence, event.

circonstanciel [sirkõstã'sjɛl], *a.* (*fem.* **-elle**) circumstantial.

circonstancier [sirkõstã'sje], *v.t.* to state circumstantially, to particularize.

circonvenir [sirkõv'ni:r], *v.t. irr.* (*conjug. like* TENIR) to circumvent, to outwit.

circonvention [sirkõvã'sjõ], *n.f.* circumvention, fraud.

circonvoisin [sirkõvwa'zɛ̃], *a.* circumjacent, neighboring, adjoining.

circonvolution [sirkõvɔly'sjõ] *n.f.* circumvolution.

circuit [sir'kɥi], *n.m.* circuit, circumference; detour; lap; (*Elec.*) **court circuit**, short circuit; **en circuit**, switched on.

circulaire [sirky'lɛ:r], *a.* circular, round.—*n.f.* circular.

circulation [sirkylɑ'sjõ], *n.f.* circulation; currency; traffic.

circulatoire [sirkyla'twa:r], *a.* circulatory, circulating.

circuler [sirky'le], *v.i.* to circulate, to revolve, to move round; to be current.

cire [si:r], *n.f.* beeswax; wax; taper.

ciré [si're], *n.m.* (*Naut.*) (suit of) oilskins.

cirer [si're], *v.t.* to wax; to black or to polish (*boots*).

claquette

cireur [si'rœːr], *n.m.* (*fem.* **cireuse** (1)) polisher; *cireuse électrique*, electric polisher.
cireux [si'rø], *a.* (*fem.* **cireuse** (2)) waxy.
ciron [si'rɔ̃], *n.m.* mite.
cirque [sirk], *n.m.* circus.
cirrus [sir'ryːs], *n.m.* cirrus (*cloud*).
cirure [si'ryːr], *n.f.* prepared wax.
cisaille [si'zaːj], *n.f.* clipping *or* shearing of metals; (*pl.*) shears; (*Bookb.*) guillotine.
cisailler [siza'je], *v.t.* to pare, to clip (*coins etc.*); to cut with shears.
cisalpin [sizal'pɛ̃], *a.* cisalpine.
ciseau [si'zo], *n.m.* (*pl.* **-eaux**) chisel; (*pl.*) scissors.
ciseler [siz'le], *v.t.* (*conjug. like* AMENER) to chisel; to chase.
ciselet [siz'lɛ], *n.m.* small chisel, graver.
ciseleur [siz'lœːr], *n.m.* chaser; carver, sculptor.
ciselure [siz'lyːr], *n.f.* chasing, sculpture, carving.
cisoires [si'zwaːr], *n.f.* (*used only in pl.*) big bench-shears (*to cut sheet iron*).
ciste [sist], *n.m.* cistus, rockrose.
citadelle [sita'dɛl], *n.f.* citadel; (*fig.*) stronghold.
citadin [sita'dɛ̃], *n.m.* (*fem.* **-e**) citizen, townsman *or* -woman.
citation [sita'sjɔ̃], *n.f.* citation, quotation; summons.
cité [si'te], *n.f.* city; town.
citer [si'te], *v.t.* to cite, to quote; to summon.
citérieur [site'rjœːr], *a.* (*Geog.*) nearer, hithermost.
citerne [si'tɛrn], *n.f.* cistern, reservoir; (*Naut.*) tanker.
cithare [si'taːr], *n.f.* zither.
citoyen [sitwa'jɛ̃], *n.m.* (*fem.* **-enne**) citizen, burgess; (*fig.*) patriot.
citrate [si'trat], *n.m.* citrate.
citrin [si'trɛ̃], *a.* citrine, lemon-colored.
citrique [si'trik], *a.* citric.
citron [si'trɔ̃], *a.* lemon-colored. —*n.m.* lemon, citron.
citronnade [sitrɔ'nad], *n.f.* lemon squash.
citronnat [sitrɔ'na], *n.m.* candied lemon peel.
citronné [sitrɔ'ne], *a.* lemon-flavored.
citronnier [sitrɔ'nje], *n.m.* citron tree.
citrouille [si'truːj], *n.f.* pumpkin, gourd.
cive [siːv], **civette** (1) [si'vɛt], [CIBOULETTE].
civet [si'vɛ], *n.m.* wine stew (*of venison*); *civet de lièvre*, jugged hare.
civette (1) [CIVE].
civette (2) [si'vɛt], *n.f.* civet cat; civet.
civière [si'vjɛːr], *n.f.* hand barrow; stretcher; bier.
civil [si'vil], *a.* civil; private; plain; polite.— *n.m.* civilian.
civilement [sivil'mɑ̃], *adv.* civilly; courteously.
civilisable [sivili'zabl], *a.* civilizable.
civilisateur [siviliza'tœːr], *a.* (*fem.* **-trice**) civilizing.
civilisation [siviliza'sjɔ̃], *n.f.* civilization.
civiliser [sivili'ze], *v.t.* to civilize. **se civiliser,** *v.r.* to become civilized.
civilité [sivili'te], *n.f.* civility, good manners; (*pl.*) compliments.
civique [si'vik], *a.* civic.
civisme [si'vism], *n.m.* good citizenship.

clabaudage [klabo'daːʒ], *n.m.* barking, bawling.
clabauder [klabo'de], *v.i.* to clamor, to bawl out.
clabaudeur [klabo'dœːr], *n.m.* (*fem.* **-euse**) brawler, scandalmonger.
claie [klɛ], *n.f.* wattle, hurdle; screen (*of a sieve*).
clair [klɛːr], *a.* clear, bright, luminous; light-colored, pure, cloudless; thin (*of liquids etc.*); plain, intelligible, obvious.—*adv.* clearly, distinctly, plainly.—*n.m.* light, clearness; (*Paint.*) highlight.
Claire [klɛːr], *f.* Clara, Cla(i)re.
clairement [klɛr'mɑ̃], *adv.* clearly, plainly, distinctly.
clairet [klɛ'rɛ], *a.* (*fem.* **clairette** (1)) palish, lightish (*of wines*).—*n.m.* light-red wine.
clairette (2) [klɛ'rɛt], *n.f.* white grape.
claire-voie [klɛr'vwa], *n.f.* (*pl.* **claires-voies**) wooden fencing; opening (*in garden wall*), wicket; skylight.
clairière [klɛ'rjɛːr], *n.f.* clearing, glade.
clair-obscur [klɛrɔps'kyːr], *n.m.* (*pl.* **clairs-obscurs**) chiaroscuro; light and shade.
clairon [klɛ'rɔ̃], *n.m.* clarion, bugle; bugler.
clairsemé [klɛrsə'me], *a.* thin, thinly sown, scattered.
clairvoyance [klɛrvwa'jɑ̃ːs], *n.f.* sharpness, perspicacity; clairvoyance.
clairvoyant [klɛrvwa'jɑ̃], *a.* clear-sighted, discerning; clairvoyant.
clamer [kla'me], *v.t.* to cry out, to shout.
clameur [kla'mœːr], *n.f.* clamor, outcry.
clan [klɑ̃], *n.m.* clan.
clandestin [klɑ̃des'tɛ̃], *a.* clandestine, secret.
clandestinement [klɑ̃destin'mɑ̃], *adv.* clandestinely, secretly.
clapement [CLAPPEMENT].
clapet [kla'pɛ], *n.m.* valve, clapper.
clapier [kla'pje], *n.m.* hutch (*for rabbits*).
clapir [kla'piːr], *v.i.* to squeak (*of rabbits*). **se clapir,** *v.r.* to hide in a hole, to squat, to cower.
clapotage [klapɔ'taːʒ], *n.m.* rippling, plashing; lapping.
clapotement [klapɔt'mɑ̃], *n.m.* [CLAPOTAGE].
clapoter [klapɔ'te], *v.i.* to plash, to chop.
clapoteux [klapɔ'tø], *a.* (*fem.* **-euse**) plashing, choppy, rough.
clapotis [klapɔ'ti], *n.m.* [CLAPOTAGE].
clappement *or* **clapement** [klap'mɑ̃], *n.m.* clacking, smacking.
clapper [kla'pe], *v.i.* to clack, to smack (*of the tongue*).
claque (1) [klak], *n.f.* slap, smack; claque (*paid applauders at theatres*); (*pl.*) (C) clogs, galoshes.
claque (2) [klak], *n.m.* opera hat, crush hat.
claquebois [klak'bwa], *n.m.* xylophone.
claquement [klak'mɑ̃], *n.m.* clapping, clap; snapping; cracking; chattering; slamming.
claquemurer [klakmy're], *v.t.* to coop up, to imprison. **se claquemurer,** *v.r.* to shut oneself up.
claquer [kla'ke], *v.t.* to slap, to crack, to slam.—*v.i.* to snap, to crack, to clap, to clack; to slam, to bang.
claqueter [klak'te], *v.i.* (*conjug. like* APPELER) to cackle (*of a hen*); to cry (*of the stork*).
claquette [kla'kɛt], *n.f.* clapper, rattle; *danseur à claquettes*, tap dancer.

claquoir [kla'kwa:r], *n.m.* [CLAQUETTE].
clarification [klarifika'sjɔ̃], *n.f.* clarification.
clarifier [klari'fje], *v.t.* to clarify; to purify, to fine. **se clarifier**, *v.r.* to clarify, to settle.
clarine [kla'rin], *n.f.* bell (*attached to cattle*).
clarinette [klari'nɛt], *n.f.* clarinet.
clarinettiste [klarinɛ'tist], *n.* clarinetist.
clarté [klar'te], *n.f.* light, splendor; clearness.
classe [kla:s], *n.f.* class, order, rank; kind, tribe; class *or* grade (*in a school*); classroom; lesson; (*pl.*) school hours; school time.
classement [klas'mã], *n.m.* classing, classification, filing.
classer [kla'se], *v.t.* to class, to classify, to sort; to file.
classeur [kla'sœ:r], *n.m.* card index; file.
classification [klasifika'sjɔ̃], *n.f.* classification.
classifier [klasi'fje], *v.t.* to classify.
classique [kla'sik], *a.* classic, classical; standard (*of authors, books etc.*); conventional.—*n.m.* classic (*author, book etc.*).
claudicant [klodi'kã], *a.* lame, limping.
claudication [klodika'sjɔ̃], *n.f.* lameness, limping, halting.
clause [klo:z], *n.f.* clause.
claustral [klos'tral], *a.* (*m. pl.* -**aux**) claustral; monastic.
claustration [klostra'sjɔ̃], *n.f.* claustration, confinement.
claustrer [klos'tre], *v.t.* to cloister, to confine.
claustrophobie [klostrɔfɔ'bi], *n.f.* claustrophobia.
clavecin [klav'sɛ̃], *n.m.* harpsichord, clavecin.
clavette [kla'vɛt], *n.f.* (*Tech.*) peg, pin; key, cotter.
claviculaire [klaviky'lɛ:r], *a.* clavicular.
clavicule [klavi'kyl], *n.f.* clavicle, collarbone.
clavier [kla'vje], *n.m.* clavier, keyboard (*piano, typewriter*), key frame.
clayère [klɛ'jɛ:r], *n.f.* oyster bed *or* breeding ground.
clayon [klɛ'jɔ̃], *n.m.* wattle; stand (*for draining cheese*).
clef or **clé** [kle], *n.f.* key; plug (*of a cock*); spanner; keystone (*of arch*); (*Mus.*) clef, tuning key.
clématite [klema'tit], *n.f.* (*Bot.*) clematis.
clémence [kle'mã:s], *n.f.* clemency, mercy.
clément [kle'mã], *a.* clement, merciful, lenient; mild (*of the weather*).
Clémentine [klemã'tin], *f.* Clementine.
clenche [klã:ʃ], **clenchette** [klã'ʃɛt], *n.f.* catch *or* latch (*of a lock*).
cleptomane [klɛptɔ'man], *n.* kleptomaniac.
cleptomanie [klɛptɔma'ni], *n.f.* kleptomania.
clerc [klɛ:r], *n.m.* clergyman; (*fig.*) scholar.
clergé [klɛr'ʒe], *n.m.* clergy.
clérical [kleri'kal], *a.* (*m. pl.* -**aux**) clerical.
cléricalisme [klerika'lism], *n.m.* clericalism.
cléricaliste [klerika'list], *n.* clericalist.
clic-clac [klik'klak], *n.m.* cracking (*of a whip*).
clichage [kli'ʃa:ʒ], *n.m.* stereotyping, stereotype.
cliché [kli'ʃe], *n.m.* stereotype plate, cliché; (*fig.*) stereotyped phrase; (*Phot.*) negative; (*Sculp.*) cast.
clicher [kli'ʃe], *v.t.* to stereotype.
client [kli'ã], *n.m.* (*fem.* -**e**) client (*of law-

yers etc.); patient (*of physicians*); customer (*of tradesmen*).
clientèle [kliã'tɛl], *n.f.* clientele; practice; connection; custom; goodwill (*of a business*).
clignement [kliɲ'mã], *n.m.* winking, blinking, wink.
cligner [kli'ɲe], *v.t., v.i.* to wink, to blink.
clignotant [kliɲɔ'tã], *a.* winking, blinking.—*n.m.* (*Motor.*) winker, flashing indicator.
clignotement [kliɲɔt'mã], *n.m.* winking, blinking.
clignoter [kliɲɔ'te], *v.i.* to wink, to blink.
climat [kli'ma], *n.m.* climate; region, country.
climatérique [klimate'rik], **climatique** [klima'tik], *a.* climatic.
climatisation [klimatiza'sjɔ̃], *n.f.* air conditioning.
climatisé [klimati'ze], *a.* air-conditioned.
climatiser [klimati'ze], *v.t.* to air-condition.
clin [klɛ̃], *n.m.* wink (*of an eye*).
clinicien [klini'sjɛ̃], *a.m.* clinical.—*n.m.* clinical physician.
clinique [kli'nik], *a.* clinical.—*n.f.* clinical surgery; clinic, nursing home.
clinquant [klɛ̃'kã], *a.* showy, gaudy, trumpery.—*n.m.* tinsel; (*fig.*) glitter, affectation.
clip [klip], *n.m.* clip-fastened jewel.
clipper [kli'pɛr], *n.m.* (*Naut.* and *Av.*) clipper.
clique [klik], *n.f.* set, coterie, party, clique.
cliquet [kli'kɛ], *n.m.* catch, pawl.
cliqueter [klik'te], *v.i.* (*conjug. like* APPELER) to click *or* jingle; (*Motor.*) to knock.
cliquetis [klik'ti], *n.m.* clanking, clash.
cliquette [kli'kɛt], *n.f.* sinker (*of net*); (*usu. pl.*) bones (*a kind of castanets*).
clissage [kli'sa:ʒ], *n.m.* wickering.
clisse [klis], *n.f.* wicker mat for draining cheese; basket-work cover for a bottle; (*Surg.*) splint.
clisser [kli'se], *v.t.* to wicker, to cover with wicker-work etc.
clivage [kli'va:ʒ], *n.m.* (*Min.*) cleavage; cleaving.
cliver [kli've], *v.t.* to cleave (*diamonds etc.*). **se cliver**, *v.r.* to split, to be cleft.
cloaque [klɔ'ak], *n.m.* drain, sewer, sink, cesspool; (*fig.*) filthy hole.
clochage [klɔ'ʃa:ʒ], *n.m.* cultivation under cloches.
clochard [klɔ'ʃa:r], *n.m.* (*fam.*) tramp, vagrant; (*Am.*) hobo.
cloche [klɔʃ], *n.f.* bell; dish cover; blister; stewpan; (*Gard.*) cloche.
clochement [klɔʃ'mã], *n.m.* hobbling, halting.
cloche-pied [klɔʃ'pje], *n.m.* hopping on one leg.
clocher (1) [klɔ'ʃe], *n.m.* steeple, belfry; (*fig.*) parish, native place.
clocher (2) [klɔ'ʃe], *v.t.* (*Gard.*) to cover with a cloche.
clocher (3) [klɔ'ʃe], *v.i.* to limp, to hobble; (*fig., fam.*) to go wrong somewhere, to be defective.
clocheton [klɔʃ'tɔ̃], *n.m.* bell turret.
clochette [klɔ'ʃɛt], *n.f.* small bell, hand bell; bellflower.
cloison [klwa'zɔ̃], *n.f.* partition, division; compartment; (*Naut.*) bulkhead.
cloisonnage [klwazɔ'na:ʒ], **cloisonnement** [klwazɔn'mã], *n.m.* partition work, wainscotting.

cloisonner [klwazɔ'ne], *v.t.* to partition.
cloître [klwɑ:tr], *n.m.* cloister.
cloîtrer [klwɑ'tre], *v.t.* to shut up in a cloister, to immure. **se cloîtrer**, *v.r.* to enter a monastery *or* convent.
cloîtrier [klwɑ'trie], *n.m.* (*fem.* **-ière**) cloistered monk *or* nun.
clopin-clopant [klɔpɛ̃klɔ'pɑ̃], *adv.* limpingly, hobbling along.
clopiner [klɔpi'ne], *v.i.* to limp, to halt, to hobble.
cloporte [klɔ'pɔrt], *n.m.* woodlouse.
cloque [klɔk], *n.f.* blister (*on skin, paint etc.*); blight, rust (*of plants*).
cloquer [klɔ'ke], *v.i.* to blister (*of paint*).
clore [klɔ:r], *v.t. irr.* (*chiefly used in p.p.*) to close, to shut; to enclose; to end.—*v.i.* to close, to shut. **se clore**, *v.r.* to close, to be closed; to end.
clos [klo], *a.* closed, sealed; completed; *à huis clos*, in camera.—*n.m.* close; enclosure, field.
closeau [klo'zo], *n.m.* (*pl.* **-eaux**) small garden.
closerie [kloz'ri], *n.f.* small enclosed farm *or* garden.
clôture [klo'ty:r], *n.f.* enclosure, fence; closing, close; closure; (*Relig.*) enclosure (*of nuns etc.*).
clôturer [kloty're], *v.t.* to close.
clou [klu], *n.m.* nail, spike, stud; (*Path.*) carbuncle, boil; *clou de girofle*, clove.
clouage [klu'a:ʒ], **clouement** [klu'mɑ̃], *n.m.* nailing.
clouer [klu'e], *v.t.* to nail; to fix; (*fig.*) to detain.
clouter [klu'te], *v.t.* to adorn with nails, to stud; *passage clouté*, pedestrian crossing.
clouterie [klu'tri], *n.f.* nail factory; nail trade.
cloutier [klu'tje], *n.m.* nail maker, nail dealer.
cloutière [klu'tjɛ:r], *n.f.* nail box.
clovisse [klɔ'vis], *n.f.* winkle; cockle.
clown [klun], *n.m.* clown.
cloyère [klwa'jɛ:r], *n.f.* oyster basket.
club [klʌb, klyb], *n.m.* club (*sporting* or *political*).
clystère [klis'tɛ:r] *n.m.* clyster, injection, enema.
coaccusé [koaky'ze], *n.m.* (*fem.* **-ée**) fellow prisoner; co-defendant.
coacquéreur [koake'rœ:r], *n.m.* (*fem.* **-euse**) co-purchaser, joint buyer.
coacquisition [koakizi'sjɔ̃], *n.f.* joint purchase.
coactif [koak'tif], *a.* (*fem.* **-tive**) coactive.
coaction [koak'sjɔ̃], *n.f.* coercion, compulsion.
coadjuteur [koadʒy'tœ:r], *n.m.* coadjutor.
coadjutrice [koadʒy'tris], *n.f.* coadjutrix.
coagulant [koagy'lɑ̃], *a.* coagulant.
coagulation [koagyla'sjɔ̃], *n.f.* coagulation.
coaguler [koagy'le], *v.t.* to coagulate. **se coaguler**, *v.r.* to coagulate.
coaliser [koali'ze], *v.t.* to unite in a coalition. **se coaliser**, *v.r.* to coalesce, to league, to unite, to combine.
coalition [koali'sjɔ̃], *n.f.* coalition, union, league.
coassement [koas'mɑ̃], *n.m.* croaking (*of frogs*).
coasser [koa'se], *v.i.* to croak (*of frogs*).

coassocié [koasɔ'sje], *n.m.* (*fem.* **-ée**) co-partner.
coauteur [koo'tœ:r], *n.m.* co-author.
cobalt [kɔ'balt], *n.m.* cobalt.
cobaye [kɔ'ba:j], *n.m.* guinea pig.
cobra [kɔ'bra], *n.m.* cobra, hooded snake.
cocagne [kɔ'kaɲ], *n.m. mât de cocagne*, greasy pole; *pays de cocagne*, land of plenty.
cocaïne [kɔka'in], *n.f.* cocaine.
cocarde [kɔ'kard], *n.f.* cockade; rosette.
cocasse [kɔ'kas], *a.* (*fam.*) odd, laughable, comical.
cocasserie [kɔkas'ri], *n.f.* drollery, foolery, farce.
coccinelle [kɔksi'nɛl], *n.f.* ladybug.
coche (1) [kɔʃ], *n.m.* coach; *c'est la mouche du coche*, he is a busybody.
coche (2) [kɔʃ], *n.f.* notch, score.
coche (3) [kɔʃ], *n.f.* sow.
cochenille [kɔʃ'ni:j], *n.f.* cochineal.
cocher (1) [kɔ'ʃe], *n.m.* coachman, driver.
cocher (2) [kɔ'ʃe], *v.t.* to notch.
cochère [kɔ'ʃɛ:r], *a.f.* for carriages; *porte cochère*, carriage entrance, gateway.
cochet [kɔ'ʃe], *n.m.* young cock, cockerel.
cochon [kɔ'ʃɔ̃], *n.m.* hog, pig; pork; *cochon d'Inde*, guinea pig.
cochonnée [kɔʃɔ'ne], *n.f.* litter (*of pigs*).
cochonner [kɔʃɔ'ne], *v.i.* to farrow, to pig.
cochonnerie [kɔʃɔn'ri], *n.f.* nastiness, filth.
cochonnet [kɔʃɔ'nɛ], *n.m.* young pig; jack (*at bowls*).
cocktail [kɔk'tɛl], *n.m.* cocktail; cocktail party.
coco [ko'ko], *n.m.* coconut.
cocon [kɔ'kɔ̃], *n.m.* cocoon.
cocotier [kɔkɔ'tje], *n.m.* coconut palm.
coction [kɔk'sjɔ̃], *n.f.* coction, boiling; digestion (*of food*).
code [kɔd], *n.m.* code (*digest* or *collection of laws*); law, rule.
codemandeur [kodəmɑ̃'dœ:r], *n.m.* (*fem.* **-eresse**) co-plaintiff.
coder [kɔ'de], *v.t.* to code (*telegram*).
codétenteur [kodetɑ̃'tœ:r], *n.m.* (*fem.* **-trice**) joint holder.
codétenu [kodet'ny], *n.m.* (*fem.* **-e**) fellow prisoner.
codicillaire [kodisi'lɛ:r], *a.* contained in a codicil.
codicille [kodi'sil], *n.m.* codicil, rider.
codifier [kodi'fje], *v.t.* to codify.
codirecteur [kodirɛk'tœ:r], *n.m.* (*fem.* **-trice**) joint manager.
codonataire [kodɔna'tɛ:r], *n.* joint donee.
codonateur [kodɔna'tœ:r], *n.m.* (*fem.* **-trice**) joint donor.
coéquipier [koeki'pje], *n.m.* fellow member (*of a crew, team etc.*).
coercer [kɔɛr'se], *v.t.* to coerce.
coercition [kɔɛrsi'sjɔ̃], *n.f.* coercion.
cœur [kœ:r], *n.m.* heart; (*fig.*) bosom, mind, soul; courage; core, middle; love, affection; hearts (*cards*).
coexistant [kɔɛgzis'tɑ̃], *a.* coexistent.
coexistence [kɔɛgzis'tɑ̃:s], *n.f.* coexistence.
coexister [kɔɛgzis'te], *v.i.* to coexist.
coffre [kɔfr], *n.m.* chest, trunk; coffer; (*Naut.*) mooring buoy; boot (*of a car*).
coffre-fort [kɔfrə'fɔ:r], *n.m.* (*pl.* **coffres-forts**) strongbox, safe.

coffret [kɔ'frɛ], *n.m.* little chest, casket.
cogitation [kɔʒita'sjɔ̃], *n.f.* cogitation, reflection.
cognac [kɔ'ɲak], *n.m.* cognac, brandy.
cognasse [kɔ'ɲas], *n.f.* wild quince.
cognassier [kɔɲa'sje], *n.m.* quince tree.
cognée [kɔ'ɲe], *n.f.* axe, hatchet.
cogner [kɔ'ɲe], *v.t.* to knock in, to drive in; to thump.—*v.i.* to hit, to bump (*contre*); to knock (*engine*). **se cogner**, *v.r.* to knock (*against*).
cohabitant [kɔabi'tɑ̃], *a.* cohabiting (*with*).
cohabitation [kɔabita'sjɔ̃], *n.f.* cohabitation.
cohabiter [kɔabi'te], *v.i.* to cohabit.
cohérence [kɔe'rɑ̃:s], *n.f.* coherence.
cohérent [kɔe'rɑ̃], *a.* coherent.
cohériter [kɔeri'te], *v.i.* to inherit conjointly.
cohéritier [kɔeri'tje], *n.m.* (*fem.* **-ière**) coheir, co-heiress.
cohésif [kɔe'zif], *a.* (*fem.* **-sive**) cohesive.
cohésion [kɔe'zjɔ̃], *n.f.* cohesion.
cohorte [kɔ'ɔrt], *n.f.* cohort; (*poet.*) troop, host; (*colloq.*) crew, gang.
cohue [kɔ'y], *n.f.* throng, mob, crush.
coi [kwa], *a.* (*fem.* **coite** (1)) quiet, calm, still.
coiffe [kwaf], *n.f.* hood, headdress.
coiffer [kwa'fe], *v.t.* to put on the head of; to dress the hair of; (*fig.*) to infatuate.—*v.i.* to dress hair; to become; to suit. **se coiffer**, *v.r.* to put one's hat on; to do one's hair.
coiffeur [kwa'fœ:r], *n.m.* (*fem.* **-euse**) hairdresser.—*n.f.* (**-euse**) lady's dressing-table.
coiffure [kwa'fy:r], *n.f.* headdress, hairstyle.
coin [kwɛ̃], *n.m.* corner, angle, nook; (*Coin. etc.*) stamp.
coincer [kwɛ̃'se], *v.t.* (*conjug. like* COMMENCER) to wedge. **se coincer**, *v.r.* to jam (*of machines*).
coïncidence [kɔɛ̃si'dɑ̃:s], *n.f.* coincidence.
coïncident [kɔɛ̃si'dɑ̃], *a.* coincident.
coïncider [kɔɛ̃si'de], *v.i.* to coincide, to be coincident.
coing [kwɛ̃], *n.m.* quince.
coïntéressé [kɔɛ̃tere'se], *a.* jointly interested.—*n.m.* (*fem.* **-ée**) associate, partner.
coite (1) [kwat], [COI].
coite (2), **coitte** [COUETTE].
cojouissance [kɔʒwi'sɑ̃:s], *n.f.* (*Law*) joint use.
coke [kɔk], *n.m.* coke.
cokéfier [kɔke'fje], *v.t.* to coke.
col [kɔl], *n.m.* neck (*of a bottle, dress etc.*); collar; pass, col (*of mountain*).
colback [kɔl'bak], *n.m.* busby.
colchique [kɔl'ʃik], *n.m.* (*Bot.*) meadow saffron, colchicum.
colégataire [kɔlega'tɛ:r], *n.* co-legatee.
coléoptère [kɔleɔp'tɛ:r], *a.* coleopterous.—*n.m.* beetle.
colère [kɔ'lɛ:r], *n.f.* anger, wrath, rage, fury.
colérique [kɔle'rik], *a.* choleric, irascible.
colibri [kɔli'bri], *n.m.* hummingbird.
colifichet [kɔlifi'ʃɛ], *n.m.* trinket, knick-knack.
colimaçon [kɔlima'sɔ̃], *n.m.* snail; *escalier en colimaçon*, spiral staircase.
colin-maillard [kɔlɛ̃ma'ja:r], *n.m. inv.* blindman's-buff.
colique [kɔ'lik], *n.f.* colic, stomach ache.
colis [kɔ'li], *n.m.* package, parcel, case.
collaborateur [kɔlabɔra'tœ:r], *n.m.* (*fem.* **-trice**) collaborator.

collaboration [kɔlabɔra'sjɔ̃], *n.f.* collaboration.
collaborer [kɔlabɔ're], *v.i.* to collaborate.
collage [kɔ'la:ʒ], *n.m.* pasting, gluing; paperhanging; (*Art*) collage.
collant [kɔ'lɑ̃], *a.* sticky; tight, close-fitting.
collatéral [kɔllate'ral], *a.* (*m. pl.* **-aux**) collateral.
collatéralement [kɔllateral'mɑ̃], *adv.* collaterally.
collation [kɔlla'sjɔ̃], *n.f.* light meal; comparison (*of documents etc.*).
collationnement [kɔllasjɔn'mɑ̃], *n.m.* collating, comparing.
collationner [kɔllasjɔ'ne], *v.t.* to collate, to compare.—*v.i.* to have a snack.
colle [kɔl], *n.f.* paste, gum; poser; sham, fib.
collecte [kɔ'lɛkt], *n.f.* collection (*of money etc.*); collect (*prayer*).
collecteur [kɔlɛk'tœ:r], *n.m.* (*fem.* **-trice**) collector.
collectif [kɔlɛk'tif], *a.* (*fem.* **-tive**) collective.
collection [kɔlɛk'sjɔ̃], *n.f.* collection; set.
collectionner [kɔlɛksjɔ'ne], *v.t.* to collect, to make collections of things.
collectionneur [kɔlɛksjɔ'nœ:r], *n.m.* (*fem.* **-euse**) collector.
collectivement [kɔlɛktiv'mɑ̃], *adv.* collectively.
collectivisme [kɔlɛkti'vism], *n.m.* collectivism.
collectiviste [kɔlɛkti'vist], *n.* collectivist.
collectivité [kɔlɛktivi'te], *n.f.* collectivity; common ownership.
collège [kɔ'lɛ:ʒ], *n.m.* college; grammar school.
collégien [kɔle'ʒjɛ̃], *n.m.* (*fem.* **-enne**) high-school boy or girl.
collègue [kɔl'lɛg], *n.* colleague.
coller [kɔ'le], *v.t.* to paste, to glue; to stick together.—*v.i.* to stick, to adhere. **se coller**, *v.r.* to stick to.
collerette [kɔl'rɛt], *n.f.* collar (*for ladies*).
collet [kɔ'lɛ], *n.m.* collar (*of gown etc.*); cape; flange; snare.
colleter [kɔl'te], *v.t.* (*conjug. like* APPELER) to collar, to seize by the neck.—*v.i.* to set snares. **se colleter**, *v.r.* to come to grips (*with someone*).
colleur [kɔ'lœ:r], *n.m.* (*fem.* **-euse**) gluer, paster, paperhanger; billposter.
collier [kɔ'lje], *n.m.* necklace; gold chain (*of knightly orders etc.*); collar (*for animals*).
colline [kɔ'lin], *n.f.* hill, hillock.
collision [kɔli'zjɔ̃], *n.f.* collision.
collocation [kɔllɔka'sjɔ̃], *n.f.* classification.
colloque [kɔl'lɔk], *n.m.* colloquy, conference.
collusion [kɔlly'zjɔ̃], *n.f.* collusion.
collusoire [kɔlly'zwa:r], *a.* collusory, collusive.
Colomb [kɔ'lɔ̃], *m.* Columbus.
colombe [kɔ'lɔ̃:b], *n.f.* (*poet.*) pigeon, dove.
Colombie [kɔlɔ̃'bi], **la**, *f.* Colombia.
colombien [kɔlɔ̃'bjɛ̃], *a.* (*fem.* **-enne**) Colombian.—*n.m.* (**Colombien**, *fem.* **-enne**) Colombian (*person*).
colombier [kɔlɔ̃'bje], *n.m.* dovecot, pigeon house.
colombin [kɔlɔ̃'bɛ̃], *a.* columbine; dove-color.
colombophile [kɔlɔ̃bɔ'fil], *a.* and *n.* pigeon fancier.

colon [kɔ'lɔ̃], *n.m.* colonist, planter; settler.
côlon [ko'lɔ̃], *n.m.* (*Anat.*) colon.
colonel [kɔlɔ'nɛl], *n.m.* colonel; (*Av.*) group captain.
colonial [kɔlɔ'njal], *a.* (*m. pl.* -**aux**) colonial. —*n.m.* (*fem.* -**e**) colonial.
colonie [kɔlɔ'ni], *n.f.* colony, settlement; *colonie de vacances,* holiday camp.
colonisation [kɔlɔniza'sjɔ̃], *n.f.* colonization.
coloniser [kɔlɔni'ze], *v.t.* to colonize.
colonnade [kɔlɔ'nad], *n.f.* (*Arch.*) colonnade.
colonne [kɔ'lɔn], *n.f.* column, pillar; column (*of units, tens etc.*).
colonnette [kɔlɔ'nɛt], *n.f.* little column.
colorant [kɔlɔ'rɑ̃], *a.* coloring.—*n.m.* dye.
coloration [kɔlɔra'sjɔ̃], *n.f.* coloration, staining.
colorer [kɔlɔ're], *v.t.* to color, to dye; to varnish. **se colorer,** *v.r.* to color (*of a thing*).
coloriage [kɔlɔ'rja:ʒ], *n.m.* (*Paint.*) coloring.
colorier [kɔlɔ'rje], *v.t.* to color, to stain (*a drawing etc.*).
coloris [kɔlɔ'ri], *n.m.* coloring, art of coloring.
coloriste [kɔlɔ'rist], *n.* colorer; colorist.
colossal [kɔlɔ'sal], *a.* (*m. pl.* -**aux**) colossal.
colosse [kɔ'lɔs], *n.m.* colossus, giant.
colportage [kɔlpɔr'ta:ʒ], *n.m.* hawking, peddling.
colporter [kɔlpɔr'te], *v.t.* to hawk about; to spread.
colporteur [kɔlpɔr'tœ:r], *n.m.* hawker, pedlar.
coltiner [kɔlti'ne], *v.t.* to carry heavy loads (*on head and back*).
coltineur [kɔlti'nœ:r], *n.m.* coal heaver, loadporter.
colza [kɔl'za], *n.m.* colza, rape, rape seed.
coma [kɔ'ma], *n.m.* coma.
comateux [kɔma'tø], *a.* (*fem.* -**euse**) comatose.
combat [kɔ̃'ba], *n.m.* combat, fight, battle, contest; struggle; *hors de combat,* disabled.
combattant [kɔ̃ba'tɑ̃], *n.m.* combatant; champion; *anciens combattants,* ex-service men.
combattre [kɔ̃'batr], *v.t.* (*conjug. like* BATTRE) to fight, to combat, to wage war against, to strive against.—*v.i.* to fight, to vie, to struggle. **se combattre,** *v.r.* to combat; to contend with each other.
combien [kɔ̃'bjɛ̃], *adv.* how much, how many; how; how far; how long.
combinaison [kɔ̃binɛ'zɔ̃], *n.f.* combination; contrivance, scheme; overalls; slip (*woman's undergarment*).
combiné [kɔ̃bi'ne], *n.m.* (*Chem.*) compound; (*Rad.*) radiogram.
combiner [kɔ̃bi'ne], *v.t.* to combine; (*fig.*) to contrive.
comble [kɔ̃bl], *n.m.* heaping up above a full measure; summit; (*fig.*) zenith; (*pl.*) roof timbers.—*a.* full, heaped up, full to the top; *salle comble,* house full.
comblement [kɔ̃blə'mɑ̃], *n.m.* filling up, heaping up.
combler [kɔ̃'ble], *v.t.* to heap up, to fill up; to complete; to overwhelm.
comburant [kɔ̃by'rɑ̃], *a.* (*Chem.*) causing burning (*of oxygen etc.*).—*n.m.* fuel.
combustibilité [kɔ̃bystibili'te], *n.f.* combustibility.

combustible [kɔ̃bys'tibl], *a.* combustible.—*n.m.* combustible; fuel, firing.
combustion [kɔ̃bys'tjɔ̃], *n.f.* combustion, flame.
comédie [kɔme'di], *n.f.* comedy; theatre; players.
comédien [kɔme'djɛ̃], *n.m.* (*fem.* -**enne**) comedian, actor, actress, player; (*fig.*) hypocrite.
comestible [kɔmɛs'tibl], *a.* edible, eatable.—*n.m.* eatable; (*pl.*) eatables.
comète [kɔ'mɛt], *n.f.* comet.
comice [kɔ'mis], *n.m.* meeting; electoral meeting; *comice agricole,* agricultural show.
comique [kɔ'mik], *a.* comic; comical, ludicrous.—*n.m.* comic art, comedy.
comiquement [kɔmik'mɑ̃], *adv.* comically.
comité [kɔmi'te], *n.m.* committee, board.
commandant [kɔmɑ̃'dɑ̃], *n.m.* commanding.— *n.m.* (*fem.* -**e**) commander, commanding officer, commandant; major.
commande [kɔ'mɑ̃:d], *n.f.* order; (*Mach.*) driving wheel.
commandement [kɔmɑ̃d'mɑ̃], *n.m.* command; authority, control; order; commandment, law.
commander [kɔmɑ̃'de], *v.t.* to command, to order; to govern; to overlook.—*v.i.* to command, to have authority. **se commander,** *v.r.* to control oneself.
commandeur [kɔmɑ̃'dœ:r], *n.m.* commander (*in orders of knighthood*).
commanditaire [kɔmɑ̃di'tɛ:r], *n.* silent partner.
commandite [kɔmɑ̃'dit], *n.f.* limited partnership.
commanditer [kɔmɑ̃di'te], *v.t.* to finance (*a commercial undertaking*).
commando [kɔmɑ̃'do], *n.m.* commando.
comme [kɔm], *adv.* as; like, such as; almost, nearly, as if; how, in what way, to what extent.—*conj.* as, since, because.
commémoraison [kɔmemɔrɛ'zɔ̃], *n.f.* (*R.-C. Ch.*) commemoration, remembrance.
commémoratif [kɔmemɔra'tif], *a.* (*fem.* -**tive**) commemorative.
commémoration [kɔmemɔra'sjɔ̃], *n.f.* commemoration.
commémorer [kɔmemɔ're], *v.t.* to commemorate, to remember.
commençant [kɔmɑ̃'sɑ̃], *n.m.* (*fem.* -**e**) beginner, novice.
commencement [kɔmɑ̃s'mɑ̃], *n.m.* beginning, commencement.
commencer [kɔmɑ̃'se], *v.t.*, *v.i.* (*see Verb Tables*) to begin, to commence; to initiate.
commensal [kɔmɑ̃'sal], *n.m.* (*m. pl.* -**aux**) habitual guest; fellow boarder, messmate.
commensurable [kɔmɑ̃sy'rabl], *a.* commensurable.
comment [kɔ'mɑ̃], *adv.* how, in what manner; why, wherefore.—*int.* what! indeed!— *n.m.* the why and wherefore.
commentaire [kɔmɑ̃'tɛ:r], *n.m.* commentary, exposition; (*fig.*) unfavorable comment.
commentateur [kɔmɑ̃ta'tœ:r], *n.m.* (*fem.* -**trice**) commentator, annotator.
commenter [kɔmɑ̃'te], *v.t.* to comment on, to explain, to annotate.—*v.i.* to criticize adversely.

commérage [kɔme'ra:ʒ], *n.m.* gossip, tittle-tattle.

commerçant [kɔmɛr'sɑ̃], *a.* commercial, mercantile, trading.—*n.m.* (*fem.* **-e**) merchant, tradesman, shopkeeper.

commerce [kɔ'mɛrs], *n.m.* commerce, trade, trading, traffic; intercourse, dealings.

commercer [kɔmɛr'se], *v.i.* (*conjug. like* COMMENCER) to trade, to deal.

commercial [kɔmɛr'sjal], *a.* (*m. pl.* **-aux**) commercial.

commercialement [kɔmɛrsjal'mɑ̃], *adv.* commercially.

commercialisation [kɔmɛrsjaliza'sjɔ̃], *n.f.* commercialization.

commercialiser [kɔmɛrsjali'ze], *v.t.* to commercialize.

commère [kɔ'mɛr], *n.f.* godmother; gossip.

commettre [kɔ'mɛtr], *v.t. irr.* (*conjug. like* METTRE) to commit, to perpetrate; to appoint, to empower; to entrust. **se commettre,** *v.r.* to commit oneself.

commis (1) [kɔ'mi], *n.m.* (*fem.* **commise**) clerk; ***commis voyageur,*** commercial traveller.

commis (2) [kɔ'mi], *a.* committed, appointed.

commisération [kɔmizera'sjɔ̃], *n.f.* commiseration, compassion, pity.

commissaire [kɔmi'sɛ:r], *n.m.* commissioner; manager, steward, trustee; purser (*of a vessel*).

commissaire-priseur [kɔmisɛrpri'zœ:r], *n.m.* auctioneer; valuer, appraiser.

commissariat [kɔmisa'rja], *n.m.* commissaryship, trusteeship; (*Mil., Navy*) commissariat; police station.

commission [kɔmi'sjɔ̃], *n.f.* commission, charge; errand; power; (*Comm.*) percentage; warrant.

commissionnaire [kɔmisjɔ'nɛ:r], *n.m.* commission agent, commissionnaire; messenger, porter.

commissionner [kɔmisjɔ'ne], *v.t.* to empower, to commission; to order (*goods*).

commode [kɔ'mɔd], *a.* convenient, commodious, handy; comfortable, suitable; easy.—*n.f.* chest of drawers, commode.

commodément [kɔmɔde'mɑ̃], *adv.* commodiously, conveniently; comfortably, suitably.

commodité [kɔmɔdi'te], *n.f.* convenience, accommodation.

commotion [kɔmɔ'sjɔ̃], *n.f.* commotion; shock; concussion.

commotionné [kɔmɔsjɔ'ne], *a.* suffering from concussion.

commuable [kɔ'mɥabl], *a.* commutable.

commun [kɔ'mœ̃], *a.* common; usual, ordinary; mean, vulgar; ***le bien commun,*** the common weal; ***lieux communs,*** commonplaces.—*n.m.* common people.

communal [kɔmy'nal], *a.* (*m. pl.* **-aux**) communal, parochial; common.—*n.m. pl.* (*biens*) ***communaux,*** communal property.

communauté [kɔmyno'te], *n.f.* community, society, corporation.

commune [kɔ'myn], *n.f.* commune (*parish, township, in France*).

communément [kɔmyne'mɑ̃], *adv.* commonly, usually.

communiant [kɔmy'njɑ̃], *n.m.* (*fem.* **-e**) communicant.

communicatif [kɔmynika'tif], *a.* (*fem.* **-tive**) communicative, open.

communication [kɔmynika'sjɔ̃], *n.f.* intercourse, communication; (*Teleph.*) call.

communicativement [kɔmynikativ'mɑ̃], *adv.* communicatively.

communier [kɔmy'nje], *v.i.* to communicate, to receive the sacrament.

communion [kɔmy'njɔ̃], *n.f.* communion, fellowship; persuasion; sacrament.

communiqué [kɔmyni'ke], *n.m.* statement, communiqué.

communiquer [kɔmyni'ke], *v.t.* to communicate, to impart; to tell, to acquaint.—*v.i.* to be in contact *or* correspondence (*with*).

communisant [kɔmyni'zɑ̃], *a.* communistic. —*n.m.* (*fem.* **-e**) fellow traveller.

communisme [kɔmy'nism], *n.m.* communism.

communiste [kɔmy'nist], *n.* communist.

commutable [kɔmy'tabl], [COMMUABLE].

commutateur [kɔmyta'tœ:r], *n.m.* (*Elec.*) switch.

compact [kɔ̃'pakt], *a.* compact, dense.

compagne [kɔ̃'paɲ], *n.f.* female companion, consort; playmate.

compagnie [kɔ̃pa'ɲi], *n.f.* society, companionship; company; (*Comm.*) company.

compagnon [kɔ̃pa'ɲɔ̃], *n.m.* companion, comrade; playmate; mate; (*Bot.*) campion.

comparable [kɔ̃pa'rabl], *a.* comparable.

comparablement [kɔ̃parablə'mɑ̃], *adv.* in comparison (*with*).

comparaison [kɔ̃parɛ'zɔ̃], *n.f.* comparison; similitude.

comparaître [kɔ̃pa'rɛ:tr], *v.i. irr.* (*conjug. like* CONNAÎTRE) to appear (*before a tribunal*).

comparant [kɔ̃pa'rɑ̃], *n.m.* (*fem.* **-e**) person appearing in court on a summons.

comparatif [kɔ̃para'tif], *a.* (*fem.* **-tive**) comparative.—*n.m.* comparative degree.

comparativement [kɔ̃parativ'mɑ̃], *adv.* comparatively.

comparer [kɔ̃pa're], *v.t.* to compare. **se comparer,** *v.r.* to be compared.

compartiment [kɔ̃parti'mɑ̃], *n.m.* compartment, division.

compas [kɔ̃'pɑ], *n.m.* pair of compasses; mariner's compass.

compassé [kɔ̃pa'se], *a.* formal, stiff, starchy.

compasser [kɔ̃pa'se], *v.t.* to measure, set out; to proportion, to regulate; (*fig.*) to weigh, to consider.

compassion [kɔ̃pa'sjɔ̃], *n.f.* compassion, pity, mercy.

compatibilité [kɔ̃patibili'te], *n.f.* compatibility.

compatible [kɔ̃pa'tibl], *a.* compatible, consistent.

compatir [kɔ̃pa'ti:r], *v.i.* to sympathize; to agree, to be compatible (*with*).

compatissant [kɔ̃pati'sɑ̃], *a.* compassionate, tender.

compatriote [kɔ̃patri'ɔt], *n.* compatriot, fellow countryman.

compendium [kɔ̃pɑ̃'djɔm], *n.m.* summary.

compensable [kɔ̃pɑ̃'sabl], *a.* that may be compensated.

compensation [kɔ̃pɑ̃sa'sjɔ̃], *n.f.* compensation, amends, reparation.

compromis

compensatoire [kɔ̃pɑ̃sa'twaːr], *a.* compensatory.
compenser [kɔ̃pɑ̃'se], *v.t.* to counterbalance, to compensate, to make up for. **se compenser,** *v.r.* to compensate each other; to be set off against.
compère [kɔ̃'pɛːr], *n.m.* godfather; (*fig.*) gossip, crony; confederate.
compétence [kɔ̃pe'tɑ̃ːs], *n.f.* competence, cognizance; (*fig.*) department, province; proficiency.
compétent [kɔ̃pe'tɑ̃], *a.* competent, qualified; (*fig.*) suitable, requisite.
compétiteur [kɔ̃peti'tœːr], *n.m.* (*fem.* **-trice**) competitor, candidate.
compétitif [kɔ̃peti'tif], *a.* (*fem.* **-tive**) competitive.
compétition [kɔ̃peti'sjɔ̃], *n.f.* competition, rivalry.
compilateur [kɔ̃pila'tœːr], *n.m.* compiler.
compilation [kɔ̃pila'sjɔ̃], *n.f.* compilation.
compiler [kɔ̃pi'le], *v.t.* to compile.
complainte [kɔ̃'plɛ̃ːt], *n.f.* tragic *or* plaintive ballad, lament; (*fig.*) lamentation.
complaire [kɔ̃'plɛːr], *v.i. irr.* (*conjug. like* PLAIRE) to be pleasing (*à*). **se complaire,** *v.r.* to delight (*dans* or *à*).
complaisamment [kɔ̃plɛza'mɑ̃], *adv.* complaisantly, obligingly.
complaisance [kɔ̃plɛ'zɑ̃ːs], *n.f.* complaisance, good nature; complacency.
complaisant [kɔ̃plɛ'zɑ̃], *a.* affable, civil, obliging, kind.—*n.m.* (*fem.* **-e**) flatterer; go-between.
complément [kɔ̃ple'mɑ̃], *n.m.* complement; (*Gram.*) object; extension (*of subject*).
complémentaire [kɔ̃plemɑ̃'tɛːr], *a.* complementary, completing.
complet [kɔ̃'plɛ], *a.* (*fem.* **-plète**) complete, whole; full, filled.—*n.m.* complement, full number; suit (*of clothes*).
complètement [kɔ̃plɛt'mɑ̃], *adv.* completely, entirely, thoroughly.
complétement [kɔ̃plet'mɑ̃], *n.m.* finishing, completion.
compléter [kɔ̃ple'te], *v.t.* (*conjug. like* CÉDER) to complete, to perfect; to fill up.
complexe [kɔ̃'plɛks], *a.* complex, complicated.—*n.m.* **complexe d'infériorité,** inferiority complex.
complexion [kɔ̃plɛk'sjɔ̃], *n.f.* constitution; disposition, humor, temper.
complexité [kɔ̃plɛksi'te], *n.f.* complexity.
complication [kɔ̃plika'sjɔ̃], *n.f.* complication, intricacy.
complice [kɔ̃'plis], *a.* accessory, privy to.—*n.* accomplice, accessory.
complicité [kɔ̃plisi'te], *n.f.* complicity, participation.
compliment [kɔ̃pli'mɑ̃], *n.m.* compliment; (*pl.*) regards, congratulations.
complimenter [kɔ̃plimɑ̃'te], *v.t.* to compliment, to congratulate.
complimenteur [kɔ̃plimɑ̃'tœːr], *a. and n.m.* (*fem.* **-euse**) over-complimentary; obsequious (person).
compliqué [kɔ̃pli'ke], *a.* complicated, intricate.
compliquer [kɔ̃pli'ke], *v.t.* to complicate, to entangle. **se compliquer,** *v.r.* to become complicated.

complot [kɔ̃'plo], *n.m.* plot, conspiracy; **chef du complot,** ringleader.
comploter [kɔ̃plɔ'te], *v.t.* to plot.
comploteur [kɔ̃plɔ'tœːr], *n.m.* plotter, schemer.
componction [kɔ̃pɔ̃k'sjɔ̃], *n.f.* compunction; solemn manners *or* expression.
comportement [kɔ̃pɔrtə'mɑ̃], *n.m.* demeanor, deportment, behavior.
comporter [kɔ̃pɔr'te], *v.t.* to permit, to allow; to require; to comprise. **se comporter,** *v.r.* to behave; to act, to manage.
composant [kɔ̃po'zɑ̃], *n.m.* (*Chem.*) component, constituent.
composé [kɔ̃po'ze], *a.* composed, compound. —*n.m.* compound.
composer [kɔ̃po'ze], *v.t.* to compose, to compound, to make up; to form, to create; to adjust, to regulate; **composer un numéro,** to dial a number.—*v.i.* to compound, to compromise, to make up.
composeuse [kɔ̃po'zøːz], *n.f.* type-setting machine.
composite [kɔ̃po'zit], *a.* composite.
compositeur [kɔ̃pozi'tœːr], *n.m.* (*fem.* **-trice**) composer (*of music*); (*Print.*) compositor.
composition [kɔ̃pozi'sjɔ̃], *n.f.* composition; chemical composition; settlement; (*fig.*) disposition; (*Print.*) composing.
compost [kɔ̃'pɔst], *n.m.* (*Agric.*) compost.
composter [kɔ̃pɔs'te], *v.t.* to compost; to date *or* obliterate (*ticket etc.*).
compote [kɔ̃'pɔt], *n.f.* stewed fruit, compote.
compotier [kɔ̃pɔ'tje], *n.m.* fruit dish.
compréhensibilité [kɔ̃preɑ̃sibili'te], *n.f.* comprehensibility.
compréhensible [kɔ̃preɑ̃'sibl], *a.* understandable, intelligible.
compréhensif [kɔ̃preɑ̃'sif], *a.* (*fem.* **-sive**) comprehensive; broadminded.
compréhension [kɔ̃preɑ̃'sjɔ̃], *n.f.* comprehension; (*fig.*) understanding, intelligence.
compréhensivité [kɔ̃preɑ̃sivi'te], *n.f.* comprehensiveness, faculty of comprehending.
comprendre [kɔ̃'prɑ̃ːdr], *v.t. irr.* (*conjug. like* PRENDRE) to include, to comprise; to understand, to conceive, to realize.
compresse [kɔ̃'prɛːs], *n.f.* (*Surg.*) compress, pledget.
compresseur [kɔ̃prɛ'sœːr], *a.* compressive.— *n.m.* compressor, roller.
compressif [kɔ̃prɛ'sif], *a.* (*fem.* **-ssive**) compressive, repressive.
compression [kɔ̃prɛ'sjɔ̃], *n.f.* compression; (*fig.*) constraint.
comprimable [kɔ̃pri'mabl], *a.* compressible.
comprimé [kɔ̃pri'me], *a.* compressed, condensed; kept under.—*n.m.* (*Pharm.*) tabloid, tablet.
comprimer [kɔ̃pri'me], *v.t.* to compress, to condense; to repress, to restrain.
compris [kɔ̃'pri], *a.* understood; included.
compromettant [kɔ̃prɔmɛ'tɑ̃], *a.* compromising; damaging.
compromettre [kɔ̃prɔ'mɛtr], *v.t. irr.* (*conjug. like* METTRE) to expose, to commit, to compromise; to jeopardize.—*v.i.* to compromise; to submit to arbitration. **se compromettre,** *v.r.* to compromise oneself.
compromis [kɔ̃prɔ'mi], *n.m.* mutual agreement, compromise.

comptabilité [kɔ̃tabili'te], *n.f.* accountancy, bookkeeping; accountant's department.
comptable [kɔ̃'tabl], *a.* responsible for accounts; accountable, responsible.—*n.m.* accountant, bookkeeper; (*Naut.*) purser.
comptant [kɔ̃'tã], *a.m.* (*of money*) ready; (*of payment*) in cash.—*n.m.* ready money, cash.
compte [kɔ̃:t], *n.m.* reckoning; account, score, statement, report; (*fig.*) profit; esteem, value; *se rendre compte de*, to realize.
compte-gouttes [kɔ̃t'gut], *n.m. inv.* (*Med.*) drop-tube, dropper; filler; (*fig.*) *au compte-gouttes*, sparingly.
compte-pas [kɔ̃tə'pa], *n.m.* pedometer.
compter [kɔ̃'te], *v.t.* to count, to calculate, to compute; to pay down; to comprise.—*v.i.* to reckon, to count; to be reckoned; to expect; to intend; to rely (*sur*). **se compter**, *v.r.* to be reckoned *or* included.
compteur [kɔ̃'tœ:r], *a.* and *n.m.* (*fem.* **-euse**) that counts; computer.—*n.m.* meter; (*C*) *compteur de stationnement*, parking meter.
comptoir [kɔ̃'twa:r], *n.m.* counter; cashier's desk; counting-house; branch bank; factory.
compulser [kɔ̃pyl'se], *v.t.* to inspect (*documents etc.*).
computation [kɔ̃pyta'sjɔ̃], *n.f.* computation.
computer [kɔ̃py'te], *v.t.* to compute.
comtal [kɔ̃'tal], *a.* (*m. pl.* **-aux**) pertaining to an earl *or* a countess.
comte [kɔ̃:t], *n.m.* count; earl.
comté [kɔ̃'te], *n.m.* county, shire; earldom.
comtesse [kɔ̃'tɛs], *n.f.* countess.
concassage [kɔ̃ka'sa:ʒ], *n.m.* pounding, crushing.
concasser [kɔ̃ka'se], *v.t.* to pound, to crush.
concasseur [kɔ̃ka'sœ:r], *n.m.* crushing-mill; steam roller.
concave [kɔ̃'ka:v], *a.* concave.
concavité [kɔ̃kavi'te], *n.f.* concave; concavity.
concéder [kɔ̃se'de], *v.t.* (*conjug. like* CÉDER) to grant, to concede, to allow.
concentration [kɔ̃sãtra'sjɔ̃], *n.f.* concentration; condensation; *camp de concentration*, concentration camp.
concentré [kɔ̃sã'tre], *a.* concentrated; (*fig.*) silent, reserved.—*n.m.* extract.
concentrer [kɔ̃sã'tre], *v.t.* to concentrate, to focus; (*fig.*) to repress, to smother (*anger etc.*). **se concentrer**, *v.r.* to concentrate; to withdraw within oneself.
concentrique [kɔ̃sã'trik], *a.* concentric.
concentriquement [kɔ̃sãtrik'mã], *adv.* concentrically.
concept [kɔ̃'sɛpt], *n.m.* concept.
conceptibilité [kɔ̃sɛptibili'te], *n.f.* conceivability.
conceptible [kɔ̃sɛp'tibl], *a.* conceivable.
conceptif [kɔ̃sɛp'tif], *a.* (*fem.* **-tive**) conceptive.
conception [kɔ̃sɛp'sjɔ̃], *n.f.* conception; thought, notion; understanding.
concernant [kɔ̃sɛr'nã], *prep.* concerning, relating to.
concerner [kɔ̃sɛr'ne], *v.t.* to relate (*to*), to concern, to regard.
concert [kɔ̃'sɛ:r], *n.m.* harmony; concert; (*fig.*) concord.
concertant [kɔ̃sɛr'tã], *a.* in concert (*of a piece of music*).—*n.m.* (*fem.* **-e**) performer in a concert.
concerté [kɔ̃sɛr'te], *a.* concerted, united; studied, stiff.
concerter [kɔ̃sɛr'te], *v.t.* to contrive, to concert; to plan, to devise; to compose (*one's demeanor etc.*). **se concerter**, *v.r.* to plan together, to concert.
concertiste [kɔ̃sɛr'tist], *n.* performer (*at a concert*).
concerto [kɔ̃sɛr'to], *n.m.* concerto.
concession [kɔ̃sɛ'sjɔ̃], *n.f.* concession, privilege.
concessionnaire [kɔ̃sɛsjɔ'nɛ:r], *a.* concessionary.—*n.* grantee.
concevable [kɔ̃s'vabl], *a.* conceivable, imaginable.
concevoir [kɔ̃sə'vwa:r], *v.t. irr.* (*conjug. like* RECEVOIR) to become pregnant, to conceive; to imagine, to understand; to comprehend.
concierge [kɔ̃'sjɛrʒ], *n.* concierge, hall-porter, caretaker.
conciergerie [kɔ̃sjɛrʒə'ri], *n.f.* caretaker's lodge; *La Conciergerie*, a prison in Paris (*during French Revolution*).
concile [kɔ̃'sil], *n.m.* an assembly of prelates and doctors, council, synod.
conciliable [kɔ̃si'ljabl], *a.* reconcilable.
conciliabule [kɔ̃silja'byl], *n.m.* conventicle, secret meeting.
conciliaire [kɔ̃si'ljɛ:r], *a.* of *or* belonging to a council.
conciliant [kɔ̃si'ljã], *a.* conciliating, reconciling.
conciliateur [kɔ̃silja'tœ:r], *a.* (*fem.* **-trice**) conciliatory.—*n.m.* (*fem.* **-trice**) conciliator.
conciliation [kɔ̃silja'sjɔ̃], *n.f.* reconciliation.
conciliatoire [kɔ̃silja'twa:r], *a.* conciliatory.
concilier [kɔ̃si'lje], *v.t.* to conciliate, to reconcile; to gain, to win, to procure. **se concilier**, *v.r.* to gain, to win.
concis [kɔ̃'si], *a.* concise, brief, short.
concision [kɔ̃si'zjɔ̃], *n.f.* brevity, conciseness.
concitoyen [kɔ̃sitwa'jɛ̃], *n.m.* (*fem.* **-enne**) fellow citizen.
conclave [kɔ̃'kla:v], *n.m.* conclave, assembly of all the cardinals.
concluant [kɔ̃kly'ã], *a.* conclusive, decisive.
conclure [kɔ̃'kly:r], *v.t. irr.* to conclude; to infer; to judge.
conclusif [kɔ̃kly'zif], *a.* (*fem.* **-sive**) conclusive.
conclusion [kɔ̃kly'zjɔ̃], *n.f.* conclusion, upshot.
concombre [kɔ̃'kɔ̃:br], *n.m.* cucumber.
concomitance [kɔ̃kɔmi'tã:s], *n.f.* concomitance.
concomitant [kɔ̃kɔmi'tã], *a.* concomitant.
concordance [kɔ̃kɔr'dã:s], *n.f.* agreement; (*Bibl. etc.*) concordance.
concordant [kɔ̃kɔr'dã], *a.* concordant.
concordat [kɔ̃kɔr'da], *n.m.* concordat, agreement; bankrupt's certificate.
concordataire [kɔ̃kɔrda'tɛ:r], *n.m.* certificated bankrupt.
concorde [kɔ̃'kɔrd], *n.f.* concord, agreement, harmony; good understanding.
concorder [kɔ̃kɔr'de], *v.i.* to be in accord, to agree, to concur.
concourir [kɔ̃ku'ri:r], *v.i. irr.* (*conjug. like* COURIR) to concur; to contribute to; to cooperate; to compete; to converge.

concours [kɔ̃'kuːr], *n.m.* concourse, meeting; coincidence; competition; co-operation; competitive examination; assistance.

concret [kɔ̃'krɛ], *a.* (*fem.* **-crète**) concrete, solid.

concubine [kɔ̃ky'bin], *n.f.* concubine.

concupiscence [kɔ̃kypi'sɑ̃ːs], *n.f.* concupiscence, lust.

concurremment [kɔ̃kyra'mɑ̃], *adv.* concurrently; jointly, together.

concurrence [kɔ̃ky'rɑ̃ːs], *n.f.* competition; rivalry, opposition.

concurrent [kɔ̃ky'rɑ̃], *n.m.* (*fem.* **-e**) competitor, rival.

concussion [kɔ̃ky'sjɔ̃], *n.f.* extortion, embezzlement.

concussionnaire [kɔ̃kysjɔ'nɛːr], *a.* guilty of peculation, of bribery *or* of extortion.— *n.m.* extortioner, peculator, embezzler.

condamnable [kɔ̃dɑ'nabl], *a.* condemnable, blamable.

condamnation [kɔ̃dɑnɑ'sjɔ̃], *n.f.* condemnation, judgment, sentence; penalty.

condamné [kɔ̃dɑ'ne], *a.* condemned, convicted.—*n.m.* (*fem.* **-ée**) convict.

condamner [kɔ̃dɑ'ne], *v.t.* to condemn, to sentence, to convict; (*fig.*) to blame, to censure.

condensateur [kɔ̃dɑ̃sa'tœːr], *n.m.* (*Phys.*) condenser.

condensation [kɔ̃dɑ̃sɑ'sjɔ̃], *n.f.* condensation.

condensé [kɔ̃dɑ̃'se], *a.* condensed.—*n.m.* digest.

condenser [kɔ̃dɑ̃'se], *v.t.* to condense.

condenseur [kɔ̃dɑ̃'sœːr], *n.m.* condenser.

condescendance [kɔ̃desɑ̃'dɑ̃ːs], *n.f.* condescension.

condescendant [kɔ̃desɑ̃'dɑ̃], *a.* condescending, complying.

condescendre [kɔ̃de'sɑ̃ːdr], *v.i.* to condescend, to comply.

condiment [kɔ̃di'mɑ̃], *n.m.* condiment, seasoning.

condisciple [kɔ̃di'sipl], *n.m.* schoolfellow.

condit [kɔ̃'di], *n.m.* candied fruit.

condition [kɔ̃di'sjɔ̃], *n.f.* condition; rank, station; domestic service; situation, circumstances; terms; *à condition* or *sous condition*, on condition, on approval.

conditionné [kɔ̃disjɔ'ne], *a.* conditioned (*bien* or *mal*); well-conditioned, sound.

conditionnel [kɔ̃disjɔ'nɛl], *a.* conditional.— *n.m.* (*Gram.*) conditional.

conditionnellement [kɔ̃disjɔnɛl'mɑ̃], *adv.* conditionally, on condition.

conditionner [kɔ̃disjɔ'ne], *v.t.* to condition; to dry (*silk*); to season (*wood*).

condoléance [kɔ̃dɔle'ɑ̃ːs], *n.f.* condolence.

condominium [kɔ̃dɔmi'njɔm], *n.m.* condominium.

condor [kɔ̃'dɔːr], *n.m.* condor.

conductance [kɔ̃dyk'tɑ̃ːs], *n.f.* (*Elec.*) conductance.

conducteur [kɔ̃dyk'tœːr], *n.m.* (*fem.* **-trice**) conductor, conductress, leader, guide; driver, drover.—*a.* (*Phys.*) conducting.

conductibilité [kɔ̃dyktibili'te], *n.f.* conductibility.

conductible [kɔ̃dyk'tibl], *a.* conductible.

conduction [kɔ̃dyk'sjɔ̃], *n.f.* (*Phys.*) conduction; (*Civic Law*) hiring.

conduire [kɔ̃'dɥiːr], *v.t. irr.* to conduct, to lead, to guide; to drive; to accompany; to bring, to take; to be at the head of.—*v.i.* to lead (*à*); to drive. **se conduire**, *v.r.* to conduct *or* behave oneself.

conduit [kɔ̃'dɥi], *n.m.* conduit, duct, pipe, passage, tube, canal.

conduite [kɔ̃'dɥit], *n.f.* conducting, leading, driving, steering; management, direction, administration; conveyance, distribution; scheme, plan; water-pipe, conduit; behavior, demeanor; prudence, discretion.

cône [koːn], *n.m.* cone; *en cône*, conical.

confection [kɔ̃fɛk'sjɔ̃], *n.f.* preparation, making; making of ready-made clothes; (*Pharm.*) confection; *vêtements de confection*, ready-made clothes.

confectionner [kɔ̃fɛksjɔ'ne], *v.t.* to make, to manufacture, to finish.

confectionneur [kɔ̃fɛksjɔ'nœːr], *n.m.* (*fem.* **-euse**) maker, finisher (*of wearing apparel*), clothier, outfitter.

confédération [kɔ̃federɑ'sjɔ̃], *n.f.* confederation, confederacy; *la Confédération Générale du Travail* (*abbr.* **C.G.T.**), the French equivalent of the C.I.O.

confédéré [kɔ̃fede're], *a.* and *n.m.* (*fem.* **-ée**) confederate, associate.

confédérer (se) [səkɔ̃fede're], *v.r.* (*conjug. like* CÉDER) to combine, to enter into confederation.

conférence [kɔ̃fe'rɑ̃ːs], *n.f.* conference; lecture.

conférencier [kɔ̃ferɑ̃'sje], *n.m.* (*fem.* **-ière**) lecturer.

conférer [kɔ̃fe're], *v.t.* (*conjug. like* CÉDER) to confer, to bestow, to grant; to compare.—*v.i.* to consult together, to confer.

confesse [kɔ̃'fɛs], *n.f.* (*always used with* **à** *or* **de**) *aller à confesse*, to go to confession; *venir de confesse*, to come from confession.

confesser [kɔ̃fɛ'se], *v.t.* to confess; to acknowledge, to admit; to shrive. **se confesser**, *v.r.* to confess one's sins, to confess (*to a priest*).

confesseur [kɔ̃fɛ'sœːr], *n.m.* (father) confessor.

confession [kɔ̃fɛ'sjɔ̃], *n.f.* confession, acknowledgment, avowal.

confessionnal [kɔ̃fɛsjɔ'nal], *n.m.* confessional.

confetti [kɔ̃fɛt'ti], *n.m. pl.* confetti.

confiance [kɔ̃'fjɑ̃ːs], *n.f.* confidence, reliance, trust.

confiant [kɔ̃'fjɑ̃], *a.* confident, unsuspecting, sanguine; self-conceited.

confidemment [kɔ̃fida'mɑ̃], *adv.* confidentially.

confidence [kɔ̃fi'dɑ̃ːs], *n.f.* confidence; secret.

confident [kɔ̃fi'dɑ̃], *n.m.* (*fem.* **-ente**) confidant, confidante.

confidentiel [kɔ̃fidɑ̃'sjɛl], *a.* confidential.

confidentiellement [kɔ̃fidɑ̃sjɛl'mɑ̃], *adv.* confidentially.

confier [kɔ̃'fje], *v.t.* to confide, to entrust, to commit (*à*). **se confier**, *v.r.* to trust in; to unbosom oneself (*à*).

configuration [kɔ̃figyrɑ'sjɔ̃], *n.f.* configuration, form, shape, lay (*of the land*).

confinement [kɔ̃fin'mɑ̃], *n.m.* confinement; overcrowding.

confiner [kɔ̃fi'ne], v.t. to confine, to imprison; **air confiné**, stuffy atmosphere.—v.i. to border upon, to be adjoining. **se confiner**, v.r. to confine or to limit oneself.

confins [kɔ'fɛ̃], n.m. (used only in pl.) confines, borders, limits.

confire [kɔ̃'fiːr]. v.t. irr. to preserve; to candy, to pickle.

confirmatif [kɔ̃firma'tif], a. (fem. -tive) confirmative.

confirmation [kɔ̃firma'sjɔ̃], n.f. confirmation, ratification.

confirmer [kɔ̃fir'me], v.t. to strengthen, to corroborate; to confirm; to ratify. **se confirmer**, v.r. to be confirmed.

confiscable [kɔ̃fis'kabl], a. confiscable, forfeitable.

confiscation [kɔ̃fiska'sjɔ̃], n.f. confiscation, forfeiture.

confiserie [kɔ̃fiz'ri], n.f. confectionery; confectioner's shop.

confiseur [kɔ̃fi'zœːr] n.m. (fem. -euse) confectioner.

confisquer [kɔ̃fis'ke], v.t. to confiscate, to forfeit, to impound; to seize.

confit (1) [kɔ'fi], p.p. [CONFIRE].

confit (2) [kɔ'fi], n.m. meat, poultry etc. preserved in fat; bran mash (for pigs etc.).

confiture [kɔ̃fi'tyːr], n.f. preserve, jam.

conflagration [kɔ̃flagra'sjɔ̃], n.f. conflagration.

conflit [kɔ'fli], n.m. conflict, collision, encounter; contention, strife, contest, rivalry; jar, clash.

confluent [kɔ̃fly'ã], n.m. confluence, junction (of rivers).

confluer [kɔ̃fly'e], v.i. to meet, to unite (of streams etc.).

confondre [kɔ'fɔ̃ːdr], v.t. to confound, to confuse; to mix, to mingle; (fig.) to amaze, to astound. **se confondre**, v.r. to mingle, to be lost in; to be confounded, to be abashed.

conformation [kɔ̃fɔrma'sjɔ̃], n.f. conformation, structure.

conforme [kɔ̃'fɔrm], a. conformable; congenial, consistent; **pour copie conforme**, certified true copy.

conformé [kɔ̃fɔr'me], a. formed, shaped (bien or mal).

conformément [kɔ̃fɔrme'mã], adv. suitably; according to.

conformer [kɔ̃fɔr'me], v.t. to give form to. **se conformer**, v.r. to conform, to comply (with).

conformisme [kɔ̃fɔr'mism], n.m. conformity, orthodoxy.

conformité [kɔ̃fɔrmi'te], n.f. likeness, conformity, compliance.

confort [kɔ'fɔːr], n.m. comfort, ease.

confortable [kɔ̃fɔr'tabl], a. cosy, comfortable.

confortablement [kɔ̃fɔrtablə'mã], adv. comfortably.

confraternité [kɔ̃fratɛrni'te], n.f. fraternity, brotherhood.

confrère [kɔ'frɛːr], n.m. colleague; fellow member.

confrérie [kɔ̃fre'ri], n.f. brotherhood, fraternity.

confrontation [kɔ̃frɔ̃ta'sjɔ̃], n.f. confrontation; comparing.

confronter [kɔ̃frɔ̃'te], v.t. to confront; to compare.

confus [kɔ'fy], a. confused, muddled, vague, indistinct, obscure; abashed, crestfallen.

confusément [kɔ̃fyze'mã], adv. confusedly, vaguely, dimly.

confusion [kɔ̃fy'zjɔ̃], n.f. confusion, disorder; bewilderment; embarrassment, shame, blush; misunderstanding.

congé [kɔ'ʒe], n.m. leave, permission; leave of absence, holiday; discharge, dismissal; notice (to quit); permit.

congédier [kɔ̃ʒe'dje], v.t. to discharge, to dismiss, to pay off; to disband.

congélateur [kɔ̃ʒela'tœːr], n.m. refrigerator.

congeler [kɔ̃ʒ'le], v.t., **se congeler**, v.r. (conjug. like AMENER) to congeal, to freeze; to coagulate.

congénère [kɔ̃ʒe'nɛːr], a. congeneric; of same species (Philol.) cognate.

congénial [kɔ̃ʒe'njal], a. (m. pl. -aux) congenial, of the same nature.

congénital [kɔ̃ʒeni'tal], a. (m. pl. -aux) congenital, hereditary.

congère [kɔ'ʒɛːr], n.f. snowdrift.

congestion [kɔ̃ʒɛs'tjɔ̃], n.f. congestion.

conglomération [kɔ̃glɔmera'sjɔ̃], n.f. conglomeration.

conglomérer [kɔ̃glɔme're], v.t. (conjug. like CÉDER) to conglomerate.

congolais [kɔ̃gɔ'lɛ], a. Congolese.— (**Congolais**, fem. -aise) Congolese (person).

congratulation [kɔ̃gratyla'sjɔ̃], n.f. congratulation.

congratulatoire [kɔ̃gratyla'twaːr], a. congratulatory.

congratuler [kɔ̃graty'le], v.t. to congratulate.

congre [kɔ̃:gr], n.m. conger, conger eel.

congrégation [kɔ̃grega'sjɔ̃], n.f. fraternity, brotherhood, general body (of an order etc.).

congrès [kɔ'grɛ], n.m. congress.

congressiste [kɔ̃grɛ'sist], n.m. (Am.) congressman.

congru [kɔ'gry], a. suitable, consistent, congruous, proper.

congruité [kɔ̃gryi'te], n.f. congruity, consistency, propriety.

congrûment [kɔ̃gry'mã], adv. congruously, properly.

conifère [kɔni'fɛːr], a. coniferous.—n.m. conifer.

conique [kɔ'nik], a. conical.

conjecture [kɔ̃ʒɛk'tyːr], n.f. conjecture, surmise, guess.

conjecturer [kɔ̃ʒɛkty're], v.t. to conjecture, to guess, to surmise.

conjoindre [kɔ̃'ʒwɛ̃ːdr], v.t. irr. (conjug. like CRAINDRE) to conjoin, to unite together; to marry.

conjoint [kɔ'ʒwɛ̃], a. conjoined, united, joint. —n.m. (fem. -e) spouse.

conjointement [kɔ̃ʒwɛ̃'mã], adv. conjointly, unitedly.

conjoncteur [kɔ̃ʒɔ̃k'tœːr], n.m. (Elec.) circuit breaker, switch key.

conjonctif [kɔ̃ʒɔ̃k'tif], a. (fem. -tive) conjunctive.

conjonction [kɔ̃ʒɔ̃k'sjɔ̃], n.f. conjunction; union, connection; coition.

conjoncture [kɔ̃ʒɔ̃k'tyːr], n.f. conjuncture, juncture.

conjugaison [kɔ̃ʒyge'zɔ̃], n.f. conjugation.

conjugal [kɔ̃ʒy'gal], *a.* (*m. pl.* **-aux**) conjugal.
conjugalement [kɔ̃ʒygal'mɑ̃], *adv.* conjugally.
conjugué [kɔ̃ʒy'ge], *a.* (*Mech.*) twin.
conjuguer [kɔ̃ʒy'ge], *v.t.* (*Gram.*) to conjugate.
conjuration [kɔ̃ʒyra'sjɔ̃], *n.f.* conspiracy, plot.
conjuré [kɔ̃ʒy're], *a.* confederate, sworn.—*n.m.* (*fem.* **-ée**) conspirator, plotter.
conjurer [kɔ̃ʒy're], *v.t.* to implore; to conspire; to swear; to conjure up; to exorcize, to ward off.
connaissable [kɔnɛ'sabl], *a.* recognizable.
connaissance [kɔnɛ'sɑ̃:s], *n.f.* knowledge, learning; consciousness (*de*); acquaintance; intercourse; (*Law*) cognizance; (*pl.*) attainments.
connaisseur [kɔnɛ'sœ:r], *a.* (*fem.* **-euse**) expert, skilled.—*n.m.* connoisseur, expert.
connaître [kɔ'nɛ:tr], *v.t. irr.* to know, to perceive; to understand; to be acquainted with.—*v.i.* to have *or* take cognizance of; to deal with (*a matter*). **se connaître**, *v.r.* to know oneself; to know each other; to be a connoisseur.
connecter [kɔnɛk'te], *v.t.* to connect; (*Elec.*) to couple (up), to group.
connétable [kɔne'tabl], *n.m.* high constable.
connexion [kɔnɛk'sjɔ̃], *n.f.* connection, affinity.
connexité [kɔnɛksi'te], *n.f.* connection.
connivence [kɔni'vɑ̃:s], *n.f.* connivance.
connotation [kɔnɔta'sjɔ̃], *n.f.* connotation.
connu [kɔ'ny], *a.* known, understood.—*n.m.* that which is known.
conque [kɔ̃:k], *n.f.* conch, sea-shell.
conquérant [kɔ̃ke'rɑ̃], *a.* conquering.—*n.m.* (*fem.* **-e**) conqueror.
conquérir [kɔ̃ke'ri:r], *v.t. irr.* (*conjug. like* ACQUÉRIR) to conquer, to subdue (*a country*); (*fig.*) to gain, to win over.
conquête [kɔ̃'kɛ:t], *n.f.* conquest, acquisition.
conquis [kɔ̃'ki], *a.* conquered.
consacrant [kɔ̃sa'krɑ̃], *a.* consecrating, officiating.—*n.m.* consecrator, officiant.
consacrer [kɔ̃sa'kre], *v.t.* to consecrate, to dedicate, to sanctify; to sanction; to authorize. **se consacrer**, *v.r.* to devote oneself.
consciemment [kɔ̃sja'mɑ̃], *adv.* consciously, knowingly.
conscience [kɔ̃'sjɑ̃:s], *n.f.* consciousness, perception; conscience, conscientiousness.
consciencieusement [kɔ̃sjɑ̃sjøz'mɑ̃], *adv.* conscientiously.
consciencieux [kɔ̃sjɑ̃'sjø], *a.* (*fem.* **-euse**) conscientious.
conscient [kɔ̃'sjɑ̃], *a.* conscious (*de*); self-conscious.
conscription [kɔ̃skrip'sjɔ̃], *n.f.* enlistment; conscription.
conscrit [kɔ̃'skri], *a.* conscript.—*n.m.* conscript; (raw) recruit.
consécrateur [kɔ̃sekra'tœ:r], [CONSACRANT].
consécration [kɔ̃sekra'sjɔ̃], *n.f.* consecration, ordination.
consécutif [kɔ̃seky'tif], *a.* (*fem.* **-tive**) consecutive, following.
consécutivement [kɔ̃sekytiv'mɑ̃], *adv.* consecutively.
conseil [kɔ̃'sɛ:j], *n.m.* counsel, advice; resolution; council, board; (*Law*) counsel;

conseil d'administration, board of directors; **Conseil d'État**, Council of State; **Conseil de Sécurité** (*de l'O.N.U.*), (U.N.) Security Council; **conseil judiciaire**, guardian; **conseil de guerre**, court-martial; council of war; **conseil municipal**, town council, corporation.
conseiller [kɔ̃sɛ'je], *v.t.* to advise, to counsel; to recommend.—*n.m.* (*fem.* **-ère**) counsellor, adviser, councillor.
consensus [kɔ̃sɑ̃'sy:s], *n.m.* consent, consensus.
consentant [kɔ̃sɑ̃'tɑ̃], *a.* consenting, willing.
consentement [kɔ̃sɑ̃t'mɑ̃], *n.m.* consent, assent.
consentir [kɔ̃sɑ̃'ti:r], *v.i. irr.* (*conjug. like* SENTIR) to consent, to agree, to acquiesce (*à*).
conséquemment [kɔ̃seka'mɑ̃], *adv.* consequently, accordingly.
conséquence [kɔ̃se'kɑ̃:s], *n.f.* consequence, sequel; issue, result; inference, conclusion.
conséquent [kɔ̃se'kɑ̃], *a.* rational, consistent.—*n.m.* (*Log., Math.*) consequent; **par conséquent**, consequently.
conservateur [kɔ̃sɛrva'tœ:r], *a.* (*fem.* **-trice**) preserving, conservative.—*n.m.* (*fem.* **-trice**) Conservative, Tory.—*n.m.* guardian, keeper, curator.
conservatif [kɔ̃sɛrva'tif], *a.* (*fem.* **-tive**) conservative, preservative.—*n.m.* preservative.
conservation [kɔ̃sɛrva'sjɔ̃], *n.f.* conservation, preservation; registration (*of mortgages etc.*).
conservatisme [kɔ̃sɛrva'tism], *n.m.* conservatism.
Conservatoire [kɔ̃sɛrva'twa:r], *n.m.* academy of music and school of elocution in Paris.
conserve [kɔ̃'sɛrv], *n.f.* preserve; tinned (*Am.* canned) food.
conserver [kɔ̃sɛr've], *v.t.* to preserve; to keep. **se conserver**, *v.r.* to be preserved; to bear one's age well; to keep (*of meat, fruit etc.*).
considérable [kɔ̃side'rabl], *a.* considerable, notable, eminent; **peu considérable**, of little importance.
considérablement [kɔ̃siderablə'mɑ̃], *adv.* considerably.
considérant [kɔ̃side'rɑ̃], *conj. phr.* **considérant que**, whereas.
considération [kɔ̃sidera'sjɔ̃], *n.f.* consideration, attention; motive, grounds; regard, respect.
considérément [kɔ̃sidere'mɑ̃], *adv.* considerately, prudently.
considérer [kɔ̃side're], *v.t.* (*conjug. like* CÉDER) to consider, to look at, to view; to ponder; to value, to esteem; to pay attention to. **se considérer**, *v.r.* to esteem oneself.
consignataire [kɔ̃siɲa'tɛ:r], *n.* trustee, depositary.
consignateur [kɔ̃siɲa'tœ:r], *n.m.* (*fem.* **-trice**) (*Comm.*) consignor, shipper.
consignation [kɔ̃siɲa'sjɔ̃], *n.f.* (*Comm.*) deposit, consignment.
consigne [kɔ̃'siɲ], *n.f.* (*Mil.*) order, password; (*fig.*) strict command, prohibition; (*Rail.*) baggage check room, cloak-room; (*sch.*) gating, detention.

consigner [kɔ̃siˈɲe], *v.t.* to deposit; to consign; to record, to register; to keep in; to refuse admittance to.

consistance [kɔ̃sisˈtãːs], *n.f.* consistency; firmness, stability; (*fig.*) credit, consideration.

consistant [kɔ̃sisˈtã], *a.* consisting of; consistent, firm, solid.

consister [kɔ̃sisˈte], *v.i.* to consist; to be composed of.

consistoire [kɔ̃sisˈtwaːr], *n.m.* consistory.

consolable [kɔ̃soˈlabl], *a.* consolable.

consolant [kɔ̃soˈlã], *a.* consoling, comforting.

consolateur [kɔ̃solaˈtœːr], *a.* (*fem.* **-trice**) consoling.—*n.m.* (*fem.* **-trice**) comforter, consoler.

consolation [kɔ̃solaˈsjɔ̃], *n.f.* consolation, comfort, solace.

console [kɔ̃ˈsɔl], *n.f.* console, bracket.

consoler [kɔ̃soˈle], *v.t.* to console, to comfort. **se consoler**, *v.r.* to console oneself.

consolidation [kɔ̃solidaˈsjɔ̃], *n.f.* consolidation; strengthening; funding (*of interest*).

consolidé [kɔ̃soliˈde], *a.* funded.—*n.m.* (*Fin.*, *used only in pl.*) consols.

consolider [kɔ̃soliˈde], *v.t.* to consolidate; to strengthen. **se consolider**, *v.r.* to consolidate, to grow firm.

consommable [kɔ̃soˈmabl], *a.* consumable, edible.

consommateur [kɔ̃somaˈtœːr], *n.m.* (*fem.* **-trice**) consumer (*as opposed to producer*), eater, drinker.

consommation [kɔ̃somaˈsjɔ̃], *n.f.* consumption; consummation; food, drinks, refreshments.

consommé [kɔ̃soˈme], *a.* consumed; consummated; consummate; accomplished.—*n.m.* clear soup.

consommer [kɔ̃soˈme], *v.t.* to consume, to use; (*fig.*) to consummate, to accomplish.—*v.i.* (*pop.*) to have a drink.

consomption [kɔ̃sɔ̃pˈsjɔ̃], *n.f.* consumption, using up; (*Path.*) phthisis, decline.

consonance [kɔ̃soˈnãːs], *n.f.* consonance; (*fig.*) concord.

consonant [kɔ̃soˈnã], *a.* consonant.

consonne [kɔ̃ˈsɔn], *n.f.* consonant.

consort [kɔ̃ˈsɔːr], *a.* consort (*of the husband or wife of a sovereign*).—*n.m.* (*used only in pl.*) consorts, confederates; (*Law*) associates.

consortium [kɔ̃sɔrˈsjɔm], *n.m.* consortium.

conspirateur [kɔ̃spiraˈtœːr], *n.m.* (*fem.* **-trice**) conspirator.—*a.* conspiring.

conspiration [kɔ̃spiraˈsjɔ̃], *n.f.* conspiracy, plot.

conspirer [kɔ̃spiˈre], *v.t.* to plot.—*v.i.* to conspire, to concur; to plot.

conspuer [kɔ̃sˈpɥe], *v.t.* to despise, to spurn; to boo, to barrack.

constamment [kɔ̃staˈmã] *adv.* steadily; continually, constantly.

constance [kɔ̃sˈtãːs], *n.f.* constancy; perseverance.

constant [kɔ̃sˈtã], *a.* constant, faithful, unshaken; persevering.

constatation [kɔ̃stataˈsjɔ̃], *n.f.* authentication; statement; findings.

constater [kɔ̃staˈte], *v.t.* to prove, to verify; to ascertain; to state, to declare.

constellation [kɔ̃stɛlaˈsjɔ̃], *n.f.* constellation.

constellé [kɔ̃stɛˈle], *a.* constellated; studded.

consteller [kɔ̃stɛˈle], *v.t.* to constellate, to stud.

consternation [kɔ̃stɛrnaˈsjɔ̃], *n.f.* consternation, dismay.

consterné [kɔ̃stɛrˈne], *a.* dismayed, overwhelmed.

consterner [kɔ̃stɛrˈne], *v.t.* to dismay, to dishearten; to astound, to amaze.

constipation [kɔ̃stipaˈsjɔ̃], *n.f.* constipation, costiveness.

constipé [kɔ̃stiˈpe], *a.* costive, constipated.

constiper [kɔ̃stiˈpe], *v.t.* to constipate, to bind.

constituant [kɔ̃stiˈtɥã], *a.* constituent.

constituer [kɔ̃stiˈtɥe], *v.t.* to constitute; to establish; to appoint; to settle, to assign. **se constituer**, *v.r.* to constitute oneself.

constitution [kɔ̃stityˈsjɔ̃], *n.f.* constitution; establishment; settlement (*of an annuity etc.*); temperament.

constitutionnel [kɔ̃stitysjoˈnɛl], *a.* (*fem.* **-elle**) constitutional.

constitutionnellement [kɔ̃stitysjonɛlˈmã], *adv.* constitutionally.

constriction [kɔ̃strikˈsjɔ̃], *n.f.* constriction.

constringent [kɔ̃strɛ̃ˈʒã], *a.* constringent.

constructeur [kɔ̃strykˈtœːr], *n.m.* constructor, builder; shipbuilder, shipwright.

construction [kɔ̃strykˈsjɔ̃], *n.f.* building, construction; erection, structure.

constructivité [kɔ̃stryktiviˈte], *n.f.* constructiveness.

construire [kɔ̃sˈtrɥiːr], *v.t.* irr. (*conjug. like* CONDUIRE) to construct, to build, to erect.

consul [kɔ̃ˈsyl], *n.m.* consul.

consulaire [kɔ̃syˈlɛːr], *a.* consular.

consulat [kɔ̃syˈla], *n.m.* consulate, consulship.

consultant [kɔ̃sylˈtã], *a.* consulting.—*n.m.* (*fem.* **-e**) consultant, consulting physician.

consultatif [kɔ̃syltaˈtif], *a.* (*fem.* **-tive**) consultative, deliberative.

consultation [kɔ̃syltaˈsjɔ̃], *n.f.* consultation; opinion, advice; ***cabinet de consultation***, surgery.

consulter [kɔ̃sylˈte], *v.t.* to consult; to refer to.—*v.i.* to deliberate, to take counsel (*together*). **se consulter**, *v.r.* to consider, to reflect, to deliberate.

consumable [kɔ̃syˈmabl], *a.* consumable.

consumant [kɔ̃syˈmã], *a.* consuming, devouring, burning.

consumer [kɔ̃syˈme], *v.t.* to consume; to destroy, to wear out, to wear away, to squander, to waste. **se consumer**, *v.r.* to decay, to waste away, to wear out; to undermine one's health.

contact [kɔ̃ˈtakt], *n.m.* contact; touch; connection; (*Motor.*) ***clé de contact***, ignition key; (*Opt.*) ***verres de contact***, contact lenses.

contagieux [kɔ̃taˈʒjø], *a.* (*fem.* **-euse**) contagious, infectious.

contagion [kɔ̃taˈʒjɔ̃], *n.f.* contagion, infection.

contamination [kɔ̃taminaˈsjɔ̃], *n.f.* contamination, pollution.

contaminé [kɔ̃tamiˈne], *a.* polluted, contaminated.

contaminer [kɔ̃tamiˈne], *v.t.* to contaminate.

conte [kɔ̃ːt], *n.m.* story, tale; (*fig.*) fib, fairytale.

contemplateur [kɔ̃tɑ̃pla'tœ:r], *n.m.* (*fem.* **-trice**) contemplator.

contemplatif [kɔ̃tɑ̃pla'tif], *a.* (*fem.* **-tive**) contemplative.

contemplation [kɔ̃tɑ̃plɑ'sjɔ̃], *n.f.* contemplation, meditation.

contempler [kɔ̃tɑ̃'ple], *v.t.* to contemplate, to survey, to gaze on.—*v.i.* to contemplate, to meditate, to reflect.

contemporain [kɔ̃tɑ̃pɔ'rɛ̃], *a.* and *n.m.* (*fem.* **-e**) contemporary.

contempteur [kɔ̃tɑ̃p'tœ:r], *a.* (*fem.* **-trice**) contemptuous, scornful, insolent, disdainful.—*n.m.* contemner, despiser, scorner.

contenance [kɔ̃t'nɑ̃:s], *n.f.* capacity; volume; (*fig.*) countenance, air, bearing.

contenant [kɔ̃t'nɑ̃], *a.* holding, containing.— *n.m.* holder, container.

contenir [kɔ̃t'ni:r], *v.t. irr.* (*conjug. like* TENIR) to contain, to comprise, to hold, to include; to restrain. **se contenir**, *v.r.* to keep within bounds, to be moderate; to control oneself.

content [kɔ̃'tɑ̃], *a.* content, satisfied; pleased, glad, gratified.

contentement [kɔ̃tɑ̃t'mɑ̃], *n.m.* contentment, satisfaction; comfort, pleasure.

contenter [kɔ̃tɑ̃'te], *v.t.* to content, to satisfy; to please, to gratify. **se contenter**, *v.r.* to be satisfied, to be content.

contentieusement [kɔ̃tɑ̃sjøz'mɑ̃], *adv.* contentiously, litigiously.

contentieux [kɔ̃tɑ̃'sjø], *a.* (*fem.* **-euse**) contentious, disputable; litigious; in dispute; quarrelsome. — *n.m.* debatable matter; *bureau du contentieux*, legal department.

contention [kɔ̃tɑ̃'sjɔ̃], *n.f.* application, vehemence; contention, contest, debate, strife.

contenu [kɔ̃t'ny], *a.* contained; (*fig.*) kept in control.—*n.m.* contents; enclosure; terms (*of a letter etc.*).

conter [kɔ̃'te], *v.t.* to tell, to relate; *en conter*, to tell fibs.

contestable [kɔ̃tɛs'tabl], *a.* disputable, debatable.

contestant [kɔ̃tɛs'tɑ̃], *a.* contending (*at law*). —*n.m.* (*fem.* **-e**) contesting party, litigant.

contestation [kɔ̃tɛsta'sjɔ̃], *n.f.* contestation, contest; dispute, debate; litigation.

contester [kɔ̃tɛs'te], *v.t.* to dispute, to contest; to contend, to debate.—*v.i.* to quarrel; to be contentious.

conteur [kɔ̃'tœ:r], *a.* (*fem.* **-euse**) who tells stories.—*n.m.* (*fem.* **-euse**) story teller; (*fig.*) fibber.

contexte [kɔ̃'tɛkst], *n.m.* context; text (*of a deed*).

contexture [kɔ̃tɛks'ty:r], *n.f.* contexture (*of the muscles etc.*); texture (*of materials*).

contigu [kɔ̃ti'gy], *a.* (*fem.* **-ë**) contiguous, adjoining.

contiguïté [kɔ̃tigɥi'te], *n.f.* contiguity.

continence [kɔ̃ti'nɑ̃:s], *n.f.* continency, chastity.

continent (1) [kɔ̃ti'nɑ̃], *a.* chaste, continent.

continent (2) [kɔ̃ti'nɑ̃], *n.m.* continent, mainland.

continental [kɔ̃tinɑ̃'tal], *a.* (*m. pl.* **-aux**) continental.

contingence [kɔ̃tɛ̃'ʒɑ̃:s], *n.f.* contingency, casualty.

contingent [kɔ̃tɛ̃'ʒɑ̃], *a.* contingent, accidental, casual.—*n.m.* quota; contingent.

continu [kɔ̃ti'ny], *a.* continuous, continual, uninterrupted; incessant.

continuation [kɔ̃tinɥɑ'sjɔ̃], *n.f.* continuation.

continuel [kɔ̃ti'nɥɛl], *a.* (*fem.* **-elle**) continual, perpetual.

continuellement [kɔ̃tinɥɛl'mɑ̃], *adv.* continually, perpetually.

continuer [kɔ̃ti'nɥe], *v.t.* to continue, to proceed with; to lengthen.—*v.i.* to continue, to keep on. **se continuer**, *v.r.* to be continued, to last.

continuité [kɔ̃tinɥi'te], *n.f.* continuity; continuance.

continûment [kɔ̃tiny'mɑ̃], *adv.* unremittingly, continuously, without cessation.

contorsion [kɔ̃tɔr'sjɔ̃], *n.f.* contortion; grimace.

contorsionniste [kɔ̃tɔrsjɔ'nist], *n.* contortionist.

contour [kɔ̃'tu:r], *n.m.* circuit, circumference; contour, outline.

contourné [kɔ̃tur'ne], *a.* distorted, bizarre.

contournement [kɔ̃turnə'mɑ̃], *n.m.* outlining, tracing; winding, convolution; *route de contournement*, by-pass (*road*).

contourner [kɔ̃tur'ne], *v.t.* to outline; to distort, to twist; to twist, turn, go *or* wind round. **se contourner**, *v.r.* to grow crooked, to become bent.

contractant [kɔ̃trak'tɑ̃], *a.* *partie contractante*, contracting party.—*n.m.* (*fem.* **-e**) stipulator.

contracté [kɔ̃trak'te], *a.* contracted, shortened.

contracter [kɔ̃trak'te], *v.t.* to contract; to covenant, to stipulate, to bargain; to make a contract; to acquire. **se contracter**, *v.r.* to contract, to shrink; to shorten; to be settled by contract.

contraction [kɔ̃trak'sjɔ̃], *n.f.* contraction.

contractuel [kɔ̃trak'tɥɛl], *a.* (*fem.* **-elle**) stipulated, done by contract.

contractuellement [kɔ̃traktɥɛl'mɑ̃], *adv.* by contract.

contradicteur [kɔ̃tradik'tœ:r], *n.m.* contradictor; (*Law*) adversary.

contradiction [kɔ̃tradik'sjɔ̃], *n.f.* contradiction, denial; opposition; discrepancy.

contradictoire [kɔ̃tradik'twa:r], *a.* contradictory, inconsistent, conflicting; *examen contradictoire*, cross-examination.

contraindre [kɔ̃'trɛ̃:dr], *v.t. irr.* (*conjug. like* CRAINDRE) to constrain, to compel, to coerce; to restrain; to squeeze. **se contraindre**, *v.r.* to restrain oneself, to refrain.

contraint [kɔ̃'trɛ̃], *a.* constrained, forced.

contrainte [kɔ̃'trɛ̃:t], *n.f.* constraint, compulsion, coercion; restraint; uneasiness.

contraire [kɔ̃'trɛ:r], *a.* contrary, opposite, inconsistent; adverse; prejudicial.—*n.m.* contrary, opposite, reverse.

contrairement [kɔ̃trɛr'mɑ̃], *adv.* contrarily, in opposition.

contralte [kɔ̃'tralt], **contralto** [kɔ̃tral'to], *n.m.* contralto, counter-tenor.

contrariant [kɔ̃tra'rjɑ̃], *a.* thwarting, annoying.

contrarier [kɔ̃tra'rje], *v.t.* to thwart, to counteract, to baffle; to annoy; to disappoint.

83

contrariété [kɔ̃trarje'te], *n.f.* contrariety, contradiction; annoyance; hindrance, disappointment; *quelle contrariété!* how annoying!

contrastant [kɔ̃tras'tɑ̃], *a.* contrasting.

contraste [kɔ̃'trast], *n.m.* contrast, opposition.

contraster [kɔ̃tras'te], *v.t., v.i.* to contrast.

contrat [kɔ̃'tra], *n.m.* contract, deed; agreement, bargain.

contravention [kɔ̃travɑ̃'sjɔ̃], *n.f.* contravention.

contre [kɔ̃:tr], *prep.* against, versus, contrary to; close up against, near; in exchange for; *ci-contre,* opposite, in the margin; *par contre,* on the other hand; *pour et contre,* pro and con.—*adv.* against.—*n.m.* the opposite side of the question; *le pour et le contre,* the pros and cons.

contre-allée [kɔ̃tra'le], *n.f.* side lane, side alley.

contre-amiral [kɔ̃trami'ral], *n.m.* (*pl.* **contre-amiraux**) rear-admiral.

contre-attaque [kɔ̃tra'tak], *n.f.* (*Mil.*) counter-attack.

contre-avions [kɔ̃tra'vjɔ̃], *a.* anti-aircraft.

contrebalancer [kɔ̃trabalɑ̃'se], *v.t.* (*conjug. like* COMMENCER) to counterbalance, to counterpoise.

contrebande [kɔ̃trə'bɑ̃:d], *n.f.* contraband, smuggling; smuggled goods.

contrebandier [kɔ̃trəbɑ̃'dje], *n.m.* smuggler, gunrunner; smuggling vessel.

contre-bas (en) [ɑ̃kɔ̃trə'ba], *adv.* downwards.

contrebasse [kɔ̃trə'bɑ:s], *n.f.* double bass.

contre-bord (à) [akɔ̃trə'bɔ:r], *adv.* (*Naut.*) on the opposite tack.

contre-boutant [kɔ̃trəbu'tɑ̃], **contre-boutement** [kɔ̃trəbut'mɑ̃], *n.m.* abutment, buttress.

contre-bouter [kɔ̃trəbu'te], *v.t.* to buttress; to shore up.

contrecarrer [kɔ̃trəka're], *v.t.* to thwart, to oppose.

contre-cœur [kɔ̃trə'kœ:r], *n.m.* chimney-back; *à contre-cœur,* reluctantly.

contre-coup [kɔ̃trə'ku], *n.m.* rebound, repercussion; (*fig.*) consequence, result; *par contre-coup,* as a consequence.

contredanse [kɔ̃trə'dɑ̃:s], *n.f.* quadrille.

contredire [kɔ̃trə'di:r], *v.t. irr.* (*conjug. like* MÉDIRE) to contradict, to gainsay; (*Law*) to disprove. **se contredire,** *v.r.* to contradict oneself; to be contradictory.

contredisant [kɔ̃tradi'zɑ̃], *a.* contradicting.

contredit [kɔ̃trə'di], *n.m.* contradiction; answer, reply; *sans contredit,* incontestably.

contrée [kɔ̃'tre], *n.f.* country, region, district.

contre-échange [kɔ̃tre'ʃɑ̃:ʒ], *n.m.* mutual exchange.

contre-écrou [kɔ̃tre'kru], *n.m.* lock nut.

contre-épreuve [kɔ̃tre'prœ:v], *n.f.* (*Engraving*) counter-proof; (*fig.*) feeble imitation.

contre-espionnage [kɔ̃trɛspjɔ'na:ʒ], *n.m.* counter-espionage.

contrefaçon [kɔ̃trəfa'sɔ̃], *n.f.* counterfeiting, forgery.

contrefacteur [kɔ̃trəfak'tœ:r], *n.m.* counterfeiter (*of coins etc.*); forger (*of bills etc.*); infringer (*of patents etc.*).

contrefaire [kɔ̃trə'fɛ:r], *v.t. irr.* (*conjug. like* FAIRE) to counterfeit, to imitate; to copy; to forge; to mimic; to disguise. **se contrefaire,** *v.r.* to dissemble, to sham.

contrefaiseur [kɔ̃trəfə'zœ:r], *n.m.* (*fem.* **-euse**) counterfeiter, mimic, imitator.

contrefait [kɔ̃trə'fɛ], *a.* counterfeit; deformed.

contre-fiche [kɔ̃trə'fiʃ], *n.f.* (*Carp.*) prop, strut.

contre-haut (en) [ɑ̃kɔ̃trə'o], *adv.* upwards.

contre-jour [kɔ̃trə'ʒu:r], *n.m.* (*Phot.*) low light; *à contre-jour,* against the light.

contremaître [kɔ̃trə'mɛ:tr], *n.m.* overseer, foreman.

contremander [kɔ̃trəmɑ̃'de], *v.t.* to countermand.

contremarche [kɔ̃trə'marʃ], *n.f.* countermarch.

contremarcher [kɔ̃trəmar'ʃe], *v.i.* to countermarch.

contremarque [kɔ̃trə'mark], *n.f.* countermark; (*Theat.*) pass-out check.

contre-mesure [kɔ̃trəmə'zy:r], *n.f.* countermeasure.

contre-offensive [kɔ̃trɔfɑ̃'si:v], *n.f.* counterattack.

contre-partie [kɔ̃trəpar'ti], *n.f.* counterpart; (*fig.*) opposite, contrary; return match.

contre-pédaler [kɔ̃trəpeda'le], *v.i.* to backpedal.

contre-pied [kɔ̃trə'pje], *n.m.* (*Hunt.*) backscent; (*fig.*) reverse way, contrary.

contre-plaqué [kɔ̃trəpla'ke], *a.* laminated. —*n.m.* two- (*or* three-) ply wood.

contrepoids [kɔ̃trə'pwa], *n.m. inv.* counterpoise, counter-balance; (*fig.*) equilibrium.

contre-poil [kɔ̃trə'pwal], *n.m.* wrong way of the hair *or* of the nap; *à contre-poil,* against the grain.

contrepoint [kɔ̃trə'pwɛ̃], *n.m.* counterpoint.

contrepoison [kɔ̃trəpwa'zɔ̃], *n.m.* antidote, counter-poison.

contre-poser [kɔ̃trəpo'ze], *v.t.* to misplace; (*Comm.*) to set down wrong.

contrer [kɔ̃'tre], *v.t.* (*Bridge*) to double.

contre-ressort [kɔ̃trərə'sɔ:r], *n.m.* shock absorber.

contre-révolution [kɔ̃trərevɔly'sjɔ̃], *n.f.* counter-revolution.

contre-saison (à) [akɔ̃trəsɛ'zɔ̃], *adv. phr.* (*flower*) produced out of season; ill-timed.

contresens [kɔ̃trə'sɑ̃:s], *n.m.* contrary sense; wrong construction *or* meaning; mistranslation; wrong side (*of material*).

contresigner [kɔ̃trəsi'ɲe], *v.t.* to countersign.

contretemps [kɔ̃trə'tɑ̃], *n.m. inv.* untoward accident, disappointment, mishap; (*Mus.*) syncopation; *à contretemps,* at the wrong time.

contre-torpilleur [kɔ̃trətɔrpi'jœ:r], *n.m.* torpedo-boat destroyer.

contrevenant [kɔ̃trəv'nɑ̃], *n.m.* (*fem.* **-e**) contravener, infringer, offender, transgressor.

contrevenir [kɔ̃trəv'ni:r], *v.i. irr.* (*conjug. like* TENIR) to contravene, infringe.

contrevent [kɔ̃trə'vɑ̃], *n.m.* outside windowshutter.

contribuable [kɔ̃tri'bɥabl], *a.* taxable. —*n.* tax-payer.

contribuer [kɔ̃tri'bɥe], *v.i.* to contribute, to pay; (*fig.*) to conduce, to be an accessory (*à*).

contributaire [kɔ̃triby'tɛːr], *a.* contributory.
contribution [kɔ̃triby'sjɔ̃], *n.f.* contribution; tax; share, portion; *contribution foncière*, land tax.
contrister [kɔ̃tris'te], *v.t.* to grieve, to vex, to sadden.
contrit [kɔ̃'tri], *a.* contrite, penitent; afflicted.
contrition [kɔ̃tri'sjɔ̃], *n.f.* contrition.
contrôlable [kɔ̃tro'labl], *a.* that may be checked, verified.
contrôle [kɔ̃'troːl], *n.m.* muster roll; roll, list; controller's office; stamp, hall-mark; (*Theat.*) ticket-checking counter; (*fig.*) control, censure.
contrôler [kɔ̃tro'le], *v.t.* to register; to stamp; to check, to verify; to audit; to censure.
contrôleur [kɔ̃tro'lœːr], *n.m.* (*fem.* **-euse**) controller; (*Taxes, Theat., Rail.*) inspector; time-keeper; ticket collector; (*fig.*) critic.
controuver [kɔ̃tru've], *v.t.* to forge, to fabricate.
controversable [kɔ̃trɔvɛr'sabl], *a.* contro-vertible, controversial.
controverse [kɔ̃trɔ'vɛrs], *n.f.* controversy, discussion, dispute.
controverser [kɔ̃trɔvɛr'se], *v.t.* to dispute, to discuss.
contumace [kɔ̃ty'mas], *n.f.* contumacy, non-appearance *or* default, contempt of court; obstinacy.—*a.* contumacious.—*n.* defaulter.
contus [kɔ̃'ty], *a.* bruised, contused.
contusion [kɔ̃ty'zjɔ̃], *n.f.* contusion, bruise.
contusionner [kɔ̃tyzjɔ'ne], *v.t.* to contuse, to bruise.
convaincant [kɔ̃vɛ̃'kɑ̃], *a.* convincing.
convaincre [kɔ̃'vɛ̃ːkr], *v.t. irr.* (*conjug. like* VAINCRE) to convince; to persuade. **se convaincre**, *v.r.* to convince oneself.
convaincu [kɔ̃vɛ̃'ky], *a.* convinced; sincere; convicted.
convalescence [kɔ̃valɛ'sɑ̃ːs], *n.f.* conva-lescence.
convalescent [kɔ̃valɛ'sɑ̃], *a.* and *n.m.* (*fem.* **-e**) convalescent (person).
convection [kɔ̃vɛk'sjɔ̃], *n.f.* convection.
convenable [kɔ̃v'nabl], *a.* suitable, fit, proper; convenient; becoming.
convenablement [kɔ̃vənablə'mɑ̃], *adv.* suit-ably, becomingly, decently.
convenance [kɔ̃v'nɑ̃ːs], *n.f.* fitness, pro-priety; seasonableness (*of time*); decency, seemliness; (*pl.*) propriety, decorum; *mariage de convenance*, marriage of convenience.
convenir [kɔ̃v'niːr], *v.i. irr.* (*conjug. like* TENIR, *but with aux.* ÊTRE) to agree; to admit, to own, to acknowledge (*de*); (*with aux.* AVOIR) to suit, to fit, to match; (*impers.*) to be fitting. **se convenir**, *v.r.* to suit each other, to agree.
convention [kɔ̃vɑ̃'sjɔ̃], *n.f.* agreement, treaty; (*social and other*) convention; (*pl.*) con-ditions (*of an agreement*).
conventionnel [kɔ̃vɑ̃sjɔ'nɛl], *a.* (*fem.* **-elle**) conventional.
conventionnellement [kɔ̃vɑ̃sjɔnɛl'mɑ̃], *adv.* by agreement.
convenu [kɔ̃v'ny], *a.* agreed; conventional; banal.
convergent [kɔ̃vɛr'ʒɑ̃], *a.* convergent.
converger [kɔ̃vɛr'ʒe], *v.i.* (*conjug. like* MANGER) to converge.

conversation [kɔ̃vɛrsa'sjɔ̃], *n.f.* conversation, converse, talk.
converse [kɔ̃'vɛrs], *a.* and *n.f.* (*Log.*) con-verse; (*Math.*) inverted.
converser [kɔ̃vɛr'se], *v.i.* to converse, to discourse.
conversible [kɔ̃vɛr'sibl], [CONVERTIBLE].
conversion [kɔ̃vɛr'sjɔ̃], *n.f.* conversion; transformation; change.
converti [kɔ̃vɛr'ti], *n.m.* (*fem.* **-e**) convert.
convertible [kɔ̃vɛr'tibl], *a.* convertible.
convertir [kɔ̃vɛr'tiːr], *v.t.* to convert, to transform, to change, to turn. **se convertir**, *v.r.* to be converted, to turn.
convertissement [kɔ̃vɛrtis'mɑ̃], *n.m.* con-version.
convexe [kɔ̃'vɛks], *a.* convex.
convexité [kɔ̃vɛksi'te], *n.f.* convexity.
conviction [kɔ̃vik'sjɔ̃], *n.f.* conviction, con-vincing proof.
convié [kɔ̃'vje], *a.* invited.—*n.m.* (*fem.* **-ée**) guest.
convier [kɔ̃'vje], *v.t.* to invite, to bid; (*fig.*) to urge.
convive [kɔ̃'viv], *n.* guest; fellow diner.
convocation [kɔ̃vɔka'sjɔ̃], *n.f.* convocation; summons.
convoi [kɔ̃'vwa], *n.m.* (*Mil., Navy*) convoy; (*Rail. etc.*) train; *convoi funèbre*, funeral procession.
convoiter [kɔ̃vwa'te], *v.t.* to covet, to hanker after.
convoitise [kɔ̃vwa'tiːz], *n.f.* covetousness; lust.
convolution [kɔ̃vɔly'sjɔ̃], *n.f.* convolution.
convolvulus [kɔ̃vɔlvy'lyːs], *n.m.* (*Bot.*) con-volvulus.
convoquer [kɔ̃vɔ'ke], *v.t.* to convoke, to con-vene; to summon.
convoyer [kɔ̃vwa'je], *v.t.* (*conjug. like* EMPLOYER) to convoy, to escort.
convoyeur [kɔ̃vwa'jœːr], *n.m.* convoy (*ship*); (*Mech.*) conveyor.
convulser [kɔ̃vyl'se], *v.t.* to convulse. **se convulser**, *v.r.* to be *or* become convulsed.
convulsif [kɔ̃vyl'sif], *a.* (*fem.* **-sive**) con-vulsive.
convulsion [kɔ̃vyl'sjɔ̃], *n.f.* convulsion.
convulsionner [kɔ̃vylsjɔ'ne], *v.t.* (*Med.*) to convulse.
convulsivement [kɔ̃vylsiv'mɑ̃], *adv.* con-vulsively.
coolie or **coulis** [ku'li], *n.m.* coolie.
coopérateur [kɔɔpera'tœːr], *n.m.* (*fem.* **-trice**) co-operator, fellow workman.—*a.* (*fem.* **-trice**) co-operating.
coopératif [kɔɔpera'tif], *a.* (*fem.* **-tive**) co-operative.
coopération [kɔɔpera'sjɔ̃], *n.f.* co-operation.
coopérer [kɔɔpe're], *v.i.* (*conjug. like* CÉDER) to co-operate.
coopter [kɔɔp'te], *v.t.* to co-opt.
coordination [kɔɔrdina'sjɔ̃], *n.f.* co-ordina-tion.
coordonné [kɔɔrdɔ'ne], *a.* co-ordinate.—*n.f. pl.* (**-ées**) (*Gram., Geom.*) co-ordinates.
coordonner [kɔɔrdɔ'ne], *v.t.* to co-ordinate.
copain [kɔ'pɛ̃], *n.m.* (*colloq.*) pal, mate.
copal [kɔ'pal], *n.m.* copal.
copeau [kɔ'po], *n.m.* (*pl.* **-eaux**) shaving, chip (*of wood*).
Copenhague [kɔpə'nag], *f.* Copenhagen.

cophte [COPTE].
copie [kɔ'pi], *n.f.* copy, transcript; reproduction; (*Print.*) 'copy'; candidate's paper.
copier [kɔ'pje], *v.t.* to copy; to imitate; to mimic.
copieusement [kɔpjøz'mã], *adv.* copiously, heartily (*of drinking, eating*).
copieux [kɔ'pjø], *a.* (*fem.* **-euse**) copious, plentiful.
co-pilote [kopi'lɔt], *n.m.* second pilot.
copiste [kɔ'pist], *n.* copier, transcriber, copyist.
copte or **cophte** [kɔpt], *a.* Coptic.—*n.* (**Copte, Cophte**) Copt.
coq [kɔk], *n.m.* cock, rooster; cock- (*as opposed to hen*); weathercock; *au chant du coq*, at cock-crow; *coq de bruyère*, grouse; *coq d'Inde*, turkey cock; *poids coq*, (*Box.*) bantam weight.
coq-à-l'âne [kɔka'lɑ:n], *n.m. inv.* nonsense, cock-and-bull story.
coque [kɔk], *n.f.* shell (*of eggs, walnuts, fruits, snails etc.*); cocoon; cockle-shell (*small boat*); (*Naut.*) hull.
coquelicot [kɔkli'ko], *n.m.* corn-poppy.
coqueluche [kɔ'klyʃ], *n.f.* the rage, favorite; (*Med.*) whooping-cough.
coquerico [kɔkri'ko], *n.m.* cock-a-doodle-doo.
coqueriquer [kɔkri'ke], *v.i.* to crow.
coquet [kɔ'kɛ], *a.* (*fem.* **-ette**) coquettish; stylish, smart.—*n.m.* (*fem.* **-ette**) coquette, flirt; dandy.
coqueter [kɔk'te], *v.i.* (*conjug. like* APPELER) to coquet, to flirt.
coquetier [kɔk'tje], *n.m.* egg merchant, poulterer; egg cup.
coquetterie [kɔkɛ'tri], *n.f.* coquettishness, flirtation; affectation (*in dress etc.*).
coquillage [kɔki'ja:ʒ], *n.m.* shell-fish; shell.
coquille [kɔ'ki:j], *n.f.* shell (*of shell-fish, egg, fruits etc.*); (*Cook.*) Dutch oven; pat (*of butter*); (*Print.*) wrong letter; thumb (*of a latch*); (*Ornament*) conch.
coquin [kɔ'kɛ̃], *a.* roguish; rascally.—*n.m.* knave, rascal, rogue, scamp.—*n.f.* (**-e**) slut, hussy, jade.
coquinerie [kɔki'nɛ], *n.f.* knavery, rascality, roguery.
coquinet [kɔki'nɛ], *n.m.* little rascal.
cor (1) [kɔ:r], *n.m.* horn, hunting horn.
cor (2) [kɔ:r], *n.m.* corn (*on the foot*).
cor (3) [kɔ:r], *n.m.* tine (*of antler*).
corail [kɔ'ra:j], *n.m.* (*pl.* **-aux**) coral.
corailleur [kɔra'jœ:r], *n.m.* coral fisher; coral-fishing boat.
Coran [kɔ'rã], *n.m.* Koran.
corbeau [kɔr'bo], *n.m.* (*pl.* **-eaux**) crow; raven.
corbeille [kɔr'bɛ:j], *n.f.* flat, wide basket.
corbillard [kɔrbi'ja:r], *n.m.* hearse.
corbillon [kɔrbi'jõ], *n.m.* small basket; crambo (*game*).
corbin [kɔr'bɛ̃], *n.m.* crow.
corbine [kɔr'bin], *n.f.* carrion crow.
corbleu! [kɔr'blø], *int.* by Jove!
cordage [kɔr'da:ʒ], *n.m.* cord, rope, cordage, rigging.
corde [kɔrd], *n.f.* cord, rope; twine, twist; string (*musical instrument, racquet*); line; (*Mus., Geom. etc.*) chord, tone, note; *corde à boyau*, catgut.
cordé (1) [kɔr'de], *a.* twisted, corded.

cordé (2) [kɔr'de], *a.* cordate, heart-shaped.
cordeau [kɔr'do], *n.m.* (*pl.* **-eaux**) cord; line; fuse; tape.
cordée [kɔr'de], *n.f.* fishing line; line of roped mountaineers.
cordeler [kɔrdə'le], *v.t.* (*conjug. like* APPELER) to twist, to twine.
cordelette [kɔrdə'lɛt], *n.f.* small cord; string.
cordelier [kɔrdə'lje], *n.m.* Franciscan friar.
cordelière [kɔrdə'ljɛ:r], *n.f.* girdle (*of dressing-gown etc.*).
cordelle [kɔr'dɛl], *n.f.* towline, tow-rope.
corder [kɔr'de], *v.t.* to twist (*into cord*); to cord; to bind with a cord; to string (*racquet*).
se corder, *v.r.* to be corded; to become stringy (*of plants etc.*).
corderie [kɔr'dri], *n.f.* rope walk.
cordial [kɔr'djal], *a.* (*m. pl.* **-aux**) cordial, hearty, sincere.—*n.m.* cordial.
cordialement [kɔrdjal'mã], *adv.* cordially, heartily, sincerely.
cordialité [kɔrdjali'te], *n.f.* cordiality, heartiness.
cordier [kɔr'dje], *n.m.* rope maker.
Cordillères [kɔrdi'jɛ:r], **les**, *f.pl.* the Cordilleras.
cordite [kɔr'dit], *n.f.* cordite.
cordon [kɔr'dõ], *n.m.* strand (*of a rope*); twist, string; cord; ribbon (*of an order*); border, edging; *cordon bleu*, blue ribbon, first-rate cook.
cordonner [kɔrdɔ'ne], *v.t.* to twist, to twine, to braid; to mill (*coins*).
cordonnerie [kɔrdɔn'ri], *n.f.* shoe-making; cobbler's shop.
cordonnet [kɔrdɔ'nɛ], *n.m.* twist; milled edge (*of coins*).
cordonnier [kɔrdɔ'nje], *n.m.* shoe-maker.
Corée [kɔ're], **la**, *f.* Korea.
coréen [kɔre'ɛ̃], *a.* (*fem.* **-enne**) Korean.— *n.m.* Korean (*language*); (**Coréen**, *fem.* **-enne**) Korean (*person*).
coriace [kɔ'rjas], *a.* tough, leathery; (*fig.*) close, niggardly; dogged.
coricide [kɔri'sid], *n.m.* corn cure.
corinthien [kɔrɛ̃'tjɛ̃], *a.* (*fem.* **-enne**) Corinthian.—*n.m.* (**Corinthien**, *fem.*-**enne**) Corinthian.
coris [CAURI].
corli [kɔr'li], **courlis** [kur'li], **corlieu** [kɔr'ljø], *n.m.* curlew.
cormoran [kɔrmɔ'rã], *n.m.* cormorant.
cornac [kɔr'nak], *n.m.* elephant driver, mahout; mentor.
corne [kɔrn], *n.f.* horn, hoof; shoe horn; dog's-ear (*on books, leaves*); *chapeau à trois cornes*, three-cornered hat.
corné [kɔr'ne], *a.* corneous, horny.
cornée [kɔr'ne], *n.f.* cornea.
corneille [kɔr'nɛ:j], *n.f.* crow, rook, jackdaw.
cornement [kɔrnə'mã], *n.m.* buzzing in the ears.
cornemuse [kɔrnə'my:z], *n.f.* bagpipes.
corner (1) [kɔr'ne], *v.t.* to blurt out, to trumpet; to dog's-ear (*a leaf*).—*v.i.* to blow, wind *or* sound a horn; to tingle (*of the ears*).
corner (2) [kɔr'nɛr], *n.m.* (*Ftb.*) corner (-kick).
cornet [kɔr'nɛ], *n.m.* horn, hooter; ink horn; cone.
cornette [kɔr'nɛt], *n.f.* mob-cap; pennant of cavalry.
corniche [kɔr'niʃ], *n.f.* cornice; ledge.

cornichon [kɔrni'ʃɔ̃], *n.m.* gherkin; (*fig.*) greenhorn.
corniste [kɔr'nist], *n.* horn player.
Cornouaille [kɔr'nwɑ:j], **la**, *f.* Cornwall.
cornu [kɔr'ny], *a.* horned; angular, cornered; (*fig.*) absurd.
cornue [kɔr'ny], *n.f.* (*Chem.*) retort.
corollaire [kɔrɔ'lɛ:r], *n.m.* corollary.
corolle [kɔ'rɔl], *n.f.* corolla.
coronaire [kɔrɔ'nɛ:r], *a.* (*Anat.*) coronary.
coronal [kɔrɔ'nal], *a.* (*m. pl.* **-aux**) (*Anat.*) coronal.
corporation [kɔrpɔrɑ'sjɔ̃], *n.f.* corporation, corporate body.
corporel [kɔrpɔ'rɛl], *a.* (*fem.* **-elle**) corporal, bodily.
corps [kɔ:r], *n.m.* body; matter, substance; thickness, consistence; chief part; corporation, company; society, college; corps; fellow creature; *à corps perdu*, desperately; *à son corps défendant*, (*fig.*) reluctantly; *corps à corps*, hand to hand, (*Box.*) in-fight(ing); *corps morts*, (*Naut.*) fixed moorings; *garde du corps*, lifeguard; *sombre corps et biens*, to founder with all hands.
corpulence [kɔrpy'lɑ̃:s], *n.f.* corpulence, stoutness.
corpulent [kɔrpy'lɑ̃], *a.* corpulent, stout.
corpuscule [kɔrpys'kyl], *n.m.* corpuscule, corpuscle.
correct [kɔ'rɛkt], *a.* correct, accurate.
correctement [kɔrɛkt'mɑ̃], *adv.* correctly, accurately.
correctif [kɔrɛk'tif], *a.* (*fem.* **-tive**) corrective. —*n.m.* corrective.
correction [kɔrɛk'sjɔ̃], *n.f.* correction; correctness, accuracy; (*Print.*) reading, alteration (*of a proof etc.*); (*fig.*) reprimand, reproof; punishment; thrashing.
correctionnel [kɔrɛksjɔ'nɛl], *a.* (*fem.* **-elle**) within the jurisdiction of the *tribunal de police correctionnelle*, court of petty sessions.
corrélation [kɔrɛlɑ'sjɔ̃], *n.f.* correlation.
correspondance [kɔrɛspɔ̃'dɑ̃:s], *n.f.* correspondence; connection; intercourse; conformity; (*Rail.*) connection.
correspondant [kɔrɛspɔ̃'dɑ̃], *a.* correspondent, corresponding.—*n.m.* (*fem.* **-e**) correspondent, corresponding member.
correspondre [kɔrɛs'pɔ̃:dr], *v.i.* to correspond, to communicate, to be in correspondence; to agree.
corridor [kɔri'dɔ:r], *n.m.* corridor, gallery, passage.
corrigé [kɔri'ʒe], *n.m.* corrected (*schoolboy's*) exercise; key (*book*), crib.
corriger [kɔri'ʒe], *v.t.* (*conjug. like* MANGER) to correct, to rectify; to repair, to amend; to reprove, to chide; to chastise. **se corriger**, *v.r.* to correct oneself, to amend, to reform.
corroboration [kɔrɔbɔrɑ'sjɔ̃], *n.f.* corroboration, strengthening.
corroborer [kɔrɔbɔ're], *v.t.* to strengthen; to corroborate.
corrodant [kɔrɔ'dɑ̃], *a.* corroding, corrosive.
corroder [kɔrɔ'de], *v.t.* to corrode.
corrompre [kɔ'rɔ̃:pr], *v.t.* (*conjug. like* ROMPRE) to corrupt; to infect; to spoil; to taint (*meat*); (*fig.*) to pervert; to bribe. **se**

corrompre, *v.r.* to grow corrupt; to become tainted.
corrompu [kɔrɔ̃'py], *a.* corrupted, unsound; bribed.
corrosif [kɔrɔ'zif], *a.* (*fem.* **-sive**) and *n.m.* corrosive.
corrosion [kɔrɔ'zjɔ̃], *n.f.* corrosion.
corroyer [kɔrwa'je], *v.t.* (*conjug. like* EMPLOYER) to curry (*leather*); to plane (*wood*).
corroyeur [kɔrwa'jœ:r], *n.m.* currier.
corrupteur [kɔryp'tœ:r], *a.* (*fem.* **-trice**) corrupting, perverting, infectious.—*n.m.* (*fem.* **-trice**) corrupter, seducer; briber.
corruptibilité [kɔryptibili'te], *n.f.* corruptibility.
corruptible [kɔryp'tibl], *a.* corruptible.
corruptif [kɔryp'tif], *a.* (*fem.* **-tive**) corruptive.
corruption [kɔryp'sjɔ̃], *n.f.* corruption; rottenness; (*fig.*) depravity; (*Polit.*) bribery.
corsage [kɔr'sa:ʒ], *n.m.* chest (*of the body*); corsage, bodice.
corsaire [kɔr'sɛ:r], *n.m.* privateer, corsair; (*fig.*) shark.
Corse [kɔrs], **la**, *f.* Corsica.—*n.* Corsican (*person*).
corse [kɔrs], *a.* Corsican.
corsé [kɔr'se], *a.* rich, full-bodied; (*colloq.*) strong, thick; (*of stories etc.*) spicy.
corser [kɔr'se], *v.t.* to stiffen; to thicken; to complicate.
corset [kɔr'sɛ], *n.m.* corset, stays.
corsetier [kɔrsə'tje], *n.m.* (*fem.* **-ière**) corset maker.
cortège [kɔr'tɛ:ʒ], *n.m.* train, retinue, suite, procession.
corvée [kɔr've], *n.f.* (*Feud.*) forced *or* statute labor; fatigue party; (*fig.*) drudgery.
corvette [kɔr'vɛt], *n.f.* corvette, sloop of war.
Cosaque [kɔ'zak], *n.m.* Cossack.
cosinus [kɔsi'ny:s], *n.m.* cosine.
cosmétique [kɔsme'tik], *a.* and *n.m.* cosmetic.
cosmique [kɔs'mik], *a.* cosmic.
cosmographie [kɔsmɔgra'fi], *n.f.* cosmography.
cosmopolite [kɔsmɔpɔ'lit], *n.* cosmopolite. —*a.* cosmopolitan.
cosmos [kɔs'mos], *n.m.* cosmos.
cosse [kɔs], *n.f.* pod, shell, husk, rind.
cossu [kɔ'sy], *a.* substantial, wealthy.
costume [kɔs'tym], *n.m.* costume, dress; uniform.
costumer [kɔsty'me], *v.t.* to dress (*in a certain style etc.*). **se costumer**, *v.r.* to dress (*oneself*) up.
costumier [kɔsty'mje], *n.m.* (*fem.* **-ière**) costumier.
cote [kɔt], *n.f.* quota, share; letter, number, figure (*to indicate order etc.*); (*St. Exch.*) quotation; (*Comm.*) price list; odds.
côte [ko:t], *n.f.* rib (*of the body, cloth, fruit etc.*); slope, hill; shore, sea coast; *à mi-côte*, half-way up.
côté [ko'te], *n.m.* side; part, quarter, hand, way, direction; face, aspect; *à côté de*, by, near; *d'à côté*, adjoining, next.
coté [kɔ'te], *a.* marked; classed; backed; *point coté*, (*on a map*) trig-point; *cheval bien coté*, well-backed horse.
coteau [kɔ'to], *n.m.* (*pl.* **-eaux**) slope; little hill.

87

côtelette [ko'tlɛt], *n.f.* cutlet, chop.

coter [ko'te], *v.t.* to number; to price; (*St. Exch.*) to quote.

coterie [ko'tri], *n.f.* coterie, set, circle, clique.

cothurne [ko'tyrn], *n.m.* buskin.

côtier [ko'tje], *a.* (*fem.* **-ière**) coasting.—*n.m.* coaster (*ship*).

cotillon [koti'jɔ̃], *n.m.* under-petticoat; cotillion.

cotisation [kotiza'sjɔ̃], *n.f.* assessment, quota, share; subscription.

cotiser [koti'ze], *v.t.* to assess, to rate. **se cotiser,** *v.r.* to club together; to get up a subscription, to subscribe.

coton [ko'tɔ̃], *n.m.* cotton; fluff, down (*of fruit, and hair on the face*);absorbent cotton.

cotonnade [koto'nad], *n.f.* cotton cloth.

cotonné [koto'ne], *a.* covered with *or* full of cotton; downy; woolly (*of hair*); padded.

cotonner [koto'ne], *v.t.* to fill *or* to stuff with cotton; to pad. **se cotonner,** *v.r.* to be covered with down.

cotonneux [koto'nø], *a.* (*fem.* **-euse**) cottony, downy; spongy, mealy.

cotonnier [koto'nje], *n.m.* cotton bush.

côtoyer [kotwa'je], *v.t.* (*conjug. like* EMPLOYER) to go by the side of, to skirt; to coast; (*fig.*) to keep close to.

cotre [ko:tr], *n.m.* cutter (*vessel*).

cotret [ko'trɛ], *n.m.* faggot; stick.

cottage [ko'ta:ʒ], *n.m.* cottage.

cotte [kot], *n.f.* short petticoat; (*engineer's*) overalls.

cotuteur [koty'tœ:r], *n.m.* (*fem.* **-trice**) joint guardian.

cou [ku], *n.m.* neck.

couac [kwak], *n.m.* false note; squawk.

couard [kwa:r], *a.* coward, cowardly.—*n.m.* (*fem.* **-e**) coward.

couardise [kwar'di:z], *n.f.* cowardice.

couchage [ku'ʃa:ʒ], *n.m.* act of lying in bed; bed, night's lodging; bedding.

couchant [ku'ʃɑ̃], *a.* setting; lying; (*fig.*) fawning; **un chien couchant,** a setter.—*n.m.* west; (*fig.*) decline.

couche [kuʃ], *n.f.* bed, couch; confinement; diaper; layer, row; (*Min.*) seam; (*Gard.*) hotbed, bed; coat (*of varnish* or *color*); (*fig.*) social stratum.

couché [ku'ʃe], *a.* in bed, gone to bed, lying down, recumbent; (*Her.*) couchant.

couchée [ku'ʃe], *n.f.* act of lying down; sleeping place; night's lodging.

coucher [ku'ʃe], *v.t.* to put to bed; to lay down; to knock down; to lay on; to stake.—*v.i.* to sleep, to lie (down), to rest; **coucher à la belle étoile,** to sleep in the open air. **se coucher,** *v.r.* to go to bed; to lie down; to set, to go down (*of the sun etc.*).—*n.m.* going to bed; bed time; setting (*of the sun etc.*).

couchette [ku'ʃɛt], *n.f.* small bed, crib; berth; bunk (*on a ship*); **wagon à couchettes,** second-class sleeper.

coucou [ku'ku], *n.m.* cuckoo; cuckoo clock; (*Bot.*) cowslip.

coude [kud], *n.m.* elbow; bend, angle; turning.

coudé [ku'de], *a.* bent, elbowed, cranked.

coudée [ku'de], *n.f.* length of arm from elbow to tip of middle finger, cubit.

cou-de-pied [kud'pje], *n.m.* (*pl.* **cous-de-pied**) instep.

couder [ku'de], *v.t.* to bend, to make an elbow in. **se couder,** *v.r.* to elbow, to form an elbow.

coudoyer [kudwa'je], *v.t.* (*conjug. like* EMPLOYER) to elbow, to jostle. **se coudoyer,** *v.r.* to elbow *or* jostle each other.

coudraie [ku'drɛ], *n.f.* hazel copse; filbert orchard.

coudre [kudr], *v.t. irr.* to sew, to stitch; (*fig.*) to attach, to connect.

coudrier [ku'drje], *n.m.* hazel tree.

couenne [kwan], *n.f.* scraped pig-skin; crackling (*of pork*); rind; (*Med.*) birthmark.

couette [kwɛt], **coit(t)e** (2) [kwat], *n.f.* feather-bed; sea-gull; (*hare's*) scut.

couguar [ku'ga:r], *n.m.* cougar, puma.

coulage [ku'la:ʒ], *n.m.* flow (*of metal in fusion*); melting, casting; leakage, waste; pilferage.

coulant [ku'lɑ̃], *a.* flowing, smooth, natural (*of style etc.*); (*fig.*) easy; **nœud coulant,** slip knot.—*n.m.* sliding ring (*for a necktie, umbrella etc.*).

coulé [ku'le], *n.m.* (*Mus.*) slur; (*Billiards*) follow through; (*Swim.*) plunge.

coulée [ku'le], *n.f.* running hand (*of writing*); (*Metal.*) tapping; flow, rush (*of a torrent etc.*); (*Hunt.*) track, path.

couler [ku'le], *v.t.* to cast; to strain; to slip (*dans*); to sink, to run down; (*Mus.*) to slur. —*v.i.* to flow; to glide; to trickle; to leak; to slip away (*of time etc.*); to founder (*of a ship etc.*). **se couler,** *v.r.* to slip, to creep, to steal, to glide; to be cast (*of metals*).

couleur [ku'lœ:r], *n.f.* color; coloring-matter, paint; coloring; (*fig.*) appearance; pretence; suit (*at cards*).

couleuvre [ku'lœ:vr], *n.f.* (grass) snake.

coulis [ku'li], *n.m.* strained juice from meat etc. slowly stewed.

coulisse [ku'lis], *n.f.* groove, channel; running string; (*Theat.*) wing; (*fig.*) behind the scenes; **porte à coulisse,** sliding door; **faire les yeux en coulisse,** to make sheep's eyes.

coulissé [kuli'se], *a.* grooved.

coulissier [kuli'sje], *n.m.* stock jobber, outside broker.

couloir [ku'lwa:r], *n.m.* passage, corridor, lobby, gangway.

couloire [ku'lwa:r], *n.f.* colander, strainer.

coup [ku], *n.m.* blow, stroke, hit, thump, knock, stab, thrust; beat (*of a drum*); draft (*of liquids*); clap (*of thunder*); (*Artill.*) charge; gust (*of wind*); throw; shot; moment; bout; attempt; deed; event; **à coup sûr,** unquestionably; (*Ftb.*) **coup d'envoi,** kick-off; **coup d'œil,** glance; **coup de téléphone,** telephone call; **le coup de grâce,** the finishing stroke; **tout à coup,** all of a sudden; **tout d'un coup,** all at once.

coupable [ku'pabl], *a.* culpable, guilty.—*n.* guilty person, culprit.

coupage [ku'pa:ʒ], *n.m.* cutting; diluting (*of wine*); blending (*of spirits*).

coupant [ku'pɑ̃], *a.* cutting, sharp.—*n.m.* edge (*of a sword etc.*).

coupe (1) [kup], *n.f.* cutting, felling (*of wood*); wood felled; the cut end; cut (*clothes etc.*); shape; (*Pros.*) cadence; (*Swim.*) overarm stroke.

coupe (2) [kup], *n.f.* cup, goblet, chalice; basin (*of a fountain etc.*).
coupé (1) [ku'pe], *a.* intersected; diluted; (*fig.*) laconic.
coupé (2) [ku'pe], *n.m.* coupé (*kind of brougham*); a dance step.

[In the following compounds *coupe* is *inv.*]

coupe-circuit [kupsir'kɥi], *n.m. inv.* cut-out, circuit breaker; fuse.
coupée [ku'pe], *n.f.* (*Naut.*) gangway; *échelle de coupée*, accommodation ladder.
coupe-file [kup'fil], *n.m. inv.* police pass.
coupe-gorge [kup'gɔrʒ], *n.m. inv.* cut-throat place, den.
coupe-jarret [kupʒa'rɛ], *n.m.* cut-throat, assassin, ruffian.
coupe-papier [kuppa'pje], *n.m. inv.* paper knife.
couper [ku'pe], *v.t.* to cut; to dock. to strike off; to clip, to pare; to geld; (*Mil.*) to intercept; to dilute (*milk, wine, with water*); to intersect; to interrupt.—*v.i.* to make an incision; to cut, to trump (*at cards*). **se couper**, *v.r.* to cut oneself; to intersect.
couperet [ku'prɛ], *n.m.* (*butcher's*) chopper; knife (*of guillotine*).
couperose [ku'pro:z], *n.f.* copperas.
couperosé [kupro'ze], *a.* blotched.
coupeur [ku'pœ:r], *n.m.* (*fem.* **-euse**) cutter. —*n.f.* (**-euse**) cutting machine.
(C) **coupe-vent** [kup'vɑ̃], *n.m.* wind breaker.
couplage [ku'plaːʒ], *n.m.* coupling.
couple [kupl], *n.f.* brace, couple.—*n.m.* married couple; pair (*of animals, male and female*); (*Naut.*) frame.
coupler [ku'ple], *v.t.* to couple, to link.
couplet [ku'plɛ], *n.m.* couplet; verse of song; (*fig.*) tirade; (*Tech.*) hinge.
coupleur [ku'plœ:r], *n.m.* (*Elec.*) make-and-break, cut-out.
coupoir [ku'pwa:r], *n.m.* cutter (*instrument*).
coupole [ku'pɔl], *n.f.* cupola; (*Naut.*) revolving gun turret.
coupon [ku'pɔ̃], *n.m.* remnant; coupon; dividend check, check; (*Theat.*) ticket.
coupure [ku'py:r], *n.f.* cut, incision, slit; cutting; suppression; drain; (*Banking*) small note.
cour [ku:r], *n.f.* court (*of a prince, of justice etc.*); yard, courtyard; (*fig.*) courtship, suit.
courage [ku'ra:ʒ], *n.m.* courage, daring; spirit, mettle; fortitude, greatness of soul.
courageusement [kuraʒøz'mɑ̃], *adv.* courageously, bravely, resolutely.
courageux [kura'ʒø], *a.* (*fem.* **-euse**) courageous, daring, fearless, plucky.
couramment [kura'mɑ̃], *adv.* fluently, readily.
courant [ku'rɑ̃], *a.* running; current, present; usual; fair, middling (*of goods*); lineal (*of measures*).—*n.m.* stream, current, tide; course (*of time etc.*); routine; present price; present (*time*).
courbage [kur'ba:ʒ], *n.m.* bending, curving.
courbatu [kurba'ty], *a.* foundered (*of horses*); stiff in the joints; (*Med.*) affected with lumbago.
courbature [kurba'ty:r], *n.f.* foundering, lameness; (*Path.*) stiffness in the limbs, lumbago.

courbaturer [kurbaty're], *v.t.* to make (*someone*) feel stiff all over.
courbe [kurb], *a.* curved, bent, crooked.—*n.f.* curve; (*Naut., Carp.*) knee; (*Vet.*) curb; (*Math.*) graph.
courber [kur'be], *v.t.* to curve, to bend, to warp, to make crooked.—*v.i.* to bend, to sag. **se courber**, *v.r.* to bend, to stoop; to bow down.
courbette [kur'bɛt], *n.f.* curvet; (*pl.*) bowing and scraping, cringing.
courbetter [kurbɛ'te], *v.i.* to curvet.
courbure [kur'by:r], *n.f.* curvature, curve; bend; sagging.
coureur [ku'rœːr], *a.* (*fem.* **-euse**) swift.— *n.m.* runner, racer; hunter (*horse*); light porter; rover; rake, libertine; (*Mil.*) scout.
courge [kurʒ], *n.f.* gourd; *courge à la moelle*, vegetable marrow; squash.
courir [ku'ri:r], *v.t. irr.* to pursue; to travel over; to hunt; to frequent; to expose oneself to.—*v.i.* to run; to hasten; to ramble, to rove; to flow; to stretch; to circulate.
courlis [kur'li], **courlieu** [kur'ljø], *n.m.* curlew.
couronne [ku'rɔn], *n.f.* crown; coronet; wreath; crown (*a coin*).
couronnement [kurɔn'mɑ̃], *n.m.* crowning, coronation; completion.
couronner [kurɔ'ne], *v.t.* to crown; to award a prize, to honor (*avec*); to consummate; to wreathe.
courre [ku:r], *v.t. only used in chasse à courre*, hunting.
courrier [ku'rje], *n.m.* messenger, courier; mail, post; letters, correspondence.
courriériste [kurje'rist], *n.m.* columnist.
courroie [ku'rwa], *n.f.* strap, thong; driving belt *or* band.
courroucer [kuru'se], *v.t.* (*conjug. like* COMMENCER) to provoke, to anger, to incense, to irritate. **se courroucer**, *v.r.* to become angry, to rage.
courroux [ku'ru], *n.m.* wrath, anger, rage.
cours [ku:r], *n.m.* course, stream, current, flow; lapse; path, orbit; vent, scope; public drive *or* walk; vogue; currency; series of lectures; (*pl.*) classes; (*St. Exch.*) market price, rate.
course [kurs], *n.f.* running, run; course; drive, walk, excursion; career; race; errand; privateering; cruise; length of the stroke (*of a piece of machinery*).
coursier [kur'sje], *n.m.* charger; (*poet.*) steed; (*Naut.*) bow gun.
coursive [kur'si:v], *n.f.* (*Naut.*) gangway.
court (1) [ku:r], *a.* short; brief; concise, curt; limited, scanty; fleeting.—*adv.* short, abruptly; *demeurer court*, to stop short; *être à court d'argent*, to be short of money.
court (2) [kɔrt], *n.m.* tennis court.
courtage [kur'ta:ʒ], *n.m.* brokerage, commission.
courtaud [kur'to], *a.* thick-set, dumpy; docked, crop-eared.—*n.m.* (*fem.* **-e**) short, thick-set person; docked *or* crop-eared horse.
courtauder [kurto'de], *v.t.* to dock, to crop (*horses etc.*).
court-circuit [kursir'kɥi], *n.m.* (*pl.* **courts-circuits**) short circuit.

89

court-circuiter

court-circuiter [kursirkɥi'te], *v.t.* to short-circuit.
courtement [kurtə'mã], *adv.* shortly, briefly.
courtepointe [kurtə'pwɛ̃:t], *n.f.* counterpane, quilt.
courtier [kur'tje], *n.m.* (*fem.* **-ière**) broker, agent.
courtil [kur'til], *n.m.* *small garden; garth.
courtisan [kurti'zã], *n.m.* courtier; fawner.
courtisane [kurti'zan], *n.f.* courtesan.
courtisanerie [kurtizan'ri], *n.f.* court flattery, toadyism.
courtisanesque [kurtiza'nɛsk], *a.* courtier-like.
courtiser [kurti'ze], *v.t.* to court; to woo; to flatter.
courtois [kur'twa] *a.* courteous, polite.
courtoisement [kurtwaz'mã], *adv.* courteously.
courtoisie [kurtwa'zi], *n.f.* courtesy; kindness, good turn.
couseur [ku'zœ:r], *n.m.* (*fem.* **-euse**) sewer, stitcher (*of books*).
cousin [ku'zɛ̃], *n.m.* (*fem.* **-e**) cousin; (*fig.*) friend, crony.
cousinage [kuzi'na:ʒ], *n.m.* cousinhood; cousins; relationship.
cousiner [kuzi'ne], *v.t.* to call cousin; to hob-nob with.—*v.i.* to live on others; to be friends *or* cronies.
coussin [ku'sɛ̃], *n.m.* cushion, hassock; pad.
coussiner [kusi'ne], *v.t.* to pad, to cushion.
coussinet [kusi'nɛ], *n.m.* small cushion, pad; iron wedge; pillion.
cousu [ku'zy], *a.* sewn, stitched.
coût [ku], *n.m.* costs, charge; *le coût de la vie,* the cost of living.
coûtant [ku'tã], *a.* costing; *à prix coûtant,* at cost price.
couteau [ku'to], *n.m.* (*pl.* **-eaux**) knife.
coutelas [kut'la], *n.m.* cutlass.
coutelier [kutə'lje], *n.m.* cutler.
coutelière [kutə'ljɛ:r], *n.f.* knife case; cutler's wife.
coutellerie [kutɛl'ri], *n.f.* cutler's shop *or* business; cutlery.
coûter [ku'te], *v.t.* to cost, to cause, to occasion.—*v.i.* to cost (*cher etc.*); to be expensive; (*fig.*) to be painful, troublesome.
coûteusement [kutøz'mã], *adv.* expensively.
coûteux [ku'tø], *a.* (*fem.* **-euse**) expensive, costly.
coutil [ku'ti], *n.m.* tick, ticking; (*Tex.*) drill.
coutre [kutr], *n.m.* plough-share, coulter, axe.
coutume [ku'tym], *n.f.* custom, habit, practice.
coutumier [kuty'mje], *a.* (*fem.* **-ière**) customary, common, ordinary; habitual.
couture [ku'ty:r], *n.f.* sewing, needlework; seam, suture; scar.
couturer [kuty're], *v.t.* to seam.
couturier [kuty'rje], *n.m.* ladies' tailor.—*a.* sartorial.
couturière [kuty'rjɛ:r], *n.f.* dressmaker, seamstress.
couvage [ku'va:ʒ], *n.f.* **couvaison** [kuvɛ'z�õ], *n.f.* brooding-time, sitting, incubation.
couvée [ku've], *n.f.* sitting (*of eggs*); brood, covey.
couvent [ku'vã], *n.m.* convent, monastery, nunnery; convent school.

couver [ku've], *v.t.* to sit on, to incubate, to hatch; to brood, to prepare in secret (*a plot etc.*); to brood over.—*v.i.* to lie hidden, to lurk; to smoulder.
couvercle [ku'vɛrkl], *n.m.* cover, lid, cap, shutter.
couvert [ku'vɛ:r], *a.* covered; clad, clothed; cloudy, overcast; obscure, ambiguous (*of words*).—*n.m.* cover (*plate, spoon, knife, fork*); shelter; cover, wrapper; covert, thicket; *le vivre et le couvert,* board and lodging.
couverte [ku'vɛrt], *n.f.* glaze, glazing.
couverture [kuvɛr'ty:r], *n.f.* covering, wrapper; blanket, rug, counterpane, quilt; cover (*of a book*); (*Comm.*) guaranty, security; *couverture chauffante,* electric blanket.
couveuse [ku'vø:z], *n.f.* broody hen; *couveuse artificielle,* incubator.
couvi [ku'vi], *a.* addled, rotten (*egg*).
couvoir [ku'vwa:r], *n.m.* incubator.

[In the following compounds **couvre** is *inv.*]

couvre-chef [kuvrə'ʃɛf], *n.m.* headgear.
couvre-feu [kuvrə'fø], *n.m. inv.* curfew; curfew-bell; fire cover, fire plate; black-out.
couvre-plat [kuvrə'pla], *n.m.* dish cover.
couvre-théière [kuvrəte'jɛ:r], *n.m.* tea cosy.
couvreur [ku'vrœ:r], *n.m.* roofer.
couvrir [ku'vri:r], *v.t. irr.* (*conjug. like* OUVRIR) to cover; to wrap up; to roof; to overwhelm; to clothe; to defend, to protect; to overrun, to overflow; to excuse; to disguise; to defray (*expenses etc.*). **se couvrir,** *v.r.* to cover oneself, to put on (*one's hat*); to get under cover; to be overcast (*of the weather*); (*Comm.*) to reimburse oneself.
coyote [kɔ'jɔt], *n.m.* prairie wolf.
crabe [kra:b], *n.m.* crab.
crac! [krak], *int.* crack! pop!
crachat [kra'ʃa], *n.m.* spittle, expectoration.
crachement [kraʃ'mã], *n.m.* spitting.
cracher [kra'ʃe], *v.t.* to spit; (*fig.*) to spit out, to come out with.—*v.i.* to spit, to splutter; (*Mach. etc.*) to spark, to backfire.
crachoir [kra'ʃwa:r], *n.m.* spittoon.
crachoter [kraʃɔ'te], *v.i.* to spit often.
Cracovie [krakɔ'vi], *f.* Cracow.
craie [krɛ], *n.f.* chalk.
craillement [kraj'mã], *n.m.* cawing (*of crows*).
crailler [kra'je], *v.i.* to caw.
craindre [krɛ̃:dr], *v.t. irr.* to fear; to dread; to dislike.
crainte [krɛ̃:t], *n.f.* fear, apprehension; dread, awe.
craintif [krɛ̃'tif], *a.* (*fem.* **-tive**) fearful, apprehensive, timid.
craintivement [krɛ̃tiv'mã], *adv.* fearfully, timorously.
cramoisi [kramwa'zi], *a.* and *n.m.* crimson.
crampe [krã:p], *n.f.* cramp; crampon.
crampon [krã'põ], *n.m.* crampon, cramp-iron, grappling iron.
cramponner [krãpɔ'ne], *v.t.* to cramp, to fasten with a cramp-iron. **se cramponner,** *v.r.* to hold fast, to cling like grim death.

90

cramponnet [krɑ̃pɔ'nɛ], *n.m.* small cramp, tack; staple (*of a lock*).

cran (1) [krɑ̃], *n.m.* notch; cog; (*Print.*) nick; (*fam.*) pluck.

cran (2) [krɑ̃], *n.m.* horse-radish.—*n.m.* skull, cranium.

crâne [krɑːn], *a.* bold, plucky.—*n.m.* skull, cranium.

crânement [krɑn'mɑ̃], *adv.* pluckily; in style, famously.

craner [krɑ'ne], *v.t.* to notch, to indent (*a clock wheel*).

crâner [krɑ'ne], *v.i.* to swagger.

cranologie [kranɔlɔ'ʒi], **craniologie** [kranjɔlɔ'ʒi], *n.f.* craniology.

crapaud [kra'po], *n.m.* toad; jumping cracker; (*fig.*) urchin, brat.

crapaudière [krapo'djɛːr], *n.f.* nest of toads; (*fig.*) low, swampy place.

crapaudine [krapo'din], *n.f.* toadstone; grating (*of an escape-pipe*); **à la crapaudine**, cut open and broiled.

crapouillot [krapu'jo], *n.m.* trench-mortar.

crapule [kra'pyl], *n.f.* low vulgar debauchery, gluttony, drunkenness; blackguards.

crapuleusement [krapyløz'mɑ̃], *adv.* dissolutely.

crapuleux [krapy'lø], *a.* (*fem.* **-euse**) low, debauched, vicious, dissolute.

craque [krak], *n.f.* fib, humbug.

craqueler [kra'kle], *v.t.* (*conjug. like* APPELER) to crackle (*china*).

craquelot [kra'klo], *n.m.* bloater.

craquelure [kra'klyːr], *n.f.* crack (*in china*).

craquement [krak'mɑ̃], *n.m.* cracking noise, creaking, snapping (*boughs*).

craquer [kra'ke], *v.i.* to crack, to crackle, to snap, to creak, to crunch.

craquètement [krakɛt'mɑ̃], *n.m.* crackling; chattering (*of the teeth*); gabbling (*of a stork and other birds*).

craqueter [krak'te], *v.i.* (*conjug. like* APPELER) to crackle, to crepitate; to gabble (*birds*).

crasse (1) [kras], *a.* gross, thick, coarse, crass.

crasse (2) [kras], *n.f.* dirt, filth, squalor; stinginess; dross.

crasser [kra'se], *v.t.* to foul, to dirty (*fire-arms etc.*). **se crasser**, *v.r.* to become foul (*of fire-arms etc.*).

crasseux [kra'sø], *a.* (*fem.* **-euse**) dirty, filthy, nasty, squalid, sordid; stingy, mean.—*n.m.* (*fem.* **-euse**) sloven, slut; skinflint.

crassier [kra'sje], *n.m.* slag heap; rubbish dump.

cratère [kra'tɛːr], *n.m.* crater (*mouth of volcano*); (*Gr. or Rom.*) bowl *or* cup.

cravache [kra'vaʃ], *n.f.* riding whip.

cravacher [krava'ʃe], *v.t.* to horse whip.

cravate [kra'vat], *n.f.* cravat, (neck-)tie.

cravater (**se**) [səkrava'te], *v.r.* to put on one's (neck-)tie.

cravatier [krava'tje], *n.m.* maker *or* vendor of neckties.

crawl [krol], *n.m.* (*Swim.*) crawl.

crawleur [kro'lœːr], *n.m.* crawl swimmer.

crayer [krɛ'je], *v.t.* (*conjug. like* PAYER) to chalk, to mark up etc. with chalk.

crayère [krɛ'jɛːr], *n.f.* chalk pit.

crayeux [krɛ'jø], *a.* (*fem.* **-euse**) chalky.

crayon [krɛ'jɔ̃], *n.m.* pencil; drawing *or* portrait in crayon; (*fig.*) style; sketch; **crayon à bille**, ball-point pen.

crayonnage [krɛjɔ'naːʒ], *n.m.* pencil drawing.

crayonner [krɛjɔ'ne], *v.t.* to draw with a pencil; to mark with a pencil; (*fig.*) to sketch.

crayonneux [krɛjɔ'nø], *a.* (*fem.* **-euse**) chalky.

créance [kre'ɑ̃ːs], *n.f.* credence, trust, belief; credit; money owing; (*Hunt.*) command.

créancier [kreɑ̃'sje], *n.m.* (*fem.* **-ière**) creditor.

créateur [krea'tœːr], *a.* (*fem.* **-trice**) creative, inventive.—*n.m.* (*fem.* **-trice**) creator, maker, author.

création [krea'sjɔ̃], *n.f.* creation; universe; establishment; (*Dress.*) design.

créature [krea'tyːr], *n.f.* creature; man, as opposed to God.

crécelle [kre'sɛl], *n.f.* child's *or* hand rattle.

crécerelle [kres'rɛl], *n.f.* (*Orn.*) kestrel.

crèche [krɛːʃ], *n.f.* manger; crib; crèche.

crédence [kre'dɑ̃ːs], *n.f.* credence table; side-board.

crédibilité [kredibili'te], *n.f.* credibility.

crédit [kre'di], *n.m.* credit; trust; authority, influence; esteem; vogue; parliamentary grant.

créditer [kredi'te], *v.t.* to credit.

créditeur [kredi'tœːr], *a.* credit.—*n.m.* (*fem.* **-trice**) creditor.

credo [kre'do], *n.m.* (*no pl.*) creed, belief.

crédule [kre'dyl], *a.* credulous.

crédulement [kredyl'mɑ̃], *adv.* credulously.

crédulité [kredyli'te], *n.f.* credulity.

créer [kre'e], *v.t.* to create; to produce; to invent, to imagine; to establish.

crémaillère [krema'jɛːr], *n.f.* pot-hook.

crémation [krema'sjɔ̃], *n.f.* cremation.

crématorium [krematɔ'rjɔm], *n.m.* (*pl.* **-ia**) crematorium.

crème [krɛːm], *n.f.* cream; custard; sweet liqueur; the best part of a thing.

crémer (1) [kre'me], *v.t.* (*conjug. like* CÉDER) to dye cream color. —*v.i.* to cream.

crémer (2) [kre'me], *v.t.* (*conjug. like* CÉDER) to cremate.

crémerie [krɛn'ri], *n.f.* creamery, dairy.

crémeux [kre'mø], *a.* (*fem.* **-euse**) creamy.

crémier [kre'mje], *n.m.* (*fem.* **-ière**) milkman, dairyman *or* -woman.—*n.f.* (**-ière**) cream pitcher.

créneau [kre'no], *n.m.* (*pl.* **-eaux**) battlement.

crénelage [kren'laːʒ], *n.m.* milling, milled edge (*on coins*), crenellation.

créneler [kren'le], *v.t.* (*conjug. like* APPELER) to embattle; to indent, to notch.

crénelure [kren'lyːr], *n.f.* crenellation; notching.

créole [kre'ɔl], *a.* Creole.—*n.* (**Créole**) Creole.

créosote [kreɔ'zɔt], *n.f.* creosote.

créosoter [kreɔzɔ'te], *v.t.* to creosote.

crêpe (1) [krɛːp], *n.m.* crape; (*fig.*) veil; crêpe rubber.

crêpe (2) [krɛːp], *n.f.* pancake.

crépelu [krɛ'ply], *a.* frizzy (*hair*).

crêper [krɛ'pe], *v.t.* to crisp, to frizz.

crépi [kre'pi], *n.m.* rough-cast, parget.

crépir [kre'piːr], *v.t.* to rough-cast, to plaster.

crépissage [krepi'saːʒ], **crépissement** [krepis'mɑ̃], *n.m.* plastering, pargeting, rough-casting.

crépissure [krepi'syːr], *n.m.* parget; rough-casting.

crépitant [krepi'tɑ̃], *a.* crepitating; crackling.
crépitation [krepitɑ'sjɔ̃], *n.f.*, **crépitement** [krepit'mɑ̃], *n.m.* crepitation; crackling.
crépiter [krepi'te], *v.i.* to crackle; to crepitate.
crépu [kre'py], *a.* crisped, frizzy; woolly.
crêpure [krɛ'py:r], *n.f.* crisping; craping.
crépusculaire [krepysky'lɛ:r], *a.* crepuscular, twilight.
crépuscule [krepys'kyl], *n.m.* twilight; dawn.
créquier [kre'kje], *n.m.* sloe tree.
cresson [krɛ'sɔ̃], *n.m.* cress.
cressonnière [krɛsɔ'njɛ:r], *n.f.* water-cress bed.
Crésus [kre'zy:s], *m.* Croesus.
crésus [kre'zy:s], *n.m. inv.* very rich man.
crétacé [kreta'se], *a.* cretaceous, chalky.
Crète [krɛ:t], **la**, *f.* Crete.
crête [krɛ:t], *n.f.* crest, comb (*of a cock or hen*); tuft; ridge; coping.
crêté [krɛ'te], *a.* crested, tufted.
crêteler [krɛ'tle], *v.i.* (*conjug. like* APPELER) to cackle (*of hens*).
crétin [kre'tɛ̃], *a.* cretinous; idiotic.—*n.m.* (*fem.* **-e**) cretin; idiot, dunce.
crétinerie [kretin'ri], *n.f.* idiotic behavior; foolishness.
crétiniser [kretini'ze], *v.t.* to make cretinous, to brutalize, to make an idiot of.
crétinisme [kreti'nism], *n.m.* cretinism.
crétois [kre'twa], *a.* Cretan.—*n.m.* (**Crétois**, *fem.* **-oise**) Cretan (*person*).
cretonne [krə'tɔn], *n.f.* cretonne.
creusage [krø'za:ʒ], **creusement** [krøz'mɑ̃], *n.m.* deepening, hollowing; excavation.
creuser [krø'ze], *v.t.* to dig, to hollow, to excavate, to scoop out; to sink, to drive (*a well, shaft etc.*); to make hollow or empty. **se creuser**, *v.r.* to become hollow.
creuset [krø'zɛ], *n.m.* crucible, melting pot; (*fig.*) test, trial.
creux [krø], *a.* (*fem.* **creuse**) hollow; cavernous; deep; empty; (*fig.*) airy, extravagant. —*n.m.* hollow, cavity; pit, hole, chasm; mold, mortar, trough.—*adv.* hollow; **sonner creux**, to sound hollow.
crevaison [krəvɛ'zɔ̃], *n.f.* puncture (*of a tire*).
crevant [krə'vɑ̃], *a.* (*vulg.*) tiresome; killing (*toil etc.*); killing (*funny*).
crevasse [krə'vas], *n.f.* crevice, rift, crack, chink, crevasse; gap, cranny; chap (*in the hands etc.*).
crevasser [krəva'se], *v.t.* to split; to crack; to chap. **se crevasser**, *v.r.* to crack, to become chapped.
crevé [krə've], *n.m.* (*Dress.*) opening, slash (*in sleeves*).
crève-cœur [krɛv'kœ:r], *n.m. inv.* heart-break; heart-breaking thing.
crever [krə've], *v.t.* (*conjug. like* AMENER) to burst, to split, to break open, to rend; to stave in; to puncture.—*v.i.* to burst; to die (*animals*); (*vulg.*) to die (*human beings*). **se crever**, *v.r.* to burst; to kill oneself.
crevette [krə'vɛt], *n.f.* shrimp, prawn.
cri [kri], *n.m.* cry; scream, roar, yell, shriek, screech, wail, outcry, clamor.
criaillement [kriɑj'mɑ̃], *n.m.* shouting, wrangling, brawling; scolding.

criailler [kriɑ'je], *v.i.* to bawl, to cry, to clamor; to scold; to brawl; to gabble (*of geese*).
criaillerie [kriɑj'ri], *n.f.* brawling, clamoring, wrangling.
criailleur [kriɑ'jœ:r], *n.m.* (*fem.* **-euse**) brawler, wrangler; shrew, scold.
criant [kri'ɑ̃], *a.* crying; (*fig.*) glaring, shocking.
criard [kri'a:r], *a.* crying, noisy, clamorous; scolding; (*fig.*) shrill, discordant, crude.— *n.m.* (*fem.* **-e**) bawler, clamorer; scold, shrew.
criblage [kri'bla:ʒ], *n.m.* sifting, screening (*of coals etc.*).
crible [kribl], *n.m.* sieve, riddle.
cribler [kri'ble], *v.t.* to sift, to riddle; to pierce all over, to riddle (*with wounds etc.*); (*fig.*) to overwhelm.
cric [kri], *n.m.* jack, screw-jack, hand-screw.
cri-cri [kri'kri], *n.m. inv.* (*fam.*) cricket (*insect*); chirping.
criée [kri'e], *n.f.* (*public*) auction.
crier [kri'e], *v.t.* to cry, to proclaim, to put up for sale; to publish; to announce.—*v.i.* to cry out; to shout, to scream, to shriek; to call out; to whine; to complain loudly, to exclaim; to chirp; to creak.
crieur [kri'jœ:r], *n.m.* (*fem.* **-euse**) bawler; crier; (*Theat.*) call-boy; auctioneer; hawker; **crieur public**, town crier; **crieur de journaux**, newsboy.
crime [krim], *n.m.* crime, offence.
Crimée [kri'me], **la**, *f.* the Crimea.
criminel [krimi'nɛl], *a.* (*fem.* **-elle**) criminal, felonious, guilty.—*n.m.* (*fem.* **-elle**) criminal, felon, culprit, offender.
criminellement [kriminɛl'mɑ̃], *adv.* criminally, culpably, guiltily.
crin [krɛ̃], *n.m.* horse-hair, bristles, fibres, mane.
crinière [kri'njɛ:r], *n.f.* mane (*of animal*).
crinoline [krinɔ'lin], *n.f.* crinoline.
crique [krik], *n.f.* creek, cove; flaw, crack.
criquet [kri'kɛ], *n.m.* locust; (*fig.*) bad horse.
criqueter [krik'te], *v.i.* (*conjug. like* APPELER) to rasp, to grate.
crise [kri:z], *n.f.* crisis; fit, convulsion; slump.
crispation [krispa'sjɔ̃], *n.f.* shrivelling, crispation; fidgets.
crisper [kris'pe], *v.t.* to shrivel; to irritate (*the nerves*), to give (*someone*) the fidgets. **se crisper**, *v.r.* to shrivel, to contract.
crissement [kris'mɑ̃], *n.m.* grating (*of teeth, of brakes etc.*).
crisser [kri'se], *v.i.* to grate, to squeak.
cristal [kris'tal], *n.m.* (*pl.* **-aux**) crystal, cut glass; (*fig.*) limpidity; **cristal de mine**, quartz; **cristal de roche**, rock crystal.
cristallerie [kristal'ri], *n.f.* glass-cutting; crystal manufactory, glass works.
cristallier [krista'lje], *n.m.* glass-cutter; glass cupboard.
cristallière [krista'ljɛ:r], *n.f.* rock-crystal mine; machine for glass-cutting.
cristallin [krista'lɛ̃], *a.* crystalline; pellucid. —*n.m.* (*Anat.*) crystalline lens (*of the eye*); (*Astron.*) crystalline heaven.
cristallisant [kristali'zɑ̃], *a.* crystallizing.
cristallisation [kristaliza'sjɔ̃], *n.f.* crystallization.

croustille

cristalliser [kristali'ze], *v.t.*, *v.i.* to crystallize. **se cristalliser**, *v.r.* to crystallize; to candy.

critère [kri'tɛːr], **critérium** [krite'rjɔm], *n.m.* criterion, standard, test.

critiquable [kriti'kabl], *a.* open to criticism, censurable, exceptionable.

critique [kri'tik], *a.* critical; censorious, carping; ticklish, momentous; critical (*in the literary sense*).—*n.m.* critic; censor, carper.—*n.f.* criticism, science of criticism; review.

critiquer [kriti'ke], *v.t.* to criticize unfavorably; to censure, to find fault with.

critiqueur [kriti'kœːr], *n.m.* (*fem.* **-euse**) criticizer, fault-finder, carper.

croassement [krɔas'mã], *n.m.* croak, croaking, cawing (*of rooks*).

croasser [krɔa'se], *v.i.* to croak, to caw (*of crows, rooks etc.*).

croate [krɔ'at], *a.* Croatian.—*n.m.* Croatian (*language*).—*n.* (**Croate**) Croat.

Croatie [krɔa'si], **la**, *f.* Croatia.

croc [krɔ], *n.m.* hook; fang (*of dog*), tusk (*of walrus*).

croc-en-jambe [krɔkã'ʒã:b], *n.m.* (*pl.* **crocs-en-jambe**) trip up; dirty trick.

croche [krɔʃ], *a.* crooked, bent.—*n.f.* (*Mus.*) quaver; (*pl.*) smith's tongs; **double croche**, semi-quaver; **triple croche**, demi-semiquaver.

crocher [krɔ'ʃe], *v.t.* to hook; to bend like a hook.

crochet [krɔ'ʃɛ], *n.m.* small hook; knitting needle, crochet hook; (*Print.*) square bracket; teeth of certain animals.

crochetable [krɔʃ'tabl], *a.* pickable (*of locks*).

crochetage [krɔʃ●a:ʒ], *n.m.* lock picking.

crocheter [krɔʃ'te], *v.t.* (*conjug. like* AMENER) to pick (*a lock*); to crochet.

crochetier [krɔʃ'tje], *n.m.* hook maker, clasp maker.

crochu [krɔ'ʃy], *a.* crooked, hooked.

crocodile [krɔkɔ'dil], *n.m.* crocodile; (*Rail.*) automatic stop.

crocus [krɔ'kyːs], *n.m.* (*Bot.*) crocus.

croire [krwaːr], *v.t. irr.* to believe; to have faith in; to think, to deem.—*v.i.* to believe, to have faith (*à*), to be a believer. **se croire**, *v.r.* to believe *or* think oneself. to consider oneself; to be believed, to be credible.

croisade [krwa'zad], *n.f.* crusade.

croisé [krwa'ze], *a.* crossed; twilled, doublemilled (*of cloth*); cross (*of breeds of animals*); **mots croisés**, a crossword.—*n.m.* crusader; twill; crossing (*a step in dancing*).

croisée [krwa'ze], *n.f.* crossing point; casement window (*opening inside*).

croisement [krwaz'mã], *n.m.* crossing (*of two roads etc.*); meeting; cross-breeding (*of animals*).

croiser [krwa'ze], *v.t.* to cross; to lay across; to cross (*breeds of animals*); to pass (*a person*); to thwart.—*v.i.* to overlap; to cruise. **se croiser**, *v.r.* to cross *or* pass each other; to be crossed; to thwart one another.

croiseur [krwa'zœːr], *n.m.* cruiser.

croisière [krwa'zjɛːr], *n.f.* cruise, cruising; (*Rail.*) crossing.

croissance [krwa'sãːs], *n.f.* growth, increase.

croissant [krwa'sã], *a.* growing, increasing.—*n.m.* the moon in her increase; crescent; pruning hook, hedging bill; crescent roll.

croît [krwa], *n.m.* increase (*from breeding*).

croître [krwaːtr], *v.i. irr.* to grow; to increase; to wax (*moon*); to spring up, to sprout; to lengthen; to swell.

croix [krwa], *n.f.* cross; the Holy Rood; (*fig.*) affliction; (*Coin.*) obverse.

cromlech [krɔm'lɛk], *n.m.* (*Archaeol.*) stone circle.

crône [kroːn], *n.m.* crane (*on a wharf*).

croquade [krɔ'kad], *n.f.* rough sketch.

croquant [krɔ'kã], *a.* crisp, crackling, short.—*n.m.* poor wretch; clodhopper.—*n.f.* crisp almond cake.

croque-au-sel (à la) [krɔkɔ'sɛl], *adv. phr.* with salt only.

croque-mitaine [krɔkmi'tɛn], *n.m.* (*pl.* **croque-mitaines**) bogy man.

croquer [krɔ'ke], *v.t.* to ˙crunch; to devour; to draft, to sketch.—*v.i.* to crackle between the teeth, to make a scrunching noise.

croquet [krɔ'kɛ], *n.m.* crisp biscuit; croquet (*game*).

croquette [krɔ'kɛt], *n.f.* croquette.

croquignole [krɔki'nɔl], *n.f.* cracknel; fillip; (*C*) doughnut.

croquis [krɔ'ki], *n.m.* first sketch, rough draft, outline.

cross [krɔs], *n.m.* (*Box.*) cross-counter; cross-country running.

crosse [krɔs], *n.f.* crooked stick, crosier (*of bishops*); butt (*of rifle*); stock; hockey stick, golf club etc.; (*C*) **jeu de crosse**, lacrosse.

crossé [krɔ'se], *a.* crosiered, mitred.

crosser [krɔ'se], *v.t.* to strike (*a ball etc.*).

crosseur [krɔ'sœːr], *n.m.* hockey player, lacrosse player.

crotale [krɔ'tal], *n.m.* rattlesnake.

crotte [krɔt], *n.f.* dung; dirt, mud, mire.

crotté [krɔ'te], *a.* dirty, muddy; (*fig.*) squalid.

crotter [krɔ'te], *v.t.* to dirty; to draggle, to bespatter. **se crotter**, *v.r.* to get dirty.

crottin [krɔ'tɛ̃], *n.m.* dung.

croulant [kru'lã], *a.* sinking, crumbling; tottering, tumbledown.

croulement [krul'mã], *n.m.* sinking, falling in, collapse.

crouler [kru'le], *v.i.* to give way, to fall in, to collapse.

croup [krup], *n.m.* (*Path.*) croup, diphtheria.

croupal [kru'pal], *a.* (*m. pl.* **-aux**) pertaining to the croup; laryngitic.

croupe [krup], *n.f.* croup, crupper, buttocks (*of a horse*), rump; top *or* brow (*of a hill*); **monter en croupe**, to ride pillion.

croupé [kru'pe], *a.* with a rump or crupper.

croupi [kru'pi], *a.* stagnant, putrid; **de l'eau croupie**, ditch water.

croupier [kru'pje], *n.m.* croupier (*at a gaming table*); partner (*of a financier etc.*).

croupière [kru'pjɛːr], *n.f.* saddle tie, crupper.

croupion [kru'pjɔ̃], *n.m.* rump; **le croupion** (*d'une volaille*), the parson's nose.

croupir [kru'piːr], *v.i.* to stagnate; to wallow.

croupissant [krupi'sã], *a.* stagnant, putrescent.

croupon [kru'pɔ̃], *n.m.* butt (*leather*).

croustillant [krusti'jã], *a.* crisp, crusty.

croustille [krus'tiːj], *n.f.* little crust; (*fig.*) snack.

93

croustiller [krusti'je], *v.i.* to bite, eat, crunch a crust, to munch.

croûte [krut], *n.f.* crust; pie crust; scab; *casser la croûte*, to have a snack; (*C*) crust (*of the snow*); (*fig.*) bad painting, daub.

croûton [kru'tɔ̃], *n.m.* bit of crust, crusty end; sippet.

croyable [krwa'jabl], *a.* credible, likely.

croyance [krwa'jɑ̃:s], *n.f.* belief; creed, faith.

croyant [krwa'jɑ̃], *a.* believing.—*n.m.* (*fem.* **-e**) believer.

cru (1) [kry], *n.m.* growth; production (*esp. of wine*).

cru (2) [kry], *a.* raw, uncooked; unwrought; (*fig.*) crude, coarse, indecent; *à cru*, on the bare skin.

cruauté [kryo'te], *n.f.* cruelty, inhumanity.

cruche [kryʃ], *n.f.* pitcher, jar, jug; (*colloq.*) blockhead.

cruchée [kry'ʃe], *n.f.* pitcherful, jugful, jarful.

cruchon [kry'ʃɔ̃], *n.m.* little pitcher; (*stone*) hot-water bottle.

crucial [kry'sjal], *a.* (*m. pl.* **-aux**) cross-shaped, crucial; (*fig.*) decisive.

crucifiement [krysifi'mɑ̃], *n.m.* crucifixion.

crucifier [krysi'fje], *v.t.* to crucify.

crucifix [krysi'fi], *n.m.* crucifix.

crucifixion [krysifik'sjɔ̃], *n.f.* crucifixion.

cruciforme [krysi'form], *a.* cruciform, cross-shaped.

crudité [krydi'te], *n.f.* crudity, rawness; coarse expression; (*pl.*) raw vegetables *or* fruit.

crue [kry], *n.f.* growth, increase; rise, swelling (*of river etc.*); flood.

cruel [kry'ɛl], *a.* (*fem.* **-elle**) cruel, merciless; bloodthirsty; hard; grievous, sad.

cruellement [kryɛl'mɑ̃], *adv.* cruelly; unmercifully; severely.

crûment [kry'mɑ̃], *adv.* roughly, coarsely; crudely.

crustacé [krysta'se], *a.* crustaceous.—*n.m.* crustacean; shell-fish.

crypte [kript], *n.f.* crypt.

cryptogramme [kriptɔ'gram], *n.m.* cryptogram, cipher.

cryptographe [kriptɔ'graf], *n.* cryptographer.

cryptographie [kriptɔgra'fi], *n.f.* cryptography.

cryptographique [kriptɔgra'fik], *a.* cryptographic.

cubage [ky'ba:ʒ], *n.m.* cubage, cubature; cubic content.

cubain [ky'bɛ̃], *a.* Cuban.—*n.m.* (**Cubain**, *fem.* **-aine**) Cuban (*person*).

cubature [kyba'ty:r], *n.f.* cubature.

cube [kyb], *a.* cubic.—*n.m.* cube (*shape and measure*).

cuber [ky'be], *v.t.* to cube.

cubique [ky'bik], *a.* cubic; cubical.

cubisme [ky'bism], *n.m.* (*Art*) cubism.

cubiste [ky'bist], *a.* and *n.* cubist.

cueillage [kœ'ja:ʒ], *n.m.*, **cueillaison** [kœje'zɔ̃], **cueille** [kœ:j], *n.f.* gathering time, gathering.

cueillette [kœ'jɛt], *n.f.* gathering of a crop; harvesting time.

cueilleur [kœ'jœːr], *n.m.* (*fem.* **-euse**) gatherer, picker.

cueillir [kœ'ji:r], *v.t. irr.* to gather, to cull, to pick, to pluck; to acquire.

cueilloir [kœj'wa:r], *n.m.* fruit basket; implement for picking fruit.

cuiller [kɥi'je], **cuillère** [kɥi'jɛːr], *n.f.* spoon; scoop.

cuillerée [kɥij're], *n.f.* spoonful.

cuilleron [kɥij'rɔ̃], *n.m.* bowl of a spoon.

cuir [kɥi:r], *n.m.* hide; leather; strop.

cuirasse [kɥi'ras], *n.f.* cuirass, breast-plate.

cuirassé [kɥira'se], *a.* armed with a cuirass; armour-plated; hardened; secret.—*n.m.* (*Naut.*) battleship.

cuirassement [kɥiras'mɑ̃], *n.m.* armor-plating.

cuirasser [kɥira'se], *v.t.* to arm with a cuirass; to armor-plate; (*fig.*) to steel, to harden. **se cuirasser**, *v.r.* to put on a cuirass; to harden *or* fortify oneself.

cuirassier [kɥira'sje], *n.m.* cuirassier.

cuire [kɥi:r], *v.t. irr.* (*conjug. like* CONDUIRE) to cook; to burn (*of the sun*); to ripen.—*v.i.* to cook, to be cooked, to be done; to bake, boil etc.; to smart.

cuisage [kɥi'za:ʒ], *n.m.* burning (*of charcoal*), charring.

cuisant [kɥi'zɑ̃], *a.* sharp, smarting; piercing.

cuiseur [kɥi'zœːr], *n.m.* pressure cooker.

cuisine [kɥi'zin], *n.f.* kitchen; cookery; cooks; fare, living; (*Naut.*) galley.

cuisiner [kɥizi'ne], *v.t., v.i.* to cook.

cuisinier [kɥizi'nje], *n.m.* (*fem.* **-ière**) cook.—*n.f.* (**-ière**) Dutch oven.

cuisse [kɥis], *n.f.* thigh; quarter (*of venison*); leg (*of poultry*).

cuisseau [kɥi'so], *n.m.* (*pl.* **-eaux**) leg (*of veal*).

cuisson [kɥi'sɔ̃], *n.f.* cooking (*baking, boiling, roasting etc.*); smart (*pain*).

cuissot [kɥi'so], *n.m.* haunch (*of venison*).

cuit [kɥi], *a.* cooked, done (*roasted, boiled, baked etc.*); (*fig.*) done for, dished.

cuite [kɥit], *n.f.* baking; burning (*of bricks etc.*); ovenful, kilnful; (*slang*) intoxication.

cuivrage [kɥi'vra:ʒ], *n.m.* coppering, copper-plating.

cuivre [kɥi:vr], *n.m.* copper; copper money; copper-plate; *cuivre battu*, wrought copper; *cuivre jaune*, brass; *cuivre rouge*, copper.

cuivré [kɥi'vre], *a.* copper-colored; (*fig.*) bronzed (*complexion*); ringing, clear.

cuivrer [kɥi'vre], *v.t.* to cover with copper.

cuivrerie [kɥivrə'ri], *n.f.* copper-works; copper wares.

cuivreux [kɥi'vrø], *a.* (*fem.* **-euse**) coppery.

cul [ky], *n.m.* (*indec.*) backside, posterior; bottom (*of bottle or bag*); stern (*of ship*).

culasse [ky'las], *n.f.* breech (*of a cannon etc.*); cylinder head (*of car engine*).

culbute [kyl'byt], *n.f.* somersault; fall, tumble; (*fig.*) ruin, bankruptcy.

culbuter [kylby'te], *v.t.* to throw over, to upset violently; to overthrow.—*v.i.* to fall head over heels.

culbutis [kylby'ti], *n.m.* confused heap, jumble.

cul de bouteille [kydbu'tɛ:j], *a.* bottle-green. —*n.m.* bottom of bottle.

cul-de-jatte [kyd'ʒat], *n.m.* (*pl.* **culs-de-jatte**) legless cripple.

cul-de-lampe [kyd'lɑ̃p], *n.m.* (*Print.*) tail-piece.

cul-de-sac [kyd'sak], *n.m.* (*pl.* **culs-de-sac**) blind alley, cul-de-sac; (*fig.*) deadlock.

culée [ky'le], *n.f.* abutment (*of bridges*); (*Naut.*) stern-way.

culer [ky'le], *v.i.* to go backwards; to fall astern.

culière [ky'ljɛːr], *n.f.* hind girth, crupper (*of harness*); gutter stone.

culinaire [kyli'nɛːr], *a.* culinary.

culminance [kylmi'nãːs], *n.f.* culmination, highest point.

culminant [kylmi'nã], *a.* culminating; prominent.

culmination [kylmina'sjɔ̃], *n.f.* culmination.

culminer [kylmi'ne], *v.i.* to culminate.

culot [ky'lo], *n.m.* bottom (*of lamps, crucibles etc.*); residuum, (*fam.*) dottle (*in a pipe*).

culottage [kylɔ'taːʒ], *n.m.* coloring, seasoning (*of pipes*).

culotte [ky'lɔt], *n.f.* breeches; (*pl.*) shorts; tights; (*Cook.*) rump (*of an ox*).

culotter [kylɔ'te], *v.t.* to breech, to put in breeches; to color (*pipes*). **se culotter,** *v.r.* to put on one's breeches; to become colored (*of pipes*).

culottier [kylɔ'tje], *n.m.* (*fem.* **-ière**) breeches maker.

culpabilité [kylpabili'te], *n.f.* culpability; guilt.

culte [kylt], *n.m.* worship, adoration; (*fig.*) cult, religion, creed; veneration, love.

cultivable [kylti'vabl], *a.* cultivable, arable.

cultivateur [kyltiva'tœːr], *a.* agricultural.— *n.m.* (*fem.* **-trice**) cultivator, farmer, agriculturist; cultivator (*implement*).

cultivé [kylti've], *a.* cultivated; (*of the mind*) cultured.

cultiver [kylti've], *v.t.* to cultivate; to till; to improve (*the mind*); to study, to practise; to cultivate the acquaintance of.

cultural [kylty'ral], *a.* (*m. pl.* **-aux**) cultural (*in relation to agriculture*).

culture [kyl'tyːr], *n.f.* culture, cultivation, tillage, husbandry; education, improvement.

culturel [kylty'rɛl], *a.* (*fem.* **-elle**) cultural (*in relation to intellectual culture*).

cumulatif [kymyla'tif], *a.* (*fem.* **-tive**) cumulative.

cumulativement [kymylativ'mã], *adv.* by accumulation.

cumuler [kymy'le], *v.t.* to accumulate; to hold several (*offices, salaries etc.*).

cumulus [kymy'lyːs], *n.m.* cumulus.

cupide [ky'pid], *a.* covetous, greedy, grasping.

cupidement [kypid'mã], *adv.* greedily, covetously.

cupidité [kypidi'te], *n.f.* cupidity, covetousness, greed.

Cupidon [kypi'dɔ̃], *n.m.* (*Myth.*) Cupid, Love.

curable [ky'rabl], *a.* curable.

curaçao [kyra'so], *n.m.* curaçao (*liqueur*).

curage [ky'raːʒ], **curement** [kyr'mã], *n.m.* cleansing.

curatelle [kyra'tɛl], *n.f.* guardianship, trusteeship.

curateur [kyra'tœːr], *n.m.* (*fem.* **-trice**) guardian, trustee.

curatif [kyra'tif], *a.* (*fem.* **-tive**) curative.— *n.m.* curative agent.

cure [kyːr], *n.f.* medical treatment, cure, healing; living, rectorship; vicarage, rectory.

curé [ky're], *n.m.* parish priest; parson, rector, vicar.

cure-dent [kyr'dã], *n.m.* (*pl.* **cure-dents**) tooth-pick.

curée [ky're], *n.f.* (*Hunt.*) quarry, chase; (*fig.*) prey, booty.

curement [CURAGE].

cure-môle [kyr'moːl], *n.m.* (*pl.* **cure-môles**) dredging machine.

cure-ongles [kyr'rɔ̃gl], *n.m. inv.* nail file.

curer [ky're], *v.t.* to cleanse, to clean out (*harbors, sewers etc.*); to pick (*teeth, ears etc.*).

curial (1) [ky'rjal], *a.* (*m. pl.* **-aux**) vicarial, rectorial.

curial (2) or **curiale** [ky'rjal], *a.* (*Rom. Ant.*) curial.

curie [ky'ri], *n.f.* (*Rom. Ant.*) curia.

curieusement [kyrjøz'mã], *adv.* curiously; inquisitively; carefully; quaintly.

curieux [ky'rjø], *a.* (*fem.* **-euse**) curious; inquisitive, prying; inquiring; careful; dainty; particular; strange.—*n.m.* (*fem.* **-euse**) interested person; inquisitive person; sightseer, looker-on.—*n.m.* curious fact.

curiosité [kyrjozi'te], *n.f.* curiosity; inquisitiveness; curio, rarity; quaintness.

cursif [kyr'sif], *a.* (*fem.* **-sive**) cursive, running; cursory.

cursivement [kyrsiv'mã], *adv.* cursively; cursorily.

curure [ky'ryːr], *n.f.* dirt, sewage.

cussonné [kysɔ'ne], *a.* worm-eaten (*of wood*).

custode [kys'tɔd], *n.m.* warden (*among monks*); custodian, inspector.

cutané [kyta'ne], *a.* cutaneous.

cuticule [kyti'kyl], *n.f.* cuticle.

cuvage [ky'vaːʒ], *n.m.*, **cuvaison** [kyvɛ'zɔ̃], *n.f.* fermenting (*of wine*).

cuve [kyːv], *n.f.* tub, vat.

cuvée [ky've], *n.f.* tubful; vatful.

cuvelage [ky'vlaːʒ], **cuvellement** [kyvɛl'mã], *n.m.* lining, casing (*of mine shafts*).

cuveler [ky'vle], *v.t.* (*conjug. like* APPELER) to line, to case (*mine shafts etc.*).

cuver [ky've], *v.t.* to ferment; (*fam.*) to sleep off the effects of (*wine*).—*v.i.* to work, to ferment, to settle.

cuvette [ky'vɛt], *n.f.* shallow basin; wash basin; lavatory bowl.

cuvier [ky'vje], *n.m.* wash tub.

cyanure [sja'nyːr], *n.m.* (*Chem.*) cyanide.

cybernétique [sibɛrne'tik], *n.f.* cybernetics.

cyclamen [sikla'mɛn], *n.m.* cyclamen, sowbread.

cycle [sikl], *n.m.* cycle (*of events*); **cycle à 4 temps** (*d'un moteur*), 4-stroke cycle (*of an engine*).

cyclique [si'klik], *a.* cyclical.

cyclisme [si'klism], *n.m.* cycling.

cycliste [si'klist], *n.* cyclist.

cyclomoteur [siklɔmɔ'tœːr], *n.m.* motorbike.

cyclonal [siklɔ'nal], *a.* (*m. pl.* **-aux**) cyclonic.

cyclone [si'klɔːn], *n.m.* cyclone.

cyclonique [siklɔ'nik], *a.* cyclonic.

Cyclope [si'klɔp], *n.m.* Cyclops.

cygne [siɲ], *n.m.* swan.

cylindrage [silɛ̃'draːʒ], *n.m.* mangling (*of linen etc.*); rolling (*of roads*).

cylindre [si'lɛ̃ːdr], *n.m.* cylinder; roller; garden roller; mangle, calender.

cylindrée

cylindrée [silɛ̃'dre], *n.f.* cubic capacity of an engine.
cylindrer [silɛ̃'dre], *v.t.* to calender; to roll.
cylindrique [silɛ̃'drik], *a.* cylindrical.
cymaise [CIMAISE].
cymbale [sɛ̃'bal], *n.f.* (*Mus.*) cymbal.
cymbalier [sɛ̃ba'lje], *n.m.* cymbal player.
cynancie [sinɑ̃'si], [ESQUINANCIE].
cynégétique [sineʒe'tik], *a.* relating to hunting and dogs.—*n.f.* the art of hunting with dogs, cynegetics.
cynique [si'nik], *a.* cynical; snarling, snappish; impudent.—*n.* cynic.
cyniquement [sinik'mɑ̃], *adv.* cynically.
cynisme [si'nism], *n.m.* cynicism; impudence.
cynodrome [sino'dro:m], *n.m.* greyhound racing track.
cynosure [sino'sy:r], *n.f.* (*Astron.*) Cynosure, Little Bear.
cyprès [si'prɛ], *n.m.* cypress, cypress tree.
cyprière [si'prjɛ:r], *n.f.* cypress grove.
cypriote [si'prjɔt], *a.* Cypriot.—*n.* (**Cypriote**) Cypriot (*person*).
cytise [si'ti:z], *n.m.* cytisus, laburnum.
czar [tsa:r], [TZAR].

D

D, d [de], *n.m.* the fourth letter of the alphabet.
d', *abbr.* [DE].
da [da], *particle* (*used after* **oui**, **non**) truly, indeed; **oui-da**, yes indeed.
d'abord [da'bɔ:r], [ABORD].
dactylo [dakti'lo], *n.f. abbr. of* [DACTYLO-GRAPHE].
dactylographe [daktilɔ'graf], *n.f.* typist.
dactylographie [daktilɔgra'fi], *n.f.* typewriting.
dactylographier [daktilɔgra'fje], *v.t.* to type(write).
dactylographique [daktilɔgra'fik], *a.* typewritten (*report*); typewriting (*material*).
dactyloptère [daktilɔp'tɛ:r], *n.m.* flying fish.
dada [da'da], *n.m.* (*childish*) horse, cockhorse; gee-gee.
dadais [da'dɛ], *n.m.* booby, clown, ninny.
dague [dag], *n.f.* dagger, dirk.
daguerréotype [dagɛreo'tip], *n.m.* daguerreotype.
dahlia [da'lja], *n.m.* dahlia.
daigner [dɛ'ne], *v.i.* to deign, to condescend.
d'ailleurs [da'jœ:r], [AILLEURS].
daim [dɛ̃], *n.m.* deer, fallow deer; buck.
daine [dɛn], *n.f.* doe.
dais [dɛ], *n.m.* canopy.
dallage [da'la:ʒ], *n.m.* paving with flagstones.
dalle [dal], *n.f.* flag, flagstone; slab.
daller [da'le], *v.t.* to pave with flagstones, to flag.
dalleur [da'lœ:r], *n.m.* pavior.
dalmate [dal'mat], *a.* Dalmatian.—*n.* (**Dalmate**) Dalmatian (*person*).
dalmatique [dalma'tik], *n.f.* dalmatic.
daltonisme [daltɔ'nism], *n.m.* color blindness.

damas [da'ma], *n.m.* damask; damson; Damascus blade.
damasquiner [damaski'ne], *v.t.* to damascene.
damassé [dama'se], *n.m.* damask linen, damask cloth.
damasser [dama'se], *v.t.* to damask.
damassin [dama'sɛ̃], *n.m.* figured linen cloth.
damassure [dama'sy:r], *n.f.* damasking (*of linen*); damask work.
dame (1) [dam], *n.f.* (*married*) lady, dame; rowlock; beetle, rammer; (*Cards, and Chess*) queen.
dame (2) [dam], *int.* **dame oui!** why, yes!
dame-jeanne [dam'ʒɑ:n], *n.f.* (*pl.* **dames-jeannes**) demijohn, carboy.
damer [da'me], *v.t.* (*Draughts*) to crown (*a man*); (*Chess*) to queen; to ram (*earth etc.*).
damier [da'mje], *n.m.* draught board.
damnable [dɑ'nabl], *a.* damnable.
damnablement [dɑnablə'mɑ̃], *adv.* damnably.
damnation [dɑnɑ'sjɔ̃], *n.f.* damnation.
damné [dɑ'ne], *a.* and *n.m.* (*fem.* **-ée**) damned (*person*).
damner [dɑ'ne], *v.t.* to damn. **se damner**, *v.r.* to damn oneself.
dancing [dɑ̃'siŋ], *n.m.* dance hall, palais de danse.
dandin [dɑ̃'dɛ̃], *n.m.* ninny.
dandinement [dɑ̃din'mɑ̃], *n.m.* swinging (*of the body*); rolling gait.
dandiner [dɑ̃di'ne], *v.i.* to swing (*of the body*) to dandle (*of a baby*). **se dandiner**, *v.r.* to waddle.
dandy [dɑ̃'di], *n.m.* dandy.
dandysme [dɑ̃'dism], *n.m.* dandyism.
Danemark [dan'mark], **le**, *m.* Denmark.
danger [dɑ̃'ʒe], *n.m.* danger, peril, risk, hazard.
dangereusement [dɑ̃ʒrøz'mɑ̃], *adv.* dangerously.
dangereux [dɑ̃'ʒrø], *a.* (*fem.* **-euse**) dangerous.
danois [da'nwa], *a.* Danish.—*n.m.* Danish (*language*); Great Dane (*dog*); (**Danois**, *fem.* **-oise**) Dane (*person*).
dans [dɑ̃], *prep.* in, within; into; with, according to; during; out of.
danse [dɑ̃:s], *n.f.* dance; dancing; (*fig.*) beating, hiding; **danse de Saint-Guy**, St. Vitus's dance.
danser [dɑ̃'se], *v.t., v.i.* to dance.
danseur [dɑ̃'sœ:r], *n.m.* (*fem.* **-euse**) dancer, ballet girl.
dard [da:r], *n.m.* dart; sting; forked tongue (*of a snake*); pistil.
darder [dar'de], *v.t.* to hurl; to spear; to shoot forth, to beam, to dart.
dardillon [dardi'jɔ̃], *n.m.* small dart; barb (*of a fish-hook*).
dare-dare [dar'da:r], *adv.* (*fam.*) in great haste, in double-quick time.
darne [darn], *n.f.* slice (*of fish*).
dartre [dartr], *n.f.* slight and dry eruption (*of the skin*), scurf.
dartreux [dar'trø], *a.* (*fem.* **-euse**) herpetic, scurfy.
date [dat], *n.f.* date.
dater [da'te], *v.t.* to date (*a letter etc.*).—*v.i.* to date (*de*); to reckon.
datif [da'tif], *n.m.* (*Gram.*) dative, dative case.

datte [dat], *n.f.* date.
dattier [da'tje], *n.m.* date palm.
datura [daty'ra], *n.m.* datura, thorn apple.
daube [do:b], *n.f.* stew.
dauber [do'be], *v.t.* to cuff, to drub; (*fig.*) to banter, to jeer at; (*Cook.*) to stew.
daubeur [do'bœ:r], *n.m.* (*fem.* **-euse**) jeerer, banterer, sneerer.
daubière [do'bjɛ:r], *n.f.* stew pan.
dauphin [do'fɛ̃], *n.m.* dolphin; dauphin (*eldest son of the king of France*).
dauphine [do'fin], *n.f.* wife of the dauphin.
dauphinelle [dofi'nɛl], *n.f.* (*Bot.*) larkspur, delphinium.
daurade [do'rad], *n.f.* gilt-head (*fish*).·
davantage [davɑ̃'ta:ʒ], *adv.* more, any more; any longer, any further.
davier [da'vje], *n.m.* dentist's forceps; cramp; (*Naut.*) davit.
de [də], *prep.* of; out of, made of, composed of, from; by, with; at, for; concerning, about.
dé (1) [de], *n.m.* die (*for playing*); (*fig.*) throw, hazard.
dé (2) [de], *n.m.* thimble.
débâcher [deba'ʃe], *v.t.* to uncover, to untilt.
débâcle [de'ba:kl], *n.f.* breaking up (*of ice*); (*fig.*) downfall, collapse.
débâcler [deba'kle], *v.i.* to break up (*of ice*).
débâcleur [deba'klœ:r], *n.m.* water *or* port bailiff.
déballage [deba'la:ʒ], *n.m.* unpacking.
déballer [deba'le], *v.t.* to unpack.
débandade [debɑ̃'dad], *n.f.* rout, stampede; *à la débandade*, in confusion.
débander [debɑ̃'de], *v.t.* to unbind; to loosen; to remove a bandage from. **se débander**, *v.r.* to slacken, to relax; to disband.
débaptiser [debati'ze], *v.t.* to change the name of.
débarbouillage [debarbu'ja:ʒ], *n.m.* washing, cleansing.
débarbouiller [debarbu'je], *v.t.* to wash, to cleanse. **se débarbouiller**, *v.r.* to wash one's face etc.; (*fig.*) to extricate oneself.
débarcadère [debarka'dɛ:r], *n.m.* landing place, wharf; (*Rail.*) station; arrival platform.
débardage [debar'da:ʒ], *n.m.* unloading (*of wood etc.*).
débarder [debar'de], *v.t.* to unload (*wood etc.*); to clear (*a wood etc.*) of felled trees.
débardeur [debar'dœ:r], *n.m.* stevedore, lighterman, docker.
débarquement [debarkə'mɑ̃], *n.m.* landing, disembarkation (*of persons*); unloading (*of goods*).
débarquer [debar'ke], *v.t.*, *v.i.* to disembark, to land.
débarras [deba'ra], *n.m.* riddance, disencumbrance; *chambre de débarras*, lumber-room, box room.
débarrasser [debara'se], *v.t.* to disencumber, to rid; to disentangle, to extricate; to clear (*the table*). **se débarrasser**, *v.r.* to extricate oneself, to rid oneself of; to shake off; to get clear.
débarrer [deba're], *v.t.* to unbar.
débat [de'ba], *n.m.* dispute, contest; debate, discussion; (*pl.*) parliamentary debates.
débateler [debata'le], *v.t.* (*conjug. like* APPELER) to unlade (*boats etc.*).

débâter [debɑ'te], *v.t.* to unsaddle; to take a packsaddle off.
débâtir [debɑ'ti:r], *v.t.* to pull down, to demolish; to unbaste, to untack (*garments*).
débattre [de'batr], *v.t.* (*conjug. like* BATTRE) to debate, to discuss, to argue. **se débattre**, *v.r.* to struggle, to strive; to flounder, to flutter.
débauche [de'bo:ʃ], *n.f.* debauchery; dissoluteness.
débauché [debo'ʃe], *n.m.* debauchee, rake.
débaucher [debo'ʃe], *v.t.* to debauch; to corrupt; to lead astray. **se débaucher**, *v.r.* to become debauched.
débet [de'bɛ], *n.m.* debit.
débile [de'bil], *a.* weak, feeble.
débilement [debil'mɑ̃], *adv.* feebly, weakly.
débilité [debili'te], *n.f.* debility, weakness.
débiliter [debili'te], *v.t.* to debilitate, to enfeeble.
débit [de'bi], *n.m.* sale; market; retail; retail shop; (*fig.*) delivery, utterance; (*Bookkeeping*) debit.
débitage [debi'ta:ʒ], *n.m.* cutting up (*of stones, timber etc.*).
débitant [debi'tɑ̃], *n.m.* (*fem.* **-e**) retailer, dealer.
débiter [debi'te], *v.t.* to sell; to retail; to supply; to debit; to cut up (*wood, stone etc.*); (*fig.*) to spread, to report, to utter.
débiteur (1) [debi'tœ:r], *n.m.* (*fem.* **-trice**) debtor.
débiteur (2) [debi'tœ:r], *n.m.* (*fem.* **-euse**) prattler, gossipmonger.
déblai [de'blɛ], *n.m.* clearing; excavation; (*pl.*) earth, stones etc. cleared away.
déblaiement *or* **déblayement** [deblɛ'mɑ̃], *n.m.* clearance; cutting, excavation, digging.
déblatérer [deblate're], *v.i.* (*conjug. like* CÉDER) to utter violent abuse, to rail (*contre*).
déblayement [DÉBLAIEMENT].
déblayer [deblɛ'je], *v.t.* (*conjug. like* PAYER) to clear away; to clear; (*fig.*) to sweep away (*obstacles etc.*).
déblocage [deblɔ'ka:ʒ], *n.m.* (*Print.*) turning letters.
débloquer [deblɔ'ke], *v.t.* to raise the blockade from; (*Print.*) to turn letters; to release.
débobiner [debɔbi'ne], *v.t.* to unwind.
déboire [de'bwa:r], *n.m.* after-taste; (*fig.*) disappointment, vexation.
déboisement [debwaz'mɑ̃], *n.m.* clearing of trees, deforestation.
déboiser [debwa'ze], *v.t.* to clear of trees.
déboîtement [debwat'mɑ̃], *n.m.* dislocation.
déboîter [debwa'te], *v.t.* to put out of joint, to dislocate; (*Elec.*) to disconnect. **se déboîter**, *v.r.* to be dislocated.
débonder [debɔ̃'de], *v.t.* to unplug, to unstopper; to loosen, to unbind.—*v.i.* or **se débonder**, *v.r.* to gush, to break out, to burst forth; to be relaxed (*of a person*).
débonnaire [debɔ'nɛ:r], *a.* good-natured, easy-tempered.
débonnairement [debɔnɛr'mɑ̃], *adv.* compliantly, easily.
débonnaireté [debɔnɛr'te], *n.f.* compliance, good nature.
débordé [debɔr'de], *a.* overflowing (*river*); overwhelmed (*man*); outflanked (*troops*).

débordement [debɔrdə′mā], *n.m.* overflowing, flood; outburst; (*fig.*) dissoluteness.

déborder [debɔr′de], *v.t.* to take off the border from; to go beyond; to outrun.—*v.i.* to overflow, to run over; to project, to jut out. **se déborder**, *v.r.* to overflow; to run over, to burst forth.

débordoir [debɔr′dwa:r], *n.m.* edging tool; spoke shave.

débosseler [debɔs′le], *v.t.* (*conjug. like* APPELER) to take the dents out of.

débotté or **débotter** (1) [debɔ′te], *n.m.* the moment of taking boots off; (*fig.*) **au débotté**, at once.

débotter (2) [debɔ′te], *v.t.* to pull off (*some-one's*) boots. **se débotter**, *v.r.* to take off one's boots.

débouché [debu′ʃe], *n.m.* outlet, issue; waterway; (*Comm.*) market, sale.

débouchage [debu′ʃa:ʒ], **débouchement** [debuʃ′mā], *n.m.* uncorking; outlet; market, sale.

déboucher [debu′ʃe], *v.t.* to open, to clear; to uncork; to unplug.—*v.i.* to emerge; to empty itself (*of rivers*); (*Mil.*) to debouch.

déboucler [debu′kle], *v.t.* to unbuckle; to uncurl.

débouler [debu′le], *v.i.* to roll down (*like a ball*); to start off suddenly (*like a hare*).

déboulonner [debulɔ′ne], *v.t.* to unrivet, to unbolt.

débourrer [debu′re], *v.t.* to draw the wad *or* wadding out of (*fire arms*); to empty the tobacco out of (*a pipe*); (*fig.*) to polish (*a person's manners*).

débours [de′bu:r], **déboursé** [debur′se], *n.m.* disbursement, outlay.

déboursement [deburs′mā], *n.m.* outlay, expenditure.

débourser [debur′se], *v.t.* to disburse, to expend, to lay out.

debout [dɔ′bu], *adv.* upright, on end, standing up; out of bed, up; in existence; (*Naut.*) ahead (*of the wind*).

déboutonner [debutɔ′ne], *v.t.* to unbutton. **se déboutonner**, *v.r.* to unbutton oneself; (*colloq.*) to unbosom oneself.

débraillé [debra′je], *a.* loosely dressed, in disorder.—*n.m.* disorder, untidiness; (*fig.*) license.

débrailler (se) [sədebra′je], *v.r.* to uncover one's breast, to be untidy *or* disordered.

débrancher [debrā′ʃe], *v.t.* (*Elec.*) to disconnect.

débrayage [debrɛ′ja:ʒ], **désembrayage** [dezābrɛ′ja:ʒ], *n.m.* disengaging gear (*of motors etc.*); declutching.

débrayer [debrɛ′je], *v.t.* (*conjug. like* PAYER) to throw out of gear, to disengage, to declutch.

débridement [debrid′mā], *n.m.* unbridling; (*fig.*) dispatch, hurry.

débrider [debri′de], *v.t. v.i.* to unbridle (*horse*); to halt.

débris [de′bri], *n.m.* (*usu. in pl.*) remains, debris; rubbish.

débrouillard [debru′ja:r], *a.* and *n.m.* (*fem.* -e) (*colloq.*) resourceful (person).

débrouiller [debru′je], *v.t.* to disentangle, to unravel; (*fig.*) to explain. **se débrouiller**, *v.r.* to be cleared up; to get out of difficulties, to manage.

débusquement [debyskə′mā], *n.m.* driving out, dislodging.

débusquer [debys′ke], *v.t.* to turn out, to oust, to expel; (*Hunt.*) to start.

début [de′by], *n.m.* lead; outset; début.

débutant [deby′tā], *n.m.* (*fem.* -e) actor *or* actress appearing for the first time; beginner.

débuter [deby′te], *v.i.* to lead, to play first; to open; to start; to make one's début.

deçà [dɔ′sa], *prep.* on this side of; short of, well within.—*adv.* here, on this side; **deçà** (*et*) **delà**, here and there.

décachetage [dekaʃ′ta:ʒ], *n.m.* unsealing, opening.

décacheter [dekaʃ′te], *v.t.* (*conjug. like* APPELER) to unseal, to open.

décadaire [deka′dɛ:r], *a.* decadal.

décade [de′kad], *n.f.* decade, group of ten.

décadenasser [dekadna′se], *v.t.* to unpadlock.

décadence [deka′dā:s], *n.f.* decadence, decline, wane.

décadent [deka′dā], *a.* and *n.m.* (*fem.* -e) decadent (person).

décaèdre [deka′ɛdr], *a.* decahedral.—*n.m.* decahedron.

décagonal [dekagɔ′nal], *a.* (*pl.* -aux) decagonal (*ten-sided*).

décagone [deka′gɔn], *n.m.* decagon.

décagramme [deka′gram], *n.m.* decagramme, ten grammes.

décaissement [dekɛs′mā], **décaissage** [dekɛ′sa:ʒ], *n.m.* uncasing, unpacking.

décaisser [dekɛ′se], *v.t.* to unpack; to pay out.

décaler [deka′le], *v.t.* to unwedge.

décalaminage [dekalami′na:ʒ], *n.m.* (*Motor.*) decarbonizing.

décalaminer [dekalami′ne], *v.t.* to decarbonize.

décalitre [deka′litr], *n.m.* decalitre (2·2 *gallons*).

décalquer [dekal′ke], *v.t.* to transfer (*a tracing*), to countertrace.

décamètre [deka′mɛtr], *n.m.* decametre.

décamper [dekā′pe], *v.i.* to decamp; (*fig.*) to bolt.

décanter [dekā′te], *v.t.* to decant, to pour off gently.

décapitation [dekapita′sjɔ̃], *n.f.* decapitation, beheading.

décapiter [dekapi′te], *v.t.* to behead, to decapitate.

décapotable [dekapɔ′tabl], *a.* (*Motor.*) convertible.

décarboniser [dekarbɔni′ze], *v.t.* to decarbonize.

décarburation [dekarbyra′sjɔ̃], *n.f.* decarbonization.

décarburer [dekarby′re], *v.t.* to decarburize, to decarbonize.

décastère [deka′stɛ:r], *n.m.* measure of 10 steres *or* cubic metres (13.1 cubic yards).

décathlon [dekat′lɔ̃], *n.m.* (*spt.*) decathlon.

decauville [dəkɔ′vil], *n.m.* narrow gauge railway.

décaver [deka′ve], *v.t.* to win the whole of the stakes from, (*fam.*) to clean out; (*fig.*) to ruin, to beggar.

décédé [dese′de], *n.m.* (*fem.* -ée) deceased (*person*).

décéder [dese′de], *v.i.* (*conjug. like* CÉDER) to die, to decease.

décèlement [desɛl'mã], *n.m.* disclosure, exposure, discovery.

déceler [des'le], *v.t.* (*conjug. like* AMENER) to disclose, to reveal, to betray. **se déceler,** *v.r.* to betray oneself.

déceleur [des'lœ:r], *n.m.* (*fem.* **-euse**) betrayer, revealer.

décembre [de'sã:br], *n.m.* December.

décemment [desa'mã], *adv.* decently.

décence [de'sã:s], *n.f.* decency, propriety.

décent [de'sã], *a.* decent, becoming; modest.

décentralisation [desãtraliza'sjɔ̃], *n.f.* decentralization.

décentraliser [desãtrali'ze], *v.t.* to decentralize.

déception [desɛp'sjɔ̃], *n.f.* disappointment; deception, deceit.

décernement [desɛrnə'mã], *n.m.* awarding.

décerner [desɛr'ne], *v.t.* to decree, to enact; to award, to confer (*an honor*); to issue (*a summons etc.*).

décès [de'sɛ], *n.m.* decease, demise, death.

décevant [des'vã], *a.* deceptive; disappointing.

décevoir [desə'vwa:r], *v.t.* irr. (*conjug. like* RECEVOIR) to deceive; to disappoint.

déchaînement [deʃɛn'mã], *n.m.* unbridling, bursting (*of storm*); outburst (*of passion*); fury, rage; invective.

déchaîner [deʃɛ'ne], *v.t.* to unchain, to let loose; to give vent to (*passion*). **se déchaîner,** *v.r.* to break loose; to burst out; to run wild (*of passions etc.*).

déchaler [deʃa'le], *v.i.* to ebb; to lie dry.

déchanter [deʃã'te], *v.i.* to lower one's key (*in singing*); (*fig.*) to lower one's pretensions, to sing another tune.

déchaperonner [deʃaprɔ'ne], *v.t.* to unhood (*a hawk etc.*); to uncope (*a wall*).

décharge [de'ʃarʒ], *n.f.* unloading; rebate (*on a tax*); outlet, discharge (*of water etc.*); (*Law*) discharge, acquittal; (*Mil.*) volley.

déchargement [deʃarʒə'mã], *n.m.* unloading, unlading.

décharger [deʃar'ʒe], *v.t.* (*conjug. like* MANGER) to unload; to empty; to disburden; to discharge; to fire (*fire-arms*); to acquit (*de*). **se décharger,** *v.r.* to be unloaded, to discharge; to give vent (*to*); to unburden oneself.

déchargeur [deʃar'ʒœ:r], *n.m.* unloader, wharf porter, heaver, lumper.

décharné [deʃar'ne], *a.* fleshless; lean, emaciated.

décharnement [deʃarnə'mã], *n.m.* emaciation.

décharner [deʃar'ne], *v.t.* to strip the flesh off; to emaciate.

déchaumage [deʃo'ma:ʒ], *n.m.* (*Agric.*) ploughing up fallow ground.

déchaumer [deʃo'me], *v.t.* to plough up the stubble on; to break up (*follow land*).

déchaussé [deʃo'se], *a.* barefooted.

déchausser [deʃo'se], *v.t.* to pull off (*someone's*) shoes and stockings; to lay bare the root *or* base (*of trees, buildings, teeth etc.*). **se déchausser,** *v.r.* to take off one's shoes and stockings.

déchéance [deʃe'ã:s], *n.f.* forfeiture; disgrace; deposition.

déchet [de'ʃɛ], *n.m.* loss, waste, offal.

décheveler [deʃə'vle], *v.t.* (*conjug. like* APPELER) to dishevel [ÉCHEVELER].

déchevêtrer [deʃəvɛ'tre], *v.t.* to unhalter (*a beast of burden*).

décheviller [deʃəvi'je], *v.t.* to unpeg, to unpin.

déchiffrable [deʃi'frabl], *a.* legible.

déchiffrement [deʃifrə'mã], *n.m.* deciphering; reading *or* playing at sight.

déchiffrer [deʃi'fre], *v.t.* to decipher, to unravel; to read *or* play at sight. **se déchiffrer,** *v.r.* to be deciphered.

déchiffreur [deʃi'frœ:r], *n.m.* (*fem.* **-euse**) decipherer; sight reader; **déchiffreur de radar,** radar scanner.

déchiqueté [deʃik'te], *a.* jagged, indented.

déchiqueter [deʃik'te], *v.t.* (*conjug. like* APPELER) to cut, to slash, to hack; to cut into long pieces.

déchiqueture [deʃik'ty:r], *n.f.* tear, slash.

déchirage [deʃi'ra:ʒ], *n.m.* ripping up, breaking up (*of a ship etc.*).

déchirant [deʃi'rã], *a.* heart-rending, piercing; excruciating.

déchirement [deʃir'mã], *n.m.* rending, tearing, laceration; (*fig.*) heart-break.

déchirer [deʃi're], *v.t.* to tear to pieces, to rend; (*fig.*) to torture; to revile. **se déchirer,** *v.r.* to tear, to be torn; to defame each other.

déchirure [deʃi'ry:r], *n.f.* rent, tear; fissure.

déchoir [de'ʃwa:r], *v.i.* irr. to decay, to fall off, to decline; to sink.

déchouer [deʃu'e], *v.t.* to get off, to set afloat.

déchu [de'ʃy], *a.* fallen, decayed; sunken; **ange déchu,** fallen angel.

décidé [desi'de], *a.* decided, determined, resolved.

décidément [deside'mã], *adv.* decidedly, positively; firmly; definitely.

décider [desi'de], *v.t.* to decide, to determine, to settle; to induce, to persuade.—*v.i.* to decide. **se décider,** *v.r.* to decide, to determine, to make up one's mind.

décigramme [desi'gram], *n.m.* decigram (*one-tenth of a gramme*, 1.54 *grains*).

décilitre [desi'litr], *n.m.* decilitre (*one-tenth of a litre*).

décimal [desi'mal], *a.* (*m.pl.* **-aux**) decimal.— *n.f.* (**-e**) a decimal.

décimalisation [desimaliza'sjɔ̃], *n.f.* decimalization.

décimaliser [desimali'ze], *v.t.* to decimalize.

décimateur [desima'tœ:r], *n.m.* tithe owner.

décime [de'sim], *n.f.* tithe.

décimer [desi'me], *v.t.* to decimate, to destroy, to annihilate.

décimètre [desi'mɛtr], *n.m.* decimetre (3.937 *inches*).

décimo [desi'mo], *adv.* tenthly.

décintrer [desɛ̃'tre], *v.t.* to remove the centerings from (*arches*).

décisif [desi'zif], *a.* (*fem.* **-sive**) decisive, conclusive.

décision [desi'zjɔ̃], *n.f.* decision, determination; resolution.

décisivement [desiziv'mã], *adv.* decisively; peremptorily, positively.

décistère [desi'stɛ:r], *n.m.* tenth of a stere (3·53 *cubic feet*).

déciviliser [desivili'ze], *v.t.* to decivilize.

déclamateur

déclamateur [deklama'tœ:r], *n.m.* (*fem.* **-trice**) declaimer; (*fig.*) tub-thumper.—*a.* (*fem.* **-trice**) declamatory, bombastic.

déclamation [deklama'sjɔ̃], *n.f.* declamation, elocution.

déclamatoire [deklama'twa:r], *a.* declamatory.

déclamer [dekla'me], *v.t., v.i.* to declaim; to spout, to mouth.

déclarant [dekla'rɑ̃], *n.m.* (*Law*) informant.

déclaration [deklara'sjɔ̃], *n.f.* declaration, proclamation; disclosure; notification; *déclaration sous serment*, affidavit.

déclaratoire [deklara'twa:r], *a.* declaratory.

déclarer [dekla're], *v.t.* to declare, to make known; to proclaim; to certify. **se déclarer**, *v.r.* to speak one's mind; to declare oneself *or* itself; to show oneself *or* itself.

déclassé [dekla'se], *a.* come down in the world.—*n.m.* (*fem.* **-ée**) one who has come down in the world; one rejected by his own class *or* sphere.

déclassement [deklas'mɑ̃], *n.m.* loss of social position.

déclasser [dekla'se], *v.t.* to alter the classing of; to transfer from one class to another (*on trains, boats etc.*); to strike off the rolls, to dismiss from the service.

déclencher [deklɑ̃'ʃe], *v.t.* to unlatch (*a door*); to unhook, to detach; to release; (*Mil.*) to launch (*an attack*).

déclic [de'klik], *n.m.* pawl, catch.

déclin [de'klɛ̃], *n.m.* decline; decay; wane (*of the moon*); ebb; close (*of day etc.*).

déclinaison [deklinɛ'zɔ̃], *n.f.* (*Gram.*) declension.

déclinant [dekli'nɑ̃], *a.* declining.

décliner [dekli'ne], *v.t.* to refuse; (*Gram.*) to decline; to state.—*v.i.* to decline, to be on the wane, to fall off.

déclive [de'kli:v], *a.* declivous, sloping.

déclivité [deklivi'te], *n.f.* declivity, slope.

décloître (**se**) [sədeklwa'tre], *v.r.* to leave the cloister, to return to the world.

déclore [de'klɔ:r], *v.t. irr.* (*conjug. like* CLORE) to unclose, to throw open.

décochement [dekɔʃ'mɑ̃], *n.m.* discharge, shooting (*of arrows, shafts etc.*).

décocher [dekɔ'ʃe], *v.t.* to discharge, to dart (*arrows etc.*); to let fly (*insults etc.*).

décoiffer [dekwa'fe], *v.t.* to remove *or* undo the coiffure of, to undress the hair of. **se décoiffer**, *v.r.* to undo one's head-dress; to take off one's hat.

décoincer (**se**) [sədekwɛ̃'se], *v.r.* (*conjug. like* COMMENCER) to work loose.

décollage [dekɔ'la:ʒ], *n.m.* (*Av.*) taking off.

décollement [dekɔl'mɑ̃], *n.m.* ungluing, unpasting; coming off; detachment (*of retina*).

décoller [dekɔ'le], *v.t.* to unglue.—*v.i.* (*Av.*) to take off. **se décoller**, *v.r.* to become unglued,to come off.

décolletage [dekɔl'ta:ʒ], *n.m.* lowness in the neck (*of dresses*); baring the neck and shoulders.

décolleté [dekɔl'te], *a.* (*Dress.*) low-necked.

décolleter [dekɔl'te], *v.t.* (*conjug. like* APPELER) to uncover the neck, shoulders etc., of; to cut (*a dress*) low. **se décolleter**, *v.r.* to bare one's shoulders; to wear a low dress.

décoloration [dekɔlɔra'sjɔ̃], *n.f.* discoloration.

décoloré [dekɔlɔ're], *a.* discolored, faded.

décolorer [dekɔlɔ're], *v.t.* to discolor. **se décolorer**, *v.r.* to become discolored, to fade.

décombres [de'kɔ̃:br], *n.m.* (*used only in pl.*) rubbish, debris, ruins.

décommander [dekɔmɑ̃'de], *v.t.* to countermand; to cancel.

décomposé [dekɔ̃po'ze], *a.* decomposed.

décomposer [dekɔ̃po'ze], *v.t.* to decompose; to break up; to distort. **se décomposer**, *v.r.* to decompose, to rot; (*fig.*) to be distorted (*of the face etc.*).

décomposition [dekɔ̃pozi'sjɔ̃], *n.f.* decomposition, analysis.

décompresseur [dekɔ̃prɛ'sœ:r], *n.m.* (*Motor.*) exhaust valve.

décompte [de'kɔ̃:t], *n.m.* deduction, discount, allowance; deficit; balance due; (*fig.*) drawback; disappointment.

décompter [dekɔ̃'te], *v.t.* to deduct.—*v.i.* (*fig.*) to be disappointed.

déconcertant [dekɔ̃sɛr'tɑ̃], *a.* disconcerting.

déconcerter [dekɔ̃sɛr'te], *v.t.* to disconcert; to baffle. **se déconcerter**, *v.r.* to be disconcerted *or* put out.

déconfiture [dekɔ̃fi'ty:r], *n.f.* discomfiture; break-down; insolvency.

décongeler [dekɔ̃'ʒle], *v.t.* (*conjug. like* AMENER) to thaw (*chilled meat*).

déconseiller [dekɔ̃sɛ'je], *v.t.* to dissuade.

déconsidération [dekɔ̃sidera'sjɔ̃], *n.f.* disrepute, discredit.

déconsidérer [dekɔ̃side're], *v.t.* (*conjug. like* CÉDER) to bring into disrepute, to discredit. **se déconsidérer**, *v.r.* to fall into disrepute.

décontenancement [dekɔ̃tnɑ̃s'mɑ̃], *n.m.* mortification, embarrassment.

décontenancer [dekɔ̃tnɑ̃'se], *v.t.* (*conjug. like* COMMENCER) to abash, to put out of countenance. **se décontenancer**, *v.r.* to be put out of countenance, to be abashed.

déconvenue [dekɔ̃v'ny], *n.f.* discomfiture; disappointment, set-back.

décor [de'kɔ:r], *n.m.* decoration; (*Theat., pl.*) scenery.

décorateur [dekɔra'tœ:r], *n.m.* (*fem.* **-trice**) ornamental painter, decorator; scene painter.

décoratif [dekɔra'tif], *a.* (*fem.* **-tive**) decorative, ornamental.

décoration [dekɔra'sjɔ̃], *n.f.* decoration, embellishment; medal, insignia (*of an order*).

décorder [dekɔr'de], *v.t.* to untwist, to untwine (*a cord etc.*); to untie the rope (*of a box*).

décoré [dekɔ're], *a.* decorated; wearing the insignia of some order *or* its ribbon in one's buttonhole.

décorer [dekɔ're], *v.t.* to decorate; to set off; to confer the Legion of Honor etc. upon.

décorner [dekɔr'ne], *v.t.* to dishorn.

décortiquer [dekɔrti'ke], *v.t.* to decorticate, to bark, to husk, to shell, to peel.

décorum [dekɔ'rɔm], *n.m.* decorum, propriety.

découcher [deku'ʃe], *v.i.* to sleep away from home; to stay out all night.

découdre [de'kudr] *v.t. irr. (conjug. like* COUDRE) to unsew, to unstitch; to rip up. **se découdre,** *v.r.* to come unstitched.

découler [deku'le], *v.i.* to trickle, to flow; to spring, to proceed *(from).*

découpage [deku'paːʒ], *n.m.* cutting out, carving out.

découpé [deku'pe], *a. (Bot.)* cut, denticulated.

découper [deku'pe], *v.t.* to cut up; to pink, to cut out; to punch. **se découper,** *v.r.* to stand out, to show up *(against).*

découpeur [deku'pœːr], *n.m. (fem.* **-euse)** carver; pinker, cutter.

découplé [deku'ple], *a.* strapping.

découpler [deku'ple], *v.t.* to uncouple, to unleash, to let loose *(in pursuit).*

découpoir [deku'pwaːr], *n.m.* punch, stamping machine, stamping press.

découpure [deku'pyːr], *n.f.* cutting out, pinking, work cut out; cut paper-work; indentation.

décourageant [dekura'ʒɑ̃], *a.* discouraging, disheartening.

découragement [dekuraʒ'mɑ̃], *n.m.* discouragement.

décourager [dekura'ʒe], *v.t. (conjug. like* MANGER) to discourage, to dishearten. **se décourager,** *v.r.* to be disheartened.

décours [de'kuːr], *n.m.* decrease; wane *(of the moon).*

décousu [deku'zy], *a.* unsewn, unstitched; *(fig.)* desultory *(of style etc.).*

décousure [deku'zyːr], *n.f.* unpicked stitching.

découvert [deku'vɛːr], *a.* uncovered; discovered; open, unguarded; bare, bareheaded.—*n.m. (Comm.)* overdraft, deficit.

découverte [deku'vɛrt], *n.f.* discovery, detection; *(Mil.)* reconnoitring; *(Naut.)* look out.

découvreur [deku'vrœːr], *n.m. (fem.* **-euse)** discoverer.

découvrir [deku'vriːr], *v.t. (conjug. like* OUVRIR) to uncover, to expose; to discover, to disclose, to detect. **se découvrir,** *v.r.* to uncover oneself, to take off one's hat; to unbosom oneself; to expose oneself; to lie open *or* bare; to clear up *(of the sky).*

décramponner (se) [sədekrɑ̃pɔ'ne], *v.r.* to let go one's hold.

décrasser [dekra'se], *v.t.* to take the dirt off, to scour; *(fig.)* to make presentable. **se décrasser,** *v.r.* to wash, to clean oneself; to become polished.

décrassoir [dekra'swaːr], *n.m.* fine-tooth comb.

décréditement [dekredit'mɑ̃], *n.m.* discrediting.

décrépi [dekre'pi], *a.* unplastered.

décrépir (se) [sədekre'piːr], *v.r.* to lose its plaster *(of a wall etc.).*

décrépit [dekre'pi], *a.* decrepit, brokendown.

décrépitude [dekrepi'tyd], *n.f.* decrepitude.

décret [de'krɛ], *n.m.* decree, order, enactment; *(Law)* writ, warrant.

décret-loi [dekrɛ'lwa], *n.m.* Order in Council.

décréter [dekre'te], *v.t. (conjug. like* CÉDER) to decree, to order, to enact.

décri [de'kri], *n.m.* official crying down *or* depreciation *(of coinage); (fig.)* discredit.

décrier [dekri'e], *v.t.* to decry, to run down;

(fig.) to discredit. **se décrier,** *v.r.* to bring oneself into disrepute; to decry one another.

décrire [de'kriːr], *v.t. irr. (conjug. like* ÉCRIRE) to describe, to depict. **se décrire,** *v.r.* to be described.

décrocher [dekrɔ'ʃe], *v.t.* to unhook, to take down, to disconnect.

décroiser [dekrwa'ze], *v.t.* to uncross *(the legs etc.).*

décroissant [dekrwa'sɑ̃], *a.* decreasing, diminishing; subsiding.

décroissement [dekrwas'mɑ̃], *n.m.,* **décroissance** [dekrwa'sɑ̃ːs], *n.f.* decrease, diminution, wane.

décroît [de'krwa], *n.m.* wane *(of the moon).*

décroître [de'krwaːtr], *v.i. irr. (conjug. like* CROÎTRE) to decrease, to diminish, to wane.

décrottage [dekrɔ'taːʒ], *n.m.* cleaning *(of boots, trousers etc.).*

décrotter [dekrɔ'te], *v.t.* to rub the dirt off; *(fig.)* to improve the manners of. **se décrotter,** *v.r.* to clean oneself; to clean one's shoes etc.

décrotteur [dekrɔ'tœːr], *n.m. (fem.* **-euse)** bootblack.

décrottoir [dekrɔ'twaːr], *n.m.* scraper *(for shoes).*

décrottoire [dekrɔ'twaːr], *n.f.* shoe brush.

décrue [de'kry], *n.f.* decrease; fall *(of water).*

décrypter [dekrip'te], *v.t.* to decipher.

déculotter [dekylɔ'te], *v.t.* to take off *(s.o.'s)* breeches, *(child's)* pants.

décuple [de'kypl], *a.* and *n.m.* tenfold.

décupler [deky'ple], *v.t.* to increase tenfold.

décuvage [deky'vaːʒ], *n.m.,* **décuvaison** [dekyvɛ'zɔ̃], *n.f.* tunning *(of wine).*

décuver [deky've], *v.t.* to tun.

dédaigner [dedɛ'ɲe], *v.t.* to disdain, to scorn, to despise.

dédaigneusement [dedɛɲøz'mɑ̃], *adv.* disdainfully, scornfully.

dédaigneux [dedɛ'ɲø], *a. (fem.* **-euse)** disdainful, scornful.

dédain [de'dɛ̃], *n.m.* disdain, scorn, disregard.

dédale [de'dal], *n.m.* labyrinth, maze.

dedans [də'dɑ̃], *adv.* within, in, inside; at home.—*n.m.* inside, interior.

dédicace [dedi'kas], *n.f.* dedication, consecration *(of a church etc.).*

dédication [dedika'sjɔ̃], *n.f. (Law)* dedication *(of a temple etc.).*

dédier [de'dje], *v.t.* to dedicate, to consecrate; to devote; to inscribe *(a book etc.).*

dédire [de'diːr], *v.t. irr. (conjug. like* MÉDIRE) to disown; gainsay, to contradict. **se dédire,** *v.r.* to recant, to retract, to go back on one's word.

dédit [de'di], *n.m.* retraction; forfeit.

dédommagement [dedɔmaʒ'mɑ̃], *n.m.* indemnification; compensation, damages.

dédommager [dedɔma'ʒe], *v.t. (conjug. like* MANGER) to make amends for; to compensate, to make up for. **se dédommager,** *v.r.* to indemnify oneself.

dédorer [dedɔ're], *v.t.* to ungild. **se dédorer,** *v.r.* to lose its gilt *(of metal etc.).*

dédouanement [dedwan'mɑ̃], *n.m. (customs)* clearance.

dédouaner [dedwa'ne], *v.t.* to clear *(goods)* from the custom house.

101

dédoublement [dedublə'mã], **dédoublage** [dedu'bla:ʒ], *n.m.* dividing into two; unlining (*of a garment*); diluting.

dédoubler [dedu'ble], *v.t.* to take out the lining of; to divide into two; *dédoubler un autocar* (*un train*), to run a relief coach (train). **se dédoubler**, *v.r.* to be divided into two.

déductif [dedyk'tif], *a.* (*fem.* **-tive**) deductive.

déduction [dedyk'sjɔ̃], *n.f.* deduction, allowance; inference.

déduire [de'dɥi:r], *v.t. irr.* (*conjug. like* CONDUIRE) to deduct, to subtract; to deduce, to infer.

déesse [de'ɛs], *n.f.* goddess, female deity.

défâcher [defa'ʃe], *v.t.* to pacify. **se défâcher**, *v.r.* to be pacified, to cool down.

défaillance [defa'jã:s], *n.f.* fainting fit, swoon, faintness; exhaustion; extinction (*of a family etc.*).

défaillant [defa'jã], *a.* failing, falling off; decaying; without heirs; weak, feeble.— *n.m.* (*fem.* **-e**) (*Law*) defaulter.

défaillir [defa'ji:r], *v.i. irr.* (*conjug. like* ASSAILLIR) to fail, to default; to decay; to swoon, to faint away.

défaire [de'fɛ:r], *v.t. irr.* (*conjug. like.* FAIRE) to undo, to unmake; to defeat; to emaciate; to embarrass; to rid. **se défaire**, *v.r.* to come undone; *se défaire de*, to get rid of, to give up.

défait [de'fɛ], *a.* undone, defeated; meager, wasted; worn out.

défaite [de'fɛt], *n.f.* defeat, overthrow; evasion, pretence, excuse.

défaitisme [defɛ'tism], *n.m.* defeatism.

défaitiste [defɛ'tist], *a.* and *n.* defeatist.

défalcation [defalka'sjɔ̃], *n.f.* deduction.

défalquer [defal'ke], *v.t.* to take off, to deduct.

défausser [defo'se], *v.t.* to straighten.

défaut [de'fo], *n.m.* absence, lack, default; defect, fault, flaw; (*Law*) non-appearance; *à défaut de*, instead of, for want of; *faire défaut*, to be wanting, to be missing.

défaveur [defa'vœ:r], *n.f.* disfavor, discredit.

défavorable [defavɔ'rabl], *a.* unfavorable.

défavorablement [defavɔrablə'mã], *adv.* unfavorably.

défectif [defɛk'tif], *a.* (*fem.* **-tive**) (*Gram.*) defective.

défection [defɛk'sjɔ̃], *n.f.* defection, falling off, disloyalty.

défectueux [defɛk'tɥø], *a.* (*fem.* **-euse**) defective, imperfect.

défectuosité [defɛktɥozi'te], *n.f.* defect, imperfection, flaw.

défendable [defã'dabl], *a.* defensible, tenable.

défendeur [defã'dœ:r], *n.m.* (*fem.* **-eresse**) defendant; respondent.

défendre [de'fã:dr], *v.t.* to defend, to protect; to shield; to support; to forbid. **se défendre**, *v.r.* to defend oneself; to clear oneself; to deny.

défense [de'fã:s], *n.f.* defense, protection; prohibition; apology, plea; (*Law*) the defense; (*Fort., pl.*) outworks; tusk, fang (*of animals*); (*Naut.*) fender; *défense de fumer*, no smoking.

défenseur [defã'sœ:r], *n.m.* defender, supporter; advocate, counsel.

défensif [defã'sif], *a.* (*fem.* **-sive**) defensive. —*n.f.* (**-sive**) defensive.

déféquer [defe'ke], *v.t.* (*conjug. like* CÉDER) to purify.—*v.i.* to defecate.

déférence [defe'rã:s], *n.f.* deference, regard, respect.

déférent [defe'rã], *a.* deferential, compliant.

déférer [defe're], *v.t.* (*conjug. like* CÉDER) * to confer, to bestow; to tender; to accuse, to inform against.—*v.i.* to defer, to yield, to comply.

déferler [defer'le], *v.t.* (*Naut.*) to unfurl.— *v.i.* to break into foam (*of the sea*).

déferrer [defe're], *v.t.* to unshoe (*a horse*). **se déferrer**, *v.r.* to come unshod, to lose a shoe.

défeuiller [defœ'je], *v.t.* to take the leaves off. **se défeuiller**, *v.r.* to shed its leaves.

défi [de'fi], *n.m.* defiance, challenge.

défiance [de'fjã:s], *n.f.* distrust, mistrust; caution.

défiant [de'fjã], *a.* distrustful, suspicious.

déficeler [defis'le], *v.t.* (*conjug. like* APPELER) to untie; to undo.

déficient [defi'sjã], *a.* deficient.

déficit [defi'sit], *n.m.* deficit, deficiency.

défier [de'fje], *v.t.* to defy, to challenge; to brave, to face; to set at defiance. **se défier**, *v.r.* to defy *or* to challenge each other; to distrust, to beware (*de*).

défiger [defi'ʒe], *v.t.* (*conjug. like* MANGER) to liquefy.

défiguration [defigyra'sjɔ̃], *n.f.*, **défigurement** [defigyr'mã], *n.m.* disfigurement, defacement.

défigurer [defigy're], *v.t.* to disfigure, to mar; to distort. **se défigurer**, *v.r.* to disfigure oneself; to become deformed.

défilade [defi'lad], *n.f.* filing off *or* past, marching past; succession.

défilé [defi'le], *n.m.* defile, narrow pass, gorge; (*fig.*) strait, difficulty; (*Mil.*) filing past; *un défilé de mannequins*, a mannequin parade.

défiler [defi'le], *v.t.* to unstring, to unthread; to untwist.—*v.i.* to file off, to march past. **se défiler**, *v.r.* to come unthreaded *or* unstrung; (*Mil.*) to take cover; to slip away.

défini [defi'ni], *a.* definite, determined, defined.

définir [defi'ni:r], *v.t.* to define; to determine; to describe.

définissable [defini'sabl], *a.* definable.

définitif [defini'tif], *a.* (*fem.* **-tive**) definitive, final; ultimate, eventual.

définition [defini'sjɔ̃], *n.f.* definition.

définitivement [definitiv'mã], *adv.* definitively, positively, decidedly; eventually.

déflation [defla'sjɔ̃], *n.f.* deflation.

défléchir [defle'ʃi:r], *v.t., v.i.* to turn from *or* aside, to deflect.

déflecteur [deflɛk'tœ:r], *n.m.* (*Motor.*) ventilating window; deflector.

défleuraison [DÉFLORAISON].

défleurir [deflœ'ri:r], *v.t.* to nip *or* strip off blossoms.—*v.i.* to lose its flowers.

déflexion [deflɛk'sjɔ̃], *n.f.* deviation; (*Gram.*) deflection.

défloraison [deflɔrɛ'zɔ̃], **défleuraison** [deflœrɛ'zɔ̃], *n.f.* fall *or* withering of the blossom.

déflorer [deflɔ're], *v.t.* to deflower, to seduce.

défonçage [defɔ̃'sa:ʒ], **défoncement** [defɔ̃s'mã], *n.m.* staving in (*of the head of casks*), breaking *or* smashing in; (*Agric.*) deep trenching.

défoncer [defɔ̃'se], *v.t.* (*conjug. like* COMMENCER) to stave in, to bilge (*a cask*); to dig deeply, to trench (*ground*). **se défoncer**, *v.r.* to give way; to break up (*of roads*); to get battered.

défonceuse [defɔ̃'sø:z], *n.f.* trenching plough.

déforestation [deforɛstɑ'sjɔ̃], *n.f.* deforestation.

déformant [defɔr'mã], *a.* distorting (*mirror etc.*).

déformation [deformɑ'sjɔ̃], *n.f.* distortion, buckling.

déformer [defɔr'me], *v.t.* to deform, to distort. **se déformer**, *v.r.* to lose its shape.

défortifier [defɔrti'fje], *v.t.* to dismantle the fortifications of.

défourner [defur'ne], *v.t.* to draw out of an oven *or* kiln.

défourrer [defu're], *v.t.* to unwrap, to take out of its cover; to thresh (*grain*).

défraîchir [defrɛ'ʃi:r], *v.t.* to tarnish, to take away the brilliancy, gloss *or* freshness of. **se défraîchir**, *v.r.* to lose its brilliancy, freshness etc., to tarnish.

défrayer [defrɛ'je], *v.t.* (*conjug. like* PAYER) to defray, to bear the cost of; to amuse.

défriche [de'friʃ], *n.f.*, **défriché** [defri'ʃe], *n.m.* piece of cleared land.

défrichement [defriʃ'mã], **défrichage** [defri'ʃa:ʒ], *n.m.* clearing, breaking up (*of land for tillage*).

défricher [defri'ʃe], *v.t.* to clear, to break up (*ground*) for tillage; to reclaim.

défricheur [defri'ʃœ:r], *n.m.* clearer; settler.

défriper [defri'pe], *v.t.* to smooth out.

défrisement [defriz'mã], *n.m.* uncurling.

défriser [defri'ze], *v.t.* to uncurl; (*fam.*) to disappoint, to ruffle.

défroque [de'frɔk], *n.f.* the effects left by a dying monk; *hence*, old things, effects, cast-off clothes, etc.

défroqué [defrɔ'ke], *a.* and *n.m.* unfrocked (*priest*).

défroquer [defrɔ'ke], *v.t.* to unfrock. **se défroquer**, *v.r.* to renounce one's order (*of monks*).

défunt [de'fœ̃], *a.* defunct, deceased, late.—*n.m.* (*fem.* -**e**) the deceased.

dégagé [dega'ʒe], *a.* free, easy, unconstrained; flippant; bold; slender, graceful.

dégagement [degaʒ'mã], *n.m.* disengagement, redemption; clearance; discharge (*of gas etc.*); (*fig.*) unconcern.

dégager [dega'ʒe], *v.t.* (*conjug. like* MANGER) to disengage, to extricate; to clear; to deliver, to rescue; to release, to emit (*fumes etc.*); to redeem, to take out of pawn. **se dégager**, *v.r.* to be liberated (*de*); to extricate, disengage *or* disentangle oneself; to get away; (*Chem.*) to be emitted.

dégaine [de'gɛ:n], *n.f.* (*colloq.*) awkward gait.

dégainer [degɛ'ne], *v.t.* to unsheathe (*one's sword etc.*).

déganter [degã'te], *v.t.* to unglove. **se déganter**, *v.r.* to take off one's gloves.

dégarnir [degar'ni:r], *v.t.* to strip; to dismantle; to thin (*trees, woods etc.*). **se dégarnir**, *v.r.* to strip oneself (*de*); to

become empty; to grow thin; to lose branches etc.

dégât [de'gɑ], *n.m.* havoc, damage, ravage.

dégauchir [dego'ʃi:r], *v.t.* to smooth, to plane, to level, to straighten; (*fig.*) to polish.

dégauchissement [degoʃis'mã], **dégauchissage** [degoʃi'sa:ʒ], *n.m.* planing, straightening, levelling, smoothing.

dégazonner [degazɔ'ne], *v.t.* to remove the turf.

dégel [de'ʒɛl], *n.m.* thaw.

dégeler [deʒ'le], *v.t.*, *v.i.* (*conjug. like* AMENER) to thaw. **se dégeler**, *v.r.* to thaw (*of persons*).

dégénération [deʒenerɑ'sjɔ̃], *n.f.* degeneration, degeneracy.

dégénéré [deʒene're], *a.* and *n.m.* (*fem.* -**ée**) degenerate (*person*).

dégénérer [deʒene're], *v.i. irr.* (*conjug. like* CÉDER) to decline, to degenerate.

dégénérescence [deʒenerɛ'sã:s], *n.f.* degeneracy, degeneration.

dégénérescent [deʒenere'sã], *a.* degenerating.

dégingandé [deʒɛ̃gã'de], *a.* ungainly, gawky, awkward in one's gait; clumsy, disjointed, irregular.

dégivrer [deʒi'vre], *v.t.* to de-ice.

dégivreur [deʒi'vrœ:r], *n.m.* (*Motor.*, *Av.*) de-icer.

déglutir [degly'ti:r], *v.t.* to swallow.

déglutition [deglyti'sjɔ̃], *n.f.* deglutition, swallowing.

dégommer [degɔ'me], *v.t.* to wash the gum out of; (*slang*) to sack.

dégonflement [degɔ̃flə'mã], *n.m.* deflating (*of tire, balloon*); collapse; reduction.

dégonfler [degɔ̃'fle], *v.t.* to cause to collapse; to deflate; to reduce (*a swelling*). **se dégonfler**, *v.r.* to go down, to be reduced; to subside; (*pop.*) to sing small.

dégorgement [degɔrʒ'mã], *n.m.* breaking out, overflow; unstopping.

dégorger [degɔr'ʒe], *v.t.* (*conjug. like* MANGER) to disgorge; to unstop, to clear; to cleanse.—*v.i.* to discharge, to overflow. **se dégorger**, *v.r.* to discharge *or* empty itself *or* oneself, to be unstopped, to be cleared.

dégourdi [degur'di], *a.* quick, sharp, acute, smart; tepid (*of water*).—*n.m.* (*fem.* -**e**) a shrewd *or* forward person.

dégourdir [degur'di:r], *v.t.* to revive, to quicken; to take the chill off; (*fig.*) to sharpen; to render shrewd; to polish. **se dégourdir**, *v.r.* to lose numbness, to feel warmer; to brighten up.

dégourdissement [degurdis'mã], *n.m.* return of circulation; quickening, reviving.

dégoût [de'gu], *n.m.* dislike, distaste; disgust, aversion; mortification.

dégoûtant [degu'tã], *a.* disgusting, distasteful, nauseous; loathsome; unpleasant.

dégoûté [degu'te], *a.* disgusted; fastidious.—*n.m.* (*fem.* -**ée**) fastidious person.

dégoûter [degu'te], *v.t.* to disgust. **se dégoûter**, *v.r.* to take a dislike to.

dégouttant [degu'tã], *a.* dripping.

dégouttement [degut'mã], *n.m.* dripping, falling in drops.

dégoutter [degu'te], *v.i.* to drip, to fall in drops, to trickle.

dégradant [degra'dã], *a.* degrading, debasing.

dégradation

dégradation [degrɑdɑ'sjɔ̃], *n.f.* degradation; debasement; (*Paint.*) gradation of light and shade; (*Law*) *dégradation nationale* or *civile*, loss of civil rights; *dégradation militaire*, cashiering.

dégrader [degrɑ'de], *v.t.* to degrade, to debase; to deface; (*Mil.*) to reduce to the ranks; to cashier; (*Paint.*) to graduate the light and shade. **se dégrader**, *v.r.* to degrade, debase *or* disgrace oneself; to become damaged *or* defaced.

dégrafer [degrɑ'fe], *v.t.* to unclasp, to unhook. **se dégrafer**, *v.r.* to come unfastened (*of garments etc.*); to unfasten one's clothes.

dégraissage [degrɛ'sa:ʒ], **dégraissement** [degrɛs'mɑ̃], *n.m.* dry-cleaning (*garments*); scouring (*wool*).

dégraisser [degrɛ'se], *v.t.* to remove greasy stains from.

dégraisseur [degrɛ'sœ:r], *n.m.* (*fem.* **-euse**) scourer (*of wool*); dry-cleaner (*of clothes etc.*).

dégraissoir [degrɛ'swa:r], *n.m.* scraper.

degré [də'gre], *n.m.* step, stair; stage, grade, degree; point, extent, height, pitch.

dégréer [degre'e], *v.t.* to unrig; to strip a mast.

dégrèvement [degrɛv'mɑ̃], *n.m.* reduction; tax allowance, relief.

dégrever [degrə've], *v.t.* (*conjug. like* AMENER) to diminish, to reduce (*a tax etc.*); to relieve (*someone of a tax*); to disencumber (*an estate etc.*); to pay off (*a mortgage*).

dégringolade [degrɛ̃gɔ'lad], *n.f.* (*fam.*) fall, tumble.

dégringoler [degrɛ̃gɔ'le], *v.i.* to tumble down, to topple over.

dégrisement [degriz'mɑ̃], *n.m.* (*colloq.*) sobering, getting sober; (*fig.*) cooling down.

dégriser [degri'ze], *v.t.* to sober; (*fig.*) to cool down, to bring to one's senses. **se dégriser**, *v.r.* to sober up; (*fig.*) to come to one's senses; to lose one's illusions.

dégrossir [degro'si:r], *v.t.* to rough-hew; (*fig.*) to make a rough sketch of.

dégrossissage [degrosi'sa:ʒ], **dégrossissement** [degrosis'mɑ̃], *n.m.* rough-hewing; (*Carp.*) dressing, trimming.

déguenillé [degəni'je], *a.* tattered, ragged.—*n.m.* (*fem.* **-ée**) ragamuffin.

déguerpir [degɛr'pi:r], *v.i.* to move off; to be gone.

déguerpissement [degɛrpis'mɑ̃], *n.m.* quitting, giving up, abandonment.

dégueuler [degœ'le], *v.t.* (*vulg.*) to spew.

déguignonner [degiɲɔ'ne], *v.t.* to lift a curse from, to bring better luck to.

déguisable [degi'zabl], *a.* disguisable.

déguisement [degiz'mɑ̃], *n.m.* disguise, concealment; *parlez sans déguisement*, speak openly.

déguiser [degi'ze], *v.t.* to disguise, to cloak; to misrepresent. **se déguiser**, *v.r.* to disguise oneself; to put on fancy dress.

dégustateur [degysta'tœ:r], *n.m.* (*fem.* **-trice**) taster (*of wines etc.*).

dégustation [degysta'sjɔ̃], *n.f.* tasting (*of wines etc.*).

déguster [degys'te], *v.t.* to taste; to sip, to savor.

déhaler [dea'le], *v.t.* (*Naut.*) to tow out; to haul off.

déhâler [dɛa'le], *v.t.* to take away sun-burn, freckles, tan etc. from. **se déhâler**, *v.r.* to clear one's complexion.

déhanché [deɑ̃'ʃe], *a.* having the hip dislocated; (*fig.*) ungainly.

déhanchement [deɑ̃ʃ'mɑ̃], *n.m.* waddling gait, waddle.

déhancher (se) [sədeɑ̃'ʃe], *v.r.* to sway one's hips; to have a waddling, loose gait.

déharnachement [dearnaʃ'mɑ̃], *n.m.* unharnessing.

déharnacher [dearna'ʃe], *v.t.* to unharness.

dehors [də'ɔ:r], *adv.* out, *without, outside; out of doors; abroad; externally; (*Naut.*) at sea; *au dedans et au dehors*, at home and abroad; *au dehors*, outwardly; *de dehors*, from without; *en dehors*, outside, *without; *mettre quelqu'un dehors*, to turn someone out.—*n.m. inv.* outside, exterior; (*pl.*) appearances; (*Fort.*) outworks; dependencies, approaches, grounds (*of a house*); *sauver les dehors*, to save appearances.

déification [deifika'sjɔ̃], *n.f.* deification.

déifier [dei'fje], *v.t.* to deify.

déisme [de'ism], *n.m.* deism.

déiste [de'ist], *a.* deistic.—*n.* deist.

déité [dei'te], *n.f.* deity (*god, goddess*), divinity.

déjà [de'ʒa], *adv.* already, before, previously.

déjection [deʒɛk'sjɔ̃], *n.f.* (*Med.*) dejection, ejection, evacuation.

déjeté [deʒ'te], *a.* awry, lopsided, off the straight.

déjeter [deʒ'te], *v.t.* (*conjug. like* APPELER) to warp. **se déjeter**, *v.r.* to warp (*of wood etc.*); (*Path.*) to deviate.

déjettement [deʒɛt'mɑ̃], *n.m.* warping; deviation.

déjeuner [deʒœ'ne], *n.m.* lunch; *petit déjeuner*, breakfast; *un déjeuner de porcelaine*, a china breakfast-set.—*v.i.* to breakfast, to lunch.

déjouer [de'ʒwe], *v.t.* to baffle, to frustrate, to foil; (*Mil.*) to outmaneuver.

déjucher [deʒy'ʃe], *v.t.* to dislodge.—*v.i.* to come down from the roost *or* from one's perch.

déjuger (se) [sədeʒy'ʒe], *v.r.* (*conjug. like* MANGER) to reverse one's opinion *or* decision.

delà [də'la], *prep.* on the other side of; beyond; *au delà, de delà, par delà*, or *en delà*, beyond; *deçà et delà*, both here and there, both this and that; *l'au-delà*, the hereafter.

délabré [delɑ'bre], *a.* tattered, shabby (*garments*); tumbledown, ramshackle (*building*).

délabrement [delabrə'mɑ̃], *n.m.* decay, dilapidation; shabbiness.

délabrer [delɑ'bre], *v.t.* to shatter, to ruin, to tear to tatters. **se délabrer**, *v.r.* to fall to pieces, to go to ruin.

délacer [dela'se], *v.t.* (*conjug. like* COMMENCER) to unlace (*shoes etc.*). **se délacer**, *v.r.* to unlace oneself; to come undone (*of shoes, strings etc.*).

délai [de'lɛ], *n.m.* delay; respite.

délaissé [delɛ'se], *a.* abandoned, friendless.

délaissement [delɛs'mã], *n.m.* desertion; destitution, helplessness.
délaisser [delɛ'se], *v.t.* to forsake, to abandon; to neglect.
délassant [delɑ'sã], *a.* refreshing, diverting.
délassement [delɑs'mã], *n.m.* relaxation; repose.
délasser [delɑ'se], *v.t.* to refresh, to relax, to divert. **se délasser**, *v.r.* to refresh oneself, to rest.
délateur [dela'tœ:r], *n.m.* (*fem.* **-trice**) informer, accuser.
délation [dela'sjõ], *n.f.* informing.
délavage [dela'va:3], *n.m.* diluting of color; soaking.
délaver [dela've], *v.t.* to dilute *or* wash (*color*); to soak into. **se délaver**, *v.r.* to become soaked; to lose color.
délayable [delɛ'jabl], *a.* dilutable.
délayage [delɛ'ja:3], *n.m.* diluting, dilution.
délayé [delɛ'je], *a.* watery.
délayer [delɛ'je], *v.t.* (*conjug. like* PAYER) to dilute; (*fig.*) to spin out.
délectable [delɛk'tabl], *a.* delectable, delightful.
délecter (se) [sədelɛk'te], *v.r.* to take delight.
délégation · [delega'sjõ], *n.f.* delegation, assignment.
délégatoire [delega'twa:r], *a.* delegatory.
délégué [dele'ge], *n.m.* (*fem.* **-ée**) delegate, deputy; proxy.
déléguer [dele'ge], *v.t.* (*conjug. like* CÉDER) to delegate; to assign. **se déléguer**, *v.r.* to be delegated.
délester [delɛs'te], *v.t.* to unballast.
délétère [dele'tɛ:r], *a.* deleterious.
délibérant [delibe'rã], *a.* deliberative.
délibératif [delibera'tif], *a.* (*fem.* **-tive**) deliberative.
délibération [delibera'sjõ], *n.f.* deliberation; resolution.
délibéré [delibe're], *a.* deliberate, determined, resolute.
délibérément [delibere'mã], *adv.* deliberately, resolutely.
délibérer [delibe're], *v.i.* (*conjug. like* CÉDER) to deliberate; to resolve.
délicat [deli'ka], *a.* delicate, dainty; nice, fastidious; frail.—*n.m.* (*fem.* **-e**) fastidious person.
délicatement [delikat'mã], *adv.* delicately, daintily, tenderly.
délicatesse [delika'tɛs], *n.f.* delicacy, fragility; tenderness; daintiness, fastidiousness; refinement, squeamishness; nicety (*of language etc.*); considerateness; (*pl.*) dainties.
délice [de'lis], *n.m. in sing.* (*used chiefly in f.pl.*) delight, pleasure.
délicieusement [delisjøz'mã], *adv.* deliciously, delightfully.
délicieux [deli'sjø], *a.* (*fem.* **-euse**) delicious, delightful.
délié [de'lje], *a.* slender, fine; sharp, shrewd; glib, flowing (*of style etc.*); untied, loose.
délier [de'lje], *v.t.* to unbind, to untie; to liberate, to release; to absolve. **se délier**, *v.r.* to come untied, to get loose.
délimitation [delimitɑ'sjõ], *n.f.* delimitation, fixing of boundaries.
délimiter [delimi'te], *v.t.* to delimit, to settle the boundaries of.

délinéation [delinea'sjõ], *n.f.* delineation.
délinéer [deline'e], *v.t.* to delineate.
délinquance [delɛ̃'kã:s], *n.f.* delinquency.
délinquant [delɛ̃'kã], *n;a.* (*fem.* **-e**) delinquent, offender.— **enfance délinquante**, juvenile delinquents.
délirant [deli'rã], *a.* delirious, frenzied, frantic; rapturous, ecstatic.—*n.m.* (*fem.* **-e**) a delirious *or* ecstatic person.
délire [de'li:r], *n.m.* delirium, frenzy, folly.
délirer [deli're], *v.i.* to be delirious, to rave, to wander.
délit [de'li], *n.m.* misdemeanor, offence; **en flagrant délit**, in the very act, red-handed.
délivrance [deli'vrã:s], *n.f.* rescue, deliverance; issue (*of tickets*); delivery (*of certificates etc.*); accouchement.
délivre [de'livr], *n.m.* (*Anat.*) after-birth, placenta.
délivrer [deli'vre], *v.t.* to deliver, to release, to set free; to hand over; to issue; to deliver (*a woman of a baby*).
délogement [delɔ3'mã], *n.m.* removal, change of quarters, decamping.
déloger [delɔ'3e], *v.t.* (*conjug. like* MANGER) to turn out (*of house etc.*), to oust; to drive away; (*Mil.*) to dislodge.—*v.i.* to remove, to go (*from one's house etc.*), to go away, to march off.
déloyal [delwa'jal], *a.* (*m.pl.* **-aux**) disloyal, false, treacherous, unfair; foul.
déloyalement [delwajal'mã], *adv.* disloyally, unfairly.
déloyauté [delwajo'te], *n.f.* disloyalty, treachery.
delta [dɛl'ta], *n.m.* delta.
déluge [de'ly:3], *n.m.* deluge, flood.
déluré [dely're], *a.* wide-awake, sharp.
délustrer [delys'tre], *v.t.* to take the luster *or* gloss from.
démagnétiser [demaɲeti'ze], *v.t.* to demagnetize.
démagogue [dema'gɔg], *n.* demagogue.
démailler [dema'je], *v.t.* to undo the meshes of (*a net etc.*).
demain [də'mɛ̃] *adv.* and *n.m.* tomorrow; **à demain!** see you tomorrow!
démancher [demã'ʃe], *v.t.* to take off the handle of; (*fig.*) to dislocate. **se démancher**, *v.r.* to lose its handle; to go wrong.
demande [də'mã:d], *n.f.* question; request, application, petition; claim; (*Comm.*) demand; order.
demander [dəmã'de], *v.t.* to ask, to beg, to request; to desire, to wish; to require, to call for; to need, to want; to inquire about; to ask to see; to seek in marriage; (*Comm.*) to order. **se demander**, *v.r.* to ask oneself, to wonder.
demandeur [dəmã'dœ:r], *a.* (*fem.* **-euse**) always asking.—*n.m.* (*fem.* **-eresse**) asker, applicant; (*Law*) plaintiff.
démangeaison [demã3e'zõ], *n.f.* itching; longing.
démanger [demã'3e], *v.i.* (*conjug. like* MANGER) to itch; to long.
démantibuler [demãtiby'le], *v.t.* to break, to dislocate.
démaquiller [demaki'je], *v.t.* to take off someone's make-up. **se démaquiller**, *v.r.* to take off one's make-up.

démarcation [demarkɑ'sjɔ̃], *n.f.* demarcation; *ligne de démarcation*, line of demarcation.

démarche [de'marʃ], *n.f.* gait, walk, bearing; proceeding, measure, step, course.

démarcheur [demar'ʃœːr], *n.m.* canvasser.

démarier [dema'rje], *v.t.* (*fam.*) to annul the marriage of; (*Hort.*) to thin out. **se démarier**, *v.r.* to be divorced.

démarrer [dema're], *v.t.* to cast off; to unfasten.—*v.i.* to leave, to slip her moorings (*of a ship*); to move, to get away, to start.

démarreur [dema'rœːr], *n.m.* (*Motor.*) self-starter.

démasquer [demas'ke], *v.t.* to unmask; to show up.

démâter [demɑ'te], *v.t.* to dismast.—*v.i.* to lose her masts (*of a ship*).

démêlage [demɛ'laːʒ], *n.m.* combing (*of wool*).

démêlé [demɛ'le], *n.m.* strife, contest, quarrel.

démêler [demɛ'le], *v.t.* to unravel, to disentangle, to separate; to clear up; to distinguish, to discern; to comb out (*hair*), to tease (*wool*). **se démêler**, *v.r.* to be disentangled; to extricate oneself; to stand out (*clearly*); to comb out one's hair.

démembrement [demɑ̃brə'mɑ̃], *n.m.* dismemberment; breaking up.

démembrer [demɑ̃'bre], *v.t.* to tear limb from limb, to dismember; to break up.

déménagement [demenaʒ'mɑ̃], *n.m.* (*household*) removal.

déménager [demena'ʒe], *v.t.* (*conjug. like* MANGER) to remove (*one's furniture*).—*v.i.* to (re)move.

déménageur [demena'ʒœːr], *n.m.* furniture mover.

démence [de'mɑ̃ːs], *n.f.* insanity, madness.

démener (se) [sədemɛ'ne], *v.r.* (*conjug. like* AMENER) to stir, to struggle, to make a great fuss, to strive hard.

démenti [demɑ̃'ti], *n.m.* denial, flat contradiction; lie.

démentir [demɑ̃'tiːr], *v.t.* (*conjug. like* SENTIR) to give the lie to, to contradict; to deny; to belie, to refute. **se démentir**, *v.r.* to contradict oneself; to fall off, to flag.

démérite [deme'rit], *n.m.* demerit.

démériter [demeri'te], *v.i.* to lose esteem or favor.

démesuré [deməzy're], *a.* inordinate, excessive, enormous.

démesurément [deməzyre'mɑ̃], *adv.* inordinately, excessively.

démettre [de'mɛtr], *v.t. irr.* (*conjug. like* METTRE) to put out of joint, to dislocate; to dismiss; (*Law*) to overrule. **se démettre**, *v.r.* to be put out of joint; to resign.

démeubler [demœ'ble], *v.t.* to strip of furniture.

demeurant [dəmœ'rɑ̃], *a.* dwelling, living.—*n.m.* remainder; *au demeurant*, after all, nevertheless.

demeure [də'mœːr], *n.f.* abode, home, dwelling; stay; (*Law*) delay.

demeurer [dəmœ're], *v.i.* to live, to lodge, to reside; to stop, to stand; to continue, to stay.

demi [də'mi], *a.* and *adv.* half.—*n.m.* (*Arith.*) half; (*Ftb. etc.*) half-back; glass of beer.—*n.f.* (**-e**) (the) half-hour.

[In the following compounds *demi* is *inv.* The noun has its regular plural, unless otherwise indicated.]

demi-bain [dəmi'bɛ̃], *n.m.* hip bath.

demi-bas [dəmi'bɑ], *n.m. inv.* knee-length stocking.

demi-botte [dəmi'bɔt], *n.f.* Wellington boot.

demi-cercle [dəmi'sɛrkl], *n.m.* semicircle.

demi-finale [dəmifi'nal], *n.f.* (*Spt.*) semi-final.

demi-fond [dəmi'fɔ̃], *n.m. inv.* middle distance (*race*).

demi-heure [dəmi'œːr], *n.f.* half-hour; *une demi-heure*, half an hour.

demi-jour [dəmi'ʒuːr], *n.m.* twilight.

demi-mot [dəmi'mo], *adv. phr. comprendre à demi-mot*, to take the hint.

déminage [demi'naːʒ], *n.m.* mine clearing.

déminer [demi'ne], *v.t.* to clear of mines.

demi-pension [dəmipɑ̃'sjɔ̃], *n.f.* half-board.

demi-pensionnaire [dəmipɑ̃sjɔ'nɛːr], *n.* day-boarder.

demi-place [dəmi'plas], *n.f.* half-fare.

demi-saison [dəmisɛ'zɔ̃], *n.f.* autumn or spring.

demi-sang [dəmi'sɑ̃], *n.m. inv.* half-bred horse.

demi-sel [dəmi'sɛl], *n.m.* slightly salted cream cheese.

demi-solde [dəmi'sɔld], *n.f.* half-pay.

démission [demi'sjɔ̃], *n.f.* resignation.

démissionnaire [demisjɔ'nɛːr], *a.* who has resigned or vacated his seat, outgoing.

démissionner [demisjɔ'ne], *v.i.* to resign.

demi-tour [dəmi'tuːr], *n.m.* half-turn; (*Mil.*) about turn; *faire demi-tour*, to turn back.

démobilisation [demɔbiliza'sjɔ̃], *n.f.* demobilization.

démobiliser [demɔbili'ze], *v.t.* to demobilize.

démocrate [demɔ'krat], *a.* democratic.—*n*) democrat.

démocratie [demɔkra'si], *n.f.* democracy.

démocratique [demɔkra'tik], *a.* democratic.

démocratiquement [demɔkratik'mɑ̃], *adv.* democratically.

démocratiser [demɔkrati'ze], *v.t.* to democratize.

démodé [demɔ'de], *a.* old-fashioned, antiquated.

demoiselle [dəmwa'zɛl], *n.f.* young lady; unmarried woman, spinster; young girl; dragon-fly; *demoiselle d'honneur*, bridesmaid.

démolir [demɔ'liːr], *v.t.* to demolish, to pull down.

démolisseur [demɔli'sœːr], *n.m.* (*fem.* **-euse**) demolisher.

démolition [demɔli'sjɔ̃], *n.f.* demolition; (*pl.*) old building materials.

démon [de'mɔ̃], *n.m.* demon; (*good* or *evil*) genius; devil, fiend.

démonétisation [demɔnetiza'sjɔ̃], *n.f.* withdrawal from circulation (*of money*).

démonétiser [demɔneti'ze], *v.t.* to withdraw from circulation, to call in (*money*).

démoniaque [demɔ'njak], *a.* demoniac(al).—*n.* demoniac, demon, devil.

démonstrateur [demɔ̃stra'tœːr], *n.m.* (*fem.* **-euse**) demonstrator, lecturer.

démonstratif [demɔ̃stra'tif], *a.* (*fem.* **-tive**) demonstrative.

démonstration [demõstra′sjõ], *n.f.* demonstration, proof; exhibition.

démontable [demõ′tabl], *a.* that can be taken to pieces; collapsible (*canoe*).

démontage [demõ′ta:ʒ], *n.m.* taking to pieces, dismantling.

démonte-pneu [demõt′pnø], *n.m.* tire lever.

démonter [demõ′te], *v.t.* to unhorse, to dismount; to take to pieces, to dismantle; (*fig.*) to nonplus, to baffle; *mer démontée,* very rough sea. **se démonter,** *v.r.* to take *or* come to pieces (*of machinery*); to lose countenance, to be nonplussed; to be getting out of order (*of machinery etc.*).

démontrer [demõ′tre], *v.t.* to demonstrate, to prove.

démoralisant [demɔrali′zã], *a.* demoralizing.

démoralisateur [demɔraliza′tœ:r], *a.* (*fem.* **-trice**) corrupting, demoralizing.

démoralisation [demɔraliza′sjõ], *n.f.* demoralization.

démoraliser [demɔrali′ze], *v.t.* to demoralize; to corrupt.

démordre [de′mɔrdr], *v.i.* to let go one's hold; to desist, to yield, to give in.

démoucheter [demuʃ′te], *v.t.* (*conjug. like* APPELER) to take off the button from (*a foil*), to uncap.

démoulage [demu′la:ʒ], *n.m.* taking from the mold.

démouler [demu′le], *v.t.* to take from the mold.

démunir [demy′ni:r], *v.t.* to strip (*of ammunition*), to leave unprovided. **se démunir,** *v.r.* to deprive oneself, to leave oneself unprovided for.

démuseler [demyz′le], *v.t.* (*conjug. like* APPELER) to unmuzzle; (*fig.*) to let loose.

dénatalité [denatali′te], *n.f.* fall in the birthrate.

dénationalisation [denasjɔnaliza′sjõ], *n.f.* denationalization.

dénationaliser [denasjɔnali′ze], *v.t.* to denationalize.

dénatter [dena′te], *v.t.* to unplait (*hair etc.*).

dénaturé [denaty′re], *a.* unnatural, barbarous, cruel.

dénaturer [denaty′re], *v.t.* to alter the nature of; to misrepresent, to distort; to disfigure; to methylate (*alcohol*).

dénégation [denega′sjõ], *n.f.* denial, denegation.

déni [de′ni], *n.m.* denial, refusal.

déniaiser [denjɛ′ze], *v.t.* to sharpen the wits of; to initiate; to seduce. **se déniaiser,** *v.r.* to learn to be sharp, to grow cunning; (*fam.*) to lose one's innocence.

dénicher [deni′ʃe], *v.t.* to take out of the nest; to hunt out, to find out.—*v.i.* to forsake its nest (*of a bird*); to make off, to run away.

dénicheur [deni′ʃœ:r], *n.m.* nest robber.

denier [də′nje], *n.m.* (*Rom. Ant.*) denarius; (*Fr. Ant.*) denier; penny; farthing, mite; (*pl.*) state revenues.

dénier [de′nje], *v.t.* to deny, to refuse.

dénigrant [deni′grã], *a.* disparaging.

dénigrement [denigrə′mã], *n.m.* disparagement.

dénigrer [deni′gre], *v.t.* to disparage; to vilify.

dénivellation [denivɛlla′sjõ], *n.f.,* **dénivellement** [denivɛl′mã], *n.m.* difference of level; unevenness.

dénombrement [denõbrə′mã], *n.m.* enumeration; census.

dénombrer [denõ′bre], *v.t.* to number, to enumerate.

dénominateur [denɔmina′tœ:r], *n.m.* (*Arith.*) denominator.

dénomination [denɔmina′sjõ], *n.f.* denomination, name.

dénommer [denɔ′me], *v.t.* to designate.

dénoncer [denõ′se], *v.t.* (*conjug. like* COMMENCER) to denounce, to inform against; to give notice of, to declare (*war etc.*). **se dénoncer,** *v.r.* to own up; to give oneself up.

dénonciateur [denõsja′tœ:r], *n.m.* (*fem.* **-trice**) informer, accuser.

dénonciation [denõsja′sjõ], *n.f.* denunciation, declaration.

dénoter [denɔ′te], *v.t.* to denote, to betoken.

dénouement *or* **dénoûment** [denu′mã], *n.m.* dénouement, unravelling (*esp. of a play etc.*).

dénouer [denu′e], *v.t.* to untie, to loosen; to solve (*difficulties etc.*); to unravel (*plots*). **se dénouer,** *v.r.* to come untied, to be unravelled; to be solved.

denrée [dã′re], *n.f.* commodity, produce provisions.

dense [dã:s], *a.* dense, close, thick.

densité [dãsi′te], *n.f.* density, thickness.

dent [dã], *n.f.* tooth; fang; notch; cog; prong; *faire ses dents,* to cut one's teeth.

dentaire [dã′tɛ:r], *a.* dental.

dental [dã′tal], *a.* (*m.pl.* **-aux**) (*Phon.*) dental.

dent-de-lion [dãdə′ljõ], *n.m.* (*pl.* **dents-de-lion**) dandelion.

denté [dã′te], *a.* toothed; (*Bot.*) dentate; *roue dentée,* cogged wheel.

dentelé [dã′tle], *a.* notched, denticulated, indented, jagged.

denteler [dã′tle], *v.t.* (*conjug. like* APPELER) to indent, to notch.

dentelle [dã′tɛl], *n.f.* lace, lace work.

dentellier [dãtɛ′lje], *n.m.* (*fem.* **-ière**) lace maker.

dentelure [dã′tly:r], *n.f.* denticulation, indenting; scallop.

denticule [dãti′kyl], *n.m.* denticle.

dentier [dã′tje], *n.m.* set of teeth (*esp. artificial*), denture.

dentifrice [dãti′fris], *n.m.* toothpaste.

dentiste [dã′tist], *n.m.* dentist.

denture [dã′ty:r], *n.f.* set of teeth; (*Horol.*) teeth of a wheel.

dénudation [denyda′sjõ], *n.f.* denudation.

dénuder [deny′de], *v.t.* to denude; to lay bare.

dénuement *or* **dénûment** [deny′mã], *n.m.* destitution, penury, want.

dénuer [de′nɥe], *v.t.* to strip, to leave destitute. **se dénuer,** *v.r.* to strip oneself; to leave oneself destitute.

dépannage [depa′na:ʒ], *n.m.* (*Mach., Elec.*) repairing; *service de dépannage,* breakdown *or* repair service.

dépanner [depa′ne], *v.t.* (*Mach., Elec.*) to repair (*a breakdown*).

dépanneuse [depa′nø:z], *n.f.* breakdown vehicle, repair car, wrecker.

dépaqueter [depak′te], *v.t.* (*conjug. like* APPELER) to unpack.

107

dépareillé

dépareillé [depars'je], *a.* unmatched, odd.
déparer [depa're], *v.t.* to strip (*of ornaments*); (*fig.*) to mar, to disfigure.
déparier [depa'rje], *v.t.* to take away one (*of a pair*); to separate (*a pair of animals*).
départ [de'pa:r], *n.m.* departure, start, setting out.
départager [departa'ʒe], *v.t.* (*conjug. like* MANGER) to settle by a vote.
département [departə'mã], *n.m.* department; line, business.
départemental [departəmã'tal], *a.* (*m. pl.* **-aux**) departmental.
départir [depar'ti:r], *v.t. irr.* (*conjug. like* SENTIR) to separate; to distribute, to divide, to endow, to bestow. **se départir**, *v.r.* to desist; to deviate (*from*).
dépassement [depas'mã], *n.m.* overstepping (*of credit etc.*); (*Motor.*) passing.
dépasser [depa'se], *v.t.* to go beyond, to pass, to overtake; to exceed, to surpass; to be taller etc. than; to show; *son jupon dépasse*, her slip is showing.
dépaver [depa've], *v.t.* to unpave, to take up the pavement of.
dépaysé [depei'ze], *a.* away from home, out of one's element.
dépayser [depei'ze], *v.t.* to send away from home; to remove from his natural sphere etc.; (*fig.*) to bewilder. **se dépayser**, *v.r.* to leave one's home; to go abroad; to get out of one's element.
dépècement [depɛs'mã], **dépeçage** [depə'sa:ʒ], *n.m.* cutting up, carving, dismemberment.
dépecer [dep'se], *v.t.* (*see Verb Tables*) to cut up (*a carcass*), to carve.
dépêche [de'pɛ:ʃ], *n.f.* dispatch (*letter on affairs of State*); communication (*esp. a telegram*).
dépêcher [depɛ'ʃe], *v.t.* to dispatch, to do quickly; to send quickly, to send by messenger; to kill. **se dépêcher**, *v.r.* to hurry, to make haste; *dépêchez-vous*, hurry up.
dépeigner [depɛ'ɲe], *v.t.* to ruffle (*hair*).
dépeindre [de'pɛ̃:dr], *v.t. irr.* (*conjug. like* CRAINDRE) to depict, to describe; to portray, to paint.
dépelotonner [depləto'ne], *v.t.* to unwind. **se dépelotonner**, *v.r.* to come unwound; to uncurl (*of cat*).
dépenaillé [depna'je], *a.* tattered, ragged.
dépendance [depã'dã:s], *n.f.* subordination; dependence; appendage, annex, outhouse, (*pl.*) out-buildings.
dépendant [depã'dã], *a.* dependent.
dépendre (1) [de'pã:dr], *v.t.* to take down; to unhang.
dépendre (2) [de'pã:dr], *v.i.* to depend, to be dependent (*de*).
dépens [de'pã], *n.m.* (*used only in pl.*) expense, cost.
dépense [de'pã:s], *n.f.* expense; expenditure, outlay; waste, flow.
dépenser [depã'se], *v.t.* to spend or consume; to waste.
dépensier [depã'sje], *a.* (*fem.* **-ière**) extravagant.—*n.m.* (*fem.* **-ière**) extravagant person, spend-thrift; bursar.
déperdition [depɛrdi'sjõ], *n.f.* loss, waste.
dépérir [depe'ri:r], *v.i.* to decline, to pine away, to wither, to dwindle, to waste away.

dépérissement [deperis'mã], *n.m.* decay, withering, wasting away.
dépêtrer [depɛ'tre], *v.t.* to disentangle, to extricate. **se dépêtrer**, *v.r.* to get clear of.
dépeuplement [depœplə'mã], *n.m.* depopulation; thinning (*of forests etc.*).
dépeupler [depœ'ple], *v.t.* to depopulate; to thin. **se dépeupler**, *v.r.* to become depopulated, to be unstocked (*of river*).
dépilage [depi'la:ʒ], *n.m.* removal of hairs, bristles, etc. (*from hides etc.*).
dépilation [depila'sjõ], *n.f.* depilation.
dépiquage [depi'ka:ʒ], *n.m.* threshing or treading out (*grain*).
dépiquer (1) [depi'ke], *v.t.* to unquilt, to unstitch.
dépiquer (2) [depi'ke], *v.t.* to tread out (*grain*).
dépister [depis'te], *v.t.* to track down; to hunt out; (*fig.*) to throw off the scent.
dépit [de'pi], *n.m.* spite; vexation.
dépiter [depi'te], *v.t.* to vex, to spite. **se dépiter**, *v.r.* to be vexed, to fret.
déplacé [depla'se], *a.* displaced, misplaced, ill-timed, unbecoming.
déplacement [deplas'mã], *n.m.* removal; displacement; *frais de déplacement*, travelling expenses.
déplacer [depla'se], *v.t.* (*conjug. like* COMMENCER) to displace; to remove, to change; to misplace. **se déplacer**, *v.r.* to move, to change one's place, to leave one's residence; to be displaced (*of things*).
déplaire [de'plɛ:r], *v.i. irr.* (*conjug. like* PLAIRE) to displease, to offend; to be disagreeable, to give offence. **se déplaire**, *v.r.* to be displeased or dissatisfied (*with*).
déplaisant [deplɛ'zã], *a.* unpleasant, disagreeable.
déplaisir [deple'zi:r], *n.m.* displeasure, annoyance; grief.
déplanter [deplã'te], *v.t.* to dig or take up (*a plant*).
déplantoir [deplã'twa:r], *n.m.* garden trowel.
dépliant [depli'ã], *n.m.* folding page; folder, prospectus, leaflet.
déplier [depli'e], *v.t.* to unfold, to open out; to lay out.
déplisser [depli'se], *v.t.* to unpleat. **se déplisser**, *v.r.* to come unpleated; to lose its pleats (*of a skirt etc.*).
déploiement or **déploîment** [deplwa'mã], *n.m.* unfolding; display, show; (*Mil.*) deployment.
déplombage [deplõ'ba:ʒ], *n.m.* unsealing; unstopping.
déplomber [deplõ'be], *v.t.* to take the custom-house seal off (*goods*); to unstop (*a tooth*).
déplorable [deplo'rabl], *a.* deplorable, lamentable.
déplorablement [deplorablə'mã], *adv.* deplorably, wretchedly.
déplorer [deplo're], *v.t.* to deplore, to bewail, to lament, to mourn.
déployer [deplwa'je], *v.t.* (*conjug. like* EMPLOYER) to unfold, to unroll, to unfurl, to spread out; to display, to show; (*Mil.*) to deploy; *à gorge déployée*, at the top of one's voice. **se déployer**, *v.r.* to unroll; to display oneself; (*Mil.*) to deploy.
déplumer [deply'me], *v.t.* to pluck; (*fig.*) to despoil; to tear the hair from. **se déplumer**, *v.r.* to molt, to shed feathers.

dépolariser [depɔlari'ze], *v.t.* to depolarize.
dépolir [depɔ'li:r], *v.t.* to make the surface (*of metal etc.*) dull, to frost (*glass*).
dépopulation [depɔpyla'sjɔ̃], *n.m.* depopulation.
déportation [depɔrta'sjɔ̃], *n.f.* deportation.
déporté [depɔr'te], *n.m.* (*fem.* **-ée**) deported person.
déportements [depɔrtə'mɑ̃], *n.m. pl.* misconduct, evil-doings.
déporter [depɔr'te], *v.t.* to deport, to transport for life; to swerve; to carry away, to drift. **se déporter**, *v.r.* (*Law*) to desist (*from*).
déposant [depo'zɑ̃], *a.* giving evidence; depositing.—*n.m.* (*fem.* **-e**) witness; depositor.
déposer [depo'ze], *v.t.* to lay down *or* aside; to divest oneself of; to depose; to deposit; to lodge (*a complaint etc.*); **marque déposée**, registered trademark.—*v.i.* to give evidence; to settle, to leave a sediment.
dépositaire [depɔzi'tɛ:r], *n.m.* depositary, trustee; agent.
déposition [depɔzi'sjɔ̃], *n.f.* deposition, evidence.
dépositoire [depɔzi'twa:r], *n.m.* depository, mortuary.
déposséder [depose'de], *v.t.* (*conjug. like* CÉDER) to dispossess, to oust.
dépossession [deposɛ'sjɔ̃], *n.f.* dispossession, deprivation.
dépôt [de'po], *n.m.* depositing; deposit; sediment; depository, warehouse; (*Mil.*) depot; (*Med.*) tumor, abscess; **dépôt d'essence**, gas station; **en dépôt**, as a deposit in trust, (*Comm.*) on sale; **mandat de dépôt**, writ of imprisonment.
dépotage [depɔ'ta:ʒ], **dépotement** [depɔt'mɑ̃], *n.m.* unpotting; decanting.
dépoter [depɔ'te], *v.t.* to take out of a pot; to decant.
dépouille [de'pu:j], *n.f.* slough, cast-off skin *or* hide; spoil; remains, wardrobe (*of persons deceased*); (*pl.*) spoils, booty; **dépouille mortelle**, mortal remains.
dépouillement [depuj'mɑ̃], *n.m.* spoliation, despoiling; scrutiny (*of a ballot box*); abstract (*of an account*).
dépouiller [depu'je], *v.t.* to strip, to skin; to unclothe; to despoil; to throw off; to cast (*of insects*); to reap (*crops*); to inspect, to count up (*a ballot-box*); to present an abstract (*of accounts*). **se dépouiller**, *v.r.* to shed its skin (*of insects and animals*), to molt; **se dépouiller de**, to divest oneself of, to strip oneself of, to renounce (*possessions etc.*).
dépourvoir [depur'vwa:r], *v.t. irr.* (*conjug. like* POURVOIR) to leave unprovided (*with*) *or* destitute (*of*). **se dépourvoir**, *v.r.* to leave oneself unequipped.
dépourvu [depur'vy], *a.* destitute, unprovided; **au dépourvu**, unawares, unexpectedly.
dépravation [depravɑ'sjɔ̃], *n.f.* vitiation, depravity.
dépravé [depra've], *a.* vitiated, depraved, corrupt.
dépraver [depra've], *v.t.* to deprave, to corrupt, to pervert. **se dépraver**, *v.r.* to become depraved *or* corrupted.

dépréciation [depresjɑ'sjɔ̃], *n.f.* depreciation.
déprécier [depre'sje], *v.t.* to depreciate, to undervalue, to underrate; to disparage. **se déprécier**, *v.r.* to underrate oneself; to fall in value (*of things*).
déprédateur [depreda'tœ:r], *n.m.* (*fem.* **-trice**) depredator, plunderer.
déprédation [depredɑ'sjɔ̃], *n.f.* plundering, depredation.
déprendre [de'prɑ̃:dr], *v.t. irr.* (*conjug. like* PRENDRE) to loosen, to detach. **se déprendre**, *v.r.* to get loose; to detach oneself (*de*).
dépression [depre'sjɔ̃], *n.f.* depression, hollow; (*fig.*) recession, slump (*of business*); **dépression nerveuse**, nervous breakdown.
déprimer [depri'me], *v.t.* to press down, to depress; (*fig.*) to discourage.
depuis [də'pɥi], *prep.* since, for; from, after; **depuis longtemps**, for a long time; **depuis peu**, lately; **depuis quand?** since when?—*adv.* since (then), afterwards, since that time.—*conj. phr.* **depuis que**, since.
députation [depytɑ'sjɔ̃], *n.f.* deputation; deputyship.
député [depy'te], *n.m.* deputy, delegate; Member of Parliament.
députer [depy'te], *v.t.* to send as representative, to depute.
déracinement [derasin'mɑ̃], *n.m.* uprooting, eradication.
déraciner [derasi'ne], *v.t.* to uproot; to eradicate, to extirpate.
déraidir [derɛ'di:r], *v.t.* to unstiffen; to make pliant. **se déraidir**, *v.r.* to grow soft *or* supple; to unbend.
déraillement [deraj'mɑ̃], *n.m.* derailment.
dérailler [deraj'je], *v.i.* to run off the rails.
déraison [derɛ'zɔ̃], *n.f.* unreasonableness, folly.
déraisonnable [derɛzɔ'nabl], *a.* unreasonable, senseless.
déraisonnablement [derɛzɔnablə'mɑ̃], *adv.* unreasonably, irrationally.
déraisonner [derɛzɔ'ne], *v.i.* to reason falsely, to talk nonsense; to rave.
dérangement [derɑ̃ʒ'mɑ̃], *n.m.* derangement; trouble; disorder, disturbance.
déranger [derɑ̃'ʒe], *v.t.* (*conjug. like* MANGER) to derange, to put out of place *or* order; to discompose, to disconcert; to disturb, to upset; to unsettle. **se déranger**, *v.r.* to move; to be deranged, to get out of order; to trouble *or* disturb oneself, to put oneself out.
déraper [dera'pe], *v.i.* to skid, to side-slip (*bicycle, car etc.*).
dératé [dera'te], *n.m. only used in* **courir comme un dératé**, to run like a greyhound.
derechef [dər'ʃɛf], *adv.* over again, afresh, anew.
déréglé [dere'gle], *a.* out of order; irregular; intemperate, (*fig.*) unruly, dissolute.
déréglement [derɛglə'mɑ̃], *n.m.* irregularity, disorder; dissoluteness, licentiousness.
dérégler [dere'gle], *v.t.* (*conjug. like* CÉDER) to put out of order. **se dérégler**, *v.r.* to get out of order, to be deranged; to lead a disorderly life.

dérider

dérider [deri'de], *v.t.* to unwrinkle, to smooth; to brighten, to cheer up. **se dérider**, *v.r.* to smooth one's brow; to cheer up.

dérision [deri'zjɔ̃], *n.f.* derision, mockery, ridicule.

dérisoire [deri'zwa:r], *a.* derisive, mocking.

dérivatif [deriva'tif], *a.* (*fem.* **-tive**) derivative.—*n.m.* (*Med.*) derivative, counter-irritant.

dérivation [deriva'sjɔ̃], *n.f.* derivation; diversion (*of water etc.*); (*Elec.*) branching, shunting; (*Naut.*) drift, leeway; (*Av.*) windage; (*Elec.*) **circuit en dérivation**, branch circuit.

dérive [de'ri:v], *n.f.* (*Naut.*) drift, leeway; (*Av.*) fin.

dérivé [deri've], *a.* drifted.—*n.m.* (*Gram.*) derivative.

dériver [deri've], *v.t.* to divert; to derive.—*v.i.* to be turned from its proper course; (*Naut.*) to drift (*from the shore*), to go adrift.

dermatite [dɛrma'tit], *n.f.* dermatitis.

dernier [dɛr'nje], *a.* (*fem.* **-ière**) last, latest; vilest, meanest; extreme (*highest, greatest etc.*); the one just past; youngest (*of a family of children*).—*n.m.* (*fem.* **-ière**) the last; the highest, lowest etc.

dernièrement [dɛrnjɛr'mɑ̃], *adv.* lately, recently.

dérobé [derɔ'be], *a.* stolen, hidden, secret; **à la dérobée**, stealthily.

dérober [derɔ'be], *v.t.* to steal; to remove; to conceal; to protect; to screen. **se dérober**, *v.r.* to steal away, to escape, to disappear.

dérogation [derɔga'sjɔ̃], *n.f.* derogation.

dérogatoire [derɔga'twa:r], *a.* derogatory.

déroger [derɔ'ʒe], *v.i.* (*conjug. like* MANGER) to derogate; to detract; to condescend, to stoop.

dérouillement [deruj'mɑ̃], *n.m.* removal of rust.

dérouiller [deru'je], *v.t.* to remove the rust from; (*fig.*) to polish. **se dérouiller**, *v.r.* to lose its *or* one's rust; to brighten up; to read a subject up again.

déroulement [derul'mɑ̃], *n.m.* unrolling, unfolding.

dérouler [deru'le], *v.t.* to unroll; to spread out, to display. **se dérouler**, *v.r.* to unroll; to open to the view; to roll in (*of the waves*); to take place (*of events*).

déroutant [deru'tɑ̃], *a.* baffling, confusing.

déroute [de'rut], *n.f.* rout, overthrow; ruin; disorder, confusion.

dérouter [deru'te], *v.t.* to lead astray; to embarrass, to disconcert; to baffle; to divert (*ship, train etc.*).

derrière [dɛ'rjɛ:r], *prep.* behind, on the other side of.—*adv.* behind, after.—*n.m.* back, hinder part; posterior; behind; **pattes de derrière**, hind legs; **porte de derrière**, back door.

derviche [dɛr'viʃ], **dervis** [dɛr'vi], *n.m.* dervish.

des [de], [*contr. of* DE LES].

dès [dɛ], *prep.* from, since, as early as.—*conj. phr.* **dès que**, when, as soon as, since.

désabonnement [dezabɔn'mɑ̃], *n.m.* withdrawal of subscription.

désabonner (se) [sədezabɔ'ne], *v.r.* to withdraw one's subscription (*to a magazine etc.*).

désabuser [dezaby'ze], *v.t.* to disabuse, to undeceive. **se désabuser**, *v.r.* to be undeceived, to face the facts.

désaccord [deza'kɔ:r], *n.m.* disagreement, discord.

désaccorder [dezakɔr'de], *v.t.* to untune; (*fig.*) to set at variance. **se désaccorder**, *v.r.* to get out of tune.

désaccouplement [dezakuplə'mɑ̃], *n.m.* uncoupling.

désaccoupler [dezaku'ple], *v.t.* to uncouple. **se désaccoupler**, *v.r.* to become uncoupled; to come asunder.

désaccoutumer [dezakuty'me], *v.t.* to disaccustom. **se désaccoutumer**, *v.r.* to break oneself of, to lose the habit of.

désaffecter [dezafɛk'te], *v.t.* to secularize (*a church*); (*Mil.*) to transfer; to put a building to another use.

désaffection [dezafɛk'sjɔ̃], *n.f.* loss of affection.

désaffectionner [dezafɛksjɔ'ne], *v.t.* to cause (*someone*) to lose his *or* her affection, to disaffect. **se désaffectionner**, *v.r.* to lose affection.

désagencement [dezaʒɑ̃s'mɑ̃], *n.m.* throwing out of gear.

désagencer [dezaʒɑ̃'se], *v.t.* (*conjug. like* COMMENCER) to throw out of gear, to disarrange.

désagréable [dezagre'abl], *a.* disagreeable, unpleasant.

désagréablement [dezagreablə'mɑ̃], *adv.* disagreeably, unpleasantly.

désagréger [dezagre'ʒe], *v.t.* (*conjug. like* ASSIÉGER) to disaggregate, to break up, to separate.

désagrément [dezagre'mɑ̃], *n.m.* disagreeableness, unpleasantness; annoyance, discomfort.

désaimanter [dezɛmɑ̃'te], *v.t.* to demagnetize.

désajustement [dezaʒystə'mɑ̃], *n.m.* disarrangement, disorder.

désajuster [dezaʒys'te], *v.t.* to disarrange, to disturb, to put out of order. **se désajuster**, *v.r.* to become disarranged, to get out of order.

désaltérant [dezalte'rɑ̃], *a.* thirst-quenching.

désaltérer [dezalte're], *v.t.* (*conjug. like* CÉDER) to quench the thirst of, to refresh. **se désaltérer**, *v.r.* to quench one's thirst.

désamorcer [dezamɔr'se], *v.t.* (*conjug. like* COMMENCER) to unprime, to uncap (*fire-arms etc.*). **se désamorcer**, *v.r.* to run down (*dynamo*); to run dry (*pump*).

désappointement [dezapwɛ̃t'mɑ̃], *n.m.* disappointment.

désappointer [dezapwɛ̃'te], *v.t.* to disappoint.

désapprendre [deza'prɑ̃:dr], *v.t. irr.* (*conjug. like* PRENDRE) to unlearn, to forget.

désapprobateur [dezaprɔba'tœ:r], *a.* (*fem.* **-trice**) disapproving, censuring, carping.—*n.m.* (*fem.* **-trice**) censurer, fault-finder.

désapprobation [dezaprɔba'sjɔ̃], *n.f.* disapprobation, disapproval.

désappropriation [dezaprɔpria'sjɔ̃], *n.f.* renunciation (*of property*).

désapprouver [dezapru've], *v.t.* to disapprove of, to blame.

désarçonner [dezarsɔ'ne], *v.t.* to unhorse; (*fig.*) to baffle, to floor.

désarmement [dezarmə'mã], *n.m.* disarming, disarmament; (*Naut.*) laying up.

désarmer [dezar'me], *v.t.* to disarm, to unarm; (*fig.*) to appease, to calm; to uncock (*a gun*); (*Naut.*) to lay up (*a vessel*).—*v.i.* to disarm; to give up maintaining troops.

désarroi [deza'rwɑ], *n.m.* disorder, disarray, confusion.

désarticulation [dezartikylɑ'sjɔ̃], *n.f.* disarticulation.

désarticuler [dezartiky'le], *v.t.* to disarticulate, to disjoint.

désassemblage [dezasɑ̃'bla:ʒ], **désassemblement** [dezasɑ̃blə'mã], *n.m.* dismantling.

désassembler [dezasɑ̃'ble], *v.t.* to take to pieces, to separate, to dismantle.

désassocier [dezasɔ'sje], *v.t.* to disassociate, to dissociate.

désassortiment [dezasɔrti'mã], *n.m.* unmatching, ill-assortment; unstocking.

désastre [de'zastr], *n.m.* disaster.

désastreusement [dezastrøz'mã], *adv.* disastrously.

désastreux [dezas'trø], *a.* (*fem.* **-euse**) disastrous, unfortunate, very sad.

désavantage [dezavɑ̃'ta:ʒ], *n.m.* disadvantage; detriment, prejudice; drawback, handicap.

désavantager [dezavɑ̃ta'ʒe], *v.t.* (*conjug. like* MANGER) to disadvantage, to handicap.

désavantageusement [dezavɑ̃taʒøz'mã], *adv.* disadvantageously; disparagingly.

désavantageux [dezavɑ̃ta'ʒø], *a.* (*fem.* **-euse**) disadvantageous; detrimental, prejudicial, unfavorable.

désaveu [deza'vø], *n.m.* (*pl.* **-eux**) disavowal; denial; retractation.

désavouer [deza'vwe], *v.t.* to disown, to disclaim, to disavow; to retract.

désaxé [deza'kse], *a.* offset, out of true (*of a wheel, etc.*); (*fig.*) out of joint.

descellement [desɛl'mã], *n.m.* loosening, unsealing.

desceller [desɛ'le], *v.t.* to unseal; to loosen (*masonry etc.*). **se desceller**, *v.r.* to become loose *or* unsealed.

descendance [desɑ̃'dɑ̃:s], *n.f.* descent, lineage.

descendant [desɑ̃'dɑ̃], *a.* descending, going down; (*Mil.*) coming off duty.—*n.m.* (*fem.* **-e**) descendant, offspring, issue.

descendre [de'sɑ̃:dr], *v.t.* (*with aux.* AVOIR) to take down, bring *or* let down; to go *or* come down (*a staircase etc.*); to drop off (*of a cab etc.*); to land.—*v.i.* (*with aux.* ÊTRE) to descend, to go down; to go downstairs; to alight, to land; to slope, to incline; to fall, to subside.

descente [de'sɑ̃:t], *n.f.* descent; taking down; subsidence (*of waters etc.*); dismounting; disembarkation; declivity; raid; (*pop.*) rupture; **descente de lit**, bedside rug; **descente de bain**, bath mat.

descriptif [deskrip'tif], *a.* (*fem.* **-tive**) descriptive.

description [deskrip'sjɔ̃], *n.f.* description; inventory.

désemballage [dezɑ̃ba'la:ʒ], *n.m.* unpacking.

désemballer [dezɑ̃ba'le], *v.t.* to unpack.

désembarquement [dezɑ̃barkə'mã], *n.m.* disembarkation, landing.

désembarquer [dezɑ̃bar'ke], *v.t.* to disembark, to land; to unship, to unload.

désemboîter [dezɑ̃bwa'te], *v.t.* to dislocate. **se désemboîter**, *v.r.* to become disjointed.

désembourber [dezɑ̃bur'be], *v.t.* to draw out of the mire.

désemparé [dezɑ̃pa're], *a.* in distress, helpless.

désemparer [dezɑ̃pa're], *v.t.* (*Naut.*) to disable.—*v.i.* to quit, to go away; **sans désemparer**, on the spot, at once.

désempeser [dezɑ̃pə'ze], *v.t.* (*conjug. like* AMENER) to unstarch. **se désempeser**, *v.r.* to become limp.

désemplir [dezɑ̃'pli:r], *v.t.* to make less full, to empty in part.—*v.i.* to become less full (*used only in negative*). **se désemplir**, *v.r.* to become less full.

désenchaîner [dezɑ̃ʃɛ'ne], *v.t.* to unchain.

désenchantement [dezɑ̃ʃɑ̃t'mã], *n.m.* disenchantment, disillusion.

désenchanter [dezɑ̃ʃɑ̃'te], *v.t.* to disenchant, to disillusion.

désenchanteur [dezɑ̃ʃɑ̃'tœ:r], *a.* (*fem.* **-eresse**) disenchanting.

désencombrement [dezɑ̃kɔ̃brə'mã], *n.m.* disencumbrance; dispersal.

désencombrer [dezɑ̃kɔ̃'bre], *v.t.* to disencumber, to clear (*a road etc.*).

désenfiler [dezɑ̃fi'le], *v.t.* to unthread, to unstring. **se désenfiler**, *v.r.* to come unthreaded *or* unstrung.

désenfler [dezɑ̃'fle], *v.t.* to reduce the swelling of.—*v.i.* and **se désenfler**, *v.r.* to become less swollen.

désenflure [dezɑ̃'fly:r], *n.f.*, **désenflement** [dezɑ̃flə'mã], *n.m.* diminution *or* disappearance of a swelling.

désengager [dezɑ̃ga'ʒe], *v.t.* (*conjug. like* MANGER) to disengage, to release from an engagement.

désengrener [dezɑ̃grə'ne], *v.t.* (*conjug. like* AMENER) to throw out of gear.

désenivrer [dezãni'vre], *v.t.*, to make sober again.—*v.i.* to sober. **se désenivrer**, *v.r.* to become sober (*again*), to sober up.

désenlaidir [dezɑ̃lɛ'di:r], *v.t.* to render less ugly.—*v.i.* to become less ugly.

désennuyer [dezɑ̃nɥi'je], *v.t.* (*conjug. like* EMPLOYER) to enliven, to cheer. **se désennuyer**, *v.r.* to find amusement, to kill time.

désenrayer [dezɑ̃rɛ'je], *v.t.* (*conjug. like* PAYER) to unlock *or* unskid (*a wheel etc.*).

désenrhumer [dezɑ̃ry'me], *v.t.* to cure (*someone*) of a cold. **se désenrhumer**, *v.r.* to get rid of a cold.

désenrôlement [dezɑ̃rol'mã], *n.m.* (*Mil.*) discharge.

désenrôler [dezɑ̃ro'le], *v.t.* to discharge.

désensevelir [dezɑ̃sə'vli:r], *v.t.* to unshroud; to exhume.

désensevelissement [dezɑ̃səvlis'mã], *n.m.* unshrouding, exhumation, disinterment.

désentortiller [dezɑ̃tɔrti'je], *v.t.* to untwist, to unravel.

désentraver [dezɑ̃tra'we], *v.t.* to untrammel, to unhobble (*a horse etc.*).

déséquilibre [dezeki'libr], *n.m.* lack of balance, unbalance; imbalance.

111

déséquilibré [dezekili'bre], *a.* and *n.m.* (*fem.* -ée) unbalanced (person).
déséquilibrer [dezekili'bre], *v.t.* to unbalance.
désert [de'zɛ:r], *a.* uninhabited, solitary; wild, waste, deserted.—*n.m.* desert, wilderness; solitary place; (*C*) clearing in a forest.
déserter [dezɛrte], *v.t.* to desert, to abandon, to forsake; to quit, to leave; (*C*) to clear land, to break up (*ground*) for tillage.—*v.i.* to desert, to go over to the enemy.
déserteur [dezɛr'tœ:r], *n.m.* deserter.
désertion [dezɛr'sjɔ̃], *n.f.* desertion.
désespérance [dezɛspe'rã:s], *n.f.* despair.
désespérant [dezɛspe'rã], *a.* desperate, hopeless; disheartening, distressing.
désespéré [dezɛspe're], *a.* hopeless, desperate; disconsolate.—*n.m.* (*fem.* -ée) person in despair; madman, madwoman.
désespérément [dezɛspere'mã], *adv.* desperately, despairingly.
désespérer [dezɛspe're], *v.t.* (*conjug. like* CÉDER) to drive to despair; to dishearten; to distress.—*v.i.* to despair. **se désespérer**, *v.r.* to be in despair.
désespoir [dezɛs'pwa:r], *n.m.* despair, hopelessness, despondency, grief; *en désespoir de cause*, as a last resource.
déshabiliter [dezabili'te], *v.t.* to disqualify.
déshabillé [dezabi'je], *n.m.* deshabille, undress; *en déshabillé*, partly *or* scantily dressed.
déshabiller [dezabi'je], *v.t.* to undress, to strip. **se déshabiller**, *v.r.* to undress oneself.
déshabituer [dezabi'tɥe], *v.t.* to disaccustom, to break off. **se déshabituer**, *v.r.* to lose the habit of; to break oneself of.
déshérence [deze'rã:s], *n.f.* (*Law*) escheat.
déshériter [dezeri'te], *v.t.* to disinherit.
déshonnête [dezɔ'nɛ:t], *a.* immodest, indecent, unseemly.
déshonnêtement [dezɔnɛt'mã], *adv.* indecently, immodestly.
déshonnêteté [dezɔnɛt'te], *n.f.* indecency, unseemliness.
déshonneur [dezɔ'nœ:r], *n.m.* dishonor, disgrace, shame.
déshonorable [dezɔnɔ'rabl], *a.* dishonorable.
déshonorablement [dezɔnɔrablə'mã], *adv.* dishonorably.
déshonorant [dezɔnɔ'rã], *a.* dishonorable, disgraceful.
déshonorer [dezɔnɔ're], *v.t.* to dishonor, to disgrace. **se déshonorer**, *v.r.* to dishonor *or* disgrace oneself.
déshydrater [dezidra'te], *v.t.* to dehydrate.
désignatif [deziɲa'tif], *a.* (*fem.* -tive) indicative.
désignation [deziɲa'sjɔ̃], *n.f.* designation, indication.
désigner [dezi'ɲe], *v.t.* to designate, to denote; to appoint, to nominate, to point out; (*Mil.*) to detail.
désillusion [dezilyzjɔ̃], *n.f.*, **désillusionnement** [dezilyzjɔn'mã], *n.m.* disillusion.
désillusionner [dezilyzjɔ'ne], *v.t.* to disillusion, to disappoint.
désinfectant [dezɛ̃fɛk'tã], *a.* disinfecting.—*n.m.* disinfectant.

désinfecter [dezɛ̃fɛk'te], *v.t.* to disinfect, to decontaminate.
désinfection [dezɛ̃fɛk'sjɔ̃], *n.f.* disinfection.
désintégration [dezɛ̃tegra'sjɔ̃], *n.f.* disintegration; fission.
désintégrer [dezɛ̃te'gre], *v.t.* (*conjug. like* CÉDER) to disintegrate; to split (*atom*).
désintéressé [dezɛ̃terɛ'se], *a.* disinterested, unselfish, unbiased.
désintéressement [dezɛ̃terɛs'mã], *n.m.* disinterestedness.
désintéresser [dezɛ̃terɛ'se], *v.t.* to indemnify.
désinvestir [dezɛ̃vɛs'ti:r], *v.t.* (*Mil.*) to raise the siege of.
désinvolte [dezɛ̃'vɔlt], *a.* free, easy; offhand.
désinvolture [dezɛ̃vɔl'ty:r], *n.f.* casual, easy bearing *or* gait; offhandedness.
désir [de'zi:r], *n.m.* desire, wish, longing.
désirable [dezi'rabl], *a.* desirable.
désirer [dezi're], *v.t.* to desire, to wish for, to long for, to want.
désireux [dezi'rø], *a.* (*fem.* -euse) desirous, anxious, eager (*to*).
désistement [dezistə'mã], *n.m.* desistance, withdrawal.
désister (se) [sədezis'te], *v.r.* to desist from, to renounce, to withdraw.
désobéir [dezobe'i:r], *v.i.* to disobey.
désobéissance [dezobei'sã:s], *n.f.* disobedience.
désobéissant [dezobei'sã], *a.* disobedient.
désobligeamment [dezobliʒa'mã], *adv.* disobligingly; unkindly.
désobligeance [dezobli'ʒã:s], *n.f.* lack of complaisance; unkindness.
désobligeant [dezobli'ʒã], *a.* disobliging; uncivil.
désobliger [dezobli'ʒe], *v.t.* (*conjug. like* MANGER) to disoblige, to displease.
désodorisant [dezɔdori'zã], *a.* and *n.m.* deodorant.
désœuvré [dezœ'vre], *a.* unoccupied, idle.
désœuvrement [dezœvrə'mã], *n.m.* want of occupation, idleness.
désolant [dezo'lã], *a.* grievous, distressing.
désolation [dezola'sjɔ̃], *n.f.* desolation, ruin; deep affliction, grief.
désolé [dezo'le], *a.* afflicted, broken-hearted; very sorry, grieved; dreary, desolate (*place*).
désoler [dezo'le], *v.t.* to devastate, to desolate, to lay waste; to afflict, to grieve; to annoy, to torment. **se désoler**, *v.r.* to grieve, to be disconsolate.
désolidariser [desolidari'ze], *v.t.* to break the ties which keep together (*a party, friends etc.*).
désopilant [dezopi'lã], *a.* very funny, sidesplitting.
désopiler [dezopi'le], *v.t.* (*Med.*) to clear of obstruction; (*fig.*) to cheer up, to enliven.
désordonné [dezordo'ne], *a.* disorderly; (*fig.*) dissolute, unruly; inordinate.
désordonner [dezordo'ne], *v.t.* to disturb; to throw into confusion.
désordre [de'zordr], *n.m.* disorder, confusion; disorderly life; perturbation; (*pl.*) disturbances, riots.
désorganisation [dezorganiza'sjɔ̃], *n.f.* disorganization.
désorganiser [dezorgani'ze], *v.t.* to disorganize. **se désorganiser**, *v.r.* to become disorganized.

désorienter [dezɔrjɑ̃'te], *v.t.* to lead astray, to mislead, to bewilder; to put out, to disconcert.

désormais [dezɔr'mɛ], *adv.* henceforth, hereafter.

désossé [dezɔ'se], *a.* boneless, flabby.

désosser [dezɔ'se], *v.t.* to bone. **se désosser**, *v.r.* to become disjointed, limp, flabby etc.

despote [dɛs'pɔt], *n.m.* despot.

despotique [dɛspɔ'tik], *a.* despotic.

despotiquement [dɛspɔtik'mɑ̃], *adv.* despotically.

despotisme [dɛspɔ'tism], *n.m.* despotism.

desquels [de'kɛl], *m.pl. (fem.* **-elles**) [DUQUEL].

dessaisir [desɛ'zi:r], *v.t.* to let go; to dispossess. **se dessaisir**, *v.r.* to give up, to part with.

dessaisissement [desɛzis'mɑ̃], *n.m.* parting with, abandonment.

dessalé [desa'le], *a.* unsalted, free from salt; (*fam.*) sharp.—*n.m. (fem.* **-ée**) sharp person.

dessaler [desa'le], *v.t.* to remove salt from (*meat etc.*); (*fig.*) to make sharp, cunning etc.

dessangler [desɑ̃'gle], *v.t.* to loosen the girth of (*a horse etc.*).

desséchant [dese'ʃɑ̃], *a.* drying, parching.

dessèchement [desɛʃ'mɑ̃], *n.m.* drying up; dryness.

dessécher [dese'ʃe], *v.t.* to dry up; to parch; (*fig.*) to wither (*the heart etc.*); to emaciate. **se dessécher**, *v.r.* to become dry, to dry up; (*fig.*) to wither, to waste away.

dessein [de'sɛ̃], *n.m.* design, plan, scheme; intention, resolution.

desseller [desɛ'le], *v.t.* to unsaddle.

desserrer [desɛ'rɛ], *v.t.* to loosen, to relax; to ease. **se desserrer**, *v.r.* to become loose, to relax.

dessert [de'sɛ:r], *n.m.* dessert.

desserte [de'sɛrt], *n.f.* leavings, remains (*of a meal*); small sideboard; parochial duty; railway service.

desservant [desɛr'vɑ̃], *n.m.* officiating minister (*of a parish etc.*).

desservir [desɛr'vi:r], *v.t. irr. (conjug. like* SENTIR) to clear (*a table*); to officiate (*of clergymen*); to ply between (*of boats etc.*); (*fig.*) to do someone a disservice.

dessiller or **déciller** [desi'je], *v.t.* to open (*someone's eyes*); to undeceive.

dessin [de'sɛ̃], *n.m.* drawing; sketch; pattern, design; *dessin animé*, (*Cine.*) cartoon.

dessinateur [desina'tœ:r], *n.m. (fem.* **-trice**) draftsman; designer.

dessiner [desi'ne], *v.t.* to draw; to sketch; to set off, to indicate; to lay out. **se dessiner**, *v.r.* to be delineated, to be visible, to stand out.

dessous [dǝ'su], *adv.* under, underneath, below.—*n.m.* lower part; under, hidden *or* wrong side; worst; lee (*of the wind*); (*pl.*) underclothing (*of women*).—*prep. phr.* **au-dessous de**, beneath.

dessus [dǝ'sy], *adv.* on, upon, over, above; *là-dessus*, thereupon; *par-dessus*, over, besides; *sens dessus dessous*, upside down.—*n.m.* top, upper part; right side; upper hand, advantage.—*prep. phr.* **au-dessus de**, above.

destin [dɛs'tɛ̃], *n.m.* destiny, fate; career.

destinataire [dɛstina'tɛ:r], *n.* addressee; recipient; (*Comm.*) consignee; payee.

destination [dɛstina'sjɔ̃], *n.f.* destination; object, end.

destinée [dɛsti'ne], *n.f.* fate, destiny, doom.

destiner [dɛsti'ne], *v.t.* to destine, to purpose; to reserve (*for a particular fate etc.*). **se destiner**, *v.r.* to be destined.

destituer [dɛsti'tɥe], *v.t.* to dismiss, to discharge.

destitution [dɛstity'sjɔ̃], *n.f.* dismissal, removal (*from office*).

destroyer [dɛstrwa'jœ:r], *n.m.* (*Navy*) destroyer.

destructeur [dɛstryk'tœ:r], *a.* (*fem.* **-trice**) destructive, deadly, ruinous.—*n.m.* (*fem.* **-trice**) ravager, spoiler.

destructif [dɛstryk'tif], *a.* (*fem.* **-tive**) destructive, destroying.

destruction [dɛstryk'sjɔ̃], *n.f.* destruction.

désuet [desɥ'ɛ], *a.* (*fem.* **-ète**) obsolete, out-of-date.

désuétude [desɥe'tyd], *n.f.* disuse, desuetude.

désunion [dezy'njɔ̃], *n.f.* disunion; disjunction.

désunir [dezy'ni:r], *v.t.* to disunite, to disjoin, to part. **se désunir**, *v.r.* to disunite, to come asunder.

détachage [deta'ʃa:ʒ], *n.m.* cleaning, scouring.

détachant [deta'ʃɑ̃], *n.m.* cleaner, stain-remover.

détachement [detaʃ'mɑ̃], *n.m.* indifference, unconcern; (*Mil.*) detachment, draft.

détacher (1) [deta'ʃe], *v.t.* to remove stains, spots etc.

détacher (2) [deta'ʃe], *v.t.* to detach, to untie, to unfasten, to undo; to cut off; (*Mil.*) to detail. **se détacher**, *v.r.* to come unfastened, to come undone; to disengage oneself; to break away; to stand out clearly.

détail [de'ta:j], *n.m.* detail, small matter, trifle; retail.

détaillant [deta'jɑ̃], *n.m.* (*fem.* **-e**) retailer, small dealer.

détailler [deta'je], *v.t.* to cut in pieces; to retail; to relate minutely.

détaxation [detaksa'sjɔ̃], *n.f.* decontrol (*of prices*).

détaxer [detak'se], *v.t.* to reduce *or* take off a tax; to decontrol.

détecter [detɛk'te], *v.t.* to detect.

détecteur [detɛk'tœ:r], *n.m.* detector.

détection [detɛk'sjɔ̃], *n.f.* detection.

détective [detɛk'ti:v], *n.m.* detective.

déteindre [de'tɛ̃:dr], *v.t. irr. (conjug. like* CRAINDRE) to take the dye *or* color out of.—*v.i.* to lose color, to run, to fade.

dételage [de'tla:ʒ], *n.m.* unharnessing.

dételer [de'tle], *v.t.* (*conjug. like* APPELER) to unharness, to unyoke.

détendre [de'tɑ̃:dr], *v.t.* to slacken, to relax; to reduce the pressure of; to take down. **se détendre**, *v.r.* to slacken, to unbend, to become easier, to relax.

détenir [det'ni:r], *v.t. irr.* (*conjug. like* TENIR) to detain, to withhold; to confine.

détente [de'tɑ̃:t], *n.f.* trigger (*of a gun etc.*); cut-off (*of an engine*); relaxation, easing.

détenteur [detɑ̃'tœ:r], *n.m.* (*fem.* **-trice**) holder, detainer.

113

détention [detɑ̃'sjɔ̃], *n.f.* detention; imprisonment.

détenu [det'ny], *a.* detained, imprisoned.—*n.m.* (*fem.* **-e**) prisoner.

détergent [detɛr'ʒɑ̃], *a.* (*Med.*) detergent.—*n.m.* detergent.

déterger [detɛr'ʒe], *v.t.* (*conjug. like* MANGER) to cleanse, to purify.

détérioration [deterjorɑ'sjɔ̃], *n.f.* deterioration; wear and tear.

détériorer [deterjɔ're], *v.t.* to impair, to make worse. **se détériorer**, *v.r.* to deteriorate.

déterminable [detɛrmi'nabl], *a.* determinable.

déterminant [detɛrmi'nɑ̃], *a.* determinative, decisive.—*n.m.* (*Math.*) determinant.

détermination [detɛrminɑ'sjɔ̃], *n.f.* determination, resolution.

déterminé [detɛrmi'ne], *a.* determined, decided, fixed; resolute, firm.

déterminer [detɛrmi'ne], *v.t.* to determine, to settle; to ascertain; to decide; to cause to take a resolution. **se déterminer**, *v.r.* to resolve, to determine.

déterré [detɛ're], *n.m.* exhumed body.

déterrer [detɛ're], *v.t.* to dig up, to disinter; to unearth, to bring to light.

détestable [detɛs'tabl], *a.* detestable, hateful, odious; wretched.

détestablement [detɛstablə'mɑ̃], *adv.* detestably, abominably.

détestation [detɛstɑ'sjɔ̃], *n.f.* detestation, abhorrence.

détester [detɛs'te], *v.t.* to detest, to hate.

détirer [deti're], *v.t.* to draw out, to stretch.

détisser [deti'se], *v.t.* to unweave.

détonateur [detɔnɑ'tœːr], *n.m.* detonator.

détonation [detɔnɑ'sjɔ̃], *n.f.* detonation, report.

détoner [detɔ'ne], *v.t., v.i.* to detonate.

détonneler [detɔn'le], *v.t.* (*conjug. like* APPELER) to draw from a cask.

détonner [detɔ'ne], *v.i.* to be out of tune; to jar.

détordre [de'tɔrdr], *v.t.* to untwist; to unravel. **se détordre**, *v.r.* to come untwisted.

détors [de'tɔːr], *a.* untwisted.

détortiller [detɔrti'je], *v.t.* to untwist; to unravel. **se détortiller**, *v.r.* to become untwisted; to be unravelled.

détour [de'tuːr], *n.m.* turning, change of direction; roundabout way; (*fig.*) shift, evasion, trick.

détourné [detur'ne], *a.* out of the way, unfrequented; indirect.

détournement [deturnə'mɑ̃], *n.m.* turning aside; embezzlement; *détournement de mineur*, (*Law*) abduction of a minor.

détourner [detur'ne], *v.t.* to turn away; to lead astray; to divert; to ward off; to embezzle; to deter.—*v.i.* to turn, to turn off. **se détourner**, *v.r.* to turn aside; to abandon (*de*).

détracteur [detrak'tœːr], *a.* (*fem.* **-trice**) detractive, detracting.—*n.m.* (*fem.* **-trice**) detractor, disparager.

détraqué [detra'ke], *a.* out of order; deranged, (*colloq.*) crazy.—*n.m.* (*fem.* **-ée**) person shattered in mind or body.

détraquement [detrak'mɑ̃], *n.m.* breakdown (*of mechanism, mind, health*).

détraquer [detra'ke], *v.t.* to spoil (*a horse's*) paces; (*fig.*) to put out of order. **se détraquer**, *v.r.* to lose its paces (*of a horse*); (*fig.*) to be disordered.

détrempe [de'trɑ̃ːp], *n.f.* calcimine (*paint*).

détremper [detrɑ̃'pe], *v.t.* to dilute, to dissolve.

détresse [de'trɛs], *n.f.* distress, grief, trouble.

détresser [detrɛ'se], *v.t.* to unravel; to unplait.

détriment [detri'mɑ̃], *n.m.* detriment, injury, prejudice.

détritus [detri'tys], *n.m.* residue, refuse; offal.

détroit [de'trwa], *n.m.* strait, channel, sound, narrow firth.

détromper [detrɔ̃'pe], *v.t.* to undeceive. **se détromper**, *v.r.* to be undeceived.

détrônement [detron'mɑ̃], *n.m.* dethronement.

détrôner [detro'ne], *v.t.* to dethrone.

détrousser [detru'se], *v.t.* to untruss, to let down; (*fig.*) to rob.

détrousseur [detru'sœːr], *n.m.* (*fem.* **-euse**) highwayman, robber.

détruire [de'trɥiːr], *v.t. irr.* (*conjug. like* CONDUIRE) to destroy, to demolish, to ruin; to exterminate, to do away with, to efface, to suppress. **se détruire**, *v.r.* to fall into ruin *or* decay; to destroy each other.

dette [dɛt], *n.f.* debt; obligation.

deuil [dœːj], *n.m.* mourning; grief, sorrow; gloom; period of mourning; bereavement; mourning clothes; funeral cortège.

Deutéronome [døterɔ'nɔm], *n.m.* Deuteronomy.

deux [dø], *a.* two, both; second.—*n.m.* two; second (*of the month*); (*Cards, Dice etc.*) deuce.

deuxième [dø'zjɛm], *a.* second.—*n.m.* second; second floor.

deuxièmement [døzjɛm'mɑ̃], *adv.* secondly.

deux-pièces [dø'pjɛs], *n.m. inv.* (*women's*) two-piece (*suit*).

deux-points [dø'pwɛ̃], *n.m. inv.* (*Print.*) colon.

dévaler [deva'le], *v.t.* to descend; to lower.—*v.i.* to descend, to slope; to go *or* rush down (*of streams etc.*).

dévaliser [devali'ze], *v.t.* to rifle, to strip, to rob.

dévaliseur [devali'zœːr], *n.m.* (*fem.* **-euse**) thief, burglar.

dévaluation [devalɥɑ'sjɔ̃], *n.f.* devaluation.

dévaluer [deva'lɥe], *v.t.* to devalue.

devancer [dəvɑ̃'se], *v.t.* (*conjug. like* COMMENCER) to precede; to outstrip; to forestall, to anticipate; to surpass.

devancier [dəvɑ̃'sje], *n.m.* (*fem.* **-ière**) predecessor; (*pl.*) ancestors, forefathers.

devant [də'vɑ̃], *prep.* before; in front of, over against.—*adv.* in front, ahead.—*n.m.* front, forepart.

devanture [dəvɑ̃'tyːr], *n.f.* front(age) (*of a building*); shop front.

dévaser [deva'ze], *v.t.* to dredge.

dévastateur [devasta'tɔːr], *a.* (*fem.* **-trice**) devastating, destructive.—*n.m.* (*fem.* **-trice**) devastator.

dévastation [devastɑ'sjɔ̃], *n.f.* devastation, ravage, havoc.

dévaster [devas'te], *v.t.* to devastate, to lay waste.

développement [devlɔp'mɑ̃], *n.m.* unfolding, opening; development, progress; (*Mil.*) deployment.

développer [devlɔ'pe], *v.t.* to open, to unwrap; to expand, to explain; to develop. **se développer**, *v.r.* to expand, to unfold; to be unravelled; to extend; to develop.

devenir [dəv'ni:r], *v.i. irr.* (*conjug. like* TENIR) to become, to grow, to get, to turn into.— *n.m.* gradual development (*of beings or of things*).

dévergondage [devɛrgɔ̃'da:ʒ], *n.m.* shamelessness; profligacy, dissoluteness.

dévergonder (se) [sədevɛrgɔ̃'de], *v.r.* to become dissolute.

déverrouillement [devɛruj'mɑ̃], *n.m.* unbolting.

déverrouiller [devɛru'je], *v.t.* to unbolt; (*fig.*) to set free.

devers [də'vɛ:r], *prep.* towards; *par devers*, in the presence of.

dévers [de'vɛ:r], *a.* inclined; out of alignment. —*n.m.* inclination; warping.

déverser [devɛr'se], *v.t.* to bend; to dump; to pour out (*water etc.*).—*v.i.* to lean, to jut out; to warp. **se déverser**, *v.r.* to empty (*of rivers, canals etc.*).

déversoir [devɛr'swa:r], *n.m.* overflow (*of a canal etc.*); outfall.

dévêtir [deve'ti:r], *v.t. irr.* (*conjug. like* VÊTIR) to undress, to strip of clothes; (*Law*) to divest. **se dévêtir**, *v.r.* to take off one's clothes, to undress.

déviation [devja'sjɔ̃], *n.f.* deviation, curvature; detour (*of a road*).

déviationnisme [devjasjɔ'nism], *n.m.* (*Polit.*) deviationism.

déviationniste [devjasjɔ'nist], *n.* deviationist.

dévidage [devi'da:ʒ], *n.m.* winding *or* reeling off.

dévider [devi'de], *v.t.* to wind off (*into skeins etc.*); (*fig.*) to explain.

dévideur [devi'dœ:r], *n.m.* (*fem.* **-euse**) winder, reeler.

dévidoir [devi'dwa:r], *n.m.* reel, skein winder, spool.

dévier [de'vje], *v.i.* and **se dévier**, *v.r.* to deviate; to swerve.

devin [də'vɛ̃], *n.m.* (*fem.* **devineresse**) diviner, augur; fortune-teller.

deviner [dəvi'ne], *v.t.* to divine, to predict; to guess. **se deviner**, *v.r.* to understand each other.

devinette [dəvi'nɛt], *n.f.* poser, riddle, conundrum.

devineur [dəvi'nœ:r], *n.m.* (*fem.* **-euse**) guesser.

devis [də'vi], *n.m.* estimate; specification.

dévisager [deviza'ʒe], *v.t.* (*conjug. like* MANGER) to disfigure; to stare at.

devise [də'vi:z], *n.f.* device, emblem; motto, slogan; (*Fin.*) currency; *des devises étrangères*, foreign currency.

deviser [dəvi'ze], *v.i.* to talk casually, to chat.

dévissage [devi'sa:ʒ], **dévissement** [devis'mɑ̃], *n.m.* unscrewing.

dévisser [devi'se], *v.t.* to unscrew. **se dévisser**, *v.r.* to come unscrewed.

dévitaliser [devitali'ze], *v.t.* to kill the nerve (*of a tooth etc.*).

dévoiement [devwa'mɑ̃], *n.m.* looseness (*of the bowels*); (*Arch.*) inclination, slope; (*fig.*) departure from the normal path.

dévoilement [devwal'mɑ̃], *n.m.* unveiling, disclosure.

dévoiler [devwa'le], *v.t.* to unveil, to reveal, to disclose. **se dévoiler**, *v.r.* to be revealed.

dévoîment [DÉVOIEMENT].

devoir [də'vwa:r], *v.t. irr.* to owe (*money, gratitude*); to be obliged to, to be bound to, to have to, must. **se devoir**, *v.r.* to owe oneself; to owe it to oneself.—*n.m.* duty; (*Sch.*) work set, homework; (*pl.*) respects, compliments.

dévoltage [devɔl'ta:ʒ], *n.m.* (*Elec.*) reduction of voltage.

dévolter [devɔl'te], *v.t.* to reduce the voltage, to step down (*current*).

dévolteur [devɔl'tœ:r], *n.m.* reducing transformer.

dévolu [devɔ'ly], *a.* (*Law*) devolved, vested. —*n.m.* choice, preference.

dévolution [devɔly'sjɔ̃], *n.f.* devolution; escheat.

dévorant [devɔ'rɑ̃], *a.* devouring, ravenous; (*fig.*) wasting.

dévorateur [devɔra'tœ:r], *a.* (*fem.* **-trice**) devouring.—*n.m.* (*fem.* **-trice**) devourer, destroyer.

dévorer [devɔ're], *v.t.* to devour; to destroy; to squander; to gaze at eagerly.

dévot [de'vo], *a.* devout, pious; sanctimonious; holy (*of books etc.*).—*n.m.* (*fem.* **-e**) devout person, devotee; bigot.

dévotement [devɔt'mɑ̃], *adv.* devoutly, piously.

dévotion [devɔ'sjɔ̃], *n.f.* devotion, piety; disposal; devoutness.

dévouement *or* **dévoûment** [devu'mɑ̃], *n.m.* self-sacrifice; devotion, devotedness; zeal.

dévouer [de'vwe], *v.t.* to devote, to dedicate. **se dévouer**, *v.r.* to devote oneself; to dedicate oneself.

dévoyé [devwa'je], *a.* stray, gone astray.—*n.m.* (*fem.* **-ée**) (*fig.*) black sheep.

dévoyer [devwa'je], *v.t.* (*conjug. like* EMPLOYER) to corrupt; to lead astray. **se dévoyer**, *v.r.* to become corrupted.

dextérité [dɛksteri'te], *n.f.* dexterity, skill.

dextrine [dɛks'trin], *n.f.* dextrin.

dextrose [dɛks'tro:z], *n.f.* dextrose, glucose.

diabète [dja'bɛt], *n.m.* diabetes.

diabétique [djabe'tik], *a.* and *n.* diabetic.

diable [dja:bl], *n.m.* devil; wayward child; jack-in-the-box; luggage-truck; drag; *un bon diable*, a good-natured fellow; *un pauvre diable*, a poor wretch.—*int.* the devil! the deuce! confound it! hang it!

diablement [djablə'mɑ̃], *adv.* devilishly.

diablerie [djablə'ri], *n.f.* deviltry, witchcraft; mischief.

diablesse [dja'blɛs], *n.f.* she-devil; shrew, vixen.

diablotin [djablɔ'tɛ̃], *n.m.* imp; (Christmas) cracker.

diabolique [djabɔ'lik], *a.* diabolical, devilish.

diaboliquement [djabɔlik'mɑ̃], *adv.* diabolically, devilishly.

diaconal [djakɔ'nal], *a.* (*m. pl.* **-aux**) diaconal.

diaconat [djakɔ'na], *n.m.* diaconate, deaconry.

diaconesse [djakɔ'nɛs], *n.f.* deaconess.
diacre [djakr], *n.m.* deacon.
diadème [dja'dɛ:m], *n.m.* diadem; coronet.
diagnose [djag'no:z], *n.f.* (*art of*) diagnosis.
diagnostic [djagnɔs'tik], *n.m.* diagnosis.
diagnostique [djagnɔs'tik], *a.* diagnostic.
diagnostiquer [djagnɔsti'ke], *v.t.* to diagnose.
diagonal [djagɔ'nal], *a.* (*m. pl.* **-aux**) diagonal.—*n.f.* (**-e**) diagonal.
diagonalement [djagɔnal'mã], *adv.* diagonally.
diagramme [dja'gram], *n.m.* diagram.
dialecte [dja'lɛkt], *n.m.* dialect.
dialecticien [djalɛkti'sjɛ̃], *n.m.* dialectician.
dialectique [djalɛk'tik], *a.* dialectical.—*n.f.* dialectics, logic.
dialogue [dja'lɔg], *n.m.* dialogue, colloquy.
dialoguer [djalɔ'ge], *v.t.* to write in dialogue form.—*v.i.* to converse, to chat.
dialoguiste [djalɔ'gist], *n.m.* (*Cine.*) script writer.
diamant [dja'mã], *n.m.* diamond.
diamantaire [djamã'tɛ:r], *a.* of diamond brilliancy.—*n.m.* diamond cutter *or* seller.
diamanter [djamã'te], *v.t.* to set with diamonds; to tinsel, to frost.
diamétral [djame'tral], *a.* (*m. pl.* **-aux**) diametrical.
diamétralement [djametral'mã], *adv.* diametrically.
diamètre [dja'mɛtr], *n.m.* diameter.
diane [djan], *n.f.* reveille.
diantre [djã:tr], *int.* the deuce! dash! blast!
diapason [djapa'zɔ̃], *n.m.* diapason, pitch; tuning fork.
diaphane [dja'fan], *a.* diaphanous, transparent.
diaphragme [dja'fragm], *n.m.* diaphragm, midriff.
diapositive [djapozi'ti:v], *n.f.* transparency, slide.
diapré [dja'pre], *a.* dappled, variegated.
diaprer [dja'pre], *v.t.* to dapple, to variegate, to mottle.
diarrhée [dja're], *n.f.* diarrhoea.
diatribe [dja'trib], *n.f.* diatribe, bitter criticism *or* dissertation.
dictamen [dikta'mɛn], *n.m.* dictate (*of one's conscience*).
dictateur [dikta'tœ:r], *n.m.* dictator.
dictatorial [diktatɔ'rjal], *a.* (*m. pl.* **-aux**) dictatorial.
dictature [dikta'ty:r], *n.f.* dictatorship.
dictée [dik'te], *n.f.* act of dictating, dictation.
dicter [dik'te], *v.t.* to dictate; (*fig.*) to suggest, to inspire.
diction [dik'sjɔ̃], *n.f.* diction; delivery.
dictionnaire [diksjɔ'nɛ:r], *n.m.* dictionary.
dicton [dik'tɔ̃], *n.m.* common saying, saw, proverb.
didactique [didak'tik], *a.* didactic.—*n.f.* didactic art.
didactiquement [didaktik'mã], *adv.* didactically.
dièse [djɛ:z], *n.m.* (*Mus.*) sharp.
diesel [djɛ'zɛl], *n.m.* diesel (*engine*).
diète (1) [djɛt], *n.f.* diet (*regimen*).
diète (2) [djɛt], *n.f.* (*Hist.*) diet.
diététicien [djeteti'sjɛ̃], *n.m.* (*fem.* **-enne**) dietician, dietist.

diététique [djete'tik], *a.* dietetical.—*n.f.* dietetics.
Dieu [djø], *n.m.* God.
dieu [djø], *n.m.* (*pl.* **dieux**) god.
diffamant [difa'mã], *a.* defamatory, libellous, slanderous.
diffamateur [difama'tœ:r], *n.m.* (*fem.* **-trice**) defamer, slanderer.
diffamation [difama'sjɔ̃], *n.f.* defamation, aspersion, calumny.
diffamatoire [difama'twa:r], *a.* defamatory, libelous, slanderous.
diffamer [difa'me], *v.t.* to defame, to slander, to libel.
différemment [difera'mã], *adv.* differently.
différence [dife'rã:s], *n.f.* difference, diversity, contrast.
différenciation [diferãsja'sjɔ̃], *n.f.* differentiation.
différencier [diferã'sje], *v.t.* to make a difference, to distinguish; (*Math.*) to differentiate.
différend [dife'rã], *n.m.* difference, quarrel, dispute.
différent [dife'rã], *a.* different, dissimilar, unlike.
différentiel [diferã'sjɛl], *a.* (*fem.* **-elle**) differential.—*n.m.* (*Motor.*) differential.
différer [dife're], *v.t.* (*conjug. like* CÉDER) to defer, to postpone, to adjourn.—*v.i.* to defer, to put off; to differ, to disagree.
difficile [difi'sil], *a.* difficult; hard, trying; hard to please, particular.
difficilement [difisil'mã], *adv.* with difficulty.
difficulté [difikyl'te], *n.f.* difficulty; obstacle; rub; objection.
difficultueux [difikyl'tɥø], *a.* (*fem.* **-euse**) prone to raise difficulties; hard to please.
difforme [di'fɔrm], *a.* deformed, misshapen.
difformité [difɔrmi'te], *n.f.* deformity; hideousness.
diffus [di'fy], *a.* diffuse, prolix, verbose.
diffusément [difyze'mã], *adv.* diffusely, wordily.
diffuser [dify'ze], *v.t.* to diffuse; (*Rad. Tel.*) to broadcast.
diffuseur [dify'zœ:r], *n.m.* diffuser, spray cone; loudspeaker.
diffusion [dify'zjɔ̃], *n.f.* diffusion; diffusiveness, wordiness; propagation; broadcasting.
digérer [diʒe're], *v.t.* (*conjug. like* CÉDER) to digest; to ponder, to discuss; to put up with.
digestible [diʒɛs'tibl], *a.* digestible.
digestif [diʒɛs'tif], *a.* (*fem.* **-tive**) and *n.m.* digestive.
digestion [diʒɛs'tjɔ̃], *n.f.* digestion.
digital [diʒi'tal], *a.* (*m. pl.* **-aux**) digital; *empreinte digitale*, finger-print.
digitale [diʒi'tal], *n.f.* foxglove.
digitaline [diʒita'lin], *n.f.* (*Pharm.*) digitalis.
digne [diɲ], *a.* deserving, worthy; dignified.
dignement [diɲ'mã], *adv.* worthily, deservedly; with dignity.
dignitaire [diɲi'tɛ:r], *n.m.* dignitary.
dignité [diɲi'te], *n.f.* dignity, nobility, seriousness; self-respect.
digresser [digrɛ'se], *v.i.* to digress, to depart from the main subject.
digressif [digrɛ'sif], *a.* (*fem.* **-ive**) digressive.
digression [digrɛ'sjɔ̃], *n.f.* digression.

digressivement [digrɛsiv'mã], *adv.* digres-sively.

digue [dig], *n.f.* dike, dam, embankment; (*fig.*) limit; security.

diguer [di'ge], *v.t.* to dam, to embank.

dilacération [dilaserɑ'sjɔ̃], *n.f.* tearing, rending.

dilacérer [dilase're], *v.t.* (*conjug. like* CÉDER) to tear to pieces.

dilapidateur [dilapida'tœːr], *a.* (*fem.* **-trice**) wasteful, extravagant.—*n.m.* (*fem.* **-trice**) squanderer.

dilapidation [dilapidɑ'sjɔ̃], *n.f.* waste; embezzlement.

dilapider [dilapi'de], *v.t.* to waste, to squander (*a fortune*); to embezzle.

dilatation [dilatɑ'sjɔ̃] *n.f.* dilatation, expansion, distension.

dilater [dila'te], *v.t.* to dilate, to distend, to expand. **se dilater**, *v.r.* to dilate, to be dilated.

dilatoire [dila'twaːr], *a.* (*Law*) dilatory.

dilemme [di'lɛm], *n.m.* dilemma.

dilettante [dilɛ'tãːt], *n.* dilettante.

dilettantisme [dilɛtã'tism], *n.m.* dilettantism, amateurism.

diligemment [diliʒa'mã], *adv.* diligently, promptly.

diligence [dili'ʒãːs], *n.f.* diligence; dispatch, application; stage-coach.

diligent [dili'ʒã], *a.* diligent, assiduous, active.

diluer [di'lɥe], *v.t.* to dilute.

dilution [dily'sjɔ̃], *n.f.* dilution.

diluvien [dily'vjɛ̃], *a.* (*fem* **-enne**) diluvian.

dimanche [di'mãːʃ], *n.m.* Sunday, Sabbath.

dîme [dim], *n.f.* tithe; (U.S.) dime.

dimension [dimã'sjɔ̃], *n.f.* dimension, size.

dîmer [di'me], *v.t.* to tithe.—*v.i.* to levy a tithe.

diminuer [dimi'nɥe], *v.t.* to diminish, to lessen; to impair.—*v.i.* to diminish, to abate, to fall (*in price etc.*); to grow shorter(*of days*).

diminutif [diminy'tif], *a.* (*fem.* ive) and *n.m.* diminutive.

diminution [diminy'sjɔ̃], *n.f.* diminution, reduction, abatement.

dinde [dɛ̃ːd], *n.f.* turkey hen; turkey.

dindon [dɛ̃'dɔ̃], *n.m.* turkey cock.

dindonneau [dɛ̃dɔ'no], *n.m.* (*pl.* **-eaux**) young turkey.

dindonner [dɛ̃dɔ'ne], *v.t.* to dupe, to take in.

dindonnier [dɛ̃dɔ'nje], *n.m.* (*fem.* **-ière**) turkey keeper.

dîné [DÎNER].

dîner [di'ne], *v.i.* to dine, to have dinner.—*n.m.* or **dîné** [di'ne], dinner; dinner party.

dînette [di'nɛt], *n.f.* child's *or* doll's dinner.

dîneur [di'nœːr], *n.m.* (*fem.* **-euse**) diner; diner-out.

diocésain [djose'zɛ̃], *a.* diocesan.

diocèse [djo'sɛːz], *n.m.* diocese.

diphasé [difa'ze], *a.* (*Elec.*) two-phase, diphasic.

diphtérie [difte'ri], *n.f.* diphtheria.

diphtongue [dif'tɔ̃ːg], *n.f.* diphthong.

diplomate [diplɔ'mat], *a.* diplomatic.—*n.* diplomatist, diplomat.

diplomatie [diplɔma'si], *n.f.* diplomacy; diplomatic service.

diplomatique [diplɔma'tik], *a.* diplomatic; tactful.

diplomatiquement [diplɔmatik'mã], *adv.* diplomatically.

diplôme [di'plɔːm], *n.m.* diploma.

diplômé [diplo'me], *a.* (*fem.* **-ée**) qualified. —*n.m.* (*fem.* **-ée**) qualified person.

dipsomane [dipsɔ'man], *n.m.* dipsomaniac.

dipsomanie [dipsɔma'ni], *n.f.* dipsomania.

dire [diːr], *v.t. irr.* to say, to speak; to tell; to recite; to order; to express. **se dire**, *v.r.* to call oneself, to be called; to say to oneself; to be said.—*n.m.* what one says, statement; (*Law*) allegation.

direct [di'rɛkt], *a.* direct, straight, immediate. —*n.m.* (*Box.*) straight blow; **un direct du gauche**, a straight left.

directement [dirɛkta'mã], *adv.* directly, point-blank.

directeur [dirɛk'tœːr], *n.m.* (*fem.* **-trice**) director, manager, superintendent, head; principal, head master, head mistress; conductor (*of orchestra*).

direction [dirɛk'sjɔ̃], *n.f.* directing, direction; management; directorship; (*Motor.*) steering.

directives [dirɛk'tiːv], *n.f. pl.* general rules, directives.

directoire [dirɛk'twaːr], *n.m.* (*Eccles.*) directory.

directorat [dirɛktɔ'ra], *n.m.* directorship, directorate.

dirigeable [diri'ʒabl], *a.* dirigible balloon *or* airship.

dirigeant [diri'ʒã], *a.* directing, leading.—*n.* ruler, leader.

diriger [diri'ʒe], *v.t.* (*conjug. like* MANGER) to direct; to control; to steer, to manage, to govern; to send, to aim. **se diriger**, *v.r.* to make for, to go (*towards*); to govern oneself.

dirigisme [diri'ʒism], *n.m.* (*Polit.*) state planning *or* controls.

discernement [disɛrnə'mã], *n.m.* discernment; discrimination; judgment.

discerner [disɛr'ne], *v.t.* to discern; to distinguish, to discriminate.

disciple [di'sipl], *n.m.* disciple, follower.

disciplinaire [displi'nɛːr], *a.* disciplinary.

discipline [disi'plin], *n.f.* discipline; education, training; (*sch.*) subject.

discipliner [disipli'ne], *v.t.* to discipline. **se discipliner**, *v.r.* to be disciplined.

discontinu [diskɔ̃ti'ny], *a.* discontinuous.

discontinuation [diskɔ̃tinɥɑ'sjɔ̃], *n.f.* discontinuance, discontinuation.

discontinuer [diskɔ̃ti'nɥe], *v.t.* to discontinue, to interrupt, to suspend.—*v.i.* to cease, to leave off.

discontinuité [diskɔ̃tinɥi'te], *n.f.* discontinuity, discontinuance, interruption.

disconvenance [diskɔ̃v'nãːs], *n.f.* incongruity, unsuitability; dissimilarity.

disconvenir [diskɔ̃v'niːr], *v.i. irr.* (*conjug. like* TENIR) to deny, to disown; to disagree.

discord [dis'kɔːr], *a.* (*Mus.*) out of tune, discordant.

discordance [diskɔr'dãːs], *n.f.* discordancy, dissonance.

discordant [diskɔr'dã], *a.* discordant, dissonant, out of tune; inharmonious, incongruous.

discorde [dis'kɔrd], *n.f.* discord, disagreement, strife.

discorder [diskɔr'de], *v.i.* (*Mus.*) to be out of tune; to be in a state of dissension.
discothèque [diskɔ'tɛk], *n.f.* record library; discothèque.
discoureur [disku'rœːr], *n.m.* (*fem.* **-euse**) talker, chatterer.
discourir [disku'riːr], *v.i.* irr. (*conjug. like* COURIR) to discourse; to descant (*sur*); to babble.
discours [dis'kuːr], *n.m.* discourse; speech, address; diction; treatise.
discourtois [diskur'twa], *a.* discourteous.
discourtoisement [diskurtwaz'mã], *adv.* discourteously.
discourtoisie [diskurtwa'zi], *n.f.* discourtesy, incivility.
discrédit [diskre'di], *n.m.* discredit, disrepute.
discréditer [diskredi'te], *v.t.* to discredit.
discret [dis'krɛ], *a.* (*fem.* **-ète**) discreet; cautious, shy; secret, close.
discrètement [diskrɛt'mã], *adv.* discreetly; warily.
discrétion [diskre'sjõ], *n.f.* circumspection, prudence; discretion; reserve; *pain à discrétion*, bread ad lib.
discrétionnaire [diskresjɔ'nɛːr], *a.* discretionary.
discrimination [diskrimina'sjõ], *n.f.* discrimination.
discriminer [diskrimi'ne], *v.t.* to discriminate.
disculper [diskyl'pe], *v.t.* to exculpate, to vindicate, to exonerate.
discursif [diskyr'sif], *a.* (*fem.* **-sive**) discursive.
discussion [disky'sjõ], *n.f.* discussion, debate; altercation, dispute.
discutable [disky'tabl], *a.* debatable, disputable, contestable.
discuter [disky'te], *v.t.* to discuss, to debate, to argue; to examine, to inquire into, to sift.
discuteur, [disky'tœːr] *n.m.* (*fem.* **-euse**) disputant.
disert [di'zɛːr], *a.* copious, fluent, eloquent.
disertement [dizɛrtə'mã], *adv.* copiously, fluently.
disette [di'zɛt], *n.f.* scarcity, dearth, famine; poverty, penury.
diseur [di'zœːr], *n.m.* (*fem.* **-euse**) sayer, teller; diseuse.
disgrâce [diz'grɑːs], *n.f.* disfavor; disgrace, misfortune; plainness (*of features*).
disgracié [dizgra'sje], *a.* out of favor; (*fig.*) ill-favored, deformed.
disgracier [dizgra'sje], *v.t.* to disgrace, to put out of favor.
disgracieusement [dizgrasjøz'mã], *adv.* awkwardly, ungracefully.
disgracieux [dizgra'sjø], *a.* (*fem.* **-euse**) awkward, uncouth, disagreeable.
disjoindre [diz'ʒwɛ̃ːdr], *v.t.* irr. (*conjug. like* CRAINDRE) to disjoin, to disunite. **se disjoindre**, *v.r.* to come apart, to disunite.
disjoncteur [dizʒõk'tœːr], *n.m.* (*Elec.*) circuit breaker.
disjonction [dizʒõk'sjõ], *n.f.* disjunction, separation.
dislocation [dislɔka'sjõ], *n.f.* dislocation, dismemberment.
disloquement [dislɔk'mã], *n.m.* dislocation.

disloquer [dislɔ'ke], *v.t.* to dislocate, to dismember; to take to pieces (*machines etc.*); (*Mil.*) to break up (*an army*). **se disloquer**, *v.r.* to dislocate one's arm etc.; to be taken to pieces; to come apart.
dispache [dis'paʃ], *n.f.* (*Maritime Insurance*) assessment; average adjustment.
dispacheur [dispa'ʃœːr], **dispatcheur** [dispa'tʃœːr], *n.m.* assessor, average adjuster.
disparaître [dispa'rɛːtr], *v.i.* irr. (*conjug. like* CONNAÎTRE) to vanish, to disappear; to abscond; to die.
disparate [dispa'rat], *a.* dissimilar, incongruous, unlike, ill-matched.—*n.f.* incongruity, dissimilarity.
disparité [dispari'te], *n.f.* disparity, dissimilarity.
disparition [dispari'sjõ], *n.f.* disappearance.
dispendieusement [dispãdjøz'mã], *adv.* expensively.
dispendieux [dispã'djø], *a.* (*fem.* **-euse**) expensively, costly.
dispensaire [dispã'sɛːr], *n.m.* dispensary; out-patients' department.
dispensateur [dispãsa'tœːr], *n.m.* (*fem.* **-trice**) dispenser; bestower, giver.
dispensation [dispãsa'sjõ], *n.f.* dispensation; distribution; dispensing.
dispense [dis'pãːs], *n.f.* dispensation (*from fasting*); exemption (*from military service*).
dispenser [dispã'se], *v.t.* to dispense, to bestow; to exempt; to dispense (*with*). **se dispenser**, *v.r.* to dispense with; to exempt *or* excuse oneself (*from*); to spare oneself.
disperser [dispɛr'se], *v.t.* to disperse, to scatter. **se disperser**, *v.r.* to be dispersed, to break up, to be scattered.
dispersion [dispɛr'sjõ], *n.f.* dispersion, breaking up.
disponibilité [dispɔnibili'te], *n.f.* (*Law*) state of being disposable, disposal (*of property*); (*Mil.*) state of being unattached.
disponible [dispɔ'nibl], *a.* disposable, available; disengaged.—*n.m.* realizable assets.
dispos [dis'po], *a.* fit and well, in good fettle, nimble; cheerful.
disposer [dispɔ'ze], *v.t.* to dispose, to arrange, to prepare; to incline, to prevail upon.—*v.i.* to dispose (*de*); to prescribe, to ordain. **se disposer**, *v.r.* to dispose oneself, to be disposed; to get ready.
disposition [dispɔzi'sjõ], *n.f.* disposition, arrangement; inclination, frame of mind; mind, intention.
disproportion [disprɔpɔr'sjõ], *n.f.* disproportion.
disproportionné [disprɔpɔrsjɔ'ne], *a.* disproportionate, inadequate.
disproportionnel [disprɔpɔrsjɔ'nɛl], *a.* (*fem.* **-elle**) disproportional.
disputable [dispy'tabl], *a.* disputable, debatable, doubtful.
dispute [dis'pyt], *n.f.* dispute, debate, controversy, wrangle; quarrel.
disputer [dispy'te], *v.t.* to contend for; to dispute, to call in question.—*v.i.* to discuss, to argue, to dispute; to contend, to wrangle. **se disputer**, *v.r.* to dispute; to contend, to quarrel.
disputeur [dispy'tœːr], *a.* (*fem.* **-euse**) contentious, quarrelsome.—*n.m.* (*fem.* **-euse**) wrangler.

distributaire

disqualification [diskalifika'sjɔ̃], *n.f.* disqualification.

disqualifier [diskali'fje], *v.t.* to disqualify.

disquaire [dis'kɛːr], *n.* phonograph record seller.

disque [disk], *n.m.* discus, quoit; disk; (*Rail.*) signal disk; phonograph record; *disque longue durée* or *microsillon*, long-playing record.

disruptif [disryp'tif], *a.* (*fem.* -**tive**) disruptive.

disrupteur [disryp'tœːr], *n.m.* (*Elec.*) interrupter.

dissecteur [disɛk'tœːr], *n.m.* dissector.

dissection [disɛk'sjɔ̃], *n.f.* dissection.

dissemblable [disã'blabl], *a.* dissimilar, unlike.

dissemblablement [disãblablə'mã], *adv.* dissimilarly.

dissemblance [disã'blãːs], *n.f.* dissimilarity, difference.

dissemblant [disã'blã], *a.* dissimilar, different.

dissémination [disemina'sjɔ̃], *n.f.* dissemination, scattering (*of seeds etc.*).

disséminer [disemi'ne], *v.t.* to disseminate, to scatter.

dissension [disã'sjɔ̃], *n.f.* dissension, discord, strife.

dissentiment [disãti'mã], *n.m.* dissent, disagreement.

disséquer [dise'ke], *v.t.* (*conjug. like* CÉDER) to dissect; to analyse.

disséqueur [dise'kœːr], [DISSECTEUR].

dissertation [disɛrta'sjɔ̃], *n.f.* dissertation, treatise; essay (*in schools*).

disserter [disɛr'te], *v.i.* to dissert.

dissidence [disi'dãːs], *n.f.* dissidence, difference of opinion, dissent.

dissident [disi'dã], *a.* dissident.—*n.m.* (*fem.* -**e**) dissenter, rebel.

dissimilaire [disimi'lɛːr], *a.* dissimilar, different, unlike.

dissimilarité [disimilari'te], *n.f.* dissimilarity.

dissimilitude [disimili'tyd], *n.f.* dissimilitude, difference.

dissimulateur [disimyla'tœːr], *n.m.* (*fem.* -**trice**) dissembler; hypocrite.

dissimulation [disimyla'sjɔ̃], *n.f.* dissimulation; double-dealing.

dissimulé [disimy'le], *a.* two-faced, artful.—*n.m.* (*fem.* -**ée**) dissembler; hypocrite.

dissimuler [disimy'le], *v.t.* to dissemble, to conceal. **se dissimuler**, *v.r.* to hide oneself, to pass unnoticed.

dissipateur [disipa'tœːr], *a.* (*fem.* -**trice**) lavish, extravagant.—*n.m.* (*fem.* -**trice**) squanderer, spendthrift.

dissipation [disipa'sjɔ̃], *n.f.* dissipation, waste; idleness.

dissipé [disi'pe], *a.* dissipated, profligate; inattentive.

dissiper [disi'pe], *v.t.* to dissipate, to dispel; to scatter, to squander. **se dissiper**, *v.r.* to be dispersed; to vanish; to be squandered; to be inattentive (*in class-room*).

dissolu [disɔ'ly], *a.* dissolute, profligate, licentious.

dissolubilité [disɔlybili'te], *n.f.* dissolubility.

dissoluble [disɔ'lybl], *a.* dissoluble, dissolvable.

dissolution [disɔly'sjɔ̃], *n.f.* dissolution; solution; dissoluteness.

dissolvant [disɔl'vã], *a.* and *n.m.* dissolvent, solutive, solvent.

dissonance [disɔ'nãːs], *n.f.* dissonance, discord.

dissonant [disɔ'nã], *a.* dissonant, discordant.

dissoudre [di'sudr], *v.t.* irr. (*conjug. like* ABSOUDRE) to dissolve; to break up; to annul. **se dissoudre**, *v.r.* to dissolve, to be dissolved; to break up.

dissous [di'su], *a.* (*fem.* -**oute**) dissolved; broken up.

dissuader [disɥa'de], *v.t.* to dissuade.

dissuasif [disɥa'zif], *a.* (*fem.* -**sive**) dissuasive.

dissymétrique [disime'trik], *a.* assymetric(al).

distance [dis'tãːs], *n.f.* distance; interval (*of place* or *time*).

distancer [distã'se], *v.t.* (*conjug. like* COMMENCER) to out-distance, to outrun; (*fig.*) to surpass, to outdo.

distant [dis'tã], *a.* distant, remote; aloof, stand-offish.

distendre [dis'tãːdr], *v.t.* to distend.

distension [distã'sjɔ̃], *n.f.* distension, strain.

distillable [disti'labl], *a.* distillable.

distillateur [distila'tœːr], *n.m.* distiller.

distillation [distila'sjɔ̃], *n.f.* distillation.

distiller [disti'le], *v.t.* to distil; to discharge; to vent.—*v.i.* to drop, to distil, to trickle.

distillerie [distil'ri], *n.f.* distillery; distilling.

distinct [dis'tɛ̃], *a.* distinct, different, separate.

distinctement [distɛ̃ktə'mã], *adv.* distinctly, clearly, plainly.

distinctif [distɛ̃k'tif], *a.* (*fem.* -**tive**) distinctive, characteristic.

distinction [distɛ̃k'sjɔ̃], *n.f.* distinction; division, difference; eminence; refinement.

distinctivement [distɛ̃ktiv'mã], *adv.* distinctively.

distingué [distɛ̃'ge], *a.* distinguished, eminent, noted; elegant, well-bred.

distinguer [distɛ̃'ge], *v.t.* to distinguish, to discern; to discriminate; to honor. **se distinguer**, *v.r.* to be conspicuous; to gain distinction.

distique [dis'tik], *n.m.* distich; couplet.

distordre [dis'tɔrdr], *v.t.* to distort; to sprain. **se distordre**, *v.r.* to become distorted.

distorsion [distɔr'sjɔ̃], *n.f.* distortion; sprain.

distraction [distrak'sjɔ̃], *n.f.* separation; absence of mind, inattention; diversion, hobby.

distraire [dis'trɛːr], *v.t.* irr. (*conjug. like* TRAIRE) to separate; to distract, to disturb; to entertain. **se distraire**, *v.r.* to be disturbed; to be diverted (*de*); to amuse oneself.

distrait [dis'trɛ], *a.* absent-minded, heedless; vacant (*person*).—*n.m.* (*fem.* -**e**) absent-minded person.

distraitement [distrɛt'mã], *adv.* absent-mindedly.

distrayant [distrɛ'jã], *a.* diverting, pleasing.

distribuable [distri'bɥabl], *a.* distributable.

distribuer [distri'bɥe], *v.t.* to distribute, to divide; to dispose; to arrange.

distributaire [distriby'tɛːr], *n.* recipient, receiver; sharer.

distributeur

distributeur [distriby'tœ:r], *a.* (*fem.* **-trice**) distributing.—*n.m.* (*fem.* **-trice**) distributer, bestower, dispenser; *distributeur automatique*, vending machine.

distributif [distriby'tif], *a.* (*fem.* **-tive**) distributive.

distribution [distriby'sjɔ̃], *n.f.* distribution; division; disposition; delivery (*of mail*).

district [dis'trikt], *n.m.* (administrative) district; region.

dit [di], *a.* said, spoken; surnamed, called; *aussitôt dit, aussitôt fait*, no sooner said than done; *autrement dit*, in other words. —*n.m.* maxim; saying.

dito [di'to], *adv.* (*Comm.*) ditto, (*abbr.*) do.

diurnal [djyr'nal], *a.* (*m. pl.* **-aux**) diurnal.—*n.m.* diurnal, daily-prayer book.

diurne [djyrn], *a.* diurnal, daily.—*n.m.* diurnal insect.

divagant [diva'gɑ̃], *a.* wandering, rambling.

divagateur [divaga'tœ:r], *a.* (*fem.* **-trice**) desultory, rambling.—*n.m.* (*fem.* **-trice**) rambling speaker.

divagation [divagɑ'sjɔ̃], *n.f.* divagation, wandering.

divaguer [diva'ge], *v.i.* to ramble, to wander from the question; to be incoherent (*in writing or speaking*).

divan [di'vɑ̃], *n.m.* divan; couch.

divergence [diver'ʒɑ̃:s], *n.f.* divergence.

divergent [diver'ʒɑ̃], *a.* divergent; different.

diverger [diver'ʒe], *v.i.* (*conjug. like* MANGER) to diverge, to branch off.

divers [di'vɛ:r], *a.* diverse, miscellaneous; changing; (*pl.*) various, divers, sundry.

diversement [diversə'mɑ̃], *adv.* diversely, variously.

diversifier [diversi'fje], *v.t.* to diversify; to variegate. **se diversifier**, *v.r.* to be varied *or* diversified.

diversion [diver'sjɔ̃], *n.f.* diversion; change.

diversité [diversi'te], *n.f.* diversity, variety, difference.

divertir [diver'ti:r], *v.t.* to amuse, to delight; to divert; to embezzle. **se divertir**, *v.r.* to amuse oneself.

divertissant [diverti'sɑ̃], *a.* diverting, entertaining.

divertissement [divertis'mɑ̃], *n.m.* diversion, amusement, entertainment; (*Law*) embezzlement.

divette [di'vɛt], *n.f.* musical comedy actress.

dividende [divi'dɑ̃:d], *n.m.* dividend.

divin [di'vɛ̃], *a.* divine, heavenly; (*fig.*) admirable, exquisite.

divinateur [divina'tœ:r], *a.* (*fem.* **-trice**) prophetic.—*n.m.* (*fem.* **-trice**) diviner, seer.

divination [divinɑ'sjɔ̃], *n.f.* divination.

divinatoire [divina'twa:r], *a.* divinatory, divining.

divinement [divin'mɑ̃], *adv.* divinely; (*fig.*) admirably, exquisitely.

diviniser [divini'ze], *v.t.* to deify; to laud to the skies.

divinité [divini'te], *n.f.* divinity, godhead, deity.

diviser [divi'ze], *v.t.* to divide, to portion out; to disunite. **se diviser**, *v.r.* to be divided; to fall (*into*), to break up (*into*).

diviseur [divi'zœ:r], *a.* divisive, dividing.—*n.m.* (*Arith.*) divisor; divider.

divisibilité [divizibili'te], *n.f.* divisibility.

divisible [divi'zibl], *a.* divisible.

division [divi'zjɔ̃], *n.f.* division, partition, dividing; (*Mil.*) division.

divisionnaire [divizjɔ'nɛ:r], *a.* divisional, divisionary.

divorce [di'vɔrs], *n.m.* divorce; (*fig.*) variance.

divorcer [divɔr'se], *v.i.* (*conjug. like* COMMENCER) to divorce oneself (*de*); to break with; to divorce *or* get a divorce from someone (*d'avec quelqu'un*).

divulgation [divylgɑ'sjɔ̃], *n.f.* divulgence; revelation.

divulguer [divyl'ge], *v.t.* to divulge, to reveal, to make public. **se divulguer**, *v.r.* to leak out (*secret*).

dix [dis], *when other words follow* [di] *or* [diz], *a.* ten; tenth.—*n.m.* ten.

dix-huit [di'zɥit], *a. and n.m.* eighteen.

dix-huitième [dizɥi'tjɛm], *a.* and *n.* eighteenth.

dixième [di'zjɛm], *a.* and *n.* tenth.

dixièmement [dizjɛm'mɑ̃], *adv.* tenthly.

dix-neuf [diz'nœf], *a.* and *n.m.* nineteen; nineteenth.

dix-neuvième [diznœ'vjɛm], *a.* and *n.* nineteenth.

dix-sept [dis'sɛt], *a.* and *n.m.* seventeen; seventeenth.

dix-septième [disse'tjɛm], *a.* and *n.* seventeenth.

dizaine [di'zɛn], *n.f.* half a score; about ten.

djinn [dʒin], *n.m.* jinn(ee).

do [do], *n.m.* (*Mus.*) do *or* ut; (the note) C.

docile [dɔ'sil], *a.* docile, tractable, submissive.

docilement [dɔsil'mɑ̃], *adv.* with docility.

docilité [dɔsili'te], *n.f.* docility, tractability.

dock [dɔk], *n.m.* dock; warehouse.

docker [dɔ'kɛːr], *n.m.* docker.

docte [dɔkt], *a.* erudite, learned.

doctement [dɔktə'mɑ̃], *adv.* learnedly; pedantically.

docteur [dɔk'tœ:r], *n.* doctor.

doctoral [dɔktɔ'ral], *a.* (*m. pl.* **-aux**) doctoral.

doctorat [dɔktɔ'ra], *n.m.* doctorate, doctor's degree.

doctrinaire [dɔktri'nɛ:r], *a.* stiff, formal, pedantic.—*n.m.* doctrinaire.

doctrinairement [dɔktrinɛr'mɑ̃], *adv.* stiffly, formally, pedantically.

doctrine [dɔk'trin], *n.f.* doctrine.

document [dɔky'mɑ̃], *n.m.* document; (*pl.*) records.

documentaire [dɔkymɑ̃'tɛ:r], *a.* documentary.—*n.m.* (*Ciné.*) documentary film.

documentation [dɔkymɑ̃tɑ'sjɔ̃], *n.f.* documentation.

documenter [dɔkymɑ̃'te], *v.t.* to give information. **se documenter**, *v.r.* to gather evidence.

dodelinement [dɔdlin'mɑ̃], *n.m.* wagging, nodding (*of head*); dandling.

dodeliner [dɔdli'ne], *v.t.* to dandle, to rock (*a child*).—*v.i.* to wag, nod (*head*).

dodiner [dɔdi'ne], *v.t.* to rock, to dandle.— *v.i.* to oscillate. **se dodiner**, *v.r.* to rock one's body; to nurse *or* coddle oneself.

dodo [do'do], *n.m.* (*Infantile*) bye-bye; (*fig.*) sleep, bed.

dodu [dɔ'dy], *a.* plump.

dogaresse [dɔga'rɛs], *n.f.* dogaressa, wife of a doge.

doge [dɔ:ʒ], *n.m.* doge.

dogmatique [dɔgma'tik], *a.* dogmatic.
dogmatiquement [dɔgmatik'mã], *adv.* dogmatically.
dogmatiser [dɔgmati'ze], *v.t.* to state dogmatically.—*v.i.* to dogmatize.
dogmatisme [dɔgma'tism], *n.m.* dogmatism.
dogmatiste [dɔgma'tist], *n.* dogmatist.
dogme [dɔgm], *n.m.* dogma, tenet.
dogue [dɔg], *n.m.* mastiff; (*fig.*) bull-dog (*of a man*).
doguin [dɔ'gɛ̃], *n.m.* pug.
doigt [dwa], *n.m.* finger, digit; toe.
doigté [dwa'te], *n.m.* (*Mus.*) fingering, touch; (*fig.*) tact, adroitness.
doigtier [dwa'tje], *n.m.* finger-stall.
dol [dɔl], *n.m.* deceit, fraud.
dolage [dɔ'la:ʒ], *n.m.* planing.
doléances [dɔle'ã:s], *n.f. pl.* complaints; grievances.
dolemment [dɔla'mã], *adv.* dolefully.
dolent [dɔ'lã], *a.* doleful, piteous, plaintive.
doler [dɔ'le], *v.t.* to smooth with the adze; to plane.
dolmen [dɔl'mɛn], *n.m.* dolmen.
doloir [dɔ'lwa:r], *n.m.* paring knife, parer.
doloire [dɔ'lwa:r], *n.f.* cooper's adze; mason's axe.
dolosif [dɔlɔ'zif], *a.* (*fem.* **-sive**) fraudulent.
domaine [dɔ'mɛ:n], *n.m.* domain, estate, property; province, sphere.
dôme [do:m], *n.m.* dome; canopy, vault.
domestication [dɔmɛstika'sjɔ̃], *n.f.* domestication.
domesticité [dɔmɛsti'te], *n.f.* domesticity; (*collect.*) domestic servants.
domestique [dɔmɛs'tik], *a.* domestic; tame, domesticated.—*n.* servant, domestic.—*n.m.* household.
domestiquer [dɔmɛsti'ke], *v.t.* to domesticate, to tame.
domicile [dɔmi'sil], *n.m.* domicile, residence.
domiciliaire [dɔmisi'ljɛ:r], *a.* domiciliary.
domicilié [dɔmisi'lje], *a.* resident, domiciled.
domicilier (se) [sədɔmisi'lje], *v.r.* to settle down in a place.
dominance [dɔmi'nã:s], *n.f.* dominance.
dominant [dɔmi'nã], *a.* dominant, predominant, prevalent.
dominateur [dɔmina'tœ:r], *a.* (*fem.* **-trice**) ruling, domineering, arrogant.—*n.m.* (*fem.* **-trice**) dominator, ruler, tyrant.
domination [dɔmina'sjɔ̃], *n.f.* domination, dominion, rule, sway.
dominer [dɔmi'ne], *v.t.* to dominate; to rule; to prevail over; to overlook, to tower over.—*v.i.* to rule, to control; to dominate, to prevail; to lord it; to tower. **se dominer** *v.r.* to control oneself.
dominicain [dɔmini'kɛ̃], *a.* (*Relig., Polit.*) Dominican.—*n.m.* (**Dominicain**, *fem.* **-aine**) (*Polit.*) Dominican (*person*), Dominican friar *or* nun; **la *République Dominicaine***, the Dominican Republic.
dominical [dɔmini'kal], *a.* (*m. pl.* **-aux**) dominical.
dominicale [dɔmini'kal], *n.f.* Sunday sermon.
dominion [dɔmi'njɔ̃], *n.m.* dominion.
domino [dɔmi'no], *n.m.* domino.
dommage [dɔ'ma:ʒ], *n.m.* damage, injury, loss; **c'est dommage**, it is a pity.

dommageable [dɔma'ʒabl], *a.* hurtful, prejudicial, injurious; damageable (*goods*).
domptable [dɔ̃'tabl], *a.* tamable, manageable.
dompter [dɔ̃'te], *v.t.* to subdue, to subjugate, to tame. **se dompter**, *v.r.* to quell *or* overcome one's passions.
dompteur [dɔ̃'tœ:r], *n.m.* (*fem.* **-euse**) subduer; tamer; breaker-in.
don [dɔ̃], *n.m.* gift, donation; (*fig.*) aptitude, talent.
donataire [dɔna'tɛ:r], *n.* donee, recipient.
donateur [dɔna'tœ:r], *n.m.* (*fem.* **-trice**) donor, giver.
donation [dɔna'sjɔ̃], *n.f.* donation, free gift.
donc [dɔ̃:k, dɔ̃], *conj.* then, therefore, accordingly, hence; consequently; of course, to be sure.
donjon [dɔ̃'ʒɔ̃], *n.m.* keep, castle keep; turret.
donnant [dɔ'nã], *a.* open-handed, generous; ***donnant donnant***, give and take.
donne [dɔn], *n.f.* deal (*at cards*).
donnée [dɔ'ne], *n.f.* given fact, datum; notion; (*Math.*) known quantity; (*pl.*) data.
donner [dɔ'ne], *v.t.* to give, to bestow; to grant; to present (*a play etc.*); to deal (*at cards*).—*v.i.* to give way; to hit, to stumble (*dans*); to be addicted to (*dans*); to attack (*of troops etc.*); to yield; to overlook. **se donner**, *v.r.* to procure; to take place (*of battles etc.*); to give oneself out (*pour*).
donneur [dɔ'nœ:r], *n.m.* (*fem.* **-euse**) giver, donor; dealer (*of cards*); ***donneur de sang***, blood donor.
don Quichotte [dɔ̃ki'ʃɔt], *n.m.* Don Quixote, quixotic person.
dont [dɔ̃], *pron.* whose, of which, of whom, from whom etc.
doper [dɔ'pe], *v.t.* (*Spt.*) to dope (*a horse etc.*).
doping [dɔ'piŋ], *n.m.* dope; doping.
dorade [dɔ'rad], *n.f.* (*Ichth.*) sea bream.
doré [dɔ're], *a.* gilt, gilded, golden.
dorénavant [dɔrena'vã], *adv.* henceforth, hereafter.
dorer [dɔ're], *v.t.* to gild; to glaze (*pastry*). **se dorer**, *v.r.* to gild; to become yellow.
doreur [dɔ'rœ:r], *n.m.* (*fem.* **-euse**) gilder.
dorien [dɔ'rjɛ̃], *a.* and *n.m.* (*fem.* **-enne**) Dorian; Doric.
dorique [dɔ'rik], *a.* and *n.m.* Doric.
dorloter [dɔrlɔ'te], *v.t.* to fondle, to pamper, to coddle, to pet. **se dorloter**, *v.r.* to coddle oneself; to indulge oneself.
dormant [dɔr'mã], *a.* sleeping, asleep; dormant, stagnant.—*n.m.* fixed frame (*of window etc.*).
dormeur [dɔr'mœ:r], *a.* (*fem.* **-euse**) sleepy, drowsy, sluggish.—*n.m.* (*fem.* **-euse**) sleeper; sluggard.—*n.f.* (**-euse** (1)) sort of chaise longue.
dormeuse (2) [dɔr'mø:z], *n.f.* stud ear-ring.
dormir [dɔr'mi:r], *v.i. irr.* (*conjug. like* SENTIR) to sleep, to be asleep; to lie still; to lie dormant (*of money*); to be stagnant (*of water*).
dormitif [dɔrmi'tif], *a.* (*fem.* **-tive**) soporific, dormitive.
Dorothée [dɔrɔ'te], *f.* Dorothy.
dorsal [dɔr'sal], *a.* dorsal.
dortoir [dɔr'twa:r], *n.m.* dormitory.
dorure [dɔ'ry:r], *n.f.* gilding; glazing (*of pastry*).

doryphore [dɔri'fɔ:r], *n.m.* Colorado beetle.
dos [do], *n.m. inv.* back; rear; top, ridge.
dosable [do'zabl], *a.* measurable.
dosage [do'za:ʒ], *n.m.* dosage; titration.
dose [do:z], *n.f.* dose; quantity; portion.
doser [do'ze], *v.t.* to dose; to proportion.
dossier [do'sje], *n.m.* back (*of chair etc.*); brief (*of a lawyer*); record, file, dossier.
dossière [do'sjɛ:r], *n.f.* back band, ridge band (*of harness*); back plate (*of a cuirass*).
dot [dɔt], *n.f.* marriage portion, dowry.
dotal [dɔ'tal], *a.* (*m. pl.* **-aux**) of or concerning dowry.
dotation [dɔta'sjɔ̃], *n.f.* endowment.
doter [dɔ'te], *v.t.* to endow; to make a grant.
douaire [dwɛ:r], *n.m.* (*widow's*) dower; jointure, marriage settlement.
douairière [dwɛ'rjɛ:r], *n.f.* dowager.
douane [dwan], *n.f.* customs; custom house; custom duty.
douanier [dwa'nje], *a.* relating to the custom house, of customs.—*n.m.* customs officer.
doublage [du'bla:ʒ], *n.m.* lining, plating; (*Cine.*) dubbing.
double [dubl], *a.* twofold, double, duplicate; (*fig.*) deceitful, downright.—*n.m.* double; carbon copy, duplicate, replica; (*Ten.*) doubles.—*adv.* double; *voir double*, to see double.
doublé [du'ble], *n.m.* gold- or silver-plated ware; (*Billiards*) carom off the cushion.
doubleau [du'blo], *n.m.* (*pl.* **-eaux**) ceiling beam.
doublement [dublə'mã], *n.m.* doubling.—*adv.* doubly.
doubler [du'ble], *v.t.* to double; to line (*clothes etc.*); to overtake, to pass; (*Theat.*) to understudy; (*Cine.*) to dub.
doublet [du'blɛ], *n.m.* doublet.
doubleur [du'blœ:r], *n.m.* (*fem.* **-euse**) doubler, twister.
doublure [du'bly:r], *n.f.* lining; (*Theat.*) understudy.
douce-amère [dusa'mɛ:r], *n.f.* (*pl.* **douces-amères**) woody nightshade, bitter-sweet.
douceâtre [du'sɑ:tr], *a.* sweetish, sickly.
doucement [dus'mã], *adv.* gently, tenderly; slowly, quietly; mildly, calmly; so-so.
doucereux [dus'rø], *a.* (*fem.* **-euse**) sweetish; mawkish, mealy-mouthed.
doucet [du'sɛ], *a. and n.m.* (*fem.* **-ette** (1)) demure, mild, affected (person).
doucette (2) [du'sɛt], *n.f.* corn salad.
doucette (3) [du'sɛt], *n.f.* Venus's-looking-glass.
douceur [du'sœ:r], *n.f.* sweetness, softness; fragrance; kindness; peacefulness; gentleness; (*pl.*) sweets; gallantries.
douche [duʃ], *n.f.* shower-bath.
doucher [du'ʃe], *v.t.* to give someone a shower-bath; to cool down (*excitement etc.*). **se doucher**, *v.r.* to take a shower.
doucir [du'si:r], *v.t.* to polish (*looking-glasses etc.*).
doucissage [dusi'sa:ʒ], *n.m.* polishing.
doucisseur [dusi'sœ:r], *n.m.* polisher.
doué [dwe], *a.* gifted.
douer [dwe], *v.t.* to endow, to bestow upon.
douille [du:j], *n.f.* socket; case or shell (*of cartridges*); *douille d'embrayage*, clutch casing; *douille de lampe*, lamp socket, lamp holder.

douillet [du'jɛ], *a.* effeminate, delicate; sensitive; soft.
douillettement [dujɛt'mã], *adv.* softly; delicately; cosily.
douleur [du'lœ:r], *n.f.* pain, suffering, ache; anguish, grief, sorrow.
douloureusement [dulurøz'mã], *adv.* painfully; grievously.
douloureux [dulu'rø], *a.* (*fem.* **-euse**) painful, smarting, sore; grievous, afflicting, sad.
doute [dut], *n.m.* doubt, irresolution; suspicion; scepticism; fear; *sans doute*, no doubt.
douter [du'te], *v.i.* (**de**) to doubt, to question; to hesitate; to distrust, to fear. **se douter**, *v.r.* (**de, que**) to suspect, to conjecture.
douteur [du'tœ:r], *a.* (*fem.* **-euse** (1)) doubting.—*n.m.* (*fem.* **-euse**) doubter.
douteusement [dutøz'mã], *adv.* doubtfully.
douteux [du'tø], *a.* (*fem.* **-euse** (2)) doubtful, questionable.
douve [du:v], *n.f.* stave (*for casks*); trench, moat.
Douvres [du:vr], *m.* Dover.
doux [du], *a.* (*fem.* **douce**) sweet; fragrant; kindly, charming; easy; gentle; calm; fresh (*of water*).—*adv.* gently; submissively.
douzaine [du'zɛn], *n.f.* dozen.
douze [du:z], *a.* twelve, twelfth.—*n.m.* twelve.
douzième [du'zjɛm], *a. and n.* twelfth.
douzièmement [duzjɛm'mã], *adv.* twelfthly.
doyen [dwa'jɛ̃], *n.m.* (*fem.* **-enne**) senior, oldest member; dean.
doyenné [dwaje'ne], *n.m.* deanship, deanery.
drachme [drakm], *n.f.* drachma; (*Pharm.*) dram.
draconien [drakɔ'njɛ̃], *a.* (*fem.* **-enne**) draconian, harsh, severe.
dragage [dra'ga:ʒ], *n.m.* dredging, dragging (*of a river etc.*).
dragée [dra'ʒe], *n.f.* sugar-almond, sugar-plum; small shot.
drageoir [dra'ʒwa:r], *n.m.* comfit dish.
drageon [dra'ʒɔ̃], *n.m.* sucker.
drageonner [draʒɔ'ne], *v.i.* to put forth suckers.
dragon [dra'gɔ̃], *a.* dragonish—*n.m.* dragon; (*fig.*) vixen; dragoon.
dragonne [dra'gɔn], *n.f.* sword-knot.
drague [drag], *n.f.* dredger; dredge net; grappling iron.
draguer [dra'ge], *v.t.* to drag, to dredge.
dragueur [dra'gœ:r], *n.m.* dredger; *dragueur de mines*, minesweeper.
drain [drɛ̃], *n.m.* drain, drain-pipe.
drainage [drɛ'na:ʒ], *n.m.* drainage.
drainer [drɛ'ne], *v.t.* to drain.
dramatique [drama'tik], *a.* dramatic.
dramatiser [dramati'ze], *v.t.* to dramatize.
dramaturge [drama'tyrʒ], *n.m.* dramatist, playwright.
drame [dram], *n.m.* drama.
drap [dra], *n.m.* cloth; (*bed*) sheet; pall.
drapeau [dra'po], *n.m.* (*pl.* **-eaux**) flag, standard, ensign, streamer, colors.
draper [dra'pe], *v.t.* to cover with cloth; to drape. **se draper**, *v.r.* to wrap oneself up; to make a show, to parade.
draperie [dra'pri], *n.f.* drapery; cloth trade, cloth making.
drapier [dra'pje], *n.m.* draper, clothier.

drastique [dras'tik], *a.* and *n.m.* (*Med.*) drastic.

(C) **drave** [drav], *n.f.* drive, log-running.

(C) **draver** [dra've], *v.t.* to drive, to drift.

(C) **draveur** [dra'vœːr], *n.m.* wood-floater, rafter.

drayage [drɛ'jaːʒ], *n.m.* fleshing (*of hides*).

drayer [drɛ'je], *v.t.* (*conjug. like* PAYER) to flesh (*hides*).

dressage [drɛ'saːʒ], *n.m.* erection; training (*of animals*); pitching (*of a tent*).

dresser [drɛ'se], *v.t.* to erect, to set up, to raise; to straighten; to lay out; to lay (*a snare*); to pitch (*a tent*); to draw up (*a report*); to prick up (*the ears*); to train (*animals*). se **dresser**, *v.r.* to stand on end (*of hair*); to stand erect; to rear.

dresseur [drɛ'sœːr], *n.m.* (*fem.* -**euse**) trainer (*of dogs etc.*).

dressoir [drɛ'swaːr], *n.m.* dresser, sideboard.

drille [dri:j], *n.f.* hand-drill, borer.

driller [dri'je], *v.t.* to drill, to bore.

drive [driv], *n.m.* (*Ten.*) drive.

drogue [drɔg], *n.f.* drug; rubbish; dope.

droguer [drɔ'ge], *v.t.* to drug; to physic. se **droguer**, *v.r.* to physic *or* doctor oneself, to dope oneself.

droguerie [drɔ'gri], *n.f.* drug-store; drug-trade, drysaltery.

droguiste [drɔ'gist], *n.* retailer in drugs and chemicals.

droguet [drɔ'gɛ], *n.m.* (*Tex.*) drugget.

droit [drwa], *a.* straight, right, direct; vertical, upright; just, sincere; right (*opposed to left*).—*adv.* straight, straight on.—*n.m.* right, equity; law; right (*to*), claim, title; fee; due (*tax*), duty, customs duty.

droite [drwat], *n.f.* right hand, right.

droitement [drwat'mã], *adv.* rightly; sincerely, straightforwardly.

droitier [drwa'tje], *a.* and *n.m.* (*fem.* -**ière**) right-handed (person).

droiture [drwa'tyːr], *n.f.* equity, justice; uprightness, integrity.

drolatique [drola'tik], *a.* amusing, laughable, facetious.

drôle [dro:l], *a.* funny, droll, ludicrous; strange, curious.—*n.* rogue, rascal, scoundrel.

drôlement [drol'mã], *adv.* comically, facetiously, jocosely.

drôlerie [drol'ri], *n.f.* drollery; buffoonery.

drôlesse [dro'lɛs], *n.f.* jade, hussy.

dromadaire [drɔma'dɛːr], *n.m.* dromedary.

dru [dry], *a.* sturdy; dense (*of rain*); brisk, lively; close-planted; fledged (*of birds*).—*adv.* thick, fast, hard.

druide [drɥid], *n.m.* druid.

druidesse [drɥi'dɛs], *n.f.* druidess.

druidique [drɥi'dik], *a.* druidical.

druidisme [drɥi'dism], *n.m.* druidism.

dryade [dri'ad], *n.f.* dryad; (*Bot.*) dryas.

du [dy], (*contraction of* DE LE) of the, from the, by the; some, any.

dû [dy], *n.m.* due, what is owed, what is owing.

dualisme [dɥa'lism], *n.m.* dualism.

dualiste [dɥa'list], *a.* and *n.* dualist.

dualité [dɥali'te], *n.f.* duality.

duc [dyk], *n.m.* duke; horned owl.

ducal [dy'kal], *a.* (*m. pl.* -**aux**) ducal.

ducat [dy'ka], *n.m.* ducat.

duché [dy'ʃe], *n.m.* dukedom, duchy.

duchesse [dy'ʃɛs], *n.f.* duchess.

ductile [dyk'til], *a.* ductile, malleable.

ductilité [dyktili'te], *n.f.* ductility.

duègne [dɥɛɲ], *n.f.* duenna, chaperon.

duel [dɥɛl], *n.m.* duel; struggle.

duelliste [dɥe'list], *n.m.* duellist.

dulcifier [dylsi'fje], *v.t.* to dulcify.

dulcinée [dylsi'ne], *n.f.* sweetheart.

dûment [dy'mã], *adv.* duly, properly.

dumping [dʌm'piŋ], *n.m.* dumping, unfair competition.

dune [dyn], *n.f.* dune, sand-hill.

dunette [dy'nɛt], *n.f.* poop-deck.

duo [dɥo], *n.m.* duet.

duodécimal [dɥɔdesi'mal], *a.* (*m. pl.* -**aux**) duodecimal.

duodénal [dɥɔde'nal], *a.* (*m. pl.* -**aux**) duodenal.

duodénum [dɥɔde'nɔm], *n.m.* duodenum.

dupe [dyp], *n.f.* dupe.

duper [dy'pe], *v.t.* to dupe, to gull, to take in.

duperie [dy'pri], *n.f.* dupery, trickery.

dupeur [dy'pœːr], *n.m.* (*fem.* -**euse**) cheat, trickster.

duplicata [dyplika'ta], *n.m.* duplicate.

duplicateur [dyplika'tœːr], *n.m.* (*Elec.*) duplicator; duplicating machine.

duplicité [dyplisi'te], *n.f.* duplicity, double-dealing, deceit.

duquel [dy'kɛl], (*contraction of* DE LEQUEL) of whom, of which.

dur [dy:r], *a.* hard; tough; (*fig.*) unyielding, harsh, unkind; difficult.—*adv.* hard; firmly; *travailler dur*, to work hard.

durabilité [dyrabili'te], *n.f.* durability.

durable [dy'rabl], *a.* durable, lasting, solid.

durablement [dyrablə'mã], *adv.* durably, lastingly.

duralumin [dyraly'mɛ̃], *n.m.* duralumin.

durant [dy'rã], *prep.* during.

durcir [dyr'siːr], *v.t.* to harden.—*v.i.* to harden, to stiffen. se **durcir**, *v.r.* to harden.

durcissement [dyrsis'mã], *n.m.* hardening, stiffening, induration.

dure [dy:r], *n.f.* hard ground *or* floor *in coucher sur la dure.*

durée [dy're], *n.f.* duration; continuance.

durement [dyr'mã], *adv.* hard; harshly, roughly.

durer [dy're], *v.i.* to last, to remain; to endure.

dureté [dyr'te], *n.f.* hardness; harshness, austerity, unkindness; (*pl.*) harsh *or* offensive words.

durillon [dyri'jɔ̃], *n.m.* callosity, corn.

duvet [dy'vɛ], *n.m.* down; wool, nap; fluff.

duveté [dyv'te], *a.* downy (*of birds etc.*); like down.

duveteux [dyv'tø], *a.* (*fem.* -**euse**) downy, fluffy.

dynamique [dina'mik], *a.* dynamic.—*n.f.* dynamics.

dynamisme [dina'mism], *n.m.* dynamism.

dynamiste [dina'mist], *n.* dynamist.

dynamitage [dinami'taːʒ], *n.m.* blasting, blowing up.

dynamite [dina'mit], *n.f.* dynamite.

dynamiter [dinami'te], *v.t.* to dynamite, to blow up.

dynamo [dina'mo], *n.f.* dynamo.

dynastie [dinas'ti], *n.f.* dynasty.

dynastique [dinas'tik], *a.* dynastic.
dysenterie [disã'tri], *n.f.* dysentery.
dyspepsie [dispɛp'si], *n.f.* dyspepsia.
dyspepsique [dispɛp'sik], **dyspeptique** [dispɛp'tik], *a.* dyspeptic.

E

E, e [ə], *n.m.* the fifth letter of the alphabet.
eau [o], *n.f.* water; rain, flood; (*pl.*) mineral *or* thermal waters; watering place; stream; track; gloss; *à fleur d'eau*, on a level with the water; (*Chem.*) *eau lourde*, heavy water.
eau-de-vie [o'dvi], *n.f.* (*pl.* **eaux-de-vie**) brandy.
ébahi [eba'i], *a.* astonished, dumbfounded.
ébahir (s') [seba'i:r], *v.r.* to wonder (at), to be amazed.
ébahissement [ebais'mã], *n.m.* amazement, astonishment.
ébats [e'ba], *n.m. pl.* pastime, sport, gambol, frolic.
ébattre (s') [se'batr], *v.r.* (*conjug. like* BATTRE) to sport, to gambol, to frolic.
ébauchage [ebo'ʃa:ʒ], *n.m.* sketching.
ébauche [e'bo:ʃ], *n.f.* rough draft, outline.
ébaucher [ebo'ʃe], *v.t.* to make the first draft of, to draw an outline of, to sketch.
ébauchoir [ebo'ʃwa:r], *n.m.* (*Sculp.*) roughing chisel; (*Carp.*) mortise chisel.
ébène [e'bɛ:n], *n.f.* ebony, ebony work.
ébéner [ebe'ne], *v.t.* (*conjug. like* CÉDER) to ebonize.
ébénier [ebe'nje], *n.m.* ebony tree.
ébéniste [ebe'nist], *n.* cabinet-maker.
ébénisterie [ebenis'tri], *n.f.* cabinet-work.
ébiseler [ebi'zle], *v.t.* (*conjug. like* APPELER) to chamfer, to bevel.
éblouir [eblu'i:r], *v.t.* to dazzle; (*fig.*) to fascinate, to amaze. **s'éblouir**, *v.r.* to be dazzled *or* fascinated.
éblouissant [eblui'sã], *a.* dazzling, resplendent.
éblouissement [ebluis'mã], *n.m.* dazzle, daze; (*fig.*) bewilderment.
ébonite [ebɔ'nit], *n.f.* ebonite; vulcanite.
ébouage [ebu'a:ʒ], *n.m.* scavenging.
ébouer [ebu'e], *v.t.* to scavenge.
éboueur [ebu'œ:r], *n.m.* (*fem.* **-euse**) road-sweeper, scavenger.—*n.f.* (**-euse**) road-sweeping machine.
ébouillanter [ebujã'te], *v.t.* to dip in hot water, to scald.
éboulement [ebul'mã], *n.m.* falling in, fall; caving in, collapse; landslide, landslip.
ébouler [ebu'le], *v.i.* to fall in, to fall down, to sink. **s'ébouler**, *v.r.* to fall in, to cave in.
éboulis [ebu'li], *n.m. inv.* debris, fallen rocks.
ébourgeonner [eburʒɔ'ne], *v.t.* to disbud.
ébouriffé [eburi'fe], *a.* disordered, ruffled, in disorder; (*fig.*) in a flutter.
ébouriffer [eburi'fe], *v.t.* to ruffle, to disorder; (*fig.*) to startle, to amaze.
ébouter [ebu'te], *v.t.* to cut off (*the end*).

ébranchage [ebrã'ʃa:ʒ], **ébranchement** [ebrãʃ'mã], *n.m.* (*Hort.*) pruning, lopping, trimming.
ébrancher [ebrã'ʃe], *v.t.* to prune, to lop, to trim.
ébranlement [ebrãl'mã], *n.m.* shock, shaking; (*fig.*) perturbation, disturbance.
ébranler [ebrã'le], *v.t.* to shake; to disturb, to unsettle. **s'ébranler**, *v.r.* to get under way, to move off.
ébrécher [ebre'ʃe], *v.t.* (*conjug. like* CÉDER) to notch, to indent; to crack, to chip; (*fig.*) to impair.
ébriété [ebrie'te], *n.f.* drunkenness, inebriety.
ébrouement [ebru'mã], *n.m.* snorting.
ébrouer (s') [sebru'e], *v.r.* to snort from fear (*of horses*).
ébruiter [ebrɥi'te], *v.t.* to make known, to spread about. **s'ébruiter**, *v.r.* to spread, to be noised abroad.
ébullition [ebyli'sjɔ̃], *n.f.* boiling, ebullition.
écaille [eka:j], *n.f.* scale; shell.
écaillé [eka'je], *a.* scaly.
écailler (1) [eka'je], *v.t.* to scale. **s'écailler** *v.r.* to peel off, to scale.
écailler (2) [eka'je], *n.m.* (*fem.* **-ère**) oyster-man, oyster-woman.
écailleux [eka'jø], *a.* (*fem.* **-euse**) scaly, squamous.
écale [e'kal], *n.f.* shell, pod (*of peas etc.*); hull, husk (*of walnut*).
écaler [eka'le], *v.t.* to shell (*beans, peas etc.*); to hull, to husk (*almonds, nuts etc.*). **s'écaler**, *v.r.* to come out of the shell.
écarlate [ekar'lat], *a. and n.f.* scarlet; hectic red.
écarquillement [ekarkij'mã], *n.m.* spreading out, opening wide (*of one's eyes, legs etc.*).
écarquiller [ekarki'je], *v.t.* to spread out, to open wide.
écart [e'ka:r], *n.m.* stepping aside, swerving; fault; deviation; *à l'écart*, aside; *faire un écart*, to step aside.
écarté (1) [ekar'te], *n.m.* écarté (*game of cards*).
écarté (2) [ekar'te], *a.* remote, lonely secluded.
écartelé [ekartə'le], *a.* (*of mind, heart, etc.*) divided, torn asunder; (*Her.*) quartered.
écartèlement [ekartel'mã], *n.m.* tearing to pieces, quartering.
écarteler [ekartə'le], *v.t.* (*conjug. like* AMENER) to tear to pieces; (*Her.*) to quarter.
écartement [ekartə'mã], *n.m.* putting aside; removal; spacing; spread.
écarter [ekar'te], *v.t.* to open, to throw wide apart; to set aside; to avert; to dispel, to deviate; to spread. **s'écarter**, *v.r.* to turn aside, to swerve; to stray; to make way.
ecchymose [ɛki'mo:z], *n.f.* (*Med.*) ecchymosis.
ecclésiastique [eklezjas'tik], *a.* ecclesiastic; clerical.—*n.m.* clergyman, ecclesiastic.
écervelé [esɛrvə'le], *a.* hare-brained, rash, giddy.—*n.m.* (*fem.* **-ée**) madcap; scatter-brain.
échafaud [eʃa'fo], *n.m.* scaffold.
échafaudage [eʃafo'da:ʒ], *n.m.* scaffolding; (*fig.*) structure.
échafauder [eʃafo'de], *v.t.* to pile up; (*fig.*) to lay out (*a plan*).—*v.i.* to erect scaffolding.

échalas [eʃaˈla], *n.m.* vine prop; hop pole.
échalassage [eʃalaˈsaːʒ], **échalassement** [eʃalasˈmã], *n.m.* propping.
échalasser [eʃalaˈse], *v.t.* to prop (*vines etc.*).
échalier [eʃaˈlje], **échalis** [eʃaˈli], *n.m.* stile; wooden fence.
échalote [eʃaˈlɔt], *n.f.* (*Bot.*) shallot.
échancrer [eʃɑ̃ˈkre], *v.t.* to make a crescent-shaped cut; to indent.
échancrure [eʃɑ̃ˈkryːr], *n.f.* notch, cut, indentation; opening.
échandole [eʃɑ̃ˈdɔl], *n.f.* shingle (*for roofing*).
échange [eˈʃãːʒ], *n.m.* exchange, barter; **libre échange**, free trade.
échangeable [eʃɑ̃ˈʒabl], *a.* exchangeable.
échanger [eʃɑ̃ˈʒe], *v.t.* (*conjug. like* MANGER) to exchange, to barter; to interchange.
échanson [eʃɑ̃ˈsõ], *n.m.* cup-bearer; butler.
échantillon [eʃɑ̃tiˈjõ], *n.m.* sample, pattern, specimen; (*fig.*) model.
échantillonner [eʃɑ̃tijɔˈne], *v.t.* to sample.
échappatoire [eʃapaˈtwaːr], *n.f.* shift, subterfuge, loop-hole, evasion.
échappé [eʃaˈpe], *a.* runaway.—*n.m.* (*fem.* **-ée** (1)) one who has escaped, runaway.
échappée (2) [eʃaˈpe], *n.f.* escapade, prank; short space of time.
échappement [eʃapˈmã], *n.m.* escape; leakage; (*Horol.*) escapement; exhaust.
échapper [eʃaˈpe], *v.t.* to escape, to avoid; **l'échapper belle**, to have a narrow escape. —*v.i.* to escape, to make good one's escape; to be overlooked. **s'échapper**, *v.r.* to escape; to vanish.
écharde [eˈʃard], *n.f.* prickle (*of a thistle etc.*); splinter.
écharner [eʃarˈne], *v.t.* to flesh *or* scrape (*hides*).
écharnoir [eʃarˈnwaːr], *n.m.* fleshing-knife.
écharpe [eˈʃarp], *n.f.* scarf, sash; arm-sling.
écharper [eʃarˈpe], *v.t.* to slash, to cut.
échasse [eˈʃaːs], *n.f.* stilt; long-legged plover.
échassier [eʃaˈsje], *n.m.* (*fem.* **-ière**) stilt-walker; (*colloq.*) long-legged person.—*n.m.* (*Orn.*) wader.
échauboulure [eʃobuˈlyːr], *n.f.* pimple, blotch.
échaudage [eʃoˈdaːʒ], *n.m.* whitewash; white-washing; scalding.
échaudé (1) [eʃoˈde], *n.m.* simnel, cracknel.
échaudé (2) [eʃoˈde], *a.* scalded.
échauder [eʃoˈde], *v.t.* to scald. **s'échauder**, *v.r.* to burn oneself.
échaudoir [eʃoˈdwaːr], *n.m.* scalding-house; scalding-tub.
échaudure [eʃoˈdyːr], *n.f.* scald.
échauffant [eʃoˈfã], *a.* heating; binding (*food*).
échauffement [eʃofˈmã], *n.m.* heating; over-excitement.
échauffer [eʃoˈfe], *v.t.* to warm, to heat, to over-heat; to excite, to irritate. **s'échauffer**, *v.r.* to grow warm, to overheat oneself; to grow angry, to chafe.
échauffourée [eʃofuˈre], *n.f.* rash *or* blundering enterprise; brush, scuffle.
échauffure [eʃoˈfyːr], *n.f.* red rash.
échauguette [eʃoˈgɛt], *n.f.* (*Mil.*) watch-tower.
échéable [eʃeˈabl], *a.* due, payable.
échéance [eʃeˈãːs], *n.f.* falling due (*of bill*); date (*of payment, of maturity*); expiration (*of tenancy*).

échéant [eʃeˈã], *a.* falling due; **le cas échéant**, in that case, if need be.
échec [eˈʃɛk], *n.m.* check, defeat, blow, loss.
échecs [eˈʃɛk], *n.m. pl.* chess; chess-men.
échelle [eˈʃɛl], *n.f.* ladder; scale; gradation.
échelon [eʃˈlõ], *n.m.* round, rung, step (*of a ladder*); degree; (*Mil.*) echelon.
échelonner [eʃlɔˈne], *v.t.* to draw up in echelon; to arrange according to gradation; to spread (*over a period of time*); to place (*at regular intervals*); **vacances échelonnées**, staggered holidays. **s'échelonner**, *v.r.* to be graduated; to slope gradually; to be arranged in echelon.
écheniller [eʃniˈje], *v.t.* to rid (*plants, trees etc.*) of caterpillars.
écheveau [eʃˈvo], *n.m.* (*pl.* **-eaux**) hank, skein.
échevelé [eʃaˈvle], *a.* dishevelled; (*fig.*) wild, extravagant.
écheveler [eʃaˈvle], *v.t.* (*conjug. like* APPELER) to dishevel.
*****échevin** [eʃˈvɛ̃], *n.m.* sheriff; alderman; (*C*) municipal magistrate.
échine [eˈʃin], *n.f.* spine, backbone, chine.
échiner [eʃiˈne], *v.t.* to beat unmercifully; to tire out. **s'échiner**, *v.r.* (*pop.*) to work oneself to death.
échiqueté [eʃikˈte], *a.* chequered.
échiquier [eʃiˈkje], *n.m.* chess-board; exchequer; square net.
écho [eˈko], *n.m.* echo.
échoir [eˈʃwaːr], *v.i. irr.* (*aux.* ÊTRE) to expire, to fall due, to lapse; to happen, to befall.
échoppe [eˈʃɔp], *n.f.* booth, covered stall.
échopper [eʃɔˈpe], *v.t.* to gouge.
échotier [ekoˈtje], *n.m.* (*fem.* **-ière**) gossip writer, columnist.
échouage [eˈʃwaːʒ], **échouement** [eʃuˈmã], *n.m.* (*Naut.*) beaching, running aground.
échouer [eˈʃwe], *v.t.* to run (*a vessel*) aground. —*v.i.* to run aground, to be stranded; (*fig.*) to miscarry, to fail.
écimer [esiˈme], *v.t.* to top (*plants etc.*), to pollard (*trees*).
éclaboussement [eklabusˈmã], *n.m.* splashing, bespattering.
éclabousser [eklabuˈse], *v.t.* to splash, to bespatter.
éclaboussure [eklabuˈsyːr], *n.f.* splash.
éclair [eˈklɛːr], *n.m.* lightning, flash of lightning; variety of chocolate cake.
éclairage [eklɛˈraːʒ], *n.m.* lighting, illumination, light.
éclaircie [eklɛrˈsi], *n.f.* opening, rift (*in clouds etc.*); glade, clearing; (*fig.*) favorable change of affairs.
éclaircir [eklɛrˈsiːr], *v.t.* to make clear *or* clearer, to brighten; to clarify; to make thin *or* thinner; to elucidate, to explain. **s'éclaircir**, *v.r.* to become clear, bright *or* fine; to grow light; to be explained.
éclaircissement [eklɛrsisˈmã], *n.m.* clearing up, explanation, solution; hint, light.
éclaire [eˈklɛːr], *n.f.* celandine.
éclairé [eklɛˈre], *a.* lighted; well-lighted; (*fig.*) well-informed; intelligent; enlightened.
éclairer [eklɛˈre], *v.t.* to light, to give light to, to illuminate; to enlighten; to observe; (*Mil.*) to reconnoitre.—*v.i.* to sparkle, to shine, to glitter. **s'éclairer**, *v.r.* to become enlightened; to instruct *or* enlighten one another; to light up.

125

éclaireur [ekle′rœːr], *n.m.* (*Mil.*) scout; boy scout.

éclanche [e′klɑ̃ːʃ], *n.f.* shoulder of mutton.

éclat [e′kla], *n.m.* burst; crash, peal; splinter (*of wood, stone, brick etc.*); brightness, glare, glitter; luster, pomp; renown; gaudiness (*of colors*); rumor, scandal; *un éclat de rire*, a burst of laughter; *un grand éclat de voix*, a loud shout; *voler en éclats*, to fly into a thousand pieces.

éclatant [ekla′tɑ̃], *a.* bright, sparkling, brilliant; striking; piercing, shrill.

éclatement [eklat′mɑ̃], *n.m.* bursting, explosion.

éclater [ekla′te], *v.i.* to split, to burst, to explode; to cry out; to shine, to sparkle, to flash; to break out (*war etc.*); *éclater de rire*, to burst out laughing.

éclectique [eklɛk′tik], *a.* and *n.* eclectic; dilettante.

éclectisme [eklɛk′tism], *n.m.* eclecticism.

éclipse [e′klips], *n.f.* eclipse; (*fig.*) disappearance.

éclipser [eklip′se], *v.t.* to eclipse; (*fig.*) to surpass. **s'éclipser**, *v.r.* (*fig.*) to disappear, to vanish.

écliptique [eklip′tik], *a.* and *n.f.* ecliptic.

éclisse [e′klis], *n.f.* (*Surg.*) splint.

éclisser [ekli′se], *v.t.* (*Surg.*) to splint.

éclopé [eklɔ′pe], *a.* crippled, footsore, lame.—*n.m.* (*fem.* -ée) cripple.

éclopper [eklɔ′pe], *v.t.* to lame, to disable.

éclore [e′klɔːr], *v.i.* irr. (*conjug. like* CLORE, *but with aux.* ÊTRE) to hatch; to open, to bloom (*of flowers*); (*fig.*) to show itself.

éclosion [eklo′zjɔ̃], *n.f.* hatching; (*fig.*) opening, blooming; appearance.

écluse [e′klyːz], *n.f.* lock (*on canals etc.*); dam, weir; *porte d'écluse*, sluice, floodgate.

écluser [ekly′ze], *v.t.* to furnish with locks; to take (*a boat etc.*) through a lock.

éclusier [ekly′zje], *n.m.* (*fem.* -ière) lock keeper.

écœurant [ekœ′rɑ̃], *a.* disgusting, nauseating.

écœurement [ekœr′mɑ̃], *n.m.* disgust; nausea.

écœurer [ekœ′re], *v.t.* to disgust, to sicken; (*fig.*) to shock, to dishearten.

école [e′kɔl], *n.f.* school, college; scholastic philosophy; sect; (*Mil.*) training; (*fig.*) manner, practice.

écolier [ekɔ′lje], *n.m.* (*fem.* -ière) schoolboy, schoolgirl, pupil, student.

éconduire [ekɔ̃′dɥiːr], *v.t.* irr. (*conjug. like* CONDUIRE) to show out, to dismiss; to refuse.

économat [ekɔnɔ′ma], *n.m.* stewardship, bursarship.

économe [ekɔ′nɔm], *a.* economical, saving, thrifty.—*n.* steward, housekeeper, bursar, treasurer (*of colleges, hospitals etc.*).

économie [ekɔnɔ′mi], *n.f.* economy; thrift, saving.

économique [ekɔnɔ′mik], *a.* (*applied to things only*) economic, economical, cheap.—*n.f.* economics.

économiquement [ekɔnɔmik′mɑ̃], *adv.* economically.

économiser [ekɔnɔmi′ze], *v.t., v.i.* to economize, to save (up).

économiste [ekɔnɔ′mist], *n.* economist.

écope [e′kɔp], *n.f.* scoop, ladle; (*Naut.*) bailer.

écorce [e′kɔrs], *n.f.* bark, rind, peel; shell; (*Geol.*) crust (*of the earth*).

écorcement [ekɔrs′mɑ̃], **écorçage** [ekɔr′saːʒ], *n.m.* barking or stripping (*of trees etc.*); peeling.

écorcer [ekɔr′se], *v.t.* (*conjug. like* COMMENCER) to bark, to strip (*trees etc.*), to peel.

écorchement [ekɔrʃə′mɑ̃], *n.m.* excoriation, flaying, skinning.

écorcher [ekɔr′ʃe], *v.t.* to flay, to skin; to graze (*skin*); to peel, to bark; (*fig.*) to strip, to fleece. **s'écorcher**, *v.r.* to graze oneself.

écorcheur [ekɔr′ʃœːr], *n.m.* (*fem.* -euse) knacker, flayer; (*fig.*) fleecer.

écorchure [ekɔr′ʃyːr], *n.f.* scratch, graze.

écorner [ekɔr′ne], *v.t.* to break the horns of; to break the corners of, to dog-ear; to curtail, to impair.

écornifler [ekɔrni′fle], *v.t.* to sponge upon.

écornure [ekɔr′nyːr], *n.f.* broken-off corner, chip.

écossais [ekɔ′sɛ], *a.* Scottish.—*n.m.* Scots (*language*); plaid, tartan cloth; (**Écossais**, *fem.* -aise) Scot, Scotsman, Scotswoman.

Écosse [e′kɔs], l', *f.* Scotland; *La Nouvelle Écosse, f.* Nova Scotia.

écosser [ekɔ′se], *v.t.* to shell, to husk (*peas or beans*).

écosseur [ekɔ′sœːr], *n.m.* (*fem.* -euse) sheller.

écot (1) [e′ko], *n.m.* share (*of a reckoning*); bill, reckoning, score (*usually in the expression payer son écot, to pay one's share*).

écot (2) [e′ko], *n.m.* stump of a tree.

écoulement [ekul′mɑ̃], *n.m.* flowing, flow, running; outlet; (*Comm.*) sale, disposal; export.

écouler [eku′le], *v.t.* to dispose of, to sell. **s'écouler**, *v.r.* to run or flow away, to pass, to slip away; (*Comm.*) to be disposed of.

écourter [ekur′te], *v.t.* to shorten, to dock, to crop.

écoutant [eku′tɑ̃], *a.* listening; *avocat écoutant*, briefless attorney.

écoute (1) [e′kut], *n.f.* hiding place for listening; *être aux écoutes*, to be on the watch.

écoute (2) [e′kut], *n.f.* (*Naut.*) sheet (*of sail*).

écouter [eku′te], *v.t.* to listen to, to hearken to; to pay attention to. **s'écouter**, *v.r.* to like the sound of one's own voice; to indulge oneself.

écouteur [eku′tœːr], *n.m.* (*fem.* -euse) listener, listener-in; (*Teleph.*) receiver; (*Teleg.*) ear-phone.

écoutille [eku′tiːj], *n.f.* (*Naut.*) hatchway.

écran [e′krɑ̃], *n.m.* screen; *vedette de l'écran*, film star.

écrasant [ekra′zɑ̃], *a.* crushing; (*fig.*) humiliating, excessive; overwhelming.

écrasé [ekra′ze], *a.* crushed, ruined.

écrasement [ekraz′mɑ̃], *n.m.* crushing, bruising; (*fig.*) overwhelming.

écraser [ekra′ze], *v.t.* to crush; to bruise; to overwhelm, to ruin; to run over.

écraseur [ekra′zœːr], *n.m.* crusher; (*Motor.*) road hog; steam-roller.

écrémer [ekre′me], *v.t.* (*conjug. like* CÉDER) to take the cream off, to skim.

écrémeuse [ekre′møːz], *n.f.* separator.

écrevisse [ekra′vis], *n.f.* crayfish; (*Am.*) crawfish; (*Astron.*) Cancer.

écrier (s') [sekri′je], *v.r.* to cry out, to exclaim.

écrin [e'krɛ̃], *n.m.* casket, jewel box *or* case.
écrire [e'kriːr], *v.t. irr.* to write; to spell. **s'écrire**, *v.r.* to be written; to be spelled; to write to each other.
écrit [e'kri], *n.m.* writing; pamphlet.
écriteau [ekri'to], *n.m.* (*pl.* **-eaux**) bill (*poster*); board.
écritoire [ekri'twaːr], *n.f.* writing desk; inkstand.
écriture [ekri'tyːr], *n.f.* writing, handwriting; scripture; (*pl.*) accounts, documents.
écrivain [ekri'vɛ̃], *n.m.* writer, author; **femme écrivain**, authoress, woman writer.
écrivassier [ekriva'sje], *n.m.* (*fem.* **-ière**) (*colloq.*) scribbler.
écrou [e'kru], *n.m.* screw nut; **écrou à oreilles**, wing nut.
écrouelles [ekru'ɛl], *n.f. pl.* king's evil, scrofula.
écrouelleux [ekruɛ'lø], *a.* (*fem.* **-euse**) scrofulous.
écrouer [ekru'e], *v.t.* to imprison, to lock up.
écroulement [ekrul'mɑ̃], *n.m.* falling in, collapse; wreck, ruin.
écrouler (s') [sekru'le], *v.r.* to fall in, to fall to pieces, to collapse.
écru [e'kry], *a.* raw, unbleached; **toile écrue**, (brown) holland.
ectoplasme [ɛkto'plasm], *n.m.* ectoplasm.
écu [e'ky], *n.m.* shield; crown (*coin*); (*fig.*) money, cash.
écueil [e'kœːj], *n.m.* reef, rock; (*fig.*) danger, stumbling-block.
écuelle [e'kɥɛl], *n.f.* porringer, bowl, basin.
écuellée [ekɥe'le], *n.f.* bowlful.
éculer [eky'le], *v.t.* to tread down at heel; **des souliers éculés**, down-at-heel shoes.
écumage [eky'maːʒ], *n.m.* skimming.
écumant [eky'mɑ̃], *a.* foaming, frothing, seething.
écume [e'kym], *n.f.* foam, froth; lather; (*fig.*) scum, dregs.
écumer [eky'me], *v.t.* to skim; to scour; **écumer la marmite**, to be a sponger.—*v.i.* to foam, to froth.
écumeur [eky'mœːr], *n.m.* (*fem.* **écumeuse** (1)) skimmer; hanger-on, parasite.
écumeux [eky'mø], *a.* (*fem.* **écumeuse** (2)) frothy, foaming.
écumoire [eky'mwaːr], *n.f.* skimmer.
écurage [eky'raːʒ], *n.m.* scouring, cleaning.
écurer [eky're], *v.t.* to scour, to cleanse.
écureuil [eky'rœːj], *n.m.* squirrel.
écurie [eky'ri], *n.f.* stable, mews; stud.
écusson [eky'sɔ̃], *n.m.* escutcheon; shield.
écuyer [ekɥi'je], *n.m.* squire; equerry; riding-master; rider; wall hand-rail (*of a staircase*).
écuyère [ekɥi'jɛːr], *n.f.* horsewoman; female equestrian performer; **bottes à l'écuyère**, top boots, riding boots.
eczéma [ɛgze'ma], *n.m.* eczema.
édenté [edɑ̃'te], *a.* toothless.
édenter [edɑ̃'te], *v.t.* to break the teeth of (*combs, saws etc.*).
édicter [edik'te], *v.t.* to enact, to decree.
édicule [edi'kyl], *n.m.* small building (*pavilion, kiosk etc.*).
édifiant [edi'fjɑ̃], *a.* edifying.
édification [edifika'sjɔ̃], *n.f.* building, erection; (*fig.*) edification.
édifice [edi'fis], *n.m.* edifice, building, pile.

édifier [edi'fje], *v.t.* to build, to erect, to construct; (*fig.*) to edify, to improve; to instruct, to enlighten; to satisfy.
édile [e'dil], *n.m.* ædile; town councillor.
Édimbourg [edɛ̃'buːr], *m.* or *f.* Edinburgh.
édit [e'di], *n.m.* edict.
éditer [edi'te], *v.t.* to publish; to edit.
éditeur [edi'tœːr], *n.m.* (*fem.* **-trice**) publisher.
édition [edi'sjɔ̃], *n.f.* edition.
éditorial [edito'rjal], *n.m.* (*pl.* **-aux**) leading article, leader, editorial.
éditorialiste [editorja'list], *n.* leader writer.
Édouard [e'dwaːr], *m.* Edward.
édredon [edrə'dɔ̃], *n.m.* eider-down; eiderdown quilt.
éducateur [edyka'tœːr], *a.* (*fem.* **-trice**) educative, instructing.—*n.m.* (*fem.* **-trice**) educator; breeder.
éducatif [edyka'tif], *a.* (*fem.* **-tive**) educational.
éducation [edyka'sjɔ̃], *n.f.* education; training; rearing (*of animals*); breeding, manners.
éduquer [edy'ke], *v.t.* to bring up, to educate (*children*).
effacement [efas'mɑ̃], *n.m.* effacement, obliteration; disappearance; humility, self-effacement.
effacer [efa'se], *v.t.* (*conjug. like* COMMENCER) to efface, to erase, to rub out, to blot out, to obliterate. **s'effacer**, *v.r.* to become obliterated; to wear away; to draw aside, to give way.
effaçure [efa'syːr], *n.f.* erasure, blotting out, obliteration.
effaré [efa're], *a.* wild, scared, bewildered; astounded.
effarement [efar'mɑ̃], *n.m.* bewilderment, terror, affright.
effarer [efa're], *v.t.* to frighten, to scare. **s'effarer**, *v.r.* to be scared, to take fright.
effarouchant [efaru'ʃɑ̃], *a.* startling, disquieting; shocking; annoying.
effaroucher [efaru'ʃe], *v.t.* to startle, to frighten away. **s'effaroucher**, *v.r.* to be scared, to be startled.
effectif [efɛk'tif], *a.* (*fem.* **-tive**) actual, real, positive.—*n.m.* effective force (*of troops etc.*); size (*of a class*).
effectivement [efɛktiv'mɑ̃], *adv.* in effect, actually, indeed, in fact; (*in answer*) that is so.
effectuer [efɛk'tɥe], *v.t.* to effect, to accomplish, to carry out. **s'effectuer**, *v.r.* to be accomplished, to take place.
effémination [efemina'sjɔ̃], *n.f.* effeminacy.
efféminé [efemi'ne], *a.* effeminate, womanish.
effervescence [efɛrvɛ'sɑ̃ːs], *n.f.* effervescence; (*fig.*) agitation, ferment.
effervescent [efɛrvɛ'sɑ̃], *a.* effervescent; (*fig.*) excitable, irascible.
effet [e'fɛ], *n.m.* effect, result; performance; impression; power (*transmitted by machinery etc.*); (*Comm.*) bill of exchange; (*pl.*) belongings; **en effet**, indeed, in fact.
effeuillaison [efœjɛ'zɔ̃], *n.f.,* **effeuillement** [efœj'mɑ̃], *n.m.* fall of the leaves.
effeuiller [efœ'je], *v.t.* to strip off leaves, to pick (*a flower*) to pieces. **s'effeuiller**, *v.r.* to lose *or* shed its leaves.
efficace [efi'kas], *a.* efficacious, effective.

efficacité [efikasi'te], *n.f.* efficacy, effectiveness; efficiency.

effigie [efi'ʒi], *n.f.* effigy.

effilé [efi'le], *a.* slender, slim; sharp, keen, trenchant.—*n.m.* fringe.

effiler [efi'le], *v.t.* to unweave, to unravel; to taper. **s'effiler**, *v.r.* to unravel; to taper, to become sharp; to fray.

effiloche [efi'lɔʃ], **effiloque** [efi'lɔk], *n.f.* floss silk, light refuse silk.

effilocher [efilɔ'ʃe], **effiloquer** [efilɔ'ke], *v.t.* to unravel, to undo.

efflanqué [eflã'ke], *a.* lean, thin, lank.

efflanquer [eflã'ke], *v.t.* to make lean, to emaciate.

effleurer [eflœ're], *v.t.* to graze, to skim the surface of, to touch lightly; (*fig.*) to touch upon.

efflorescence [eflɔrɛ'sã:s], *n.f.* efflorescence.

efflorescent [eflɔrɛ'sã], *a.* efflorescent.

effluent [efly'ã], *a.* effluent.

effluve [ef'fly:v], *n.m.* effluvium.

effondrement [efɔ̃drə'mã], *n.m.* (*Agric.*) trenching; falling in, sinking; collapse.

effondrer [efɔ̃'dre], *v.t.* to dig deeply; to break in; to overwhelm. **s'effondrer**, *v.r.* to fall in, to collapse.

efforcer (s') [sefɔr'se], *v.r.* (*conjug. like* COMMENCER) to exert oneself, to strain, to strive.

effort [e'fɔ:r], *n.m.* effort, exertion, endeavor; stress; (*Med.*) strain, rupture.

effraction [efrak'sjɔ̃], *n.f.* breaking into, house-breaking; *vol avec effraction*, burglary.

effraie [e'frɛ], *n.f.* barn owl, screech owl.

effrayant [efrɛ'jã], *a.* frightful, dreadful.

effrayer [efrɛ'je], *v.t.* (*conjug. like* PAYER) to frighten, to alarm, to terrify. **s'effrayer**, *v.r.* to be frightened, to be startled.

effréné [efre'ne], *a.* unrestrained; lawless; wild.

effritement [efrit'mã], *n.m.* crumbling into dust.

effriter (s') [sefri'te], *v.r.* to crumble.

effroi [e'frwa], *n.m.* fright, terror, dread.

effronté [efrɔ̃'te], *a.* and *n.m.* (*fem.* **-ée**) shameless, brazen, impudent (person).

effrontément [efrɔ̃te'mã], *adv.* impudently, shamelessly.

effronterie [efrɔ̃'tri], *n.f.* effrontery, impudence.

effroyable [efrwa'jabl], *a.* frightful, dreadful, hideous.

effroyablement [efrwajablə'mã], *adv.* frightfully, horribly, dreadfully.

effusion [efy'zjɔ̃], *n.f.* effusion; overflowing.

égal [e'gal], *a.* (*m. pl.* **-aux**) equal, alike; even, level, smooth; all the same.—*n.m.* (*fem.* **-e**) equal.

également [egal'mã], *adv.* equally, alike.

égaler [ega'le], *v.t.* to equal; to make equal; to compare. **s'égaler**, *v.r.* to equal; to compare oneself (*à*).

égalisation [egaliza'sjɔ̃], *n.f.* equalization.

égaliser [egali'ze], *v.t.* to equalize; to level.

égalitaire [egali'tɛːr], *a.* and *n.* egalitarian.

égalité [egali'te], *n.f.* equality, parity; uniformity.

égard [e'ga:r], *n.m.* regard, consideration, respect.

égaré [ega're], *a.* wandering, strayed; misled; mislaid; distracted.

égarement [egar'mã], *n.m.* straying, losing one's way; mistake; ill-conduct.

égarer [ega're], *v.t.* to mislead; to lose; to lead astray; to bewilder; to impair (*intellect*). **s'égarer**, *v.r.* to lose one's way, to stray; to err.

égayer [egɛ'je], *v.t.* (*conjug. like* PAYER) to enliven, to cheer up; (*Hort.*) to prune (*trees*). **s'égayer**, *v.r.* to brighten up; to make merry.

églantier [eglã'tje], *n.m.* eglantine, briar, dog-rose (*bush*).

églantine [eglã'tin], *n.f.* eglantine, dog-rose (*flower*).

église [e'gli:z], *n.f.* church.

églogue [e'glɔg], *n.f.* eclogue.

égocentrique [egosã'trik], *a.* egocentric, self-centered.

égoïsme [ego'ism], *n.m.* egoism, selfishness.

égoïste [ego'ist], *a.* egoistic, selfish.—*n.* egoist, selfish person.

égorger [egɔr'ʒe], *v.t.* (*conjug. like* MANGER) to cut the throat of, to slaughter.

égorgeur [egɔr'ʒœ:r], *n.m.* (*fem.* **-euse**) slaughterer, murderer.

égosiller (s') [segozi'je], *v.r.* to make oneself hoarse; to bawl.

égotisme [ego'tism], *n.m.* egotism.

égotiste [ego'tist], *a.* egotistic(al).—*n.* egotist.

égout [e'gu], *n.m.* running or falling of water; sink, drain, sewer.

égouttage [egu'ta:ʒ], **égouttement** [egut'mã], *n.m.* drainage, draining; dripping.

égoutter [egu'te], *v.t., v.i.* to drain, to drip. **s'égoutter**, *v.r.* to drip, to drain.

égouttoir [egu'twa:r], *n.m.* drainer (*plate-rack etc.*).

égrapper [egra'pe], *v.t.* to pick (*grapes, currants etc.*) from the bunch.

égratigner [egrati'ɲe], *v.t.* to scratch.

égratignure [egrati'ɲy:r], *n.f.* scratch; slight wound.

égrenage [egrə'na:ʒ], *n.m.* picking off (*of grapes etc.*).

égrener [egrə'ne], *v.t.* (*conjug. like* AMENER) to tell (*beads*); to unstring (*beads etc.*); to pick off (*grapes etc.*) from the bunch. **s'égrener**, *v.r.* to fall from the stalk, to drop one by one.

égrillard [egri'ja:r], *a.* lewd, broad, naughty; *propos égrillards*, spicy talk.

égrilloir [egri'jwa:r], *n.m.* weir; grate (*to confine fish in a pond*).

égrisé, *n.m.* or **égrisée** [egri'ze], *n.f.* diamond dust.

égriser [egri'ze], *v.t.* to grind, to polish (*diamonds etc.*).

égrugeoir [egry'ʒwa:r], *n.m.* mortar.

égruger [egry'ʒe], *v.t.* (*conjug. like* MANGER) to pound, to grind in a mortar.

égueuler [egœ'le], *v.t.* to break off the mouth or neck (*of glass and other vessels*).

Égypte [e'ʒipt], **l'**, *f.* Egypt.

égyptien [eʒip'sjɛ̃], *a.* (*fem.* **-enne**) Egyptian.—*n.m.* (**Égyptien**, *fem.* **-enne**) Egyptian (*person*).

eh! [e], *int.* ah! well! hey! *eh bien !* well!

éhonté [eɔ̃'te], *a.* shameless.

éjaculation [eʒakylɑ'sjɔ̃], *n.f.* throwing out with force, discharge; ejaculation.
éjaculer [eʒaky'le], *v.t.* to discharge, to ejaculate.
éjecter [eʒɛk'te], *v.t.* to eject.
éjecteur [eʒɛk'tœːr], *a.* (*fem.* **-trice**) ejecting; (*Av.*) **siège éjecteur**, ejector seat.—*n.m.* ejector (*of firearm*).
élaboration [elabɔrɑ'sjɔ̃], *n.f.* elaboration.
élaboré [elabɔ're], *a.* wrought; elaborate.
élaborer [elabɔ're], *v.t.* to elaborate, to work out.
élaguer [ela'ge], *v.t.* to lop, to prune; (*fig.*) to curtail, to cut down.
élagueur [ela'gœːr], *n.m.* (*Hort.*) pruner.
élan (1) [e'lɑ̃], *n.m.* start, spring, bound; flight; burst; dash.
élan (2) [e'lɑ̃], *n.m.* elk; moose, wapiti (*Canada*), eland (*S. Africa*).
élancé [elɑ̃'se], *a.* slender, slim.
élancement [elɑ̃s'mɑ̃], *n.m.* darting forward; shooting pain, twinge; (*pl.*) transports.
élancer [elɑ̃'se], *v.t.* (*conjug. like* COMMENCER) to dart, to hurl.—*v.i.* to shoot, to twitch (*of pain*). **s'élancer**, *v.r.* to bound, to shoot *or* dart forth, to rush, to dash; to soar up.
élargir [elar'ʒiːr], *v.t.* to widen, to enlarge; to release. **s'élargir**, *v.r.* to widen; to stretch; to enlarge one's estate.
élargissement [elarʒis'mɑ̃], *n.m.* widening, enlarging; discharge (*from prison etc.*).
élasticité [elastisi'te], *n.f.* elasticity, springiness.
élastique [elas'tik], *a.* elastic, springy.—*n.m.* India rubber; elastic band.
électeur [elɛk'tœːr], *n.m.* (*fem.* **-trice**) (*Hist.*) elector, electress; (*Polit.*) voter.
élection [elɛk'sjɔ̃], *n.f.* election, polling; choice; appointment.
électoral [elɛktɔ'ral], *a.* (*m. pl.* **-aux**) electoral.
électorat [elɛktɔ'ra], *n.m.* electorate.
électricien [elɛktri'sjɛ̃], *n.m.* electrician.
électricité [elɛktrisi'te], *n.f.* electricity.
électrification [elɛktrifika'sjɔ̃], *n.f.* electrification.
électrifier [elɛktri'fje], *v.t.* to provide with current, to electrify.
électrique [elɛk'trik], *a.* electric; **secousse électrique**, electric shock.
électriquement [elɛktrik'mɑ̃], *adv.* electrically.
électriser [elɛktri'ze], *v.t.* to electrify.
électro-aimant [elɛktrɔɛ'mɑ̃], *n.m.* (*pl.* **électro-aimants**) electro-magnet.
électrocuter [elɛktrɔky'te], *v.t.* to electrocute.
électrocution [elɛktrɔky'sjɔ̃], *n.f.* electrocution.
électron [elɛk'trɔ̃], *n.m.* electron.
électronique [elɛktrɔ'nik], *a.* electronic.
élégamment [elega'mɑ̃], *adv.* elegantly, stylishly.
élégance [ele'gɑ̃ːs], *n.f.* elegance, style.
élégant [ele'gɑ̃], *a.* elegant, smart, fashionable, stylish.—*n.m.* (*fem.* **-ée**) gentleman *or* lady of fashion.
élégiaque [ele'ʒjak], *a.* elegiac.—*n.* elegist.
élégie [ele'ʒi], *n.f.* elegy.
élément [ele'mɑ̃], *n.m.* element, component part.

élémentaire [elemɑ̃'tɛːr], *a.* elementary, elemental.
éléphant [ele'fɑ̃], *n.m.* elephant.
éléphantin [elefɑ̃'tɛ̃], *a.* elephantine.
élevage [el'vaːʒ], *n.m.* breeding, rearing (*of cattle*); stud.
élévateur [eleva'tœːr], *a.* (*fem.* **-trice**) raising, lifting.—*n.m.* elevator, lift, hoist.
élévation [elevɑ'sjɔ̃], *n.f.* elevation, raising; eminence, height; promotion; greatness (*of soul*); rise (*in prices etc.*).
élève [e'lɛːv], *n.* pupil; student, disciple; apprentice.
élevé [el've], *a.* raised, grand; reared; heroic, eminent; high (*of prices etc.*); exalted; **bien élevé**, well-bred; **mal élevé**, ill-bred.
élever [el've], *v.t.* (*conjug. like* AMENER) to raise, to lift up; to erect; to exalt; to run up (*accounts etc.*); to bring up, to rear; to educate; to foster. **s'élever**, *v.r.* to rise, to ascend, to go up; to be constructed; to increase; to break out.
éleveur [ele'vœːr], *n.m.* (*fem.* **-euse**) raiser; cattle breeder.—*n.f.* (**-euse**) incubator.
elfe [ɛlf], *n.m.* elf, brownie.
élider [eli'de], *v.t.* (*Gram.*) to cut off, to elide. **s'élider**, *v.r.* to be elided.
éligibilité [eliʒibili'te], *n.f.* eligibility.
éligible [eli'ʒibl], *a.* eligible.
élimer [eli'me], *v.t.* to wear out. **s'élimer**, *v.r.* to wear threadbare (*of clothes etc.*).
élimination [eliminɑ'sjɔ̃], *n.f.* elimination.
éliminatoire [elimina'twaːr], *a.* and *n.f.* (*Spt.*) eliminating (heat); disqualifying.
éliminer [elimi'ne], *v.t.* to eliminate; to expel; to remove.
élire [e'liːr], *v.t. irr.* (*conjug. like* LIRE) to elect, to choose; to return, to appoint.
élision [eli'zjɔ̃], *n.f.* elision.
élite [e'lit], *n.f.* choice, pick, select few, élite.
élixir [elik'siːr], *n.m.* elixir.
elle [ɛl], *pron.* (*pl.* **elles**) she, her, it; (*pl.*) they.
ellébore [ele'bɔːr], *n.m.* hellebore.
ellipse [ɛ'lips], *n.f.* ellipse; (*Gram.*) ellipsis.
elliptique [ɛlip'tik], *a.* elliptical.
élocution [elɔky'sjɔ̃], *n.f.* elocution.
éloge [e'lɔːʒ], *n.m.* eulogy, praise; panegyric.
élogieux [elɔ'ʒjø], *a.* (*fem.* **-euse**) laudatory, eulogistic, flattering.
éloigné [elwa'ɲe], *a.* removed, distant, remote; absent.
éloignement [elwaɲ'mɑ̃], *n.m.* removal; remoteness; dislike; unwillingness.
éloigner [elwa'ɲe], *v.t.* to remove; to dismiss; to set aside, to repudiate; to waive; to banish; to put off; to alienate. **s'éloigner**, *v.r.* to go away, to withdraw; to digress; to deviate; to be alienated.
éloquemment [elɔka'mɑ̃], *adv.* eloquently.
éloquence [elɔ'kɑ̃ːs], *n.f.* eloquence, oratory.
éloquent [elɔ'kɑ̃], *a.* eloquent.
élu [e'ly], *a.* elected, chosen, elect; appointed.—*n.m.* (*fem.* **-e**) elected *or* chosen person.
élucidation [elysidɑ'sjɔ̃], *n.f.* elucidation.
élucider [elysi'de], *v.t.* to elucidate, to clear up.
éluder [ely'de], *v.t.* to elude, to evade.
Élysée [eli'ze], *n.m.* Elysium; **l'Élysée**, the residence (*in Paris*) of the President of the Republic.
émaciation [emasjɑ'sjɔ̃], *n.f.* emaciation.
émacié [ema'sje], *a.* emaciated.

émail [e'ma:j], *n.m.* (*pl.* **émaux**) enamel.
émaillage [ema'ja:ʒ], *n.m.* enamelling.
émailler [ema'je], *v.t.* to enamel; (*fig.*) to adorn.
émailleur [ema'jœr], *n.m.* enameller.
émaillure [ema'jy:r], *n.f.* enamelling.
émanation [emana'sjɔ̃], *n.f.* emanation.
émancipation [emɑ̃sipa'sjɔ̃], *n.f.* emancipation.
émanciper [emɑ̃si'pe], *v.t.* to emancipate. **s'émanciper**, *v.r.* to gain one's liberty; to overstep the mark, to forget oneself.
émaner [ema'ne], *v.i.* to emanate.
émargement [emarʒ'mɑ̃], *n.m.* writing in the margin, marginal note; signature in the margin.
émarger [emar'ʒe], *v.t.* (*conjug. like* MANGER) to write *or* sign in the margin, *esp. on receipt*; *hence,* to draw one's salary.
embâcle [ɑ̃'ba:kl], *n.m.* ice-pack (*in a river etc.*).
emballage [ɑ̃ba'la:ʒ], *n.m.* packing up, packing; package; (*Spt.*) spurt.
emballement [ɑ̃bal'mɑ̃], *n.m.* excitement; flying into a temper; burst of enthusiasm.
emballer [ɑ̃ba'le], *v.t.* to pack up, to wrap up; (*colloq.*) to pack off; to arrest; to tell (*someone*) off. **s'emballer**, *v.r.* to bolt (*of a horse etc.*); to wrap oneself up; to be carried away (*by rage, enthusiasm etc.*), to race (*of an engine*).
emballeur [ɑ̃ba'lœr], *n.m.* packer.
embarbouiller [ɑ̃barbu'je], *v.t.* to besmear. **s'embarbouiller**, *v.r.* to get muddled.
embarcadère [ɑ̃barka'dɛr], *n.m.* wharf, pier, landing-stage.
embarcation [ɑ̃barka'sjɔ̃], *n.f.* small boat, craft.
embardée [ɑ̃bar'de], *n.f.* lurch (*of a boat, a car etc.*); **faire une embardée**, to lurch (*of boat*); to swerve, to skid (*of car*).
embargo [ɑ̃bar'go], *n.m.* embargo.
embarquement [ɑ̃barkə'mɑ̃], *n.m.* embarkation, embarking; shipment.
embarquer [ɑ̃bar'ke], *v.t.* to embark, to take on board; to ship (*water etc.*). **s'embarquer**, *v.r.* to embark, to go on board; **s'embarquer dans**, (*fig.*) to embark upon.
embarras [ɑ̃ba'ra], *n.m.* encumbrance, hindrance; difficulty, fuss; (*pl.*) embarrassing circumstances; trouble, nervousness.
embarrassant [ɑ̃bara'sɑ̃], *a.* embarrassing, puzzling, awkward; troublesome.
embarrassé [ɑ̃bara'se], *a.* embarrassed, perplexed.
embarrasser [ɑ̃bara'se], *v.t.* to embarrass, to obstruct; to trouble, to confound, to puzzle. **s'embarrasser**, *v.r.* to entangle oneself; to be embarrassed; to concern oneself (*with*).
embâter [ɑ̃ba'te], *v.t.* to put a pack-saddle on, to saddle.
embauchage [ɑ̃bo'ʃa:ʒ], *n.m.*, **embauche** [ɑ̃'boʃ], *n.f.* hiring, engaging (*of workmen*); enlisting, recruiting (*soldiers*).
embaucher [ɑ̃bo'ʃe], *v.t.* to hire, to engage, to sign on (*workmen*); to enlist (*soldiers*).
embaucheur [ɑ̃bo'ʃœr], *n.m.* (*fem.* -**euse**) hirer, recruiting officer.
embauchoir [ɑ̃bo'ʃwa:r], *n.m.* boot tree, boot last.

embaumement [ɑ̃bom'mɑ̃], *n.m.* embalming.
embaumer [ɑ̃bo'me], *v.t.* to embalm; to perfume.—*v.i.* to smell sweet.
embaumeur [ɑ̃bo'mœr], *n.m.* embalmer.
embecquer [ɑ̃bɛ'ke], *v.t.* to feed (*a bird*); to bait (*a hook*).
embéguiner [ɑ̃begi'ne], *v.t.* to muffle up. **s'embéguiner**, *v.r.* to wrap oneself up; (*fig.*) to be infatuated with.
embellir [ɑ̃bɛ'li:r], *v.t.* to embellish, to beautify.—*v.i.* to grow more beautiful. **s'embellir**, *v.r.* to grow more beautiful; to enhance one's looks.
embellissement [ɑ̃bɛlis'mɑ̃], *n.m.* embellishment; improvement.
embêtant [ɑ̃bɛ'tɑ̃], *a.* (*colloq.*) boring, annoying.
embêtement [ɑ̃bɛt'mɑ̃], *n.m.* (*colloq.*) annoyance; nuisance, bore.
embêter [ɑ̃bɛ'te], *v.t.* to bore; to annoy, to rile; to worry. **s'embêter**, *v.r.* to feel dull *or* bored.
emblée (d') [dɑ̃'ble], *adv.* at the first, at the first attempt, immediately.
emblématique [ɑ̃blema'tik], *a.* emblematical.
emblème [ɑ̃'blɛ:m], *n.m.* emblem.
emboîtage [ɑ̃bwa'ta:ʒ], *n.m.* boards, cover (*book*).
emboîtement [ɑ̃bwat'mɑ̃], *n.m.* fitting in, jointing, clamping.
emboîter [ɑ̃bwa'te], *v.t.* to fit in, to put (*a book*) into its boards; to clamp. **s'emboîter**, *v.r.* to fit, to fit in; (*fig.*) to model oneself upon.
emboîture [ɑ̃bwa'ty:r], *n.f.* socket, clamp.
embolie [ɑ̃bo'li], *n.f.* (*Path.*) embolism.
embonpoint [ɑ̃bɔ̃'pwɛ̃], *n.m.* plumpness, stoutness, obesity.
emboucher [ɑ̃bu'ʃe], *v.t.* to put to one's mouth, to sound (*wind instruments*); to bit (*a horse*).
embouchure [ɑ̃bu'ʃy:r], *n.f.* mouth (*of a river, harbor etc.*); mouth-piece (*of wind instruments*); opening (*of a receptacle*).
embourber [ɑ̃bur'be], *v.t.* to put in the mire; (*fig.*) to implicate in a dirty affair. **s'embourber**, *v.r.* to stick in the mire, to get bogged down; (*fig.*) to be involved (*in some trouble*); to put one's foot in it.
embourser [ɑ̃bur'se], *v.t.* to receive, to swallow (*affronts etc.*).
embout [ɑ̃'bu], *n.m.* ferrule.
embouteillage [ɑ̃butɛ'ja:ʒ], *n.m.* bottling; traffic jam.
embouteiller [ɑ̃butɛ'je], *v.t.* to bottle; to bottle up; to block up.
embouterr [ɑ̃bu'ti:r], *v.t.* to beat out (*coppersmith's work etc.*); to scoop out, to stamp; (*fam.*) to bump into. **s'emboutir**, *v.r.* to crash into, to collide with.
embranchement [ɑ̃brɑ̃ʃ'mɑ̃], *n.m.* branching off; branch road, branch line etc.; junction.
embrancher [ɑ̃brɑ̃'ʃe], *v.t.* to put together, to join up (*roads, railways, pipes etc.*). **s'embrancher**, *v.r.* to join (*of a minor road or line joining a major one*).
embrasement [ɑ̃braz'mɑ̃], *n.m.* conflagration; illumination.

embraser [ābrɑ'ze], v.t. to fire, to set on fire; (fig.) to inflame; to illuminate. **s'embraser**, v.r. to kindle, to catch fire; to glow.
embrassade [ābrɑ'sad], n.f. embrace, hug; kissing, kiss.
embrasse [ā'bras], n.f. curtain loop.
embrassement [ābras'mā], n.m. embrace, embracing.
embrasser [ābra'se], v.t. to embrace, to clasp; to kiss; (fig.) to encircle; to comprise. **s'embrasser**, v.r. to embrace or kiss one another; to be included.
embrassure [ābras'syːr], n.f. band of iron.
embrasure [ābrɑ'zyːr], n.f. embrasure, recess.
embrayage [ābrɛ'jaːʒ], n.m. (Motor.) coupling gear, clutch.
embrayer [ābrɛ'je], v.t. (conjug. like PAYER) to connect up, to throw into gear.—v.i. to let in the clutch.
embrèvement [ābrɛv'mā], n.m. (Carp.) mortise.
embrocation [ābrɔka'sjɔ̃], n.f. embrocation.
embrocher [ābrɔ'ʃe], v.t. to put on the spit.
embrouillement [ābruj'mā], n.m. embroilment, entanglement, perplexity.
embrouiller [ābru'je], v.t. to embroil, to confuse; to perplex; to obscure. **s'embrouiller**, v.r. to become intricate or entangled; to get confused or muddled.
embrouilleur [ābru'jœːr], n.m. (fem. -euse) muddler, blunderer.
embrumer (s') [sābry'me], v.r. to be covered with fog etc; to become misty or hazy; (fig.) to grow somber or gloomy.
embrun [ā'brœ̃], n.m. (usu. pl.) spray, spindrift.
embrunir [ābry'niːr], v.t. to brown.
embryon [ābri'jɔ̃], n.m. embryo; germ; (fig.) dwarf, shrimp.
embryonnaire [ābrijɔ'nɛːr], a. embryonic, in embryo.
embûche [ā'byʃ], n.f. ambush, snare.
embuscade [ābys'kad], n.f. ambuscade, ambush.
embusqué [ābys'ke], n.m. (Mil. slang) shirker.
embusquer [ābys'ke], v.t. to place in ambuscade, to post. **s'embusquer**, v.r. to lie in wait.
émender [emā'de], v.t. (Law) to amend, to correct.
émeraude [em'roːd], n.f. emerald.
émergence [emɛr'ʒãːs], n.f. emergence; emersion.
émergent [emɛr'ʒã], a. emergent.
émerger [emɛr'ʒe], v.i. (conjug. like MANGER) to emerge, to rise out.
émeri [em'ri], n.m. emery.
émerillon [emri'jɔ̃], n.m. (Orn.) merlin.
émeriser [emri'ze], v.t. to cover with emery; **papier émerisé**, emery paper.
émérite [eme'rit], a. emeritus; practised, perfect; eminent.
émersion [emɛr'sjɔ̃], n.f. emersion.
émerveillement [emɛrvɛj'mā], n.m. wonder, astonishment.
émerveiller [emɛrvɛ'je], v.t. to astonish, to amaze. **s'émerveiller**, v.r. to marvel, to be astonished.
émétique [eme'tik], a. and n.m. emetic.
émetteur [emɛ'tœːr] a. (fem. -trice)

(Rad., Tel.) **poste émetteur** or **station émettrice**, broadcasting station.—n.m. transmitter; **émetteur-récepteur**, transmitter-receiver, (fam.) walkie-talkie.
émettre [e'mɛtr], v.t. irr. (conjug. like METTRE) to emit, to give out; to utter, to express; (Rad., Tel.) to broadcast.
émeu [e'mø], n.m. (Orn.) emu.
émeute [e'møːt], n.f. riot, disturbance, tumult, rising; **chef d'émeute**, ringleader.
émeuter [emø'te], v.t. to rouse, to stir up, to excite.
émeutier [emø'tje], n.m. (fem. -ière) rioter.
émiettement [emjɛt'mā], n.m. crumbling.
émietter [emjɛ'te], v.t. to crumble. **s'émietter**, v.r. to crumble.
émigrant [emi'grā], a. emigrating.—n.m. (fem. -e) emigrant.
émigration [emigrɑ'sjɔ̃], n.f. emigration, migration.
émigré [emi'gre], n.m. (fem. -ée) emigrant; refugee.
émigrer [emi'gre], v.i. to emigrate; to migrate.
émincé [emɛ̃'se], n.m. (Cook.) thin slices (of meat).
émincer [emɛ̃'se], v.t. (conjug. like COMMENCER) to slice (meat).
éminemment [emina'mā], adv. eminently.
éminence [emi'nāːs], n.f. eminence, elevation, rising ground, height.
éminent [emi'nā], a. eminent, high, lofty.
émissaire [emi'sɛːr], n.m. emissary, messenger; **bouc émissaire**, scapegoat.
émission [emi'sjɔ̃], n.f. emission; issue, uttering; broadcasting.
emmagasinage [āmagazi'naːʒ], n.m. storage, warehousing.
emmagasiner [āmagazi'ne], v.t. to warehouse, to store.
emmaillotement [āmajɔt'mā], n.m. swaddling, swathing.
emmailloter [āmajo'te], v.t. to swaddle, to swathe.
emmanchement [āmāʃ'mā], n.m. hafting, helving (putting a handle on); (fig.) joining.
emmancher [āmā'ʃe], v.t. to put a handle to, to haft, to helve. **s'emmancher**, v.r. to fit on a handle; (fig.) to start (of an affair).
emmanchure [āmā'ʃyːr], n.f. armhole.
emmarchement [āmarʃə'mā], n.m. tread (of stair).
emmêlement [āmɛl'mā], n.m. tangle, muddle.
emmêler [āmɛ'le], v.t. to entangle. **s'emmêler**, v.r. to get entangled.
emménagement [āmenaʒ'mā], n.m. moving into (a new house), installation.
emménager [āmena'ʒe], v.t. (conjug. like MANGER) to move in; to fit out (a ship etc.).—v.i. and **s'emménager**, v.r. to move in.
emmener [ām'ne], v.t. (conjug. like AMENER) to take away, to lead away, to fetch away, to convey away.
emmenotter [āmnɔ'te], v.t. to handcuff.
emmeuler [āmø'le], v.t. to stack (hay etc.).
emmiellé [āmjɛ'le], a. honeyed, sweet.
emmieller [āmjɛ'le], v.t. to honey, to sweeten with or as with honey.
emmitoufler [āmitu'fle], v.t. to wrap up warmly.

émoi

émoi [e'mwa], *n.m.* emotion, anxiety, flutter.
émollient [emɔ'ljā], *a.* emollient, softening. —*n.m.* emollient.
émolument [emɔly'mā], *n.m.* emolument, fee; (*pl.*) salary.
émondage [emɔ̃'da:ʒ], *n.m.* pruning, lopping, trimming.
émonder [emɔ̃'de], *v.t.* to prune, to lop.
émondeur [emɔ̃'dœ:r], *n.m.* (*fem.* **-euse**) pruner, trimmer.
émotion [emo'sjɔ̃], *n.f.* emotion; stir, commotion.
émotter [emɔ'te], *v.t.* to break up (*soil, a field etc.*).
émoucher [emu'ʃe], *v.t.* to drive flies away from. **s'émoucher**, *v.r.* to whisk away the flies.
émouchet [emu'ʃɛ], *n.m.* sparrow hawk.
émouchette [emu'ʃɛt], *n.f.* fly net (*for horses etc.*).
émouchoir [emu'ʃwa:r], *n.m.* fly whisk.
émoudre [e'mudr], *v.t. irr.* (*conjug. like* MOUDRE) to grind, to sharpen.
émouleur [emu'lœ:r], *n.m.* knifegrinder.
émoulu [emu'ly], *a.* sharpened, sharp.
émousser [emu'se], *v.t.* to blunt, to take the edge off; (*fig.*) to dull; to deaden. **s'émousser**, *v.r.* to get blunt; to become dull.
émoustiller [emusti'je], *v.t.* (*colloq.*) to exhilarate, to put into good spirits; (*fam.*) to ginger up. **s'émoustiller**, *v.r.* to bestir oneself.
émouvant [emu'vā], *a.* touching, moving, stirring.
émouvoir [emu'vwa:r], *v.t. irr.* (*conjug. like* MOUVOIR) to move, to affect; to excite, to rouse. **s'émouvoir**, *v.r.* to be roused *or* moved; to be agitated.
empaillage [āpa'ja:ʒ], **empaillement** [āpaj'mā], *n.m.* bottoming (*with straw*); stuffing (*of animals*).
empaillé [āpa'je], *a.* stuffed; (*fam.*) **avoir l'air empaillé**, to be slow *or* dull-witted.
empailler [āpa'je], *v.t.* to pack in straw; to straw-bottom; to stuff (*birds etc.*).
empailleur [āpa'jœ:r], *n.m.* (*fem.* **-euse**) chair mender; bird *or* animal stuffer, taxidermist.
empaler [āpa'le], *v.t.* to impale.
empanacher [āpana'ʃe], *v.t.* to adorn with a plume; (*colloq.*) to touch up.
empaquetage [āpak'ta:ʒ], *n.m.* packing.
empaqueter [āpak'te], *v.t.* (*conjug. like* APPELER) to pack up, to make up into a bundle, to do up. **s'empaqueter**, *v.r.* to wrap oneself up.
emparer (**s'**) [sāpa're], *v.r.* to possess oneself (*of*), to get hold (*of*); to seize, to secure.
empâtement [āpat'mā], *n.m.* stickiness, clamminess.
empâter [āpa'te], *v.t.* to make clammy *or* sticky; to cram (*fowls*).
empattement [āpat'mā], *n.m.* footing, foundation, base; (*Motor. etc.*) wheel-base.
empaumer [āpo'me], *v.t.* to catch *or* strike (*a ball etc.*) in *or* with the palm of the hand; (*fig.*) to get hold of, to grasp, to take possession of.
empêchement [āpɛʃ'mā], *n.m.* hindrance, obstacle, impediment; objection.
empêcher [āpɛ'ʃe], *v.t.* to oppose, to prevent; to hinder. **s'empêcher**, *v.r.* (*always in the negative*) to forbear, to refrain from; **je ne peux m'empêcher de rire**, I cannot help laughing.

empeigne [ā'pɛɲ], *n.f.* upper (leather) (*of shoe*).
empenner [āpɛ'ne], *v.t.* to feather (*arrows*); to fit on (*fins*).
empereur [ā'prœ:r], *n.m.* emperor.
empesage [āpə'za:ʒ], *n.m.* starching.
empesé [āpə'ze], *a.* starched; stiff (*of style etc.*), formal.
empeser [āpə'ze], *v.t.* (*conjug. like* AMENER) to starch.
empester [āpɛs'te], *v.t.* to infect, to taint; to cause to stink horribly; (*fig.*) to corrupt.
empêtrer [āpɛ'tre], *v.t.* to entangle; to embarrass. **s'empêtrer**, *v.r.* to become entangled.
emphase [ā'fa:z], *n.f.* grandiloquence; emphasis, stress.
emphatique [āfa'tik], *a.* bombastic, affected; emphatic.
empiècement [āpjɛs'mā], *n.m.* yoke (*of blouse*).
empierrement [āpjɛr'mā], *n.m.* stoning, metalling, surfacing (*a road etc.*).
empierrer [āpjɛ're], *v.t.* to stone, to metal, to surface (*roads etc.*).
empiétement [āpjet'mā], *n.m.* encroaching, infringement.
empiéter [āpje'te], *v.t.* (*conjug. like* CÉDER) to encroach upon, to invade, to trespass upon.—*v.i.* to encroach (*sur*).
empilement [āpil'mā], *n.m.* piling, stacking.
empiler [āpi'le], *v.t.* to pile up, to stack.
empire [ā'pi:r], *n.m.* empire, sovereignty, control, authority, dominion; (*fig.*) prestige, sway, mastery.
empirer [āpi're], *v.t.* to make worse.—*v.i.* to grow worse.
empirique [āpi'rik], *a.* empiric(al).
empirisme [āpi'rism], *n.m.* empiricism.
emplacement [āplas'mā], *n.m.* site, place, piece of ground.
emplâtre [ā'pla:tr], *n.m.* plaster, ointment; (*fig.*) palliative; (*colloq.*) helpless creature.
emplette [ā'plɛt], *n.f.* purchase; **faire des emplettes**, to go shopping.
emplir [ā'pli:r], *v.t.* to fill. **s'emplir**, *v.r.* to fill; to be filled.
emploi [ā'plwa], *n.m.* employ, employment; use, function; situation, post.
employé [āplwa'je], *a.* employed.—*n.m.* (*fem.* **-ée**) employee, assistant, clerk.
employer [āplwa'je], *v.t.* (*see Verb Tables*) to employ, to use; to give employment to; to spend, to invest. **s'employer**, *v.r.* to employ oneself, to exert *or* busy oneself; to use one's interest; to be used.
employeur [āplwa'jœ:r], *n.m.* (*fem.* **-euse**) employer.
emplumer (**s'**) [sāply'me], *v.r.* to become fledged.
empocher [āpɔ'ʃe], *v.t.* to pocket.
empoignade [āpɔ'ɲad, āpwa'ɲad], *n.f.* (*colloq.*) dispute, row, set-to.
empoignant [āpɔ'ɲā, āpwa'ɲā], *a.* thrilling, poignant.
empoigner [āpɔ'ɲe, āpwa'ɲe], *v.t.* to grasp, to seize. **s'empoigner**, *v.r.* to lay hold of each other, to grapple.
empois [ā'pwa], *n.m.* starch.

empoisonné [ãpwazɔ'ne], *a.* poisoned; (*fig.*) poisonous.

empoisonner [ãpwazɔ'ne], *v.t.* to poison; (*fig.*) to infect; to corrupt; to embitter; (*slang*) to bore to death. **s'empoisonner**, *v.r.* to poison oneself.

empoisonneur [ãpwazɔ'nœːr], *a.* (*fem.* **-euse**) poisonous; (*fig.*) corrupting.—*n.m.* (*fem.* **-euse**) poisoner; (*fig.*) corrupter.

empoissonner [ãpwasɔ'ne], *v.t.* to stock with fish.

emporté [ãpɔr'te], *a.* fiery, passionate, hotheaded; runaway, unmanageable.

emportement [ãpɔrt'mã], *n.m.* transport, fit of passion, outburst (*of anger, rage etc.*).

emporte-pièce [ãpɔrtə'pjɛs], *n.m.* punch (*instrument*), cutting-out machine; *c'est une réponse à l'emporte-pièce*, it is a very cutting answer.

emporter [ãpɔr'te], *v.t.* to carry away, to take away; to remove (*stains etc.*); to transport (*of emotion etc.*); to entail, to involve; to gain, to obtain. **s'emporter**, *v.r.* to fly into a passion, to flare up; to declaim (*contre*); to bolt (*of horses*).

empotage [ãpɔ'taːʒ], *n.m.* potting (*of plants*).

empoter [ãpɔ'te], *v.t.* to pot (*plants*).

empourpré [ãpur'pre], *a.* crimson.

empourprer [ãpur'pre], *v.t.* to color red *or* purple. **s'empourprer**, *v.r.* to turn red *or* purple; to flush, to blush.

empreindre [ã'prɛ̃ːdr], *v.t. irr.* (*conjug. like* CRAINDRE) to imprint, to stamp, to impress. **s'empreindre**, *v.r.* to become tinged.

empreinte [ã'prɛ̃ːt], *n.f.* stamp, print, impression; mark; *empreintes digitales*, fingerprints.

empressé [ãprɛ'se], *a.* eager, earnest; assiduous.

empressement [ãprɛs'mã], *n.m.* alacrity, eagerness; haste, hurry.

empresser (s') [sãprɛ'se], *v.r.* to be eager (*to*); to crowd, to press.

emprisonnement [ãprizɔn'mã], *n.m.* imprisonment.

emprisonner [ãprizɔ'ne], *v.t.* to imprison, to confine.

emprunt [ã'prœ̃], *n.m.* borrowing; loan.

emprunter [ãprœ̃'te], *v.t.* to borrow; to assume.

emprunteur [ãprœ̃'tœːr], *a.* (*fem.* **-euse**) borrowing.—*n.m.* (*fem.* **-euse**) borrower.

empuantir [ãpɥã'tiːr], *v.t.* to give an ill smell to, to infect.

ému [e'my], *a.* moved, affected.

émulation [emyla'sjɔ̃], *n.f.* emulation, rivalry.

émule [e'myl], *n.* rival, competitor.

émulgent [emyl'ʒã], *a.* (*Physiol.*) emulgent.

émulsif [emyl'sif], *a.* (*fem.* **-sive**) emulsive.

émulsion [emyl'sjɔ̃], *n.f.* emulsion.

en (1) [ã], *prép.* in; to; within; into; at; like, in the form of, as; out of, by, through, from; for, on.

en (2) [ã], *pron. inv.* of him, of her, of it, its, of them, their; from him, by him, about him etc.; thence, from thence; some of it, any.

enamourer (s') [sãnamu're], *v.r.* to fall in love; to be enamored (*de*).

encadrement [ãkadrə'mã], *n.m.* framing, frame; border; (*fig.*) environment.

encadrer [ãka'dre], *v.t.* to frame; to surround; to insert; (*Mil.*) to bracket (*target*);

to officer (*troops*). **s'encadrer**, *v.r.* to be inserted *or* enclosed.

encadreur [ãka'drœːr], *n.m.* (*fem.* **-euse**) picture-frame maker.

encager [ãka'ʒe], *v.t.* (*conjug. like* MANGER) to cage, to put in a cage.

encaissage [ãkɛ'saːʒ], *n.m.* encasing.

encaisse [ã'kɛs], *n.f.* cash in hand, cash balance.

encaissé [ãkɛ'se], *a.* encased; sunk, hollow; steeply *or* deeply embanked.

encaissement [ãkɛs'mã], *n.m.* packing, putting in boxes etc.; embankment; paying in (*of money*).

encaisser [ãkɛ'se], *v.t.* to encase, to pack; to bank, pay in; to collect, to receive (*money*).

encaisseur [ãkɛ'sœːr], *n.m.* (*fem.* **-euse**) cashier.

encan [ã'kã], *n.m.* public auction.

encapuchonner (s') [sãkapyʃɔ'ne], *v.r.* to put on a cowl; to wrap one's head up; to arch the neck (*of horses*).

encarter [ãkar'te], *v.t.* to card-index.

en-cas [ã'kɑ], *n.m. inv.* anything kept for use in emergency; small umbrella; light meal prepared in case of need.

encastrement [ãkastrə'mã], *n.m.* fitting, fitting in.

encastrer [ãkas'tre], *v.t.* to fit in, to imbed.

encaustiquage [ãkosti'ka:ʒ], *n.m.* waxpolishing.

encavement [ãkav'mã], *n.m.* storing (*in cellar*), cellaring.

encaver [ãka've], *v.t.* to put *or* store in a cellar.

enceindre [ã'sɛ̃ːdr], *v.t. irr.* (*conjug. like* CRAINDRE) to surround, to enclose.

enceinte [ã'sɛ̃ːt], *n.f.* circuit, enclosure; (*Fort.*) enceinte. *a.* pregnant

encens [ã'sã], *n.m.* incense; (*fig.*) fragrance; flattery.

encensement [ãsãs'mã], *n.m.* incensing; (*fig.*) flattery.

encenser [ãsã'se], *v.t.* to incense; (*fig.*) to flatter.

encenseur [ãsã'sœːr], *n.m.* (*fem.* **-euse**) burner of incense; (*fig.*) flatterer.

encensoir [ãsã'swaːr], *n.m.* censer; (*fig.*) flattery.

encerclement [ãsɛrklə'mã], *n.m.* encircling; (*Polit.*) encirclement.

encercler [ãsɛr'kle], *v.t.* to encircle.

enchaînement [ãʃɛn'mã], *n.m.* chaining, linking; series, connection.

enchaîner [ãʃɛ'ne], *v.t.* to chain up, to bind in chains; (*Cine.*) to fade in; (*fig.*) to restrain; to captivate; to link. **s'enchaîner**, *v.r.* to be connected *or* linked together.

enchanté [ãʃã'te], *a.* enchanted; (*fig.*) charmed, delighted.

enchantement [ãʃãt'mã], *n.m.* enchantment, magic; (*fig.*) charm, delight.

enchanter [ãʃã'te], *v.t.* to enchant; (*fig.*) to fascinate, to charm.

enchanteur [ãʃã'tœːr], *a.* (*fem.* **-eresse**) enchanting, entrancing, captivating.—*n.m.* (*fem.* **-eresse**) enchanter, enchantress, charmer.

enchâsser [ãʃã'se], *v.t.* to enchase; to enshrine; to insert.

enchâssure [ãʃã'syːr], *n.f.* setting, mount; insertion.

133

enchère

enchère [ã'ʃɛːr], *n.f.* bid (*at an auction*); auction.

enchérir [ãʃe'riːr], *v.t.* to bid for, to outbid; to raise (*prices etc.*).—*v.i.* to rise (*in price*); (*fig.*) to surpass, to outdo; to bid, to outbid (*sur*).

enchérissement [ãʃeris'mã], *n.m.* rise, increase.

enchérisseur [ãʃeri'sœːr], *n.m.* bidder (*at an auction*).

enchevêtrement [ãʃvɛtrə'mã], *n.m.* entanglement.

enchevêtrer [ãʃvɛ'tre], *v.t.* to halter (*a horse etc.*); to entangle. **s'enchevêtrer**, *v.r.* to get entangled, confused *or* embarrassed.

enclave [ã'klaːv], *n.f.* enclave, piece of enclosed land.

enclaver [ãkla've], *v.t.* to enclose, to hem in.

enclenchement [ãklãʃ'mã], *n.m.* throwing into gear; automatic clutch.

enclin [ã'klɛ̃], *a.* inclined; prone, addicted, apt, given to.

enclore [ã'kloːr], *v.t. irr.* (*conjug. like* CLORE) to enclose, to fence in, to take in, to shut in.

enclos [ã'klo], *n.m.* enclosure, yard; paddock; fencing, wall.

enclume [ã'klym], *n.f.* anvil.

encoche [ã'kɔʃ], *n.f.* notch.

encoffrer [ãkɔ'fre], *v.t.* to shut in a coffer; (*fig.*) to cage.

encoignure [ãkɔ'ɲyːr], *n.f.* corner, angle (*of a street*); corner piece; corner cupboard.

encollage [ãkɔ'laːʒ], *n.m.* sizing, gluing; glue, size.

encoller [ãkɔ'le], *v.t.* to size, to glue.

encolure [ãkɔ'lyːr], *n.f.* neck and shoulders (*of a horse*); neck-line (*of a garment*); size (*of collars*); (*fig.*) appearance (*of a person*).

encombrant [ãkɔ̃'brã], *a.* cumbersome.

encombre [ã'kɔ̃:br], *n.m.* (*now only used after sans*) impediment, hindrance.

encombrement [ãkɔ̃brə'mã], *n.m.* obstruction; crowding, congestion (*of traffic*).

encombrer [ãkɔ̃'bre], *v.t.* to obstruct; to crowd, to throng.

encontre (à l' . . . de) [alã'kɔ̃:trdə], *prep. phr.* against, counter to.

encore [ã'kɔːr], *adv.* yet, still, as yet; anew, again, once more; further, moreover, besides; even, but, only.

encorner [ãkɔr'ne], *v.t.* to gore, to toss.

encourageant [ãkura'ʒã], *a.* encouraging, cheering.

encouragement [ãkuraʒ'mã], *n.m.* encouragement.

encourager [ãkura'ʒe]. *v.t.* (*conjug. like* MANGER) to encourage, to stimulate. **s'encourager**, *v.r.* to encourage each other, to take courage.

encourir [ãku'riːr], *v.t. irr.* (*conjug. like* COURIR) to incur (*disgrace, reproach, obligation etc.*).

encrasser [ãkra'se], *v.t.* to make dirty, to foul. **s'encrasser**, *v.r.* to become dirty.

encre [ã:kr], *n.f.* ink.

encrier [ãkri'e], *n.m.* ink-stand, ink-pot.

encroûté [ãkru'te], *a.* covered with a crust; (*fig.*) full of prejudices.—*n.m.* (*fem.* **-ée**) old fogy.

encroûter (s') [sãkru'te], *v.r.* to crust, to get hard; to become dull, stupid *or* hide-bound.

encuvage [ãky'va:ʒ], **encuvement** [ãkyv'mã], *n.m.* tubbing.

encuver [ãky've], *v.t.* to put into a vat, to tub.

encyclopédie [ãsiklɔpe'di], *n.f.* encyclopaedia.

endémique [ãde'mik], *a.* endemic.

endenté [ãdã'te], *a.* indented.

endenter [ãdã'te], *v.t.* to cog, to tooth.

endetter [ãdɛ'te], *v.t.* to get (*a person*) into debt. **s'endetter**, *v.r.* to run into debt.

endeuiller [ãdœ'je], *v.t.* to put into mourning; ʼo sadden.

endiablé [ãdja'ble], *a.* possessed; (*fig.*) devilish.

endiabler [ãdja'ble], *v.i.* to be furious; **faire endiabler**, to torment.

endiguement [ãdig'mã], *n.m.* damming up.

endiguer [ãdi'ge], *v.t.* to dam up, to embank.

endimancher (s') [sãdimã'ʃe], *v.r.* to put on one's Sunday best.

endive [ã'diːv], *n.f.* (*broad-leaved*) chicory.

endoctrinement [ãdɔktrin'mã], *n.m.* indoctrination.

endoctriner [ãdɔktri'ne], *v.t.* to indoctrinate.

endolorir [ãdɔlɔ'riːr], *v.t.* to make sore; to make (*the heart etc.*) ache. **s'endolorir**, *v.r.* to become sore.

endolorissement [ãdɔlɔris'mã], *n.m.* pain, soreness.

endommagement [ãdɔmaʒ'mã], *n.m.* loss, injury, damage.

endommager [ãdɔma'ʒe], *v.t.* (*conjug. like* MANGER) to damage, to injure.

endormeur [ãdɔr'mœːr], *n.m.* (*fem.* **-euse**) cajoler, flatterer; bore.

endormi [ãdɔr'mi], *a.* asleep; sleepy; benumbed.—*n.m.* (*fem.* **-e**) sleepy-head.

endormir [ãdɔr'miːr], *v.t. irr.* (*conjug. like* SENTIR) to send to sleep, to rock to sleep; to anesthetize; to wheedle, to deceive; to benumb; to bore. **s'endormir**, *v.r.* to fall asleep.

endos [ã'do], **endossement** [ãdɔs'mã], *n.m.* endorsement.

endosser [ãdo'se], *v.t.* to put on one's back, to put on; to saddle oneself with (*an obligation etc.*); to endorse.

endroit [ã'drwa], *n.m.* place, spot; point; right side (*of a material*); part, passage (*of a book etc.*).

enduire [ã'dɥiːr], *v.t. irr.* (*conjug. like* CONDUIRE) to do over, to coat, to smear.

enduit [ã'dɥi], *n.m.* coating, layer, plaster, glaze, varnish, polish.

endurance [ãdy'rã:s], *n.f.* endurance, fortitude; **épreuve d'endurance**, endurance *or* reliability test.

endurant [ãdy'rã], *a.* patient, tolerant.

endurci [ãdyr'si], *a.* hardened; inured, callous.

endurcir [ãdyr'siːr], *v.t.* to harden, to toughen, to inure; to render callous. **s'endurcir**, *v.r.* to harden, to grow hard; to become callous.

endurcissement [ãdyrsis'mã], *n.m.* hardening, obduracy; callousness.

endurer [ãdy're], *v.t.* to endure, to bear; to put up with.

énergie [enɛr'ʒi], *n.f.* energy, strength, vigor, power.

énergique [enɛr'ʒik], *a.* energetic, vigorous.

énergiquement [enɛrʒik'mã], *adv.* energetically, vigorously.
énervant [enɛr'vã], *a.* enervating; debilitating, nerve-racking.
énervé [enɛr've], *a.* nerveless; on edge, fidgety.
énervement [enɛrv'mã], *n.m.* nervous tension.
énerver [enɛr've], *v.t.* to enervate, to debilitate; to weaken; to unnerve; (*fam.*) to get on the nerves. **s'énerver,** *v.r.* to become enervated, unnerved, irritable *or* fidgety.
enfance [ã'fãːs], *n.f.* infancy, childhood; childishness.
enfant [ã'fã], *n.* child; infant, baby; descendant; citizen, native.
enfantement [ãfãt'mã], *n.m.* childbirth.
enfanter [ãfã'te], *v.t.* to bring forth, to bear; (*fig.*) to beget, to give birth to.
enfantillage [ãfãti'jaːʒ], *n.m.* child's-play, childishness.
enfantin [ãfã'tɛ̃], *a.* infantile, childish.
enfariner [ãfari'ne], *v.t.* to flour, to sprinkle with flour.
enfer [ã'fɛːr], *n.m.* hell; (*fig.*) torment, misery.
enfermer [ãfɛr'me], *v.t.* to shut in *or* up; to lock up; to enclose; to conceal; to comprise. **s'enfermer,** *v.r.* to lock oneself in.
enficeler [ãfis'le], *v.t.* (*conjug. like* APPELER) to tie with string etc.
enfièvrement [ãfjɛvrə'mã], *n.m.* feverishness.
enfilade [ãfi'lad], *n.f.* suite (*of chambers etc.*); string (*of phrases etc.*); (*Mil.*) enfilade.
enfiler [ãfi'le], *v.t.* to thread (*a needle*); to string (*beads*); to pierce; to pass through; (*Mil.*) to enfilade; to slip on (*clothes*). **s'enfiler,** *v.r.* to be threaded; to be pierced; to get involved in.
enfin [ã'fɛ̃], *adv.* at last, finally, at length, after all, lastly; in short, in a word.
enflammé [ãfla'me], *a.* on fire, in flames, ignited.
enflammer [ãfla'me], *v.t.* to set on fire, to kindle; (*fig.*) to incense, to provoke. **s'enflammer,** *v.r.* to catch fire, to blaze; (*fig.*) to be incensed.
enflé [ã'fle], *a.* swollen, puffed up; (*fig.*) bombastic, high-flown (*style etc.*).
enfler [ã'fle], *v.t.* to swell out, to puff up, to distend; (*fig.*) to excite; to exaggerate. **s'enfler,** *v.r.* to swell; (*fig.*) to be puffed up.
enflure [ã'flyːr], *n.f.* bloatedness, swelling; bombast.
enfoncé [ãfõ'se], *a.* broken open; sunken; (*pop.*) done for.
enfoncement [ãfõs'mã], *n.m.* breaking in; sinking; recess; (*Paint.*) background.
enfoncer [ãfõ'se], *v.t.* (*conjug. like* COMMENCER) to push *or* drive in, down etc.; to sink; to break in; to get the better of.—*v.i.* to sink, to founder. **s'enfoncer,** *v.r.* to sink; to bury oneself; to plunge; (*fig.*) to fail.
enfonçure [ãfõ'syːr], *n.f.* cavity, hole, hollow.
enforcir [ãfor'siːr], *v.t.* to strengthen.—*v.i.* and **s'enforcir,** *v.r.* to gather strength; to grow stronger.
enfouir [ã'fwiːr], *v.t.* to put *or* bury in the ground; (*fig.*) to hide. **s'enfouir,** *v.r.* to bury oneself (*in an out-of-the-way place etc.*).
enfourcher [ãfur'ʃe], *v.t.* to bestride, to straddle; to pierce with a pitch-fork etc.

enfourchure [ãfur'ʃyːr], *n.f.* fork; crotch.
enfourner [ãfur'ne], *v.t.* to put in the oven. **s'enfourner,** *v.r.* to get into a blind alley, a scrape etc.
enfreindre [ã'frɛ̃ːdr], *v.t. irr.* (*conjug. like* CRAINDRE) to infringe, to break, to violate.
enfuir (s') [sã'fɥiːr], *v.r. irr.* (*conjug. like* FUIR) to run away, to escape.
enfumer [ãfy'me], *v.t.* to smoke, to fill with smoke, to smoke (*vermin etc.*) out.
enfûtage [ãfy'taːʒ], *n.m.* casking.
enfutailler [ãfyta'je], **enfuter** [ãfy'te], *v.t.* to cask, to barrel, to tun (*wine etc.*).
engagé [ãga'ʒe], *a.* pledged; engaged, enlisted; in action; (*Naut.*) water-logged.
engageant [ãga'ʒã], *a.* engaging, winning.
engagement [ãgaʒ'mã], *n.m.* engagement, commitment, pledging; mortgage; appointment; (*Mil.*) enlisting; action; entry (*for a sporting event*); (*pl.*) liabilities.
engager [ãga'ʒe], *v.t.* (*conjug. like* MANGER) to pledge, to pawn; to engage; to begin; to invite, to induce, to urge; to involve. **s'engager,** *v.r.* to engage oneself, to undertake, to promise; to stand security; to begin; to enter; to enlist; to get involved.
engeance [ã'ʒãːs], *n.f.* breed; brood (*esp. of poultry*).
engelure [ãʒ'lyːr], *n.f.* chilblain.
engendrer [ãʒã'dre], *v.t.* to beget, to engender; (*fig.*) to produce.
engin [ã'ʒɛ̃], *n.m.* machine, engine; snare; tool; *engin téléguidé,* guided missile.
englober [ãglo'be], *v.t.* to unite, to put together; (*fig.*) to include, to embrace.
engloutir [ãglu'tiːr], *v.t.* to swallow, to devour. **s'engloutir,** *v.r.* to be swallowed up.
engloutissement [ãglutis'mã], *n.m.* engulfing, swallowing up.
engoncé [ãgõ'se], *a. avoir l'air engoncé,* to look awkward and stiff.
engorgement [ãgorʒə'mã], *n.m.* obstruction, stopping up (*of a pipe etc.*); (*Med.*) congestion; (*Econ.*) glut.
engorger [ãgor'ʒe], *v.t.* (*conjug. like* MANGER) to obstruct, to block. **s'engorger,** *v.r.* to be obstructed *or* choked up.
engouement *or* **engoûment** [ãgu'mã], *n.m.* (*Med.*) choking, obstruction; (*fig.*) infatuation.
engouer [ã'gwe], *v.t.* to obstruct (*the throat etc.*); (*fig.*) to infatuate. **s'engouer,** *v.r.* to half choke oneself; (*fig.*) to be infatuated.
engouffrer [ãgu'fre], *v.t.* to engulf; (*fig.*) to swallow up. **s'engouffrer,** *v.r.* to be engulfed; to be swallowed up; to blow hard (*of the wind*).
engourdi [ãgur'di], *a.* torpid; benumbed.
engourdir [ãgur'diːr], *v.t.* to benumb; to dull, to enervate. **s'engourdir,** *v.r.* to get benumbed; to become sluggish.
engourdissement [ãgurdis'mã], *n.m.* numbness; torpor, enervation.
engrais [ã'grɛ], *n.m.* manure, fertilizer; fattening (*cattle*).
engraissant [ãgrɛ'sã], *a.* fattening.
engraissement [ãgrɛs'mã], *n.m.* fattening.
engraisser [ãgrɛ'se], *v.t.* to fatten; to manure; (*fig.*) to enrich.—*v.i.* to grow fat; (*fig.*) to thrive. **s'engraisser,** *v.r.* to grow fat *or* stout.

engrenage

engrenage [āgrə′na:ʒ], n.m. gear, gearing etc.; action of these; (fig.) correlation (of circumstances etc.).

engrener (1) [āgrə′ne], v.t. (conjug. like AMENER) to put corn into (the mill-hopper); to feed with corn.

engrener (2) [āgrə′ne], v.t. (conjug. like AMENER) (Mach.) to throw into gear. s'engrener, v.r. to work into each other (of toothed wheels); to be put in gear.

engrenure [āgrə′ny:r], n.f. engagement of teeth, cogs etc.

engrumeler (s') [sāgrym′le], v.r. (conjug. like APPELER) to clot, to coagulate.

enhardir [āar′di:r], v.t. to embolden, to encourage. s'enhardir, v.r. to grow bold.

enherber [ānɛr′be], v.t. to put land under grass.

énigmatique [enigma′tik], a. enigmatical.

énigmatiquement [enigmatik′mā], adv. enigmatically.

énigme [e′nigm], n.f. enigma, riddle.

enivrant [āni′vrā], a. intoxicating.

enivrement [ānivrə′mā], n.m. intoxication; (fig.) elation.

enivrer [āni′vre], v.t. to intoxicate, to inebriate; (fig.) to elate. s'enivrer, v.r. to get intoxicated; (fig.) to be elated.

enjambée [āʒā′be], n.f. stride.

enjambement [āʒāb′mā], n.m. (Pros.) run-on line, enjambment.

enjamber [āʒā′be], v.t. to skip or leap over; to stride; (fig.) to encroach upon; (Pros.) to make enjambment.

enjeu [ā′ʒø], n.m. (pl. -eux) stake (gaming and fig.).

enjoindre [ā′ʒwɛ̃:dr], v.t. irr. (conjug. like CRAINDRE) to enjoin, to charge, to direct, to prescribe.

enjôlement [āʒol′mā], n.m. wheedling, coaxing, cajoling.

enjôler [āʒo′le], v.t. to coax, to wheedle.

enjôleur [āʒo′lœ:r], n.m. (fem. -euse) wheedler, coaxer.

enjolivement [āʒoliv′mā], n.m. embellishment, decoration, ornament.

enjoliver [āʒoli′ve], v.t. to embellish, to set off.

enjoliveur [āʒoli′vœ:r], n.m. (fem. -euse) embellisher.

enjolivure [āʒoli′vy:r], n.f. (small) embellishment.

enjoué [ā′ʒwe], a. playful, sprightly, lively, jovial, sportive.

enjouement or enjoûment [āʒu′mā], n.m. playfulness, sportiveness, sprightliness.

enlacement [ālas′mā], n.m. lacing, interlacing, entwining.

enlacer [āla′se], v.t. (conjug. like COMMENCER) to lace; to entwine; to clasp. s'enlacer, v.r. to entwine, to be interlaced.

enlaidir [ālɛ′di:r], v.t. to make ugly; to disfigure.—v.i. to grow ugly, to be disfigured.

enlaidissement [ālɛdis′mā], n.m. disfigurement.

enlèvement [ālɛv′mā], n.m. carrying off; removal; wiping off; kidnapping.

enlever [ālə′ve], v.t. (conjug. like AMENER) to remove, to take off; to carry off; to kidnap; to wipe off; to charm. s'enlever, v.r. to rise, to be lifted; to come off, to peel off; to come

out; to be snapped up (of goods on sale); to get into a passion.

enlève-taches [ālɛv′taʃ], n.m. inv. stain remover.

enliasser [ālja′se], v.t. to tie up in a bundle.

enlignement [āliɲ′mā], n.m. alignment.

enligner [āli′ɲe], v.t. to put in line.

enlisement [āliz′mā], n.m. sinking, swallowing up (in quicksand).

enliser [āli′ze], v.t. to engulf. s'enliser, v.r. to be engulfed or swallowed up.

enluminer [ālymi′ne], v.t. to color; to illuminate. s'enluminer, v.r. to rouge, to paint; to flush.

enlumineur [ālymi′nœ:r], n.m. (fem. -euse) colorer of maps, prints etc.

enluminure [ālymi′ny:r], n.f. coloring; colored print; tinsel (of style).

enneigé [āne′ʒe], a. snow-covered.

ennemi [ɛn′mi], a. hostile; injurious.—n.m. (fem. -e) enemy, foe.

ennoblir [āno′bli:r], v.t. to dignify, to exalt. s'ennoblir, v.r. to be ennobled or exalted.

ennoblissement [ānoblis′mā], n.m. ennoblement, exaltation.

ennui [ā′nɥi], n.m. trouble, worry; nuisance; boredom.

ennuyer [ānɥi′je], v.t. (conjug. like EMPLOYER) to bore, to weary; to pester; (fig.) to annoy. s'ennuyer, v.r. to be bored, to feel dull; to miss.

ennuyeusement [ānɥijøz′mā], adv. tediously, irksomely.

ennuyeux [ānɥi′jø], a. (fem. -euse) boring, tedious, dull, tiresome; annoying.—n.m. (fem. -euse) tiresome person, bore.

énoncé [enɔ̃′se], n.m. statement.

énoncer [enɔ̃′se], v.t. (conjug. like COMMENCER) to state, to express, to enunciate. s'énoncer, v.r. to be worded or expressed.

énonciatif [enɔ̃sja′tif], a. (fem. -tive) enunciative.

énonciation [enɔ̃sja′sjɔ̃], n.f. enunciation; delivery; statement; wording.

enorgueillir [ānɔrgœ′ji:r], v.t. to make proud, to elate. s'enorgueillir, v.r. to be or grow proud of, to be elated, to glory in (de).

énorme [e′nɔrm], a. enormous, huge.

énormément [enɔrme′mā], adv. enormously, beyond measure.

énormité [enɔrmi′te], n.f. hugeness, vastness; enormity.

enquérir (s') [sāke′ri:r], v.r. irr. (conjug. like ACQUÉRIR) to inquire, to make inquiries.

enquête [ā′kɛ:t], n.f. inquiry, investigation; inquest.

enquêter [āke′te], v.i. to inquire into a matter (sur); to conduct an inquiry.

enquêteur [āke′tœ:r], n.m. (fem. -euse) investigator.

enraciner [ārasi′ne], v.t. to root; (fig.) to implant. s'enraciner, v.r. to take root.

enragé [āra′ʒe], a. mad, rabid; (fig.) enthusiastic.—n.m. (fem. -ée) madman, mad woman; desperate person.

enrageant [āra′ʒā], a. maddening, vexing.

enrager [āra′ʒe], v.i. (conjug. like MANGER) to be mad, to go mad; to be enraged, to fume.

enrayage [ārɛ′ja:ʒ], n.m. (Mil.) jam (in rifle).

enrayement or **enraiement** [ãrɛj'mã], *n.m.* skidding, locking.

enrayer (1) [ãrɛ'je], *v.t.* (*conjug. like* PAYER) to put spokes to (*a wheel*); to skid (*a wheel*), to apply brakes to; (*fig.*) to check, to slow up (*an attack*); to stem (*an epidemic*); to jam (*a machine-gun*).

enrayer (2) [ãrɛ'je], *v.t.* (*conjug. like* PAYER) (*Agric.*) to plough the first furrow in.

enrayure (1) [ãrɛ'jyːr], *n.f.* drag, skid, lock-chain.

enrayure (2) [ãrɛ'jyːr], *n.m.* (*Agric.*) first furrow.

enrégimenter [ãreʒimã'te], *v.t.* to form into regiments; (*fig.*) to enroll.

enregistrement [ãrəʒistrə'mã], *n.m.* registration, recording; checking(*of luggage*).

enregistrer [ãrəʒis'tre], *v.t.* to register, to record; to check(*luggage*).

enregistreur [ãrəʒis'trœːr], *n.m.* registrar; recording machine.

enrêner [ãrɛ'ne], *v.t.* to rein in; to tie up by the reins.

enrhumer [ãry'me], *v.t.* to give a cold to (*someone*). **s'enrhumer**, *v.r.* to catch a cold.

enrichi [ãri'ʃi], *n.m.* (*fem.* -e) upstart, parvenu, new rich.

enrichir [ãri'ʃiːr], *v.t.* to enrich; (*fig.*) to embellish. **s'enrichir**, *v.r.* to enrich oneself, to thrive.

enrichissement [ãriʃis'mã], *n.m.* enrichment; (*fig.*) embellishment.

enrôlement [ãrol'mã], *n.m.* enrolment; (*Mil.*) enlistment.

enrôler [ãro'le], *v.t.* to enlist; to enroll. **s'enrôler**, *v.r.*to enroll oneself, to enlist.

enroué [ã'rwe], *a.* hoarse, husky.

enrouement [ãru'mã], *n.m.* hoarseness, huskiness.

enrouer [ã'rwe], *v.t.* to make hoarse. **s'enrouer**, *v.r.* to become hoarse or husky.

enroulement [ãrul'mã], *n.m.* rolling up; (*Arch.*) scroll.

enrouler [ãru'le], *v.t.* to roll up, to coil. **s'enrouler**, *v.r.* to roll oneself up; to twine (*of plants etc.*).

enrubanner [ãryba'ne], *v.t.* to deck out with ribbons. **s'enrubanner**, *v.r.* to beribbon oneself.

ensablement [ãsablə'mã], *n.m.* sand-bank; ballasting; stranding (*of a ship*).

ensabler [ãsa'ble], *v.t.* to ballast; to run aground, to strand. **s'ensabler**, *v.r.* to run aground; to sink in sand; to silt up.

ensacher [ãsa'ʃe], *v.t.* to put in bags or sacks.

ensanglanter [ãsãglã'te], *v.t.* to make bloody, to stain with blood.

enseignant [ãsɛ'ɲã], *a.* teaching.—*n.m.* (*pl.*) teachers.

enseigne [ã'sɛɲ], *n.f.* sign, signboard; mark, token; ensign, flag.—*n.m.* (*Navy*) sub-lieutenant; (*U.S.*) ensign.

enseignement [ãsɛɲ'mã], *n.m.* teaching, education; teaching profession.

enseigner [ãsɛ'ɲe], *v.t.* to teach, to instruct; to inform, to direct.

ensemble [ã'sã:bl], *adv.* together, at the same time.—*n.m.* whole, general effect, mass; two- or three-piece (*clothing*); suite (*furniture*); (*Math.*) set.

ensemencement [ãsmãs'mã], *n.m.* sowing.

ensemencer [ãsmã'se], *v.t.* (*conjug. like* COMMENCER) to sow.

enserrer [ãsɛ'rɛ], *v.t.* to enclose; to lock up; to hem in.

ensevelir [ãsə'vliːr], *v.t.* to shroud; (*fig.*) to bury; to swallow up, to entomb; to absorb. **s'ensevelir**, *v.r.* to bury oneself.

ensevelissement [ãsəvlis'mã], *n.m.* putting in a shroud; burial.

ensoleillé [ãsɔlɛ'je], *a.* sunny.

ensoleiller [ãsɔlɛ'je], *v.t.* to light up with sunshine; (*fig.*) to brighten.

ensommeillé [ãsɔmɛ'je], *a.* heavy with sleep; (*fig.*) torpid.

ensorceler [ãsɔrsə'le], *v.t.* (*conjug. like* APPELER) to bewitch.

ensorceleur [ãsɔrsə'lœːr], *a.* (*fem.* -euse) bewitching.—*n.m.* (*fem.* -euse) enchanter, enchantress.

ensorcellement [ãsɔrsɛl'mã], *n.m.* bewitchment.

ensuite [ã'sɥit], *adv.* after, afterwards, then, in the next place; what then? what next? well!

ensuivre (s') [sã'sɥiːvr], *v.r. irr.* (*conjug. like* SUIVRE) to follow, to result, to ensue.

entacher [ãta'ʃe], *v.t.* to sully; to taint, to cast a slur on.

entaille [ã'taːj], *n.f.* notch; cut; gash; groove.

entailler [ãta'je], *v.t.* to notch, to cut.

entamer [ãta'me], *v.t.* to make the first cut in; to make an incision in; to broach; to break into.

entartrer (s') [sãtar'tre], *v.r.* to scale, to become furred.

entassement [ãtas'mã], *n.m.* accumulation; heap, pile; crowding together.

entasser [ãta'se], *v.t.* to heap or pile up, to accumulate; to hoard up; to pack together. **s'entasser**, *v.r.* to heap up; to crowd together.

entendement [ãtãd'mã], *n.m.* understanding; judgment, sense.

entendre [ã'tãːdr], *v.t.* to hear; to understand; to know; to intend; to mean. **s'entendre**, *v.r.* to hear each other; to hear one's own voice; to be heard; to be understood; to understand one another; to act in concert; to come to terms (*avec*); to agree with; to be skilful in.

entendu [ãtã'dy], *a.* heard; understood; agreed; skilful.

enténébrer [ãtene'bre], *v.t.* (*conjug. like* CÉDER) to plunge or wrap in darkness.

entente [ã'tãːt], *n.f.* meaning; skill, judgment; understanding, agreement.

enter [ã'te], *v.t.* to graft upon, to engraft; to join.

entériner [ãteri'ne], *v.t.* to ratify, to confirm.

entérique [ãte'rik], *a.* enteric.

entérite [ãte'rit], *n.f.* enteritis.

enterrement [ãtɛr'mã], *n.m.* burial, interment, funeral.

enterrer [ãtɛ're], *v.t.* to bury, to inter; (*fig.*) to survive, to outlive; to end. **s'enterrer**, *v.r.* to bury oneself.

en-tête [ã'tɛːt], *n.m.* (*pl.* -têtes) heading, headline.

entêté [ãtɛ'te], *a.* stubborn, obstinate.—*n.m.* (*fem.* -ée) stubborn person.

entêtement [ātɛt'mā], *n.m.* stubbornness, obstinacy; infatuation.
entêter [ātɛ'te], *v.t.* to give a headache to; to make giddy, to intoxicate. **s'entêter,** *v.r.* to be stubborn, to persist (*in*); to be infatuated (*de*).
enthousiasme [ātu'zjasm], *n.m.* enthusiasm, rapture, ecstasy.
enthousiasmer [ātuzjas'me], *v.t.* to render enthusiastic, to enrapture. **s'enthousiasmer,** *v.r.* to be enthusiastic, to be in raptures (*de*).
enthousiaste [ātu'zjast], *a.* enthusiastic.—*n.* enthusiast.
entiché [āti'ʃe], *a.* infatuated, keen on.
entichement [ātiʃ'mā], *n.m.* infatuation, addiction.
enticher [āti'ʃe], *v.t.* to infatuate. **s'enticher,** *v.r.* to be infatuated with (*de*).
entier [ā'tje], *a.* (*fem.* **-ière**) entire, whole; total; positive.—*n.m.* entirety, totality; (*Arith.*) integral.
entièrement [ātjɛr'mā], *adv.* entirely, wholly.
entité [āti'te], *n.f.* entity.
entonner (1) [ātɔ'ne], *v.t.* to tun, to put into casks.
entonner (2) [ātɔ'ne], *v.t.* to begin to sing, to strike up.
entonnoir [ātɔ'nwa:r], *n.m.* funnel; shell hole.
entorse [ā'tɔrs], *n.f.* sprain; strain, twist.
entortillage [ātɔrti'ja:ʒ], **entortillement** [ātɔrtij'mā], *n.m.* entanglement; winding, coiling; abstruseness; subterfuge; equivocation.
entortiller [ātɔrti'je], *v.t.* to wrap, to roll round; to distort; to entangle. **s'entortiller,** *v.r.* to twist oneself round; to twine; to be obscure.
entour [ā'tu:r], *n.m.* (*used only in pl. except in the adverbial expression* **à l'entour,** around) environs, adjacent parts.
entourage [ātu'ra:ʒ], *n.m.* frame; entourage, friends, relations, circle, attendants.
entourer [ātu're], *v.t.* to surround; to gather round.
entournure [ātur'ny:r], *n.f.* arm-hole.
entracte [ā'trakt], *n.m.* intermission (*Theat.*); interlude.
entraide [ā'trɛd], *n.f.* (*no pl.*) mutual aid.
entraider (**s'**) or **entr'aider** (**s'**) [sātrɛ'de], *v.r.* to help one another.
entrailles [ā'tra:j], *n.f. pl.* intestines, entrails, bowels; (*fig.*) feelings, tenderness, pity.
entrain [ā'trɛ̃], *n.m.* warmth, heartiness; spirit, animation, life, go.
entraînant [ātrɛ'nā], *a.* captivating, seductive.
entraînement [ātrɛn'mā], *n.m.* enthusiasm, rapture; impulse, temptation; (*Spt.*) coaching, training.
entraîner [ātrɛ'ne], *v.t.* to drag along; to carry away; to win over; to involve; to train.
entraîneur [ātrɛ'nœ:r], *n.m.* (*fem.* **-euse**) trainer (*esp. of horses*); pace-maker; coach (*of teams*).
entrant [ā'trā], *a.* ingoing, incoming.—*n.m.* (*fem.* **-e**) person going *or* coming in.
entr'apercevoir [ātrapɛrsə'vwa:r], *v.t. irr.* (*conjug. like* RECEVOIR) to catch a quick glimpse of.
entr'appeler (**s'**) [sātra'ple], *v.r.* (*conjug. like* APPELER) to call one another.

entrave [ā'tra:v], *n.f.* clog, fetter, hobble; (*fig.*) hindrance, impediment.
entraver [ātra've], *v.t.* to shackle; to hinder, to thwart.
entre [ā:tr], *prep.* between, betwixt; among, amongst; into.
entrebâillé [ātrəba'je], *a.* ajar, half-open.
entrebâillement [ātrəbaj'mā], *n.m.* small opening, gap, chink.
entrebâiller [ātrəba'je], *v.t.* to half-open.
entrechat [ātrə'ʃa], *n.m.* caper in dancing, entrechat.
entrechoquement [ātrəʃɔk'mā], *n.m.* clash, collision, conflict.
entrechoquer (**s'**) [sātrəʃɔ'ke], *v.r.* to knock, to run *or* dash against each other.
entre-clos [ātrə'klo], *a.* half-closed; half-drawn.
entr'éclos [ātre'klo], *a.* half-opened (*flower*).
entrecôte [ātrə'ko:t], *n.f.* steak cut from between the ribs.
entrecoupé [ātrəku'pe], *a.* broken (*of words, speech etc.*).
entrecouper [ātrəku'pe], *v.t.* to intersect; to interrupt; to intersperse.
entrecroisement [ātrəkrwaz'mā], *n.m.* intersection, crossing.
entrecroiser [ātrəkrwa'ze], *v.t.* to intersect. **s'entrecroiser,** *v.r.* to cross one other, to intersect.
entre-deux [ātrə'dø], *n.m. inv.* partition; insertion (*of lace etc.*).
entrée [ā'tre], *n.f.* entry, entrance; mouth; reception; beginning; first course.
entrefaites [ātrə'fɛt], *n.f. pl.* interval, meantime; *sur ces entrefaites,* meanwhile.
entrefilet [ātrəfi'lɛ], *n.m.* (short) paragraph, note (*in a newspaper*).
entregent [ātrə'ʒā], *n.m.* tact, cleverness (*in dealing with people*).
entrelacement [ātrəlas'mā], *n.m.* interlacing, interweaving, entertwining.
entrelacer [ātrəla'se], *v.t.* (*conjug. like* COMMENCER) to interlace, to intertwine. **s'entrelacer,** *v.r.* to entwine, to twist round each other.
entrelardé [ātrəlar'de], *a.* interlarded; streaky.
entrelarder [ātrəlar'de], *v.t.* to lard.
entremêlement [ātrəmɛl'mā] *n.m.* intermixing, intermingling.
entremêler [ātrəmɛ'le], *v.t.* to intermingle, to intermix. **s'entremêler,** *v.r.* to intermingle, to meddle.
entremets [ātrə'mɛ], *n.m. inv.* side dish, sweet.
entremetteur [ātrəmɛ'tœ:r], *n.m.* (*fem.* **-euse**) go-between, mediator.
entremettre (**s'**) [sātrə'mɛtr], *v.r. irr.* (*conjug. like* METTRE) to interpose; to interfere, to meddle.
entremise [ātrə'mi:z], *n.f.* intervention, mediation.
entrepont [ātrə'pɔ̃], *n.m.* (*Naut.*) between decks; *passagers d'entrepont,* steerage passengers.
entreposer [ātrəpo'ze], *v.t.* to store, to warehouse; to put in bond.
entrepositaire [ātrəpozi'tɛ:r], *n.* bonder; depositor (*of goods*).
entrepôt [ātrə'po], *n.m.* bonded warehouse, store; mart, emporium, depot.

entreprenant [ãtrəprə'nã], *a.* enterprising, adventurous; daring, bold.

entreprendre [ãtrə'prã:dr], *v.t. irr.* (*conjug. like* PRENDRE) to undertake, to attempt; to contract for *or* to; to venture.—*v.i.* to encroach, to infringe (*sur*).

entrepreneur [ãtrəprə'nœ:r], *n.m.* (*fem.* **-euse**) contractor; master builder; *entrepreneur de pompes funèbres*, undertaker.

entreprise [ãtrə'pri:z], *n.f.* enterprise, undertaking; concern, company.

entrer [ã'tre], *v.i.* (*with aux.* ÊTRE) to enter, to come *or* go in; to run into.

entre-rail [ãtrə'ra:j], *n.m.* (*pl.* **-rails**) (Rail.) gauge.

entresol [ãtrə'sɔl], *n.m.* mezzanine, entresol (*rooms between the ground floor and the first floor*).

entre-temps [ãtrə'tã], *n.m. inv.* interval; *dans l'entre-temps*, meanwhile.—*adv.* meanwhile.

entretenir [ãtrət'ni:r], *v.t. irr.* (*conjug. like* TENIR) to hold together, to keep up, to keep in good order; to maintain, to support; to entertain. **s'entretenir**, *v.r.* to be kept up, to be maintained; to subsist; to converse.

entretien [ãtrə'tjɛ̃], *n.m.* maintenance, servicing (*of car etc.*); preservation; living, livelihood; conversation, interview, conference.

entrevoir [ãtrə'vwa:r], *v.t. irr.* (*conjug. like* VOIR) to catch a glimpse of; to foresee confusedly.

entrevue [ãtrə'vy], *n.f.* interview.

entr'ouvert [ãtru'vɛ:r], *a.* partly open, ajar; gaping.

entr'ouvrir [ãtru'vri:r], *v.t. irr.* (*conjug. like* OUVRIR) to open a little, to half-open. **s'entr'ouvrir**, *v.r.* to be ajar; to open up.

énumérateur [enymera'tœ:r], *n.m.* (*fem.* **-trice**) enumerator.

énumératif [enymera'tif], *a.* (*fem.* **-tive**) enumerative.

énumération [enymera'sjɔ̃], *n.f.* enumeration.

énumérer [enyme're] *v.t.* (*conjug. like* CÉDER) to enumerate, to count, to reckon.

envahir [ãva'i:r], *v.t.* to invade, to overrun; to encroach upon.

envahissant [ãvai'sã], *a.* invading, encroaching.

envahissement [ãvais'mã], *n.m.* invasion, overrunning; encroachment.

envahisseur [ãvai'sœ:r], *a.* (*fem.* **-euse**) invading, encroaching.—*n.m.* (*fem.* **-euse**) invader.

envaser [ãva'ze], *v.t.* to fill up *or* choke with silt. **s'envaser**, *v.r.* to stick fast in the mud; to silt up.

enveloppe [ã'vlɔp], *n.f.* wrapper, cover; envelope; exterior; tire casing.

enveloppement [ãvlɔp'mã], *n.m.* enveloping, wrapping up.

envelopper [ãvlɔ'pe], *v.t.* to envelop, to wrap up, to cover; to surround; to disguise. **s'envelopper**, *v.r.* to cover *or* wrap oneself up.

envenimement [ãvnima'mã], *n.m.* poisoning; aggravation (*of a quarrel*).

envenimer [ãvni'me], *v.t.* to poison; to inflame, to exasperate. **s'envenimer**, *v.r.* to be envenomed; to fester, to rankle.

envergure [ãvɛr'gy:r], *n.f.* spread (*of sail*); spread, span (*of a bird's wings, of an airplane*).

envers [ã'vɛ:r], *prep.* towards, to (*in respect of*).—*n.m.* wrong side, reverse side, back; *à l'envers*, on the wrong side, inside out.

envi (à l') [alã'vi], *adv. phr.* emulously, vying with each other.

enviable [ã'vjabl], *a.* enviable, to be envied.

envie [ã'vi], *n.f.* envy; desire, longing; birthmark; *avoir envie de*, to have a mind to, to long for, to feel like.

envier [ã'vje], *v.t.* to envy; to long for; to grudge.

envieux [ã'vjø], *a.* and *n.m.* (*fem.* **-euse**) envious, jealous (person).

environ [ãvi'rɔ̃], *adv.* about, nearly, thereabouts.—*n.m.* (*pl.*) environs, vicinity, neighborhood.

environnant [ãviro'nã], *a.* surrounding.

environner [ãviro'ne], *v.t.* to surround, to stand round, to encircle, to enclose.

envisager [ãviza'ʒe], *v.t.* (*conjug. like* MANGER) to look, to stare in the face; to face; to consider, to envisage.

envoi [ã'vwa], *n.m.* sending (*of thing sent*); packet, parcel, consignment, shipment; (*Pros.*) envoy.

envol [ã'vɔl], *n.m.* taking wing (*of birds*), taking off (*of airplanes*), start; *piste d'envol*, runway.

envolée [ãvɔ'le], *n.f.* flight; (*fig.*) élan.

envoler (s') [sãvɔ'le], *v.r.* to fly away; to take off; (*fig.*) to be carried off (*by the wind etc.*); (*fig.*) to disappear.

envoûtement [ãvut'mã], *n.m.* spell, magical charm.

envoûter [ãvu'te], *v.t.* to cast a spell on (*someone*).

envoyé [ãvwa'je], *n.m.* (*fem.* **-ée**) envoy; delegate, messenger; *envoyé spécial* (*of a paper*), special correspondent.

envoyer [ãvwa'je], *v.t. irr.* to send, to forward, to dispatch.

envoyeur [ãvwa'jœ:r], *n.m.* (*fem.* **-euse**) sender.

enzyme [ã'ʒim], *n.f.* enzyme.

éon [e'ɔ̃], *n.m.* eon.

épagneul [epa'nœl], *n.m.* spaniel.

épais [e'pɛ], *a.* thick, dense; thickset; (*fig.*) dull, gross.—*adv.* thick, thickly.

épaisseur [epɛ'sœ:r], *n.f.* thickness, density; stoutness; dullness.

épaissir [epɛ'si:r], *v.t.* to thicken.—*v.i.* and **s'epaissir**, *v.r.* to become thick, to grow big; to become heavy.

épaississement [epɛsis'mã], *n.m.* thickening.

épanchement [epãʃ'mã], *n.m.* pouring out, discharge; (*fig.*) outpouring (*emotion etc.*).

épancher [epã'ʃe], *v.t.* to pour out, to shed; to discharge. **s'épancher**, *v.r.* to be discharged, to overflow; to open one's heart.

épanchoir [epã'ʃwa:r], *n.m.* outlet, overflow.

épandre [e'pã:dr], *v.t.* to scatter, to strew; to shed (*light etc.*). **s'épandre**, *v.r.* to spread; (*fig.*) to stretch (*of a sheet of water etc.*).

épanoui [epa'nwi], *a.* in full bloom; (*fig.*) beaming.

épanouir [epa'nwi:r], *v.t.* to cause to open *or* expand; (*fig.*) to gladden. **s'épanouir**, *v.r.* to blossom, to open (*of flowers*); to brighten up (*of the face etc.*).

épanouissement

épanouissement [epanwis'mã], *n.m.* blossoming, opening (*of flowers*); (*fig.*) brightness, glow.

épargnant [epar'ɲã], *a.* sparing, saving; parsimonious.—*n.m.* (*fem.* **-e**) small investor.

épargne [e'parɲ], *n.f.* saving, thrift; parsimony; **caisse d'épargne**, savings bank.

épargner [epar'ɲe], *v.t.* to save; to spare; to economize.

éparpillement [eparpij'mã], *n.m.* scattering, dispersion.

éparpiller [eparpi'je], *v.t.* to scatter, to spread, to disperse; to squander.

épars [e'pa:r], *a.* scattered, dispersed, sparse; dishevelled (*of hair*).

épaté [epa'te], *a.* flat (*of noses*); (*fam.*) amazed.

épaule [e'po:l], *n.f.* shoulder.

épaulement [epol'mã], *n.m.* shoulder; (*Naut.*) bows; (*Fort.*) breast-work.

épauler [epo'le], *v.t.* to splay the shoulder (*a horse etc.*); to bring (*a rifle*) to the shoulder.

épaulette [epo'lɛt], *n.f.* shoulder strap; epaulet.

épave [e'pa:v], *n.f.* wreck; flotsam, jetsam; waif.

épée [e'pe], *n.f.* sword; (*fig.*) brand, steel.

épeler [e'ple], *v.t.* (*conjug. like* APPELER) to spell.

épellation [epɛla'sjõ], *n.f.* spelling.

éperdu [epɛr'dy], *a.* distracted, bewildered.

éperdument [epɛrdy'mã], *adv.* madly, distractedly.

éperon [e'prõ], *n.m.* spur; (*Arch.*) buttress, starling (*of a bridge etc.*); (*Naut.*) prow.

éperonné [epro'ne], *a.* spurred.

éperonner [epro'ne], *v.t.* to spur; to urge forward.

éperonnière [epro'njɛ:r], *n.f.* (*Bot.*) larkspur.

épervier [epɛr'vje], *n.m.* sparrow hawk; casting net.

épeuré [epø're], *a.* scared.

éphélide [efe'lid], *n.f.* sunburn; freckle.

éphémère [efe'mɛ:r], *a.* ephemeral, short-lived.—*n.m.* ephemera, May fly.

épi [e'pi], *n.m.* ear of corn; (*Rail.*) system of marshalling tracks, spur tracks.

épice [e'pis], *n.f.* spice.

épicé [epi'se], *a.* spiced; seasoned.

épicer [epi'se], *v.t.* (*conjug. like* COMMENCER) to spice.

épicerie [epi'sri], *n.f.* spices; grocery.

épicier [epi'sje], *n.m.* (*fem.* **-ière**) grocer.

épicurien [epiky'rjɛ̃], *a.* (*fem.* **-enne**) epicurean, voluptuous.—*n.m.* (*fem.* **-enne**) epicure.

épicurisme [epiky'rism], *n.m.* epicureanism, epicurism.

épidémie [epide'mi], *n.f.* epidemic.

épidémique [epide'mik], *a.* epidemic.

épiderme [epi'dɛrm], *n.m.* epidermis, cuticle.

épidermique [epidɛr'mik], *a.* epidermic, epidermal.

épier (1) [e'pje], *v.i.* to ear (*of grain*).

épier (2) [e'pje], *v.t.* to watch; to spy upon; to lie in wait for.

épieu [e'pjø], *n.m.* (*pl.* **-eux**) boar spear, hunting pole.

épigrammatique [epigrama'tik], *a.* epigrammatical.

épigrammatiste [epigrama'tist], *n.* epigrammatist.

épigramme [epi'gram], *n.f.* epigram.

épigraphe [epi'graf], *n.f.* epigraph.

épilation [epila'sjõ], *n.f.* depilation.

épilatoire [epila'twa:r], *a.* depilatory.

épilepsie [epilɛp'si], *n.f.* epilepsy.

épileptique [epilɛp'tik], *a.* and *n.* epileptic.

épiler [epi'le], *v.t.* to depilate. **s'épiler**, *v.r.* to pluck out one's hairs.

épileur [epi'lœ:r], *n.m.* (*fem.* **-euse**) depilator (*person*).

épilogue [epi'lɔg], *n.m.* epilogue.

épiloguer [epilɔ'ge], *v.t.* to censure, to criticize.—*v.i.* to carp, to find fault.

épilogueur [epilɔ'gœ:r], *a.* (*fem.* **-euse**) fault-finding.—*n.m.* (*fem.* **-euse**) critic, fault-finder, carper.

épiloir [epi'lwa:r], *n.m.* tweezers.

épinaie [epi'nɛ], *n.f.* brake, thorny thicket.

épinard [epi'na:r], *n.m.* spinach.

épine [e'pin], *n.f.* thorn, prickle; (*fig.*) obstacle, difficulty; (*Anat.*) spine.

épinette [epi'nɛt], *n.f.* *spinet; (*Bot.*) spruce.

épineux [epi'nø], *a.* (*fem.* **-euse**) thorny, prickly; (*fig.*) irritable; ticklish, intricate.

épingle [e'pɛ̃gl], *n.f.* pin; scarf pin, breast-pin.

épinglé [epɛ̃'gle], *a.* pinned; corded, terry.—*n.m.* terry velvet.

épingler [epɛ̃'gle], *v.t.* to pin.

épinglier [epɛ̃'glje], *n.m.* pin tray; (*fem.* **-ière**) pin maker.

épinière [epi'njɛ:r], *a.* (*Anat.*) spinal.

Épiphanie [epifa'ni], *n.f.* Epiphany.

épique [e'pik], *a.* epic(al).

épiscopal [episkɔ'pal], *a.* (*m.pl.* **-aux**) episcopal.

épiscopalien [episkɔpa'ljɛ̃], *a.* and *n.m.* (*fem.* **-enne**) episcopalian.

épiscopat [episkɔ'pa], *n.m.* episcopate, episcopacy.

épisode [epi'zɔd], *n.m.* episode.

épistolaire [epistɔ'lɛ:r], *a.* epistolary.

épitaphe [epi'taf], *n.f.* epitaph.

épithète [epi'tɛt], *n.f.* epithet.

épitomé [epito'me], *n.m.* epitome, abridgment.

épître [e'pi:tr], *n.f.* epistle, letter, missive.

éploré [eplɔ're], *a.* in tears, distressed.

épluchage [eply'ʃa:ʒ], **épluchement** [eplyʃ'mã], *n.m.* cleaning; picking; peeling.

éplucher [eply'ʃe], *v.t.* to pick; to clean; to peel; (*fig.*) to sift.

éplucheur [eply'ʃœ:r], *n.m.* (*fem.* **-euse**) picker; fault-finder, hair-splitter.

épluchures [eply'ʃy:r], *n.f. pl.* parings, peelings.

épointé [epwɛ̃'te], *a.* blunt (*pencil, needle*).

épointement [epwɛ̃t'mã], *n.m.* bluntness.

épointer [epwɛ̃'te], *v.t.* to break the point off, to blunt. **s'épointer**, *v.r.* to have its point broken off.

éponge [e'põ:ʒ], *n.f.* sponge.

épongeage [epõ'ʒa:ʒ], *n.m.* sponging.

éponger [epõ'ʒe], *v.t.* (*conjug. like* MANGER) to sponge.

épopée [epɔ'pe], *n.f.* epic.

époque [e'pɔk], *n.f.* epoch, period, era; time.

époumoner [epumɔ'ne], *v.t.* to tire the lungs of, to exhaust. **s'époumoner**, *v.r.* to tire one's lungs; (*fig.*) to shout oneself hoarse.

épouse [e'pu:z], *n.f.* spouse, bride, wife.

épouser [epu'ze], *v.t.* to marry, to wed; (*fig.*) to take up. **s'épouser**, *v.r.* to marry (*each other*).

épousetage [epus'ta:ʒ], *n.m.* dusting.
épousseter [epus'te], *v.t.* (*conjug. like* AP-PELER) to dust.
époussette [epu'sɛt], *n.f.* dusting brush, duster.
épouvantable [epuvɑ̃'tabl], *a.* frightful, dreadful, horrible, appalling.
épouvantablement [epuvɑ̃tablə'mɑ̃], *adv.* frightfully; dreadfully.
épouvantail [epuvɑ̃'ta:j], *n.m.* scarecrow; (*fig.*) bugbear.
épouvante [epu'vɑ̃:t], *n.f.* terror, fright; dismay.
épouvanter [epuvɑ̃'te], *v.t.* to terrify, to frighten. **s'épouvanter**, *v.r.* to be frightened *or* terrified.
époux [e'pu], *n.m.* husband, bridegroom; (*pl.*) married couple.
épreindre [e'prɛ̃:dr], *v.t. irr.* (*conjug. like* CRAINDRE) to squeeze out, to press.
éprendre (**s'**) [se'prɑ̃:dr], *v.r. irr.* (*conjug. like* PRENDRE) to fall in love (*de*).
épreuve [e'prœ:v], *n.f.* proof, test; ordeal; examination; (*Print.*) proof sheet; (*Phot.*) print.
épris [e'pri], *a.* in love, taken with.
éprouvé [epru've], *a.* tried, tested; stricken with misfortune.
éprouver [epru've], *v.t.* to try, to test; to put to the proof; (*fig.*) to feel, to experience.
éprouvette [epru'vɛt], *n.f.* gauge; test tube; eprouvette (*for testing gunpowder*); (*Surg.*) probe.
épuisable [epɥi'zabl], *a.* exhaustible.
épuisement [epɥiz'mɑ̃], *n.m.* exhaustion, draining; enervation.
épuiser [epɥi'ze], *v.t.* to exhaust, to drain; to use up; to tire out, to wear out. **s'épuiser**, *v.r.* to be exhausted; to use up one's strength.
épuisette [epɥi'zɛt], *n.f.* landing-net; scoop.
épurateur [epyra'tœ:r], *a.* (*fem.* **-trice**) purifying.—*n.m.* purifier.
épuratif [epyra'tif], *a.* (*fem.* **-tive**) purifying, refining.
épuration [epyra'sjɔ̃], *n.f.* purification; refining; (*Polit.*) purge.
épuratoire [epyra'twa:r], *a.* purifying.
épurement [epyr'mɑ̃], *n.m.* purifying.
épurer [epy're], *v.t.* to purify; to clarify; to refine; to purge. **s'épurer**, *v.r.* to be purified, to become pure.
équanime [ekwa'nim], *a.* even-tempered.
équanimité [ekwanimi'te], *n.f.* equanimity.
équarrir [eka'ri:r], *v.t.* to square; to cut up (*a carcass*).
équarrissage [ekari'sa:ʒ], **équarrissement** [ekaris'mɑ̃], *n.m.* squaring; squareness; flaying and cutting up (*of horses etc.*).
équarrisseur [ekari'sœ:r], *n.m.* knacker.
Équateur [ekwa'tœ:r], **l'**, *m.* Ecuador.
équateur [ekwa'tœ:r], *n.m.* equator.
équation [ekwa'sjɔ̃], *n.f.* equation.
équatorial [ekwatɔ'rjal], *a.* (*m. pl.* **-aux**) equatorial.
équatorien [ekwatɔ'rjɛ̃], *a.* (*fem.* **-enne**) Ecuadorean.—*n.m.* (**Équatorien**, *fem.* **-enne**) Ecuadorean (*person*).
équerre [e'kɛ:r], *n.f.* square, set-square.
équerrer [ekɛ're], *v.t.* to square, to bevel.
équestre [e'kɛstr], *a.* equestrian.

équilibre [eki'libr], *n.m.* equilibrium, poise, balance; (*Hist.*) balance of power.
équilibrer [ekili'bre], *v.t.* to equilibrate, to balance.
équilibriste [ekili'brist], *n.* tight-rope walker, acrobat.
équin [e'kɛ̃], *a.* equine; **pied équin**, club foot.
équinoxe [eki'nɔks], *n.m.* equinox.
équinoxial [ekinɔk'sjal], *a.* (*m. pl.* **-aux**) equinoctial.
équipage [eki'pa:ʒ], *n.m.* equipage; carriage; dress; gear, tackle; personnel, crew.
équipe [e'kip], *n.f.* train of boats; gang (*of workmen etc.*); team (*of sportsmen*).
équipement [ekip'mɑ̃], *n.m.* outfit, fitting out; equipment.
équiper [eki'pe], *v.t.* to equip, to fit out; to furnish; to man. **s'équiper**, *v.r.* to fit oneself out; to rig oneself out.
équitable [eki'tabl], *a.* equitable, just, fair.
équitablement [ekitablə'mɑ̃], *adv.* equitably, justly, fairly.
équitation [ekita'sjɔ̃], *n.f.* horsemanship, riding.
équité [eki'te], *n.f.* equity, fairness.
équivalence [ekiva'lɑ̃:s], *n.f.* equivalence.
équivalent [ekiva'lɑ̃], *a.* equivalent; tantamount (to).—*n.m.* equivalent.
équivaloir [ekiva'lwa:r], *v.i. irr.* (*conjug. like* VALOIR) to be equivalent, to be tantamount (*à*).
équivoque [eki'vɔk], *a.* equivocal, ambiguous; doubtful.—*n.f.* equivocation, ambiguity; evasion.
équivoquer [ekivɔ'ke], *v.t.* to equivocate, to speak ambiguously, to quibble.
érable [e'rabl], *n.m.* maple, maple tree.
éradication [eradika'sjɔ̃], *n.f.* eradication.
érafler [era'fle], *v.t.* to scratch slightly, to graze.
éraflure [era'fly:r], *n.f.* slight scratch, graze.
éraillé [era'je], *a.* frayed; wrinkled; bloodshot (*of the eyes*); raucous, hoarse (*of the voice*).
éraillement [eraj'mɑ̃], *n.m.* eversion of the eyelids; fraying; huskiness.
érailler [era'je], *v.t.* to unravel; to fray. **s'érailler**, *v.r.* to fray; to become bloodshot (*of the eyes*); to become husky (*of the voice*).
éraillure [era'jy:r], *n.f.* fret, fraying; scratch.
ère [ɛ:r], *n.f.* era, epoch.
érection [erɛk'sjɔ̃], *n.f.* erection, erecting.
éreinter [erɛ̃'te], *v.t.* to break the back (*of*); to tire out; to beat unmercifully; (*fig.*) to slate, to lash (*satire etc.*). **s'éreinter**, *v.r.* to break one's back, to tire oneself out, to drudge.
érésipèle [ERYSIPÈLE].
ergot [ɛr'go], *n.m.* spur (*of certain birds etc.*); catch, stop (*of machine*).
ergotage [ɛrgɔ'ta:ʒ], **ergotement** [ɛrgɔt'mɑ̃] *n.m.*, **ergoterie** [ɛrgɔ'tri], *n.f.* cavilling, quibbling.
ergoter [ɛrgɔ'te], *v.i.* (*colloq.*) to cavil; to wrangle.
ergoteur [ɛrgɔ'tœ:r], *a.* (*fem.* **-euse**) cavilling. —*n.m.* (*fem.* **-euse**) caviller, quibbler.
ériger [eri'ʒe], *v.t.* (*conjug. like* MANGER) to erect, to raise, to rear; to set up; to exalt. **s'ériger**, *v.r.* to set up for, to pose (*en*); to be erected.
ermitage [ɛrmi'ta:ʒ], *n.m.* hermitage.

ermite [εr'mit], *n.* hermit, recluse.
éroder [ero'de], *v.t.* to erode.
érosif [ero'zif], *a.* (*fem.* **-sive**) erosive.
érosion [ero'zjɔ̃], *n.f.* erosion.
érotique [ero'tik], *a.* erotic.
errant [ε'rɑ̃], *a.* wandering, roving, errant; erring; *chevalier errant,* knight errant.
erratique [εra'tik], *a.* erratic.
erre [ε:r], *n.f.* course, way; (*pl.*) track (*of a stag etc.*).
errements [εr'mɑ̃], *n.m.* (*used only in pl.*) manner, way; vagaries, follies.
errer [ε'rε], *v.i.* to wander, to stray; to range to rove; to err, to go astray.
erreur [ε'rœ:r], *n.f.* error, mistake.
erroné [εro'ne], *a.* erroneous, mistaken, false.
erronément [εrone'mɑ̃], *adv.* erroneously.
érudit [ery'di], *a.* erudite, learned.—*n.m.* (*fem.* **-e**) scholar, learned person.
érudition [erydi'sjɔ̃], *n.f.* erudition, scholarship.
éruptif [eryp'tif], *a.* (*fem.* **-tive**) eruptive.
éruption [eryp'sjɔ̃], *n.f.* eruption; cutting (*of teeth*); breaking out (*of a rash*).
érysipèle [erizi'pεl], **érésipèle** [erezi'pεl], *n.m.* erysipelas.
ès [εs], *contraction of* EN (I) LES (*survives only in a few set expressions*) in, of; *licencié ès lettres,* bachelor of arts.
escabeau [εska'bo], *n.m.* (*pl.* **-eaux**) stool; step ladder.
escabelle [εska'bεl], *n.f.* three-legged stool.
escadre [εs'ka:dr], *n.f.* (*Naut.*) squadron; (*Av.*) wing.
escadrille [εska'dri:j], *n.f.* small squadron, flotilla.
escadron [εska'drɔ̃], *n.m.* squadron (*of horse*).
escalade [εska'lad], *n.f.* scaling (*a wall*); rockclimbing; escalation (*of a war etc.*).
escalader [εskala'de], *v.t.* to scale, to climb over.
escale [εs'kal], *n.f.* port of call, stopping place.
escalier [εska'lje], *n.m.* staircase, stairs, steps; *escalier roulant,* escalator.
escalope [εska'lɔp], *n.f.* escalope, collop (*of veal*); steak (*of fish*).
escamotable [εskamɔ'tabl], *a.* which can be tucked away; (*Av.*) *train escamotable,* retractable landing-gear.
escamotage [εskamɔ'ta:ʒ], *n.m.* juggling, sleight of hand; (*fig.*) filching.
escamoter [εskamɔ'te], *v.t.* to conjure away; to pilfer, to make away with; (*Av.*) to retract (*the undercarriage*).
escamoteur [εskamɔ'tœ:r], *n.m.* (*fem.* **-euse**) juggler, conjurer; pilferer, pickpocket.
escapade [εska'pad], *n.f.* escapade, prank.
escarbille [εskar'bi:j], *n.f.* cinder (*of coal*).
escarboucle [εskar'bukl], *n.f.* carbuncle (*precious stone*).
escargot [εskar'go], *n.m.* snail (*edible*).
escarmouche [εskar'muʃ], *n.f.* skirmish; brush; (*fig.*) bickering.
escarmoucher [εskarmu'ʃe], *v.i.* to skirmish; (*fig.*) to bicker.
escarpé [εskar'pe], *a.* scarped, steep, precipitous; (*fig.*) difficult.
escarpement [εskarpə'mɑ̃], *n.m.* escarpment; steep face *or* slope.
escarpin [εskar'pɛ̃], *n.m.* pump, dancing shoe.

escarpolette [εskarpɔ'lεt], *n.f.* (*child's*) swing.
escarre *or* **eschare** [εs'ka:r], *n.f.* scab.
escient [ε'sjɑ̃], *n.m. used only in* **à bon escient**, wittingly, knowingly.
esclaffer (s') [sεskla'fe], *v.r.* to laugh noisily, to guffaw.
esclandre [εs'klɑ̃:dr], *n.m.* scandal, exposure, scene.
esclavage [εskla'va:ʒ], *n.m.* slavery; bondage.
esclave [εs'kla:v], *a.* slavish.—*n.* slave, bondsman; drudge.
escogriffe [εskɔ'grif], *n.m.* (*colloq.*) tall, lanky, ungainly fellow.
escompte [εs'kɔ̃:t], *n.m.* discount, rebate.
escompter [εskɔ̃'te], *v.t.* to discount; (*fig.*) to anticipate; *escompter un billet,* to cash a bill.
escorte [εs'kɔrt], *n.f.* escort; (*Navy*) convoy; (*fig.*) retinue, attendants.
escorter [εskɔr'te], *v.t.* to escort, to accompany, to attend.
escorteur [εskɔr'tœ:r], *n.m.* escort vessel.
escouade [εs'kwad], *n.f.* squad, small party (*of soldiers*); gang (*of workmen*).
escrime [εs'krim], *n.f.* fencing.
escrimer [εskri'me], *v.i.* to fence; (*fig.*) to have a trial of skill etc. **s'escrimer,** *v.r.* (*colloq.*) to strive; to try hard.
escrimeur [εskri'mœ:r], *n.m.* (*fem.* **-euse**) fencer.
escroc [εs'kro], *n.m.* sharper, swindler.
escroquer [εskro'ke], *v.t.* to swindle out of; to cheat.
escroquerie [εskro'kri], *n.f.* swindling.
espace [εs'pa:s], *n.m.* space, room; duration. —*n.f.* (*Print.*) space.
espacement [εspas'mɑ̃], *n.m.* interval; (*Print.*) spacing.
espacer [εspa'se], *v.t.* (*conjug. like* COMMENCER) to leave a space between; to separate. **s'espacer,** *v.r.* to become less frequent *or* numerous.
espadrille [εspa'dri:j], *n.f.* canvas shoe with cord soles.
Espagne [εs'paɲ], **l',** *f.* Spain.
espagnol [εspa'ɲɔl], *a.* Spanish.—*n.m.* Spanish (*language*); (**Espagnol,** *fem.* **-ole**) Spaniard.
espagnolette [εspaɲɔ'lεt], *n.f.* bolt of French window.
espalier [εspa'lje], *n.m.* espalier (*tree or wall*).
espèce [εs'pεs], *n.f.* species; sort, nature; (*pl.*) ready money, hard cash.
espérance [εspe'rɑ̃:s], *n.f.* hope, trust, expectation.
espéranto [εsperɑ̃'to], *n.m.* Esperanto.
espérer [εspe're], *v.t.* (*conjug. like* CÉDER) to hope for; to expect; to trust.—*v.i.* to hope; to put one's trust in.
espiègle [εs'pjεgl], *a.* and *n.* mischievous, roguish (person).
espièglerie [εspjεglə'ri], *n.f.* frolic, roguish trick, prank.
espion [εs'pjɔ̃], *n.m.* (*fem.* **-onne**) spy.
espionnage [εspjɔ'na:ʒ], *n.m.* espionage.
espionner [εspjɔ'ne], *v.t.* to spy, to pry into.
esplanade [εspla'nad], *n.f.* esplanade, parade.
espoir [εs'pwa:r], *n.m.* hope.
esprit [εs'pri], *n.m.* spirit, ghost; soul; mind, sense, intellect; wit; humor, character.
esquif [εs'kif], *n.m.* small boat.
esquille [εs'ki:j], *n.f.* splinter (*of a bone*).

esquimau [ɛski'mo], *a.* (*pl.* **-aux**) and *n.* (**Esquimau** or **Eskimo**) Eskimo.
esquinancie [ɛskinã'si], **cynancie** [sinã'si], *n.f.* quinsy.
esquisse [ɛs'kis], *n.f.* sketch, outline, rough draft *or* plan.
esquisser [ɛski'se], *v.t.* to sketch, to outline.
esquiver [ɛski've], *v.t.* to avoid, to elude; to duck; to dodge. **s'esquiver**, *v.r.* to escape; to give the slip.
essai [ɛ'sɛ], *n.m.* trial; attempt; experiment, testing; (*Rugby*) try; (*Lit.*) essay.
essaim [ɛ'sɛ̃], *n.m.* swarm; (*fig.*) crowd, host.
essaimer [ɛsɛ'me], *v.i.* to swarm; to hive off.
essarter [ɛsar'te], *v.t.* to clear, to grub (*land*).
essayage [ɛsɛ'jaːʒ] *n.m.* trying, testing; trying-on (*of clothes*).
essayer [ɛsɛ'je], *v.t.* (*conjug. like* PAYER) to try; to try on; to attempt; to assay.—*v.i.* to try, to make an attempt. **s'essayer**, *v.r.* to try one's strength *or* skill.
essayeur [ɛsɛ'jœːr], *n.m.* (*fem.* **-euse**) assayer; (*cloth*) fitter.
essayiste [ɛsɛ'jist], *n.* essayist.
essence [ɛ'sãːs], *n.f.* essence; gasoline; attar (*of roses*).
essentiel [ɛsã'sjɛl], *a.* (*fem.* **-elle**) essential, material.—*n.m.* essential, main point.
essentiellement [ɛsãsjɛl'mã], *adv.* essentially, absolutely, above all.
essieu [ɛ'sjø], *n.m.* (*pl.* **-eux**) axle-tree; spindle; pin (*of a block*); *écartement des essieux*, wheel base (*motor*); *essieu moteur*, driving-shaft.
essor [ɛ'sɔːr], *n.m.* flight, soaring; (*fig.*) impulse, vigor.
essorer [ɛsɔ're], *v.t.* to hang in the air to dry, to wring out (*washing*).
essoreuse [ɛsɔ'røːz], *n.f.* wringer, mangle.
essoriller [ɛsɔri'je], *v.t.* to cut the ears (*of a dog etc.*); to crop.
essoufflement [ɛsuflə'mã], *n.m.* panting, breathlessness.
essouffler [ɛsu'fle], *v.t.* to wind (*horses etc.*). **s'essouffler**, *v.r.* to be out of breath; to be winded.
essuie-glaces [ɛsɥi'glas], *n.m. pl.* windshield wipers.
essuie-main(s) [ɛsɥi'mɛ̃], *n.m. inv.* hand towel.
essuie-pieds [ɛsɥi'pje], *n.m. inv.* doormat.
essuyage [ɛsɥi'jaːʒ], *n.m.* wiping, drying.
essuyer [ɛsɥi'je], *v.t.* (*conjug. like* EMPLOYER) to wipe; to dry; to sustain, to endure, to undergo. **s'essuyer**, *v.r.* to dry oneself; *s'essuyer les mains, la figure etc.*, to dry one's hands, one's face etc.
est [ɛ], *n.m.* east.
estacade [ɛsta'kad], *n.f.* breakwater; pier *or* boom made of timbers.
estafette [ɛsta'fɛt], *n.f.* courier, express messenger; dispatch rider.
estafilade [ɛstafi'lad], *n.f.* cut, gash; slash, rent.
estaminet [ɛstami'nɛ], *n.m.* coffee house *or* room; tavern.
estampage [ɛstã'paːʒ], *n.m.* stamping (*of metal etc.*).
estampe [ɛs'tãp], *n.f.* print, engraving.
estamper [ɛstã'pe], *v.t.* to stamp, to punch.
estampeur [ɛstã'pœːr], *a.* (*fem.* **-euse**) stamp-

ing.—*n.m.* (*fem.* **-euse**) stamper.—*n.f.* (**-euse**) stamping machine.
estampillage [ɛstãpi'jaːʒ], *n.m.* stamping, marking.
estampille [ɛstã'piːj], *n.f.* stamp, mark, trade mark.
estampiller [ɛstãpi'je], *v.t.* to stamp, to mark.
esthétique [ɛste'tik], *a.* esthetic.—*n.f.* esthetics.
Esthonie [ɛstɔ'ni], l', *f.* Estonia.
esthonien [ɛstɔ'njɛ̃], *a.* (*fem.* **-enne**) Estonian.—*n.m.* Estonian (*language*); (**Esthonien**, *fem.* **-enne**) Estonian (*person*).
estimable [ɛsti'mabl], *a.* estimable.
estimateur [ɛstima'tœːr], *n.m.* (*fem.* **-trice**) appraiser, valuer.
estimation [ɛstima'sjɔ̃], *n.f.* estimation, appraising, valuation, estimate.
estime [ɛs'tim], *n.f.* esteem, regard, estimation; (*Naut.*) reckoning.
estimer [ɛsti'me], *v.t.* to estimate, to value, to assess; to esteem; to deem. **s'estimer**, *v.r.* to esteem oneself; to deem oneself.
estival [ɛsti'val], *a.* (*m. pl.* **-aux**) estival, summer (*plant, resort etc.*).
estivant [ɛsti'vã], *n.m.* (*fem.* **-e**) summer visitor.
estomac [ɛstɔ'ma], *n.m.* stomach; (*fig.*) pluck.
estompage [ɛstɔ̃'paːʒ], *n.m.* (*Drawing*) stumping.
estompe [ɛ'stɔ̃ːp], *n.f.* (*Drawing*) stump.
estomper [ɛstɔ̃'pe], *v.t.* (*Drawing*) to stump; to shade off, to blur. **s'estomper**, *v.r.* to become blurred.
Estonie [ESTHONIE].
estonien [ESTHONIEN].
estrade [ɛs'trad], *n.f.* platform, stand, stage.
estragon [ɛstra'gɔ̃], *n.m.* (*Bot.*) tarragon.
estropié [ɛstrɔ'pje], *a.* crippled, lame, disabled.—*n.m.* (*fem.* **-ée**) cripple.
estropier [ɛstrɔ'pje], *v.t.* to cripple, to maim, to disable; (*fig.*) to distort, to mangle.
estuaire [ɛs'tɥɛːr], *n.m.* estuary.
esturgeon [ɛstyr'ʒɔ̃], *n.m.* sturgeon.
et [e], *conj.* and.
étable [e'tabl], *n.f.* shed (*for oxen, sheep, goats etc.*); stall; pigsty, sty.
établi [eta'bli], *n.m.* bench (*tailor's etc.*).
établir [eta'bliːr], *v.t.* to fix, to erect, to set up; to establish, to found; to assert. **s'établir**, *v.r.* to establish oneself; to take up one's residence; to settle down; to set up in business.
établissement [etablis'mã], *n.m.* establishment, setting up; placing, erecting; proving; imposition (*of taxes*).
étage [e'taːʒ], *n.m.* storey, floor, flight (*of stairs*); (*fig.*) stage; tier; (*Geol., Mining*) layer, stratum.
étager [eta'ʒe], *v.t.* (*conjug. like* MANGER) to dispose in tiers. **s'étager**, *v.r.* to rise tier upon tier.
étagère [eta'ʒɛːr], *n.f.* whatnot, set of shelves, shelf.
étai [e'tɛ], *n.m.* stay, shore, prop, strut.
étaiement [ÉTAYAGE].
étain [e'tɛ̃], *n.m.* tin; pewter.
étal [e'tal], *n.m.* (*pl.* **-aux** *or* **-als**) butcher's stall, butcher's shop.
étalage [eta'laːʒ], *n.m.* laying out of goods for sale; goods exposed for sale; shop window, frontage; (*fig.*) showing off.

étalager [etala'ʒe], *v.t.* (*conjug. like* MANGER) to display (*goods*) for sale.

étalagiste [etala'ʒist], *n.* stall keeper; window dresser.

étale [e'tal], *a.* slack (*of water or wind*).

étalement [etal'mã] *n.m.* display, parade; staggering (*of holidays*).

étaler [eta'le], *v.t.* to expose for sale; to spread out; to display; (*Naut.*) to stem (*current*); to weather (*gale*). **s'étaler**, *v.r.* to stretch oneself out, to sprawl; to show off.

étalon (1) [eta'lɔ̃], *n.m.* stallion.

étalon (2) [eta'lɔ̃]. *n.m.* standard (*of weights and measures*).

étalonnage [etalɔ'na:ʒ], **étalonnement** [etalɔn'mã], *n.m.* standardization; stamping (*of weights etc.*); gauging.

étalonner [etalɔ'ne], *v.t.* to standardize; to gauge.

étalonneur [etalɔ'nœ:r], *n.m.* inspector of weights and measures.

étamage [eta'ma:ʒ], *n.m.* tinning; quick-silvering (*of glass*).

étamer [eta'me], *v.t.* to tin; to quicksilver.

étameur [eta'mœ:r], *n.m.* tinner; silverer (*of mirrors*).

étamine (1) [eta'min], *n.f.* sieve, strainer; (*Naut.*) bunting.

étamine (2) [eta'min], *n.f.* (*Bot.*) stamen.

étampe [e'tã:p], *n.f.* die; punch.

étamper [etã'pe], *v.t.* to punch (*horse-shoes etc.*); to stamp (*sheet metal etc.*).

étanche [e'tã:ʃ], *a.* water-tight, air-tight etc.

étanchement [etãʃ'mã], *n.m.* stanching, stopping; slaking; quenching.

étancher [etã'ʃe], *v.t.* to stanch, to stop; to render water-tight; (*fig.*) to quench.

étang [e'tã], *n.m.* pond, mere, pool.

étape [e'tap], *n.f.* halting-place, stage, station; day's march.

état [e'ta], *n.m.* state, case, condition; circumstance, predicament; statement; list, estimate; profession.

étatique [eta'tik], *a.* nationalized.

étatiser [etati'ze], *v.t.* to nationalize.

étatisme [eta'tism], *n.m.* State socialism, State control, nationalization.

état-major [etama'ʒɔ:r], *n.m.* (*pl.* **états-majors**) (*Mil.*) staff, general staff.

étau [e'to], *n.m.* (*pl.* **-aux**) (*Tech.*) vise.

étayage [etɛ'ja:ʒ], **étayement** [etej'mã], **étaiement** [etɛ'mã], *n.m.* staying, shoring, supporting.

étayer [etɛ'je], *v.t.* (*conjug. like* PAYER) to stay, to shore; to support (*a theory etc.*).

été [e'te], *n.m.* summer; (*C*) **Été des Sauvages**, Indian summer.

éteignoir [etɛ'ɲwa:r], *n.m.* extinguisher (*for candles*).

éteindre [e'tɛ̃:dr], *v.t.* irr. (*conjug. like* CRAINDRE) to put out, to extinguish; to appease; to destroy. **s'éteindre**, *v.r.* to be extinguished, to be put out; to die out; to become extinct.

éteint [e'tɛ̃], *a.* extinguished; extinct; (*fig.*) dull.

étendard [etã'da:r], *n.m.* standard, banner, flag.

étendre [e'tã:dr], *v.t.* to extend, to spread out; to stretch; to dilute; to prolong; to lay (down) (*a person*). **s'étendre**, *v.r.* to stretch oneself out; to reach, to extend; to dwell on.

étendu [etã'dy], *a.* outstretched, outspread; extensive; diluted.

étendue [etã'dy], *n.f.* extent; scope, length.

éternel [etɛr'nɛl], *a.* (*fem.* **-elle**) eternal, everlasting.—*n.m.* (**l'Éternel**) God, the Eternal.

éternellement [etɛrnɛl'mã], *adv.* eternally.

éterniser [etɛrni'ze], *v.t.* to perpetuate. **s'éterniser**, *v.r.* to be perpetuated, to last forever.

éternité [etɛrni'te], *n.f.* eternity.

éternuement or **éternûment** [etɛrny'mã], *n.m.* sneezing, sneeze.

éternuer [etɛr'nɥe], *v.i.* to sneeze.

éternueur [etɛr'nɥœ:r], *n.m.* (*fem.* **-euse**) sneezer.

éteule [e'tœ:l], *n.f.* stubble.

éther [e'tɛ:r], *n.m.* ether.

éthéré [ete're], *a.* ethereal.

éthériser [eteri'ze], *v.t.* to etherize.

Éthiopie [etjɔ'pi], **l'**, *f.* Ethiopia.

éthiopien [etjɔ'pjɛ̃], *a.* (*fem.* **-enne**) Ethiopian.—*n.m.* (**Éthiopien**, *fem.* **-enne**) Ethiopian (*person*).

éthique [e'tik], *a.* ethic(al).—*n.f.* ethics, morals.

ethnique [ɛt'nik], *a.* ethnic(al).

ethnographe [ɛtnɔ'graf], *n.* ethnographer.

ethnographie [ɛtnɔgra'fi], *n.f.* ethnography.

ethnographique [ɛtnɔgra'fik], *a.* ethnographic.

ethnologie [ɛtnɔlɔ'ʒi], *n.f.* ethnology.

ethnologique [ɛtnɔlɔ'ʒik], *a.* ethnological.

ethnologue [ɛtnɔ'lɔg], **ethnologiste** [ɛtnɔlɔ'ʒist], *n.* ethnologist.

éthologie [etɔlɔ'ʒi], *n.f.* ethology.

éthyle [e'ti:l], *n.m.* ethyl.

étiage [e'tja:ʒ], *n.m.* low-water mark; (*fig.*) level.

Étienne [e'tjɛn], *m.* Stephen.

étincelant [etɛ̃s'lã], *a.* sparkling, glittering, glistening.

étinceler [etɛ̃s'le], *v.i.* (*conjug. like* APPELER) to sparkle, to flash; to gleam, to glitter.

étincelle [etɛ̃'sɛl], *n.f.* spark, flash; brilliance.

étincellement [etɛ̃sɛl'mã], *n.m.* sparkling, twinkling, scintillation.

étiolement [etjɔl'mã], *n.m.* etiolation, sickliness (*of plants etc.*); paleness, emaciation.

étioler [etjɔ'le], *v.t.* to etiolate (*plants*); (*fig.*) to enervate. **s'étioler**, *v.r.* to become etiolated (*of plants*); (*fig.*) to waste away.

étique [e'tik], *a.* consumptive; emaciated.

étiqueter [etik'te], *v.t.* (*conjug. like* APPELER) to label, to ticket.

étiquette [eti'kɛt], *n.f.* ticket, label, tag; etiquette.

étirage [eti'ra:ʒ], *n.m.* stretching.

étirer [eti're], *v.t.* to stretch; to lengthen. **s'étirer**, *v.r.* to stretch one's limbs.

étisie [eti'zi], *n.f.* consumption.

étoffe [e'tɔf], *n.f.* material; stuff, cloth; quality, worth; (*C*) **étoffe du pays**, homespun.

étoffé [etɔ'fe], *a.* stuffed full; upholstered; stout, substantial.

étoffer [etɔ'fe], *v.t.* to stuff; to upholster.

étoile [e'twal], *n.f.* star; (*fig.*) fate, destiny; blaze (*on horse's head*); star (*crack in glass*).

étoilé [etwa'le], *a.* starry; star-shaped.

étoiler [etwa'le], *v.t.* to star, to stud with stars; to crack (*of glass*). **s'étoiler**, *v.r.* to star, to crack (*of glass*).

étole [e′tɔl], *n.f.* stole.
étonnamment [etɔna′mã], *adv.* astonishingly, wonderfully, amazingly.
étonnant [etɔ′nã], *a.* astonishing, wonderful, marvellous.
étonnement [etɔn′mã], *n.m.* astonishment, amazement; wonder; crack, fissure.
étonner [etɔ′ne], *v.t.* to astonish, to amaze, to astound; to shock; to cause to crack. **s'étonner**, *v.r.* to be astonished, to wonder; to become cracked.
étouffant [etu′fã], *a.* suffocating, sultry, close.
étouffement [etuf′mã], *n.m.* suffocation.
étouffer [etu′fe], *v.t.* to suffocate, to choke, to smother; (*fig.*) to stifle, to hush up; to deaden (*sound etc.*).—*v.i.* to choke, to suffocate. **s'étouffer**, *v.r.* to be choking, to be suffocated; to swelter.
étoupe [e′tup], *n.f.* tow, oakum.
étouper [etu′pe], *v.t.* to stop (*with tow or oakum*); to caulk.
étoupiller [etupi′je], *v.t.* to prime (*a friction tube*).
étourderie [eturdə′ri], *n.f.* heedlessness, thoughtlessness; blunder.
étourdi [etur′di], *a.* giddy, thoughtless, heedless.—*n.m.* (*fem.* **-e**) madcap.
étourdiment [eturdi′mã], *adv.* heedlessly, thoughtlessly.
étourdir [etur′di:r], *v.t.* to stun, to deafen, to make giddy; to din; to astound. **s'étourdir**, *v.r.* to divert one's thoughts; to try to forget something.
étourdissant [eturdi′sã], *a.* deafening; stunning, astounding.
étourdissement [eturdis′mã], *n.m.* dizziness, giddiness; stupefaction; shock.
étourneau [etur′no], *n.m.* (*pl.* **-eaux**) starling; (*fig.*) giddy fellow.
étrange [e′trã:ʒ], *a.* strange, odd, queer.
étrangement [etrãʒ′mã], *adv.* strangely, queerly, extraordinarily.
étranger [etrã′ʒe], *a.* (*fem.* **-ère**) foreign; strange; unknown; irrelevant.—*n.m.* (*fem.* **-ère**) foreigner, alien; stranger; *à l'étranger*, abroad.
étrangeté [etrãʒ′te], *n.f.* strangeness, oddness.
étranglé [etrã′gle], *a.* strangled; restricted, scanty, too narrow.
étranglement [etrãglə′mã], *n.m.* strangling; garotting; constriction.
étrangler [etrã′gle], *v.t.* to strangle, to choke, to stifle; to constrict, to confine; (*fig.*) to smother, to suppress.—*v.i.* to be choked, to be short of breath. **s'étrangler**, *v.r.* to strangle oneself; to choke.
étrangleur [etrã′glœ:r], *n.m.* (*fem.* **-euse**) strangler; garotter.
être [ɛ:tr], *v.i. irr.* to be, to exist; to belong (*à*); to stand; to take part (*à*); to be a member (*de*).—*n.m.* being, existence; creature.
étreindre [e′trẽ:dr], *v.t. irr.* (*conjug. like* CRAINDRE) to embrace, to clasp, to grip.
étreinte [e′trẽ:t], *n.f.* embrace, hug; grip.
étrenne [e′trɛn], *n.f.* New Year's gift (*usually in pl.*); gift, present.
étrenner [etrɛ′ne], *v.t.* to give a New Year's gift; to handsel; to try *or* put on for the first time; to buy the first lot from.
étrier [etri′e], *n.m.* stirrup; (*Surg.*) caliper.
étrille [e′tri:j], *n.f.* curry-comb.

étriller [etri′je], *v.t.* to curry, to comb (*a horse*); (*fig.*) to fleece; to drub.
étriper [etri′pe], *v.t.* to gut (*an animal*).
étriqué [etri′ke], *a.* scanty, narrow, curtailed.
étriquer [etri′ke], *v.t.* to shorten, to curtail, to make too small.
étrivière [etri′vjɛ:r], *n.f.* stirrup leather.
étroit [e′trwa], *a.* narrow, tight, strait; limited; (*fig.*) strict, rigorous.
étroitement [etrwat′mã], *adv.* narrowly, tightly; intimately, closely.
étroitesse [etrwa′tɛs], *n.f.* narrowness, straitness; tightness, closeness.
Étrurie [etry′ri], **l'**, *f.* Etruria.
étrusque [e′trysk], *a.* Etruscan.—*n.m.* Etruscan (*language*).—*n.* (**Étrusque**) Etruscan (*person*).
étude [e′tyd], *n.f.* study; room for study; time of preparation; office, practice (*of attorneys*); essay, article.
étudiant [ety′djã], *n.m.* (*fem.* **-e**) student; undergraduate.
étudié [ety′dje], *a.* studied; affected.
étudier [ety′dje], *v.t.* to study, to learn; to practice (*music*); to rehearse (*a play*); to observe.—*v.i.* to study, to learn; to practice (*music*). **s'étudier**, *v.r.* to make (*it*) one's study, to school oneself.
étui [e′tɥi], *n.m.* case, box, sheath.
étuve [e′ty:v], *n.f.* sweating room; stove; drying room; incubator.
étuvée [ety′ve], *n.f.* stew.
étuver [ety′ve], *v.t.* to stew; (*Med.*) to bathe, to foment.
étymologie [etimɔlɔ′ʒi], *n.f.* etymology.
étymologique [etimɔlɔ′ʒik], *a.* etymological.
étymologiste [etimɔlɔ′ʒist], *n.* etymologist.
eucharistie [økaris′ti], *n.f.* eucharist.
eucharistique [økaris′tik], *a.* eucharistic.
eugénique [øʒe′nik], *n.f.*, **eugénisme** [øʒe′nism], *n.m.* eugenics.
euh [ø], *int.* aha! oh! hum!
eunuque [ø′nyk], *n.m.* eunuch.
euphémique [øfe′mik], *a.* euphemistic.
euphémisme [øfe′mism], *n.m.* euphemism.
euphonie [øfɔ′ni], *n.f.* euphony.
euphonique [øfɔ′nik], *a.* euphonious.
Euphrate [ø′frat], **l'**, *m.* the Euphrates.
euphuïsme [øfy′ism], *n.m.* euphuism.
eurasien [øra′zjẽ], *a.* (*fem.* **-enne**) Eurasian.—*n.m.* (**Eurasien**, *fem.* **-enne**) Eurasian (*person*).
Euripide [øri′pid], *m.* Euripides.
Europe [ø′rɔp], *f.* (*Myth.*) Europa; *l'Europe*, (*Geog.*) Europe.
européaniser [ørɔpeani′ze], *v.t.* to Europeanize.
européen [ørɔpe′ɛ̃], *a.* (*fem.* **-éenne**) European.—*n.m.* (**Européen**, *fem.* **-éenne**) European (*person*).
euthanasie [øtana′zi], *n.f.* euthanasia.
eux [ø], *pron. pers. m. pl.* (*fem.* **-elles**) they; them.
évacuant [eva′kɥã], **évacuatif** [evakɥa′tif] (*fem.* **-tive**), *a.* and *n.m.* evacuant.
évacuation [evakɥa′sjɔ̃], *n.f.* evacuation; ejection.
évacué [eva′kɥe], *n.m.* (*fem.* **-ée**) evacuee.
évacuer [eva′kɥe], *v.t.* to evacuate; to throw off, to eject, to clear. **s'évacuer**, *v.r.* to discharge (*into*).

évadé [eva'de], *a.* and *n.m.* (*fem.* **-ée**) escaped (*person*); escapee.

évader (s') [seva'de], *v.r.* to escape; to get away *or* out of (*de*).

évaluable [eva'lɥabl], *a.* appraisable.

évaluateur [evalɥa'tœ:r], *n.m.* (*fem.* **-trice**) valuer, appraiser.

évaluation [evalɥa'sjɔ̃], *n.f.* valuation, estimate.

évaluer [eva'lɥe], *v.t.* to value, to estimate, to appreciate.

évangélique [evɑ̃ʒe'lik], *a.* evangelical.

évangéliser [evɑ̃ʒeli'ze], *v.t.* to evangelize, to preach the Gospel to.

évangélisme [evɑ̃ʒe'lism], *n.m.* evangelism.

évangéliste [evɑ̃ʒe'list], *n.m.* evangelist.

évangile [evɑ̃'ʒil], *n.m.* Gospel.

évanouir (s') [seva'nwi:r], *v.r.* to faint, to swoon, to lose consciousness; (*fig.*) to vanish, to disappear.

évanouissement [evanwis'mɑ̃], *n.m.* swoon, fainting fit; disappearance; (*Math.*) cancelling out.

évaporatif [evapɔra'tif], *a.* (*fem.* **-tive**) evaporative.

évaporation [evapɔra'sjɔ̃], *n.f.* evaporation.

évaporé [evapɔ're], *a.* and *n.m.* (*fem.* **-ée**) frivolous, thoughtless (person).

évaporer [evapɔ're], *v.t.* to evaporate; (*fig.*) to exhale, to give vent to; *évaporer son chagrin,* to give vent to one's grief. **s'évaporer,** *v.r.* to evaporate; (*fig.*) to get giddy.

évasé [eva'ze], *a.* wide, bell-shaped; flared (*skirt*).

évasement [evɑz'mɑ̃], *n.m.* width, widening (*at the mouth of a vase etc.*); flare (*of a skirt*).

évaser [eva'ze], *v.t.* to widen (*an opening*); to flare (*a skirt*). **s'évaser,** *v.r.* to be widened; to extend, to spread.

évasif [eva'zif], *a.* (*fem.* **-sive**) evasive.

évasion [eva'zjɔ̃], *n.f.* escape, flight; evasion; escapism.

évasivement [evaziv'mɑ̃], *adv.* evasively.

évêché [evɛ'ʃe], *n.m.* bishopric, episcopate, see; bishop's palace.

éveil [e've:j], *n.m.* awakening; warning, hint, alarm.

éveillé [evɛ'je], *a.* wide-awake; lively, sprightly; sharp, intelligent.

éveiller [evɛ'je], *v.t.* to awaken, to rouse; to excite, to enliven. **s'éveiller,** *v.r.* to wake up; to become animated.

événement [evɛn'mɑ̃], *n.m.* event, occurrence; result; climax; emergency.

évent [e'vɑ̃], *n.m.* open air; vent hole, air hole; (*fig.*) flatness, vapidness.

éventail [evɑ̃'ta:j], *n.m.* (*pl.* **éventails**) fan; fan-light.

éventaire [evɑ̃'tɛ:r], *n.m.* flat tray (*carried by hawkers*); street stall.

éventé [evɑ̃'te], *a.* fanned, aired; flat, stale (*beer etc.*); (*fig.*) giddy, thoughtless.

éventer [evɑ̃'te], *v.t.* to fan; to winnow(*grain*); to air; to let (*wine etc.*) get flat; to get wind of; to divulge. **s'éventer,** *v.r.* to fan oneself; to evaporate; to become flat; to be divulged.

éventrer [evɑ̃'tre], *v.t.* to disembowel, to gut (*fish etc.*); to rip up, to break open. **s'éventrer,** *v.r.* to rip one's bowels open; to commit hara-kiri.

éventualité [evɑ̃tɥali'te], *n.f.* contingency, eventuality.

éventuel [evɑ̃'tɥɛl], *a.* (*fem.* **-elle**) contingent, possible.

éventuellement [evɑ̃tɥɛl'mɑ̃], *adv.* possibly; on occasion.

évêque [e'vɛ:k], *n.m.* bishop.

évertuer (s') [sevɛr'tɥe], *v.r.* to strive, to exert *or* bestir oneself.

éviction [evik'sjɔ̃], *n.f.* eviction, ejectment.

évidemment [evida'mɑ̃], *adv.* evidently.

évidence [evi'dɑ̃:s], *n.f.* obviousness, clearness; conspicuousness.

évident [evi'dɑ̃], *a.* evident, plain, clear, obvious.

évider [evi'de], *v.t.* to hollow, to groove, to scoop out.

évier [e'vje], *n.m.* sink.

évincer [evɛ̃'se], *v.t.* (*conjug. like* COMMENCER) to evict, to eject, to oust.

éviscérer [evise're], *v.t.* (*conjug. like* CÉDER) to disembowel.

évitable [evi'tabl], *a.* avoidable.

évitement [evit'mɑ̃], *n.m.* (*Rail.*) siding, shunting; by-pass.

éviter [evi'te], *v.t.* to shun, to avoid, to evade; to abstain from.

évocateur [evɔka'tœ:r], *a.* (*fem.* **-trice**) evocative.

évocation [evɔka'sjɔ̃], *n.f.* evocation; recollection.

évolué [evɔ'lɥe], *a.* highly civilized.

évoluer [evɔ'lɥe], *v.i.* to evolve; to develop.

évolution [evɔly'sjɔ̃], *n.f.* evolution.

évoquer [evɔ'ke], *v.t.* to evoke; to allude to.

exacerbation [ɛgzasɛrba'sjɔ̃], *n.f.* exacerbation.

exacerber [ɛgzasɛr'be], *v.t.* to exacerbate.

exact [eg'zakt], *a.* exact, correct; punctual.

exactement [ɛgzaktə'mɑ̃], *adv.* exactly, accurately; punctually.

exaction [ɛgzak'sjɔ̃], *n.f.* exaction, impost, extortion.

exactitude [ɛgzakti'tyd], *n.f.* exactness, accuracy; punctuality.

exagération [ɛgzaʒera'sjɔ̃], *n.f.* exaggeration; overrating.

exagérer [ɛgzaʒe're], *v.t.* (*conjug. like* CÉDER) to exaggerate, to magnify.

exaltation [ɛgzalta'sjɔ̃], *n.f.* exaltation; extolling.

exalté [ɛgzal'te], *a.* exalted, feverish.—*n.m.* (*fem.* **-ée**) enthusiast, fanatic.

exalter [ɛgzal'te], *v.t.* to exalt, to magnify; to excite, to inflame. **s'exalter,** *v.r.* to become excited, to be elated.

examen [ɛgza'mɛ̃], *n.m.* examination; inspection; research.

examinateur [ɛgzamina'tœ:r], *n.m.* (*fem.* **-trice**) examiner.

examiner [ɛgzami'ne], *v.t.* to examine, to inspect, to survey; to discuss, to investigate. **s'examiner,** *v.r.* to examine or search oneself; to observe each other attentively.

exaspération [ɛgzaspera'sjɔ̃], *n.f.* exasperation, aggravation.

exaspérer [ɛgzaspe're], *v.t.* (*conjug. like* CÉDER) to exasperate, to incense, to inflame; to aggravate (*pain etc.*). **s'exaspérer,** *v.r.* to become exasperated *or* incensed; to become aggravated (*pain etc.*).

exaucer [ɛgzo'se], *v.t.* (*conjug. like* COM-MENCER) to hearken to, to grant.

excavateur [ɛkskava'tœːr], *n.m.* excavator, digging machine.

excavation [ɛkskava'sjɔ̃], *n.f.* excavation.

excaver [ɛkska've], *v.t.* to excavate, to hollow out.

excédant [ɛkse'dɑ̃], *a.* exceeding, excessive; unbearable.

excédent [ɛkse'dɑ̃], *n.m.* surplus, excess.

excéder [ɛkse'de], *v.t.* (*conjug. like* CÉDER) to exceed, to surpass, to rise above (*in level, price etc.*); (*fig.*) to wear out, to tire out.

excellemment [ɛksɛla'mɑ̃], *adv.* excellently, surpassingly.

Excellence [ɛksɛ'lɑ̃ːs], *f.* (*title*) Excellency.

excellence [ɛksɛ'lɑ̃ːs], *n.f.* excellence; *par excellence*, pre-eminently, above all.

excellent [ɛksɛ'lɑ̃], *a.* excellent; delightful.

excellentissime [ɛksɛlɑ̃ti'sim], *a.* most excellent.

exceller [ɛksɛ'le], *v.i.* to excel, to be eminent; to surpass.

excentricité [ɛksɑ̃trisi'te], *n.f.* eccentricity.

excentrique [ɛksɑ̃'trik], *a.* eccentric, odd.

excepté [ɛksɛp'te], *prep.* except, excepting, but.

excepter [ɛksɛp'te], *v.t.* to except.

exception [ɛksɛp'sjɔ̃], *n.f.* exception.

exceptionnel [ɛksɛpsjɔ'nɛl], *a.* (*fem.* **-elle**) exceptional; rare, infrequent.

excès [ɛk'sɛ], *n.m. inv.* excess; (*pl.*) riot, out-rages, violence.

excessif [ɛksɛ'sif], *a.* (*fem.* **-ive**) excessive, exorbitant; intemperate.

excessivement [ɛksɛsiv'mɑ̃], *adv.* excessively, to excess.

excise [ɛk'siːz], *n.f.* excise; excise office.

excitabilité [ɛksitabili'te], *n.f.* excitability.

excitable [ɛksi'tabl], *a.* excitable.

excitant [ɛksi'tɑ̃], *a.* exciting.—*n.m.* (*Med.*) excitant.

excitateur [ɛksita'tœːr], *a.* (*fem.* **-trice**) provocative.—*n.m.* (*fem.* **-trice**) instigator.

excitation [ɛksita'sjɔ̃], *n.f.* exciting, excita-tion; excitement.

exciter [ɛksi'te], *v.t.* to excite, to stir up, to rouse; to stimulate, to animate; to instigate, to prompt; to irritate. **s'exciter**, *v.r.* to excite oneself, to work oneself up; to encourage each other; to be excited.

exclamation [ɛksklamɑ'sjɔ̃], *n.f.* exclamation; *point d'exclamation*, exclamation mark.

exclamer (s') [ɛkskla'me], *v.r.* to exclaim, to cry out; to protest.

exclure [ɛks'klyːr], *v.t. irr.* (*conjug. like* CONCLURE) to exclude, to debar, to shut out; to bar; to be incompatible with.

exclusif [ɛkskly'zif], *a.* (*fem.* **-sive**) exclusive; intolerant.

exclusion [ɛkskly'zjɔ̃], *n.f.* exclusion.

exclusivement [ɛksklyziv'mɑ̃], *adv.* exclu-sively.

excommunication [ɛkskɔmynikɑ'sjɔ̃], *n.f.* excommunication.

excommunié [ɛkskɔmy'nje], *a.* excom-municated.—*n.m.* (*fem.* **-ée**) excommuni-cated person.

excommunier [ɛkskɔmy'nje], *v.t.* to excom-municate.

excrément [ɛkskre'mɑ̃], *n.m.* excrement.

excréter [ɛkskre'te], *v.t.* (*conjug. like* CÉDER) to excrete.

excrétion [ɛkskre'sjɔ̃], *n.f.* excretion.

excroissance [ɛkskrwa'sɑ̃ːs], *n.f.* excrescence (*tumor etc.*).

excursion [ɛkskyr'sjɔ̃], *n.f.* excursion, ramble, tour, trip; raid; (*fig.*) digression.

excursionniste [ɛkskyrsjɔ'nist], *n.* tripper.

excusable [ɛksky'zabl], *a.* excusable, pardon-able.

excuse [ɛks'kyːz], *n.f.* excuse, (*pl.*) apology.

excuser [ɛksky'ze], *v.t.* to excuse, to pardon; to bear with; to apologize for. **s'excuser**, *v.r.* to excuse *or* exculpate oneself; to apologize; to decline; *qui s'excuse, s'accuse*, excuses indicate a guilty con-science.

exécrable [ɛgze'krabl], *a.* execrable; abomin-able.

exécrablement [ɛgzekrablə'mɑ̃], *adv.* exe-crably.

exécration [ɛgzekrɑ'sjɔ̃], *n.f.* execration.

exécrer [ɛgze'kre], *v.t.* (*conjug. like* CÉDER) to execrate, to abhor.

exécutable [ɛgzeky'tabl], *a.* feasible, practi-cable.

exécutant [ɛgzeky'tɑ̃], *n.m.* (*fem.* **-e**) per-former, player (*esp. of music*).

exécuter [ɛgzeky'te], *v.t.* to execute, to per-form, to accomplish; to carry out, to fulfil. **s'exécuter**, *v.r.* to be performed, to be done, to take place; to yield, to comply, to submit; *allons, exécutez-vous*, come, do the needful.

exécuteur [ɛgzeky'tœːr], *n.m.* (*fem.* **-trice**) executor, executrix; *exécuteur (des hautes œuvres)*, executioner.

exécutif [ɛgzeky'tif], *a.* (*fem.* **-tive**) execu-tive.—*n.m.* the executive.

exécution [ɛgzeky'sjɔ̃], *n.f.* execution, accom-plishment, performance, fulfilment; (*St. Exch.*) suspension (*of defaulter*).

exemplaire [ɛgzɑ̃'plɛːr], *a.* exemplary.—*n.m.* model, pattern; copy (*of printed books, engravings etc.*); specimen.

exemplairement [ɛgzɑ̃plɛr'mɑ̃], *adv.* in an exemplary manner.

exemple [ɛg'zɑ̃ːpl], *n.m.* example, pattern, model; precedent, parallel, instance; *à l'exemple de*, in imitation of; *par exemple*, for instance; upon my word! *sans exemple*, unparalleled.

exempt [ɛg'zɑ̃], *a.* exempt, free (*from*).

exempté [ɛgzɑ̃'te], *a. and n.m.* (*fem.* **-ée**) exempt(ed) (person).

exempter [ɛgzɑ̃'te], *v.t.* to exempt, to free; to dispense, to exonerate.

exemption [ɛgzɑ̃'sjɔ̃], *n.f.* exemption, im-munity; dispensation.

exercer [ɛgzɛr'se], *v.t.* (*conjug. like* COM-MENCER) to exercise, to train; to fulfil (*an office etc.*); to follow, to practice (*a trade or profession*); (*fig.*) to try (*one's patience etc.*). **s'exercer**, *v.r.* to exercise, to practice; to exert oneself.

exercice [ɛgzɛr'sis], *n.m.* exercise, practice, use; (*Customs*) inspection; (*Administration*) financial year; (*Mil.*) drill.

exerciseur [ɛgzɛrsi'zœːr], *n.m.* (*Gym.*) chest expander.

exhalaison [ɛgzalɛ'zɔ̃], *n.f.* exhalation, effluvium.

exhalation [ɛgzalɑ'sjɔ̃], *n.f.* exhalation.

exhaler

exhaler [egza'le], *v.t.* to send forth, to exhale; to give vent to, to emit. **s'exhaler**, *v.r.* to be emitted, to be exhaled; to give vent to.
exhausser [egzo'se], *v.t.* to raise, to make higher.
exhaustif [egzos'tif], *a.* (*fem.* **-tive**) exhaustive.
exhaustion [egzos'tjɔ̃], *n.f.* exhaustion.
exhiber [egzi'be], *v.t.* to exhibit (*in a law court*); to produce, to show. **s'exhiber,** *v.r.* (*pej.*) to show off.
exhibition [egzibi'sjɔ̃], *n.f.* producing, show, exhibiting, exhibition.
exhilarant [egzila'rɑ̃], *a.* exhilarating.
exhortation [egzɔrta'sjɔ̃], *n.f.* exhortation.
exhorter [egzɔr'te], *v.t.* to exhort, to encourage.
exhumation [egzyma'sjɔ̃], *n.f.* exhumation, disinterment.
exhumer [egzy'me], *v.t.* to exhume, to disinter; (*fig.*) to rake up.
exigeant [egzi'ʒɑ̃], *a.* exacting, hard to please.
exigence [egzi'ʒɑ̃ːs], *n.f.* unreasonableness; exigency; demand, requirement.
exiger [egzi'ʒe], *v.t.* (*conjug. like* MANGER) to exact, to require, to demand.
exigu [egzi'gy], *a.* (*fem.* **-uë**) very small; scanty, slender, slight.
exiguïté [egzigqi'te], *n.f.* scantiness, slenderness, slightness.
exil [eg'zil], *n.m.* exile, banishment.
exilé [egzi'le], *a.* exiled.—*n.m.* (*fem.* **-ée**) exile.
exiler [egzi'le], *v.t.* to exile, to banish. **s'exiler,** *v.r.* to go into exile.
existant [egzis'tɑ̃], *a.* existing, in being, existent; extant.
existence [egzis'tɑ̃ːs], *n.f.* existence; subsistence, living; (*pl.*) (*Comm.*) stock on hand.
existentialisme [egzistɑ̃sja'lism], *n.m.* existentialism.
exister [egzis'te], *v.i.* to exist, to live; to be extant.
exocet [egzɔ'sɛ], *n.m.* flying fish.
exode [eg'zɔd], *n.m.* exodus.
exonération [egzɔnera'sjɔ̃], *n.f.* exoneration.
exonérer [egzɔne're], *v.t.* (*conjug. like* CÉDER) to exonerate, to discharge.
exorable [egzɔ'rabl], *a.* lenient, merciful.
exorbitant [egzɔrbi'tɑ̃], *a.* exorbitant.
exorciser [egzɔrsi'ze], *v.t.* to exorcize.
exorde [eg'zɔrd], *n.m.* exordium, beginning (*of a speech etc.*).
exotique [egzɔ'tik], *a.* exotic; foreign, outlandish.
expansif [ekspɑ̃'sif], *a.* (*fem.* **-sive**) expansive; (*fig.*) unreserved, open-hearted.
expansion [ekspɑ̃'sjɔ̃], *n.f.* expansion; (*fig.*) unreservedness.
expatriation [ekspatria'sjɔ̃], *n.f.* expatriation; self-banishment.
expatrier [ekspatri'e], *v.t.* to expatriate, to exile. **s'expatrier,** *v.r.* to leave one's country.
expectant [ekspɛk'tɑ̃], *a.* expectant.
expectative [ekspɛkta'tiːv], *n.f.* expectation, hope, expectancy.
expectoration [ekspɛktɔra'sjɔ̃], *n.f.* expectoration; sputum.

expectorer [ekspɛktɔ're], *v.t.* to expectorate, to spit.
expédient [ekspe'djɑ̃], *a.* expedient, fit, meet.—*n.m.* expedient, device; shift.
expédier [ekspe'dje], *v.t.* to dispatch, to send off, to forward; to do quickly; to clear (*at the customs*); to draw up (*a deed etc.*).
expéditeur [ekspedi'tœːr], *n.m.* (*fem.* **-trice**) sender (*by post*); shipper, consigner.
expéditif [ekspedi'tif], *a.* (*fem.* **-tive**) expeditious, quick.
expédition [ekspedi'sjɔ̃], *n.f.* expedition, dispatch; shipment; thing sent; performance; (*Law*) copy (*of a deed etc.*).
expéditionnaire [ekspedisjɔ'nɛːr], *a.* expeditionary.—*n.* sender, shipper; commission-agent; copying clerk.
expérience [ekspe'rjɑ̃ːs], *n.f.* experience; experiment, test.
expérimental [eksperimɑ̃'tal], *a.* (*m.pl.* **-aux**) experimental.
expérimenté [eksperimɑ̃'te], *a.* experienced.
expérimenter [eksperimɑ̃'te], *v.t.* to try out, to test; to experience.
expert [eks'pɛːr], *a.* expert, skillful.—*n.m.* connoisseur; valuer, surveyor; expert; **expert comptable,** C. P. A., accountant.
expertement [ekspɛrt'mɑ̃], *adv.* expertly skilfully.
expertise [ekspɛr'tiːz], *n.f.* survey, valuation; appraisal.
expertiser [ekspɛrti'ze], *v.t.* to make a survey of; to appraise, to value, to assess.
expiation [ekspja'sjɔ̃], *n.f.* expiation, atonement.
expiatoire [ekspja'twaːr], *a.* expiatory.
expier [eks'pje], *v.t.* to expiate, to atone for.
expirant [ekspi'rɑ̃], *a.* expiring, dying.
expiration [ekspira'sjɔ̃], *n.f.* expiration.
expirer [ekspi're], *v.t.* to breathe out; exhale.—*v.i.* to expire, to die; to come to an end.
explicable [ekspli'kabl], *a.* explicable.
explicatif [eksplika'tif], *a.* (*fem.* **-tive**) explicative, explanatory.
explication [eksplika'sjɔ̃], *n.f.* explanation; interpretation; meaning.
explicite [ekspli'sit], *a.* explicit, clear, express.
explicitement [eksplisit'mɑ̃], *adv.* explicitly, clearly.
expliquer [ekspli'ke], *v.t.* to explain, to expound; to interpret; to make known. **s'expliquer,** *v.r.* to explain oneself; to be explained.
exploit [eks'plwa], *n.m.* exploit, achievement, feat; (*Law*) writ, process.
exploitable [eksplwa'tabl], *a.* workable; (*Law*) distrainable.
exploitant [eksplwa'tɑ̃], *n.m.* operator (*of mines etc.*); farmer, grower.
exploitation [eksplwata'sjɔ̃], *n.f.* working, improving (*of lands etc.*); employing, using; taking advantage of, exploitation.
exploiter [eksplwa'te], *v.t.* to work, to improve, to cultivate; to use; to exploit, to take (*unfair*) advantage of.
exploiteur [eksplwa'tœːr], *n.m.* (*fem.* **-euse**) exploiter, person who takes advantage (*of others*).
explorateur [eksplɔra'tœːr], *a.* (*fem.* **-trice**) exploratory.—*n.m.* (*fem.* **-trice**) explorer.

148

exploration [εksplɔra'sjɔ̃], *n.f.* exploration.
explorer [εksplɔ're], *v.t.* to explore.
exploser [εksplɔ'ze], *v.i.* to explode, to blow up.
explosible [εksplɔ'zibl], *a.* explosive.
explosif [εksplɔ'zif], *a.* (*fem.* -**sive**) and *n.m.* explosive.
explosion [εksplɔ'zjɔ̃], *n.f.* explosion; (*fig.*) outbreak.
exportateur [εkspɔrta'tœːr], *a.* (*fem.* -**trice**) exporting.—*n.m.* (*fem.* -**trice**) exporter.
exportation [εkspɔrta'sjɔ̃], *n.f.* exportation, export.
exporter [εkspɔr'te], *v.t.* to export.
exposant [εkspo'zɑ̃], *n.m.* (*fem.* -**e**) exhibitor; (*Law*) petitioner.—*n.m.* (*Math.*) exponent.
exposé [εkspo'ze], *a.* exposed, on view; dangerous (*position*).—*n.m.* statement, explanation; account, report.
exposer [εkspo'ze], *v.t.* to expose, to show, to exhibit; to lay bare; to state, to explain; to endanger.—*v.i.* to explain; to exhibit.
s'exposer, *v.r.* to expose oneself; to be liable.
exposition [εkspozi'sjɔ̃], *n.f.* exhibition; exposure; situation, aspect; explanation, account.
exprès [εks'prεs], *a.* (*fem.* -**presse**) express, formal, positive.—[εks'prε], *adv.* expressly, on purpose.—*n.m.* express (*messenger*).
express [εks'prεs], *a.* (*Rail.*) express.—*n.m.* express train.
expressément [εksprεse'mɑ̃], *adv.* expressly, positively.
expressif [εksprε'sif], *a.* (*fem.* -**ive**) expressive.
expression [εksprε'sjɔ̃], *n.f.* expression; expressiveness.
exprimer [εkspri'me], *v.t.* to express; to press *or* squeeze out; to utter; to betoken.
s'exprimer, *v.r.* to express oneself.
expropriation [εksprɔpria'sjɔ̃], *n.f.* expropriation, dispossession, compulsory purchase.
exproprier [εksprɔpri'e], *v.t.* to expropriate, to dispossess; to requisition (*buildings*).
expulser [εkspyl'se], *v.t.* to expel, to turn out; to evict.
expulsion [εkspyl'sjɔ̃], *n.f.* expulsion; (*Law*) ejection.
expurger [εkspyr'ʒe], *v.t.* (*conjug. like* MANGER) to expurgate, to bowdlerize (*a book*).
exquis [εks'ki], *a.* exquisite, nice, refined.
exquisement [εkskiz'mɑ̃], *adv.* exquisitely.
exsangue [εk'sɑ̃ːg], *a.* bloodless, anaemic.
extase [εks'tɑːz], *n.f.* ecstasy, rapture.
extasier (s') [sεksta'zje], *v.r.* to be enraptured, to go into raptures.
extatique [εksta'tik], *a.* ecstatic, rapturous.
extenseur [εkstɑ̃'sœːr], *a.* extensor.—*n.m.* (*Anat.*) extensor; chest-expander.
extension [εkstɑ̃'sjɔ̃], *n.f.* extension, stretching; extent; increase.
exténuant [εkste'nɥɑ̃], *a.* extenuating.
exténuation [εkstenɥa'sjɔ̃], *n.f.* extenuation, debility.
exténuer [εkste'nɥe], *v.t.* to extenuate, to enfeeble.

extérieur [εkste'rjœːr], *a.* exterior, external, outward; foreign.—*n.m.* exterior; outward appearance; abroad.
extérieurement [εksterjœr'mɑ̃], *adv.* externally, outwardly.
exterminateur [εkstεrmina'tœːr], *a.* (*fem.* -**trice**) exterminating, destroying.—*n.m.* (*fem.* -**trice**) destroyer, exterminator.
extermination [εkstεrmina'sjɔ̃], *n.f.* extermination.
exterminer [εkstεrmi'ne], *v.t.* to exterminate, to destroy.
externat [εkstεr'na], *n.m.* day school.
externe [εks'tεrn], *a.* external, exterior, outer.—*n.* day scholar.
extincteur [εkstɛk'tœːr], *a.* (*fem.* -**trice**) extinguishing (*fire*).—*n.m.* fire extinguisher.
extinction [εkstɛk'sjɔ̃], *n.f.* extinction, destruction; liquidation; quelling; quenching (*of thirst*); slaking (*of lime*).
extinguible [εkstɛ̃'gibl], *a.* extinguishable.
extirpateur [εkstirpa'tœːr], *n.m.* extirpator, destroyer; (*Agric.*) scarifier, weeder.
extirpation [εkstirpa'sjɔ̃], *n.f.* extirpation.
extirper [εkstir'pe], *v.t.* to extirpate.
extorquer [εkstɔr'ke], *v.t.* to extort, to wrest.
extorsion [εkstɔr'sjɔ̃], *n.f.* extortion.
extra [εks'tra], *n.m. inv.* extra.
extra-conjugal [εkstrakɔ̃ʒy'gal], *a.* (*m.pl.* -**aux**) extra-marital.
extracteur [εkstrak'tœːr], *n.m.* extractor.
extraction [εkstrak'sjɔ̃], *n.f.* extraction; origin, descent.
extrader [εkstra'de], *v.t.* to extradite.
extradition [εkstradi'sjɔ̃], *n.f.* extradition.
extraire [εks'trɛːr], *v.t. irr.* (*conjug. like* TRAIRE) to extract, to take out; to make extracts from.
extrait [εks'trɛ], *n.m.* extract; selection; abstract; certificate.
extraordinaire [εkstraɔrdi'nɛːr], *a.* extraordinary, unusual.—*n.m.* extraordinary thing.
extraordinairement [εkstraɔrdinɛr'mɑ̃], *adv.* extraordinarily, unusually; oddly.
extrapolation [εkstrapɔla'sjɔ̃], *n.f.* (*Math.*) extrapolation.
extra-scolaire [εkstraskɔ'lɛːr], *a.* out-of-school (*activities*).
extravagamment [εkstravaga'mɑ̃], *adv.* extravagantly, unreasonably.
extravagance [εkstrava'gɑ̃ːs], *n.f.* extravagance, folly.
extravagant [εkstrava'gɑ̃], *a.* and *n.m.* (*fem.* -**e**) extravagant (person).
extravaguer [εkstrava'ge], *v.i.* to talk wildly.
extrême [εks'trɛːm], *a.* extreme, utmost; excessive.—*n.m.* extreme *or* utmost point.
extrêmement [εkstrεm'mɑ̃], *adv.* extremely.
Extrême-Orient [εkstrεmɔ'rjɑ̃], l', *m.* Far East.
extrémiste [εkstre'mist], *n.* extremist, diehard.
extrémité [εkstremi'te], *n.f.* extremity, end; last moment; (*fig.*) border, brink.
exubérance [εgzybe'rɑ̃ːs], *n.f.* exuberance.
exubérant [εgzybe'rɑ̃], *a.* exuberant, luxuriant.
exultation [εgzylta'sjɔ̃], *n.f.* exultation, rapture.

F, f

F

F, f (1) [ɛf], *n.m.* the sixth letter of the alphabet.
f. (2) or **fr.**, (*abbr.*) franc.
fa [fa], *n.m.* (*Mus.*) fa; F.
fable [faːbl], *n.f.* fable; story, tale; (*fig.*) untruth; byword.
fablier [fɑbli'e], *n.m.* book of fables; fabulist.
fabricant [fabri'kɑ̃], *n.m.* (*fem.* **-e**) manufacturer, maker.
fabricateur [fabrika'tœːr], *n.m.* (*fem.* **-trice**) fabricator; counterfeiter; forger.
fabrication [fabrika'sjɔ̃], *n.f.* fabrication, manufacture.
fabrique [fa'brik], *n.f.* building and maintenance (*esp. of churches*); factory; fabrication.
fabriquer [fabri'ke], *v.t.* to manufacture, to make; to fabricate.
fabuleusement [fabyløz'mɑ̃], *adv.* fabulously; (*fig.*) incredibly.
fabuleux [faby'lø], *a.* (*fem.* **-euse**) fabulous, fictitious; (*fig.*) incredible.
fabuliste [faby'list], *n.* fabulist.
façade [fa'sad], *n.f.* façade, front (*of an edifice*); (*fig.*) appearance.
face [fas], *n.f.* face; front; side (*of a record*); (*fig.*) state, appearance; turn (*of affairs*); **en face de**, opposite.
facétie [fase'si], *n.f.* facetiousness; jest, joke.
facétieusement [fasesjøz'mɑ̃], *adv.* facetiously.
facétieux [fase'sjø], *a.* (*fem.* **-euse**) facetious, humorous.
facette [fa'sɛt], *n.f.* facet, face.
fâcher [fɑ'ʃe], *v.t.* to anger, to offend, to displease; **être fâché avec**, to be on bad terms with; **fâché** (*contre*), angry (*with*); **fâché** (*de*), sorry. **se fâcher**, *v.r.* to get angry, to be offended.
fâcherie [fɑ'ʃri], *n.f.* angry feeling; quarrel.
fâcheusement [fɑʃøz'mɑ̃], *adv.* unfortunately, unpleasantly; inopportunely, disagreeably; awkwardly.
fâcheux [fɑ'ʃø], *a.* (*fem.* **-euse**) troublesome, vexatious; unfortunate; cross.—*n.m.* (*fem.* **-euse**) troublesome *or* disagreeable person *or* thing, pesterer, bore.
facial [fa'sjal], *a.* (*m. pl.* **-aux**) (*Anat.*) facial.
facile [fa'sil] *a.* easy; facile; fluent; ready, quick; weak.
facilement [fasil'mɑ̃], *adv.* easily, readily.
facilité [fasili'te], *n.f.* facility, ease; readiness; (*pl.*) easy terms (*for payment*).
faciliter [fasili'te], *v.t.* to facilitate, to make easy.
façon [fa'sɔ̃], *n.f.* make, shape, fashion; making, workmanship; (*fig.*) manner; appearance; sort; affectation; fuss; (*pl.*) ceremony.
faconde [fa'kɔ̃ːd], *n.f.* talkativeness, loquacity.
façonné [fasɔ'ne], *a.* figured (*of materials*); wrought.
façonnement [fasɔn'mɑ̃], **façonnage** [fasɔ'naːʒ], *n.m.* fashioning, making.
façonner [fasɔ'ne], *v.t.* to make, to fashion, to form; to work, to mold; to accustom, to use (*to discipline etc.*).
façonnier [fasɔ'nje], *a.* (*fem.* **-ière**) ceremonious, affected.—*n.m.* custom tailor.
fac-similé [faksimi'le], *n.m.* facsimile.

factage [fak'taːʒ], *n.m.* porterage, carriage.
facteur [fak'tœːr], *n.m.* (*fem.* **-trice**) maker (*of musical instruments*); agent; postman; railway porter; (*Math., Biol.*) factor.
factice [fak'tis], *a.* factitious, artificial; unnatural.
factieux [fak'sjø], *a.* (*fem.* **-euse**) factious, mutinous.—*n.m.* (*fem.* **-euse**) rebel.
faction [fak'sjɔ̃], *n.f.* watch, sentry duty; faction.
factionnaire [faksjɔ'nɛːr], *n.m.* sentry.
factorerie [faktɔrə'ri], *n.f.* trading depot, factory (*in a colony etc.*).
facture [fak'tyːr], *n.f.* composition, workmanship (*of music, verse etc.*); (*Comm.*) bill (of sale), invoice.
facturer [fakty're], *v.t.* to invoice.
facultatif [fakylta'tif], *a.* (*fem.* **-tive**) optional; **arrêt facultatif**, request stop.
faculté [fakyl'te], *n.f.* faculty, ability, power; quality; option, right; (*pl.*) mental faculties.
fadaise [fa'dɛːz], *n.f.* trifle, stuff, nonsense, twaddle.
fade [fad], *a.* insipid, tasteless, dull; (*fig.*) flat, stale.
fadement [fad'mɑ̃], *adv.* insipidly, tastelessly; mawkishly.
fadeur [fa'dœːr], *n.f.* insipidity, tastelessness; (*fig.*) pointlessness.
fagot [fa'go], *n.m.* faggot, bundle of sticks etc.
fagoter [fagɔ'te], *v.t.* to tie into faggots; (*fig.*) to jumble together; to dress in a slovenly manner; **comme le voilà fagoté**, what a sight he looks. **se fagoter**, *v.r.* to dress in a slovenly manner.
faible [fɛːbl], *a.* and *n.m.* weak, feeble (person). —*n.m.* weak part; defect, failing; partiality, weakness (*for*).
faiblement [fɛblə'mɑ̃], *adv.* weakly, feebly.
faiblesse [fɛ'blɛs], *n.f.* weakness, feebleness; faintness; deficiency; backwardness; defect; partiality.
faiblir [fɛ'bliːr], *v.i.* to become weak, to flag, to yield, to abate; to relax.
faïence [fa'jɑ̃ːs], *n.f.* crockery, earthenware.
faïencier [fajɑ̃'sje], *n.m.* (*fem.* **-ière**) dealer in *or* maker of crockery.
faille [fɑːj], *n.f.* (*Geol.*) fault.
failli [fa'ji], *a.* and *n.m.* (*fem.* **-e**) bankrupt, insolvent (person).
faillibilité [fajibili'te], *n.f.* fallibility.
faillible [fa'jibl], *a.* fallible.
faillir [fa'jiːr], *v.i. irr.* to err, to transgress; to yield; to fail; to be on the point of; **j'ai failli tomber**, I nearly fell.
faillite [fa'jit], *n.f.* bankruptcy, insolvency; **faire faillite**, to become bankrupt.
faim [fɛ̃], *n.f.* hunger, appetite; (*fig.*) longing; **avoir faim**, to be hungry.
faîne [fɛːn], *n.f.* beechnut; beechmast.
fainéant [fɛne'ɑ̃], *a.* idle, lazy.—*n.m.* (*fem.* **-e**) idler.
fainéanter [fɛneɑ̃'te], *v.i.* (*colloq.*) to be idle, to loaf.
fainéantise [fɛneɑ̃'tiːz], *n.f.* idleness, laziness, sloth.
faire (1) [fɛːr], *v. irr.* (*The most frequently used verb in the language; faire not only translates* to do *or* to make, *but, followed by a noun or an infinitive, it may take the place of practically any verb; followed by an adjective*

or an adverb it forms many current idioms.)
I. *v.t.* to do; to make; to form; to be;
cela fait mon affaire, this is exactly what
I want; *cela fait beaucoup,* that makes a
great difference; *cela ne fait rien,* that
makes no difference; *faire accueil à,* to
welcome; *faire attention,* to pay attention; *faire bâtir,* to have built; *faire cas
de,* to have a high opinion of; (*Motor.*)
faire du 50 à l'heure, to do 50 kilometres
an hour; *faire le mort,* to sham dead;
faire part de, to inform, to announce;
faire peu de cas de, to set little store by;
faire ses dents, to cut one's teeth; *faire
une promenade,* to take a walk; *faire
venir,* to send for; *faire voir,* to show;
faites-le entrer, show him in; *il ne fait
que d'arriver,* he has only just arrived; *je
n'ai que faire de lui,* I am in no way
interested in him; *qu'est-ce que cela vous
fait?* what is that to you? *que faire?* what
is to be done? *se laisser faire,* to offer no
resistance.
II. *v.i.* to do; to mean, to signify, to look;
to fit, to suit; to deal (*at cards*); to arrange,
to manage; *avoir à faire,* to have work to
do; *c'en est fait de,* it is all up with.
III. *v. impers.* to be; *il fait beau,* it is
fine; *quel temps fait-il?* what sort of
weather is it?
IV. **se faire,** *v.r.* to be done, to be made;
to happen, to become; to pretend to be; to
have, make *or* get oneself; to be used (*à*),
to accustom oneself (*à*); to improve; *cela
ne se fait pas,* that is not done.
faire (2) [fɛːr], *n.m.* doing, making; (*Paint.
etc.*) execution, style.
faire-part [fɛr'paːr], *n.m. inv.* **un faire-
part** *or* **une lettre de faire-part de
décès** *or* **de mariage,** notification of death,
wedding-card.
faisable [fə'zabl], *a.* practicable, feasible.
faisan [fə'zɑ̃], *n.m.* pheasant.
faisandé [fəzɑ̃'de], *a.* gamy, high.
faisandeau [fəzɑ̃'do], *n.m.* (*pl.* **-eaux**) young
pheasant.
faisceau [fɛ'so], *n.m.* (*pl.* **-eaux**) bundle;
sheaf (*of arrows etc.*); pile (*of arms etc.*);
(*fig.*) union; (*Elec.*) beam; (*Antiq.,* *pl.*)
fasces.
faiseur [fə'zœːr], *n.m.* (*fem.* **-euse**) maker;
doer; charlatan, quack.
fait [fɛ, fɛt], *a.* made; done; fit, qualified;
dressed, got up; full grown; mature.—*n.m.*
act, deed; fact, actual event; case, matter
point in business; *tout à fait,* quite.
faîte [fɛːt], *n.m.* top, pinnacle; ridge, coping
(*of a building*); (*fig.*) zenith, height.
faits divers [fɛdi'vɛr], *n.m. pl.* news items,
news in brief.
faix [fɛ], *n.m. inv.* weight, burden, load.
falaise [fa'lɛːz], *n.f.* cliff.
fallacieusement [falasjøz'mɑ̃], *adv.* falla-
ciously, falsely.
fallacieux [fala'sjø], *a.* (*fem.* **-euse**) fallacious,
deceptive.
falloir [fa'lwaːr], *v. impers. irr.* to be necessary, to be obligatory, proper *or* expedient
(*should,* *must*); to be needful, to be
wanting *or* lacking; *comme il faut,*
properly, well-bred (*of people*); *peu s'en

faut, very nearly; *tant s'en faut,* far from
it.
falot [fa'lo], *n.m.* large hand-lantern.
falsification [falsifika'sjɔ̃], *n.f.* falsification;
adulteration, debasement.
falsifier [falsi'fje], *v.t.* to falsify; to alter (*texts
etc.*); to adulterate (*milk, metals*); to tamper
with.
faluche [fa'lyʃ], *n.f.* student's beret.
famé [fa'me], *a. used only in* **bien** *or* **mal
famé,** of good *or* evil repute.
famélique [fame'lik], *a.* starving.—*n.* starveling.
fameux [fa'mø], *a.* (*fem.* **-euse**) famous,
celebrated; first-rate; (*iron. adj. before
noun*) perfect.
familial [fami'ljal], *a.*(*m. pl.* **-aux**) pertaining
to family.
familiariser [familjari'ze], *v.t.* to accustom
to, to familiarize. **se familiariser,** *v.r.* to
familiarize oneself (*avec*), to become
accustomed; to grow familiar.
familiarité [familjari'te], *n.f.* familiarity,
familiar terms, intimacy; (*pl.*) liberties.
familier [fami'lje], *a.* (*fem.* **-ière**) familiar,
intimate; free; homely.—*n.m.* familiar.
familièrement [familjɛr'mɑ̃], *adv.* familiarly.
famille [fa'miːj], *n.f.* family, kindred, kin;
race, tribe; (*fig.*) set.
famine [fa'min], *n.f.* famine, dearth.
fanal [fa'nal], *n.m.* (*pl.* **-aux**) signal light;
ship's lantern.
fanatique [fana'tik], *a.* fanatical.—*n.* fanatic,
enthusiast.
fanatiquement [fanatik'mɑ̃], *adv.* fanatically.
fanatisme [fana'tism], *n.m.* fanaticism.
faner [fa'ne], *v.t.* to toss *or* ted (*hay*); to
cause to fade; to tarnish. **se faner,** *v.r.* to
fade, to droop, to wither; to tarnish.
faneur [fa'nœːr], *n.m.* (*fem.* **-euse**) haymaker.
—*n.f.* (**-euse**) haymaking machine.
fanfare [fɑ̃'faːr], *n.f.* flourish (*of trumpets*);
fanfare; brass band.
fanfaron [fɑ̃fa'rɔ̃], *a.* (*fem,* **-onne**) blustering,
swaggering, boasting.—*n.m.* (*fem.* **-onne**)
blusterer, swaggerer; braggart.
fanfreluche [fɑ̃frə'lyʃ], *n.f.* bauble, gewgaw.
fange [fɑ̃ːʒ], *n.f.* mire, mud, dirt; vileness.
fangeux [fɑ̃'ʒø], *a.* (*fem.* **-euse**) miry, muddy,
dirty.
fanon [fa'nɔ̃], *n.m.* dewlap (*oxen*); fetlock
(*horse*); horny strip (*in whales*); (*Mil.*)
pennon (*of lance*).
fantaisie [fɑ̃tɛ'zi], *n.f.* imagination; fancy;
whim, caprice; (*Mus.*) fantasia.
fantaisiste [fɑ̃tɛ'zist], *a.* whimsical, fantastic.
—*n.* whimsical painter, writer *or* other
artist.
fantasmagorie [fɑ̃tasmagɔ'ri], *n.f.* phantas-
magoria.
fantasque [fɑ̃'task], *a.* fantastic, whimsical;
strange, odd.
fantassin [fɑ̃ta'sɛ̃], *n.m.* foot soldier, infantry-
man.
fantastique [fɑ̃tas'tik], *a.* fantastic, fanciful.
—*n.m.* uncanny.
fantastiquement [fɑ̃tastik'mɑ̃], *adv.* fantasti-
cally.
fantoche [fɑ̃'tɔʃ], *n.m.* marionette, puppet.
fantôme [fɑ̃'toːm], *n.m.* phantom, specter,
ghost.

faon [fɑ̃], *n.m.* fawn, calf of deer.
faquin [fa'kɛ̃], *n.m.* cad, rascal.
farandole [farɑ̃'dɔl], *n.f.* farandole (*Provençal dance*).
farce [fars], *n.f.* stuffing, force-meat; farce; buffoonery; practical joke; prank.
farceur [far'sœ:r], *a.* (*fem.* **-euse**) waggish, facetious.—*n.m.* (*fem.* **-euse**) practical joker; humbug.
farcir [far'si:r], *v.t.* to stuff with force-meat etc.; to cram.
fard [fa:r], *n.m.* paint (*for the complexion*), rouge, make-up; (*fig.*) varnish, disguise; *sans fard*, plainly, frankly.
fardeau [far'do], *n.m.* (*pl.* **-eaux**) burden, load; mash (*for brewing*); (*Mining*) mass.
farder [far'de], *v.t.* to paint (*the face*), to make up; (*fig.*) to varnish, to gloss over. **se farder**, *v.r.* to paint one's face, to make up.
(*C*) **fardoches** [far'dɔʃ], *n.f. pl.* brushwood.
farfadet [farfa'dɛ], *n.m.* goblin, elf.
farfouiller [farfu'je], *v.i.* (*fam.*) to rummage.
faribole [fari'bɔl], *n.f.* idle story; trifle.
farine [fa'rin], *n.f.* flour; meal.
farineux [fari'nø], *a.* (*fem.* **-euse**) mealy, farinaceous; white with flour.
farouche [fa'ruʃ], *a.* wild; fierce; sullen; shy.
fascicule [fasi'kyl], *n.m.* fascicle.
fascinateur [fasinɑ'tœ:r], *a.* (*fem.* **-trice**) fascinating.
fascination [fasinɑ'sjɔ̃], *n.f.* fascination.
fasciner [fasi'ne], *v.t.* to fascinate.
fascisme [fa'ʃism], *n.m.* fascism.
fasciste [fa'ʃist], *a.* and *n.* fascist.
faste [fast], *a.* favourable, lucky.—*n.m.* (*used only in sing.*) pomp, ostentation.
fastidieusement [fastidjøz'mɑ̃], *adv.* tediously.
fastidieux [fasti'djø], *a.* (*fem.* **-euse**) irksome, tedious.
fastueusement [fastɥøz'mɑ̃], *adv.* ostentatiously, pompously; splendidly.
fastueux [fas'tɥø], *a.* (*fem.* **-euse**) ostentatious, pompous, showy; stately.
fat [fat], *a.* conceited, vain, foppish.—*n.m.* fop, coxcomb.
fatal [fa'tal], *a.* fatal; inevitable; *une femme fatale*, a vamp.
fatalement [fatal'mɑ̃], *adv.* fatally; inevitably.
fatalisme [fata'lism], *n.m.* fatalism.
fataliste [fata'list], *n.* fatalist.
fatalité [fatali'te], *n.f.* fatality.
fatigant [fati'gɑ̃], *a.* fatiguing, tiring, wearisome.
fatigue [fa'tig], *n.f.* fatigue, weariness; toil, hardship; *habits de fatigue*, working clothes.
fatigué [fati'ge], *a.* fatigued, tired; (*fig.*) worn out.
fatiguer [fati'ge], *v.t.* to fatigue; to tire.—*v.i.* to tire; to be fatiguing. **se fatiguer**, *v.r.* to tire oneself out, to get tired, to be jaded.
fatras [fa'trɑ], *n.m.* jumble; rubbish, trash.
fatuité [fatɥi'te], *n.f.* fatuity, self-conceit.
faubourg [fo'bu:r], *n.m.* outskirts, suburb.
faubourien [fobu'rjɛ̃], *a.* (*fem.* **-enne**) suburban, working-class; common.—*n.m.* (*fem.* **-enne**) person living in the suburbs; (*pej.*) common person.
fauchage [fo'ʃa:ʒ], *n.m.* mowing.
fauchaison [foʃɛ'zɔ̃], *n.f.* mowing time.
fauché [fo'ʃe], *a.* mown; (*slang*) broke.

faucher [fo'ʃe], *v.t.* to mow, to reap.
faucheur [fo'ʃœ:r], *n.m.* (*fem.* **-euse**) mower, reaper.—*n.f.* (**-euse**) (*mechanical*) mower.
faucille [fo'si:j], *n.f.* sickle, reaping-hook.
faucon [fo'kɔ̃], *n.m.* falcon, hawk.
fauconnerie [fokɔn'ri], *n.f.* falconry.
fauconnier [fokɔ'nje], *n.m.* falconer.
faufiler [fofi'le], *v.t.* to tack, to baste (*needlework*). **se faufiler**, *v.r.* to insinuate oneself, to sneak in; to find a way in.
faune (1) [fo:n], *n.m.* faun.
faune (2) [fo:n], *n.f.* (*Zool.*) fauna.
faussaire [fo'sɛ:r], *n.* forger.
fausse [fos], [FAUX].
faussement [fos'mɑ̃], *adv.* falsely, wrongfully.
fausser [fo'se], *v.t.* to bend; to falsify, to pervert; to break, to force *or* strain (*a lock*).
fausset [fo'sɛ], *n.m.* (*Mus.*) falsetto.
fausseté [fos'te], *n.f.* falsity, falsehood; duplicity.
faute [fo:t], *n.f.* want; defect; fault, mistake, error; *faute de*, for want of.
fauteuil [fo'tœ:j], *n.m.* arm-chair; chair (*speaker's, president's seat*).
fauteur [fo'tœ:r], *n.m.* abettor, favorer.
fautif [fo'tif], *a.* (*fem.* **-tive**) faulty, at fault, defective.
fauve [fo:v], *a.* fawn-colored; tawny.—*n.m.* wild animal; *Les Fauves*, group of French painters at the beginning of this century.
fauvette [fo'vɛt], *n.f.* warbler.
faux (1) [fo], *n.f. inv.* scythe.
faux (2) [fo], *a.* (*fem.* **fausse**) false, untrue, wrong; base, counterfeit, forged (*coinage*); sham; insincere; (*Mus.*) out of tune; *faire un faux pas*, to stumble; (*fig.*) to make a slip.—*n.m.* falsehood; error; forgery.—*adv.* falsely, erroneously; (*Mus.*) out of tune.
faux-filet [fofi'lɛ], *n.m.* sirloin.
faux-fuyant [fofɥi'jɑ̃], *n.m.* subterfuge, evasion.
faux-monnayeur [fomɔne'jœ:r], *n.m.* counterfeiter.
faveur [fa'vœ:r], *n.f.* favor, boon; grace; vogue; (*narrow*) silk ribbon; *à la faveur de*, by means of; *en faveur de*, on behalf of.
favorable [favɔ'rabl], *a.* favorable, propitious.
favorablement [favɔrablə'mɑ̃], *adv.* favorably.
favori [favɔ'ri], *a.* and *n.m.* (*fem.* **-ite**) favorite.—*n.m.* (*pl.*) side whiskers.
favoriser [favɔri'ze], *v.t.* to favor, to befriend; to assist, to protect.
favoritisme [favɔri'tism], *n.m.* favoritism.
fébrile [fe'bril], *a.* febrile, feverish.
fécond [fe'kɔ̃], *a.* fruitful, prolific; copious, abundant, fertile.
fécondation [fekɔ̃dɑ'sjɔ̃], *n.f.* impregnation; fertilization.
féconder [fekɔ̃'de], *v.t.* to make fruitful, to fertilize.
fécondité [fekɔ̃di'te], *n.f.* fecundity, fruitfulness, fertility.
fécule [fe'kyl], *n.f.* faecula, starch.
féculent [feky'lɑ̃], *a.* feculent.—*n.m.* starchy food.
fédéral [fede'ral], *a.* (*m. pl.* **-aux**) federal.
fédéralisme [federa'lism], *n.m.* federalism.
fédéraliste [federa'list], *a.* and *n.* federalist.

fédération [federɑ'sjɔ̃], *n.f.* federation, alliance.
fédéré [fede're], *a.* federate, confederate; amalgamated.
fédérer (**se**) [səfede're], *v.r.* (*conjug. like* CÉDER) to federate, to band together.
fée [fe], *n.f.* fairy, fay.
féerie [feə'ri], *n.f.* enchantment; fairy scene; fairy-land.
féerique [feə'rik], *a.* fairy-like; wonderful.
feindre [fɛ̃:dr], *v.t. irr* (*conjug. like* CRAINDRE) to feign, to simulate, to sham, to pretend.—*v.i.* to feign, to sham.
feint [fɛ̃], *a.* feigned, pretended, sham.
feinte [fɛ̃:t], *n.f.* feint; pretence, dissimulation.
feld-maréchal [fɛldmare'ʃal], *n.m.* (*pl.* **-aux**) field marshal.
feldspath [fɛls'pat], *n.m.* feldspar.
fêlé [fɛ'le], *a.* cracked (*of glass*); (*fig.*) crackbrained.
fêler [fɛ'le], *v.t.* and **se fêler**, *v.r.* to crack (*of glass etc.*).
félicitation [felisitɑ'sjɔ̃], *n.f.* felicitation, congratulation.
félicité [felisi'te], *n.f.* felicity, bliss.
féliciter [felisi'te], *v.t.* to congratulate, to felicitate. **se féliciter**, *v.r.* to congratulate oneself.
félin [fe'lɛ̃], *a.* and *n.m.* (*fem.* **-e**) feline.
félon [fe'lɔ̃], *a.* (*fem.* **-onne**) disloyal, traitorous.—*n.m.* (*fem.* **-onne**) traitor, caitiff.
félonie [felɔ'ni], *n.f.* (*Feud.*) felony, treason.
fêlure [fɛ'ly:r], *n.f.* crack, fissure.
femelle [fə'mɛl], *a.* female, feminine, she-.—*n.f.* female, (*pej.*) woman.
féminin [femi'nɛ̃], *a.* feminine, female, womanish, womanly, effeminate.—*n.m.* (*Gram.*) feminine.
femme [fam], *n.f.* woman; married woman; wife; female attendant; lady.
femme-agent [fama'ʒɑ̃], *n.f.* police-woman.
femmelette [fam'lɛt], *n.f.* silly, weak woman; effeminate man.
femme-soldat [famsɔl'da], *n.f.* service-woman.
fémur [fe'my:r], *n.m.* femur, thigh-bone.
fenaison [fənɛ'zɔ̃], *n.f.* hay time, haymaking.
fendiller (**se**) [səfɑ̃di'je], *v.r.* to be covered with small cracks, to crack, to split.
fendre [fɑ̃:dr], *v.t.* to cleave, to split, to crack, to cut open; to plough (*the sea*). **se fendre**, *v.r.* to burst asunder, to split, to be ready to burst.
fendu [fɑ̃'dy], *a.* cleft, split, cloven.
fenêtre [fə'nɛ:tr], *n.f.* window, casement.
fenil [fə'ni], *n.m.* hayloft.
fenouil [fə'nu:j], *n.m.* fennel.
fente [fɑ̃:t], *n.f.* slit, chink, cleft; gap, crevice.
féodal [feɔ'dal], *a.* (*m. pl.* **-aux**) feudal.
féodalisme [feɔda'lism], *n.m.* feudalism.
fer [fɛ:r], *n.m.* iron; iron tool; horseshoe; head, point, etc.; (*fig.*) sword, brand; (*Golf*) club; (*pl.*) irons, chains, fetters; **fer battu** or **forgé**, wrought iron; **fil de fer**, wire.
fer-blanc [fɛr'blɑ̃], *n.m.* (*pl.* **fers-blancs**) tin, tin plate.
férié [fe'rje], *a.* holiday; **jour férié**, holiday, general holiday, bank holiday.
férir [fe'ri:r], *v.t.* used only in **sans coup férir**, without striking a blow.

ferler [fɛr'le], *v.t.* to furl (*sails*).
fermage [fɛr'ma:ʒ], *n.m.* rent (*of a farm*).
fermail [fɛr'ma:j], *n.m.* clasp, buckle.
ferme (1) [fɛrm], *a.* firm; fixed, stable; strong, stout, stiff, steady; resolute.—*adv.* firmly, fast, hard.
ferme (2) [fɛrm], *n.f.* farm, farmhouse, farmstead; farming (*of taxes*); letting out on lease.
ferme (3) [fɛrm], *n.f.* framework of beams.
fermement [fɛrmə'mɑ̃], *adv.* firmly, steadily; resolutely.
ferment [fɛr'mɑ̃], *n.m.* ferment, leaven.
fermentation [fɛrmɑ̃tɑ'sjɔ̃], *n.f.* fermentation, working; (*fig.*) ferment.
fermenter [fɛrmɑ̃'te], *v.i.* to ferment, to rise, to work.
fermer [fɛr'me], *v.t.* to shut, to close; to fasten; to turn off (*water, gas etc.*); to put an end to (*a discussion etc.*); to enclose.—*v.i.* to shut, to be shut. **se fermer**, *v.r.* to shut, to close, to be closed; to lock.
fermeté [fɛrmə'te], *n.f.* firmness; steadiness; resolution.
fermeture [fɛrmə'ty:r], *n.f.* closing, shutting; **fermeture à glissière**, zip fastener.
fermier [fɛr'mje], *n.m.* (tenant) farmer.
fermière [fɛr'mjɛ:r], *n.f.* farmer's wife.
fermoir [fɛr'mwa:r], *n.m.* clasp, fastener.
féroce [fe'rɔs], *a.* ferocious, fierce, savage.
férocement [ferɔs'mɑ̃], *adv.* ferociously.
férocité [ferɔsi'te], *n.f.* ferocity, fierceness.
ferraille [fɛ'rɑ:j], *n.f.* old iron, scrap iron.
ferrailler [fɛrɑ'je], *v.i.* (*Spt.*) to fence clumsily; (*fig.*) to squabble.
ferrailleur [fɛrɑ'jœ:r], *n.m.* dealer in old iron, scrap merchant; (*Spt.*) clumsy fencer.
ferrant [fɛ'rɑ̃], *a.* **maréchal ferrant**, farrier, shoeing-smith.
ferré [fɛ're], *a.* bound, shod etc., with iron; metalled; (*colloq.*) skilled; **voie ferrée**, railway.
ferrer [fɛ're], *v.t.* to bind, hoop, etc., with iron; to shoe (*a horse etc.*).
ferret [fɛ'rɛ], *n.m.* tag (*of a lace*).
ferronnerie [fɛrɔn'ri], *n.f.* iron foundry; ironmongery; wrought iron.
ferronnier [fɛrɔ'nje], *n.m.* (*fem.* **-ière**) ironmonger, iron worker.
ferroviaire [fɛrɔ'vjɛ:r], *a.* pertaining to railways.
ferrure [fɛ'ry:r], *n.f.* iron work; shoeing (*of a horse etc.*).
fertile [fɛr'til], *a.* fertile, fruitful.
fertilement [fɛrtil'mɑ̃], *adv.* fertilely, abundantly.
fertilisant [fɛrtili'zɑ̃], *a.* fertilizing.
fertiliser [fɛrtili'ze], *v.t.* to fertilize, to manure.
fertilité [fɛrtili'te], *n.f.* fertility, fruitfulness.
féru [fe'ry], *a.* smitten; keen on (*something or someone*).
férule [fe'ryl], *n.f.* (*Sch.*) cane, ferule, rod; stroke, cut.
fervent [fɛr'vɑ̃], *a.* fervent.—*n.m.* (*fem.* **-e**) enthusiast, devotee, fan.
ferveur [fɛr'vœ:r], *n.f.* fervor, ardor.
fesse [fɛs], *n.f.* buttock, rump; (*pl.*) bottom.
fessée [fɛ'se], *n.f.* spanking.
fesse-mathieu [fɛsma'tjø], *n.m.* (*pl.* **fesse-mathieux**) miser, skinflint.
fesser [fɛ'se], *v.t.* to spank, to smack.

fessier [fɛ'sje], *n.m.* buttocks, bottom.
festin [fɛs'tɛ̃], *n.m.* feast, banquet.
***festiner** [fɛsti'ne], *v.i.* to banquet, to carouse.
festival [fɛsti'val], *n.m.* festival.
festivité [fɛstivi'te], *n.f.* festivity.
feston [fɛs'tɔ̃], *n.m.* festoon; scallop.
festonner [fɛstɔ'ne], *v.t.* to festoon; to cut in festoons, to scallop.
festoyer [fɛstwa'je], *v.t.* (*conjug. like* EM-PLOYER) to entertain, to feast.
fête [fɛːt], *n.f.* holiday, festival; saint's day; feast; birthday; festivity, merry-making.
fête-Dieu [fɛːt'djø], *n.f.* Corpus Christi day.
fêter [fɛ'te], *v.t.* to keep (as a holiday); to entertain, to feast.
fétiche [fe'tiʃ], *n.m.* fetish.
fétide [fe'tid], *a.* fetid, rank, offensive.
fétidité [fetidi'te], *n.f.* fetidity, offensive smell.
fétu [fe'ty], *n.m.* straw; (*fig.*) pin, rap.
feu (1) [fø], *n.m.* (*pl.* **feux**) fire; burning; heat; discharge of fire-arms; fire-place; (*fig.*) light; brilliancy; passion; vivacity; *crier 'au feu'*, to cry 'fire!'; *faire feu*, to fire; *feu d'artifice*, fireworks; *feu de joie*, bonfire; *feux de position*, (*Motor.*) parking lights; *le coin du feu*, the fire-side; *prendre feu*, to catch fire.
feu (2) [fø], *a.* late, deceased.
feuillage [fœ'jaːʒ], *n.m.* foliage, leaves.
feuille [fœːj], *n.f.* leaf; sheet (*of paper, metal etc.*); newspaper; list; foïl (*of mirrors*).
feuillet [fœ'jɛ], *n.m.* leaf (*of a book*).
feuilleter [fœj'te], *v.t.* (*conjug. like* APPELER) to turn over; to peruse rapidly; *gâteau feuilleté*, flaky puff.
feuillu [fœ'jy], *a.* leafy.
feutrage [fø'traːʒ], *n.m.* felting.
feutre [fø:tr], *n.m.* felt; felt hat.
feutrer [fø'tre], *v.t.* to felt; to pad, to pack.
feutrier [føtri'e], *n.m.* (*fem.* **-ière**) felt maker.
fève [fɛːv], *n.f.* bean, broad bean.
février [fevri'e], *n.m.* February.
fez [fɛːz], *n.m. inv.* fez (*Turkish cap*).
fi! [fi], *int.* fie!
fiacre [fjakr], *n.m.* hackney-coach, cab.
fiançailles [fjɑ̃'saːj], *n.f.* (*used only in pl.*) betrothal, engagement.
fiancé [fjɑ̃'se], *n.m.* (*fem.* **-ée**) betrothed, fiancé, fiancée.
fiancer [fjɑ̃'se], *v.t.* (*conjug. like* COMMENCER) to betroth, to affiance. **se fiancer**, *v.r.* to become engaged to each other.
fiasco [fjas'ko], *n.m. inv.* fiasco, failure.
fibre [fibr], *n.f.* fiber, filament; (*fig.*) feeling.
fibreux [fi'brø], *a.* (*fem.* **-euse**) fibrous, stringy.
ficeler [fis'le], *v.t.* (*conjug. like* APPELER) to bind *or* tie up with string; to do up; to dress up.
ficeleur [fis'lœːr], *n.m.* (*fem.* **-euse**) packer.
ficelle [fi'sɛl], *n.f.* string, packthread, twine; (*fig.*) dodge.
fiche [fiʃ], *n.f.* peg, pin (*for a hinge etc.*); (*Teleph.*) plug; small card; (*Whist*) booby prize; (*colloq.*) slip of paper, memo.
ficher [fi'ʃe], *v.t.* to drive in, to fasten in. **se ficher**, *v.r.* (*colloq.*) to laugh at (*de*).
fichier [fi'ʃje], *n.m.* card index (*cabinet*).
fichoir [fi'ʃwaːr], *n.m.* clothespin.
fichtre! [fiʃtr], *int.* (*colloq.*) dash it! hang it!
fichu (1) [fi'ʃy], *n.m.* neckerchief.

fichu (2) [fi'ʃy], *a.* sorry, pitiful; got up (*dressed*); (*slang*) done for.
fictif [fik'tif], *a.* (*fem.* **-tive**) supposed, fictitious.
fiction [fik'sjɔ̃], *n.f.* fiction; fable.
fictivement [fiktiv'mɑ̃], *adv.* fictitiously.
fidèle [fi'dɛl], *a.* faithful, loyal, true.—*n.* faithful friend etc.; (*pl.*) worshippers, faithful.
fidèlement [fidɛl'mɑ̃], *adv.* faithfully, truly.
fidélité [fideli'te], *n.f.* fidelity, faithfulness, loyalty; accuracy.
fief [fjɛf], *n.m.* fief, fee.
fieffé [fje'fe], *a.* (*colloq.*) arrant, downright.
fiel [fjɛl], *n.m.* gall; (*fig.*) hatred, bitterness, rancour.
fier [fje], *v.t.* to trust, to entrust. **se fier**, *v.r.* to trust to *or* in, to depend upon (*à*).
fier [fjɛːr], *a.* (*fem.* **fière**) proud, haughty; bold; (*colloq.*) fine, capital.
fièrement [fjɛr'mɑ̃], *adv.* proudly, arrogantly, haughtily; boldly.
fierté [fjɛr'te], *n.f.* pride, arrogance; dignity.
fièvre [fjɛːvr], *n.f.* fever, feverishness; (*fig.*) restlessness, excitement.
fiévreux [fje'vrø], *a.* (*fem.* **-euse**) feverish; (*fig.*) restless.—*m.* (*fem.* **-euse**) fever patient.
fifre [fifr], *n.m.* fife; fifer.
figé [fi'ʒe], *a.* stiff, cold, set (*features, smile etc.*).
figement [fiʒ'mɑ̃], *n.m.* congealment, coagulation, curdling.
figer [fi'ʒe], *v.t.* and **se figer**, *v.r.* (*conjug. like* MANGER) to congeal, to coagulate, to curdle.
figue [fig], *n.f.* fig.
figuier [fi'gje], *n.m.* fig tree.
figurant [figy'rɑ̃], *n.m.* (*fem.* **-e**) (*Theat.*, *Cine.*) figurant; extra.
figuratif [figyra'tif], *a.* (*fem.* **-tive**) figurative.
figurativement [figyrativ'mɑ̃], *adv.* figuratively.
figure [fi'gyːr], *n.f.* figure, shape; face, appearance; symbol, type.
figuré [figy're], *a.* figured; figurative.
figurer [figy're], *v.t.* to figure, to represent.—*v.i.* to figure, to appear. **se figurer**, *v.r.* to imagine, fancy *or* picture to oneself.
figurine [figy'rin], *n.f.* figurine, statuette.
fil [fil], *n.m.* thread; wire; yarn; (*cutting*) edge; grain, vein (*in stones etc.*); course (*of a stream etc.*); chain, series; *de fil en aiguille*, one thing leading to another; *donner un coup de fil*, to give a ring; *être au bout du fil*, to be speaking (*on the phone*); *fil à coudre*, sewing thread; *fil de la Vierge*, gossamer; *laine deux fils*, two-ply wool.
filage [fi'laːʒ], *n.m.* spinning.
filament [fila'mɑ̃], *n.m.* filament, thread.
filamenteux [filamɑ̃'tø], *a.* (*fem.* **-euse**) thready, stringy.
filandière [filɑ̃'djɛːr], *n.f.* spinner.
filandreux [filɑ̃'drø], *a.* (*fem.* **-euse**) fibrous, stringy, thready.
filant [fi'lɑ̃], *a.* flowing; ropy; shooting (*of stars*).
filasse [fi'las], *n.f.* harl, tow (*of flax, hemp etc.*); oakum.
filateur [fila'tœːr], *n.m.* spinning-mill owner; spinner.

filature [fila'ty:r], *n.f.* spinning-mill; spinning; shadowing (*by a detective*).
file [fil], *n.f.* file; *à la file*, one after another; *prendre la file*, to take one's place in the line.
filé [fi'le], *a.* drawn out, sustained.—*n.m.* gold *or* silver thread.
filer [fi'le], *v.t.* to spin; (*fig.*) to carry on; to spin out (*a story etc.*); (*Naut.*) to pay out (*a rope*); to trail, to shadow.—*v.i.* to become ropy; to go, to travel; to shoot (*of stars*); to flare (*of a lamp etc.*); to take oneself off; *filer à l'anglaise*, to take French leave; *filer doux*, to sing small.
filet [fi'lɛ], *n.m.* slender thread, string; net; (*Rail.*) rack; filament, fiber; (*Bot., Arch. etc.*) fillet; drop (*of water etc.*); (*fig.*) streak; trickle, streamlet; snaffle-bridle; (*fig.*) snare.
fileur [fi'lœ:r], *n.m.* (*fem.* **-euse**) spinner; wire-drawer.
filial [fi'ljal], *a.* (*m. pl.* **-aux**) filial.
filiale [fi'ljal], *n.f.* subsidiary company, branch.
filiation [filja'sjɔ̃], *n.f.* filiation; (*fig.*) connection, relationship.
filière [fi'ljɛ:r], *n.f.* draw-plate; screw-plate; (*Carp.*) purlin; (*fig.*) channel, series.
filigrane [fili'gran], *n.m.* filigree, filigree work; water-mark (*in paper*); embossing.
filigraner [filigra'ne], *v.t.* to work in filigree; to emboss.
fille [fi:j], *n.f.* daughter; girl, young unmarried woman; maiden; servant-maid; *arrière-petite-fille*, great-granddaughter; *belle-fille*, daughter-in-law, stepdaughter; *jeune fille*, girl; *petite-fille*, granddaughter; *vieille fille*, old maid.
fillette [fi'jɛt], *n.f.* little girl; lass.
filleul [fi'jœ:l], *n.m.* godson.
filleule [fi'jœ:l], *n.f.* goddaughter.
film [film], *n.m.* film; *film fixe*, film strip.
filmer [fil'me], *v.t.* to film.
filon [fi'lɔ̃], *n.m.* metallic vein; (*fig.*) good job; tip.
filou [fi'lu], *n.m.* pickpocket, thief; swindler.
filouter [filu'te], *v.t.* to steal; to cheat, to swindle.
filouterie [filu'tri], *n.f.* picking pockets; swindling, cheating.
fils [fis], *n.m. inv.* son, male child; offspring; *arrière-petit-fils*, great-grandson; *beau-fils*, stepson, son-in-law; *petit-fils*, grandson.
filtrage [fil'tra:ʒ], *n.m.* filtering, straining.
filtrant [fil'trɑ̃], *a.* filtering, straining; *bout filtrant*, filter-tip.
filtration [filtra'sjɔ̃], *n.f.* filtration, straining; percolation.
filtre (1) [filtr], *n.m.* filter; cup of filtered coffee; *filtre à café*, percolator.
filtre (2) [PHILTRE].
filtrer [fil'tre], *v.t.* to filter, to strain.—*v.i.* and **se filtrer**, *v.r.* to filter; to percolate.
filure [fi'ly:r], *n.f.* texture of a spun fabric.
fin (1) [fɛ̃], *n.f.* end, conclusion, close; death; destination; aim, design.
fin (2) [fɛ̃], *a.* fine, thin, slender; delicate; refined, polite; acute; cunning.—*n.m.* sharp fellow; main point.—*n.f.* **(-e)** type of liqueur brandy.
final [fi'nal], *a.* final, last, ultimate.

finale [fi'nal], *n.m.* (*Mus.*) finale.—*n.f.* (*Spt.*) final.
finalement [final'mɑ̃], *adv.* finally, lastly.
finalité [finali'te], *n.f.* finality.
finance [fi'nɑ̃:s], *n.f.* ready money; (*pl.*) (*public*) finances, exchequer, treasury.
financer [finɑ̃'se], *v.t.* (*conjug. like* COMMENCER) to finance—*v.i.* to lay out money.
financier [finɑ̃'sje], *a.* (*fem.* **-ière**) financial.—*n.m.* financier.
financièrement [finɑ̃sjɛr'mɑ̃], *adv.* financially.
finaud [fi'no], *a.* sly, artful, cunning.—*n.m.* (*fem.* **-e**) sly, artful person.
fine [fin], [FIN (2)].
finement [fin'mɑ̃], *adv.* finely, delicately; ingeniously; artfully.
finesse [fi'nɛs], *n.f.* fineness, delicacy; ingenuity; finesse, artifice, slyness.
finette [fi'nɛt], *n.f.* thin material of wool *or* cotton, flannelette.
fini [fi'ni], *a.* finished, ended.—*n.m.* finish, high finish, perfection.
finir [fi'ni:r], *v.t.* to finish, to complete; to end, to terminate.—*v.i.* to end, to conclude, to be over; to expire.
finissage [fini'sa:ʒ], *n.m.* finishing touches.
finissant [fini'sɑ̃], *a.* declining, dying.
finlandais [fɛ̃lɑ̃'dɛ], *a.* Finnish.—*n.m.* Finnish (*language*); (**Finlandais**, *fem.* **-aise**) Finn.
Finlande [fɛ̃'lɑ̃:d], **la**, *f.* Finland.
finnois [fi'nwa], *a.* Finnish.—*n.m.* Finnish (*language*); (**Finnois**, *fem.* **-oise**) Finn.
fiole [fjɔl], *n.f.* phial.
firmament [firma'mɑ̃], *n.m.* firmament, sky.
fisc [fisk], *n.m.* public treasury, fisc.
fiscal [fis'kal], *a.* (*m. pl.* **-aux**) fiscal, financial.
fissible [fi'sibl], *a.* fissile (*of radio-active materials*).
fission [fi'sjɔ̃], *n.f.* fission, splitting (*of atom*); *fission de l'atome*, nuclear fission.
fissure [fi'sy:r], *n.f.* fissure, crack, rent.
fissurer (**se**) [səfisy're], *v.r.* to become fissured.
five-o'clock [faivɔ'klɔk], *n.m.* afternoon tea.
fixation [fiksa'sjɔ̃], *n.f.* fixation, fixing; settlement; rating, assessment.
fixe [fiks], *a.* fixed; settled; appointed, regular.—*n.m.* fixed salary.—*int.* (*Mil.*) eyes front! steady!
fixement [fiksə'mɑ̃], *adv.* fixedly, steadily.
fixer [fik'se], *v.t.* to fix, to fasten; to settle; to establish; to stare at; to attract. **se fixer**, *v.r.* to be fixed; to settle down.
fixité [fiksi'te], *n.f.* fixity, stability.
flac [flak], *int.* slap! bang! plop!—*n.m.* anti-aircraft gunfire, flak.
flaccidité [flaksidi'te], *n.f.* flaccidity.
flacon [fla'kɔ̃], *n.m.* bottle; decanter; phial.
flagellant [flaʒɛ'lɑ̃], *n.m.* flagellant.
flagellation [flaʒɛla'sjɔ̃], *n.f.* flagellation, flogging.
flageller [flaʒɛ'le], *v.t.* to flagellate, to scourge, to flog; (*fig.*) to lash with words.
flageoler [flaʒɔ'le], *v.i.* to tremble, to shake (*of legs*).
flageolet [flaʒɔ'lɛ], *n.m.* flageolet (*music*); (*small*) green kidney bean.
flagorner [flagɔr'ne], *v.t.* to flatter servilely, to toady to.

flagornerie [flagɔrnə'ri], *n.f.* sycophancy, base flattery.

flagorneur [flagɔr'nœːr], *n.m.* (*fem.* **-euse**) sycophant, toady.

flagrant [fla'grã], *a.* flagrant, gross; *en flagrant délit*, red-handed.

flair [flɛːr], *n.m.* (*Hunt.*) nose; (*fig.*) perspicacity.

flairer [flɛ're], *v.t.* to smell, to scent; (*colloq.*) to smell of; to find out.

flamand [fla'mã], *a.* Flemish.—*n.m.* Flemmish (*language*); (**Flamand**, *fem.* **-ande**) Fleming.

flamant (rose) [fla'mã(roːz)], *n.m.* flamingo.

flambant [flã'bã], *a.* blazing, flaming; (*pop.*) smart, flashy; *flambant neuf*, brand new.

flambeau [flã'bo], *n.m.* (*pl.* **-eaux**) torch, link; candle, candlestick.

flambée [flã'be], *n.f.* blaze.

flamber [flã'be], *v.t.* to singe; to fumigate, to disinfect.—*v.i.* to blaze, to flame, to flare.

flamboiement [flãbwa'mã], *n.m.* flaming, blaze.

flamboyant [flãbwa'jã], *a.* flaming, blazing; flashing.

flamboyer [flãbwa'je], *v.i.* (*conjug. like* EMPLOYER) to flame, to blaze, to flare.

flamme [flɑːm], *n.f.* flame; (*fig.*) fire; glow; ardor, passion.

flammèche [flɑ'mɛʃ], *n.f.* flake of fire, spark.

flammer [flɑ'me], *v.t.* to singe (*material*).

flan [flã], *n.m.* (*baked*) custard tart; flan.

flanc [flã], *n.m.* flank, side; (*fig.*) womb, bowels.

flancher [flã'ʃe], *v.i.* (*fam.*) to give in, to rat, to scab; (*Motor.*) to stop, to break down.

flandrin [flã'drɛ̃], *n.m.* (*colloq.*) *un grand flandrin*, a long, lanky fellow.

flanelle [fla'nɛl], *n.f.* flannel.

flâner [flɑ'ne], *v.i.* to lounge, to stroll, to loaf.

flânerie [flɑ'nri], *n.f.* lounging; stroll; loafing.

flâneur [flɑ'nœːr], *n.m.* (*fem.* **-euse**) stroller; lounger, loafer.

flanquer [flã'ke], *v.t.* to flank; (*Mil.*) to defend, to guard; (*colloq.*) to deal (*a blow*); to fling. **se flanquer**, *v.r. se flanquer par terre*, to throw oneself down.

flaque [flak], *n.f.* small pool, puddle.

flash [flaʃ], *n.m.* (*Phot.*) flash-light; (*Cine.*) flash.

flasque (1) [flask], *a.* limp, slack, flabby, flaccid.

flasque (2) [flask], *n.f.* powder horn.

flatter [fla'te], *v.t.* to stroke, to caress; to flatter; to soothe; to cajole. **se flatter**, *v.r.* to flatter oneself; to pride oneself; to hope, to expect.

flatterie [fla'tri], *n.f.* flattery, adulation.

flatteur [fla'tœːr], *a.* (*fem.* **-euse**) flattering, complimentary.—*n.m.* (*fem.* **-euse**) flatterer.

flatteusement [flatøz'mã], *adv.* flatteringly.

flatulence [flaty'lãːs], *n.f.* flatulence, wind.

flatulent [flaty'lã], *a.* flatulent, windy.

fléau [fle'o], *n.m.* (*pl.* **fléaux**) flail; (*fig.*) scourge, plague; beam (*of a balance*).

flèche [flɛʃ], *n.f.* arrow, dart; shaft; (*Arch.*) slender spire; *faire flèche de tout bois*, to leave no stone unturned.

fléchette [fle'ʃɛt], *n.f.* dart (*game*).

fléchir [fle'ʃiːr], *v.t.* to bend, to bow; (*fig.*) to move, to persuade.—*v.i.* to bend, to bow, to yield; to stagger.

fléchissement [fleʃis'mã], *n.m.* bending, giving way.

flegmatique [flɛgma'tik], *a.* (*Med.*) phlegmatic; (*fig.*) stolid, sluggish.

flegme [flɛgm], *n.m.* phlegm; (*fig.*) coolness, impassivity.

flet [flɛ], **flétan** [fle'tã], *n.m.* **grand flétan**, halibut; *petit flétan* or *flet*, flounder.

flétrir [fle'triːr], *v.t.* to wither; (*fig.*) to blight, to tarnish, to blemish. **se flétrir**, *v.r.* to fade, to wither.

flétrissant [fletri'sã], *a.* dishonoring, blighting.

flétrissure [fletri'syːr], *n.f.* fading, withering; stigma, disgrace.

fleur [flœːr], *n.f.* flower, blossom; bloom; (*fig.*) best, pick; surface; *à fleur d'eau*, at water level; *à fleur de peau*, superficially; *yeux à fleur de tête*, prominent or goggle eyes.

fleurer [flœ're], *v.i.* to smell, to exhale.

fleuret [flœ'rɛ], *n.m.* (*Fenc.*) foil; miner's drill.

fleurette [flœ'rɛt], *n.f.* little flower, floweret; amorous discourse, gallant speech.

fleuri [flœ'ri], *a.* flowery; florid.

fleurir [flœ'riːr], *v.t.* to decorate with flowers. —*v.i.* to flower, to blossom; to flourish. **se fleurir**, *v.r.* to adorn oneself with flowers.

fleurissant [flœri'sã], *a.* blossoming, blooming.

fleuriste [flœ'rist], *a. and n.* florist; artificial flower maker *or* seller.

fleuron [flœ'rɔ̃], *n.m.* carved *or* painted flower; (*fig.*) flower work; jewel.

fleuve [flœːv], *n.m.* river (*flowing into the sea*), large stream.

flexibilité [flɛksibili'te], *n.f.* flexibility, pliancy.

flexible [flɛk'sibl], *a.* flexible, pliable, supple.

flexion [flɛk'sjɔ̃], *n.f.* flexion, bending.

flibuster [flibys'te], *v.i.* to buccaneer, to filibuster, to freeboot.

flibusterie [flibys'tri], *n.f.* filibustering; robbery, theft.

flibustier [flibys'tje], *n.m.* buccaneer, pirate; filibuster.

flirt [flœrt], *n.m.* flirtation, flirting.

flirter [flœr'te], *v.i.* to flirt.

floc [flɔk], *n.m.* tuft, tassel.—*int.* flop!

floche [flɔʃ], *a.* flossy, shaggy.

flocon [flɔ'kɔ̃], *n.m.* flock, tuft; flake (*of snow*).

floconneux [flɔkɔ'nø], *a.* (*fem.* **-euse**) flaky.

floraison [flɔrɛ'zɔ̃], *n.f.* efflorescence, flowering.

floral [flɔ'ral], *a.* (*m. pl.* **-aux**) floral.

flore [flɔːr], *n.f.* flora.

florentin [flɔrã'tɛ̃], *a.* Florentine.

florin [flɔ'rɛ̃], *n.m.* florin.

florir [flɔ'riːr], [FLEURIR].

florissant [flɔri'sã], *a.* prosperous, flourishing.

floriste [flɔ'rist], *n.* florist.

flot [flo], *n.m.* wave, billow; (*fig.*) tide, flood; crowd; (*pl.*) sea, stream, torrent.

flottage [flɔ'taːʒ], *n.m.* floating of wood, rafting.

flottaison [flɔtɛ'zɔ̃], *n.f.* floating.

flottant [flɔ'tã], *a.* floating, waving; (*fig.*) irresolute.

flotte [flɔt], *n.f.* fleet; navy.

flottement [flɔt'mã], *n.m.* floating; (*fig.*) wavering, irresolution.

flotter [flɔ'te], v.i. to float; to flutter (of flag); to be irresolute.
flotteur [flɔ'tœːr], n.m. raftsman; fishing-float; cable-buoy.
flottille [flɔ'tiːj], n.f. flotilla.
flou [flu], a. hazy, soft, blurred, out of focus. —n.m. softness, haziness (of outlines); (Dress.) looseness.
fluctuation [flyktɥa'sjɔ̃], n.f. fluctuation.
fluctuer [flyk'tɥe], v.i. to fluctuate.
fluctueux [flyk'tɥø], a. (fem. -euse) fluctuating, agitated, boisterous.
fluet [flɥ'ɛ], a. (fem. -ette) slender, thin, slim.
fluide [flɥ'id], a. fluid (liquid).—n.m. fluid.
fluidité [flyidi'te], n.f. fluidity.
fluorescence [flyɔrɛ'sãːs], n.f. fluorescence.
fluorescent [flyɔrɛ'sã], a. fluorescent.
fluorure [flyɔ'ryːr], n.m. fluoride.
flûte [flyt], n.f. flute; long French roll; tall glass (for champagne).
flûté [fly'te], a. soft, fluted, fluty (of a voice).
flûtiste [fly'tist], n. flautist, flute player.
fluvial [fly'vjal], a. (m. pl. -aux) fluvial.
flux [fly], n.m. flux, flow, flood, rising.
fluxion [flyk'sjɔ̃], n.f. inflammation, swelling.
foc [fɔk], n.m. (Naut.) jib.
focal [fɔ'kal], a. (m. pl. -aux) focal.
foi [fwa], n.f. faith, belief; trust; fidelity, honor; proof, testimony.
foie [fwa], n.m. liver.
foin [fwɛ̃], n.m. hay.
foire [fwaːr], n.f. fair (market); fairing.
fois [fwa], n.f. inv. time (turn, occasion); **une fois**, once; **trois fois**, three times.
foison [fwa'zɔ̃], n.f. plenty, abundance.
foisonner [fwazɔ'ne], v.i. to abound, to increase, to multiply.
fol [fɔl], [FOU].
folâtre [fɔ'laːtr], a. playful, gay, frolicsome.
folâtrer [fɔla'tre], v.i. to play, to sport, to frolic.
folâtrerie [fɔlatrə'ri], n.f. frolic, prank, gambol.
foliacé [fɔlja'se], a. (Bot.) foliaceous.
foliation [fɔlja'sjɔ̃], n.f. foliation.
folichon [fɔli'ʃɔ̃], a. (fam.) frolicsome, waggish, wanton.
folie [fɔ'li], n.f. madness, distraction, folly; foolery, jest; mania; hobby.
folio [fɔ'ljo], n.m. folio.
folle [fɔl], [FOU].
follement [fɔl'mã], adv. madly, foolishly.
follet [fɔ'lɛ], a. (fem. -ette) wanton, playful, frolicsome; **feu follet**, will o' the wisp.
fomentation [fɔmãta'sjɔ̃], n.f. fomentation.
fomenter [fɔmã'te], v.t. to foment; (fig.) to feed, to excite.
foncé [fɔ̃'se], a. dark, deep (of color).
foncer [fɔ̃'se], v.t. (conjug. like COMMENCER) to fit a bottom to (a cask etc.); to sink (wells etc.); to deepen (colors). —v.i. to dash, to swoop (sur).
foncier [fɔ̃'sje], a. (fem. -ière) landed; based on or derived from land; (fig.) thorough.—n.m. land tax.
foncièrement [fɔ̃sjɛr'mã], adv. thoroughly, completely, fundamentally.
fonction [fɔ̃k'sjɔ̃], n.f. function, office; occupation.
fonctionnaire [fɔ̃ksjɔ'nɛːr], n.m. civil servant, officer, official.

fonctionnel [fɔ̃ksjɔ'nɛl], a. (fem. -elle) functional.
fonctionnement [fɔ̃ksjɔn'mã], n.m. operation, working, action.
fonctionner [fɔ̃ksjɔ'ne], v.i. to work, to act, to operate.
fond [fɔ̃], n.m. bottom; bed, ground; farther end; foundation; (fig.) essence; basis; subject matter; (Paint.) background; (Theat.) back-cloth.
fondage [fɔ̃'daːʒ], n.m. casting, smelting.
fondamental [fɔ̃dama'tal], a. (m. pl. -aux) fundamental, essential.
fondamentalement [fɔ̃damãtal'mã], adv. fundamentally, essentially, radically.
fondant [fɔ̃'dã], a. melting, dissolving; luscious.—n.m. fondant (sweetmeat); flux (for metals).
fondateur [fɔ̃da'tœːr], n.m. (fem. -trice) founder; promoter.
fondation [fɔ̃da'sjɔ̃], n.f. foundation; ground-work; founding; endowment.
fondé [fɔ̃'de], a. founded, well-founded; (Fin.) consolidated.—n.m. proxy.
fondement [fɔ̃d'mã], n.m. foundation; basis, ground, cause.
fonder [fɔ̃'de], v.t. to lay the foundation of, to establish; to institute; to base; to endow. **se fonder**, v.r. to rely or rest (upon), to be founded (sur).
fonderie [fɔ̃'dri], n.f. foundry; smelting-house; casting.
fondeur [fɔ̃'dœːr], n.m. founder, caster, smelter.
fondre [fɔ̃dr], v.t. to melt; to dissolve; to smelt; to cast.—v.i. to melt; to pounce (sur); to vanish; to blow (of a fuse); **fondre en larmes**, to burst into tears. **se fondre**, v.r. to melt; to dissolve; to be cast; to blend; to diminish, to melt away.
fondrière [fɔ̃dri'ɛːr], n.f. bog, quagmire; rut, pothole; slough.
fonds [fɔ̃], n.m. land, soil; landed property; funds, capital; business assets; (pl.) funds, stocks etc.
fondue [fɔ̃'dy], n.f. dish of melted cheese and eggs.
fongicide [fɔ̃ʒi'sid], a. fungicide.
fongoïde [fɔ̃gɔ'id], a. fungoid.
fongueux [fɔ̃'gø], a. (fem. -euse) fungous.
fongus [fɔ̃'gys], n.m. (Med.) fungus.
fontaine [fɔ̃'tɛːn], n.f. fountain, spring; cistern.
fonte [fɔ̃ːt], n.f. melting, smelting; cast-iron; casting; holster (of saddles).
fonts [fɔ̃], n.m. pl. (no sing.) font.
football [fut'bol], n.m. Association Football.
footballeur [futbɔ'lœːr], n.m. football player.
footing [fu'tiŋ], n.m. walking (for training or exercise).
forage [fɔ'raːʒ], n.m. boring, drilling; sinking (of well).
forain [fɔ'rɛ̃], a. non-resident, travelling, itinerant; **marchand forain**, hawker, pedlar.
forban [fɔr'bã], n.m. pirate, corsair, free-booter.
forçat [fɔr'sa], n.m. convict.
force [fɔrs], n.f. strength, might, power; authority; violence, constraint; vigor; resolution; skill; (pl.) troops, forces.— *adv. a great deal, a great many.

forcé [fɔr'se], *a.* forced, compulsory; unnatural, strained, far-fetched.

forcément [fɔrse'mā], *adv.* forcibly; necessarily, inevitably.

forcené [fɔrsə'ne], *a.* mad, furious; passionate, infuriated.—*n.m.* (*fem.* **-ée**) mad person.

forceps [fɔr'sɛps], *n.m. inv.* forceps.

forcer [fɔr'se], *v.t.* (*conjug. like* COMMENCER) to force; to compel; to impel; to strain; to break open; to storm; to outrage. **se forcer**, *v.r.* to strain oneself; to do violence to one's feelings.

forer [fɔ're], *v.t.* to bore, to drill, to perforate.

forestier [fɔrɛs'tje], *a.* (*fem.* **-ière**) pertaining to forests.—*n.m.* ranger, keeper, forester.

foret [fɔ're], *n.m.* borer, drill.

forêt [fɔ're], *n.f.* forest; woodland.

forfaire [fɔr'fɛːr], *v.t. irr.* to forfeit (*a fief*).—*v.i.* (*used only in inf.*, *p.p.* **(forfait** (1) *and compound tenses*) to fail (*in one's duty*); to trespass, to be false to.

forfait (2) [fɔr'fɛ], *n.m.* crime, heinous offence.

forfait (3) [fɔr'fɛ], *n.m.* contract.

forfaiture [fɔrfɛ'tyːr], *n.f.* forfeiture; breach of duty.

forfanterie [fɔrfā'tri], *n.f.* romancing, bragging, boasting.

forge [fɔrʒ], *n.f.* forge, smithy; iron-works.

forger [fɔr'ʒe], *v.t.* (*conjug. like* MANGER) to forge, to hammer; (*fig.*) to invent, to fabricate. **se forger**, *v.r.* to imagine, to conjure up, to fancy.

forgeron [fɔrʒə'rō], *n.m.* smith, blacksmith.

formaliser (**se**) [səfɔrmali'ze], *v.r.* to take exception *or* offence (*de*).

formalisme [fɔrma'lism], *n.m.* formalism.

formaliste [fɔrma'list], *a.* formal, precise.—*n.* formalist; quibbler.

formalité [fɔrmali'te], *n.f.* formality; form, ceremony.

format [fɔr'ma], *n.m.* format (*size, shape etc.*, *of a book*).

formateur [fɔrma'tœːr], *a.* (*fem.* **-trice**) formative, creative.

formation [fɔrma'sjō], *n.f.* formation; education; (*Geol.*) structure.

forme [fɔrm], *n.f.* form, shape, figure; etiquette; crown (*of a hat*).

formé [fɔr'me], *a.* formed, mature.

formel [fɔr'mɛl], *a.* (*fem.* **-elle**) formal; express, precise.

formellement [fɔrmɛl'mā], *adv.* formally; expressly, precisely, strictly.

former [fɔr'me], *v.t.* to form, to frame; to make up; to bring up; to train; to mold. **se former**, *v.r.* to be formed; to take shape.

formidable [fɔrmi'dabl], *a.* formidable, fearful; (*fam.*) terrific.

Formose [fɔr'moːz], **la**, *f.* Formosa, Taiwan.

formule [fɔr'myl], *n.f.* formula, form; model; recipe.

formuler [fɔrmy'le], *v.t.* to formulate; to detail; (*Med.*) to write (*a prescription*).

fort [fɔːr], *a.* strong, sturdy, powerful; clever; plentiful; shocking; painful; high (*wind*); heavy (*ground, rain*).—*n.m.* strong part; stronghold, fort; strength; depth, heat, height; centre.—*adv.* very, very much, extremely; hard.

fortement [fɔrtə'mā], *adv.* strongly, vigorously; much, exceedingly.

forteresse [fɔrtə'rɛs], *n.f.* fortress, stronghold.

fortifiant [fɔrti'fjā], *a.* strengthening, bracing.—*n.m.* (*Med.*) tonic.

fortification [fɔrtifika'sjō], *n.f.* fortification; fort, redoubt.

fortifier [fɔrti'fje], *v.t.* to strengthen, to invigorate; to fortify; to confirm. **se fortifier**, *v.r.* to fortify oneself, to grow strong.

fortuit [fɔr'tɥi], *a.* fortuitous, casual.

fortuitement [fɔrtɥit'mā], *adv.* fortuitously, casually, by chance.

fortune [fɔr'tyn], *n.f.* fortune, chance, hazard, risk; success, luck; wealth.

fortuné [fɔrty'ne], *a.* fortunate, lucky; happy; well-to-do.

fosse [foːs], *n.f.* hole, pit; grave; (*Hort.*) trench.

fossé [fo'se], *n.m.* ditch, drain, trench; moat.

fossette [fo'sɛt], *n.f.* dimple.

fossile [fo'sil], *a.* fossilized.—*n.m.* fossil.

fossiliser [fɔsili'se], *v.t.* to fossilize. **se fossiliser**, *v.r.* to become fossilized.

fossoyage [foswa'jaːʒ], *n.m.* ditching; gravedigging.

fossoyer [foswa'je], *v.t.* (*conjug. like* EMPLOYER) to ditch, to dig a trench round.

fossoyeur [foswa'jœːr], *n.m.* grave digger; sexton beetle.

fou [fu], *a.* (*before vowels* **fol**, *fem.* **folle**) mad, demented; wild, foolish; tremendous.—*n.m.* (*fem.* **folle**) madman, madwoman.—*n.m* jester, fool; (*Chess*) bishop.

foudre (1) [fudr], *n.f.* lightning; thunder, thunderbolt; (*fig.*) sudden calamity; *coup de foudre*, clap of thunder.—*n.m.* (*fig.*) *un foudre de guerre* a great captain; *un foudre d'éloquence*, a mighty speaker.

foudre (2) [fudr], *n.m.* large cask, tun.

foudroiement [fudrwa'mā], *n.m.* striking, blasting (*by thunder* or *lightning*); (*fig.*) destruction.

foudroyant [fudrwa'jā], *a.* thundering; terrible, crushing (*news*).

foudroyer [fudrwa'je], *v.t.* (*conjug. like* EMPLOYER) to strike (*thunder* or *lightning*); to riddle with shot; (*fig.*) to blast, to crush.—*v.i.* to thunder; (*fig.*) to fulminate.

fouet [fwɛ], *n.m.* whip; lash; whipping; slating (*criticism*).

fouetter [fwɛ'te], *v.t.* to whip, to flog; to beat (*eggs etc.*); to flick; (*fig.*) to excite.—*v.i.* to beat, to patter (*of hail, rain*).

fougeraie [fuʒ're], *n.f.* fern patch, fernery.

fougère [fu'ʒɛːr], *n.f.* fern.

fougue [fug], *n.f.* ardor, impetuosity; fire, spirit, mettle; (*Naut.*) mizzen-top.

fougueux [fu'gø], *a.* (*fem.* **-euse**) fiery, impetuous, ardent, passionate, high-mettled.

fouille [fuːj], *n.f.* excavation, digging; search.

fouiller [fu'je], *v.t.* to excavate; (*fig.*) to pry into, to rummage, to ransack; to search; to think out (*problems etc.*).—*v.i.* to dig, to search; (*fig.*) to rummage.

fouillis [fu'ji], *n.m.* medley, jumble; confused mass (*of foliage etc.*).

fouine (1) [fwin], *n.f.* marten.

fouine (2) [fwin], *n.f.* pitchfork; fish spear.
fouiner [fwi'ne], *v.i.* (*colloq.*) to nose about, to ferret; to slink off.
fouir [fwi:r], *v.t.* to dig; to burrow.
fouissement [fwis'mã], *n.m.* digging; burrowing.
fouisseur [fwi'sœr], *a.* (*fem.* **-euse**) burrowing (*animal*).
foulage [fu'la:ʒ], *n.m.* fulling; treading, pressing (*of grapes*).
foulant [fu'lã], *a.* pressing; forcing; *pompe foulante*, force pump.
foulard [fu'la:r], *n.m.* silk neckerchief; scarf.
foule [ful], *n.f.* crowd, throng, multitude; mob.
foulée [fu'le], *n.f.* tread (*of steps*); stride (*of a horse* or *runner*).
fouler [fu'le], *v.t.* to tread; to trample down; to press; to oppress; to sprain (*ankle*).—*v.i.* (*Print.*) to press. **se fouler**, *v.r. se fouler le pied*, to sprain one's foot.
fouleur [fu'lœ:r], *n.m.* (*fem.* **-euse**) fuller; wine presser.
foulure [fu'ly:r], *n.f.* sprain, wrench, strain.
four [fu:r], *n.m.* oven; bakehouse; furnace; kiln; *des petits fours*, fancy biscuits, small cakes.
fourbe [furb], *a.* cheating, deceitful.—*n.* cheat, swindler, impostor.
fourberie [furbə'ri], *n.f.* cheating, knavery, imposture, deceit.
fourbir [fur'bi:r], *v.t.* to furbish, to polish.
fourbisseur [furbi'sœ:r], *n.m.* furbisher; sword-cutler.
fourbissure [furbi'sy:r], *n.f.* furbishing, polishing.
fourbu [fur'by], *a.* foundered, run down (*of horses*); dead tired (*of persons*).
fourbure [fur'by:r], *n.f.* foundering, inflammation of the feet.
fourche [furʃ], *n.f.* pitchfork, (garden) fork, fork (*of roads*).
fourchée [fur'ʃe], *n.f.* pitchforkful.
fourcher [fur'ʃe], *v.i.* to fork; to divide. **se fourcher**, *v.r.* to fork, to branch off.
fourchetée [furʃ'te], *n.f.* table-forkful.
fourchette [fur'ʃet], *n.f.* table fork; breast bone (*of birds*).
fourchu [fur'ʃy], *a.* forked; cloven; furcate.
fourgon (1) [fur'gõ], *n.m.* van, truck, freight *or* baggage car.
fourgon (2) [fur'gõ], *n.m.* poker, fire-iron (*for ovens etc.*).
fourgonner [furgɔ'ne], *v.i.* to poke the fire (*of an oven*); (*colloq.*) to poke, to rummage.
fourmi [fur'mi], *n.f.* ant.
fourmilière [furmi'lje:r], *n.f.* ant hill, ants' nest; (*fig.*) swarm; crowd.
fourmillement [furmij'mã], *n.m.* tingling, pins and needles; swarming.
fourmiller [furmi'je], *v.i.* to swarm, to be full (*de*); to have pins and needles (*in one's limbs etc.*).
fournaise [fur'ne:z], *n.f.* (*Lit.*) furnace; (*fig.*) oven.
fourneau [fur'no], *n.m.* (*pl.* **-eaux**) stove, cooker, cooking range; furnace.
fournée [fur'ne], *n.f.* batch, baking; kilnful (*of bricks*).
fournil [fur'ni], *n.m.* bakehouse.
fourniment [furni'mã], *n.m.* (*Mil.*) equipment.

fournir [fur'ni:r], *v.t.* to furnish, to supply, to stock, to provide; to make up (*a sum of money*).—*v.i.* to contribute (*à*); to suffice.
fournisseur [furni'sœ:r], *n.m.* army contractor; purveyor; tradesman.
fourniture [furni'ty:r], *n.f.* furnishing; supply, provision; equipment.
fourrage [fu'ra:ʒ], *n.m.* fodder; forage; foraging party.
fourrager [fura'ʒe], *v.t.* (*conjug. like* MANGER) to ravage; to upset.—*v.i.* to forage; to plunder, to ravage; (*fig.*) to rummage.
fourrageur [fura'ʒœ:r], *n.m.* forager; (*fig.*) marauder; rummager.
fourré [fu're], *a.* thick, furry; wooded; (*fig.*) underhand (*of a blow etc.*).—*n.m.* thicket, brake.
fourreau [fu'ro], *n.m.* (*pl.* **-eaux**) sheath, case; scabbard; cover; tight-fitting *or* sheath dress.
fourrer [fu're], *v.t.* to line with fur; to poke; to cram, to stuff. **se fourrer**, *v.r.* to thrust oneself in, to intrude; to wrap oneself up warmly.
fourreur [fu'rœ:r], *n.m.* furrier.
fourrier [fu'rje], *n.m.* quartermaster-sergeant; (*fig.*) harbinger.
fourrière [fu'rjɛ:r], *n.f.* pound (*for vehicles, strayed animals*).
fourrure [fu'ry:r], *n.f.* fur, furred gown.
fourvoyer [furvwa'je], *v.t.* (*conjug. like* EMPLOYER) to lead astray, to mislead; (*fig.*) to baffle. **se fourvoyer**, *v.r.* to go astray, to lose one's way; (*fig.*) to blunder badly.
fox (1) [fɔks], *n.m.* fox terrier.
fox (2) [fɔks], *n.m.* foxtrot.
foyer [fwa'je], *n.m.* hearth; fire; fire box (*of an engine*); (*fig.*) home, family; (*Theat.*) foyer; focus, source.
frac [frak], *n.m.* frock coat.
fracas [fra'kɑ], *n.m.* noise, din; disturbance; fuss.
fracasser [fraka'se], *v.t.* to break into pieces, to shatter. **se fracasser**, *v.r.* to crash to pieces.
fraction [frak'sjõ], *n.f.* breaking; fraction, portion.
fractionnaire [fraksjɔ'nɛ:r], *a.* fractional.
fracture [frak'ty:r], *n.f.* breaking (*with violence*), rupture; (*Surg.*) fracture.
fracturer [frakty're], *v.t.* to break, to smash; (*Surg.*) to fracture. **se fracturer**, *v.r.* to fracture oneself; to be fractured.
fragile [fra'ʒil], *a.* fragile, brittle; frail.
fragilité [fraʒili'te], *n.f.* fragility, brittleness; frailty.
fragment [frag'mã], *n.m.* fragment, piece, remnant.
fragmentaire [fragmã'tɛ:r], *a.* fragmentary.
fragmentation [fragmãta'sjõ], *n.f.* fragmenting, fragmentation.
fragmenter [fragmã'te], *v.t.* to reduce to fragments.
fragrance [fra'grã:s], *n.f.* fragrance.
fragrant [fra'grã], *a.* fragrant.
frai [frɛ], *n.m.* fraying; spawning (*of fish*).
fraîche [freʃ], [FRAIS (1)].
fraîchement [frɛʃ'mã], *adv.* coolly, freshly; newly, recently.
fraîcheur [frɛ'ʃœ:r], *n.f.* coolness, freshness, coldness; ruddiness; brilliancy.
fraîchir [frɛ'ʃi:r], *v.i.* to freshen; to get cool.

159

frais

frais (1) [frɛ], *a.* (*fem.* **fraîche**) cool; fresh; new; youthful; ruddy; new-laid (*of eggs*).— *n.m.* coolness, freshness; cool spot.—*adv.* freshly, newly, recently, just.

frais (2) [frɛ], *n.m.* (*used only in pl.*) expense, expenses; charge, charges, cost, outlay; *menus frais*, petty expenses; *sans frais*, free of charge.

fraise (1) [frɛːz], *n.f.* strawberry; strawberry mark, birthmark; ruff.

fraise (2) [frɛːz], *n.f.* fraise (*tool for enlarging a drill hole etc.*); (dentist's) drill.

fraiser [frɛ'ze], *v.t.* to plait, to ruffle; to countersink.

fraisier [frɛ'zje], *n.m.* strawberry plant; strawberry grower.

framboise [frã'bwaːz], *n.f.* raspberry.

framboiser [frãbwa'ze], *v.t.* to give a raspberry flavor to.

framboisier [frãbwa'zje], *n.m.* raspberrybush.

franc (1) [frã], *n.m.* franc (*French coin*); new franc (*of 1960*).

franc (2) [frã], *a.* (*fem.* **franche**) free; exempt; frank, candid, sincere; clear.— *adv.* frankly, openly, sincerely; clean; quite, completely.

franc (3) [frã], *a.* (*fem.* **franque**) Frankish.— *n.m.* Frankish (*language*); (**Franc,** *fem.* **Franque**) Frank.

français [frã'sɛ], *a.* French.—*n.m.* French (*language*); (**Français,** *fem.* **-aise**) Frenchman, Frenchwoman.

France [frãːs], **la,** *f.* France.

franche [frãʃ], [FRANC (2)].

franchement [frãʃ'mã], *adv.* frankly, sincerely; plainly; boldly.

franchir [frã'ʃiːr], *v.t.* to leap, to jump over; to clear; to pass over; to surmount.

franchise [frã'ʃiːz], *n.f.* exemption, immunity; freedom (*of a city*); (*fig.*) frankness, sincerity.

franchissable [frãʃi'sabl], *a.* passable, capable of being crossed.

franchissement [frãʃis'mã], *n.m.* leaping over, crossing.

francisation [frãsiza'sjɔ̃], *n.f.* Gallicizing of foreign word; registration as a French ship.

franciscain [frãsis'kɛ̃], *a.* and *n.m.* (*fem.* **-e**) Franciscan, grey friar, Franciscan nun.

franciser [frãsi'ze], *v.t.* to Gallicize; to Frenchify. **se franciser,** *v.r.* to become French *or* Frenchified.

franc-maçon [frãma'sɔ̃], *n.m.* (*pl.* **francs-maçons**) freemason.

franc-maçonnerie [frãmasɔn'ri], *n.f.* freemasonry.

franco [frã'ko], *adv.* free of charge; prepaid.

François [frã'swa], *m.* Francis.

Françoise [frã'swaːz], *f.* Frances.

francophile [frãko'fil], *a.* and *n.* Francophile.

francophobe [frãko'fɔb], *a.* and *n.* Francophobe.

franc-parler [frãpar'le], *n.m.* frankness *or* freedom of speech.

franc-tireur [frãti'rœːr], *n.m.* franc-tireur; sniper.

frange [frãːʒ], *n.f.* fringe.

franger [frã'ʒe], *v.t.* (*conjug. like* MANGER) to fringe.

franque [frãk], [FRANC (3)].

frappant [fra'pã], *a.* striking, impressive.

frappé [fra'pe], *a.* struck, astounded; iced (*of liquids etc.*); (*fig.*) powerful.

frappement [frap'mã], *n.m.* striking, stamping; clapping (*of hands*).

frapper [fra'pe], *v.t.* to strike, to slap, to hit; to make an impression on, to affect; to surprise, to frighten; to ice (*liquids*).—*v.i.* to knock, to rap. **se frapper,** *v.r.* to strike oneself; to strike each other; to be impressed.

frappeur [fra'pœːr], *a.* (*fem.* **-euse**) striking, rapping.—*n.m.* (*fem.* **-euse**) beater, striker.

frasque [frask], *n.f.* prank, escapade.

fraternel [frater'nɛl], *a.* (*fem.* **-elle**) fraternal, brotherly.

fraternellement [fraternɛl'mã], *adv.* fraternally.

fraternisation [fraterniza'sjɔ̃], *n.f.* fraternization.

fraterniser [fraterni'ze], *v.t.* to fraternize.

fraternité [fraterni'te], *n.f.* fraternity, brotherhood.

fratricide [fratri'sid], *a.* fratricidal.—*n.m.* fratricide.

fraude [froːd], *n.f.* fraud, deceit.

frauder [fro'de], *v.t.* to defraud.—*v.i.* to smuggle.

fraudeur [fro'dœːr], *n.m.* (*fem.* **-euse**) defrauder; smuggler.

frauduleusement [frodyløz'mã], *adv.* fraudulently.

frauduleux [frody'lø], *a.* (*fem.* **-euse**) fraudulent.

frayer [frɛ'je], *v.t.* to trace out, to open out; to make (*a way etc.*); to rub against, to graze.—*v.i.* to wear away; to spawn (*of fish*); (*fig.*) to frequent, to be on good terms (*avec*). **se frayer,** *v.r.* to open for oneself; to prepare *or* carve out (*a way*) for oneself.

frayeur [frɛ'jœːr], *n.f.* fright, terror, fear.

fredaine [frə'dɛn], *n.f.* (*colloq.*) frolic, prank; freak.

Frédéric [frede'rik], *m.* Frederick.

Frédérique [frede'rik], *f.* Frederica.

fredon [frə'dɔ̃], *n.m.* song, refrain.

fredonnement [frədɔn'mã], *n.m.* humming.

fredonner [frədɔ'ne], *v.t.*, *v.i.* to hum.

frégate [fre'gat], *n.f.* frigate; frigate bird; (*Navy*) *capitaine de frégate,* commander.

frein [frɛ̃], *n.m.* bit, bridle; curb, check; brake.

freinage [frɛ'naːʒ], *n.m.* braking.

freiner [frɛ'ne], *v.t.* to brake; to curb.

frelatage [frəla'taːʒ], **frelatement** [frəlat'mã], *n.m.*, **frelaterie** [frəla'tri], **frelatation** [frəlata'sjɔ̃], *n.f.* adulteration.

frelater [frəla'te], *v.t.* to adulterate.

frêle [frɛːl], *a.* frail, fragile, weak.

frelon [frə'lɔ̃], *n.m.* hornet.

freluquet [frəly'kɛ], *n.m.* conceited young man, puppy.

frémir [fre'miːr], *v.i.* to quiver, to shudder, to tremble; to vibrate; to rustle.

frémissant [fremi'sã], *a.* quivering, trembling.

frémissement [fremis'mã], *n.m.* quivering, trembling, shuddering; thrill, vibration; rustling.

frênaie [frɛ'nɛ], *n.f.* ash grove.

frêne [frɛːn], *n.m.* ash, ash tree.

frénésie [frene'zi], *n.f.* frenzy, madness.

frénétique [frene'tik], a. frantic, frenzied.—
n. raving, frantic person.
frénétiquement [frenetik'mã], adv. frantically.
fréquemment [freka'mã], adv. frequently.
fréquence [fre'kã:s], n.f. frequency.
fréquent [fre'kã], a. frequent.
fréquentation [frekãta'sjõ], n.f. frequenta-
tion, company.
fréquenter [frekã'te], v.t. to frequent, to
keep company with; to haunt.—v.i. to
associate (chez); to be a frequent caller
(at).
frère [frɛ:r], n.m. brother; fellow member;
monk.
fresque [frɛsk], n.f. fresco.
fret [frɛ], n.m. freight, cargo.
fréter [fre'te], v.t. (conjug. like CÉDER) to
charter; to freight; to hire (a car).
fréteur [fre'tœ:r], n.m. freighter, charterer.
frétillant [freti'jã], a. wriggling, lively;
frisky.
frétillement [fretij'mã], n.m. wriggling;
frisking.
frétiller [freti'je], v.i. to wriggle, to jump
about; to frisk.
fretin [frə'tɛ̃], n.m. fry, young fish; (fig.)
trash.
freudien [frø'djɛ̃], a. (fem. -enne) Freudian.
freux [frø], n.m. inv. (Orn.) rook.
friable [fri'abl], a. friable; crisp, short.
friand [fri'ã], a. dainty, nice; partial to;
appetizing.
friandise [friã'di:z], n.f. daintiness; dainty,
titbit.
fricassée [frika'se], n.f. fricassee.
fricasser [frika'se], v.t. to fricassee.
friche [friʃ], n.f. waste or fallow land.
fricot [fri'ko], n.m. (colloq.) ragout, stew.
fricoter [friko'te], v.t. to squander.—v.i. to
cook.
fricoteur [friko'tœ:r], n.m. (fem. -euse)
feaster; fast liver.
friction [frik'sjõ], n.f. friction, rubbing.
frictionner [friksjo'ne], v.t. to rub.
frigide [fri'ʒid], a. frigid.
frigidité [friʒidi'te], n.f. frigidity.
frigorifier [frigori'fje], v.t. to chill, to freeze
(meat etc.).
frileux [fri'lø], a. (fem. -euse) chilly; susceptible to cold.—n.m. redbreast, robin.
frimas [fri'mɑ], n.m. *rime, hoar-frost.
frime [frim], n.f. (pop.) show, pretence, sham.
fringant [frɛ̃'gã], a. brisk, frisky; smart.
fringuer [frɛ̃'ge], v.i. to skip; to prance (of a
horse).
fripe [frip], n.f. rag, scrap (of cloth etc.).
friper [fri'pe], v.t. to crumple, to rumple. se
friper, v.r. to become rumpled or shabby.
friperie [fri'pri], n.f. frippery, old clothes;
junk shop.
fripier [fri'pje], n.m. (fem. -ière) dealer in
old clothes, furniture etc.
fripon [fri'põ], a. (fem. -onne) cheating,
rascally.—n.m. (fem. -onne) rogue, cheat.
friponnerie [fripon'ri], n.f. cheating, roguery,
knavery.
friquet [fri'kɛ], n.m. tree sparrow.
frire [fri:r], v.t., v.i. irr. to fry.
frisage [fri'za:ʒ], n.m. curling, frizzing (of
hair etc.).
frise [fri:z], n.f. (Arch. etc.) frieze.

friser [fri'ze], v.t. to curl, to frizz (hair); to
graze; to border upon.—v.i. to curl. se
friser, v.r. to curl; to curl one's hair.
frisson [fri'sõ], n.m. shiver, shudder; thrill.
frissonnant [friso'nã], a. shuddering, shivering.
frissonnement [frisõ'mã], n.m. shivering,
shudder; thrill.
frissonner [friso'ne], v.i. to shiver, to
shudder; to feel a thrill; to tremble.
frisure [fri'zy:r], n.f. crisping; curling.
frit [fri], a. fried.—n.f. pl. des frites, chips,
French fried potatoes.
friture [fri'ty:r], n.f. frying; fried fish etc.;
grease (for frying).
frivole [fri'vol], a. frivolous, trifling; futile.
frivolité [frivoli'te], n.f. frivolity; trifle.   '
froc [frok], n.m. cowl, monk's gown.
froid [frwa], a. cold; (fig.) indifferent, lifeless;
reserved.—n.m. cold, coldness; chilliness;
(fig.) unconcern, dullness; reserve.
froidement [frwad'mã], adv. coldly, frigidly;
dispassionately.
froideur [frwa'dœ:r], n.f. coldness; chilliness; (fig.) indifference, coolness.
froidure [frwa'dy:r], n.f. coldness (of the
weather); cold; (fig.) winter.
froissement [frwas'mã], n.m. rumpling;
bruising; (fig.) clash; slight, affront, annoyance.
froisser [frwa'se], v.t. to rumple; to crease;
to bruise slightly; (fig.) to offend, to wound.
se froisser, v.r. to become bruised (of a
muscle); to take offence.
froissure [frwa'sy:r], n.f. crease; bruise.
frôlement [frol'mã], n.m. grazing; rustle.
frôler [fro'le], v.t. to graze, to touch slightly in
passing; to brush past.
fromage [fro'ma:ʒ], n.m. cheese; (fig.) un
(bon) fromage, a nice soft job.
fromagerie [fromaʒ'ri], n.f. cheese farm or
dairy; cheese trade.
fromageux [froma'ʒø], a. (fem. -euse)
cheesy.
froment [fro'mã], n.m. wheat.
fronce [frõ:s], n.f. gather, pucker (in needlework etc.); crease (in paper).
froncement [frõs'mã], n.m. contraction,
knitting (of the brows etc.); (fig.) frown.
froncer [frõ'se], v.t. (conjug. like COMMENCER)
to contract; to wrinkle; to purse (the
lips); to gather (needlework); froncer les
sourcils, to frown. se froncer, v.r. to contract, to pucker; to wrinkle.
frondaison [frõde'zõ], n.f. foliation; foliage.
fronde [frõ:d], n.f. sling; frond; (Surg.)
bandage.
fronder [frõ'de], v.t. to sling, to fling with a
sling; to banter; to jeer at.
frondeur [frõ'dœ:r], n.m. (fem. -euse) slinger;
censurer, fault-finder; rioter.
front [frõ], n.m. forehead, brow; face; (fig.)
boldness, impudence; (Polit.) Front populaire, Popular Front.
frontal [frõ'tal], a. (m. pl. -aux) (Anat.)
frontal.—n.m. headband.
frontière [frõ'tje:r], n.f. frontier, border.
frontispice [frõtis'pis], n.m. frontispiece;
title page.
fronton [frõ'tõ], n.m. (Arch.) fronton, pediment.
frottage [fro'ta:ʒ], n.m. rubbing; polishing.

frottée

frottée [froˈte], *n.f.* (*colloq.*) drubbing.
frottement [frotˈmã], *n.m.* rubbing, friction; (*fig.*) interaction.
frotter [froˈte], *v.t.* to rub; to polish; (*fig.*) to pommel, to warm (*the ears of*).—*v.i.* to rub. **se frotter**, *v.r.* to rub oneself; to provoke, to meddle (*à*).
frotteur [froˈtœːr], *n.m.* (*fem.* **-euse**) rubber; scrubber; floor polisher.
frottoir [froˈtwaːr], *n.m.* rubbing cloth; (*Elec.*) brush (*of dynamo*).
frou-frou [fruˈfru], *n.m.* (*pl.* **-frous**) rustling (*of silk etc.*).
fructification [fryktifikaˈsjõ], *n.f.* fructification.
fructifier [fryktiˈfje], *v.i.* to fructify, to bear fruit; (*fig.*) to thrive.
fructueusement [fryktɥøzˈmã], *adv.* fruitfully, profitably.
fructueux [frykˈtɥø], *a.* (*fem.* **-euse**) fruitful, profitable.
frugal [fryˈgal], *a.* (*m. pl.* **-aux**) frugal.
frugalement [frygalˈmã], *adv.* frugally.
frugalité [frygaliˈte], *n.f.* frugality.
fruit [frɥi], *n.m.* fruit; (*fig.*) offspring; advantage, utility; (*pl.*) fruits; result.
fruiterie [frɥiˈtri], *n.f.* fruit loft; fruit trade.
fruitier [frɥiˈtje], *a.* (*fem.* **-ière**) fruit-bearing.—*n.m.* (*fem.* **-ière**) fruiterer, greengrocer.
fruste [fryst], *a.* worn, defaced; unpolished (*person*).
frustration [frystraˈsjõ], *n.f.* frustration.
frustrer [frysˈtre], *v.t.* to defraud; to frustrate, to disappoint; to baffle.
fuchsia [fykˈsja], *n.m.* fuchsia.
fugace [fyˈgas], *a.* fugitive, fleeting, transient.
fugitif [fyʒiˈtif], *a.* (*fem.* **-tive**) fugitive, fleeting.—*n.m.* (*fem.* **-tive**) fugitive, runaway.
fugue [fyg], *n.f.* fugue; (*colloq.*) flight, escapade.
fuir [fɥiːr], *v.t. irr.* to fly, to avoid; to shun.—*v.i.* to fly, to flee, to run away; to elude; to leak. **se fuir**, *v.r.* to fly from oneself; to shun *or* avoid each other.
fuite [fɥit], *n.f.* flight, escaping; avoiding; evasion, shift; leakage.
fulgurant [fylgyˈrã], *a.* flashing, vivid, sharp.
fulguration [fylgyraˈsjõ], *n.f.* (*Chem.*) fulguration; lightning.
fuligineux [fyliʒiˈnø], *a.* (*fem.* **-euse**) fuliginous.
fulminant [fylmiˈnã], *a.* fulminant, fulminating.
fulminer [fylmiˈne], *v.t.* to fulminate, to send forth (*maledictions or religious decrees*).—*v.i.* to explode; (*fig.*) to storm, to thunder, to inveigh (*against*).
fumage [fyˈmaːʒ], *n.m.*, **fumaison** [fymɛˈzõ], **fumure** [fyˈmyːr], *n.f.* manuring, spreading of dung on land.
fumant [fyˈmã], *a.* smoking, reeking, fuming.
fumé [fyˈme], *a.* smoked; manured.
fumée [fyˈme], *n.f.* smoke; steam; fume, reek; phantom, dream.
fumer [fyˈme], *v.t.* to smoke (*a cigarette etc.*); to smoke-dry; to manure.—*v.i.* to smoke; to reek, to steam; (*fig.*) to fret, to fume.
fumerolle [fymˈrɔl], *n.f.* fumarole.
fumet [fyˈmɛ], *n.m.* flavor (*of meat*); bouquet (*of wines*); (*fig.*) raciness; (*Hunt.*) scent.

fumeur [fyˈmœːr], *n.m.* (*fem.* **-euse** (1)) smoker.
fumeux [fyˈmø], *a.* (*fem.* **-euse** (2)) smoky, fumy; hazy (*of brain, ideas etc.*).
fumier [fyˈmje], *n.m.* manure, dung, dunghill; (*fig.*) trash.
fumigateur [fymigaˈtœːr], *n.m.* fumigator.
fumigation [fymigaˈsjõ], *n.f.* fumigation.
fumiger [fymiˈʒe], *v.t.* (*conjug. like* MANGER) to fumigate.
fumiste [fyˈmist], *n.m.* stove *or* chimney repairer; (*fig.*) practical joker; humbug, trickster.
fumisterie [fymisˈtri], *n.f.* (*fig.*) practical joke.
fumoir [fyˈmwaːr], *n.m.* smoking shed (*for curing fish etc.*); smoking room.
fumure [FUMAGE].
funèbre [fyˈnɛbr], *a.* funeral; funereal, mournful; dismal.
funérailles [fyneˈraːj], *n.f. pl.* funeral ceremonies, obsequies.
funéraire [fyneˈrɛːr], *a.* funeral, funereal.
funeste [fyˈnɛst], *a.* fatal, deadly; (*fig.*) disastrous; distressing.
funestement [fynɛstˈmã], *adv.* fatally, disastrously.
funiculaire [fynikyˈlɛːr], *a.* funicular.—*n.m.* funicular railway.
fur [fyːr], *n.m.*, *used only in the expression* **au fur et à mesure** (*que*), gradually (as), in proportion (as).
furet [fyˈrɛ], *n.m.* ferret; inquisitive, prying person.
fureter [fyrˈte], *v.i.* (*conjug. like* AMENER) to ferret, to hunt with a ferret; (*fig.*) to rummage.
fureteur [fyrˈtœːr], *n.m.* (*fem.* **-euse**) ferreter; (*fig.*) Nosey Parker.
fureur [fyˈrœːr], *n.f.* rage, fury; passion, frenzy.
furibond [fyriˈbõ], *a.* furious, raging, wild.—*n.m.* (*fem.* **-e**) furious person.
furie [fyˈri], *n.f.* fury, rage; ardour, intensity.
furieusement [fyrjøzˈmã], *adv.* furiously.
furieux [fyˈrjø], *a.* (*fem.* **-euse**) furious; mad, fierce, impetuous; (*colloq.*) monstrous.—*n.m.* (*fem.* **-euse**) mad person.
furoncle [fyˈrõːkl], *n.m.* (*Med.*) furuncle, boil.
furtif [fyrˈtif], *a.* (*fem.* **-tive**) furtive, stealthy, secret.
furtivement [fyrtivˈmã], *adv.* furtively.
fusain [fyˈzɛ̃], *n.m.* spindle-tree; charcoal (*for drawing*).
fuseau [fyˈzo], *n.m.* (*pl.* **-eaux**) spindle; distaff.
fusée [fyˈze], *n.f.* spindleful; spindle (*of axle*); (*Motor.*) stub axle; (*Mil. etc.*) fuse; rocket; (*Vet.*) splint.
fuselage [fyzˈlaːʒ], *n.m.* framework, fuselage (*of an aeroplane*).
fuselé [fyzˈle], *a.* slender, tapering (*fingers*); streamlined.
fuser [fyˈze], *v.i.* to spirt; to liquefy, to dissolve, to fuse.
fusibilité [fyzibiliˈte], *n.f.* fusibility.
fusible [fyˈzibl], *a.* fusible.—*n.m.* (*Elec.*) fuse.
fusil [fyˈzi], *n.m.* gun, rifle; steel (*for sharpening knives*).
fusilier [fyziˈlje], *n.m.* fusilier; *fusilier marin*, marine.
fusillade [fyziˈjad], *n.f.* discharge of musketry, fusillade; execution by shooting.

162

fusiller [fyzi′je], *v.t.* to shoot (down); to execute by shooting.

fusil-mitrailleur [fyzimitra′jœːr], *n.m.* sub-machine gun.

fusion [fy′zjɔ̃], *n.f.* fusion, melting; (*fig.*) blending, merger.

fusionner [fyzjɔ′ne], *v.t., v.i.* to amalgamate, to unite, to merge; to blend.

fustigation [fystiga′sjɔ̃], *n.f.* fustigation, whipping, flogging.

fustiger [fysti′ʒe], *v.t.* (*conjug. like* MANGER) to flog, to whip.

fût [fy], *n.m.* stock (*of a gun or pistol*); shaft (*of a column*); cask; barrel (*of a drum*).

futaie [fy′tɛ], *n.f.* forest of high trees; high forest tree.

futaille [fy′taːj], *n.f.* cask, barrel.

futaine [fy′tɛːn], *n.f.* fustian.

futé [fy′te], *a.* (*colloq.*) sharp, cunning, sly.

futile [fy′til], *a.* futile, frivolous, trifling.

futilité [fytili′te], *n.f.* futility; trifle.

futur [fy′tyːr], *a.* future.—*n.m.* (*Gram.*) future. —*n.m.* (*fem.* **-e**) intended husband *or* wife.

futurisme [fyty′rism], *n.m.* futurism.

futuriste [fyty′rist], *a.* futuristic.—*n.* futurist.

fuyant [fɥi′jɑ̃], *a.* flying, fleeing, retreating; receding (*of the forehead etc.*); fleeting.—*n.m.* perspective.

fuyard [fɥi′jaːr], *a.* and *n.m.* (*fem.* **-e**) fugitive, runaway.

G

G, g [ʒe], *n.m.* the seventh letter of the alphabet.

gabardine [gabar′din], *n.f.* gabardine.

gabare [ga′baːr], *n.f.* lighter, flat-bottomed barge; store ship.

gabarier [gaba′rje], *n.m.* lighterman.

gabelle [ga′bɛl], *n.f.* gabelle, salt tax.

gâche (1) [gɑːʃ], *n.f.* staple, wall hook.

gâche (2) [gɑːʃ], *n.f.* trowel; (baker's) spatula.

gâcher [gɑ′ʃe], *v.t.* to mix (*mortar*); (*fig.*) to bungle, to botch.

gâchette [gɑ′ʃɛt], *n.f.* tumbler, sear (*of a gun-lock*); follower, catch (*of a lock*); (*fam.*) trigger.

gâcheur [gɑ′ʃœːr], *n.m.* mason's helper; (*fig.*) bungler.

gâchis [gɑ′ʃi], *n.m.* wet mortar; sludge; (*fig.*) mess.

gaélique [gae′lik], *a.* Gaelic.—*n.m.* Gaelic (*language*).

gaffe [gaf], *n.f.* boat-hook, gaff; (*fam.*) gross blunder, howler.

gaffer [ga′fe], *v.t.* to hook with a gaff.—*v.i.* (*fam.*) to blunder; (*Row.*) to catch a crab.

gage [ga:ʒ], *n.m.* pawn, pledge; security, deposit; stake, token; (*pl.*) wages.

gager [ga′ʒe], *v.t.* (*conjug. like* MANGER) to wager, to bet, to stake; to pay wages to; to engage.

gageur [ga′ʒœːr], *n.m.* (*fem.* **-euse**) bettor, one who wagers, punter.

gageure [ga′ʒyːr], *n.f.* wager, stake.

gagnant [ga′nɑ̃], *a.* winning.—*n.m.* (*fem.* **-e**) winner.

gagne-pain [gan′pɛ̃], *n.m. inv.* livelihood, daily bread; bread-winner.

gagner [ga′ne], *v.t.* to gain, to earn; to win; to deserve; to prevail upon, to gain over; to allure; to seize; to overtake.—*v.i.* to spread; to gain (*à*); to improve. **se gagner**, *v.r.* to be gained; to be contagious.

gai [ge], *a.* gay, merry; exhilarating; vivid (*of colors*).

gaiement *or* **gaîment** [ge′mɑ̃], *adv.* gaily, merrily, cheerfully; briskly, willingly.

gaieté *or* **gaîté** [ge′te], *n.f.* gaiety, cheerfulness, good humor.

gaillard (1) [ga′jaːr], *n.m.* (*Naut.*) castle; **gaillard d'arrière**, quarter-deck; **gaillard d'avant**, forecastle.

gaillard (2) [ga′jaːr], *a.* strong; jolly, lively; wanton; gallant.—*n.m.* (*fem.* **-e**) lively, merry, strapping fellow *or* girl.

gaillardement [gajardə′mɑ̃], *adv.* joyously, merrily; boldly.

gaillardise [gajar′diːz], *n.f.* sprightliness, liveliness, jollity; broad language, risky story.

gaîment [GAIEMENT].

gain [gɛ̃], *n.m.* gain, profit; earnings; winnings.

gaine [gɛːn], *n.f.* sheath; foundation garment; case (*of a clock etc.*).

gaîté [GAIETÉ].

gala [ga′la], *n.m.* gala.

galamment [gala′mɑ̃], *adv.* gallantly, courteously; gracefully, handsomely.

galant [ga′lɑ̃], *a.* attentive to ladies; elegant; correct, courteous; complimentary, flattering; **c'est un galant homme**, he is a man of honor; **femme galante**, courtesan.—*n.m.* gallant; sweetheart, suitor; **faire le galant**, to court the ladies.

galanterie [galɑ̃′tri], *n.f.* politeness; gallantry (*towards the ladies*); intrigue; love affair.

galantin [galɑ̃′tɛ̃], *n.m.* fop, coxcomb.

galbe [galb], *n.m.* graceful curve *or* contour.

gale [gal], *n.f.* scabies; itch; scab; mange.

galène [ga′lɛːn], *n.f.* galena; **poste à galène**, crystal set.

galère [ga′lɛːr], *n.f.* galley; (*pl.*) galleys, imprisonment with hard labor.

galerie [gal′ri], *n.f.* gallery; corridor; picture gallery; (*Theat.*) upper circle, gallery; (*fig.*) spectators; (*Mining*) drift.

galérien [gale′rjɛ̃], *n.m.* galley slave, convict.

galet [ga′lɛ], *n.m.* pebble, shingle; friction roller.

galetas [gal′tɑ], *n.m. inv.* garret, attic; (*fig.*) hole, hovel.

galette [ga′lɛt], *n.f.* broad thin cake; sea biscuit.

galeux [ga′lø], *a.* (*fem.* **-euse**) itchy; scabby; mangy; **brebis galeuse**, (*fig.*) black sheep.

Galilée [gali′le], *m.* Galileo.

Galilée [gali′le], *f.* Galilee.

galimatias [galima′tja], *n.m.* balderdash; rigmarole.

galion [ga′ljɔ̃], *n.m.* galleon.

galiote [ga′ljɔt], *n.f.* galliot, half galley.

galle [gal], *n.f.* gall.

Galles, le Pays de [ləpeidə′gal], *m.* Wales.

gallican [gali'kɑ̃], a. gallican.
gallicisme [gali'sism], n.m.Gallicism, French idiom.
gallois [ga'lwa], a. Welsh.—n.m. Welsh (*language*); (**Gallois**, *fem.* **-oise**) Welshman, Welshwoman.
galoche [ga'lɔʃ], n.f. clog.
galon [ga'lɔ̃], n.m. braid; lace; (*pl.*) (*Mil.*) bands *or* stripes (*officers and N.C.O.s*).
galonner [galɔ'ne], v.t. to lace, to adorn with gold *or* silver lace.
galonnier [galɔ'nje], n.m. gold *or* silver lace maker.
galop [ga'lo], n.m. gallop, galloping.
galopade [galɔ'pad], n.f. galloping, gallop.
galoper [galɔ'pe], v.t. to gallop (*a horse etc.*); to run after.—v.i. to gallop; (*fig.*) to run on.
galopin [galɔ'pɛ̃], n.m. errand boy; (*fig.*) urchin, rogue, imp.
galvanique [galva'nik], a. galvanic.
galvaniser [galvani'ze], v.t. to galvanize; (*fig.*) to stimulate.
galvanisme [galva'nism], n.m. galvanism.
galvanomètre [galvanɔ'mɛːtr], n.m. galvanometer.
galvanoplastie [galvanɔplas'ti], n.f. electroplating.
galvauder [galvo'de], v.t. to muddle; to lower, to dishonor.
gambade [gɑ̃'bad], n.f. skip, gambol.
gambader [gɑ̃ba'de], v.i. to skip, to gambol, to romp, to frisk about.
Gambie [gɑ̃'bi], **la**, f. Gambia.
gambit [gɑ̃'bi], n.m. gambit.
gamelle [ga'mɛl], n.f. (*Mil.*, *Naut.*) mess tin *or* pot;(*fig.*) company-mess.
gamète [ga'mɛt], n.m. (*Biol.*) gamete.
gamin [ga'mɛ̃], n.m. boy, youngster, urchin.
gamine [ga'min], n.f. hoyden, chit of a girl.
gamme [gam], n.f. gamut, scale.
gammée [ga'me], a. *used in* '**croix gammée**', swastika.
ganache [ga'naʃ], n.f. lower jaw (*of a horse*); (*colloq.*) booby, blockhead.
gandin [gɑ̃'dɛ̃], n.m. dandy, swell.
gang [gɑ̃g], n.m. gang (*of thieves*).
Gange [gɑ̃ːʒ], **le**, m. Ganges.
gangrène [gɑ̃'grɛːn], n.f. gangrene; (*fig.*) corruption.
gangrené [gɑ̃grə'ne], a. gangrened; (*fig.*) cankered, corrupt.
gangrener [gɑ̃grə'ne], v.t. (*conjug. like* AMENER) to gangrene, to mortify; (*fig.*) to corrupt.
gangreneux [gɑ̃grə'nø], a. (*fem.* **-euse**) gangrenous, cankered.
gangster [gɑ̃gs'tɛːr], n.m. gangster.
ganse [gɑ̃ːs], n.f. braid; cord, twist; edging; string.
gant [gɑ̃], n.m. glove, gauntlet.
gantelet [gɑ̃'tle], n.m. gauntlet; handleather; (*Surg.*) glove bandage.
ganter [gɑ̃'te], v.t. to glove, to put gloves on; (*fig.*) to fit, to suit. **se ganter**, v.r. to put on one's gloves.
ganterie [gɑ̃'tri], n.f. glove-making; glove trade; glove shop.
gantier [gɑ̃'tje], n.m. (*fem.* **-ière**) glover.
garage [ga'raːʒ], n.m. parking, storing away; (*Rail.*) shunting; siding; (*on rivers, canals etc.*) putting into wet dock; (*Motor. etc.*) garage; (*Row.*) boat-house.

garagiste [gara'ʒist], n.m. garage keeper; garage mechanic *or* owner.
garance [ga'rɑ̃ːs], a. madder-colored. —n.f. madder; madder root.
garant [ga'rɑ̃], n.m. (*fem.* **-e**) guarantor, surety.—n.m. guaranty, voucher, proof.
garanti [garɑ̃'ti], a. guaranteed, warranted.
garantie [garɑ̃'ti], n.f. guarantee, guaranty; indemnity; security; voucher, pledge.
garantir [garɑ̃'tiːr], v.t. to guarantee, to vouch for; to ensure; to indemnify; to protect, to shield. **se garantir**, v.r. to secure oneself, to preserve oneself.
garantisseur [garɑ̃ti'sœːr], n.m. warranter.
garçon [gar'sɔ̃], n.m. boy, lad; bachelor; workman; porter; waiter; stable boy; steward (*on ship*).
garçonnet [garsɔ'nɛ], n.m. little boy.
garçonnière [garsɔ'njɛːr], n.f. bachelor's flat.
garde [gard], n.f. keeping; defense, guard; custody, watch; heed; nurse; hilt (*of sword*).—n.m. guard, guardsman, keeper, warder; watchman.
garde-à-vous [garda'vu], n.m. inv. (*Mil.*) position at attention.
garde-barrière [gardba'rjɛːr], n.m. (*pl. unchanged* or **gardes-barrières**) (*Rail.*) signalman at level crossing.
garde-boue [gard'bu], n.m. inv. mudguard.
garde-cendre(s) [gard'sɑ̃ːdr], n.m. inv. fender, fire guard.
garde-chasse [gard'ʃas], n.m. (*pl. unchanged* or **gardes-chasses**) game-keeper.
garde-chiourme [gard'ʃjurm], n.m. (*pl. unchanged* or **gardes-chiourme**) overseer of convict gangs; warder.
garde-corps [gard'kɔːr], n.m. inv. rail, handrail; (*Naut.*) life-line.
garde-côte(s) [gard'kot], n.m. (*pl.* **gardecôtes** or **gardes-côtes**) guard ship, coast guard.
garde-crotte [gard'krɔt], n.m. inv. mudguard.
garde-feu [gard'fø], n.m. (*pl. unchanged* or **garde-feux**) fire-guard; fender.
garde-fou [gard'fu], n.m. (*pl.* **-fous**) parapet; railings.
garde-frein [gard'frɛ̃], n.m. (*pl.* **garde-freins** or **gardes-freins**) brakeman.
garde-magasin [gardmaga'zɛ̃], n.m. (*pl. unchanged* or **gardes-magasins**) warehouse keeper, storekeeper.
garde-malade [gardma'lad], n. (*pl. unchanged* or **gardes-malades**) sick-nurse, attendant.
garde-manger [gardmɑ̃'ʒe], n.m. inv. larder, pantry, meat safe.
garde-meuble(s) [gard'mœbl], n.m. inv. furniture repository.
garde-pêche [gard'pɛːʃ], n.m. (*pl.* **gardespêche**) river keeper, water bailiff.
garde-port [gard'pɔːr], n.m. (*pl.* **gardesport** or **gardes-ports**) harbor-master.
garder [gar'de], v.t. to keep, to preserve; to retain; to watch over, to take care of, to nurse; to guard, to defend; to observe (*silence etc.*); to keep up. **se garder**, v.r. to keep, to last; to beware, to take care not to; to refrain (*de*); to guard.
garderie [gardə'ri], n.f. day nursery.

garde-robe (1) [gard′rɔb], *n.m.* (*pl.* **-robes**) apron; overall.

garde-robe (2) [gard′rɔb], *n.f.* (*pl.* **-robes**) wardrobe (*cupboard for clothes*).

gardeur [gar′dœːr], *n.m.* (*fem.* **-euse**) herd-boy *or* -girl, keeper.

gardien [gar′diɛ̃], *a.* (*fem.* **-enne**) tutelary, guardian.—*n.m.* (*fem.* **-enne**) guardian, keeper, door-keeper; trustee; **gardien de but**, goalkeeper.

gardon [gar′dɔ̃], *n.m.* roach.

gare! (1) [gaːr], *int.* beware! take care! look out!

gare (2) [gaːr], *n.f.* railway station, terminus; (*wet*) dock; **gare routière**, coach station.

garenne [ga′rɛn], *n.f.* warren.

garer [ga′re], *v.t.* to side-track (*a train*); to garage, to park. **se garer**, *v.r.* to keep *or* get out of the way; to take cover; to park.

Gargantua [gargɑ̃′tɥa], *n.m.* Gargantua; glutton.

gargantuesque [gargɑ̃′tɥɛsk], *a.* gluttonous.

gargariser (se) [səgargari′ze], *v.r.* to gargle.

gargarisme [garga′rism], *n.m.* gargle, gargling.

gargote [gar′gɔt], *n.f.* cheap eating-house, cook-shop.

gargotier [gargɔ′tje]. *n.m.* (*fem.* **-ière**) keeper of a cook-shop; bad cook.

gargouille [gar′guːj], *n.f.* gargoyle, water-spout.

gargouillement [garguj′mɑ̃], *n.m.* rumbling (*in the stomach*); gurgling, bubbling (*of water*).

gargouiller [gargu′je], *v.i.* to rumble, to gurgle.

gargouillis [gargu′ji], *n.m.* gurgling (*of water*).

gargousse [gar′gus], *n.f.* cannon cartridge; **papier à gargousse**, cartridge paper.

garnement [garnə′mɑ̃], *n.m.* scapegrace, scamp, (*young*) rogue.

garni [gar′ni], *a.* furnished; trimmed, garnished.—*n.m.* furnished lodgings *or* house.

garnir [gar′niːr], *v.t.* to furnish, to stock; to trim, to garnish; to adorn; to fill. **se garnir**, *v.r.* to furnish *or* provide oneself (*with*).

garnison [garni′zɔ̃], *n.f.* garrison, station.

garnissage [garni′saːʒ], **garnissement** [garnis′mɑ̃], *n.m.* trimming (*of clothes etc.*).

garnisseur [garni′sœːr], *n.m.* (*fem.* **-euse**) trimmer.

garniture [garni′tyːr], *n.f.* furniture, trimmings; ornaments.

garrot (1) [ga′ro], *n.m.* withers (*of a horse etc.*).

garrot (2) [ga′ro], *n.m.* tightener, garrot; (*Surg.*) tourniquet.

garrotte [ga′rɔt], *n.f.* garrotting, strangulation.

garrotter [garɔ′te], *v.t.* to tie down, to pinion; to strangle.

gars [gɑ], *n.m.* lad, stripling, young fellow.

Gascogne [gas′kɔɲ], **la**, *f.* Gascony; **le Golfe de Gascogne**, the Bay of Biscay.

gascon [gas′kɔ̃], *a.* (*fem.* **-onne**) Gascon.—*n.m.* Gascon (*dialect*); (**Gascon**, *fem.* **-onne**) Gascon (*person*); (*fig.*) boaster, braggart.

gasconnade [gaskɔ′nad], *n.f.* gasconade, boast, brag.

gasconner [gaskɔ′ne], *v.i.* to speak with a Gascon accent; to brag.

gaspillage [gaspi′jaːʒ], *n.m.* waste, squandering.

gaspiller [gaspi′je], *v.t.* to waste, to squander.

gaspilleur [gaspi′jœːr], *a.* (*fem.* **-euse**) wasting, squandering.—*n.m.* (*fem.* **-euse**) waster, squanderer, spendthrift.

gastrique [gas′trik], *a.* gastric.

gastrite [gas′trit], *n.f.* gastritis.

gastro-entérite [gastroɑ̃te′rit], *n.f.* gastro-enteritis.

gâté [gɑ′te], *a.* marred, damaged, tainted; (*fig.*) spoiled.

gâteau [gɑ′to], *n.m.* (*pl.* **-eaux**) cake.

gâte-métier [gɑtme′tje], *n.m.* (*pl. unchanged* or **gâte-métiers**) underseller.

gâte-papier [gɑtpa′pje], *n. inv.* scribbler, poor writer.

gâter [gɑ′te], *v.t.* to spoil, to damage, to injure, to mar; to corrupt. **se gâter**, *v.r.* to taint, to spoil, to get spoiled; to break up (*of weather*).

gâterie [gɑ′tri], *n.f.* spoiling (*of children*), foolish indulgence.

gâte-sauce [gɑt′soːs], *n.m.* (*pl. unchanged* or **gâte-sauces**) scullion; (*colloq.*) bad cook.

gâteux [gɑ′tø], *a. and n.m.* (*fem.* **-euse**) idiot.

gauche [goːʃ], *a.* left; (*fig.*) crooked, ugly; clumsy.—*n.f.* left hand, left side; (*Mil.*) left wing, left flank.

gauchement [goʃ′mɑ̃], *adv.* awkwardly, clumsily.

gaucher [go′ʃe], *a. and n.m.* (*fem.* **-ère**) left-handed (person).

gaucherie [go′ʃri], *n.f.* awkwardness, clumsiness.

gauchir [go′ʃiːr], *v.t.* to warp.—*v.i.* to turn aside; to flinch; to become warped; (*fig.*) to dodge.

gaudriole [godri′ɔl], *n.f.* broad joke, coarse jest.

gaufrage [go′fraːʒ], *n.m.* goffering.

gaufre [goːfr], *n.f.* wafer, waffle (*thin cake*); honeycomb.

gaufrer [go′fre], *v.t.* to goffer.

gaufrette [go′frɛt], *n.f.* small wafer.

gaufreur [go′frœːr], *n.m.* (*fem.* **-euse**) gofferer.

gaufrier [gofri′e], *n.m.* waffle iron.

gaufrure [go′fryːr], *n.f.* goffering.

Gaule [goːl], **la**, *f.* Gaul.

gaule [goːl], *n.f.* pole, switch, long stick.

gauler [go′le], *v.t.* to beat (*trees*) with a long pole; to knock down (*fruit*).

gaullisme [go′lism], *n.m.* policy *or* partisan-ship of General de Gaulle.

gaulliste [go′list], *a. and n.* follower of General de Gaulle.

gaulois [go′lwa], *a.* Gaulish, Gallic; (*fig.*) free.—*n.m.* Gallic (*language*); (**Gaulois**, *fem.* **-oise**) Gaul (*person*).

gausser (se) [səgo′se], *v.r.* (*colloq.*) to banter, to chaff.

Gauthier [go′tje], *m.* Walter.

gave (1) [gaːv], *n.m.* torrent, mountain stream (*in the Pyrenees*).

gave (2) [gaːv], *n.f.* crop (*of birds*).

gaver [ga′ve], *v.t.* (*colloq.*) to cram, to gorge.

gavotte [ga′vɔt], *n.f.* gavotte (*dance*).

gavroche [ga′vrɔʃ], *n.m.* Parisian urchin.

gaz [gɑːz], *n.m.* gas; **bec de gaz**, gas burner.

gaze [gɑːz], *n.f.* gauze.
gazé [gɑ'ze], *a.* covered with gauze, veiled; softened, toned down; (*Mil.*) gassed (*soldier*).
gazelle [gɑ'zɛl], *n.f.* gazelle.
gazer (1) [gɑ'ze], *v.t.* to cover with gauze; (*fig.*) to veil, to tone down.
gazer (2) [gɑ'ze], *v.t.* (*Mil.*) to gas (*men*).
gazette [gɑ'zɛt], *n.f.* gazette, newspaper; (*fig.*) gossipmonger.
gazeux [gɑ'zø], *a.* (*fem.* **-euse**) gaseous; aerated.
gazier (1) [gɑ'zje], *n.m.* gas-fitter.
gazier (2) [gɑ'zje], *n.m.* (*fem.* **-ière**) gauze maker.
gazolène [gɑzɔ'lɛn], **gazoléine** [gɑzɔle'in], **gazoline** [gɑzɔ'lin], *n.f.* gasoline.
gazomètre [gɑzɔ'mɛtr], *n.m.* gasometer.
gazon [gɑ'zɔ̃], *n.m.* grass; sod, turf; lawn.
gazonnant [gɑzɔ'nɑ̃], *a.* producing grass; grassy.
gazonner [gɑzɔ'ne], *v.t.* to cover with turf, to turf.
gazonneux [gɑzɔ'nø], *a.* (*fem.* **-euse**) turfy, swarded.
gazouillement [gɑzuj'mɑ̃], *n.m.* chirping, warbling (*of birds*); babbling (*of a brook etc.*); prattle.
gazouiller [gɑzu'je], *v.i.* to chirp, to warble; to twitter; to prattle; to babble.
gazouillis [gɑzu'ji], *n.m.* warbling, twittering.
geai [ʒe], *n.m.* jay.
géant [ʒe'ɑ̃], *a.* gigantic.—*n.m.* (*fem.* **-e**) giant.
geignard [ʒɛ'ɲaːr], *a.* always whining, querulous.
geignement [ʒɛɲ'mɑ̃], *n.m.* moan, whine.
geindre [ʒɛ̃ːdr], *v.i. irr.* (*conjug. like* CRAINDRE) to moan, to whine, to fret, to complain.
gel [ʒɛl], *n.m.* frost, freezing.
gélatine [ʒela'tin], *n.f.* gelatine.
gélatiner [ʒelati'ne], *v.t.* to gelatinize.
gélatineux [ʒelati'nø], *a.* (*fem.* **-euse**) gelatinous.
gelé [ʒə'le], *a.* frozen, cold.
gelée [ʒə'le], *n.f.* frost; jelly; aspic.
geler [ʒə'le], *v.t., v.i.* (*conjug. like* AMENER) and **se geler**, *v.r.* to freeze.
gélignite [ʒeli'nit], *n.f.* gelignite.
gelinotte [ʒəli'nɔt], *n.f.* grouse (*bird*).
gémir [ʒe'miːr], *v.i.* to groan, to moan; to lament; (*fig.*) to suffer.
gémissant [ʒemi'sɑ̃], *a.* groaning, moaning; lamenting.
gémissement [ʒemis'mɑ̃], *n.m.* groan, moan; (*fig.*) lament, cooing.
gemme [ʒɛm], *n.f.* gem; resin; (*Bot.*) bud.
gemmer [ʒɛ'me], *v.i.* to bud.
gênant [ʒɛ'nɑ̃], *a.* troublesome, inconvenient, embarrassing.
gencive [ʒɑ̃'siːv], *n.f.* gum (*of the teeth*).
gendarme [ʒɑ̃'darm], *n.m.* gendarme (*armed policeman*); constable; virago (*woman*).
gendarmerie [ʒɑ̃darm'ri], *n.f.* gendarmery (*armed police*); constabulary; barracks (*of gendarmes*).
gendre [ʒɑ̃ːdr], *n.m.* son-in-law.
gêne [ʒɛːn], *n.f.* constraint, uneasiness, annoyance; difficulty; financial difficulties, penury.
gêné [ʒɛ'ne], *a.* constrained, ill at ease; hard up.

généalogie [ʒenealɔ'ʒi], *n.f.* genealogy; pedigree.
généalogique [ʒenealɔ'ʒik], *a.* genealogical.
généalogiste [ʒenealɔ'ʒist], *n.m.* genealogist.
gêner [ʒɛ'ne], *v.t.* to constrain, to constrict; to impede; to obstruct; to thwart, to restrain; to inconvenience, to embarrass; to annoy. **se gêner**, *v.r.* to constrain oneself, to put oneself out.
général [ʒene'ral], *a.* (*m. pl.* **-aux**) general, universal; vague.—*adv. phr.* **en général**, in general.—*n.m.* (*Mil.*) general.
générale [ʒene'ral], *n.f.* general's wife; drum-beat (*to give alarm of fire etc.*).
généralement [ʒeneral'mɑ̃], *adv.* generally, in general.
généralisation [ʒeneralizɑ'sjɔ̃], *n.f.* generalization.
généraliser [ʒenerali'ze], *v.t.* to generalize.
généralissime [ʒenerali'sim], *n.m.* generalissimo, commander-in-chief of allied armies.
généralité [ʒenerali'te], *n.f.* generality.
générateur [ʒenera'tœːr], *a.* (*fem.* **-trice**) generating, generative.—*n.m.* generator.
génératif [ʒenera'tif], *a.* (*fem.* **-tive**) generative.
génération [ʒenera'sjɔ̃], *n.f.* generation; procreation.
générer [ʒene're], *v.t.* (*conjug. like* CÉDER) to generate.
généreusement [ʒenerøz'mɑ̃], *adv.* generously, bountifully; nobly, bravely.
généreux [ʒene'rø], *a.* (*fem.* **-euse**) generous, liberal, bountiful; noble; courageous.
générique [ʒene'rik], *a.* generic.—*n.m.* (*Cine.*) credits.
générosité [ʒenerozi'te], *n.f.* generosity, liberality; magnanimity.
Gênes [ʒɛːn], *f.* Genoa.
genèse [ʒə'nɛːz], *n.f.* genesis.
genêt [ʒə'nɛ], *n.m.* (*Bot.*) broom.
genette [ʒə'nɛt], *n.f.* genet, civet cat.
gêneur [ʒɛ'nœːr], *n.m.* (*fem.* **-euse**) intruder; spoil-sport.
Genève [ʒə'nɛːv], *f.* Geneva.
genevois [ʒən'vwa], *a.* Genevese.
genévrier [ʒənevri'e], *n.m.* juniper tree.
génie [ʒe'ni], *n.m.* genius; spirit, nature, bent, talent; (*Mil.*) corps of engineers.
genièvre [ʒə'njɛːvr], *n.m.* juniper berry; juniper tree; gin.
génisse [ʒe'nis], *n.f.* heifer.
génital [ʒeni'tal], *a.* (*m. pl.* **-aux**) genital.
génitif [ʒeni'tif], *n.m.* (*Gram.*) genitive.
génocide [ʒeno'sid], *n.m.* genocide.
génois [ʒe'nwa], *a.* Genoese.
genou [ʒə'nu], *n.m.* (*pl.* **-oux**) knee; (*Mech.*) ball and socket; (*pl.*) lap.
genouillère [ʒənu'jɛːr], *n.f.* knee piece (*of armor*); top (*of a high boot*); knee-cap; ball-and-socket joint.
genre [ʒɑ̃ːr], *n.m.* genus; species, kind, sort; fashion, style; (*Gram.*) gender.
gens [ʒɑ̃]. *n.m. pl.* (*but adjectives directly preceding the word take the feminine form*) people, persons, folk; men, hands; servants.
gent [ʒɑ̃], *n.f.* brood, race, tribe.
gentiane [ʒɑ̃'sjan], *n.f.* (*Bot.*) gentian.
gentil (1) [ʒɑ̃'ti], *n.m.* Gentile.
gentil (2) [ʒɑ̃'ti], *a.* (*fem.* **-ille**) noble, gentle; pretty, nice, graceful; amiable, pleasing.

gentilhomme [ʒãti'jɔm], *n.m.* (*pl.* **gentils-hommes**) nobleman, gentleman.
gentillesse [ʒãti'jɛs], *n.f.* kindness, sweetness (*of temperament*); prettiness, gracefulness; pretty thing, thought etc.
gentiment [ʒãti'mã], *adv.* prettily, gracefully, like a good boy *or* girl.
génuflexion [ʒenyflɛk'sjõ], *n.f.* genuflexion.
géocentrique [ʒeosã'trik], *a.* geocentric.
Geoffroy [ʒɔ'frwa], *m.* Geoffrey, Jeffrey.
géographe [ʒeo'graf], *n.m.* geographer.
géographie [ʒeogra'fi], *n.f.* geography.
géographique [ʒeogra'fik], *a.* geographical.
geôle [ʒo:l], *n.f.* jail, prison.
geôlier [ʒo'lje], *n.m.* jailer.
géologie [ʒeolo'ʒi], *n.f.* geology.
géologique [ʒeolo'ʒik], *a.* geological.
géologue [ʒeo'lɔg], *n.m.* geologist.
géométral [ʒeome'tral], *a.* (*m. pl.* **-aux**) geometrical.
géomètre [ʒeo'mɛtr], *n.m.* geometrician; geometer.
géométrie [ʒeome'tri], *n.f.* geometry.
géométrique [ʒeome'trik], *a.* geometrical.
Georges [ʒɔrʒ], *m.* George.
gérance [ʒe'rã:s], *n.f.* management, managership; editorship.
géranium [ʒera'njɔm], *n.m.* geranium.
gérant [ʒe'rã], *n.m.* (*fem.* **-e**) manager; editor; *rédacteur gérant*, managing editor.
gerbe [ʒɛrb], *n.f.* sheaf, bundle; bunch of flowers.
gerber [ʒɛr'be], *v.t.* to make up *or* bind into sheaves.
gerbier [ʒɛr'bje], *n.m.* cornstack.
gerce [ʒɛrs], *n.f.* chap, crack.
gercé [ʒɛr'se], *a.* chapped (*hands*).
gercer [ʒɛr'se], *v.t.,* *v.i.,* (*conjug. like* COMMENCER) and **se gercer**, *v.r.* to chap, to crack.
gerçure [ʒɛr'sy:r], *n.f.* chap, crack; chink, cleft.
gérer [ʒe're], *v.t.* (*conjug. like* CÉDER) to manage, to administer.
gerfaut [ʒɛr'fo], *n.m.* gerfalcon.
germain [ʒɛr'mɛ̃], *a.* german, first (*of cousins etc.*); (*Law*) full (*brother etc.*).
germanique [ʒɛrma'nik], *a.* Germanic.
germe [ʒɛrm], *n.m.* germ, embryo; seed; bud, sprout, shoot; (*fig.*) origin.
germer [ʒɛr'me], *v.i.* to shoot, to sprout, to germinate.
germination [ʒɛrmina'sjõ], *n.f.* germination.
gésier [ʒe'zje], *n.m.* gizzard.
***gésir** [ʒe'zi:r], *v.i. irr.* to lie; *ci-gît*, here lies.
gestation [ʒɛsta'sjõ], *n.f.* gestation.
gestatoire [ʒɛsta'twa:r], *a.* gestatory.
geste [ʒɛst], *n.m.* gesture, action; sign.
gesticulateur [ʒɛstikyla'tœːr], *n.m.* (*fem.* **-trice**) gesticulator.
gesticulation [ʒɛstikyla'sjõ], *n.f.* gesticulation.
gesticuler [ʒɛstiky'le], *v.i.* to gesticulate.
gestion [ʒɛs'tjõ], *n.f.* management, administration.
geyser [ge'zɛːr], *n.m.* geyser.
Ghana [ga'na], **le**, *m.* Ghana.
ghetto [ge'to], *n.m.* Jewish quarter, ghetto.
gibbeux [ʒi'bø], *a.* (*fem.* **-euse**) gibbous, hump-backed.
gibbon [ʒi'bõ], *n.m.* gibbon (*ape*).
gibbosité [ʒibozi'te], *n.f.* gibbosity; hump.

gibecière [ʒib'sjɛːr], *n.f.* game bag, satchel; juggler's pocket.
gibelet [ʒi'ble], *n.m.* gimlet.
giberne [ʒi'bɛrn], *n.f.* cartridge box *or* pouch.
gibet [ʒi'bɛ], *n.m.* gibbet, gallows.
gibier [ʒi'bje], *n.m.* (*Hunt.*) game.
giboulée [ʒibu'le], *n.f.* sudden shower, hail storm
gibus [ʒi'by:s], *n.m. inv.* gibus (*crush-hat, opera hat*).
giclage [ʒi'kla:ʒ], *n.m.* spraying; *carburateur à giclage*, jet carburetor.
giclée [ʒi'kle], *n.f.* squirt, spirt.
gicleur [ʒi'klœːr], *n.m.* spray nozzle, jet.
gicler [ʒi'kle], *v.i.* to spout, to squirt.
gifle [ʒifl], *n.f.* slap in the face, box on the ear.
gifler [ʒi'fle], *v.t.* to slap in the face, to box the ears of.
gigantesque [ʒigã'tɛsk], *a.* gigantic, colossal.
gigot [ʒi'go], *n.m.* leg of mutton.
gigue [ʒig], *n.f.* shank, leg, haunch (*of venison*); jig (*dance*).
gilet [ʒi'le], *n.m.* waistcoat; vest.
Gilles [ʒil], *m.* Giles.
gingembre [ʒɛ̃'ʒã:br], *n.m.* ginger.
gingivite [ʒɛ̃ʒi'vit], *n.f.* gingivitis.
ginguet [ʒɛ̃'gɛ], *a.* (*fem.* **-ette**) (*colloq.*) weak, worthless, scanty.—*n.m.* thin wine.
girandole [ʒirã'dɔl], *n.f.* girandole, epergne.
giration [ʒira'sjõ], *n.f.* gyration.
giratoire [ʒira'twa:r], *a.* gyratory.
girofle [ʒi'rɔfl], *n.m.* clove.
giroflée [ʒiro'fle], *n.f.* gillyflower, stock; *giroflée jaune*, wallflower.
giron [ʒi'rõ], *n.m.* lap; (*fig.*) bosom.
girouette [ʒi'rwɛt], *n.f.* weathercock, vane.
gisant [ʒi'zã], *a.* lying (*ill, dead etc.*); outstretched [GÉSIR].
gisement [ʒiz'mã], *n.m.* (*Geol. etc.*) lie (*of strata*); layer, bed; (*Naut.*) bearing (*of coast etc.*).
gitan [ʒi'tã], *n.m.* (*fem.* **-e**) gipsy.
gîte [ʒit], *n.m.* home, lodging; refuge; lair (*of deer*); (*Min.*) seam, layer.—*n.f.* (*Naut.*) list.
gîter [ʒi'te], *v.t.* to lodge, to house, to put up, to shelter.—*v.i.* to lie, to lodge; (*Naut.*) to list; to run aground. **se gîter**, *v.r.* to lodge, to sleep.
givrage [ʒi'vra:ʒ], *n.m.* (*Av.*) frosting, icing.
givre [ʒi:vr], *n.m.* hoar-frost, *rime.
givré [ʒi'vre], *a.* rimed, rimy.
glabre [gla:br], *a.* (*Bot.*) glabrous, smooth, without down; hairless.
glaçage [gla'sa:ʒ], *n.m.* frosting, glazing.
glaçant [gla'sã], *a.* freezing; icy, chilling.
glace [glas], *n.f.* ice; ice cream; glass, plate glass; mirror; carriage window; flaw (*in a diamond etc.*); icing (*on cakes etc.*).
glacé [gla'se], *a.* frozen, freezing; icy-cold; iced; glazed; glossy (*paper*); candied.
glacer [gla'se], *v.t.* (*conjug. like* COMMENCER) to freeze; to ice; (*fig.*) to paralyze; to glaze. —*v.i.* and **se glacer**, *v.r.* to freeze.
glaciaire [gla'sjɛːr], *a.* of glaciers, glacial.
glacial [gla'sjal], *a.* frozen, glacial, icy.
glaciale [gla'sjal], *n.f.* (*Bot.*) ice-plant.
glacier [gla'sje], *n.m.* glacier, field of ice; ice-cream vendor.
glaçon [gla'sõ], *n.m.* block of ice; floe; ice cube; *petit glaçon*, icicle.
gladiateur [gladja'tœːr], *n.m.* gladiator.

glaïeul [glaˈjœl], *n.m.* gladiolus; iris.

glaire [glɛːr], *n.f.* glair, white of egg; phlegm, mucus.

glaise [glɛːz], *a.* clayey.—*n.f.* clay, loam; potter's earth.

glaiseux [glɛˈzø], *a.* (*fem.* **-euse**) clayey, loamy.

glaisière [glɛˈzjɛːr], *n.f.* clay pit.

glaive [glɛːv], *n.m.* sword, blade, steel.

gland [glɑ̃], *n.m.* acorn; tassel.

glande [glɑ̃ːd], *n.f.* (*Anat.*) gland; (*pop.*) tumor; kernel.

glanduleux [glɑ̃dyˈlø], *a.* (*fem.* **-euse**) glandulous, glandular.

glaner [glaˈne], *v.t., v.i.* to glean.

glaneur [glaˈnœːr], *n.m.* (*fem.* **-euse**) gleaner.

glapir [glaˈpiːr], *v.i.* to yelp (*of puppies etc.*); to screech, to scream (*of persons*).

glapissant [glapiˈsɑ̃], *a.* yelping; screeching, shrill.

glapissement [glapisˈmɑ̃], *n.m.* yelping; screeching.

glas [glɑ], *n.m.* knell.

glauque [gloːk], *a.* glaucous, sea-green.

glèbe [glɛb], *n.f.* glebe; land, soil.

glissade [gliˈsad], *n.f.* sliding, slide; slipping.

glissant [gliˈsɑ̃], *a.* slippery; (*fig.*) ticklish, delicate.

glissement [glisˈmɑ̃], *n.m.* slipping, sliding, gliding; (*Polit.*) landslide.

glisser [gliˈse], *v.t.* to slip, to slide; to insinuate.—*v.i.* to slip, to slide; to glide. **se glisser**, *v.r.* to slip, to slide, to creep, to steal, to insinuate oneself (*dans*).

glissière [gliˈsjɛːr], *n.f.* slide; *porte à glissière*, sliding door.

glissoire [gliˈswaːr], *n.f.* slide on ice.

global [glɔˈbal], *a.* (*m. pl.* **-aux**) in a mass, entire; *somme globale*, lump sum.

globe [glɔb], *n.m.* globe, sphere, orb; glass shade.

globulaire [glɔbyˈlɛːr], *a.* globular.

globule [glɔˈbyl], *n.m.* globule.

gloire [glwaːr], *n.f.* glory, fame.

gloriette [glɔˈrjɛt], *n.f.* arbor, summer-house.

glorieusement [glɔrjøzˈmɑ̃], *adv.* gloriously.

glorieux [glɔˈrjø], *a.* (*fem.* **-euse**) glorious; vainglorious.—*n.m.* braggart, boaster.

glorification [glɔrifikaˈsjɔ̃], *n.f.* glorification.

glorifier [glɔriˈfje], *v.t.* to glorify, to honor. **se glorifier**, *v.r.* to glory in, to boast (*de*).

gloriole [glɔˈrjɔl], *n.f.* vainglory, petty vanity.

glose [gloːz], *n.f.* gloss; criticism; comment; parody.

gloser [gloˈze], *v.t.* to gloss; to criticize.—*v.i.* to carp, to find fault.

gloseur [gloˈzœːr], *n.m.* (*fem.* **-euse**) carper, fault-finder.

glossaire [glɔˈsɛːr], *n.m.* glossary, vocabulary.

glouglou [gluˈglu], *n.m.* gurgling, gurgle.

glouglouter [glugluˈte], *v.i.* to gurgle.

gloussement [glusˈmɑ̃], *n.m.* clucking.

glousser [gluˈse], *v.i.* to cluck (*of hens*).

glouton [gluˈtɔ̃], *a.* (*fem.* **-onne**) gluttonous, greedy.—*n.m.* (*fem.* **-onne**) glutton.

gloutonnement [glutɔnˈmɑ̃], *adv.* gluttonously, greedily.

gloutonnerie [glutɔnˈri], *n.f.* gluttony, greediness.

glu [gly], *n.f.* bird-lime, glue.

gluant [glyˈɑ̃], *a.* glutinous, sticky; slimy.

glucose [glyˈkoːz], *n.m.* glucose.

glutineux [glytiˈnø], *a.* (*fem.* **-euse**) glutinous, viscous.

glycérine [gliseˈrin], *n.f.* glycerine.

glycine [gliˈsin], *n.f.* wistaria.

gnome [gnoːm], *n.m.* (*fem.* **gnomide**) gnome.

gnou [gnu], *n.m.* gnu.

gobelet [gɔˈblɛ], *n.m.* goblet, mug; dice box; *tour de gobelet*, juggler's trick.

gobelin [gɔˈblɛ̃], *n.m.* goblin, imp.

gobe-mouches [gɔbˈmuʃ], *n.m. inv.* fly-catcher (*bird*); fly-trap (*plant*); (*fig.*) simpleton.

gober [gɔˈbe], *v.t.* to gulp down, to swallow; (*colloq.*) to believe easily; to have a liking for (*a person*).

(C) **godendard** [gɔdɑ̃ˈdaːr], *n.m.* cross-cut saw, whip-saw, two-handle saw.

goder [gɔˈde], *v.i.* to crease, to bag (*of clothes*), to pucker (*of needlework etc.*).

godiche [gɔˈdiʃ], *a.* clumsy, boobyish, simple.

godille [gɔˈdiːj], *n.f.* stern oar; scull.

goéland [gɔeˈlɑ̃], *n.m.* gull, sea-gull.

goélette [gɔeˈlɛt], *n.f.* schooner.

goémon [gɔeˈmɔ̃], *n.m.* seaweed.

gogo [gɔˈgo] (*in adv. phr.*) *à gogo*, galore.

goguenard [gɔgˈnaːr], *a.* bantering, jeering, mocking, scoffing.—*n.m.* (*fem.* **-e**) banterer, jeerer, chaffer.

goguenarder [gɔgnarˈde], *v.i.* to jeer, to banter, to chaff.

goguette [gɔˈgɛt], *n.f. être en goguette*, to be in a merry mood, to be on the spree.

goinfre [gwɛ̃ːfr], *n.m.* (*fam.*) guzzler, gormandizer.

goinfrer [gwɛ̃ˈfre], *v.i.* to gorge, to gormandize.

goinfrerie [gwɛ̃frəˈri], *n.f.* gluttony.

goître [gwaːtr], *n.m.* goitre; wen.

goîtreux [gwaˈtrø], *a.* (*fem.* **-euse**) goitrous.—*n.m.* (*fem.* **-euse**) goitrous person, (*colloq.*) imbecile, idiot.

golfe [gɔlf], *n.m.* gulf, bay.

gommage [gɔˈmaːʒ], *n.m.* gumming.

gomme [gɔm], *n.f.* gum; rubber, eraser.

gommer [gɔˈme], *v.t.* to gum; to rub out.

gommeux [gɔˈmø], *a.* (*fem.* **-euse**) gummy.

gommier [gɔˈmje], *n.m.* gum tree.

gond [gɔ̃], *n.m.* hinge; *hors des gonds*, unhinged, (*fig.*) enraged, beside oneself.

gondole [gɔ̃ˈdɔl], *n.f.* gondola; car *or* gondola (*of a balloon etc.*); eye-bath.

gondoler [gɔ̃dɔˈle], *v.i.* to bulge; to warp (*of wood*); to buckle.

gondolier [gɔ̃dɔˈlje], *n.m.* gondolier.

gonflement [gɔ̃fləˈmɑ̃], *n.m.* swelling, inflation.

gonfler [gɔ̃ˈfle], *v.t.* to swell, to inflate; to pump up (*a tire*).—*v.i.* to swell, to be swollen. **se gonfler**, *v.r.* to swell, to be swollen, to be puffed up; (*fam.*) to swank.

gonfleur [gɔ̃ˈflœːr], *n.m.* air-pump, inflator.

gong [gɔ̃ːg], *n.m.* gong.

gorge [gɔrʒ], *n.f.* throat, gullet; bosom; neck; defile, strait; (*Bot.*) mouth; (*Arch., Fort.*) gorge; *avoir mal à la gorge*, to have a sore throat; *avoir la gorge serrée*, to have a lump in one's throat; *rendre gorge*, to refund, to pay up; *faire des gorges chaudes*, to gloat over.

gorge-de-pigeon [gɔrʒdəpiˈʒɔ̃], *a. inv.* iridescent, shot (*of colors*).

gorgée [gɔr'ʒe], *n.f.* draft, gulp; *petite gorgée*, sip.

gorger [gɔr'ʒe], *v.t.* (*conjug. like* MANGER) to gorge, to cram. **se gorger**, *v.r.* to gorge oneself.

gorille [gɔ'ri:j], *n.m.* gorilla.

gosier [go'zje], *n.m.* throat, gullet; (*fig.*) voice.

gosse [gɔs], *n.* (*fam.*) brat, urchin, kid.

gothique [gɔ'tik], *a.* Gothic.—*n.f.* (*Print.*) Old English.

gouache [gwaʃ], *n.f.* gouache; painting in this.

goudron [gu'drɔ̃], *n.m.* tar.

goudronnage [gudrɔ'naːʒ], *n.m.* tarring.

goudronner [gudrɔ'ne], *v.t.* to tar.

goudronneux [gudrɔ'nø], *a.* (*fem.* -**euse**) tarry.

gouffre [gufr], *n.m.* gulf, abyss, pit.

gouge [gu:ʒ], *n.f.* gouge.

goujat [gu'ʒa], *n.m.* (*fig.*) cad, vulgar fellow.

goujon [gu'ʒɔ̃], *n.m.* gudgeon (*pin or fish*).

goule [gul], *n.f.* ghoul.

goulet [gu'lɛ], *n.m.* narrow entrance (*to a harbour etc.*); inlet; mouth, neck (*of a bottle etc.*); gully, gorge (*between mountains etc.*).

goulot [gu'lo], *n.m.* neck (*of a bottle etc.*).

goulu [gu'ly], *a.* gluttonous, greedy.—*n.m.* (*fem.* -**e**) glutton, greedy person.

goulûment [guly'mɑ̃], *adv.* greedily.

goupille [gu'pi:j], *n.f.* (cotter) pin, peg, bolt.

goupiller [gupi'je], *v.t.* to pin, to bolt.

gourd [gu:r], *a.* benumbed, numb.

gourde [gurd], *n.f.* gourd; flask, wineskin.

gourdin [gur'dɛ̃], *n.m.* cudgel, club, thick stick.

gourmade [gur'mad], *n.f.* smack in the face.

gourmand [gur'mɑ̃], *a.* greedy.—*n.m.* (*fem.* -**e**) glutton.

gourmander [gurmɑ̃'de], *v.t.* to chide, to reprimand; to prune (*trees*).

gourmandise [gurmɑ̃'diːz], *n.f.* gluttony, greediness; (*pl.*) sweetmeats.

gourmé [gur'me], *a.* stiff, stuck-up, formal, solemn.

gourmer [gur'me], *v.t.* to box, to thump; to curb (*a horse*). **se gourmer**, *v.r.* to thump, to pummel each other.

gourmet [gur'mɛ], *n.m.* connoisseur in wines etc.; epicure.

gourmette [gur'mɛt], *n.f.* bit, curb chain.

gousse [gus], *n.f.* shell, pod, husk; *gousse d'ail*, clove of garlic.

gousset [gu'sɛ], *n.m.* armpit; fob, (waistcoat-) pocket; gusset (*of a shirt etc.*); bracket.

goût [gu], *n.m.* taste, flavor, relish; savor; inclination, liking; style, manner; *chacun à son goût*, every man to his taste; *chacun son goût*, tastes differ; *viande de haut goût*, highly seasoned meat.

goûter [gu'te], *v.t.* to taste, to try; to like; to enjoy; to feel.—*v.i.* to taste; to try; to have a snack.—*n.m.* a snack taken between lunch and dinner (*the equivalent of English tea*).

goutte (1) [gut], *n.f.* drop, small quantity; sip, dram; (*Arch., Pharm.*) drop.—*adv. phr. ne ... goutte*, *n'entendre goutte*, not to hear *or* understand in the least; *n'y voir goutte*, not to make it out at all.

goutte (2) [gut], *n.f.* gout.

gouttelette [gut'lɛt], *n.f.* small drop, drip.

goutter [gu'te], *v.i.* to drip.

goutteux [gu'tø], *a.* and *n.m.* (*fem.* -**euse**) gouty (person).

gouttière [gu'tjɛːr], *n.f.* gutter of a roof; shoot, spout (*for rain water*); cradle splint.

gouvernable [guvɛr'nabl], *a.* governable, manageable.

gouvernail [guvɛr'naːj], *n.m.* rudder, helm.

gouvernant [guvɛr'nɑ̃], *a.* governing, ruling.—*n.m.* governor, ruler.—*n.f.* (-**e**) governor's wife; governess; housekeeper (*of bachelor*).

gouverne [gu'vɛrn], *n.f.* guidance, guide, direction; (*pl.*) (*Av.*) rudders and ailerons.

gouvernement [guvɛrnə'mɑ̃], *n.m.* government, rule, sway; management; governorship.

gouvernemental [guvɛrnəmɑ̃'taɪj], *a.* (*m. pl.* -**aux**) governmental.

gouverner [guvɛr'ne], *v.t.* to control, to govern, to direct, to steer; to rule, to command, to manage, to regulate.—*v.i.* to steer, to answer the helm.

gouverneur [guvɛr'nœːr], *n.m.* governor; manager; tutor.

grabat [gra'ba], *n.m.* pallet, litter (*of straw etc.*), trundle bed.

grabuge [gra'byːʒ], *n.m.* (*fam.*) wrangling, squabble, brawl.

grâce [graːs], *n.f.* grace, favor, mercy, forgiveness; gracefulness, elegance; (*pl.*) thanks; (*Myth.*) *les Grâces*, the Graces.

graciable [gra'sjabl], *a.* pardonable.

gracier [gra'sje], *v.t.* to pardon, to reprieve.

gracieusement [grasjøz'mɑ̃], *adv.* graciously, kindly, gracefully.

gracieuseté [grasjøz'te], *n.f.* graciousness, kindness; act of courtesy; gratuity.

gracieux [gra'sjø], *a.* (*fem.* -**euse**) graceful, gracious, obliging.

gracilité [grasili'te], *n.f.* slimness, slenderness.

gradation [grada'sjɔ̃], *n.f.* gradation; climax.

grade [grad], *n.m.* grade, rank; degree; *monter en grade*, to be promoted.

gradé [gra'de], *n.m.* (*Mil.*) non-commissioned officer.

gradin [gra'dɛ̃], *n.m.* step; tier.

graduation [gradɥa'sjɔ̃], *n.f.* graduation; scale.

gradué [gra'dɥe], *a.* graduated; progressive (*exercises*).—*n.m.* (*fem.* -**ée**) graduate (*of a university*).

graduel [gra'dɥɛl], *a.* (*fem.* -**elle**) gradual.

graduellement [gradɥɛl'mɑ̃], *adv.* gradually.

graduer [gra'dɥe], *v.t.* to graduate, to proportion.

graillon [gra'jɔ̃], *n.m.* smell of burnt meat *or* fat; (*pl.*) scraps (*of meat etc.*) from a meal.

grain (1) [grɛ̃], *n.m.* grain, berry; bead; jot, bit; *avoir un grain*, to have a bee in one's bonnet; *grain de beauté*, mole, beauty-spot; *grain de café*, coffee bean; *grain de poivre*, peppercorn; *grain de raisin*, grape.

grain (2) [grɛ̃], *n.m.* (*Naut.*) squall.

graine [grɛːn], *n.f.* seed; breed; *c'est une mauvaise graine*, he is a bad lot.

grainetier [grɛn'tje], **grainier** [grɛ'nje], *n.m.* (*fem.* -**ière**) seedsman, seedswoman; grain and seed dealer.

graissage [grɛ'saːʒ], *n.m.* greasing, oiling, lubrication.

graisse

graisse [grɛ:s], *n.f.* fat, grease.
graisser [grɛ'se], *v.t.* to grease; to make greasy; to lubricate, to oil.
graisseur [grɛ'sœːr], *n.m.* greaser, oiler.
graisseux [grɛ'sø], *a.* (*fem.* **-euse**) greasy; oily; fatty.
grammaire [gra'mɛːr], *n.f.* grammar.
grammairien [grame'rjɛ̃], *n.m.* (*fem.* **-enne**) grammarian.
grammatical [gramati'kal], *a.* (*m. pl.* **-aux**) grammatical.
grammaticalement [gramatikal'mɑ̃], *adv.* grammatically.
gramme [gram], *n.m.* gramme *or* gram.
grand [grɑ̃], *a.* great, big; large, big; high, tall; wide, spacious; grown-up; capital (*of letters*); broad (*of daylight*); grand, noble.— *adv.* **voir grand**, to have big ideas; **en grand**, on a large scale; (*of portraits*) full length.—*n.m.* the grand, the sublime.— *n.m.* (*fem.* **-e**) great person; grown-up person; **grand d'Espagne**, Spanish grandee; (*pl.*) the great, the great people; (*sch.*) the big (*or senior*) boys *or* girls.
(C) **grand-bois** [grɑ̃'bwa], *n.m.* virgin forest.
grand-duc [grɑ̃'dyk], *n.m.* (*pl.* **grands-ducs**) grand duke; eagle-owl.
grand-duché [grɑ̃dy'ʃe], *n.m.* (*pl.* **grands-duchés**) grand duchy.
grande-duchesse [grɑ̃ddy'ʃɛs], *n.f.* (*pl.* **grandes-duchesses**) grand duchess.
grandement [grɑ̃d'mɑ̃], *adv.* greatly, extremely, very much; grandly, nobly, handsomely.
grandeur [grɑ̃'dœːr], *n.f.* extent, size; height; length; breadth; bulk; greatness, magnitude; tallness; grandeur, magnificence; grace, highness (*titles*).
grandiose [grɑ̃'djoːz], *a.* grandiose.
grandir [grɑ̃'diːr], *v.t.* to increase; to magnify.—*v.i.* to grow; to grow (tall, big, up etc.). **se grandir**, *v.r.* to make oneself appear taller; to grow taller; to raise oneself, to rise.
grandissement [grɑ̃dis'mɑ̃], *n.m.* growth, increase; rise; (*Opt.*) magnification.
grand-maman [grɑ̃ma'mɑ̃], *n.f.* (*pl.* **-mamans**) granny.
grand-mère [grɑ̃'mɛːr], *n.f.* (*pl.* **-mères**) grandmother.
grand-père [grɑ̃'pɛːr], *n.m.* (*pl.* **grands-pères**) grandfather.
grand-route [grɑ̃'rut], *n.f.* (*pl.* **-routes**) high-road, main road.
grand-rue [grɑ̃'ry], *n.f.* (*pl.* **-rues**) high street, main street.
grange [grɑ̃:ʒ], *n.f.* barn.
granit [gra'nit, gra'ni], **granite** [gra'nit], *n.m.* granite.
granulaire [grany'lɛːr], *a.* granular.
granule [gra'nyl], *n.m.* granule.
granulé [grany'le], *a.* granulated, granular.
graphique [gra'fik], *a.* graphic.—*n.m.* diagram; graph.
graphiquement [grafik'mɑ̃], *adv.* graphically.
graphite [gra'fit], *n.m.* graphite; plumbago.
grappe [grap], *n.f.* bunch (*of grapes, currants etc.*); cluster (*of fruit etc.*); (*Artill.*) grapeshot.
grappillage [grapi'ja:ʒ], *n.m.* vine gleaning *or* pickings.

grappiller [grapi'je], *v.t.* to glean.—*v.i.* to glean; to get pickings, to make a little profit.
grappilleur [grapi'jœːr], *n.m.* (*fem.* **-euse**) gleaner; petty thief, profiteer.
grappin [gra'pɛ̃], *n.m.* grapnel, grappling iron; grab.
gras [grɑ], *a.* (*fem.* **grasse**) fat; fleshy, corpulent; greasy, oily, unctuous; rich; broad, indecent; **eaux grasses**, dishwater; **faire la grasse matinée**, to get up late; **mardi gras**, Shrove Tuesday; **matières grasses**, fats.—*n.m.* fat, fat part (*of meat etc.*); meat, flesh; meat diet.
gras-double [grɑ'dubl], *n.m.* tripe.
grassement [grɑs'mɑ̃], *adv.* plentifully, liberally; in affluence.
grasseyement [grasɛj'mɑ̃], *n.m.* exaggerated rolling of uvular r.
grasseyer [grasɛ'je], *v.i.* to roll one's r's.
grassouillet [grasu'jɛ], *a.* (*fem.* **-ette**) (*fam.*) plump, chubby.
gratification [gratifika'sjɔ̃], *n.f.* gratuity, extra pay, reward.
gratifier [grati'fje], *v.t.* to confer (*a favor*) on; to ascribe.
gratin [gra'tɛ̃], *n.m.* burnt part; **au gratin**, (*Cook.*) dressed with crust of bread-crumbs.
gratis [gra'tis], *adv.* gratis, for nothing.
gratitude [grati'tyd], *n.f.* gratitude.
gratte-ciel [grat'sjɛl], *n.m. inv.* skyscraper.
grattelle [gra'tɛl], *n.f.* rash, itching.
gratte-papier [gratpa'pje], *n.m. inv.* scribbler, pen pusher.
gratter [gra'te], *v.t.* to scratch; to scrape. **se gratter**, *v.r.* to scratch oneself.
grattoir [gra'twaːr], *n.m.* scraper; eraser, paint scraper.
gratuit [gra'tyi], *a.* free (of charge); gratuitous.
gratuité [gratyi'te], *n.f.* gratuitousness.
gratuitement [gratyit'mɑ̃], *adv.* for nothing; gratuitously.
gravats [gra'va], *n.m. pl.* rubbish, debris (*of a building*).
grave [graːv], *a.* heavy, grave, serious; weighty; dangerous; low, deep (*of voice*); (*Mus.*) low-pitched.
gravé [gra've], *a.* pitted; engraved.
graveleux [gra'vlø], *a.* (*fem.* **-euse**) gravelly, sandy, gritty; (*fig.*) smutty.
gravelle [gra'vɛl], *n.f.* (*Path.*) gravel.
gravement [grav'mɑ̃], *adv.* gravely, seriously.
graver [gra've], *v.t.* to engrave; to impress, to imprint. **se graver**, *v.r.* to be engraved, to be impressed *or* imprinted.
graveur [gra'vœːr], *n.m.* engraver.
gravier [gra'vje], *n.m.* gravel, grit; (*Path.*) gravel.
gravir [gra'viːr], *v.t.* to clamber up, to climb, to ascend.
gravitation [gravita'sjɔ̃], *n.f.* gravitation.
gravité [gravi'te], *n.f.* gravity; seriousness, solemnity; weight, importance.
graviter [gravi'te], *v.i.* to gravitate.
gravure [gra'vyːr], *n.f.* engraving, print; illustration (*in book*).
gré [gre], *n.m.* will, wish; liking, pleasure; mind, taste; accord, consent **bon gré mal gré** *or* **de gré ou de force**, willy nilly; **de bon gré**, willingly; **de mauvais gré**, unwillingly; **savoir (bon) gré**, to be thankful; **vendre de gré à gré**, to sell by private contract.

grèbe [grɛb], *n.m.* (*Orn.*) grebe.
grec [grɛk], *a.* (*fem.* **grecque**) Greek; Grecian.—*n.m.* Greek (*language*); (**Grec**, *fem.* **Grecque**) Greek (*person*).
Grèce [grɛs], **la**, *f.* Greece.
gredin [grə'dɛ̃], *n.m.* rascal, scoundrel.
gréer [gre'e], *v.t.* to rig.
greffe (1) [grɛf], *n.m.* (*Law*) registry, record office.
greffe (2) [grɛf], *n.f.* graft; grafting.
greffer [grɛ'fe], *v.t.* to graft.
greffier [grɛ'fje], *n.m.* registrar, recorder, clerk of the court.
greffoir [grɛ'fwa:r], *n.m.* grafting knife.
greffon [grɛ'fɔ̃], *n.m.* graft, scion, slip.
grégaire [gre'gɛ:r], **grégarien** [grega'rjɛ̃] (*fem.* **-enne**), *a.* gregarious.
grêle (1) [grɛ:l], *a.* slender, slim; shrill.
grêle (2) [grɛ:l], *n.f.* hail; hailstorm.
grêlé [grɛ'le], *a.* ravaged by hail; pock-marked.
grêler [grɛ'le], *v. impers.* to hail.—*v.t.* to ravage, ruin *or* spoil by hail.
grêlon [grɛ'lɔ̃], *n.m.* hailstone.
grelot [grə'lo], *n.m.* small (*round*) bell.
grelotter [grələ'te], *v.i.* to tremble, to shake, to shiver (*with cold, fear*); to tinkle.
grenade [grə'nad], *n.f.* pomegranate; (*Mil.*) grenade.
grenadier [grəna'dje], *n.m.* pomegranate tree; (*Mil.*) grenadier.
grenadine [grəna'din], *n.f.* grenadine (*silk or syrup*).
grenat [grə'na], *n.m.* garnet.—*a.* garnet-red.
grener [grə'ne], *v.t.* (*conjug. like* AMENER) to granulate; to grain (*leather etc.*); (*Engr.*) to stipple.—*v.i.* to seed, to run to seed.
grènetis [grɛn'ti], *n.m.* milling, milled edge.
grenier [grə'nje], *n.m.* loft; attic; corn loft, granary.
grenouille [grə'nu:j], *n.f.* frog.
grenu [grə'ny], *a.* full of grains, rough-grained.
grès [grɛ], *n.m.* sandstone, stoneware.
grésil [gre'zi], *n.m.* sleet.
grésillement [grezij'mã], *n.m.* pattering (*like sleet*); shrivelling, crackling; chirping.
grésiller [grezi'je], *v. impers.* to sleet, to patter.—*v.t.* to shrivel up.—*v.i.* to crackle.
grève [grɛ:v], *n.f.* strand, beach of sand *or* shingle; strike of workmen; **grève du zèle**, slowdown (*strike*).
grever [grə've], *v.t.* (*conjug. like* AMENER) to wrong, to injure; to burden; to encumber (*with debt etc.*).
gréviste [gre'vist], *n.* striker.
gribouillage [gribu'ja:ʒ], *n.m.* (*Paint.*) daub; scrawl.
gribouiller [gribu'je], *v.t.*, *v.i.* to daub; to scrawl, to scribble.
gribouilleur [gribu'jœ:r], *n.m.* (*fem.* **-euse**) dauber; scrawler, scribbler.
grief [gri'ɛf], *n.m.* wrong, injury, grievance.
grièvement [griɛv'mã], *adv.* grievously, gravely.
grièveté [griɛv'te], *n.f.* gravity, seriousness.
griffade [gri'fad], *n.f.* clawing, scratch.
griffe [grif], *n.f.* claw, talon; (*pl.*) clutches; paper-clip, clamp; **griffe d'asperge**, root of asparagus.
griffer [gri'fe], *v.t.* to claw, to scratch (*of cats etc.*); to stamp (*with signature etc.*).

griffon [gri'fɔ̃], *n.m.* griffin; griffon.
griffonnage [grifɔ'na:ʒ], *n.m.* scrawl, scribble.
griffonner [grifɔ'ne], *v.t.* to scrawl, to scribble.
griffonneur [grifɔ'nœ:r], *n.m.* (*fem.* **-euse**) scrawler, scribbler.
grignoter [griɲɔ'te], *v.t.* to nibble; (*fig.*) to get pickings out of.
gril [gri], *n.m.* gridiron, grill.
grillade [gri'jad], *n.f.* grilling, broiling; grill, grilled steak.
grillage [gri'ja:ʒ], *n.m.* grilling, broiling, toasting; wire guard *or* mesh; light iron railing.
grille [gri:j], *n.f.* railing, grating; grill; iron gate *or* bars; (*Elec.*) grid.
grille-pain [grij'pɛ̃], *n.m. inv.* toaster.
griller (1) [gri'je], *v.t.* to broil, to grill (*meat*); to roast (*coffee*); to toast (*bread*).—*v.i.* to broil, to be burned up *or* scorched; to burn out (*electric bulbs*); (*fig.*) to be itching (*to do something*). **se griller**, *v.r.* to be scorched, to be parched.
griller (2) [gri'je], *v.t.* to enclose with iron rails.
grillon [gri'jɔ̃], *n.m.* cricket.
grimaçant [grima'sã], *a.* grimacing, grinning; (*fig.*) gaping, ill-fitting.
grimace [gri'mas], *n.f.* grimace, wry face; (*fig.*) (*pl.*) affectations, airs and graces.
grimacer [grima'se], *v.i.* (*conjug. like* COMMENCER) to make faces, to grimace, to grin; to simper; to pucker.
grimer (se) [səgri'me], *v.r.* to make up.
grimpant [grɛ̃'pã], *a.* climbing, creeping (*of plants*).
grimper [grɛ̃'pe], *v.i.* to climb, to clamber up; to creep up (*of plants*).
grimpeur [grɛ̃'pœ:r], *a.* (*fem.* **-euse**) climbing, twining.—*n.m.* (*fem.* **-euse**) (*Orn.*) climber.
grincement [grɛ̃s'mã], *n.m.* gnashing, grinding (*of the teeth etc.*); grating.
grincer [grɛ̃'se], *v.i.* (*conjug. like* COMMENCER) to grind, to gnash, to grate.
grincheux [grɛ̃'ʃø], *a.* (*fem.* **-euse**) ill-tempered, peevish, crabbed, surly.—*n.m.* (*fem.* **-euse**) grumbler.
gringalet [grɛ̃ga'lɛ], *n.m.* weak, puny man.
griotte [gri'ɔt], *n.f.* morello cherry.
grippage [gri'pa:ʒ], **grippement** [grip'mã], *n.m.* friction (*of two surfaces*); seizing, jamming (*of bearing*).
grippe [grip], *n.f.* influenza, flu; (*colloq.*) dislike.
grippé [gri'pe], *a.* shrunk, contracted (*of the face*); ill with influenza; run hot, seized up (*of motors*).
gripper [gri'pe], *v.t.* to pounce upon, to clutch, to seize.—*v.i.* to run hot, to seize up, to jam. **se gripper**, *v.r.* to shrivel, to shrink.
grippe-sou [grip'su], *n.m.* (*pl. unchanged or* **grippe-sous**) miser, money-grubber.
gris [gri], *a.* grey; grey-haired; dull (*of the weather*); (*fig.*) tipsy; **papier gris**, brown paper.—*n.m.* grey.
grisaille [gri'za:j], *n.f.* sketch *or* painting in tones of grey; greyness (*of weather*).
grisâtre [gri'za:tr], *a.* grayish.
griser [gri'ze], *v.t.* to give a gray tint to; to intoxicate. **se griser**, *v.r.* to get tipsy.
grisette [gri'zɛt], *n.f.* gray gown; (*Orn.*) whitethroat.

grison

grison [gri'zɔ̃], *a.* (*fem.* **-onne**) gray, gray-haired.—*n.m.* (*colloq.*) gray-beard (*old man*); donkey.

grisonnant [grizɔ'nɑ̃], *a.* turning gray.

grisonner [grizɔ'ne], *v.i.* to grow gray (*of hair etc.*).

grisou [gri'zu], *n.m.* fire-damp.

grive [gri:v], *n.f.* thrush.

grivelé [gri'vle], *a.* speckled.

grivois [gri'vwa], *a.* loose, broad, obscene.

grivoiserie [grivwaz'ri], *n.f.* smutty story.

Groenland [grɔen'lɑ̃d], **le**, *m.* Greenland.

groenlandais [grɔenlɑ̃de], *a.* of Greenland.—*n.m.* (**Groenlandais**, *fem.* **-aise**) Greenlander.

grognard [grɔ'naːr], *a.* grumbling, growling.—*n.* grumbler, grouser; veteran of Napoleon's Old Guard.

grognement [grɔɲ'mɑ̃], *n.m.* grunt, grunting; growling, grumbling.

grogner [grɔ'ɲe], *v.i.* to grunt; to growl, to grumble, to grouse.

grognon [grɔ'nɔ̃], *a.* (*fem.* **-onne**, *but usu. unchanged*) grumbling, querulous.—*n.m.* (*fem.* **-onne**) grumbler, growler.

groin [grwɛ̃], *n.m.* snout (*of a hog*).

grommeler [grɔm'le], *v.t.*, *v.i.* (*conjug. like* APPELER) to mutter, to grumble.

grondant [grɔ̃'dɑ̃], *a.* scolding; roaring, rumbling.

grondement [grɔ̃d'mɑ̃], *n.m.* rumbling, growling, snarling; roar.

gronder [grɔ̃'de], *v.t.* to chide, to scold.—*v.i.* to growl, to mutter; to snarl, to rumble, to roar.

gronderie [grɔ̃'dri], *n.f.* scolding, chiding.

grondeur [grɔ̃'dœːr], *a.* (*fem.* **-euse**) grumbling, scolding.—*n.m.* (*fem.* **-euse**) scold; grumbler.

grondin [grɔ̃'dɛ̃], *n.m.* (*Ichth.*) gurnard, gurnet.

groom [grum], *n.m.* page, (*U.S.*) bell-boy; stable lad.

gros [gro], *a.* (*fem.* **grosse** (1)) big, large, bulky; stout; coarse; pregnant; loud (*of laughter*); gruff (*of the voice*); substantial; foul (*of the weather*); high (*of the sea etc.*); dark, deep (*in color*); (*Cine.*) **gros plan**, close-up.—*n.m.* large *or* main part; bulk, mass; main body (*of an army*); **en gros et en détail**, wholesale and retail.—*adv.* much.

groseille [gro'zɛːj], *n.f.* currant; **groseille à maquereau**, gooseberry.

groseillier [grozɛ'je], *n.m.* currant bush.

grosse (1) [gros], [GROS].

grosse (2) [gros], *n.f.* gross (*twelve dozen*).

grossement [gros'mɑ̃], *adv.* grossly, coarsely.

grossesse [gro'sɛs], *n.f.* pregnancy.

grosseur [gro'sœːr], *n.f.* size, bulk; bigness; swelling, tumor.

grossier [gro'sje], *a.* (*fem.* **-ière**) gross, coarse, thick; plain, common; rough, rude, unpolished, unmannerly, boorish.

grossièrement [grosjɛr'mɑ̃], *adv.* coarsely, rudely, roughly, uncouthly.

grossièreté [grosjɛr'te], *n.f.* coarseness, grossness; rudeness; coarse language.

grossir [gro'siːr], *v.t.* to make bigger *or* greater.—*v.i.* to grow bigger; to put on weight.

grossissant [grosi'sɑ̃], *a.* magnifying.

grossissement [grosis'mɑ̃], *n.m.* magnifying, magnifying power; increase; exaggeration.

grosso-modo [grosɔmɔ'do], *adv.* summarily.

grotesque [grɔ'tɛsk], *a.* and *n.m.* grotesque.

grotte [grɔt], *n.f.* grotto, cave.

grouillant [gru'jɑ̃], *a.* stirring, swarming, crawling.

grouillement [gruj'mɑ̃], *n.m.* stirring, swarming; rumbling (*of the intestines*).

grouiller [gru'je], *v.i.* to stir, to move; to swarm; to rumble (*of the intestines*).

groupe [grup], *n.m.* group, party (*of people*); cluster (*of stars*); clump (*of trees etc.*).

groupement [grup'mɑ̃], *n.m.* grouping.

grouper [gru'pe], *v.t.* to group. **se grouper**, *v.r.* to form groups, to gather.

gruau [gry'o], *n.m.* flour of wheat; **gruau d'avoine**, groats; oatmeal; **tisane de gruau**, gruel.

grue [gry], *n.f.* (*Orn.*, *Eng.*) crane.

gruger [gry'ʒe], *v.t.* (*conjug. like* MANGER) to crunch; to eat, to devour.

grume [grym], *n.f.* bark (*of tree*); **bois de** *or* **en grume**, wood with the bark on.

grumeau [gry'mo], *n.m.* (*pl.* **-eaux**) clot, small lump.

grumeler (**se**) [səgry'mle], *v.r.* (*conjug. like* APPELER) to clot.

grumeleux [gry'mlø], *a.* (*fem.* **-euse**) clotted, rough.

gruyère [gry'jɛːr], *n.m.* Gruyère cheese.

guano [gwa'no], *n.m.* guano.

Guatémala [gwatema'la], **le**, *m.* Guatemala.

guatémaltèque [gwatemal'tɛk], *a.* Guatemalan.—*n.* (**Guatémaltèque**) Guatemalan (*person*).

gué [ge], *n.m.* ford.

guéable [ge'abl], *a.* fordable.

guéer [ge'e], *v.t.* to ford.

guenille [gə'niːj], *n.f.* rag, tatter; (*pl.*) tattered clothes.

guenilleux [gəni'jø], *a.* (*fem.* **-euse**) tattered, ragged.

guenon [gə'nɔ̃], *n.f.* monkey, ape; she-monkey; (*fig.*) fright, ugly woman.

guépard [ge'paːr], *n.m.* cheetah.

guêpe [gɛːp], *n.f.* wasp.

guêpier [gɛ'pje], *n.m.* wasps' nest; bee-eater (*bird*); scrape, difficulty.

guère [gɛːr], *adv.* but little, not much, not very; not long; hardly, scarcely.

guères (*poet.*) [GUÈRE].

guéret [ge'rɛ], *n.m.* ploughed but unsown land; fallow land; (*pl.*, *poet.*) fields.

guéridon [geri'dɔ̃], *n.m.* (small) round table.

guérilla [geri'ja], *n.f.* guerrilla war *or* troops.

guérir [ge'riːr], *v.t.* to heal, to cure.—*v.i.* to heal, to heal up; to recover, to be cured.

guérison [geri'zɔ̃], *n.f.* recovery, healing, cure.

guérissable [geri'sabl], *a.* curable.

guérisseur [geri'sœːr], *n.m.* (*fem.* **-euse**) healer, faith healer; quack.

guérite [ge'rit], *n.f.* sentry box; look-out turret.

Guernesey [gɛrnə'zɛ], *f.* Guernsey.

guerre [gɛːr], *n.f.* war; warfare, hostilities; strife.

guerrier [gɛ'rje], *a.* (*fem.* **-ière**) warlike, martial.—*n.m.* (*fem.* **-ière**) warrior, fighting man *or* woman.

guerroyant [gɛrwɑ'jɑ̃], *a.* bellicose, pugnacious.

guerroyer [gɛrwɑ'je], *v.i.* (*conjug. like* EMPLOYER) to make war, to wage war.

guet [gɛ], *n.m.* watch; watching; *au guet*, on the look-out.

guet-apens [gɛta'pɑ̃], *n.m.* (*pl.* **guets-apens**) ambush; trap.

guêtre [gɛ:tr], *n.f.* gaiter; *grandes guêtres*, leggings; *petites guêtres*, spats.

guetter [gɛ'te], *v.t.* to lie in wait for, to watch for, to waylay.

guetteur [gɛ'tœ:r], *n.m.* signalman, look-out man.

gueulard [gœ'la:r], *a.* (*pop.*) bawling, mouthing; gluttonous; hard-mouthed (*of horses*). —*n.m.* (*fem.* **-e**) bawler; glutton.—*n.m.* mouth of a furnace.

gueule [gœl], *n.f.* mouth (*of animals*); (*vulg.*) mouth, face, mug (*of human*).

gueule-de-lion [gœldə'ljɔ̃], *n.f.* (*pl.* **gueules-de-lion**) antirrhinum.

gueule-de-loup [gœldə'lu], *n.f.* (*pl.* **gueules-de-loup**) snapdragon; chimney cowl.

gueuler [gœ'le], *v.i.* (*pop.*) to bawl.

gueuse (1) [gø:z], *n.f.* pig iron.

gueuser [gø'ze], *v.t.*, *v.i.* to beg.

gueuserie [gø'zri], *n.f.* beggary; destitution; (*fig.*) trash.

gueux [gø], *a.* (*fem.* **-euse**) poor, destitute; wretched.—*n.m.* beggar, tramp; knave, rascal.—*n.f.* (**-euse** (2)) wench, bitch.

gui [gi], *n.m.* mistletoe.

guichet [gi'ʃɛ], *n.m.* wicket gate (*of prison*); spyhole (*of door*); position at counter (*banks, post office*), pay desk; ticket office (*railways*).

guichetier [giʃ'tje], *n.m.* turnkey.

guide [gid], *n.m.* guide; guide-book.—*n.f.* girl scout; rein.

guider [gi'de], *v.t.* to guide, to lead; to direct.

guidon [gi'dɔ̃], *n.m.* (*Mil.*) guidon; (*Navy*) burgee; (fore)sight, bead (*of fire-arms*); reference mark (*in a book*); handle-bar (*of bicycle*).

guigner [gi'ɲe], *v.t.* to peer or peep at; to ogle; to covet.—*v.i.* to peep, to peer.

guignol [gi'ɲɔl], *n.m.* Punch; puppet show, Punch and Judy show.

guignolet [giɲɔ'lɛ], *n.m.* cherry brandy.

guignon [gi'ɲɔ̃], *n.m.* bad luck, ill-luck.

Guillaume [gi'jo:m], *m.* William.

guillemet [gij'mɛ], *n.m.* quotation mark, inverted comma.

guillemot [gij'mo], *n.m.* (*Orn.*) guillemot.

guilleret [gij'rɛ], *a.* (*fem.* **-ette**) brisk, lively.

guilleri [gij'ri], *n.m.* chirping (*of sparrows*).

guillotine [gijɔ'tin], *n.f.* guillotine; *fenêtre à guillotine*, sash-window.

guillotiner [gijɔti'ne], *v.t.* to guillotine.

guimauve [gi'mo:v], *n.f.* marsh-mallow.

guimbarde [gɛ̃'bard], *n.f.* Jew's harp; (*colloq.*) rickety old vehicle, boneshaker.

guimpe [gɛ̃:p], *n.f.* stomacher; wimple (*for nuns etc.*).

guindé [gɛ̃'de], *a.* stiff, forced, unnatural; formal (*of style*).

guindeau [gɛ̃'do], *n.m.* (*pl.* **-eaux**) windlass.

guinder [gɛ̃'de], *v.t.* to hoist; to strain, to force. **se guinder**, *v.r.* to hoist oneself up; to be strained, to be forced.

Guinée [gi'ne], **la**, *f.* Guinea.

guinéen [gine'ɛ̃], *a.* (*fem.* **-éenne**) Guinean.— *n.m.* (**Guinéen**, *fem.* **-éenne**) Guinean (*person*).

guingan [gɛ̃'gɑ̃], *n.m.* gingham.

guingois [gɛ̃'gwa], *n.m.* crookedness; *de guingois*, awry, askew.

guinguette [gɛ̃'gɛt], *n.f.* small suburban tavern (*usually with pleasure garden*).

guirlande [gir'lɑ̃:d], *n.f.* garland, wreath.

guise [gi:z], *n.f.* manner, way, guise; fancy; *en guise de*, by way of.

guitare [gi'ta:r], *n.f.* guitar.

guitariste [gita'rist], *n.* guitarist, guitar player.

gustatif [gysta'tif], *a.* (*fem.* **-tive**) gustatory.

gustation [gystɑ'sjɔ̃], *n.f.* tasting, gustation.

guttural [gyty'ral], *a.* (*m. pl.* **-aux**) guttural.

guyanais [gɥija'nɛ], *a.* (*fem.* **-aise**) Guyanese. —*n.m.* (**Guyanais**, *fem.* **-aise**) Guyanese (*person*).

Guyane [gɥi'jan], **la**, *f.* Guyana.

gymnase [ʒim'nɑ:z], *n.m.* gymnasium.

gymnaste [ʒim'nast], *n.* gymnast.

gymnastique [ʒimnas'tik], *a.* gymnastic.— *n.f.* gymnastics.

gynécologie [ʒinekɔlɔ'ʒi], *n.f.* gynecology.

gynécologiste [ʒinekɔlɔ'ʒist], **gynécologue** [ʒineko'lɔg], *n.* gynecologist.

gypse [ʒips], *n.m.* gypsum; plaster of Paris.

gyroscope [ʒirɔs'kɔp], *n.m.* gyroscope.

H

[In words marked thus † the *h* is 'aspirated'.]

H, h [aʃ], *n.m.* or *f.* the eighth letter of the alphabet. *H* is mute or aspirated. The socalled aspirated *h* is a graphic symbol which indicates that there is neither elision nor liaison; *e.g.* **la halle** [la'al], **les halles** [lɛ'al]; *l'heure H*, (*Mil.*) zero hour.

habile [a'bil], *a.* able, clever; capable; skilful; sharp, cunning.

habilement [abil'mɑ̃], *adv.* cleverly, skilfully.

habileté [abil'te], *n.f.* ability, skill, cleverness.

habilité [abili'te], *a.* entitled, qualified.—*n.f.* (*Law*) competency, qualification.

habiliter [abili'te], *v.t.* to qualify, to enable, to entitle.

habillage [abi'ja:ʒ], *n.m.* dressing; trussing (*poultry*).

habillant [abi'jɑ̃], *a.* dressy or suiting well (*of clothes etc.*).

habillé [abi'je], *a.* dressed, clad, decked out.

habillement [abij'mɑ̃], *n.m.* clothes, dress, attire.

habiller [abi'je], *v.t.* to dress; to make clothes for; to become, to fit; to wrap up; (*Cook.*) to truss (*fowls, fish etc.*); (*fig.*) to adorn. **s'habiller**, *v.r.* to dress; to have one's clothes made.

habilleur [abi'jœ:r], *n.m.* (*fem.* **-euse**) (*Theat.*) dresser.

habit

habit [a'bi], *n.m.* clothes; dress coat; *habit complet*, suit of clothes.
habitable [abi'tabl], *a.* habitable.
habitant [abi'tɑ̃], *n.m.* (*fem.* **-e**) inhabitant, resident; occupier; denizen; (*C*) farmer.
habitation [abita'sjɔ̃], *n.f.* habitation, residence, abode.
habiter [abi'te], *v.t.* to inhabit, to dwell in, to live in; to frequent; *habiter un lieu*, to live in a place.—*v.i.* to inhabit, to dwell, to reside; *habiter avec*, (*Law*) to cohabit.
habitude [abi'tyd], *n.f.* habit, custom, practice; *d'habitude*, usually.
habitué [abi'tɥe], *n.m.* (*fem.* **-ée**) frequenter, customer.
habituel [abi'tɥɛl], *a.* (*fem.* **-elle**) habitual, usual.
habituellement [abitɥɛl'mɑ̃], *adv.* habitually, usually.
habituer [abi'tɥe], *v.t.* to accustom. **s'habituer**, *v.r.* to accustom oneself; to get used (*à*).
†**hâbler** [ɑ'ble], *v.i.* to brag, to boast.
†**hâblerie** [ɑblə'ri], *n.f.* bragging, boasting.
†**hâbleur** [ɑ'blœːr], *n.m.* (*fem.* **-euse**) braggart, boaster.
†**hache** [aʃ], *n.f.* axe, hatchet.
†**haché** [a'ʃe], *a.* chopped up, mixed; (*fig.*) abrupt.
†**hacher** [a'ʃe], *v.t.* to chop, to cut to pieces; to hash, to mince; to hack; to cross-hatch.
†**hachis** [a'ʃi], *n.m.* minced meat, hash.
†**hachoir** [a'ʃwaːr], *n.m.* chopping board; chopping knife; mincer.
†**hachure** [a'ʃyːr], *n.f.* (*Engr.*) hatching, hachure.
†**hagard** [a'gaːr], *a.* wild-looking, haggard.
†**haie** [ɛ], *n.f.* hedge, hedgerow; hurdle; row, line.
†**haillon** [ɑ'jɔ̃], *n.m.* rag, tatter.
†**haine** [ɛːn], *n.f.* hate, hatred; dislike; spite.
†**haineusement** [ɛnøz'mɑ̃], *adv.* hatefully, spitefully.
†**haineux** [ɛ'nø], *a.* (*fem.* **-euse**) hating, spiteful.
†**haïr** [a'iːr], *v.t.* irr. to hate, to detest, to loathe.
†**haire** [ɛːr], *n.f.* hair shirt.
†**haïssable** [ai'sabl], *a.* hateful, odious.
†**Haïti** [ai'ti], *m.* or *f.* Haiti.
†**haïtien** [ai'sjɛ̃], *a.* (*fem.* **-enne**) Haitian.—*n.m.* (**Haïtien**, *fem.* **-enne**) Haitian (*person*).
†**halage** [a'laːʒ], *n.m.* towage, hauling.
†**hale** [a:l], *n.m.* tow-line, tow-rope.
†**hâle** [ɑ:l], *n.m.* heat of the sun; sunburn.
†**hâlé** [ɑ'le], *a.* sunburnt; tanned; swarthy.
haleine [a'lɛn], *n.f.* breath, wind.
†**haler** [a'le], *v.t.* (*Naut.*) to haul, to tow.
†**hâler** [ɑ'le], *v.t.* to tan, to burn (*of the sun*). **se hâler**, *v.r.* to become sunburnt or tanned.
†**haletant** [al'tɑ̃], *a.* out of breath, panting.
†**haleter** [al'te], *v.i.* (*conjug. like* AMENER) to pant, to gasp for breath.
†**hall** [ɔl], *n.m.* large entrance hall (*of hotel, station*).
†**halle** [al], *n.f.* market; market hall, market-place.
†**hallebarde** [al'bard], *n.f.* halberd; *pleuvoir des hallebardes*, to rain cats and dogs.
†**hallebardier** [albar'dje], *n.m.* halberdier.
†**hallier** [a'lje], *n.m.* thicket, coppice.

hallucination [alysinɑ'sjɔ̃], *n.f.* hallucination, delusion.
halluciné [alysi'ne], *a.* hallucinated; (*fig.*) deluded.—*n.m.* (*fem.* **-ée**) person suffering from delusions.
halluciner [alysi'ne], *v.t.* to hallucinate; (*fig.*) to delude.
†**halo** [a'lo], *n.m.* halo; (*Phot.*) halation.
†**halot** [a'lo], *n.m.* rabbit-burrow.
†**halte** [alt], *n.f.* halt; stand, stop; halting-place.—*int.* halt! stop!
haltère [al'tɛːr], *n.m.* dumb-bell.
†**hamac** [a'mak], *n.m.* hammock.
†**hameau** [a'mo], *n.m.* (*pl.* **-eaux**) hamlet.
hameçon [am'sɔ̃], *n.m.* hook, fish-hook; bait.
†**hampe** [ɑ̃:p], *n.f.* staff (*of a lance, flag etc.*); stem, flower stalk.
†**hamster** [ams'tɛːr], *n.m.* hamster.
†**hanche** [ɑ̃:ʃ], *n.f.* hip; haunch (*of horse*).
†**handicap** [ɑ̃di'kap], *n.m.* handicap.
†**hangar** [ɑ̃'gaːr], *n.m.* outhouse, shed, cart shed; hangar (*for airplanes*).
†**hanneton** [an'tɔ̃], *n.m.* May-bug, cockchafer; (*fig.*) thoughtless person.
†**hanter** [ɑ̃'te], *v.t.* to haunt; to frequent.
†**hantise** [ɑ̃'tiːz], *n.f.* obsession.
†**happer** [a'pe], *v.t.* to snap up, to snatch; to seize.
†**happeur** [a'pœːr], *n.m.* paper-clip.
†**haquenée** [ak'ne], *n.f.* hack, quiet horse; (*fig.*) ungainly woman.
†**haquet** [a'kɛ], *n.m.* dray.
†**harangue** [a'rɑ̃:g], *n.f.* harangue, speech; (*boring*) address.
†**haranguer** [arɑ̃'ge], *v.t., v.i.* to harangue.
†**harangueur** [arɑ̃'gœːr], *n.m.* (*fem.* **-euse**) haranguer, orator, speechifier.
†**haras** [a'rɑ], *n.m.* stud, breeding-stud.
†**harasser** [ara'se], *v.t.* to harass, to tire out, to weary.
†**harceler** [arsə'le], *v.t.* (*conjug. like* APPELER) to worry, to pester, to torment; to harass.
†**harde** [ard], *n.f.* herd (*of deer etc.*); leash (*for hounds*).
†**hardes** [ard], *n.f.* (*used only in pl.*) wearing apparel, attire; worn clothes.
†**hardi** [ar'di], *a.* bold, daring, fearless; rash; impudent.
†**hardiesse** [ar'djɛs], *n.f.* boldness, daring; rashness; assurance, impudence.
†**hardiment** [ardi'mɑ̃], *adv.* boldly, daringly; impudently.
†**harem** [a'rɛm], *n.m.* harem.
†**hareng** [a'rɑ̃], *n.m.* herring.
†**harengère** [arɑ̃'ʒɛːr], *n.f.* fish-wife.
†**harenguet** [arɑ̃'gɛ], *n.m.* sprat.
†**hargneux** [ar'nø], *a.* (*fem.* **-euse**) cross, cross-grained, peevish, surly.
†**haricot** [ari'ko], *n.m.* kidney bean; *haricot de mouton*, Irish stew; *haricots d'Espagne*, scarlet runners; *haricots verts*, French beans.
†**haridelle** [ari'dɛl], *n.f.* jade, hack; (*fig.*) gawky woman.
†**harle** [arl], *n.m.* (*Orn.*) merganser.
harmonica [armɔni'ka], *n.m.* harmonica, mouth-organ.
harmonie [armɔ'ni], *n.f.* harmony; concord; (*Mus.*) harmonics.
harmonieusement [armɔnjøz'mɑ̃], *adv.* harmoniously.

harmonieux [armɔ'njø], *a.* (*fem.* **-euse**) harmonious; musical, melodious; in keeping; blending (*of colors*).

harmonique [armɔ'nik], *a.* harmonic.—*n.f.* harmonics.

harmoniser [armɔni'ze], *v.t.* and **s'harmoniser**, *v.r.* to harmonize.

harmonium [armɔ'njɔm], *n.m.* harmonium.

†**harnachement** [arnaʃ'mã], *n.m.* harness, trappings.

†**harnacher** [arna'ʃe], *v.t.* to harness; to rig out.

†**harnais** [ar'nɛ], *n.m.* harness; horse-trappings; armor; equipment, tackle.

†**haro** [a'ro], *n.m.* hue and cry.

†**harpagon** [arpa'gɔ̃], *n.m.* miser, skinflint.

†**harpe** [arp], *n.f.* harp.

†**harper** [ar'pe], *v.t.* to grasp, to clutch.

†**harpie** [ar'pi], *n.f.* harpy, vixen, shrew.

†**harpiste** [ar'pist], *n.* harpist.

†**harpon** [ar'pɔ̃], *n.m.* harpoon.

†**harponner** [arpɔ'ne], *v.t.* to harpoon.

†**hasard** [a'za:r], *n.m.* chance; hazard; risk, danger; *à tout hasard*, on the off chance; *au hasard*, at random; *par hasard*, by chance.

†**hasardé** [azar'de], *a.* hazarded, ventured; hazardous, bold.

†**hasarder** [azar'de], *v.t.* to hazard, to risk, to venture. **se hasarder**, *v.r.* to hazard, to venture, to take the risk.

†**hasardeusement** [azardøz'mã], *adv.* hazardously.

†**hasardeux** [azar'dø], *a.* (*fem.* **-euse**) venturesome, daring; hazardous, unsafe.

†**hâte** [a:t], *n.f.* hurry, haste; *à la hâte*, in a hurry.

†**hâter** [a'te], *v.t.* to hasten, to forward, to hurry, to urge on; to expedite; to force (*fruit*). **se hâter**, *v.r.* to make haste, to hurry.

†**hâtif** [a'tif], *a.* (*fem.* **-tive**) forward; precocious, premature; (*Hort.*) early.

†**hâtivement** [ativ'mã], *adv.* early, prematurely; hastily.

†**hauban** [o'bã], *n.m.* (*Naut.*) shroud, guy, stay.

†**hausse** [o:s], *n.f.* lift, block (*for raising anything*); (*Comm.*) rise, advance; (back) sight (*of a rifle*).

†**haussement** [os'mã], *n.m.* raising, lifting; *haussement d'épaules*, shrugging of the shoulders.

†**hausser** [o'se], *v.t.* to raise, to lift up; to increase; to shrug; (*Comm.*) to advance.—*v.i.* to rise; to get higher; to increase. **se hausser**, *v.r.* to be raised, to rise; to raise oneself; to clear up (*of the weather*); to increase.

†**haussier** [o'sje], *n.m.* (*St. Exch.*) bull.

†**haussière** [o'sjɛ:r], *n.f.* hawser.

†**haut** [o], *a.* high, tall, lofty; elevated; upper; principal; eminent; haughty; loud (*of sound*); *lire à haute voix*, to read aloud; *pousser les hauts cris*, to complain loudly.—*n.m.* height; top; summit; upper part; from above.—*n.f.* (*colloq.*) *la haute*, the wealthy, the upper crust.—*adv.* high; loud, aloud, loudly; haughtily; *ainsi qu'il a été dit plus haut*, as has already been said; *parlez plus haut*, speak louder.—*adv. phr.* **en haut**, upstairs.

†**hautain** [o'tɛ], *a.* haughty, proud.

†**hautainement** [otɛn'mã], *adv.* haughtily, superciliously, proudly.

†**hautbois** [o'bwa], *n.m.* hautboy, oboe; oboe player.

†**haut-de-forme** [od'fɔrm], *n.m.* (*pl.* **hauts-de-forme**) top hat.

†**hautement** [ot'mã], *adv.* boldly, resolutely, proudly; aloud.

†**hauteur** [o'tœ:r], *n.f.* height, elevation, altitude; depth; rising ground; haughtiness, arrogance; pitch (*of the voice etc.*); (*Naut.*) bearing; *être à la hauteur de quelqu'un*, to be a match for someone; *être à la hauteur d'une tâche*, to be equal to a task.

†**haut-fond** [o'fɔ̃], *n.m.* (*pl.* **hauts-fonds**) shoal, shallow.

†**haut-le-corps** [ol'kɔ:r] *n.m. inv.* spring, bound; start.

†**haut-le-pied** [ol'pje], *a. inv. cheval haut-le-pied*, spare horse; *locomotive haut-le-pied*, engine running light.

†**haut-parleur** [opar'lœ:r], *n.m.* (*pl.* **-parleurs**) loud-speaker; amplifier.

†**Havane** [a'van], **la**, *f.* Havana.

†**havane** [a'van], *a.* brown, tan.—*n.m.* Havana cigar.

†**hâve** [a:v], *a.* pale, wan, emaciated.

†**havre** [a:vr], *n.m.* haven, harbor, port.

†**havresac** [avrə'sak], *n.m.* knapsack, pack.

†**Haye** [ɛ],**La**, *f.*The Hague.

†**hé!** [e], *int.* hoy! (*for calling, warning etc.*); why! well! I say! (*emphat.*).

†**heaume** [o:m], *n.m.* helmet.

hebdomadaire [ɛbdɔma'dɛ:r], *a.* weekly.—*n.m.* weekly newspaper.

hébergement [ɛbɛrʒə'mã], *n.m.* lodging.

héberger [ebɛr'ʒe], *v.t.* (*conjug. like* MANGER) to lodge.

hébété [ebe'te], *a.* dazed, stupid, bewildered.

hébéter [ebe'te], *v.t.* (*conjug. like* CÉDER) to make stupid, to besot.

hébraïque [ebra'ik], *a.* Hebrew, Hebraic.

hébreu [e'brø], *a.* (*fem.* **hébraïque**) Hebrew.—*n.m.* Hebrew (*language*); (**Hébreu,** *fem.* **Juive,** *pl.* **Hébreux**) Hebrew (*person*).

hécatombe [eka'tɔ̃:b], *n.f.* hecatomb.

hectare [ɛk'ta:r], *n.m.* hectare (*2 acres, 1 rood, 35 perches or 2.4711 acres*).

hectogramme [ɛktɔ'gram], **hecto** [ɛk'to], *n.m.* hectogramme (*3.527 oz. avoirdupois*).

hectolitre [ɛktɔ'litr], *n.m.* hectolitre (*22.009668 imperial gallons*).

hectomètre [ɛktɔ'mɛtr], *n.m.* hectometre (*109.936 yds.*).

hégire [e'ʒi:r], *n.f.* Hegira (*Mohammedan era*).

†**hein!** [ɛ], *int.* (*before a sentence*) hey! what! (*after a sentence* = *n'est-ce pas*) isn't it etc.?

hélas! [e'la:s], *int.* alas!

Hélène [e'lɛn], *f.* Helen.

†**héler** [e'le], *v.t.* (*conjug. like* CÉDER) to hail, to call (*a taxi, a boat etc.*).

hélice [e'lis], *n.f.* screw; propeller.

hélicoptère [elikɔp'tɛ:r], *n.m.* helicopter.

héliport [eli'pɔ:r], *n.m.* heliport, helicopter landing-ground.

hélium [e'ljɔm], *n.m.* helium.

helvétique [ɛlve'tik], *a.* Helvetic, Helvetian, Swiss.

hémisphère [emis'fɛ:r], *n.m.* hemisphere.

hémisphérique

hémisphérique [emisfe′rik], *a.* hemispheric.
hémistiche [emis′tiʃ], *n.m.* hemistich.
hémoglobine [emɔglɔ′bin], *n.f.* hemoglobin.
hémophylie [emofi′li], *n.f.* hemophilia.
hémorragie [emɔra′ʒi], *n.f.* hemorrhage.
hémorroïdes [emɔrɔ′id], *n.f. pl.* hemorrhoids, piles.
†**henné** [ε′ne], *n.m.* (*Bot.*) henna.
†**hennir** [ε′niːr], *v.i.* to neigh, to whinny.
†**hennissement** [enis′mɑ̃], *n.m.* neighing.
Henri [ɑ̃′ri], *m.* Henry.
hépatique [epa′tik], *a.* hepatic.—*n.f.* (*Bot.*) liverwort.
hépatite [epa′tit], *n.f.* hepatitis (*inflammation of the liver*); (*Min.*) hepatite (*liver stone*).
heptagone [epta′gɔn], *a.* heptagonal.—*n.m.* heptagon.
héraldique [eral′dik], *a.* heraldic.—*n.f.* heraldry.
†**héraut** [e′ro], *n.m.* herald.
herbacé [εrba′se], *a.* (*Bot.*) herbaceous.
herbage [εr′baːʒ], *n.m.* herbage, grass-land; pasture.
herbager [εrba′ʒe] *v.t.* (*conjug. like* MANGER) to graze (*cattle*).
herbe [εrb], *n.f.* herb, grass, wort; *blé en herbe*, grain in the blade; *brin d'herbe*, blade of grass; *fines herbes*, herbs for seasoning; *mauvaise herbe*, weed; (*fig.*) scamp.
herbette [εr′bεt], *n.f.* (*Poet.*) short grass, green-sward.
herbeux [εr′bø], *a.* (*fem.* **-euse**) grassy, herbous.
herbicide [εrbi′sid], *a.* weed-killing.—*n.m.* weed-killer.
herbivore [εrbi′vɔːr], *a.* herbivorous.—*n.m.* herbivore.
herboriste [εrbɔ′rist], *n.* herbalist, dealer in medicinal herbs.
herbu [εr′by], *a.* grassy, covered with grass.
Hercule [εr′kyl], *m.* Hercules.
hercule [εr′kyl], *n.m.* man of herculean strength; strong-arm man.
herculéen [εrkyle′ɛ̃], *a.* (*fem.* **-éenne**) herculean.
†**hère** [ε:r], *n.m.* *un pauvre hère*, a sorry fellow, a poor devil.
héréditaire [eredi′tεːr], *a.* hereditary.
hérédité [eredi′te], *n.f.* hereditary transmission, inheritance *or* succession, hereditary right; heredity.
hérésie [ere′zi], *n.f.* heresy.
hérétique [ere′tik], *a.* heretical.—*n.* heretic.
†**hérissé** [eri′se], *a.* bristling, on end; rough, shaggy; (*Bot.*) hairy, prickly.
†**hérissement** [eris′mɑ̃], *n.m.* bristling, shagginess.
†**hérisser** [eri′se], *v.t.* to bristle, to erect. **se hérisser**, *v.r.* to stand on end, to bristle up; to be bristling with.
†**hérisson** [eri′sɔ̃], *n.m.* hedgehog; (*fig.*) cross-grained person; *hérisson de mer*, sea-urchin.
héritage [eri′taːʒ], *n.m.* heritage, inheritance, legacy.
hériter [eri′te], *v.t.* to inherit.—*v.i.* to inherit, to be heir (*de*); to succeed.
héritier [eri′tje], *n.m.* (*fem.* **-ière**) heir, heiress.
hermétique [εrme′tik], *a.* hermetic, airtight, water-tight.

hermétiquement [εrmetik′mɑ̃], *adv.* hermetically.
hermine [εr′min], *n.f.* ermine.
hermitage [εrmi′taːʒ], [ERMITAGE].
†**herniaire** [εr′njεːr], *a.* hernial; *bandage herniaire*, truss.
†**hernie** [εr′ni], *n.f.* hernia, rupture.
héroïne [erɔ′in], *n.f.* heroine; (*Chem.*) heroin.
héroïque [erɔ′ik], *a.* heroic.
héroïquement [erɔik′mɑ̃], *adv.* heroically.
héroïsme [erɔ′ism], *n.m.* heroism.
†**héron** [e′rɔ̃], *n.m.* heron.
†**héros** [e′ro], *n.m.* hero.
†**hersage** [εr′saːʒ], *n.m.* harrowing.
†**herse** [εrs], *n.f.* harrow; portcullis,*herse; (*pl.*) (*Theat.*) battens, lights (*above stage*).
†**hersé** [εr′se], *a.* harrowed; (*Her.*) represented with a herse.
†**herser** [εr′se], *v.t.* to harrow.
†**hésitant** [ezi′tɑ̃], *a.* hesitating, wavering.
hésitation [ezitɑ′sjɔ̃], *n.f.* hesitation.
hésiter [ezi′te], *v.i.* to hesitate, to falter, to pause, to waver.
†**hessois** [e′swa], *a.* Hessian.—*n.m.* (**Hessois**, *fem.* **-oise**) Hessian (*person*).
hétéroclite [eterɔ′klit], *a.* heteroclite, anomalous; irregular.
hétérodoxe [eterɔ′dɔks], *a.* heterodox.
hétérodyne [eterɔ′din], *a.* and *n.f.* (*Rad.*) heterodyne.
hétérogène [eterɔ′ʒεːn], *a.* heterogeneous; incongruous.
†**hêtre** [εːtr], *n.m.* beech, beech tree.
heure [œːr], *n.f.* hour; o'clock; time of day; moment; (*pl.*) primer (*prayer-book*); *heures d'affluence* or *de pointe*, rush hours, peak periods; (*nouvelles de la*) *dernière heure*, latest news; *quelle heure est-il?* what time is it? *tout à l'heure*, in a few minutes, just now; *de bonne heure*, early.
heureusement [œrøz′mɑ̃], *adv.* happily, luckily, fortunately; successfully.
heureux [œ′rø], *a.* (*fem.* **-euse**) happy, blissful; blessed, lucky; successful; pleasing; delighted.
†**heurt** [œːr], *n.m.* blow; knock, shock, collision; bruise.
†**heurté** [œr′te], *a.* abrupt, harsh, jerky (*of style*).
†**heurtement** [œrtə′mɑ̃], *n.m.* clash, collision; hiatus.
†**heurter** [œr′te], *v.t.* to knock against, to strike against; to jostle; to shock, to offend; to jar with.—*v.i.* to strike, to knock, to hit. **se heurter**, *v.r.* to strike *or* hit oneself; to strike against each other; to jostle each other, to clash.
hiatus [ja′tyːs], *n.m.* hiatus; gap.
hibernal [iber′nal], *a.* (*m. pl.* **-aux**) hibernal.
hibernant [iber′nɑ̃], *a.* hibernating.
hibernation [ibεrnɑ′sjɔ̃], *n.f.* hibernation.
hiberner [ibεr′ne], *v.i.* to hibernate.
†**hibou** [i′bu], *n.m.* (*pl.* **-oux**) owl; (*fig.*) moper.
†**hic** [ik], *n.m.* knot, difficulty, rub.
†**hideur** [i′dœːr], *n.f.* hideousness.
†**hideusement** [idøz′mɑ̃], *adv.* hideously.
†**hideux** [i′dø], *a.* (*fem.* **-euse**) hideous, frightful, shocking.
hier [jεːr], *adv.* yesterday; *avant-hier*, the day before yesterday; *hier matin*, yesterday morning; *hier* (*au*) *soir*, last night.

†**hiérarchie** [jerar′ʃi], *n.f.* hierarchy.
†**hiérarchique** [jerar′ʃik], *a.* hierarchical.
hiératique [jera′tik], *a.* hieratic.
hiéroglyphe [jerɔ′glif], *n.m.* hieroglyph.
hiéroglyphique [jerɔgli′fik], *a.* hieroglyphical.
Hilaire [i′lɛːr], *m.* Hilary.
hilarant [ila′rã], *a.* screamingly funny, rollicking; *gaz hilarant*, laughing-gas.
hilare [i′laːr], *a.* hilarious.
hilarité [ilari′te], *n.f.* hilarity, mirth, laughter.
hindou [ɛ̃′du], *a.* Hindu; Indian (*of India*).— *n.m.* (**Hindou**, *fem.* **-oue**) Hindu; Indian (*of India*).
hindouisme [ɛ̃du′ism], *n.m.* Hinduism.
hindoustani [ɛ̃dusta′ni], *n.m.* Hindustani, Urdu (*language*).
hippique [i′pik], *a.* hippic; *concours hippique*, horse show.
hippodrome [ipɔ′drom], *n.m.* hippodrome, circus; race-course.
hippopotame [ipɔpɔ′tam], *n.m.* hippopotamus.
hirondelle [irɔ̃′dɛl], *n.f.* swallow.
hirsute [ir′syt], *a.* hirsute, hairy; shaggy, dishevelled; (*fig.*) boorish.
†**hisser** [i′se], *v.t.* to hoist, to lift, to run up, to raise. **se hisser**, *v.r.* to raise, hoist *or* lift oneself up.
histoire [is′twaːr], *n.f.* history; tale, story; idle story, untruth, falsehood; trifle; (*pl.*) fuss.
historien [istɔ′rjɛ̃], *n.m.* historian.
historier [istɔ′rje], *v.t.* to illustrate, to embellish, to adorn.
historiette [istɔ′rjɛt], *n.f.* little story, short tale.
historiographe [istɔrjɔ′graf], *n.* historiographer.
historique [istɔ′rik], *a.* historic(al).—*n.m.* historical account.
historiquement [istɔrik′mã], *adv.* historically.
histrion [istri′jɔ̃], *n.m.* histrion, actor; mountebank.
histrionique [istriɔ′nik], *a.* histrionic.
hitlérien [itle′rjɛ̃], *a.* (*fem.* **-enne**) Hitlerite.
hitlérisme [itle′rism], *n.m.* Hitlerism.
hiver [i′vɛːr], *n.m.* winter.
hivernage [ivɛr′naːʒ], *n.m.* winter season, winter-time; wintering place.
hivernal [ivɛr′nal], *a.* (*m. pl.* **-aux**) wintry.
hiverner [ivɛr′ne], *v.t.* (*Agric.*) to winterfallow.—*v.i.* to winter.
†**hobereau** [ɔ′bro], *n.m.* (*pl.* **-eaux**) hobby (*bird*); country squire, squireen.
†**hochement** [ɔʃ′mã], *n.m.* shaking, tossing, wagging (*of the head*).
†**hochequeue** [ɔʃ′kø], *n.m.* (*Orn.*) wagtail.
†**hocher** [ɔ′ʃe], *v.t.* to shake, to toss; to wag (*the tail etc.*).
†**hochet** [ɔ′ʃɛ], *n.m.* rattle (*for children*); (*fig.*) toy, bauble, plaything.
†**hockey** [ɔ′kɛ], *n.m.* hockey; (*C*) hockey, hockey stick; *hockey sur glace*, ice hockey.
†**holà!** [ɔ′la], *int.* stop! hold on! hallo, there! —*n.m.* stop, end; *mettre le holà*, to put a stop to (*a quarrel*).
†**hollandais** [ɔlã′dɛ], *a.* Dutch.—*n.m.* Dutch (*language*); (**Hollandais**, *fem.* **-aise**) Dutchman, Dutchwoman.

†**Hollande** [ɔ′lãːd], **la**, *f.* Holland, the Netherlands.
holocauste [ɔlɔ′koːst], *n.m.* holocaust, burnt offering; sacrifice.
†**homard** [ɔ′maːr], *n.m.* lobster.
homélie [ɔme′li], *n.f.* homily, familiar sermon.
homéopathe [ɔmeɔ′pat], *a.* homeopathic.— *n.* homoeopath.
homéopathie [ɔmeɔpa′ti], *n.f.* homeopathy.
homéopathique [ɔmeɔpa′tik], *a.* homeopathic.
Homère [ɔ′mɛːr], *m.* Homer.
homérique [ɔme′rik], *a.* Homeric.
homicide [ɔmi′sid], *a.* murderous.—*n.m.* homicide, manslaughter.—*n.* murderer.
hommage [ɔ′maːʒ]. *n.m.* homage; respect; service; acknowledgment; token, gift; (*pl.*) respects.
homme [ɔm], *n.m.* man; (*colloq.*) husband, old man.
homme-grenouille [ɔmgrə′nuːj], *n.m.* (*pl.* **hommes-grenouilles**) frogman.
homme-sandwich [ɔmsã′dwitʃ], *n.m.* (*pl.* **hommes-sandwich(e)s**) sandwich man.
homogène [ɔmɔ′ʒɛːn], *a.* homogeneous.
homogénéité [ɔmɔʒenei′te], *n.f.* homogeneity.
homonyme [ɔmɔ′nim], *a.* homonymous.— *n.m.* homonym; namesake.
†**Honduras** [ɔ̃dy′ras], **le**, *m.* Honduras.
†**hondurien** [ɔ̃dy′rjɛ̃], *a.* (*fem.* **-enne**) Honduran.—*n.m.* (**Hondurien**, *fem.* **-enne**) Honduran (*person*).
†**hongre** [ɔ̃:gr], *a.* gelded.—*n.m.* gelding.
†**hongrer** [ɔ̃′gre], *v.t.* to geld (*a horse*).
†**Hongrie** [ɔ̃′gri], **la**, *f.* Hungary.
†**hongrois** [ɔ̃′grwa], *a.* Hungarian.—*n.m.* Hungarian (*language*); (**Hongrois**, *fem.* **-oise**) Hungarian (*person*).
honnête [ɔ′nɛːt], *a.* honest, upright; modest (*of women*); respectable; decorous; proper; handsome; reasonable.—*n.m.* honesty, probity.
honnêtement [ɔnɛt′mã], *adv.* honestly, honorably; virtuously; becomingly; handsomely; suitably; reasonably.
honnêteté [ɔnɛt′te], *n.f.* honesty, integrity; modesty, chastity, virtue; propriety; respectability.
honneur [ɔ′nœːr], *n.m.* honor; virtue; integrity; repute; credit; distinction; respect; (*Cards*) honor.
†**honnir** [ɔ′niːr], *v.t.* to dishonor, to disgrace, to cover with shame.
honorabilité [ɔnɔrabili′te], *n.f.* honor, respectability.
honorable [ɔnɔ′rabl], *a.* honorable; respectable, creditable; suitable.
honorablement [ɔnɔrablə′mã], *adv.* honorably, respectably, creditably; nobly.
honoraire [ɔnɔ′rɛːr], *a.* honorary, titular.— *n.m.* (*pl.*) honorarium, fee.
honorer [ɔnɔ′re], *v.t.* to honor; to do credit to, to be an honor to; *honorer une traite*, to meet a bill. **s'honorer**, *v.r.* to do oneself honor; to acquire honor; to deem it an honor; to pride oneself.
honorifique [ɔnɔri′fik], *a.* honorary, titular, gratuitous.

177

honte

†**honte** [ɔ̃:t], *n.f.* shame; disgrace, infamy; reproach; scandal; *avoir honte de*, to be ashamed of; *mauvaise honte* or *fausse honte*, self-consciousness, bashfulness.
†**honteusement** [ɔ̃tøz'mɑ̃], *adv.* shamefully, disgracefully; infamously.
†**honteux** [ɔ̃'tø], *a.* (*fem.* **-euse**) ashamed; bashful, shy; shameful, disgraceful.
hôpital [ɔpi'tal], *n.m.* (*pl.* **-aux**) hospital.
†**hoquet** [ɔ'kɛ], *n.m.* hiccup.
hoqueter [ɔk'te], *v.i.* (*conjug. like* APPELER) to hiccup.
horaire [ɔ'rɛ:r], *a.* hourly; horary, horal.— *n.m.* time-table, schedule.
†**horde** [ɔrd], *n.f.* horde; pack; rabble.
horizon [ɔri'zɔ̃], *n.m.* horizon, sky-line.
horizontal [ɔrizɔ̃'tal], *a.* (*m. pl.* **-aux**) horizontal.
horizontalement [ɔrizɔ̃tal'mɑ̃], *adv.* horizontally.
horloge [ɔr'lɔ:ʒ], *n.f.* clock; time-keeper.
horloger [ɔrlɔ'ʒe], *a.* (*fem.* **-ère**) pertaining to clock-making.—*n.m.* (*fem.* **-ère**) clock-maker, watch-maker.
horlogerie [ɔrlɔ'ʒri], *n.f.* watch- and clock-making; clocks and watches.
hormis [ɔr'mi], *prep.* except, excepting, but.
hormone [ɔr'mɔn], *n.f.* hormone.
horoscope [ɔrɔs'kɔp], *n.m.* horoscope.
horreur [ɔ'rœ:r], *n.f.* horror, dread; detestation; enormity.
horrible [ɔ'ribl], *a.* horrible, dreadful; hideous, frightful, shocking.
horriblement [ɔribl(ə)'mɑ̃], *adv.* horribly, awfully.
horrifier [ɔri'fje], *v.t.* to horrify.
horrifique [ɔri'fik], *a.* hair-raising.
horripilant [ɔripi'lɑ̃], *a.* exasperating.
horripiler [ɔripi'le], *v.t.* to horripilate; to exasperate.
†**hors** [ɔ:r], *prep.* out of, outside of; beyond, past; but, except, save; *hors d'affaire*, out of danger; *hors de combat*, disabled; *hors de doute*, beyond doubt; *hors d'ici!* away with you! out of my sight! *hors de prix*, exorbitant; *hors de service*, unserviceable, out of order; *hors la loi*, outlawed.
†**hors-bord** [ɔr'bɔr], *n.m. inv.* outboard; speed-boat.
†**hors-caste** [ɔr'kast], *a.* and *n. inv.* outcaste, untouchable.
†**hors-d'œuvre** [ɔr'dœ:vr], *n.m. inv.* (*Arch.*) outwork, outbuilding; (*Lit.*) digression, episode; (*Cook.*) dish served at the beginning of a meal.
†**hors-jeu** [ɔr'ʒø], *n.m. inv.* (*Ftb.*) off-side.
†**hors-la-loi** [ɔrla'lwa], *n.m. inv.* outlaw.
hortensia [ɔrtɑ̃'sja], *n.m.* hydrangea.
horticulteur [ɔrtikyl'tœ:r], *n.m.* horticulturist.
horticultural [ɔrtikylty'ral], *a.* (*m. pl.* **-aux**) horticultural.
horticulture [ɔrtikyl'tyr], *n.f.* horticulture.
hospice [ɔs'pis], *n.m.* refuge; asylum; alms-house.
hospitalier [ɔspita'lje], *a.* (*fem.* **-ière**) hospitable.—*n.m.* (*fem.* **-ière**) hospitaller.
hospitalièrement [ɔspitaljɛr'mɑ̃], *adv.* hospitably.
hospitalité [ɔspitali'te], *n.f.* hospitality.

hostellerie [ɔstɛl'ri], *n.f.* inn.
hostie [ɔs'ti], *n.f.* (*Jewish Ant.*) offering, victim, sacrifice; (*R.-C. Ch.*) host.
hostile [ɔs'til], *a.* hostile, adverse.
hostilement [ɔstil'mɑ̃], *adv.* hostilely, adversely.
hostilité [ɔstili'te], *n.f.* hostility, enmity.
hôte [o:t], *n.m.* (*fem.* **-esse**) host, hostess; landlord, innkeeper; guest; lodger; occupier, inmate.
hôtel [o'tɛl], *n.m.* town mansion, large house; hotel, inn; *hôtel de ville*, town hall; *hôtel des ventes*, auction mart; *hôtel meublé*, furnished lodgings, lodging-house.
hôtelier [otə'lje], *n.m.* (*fem.* **-ière**) innkeeper, host, hostess.
hôtellerie [otɛl'ri], *n.f.* inn, hotel; hotel trade.
hôtesse [o'tɛs], [HÔTE].
†**hotte** [ɔt], *n.f.* basket (*carried on the back*); dosser, hod.
†**hottée** [ɔ'te], *n.f.* basketful.
†**hottentot** [ɔtɑ̃'to], *a.* Hottentot.—*n.m.* (**Hottentot**, *fem.* **-e**) Hottentot (*person*).
†**houage** [wa:ʒ], *n.m.* hoeing.
†**houblon** [u'blɔ̃], *n.m.* (*Bot.*) hop.
†**houblonnière** [ublɔ'njɛ:r], *n.f.* hop field.
†**houe** [u], *n.f.* hoe.
†**houer** [u'e], *v.t.* to hoe.
†**houille** [u:j], *n.f.* coal.
†**houiller** [u'je], *a.* (*fem.* **-ère**) coal-bearing. —*n.f.* (**-ère**) coal mine, colliery.
†**houilleur** [u'jœ:r], *n.m.* collier, coal miner.
†**houilleux** [u'jø], *a.* (*fem.* **-euse**) containing coal.
†**houle** [ul], *n.f.* swell, surge.
†**houlette** [u'lɛt], *n.f.* (shepherd's) crook; crosier.
†**houleux** [u'lø], *a.* (*fem.* **-euse**) swelling, rough (*of sea*).
†**houppe** [up], *n.f.* tuft; top-knot; tassel.
†**houppé** [u'pe], *a.* tufted, crested.
†**houppelande** [u'plɑ̃:d], *n.f.* overcoat, cloak.
†**houpper** [u'pe], *v.t.* to tuft; to comb (*wool*).
†**houppette** [u'pɛt], *n.f.* powder puff.
†**hourdage** [ur'da:ʒ], †**hourdis** [ur'di], *n.m.* rough-walling; pugging.
†**hourder** [ur'de], *v.t.* to rough-wall; to pug.
†**hourdis** [HOURDAGE].
†**hourra** [u'ra], *n.m.* hurrah.
†**houspiller** [uspi'je], *v.t.* to manhandle, to rough-house; to abuse.
†**housse** [us], *n.f.* housing, horse-cloth; dust-sheet, loose cover.
†**housser** [u'se], *v.t.* to cover up.
†**houssine** [u'sin], *n.f.* switch; riding-whip.
†**houssiner** [usi'ne], *v.t.* to switch; to beat.
†**houx** [u], *n.m.* holly, holly tree.
†**hoyau** [wa'jo], *n.m.* (*pl.* **-aux**) mattock, grubbing-hoe.
†**huard** [ɥa:r], *n.m.* osprey; sea-eagle.
†**hublot** [y'blo], *n.m.* (*Naut.*) side-light, port-hole.
†**huche** [yʃ], *n.f.* kneading trough; bread pan.
†**hue!** [y], *int.* gee! gee up!
†**huée** [ɥe], *n.f.* whoop, shouting; hooting, booing.
†**huer** [ɥe], *v.t.* to shout after; to hoot at, to boo.—*v.i.* to boo.

†**huguenot** [yg'no], *a.* Huguenot.—*n.m.* (**Huguenot**, *fem.* **-e**) Huguenot (*person*).

huilage [ɥi'la:ʒ], *n.m.* oiling.

huile [ɥil], *n.f.* oil.

huiler [ɥi'le], *v.t.* to oil; to anoint with oil; to lubricate.—*v.i.* (*Bot.*) to exude oil.

huilerie [ɥil'ri], *n.f.* oil works.

huileux [ɥi'lø], *a.* (*fem.* **-euse**) oily, greasy.

huilier [ɥi'lje], *n.m.* cruet-stand; oil merchant.

†*huis** [ɥi], *n.m.* door; *à huis clos*, behind closed doors, in camera.

huisserie [ɥis'ri], *n.f.* door frame.

huissier [ɥi'sje], *n.m.* usher; gentleman-usher; door-keeper; sheriff's officer, bailiff.

†**huit** [ɥit], *a.* and *n.m.* eight; eighth.

†**huitaine** [ɥi'tɛn], *n.f.* eight days, week.

†**huitième** [ɥi'tjɛm], *a.* eighth.—*n.m.* eighth, eighth part.

†**huitièmement** [ɥitjɛm'mã], *adv.* eighthly.

huître [ɥitr], *n.f.* oyster; (*fig.*) blockhead, dunce.

huîtrier [ɥit'rje], *n.m.* (*Orn.*) oyster-catcher.

huîtrière [ɥitri'ɛ:r], *n.f.* oyster bed.

hululer [ULULER].

humain [y'mɛ̃], *a.* human; humane, benevolent.—*n.m.* humanity, mankind.

humainement [ymɛn'mã], *adv.* humanly; humanely.

humaniser [ymani'ze], *v.t.* to humanize, to civilize. **s'humaniser**, *v.r.* to become humanized.

humanisme [yma'nism], *n.m.* humanism.

humaniste [yma'nist], *a.* and *n.* humanist; classical scholar.

humanitaire [ymani'tɛ:r], *a.* and *n.* humanitarian.

humanité [ymani'te], *n.f.* humanity; human nature; mankind.

humble [œ̃:bl], *a.* humble, meek, modest.

humblement [œ̃mblə'mã], *adv.* humbly, meekly.

humectant [ymɛk'tã], *a.* refreshing, moistening.—*n.m.* humectant.

humectation [ymɛkta'sjɔ̃], *n.f.* moistening.

humecter [ymɛk'te], *v.t.* to damp, to moisten, to refresh. **s'humecter**, *v.r.* to be moistened; to refresh oneself.

†**humer** [y'me], *v.t.* to inhale.

humeur [y'mœ:r], *n.f.* humor; temperament, disposition; mood, fancy; ill-humor.

humide [y'mid], *a.* damp, wet, moist, humid.

humidité [ymidi'te], *n.f.* humidity, moisture, dampness.

humiliant [ymi'ljã], *a.* humiliating, degrading.

humiliation [ymilja'sjɔ̃], *n.f.* humiliation, abasement.

humilier [ymi'lje], *v.t.* to humble, to humiliate. **s'humilier**, *v.r.* to humble *or* abase oneself.

humilité [ymili'te], *n.f.* humility, meekness, lowliness.

humoriste [ymɔ'rist], *a.* humorous.—*n.* humorist.

humoristique [ymɔris'tik] *a.* humorous (*writer etc.*).

humour [y'mur], *n.m.* humor.

humus [y'mys], *n.m.* humus, mold.

†**hune** [yn], *n.f.* (*Naut.*) top.

†**hunier** [y'nje], *n.m.* topsail.

†**huppe** [yp], *n.f.* hoopoe; tuft, crest.

†**huppé** [y'pe], *a.* tufted, crested (*of birds*); (*colloq.*) well off, smartly dressed.

†**hurlement** [yrlə'mã], *n.m.* howling; howl, roar, yell.

†**hurler** [yr'le], *v.i.* to howl, to yell; to roar; *hurler avec les loups*, to do as others do.

†**hurleur** [yr'lœ:r], *a.* (*fem.* **-euse**) howling.—*n.m.* (*fem.* **-euse**) howler.

hurluberlu [yrlybɛr'ly], *n.* hare-brained person, harum-scarum.

†**hussard** [y'sa:r], *n.m.* hussar.

†**hutte** [yt], *n.f.* hut, cabin, shanty.

hyacinthe [ja'sɛ̃:t], *n.f.* jacinth; hyacinth.

hybride [i'brid], *a.* and *n.m.* hybrid, mongrel.

hydrangée [iurã'ʒe], *n.f.* (*Bot.*) hydrangea.

hydrater [idra'te], *v.t.* to hydrate.

hydraulique [idro'lik], *a.* hydraulic.—*n.f.* hydraulics.

hydravion [idra'vjɔ̃], *n.m.* flying boat, seaplane.

hydre [idr], *n.f.* hydra.

hydro-électrique [idrɔelɛk'trik], *a.* hydro-electric.

hydrogène [idrɔ'ʒɛ:n], *n.m.* hydrogen.

hydrophobe [idrɔ'fɔb], *a.* and *n.* hydrophobic (*person*).

hydrophobie [idrɔfɔ'bi], *n.f.* hydrophobia, rabies.

hydropique [idrɔ'pik], *a.* and *n.* dropsical (*person*).

hydropisie [idrɔpi'zi], *n.f.* dropsy.

hydroplane [idrɔ'plan], *n.m.* hydroplane.

hydroscope [idrɔs'kɔp], *n.m.* water diviner.

hyène [jɛ:n], *n.f.* hyena.

hygiène [i'ʒjɛ:n], *n.f.* hygiene.

hygiénique [iʒje'nik], *a.* hygienic; sanitary.

hymen [i'mɛn], **hyménée** [ime'ne], *n.m.* hymen, marriage, wedlock.

hymnaire [im'nɛ:r], *n.m.* hymn book, hymnal.

hymne [imn], *n.m.* (*patriotic*) song, anthem.—*n.f.* hymn.

hyperbole [ipɛr'bɔl], *n.f.* hyperbole, exaggeration; (*Math.*) hyperbola.

hyperbolique [ipɛrbɔ'lik], *a.* hyperbolic.

hypermétrope [ipɛrme'trɔp], *a.* long-sighted.

hypersensible [ipɛrsã'sibl], *a.* over-sensitive.

hypertension [ipɛrtã'sjɔ̃], *n.f.* high blood pressure.

hypnose [ip'no:z], *n.f.* hypnosis.

hypnotique [ipnɔ'tik], *a.* and *n.m.* hypnotic.

hypnotiser [ipnɔti'ze], *v.t.* to hypnotize; to fascinate.

hypnotiseur [ipnɔti'zœ:r], *n.m.* (*fem.* **-euse**) hypnotist.

hypnotisme [ipnɔ'tism], *n.m.* hypnotism.

hypocondriaque [ipɔkɔ̃'driak], *a.* and *n.* hypochondriac.

hypocondrie [ipɔkɔ̃'dri], *n.f.* hypochondria.

hypocrisie [ipɔkri'zi], *n.f.* hypocrisy.

hypocrite [ipɔ'krit], *a.* hypocritical.—*n.* hypocrite.

hypodermique [ipɔdɛr'mik], *a.* hypodermic, under the skin.

hypotension [ipɔtã'sjɔ̃], *n.f.* low blood pressure.

hypothécaire [ipɔte'kɛ:r], *a.* on mortgage.

hypothèque [ipɔ'tɛk], *n.f.* mortgage.

hypothéquer [ipɔte'ke], *v.t.* (*conjug. like* CÉDER) to mortgage.

hypothèse [ipɔ'tɛ:z], *n.f.* hypothesis, supposition.

hypothétique [ipɔte'tik], *a.* hypothetical.
hystérie [iste'ri], *n.f.* hysteria.
hystérique [iste'rik], *a.* hysteric, hysterical.

I

I, i [i], *n.m.* the ninth letter of the alphabet.
iceberg [is'bɛrg], *n.m.* iceberg.
ici [i'si], *adv.* here, in this place; hither; now, this time.
iconoclaste [ikɔnɔ'klast], *a.* iconoclastic.— *n.* iconoclast.
iconolâtre [ikɔnɔ'la:tr], *n.m.* image-worshipper.
iconolâtrie [ikɔnɔla'tri], *n.f.* image-worship.
idéal [ide'al], *a.* (*m. pl.* **-aux**) ideal; unreal, imaginary.—*n.m.* (*pl.* **-als** or **-aux**) ideal.
idéalement [ideal'mã], *adv.* ideally.
idéaliser [ideali'ze], *v.t.* to idealize.
idéalisme [idea'lism], *n.m.* idealism.
idéaliste [idea'list], *a.* idealistic.—*n.* idealist.
idée [i'de], *n.f.* idea; notion; conception; opinion; plan; fancy; sketch, suggestion.
idem [i'dɛm], *adv.* idem, ditto.
identification [idãtifika'sjɔ̃], *n.f.* identification.
identifier [idãti'fje], *v.t.* to identify. **s'identifier,** *v.r.* to identify oneself.
identique [idã'tik], *a.* identical, the same.
identiquement [idãtik'mã], *adv.* identically.
identité [idãti'te], *n.f.* identity.
idéologie [ideɔlɔ'ʒi], *n.f.* ideology.
idéologique [ideɔlɔ'ʒik], *a.* ideological.
idéologue [ideɔ'lɔg], *n.m.* ideologue.
ides [id], *n.f. pl.* Ides (15 March etc.).
idiomatique [idjɔma'tik], *a.* idiomatic.
idiome [i'djɔ:m], *n.m.* idiom, dialect.
idiosyncrasie [idjɔsɛkra'zi], *n.f.* idiosyncrasy.
idiot [i'djo], *a.* idiotic, absurd.—*n.m.* (*fem.* **-e**) idiot, imbecile, fond.
idiotie [idjɔ'si], *n.f.* idiocy, imbecility.
idiotisme [idjɔ'tism], *n.m.* (*Gram.*) idiom; (*Path.*) idiocy.
idolâtre [idɔ'la:tr], *a.* idolatrous.—*n.* idolater.
idolâtrer [idɔla'tre], *v.t.* to idolize, to dote upon.
idolâtrie [idɔla'tri], *n.f.* idolatry.
idole [i'dɔl], *n.f.* idol.
idylle [i'dil], *n.f.* idyll.
idyllique [idi'lik], *a.* idyllic.
if [if], *n.m.* yew, yew tree.
igloo or **iglou** [i'glu], *n.m.* igloo.
ignare [i'ɲa:r], *a.* illiterate, ignorant.—*n.* dunce, ignoramus.
igné [ig'ne], *a.* igneous.
ignifuge [igni'fy:ʒ], *a.* fire-resisting, fire-proof; **grenade ignifuge,** fire extinguisher.
ignifuger [ignify'ʒe], *v.t.* (*conjug. like* MANGER) to fireproof.
ignition [igni'sjɔ̃], *n.f.* ignition.
ignoble [i'ɲɔbl], *a.* ignoble; vile, base; beastly, filthy.
ignoblement [iɲɔblə'mã], *adv.* ignobly, vilely, basely.

ignominie [iɲɔmi'ni], *n.f.* ignominy, shame, dishonor.
ignominieusement [iɲɔminjøz'mã], *adv.* ignominiously.
ignominieux [iɲɔmi'njø], *a.* (*fem.* **-euse**) ignominious.
ignorance [iɲɔ'rã:s], *n.f.* ignorance; error, mistake, blunder.
ignorant [iɲɔ'rã], *a.* ignorant, illiterate, unlearned.—*n.m.* (*fem.* **-e**) ignoramus.
ignorer [iɲɔ're], *v.t.* to be ignorant of, not to know, not to be aware of. **s'ignorer,** *v.r.* not to know oneself; to be ignorant of one's own capabilities.
iguane [i'gwan], *n.m.* iguana.
il [il], *pron. m.* (*pl.* **ils**) he; it; there; (*pl.*) they.
île [il], *n.f.* island, isle.
illégal [ille'gal], *a.* (*m. pl.* **-aux**) illegal, unlawful.
illégalement [illegal'mã], *adv.* illegally.
illégalité [illegali'te], *n.f.* illegality.
illégitime [illeʒi'tim], *a.* illegitimate; unlawful, unjust.
illégitimement [illeʒitim'mã], *adv.* illegitimately, unlawfully.
illégitimité [illeʒitimi'te], *n.f.* illegitimacy; unlawfulness; spuriousness.
illettré [ille'tre], *a.* and *n.m.* (*fem.* **-ée**) illiterate, unlettered (person).
illicite [illi'sit], *a.* illicit, unlawful.
illicitement [illisit'mã], *adv.* illicitly, unlawfully.
illimitable [illimi'tabl], *a.* illimitable.
illimité [illimi'te], *a.* unlimited, unbounded, boundless.
illisibilité [illizibili'te], *n.f.* illegibility.
illisible [illi'zibl], *a.* illegible.
illisiblement [illiziblə'mã], *adv.* illegibly.
illogique [illɔ'ʒik], *a.* illogical.
illogiquement [illɔʒik'mã], *adv.* illogically.
illuminant [illymi'nã], *a.* illuminating.—*n.m.* illuminant.
illuminateur [illymina'tœ:r], *n.m.* illuminator, enlightener.
illumination [illymina'sjɔ̃], *n.f.* illumination.
illuminé [illymi'ne], *a.* illuminated, enlightened.—*n.m.* (*fem.* **-ée**) visionary, fanatic.
illuminer [illymi'ne], *v.t.* to illuminate, to illumine, to light up; to enlighten (*the mind etc.*). **s'illuminer,** *v.r.* to light *or* brighten up.
illusion [illy'zjɔ̃], *n.f.* illusion, self-deception, delusion; fallacy, chimera.
illusionner [illyzjɔ'ne], *v.t.* to delude, to deceive.
illusionniste [illyzjɔ'nist], *n.m.* conjurer.
illusoire [illy'zwa:r], *a.* illusive, illusory, delusive.
illusoirement [illyzwar'mã], *adv.* illusively.
illustration [illystra'sjɔ̃], *n.f.* illustriousness, renown; explanation; illustration.
illustre [il'lystr], *a.* illustrious, famous.
illustrer [illys'tre], *v.t.* to do honor to; to illustrate, to make clear. **s'illustrer,** *v.r.* to win fame.
illustrissime [illystri'sim], *a.* most illustrious.
îlot [i'lo], *n.m.* islet (*in sea*); holm (*in river*); block (*of houses*).
ilote [i'lɔt], *n.m.* helot.
ils [il], *pl. pron.* [IL].
image [i'ma:ʒ], *n.f.* image; likeness; picture; statue.

imaginable [imaʒi'nabl], *a.* imaginable.
imaginaire [imaʒi'nɛːr], *a.* imaginary, visionary, unreal, fantastic.
imaginatif [imaʒina'tif], *a.* (*fem.* **-tive**) imaginative.
imagination [imaʒina'sjɔ̃], *n.f.* imagination; conception, thought; fancy.
imaginer [imaʒi'ne], *v.t.* to imagine, to conceive; to fancy, to suppose; to devise. **s'imaginer**, *v.r.* to imagine oneself; to imagine, to fancy, to surmise.
imbécile [ɛ̃be'sil], *a.* imbecile; foolish, idiotic.—*n.* imbecile, idiot; fool.
imbécilement [ɛ̃besil'mɑ̃], *adv.* foolishly.
imbécillité [ɛ̃besili'te], *n.f.* imbecility, idiocy; stupidity.
imberbe [ɛ̃'bɛrb], *a.* beardless; (*fig.*) green.
imbiber [ɛ̃bi'be], *v.t.* to imbibe; to imbue; to steep. **s'imbiber**, *v.r.* to imbibe, to drink in.
imbroglio [ɛ̃brɔ'ljo], *n.m.* imbroglio, intricacy.
imbu [ɛ̃'by], *a.* imbued, saturated.
imbuvable [ɛ̃by'vabl], *a.* undrinkable.
imitable [imi'tabl], *a.* imitable.
imitateur [imita'tœːr], *a.* (*fem.* **-trice**) imitative.—*n.m.* (*fem.* **-trice**) imitator.
imitatif [imita'tif], *a.* (*fem.* **-tive**) imitative.
imitation [imita'sjɔ̃], *n.f.* imitation.
imiter [imi'te], *v.t.* to imitate, to copy; to mimic; to resemble.
immaculé [immaky'le], *a.* immaculate, spotless.
immanent [imma'nɑ̃], *a.* immanent.
immangeable [ɛ̃mɑ̃'ʒabl, imɑ̃'ʒabl], *a.* uneatable.
immanquable [ɛ̃mɑ̃'kabl], *a.* infallible, certain, sure.
immanquablement [ɛ̃mɑ̃kablə'mɑ̃], *adv.* infallibly, certainly, without fail.
immatériel [immate'rjɛl], *a.* (*fem.* **-elle**) immaterial, incorporeal.
immatriculation [immatrikyla'sjɔ̃], *n.f.* matriculation; registering; enrolment; (*Motor.*) **plaque d'immatriculation**, license plate.
immatriculé [immatriky'le], *a.* registered; matriculated.
immatriculer [immatriky'le], *v.t.* to matriculate; to register.
immaturité [immatyri'te], *n.f.* unripeness; immaturity.
immédiat [imme'dja], *a.* immediate.
immédiatement [immedjat'mɑ̃] *adv.* immediately.
immémorial [immemɔ'rjal], *a.* (*m. pl.* **-aux**) immemorial.
immense [im'mɑ̃ːs], *a.* immense, immeasurable; boundless, huge.
immensément [immɑ̃se'mɑ̃], *adv.* immensely.
immensité [immɑ̃si'te], *n.f.* immensity.
immerger [immɛr'ʒe], *v.t.* (*conjug. like* MANGER) to immerse, to plunge.
immérité [immeri'te], *a.* undeserved, unmerited, unjust.
immersion [immɛr'sjɔ̃], *n.f.* immersion; submergence; committal to the deep.
immesurable [immǝzy'rabl], *a.* unmeasurable, immeasurable.
immeuble [im'mœbl], *a.* fixed, real (*of estate*).—*n.m.* real estate; property; premises.

immigrant [immi'grɑ̃], *a.* and *n.m.* (*fem.* **-e**) immigrant.
immigration [immigrɑ'sjɔ̃], *n.f.* immigration.
immigrer [immi'gre], *v.i.* to immigrate.
imminence [immi'nɑ̃ːs], *n.f.* imminence.
imminent [immi'nɑ̃], *a.* imminent, impending.
immiscer (s') [simmi'se], *v.r.* (*conjug. like* COMMENCER) to interfere.
immobile [immɔ'bil], *a.* motionless, still; (*fig.*) firm, immovable, unshaken.
immobilier [immɔbi'lje], *a.* (*fem.* **-ière**) real, landed (*of estate*); **agent immobilier**, real estate agent; **société immobilière**, building society.
immobilisation [immɔbiliza'sjɔ̃], *n.f.* immobilization; (*Law*) conversion of movable property into real estate.
immobiliser [immɔbili'ze], *v.t.* to immobilize; to convert into real estate, to tie up (*capital*).
immobilité [immɔbili'te], *n.f.* immobility, immovability.
immodération [immɔderɑ'sjɔ̃], *n.f.* immoderation.
immodéré [immɔde're], *a.* immoderate, excessive, violent.
immodérément [immɔdere'mɑ̃], *adv.* immoderately, intemperately; excessively.
immodeste [immɔ'dɛst], *a.* immodest, indecent.
immodestement [immɔdɛstǝ'mɑ̃], *adv.* immodestly.
immodestie [immɔdɛs'ti], *n.f.* immodesty.
immolation [immɔlɑ'sjɔ̃], *n.f.* immolation; (*fig.*) sacrifice.
immoler [immɔ'le], *v.t.* to immolate, to sacrifice; to slay. **s'immoler**, *v.r.* to immolate *or* sacrifice oneself.
immonde [im'mɔ̃ːd], *a.* unclean, impure.
immondice [immɔ̃'dis], *n.f.* (*usu. in pl.*) filth, dirt; rubbish.
immoral [immɔ'ral], *a.* (*m. pl.* **-aux**) immoral.
immoralité [immɔrali'te], *n.f.* immorality.
immortaliser [immɔrtali'ze], *v.t.* to immortalize. **s'immortaliser**, *v.r.* to immortalize oneself.
immortalité [immɔrtali'te], *n.f.* immortality.
immortel [immɔr'tɛl], *a.* (*fem.* **-elle**) immortal, everlasting.
immuable [im'mɥabl], *a.* immutable, unalterable, unchangeable.
immuablement [immɥablǝ'mɑ̃], *adv.* immutably, unalterably, unchangeably.
immunisation [immyniza'sjɔ̃], *n.f.* (*Med.*) immunization.
immuniser [immyni'ze], *v.t.* to immunize.
immunité [immyni'te], *n.f.* immunity; privilege; exemption.
immutabilité [immytabili'te], *n.f.* immutability, unchangeableness, fixity.
impact [ɛ̃'pakt], *n.m.* impact; hit.
impaction [ɛ̃pak'sjɔ̃], *n.f.* (*Surg.*) impaction.
impair [ɛ̃'pɛːr], *a.* odd, uneven.—*n.m.* blunder, bloomer.
impalpabilité [ɛ̃palpabili'te], *n.f.* impalpability.
impalpable [ɛ̃pal'pabl], *a.* impalpable.
impardonnable [ɛ̃pardɔ'nabl], *a.* unpardonable, unforgivable.

181

imparfait

imparfait [ɛ̃parˈfɛ], *a.* imperfect, incomplete, defective.—*n.m.* (*Gram.*) imperfect (tense).
imparfaitement [ɛ̃parfɛtˈmã], *adv.* imperfectly.
imparité [ɛ̃pariˈte], *n.f.* imparity, inequality; oddness.
impartageable [ɛ̃partaˈʒabl], *a.* indivisible.
impartial [ɛ̃parˈsjal], *a.* (*m. pl.* **-aux**) impartial.
impartialement [ɛ̃parsjalˈmã], *adv.* impartially, even-handedly.
impartialité [ɛ̃parsjaliˈte], *n.f.* impartiality.
impasse [ɛ̃ˈpɑːs], *n.f.* blind alley, cul-de-sac; deadlock, dilemma.
impassibilité [ɛ̃pɑsibiliˈte], *n.f.* impassibility, insensibility.
impassible [ɛ̃pɑˈsibl], *a.* impassive, unmoved.
impassiblement [ɛ̃pɑsibləˈmã], *adv.* impassively, impassibly.
impatiemment [ɛ̃pasjaˈmã], *adv.* impatiently, eagerly.
impatience [ɛ̃paˈsjãːs], *n.f.* impatience; restlessness; eagerness, longing.
impatient [ɛ̃paˈsjã], *a.* impatient; anxious, restless, eager.
impatientant [ɛ̃pasjãˈtã], *a.* provoking, vexing, tiresome.
impatienter [ɛ̃pasjãˈte], *v.t.* to make impatient, to put out of patience; to provoke. **s'impatienter**, *v.r.* to lose one's patience; to fret, to worry.
impayable [ɛ̃pɛˈjabl], *a.* invaluable, priceless; inimitable, extraordinarily funny.
impayé [ɛ̃pɛˈje], *a.* unpaid.
impeccabilité [ɛ̃pɛkabiliˈte], *n.f.* impeccability.
impeccable [ɛ̃pɛˈkabl], *a.* impeccable, faultless.
impécunieux [ɛ̃pekyˈnjø], *a.* (*fem.* **-euse**) impecunious.
impénétrabilité [ɛ̃penetrabiliˈte], *n.f.* impenetrability, imperviousness.
impénétrable [ɛ̃peneˈtrabl], *a.* impenetrable, impervious; inscrutable.
impénitence [ɛ̃peniˈtãːs], *n.f.* impenitence, obduracy.
impénitent [ɛ̃peniˈtã], *a.* and *n.m.* (*fem.* **-e**) impenitent, obdurate (person).
impératif [ɛ̃peraˈtif], *a.* (*fem.* **-tive**) imperative, peremptory.—*n.m.* (*Gram.*) imperative.
impérativement [ɛ̃perativˈmã], *adv.* imperatively.
impératrice [ɛ̃peraˈtris], *n.f.* empress.
imperceptible [ɛ̃pɛrsɛpˈtibl], *a.* imperceptible, unperceivable.
imperceptiblement [ɛ̃pɛrsɛptibləˈmã], *adv.* imperceptibly.
imperfectible [ɛ̃pɛrfɛkˈtibl], *a.* imperfectible.
imperfection [ɛ̃pɛrfɛkˈsjɔ̃], *n.f.* imperfection, defect, flaw.
impérial [ɛ̃peˈrjal], *a.* (*m. pl.* **-aux**) imperial.
impériale [ɛ̃peˈrjal], *n.f.* top, outside (*of a coach*); imperial (*small beard under the lip*).
impérieusement [ɛ̃perjøzˈmã], *adv.* imperiously.
impérieux [ɛ̃peˈrjø], *a.* (*fem.* **-euse**) imperious, supercilious, haughty, lordly.
impérissable [ɛ̃periˈsabl], *a.* imperishable.

impérissablement [ɛ̃perisabləˈmã], *adv.* imperishably.
impéritie [ɛ̃periˈsi], *n.f.* incapacity, incompetence.
imperméabilité [ɛ̃pɛrmeabiliˈte], *n.f.* impermeability.
imperméable [ɛ̃pɛrmeˈabl], *a.* impermeable, impervious.—*n.m.* raincoat, mackintosh.
impersonnalité [ɛ̃pɛrsɔnaliˈte], *n.f.* impersonality.
impersonnel [ɛ̃pɛrsɔˈnɛl], *a.* (*fem.* **-elle**) impersonal.—*n.m.* (*Gram.*) impersonal verb.
impersonnellement [ɛ̃pɛrsɔnɛlˈmã], *adv.* impersonally.
impertinemment [ɛ̃pɛrtina mã], *adv.* impertinently.
impertinence [ɛ̃pɛrtiˈnãːs], *n.f.* impertinence, insolence; silliness.
impertinent [ɛ̃pɛrtiˈnã], *a.* impertinent, insolent, pert.—*n.m.* (*fem.* **-e**) impertinent, saucy person.
imperturbabilité [ɛ̃pɛrtyrbabiliˈte], *n.f.* imperturbability.
imperturbable [ɛ̃pɛrtyrˈbabl], *a.* imperturbable.
imperturbablement [ɛ̃pɛrtyrbabləˈmã], *adv.* imperturbably.
impétigo [ɛ̃petiˈgo], *n.m.* (*Med.*) impetigo.
impétueusement [ɛ̃petɥøzˈmã], *adv.* impetuously.
impétueux [ɛ̃peˈtɥø], *a.* (*fem.* **-euse**) impetuous, vehement, violent.
impétuosité [ɛ̃petɥoziˈte], *n.f.* impetuosity, vehemence; impetus.
impie [ɛ̃ˈpi], *a.* impious, godless; irreligious.—*n.* impious, ungodly *or* irreligious person.
impiété [ɛ̃pjeˈte], *n.f.* impiety, godlessness.
impitoyable [ɛ̃pitwaˈjabl], *a.* pitiless, merciless, ruthless; unrelenting.
impitoyablement [ɛ̃pitwajabləˈmã], *adv.* pitilessly.
implacabilité [ɛ̃plakabiliˈte], *n.f.* implacability.
implacable [ɛ̃plaˈkabl], *a.* implacable.
implacablement [ɛ̃plakabləˈmã], *adv.* implacably.
implantation [ɛ̃plãtaˈsjɔ̃], *n.f.* implantation.
implanter [ɛ̃plãˈte], *v.t.* to implant; to plant. **s'implanter**, *v.r.* to be implanted, fixed, rooted *or* lodged.
implication [ɛ̃plikaˈsjɔ̃], *n.f.* implication, involving; discrepancy.
implicite [ɛ̃pliˈsit], *a.* implicit.
implicitement [ɛ̃plisitˈmã], *adv.* implicitly.
impliquer [ɛ̃pliˈke], *v.t.* to implicate, to involve, to entangle; to imply.
implorateur [ɛ̃plɔraˈtœːr], *n.m.* (*fem.* **-trice**) implorer, suppliant.
imploration [ɛ̃plɔraˈsjɔ̃], *n.f.* supplication, imploration.
implorer [ɛ̃plɔˈre], *v.t.* to implore, to entreat, to beseech; to crave.
imployable [ɛ̃plwaˈjabl], *a.* unbending.
impoli [ɛ̃pɔˈli], *a.* impolite, discourteous, uncivil, rude.
impoliment [ɛ̃pɔliˈmã], *adv.* impolitely, discourteously.
impolitesse [ɛ̃pɔliˈtɛs], *n.f.* impoliteness, incivility; rudeness.
impolitique [ɛ̃pɔliˈtik], *a.* impolitic, ill-advised.

impolitiquement [ɛ̃pɔlitik'mɑ̃], *adv.* unwisely.

impopulaire [ɛ̃pɔpy'lɛːr], *a.* unpopular.

impopularité [ɛ̃pɔpylari'te], *n.f.* unpopularity.

importable [ɛ̃pɔr'tabl], *a.* importable.

importance [ɛ̃pɔr'tɑ̃ːs], *n.f.* importance, consequence; authority, credit; self-conceit.

important [ɛ̃pɔr'tɑ̃], *a.* important, of consequence, weighty.—*n.m.* the essential, the main point; (*fem.* **-e**) person of importance.

importateur [ɛ̃pɔrta'tœːr], *a.* (*fem.* **-trice**) importing.—*n.m.* (*fem.* **-trice**) importer.

importation [ɛ̃pɔrta'sjɔ̃], *n.f.* importation; (*pl.*) imports.

importer [ɛ̃pɔr'te], *v.t.* to import; (*fig.*) to introduce.—*v.i.* to import, to be of moment, to matter; **n'importe**, no matter, never mind; **n'importe où**, anywhere; **n'importe qui**, anyone; **n'importe quoi**, anything; **peu importe**, it does not much matter; **venez n'importe quand**, come when you like.

importun [ɛ̃pɔr'tœ̃], *a.* importunate, tiresome, obtrusive, irksome.—*n.m.* (*fem.* **-e**) tiresome person; intruder, bore.

importuner [ɛ̃pɔrty'ne], *v.t.* to importune, to pester; to inconvenience; to tease.

importunité [ɛ̃pɔrtyni'te], *n.f.* importunity.

imposable [ɛ̃po'zabl], *a.* taxable.

imposant [ɛ̃po'zɑ̃], *a.* imposing, impressive, striking.

imposer [ɛ̃po'ze], *v.t.* to lay on (*hands*); to impose, to tax; to force (*à*).—*v.i.* or **en imposer**, to awe, to overawe. **s'imposer**, *v.r.* to assert oneself; to thrust oneself (*upon somebody*); to be indispensable.

imposition [ɛ̃pozi'sjɔ̃], *n.f.* imposition, laying on (*of hands*); tax, assessment.

impossibilité [ɛ̃pɔsibili'te], *n.f.* impossibility.

impossible [ɛ̃pɔ'sibl], *a.* impossible.—*n.m.* one's utmost, a great deal.

imposte [ɛ̃'pɔst], *n.f.* (*Arch.*) impost, fanlight.

imposteur [ɛ̃pɔs'tœːr], *n.m.* impostor, cheat.

imposture [ɛ̃pɔs'tyːr], *n.f.* imposture, deception.

impôt [ɛ̃'po], *n.m.* tax, duty, impost; **percevoir les impôts**, to collect the taxes.

impotence [ɛ̃pɔ'tɑ̃ːs], *n.f.* helplessness, infirmity.

impotent [ɛ̃pɔ'tɑ̃], *a.* infirm, crippled.—*n.m.* (*fem.* **-e**) cripple, helpless invalid.

impraticabilité [ɛ̃pratikabili'te], *n.f.* impracticability.

impraticable [ɛ̃prati'kabl], *a.* impracticable; impassable; unmanageable.

imprécation [ɛ̃preka'sjɔ̃], *n.f.* imprecation, curse.

imprécatoire [ɛ̃preka'twaːr], *a.* imprecatory.

imprécis [ɛ̃pre'si], *a.* unprecise, indefinite (*words*); (*Mil.*) inaccurate (*fire*).

imprécision [ɛ̃presi'zjɔ̃], *n.f.* lack of precision, vagueness (*of statement*); looseness (*of terms*); (*Mil.*) inaccuracy (*in firing*).

imprégnation [ɛ̃preɲa'sjɔ̃], *n.f.* impregnation.

imprégner [ɛ̃pre'ɲe], *v.t.* (*conjug. like* CÉDER) to impregnate; (*fig.*) to imbue. **s'imprégner**, *v.r.* to become impregnated; to be imbued.

imprenable [ɛ̃prə'nabl], *a.* impregnable.

impressif [ɛ̃prɛ'sif], *a.* (*fem.* **-ive**) impressive, striking.

impression [ɛ̃prɛ'sjɔ̃], *n.f.* impression; mark, stamp; print; edition; *faute d'impression*, misprint.

impressionnable [ɛ̃prɛsjɔ'nabl], *a.* impressionable, sensitive.

impressionnant [ɛ̃prɛsjɔ'nɑ̃], *a.* impressive.

impressionner [ɛ̃prɛsjɔ'ne], *v.t.* to move, to affect, to impress.

impressionnisme [ɛ̃prɛsjɔ'nism], *n.m.* impressionism.

impressionniste [ɛ̃prɛsjɔ'nist], *a.* and *n.* impressionist.

imprévisible [ɛ̃previ'zibl], *a.* unforeseeable.

imprévoyance [ɛ̃prevwa'jɑ̃ːs], *n.f.* want of foresight, improvidence.

imprévoyant [ɛ̃prevwa'jɑ̃], *a.* improvident.

imprévu [ɛ̃pre'vy], *a.* unforeseen, unexpected.

imprimable [ɛ̃pri'mabl], *a.* fit to be printed.

imprimé [ɛ̃pri'me], *n.m.* printed book, paper, document etc.; *service des imprimés*, book post.

imprimer [ɛ̃pri'me], *v.t.* to imprint, to impress, to stamp; to print; to instil; to impart. **s'imprimer**, *v.r.* to be printed.

imprimerie [ɛ̃prim'ri], *n.f.* printing; printing office, printing establishment.

imprimeur [ɛ̃pri'mœːr], *n.m.* printer; (*Print.*) press-man.

improbabilité [ɛ̃prɔbabili'te], *n.f.* improbability, unlikelihood.

improbable [ɛ̃prɔ'babl], *a.* improbable, unlikely.

improbablement [ɛ̃prɔbablə'mɑ̃], *adv.* improbably.

improbité [ɛ̃prɔbi'te], *n.f.* improbity, dishonesty.

improductible [ɛ̃prɔdyk'tibl], *a.* unproducible.

improductif [ɛ̃prɔdyk'tif], *a.* (*fem.* **-tive**) unproductive, idle.

impromptu [ɛ̃prɔp'ty], *a. inv.* impromptu, extemporary.—*n.m.* impromptu.—*adv.* offhand, extempore.

imprononçable [ɛ̃prɔnɔ̃'sabl], *a.* unpronounceable (*word*).

impropre [ɛ̃'prɔpr], *a.* improper, wrong; unfit.

improprement [ɛ̃prɔprə'mɑ̃], *adv.* improperly.

impropriété [ɛ̃prɔprie'te], *n.f.* impropriety; unfitness.

improvisateur [ɛ̃prɔviza'tœːr], *n.m.* (*fem.* **-trice**) improviser, extempory speaker.

improvisation [ɛ̃prɔviza'sjɔ̃], *n.f.* improvisation; (*Mus.*) voluntary.

improviser [ɛ̃prɔvi'ze], *v.t.* to improvise, to extemporize.

improviste (à l') [alɛ̃prɔ'vist], *adv. phr.* all of a sudden, unawares, unexpectedly.

imprudemment [ɛ̃pryda'mɑ̃], *adv.* imprudently, indiscreetly.

imprudence [ɛ̃pry'dɑ̃ːs], *n.f.* imprudence, rashness; indiscretion.

imprudent [ɛ̃pry'dɑ̃], *a.* imprudent, foolhardy, unwise, incautious.

impudemment [ɛ̃pyda'mɑ̃], *adv.* impudently, shamelessly.

impudence [ɛ̃py'dɑ̃ːs], *n.f.* impudence, shamelessness.

impudent

impudent [ɛ̃py'dɑ̃], *a.* impudent, shameless, saucy.—*n.m.* (*fem.* **-e**) impudent person.
impudeur [ɛ̃py'dœːr], *n.f.* immodesty, indecency; effrontery.
impudicité [ɛ̃pydisi'te], *n.f.* impudicity, immodesty, lewdness.
impudique [ɛ̃py'dik], *a.* unchaste, lewd, immodest.
impudiquement [ɛ̃pydik'mɑ̃], *adv.* immodestly, unchastely, lewdly.
impuissance [ɛ̃pɥi'sɑ̃ːs], *n.f.* impotence, incapacity, powerlessness.
impuissant [ɛ̃pɥi'sɑ̃], *a.* impotent, powerless, unable.
impulsif [ɛ̃pyl'sif], *a.* (*fem.* **-sive**) impulsive.
impulsion [ɛ̃pyl'sjɔ̃], *n.f.* impulsion, impulse; impetus; motive.
impunément [ɛ̃pyne'mɑ̃], *adv.* with impunity.
impuni [ɛ̃py'ni], *a.* unpunished.
impunité [ɛ̃pyni'te], *n.f.* impunity.
impur [ɛ̃'pyːr], *a.* impure, foul; unchaste, immodest; unclean.
impurement [ɛ̃pyr'mɑ̃], *adv.* impurely; immodestly.
impureté [ɛ̃pyr'te], *n.f.* impurity, foulness; immodesty; obscenity.
imputabilité [ɛ̃pytabili'te], *n.f.* imputability.
imputable [ɛ̃py'tabl], *a.* imputable, chargeable; to be deducted.
imputation [ɛ̃pytɑ'sjɔ̃], *n.f.* imputation, charge; deduction.
imputer [ɛ̃py'te], *v.t.* to impute, to attribute; to deduct.
imputrescible [ɛ̃pytrɛ'sibl], *a.* not liable to putrefaction; rot-proof.
inabordable [inabor'dabl], *a.* inaccessible, unapproachable.
inabrité [inabri'te], *a.* unsheltered, open.
inabrogé [inabrɔ'ʒe], *a.* unrepealed.
inacceptable [inaksɛp'tabl], *a.* unacceptable.
inaccessibilité [inaksɛsibili'te], *n.f.* inaccessibility.
inaccessible [inaksɛ'sibl], *a.* inaccessible.
inaccordable [inakɔr'dabl], *a.* irreconcilable; unallowable, inadmissible.
inaccoutumé [inakuty'me], *a.* unaccustomed, unusual.
inachevé [inaʃ've], *a.* unfinished.
inactif [inak'tif], *a.* (*fem.* **-tive**) inactive; inert, indolent.
inaction [inak'sjɔ̃], *n.f.* inaction; indolence, inertness.
inactivement [inaktiv'mɑ̃], *adv.* inactively.
inactivité [inaktivi'te], *n.f.* inactivity.
inadaptation [inadaptɑ'sjɔ̃], *n.f.* maladjustment.
inadapté [inadap'te], *a.* maladjusted.—*n.m.* (*fem.* **-ée**) social misfit.
inadmissible [inadmi'sibl], *a.* inadmissible.
inadmission [inadmi'sjɔ̃], *n.f.* non-admission.
inadvertance [inadvɛr'tɑ̃ːs], *n.f.* inadvertence, oversight.
inaliénable [inalje'nabl], *a.* inalienable.
inaliéné [inalje'ne], *a.* unalienated.
inalliable [ina'ljabl], *a.* that cannot be alloyed; incompatible.
inaltérable [inalte'rabl], *a.* unalterable, invariable.
inamical [inami'kal], *a.* (*m. pl.* **-aux**) unfriendly.

inamovibilité [inamɔvibili'te], *n.f.* irremovability, fixity of tenure.
inamovible [inamɔ'vibl], *a.* irremovable, permanent; built in.
inanimé [inani'me], *a.* inanimate, lifeless.
inanité [ɪ�'te], *n.f.* inanity, emptiness.
inanition [inani'sjɔ̃], *n.f.* inanition, starvation.
inapaisé [inapɛ'ze], *a.* unappeased; unquenched.
inaperçu [inapɛr'sy], *a.* unperceived, unobserved, unnoticed.
inapparent [inapa'rɑ̃], *a.* unapparent; inconspicuous.
inapplicable [inapli'kabl], *a.* inapplicable.
inappliqué [inapli'ke], *a.* inattentive, heedless.
inappréciable [inapre'sjabl], *a.* inappreciable; invaluable.
inappréciablement [inapresjablə'mɑ̃], *adv.* inappreciably.
inapprécié [inapre'sje], *a.* unappreciated.
inapprêté [inaprɛ'te], *a.* unprepared, undressed, uncooked.
inapprochable [inaprɔ'ʃabl], *a.* unapproachable.
inapte [i'napt], *a.* inapt, unfit, unqualified.
inaptitude [inapti'tyd], *n.f.* inaptitude, unfitness; disqualification.
inarticulé [inartiky'le], *a.* inarticulate.
inassouvi [inasu'vi], *a.* unsatiated.
inassouvissable [inasuvi'sabl], *a.* insatiable.
inattaquable [inata'kabl], *a.* unassailable; (*fig.*) unimpeachable, irreproachable.
inattendu [inatɑ̃'dy], *a.* unexpected, unforeseen; unhoped for.
inattentif [inatɑ̃'tif], *a.* (*fem.* **-tive**) inattentive, unmindful.
inattention [inatɑ̃'sjɔ̃], *n.f.* inattention, carelessness; *faute d'inattention*, slip.
inaudible [ino'dibl], *a.* inaudible.
inaugural [inogy'ral], *a.* (*m. pl.* **-aux**) inaugural.
inauguration [inogyrɑ'sjɔ̃], *n.f.* inauguration.
inaugurer [inogy're], *v.t.* to inaugurate, to open; to usher in.
inavouable [ina'vwabl], *a.* unavowable; shameful.
incalculable [ɛ̃kalky'labl], *a.* incalculable, numberless.
incandescence [ɛ̃kɑ̃dɛ'sɑ̃ːs], *n.f.* incandescence.
incandescent [ɛ̃kɑ̃dɛ'sɑ̃], *a.* incandescent.
incapable [ɛ̃ka'pabl], *a.* incapable, unable (*de*); unfit, incompetent.
incapacité [ɛ̃kapasi'te], *n.f.* incapacity, incapability; inability, unfitness; incompetence, disability; disqualification, (*Mil.*) disablement; *frapper d'incapacité*, to incapacitate.
incarcération [ɛ̃karserɑ'sjɔ̃], *n.f.* incarceration.
incarcérer [ɛ̃karse're], *v.t.* (*conjug. like* CÉDER) to incarcerate, to imprison.
incarnat [ɛ̃kar'na], *a.* flesh-colored, rosy.—*n.m.* carnation, flesh-color.
incarnation [ɛ̃karnɑ'sjɔ̃], *n.f.* incarnation.
incarné [ɛ̃kar'ne], *a.* incarnate; ingrowing (*nail*).

incarner [ɛ̃kar′ne], *v.t.* to incarnate, to embody. **s'incarner**, *v.r.* to become incarnate; to grow in (*of nails*).
incartade [ɛ̃kar′tad], *n.f.* thoughtless insult; prank, folly.
incassable [ɛ̃ka′sabl], *a.* unbreakable.
incendiaire [ɛ̃sɑ̃′djɛ:r], *a.* and *n.* incendiary.
incendie [ɛ̃sɑ̃′di], *n.m.* fire, conflagration.
incendié [ɛ̃sɑ̃′dje], *a.* burnt-out, gutted.— *n.m.* (*fem.* **-ée**) sufferer by fire.
incendier [ɛ̃sɑ̃′dje], *v.t.* to set fire to, to burn down.
incertain [ɛ̃sɛr′tɛ̃], *a.* uncertain; unsettled, inconstant; vague.
incertitude [ɛ̃sɛrti′tyd], *n.f.* uncertainty, doubt, suspense; instability, fickleness.
incessamment [ɛ̃sɛsa′mɑ̃], *adv.* immediately, at once; incessantly.
incessant [ɛ̃sɛ′sɑ̃], *a.* incessant, ceaseless, unremitting.
inceste [ɛ̃′sɛst], *a.* incestuous.—*n.m.* incest. —*n.* incestuous person.
incestueusement [ɛ̃sɛstɥøz′mɑ̃], *adv.* incestuously.
incestueux [ɛ̃sɛs′tɥø], *a.* (*fem.* **-euse**) incestuous.—*n.m.* (*fem.* **-euse**) incestuous person.
incidemment [ɛ̃sida′mɑ̃], *adv.* incidentally.
incidence [ɛ̃si′dɑ̃:s], *n.f.* incidence.
incident [ɛ̃si′dɑ̃] *a.* incidental; incident.— *n.m.* incident, occurrence.
incinération [ɛ̃sinera′sjɔ̃], *n.f.* incineration; cremation.
incinérer [ɛ̃sine′re], *v.t.* (*conjug. like* CÉDER) to incinerate; to cremate.
inciser [ɛ̃si′ze], *v.t.* to make an incision in, to notch, to gash; to tap (*a tree*).
incisif [ɛ̃si′zif], *a.* (*fem.* **-sive**) sharp, cutting, incisive.—*n.f.* (**-sive**) incisive tooth, incisor.
incision [ɛ̃si′zjɔ̃], *n.f.* incision.
incitation [ɛ̃sita′sjɔ̃], *n.f.* incitement, instigation; (*Med.*) stimulus.
inciter [ɛ̃si′te], *v.t.* to incite; to instigate, to induce.
incivil [ɛ̃si′vil], *a.* uncivil, unmannerly.
incivilement [ɛ̃sivil′mɑ̃], *adv.* uncivilly.
incivilisé [ɛ̃sivili′ze], *a.* uncivilized.
incivilité [ɛ̃sivili′te], *n.f.* incivility; rude remark.
inclémence [ɛ̃kle′mɑ̃:s], *n.f.* inclemency.
inclément [ɛ̃kle′mɑ̃], *a.* inclement.
inclinaison [ɛ̃klinɛ′zɔ̃], *n.f.* inclination; incline, gradient; pitch, slant.
inclination [ɛ̃klinɑ′sjɔ̃], *n.f.* bow, bending; proneness, propensity; attachment, passion.
incliner [ɛ̃kli′ne], *v.t.* to incline, to slope; to bow; to bend; (*fig.*) to dispose, to turn.— *v.i.* to incline, to lean; to be inclined (*à* or *vers*). **s'incliner**, *v.r.* to incline, to lean; to bow to bend, to yield.
inclure [ɛ̃′kly:r] *v.t. irr.* (*conjug. like* CONCLURE *but p.p.* **inclus**) to include, to enclose, to insert.
inclus [ɛ̃′kly], *a.* enclosed, included.
inclusif [ɛ̃kly′zif], *a.* (*fem.* **-sive**) inclusive.
inclusion [ɛ̃kly′zjɔ̃], *n.f.* enclosing; inclusion.
inclusivement [ɛ̃klyziv′mɑ̃], *adv.* inclusively.
incognito [ɛ̃kɔɲi′to], *adv.* incognito.
incohérence [ɛ̃kɔe′rɑ̃:s], *n.f.* incoherence.
incohérent [ɛ̃kɔe′rɑ̃], *a.* incoherent.
incolore [ɛ̃kɔ′lɔ:r], *a.* colorless.
incomber [ɛ̃kɔ̃′be], *v.i.* to be incumbent (*on anyone*).

incombustible [ɛ̃kɔ̃bys′tibl], *a.* incombustible, fire-proof.
incomestible [ɛ̃kɔmɛs′tibl], *a.* inedible.
incommode [ɛ̃kɔ′mɔd], *a.* inconvenient, uncomfortable; annoying, disagreeable.
incommodé [ɛ̃kɔmɔ′de], *a.* indisposed, unwell, poorly.
incommodément [ɛ̃kɔmɔde′mɑ̃], *adv.* incommodiously, inconveniently.
incommoder [ɛ̃kɔmɔ′de], *v.t.* to inconvenience, to trouble; to disturb, to annoy; to make unwell.
incommodité [ɛ̃kɔmɔdi′te], *n.f.* inconvenience, incommodiousness; annoyance; indisposition.
incommunicable [ɛ̃kɔmyni′kabl], *a.* incommunicable.
incomparable [ɛ̃kɔ̃pa′rabl], *a.* incomparable, unequalled, peerless.
incomparablement [ɛ̃kɔ̃parablə′mɑ̃], *adv.* incomparably.
incompatibilité [ɛ̃kɔ̃patibili′te], *n.f.* incompatibility.
incompatible [ɛ̃kɔ̃pa′tibl], *a.* incompatible, inconsistent.
incompétence [ɛ̃kɔ̃pe′tɑ̃:s] *n.f.* incompetence.
incompétent [ɛ̃kɔ̃pe′tɑ̃], *a.* imcompetent.
incomplet [ɛ̃kɔ̃′plɛ], *a.* (*fem.* **-ète**) incomplete.
incomplètement [ɛ̃kɔ̃plɛt′mɑ̃], *adv.* incompletely.
incompréhensible [ɛ̃kɔ̃preɑ̃′sibl], *a.* incomprehensible, inscrutable.
incompréhension [ɛ̃kɔ̃preɑ̃′sjɔ̃], *n.f.* lack of understanding; obtuseness.
incompressible [ɛ̃kɔ̃prɛ′sibl], *a.* incompressible.
incompris [ɛ̃kɔ̃′pri], *a.* and *n.m.* (*fem.* **-e**) misunderstood, unappreciated (person).
inconcevable [ɛ̃kɔ̃s′vabl], *a.* inconceivable, unthinkable.
inconcevablement [ɛ̃kɔ̃svablə′mɑ̃], *adv.* inconceivably.
inconciliable [ɛ̃kɔ̃si′ljabl], *a.* irreconcilable, incompatible.
inconduite [ɛ̃kɔ̃′dɥit], *n.f.* misconduct.
inconfort [ɛ̃kɔ̃′fɔ:r], *n.m.* discomfort, lack of comfort.
inconfortable [ɛ̃kɔ̃fɔr′tabl], *a.* uncomfortable.
incongru [ɛ̃kɔ̃′gry], *a.* incongruous, improper, unseemly.
incongruité [ɛ̃kɔ̃gryi′te], *n.f.* incongruity, impropriety.
incongrûment [ɛ̃kɔ̃gry′mɑ̃], *adv.* incongruously, improperly.
inconnu [ɛ̃kɔ′ny], *a.* unknown.—*n.m.* the unknown.—*n.m.* (*fem.* **-e**) stranger. —*n.f.* (**-e**) (*Math.*) unknown quantity.
inconquis [ɛ̃kɔ̃′ki], *a.* unconquered.
inconsciemment [ɛ̃kɔ̃sja′mɑ̃], *adv.* unconsciously, unawares.
inconscience [ɛ̃kɔ̃′sjɑ̃:s], *n.f.* unconsciousness; failure to realize.
inconscient [ɛ̃kɔ̃′sjɑ̃], *a.* unconscious.—*n.m.* the unconscious.
inconséquemment [ɛ̃kɔ̃seka′mɑ̃], *adv.* inconsistently, inconsequentially.
inconséquence [ɛ̃kɔ̃se′kɑ̃:s], *n.f.* inconsistency, inconsequence.
inconséquent [ɛ̃kɔ̃se′kɑ̃], *a.* inconsistent; inconsequential.

inconsidéré [ɛ̃kɔ̃side're], *a.* inconsiderate, thoughtless.

inconsistance [ɛ̃kɔ̃sis'tɑ̃s], *n.f.* inconsistency.

inconsistant [ɛ̃kɔ̃sis'tɑ̃], *a.* inconsistent.

inconsolable [ɛ̃kɔ̃sɔ'labl], *a.* disconsolate; inconsolable.

inconsolablement [ɛ̃kɔ̃sɔlablə'mɑ̃], *adv.* disconsolately, inconsolably.

inconsolé [ɛ̃kɔ̃sɔ'le], *a.* unconsoled, uncomforted.

inconstamment [ɛ̃kɔ̃sta'mɑ̃], *adv.* inconstantly; unsteadily.

inconstance [ɛ̃kɔ̃s'tɑ̃s], *n.f.* inconstancy, fickleness; instability.

inconstant [ɛ̃kɔ̃s'tɑ̃], *a.* inconstant, fickle; changeable; unsettled, unsteady.—*n.m.* (*fem.* **-e**) fickle person.

inconstitutionnel [ɛ̃kɔ̃stitysjɔ'nɛl], *a.* (*fem.* **-elle**) unconstitutional.

incontestable [ɛ̃kɔ̃tɛs'tabl], *a.* incontestable, indisputable.

incontestablement [ɛ̃kɔ̃tɛstablə'mɑ̃], *adv.* incontestably.

incontesté [ɛ̃kɔ̃tɛs'te], *a.* uncontested, unquestioned, undisputed.

incontinence [ɛ̃kɔ̃ti'nɑ̃s], *n.f.* incontinence.

incontinent (1) [ɛ̃kɔ̃ti'nɑ̃], *a.* incontinent, unchaste.

incontinent (2) [ɛ̃kɔ̃ti'nɑ̃], *adv.* at once, immediately, forthwith.

incontrôlable [ɛ̃kɔ̃tro'labl], *a.* that cannot be checked *or* verified.

inconvenance [ɛ̃kɔ̃v'nɑ̃s], *n.f.* impropriety, unseemliness; indecorum; *quelle inconvenance!* how very improper!

inconvenant [ɛ̃kɔ̃v'nɑ̃], *a.* improper, unbecoming, unseemly.

inconvénient [ɛ̃kɔ̃ve'njɑ̃], *n.m.* inconvenience, harm; drawback, objection.

inconvertible [ɛ̃kɔ̃vɛr'tibl], *a.* unconvertible.

incorporation [ɛ̃kɔrpɔra'sjɔ̃], *n.f.* incorporation.

incorporer [ɛ̃kɔrpɔ're], *v.t.* to incorporate, to embody; to fuse. **s'incorporer**, *v.r.* to be embodied; to unite, to be blended.

incorrect [ɛ̃kɔ'rɛkt], *a.* incorrect, inaccurate.

incorrectement [ɛ̃kɔrɛktə'mɑ̃], *adv.* incorrectly, inaccurately.

incorrection [ɛ̃kɔrɛk'sjɔ̃], *n.f.* incorrectness, inaccuracy.

incorrigible [ɛ̃kɔri'ʒibl], *a.* incorrigible.

incorrigiblement [ɛ̃kɔriʒiblə'mɑ̃], *adv.* incorrigibly.

incorruptible [ɛ̃kɔryp'tibl], *a.* incorruptible, unbribable.

incrédibilité [ɛ̃kredibili'te], *n.f.* incredibility.

incrédule [ɛ̃kre'dyl], *a.* incredulous, unbelieving.—*n.* incredulous, infidel.

incrédulité [ɛ̃kredyli'te], *n.f.* incredulity, unbelief.

incriminer [ɛ̃krimi'ne], *v.t.* to incriminate, to accuse.

incroyable [ɛ̃krwa'jabl], *a.* incredible, past belief.

incroyablement [ɛ̃krwajablə'mɑ̃], *adv.* incredibly.

incroyance [ɛ̃krwa'jɑ̃s], *n.f.* unbelief.

incroyant [ɛ̃krwa'jɑ̃], *a.* unbelieving. —*n.m.* (*fem.* **-e**) unbeliever.

incruster [ɛ̃krys'te], *v.t.* to encrust, to inlay. **s'incruster**, *v.r.* to become encrusted.

incubateur [ɛ̃kyba'tœːr], *a.* (*fem.* **-trice**) incubating.—*n.m.* incubator.

incubation [ɛ̃kyba'sjɔ̃], *n.f.* incubation, hatching.

incuber [ɛ̃ky'be], *v.t.* to incubate.

inculcation [ɛ̃kylka'sjɔ̃], *n.f.* inculcation.

inculpation [ɛ̃kylpa'sjɔ̃], *n.f.* indictment, charge.

inculpé [ɛ̃kyl'pe], *n.m.* (*fem.* **-ée**) defendant, accused.

inculper [ɛ̃kyl'pe], *v.t.* to indict, to inculpate, to charge.

inculquer [ɛ̃kyl'ke], *v.t.* to inculcate, to impress.

inculte [ɛ̃'kylt], *a.* uncultivated; untilled; unpolished; unkempt.

incultivable [ɛ̃kylti'vabl], *a.* untillable, uncultivable.

incultivé [ɛ̃kylti've], *a.* uncultivated; (*fig.*) uncultured.

incurable [ɛ̃ky'rabl], *a.* and *n.* incurable.

incurablement [ɛ̃kyrablə'mɑ̃], *adv.* incurably.

incurie [ɛ̃ky'ri], *n.f.* carelessness, heedlessness; negligence.

incursion [ɛ̃kyr'sjɔ̃], *n.f.* incursion, inroad, irruption; expedition.

incurver [ɛ̃kyr've], *v.t.* to curve (*something*) inwards.

Inde [ɛ̃ːd], **l'**, *f.* India; *les Indes*, the Indies; *les Indes occidentales*, the West Indies.

indécemment [ɛ̃desa'mɑ̃], *adv.* indecently.

indécence [ɛ̃de'sɑ̃s], *n.f.* indecency, impropriety.

indécent [ɛ̃de'sɑ̃], *a.* indecent; unseemly.

indéchiffrable [ɛ̃deʃi'frabl], *a.* undecipherable, illegible; obscure, incomprehensible.

indéchirable [ɛ̃deʃi'rabl], *a.* untearable.

indécis [ɛ̃de'si], *a.* undecided, doubtful; irresolute.

indécision [ɛ̃desi'zjɔ̃], *n.f.* indecision, irresolution.

indécrottable [ɛ̃dekrɔ'tabl], *a.* uncleanable; (*fig.*) incorrigible.

indéfendable [ɛ̃defɑ̃'dabl], *a.* indefensible, untenable.

indéfini [ɛ̃defi'ni], *a.* indefinite, unlimited.

indéfiniment [ɛ̃defini'mɑ̃], *adv.* indefinitely.

indéfinissable [ɛ̃defini'sabl], *a.* undefinable; nondescript.

indéfrichable [ɛ̃defri'ʃabl], *a.* unclearable (*of land*).

indéfrisable [ɛ̃defri'zabl], *n.f.* permanent wave.

indélébile [ɛ̃dele'bil], *a.* indelible, ineffaceable.

indélicat [ɛ̃deli'ka], *a.* indelicate; unhandsome.

indélicatement [ɛ̃delikat'mɑ̃], *adv.* indelicately; unhandsomely.

indélicatesse [ɛ̃delika'tɛs], *n.f.* tactlessness; unscrupulousness; objectionable action.

indémaillable [ɛ̃dema'jabl], *a.* run-proof (*stocking*).

indemne [ɛ̃'dɛmn], *a.* uninjured.

indemnisation [ɛ̃dɛmniza'sjɔ̃], *n.f.* indemnification, compensation.

indemniser [ɛ̃dɛmni'ze], *v.t.* to indemnify; to make good.

indemnité [ɛdɛmni'te], *n.f.* indemnity; *indemnité de charges de famille*, family allowance; *indemnité de chômage*, unemployment benefit; *indemnité de vie chère*, cost of living bonus.

indéniable [ɛde'njabl], *a.* undeniable; self-evident.

indépendamment [ɛdepɑ̃da'mɑ̃], *adv.* independently.

indépendance [ɛdepɑ̃'dɑ̃:s], *n.f.* independence.

indépendant [ɛdepɑ̃'dɑ̃], *a.* independent.

indescriptible [ɛdɛskrip'tibl], *a.* indescribable.

indésirable [ɛdezi'rabl], *a.* and *n.* undesirable.

indestructible [ɛdɛstryk'tibl], *a.* indestructible.

indéterminable [ɛdetɛrmi'nabl], *a.* indeterminable.

indétermination [ɛdetɛrmina'sjɔ̃], *n.f.* indetermination, irresolution.

indéterminé [ɛdetɛrmi'ne], *a.* undetermined, irresolute.

index [ɛ'dɛks], *n.m. inv.* fore-finger; index.

indicateur [ɛdika'tœ:r], *a.* (*fem.* **-trice**) indicating, indicatory.—*n.m.* indicator, guide; time-table; (*fem.* **-trice**) (*fig.*) informer.

indicatif [ɛdika'tif], *a.* (*fem.* **-tive**) indicative.—*n.m.* (*Gram.*) indicative mood; call-sign; signature tune.

indication [ɛdika'sjɔ̃], *n.f.* indication, information; sign, mark.

indice [ɛ'dis], *n.m.* indication, sign, mark, clue.

indicible [ɛdi'sibl], *a.* inexpressible, unspeakable, indescribable.

indiciblement [ɛdisiblə'mɑ̃], *adv.* inexpressibly.

indien [ɛ'djɛ̃], *a.* (*fem.* **-enne**) Indian.—*n.m.* (**Indien**, *fem.* **-enne**) Indian (*person*).—*n.f.* (**-enne**) printed calico, printed cotton.

indifféremment [ɛdifera'mɑ̃], *adv.* indifferently; alike.

indifférence [ɛdife'rɑ̃:s], *n.f.* indifference, unconcern.

indifférent [ɛdife'rɑ̃], *a.* indifferent, immaterial; unconcerned, heedless.—*n.m.* (*fem.* **-e**) indifferent person.

indigence [ɛdi'ʒɑ̃:s], *n.f.* indigence, poverty, need.

indigène [ɛdi'ʒɛ:n], *a.* indigenous, native.—*n.* native.

indigent [ɛdi'ʒɑ̃], *a.* indigent, needy.—*n.m.* (*fem.* **-e**) pauper, destitute person.

indigéré [ɛdiʒe're], *a.* undigested, crude.

indigeste [ɛdi'ʒɛst], *a.* indigestible; undigested.

indigestion [ɛdiʒɛs'tjɔ̃], *n.f.* indigestion, surfeit.

indignation [ɛdiɲa'sjɔ̃], *n.f.* indignation.

indigne [ɛ'diɲ], *a.* unworthy; infamous, worthless.

indigné [ɛdi'ɲe], *a.* indignant; shocked.

indignement [ɛdiɲə'mɑ̃], *adv.* unworthily; scandalously.

indigner [ɛdi'ɲe], *v.t.* to render indignant; to shock. **s'indigner**, *v.r.* to be indignant; to be shocked.

indignité [ɛdiɲi'te], *n.f.* unworthiness, worthlessness; indignity; infamy.

indigo [ɛdi'go], *a. inv.* and *n.m.* indigo.

indigotier [ɛdigɔ'tje], *n.m.* indigo plant *or* manufacturer.

indiquer [ɛdi'ke], *v.t.* to indicate, to point out; to mention; to denote; to appoint, to recommend; to outline.

indirect [ɛdi'rɛkt], *a.* indirect; circumstantial (*of evidence*); collateral (*of heirs*).

indirectement [ɛdirɛktə'mɑ̃], *adv.* indirectly.

indiscipline [ɛdisi'plin], *n.f.* indiscipline, insubordination.

indiscipliné [ɛdisipli'ne], *a.* undisciplined.

indiscret [ɛdis'krɛ], *a.* (*fem.* **-ète**) indiscreet, inconsiderate; inquisitive; tell-tale.—*n.m.* (*fem.* **-ète**) babbler.

indiscrètement [ɛdiskrɛt'mɑ̃], *adv.* indiscreetly, inconsiderately.

indiscrétion [ɛdiskre'sjɔ̃], *n.f.* indiscretion; unwariness.

indiscutable [ɛdisky'tabl], *a.* incontestable, indisputable, obvious.

indispensable [ɛdispɑ̃'sabl], *a.* indispensable.

indispensablement [ɛdispɑ̃sablə'mɑ̃], *adv.* indispensably.

indisponible [ɛdispɔ'nibl], *a.* unavailable.

indisposé [ɛdispo'ze], *a.* unwell; unfriendly.

indisposer [ɛdispo'ze], *v.t.* to indispose, to make unwell; to disincline, to set against (*contre*).

indisposition [ɛdispozi'sjɔ̃], *n.f.* indisposition; disinclination.

indisputé [ɛdispy'te], *a.* unquestioned.

indissoluble [ɛdisɔ'lybl], *a.* indissoluble.

indissolublement [ɛdisɔlyblə'mɑ̃], *adv.* indissolubly.

indistinct [ɛdis'tɛ̃:kt], *a.* indistinct.

indistinctement [ɛdistɛ̃ktə'mɑ̃], *adv.* indistinctly.

individu [ɛdivi'dy], *n.m.* individual; (*colloq.*) fellow.

individualisme [ɛdividqa'lism], *n.m.* individualism.

individualiste [ɛdividqa'list], *a.* individualistic.—*n.* individualist.

individualité [ɛdividqali'te], *n.f.* individuality.

individuel [ɛdivi'dqɛl], *a.* (*fem.* **-elle**) individual.

individuellement [ɛdividqɛl'mɑ̃], *adv.* individually.

indivisé [ɛdivi'ze], *a.* undivided.

indivisément [ɛdivize'mɑ̃], *adv.* jointly.

indivisibilité [ɛdivizibili'te], *n.f.* indivisibility.

indivisible [ɛdivi'zibl], *a.* indivisible.

indivisiblement [ɛdiviziblə'mɑ̃], *adv.* indivisibly.

indivision [ɛdivi'zjɔ̃], *n.f.* joint possession.

Indochine [ɛdɔ'ʃin], **l'**, *f.* Indo-China.

indochinois [ɛdɔʃi'nwa], *a.* Indo-Chinese.—*n.m.* (**Indochinois**, *fem.* **-oise**) Indo-Chinese (*person*).

indocile [ɛdɔ'sil], *a.* indocile, unmanageable.

indocilité [ɛdɔsili'te], *n.f.* indocility, intractability.

indolemment [ɛdɔla'mɑ̃], *adv.* indolently.

indolence [ɛdɔ'lɑ̃:s], *n.f.* indolence, sloth.

indolent [ɛdɔ'lɑ̃], *a.* indolent, slothful.—*n.m.* (*fem.* **-e**) sluggard.

indolore [ɛdɔ'lɔ:r], *a.* painless.

indomptable [ɛdɔ̃'tabl], *a.* indomitable, untamable; unmanageable.

indompté [ɛ̃dɔ̃'te], *a.* untamed, wild; unsubdued.

Indonésie [ɛ̃dɔne'zi], l', *f.* Indonesia.

indonésien [ɛ̃dɔne'zjɛ̃], *a.* Indonesian.—*n.m.* Indonesian (*language*); (**Indonésien**, *fem.* **-enne**) Indonesian (*person*).

indou [HINDOU].

indu [ɛ̃'dy], *a.* undue, unseasonable, late.

indubitable [ɛ̃dybi'tabl], *a.* indubitable, certain.

indubitablement [ɛ̃dybitablə'mɑ̃], *adv.* undoubtedly.

inductif [ɛ̃dyk'tif], *a.* (*fem.* **-tive**) inductive.

induction [ɛ̃dyk'sjɔ̃], *n.f.* induction, inference.

induire [ɛ̃'dɥi:r], *v.t. irr.* (*conjug. like* CONDUIRE) to induce, to lead; to infer.

indulgence [ɛ̃dyl'ʒɑ̃:s], *n.f.* indulgence, leniency.

indulgent [ɛ̃dyl'ʒɑ̃], *a.* indulgent, forbearing.

indûment [ɛ̃dy'mɑ̃] *adv.* unduly.

industrialiser [ɛ̃dystriali'ze], *v.t.* to industrialize.

industrialisme [ɛ̃dystria'lism], *n.m.* industrialism.

industrie [ɛ̃dys'tri], *n.f.* skill, ingenuity; business; manufacturing; industry, work; *chevalier d'industrie*, swindler, sharper; *industrie de base* or *industrie clef*, key industry.

industriel [ɛ̃dystri'ɛl], *a.* (*fem.* **-elle**) industrial, manufacturing.—*n.m.* manufacturer, mill owner.

industrieusement [ɛ̃dystriøz'mɑ̃], *adv.* ingeniously, skilfully; industriously.

industrieux [ɛ̃dystri'ø], *a.* (*fem.* **-euse**) ingenious, skilful; industrious.

inébranlable [inebrɑ̃'labl], *a.* immovable; firm, resolute.

inébranlablement [inebrɑ̃lablə'mɑ̃], *adv.* immovably, steadily; resolutely.

inédit [ine'di], *a.* unpublished; new.

ineffable [inɛ'fabl], *a.* ineffable, inexpressible, unutterable.

ineffaçable [inɛfa'sabl], *a.* indelible, ineffaceable.

inefficace [inɛfi'kas], *a.* ineffectual, ineffective.

inefficacité [inɛfikasi'te], *n.f.* inefficacy, ineffectiveness.

inégal [ine'gal], *a.* (*m. pl.* **-aux**) unequal; rough; (*fig.*) ill-matched; irregular.

inégalement [inegal'mɑ̃], *adv.* unequally, unevenly.

inégalité [inegali'te], *n.f.* inequality; unevenness; irregularity.

inélégance [inele'gɑ̃:s], *n.f.* inelegance.

inélégant [inele'gɑ̃], *a.* inelegant.

inéligible [ineli'ʒibl], *a.* ineligible.

inéluctable [inelyk'tabl], *a.* unavoidable; unescapable.

inénarrable [inena'rabl], *a.* untellable; incredible.

inepte [i'nɛpt], *a.* foolish, silly, inept, absurd.

ineptie [inɛp'si], *n.f.* ineptitude, foolishness, absurdity.

inépuisable [inepɥi'zabl], *a.* inexhaustible.

inépuisablement [inepɥizablə'mɑ̃], *adv.* inexhaustibly.

inéquitable [ineki'tabl], *a.* unfair.

inerte [i'nɛrt], *a.* inert, sluggish, inactive.

inertie [inɛr'si], *n.f.* inertia; indolence.

inespéré [inɛspe're], *a.* unhoped for, unexpected.

inestimable [inɛsti'mabl], *a.* inestimable.

inévitable [inevi'tabl], *a.* inevitable, unavoidable.

inévitablement [inevitablə'mɑ̃], *adv.* inevitably, unavoidably.

inexact [inɛg'zakt], *a.* inexact, inaccurate, incorrect.

inexactement [inɛgzaktə'mɑ̃], *adv.* inaccurately, incorrectly.

inexactitude [inɛgzakti'tyd], *n.f.* incorrectness; inaccuracy, slip.

inexcusable [inɛksky'zabl], *a.* inexcusable, unwarrantable.

inexécutable [inɛgzeky'tabl], *a.* impracticable.

inexercé [inɛgzɛr'se], *a.* untrained.

inexistant [inɛgzis'tɑ̃], *a.* non-existent.

inexorable [inɛgzɔ'rabl], *a.* inexorable, inflexible; pitiless.

inexorablement [inɛgzɔrablə'mɑ̃], *adv.* inexorably.

inexpérience [inɛkspe'rjɑ̃:s], *n.f.* inexperience.

inexpérimenté [inɛksperimɑ̃'te], *a.* inexperienced; untried (*of things*).

inexplicable [inɛkspli'kabl], *a.* inexplicable, unaccountable.

inexpliqué [inɛkspli'ke], *a.* unexplained.

inexploitable [inɛksplwa'tabl], *a.* unworkable, useless.

inexploité [inɛksplwa'te], *a.* uncultivated (*of land*); unworked (*of mines etc.*); untapped (*resources*).

inexploré [inɛksplɔ're], *a.* unexplored.

inexplosible [inɛksplo'zibl], *a.* unexplosive.

inexpressible [inɛksprɛ'sibl], *a.* inexpressible.

inexpressif [inɛksprɛ'sif], *a.* (*fem.* **-ive**) inexpressive, lacking expression.

inexprimable [inɛkspri'mabl], *a.* inexpressible, unspeakable.

inextinguible [inɛkstɛ̃'gibl], *a.* inextinguishable; unquenchable (*thirst, fire*); irrepressible (*laughter*).

inextricable [inɛkstri'kabl], *a.* inextricable.

inextricablement [inɛkstrikablə'mɑ̃], *adv.* inextricably.

infaillibilité [ɛ̃fajibili'te], *n.f.* infallibility.

infaillible [ɛ̃fa'jibl], *a.* infallible.

infailliblement [ɛ̃fajiblə'mɑ̃], *adv.* infallibly.

infaisable [ɛ̃fə'zabl], *a.* impracticable.

infamant [ɛ̃fa'mɑ̃], *a.* infamous, ignominious.

infâme [ɛ̃'fɑ:m], *a.* infamous; squalid, sordid.—*n.* infamous person, wretch.

infamie [ɛ̃fa'mi], *n.f.* infamy, ignominy; baseness.

infant [ɛ̃'fɑ̃], *n.m.* (*fem.* **-e**) infante, infanta (*Spanish prince or princess*).

infanterie [ɛ̃fɑ̃'tri], *n.f.* infantry.

infanticide [ɛ̃fɑ̃ti'sid], *n.m.* infanticide.—*n.* child-murderer.

infantile [ɛ̃fɑ̃'til], *a.* infantile.

infatigable [ɛ̃fati'gabl], *a.* indefatigable, untiring.

infatuation [ɛ̃fatɥa'sjɔ̃], *n.f.* infatuation.

infatuer [ɛ̃fa'tɥe], *v.t.* to infatuate. **s'infatuer**, *v.r.* to become infatuated.

infécond [ɛ̃fe'kɔ̃], *a.* unfruitful, barren, sterile.

infécondité [ɛ̃fekɔ̃di'te], *n.f.* unfruitfulness, barrenness, sterility.
infect [ɛ̃'fɛkt], *a.* infected, foul, noisome, stinking.
infectant [ɛ̃fɛk'tɑ̃], *a.* infecting.
infecter [ɛ̃fɛk'te], *v.t.* to infect, to contaminate; to taint.—*v.i.* to stink.
infectieux [ɛ̃fɛk'sjø], *a.* (*fem.* **-euse**) infectious.
infection [ɛ̃fɛk'sjɔ̃], *n.f.* infection; infectious disease; stench; *foyer d'infection*, hotbed of disease.
inférence [ɛ̃fe'rɑ̃:s], *n.f.* conclusion, inference.
inférer [ɛ̃fe're], *v.t.* (*conjug. like* CÉDER) to infer, to conclude.
inférieur [ɛ̃fe'rjœ:r], *a.* inferior, lower.—*n.m.* (*fem.* **-e**) inferior; subordinate.
infériorité [ɛ̃ferjɔri'te], *n.f.* inferiority.
infernal [ɛ̃fɛr'nal], *a.* (*m. pl.* **-aux**) infernal, hellish.
infernalement [ɛ̃fɛrnal'mɑ̃], *adv.* infernally.
infertile [ɛ̃fɛr'til], *a.* infertile, unfruitful; sterile, barren.
infertilité [ɛ̃fɛrtili'te], *n.f.* unfruitfulness.
infester [ɛ̃fɛs'te], *v.t.* to infest, to overrun; to haunt.
infidèle [ɛ̃fi'dɛl], *a.* unfaithful, disloyal; unbelieving.—*n.* unfaithful person; infidel.
infidèlement [ɛ̃fidɛl'mɑ̃], *adv.* unfaithfully; inaccurately.
infidélité [ɛ̃fideli'te], *n.f.* infidelity; unbelief; dishonesty.
infiltration [ɛ̃filtra'sjɔ̃], *n.f.* infiltration.
infiltrer (s') [sɛ̃fil'tre], *v.r.* to infiltrate, to percolate.
infime [ɛ̃'fim], *a.* lowest (*of ranks*); tiny.
infini [ɛ̃fi'ni], *a.* infinite, boundless.—*n.m.* infinite, infinity.
infiniment [ɛ̃fini'mɑ̃], *adv.* infinitely, without end; exceedingly, extremely.
infinité [ɛ̃fini'te], *n.f.* infinity, infiniteness; (*fig.*) crowd; no end.
infinitif [ɛ̃fini'tif], *a.* (*fem.* **-tive**) and *n.m.* infinitive (mood).
infirme [ɛ̃'firm], *a.* crippled, invalid; infirm; feeble.—*n.* invalid, cripple.
infirmerie [ɛ̃firm'ri], *n.f.* infirmary, sick ward; (*sch.*) sanatorium, sick-bay.
infirmier [ɛ̃fir'mje], *n.m.* (*fem.* **-ière**) hospital attendant; nurse.
infirmité [ɛ̃firmi'te], *n.f.* infirmity, weakness, failing.
inflammable [ɛ̃fla'mabl], *a.* inflammable.
inflammation [ɛ̃flamma'sjɔ̃], *n.f.* inflammation.
inflammatoire [ɛ̃flamma'twa:r], *a.* inflammatory.
inflation [ɛ̃fla'sjɔ̃], *n.f.* inflation, swelling.
inflexible [ɛ̃flɛk'sibl], *a.* inflexible; unyielding, unbending.
inflexiblement [ɛ̃flɛksiblə'mɑ̃], *adv.* inflexibly.
inflexion [ɛ̃flɛk'sjɔ̃], *n.f.* inflexion; modulation, variation.
infliction [ɛ̃flik'sjɔ̃], *n.f.* infliction.
infliger [ɛ̃fli'ʒe], *v.t.* (*conjug. like* MANGER) to inflict, to impose.
influence [ɛ̃fly'ɑ̃:s], *n.f.* influence; sway, power, authority.
influencer [ɛ̃flyɑ̃'se], *v.t.* (*conjug. like* COMMENCER) to influence, to sway, to bias.

influent [ɛ̃fly'ɑ̃], *a.* influential.
influenza [ɛ̃flyɑ̃'za], *n.f.* influenza.
influer [ɛ̃fly'e], *v.i.* to have an influence (*sur, on*).
informateur [ɛ̃fɔrma'tœ:r], *n.m.* (*fem.* **-trice**) informant.
information [ɛ̃fɔrma'sjɔ̃], *n.f.* inquiry; information; (*pl.*) news (bulletin).
informe [ɛ̃'fɔrm], *a.* shapeless; misshapen; crude, imperfect.
informer [ɛ̃fɔr'me], *v.t.* to inform, to acquaint, to apprise. **s'informer**, *v.r.* to inquire, to make inquiries, to investigate.
infortune [ɛ̃fɔr'tyn], *n.f.* misfortune, adversity.
infortuné [ɛ̃fɔrty'ne], *a.* unfortunate, unhappy, ill-fated, wretched.—*n.m.* (*fem.* **-ée**) unfortunate, unhappy *or* wretched person.
infraction [ɛ̃frak'sjɔ̃], *n.f.* infringement, breach, violation.
infranchissable [ɛ̃frɑ̃ʃi'sabl], *a.* insurmountable, insuperable.
infra-rouge [ɛ̃fra'ruʒ], *a.* infra-red.
infréquenté [ɛ̃freka'te], *a.* unfrequented.
infructueusement [ɛ̃fryktɥøz'mɑ̃], *adv.* fruitlessly, to no purpose, in vain.
infructueux [ɛ̃fryk'tɥø], *a.* (*fem.* **-euse**) unfruitful, vain, unavailing.
infus [ɛ̃'fy], *a.* infused, innate, native (*of knowledge etc.*).
infuser [ɛ̃fy'ze], *v.t.* to infuse, to instill; to steep.
infusion [ɛ̃fy'zjɔ̃], *n.f.* infusion, decoction.
ingambe [ɛ̃'gɑ̃:b], *a.* nimble, brisk, active.
ingénier (s') [sɛ̃ʒe'nje], *v.r.* to tax one's ingenuity, to contrive.
ingénieur [ɛ̃ʒe'njœ:r], *n.m.* engineer.
ingénieusement [ɛ̃ʒenjøz'mɑ̃], *adv.* ingeniously.
ingénieux [ɛ̃ʒe'njø], *a.* (*fem.* **-euse**) ingenious, clever, witty.
ingéniosité [ɛ̃ʒenjozi'te], *n.f.* ingenuity; cleverness.
ingénu [ɛ̃ʒe'ny], *a.* ingenuous; guileless, unsophisticated; simple, artless.—*n.m.* (*fem.* **-e**) ingenuous person, artless *or* simple-minded person.
ingénuité [ɛ̃ʒenɥi'te], *n.f.* ingenuousness.
ingénument [ɛ̃ʒeny'mɑ̃], *adv.* ingenuously.
ingérence [ɛ̃ʒe'rɑ̃:s], *n.f.* interference, meddling.
ingérer (s') [sɛ̃ʒe're], *v.r.* (*conjug. like* CÉDER) to meddle with, to interfere, to obtrude.
inglorieux [ɛ̃glɔ'rjø], *a.* (*fem.* **-euse**) inglorious.
ingouvernable [ɛ̃guvɛr'nabl], *a.* ungovernable, uncontrollable.
ingrat [ɛ̃'gra], *a.* unthankful, ungrateful; thankless, unprofitable.
ingratitude [ɛ̃grati'tyd], *n.f.* ingratitude, thanklessness.
ingrédient [ɛ̃gre'djɑ̃], *n.m.* ingredient.
inguérissable [ɛ̃geri'sabl], *a.* incurable.
inhabile [ina'bil], *a.* unskillful, unskilled, inexpert.
inhabilement [inabil'mɑ̃], *adv.* unskillfully.
inhabileté [inabil'te], *n.f.* unskillfulness, incompetence, inability.
inhabitable [inabi'tabl], *a.* uninhabitable.
inhabité [inabi'te], *a.* uninhabited.
inhabitué [inabi'tɥe], *a.* unaccustomed, unused.

189

inhalation [inala'sjɔ̃], *n.f.* inhalation.
inhaler [ina'le], *v.t.* to inhale.
inharmonieux [inarmɔ'njø], *a.* (*fem.* **-euse**) inharmonious, unmusical.
inhérent [ine'rɑ̃], *a.* inherent.
inhospitalier [inɔspita'lje], *a.* (*fem.* **-ière**) inhospitable; (*fig.*) unfriendly, forbidding.
inhumain [iny'mɛ̃], *a.* inhuman, cruel.
inhumainement [inymɛn'mɑ̃], *adv.* inhumanly.
inhumanité [inymani'te], *n.f.* inhumanity, cruelty.
inhumation [inyma'sjɔ̃], *n.f.* inhumation, interment.
inhumer [iny'me], *v.t.* to bury, to inter.
inimaginable [inimaʒi'nabl], *a.* unimaginable, inconceivable.
inimitable [inimi'tabl], *a.* inimitable.
inimitié [inimi'tje], *n.f.* enmity, antipathy, aversion.
ininflammable [inɛ̃fla'mabl], *a.* non-inflammable, fire-proof.
inintelligemment [inɛ̃tɛliʒa'mɑ̃], *adv.* unintelligently.
inintelligence [inɛ̃tɛli'ʒɑ̃:s], *n.f.* lack of intelligence.
inintelligent [inɛ̃tɛli'ʒɑ̃], *a.* unintelligent.
inintelligible [inɛ̃tɛli'ʒibl], *a.* unintelligible.
inintéressant [inɛ̃tere'sɑ̃], *a.* uninteresting.
ininterrompu [inɛ̃tɛrɔ̃'py], *a.* uninterrupted.
inique [i'nik], *a.* iniquitous; unrighteous.
iniquement [inik'mɑ̃], *adv.* iniquitously.
iniquité [iniki'te]. *n.f.* iniquity, unrighteousness; injustice.
initial [ini'sjal], *a.* (*m. pl.* **-aux**) initial.
initiale [ini'sjal], *n.f.* initial.
initialement [inisjal'mɑ̃], *adv.* initially.
initiateur [inisja'tœ:r], *n.m.* (*fem.* **-trice**) initiator.
initiation [inisja'sjɔ̃], *n.f.* initiation.
initiative [inisja'ti:v], *n.f.* initiative.
initier [ini'sje], *v.t.* to initiate, to admit.
injecté [ɛ̃ʒɛk'te], *a.* injected; bloodshot; creosoted.
injecter [ɛ̃ʒɛk'te], *v.t.* to inject.
injection [ɛ̃ʒɛk'sjɔ̃], *n.f.* injection.
injonction [ɛ̃ʒɔ̃k'sjɔ̃], *n.f.* injunction, order.
injudicieux [ɛ̃ʒydi'sjø], *a.* (*fem.* **-euse**) injudicious.
injure [ɛ̃'ʒy:r], *n.f.* injury; insult; (*pl.*) abuse, abusive language; slander.
injurier [ɛ̃ʒy'rje], *v.t.* to abuse, to insult.
injurieux [ɛ̃ʒy'rjø], *a.* (*fem.* **-euse**) wrongful; abusive, insulting.
injuste [ɛ̃'ʒyst], *a.* unjust, unfair, wrong.
injustement [ɛ̃ʒystə'mɑ̃], *adv.* unjustly, wrongly.
injustice [ɛ̃ʒys'tis], *n.f.* injustice; wrong.
injustifiable [ɛ̃ʒysti'fjabl], *a.* unjustifiable.
injustifié [ɛ̃ʒysti'fje], *a.* unjustified, groundless.
inlassable [ɛ̃la'sabl], *a.* untirable.
inné [in'ne]. *a.* innate, inborn.
innocemment [inɔsa'mɑ̃], *adv.* innocently.
innocence [inɔ'sɑ̃:s], *n.f.* innocence; inoffensiveness; simplicity.
innocent [inɔ'sɑ̃], *a.* innocent; harmless, inoffensive; guileless, simple.—*n.m.* (*fem.* **-e**) simpleton; idiot.
innocenter [inɔsɑ̃'te], *v.t.* to acquit.
innombrable [innɔ̃'brabl], *a.* innumerable, numberless.

innombrablement [inɔ̃brablə'mɑ̃], *adv.* innumerably.
innovateur [innɔva'tœ:r], *n.m.* (*fem.* **-trice**) innovator.
innovation [innɔva'sjɔ̃], *n.f.* innovation.
innover [innɔ've], *v.i.* to make innovations.
inobservable [inɔpsɛr'vabl], *a.* inobservable.
inobservance [inɔpsɛr'vɑ̃:s], **inobservation** [inɔpsɛrva'sjɔ̃], *n.f.* non-observance.
inobservé [inɔpsɛr've], *a.* unobserved, unnoticed.
inoccupé [inɔky'pe], *a.* unoccupied; idle; vacant.
inoculateur [inɔkyla'tœ:r], *n.m.* (*fem.* **-trice**) inoculator.
inoculation [inɔkyla'sjɔ̃], *n.f.* inoculation.
inoculer [inɔky'le], *v.t.* to inoculate.
inodore [inɔ'dɔ:r], *a.* odorless.
inoffensif [inɔfɑ̃'sif], *a.* (*fem.* **-sive**) inoffensive; innocuous.
inoffensivement [inɔfɑ̃siv'mɑ̃], *adv.* inoffensively.
inofficiel [inɔfi'sjɛl], *a.* (*fem.* **-elle**) unofficial.
inofficiellement [inɔfisjɛl'mɑ̃], *adv.* unofficially.
inondation [inɔ̃da'sjɔ̃], *n.f.* inundation, flood, deluge.
inonder [inɔ̃'de], *v.t.* to inundate, to overflow; (*fig.*) to overrun.
inopérant [inɔpe'rɑ̃], *a.* inoperative; inefficient.
inopiné [inɔpi'ne] *a.* unforeseen, unexpected, sudden.
inopinément [inɔpine'mɑ̃], *adv.* unawares, unexpectedly, suddenly.
inopportun [inɔpɔr'tœ̃], *a.* inopportune, untimely.
inorganique [inɔrga'nik], *a.* inorganic.
inoubliable [inu'bljabl], *a.* unforgettable.
inoublié [inu'blje], *a.* unforgotten, well-remembered.
inouï [i'nwi], *a.* unheard of, unprecedented.
inoxydable [inɔksi'dabl], *a.* rustless, stainless.
inqualifiable [ɛ̃kali'fjabl], *a.* unspeakable.
inquiet [ɛ̃'kjɛ], *a.* (*fem.* **-ète**) anxious; restless.
inquiétant [ɛ̃kje'tɑ̃], *a.* disquieting, alarming.
inquiéter [ɛ̃kje'te], *v.t.* (*conjug. like* CÉDER) to disquiet; to worry; to disturb. **s'inquiéter**, *v.r.* to be anxious, to be uneasy; to worry.
inquiétude [ɛ̃kje'tyd], *n.f.* anxiety, uneasiness, concern.
inquisiteur [ɛ̃kizi'tœ:r], *a.* inquisitorial; inquisitive.—*n.m.* inquisitor.
inquisitif [ɛ̃kizi'tif], *a.* (*fem.* **-tive**) inquisitive.
inquisition [ɛ̃kizi'sjɔ̃], *n.f.* inquisition.
insaisissable [ɛ̃sezi'sabl], *a.* unseizable, imperceptible.
insalubre [ɛ̃sa'lybr], *a.* insalubrious, unhealthy, unwholesome.
insalubrement [ɛ̃salybrə'mɑ̃], *adv.* insalubriously, unhealthily.
insalubrité [ɛ̃salybri'te], *n.f.* insalubrity, unhealthiness.
insanité [ɛ̃sani'te], *n.f.* insanity.
insatiabilité [ɛ̃sasjabili'te], *n.f.* insatiability.
insatiable [ɛ̃sa'sjabl], *a.* insatiable.
insciemment [ɛ̃sja'mɑ̃], *adv.* unwittingly.
inscription [ɛ̃skrip'sjɔ̃], *n.f.* inscription; registration, enrolment; matriculation.

inscrire [ɛ̃s'kriːr], *v.t. irr. (conjug. like* ÉCRIRE*)* to inscribe, to set down, to register. **s'inscrire**, *v.r.* to inscribe oneself; to enter one's name; to register, to enroll.

inscrutable [ɛ̃skry'tabl], *a.* inscrutable, unfathomable.

insecte [ɛ̃'sɛkt], *n.m.* insect.

insecticide [ɛ̃sɛkti'sid], *a.* insecticidal.—*n.m.* insecticide.

insectivore [ɛ̃sɛkti'vɔːr], *a.* insectivorous.

insécurité [ɛ̃sekyri'te], *n.f.* insecurity.

insémination [ɛ̃semina'sjɔ̃], *n.f.* insemination (*cows, ewes etc.*).

inséminer [ɛ̃semi'ne], *v.t.* to inseminate.

insensé [ɛ̃sɑ̃'se], *a.* insane, mad; foolish, senseless.—*n.m. (fem.* **-ée***)* madman, mad woman, maniac.

insensibiliser [ɛ̃sɑ̃sibili'ze], *v.t.* to anesthetize.

insensibilité [ɛ̃sɑ̃sibili'te], *n.f.* insensibility; callousness.

insensible [ɛ̃sɑ̃'sibl], *a.* insensible, unconscious; hard-hearted, insensitive.

insensiblement [ɛ̃sɑ̃siblə'mɑ̃], *adv.* insensibly; gradually, imperceptibly.

inséparable [ɛ̃sepa'rabl], *a.* inseparable.—*n.m. (pl.) (Orn.)* love-birds.

inséparablement [ɛ̃separablə'mɑ̃], *adv.* inseparably.

insérer [ɛ̃se're], *v.t. (conjug. like* CÉDER*)* to insert, to put in.

insertion [ɛ̃sɛr'sjɔ̃], *n.f.* insertion.

insidieusement [ɛ̃sidjøz'mɑ̃], *adv.* insidiously.

insidieux [ɛ̃si'djø], *a. (fem.* **-euse***)* insidious.

insigne [ɛ̃'siɲ], *a.* distinguished; conspicuous; notorious.—*n.m.* badge, mark; (*pl.*) insignia.

insignifiance [ɛ̃siɲi'fjɑ̃s], *n.f.* insignificance.

insignifiant [ɛ̃siɲi'fjɑ̃], *a.* insignificant, trivial.

insincère [ɛ̃sɛ̃'sɛːr], *a.* insincere.

insinuant [ɛ̃si'nɥɑ̃], *a.* insinuating; ingratiating.

insinuation [ɛ̃sinɥa'sjɔ̃], *n.f.* insinuation, hint, innuendo.

insinuer [ɛ̃si'nɥe], *v.t.* to insinuate; to hint, to suggest. **s'insinuer**, *v.r.* to insinuate oneself (*dans*), to creep *or* worm one's way (*into*).

insipide [ɛ̃si'pid], *a.* insipid, tasteless; dull.

insipidité [ɛ̃sipidi'te], *n.f.* insipidity.

insistance [ɛ̃sis'tɑ̃s], *n.f.* insistence, persistence.

insister [ɛ̃sis'te], *v.i.* to insist, to lay stress (*sur*).

insociable [ɛ̃sɔ'sjabl], *a.* unsociable; difficult to live with.

insolation [ɛ̃sɔla'sjɔ̃], *n.f.* insolation, sunstroke.

insolemment [ɛ̃sɔla'mɑ̃], *adv.* insolently.

insolence [ɛ̃sɔ'lɑ̃s], *n.f.* insolence, impertinence.

insolent [ɛ̃sɔ'lɑ̃], *a.* insolent, impudent, rude.—*n.m. (fem.* **-e***)* insolent person.

insolite [ɛ̃sɔ'lit], *a.* unusual, unwonted.

insolubilité [ɛ̃sɔlybili'te], *n.f.* insolubility.

insoluble [ɛ̃sɔ'lybl], *a.* insoluble.

insolvabilité [ɛ̃sɔlvabili'te], *n.f.* insolvency.

insolvable [ɛ̃sɔl'vabl], *a.* insolvent.

insomnie [ɛ̃sɔm'ni], *n.f.* insomnia.

insondable [ɛ̃sɔ̃'dabl], *a.* unfathomable.

insonore [ɛ̃sɔ'nɔːr], *a.* sound-proof.

insouciance [ɛ̃su'sjɑ̃s], *n.f.* carelessness, thoughtlessness.

insouciant [ɛ̃su'sjɑ̃], **insoucieux** [ɛ̃su'sjø] (*fem.* **-euse***)*, *a.* careless, thoughtless; unconcerned, easy-going.

insoumis [ɛ̃su'mi], *a.* unsubdued; refractory, unruly.—*n.m. (Mil.)* defaulter.

insoumission [ɛ̃sumi'sjɔ̃], *n.f.* insubordination.

insoutenable [ɛ̃sut'nabl], *a.* indefensible; unbearable.

inspecter [ɛ̃spɛk'te], *v.t.* to inspect, to survey, to scan.

inspecteur [ɛ̃spɛk'tœːr], *n.m. (fem.* **-trice***)* inspector, superintendent, surveyor.

inspection [ɛ̃spɛk'sjɔ̃], *n.f.* inspection, survey; superintendence; *faire l'inspection de*, to inspect; *passer à l'inspection*, to undergo inspection.

inspirateur [ɛ̃spira'tœːr], *a. (fem.* **-trice***)* inspiring; (*Anat.*) inspiratory.—*n.m. (fem.* **-trice***)* inspirer.

inspiration [ɛ̃spira'sjɔ̃], *n.f.* inspiration; suggestion; inhaling.

inspiré [ɛ̃spi're], *a.* and *n.m. (fem.* **-ée***)* inspired (person).

inspirer [ɛ̃spi're], *v.t.* to inspire, to breathe in; (*fig.*) to suggest, to instill. **s'inspirer**, *v.r.* to draw one's inspiration (*de*).

instabilité [ɛ̃stabili'te], *n.f.* instability, fickleness.

instable [ɛ̃'stabl], *a.* unstable; unsteady, wobbly.

installation [ɛ̃stala'sjɔ̃], *n.f.* installation; equipment.

installer [ɛ̃sta'le], *v.t.* to install; to inaugurate, to establish. **s'installer**, *v.r.* to install oneself; to settle.

instamment [ɛ̃sta'mɑ̃], *adv.* earnestly, urgently.

instance [ɛ̃s'tɑ̃s], *n.f.* entreaty; urgency, earnestness; (*Law*) instance; (*pl.*) entreaties.

instant (1) [ɛ̃s'tɑ̃], *n.m.* instant, moment; *à l'instant*, in an instant, immediately.

instant (2) [ɛ̃s'tɑ̃], *a.* pressing, urgent; imminent.

instantané [ɛ̃stɑ̃ta'ne], *a.* instantaneous.—*n.m.* snapshot.

instantanément [ɛ̃stɑ̃tane'mɑ̃], *adv.* instantaneously.

instar (à l') [alɛ̃s'taːr], *prep. phr. à l'instar de*, like; in imitation of.

instigateur [ɛ̃stiga'tœːr], *n.m. (fem.* **-trice***)* instigator.

instigation [ɛ̃stiga'sjɔ̃], *n.f.* instigation.

instiller [ɛ̃sti'le], *v.t.* to instil.

instinct [ɛ̃s'tɛ̃], *n.m.* instinct.

instinctif [ɛ̃stɛ̃k'tif], *a. (fem.* **-tive***)* instinctive.

instinctivement [ɛ̃stɛ̃ktiv'mɑ̃], *adv.* instinctively.

instituer [ɛ̃sti'tɥe], *v.t.* to institute, to establish.

institut [ɛ̃sti'ty], *n.m.* institution; institute; order (*of monks*).

instituteur [ɛ̃stity'tœːr], *n.m. (fem.* **-trice***)* teacher, schoolmaster, schoolmistress (*in primary schools*); *institutrice (particulière)*, governess.

institution [ɛ̃stity'sjɔ̃], *n.f.* institution; establishment; (*Law*) appointment.

instructeur [ɛ̃stryk'tœːr], *n.m.* instructor, drill-master.
instructif [ɛ̃stryk'tif], *a.* (*fem.* **-tive**) instructive.
instruction [ɛ̃stryk'sjɔ̃], *n.f.* instruction, tuition, education, learning; (*Law*) inquiry, examination; (*pl.*) directions.
instruire [ɛ̃s'trɥiːr], *v.t. irr.* (*conjug. like* CONDUIRE) to instruct, to teach, to educate; to inform (*de*). **s'instruire,** *v.r.* to instruct, inform *or* improve oneself.
instruit [ɛ̃'strɥi], *a.* instructed, informed; aware; educated.
instrument [ɛ̃stry'mɑ̃], *n.m.* instrument, tool; document.
instrumental [ɛ̃strymɑ̃'tal], *a.* (*m. pl.* **-aux**) instrumental.
instrumentiste [ɛ̃strymɑ̃'tist], *n.* instrumentalist.
insu [ɛ̃'sy], *prep. phr.* **à l'insu de,** unknown to; **à mon insu,** unknown to me.
insubmersible [ɛ̃sybmɛr'sibl]. *a.* unsinkable.
insubordination [ɛ̃sybɔrdina'sjɔ̃], *n.f.* insubordination.
insubordonné [ɛ̃sybɔrdɔ'ne], *a.* insubordinate.
insuccès [ɛ̃syk'sɛ], *n.m. inv.* failure, lack of success.
insuffisamment [ɛ̃syfiza'mɑ̃], *adv.* insufficiently.
insuffisance [ɛ̃syfi'zɑ̃ːs], *n.f.* insufficiency.
insuffisant [ɛ̃syfi'zɑ̃], *a.* insufficient, inadequate.
insulaire [ɛ̃sy'lɛːr], *a.* insular.—*n.* islander.
insularité [ɛ̃sylari'te], *n.f.* insularity.
insuline [ɛ̃sy'lin], *n.f.* insulin.
insultant [ɛ̃syl'tɑ̃], *a.* insulting.
insulte [ɛ̃'sylt], *n.f.* insult.
insulter [ɛ̃syl'te], *v.t.* to insult, to affront.
insupportable [ɛ̃sypɔr'tabl], *a.* intolerable, unbearable.
insupportablement [ɛ̃sypɔrtablə'mɑ̃], *adv.* intolerably, unbearably.
insurgé [ɛ̃syr'ʒe], *a.* and *n.m.* (*fem.* **-ée**) rebel, insurgent.
insurger (**s'**) [sɛ̃syr'ʒe], *v.r.* (*conjug. like* MANGER) to revolt, to rebel.
insurmontable [ɛ̃syrmɔ̃'tabl], *a.* insurmountable, insuperable.
insurrection [ɛ̃syrɛk'sjɔ̃], *n.f.* insurrection, rising.
intact [ɛ̃'takt], *a.* intact, entire, whole.
intangible [ɛ̃tɑ̃'ʒibl], *a.* intangible.
intarissable [ɛ̃tari'sabl], *a.* inexhaustible.
intégral [ɛ̃te'gral], *a.* (*m. pl.* **-aux**) integral, whole, entire.
intégrale [ɛ̃te'gral], *n.f.* (*Math.*) integral.
intégralement [ɛ̃tegral'mɑ̃], *adv.* integrally, entirely, in full.
intègre [ɛ̃'tɛgr], *a.* honest, upright, just.
intègrement [ɛ̃tegrə'mɑ̃], *adv.* honestly, uprightly.
intégrer [ɛ̃te'gre], *v.t.* (*conjug. like* CÉDER) to integrate. **s'intégrer,** *v.r.* to combine into; to form an integral part of.
intégrité [ɛ̃tegri'te], *n.f.* integrity, uprightness, probity.
intellect [ɛ̃te'lɛkt], *n.m.* intellect, understanding.
intellectuel [ɛ̃telɛk'tɥel], *a.* (*fem.* **-elle**) and *n.m.* (*fem.* **-elle**) intellectual.

intellectuellement [ɛ̃telɛktɥɛl'mɑ̃], *adv.* intellectually.
intelligemment [ɛ̃teliʒa'mɑ̃] *adv.* intelligently.
intelligence [ɛ̃teli'ʒɑ̃ːs], *n.f.* intelligence, intellect; clear comprehension; cleverness, skill, ability; mutual understanding; **avec intelligence,** skillfully, cleverly; **en bonne intelligence avec,** on good terms with; **être d'intelligence avec,** to be in collusion with.
intelligent [ɛ̃teli'ʒɑ̃], *a.* intelligent; bright, clever, sharp.
intelligible [ɛ̃teli'ʒibl], *a.* intelligible; distinct, clear.
intelligiblement [ɛ̃teliʒiblə'mɑ̃], *adv.* intelligibly, clearly.
intempérance [ɛ̃tɑ̃pe'rɑ̃ːs], *n.f.* intemperance, insobriety.
intempérant [ɛ̃tɑ̃pe'rɑ̃], *a.* intemperate.
intempérie [ɛ̃tɑ̃pe'ri], *n.f.* (*usu. in pl.*) inclemency (*of the weather*).
intempestif [ɛ̃tɑ̃pɛs'tif], *a.* (*fem.* **-tive**) unseasonable, untimely.
intenable [ɛ̃tə'nabl], *a.* untenable; insufferable.
intendance [ɛ̃tɑ̃'dɑ̃ːs], *n.f.* stewardship (*of an estate*); (*Mil.*) commissariat; the Army Service Corps.
intendant [ɛ̃tɑ̃'dɑ̃], *n.m.* intendant, steward; major-domo; (*Mil.*) administrative officer (*having the rank of a general*).
intense [ɛ̃'tɑ̃ːs], *a.* intense, violent; severe.
intensité [ɛ̃tɑ̃si'te], *n.f.* intensity, violence, severity.
intensivement [ɛ̃tɑ̃siv'mɑ̃], *adv.* intensively.
intenter [ɛ̃tɑ̃'te], *v.t.* (*Law*) **intenter une action** *or* **un procès à** *or* **contre quelqu'un,** to enter *or* bring an action against someone.
intention [ɛ̃tɑ̃'sjɔ̃], *n.f.* intention; (*Law*) intent; purpose; **à l'intention de,** for the sake of; **avec intention,** on purpose; **avoir l'intention de,** to intend to; **sans intention,** unintentionally.
intentionné [ɛ̃tɑ̃sjɔ'ne], *a.* intentioned, disposed, meaning.
intentionnel [ɛ̃tɑ̃sjɔ'nɛl], *a.* (*fem.* **-elle**) intentional.
inter [ɛ̃'tɛr], *n.m.* (*Ftb.*) inside-forward.
interaction [ɛ̃tɛrak'sjɔ̃], *n.f.* interaction.
intercaler [ɛ̃tɛrka'le], *v.t.* to intercalate; to interpolate; (*Elec.*) to switch in.
intercéder [ɛ̃tɛrse'de], *v.i.* (*conjug. like* CÉDER) to intercede, to plead.
intercepter [ɛ̃tɛrsɛp'te], *v.t.* to intercept.
intercession [ɛ̃tɛrse'sjɔ̃], *n.f.* intercession; mediation.
intercontinental [ɛ̃tɛrkɔ̃tinɑ̃'tal], *a.* (*m. pl.* **-aux**) intercontinental.
interdépartemental [ɛ̃tɛrdepartəmɑ̃'tal], *a.* (*m. pl.* **-aux**) interdepartmental.
interdiction [ɛ̃tɛrdik'sjɔ̃], *n.f.* interdiction, prohibition.
interdire [ɛ̃tɛr'diːr], *v.t. irr.* (*conjug. like* MÉDIRE) to interdict, to prohibit; to forbid; to suspend; (*fig.*) to confound, to nonplus.
interdit [ɛ̃tɛr'di], *a.* forbidden, prohibited; (*fig.*) abashed, confused; **entrée interdite,** no admittance; **passage interdit,** no thoroughfare.—*n.m.* interdict.—*n.m.* (*fem.* **-e**) person interdicted.

intéressant [ɛ̃tɛrɛ'sā], *a.* interesting; attractive (*price*).
intéressé [ɛ̃tɛrɛ'se], *a.* interested; selfish.—*n.m.* (*fem.* **-ée**) interested party.
intéresser [ɛ̃tɛrɛ'se], *v.t.* to interest; to concern, to affect. **s'intéresser**, *v.r.* to take an interest in, to be interested (*à*).
intérêt [ɛ̃te'rɛ], *n.m.* interest, concern; share.
interférence [ɛ̃tɛrfe'rā:s], *n.f.* interference; (*pl.*) (*Rad., Tel.*) interference.
interférer [ɛ̃tɛrfe're], *v.i.* (*conjug. like* CÉDER) to interfere.
intérieur [ɛ̃te'rjœ:r], *a.* inner, inward, internal, interior; inland.—*n.m.* interior; home, private life; *à l'intérieur*, inside; *Ministre de l'Intérieur*, Home Secretary.
interlocuteur [ɛ̃tɛrlɔky'tœ:r], *n.m.* (*fem.* **-trice**) speaker (*in a conversation*).
interloquer [ɛ̃tɛrlɔ'ke], *v.t.* to nonplus, to disconcert.
intermède [ɛ̃tɛr'mɛd], *n.m.* interlude.
intermédiaire [ɛ̃tɛrme'djɛ:r], *a.* intermediate, intervening.—*n.m.* medium, agency; intermediary, middleman, agent.
interminable [ɛ̃tɛrmi'nabl], *a.* interminable, endless.
intermission [ɛ̃tɛrmi'sjɔ̃], *n.f.* intermission, pause.
intermittence [ɛ̃tɛrmi'tā:s], *n.f.* intermission, cessation.
intermittent [ɛ̃tɛrmi'tā], *a.* intermittent.
internat [ɛ̃tɛr'na], *n.m.* boarding school; house-surgeonship (*of hospitals*).
international [ɛ̃tɛrnasjɔ'nal], *a.* (*m, pl.* **-aux**) international.
interne [ɛ̃'tɛrn], *a.* internal, inward, resident. —*n.* boarder (*in schools*).
interné [ɛ̃tɛr'ne], *a.* interned.—*n.m.* (*fem.* **-ée**) internee.
interner [ɛ̃tɛr'ne], *v.t.* to intern.
interpellation [ɛ̃tɛrpɛla'sjɔ̃], *n.f.* interpellation.
interpeller [ɛ̃tɛrpɛ'le], *v.t.* to hail, to call upon, to challenge; (*Polit.*) to interpellate.
interplanétaire [ɛ̃tɛrplane'tɛ:r], *a.* interplanetary.
interpoler [ɛ̃tɛrpɔ'le], *v.t.* to interpolate.
interposer [ɛ̃tɛrpɔ'ze], *v.t.* to interpose. **s'interposer**, *v.r.* to interpose, to come between.
interprétation [ɛ̃tɛrpreta'sjɔ̃], *n.f.* interpretation; rendering (*of a play*).
interprète [ɛ̃tɛr'prɛt], *n.* interpreter, expounder; artist, actor, actress.
interpréter [ɛ̃tɛrpre'te], *v.t.* (*conjug. like* CÉDER) to interpret, to explain; to construe.
interrègne [ɛ̃tɛr'rɛɲ], *n.m.* interregnum.
interrogateur [ɛ̃tɛrɔga'tœr], *n.m.* (*fem.* **-trice**) interrogator, questioner, examiner.
interrogatif [ɛ̃tɛrɔga'tif], *a.* (*fem.* **-tive**) interrogative.
interrogation [ɛ̃tɛrɔga'sjɔ̃], *n.f.* interrogation, question; *point d'interrogation*, question mark.
interrogatoire [ɛ̃tɛrɔga'twa:r], *n.m.* examination.
interroger [ɛ̃tɛrɔ'ʒe], *v.t.* (*conjug. like* MANGER) to interrogate, to question; to examine.
interrompre [ɛ̃te'rɔ̃:pr], *v.t.* (*conjug. like* RÓMPRE) to interrupt, to break off; to stop.
interrupteur [ɛ̃tɛryp'tœ:r], *a.* and *n.m.* (*fem.*

-trice) interrupting; interrupter.—*n.m.* (*Elec.*) switch, cut-out.
interruption [ɛ̃tɛryp'sjɔ̃], *n.f.* interruption; (*Elec.*) disconnection.
interscolaire [ɛ̃tɛrskɔ'lɛ:r], *a.* inter-school (*competition etc.*).
intersection [ɛ̃tɛrsɛk'sjɔ̃], *n.f.* intersection.
interstice [ɛ̃tɛr'stis], *n.m.* interstice, chink, crack.
intervalle [ɛ̃tɛr'val], *n.m.* interval; distance, gap; *dans l'intervalle*, in the meantime.
intervenir [ɛ̃tɛrvə'ni:r], *v.i. irr.* (*conjug. like* TENIR) to intervene, to interfere; to happen.
intervention [ɛ̃tɛrvā'sjɔ̃], *n.f.* intervention, interference.
interversion [ɛ̃tɛrvɛr'sjɔ̃], *n.f.* inversion.
intervertir [ɛ̃tɛrvɛr'ti:r], *v.t.* to invert, to reverse.
intestin [ɛ̃tɛs'tɛ̃], *a.* intestine; internal, domestic, civil.—*n.m.* intestine.
intimation [ɛ̃tima'sjɔ̃], *n.f.* notification.
intime [ɛ̃'tim], *a.* intimate, inmost, secret; close.—*n.* intimate.
intimement [ɛ̃tim'mā], *adv.* intimately.
intimider [ɛ̃timi'de], *v.t.* to intimidate, to frighten.
intimité [ɛ̃timi'te], *n.f.* intimacy, closeness.
intitulé [ɛ̃tity'le], *a.* entitled.—*n.m.* title (*of deeds, books etc.*).
intituler [ɛ̃tity'le], *v.t.* to entitle, to call, to name. **s'intituler**, *v.r.* to entitle or call oneself.
intolérable [ɛ̃tɔle'rabl], *a.* intolerable, insufferable.
intolérablement [ɛ̃tɔlerablə'mā], *adv.* unbearably.
intolérance [ɛ̃tɔle'rā:s], *n.f.* intolerance.
intolérant [ɛ̃tɔle'rā], *a.* intolerant.
intonation [ɛ̃tɔna'sjɔ̃], *n.f.* intonation; pitch.
intoxicant [ɛ̃tɔksi'kā], *a.* poisonous.
intoxication [ɛ̃tɔksika'sjɔ̃], *n.f.* poisoning.
intoxiquer [ɛ̃tɔksi'ke], *v.t.* to poison.
intraduisible [ɛ̃tradɥi'zibl], *a.* untranslatable.
intraitable [ɛ̃trɛ'tabl], *a.* intractable, unmanageable.
intransigeant [ɛ̃trāzi'ʒā], *a.* intransigent, uncompromising.—*n.m.* (*fem.* **-e**) intransigent, diehard.
intransitif [ɛ̃trāzi'tif], *a.* (*fem.* **-tive**) (*Gram.*) intransitive.
intraversable [ɛ̃traver'sabl], *a.* impassable.
intrépide [ɛ̃tre'pid], *a.* intrepid, dauntless, fearless.
intrigant [ɛ̃tri'gā], *a.* intriguing.—*n.m.* (*fem.* **-e**) intriguer, schemer.
intrigue [ɛ̃'trig], *n.f.* intrigue; plot (*of a novel etc.*).
intrigueur [ɛ̃tri'gœ:r], *n.m.* (*fem.* **-euse**) intriguer, plotter.
intrinsèque [ɛ̃trɛ̃'sɛk], *a.* intrinsic.
introduction [ɛ̃trɔdyk'sjɔ̃], *n.f.* introduction; preamble.
introductoire [ɛ̃trɔdyk'twa:r], *a.* introductory, preliminary.
introduire [ɛ̃trɔ'dɥi:r], *v.t. irr.* (*conjug. like* CONDUIRE) to show or bring in, to introduce. **s'introduire**, *v.r.* to get in, to find one's way in; to intrude.
introniser [ɛ̃trɔni'ze], *v.t.* to install, to enthrone; (*fig.*) to establish (*a fashion*).
introspectif [ɛ̃trɔspɛk'tif], *a.* (*fem.* **-tive**) introspective.

introuvable [ɛ̃tru'vabl], *a.* not to be found; matchless.
introverti [ɛ̃trɔvɛr'ti], *a.* introverted.—*n.m.* (*fem.* **-e**) introvert.
intrus [ɛ̃'try], *a.* intruding, intruded.—*n.m.* (*fem.* **-e**) intruder.
intrusion [ɛ̃try'zjɔ̃], *n.f.* intrusion.
intuitif [ɛ̃tɥi'tif], *a.* (*fem.* **-tive**) intuitive.
intuition [ɛ̃tɥi'sjɔ̃], *n.f.* intuition.
inusable [iny'zabl], *a.* durable, everlasting.
inusité [inyzi'te], *a.* unused; unusual; obsolete.
inutile [iny'til], *a.* useless, unnecessary.
inutilement [inytil'mɑ̃], *adv.* uselessly, to no purpose, needlessly.
inutilisable [inytili'zabl], *a.* that cannot be utilized, worthless.
inutilité [inytili'te], *n.f.* uselessness; useless thing.
invaincu [ɛ̃vɛ̃'ky], *a.* unvanquished, unconquered.
invalidation [ɛ̃valida'sjɔ̃], *n.f.* invalidation.
invalide [ɛ̃va'lid], *a.* disabled, crippled, infirm, invalid; (*Law*) not valid.—*n.* invalid, pensioner; *Hôtel des Invalides*, the veterans hospital of France.
invalider [ɛ̃vali'de], *v.t.* to invalidate, to annul.
invariable [ɛ̃va'rjabl], *a.* invariable, unchangeable.
invariablement [ɛ̃varjablə'mɑ̃], *adv.* invariably.
invasion [ɛ̃va'zjɔ̃], *n.f.* invasion; inroad.
invective [ɛ̃vɛk'ti:v], *n.f.* invective, (*pl.*) abuse.
invectiver [ɛ̃vɛkti've] *v.t.* to abuse.—*v.i.* to inveigh against, to revile (**contre**).
inventaire [ɛ̃vɑ̃'tɛ:r], *n.m.* inventory; stock-taking.
inventer [ɛ̃vɑ̃'te], *v.t.* to invent, to devise; to find out; to imagine; to forge.
inventeur [ɛ̃vɑ̃'tœ:r], *n.m.* (*fem.* **-trice**) inventor.
inventif [ɛ̃vɑ̃'tif], *a.* (*fem.* **-tive**) inventive.
invention [ɛ̃vɑ̃'sjɔ̃], *n.f.* invention; inventiveness; device, trick; falsehood; *brevet d'invention*, patent.
inventorier [ɛ̃vɑ̃tɔ'rje], *v.t.* to draw up an inventory of; to schedule, to catalogue.
inversable [ɛ̃vɛr'sabl], *a.* that cannot be upset.
inverse [ɛ̃'vɛrs], *a.* inverse, inverted.—*n.m.* reverse, contrary.
inversement [ɛ̃vɛrs'mɑ̃], *adv.* inversely.
invertébré [ɛ̃vɛrte'bre], *a.* and *n.m.* (*fem.* **-ée**) invertebrate.
inverti [ɛ̃vɛr'ti], *a.* inverted, reversed.
investigateur [ɛ̃vɛstiga'tœ:r], *a.* (*fem.* **-trice**) searching, inquiring.—*n.m.* (*fem.* **-trice**) investigator.
investigation [ɛ̃vɛstiga'sjɔ̃], *n.f.* investigation, inquiry.
investir [ɛ̃vɛs'ti:r], *v.t.* to invest; to surround, to lay siege to.
investiture [ɛ̃vɛsti'ty:r], *n.f.* investiture.
invétéré [ɛ̃vete're], *a.* inveterate.
invincibilité [ɛ̃vɛ̃sibili'te], *n.f.* invincibility.
invincible [ɛ̃vɛ̃'sibl], *a.* invincible, unconquerable.
inviolable [ɛ̃vjɔ'labl], *a.* inviolable.
inviolé [ɛ̃vjɔ'le], *a.* inviolate.
invisible [ɛ̃vi'zibl], *a.* invisible.

invisiblement [ɛ̃viziblə'mɑ̃], *adv.* invisibly.
invitation [ɛ̃vita'sjɔ̃], *n.f.* invitation.
invité [ɛ̃vi'te], *n.m.* (*fem.* **-ée**) guest.
inviter [ɛ̃vi'te], *v.t.* to invite, to request; to incite, to tempt.
invocation [ɛ̃vɔka'sjɔ̃], *n.f.* invocation.
involontaire [ɛ̃vɔlɔ̃'tɛ:r], *a.* involuntary, unwilling.
involontairement [ɛ̃vɔlɔ̃tɛr'mɑ̃], *adv.* involuntarily.
invoquer [ɛ̃vɔ'ke], *v.t.* to invoke, to call upon; to appeal to.
invraisemblable [ɛ̃vrɛsɑ̃'blabl], *a.* unlikely, improbable.
invraisemblablement [ɛ̃vrɛsɑ̃blablə'mɑ̃], *adv.* improbably.
invraisemblance [ɛ̃vrɛsɑ̃'blɑ̃:s], *n.f.* unlikelihood, improbability.
invulnérable [ɛ̃vylne'rabl], *a.* invulnerable.
iode [jɔd], *n.m.* iodine.
ion [jɔ̃], *n.m.* (*Phys.*) ion.
ionisation [jɔniza'sjɔ̃], *n.f.* ionization.
ionosphère [jɔnɔs'fɛ:r], *n.f.* ionosphere.
iota [jɔ'ta], *n.m.* iota, jot, tittle.
Irak [i'rak], *l'*, *m.* Iraq.
irakien [ira'kjɛ̃], *a.* (*fem.* **-enne**) Iraqi.—*n.m.* (**Irakien**, *fem.* **-enne**) Iraqi (*person*).
Iran [i'rɑ̃] *l'*, *m.* Iran.
iranien [ira'njɛ̃], *a.* (*fem.* **-enne**) Iranian.—*n.m.* (**Iranien**, *fem.* **-enne**) Iranian (*person*).
irascibilite [irasibili'te], *n.f.* irascibility.
irascible [ira'sibl], *a.* irascible, irritable.
iridescence [iridɛ'sɑ̃:s], *n.f.* iridescence.
iridescent [iride'sɑ̃], *a.* iridescent.
iris [i'ri:s], *n.m. inv.* iris; rainbow.
irisé [iri'ze], *a.* rainbow-colored, iridescent.
irlandais [irlɑ̃'dɛ], *a.* Irish.—*n.m.* Irish (*language*); (**Irlandais**, *fem.* **-aise**) Irishman, Irishwoman.
Irlande [ir'lɑ̃d], *l'*, *m.* Ireland.
ironie [irɔ'ni], *n.f.* irony, mockery, raillery.
ironique [irɔ'nik], *a.* ironical.
irradiation [irradja'sjɔ̃], *n.f.* irradiation.
irradier [irra'dje], *v.t.* to radiate through; (*C*) to broadcast.
irraisonnable [irrɛzɔ'nabl], *a.* irrational.
irraisonnablement [irrɛzɔnablə'mɑ̃], *adv.* irrationally.
irrationnel [irrasjɔ'nɛl], *a.* (*fem.* **-elle**) irrational.
irrationnellement [irrasjɔnɛl'mɑ̃], *adv.* irrationally.
irréalisable [irreali'zabl], *a.* impossible, impracticable.
irréconciliable [irrekɔ̃si'ljabl], *a.* irreconcilable.
irrécusable [irreky'zabl], *a.* unexceptionable, unimpeachable.
irréductible [irredyk'tibl], *a.* irreducible; (*fig.*) unyielding.
irréel [irre'ɛl], *a.* (*fem.* **-éelle**) unreal.—*n.m.* unreality.
irréfléchi [irrefle'ʃi], *a.* thoughtless, inconsiderate.
irréflexion [irreflɛk'sjɔ̃], *n.f.* thoughtlessness, heedlessness.
irréfutable [irrefy'tabl], *a.* irrefutable.
irrégularité [irregylari'te], *n.f.* irregularity.
irrégulier [irreg/'lje], *a.* (*fem.* **-ière**) irregular.
irrégulièrement [irregyljɛr'mɑ̃], *adv.* irregularly.

irréligieux [irreli'ʒjø], *a.* (*fem.* **-euse**) irreligious.

irrémédiable [irreme'djabl], *a.* irremediable, irreparable, irretrievable.

irrémédiablement [irremedjablə'mã], *adv.* irremediably, irreparably.

irrémissible [irremi'sibl], *a.* irremissible, unpardonable.

irremplaçable [irrãpla'sabl], *a.* irreplaceable.

irréparable [irrepa'rabl], *a.* irreparable.

irrépressible [irrepre'sibl], *a.* irrepressible.

irréprochable [irrepro'ʃabl], *a.* irreproachable.

irrésistible [irrezis'tibl], *a.* irresistible.

irrésistiblement [irrezistiblə'mã], *adv.* irresistibly.

irrésolu [irrezo'ly], *a.* irresolute, wavering.

irrésolument [irrezoly'mã], *adv.* irresolutely.

irrésolution [irrezoly'sjõ], *n.f.* irresolution, indecision.

irrespectueusement [irrespektɥøz'mã], *adv.* disrespectfully.

irrespectueux [irrespek'tɥø], *a.* (*fem.* **-euse**) disrespectful.

irresponsabilité [irrespõsabili'te], *n.f.* irresponsibility.

irresponsable [irrespõ'sabl], *a.* irresponsible.

irrétrécissable [irretresi'sabl], *a.* unshrinkable.

irrévérence [irreve'rã:s], *n.f.* irreverence, disrespect.

irrévocable [irrevo'kabl], *a.* irrevocable.

irrévocablement [irrevokablə'mã], *adv.* irrevocably.

irrigateur [irriga'tœ:r], *n.m.* watering engine; garden hose.

irrigation [irriga'sjõ], *n.f.* irrigation.

irriguer [irri'ge], *v.t.* to irrigate, to water.

irritabilité [irritabili'te], *n.f.* irritability.

irritable [irri'tabl], *a.* irritable.

irritant [irri'tã], *a.* irritating, provoking.

irritation [irrita'sjõ], *n.f.* irritation, exasperation.

irriter [irri'te], *v.t.* to irritate, to incense, to anger; to provoke, to excite. **s'irriter**, *v.r.* to grow angry; to become irritated.

irruption [irryp'sjõ], *n.f.* irruption, raid; overflow, flood; **faire irruption dans**, to invade.

Isaïe [iza'i], *m.* Isaiah.

Islam [is'lam], *n.m.* Islam.

islandais [islã'dɛ], *a.* Icelandic.—*n.m.* Icelandic (*language*); (**Islandais**, *fem.* **-aise**) Icelander.

Islande [is'lãd], **l'**, *f.* Iceland.

isobare [izo'bar], *n.f.* isobar.

isocèle or **isoscèle** [izo'sɛl], *a.* (*Geom.*) isosceles.

isolant [izo'lã], *a.* insulating; **bouteille isolante**, vacuum flask.

isolateur [izola'tœ:r], *a.* (*fem.* **-trice**) insulating.—*n.m.* insulator.

isolation [izola'sjõ], *n.f.* insulation; isolation.

isolé [izo'le], *a.* isolated; lonely, solitary; detached; insulated; apart.

isolement [izol'mã], *n.m.* loneliness, isolation; insulation.

isolément [izole'mã], *adv.* separately.

isoler [izo'le], *v.t.* to isolate; to insulate; to detach; to separate.

isotope [izo'tɔp], *n.m.* isotope.

Israël [isra'ɛl], **l'**, *m.* Israel.

israélien [israe'ljɛ̃], *a.* (*fem.* **-enne**) Israeli(i). —*n.m.* (**Israélien**, *fem.* **-enne**) Israeli (*person*).

issu [i'sy], *a.* born, descended, sprung from.

issue [i'sy], *n.f.* issue, outlet; escape; (*fig.*) end, event.

isthme [ism], *n.m.* isthmus.

Italie [ita'li], **l'**, *f.* Italy.

italien [ita'ljɛ̃] *a.* (*fem.* **-enne**) Italian.— *n.m.* Italian (*language*); (**Italien**, *fem.* **-enne**) Italian (*person*).

italique [ita'lik], *a.* and *n.m.* italic.

itinéraire [itine'rɛ:r], *a.* pertaining to roads etc.—*n.m.* itinerary, route; guide-book.

itinérant [itine'rã], *a.* itinerant.

ivoire [i'vwa:r], *n.m.* ivory; (*fig.*) whiteness; **la Côte d'Ivoire**, Ivory Coast.

ivraie [i'vrɛ], *n.f.* darnel, tare.

ivre [i:vr], *a.* drunk; intoxicated; (*fig.*) transported; **ivre mort**, dead drunk.

ivresse [i'vrɛs], *n.f.* drunkenness, intoxication; (*fig.*) frenzy, rapture.

ivrogne [i'vrɔɲ], *a.* drunken.—*n.* drunkard.

ivrognerie [ivro'ɲri], *n.f.* habitual drunkenness.

J

J, j [ʒi], *n.m.* the tenth letter of the alphabet.

jabot [ʒa'bo], *n.m.* crop (*of a bird*); frill (*of a shirt* or *blouse*); jabot.

jaboter [ʒabo'te], *v.i.* (*colloq.*) to prattle, to chatter.

jacasser [ʒaka'se], *v.i.* to chatter (*of the magpie*); (*fig.*) to chatter, to jabber.

jachère [ʒa'ʃɛ:r], *n.f.* fallow.

jacinthe [ʒa'sɛ̃:t], *n.f.* jacinthe; hyacinth.

Jacques [ʒɑ:k], *m.* James.

jade [ʒad], *n.m.* jade.

jadis [ʒɑ'dis], *adv.* of old, formerly.

jaguar [ʒa'gwa:r], *n.m.* jaguar.

jaillir [ʒa'ji:r], *v.i.* to spout, to gush; to shoot out *or* up.

jaillissant [ʒaji'sã], *a.* spouting, gushing.

jaillissement [ʒajis'mã], *n.m.* gushing, spouting, flashing.

jais [ʒɛ], *n.m.* jet.

jalon [ʒa'lõ], *n.m.* levelling staff, surveying staff; (*fig.*) landmark, beacon.

jalonnement [ʒalon'mã], *n.m.* (*Land surveying*) staking out, marking out.

jalonner [ʒalo'ne], *v.t.* to mark *or* stake out.—*v.i.* to place land marks etc.

jalousement [ʒaluz'mã], *adv.* jealously.

jalouser [ʒalu'ze], *v.t.* to be jealous of, to envy.

jalousie [ʒalu'zi], *n.f.* jealousy, envy; Venetian blind; (*Bot.*) sweet william.

jaloux [ʒa'lu], *a.* (*fem.* **-ouse**) jealous; envious; desirous, anxious.—*n.m.* (*fem.* **-ouse**) jealous person.

jamaïquain [ʒamai'kɛ̃], *a.* Jamaican.—*n.m.* (**Jamaïquain,** *fem.* **-aine**) Jamaican (*person*).
Jamaïque [ʒama'ik], **la,** *f.* Jamaica.
jamais [ʒa'mɛ], *adv.* (*neg.*) never, (*affirm.*) ever; *à jamais,* for ever; *jamais de la vie,* not on your life!; *mieux vaut tard que jamais,* better late than never.
jambage [ʒɑ̃'baːʒ], *n.m.* jamb (*of a door etc.*); down-stroke, pot-hook (*in writing*).
jambe [ʒɑ̃:b], *n.f.* leg; shank; *courir à toutes jambes,* to run as fast as one can; *prendre ses jambes à son cou,* to take to one's heels.
jambière [ʒɑ̃'bjɛːr], *n.f.* legging, leg guard.
jambon [ʒɑ̃'bɔ̃], *n.m.* ham.
jamboree [ʒɑ̃bɔ'ri], *n.m.* jamboree.
jante [ʒɑ̃:t], *n.f.* felloe, rim (*of a wheel*).
janvier [ʒɑ̃'vje], *n.m.* January.
Japon [ʒa'pɔ̃], **le,** *m.* Japan.
japonais [ʒapɔ'nɛ], *a.* Japanese.—*n.m.* Japanese (*language*); (**Japonais,** *fem.* **-aise**) Japanese (*person*).
japper [ʒa'pe], *v.i.* to yelp, to yap.
jaquette [ʒa'kɛt], *n.f.* morning coat, tail coat; woman's jacket; dust cover (*of book*).
jardin [ʒar'dɛ̃], *n.m.* garden.
jardinage [ʒardi'naːʒ], *n.m.* gardening; garden produce.
jardiner [ʒardi'ne], *v.i.* to garden.
jardinier [ʒardi'nje], *a.* (*fem.* **-ière**) (of the) garden.—*n.m.* (*fem.* **-ière**) gardener.—*n.f.* (**-ière**) flower-stand, jardinière.
jardiniste [ʒardi'nist], *n.* landscape-gardener.
jargon [ʒar'gɔ̃], *n.m.* jargon, gibberish; lingo.
jarre [ʒaːr], *n.f.* jar.
jarret [ʒa'rɛ], *n.m.* ham (*of man*); hough, hock (*of horse*).
jarretière [ʒar'tjɛr], *n.f.* (lady's) garter.
jars (1) [ʒaːr], *n.m.* gander.
jars (2) [ʒaːr], *n.m.* (*another form of* **jargon**) slang.
jaser [ʒa'ze], *v.i.* to chatter, to gossip.
jaserie [ʒaz'ri], *n.f.* chatter; gossip.
jaseur [ʒa'zœːr], *a.* (*fem.* **-euse**) talkative.—*n.m.* (*fem.* **-euse**) chatterer, chatterbox.
jasmin [ʒas'mɛ̃], *n.m.* jasmine.
jaspe [ʒasp], *n.m.* jasper.
jasper [ʒas'pe], *v.t.* to marble, to vein, to variegate.
jaspure [ʒas'pyːr], *n.f.* marbling, veining.
jatte [ʒat], *n.f.* bowl, platter; dog's bowl.
jauge [ʒoːʒ], *n.f.* gauge; (*Naut.*) tonnage.
jaugeage [ʒo'ʒaːʒ], *n.m.* gauging.
jauger [ʒo'ʒe], *v.t.* (*conjug. like* MANGER) to gauge, to measure the capacity of; (*Naut.*) to draw (*so many feet of water*).
jaunâtre [ʒo'naːtr], *a.* yellowish.
jaune [ʒoːn], *a.* yellow; *rire jaune,* to give a sickly smile.—*n.m.* yellow; *jaune d'œuf,* egg yolk.
jaunir [ʒo'niːr], *v.t.* to make yellow, to dye yellow.—*v.i.* to grow yellow, to turn yellow.
jaunissant [ʒoni'sɑ̃], *a.* turning yellow, yellowing; ripening.
jaunisse [ʒo'nis], *n.f.* jaundice.
javanais [ʒava'nɛ], *a.* Javanese.—*n.m.* (**Javanais,** *fem.* **-aise**) Javanese (*person*).
javeau [ʒa'vo], *n.m.* (*pl.* **-eaux**) sandbank.
javeline [ʒav'lin], *n.f.* javelin.
javelle [ʒa'vɛl], *n.f.* swathe, loose sheaf.
javelot [ʒav'lo], *n.m.* javelin.

jazz [(d)ʒaːz], *n.m.* jazz.
je [ʒə], (**j'**, *before a vowel sound*), *pron.* I.
Jean [ʒɑ̃], *m.* John [JEANNOT].
Jeanne [ʒa(ː)n], *f.* Joan, Jane, Jean.
Jeannot [ʒa'no], *m.* Johnny, Jock.
jeep [(d)ʒip], *n.f.* jeep.
jésuite [ʒe'zɥit], *a.* Jesuit.—*n.m.* (**Jésuite**) Jesuit.
Jésus [ʒe'zy], *m.* Jesus.
jet [ʒɛ], *n.m.* casting, cast, throw; jet, gush, spurt (*of water*); sudden ray (*of light*); casting (*of metal*); shoot, sprout (*of plants*); spout (*of pump etc.*); new swarm (*of bees*); *arme de jet,* missile weapon.
jetée [ʒə'te], *n.f.* jetty, pier; breakwater.
jeter [ʒə'te], *v.t.* (*conjug. like* APPELER) to throw, to fling, to hurl; to throw up; to throw down, to knock down; to throw out; to mold; to shoot out; to send forth; to empty; to discharge. **se jeter,** *v.r.* to throw oneself, to fling oneself; to fall upon (*attack*); to flow (*of rivers etc.*).
jeton [ʒə'tɔ̃], *n.m.* token, counter; voucher.
jeu [ʒø], *n.m.* (*pl.* **jeux**) play, sport; game; fun; gambling; (*fig.*) stake; manner of playing; performance (*of players*); (*Mach.*) working; clearance; play.
jeudi [ʒø'di], *n.m.* Thursday.
jeun (à) [a'ʒœ̃], *adv.* fasting, sober, on an empty stomach.
jeune [ʒœn], *a.* young, youthful; junior; new; early, unripe, green.—*n.* young person *or* animal.
jeûne [ʒøːn], *n.m.* fasting; fast, abstinence.
jeûner [ʒø'ne], *v.i.* to fast.
jeunesse [ʒœ'nɛs], *n.f.* youth, young days; youthfulness; freshness, prime; young people.
jeunet [ʒœ'nɛ], *a.* (*fem.* **-ette**) (*colloq.*) very young.
jiu-jitsu [(d)ʒy'ʒi'tsy], *n.m.* ju-jitsu.
joaillerie [ʒwaj'ri], *n.f.* jeweller's trade *or* business; jewelry, jewels.
joaillier [ʒwa'je], *n.m.* (*fem.* **-ière**) jeweller.
jobard [ʒo'baːr], *n.m.* (*colloq.*) sucker, mug, fool.
jockey [ʒo'kɛ], *n.m.* jockey.
jocrisse [ʒo'kris], *n.m.* dolt, simpleton.
joie [ʒwa], *n.f.* joy, happiness, joyfulness, gladness; glee, mirth.
joignant [ʒwa'ɲɑ̃], *a.* and *prep.* next to, adjoining.
joindre [ʒwɛ̃:dr], *v.t. irr.* (*conjug. like* CRAINDRE) to join, to put together, to unite, to combine; to add; to meet; to overtake.—*v.i.* to join, to meet. **se joindre,** *v.r.* to join, to be joined, to be united; to be adjoining, to be adjacent; to be added.
joint [ʒwɛ̃], *a.* joined, united; added.—*n.m.* joint; seam, junction.
jointé [ʒwɛ̃'te], *a.* jointed.
jointure [ʒwɛ̃'tyːr], *n.f.* joint, jointing, articulation.
joli [ʒo'li], *a.* pretty, pleasing, neat; fine; nice. —*n.m.* what is pretty; *le joli de la chose c'est que . . . ,* the best of the thing is that . . . .
joliment [ʒoli'mɑ̃], *adv.* prettily; (*iron.*) nicely, finely; (*colloq.*) awfully, jolly, much, very.
jonc [ʒɔ̃], *n.m.* (*Bot.*) rush; cane, Malacca cane; keeper, guard (*ring*).

jonchée [ʒɔ̃'ʃe], *n.f.* strewing (*of flowers*).
joncher [ʒɔ̃'ʃe], *v.t.* to strew; to heap; to scatter.
jonction [ʒɔ̃k'sjɔ̃], *n.f.* junction, joining.
jongler [ʒɔ̃'gle], *v.i.* to juggle.
jonglerie [ʒɔ̃glə'ri], *n.f.* juggling.
jongleur [ʒɔ̃'glœːr], *n.m.* juggler; (*fig.*) trickster.
jonque [ʒɔ̃:k], *n.f.* junk (*Chinese vessel*).
jonquille [ʒɔ̃'ki:j], *n.f.* jonquil.—*a. inv.* and *n.m.* pale yellow, jonquil (*color*).
Jordanie [ʒɔrda'ni], **la**, *f.* Jordan.
jordanien [ʒɔrda'njɛ̃], *a.* Jordanian.—*n.m.* (**Jordanien**, *fem.* **-enne**) Jordanian (*person*).
Joseph [ʒo'zef], *m.* Joseph.
jouable [ʒwabl], *a.* playable.
joue [ʒu]. *n.f.* cheek; **coucher** or **mettre en joue**, to take aim at.
jouer [ʒwe], *v.t.* to play; to stake; to gamble away; to move (*a piece*); to perform, to act; to pretend to be, to imitate; to ridicule; to deceive.—*v.i.* to play, to amuse oneself; to gambol, to frolic; to gamble, to run the risk; to speculate (*on the funds*); to work, to work loose (*of machinery etc.*); to act, to perform. **se jouer**, *v.r.* to sport, to play; to make game (*of*); to make light of.
jouet [ʒwɛ], *n.m.* plaything, toy; laughing-stock, jest, sport.
joueur [ʒwœːr], *n.m.* (*fem.* **-euse**) player; gambler; speculator; performer (*on an instrument*).
joufflu [ʒu'fly], *a.* chubby, chubby-cheeked.
joug [ʒu(g)], *n.m.* yoke; bondage, slavery.
jouir [ʒwiːr], *v.i.* to enjoy, to revel; to be in possession (*de*).
jouissance [ʒwi'sãːs], *n.f.* enjoyment; possession, use; delight; interest payable.
jouissant [ʒwi'sã], *a.* enjoying, in possession (*de*).
joujou [ʒu'ʒu], *n.m.* (*pl.* **-oux**) plaything, toy.
jour [ʒuːr], *n.m.* day, daylight; light; daybreak; day time; opening, gap; **broderie à jours**, open-work embroidery; **donner le jour à**, to give birth to; **plat du jour**, today's special; **se faire jour**, to force one's way through; **un jour de fête**, a holiday.
Jourdain [ʒur'dɛ̃], **le**, *m.* Jordan (*river*).
journal [ʒur'nal], *n.m.* (*pl.* **-aux**) journal, diary; newspaper; (*Comm.*) day-book.
journalier [ʒurna'lje], *a.* (*fem.* **-ière**) daily, diurnal.—*n.m.* journeyman, day laborer.
journalisme [ʒurna'lism], *n.m.* journalism.
journaliste [ʒurna'list], *n.* journalist.
journée [ʒur'ne], *n.f.* day (time), day's work *or* wages; day's journey; battle; historic day; **toute la journée**, all day (long).
journellement [ʒurnɛl'mã], *adv.* daily, every day.
joute [ʒut], *n.f.* joust, tilting match; contest; (*C*) game.
jouter [ʒu'te], *v.i.* to joust, to tilt.
jouteur [ʒu'tœːr], *n.m.* tilter; (*fig.*) antagonist, adversary.
jovial [ʒɔ'vjal], *a.* (*m. pl.* **-aux**) jovial, jolly, merry.
jovialement [ʒɔvjal'mã], *adv.* jovially.
jovialité [ʒɔvjali'te], *n.f.* joviality, jollity.
joyau [ʒwa'jo], *n.m.* (*pl.* **-aux**) jewel.
joyeusement [ʒwajøz'mã], *adv.* cheerfully, joyfully.
joyeuseté [ʒwajøz'te], *n.f.* (*fam.*) joke, jest.

joyeux [ʒwa'jø], *a.* (*fem.* **-euse**) joyful, merry; cheerful.
jubilaire [ʒybi'lɛːr], *a.* jubilee; (*fig.*) of fifty years' standing (*of persons etc.*).
jubilant [ʒybi'lã], *a.* jubilant, delighted.
jubilation [ʒybila'sjɔ̃], *n.f.* jubilation, rejoicing.
jubilé [ʒybi'le], *n.m.* jubilee; (*fig.*) golden wedding.
jubiler [ʒybi'le], *v.i.* to jubilate, to exult.
jucher [ʒy'ʃe], *v.i.* to roost, to perch; to lodge (*at the top of a house etc.*). **se jucher**, *v.r.* to go to roost; to perch (*oneself*).
juchoir [ʒy'ʃwaːr], *n.m.* roosting-place, perch.
judaïque [ʒyda'ik], *a.* Judaical, Jewish.
judaïsme [ʒyda'ism], *n.m.* Judaism.
judas [ʒy'da], *n.m.* Judas, traitor; peep-hole (*in a door etc.*).
Judée [ʒy'de], **la**, *f.* Judaea.
judicature [ʒydika'tyːr], *n.f.* judicature, magistracy.
judiciaire [ʒydi'sjɛːr], *a.* judiciary, judicial; legal.
judiciairement [ʒydisjɛr'mã], *adv.* judicially, by authority of justice.
judicieusement [ʒydisjøz'mã], *adv.* judiciously, discreetly.
judicieux [ʒydi'sjø], *a.* (*fem.* **-euse**) judicious, wise, discreet.
juge [ʒy:ʒ], *n.m.* judge; magistrate, justice; (*pl.*) bench.
jugé [ʒy'ʒe], *a.* judged.—*n.m.* **au jugé**, at a guess.
jugement [ʒyʒ'mã], *n.m.* judgment; opinion; trial; sentence; good sense; **jugement arbitral**, award; **jugement provisoire**, decree nisi; **jugement définitif**, decree absolute.
juger [ʒy'ʒe], *v.t.* (*conjug. like* MANGER) to judge; to try; to pass sentence on; to consider, to think.—*v.i.* to judge (*de*), to give judgment, to deem. **se juger**, *v.r.* to judge oneself; to deem oneself; to be judged.
jugulaire [ʒygy'lɛːr], *a.* (*Anat.*) jugular.—*n.f.* jugular vein; chin strap.
juguler [ʒygy'le], *v.t.* to strangle; (*fig.*) to torment; to fleece.
juif [ʒɥif], *a.* (*fem.* **juive**) Jewish.—*n.m.* (**Juif**, *fem.* **Juive**) Jew, Jewess.
juillet [ʒɥi'jɛ], *n.m.* July.
juin [ʒɥɛ̃], *n.m.* June.
juiverie [ʒɥi'vri], *n.f.* ghetto (*Jews' quarter*).
jujube [ʒy'ʒyb], *n.f.* jujube (*fruit*).—*n.m.* or **pâte de jujube**, jujube (*lozenge*).
julep [ʒy'lɛp], *n.m.* julep.
julienne [ʒy'ljɛn], *n.f.* julienne (*vegetable soup*).
jumeau [ʒy'mo], *a.* (*fem.* **-elle**, *m. pl.* **-eaux**) twin; double (*of fruit etc.*).—*n.m.* twin (brother).
jumelage [ʒym'la:ʒ], *n.m.* twinning (*of towns etc.*).
jumelé [ʒym'le], *a.* twin, in couples; **maison jumelée**, semi-detached house; (*horse racing*) **pari jumelé**, each-way bet.
jumelle [ʒy'mɛl], *n.f.* twin (sister); (*pl.*) binoculars; **jumelles de campagne**, field glasses; **jumelles de théâtre**, opera glasses; **jumelles de manchettes**, cuff links.
jument [ʒy'mã], *n.f.* mare.
jungle [ʒɔ̃:gl], *n.f.* jungle.
jupe [ʒyp], *n.f.* skirt.

Jupiter [ʒypi'tɛr], *m.* Jupiter, Jove.
jupon [ʒy'pɔ̃], *n.m.* petticoat.
juré [ʒy're], *a.* sworn.—*n.m.* juror, juryman.
jurement [ʒyr'mɑ̃], *n.m.* oath; swearing.
jurer [ʒy're], *v.t.* to swear by; to swear, to vow, to take an oath that; to blaspheme.—*v.i.* to swear, to take an oath; to blaspheme; (*fig.*) to contrast, to jar, to clash (*of colors etc.*).
juridiction [ʒyridik'sjɔ̃], *n.f.* jurisdiction; department, province.
juridique [ʒyri'dik], *a.* juridical, judicial, legal.
juridiquement [ʒyridik'mɑ̃], *adv.* juridically, judicially.
jurisprudence [ʒyrispry'dɑ̃:s], *n.f.* jurisprudence.
juriste [ʒy'rist], *n.m.* jurist.
juron [ʒy'rɔ̃], *n.m.* oath, curse, swear word.
jury [ʒy'ri], *n.m.* jury; board, committee.
jus [ʒy], *n.m.* juice; gravy.
jusque or **jusques** [ʒysk], *prep.* even to, as far as; till, until; down to; up to.
juste [ʒyst], *a.* just, equitable; fair, legitimate, lawful; proper, fit; exact; well-fitting; tight; *au plus juste prix*, at the lowest price; *un homme juste*, a righteous man.—*n.m.* upright man, virtuous man; what is just.—*adv.* just, exactly, precisely; (*Mus.*) true.
justement [ʒystə'mɑ̃], *adv.* justly, precisely; justifiably.
justesse [ʒys'tɛs], *n.f.* justness, exactness, precision, accuracy; appropriateness.
justice [ʒys'tis], *n.f.* justice; righteousness, probity; fairness, impartiality; reason; courts of justice, judges; *palais de justice*, law court.
justifiable [ʒysti'fjabl], *a.* justifiable; warrantable.
justification [ʒystifika'sjɔ̃], *n.f.* justification, vindication, proof.
justifier [ʒysti'fje], *v.t.* to justify, to vindicate, to make good. **se justifier**, *v.r.* to justify, clear *or* vindicate oneself.
jute [ʒyt], *n.m.* jute.
juteux [ʒy'tø], *a.* (*fem.* **-euse**) juicy.
juvénile [ʒyve'nil], *a.* juvenile, youthful.
juvénilement [ʒyvenil'mɑ̃], *adv.* boyishly, in a juvenile manner.
juxtaposer [ʒykstapo'ze], *v.t.* to place side by side. **se juxtaposer**, *v.r.* to be in juxtaposition.
juxtaposition [ʒykstapozi'sjɔ̃], *n.f.* juxtaposition.

K

K, k [kɑ], *n.m.* the eleventh letter of the alphabet; *Échelle K* (*viz. Kelvin*), absolute scale (*of temperature*).
kakatoès [kakatɔ'ɛs], [CACATOIS].
kaki [ka'ki], *a. inv.* khaki (*color*).
kaléidoscope [kaleidɔs'kɔp], *n.m.* kaleidoscope.
kangourou [kɑ̃gu'ru], *n.m.* kangaroo.

kaolin [kaɔ'lɛ̃], *n.m.* kaolin, porcelain clay, china clay.
kapok or **kapoc** [ka'pɔk], *n.m.* kapok.
kascher or **kacher** [ka'ʃer], **kachir** [ka'ʃir], *a.* (*Jew. Relig.*) kosher.
kayac [ka'jak], *n.m.* kayak.
Kénia [ke'nja], **le**, *m.* Kenya.
képi [ke'pi], *n.m.* kepi, military cap; peak cap.
kermesse [kɛr'mɛs], *n.f.* kermis (*in the Netherlands*); kermesse; village fair.
kérosène [kero'zɛ:n], *n.m.* kerosene, coal oil.
kidnapper [kidna'pe], *v.t.* to kidnap.
kilo [ki'lo], *n.m.* (*abbr.*) kilogramme.
kilocycle [kilɔ'sikl], *n.m.* kilocycle.
kilogramme [kilɔ'gram], *n.m.* kilogramme (*2.2 lb. avoirdupois*).
kilomètre [kilɔ'mɛtr], *n.m.* kilometre (*1093.6 yards*).
kilowatt [kilɔ'wat], *n.m.* kilowatt.
kimono [kimɔ'no], *n.m.* kimono.
kiosque [kjɔsk], *n.m.* kiosk; (*Naut.*) house; *kiosque à journaux*, newspaper stand; *kiosque à musique*, bandstand.
klakson or **klaxon** [klak'sɔ̃], *n.m.* klaxon, hooter, horn.
kleptomane [klɛptɔ'man], *a.* and *n.* kleptomaniac.
kleptomanie [klɛptɔma'ni], *n.f.* kleptomania.
kola or **cola** [kɔ'la], *n.m.* kola.
Kominform [kɔmɛ̃'fɔrm], *n.m.* Cominform.
Komintern [kɔmɛ̃'tɛrn], *n.m.* Comintern.
Koweit [kɔ'weit], **le**, *m.* Kuwait.
kyrielle [ki'rjɛl], *n.f.* litany; (*fig.*) long string (*of words etc.*), long tedious story.
kyste [kist], *n.m.* (*Path.*) cyst.

L

L, l [ɛl], *n.m.* or *f.* the twelfth letter of the alphabet.
l', *art.* and *pron.* (*by elision of* **le** or **la**) the; him, her, it.
la (1) [la], *art* and *pron. f.* the; her, it.
la (2) [la], *n.m.* (*Mus.*) la; the note A.
là [la], *adv.* and *int.* there, thither; then (*of time*); *çà et là*, here and there; *là là*, now now! there! there now! *là où*, where; *par là*, that way.
là-bas [la'ba], *adv.* there, over there.
labbe [lab], *n.m.* (*Orn.*) skua.
label [la'bɛl], *n.m.* (*Ind.*) label; brand, mark.
labeur [la'bœ:r], *n.m.* labor, work, toil.
laboratoire [labɔra'twa:r], *n.m.* laboratory.
laborieusement [labɔrjøz'mɑ̃], *adv.* laboriously; painfully.
laborieux [labɔ'rjø], *a.* (*fem.* **-euse**) laborious, hard-working.
labour [la'bu:r], *n.m.* ploughing, tillage; arable land.
labourable [labu'rabl], *a.* arable.
labourage [labu'ra:ʒ], *n.m.* tillage, ploughing; dressing.
labourer [labu're], *v.t.* to plough, to till; to dig, to turn up; to dress; to toil through.

laboureur [labu'rœːr], *n.m.* husbandman, plowman.

laboureuse [labu'røːz], *n.f.* tractor plow.

laburne [la'byrn], *n.m.* laburnum.

labyrinthe [labi'rɛ̃ːt], *n.m.* labyrinth, maze.

lac [lak], *n.m.* lake.

laçage [la'saːʒ], *n.m.* lacing.

lacer [la'se], *v.t.* (*conjug. like* COMMENCER) to lace.

lacération [lasera'sjɔ̃], *n.f.* laceration.

lacérer [lase're], *v.t.* (*conjug. like* CÉDER) to lacerate, to tear.

lacet [la'sɛ], *n.m.* lace, shoe-lace; noose; bow-string (*for strangling*); winding, hairpin bend (*of road etc.*); (*pl.*) toils.

lâche [lɑːʃ], *a.* loose, slack; faint-hearted, cowardly; base, mean, shameful.—*n.* coward, craven; dastard.—*adv.* loosely.

lâché [lɑ'ʃe], *a.* slovenly, slipshod.

lâchement [lɑʃ'mɑ̃], *adv.* in a dastardly *or* cowardly manner; loosely; shamefully.

lâcher [lɑ'ʃe], *v.t.* to loosen, to slacken; to let go, to release; to unbind; to blurt out; to let fly, to discharge; to let down (*someone*).—*v.i.* to slacken, to become loose; to slip; (*Spt.*) to give up.

lâcheté [lɑʃ'te], *n.f.* cowardice; baseness, meanness.

lacis [la'si], *n.m.* network.

laconique [lakɔ'nik], *a.* laconic.

laconiquement [lakɔnik'mɑ̃], *adv.* laconically.

lacs [lɑ], *n.m. inv.* string; noose; trap; *lacs d'amour*, love-knot.

lacté [lak'te], *a.* lacteous, milky; *la voie lactée*, the Milky Way.

lacune [la'kyn], *n.f.* gap, break, hiatus, blank.

là-dedans [ladə'dɑ̃], *a.* in there.

là-dehors [ladə'ɔːr], *adv.* outside.

là-dessous [la'tsu], *adv.* under there.

là-dessus [la'tsy], *adv.* on that; thereupon.

ladite [la'dit], [LEDIT].

ladre [lɑːdr], *a.* leprous; (*fig.*) mean, sordid, stingy; unfeeling.—*n.m.* (*fem.* **-esse**) leper; (*fig.*) sordid person.

ladrerie [lɑdrə'ri], *n.f.* sordid avarice, stinginess.

lagune [la'gyn], *n.f.* lagoon.

là-haut [la'o], *adv.* up there; upstairs.

lai [lɛ], *n.m.* lay (*poem, song*).

laïc [LAÏQUE].

laid [lɛ], *a.* ugly, unsightly; unseemly, unbecoming.—*n.m.* ugliness; (*fem.* **-e**) ugly person, creature etc.; naughty boy *or* girl.

laidement [lɛd'mɑ̃], *adv.* in an ugly way.

laideron [lɛd'rɔ̃], *n.m.* (*fem.* **-onne**) ugly creature.

laideur [lɛ'dœːr], *n.f.* ugliness, uncomeliness; unseemliness.

laie [lɛ], *n.f.* path (*in a forest*).

lainage [lɛ'naːʒ], *n.m.* woollens, woollen goods.

laine [lɛn], *n.f.* wool; *laine filée*, yarn; *laine peignée*, worsted; *tapis de haute laine*, thick-pile carpet; *tout laine*, pure wool.

lainerie [lɛn'ri], *n.f.* woollen goods, woollens; wool trade, shop etc.

laineux [lɛ'nø], *a.* (*fem.* **-euse**) woolly, fleecy.

lainier [lɛ'nje], *a.* (*fem.* **-ière**) of wool, woollen.—*n.m.* (*fem.* **-ière**) wool merchant; wool worker.

laïque *or* **laïc** [la'ik], *a.* lay, secular.—*n.* layman, lay person.

laisse [lɛːs], *n.f.* string, leash, lead.

laisser [lɛ'se], *v.t.* to leave, to quit; to leave behind, to part with; to bequeath; to permit, to let, to allow; to let alone; to leave off; to give up. **se laisser**, *v.r.* to allow oneself, to let oneself.

laisser-aller [lɛsea'le], *n.m.* unconstraint, negligence; slovenliness; indolence.

laisser-faire [lɛse'fɛːr], *n.m.* non-interference.

laissez-passer [lɛsepɑ'se], *n.m. inv.* permit, leave, pass.

lait [lɛ], *n.m.* milk; *au lait*, with milk; *lait de chaux*, whitewash; *lait de poule*, eggflip; *petit-lait* *or* *lait clair*, whey.

laitage [lɛ'taːʒ], *n.m.* milk puddings; milk products.

laiterie [lɛ'tri], *n.f.* dairy, dairy-farm.

laiteux [lɛ'tø], *a.* (*fem.* **-euse**) lacteous, milky.

laitier [lɛ'tje], *a.* (*fem.* **-ière**) pertaining to milk; having milk, milch (*of cows*).—*n.m.* (*fem.*-**ière**) milkman; milkmaid, dairy maid. —*n.f.* (**-ière**) milch cow; milk truck *or* cart.

laiton [lɛ'tɔ̃], *n.m.* brass, latten.

laitue [lɛ'ty], *n.f.* lettuce.

lama [la'ma], *n.m.* lama (*priest*); llama.

lambeau [lɑ̃'bo], *n.m.* (*pl.* **-eaux**) shred; rag; fragment, scrap.

lambin [lɑ̃'bɛ̃], *a.* slow, dawdling.—*n.m.* (*fem.* **-e**) dawdler, slowcoach.

lambiner [lɑ̃bi'ne], *v.i.* to dawdle, to dilly-dally.

lambrequin [lɑ̃brə'kɛ̃], *n.m.* valance, cut-out, pelmet.

lambris [lɑ̃'bri] *n.m.* panelling; wainscot; ceiling; (*fig.*) mansion, palace; canopy.

lambrissage [lɑ̃bri'saːʒ], *n.m.* wainscoting, panelling.

lambrisser [lɑ̃bri'se], *v.t.* to panel, to wainscot.

lame [lam], *n.f.* thin plate, leaf of metal; foil; knife (*of mower etc.*), blade; (*fig.*) sword; wave, billow.

lamé [la'me], *a.* spangled with gold *or* silver.

lamentable [lamɑ̃'tabl], *a.* lamentable, sad, distressing; pitiful.

lamentablement [lamɑ̃tablə'mɑ̃], *adv.* woefully.

lamentation [lamɑ̃ta'sjɔ̃], *n.f.* lamentation, wailing; lament; whining.

lamenter (se) [sǝlamɑ̃'te], *v.r.* to lament, to bewail.

laminage [lami'naːʒ], *n.m.* laminating; rolling (*of gold etc.*).

laminer [lami'ne], *v.t.* to laminate, to roll.

laminoir [lami'nwaːr], *n.m.* flattening mill; rolling mill.

lampe [lɑ̃ːp], *n.f.* lamp; (*Rad. Tel.*) tube; *lampe de bord*, (*Motor.*) dashboard light; *lampe de poche*, electric flashlight.

lampion [lɑ̃'pjɔ̃], *n.m.* illumination lamp, fairy-light; Chinese lantern; (*slang*) cocked hat.

lampiste [lɑ̃'pist], *n.m.* lamp maker; lamp lighter.

lampisterie [lɑ̃pis'tri], *n.f.* lamp room.

lamproie [lɑ̃'prwa], *n.f.* lamprey.

lance [lɑ̃ːs], *n.f.* lance, spear; staff, flagstaff; nozzle (*of a fire-hose*).

lance-flammes [lɑ̃s'flɑm], *n.m. inv.* flame-thrower.
lancement [lɑ̃s'mɑ̃], *n.m.* throwing, darting; launching, launch.
lance-pierres [lɑ̃s'pjɛ:r], *n.m. inv.* catapult.
lancer [lɑ̃'se], *v.t. (conjug. like* COMMENCER) to fling, to hurl, to throw; to launch; to shoot forth, to dart; to issue (*a warrant etc.*). **se lancer**, *v.r.* to dart, to spring; to rush, to fly; to launch out; (*fig.*) to make a start.
lancette [lɑ̃'sɛt], *n.f.* lancet.
lancier [lɑ̃'sje], *n.m.* lancer.
lancinant [lɑ̃si'nɑ̃], *a.* shooting (*of pains*).
lande [lɑ̃:d], *n.f.* waste land, moor, heath.
langage [lɑ̃'ga:ʒ], *n.m.* language; speech, diction.
lange [lɑ̃:ʒ], *n.m.* diaper; swaddling-cloth; (*pl.*) swaddling clothes.
langoureusement [lɑ̃gurøz'mɑ̃], *adv.* languishingly, languidly.
langoureux [lɑ̃gu'rø], *a.* (*fem.* **-euse**) languishing, languid.
langouste [lɑ̃'gust], *n.f.* spiny lobster.
langoustine [lɑ̃gus'tin], *n.f.* large Brittany prawn; Dublin Bay prawn.
langue [lɑ̃:g] *n.f.* tongue; language; strip (*of land*); **avoir la langue bien pendue** or **bien affilée**, to have the gift of the gab; **avoir la langue liée**, to be tongue-tied.
languette [lɑ̃'gɛt], *n.f.* small tongue; tongue-like strip; partition; tongue (*of instruments*); index (*of a balance*); tongue (*of shoe*).
langueur [lɑ̃'gœ:r], *n.f.* apathy, languor; weakness, weariness; debility.
languir [lɑ̃'gi:r], *v.i.* to languish, to pine away, to droop; to linger; to flag.
languissant [lɑ̃gi'sɑ̃], *a.* languid, languishing, pining; (*Comm.*) dull, inactive.
lanière [la'njɛ:r], *n.f.* thong, lash.
lanoline [lanɔ'lin], *n.f.* lanoline.
lanterne [lɑ̃'tɛrn], *n.f.* lantern; street lamp; (*Arch.*) skylight; dawdler; **lanterne vénitienne**, Chinese lantern.
lanterner [lɑ̃tɛr'ne], *v.i.* to dawdle, to trifle away one's time.
Laos [laɔs], le, *m.* Laos.
laotien [laɔ'sjɛ̃], *a.* (*fem.* **-enne**) Laotian.— *n.m.* (**Laotien**, *fem.* **-enne**) Laotian (*person*).
lapement [lap'mɑ̃], *n.m.* lapping.
laper [la'pe], *v.t., v.i.* to lap (up).
lapidaire [lapi'dɛ:r], *a.* and *n.m.* lapidary.
lapidation [lapida'sjɔ̃], *n.f.* lapidation, stoning.
lapider [lapi'de], *v.t.* to lapidate, to stone to death; (*fig.*) to pelt, to abuse.
lapin [la'pɛ̃], *n.m.* rabbit.
lapis [la'pi:s], **lapis lazuli** [lapislazy'li], *n.m. inv.* lapis lazuli.
lapon [la'pɔ̃], *a.* (*fem.* **-onne**) Lapp.—*n.m.* Lappish (*language*); (**Lapon**, *fem.* **-onne**) Laplander.
Laponie [lapɔ'ni], **la**, *f.* Lapland.
laps (1) [laps], *n.m.* lapse (*of time*).
laps (2) [laps], *a.* *lapsed, fallen into heresy.
lapsus [lap'sy:s], *n.m. inv.* slip, mistake.
laquais [la'kɛ], *n.m. inv.* lackey, footman?
laque [lak], *n.f.* lacquer, lac, lake (*paint*).— *n.m.* lacquer.
laquelle [la'kɛl], [LEQUEL].
laquer [la'ke], *v.t.* to lacquer, to japan.
larcin [lar'sɛ̃], *n.m.* larceny, pilfering; petty theft; **larcin littéraire**, plagiarism.

lard [la:r], *n.m.* fat (*esp. of pigs*); bacon; **flèche de lard**, flitch of bacon; **tranche de lard**, rasher of bacon.
larder [lar'de], *v.t.* to lard; to pink, to run through, to pierce.
lardon [lar'dɔ̃], *n.m.* thin slice of bacon; (*fam.*) child, kid, brat.
large [larʒ], *a.* broad, wide; large, great, extensive; generous, liberal; lax, loose.— *n.m.* breadth, width; offing, open sea; **au large !** keep off! sheer off! **au large de Dieppe**, off Dieppe.
largement [larʒ'mɑ̃], *adv.* largely, abundantly; fully; liberally.
largesse [lar'ʒɛs], *n.f.* largess, bounty, munificence.
largeur [lar'ʒœ:r], *n.f.* breadth, width; amplitude.
larme [larm] *n.f.* tear; drop; **fondre en larmes**, to burst into tears.
larmoiement [larmwa'mɑ̃], *n.m.* watering of the eyes.
larmoyant [larmwa'jɑ̃], *a.* weeping, in tears; tearful, whining.
larmoyer [larmwa'je], *v.i.* (*conjug. like* EMPLOYER) to shed tears; to whine, to snivel; to water (*of the eyes*).
larron [la'rɔ̃], *n.m.* thief.
larve [larv], *n.f.* larva, grub.
laryngite [larɛ̃'ʒit], *n.f.* laryngitis.
larynx [la'rɛ̃:ks], *n.m. inv.* larynx.
las! (1) [lɑ], *int.* alas!
las (2) [lɑ], *a.* (*fem.* **lasse**) tired, weary, fatigued; bored; disgusted.
lascif [la'sif], *a.* (*fem.* **-cive**) lascivious, lewd, wanton.
lascivement [lasiv'mɑ̃], *adv.* lasciviously.
lassant [lɑ'sɑ̃], *a.* tiresome, wearisome, tedious.
lasser [lɑ'se], *v.t.* to tire, to weary, to fatigue, to wear out. **se lasser**, *v.r.* to tire, to grow tired, to be wearied.
lassitude [lɑsi'tyd], *n.f.* lassitude, weariness.
lasso [la'so], *n.m.* lasso.
latent [la'tɑ̃], *a.* latent, concealed, secret.
latéral [late'ral], *a.* (*m. pl.* **-aux**) lateral, side.
latéralement [lateral'mɑ̃], *adv.* laterally.
latin [la'tɛ̃], *a.* Latin.—*n.m.* Latin (*language*); **latin de cuisine**, dog Latin.—*n.m.* (**Latin**, *fem.* **-ine**) Latin (*person*).
latitude [lati'tyd], *n.f.* latitude; room, space, margin.
latte [lat], *n.f.* lath.
latter [la'te], *v.t.* to lath.
lattis [la'ti], *n.m.* lathing, lath-work; laths.
laudanum [loda'nɔm], *n.m.* laudanum.
laudatif [loda'tif], *a.* (*fem.* **-tive**) laudatory.
lauréat [lɔre'a], *a.* laureate.—*n.m.* (*fem.* **-e**) prize-winner.
laurier [lɔ'rje], *n.m.* laurel, bay tree; (*fig.*) glory, honor.
lavable [la'vabl], *a.* washable.
lavabo [lava'bo], *n.m.* wash-basin; washstand; (*pl.*) conveniences.
lavage [la'va:ʒ], *n.m.* washing; dilution.
lavande [la'vɑ̃:d], *n.f.* lavender.
lavandière [lavɑ̃'djɛ:r], *n.f.* laundress, washerwoman; (*Orn.*) gray wagtail.
lavasse [la'vas], *n.f.* washy soup or wine.
lave [la:v], *n.f.* lava.
lavé [la've], *a.* washed out, faint.

lave-dos [lav'do], *n.m. inv.* back brush.
lavement [lav'mɑ̃], *n.m.* (*Med.*) enema.
laver [la've], *v.t.* to wash, to cleanse; to purify; to expiate; *laver à grande eau*, to swill; *laver la vaisselle*, to wash up; *machine à laver*, washing machine. **se laver**, *v.r.* to wash, to wash oneself; to clear oneself (*of an accusation*).
lavette [la'vɛt], *n.f.* dish mop.
laveur [la'vœ:r], *n.m.* (*fem.* **-euse**) washer, scourer; *laveuse de vaisselle*, scullery maid.
lavoir [la'vwa:r], *n.m.* wash house.
laxatif [laksa'tif], *a.* (*fem.* **-tive**) laxative, opening.—*n.m.* laxative.
layette [lɛ'jɛt], *n.f.* box; baby's trousseau *or* outfit.
le [lə], *art.* and *pron. m.* the; him, it; so; *je le crois*, I think so.
lécher [le'ʃe], *v.t.* (*conjug. like* CÉDER) to lick; to lick up; (*fig.*) to labor, to polish, to elaborate, to overdo; *lécher les vitrines*, to go window-shopping.
leçon [lə'sɔ̃], *n.f.* lesson; reading (*of a text*).
lecteur [lɛk'tœ:r], *n.m.* (*fem.* **-trice**) reader, lector.
lecture [lɛk'ty:r], *n.f.* reading; perusal.
ledit [lə'di], *a.* (*fem.* **ladite**, *pl.* **lesdit(e)s**) the (afore)said, the same.
légal [le'gal], *a.* (*m. pl.* **-aux**) legal, lawful, legitimate.
légalement [legal'mɑ̃], *adv.* legally, lawfully.
légaliser [legali'ze], *v.t.* to legalize.
légalité [legali'te], *n.f.* legality, lawfulness.
légataire [lega'tɛ:r], *n.* legatee.
légation [lega'sjɔ̃], *n.f.* legateship; legation.
légendaire [leʒɑ̃'dɛ:r], *a.* and *n.m.* legendary.
légende [le'ʒɑ̃:d], *n.f.* legend; inscription; caption; key (*to map etc.*).
léger [le'ʒe], *a.* (*fem.* **-ère**) light; slight; buoyant; fleet, fast; nimble; fickle; faint; thoughtless.
légèrement [leʒɛr'mɑ̃], *adv.* lightly, slightly; swiftly; thoughtlessly.
légèreté [leʒɛr'te], *n.f.* lightness; swiftness; fickleness; frivolity; thoughtlessness.
légiférer [leʒife're], *v.i.* (*conjug. like* CÉDER) to legislate.
légion [le'ʒjɔ̃], *n.f.* legion; great number, host.
légionnaire [leʒjɔ'nɛ:r], *n.m.* legionary; member of the Legion of Honor; soldier of the Foreign Legion.
législateur [leʒisla'tœ:r], *a.* (*fem.* **-trice**) legislative, lawgiving.—*n.m.* (*fem.* **-trice**) legislator.
législatif [leʒisla'tif], *a.* (*fem.* **-tive**) legislative.
législation [leʒisla'sjɔ̃], *n.f.* legislation.
législature [leʒisla'ty:r], *n.f.* legislature.
légitime [leʒi'tim], *a.* lawful, legitimate, rightful; justifiable.
légitimement [leʒitim'mɑ̃], *adv.* legitimately, lawfully; justifiably.
légitimer [leʒiti'me], *v.t.* to legitimate; to justify; to recognize.
légitimité [leʒitimi'te], *n.f.* legitimacy, lawfulness.
legs [lɛ], *n.m.* legacy, bequest.
léguer [le'ge], *v.t.* (*conjug. like* CÉDER) to leave by will, to bequeath.
légume [le'gym], *n.m.* vegetable.—*n.f. pl.* (*fam.*) *les grosses légumes*, the bigwigs.

légumier [legy'mje], *a.* (*fem.* **-ière**) of vegetables.—*n.m.* vegetable dish.
lendemain [lɑ̃d'mɛ̃], *n.m.* morrow, next day, day after.
lent [lɑ̃], *a.* slow, tardy; backward; sluggish, slack.
lentement [lɑ̃t'mɑ̃], *adv.* slowly, tardily; sluggishly.
lenteur [lɑ̃'tœ:r], *n.f.* slowness; tardiness.
lenticulaire [lɑ̃tiky'lɛ:r], **lenticulé** [lɑ̃tiky'le], *a.* lenticular.
lentille [lɑ̃'ti:j], *n.f.* lentil; lens; (*pl.*) freckles; *lentille d'eau*, duckweed.
léonin [leɔ'nɛ̃], *a.* leonine.
léopard [leɔ'pa:r], *n.m.* leopard.
lèpre [lɛpr], *n.f.* leprosy.
lépreux [le'prø], *a.* (*fem.* **-euse**) leprous.—*n.m.* (*fem.* **-euse**) leper.
léproserie [lepro'zri], *n.f.* leper hospital.
lequel [lə'kɛl], *pron. m.* (*fem.* **laquelle**, *m. pl.* **lesquels**, *f. pl.* **lesquelles**) who, whom, that, which; (*inter.*) which one, which ?
les [le], *art.* and *pron. pl.* the; them.
lèse-majesté [lɛzmaʒɛs'te], *n.f.* high treason, lese-majesty.
léser [le'ze], *v.t.* (*conjug. like* CÉDER) to wrong; to injure, to hurt.
lésine [le'zin], *n.f.* niggardliness, stinginess.
lésiner [lezi'ne], *v.i.* to be stingy *or* mean; to haggle.
lésinerie [lezin'ri], *n.f.* stinginess, meanness.
lésion [le'zjɔ̃], *n.f.* (*Law*) wrong, injury; (*Surg.*) lesion.
lessive [lɛ'si:v], *n.f.* wash, linen washed *or* to be washed, washing.
leste [lɛst], *a.* brisk, nimble, active; light; smart; sharp; improper, free.
lestement [lɛst'mɑ̃], *adv.* briskly, cleverly; flippantly; freely.
lester [lɛs'te], *v.t.* to ballast. **se lester**, *v.r.* (*fam.*) to take in ballast; to line one's stomach.
léthargie [letar'ʒi], *n.f.* lethargy.
léthargique [letar'ʒik], *a.* lethargic.
lette [lɛt], **letton** [lɛ'tɔ̃] (*fem.* **-onne**), *a.* Latvian.—*n.m.* Latvian (*language*); (**Lette, Letton,** *fem.* **-onne**) Latvian (*person*).
Lettonie [lɛtɔ'ni], **la,** *f.* Latvia.
lettre [lɛtr], *n.f.* letter, note; (*Print.*) character, type; (*pl.*) literature, letters; *les belles-lettres*, humanities; *lettre de change*, bill of exchange; *lettre d'envoi*, covering letter; *lettre de voiture*, way-bill.
lettré [lɛ'tre], *a.* cultured, literate, well-read; literary.—*n.m.* (*fem.* **-ée**) scholar.
leur [lœ:r], *a. poss.* their.—*poss. pron. le leur, la leur* or *les leurs*, theirs.—*pers. pron.* to them, them.
leurre [lœ:r], *n.m.* lure, decoy; bait; snare, trap.
leurrer [lœ're], *v.t.* to lure, to entice, to decoy; to ensnare. **se leurrer**, *v.r.* to delude oneself.
levage [lə'va:ʒ], *n.m.* raising, lifting.
levain [lə'vɛ̃], *n.m.* leaven; (*fig.*) germ.
levant [lə'vɑ̃], *a.* rising.—*n.m.* east; rising sun; Levant.
levantin [lavɑ̃'tɛ̃], *a.* Levantine.—*n.m.* (**Levantin,** *fem.* **-ine**) Levantine (*person*).
levé [lə've], *a.* lifted up, raised; up, out of bed.

levée [lə've], *n.f.* raising, lifting; levying; gathering (*crop, fruit etc.*); collection (*post-office*); embankment; swell (*of the sea*); (*Cards*) trick.
lever [lə've], *v.t.* (*conjug. like* AMENER) to lift, to lift up, to raise; to heave; to pull up; to weigh (*anchor*); to take away; to take out; to collect; to levy.—*v.i.* to come up; to spring up, to rise. **se lever**, *v.r.* to rise, to get up; to stand up; to heave (*of the sea*); to clear up (*of the weather*).
lever [lə've], *n.m.* rising, getting up; levee (*of king*).
levier [lə'vje], *n.m.* lever; crowbar, hand-spike.
levraut [lə'vro], *n.m.* leveret, young hare.
lèvre [lɛːvr], *n.f.* lip; rim.
lévrier [levri'e], *n.m.* greyhound.
levure [lə'vyːr], *n.f.* yeast.
lexique [lɛk'sik], *n.m.* lexicon; abridged dictionary.
lézard [le'zaːr], *n.m.* lizard.
lézarde [le'zard], *n.f.* crevice, crack, chink.
lézardé [lezar'de], *a.* cracked (*of walls etc.*).
lézarder [lezar'de], *v.t.* to crack (*walls etc.*). **se lézarder**, *v.r.* to crack, to become cracked.
liais [ljɛ], *n.m.* lias; blue limestone.
liaison [ljɛ'zõ], *n.f.* joining; connection, acquaintance; intimacy; (*Mil.*) liaison.
liane [ljan], *n.f.* liana, tropical creeper.
liant [ljɑ̃], *a.* supple, flexible; affable, sociable. —*n.m.* suppleness; sociability; gentleness.
liard [lja:r], *n.m.* liard (*half-farthing*).
liasse [ljas], *n.f.* bundle, file (*of papers*); wad (*of banknotes*).
Liban [li'bɑ̃], **le**, *m.* Lebanon.
libanais [liba'nɛ], *a.* Lebanese.—*n.m.* (**Libanais**, *fem.* **-aise**) Lebanese (*person*).
libation [liba'sjõ], *n.f.* libation; (*fig.*) potation.
libelle [li'bɛl], *n.m.* libel, lampoon.
libellé [libɛl'le], *a.* drawn up, specified.— *n.m.* wording, contents.
libellule [libɛl'lyl], *n.f.* dragon-fly.
libéral [libe'ral], *a.* (*m. pl.* **-aux**) liberal, generous, bountiful; (*Polit.*) liberal.
libéralement [liberal'mɑ̃], *adv.* liberally, bountifully, generously.
libéralisme [libera'lism], *n.m.* liberalism.
libéralité [liberali'te], *n.f.* generosity, open-handedness.
libérateur [libera'tœːr], *n.m.* (*fem.* **-trice**) deliverer, liberator, rescuer.
libération [libera'sjõ], *n.f.* liberation, deliverance; rescue, discharge.
libéré [libe're], *a.* liberated, discharged.
libérer [libe're], *v.t.* (*conjug. like* CÉDER) to liberate, to free; to discharge. **se libérer**, *v.r.* to free oneself, to clear oneself (*de*); to pay off one's debts.
Libéria [libe'rja], **le**, *m.* Liberia.
libérien [libe'rjɛ̃], *a.* (*fem.* **-enne**) Liberian. —*n.m.* (**Libérien**, *fem.* **-enne**) Liberian (*person*).
liberté [libɛr'te], *n.f.* liberty, freedom, ease.
libertin [libɛr'tɛ̃], *a.* libertine, licentious; dissolute.—*n.m.* (*fem.* **-e**) libertine, rake.
libertinage [liberti'naːʒ], *n.m.* libertinism, debauchery.
libraire [li'brɛːr], *n.* bookseller; **libraire-éditeur**, publisher and bookseller.

librairie [librɛ'ri], *n.f.* book trade; bookseller's shop.
libre [librə], *a.* free; at liberty; independent; undisciplined, unconfined; bold, broad; exempt; irregular (*of verse*).
libre-échange [librɛ'ʃɑ̃:ʒ], *n.m.* free trade.
libre-échangiste [librɛʃɑ̃'ʒist], *n.m.* (*pl.* **libre-échangistes**) free-trader.
librement [librə'mɑ̃], *adv.* freely, without restraint; boldly.
librettiste [librɛ'tist], *n.m.* librettist.
Libye [li'bi], **la**, *f.* Libya.
libyen [li'bjɛ̃], *a.* (*fem.* **-enne**) Libyan.—*n.m.* (**Libyen**, *fem.* **-enne**) Libyan (*person*).
lice [lis], *n.f.* lists, tilt yard.
licence [li'sɑ̃:s], *n.f.* license, leave, permission; licentiousness; licentiate's degree.
licencié [lisɑ̃'sje], *a.* licentiate; (*C*) **épicier licencié**, licensed grocer.—*n.m.* (*fem.* **-ée**) licenciate.
licenciement [lisɑ̃si'mɑ̃], *n.m.* disbanding.
licencier [lisɑ̃'sje], *v.t.* to disband (*troops*); to declare redundant, to lay off; to dismiss.
licencieusement [lisɑ̃sjøz'mɑ̃], *adv.* licentiously, dissolutely.
licencieux [lisɑ̃'sjø], *a.* (*fem.* **-euse**) licentious, dissolute.
licite [li'sit], *a.* licit, lawful, allowable.
licitement [lisit'mɑ̃], *adv.* lawfully, licitly.
licol [LICOU].
licorne [li'kɔrn], *n.f.* unicorn.
licou [li'ku], **licol** [li'kɔl], *n.m.* halter.
licteur [lik'tœːr], *n.m.* (*Rom. Ant.*) lictor.
lie [li], *n.f.* lees, dregs; (*fig.*) scum, refuse.
liège [ljɛ:ʒ], *n.m.* cork; cork tree.
lien [ljɛ̃], *n.m.* bond, tie, link; (*pl.*) bonds, shackles.
lier [lje], *v.t.* to fasten, to tie; to bind, to tie up; to join, to connect (*avec*); to engage in; (*Mus.*) to slur; to thicken (*a sauce etc.*). **se lier**, *v.r.* to become acquainted; to thicken (*of sauce etc.*).
lierre [ljɛ:r], *n.m.* ivy.
lieu [ljø], *n.m.* (*pl.* **lieux**) place, spot; position; cause; (*pl.*) premises, apartments; **au lieu de**, instead of; **avoir lieu**, to take place; **lieu commun**, commonplace.
lieue [ljø], *n.f.* league (*4 kilometres, 2¼ miles*).
lieur [ljœːr], *n.m.* (*fem.* **-euse**) (*Agric.*) binder (*person*).—*n.f.* (**-euse**) binder (*machine*).
lieutenance [ljøt'nɑ̃:s], *n.f.* lieutenancy.
lieutenant [ljøt'nɑ̃], *n.m.* lieutenant; right-hand man.
lièvre [ljɛ:vr], *n.m.* hare.
liftier [lif'tje], *n.m.* (*fem.* **-ière**) elevator operator.
ligament [liga'mɑ̃], *n.m.* ligament.
ligature [liga'tyːr], *n.f.* ligature.
ligaturer [ligaty're], *v.t.* to ligature, to splice.
lignage [li'naːʒ], *n.m.* lineage.
ligne [lin], *n.f.* line; row; path, way; cord; fishing line; order.
lignée [li'ne], *n.f.* issue, progeny, offspring.
ligoter [ligo'te], *v.t.* to bind, to tie up.
ligue [lig], *n.f.* league, confederacy.
liguer [li'ge], *v.t.* to unite in a league. **se liguer**, *v.r.* to league, to combine.
ligueur [li'gœːr], *n.m.* (*fem.* **-euse**) leaguer; plotter.
lilas [li'la], *a. inv.* lilac-colored. —*n.m.* lilac.
lilliputien [lilipy'sjɛ̃], *a.* (*fem.* **-enne**) Lilliputian.

limace [li'mas], *n.f.* slug; Archimedean screw.
limaçon [lima'sɔ̃], *n.m.* snail.
limbe [lɛ̃:b], *n.m.* (*Math.*, *Bot.* etc.) limb; (*Astron.*) border, halo; (*pl.*) limbo.
lime (1) [lim], *n.f.* file.
lime (2) [lim], *n.f.* lime, citron.
limer [li'me], *v.t.* to file, to smooth.
limeur [li'mœ:r], *n.m.* (*fem.* **-euse**) filer.— *n.f.* (**-euse**) finishing tool *or* machine.
limier [li'mje], *n.m.* bloodhound; (*fig.*) police spy, detective.
liminaire [limi'nɛ:r], *a.* prefatory.
limitatif [limita'tif], *a.* (*fem.* **-tive**) limiting, restrictive.
limitation [limitɑ'sjɔ̃], *n.f.* limitation.
limite [li'mit], *n.f.* limit, boundary; border; landmark.
limiter [limi'te], *v.t.* to limit, to bound; to confine.
limitrophe [limi'trɔf], *a.* neighboring, bordering.
limon [li'mɔ̃], *n.m.* silt, ooze, mud; shaft (*of a carriage*); sour lime (*fruit*).
limonade [limɔ'nad], *n.f.* lemonade.
limonadier [limɔna'dje], *n.m.* (*fem.* **-ière**) seller of lemonade.
limoneux [limɔ'nø], *a.* (*fem.* **-euse**) muddy, turbid, slimy; alluvial.
limonier [limɔ'nje], *n.m.* carriage horse; lime tree.
limonière [limɔ'njɛ:r], *n.f.* pair of shafts (*of wagon* etc.); wagon with two shafts.
limousin [limu'zɛ̃], *n.m.* stonemason.
limousine [limu'zin], *n.f.* limousine (*car*); coarse woollen cloak.
limpide [lɛ̃'pid], *a.* limpid, clear.
limpidité [lɛ̃pidi'te], *n.f.* limpidity.
lin [lɛ̃], *n.m.* flax; **graine de lin**, linseed; **huile de lin**, linseed oil; **toile de lin**, linen cloth.
linceul [lɛ̃'sœl], *n.m.* winding-sheet, shroud.
linéaire [line'ɛ:r], *a.* linear.
linéal [line'al], *a.* (*m. pl.* **-aux**) lineal, in a direct line.
linéament [linea'mã], *n.m.* lineament, feature; (*fig.*) trace, vestige.
linge [lɛ̃:ʒ], *n.m.* linen; piece, rag.
linger [lɛ̃'ʒe], *n.m.* (*fem.* **-ère**) linen dealer; maker of linen goods; seamstress (*of same*). —*n.f.* (**-ère**) wardrobe woman.
lingerie [lɛ̃'ʒri], *n.f.* linen trade; linen room; linen goods.
lingot [lɛ̃'go], *n.m.* ingot; bullion.
lingue [lɛ̃:g], *n.f.* (*Ichth.*) ling.
linguiste [lɛ̃'gɥist], *n.* linguist.
linguistique [lɛ̃gɥis'tik], *a.* linguistic.—*n.f.* linguistics.
linier [li'nje], *a.* (*fem.* **-ière**) of flax *or* linen.— *n.f.* (**-ière**) flax field.
linoléum [linɔle'ɔm], *n.m.* linoleum.
linon [li'nɔ̃], *n.m.* lawn (*fine linen*).
linot [li'no], *n.m.*, **linotte** [li'nɔt], *n.f.* linnet.
linotype [linɔ'tip], *n.f.* linotype.
linotypiste [linɔti'pist], *n.* linotype operator.
linteau [lɛ̃'to], *n.m.* (*pl.* **-eaux**) lintel.
lion [ljɔ̃], *n.m.* (*fem.* **lionne**) lion, lioness; (*fig.*) a bold, brave fellow.
lionceau [ljɔ̃'so], *n.m.* (*pl.* **-eaux**) young lion, lion's cub.
lippe [lip], *n.f.* thick lower lip; pouting lip.
lippu [li'py], *a.* thick-lipped.

liquéfaction [likefak'sjɔ̃], *n.f.* liquefaction.
liquéfiable [like'fjabl], *a.* liquefiable.
liquéfier [like'fje], *v.i.* and **se liquéfier**, *v.r.* to liquefy.
liqueur [li'kœ:r], *n.f.* liquid; liqueur, cordial; (*Chem.*) spirit.
liquidateur [likida'tœ:r], *n.m.* liquidator.
liquidation [likida'sjɔ̃], *n.f.* liquidation; settlement (*of debts* etc.); winding up (*of a business*); clearance sale.
liquide [li'kid], *a.* liquid; clear, net (*of money*).—*n.m.* liquid, fluid; drink.
liquider [liki'de], *v.t.* to liquidate, to settle; to wind up; to sell off; (*fam.*) to get rid of.
liquidité [likidi'te], *n.f.* liquidity, fluidity.
liquoreux [likɔ'rø], *a.* (*fem.* **-euse**) luscious, sweet.
liquoriste [likɔ'rist], *n.m.* wine and spirit merchant.
lire [li:r], *v.t. irr.* to read, to peruse, to study.
lis [lis], *n.m.* lily.
liseré [lizə're], *n.m.* piping; border, edge.
lisérer [lize're], *v.t.* (*conjug. like* CÉDER) to trim (*a dress* etc.) with piping.
liseron [liz'rɔ̃], **liset** [li'zɛ], *n.m.* (*Bot.*) convolvulus.
liseur [li'zœ:r], *n.m.* (*fem.* **-euse**) reader.
lisibilité [lizibili'te], *n.f.* legibility, readableness.
lisible [li'zibl], *a.* legible, readable.
lisiblement [lizibla'mã], *adv.* legibly.
lisière [li'zjɛ:r], *n.f.* selvedge, edge (*of cloth* etc.); border, verge, outskirts.
lissage [li'sa:ʒ], *n.m.* smoothing, glossing.
lisse (1) [lis], *a.* smooth; sleek; glossy.—*n.m.* smoothness, gloss.
lisse (2) [lis], *n.f.* rail, railing (*of ship*).
lisser [li'se], *v.t.* to smooth, to polish.
lisseur [li'sœ:r], *n.m.* (*fem.* **-euse**) polisher.
liste [list], *n.f.* list, roll; catalogue; schedule.
lit [li], *n.m.* bed; layer (*of clay, mortar*); direction, set (*of tide, current*); (*fig.*) marriage.
litanie [lita'ni], *n.f.* (*fig.*) rigmarole; (*pl.*) litany.
litée [li'te], *n.f.* litter (*of animals*).
literie [li'tri], *n.f.* bedding.
lithographe [litɔ'graf], *n.m.* lithographer.
lithographie [litɔgra'fi], *n.f.* lithography; lithograph.
lithographier [litɔgra'fje], *v.t.* to lithograph.
lithographique [litɔgra'fik] *a.* lithographic.
Lithuanie [LITUANIE].
lithuanien [LITUANIEN].
litière [li'tjɛ:r], *n.f.* stable litter; litter (*for carrying sick persons* etc.).
litigant [liti'gã], *a.* litigant.
litige [li'ti:ʒ], *n.m.* litigation, legal dispute; (*fig.*) strife.
litigieux [liti'ʒjø], *a.* (*fem.* **-euse**) litigious, given to lawsuits.
litre [litr], *n.m.* litre (*1.76 pints*).
littéraire [lite're:r], *a.* literary; **propriété littéraire**, copyright.
littérairement [literɛr'mã], *adv.* in a literary manner *or* way.
littéral [lite'ral], *a.* (*m. pl.* **-aux**) literal.
littéralement [literal'mã], *adv.* literally, word for word.
littérateur [litera'tœ:r], *n.m.* literary man, author, man of letters.
littérature [litera'ty:r], *n.f.* literature.

littoral

littoral [lito'ral], *a. (m. pl.* **-aux**) littoral, coastal.—*n.m.* littoral, seaboard.
Lituanie [litɥa'ni], **la,** *f.* Lithuania.
lituanien [litɥa'njɛ̃], *a.* Lithuanian.—*n.m.* Lithuanian (*language*); (**Lituanien,** *fem.* **-enne**) Lithuanian (*person*).
liturgie [lityr'ʒi], *n.f.* liturgy.
liturgique [lityr'ʒik], *a.* liturgic, liturgical.
liturgiste [lityr'ʒist], *n.* liturgist.
livide [li'vid], *a.* livid, ghastly.
lividité [lividi'te], *n.f.* lividness.
livrable [li'vrabl], *a.* deliverable.
livraison [livrɛ'zɔ̃], *n.f.* delivery (*of goods*); part, number, issue (*of a magazine etc.*).
livre (1) [li:vr], *n.m.* book; register, account book.
livre (2) [li:vr], *n.f.* pound (*1.1 lb. avoirdupois*); **livre sterling,** pound sterling.
livrée [li'vre], *n.f.* livery; livery servants.
livrer [li'vre], *v.t.* to deliver; to give up, to hand over; to betray (*a secret*). **se livrer,** *v.r.* to give oneself up (*à*); to surrender; to devote oneself; to entrust oneself to; to indulge in (*a vice*).
livret [li'vrɛ], *n.m.* little book; memorandum book; libretto.
livreur [li'vrœːr], *n.m.* (*fem.* **-euse**) deliverer (*of goods*); delivery man, van man.—*n.f.* (**-euse**) delivery van.
lobe [lɔb], *n.m.* lobe (*of ear, liver etc.*).
lobélie [lɔbe'li], *n.f.* (*Bot.*) lobelia.
local [lɔ'kal], *a. (m. pl.* **-aux**) local.—*n.m.* place, premises; quarters.
localement [lɔkal'mɑ̃], *adv.* locally.
localisation [lɔkaliza'sjɔ̃], *n.f.* localization.
localiser [lɔkali'ze], *v.t.* to localize. **se localiser,** *v.r.* to become localized.
localité [lɔkali'te], *n.f.* locality.
locataire [lɔka'tɛ:r], *n.* tenant, lodger, occupier.
location [lɔka'sjɔ̃], *n.f.* letting out; hiring, renting; (*Theat.*) booking of seat.
lock-out [lɔ'kaut], *n.m. inv.* lock-out.
lock-outer [lɔkau'te], *v.t.* to lock-out.
locomoteur [lɔkɔmɔ'tœːr], *a.* (*fem.* **-trice**) locomotor.
locomotif [lɔkɔmɔ'tif], *a.* (*fem.* **-tive**) locomotive.—*n.f.* (**-tive**) locomotive, engine.
locomotion [lɔkɔmɔ'sjɔ̃], *n.f.* locomotion.
locomotive [LOCOMOTIF].
locuste [lɔ'kyst], *n.f.* locust.
locution [lɔky'sjɔ̃], *n.f.* locution, expression, form of speech; term, phrase.
logarithme [lɔga'ritm], *n.m.* logarithm.
loge [lɔ:ʒ], *n.f.* hut; lodge; (*Theat.*) box, dressing-room; stand, stall; kennel; booth.
logeable [lɔ'ʒabl], *a.* tenantable, fit to live in.
logement [lɔʒ'mɑ̃], *n.m.* lodgings; dwelling; house-room, accommodation; quarters.
loger [lɔ'ʒe], *v.t.* (*conjug. like* MANGER) to lodge; to put up, to accommodate, to house; to quarter; to stable.—*v.i.* to lodge, to live; to put up. **se loger,** *v.r.* to lodge, to take up one's abode; to lodge itself.
logette [lɔ'ʒɛt], *n.f.* small lodge.
logeur [lɔ'ʒœːr], *n.m.* (*fem.* **-euse**) lodging-house keeper.
logicien [lɔʒi'sjɛ̃], *n.m.* (*fem.* **-enne**) logician.
logique [lɔ'ʒik], *a.* logical.—*n.f.* logic.
logiquement [lɔʒik'mɑ̃], *adv.* logically.
logis [lɔ'ʒi], *n.m.* (*rare*) house, dwelling.

loi [lwɑ], *n.f.* law, statute, act; rule.
loin [lwɛ̃], *adv.* far, at a distance; remote, distant; **au loin,** far away, far and wide; **de loin,** from afar, from a distance; **de loin en loin,** at long intervals.
lointain [lwɛ̃'tɛ̃], *a.* remote, far off, distant.—*n.m.* distance, distant prospect.
loir [lwa:r], *n.m.* dormouse.
loisible [lwa'zibl], *a.* optional, lawful, allowable.
loisir [lwa'zi:r], *n.m.* leisure, spare time.
lombes [lɔ̃:b], *n.m. pl.* (*Anat.*) lumbar region, loins.
londonien [lɔ̃dɔ'njɛ̃], *a.* (*fem.* **-enne**) of *or* pertaining to London.—*n.m.* (**Londonien,** *fem.* **-enne**) Londoner.
Londres ['lɔ̃drə], *f.* London.
long [lɔ̃], *a.* (*fem.* **longue**) long; slow, tedious; diffuse, drawn out.—*n.m.* length; extent; (*tout*) **au long,** in full; **de long en large,** up and down, to and fro.—*n.f. à la longue,* in the long run.—*adv.* much, great deal.
longanimité [lɔ̃ganimi'te], *n.f.* longanimity, forbearance, long-suffering.
long-courrier [lɔ̃ku'rje], *n.m.* (*pl.* **-courriers**) ocean-going ship.
longe (1) [lɔ̃:ʒ], *n.f.* tether, leading-rein; thong.
longe (2) [lɔ̃:ʒ], *n.f. longe de veau,* loin of veal.
longer [lɔ̃'ʒe], *v.t.* (*conjug. like* MANGER) to go, to run along; to skirt; to extend along.
longévité [lɔ̃ʒevi'te], *n.f.* longevity.
longitude [lɔ̃ʒi'tyd], *n.f.* longitude.
longitudinal [lɔ̃ʒitydi'nal], *a.* (*m. pl.* **-aux**) longitudinal.
longitudinalement [lɔ̃ʒitydinal'mɑ̃], *adv.* lengthwise.
longtemps [lɔ̃'tɑ̃], *adv.* long, a long while.
longuement [lɔ̃g'mɑ̃], *adv.* long, a long time, for a great while.
longueur [lɔ̃'gœːr], *n.f.* length, extent in time; slowness; prolixity.
longue-vue [lɔ̃g'vy], *n.f.* (*pl.* **longues-vues**) telescope, spy-glass.
lopin [lɔ'pɛ̃], *n.m.* small piece *or* share; **lopin de terre,** plot of ground.
loquace [lɔ'kwas], *a.* loquacious, talkative.
loquacement [lɔkwas'mɑ̃], *adv.* talkatively, loquaciously.
loquacité [lɔkwasi'te], *n.f.* loquacity, talkativeness.
loque [lɔk], *n.f.* rag, tatter.
loquet [lɔ'kɛ], *n.m.* latch; **fermé au loquet,** on the latch.
loqueteau [lɔk'to], *n.m.* (*pl.* **-eaux**) small latch.
loqueteux [lɔk'tø], *a.* (*fem.* **-euse**) in rags.—*n.m.* (*fem.* **-euse**) ragged person.
lorgner [lɔr'ɲe], *v.t.* to leer at, to ogle.
lorgnette [lɔr'ɲɛt], *n.f.* field *or* opera glasses.
lorgnon [lɔr'ɲɔ̃], *n.m.* (*sometimes pl.*) eye-glasses; lorgnette.
lorry [lɔ'ri], *n.m.* (*Rail.*) trolley, repair *or* construction car.
lors [lɔːr], *adv.* then; **depuis** *or* **dès lors,** from that time, since then; **lors de,** at the time of; **lors même que,** even though; **pour lors,** then, at the time; so, therefore.
lorsque [lɔrsk, 'lɔrskə], *conj.* when; at the time *or* moment of.

losange [lɔ'zɑ̃:ʒ], *n.m.* diamond-shape, lozenge.

losangé [lɔzɑ̃'ʒe], *a.* in lozenges.

lot [lo], *n.m.* lot; portion, share; prize (*in a lottery*); (*fig.*) fate.

loterie [lɔ'tri], *n.f.* lottery, raffle.

lotion [lo'sjɔ̃], *n.f.* lotion; ablution.

lotir [lɔ'ti:r], *v.t.* to divide into lots, to portion off.

lotissement [lɔtis'mɑ̃], *n.m.* dividing into lots; building plot.

loto [lɔ'to], *n.m.* lotto (*game of chance*); bingo.

lotus [lɔ'ty:s], *n.m. inv.* lotus.

louable [lwabl], *a.* laudable, praiseworthy, commendable.

louablement [lwablə'mɑ̃], *adv.* commendably.

louage [lwa:ʒ], *n.m.* letting out, hiring, renting; hire.

louange [lwɑ̃:ʒ], *n.f.* praise, commendation, eulogy.

louanger [lwɑ̃'ʒe], *v.t.* (*conjug. like* MANGER) to praise, to flatter, to extol.

louangeur [lwɑ̃'ʒœ:r], *a.* (*fem.* **-euse**) laudatory, eulogistic.—*n.m.* (*fem.* **-euse**) praiser, flatterer.

louche (1) [luʃ], *n.f.* (*soup*) ladle; scoop; countersink bit.

louche (2) [luʃ], *a.* squint-eyed; dubious, ambiguous; suspicious, shady.

loucher [lu'ʃe], *v.i.* to squint.

loucheur [lu'ʃœ:r], *a.* (*fem.* **-euse**) squinting.—*n.m.* (*fem.* **-euse**) squinter.

louer (1) [lwe], *v.t.* to let *or* hire out; to lease, to rent, to hire; to book. **se louer** (1), *v.r.* to hire oneself out; to be let *or* rented.

louer (2) [lwe], *v.t.* to praise, to commend, to extol. **se louer** (2), *v.r.* to praise oneself; to rejoice.

loueur [lwœ:r], *n.m.* (*fem.* **-euse**) hirer, letter out.

lougre [lugr], *n.m.* lugger.

Louis [lwi], *m.* Lewis, Louis.

louis [lwi], *n.m. inv.* louis (*a French coin worth 20 gold francs*).

loup [lu], *n.m.* wolf; black velvet mask.

loup-cervier [luser'vje] *n.m.* (*pl.* **loups-cerviers**) lynx; (*fig.*) profiteer.

loupe (1) [lup], *n.f.* magnifying glass.

loupe (2) [lup], *n.f.* wen; gnarl (*on trees*).

louper [lu'pe], *v.t.* (*pop.*) to botch (*a piece of work*); (*Exam.*) to fail; to miss (*train*).

loupeux [lu'pø], *a.* (*fem.* **-euse**) wenny, knobby.

loup-garou [luga'ru], *n.m.* (*pl.* **loups-garous**) wer(e)wolf; bugbear.

lourd [lu:r], *a.* heavy, clumsy; stupid; sultry.

lourdaud [lur'do], *a.* loutish.—*n.m.* (*fem.* **-e**) blockhead.

lourdement [lurdə'mɑ̃], *adv.* heavily; clumsily.

lourdeur [lur'dœ:r], *n.f.* heaviness; clumsiness; stupidity; sultriness.

loutre [lutr], *n.f.* otter; otter fur.

louve [lu:v], *n.f.* she-wolf.

louveteau [luv'to], *n.m.* (*pl.* **-eaux**) wolf cub.

louveterie [luv'tri], *n.f.* wolf-hunting equipage; wolf hunting.

louvetier [luv'tje], *n.m.* wolf hunter.

louvoyer [luvwa'je], *v.i.* (*conjug. like* EM-PLOYER) to tack, to tack about; (*fig.*) to maneuver, to dodge.

lover [lɔ've], *v.t.* to coil (*rope etc.*). **se lover**, *v.r.* to coil up (*of snakes*).

loyal [lwa'jal], *a.* (*m. pl.* **-aux**) fair, honest, upright; loyal; (*Comm.*) unadulterated.

loyalement [lwajal'mɑ̃] *adv.* fairly, honestly; loyally.

loyauté [lwajo'te], *n.f.* honesty, fairness; loyalty, faithfulness.

loyer [lwa'je], *n.m.* hire, rent.

lubie [ly'bi] *n.f.* crotchet, whim, fad.

lubrifiant [lybri'fjɑ̃], *a.* lubricating.—*n.m.* lubricant.

lubrification [lybrifika'sjɔ̃], *n.f.* lubrication.

lubrifier [lybri'fje], *v.t.* to lubricate.

Luc [lyk], *m.* Luke.

lucarne [ly'karn], *n.f.* dormer window, skylight.

lucide [ly'sid], *a.* lucid, clear.

lucidement [lysid'mɑ̃], *adv.* lucidly.

lucidité [lysidi'te], *n.f.* lucidity, clearness.

luciole [ly'sjɔl], *n.f.* (*Ent.*) fire-fly; winged glow-worm.

lucratif [lykra'tif], *a.* (*fem.* **-tive**) lucrative.

lucre [lykr], *n.m.* lucre, gain.

lueur [lɥœ:r], *n.f.* glimmer, gleam; flash.

luffa [ly'fa], *n.m. or f.* loofah.

lugubre [ly'gybr], *a.* lugubrious, doleful, dismal.

lugubrement [lygybrə'mɑ̃], *adv.* ominously; dismally.

lui [lɥi], *pers. pron.* he, it; to him, to her, to it.

luire [lɥi:r], *v.i. irr.* to shine; to glitter, to gleam, to glisten; to dawn.

luisant [lɥi'zɑ̃], *a.* glistening, glittering, bright; glossy.—*n.m.* gloss, shine.

lumbago [lɔ̃ba'go], *n.m.* lumbago.

lumière [ly'mjɛ:r], *n.f.* light; daylight, day; (*fig.*) enlightenment; knowledge, wisdom.

luminaire [lymi'nɛ:r], *n.m.* luminary, light.

lumineux [lymi'nø], *a.* (*fem.* **-euse**) luminous; bright.

lunaire [ly'nɛ:r], *a.* lunar.

lunatique [lyna'tik], *a.* fantastical, whimsical. —*n.* incalculable *or* whimsical person.

lundi [lœ̃'di], *n.m.* Monday.

lune [lyn], *n.f.* moon.

lunetier [lyn'tje], *n.m.* (*fem.* **-ière**) spectacle maker; optician.

lunette [ly'nɛt], *n.f.* telescope, field glass; (*pl.*) spectacles.

lupin [ly'pɛ̃], *n.m.* (*Bot.*) lupin(e).

lupus [ly'py:s], *n.m.* lupus.

luron [ly'rɔ̃], *n.m.* (*fem.* **-onne**) jolly fellow, gay dog; carefree type of girl.

lustrage [lys'tra:ʒ], *n.m.* glossing.

lustral [lys'tral], *a.* (*m. pl.* **-aux**) lustral.

lustration [lystra'sjɔ̃], *n.f.* lustration.

lustre (1) [lystr], *n.m.* luster, brilliancy, brightness; (*fig.*) distinction; chandelier.

lustre (2) [lystr], *n.m.* (*Rom. Ant.*) lustrum, space of five years.

lustré [lys'tre], *a.* glossy, shiny.

lustrer [lys'tre], *v.t.* to give a luster *or* gloss to, to glaze.

lustrine [lys'trin], *n.f.* lustering, cotton luster.

luth [lyt], *n.m.* lute.

luthérien [lyte'rjɛ̃], *a.* Lutheran.—*n.m.* (**Luthérien**, *fem.* **-enne**) Lutheran (*person*).

lutin

lutin [ly'tɛ̃], *a.* roguish, sprightly.—*n.m.* goblin, sprite, elf, imp.

lutiner [lyti'ne], *v.t.* to plague, to tease, to pester.—*v.i.* to be mischievous, to play the imp.

lutrin [ly'trɛ̃], *n.m.* music lectern *or* desk; choir.

lutte [lyt], *n.f.* wrestling; struggle, contest, strife; *de bonne lutte*, by fair play; *de haute lutte*, by force.

lutter [ly'te], *v.i.* to wrestle; to struggle, to contend.

lutteur [ly'tœ:r], *n.m.* (*fem.* **-euse**) wrestler.

luxation [lyksɑ'sjɔ̃], *n.f.* luxation, dislocation.

luxe [lyks], *n.m.* luxury; profusion; extravagance, excess.

Luxembourg [lyksɑ̃'bu:r], **le**, *m.* Luxembourg.

luxembourgeois [lyksɑbur'ʒwa], *a.* (of) Luxembourg.—*n.m.* (**Luxembourgeois,** *fem.* **-oise**) citizen of Luxembourg.

luxer [lyk'se], *v.t.* to luxate, to dislocate.

luxueusement [lyksɥøz'mɑ̃], *a.* luxuriously, sumptuously, richly.

luxueux [lyk'sɥø], *a.* (*fem.* **-euse**) luxurious; magnificent, rich, sumptuous.

luxure [lyk'sy:r], *n.f.* lust.

luxuriance [lyksy'rjɑ:s], *n.f.* luxuriance.

luxuriant [lyksy'rjɑ̃], *a.* luxuriant.

luxurieux [lyksy'rjø], *a.* (*fem.* **-euse**) lustful, lecherous.

lycée [li'se], *n.m.* French grammar *or* high school.

lycéen [lise'ɛ̃], *n.m.* (*fem.* **-éenne**) grammar-school pupil.

lymphatique [lɛ̃fa'tik], *a.* lymphatic.

lymphe [lɛ̃:f] *n.f.* lymph; (*Bot.*) sap.

lynchage [lɛ̃'ʃa:ʒ], *n.m.* lynching.

lyncher [lɛ̃'ʃe], *v.t.* to lynch.

lynx [lɛ̃:ks], *n.m. inv.* lynx.

Lyon [ljɔ̃], *m.* Lyons.

lyre [li:r], *n.f.* lyre; (*fig.*) poetry.

lyrique [li'rik], *a.* lyric, lyrical.

lyrisme [li'rism], *n.m.* lyric poetry; poetic fire.

M

M m [ɛm], *n.m. or f.* the thirteenth letter of the alphabet; *M*, 1000; *M. MM.*, abbr. of *Monsieur, Messieurs.*

m' [ME].

ma [ma], *a. poss. f.* [MON].

macabre [ma'kɑ:br], *a.* gruesome, macabre, deathly, ghastly; *la danse macabre*, the dance of death.

macadam [maka'dam], *n.m.* macadam.

macadamiser [makadami'ze], *v.t.* to macadamize.

macaque [ma'kak], *n.m.* macaco (*monkey*).

macaron [maka'rɔ̃], *n.m.* macaroon.

macaroni [makarɔ'ni], *n.m.* macaroni.

Macédoine [mase'dwan], **la**, *f.* Macedonia.

macédoine [mase'dwan], *n.f.* vegetable hotchpotch; fruit salad; (*fig.*) medley, hotchpotch.

macédonien [masedɔ'njɛ̃], *a.* Macedonian.—*n.m.* (**Macédonien,** *fem.* **-enne**) Macedonian (*person*).

macération [maserɑ'sjɔ̃], *n.f.* maceration.

macérer [mase're], *v.t.* (*conjug. like* CÉDER) to macerate; (*fig.*) to mortify.—*v.i.* to soak. **se macérer,** *v.r.* to macerate one's body; (*fig.*) to mortify oneself.

mâcher [ma'ʃe], *v.t.* to chew, to masticate; *ne pas mâcher ses mots,* not to mince matters.

machiavélique [makjave'lik], *a.* Machiavellian.

machiavélisme [makjave'lism], *n.m.* Machiavellism.

machiavéliste [makjave'list], *n.* Machiavellian.

machinal [maʃi'nal], *a.* (*m. pl.* **-aux**) mechanical, automatic, instinctive.

machinalement [maʃinal'mɑ̃], *adv.* mechanically, automatically, instinctively.

machinateur [maʃina'tœ:r], *n.m.* (*fem.* **-trice**) plotter, schemer.

machination [maʃinɑ'sjɔ̃], *n.f.* machination, plot, scheme.

machine [ma'ʃin], *n.f.* machine, engine, piece of machinery; apparatus; scheme, plot; *machine à coudre,* sewing machine; *machine à écrire,* typewriter; *machine à laver,* washing machine; *machine pneumatique,* air pump.

machine-outil [maʃinu'ti], *n.f.* (*pl.* **machines-outils**) machine tool.

machiner [maʃi'ne], *v.t.* to contrive, to plot.

machiniste [maʃi'nist], *n.m.* machinist, engine man; (*Theat.*) scene shifter.

mâchoire [ma'ʃwa:r], *n.f.* jaw; jawbone.

mâchonner [maʃɔ'ne], *v.t.* to chew with difficulty; to munch; to mumble; to champ (*the bit*).

mâchurer [maʃy're], *v.t.* to daub, to smudge; to bruise.

maçon [ma'sɔ̃], *n.m.* mason, bricklayer; freemason.

maçonnage [masɔ'na:ʒ], *n.m.* mason's work, stonework.

maçonner [masɔ'ne], *v.t.* to build; to wall up.

maçonnerie [masɔn'ri], *n.f.* masonry, mason's work, stone work; freemasonry.

maçonnique [masɔ'nik], *a.* masonic.

macule [ma'kyl], *n.f.* stain, spot.

maculer [maky'le], *v.t.* to blot, to spot.

Madagascar [madagas'ka:r], **le**, *n.m.* Malagasy Republic.

madame [ma'dam], *n.f.* (*pl.* **mesdames**) madam, ma'am; Mrs.; your ladyship.

madécasse [made'kas], *a.* Madagascan.—*n.* (**Madécasse**) Madagascan (*person*).

madeleine [ma'dlɛn], *n.f.* shell-shaped sponge-cake; early pear.

Madelon [ma'dlɔ̃], *f.* Maud.

mademoiselle [madmwa'zɛl], *n.f.* (*pl.* **mesdemoiselles**) Miss; young lady.

Madère [ma'dɛ:r], **la**, *f.* Madeira.

madère [ma'dɛ:r], *n.m.* Madeira wine.

madone [ma'dɔn], *n.f.* Madonna.

madré [ma'dre], *a.* veined, mottled; (*fig.*) cunning, sly, sharp.—*n.m.* (*fem.* **-ée**) cunning, sharp *or* sly person.

madrier [madri'e], *n.m.* thick plank.

maestria [maɛs'tria], *n.f.* masterliness; *avec maestria,* in a masterly manner.

magasin [maga′zɛ̃], *n.m.* warehouse, storehouse; shop, store; magazine (*of fire-arm, camera etc.*).

(C) **magasiner** [magazi′ne], *v.i.* to shop.

magasinier [magazi′nje], *n.m.* warehouse keeper, storeman.

magazine [maga′zin], *n.m.* magazine (*usu. illustrated*).

mage [ma:ʒ], *n.m.* mage, magus; seer; *les rois mages*, the three wise men.

magicien [maʒi′sjɛ̃], *n.m.* (*fem.* **-enne**) magician, wizard, sorcerer, sorceress.

magie [ma′ʒi], *n.f.* magic.

magique [ma′ʒik], *a.* magic(al).

magister [maʒis′tɛ:r], *n.m.* village schoolmaster; pedant.

magistral [maʒis′tral], *a.* (*m. pl.* **-aux**) magisterial; masterly, authoritative, sovereign.

magistralement [maʒistral′mɑ̃], *adv.* magisterially; in a masterly fashion.

magistrat [maʒis′tra], *n.m.* magistrate, justice; civic officer.

magistrature [maʒistra′ty:r], *n.f.* magistracy; bench.

magnanime [maɲa′nim], *a.* magnanimous, high-minded.

magnanimement [maɲanim′mɑ̃], *adv.* magnanimously.

magnanimité [maɲanimi′te], *n.f.* magnanimity.

magnat [mag′na], *n.m.* magnate.

magnésie [maɲe′zi], *n.f.* magnesia.

magnétique [maɲe′tik], *a.* magnetic.

magnétiser [maɲeti′ze], *v.t.* to magnetize.

magnetiseur [maɲeti′zœ:r], *n.m.* magnetizer.

magnétisme [maɲe′tism], *n.m.* magnetism; (*fig.*) attraction.

magnétophone [maɲeto′fɔn], *n.m.* (*Reg. trade mark*) tape recorder.

magnificence [maɲifi′sɑ̃:s], *n.f.* magnificence, splendo r.

magnifier [maɲi′fje], *v.t.* to magnify, to glorify.

magnifique [maɲi′fik], *a.* magnificent, splendid; gorgeous.

magnifiquement [maɲifik′mɑ̃], *adv.* magnificently.

magot [ma′go], *n.m.* magot, ape; grotesque figure (*of china*); (*fig.*) ugly person; (*fam.*) hoard, hidden savings.

Mahomet [maɔ′mɛ], *m.* Mohammed.

mahométan [maɔme′tɑ̃], *a.* Mohammedan. —*n.m.* (**Mahométan**. *fem.* **-ane**) Mohammedan (*person*).

mahométisme [maɔme′tism], *n.m.* Mohammedanism.

mai [mɛ], *n.m.* May; maypole.

maigre [mɛ:gr], *a.* meager, lean, thin; poor, scanty; barren; fasting; *repas maigre*, meatless meal; *maigre repas*, slender meal.

maigrement [mɛgrə′mɑ̃], *adv.* meagerly; poorly; sparingly.

maigreur [mɛ′grœ:r], *n.f.* leanness, meagerness; thinness, poorness, barrenness.

maigrir [mɛ′gri:r], *v.i.* to grow thin, to lose weight.

mail [ma:j], *n.m.* mall (*game, promenade, avenue of trees*).

maille [mɑ:j], *n.f.* mesh; ring of cable; link of mail; stitch.

maillé [mɑ′je], *a.* stitched; mailed.

mailler [mɑ′je], *v.t.* to make with meshes, to lattice; to mail.

maillet [ma′jɛ], *n.m.* mallet.

maillon [mɑ′jɔ̃], *n.m.* link (*of chain*) .

maillot [ma′jo], *n.m.* swaddling-band; swaddling clothes; pair of tights (*for theatre*); bathing suit, (*Spt.*) jersey, vest; *enfant au maillot*, baby in arms.

main [mɛ̃], *n.f.* hand; handwriting; lead, deal (*at cards*); handle; quire (*of paper*); *à la main*, in his *or* her hand, by hand; *à la portée de la main*, within reach; *à main armée*, by force of arms, armed; *à pleines mains*, by handfuls, liberal; *vol à main armée*, armed robbery.

main-d'œuvre [mɛ̃′dœ:vr], *n.f.* (*pl.* **mains-d'œuvre**) man-power, labor; workmanship.

main-forte [mɛ̃′fɔrt], *n.f.* assistance, help.

maint [mɛ̃], *a.* many; *maintes fois*, many a time.

maintenant [mɛ̃t′nɑ̃], *adv.* now, at this moment, at present, nowadays.

maintenir [mɛ̃t′ni:r], *v.t. irr.* (*conjug. like* TENIR) to uphold, to sustain; to maintain; to enforce. **se maintenir**, *v.r.* to keep up; to subsist; to hold out, to stand one's ground; to remain in force.

maintien [mɛ̃′tjɛ̃], *n.m.* maintenance, keeping up; deportment; attitude.

maire [mɛ:r], *n.m.* mayor.

mairesse [mɛ′rɛs], *n.f.* mayoress.

mairie [mɛ′ri], *n.f.* mayoralty; town hall.

mais [mɛ], *conj.* but; why.

maïs [ma′is], *n.m.* maize, Indian corn.

maison [mɛ′zɔ̃], *n.f.* house; home; housekeeping; family; (*Comm.*) firm; *à la maison*, at home.

maisonnée [mɛzɔ′ne], *n.f.* (*fam.*) whole house *or* family, household.

maisonnette [mɛzɔ′nɛt], *n.f.* small house, cottage, lodge.

maître [me:tr], *n.m.* master; ruler, lord; proprietor, landlord; teacher, tutor; (*Naut.*) chief petty officer; *coup de maître*, masterly stroke; *maître chanteur*, blackmailer.

maître-autel [metro′tɛl], *n.m.* (*pl.* **maîtres-autels**) high altar.

maîtresse [me′trɛs], *a.* chief, leading, main.— *n.f.* mistress; ruler, lady; proprietress; teacher; sweetheart.

maîtrise [me′tri:z], *n.f.* mastery; control; music school (*in a cathedral*).

maîtriser [metri′ze], *v.t.* to master, to control; to lord (it) over.

majesté [maʒɛs′te], *n.f.* majesty; stateliness.

majestueusement [maʒɛstɥøz′mɑ̃], *adv.*- majestically.

majestueux [maʒɛs′tɥø], *a.* (*fem.* **-euse**) majestic.

majeur [ma′ʒœ:r], *a.* major, greater; superior, main, chief, most important; of full age.— *n.m.* (*fem.* **-e**) a male *or* female of full age, major.—*n.m.* middle finger.

majolique [maʒɔ′lik], *n.f.* majolica.

major [ma′ʒɔ:r], *n.m.* major; medical officer.

majordome [maʒɔr′dɔm], *n.m.* major-domo.

majorer [maʒɔ′re], *v.t.* to raise (*the price*).

majorité [maʒɔri′te], *n.f.* majority.

majuscule [maʒys′kyl], *a.* capital, large.— *n.f.* capital letter.

mal

mal [mal], *n.m.* (*pl.* **maux**) evil, ill; harm; pain, ache, sickness; hardship, misfortune; trouble; repugnance.—*adv.* wrong, badly; **mal à propos**, improperly.

malade [ma'lad], *a.* sick, ill; unhealthy.—*n.* sick person, invalid; patient.

maladie [mala'di], *n.f.* illness, sickness, malady.

maladif [mala'dif], *a.* (*fem.* **-dive**) sickly, puny, ailing, unhealthy.

maladivement [maladiv'mā], *adv.* morbidly.

maladresse [mala'drɛs], *n.f.* awkwardness, clumsiness; blunder.

maladroit [mala'drwa], *a.* and *n.m.* (*fem.* **-e**) awkward, clumsy, stupid (person).

maladroitement [maladrwat'mā], *adv.* clumsily.

malais [ma'lɛ], *a.* Malay, Malayan, Malaysian.—*n.m.* Malay (*language*); (**Malais**, *fem.* **-aise**) Malay, Malayan, Malaysian (*person*).

malaise [ma'lɛ:z], *n.m.* uneasiness, discomfort; indisposition.

malaisé [malɛ'ze], *a.* hard, difficult, rough, arduous.

malaisément [malɛze'mā], *adv.* with difficulty, painfully.

Malaisie [malɛ'zi], **la**, *f.* Malaysia.

malappris [mala'pri], *a.* unmannerly, ill-bred.—*n.m.* (*fem.* **-e**) ill-bred person, lout.

malard [ma'la:r], *n.m.* mallard, wild drake.

malaria [mala'rja], *n.f.* malaria.

malart [MALARD].

malavisé [malavi'ze], *a.* ill-advised, imprudent, unwise, indiscreet.

malaxer [malak'ze], *v.t.* to mix, knead *or* work up; to massage.

malbâti [malba'ti], *a.* ill-shaped, gawky.—*n.m.* (*fem.* **-e**) ill-favored person.

malchance [mal'ʃā:s], *n.f.* ill-luck, mishap, mischance.

malchanceux [malʃā'sø], *a.* (*fem.* **-euse**) unlucky.

mâle [ma:l], *a.* male; manly, virile; masculine.—*n.m.* male; cock.

malédiction [maledik'sjɔ̃], *n.f.* malediction, curse.

maléfice [male'fis], *n.m.* evil spell, sorcery.

maléfique [male'fik], *a.* harmful, malefic, baleful.

malencontre [malā'kɔ̃:tr], *n.f.* mishap, mischance.

malencontreusement [malākɔ̃trøz'mā], *adv.* unluckily, untowardly.

malencontreux [malākɔ̃'trø], *a.* (*fem.* **-euse**) unlucky, untoward.

mal-en-point [malā'pwɛ̃], *adv.* badly off; in a sorry plight.

malentendu [malātā'dy], *n.m.* misunderstanding, misapprehension, mistake.

malfaçon [malfa'sɔ̃], *n.f.* bad work; malpractice, illicit profit.

malfaire [mal'fɛ:r], *v.i.* (*used only in the inf.*) to do evil.

malfaisant [malfə'zā], *a.* mischievous; spiteful, malevolent.

malfaiteur [malfɛ'tœ:r], *n.m.* (*fem.* **-trice**) malefactor, evil-doer; offender; thief.

malfamé [malfa'me], *a.* ill-famed, of bad repute.

malformation [malfɔrma'sjɔ̃], *n.f.* malformation.

malgache [mal'gaʃ], *a.* Madagascan.—*n.* (**Malgache**) Malagasy, Madagascan.

malgracieusement [malgrasjøz'mā], *adv.* ungraciously, rudely, uncivilly.

malgracieux [malgra'sjø], *a.* (*fem.* **-euse**) rude, ungracious, uncivil.

malgré [mal'gre], *prep.* in spite of, notwithstanding.

malhabile [mala'bil], *a.* unskilled, awkward.

malhabilement [malabil'mā], *adv.* unskilfully, awkwardly.

malhabileté [malabil'te], *n.f.* unskilfulness, awkwardness, clumsiness.

malheur [ma'lœ:r], *n.m.* unhappiness, misfortune, bad luck; mischance; calamity, disaster; woe, adversity; poverty.

malheureusement [malœrøz'mā], *adv.* unfortunately.

malheureux [malœ'rø], *a.* (*fem.* **-euse**) unfortunate, unlucky; unsuccessful; unpleasant; unhappy, miserable, wretched.—*n.m.* (*fem.* **-euse**) unhappy person.

malhonnête [malɔ'nɛ:t], *a.* dishonest; uncivil, rude.—*n.* rude person.

malhonnêtement [malɔnɛt'mā], *adv.* dishonestly; rudely.

malhonnêteté [malɔnɛt'te], *n.f.* rudeness, incivility; dishonesty.

malice [ma'lis], *n.f.* malice, spite; mischievousness; prank, trick.

malicieusement [malisjøz'mā], *adv.* maliciously; mischievously; slyly.

malicieux [mali'sjø], *a.* (*fem.* **-euse**) malicious, spiteful; mischievous; roguish.

malignement [maliɲ'mā], *adv.* malignantly; maliciously.

malignité [maliɲi'te], *n.f.* malignity, spite.

malin [ma'lɛ̃], *a.* (*fem.* **maligne**) malicious, mischievous; malignant; waggish, roguish; cunning, clever.—*n.m.* (*fem.* **maligne**) malignant *or* malicious person.—*n.m.* devil, evil spirit, fiend.

maline [ma'lin], *n.f.* spring tide.

malingre [ma'lɛ̃:gr], *a.* sickly, weakly, puny.

malintentionné [malɛ̃tāsjɔ'ne], *a.* evil-minded, ill-disposed.

malle [mal], *n.f.* trunk, box; mail car, mail boat.

malléabilité [maleabili'te], *n.f.* malleability; pliability.

malléable [male'abl], *a.* malleable.

malle-poste [mal'pɔst], *n.f.* (*pl.* **malles-poste(s)**) mail car.

mallette [ma'lɛt], *n.f.* small case, suitcase, attaché-case.

malmener [malmə'ne], *v.t.* (*conjug. like* AMENER) to ill-treat, to handle roughly; to abuse.

malodorant [malɔdɔ'rā], *a.* malodorous, ill-smelling.

malotru [malɔ'try], *a.* coarse, uncouth, vulgar.—*n.m.* (*fem.* **-e**) ill-bred person; lout.

Malouines [ma'lwin], **les Îles**, *f. pl.* the Falkland Islands.

malpeigné [malpɛ'ɲe], *a.* unkempt.—*n.m.* (*fem.* **-ée**) unkempt *or* dirty person.

malplaisant [malplɛ'zā], *a.* unpleasant, disagreeable.

malpropre [mal'prɔpr], *a.* slovenly, dirty; dishonest; unfit (*à*).

malproprement [malprɔprə'mā], *adv.* in a slovenly way, dirtily; improperly.

malpropreté [malprɔprəˈte], *n.f.* dirtiness.
malsain [malˈsɛ̃], *a.* unhealthy; unwholesome, injurious.
malséant [malseˈɑ̃], *a.* unbecoming, unseemly, improper.
malsonnant [malsɔˈnɑ̃], *a.* ill-sounding; offensive.
malt [malt], *n.m.* malt.
maltais [malˈtɛ], *a.* Maltese.—*n.m.* Maltese (*language*); (**Maltais**, *fem.* **-aise**) Maltese (*person*).
Malte [malt], **la**, *f.* Malta.
maltraiter [maltrɛˈte], *v.t.* to ill-use, to maltreat, to abuse.
malveillamment [malvɛjaˈmɑ̃], *adv.* malevolently.
malveillance [malvɛˈjɑ̃:s], *n.f.* malevolence, ill-will, malice.
malveillant [malvɛˈjɑ̃], *a.* malevolent, malignant, ill-disposed, spiteful.—*n.m.* (*fem.* **-e**) evil-minded person.
malversation [malvɛrsaˈsjɔ̃], *n.f.* malversation, peculation, embezzlement.
maman [maˈmɑ̃], *n.f.* mamma, mummy.
mamelle [maˈmɛl], *n.f.* breast; udder.
mamelon [mamˈlɔ̃], *n.m.* nipple, teat; dug (*of animals*); pap, hillock, knoll.
mameluk [mamˈluk], *n.m.* Mameluke.
mammouth [maˈmut], *n.m.* mammoth.
manant [maˈnɑ̃], *n.m.* peasant, clodhopper.
manche (1) [mɑ̃:ʃ], *n.m.* handle; neck (*of violin etc.*).
manche (2) [mɑ̃:ʃ], *n.f.* sleeve; hose; channel; (*Spt.*) rubber, game, heat.
Manche [mɑ̃:ʃ], **la**, *f.* The (English) Channel. *Les Îles de la Manche*, the Channel Islands.
manchette [mɑ̃ˈʃɛt], *n.f.* cuff; ruffle; wristband.
manchon [mɑ̃ˈʃɔ̃], *n.m.* muff.
manchot [mɑ̃ˈʃo], *a.* ône-handed, one-armed.—*n.m.* penguin; (*fem.* **-e**) one-handed, one-armed person.
mandarin [mɑ̃daˈrɛ̃], *a.* and *n.m.* (*fem.* **-ine** (1)) mandarin.
mandarine (2) [mɑ̃daˈrin], *n.f.* tangerine.
mandat [mɑ̃ˈda], *n.m.* mandate, authority; warrant, writ; money order, order.
mandataire [mɑ̃daˈtɛ:r], *n.m.* mandatory; proxy, attorney, agent.
mandchou [mɑ̃tˈʃu], *a.* Manchu(rian).—*n.m.* Manchu(rian) (*language*); (**Mandchou**, *fem.* **-oue**) Manchu(rian) (*person*).
Mandchourie [mɑ̃tʃuˈri], **la**, *f.* Manchuria.
mandement [mɑ̃dˈmɑ̃], *n.m.* mandate; bishop's letter.
mander [mɑ̃ˈde], *v.t.* to write, to send word, to inform; to send for.
mandoline [mɑ̃dɔˈlin], *n.f.* mandolin.
mandoliniste [mɑ̃dɔliˈnist], *n.* mandolin player.
manège [maˈnɛ:ʒ], *n.m.* horsemanship; riding school; merry-go-round; (*fig.*) trick, intrigue.
mânes [mɑ:n], *n.m. pl.* manes, shades.
manette [maˈnɛt], *n.f.* hand lever, grip; (*Hort.*) trowel.
mangeable [mɑ̃ˈʒabl], *a.* eatable, edible.
mangeoire [mɑ̃ˈʒwa:r], *n.f.* manger, crib.
manger [mɑ̃ˈʒe], *v.t.* (*see Verb Tables*) to eat; (*fig.*) to squander, to run through.—*v.i.* to eat; to feed.—*n.m.* eating; victuals, food.

se manger, *v.r.* to eat each other; to hurt each other; to be edible.
mangeur [mɑ̃ˈʒœ:r], *n.m.* (*fem.* **-euse**) eater; spendthrift.
mangouste [mɑ̃ˈgust], *n.f.* mongoose.
maniable [maˈnjabl], *a.* easy to handle; tractable, supple, pliable.
maniaque [maˈnjak], *a.* eccentric, having a mania.—*n.* crank, faddist.
manicure [maniˈky:r], [MANUCURE].
manie [maˈni], *n.f.* mania; fad, hobby; inveterate habit, craze.
maniement [maniˈmɑ̃], *n.m.* handling; management, use.
manier [maˈnje], *v.t.* to handle; to touch; to use, to wield; to manage, to govern.
manière [maˈnjɛ:r], *n.f.* manner, way, style; sort; affectation; (*pl.*) manners; *de manière à*, so as to; *de quelle manière*, how; *manière d'être*, bearing, attitude.
maniéré [manjeˈre], *a.* affected, unnatural, forced.
maniérisme [manjeˈrism], *n.m.* mannerism.
manifestation [manifɛstaˈsjɔ̃], *n.f.* manifestation; (*Polit.*) demonstration.
manifeste [maniˈfɛst], *a.* manifest, obvious.—*n.m.* manifesto.
manifestement [manifɛstəˈmɑ̃], *adv.* manifestly.
manifester [manifɛsˈte], *v.t.* to manifest, to display, to show.—*v.i.* to attend a (*political*) demonstration. **se manifester**, *v.r.* to manifest oneself, to make oneself known.
manigance [maniˈgɑ̃:s], *n.f.* (*fam.*) maneuver, intrigue.
manigancer [manigɑ̃ˈse], *v.t.* (*conjug. like* COMMENCER) to contrive, to plot.
Manille [maˈni:j], **la**, *f.* Manila.
manipulateur [manipylaˈtœ:r], *n.m.* (*fem.* **-trice**) manipulator.
manipulation [manipylaˈsjɔ̃], *n.f.* manipulation.
manipuler [manipyˈle], *v.t.* to manipulate; (*Teleg.*) to operate.
manivelle [maniˈvɛl], *n.f.* crank; handle.
manne (1) [ma:n], *n.f.* manna.
manne (2) [ma:n], *n.f.* hamper, flat basket.
mannequin (1) [manˈkɛ̃], *n.m.* small hamper.
mannequin (2) [manˈkɛ̃], *n.m.* lay figure; tailor's dummy; model girl; mannequin.
manœuvre [maˈnœ:vr], *n.f.* working; drilling (*of soldiers*); maneuver; scheme; move; (*Rail.*) marshalling.—*n.m.* unskilled workman, laborer.
manœuvrer [manœˈvre], *v.t.* to maneuver; to work (*a machine*); to shunt (*trains*).
manœuvrier [manœvriˈe], *a.* (*fem.* **-ière**) highly trained.—*n.m.* expert seaman; tactician.
manoir [maˈnwa:r], *n.m.* manor; country house.
manouvrier [manuvriˈe], *n.m.* (*fem.* **-ière**) day laborer.
manquant [mɑ̃ˈkɑ̃], *a.* missing, absent, wanting.—*n.m.* (*fem.* **-e**) absentee, defaulter. —*n.m.* (*pl.*) shortages, deficiencies.
manque [mɑ̃:k], *n.m.* want, lack; defect; deficiency.
manqué [mɑ̃ˈke], *a.* missed; defective; unsuccessful, abortive.
manquement [mɑ̃kəˈmɑ̃], *n.m.* omission, oversight; failure; breach.

manquer [mɑ̃'ke], *v.t.* to miss, to lose; to spoil.—*v.i.* to miss, to fail; to be wanting; to be deficient; to slip; to misfire; to go bankrupt; to miscarry.

mansarde [mɑ̃'sard], *n.f.* roof window, dormer; garret.

mansardé [mɑ̃sar'de], *a.* with attics.

mansuétude [mɑ̃sye'tyd], *n.f.* mildness, gentleness, forbearance.

mante (1) [mɑ̃:t], *n.f.* mantle (*woman's*).

mante (2) [mɑ̃:t], *n.f.* mantis; *mante religieuse*, praying mantis.

manteau [mɑ̃'to], *n.m.* (*pl.* **-eaux**) cloak, mantle; overcoat; (*fig.*) pretence.

mantille [mɑ̃'ti:j], *n.f.* mantilla.

manucure [many'ky:r], **manicure** [mani'ky:r], *n.* manicure (*person*), manicurist.

manuel [ma'nɥɛl], *a.* (*fem.* **-elle**) manual, portable.—*n.m.* manual, textbook.

manuellement [manɥɛl'mɑ̃], *adv.* by hand, manually.

manufacture [manyfak'ty:r], *n.f.* manufacture, making; factory, mill, works.

manufacturer [manyfakty're], *v.t.* to manufacture.

manufacturier [manyfakty'rje], *a.* (*fem.* **-ière**) manufacturing.—*n.m.* manufacturer.

manuscrit [manys'kri], *a.* handwritten.—*n.m.* manuscript.

manutention [manytɑ̃'sjɔ̃], *n.f.* management, administration; manipulation; handling (*of goods etc.*); army bakery.

mappemonde [map'mɔ̃:d], *n.f.* map of the world, planisphere.

maquereau [ma'kro], *n.m.* (*pl.* **-eaux**) mackerel.

maquette [ma'kɛt], *n.f.* (*Sculp.*) small rough model (*in clay, wax etc.*); (*Paint.*) rough sketch; lay figure; (*Theat., Cine.*) model.

maquignon [maki'ɲɔ̃], *n.m.* (*fem.* **-onne**) horse dealer, jobber.

maquignonnage [makiɲɔ'na:ʒ], *n.m.* horse-dealing; underhand work, jobbery.

maquignonner [makiɲɔ'ne], *v.t.* to jockey to bishop (*a horse for sale*); to job.

maquillage [maki'ja:ʒ], *n.m.* make-up.

maquiller [maki'je], *v.t.* to make up; to fake up. **se maquiller**, *v.r.* to make up *or* paint oneself.

maquilleur [maki'jœ:r], *n.m.* (*fem.* **-euse**) (*Theat.*) maker-up; faker (*of paintings etc.*).

maquis [ma'ki], *n.m. inv.* scrub (*in Corsica*); (*1941-44*) underground forces.

maquisard [maki'za:r], *n.m.* free fighter in the maquis.

maraîcher [marɛ'ʃe], *a.* (*fem.* **-ère**) of market gardening.—*n.m.* market gardener.

marais [ma'rɛ], *n.m.* marsh, fen, bog, swamp.

marasme [ma'rasm], *n.m.* emaciation; (*fig.*) depression; stagnation, slump.

marâtre [ma'rɑ:tr], *n.f.* stepmother; (*fig.*) harsh mother.

maraudage [maro'da:ʒ], *n.m.* marauding.

maraude [ma'ro:d], *n.f.* pilfering.

marauder [maro'de], *v.i.* to pilfer, to go scrounging.

maraudeur [maro'dœ:r], *n.m.* (*fem.* **-euse**) marauder; plunderer.

marbre [marbr], *n.m.* marble.

marbré [mar'bre], *a.* marbled.

marbrer [mar'bre], *v.t.* to marble, to vein.

marbrerie [marbrə'ri], *n.f.* marble-cutting; marble works.

marbrier [marbri'e], *a.* (*fem.* **-ière**) of marble.—*n.m.* marble cutter, marble polisher; dealer in marble.—*n.f.* (**-ière**) marble quarry.

marbrure [mar'bry:r], *n.f.* marbling; mottling (*on the skin*).

marc [ma:r], *n.m.* residuum (*of fruit etc. squeezed, boiled or strained*); dregs, grounds.

Marc [mark], *m.* Mark.

marchand [mar'ʃɑ̃], *a.* saleable, trading.—*n.m.* (*fem.* **-e**) dealer, tradesman, shopkeeper; merchant; *marchand des quatre saisons*, hawker of fruits etc.; *marchand au détail*, retail merchant; *marchand en gros*, wholesale dealer.

marchandage [marʃɑ̃'da:ʒ] *n.m.* bargaining, haggling; piece-work.

marchander [marʃɑ̃'de], *v.t.* to bargain for; to haggle over; (*fig.*) to spare; to grudge.—*v.i.* to haggle; to hesitate.

marchandeur [marʃɑ̃'dœ:r], *n.m.* (*fem.* **-euse**) bargainer, haggler; contractor on small scale.

marchandise [marʃɑ̃'di:z], *n.f.* merchandise; goods, wares, commodities.

marche (1) [marʃ], *n.f.* walk; gait; march, journey; procession; movement; conduct; *marche arrière*, reversing (*of a car*); *mettre en marche*, to set going.

marche (2) [marʃ], *n.f.* step, stair; treadle.

marché [mar'ʃe], *n.m.* market; market-place; bargain, purchase; price, rate; contract; *à bon marché*, cheaply; *bon marché*, cheap, cheapness.

marchepied [marʃə'pje], *n.m.* step (*of a coach, altar etc.*); step-ladder; running-board.

marcher [mar'ʃe], *v.i.* to walk; to progress; to step, to tread; to march; to run, to ply; to work (*of a machine*).

marcheur [mar'ʃœ:r], *n.m.* (*fem.* **-euse**) walker.

mardi [mar'di], *n.m.* Tuesday; *mardi gras*, Shrove Tuesday.

mare [ma:r], *n.f.* pool, pond.

marécage [mare'ka:ʒ], *n.m.* marsh, bog, fen, swamp.

marécageux [mareka'ʒø], *a.* (*fem.* **-euse**) marshy, swampy, boggy.

maréchal [mare'ʃal], *n.m.* (*pl.* **-aux**) marshal, field marshal.

maréchalerie [mareʃal'ri], *n.f.* farriery, smithy.

maréchal-ferrant [mareʃalfɛ'rɑ̃], *n.m.* (*pl.* **maréchaux-ferrants**) farrier, shoeing smith.

marée [ma're], *n.f.* tide, flood; fresh sea-fish.

marelle [ma'rɛl], *n.f.* hopscotch.

mareyeur [marɛ'jœ:r] *n.m.* fish dealer, fish-salesman.

margarine [marga'rin], *n.f.* margarine.

marge [marʒ], *n.f.* margin, border, edge; (*fig.*) freedom, latitude, scope; means.

margelle [mar'ʒɛl], *n.f.* curb, edge (*of a well etc.*).

Marguerite [margə'rit], *f.* Margaret.

marguerite [margə'rit], *n.f.* daisy.

marguillier [margi'je], *n.m.* churchwarden.

mari [ma'ri], *n.m.* husband.

mariable [ma'rjabl], *a.* marriageable.

mariage [ma'rja:ʒ], *n.m.* marriage; matrimony; wedding; union, blending.

Marie [ma'ri], *f.* Mary, Maria.

marié [ma'rje], *a.* married.—*n.m.* (*fem.* **-ée**) married man; bridegroom; married woman; bride.

marier [ma'rje], *v.t.* to give in marriage, to marry off; to match. **se marier**, *v.r.* to marry, to get married (*avec*).

marieur [ma'rjœ:r], *n.m.* (*fem.* **-euse**) matchmaker.

marin [ma'rɛ̃], *a.* marine; sea-going.—*n.m.* sailor.

marinade [mari'nad], *n.f.* pickle, souse.

marine [ma'rin], *n.f.* sea service; Admiralty; navy.

mariner [mari'ne], *v.t.* to pickle, to souse.

marinier [mari'nje], *a.* (*fem.* **-ière** (1)) *officiers mariniers*, petty officers.—*n.m.* bargeman, lighter-man.—*n.f.* (**-ière**) (*Swim.*) side stroke.

marinière (2) [mari'njɛ:r], *n.f.* (*Cook.*) onion sauce.

marionnette [marjɔ'nɛt], *n.f.* puppet, marionette; (*pl.*) puppet show.

marital [mari'tal], *a.* (*m. pl.* **-aux**) marital.

maritalement [marital'mã], *adv.* maritally, as man and wife.

maritime [mari'tim], *a.* maritime, naval.

marmaille [mar'ma:j], *n.f.* (*colloq.*) brats.

marmelade [marmə'lad], *n.f.* compote; (*fig.*) jelly, soup.

marmite [mar'mit], *n.f.* cooking pot.

marmiteux [marmi'tø], *a.* (*fem.* **-euse**) pitiful, wretched, miserable.—*n.m.* (*fem.* **-euse**) poor devil.

marmiton [marmi'tɔ̃], *n.m.* scullion.

marmonner [marmɔ'ne], *v.t.* to mutter.

marmoréen [marmɔre'ɛ̃], *a.* (*fem.* **-éenne**) marmorean.

marmot [mar'mo], *n.m.* kid, brat, urchin.

marmotte [mar'mɔt], *n.f.* marmot.

marmotter [marmɔ'te], *v.t., v.i.* to mutter, to mumble.

marmouset [marmu'zɛ], *n.m.* grotesque figure; young monkey (*little boy*); fire-dog.

marne [marn], *n.f.* marl, chalk, clay.

marner [mar'ne], *v.t.* to marl.

marneux [mar'nø], *a.* (*fem.* **-euse**) marly.

marnière [mar'njɛ:r], *n.f.* marlpit.

Maroc [ma'rɔk], **le**, *m.* Morocco.

marocain [marɔ'kɛ̃], *a.* Moroccan.—*n.m.* (**Marocain**, *fem.* **-aine**) Moroccan (*person*).

maroquin [marɔ'kɛ̃], *n.m.* morocco leather.

maroquiner [marɔki'ne], *v.t.* to morocco.

maroquinerie [marɔkin'ri], *n.f.* morocco leather manufacture *or* factory.

maroquinier [marɔki'nje], *n.m.* morocco leather tanner.

marotte [ma'rɔt], *n.f.* cap and bells; hairdresser's dummy head; (*fig.*) fancy, hobby.

marquant [mar'kã], *a.* conspicuous, striking.

marque [mark], *n.f.* mark, imprint, stamp; cipher, trade mark, make; badge, sign, token; proof; distinction.

marqué [mar'ke], *a.* marked, conspicuous, obvious; determined.

marquer [mar'ke], *v.t.* to mark; to stamp; to brand; to indicate; to denote; to testify; to score.—*v.i.* to mark, to be remarkable; to show off.

marqueter [markə'te], *v.t.* (*conjug. like* APPELER) to speckle, to spot; to inlay.

marqueterie [markə'tri], *n.f.* marquetry, inlaid work, inlaying.

marqueur [mar'kœ:r], *n.m.* (*fem.* **-euse**) marker; scorer.

marquis [mar'ki], *n.m.* marquess, marquis.

marquise [mar'ki:z], *n.f.* marchioness; marquee, glass porch *or* roof.

marraine [ma'rɛn], *n.f.* godmother; sponsor.

marron (1) [ma'rɔ̃], *a. inv.* maroon, chestnut-color. —*n.m.* chestnut; cracker (*fireworks*); *marron d'Inde*, horse chestnut.

marron (2) [ma'rɔ̃] *a.* (*fem.* **-onne**) fugitive, runaway (*of slaves*); (*Comm.*) unlicensed; unqualified (*doctor etc.*).

marronnier [marɔ'nje], *n.m.* chestnut tree; *marronnier d'Inde*, horse chestnut tree.

mars [mars]; *n.m.* March.

Marseillaise [marsɛ'jɛ:z], *n.f.* Marseillaise (*French national anthem*).

marsouin [mar'swɛ̃], *n.m.* porpoise.

marte [MARTRE].

marteau [mar'to], *n.m.* (*pl.* **-eaux**) hammer; *marteau de porte*, knocker; *marteau pneumatique*, pneumatic drill.

marteau-pilon [martopi'lɔ̃], *n.m.* (*pl.* **marteaux-pilons**) steam hammer.

martelage [martə'la:ʒ], *n.m.* hammering; marking (*of trees*).

martelé [martə'le], *a.* hammered; (*Mus.*) brilliant and distinct.

marteler [martə'le], *v.t.* (*conjug. like* AMENER) to hammer; to mark (*trees*).

Marthe [mart], *f.* Martha.

martial [mar'sjal], *a.* (*m. pl.* **-aux**) martial, warlike, soldierly.

martinet (1) [marti'nɛ], *n.m.* (*Orn.*) swift, martlet.

martinet (2) [mɛrti'nɛ], *n.m.* tilt hammer; cat-o'-nine-tails.

martingale [martɛ̃'gal], *n.f.* martingale; *jouer la martingale*, to play double or quits.

martin-pêcheur [martɛ̃pɛ'ʃœ:r], *n.m.* (*pl.* **martins-pêcheurs**) kingfisher; *martin-pêcheur d'Australie*, laughing jackass.

martre [martr], **marte** [mart], *n.f.* marten.

martyr [mar'ti:r], *n.m.* (*fem.* **martyre** (1)) martyr.

martyre (2) [mar'ti:r], *n.m.* martyrdom.

martyriser [martiri'ze], *v.t.* to martyrize; to torment, to torture.

marxisme [mark'sism], *n.m.* Marxism.

marxiste [mark'sist], *a.* and *n.* Marxist.

mascarade [maska'rad], *n.f.* masquerade.

mascotte [mas'kɔt], *n.f.* mascot, charm.

masculin [masky'lɛ̃], *a.* masculine, male.—*n.m.* (*Gram.*) masculine.

masculiniser [maskylini'ze], *v.t.* to make masculine.

masculinité [maskylini'te], *n.f.* masculinity.

masque [mask], *n.m.* mask; (*fig.*) blind, cloak, pretence; masquerader, mummer; (*Fenc.*) face guard.

masqué [mas'ke], *a.* masked; disguised; concealed; *virage masqué*, blind corner.

masquer [mas'ke], *v.t.* to mask; to cloak, to disguise; to conceal.

massacrant [masa'krã], *a.* used chiefly in *être d'une humeur massacrante*, to be in an awful temper.

massacre [ma'sakr], *n.m.* massacre, butchery, slaughter; (*fig.*) havoc, waste.

massacrer [masa'kre], *v.t.* to massacre, to butcher, to murder, to slaughter; (*fig.*) to bungle.

massacreur [masa'krœːr], *n.m.* (*fem.* **-euse**) slaughterer, slayer; (*fig.*) bungler.

massage [ma'saːʒ], *n.m.* massage.

masse (1) [mas], *n.f.* mass, heap, lump; mob; stock; (*Elec.*) ground.

masse (2) [mas], *n.f.* sledge-hammer.

massepain [mas'pɛ̃], *n.m.* marzipan.

masser [ma'se], *v.t.* to mass (*troops etc.*); to massage.

masseur [ma'sœːr], *n.m.* (*fem.* **-euse**) masseur, masseuse.

massier [ma'sje], *n.m.* mace bearer.

massif [ma'sif], *a.* (*fem.* **-ive**) massive, bulky, massy, solid; lumpish, heavy.—*n.m.* clump (*of trees, flowers etc.*); solid mass *or* block (*of masonry*); (*Geog.*) massif.

massivement [masiv'mã], *adv.* massively, heavily, solidly.

massiveté [masiv'te], *n.f.* massiveness.

massue [ma'sy], *n.f.* club (*weapon*).

mastic [mas'tik], *n.m.* mastic; cement; putty; filling(*for teeth*); plastic wood.

masticage [masti'kaːʒ], *n.m.* cementing, puttying; filling.

mastication [mastika'sjõ], *n.f.* mastication, chewing.

mastiquer (1) [masti'ke], *v.t.* to masticate.

mastiquer (2) [masti'ke], *v.t.* to putty, to cement.

mastodonte [mastɔ'dõːt], *n.m.* mastodon.

mastoïde [mastɔ'id], *a.* mastoid.

masure [ma'zyːr], *n.f.* hovel, tumbledown cottage.

mat (1) [mat], *n.m.* (*Chess*) mate.

mat (2) [mat], *a.* mat, dull, unpolished; dull-sounding; heavy, sodden.

mât [mɑ], *n.m.* mast; pole.

matador [mata'doːr], *n.m.* matador.

matamore [mata'mɔːr], *n.m.* blusterer, braggart.

match [matʃ], *n.m.* (*pl.* **matches**) (*Spt.*) match; *match nul*, draw.

matelas [ma'tlɑ], *n.m.* mattress; pad, cushion; *toile à matelas*, ticking.

matelasser [matla'se], *v.t.* to stuff, to pad.

matelot [ma'tlo], *n.m.* sailor, seaman.

matelote [ma'tlɔt], *n.f.* sailor's wife; fish stew.

mater (1) [ma'te], *v.t.* to checkmate; to bring down, to subdue.

mater (2) [ma'te], *v.t.* to make mat *or* dull, to deaden.

matérialiser [materjali'ze], *v.t.* to materialize.

matérialisme [materja'lism], *n.m.* materialism.

matérialiste [materja'list], *a.* materialistic.—*n.* materialist.

matériaux [mate'rjo], *n.m. pl.* materials.

matériel [mate'rjɛl], *a.* (*fem.* **-elle**) material; gross, rough; heavy, dull.—*n.m.* material, working stock, implements, plant.

matériellement [materjɛl'mã], *adv.* materially; positively; sensually.

maternel [matɛr'nɛl], *a.* (*fem.* **-elle**) maternal, motherly; *école maternelle*, nursery school.

maternité [matɛrni'te], *n.f.* maternity.

mathématicien [matemati'sjɛ̃], *n.m.* (*fem.* **-enne**) mathematician.

mathématique [matema'tik], *a.* mathematical.—*n.f.* (*usu. in pl.*) mathematics.

mathématiquement [matematik'mã], *adv.* mathematically.

matière [ma'tjɛːr], *n.f.* matter; material; subject matter; cause, motive; contents; *matière première*, raw material.

matin [ma'tɛ̃], *n.m.* morning, forenoon; prime, dawn.—*adv.* early, early in the morning.

mâtin [mɑ'tɛ̃], *n.m.* mastiff; big mongrel dog.

matinal [mati'nal], *a.* (*m. pl.* **-aux**) morning, early; early-rising.

matinée [mati'ne], *n.f.* morning, forenoon; afternoon performance, matinée.

matines [ma'tin], *n.f. pl.* matins.

matineux [mati'nø], *a.* (*fem.* **-euse**) rising early.

matois [ma'twa], *a.* cunning, artful, sly.—*n.m.* (*fem.* **-e**) cunning person, sly dog.

matoisement [matwaz'mã], *adv.* cunningly, slyly.

matoiserie [matwaz'ri], *n.f.* cunning; wile.

matou [ma'tu], *n.m.* tom-cat; (*fam.*) curmudgeon.

matraque [ma'trak], *n.f.* bludgeon; truncheon.

matriarcal [matriar'kal], *a.* (*m. pl.* **-aux**) matriarchal.

matriarcat [matriar'ka], *n.m.* matriarchy.

matrice [ma'tris], *n.f.* womb, matrix.

matricide [matri'sid], *a.* matricidal.—*n.* matricide (*person*).—*n.m.* matricide (*crime*).

matricule [matri'kyl], *n.f.* register, roll; matriculation.—*n.m.* regimental number (*of a soldier*); number (*of a rifle etc.*).

matrimonial [matrimɔ'njal], *a.* (*m. pl.* **-aux**) matrimonial.

Matthieu [ma'tjø], *m.* Matthew.

maturation [matyra'sjõ], *n.f.* maturation.

mâture [mɑ'tyːr], *n.f.* masting, masts and spars.

maturité [matyri'te], *n.f.* maturity, ripeness.

maudire [mo'diːr], *v.t. irr.* to curse; to detest.

maudissable [modi'sabl], *a.* execrable, detestable.

maudit [mo'di], *a.* cursed, accursed; wretched.

maugréer [mogre'e], *v.i.* to fret and fume, to curse and swear.

maure [MORE].

Maurice [mɔ'ris], *m.* Maurice; *l'île Maurice*, Mauritius.

Mauritanie [mɔrita'ni], **la**, *f.* Mauritania.

mauritanien [mɔrita'njɛ̃], *a.* (*fem.* **-enne**) Mauritanian.—*n.m.* (**Mauritanien**, *fem.* **-enne**) Mauritanian (*person*).

mausolée [mozo'le], *n.m.* mausoleum.

maussade [mo'sad], *a.* sulky, sullen, cross; disagreeable, dull.

maussadement [mosad'mã], *adv.* disagreeably, sullenly, peevishly.

maussaderie [mosa'dri], *n.f.* sullenness, sulkiness.

mauvais [mɔ'vɛ], *a.* bad, ill, evil; naughty, mischievous; hurtful; wrong; unpleasant; wretched; nasty.—*n.m.* bad.—*adv.* bad, badly, wrong.

mauve [moːv], *a.* mauve.—*n.f.* (*Bot.*) mallow.

maxillaire [maksi′lɛːr], *a.* maxillary.—*n.m.*
jaw-bone.
maxime [mak′sim]. *n.f.* maxim.
maximum [maksi′nɔm], *a.* (*fem.* **maxima**)
maximum.—*n.m.* (*pl.* **maxima** or **max-
imums**) maximum; acme.
mayonnaise [majɔ′nɛːz], *n.f.* mayonnaise.
mazout [ma′ʒut], *n.m.* fuel oil.
me [mə], *pron. pers.* me; to me.
méandre [me′ɑːdr], *n.m.* meander, winding.
mécanicien [mekani′sjɛ̃], *n.m.* mechanic;
engine driver, (*Am.*) engineer; *ingénieur
mécanicien*, mechanical engineer.
mécanique [meka′nik], *a.* mechanical.—
n.f. mechanics; mechanism, machinery;
machine.
mécaniquement [mekanik′mɑ̃], *adv.* mechanically.
mécanisation [mekaniza′sjɔ̃], *n.f.* mechanization.
mécaniser [mekani′ze], *v.t.* to mechanize.
mécanisme [meka′nism], *n.m.* mechanism,
machinery.
méchamment [meʃa′mɑ̃], *adv.* wickedly;
maliciously.
méchanceté [meʃɑ̃s′te], *n.f.* wickedness;
spitefulness; naughtiness.
méchant [me′ʃɑ̃], *a.* wicked, evil, bad; spiteful, malicious; naughty; paltry; vicious
(*of an animal*); nasty.—*n.m.* (*fem.* **-e**) wicked
person, evil-doer; naughty child.
mèche [mɛːʃ], *n.f.* wick (*of candle*); fuse;
bit, drill; worm (*of screws*); lock (*of hair*).
mécompte [me′kɔ̃ːt], *n.m.* miscalculation;
mistake; disappointment.
méconnaissable [mekɔnɛ′sabl], *a.* unrecognizable.
méconnaissance [mekɔnɛ′sɑ̃ːs], *n.f.* mis-
appreciation, misreading; ingratitude.
méconnaître [mekɔ′nɛːtr], *v.t. irr.* (*conjug.
like* CONNAÎTRE) not to recognize; to disown;
to disregard, to ignore; to misjudge. **se
méconnaître**, *v.r.* to forget oneself.
méconnu [mekɔ′ny], *a.* unrecognized, unacknowledged; ignored, disowned.
mécontent [mekɔ̃′tɑ̃], *a.* displeased, dissatisfied.—*n.m.* (*fem.* **-e**) malcontent.
mécontentement [mekɔ̃tɑ̃t′mɑ̃], *n.m.* dissatisfaction, discontent.
mécontenter [mekɔ̃tɑ̃′te], *v.t.* to displease.
Mecque [mɛk], **la**, *f.* Mecca.
mécréant [mekre′ɑ̃], *n.m.* (*fem.* **-e**) unbeliever, infidel.
médaille [me′daːj], *n.f.* medal; (*Arch.*)
medallion.
médaillé [meda′je], *a.* with a medal as a
reward; having a badge (*of hawker, porter
etc.*).—*n.m.* (*fem.* **-ée**) holder of a medal.
médaillon [meda′jɔ̃], *n.m.* medallion; locket.
médecin [med′sɛ̃], *n.m.* physician, doctor;
faire venir le médecin, to send for the
doctor.
médecine [med′sin], *n.f.* medicine.
médiateur [medja′tœːr], *a.* (*fem.* **-trice**)
mediatory.—*n.m.* (*fem.* **-trice**) mediator.
médiation [medja′sjɔ̃], *n.f.* mediation.
médical [medi′kal], *a.* (*m. pl.* **-aux**) medical.
médicament [medika′mɑ̃], *n.m.* medicine,
drug.
médicamenter [medikamɑ̃′te], *v.t.* to physic,
to doctor.
médication [medika′sjɔ̃], *n.f.* medication.

médicinal [medisi′nal], *a.* (*m. pl.* **-aux**)
medicinal.
médiéval [medje′val], *a.* (*m. pl.* **-aux**) medi-
(a)eval.
médiocre [me′djɔkr], *a.* mediocre, middling;
moderate.—*n.m.* mediocrity.
médiocrement [medjɔkrə′mɑ̃], *adv.* mid-
dlingly, indifferently; poorly; barely.
médiocrité [medjɔkri′te], *n.f.* mediocrity.
médire [me′diːr], *v.i. irr.* to slander, to speak
ill of, to traduce.
médisance [medi′zɑ̃ːs], *n.f.* slander, scandal.
médisant [medi′zɑ̃], *a.* slanderous, scandalous.—*n.m.* (*fem.* **-e**) slanderer, scandal-
monger.
méditatif [medita′tif], *a.* (*fem.* **-tive**) meditative, pensive.
méditation [medita′sjɔ̃], *n.f.* meditation.
méditer [medi′te], *v.t.* to meditate, to think
over; to plan.—*v.i.* to meditate, to muse.
méditerrané [meditera′ne], *a.* inland; *la
(Mer) Méditerranée*, the Mediterranean
(Sea).
méditerranéen [meditɛrane′ɛ̃], *a.* (*fem.*
-enne) Mediterranean.
médium [me′djɔm], *n.m.* medium.
médoc [me′dɔk], *n.m.* or *vin de Médoc*,
Médoc (*claret*).
meeting [mi′tiŋ], *n.m.* (*Polit., Spt.*) meeting.
méfait [me′fɛ], *n.m.* misdeed, crime.
méfiance [me′fjɑ̃ːs], *n.f.* mistrust, distrust,
suspicion.
méfiant [me′fjɑ̃], *a.* distrustful, suspicious.
méfier (se) [səme′fje], *v.r.* to mistrust, to
distrust, to be suspicious of (*de*).
mégaphone [mega′fɔn], *n.m.* megaphone.
mégarde [me′gard], *n.f.* inadvertence; *par
mégarde*, inadvertently.
mégère [me′ʒɛːr], *n.f.* shrew, vixen.
mégot [me′go], *n.m.* (*pop.*) cigar stump,
cigarette end.
meilleur [mɛ′jœːr], *a.* better; preferable; *le
meilleur*, the best; *meilleur marché*,
cheaper; *de meilleure heure*, earlier.—
n.m. best.
mélancolie [melɑ̃kɔ′li], *n.f.* melancholy, sadness, gloom, dejection.
mélancolique [melɑ̃kɔ′lik], *a.* melancholy;
dismal, gloomy.
mélancoliquement [melɑ̃kɔlik′mɑ̃], *adv.*
gloomily.
mélange [me′lɑ̃ːʒ], *n.m.* mixture, mingling;
blending (*of tea*); medley, mash (*for
brewing*).
mélanger [melɑ̃′ʒe], *v.t.* and **se mélanger**,
v.r. (*conjug. like* MANGER) to mix, to mingle,
to blend.
mélasse [me′laːs], *n.f.* molasses treacle.
mêlé [mɛ′le], *a.* mixed; miscellaneous.
mêlée [me′le], *n.f.* conflict, fray; scramble,
scuffle, free fight.
mêler [mɛ′le], *v.t.* to mingle, to mix; to blend;
to jumble; to entangle, to involve; to
shuffle (*cards*). **se mêler**, *v.r.* to mingle to
blend, to intermingle; to trouble oneself
(*de*); to interfere (*de*); to have a hand in; to
get entangled, to get mixed up (*dans*);
mêlez-vous de vos affaires, mind your
own business.
mélèze [me′lɛːz], *n.m.* larch.
mélodie [melɔ′di], *n.f.* melody; melodious-
ness.

mélodieusement [melɔdjøz'mã], *adv.* tunefully.

mélodieux [melɔ'djø], *a.* (*fem.* **-euse**) melodious, musical, tuneful.

mélodramatique [melɔdrama'tik], *a.* melodramatic.

mélodrame [melɔ'dram], *n.m.* melodrama.

melon [mə'lɔ̃], *n.m.* melon; derby (hat).

membrane [mã'bran], *n.f.* membrane; web (*of duck's foot etc.*).

membraneux [mãbra'nø], *a.* (*fem.* **-euse**) membranous.

membre [mã:br], *n.m.* limb; member.

membrure [mã'bry:r], *n.f.* limbs, frame (*of a person etc.*); ribs, timbers (*of a ship*).

même [mɛ:m], *a.* same; self, self-same, very same; *moi-même*, myself.—*adv.* even, also; *à même de*, in a position to, able to; *de même*, likewise; *quand même*, even though; *tout de même*, all the same.

mémoire (1) [me'mwa:r], *n.f.* memory; remembrance; commemoration; fame; *de mémoire* from memory; *de mémoire d'homme*, within living memory.

mémoire (2) [me'mwa:r], *n.m.* memorandum, bill, statement of account; (*Sci., Lit.*) treatise; memorial; (*pl.*) memoirs.

mémorable [memɔ'rabl], *a.* memorable.

mémorandum [memɔrã'dɔm], *n.m.* memorandum; notebook.

mémorial [memɔ'rjal], *n.m.* (*pl.* **-aux**) memorial; memoirs; (*Comm.*) daybook.

menaçant [məna'sã], *a.* menacing, threatening.

menace [mə'nas], *n.f.* menace, threat.

menacer [məna'se], *v.t.* (*conjug. like* COMMENCER) to threaten, to menace; to forebode; to impend.

ménage [me'na:ʒ], *n.m.* housekeeping; household, family, married couple; household equipment; economy; *faire bon ménage*, to live happily together; *faire des ménages*, to do housework by the day; *femme de ménage*, housemaid.

ménagement [menaʒ'mã], *n.m.* regard, circumspection, caution, discretion.

ménager [mena'ʒe], *v.t.* (*conjug. like* MANGER) to be sparing of, to save; to be careful of, to treat with caution, to humor; to procure; to contrive. **se ménager**, *v.r.* to take care of oneself; to spare oneself.—*a.* (*fem.* **-ère**) thrifty, sparing, frugal; household.—*n.f.* (**-ère**) housewife, housekeeper; cruet stand; tableware.

ménagerie [menaʒ'ri], *n.f.* menagerie.

mendiant [mã'djã], *n.m.* (*fem.* **-e**) beggar, mendicant.

mendicité [mãdisi'te], *n.f.* begging, mendicity.

mendier [mã'dje], *v.t.* to beg for.—*v.i.* to beg.

mener [mə'ne], *v.t.* (*conjug. like* AMENER) to guide, to conduct, to lead; to drive (*a carriage*); to steer (*a boat etc.*); to bring, to take; to manage.—*v.i.* to lead, to conduct, to go.

ménestrel [menɛs'trɛl], *n.m.* minstrel.

meneur [mə'nœ:r], *n.m.* (*fem.* **-euse**) driver, leader; agitator, ringleader.

méningite [menɛ̃'ʒit], *n.f.* meningitis.

menotte [mə'nɔt], *n.f.* (*colloq.*) little hand (*of a child*); (*pl.*) handcuffs.

menotter [mənɔ'te], *v.t.* to handcuff.

mensonge [mã'sɔ̃:ʒ], *n.m.* lie, falsehood, untruth.

mensonger [mãsɔ̃'ʒe], *a.* (*fem.* **-ère**) lying, untrue, false.

menstruation [mãstrɥa'sjɔ̃], *n.f.* menstruation.

menstrues [mã'stry], *n.f. pl.* menses, periods.

mensualité [mãsɥali'te], *n.f.* monthly payment.

mensuel [mã'sɥel], *a.* (*fem.* **-elle**) monthly.

mensuellement [mãsɥel'mã], *adv.* · onthly.

mensuration [mãsyra'sjɔ̃], *n.f.* measurement.

mental [mã'tal], *a.* (*m. pl.* **-aux**) mental.

mentalement [mãtal'mã], *adv.* mentally.

mentalité [mãtali'te], *n.f.* mentality.

menteur [mã'tœ:r], *a.* (*fem.* **-euse**) lying, false, deceitful.—*n.m.* (*fem.* **-euse**) liar, story-teller.

menthe [mã:t], *n.f.* mint.

mention [mã'sjɔ̃], *n.f.* mention; (*sch.*) *reçu avec mention*, passed with distinction.

mentionner [mãsjɔ'ne], *v.t.* to mention, to name.

mentir [mã'ti:r], *v.i. irr.* (*conjug. like* SENTIR) to lie, to tell a lie *or* untruth.

menton [mã'tɔ̃], *n.m.* chin.

mentor [mã'tɔ:r], *n.m.* mentor, guide, tutor.

menu [mə'ny], *a.* slender, spare, thin, small; petty.—*n.m.* minute detail, particulars; menu, bill of fare; *par le menu*, in detail.—*adv.* small, fine, minutely, in small pieces; *hacher menu*, to mince.

menuet [mə'nɥɛ], *n.m.* minuet.

menuiser [mənɥi'ze], *v.t.* to saw, to cut etc. (*wood*).—*v.i.* to do carpenter's work.

menuiserie [mənɥiz'ri], *n.f.* woodwork, joinery, carpentry.

menuisier [mənɥi'zje], *n.m.* joiner, carpenter.

méprendre (se) [səme'prã:dr], *v.r. irr.* (*conjug. like* PRENDRE) to mistake, to be mistaken.

mépris [me'pri], *n.m.* contempt, scorn.

méprisable [mepri'zabl], *a.* contemptible, despicable.

méprisant [mepri'zã], *a.* contemptuous, scornful.

méprise [me'pri:z], *n.f.* mistake, misunderstanding.

mépriser [mepri'ze], *v.t.* to despise, to scorn.

mer [mɛ:r], *n.f.* sea; *aller au bord de la mer*, to go to the seaside; *en pleine mer*, on the open sea; *mal de mer*, seasickness.

mercantile [mɛrkã'til], *a.* mercantile, commercial; (*fig.*) mercenary.

mercenaire [mɛrsə'nɛ:r], *a.* mercenary, venal.—*n.m.* mercenary, hireling.

mercerie [mɛrsə'ri], *n.f.* notions (store).

merci [mɛr'si], *n.f.* (*no pl.*) mercy, discretion, will.—*n.m.* thanks.—*int.* thank you, thanks.

mercier [mɛr'sje], *n.m.* (*fem.* **-ière**) dealer in notions.

mercredi [mɛrkrə'di], *n.m.* Wednesday; *mercredi des Cendres*, Ash Wednesday.

mercure [mɛr'ky:r], *n.m.* mercury, quicksilver.

mercuriel [mɛrky'rjɛl], *a.* (*fem.* **-elle**) mercurial.

mère [mɛ:r], *n.f.* mother; dam (*of animals*); (*fig.*) cause, reason.

méridien [meri'djɛ̃], *a.* (*fem.* **-enne**) and *n.m.* meridian.—*n.f.* (**-enne**) siesta.

méridional [meridjɔ'nal], a. (m. pl. **-aux**) meridional, southern.—*n.m.* (*fem.* **-e**) person of the Midi, southerner.

meringue [mə'rɛ̃:g], *n.f.* meringue (*confection*).

mérinos [meri'nɔ:s], *n.m.* merino sheep; merino wool; merino (*material*).

merise [mə'ri:z], *n.f.* wild cherry.

merisier [məri'zje], *n.m.* wild-cherry tree.

méritant [meri'tɑ̃], a. meritorious, worthy.

mérite [me'rit], *n.m.* merit, worth; desert.

mériter [meri'te], *v.t.* to deserve, to merit; to earn.—*v.i.* to be deserving (**de**).

méritoire [meri'twa:r], a. meritorious.

méritoirement [meritwar'mɑ̃], adv. meritoriously, deservingly.

merlan [mɛr'lɑ̃], *n.m.* whiting.

merle [mɛrl], *n.m.* blackbird.

merluche [mɛr'lyʃ], *n.f.* hake; dried cod.

merveille [mɛr'vɛ:j], *n.f.* wonder, marvel, prodigy; **à merveille**, wonderfully well.

merveilleusement [mɛrvejøz'mɑ̃], adv. wonderfully, admirably.

merveilleux [mɛrvɛ'jø], a. (*fem.* **-euse**) wonderful, marvellous.—*n.m.* the wonderful, the marvellous part.

mes [me], *pl.* [MON].

mésalliance [meza'ljɑ̃:s], *n.f.* misalliance, bad match.

mésallier [meza'lje], *v.t.* to marry off (*somebody*) badly; (*fig.*) to disparage. **se mésallier**, *v.r.* to marry beneath one.

mésange [me'zɑ̃:ʒ], *n.f.* (*Orn.*) tit.

mésangette [mezɑ̃'ʒɛt], *n.f.* bird trap.

mésaventure [mezavɑ̃'ty:r], *n.f.* mischance, misadventure, misfortune.

mésentente [mezɑ̃'tɑ̃:t], *n.f.* misunderstanding; disagreement.

mésestime [mezɛs'tim], *n.f.* low esteem.

mésestimer [mezɛsti'me], *v.t.* to underestimate, to underrate.

mésintelligence [mezɛ̃tɛli'ʒɑ̃:s], *n.f.* misunderstanding, variance, disagreement.

mesmérisme [mɛsme'rism], *n.m.* mesmerism.

mesquin [mɛs'kɛ̃], a. shabby; paltry; mean.

mesquinement [mɛskin'mɑ̃], adv. shabbily, meanly.

mesquinerie [mɛskin'ri], *n.f.* meanness, shabbiness.

mess [mɛs], *n.m. inv.* (*Mil.*) mess.

message [me'sa:ʒ], *n.m.* message.

messager [mesa'ʒe], *n.m.* (*fem.* **-ère**) messenger; carrier; (*fig.*) forerunner.

messagerie [mesa'ʒri], *n.f.* shipping office; carriage of goods; goods department; parcels office; **messageries maritimes**, shipping service.

messe [mɛs], *n.f.* (*R.-C. Ch.*) mass.

messéance [mese'ɑ̃:s], *n.f.* unseemliness, impropriety.

messéant [mese'ɑ̃], a. unseemly, unbecoming, improper.

messeigneurs [mesɛ'nœ:r], *pl.* [MONSEIGNEUR].

Messie [me'si], *m.* Messiah.

messieurs [me'sjø], *pl.* [MONSIEUR].

mesurable [məzy'rabl], a. measurable.

mesurage [məzy'ra:ʒ], *n.m.* measurement, measuring.

mesure [mə'zy:r], *n.f.* measure; gauge, standard; measurement, extent, limit; (*fig.*) moderation; dimension; (*Mus.*) bar; (*Pros.*) metre; **à mesure que**, in proportion as, as; **outre mesure**, excessively; **se mettre en mesure de**, to prepare to, to get ready to.

mesuré [məzy're], a. measured, regular; cautious.

mesurer [məzy're], *v.t.* to measure; to proportion; to calculate; to compare, to consider. **se mesurer**, *v.r.* to try one's strength; (*fig.*) to vie, to contend, to cope.

mesureur [məzy'rœ:r], *n.m.* measurer; meter.

mésusage [mezy'za:ʒ], *n.m.* misuse, abuse.

mésuser [mezy'ze], *v.i.* to misuse, to abuse (**de**).

métabolisme [metabɔ'lism], *n.m.* metabolism.

métairie [mete'ri], *n.f.* land, small farm.

métal [me'tal], *n.m.* (*pl.* **-aux**) metal.

métallique [meta'lik], a. metallic.

métallurgie [metalyr'ʒi], *n.f.* metallurgy.

métallurgiste [metalyr'ʒist], *n.m.* metallurgist.

métamorphose [metamɔr'fo:z], *n.f.* metamorphosis, transformation.

métaphore [meta'fɔ:r], *n.f.* metaphor.

métaphorique [metafɔ'rik], a. metaphorical.

métaphoriquement [metafɔrik'mɑ̃], adv. metaphorically.

métaphysique [metafi'zik], a. metaphysical. —*n.f.* metaphysics.

métatarse [meta'tars], *n.m.* (*Anat.*) metatarsus.

métayage [mete'ja:ʒ], *n.m.* metayage.

métayer [mete'je], *n.m.* (*fem.* **-ère**) small farmer.

météo [mete'o], *n.f.* (*fam.*) meteorology; weather report; meteorological office.

météore [mete'ɔ:r], *n.m.* meteor.

météorique [meteɔ'rik], a. meteoric.

météorite [meteɔ'rit], *n.m.* or *f.* meteorite.

météorologie [meteɔrɔlɔ'ʒi], *n.f.* meteorology.

météorologique [meteɔrɔlɔ'ʒik], a. meteorological.

météorologiste [meteɔrɔlɔ'ʒist], **météorologue** [meteɔrɔ'lɔg], *n.* meteorologist.

méthane [me'tan], *n.m.* marsh gas, methane.

méthode [me'tɔd], *n.f.* method, system; way.

méthodique [metɔ'dik], a. methodical, systematic.

méthodiquement [metɔdik'mɑ̃], adv. methodically.

méthodisme [metɔ'dism], *n.m.* Methodism.

méthodiste [metɔ'dist], a. and n. Methodist.

méticuleusement [metikyløz'mɑ̃], adv. meticulously.

méticuleux [metiky'lø], a. (*fem.* **-euse**) meticulous, fastidious.

méticulosité [metikylɔzi'te], *n.f.* meticulousness.

métier [me'tje], *n.m.* trade, business, calling, craft, profession; loom, frame; **arts et métiers**, arts and crafts; **corps de métier**, corporation, guild; **gens de métier**, professionals; **homme de métier**, craftsman; **métier manuel**, handicraft.

métis [me'ti:s], a. (*fem.* **-isse**) half-caste, cross-bred; hybrid (*plant*); mongrel (*dog*).— *n.m.* (*fem.* **-isse**) half-caste; mongrel (*dog*).

métissage [meti'sa:ʒ], *n.m.* cross-breeding.

métisser [meti'se], *v.t.* to cross-breed.

métrage [me′traːʒ], *n.m.* measurement (*in metres*); (*Cine.*) **court métrage**, short film.
mètre [mɛtr], *n.m.* metre (*1.09 yards*); rule, measure (*of 1 metre*); (*Pros.*) metre.
métrer [me′tre], *v.t.* (*conjug. like* CÉDER) to measure (*by the metre*).
métreur [me′trœːr], *n.m.* quantity surveyor.
métrique [me′trik], *a.* metric (*system etc.*); (*Pros.*) metrical.—*n.f.* scansion.
métro [me′tro], *n.m.* (*collog. abbr. of* **chemin de fer métropolitain**) the underground (railway), the tube (*in Paris*), (*Am.*) the subway.
métropole [metro′pɔl], *n.f.* mother country; metropolis.
métropolitain [metrɔpɔli′tɛ̃], *a.* metropolitan.—*n.m.* metropolitan, archbishop; underground railway, subway.
mets [mɛ], *n.m.* dish, food, viands.
mettable [me′tabl], *a.* fit to be worn, wearable.
metteur [mɛ′tœːr], *n.m.* **metteur en scène**, (*Theat.*) producer, (*Cine.*) director.
mettre [mɛtr], *v.t. irr.* to put, to set, to place; to put on, to wear; to employ; to contribute, to expend; to suppose, to imagine; **mettre en marche** or **en mouvement**, to start up, to set going; **mettre quelqu'un en état de**, to enable someone to; **mettre un habit**, to put on a coat. **se mettre**, *v.r.* to put *or* place oneself; to dress; to begin (*à*); to take to; **se mettre à parler**, to begin to speak; **se mettre à table**, to sit down to table; **se mettre bien**, to dress well; **se mettre en route**, to start.
meuble [mœbl], *a.* movable; **biens meubles**, (*Law*) personal property.—*n.m.* piece of furniture; (*pl.*) furniture.
meublé [mœ′ble], *a.* furnished.—*n.m.* a furnished room *or* flat.
meubler [mœ′ble], *v.t.* to furnish; to stock, to store. **se meubler**, *v.r.* to furnish one's home.
meule [mø:l], *n.f.* millstone, grindstone; (*Agric.*) stack, rick (*of grain, hay etc.*); (*Hort.*) hotbed.
meunerie [møn′ri], *n.f.* miller's trade; (*collect.*) millers.
meunier [mø′nje], *n.m.* miller; chub (*fish*).
meunière [mø′njɛːr], *n.f.* miller's wife.
meurtre [mœrtr], *n.m.* murder.
meurtrier [mœrtri′e], *a.* (*fem.* **-ière**) murdering, murderous, deadly; killing.—*n.m.* (*fem.* **-ière** (1)) murderer, murderess.
meurtrière (2) [mœrtri′ɛːr], *n.f.* (*Fort.*) loophole.
meurtrir [mœr′triːr], *v.t.* to bruise, to make black and blue.
meurtrissure [mœrtri′syːr], *n.f.* bruise.
meute [mø:t], *n.f.* pack (*of hounds etc.*).
mévendre [me′vãːdr], *v.t.* to sell at a loss.
mévente [me′vãːt], *n.f.* selling at a loss; slump.
mexicain [mɛksi′kɛ̃], *a.* Mexican.—*n.m.* (**Mexicain** *fem.* **-aine**) Mexican (*person*).
Mexico [mɛksi′ko], *m.* Mexico City.
Mexique [mɛk′sik], **le**, *m.* Mexico.
mi [mi], *n.m.* (*Mus.*) mi; the note E.
mi- [mi], *comb. form.* half, demi-, semi-; mid, middle; **à mi-chemin**, half-way; **à mi-corps**, up to the waist; **à mi-côte**, half-way

up the hill; **à mi-jambe**, half-way up the leg; **la mi-août**, the middle of August.
miaou [mjau], *n.m. inv.* (*fam.*) mew, miaow; cat.
miaulement [mjol′mã], *n.m.* mewing.
miauler [mjo′le], *v.i.* to mew; to caterwaul.
mica [mi′ka], *n.m.* mica.
miche [miʃ], *n.f.* round loaf.
Michel [mi′ʃɛl], *m.* Michael; **la Saint-Michel**, Michaelmas.
Michel-Ange [mikɛl′ãːʒ], *m.* Michelangelo.
Micheline [miʃ′lin], *n.f.* rail-car, autorail.
micro [mi′kro], *n.m.* (*fam. abbr. of* **microphone**) mike.
microbe [mi′krɔb], *n.m.* microbe.
microcosme [mikro′kɔsm], *n.m.* microcosm.
microfilm [mikro′film], *n.m.* microfilm.
micromètre [mikro′mɛtr], *n.m.* micrometer.
micro-organisme [mikroorga′nism], *n.m.* micro-organism.
microphone [mikro′fɔn], *n.m.* microphone.
microscope [mikros′kɔp], *n.m.* microscope.
microscopique [mikrosko′pik], *a.* microscopic.
midi [mi′di], *n.m.* noon, midday, twelve o'clock (*in the day*); meridian; south; **le Midi (de la France)**, the South of France.
midinette [midi′nɛt], *n.f.* (*fam.*) young dressmaker *or* milliner in Paris.
mie [mi], *n.f.* crumb; soft part of loaf.
miel [mjɛl], *n.m.* honey; **lune de miel**, honeymoon.
miellé [mjɛ′le], *a.* honeyed; like honey; (*fig.*) sweet, bland.
miellée [mjɛ′le], **miellure** [mjɛ′lyːr], *n.f.* honeydew.
mielleusement [mjɛløz′mã], *adv.* sweetly, blandly, honey-like.
mielleux [mjɛ′lø], *a.* (*fem.* **-euse**) honeyed; sweet, bland.
mien [mjɛ̃], *a. poss. and pron. poss.* (*fem.* **mienne**) mine; **le mien, la mienne, les miens, les miennes**, mine, my own.
miette [mjɛt], *n.f.* crumb, bit, morsel.
mieux [mjø], *adv.* better; correctly; more agreeably, more comfortably etc.; rather, more; **faute de mieux**, for want of better; **mieux vaut tard que jamais**, better late than never; **tant mieux**, so much the better; **valoir mieux**, to be better, to be worth more.—*n.m.* best thing; improvement.
mièvre [mjɛːvr], *a.* finical, affected; delicate (*child*), fragile.
mièvrerie [mjɛvrə′ri], **mièvreté** [mjɛvrə′te], *n.f.* affectation.
mignard [mi′naːr], *a.* delicate, pretty, dainty; mincing, affected.
mignardement [miɲardə′mã], *adv.* delicately, daintily; mincingly.
mignarder [miɲar′de], *v.t.* to fondle, to pet; to indulge.
mignardise [miɲar′diːz], *n.f.* delicacy, prettiness, daintiness; affectation, mincing ways.
mignon [mi′nɔ̃], *a.* (*fem.* **-onne**) delicate, pretty, dainty; sweet; neat, tiny.—*n.m.* (*fem.* **-onne**) darling, pet, favorite.
mignonnement [miɲɔn′mã], *adv.* daintily, prettily.
migraine [mi′grɛn], *n.f.* sick headache; migraine.

migrateur [migra'tœːr], *a.* (*fem.* **-trice**) migratory.

migration [migra'sjɔ̃], *n.f.* migration.

migratoire [migra'twaːr], *a.* migratory.

mijoter [miʒɔ'te], *v.t., v.i.* to cook slowly, to stew; to simmer; (*fig.*) to plot, to brew.

mil (1) [MILLE (2)].

mil (2) [mil], *n.m.* millet.

milan [mi'lɑ̃], *n.m.* kite (*bird*).

milice [mi'lis], *n.f.* militia; (*fig.*) troops, soldiery.

milicien [mili'sjɛ̃], *n.m.* militiaman.

milieu [mi'ljø], *n.m.* (*pl.* **-eux**) middle, midst; heart, center; mean; environment, surroundings; *au beau milieu*, in the very middle.

militaire [mili'tɛːr], *a.* military.—*n.m.* soldier.

militairement [militɛr'mɑ̃], *adv.* in a soldier-like manner.

militant [mili'tɑ̃], *a.* militant.

militer [mili'te], *v.i.* to militate (*pour* or *contre*).

(*C*) **millage** [mi'laːʒ], *n.m.* mileage.

mille (1) [mil], *n.m.* mile (*English, American mile, 1609.35 metres*).

mille (2) [mil], *a. inv.* and *n.m. inv.* (**mil** *in dates of the Christian era*) thousand, a thousand, one thousand.

millénaire [mille'nɛːr], *a.* millenary.—*n.m.* millennium.

mille-pattes [mil'pat], *n.m. inv.* centipede.

millésime [mile'zim], *n.m.* date (*on a coin, monument etc.*).

millet [mi'jɛ], *n.m.* millet, millet grass.

milliard [mi'ljaːr], *n.m.* one thousand millions, (*Am.*) one billion.

milliardaire [miljar'dɛːr], *a.* and *n.* multi-millionaire(ss).

millibar [milli'bar], *n.m.* (*Meteor.*) millibar.

millième [mi'ljɛm], *a.* and *n.m.* thousandth.

millier [mi'lje], *n.m.* thousand.

milligramme [milli'gram], *n.m.* milligramme (*.01 54 grain*).

millimètre [milli'mɛtr], *n.m.* millimetre (*.03937 in.*).

million [mi'ljɔ̃], *n.m.* million.

millionième [miljɔ'njɛːm], *a.* and *n.m.* millionth.

millionnaire [miljɔ'nɛːr], *a.* and *n.* millionaire(ss).

mime [mim], *n.m.* mime; mimic.

mimer [mi'me], *v.t., v.i.* to mimic, to mime.

mimi [mi'mi], *n.m.* (*Childish*) cat, pussy; darling, ducky.

mimique [mi'mik], *a.* mimic, mimetic.—*n.f.* art of mimicry.

mimosa [mimo'za], *n.m.* mimosa.

minable [mi'nabl], *a.* (*colloq.*) seedy, shabby.

minaret [mina'rɛ], *n.m.* minaret.

minauder [mino'de], *v.i.* to smirk, to simper.

minauderie [mino'dri], *n.f.* affected *or* mincing manners, simpering, smirking.

minaudier [mino'dje], *a.* (*fem.* **-ière**) affected, lackadaisical.—*n.m.* (*fem.* **-ière**) affected person.

mince [mɛ̃ːs], *a.* thin, slender, slim; puny, slight, trivial; scanty, small.—*int.* (*pop.*) *ah! mince!* or *mince alors!* my word! well, I never!

minceur [mɛ̃'sœːr], *n.f.* slenderness, slimness.

mine (1) [min], *n.f.* look, bearing; face, expression; appearance, aspect; (*pl.*) airs.

mine (2) [min], *n.f.* (*Min.*) mine; (*fig.*) source, store.

mine (3) [min], *n.f.* (*Mil., Pyro.*) mine.

miner [mi'ne], *v.t.* to mine, to undermine, to sap; to wear away.

minerai [min'rɛ], *n.m.* ore.

minéral [mine'ral], *a.* (*m. pl.* **-aux**) mineral. —*n.m.* (*pl.* **-aux**) mineral; ore.

minéralogie [mineralɔ'ʒi], *n.f.* mineralogy.

minéralogique [mineralɔ'ʒik], *a.* mineralogical.

minéralogiste [mineralɔ'ʒist], *n.* mineralogist.

Minerve [mi'nɛrv], *f.* Minerva.

minet [mi'nɛ], *n.m.* (*fem.* **-ette**) (*colloq.*) puss, kitten.

mineur (1) [mi'nœːr], *n.m.* miner, pitman; (*Mil.*) sapper.

mineur (2) [mi'nœːr], *a.* lesser, minor; under age.—*n.m.* (*fem.* **-e**) minor; (*Law*) infant.

miniature [minja'tyːr], *n.f.* miniature.

miniaturiste [minjaty'rist], *a.* of miniatures. —*n.* miniature painter.

minier [mi'nje], *a.* (*fem.* **-ière**) pertaining to mines, mining.—*n.f.* (**-ière**) open mine.

minime [mi'nim], *a.* very small, trifling.

minimum [mini'mɔm], *a.* (*usu. inv.*) minimum.—*n.m.* (*pl.* **minimums** *or* **minima**) minimum.

ministère [minis'tɛːr], *n.m.* ministry; department; minister's office; offices, services; administration.

ministériel [ministe'rjɛl], *a.* (*fem.* **-elle**) ministerial.

ministre [mi'nistr], *n.m.* (*Polit., Ch.*) minister; clergyman.

minois [mi'nwa], *n.m. inv.* pretty face; looks, appearance.

minoritaire [minɔri'tɛːr], *a.* minority.

minorité [minɔri'te], *n.f.* minority; (*Law*) infancy.

Minorque [mi'nɔrk], *f.* Minorca.

minoterie [minɔ'tri] *n.f.* flour mill; flour trade.

minotier [minɔ'tje], *n.m.* flour dealer, grain dealer.

minuit [mi'nɥi], *n.m.* midnight.

minuscule [minys'kyl], *a.* small (*of letters*), minute, tiny.—*n.f.* small letter.

minute [mi'nyt], *n.f.* minute (*of time*), moment, instant; rough draft; minute, record; *minute !* (*fam.*) just a moment!

minuter [miny'te], *v.t.* to record; to time.

minuterie [minyt'ri], *n.f.* time switch.

minutie [miny'si], *n.f.* trifle, (*pl.*) minutiae.

minutieusement [minysjøz'mɑ̃], *adv.* minutely.

minutieux [miny'sjø], *a.* (*fem.* **-euse**) minute; meticulous.

mioche [mjɔʃ], *n.* (*colloq.*) brat, urchin.

mi-parti [mipar'ti], *a.* bipartite, half and half.

mirabelle [mira'bɛl], *n.f.* yellow variety of plum.

miracle [mi'raːkl], *n.m.* miracle; (*fig.*) wonder; *à miracle*, wonderfully well.

miraculeusement [mirakyløz'mɑ̃], *adv.* miraculously; wonderfully.

miraculeux [miraky'lø], *a.* (*fem.* **-euse**) miraculous; wonderful, marvellous.

mirage

mirage [mi'ra:ʒ], *n.m.* mirage; (*Naut.*) looming; (*fig.*) shadow.

mire [mi:r], *n.f.* land-surveyor's pole; (*Artill.*) aim; sight (*of fire-arms*).

mirer [mi're], *v.t.* to aim at; to have in view, to look at; to covet. **se mirer**, *v.r.* to look at oneself; to admire oneself; to be reflected.

mirliton [mirli'tɔ̃], *n.m.* reed pipe.

mirobolant [mirɔbɔ'lɑ̃], *a.* (*colloq.*) wonderful, prodigious.

miroir [mi'rwa:r], *n.m.* mirror, looking-glass.

miroitant [mirwa'tɑ̃], *a.* reflecting (*like a mirror*), glistening.

miroité [mirwa'te], *a.* shot, shiny; dappled (*of horses*).

miroitement [mirwat'mɑ̃], *n.m.* reflection of the light by polished surfaces; sheen, brilliancy.

miroiter [mirwa'te], *v.i.* to reflect light, to shine, to glisten, to shimmer.

mis [mi], *p.p.* [METTRE] **bien** or **mal mis**, well *or* badly dressed.

misaine [mi'zɛ:n], *n.f.* **mât de misaine**, foremast; **voile de misaine**, foresail.

misanthrope [mizɑ̃'trɔp], *n.* misanthrope.

misanthropie [mizɑ̃trɔ'pi], *n.f.* misanthropy.

misanthropique [mizɑ̃trɔ'pik], *a.* misanthropic.

miscellanées [misɛla'ne], *n.f. pl.* miscellanea, miscellany.

mise [mi:z], *n.f.* placing; stake; investment; bidding (*at auctions*); capital; dress; **mise en marche**, starting; starting-handle; **mise en marche automatique**, self-starter; **mise en scène**, (*Theat.*) production, (*Cine.*) direction.

misérable [mize'rabl], *a.* miserable, pitiable; worthless; despicable.—*n.* wretch, miserable person; miscreant.

misérablement [mizerablə'mɑ̃], *adv.* miserably.

misère [mi'zɛ:r], *n.f.* misery, wretchedness, distress; poverty; trouble; trifling thing.

miséreux [mize'rø], *a.* and *n.m.* (*fem.* **-euse**) poor, destitute; seedy looking (person).

miséricorde [mizeri'kɔrd], *n.f.* mercy, pardon, grace.

miséricordieux [mizerikɔr'djø], *a.* (*fem.* **-euse**) merciful, compassionate.

missel [mi'sɛl], *n.m.* missal, mass book.

mission [mi'sjɔ̃], *n.f.* mission.

missionnaire [misjɔ'nɛ:r], *n.* missionary.

missive [mi'si:v], *a.f.* and *n.f.* missive.

mistral [mis'tral], *n.m.* mistral (*cold north wind in southern France*).

mitaine [mi'tɛn], *n.f.* mitten.

mite [mit], *n.f.* mite; moth; **mangé des mites**, moth-eaten.

mité [mi'te], *a.* moth-eaten, maggoty.

mi-temps [mi'tɑ̃], *n.f.* (*Ftb.*) half-time.

miteux [mi'tø], *a.* (*fem.* **-euse**) full of mites; (*fig.*) shabby, poverty-stricken.

mitigation [mitiga'sjɔ̃], *n.f.* mitigation.

mitiger [miti'ʒe], *v.t.* (*conjug. like* MANGER) to mitigate, to alleviate, to modify.

mitonner [mitɔ'ne], *v.t.* to coddle, to fondle; to nurse.—*v.i.* to let slices of bread simmer in the broth, to simmer.

mitoyen [mitwa'jɛ̃], *a.* (*fem.* **-enne**) middle; intermediate; party, joint; **mur mitoyen**, party wall.

mitraille [mi'trɑ:j], *n.f.* grape-shot.

mitrailler [mitrɑ'je], *v.t.*, *v.i.* to machine-gun.

mitraillette [mitrɑ'jɛt], *n.f.* Tommy gun.

mitrailleuse [mitrɑ'jø:z], *n.f.* machine gun.

mitre [mitr], *n.f.* miter.

mitré [mi'tre], *a.* mitered.

mitron [mi'trɔ̃], *n.m.* journeyman baker; pastry-cook's boy.

mixte [mikst], *a.* mixed.

mixture [miks'ty:r], *n.f.* mixture.

mobile [mɔ'bil], *a.* mobile, movable; unsteady, variable.—*n.m.* body in motion; mover, motive power.

mobilier [mɔbi'lje], *a.* (*fem.* **-ière**) movable; personal (*of property*).—*n.m.* furniture.

mobilisation [mɔbiliza'sjɔ̃], *n.f.* mobilization; liquidation (*of capital*).

mobiliser [mɔbili'ze], *v.t.* (*Law*) to liquidate; (*Mil.*) to mobilize.

mobilité [mɔbili'te], *n.f.* mobility; variability; instability.

mode (1) [mɔd], *n.f.* fashion; manner, way, custom; (*pl.*) millinery.

mode (2) [mɔd], *n.m.* (*Mus. etc.*) mode; (*Gram.*) mood; method; **mode d'emploi**, directions for use.

modelage [mɔ'dla:ʒ], *n.m.* modelling.

modèle [mɔ'dɛl], *a.* exemplary.—*n.m.* model; pattern, design.

modelé [mɔ'dle], *n.m.* (*Sculp., Paint.*) relief; reproduction.

modeler [mɔ'dle], *v.t.* (*conjug. like* AMENER) to model; to shape; to mold (*clay*). **se modeler**, *v.r.* to model oneself (*sur*).

modeleur [mɔ'dlœ:r], *n.m.* modeller.

modérateur [mɔdera'tœ:r], *a.* (*fem.* **-trice**) moderating.—*n.m.* (*fem.* **-trice**) moderator.—*n.m.* (*Mech.*) regulator.

modération [mɔdera'sjɔ̃], *n.f.* moderation; abatement.

modéré [mɔde're], *a.* moderate, reasonable.—*n.m.* (*fem.* **-e**) (*Polit.*) moderate.

modérément [mɔdere'mɑ̃], *adv.* moderately, in moderation.

modérer [mɔde're], *v.t.* (*conjug. like* CÉDER) to moderate, to mitigate; to restrain. **se modérer**, *v.r.* to keep one's temper; to restrain oneself.

moderne [mɔ'dɛrn], *a.* modern, up-to-date. —*n.m.* modern style.

modernisation [mɔderniza'sjɔ̃], *n.f.* modernization.

moderniser [mɔderni'ze], *v.t.* to modernize.

modeste [mɔ'dɛst], *a.* modest, unassuming; quiet; simple.

modestement [mɔdɛstə'mɑ̃], *adv.* modestly, quietly, simply.

modestie [mɔdɛs'ti], *n.f.* modesty, simplicity.

modicité [mɔdisi'te], *n.f.* smallness; modicum.

modification [mɔdifika'sjɔ̃], *n.f.* modification.

modifier [mɔdi'fje], *v.t.* to modify, to change, to alter. **se modifier**, *v.r.* to become modified.

modique [mɔ'dik], *a.* moderate; small.

modiquement [mɔdik'mɑ̃], *adv.* moderately.

modiste [mɔ'dist], *n.* modiste, milliner.

modulation [mɔdyla'sjɔ̃], *n.f.* modulation; (*Rad.*) **modulation de fréquence**, very high frequency, V.H.F.

moduler [mɔdy'le], *v.t.* to modulate.
moelle [mwal], *n.f.* marrow (*of bone*); (*Bot.*) pith.
moelleusement [mwaløz'mã], *adv.* softly; (*Paint.*) with mellowness.
moelleux [mwa'lø], *a.* (*fem.* **-euse**) full of marrow; pithy; soft; mellow.—*n.m.* softness; mellowness.
moellon [mwa'lɔ̃], *n.m.* rubble; building stone.
mœurs [mœrs], *n.f. pl.* morals; manners, habits, ways, customs; *certificat de bonne vie et mœurs*, certificate of good character.
Mogol [mɔ'gɔl], *m.* Mogul.
moi [mwa], *pron. pers.* I; me, to me; *moi-même*, myself.—*n.m.* self, ego.
moignon [mwa'ɲɔ̃], *n.m.* stump (*of limbs, trees etc.*).
moindre [mwɛ̃:dr], *a.* lesser; least.
moine [mwan], *n.m.* monk, friar; bed-warmer.
moineau [mwa'no], *n.m.* (*pl.* **-eaux**) sparrow.
moins [mwɛ̃], *adv.* less; fewer (*de* or *que*); not so; *à moins de* (or *que*), unless; *du moins*, at least, at any rate; *les moins de seize ans*, the under sixteens.—*prep.* less, minus.—*n.m.* (*Math.*) minus sign; (*Print.*) dash.
moire [mwar], *n.f.* watering; moire, watered silk.
moiré [mwa're], *a.* watered, moiré.—*n.m.* watered effect.
moirer [mwa're], *v.t.* to moiré, to give a watered appearance to.
mois [mwa], *n.m.* month; monthly allowance, month's pay.
Moïse [mɔ'i:z], *m.* Moses.
moisi [mwa'zi], *a.* moldy, musty.—*n.m.* moldiness, mustiness.
moisir [mwa'zi:r], *v.t.* to make moldy *or* musty.—*v.i.* and **se moisir**, *v.r.* to grow moldy *or* musty.
moisissure [mwazi'sy:r], *n.f.* moldiness, mustiness, mildew.
moisson [mwa'sɔ̃], *n.f.* harvest, harvest time.
moissonner [mwasɔ'ne], *v.t.* to reap, to gather in, to mow.
moissonneur [mwasɔ'nœ:r], *n.m.* (*fem.* **-euse**) reaper, harvester.—*n.f.* (**-euse**) reaping machine.
moissonneuse-batteuse [mwasɔ'nøzba'tø:z] *n.f.* (*pl.* **moissonneuses-batteuses**) combine harvester.
moite [mwat], *a.* moist, damp; clammy.
moiteur [mwa'tœ:r], *n.f.* moistness, dampness.
moitié [mwa'tje], *n.f.* half; (*colloq.*) better half, wife.—*adv.* half; *à moitié fait*, half done; *trop cher de moitié*, too dear by half.
moka [mɔ'ka], *n.m.* mocha (*coffee* or *cake*).
mol [mɔl], [MOU].
molaire [mɔ'lɛ:r], *a.* molar.—*n.f.* molar (tooth).
môle [mo:l], *n.m.* mole, pier.
moléculaire [mɔleky'lɛ:r], *a.* molecular.
molécule [mɔle'kyl], *n.f.* molecule.
molestation [mɔlɛsta'sjɔ̃], *n.f.* molestation, annoyance.
molester [mɔlɛs'te], *v.t.* to molest, to trouble.

mollasse [mɔ'las], *a.* flabby; spineless.
molle [mɔl], [MOU].
mollement [mɔl'mã], *adv.* softly; feebly; indolently.
mollesse [mɔ'lɛs], *n.f.* softness; flabbiness; slackness; indolence.
mollet [mɔ'lɛ], *a.* (*fem.* **-ette**) soft; light (*of bread*).—*n.m.* calf (*of the leg*).
molletière [mɔl'tjɛ:r], *n.f.* legging, puttee.
molleton [mɔl'tɔ̃], *n.m.* thick flannel, duffel.
mollir [mɔ'li:r], *v.i.* to soften; to mellow (*of fruit*); to slacken, to give way.
mollusque [mɔ'lysk], *n.m.* mollusc.
molosse [mɔ'lɔs], *n.m.* mastiff, watch-dog.
môme [mo:m], *n.* (*pop.*) brat, urchin.
moment [mɔ'mã], *n.m.* moment, instant; favorable occasion; *au moment de*, just as; *du moment que*, since.
momentané [mɔmãta'ne], *a.* momentary.
momentanément [mɔmãtane'mã], *adv.* momentarily.
momie [mɔ'mi], *n.f.* mummy; (*fig.*) old fogy.
momifier [mɔmi'fje], *v.t.* to mummify.
mon [mɔ̃], *a.poss.m.* (*fem.* **ma**, *pl.* **mes**) my.
monarchie [mɔnar'ʃi], *n.f.* monarchy.
monarchique [mɔnar'ʃik], *a.* monarchical.
monarchiste [mɔnar'ʃist], *a.* and *n.* monarchist.
monarque [mɔ'nark], *n.m.* monarch.
monastère [mɔnas'tɛ:r], *n.m.* monastery, convent.
monastique [mɔnas'tik], *a.* monastic.
monceau [mɔ̃'so], *n.m.* (*pl.* **-eaux**) heap, pile.
mondain [mɔ̃'dɛ̃], *a.* worldly, mundane.—*n.m.* (*fem.* **-e**) worldly person.
mondanité [mɔ̃dani'te], *n.f.* worldliness; (*pl.*) social events.
monde [mɔ̃:d], *n.m.* world; universe; mankind; people; society; company, set; men; customers; *tout le monde*, everybody.
monder [mɔ̃'de], *v.t.* to cleanse; to hull (*barley*), to blanch (*almonds*).
mondial [mɔ̃'djal], *a.* (*m. pl.* **-aux**) world, world-wide.
monétaire [mɔne'tɛ:r], *a.* monetary.
mongol [mɔ̃'gɔl], *a.* Mongolian.—*n.m.* Mongolian (*language*); (**Mongol**, *fem.* **-ole**) Mongol(ian) (*person*).
Mongolie [mɔ̃go'li], **la**, *f.* Mongolia.
Monique [mɔ'nik], *f.* Monica.
moniteur [mɔni'tœ:r], *n.m.* (*fem.* **-trice**) (*sch.*) prefect, monitor; instructor.
monnaie [mɔ'nɛ], *n.f.* coin, money; change; mint; *monnaie forte*, hard currency; *monnaie légale*, legal tender.
monnayage [mɔnɛ'ja:ʒ], *n.m.* coining, minting.
monnayer [mɔnɛ'je], *v.t.* (*conjug. like* PAYER) to coin into money, to mint; (*fig.*) to make money out of, to sell.
monnayeur [mɔnɛ'jœ:r], *n.m.* coiner, minter; *faux monnayeur*, counterfeiter, forger.
monochrome [mɔnɔ'krɔm], *a.* monochrome.
monocle [mɔ'nɔkl], *n.m.* monocle, eyeglass.
monogramme [mɔnɔ'gram], *n.m.* monogram.
monologue [mɔnɔ'lɔg], *n.m.* monologue, soliloquy.
monopole [mɔnɔ'pɔl], *n.m.* monopoly.
monopoliser [mɔnɔpɔli'ze], *v.t.* to monopolize.
monorail [mɔnɔ'ra:j], *a.* and *n.m.* monorail.

monosyllabe [monosil'lab], *a.* monosyllabic. —*n.f.* monosyllable.

monosyllabique [monosilla'bik], *a.* monosyllabic.

monotone [mono'ton], *a.* monotonous.

monotonie [monoto'ni], *n.f.* monotony.

monseigneur [mɔ̃sɛ'nœːr], *n.m.* (*pl.* **messeigneurs** or **nosseigneurs**) my lord; your Grace; your Royal *or* Imperial Highness.

monsieur [mə'sjø, msjø], *n.m.* (*pl.* **messieurs**) sir; gentleman; Mr.

monstre [mɔ̃:str], *a.* (*fam.*) huge.—*n.m.* monster.

monstrueusement [mɔ̃strɥøz'mã], *adv.* monstrously, prodigiously.

monstrueux [mɔ̃s'trɥø], *a.* (*fem.* **-euse**) monstrous, prodigious.

monstruosité [mɔ̃strɥozi'te], *n.f.* monstrosity.

mont [mɔ̃], *n.m.* hill, mount, mountain.

montage [mɔ̃'ta:ʒ], *n.m.* carrying up; mounting, setting; assembling; (*Cine.*) editing (*of film*); (*Ind.*) **châine de montage**, assembly line.

montagnard [mɔ̃ta'ɲaːr], *a.* mountain, highland.—*n.m.* (*fem.* **-e**) mountaineer, highlander.

montagne [mɔ̃'taɲ], *n.f.* mountain; hill.

montagneux [mɔ̃ta'ɲø], *a.* (*fem.* **-euse**) mountainous, hilly.

montant (1) [mɔ̃'tã], *n.m.* upright (*of a ladder etc.*); post (*of door etc.*); (*Naut.*) stanchion; amount, sum total; rising tide; high flavor, pungency; (*Ftb.*) goal post.

montant (2) [mɔ̃'tã], *a.* rising; ascending; flowing, coming in; high-necked (*of dresses*).

monte [mɔ̃:t], *n.f.* mounting, mount (*of a jockey*); serving (*of animals*), covering season.

monte-charge [mɔ̃t'ʃarʒ], *n.m. inv.* hoist, goods lift; (*Am.*) freight elevator.

montée [mɔ̃'te], *n.f.* gradient, slope; ascent; (*Arch. etc.*) height.

monter [mɔ̃'te], *v.t.* to mount, to ascend, to go up: to walk, ride, row etc. up; to get up on, to ride; to raise; to wind up; to equip; to make up; to rouse.—*v.i.* (*with aux.* AVOIR *or* ÊTRE *according as action or condition is meant*) to go (*or* come) up, to mount; to climb; to rise; to increase; to amount. **se monter**, *v.r.* to amount, to rise; to get excited; to supply oneself with (*en*).

monteur [mɔ̃'tœːr], *n.m.* (*fem.* **-euse**) setter, mounter (*of jewels, machinery etc.*); (*Cine.*) (film-)editor.

monticule [mɔ̃ti'kyl], *n.m.* hillock, knoll.

montoir [mɔ̃'twaːr], *n.m.* horse-block; *côté du montoir*, near side; *côté hors montoir*, off side.

montre (1) [mɔ̃:tr], *n.f.* show-case, shopwindow; show, display, exhibition.

montre (2) [mɔ̃:tr], *n.f.* watch.

montre-bracelet [mɔ̃trabras'lɛ], *n.f.* (*pl.* **montres-bracelets**) wrist watch.

montrer [mɔ̃'tre], *v.t.* to show, to display; to demonstrate; to teach; to indicate. **se montrer**, *v.r.* to show oneself; to appear; to prove oneself to be, to turn out.

montreur [mɔ̃'trœːr], *n.m.* (*fem* **-euse**) showman, exhibitor.

montueux [mɔ̃'tɥø], *a.* (*fem.* **-euse**) hilly.

monture [mɔ̃'tyːr], *n.f.* animal for riding, mount; setting (*of gems etc.*); frame.

monument [mɔny'mã], *n.m.* monument; memorial.

monumental [mɔnymã'tal], *a.* (*m. pl.* **-aux**) monumental.

moquer (se) [səmɔ'ke], *v.r.* (*de*) to mock, to jeer, to laugh at; to make fun of.

moquerie [mɔ'kri], *n.f.* mockery, derision; jest.

moquette [mɔ'kɛt], *n.f.* carpet; fitted carpet; velvet pile.

moqueur [mɔ'kœːr], *a.* (*fem.* **-euse**) mocking, jeering, derisive.—*n.m.* (*fem.* **-euse**) mocker, scoffer; wag.

moral [mɔ'ral], *a.* (*m. pl.* **-aux**) moral; mental.—*n.m.* mind, mental faculties, spirit, morale.

morale [mɔ'ral], *n.f.* ethics, moral philosophy; morals, morality; rebuke, lecture; moral (*of a story etc.*).

moralement [mɔral'mã], *adv.* morally.

moraliste [mɔra'list], *a.* and *n.* moralist.

moralité [mɔrali'te], *n.f.* morality; morals.

morbide [mɔr'bid], *a.* morbid.

morbleu! [mɔr'blø], *int.* the devil! hang it!

morceau [mɔr'so], *n.m.* (*pl.* **-eaux**) bit, piece, morsel, fragment.

morceler [mɔrsə'le], *v.t.* (*conjug. like* APPELER) to parcel out, to cut up.

mordant [mɔr'dã], *a.* biting; cutting, sarcastic.—*n.m.* mordant; pungency, keenness.

mordiller [mɔrdi'je], *v.t.* to nibble, to bite at.

mordoré [mɔrdɔ're], *a.* and *n.m.* reddish brown.

mordre [mɔrdr], *v.t.* to bite; to gnaw; to eat into.—*v.i.* to bite, to nibble; to take hold; to succeed; to criticize. **se mordre**, *v.r.* to bite oneself; *s'en mordre les doigts*, to repent of a thing.

more [mɔ:r], **moresque** [mɔ'rɛsk], *a.* Moorish.—*n.* (**More**) Moor; Negro.

morfondre [mɔr'fɔ̃:dr], *v.t.* to chill. **se morfondre**, *v.r.* to be chilled, to shiver; to kick one's heels; (*fig.*) to mope.

morfondu [mɔrfɔ̃'dy], *a.* chilled, shivering, benumbed.

morganatique [mɔrgana'tik], *a.* morganatic.

morgue (1) [mɔrg], *n.f.* haughtiness, arrogance.

morgue (2) [mɔrg], *n.f.* morgue, mortuary.

moribond [mɔri'bɔ̃], *a.* moribund, dying.—*n.m.* (*fem.* **-e**) person in a dying state.

moricaud [mɔri'ko], *a.* dark, darkish.—*n.m.* (*fem.* **-e**) (*pej.*) blackamoor, (*pej.*) Negro.

morigéner [mɔriʒe'ne], *v.t.* (*conjug. like* CÉDER) to scold, to reprimand.

mormon [mɔr'mɔ̃], *a.* Mormon.—*n.m.* (**Mormon**, *fem.* **-e**) Mormon (*person*)

morne [mɔrn], *a.* gloomy, dejected, dreary.

morose [mɔ'ro:z], *a.* morose, sullen, surly.

morosité [mɔrozi'te], *n.f.* moroseness, sullenness, surliness.

Morphée [mɔr'fe], *m.* Morpheus.

morphine [mɔr'fin], *n.f.* morphia.

morphologie [mɔrfɔlɔ'ʒi], *n.f.* morphology.

mors [mɔ:r], *n.m. inv.* bit (*of a bridle*); (*fig.*) curb, check.

morse (1) [mɔrs], *n.m.* morse, walrus.

morse (2) [mɔrs], *n.m.* Morse (code).

morsure [mɔr'syːr], *n.f.* bite, biting.

moutarde

mort [mɔːr], *a.* dead; lifeless, inanimate; dormant; stagnant; out (*of a candle etc.*); *nature morte*, still life; *au point mort*, at a standstill, in neutral (gear) (*of a car*).—*n.m.* (*fem.* **-e**) dead person, corpse.—*n.m.* dummy (*at cards*).—*n.f.* death; *à mort*, mortally, to the death.

mortalité [mɔrtali'te], *n.f.* mortality.

mort-bois [mɔr'bwɑ], *n.m.* (*no pl.*) brushwood, undergrowth.

morte-eau [mɔr'to], *n.f.* (*pl.* **mortes-eaux**) neap tide.

mortel [mɔr'tɛl], *a.* (*fem.* **-elle**) mortal, deadly; grievous.—*n.m.* (*fem.* **-elle**) mortal.

mortellement [mɔrtɛl'mɑ̃], *adv.* fatally, deadly.

morte-saison [mɔrtsɛ'zɔ̃], *n.f.* (*pl.* **mortes-saisons**) slack time, off season.

mortier [mɔr'tje], *n.m.* mortar (*cement, artillery, vessel*).

mortifiant [mɔrti'fjɑ̃], *a.* mortifying, humiliating.

mortification [mɔrtifika'sjɔ̃], *n.f.* mortification, humiliation.

mortifier [mɔrti'fje], *v.t.* to mortify; to humiliate. **se mortifier**, *v.r.* to mortify oneself.

mort-né [mɔr'ne], *a.* and *n.m.* (*fem.* **mort-née**, *pl.* **mort-nés, mort-nées**) stillborn (child).

mortuaire [mɔr'tɥɛːr], *a.* mortuary; *drap mortuaire*, pall.

morue [mɔ'ry], *n.f.* cod, codfish; *huile de foie de morue*, cod-liver oil.

morveux [mɔr'vø], *a.* (*fem.* **-euse**) snotty; *qui se sent morveux se mouche*, if the cap fits, wear it.

mosaïque [mɔza'ik], *a.* and *n.f.* mosaic.

Moscou [mɔs'ku], **le,** *m.* Moscow.

mosquée [mɔs'ke], *n.f.* mosque.

mot [mo], *n.m.* word; remark, saying, sentence; motto; note; (*Mil.*) parole, watchword; *au bas mot*, at the least; *bon mot*, witticism; *mots croisés*, crossword.

motel [mɔ'tɛl], *n.m.* motel.

moteur [mɔ'tœːr], *a.* (*fem.* **-trice**) motive, driving.—*n.m.* mover; motor, engine; motive power.

motif [mɔ'tif], *a.* (*fem.* **-tive**) moving, inciting.—*n.m.* motive, incentive; cause; (*Mus. etc.*) motif, design.

motion [mo'sjɔ̃], *n.f.* (*Polit.*) motion.

motiver [mɔti've], *v.t.* to justify; to allege as a motive; to be the cause of, to bring about.

moto [mɔ'to], *n.f.* (*fam.*) motor bike.

motocyclette [mɔtosi'klɛt], *n.f.* motor-cycle.

motte [mɔt], *n.f.* clod; *motte de beurre*, pat of butter.

motus! [mɔ'tyːs], *int.* (*colloq.*) mum's the word!

mou [mu], *a.* (**mol** before vowel or *h* mute, *fem.* **molle**) soft; limp; flabby; weak; slack, sluggish, indolent.—*n.m.* soft part of thing; slack (*of a rope*); lights (*of animals*).

mouchard [mu'ʃaːr], *n.m.* sneak, *esp.* police spy, nark, informer.

moucharder [muʃar'de], *v.t., v.i.* to inform (*on*), to spy (*on*); to sneak.

mouche [muʃ], *n.f.* fly; patch (*on the face*), beauty spot; button (*of foil*); bull's-eye (*of a target*); river passenger-steamer.

(*C*) **mouche à feu** [muʃa'fø], *n.f.* firefly.

moucher [mu'ʃe], *v.t.* to wipe the nose of; to snuff. **se moucher**, *v.r.* to blow one's nose.

moucheron [muʃ'rɔ̃], *n.m.* gnat, very small fly.

moucheté [muʃ'te], *a.* spotted, speckled, flecked; capped (*of foils*).

moucheter [muʃ'te], *v.t.* (*conjug. like* APPELER) to spot, to speckle, to fleck; to cap (*foils*).

mouchoir [mu'ʃwaːr], *n.m.* handkerchief.

moudre [mudr], *v.t. irr.* to grind, to crush.

moue [mu], *n.f.* pout; *faire la moue*, to pout.

mouette [mwɛt], *n.f.* gull, sea-mew.

moufle [mufl], *n.f.* mitten; tackle-block.

mouillage [mu'jaːʒ], *n.m.* soaking, wetting; anchorage.

mouillé [mu'je], *a.* wet, watery; liquid (*of the letter l*); at anchor.

mouiller [mu'je], *v.t.* to wet, to moisten.—*v.i.* to drop anchor; to moor.

moulage [mu'laːʒ], *n.m.* molding, casting; mold; cast; grinding, milling.

moule (1) [mul], *n.m.* mold, matrix; pattern.

moule (2) [mul], *n.f.* mussel.

moulé [mu'le], *a.* molded, cast; well-formed; *lettre moulée*, block letter.

mouler [mu'le], *v.t.* to cast, to mold; to shape. **se mouler**, *v.r.* to model oneself (*sur*).

mouleur [mu'lœːr], *n.m.* molder.

moulin [mu'lɛ̃], *n.m.* mill; grinder; (*Geol.*) pothole; *jeter son bonnet par-dessus les moulins*, to throw off all restraint.

moulinet [muli'nɛ], *n.m.* small mill; winch; turnstile; fishing reel.

moulu [mu'ly], *a.* ground; bruised.

moulure [mu'lyːr], *n.f.* (*Arch.*) molding.

mourant [mu'rɑ̃], *a.* dying, expiring; fading.—*n.m.* (*fem.* **-e**) dying person.

mourir [mu'riːr], *v.i. irr.* (*with aux.* ÊTRE) to die, to expire; to perish; to stop; to go out (*of fire*); to be out (*at play*). **se mourir**, *v.r.* (*Poet., only used in pres. and imp. indic.*) to be dying.

mouron [mu'rɔ̃], *n.m.* (*Bot.*) *mouron rouge*, scarlet pimpernel; *mouron des oiseaux*, chickweed.

mousquet [mus'kɛ], *n.m.* musket; *mousquet à pierre*, flintlock.

mousquetaire [muskə'tɛːr], *n.m.* musketeer.

mousse (1) [mus], *a.* blunt (*of tools*).

mousse (2) [mus], *n.f.* moss; froth, foam; lather; whipped cream.

mousse (3) [mus], *n.m.* ship's boy.

mousseline [mus'lin], *n.f.* muslin.

mousser [mu'se], *v.i.* to froth, to foam; to sparkle (*of wine*).

mousseux [mu'sø], *a.* (*fem.* **-euse**) foaming, frothy; sparkling (*of wine etc.*). **se mousser**, ...

mousson [mu'sɔ̃], *n.f.* monsoon.

moussu [mu'sy], *a.* mossy.

moustache [mus'taʃ], *n.f.* moustache; whiskers (*of animals*).

moustiquaire [musti'kɛːr], *n.f.* mosquito net.

moustique [mus'tik], *n.m.* mosquito.

moût [mu], *n.m.* must (*wine not fermented*); wort (*of beer*).

moutarde [mu'tard], *n.f.* mustard.

moutardier [mutar'dje], *n.m.* mustard pot; mustard maker.

mouton [mu'tɔ̃], *n.m.* sheep; mutton; sheepskin (*leather*); ram; (*fig.*) ninny; (*slang*) decoy, prison spy; (*pl.*) white-crested waves; *revenons à nos moutons*, let us return to the subject.

moutonné [mutɔ'ne], *a.* fleecy, curled; white with foam (*of the sea*).

moutonner [mutɔ'ne], *v.t.* to make woolly *or* fleecy; to curl, to frizzle.—*v.i.* to be ruffled, to foam.

moutonneux [mutɔ'nø], *a.* (*fem.* **-euse**) fleecy; foaming (*of waves*).

moutonnier [mutɔ'nje], *a.* (*fem.* **-ière**) sheep-like.

mouvant [mu'vɑ̃], *a.* moving, shifting; unstable.

mouvement [muv'mɑ̃], *n.m.* movement, motion; march; animation, bustle; emotion, commotion; spirit, impulse; (*Mus.*) time; (*Mil.*) maneuver.

mouvementé [muvmɑ̃'te], *a.* animated, lively; undulating (*ground*).

mouvoir [mu'vwɑːr], *v.t. irr.* to move, to stir; to prompt. **se mouvoir**, *v.r.* to move, to stir.

moyen [mwa'jɛ̃], *a.* (*fem.* **-enne**) mean, middle, medium; average.—*n.m.* means; way, manner, medium; (*pl.*) resources; talents.

moyennant [mwajɛ'nɑ̃], *prep.* by means of; in consideration of.—*conj. phr.* **moyennant que**, on condition that.

moyenne [mwa'jɛn], *n.f.* average; (*sch.*) passing mark.

moyeu [mwa'jø], *n.m.* (*pl.* **-eux**) nave (*of cartwheel*); hub (*of bicycle*).

muable [mɥabl], *a.* mutable, changeable.

mucosité [mykozi'te], *n.f.* mucus.

mucus [my'kyːs], *n.m.* mucus.

mue [my], *n.f.* molting; skin, slough; mew, coop (*cage*).

muer [mɥe], *v.i.* to molt, to cast *or* slough horns etc.; to break (*of the voice*).

muet [mɥe], *a.* (*fem.* **muette**) dumb, mute; silent (*of letters*); blank (*of maps*).—*n.m.* (*fem.* **muette** (1)) dumb man *or* woman.

muette (2) [mɥet], *n.f.* mews; hunting lodge.

mufle [myfl], *n.m.* snout, muzzle (*of animals*); (*pop.*) beast, cad.

muflier [myfli'e], *n.m.* (*Bot.*) antirrhinum.

mugir [my'ʒiːr], *v.i.* to bellow, to low; (*fig.*) to roar; to sough (*of the wind*).

mugissement [myʒis'mɑ̃], *n.m.* bellowing, lowing, roaring; soughing (*of the wind*).

muguet [my'gɛ], *n.m.* lily of the valley.

mulâtre [my'lɑːtr], *a* and *n.m.* (*fem. inv.* or **-esse**) mulatto, half-caste.

mule [myl], *n.f.* mule, slipper; she-mule.

mulet [my'lɛ], *n.m.* he-mule; mullet.

muletier [myl'tje], *a.* (*fem.* **-ière**) pertaining to mules.—*n.m.* muleteer.

mulot [my'lo], *n.m.* field-mouse.

multicolore [myltikɔ'lɔːr], *a.* many-colored; motley; variegated.

multiforme [mylti'fɔrm], *a.* multiform.

multilatéral [myltilate'ral], *a.* (*m. pl.* **-aux**) multilateral.

multiple [myl'tipl], *a.* multiple; multifarious. —*n.m.* multiple.

multiplicateur [myltiplika'tœːr], *a.* (*fem.* **-trice**) multiplying.—*n.m.* (*Arith.*) multiplier, multiplicator.

multiplication [myltiplikɑ'sjɔ̃], *n.f.* multiplication; gearing (-ratio).

multiplicité [myltiplisi'te], *n.f.* multiplicity.

multiplié [myltipli'e], *a.* multiplied; manifold; frequent.

multiplier [myltipli'e], *v.t., v.i.* to multiply; to gear up to. **se multiplier**, *v.r.* to multiply; to be repeated.

multitude [mylti'tyd], *n.f.* multitude; crowd.

muni [my'ni], *a.* supplied, provided (*de*); fortified.

municipal [mynisi'pal], *a.* (*m. pl.* **-aux**) municipal.—*n.m.* soldier of the municipal guard.

municipalité [mynisipali'te], *n.f.* municipality; town council and staff.

munificence [mynifi'sɑ̃ːs], *n.f.* bounty, munificence.

munificent [mynifi'sɑ̃], *a.* bountiful.

munir [my'niːr], *v.t.* to provide, to supply; to arm, to secure. **se munir**, *v.r.* to provide oneself, to be provided (*de*).

munitions [myni'sjɔ̃], *n.f. pl.* ammunition, munitions; military stores.

muqueux [my'kø], *a.* (*fem.* **-euse** (1)) mucous.

muqueuse (2) [my'køːz], *n.f.* mucous membrane.

mur [myːr], *n.m.* wall; *le mur du son*, the sound barrier.

mûr [myːr], *a.* ripe, mature, matured.

murage [my'raːʒ], *n.m.* walling.

muraille [my'raːj], *n.f.* thick, high wall; (*pl.*) ramparts.

mural [my'ral], *a.* (*m. pl.* **-aux**) mural; *peinture murale*, mural.

mûre [myːr], *n.f.* mulberry.

mûrement [myr'mɑ̃], *adv.* maturely.

murer [my're], *v.t.* to wall in, to brick up; (*fig.*) to screen.

mûrier [my'rje], *n.m.* mulberry tree, bramble bush.

mûrir [my'riːr], *v.t.* to ripen, to mature.— *v.i.* to ripen, to grow ripe, to mature.

murmurant [myrmy'rɑ̃], *a.* murmuring; babbling; grumbling.

murmure [myr'myːr], *n.m.* murmur; grumbling; whispering; babbling; soughing (*of the wind*).

murmurer [myrmy're], *v.t.* to mutter, to whisper.—*v.i.* to murmur, to whisper; to grumble; to gurgle, to prattle, to babble; to sough.

musard [my'zaːr], *a.* loitering, dawdling.— *n.m.* (*fem.* **-e**) (*colloq.*) loiterer, dawdler.

musarder [myzar'de], *v.i.* to dawdle.

musarderie [myzar'dri], **musardise** [myzar 'diːz], *n.f.* loitering, dawdling, trifling.

musc [mysk], *n.m.* musk deer, musk.

muscade [mys'kad], *n.f.* nutmeg; juggler's ball.

muscadier [myska'dje], *n.m.* nutmeg tree.

muscat [mys'ka], *a.* and *n.m.* muscat (grape), muscadine; dried muscatel wine; variety of pear.

muscle [myskl], *n.m.* muscle.

musculaire [mysky'lɛːr], *a.* muscular.

musculeux [mysky'lø], *a.* (*fem.* **-euse**) muscular, brawny.

muse [myz], *n.f.* muse.

museau [myz'zo], *n.m.* (*pl.* **-eaux**) muzzle, snout, nose.
musée [my'ze], *n.m.* museum, art gallery.
museler [myz'le], *v.t.* (*conjug. like* APPELER) to muzzle; (*fig.*) to gag, to silence.
muselière [myz'lje:r], *n.f.* muzzle.
musellement [myzɛl'mɑ̃], *n.m.* muzzling; (*fig.*) gagging, silencing.
muser [my'ze], *v.i.* to loiter, to moon, to dawdle.
musette [my'zɛt], *n.f.* bagpipe; (*Mil.*) haversack; nosebag (*for horses*).
muséum [myze'ɔm], *n.m.* natural history museum.
musical [myzi'kal], *a.* (*m. pl.* **-aux**) musical.
musicalement [myzikal'mɑ̃], *adv.* musically.
musicien [myzi'sjɛ̃], *n.m.* (*fem.* **-enne**) musician.
musique [my'zik], *n.f.* music; band, musicians.
musoir [my'zwa:r], *n.m.* pier head, jetty head.
musqué [mys'ke], *a.* musked, perfumed; (*fig.*) affected (*language etc.*).
musquer [mys'ke], *v.t.* to perfume with musk.
musulman [myzyl'mɑ̃], *a.* Moslem.—*n.m.* (**Musulman**, *fem.* **-ane**) Moslem (*person*).
mutabilité [mytabili'te], *n.f.* mutability, changeableness.
mutation [myta'sjɔ̃], *n.f.* change; (*Biol.*) mutation.
muter [my'te], *v.t.* (*Mil., Adm.*) to transfer.
mutilateur [mytila'tœ:r], *n.m.* (*fem.* **-trice**) mutilator, maimer, defacer.
mutilation [mytila'sjɔ̃], *n.f.* mutilation, maiming.
mutiler [myti'le], *v.t.* to mutilate, to maim; (*fig.*) to disfigure.
mutin [my'tɛ̃], *a.* obstinate; fractious; pert.—*n.m.* (*fem.* **-e**) mutineer, rebel.
mutiné [myti'ne], *a.* mutinous, riotous.
mutiner (se) [səmyti'ne], *v.r.* to mutiny.
mutinerie [mytin'ri], *n.f.* unruliness; mutiny, riot; pertness.
mutisme [my'tism], *n.m.* dumbness; speechlessness.
mutualité [mytɥali'te], *n.f.* mutuality.
mutuel [my'tɥɛl], *a.* (*fem.* **-elle**) mutual, reciprocal; **société de secours mutuels**, mutual benefit society.
mutuellement [mytɥɛl'mɑ̃], *adv.* mutually.
myope [mjɔp], *a.* myopic, short-sighted.—*n.* short-sighted person.
myopie [mjɔ'pi], *n.f.* myopia, short-sightedness.
myosotis [mjɔzɔ'ti:], *n.m.* myosotis, forget-me-not.
myriade [mi'rjad], *n.f.* myriad.
myrrhe [mi:r], *n.f.* myrrh.
myrte [mirt], *n.m.* myrtle.
myrtille [mir'ti:j], *n.f.* bilberry.
mystère [mis'tɛ:r], *n.m.* mystery; secret; (*fig.*) fuss.
mystérieusement [misterjøz'mɑ̃], *adv.* mysteriously.
mystérieux [miste'rjø], *a.* (*fem.* **-euse**) mysterious.
mysticisme [misti'sism], *n.m.* mysticism.
mystificateur [mistifika'tœ:r], *a.* (*fem.*

-trice) mystifying, hoaxing.—*n.m.* (*fem.* **-trice**) mystifier, hoaxer.
mystification [mistifika'sjɔ̃], *n.f.* hoax.
mystifier [misti'fje], *v.t.* to mystify; to hoax.
mystique [mis'tik], *a.* mystical, mystic.—*n.* mystic.
mythe [mit], *n.m.* myth; fable, fiction.
mythique [mi'tik], *a.* mythical.
mythologie [mitɔlɔ'ʒi], *n.f.* mythology.
mythologique [mitɔlɔ'ʒik], *a.* mythological.
mythologiste [mitɔlɔ'ʒist], **mythologue** [mitɔ'lɔg], *n.* mythologist.
myxomatose [miksɔma'to:z], *n.f.* myxomatosis.

N

N, n [ɛn], *n.m.* the fourteenth letter of the alphabet.
nabab [na'bab], *n.m.* nabob.
nacelle [na'sɛl], *n.f.* wherry, skiff; gondola (*of airship etc.*).
nacre [nakr], *n.f.* mother-of-pearl.
nacré [na'kre], *a.* nacreous, pearly.
nage [na:ʒ], *n.f.* swimming; rowing, sculling; (*fam.*) **être en nage**, to be bathed in perspiration.
nageoire [na'ʒwa:r], *n.f.* fin (*of a fish*).
nager [na'ʒe], *v.i.* (*conjug. like* MANGER) to swim; to float; to row.
nageur [na'ʒœ:r], *a.* (*fem.* **-euse**) swimming.—*n.m.* (*fem.* **-euse**) swimmer; rower, oarsman.
naguère [na'gɛ:r], *adv.* lately, not long ago.
naïade [na'jad], *n.f.* naiad, water nymph.
naïf [na'if], *a.* (*fem.* **naïve**) naïve, artless, ingenuous, unaffected; simple.
nain [nɛ̃], *a.* dwarfish.—*n.m.* (*fem.* **-e**) dwarf.
naissance [nɛ'sɑ̃:s], *n.f.* birth; descent; (*fig.*) beginning, dawn, rise.
naissant [nɛ'sɑ̃], *a.* new-born, in its infancy; beginning, rising.
naître [nɛ:tr], *v.i. irr.* (*with aux.* ÊTRE) to be born, (*fig.*) to originate; to dawn.
naïvement [naiv'mɑ̃], *adv.* naïvely, ingenuously, artlessly.
naïveté [naiv'te], *n.f.* artlessness, simplicity, naïvety.
nantir [nɑ̃'ti:r], *v.t.* to give as a pledge, to secure; (*fig.*) to furnish. **se nantir**, *v.r.* to provide oneself (**de**); to take possession (**de**).
nantissement [nɑ̃tis'mɑ̃], *n.m.* security, pledge.
naphte [naft], *n.m.* naphtha.
napolitain [napɔli'tɛ̃], *a.* Neapolitan.—*n.m.* (**Napolitain**, *fem.* **-aine**) Neapolitan (*person*).
nappe [nap], *n.f.* table-cloth, cover; sheet (*of water etc.*).
napperon [na'prɔ̃], *n.m.* tray cloth; doily.
narcisse [nar'sis], *n.m.* (*Bot.*) narcissus.
narcotique [narkɔ'tik], *a.* and *n.m.* narcotic.
narcotisme [narkɔ'tism], *n.m.* narcotism.
narguer [nar'ge], *v.t.* to defy, to flout.

narine [na´rin], *n.f.* nostril.
narquois [nar´kwa], *a.* cunning, sly; chaffing.
narquoisement [narkwaz´mã], *adv.* slyly, quizzingly.
narrateur [nara´tœːr], *n.m.* (*fem.* **-trice**) narrator, relater.
narratif [nara´tif], *a.* (*fem.* **-tive**) narrative.
narration [nara´sjɔ̃], *n.f.* narration, narrative.
narrer [na´re], *v.t.* to narrate, to tell.
nasal [na´zal], *a.* (*m. pl.* **-aux**) nasal.
nasalement [nazal´mã], *adv.* nasally, with a nasal sound.
naseau [na´zo], *n.m.* (*pl.* **-eaux**) nostril (*of animals*).
nasillant [nazi´jã], *a.* speaking through the nose.
nasillard [nazi´jaːr], *a.* snuffling, nasal.
nasillement [nazij´mã], *n.m.* speaking through the nose, snuffling; twang.
nasiller [nazi´je], *v.i.* to speak through the nose, to snuffle.
nasse [naːs], *n.f.* bow net, weir, eel pot.
natal [na´tal], *a.* (*m. pl.* **-als** (*rare*)) natal, native.
natalité [natali´te], *n.f.* birth-rate.
natation [nata´sjɔ̃], *n.f.* swimming.
natif [na´tif], *a.* (*fem.* **-tive**) native; natural. —*n.m.* native.
nation [na´sjɔ̃], *n.f.* nation.
national [nasjɔ´nal], *a.* (*m. pl.* **-aux**) national.
nationalement [nasjonal´mã], *adv.* nationally.
nationalisation [nasjɔnaliza´sjɔ̃], *n.f.* nationalization.
nationaliser [nasjɔnali´ze], *v.t.* to nationalize.
nationaliste [nasjɔna´list], *n.* nationalist.
nationalité [nasjɔnali´te], *n.f.* nationality.
nativité [nativi´te], *n.f.* nativity, birth.
natte [nat], *n.f.* mat, matting (*of straw*); plait.
natter [na´te], *v.t.* to mat; to plait, to twist.
naturalisation [natyraliza´sjɔ̃], *n.f.* naturalization; taxidermy.
naturaliser [natyrali´ze], *v.t.* to naturalize; to stuff (*animal*).
naturalisme [natyra´lism], *n.m.* naturalness; naturalism.
naturaliste [natyra´list], *a.* naturalistic.—*n.* naturalist; taxidermist.
nature [na´tyːr], *n.f.* nature; kind, sort; temperament; life, life-size; *de nature à*, likely to; *dessiner d'après nature*, to draw from life; *nature morte*, still life; *payer en nature*, to pay in kind.
naturel [naty´rɛl], *a.* (*fem.* **-elle**) natural; native, innate; artless, plain; *enfant naturel*, illegitimate child.—*n.m.* (*fem.* **-elle**) native (*of a country*).—*n.m.* disposition, nature; genuineness, simplicity.
naturellement [natyrɛl´mã], *adv.* naturally. —*int.* of course!
naturiste [naty´rist], *a.* naturistic.—*n.* naturist.
naufrage [no´fraːʒ], *n.m.* shipwreck.
naufragé [nofra´ʒe], *a.* shipwrecked, wrecked. —*n.m.* (*fem.* **-ée**) shipwrecked person, castaway.
nauséabond [nozea´bɔ̃], *a.* nauseating, loathsome, disgusting.
nausée [no´ze], *n.f.* nausea, sickness; (*fig.*) loathing, disgust.
nauséeux [noze´ø], *a.* (*fem.* **-éeuse**) nauseating.

nautique [no´tik], *a.* nautical.
naval [na´val], *a.* (*m. pl.* **-als**) naval, nautical.
navet [na´vɛ], *n.m.* turnip.
navette [na´vɛt], *n.f.* incense box; weaver's shuttle; (*Bot.*) rape; *faire la navette*, to run a shuttle service.
navigabilité [navigabili´te], *n.f.* airworthiness, seaworthiness.
navigable [navi´gabl], *a.* navigable; seaworthy, airworthy.
navigateur [naviga´tœːr], *n.m.* navigator.— *a.m.* seafaring; swimming (*birds etc.*).
navigation [naviga´sjɔ̃], *n.f.* navigation; voyage, sailing.
naviguer [navi´ge], *v.i.* to navigate; to row, to sail etc.
navire [na´viːr], *n.m.* vessel, ship.
navrant [nɑ´vrã], *a.* heartrending, harrowing, distressing.
navrer [nɑ´vre], *v.t.* to distress, to rend (*the heart*).
nazaréen [nazare´ɛ̃], *a.* (*fem.* **-éenne**) of Nazareth.—*n.m.* (**Nazaréen**, *fem.* **-éenne**) Nazarene; Nazarite.
nazi [na´zi], *a.* Nazi.—*n.* (**Nazi**) Nazi.
nazisme [na´zism], *n.m.* Nazism.
ne [nə], *adv.* no, not.
né [ne], *a.* born.
néanmoins [neɑ̃´mwɛ̃], *adv.* nevertheless, for all that.
néant [ne´ɑ̃], *n.m.* naught, nothingness; nil.
nébuleux [neby´lø], *a.* (*fem.* **-euse**) cloudy, misty; nebulous; (*fig.*) obscure.—*n.f.* (**-euse**) nebula.
nébulosité [nebylozi´te], *n.f.* patch of haze.
nécessaire [nesɛ´sɛːr], *a.* necessary; inevitable.—*n.m.* the needful; necessities (*of life etc.*); dressing-case, work-box.
nécessairement [nesɛsɛr´mã], *adv.* necessarily; inevitably, of course.
nécessité [nesɛsi´te], *n.f.* necessity; need, want.
nécessiter [nesɛsi´te], *v.t.* to necessitate; to compel, to oblige.
nécessiteux [nesɛsi´tø], *a.* (*fem.* **-euse**) necessitous, needy.—*n.m.* (*fem.* **-euse**) pauper.
nécrologe [nekrɔ´lɔːʒ], *n.m.* obituary list; death roll.
nécrologie [nekrɔlɔ´ʒi], *n.f.* necrology, obituary.
nécrologique [nekrɔlɔ´ʒik], *a.* necrological.
nécromancie [nekrɔmɑ̃´si], *n.f.* necromancy.
nécromancien [nekrɔmɑ̃´sjɛ̃], *n.m.* (*fem.* **-enne**) necromancer.
nécropole [nekrɔ´pɔl], *n.f.* necropolis.
nectar [nɛk´taːr], *n.m.* nectar.
néerlandais [neɛrlɑ̃´dɛ], *a.* Dutch.—*n.m.* Dutch (*language*); (**Néerlandais**, *fem.* **-aise**) Dutchman, Dutchwoman.
nef [nɛf], *n.f.* nave (*of a church*).
néfaste [ne´fast], *a.* inauspicious; disastrous.
nèfle [nɛfl], *n.f.* medlar.
néflier [ne´flje], *n.m.* medlar tree.
négatif [nega´tif], *a.* (*fem.* **-tive**) negative.— *n.m.* (*Phot.*) negative.—*n.f.* (**-tive**) negative, refusal.
négation [nega´sjɔ̃], *n.f.* negation; (*Gram.*) negative.
négativement [negativ´mã], *adv.* negatively.

négligé [negli'ʒe], *a.* neglected, unnoticed; careless; slovenly.—*n.m.* undress, negligee.
négligeable [negli'ʒabl], *a.* negligible; trifling, unimportant.
négligemment [negliʒa'mã], *adv.* nonchalantly; negligently.
négligence [negli'ʒã:s], *n.f.* negligence, neglect, oversight.
négligent [negli'ʒã], *a.* negligent, careless.— *n.m.* (*fem.* **-e**) negligent person.
négliger [negli'ʒe], *v.t.* (*conjug. like* MANGER) to neglect; to omit. **se négliger,** *v.r.* to neglect oneself; to be careless.
négoce [ne'gɔs], *n.m.* trade, business; trafficking.
négociabilité [negɔsjabili'te], *n.f.* negotiability.
négociable [negɔ'sjabl], *a.* negotiable, transferrable.
négociant [negɔ'sjã], *n.m.* (*fem.* **-e**) merchant (*wholesale*).
négociateur [negɔsja'tœ:r], *n.m.* (*fem.* **-trice**) negotiator, transactor.
négociation [negɔsja'sjõ], *n.f.* negotiation, transaction.
négocier [negɔ'sje], *v.t.* to negotiate.—*v.i.* to trade.
nègre [nɛ:gr], *a.* and *n.m.* (*fem.* **négresse**) (*pej.*) Negro; (*pl.*) (*pej.*) blacks.
négrier [negri'e], *n.m.* slave ship; slaver; slave dealer.
négrillon [negri'jõ], *n.m.* (*fem.* **-onne**) (*pej.*) little Negro, Negro boy *or* girl.
neige [nɛ:ʒ], *n.f.* snow; **boule de neige,** snowball.
neiger [nɛ'ʒe], *v. impers.* (*conjug. like* MANGER) to snow.
neigeux [nɛ'ʒø], *a.* (*fem.* **-euse**) snowy, snow-covered.
nénuphar [neny'fa:r], *n.m.* water lily.
néon [ne'õ], *n.m.* neon.
néo-zélandais [neozelã'dɛ], *a.* New Zealand (*butter, cheese etc.*).—*n.m.* (**Néo-Zélandais,** *fem.* **-aise**) New Zealander.
Népal [ne'pa:l], **le,** *m.* Nepal.
népalais [nepa'lɛ], *a.* Nepalese.—*n.m.* (**Népalais,** *fem.* **-aise**) Nepalese (*person*).
népotisme [nepɔ'tism], *n.m.* nepotism.
nerf [nɛ:r], *n.m.* nerve; sinew; fortitude, strength.
nerveusement [nɛrvøz'mã], *adv.* impatiently; nervously.
nerveux [nɛr'vø], *a.* (*fem.* **-euse**) nervous; excitable; muscular.
nervosité [nɛrvozi'te], *n.f.* nervousness.
nervure [nɛr'vy:r], *n.f.* (*Bot. etc.*) nervure, nerve; (*Arch.*) molding; (*Carp.*) rib, fillet; (*Bookb.*) tapes, cording; (*Needlework*) piping.
net [nɛt], *a.* (*fem.* **nette**) clean; pure; clear, distinct; flat, frank, pointblank; net (*of prices*).—*n.m.* fair copy; **mettre au net,** to make a fair copy.—*adv.* clean off, at once; flatly, point-blank.
nettement [nɛt'mã], *adv.* cleanly; clearly; plainly, flatly.
netteté [nɛt'te], *n.f.* cleanness; clearness, distinctness.
nettoiement [nɛtwa'mã], **nettoyage** [nɛtwa'ja:ʒ], *n.m.* cleaning; clearing; wiping.
nettoyer [nɛtwa'je], *v.t.* (*conjug. like* EMPLOYER) to clean; to wipe; to rid (*de*).

neuf (1) [nœf], *a.* and *n.m.* nine, ninth.
neuf (2) [nœf], *a.* (*fem.* **neuve**) new, brandnew; young, raw.—*n.m.* something new.
neurologie [nørɔlɔ'ʒi], *n.f.* neurology.
neutralisation [nøtraliza'sjõ], *n.f.* neutralization.
neutraliser [nøtrali'ze], *v.t.* to neutralize. **se neutraliser,** *v.r.* to neutralize each other.
neutralité [nøtrali'te], *n.f.* neutrality.
neutre [nø:tr], *a.* and *n.m.* neuter; neutral.
neutron [nø'trõ], *n.m.* neutron.
neuvième [nœ'vjɛm], *a.* and *n.* ninth.
neveu [na'vø], *n.m.* (*pl.* **-eux**) nephew; (*pl. poet.*) descendants.
névralgie [nevral'ʒi], *n.f.* neuralgia.
névralgique [nevral'ʒik], *a.* neuralgic.
névrite [ne'vrit], *n.f.* neuritis.
névritique [nevri'tik], *a.* neuritic.
névrose [ne'vro:z], *n.f.* neurosis, nervous disorder.
névrosé [nevro'ze], *a.* and *n.m.* (*fem.* **-ée**) neurotic.
nez [ne], *n.m. inv.* nose; face; scent (*of dogs etc.*).
ni [ni], *conj.* nor, neither . . . nor; (*after* **sans,** **sans que,** *etc.*) either . . . or.
niable [njabl], *a.* deniable.
niais [njɛ], *a.* silly, foolish.—*n.m.* (*fem.* **-e**) ninny, simpleton.
niaisement [njɛz'mã], *adv.* foolishly.
niaiser [njɛ'ze], *v.i.* to play the fool.
niaiserie [njɛz'ri], *n.f.* foolishness; nonsense.
Nicaragua [nikara'gwa], **le,** *m.* Nicaragua.
nicaraguayen [nikaragwa'jɛ̃], *a.* (*fem.* **-enne**) Nicaraguan.—*n.m.* (**Nicaraguayen,** *fem.* **-enne**) Nicaraguan (*person*).
niche [niʃ], *n.f.* niche, nook; recess; kennel; (*fam.*) prank.
nichée [ni'ʃe], *n.f.* nestful (*of young birds*); brood (*of animals, children etc.*).
nicher [ni'ʃe], *v.t.* to lodge, to put.—*v.i.* to build a nest; to nestle. **se nicher,** *v.r.* to nest, to nestle; to hide oneself.
nickel [ni'kɛl], *n.m.* nickel.
nickelage [ni'kla:ʒ], *n.m.* nickel-plating.
nickeler [ni'kle], *v.t.* (*conjug. like* APPELER) to nickel-plate.
Nicolas [niko'la], *m.* Nicholas.
nicotine [niko'tin], *n.f.* nicotine.
nid [ni], *n.m.* nest; berth, post.
nièce [njɛs], *n.f.* niece.
nier [nje], *v.t.* to deny; to repudiate, to disown.
nigaud [ni'go], *a.* (*colloq.*) silly, simple.—*n.m.* (*fem.* **-e**) booby, simpleton.
Nigéria [niʒe'rja], **le,** *m.* Nigeria.
nigérien [niʒe'rjɛ̃], *a.* (*fem.* **-enne**) Nigerian. —*n.m.* (**Nigérien,** *fem.* **-enne**) Nigerian (*person*).
nihilisme [nii'lism], *n.m.* nihilism.
nihiliste [nii'list], *a.* nihilistic.—*n.* nihilist.
Nil [nil], **le,** *m.* the Nile.
nimbe [nɛ̃:b], *n.m.* nimbus, halo.
nippe [nip], *n.f. usu. pl.* (*colloq.*) old clothes, togs.
nipper [ni'pe], *v.t.* (*colloq.*) to fit out, to rig out. **se nipper,** *v.r.* to rig oneself out.
nippon [ni'põ], *a.* Japanese.—*n.m.* (**Nippon,** *fem.* **-one**) Japanese (*person*).
nitrate [ni'trat], *n.m.* nitrate.
nitre [nitr], *n.m.* nitre, saltpeter.
nitrique [ni'trik], *a.* nitric.

225

nitrogène [nitrɔ'ʒɛn], *n.m.* nitrogen.

niveau [ni'vo], *n.m.* (*pl.* **-eaux**) level; standard; *passage à niveau*, level crossing.

niveler [ni'vle], *v.t.* (*conjug. like* APPELER) to level, to flatten (out).

niveleur [ni'vlœːr], *a.* (*fem.* **-euse**) levelling. —*n.* (*fem.* **-euse**) leveller.

nivellement [nivɛl'mã], *n.m.* levelling.

nobiliaire [nɔbi'ljɛːr], *a.* of the nobility, nobiliary.

noble [nɔbl], *a.* noble; great, high, exalted.— *n.* noble, nobleman, noblewoman.

noblement [nɔblə'mã], *adv.* nobly; honorably.

noblesse [nɔ'blɛs], *n.f.* nobility; nobleness, loftiness.

noce [nɔs], *n.f.* wedding; wedding party; (*colloq.*) jollification.

noceur [nɔ'sœːr], *n.m.* (*fem.* **-euse**) gay dog, gay woman, rake.

nocif [nɔ'sif], *a.* (*fem.* **-cive**) injurious, noxious.

noctambule [nɔktã'byl], *a.* noctambulant, noctambulous.—*n.* sleep-walker.

noctambulisme [nɔktãby'lism], *n.m.* noctambulism, sleep-walking.

nocturne [nɔk'tyrn], *a.* nocturnal, nightly.— *n.m.* (*Mus.*) nocturne.

Noël [nɔ'ɛl], *n.m.* Christmas, Yule-tide; (**noël**) Christmas carol.

nœud [nø], *n.m.* knot; bow; difficulty, intricacy; (*fig.*) tie; bond.

noir [nwaːr], *a.* black; swarthy; gloomy, dismal; foul; *bête noire*, pet aversion.— *n.m.* black (*color*); (*fem.* **-e**) Negro.

noirâtre [nwa'raːtr], *a.* blackish.

noiraud [nwa'ro], *a.* dark, swarthy-looking.

noirceur [nwar'sœːr], *n.f.* blackness; baseness; foul deed.

noircir [nwar'siːr], *v.t.* to blacken; to sully; to defame; to darken.—*v.i.* and **se noircir**, *v.r.* to blacken, to darken, to grow black or dark.

noircissure [nwarsi'syːr], *n.f.* black spot, smudge.

noire (2) [nwaːr], *n.f.* (*Mus.*) crotchet.

noisetier [nwaz'tje], *n.m.* hazel (*tree or bush*).

noisette [ɾwa'zɛt], *n.f.* hazel-nut.

noix [nwɑ], *n.f. inv.* walnut; nut.

nom [nɔ̃], *n.m.* name; fame, celebrity; noun.

nomade [nɔ'mad], *a.* nomad, nomadic, wandering.—*n.* nomad.

nombre [nɔ̃ːbr], *n.m.* number; quantity; numbers.

nombrer [nɔ̃'bre], *v.t.* to number, to reckon.

nombreux [nɔ̃'brø], *a.* (*fem.* **-euse**) numerous; harmonious (*prose*, *style*).

nombril [nɔ̃'bri], *n.m.* navel.

nomenclature [nɔmãkla'tyːr], *n.f.* nomenclature; list, catalogue.

nominal [nɔmi'nal], *a.* (*m. pl.* **-aux**) nominal.

nominalement [nɔminal'mã], *adv.* nominally.

nominatif [nɔmina'tif], *a.* (*fem.* **-tive**) and *n.m.* nominative.

nomination [nɔmina'sjɔ̃], *n.f.* nomination; appointment.

nominativement [nɔminativ'mã], *adv.* by name.

nommé [nɔ'me], *a.* named, called; appointed.

nommément [nɔme'mã], *adv.* namely; particularly, especially.

nommer [nɔ'me], *v.t.* to name, to call; to mention; to nominate, to appoint. **se nommer**, *v.r.* to state one's name; to be called.

non [nɔ̃], *adv.* no, not.

non-activité [nɔ̃naktivi'te], *n.f.* state of being unattached or unemployed.

nonagénaire [nɔnaʒe'nɛːr], *a.* ninety years of age.—*n.* nonagenarian.

non-agression [nɔ̃nagrɛ'sjɔ̃], *n.f.* non-aggression.

nonce [nɔ̃ːs], *n.m.* nuncio.

nonchalamment [nɔ̃ʃala'mã], *adv.* nonchalantly, carelessly, heedlessly.

nonchalance [nɔ̃ʃa'lãːs], *n.f.* carelessness, heedlessness, nonchalance.

nonchalant [nɔ̃ʃa'lã], *a.* nonchalant, careless; listless.—*n.m.* (*fem.* **-e**) such a person.

non-lieu [nɔ̃'ljø], *n.m.* (*Law*) no true bill.

nonne [nɔn], *n.f.* nun.

nonobstant [nɔnɔps'tã], *prep.* notwithstanding, in spite of.—*adv.* nevertheless.

nonpareil [nɔ̃pa'rɛːj], *a.* (*fem.* **-eille**) nonpareil, matchless.

non-sens [nɔ̃'sãːs], *n.m.* meaningless sentence, translation, or action.

nord [nɔːr], *a. inv.* north, *Pôle nord*, North Pole.—*n.m.* north; north-wind; *nord-est*, north-east; *nord-ouest*, north-west.

nordique [nɔr'dik], *a.* Nordic, Scandinavian. —*n.* (**Nordique**) Nordic, Scandinavian (*person*).

normal [nɔr'mal], *a.* (*m. pl.* **-aux**) normal; (*Geom.*) perpendicular.

normalement [nɔrmal'mã], *adv.* normally.

normalien [nɔrma'ljɛ̃], *n.m.* (*fem.* **-enne**) training-college student or ex-student.

normalité [nɔrmali'te], *n.f.* normality.

normand [nɔr'mã], *a.* Norman.—*n.m.* (**Normand**, *fem.* **-ande**) Norman (*person*).

Normandie [nɔrmã'di], **la**, *f.* Normandy.

norme [nɔrm], *n.f.* norm, average.

Norvège [nɔr'vɛːʒ], **la**, *f.* Norway.

norvégien [nɔrve'ʒjɛ̃], *a.* (*fem.* **-enne**) Norwegian.—*n.m.* Norwegian (*language*); (**Norvégien**, *fem.* **-enne**) Norwegian (*person*).

nos [no], *pl.* [NOTRE].

nostalgie [nɔstal'ʒi], *n.f.* nostalgia, homesickness.

nostalgique [nɔstal'ʒik], *a.* nostalgic; sad.

notabilité [nɔtabili'te], *n.f.* respectability; person of note.

notable [nɔ'tabl], *a.* notable, of influence.— *n.* notable, person of note.

notablement [nɔtablə'mã], *adv.* notably.

notaire [nɔ'tɛːr], *n.m.* notary; solicitor.

notamment [nɔta'mã], *adv.* specially; more particularly.

notariat [nɔta'rja], *n.m.* profession, business or function of notary.

notation [nɔta'sjɔ̃], *n.f.* notation.

note [nɔt], *n.f.* note, memorandum; mark; statement; bill.

noter [nɔ'te], *v.t.* to note; to mark; to note down; to observe, to notice.

notice [nɔ'tis], *n.f.* notice, account; review (*of a book*); notification.

notification [nɔtifika'sjɔ̃], *n.f.* notification, notice, intimation.

notifier [nɔti'fje], *v.t.* to notify; to intimate.

notion [nɔ'sjɔ̃], *n.f.* notion, idea; (*pl.*) elements, rudiments.

notoire [nɔ'twaːr], *a.* notorious; well-known.
notoirement [nɔtwar'mɑ̃], *adv.* notoriously.
notoriété [nɔtɔrje'te], *n.f.* notoriety (*of fact*); repute (*of person*).
notre [nɔtr], *a. poss.* (*pl.* **nos**) our.
nôtre [noːtr], *pron. poss.* (*pl.* **nôtres**) ours; our own; our things, friends, relatives etc.
noué [nwe], *a.* knotty, tied; rickety.
nouer [nwe], *v.t.* to tie, to knot; (*fig.*) to devise; to establish. **se nouer**, *v.r.* to be twisted *or* tied; to fasten oneself.
noueux [nu'ø], *a.* (*fem.* **-euse**) knotty, gnarled.
nougat [nu'ga], *n.m.* nougat; almond cake.
nouilles [nuːj], *n.f. pl.* noodles, spaghetti.
nourri [nu'ri], *a.* nourished, fed; full, rich, copious; brisk (*fire*).
nourrice [nu'ris], *n.f.* nurse; wet-nurse; (*Motor., Av.*) feed-tank.
nourricier [nuri'sje], *a.* (*fem.* **-ière**) life-giving, nourishing; producing food.—*n.m.* (*fem.* **-ière**) foster parent.
nourrir [nu'riːr], *v.t.* to nourish, to feed; to keep, to maintain; to nurse; to foster; to rear; to cherish. **se nourrir** *v.r.* to feed, to live upon.
nourrissage [nuri'saːʒ], *n.m.* rearing, feeding (*of cattle*).
nourrissant [nuri'sɑ̃], *a.* nutritious; nourishing; sustaining.
nourrisseur [nuri'sœːr], *n.m.* cow keeper; stock raiser.
nourrisson [nuri'sɔ̃], *n.m.* (*fem.* **-onne**) infant; foster child; nursling.
nourriture [nuri'tyːr], *n.f.* nourishment, food; livelihood.
nous [nu], *pers. pron.* we; us; to us; ourselves; each other.
nouveau [nu'vo] (*before a vowel or unaspirated* h, **nouvel**), *a.* (*fem.* **-elle** (1)) new; recent, novel; additional; inexperienced.—*n.m.* (*pl.* **-eaux**) new, something new; **à nouveau**, afresh; **de nouveau**, again.
nouveau-né [nuvo'ne], *n.m.* (*fem.* **nouveau-née**, *pl.* **nouveau-né(e)s**) new-born child.
nouveauté [nuvo'te], *n.f.* novelty; change, innovation; (*pl.*) fancy articles; (*fig.*) new book, new play.
nouvelle (2) [nu'vɛl], *n.f.* (*often in pl.*) news, tidings; short story, short novel.
nouvellement [nuvɛl'mɑ̃], *adv.* newly, lately, recently.
Nouvelle-Zélande [nuvɛlze'lɑ̃ːd], **la**, *f.* New Zealand.
nouvelliste [nuvɛ'list], *n.* newswriter; short story writer.
novateur [nɔva'tœːr], *a.* (*fem.* **-trice**) innovating.—*n.m.* (*fem.* **-trice**) innovator.
novembre [nɔ'vɑ̃ːbr], *n.m.* November.
novice [nɔ'vis], *a.* novice, inexperienced.—*n.* novice, probationer.
noviciat [nɔvi'sja], *n.m.* noviciate.
noyade [nwa'jad], *n.f.* drowning.
noyau [nwa'jo], *n.m.* (*pl.* **-aux**) stone (*of fruit*), nucleus; core (*of statues, casts etc.*).
noyé [nwa'je], *a.* drowned.—*n.m.* (*fem.* **-ée**) drowned person.
noyer (1) [nwa'je], *n.m.* walnut tree; walnut (*wood*).
noyer (2) [nwa'je], *v.t.* (*conjug. like* EMPLOYER) to drown; to swamp; to deluge. **se noyer**, *v.r.* to be drowned; to be plunged (*dans*).

nu [ny], *a.* naked, nude, bare; uncovered; unadorned; destitute.—*n.m.* the nude, nudity.
nuage [nɥa:ʒ], *n.m.* cloud; mist; (*fig.*) gloom, dejection.
nuageux [nɥa'ʒø], *a.* (*fem.* **-euse**) cloudy, overcast.
nuance [nɥɑ̃ːs], *n.f.* shade, hue; gradation; tinge.
nuancer [nɥɑ̃'se], *v.t.* (*conjug. like* COMMENCER) to shade; to vary slightly.
nubile [ny'bil], *a.* nubile, marriageable.
nubilité [nybili'te], *n.f.* nubility, marriageable age.
nucléaire [nykle'ɛːr], *a.* nuclear.
nudité [nydi'te], *n.f.* nudity, nakedness.
nuée [nɥe], *n.f.* cloud; (*fig.*) swarm, host, multitude, flock.
nues [ny], *n.f. pl.* (*Poet.*) skies.
nuire [nɥiːr], *v.i. irr.* to be hurtful, to jeopardize, to harm (*à*).
nuisible [nɥi'zibl], harmful, noxious, prejudicial.
nuit [nɥi], *n.f.* night, night-time; darkness; **il fait nuit**, it is dark; **nuit blanche**, sleepless night.
nuitamment [nɥita'mɑ̃], *adv.* by night, in the night.
nul [nyl], *a.* (*fem.* **nulle**) no, not any; void, null.—*pron.* no one, nobody, not one.
nullement [nyl'mɑ̃], *adv.* not at all, by no means.
nullifier [nyli'fje], *v.t.* to nullify.
nullité [nyli'te], *n.f.* nullity; nonentity; (*fig.*) incapacity.
numéraire [nyme'rɛːr], *a.* legal (*of coin*).—*n.m.* metallic currency, cash.
numéral [nyme'ral], *a.* (*m. pl.* **-aux**) numeral.
numérateur [nymera'tœːr], *n.m.* (*Arith.*) numerator.
numération [nymera'sjɔ̃], *n.f.* numeration, notation.
numérique [nyme'rik], *a.* numerical.
numériquement [nymerik'mɑ̃], *adv.* numerically.
numéro [nyme'ro], *n.m.* number.
numérotage [nymerɔ'taːʒ], *n.m.*, **numérotation** [nymerɔta'sjɔ̃], *n.f.* numbering.
numéroter [nymerɔ'te], *v.t.* to number.
numismate [nymis'mat], **numismatiste** [nymisma'tist], *n.* numismatist.
numismatique [nymisma'tik], *a.* numismatic.—*n.f.* numismatics.
nuptial [nyp'sjal], *a.* (*m. pl.* **-aux**) nuptial, bridal.
nuque [nyk], *n.f.* nape (*of the neck*).
nutritif [nytri'tif], *a.* (*fem.* **-tive**) nutritious, nourishing.
nutrition [nytri'sjɔ̃], *n.f.* nutrition.
nylon [ni'lɔ̃], *n.m.* nylon; **des bas nylon**, nylon stockings.
nymphe [nɛ̃ːf], *n.f.* nymph.

O

O, o [o], *n.m.* the fifteenth letter of the alphabet.
ô! [o] *int.* oh!

oasis [oa′zi:s], *n.f. inv.* oasis.
obéir [ɔbe′i:r], *v.i.* to obey; to comply, to yield, to submit (*à*).
obéissance [ɔbei′sã:s], *n.f.* obedience; allegiance.
obéissant [ɔbei′sã], *a.* obedient; docile.
obélisque [ɔbe′lɪsk], *n.m.* obelisk, needle.
obérer [ɔbe′re], *v.t.* (*conjug. like* CÉDER) to encumber *or* involve in debt.
obèse [ɔ′bɛ:z], *a.* obese, stout.
obésité [ɔbezi′te], *n.f.* obesity, stoutness.
obituaire [ɔbitɥ′ε:r], *a.* and *n.m.* obituary, register of deaths; mortuary.
objecter [ɔbʒɛk′te], *v.t.* to object; to allege.
objecteur [ɔbʒɛk′tœ:r], *n.m.* objector.
objectif [ɔbʒɛk′tif], *a.* (*fem.* **-tive**) objective. —*n.m.* objective, aim; lens; (*Mil.*) target.
objection [ɔbʒɛk′sjɔ̃], *n.f.* objection.
objectivement [ɔbʒɛktiv′mã], *adv.* objectively.
objectivité [ɔbʒɛktivi′te], *n.f.* objectivity.
objet [ɔb′ʒɛ], *n.m.* object; subject, matter; aim; (*pl.*) articles, goods.
obligation [ɔbliga′sjɔ̃], *n.f.* obligation; (*Law*) bond; (*Comm.*) debenture.
obligatoire [ɔbliga′twa:r], *a.* compulsory, obligatory, incumbent.
obligatoirement [ɔbligatwar′mã], *adv.* compulsorily.
obligeamment [ɔbliʒa′mã], *adv.* obligingly.
obligeance [ɔbli′ʒã:s], *n.f.* obligingness; kindness.
obligeant [ɔbli′ʒã], *a.* obliging, kind, helpful.
obliger [ɔbli′ʒe], *v.t.* (*conjug. like* MANGER) to oblige, to bind; to compel; to gratify. **s'obliger**, *v.r.* to put oneself under an obligation.
oblique [ɔ′blik], *a.* oblique, slanting; (*fig.*) indirect, underhand.
obliquement [ɔblik′mã], *adv.* obliquely, indirectly; unfairly.
obliquer [ɔbli′ke], *v.i.* to slant, to swerve.
obliquité [ɔbliki′te], *n.f.* obliquity.
oblitération [ɔblitera′sjɔ̃], *n.f.* obliteration.
oblitérer [ɔblite′re], *v.t.* (*conjug. like* CÉDER) to obliterate; to cancel (*stamps*).
oblong [ɔ′blɔ̃], *a.* (*fem.* **-ue**) oblong.
obole [ɔ′bɔl], *n.f.* obolus; (*fig.*) farthing, mite.
obscène [ɔp′sɛ:n], *a.* obscene.
obscénité [ɔpseni′te], *n.f.* obscenity, lewdness.
obscur [ɔps′ky:r], *a.* obscure; dark, gloomy; (*fig.*) humble; mean.
obscurcir [ɔpskyr′si:r], *v.t.* to obscure, to darken, to dim; to tarnish. **s'obscurcir**, *v.r.* to grow dim.
obscurcissement [ɔpskyrsis′mã], *n.m.* darkening; (*Mil.*) black-out.
obscurément [ɔpskyre′mã], *adv.* obscurely, dimly.
obscurité [ɔpskyri′te], *n.f.* obscurity, darkness.
obséder [ɔpse′de], *v.t.* (*conjug. like* CÉDER) to beset; to haunt, to importune, to obsess.
obsèques [ɔp′sɛk], *n.f. pl.* obsequies, funeral.
obséquieusement [ɔpsekjøz′mã], *adv.* obsequiously.
obséquieux [ɔpse′kjø], *a.* (*fem.* **-euse**) obsequious, fawning.
observable [ɔpsɛr′vabl], *a.* observable.
observance [ɔpsɛr′vã:s], *n.f.* observance.

observateur [ɔpsɛrva′tœ:r], *a.* (*fem.* **-trice**) observant.—*n.m.* (*fem.* **-trice**) observer, onlooker.
observation [ɔpsɛrva′sjɔ̃], *n.f.* observation; observance; remark.
observatoire [ɔpsɛrva′twa:r], *n.m.* observatory; look-out.
observer [ɔpsɛr′ve], *v.t.* to observe, to notice; to watch; to remark; to perform. **s'observer**, *v.r.* to be circumspect, to be on one's guard; to observe each other.
obsession [ɔpsɛ′sjɔ̃], *n.f.* obsession.
obstacle [ɔps′takl], *n.m.* obstacle, bar, hindrance.
obstination [ɔpstina′sjɔ̃], *n.f.* obstinacy, stubbornness, wilfulness.
obstiné [ɔpsti′ne], *a.* obstinate, self-willed, stubborn; persistent.
obstinément [ɔpstine′mã], *adv.* obstinately, stubbornly.
obstiner (s') [sɔpsti′ne], *v.r.* to be obstinately resolved (*à*), to insist; to persist.
obstructif [ɔpstryk′tif], *a.* (*fem.* **-tive**) obstructive.
obstruction [ɔpstryk′sjɔ̃], *n.f.* obstruction; stoppage.
obstruer [ɔpstrɥ′e], *v.t.* to obstruct, to block.
obtempérer [ɔptãpe′re], *v.i.* (*conjug. like* CÉDER) to obey, to comply (*à*).
obtenir [ɔptə′ni:r], *v.t. irr.* (*conjug. like* TENIR) to obtain, to procure, to get. **s'obtenir**, *v.r.* to be obtained; to be obtainable.
obtention [ɔptã′sjɔ̃], *n.f.* obtaining, getting.
obturer [ɔpty′re], *v.t.* to seal, to obturate; to fill (*gap*), to fill (*a tooth etc.*).
obtus [ɔp′ty], *a.* obtuse; dull, blunt.
obus [ɔ′by], *n.m.* (*Artill.*) shell.
obusier [ɔby′zje], *n.m.* howitzer.
obvier [ɔb′vje], *v.i.* to obviate, to prevent (*à*).
occasion [ɔka′zjɔ̃], *n.f.* opportunity, occasion; cause; bargain, job lot; *livres d'occasion*, second-hand books.
occasionnel [ɔkazjɔ′nɛl], *a.* (*fem.* **-elle**) occasional.
occasionnellement [ɔkazjɔnɛl′mã], *adv.* occasionally.
occasionner [ɔkazjɔ′ne], *v.t.* to occasion, to cause.
occident [ɔksi′dã], *n.m.* west.
occidental [ɔksidã′tal], *a.* (*m. pl.* **-aux**) occidental, western.
Occidentaux [ɔksidã′to], *n.m. pl.* natives *or* inhabitants of the western countries, members of the western *bloc*.
occulte [ɔ′kylt], *a.* occult.
occupant [ɔky′pã], *a.* occupying.—*n.m.* (*fem.* **-e**) occupant, occupier.
occupation [ɔkypa′sjɔ̃], *n.f.* occupation; occupancy; capture.
occupé [ɔky′pe], *a.* occupied, busy, engaged; seized.
occuper [ɔky′pe], *v.t.* to occupy; to employ; to inhabit. **s'occuper**, *v.r.* to occupy oneself; to be busy; to look after; to see to (*de*).
occurrence [ɔky′rã:s], *n.f.* occurrence; event; *en l'occurrence*, under the circumstances.
océan [ɔse′ã], *n.m.* ocean, high sea.
océanique [ɔsea′nik], *a.* oceanic.
ocre [ɔkr], *n.f.* ochre.
octane [ɔk′tan], *n.m.* octane.
octave [ɔk′ta:v], *n.f.* octave.

octavo [ɔkta'vo], *adv.* eighthly.—*n.m.* octavo.
octobre [ɔk'tɔbr], *n.m.* October.
octogénaire [ɔktɔʒe'nɛːr], *a.* and *n.* octogenarian.
octogone [ɔktɔ'gɔn], *a.* octagonal, eightsided.—*n.m.* octagon.
octroi [ɔk'trwa], *n.m.* grant, concession; town dues, toll; toll house *or* office.
octroyer [ɔktrwa'je], *v.t.* (*conjug. like* EMPLOYER) to grant, to concede.
oculaire [ɔky'lɛːr], *a.* ocular; *témoin oculaire*, eyewitness.—*n.m.* eye-piece.
oculiste [ɔky'list], *n.m.* oculist.
odalisque [ɔda'lisk], *n.f.* odalisque.
ode [ɔd], *n.f.* ode.
odeur [o'dœːr], *n.f.* odor, smell; scent.
odieusement [ɔdjøz'mɑ̃], *adv.* odiously, hatefully.
odieux [o'djø], *a.* (*fem.* **-euse**) odious, hateful, loathsome.—*n.m.* odiousness, hatefulness.
odorant [ɔdɔ'rɑ̃], *a.* fragrant, sweet-smelling.
odorat [ɔdɔ'ra], *n.m.* smell, sense of smell.
odoriférant [ɔdɔrife'rɑ̃], *a.* sweet-smelling.
Odyssée [ɔdi'se], *n.f.* Odyssey.
œil [œːj], *n.m.* (*pl.* **yeux**) eye; look; luster; bud; dint, hole (*in bread, cheese*); *des yeux à fleur de tête*, prominent eyes; *d'un coup d'œil*, at a glance; *en un clin d'œil*, in the twinkling of an eye.
œil-de-bœuf [œjdə'bœf], *n.m.* (*pl.* **œils-de-bœuf**) round *or* oval window.
œillade [œ'jad], *n.f.* glance; ogle, leer; wink.
œillère [œ'jɛːr], *n.f.* blinker; canine tooth; eye bath.
œillet [œ'jɛ], *n.m.* eyelet; (*Bot.*) dianthus, pink; *œillet des fleuristes*, carnation; *œillet de poète*, sweet william; *petit œillet d'Inde*, French marigold.
œuf [œf], *n.m.* (*pl.* **œufs**) egg; ovum; spawn, roe (*of fish*).
œuvre [œːvr], *n.f.* work; performance; production; (*pl.*) works (*of an author*).—*n.m.* (no *pl.*) work (*of an author, painter, musician etc.*)
œuvrer [œ'vre], [OUVRER]
offensant [ɔfɑ̃'sɑ̃], *a.* offensive, insulting.
offense [ɔ'fɑ̃ːs], *n.f.* offense; injury, wrong, trespass.
offensé [ɔfɑ̃'se], *n.m.* (*fem.* **-ée**) offended party.
offenser [ɔfɑ̃'se], *v.t.* to offend; to sin against; to hurt, to injure (*feelings*); to shock. **s'offenser**, *v.r.* to be offended, to take offense.
offenseur [ɔfɑ̃'sœːr], *n.m.* offender.
offensif [ɔfɑ̃'sif], *a.* (*fem.* **-sive**) offensive.—*n.f.* (**-sive**) offensive (*attack*).
offensivement [ɔfɑ̃siv'mɑ̃], *adv.* offensively.
office [ɔ'fis], *n.m.* office; duty; employment; service; Divine worship.—*n.f.* servants' hall, pantry, larder.
officiant [ɔfi'sjɑ̃], *a.* officiating.—*n.m.* officiating priest.
officiel [ɔfi'sjɛl], *a.* (*fem.* **-elle**) official, formal.
officiellement [ɔfisjɛl'mɑ̃], *adv.* officially.
officier (1) [ɔfi'sje], *v.i.* to officiate (*at divine service*).
officier (2) [ɔfi'sje], *n.m.* officer.
officieusement [ɔfisjøz'mɑ̃], *adv.* officiously.
officieux [ɔfi'sjø], *a.* (*fem.* **-euse**) officious; semi-official; obliging.—*n.m.* (*fem.* **-euse**) busybody.

offrande [ɔ'frɑ̃ːd], *n.f.* offertory; offering.
offre [ɔfr], *n.f.* offer, tender.
offrir [ɔ'friːr], *v.t.* (*conjug. like* OUVRIR) to offer, to tender; to present, to give. **s'offrir**, *v.r.* to offer oneself; to present itself.
offusquer [ɔfys'ke], *v.t.* to obscure; to dazzle; to offend. **s'offusquer**, *v.r.* (*rare*) to become darkened; (*fig.*) to take offense.
ogival [ɔʒi'val], *a.* (*m. pl.* **-aux**) (*Arch.*) pointed; gothic.
ogive [ɔ'ʒiːv], *n.f.* ogive, pointed arch; nose (*of missile, rocket*).
ogre [ɔgr], *n.m.* (*fem.* **-esse**) ogre, ogress.
oh! [o], *int.* O! ho!
ohm [om], *n.m.* ohm.
oie [wa], *n.f.* goose; (*fig.*) simpleton.
oignon [ɔ'ɲɔ̃], *n.m.* onion; bulb; bunion.
oindre [wɛ̃ːdr], *v.t. irr.* to anoint.
oiseau [wa'zo], *n.m.* (*pl.* **-eaux**) bird; hod; (*colloq.*) fellow, chap; *à vol d'oiseau*, as the crow flies.
oiseau-mouche [wazo'muʃ], *n.m.* (*pl.* **oiseaux-mouches**) humming-bird.
oiselet [wa'zlɛ], *n.m.* small bird.
oiseleur [wa'zlœːr], *n.m.* bird-catcher; fowler.
oiselier [waz'lje], *n.m.* bird seller; bird fancier.
oiseux [wa'zø], *a.* (*fem.* **-euse**) idle; useless, trifling.
oisif [wa'zif], *a.* (*fem.* **-sive**) idle, unoccupied; lying dead (*money*).—*n.m.* (*fem.* **-sive**) idler.
oisillon [wazi'jɔ̃], *n.m.* young bird, fledg(e)ling.
oisivement [waziv'mɑ̃], *adv.* idly.
oisiveté [waziv'te], *n.f.* idleness; hours of ease.
oison [wa'zɔ̃], *n.m.* gosling; (*fig.*) simpleton.
oléagineux [ɔleaʒi'nø], *a.* (*fem.* **-euse**) oleaginous, oily.
oléoduc [ɔleo'dyk], *n.m.* pipeline.
oligarchie [ɔligar'ʃi], *n.f.* oligarchy.
oligarchique [ɔligar'ʃik], *a.* oligarchical.
oligarque [ɔli'gark], *n.* oligarch.
olivâtre [ɔli'vɑːtr], *a.* olivaceous, olive-hued; sallow.
olive [ɔ'liːv], *a. inv.* olive-colored.—*n.f.* olive.
Olivier [ɔli'vje], *m.* Oliver.
olivier [ɔli'vje], *n.m.* olive tree; olive wood.
olographe [ɔlɔ'graf], *a.* holograph(ic) (*will*).
Olympe [ɔ'lɛ̃ːp], *n.m.* Olympus; (*fig.*) heaven.
olympien [ɔlɛ̃'pjɛ̃], *a.* (*fem.* **-enne**) Olympian. —*n.m.* (**Olympien**, *fem.* **-enne**) Olympian.
olympique [ɔlɛ̃'pik], *a.* Olympic.
ombrage [ɔ̃'braːʒ], *n.m.* shade; umbrage, suspicion.
ombrager [ɔ̃bra'ʒe], *v.t.* (*conjug. like* MANGER) to shade; (*fig.*) to protect.
ombrageux [ɔ̃bra'ʒø], *a.* (*fem.* **-euse**) skittish (*of horses*); suspicious, touchy.
ombre [ɔ̃ːbr], *n.f.* shadow; shade; darkness; ghost; *à l'ombre*, in the shade.
ombré [ɔ̃'bre], *a.* tinted, shaded.
ombrelle [ɔ̃'brɛl], *n.f.* parasol, sunshade.
ombrer [ɔ̃'bre], *v.t.* to shade; to darken.
ombreux [ɔ̃'brø], *a.* (*fem.* **-euse**) shady.
omelette [ɔm'lɛt], *n.f.* omelet(te).
omettre [ɔ'mɛtr], *v.t. irr.* (*conjug. like* METTRE) to omit.
omission [ɔmi'sjɔ̃], *n.f.* omission.
omnibus [ɔmni'byːs], *a.* suitable for all; *train omnibus*, slow train, local train. —*n.m. inv.* omnibus, bus.

229

omnipotence [ɔmnipɔ'tɑ̃:s], *n.f.* omnipotence.

omnipotent [ɔmnipɔ'tɑ̃], *a.* omnipotent.

omnivore [ɔmni'vɔ:r], *a.* omnivorous.—*n.m.* omnivore.

omoplate [ɔmo'plat], *n.f.* shoulder-blade; scapula.

on [ɔ̃], *indef. pron.* one, they, we, you, people, men, somebody.

once (1) [ɔ̃:s], *n.f.* ounce (*weight*).

once (2) [ɔ̃:s], *n.f.* ounce, snow leopard.

oncle [ɔ̃:kl], *n.m.* uncle.

onction [ɔ̃k'sjɔ̃], *n.f.* unction, anointing; (*fig.*) unctuousness.

onctueusement [ɔ̃ktɥøz'mɑ̃], *adv.* unctuously.

onctueux [ɔ̃k'tɥø], *a.* (*fem.* **-euse**) unctuous, oily.

onctuosité [ɔ̃ktɥozi'te], *n.f.* unctuousness; smoothness.

onde [ɔ̃:d], *n.f.* wave, billow; (*fig.*) sea.

ondé [ɔ̃'de], *a.* undulating, wavy; watered (*of silk etc.*).

ondée [ɔ̃'de], *n.f.* shower (*of rain*).

ondoyant [ɔ̃dwa'jɑ̃], *a.* undulating; (*fig.*) changeable.

ondoyer [ɔ̃dwa'je], *v.t.* (*conjug. like* EMPLOYER) to baptize privately.—*v.i.* to undulate; to ripple (*water*).

ondulant [ɔ̃dy'lɑ̃], *a.* undulating; waving, flowing.

ondulation [ɔ̃dyla'sjɔ̃], *n.f.* undulation; wave (*of hair*).

ondulé [ɔ̃dy'le], *a.* rolling, undulating; waved (*hair*); corrugated (*iron*).

onduler [ɔ̃dy'le], *v.t.* to wave (*hair*).—*v.i.* to undulate; to ripple.

onduleux [ɔ̃dy'lø], *a.* (*fem.* **-euse**) sinuous, wavy.

onéreux [ɔne'rø], *a.* (*fem.* **-euse**) burdensome, onerous; expensive.

ongle [ɔ̃:gl], *n.m.* nail (*of fingers, claws etc.*); claw, talon; hoof.

onglée [ɔ̃'gle], *n.f.* numbness of the fingers (*from cold*).

onglet [ɔ̃'glɛ], *n.m.* miter, miter-joint.

onglier [ɔ̃'glje], *n.m.* manicure case; (*pl.*) (*curved*) nail scissors.

onguent [ɔ̃'gɑ̃], *n.m.* ointment, salve.

ongulé [ɔ̃gy'le], *a.* hoofed, ungulate.

onyx [ɔ'niks], *a.* and *n.m. inv.* onyx.

onze [ɔ̃:z], *a.* and *n.m.* eleven, eleventh.

onzième [ɔ̃'zjɛm], *a.* and *n.m.* eleventh.

onzièmement [ɔ̃zjɛm'mɑ̃], *adv.* eleventhly, in the eleventh place.

opacité [ɔpasi'te], *n.f.* opacity; (*fig.*) darkness.

opale [ɔ'pal], *n.f.* opal.

opalescence [ɔpalɛ'sɑ̃:s], *n.f.* opalescence.

opalescent [ɔpalɛ'sɑ̃], *a.* opalescent.

opaque [ɔ'pak], *a.* opaque.

opéra [ɔpe'ra], *n.m.* opera; opera house.

opéra-bouffe [ɔpera'buf], *n.m.* comic opera; musical comedy.

opérateur [ɔpera'tœ:r], *n.m.* (*fem.* **-trice**) operator; operative.

opératif [ɔpera'tif], *a.* (*fem.* **-tive**) operative.

opération [ɔpera'sjɔ̃], *n.f.* operation, working, performance; (*Comm.*) transaction.

opératoire [ɔpera'twa:r], *a.* operative, surgical.

opérer [ɔpe're], *v.t.* (*conjug. like* CÉDER) to operate, to bring about, to perform; to

operate upon.—*v.i.* to work, to operate.

s'opérer, *v.r.* to take place, to be brought about.

opérette [ɔpe'rɛt], *n.f.* operetta, light opera.

ophtalmie [ɔftal'mi], *n.f.* ophthalmia.

ophtalmique [ɔftal'mik], *a.* ophthalmic.

opiner [ɔpi'ne], *v.i.* to opine, to give *or* be of opinion; to speak.

opiniâtre [ɔpi'nja:tr], *a.* stubborn, obstinate. —*n.* stubborn person.

opiniâtrement [ɔpinjatrə'mɑ̃], *adv.* doggedly.

opiniâtrer (s') [sɔpinja'tre], *v.r.* to be obstinate, to insist.

opiniâtreté [ɔpinjatrə'te], *n.f.* obstinacy.

opinion [ɔpi'njɔ̃], *n.f.* opinion; judgment, view; (*pl.*) votes.

opium [ɔ'pjɔm], *n.m.* opium.

opossum [ɔpɔ'sɔm], *n.m.* opossum.

opportun [ɔpɔr'tœ̃], *a.* opportune, timely; expedient.

opportunément [ɔpɔrtyne'mɑ̃], *adv.* seasonably.

opportunisme [ɔpɔrty'nism], *n.m.* opportunism.

opportuniste [ɔpɔrty'nist], *a.* and *n.* opportunist.

opportunité [ɔpɔrtyni'te], *n.f.* opportuneness, expediency.

opposant [ɔpo'zɑ̃], *a.* opposing, adverse.— *n.m.* (*fem.* **-e**) opponent, adversary.

opposé [ɔpo'ze], *a.* opposite, contrary.—*n.m.* the opposite, the reverse, the contrary.

opposer [ɔpo'ze], *v.t.* to oppose; to object; to urge. **s'opposer**, *v.r.* to be opposed *or* contrary (*à*), to set oneself against, to resist.

opposition [ɔpozi'sjɔ̃], *n.f.* opposition, resistance; contrast.

oppresser [ɔprɛ'se], *v.t.* (*fig.*) to depress; *to oppress.

oppresseur [ɔprɛ'sœ:r], *a.m.* oppressive.— *n.m.* oppressor.

oppressif [ɔprɛ'sif], *a.* (*fem.* **-ive**) oppressive.

oppression [ɔprɛ'sjɔ̃], *n.f.* oppression.

oppressivement [ɔprɛsiv'mɑ̃], *adv.* tyrannically, oppressively (*person*).

opprimant [ɔpri'mɑ̃], *a.* oppressing.

opprimé [ɔpri'me], *a.* oppressed.—*n.m.* (*fem.* **-ée**) the oppressed.

opprimer [ɔpri'me], *v.t.* to oppress, to crush.

opprobre [ɔ'prɔbr], *n.m.* opprobrium, shame, disgrace.

opter [ɔp'te], *v.i.* to choose, to decide.

opticien [ɔpti'sjɛ̃], *n.m.* optician.

optimisme [ɔpti'mism], *n.m.* optimism.

optimiste [ɔpti'mist], *a.* optimistic.—*n.* optimist.

option [ɔp'sjɔ̃], *n.f.* option, choice.

optique [ɔp'tik], *a.* optic, optical.—*n.f.* optics; perspective.

opulence [ɔpy'lɑ̃:s], *n.f.* opulence, wealth.

opulent [ɔpy'lɑ̃], *a.* opulent, wealthy.

or (1) [ɔ:r], *n.m.* gold; (*Her.*) or.

or (2) [ɔ:r], *conj.* but, now; well.

oracle [ɔ'ra:kl], *n.m.* oracle.

orage [ɔ'ra:ʒ], *n.m.* storm; thunder-storm; (*fig.*) tumult, disorder.

orageusement [ɔraʒøz'mɑ̃], *adv.* tempestuously; boisterously.

orageux [ɔra'ʒø], *a.* (*fem.* **-euse**) stormy, tempestuous; restless.

oraison [ɔrɛ'zɔ̃], *n.f.* speech, oration; prayer.
oral [ɔ'ral], *a.* (*m. pl.* **-aux**) oral, by word of mouth.
oralement [ɔral'mã], *adv.* orally, by word of mouth.
orange [ɔ'rãːʒ], *n.f.* orange (*fruit*).—*a. inv.* and *n.m.* orange (*color*).
orangé [ɔrã'ʒe], *a.* orange(-colored).
orangeade [ɔrã'ʒad], *n.f.* orangeade, orange squash.
oranger [ɔrã'ʒe], *n.m.* orange tree.
orangerie [ɔrã'ʒri], *n.f.* orange house; orange grove, orangery.
orang-outan(g) [ɔrãu'tã], *n.m.* (*pl.* **orangs-outans**) orang-utan.
orateur [ɔra'tœːr], *n.m.* (*fem.* **-trice**) orator, speaker.
oratoire [ɔra'twaːr], *a.* oratorical; oratorial.—*n.m.* oratory; private chapel.
orbe [ɔrb], *n.m.* orb, orbit; globe; sphere; coil (*snake*).
orbite [ɔr'bit], *n.f.* orbit; (*Anat.*) socket; (*fig.*) sphere (*of action*).
Orcades [ɔr'kad], **les**, *f. pl.* the Orkneys.
orchestral [ɔrkɛs'tral], *a.* (*m. pl.* **-aux**) orchestral.
orchestration [ɔrkɛstra'sjɔ̃], *n.f.* scoring, orchestration.
orchestre [ɔr'kɛstr], *n.m.* orchestra; band.
orchestrer [ɔrkɛs'tre], *v.t.* to score, to orchestrate.
orchidée [ɔrki'de], *n.f.* orchid; (*pl.*) Orchidaceae.
ordinaire [ɔrdi'nɛːr], *a.* ordinary, common, usual.—*n.m.* ordinary practice; usual fare.
ordinairement [ɔrdinɛr'mã], *adv.* usually.
ordinal [ɔrdi'nal], *a.* (*m. pl.* **-aux**) ordinal.
ordination [ɔrdina'sjɔ̃], *n.f.* ordination.
ordonnance [ɔrdɔ'nãːs], *n.f.* order, ordinance, regulation; disposition, arrangement; (*Med.*) prescription.—*n.* (*usu. fem.*) (*Mil.*) orderly.
ordonnateur [ɔrdɔna'tœːr], *a.* (*fem.* **-trice**) ordaining, ordering.—*n.m.* (*fem.* **-trice**) organizer, manager; master of ceremonies.
ordonné [ɔrdɔ'ne], *a.* ordered; tidy; ordained (*priest*).
ordonner [ɔrdɔ'ne], *v.t.* to order, to regulate; to direct, to command; to ordain; (*Med.*) to prescribe.
ordre [ɔrdr], *n.m.* order, command; class, tribe; (*pl.*) holy orders.
ordure [ɔr'dyːr], *n.f.* filth, dirt; (*pl.*) sweepings, refuse, garbage.
ordurier [ɔrdy'rje], *a.* (*fem.* **-ière**) filthy, ribald, lewd.
oreille [ɔ'rɛːj], *n.f.* ear; hearing; flange; handle (*of a vase etc.*); *avoir l'oreille basse*, to be crestfallen; *avoir mal aux oreilles*, to have ear-ache; *faire la sourde oreille*, to turn a deaf ear; *prêter l'oreille à*, to listen to.
oreiller [ɔrɛ'je], *n.m.* pillow.
oreillons [ɔrɛ'jɔ̃], *n.m. pl.* mumps.
orfèvre [ɔr'fɛːvr], *n.m.* goldsmith, silversmith.
orfraie [ɔr'frɛ], *n.f.* osprey.
organdi [ɔrgã'di], *n.m.* organdie.
organe [ɔr'gan], *n.m.* organ; voice; agent, agency; spokesman.
organique [ɔrga'nik], *a.* organic.

organisateur [ɔrganiza'tœːr], *a.* (*fem.* **-trice**) organizing.—*n.m.* (*fem.* **-trice**) organizer.
organisation [ɔrganiza'sjɔ̃], *n.f.* organization; (*fig.*) set-up; constitution.
organisé [ɔrgani'ze], *a.* organized.
organiser [ɔrgani'ze], *v.t.* to organize; to get up, to arrange. **s'organiser**, *v.r.* to become organized.
organisme [ɔrga'nism], *n.m.* organism.
organiste [ɔrga'nist], *n.* organist.
orge [ɔrʒ], *n.f.* barley; (*masc. in orge mondé*, hulled barley, *and orge perlé*, pearl barley).
orgelet [ɔrʒ'lɛ], *n.m.* sty (*in the eye*).
orgie [ɔr'ʒi], *n.f.* orgy; (*fig.*) profusion.
orgue [ɔrg], *n.m.* (*fem. in pl.*) (*Mus.*) organ.
orgueil [ɔr'gœːj], *n.m.* pride; arrogance.
orgueilleusement [ɔrgœjøz'mã], *adv.* proudly, haughtily.
orgueilleux [ɔrgœ'jø], *a.* (*fem.* **-euse**) proud, haughty, arrogant.—*n.m.* (*fem.* **-euse**) proud and haughty person.
orient [ɔ'rjã], *n.m.* East, Orient; rise; water (*of pearls*).
oriental [ɔrjã'tal], *a.* (*m. pl.* **-aux**) oriental, eastern.—*n.m.* (*fem.* **-e**) oriental (*person*).
orientation [ɔrjãta'sjɔ̃], *n.f.* orientation.
orienter [ɔrjã'te], *v.t.* to orientate; to set (*a map*) by the compass; (*fig.*) to guide; (*Naut.*) to trim (*sails*). **s'orienter**, *v.r.* to take one's bearings, to ascertain one's position; (*fig.*) to see what one is about.
orifice [ɔri'fis], *n.m.* orifice, aperture, hole.
originaire [ɔriʒi'nɛːr], *a.* originally (*coming*) from; native (*de*); primitive.
originairement [ɔriʒinɛr'mã], *adv.* originally, primitively.
original [ɔriʒi'nal], *a.* (*m. pl.* **-aux**) original; singular, odd, peculiar, quaint.—*n.m.* original manuscript, drawing etc. (*not a copy*).—*n.m.* (*fem.* **-e**) queer person, character, oddity.
originalement [ɔriʒinal'mã], *adv.* originally; singularly, oddly.
originalité [ɔriʒinali'te], *n.f.* originality; eccentricity.
origine [ɔri'ʒin], *n.f.* origin, source; descent, derivation, extraction; *d'origine*, authentic; vintage (*wine*).
originel [ɔriʒi'nɛl], *a.* (*fem.* **-elle**) original, primitive.
originellement [ɔriʒinɛl'mã], *adv.* originally.
orignal [ɔri'nal], *n.m.* elk (*of Canada*), moose.
Orion [ɔ'rjɔ̃], *n.m.* (*Astron.*) Orion.
oripeau [ɔri'po], *n.m.* (*pl.* **-eaux**) tinsel; foil; (*pl.*) tawdry finery; (*more usually*) rags.
orme [ɔrm], *n.m.* elm.
ormeau [ɔr'mo], *n.m.* (*pl.* **-eaux**) young elm.
orné [ɔr'ne], *a.* ornate.
ornement [ɔrnə'mã], *n.m.* ornament, embellishment.
ornemental [ɔrnəmã'tal], *a.* (*m. pl.* **-aux**) ornamental.
ornementation [ɔrnəmãta'sjɔ̃], *n.f.* ornamentation.
orner [ɔr'ne], *v.t.* to adorn, to decorate, to deck, to embellish. **s'orner**, *v.r.* to adorn oneself; to be adorned.
ornière [ɔr'njɛːr], *n.f.* rut.
ornithologie [ɔrnitɔlɔ'ʒi], *n.f.* ornithology.
ornithologiste [ɔrnitɔlɔ'ʒist], **ornithologue** [ɔrnitɔ'lɔg], *n.m.* ornithologist.

Orphée [ɔr′fe], *m.* Orpheus.
orphelin [ɔrfə′lɛ̃], *a.* and *n.m.* (*fem.* **-e**) orphan.
orphelinat [ɔrfəli′na], *n.m.* orphanage.
orphéon [ɔrfe′ɔ̃], *n.m.* male-voice choir.
ort [ɔ:r], *a. inv.* and *adv.* (*Comm.*) gross, gross weight.
orteil [ɔr′tɛ:j], *n.m.* toe, *esp.* the big toe.
orthodoxe [ɔrtɔ′dɔks], *a.* orthodox.
orthodoxie [ɔrtɔdɔk′si], *n.f.* orthodoxy.
orthographe [ɔrtɔ′graf], *n.f.* orthography, spelling.
orthopédie [ɔrtɔpe′di], *n.f.* orthopedics.
ortie [ɔr′ti], *n.f.* nettle.
orvet [ɔr′vɛ], *n.m.* slow-worm.
os [ɔs; *pl.* o], *n.m. inv.* bone.
oscillant [ɔsi′lɑ̃], *a.* oscillating.
oscillation [ɔsila′sjɔ̃], *n.f.* oscillation, vibration.
oscillatoire [ɔsila′twa:r], *a.* oscillatory.
osciller [ɔsi′le], *v.i.* to oscillate, to swing, to vibrate; (*fig.*) to fluctuate.
oscillographe [ɔsilɔ′graf], *n.m.* (*Elec.*) oscillograph.
osé [o′ze], *a.* bold, daring.
oseille [o′zɛ:j], *n.f.* sorrel.
oser [o′ze], *v.t., v.i.* to dare, to venture.
oseraie [oz′rɛ], *n.f.* osier bed.
osier [o′zje] *n.m.* osier, withy, wicker.
osselet [ɔs′lɛ], *n.m.* knuckle bone (*of sheep*); ossicle (*of ear*).
ossements [ɔs′mɑ̃], *n.m. pl.* bones (*of the dead*).
osseux [ɔ′sø], *a.* (*fem.* **-euse**) bony, osseous.
ossification [ɔsifika′sjɔ̃], *n.f.* ossification.
ossifier [ɔsi′fje], *v.t.* to ossify. **s'ossifier**, *v.r.* to become ossified.
ossuaire [ɔ′sɥɛ:r], *n.m.* ossuary, charnel-house.
ostensible [ɔstɑ̃′sibl], *a.* open; above-board.
ostensiblement [ɔstɑ̃siblə′mɑ̃], *adv.* openly, publicly.
ostensoir [ɔstɑ̃′swa:r], *n.m.* monstrance.
ostentateur [ɔstɑ̃ta′tœ:r], *a.* (*fem.* **-trice**) ostentatious.
ostentation [ɔstɑ̃ta′sjɔ̃], *n.f.* ostentation, show.
ostraciser [ɔstrasi′ze], *v.t.* to ostracize.
ostracisme [ɔstra′sism], *n.m.* ostracism.
ostréiculture [ɔstreikyl′ty:r], *n.f.* oyster culture.
otage [ɔ′ta:ʒ], *n.m.* hostage; pledge.
ôter [o′te], *v.t.* to take away; to remove; to take off; to deprive of; to deduct; to rid of. **s'ôter**, *v.r.* to remove oneself, to get away; to rid oneself; *ôtez-vous de mon chemin*, stand aside.
ou [u], *conj.* or, either, else; *ou bien*, or else; *ou . . . ou*, either . . . or.
où [u], *adv.* where; whither; at which, in which,- to which, through which; when, that; *par où?* which way ?
ouais! [wɛ], *int.* well now! my word!
ouate [wat], *n.f. l'ouate* or *la ouate*, wadding, padding; cotton-wool.
ouater [wa′te], *v.t.* to wad, to pad; to coddle.
oubli [u′bli], *n.m.* forgetfulness; oblivion; oversight, slip; pardon.
oubliable [u′bljabl], *a.* liable *or* deserving to be forgotten.
oublier [u′blje], *v.t.* to forget, to omit, to

neglect; to pardon. **s'oublier**, *v.r.* to forget oneself; to be forgotten.
oubliettes [u′bljɛt], *n.f. pl.* oubliette, trap-dungeon.
oublieux [u′bljø], *a.* (*fem.* **-euse**) forgetful, unmindful.
ouest [wɛst], *a. inv.* westerly, western.—*n.m.* west.
ouf! [uf], *int.* oh! (*of relief*).
Ouganda [ugɑ̃′da], **l'**, *m.* Uganda.
oui [wi], *adv.* yes.—*n.m.* yes.
ouï [wi], *p.p.* [OUÏR].
ouï-dire [wi′di:r], *n.m. inv.* hearsay.
ouïe [wi], *n.f.* *hearing; hole (*of a violin etc.*); (*pl.*) gills (*of fish*).
ouïr [wi:r], *v.t. irr.* (*rarely used except in the infinitive and compound tenses*) to hear; *j'ai ouï dire*, I have heard say.
ouragan [ura′gɑ̃], *n.m.* hurricane; (*fig.*) storm.
ourdir [ur′di:r], *v.t.* to warp (*cloth*); (*fig.*) to weave, to plot, to concoct.
ourdissage [urdi′sa:ʒ], *n.m.* warping.
ourdou [ur′du], *n.m.* Urdu (*language*), Hindustani.
ourler [ur′le], *v.t.* to hem; *ourler à jour*, to hemstitch.
ourlet [ur′lɛ], *n.m.* hem.
ours [urs], *n.m.* bear.
ourse [urs], *n.f.* she-bear.
oursin [ur′sɛ̃], *n.m.* sea-urchin.
ourson [ur′sɔ̃], *n.m.* bear cub.
outil [u′ti], *n.m.* tool, implement.
outillage [uti′ja:ʒ], *n.m.* stock of tools; equipment.
outillé [uti′je], *a.* furnished with tools.
outiller [uti′je], *v.t.* to furnish with tools; to equip.
outrage [u′tra:ʒ], *n.m.* outrage, gross insult; injury, wrong.
outrageant [utra′ʒɑ̃], *a.* outrageous; insulting, abusive.
outrager [utra′ʒe], *v.t.* (*conjug. like* MANGER) to outrage; to insult, to offend.
outrageusement [utraʒøz′mɑ̃], *adv.* insultingly.
outrageux [utra′ʒø], *a.* (*fem.* **-euse**) outrageous.
outrance [u′trɑ̃:s], *n.f.* extreme; excess; *à outrance*, to the death.
outre (1) [utr], *n.f.* goatskin *or* leather bottle.
outre (2) [utr], *adv.* further, beyond; *en outre*, besides; *passer outre*, to go on, to take no notice of a thing.—*prep.* beyond; besides, in addition to; *outre que*, besides.
outré [u′tre], *a.* exaggerated, strained, excessive; incensed.
outrecuidance [utrəkɥi′dɑ̃:s], *n.f.* presumption.
outrecuidant [utrəkɥi′dɑ̃], *a.* presumptuous, bumptious.
outre-Manche [utrə′mɑ̃:ʃ], *adv.* across the Channel.
outremer [utrə′mɛ:r], *n.m.* ultramarine (*color*).
outre-mer [utrə′mɛ:r], *adv.* overseas.
outrepasser [utrəpa′se], *v.t.* to go beyond, to transgress.
outrer [u′tre], *v.t.* to overdo; to exaggerate.
ouvert [u′vɛ:r], *a.* open; unfortified (*of towns*); (*fig.*) frank.

ouvertement [uvɛrtə'mã], *adv.* openly, frankly.

ouverture [uvɛr'ty:r], *n.f.* opening; aperture, gap, hole; (*Mus.*) overture; (*Arch.*) span, width (*of a doorway etc.*); (*Av.*) (parachute) drop.

ouvrable [u'vrabl], *a.* working, workable; *jour ouvrable*, working day.

ouvrage [u'vra:ʒ], *n.m.* work, piece of work; performance, workmanship.

ouvragé [uvra'ʒe], *a.* wrought, figured.

ouvrager [uvra'ʒe], *v.t.* (*conjug. like* MANGER) to work, to figure.

ouvrant [u'vrã], *a.* opening.

ouvré [u'vre], *a.* wrought; diapered, figured.

ouvre-boîte [uvrə'bwa:t], *n.m.* (*pl.* **-boîtes**) can opener.

ouvrer [u'vre], *v.t.* to work (*material*); to diaper (*linen*).—*v.i.* to work.

ouvrier [uvri'e], *a.* (*fem.* **-ière**) operative, working.—*n.m.* (*fem.* **-ière**) workman, (female) worker, hand, operative; laborer.

ouvrir [u'vri:r], *v.t. irr.* to open, to unlock; to sharpen (*the appetite*); to broach (*opinions etc.*).—*v.i.* to open; to expand. **s'ouvrir**, *v.r.* to open; to open for oneself; to open one's mind.

ouvroir [u'vrwa:r], *n.m.* charity workshop; workroom.

ovaire [ɔ'vɛ:r], *n.m.* ovary.

ovalaire [ɔva'lɛ:r], *a.* (*Anat.*) oval.

ovale [ɔ'val], *a.* and *n.m.* oval.

ovation [ɔva'sjõ], *n.f.* ovation.

ovoïde [ɔvɔ'id], *a.* ovoid, egg-shaped.

ovule [ɔ'vyl], *n.m.* ovule.

oxalique [ɔksa'lik], *a.* oxalic.

oxyacétylénique [ɔksiasetile'nik], *a.* oxyacetylene (*welding etc.*).

oxyde [ɔk'sid], *n.m.* oxide.

oxyder [ɔksi'de], *v.t.* to oxidize.

oxygène [ɔksi'ʒɛ:n], *n.m.* oxygen.

oxygéné [ɔksiʒe'ne], *a.* *eau oxygénée*, hydrogen peroxide.

ozone [ɔ'zɔn], *n.m.* ozone.

P

P, p [pe], *n.m.* the sixteenth letter of the alphabet.

pacage [pa'ka:ʒ], *n.m.* pasture land; *droit de pacage*, grazing rights.

pacificateur [pasifika'tœ:r], *a.* (*fem.* **-trice**) pacifying, peace-making.—*n.m.* (*fem.* **-trice**) peacemaker.

pacification [pasifika'sjõ], *n.f.* pacification.

pacifier [pasi'fje], *v.t.* to pacify, to appease.

pacifique [pasi'fik], *a.* pacific, peaceful.

pacifiquement [pasifik'mã], *adv.* peaceably, quietly.

pacifisme [pasi'fism], *n.m.* pacifism.

pacifiste [pasi'fist], *a.* and *n.* pacifist.

pacotille [pakɔ'ti:j], *n.f.* goods carried free of charge by passengers *or* seamen; shoddy goods; pack, bale.

pacte [pakt], *n.m.* compact, contract, pact, agreement; *pacte de préférence*, preference clause.

pactiser [pakti'ze], *v.i.* to covenant, to make a compact (*avec*).

paf! [paf], *int.* slap! bang!

pagaie [pa'gɛ], *n.f.* paddle (*for canoe etc.*).

pagaïe or **pagaille** [pa'gaj], *n.f.* hurry; disorder; *en pagaïe*, (*pop.*) higgledy-piggledy.

paganisme [paga'nism], *n.m.* paganism.

pagayer [page'je], *v.t.*, *v.i.* (*conjug. like* PAYER) to paddle.

page (1) [pa:ʒ], *n.m.* page (boy).

page (2) [pa:ʒ], *n.f.* page (*of a book*).

pagode [pa'gɔd], *n.f.* pagoda.

paiement [PAYEMENT].

païen [pa'jɛ̃], *a.* and *n.m.* (*fem.* **-enne**) pagan, heathen.

paillard [pɑ'ja:r], *a.* lecherous, lewd.—*n.m.* (*fem.* **-e**) wanton, sensual person, bawd.

paillasse (1) [pɑ'jas], *n.f.* straw mattress.

paillasse (2) [pɑ'jas], *n.m.* clown, buffoon.

paillasson [pɑja'sõ], *n.m.* straw mat; doormat.

paille [pɑ:j], *a. inv.* straw-colored. —*n.f.* straw; flaw (*in gems, metals etc.*); *botte de paille*, bale of straw.

paillé [pɑ'je], *a.* straw-colored; faulty (*of metals etc.*).

pailler (1) [pɑ'je], *n.m.* farm yard; heap *or* stack of straw.

pailler (2) [pɑ'je], *v.t.* to mulch (*plants*).

pailleter [pɑj'te], *v.t.* (*conjug. like* APPELER) to spangle.

paillette [pɑ'jɛt], *n.f.* spangle; flaw (*in a gem*); *savon en paillettes*, soap flakes.

paillis [pɑ'ji], *n.m.* mulch.

paillon [pɑ'jõ], *n.m.* large spangle, tinsel; wisp of straw; straw wrapper (*for bottle*).

pain [pɛ̃], *n.m.* bread; loaf; cake (*of soap etc.*); (*pop.*) blow, punch; *pain grillé*, toast; *un pain*, a loaf; *un petit pain*, a roll.

pair [pɛ:r], *a.* equal, even (*of numbers*).—*n.m.* peer; equal; mate (*of birds*); par, equality; *au pair*, at par, even (*with*), 'au pair'; *de pair*, on a par; *hors (de) pair*, beyond comparison.

paire [pɛ:r], *n.f.* pair, brace, couple.

pairesse [pɛ'rɛs], *n.f.* peeress.

pairie [pɛ'ri], *n.f.* peerage.

paisible [pe'zibl], *a.* peaceful, quiet, calm.

paisiblement [peziblə'mã], *adv.* peacefully.

paître [pɛ:tr], *v.t., v.i. irr.* to graze, to feed.

paix [pɛ], *n.f.* peace; quiet; stillness; rest.—*int.* be quiet!

Pakistan [pakis'tã], **le**, *m.* Pakistan.

pakistanais [pakista'nɛ], *a.* Pakistani.—*n.m.* (**Pakistanais**, *fem.* **-aise**) Pakistani (*person*).

paladin [pala'dɛ̃], *n.m.* paladin, champion.

palais (1) [pa'lɛ], *n.m.* palace; (*fig.*) the bar, the law; *palais de justice*, law-courts.

palais (2) [pa'lɛ], *n.m.* palate, roof (*of the mouth*).

palan [pa'lã], *n.m.* tackle, pulley block.

pale [pal], *n.f.* blade (*of oar, propeller etc.*); sluice, flood-gate.

pâle [pɑ:l], *a.* pale, wan, pallid, ghastly.

palefrenier [palfrə'nje], *n.m.* groom, ostler.

palefroi [pal'frwa], *n.m.* palfrey.

Palestine [palɛs'tin], **la**, *f.* Palestine.

palestinien [palɛsti'njɛ̃], *a.* (*fem.* **-enne**) Palestinian.

palet

palet [pa'lɛ], *n.m.* quoit.
palette [pa'lɛt], *n.f.* paddle (*of paddle-wheel*); bat (*ping-pong*); palette (*of painter*).
pâleur [pa'lœːr], *n.f.* pallor, wanness.
pâli [pa'li], *a.* grown pale.
palier [pa'lje], *n.m.* landing (*on a staircase*), floor; stage, degree; level stretch; *vitesse en palier*, speed on the flat.
pâlir [pa'liːr], *v.t.* to make pale, to bleach.— *v.i.* to (grow, turn *or* become) pale; to grow dim.
palis [pa'li], *n.m.* stake, pale; paling, enclosure.
palissade [pali'sad], *n.f.* palisade, paling; wooden fence; hedgerow; stockade.
palissader [palisa'de], *v.t.* to palisade; to stockade; to fence in.
pâlissant [pali'sã], *a.* turning pale, fading.
pallier [pa'lje], *n.f.* to palliate, to excuse.
palmarès [palma'rɛːs], *n.m. inv.* prize list, list of honors.
palme [palm], *n.f.* palm, palm branch; palm tree; (*fig.*) victory, triumph.
palmé [pal'me], *a.* palmate; web-footed.
palmier [pal'mje], *n.m.* palm tree, palm.
palombe [pa'lɔ̃:b], *n.f.* wood pigeon, ringdove.
palonnier [palɔ'nje], *n.m.* pole (*of a coach*); (*Motor.*) compensator (*of brake*); (*Av.*) rudder bar.
pâlot [pa'lo], *a.* (*fem.* **-otte**) palish, rather pale.
palourde [pa'luːrd], *n.f.* clam.
palpable [pal'pabl], *a.* palpable.
palpablement [palpablə'mã], *adv.* palpably.
palper [pal'pe], *v.t.* to feel, to touch; (*colloq.*) to pocket.
palpitant [palpi'tã], *a.* palpitating; thrilling.
palpitation [palpita'sjɔ̃], *n.f.* palpitation; throbbing; thrill, flutter.
palpiter [palpi'te], *v.i.* to palpitate, to throb; to quiver, to flutter.
paludéen [palyde'ɛ̃], *a.* (*fem.* **-éenne**) paludal, marshy.
pâmer [pa'me], *v.i.* and *se pâmer*, *v.r.* to swoon.
pâmoison [pɑmwa'zɔ̃], *n.f.* swoon, fainting fit.
pamphlet [pã'flɛ], *n.m.* satirical booklet, lampoon.
pamphlétaire [pãfle'tɛːr], *n.* pamphleteer.
pamplemousse [pãplə'mus], *n.m. or f.* grapefruit.
pampre [pã:pr], *n.m.* vine branch.
pan (1) [pã], *n.m.* flap, coat tails, panel (*of dress*); side, section (*of a wall etc.*); *pan de ciel*, stretch *or* patch of sky; *pan de mur*, bare wall, piece of wall.
pan! (2) [pã], *int.* slap! bang! smack!
panacée [pana'se], *n.f.* panacea.
panache [pa'naʃ], *n.m.* plume, bunch of feathers etc.; (*fig.*) show, swagger.
panaché [pana'ʃe], *a.* plumed, tufted; striped; (*colloq.*) variegated, motley; *glace panachée*, mixed ice-cream.
panacher [pana'ʃe], *v.t.* to plume; to streak, to variegate, to mix.
panais [pa'nɛ], *n.m.* parsnip.
Panama [pana'ma], **le**, *m.* Panama.
panama [pana'ma], *n.m.* panama hat.
panamien [pana'mjɛ̃], *a.* (*fem.* **-enne**) Panama(nian).—*n.m.* (**Panamien**, *fem.* **-enne**) Panamanian (*person*).

panaris [pana'ri], *n.m.* whitlow.
pancarte [pã'kart], *n.f.* large placard *or* bill.
pancréas [pãkre'a:s], *n.m. inv.* pancreas; sweetbread.
panda [pã'da], *n.m.* panda.
pandémonium [pãdemɔ'njɔm], *n.m.* pandemonium.
pandit [pã'di], *n.m.* pundit.
Pandore [pã'dɔːr], *f.* Pandora.
pané [pa'ne], *a.* covered *or* fried, in breadcrumbs.
panégyrique [paneʒi'rik], *n.m.* panegyric.
paner [pa'ne], *v.t.* to cover with breadcrumbs.
panier [pa'nje], *n.m.* basket, hamper, pannier; hoop-petticoat; *le dessus du panier*, the pick of the basket; *panier à salade*, (*wire*) salad washer; (*slang*) black Maria; *panier percé*, spendthrift.
panique [pa'nik], *a.* and *n.f.* panic.
panne [pan], *n.f.* plush; fat, lard; purlin; breakdown, mishap; *panne d'allumage*, (*Motor.*) ignition trouble; *rester en panne* (*Motor.*) to have a breakdown.
panneau [pa'no], *n.m.* (*pl.* **-eaux**) panel; snare, trap; (*Naut.*) hatch; (*Hort.*) glass frame.
panoplie [panɔ'pli], *n.f.* panoply; trophy (*of arms*).
panorama [panɔra'ma], *n.m.* panorama.
panoramique [panɔra'mik], *a.* panoramic.
pansage [pã'sa:ʒ], *n.m.* grooming (*of horses etc.*).
panse [pã:s], *n.f.* belly, paunch.
pansement [pãs'mã], *n.m.* dressing (*of wounds*); *pansement sommaire*, first aid; dressing.
panser [pã'se], *v.t.* to dress (*wounds*); to groom (*a horse*).
pansu [pã'sy], *a.* and *n.m.* (*fem.* **-e**) pot-bellied (*person*); bulging.
pantalon [pãta'lɔ̃], *n.m.* (pair of) trousers; *pantalon de femme*, women's drawers, panties.
pantelant [pã'tlã], *a.* panting, gasping.
panteler [pã'tle], *v.i.* (*conjug. like* APPELER) to gasp, to pant.
panthère [pã'tɛːr], *n.f.* panther.
pantin [pã'tɛ̃], *n.m.* nonentity, puppet; (*fig.*) jumping-jack.
pantois [pã'twa], *a.* (*fig.*) astonished, flabbergasted.
pantomime [pãtɔ'mim], *a.* pantomimic.— *n.f.* dumb-show, pantomime.—*n.m.* pantomime (*actor*).
pantoufle [pã'tufl], *n.f.* slipper; *en pantoufles*, slipshod.
paon [pã], *n.m.* peacock; emperor moth; (*fig.*) vain person.
paonne [pan], *n.f.* peahen.
papa [pa'pa], *n.m.* papa, daddy.
papal [pa'pal], *a.* (*m. pl.* **-aux**) papal.
papauté [papo'te], *n.f.* papacy.
pape [pap], *n.m.* pope.
paperasse [pa'pras], *n.f.* useless papers, documents; red tape; paper work.
paperasser [papra'se], *v.i.* to rummage among old papers; to scribble.
paperasserie [papras'ri], *n.f.* red tape.
paperassier [papra'sje], *a.* (*fem.* **-ière**) redtape; formal.—*n.m.* (*fem.* **-ière**) everlasting scribbler; rummager through old papers.

papeterie [pap'tri], *n.f.* paper mill, paper trade; stationery; stationer's shop; stationery case.

papetier [papə'tje], *a.* (*fem.* **-ière**) paper (*industry etc.*).—*n.m.* (*fem.* **-ière**) paper maker; stationer.

papier [pa'pje], *n.m.* paper; *papier buvard*, blotting paper; *papier d'emballage*, brown paper; *papier de verre*, glass-paper, sand-paper; *papier hygiénique*, toilet paper.

papillon [papi'jɔ̃], *n.m.* butterfly.

papillonner [papijɔ'ne], *v.i.* to flutter about, to hover; (*fig.*) to trifle, to flirt.

papillotage [papijɔ'ta:ʒ], *n.m.* blinking (*of the eyes*); dazzle, glitter, tinsel (*of style*).

papillote [papi'jɔt], *n.f.* curl paper; bonbon; *fer à papillotes*, curling irons; *papillotes à pétard*, Christmas crackers.

papilloter [papijɔ'te], *v.t.* to put (*hair etc.*) in paper.—*v.i.* to blink; to dazzle, to be gaudy.

papisme [pa'pism], *n.m.* papism, popery.

papiste [pa'pist], *a.* popish.—*n.* papist.

papou [pa'pu], *a.* Papuan.—*n.m.* (**Papou**, *fem.* **-oue**) Papuan (*person*).

Papouasie [papwa'zi], **la**, *f.* Papua.

papyrus [papi'ry:s], *n.m.* papyrus.

pâque [pɑ:k], *n.f.* Passover (*among Jews*).

paquebot [pak'bo], *n.m.* packet boat, steamer, liner.

pâquerette [pɑ'krɛt], *n.f.* daisy.

Pâques [pɑ:k], *n.m.* Easter.

paquet [pa'kɛ], *n.m.* package, bundle, parcel; packet; (*fig.*) clumsy lout.

paqueter [pak'te], *v.t.* (*conjug. like* APPELER) to make into a packet, parcel etc.

par [pa:r], *prep.* by, through, out of, from; about, in, into; for, for the sake of.

parabole [para'bɔl], *n.f.* parabola; parable.

parabolique [parabɔ'lik], *a.* parabolic.

parachutage [paraʃy'ta:ʒ], *n.m.* parachuting; parachute landing.

parachute [para'ʃyt], *n.m.* parachute; *sauter en parachute*, to bale out.

parachuter [paraʃy'te], *v.t., v.i.* to parachute, to drop (by parachute).

parachutiste [paraʃy'tist], *n.* parachutist, paratrooper.

parade [pa'rad], *n.f.* parade, show, display; pageantry; (*Fenc.*) parry.

parader [para'de], *v.i.* to show off.

paradis [para'di], *n.m.* paradise; (*Theat.*) upper gallery, the gods.

paradoxal [paradɔk'sal], *a.* (*m. pl.* **-aux**) paradoxical.

paradoxe [para'dɔks], *n.m.* paradox.

parafe or **paraphe** [pa'raf], *n.m.* paraph; flourish (*after one's signature*); initials and flourish.

parafer or **parapher** [para'fe], *v.t.* to paraph, to put one's flourish, dash or initials to.

paraffine [para'fin], *n.f.* paraffin, paraffin wax; *huile de paraffine*, liquid paraffin.

parage [pa'ra:ʒ], *n.m.* extraction, descent, lineage; (*usually in pl.*) localities, latitudes, waters; *dans ces parages*, in these parts.

paragraphe [para'graf], *n.m.* paragraph.

Paraguay [para'gwɛ], **le**, *m.* Paraguay.

paraguayen [paragwɛ'jɛ̃], *a.* (*fem.* **-enne**)

Paraguayan.—*n.m.* (**Paraguayen**, *fem.* **-enne**) Paraguayan (*person*).

paraître [pa'rɛ:tr], *v.i. irr.* (*conjug. like* CONNAÎTRE) to appear, to come into sight; to make a show, to seem, to look like; to come out, to be published; *à ce qu'il paraît*, as it would seem.

parallèle [para'lɛl], *a.* parallel.—*n.f.* parallel line.—*n.m.* parallel, comparison; (*Geog.*) parallel of latitude.

parallèlement [paralɛl'mɑ̃], *adv.* in a parallel way or direction.

parallélogramme [paralelɔ'gram], *n.m.* parallelogram.

paralysateur [paraliza'tœ:r], (*fem.* **-trice**), **paralysant** [parali'zɑ̃], *a.* paralysing.

paralyser [parali'ze], *v.t.* to paralyse.

paralysie [parali'zi], *n.f.* paralysis, palsy.

paralytique [parali'tik], *a.* and *n.* paralytic.

parangon [parɑ̃'gɔ̃], *n.m.* model, paragon; comparison; flawless precious stone.

paranoïa [paranɔ'ja], *n.f.* (*Med.*) paranoia.

parapet [para'pɛ], *n.m.* parapet.

paraphrase [para'fra:z], *n.f.* paraphrase, amplification.

paraphraser [parafrɑ'ze], *v.t.* to paraphrase; to amplify.

parapluie [para'plɥi], *n.m.* umbrella.

parasite [para'zit], *a.* parasitic; superfluous; extraneous.—*n.m.* parasite; (*fig.*) hanger-on; (*pl.*) (*Rad.*) atmospherics.

parasol [para'sɔl], *n.m.* sunshade.

paratonnerre [paratɔ'nɛ:r], *n.m.* lightning-conductor.

paratyphoïde [paratifɔ'id], *a.* and *n.f.* (*Med.*) paratyphoid (fever).

paravent [para'vɑ̃], *n.m.* folding screen; (*fig.*) screen.

parbleu! [par'blø], *int.* by Jove! why, of course!

parc [park], *n.m.* park; pen; *parc à huîtres*, oyster-bed; *parc d'attractions*, carnival.

parcage [par'ka:ʒ], *n.m.* folding (*of sheep*); penning (*of cattle*); parking (*of cars*).

parcellaire [parsɛ'lɛ:r], *a.* by small portions, by lots, in detail.

parcelle [par'sɛl], *n.f.* portion; particle; piece (*of land*).

parceller [parsɛ'le], *v.t.* to portion or parcel out.

parce que [parsə'kə, pars'kə], *conj.* because, as.—*n.m. inv.* **les pourquoi et les parce que**, the whys and the wherefores.

parchemin [parʃə'mɛ̃], *n.m.* parchment; (*fam.*) diploma; (*pl.*) titles of nobility.

parcimonie [parsimɔ'ni], *n.f.* parsimony.

parcimonieusement [parsimɔnjøz'mɑ̃], *adv.* parsimoniously.

parcimonieux [parsimɔ'njø], *a.* (*fem.* **-euse**) parsimonious, stingy.

(C) **parcomètre** [parkɔ'mɛtr], *n.m.* parking meter.

parcourir [parku'ri:r], *v.t. irr.* (*conjug. like* COURIR) to travel through; to run over or through, to scour; to look over; to peruse, to glance through (*a book*).

parcours [par'ku:r], *n.m.* line, course, road, way; route (*of bus*); distance; course (*golf*).

par-dessous [pardə'su], *prep.* and *adv.* under, beneath, underneath.

par-dessus [pardə'sy], *prep.* and *adv.* over, above.

235

pardessus [pardə'sy], *n.m.* overcoat.
pardon [par'dɔ̃], *n.m.* pardon, forgiveness; pilgrimage (*in Brittany*); *pardon!* excuse me!
pardonnable [pardɔ'nabl] *a.* pardonable, excusable.
pardonner [pardɔ'ne], *v.t.* to pardon, to forgive; to overlook; to excuse.
paré [pa're], *a.* adorned, got up; dressed.
pare-boue [par'bu], *n.m. inv.* fender.
pare-brise [par'bri:z], *n.m. inv.* windshield (*of motor-car*).
pare-chocs [par'ʃɔk], *n.m. inv.* bumper (*of car*).
pare-étincelles [paretɛ̃'sɛl], *n.m. inv.* fire-screen, fire-guard.
pareil [pa'rɛ:j], *a.* (*fem.* **-eille**) like, equal, similar; such, like that; same, identical.—*n.m.* (*fem.* **-eille**) similar *or* equal person.—*n.m.* equal, fellow.—*n.f.* (**-eille**) the like, tit for tat.
pareillement [parɛj'mã], *adv.* in like manner; likewise, also.
parement [par'mã], *n.m.* ornament; facing (*of dress*); cuff (*of sleeves*); (*Build.*) curb-stone.
parent [pa'rã], *n.m.* (*fem.* **-e**) relative, kinsman, kinswoman; (*pl.*) parents, relations, relatives; *être parent*, to be related; *parents par alliance*, related by marriage.
parenté [parã'te], *n.f.* relationship, kinship; relatives, kith and kin.
parenthèse [parã'tɛ:z], *n.f.* parenthesis, digression; (*Print.*) bracket.
parer [pa're], *v.t.* to adorn, to set off, to embellish; to attire, to trim; (*Box.*) to parry; to shelter, to guard.—*v.i.* to fend, to guard (*against*). **se parer**, *v.r.* to adorn oneself; to deck oneself out; to screen *or* guard oneself, to ward off.
pare-soleil [parsɔ'lɛ:j], *n.m. inv.* (*Motor.*) sun visor.
paresse [pa'rɛs], *n.f.* idleness, sloth, laziness, indolence.
paresser [parɛ'se], *v.i.* to idle, to fritter away one's time.
paresseusement [parɛsøz'mã], *adv.* lazily, idly.
paresseux [parɛ'sø], *a.* (*fem.* **-euse**) lazy, idle, slothful.—*n.m.* (*fem.* **-euse**) sluggard, lazy person.—*n.m.* (*Zool.*) sloth.
parfaire [par'fɛ:r], *v.t. irr.* (*conjug. like* FAIRE) to complete, to perfect.
parfait [par'fɛ], *a.* perfect, faultless; complete, full.—*n.m.* perfection; (*Gram.*) perfect; *un parfait au café*, a coffee ice-cream.
parfaitement [parfɛt'mã], *adv.* perfectly, completely; exactly, just so, decidedly.
parfilage [parfi'la:ʒ], *n.m.* unravelling.
parfois [par'fwa], *adv.* sometimes, occasionally.
parfum [par'fœ̃], *n.m.* perfume, odor, scent.
parfumer [parfy'me], *v.t.* to perfume, to sweeten, to scent; to fumigate. **se parfumer** *v.r.* to use perfume, to scent oneself.
parfumerie [parfym'ri], *n.f.* perfumery.
pari [pa'ri], *n.m.* bet, wager, stake; *pari mutuel*, totalizator; (*fam.*) tote.
paria [pa'rja], *n.m.* pariah, outcast.

parier [pa'rje], *v.t.* to bet, to stake.
parieur [pa'rjœ:r], *n.m.* (*fem.* **-euse**) bettor; backer.
parisien [pari'zjɛ̃], *a.* (*fem.* **-enne**) Parisian.—*n.m.* (**Parisien**, *fem.* **-enne**) Parisian (*person*).
parité [pari'te], *n.f.* parity, likeness, equality; (*Fin.*) par.
parjure [par'ʒy:r], *a.* perjured.—*n.m.* perjury, false oath.—*n.m.* perjurer.
parjurer (**se**) [səparʒy're], *v.r.* to perjure oneself.
parking [par'kiŋ], *n.m.* parking place, parking lot.
parlant [par lã], *a.* speaking; (*colloq.*) talkative.
parlement [parlə'mã], *n.m.* parliament.
parlementaire [parləmã'tɛ:r], *a.* parliamentary.—*n.m.* bearer of a flag of truce; parliamentarian.
parlementer [parləmã'te], *v.i.* to parley to come to terms.
parler [par'le], *v.t.* to speak, to talk.—*v.i.* to speak, to talk; to discourse, to converse, to treat (*de*); (*pop.*) *tu parles!* you're telling me! **se parler**, *v.r.* to be spoken; to talk to oneself; to talk to each other.—*n.m.* speech.
parleur [par'lœ:r], *n.m.* (*fem.* **-euse**) glib talker.
parloir [par'lwa:r], *n.m.* parlor (*of convent, school, prison*).
parmentier [parmã'tje], *a.* and *n.m. potage parmentier*, thick potato soup.
parmesan [parmə'zã], *n.m.* Parmesan (*cheese*).
parmi [par'mi], *prep.* among, amongst, amid, amidst.
parodie [parɔ'di], *n.f.* parody.
parodier [parɔ'dje], *v.t.* to parody, to burlesque.
paroi [pa'rwa], *n.f.* wall; partition; inner surface; lining; (*Theat.*) flat.
paroisse [pa'rwas], *n.f.* parish; (*collect.*) parishioners.
paroissial [parwa'sjal], *a.* (*m. pl.* **-aux**) parochial, parish.
paroissien [parwa'sjɛ̃], *n.m.* (*fem.* **-enne**) parishioner.—*n.m.* prayer book.
parole [pa'rɔl], *n.f.* (spoken) word; speech, utterance, voice; eloquence; promise; parole; *engager sa parole*, to pledge one's word; *manquer à sa parole*, to break one's word; *tenir parole*, to keep one's word.
paroxysme [parɔk'sism], *n.m.* paroxysm; culminating point.
parpaing [par'pɛ̃], *n.m.* (*Build.*) through stone, bondstone.
parquer [par'ke], *v.t.* to fold, to pen; to enclose; (*Motor.*) to park.—*v.i.* to be penned up (*of cattle etc.*). **se parquer**, *v.r.* to be placed in an enclosure.
parquet [par'kɛ], *n.m.* well (*of a court of justice*); prosecuting magistrates; (inlaid) floor.
parquetage [parkə'ta:ʒ], *n.m.* making a floor; flooring.
parqueter [parkə'te], *v.t.* (*conjug. like* AP-PELER) to floor, to lay a floor.
parqueterie [parkə'tri], *n.f.* floor-making; inlaid flooring.

parrain [pa'rɛ̃], *n.m.* godfather, sponsor; proposer.

parricide [pari'sid], *a.* parricidal.—*n.* parricide (*person*).—*n.m.* parricide *crime*).

parsemer [parsə'me], *v.t.* (*conjug. like* AMENER) to strew, to sprinkle; to be strewn on, to stud, to spangle.

parsi [par'si], *a.* Parsee.—*n.m.* (**Parsi,** *fem.* **-ie**) Parsee (*person*).

part [pa:r], *n.f.* share, part; concern, interest; place (*where*); *à part,* aside; apart from; *de part en part,* through and through; *de toutes parts,* on all sides; *dites-lui de ma part,* tell him from me; *nulle part,* nowhere; *quelque part,* somewhere (or other).

partage [par'ta:ʒ], *n.m.* sharing, share; partition.

partageable [parta'ʒabl], *a.* divisible into shares.

partageant [parta'ʒɑ̃], *n.m.* (*fem.* **-e**) (*Law*) sharer.

partager [parta'ʒe], *v.t.* (*conjug. like* MANGER) to divide, to share out; to participate in; to endow.—*v.i.* to share, to receive a share. **se partager,** *v.r.* to divide, to be divided.

partance [par'tɑ̃:s], *n.f.* (*Naut.*) sailing, departure; *en partance pour,* bound for.

partant [par'tɑ̃], *adv.* consequently, hence, therefore.—*n.m.* (*Turf*) starter.

partenaire [partə'nɛ:r], *n.* (*Spt. etc.*) partner.

parterre [par'tɛ:r], *n.m.* flower bed; (*Theat.*) pit.

parti [par'ti], *n.m.* (*Polit.*) party; part, cause; resolution, course; profit, advantage; match (*marriage*); (*Mil.*) detachment; *parti pris,* set purpose; rank prejudice; *le parti conservateur,* the Conservative party; *le parti travailliste,* the Labour party.

partial [par'sjal], *a.* (*m. pl.* **-aux**) partial, biased.

partialement [parsjal'mɑ̃], *adv.* partially, with partiality.

partialité [parsjali'te], *n.f.* partiality, bias.

participant [partisi'pɑ̃], *a.* participating.—*n.m.* (*fem.* **-e**) participant, sharer.

participation [partisipa'sjɔ̃], *n.f.* participation, share.

participe [parti'sip], *n.m.* (*Gram.*) participle.

participer [partisi'pe], *v.i.* to participate in, to share in; to be a party to (*à*); to partake of (*de*).

particularité [partikylari'te], *n.f.* peculiarity; particular circumstance.

particule [parti'kyl], *n.f.* particle.

particulier [partiky'lje], *a.* (*fem.* **-ière**) particular, peculiar; private; special; singular; personal.—*n.m.* (*fem.* **-ière**) private person, individual; (*colloq.*) fellow.

particulièrement [partikyljɛr'mɑ̃], *adv.* particularly, especially.

partie [par'ti] *n.f.* part (*of a whole*); line of business; party, amusement; game, match; client; opponent; (*Law*) party; (*Comm.*) parcel; *partie nulle,* drawn game.

partiel [par'sjɛl], *a.* (*fem.* **-elle**) partial.

partiellement [parsjɛl'mɑ̃], *adv.* partially, in part.

partir [par'ti:r], *v.i. irr.* (*with aux.* ÊTRE) to set out, to start, to depart, to leave; to rise (*of birds*); to proceed, to emanate (*from*); to go

off (*of firearms*); *à partir d'aujourd'hui,* from this day forward.

partisan [parti'zɑ̃], *n.m.* (*fem.* **-e**) partisan.

partition [parti'sjɔ̃], *n.f.* (*Her.*) partition; (*Mus.*) score.

partout [par'tu], *adv.* everywhere, on all sides.

parure [pa'ry:r]. *n.f.* attire, dress, finery, ornament.

parvenir [parvə'ni:r], *v.i. irr.* (*conjug. like* TENIR *but with aux.* ÊTRE) to attain,to reach; to succeed; to get; to arrive; to rise in the world.

parvenu [parvə'ny], *n.m.* (*fem.* **-e**) upstart, self-made person.

parvis [par'vi], *n.m.* parvis, open space (*in front of a church*); (*Poet.*) hall, temple.

pas (1) [pɑ], *n.m. inv.* step, pace; footprint; gait; dance; precedence; threshold; step of stair; strait, pass; thread (*of screw*); *aller à pas mesurés,* to proceed with circumspection; *au pas,* at a walking pace; in step; *faire un faux pas,* to stumble, (*fig.*) to blunder; *le pas de Calais,* the Straits of Dover; *pas à pas,* slowly, little by little.

pas (2) [pɑ], *adv.* no; not; *pas du tout,* not at all.

pascal [pas'kal], *a.* (*m. pl.* **-aux**) paschal.

passable [pɑ'sabl], *a.* passable, tolerable; (*fig.*) middling, so-so.

passablement [pɑsablə'mɑ̃], *adv.* fairly, passably.

passade [pɑ'sad], *n.f.* short stay; (*fig.*) passing fancy.

passage [pɑ'sa:ʒ], *n.m.* passage, transit; thoroughfare; arcade; crossing (*on railway etc.*); *passage clouté,* pedestrian crossing.

passager [pɑsa'ʒe], *a.* (*fem.* **-ère**) passing, transitory, short-lived; migratory.—*n.m.(fem.* **-ère**) passenger (*by sea or air*); passer-by.

passagèrement [pɑsaʒɛr'mɑ̃], *adv.* transiently.

passant [pɑ'sɑ̃], *a.* much-frequented.—*n.m.* (*fem.* **-e**) passer-by, wayfarer.

passavant [pɑsa'vɑ̃], *n.m.* pass, permit; (*Naut.*) gangway.

passe [pɑs], *n.f.* passing, passage; permit, pass; situation, state; (*Fenc.*) thrust; channel, narrow passage (*of harbors, rivers etc.*); stake (*at play*); (*Ftb.*) pass; *être dans une mauvaise passe,* to be in a fix; *en passe de,* in a fair way to.

passé [pɑ'se], *a.* past, bygone; faded, worn, withered.—*n.m.* past, past life, time past.—*prep.* after, beyond.

passée [pɑ'se], *n.f.* (*Hunt.*) flight, passage (*of woodcock etc.*).

passefiler [pɑsfi'le], *v.t.* to darn.

passement [pɑs'mɑ̃], *n.m.* lace (*of gold, silk etc.*).

passe-partout [pɑspar'tu], *n.m. inv.* master key; latch-key; passe-partout (*frame*); cross-cut saw.

passeport [pɑs'pɔ:r], *n.m.* passport.

passer [pɑ'se], *v.t.* (*takes the auxiliary* AVOIR *or* ÊTRE *according as action or condition is implied*) to pass; to cross, to go over; to transport; to strain (*liquids*); to sift (*flour*); to put on (*wearing apparel*); to omit; to waive; to allow; to spend (*time*); to take (*an examination*).—*v.i.* to pass to pass on

to pass away; to die; to pass for; to fade. **se passer**, *v.r.* to pass, to pass away; to fade; to happen; to do without (*de*).
passereau [pɑs'ro], *n.m.* (*pl.* **-eaux**) sparrow.
passerelle [pɑs'rɛl], *n.f.* foot bridge; (*Naut.*) bridge, gangway.
passe-temps [pɑs'tɑ̃], *n.m. inv.* pastime, hobby.
passeur [pɑ'sœːr], *n.m.* (*fem.* **-euse**) ferryman, ferrywoman.
passibilité [pɑsibili'te], *n.f.* liability.
passible [pɑ'sibl], *a.* passible; liable (*to*).
passif [pɑ'sif], *a.* (*fem.* **-ive**) passive; (*Comm.*) on debit side.—*n.m.* (*Gram.*) passive; (*Comm.*) liabilities.
passion [pɑ'sjɔ̃], *n.f.* suffering, agony; passion, *esp.* love; (*fig.*) fondness.
passionnant [pɑsjɔ'nɑ̃], *a.* exciting, thrilling.
passionné [pɑsjɔ'ne], *a.* passionate, impassioned, very fond of (*de*).
passionnel [pɑsjɔ'nɛl], *a.* (*fem.* **-elle**) *crime passionnel*, crime due to jealous love.
passionnément [pɑsjɔne'mɑ̃], *adv.* passionately, fondly.
passionner [pɑsjɔ'ne], *v.t.* to impassion, to interest deeply. **se passionner**, *v.r.* to be passionately fond of; to become enamored of.
passivement [pɑsiv'mɑ̃], *adv.* passively.
passiveté [pɑsiv'te], **passivité** [pɑsivi'te], *n.f.* passivity.
passoire [pɑ'swaːr], *n.f.* strainer.
pastel [pɑs'tɛl], *n.m.* pastel, crayon.
pastèque [pɑs'tɛk], *n.f.* water-melon.
pasteur [pɑs'tœːr], *n.m.* pastor, (*Protestant*) minister; clergyman.
pasteurisation [pɑstœriza'sjɔ̃], *n.f.* pasteurization.
pasteuriser [pɑstœri'ze], *v.t.* to pasteurize.
pastiche [pɑs'tiʃ], *n.m.* pastiche; (*Mus.*) medley.
pastille [pɑs'tiːj], *n.f.* pastille; lozenge; rubber patch (*for tubes of tire*).
pastoral [pɑstɔ'ral] *a.* (*m. pl.* **-aux**) pastoral. —*n.f.* (**-e**) pastoral (*play or poem*).
patapouf [pɑta'puf], *int.* **faire patapouf**, to fall flat.—*n.m.* **gros patapouf**, fat fellow, fatty.
patate [pɑ'tat], *n.f.* sweet potato.
patati [pɑta'ti], *only used in the phrase*, **et patati et patata**, and so on and so forth.
patatras! [pɑta'trɑ], *int.* crack! slap! bang!
pataud [pɑ'to], *a.* awkward, clumsy.—*n.m.* (*fem.* **-e**) pup with large paws; (*fig.*) lout, clumsy person.
patauger [pɑto'ʒe], *v.i.* (*conjug. like* MANGER) to splash, to flounder.
pâte [pɑːt], *n.f.* paste; dough, batter; (*fig.*) kind sort; (*Print.*) pie.
pâté [pɑ'te], *n.m.* pie, pasty, patty; blot (*of ink*); block (*of buildings*); (*Print.*) pie.
pâtée [pɑ'te], *n.f.* mash (*to fatten poultry*); mess (*for dogs or cats*).
patelin [pɑ'tlɛ̃], *a.* smooth-tongued, wheedling.—*n.m.* (*fem.* **-e**) wheedler.—*n.m.* (*fam.*) village.
patent [pɑ'tɑ̃], *a.* patent; obvious, manifest.
patenté [pɑtɑ̃'te], *a.* licensed.—*n.m.* (*fem.* **-ée**) licensed dealer.
patenter [pɑtɑ̃'te], *v.t.* to license.
patère [pɑ'tɛːr], *n.f.* coat hook; curtain hook.
paternel [pɑtɛr'nɛl], *a.* (*fem.* **-elle**) paternal, fatherly.

paternité [pɑtɛrni'te], *n.f.* paternity, fatherhood.
pâteux [pɑ'tø], *a.* (*fem.* **-euse**) pasty, clammy, sticky.
pathétique [pɑte'tik], *a.* pathetic, moving.—*n.m.* pathos.
pathétiquement [pɑtetik'mɑ̃], *adv.* pathetically.
pathologie [pɑtɔlɔ'ʒi], *n.f.* pathology.
pathologiste [pɑtɔlɔ'ʒist], *n.m.* pathologist.
pathos [pɑ'tɔːs], *n.m.* bathos; (*fig.*) bombast.
patiemment [pɑsja'mɑ̃], *adv.* patiently.
patience [pɑ'sjɑːs], *n.f.* patience, endurance.
patient [pɑ'sjɑ̃], *a.* patient, enduring, forbearing.—*n.m.* (*fem.* **-e**) sufferer; (*Med.*) patient.
patienter [pɑsjɑ̃'te], *v.i.* to be patient.
patin [pɑ'tɛ̃], *n.m.* skate; flange (*of rail*); skid (*of airplane*); shoe (*of brake*); **patins à roulettes**, roller skates.
patinage [pɑti'naːʒ], *n.m.* skating; skidding (*of locomotive, car etc.*).
patine [pɑ'tin], *n.f.* patina (*of bronze*).
patiner [pɑti'ne], *v.i.* to skate; to skid (*of wheels*).
patinette [pɑti'nɛt], *n.f.* scooter.
patineur [pɑti'nœːr], *n.m.* (*fem.* **-euse**) skater.
patinoire [pɑti'nwaːr], *n.f.* skating rink.
pâtir [pɑ'tiːr], *v.i.* to suffer; to be in distress.
pâtisser [pɑti'se], *v.t.*, to knead (*flour*).—*v.i.* to knead; to make pastry.
pâtisserie [pɑtis'ri], *n.f.* pastry, fancy cake; pastry-cook's shop *or* business.
pâtissier [pɑti'sje], *n.m.* (*fem.* **-ière**) pastry-cook.—*a.f.* (**-ière**) *crème patissière*, custard.
patois [pɑ'twa], *n.m. inv.* patois, provincial dialect; brogue; jargon.
patouiller [pɑtu'je], [PATAUGER].
patraque [pɑ'trak], *a.* seedy, broken-down.—*n.f.* broken-down person *or* machine.
pâtre [pɑːtr], *n.m.* herdsman, shepherd.
patriarcal [pɑtriar'kal], *a.* (*m. pl.* **-aux**) patriarchal.
patriarche [pɑtri'arʃ], *n.m.* patriarch.
Patrice [pɑ'tris], *m.* Patrick.
patrice [pɑ'tris], *n.m.* patrician.
patricien [pɑtri'sjɛ̃], *a.* and *n.m.* (*fem.* **-enne**) patrician.
patrie [pɑ'tri], *n.f.* native land, fatherland.
patrimoine [pɑtri'mwan], *n.m.* patrimony, inheritance.
patriote [pɑtri'ɔt], *a.* patriotic (*person*).—*n.* patriot.
patriotique [pɑtriɔ'tik], *a.* patriotic (*song, speech etc.*).
patriotisme [pɑtriɔ'tism], *n.m.* patriotism.
patron (1) [pɑ'trɔ̃], *n.m.* pattern, model.
patron (2) [pɑ'trɔ̃], *n.m.* (*fem.* **-onne**) patron; master, mistress, employer; proprietor; (*colloq.*) boss; (*Naut.*) skipper, coxswain.
patronage [pɑtrɔ'naːʒ], *n.m.* patronage.
patronat [pɑtrɔ'na], *n.m.* management.
patronner [pɑtrɔ'ne], *v.t.* to patronize; to support.
patrouille [pɑ'truːj], *n.f.* patrol.
patrouiller [pɑtru'je], *v.i.* to patrol.
patrouilleur [pɑtru'jœːr], *n.m.* (*Naut.*) patrol boat.
patte [pat], *n.f.* paw (*of quadruped*); foot (*of bird*); leg (*of insect*); bracket, cramp; flap (*of pocket etc.*); tab, strap (*of clothes*); (*fig.*) claws, clutches.

pâturage [pɑty'ra:ʒ], *n.m.* pasture.
pâture [pɑ'ty:r], *n.f.* food (*for animals*); pasture; fodder.
pâturer [pɑty're], *v.t.* to graze on.—*v.i.* to pasture, to graze, to feed.
pâturon or **paturon** [pɑty'rɔ̃], *n.m.* pastern.
paume [po:m], *n.f.* palm (*of the hand*); **jeu de paume**, (*court*) tennis, 'real' tennis.
paupérisme [pope'rism], *n.m.* pauperism.
paupière [po'pjɛ:r], *n.f.* eyelid; (*fig.*) eye(s).
pause [po:z], *n.f.* pause, stop; (*Mus.*) rest.
pauser [po'ze]. *v.i.* to pause.
pauvre [po:vr], *a.* poor, needy; wretched, paltry, mean.—*n.m.* poor person pauper; beggar.
pauvrement [povrə'mɑ̃], *adv.* poorly, wretchedly.
pauvresse [po'vrɛs], *n.f.* poor woman, beggar-woman.
pauvret [po'vrɛ], *n.m.* (*fem.* **-ette**) poor creature, poor little thing.
pauvreté [povrə'te], *n.f.* poverty; wretchedness; sorry thing.
pavage [pa'va:ʒ], *n.m.* paving; pavement.
pavane [pa'van], *n.f.* pavan (*dance*).
pavaner (se) [səpava'ne], *v.r.* to strut, to stalk proudly.
pavé [pa've], *a.* paved.—*n.m.* paving stone; paved part of road; (*fig.*) road, street(s).
pavement [pav'mɑ̃], *n.m.* paving; flooring.
paver [pa've], *v.t.* to pave.
paveur [pa'vœ:r], *n.m.* pavior.
pavillon [pavi'jɔ̃], *n.m.* pavilion, tent; summerhouse; detached house; wing (*of a house*), outhouse, lodge; (*Naut.*) flag.
pavoiser [pavwa'ze], *v.t.* to deck with flags, to dress (*ship*).
pavot [pa'vo], *n.m.* poppy.
payable [pɛ'jabl], *a.* payable.
payant [pɛ'jɑ̃], *a.* paying; to be paid for.—*n.m.* (*fem.* **-e**) payer.
paye [pɛ:j], **paie** [pɛ], *n.f.* pay, wages.
payement or **paiement** [pɛ'mɑ̃], *n.m.* payment.
payer [pɛ'je], *v.t.* (*see Verb Tables*) to pay (for); to reward; to expiate, to atone for. **se payer**, *v.r.* to be paid *or* satisfied; to treat oneself to.
payeur [pɛ'jœ:r], *n.m.* (*fem.* **-euse**) payer; pay-clerk; (*Mil.*) pay-master.
pays [pe'i], *n.m. inv.* country, land; region, district; fatherland, home; **avoir le mal du pays**, to be home-sick; **pays perdu**, out-of-the-way place.
paysage [pei'za:ʒ], *n.m.* landscape, scenery.
paysagiste [peiza'ʒist], *a.* and *n.m.* landscape (painter).
paysan [pei'zɑ̃], *a.* (*fem.* **-anne**) rustic.—*n.m.* (*fem.* **-anne**) peasant, country man, country woman; farmer.
paysannerie [peizan'ri], *n.f.* rusticity; peasantry.
Pays-Bas [pei'bɑ], **les**, *m.pl.* the Netherlands.
péage [pe'a:ʒ], *n.m.* toll; toll house.
péan or **pæan** [pe'ɑ̃], *n.m.* pæan, song of triumph *or* joy.
peau [po] *n.f.* (*pl.* **peaux**) skin; hide; peel, rind.
Peau-Rouge [po'ru:ʒ], *n.* (*pl.* **Peaux-Rouges**) Redskin, Red Indian.
peccadille [pɛka'di:j], *n.f.* peccadillo.
pêche (I) [pɛ:ʃ], *n.f.* peach.

pêche (2) [pɛ:ʃ], *n.f.* fishing, angling.
péché [pe'je], *n.m.* sin, transgression.
pécher [pe'je], *v.i.* (*conjug. like* CÉDER) to sin, to transgress; to offend; to be deficient.
pêcher (I) [pe'je], *n.m.* peach tree.
pêcher (2) [pe'je] *v.t.* to fish for; to drag out; (*fig.*) to get hold of.—*v.i.* to fish, to angle.
pêcheresse [peʃ'rɛs], [PÉCHEUR].
pêcherie [peʃ'ri], *n.f.* fishing ground, fishery.
pécheur [pe'jœ:r], *n.m.* (*fem.* **-eresse**) sinner.
pêcheur [pɛ'jœ:r], *n.m.* (*fem.* **-euse**) fisher, fisherman, fisherwoman.
pécore [pe'kɔ:r], *n.f.* stupid creature, blockhead; *esp.* silly girl.
pécule [pe'kyl], *n.m.* savings; earnings (*of a prisoner*)
pécuniaire [peky'njɛ:r], *a.* pecuniary.
pédagogie [pedagɔ'ʒi], *n.f.* pedagogy.
pédagogue [peda'gɔg], *n.* pedagogue.
pédale [pe'dal], *n.f.* pedal; treadle.
pédaler [peda'le], *v.i.* to pedal; (*colloq.*) to cycle.
pédant [pe'dɑ̃], *a.* pedantic.—*n.m.* (*fem.* **-e**) pedant.
pédanterie [pedɑ̃'tri], *n.f.* pedantry.
pédantesque [pedɑ̃'tɛsk], *a.* pedantic.
pédantisme [pedɑ̃'tism], *n.m.* pedantry.
pédestre [pe'dɛstr], *a.* pedestrian, on foot.
pédestrement [pedɛstrə'mɑ̃], *adv.* on foot.
pédicure [pedi'ky:r], *n.* chiropodist.
Pégase [pe'gɑ:z], *m.* Pegasus.
peignage [pɛ'ɲa:ʒ], *n.m.* combing, woolcombing.
peigne [pɛɲ], *n.m.* comb.
peigné [pe'ɲe], *a.* combed; (*fig.*) arranged.—*n.m.* worsted.
peigner [pe'ɲe], *v.t.* to comb; to card; (*fig.*) to polish (*style*). **se peigner**, *v.r.* to comb one's hair.
peignoir [pɛ'ɲwa:r], *n.m.* dressing-gown; (*Am.*) bath-robe.
peindre [pɛ̃:dr], *v.t.* irr. (*conjug. like* CRAINDRE) to paint, to portray; to represent, to express; **se faire peindre**, to sit for one's portrait. **se peindre**, *v.r.* to paint oneself; to be represented.
peine [pɛn], *n.f.* punishment, penalty; pain, grief, sorrow; anxiety; trouble; difficulty; reluctance; **à peine**, hardly, scarcely; **un homme de peine**, an unskilled laborer.
peiné [pe'ne], *a.* pained, grieved; labored; elaborate.
peiner [pe'ne], *v.t.* to pain, to trouble, to grieve; (*fig.*) to elaborate.—*v.i.* to labor, to toil; to be reluctant.
peintre [pɛ̃:tr], *n.m.* painter.
peinture [pɛ̃'ty:r], *n.f.* painting; picture; description, appearance; paint, color.
péjoratif [peʒɔra'tif], *a.* (*fem.* **-tive**) pejorative.
Pékin [pe'kɛ̃], *m.* Peking.
pékinois [peki'nwa], *a.* Pekinese.—*n.m.* Pekinese (*dog*); (**Pékinois**, *fem.* **-oise**) Pekinese (*person*).
pelage [pə'la:ʒ], *n.m.* hair, fur, coat (*of animal*).
pelé [pə'le], *a.* bald; which has lost its hair (*animals*).—*n.m.* (*fem.* **-ée**) bald-headed person.
pêle-mêle [pɛl'mɛl], *adv.* pell-mell, higgledypiggledy.—*n.m. inv.* disorder, jumble.

peler [pə'le], *v.t.* (*conjug. like* AMENER) to skin, to peel.—*v.i.* to peel off (*of the skin etc.*). **se peler,** *v.r.* to come off, to peel.

pèlerin [pɛl'rɛ̃], *n.m.* (*fem.* **-ine** (1)) pilgrim; peregrine falcon; basking shark.

pèlerinage [pɛlri'na:ʒ], *n.m.* pilgrimage.

pèlerine (2) [pɛl'rin], *n.f.* tippet, cape (*with hood*).

pélican [peli'kɑ̃], *n.m.* pelican.

pelisse [pə'lis], *n.f.* pelisse; fur-lined coat.

pelle [pɛl], *n.f.* shovel, scoop, blade (*of an oar*); (*fam.*) spill, cropper.

pelletée [pɛl'te], *n.f.* shovelful.

pelleter [pɛl'te], *v.t.* (*conjug. like* APPELER) to shovel.

pelletier [pɛl'tje], *n.m.* (*fem.* **-ière**) furrier.

pellicule [peli'kyl], *n.f.* pellicle; (*Phot.*) film; (*pl.*) scurf (*of scalp*), dandruff.

pelotage [pələ'ta:ʒ], *n.m.* winding skeins into balls; (*Billiards*, *Ten.*) warmup.

pelote [pə'lɔt], *n.f.* ball; ball of thread; pellet; pin-cushion; (*Spt.*) **pelote basque,** pelota.

peloter [pələ'te], *v.t.* to make *or* wind into a ball.—*v.i.* (*Spt.*) to warm up.

peloton [pələ'tɔ̃], *n.m.* ball; cluster (*of bees*); (*Mil.*) squad; (*Racing*) bunch (*of runners*).

pelotonner [pələtɔ'ne], *v.t.* to wind into balls. **se pelotonner,** *v.r.* to roll oneself up; to curl up.

pelouse [pə'lu:z], *n.f.* lawn, greensward.

peluche [pə'lyʃ], *n.f.* plush.

peluché [pəly'ʃe], *a.* shaggy.

pelucher [pəly'ʃe], *v.i.* to become shaggy, to wear rough.

pelucheux [pəly'ʃø], *a.* (*fem.* **-euse**) shaggy; fluffy.

pelure [pə'ly:r], *n.f.* paring; peel, skin; rind.

pénal [pe'nal], *a.* (*m. pl.* **-aux**) penal.

pénaliser [penali'ze], *v.t.* to penalize.

pénalité [penali'te], *n.f.* penal law; penalty.

pénates [pe'nat], *n.m. pl.* penates, household gods; (*fig.*) home.

penaud [pə'no], *a.* abashed, sheepish, crestfallen.

penchant [pɑ̃'ʃɑ̃], *a.* inclined, sloping, leaning.—*n.m.* declivity, slope; inclination, bent.

pencher [pɑ̃'ʃe], *v.t.* to incline, to bend.—*v.i.* to lean; to tilt, to slope. **se pencher,** *v.r.* to bend, to stoop; to slope, to be inclined.

pendable [pɑ̃'dabl], *a.* deserving hanging, abominable.

pendaison [pɑ̃dɛ'zɔ̃], *n.f.* hanging (*on the gallows*), death by hanging.

pendant [pɑ̃'dɑ̃], *a.* pendent, hanging; pending; depending.—*n.m.* thing hanging, pendant; counterpart.—*prep.* during; for; **pendant que,** while.

pendard [pɑ̃'da:r], *n.m.* (*fem.* **-e**) (*colloq.*) rascal, rogue, jade.

pendeloque [pɑ̃'dlɔk], *n.f.* ear-drop; pendant.

pendiller [pɑ̃di'je], *v.i.* to hang loose, to dangle.

pendre [pɑ̃:dr], *v.t.* to hang, to hang up, to suspend.—*v.i.* to hang; to dangle, to droop. **se pendre,** *v.r.* to hang oneself.

pendu [pɑ̃'dy], *a.* hanging; hanged; hung.—*n.m.* (*fem.* **-e**) one that has been hanged.

pendule [pɑ̃'dyl], *n.f.* clock, time-piece.—*n.m.* pendulum.

pêne [pɛ:n], *n.m.* bolt (*of a lock*).

pénétrabilité [penetrabili'te], *n.f.* penetrability.

pénétrable [pene'trabl], *a.* penetrable.

pénétrant [pene'trɑ̃], *a.* penetrating; piercing, keen; acute; impressive.

pénétration [penetra'sjɔ̃], *n.f.* penetration; acuteness, shrewdness.

pénétré [pene'tre], *a.* penetrated; moved, impressed.

pénétrer [pene'tre], *v.t.* (*conjug. like* CÉDER) to penetrate, to go through; to pierce; to pervade; to fathom; to impress, to affect.—*v.i.* to penetrate (*dans*); to reach (*à*). **se pénétrer,** *v.r.* to penetrate each other; to be impressed.

pénible [pe'nibl], *a.* painful, laborious; troublesome.

péniblement [peniblə'mɑ̃], *adv.* laboriously.

pénicilline [penisi'lin], *n.f.* penicillin.

péninsulaire [penɛ̃sy'lɛ:r], *a.* peninsular.

péninsule [penɛ̃'syl], *n.f.* peninsula.

pénitence [peni'tɑ̃:s], *n.f.* penitence, repentance; penance; punishment.

pénitencier [penitɑ̃'sje], *a.* penitentiary.—*n.m.* penitentiary, reformatory.

pénitent [peni'tɑ̃], *a.* penitent, repentant.—*n.m.* (*fem.* **-e**) penitent.

pénitentiaire [penitɑ̃'sjɛ:r], *a.* penitentiary.

penne [pɛn], *n.f.* tail feather, wing feather.

penniforme [peni'fɔrm], *a.* penniform.

pennon [pe'nɔ̃], *n.m.* pennon.

pénombre [pe'nɔ̃:br], *n.f.* penumbra; semidarkness, half-light.

pensée [pɑ̃'se], *n.f.* thought; opinion; idea, conception; meaning; (*Bot.*) pansy.

penser [pɑ̃'se], *v.t.* to think, to think of (*à* or *de*).—*v.i.* to think, to reflect, to consider; to expect; to take heed, to take care.—*n.m.* (*poet.*) inward reasoning, thought.

penseur [pɑ̃'sœ:r], *a.* (*fem.* **-euse**) thinking, thoughtful.—*n.m.* (*fem.* **-euse**) thinker.

pensif [pɑ̃'sif], *a.* (*fem.* **-sive**) pensive, thoughtful.

pension [pɑ̃'sjɔ̃], *n.f.* board and lodging; boarding house; boarding school; pension, allowance, annuity.

pensionnaire [pɑ̃sjɔ'nɛ:r], *n.* boarder; schoolboy *or* -girl; pensioner, resident.

pensionnat [pɑ̃sjɔ'na], *n.m.* private boarding school.

pensionné [pɑ̃sjɔ'ne], *a.* pensioned.—*n.m.* (*fem.* **-ée**) pensioner.

pensionner [pɑ̃sjɔ'ne], *v.t.* to pension, to grant a pension to.

pensum [pɛ̃'sɔm], *n.m.* imposition, extra task (*at school*).

pente [pɑ̃:t], *n.f.* declivity, slope; acclivity, ascent; gradient; pitch (*of roofs*); (*fig.*) propensity, bent.

Pentecôte [pɑ̃t'ko:t], *n.f.* Pentecost, Whitsuntide.

pénultième [penyl'tjɛm], *a.* last but one, penultimate.

pénurie [peny'ri], *n.f.* scarcity, dearth; penury, want.

pépier [pe'pje], *v.i.* to chirp, to cheep.

pépin [pe'pɛ̃], *n.m.* pip (*of apple etc.*); stone (*of grape*).

pépinière [pepi'njɛ:r], *n.f.* nursery (*of trees*).

pépiniériste [pepinje'rist], *n.m.* nurseryman.

pépite [pe'pit], *n.f.* nugget (*of gold*).

pepsine [pɛp'sin], *n.f.* pepsine.

peptique [pɛp'tik], *a.* peptic.
percale [pɛr'kal], *n.f.* cotton cambric, percale.
percaline [pɛrka'lin], *n.f.* glazed calico *or* lining, percaline.
perçant [pɛr'sã], *a.* piercing; sharp; shrill, acute.
perce [pɛrs], *n.f.* piercer, borer.
percé [pɛr'se], *a.* pierced, bored, in holes.
percée [pɛr'se], *n.f.* opening, cutting (*in a wood*), vista, glade; (*fig.*) break-through.
percement [pɛrsə'mã], *n.m.* piercing, boring, perforation.
perce-neige [pɛrs'nɛ:ʒ], *n.f. inv.* snowdrop.
perce-oreille [pɛrsɔ'rɛ:j], *n.m.* (*pl.* **-oreilles**) earwig.
percepteur [pɛrsɛp'tœ:r], *n.m.* collector of taxes.
perceptible [pɛrsɛp'tibl], *a.* collectible; perceptible.
perceptiblement [pɛrsɛptiblə'mã], *adv.* perceptibly.
perceptif [pɛrsɛp'tif], *a.* (*fem.* **-tive**) perceptive.
perception [pɛrsɛp'sjɔ̃], *n.f.* perception; collecting, receipt; collectorship, collector's office.
percer [pɛr'se], *v.t.* (*conjug. like* COMMENCER) to pierce, to bore, to drill; to make an opening; to tunnel; to wet through (*of rain etc.*).—*v.i.* to pierce through, to come through; to transpire; to manifest itself. **se percer**, *v.r.* to pierce oneself, to be pierced.
perceur [pɛr'sœ:r], *n.m.* (*fem.* **-euse**) borer.— *n.f.* (**-euse**) boring machine, drill.
percevoir [pɛrsə'vwa:r], *v.t. irr.* (*conjug. like* RECEVOIR) to collect (*taxes etc.*); (*Phil.*) to perceive.
perche [pɛrʃ], *n.f.* perch, pole; (*Ichth.*) perch.
perché [pɛr'ʃe], *a.* perched, perched up, roosting.
percher [pɛr'ʃe], *v.i.* and **se percher**, *v.r.* to perch, to roost.
percheur [pɛr'ʃœ:r], *a.* (*fem.* **-euse**) perching, roosting (*of birds*).
perchoir [pɛr'ʃwa:r], *n.m.* roost.
perclus [pɛr'kly], *a.* crippled, impotent.
percolateur [pɛrkola'tœ:r], *n.m.* percolator.
percussion [pɛrky'sjɔ̃], *n.f.* percussion.
percutant [pɛrky'tã], *a.* producing percussion; (*colloq.*) fabulous.
percuter [pɛrky'te], *v.t.* to strike; to percuss. —*v.t.* to crash.
perdable [pɛr'dabl], *a.* losable.
perdant [pɛr'dã], *a.* losing.—*n.m.* (*fem.* **-e**) loser.
perdition [pɛrdi'sjɔ̃], *n.f.* perdition.
perdre [pɛrdr], *v.t.* to lose, to be deprived of; to waste, to ruin, to corrupt, to lead astray. —*v.i.* to lose, to be a loser; to leak. **se perdre**, *v.r.* to be lost; to lose one's way, to be bewildered; to disappear.
perdreau [pɛr'dro], *n.m.* (*pl.* **-eaux**) young partridge.
perdrix [pɛr'dri], *n.f. inv.* partridge.
perdu [pɛr'dy], *a.* lost; ruined; spoilt; stray; obsolete; out of the way; bewildered; **salle des pas perdus**, waiting hall (*in courts of law*).
père [pɛ:r], *n.m.* father; sire.

pérégrination [peregrinɑ'sjɔ̃], *n.f.* peregrination.
péremptoire [perãp'twa:r], *a.* peremptory.
péremptoirement [perãptwar'mã], *adv.* peremptorily.
pérennité [perɛni'te], *n.f.* perpetuity.
perfectibilité [pɛrfɛktibili'te], *n.f.* perfectibility.
perfectible [pɛrfɛk'tibl], *a.* perfectible.
perfection [pɛrfɛk'sjɔ̃], *n.f.* perfection; faultlessness; completeness.
perfectionnement [pɛrfɛksjɔn'mã], *n.m.* improvement, perfecting.
perfectionner [pɛrfɛksjɔ'ne], *v.t.* to perfect; to improve. **se perfectionner**, *v.r.* to perfect oneself; to improve.
perfide [pɛr'fid], *a.* perfidious, treacherous, false.—*n.* perfidious *or* treacherous person.
perfidement [pɛrfid'mã], *adv.* perfidiously, falsely, treacherously.
perfidie [pɛrfi'di], *n.f.* perfidy, treachery.
perforage [pɛrfɔ'ra:ʒ], *n.m.* boring, perforation.
perforant [pɛrfɔ'rã], *a.* perforating, penetrating.
perforateur [pɛrfɔra'tœ:r], *a.* (*fem.* **-trice** (1)) perforative.—*n.m.* perforator.
perforation [pɛrfɔra'sjɔ̃], *n.f.* perforation.
perforatrice (2) [pɛrfɔra'tris], *n.f.* drilling machine.
perforer [pɛrfɔ're], *v.t.* to perforate, to bore, to drill.
péricliter [perikli'te], *v.i.* to be in jeopardy.
péril [pe'ril], *n.m.* peril, danger, hazard, risk.
périlleusement [perijøz'mã], *adv.* perilously.
périlleux [peri'jø], *a.* (*fem.* **-euse**) perilous, dangerous.
périmé [peri'me], *a.* out-of-date, no longer valid.
période [pe'rjɔd], *n.f.* period of time, era; (*Gram.*) period, sentence; (*Mus.*) phrase.— *n.m.* pitch, summit, degree, acme.
périodicité [perjɔdisi'te], *n.f.* periodicity.
périodique [perjɔ'dik], *a.* periodic, periodical.—*n.m.* periodical.
périodiquement [perjɔdik'mã], *adv.* periodically.
péripétie [peripe'si], *n.f.* sudden turn of fortune; (*pl.*) vicissitudes.
périr [pe'ri:r], *v.i.* to perish, to die; to be wrecked; to decay.
périscope [peris'kɔp], *n.m.* periscope.
périssable [peri'sabl], *a.* perishable.
péristyle [peris'til], *a.* and *n.m.* peristyle.
péritoine [peri'twan], *n.m.* peritoneum.
péritonite [peritɔ'nit], *n.f.* peritonitis.
perle [pɛrl], *n.f.* pearl; bead, bugle (*for bracelets, necklaces etc.*); (*fig.*) gem, jewel, the best.
perlé [pɛr'le], *a.* pearled, set with pearls; pearly.
perler [pɛr'le], *v.t.* to bead, to form into beads; to pearl.—*v.i.* to form beads (*of sweat etc.*).
perlier [pɛr'lje], *a.* (*fem.* **-ière**) of pearl.
permanence [pɛrma'nã:s], *n.f.* permanence; headquarters (*of a political party*).
permanent [pɛrma'nã], *a.* permanent, lasting.
permanente [pɛrma'nã:t], *n.f.* (*Hairdressing*) permanent wave.

perméabilité [pɛrmeabili'te], *n.f.* permeability.

perméable [pɛrme'abl], *a.* permeable, pervious (*to*).

permettre [pɛr'mɛtr], *v.t. irr.* (*conjug. like* METTRE) to permit, to allow; to enable, to afford room for. **se permettre,** *v.r.* to permit oneself; to indulge, to venture, to take the liberty (*de*).

permis [pɛr'mi], *a.* allowed, permitted, lawful.—*n.m.* permission, leave; permit, license, pass.

permission [pɛrmi'sjɔ̃], *n.f.* permission, leave, permit.

permutant [pɛrmy'tɑ̃], *n.m.* permuter, exchanger.

permutation [pɛrmytɑ'sjɔ̃], *n.f.* permutation, exchange; (*Mil.*) transfer.

permuter [pɛrmy'te], *v.t.* to exchange, to permute, to transpose.

pernicieusement [pɛrnisjøz'mɑ̃], *adv.* perniciously, mischievously, injuriously.

pernicieux [pɛrni'sjø], *a.* (*fem.* **-euse**) pernicious, mischievous, hurtful.

péronnelle [perɔ'nɛl], *n.f.* pert hussy, saucy baggage.

péroraison [perɔrɛ'zɔ̃], *n.f.* peroration.

pérorer [perɔ're], *v.i.* to hold forth, to speechify.

péroreur [perɔ'rœːr], *n.m.* (*fem.* **-euse**) speechifier, spouter.

Pérou [pe'ru], **le,** *m.* Peru.

perpendiculaire [pɛrpɑ̃diky'lɛːr], *a.* and *n.f.* perpendicular.

perpendiculairement [pɛrpɑ̃dikylɛr'mɑ̃], *adv.* perpendicularly.

perpétration [pɛrpetrɑ'sjɔ̃], *n.f.* perpetration.

perpétrer [pɛrpe'tre], *v.t.* (*conjug. like* CÉDER) to perpetrate, to commit.

perpétuation [pɛrpetɥɑ'sjɔ̃], *n.f.* perpetuation.

perpétuel [pɛrpe'tɥɛl], *a.* (*fem.* **-elle**) perpetual, permanent; for life.

perpétuellement [pɛrpetɥɛl'mɑ̃], *adv.* perpetually; everlastingly.

perpétuer [pɛrpe'tɥe], *v.t.* to perpetuate. **se perpétuer,** *v.r.* to be perpetuated, to continue.

perpétuité [pɛrpetɥi'te], *n.f.* perpetuity; *à perpétuité,* for ever, for life.

perplexe [pɛr'plɛks], *a.* perplexed, embarrassed, irresolute; perplexing.

perplexité [pɛrplɛksi'te], *n.f.* perplexity.

perquisition [pɛrkizi'sjɔ̃], *n.f.* perquisition, search; investigation.

perquisitionner [pɛrkizisjɔ'ne], *v.i.* to make a search.

perron [pɛ'rɔ̃], *n.m.* steps (*before a house*).

perroquet [perɔ'kɛ], *n.m.* parrot.

perruche [pe'ryʃ], *n.f.* parakeet, budgerigar; (*pop.*) hen-parrot.

perruque [pe'ryk], *n.f.* wig, periwig.

perruquier [pery'kje], *n.m.* wig-maker; (*obs.*) hair-dresser, barber.

persan [pɛr'sɑ̃], *a.* Persian.—*n.m.* Persian (*language*); (**Persan,** *fem.* **-ane**) Persian (*person*).

Perse [pɛrs], **la,** *f.* Persia.

perse [pɛrs], *n.f.* chintz.

persécuter [pɛrseky'te], *v.t.* to persecute; (*fig.*) to bore, to dun.

persécuteur [pɛrseky'tœːr], *a.* (*fem.* **-trice**) persecuting; troublesome.—*n.m.* (*fem.* **-trice**) persecutor; troublesome person.

persécution [pɛrseky'sjɔ̃], *n.f.* persecution; annoyance, importunity.

persévérance [pɛrseve'rɑ̃ːs], *n.f.* perseverance; firmness, steadiness.

persévérant [pɛrseve'rɑ̃], *a.* persevering; steady, resolute.

persévérer [pɛrseve're], *v.i.* (*conjug. like* CÉDER) to persevere; to be steadfast; to persist.

persienne [pɛr'sjɛn], *n.f.* Venetian shutter.

persiflage [pɛrsi'flaːʒ], *n.m.* banter, chaff, persiflage.

persifler [pɛrsi'fle], *v.t.*, *v.i.* to rally, to banter, to chaff.

persifleur [pɛrsi'flœːr], *a.* (*fem.* **-euse**) bantering, chaffing.—*n.m.* (*fem.* **-euse**) banterer, tease.

persil [pɛr'si], *n.m.* parsley.

persillé [pɛrsi'je], *a.* spotted; blue-molded (*cheese*).

persique [pɛr'sik], *a.* ancient Persian; **le Golfe Persique,** Persian Gulf.

persistance [pɛrsis'tɑ̃ːs], *n.f.* persistence.

persistant [pɛrsis'tɑ̃], *a.* persistent.

persister [pɛrsis'te], *v.i.* to persist.

personnage [pɛrsɔ'naːʒ], *n.m.* personage, person; (*Theat.*) character, part.

personnalité [pɛrsɔnali'te], *n.f.* personality, personal character; person; selfishness.

personne [pɛr'sɔn], *n.f.* person; own self; appearance.—*pron. indef.* anyone, no one, nobody.

personnel [pɛrsɔ'nɛl], *a.* (*fem.* **-elle**) personal; selfish.—*n.m.* personnel, staff.

personnellement [pɛrsɔnɛl'mɑ̃], *adv.* personally.

personnification [pɛrsɔnifikɑ'sjɔ̃], *n.f.* personification.

personnifier [pɛrsɔni'fje], *v.t.* to personify; to embody.

perspectif [pɛrspɛk'tif], *a.* (*fem.* **-tive**) perspective.—*n.f.* (**-tive**) perspective; view, prospect, distance, vista.

perspicace [pɛrspi'kas], *a.* perspicacious, shrewd.

perspicacité [pɛrspikasi'te], *n.f.* perspicacity, insight.

persuader [pɛrsɥa'de], *v.t.* to persuade; to convince, to satisfy. **se persuader,** *v.r.* to persuade *or* convince oneself; to be persuaded.

persuasible [pɛrsɥa'zibl], *a.* persuadable.

persuasif [pɛrsɥa'zif], *a.* (*fem.* **-sive**) persuasive; convincing.

persuasion [pɛrsɥa'zjɔ̃], *n.f.* persuasion; conviction, belief, opinion.

persuasivement [pɛrsɥaziv'mɑ̃], *adv.* persuasively.

perte [pɛrt], *n.f.* loss; waste; ruin, fall, doom; *à perte,* at a loss; *en pure perte,* in vain.

pertinemment [pɛrtina'mɑ̃], *adv.* pertinently.

pertinence [pɛrti'nɑ̃ːs], *n.f.* pertinence.

pertinent [pɛrti'nɑ̃], *a.* pertinent, relevant.

pertuis [pɛr'tɥi], *n.m.* opening, sluice; straits.

perturbateur [pɛrtyrba'tœːr], *a.* (*fem.* **-trice**) disturbing.—*n.m.* (*fem.* **-trice**) disturber.

perturbation [pɛrtyrbɑ'sjɔ̃], *n.f.* perturbation, disturbance.

perturber [pɛrtyr'be], *v.t.* to perturb, to disturb.

péruvien [pery'vjɛ̃], *a.* (*fem.* **-enne**) Peruvian.—*n.m.* (**Péruvien**, *fem.* **-enne**) Peruvian (*person*).

pervenche [pɛr'vã:ʃ], *n.f.* (*Bot.*) periwinkle.

pervers [pɛr'vɛ:r], *a.* perverse, wicked, depraved.—*n.m.* (*-e*) perverse person; wrongdoer.

perversion [pɛrvɛr'sjɔ̃], *n.f.* perversion.

perversité [pɛrvɛrsi'te], *n.f.* perverseness.

pervertir [pɛrvɛr'ti:r], *v.t.* to pervert.

pervertissement [pɛrvɛrtis'mã], *n.m.* perversion.

pervertisseur [pɛrvɛrti'sœ:r], *a.* (*fem.* **-euse**) perverting.—*n.m.* (*fem.* **-euse**) perverter, corrupter.

pesage [pə'za:ʒ], *n.m.* weighing; (*Turf.*) weighing-in room; paddock (*on race-course*), the enclosure.

pesamment [pəza'mã], *adv.* heavily, ponderously; clumsily.

pesant [pə'zã], *a.* heavy, ponderous, unwieldy; sluggish.—*n.m.* weight.—*adv.* in weight.

pesanteur [pəzã'tœ:r], *n.f.* weight; heaviness; unwieldiness; dullness, ponderousness; (*Phys.*) gravity.

pesée [pə'ze], *n.f.* weighing.

pèse-lettre [pɛz'lɛtr], *n.m.* (*pl.* **-lettres**) letter-scales.

peser [pə'ze], *v.t.* (*conjug. like* AMENER) to weigh; (*fig.*) to ponder, to estimate.—*v.i.* to weigh; to be heavy; to be of importance; to lie heavy; to dwell (*sur*).

peseur [pə'zœ:r], *n.m.* (*fem.* **-euse**) weigher.

pessimisme [pɛsi'mism], *n.m.* pessimism.

pessimiste [pɛsi'mist], *a.* pessimistic.—*n.* pessimist.

peste [pɛst], *n.f.* plague, pestilence; (*fig.*) pest, bore, nuisance.—*int.* the deuce! hang it!

pester [pɛs'te], *v.i.* to inveigh, to storm, to rave.

pestiféré [pɛstife're], *a.* and *n.m.* (*fem.* **-ée**) plague-stricken (person).

pestilence [pɛsti'lã:s], *n.f.* pestilence.

pestilent [pɛsti'lã], *a.* pestilent.

pestilentiel [pɛstilã'sjɛl], *a.* (*fem.* **-elle**) pestilential.

pétale [pe'tal], *n.m.* petal.

pétarade [peta'rad], *n.f.* cracking (*noise*); back-fire (*of car*).

pétard [pe'ta:r], *n.m.* petard; cracker (*fire-work*); (*Rail.*) detonator, fog signal.

pétaudière [peto'djɛ:r], *n.f.* noisy *or* disorderly assembly.

pétillant [peti'jã], *a.* crackling; sparkling.

pétillement [petij'mã], *n.m.* crackling; sparkling.

pétiller [peti'je], *v.i.* to crackle (*of burning wood*); to sparkle.

petiot [pə'tjo], *a.* (*fam.*) tiny, wee.—*n.m.* (*fem.* **-e**) little one; darling.

petit [pə'ti], *a.* little, small; short; very young; petty, slight; shabby; humble.—*n.m.* (*fem.* **-e**) little child, little one; young one; whelp, pup, kitten, cub.

petite-fille [pətit'fij], *n.f.* (*pl.* **petites-filles**) granddaughter.

petitement [pətit'mã], *adv.* in small quantity; not much, poorly, meanly.

petitesse [pəti'tɛs], *n.f.* smallness, littleness; insignificance; meanness; narrowness.

petit-fils [pəti'fis], *n.m.* (*pl.* **petits-fils**) grandson.

pétition [peti'sjɔ̃], *n.f.* petition, request.

pétitionnaire [petisjɔ'nɛ:r], *n.* petitioner.

pétitionnement [petisjɔn'mã], *n.m.* petitioning.

pétitionner [petisjɔ'ne], *v.i.* to make a request, to petition.

petit-lait [pəti'lɛ], *n.m.* whey.

petits-enfants [pətizã'fã], *n.m. pl.* grandchildren.

pétrel [pe'trɛl], *n.m.* petrel.

pétri [pe'tri], *a.* kneaded.

pétrifiant [petri'fjã], *a.* petrifying.

pétrification [petrifika'sjɔ̃], *n.f.* petrifaction.

pétrifier [petri'fje], *v.t.* to petrify. **se pétrifier**, *v.r.* to turn into stone.

pétrin [pe'trɛ̃], *n.m.* kneading trough; (*fig.*) scrape.

pétrir [pe'tri:r], *v.t.* to knead; (*fig.*) to mold, to form.

pétrissable [petri'sabl], *a.* that can be kneaded; (*fig.*) yielding, pliant.

pétrissage [petri'sa:ʒ], **pétrissement** [petris'mã], *n.m.* kneading; (*fig.*) forming.

pétrisseur [petri'sœ:r], *n.m.* (*fem.* **-euse**) kneader.—*n.f.* (**-euse**) kneading-machine.

pétrole [pe'trɔl], *n.m.* petroleum, (mineral) oil; kerosene.

pétrolier [petrɔ'lje], *a.* (*fem.* **-ière**) pertaining to oil.—*n.m.* oil tanker.

pétulance [pety'lã:s], *n.f.* liveliness, ebulliency; friskiness.

pétulant [pety'lã], *a.* lively, ebullient, frisky.

pétunia [pety'nja], *n.m.* petunia.

peu [pø], *adv.* little, not much; few, not many; not very.—*n.m.* little; bit.

peuplade [pœ'plad], *n.f.* clan, tribe, horde.

peuple [pœpl], *a.* plebeian, common, vulgar.—*n.m.* people, nation; the people, the multitude, the lower classes.

peuplé [pœ'ple], *a.* heavily populated, populous.

peuplement [pœplə'mã], *n.m.* peopling; stocking of a poultry yard, pond etc.

peupler [pœ'ple], *v.t.* to people; to stock with animals etc.; to populate; to throng.—*v.i.* to multiply, to breed. **se peupler**, *v.r.* to become peopled; to be populated.

peuplier [pœ'plje], *n.m.* poplar.

peur [pœ:r], *n.f.* fear, dread, terror; apprehension; **avoir peur**, to be afraid; **de peur de**, for fear of.

peureusement [pœrøz'mã], *adv.* timorously.

peureux [pœ'rø], *a.* (*fem.* **-euse**) fearful, timid, timorous.—*n.m.* (*fem.* **-euse**) timid person.

peut-être [pø'tɛ:tr], *adv.* perhaps, maybe.

phalange [fa'lã:ʒ], *n.f.* phalanx; (*poet.*) army, host.

phalène [fa'lɛ:n], *n.f.* moth.

pharaon [fara'ɔ̃], *n.m.* Pharaoh.

phare [fa:r], *n.m.* lighthouse; beacon; (*Motor.*) head-light.

pharisien [fari'zjɛ̃], *n.m.* Pharisee; (*fig.*) hypocrite; self-righteous person.

pharmaceutique [farmasø'tik], *a.* pharmaceutical.—*n.f.* pharmaceutics.

pharmacie [farmaˈsi], *n.f.* pharmacy, druggist's shop, dispensary; medicine chest.
pharmacien [farmaˈsjɛ̃], *n.m.* (*fem.* **-enne**) pharmacist.
phase [faːz], *n.f.* phasis (*of planet*); phase; aspect, period.
phénicien [feniˈsjɛ̃], *a.* (*fem.* **-enne**) Phoenician.—*n.m.* (**Phénicien,** *fem.* **-enne**) Phoenician (*person*).
phénix [feˈniks], *n.m.* phoenix; paragon.
phénoménal [fenomeˈnal], *a.* (*m. pl.* **-aux**) phenomenal; (*colloq.*) extraordinary.
phénomène [fenoˈmɛːn], *n.m.* phenomenon; (*colloq.*) remarkable person *or* thing; freak.
philanthrope [filɑ̃ˈtrɔp], *n.* philanthropist.
philanthropie [filɑ̃trɔˈpi], *n.f.* philanthropy.
philanthropique [filɑ̃trɔˈpik], *a.* philanthropic.
philatélie [filateˈli], *n.f.* philately, stamp collecting.
philatéliste [filateˈlist], *n.* stamp collector.
Philippe [fiˈlip], *m.* Philip.
philippine [filiˈpin], *a.* Philippine, Filipino.—*n.* (**Philippine**) Filipino (*person*).
Philippines [filiˈpin], **les,** *f. pl.* Philippines, Philippine Islands.
Philistin [filisˈtɛ̃], *n.m.* (*fem.* **-e**) Philistine, person of vulgar taste.
philosophale [filozɔˈfal], *a.* **la pierre philosophale,** the philosopher's stone.—*n.*
philosophe [filɔˈzɔf], *a.* philosophical.—*n.* philosopher.
philosopher [filozɔˈfe], *v.i.* to philosophize.
philosophie [filozɔˈfi], *n.f.* philosophy; class in French school roughly equivalent to English sixth.
philosophique [filozɔˈfik], *a.* philosophical.
philosophiquement [filozɔfikˈmɑ̃], *adv.* philosophically.
philtre *or* **filtre** [filtr], *n.m.* philtre.
phlébite [fleˈbit], *n.f.* phlebitis.
phlegmatique [FLEGMATIQUE].
phobie [fɔˈbi], *n.f.* phobia, morbid dread.
phonétique [foneˈtik], *a.* phonetic.—*n.f.* phonetics.
phonique [fɔˈnik], *a.* phonic.
phonographe [fonɔˈgraf], *n.m.* phonograph, gramophone.
phonographie [fonɔgraˈfi], *n.f.* phonography, sound recording.
phonographique [fonɔgraˈfik], *a.* phonographic.
phoque [fɔk], *n.m.* (*Zool.*) seal.
phosphate [fɔsˈfat], *n.m.* phosphate.
phosphore [fɔsˈfɔːr], *n.m.* phosphorus.
phosphorescence [fɔsfɔrɛˈsɑ̃ːs], *n.f.* phosphorescence.
phosphorescent [fɔsfɔrɛˈsɑ̃], *a.* phosphorescent.
phosphoreux [fɔsfɔˈrø], *a.m.* phosphorous.
phosphorique [fɔsfɔˈrik], *a.* phosphoric.
photo [fɔˈto], *n.f. abbr.* [PHOTOGRAPHIE].
photocopie [fɔtokɔˈpi], *n.f.* photocopy, photostat.
photogénique [fɔtoʒeˈnik], *a.* photogenic.
photographe [fɔtɔˈgraf], *n.* photographer.
photographie [fɔtɔgraˈfi], *n.f.* photography; photograph.
photographier [fɔtɔgraˈfje], *v.t.* to photograph.
photographique [fɔtɔgraˈfik], *a.* photo-

graphic; **appareil photographique,** camera.
photogravure [fɔtogravyːr], *n.f.* photogravure.
phrase [fraːz], *n.f.* sentence; (*Mus.*) phrase; **phrase toute faite,** commonplace, stock phrase.
phraséologie [frazeɔlɔˈzi], *n.f.* phraseology.
phraser [frɑˈze], *v.t.* to express in phrases; (*Mus.*) to phrase.—*v.i.* to phrase.
phraseur [frɑˈzœːr], *n.m.* (*fem.* **-euse**) (*fam.*) verbose writer *or* talker.
phtisie [ftiˈzi], *n.f.* phthisis, consumption.
phtisique [ftiˈzik], *a.* consumptive.—*n.* consumptive person.
physicien [fiziˈsjɛ̃], *n.m.* (*fem.* **-enne**) physicist.
physionomie [fizjonɔˈmi], *n.f.* physiognomy, countenance, aspect, look.
physionomiste [fizjonɔˈmist], *n.* physiognomist.
physiothérapie [fizjɔteraˈpi], *n.f.* (*Med.*) physiotherapy.
physiothérapiste [fizjɔteraˈpist], *n.* physiotherapist.
physique [fiˈzik], *a.* physical, material, bodily.—*n.f.* physics.—*n.m.* physique, natural constitution; outward appearance.
physiquement [fizikˈmɑ̃], *adv.* physically.
piaffer [pjaˈfe], *v.i.* to paw the ground, to prance (*of horses*).
piaffeur [pjaˈfœːr], *a.* (*fem.* **-euse**) pawing, prancing.—*n.m.* (*fem.* **-euse**) pawer, prancer.
piailler [pjaˈje], *v.i.* to cheep (*of small birds*); (*fig.*) to squall; to rant.
piaillerie [pjɑjˈri], *n.f.* cheeping; squealing.
piailleur [pjaˈjœːr], *n.m.* (*fem.* **-euse**) cheeper; squaller.
pianiste [pjaˈnist], *n.* pianist.
piano [pjaˈno], *n.m.* piano, pianoforte; **piano à queue,** grand piano.
piaulement [pjolˈmɑ̃], *n.m.* whining, puling; cheeping (*of chickens*).
piauler [pjoˈle], *v.i.* to cheep (*of chickens etc.*); (*fig.*) to pule, to whine.
pic [pik], *n.m.* pick, pickaxe; gaff; peak (*of a mountain*); woodpecker.
pick-up [piˈkœp], *n.m. inv.* record player.
picoté [pikɔˈte], *a.* pricked, marked.
picotement [pikɔtˈmɑ̃], *n.m.* pricking, tingling.
picoter [pikɔˈte], *v.t.* to cause to tingle; to prick; to peck (*of birds*).
picvert *or* **pivert** [piˈvɛːr], *n.m.* green woodpecker.
pie [pi], *a. inv.* and *n.* piebald (horse).—*n.f.* magpie.
pièce [pjɛs], *n.f.* piece; patch; cask (*of wine etc.*); head (*of cattle, poultry etc.*); apartment, room; piece of ordnance, cannon; (*Theat.*) play; coin; joint (*of meat*).
pied [pje], *n.m.* foot; footing; footprint, track; leg (*of furniture*); stand, rest; stalk (*of plants*).
pied-à-terre [pjetaˈtɛːr], *n.m. inv.* occasional lodging.
pied-de-biche [pjedˈbiʃ], *n.m.* (*pl.* **pieds-de-biche**) bell-pull; (*Surg.*) forceps; nailclench.
piédestal [pjedɛsˈtal], *n.m.* (*pl.* **-aux**) pedestal.

piège [pjɛ:ʒ], *n.m.* trap, snare.
piéger [pje'ʒe], *v.t.* (*conjug. like* CÉDER) to trap (*animals*); (*Mil.*) to set a booby trap.
pie-grièche [pigri'ɛʃ], *n.f.* (*pl.* **pies-grièches**) (*Orn.*) shrike; (*fig.*) shrew.
pierraille [pjɛ'rɑ:j], *n.f.* rubble, ballast.
Pierre [pjɛ:r], *m.* Peter.
pierre [pjɛ:r], *n.f.* stone; (*Path.*) calculus.
pierreries [pjɛr'ri], *n.f. pl.* precious stones, gems.
pierreux [pjɛ'rø], *a.* (*fem.* **-euse**) stony, flinty, gritty, gravelly; calculous.
pierrot [pjɛ'ro], *n.m.* pierrot, merry-andrew; house sparrow.
piété [pje'te], *n.f.* piety, godliness; affection.
piétinement [pjetin'mɑ̃], *n.m.* stamping, trampling.
piétiner [pjeti'ne], *v.t.* to tread *or* trample under foot.—*v.i.* to stamp; to paw the ground (*of horses*).
piéton [pje'tɔ̃], *n.m.* (*fem.* **-onne**) pedestrian.
piètre [pjɛtr], *a.* poor, paltry, pitiful.
piètrement [pjɛtrə'mɑ̃], *adv.* pitifully, wretchedly.
pieu [pjø], *n.m.* (*pl.* **pieux** (1)) stake, pile, post.
pieusement [pjøz'mɑ̃], *adv.* piously, devoutly; obediently; reverently.
pieuvre [pjœ:vr], *n.f.* octopus, poulpe.
pieux (2) [pjø], *a.* (*fem.* **pieuse**) pious, godly.
pigeon [pi'ʒɔ̃], *n.m.* pigeon, dove; (*slang*) dupe, gull.
pigeonneau [piʒɔ'no], *n.m.* (*pl.* **-eaux**) young pigeon, squab.
pigeonnier [piʒɔ'nje], *n.m.* pigeon house, dove-cot.
pigment [pig'mɑ̃], *n.m.* (*Anat.*) pigment.
pignon [pi'nɔ̃], *n.m.* gable end; pinion; kernel (*of fir cone*).
pilaire [pi'lɛ:r], *a.* pilous, pilose.
pilastre [pi'lastr], *n.m.* (*Arch.*) pilaster.
pilchard [pil'ʃa:r], *n.m.* pilchard.
pile [pil], *n.f.* pile, heap; pier (*of a bridge etc.*); mole (*masonry*); (*Elec.*) battery; reverse (*of coins*); **pile atomique**, atomic pile.
piler [pi'le], *v.t.* to pound, to crush, to powder.
pileur [pi'lœ:r], *n.m.* (*fem.* **-euse** (1)) pounder, beater.
pileux [pi'lø], *a.* (*fem.* **-euse** (2)) pilous, hairy.
pilier [pi'lje], *n.m.* pillar, column, post; (*fig.*) supporter, prop.
pillage [pi'ja:ʒ], *n.m.* pillage, plunder; (*fig.*) pilfering.
pillard [pi'ja:r], *a.* plundering; predatory.—*n.m.* (*fem.* **-e**) pillager, plunderer.
piller [pi'je], *v.t.* to pillage, to plunder; to ransack; to pilfer.
pillerie [pij'ri], *n.f.* pillage, plunder; extortion.
pilleur [pi'jœ:r], *n.m.* (*fem.* **-euse**) pillager, plunderer, pilferer.
pilon [pi'lɔ̃], *n.m.* pestle; rammer, stamper; wooden leg.
pilonnage [pilɔ'na:ʒ], *n.m.* ramming, pounding, stamping, milling.
pilonner [pilɔ'ne], *v.t.* to ram, to pound, to mill; to stamp (*ore*).
pilori [pilɔ'ri], *n.m.* pillory.
pilorier [pilɔ'rje], *v.t.* to pillory.
pilotage [pilɔ'ta:ʒ], *n.m.* (*Civ. Eng.*) pile-driving; (*Naut.*) piloting.
pilote [pi'lɔt], *n.m.* pilot; guide; pilot fish.

piloter [pilɔ'te], *v.t.* to pile, to drive piles into; (*Naut., Av.*) to pilot; (*fig.*) to guide.
pilotis [pilɔ'ti], *n.m.* pilework.
pilule [pi'lyl], *n.f.* pill.
pimbêche [pɛ̃'bɛʃ], *n.f.* uppish and impertinent woman.
piment [pi'mɑ̃], *n.m.* pimento, allspice.
pimenter [pimɑ̃'te], *v.t.* to flavor with pimento.
pimpant [pɛ̃'pɑ̃], *a.* natty, spruce, smart.
pin [pɛ̃], *n.m.* pine tree; **pomme de pin**, fir cone.
pinacle [pi'nakl], *n.m.* pinnacle.
pince [pɛ̃:s], *n.f.* pinching, nipping; hold, grip; pincers, pliers, forceps; tongs, clip; crowbar (*lever*); toe (*of a horse's foot*); claw (*of a lobster etc.*).
pincé [pɛ̃'se], *a.* affected, stiff, prim.
pinceau [pɛ̃'so], *n.m.* (*pl.* **-eaux**) paint-brush.
pincée [pɛ̃'se], *n.f.* pinch (*of snuff, salt etc.*).
pince-nez [pɛ̃s'ne], *n.m. inv.* pince-nez, (*folding*) eye glasses.
pince-notes [pɛ̃s'nɔt], *n.m. inv.* paper clip.
pincer [pɛ̃'se], *v.t.* (*conjug. like* COMMENCER) to pinch, to nip; to grip; to bite (*of cold etc.*); to pluck (*a musical instrument*); (*Naut.*) to hug (*the wind*).
pince-sans-rire [pɛ̃ssɑ̃'ri:r], *n.m. inv.* sly *or* malicious person, dry joker.
pincette(s) [pɛ̃'sɛt], *n.f.* (*pl.*) tongs; tweezers, nippers.
pinçure [pɛ̃'sy:r], *n.f.* pinching; crease in cloth.
pingouin [pɛ̃'gwɛ̃], *n.m.* auk.
pingre [pɛ̃:gr], *a.* avaricious, stingy.—*n.* miser, skinflint.
pinson [pɛ̃'sɔ̃], *n.m.* finch, chaffinch.
pintade [pɛ̃'tad], *n.f.* guinea fowl.
piochage [pjɔ'ʃa:ʒ], *n.m.* digging; (*fig.*) working, fagging.
pioche [pjɔʃ], *n.f.* pickaxe.
piocher [pjɔ'ʃe], *v.t.* to dig.—*v.i.* to dig; (*fig.*) to fag, to work hard, to grind.
piocheur [pjɔ'ʃœ:r], *n.m.* (*fem.* **-euse**) digger; (*slang*) hard-working student, grind. —*n.f.* (**-euse**) (*Civ. Eng.*) excavator.
piolet [pjɔ'lɛ], *n.m.* piolet, ice axe.
pion [pjɔ̃], *n.m.* pawn (*at chess*); piece (*at checkers*);(*Sch. slang*) assistant teacher.
pionnier [pjɔ'nje], *n.m.* pioneer.
pipe [pip], *n.f.* pipe; tobacco-pipe; pipe (*cask*).
pipeau [pi'po], *n.m.* (*pl.* **-eaux**) pipe, reed-pipe; bird-call; limed twig, snare.
pipée [pi'pe], *n.f.* bird-catching (*with a bird-call*); (*fig.*) deceit, trickery.
piper [pi'pe], *v.t.* to catch (*birds*) with a bird-call etc.; (*fig.*) to trick, to decoy.
pipeur [pi'pœ:r], *a.* (*fem.* **-euse**) cheating, deceitful.—*n.m.* (*fem.* **-euse**) one who decoys birds; cheat, trickster (*at play*).
piquant [pi'kɑ̃], *a.* prickling, stinging; pungent; biting; cutting, keen; piquant, pointed; smart.—*n.m.* prickle; quill (*of porcupine*); pungency, point, piquancy.
pique [pik], *n.f.* pike (*weapon*); pique, spite, quarrel.—*n.m.* (*Cards*) spade(s).
piqué [pi'ke], *a.* quilted, pinked; worm-eaten; sour (*wine*).—*n.m.* quilting; piqué; nose-dive; **bombardement en piqué**, dive-bombing.

pique-nique [pik'nik], *n.m.* (*pl.* **-niques**) picnic.

piquer [pi'ke], *v.t.* to prick; to sting; to goad, to spur; to puncture; to bite (*of insects*); to quilt; to lard; to prick off; to excite, to stimulate; to nettle, to rouse; (*Med.*) to inject.—*v.i.* to turn sour (*of wine etc.*). **se piquer**, *v.r.* to prick oneself; to be offended, to be piqued; to pride oneself; to turn sour.

piquet [pi'kɛ], *n.m.* peg, stake; (*Mil.*) picket; piquet (*card game*).

piqueter [pik'te], *v.t.* (*conjug. like* APPELER) to mark out with stakes *or* pegs; to mark with little points.

piquette [pi'kɛt], *n.f.*, **piqueton** [pik'tɔ̃], *n.m.* thin wine.

piqueur (1) [pi'kœːr], *n.m.* outrider; overseer (*of workmen*); stud groom; huntsman.

piqueur (2)• [pi'kœːr], *n.m.* (*fem.* **-euse**) stitcher.

piqûre [pi'kyːr], *n.f.* prick; sting; bite; puncture; (*Needlework*) quilting, stitching; (*Med.*) injection, shot.

pirate [pi'rat], *n.m.* pirate; (*fig.*) extortioner, plagiarist.

pirater [pira'te], *v.i.* to commit piracy.

piraterie [pira'tri], *n.f.* piracy; act of piracy *or* plagiarism.

pire [piːr], *a.* and *n.m.* worse; the worst.

pirogue [pi'rog], *n.f.* pirogue, dug-out, canoe.

pirouette [pi'rwɛt], *n.f.* pirouette, whirligig.

pirouetter [pirwɛ'te], *v.i.* to pirouette, to whirl about.

pis (1) [pi], *n.m.* udder, dug (*of cow*).

pis (2) [pi], *adv.* and *n.m.* worse.—*n.m. inv.* **pis-aller**, the worst, last resource, makeshift.

pisciculture [pisikyl'tyːr], *n.f.* fish culture.

piscine [pi'sin], *n.f.* piscina; swimming pool.

pissenlit [pisɑ̃'li], *n.m.* dandelion.

pistache [pis'taʃ], *n.f.* pistachio, pistachio nut.

pistachier [pista'ʃje], *n.m.* pistachio tree.

piste [pist], *n.f.* track, footprint, trail, scent; course, race-course.

pistolet [pisto'lɛ], *n.m.* pistol; spray gun.

piston [pis'tɔ̃], *n.m.* piston; sucker (*of a pump*); press button; (*Mus.*) cornet.

pitance [pi'tɑ̃ːs], *n.f.* pittance; allowance (*of food*), dole.

piteusement [pitøz'mɑ̃], *adv.* piteously, woefully, sadly.

piteux [pi'tø], *a.* (*fem.* **-euse**) piteous, pitiable, woeful.

pitié [pi'tje], *n.f.* pity, compassion; object of pity.

piton [pi'tɔ̃], *n.m.* eye-bolt, screw-ring, ring-bolt; peak (*of mountain*).

pitoyable [pitwa'jabl], *a.* pitiful, piteous, paltry.

pitoyablement [pitwajablə'mɑ̃], *adv.* pitifully.

pittoresque [pito'rɛsk], *a.* picturesque; graphic.—*n.m.* the picturesque, picturesqueness.

pittoresquement [pitorɛsk'mɑ̃], *adv.* picturesquely.

pivert [PICVERT].

pivoine [pi'vwan], *n.m.* bullfinch.—*n.f.* peony.

pivot [pi'vo], *n.m.* pivot, pin, spindle, hinge.

pivoter [pivɔ'te], *v.i.* to pivot, to turn on a pivot, to revolve, to turn.

placage [pla'kaːʒ], *n.m.* plating (*metal-work*); veneering (*of wood*); (*Lit.*) patchwork.

placard [pla'kaːr], *n.m.* placard, poster, bill; (*Print.*) slip; cupboard (*in a wall*).

placarder [plakar'de], *v.t.* to placard, to post up.

place [plas], *n.f.* place; room; seat; stead; post, job, situation; town; public square; **faire place**, to make room; **retenir des places**, to book seats; **sur place**, on the spot.

placement [plas'mɑ̃], *n.m.* placing; sale; employment; investment.

placer [pla'se], *v.t.* (*conjug. like* COMMENCER) to place, to put; to find a place *or* situation for; to invest; to deposit; to sell. **se placer** *v.r.* to place oneself; to find a job.

placet [pla'sɛ], *n.m.* petition, address.

placide [pla'sid], *a.* placid, calm.

placidement [plasid'mɑ̃], *adv.* placidly, calmly.

placidité [plasidi'te], *n.f.* placidity.

plafond [pla'fɔ̃], *n.m.* ceiling.

plafonnage [plafɔ'naːʒ], *n.m.* ceiling (*action, work*); (*Av.*) visibility.

plafonner [plafɔ'ne], *v.t.* to ceil, to put a ceiling to.—*v.i.* to reach the highest point (*of prices etc.*); (*Av.*) to fly at the ceiling; (*Motor.*) to travel at maximum speed.

plafonneur [plafɔ'nœːr], *n.m.* plasterer.

plafonnier [plafɔ'nje], *n.m.* ceiling light.

plage [plaːʒ], *n.f.* beach, shore; sea-side resort.

plagiaire [pla'ʒjɛːr], *a.* and *n.* plagiarist.

plagiat [pla'ʒja], *n.m.* plagiarism.

plagier [pla'ʒje], *v.t.* to plagiarize.

plaid [plɛd], *n.m.* plaid, travelling rug.

plaidant [plɛ'dɑ̃], *a.* pleading, litigant.

plaider [plɛ'de], *v.t.* to defend; to allege.—*v.i.* to go to law, to litigate; to plead, to argue.

plaideur [plɛ'dœːr], *n.m.* (*fem.* **-euse**) litigant, suitor.

plaidoirie [plɛdwa'ri], *n.f.* pleading; counsel's speech.

plaidoyer [plɛdwa'je], *n.m.* speech for the defence, counsel's address.

plaie [plɛ], *n.f.* wound; sore; (*fig.*) plague; evil.

plaignant [plɛ'nɑ̃], *a.* complaining; **la partie plaignante**, the plaintiff.—*n.m.* (*fem.* **-e**) plaintiff, prosecutor.

plain [plɛ], *a.* plain, even, flat, level.

plaindre [plɛ̃ːdr], *v.t. irr.* (*conjug. like* CRAINDRE) to pity, to be sorry for. **se plaindre**, *v.r.* to complain; to grumble.

plaine [plɛn], *n.f.* plain; flat country.

plain-pied (de) [daplɛ̃'pje], *adv. phr.* on a level; (*fig.*) without difficulty.

plainte [plɛ̃ːt], *n.f.* complaint, plaint; lamentation, wail; plaint at law.

plaintif [plɛ̃'tif], *a.* (*fem.* **-tive**) plaintive, complaining; querulous.

plaintivement [plɛtiv'mɑ̃], *adv.* dolefully, querulously.

plaire [plɛːr], *v.i. irr.* to please; to be pleasant *or* agreeable (*à*); **s'il vous plaît**, please. **se plaire**, *v.r.* to delight, to take pleasure; to like.

plaisamment [plɛza'mɑ̃], *adv.* humorously, amusingly; ludicrously.

plaisance [plɛ'zɑ̃:s], *n.f.* pleasure.

plaisant [plɛ'zɑ̃], *a.* humorous, amusing, funny; (*iron.*) odd, strange.—*n.m.* jester, wag; the funny side; *un mauvais plaisant*, a practical joker.

plaisanter [plɛzɑ̃'te], *v.t.* to chaff, to banter. —*v.i.* to jest, to joke.

plaisanterie [plɛzɑ̃'tri], *n.f.* jest, joke, witticism; mockery, trifle.

plaisir [plɛ'zi:r], *n.m.* pleasure; delight; diversion, entertainment; favor.

plan [plɑ̃], *a.* even, level, flat.—*n.m.* plane; plan; drawing; scheme, project; (*Paint.*) ground.

planche [plɑ̃:ʃ], *n.f.* board, plank; shelf; (*Engr.*) plate; (*Gard.*) bed, border.

planchéiage [plɑ̃ʃe'ja:ʒ], *n.m.* boarding, planking; flooring.

planchéier [plɑ̃ʃe'je], *v.t.* to board over, to floor.

plancher [plɑ̃'ʃe], *n.m.* floor, deck planking.

planchette [plɑ̃'ʃɛt], *n.f.* small board; (*Math.*) plane table.

plancton [plɑ̃k'tɔ̃], *n.m.* plankton.

plane [plan], *n.f.* drawing-knife; planisher.

plané [pla'ne], *a.* soaring, gliding; *un vol plané*, gliding descent.

planer [pla'ne], *v.t.* to make smooth, to plane. —*v.i.* to hover, to soar; to look down (*on*) (*sur*); (*Av.*) to glide.

planétaire [plane'tɛ:r], *a.* planetary.

planète [pla'nɛ:t], *n.f.* planet.

planeur [pla'nœ:r], *n.m.* planisher; glider (*airplane*).

planeuse [pla'nø:z], *n.f.* planing machine.

planification [planifika'sjɔ̃], *n.f.* (*Polit. Econ.*) planning.

planifier [plani'fje], *v.t.* to plan.

plant [plɑ̃], *n.m.* young plant, seedling; slip; sapling; plantation.

plantation [plɑ̃ta'sjɔ̃], *n.f.* planting; plantation.

plante [plɑ̃:t], *n.f.* plant; *la plante du pied*, (*Anat.*) the sole of the foot.

planter [plɑ̃'te], *v.t.* to plant; to set, to drive in; to set up, to erect. **se planter**, *v.r.* to station oneself.

planteur [plɑ̃'tœ:r], *n.m.* planter.

planteuse [plɑ̃'tø:z], *n.f.* potato-planting machine.

plantoir [plɑ̃'twa:r], *n.m.* dibble.

planton [plɑ̃'tɔ̃], *n.m.* (*Mil.*) orderly.

plantureusement [plɑ̃tyrøz'mɑ̃], *adv.* copiously, abundantly, luxuriantly.

plantureux [plɑ̃ty'rø], *a.* (*fem.* **-euse**) plentiful, copious; fertile.

plaquage [pla'ka:ʒ], *n.m.* (*Ftb.*) rugby tackle.

plaque [plak], *n.f.* plate, slab; plaque; badge, star; *plaque tournante*, (*Rail.*) turn-table.

plaqué [pla'ke], *a.* plated, covered with.

plaquer [pla'ke], *v.t.* to plate (*metal*); to veneer (*wood*); (*Ftb.*) to tackle.

plaquette [pla'kɛt], *n.f.* small thin book; small plate; thin slab.

plasticité [plasti'te], *n.f.* plasticity.

plastique [plas'tik], *a.* plastic.—*n.m.* plastics. —*n.f.* plastic art; figure.

plastron [plas'trɔ̃], *n.m.* breast-plate; fencing pad; shirt front.

plastronner [plastro'ne], *v.i.* to strut, to swagger.

plat (1) [pla], *a.* flat; level; regular, (*fig.*) dull, insipid.—*n.m.* flat part, side; flat racing.

plat (2) [pla], *n.m.* dish (*the vessel and the food*), (*Naut.*) mess; course (*of a meal*).

platane [pla'tan], *n.m.* plane-tree, platan.

plateau [pla'to], *n.m.* (*pl.* **-eaux**) scale (*of a balance*); tray; table-land, plateau; turn-table (*of gramophone*).

plate-bande [plat'bɑ̃:d], *n.f.* (*pl.* **plates-bandes**) border, flower bed.

plate-forme [plat'fɔrm], *n.f.* (*pl.* **plates-formes**) platform (*of a bus etc.*).

platement [plat'mɑ̃], *adv.* flatly, dully.

platine [pla'tin], *n.f.* lock (*of fire-arms*); plate (*of lock, watch, machine*); platen (*of type-writer*).—*n.m.* platinum.

platiné [plati'ne], *a.* platinum-plated; platinum-colored (*of hair*).

platitude [plati'tyd], *n.f.* platitude; flatness, dullness.

Platon [pla'tɔ̃], *m.* Plato.

platonique [plato'nik], *a.* Platonic.

platonisme [plato'nism], *n.m.* Platonism.

plâtrage [plɑ'tra:ʒ], *n.m.* plaster work, plastering.

plâtras [plɑ'trɑ], *n.m.* debris of plaster work; rubbish.

plâtre [plɑ:tr], *n.m.* plaster.

plâtré [plɑ'tre], *a.* plastered.

plâtrer [plɑ'tre], *v.t.* to plaster; (*fig.*) to patch up, to disguise.

plâtreux [plɑ'trø], *a.* (*fem.* **-euse**) chalky.

plâtrier [plɑtri'je], *n.m.* plasterer.

plâtrière [plɑtri'jɛ:r], *n.f.* chalk pit; plaster kiln.

plâtroir [plɑ'trwa:r], *n.m.* plasterer's trowel.

plausibilité [plozibili'te], *n.f.* plausibility.

plausible [plo'zibl], *a.* plausible (*never of person*).

plausiblement [plozibl'mɑ̃], *adv.* plausibly.

plèbe [plɛb], *n.f.* common people.

plébéien [plebe'jɛ̃], *a.* and *n.m.* (*fem.* **-enne**) plebeian.

plébiscite [plebi'sit], *n.m.* plebiscite.

plein [plɛ̃], *a.* full; fraught (*de*); filled, replete; entire, whole; thorough; copious; solid; *en plein air*, in the open air; *en plein hiver*, in the heart of winter.—*n.m.* full part; plenum.—*adv.* full.

pleinement [plɛn'mɑ̃], *adv.* fully, entirely, thoroughly.

plénier [ple'nje], *a.* (*fem.* **-ière**) plenary; full, complete.

plénipotentiaire [plenipotɑ̃'sjɛ:r], *a.* and *n.m.* plenipotentiary.

plénitude [pleni'tyd], *n.f.* plenitude, fullness.

pleur [plœ:r], *n.m.* (*poet.*) tear; lament.

pleurard [plœ'ra:r], *a.* whimpering, tearful.— *n.m.* (*fem.* **-e**) whimperer, blubberer.

pleurer [plœ're], *v.t.* to weep, to bewail, to mourn, to deplore the loss of.—*v.i.* to weep, to cry, to shed tears; to mourn; to run (*of the eyes*); to drip (*of a tap*).

pleurésie [plœre'zi], *n.f.* pleurisy.

pleureur [plœ'rœ:r], *a.* (*fem.* **-euse**) whimpering, tearful; *saule pleureur*, weeping willow.—*n.m.* (*fem.* **-euse**) whimperer, weeper.—*n.f.* (**-euse**) paid mourner.

pleurnichement

pleurnichement [plœrniʃ'mɑ̃], *n.m.* whimpering, snivelling.
pleurnicher [plœrni'ʃe], *v.i.* to whimper, to whine, to snivel.
pleurnicheur [plœrni'ʃœ:r], *a. (fem.* **-euse**) whimpering, snivelling.—*n.m. (fem.* **-euse**) whimperer, sniveller.
pleutre [plø:tr], *n.m.* contemptible fellow.
pleuvoir [plœ'vwa:r], *v. impers. irr.* to rain; *il pleut à verse* or *à seaux*, it is pouring in buckets; *pleuvoir des hallebardes*, to rain cats and dogs.
pli [pli], *n.m.* fold; wrinkle; coil; bend; undulation, depression; cover, envelope; habit; *(Cards)* trick; *mise en pli*, setting *(the hair)*; *sous pli recommandé*, in a registered envelope; *un faux pli*, a crease.
pliable [pli'jabl], *a.* pliable, flexible, supple.
pliage [pli'ja:ʒ], **pliement** [pli'mɑ̃], *n.m.* folding.
pliant [pli'jɑ̃], *a.* pliant, docile; folding, collapsible.—*n.m.* folding chair, deck chair.
plie [pli], *n.f.* plaice.
plier [pli'je], *v.t.* to fold, to fold up; to bend.—*v.i.* to bend, to bow; to give way. **se plier,** *v.r.* to bow, to bend, to yield.
plieur [pli'jœ:r], *n.m. (fem.* **-euse**) folder.— *n.f.* (**-euse**) folding-machine.
plinthe [plɛ̃:t], *n.f.* plinth; skirting-board.
plissage [pli'sa:ʒ], *n.m.* pleating, kilting.
plissé [pli'se], *a.* kilted, pleated.—*n.m.* kilting, pleats.
plissement [plis'mɑ̃], *n.m.* folding, doubling over; crumpling.
plisser [pli'se], *v.t.* to fold; to crumple, to wrinkle; to pleat.—*v.i.* and **se plisser,** *v.r.* to be wrinkled, to pucker.
plissure [pli'sy:r], *n.f.* pleating; pleats.
ploiement [plwa'mɑ̃], *n.m.* folding, bending.
plomb [plɔ̃], *n.m.* lead; bullet, shot; plumb-line; sinker; custom-house seal; fuse; *à plomb*, vertically.
plombage [plɔ̃'ba:ʒ], *n.m.* leading, plumbing; filling *(of teeth)*.
plombagine [plɔ̃ba'ʒin], *n.f.* plumbago, blacklead, graphite.
plomber [plɔ̃'be], *v.t.* to cover with lead, to seal; to fill *(a tooth)*; to plumb.
plomberie [plɔ̃'bri], *n.f.* plumber's shop; plumbing; lead-making; lead works.
plombier [plɔ̃'bje], *n.m.* lead worker; plumber.
plongée [plɔ̃'ʒe], *n.f.* slope; dive.
plongeoir [plɔ̃'ʒwa:r], *n.m.* diving-board.
plongeon [plɔ̃'ʒɔ̃], *n.m.* plunge, dive; *(Orn.)* diver.
plonger [plɔ̃'ʒe], *v.t. (conjug. like* MANGER) to plunge, to dip, to immerse; to throw, to involve.—*v.i.* to dive, to plunge; to submerge *(of submarine)*; to pitch *(of ships)*. **se plonger,** *v.r.* to be plunged; to immerse oneself *(in)*.
plongeur [plɔ̃'ʒœ:r], *a. (fem.* **-euse**) plunging, diving *(bird)*.—*n.m. (fem.* **-euse**) diver; dish washer *(in hotels etc.)*.
ploutocrate [pluto'krat], *n.m.* plutocrat.
ploutocratie [plutokra'si], *n.f.* plutocracy.
ploutocratique [plutokra'tik], *a.* plutocratic.
ployable [plwa'jabl], *a.* pliable, flexible.
ployer [plwa'je], *v.t. (conjug. like* EMPLOYER) to bend; to fold up.—*v.i.* and **se ployer,**

v.r. to bend, to be folded; to yield, to give way.
pluie [plɥi], *n.f.* rain; *(fig.)* shower.
plumage [ply'ma:ʒ], *n.m.* plumage, feathers.
plumassier [plyma'sje], *n.m. (fem.* **-ière**) feather merchant *or* dresser.
plume [plym], *n.f.* feather; plume; quill, pen; nib.
plumeau [ply'mo], *n.m. (pl.* **-eaux**) feather broom; feather duster.
plumée [ply'me], *n.f.* penful *(of ink)*; plucking *(of poultry)*.
plumer [ply'me], *v.t.* to pluck, to plume; *(fig.)* to fleece.
plumet [ply'mɛ], *n.m.* plume.
plumetis [plym'ti], *n.m.* feather-stitch.
plumier [ply'mje], *n.m.* pen box, pen tray.
plupart [ply'pa:r], *n.f. la plupart*, most, most part, the majority *(de)*, most people.
pluralité [plyrali'te], *n.f.* plurality; pluralism.
pluriel [ply'rjɛl], *a. (fem.* **-elle**) plural.—*n.m.* plural.
plus [ply], *adv.* more, -er *(que*, than); -est, the most; also, moreover, further, besides; *(with* **ne**) no more, no longer, never again; *de plus*, besides, moreover.—*n.m.* the most, the maximum; the more.
plusieurs [ply'zjœ:r], *a. pl.* and *pron. indef.* several, some.
plus-que-parfait [plyskəpar'fɛ], *n.m.* pluperfect.
plutonium [plyto'njɔm], *n.m.* plutonium.
plutôt [ply'to], *adv.* rather, sooner *(que)*.
pluvial [ply'vjal], *a. (m. pl.* **-aux**) pluvial, of rain, rainy.
pluvier [ply'vje], *n.m.* plover.
pluvieux [ply'vjø], *a. (fem.* **-euse**) rainy, wet, pluvious.
pluviomètre [plyvjo'mɛtr], *n.m.* rain gauge.
pluviosité [plyvjozi'te], *n.f.* rainfall.
pneu [pnø], *n.m. (pl.* **pneus**) *fam. abbr.* [PNEUMATIQUE].
pneumatique [pnøma'tik], *a.* pneumatic.— *n.m.* tire; express letter *(in Paris)*.—*n.f.* pneumatics.
pneumonie [pnømo'ni], *n.f.* pneumonia.
pochade [po'ʃad], *n.f.* rough sketch; *(fig.)* hurried piece of writing etc.
poche [poʃ], *n.f.* pocket; pouch; sack, bag; wrinkle *(in clothes)*; crop *(of a bird)*.
pocher [po'ʃe], *v.t.* to poach *(eggs)*; to give a black eye to; to stencil; to make a rough sketch of.—*v.i.* to become baggy, to bag.
pochet [po'ʃɛ], *n.m.* nosebag *(of horse)*.
pochette [po'ʃɛt], *n.f.* small pocket; small net; folder, jacket *(containers)*; fancy handkerchief.
pochoir [po'ʃwa:r], *n.m.* stencil.
podagre [po'dagr], *a.* gouty.—*n.f.* gout.—*n.* gouty person.
podomètre [podo'mɛtr], *n.m.* pedometer.
poêle [pwa:l], *n.f.* frying pan.—*n.m.* stove; pall *(at a funeral)*.
poêlée [pwa'le], *n.f.* panful.
poêlon [pwa'lɔ̃], *n.m.* small saucepan.
poème [po'ɛm], *n.m.* poem.
poésie [poe'zi], *n.f.* poetry, verse; poem.
poète [po'ɛ:t], *n.m.* poet.
poétesse [poe'tɛs], *n.f.* poetess.
poétique [poe'tik], *a.* poetical.—*n.f.* poetics.
poétiquement [poetik'mɑ̃], *adv.* poetically.

poétiser [pɔeti′ze], *v.t.* to make poetical, to idealize, to poeticize.
pogrom [pɔ′grɔm], *n.m.* pogrom.
poids [pwɑ], *n.m. inv.* weight; heaviness; gravity; load; (*fig.*) importance, consequence; **les poids lourds**, heavy vehicles.
poignant [pwa′nɑ̃], *a.* poignant; sharp, acute, keen.
poignard [pwa′naːr], *n.m.* dagger.
poignarder [pwaɲar′de], *v.t.* to stab; to knife; (*fig.*) to grieve to the heart.
poigne [pwaɲ], *n.f.* (*colloq.*) grasp, grip; (*fig.*) strength.
poignée [pwa′ɲe], *n.f.* handful; handle, hilt; shake (*of the hand*).
poignet [pwa′ɲɛ], *n.m.* wrist; wristband, cuff.
poil [pwal], *n.m.* hair (*of animals*); hair (*of persons, other than that of the head*); (*fig.*) beard; nap (*of cloth, of hats etc.*); **à contre-poil**, against the grain.
poilu [pwa′ly], *a.* hairy, shaggy.
poinçon [pwɛ̃′sɔ̃], *n.m.* punch; point, stiletto; awl, stamp, die.
poinçonnage [pwɛ̃sɔ′naːʒ], **poinçonnement** [pwɛ̃sɔn′mɑ̃], *n.m.* stamping, punching.
poinçonner [pwɛ̃sɔ′ne], *v.t.* to punch, to stamp.
poinçonneuse [pwɛ̃sɔ′nøːz], *n.f.* stamping *or* punching machine.
poindre [pwɛ̃:dr], *v.i. irr.* to dawn, to break; (*fig.*) to appear.
poing [pwɛ̃], *n.m.* fist, hand; (*fig.*) force, brute strength; (*fig.*) **dormir à poings fermés**, to sleep like a log.
point [pwɛ̃], *adv.* (*used with negative*) no, not at all; none (*more emphatic than* **pas**).—*n.m.* point; speck; dot, mark; (*Sch.*) mark; full stop; hole (*of a strap etc.*); (*Needlework*) stitch; matter, question; particular; state, case; degree; place; **à point**, in the nick of time; well done (*of meat*); **en tout point**, in every respect; **sur ce** *or* **en ce point**, on that score.
pointage [pwɛ̃′taːʒ], **pointement** [pwɛ̃t′mɑ̃], *n.m.* pointing, levelling (*of guns*); checking; scrutiny (*of votes*), tally.
pointe [pwɛ̃:t], *n.f.* point (*sharp end*); tip, head (*of an arrow etc.*); nose (*of a bullet*); cape; peak; etching needle; nail, tack; (*Print.*) bodkin; (*fig.*) dash, flavor; pungency, sharpness; witticism.
pointement [POINTAGE].
pointer [pwɛ̃′te], *v.t.* to point, to aim (*a gun etc.*); to pierce, to stab, to prick; to mark; to tally, to scrutinize (*votes*); to prick up (*ears etc.*); to sharpen.—*v.i.* to point; to spring, to soar; to rear; to sprout.
pointeur [pwɛ̃′tœːr], *n.m.* (*fem.* **-euse**) pointer, marker, checker; (*Artill.*) gun layer.
pointillage [pwɛ̃ti′jaːʒ], **pointillement** [pwɛ̃tij′mɑ̃], *n.m.* dotting, stippling; dotted line.
pointillé [pwɛ̃ti′je], *n.m.* stipple drawing *or* engraving; dotted line.
pointiller [pwɛ̃ti′je], *v.t.* to dot, to stipple; (*fig.*) to tease.—*v.i.* to bicker, to cavil.
pointilleux [pwɛ̃ti′jø], *a.* (*fem.* **-euse**) cavilling, captious; fastidious.
pointu [pwɛ̃′ty], *a.* pointed, sharp; (*fig.*) subtle, captious.

pointure [pwɛ̃′tyːr], *n.f.* (*Print.*) point; size, number (*of shoes, gloves etc.*).
poire [pwaːr], *n.f.* pear; bulb (*rubber*).
poiré [pwa′re], *n.m.* perry.
poireau [pwa′ro], **porreau** [pɔ′ro], *n.m.* (*pl.* **-eaux**) leek; wart.
poirée [pwa′re], *n.f.* white beet.
poirier [pwa′rje], *n.m.* pear tree.
pois [pwɑ], *n.m. inv.* pea, peas.
poison [pwa′zɔ̃], *n.m.* poison.
poissard [pwa′saːr], *a.* vulgar, low.
poisser [pwa′se], *v.t.* to pitch; to make sticky.
poisseux [pwa′sø], *a.* (*fem.* **-euse**) pitchy, gluey, sticky.
poisson [pwa′sɔ̃], *n.m.* fish; **poisson d'avril**, April fool.
poissonnerie [pwasɔn′ri], *n.f.* fishmarket; fish shop.
poissonneux [pwasɔ′nø], *a.* (*fem.* **-euse**) abounding in fish.
poissonnier [pwasɔ′nje], *n.m.* (*fem.* **-ière**) fishmonger, fishwife.—*n.f.* (**-ière**) fishkettle.
poitrail [pwa′traːj], *n.m.* breast (*of a horse*); breast piece (*of harness*).
poitrinaire [pwatri′nɛːr], *a.* and *n.* consumptive.
poitrine [pwa′trin], *n.f.* chest, breast; breasts; lungs; brisket.
poivrade [pwa′vrad], *n.f.* pepper sauce.
poivre [pwa:vr], *n.m.* pepper.
poivrer [pwa′vre], *v.t.* to pepper.
poivrier [pwavri′je], *n.m.* pepper plant; pepper box.
poivrière [pwavri′jɛːr], *n.f.* pepper plantation; (*Fort.*) corner turret; pepper box.
poix [pwɑ], *n.f.* pitch; shoemakers' wax.
polaire [pɔ′lɛːr], *a.* polar.
polariser [pɔlari′ze], *v.t.* to polarize.
pôle [poːl], *n.m.* (*Astron., Geog.*) pole.
polémique [pɔle′mik], *a.* polemical.—*n.f.* polemics, controversy.
poli [pɔ′li], *a.* polished, glossy, sleek; polite, civil; refined.—*n.m.* polish, finish, gloss.
police [pɔ′lis], *n.f.* police; police regulations; insurance policy; **agent de police**, police constable.
policer [pɔli′se], *v.t.* (*conjug. like* COMMENCER) to establish law and order in; to civilize, to polish, to refine.
polichinelle [pɔliʃi′nɛl], *n.m.* Punch; buffoon; Punch and Judy show.
policier [pɔli′sje], *a.* (*fem.* **-ière**) pertaining to the police; **roman policier**, detective story.—*n.m.* policeman; detective.
policlinique [pɔlikli′nik], *n.f.* out-patients' department.
poliment [pɔli′mɑ̃], *adv.* politely.
poliomyélite [pɔljɔmje′lit], *n.f.* poliomyelitis.
polir [pɔ′liːr], *v.t.* to polish, to burnish; (*fig.*) to civilize, to refine. **se polir**, *v.r.* to become polished; to become refined.
polissage [pɔli′saːʒ], **polissement** [pɔlis′mɑ̃], *n.m.* polishing, finishing.
polisseur [pɔli′sœːr], *n.m.* (*fem.* **-euse**) polisher.
polissoir [pɔli′swaːr], *n.m.* polisher (*tool*).
polisson [pɔli′sɔ̃], *a.* (*fem.* **-onne**) loose, naughty, licentious, smutty.—*n.m.* (*fem.* **-onne**) mischievous child, scamp; loose person.

polissonner [pɔlisɔ'ne], *v.i.* to run about the streets (*of children*).
polissonnerie [pɔlisɔn'ri], *n.f.* smutty joke, lewd act.
polissure [pɔli'sy:r], *n.f.* polishing.
politesse [pɔli'tɛs], *n.f.* politeness, civility, polite attention; compliment.
politicien [pɔliti'sjɛ̃], *n.m.* (*fem.* **-enne**) (*usu. pej.*) politician.
politique [pɔli'tik], *a.* political; (*fig.*) politic, prudent, wise.—*n.f.* politics; policy, discretion.—*n.m.* politician, statesman.
politiquement [pɔlitik'mã], *adv.* politically; (*fig.*) shrewdly.
polka [pɔl'ka], *n.f.* polka.
pollen [pɔl'lɛn], *n.m.* pollen.
pollinisation [pɔlliniza'sjɔ̃], *n.f.* pollinization.
polluer [pɔl'lɥe], *v.t.* to pollute; to defile; to profane.
pollution [pɔly'sjɔ̃], *n.f.* pollution; profanation.
polo [pɔ'lo], *n.m.* polo.
Pologne [pɔ'lɔɲ], **la**, *f.* Poland.
polonais [pɔlɔ'nɛ], *a.* Polish.—*n.m.* Polish (*language*); (**Polonais**, *fem.* **-aise**) Pole.— *n.f.* (**-aise**) Polonaise (*dress, dance, tune*).
poltron [pɔl'trɔ̃], *a.* (*fem.* **-onne**) cowardly, chicken-hearted. — *n.m.* (*fem.* **-onne**) coward, poltroon.
poltronnerie [pɔltrɔn'ri], *n.f.* cowardice, poltroonery.
polycopier [pɔlikɔ'pje], *v.t.* to cyclostyle.
polygamie [pɔliga'mi], *n.f.* polygamy.
polyglotte [pɔli'glɔt], *a.* and *n.* polyglot.
polytechnique [pɔlitɛk'nik], *a.* polytechnic.
pommade [pɔ'mad], *n.f.* pomade; ointment.
pomme [pɔm], *n.f.* apple; ball, knob; head (*of a cabbage, lettuce, walking-stick etc.*); (*pop.*) head, nut; **pomme de pin**, fir cone; **pomme de terre**, potato.
pommé [pɔ'me], *a.* grown to a round head; (*colloq.*) complete, downright.
pommeau [pɔ'mo], *n.m.* (*pl.* **-eaux**) pommel (*of a saddle, sword etc.*); head, knob.
pommelé [pɔm'le], *a.* dappled, mottled.
pommeler (se) [sapɔ'mle], *v.r.* (*conjug. like* APPELER) to become dappled.
pommer [pɔ'me], *v.i.* and **se pommer**, *v.r.* to grow to a firm round head (*of cabbage, lettuce etc.*).
pommette [pɔ'mɛt], *n.f.* apple-like ball *or* knob; cheek bone; (*C*) crab apple.
pommier [pɔ'mje], *n.m.* apple tree.
pompe [pɔ̃:p], *n.f.* pomp, ceremony; display; pump, inflator; **pompe à incendie**, fire-engine.
pomper [pɔ̃'pe], *v.t.* to pump; (*fig.*) to suck up.—*v.i.* to pump.
pompeusement [pɔ̃pøz'mã], *adv.* solemnly, with pomp.
pompeux [pɔ̃'pø], *a.* (*fem.* **-euse**) stately, solemn; pompous.
pompier [pɔ̃'pje], *a. inv.* conventional (*art, style*).—*n.m.* fireman.
pompiste [pɔ̃'pist], *n.* pump attendant (*at gas pump etc.*).
pompon [pɔ̃'pɔ̃], *n.m.* pompon, top-knot.
pomponner [pɔ̃pɔ'ne], *v.t.* to ornament with pompons, to deck out. **se pomponner**, *v.r.* to dress oneself up.
ponce [pɔ̃:s], *n.f.* pumice; (*Drawing*) pounce.
ponceau (1) [pɔ̃'so], *n.m.* (*pl.* **-eaux**) small bridge, culvert.

ponceau (2) [pɔ̃'so], *a.* poppy-red.—*n.m.* (*pl.* **-eaux**) corn poppy.
Ponce Pilate [pɔ̃spi'lat], *m.* Pontius Pilate.
poncer [pɔ̃'se], *v.t.* (*conjug. like* COMMENCER) to pumice; (*Drawing*) to pounce.
poncif [pɔ̃'sif], *n.m.* pounced drawing; (*fig.*) commonplace piece of work.
ponctualité [pɔ̃ktɥali'te], *n.f.* punctuality.
ponctuation [pɔ̃ktɥa'sjɔ̃], *n.f.* punctuation.
ponctué [pɔ̃k'tɥe], *a.* punctuated; dotted; **ligne ponctuée**, dotted line.
ponctuel [pɔ̃k'tɥɛl], *a.* (*fem.* **-elle**) punctual, exact.
ponctuellement [pɔ̃ktɥɛl'mã], *adv.* punctually.
ponctuer [pɔ̃k'tɥe], *v.t.* to punctuate; to point.
pondéré [pɔ̃de're], *a.* poised, calm, self-controlled.
pondérer [pɔ̃de're], *v.t.* (*conjug. like* CÉDER) to poise, to balance.
pondeur [pɔ̃'dœ:r], *a.* (*fem.* **-euse**) good laying (*of poultry etc.*); (*colloq.*) productive.—*n.f.* (**-euse**) good layer.
pondre [pɔ̃:dr], *v.t.* to lay (*eggs*).
poney [pɔ'ne], *n.m.* pony.
pont [pɔ̃], *n.m.* bridge; deck; **Ponts et Chaussées**, (*France*) Department of Bridges and Highways.
ponte (1) [pɔ̃:t], *n.f.* laying of eggs.
ponte (2) [pɔ̃:t], *n.m.* better; (*fam.*) V.I.P.
ponté [pɔ̃'te], *a.* decked (*of ship*); **non ponté**, open (*boat*).
ponter [pɔ̃'te], *v.i.* to punt, to gamble.
pontet [pɔ̃'tɛ], *n.m.* trigger guard; saddle-tree.
pontife [pɔ̃'tif], *n.m.* pontiff.
pontifier [pɔ̃ti'fje], *v.i.* (*fam.*) to act *or* speak solemnly *or* pompously; to pontificate, to lay down the law.
pont-levis [pɔ̃l'vi], *n.m.* (*pl.* **ponts-levis**) drawbridge.
ponton [pɔ̃'tɔ̃], *n.m.* bridge of boats; pontoon.
popeline [pɔ'plin], *n.f.* poplin.
populace [pɔpy'las], *n.f.* populace, mob, rabble.
populacier [pɔpyla'sje], *a.* (*fem.* **-ière**) low, vulgar.
populaire [pɔpy'lɛ:r], *a.* popular; common. —*n.m.* populace, rabble.
populairement [pɔpylɛr'mã], *adv.* popularly.
populariser [pɔpylari'ze], *v.t.* to popularize.
popularité [pɔpylari'te], *n.f.* popularity.
population [pɔpyla'sjɔ̃], *n.f.* population.
populeux [pɔpy'lø], *a.* (*fem.* **-euse**) populous.
porc [pɔ:r], *n.m.* pig; swine; pork.
porcelaine [pɔrsə'lɛn], *n.f.* porcelain, china, chinaware.
porcelet [pɔrsə'lɛ], *n.m.* young pig, piglet.
porc-épic [pɔrke'pik], *n.m.* (*pl.* **porcs-épics**) porcupine; (*Am.*) hedgehog.
porche [pɔrʃ], *n.m.* porch.
porcher [pɔr'ʃe], *n.m.* (*fem.* **-ère**) swineherd.
porcherie [pɔrʃ'ri], *n.f.* pigsty, piggery.
porcin [pɔr'sɛ̃], *a.* porcine.—*n.m.* (*pl.*) pigs.
pore [pɔ:r], *n.m.* pore.
poreux [pɔ'rø], *a.* (*fem.* **-euse**) porous.
pornographie [pɔrnɔgra'fi], *n.f.* pornography.
pornographique [pɔrnɔgra'fik], *a.* pornographic.

positif

porphyre [pɔr'fiːr], *n.m.* porphyry.
porphyriser [pɔrfiri'ze], *v.t.* to porphyrize; to pulverize.
porreau [POIREAU].
port (1) [pɔːr], *n.m.* haven, harbor, port; seaport town; *arriver à bon port*, to arrive safely; (*fig.*) to end happily; *port d'escale*, port of call.
port (2) [pɔːr], *n.m.* carrying, carriage; postage; bearing, gait; (*Naut.*) tonnage.
portable [pɔr'tabl], *a.* portable; wearable.
portage [pɔr'taːʒ], *n.m.* carriage, transport.
portail [pɔr'taːj], *n.m.* (*pl.* -s) portal, front gate (*of a church etc.*).
portant [pɔr'tã], *a.* bearing, carrying; *être bien portant*, to be in good health.
portatif [pɔrta'tif], *a.* (*fem.* -tive) portable.
porte [pɔrt], *n.f.* doorway, gateway; door; gate; entrance; eye (*of hooks etc.*); defile.
porté [pɔr'te], *a.* carried; inclined, prone, disposed (*à*); projected (*of shadows*).
porte-à-faux [pɔrta'fo], *n.m. inv.* overhang; *en porte-à-faux*, overhanging; unsteady.
porte-affiches [pɔrta'fiʃ], *n.m. inv.* advertising board.
porte-avions [pɔrta'vjɔ̃], *n.m. inv.* aircraft carrier.
porte-bagages [pɔrtba'gaːʒ], *n.m. inv.* luggage rack.
porte-billets [pɔrtbi'jɛ], *n.m. inv.* note case; (*Am.*) bill-fold.
porte-bonheur [pɔrtbɔ'nœːr], *n.m. inv.* good-luck charm; mascot.
porte-bouteilles [pɔrtbu'tɛːj], *n.m. inv.* bottle rack, wine bin.
porte-chapeaux [pɔrtʃa'po], *n.m. inv.* hat-stand.
porte-cigarettes [pɔrtsiga'rɛt], *n.m. inv.* cigarette case.
porte-clefs [pɔrtə'kle], *n.m. inv.* key ring.
porte-couteau [pɔrtku'to], *n.m. inv.* knife rest.
porte-crayon [pɔrtəkrɛ'jɔ̃], *n.m. inv.* pencil case.
porte-documents [pɔrtdɔky'mã], *n.m. inv.* dispatch case.
porte-drapeau [pɔrtdra'po], *n.m. inv.* ensign, color bearer.
portée [pɔr'te], *n.f.* brood, litter; reach (*of the hand, arm etc.*); hearing; range, shot; scope; capacity; import, significance; bearing; resting-point; (*Mus.*) stave.
porte-étendard [pɔrtetã'daːr], *n.m. inv.* standard bearer.
porte-fenêtre [pɔrtfə'nɛːtr], *n.f.* (*pl.* portes-fenêtres) French window.
portefeuille [pɔrtə'fœːj], *n.m.* wallet; (*fig.*) portfolio; office.
porte-flambeau [pɔrtflã'bo], *n.m. inv.* torch bearer, linkman.
porte-jupe [pɔrtə'ʒyp], *n.m. inv.* skirt-hanger.
porte-livres [pɔrtə'liːvr], *n.m. inv.* book rest.
porte-malheur [pɔrtma'lœːr], *n.m. inv.* bird of ill omen, bearer of ill luck.
portemanteau [pɔrtmã'to], *n.m.* (*pl.* -eaux) coat stand, coat rail; peg.
porte-masse [pɔrtə'mas], *n.m. inv.* mace bearer.
porte-mine(s) [pɔrtə'min], *n.m. inv.* mechanical pencil.

porte-monnaie [pɔrtmɔ'nɛ], *n.m. inv.* purse.
porte-musique [pɔrtmy'zik], *n.m. inv.* music case.
porte-parapluies [pɔrtpara'plɥi], *n.m. inv.* umbrella stand.
porte-parole [pɔrtpa'rɔl], *n.m. inv.* mouthpiece, spokesman.
porte-plume [pɔrtə'plym], *n.m. inv.* pen holder.
porte-queue [pɔrtə'kø], *n.m. inv.* train bearer; swallowtail butterfly.
porter [pɔr'te], *v.t.* to carry, to bear, to support; to endure; to bring, to take; to wear; to deal (*blows etc.*); to turn (*the eyes etc.*); to entertain (*affection etc.*); to incline; to produce; to declare, to show.—*v.i.* to bear; to rest, to lie; to take effect; to hit; to reach; to carry (*of a gun etc.*); (*Naut.*) to stand, to bear off; to be with young (*of animals*). **se porter**, *v.r.* to go, to repair, to move; to resort, to flock; to be inclined *or* disposed, to tend; to be, to do (*of health*); to be worn; to present oneself, to stand forth; to turn, to be directed.
porte-rame [pɔrt'ram], *n.m. inv.* oarlock.
porte-serviette(s) [pɔrtsɛr'vjɛt], *n.m. inv.* towel rail.
porteur [pɔr'tœːr], *n.m.* (*fem.* -euse) porter, carrier, bearer; holder; sleeper (*on railway track*).
porte-voix [pɔrt'vwa], *n.m. inv.* megaphone.
portier [pɔr'tje], *n.m.* (*fem.* -ière (1)) porter, door-keeper.
portière (2) [pɔr'tjɛːr], *n.f.* door-curtain, door (*of vehicle*).
portion [pɔr'sjɔ̃], *n.f.* portion, part, share, allowance.
portionner [pɔrsjɔ'ne], *v.t.* to share out.
portique [pɔr'tik], *n.m.* portico; porch.
porto [pɔr'to], *n.m.* port (wine).
portrait [pɔr'trɛ], *n.m.* portrait, likeness, picture.
portraitiste [pɔrtrɛ'tist], *n.* portrait painter.
portugais [pɔrty'gɛ], *a.* Portuguese.—*n.m.* Portuguese (*language*); (**Portugais**, *fem.* -aise) Portuguese (*person*).
Portugal [pɔrty'gal], **le**, *m.* Portugal.
pose [poːz], *n.f.* laying, setting; pose, posture, attitude; posing, affectation; sitting (*for one's portrait etc.*); hanging (*of bells*); (*Mil.*) posting (*of sentries*); (*Phot.*) (time) exposure.
posé [po'ze], *a.* laid, set, poised; bearing, resting; sedate, staid, sober; *cela posé*, this being granted.
posément [poze'mã], *adv.* calmly; sedately.
poser [po'ze], *v.t.* to put, to put in (*a lock, a window pane*); to place, to lay down; to hang; to suppose, to grant; to post (*sentries etc.*); to lay down, to state; (*Mus.*) to pitch; to sit (*for portrait*); *poser une question*, to ask a question.—*v.i.* to lie, to rest (*sur*); to stand, to pose, to sit (*for one's portrait*); to show off. **se poser**, *v.r.* to perch (*of birds etc.*); to come down, to land (*plane*); to set up (*en*), to play the part (*en*).
poseur [po'zœːr], *n.m.* (*Rail.*) track layer.—*n.m.* (*fem.* -euse) (*colloq.*) poseur, snob, prig.
positif [pozi'tif], *a.* (*fem.* -tive) positive, certain; practical, actual, matter-of-fact.—*n.m.* positive reality; certainty, fact; (*Phot., Ciné., Gram.*) positive.

position [pɔzi'sjɔ̃], *n.f.* position, situation; status, standing; case, state, circumstances.

positivement [pɔzitiv'mɑ̃], *adv.* positively, exactly.

possédé [pose'de], *a.* possessed.—*n.m.* (*fem.* **-ée**) person possessed, madman, maniac.

posséder [pose'de], *v.t.* (*conjug. like* CÉDER) to possess, to be possessed of, to own; to be master of; to be conversant with; to dominate (*a person*); (*pop.*) to deceive. **se posséder**, *v.r.* to master one's passions, to contain oneself.

possesseur [pose'sœ:r], *n.m.* possessor, owner, occupier.

possessif [pose'sif], *a.* (*fem.* **-ive**) possessive. —*n.m.* (*Gram.*) possessive adjective *or* pronoun.

possession [pose'sjɔ̃], *n.f.* possession, property.

possibilité [pɔsibili'te], *n.f.* possibility; (*pl.*) facilities.

possible [pɔ'sibl], *a.* possible.—*n.m.* possibility; **au possible**, extremely; **je ferai tout mon possible**, I'll do the best I can.

postal [pɔs'tal], *a.* (*m. pl.* **-aux**) postal, of the post.

poste (1) [pɔst], *n.m.* post, station; guard-house; place, employment, post; (*Naut.*) berth; (*Teleph.*) extension; entry (*in books*); **poste de radio**, radio set; **poste d'incendie**, fire station.

poste (2) [pɔst], *n.f.* post (*relay*); post stage; postal service; post office, mail; **bureau de poste**, post office.

poster [pɔs'te], *v.t.* to station, to post (*sentry* or *letter*).

postérieur [pɔste'rjœ:r], *a.* posterior, later; behind.—*n.m.* (*colloq.*) posterior.

postérieurement [pɔsterjœr'mɑ̃], *adv.* subsequently.

postérité [pɔsteri'te], *n.f.* posterity.

posthume [pɔs'tym], *a.* posthumous.

postiche [pɔs'tiʃ], *a.* superadded; false, artificial.—*n.m.* wig.

postier [pɔs'tje], *n.m.* (*fem.* **-ière**) post-office employee.

postillon [pɔsti'jɔ̃], *n.m.* postilion; post boy.

postscolaire [pɔstskɔ'lɛ:r], *a.* continuation (*class*); **enseignement postscolaire**, adult education.

post-scriptum [pɔstskrip'tɔm] (*abbr.* **P.S.**), *n.m. inv.* postscript.

postulant [pɔsty'lɑ̃], *n.m.* (*fem.* **-e**) candidate, applicant; postulant.

postuler [pɔsty'le], *v.t.* to solicit, to apply for.—*v.i.* (*Law*) to act on behalf of a client.

posture [pɔs'ty:r], *n.f.* posture, attitude; situation.

pot [po], *n.m.* pot; jug, tankard, flagon, can, jar; (C) half a gallon.

potable [pɔ'tabl], *a.* drinkable (*water*).

potage [pɔ'ta:ʒ], *n.m.* soup.

potager (1) [pɔta'ʒe], *n.m.* kitchen garden; kitchen stove.

potager (2) [pɔta'ʒe], *a.* (*fem.* **-ère**) culinary; **jardin potager**, kitchen garden.

potasse [pɔ'tas], *n.f.* potash.

potassium [pɔta'sjɔm], *n.m.* potassium.

pot-au-feu [pɔto'fø], *n.m. inv.* beef boiled with carrots etc.; broth of this.

pot-de-vin [pod'vɛ̃], *n.m.* (*pl.* **pots-de-vin**) gratuity; bribe; hush money.

poteau [pɔ'to], *n.m.* (*pl.* **-eaux**) post, stake.

potée [pɔ'te], *n.f.* potful; (*colloq.*) swarm (*of children etc.*); putty; (*Metal.*) molding.

potelé [pɔ'tle], *a.* plump, chubby.

potence [pɔ'tɑ̃:s], *n.f.* gallows, gibbet; bracket; crutch; **gibier de potence**, jail-bird.

potentat [pɔtɑ̃'ta], *n.m.* potentate.

potentiel [pɔtɑ̃'sjɛl], *a.* (*fem.* **-elle**) potential, —*n.m.* potentialities.

potentiellement [pɔtɑ̃sjɛl'mɑ̃], *adv.* potentially.

poterie [pɔ'tri], *n.f.* pottery, earthenware.

poterne [pɔ'tɛrn], *n.f.* postern.

potiche [pɔ'tiʃ], *n.f.* China *or* Japan porcelain vase.

potier [pɔ'tje], *n.m.* potter.

potin [pɔ'tɛ̃], *n.m.* pinchbeck; (*pl.*) gossip.

potion [po'sjɔ̃], *n.f.* potion, draft.

potiron [pɔti'rɔ̃], *n.m.* pumpkin.

pou [pu], *n.m.* (*pl.* **poux**) louse.

pouah! [pwa], *int.* ugh! disgusting!

poubelle [pu'bɛl], *n.f.* dustbin; (*Am.*) ash-can.

pouce [pus], *n.m.* thumb; big toe; inch; **un morceau sur le pouce**, a snack; (C) **faire du pouce**, to hitch-hike.

poucet [pu'sɛ], *n.m.* **le petit Poucet**, Tom Thumb.

pouding [pu'diŋ], *n.m.* plum pudding.

poudre [pudr], *n.f.* powder; gunpowder; dust; **sucre en poudre**, powdered sugar.

poudrer [pu'dre], *v.t.* to powder, to sprinkle with powder.

poudrerie [pudrə'ri], *n.f.* gunpowder-factory; (C) blizzard.

poudreux [pu'drø], *a.* (*fem.* **-euse**) dusty, powdery.

poudrier [pudri'e], *n.m.* (powder) compact.

poudrière [pudri'ɛ:r], *n.f.* powder mill, magazine; sand box.

poudroyer [pudrwa'je], *v.i.* (*conjug. like* EMPLOYER) to rise in dust; to be dusty (*of roads etc.*).

pouf! (1) [puf], *int.* plop! flop! phew!

pouf (2) [puf], *n.m.* ottoman (*seat*), pouf; blurb(*advertisement*).

pouffer [pu'fe], *v.i.* **pouffer de rire**, to burst out laughing, to guffaw.

pouilleux [pu'jø], *a.* and *n.m.* (*fem.* **-euse**) lousy; wretched, mean (person).

poulailler [pula'je], *n.m.* hen house; (*of persons*) poulterer; (*Theat.*) gods, gallery.

poulain [pu'lɛ̃], *n.m.* foal, colt.

poularde [pu'lard], *n.f.* fat pullet.

poulbot [pul'bo], *n.m.* Paris street urchin.

poule [pul], *n.f.* hen; fowl; pool (*at games*); eliminating round (*in a competition*).

poulet [pu'lɛ], *n.m.* chicken; love letter.

poulette [pu'lɛt], *n.f.* pullet.

pouliche [pu'liʃ], *n.f.* filly.

poulie [pu'li], *n.f.* pulley; (*Naut.*) block.

pouliner [puli'ne], *v.i.* to foal (*of mares*).

poulinière [puli'njɛ:r], *a.f.* and *n.f.* (*jument*) **poulinière**, brood mare.

poulpe [pulp], *n.m.* octopus, devil-fish.

pouls [pu], *n.m.* pulse; **se tâter le pouls**, to feel one's pulse.

poumon [pu'mɔ̃], *n.m.* lung; **poumon d'acier**, iron lung.

poupard [pu'pa:r], *a.* chubby.—*n.m.* baby; doll.

poupe [pup], *n.f.* stern, poop.

poupée [pu'pe], *n.f.* doll; puppet; tailor's dummy.

poupin [pu'pɛ̃], *a.* fresh-colored; rosy.

poupon [pu'põ], *n.m.* (*fem.* **-onne**) baby; plump, chubby-cheeked boy *or* girl.

pouponnière [pupɔ'njɛːr], *n.f.* (*public*) day nursery.

pour [pu:r], *prep.* for; on account of; on behalf of; as regards, as for; in order; although.—*n.m.* for, pro.

pourboire [pur'bwa:r], *n.m.* tip, gratuity.

pourceau [pur'so], *n.m.* (*pl.* **-eaux**) hog, pig, swine.

pour-cent [pur'sã], **pourcentage** [pursã'ta:ʒ], *n.m.* percentage.

pourchasser [purʃa'se], *v.t.* to pursue, to chase, to badger.

pourfendre [pur'fã:dr], *v.t.* to cleave asunder.

pourlécher [purle'ʃe], *v.t.* (*conjug. like* CÉDER) to lick all over. **se pourlécher**, *v.r.* to lick one's lips.

pourparler [purpar'le], *n.m.* (*usu. in pl.*) parley, negotiations; talks.

pourpoint [pur'pwɛ̃], *n.m.* doublet.

pourpre [purpr], *a.* purple, dark red.—*n.f.* purple (*stuff*); (*fig.*) sovereign dignity; cardinalate.—*n.m.* purple, crimson (*color*).

pourpré [pur'pre], *a.* purple.

pourquoi [pur'kwa], *adv.* and *conj.* why, wherefore; *pourquoi pas?* why not?—*n.m. inv.* the reason why.

pourri [pu'ri], *a.* rotten; *temps pourri,* muggy weather.—*n.m.* the rotten part; rottenness.

pourrir [pu'ri:r], *v.t.* to make rotten, to corrupt.—*v.i.* to rot; (*fig.*) to perish. **se pourrir**, *v.r.* to become rotten, to go bad.

pourrissable [puri'sabl], *a.* perishable.

pourrissant [puri'sã], *a.* rotting, causing rot.

pourriture [puri'ty:r], *n.f.* rot, rottenness, putrefaction; (*fig.*) corruption.

poursuite [pur'sɥit], *n.f.* pursuit, chase; prosecution; (*Law*) suit, proceedings.

poursuivable [pursɥi'vabl], *a.* actionable.

poursuivant [pursɥi'vã], *a.* suing, prosecuting.—*n.m.* suitor.—*n.m.* (*fem.* **-e**) prosecutor, plaintiff.

poursuivre [pur'sɥi:vr], *v.t. irr.* (*conjug. like* SUIVRE) to pursue; to seek; to persecute; to haunt; to go on with; to follow up; (*Law*) to sue, to prosecute.—*v.i.* to pursue, to go on, to continue. **se poursuivre**, *v.r.* to continue, to follow its course.

pourtant [pur'tã], *adv.* however, yet, still, nevertheless.

pourtour [pur'tu:r], *n.m.* periphery, circumference; aisle (*in a theatre etc.*); precincts (*of cathedral*).

pourvoi [pur'vwa], *n.m.* (*Law*) appeal.

pourvoir [pur'vwa:r], *v.t. irr.* to invest with, to appoint; to provide, to supply, to endow. —*v.i.* (*followed by* à) to see to, to attend to, to provide for; to make an appointment to. **se pourvoir**, *v.r.* to provide oneself; to appeal.

pourvoyeur [purvwa'jœ:r], *n.m.* (*fem.* **-euse**) purveyor, provider, caterer.

pourvu que [pur'vykə], *conj. phr.* provided that, provided.

pousse [pus], *n.f.* shoot, sprout.

pousse-café [puska'fe], *n.m. inv.* (*fam.*) liqueur (*after coffee*).

poussée [pu'se], *n.f.* pushing; shove; thrust (*of arches etc.*); pressure (*of business etc.*).

pousse-pousse [pus'pus], *n.m. inv.* rickshaw (*carriage or man*).

pousser [pu'se], *v.t.* to push, to thrust, to shove; to drive on; to carry on, to extend; to grow, to send forth (*of plants etc.*); to urge, to provoke; to assist, to help on; to utter, to heave (*a sigh etc.*); to deal (*a blow etc.*).—*v.i.* to sprout, to shoot (*of plants*); to grow (*of the hair, nails etc.*); to push on, to go on; to bulge; to be broken-winded (*of horses*). **se pousser**, *v.r.* to push forward, to push oneself forward; to push each other, to jostle.

poussette [pu'sɛt], *n.f.* go-cart; movement in dancing.

poussier [pu'sje], *n.m.* coal dust, screenings.

poussière [pu'sjɛ:r], *n.f.* dust; spray (*of water*).

poussiéreux [pusje'rø], *a.* (*fem.* **-euse**) dusty.

poussif [pu'sif], *a.* (*fem.* **-ive**) shortwinded.

poussin [pu'sɛ̃], *n.m.* chick, chicken just hatched.

poussinière [pusi'njɛ:r], *n.f.* chicken-coop; incubator.

poutre [putr], *n.f.* beam; girder.

poutrelle [pu'trɛl], *n.f.* small beam.

pouvoir [pu'vwa:r], *v.t.i. irr.* to be able to do.— *v.i.* to be able (*can etc.*); to have power; to be allowed (*may etc.*); (*impers.*) to be possible; *il peut arriver que,* it may happen that; *il se peut que,* it is possible that; *on ne peut plus,* (*followed by adj.*) exceedingly; *sauve qui peut,* every man for himself.—*n.m.* power; might; authority; command, commission.

prairie [pre'ri], *n.f.* meadow, grass-land, grass field; (*U.S.*) prairie.

praline [pra'lin], *n.f.* burnt almond.

praliner [prali'ne], *v.t.* to brown in sugar (*like burnt almonds*).

praticabilité [pratikabili'te], *n.f.* practicability, feasibility.

praticable [prati'kabl], *a.* practicable, feasible; passable (*of roads*); accessible; (*Theat.*) real, usable.

praticien [prati'sjɛ̃], *a.* (*fem.* **-enne**) practicing.—*n.m.* (*fem.* **-enne**) practitioner.

pratiquant [prati'kã], *a.* church-going.— *n.m.* (*fem.* **-e**) church-goer.

pratique [pra'tik], *a.* practical; experienced. —*n.f.* practice; execution; method; experience; usage; custom (*of tradesman*), practice (*of attorneys, physicians etc.*); customer; (*pl.*) dealings.

pratiquement [pratik'mã], *adv.* in actual fact, practically; in a practical way.

pratiquer [prati'ke], *v.t.* to practice, to exercise; to frequent; to tamper with, to bribe; to obtain; (*Arch.*) to contrive. **se pratiquer**, *v.r.* to be in use, to be practiced.

pré [pre], *n.m.* meadow.

préalable [prea'labl], *a.* preliminary; previous.—*n.m. au préalable,* previously, first of all.

préalablement [prealablə'mã], *adv.* previously, first, to begin with.

préambule [preã′byl], *n.m.* preamble, preface.

préau [pre′o], *n.m.* (*pl.* **-aux**) courtyard (*of a convent* or *prison*); (*sch.*) covered playground.

préavis [prea′vi], *n.m. inv.* (previous) notice.

précaire [pre′kɛːr], *a.* precarious; uncertain.

précairement [prekɛr′mã], *adv.* precariously.

précaution [preko′sjɔ̃], *n.f.* precaution; caution, care.

précautionner [prekosjo′ne], *v.t.* to warn, to caution. **se précautionner,** *v.r.* to take precautions.

précédemment [preseda′mã], *adv.* before, previously.

précédent [prese′dã], *a.* preceding, former.—*n.m.* precedent.

précéder [prese′de], *v.t.* (*conjug. like* CÉDER) to precede, to go before; to take precedence (*of*).

précepte [pre′sɛpt], *n.m.* precept, rule.

précepteur [presɛp′tœːr], *n.m.* (*fem.* **-trice**) tutor, teacher.

prêche [prɛːʃ], *n.m.* sermon (*Protestant*); Protestant church.

prêcher [pre′ʃe], *v.t.* to preach; to exhort; to extol, to praise.—*v.i.* to preach.

prêcheur [prɛ′ʃœːr], *n.m.* (*fem.* **-euse**) preacher.

précieusement [presjøz′mã], *adv.* preciously; carefully; affectedly.

précieux [pre′sjø], *a.* (*fem.* **-euse**) precious, valuable; affected.—*n.m.* affectation.—*n.m.* (*fem.* **-euse**) affected person.

préciosité [presjozi′te], *n.f.* affectation.

précipice [presi′pis], *n.m.* precipice.

précipitamment [presipita′mã], *adv.* precipitately, hurriedly, rashly.

précipitation [presipita′sjɔ̃], *n.f.* haste, hurry; (*Chem.*) precipitation.

précipité [presipi′te], *a.* precipitated, hurled; precipitate, hasty, sudden.—*n.m.* (*Chem.*) precipitate.

précipiter [presipi′te], *v.t.* to precipitate, to hurl; to hasten, to accelerate; (*Chem.*) to precipitate. **se précipiter,** *v.r.* to precipitate, throw or hurl oneself; to rush forward, to spring forth, to dart.

précis [pre′si], *a.* fixed, precise, exact; formal, terse, concise.—*n.m.* summary, abstract.

précisément [presize′mã], *adv.* precisely, exactly; quite; just so.

préciser [presi′ze], *v.t.* to state precisely, to specify.

précision [presi′zjɔ̃], *n.f.* precision, preciseness.

précité [presi′te], *a.* afore-mentioned.

précoce [pre′kɔs], *a.* precocious, early, forward.

précocité [prekɔsi′te], *n.f.* precocity.

préconçu [prekɔ̃′sy], *a.* preconceived.

préconiser [prekɔni′ze], *v.t.* to advocate, to recommend.

préconnaissance [prekɔnɛ′sãːs], *n.f.* foreknowledge.

précurseur [prekyr′sœːr], *n.m.* forerunner, precursor, harbinger.

prédateur [preda′tœːr], *a.* (*fem.* **-trice**) (*Ent.*) predatory.

prédécéder [predese′de], *v.i.* (*conjug. like* CÉDER) to predecease (*someone*).

prédestination [predɛstina′sjɔ̃], *n.f.* predestination.

prédestiné [predɛsti′ne], *a.* predestined; predetermined.—*n.m.* (*fem.* **-ée**) one of the elect.

prédicateur [predika′tœːr], *n.m.* (*fem.* **-trice**) preacher.

prédiction [predik′sjɔ̃], *n.f.* prediction, forecast.

prédilection [predilɛk′sjɔ̃], *n.f.* predilection, preference.

prédire [pre′diːr], *v.t. irr.* (*conjug. like* MÉDIRE) to predict, to foretell.

prédisposer [predispo′ze], *v.t.* to predispose.

prédisposition [predispozi′sjɔ̃], *n.f.* predisposition.

prédominance [predɔmi′nãːs], *n.f.* predominance, ascendancy.

prédominant [predɔmi′nã], *a.* predominant.

prédominer [predɔmi′ne], *v.t.* to prevail over.—*v.i.* to predominate.

prééminence [preemi′nãːs], *n.f.* pre-eminence.

prééminent [preemi′nã], *a.* pre-eminent.

préemption [preãp′sjɔ̃], *n.f.* pre-emption.

préfabriqué [prefabri′ke], *a.* prefabricated.

préface [pre′fas], *n.f.* preface; foreword.

préfecture [prefɛk′tyːr], *n.f.* prefecture; *préfecture de police,* Paris police headquarters.

préférable [prefe′rabl], *a.* preferable.

préférablement [preferablə′mã], *adv.* preferably.

préféré [prefe′re], *a.* favorite.

préférence [prefe′rãːs], *n.f.* preference.

préférer [prefe′re], *v.t.* (*conjug. like* CÉDER) to prefer.

préfet [pre′fɛ], *n.m.* prefect; chief administrator of a department in France; *préfet de police,* chief commissioner of Parisian police.

préhensile [preã′sil], *a.* prehensile.

préhistorique [preisto′rik], *a.* prehistoric.

préjudice [preʒy′dis], *n.m.* detriment, injury, damage, prejudice.

préjudiciable [preʒydi′sjabl], *a.* prejudicial, detrimental.

préjudicier [preʒydi′sje], *v.i.* to be prejudicial or detrimental.

préjugé [preʒy′ʒe], *n.m.* presumption, prejudice; (*Law*) precedent.

préjuger [preʒy′ʒe], *v.t.* (*conjug. like* MANGER) to prejudge.

prélasser (se) [səprela′se], *v.r.* to strut, to stalk along.

prélat [pre′la], *n.m.* prelate.

prélèvement [prelɛv′mã], *n.m.* deduction; sample; (*Med.*) swab.

prélever [prela′ve], *v.t.* (*conjug. like* AMENER) to deduct; to appropriate.

préliminaire [prelimi′nɛːr], *a.* and *n.m.* preliminary.

prélude [pre′lyd], *n.m.* prelude.

prématuré [prematy′re], *a.* premature, untimely.

prématurément [prematyre′mã], *adv.* prematurely.

préméditation [predmedita′sjɔ̃], *n.f.* premeditation.

préméditer [premedi′te], *v.t.* to premeditate.

prémices [pre'mis], *n.f. pl.* first-fruits; (*fig.*) beginning.

premier [prə'mje], *a.* (*fem.* **-ière**) first; foremost, best, chief; former (*of two*); early, pristine, primeval; (*Arith.*) prime; *au premier abord*, at first sight; *le premier rang*, the front rank; *matières premières*, raw materials.—*n.m.* (*fem.* **-ière**) chief, head, leader.—*n.m.* first floor; first of the month etc.—*n.f.* (**-ière**) (*Theat.*) first night.

premièrement [prəmjɛr'mā], *adv.* firstly, in the first place.

prémonition [premoni'sjɔ̃], *n.f.* premonition.

prémunir [premy'ni:r], *v.t.* to forewarn, to caution, to secure beforehand. **se prémunir**, *v.r.* to provide (*contre*).

prenant [prə'nā], taking, prehensile; (*fig.*) fascinating; *partie prenante*, payee.

prendre [prā:dr], *v.t. irr.* to take; to take up; to snatch; to seize; to capture; to contract, to catch (*a cold etc.*); to choose; to fetch; to assume; to collect (*votes etc.*); to help oneself to; to conduct (*an affair etc.*); to entertain (*a feeling etc.*); *en prendre à son aise*, to take it easy; *prendre pour dit*, to take for granted; *que je t'y prenne un peu!* just let me catch you at it!—*v.i.* to take; to take root; to congeal, to freeze; to curdle (*of milk etc.*); to succeed; to begin to burn. **se prendre**, *v.r.* to be taken, to be caught; to catch; to freeze, to congeal (*of liquids*); to begin.

preneur [prə'nœ:r], *n.m.* (*fem.* **-euse**) taker; lessee; purchaser; catcher (*of animals*).

prénom [pre'nɔ̃], *n.m.* Christian name.

prénommé [prenɔ'me], *a.* and *n.m.* (*fem.* **-ée**) (the) above-named, aforesaid; named.

préoccupation [preɔkypa'sjɔ̃], *n.f.* preoccupation; anxiety, concern.

préoccupé [preɔky'pe], *a.* preoccupied, absorbed; worried.

préoccuper [preɔky'pe], *v.t.* to engross, to preoccupy; to worry. **se préoccuper**, *v.r.* to see to, to be engaged in (*de*), to be anxious about.

préparateur [prepara'tœ:r], *n.m.* (*fem.* **-trice**) preparer, assistant (*in laboratory or in a dispensing druggist's*).

préparatif(s) [prepara'tif], *n.m. sing. or pl.* preparation.

préparation [prepara'sjɔ̃], *n.f.* preparation; *sans préparation*, extempore.

préparatoire [prepara'twa:r], *a.* preparatory.

préparer [prepa're], *v.t.* to prepare, to make ready; to fit; to make up, to manufacture. **se préparer**, *v.r.* to prepare, to prepare oneself, to get ready.

prépondérance [prepɔ̃de'rā:s], *n.f.* preponderance.

prépondérant [prepɔ̃de'rā], *a.* preponderant; *voix prépondérante*, casting-vote.

préposé [prepo'ze], *n.m.* (*fem.* **-ée**) officer in charge, superintendent, agent.

préposer [prepo'ze], *v.t.* to set over, to appoint to, to put in charge of.

préposition [prepozi'sjɔ̃], *n.f.* preposition.

prérogative [preroga'ti:v], *n.f.* prerogative.

près [prɛ], *adv.* by, near, hard by; nearly, almost, about; on the point of; *à beaucoup près*, by a great deal; *à cela près*, with

that exception; *à peu près*, pretty near, nearly so; *de près*, close, near; *tout près*, very near.—*prep.* (*usu.* **près de**) near, close to.

présage [pre'za:ʒ], *n.m.* presage, omen, foreboding.

présager [preza'ʒe], *v.t.* (*conjug. like* MANGER) to presage, to portend.

pré-salé [presa'le], *n.m.* (*pl.* **prés-salés**) salt-marsh sheep *or* mutton.

presbyte [prɛz'bit], *a.* long-sighted.—*n.* long-sighted person.

presbytère [prɛzbi'tɛ:r], *n.m.* parsonage, vicarage, rectory; presbytery (*R.-C. Ch.*).

presbytérien [prɛzbite'rjɛ̃], *a.* and *n.m.* (*fem.* **-enne**) Presbyterian.

presbytie [prɛzbi'si], *n.f.* far- *or* long-sightedness.

prescience [pre'sjā:s], *n.f.* prescience, foreknowledge.

prescription [prɛskrip'sjɔ̃], *n.f.* prescription; regulation.

prescrire [prɛs'kri:r], *v.t. irr.* (*conjug. like* ÉCRIRE) to prescribe, to stipulate; (*Law*) to bar.

préséance [prese'ā:s], *n.f.* precedence.

présence [pre'zā:s], *n.f.* presence, attendance, appearance; *mettre en présence*, to bring face to face.

présent [pre'zā], *a.* present; *présent !* here! —*n.m.* present, present time; gift; *dès à présent*, from now on.

présentable [prezā'tabl], *a.* presentable, fit to be seen.

présentation [prezātɑ'sjɔ̃], *n.f.* presentation, introduction.

présentement [prezāt'mā], *adv.* now, at present.

présenter [prezā'te], *v.t.* to present, to offer; to show; to introduce. **se présenter**, *v.r.* to present oneself, to appear.

préservateur [prezɛrva'tœ:r], *a.* (*fem.* **-trice**) preservative.

préservatif [prezɛrva'tif], *a.* (*fem.* **-tive**) preservative.

préservation [prezɛrva'sjɔ̃], *n.f.* preservation.

préserver [prezɛr've], *v.t.* to preserve; to defend, to keep safe; *le ciel m'en préserve !* heaven forbid! **se préserver**, *v.r.* to preserve oneself, to guard against.

présidence [prezi'dā:s], *n.f.* presidency, chairmanship.

président [prezi'dā], *n.m.* president (*of tribunal*), presiding judge; speaker (*of the House of Commons*), chairman.

présidente [prezi'dā:t], *n.f.* lady president; president's wife.

présider [prezi'de], *v.t.* to preside over, to be president *or* chairman of.—*v.i.* to preside, to be president, to be in the chair.

présomptif [prezɔ̃p'tif], *a.* (*fem.* **-tive**) presumptive, apparent, presumed (*of heirs*).

présomption [prezɔ̃p'sjɔ̃], *n.f.* presumption, self-conceit.

présomptueusement [prezɔ̃ptɥøz'mā], *adv.* presumptuously.

présomptueux [prezɔ̃p'tɥø], *a.* (*fem.* **-euse**) presumptuous.

presque [prɛsk], *adv.* almost, nearly, all but; hardly, scarcely; *presque jamais*, hardly ever; *presque plus (de)*, scarcely any left; *presque rien*, hardly anything.

presqu'île [prɛs′kil], *n.f.* peninsula.
pressage [prɛ′saːʒ], *n.m.* pressing.
pressant [prɛ′sɑ̃], *a.* pressing, urgent, earnest.
presse [prɛs], *n.f.* throng, crowd; hurry; urgency; (*Navy*) press-gang; press (*newspapers*); printing-press.
pressé [prɛ′se], *a.* pressed; crowded; close, thick; in haste, hurried; urgent; eager; very busy; (*fig.*) condensed, concise.
presse-citron [prɛssi′trɔ̃], *n.m.* (*pl. unchanged* or **-citrons**) lemon-squeezer.
pressée [prɛ′se], *n.f.* pressing, pressure; pressful (*of print etc.*).
pressentiment [prɛsɑ̃ti′mɑ̃], *n.m.* presentiment; foreboding.
pressentir [prɛsɑ̃′tiːr], *v.t. irr.* (*conjug. like* SENTIR) to have a presentiment of; to sound.
presse-papiers [prɛspa′pje], *n.m. inv.* paperweight.
presse-purée [prɛspy′re], *n.m. inv.* potato masher.
presser [prɛ′se], *v.t.* to press, to squeeze; to tread down; to crowd; to hasten; to entreat, to urge.—*v.i.* to be urgent. **se presser**, *v.r.* to press, to squeeze, to crowd; to make haste, to hurry.
pression [prɛ′sjɔ̃], *n.f.* pressure.
pressoir [prɛ′swaːr], *n.m.* press (*wine etc.*).
pressurer [prɛsy′re], *v.t.* to press (*grapes, apples etc.*); (*fig.*) to squeeze money etc. out of; to oppress.
pressureur [prɛsy′rœːr], *n.m.* (*fem.* **-euse**) presser (*of fruit etc.*); (*fig.*) squeezer, sponger; oppressor.
prestance [prɛs′tɑ̃ːs], *n.f.* commanding appearance, fine presence.
prestation [prɛsta′sjɔ̃], *n.f.* taking (*of an oath*); prestation (*payment of toll etc.*).
preste [prɛst], *a.* agile, nimble; smart.
prestement [prɛstə′mɑ̃], *adv.* nimbly, quickly.
prestesse [prɛs′tɛs], *n.f.* agility, quickness.
prestidigitateur [prɛstidiʒita′tœːr], *n.m.* conjurer, juggler.
prestidigitation [prɛstidiʒita′sjɔ̃], *n.f.* conjuring, sleight of hand.
prestige [prɛs′tiːʒ], *n.m.* marvel; illusion; magic spell; prestige.
prestigieux [prɛsti′ʒjø], *a.* (*fem.* **-euse**) marvellous, amazing.
(*C*) **presto** [prɛs′to], *n.m.* pressure cooker.
présumer [prezy′me], *v.t.* to presume, to suppose.
présure [pre′zyːr], *n.f.* rennet.
prêt (1) [prɛ], *a.* ready, prepared.
prêt (2) [prɛ], *n.m.* loan; (*Mil.*) pay.
prétantaine [pretɑ̃′tɛn], *n.f.* **courir la prétantaine**, to gad about.
prêté [prɛ′te], *a.* lent.
prétendant [pretɑ̃′dɑ̃], *n.m.* (*fem.* **-e**) claimant.—*n.m.* suitor; pretender (*to the throne*).
prétendre [pre′tɑ̃ːdr], *v.t.* to claim, to lay claim to; to mean; affirm.—*v.i.* to lay claim (*to*); to aspire (*à*).
prétendu [pretɑ̃′dy], *a.* pretended, supposed, sham, so-called, would-be.—*n.m.* (*fem.* **-e**) future husband *or* wife.
prétentieux [pretɑ̃′sjø], *a.* (*fem.* **-euse**) pretentious, assuming.
prétention [pretɑ̃′sjɔ̃], *n.f.* pretension, claim; intention, wish; expectation.

prêter [prɛ′te], *v.t.* to lend; to impart; to attribute; to bestow.—*v.i.* to give, to stretch; to invite, to give rise to. **se prêter**, *v.r.* to give way; to lend oneself *or* itself; to countenance, to favor.
prêteur [prɛ′tœːr], *n.m.* (*fem.* **-euse**) lender.
prétexte [pre′tɛkst], *n.m.* pretext, pretence; plea.
prétexter [pretɛks′te], *v.t.* to allege (*as pretext*), to pretend, to feign.
prétoire [pre′twaːr], *n.m.* (*Rom. Ant.*) praetorium.
prétorien [preto′rjɛ̃], *a.* (*fem.* **-enne**) praetorian.
prêtre [prɛtr], *n.m.* priest.
prêtresse [prɛ′trɛs], *n.f.* priestess.
prêtrise [prɛ′triːz], *n.f.* priesthood.
preuve [prœːv], *n.f.* proof; evidence, testimony.
preux [prø], *a. inv.* gallant, doughty, valiant.—*n.m.* valiant knight.
prévaloir [preva′lwaːr], *v.i. irr.* (*conjug. like* VALOIR) to prevail. **se prévaloir**, *v.r.* to take advantage, to avail oneself; to boast.
prévaricateur [prevarika′tœːr], *a.* (*fem.* **-trice**) dishonest, unjust.—*n.m.* (*fem.* **-trice**) betrayer of trust.
prévarication [prevarika′sjɔ̃], *n.f.* betrayal of trust, maladministration of justice.
prévariquer [prevari′ke], *v.i.* to betray one's trust.
prévenance [prev′nɑ̃ːs], *n.f.* (*pl.*) kind attentions.
prévenant [prev′nɑ̃], *a.* obliging, kind; prepossessing, engaging.
prévenir [prev′niːr], *v.t. irr.* (*conjug. like* TENIR) to precede; to forestall; to prevent; to prepossess, to predispose; to warn. **se prévenir**, *v.r.* to be prejudiced.
préventif [prevɑ̃′tif], *a.* (*fem.* **-tive**) preventive.
prévention [prevɑ̃′sjɔ̃], *n.f.* prepossession, prejudice; suspicion; accusation.
préventivement [prevɑ̃tiv′mɑ̃], *adv.* by way of prevention; while awaiting trial.
prévenu [prev′ny], *a.* forestalled, anticipated; prejudiced; accused.—*n.m.* (*fem.* **-e**) the accused.
prévisible [previ′zibl], *a.* foreseeable.
prévision [previ′zjɔ̃], *n.f.* forecast; estimate, expectation.
prévoir [pre′vwaːr], *v.t. irr.* to foresee, to anticipate.
prévôt [pre′vo], *n.m.* provost.
prévôté [prevo′te], *n.f.* provostship; military police.
prévoyance [prevwa′jɑ̃ːs], *n.f.* foresight, forethought, prudence.
prévoyant [prevwa′jɑ̃], *a.* provident, prudent, careful.
prié [pri′je], *a.* invited (*to a feast etc.*).
prie-Dieu [pri′djø], *n.m. inv.* praying-stool.
prier [pri′je], *v.t.* to pray, to beseech; to request; to invite.
prière [pri′jɛːr], *n.f.* prayer; request, entreaty; invitation.
prieur [pri′jœːr], *n.m.* prior (*superior of a convent*).
prieure [pri′jœːr], *n.f.* prioress.
prieuré [prijœ′re], *n.m.* priory.
primaire [pri′mɛːr], *a.* primary.

primat [pri′ma], *n.m.* primate, metropolitan.
primauté [primo′te], *n.f.* primacy, priority, pre-eminence; the lead (*at cards, dice etc.*).
prime [prim], *a.* first.—*n.f.* premium; subsidy; (*Mil.*) bounty; bonus, prize; (*Fenc.*) prime; (*Comm.*) free gift; *certificat de primes*, debenture; *faire prime*, to be at a premium.
primer [pri′me], *v.t.* to surpass, to excel.— *v.i.* to play first, to lead (*at games*); to excel.
primeur [pri′mœːr], *n.f.* early vegetables, fruit, flowers, etc.; early sentiment, love etc.; freshness, bloom.
primevère [prim′vɛːr], *n.f.* (*Bot.*) primula, primrose, cowslip.
primitif [primi′tif], *a.* (*fem.* **-tive**) first, early, primitive, aboriginal; pristine.—*n.m.* (*Gram., Paint.*) primitive.
primitivement [primitiv′mɑ̃], *adv.* primitively, originally.
primo [pri′mo], *adv.* first, in the first place.
primordial [primɔr′djal], *a.* (*m. pl.* **-aux**) primordial.
prince [prɛ̃ːs], *n.m.* prince.
princeps [prɛ̃′sɛps], *a. inv. édition princeps*, first edition.
princesse [prɛ̃′sɛs], *n.f.* princess.
princier [prɛ̃′sje], *a.* (*fem.* **-ière**) princely, like a prince.
principal [prɛ̃si′pal], *a.* (*m. pl.* **-aux**) principal, chief, most important.—*n.m.* chief thing, principal point; principal, capital (*money*); headmaster (*of a collège*); (*pl.*) chief personages (*of a town etc.*).
principalement [prɛ̃sipal′mɑ̃], *adv.* principally, chiefly.
principauté [prɛ̃sipo′te], *n.f.* principality, princedom.
principe [prɛ̃′sip], *n.m.* beginning, source, basis; principle; (*pl.*) principles, rudiments; *dès le principe*, from the very first; *en principe*, as a rule.
printanier [prɛ̃ta′nje], *a.* (*fem.* **-ière**) springlike, vernal; (*fig.*) youthful, early.
printemps [prɛ̃′tɑ̃], *n.m.* spring, spring-time; (*fig.*) prime, bloom.
priorité [priɔri′te], *n.f.* priority.
pris [pri], *a.* taken, caught, seized; frozen.
prisable [pri′zabl], *a.* estimable, worthy of esteem.
prise [priːz], *n.f.* taking, capture; prize; hold, purchase; grip; quarrel; dose; pinch (*of snuff etc.*); (*pl.*) fighting.
priser (1) [pri′ze], *v.t., v.i.* to (take) snuff.
priser (2) [pri′ze], *v.t.* to appraise, to estimate; to esteem.
priseur [pri′zœːr], *n.m.* *commissaire priseur*, auctioneer, valuer.
prismatique [prisma′tik], *a.* prismatic.
prisme [prism], *n.m.* prism.
prison [pri′zɔ̃], *n.f.* prison, jail; imprisonment.
prisonnier [prizo′nje], *n.m.* (*fem.* **-ière**) prisoner.
privation [priva′sjɔ̃], *n.f.* privation; want, need.
privauté [privo′te], *n.f.* extreme familiarity *or* liberty.
privé [pri′ve], *a.* and *n.m.* (*fem.* **-ée**) private; familiar, intimate; tame (*of animals*).

priver [pri′ve], *v.t.* to deprive, to bereave; to tame (*animals etc.*). **se priver**, *v.r.* to deprive *or* stint oneself; to abstain (*de*).
privilège [privi′lɛːʒ], *n.m.* privilege; license; prerogative, grant.
privilégié [privile′ʒje], *a.* privileged; licensed; entitled to preference (*of creditors*); preference (*of shares*).—*n.m.* (*fem.* **-ée**) privileged person.
privilégier [privile′ʒje], *v.t.* to privilege; to license.
prix [pri], *n.m. inv.* price, cost, value; rate, return; reward, prize; stakes (*race for prize*); *à prix d'argent*, for money; *à vil prix*, dirt cheap; *prix coûtant*, cost price; *prix de gros*, wholesale price; *remporter le prix*, to carry off the prize.
probabilité [prɔbabili′te], *n.f.* probability, likelihood.
probable [prɔ′babl], *a.* probable, likely, credible.
probablement [prɔbablə′mɑ̃], *adv.* probably.
probant [prɔ′bɑ̃], *a.* convincing, conclusive.
probation [prɔba′sjɔ̃], *n.f.* (*Eccles.*) probation.
probe [prɔb], *a.* honest, upright.
probité [prɔbi′te], *n.f.* probity, honesty, integrity.
problématique [prɔblema′tik], *a.* problematical; questionable, doubtful.
problématiquement [prɔblematik′mɑ̃], *adv.* problematically.
problème [prɔ′blɛm], *n.m.* problem.
procédé [prɔse′de], *n.m.* behavior, proceeding, conduct; process, operation; (*Billiards*) cue tip.
procéder [prɔse′de], *v.i.* (*conjug. like* CÉDER) to proceed, to arise, to originate (*de*); to behave.
procédure [prɔse′dyːr], *n.f.* procedure; proceedings.
procès [prɔ′sɛ], *n.m.* lawsuit, action, trial; (*Anat.*) process.
procession [prɔse′sjɔ̃], *n.f.* procession.
processionnel [prɔsesjɔ′nɛl], *a.* (*fem.* **-elle**) processional.
procès-verbal [prɔsɛvɛr′bal], *n.m.* (*pl.* **-verbaux**) official report; minute of proceedings; police report.
prochain [prɔ′ʃɛ̃], *a.* near, nearest, next.— *n.m.* neighbor, fellow creature.
prochainement [prɔʃɛn′mɑ̃], *adv.* shortly, soon.
proche [prɔʃ], *a.* near, neighboring; nigh, approaching.—*prep.* and *adv.* near, nigh; *de proche en proche*, gradually.—*n.m.* (*usu. in pl.*) near relation, kin, kindred.
proclamation [prɔklama′sjɔ̃], *n.f.* proclamation.
proclamer [prɔkla′me], *v.t.* to proclaim, to announce, to publish); to disclose.
proclivité [prɔklivi′te], *n.f.* proclivity, slope.
procréateur [prɔkrea′tœːr], *a.* (*fem.* **-trice**) procreative.—*n.m.* (*fem.* **-trice**) procreator.
procréation [prɔkrea′sjɔ̃], *n.f.* procreation.
procréer [prɔkre′e], *v.t.* to procreate, to beget.
procurateur [prɔkyra′tœːr], *n.m.* (*Hist.*) procurator.
procuration [prɔkyra′sjɔ̃], *n.f.* procuration, power of attorney, proxy (*deed*).

procurer [prɔky're], *v.t.* to procure, to obtain. **se procurer**, *v.r.* to procure, to get for oneself.

procureur [prɔky'rœːr], *n.m.* (*fem.* **procuratrice**) attorney, procurator, proxy.

prodigalement [prɔdigal'mã], *adv.* prodigally, extravagantly.

prodigalité [prɔdigali'te], *n.f.* prodigality, lavishness.

prodige [prɔ'diːʒ], *n.m.* prodigy, marvel.

prodigieusement [prɔdiʒjøz'mã], *adv.* prodigiously.

prodigieux [prɔdi'ʒjø], *a.* (*fem.* **-euse**) prodigious, wonderful; stupendous.

prodigue [prɔ'dig], *a.* prodigal, lavish; wasteful.—*n.* prodigal, spendthrift.

prodiguer [prɔdi'ge], *v.t.* to be prodigal of; to waste, to squander. **se prodiguer**, *v.r.* to make oneself cheap; not to spare oneself.

prodrome [prɔ'droːm], *n.m.* introduction, preface, preamble.

producteur [prɔdyk'tœːr], *a.* (*fem.* **-trice**) productive.—*n.m.* (*fem.* **-trice**) producer.

productif [prɔdyk'tif], *a.* (*fem.* **-tive**) productive.

production [prɔdyk'sjõ], *n.f.* production; produce, product (*of nature*); yield, output.

productivité [prɔdyktivi'te], *n.f.* productivity; productiveness.

produire [prɔ'dɥiːr], *v.t. irr.* (*conjug. like* CONDUIRE) to produce; to bear; to exhibit; to introduce. **se produire**, *v.r.* to put oneself forward; to occur, to happen.

produit [prɔ'dɥi], *n.m.* produce, product, production; proceeds.

proéminence [prɔemi'nãːs], *n.f.* prominence; protuberance.

proéminent [prɔemi'nã], *a.* prominent, protuberant.

profanateur [prɔfana'tœːr], *n.m.* (*fem.* **-trice**) profaner.

profanation [prɔfana'sjõ], *n.f.* profanation.

profane [prɔ'fan], *a.* profane; secular.—*n.* profane person; outsider; layman.

profaner [prɔfa'ne], *v.t.* to profane, to desecrate; to defile.

proférer [prɔfe're], *v.t.* (*conjug. like* CÉDER) to utter, to pronounce.

professer [prɔfɛ'se], *v.t.* to profess; to exercise, to practice; to teach, to lecture on. —*v.i.* to lecture, to teach.

professeur [prɔfɛ'sœːr], *n.m.* (*fem.* **femme professeur**) professor, lecturer (*at university*); teacher in secondary schools.

profession [prɔfɛ'sjõ], *n.f.* profession, declaration; calling, business.

professionnel [prɔfɛsjɔ'nɛl], *a.* and *n.m.* (*fem.* **-elle**) (*Spt. etc.*) professional.

professoral [prɔfɛsɔ'ral], *a.* (*m. pl.* **-aux**) professorial.

professorat [prɔfɛsɔ'ra], *n.m.* professorship, lectureship; mastership (*of* **lycée** or **collège**).

profil [prɔ'fil], *n.m.* profile, side view; outline; (*Drawing*) section.

profiler [prɔfi'le], *v.t.* to represent *or* show in profile. **se profiler**, *v.r.* to appear in profile, to be outlined.

profit [prɔ'fi], *n.m.* profit, gain; benefit, utility, use; (*pl.*) perquisites.

profitable [prɔfi'tabl], *a.* profitable, advantageous.

profiter [prɔfi'te], *v.i.* to profit, to gain, to benefit; to take advantage of (*de*).

profiteur [prɔfi'tœːr], *n.m.* (*fem.* **-euse**) (*pej.*) profiteer.

profond [prɔ'fõ], *a.* deep; profound; vast; sound (*of sleep etc.*); downright; dark (*of night etc.*).—*n.m.* depth, abyss.

profondément [prɔfõde'mã], *adv.* deeply, profoundly, greatly; soundly.

profondeur [prɔfõ'dœːr], *n.f.* depth; profundity; penetration; extent.

profus [prɔ'fy], *a.* profuse.

profusément [prɔfyze'mã], *adv.* profusely.

profusion [prɔfy'zjõ], *n.f.* profusion.

progéniture [prɔʒeni'tyːr], *n.f.* progeny.

prognostique [prɔgnɔs'tik], *a.* (*Med.*) prognostic.

programmation [prɔgrama'sjõ], *n.f.* programming.

programme [prɔ'gram], *n.m.* (*Theat. etc.*) program; (*sch.*) curriculum, syllabus.

progrès [prɔ'grɛ], *n.m.* progress; advancement, improvement, development.

progresser [prɔgrɛ'se], *v.i.* to progress, to get on.

progressif [prɔgrɛ'sif], *a.* (*fem.* **-ive**) progressive.

progression [prɔgrɛ'sjõ], *n.f.* progression.

progressiste [prɔgrɛ'sist], *a.* progressive.— *n.* progressist, progressive.

progressivement [prɔgrɛsiv'mã], *adv.* progressively.

prohiber [prɔi'be], *v.t.* to forbid, to prohibit.

prohibitif [prɔibi'tif], *a.* (*fem.* **-tive**) prohibitive, exorbitant.

prohibition [prɔibi'sjõ], *n.f.* prohibition.

proie [prwa], *n.f.* prey, prize, booty.

projecteur [prɔʒɛk'tœːr], *n.m.* searchlight; projector; floodlight.

projectile [prɔʒɛk'til], *a.* and *n.m.* projectile, missile.

projection [prɔʒɛk'sjõ], *n.f.* projection; (*Cine.*) **appareil de projection**, projector.

projectionniste [prɔʒɛksjɔ'nist], *n.* (*Cine.*) projectionist.

projet [prɔ'ʒɛ], *n.m.* project, plan, idea; rough draft; **homme à projets**, schemer.

projeter [prɔʒ'te], *v.t.* (*conjug. like* APPELER) to project, to throw; to delineate, to plan, to design; to contemplate, to intend.—*v.i.* to scheme, to form projects. **se projeter**, *v.r.* to project, to stand out.

prolétaire [prɔle'tɛːr], *a.* and *n.m.* proletarian.

prolétariat [prɔleta'rja], *n.m.* proletariat.

prolifique [prɔli'fik], *a.* prolific.

prolixe [prɔ'liks], *a.* verbose.

prologue [prɔ'log], *n.m.* prologue.

prolongation [prɔlõga'sjõ], *n.f.* prolongation; extension.

prolongement [prɔlõʒ'mã], *n.m.* prolongation, extension.

prolonger [prɔlõ'ʒe], *v.t.* (*conjug. like* MANGER) to prolong, to lengthen, to protract; to draw out. **se prolonger**, *v.r.* to be protracted; to extend; to continue.

promenade [prɔm'nad], *n.f.* walk; walking; promenade; drive, excursion, pleasure trip.

promener [prɔm'ne], *v.t.* to take out for a walk, for a drive, for a ride, for an airing; to cast (*one's eyes*) over; to run or pass (*one's hand, fingers*) over. **se promener**, *v.r.* to

walk, to go for a walk, ramble, drive, row, sail etc.; to stroll.
promeneur [prɔm'nœ:r], *n.m.* (*fem.* **-euse**) walker; rider; person taking a drive.
promenoir [prɔm'nwa:r], *n.m.* covered walk; promenade (*in a concert hall etc.*).
promesse [prɔ'mɛs], *n.f.* promise; promissory note.
promettre [prɔ'mɛtr], *v.t. irr.* (*conjug. like* METTRE) to promise; to forebode.—*v.i.* to be promising. **se promettre**, *v.r.* to promise oneself; to purpose; to promise each other.
promis [prɔ'mi], *a.* promised; intended, engaged.—*n.m.* (*fem.* **-e**) fiancé *or* fiancée.
promiscuité [prɔmiskɥi'te], *n.f.* promiscuity.
promontoire [prɔmɔ̃'twa:r], *n.m.* promontory, headland.
promoteur [prɔmɔ'tœ:r], *n.m.* (*fem.* **-trice**) promoter.
promotion [prɔmo'sjɔ̃], *n.f.* promotion, preferment.
promouvoir [prɔmu'vwa:r], *v.t. irr.* (*conjug. like* MOUVOIR) to promote, to advance.
prompt [prɔ̃], *a.* prompt, quick, active; sudden, swift; hasty.
promptement [prɔ̃t'mã], *adv.* promptly.
promptitude [prɔ̃ti'ty:d], *n.f.* promptitude, promptness; suddenness; hastiness.
promulgation [prɔmylga'sjɔ̃], *n.f.* promulgation.
promulguer [prɔmyl'ge], *v.t.* to promulgate.
prône [pro:n], *n.m.* sermon (*at Mass*); (*fig.*) lecture, rebuke.
prôner [pro'ne], *v.t.* to lecture, to sermonize; to extol.—*v.i.* to sermonize.
prôneur [pro'nœ:r], *n.m.* (*fem.* **-euse**) long-winded preacher.
pronom [prɔ'nɔ̃], *n.m.* (*Gram.*) pronoun.
prononçable [prɔnɔ̃'sabl], *a.* pronounceable.
prononcé [prɔnɔ̃'se], *a.* pronounced, decided, marked; (*Paint. etc.*) prominent; broad (*of speech*).—*n.m.* judgment delivered, sentence.
prononcer [prɔnɔ̃'se], *v.t.* (*conjug. like* COMMENCER) to pronounce, to utter, to say, to declare; to pass (*a verdict etc.*).—*v.i.* to declare one's sentiments, to decide with authority. **se prononcer**, *v.r.* to declare oneself, to express one's opinion, to give a verdict; to be pronounced.
prononciation [prɔnɔ̃sja'sjɔ̃], *n.f.* pronunciation; utterance.
pronostic [prɔnɔs'tik], *n.m.* prognostic; prognostication; (*Med.*) prognosis; weather forecast; (*racing*) tip.
propagande [prɔpa'gã:d], *n.f.* propaganda.
propagandiste [prɔpagã'dist], *n.* propagandist.
propagateur [prɔpaga'tœ:r], *a.* (*fem.* **-trice**) propagating, spreading.—*n.m.* (*fem.* **-trice**) propagator.
propagation [prɔpaga'sjɔ̃], *n.f.* propagation, spreading, diffusion.
propager [prɔpa'ʒe], *v.t.* (*conjug. like* MANGER) to propagate, to spread abroad, to diffuse. **se propager**, *v.r.* to be propagated, to spread.
propension [prɔpã'sjɔ̃], *n.f.* propensity, tendency.
prophète [prɔ'fɛ:t], *n.m.* prophet, seer.
prophétesse [prɔfe'tɛs], *n.f.* prophetess.

prophétie [prɔfe'si], *n.f.* prophecy, prophesying.
prophétique [prɔfe'tik], *a.* prophetic.
prophétiser [prɔfeti'ze], *v.t.* to prophesy, to foretell.
propice [prɔ'pis], *a.* propitious, favorable.
propitiation [prɔpisja'sjɔ̃], *n.f.* propitiation.
propitiatoire [prɔpisja'twa:r], *a.* propitiatory.
proportion [prɔpɔr'sjɔ̃], *n.f.* proportion, ratio.
proportionné [prɔpɔrsjɔ'ne], *a.* proportioned, suited.
proportionnel [prɔpɔrsjɔ'nɛl], *a.* (*fem.* **-elle**) proportional.
proportionner [prɔpɔrsjɔ'ne], *v.t.* to proportion, to adjust, to adapt.
propos [prɔ'po], *n.m.* talk, words; remark; purpose, resolution; (*pl.*) idle remarks, tittle-tattle; **à propos**, apt, to the purpose; by the way; **à propos de**, with respect to; **à quel propos?** what about? **de propos délibéré**, of set purpose; **mal à propos**, ill-timed; **propos de table**, table-talk; **venir fort à propos**, to come in the nick of time.
proposer [prɔpo'ze], *v.t.* to propose; to propound, to move; to designate, to set up.—*v.i.* to propose. **se proposer**, *v.r.* to propose oneself; to intend, to have in view.
proposeur [prɔpo'zœ:r], *n.m.* (*fem.* **-euse**) proposer, propounder.
proposition [prɔpozi'sjɔ̃], *n.f.* proposal, proposition; motion; (*Gram.*) clause.
propre [prɔpr], *a.* own; very, same, selfsame; proper; appropriate, suitable; good, right, correct; clean, neat, tidy; **le mot propre**, the right word; **peu propre**, inappropriate; dirty.—*n.m.* characteristic, property; proper sense; (*Law*) real property.
propre à rien [prɔpra'rjɛ̃], *n. inv.* good for nothing.
proprement [prɔprə'mã], *adv.* properly, correctly; cleanly, neatly.
propret [prɔ'prɛ], *a.* (*fem.* **-ette**) spruce, neat, tidy.
propreté [prɔprə'te], *n.f.* cleanliness; neatness.
propriétaire [prɔprie'tɛ:r], *n.* owner, proprietor, proprietress; landlord, householder.
propriété [prɔprie'te], *n.f.* property; estate; characteristic; **propriété littéraire**, copyright.
propulser [prɔpyl'se], *v.t.* (*Naut., Av.*) to propel.
propulseur [prɔpyl'sœ:r], *n.m.* propeller.
propulsif [prɔpyl'sif], *a.* (*fem.* **-sive**) propelling, propellent.
propulsion [prɔpyl'sjɔ̃], *n.f.* propulsion.
prorogation [prɔrɔga'sjɔ̃], *n.f.* adjournment, prorogation (*of Parliament etc.*); extension.
proroger [prɔrɔ'ʒe], *v.t.* (*conjug. like* MANGER) to prolong the time of; to prorogue (*Parliament etc.*).
prosaïque [prɔza'ik], *a.* prosaic; banal; prosy.
prosaïquement [prɔzaik'mã], *adv.* prosaically.
prosateur [prɔza'tœ:r], *n.m.* prose writer.
proscription [prɔskrip'sjɔ̃], *n.f.* proscription.
proscrire [prɔs'kri:r], *v.t. irr.* (*conjug. like* ÉCRIRE) to proscribe, to outlaw; to banish.

proscrit

proscrit [prɔs'kri], *a.* proscribed, forbidden. —*n.m.* (*fem.* **-e**) proscribed person, outlaw; exile.

prose [proːz], *n.f.* prose.

prosodie [prɔzɔ'di], *n.f.* prosody.

prospecter [prɔspɛk'te], *v.t.* to prospect (*for oil, minerals*).

prospecteur [prɔspɛk'tœːr], *n.m.* prospector.

prospectus [prɔspɛk'tyːs], *n.m. inv.* prospectus; handbill.

prospère [prɔs'pɛːr], *a.* prosperous, thriving.

prospérer [prɔspe're], *v.i.* (*conjug. like* CÉDER) to prosper, to be prosperous, to thrive.

prospérité [prɔsperi'te], *n.f.* prosperity.

prostate [prɔs'tat], *n.f.* (*Anat.*) prostate.

prosternation [prɔstɛrna'sjɔ̃], *n.f.*, **prosternement** [prɔstɛrnə'mã], *n.m.* prostration, obeisance.

prosterner [prɔstɛr'ne], *v.t.* to prostrate. **se prosterner**, *v.r.* to prostrate oneself, to bow low.

prostituée [prɔsti'tɥe], *n.f.* prostitute.

prostituer [prɔsti'tɥe], *v.t.* to prostitute. **se prostituer**, *v.r.* to prostitute oneself.

prostitution [prɔstity'sjɔ̃], *n.f.* prostitution.

prostration [prɔstra'sjɔ̃], *n.f.* prostration.

protagoniste [prɔtagɔ'nist], *n.m.* protagonist.

protecteur [prɔtɛk'tœːr], *a.* (*fem.* **-trice**) protective; patronizing.—*n.m.* (*fem.* **-trice**) protector, protectress; patron, patroness.—*n.m.* (*Eng.*) guard (*for machine tool*).

protection [prɔtɛk'sjɔ̃], *n.f.* protection, shelter; support, patronage.

protectorat [prɔtɛktɔ'ra], *n.m.* protectorate.

protégé [prɔte'ʒe], *n.m.* (*fem.* **-ée**) favorite, dependant.

protéger [prɔte'ʒe], *v.t.* (*conjug. like* ASSIÉGER) to protect, to defend; to patronize, to favor.

protège-vue [prɔtɛʒ'vy], *n.m. inv.* eye-shade.

protéine [prɔte'in], *n.f.* protein.

protestant [prɔtɛs'tã], *a. and n.m.* (*fem.* **-e**) Protestant.

protestantisme [prɔtɛstã'tism], *n.m.* Protestantism.

protestation [prɔtɛsta'sjɔ̃], *n.f.* protestation, protest.

protester [prɔtɛs'te], *v.t.* to protest, to affirm.—*v.i.* to protest.

protocole [prɔtɔ'kɔl], *n.m.* protocol.

proton [prɔ'tɔ̃], *n.m.* proton.

protoplasma [prɔtɔplas'ma], **protoplasme** [prɔtɔ'plasm], *n.m.* protoplasm.

prototype [prɔtɔ'tip], *n.m.* prototype.

protubérance [prɔtybe'rãːs], *n.f.* protuberance.

protubérant [prɔtybe'rã], *a.* protuberant.

proue [pru], *n.f.* prow, stem, bows (*of ship*).

prouesse [pru'ɛs], *n.f.* prowess, valor; feat.

prouver [pru've], *v.t.* to prove; to substantiate; to show.

provenance [prɔv'nãːs], *n.f.* origin, source; (*pl.*) produce, commodities.

provençal [prɔvã'sal], *a.* (*m. pl.* **-aux**) Provençal.—*n.m.* Provençal (*language*). (**Provençal**, *fem.* **-ale**) Provençal (*person*).

provenir [prɔv'niːr], *v.i. irr.* (*conjug. like* TENIR *but with aux.* ÊTRE) to issue, proceed, spring, originate *or* come from (*de*).

proverbe [prɔ'vɛrb], *n.m.* proverb, saying.

proverbial [prɔvɛr'bjal], *a.* (*m. pl.* **-aux**) proverbial.

providence [prɔvi'dãːs], *n.f.* providence.

providentiel [prɔvidã'sjɛl], *a.* (*fem.* **-elle**) providential.

provigner [prɔvi'ɲe], *v.t.* to layer (*vines*).

provin [prɔ'vɛ̃], *n.m.* layer (*of a vine*).

province [prɔ'vɛ̃ːs], *n.f.* province, shire; country; **en province**, in the country, in the provinces.

provincial [prɔvɛ̃'sjal], *a.* (*m. pl.* **-aux**) provincial; countrified.—*n.m.* (*fem.* **-e**) provincial, country person.

proviseur [prɔvi'zœːr], *n.m.* headmaster (*of a lycée*).

provision [prɔvi'zjɔ̃], *n.f.* provision, stock, store, supply; deposit; (*Comm.*) reserve funds.

provisionnel [prɔvizjɔ'nɛl], *a.* (*fem.* **-elle**) provisional.

provisoire [prɔvi'zwaːr], *a.* provisional, temporary.—*n.m.* provisional nature (*of something*).

provisoirement [prɔvizwar'mã], *adv.* provisionally, temporarily.

provocant [prɔvɔ'kã], *a.* provoking, provocative; exciting.

provocateur [prɔvɔka'tœːr], *a.* (*fem.* **-trice**) provoking, provocative; **agent provocateur**, agent hired to instigate a riot etc.—*n.m.* (*fem.* **-trice**) provoker; aggressor.

provocation [prɔvɔka'sjɔ̃], *n.f.* provocation.

provoquer [prɔvɔ'ke], *v.t.* to provoke, to incite, to call forth; to instigate.

proximité [prɔksimi'te], *n.f.* proximity, nearness.

prude [pryd], *a.* prudish.—*n.f.* prude.

prudemment [pryda'mã], *adv.* prudently, discreetly, cautiously.

prudence [pry'dãːs], *n.f.* carefulness, prudence.

prudent [pry'dã], *a.* prudent, discreet; advisable.

pruderie [pry'dri], *n.f.* prudery, prudishness.

prud'homme [pry'dɔm], *n.m.* upright, honest man; (*Ind.*) arbitrator.

pruine [prɥin], *n.f.* bloom (*on fruits*).

prune [pryn], *n.f.* plum.

pruneau [pry'no], *n.m.* (*pl.* **-eaux**) prune.

prunelle (1) [pry'nɛl], *n.f.* sloe; sloe gin.

prunelle (2) [pry'nɛl], *n.f.* pupil, apple (*of the eye*), eyeball.

prunellier [prynɛ'lje], *n.m.* sloe tree, blackthorn.

prunier [pry'nje], *n.m.* plum tree.

Prusse [prys], *la, f.* Prussia.

prussien [pry'sjɛ̃], *a.* (*fem.* **-enne**) Prussian. —*n.m.* (**Prussien**, *fem.* **-enne**) Prussian (*person*).

prussique [pry'sik], *a.* (*Chem.*) prussic.

psalmiste [psal'mist], *n.m.* psalmist.

psalmodie [psalmɔ'di], *n.f.* psalmody, intoning; (*fig.*) sing-song.

psalmodier [psalmɔ'dje], *v.t., v.i.* to recite, to chant (*as the psalms*); to read *or* recite in a sing-song manner.

psaume [psoːm], *n.m.* psalm.

psautier [pso'tje], *n.m.* psalter, psalm book.

pseudonyme [psødɔ'nim], *a.* pseudonymous. —*n.m.* pseudonym, nom-de-plume.

psychanalyse [psikana'liːz], *n.f.* psychoanalysis.

psychanalyste [psikana'list], *n.m.* psycho-analyst.
psychiatre [psi'kja:tr], *n.m.* psychiatrist.
psychiatrie [psikja'tri], *n.f.* psychiatry.
psychologie [psikɔlɔ'ʒi], *n.f.* psychology.
psychologique [psikɔlɔ'ʒik], *a.* psychological.
psychologue [psikɔ'lɔg], *n.* psychologist.
puant [pɥɑ̃], *a.* stinking; foul.
puanteur [pɥɑ̃'tœ:r], *n.f.* stench, stink.
pubère [py'bɛ:r], *a.* pubescent, puberal.
puberté [pybɛr'te], *n.f.* puberty.
public [py'blik], *a.* (*fem.* **-ique**) public; notorious; *la chose publique*, the common weal, the State.—*n.m.* public.
publication [pyblika'sjɔ̃], *n.f.* publication; publishing, proclamation.
publiciste [pybli'sist], *n.m.* publicist, journalist.
publicité [pyblisi'te], *n.f.* publicity; advertising.
publier [py'blje], *v.t.* to publish, to make public, to proclaim; to issue.
publiquement [pyblik'mã], *adv.* in public.
puce (1) [pys], *a. inv.* puce, puce-colored.
puce (2) [pys], *n.f.* flea.
puceron [pys'rɔ̃], *n.m.* plant louse, greenfly.
pudeur [py'dœ:r], *n.f.* modesty; bashfulness, shame; reserve.
pudibond [pydi'bɔ̃], *a.* bashful; prudish.
pudicité [pydisi'te], *n.f.* modesty, chastity.
pudique [py'dik], *a.* chaste, modest, bashful.
pudiquement [pydik'mã], *adv.* modestly.
puer [pɥe], *v.t.* (*fam.*) to smell of, to reek of.—*v.i.* to stink.
puéril [pɥe'ril], *a.* juvenile, childish, puerile.
puérilement [pɥeril'mã], *adv.* childishly.
puérilité [pɥerili'te], *n.f.* puerility, childishness.
pugilat [pyʒi'la], *n.m.* pugilism, boxing.
pugiliste [pyʒi'list], *n.m.* pugilist, boxer.
pugnace [pyg'nas], *a.* pugnacious.
pugnacité [pygnasi'te], *n.f.* pugnacity.
puîné [pɥi'ne], *a.* (*fem.* **-ée**) younger (*brother* or *sister*).
puis [pɥi], *adv.* then, afterwards, after that, next; besides.
puisage [pɥi'za:ʒ], **puisement** [pɥiz'mã], *n.m.* drawing up; drawing water.
puisard [pɥi'za:r], *n.m.* cesspool; sump, water-sump.
puisatier [pɥiza'tje], *n.m.* well-sinker; shaft-sinker (*in mining*).
puisement [PUISAGE].
puiser [pɥi'ze], *v.t.* to draw, to fetch up (*a liquid*); (*fig.*) to imbibe.
puisque [pɥisk], *conj.* since, as, seeing that.
puissamment [pɥisa'mã], *adv.* powerfully; extremely, very.
puissance [pɥi'sã:s], *n.f.* power; force; dominion, sway; influence.
puissant [pɥi'sã], *a.* powerful, mighty; lusty, stout; strong.
puits [pɥi], *n.m. inv.* well; pit, shaft.
pullulation [pylyla'sjɔ̃], *n.f.*, **pullulement** [pylyl'mã], *n.m.* pullulation, swarming.
pulluler [pyly'le], *v.i.* to multiply, to pullulate, to swarm.
pulmonaire [pylmɔ'nɛ:r], *a.* pulmonary; *phthisie pulmonaire*, consumption.
pulmonique [pylmɔ'nik], *a.* and *n.* consumptive.
pulpe [pylp], *n.f.* pulp.

pulper [pyl'pe], *v.t.* to pulp.
pulpeux [pyl'pø], *a.* (*fem.* **-euse**) pulpous, pulpy.
pulsatif [pylsa'tif], *a.* (*fem.* **-tive**) pulsatory, throbbing.
pulsation [pylsɑ'sjɔ̃], *n.f.* beating of the pulse, pulsation, throbbing.
pulvérin [pylve'rɛ̃], *n.m.* spray (*from waterfalls*).
pulvérisateur [pylveriza'tœ:r], *n.m.* pulverizator, vaporizer; spray, atomiser.
pulvérisation [pylveriza'sjɔ̃], *n.f.* pulverization.
pulvériser [pylveri'ze], *v.t.* to reduce to powder *or* dust, to pulverize; to atomize; (*fig.*) to annihilate.
pulvérulent [pylvery'lã], *a.* pulverulent, powdery.
puma [py'ma], *n.m.* puma, cougar.
pumicin [pymi'sɛ̃], *n.m.* palm oil.
punaise [py'nɛ:z], *n.f.* bug; thumbtack.
punch [pɔ̃:ʃ], *n.m.* (*Box.*) punch; punch (*beverage*).
punique [py'nik], *a.* Punic.
punir [py'ni:r], *v.t.* to punish, to chastise.
punissable [pyni'sabl], *a.* punishable.
punisseur [pyni'sœ:r], *a.* (*fem.* **-euse**) punishing, avenging.—*n.m.* (*fem.* **-euse**) punisher; avenger.
punitif [pyni'tif], *a.* (*fem.* **-tive**) punitive.
punition [pyni'sjɔ̃], *n.f.* punishment.
pupille [py'pil], *n.* ward, minor in charge of guardian.—*n.f.* pupil (*of the eye*).
pupitre [py'pitr], *n.m.* desk; music stand.
pur [py:r], *a.* pure, unalloyed; unadulterated; unblemished; innocent, chaste; mere, sheer; neat (*of liquor*); *en pure perte*, to no purpose.
purée [py're], *n.f.* mash, purée, thick soup.
purement [pyr'mã], *adv.* purely; merely.
pureté [pyr'te], *n.f.* purity, guilelessness, innocence; chastity.
purgatif [pyrga'tif], *a.* (*fem.* **-tive**) purgative, purging.—*n.m.* (*Med.*) purgative.
purgation [pyrgɑ'sjɔ̃], *n.f.* purgation, purge.
purgatoire [pyrga'twa:r], *n.m.* purgatory.
purge [pyrʒ], *n.f.* purge; cleansing; disinfection.
purger [pyr'ʒe], *v.t.* (*conjug. like* MANGER) to purge; to cleanse, to purify. **se purger,** *v.r.* to purge oneself; to clear oneself (*of*).
purificateur [pyrifika'tœ:r], *a.* (*fem.* **-trice**) purifying.—*n.m.* (*fem.* **-trice**) purifier.
purification [pyrifika'sjɔ̃], *n.f.* purification.
purifier [pyri'fje], *v.t.* to purify, to cleanse; to refine (*metals etc.*). **se purifier,** *v.r.* to purify oneself, to become refined.
puritain [pyri'tɛ̃], *a.* and *n.m.* (*fem.* **-e**) Puritan, puritan.
puritanisme [pyrita'nism], *n.m.* puritanism.
purpurin [pyrpy'rɛ̃], *a.* purplish.
pur-sang [pyr'sã], *n.m. inv.* thoroughbred.
pus [py], *n.m.* pus, matter.
pusillanime [pyzila'nim], *a.* pusillanimous, faint-hearted.
pusillanimité [pyzilanimi'te], *n.f.* pusillanimity.
pustule [pys'tyl], *n.f.* pustule, pimple, blotch.
putatif [pyta'tif], *a.* (*fem.* **-tive**) putative, reputed, supposed.
putativement [pytativ'mã], *adv.* reputedly.
putois [py'twa], *n.m.* polecat, skunk.

putréfaction [pytrefak'sjɔ̃], *n.f.* putrefaction; putrescence.

putréfier [pytre'fje], *v.t.* to putrefy; to rot. **se putréfier,** *v.r.* to putrefy; to rot; to decompose.

putride [py'trid], *a.* putrid.

pygmée [pig'me], *n.m.* pygmy.

pyjama [piʒa'ma], *n.m.* pajamas.

pylône [pi'loːn], *n.m.* pylon; mast.

pyorrhée [piɔ're], *n.f.* pyorrhœa.

pyramidal [pirami'dal], *a.* (*m. pl.* **-aux**) pyramidal.

pyramide [pira'mid], *n.f.* pyramid.

python [pi'tɔ̃], *n.m.* python (*snake*).

Q

Q, q [ky] *n.m.* the seventeenth letter of the alphabet.

qu' [k], *elision* [QUE].

quadragénaire [kwadraʒe'nɛːr], *a.* forty years of age.—*n.* person forty years old.

quadrangle [kwa'drɑ̃ːgl], *n.m.* quadrangle.

quadrangulaire [kwadrɑ̃gy'lɛːr], *a.* quadrangular, four-cornered.

quadrillage [kadri'jaːʒ], *n.m.* checker-work, pattern in squares; map grid.

quadrille [ka'driːj], *n.m.* quadrille (*card game*); quadrille (*dance*); check (*in tapestry*).

quadrillé [kadri'je], *a.* checkered (*of cloth*); ruled in squares (*of paper*).

quadriréacteur [kwadrireak'tœːr], *n.m.* four-engined jet plane.

quadrupède [kwadry'pɛd], *a.* and *n.m.* quadruped.

quadruple [kwa'drypl], *a.* quadruple, fourfold.

quadruplé [kwadry'ple], *n.m.* (*fem.* **-ée**) quadruplet, (*fam.*) quad.

quadrupler [kwadry'ple], *v.t., v.i.* to quadruple, to increase fourfold.

quai [ke], *n.m.* quay, wharf, pier; embankment (*along river*); platform (*railway*).

qualifiable [kali'fjabl], *a.* qualifiable, characterized (*as*).

qualification [kalifika'sjɔ̃], *n.f.* title; designation, qualification.

qualifié [kali'fje], *a.* qualified; named.

qualifier [kali'fje], *v.t.* to qualify; to style. **se qualifier,** *v.r.* to style oneself; to qualify (*for*).

qualité [kali'te], *n.f.* quality; property; excellence; talent; qualification; title; *en qualité de,* in the capacity of.

quand [kɑ̃], *adv.* when, whenever, what time; while.—*conj.* though; *quand même,* even though; all the same.

quant [kɑ̃], *adv.* (*followed by* **à**) as for, with regard to.

quant-à-soi [kɑ̃ta'swa], *n.m.* reserve, dignity.

quantième [kɑ̃'tjɛm], *n.m.* which (*day of the month etc.*).

quantité [kɑ̃ti'te], *n.f.* quantity; abundance, plenty; variety.

quarantaine [karɑ̃'tɛn], *n.f.* about forty; age of forty; quarantine.

quarante [ka'rɑ̃t], *a.* and *n.m.* forty.

quarantième [karɑ̃'tjɛm], *a.* and *n.* fortieth.

quart [kaːr], *a.* fourth.—*n.m.* quarter, fourth part; point (*of the compass*); quart (*measure*); (*Mil.*) tin cup; (*Naut.*) watch.

quarte [kart], *n.f.* (*Mus.*) fourth; (*Fenc., Piquet*) carte.

quartier [kar'tje], *n.m.* quarter, fourth part; piece, part; ward, district; gammon; (*Mil.*) quarters, barracks.

quartier-maître [kartje'mɛːtr], *n.m.* (*pl.* **quartiers-maîtres**) (*Naut.*) leading seaman.

quarto [kwar'to], *adv.* fourthly, in the fourth place.

quartz [kwaːrts], *n.m.* quartz.

quasi [ka'zi], *adv.* almost, as if, quasi.

quasiment [kazi'mɑ̃], *adv.* (*dial.*) almost, nearly, as you might say.

quaternaire [kwatɛr'nɛːr], *a.* quaternary.

quatorze [ka'tɔrz], *a.* and *n.m.* fourteen; fourteenth.

quatorzième [katɔr'zjɛm], *a.* and *n.* fourteenth.

quatrain [ka'trɛ̃], *n.m.* quatrain.

quatre [ˈkatrə, katr], *a.* and *n.m. inv.* four, fourth.

quatre-temps [katrə'tɑ̃], *n.m. pl.* Ember days.

quatre-vingtième [katrəvɛ̃'tjɛm], *a.* and *n.m.* eightieth.

quatre-vingt(s) [katrə'vɛ̃], *a.* and *n.m.* eighty.

quatrième [kat'rjɛm], *a.* and *n.* fourth.—*n.m.* fourth floor, fourth storey. —*n.f.* (*Piquet*) quart.

quatrièmement [katrjɛm'mɑ̃], *adv.* fourthly.

quatuor [kwaty'ɔr], *n.m.* (*Mus.*) quartet.

que (1) [kə, k], *pron. rel.* whom, that; which; what ? on which; *qu'est-ce que c'est?* what is it ?

que (2) [kə, k], *conj.* that; than; than that; as, if, whether; when; without; yet; lest; in order that; oh that, may; let; before; so; only, but; *afin que,* in order that; *attendez qu'il vienne,* wait till he comes; *de sorte que,* so that.—*adv.* how, how much, how many; why, wherefore ?

quel [kɛl], *a.* (*fem.* **quelle**) what, which, what sort of.

quelconque [kɛl'kɔ̃ːk], *a. indef.* any; any whatsoever; mediocre.

quelque [ˈkɛlkə, kɛlk], *adj.* some, any; a few; whatever, whatsoever.—*adv.* however, howsoever; some, about.

quelquefois [kɛlkə'fwa], *adv.* sometimes.

quelqu'un [kɛl'kœ̃], *pron. indef. m.* someone, somebody; anyone, anybody.—*n.m.* (*fem.* **quel-qu'une,** *pl.* **quelques-uns, quelques-unes,** one (or other), some.

quémander [kemɑ̃'de], *v.t., v.i.* to beg, to solicit.

quémandeur [kemɑ̃'dœːr], *n.m.* (*fem.* **-euse**) importunate beggar.

qu'en-dira-t-on [kɑ̃dira'tɔ̃], *n.m. inv.* public talk, tittle-tattle.

quenelle [kə'nɛl], *n.f.* forcemeat *or* fish ball.

quenotte [kə'nɔt], *n.f.* (*colloq.*) tooth (*of young children*).

quenouille [kə'nuːj], *n.f.* distaff; bed-post.

querelle [kə'rɛl], *n.f.* quarrel; row, brawl; feud; cause of dispute; *chercher querelle à*, to pick a quarrel with.

quereller [kərɛ'le], *v.t.* to quarrel with; to scold. **se quereller**, *v.r.* to quarrel, to wrangle, to have words.

querelleur [kərɛ'lœːr], *a.* (*fem.* **-euse**) quarrelsome.—*n.m.* (*fem.* **-euse**) quarreller, wrangler.

quérir [ke'riːr], *v.t.* to fetch (*employed only in the infinitive with aller, envoyer, venir*).

questeur [kɥɛs'tœːr], *n.m.* quaestor.

question [kɛs'tjɔ̃], *n.f.* question, interrogation; query, point, issue; rack, torture.

questionnaire [kɛstjɔ'nɛːr], *n.m.* questionnaire; book of questions.

questionner [kɛstjɔ'ne], *v.t.* to question, to interrogate.

questionneur [kɛstjɔ'nœːr], *a.* (*fem.* **-euse**) inquisitive.—*n.m.* (*fem.* **-euse**) questioner.

questure [kɥɛs'tyːr], *n.f.* quaestorship; quaestors' office.

quête [kɛːt], *n.f.* quest, search; collection, offertory; (*Hunt.*) beating about.

quêter [kɛ'te], *v.t.* to look for, to seek, to go in quest of, to gather.—*v.i.* to beg.

quêteur [kɛ'tœːr], *n.m.* (*fem.* **-euse**) collector; mendicant (friar).

queue [kø], *n.f.* tail; stalk; stem; end; rear; billiard cue; handle; train (*of robes etc.*); queue, line.

queue-d'aronde [køda'rɔ̃ːd], *n.f.* (*pl.* **queues-d'aronde**) dovetail.

qui [ki], *pron. rel.* and *inter.* who, that, whom, which; whoever, whomsoever, whatever; what; some.

quiconque [ki'kɔ̃ːk], *pron. indef.* whoever, whosoever; whomsoever, whichever.

quiétude [kɥie'tyd], *n.f.* quietude.

quignon [ki'ɲɔ̃], *n.m.* hunch, chunk, hunk (*of bread*).

quille [kiːj], *n.f.* keel; skittle, ninepin.

quiller [ki'je], *v.i.* to throw for partners *or* for first play (*at skittles*).

quillier [ki'je], *n.m.* skittle alley.

quincaillerie [kɛ̃kaj'ri], *n.f.* ironmongery, hardware.

quincaillier [kɛ̃ka'je], *n.m.* hardware dealer.

quinconce [kɛ̃'kɔ̃ːs], *n.m.* quincunx.

quine [kin], *n.m.* two fives (*at trictrac*); five winning numbers (*in a lottery*).

quinine [ki'nin], *n.f.* quinine.

quinquagénaire [kɥɛ̃kwaʒe'nɛːr], *a.* fifty years old.—*n.* person of fifty.

quinquennal [kɥɛ̃kɥɛ'nal], *a.* (*m. pl.* **-aux**) quinquennial.

quinquet [kɛ̃'kɛ], *n.m.* Argand lamp.

quinquina [kɛ̃ki'na], *n.m.* Peruvian bark.

quintal [kɛ̃'tal], *n.m.* (*pl.* **-aux**) quintal, hundredweight; 100 kilogr.

quinte [kɛ̃ːt], *n.f.* (*Mus.*) fifth; (*Piquet*) quint; (*fig.*) freak, whim; (*Fenc.*) quinte; *quinte de toux*, fit of coughing.

quintessence [kɛ̃tɛ'sɑ̃ːs], *n.f.* quintessence; (*fig.*) pith, essential part.

quintette [kɛ̃'tɛt], *n.m.* quintet.

quinteux [kɛ̃'tø], *a.* (*fem.* **-euse**) whimsical, crotchety; jibbing (*of a horse*).

quintuple [kɛ̃'typl], *a.* and *n.m.* quintuple.

quintuplé [kɛ̃ty'ple], *n.m.* quintuplet.

quintupler [kɛ̃ty'ple], *v.t.* to quintuple.

quinzaine [kɛ̃'zɛn], *n.f.* about fifteen; fortnight.

quinze [kɛ̃ːz], *a.* and *n.m.* fifteen; fifteenth.

quinzième [kɛ̃'zjɛm], *a.* and *n.* fifteenth.

quinzièmement [kɛ̃zjɛm'mɑ̃], *adv.* fifteenthly, in the fifteenth place.

quiproquo [kipro'ko], *n.m.* mistake; substitution.

quittance [ki'tɑ̃ːs], *n.f.* receipt, discharge.

quittancer [kitɑ̃'se], *v.t.* (*conjug. like* COMMENCER) to receipt.

quitte [kit], *a.* discharged (*from debt*); clear, free.

quitter [ki'te], *v.t.* to leave; to discharge; to give up; to leave off, to lay aside; to depart (*life*); *ne quittez pas !* (*Teleph.*) hold the line! **se quitter**, *v.r.* to part company, to separate.

qui va là? [kiva'la], *inter. phr.* who goes there?

qui-vive [ki'viːv], *n.m.* who goes there? (*challenge of a sentry*); *être sur le qui-vive*, to be on the alert.

quoi [kwa], *pron. rel.* and *inter.* which; what; *il n'y a pas de quoi*, don't mention it! *le je ne sais quoi*, the indefinable something; *quoi que*, whatever.—*int.* what!

quoique [ˈkwakə], *conj.* although, though.

quolibet [kɔli'bɛ], *n.m.* gibe, jeer.

quote-part [kɔt'paːr], *n.f.* (*pl.* **quotes-parts**) quota, portion, share.

quotidien [kɔti'djɛ̃], *a.* (*fem.* **-enne**) daily, quotidian.—*n.m.* daily (newspaper).

quotidiennement [kɔtidjɛn'mɑ̃], *adv.* daily.

quotient [kɔ'sjɑ̃], *n.m.* quotient.

quotité [kɔti'te], *n.f.* (*Fin.*) quota, share; proportion.

R

R, r [ɛːr], *n.m.* the eighteenth letter of the alphabet.

rabâchage [rabɑ'ʃaːʒ], *n.m.* tiresome repetition; drivel.

rabâcher [rabɑ'ʃe], *v.t., v.i.* to repeat (*the same thing*) over and over again.

rabâcheur [rabɑ'ʃœːr], *n.m.* (*fem.* **-euse**) eternal repeater, twaddler.

rabais [ra'bɛ], *n.m. inv.* abatement, reduction; discount.

rabaissement [rabɛs'mɑ̃], *n.m.* lowering, depreciation; (*fig.*) humiliation.

rabaisser [rabɛ'se], *v.t.* to lower; to abate, to lessen; to depreciate; to humble, to disparage.

rabat [ra'ba], *n.m.* clerical *or* academic band, Geneva bands; beating (*for game*).

rabat-joie [raba'ʒwa], *n.m. inv.* damper, wet blanket, spoil-sport.

rabattage [raba'taːʒ], *n.m.* cutting down, diminution; beating (*for game*).

rabattre [ra'batr], *v.t.* (*conjug. like* BATTRE) to beat down, to bring *or* cut down; to smooth down; to humble; (*Hunt.*) to beat up; to abate.—*v.i.* to reduce one's pretensions. **se**

263

rabattre, *v.r.* to turn off, to change one's road; to come down; to fall back on.

rabbin [ra′bɛ̃], *n.m.* rabbi.

rabbinique [rabi′nik], *a.* rabbinical.

rabique [ra′bik], *a.* rabid, rabic.

râble [rɑːbl], *n.m.* back (*of hare, rabbit etc.*); fire rake.

râblé [rɑ′ble], *a.* broad-backed; (*fig.*) vigorous, strapping.

rabonnir [rabɔ′niːr], *v.t., v.i.* to improve (*wine*).

rabot [ra′bo], *n.m.* plane.

rabotage [rabɔ′taːʒ], **rabotement** [rabɔt′mã], *n.m.* planing.

raboter [rabɔ′te], *v.t.* to plane; (*fig.*) to polish; (*slang*) to pilfer, to filch.

raboteur [rabɔ′tœːr], *n.m.* planer.

raboteuse (1) [rabɔ′tøːz], *n.f.* planing machine.

raboteux [rabɔ′tø], *a.* (*fem.* **-euse** (2)) knotty; rough, rugged, uneven; (*fig.*) harsh (*of style*).

rabougri [rabu′gri], *a.* stunted, dwarfed.

rabougrir [rabu′griːr], *v.t.* to stunt.

raboutir [rabu′tiːr], **rabouter** [rabu′te], *v.t.* to join end to end, to join on.

rabrouer [rabru′e], *v.t.* to snub, to rebuke sharply.

rabroueur [rabru′œːr], *n.m.* (*fem.* **-euse**) snappish person, scold.

racaille [ra′kɑːj], *n.f.* rabble, riffraff; rubbish, trash.

raccommodage [rakɔmɔ′daːʒ], *n.m.* mending, repairing; darning.

raccommodement [rakɔmɔd′mã], *n.m.* reconciliation.

raccommoder [rakɔmɔ′de], *v.t.* to mend, to repair; to darn; to patch; to set right, to correct; to reconcile. **se raccommoder**, *v.r.* to be reconciled.

raccommodeur [rakɔmɔ′dœːr], *n.m.* (*fem.* **-euse**) mender.

raccompagner [rakɔpa′ɲe], *v.t.* to accompany back.

raccord [ra′kɔːr], *n.m.* joining, fitting; joint, connection.

raccordement [rakɔrdə′mã], *n.m.* joining, union, junction; levelling; *voie de raccordement*, loop *or* junction line.

raccorder [rakɔr′de], *v.t.* to join, to unite, to connect. **se raccorder**, *v.r.* to fit together, to blend.

raccourci [rakur′si], *a.* shortened, abridged. —*n.m.* abridgment, epitome; short cut.

raccourcir [rakur′siːr], *v.t.* to shorten, to curtail, to abridge.—*v.i.* to become shorter; to take a short cut. **se raccourcir**, *v.r.* to grow shorter, to contract, to shrink.

raccourcissement [rakursis′mã], *n.m.* shortening, abridgment, shrinking.

raccoutrage [raku′traːʒ], **raccoutrement** [rakutra′mã], *n.m.* mending (*of clothes etc.*).

raccoutrer [raku′tre], *v.t.* to mend, to repair (*garment*).

raccoutumer (se) [sərakuty′me], *v.r.* to reaccustom oneself, to get used to again.

raccroc [ra′kro], *n.m.* chance, lucky stroke (*esp. at billiards*); fluke.

raccrocher [rakrɔ′ʃe], *v.t.* to hook up again, to hang up again; (*colloq.*) to recover.—*v.i.* to make flukes (*at play*); (*Teleph.*) to ring off. **se raccrocher**, *v.r.* to cling; to retrieve one's losses; to grasp *or* snatch at.

race [ras], *n.f.* race; stock, breed; family, ancestry; generation; *un cheval de race*, a thoroughbred horse.

rachat [ra′ʃa], *n.m.* repurchase, redemption.

rachetable [raʃ′tabl], *a.* redeemable.

racheter [raʃ′te], *v.t.* (*conjug. like* AMENER) to buy back, to repurchase; to redeem; to ransom; to compensate; to atone for. **se racheter**, *v.r.* to redeem oneself; to be made up for.

rachitique [raʃi′tik], *a.* rachitic, rickety.—*n.* rickety person.

rachitis [raʃi′tis], **rachitisme** [raʃi′tism], *n.m.* rachitis, rickets; (*Bot.*) blight.

racial [ra′sjal], *a.* (*m. pl.* **-aux**) racial.

racine [ra′sin], *n.f.* root; (*fig.*) principle, origin.

racisme [ra′sism], *n.m.* racialism, racism.

raciste [ra′sist], *a.* racial.—*n.* racialist, racist.

raclage [rɑ′klaːʒ], *n.m.* scraping, raking.

racle [rɑːkl], *n.f.* scraper.

raclée [rɑ′kle], *n.f.* (*fam.*) thrashing, hiding.

racler [rɑ′kle], *v.t.* to scrape, to rake; to rasp.

racleur [rɑ′klœːr], *n.m.* (*fem.* **-euse**) scraper; (*fam.*) bad violinist.

racloir [rɑ′klwaːr], *n.m.* scraper, road scraper.

raclure [rɑ′klyːr], *n.f.* scrapings.

racolage [rakɔ′laːʒ], *n.m.* impressing; recruiting.

racoler [rakɔ′le], *v.t.* to enlist.

racoleur [rakɔ′lœːr], *n.m.* tout.

racontable [rakɔ̃′tabl], *a.* relatable.

racontar [rakɔ̃′taːr], *n.m.* gossip, tittle-tattle.

raconter [rakɔ̃′te], *v.t.* to relate, to tell, to narrate.

raconteur [rakɔ̃′tœːr], *n.m.* (*fem.* **-euse**) story-teller, narrator, raconteur.

racornir [rakɔr′niːr], *v.t.* to harden; to dry up, to shrivel up. **se racornir**, *v.r.* to grow hard; to shrivel up; to grow callous.

racornissement [rakɔrnis′mã], *n.m.* hardening.

racquit [ra′ki], *n.m.* winning back.

racquitter [raki′te], *v.t.* to indemnify, to recoup. **se racquitter**, *v.r.* to retrieve one's losses.

radar [ra′dar], *n.m.* radar.

radariste [rada′rist], *n.* radar operator.

rade [rad], *n.f.* (*Naut.*) roads, roadstead.

radeau [ra′do], *n.m.* (*pl.* **-eaux**) raft.

radiance [ra′djãːs], *n.f.* radiance, luster.

radiant [ra′djã], *a.* radiant.

radiateur [radja′tœːr], *a.* (*fem.* **-trice**) radiating.—*n.m.* radiator.

radiation [radja′sjɔ̃], *n.f.* radiation, irradiation; obliteration.

radical [radi′kal], *a.* (*m. pl.* **-aux**) radical; complete.—*n.m.* radical; root.

radicalement [radikal′mã], *adv.* radically.

radicalisme [radika′lism], *n.m.* radicalism.

radier (1) [ra′dje], *n.m.* floor *or* apron (*of docks, locks, basins etc.*); invert (*of tunnel*).

radier (2) [ra′dje], *v.t.* to strike out, to erase.— *v.i.* to radiate, to beam (*with satisfaction*).

radieux [ra′djø], *a.* (*fem.* **-euse**) radiant, beaming, shining.

radio [ra′djo], *n.f.* broadcasting, radio; radio set; radiography.—*n.m.* radio message; radio operator.

radio-actif [radjoak′tif], *a.* (*fem.* **-tive**) radio-active.

radio-activité [radjoaktivi'te], *n.f.* radio-activity.

radiodiffuser [radjɔdify'ze], *v.t.* to broadcast.

radiodiffusion [radjɔdify'zjɔ̃], *n.f.* broadcasting.

radiographie [radjɔgra'fi], *n.f.* radiography.

radio-reporter [radjɔrəpɔr'tɛ:r], *n.m.* commentator.

radio-thérapie [radjɔtera'pi], *n.f.* X-ray treatment, radio-therapy.

radis [ra'di], *n.m.* radish.

radium [ra'djɔm], *n.m.* radium.

radotage [radɔ'ta:ʒ], *n.m.* nonsense, drivel; dotage.

radoter [radɔ'te], *v.i.* to talk idly, to talk drivel; to dote.

radoteur [radɔ'tœ:r], *n.m.* (*fem.* **-euse**) driveller; dotard.

radoucir [radu'si:r], *v.t.* to soften; to appease, to pacify. **se radoucir**, *v.r.* to grow milder; to soften, to be appeased, to relent, to relax.

radoucissement [radusis'mɑ̃], *n.m.* softening; getting milder (*of the weather*); mitigation, appeasement.

rafale [ra'fal], *n.f.* squall; gust of wind; (*Mil.*) burst of fire.

raffermir [rafɛr'mi:r], *v.t.* to make firm, to secure, to strengthen; to confirm. **se raffermir**, *v.r.* to grow stronger; to be established; to improve in strength *or* health.

raffermissement [rafɛrmis'mɑ̃], *n.m.* hardening; securing; strengthening; confirmation.

raffinage [rafi'na:ʒ], *n.m.* refining.

raffiné [rafi'ne], *a.* refined, delicate; subtle, clever; polished.—*n.m.* (*fem.* **-ée**) exquisite; sophisticated person.

raffinement [rafin'mɑ̃], *n.m.* refinement, affectation.

raffiner [rafi'ne], *v.t.* to refine.—*v.i.* to split hairs. **se raffiner**, *v.r.* to become refined.

raffinerie [rafin'ri], *n.f.* refinery.

raffineur [rafi'nœ:r], *n.m.* (*fem.* **-euse**) refiner.

raffoler [rafɔ'le], *v.i.* to dote, to be passionately fond (*de*).

rafistolage [rafistɔ'la:ʒ], *n.m.* (*colloq.*) patching up, mending.

rafistoler [rafistɔ'le], *v.t.* to mend, to patch up.

rafle [rɑ:fl], *n.f.* clean sweep (*by thieves*); raid, round-up in the streets by police.

rafler [rɑ'fle], *v.t.* to sweep off, to carry off; to round up (*of police*).

rafraîchir [rafrɛ'ʃi:r], *v.t.* to cool; to refresh, to restore, to renew; to rub up; to trim.—*v.i.* to cool; to freshen. **se rafraîchir**, *v.r.* to cool, to take refreshment; to be refreshed, to rest.

rafraîchissant [rafrɛʃi'sɑ̃], *a.* cooling, refreshing; laxative.

rafraîchissement [rafrɛʃis'mɑ̃], *n.m.* cooling; (*pl.*) cool drinks.

ragaillardir [ragaiar'di:r], *v.t.* to enliven, to cheer up, to buck up.

rage [ra:ʒ], *n.f.* rabies; hydrophobia; violent pain; rage, fury; passion; mania.

rager [ra'ʒe], *v.i.* (*conjug. like* MANGER) (*colloq.*) to be in a passion; to be angry, to fume.

rageur [ra'ʒœ:r], *a. and n.m.* (*fem.* **-euse**) ill-tempered (person).

ragot [ra'go], *a.* thick-set.—*n.m.* tittle-tattle.

ragoût [ra'gu], *n.m.* ragout; stew; (*fig.*) relish.

ragoûtant [ragu'tɑ̃], *a.* relishing, savory, (*fig.*) inviting, tempting.

ragoûter [ragu'te], *v.t.* to restore the appetite of; to stimulate, to stir up.

ragrafer [ragra'fe], *v.t.* to reclasp, to hook again.

ragréer [ragre'e], *v.t.* to give the finishing touch to (*wall, building*); to renovate (*building*).

ragrément *or* **ragréement** [ragre'mɑ̃], *n.m.* finishing; restoration, renovation.

rai [RAIS].

raid [rɛd], *n.m.* long-distance run *or* flight; raid; **un raid aérien**, an air-raid.

raide [rɛd], *a.* stiff, rigid; taut; steep; firm; rapid.—*adv.* quickly, swiftly, suddenly.

raideur [rɛ'dœ:r], *n.f.* stiffness; inflexibility; steepness; harshness.

raidillon [rɛdi'jɔ̃], *n.m.* stiff ascent.

raidir [rɛ'di:r], *v.t.* to stiffen; to tighten; to make inflexible.—*v.i. and* **se raidir**, *v.r.* to stiffen; to be inflexible; (*fig.*) to harden oneself (*contre*).

raidissement [rɛdis'mɑ̃], *n.m.* stiffening, tautening.

raie [rɛ], *n.f.* line, stroke; stripe; parting (*of hair*); (*Ichth.*) ray.

raifort [rɛ'fɔ:r], *n.m.* horse-radish.

rail [rɑ:j, ra:j], *n.m.* (*Rail.*) rail.

railler [rɑ'je], *v.t.* to chaff; to scoff at.—*v.i.* to banter, to jest. **se railler**, *v.r.* to jest, to mock, to make game (*de*).

raillerie [rɑj'ri], *n.f.* raillery, bantering, jesting.

railleur [rɑ'jœ:r], *a.* (*fem.* **-euse**) bantering, joking; jeering, scoffing.—*n.m.* (*fem.* **-euse**) banterer, joker; scoffer.

rainette [rɛ'nɛt], *n.f.* (*Zool.*) tree toad.

rainure [rɛ'ny:r], *n.f.* groove, rabbet, slot.

rais *or* **rai** [rɛ], *n.m.* spoke (*of a wheel*); ray (*of light*).

raisin [rɛ'zɛ̃], *n.m.* grapes; **des raisins secs**, raisins.

raisiné [rɛzi'ne], *n.m.* grape jam.

raison [rɛ'zɔ̃], *n.f.* reason; sense, judgment; satisfaction; justice, right; proof, ground; motive; **avoir raison**, to be right.

raisonnable [rɛzɔ'nabl], *a.* rational, reasonable, sensible; just, right; adequate, moderate, fair.

raisonnablement [rɛzɔnablə'mɑ̃], *adv.* reasonably, sensibly; fairly, justly; moderately; tolerably.

raisonné [rɛzɔ'ne], *a.* rational, intelligent; systematic; classified, analytical.

raisonnement [rɛzɔn'mɑ̃], *n.m.* reasoning, argument.

raisonner [rɛzɔ'ne], *v.t.* to study; to talk *or* discourse upon.—*v.i.* to reason; to argue; to answer, to murmur. **se raisonner**, *v.r.* to reason with oneself.

raisonneur [rɛzɔ'nœ:r], *a.* (*fem.* **-euse**) reasoning; argumentative.—*n.m.* (*fem.* **-euse**) reasoner, logician; argufier, pertinacious answerer.

rajeunir [raʒœ'ni:r], *v.t.* to rejuvenate; to make look young *or* younger; to renew; to modernize.—*v.i.* to grow young again. **se**

rajeunir, *v.r.* to make oneself look young again.

rajeunissant [raʒœni'sã], *a.* that makes one look younger, rejuvenating.

rajeunissement [raʒœnis'mã], *n.m.* rejuvenation; renewal, renovation.

rajouter [raʒu'te], *v.t.* to add again; to add more of.

rajustement [raʒystə'mã], *n.m.* readjustment, setting in order; (*fig.*) reconciliation.

rajuster [raʒys'te], *v.t.* to readjust; (*fig.*) to settle, to reconcile. **se rajuster**, *v.r.* to readjust *or* straighten one's dress; to be reconciled.

râle (1) [rɑːl], **râlement** [rɑːl'mã], *n.m.* rattling in the throat; death rattle.

râle (2) [rɑːl], *n.m.* (*Orn.*) rail.

ralenti [ralã'ti], *a.* slower.—*n.m.* (*Cine.*) slow motion; *tourner au ralenti*, (*Motor.*) to idle.

ralentir [ralã'tiːr], *v.t., v.i.* to slow down, to ease up; to lessen, to moderate. **se ralentir**, *v.r.* to slacken, to slow up; to abate, to relax.

ralentissement [ralãtis'mã], *n.m.* slackening; decrease; cooling (*of zeal*).

râler [rɑ'le], *v.i.* to be at one's last gasp.

ralliement [rali'mã], *n.m.* rallying, rally; winning over; *mot de ralliement*, (*Mil.*) password.

rallier [ra'lje], *v.t.* to rally; to rejoin; to win over. **se rallier**, *v.r.* to rally; to join.

rallonge [ra'lõːʒ], *n.f.* lengthening-piece, leaf; *table à rallonges*, draw-table.

rallongement [ralõʒ'mã], *n.m.* lengthening, extension.

rallonger [ralõ'ʒe], *v.t.* (*conjug. like* MANGER) to lengthen; to let out (*skirt*).

rallumer [raly'me], *v.t.* to relight; to re-kindle; to revive. **se rallumer**, *v.r.* to light again; (*fig.*) to rekindle.

rallye [ra'li], *n.m.* (*Motor.*) race meeting, rally.

ramage [ra'maːʒ], *n.m.* floral pattern (*on materials*); chirping, warbling (*of birds*); (*fig.*) prattle (*of children*).

ramaigrir [ramɛ'griːr], *v.t.* to make lean *or* thin again.—*v.i.* to grow thin again.

ramaigrissement [ramɛgris'mã], *n.m.* emaciation, leanness.

ramas [ra'mɑ], *n.m. inv.* heap, disorderly collection; set, troop, lot, rabble.

ramassé [rama'se], *a.* thick-set, stocky; compact.

ramasser [rama'se], *v.t.* to collect, to gather; to pick up, to take up. **se ramasser**, *v.r.* to assemble, to gather together; to roll itself up (*of an animal*); to crouch; to pick oneself up (*after a spill*).

ramasseur [rama'sœːr], *n.m.* (*fem.* **-euse**) gatherer, collector.

ramassis [rama'si], [RAMAS].

rame [ram], *n.f.* scull, oar; (*Hort.*) stick, prop; (*Manuf.*) tenter frame; ream (*of paper*); made-up train *or* portion of train; *une rame de Métro*, an Underground train, a subway train.

ramé [ra'me], *a.* supported with sticks (*of peas*), staked (*of plants*).

rameau [ra'mo], *n.m.* (*pl.* **-eaux**) bough, small branch (*of a tree*); subdivision.

ramée [ra'me], *n.f.* green boughs, green arbor.

ramener [ram'ne], *v.t.* (*conjug. like* AMENER) to bring back; to take home; to restore; to reclaim; to recall.

ramer (1) [ra'me], *v.t.* to stick (*peas*), to stake (*plants*).

ramer (2) [ra'me], *v.i.* to row, to scull.

rameur [ra'mœːr], *n.m.* (*fem.* **-euse**) rower.

ramier [ra'mje], *n.m.* wood pigeon, ring dove.

ramification [ramifika'sjõ], *n.f.* ramification.

ramifier [rami'fje], *v.t.* to ramify. **se ramifier**, *v.r.* to ramify, to divide.

ramille [ra'miːj], *n.f.*, **ramillon** [rami'jõ], *n.m.* twig.

ramollir [ramɔ'liːr], *v.t.* to soften, (*fig.*) to enervate, to unman. **se ramollir**, *v.r.* to soften; (*fig.*) to relent.

ramollissant [ramɔli'sã], *a.* softening, emollient.

ramollissement [ramɔlis'mã], *n.m.* softening.

ramonage [ramɔ'naːʒ], *n.m.* chimney sweeping.

ramoner [ramɔ'ne], *v.t.* to sweep (*a chimney*).

ramoneur [ramɔ'nœːr], *n.m.* chimney sweeper, sweep.

rampant [rã'pã], *a.* creeping, crawling; (*fig.*) cringing, servile.

rampe [rãːp], *n.f.* banister; flight of stairs; slope, ramp, incline, gradient; (*Theat.*) footlights.

rampement [rãp'mã], *n.m.* creeping, crawling.

ramper [rã'pe], *v.i.* to creep, to crawl; (*fig.*) to crouch, to grovel.

ramure [ra'myːr], *n.f.* branches, boughs; antlers (*of a stag*).

rancart [rã'kaːr], *n.m. mettre au rancart*, to throw aside, to cast off; to put on the shelf.

rance [rãːs], *a.* rancid, rank.—*n.m.* rancidness.

ranci [rã'si], *a.* rancid.

rancidité [rãsidi'te], **rancissure** [rãsi'syːr], *n.f.*, **rancissement** [rãsis'mã], *n.m.* rancidity.

rancir [rã'siːr], *v.i.* to grow rancid.

rancœur [rã'kœːr], *n.f.* rancor, bitterness.

rançon [rã'sõ], *n.f.* ransom.

rançonnement [rãsɔn'mã], *n.m.* ransoming; (*fig.*) extortion.

rançonner [rãsɔ'ne], *v.t.* to ransom; (*fig.*) to fleece.

rancune [rã'kyn], *n.f.* rancor, spite, grudge, malice.

rancunier [rãky'nje], *a.* and *n.m.* (*fem.* **-ière**) rancorous, spiteful (person).

randonnée [rãdɔ'ne], *n.f.* outing, run, ramble, tour.

rang [rã], *n.m.* row, line; order, class; rank.

rangé [rã'ʒe], *a.* tidy; steady; *en bataille rangée*, in a pitched battle.

rangée [rã'ʒe], *n.f.* row, range, line, tier, set.

rangement [rãʒ'mã], *n.m.* arranging, putting in order.

ranger [rã'ʒe], *v.t.* (*conjug. like* MANGER) to put in order, to set to rights; to draw up; to arrange; to range; to rank; to reduce, to subdue. **se ranger**, *v.r.* to make room, to make way (*for*); to draw up (*of carriages*, *troops etc.*), to pull up (*at curb*); to fall in (*of soldiers*).

ranimer [rani'me], *v.t.* to restore to life, to revive; to rouse, to enliven; to cheer up. **se ranimer**, *v.r.* to revive, to brighten up, to be enlivened; to cheer up.

Raoul [ra'ul], *m.* Ralph.

rapace [ra'pas], *a.* rapacious; grasping (*of person*).—*n.m.* rapacious bird, bird of prey.

rapacement [rapas'mã], *adv.* rapaciously.

rapacité [rapasi'te], *n.f.* rapacity; cupidity.

râpage [rɑ'pa:ʒ], *n.m.* rasping; grating.

rapatriement [rapatri'mã], *n.m.* repatriation.

rapatrier [rapatri'je], *v.t.* to repatriate; (*dial.*) to reconcile.

râpe [rɑ:p], *n.f.* grater; rasp; stalk (*of grapes*).

râpé [rɑ'pe], *a.* grated; rasped; threadbare (*of clothes*).

râper [rɑ'pe], *v.t.* to grate (*cheese*), to rasp; to make threadbare.

rapetassage [rapta'sa:ʒ], *n.m.* patching up, mending, cobbling.

rapetasser [rapta'se], *v.t.* to patch, to mend, to cobble.

rapetasseur [rapta'sœ:r], *n.m.* (*fem.* **-euse**) piecer, patcher; cobbler; (*fig.*) compiler, adapter.

rapetissement [raptis'mã], *n.m.* shortening, shrinking; (*fig.*) belittling.

rapetisser [rapti'se], *v.t.* to shorten, to make smaller; (*fig.*) to belittle.—*v.i.* to grow less, to shorten, to shrink.

raphia [ra'fja], *n.m.* raffia.

rapide [ra'pid], *a.* rapid, quick, fast; sudden; steep.—*n.m.* rapid; fast train.

rapidement [rapid'mã], *adv.* rapidly, swiftly; steeply.

rapidité [rapidi'te], *n.f.* rapidity, speed; steepness.

rapiéçage [rapje'sa:ʒ], **rapiècement** [rapjɛs 'mã], *n.m.* piecing, patching.

rapiécer [rapje'se] (*see Verb Tables*), **rapiéceter** [rapjɛs'te] (*conjug. like* AMENER), *v.t.* to piece, to patch.

rapière [ra'pjɛ:r], *n.f.* rapier.

rapin [ra'pɛ̃], *n.m.* art student; (*fig.*) dauber.

rapine [ra'pin], *n.f.* rapine, robbery; plunder; graft.

rapiner [rapi'ne], *v.t., v.i.* to pillage, to plunder.

rapineur [rapi'nœ:r], *n.m.* (*fem.* **-euse**) plunderer, pillager, pilferer.

rappareiller [raparɛ'je], **rapparier** [rapa'rje], *v.t.* to match, to complete.

rappel [ra'pɛl], *n.m.* recall, reminder, call (*to order*); tattoo, assembly; revocation; back pay; (*Theat.*) curtain call.

rappeler [ra'ple], *v.t.* (*conjug. like* APPELER) to call back, to recall; to restore (*to life etc.*); to muster; to retract; to recall to mind; to remind. **se rappeler**, *v.r.* to recollect, to remember.

rapport [ra'pɔ:r], *n.m.* revenue, profit; produce; productiveness; report, account, information, tale; return, statement; resemblance, conformity; agreement; connection; communication; proportion; reimbursement; *faire un rapport*, to draw up a report; *maison de rapport*, tenement house; *sous tous les rapports*, in every respect.

rapporter [rapɔr'te], *v.t.* to bring back; to bring home; to yield; to retrieve (*of dog*); to refund; to recall; to give an account of; to attribute.—*v.i.* to retrieve (*of dog*); (*sch.*) to tell tales; to be profitable. **se rapporter**, *v.r.* to agree, to correspond, to tally; to be related.

rapporteur [rapɔr'tœ:r], *n.m.* (*fem.* **-euse**) tale-bearer; reporter.—*n.m.* (*Geom.*) protractor.

rapprendre [ra'prã:dr], *v.t. irr.* (*conjug. like* PRENDRE) to learn anew; to teach again.

rapprochement [raprɔʃ'mã], *n.m.* drawing closer, bringing together; reconciliation; junction; comparison.

rapprocher [raprɔ'ʃe], *v.t.* to bring near again; to bring together; to reconcile; to compare. **se rapprocher**, *v.r.* to come near again; to draw nearer; to be brought together; to become reconciled; to approximate (*de*).

rapsodie [rapsɔ'di], *n.f.* rhapsody.

rapt [rapt], *n.m.* abduction; kidnapping.

raquette [ra'kɛt], *n.f.* racket, battledore; snow-shoe.

rare [ra:r], *a.* rare, uncommon; scarce; thin, scanty.

raréfaction [rarefak'sjɔ̃], *n.f.* rarefaction.

raréfiant [rare'fjã], *a.* rarefying.

raréfier [rare'fje], *v.t.* to rarefy. **se raréfier**, *v.r.* to become rare; to become rarefied.

rarement [rar'mã], *adv.* rarely, seldom.

rareté [rar'te], *n.f.* rarity; scarcity.

rarissime [rari'sim], *a.* very rare, most rare.

ras [rɑ], *a.* close-shaven, shorn; bare, smooth; open, flat, low; *faire table rase*, to sweep away all preconceptions; *rase campagne*, open country.—*n.m.* short-nap cloth; level; raft; race (*of a mill*) [RAZ].

rasade [rɑ'zad], *n.f.* brimful glass (*of wine*).

rasant [rɑ'zã], *a.* shaving, grazing; sweeping; (*fam.*) boring.

raser [rɑ'ze], *v.t.* to shave; to demolish; to graze, to skim over; (*fam.*) to bore. **se raser**, *v.r.* to shave, to be shaved.

rasoir [rɑ'zwa:r], *n.m.* razor; (*fam.*) bore.

rassasiant [rasa'zjã], *a.* satiating, filling (*food*).

rassasiement [rasazi'mã], *n.m.* satiety.

rassasier [rasa'zje], *v.t.* to satisfy, to fill; to satiate; to surfeit. **se rassasier**, *v.r.* to be cloyed; to take one's fill.

rassemblement [rasãbla'mã], *n.m.* assembly, muster, crowd, mob; political group.

rassembler [rasã'ble], *v.t.* to gather together, to collect; to put together; to assemble. **se rassembler**, *v.r.* to assemble, to congregate, to muster.

rasseoir [ra'swa:r], *v.t. irr.* (*conjug. like* ASSEOIR) to seat again, to reseat; to replace; to calm, to compose. **se rasseoir**, *v.r.* to sit down again; to settle (*of liquids*); to become composed again.

rasséréner [rasere'ne], *v.t.* (*conjug. like* CÉDER) to clear up; to restore serenity to. **se rasséréner**, *v.r.* to clear up; to recover one's serenity.

rassis [ra'si], *a.* settled; calm, staid, sedate; stale.

rassortiment [rasɔrti'mã], **réassortiment** [reasɔrti'mã], *n.m.* rematching (*of colors, materials etc.*), resorting; restocking.

267

rassortir [rasɔr'ti:r], **réassortir** [reasɔr'ti:r], *v.t.* to sort *or* match again; to stock (*a shop etc.*).

rassurant [rasy'rɑ̃], *a.* tranquillizing; encouraging, reassuring.

rassurer [rasy're], *v.t.* to make firm; to strengthen; to tranquillize, to reassure. **se rassurer**, *v.r.* to be reassured; to reassure oneself; to clear up (*of the weather*); *rassurez-vous*, set your mind at rest.

rat [ra], *n.m.* rat; *rat des champs*, field mouse; *rat d'hôtel*, hotel thief.

ratafia [rata'fja], *n.m.* ratafia.

ratatiné [ratati'ne], *a.* shrivelled, shrunken.

ratatiner (se) [səratati'ne], *v.r.* to shrink, to shrivel up.

rate (1) [rat], *n.f.* spleen.

rate (2) [rat], *n.f.* female rat.

râteau [rɑ'to], *n.m.* (*pl.* **-eaux**) rake.

râtelage [rɑt'la:ʒ], *n.m.* raking.

râtelée [rɑt'le], *n.f.* rakeful, raking.

râteler [rɑt'le], *v.t.* (*conjug. like* APPELER) to rake.

râteleur [rɑt'lœ:r], *n.m.* (*fem.* **-euse**) raker.

râtelier [rɑtə'lje], *n.m.* rack; set of teeth, denture.

rater [ra'te], *v.t.* to miss; (*fig.*) to fail to obtain.—*v.i.* to misfire, to miss (*one's shot*); (*fig.*) to miscarry.

ratière [ra'tjɛ:r], *n.f.* rat trap.

ratification [ratifika'sjɔ̃], *n.f.* ratification.

ratifier [rati'fje], *v.t.* to ratify.

ratine [ra'tin], *n.f.* ratteen, petersham (*cloth*).

ration [rɑ'sjɔ̃], *n.f.* ration, allowance.

rationaliser [rasjonali'ze], *v.t.* to rationalize.

rationalisme [rasjona'lism], *n.m.* rationalism.

rationaliste [rasjona'list], *a.* and *n.* rationalist.

rationalité [rasjonali'te], *n.f.* rationality.

rationnel [rasjo'nɛl], *a.* (*fem.* **-elle**) rational.

rationnement [rasjon'mɑ̃], *n.m.* rationing.

rationner [rasjo'ne], *v.t.* to ration.

ratissage [rati'sa:ʒ], *n.m.* scraping; raking.

ratisser [rati'se], *v.t.* to rake; to scrape.

ratissoire [rati'swa:r], *n.f.* scraper, light rake, hoe.

ratissure [rati'sy:r], *n.f.* scrapings.

raton [ra'tɔ̃], *n.m.* little rat; (*fig.*) little pet, darling.

rattacher [rata'ʃe], *v.t.* to refasten; to attach; (*fig.*) to link. **se rattacher**, *v.r.* to be attached *or* connected; to be linked up (*with*).

ratteindre [ra'tɛ̃:dr], *v.t.* irr. (*conjug. like* CRAINDRE) to retake, to catch again; to overtake.

rattendrir [ratɑ̃'dri:r], *v.t.* to soften again.

rattraper [ratra'pe], *v.t.* to catch again, to retake; to overtake; to recover. **se rattraper**, *v.r.* to catch hold (*à*); to be caught again; to make up for one's losses.

rature [ra'ty:r], *n.f.* erasure.

raturer [raty're], *v.t.* to erase.

raucité [rosi'te], *n.f.* raucity, hoarseness.

rauque [ro:k], *a.* hoarse, raucous, rough.

ravage [ra'va:ʒ], *n.m.* ravage, havoc.

ravager [rava'ʒe], *v.t.* (*conjug. like* MANGER) to ravage, to lay waste; to spoil, to ruin.

ravageur [rava'ʒœ:r], *n.m.* (*fem.* **-euse**) ravager, spoiler.

ravalement [raval'mɑ̃], *n.m.* scraping and pointing (*of a wall*); rough-casting; repainting.

ravaler [rava'le], *v.t.* to swallow again; (*fig.*) to disparage; to point (*stonework*); to roughcast (*wall*). **se ravaler**, *v.r.* to debase oneself, to lower oneself.

ravaudage [ravo'da:ʒ], *n.m.* mending (*of old clothes etc.*).

ravauder [ravo'de], *v.t.* to mend, to darn; (*dial.*) to scold.

ravaudeur [ravo'dœ:r], *n.m.* (*fem.* **-euse**) mender (*of stockings, old clothes etc.*).

rave [ra:v], *n.f.* (*Bot.*) **grosse rave**, French turnip; *petite rave*, radish.

ravenelle [rav'nɛl], *n.f.* wallflower.

ravi [ra'vi], *a.* carried away, enraptured, delighted.

ravier [ra'vje], *n.m.* radish dish.

ravière [ra'vjɛ:r], *n.f.* radish bed.

ravigote [ravi'gɔt], *n.f.* ravigote sauce.

ravigoter [ravigɔ'te], *v.t.* to revive, to refresh, to buck up. **se ravigoter**, *v.r.* to recover one's spirits, to perk up.

ravilir [ravi'li:r], *v.t.* to degrade, to lower.

ravin [ra'vɛ̃], *n.m.* ravine; gully.

ravine [ra'vi:n], *n.f.* mountain torrent; small gully.

ravinement [ravin'mɑ̃], *n.m.* hollowing out *or* furrowing (*by waters*).

raviner [ravi'ne], *v.t.* to channel, to furrow.

ravir [ra'vi:r], *v.t.* to carry off, to ravish; (*fig.*) to charm, to enrapture.

raviser (se) [səravi'ze], *v.r.* to change one's mind; to think better of it.

ravissant [ravi'sɑ̃], *a.* ravishing, delightful, charming.

ravissement [ravis'mɑ̃], *n.m.* carrying off; *rape; rapture, delight.

ravisseur [ravi'sœ:r], *n.m.* (*fem.* **-euse**) ravisher; kidnapper.

ravitaillement [ravitaj'mɑ̃], *n.m.* revictualling; supplying; supplies; food.

ravitailler [ravita'je], *v.t.* to provision; to supply.

raviver [ravi've], *v.t.* to revive, to cheer; to freshen up (*colors*).

ravoir [ra'vwa:r], *v.t.* (*usu. in infin.*) to get back again, to recover.

rayé [rɛ'je], *a.* striped (*garment*); rifled (*gun*); scratched (*glass*); struck off (*a list*).

rayer [rɛ'je], *v.t.* (*conjug. like* PAYER) to scratch (*dishes etc.*); to streak, to stripe; to erase; (*Artill.*) to rifle.

rayon [rɛ'jɔ̃], *n.m.* ray; beam, gleam; radius; spoke (*of a wheel*); shelf; department (*of a shop*); *rayon de miel*, honeycomb.

rayonnant [rɛjo'nɑ̃], *a.* radiant, beaming.

rayonne [rɛ'jɔn], *n.f.* rayon.

rayonnement [rɛjon'mɑ̃], *n.m.* radiance; radiation.

rayonner [rɛjo'ne], *v.i.* to radiate; to shine, to beam; to sparkle.

rayure [rɛ'jy:r], *n.f.* stripe; streak, scratch; rifling (*of fire-arms*); erasure.

raz or **ras** [rɑ], *n.m. inv.* race (*a violent current*); *raz de marée*, tidal wave.

razzia [ra'zja], *n.f.* (*Algerian*) razzia, raid, inroad, foray.

ré [re], *n.m.* (*Mus.*) re, D.

réabonnement [reabon'mɑ̃], *n.m.* renewed subscription.

réabonner (se) [sɔreabɔ'ne], *v.r.* to renew one's subscription.

réacteur [reak'tœːr], *n.m.* reactor; (*Av.*) jet engine.

réaction [reak'sjɔ̃], *n.f.* reaction; *les avions à réaction*, jet aircraft.

réactionnaire [reaksjɔ'nɛːr], *a.* and *n.* reactionary.

réactionner [reaksjɔ'ne], *v.t.* to sue again.— *v.i.* (*St. Exch.*) to react against a rise.

réadmettre [read'mɛtr], *v.t. irr.* (*conjug. like* METTRE) to admit again, to readmit.

réadmission [readmi'sjɔ̃], *n.f.* readmission.

réagir [rea'ʒiːr], *v.i.* to react.

réajourner [reaʒur'ne], *v.t.* to readjourn.

réalisable [reali'zabl], *a.* realizable; feasible.

réalisateur [realiza'tœːr], *n.m.* (*Cine.*) film director.

réalisation [realiza'sjɔ̃], *n.f.* realization; achievement; conversion into money; clearance sale.

réaliser [reali'ze], *v.t.* to realize; to achieve; to convert into money. **se réaliser**, *v.r.* to be realized, to come true.

réalisme [rea'lism], *n.m.* realism.

réaliste [rea'list], *a.* realistic.—*n.* realist.

réalité [reali'te], *n.f.* reality.

réapparaître [reapa'rɛːtr], *v.i. irr.* (*conjug. like* CONNAÎTRE) to reappear.

réapparition [reapari'sjɔ̃], *n.f.* reappearance.

réarmement [rearma'mɑ̃], *n.m.* rearmament.

réarmer [rear'me], *v.t.* to rearm; (*Navy*) to refit.

réassortiment [RASSORTIMENT].

rebaisser [rəbɛ'se], *v.t.* to lower again.

rébarbatif [rebarba'tif], *a.* (*fem.* **-tive**) stern, surly, forbidding.

rebâtir [rəba'tir], *v.t.* to rebuild.

rebattre [rə'batr], *v.t.* (*conjug. like* BATTRE) to beat again; to repeat; to shuffle (*cards*) again.

rebattu [rəba'ty], *a.* hackneyed, trite.

rebelle [rə'bɛl], *a.* rebellious; disobedient; unyielding; refractory.—*n.* rebel.

rebeller (se) [sərəbɛ'le], *v.r.* to rebel, to revolt.

rébellion [rebɛ'ljɔ̃], *n.f.* rebellion; resistance.

rebiffer (se) [sərəbi'fe], *v.r.* (*fam.*) to bridle up, to kick over the traces.

reblanchir [rəblɑ̃'ʃiːr], *v.t.* to bleach again; to whitewash again.

reboire [rə'bwaːr], *v.t. irr.* (*conjug. like* BOIRE) to drink again.

reboisement [rəbwaz'mɑ̃], *n.m.* retimbering, reforestation.

reboiser [rəbwa'ze], *v.t.* to retimber, to reforest.

rebond [rə'bɔ̃], *n.m.* rebound; bounce (*of ball*).

rebondi [rəbɔ̃'di], *a.* plump, chubby.

rebondir [rəbɔ̃'diːr], *v.i.* to rebound; to bounce.

rebondissement [rəbɔ̃dis'mɑ̃], *n.m.* rebounding; bounce.

rebord [rə'bɔːr], *n.m.* edge, brink; sill (*of window*); border, hem.

reborder [rəbɔr'de], *v.t.* to border again, to re-hem.

rebouillir [rəbu'jiːr], *v.i. irr.* (*conjug. like* BOUILLIR) to boil again.

rebours [rə'buːr], *a.* cross-grained (*wood*); intractable (*horse*).—*n.m.* wrong side (*of material etc.*); wrong way (*of the grain*); contrary, reverse; *à rebours* or *au rebours* the wrong way, against the grain, backwards.

reboutage [rəbu'taːʒ], *n.m.* bone-setting.

rebouter [rəbu'te], *v.t.* to set (*bones*).

rebouteur [rəbu'tœːr], **rebouteux** [rəbu'tø], *n.m.* (*fem.* **-euse**) bone setter.

reboutonner [rəbutɔ'ne], *v.t.* to rebutton. **se reboutonner**, *v.r.* to button up one's clothes again.

rebroussement [rəbrus'mɑ̃], *n.m.* turning back, turning up.

rebrousse-poil (à) [arəbrus'pwal], *adv. phr.* against the grain; the wrong way.

rebrousser [rəbru'se], *v.t.* to turn up (*the hair*); *rebrousser chemin*, to turn back.

rebuffade [rəby'fad], *n.f.* rebuff, repulse; snub.

rébus [re'byːs], *n.m.* rebus; riddle.

rebut [rə'by], *n.m.* repulse, rebuff; refuse, rubbish; scum.

rebutant [rəby'tɑ̃], *a.* repulsive, disgusting, forbidding.

rebuter [rəby'te], *v.t.* to repulse, to rebuff, to reject, to snub; to disgust. **se rebuter**, *v.r.* to become discouraged.

récalcitrant [rekalsi'trɑ̃], *a.* refractory, recalcitrant; rebellious.

récalcitrer [rekalsi'tre], *v.i.* to kick (*of horses*); (*fig.*) to be refractory.

recaler [rəka'le], *v.t.* to wedge up again, to refix; (*Sch.*) to fail (*s. o. in an examination*).

récapitulation [rekapityla'sjɔ̃], *n.f.* recapitulation, summing up; summary.

récapituler [rekapity'le], *v.t.* to recapitulate, to sum up; (*colloq.*) to recap.

recel [rə'sɛl], **recèlement** [rəsɛl'mɑ̃], *n.m.* receiving of stolen goods.

receler [rəs'le] (*conjug. like* AMENER), **recéler** [rəsə'le] (*conjug. like* CÉDER), *v.t.* to receive (*stolen goods*); to embezzle; to conceal from justice; to contain.

receleur [rəs'lœːr], *n.m.* (*fem.* **-euse**) receiver of stolen goods, fence.

récemment [resa'mɑ̃], *adv.* recently, newly.

recensement [rəsɑ̃s'mɑ̃], *n.m.* census; return, inventory; verification.

recenser [rəsɑ̃'se], *v.t.* to take the census of; to record; to verify.

recenseur [rəsɑ̃'sœːr], *n.m.* (*fem.* **-euse**) census taker; enumerator.

recension [rəsɑ̃'sjɔ̃], *n.f.* recension; collation (*of books etc.*).

récent [re'sɑ̃], *a.* recent, new, fresh, late.

receper [rəsə'pe] (*conjug. like* AMENER), **recéper** [rəse'pe] (*conjug. like* CÉDER), *v.t.* to cut back; to clear (*a wood*).

récépissé [resepi'se], *n.m.* receipt, acknowledgment (*for documents, papers etc.*).

réceptacle [resɛp'takl], *n.m.* receptacle; repository.

récepteur [resɛp'tœːr], *a.* (*fem.* **-trice**) receiving; *poste récepteur*, receiving set. —*n.m.* receiver; reservoir (*in a machine, etc.*); receiving instrument (*of telegraphs*).

réception [resɛp'sjɔ̃], *n.f.* receiving, receipt; admission; (*hotel*) reception desk; reception, party.

réceptionnaire [resɛpsjɔ'nɛːr], *a.* receiving. —*n.* receiver, receiving clerk; consignee.

réceptionniste [resɛpsjɔ'nist], *n.* receptionist.

recette

recette [rə'sɛt], n.f. receipts, returns; takings; (Cook.) recipe; receiver's office; *faire recette*, to be a hit (of a play).

recevable [rəsə'vabl], a. receivable, admissible.

receveur [rəsə'vœːr], n.m. (fem. **-euse**) receiver, collector (of taxes etc.); (bus) conductor.

recevoir [rəsə'vwaːr], v.t. irr. to receive, to accept, to take, to let in; to admit; to welcome; to entertain.—v.i. to receive, to be at home to visitors.

rechange [rə'ʃɑ̃ːʒ], n.m. change (of anything), replacement; spare things; (Comm.) re-exchange; *roue de rechange*, spare wheel.

rechanter [rəʃɑ̃'te], v.t. to sing again; to retell.

rechaper [rəʃa'pe], v.t. to retread (a tire).

réchapper [reʃa'pe], v.i. to escape; *réchapper d'une maladie*, to recover from an illness.

recharge [rə'ʃarʒ], n.f. fresh or second charge.

rechargement [rəʃarʒə'mɑ̃], n.m. reloading, relading; reballasting.

recharger [rəʃar'ʒe], v.t. (conjug. like MANGER) to load again; to recharge.

réchaud [re'ʃo], n.m. small portable stove; chafing dish; dish warmer.

réchauffage [reʃo'faːʒ], n.m. warming up again, reheating.

réchauffé [reʃo'fe], n.m. dish or food warmed up again; rehash, stale stuff or news.

réchauffer [reʃo'fe], v.t. to warm up, to reheat; to reanimate, to stir up. **se réchauffer**, v.r. to warm oneself, to get warm.

réchauffoir [reʃo'fwaːr], n.m. plate warmer, hot plate.

rechausser [rəʃo'se], v.t. to put shoes or stockings on (a person) again; (Build.) to underpin.

rêche [rɛːʃ], a. rough (to the taste, touch etc.); (fig.) sour, crabbed (of persons).

recherche [rə'ʃɛrʃ], n.f. search, pursuit; inquiry, investigation; research; (fig.) studied elegance or refinement, affectation.

recherché [rəʃɛr'ʃe], a. choice, exquisite; affected; far-fetched; in great demand.

rechercher [rəʃɛr'ʃe], v.t. to seek again; to seek, to search for; to investigate, to pry into; to desire; to court, to woo.

rechigné [rəʃi'ɲe], a. sour-faced, surly, crabbed.

rechignement [rəʃiɲə'mɑ̃], n.m. sulking, sullenness.

rechigner [rəʃi'ɲe], v.i. to look sulky, sullen, grim etc; to balk (at something).

rechute [rə'ʃyt], n.f. relapse, set-back.

rechuter [rəʃy'te], v.i. to have a relapse; to backslide.

récidive [resi'diːv], n.f. recidivism; second offence.

récidiver [residi've], v.i. to repeat the offence; to relapse; to recur (of disease).

récidiviste [residi'vist], n. recidivist, old lag.

récif [re'sif], n.m. reef (of rocks).

récipé [resi'pe], n.m. recipe, prescription.

récipient [resi'pjɑ̃], n.m. container, receptacle; reservoir.

réciprocité [resiprɔsi'te], n.f. reciprocity, reciprocation.

réciproque [resi'prɔk], a. reciprocal, mutual.

réciproquement [resiprɔk'mɑ̃], adv. reciprocally, mutually; vice versa.

récit [re'si], n.m. recital, account, story narrative, report.

récital [resi'tal], n.m. (pl. **-als**) musical recital.

récitant [resi'tɑ̃], a. (Mus.) solo (instrument, voice).—n.m. (fem. **-e**) soloist; narrator.

récitateur [resita'tœːr], n.m. (fem. **-trice**) reciter, repeater.

récitatif [resita'tif], n.m. (Mus.) recitative.

récitation [resita'sjɔ̃], n.f. recitation, reciting; repetition.

réciter [resi'te], v.t. to recite, to rehearse; to repeat, to say; to tell, to relate, to recount.

réclamant [rekla'mɑ̃], a. claiming.—n.m. (fem. **-e**) claimant.

réclamation [reklama'sjɔ̃], n.f. claim, request, demand; complaint.

réclame [re'klaːm], n.f. advertisement; publicity; (Print.) catch-word; blurb.

réclamer [rekla'me], v.t. to crave, to entreat; to beseech; to claim.—v.i. to object, to complain; to protest (contre). **se réclamer**, v.r. to refer to.

reclus [rə'kly], a. shut up, secluded.—n.m. (fem. **-e**) recluse; monk, nun.

reclusion [rəkly'zjɔ̃], **réclusion** [rekly'zjɔ̃], n.f. reclusion, confinement; (Law) solitary confinement (with hard labor).

recoin [rə'kwɛ̃], n.m. corner, nook; *coins et recoins*, nooks and crannies.

récolte [re'kɔlt], n.f. harvest, crop, vintage.

récolter [rekɔl'te], v.t. to reap, to gather in; to get in.

recommandable [rəkɔmɑ̃'dabl], a. respectable; commendable.

recommandation [rəkɔmɑ̃da'sjɔ̃], n.f. recommendation; reference; (fig.) esteem; (Post) registration.

recommander [rəkɔmɑ̃'de], v.t. to recommend; to enjoin; to request; to commend; (Post) to register. **se recommander**, v.r. to recommend oneself; to refer to.

recommencement [rəkɔmɑ̃s'mɑ̃], n.m. recommencement, fresh start.

recommencer [rəkɔmɑ̃'se], v.t., v.i. (conjug. like COMMENCER) to recommence, to begin again; to do (it) again.

récompense [rekɔ̃'pɑ̃ːs], n.f. reward, recompense; prize; compensation; *en récompense de*, in return for.

récompenser [rekɔ̃pɑ̃'se], v.t. to reward; to compensate; to repay.

recomposer [rəkɔ̃po'ze], v.t. to recompose.

recomposition [rəkɔ̃pozi'sjɔ̃], n.f. recomposition.

réconciliable [rekɔ̃si'ljabl], a. reconcilable.

réconciliateur [rekɔ̃silja'tœːr], n.m. (fem. **-trice**) reconciler.

réconciliation [rekɔ̃silja'sjɔ̃], n.f. reconciliation.

réconcilier [rekɔ̃si'lje], v.t. to reconcile. **se réconcilier**, v.r. to be(come) reconciled; (colloq.) to make it up.

reconduire [rəkɔ̃'dɥiːr], v.t. irr. (conjug. like CONDUIRE) to lead back, to see home; to show out.

reconduite [rəkɔ̃'dɥit], n.f. showing out, seeing out, seeing home.

réconfort [rekɔ̃'fɔːr], n.m. comfort, relief.

réconforter [rekɔ̃fɔr'te], *v.t.* to comfort, to cheer up; to fortify.

reconnaissable [rəkɔnɛ'sabl], *a.* recognizable.

reconnaissance [rəkɔnɛ'sãːs], *n.f.* recognition; discovery; gratitude, thankfulness; survey; acknowledgment, confession; reward; recognizance; pawn ticket; (*Mil.*) reconnaissance.

reconnaissant [rəkɔnɛ'sã], *a.* grateful, thankful.

reconnaître [rəkɔ'nɛːtr], *v.t. irr.* (*conjug. like* CONNAÎTRE) to recognize, to identify; to discover; to acknowledge, to admit; to be grateful for; to reconnoitre. **se reconnaître**, *v.r.* to recognize oneself; to be recognizable; to make out where one is.

reconquérir [rəkɔ̃ke'riːr], *v.t. irr.* (*conjug. like* ACQUÉRIR) to reconquer; to regain.

reconstituer [rəkɔ̃sti'tɥe], *v.t.* to reconstitute, to restore.

reconstitution [rəkɔ̃stity'sjɔ̃], *n.f.* reconstitution, reorganization; reconstruction (*of a murder*).

reconstruction [rəkɔ̃stryk'sjɔ̃], *n.f.* reconstruction, rebuilding.

reconstruire [rəkɔ̃s'trɥiːr], *v.t. irr.* (*conjug. like* CONDUIRE) to rebuild, to reconstruct; to rehabilitate.

recopier [rəkɔ'pje], *v.t.* to make a copy of.

recoquillement [rəkɔkij'mã], *n.m.* curling up, dog('s)-earing (*of pages of book*).

recoquiller [rəkɔki'je], *v.t.* to turn up *or* back. **se recoquiller**, *v.r.* to curl up, to shrivel.

record [rə'kɔːr], *n.m.* record (*in sports etc.*).

recorder [rəkɔr'de], *v.t.* to learn by heart; to tie up again.

recors [rə'kɔːr], *n.m.* local magistrate's helper.

recoucher [rəku'ʃe], *v.t.* to put to bed again; to lay down again. **se recoucher**, *v.r.* to go to bed again, to lie down again.

recoudre [rə'kudr], *v.t. irr.* (*conjug. like* COUDRE) to sew again, to sew up.

recoupement [rəkup'mã], *n.m.* (*Build.*) offset; cross-checking.

recouper [rəku'pe], *v.t.* to cut again; to cross-check.

recourbé [rəkur'be], *a.* curved, bent (back).

recourber [rəkur'be], *v.t.* to bend back, to bend round. **se recourber**, *v.r.* to be curved, to bend.

recourir [rəku'riːr], *v.i. irr.* (*conjug. like* COURIR) to run again; to resort (*à*); (*Law*) to appeal

recours [rə'kur], *n.m.* recourse; (*fig.*) resource, remedy; (*Law*) appeal.

recousu [rəku'zy], *a.* sewn *or* stitched again.

recouvrement [rəkuvrə'mã], *n.m.* recovery, regaining; recovering (*of debts etc.*); covering up, overlapping; cap (*of a watch*).

recouvrer [rəku'vre], *v.t.* to recover, to retrieve, to collect.

recouvrir [rəku'vriːr], *v.t. irr.* (*conjug. like* OUVRIR) to cover up, to cover over, to overlay; to hide. **se recouvrir**, *v.r.* to cover oneself again; to cloud over.

recracher [rəkra'ʃe], *v.t.* to spit out again; to disgorge.—*v.i.* to spit again.

récréatif [rekrea'tif], *a.* (*fem.* -tive) recreative, entertaining.

récréation [rekrea'sjɔ̃], *n.f.* recreation, amusement; (*Sch.*) playtime, break.

recréer [rəkre'e], *v.t.* to re-create, to create again.

récréer [rekre'e], *v.t.* to entertain; to amuse. **se récréer**, *v.r.* to amuse oneself, to take recreation.

recrépir [rəkre'piːr], *v.t.* to give a fresh coat of plaster to; to repoint (*a wall*); (*fig. and fam.*) to paint (*one's face*); to recast.

recrépissement [rəkrepis'mã], **recrépissage** [rəkrepi'saːʒ], *n.m.* replastering; repatching.

récrier (**se**) [sərekri'je], *v.r.* to exclaim, to cry out; to protest (*contre*); to be amazed.

récrimination [rekriminɑ'sjɔ̃], *n.f.* recrimination.

récriminatoire [rekriminɑ'twaːr], *a.* recriminatory.

récriminer [rekrimi'ne], *v.i.* to recriminate.

récrire [re'kriːr], *v.t. irr.* (*conjug. like* ÉCRIRE) to rewrite; to write back.

recroqueviller (**se**) [sərəkrɔkvi'je], *v.r.* to curl up, to shrivel.

recru [rə'kry], *a.* tired out, worn out.

recrudescence [rəkrydɛ'sãːs], *n.f.* recrudescence.

recrudescent [rəkrydɛ'sã], *a.* recrudescent.

recrue [rə'kry], *n.f.* recruiting; recruit.

recrutement [rəkryt'mã], *n.m.* recruiting, recruitment.

recruter [rəkry'te], *v.t.* to recruit; to enroll. **se recruter**, *v.r.* to be recruited.

recruteur [rəkry'tœːr], *n.m.* recruiter; recruiting officer.

rectangle [rɛk'tãːgl], *n.m.* rectangle.

rectangulaire [rɛktãgy'lɛːr], *a.* rectangular, right-angled.

recteur [rɛk'tœːr], *n.m.* rector, vice-chancellor (*of a University*); parish priest (*in Brittany*).

rectifiable [rɛkti'fjabl], *a.* rectifiable.

rectification [rɛktifikɑ'sjɔ̃], *n.f.* rectification; adjustment.

rectifier [rɛkti'fje], *v.t.* to rectify; to adjust; to reform.

rectiligne [rɛkti'liɲ], *a.* rectilinear.

rectitude [rɛkti'tyd], *n.f.* rectitude, uprightness.

recto [rɛk'to], *n.m.* first page of a leaf, right-hand page, recto.

rectorat [rɛktɔ'ra], *n.m.* rectorship.

reçu [rə'sy], *a.* received; admitted, recognized; **être reçu** (**à un examen**), to pass (an examination).—*n.m.* receipt.

recueil [rə'kœj], *n.m.* collection, selection; anthology.

recueillement [rəkœj'mã], *n.m.* meditation; peaceful contemplation.

recueilli [rəkœ'ji], *a.* meditative, calm, rapt.

recueillir [rəkœ'jiːr], *v.t. irr.* (*conjug. like* CUEILLIR) to gather, to collect; to reap; to receive; to shelter. **se recueillir**, *v.r.* to collect one's thoughts; to be plunged in meditation.

recuire [rə'kɥiːr], *v.t. irr.* (*conjug. like* CONDUIRE) to cook again.

recuit [rə'kɥi], *a.* cooked, baked *or* roasted again.

recul [rə'kyl], *n.m.* recoil (*of cannon*), kick (*of rifle*); backing (*of horse, car*).

reculade [rəky'lad], *n.f.* falling back, retreat.

reculé [rəky'le], *a.* distant, remote.

reculement [rəkyl'mā], *n.m.* drawing back, backing (*of carriages etc.*); breech (*of saddles*).

reculer [rəky'le], *v.t.* to draw back, to move back, to back; (*fig.*) to put off, to defer.— *v.i.* to go back, to draw back, to retreat; to recoil; to give way. **se reculer**, *v.r.* to draw back, to become more remote.

reculons (à) [arəky'lɔ̃], *adv. phr.* backwards.

récupérage [rekype'ra:ʒ], *n.m.*, **récupération** [rekypera'sjɔ̃], *n.f.* recovery, recuperation.

récupérer [rekype're], *v.t.* (*conjug. like* CÉDER) to recover, to retrieve, to recuperate.

récurer [reky're], *v.t.* to scour, to clean.

récusable [reky'zabl], *a.* (*Law*) exceptionable, doubtful (*of witnesses etc.*).

récusation [rekyza'sjɔ̃], *n.f.* (*Law*) challenge; exception.

récuser [reky'ze], *v.t.* to challenge, to object to (*witnesses, jurors etc.*); to reject. **se récuser**, *v.r.* to excuse oneself, to decline; to decline, to give a decision (*of judges, jurors etc.*).

rédacteur [redak'tœ:r], *n.m.* (*fem.* **-trice**) writer, inditer (*of deed*); clerk (*in public office*); **rédacteur en chef**, editor.

rédaction [redak'sjɔ̃], *n.f.* drawing up (*deeds etc.*); wording; editing (*periodicals*); essay.

reddition [rɛdi'sjɔ̃], *n.f.* surrender; rendering (*of accounts*).

rédempteur [redāp'tœ:r], *a.* (*fem.* **-trice**) redeeming, redemptory.—*n.m.* redeemer, savior.

rédemption [redāp'sjɔ̃], *n.m.* redemption; redeeming.

redescendre [rədɛ'sā:dr], *v.t.* (*with aux.* AVOIR) to carry *or* take down again.—*v.i.* (*with aux.* ÊTRE) to come, go *or* step down again.

redevable [rəd'vabl], *a.* indebted, owing.

redevance [rəd'vā:s], *n.f.* rent, due, tax.

redevenir [rədəv'ni:r], *v.i.* (*conjug. like* TENIR, *but with aux.* ÊTRE) to become again.

redevoir [rədə'vwa:r], *v.t. irr.* (*conjug. like* DEVOIR) to owe still.

rédiger [redi'ʒe], *v.t.* (*conjug. like* MANGER) to draw up, to draft; to edit.

redingote [rədɛ̃'gɔt], *n.f.* frock coat.

redire [rə'di:r], *v.t. irr.* (*conjug. like* DIRE) to repeat, to reveal.—*v.i.* to criticize; **trouver à redire à**, to find fault with.

redondance [rədɔ̃'dā:s], *n.f.* superfluity of words, redundancy.

redondant [rədɔ̃'dā], *a.* redundant.

redonner [rədɔ'ne], *v.t.* to give back again, to restore.—*v.i.* to fall again; to begin again; to charge again.

redoublé [radu'ble], *a.* redoubled, increased.

redoublement [rədublə'mā], *n.m.* redoubling, increase; (*Med.*) paroxysm.

redoubler [radu'ble], *v.t.* to redouble, to reiterate; to increase; to reline (*dress*).—*v.i.* to increase, to redouble.

redoutable [rədu'tabl], *a.* formidable, redoubtable.

redoute [rə'dut], *n.f.* redoubt.

redouter [rədu'te], *v.t.* to dread, to fear.

redressement [rədrɛs'mā], *n.m.* straightening; rectification, redress.

redresser [rədrɛ'se], *v.t.* to make straight; to set up again; to put right; (*colloq.*) to rebuke. **se redresser**, *v.r.* to become straight again; to right itself (*of a ship etc.*); to be redressed; **redressez-vous**, sit up.

redû [rə'dy], *n.m.* balance due.

réducteur [redyk'tœ:r], *a.* (*fem.* **-trice**) reducing.—*n.m.* (*Chem.*) reducer.

réductible [redyk'tibl], *a.* reducible.

réduction [redyk'sjɔ̃], *n.f.* reduction; subjugation; allowance.

réduire [re'dɥi:r], *v.t. irr.* (*conjug. like* CONDUIRE) to reduce, to diminish; to subdue; to compel, to oblige. **se réduire**, *v.r.* to be reduced, to diminish, to abate; to vanish; to be subdued; to amount to.

réduit [re'dɥi], *a.* reduced; dimmed (*of light*).—*n.m.* retreat, nook; hovel; (*Fort.*) keep.

réédification [reedifika'sjɔ̃], *n.f.* rebuilding.

réédifier [reedi'fje], *v.t.* to rebuild.

rééducatif [reedyka'tif], *a.* (*fem.* **-tive**) **thérapie rééducative**, occupational therapy.

réel [re'ɛl], *a.* (*fem.* **-elle**) real, actual; genuine.—*n.m.* reality.

réélection [reelɛk'sjɔ̃], *n.f.* re-election.

réélire [ree'li:r], *v.t. irr.* (*conjug. like* LIRE) to re-elect.

réellement [reɛl'mā], *adv.* really, in reality.

réembobiner [reābobi'ne], *v.t.* to rewind.

réemploi [reā'plwa], *n.m.* re-employment.

réexpédier [reɛkspe'dje], *v.t.* to send on, to (re)forward; to send back.

refaçonner [rəfaso'ne], *v.t.* to make again, to refashion.

réfaction [refak'sjɔ̃], *n.f.* rebate, allowance.

refaire [rə'fɛ:r], *v.t. irr.* (*conjug. like* FAIRE) to do again, to remake; to recommence; to do up; to deal again (*at cards*); to revive; (*slang*) to cheat. **se refaire**, *v.r.* to recover one's strength; to recoup oneself.

refait [rə'fɛ], *a.* set up, done again; (*slang*) **j'ai été refait(e)**, I have been had.—*n.m.* drawn game.

réfection [refɛk'sjɔ̃], *n.f.* repairs (*to buildings etc.*).

réfectoire [refɛk'twa:r], *n.m.* refectory, dining room *or* hall (*in college, convent etc.*).

refend [rə'fā], *n.m.* splitting, sawing, dividing; **mur de refend**, partition wall.

refendre [rə'fā:dr], *v.t.* to cleave *or* split again; to quarter (*timber*); to saw (*stone*) into slabs.

référence [refe'rā:s], *n.f.* reference.

referendum [rəfərā'dɔm], **référendum** [referā'dɔm], *n.m.* referendum.

référer [refe're], *v.t.* (*conjug. like* CÉDER) to refer; to ascribe.—*v.i.* to refer; **en référer à**, to refer to. **se référer**, *v.r.* to refer, to have reference; to leave it (*à*); to trust (*à*).

refermer [rəfɛr'me], *v.t.* to shut again; to close up. **se refermer**, *v.r.* to shut itself; to close up; to heal up (*of wound*).

réfléchi [refle'ʃi], *a.* reflected; deliberate; reflective, thoughtful; wary; (*Gram.*) reflexive.

réfléchir [refle'ʃi:r], *v.t.* to reflect, to throw back; to reverberate.—*v.i.* to reflect, to consider, to ponder. **se réfléchir**, *v.r.* to be reflected.

réfléchissant [refleʃi'sā], *a.* reflecting.

réflecteur [reflɛk'tœ:r], *a.* reflecting.—*n.m.* reflector.

reflet [rə'flɛ], n.m. reflection, reflex; reflected light.

refléter [rəfle'te], v.t. (conjug. like CÉDER) to reflect (light etc.).—v.i. and **se refléter**, v.r. to be reflected.

refleurir [rəflœ'ri:r], v.i. to blossom again.

réflexe [re'flɛks], a. and n.m. reflex.

réflexion [reflɛk'sjɔ̃], n.f. reflection; thought, consideration.

refluer [rə'flɥe], v.i. to reflow, to ebb; (fig.) to swing back.

reflux [rə'fly], n.m. reflux, ebb; flowing back.

refondre [rə'fɔ̃:dr], v.t. to refound (metal), to melt down again, to cast again; (fig.) to remodel.

refonte [rə'fɔ̃:t], n.f. refounding, recasting; recoining; remodelling.

réformateur [reforma'tœ:r], a. (fem. -trice) reforming.—n.m. (fem. -trice) reformer.

réformation [reforma'sjɔ̃], n.f. reformation.

réforme [re'form], n.f. reform, reformation, amendment; (Mil.) reduction, discharge.

réformé [refor'me], a. reformed; (Mil.) invalided out of the service.

réformer [refor'me], v.t. to reform, to improve; (Mil.) to invalid. **se réformer**, v.r. to reform, to mend one's ways.

reformer [rəfor'me], v.t. to form again. **se reformer**, v.r. to form anew, to re-form (of troops etc.).

réformiste [refor'mist], a. and n. reformist.

refoulement [rəful'mɑ̃], n.m. driving back; (Psych.) inhibition, repression.

refouler [rəfu'le], v.t. to drive back; to compress; to suppress; to expel (aliens); to stem (the tide).—v.i. to ebb, to flow back; **la marée refoule**, the tide is ebbing.

réfractaire [refrak'tɛ:r], a. refractory, obstinate, rebellious; **terre réfractaire**, fireproof clay.—n.m. defaulter.

réfracter [refrak'te], v.t. to refract. **se réfracter**, v.r. to be refracted.

réfraction [refrak'sjɔ̃], n.f. refraction.

refrain [rə'frɛ̃], n.m. refrain, chorus; (fig.) constant theme.

refréner [rəfre'ne], v.t. (conjug. like CÉDER) to curb, to control (passions); to bridle, to restrain.

réfrigérant [refriʒe'rɑ̃], a. refrigerant, cooling.—n.m. refrigerator.

réfrigérateur [refriʒera'tœ:r], n.m. refrigerating chamber; refrigerator, (colloq.) fridge; (Am.) icebox.

réfrigération [refriʒera'sjɔ̃], n.f. refrigeration.

réfrigérer [refriʒe're], v.t. (conjug. like CÉDER) to chill, to freeze (food etc.).

refroidir [rəfrwa'di:r], v.t. to cool, to chill.—v.i. to cool, to become cold. **se refroidir**, v.r. to cool, to grow cold; to catch cold; to slacken, to relax.

refroidissement [rəfrwadis'mɑ̃], n.m. cooling, refrigeration; coldness; chill, cold.

refuge [rə'fy:ʒ], n.m. refuge, shelter; (street-) island; lay-by.

réfugié [refy'ʒje], n.m. (fem. -ée) refugee.

réfugier (se) [sərefy'ʒje], v.r. to take refuge; (fig.) to have recourse (to) (dans).

refus [rə'fy], n.m. inv. refusal, denial.

refuser [rəfy'ze], v.t. to refuse, to deny, to decline, to reject.—v.i. to refuse; to decline.

se refuser, v.r. to deny oneself; to shun; to resist.

réfuter [refy'te], v.t. to refute, to disprove.

regagner [rəga'ɲe], v.t. to regain, to recover, to retrieve; to rejoin, to reach.

regain [rə'gɛ̃], n.m. aftermath; second crop; (fig.) revival, new lease (of life).

régal [re'gal], n.m. feast, entertainment, treat.

régalade [rega'lad], n.f. giving a treat, regaling; blazing fire.

régalant [rega'lɑ̃], a. pleasant, entertaining.

régaler [rega'le], v.t. to regale, to treat, to entertain. **se régaler**, v.r. to regale oneself; to enjoy oneself; to entertain or treat each other.

regard [rə'ga:r], n.m. look; glance; gaze, notice, attention; inspection hole; (pl.) eyes; **au regard de**, in comparison with; **d'un seul regard**, at one glance; **en regard**, opposite; **un regard de côté**, a sidelong glance.

regardant [rəgar'dɑ̃], a. particular, meticulous; stingy, niggardly.

regarder [rəgar'de], v.t. to look at, to behold; to look into, to consider; to face, to be opposite; to concern; **cela vous regarde**, that concerns you.—v.i. to look; to mind, to pay heed. **se regarder**, v.r. to look at oneself; to look at each other; to look upon oneself (comme); to consider one another (comme); to face each other.

regarnir [rəgar'ni:r], v.t. to furnish again; to retrim (dress); to re-cover (furniture) etc.

régate [re'gat], n.f. regatta, boat race.

régence [re'ʒɑ̃:s], n.f. regency.

régénérateur [reʒenera'tœ:r], a. (fem. -trice) regenerating.—n.m. regenerator.

régénération [reʒenera'sjɔ̃], n.f. regeneration; reclamation (of land).

régénérer [reʒene're], v.t. (conjug. like CÉDER) to regenerate.

régent [re'ʒɑ̃], a. and n.m. (fem. -e) regent.

régenter [reʒɑ̃'te], v.t. to domineer, to lord it over.

régie [re'ʒi], n.f. administration; (public) corporation; excise.

regimbement [rəʒɛ̃bə'mɑ̃], n.m. kicking (of horses); resistance, recalcitrance.

regimber [rəʒɛ̃'be], v.i. to kick (of horses); (fig.) to resist, to jib.

régime [re'ʒim], n.m. regimen; diet; form of government; rules, regulations; régime, system; speed (of motor etc.); bunch (of bananas etc.).

régiment [reʒi'mɑ̃], n.m. regiment.

régimentaire [reʒimɑ̃'tɛ:r], a. regimental.

région [re'ʒjɔ̃], n.f. region; district.

régional [reʒjo'nal], a. (m. pl. -aux) local.

régir [re'ʒi:r], v.t. to govern, to rule; to administer.

régisseur [reʒi'sœ:r], n.m. manager, steward; (Theat.) stage manager.

registre [rə'ʒistr], n.m. register; account book; damper (in chimneys).

réglable [re'glabl], a. adjustable.

réglage [re'gla:ʒ], n.m. ruling (of paper); regulating, adjusting, tuning.

règle [rɛgl], n.f. ruler, rule; order, regularity; model.

réglé [re'gle], a. regular, steady; ruled; paid.

règlement [rɛglə'mã], *n.m.* regulation; settlement (*of accounts*).

réglementaire [rɛgləmã'tɛːr], *a.* according to regulations, lawful; usual.

réglementer [rɛgləmã'te], *v.t.* to regulate.— *v.i.* to make regulations.

régler [re'gle], *v.t.* (*conjug. like* CÉDER) to rule (*paper etc.*); to regulate, to order, to adjust, to time (*a watch etc.*); to settle (*an account*). **se régler**, *v.r.* to regulate oneself, to be regulated; to be guided (*sur*).

régleur [re'glœːr], *n.m.* (*fem.* **-euse**) regulator (*of clocks etc.*).

réglisse [re'glis], *n.f.* liquorice.

réglure [re'glyːr], *n.f.* ruling (*of paper*).

régnant [re'nã], *a.* reigning; (*fig.*) prevailing, predominant.

règne [rɛɲ], *n.m.* reign; prevalence, vogue; (*Nat. Hist.*) kingdom.

régner [re'ɲe], *v.i.* (*conjug. like* CÉDER) to reign, to rule; to prevail, to be in fashion.

regonfler [rəgɔ̃'fle], *v.t.* to swell again; to pump up (*tire*).—*v.i.* to swell again.

regorgeant [rəgɔr'ʒã], *a.* overflowing; abounding.

regorger [rəgɔr'ʒe], *v.t.* (*conjug. like* MANGER) to regurgitate, to disgorge.—*v.i.* to overflow, to run over; to be crammed (*with*); to be plentiful, to abound.

régressif [regrɛ'sif], *a.* (*fem.* **-ive**) regressive, retrogressive.

régression [regrɛ'sjɔ̃], *n.f.* regression, recession; retrogression; (*fig.*) decline.

regret [rə'grɛ], *n.m.* regret; **à regret**, with reluctance.

regrettable [rəgrɛ'tabl], *a.* regrettable, deplorable.

regrettablement [rəgrɛtablə'mã], *adv.* regrettably.

regretter [rəgrɛ'te], *v.t.* to regret; to grieve; to be sorry for, to repent; to miss.

régularisation [regylariza'sjɔ̃], *n.f.* putting in order, regularization.

régulariser [regylari'ze], *v.t.* to put in order, to regularize.

régularité [regylari'te], *n.f.* regularity.

régulateur [regyla'tœːr], *a.* (*fem.* **-trice**) regulating.—*n.m.* regulator; (*Eng. etc.*) governor.

régulier [regy'lje], *a.* (*fem.* **-ière**) regular; steady, exact.—*n.m.* regular (*monk, soldier etc.*).

régulièrement [regyljɛr'mã], *adv.* regularly.

régurgitation [regyrʒita'sjɔ̃], *n.f.* regurgitation.

régurgiter [regyrʒi'te], *v.t.* to regurgitate.

réhabilitation [reabilita'sjɔ̃], *n.f.* rehabilitation.

réhabiliter [reabili'te], *v.t.* to rehabilitate; to reinstate. **se réhabiliter**, *v.r.* to rehabilitate oneself, to recover one's good name.

rehaussement [rəos'mã], *n.m.* raising; heightening, enhancing; increase of value (*of coin*).

rehausser [rəo'se], *v.t.* to raise; to heighten, to enhance; to raise the value of; to enrich; to set off.

réimposer [reɛ̃po'ze], *v.t.* to reassess (*tax*); (*Print.*) to reimpose.

réimpression [reɛ̃prɛ'sjɔ̃], *n.f.* reprinting; reprint.

réimprimer [reɛ̃pri'me], *v.t.* to print again, to reprint.

rein [rɛ̃], *n.m.* kidney; (*pl.*) loins, back.

réincarnation [reɛ̃karna'sjɔ̃], *n.f.* reincarnation.

reine [rɛːn], *n.f.* queen.

reine-claude [rɛːn'kloːd], *n.f.* (*pl.* **reines-claude**) greengage.

reine-des-prés [rɛːnde'pre], *n.f.* (*pl.* **reines-des-prés**) meadowsweet.

réinstallation [reɛ̃stala'sjɔ̃], *n.f.* reinstallment, re-establishment.

réinstaller [reɛ̃sta'le], *v.t.* to reinstall.

réintégration [reɛ̃tegra'sjɔ̃], *n.f.* reinstatement.

réintégrer [reɛ̃te'gre], *v.t.* (*conjug. like* CÉDER) to reinstate.

réitératif [reitera'tif], *a.* (*fem.* **-tive**) reiterative.

réitération [reitera'sjɔ̃], *n.f.* reiteration, repetition.

réitérer [reite're], *v.t.* (*conjug. like* CÉDER) to reiterate, to repeat.

rejaillir [rəʒa'jiːr], *v.i.* to gush, to spurt out; to spring, to spout; (*fig.*) to flash; to reflect; to rebound.

rejaillissement [rəʒajis'mã], *n.m.* gushing out; spouting, springing; reflection, flashing; rebound.

réjection [reʒɛk'sjɔ̃], *n.f.* rejection.

rejet [rə'ʒɛ], *n.m.* rejection; throwing out; young shoot, sprout.

rejeter [rəʒ'te], *v.t.* (*conjug. like* APPELER) to throw again; to throw back; to tilt back (*one's hat*); to repel; to throw away; to throw up (*of plants*); to reject; to deny.— *v.i.* to shoot (*of plants*). **se rejeter**, *v.r.* to have recourse to; to fall back (*upon*).

rejeton [rəʒ'tɔ̃], *n.m.* shoot, sprout; (*fig.*) scion.

rejoindre [rə'ʒwɛ̃ːdr], *v.t. irr.* (*conjug. like* CRAINDRE) to rejoin, to join; to reunite; to overtake, to catch up. **se rejoindre**, *v.r.* to reunite; to meet; to catch each other up again.

rejouer [rə'ʒwe], *v.t., v.i.* to play again, to replay.

réjoui [re'ʒwi], *a.* and *n.m.* (*fem.* **-e**) jovial, joyous, merry (person).

réjouir [re'ʒwiːr], *v.t.* to rejoice, to delight, to cheer. **se réjouir**, *v.r.* to be *or* to make merry; to rejoice, to be delighted (*de*).

réjouissance [reʒwi'sãːs], *n.f.* rejoicing; (*pl.*) merry-making.

réjouissant [reʒwi'sã], *a.* cheering; diverting; amusing.

relâchant [rəla'ʃã], *a.* relaxing; laxative, loosening.—*n.m.* (*Med.*) laxative.

relâche (1) [rə'laːʃ], *n.m.* intermission, discontinuance, respite; relaxation; (*Theat.*) suspension of performance; **relâche ce soir**, no performance this evening.

relâche (2) [rə'laːʃ], *n.f.* (*Naut.*) putting into a port; port of call.

relâché [rəla'ʃe], *a.* lax, relaxed; loose, remiss.

relâchement [rəlaʃ'mã], *n.m.* slackening; slackness; laxity (*of morals*); looseness (*of bowels*).

relâcher [rəla'ʃe], *v.t.* to slacken, to loosen, to relax; to release; to unbend (*the mind etc.*); to yield, to abate.—*v.i.* (*Naut.*) to put into port. **se relâcher**, *v.r.* to grow slack *or* loose; to abate; to relax, to unbend.

relais [rə'lɛ], *n.m.* relay (*fresh horses*); stage; shift (*of workmen*).

relancer [rəlɑ̃'se], *v.t.* (*conjug. like* COMMENCER) to throw back; (*Ten.*) to return (*the ball*); (*Cards*) to raise (*a bid*); (*fig.*) to harry (*someone*).

relaps [rə'laps], *a.* relapsed, relapsed into heresy.—*n.m.* (*fem.* **-e**) relapsed heretic.

rélargir [relar'ʒiːr], *v.t.* to widen, to let out (*clothes etc.*).

relater [rəla'te], *v.t.* to state, to tell.

relatif [rəla'tif], *a.* (*fem.* **-tive**) relative; relating (*à*).

relation [rəlɑ'sjɔ̃], *n.f.* relation, account; statement; respect; connection; communication, correspondence; (*pl.*) connections.

relativement [rəlativ'mã], *adv.* relatively.

relativité [rəlativi'te], *n.f.* relativity.

relaxation [rəlaksɑ'sjɔ̃], *n.f.* release; relaxation (*of muscles*).

relaxer [rəlak'se], *v.t.* to release (*a prisoner*); to relax (*muscles*).

relayer [rəlɛ'je] *v.t.* (*conjug. like* PAYER) to take the place of, to relieve; (*Elec. Eng., Rad., Teleg. etc.*) to relay.—*v.i.* to change horses. **se relayer**, *v.r.* to relieve each other; to work in shifts.

relégation [rəlegɑ'sjɔ̃], *n.f.* relegation; deportation (*of convict*).

reléguer [rəle'ge], *v.t.* (*conjug. like* CÉDER) to deport (*for life*); to shut up; to relegate, to consign (*à*). **se reléguer**, *v.r.* to shut oneself up.

relent [rə'lɑ̃], *a.* moldy, musty.—*n.m.* mustiness, moldiness.

relève [rə'lɛːv], *n.f.* (*Mil.*) relief.

relevé [rəl've], *a.* raised, erect; exalted, lofty; refined; highly seasoned.—*n.m.* abstract; statement, return; survey.

relèvement [rəlɛv'mã], *n.m.* raising again; recovery (*of business*); relieving (*of sentry*); raise, increase (*of salary*); (*Naut.*) bearing.

relever [rəl've], *v.t.* (*conjug. like* AMENER) to raise again, to lift up again; to turn up; to restore; to relieve (*troops*), to change (*sentry*); to raise (*prices, salary*); to set off, to enhance; to extol; to remark; to note, take down (*name, address etc.*); to release (*from vows, oath*); to survey; (*Naut.*) to take the bearings of.—*v.i.* to recover; to turn up; to depend. **se relever**, *v.r.* to rise again; to get up, to pick oneself up; to recover; to be raised; to relieve each other.

relief [rə'ljɛf], *n.m.* relief, embossment, enhancement; (*pl.*) scraps (*from the table*).

relier [rə'lje], *v.t.* to connect; to hoop (*casks*); to bind (*books*).

relieur [rə'ljœːr], *n.m.* (*fem.* **-euse**) binder, book-binder.

religieusement [rəliʒjøz'mã], *adv.* religiously; scrupulously.

religieux [rəli'ʒjø], *a.* (*fem.* **-euse**) religious, strict.—*n.m.* (*fem.* **-euse**) monk, nun.

religion [rəli'ʒjɔ̃], *n.f.* religion.

reliquaire [rəli'kɛːr], *n.m.* reliquary, shrine.

reliquat [rəli'ka], *n.m.* balance, remainder (*of an account*); after-effects (*of a disease etc.*).

relique [rə'lik], *n.f.* relic (*of a saint*).

relire [rə'liːr], *v.t. irr.* (*conjug. like* LIRE) to re-read.

reliure [rə'ljyːr], *n.f.* binding (*of books*).

relouer [rəlu'e], *v.t.* to relet, to sub-let.

reluire [rəlɥiːr], *v.i. irr.* (*conjug. like* LUIRE) to shine, to glitter.

reluisant [rəlɥi'zɑ̃], *a.* gleaming, shining, glittering.

reluquer [rəly'ke], *v.t.* (*colloq.*) to ogle, to leer at; (*fig.*) to have an eye on.

remâcher [rəmɑ'ʃe], *v.t.* to chew again; (*fig.*) to turn over in one's mind.

remailler [rəmɑ'je], *v.t.* to repair the meshes (*of fishing nets etc.*); to mend a run (*in stocking*).

remaniement *or* **remaniment** [rəmani'mã], *n.m.* (*Polit.*) shakeup; handling again, touching up; repairing; changing.

remanier [rəmɑ'nje], *v.t.* to handle again; to remodel; to adapt, to revise.

remariage [rəmɑ'rjaːʒ], *n.m.* re-marriage.

remarier [rəmɑ'rje], *v.t.* to remarry. **se remarier**, *v.r.* to marry again, to remarry.

remarquable [rəmar'kabl], *a.* remarkable, notable.

remarquablement [rəmarkablə'mã], *adv.* remarkably.

remarque [rə'mark], *n.f.* remark; notice.

remarquer [rəmar'ke], *v.t.* to mark again; to notice; to distinguish; **faire remarquer**, to point out. **se remarquer**, *v.r.* to be remarked.

remballer [rɑ̃ba'le], *v.t.* to pack up again.

rembarquement [rɑ̃barkə'mã], *n.m.* re-embarkation.

rembarquer [rɑ̃bar'ke], *v.t.* to re-embark; to ship again. **se rembarquer**, *v.r.* to go on board again.

rembarrer [rɑ̃ba're], *v.t.* to repulse; to snub; (*fam.*) to tell someone off.

remblai [rɑ̃'blɛ], *n.m.* filling up; embankment.

remblayer [rɑ̃blɛ'je], *v.t.* (*conjug. like* PAYER) to embank, to fill up (*with earth*).

remboîter [rɑ̃bwa'te], *v.t.* to fit in again; to reassemble; to reset (*a bone*).

rembourrage [rɑ̃bu'raːʒ], **rembourrement** [rɑ̃bur'mã], *n.m.* stuffing, padding.

rembourrer [rɑ̃bu're], *v.t.* to stuff, to pad; to upholster.

remboursable [rɑ̃bur'sabl], *a.* repayable; redeemable.

remboursement [rɑ̃bursə'mã], *n.m.* reimbursement, repayment.

rembourser [rɑ̃bur'se], *v.t.* to repay; to reimburse; to redeem (*an annuity etc.*).

rembruni [rɑ̃bry'ni], *a.* dark, gloomy.

rembrunir [rɑ̃bry'niːr], *v.t.* to darken; to cloud over; (*fig.*) to sadden. **se rembrunir**, *v.r.* to grow darker; to become cloudy *or* gloomy.

remède [rə'mɛd], *n.m.* remedy, medicine.

remédiable [rəme'djabl], *a.* remediable.

remédier [rəme'dje], *v.i.* to remedy, to cure (*à*).

remêler [rəmɛ'le], *v.t.* to mix again, to reshuffle.

remembrement [rəmɑ̃brə'mã], *n.m.* consolidation (*of land*).

remémoratif [rəmeməra'tif], *a.* (*fem.* **-tive**) commemorative.

remémorer [rəmemo're], *v.t.* to bring (*a thing*) to someone's mind. **se remémorer**, *v.r.* to recollect.

remerciement or **remercîment** [rəmɛrsi'mã], *n.m.* thanking; (*pl.*) thanks; *faire des remerciements*, to thank.

remercier [rəmɛr'sje], *v.t.* to thank; to dismiss; *non, je vous remercie*, no, thank you.

remettre [rə'mɛtr], *v.t. irr.* (*conjug. like* METTRE) to put back; to put on again; to lay down again; to make well again; to deliver; to postpone; to entrust; to forgive; to remember; (*Ten.*) (*balle*) *à remettre*, let (ball); *je vous remets*, I remember your face; *remettre dans l'esprit*, to remind. **se remettre**, *v.r.* to recover (*oneself*); to resume; to start again; to recollect; to refer; to improve (*of weather*).

réminiscence [remini'sã:s], *n.f.* reminiscence.

remis [rə'mi], *a.* put back, put off, postponed.

remisage [rəmi'za:ʒ], *n.m.* housing, putting away (*vehicle*).

remise [rə'mi:z], *n.f.* delivery; remittance; discount; commission; delay; coach house, mews, shed.

remiser [rəmi'ze], *v.t.* to put up, to put away (*vehicle*); to house; (*colloq.*) to put by.

rémissible [remi'si:bl], *a.* remissible, pardonable.

rémission [remi'sjɔ̃], *n.f.* remission, forgiveness.

remmener [rãm'ne], *v.t.* (*conjug. like* AMENER) to take back, to lead back.

remodeler [rəmɔ'dle], *v.t.* (*conjug. like* AMENER) to remodel.

remontage [rəmɔ̃'ta:ʒ], *n.m.* going up; winding up (*of clock etc.*); assembling; refitting (*of parts of machinery*); restocking (*of shop*).

remonte [rə'mɔ̃:t], *n.f.* remounting, going upstream; run (*of fish*); (*Mil.*) remount.

remonter [rəmɔ̃'te], *v.t.* (*with aux.* AVOIR *or* ÊTRE *according as action or condition is meant*) to go up again; to take up again; to raise; to stock; to wind up (*clock etc.*); to re-string (*instruments*).—*v.i.* to go up again; to go back; to rise or increase (*in value etc.*); to date back; to remount (*cavalry*). **se remonter**, *v.r.* to take in a fresh supply (*de*); to be wound up (*of watches etc.*); to recover one's strength *or* spirits.

remontoir [rəmɔ̃'twa:r], *n.m.* winder, key (*of clock, watch*).

remontrance [rəmɔ̃'trã:s], *n.f.* remonstrance.

remontrer [rəmɔ̃'tre], *v.t.* to show again; to point out; to represent.—*v.i. en remontrer*, (*fig.*) to give advice.

remordre [rə'mɔrdr], *v.t.* to bite again.—*v.i.* to try again.

remords [rə'mɔ:r], *n.m.* remorse.

remorquage [rəmɔr'ka:ʒ], *n.m.* towing, hauling.

remorque [rə'mɔrk], *n.f.* towing; tow; tow-line; trailer (*car*).

remorquer [rəmɔr'ke], *v.t.* to tow, to haul.

remorqueur [rəmɔr'kœ:r], *a.* (*fem.* **-euse**) towing, hauling.—*n.m.* tug-boat, tug.

rémoulade [remu'lad], *n.f.* sharp sauce.

rémouleur [remu'lœ:r], *n.m.* knife-grinder.

remous [rə'mu], *n.m.* eddy; back-wash (*of ship*); slip-stream.

rempailler [rãpa'je], *v.t.* to re-seat (*a straw-bottomed chair*); to re-stuff with straw.

rempailleur [rãpa'jœ:r], *n.m.* (*fem.* **-euse**) chair mender.

rempaqueter [rãpak'te], *v.t.* (*conjug. like* APPELER) to pack up again.

rempart [rã'pa:r], *n.m.* rampart; (*fig.*) bulwark.

remplaçable [rãpla'sabl], *a.* replaceable.

remplaçant [rãpla'sã], *n.m.* (*fem.* **-e**) substitute; locum.

remplacement [rãplas'mã], *n.m.* replacing, replacement.

remplacer [rãpla'se], *v.t.* (*conjug. like* COMMENCER) to take the place of, to replace; to reinvest. **se remplacer**, *v.r.* to be replaced.

rempli [rã'pli], *a.* filled, full.—*n.m.* tuck, take-up.

remplier [rãpli'je], *v.t.* to make a tuck in; to turn in.

remplir [rã'pli:r], *v.t.* to refill, to replenish; to fill, to fill up; to fill in (*form*); to cram; to supply; to occupy (*time etc.*); to fulfil. **se remplir**, *v.r.* to fill oneself; to become full.

remplissage [rãpli'sa:ʒ], *n.m.* filling, filling up (*of casks etc.*); (*fig.*) rubbish, padding.

remploi [rã'plwa], *n.m.* reinvestment.

remployer [rãplwa'je], *v.t.* (*conjug. like* EMPLOYER) to use again; to reinvest.

remplumer [rãply'me], *v.t.* to feather again. **se remplumer**, *v.r.* to get new feathers; (*fig.*) to retrieve one's losses; to get plump again.

rempocher [rãpɔ'ʃe], *v.t.* to put (*something*) back in one's pocket.

remporter [rãpɔr'te], *v.t.* to carry *or* take back; to carry off, to take away with one; to get; to win.

rempoter [rãpɔ'te], *v.t.* to repot.

remuant [rə'mɥã], *a.* restless; bustling; (*fam.*) on the go.

remue-ménage [rəmyme'na:ʒ], *n.m. inv.* stir, disturbance, bustle.

remuement or **remûment** [rəmy'mã], *n.m.* stir, stirring; removal; disturbance.

remuer [rə'mɥe], *v.t.* to move, to stir; to rouse; to turn up; to shake.—*v.i. and se remuer*, *v.r.* to stir, to move; to fidget.

rémunérateur [remynera'tœ:r], *a.* (*fem.* **-trice**) remunerative, profitable.—*n.m.* (*fem.* **-trice**) rewarder.

rémunération [remynera'sjɔ̃], *n.f.* remuneration, reward.

rémunératoire [remynera'twa:r], *a.* remunerative.

rémunérer [remyne're], *v.t.* (*conjug. like* CÉDER) to remunerate; to reward.

renâcler [rənɑ'kle], *v.i.* to snort; (*fam.*) to turn up one's nose; to balk (*at something*).

renaissance [rənɛ'sã:s], *n.f.* rebirth; renaissance.

renaissant [rənɛ'sã], *a.* springing up again, reviving.

renaître [rə'nɛ:tr], *v.i. irr.* (*conjug. like* NAÎTRE, *but no p.p.*) to be born again; to grow again; to appear again; to revive.

rénal [re'nal], *a.* (*m. pl.* **-aux**) (*Anat.*) renal.

renard [rə'na:r], *n.m.* fox; (*fig.*) sly fellow; (*pop.*) strikebreaker.

renarde [rə'nard], *n.f.* vixen.

renardeau [rənar'do], *n.m.* (*pl.* **-eaux**) fox cub.

Renaud [rə'no], *m.* Reginald.

renchéri [rɑ̃ʃeˈri], *a.* particular, over-nice (*of a person*).—*n.m.* (*fem.* **-e**) fastidious person; **faire le renchéri**, to put on airs.
renchérir [rɑ̃ʃeˈriːr], *v.t.* to raise the price of. —*v.i.* to get dearer, to rise in price; **renchérir sur**, to improve upon.
renchérissement [rɑ̃ʃeriˈmɑ̃], *n.m.* rise in price.
rencogner (se) [sərɑ̃koˈɲe], *v.r.* to retreat,to crouch in a corner.
rencontre [rɑ̃ˈkɔ̃ːtr], *n.f.* meeting, encounter; duel; accidental meeting, discovery etc.; collision; chance, coincidence.
rencontrer [rɑ̃kɔ̃ˈtre], *v.t.* to meet, to meet with; to light upon, to encounter. **se rencontrer**, *v.r.* to meet, to meet each other; to be met with; to agree, to coincide.
rendement [rɑ̃dˈmɑ̃], *n.m.* produce, yield, output; efficiency (*of a machine etc.*); (*Spt.*) handicap; (*Comm.*) return, profit.
rendez-vous [rɑ̃deˈvu], *n.m. inv.* rendezvous, appointment; engagement; place of meeting.
rendormir [rɑ̃dɔrˈmiːr], *v.t. irr.* (*conjug. like* SENTIR) to put to sleep again. **se rendormir**, *v.r.* to fall asleep again.
rendre [rɑ̃ːdr], *v.t.* to return, to restore, to give back; to repay; to deliver; to give up; to pay; to produce; to reward; to carry; to eject, to emit; to express; to translate; **rendre visite**, to pay a visit.—*v.i.* to lead (*of roads*); to be lucrative; to function, to work. **se rendre**, *v.r.* to go; to resort; to make oneself, to render oneself; to become; to surrender, to give up; to be worn out.
rendu [rɑ̃ˈdy], *a.* rendered, delivered; exhausted, tired out; arrived.—*n.m.* return, tit for tat.
rendurcir [rɑ̃dyrˈsiːr], *v.t.* to make harder. **se rendurcir**, *v.r.* to become harder.
rêne [rɛːn], *n.f.* rein.
renégat [rəneˈga], *a.* and *n.m.* (*fem.* **-e**) renegade, turncoat.
rêner [rɛˈne], *v.t.* to bridle (*a horse*).
renfermé [rɑ̃fɛrˈme], *a.* **personne renfermée**, close, uncommunicative person.—*n.m.* **odeur de renfermé**, fustiness; musty smell; **sentir le renfermé**, to smell close, fusty *or* stuffy.
renfermer [rɑ̃fɛrˈme], *v.t.* to shut up; to contain; to include, to comprise; to conceal. **se renfermer**, *v.r.* to shut oneself up; to confine oneself.
renfiler [rɑ̃fiˈle], *v.t.* to thread, to string again.
renflammer [rɑ̃flaˈme], *v.t.* to rekindle. **se renflammer**, *v.r.* to flare up again.
renflé [rɑ̃ˈfle], *a.* swollen, swelling; (*Bot.*) inflated.
renflement [rɑ̃fləˈmɑ̃], *n.m.* swelling, bulge.
renfler [rɑ̃ˈfle], *v.t., v.i.* to swell.
renflouage [rɑ̃fluˈaːʒ], **renflouement** [rɑ̃fluˈmɑ̃], *n.m.* refloating (*a ship*).
renflouer [rɑ̃fluˈe], *v.t.* to refloat, to raise (*a ship*); (*fig.*) to salvage (*firm, company etc.*).
renfoncement [rɑ̃fɔ̃sˈmɑ̃], *n.m.* cavity, hollow, recess.
renfoncer [rɑ̃fɔ̃ˈse], *v.t.* (*conjug. like* COMMENCER) to drive deeper; to pull (*a hat etc.*) further on.
renforçage [rɑ̃fɔrˈsaːʒ], *n.m.* strengthening.

renforcé [rɑ̃fɔrˈse], *a.* downright, regular; reinforced.
renforcement [rɑ̃fɔrsəˈmɑ̃], *n.m.* strengthening; reinforcement.
renforcer [rɑ̃fɔrˈse], *v.t.* (*conjug. like* COMMENCER) to strengthen, to reinforce; to increase. **se renforcer**, *v.r.* to gather strength, to grow stronger; (*Mil.*) to be reinforced.
renfort [rɑ̃ˈfɔːr], *n.m.* reinforcement; (*fig.*) help, aid, relief; strengthening-piece.
renfrogné [rɑ̃frɔˈɲe], *a.* frowning, scowling, surly.
renfrognement [rɑ̃frɔɲəˈmɑ̃], *n.m.* frown, scowl.
renfrogner (se) [sərɑ̃frɔˈɲe], *v.r.* to frown.
rengagement [rɑ̃gaʒˈmɑ̃], *n.m.* re-engagement; (*Mil.*) re-enlistment.
rengager [rɑ̃gaˈʒe], *v.t.* (*conjug. like* MANGER) to re-engage.—*v.i.* (*Mil.*) to re-enlist. **se rengager**, *v.r.* to re-engage; to begin afresh; to re-enlist.
rengaine [rɑ̃ˈgɛːn], *n.f.* catch phrase; (*fam.*) hackneyed story; popular tune.
rengainer [rɑ̃gɛˈne], *v.t.* to sheathe, to put up (*one's sword*); to withdraw, to put away.
rengorgement [rɑ̃gɔrʒəˈmɑ̃], *n.m.* swaggering, puffing out the neck (*of peacock*).
rengorger (se) [sərɑ̃gɔrˈʒe], *v.r.* to carry one's head high; (*fig.*) to give oneself airs.
reniable [rəˈnjabl], *a.* deniable.
reniement *or* **reniment** [rəniˈmɑ̃], *n.m.* denying, disowning.
renier [rəˈnje], *v.t.* to disown (*son, friend etc.*); to deny (*God, doctrine*).
reniflement [rəniflˈmɑ̃], *n.m.* sniffing, snuffing, snivelling.
renifler [rəniˈfle], *v.i.* to sniff, to snivel; (*fig.*) to turn up one's nose (*sur*); to hang back.
renne [rɛn], *n.m.* reindeer.
renom [rəˈnɔ̃], *n.m.* renown, fame, reputation.
renommé [rənɔˈme], *a.* renowned, famed.
renommée [rənɔˈme], *n.f.* renown, fame reputation; rumor.
renommer [rənɔˈme], *v.t.* to name again, to re-elect; to make famous, to praise.
renoncement [rənɔ̃sˈmɑ̃], *n.m.* renouncement; renunciation.
renoncer [rənɔ̃ˈse], *v.t.* (*conjug. like* COMMENCER) to renounce, to disclaim, to disown.—*v.i.* to give up, to renounce (*à*).
renonciation [rənɔ̃sjaˈsjɔ̃], *n.f.* renunciation, self-denial.
renoncule [rənɔ̃ˈkyl], *n.f.* (*Bot.*) ranunculus, buttercup, crowfoot.
renouer [rənuˈe], *v.t.* to tie again, to knot again; to put together; to resume.—*v.i.* to resume relations (*avec*).
renouveau [rənuˈvo], *n.m.* (*pl.* **-eaux**) (*poet.*) spring.
renouvelable [rənuˈvlabl], *a.* renewable.
renouveler [rənuˈvle], *v.t.* (*conjug. like* APPELER) to renew; to renovate; to revive; to recommence; to repeat. **se renouveler**, *v.r.* to be renewed, to be revived; to occur again.
renouvellement [rənuvɛlˈmɑ̃], *n.m.* renewal, revival, renovation; increase.
rénovateur [renɔvaˈtœːr], *a.* (*fem.* **-trice**) renovating.—*n.m.* (*fem.* **-trice**) renovator, restorer.

rénovation [renɔvaˈsjɔ̃], *n.f.* renovation, renewal.

renseignement [rɑ̃sɛɲˈmɑ̃], *n.m.* (piece of) information, (piece of) intelligence, account; (*pl.*) information; references; *bureau de renseignements,* information bureau, inquiry office.

renseigner [rɑ̃sɛˈɲe], *v.t.* to give information to; to direct. **se renseigner,** *v.r.* to seek information, to make inquiries.

rente [rɑ̃:t], *n.f.* yearly income; revenue; stock, funds.

renté [rɑ̃ˈte], *a.* of independent means; endowed (*of hospital etc.*).

renter [rɑ̃ˈte], *v.t.* to allow a yearly income to, to endow (*public services etc.*).

rentier [rɑ̃ˈtje], *n.m.* (*fem.* **-ière**) stockholder; person of independent means.

rentrant [rɑ̃ˈtrɑ̃], *a.* re-entering, returning; (*Av.*) retractable.—*n.m.* recess (*in a wall*); (*fem.* **-e**) new player.

rentré [rɑ̃ˈtre], *a.* returned; suppressed; depressed.

rentrée [rɑ̃ˈtre], *n.f.* re-entrance; return, home-coming; reopening (*of schools etc.*); reappearance; ingathering (*of crops etc.*); receipt, collection.

rentrer [rɑ̃ˈtre], *v.t.* (*aux.* AVOIR) to take in, to bring in; to suppress.—*v.i.* (*aux.* ÊTRE) to re-enter, to go in again; to return home; to join again; to reopen (*of schools etc.*).

renversable [rɑ̃vɛrˈsabl], *a.* liable to be upset; reversible.

renversant [rɑ̃vɛrˈsɑ̃], *a.* (*colloq.*) amazing, stunning.

renverse [rɑ̃ˈvɛrs], *n.f. à la renverse,* backwards.

renversé [rɑ̃vɛrˈse], *a.* thrown down, thrown back; upside-down.

renversement [rɑ̃vɛrsəˈmɑ̃], *n.m.* reversing; overturning, overthrow; turning upside down; confusion; subversion.

renverser [rɑ̃vɛrˈse], *v.t.* to turn upside down, to upset; to reverse; to knock over; to spill (*a liquid*); to destroy; to confuse; to turn (*the brain*); (*fam.*) to astound; to rout; (*Arith., Mus.*) to invert. **se renverser,** *v.r.* to fall back; to fall down; to capsize; to be spilt.

renvoi [rɑ̃ˈvwa], *n.m.* sending back, return; dismissal; referring (*to a committee etc.*).

renvoyer [rɑ̃vwaˈje], *v.t. irr.* (*conjug. like* ENVOYER) to send again; to send back, to return; to dismiss; to refer; to postpone; to throw back; to reflect (*light, heat etc.*); to reverberate (*sound*). **se renvoyer,** *v.r.* to be sent back *or* returned; to send from one to the other.

réoccupation [reɔkypaˈsjɔ̃], *n.f.* reoccupation.

réoccuper [reɔkyˈpe], *v.t.* to reoccupy.

réorganisation [reɔrganizaˈsjɔ̃], *n.f.* reorganization.

réorganiser [reɔrganiˈze], *v.t.* to reorganize.

réouverture [reuvɛrˈty:r], *n.f.* reopening (*of a theatre*).

repaire (1) [rəˈpɛ:r], *n.m.* haunt (*of criminals*); den, lair (*of animals*).

repaire (2) [REPÈRE].

repaître [rəˈpɛ:tr], *v.t. irr.* (*conjug. like* PAÎTRE) to feed, to nourish. **se repaître,** *v.r.*

to feed on, to feast on; to delight in, to indulge in.

répandre [reˈpɑ̃:dr], *v.t.* to pour out, to shed; to spill; to scatter; to distribute; to exhale; to spread abroad. **se répandre,** *v.r.* to be poured out, to be shed, to be spilt; to be spread; to be exhaled; to be spread abroad; to be current; to go into society.

répandu [repɑ̃ˈdy], *a.* spilt, shed; widespread.

réparable [repaˈrabl], *a.* reparable; rectifiable.

reparaître [rəpaˈrɛ:tr], *v.i. irr.* (*conjug. like* CONNAÎTRE) to reappear.

réparateur [reparaˈtœ:r], *a.* (*fem.* **-trice**) restorative, refreshing.—*n.m.* (*fem.* **-trice**) repairer, restorer.

réparation [reparaˈsjɔ̃], *n.f.* repairing, mending; amends; compensation; *en réparation,* under repair.

réparer [repaˈre], *v.t.* to repair, to mend; to make amends for, to make up for.

répareur [repaˈrœ:r], *n.m.* (*fem.* **-euse**) repairer.

reparler [rəparˈle], *v.i.* to speak again.

repartie [rəparˈti], *n.f.* repartee, retort.

repartir (1) [rəparˈti:r], *v.t., v.i.* (*conjug. like* SENTIR) to answer, to retort.

repartir (2) [rəparˈti:r], *v.i. irr.* (*conjug. like* SENTIR, *but with aux.* ÊTRE) to set out again, to go away again.

répartir [reparˈti:r], *v.t.* to divide, to distribute; to assess.

répartissable [repartiˈsabl], *a.* divisible; assessable.

répartiteur [repartiˈtœ:r], *n.m.* (*fem.* **-trice**) distributor; assessor (*of taxes etc.*).

répartition [repartiˈsjɔ̃], *n.f.* distribution; assessment.

repas [rəˈpɑ], *n.m. inv.* meal, repast.

repassage [rəpaˈsa:ʒ], *n.m.* repassing; grinding, sharpening (*of cutlery*); ironing (*of linen etc.*).

repasser [rəpaˈse], *v.t.* (*aux.* AVOIR) to pass again; to cross again; to think over; to sharpen, to grind (*tools*); to iron; to repeat; to look over again.—*v.i.* (*aux.* ÊTRE) to pass again; to go, come, call etc., again.

repasseur [rəpaˈsœ:r], *n.m.* (*fem.* **-euse**) (*Ind.*) examiner; grinder.—*n.f.* (**-euse**) ironer (*person* or *machine*).

repavage [rəpaˈva:ʒ], **repavement** [rəpavˈmɑ̃], *n.m.* repaving.

repaver [rəpaˈve], *v.t.* to repave.

repêchage [rəpɛˈʃa:ʒ], *n.m.* rescuing; (*Spt.*) *épreuve de repêchage,* supplementary heat; (*Sch.*) second chance (*for candidate who has failed an examination*).

repêcher [rəpɛˈʃe], *v.t.* to fish up *or* out again; (*fig.*) to recover, to retrieve.

repeindre [rəˈpɛ̃:dr], *v.t. irr.* (*conjug. like* CRAINDRE) to repaint.

repenser [rəpɑ̃ˈse], *v.t., v.i.* to think over; to think again (of).

repentance [rəpɑ̃ˈtɑ̃:s], *n.f.* repentance, contrition.

repentant [rəpɑ̃ˈtɑ̃], *a.* repentant.

repenti [rəpɑ̃ˈti], *a.* penitent.

repentir [rəpɑ̃ˈti:r], *n.m.* repentance, contrition, regret.

repentir (**se**) [sərəpɑ̃ˈti:r], *v.r. irr.* (*conjug. like* SENTIR) to repent; to rue (*de*).

repérage [rəpe'ra:ʒ], *n.m.* locating; (*Cine.*) synchronization; (*Mil.*) spotting.

répercussion [repɛrky'sjɔ̃], *n.f.* repercussion, reverberation.

répercuter [repɛrky'te], *v.t.* to reverberate, to echo; to reflect. **se répercuter**, *v.r.* to be reflected (*light*); to reverberate (*sound*); (*fig.*) to have repercussions.

repère or **repaire** [rə'pɛ:r], *n.m.* mark; benchmark; (*fig.*) landmark.

repérer [rəpe'rel], *v.t.* (*conjug. like* CÉDER) to locate, to spot; to make a guiding mark upon. **se repérer**, *v.r.* to find one's bearings.

répertoire [repɛr'twa:r], *n.m.* table, list, catalogue; repertory.

répéter [repe'te], *v.t.* (*conjug. like* CÉDER) to repeat, to tell again; to rehearse; to reflect; (*Law*) to demand back. **se répéter**, *v.r.* to be repeated; to repeat oneself.

répétiteur [repeti'tœ:r], *n.m.* (*fem.* **-trice**) private teacher, tutor.

répétition [repeti'sjɔ̃], *n.f.* repetition; recurrence; private lesson; (*Theat.*) rehearsal.

repétrir [rəpe'tri:r], *v.t.* to remold; to refashion.

repeupler [rəpœ'ple], *v.t.* to repeople; to restock. **se repeupler**, *v.r.* to be repeopled; to be restocked.

repiquage [rəpi'ka:ʒ], *n.m.* transplanting, pricking *or* planting out (again); repairing (*of road*).

repiquer [rəpi'ke], *v.t.* to prick again; to prick out, to transplant; to repair (*road*).

répit [re'pi], *n.m.* respite; (*fig.*) rest, breathing space.

replacement [rəplas'mã], *n.m.* replacing, putting *or* setting again; reinvestment (*of funds*).

replacer [rəpla'se], *v.t.* (*conjug. like* COMMENCER) to replace, to put in place again; to bring back; to reinvest (*funds*). **se replacer**, *v.r.* to find oneself a new situation.

replanir [rəpla'ni:r], *v.t.* to plane down (*wood*).

replanter [rəplã'te], *v.t.* to replant.

replâtrer [rəpla'tre], *v.t.* to replaster; to patch up (*temporarily*).

replet [rə'plɛ], *a.* (*fem.* **-ète**) obese, stout; (*fam.*) pudgy.

réplétion [reple'sjɔ̃], *n.f.* stoutness; repletion; surfeit.

repli [rə'pli], *n.m.* fold, crease; (*fig.*) winding, coil, meander (*of river*); (*Mil.*) withdrawal.

repliable [rəpli'jabl], *a.* folding, collapsible.

replier [rəpli'je], *v.t.* to fold again, to fold up; to bend back; to coil (*a rope etc.*). **se replier**, *v.r.* to twist oneself, to writhe, to wind, to coil; (*Mil.*) to retreat.

réplique [re'plik], *n.f.* reply, answer, retort; (*Mus.*) repeat; (*Theat.*) cue.

répliquer [repli'ke], *v.t.*, *v.i.* to reply, to retort.

replonger [rəplɔ̃'ʒe], *v.t.* (*conjug. like* MANGER) to plunge again, to dip again.—*v.i.* and **se replonger**, *v.r.* to plunge again; to dive again.

répondant [repɔ̃'dã], *n.m.* candidate (*at an examination*); bail, surety.

répondre [re'pɔ̃:dr], *v.t.* to answer, to reply. —*v.i.* to answer, to reply; to write back; to come up (*à*); to correspond; to re-echo; to be answerable (*de*); to pledge oneself (*pour*); *je vous en réponds*, take my word for it.

répons [re'pɔ̃], *n.m.* response (*in church*).

réponse [re'pɔ̃:s], *n.f.* answer, reply, response.

report [rə'pɔ:r], *n.m.* (*Book-keeping*) carrying forward, bringing forward; amount brought forward.

reportage [rəpɔr'ta:ʒ], *n.m.* (*Journ.*) reporting; feature article.

reporter (1) [rəpɔr'tɛ:r], *n.m.* (*Journ.*) reporter.

reporter (2) [rəpɔr'te], *v.t.* to carry back; take back; (*Book-keeping*) to carry forward. **se reporter**, *v.r.* to go back; to refer; *se reporter à*, please refer to.

repos [rə'po], *n.m.* rest, repose; sleep; quiet, resting place; *en repos*, at rest; (*Mil.*) *repos !* stand at ease!

reposant [rəpo'zã], *a.* restful, refreshing.

reposé [rəpo'ze], *a.* rested, refreshed; quiet, calm, cool.

reposer [rəpo'ze], *v.t.* to place again, to lay again, to replace; to rest (*on anything*); to refresh.—*v.i.* to rest, to lie down; to sleep; to be at rest. **se reposer**, *v.r.* to rest, to lie down; to settle down; to alight again (*of birds*); *se reposer sur*, to rely on.

reposoir [rəpo'zwa:r], *n.m.* resting place; pause.

repoussant [rəpu'sã], *a.* repulsive, loathsome.

repoussé [rəpu'se], *a.* chased (*silver*), embossed.

repousser [rəpu'se], *v.t.* to push back, to repel; to spurn, to reject; to rebuff; to shoot out (*branches etc.*) again; *repousser du cuir*, to emboss leather; *repousser du cuivre*, to chase copper.—*v.i.* to recoil; to spring up again (*of plants etc.*); to grow again (*of hair*); to be repulsive.

repoussoir [rəpu'swa:r], *n.m.* (*Paint.*) foil.

répréhensible [repreã'sibl], *a.* reprehensible.

répréhension [repreã'sjɔ̃], *n.f.* reprehension, reproof.

reprendre [rə'prã:dr], *v.t. irr.* (*conjug. like* PRENDRE) to recover, to recapture; to take up again; to reprove; to repair.—*v.i.* to take root again; to freeze again; to close up again (*of wounds etc.*); to begin again, to return to; to improve; to reply; to resume. **se reprendre**, *v.r.* to correct oneself; to be caught again; to begin again.

représaille [repre'za:j], *n.f.* (*usu. pl.*) reprisal; *user de représailles*, to retaliate.

représentant [rəprezã'tã], *n.m.* (*fem.* **-e**) representative.

représentatif [rəprezãta'tif], *a.* (*fem.* **-tive**) representative.

représentation [rəprezãta'sjɔ̃], *n.f.* representation; performance; show; remonstrance; agency.

représenter [rəprezã'te], *v.t.* to present again; to show, to produce; to represent; to resemble; to act (*a play*); to be the representative of.—*v.i.* to have an imposing appearance; to make a good show. **se représenter**, *v.r.* to present oneself again; to picture to oneself; to occur.

répressible [repre'sibl], *a.* repressible.

répressif [repre'sif], *a.* (*fem.* **-ive**) repressive.

répression [repre'sjɔ̃], *n.f.* repression.

réprimande [repri'mã:d], *n.f.* reprimand, rebuke.

réprimander [reprimã'de], *v.t.* to reprimand, to reprove.

réprimant [repri'mã], *a.* repressive.

réprimer [repri'me], *v.t.* to repress, to restrain.

repris [rə'pri], *a.* retaken, taken up again; reset (*of a bone*).—*n.m.* **repris de justice**, old offender. (*fam.*) old lag.

reprisage [rəpri'za:ʒ], *n.m.* darn; darning.

reprise [rə'pri:z], *n.f.* resumption; recapture, recovery; revival; darn; (*Mus.*) repetition; refrain (*of a song*); (*Ftb. etc.*) second half; (*Fenc.*) bout; (*Box.*) round; **à plusieurs reprises**, several times, repeatedly.

repriser [rəpri'ze], *v.t.* to darn.

réprobateur [reprɔba'tœ:r], *a.* (*fem.* **-trice**) reproving.

réprobation [reprɔba'sjɔ̃], *n.f.* reprobation.

reprochable [rəprɔ'ʃabl], *a.* reproachable.

reproche [rə'prɔʃ], *n.m.* reproach.

reprocher [rəprɔ'ʃe], *v.t.* to reproach, to upbraid; to taunt. **se reprocher**, *v.r.* to reproach oneself; to blame oneself.

reproducteur [rəprɔdyk'tœ:r], *a.* (*fem.* **-trice**) reproductive.

reproductif [rəprɔdyk'tif], *a.* (*fem.* **-tive**) reproductive.

reproduction [rəprɔdyk'sjɔ̃], *n.f.* reproduction; copy.

reproduire [rəprɔ'dɥi:r], *v.t. irr.* (*conjug. like* CONDUIRE) to reproduce; to reprint. **se reproduire**, *v.r.* to reproduce; to breed; to recur.

réprouvable [repru'vabl], *a.* censurable, reprehensible.

réprouvé [repru've], *a.* and *n.m.* (*fem.* **-ée**) reprobate.

réprouver [repru've], *v.t.* to disapprove of; (*Theol.*) to condemn.

reps [rɛps], *n.m.* rep (*silk* or *woollen fabric*).

reptile [rɛp'til], *a.* creeping, crawling.—*n.m.* reptile.

repu [rə'py], *a.* and *p.p.* of **repaître**, full, satiated.

républicain [repybli'kɛ̃], *a.* and *n.m.* (*fem.* **-e**) republican.

republier [rəpybli'je], *v.t.* to republish.

république [repy'blik], *n.f.* republic; commonwealth.

répudiation [repydja'sjɔ̃], *n.f.* repudiation.

répudier [repy'dje], *v.t.* to repudiate.

répugnance [repy'nã:s], *n.f.* repugnance; reluctance.

répugnant [repy'nã], *a.* repugnant.

répugner [repy'ne], *v.i.* to be repugnant; to feel repugnance; to clash with.

répulsif [repyl'sif], *a.* (*fem.* **-sive**) repulsive, repellent; (*fig.*) disgusting.

répulsion [repyl'sjɔ̃], *n.f.* repulsion; (*fig.*) aversion, disgust.

réputation [repyta'sjɔ̃], *n.f.* reputation, character; fame.

réputé [repy'te], *a.* well-known.

réputer [repy'te], *v.t.* to repute, to consider, to deem.

requérant [rəke'rã], *n.m.* (*fem.* **-e**) plaintiff, petitioner.

requérir [rəke'ri:r], *v.t. irr.* (*conjug. like* ACQUÉRIR) to request; to require; to claim; to requisition.

requête [rə'kɛ:t], *n.f.* request, petition, demand.

requiem [rekɥi'ɛm], *n.m.* requiem.

requin [rə'kɛ̃], *n.m.* shark.

requis [rə'ki], *a.* required, requisite, necessary.

réquisition [rekizi'sjɔ̃], *n.f.* requisition; summons; levy.

réquisitionner [rekizisjɔ'ne], *v.t.* to requisition, to commandeer.

rescapé [rɛska'pe], *a.* and *n.m.* (*fem.* **-ée**) survivor of a disaster.

rescousse [rɛs'kus], *n.f.* **venir** (**aller**) **à la rescousse**, to come (to go) to the rescue.

réseau [re'zo], *n.m.* (*pl.* **-eaux**) net; network; (*fig.*) web, tangle; (*Rail., Elec. etc.*) network, system.

réséda [reze'da], *n.m.* reseda; mignonette.

réservation [rezerva'sjɔ̃], *n.f.* reservation, reserving; booking (*of seats*).

réserve [re'zɛrv], *n.f.* reserve; reservation, caution; modesty; stock, store; preserve (*for game*).

réservé [rezɛr've], *a.* reserved; cautious.

réserver [rezɛr've], *v.t.* to reserve; to keep (**pour**). **se réserver**, *v.r.* to reserve for oneself; to reserve oneself, to wait.

réserviste [rezɛr'vist], *n.m.* (*Mil.*) reservist.

réservoir [rezɛr'vwa:r], *n.m.* reservoir; tank, cistern, well.

résidant [rezi'dã], *a.* resident.

résidence [rezi'dã:s], *n.f.* residence, dwelling.

résident [rezi'dã], *n.m.* (*fem.* **-e**) resident.

résidentiel [rezidã'sjɛl], *a.* (*fem.* **-elle**) residential.

résider [rezi'de], *v.i.* to reside, to dwell.

résidu [rezi'dy], *n.m.* residue; remainder.

résiduaire [rezi'dɥɛ:r], *a.* waste.

résignation [rezina'sjɔ̃], *n.f.* resignation.

résigné [rezi'ne], *a.* resigned, submissive.

résigner [rezi'ne], *v.t.* to resign, to give up. **se résigner**, *v.r.* to resign oneself, to submit.

résiliation [rezilja'sjɔ̃], *n.f.*, **résiliement** or **résilîment** [rezili'mã], *n.m.* cancelling, annulment.

résilience [rezi'ljã:s], *n.f.* resilience (*in metals*).

résilier [rezi'lje], *v.t.* to cancel, to annul.

résille [re'zi:j], *n.f.* hair net.

résine [re'zin], *n.f.* resin, rosin.

résineux [rezi'nø], *a.* (*fem.* **-euse**) resinous.

résistance [rezis'tã:s], *n.f.* resistance, opposition; **la Résistance**, the Resistance Movement (1940–45).

résistant [rezis'tã], *a.* unyielding; resistant, tough.—*n.m.* (*fem.* **-e**) member of the Resistance Movement.

résister [rezis'te], *v.i.* to resist, to withstand (**à**).

résistible [rezis'tibl], *a.* resistible.

résistivité [rezistivi'te], *n.f.* (*Elec.*) resistivity.

résolu [rezɔ'ly], *a.* resolved, resolute, determined; solved.

résoluble [rezɔ'lybl], *a.* soluble.

résolument [rezɔly'mã], *adv.* resolutely, boldly.

résolution [rezɔly'sjɔ̃], *n.f.* resolution, solution; decision, determination; resolve.

résonance [rezɔ'nã:s], *n.f.* resonance.

résonnant [rezɔ'nã], *a.* resonant, resounding, sonorous.

résonnement [rezɔn'mā], *n.m.* resounding, re-echoing.

résonner [rezo'ne], *v.i.* to resound, to reverberate, to re-echo.

résoudre [re'zu:dr], *v.t. irr.* to resolve; to dissolve; to solve; to decide upon; to cancel; to persuade. **se résoudre**, *v.r.* to resolve, to determine; to be resolved, to be solved; to dissolve.

respect [rɛs'pɛ], *n.m.* respect, regard, reverence.

respectabilité [rɛspɛktabili'te], *n.f.* respectability.

respectable [rɛspɛk'tabl], *a.* respectable.

respectablement [rɛspɛktablə'mā], *adv.* respectably.

respecter [rɛspɛk'te], *v.t.* to respect, to revere; to spare.

respectif [rɛspɛk'tif], *a. (fem. -tive)* respective.

respectivement [rɛspɛktiv'mā], *adv.* respectively.

respectueusement [rɛspɛktyøz'mā], *adv.* respectfully, deferentially.

respectueux [rɛspɛk'tyø], *a. (fem. -euse)* respectful, deferential.

respirable [rɛspi'rabl], *a.* respirable, breathable.

respirateur [rɛspira'tœːr], *a.m.* respiratory. —*n.m.* respirator.

respiration [rɛspira'sjɔ̃], *n.f.* respiration, breathing.

respiratoire [rɛspira'twa:r], *a.* respiratory, breathing.

respirer [rɛspi're], *v.t.* to breathe; *(fig.)* to express; to long for.—*v.i.* to breathe; to catch one's breath, to rest.

resplendir [rɛsplā'di:r], *v.i.* to shine brightly; to glitter.

resplendissant [rɛsplādi'sā], *a.* resplendent, glittering.

resplendissement [rɛsplādis'mā], *n.m.* splendor, refulgence.

responsabilité [rɛspɔ̃sabili'te], *n.f.* responsibility, liability.

responsable [rɛspɔ̃'sabl], *a.* responsible, accountable.

resquillage [rɛski'ja:ʒ], *n.m.*, **resquille** [rɛs'ki:j], *n.f. (slang)* gate-crashing; **entrer à la resquille**, to gate-crash.

resquiller [rɛski'je], *v.i.* to gate-crash; to wangle.

ressac [rə'sak], *n.m.* surf.

ressaisir [rəsɛ'zi:r], *v.t.* to seize again. **se ressaisir**, *v.r.* to regain one's self-control.

ressasser [rəsa'se], *v.t. (fig.)* to scrutinize; *(fig.)* to repeat tediously, to harp on.

ressaut [rə'so], *n.m.* projection; abrupt fall, dip.

ressauter [rəso'te], *v.t.* to leap over again.—*v.i.* to leap again; *(Arch.)* to project.

ressemblance [rəsā'blā:s], *n.f.* resemblance, likeness.

ressemblant [rəsā'blā], *a.* like, similar.

ressembler [rəsā'ble], *v.i.* to look like, to resemble *(à)*. **se ressembler**, *v.r.* to be like each other; to look alike.

ressemelage [rəsəm'la:ʒ], *n.m.* resoling *(of shoes)*.

ressemeler [rəsə'mle], *v.t. (conjug. like APPELER)* to re-sole *(shoes etc.)*.

ressenti [rəsā'ti], *a.* felt; *(Paint.)* strongly expressed.

ressentiment [rəsāti'mā], *n.m.* resentment.

ressentir [rəsā'ti:r], *v.t. irr. (conjug. like SENTIR)* to feel, to experience; to manifest; to resent. **se ressentir**, *v.r.* to feel the effects *(de)*; to be felt.

resserrement [rəsɛr'mā], *n.m.* contraction, tightening; restriction.

resserrer [rəsɛ're], *v.t.* to tighten; to pen in; to restrain; to abridge; to close up; to lock up again. **se resserrer**, *v.r.* to contract, to be contracted; to confine oneself; to curtail one's expenses.

ressort (1) [rə'so:r], *n.m.* spring; elasticity; energy, activity, strength; means.

ressort (2) [rə'so:r], *n.m.* extent of jurisdiction; *(fig.)* department, line.

ressortir (1) [rəsɔr'ti:r], *v.i. irr. (conjug. like SENTIR, but with aux. ÊTRE)* to go or come out again; *(fig.)* to stand out; to result *(de)*; **faire ressortir**, to throw into relief.

ressortir (2) [rəsɔr'ti:r], *v.i.* to be under the jurisdiction of, to be dependent on.

ressortissant [rəsɔrti'sā], *n.m. (fem. -e)* national.

ressource [rə'surs], *n.f.* resource, resort, expedient, shift; *(pl.)* resources; **il n'y a point de ressource**, there's no help for it; **ressources personnelles**, private means.

ressouvenir [rəsuv'ni:r], *n.m.* remembrance, recollection, reminiscence.

ressouvenir (se) [sərəsuv'ni:r], *v.r. irr. (conjug. like TENIR, but with aux. ÊTRE)* to recollect, to remember.

ressuscitation [resysita'sjɔ̃], *n.f.* resuscitation, revival.

ressusciter [resysi'te], *v.t.* to resuscitate; to revive *(a custom etc.)*.—*v.i.* to come to life again.

restant [rɛs'tā], *a.* remaining, left.—*n.m.* remainder, rest.

restaurant [rɛstɔ'rā], *n.m.* restaurant; restorative.

restaurateur [rɛstɔra'tœ:r], *n.m. (fem. -trice)* restorer; restaurant keeper.

restauration [rɛstɔra'sjɔ̃], *n.f.* restoration, repair.

restaurer [rɛstɔ're], *v.t.* to restore; to refresh. **se restaurer**, *v.r.* to take refreshment; to build up one's strength *(after illness)*.

reste [rɛst], *n.m.* rest, remainder; trace, vestige; *(pl.)* remnants, relics; remains; **au reste** or **du reste**, besides, moreover; **de reste**, over and above; **et le reste**, and so on, and so forth; **être en reste**, to be in arrears; **les restes**, remnants *(of meal)*; mortal remains.

rester [rɛs'te], *v.i. (aux. ÊTRE)* to remain; to stay; to last; to pause; **rester court**, to stop short.

restituable [rɛsti'tɥabl], *a.* repayable, returnable.

restituer [rɛsti'tɥe], *v.t.* to restore; to return, to refund.

restitution [rɛstity'sjɔ̃], *n.f.* restitution, restoration.

restreindre [rɛs'trɛ̃:dr], *v.t. irr. (conjug. like CRAINDRE)* to restrict; to limit; to restrain. **se restreindre**, *v.r.* to restrain oneself; to curtail one's expenses.

restreint [rɛs'trɛ̃], *a.* restricted, limited.

restrictif [rɛstrik'tif], *a. (fem. -tive)* restrictive.

281

restriction [rɛstrik'sjɔ̃], *n.f.* restriction, restraint; *restriction mentale*, mental reservation.

restringent [rɛstrɛ̃'ʒɑ̃], *a.* and *n.m.* (*Med.*) astringent.

résultant [rezyl'tɑ̃], *a.* resulting.

résultat [rezyl'ta], *n.m.* result.

résulter [rezyl'te], *v.i.* to result.

résumé [rezy'me], *n.m.* recapitulation, summary; *en résumé*, to sum up.

résumer [rezy'me], *v.t.* to summarize. **se résumer**, *v.r.* to recapitulate, to sum up.

résurrection [rezyrɛk'sjɔ̃], *n.f.* resurrection, revival.

rétablir [reta'bli:r], *v.t.* to re-establish, to restore; to repair; to recover; to retrieve. **se rétablir**, *v.r.* to recover one's health; to be restored.

rétablissement [retablis'mɑ̃], *n.m.* re-establishment, restoration; repair; recovery.

retailler [retɑ'je], *v.t.* to cut again, to prune again.

rétamer [reta'me], *v.t.* to tin over again; to resilver.

rétameur [reta'mœ:r], *n.m.* tinker.

retaper [reta'pe], *v.t.* (*colloq.*) to do up (*a hat etc.*), to straighten (*bedclothes*). **se retaper**, *v.r.* (*fam.*) to buck up.

retard [rə'ta:r], *n.m.* delay; slowness (*of a clock etc.*); *être en retard*, to be late.

retardataire [rətarda'tɛ:r], *a.* in arrears, late; backward.—*n.* late-comer; defaulter.

retardement [rətardə'mɑ̃], *n.m.* delay, retardment.

retarder [rətar'de], *v.t.* to retard, to delay; to defer (*payment*); to set back (*clocks and watches*).—*v.i.* to lose time; to be slow (*of clocks and watches*); to be behind the times.

retenir [rət'ni:r] *v.t. irr.* (*conjug. like* TENIR) to hold back; to retain; to detain; to remember; to reserve; to hold in, to restrain; to engage; to prevent; to get hold of again; (*Arith.*) to carry. **se retenir**, *v.r.* to control oneself; to refrain; to catch hold.

retenteur [rətɑ̃'tœ:r], *a.* (*fem.* **-trice**) retaining.

rétentif [retɑ̃'tif], *a.* (*fem.* **-tive**) retentive.

rétention [retɑ̃'sjɔ̃], *n.f.* reservation.

retentir [rətɑ̃'ti:r], *v.i.* to resound, to re-echo, to ring.

retentissant [rətɑ̃ti'sɑ̃], *a.* resounding, echoing; ringing, loud; (*fig.*) famous.

retentissement [rətɑ̃tis'mɑ̃], *n.m.* resounding, echo; ringing; (*fig.*) fame, celebrity.

retenu [rət'ny], *a.* reserved, cautious, wary.

retenue [rət'ny], *n.f.* discretion, circumspection, caution; detention; (*Comm.*) deduction; guy rope.

réticence [reti'sɑ̃:s], *n.f.* reserve, silence; concealment (*of some particular*).

rétif [re'tif], *a.* (*fem.* **-tive**) restive; stubborn.

rétine [re'tin], *n.f.* retina (*of the eye*).

retirable [rəti'rabl], *a.* withdrawable.

retiré [rəti're], *a.* retired, secluded; in retirement.

retirement [rətir'mɑ̃], *n.m.* contraction; shrinking.

retirer [rəti're], *v.t.* to draw again; to pull back, to withdraw; to take away; to retract; to derive. **se retirer**, *v.r.* to retire, to withdraw; to subside (*of waters*); to contract.

retombée [rətɔ̃'be], *n.f.* fall, fall-out;

retombée de particules radioactives, radio-active fall-out.

retomber [rətɔ̃'be], *v.i.* (*aux.* ÊTRE) to fall again; to have a relapse; to subside.

retordre [rə'tɔrdr], *v.t.* to twist again; to twist (*silk, thread etc.*).

rétorquer [retor'ke], *v.t.* to retort.

retors [rə'tɔ:r], *a.* twisted; artful, cunning, crafty.—*n.m.* twisted thread; crafty person.

retouche [rə'tuʃ], *n.f.* retouching, touching up.

retoucher [rətu'ʃe], *v.t.* to retouch; to touch up.

retour [rə'tu:r], *n.m.* return; repetition, recurrence; sending back; (*fig.*) change; reverse; turning, winding; (*Law*) reversion; *billet d'aller et retour*, return ticket.

retourne [rə'turn], *n.f.* trump card.

retourner [rətur'ne], *v.t.* (*aux.* AVOIR) to turn, to turn up, to turn over, round, about etc.; to send back.—*v.i.* (*aux.* ÊTRE) to return, to go again, to go back (again); to recoil upon; to turn up (*cards*). **se retourner**, *v.r.* to turn, to turn round, to look round.

retracer [rətra'se], *v.t.* (*conjug. like* COMMENCER) to trace again, to retrace; to relate. **se retracer**, *v.r.* to recall to mind; to recur, to be retraced (*in mind*).

rétracter [retrak'te], *v.t.* and **se rétracter** *v.r.* to retract; to recant.

retrait [rə'trɛ], *a.* shrunk (*of grain, wood etc.*).—*n.m.* shrinkage; recess (*in wall*), closet; withdrawal.

retraite [rə'trɛt], *n.f.* retreat, retiring; privacy; refuge; haunt; retirement (*from office*); superannuation; retiring pension; *battre en retraite*, to beat a retreat.

retraité [rətrɛ'te], *a.* superannuated, retired, pensioned off.

retraiter [rətrɛ'te], *v.t.* to retire, to pension off.

retranchement [rətrɑ̃ʃ'mɑ̃], *n.m.* retrenchment, curtailment; (*Mil.*) entrenchment.

retrancher [rətrɑ̃'ʃe], *v.t.* to retrench, to curtail, to cut short; to cut out; to abridge; (*Arith.*) to subtract; (*Mil.*) to entrench. **se retrancher**, *v.r.* to restrain oneself; to curtail one's expenses; (*Mil.*) to entrench oneself; (*fig.*) to fall back upon.

rétrécir [retre'si:r], *v.t.* to take in, to contract; to narrow, to limit.—*v.i.* and **se rétrécir**, *v.r.* to grow narrower; to shrink, to contract.

rétrécissement [retresis'mɑ̃], *n.m.* narrowing; shrinking.

retremper [rətrɑ̃'pe], *v.t.* to soak again; to temper again; (*fig.*) to strengthen. **se retremper**, *v.r.* to be strengthened **or** invigorated.

rétribuer [retri'bɥe], *v.t.* to remunerate.

rétribution [retriby'sjɔ̃], *n.f.* payment, reward.

rétroactif [retroak'tif], *a.* (*fem.* **-tive**) retro-active.

rétroaction [retroak'sjɔ̃], *n.f.* retroaction; (*Rad. Teleg.*) feed-back.

rétrograde [retro'grad], *a.* retrograde; backward.

rétrograder [retrogra'de], *v.i.* to retrograde; to go back, (*Mil.*) to fall back.

rétrogressif [retrogrɛ'sif], *a.* (*fem.* **-ive**) retrogressive.

rétrogression [retrɔgrɛ'sjɔ̃], *n.f.* retrogression.

rétrospectif [retrɔspɛk'tif], *a.* (*fem.* **-tive**) retrospective.

retroussé [rətru'se], *a.* turned up; tucked up; *nez retroussé*, turned-up nose, snub nose.

retrousser [rətru'se], *v.t.* to turn up, to roll up (*trousers*); to tuck up; to cock (*one's hat*). **se retrousser**, *v.r.* to tuck up one's skirt *or* other garment.

retroussis [rətru'si], *n.m.* cock (*of a hat*); top (*of a shoe*); facing (*of a uniform*).

retrouver [rətru've], *v.t.* to find again, to regain, to recover. **se retrouver**, *v.r.* to find each other again; to be oneself again.

rétroviseur [retrɔvi'zœ:r], *n.m.* (*Motor.*) rearview mirror.

rets [rɛ], *n.m. inv.* net; (*fig.*) snare, toils.

réunion [rey'njɔ̃], *n.f.* reunion; reconciliation; junction; meeting, assembly, gathering; reception.

réunir [rey'ni:r], *v.t.* to reunite, to join again, to bring together again, to reconcile; to connect; to collect. **se réunir**, *v.r.* to assemble again, to reunite; to meet; to amalgamate.

réussi [rey'si], *a.* successful, brilliant.

réussir [rey'si:r], *v.t.* to carry out well, to accomplish, to perform successfully.—*v.i.* to succeed, to be successful, to prosper, to thrive; to pass (*Exam.*).

réussite [rey'sit], *n.f.* success; (*happy*) issue *or* result; (*Cards*) solitaire.

revaloir [rəva'lwa:r], *v.t. irr.* (*conjug. like* VALOIR) to return like for like, to be even with.

revanche [rə'vã:ʃ], *n.f.* revenge; return match.

rêvasser [rɛva'se], *v.i.* to day-dream, to muse.

rêvasserie [rɛvas'ri], *n.f.* day-dreams; idle musing.

rêvasseur [rɛva'sœ:r], *n.m.* (*fem.* **-euse**) (*colloq.*) dreamer, muser.

rêve [rɛ:v], *n.m.* dream; day-dream, illusion.

revêche [rə'vɛ:ʃ], *a.* rough; cross, ill-natured, cantankerous.

réveil [re'vɛ:j], *n.m.* waking, awaking; alarm clock; (*Mil.*) reveille.

réveille-matin [revɛjma'tɛ̃], *n.m. inv.* alarm clock.

réveiller [revɛ'je], *v.t.* to awake, to arouse; to recall. **se réveiller**, *v.r.* to awake, to wake up; to be roused; to revive.

réveillon [revɛ'jɔ̃], *n.m.* midnight repast, *esp.* Christmas Eve revel.

réveillonner [revɛjɔ'ne], *v.i.* to take part in a *réveillon*.

révélateur [revela'tœ:r], *a.* (*fem.* **-trice**) revealing, tell-tale.—*n.m.* (*fem.* **-trice**) revealer, informer.—*n.m.* (*Phot.*) developer.

révélation [revela'sjɔ̃], *n.f.* revelation, disclosure.

révéler [reve'le], *v.t.* (*conjug. like* CÉDER) to reveal, to disclose; to betray; (*Phot.*) to develop. **se révéler**, *v.r.* to reveal oneself; to prove (to be).

revenant [rəvə'nã], *a.* pleasing, prepossessing. —*n.m.* ghost.

revendeur [rəvã'dœ:r], *n.m.* (*fem.* **-euse**) retail dealer, dealer in old clothes etc.

revendicable [rəvãdi'kabl], *a.* claimable.

revendicateur [rəvãdika'tœ:r], *n.m.* (*fem.* **-trice**) claimant.

revendication [rəvãdika'sjɔ̃], *n.f.* claim, demand.

revendiquer [rəvãdi'ke], *v.t.* to claim.

revendre [rə'vã:dr], *v.t.* to sell again, to resell.

revenir [rəv'ni:r], *v.i. irr.* (*conjug. like* TENIR but with aux. ÊTRE) to come again, to come back, to return; to reappear, to haunt, to walk (*of ghosts*); to recur; to recover; to amount, to cost; to retract; to please.

revente [rə'vã:t], *n.f.* resale.

revenu [rəv'ny], *n.m.* revenue, income.

revenue [rəv'ny], *n.f.* young wood, aftergrowth.

rêver [rɛ've], *v.t.* to dream, to dream of.—*v.i.* to dream; to have day-dreams; to muse.

réverbérant [reverbe'rã], *a.* reverberating.

réverbération [reverbera'sjɔ̃], *n.f.* reverberation; reflection (*of light, heat*).

réverbère [rever'bɛ:r], *n.m.* reflector; street lamp.

réverbérer [reverbe're], *v.t., v.i.* (*conjug. like* CÉDER) to reverberate; to reflect (*light, heat*).

reverdir [rəver'di:r], *v.t.* to make green again, to revive.—*v.i.* to become green again; (*fig.*) to grow young again.

reverdissement [rəverdis'mã], *n.m.* growing green again.

révéremment [revera'mã], *adv.* reverently.

révérence [reve'rã:s], *n.f.* reverence; bow, curtsy.

révérenciel [reverã'sjɛl], *a.* (*fem.* **-elle**) reverential.

révérencieusement [reverãsjøz'mã], *adv.* reverentially.

révérencieux [reverã'sjø], *a.* (*fem.* **-euse**) ceremonious, obsequious.

révérend [reve'rã], *a.* reverend.

révérendissime [reverãdi'sim], *a.* most reverend, right reverend.

révérer [reve're], *v.t.* (*conjug. like* CÉDER) to revere.

rêverie [rɛv'ri], *n.f.* reverie, musing, dreaming.

revers [rə've:r], *n.m.* back, reverse; facing (*of clothes*); lapel (*of a coat*); turn-up (*of trousers*); top (*of shoes*); (*Ten.*) back-hand stroke; misfortune, set back.

reverser [rəver'se], *v.t.* to pour out again; to pour back; to transfer; to pay back.

réversible [rever'sibl], *a.* reversible; revertible.

réversion [rever'sjɔ̃], *n.f.* reversion.

reversoir [rəver'swa:r], *n.m.* weir.

revêtement [rəvɛt'mã], *n.m.* facing (*of masonry etc.*); surface (*of road*).

revêtir [rəve'ti:r], *v.t. irr.* (*conjug. like* VÊTIR) to give clothes to, to dress; to put on; to assume; to cover; (*fig.*) to invest *or* endow with. **se revêtir**, *v.r.* to clothe oneself, to array oneself; to put on, to assume.

rêveur [rɛ'vœ:r], *a.* (*fem.* **-euse**) dreaming; (*fig.*) pensive, dreamy.—*n.m.* (*fem.* **-euse**) dreamer; muser.

revient [rə'vjɛ̃], *n.m. prix de revient*, net cost.

revirement [rəvir'mã], *n.m.* tacking about; (*fig.*) sudden change.

revirer [rəvi're], *v.i.* to tack, to put about; (*fig.*) to change sides.

revisable [rəvi'zabl], **révisable** [revi'zabl], *a.* revisable.

reviser [rəvi'ze], **réviser** [revi'ze], *v.t.* to revise, to review, to examine; to overhaul (*engine*).

reviseur [rəvi'zœ:r], **réviseur** [revi'zœ:r], *n.m.* reviser, examiner; auditor; proof-reader.

revision [rəvi'zjɔ̃], **révision** [revi'zjɔ̃], *n.f.* revision, review; overhaul (*of engine*).

revivifier [rəvivi'fje], *v.t.* to revivify, to regenerate, to revive.

revivre [rə'vi:vr], *v.t. irr.* (*conjug. like* VIVRE) to relive.—*v.i.* to come to life again, to live again.

révocable [revɔ'kabl], *a.* revocable; removable (*of an official*).

révocation [revɔka'sjɔ̃], *n.f.* revocation (*of will*), repeal; dismissal (*of an official*).

revoici [rəvwa'si], **revoilà** [rəvwa'la], *adv.* (*colloq.*) **me revoici**, here I am again; **le revoilà**, there he is again.

revoir [rə'vwa:r], *v.t. irr.* (*conjug. like* VOIR) to see again; to meet again; to revise, to review. **se revoir**, *v.r.* to see *or* meet each other again.—*n.m. inv.* **au revoir**, good-bye (*for the present*).

revoler (I) [rəvɔ'le], *v.t.* to steal again.

revoler (2) [rəvɔ'le], *v.i.* to fly again; to fly back.

révoltant [revɔl'tɑ̃], *a.* revolting, shocking.

révolte [re'vɔlt], *n.f.* revolt, rebellion.

révolté [revɔl'te], *n.m.* (*fem.* **-ée**) rebel; mutineer.

révolter [revɔl'te], *v.t.* to stir up, to rouse; to shock, to disgust. **se révolter**, *v.r.* to revolt, to rebel; to be indignant, to be shocked.

révolu [revɔ'ly], *a.* accomplished, completed; elapsed.

révolution [revɔly'sjɔ̃], *n.f.* revolution.

révolutionnaire [revɔlysjɔ'nɛ:r], *a.* revolutionary.—*n.* revolutionary; revolutionist.

révolutionner [revɔlysjɔ'ne], *v.t.* to revolutionize.

revolver [revɔl'vɛ:r], *n.m.* revolver.

révoquer [revɔ'ke], *v.t.* to dismiss (*an official etc.*); to recall (*an ambassador etc.*); to repeal, to cancel.

revue [rə'vy], *n.f.* review, survey; revision; magazine; review (*critical article*); (*Mil.*) review; (*Theat.*) revue.

révulsion [revyl'sjɔ̃], *n.f.* revulsion.

rez [re], *prep.* on a level with, even with.

rez-de-chaussée [redʃo'se], *n.m. inv.* ground-level; ground floor.

rhabillage [rabi'ja:ʒ], *n.m.* mending, overhaul.

rhabiller [rabi'je], *v.t.* to dress again; to mend.

rhétoricien [retɔri'sjɛ̃], *n.m.* rhetorician.

rhétorique [retɔ'rik], *n.f.* rhetoric.

Rhin [rɛ̃], **le**, *m.* the Rhine.

rhinocéros [rinɔse'rɔs], *n.m. inv.* rhinoceros.

rhododendron [rɔdɔdɛ̃'drɔ̃], *n.m.* rhododendron.

rhombe [rɔ̃:b], *a.* rhombic.—*n.m.* rhomb; rhombus.

rhubarbe [ry'barb], *n.f.* rhubarb.

rhum [rɔm], *n.m.* rum.

rhumatisant [rymati'zɑ̃], *a.* suffering from rheumatism, rheumatic.—*n.m.* (*fem.* **-e**) sufferer from rheumatism.

rhumatismal [rymatis'mal], *a.* (*m. pl.* **-aux**) rheumatic.

rhumatisme [ryma'tism], *n.m.* rheumatism.

rhume [rym], *n.m.* cold (*illness*).

riant [ri'jɑ̃], *a.* smiling, cheerful, pleasant, pleasing.

ribambelle [ribɑ̃'bɛl], *n.f.* (*colloq.*) swarm, string, lot.

ribaud [ri'bo], *a.* and *n.m.* (*fem.* **-e**) ribald.

ribauderie [ribod'ri], *n.f.* ribaldry.

ricanement [rikan'mɑ̃], *n.m.* sneering, sneer; mocking laughter.

ricaner [rika'ne], *v.i.* to sneer, to snigger.

ricaneur [rika'nœ:r], *a.* (*fem.* **-euse**) sneering, derisive.—*n.m.* (*fem.* **-euse**) sneerer.

Richard [ri'ʃa:r], *m.* Richard.

richard [ri'ʃa:r], *n.m.* (*fam. and pej.*) moneyed person, capitalist.

riche [riʃ], *a.* rich, wealthy; copious; valuable. —*n.* rich person.

richement [riʃ'mɑ̃], *adv.* richly; splendidly.

richesse [ri'ʃɛs], *n.f.* riches, wealth; copiousness; richness.

richissime [riʃi'sim], *a.* (*colloq.*) rolling in money.

ricin [ri'sɛ̃], *n.m.* castor-oil plant.

ricocher [rikɔ'ʃe], *v.i.* to rebound; to ricochet.

ricochet [rikɔ'ʃɛ], *n.m.* rebound (*on the water*); (*Artill.*) ricochet; (*fig.*) chain (*of events*).

rictus [rik'ty:s], *n.m. inv.* grin; rictus.

ride [rid], *n.f.* wrinkle; ripple.

ridé [ri'de], *a.* wrinkled; rippling; corrugated.

rideau [ri'do], *n.m.* (*pl.* **-eaux**) curtain; screen (*of trees etc.*).

rider [ri'de], *v.t.* to wrinkle; to corrugate; to shrivel; to ruffle (*water*). **se rider**, *v.r.* to be wrinkled; to shrivel up; to ripple (*of water*).

ridicule [ridi'kyl], *a.* ridiculous.—*n.m.* ridicule; ridiculousness.

ridiculement [ridikyl'mɑ̃], *adv.* ridiculously.

ridiculiser [ridikyli'ze], *v.t.* to ridicule, to make fun of.

rien [rjɛ̃], *n.m.* trifle, mere nothing.—*indef. pron.* nothing, nought, not anything; anything.

rieur [ri'jœ:r], *a.* (*fem.* **rieuse**) laughing, joking.

rigide [ri'ʒid], *a.* rigid, stiff; strict, severe.

rigidement [riʒid'mɑ̃], *adv.* rigidly, strictly.

rigidité [riʒidi'te], *n.f.* rigidity, stiffness; strictness, severity.

rigole [ri'gɔl], *n.f.* trench, small ditch *or* channel; gutter.

rigoler [rigɔ'le], *v.i.* (*pop.*) to laugh; to have fun; to joke.

rigorisme [rigɔ'rism], *n.m.* rigorism, austerity.

rigoriste [rigɔ'rist], *a.* over-severe.—*n.* rigorist, stickler.

rigoureusement [rigurøz'mɑ̃], *adv.* rigorously, severely, strictly.

rigoureux [rigu'rø], *a.* (*fem.* **-euse**) rigorous, harsh; strict; stern; inclement.

rigueur [ri'gœ:r], *n.f.* rigor, strictness; precision; severity; inclemency; **à la rigueur**, at a pinch; if necessary; **de rigueur**, indispensable, compulsory.

rimailler [rima'je], *v.i.* to write doggerel.

rimailleur [rima'jœːr], *n.m.* (*fem.* **-euse**) sorry rhymer, rhymester.

rime [rim], *n.f.* rhyme; (*fig.*) verse.

rimer [ri'me], *v.i.* to rhyme; to write verses.

rimeur [ri'mœːr], *n.m.* rhymer, versifier.

rinçage [rɛ̃'saːʒ], *n.m.* rinsing, washing.

rincer [rɛ̃'se], *v.t.* (*conjug. like* COMMENCER) to rinse, to wash. **se rincer,** *v.r.* to rinse.

ripaille [ri'paːj], *n.f.* feasting, junketing.

riposte [ri'post], *n.f.* (*Fenc.*) ripost, return; (*fig.*) retort, repartee.

riposter [ripɔs'te], *v.i.* (*Fenc.*) to ripost, to parry and thrust; (*fig.*) to make a smart reply.

rire [riːr], *v.i. irr.* to laugh; to smile; to be favorable; to joke; to mock. **se rire,** *v.r.* to make sport, to scoff (*de*).—*n.m.* laughter, laughing.

ris [ri], *n.m. inv.* laugh, smile, laughter; (*Naut.*) reef (*of sails*); sweetbread.

risée [ri'ze], *n.f.* laugh, laughter; mockery; laughing-stock.

risette [ri'zɛt], *n.f.* pleasant little laugh, smile.

risible [ri'zibl], *a.* comical, laughable; ridiculous.

risiblement [rizibl'mɑ̃], *adv.* laughably, ludicrously.

risque [risk], *n.m.* risk, hazard.

risqué [ris'ke], *a.* risky; **une plaisanterie risquée,** a doubtful joke.

risquer [ris'ke], *v.t.* to risk, to venture; (*fam.*) to chance. **se risquer,** *v.r.* to risk, to venture.

risque-tout [riskə'tu], *n.m. inv.* (*colloq.*) dare-devil.

rissole [ri'sɔl], *n.f.* rissole.

rissoler [risɔ'le], *v.t.* (*Cook.*) to brown.

ristourne [ris'turn], *n.f.* refund; rebate.

rit or **rite** [rit], *n.m.* rite.

ritournelle [ritur'nɛl], *n.f.* (*Mus.*) ritornello, flourish.

rituel [ri'tɥɛl], *a.* (*fem.* **-elle**) ritual.—*n.m.* ritual (*prayer book*).

rivage [ri'vaːʒ], *n.m.* shore, strand, beach; bank, waterside.

rival [ri'val], *a.* (*m. pl.* **-aux**) rival, competitive.—*n.m.* (*fem.* **-e,** *m. pl.* **-aux**) rival.

rivaliser [rivali'ze], *v.i.* to rival, to vie, to compete.

rivalité [rivali'te], *n.f.* rivalry, emulation.

rive [riːv], *n.f.* bank, shore (*of rivers, lakes etc.*); (*fig.*) seashore; border.

rivement [riv'mɑ̃], *n.m.* riveting.

river [ri've], *v.t.* to clinch, to rivet.

riverain [ri'vrɛ̃], *a.* riparian; bordering (*on rivers or woods*).—*n.m.* (*fem.* **-e**) riverside resident; borderer.

rivet [ri'vɛ], *n.m.* rivet; clinch.

rivetage [riv'taːʒ], *n.m.* riveting.

riveter [riv'te], *v.t.* (*conjug. like* APPELER) to rivet.

riveteur [riv'tœːr], **riveur** [ri'vœːr], *n.m.* riveter.

rivière [ri'vjɛːr], *n.f.* river, stream.

rivoir, *n.m.* or **rivoire** [ri'vwaːr], *n.f.* riveting hammer *or* machine.

rivure [ri'vyːr], *n.f.* clinching, riveting.

rixe [riks], *n.f.* fight, scuffle; brawl, affray.

riz [ri], *n.m.* rice.

rizière [ri'zjɛːr], *n.f.* rice field, paddy field, rice plantation; rice swamp.

robe [rɔb], *n.f.* gown, dress, frock; robe; long robe (*lawyers*), the cloth (*clergy*); coat (*of certain animals*); skin, husk, peel (*of certain fruits etc.*).

robinet [rɔbi'nɛ], *n.m.* tap; cock; **ouvrir** (**fermer**) **le robinet,** to turn on (off) the tap.

robot [rɔ'bo], *a. inv.* **avion robot,** pilotless plane; **fusée, satellite robot,** unmanned rocket, satellite.—*n.m.* automaton, robot.

robuste [rɔ'byst], *a.* robust, sturdy; hardy, strong.

robustement [rɔbystə'mɑ̃], *adv.* robustly, athletically.

robustesse [rɔbys'tɛs], *n.f.* robustness, strength, vigor.

roc [rɔk], *n.m.* rock.

rocaille [rɔ'kaːj], *n.f.* rock work, grotto work.

rocailleux [rɔka'jø], *a.* (*fem.* **-euse**) pebbly, stony; rugged, rough.

roche [rɔʃ], *n.f.* rock; boulder; stony mass.

rocher [rɔ'ʃe], *n.m.* rock, crag.

rochet [rɔ'ʃɛ], *n.m.* rochet (*surplice*); ratchet.

rocheux [rɔ'ʃø], *a.* (*fem.* **-euse**) rocky, stony.

rococo [rɔkɔ'ko], *a. inv.* rococo; antiquated.—*n.m.* rococo, antiquated style.

rodage [rɔ'daːʒ], *n.m.* grinding in; polishing; **en rodage,** breaking in (*engine*).

roder [rɔ'de], *v.t.* to break in (*car*); to grind, to polish.

rôder [ro'de], *v.i.* to prowl.

rôdeur [ro'dœːr], *a.* (*fem.* **-euse**) prowling.—*n.m.* (*fem.* **-euse**) prowler; vagrant.

rodomontade [rɔdɔmɔ̃'tad], *n.f.* bluster, swagger.

Rodrigue [rɔ'drig], *m.* Roderick.

rogaton [rɔga'tɔ̃], *n.m.* (*pl.*) scraps, odds and ends.

Roger [rɔ'ʒe], *m.* Roger; **c'est un vrai Roger Bontemps,** he is a happy-go-lucky sort of chap.

rogner [rɔ'ne], *v.t.* to cut, to pare, to crop; to clip, to prune.

rogneux [rɔ'nø], *a.* (*fem.* **-euse**) mangy, scabby.

rognon [rɔ'nɔ̃], *n.m.* kidney (*as food*).

rognure [rɔ'nyːr], *n.f.* a paring, a clipping; (*pl.*) scraps, refuse, leavings.

rogue [rɔg], *a.* arrogant, haughty.

roi [rwa], *n.m.* king.

roitelet [rwa'tlɛ], *n.m.* petty king; wren.

rôle [roːl], *n.m.* roll; list, roster, catalogue; (*Theat.*) part, character.

romain [rɔ'mɛ̃], *a.* Roman.—*n.m.* (**Romain,** *fem.* **-aine**) Roman (*person*).

roman (1) [rɔ'mɑ̃], *a.* Romance, Romanic.

roman (2) [rɔ'mɑ̃], *n.m.* novel, romance, fiction.

romance [rɔ'mɑ̃ːs], *n.f.* (*Mus.*) ballad, sentimental song.

romancier [rɔmɑ̃'sje], *n.m.* (*fem.* **-ière**) novelist.

romanesque [rɔma'nɛsk], *a.* romantic.—*n.m.* the romantic.

roman-feuilleton [rɔmɑ̃fœj'tɔ̃], *n.m.* (*pl.* **romans-feuilletons**) newspaper serial (story).

romantique [rɔmɑ̃'tik], *a.* romantic.—*n.* romanticist.

romantiquement [rɔmɑ̃tik'mɑ̃], *adv.* romantically.

romantisme [rɔmɑ̃'tism], *n.m.* (*Lit. Hist.*) romanticism.

romarin

romarin [rɔma'rɛ̃], *n.m.* rosemary.
rompre [rɔ̃:pr], *v.t.* (*see Verb Tables*) to break, to snap; to break off; to rout; to dissolve; to break in; to divert; to interrupt. —*v.i.* to break; to fall out. **se rompre**, *v.r.* to break off, to snap.
rompu [rɔ̃'py], *a.* broken, snapped; broken in.
romsteck [rɔm'stɛk], *n.m.* rump steak.
ronce [rɔ̃:s], *n.f.* bramble, blackberry bush.
ronceraie [rɔ̃s'rɛ], *n.f.* brake, brambly ground.
ronchonner [rɔ̃ʃɔ'ne], *v.i.* (*fam.*) to grumble.
rond [rɔ̃], *a.* round; plump, rotund; frank; even (*of money or accounts*).—*adv.* normally, true (*of motor*).—*n.m.* round, ring, orb, circle, disk.
ronde [rɔ̃:d], *n.f.* round; patrol; beat; (*Mus.*) whole note; roundelay; round-hand (*writing*).
rondeau [rɔ̃'do], *n.m.* (*pl.* **-eaux**) rondeau (*French poem*); (*Mus.*) rondo; roller.
rondelet [rɔ̃'dlɛ], *a.* (*fem.* **-ette**) roundish, plump, pudgy.
rondelle [rɔ̃'dɛl], *n.f.* rondelle, washer; rundle, ring.
rondement [rɔ̃d'mɑ̃], *adv.* roundly; briskly; frankly, bluntly.
rondeur [rɔ̃'dœːr], *n.f.* roundness, rotundity; fullness; plain dealing.
rondin [rɔ̃'dɛ̃], *n.m.* round log; cudgel.
rond-point [rɔ̃'pwɛ̃], *n.m.* (*pl.* **ronds-points**) (*Arch.*) apsis; circle (*place where several roads etc. meet*); traffic circle.
ronflant [rɔ̃'flɑ̃], *a.* snoring; humming, whirring; sonorous.
ronflement [rɔ̃flə'mɑ̃], *n.m.* snoring; roaring, rumbling; boom; snorting (*of horses*).
ronfler [rɔ̃'fle], *v.i.* to snore; to snort (*of horses*); to roar (*cannon, thunder etc.*); to boom; to peal (*organs*); to hum (*spinning-tops*).
ronfleur [rɔ̃'flœːr], *n.m.* (*fem.* **-euse**) snorer.
rongeant [rɔ̃'ʒɑ̃], *a.* gnawing, corroding; (*fig.*) tormenting.
ronger [rɔ̃'ʒe], *v.t.* (*conjug. like* MANGER) to gnaw, to nibble; to consume; to corrode; to prey upon (*the mind etc.*); **ronger son frein**, to champ the bit. **se ronger**, *v.r.* to fret.
rongeur [rɔ̃'ʒœːr], *a.* (*fem.* **-euse**) gnawing, biting; corroding; consuming.—*n.m.* (*Zool.*) rodent.
ronron [rɔ̃'rɔ̃], *n.m.* purr, purring.
ronronner [rɔ̃rɔ'ne], *v.i.* to purr, to hum.
roquet [rɔ'kɛ], *n.m.* pug dog; cur, mongrel.
rosace [ro'zas], *n.f.* (*Arch.*) rose; rose window.
rosage [ro'za:ʒ], *n.m.* rhododendron; azalea.
rosaire [ro'zɛːr], *n.m.* (*R.-C. Ch.*) rosary.
rosâtre [ro'zɑːtr], *a.* pinkish.
rosbif [rɔs'bif], *n.m.* roast beef.
rose [ro:z], *a.* rosy; pink, rose-colored. —*n.f.* rose; rose window; **rose trémière**, hollyhock.—*n.m.* rose-color, pink.
rosé [ro'ze], *a.* rosy, roseate; **vin rosé**, light-red wine.
roseau [ro'zo], *n.m.* (*pl.* **-eaux**) reed.
rosée [ro'ze], *n.f.* dew.
roselière [rozə'ljɛːr], *n.f.* reed bed.
roséole [roze'ɔl], *n.f.* scarlet rash; German measles.
roser [ro'ze], *v.t.* to make pink.

roseraie [roz'rɛ], *n.f.* rosery, rose garden.
rosette [ro'zɛt], *n.f.* small rose; rosette.
rosier [ro'zje], *n.m.* rose tree, rose-bush.
rosière [ro'zjɛːr], *n.f.* rose queen; queen of the May.
rosiériste [rozje'rist], *n.* rose grower.
rosse [rɔs], *a.* bad, malicious.—*n.f.* old horse; (*fig.* and *fam.*) worthless *or* nasty person.
rossée [ro'se], *n.f.* shower of blows, thrashing.
rosser [ro'se], *v.t.* (*colloq.*) to thrash, to beat up.
rossignol [rɔsi'nɔl], *n.m.* nightingale; picklock, skeleton key; (*Carp.*) wedge; (*fig.*) unsaleable article (*in a shop*).
rot [ro], *n.m.* (*pop.*) belch, eructation.
rôt [ro], *n.m.* roast, roast meat.
rotarien [rɔta'rjɛ̃], *n.m.* member of a Rotary Club.
rotateur [rɔta'tœːr], *a.* (*fem.* **-trice**) (*Anat.*) rotatory.—*n.m.* (*Anat.*) rotator.
rotatif [rɔta'tif], *a.* (*fem.* **-tive**) rotary.
rotation [rɔta'sjɔ̃], *n.f.* rotation.
rotatoire [rɔta'twaːr], *a.* rotatory.
roter [rɔ'te], *v.i.* to belch.
rôti [ro'ti], *n.m.* roast, roast meat.
rôtie [ro'ti], *n.f.* slice of toast.
rôtir [ro'tiːr], *v.t.*, *v.i.* to roast; to broil; to toast (*bread etc.*); (*fig.*) to parch.
rôtissage [roti'saːʒ], *n.m.* roasting.
rôtisserie [rotis'ri], *n.f.* cook-shop.
rôtisseur [roti'sœːr], *n.m.* (*fem.* **-euse**) cook-shop keeper.
rôtissoire [roti'swaːr], *n.f.* roaster, Dutch oven.
rotonde [rɔ'tɔ̃:d], *n.f.* rotunda; long sleeveless cloak.
rotondité [rɔtɔ̃di'te], *n.f.* rotundity; plumpness.
rotor [rɔ'tɔːr], *n.m.* rotor.
roturier [rɔty'rje], *a.* (*fem.* **-ière**) plebeian; vulgar, mean.—*n.m.* (*fem.* **-ière**) commoner.
rouage [rwa:ʒ], *n.m.* wheelwork; cog-wheel; machinery; (*Horol.*) movement.
rouan [rwɑ̃], *a.* (*fem.* **rouanne**) roan (*of horses, cattle, etc.*).—*n.m.* roan horse.
roublard [ru'blaːr], *a.* and *n.m.* (*fem.* **-e**) (*fam.*) wily, crafty (person).
rouble [rubl], *n.m.* rouble (*Russian coin*).
roucoulement [rukul'mɑ̃], *n.m.* cooing; gurgling (*of babies*).
roucouler [ruku'le], *v.t.*, *v.i.* to coo.
roue [ru], *n.f.* wheel; paddle-wheel; **faire la roue**, to spread (out) its tail (*of peacocks etc.*); to show off; **mettre** *or* **jeter des bâtons dans les roues**, to put spokes into the wheel (*of*), to interfere.
roué [rwe], *a.* cunning, sharp, artful; exhausted.—*n.m.* rake, profligate; (*fem.* **-ée**) cunning or unscrupulous person.
rouelle [rwɛl], *n.f.* round slice (*meat*).
rouer [rwe], *v.t.* to break upon the wheel; **rouer de coups**, to beat unmercifully.
rouerie [ru'ri], *n.f.* piece of knavery, trick, sharp practice.
rouet [rwɛ], *n.m.* spinning-wheel.
rouge [ru:ʒ], *a.* red; red-hot; bloodshot.—*n.m.* rouge; redness.—*n.* (*fam.*) left-winger, communist.
rougeâtre [ru'ʒɑːtr], *a.* reddish.
rougeaud [ru'ʒo], *a.* (*colloq.*) red-faced, ruddy.—*n.m.* (*fem.* **-e**) red-faced person.

rouge-gorge [ruʒ'gɔrʒ], *n.m.* (*pl.* **rouges-gorges**) red-breast, robin redbreast.

rougeole [ru'ʒɔl], *n.f.* measles.

rougeoyer [ruʒwɑ'je], *v.i.* (*conjug. like* EMPLOYER) to turn red; to glow.

rouget [ru'ʒɛ], *a.* (*fem.* **-ette**) reddish.—*n.m.* (*Ichth.*) red mullet.

rougeur [ru'ʒœːr], *n.f.* redness; flush, glow, blush.

rougir [ru'ʒiːr], *v.t.* to redden, to tinge with red.—*v.i.* to redden, to grow red, to color, to blush.

rouille [ru:j], *n.f.* rust, rustiness; (*Agric.*) mildew, blight.

rouillé [ru'je], *a.* rusty; blighted (*of grain*).

rouiller [ru'je], *v.t., v.i.* to rust; to blight; to impair. **se rouiller**, *v.r.* to rust; to grow rusty; to be impaired.

rouilleux [ru'jø], *a.* (*fem.* **-euse**) rust-colored.

rouillure [ru'jyːr], *n.f.* rustiness; (*Agric.*) rust.

rouir [rwi:r], *v.t.* to steep, to soak, to ret.

rouissage [rwi'saːʒ], *n.m.* steeping, retting.

roulade [ru'lad], *n.f.* roll, rolling down; (*Mus.*) trill.

roulage [ru'laːʒ], *n.m.* rolling; haulage, carriage (*in wagons etc.*); road traffic.

roulant [ru'lɑ̃], *a.* rolling; travelling (*crane*); easy (*of roads*); (*Print.*) at work.

rouleau [ru'lo], *n.m.* (*pl.* **-eaux**) roll; roller; rolling-pin; coil (*rope*).

roulement [rul'mɑ̃], *n.m.* rolling, roll; rumbling, rattle; rotation; *par roulement*, in rotation; *roulement à billes*, ball-bearing.

rouler [ru'le], *v.t.* to roll; to roll up; to wind up; to revolve; (*colloq.*) to cheat; (*Golf*) *coup roulé*, putt.—*v.i.* to roll, to roll along; to revolve; to ride (*en*); to ramble; to keep going. **se rouler**, *v.r.* to roll; to tumble, to wallow.

roulette [ru'lɛt], *n.f.* small wheel; roller; castor, truckle; roulette (*game*).

roulier [ru'lje], *a.* carrying (*trade*).—*n.m.* wagoner, carter, carrier.

roulis [ru'li], *n.m.* rolling, roll (*waves or ships*), lurch.

roulotte [ru'lɔt], *n.f.* gipsy van; (*Motor.*) trailer.

roumain [ru'mɛ̃], *a.* Rumanian.—*n.m.* Rumanian (*language*); (**Roumain**, *fem.* **-aine**) Rumanian (*person*).

Roumanie [ruma'ni], **la**, *f.* Rumania.

roupie [ru'pi], *n.f.* rupee.

roupiller [rupi'je], *v.i.* (*colloq.*) to doze, to snooze.

rouquin [ru'kɛ̃], *a.* (*pop.*) ginger-haired, carroty-haired.

roussâtre [ru'sɑːtr], *a.* reddish, russet.

rousseur [ru'sœːr], *n.f.* redness.

roussi [ru'si], *a.* browned, scorched.—*n.m.* burnt smell; burning.

roussir [ru'siːr], *v.t., v.i.* to redden; to singe, to scorch; *faire roussir*, to brown (*meat etc.*).

roussissage [rusi'saːʒ], **roussissement** [rusis'mɑ̃], *n.m.* reddening; browning; scorching.

routage [ru'taːʒ], *n.m.* sorting (*of mail*).

route [rut], *n.f.* road, way; route, path, course; track (*of a ship etc.*); highway.

router [ru'te], *v.t.* to sort (*mail*).

routier [ru'tje], *a.* (*fem.* **-ière**) of roads;

carte routière, road map.—*n.m.* truck driver; (*fig.*) old hand; road racer (*cyclist*).

routine [ru'tin], *n.f.* routine, habit, practice.

routinier [ruti'nje], *a.* (*fem.* **-ière**) routine, following a routine.—*n.m.* (*fem.* **-ière**) person following a routine; stick-in-the-mud.

rouvrir [ru'vriːr], *v.t., v.i. irr.* (*conjug. like* OUVRIR) to reopen.

roux [ru], *a.* (*fem.* **rousse**) reddish; red-haired, sandy.—*n.m.* (*fem.* **rousse**) red-haired *or* sandy person.—*n.m.* reddish color.

royal [rwɑ'jal], *a.* (*m. pl.* **-aux**) royal; regal, kingly.

royalement [rwajal'mɑ̃], *adv.* royally; regally.

royalisme [rwaja'lism], *n.m.* royalism.

royaliste [rwaja'list], *a.* and *n.* royalist.

royaume [rwɑ'joːm], *n.m.* kingdom, realm; *le Royaume-Uni*, the United Kingdom.

royauté [rwajo'te], *n.f.* royalty, kingship, monarchy.

ruade [rɥad], *n.f.* kick (*by horse etc.*); lashing out.

Ruanda [RWANDA].

ruban [ry'bɑ̃], *n.m.* ribbon; (*fig.*) strip; tape.

rubané [ryba'ne], *a.* covered with ribbons.

rubaner [ryba'ne], *v.t.* to trim with ribbons; to cut into ribbons.

rubanerie [ryban'ri], *n.f.* ribbon-weaving; ribbon trade.

rubéole [rybe'ɔl], *n.f.* rubeola, German measles.

rubescent [rybɛ'sɑ̃], *a.* reddish; growing red.

rubicond [rybi'kɔ̃], *a.* rubicund.

rubis [ry'bi], *n.m. inv.* ruby.

rubrique [ry'brik], *n.f.* red chalk; (*pl.*) rubric; (*fig.*) heading (*of article*).

ruche [ryʃ], *n.f.* hive; (*Needlework*) frilling, ruche.

ruchée [ry'ʃe], *n.f.* hiveful.

rucher (1) [ry'ʃe], *n.m.* stand *or* shed for bee-hives; apiary.

rucher (2) [ry'ʃe], *v.t.* (*Needlework*) to ruche, to frill.

rude [ryd], *a.* harsh, rough, rugged; violent; severe; uncouth; churlish; arduous, difficult.

rudement [ryd'mɑ̃], *adv.* roughly, harshly, severely, violently; (*pop.*) awfully, very.

rudesse [ry'dɛs], *n.f.* roughness, coarseness; ruggedness, uncouthness; harshness; unkindness.

rudiment [rydi'mɑ̃], *n.m.* rudiment; primer.

rudimentaire [rydimɑ̃'tɛːr], *a.* rudimentary.

rudoiement [rydwa'mɑ̃], *n.m.* bullying, brow-beating.

rudoyer [rydwa'je], *v.t.* (*conjug. like* EMPLOYER) to treat roughly; to bully, to ill-treat.

rue [ry], *n.f.* street; rue (*plant*).

ruée [rɥe], *n.f.* rush; onslaught.

ruelle [rɥɛl], *n.f.* lane, alley.

ruer [rɥe], *v.i.* to kick (*of horses etc.*). **se ruer**, *v.r.* to throw oneself, to rush (*sur*).

rugby [ryg'bi], *n.m.* rugby football, rugger.

rugir [ry'ʒiːr], *v.i.* to roar, to bellow.

rugissant [ryʒi'sɑ̃], *a.* roaring.

rugissement [ryʒis'mɑ̃], *n.m.* roaring, roar.

rugosité [rygozi'te], *n.f.* rugosity, roughness.

rugueux [ry'gø], *a.* (*fem.* **-euse**) rugose, rough.

ruine [rɥin], *n.f.* ruin; decay, destruction.
ruiner [rɥi′ne], *v.t.* to ruin, to lay waste; to destroy; to spoil. **se ruiner**, *v.r.* to ruin oneself; to fall into decay.
ruineux [rɥi′nø], *a.* (*fem.* **-euse**) ruinous.
ruisseau [rɥi′so], *n.m.* (*pl.* **-eaux**) brook, stream; gutter.
ruisselant [rɥi′slɑ̃], *a.* streaming, dripping.
ruisseler [rɥi′sle], *v.i.* (*conjug. like* APPELER) to run, to be very wet, to stream (with) (*de*).
rumeur [ry′mœːr], *n.f.* clamor, uproar; (*fig.*) report, rumor.
ruminant [rymi′nɑ̃], *a.* ruminant, ruminating.—*n.m.* ruminant.
rumination [ryminɑ′sjɔ̃], *n.f.* rumination (*chewing the cud*).
ruminer [rymi′ne], *v.t.* to ruminate on; (*fig.*) to think over.—*v.i.* to ruminate, to chew the cud; (*fig.*) to ponder, to muse.
rupture [ryp′tyːr], *n.f.* breaking, rupture; annulment; hernia.
rural [ry′ral], *a.* (*m. pl.* **-aux**) rural, rustic.
ruse [ryːz], *n.f.* guile, cunning; trick, wile, ruse.
rusé [ry′ze], *a.* artful, crafty, sly.—*n.m.* (*fem.* **-ée**) artful, crafty or sly person.
ruser [ry′ze], *v.i.* to use deceit, craft or guile.
russe [rys], *a.* Russian.—*n.m.* Russian (*language*).—*n.* (**Russe**) Russian (*person*).
Russie [ry′si], **la**, *f.* Russia.
rustaud [rys′to], *a.* rustic, boorish, uncouth.—*n.m.* (*fem.* **-e**) rustic, clodhopper.
rusticité [rystisi′te], *n.f.* rusticity, simplicity.
rustique [rys′tik], *a.* rustic, rural; homely, simple.
rustiquement [rystik′mɑ̃], *adv.* rustically; boorishly, uncouthly.
rustre [rystr], *a.* boorish, rude.—*n.m.* boor, lout.
rutabaga [rytaba′ga], *n.m.* rutabaga, Swedish turnip.
rutilant [ryti′lɑ̃], *a.* glowing, gleaming, rutilant.
rutiler [ryti′le], *v.i.* to glow, to gleam (*red*).
Rwanda, Ruanda [rwɑ̃′da], **le**, *m.* Rwanda.
rythme [ritm], *n.m.* rhythm.
rythmique [rit′mik], *a.* rhythmical.

S

S, s [ɛs], *n.m.* the nineteenth letter of the alphabet.
s' [s], *elision*, [SE].
sa [sa], [SON (I)].
sabbat [sa′ba], *n.m.* Sabbath.
sable [sɑːbl], *n.m.* sand; gravel; (*Zool.*, *Her.*) sable.
sablé [sɑ′ble], *a.* covered with sand or gravel.
sabler [sɑ′ble], *v.t.* to sand, to gravel; (*fig.*) to drink off.
sableux [sɑ′blø], *a.* (*fem.* **-euse**) sandy.
sablier [sɑbli′je], *n.m.* sand-glass, hour-glass; egg-timer.
sablière [sɑbli′jɛːr], *n.f.* sand pit; gravel pit.

sablon [sɑ′blɔ̃], *n.m.* fine sand, scouring sand.
sablonner [sɑblɔ′ne], *v.t.* to scour with sand.
sablonneux [sɑblɔ′nø], *a.* (*fem.* **-euse**) sandy, gritty.
sablonnière [sɑblɔ′njɛːr], *n.f.* sand pit.
sabord [sa′bɔːr], *n.m.* (*Naut.*) port-hole.
saborder [sabɔr′de], *v.t.* to scuttle.
sabot [sa′bo], *n.m.* sabot, clog; hoof (*of horse etc.*); trig (*of carriages*); **dormir comme un sabot**, to sleep like a top.
sabotage [sabɔ′taːʒ], *n.m.* sabotage.
saboter [sabɔ′te], *v.t.* (*colloq.*) to bungle; to damage wilfully, to sabotage.
saboteur [sabɔ′tœːr], *n.m.* (*fem.* **-euse**) bungler; saboteur.
sabotier [sabɔ′tje], *n.m.* (*fem.* **-ière**) sabot maker.
sabre [sɑːbr], *n.m.* saber; broadsword.
sabrer [sɑ′bre], *v.t.* to strike or cut with a saber, to saber; (*colloq.*) to hurry over, to botch.
sabreur [sɑ′brœːr], *n.m.* swashbuckler; (*colloq.*) botcher.
sac (I) [sak], *n.m.* sack, bag; pouch (*of certain animals*).
sac (2) [sak], *n.m.* sack (*plunder*), pillage.
saccade [sa′kad], *n.f.* jerk, jolt.
saccadé [saka′de], *a.* jerky, broken, abrupt, irregular.
saccader [saka′de], *v.t.* to jerk.
saccage [sa′kaːʒ], *n.m.* upset, confusion; pillage.
saccager [saka′ʒe], *v.t.* (*conjug. like* MANGER) to sack, to plunder; (*fig.*) to play havoc with.
saccharine [saka′rin], *n.f.* saccharine.
sacerdoce [sasɛr′dɔs], *n.m.* priesthood.
sacerdotal [sasɛrdɔ′tal], *a.* (*m. pl.* **-aux**) sacerdotal.
sachée [sa′ʃe], *n.f.* sackful, bagful.
sachet [sa′ʃɛ], *n.m.* small bag, sachet.
sacoche [sa′kɔʃ], *n.f.* (*Mil.*) saddle-bag; money-bag; tool-bag.
sacramental [sakramɑ̃′tal] (*m. pl.* **-aux**), **sacramentel** [sakramɑ̃′tɛl] (*fem.* **-elle**), *a.* sacramental.
sacre [sakr], *n.m.* anointing and coronation of a king; consecration of a bishop.
sacré [sa′kre], *a.* holy, consecrated; sacred, inviolable.
sacrebleu! [sakrə′blø], *int.* confound it! curse it!
sacrement [sakrə′mɑ̃], *n.m.* sacrament, *esp.* matrimony.
sacrer [sa′kre], *v.t.* to anoint, to crown; to consecrate.—*v.i.* to curse and swear.
sacrificateur [sakrifika′tœːr], *n.m.* (*fem.* **-trice**) sacrificer.
sacrificatoire [sakrifika′twaːr], *a.* sacrificial.
sacrifice [sakri′fis], *n.m.* sacrifice; renunciation.
sacrifier [sakri′fje], *v.t.* to sacrifice; to devote; to give up.—*v.i.* to sacrifice.
sacrilège [sakri′lɛːʒ], *a.* sacrilegious.—*n.m.* sacrilege.
sacrilègement [sakrilɛʒ′mɑ̃], *adv.* sacrilegiously.
sacripant [sakri′pɑ̃], *n.m.* rascal, scoundrel.
sacristain [sakris′tɛ̃], *n.m.* sacristan, sexton.
sacristie [sakris′ti], *n.f.* sacristy, vestry; church plate.
sacristine [sakris′tin], *n.f.* vestry nun, sacristine.

salpêtrerie

sacro-saint [sakrɔ'sɛ̃], *a.* sacrosanct.
sadique [sa'dik], *a.* sadistic.—*n.* sadist.
sadisme [sa'dism], *n.m.* sadism.
saducéen [sadyse'ɛ̃], *a.* (*fem.* **-éenne**) Sadducean.—*n.m.* (*fem.* **-éenne**) Sadducee.
safran [sa'frɑ̃], *n.m.* saffron; crocus.
safrané [safra'ne], *a.* saffron-colored.
saga [sa'ga], *n.f.* saga.
sagace [sa'gas], *a.* sagacious, shrewd.
sagacité [sagasi'te], *n.f.* sagacity.
sage [sa:ʒ], *a.* wise; sage, sensible, prudent; sober, well-behaved, good; virtuous, modest; gentle (*of animals*).—*n.m.* wise man, sage.
sage-femme [saʒ'fam], *n.f.* (*pl.* **sages-femmes**) midwife.
sagement [saʒ'mɑ̃] *adv.* wisely; prudently; soberly, steadily.
sagesse [sa'ʒɛs], *n.f.* wisdom; prudence; steadiness; chastity; good behavior (*of children*); gentleness (*of animals*).
sagittaire [saʒi'tɛ:r], *n.m.* (*Rom. Ant.*) archer; (*Astron.*) Sagittarius.
sagou [sa'gu], *n.m.* sago.
sagouier [sagu'je] or (*preferably*) **sagoutier** [sagu'tje], *n.m.* sago tree.
sagouin [sa'gwɛ̃], *n.m.* squirrel-monkey; (*fem.* **-e**) (*fig.*) slovenly fellow *or* woman.
Sahara [saa'ra], **le**, *m.* the Sahara.
saignant [sɛ'ɲɑ̃], *a.* bleeding, bloody; underdone (*of meat*).
saignée [sɛ'ɲe] *n.f.* blood-letting, phlebotomy; small of the arm; (*fig.*) drain on the purse.
saignement [sɛɲə'mɑ̃], *n.m.* bleeding.
saigner [sɛ'ɲe], *v.t.* to bleed; to stick (*an animal*); (*fig.*) to drain.—*v.i.* to bleed. **se saigner**, *v.r.* to bleed oneself; to drain oneself *or* one's purse.
saigneux [sɛ'ɲø], *a.* (*fem.* **-euse**) bloody.
saillant [sa'jɑ̃], *a.* jutting out, projecting; (*fig.*) striking, remarkable.—*n.m.* (*Fort.*) salient.
saillie [sa'ji], *n.f.* start, sudden spurt; sally; (*fig.*) witticism; projection.
saillir [sa'ji:r], *v.i.* to gush (*of liquids*); to ripple (*of muscles*).
sain [sɛ̃], *a.* hale, healthy; sound; sane; **sain et sauf**, safe and sound.
saindoux [sɛ̃'du], *n.m. inv.* lard.
sainement [sɛn'mɑ̃], *adv.* wholesomely; healthily, soundly; judiciously.
sainfoin [sɛ̃'fwɛ̃], *n.m.* sainfoin.
saint [sɛ̃], *a.* holy, sacred; godly, saintly; sanctified, consecrated.—*n.m.* (*fem.* **-e**) saint; patron saint.
saintement [sɛ̃t'mɑ̃], *adv.* sacredly; piously, religiously.
sainteté [sɛ̃tə'te], *n.f.* holiness, sanctity, sacredness, saintliness; **Sa Sainteté le Pape**, His Holiness the Pope.
saisi [sɛ'zi], *a.* seized, possessed, struck (*de*).
saisie [sɛ'zi], *n.f.* (*Law*) seizure; distraint, execution.
saisir [sɛ'zi:r], *v.t.* to seize, to take hold of; to understand; (*fig.*) to impress, to shock, to startle; to distrain. **se saisir**, *v.r.* to seize, to catch hold (*de*); to take possession (*de*); to arrest.
saisissable [sɛzi'sabl], *a.* distrainable, seizable.
saisissant [sɛzi'sɑ̃], *a.* keen, sharp, piercing (*of cold*); striking, impressive.

saisissement [sɛzis'mɑ̃], *n.m.* shock, violent impression, seizure.
saison [sɛ'zɔ̃], *n.f.* season; **marchand des quatre saisons**, street vendor (*of produce*).
saisonnier [sɛzɔ'nje], *a.* (*fem.* **-ière**) seasonal.
salade [sa'lad], *n.f.* salad, herb grown for salad; (*fig.*) medley, confusion.
saladier [sala'dje], *n.m.* salad bowl.
salage [sa'la:ʒ], *n.m.* salting.
salaire [sa'lɛ:r], *n.m.* wages, pay, hire; reward.
salaison [salɛ'zɔ̃], *n.f.* salting; salt provisions; curing (*of bacon etc.*).
salamalec [salama'lɛk], *n.m.* (*used chiefly in pl.*) salaam; (*fig.*) exaggerated politeness.
salamandre [sala'mɑ̃:dr], *n.f.* salamander; slow-combustion stove.
salant [sa'lɑ̃], *a.m.* **marais salant**, salt-marsh.
salarié [sala'rje], *a.* paid, wage-earning.—*n.m.* (*fem.* **-ée**) wage-earner.
salarier [sala'rje], *v.t.* to pay, to give wages to.
salaud [sa'lo], *n.m.* (*fem.* **-e**) (*pop.* and *rude*) sloven, dirty person, slut; **quel salaud!** dirty beast! dirty dog!
sale [sal], *a.* dirty; nasty, foul; coarse, obscene; squalid.
salé [sa'le], *a.* salted, salt; briny; (*fig.*) keen, biting; coarse; spicy.—*n.m.* salt pork; **du petit salé**, pickled pork.
salement [sal'mɑ̃], *adv.* dirtily; nastily.
saler [sa'le], *v.t.* to salt; (*fig.*) to overcharge for; to fleece (*customers*).
saleté [sal'te], *n.f.* dirtiness, filthiness; filth, dirt; dirty trick; obscenity.
saleur [sa'lœ:r], *n.m.* (*fem.* **-euse**) salter, curer.
salière [sa'ljɛ:r], *n.f.* salt-cellar; salt box; eyepit (*in horses*).
salin [sa'lɛ̃], *a.* salt, saline, briny.—*n.m.* salt works; salt marsh.
saline [sa'lin], *n.f.* salt marsh, salt mine, salt pit.
salinier [sali'nje], *n.m.* owner of salt works; salt worker *or* vendor.
salique [sa'lik], *a.* **loi salique**, Salic law.
salir [sa'li:r], *v.t.* to dirty, to soil; to taint, to sully. **se salir**, *v.r.* to get dirty; to sully one's reputation.
salissant [sali'sɑ̃], *a.* that soils *or* gets dirty easily; dirty (*of job, work etc.*).
salive [sa'li:v], *n.f.* saliva, spittle.
saliver [sali've], *v.i.* to salivate.
salle [sal], *n.f.* hall; large room; gallery (*of museum*); ward (*in hospitals*); (*Theat.*) house; **salle à manger**, dining room; **salle d'attente**, waiting room; **salle de bain(s)**, bathroom; **salle de spectacle**, playhouse.
saloir [sa'lwa:r], *n.m.* salt box; salting-tub.
salon [sa'lɔ̃], *n.m.* drawing-room, parlor; lounge; saloon; exhibition (*art*); (*pl.*) world of fashion.
salopette [salɔ'pɛt], *n.f.* overall, dungarees.
salpêtrage [salpɛ'tra:ʒ], *n.m.* saltpeter-making; nitrification.
salpêtre [sal'pɛ:tr], *n.m.* saltpeter.
salpêtrer [salpɛ'tre], *v.t.* to cover with saltpeter.
salpêtrerie [salpɛtrə'ri], *n.f.* saltpeter-works.

salpêtreux [salpɛ'trø], a. (fem. **-euse**) salt-petrous.

salpêtrière [salpɛtri'jɛːr], n.f. saltpeter works.

salsepareille [salspa'rɛːj], n.f. sarsaparilla.

saltimbanque [saltɛ̃'bãːk], n.m. mountebank, buffoon; (fig.) humbug.

salubre [sa'lybr], a. salubrious, healthy (climate).

salubrité [salybri'te], n.f. salubrity, healthfulness, wholesomeness.

saluer [sa'lɥe], v.t. to salute, to bow to; to greet; to cheer; to proclaim. **se saluer**, v.r. to bow to or salute each other.

salure [sa'lyːr], n.f. saltness, salinity.

salut [sa'ly], n.m. safety; salvation; welfare; escape; salutation, greeting; hail, cheers.

salutaire [saly'tɛːr], a. salutary, advantageous, beneficial.

salutairement [salytɛr'mã], adv. beneficially.

salutation [salyta'sjɔ̃], n.f. salutation, greeting; (pl.) compliments.

Salvador [salva'dɔr], **le**, m. El Salvador.

salvadorègne [salvadɔ'rɛɲ], a. Salvadorean. —n. (**Salvadorègne**) Salvadorean (person).

salve [salv], n.f. salvo, volley; salute (of artillery).

samedi [sam'di], n.m. Saturday.

sanatorium [sanatɔ'rjɔm], n.m. sanatorium.

sanctifiant [sãkti'fjã], a. sanctifying.

sanctificateur [sãktifika'tœːr], a. (fem. **-trice**) sanctifying.—n.m. sanctifier.

sanctification [sãktifika'sjɔ̃], n.f. sanctification.

sanctifier [sãk'sjɔ̃], v.t. to sanctify, to hallow.

sanction [sãk'sjɔ̃], n.f. sanction; approbation; penalty.

sanctionner [sãksjɔ'ne], v.t. to sanction, to approve; to penalize.

sanctuaire [sãk'tɥɛːr], n.m. sanctuary (of the temple etc.), shrine; chancel (of church).

sandale [sã'dal], n.f. sandal; fencing shoe.

sandalier [sãda'lje], n.m. sandal-maker.

sandow [sã'dɔf], n.m. chest-expander; rubber shock-absorber.

sandwich [sã'dwitʃ], n.m. (pl. **sandwichs** or **sandwiches**) sandwich.

sang [sã], n.m. blood; race; kindred; **pur sang**, thoroughbred.

sang-froid [sã'frwa], n.m. coolness, composure, sang-froid.

sanglade [sã'glad], n.f. lash, cut (with a whip).

sanglant [sã'glã], a. bloody, bleeding; (fig.) biting, outrageous.

sangle [sãːgl], n.f. strap, belt; saddle-girth; **lit de sangle**, camp bed.

sangler [sã'gle], v.t. to girth, to strap; to lace too tightly; to deal (a slashing blow). **se sangler**, v.r. to lace oneself tightly.

sanglier [sã'glje], n.m. wild boar.

sanglot [sã'glo], n.m. sob.

sangloter [sãglɔ'te], v.i. to sob.

sang-mêlé [sãme'le], n.m. inv. half-caste.

sangsue [sã'sy], n.f. leech; (fig.) extortioner.

sanguin [sã'gɛ̃], a. of blood; full-blooded; blood-red.

sanguinaire [sãgi'nɛːr], a. sanguinary, bloody, blood-thirsty.

sanitaire [sani'tɛːr], a. sanitary.

sans [sã], prep. without; free from; but for, had it not been for, were it not for; **cela va sans dire**, of course; **sans abri**, **sans gîte**, **sans logis**, homeless; **sans cela**, otherwise; **sans quoi**, otherwise.

sans-atout [sãza'tu], n.m. no trumps.

sans-cœur [sã'kœːr], n. inv. heartless, unfeeling person.

sanscrit [sãs'kri], n.m. Sanskrit.

sans-façon [sãfa'sɔ̃], n.m. bluntness; offhandedness.

sans-gêne [sã'ʒɛːn], n.m. unceremoniousness, coolness; (fam.) cheek.

sansonnet [sãsɔ'nɛ], n.m. (Orn.) starling.

sans-patrie [sãpa'tri], n. inv. stateless person.

sans-souci [sãsu'si], a. carefree, happy-go-lucky.—n. inv. (colloq.) carefree, easy-going person.—n.m. inv. free-and-easy manners.

sans-travail [sãtra'vaj], n.m. inv. **les sans-travail**, the unemployed.

santal [sã'tal], n.m. (pl. **-als**) sandalwood, santal.

santé [sã'te], n.f. health, healthiness; state of health.

saoul [suːl].

sape [sap], n.f. sapping, undermining; mine; trench.

saper [sa'pe], v.t. to sap, to undermine.

sapeur [sa'pœːr], n.m. sapper.

sapeur-pompier [sapœrpɔ̃'pje], n.m. (pl. **sapeurs-pompiers**) fireman.

sapeur-télégraphiste [sapœrtelegra'fist], n.m. (pl. **sapeurs-télégraphistes**) soldier of the signal corps; (pl.) (fam.) signals.

saphir [sa'fiːr], n.m. sapphire.

sapin [sa'pɛ̃], n.m. fir, fir tree; (bois de) **sapin**, deal.

sapinette [sapi'nɛt], n.f. spruce.

sapinière [sapi'njɛːr], n.f. fir wood, fir plantation.

sarabande [sara'bãːd], n.f. saraband (dance); (fam.) song-and-dance.

sarcasme [sar'kasm], n.m. sarcasm, sarcastic remark.

sarcastique [sarkas'tik], a. sarcastic.

sarcelle [sar'sɛl], n.f. (Orn.) teal.

sarclage [sar'klaːʒ], n.m. weeding.

sarcler [sar'kle], v.t. to weed; to hoe; (fig.) to extirpate.

sarcleur [sar'klœːr], n.m. (fem. **-euse**) weeder.

sarcloir [sar'klwaːr], n.m. hoe.

sarcophage (1) [sarkɔ'faːʒ], n.m. sarcophagus.

sarcophage (2) [sarkɔ'faːʒ], n.f. (Ent.) blow-fly.

Sardaigne [sar'dɛɲ], **la**, f. Sardinia.

sarde [sard], a. Sardinian.—n. (**Sarde**) Sardinian (person).

sardine [sar'din], n.f. sardine.

sardinerie [sardin'ri], n.f. sardine packing and curing factory.

sardinier [sardi'nje], n.m. (fem. **-ière**) sardine fisher; sardine packer or · curer. —n.m. sardine net; sardine boat.

sardoine [sar'dwan], n.f. sardonyx.

sardonique [sardɔ'nik], a. sardonic.

sarigue [sa'rig], n. sarigue (opossum).

sarment [sar'mã], n.m. vine shoot, vine branch.

sarmenteux [sarmã'tø], a. (fem. **-euse**) branchy, climbing; rambling (of roses).

sarrasin [sara'zɛ̃], n.m. buckwheat.

sarrau [saˈro], *n.m.* (*pl.* -**aux**) smock frock; child's blouse.

sas [sɑ], *n.m. inv.* sieve, screen; (*Naut.*) floating chamber (*of submarine*).

Satan [saˈtɑ̃], *m.* Satan.

satané [sataˈne], *a.* (*collog.*) devilish, confounded.

satanique [sataˈnik], *a.* satanic, diabolical.

sataniquement [satanikˈmɑ̃], *adv.* fiendishly, diabolically.

satellite [sateˈlit], *a.* satellite.—*n.m.* satellite.

satiété [sasjeˈte], *n.f.* satiety, repletion.

satin [saˈtɛ̃], *n.m.* satin.

satiné [satiˈne], *a.* satin-like, satiny; glazed (*of paper etc.*).

satiner [satiˈne], *v.t.* to satin; to glaze (*paper etc.*).—*v.i.* to look like satin.

satire [saˈtiːr], *n.f.* satire; lampoon.

satirique [satiˈrik], *a.* satirical.—*n.m.* satirist.

satiriquement [satirikˈmɑ̃], *adv.* satirically.

satiriser [satiriˈze], *v.t.* to satirize.

satisfaction [satisfakˈsjɔ̃]. *n.f.* satisfaction; gratification; atonement.

satisfaire [satisˈfɛːr], *v.t. irr.* (*conjug. like* FAIRE) to satisfy; to gratify; to answer; to give satisfaction to, to make amends to.—*v.i.* to be satisfactory (*à*); to fulfil (*à*). **se satisfaire**, *v.r.* to satisfy oneself, to indulge oneself.

satisfaisant [satisfəˈzɑ̃], *a.* satisfactory.

satisfait [satisˈfɛ], *a.* satisfied, contented, pleased.

saturant [satyˈrɑ̃], *a.* saturating.

saturation [satyraˈsjɔ̃], *n.f.* saturation.

saturer [satyˈre], *v.t.* to saturate; (*fig.*) to surfeit.

saturnales [satyrˈnal], *n.f. pl.* saturnalia.

Saturne [saˈtyrn], *m.* Saturn.

satyre [saˈtiːr], *n.m.* satyr.

sauce [soːs], *n.f.* sauce; *sauce hollandaise*, egg yolks and melted butter.

saucé [soˈse], *a.* soused, wet through.

saucer [soˈse], *v.t.* (*conjug. like* COMMENCER) to dip in sauce; to sop, to souse.

saucière [soˈsjɛːr], *n.f.* sauce dish.

saucisse [soˈsis], *n.f.* (*fresh*) sausage.

saucisson [sosiˈsɔ̃], *n.m.* large dry sausage; salami.

sauf (1) [sof], *a.* (*fem.* **sauve**) safe; unhurt, unscathed; *sain et sauf*, safe and sound.

sauf (2) [sof], *prep.* save, except; unless.

sauf-conduit [sofkɔ̃ˈdɥi], *n.m.* (*pl.* -**conduits**) safe-conduct.

sauge [soːʒ], *n.f.* sage (*herb*).

saugrenu [sogrəˈny], *a.* absurd, ridiculous, preposterous.

saulaie [soˈlɛ], *n.f.* willow grove.

saule [soːl], *n.m.* willow.

saumâtre [soˈmɑːtr], *a.* brackish, briny.

saumon [soˈmɔ̃], *n.m.* salmon.

saumoné [somoˈne], *a.* salmon-colored; *truite saumonée*, salmon trout.

saumurage [somyˈraːʒ], *n.m.* pickling (*in brine*), brining.

saumure [soˈmyːr], *n.f.* brine, pickle.

saumuré [somyˈre], *a.* pickled, brined.

saunage [soˈnaːʒ], *n.m.*, **saunaison** [sonɛˈzɔ̃], *n.f.* salt-making; salt trade.

sauner [soˈne], *v.i.* to make salt.

saunerie [sonˈri], *n.f.* saltworks.

saunier [soˈnje], *n.m.* salt-maker; salt merchant.

saunière [soˈnjɛːr], *n.f.* salt bin.

saupoudrage [sopuˈdraːʒ], *n.m.* salting; sprinkling, powdering.

saupoudrer [sopuˈdre], *v.t.* to sprinkle with salt, pepper etc.; to powder, to sprinkle.

saur or **sor** [soːr], *a.m.* smoked and salted; red (*of herrings*).

saure [sor], *a.* yellowish-brown; sorrel (*of horses*); red, smoked (*of herrings*).

saurer [soˈre], *v.t.* to smoke (*herrings*).

saurin [soˈrɛ̃], *n.m.* freshly smoked herring, bloater.

saurisserie [sorisˈri], *n.f.* kippering factory.

saut [so], *n.m.* leap, jump, hop, bound; *de plein saut*, at once, suddenly; *saut périlleux*, somersault.

sautage [soˈtaːʒ], *n.m.* exploding (*mines*).

saut-de-mouton [sodmuˈtɔ̃], *n.m.* (*pl.* **sauts-de-mouton**) overpass.

saute [sot], *n.f.* (*Naut.*) sudden shift or change (*of wind*).

sauté [soˈte], *a.* fried, tossed in the pan.

saute-mouton [sotmuˈtɔ̃], *n.m.* leap-frog (*game*).

sauter [soˈte], *v.t.* to leap over; to leave out, to skip; to toss in the pan.—*v.i.* to leap, to jump; to explode; to spring; to blow out (*of fuse*).

sauterelle [soˈtrɛl], *n.f.* grasshopper, locust.

sauterie [sotˈri], *n.f.* (*fam.*) informal dance, hop.

saute-ruisseau [sotrɥiˈso], *n.m. inv.* messenger boy (*in offices*).

sauteur [soˈtœːr], *a.* (*fem.* -**euse**) jumping, leaping.—*n.m.* (*fem.* -**euse**) leaper, jumper; vaulter.

sautillant [sotiˈjɑ̃], *a.* hopping, skipping.

sautiller [sotiˈje], *v.i.* to hop, to skip, to jump about.

sautoir [soˈtwaːr], *n.m.* Saint Andrew's cross.

sauvage [soˈvaːʒ], *a.* savage, wild; uncivilized; brutal; shy; unsociable.—*n.* savage; unsociable person.

sauvagement [sovaʒˈmɑ̃], *adv.* wildly, savagely; barbarously, fiercely.

sauvageon [sovaˈʒɔ̃], *n.m.* (*Agric.*) wild stock (*for grafting*); briar (*of roses*).

sauvagerie [sovaʒˈri], *n.f.* unsociableness, shyness; wildness.

sauvagesse [sovaˈʒɛs], *n.f.* uncivilized woman; hoyden.

sauvagin [sovaˈʒɛ̃], *a.* fishy (*in taste, smell, etc.*).—*n.m.* fishy taste or smell.—*n.f.* (-**e**) wild waterfowl.

sauvegarde [sovˈgard], *n.f.* safe-keeping, safeguard; safe-conduct; (*Naut.*) life-line.

sauvegarder [sovgarˈde], *v.t.* to watch over, to protect, to safeguard.

sauve-qui-peut [sovkiˈpø], *n.m. inv.* headlong flight, stampede; every man for himself.

sauver [soˈve], *v.t.* to save, to rescue; to preserve; to exempt; to conceal. **se sauver**, *v.r.* to escape, to make off; (*fam.*) to abscond; to take refuge.

sauvetage [sovˈtaːʒ], *n.m.* salvage; life-saving, rescue; *appareil de sauvetage*, rescue apparatus, fire escape; *bouée de*

sauvetage, life buoy; *canot de sauvetage*, life-boat; *ceinture de sauvetage*, life belt.
sauveteur [sov'tœ:r], *n.m.* rescuer, lifeboat man.
sauveur [so'vœ:r], *a.* saving, redeeming.—*n.m.* saver, deliverer; Saviour.
savamment [sava'mã], *adv.* learnedly; knowingly.
savane [sa'van], *n.f.* savanna; (*C*) swamp.
savant [sa'vã], *a.* learned, expert (*en*); scholarly; clever.—*n.m.* (*fem.* **-e**) scholar, scientist.
savarin [sava'rɛ̃], *n.m.* round, hollow cake.
savate [sa'vat], *n.f.* old shoe; clumsy person.
savetier [sav'tje], *n.m.* cobbler; (*fig.*) bungler.
saveur [sa'vœ:r], *n.f.* savor, flavor, relish.
savoir [sa'vwa:r], *v.t. irr.* to be aware of; to understand; to know how (*can*), to be able. **se savoir**, *v.r.* to get known.—*n.m.* knowledge, learning, scholarship.
savoir-faire [savwar'fɛ:r], *n.m.* tact; savoir-faire; cleverness.
savoir-vivre [savwar'vi:vr], *n.m.* good manners, good breeding.
savon [sa'vɔ̃], *n.m.* soap; (*colloq.*) scolding.
savonnage [savɔ'na:ʒ], *n.m.* soaping, washing with soap.
savonner [savɔ'ne], *v.t.* to soap; to lather; (*colloq.*) to scold. **se savonner**, *v.r.* to be washable, to wash (*of fabrics*); to lather (*oneself*).
savonnerie [savɔn'ri], *n.f.* soap manufacture; soap trade; soap works.
savonnette [savɔ'nɛt], *n.f.* cake of toilet soap.
savonneux [savɔ'nø], *a.* (*fem.* **-euse**) soapy.
savourer [savu're], *v.t.* to savor, to relish; (*fig.*) to enjoy.
savoureusement [savurøz'mã], *adv.* with relish.
savoureux [savu'rø], *a.* (*fem.* **-euse**) savory, tasty (*dish*); racy (*story*).
savoyard [savwa'ja:r], *a.* of Savoy.—*n.m.* (**Savoyard**, *fem.* **-arde**) Savoyard (*person*); *petit Savoyard*, little chimney-sweep.
saxifrage [saksi'fra:ʒ], *a.* saxifragous.—*n.f.* saxifrage.
saxon [sak'sɔ̃], *a.* (*fem.* **-onne**) Saxon.—*n.m.* (**Saxon**, *fem.* **-onne**) Saxon (*person*).
saxophone [saksɔ'fɔn], *n.m.* saxophone.
saynète [sɛ'nɛt], *n.f.* playlet, sketch.
scabieux [ska'bjø], *a.* (*fem.* **-euse**) scabious, scabby.—*n.f.* (**-euse**) scabious (*plant*).
scabreux [ska'brø], *a.* (*fem.* **-euse**) scabrous, rugged, rough; (*fig.*) dangerous, difficult, ticklish; improper.
scalp [skalp], *n.m.* scalp (*of an enemy*).
scalpel [skal'pɛl], *n.m.* scalpel.
scalper [skal'pe], *v.t.* to scalp.
scandale [skã'dal], *n.m.* scandal; shame, dismay, disgust.
scandaleusement [skãdaløz'mã], *adv.* scandalously.
scandaleux [skãda'lø], *a.* (*fem.* **-euse**) scandalous.
scandaliser [skãdali'ze], *v.t.* to scandalize, to shock. **se scandaliser**, *v.r.* to be shocked.
scander [skã'de], *v.t.* to scan; to stress (*a phrase*).
scandinave [skãdi'na:v], *a.* Scandinavian.—*n.* (**Scandinave**) Scandinavian (*person*).
Scandinavie [skãdina'vi], **la**, *f.* Scandinavia.

scansion [skã'sjɔ̃], *n.f.* scansion.
scaphandre [ska'fã:dr], *n.m.* diving suit.
scaphandrier [skafãdri'je], *n.m.* diver.
scapulaire [skapy'lɛ:r], *a.* and *n.m.* scapular.
scarabée [skara'be], *n.m.* scarabaeus (*beetle*); scarab.
scarlatine [skarla'tin], *a.* and *n.f.* (*fièvre*) *scarlatine*, scarlet fever.
sceau [so], *n.m.* (*pl.* **sceaux**) seal; (*fig.*) sanction; *mettre le sceau à*, to seal, (*fig.*) to complete.
scélérat [sele'ra], *a.* wicked, villainous, criminal, vile.—*n.m.* (*fem.* **-e**) scoundrel, villain, miscreant, jade.
scélératesse [selera'tɛs], *n.f.* villainy.
scellé [sɛ'le], *n.m.* seal.
scellement [sɛl'mã], *n.m.* sealing; fastening.
sceller [sɛ'le], *v.t.* to put an official seal on, to seal; (*Build.*) to fasten; (*fig.*) to ratify.
scénario [sena'rjo], *n.m.* (*pl.* **scénarios** or **scénarii**) scenario (*of ballet etc.*); film script.
scénariste [sena'rist], *n.* script writer, scenario writer.
scène [sɛ:n], *n.f.* stage; scenery; (*colloq.*) scene, quarrel.
scénique [se'nik], *a.* scenic, theatrical; *indications scéniques*, stage directions.
scepticisme [sɛpti'sism], *n.m.* scepticism.
sceptique [sɛp'tik], *a.* sceptical.—*n.* sceptic.
sceptre [sɛptr], *n.m.* scepter; (*fig.*) sway, dominion.
schah [ʃa], *n.m.* shah (*of Persia*).
scheik or **cheik** [ʃɛk], *n.m.* sheik.
schéma [ʃe'ma], **schème** [ʃɛm], *n.m.* diagram; rough sketch.
schématique [ʃema'tik], *a.* diagrammatic; *dessin schématique*, draft, diagram.
schibboleth [ʃibɔ'lɛt], *n.m.* catchword, shibboleth.
schisme [ʃism], *n.m.* schism.
schiste [ʃist], *n.m.* schist, slaty rock, shale.
schizophrène [skizɔ'frɛn], *a.* and *n.* schizophrenic.
schizophrénie [skizɔfre'ni], *n.f.* schizophrenia.
schnorkel [ʃnɔr'kɛl], *n.m.* snorkel; submarine's air-tube.
schooner [ʃu'nœ:r], *n.m.* schooner.
sciage [sja:ʒ], *n.m.* sawing.
sciatique [sja'tik], *a.* sciatic.—*n.m.* sciatic nerve.—*n.f.* sciatica.
scie [si], *n.f.* saw; (*pop.*) bore, nuisance.
sciemment [sja'mã], *adv.* wittingly, knowingly.
science [sjã:s], *n.f.* science, knowledge, learning; skill.
scientifique [sjãti'fik], *a.* scientific.
scientifiquement [sjãtifik'mã], *adv.* scientifically.
scier [sje], *v.t.* to saw; to cut down.—*v.i.* (*Row.*) to back water.
scierie [si'ri], *n.f.* sawmill.
scieur [sjœ:r], *n.m.* sawyer.
scinder [sɛ̃'de], *v.t.* to divide, to split up.
scintillant [sɛ̃ti'jã], *a.* scintillating; twinkling.
scintillation [sɛ̃tija'sjɔ̃] *n.f.*, **scintillement** [sɛ̃tij'mã], *n.m.* scintillation, sparkling; twinkling.
scintiller [sɛ̃ti'je], *v.i.* to scintillate, to sparkle; to twinkle (*of star*); to flicker.

scion [sjø], *n.m.* scion, shoot.
scission [si'sjɔ̃], *n.f.* scission; split, secession.
scissure [si'sy:r], *n.f.* fissure, crack, cleft.
sciure [sjy:r], *n.f.* **sciure de bois**, sawdust.
sclérose [skle'ro:z], *n.f.* sclerosis.
scolaire [skɔ'lɛ:r], *a.* of schools; **année scolaire**, school year.
scolarité [skɔlari'te], *n.f.* course of study; school attendance.
scolastique [skɔlas'tik], *a.* scholastic.—*n.m.* scholastic; schoolman.—*n.f.* scholasticism.
scolastiquement [skɔlastik'mɑ̃], *adv.* scholastically.
scooter [sku'tɛːr], *n.m.* motor-scooter; *autos scooters*, 3-wheeled delivery vehicles.
scorbut [skɔr'byt], *n.m.* scurvy.
scorbutique [skɔrby'tik], *a.* and *n.* scorbutic.
scorie [skɔ'ri], *n.f.* scoria, slag, dross.
scorifier [skɔri'fje], *v.t.* to scorify.
scorpion [skɔr'pjɔ̃], *n.m.* scorpion.
scout [skut], *a.* of scouting.—*n.m.* (boy) scout.
scoutisme [sku'tism], *n.m.* scouting, boy-scout movement.
scratch [skratʃ], *n.m.* (*Spt.*) **être** or **partir scratch**, to start at scratch.
scratcher [skrat'ʃe], *v.t.* (*Spt.*) to scratch (*horse, competitor etc.*).
scribe [skrib], *n.m.* scribe; copyist.
script [skript], *n.m.* script (*film* or *play*).
scriptural [skripty'ral], *a.* (*m. pl.* **-aux**) scriptural.
scrofule [skrɔ'fyl], *n.f.* scrofula, king's evil.
scrofuleux [skrɔfy'lø], *a.* and *n.m.* (*fem.* **-euse**) scrofulous (person).
scrupule [skry'pyl], *n.m.* scruple, qualm, 'doubt; scrupulousness.
scrupuleusement [skrypyløz'mɑ̃], *adv.* scrupulously.
scrupuleux [skrypy'lø], *a.* (*fem.* **-euse**) scrupulous, strict, punctilious.
scrutateur [skryta'tœːr], *a.* (*fem.* **-trice**) searching, scrutinizing.—*n.m.* (*fem.* **-trice**) investigator, scrutinizer; scrutineer, teller (*of a ballot etc.*).
scruter [skry'te], *v.t.* to scrutinize, to investigate.
scrutin [skry'tɛ̃], *n.m.* ballot, balloting, poll.
sculpter [skyl'te], *v.t.* to sculpture, to carve.
sculpteur [skyl'tœːr], *n.m.* sculptor, carver.
sculptural [skylty'ral], *a.* (*m. pl.* **-aux**) sculptural.
sculpture [skyl'ty:r], *n.f.* sculpture, carving.
se [sə], **s'** [s], *pron. inv.* oneself, himself, herself, itself, themselves; to oneself etc.; one another, each other; *cela se peut*, that may be.
séance [se'ɑ̃:s], *n.f.* seat (*right to sit*); session, duration, meeting; sitting (*for one's portrait etc.*); seance; *être en séance*, to be in session; *lever la séance*, to close the meeting; *séance tenante*, there and then, forthwith.
séant [se'ɑ̃], *a.* sitting; fitting, seemly, becoming.—*n.m.* sitting posture; seat.
seau [so], *n.m.* (*pl.* **seaux**) pail, bucket.
sébile [se'bil], *n.f.* small wooden bowl (*used by beggars*); pan (*in gold mining*).
sec [sɛk], *a.* (*fem.* **sèche**) dry, arid; withered; lean; plain; unfeeling, sharp; *à pied sec*, dry-shod; *coup sec*, sharp stroke; *perte*

sèche, dead loss.—*n.m.* dryness.—*adv.* dryly, sharply.
sécateur [seka'tœːr], *n.m.* (*Gard.*) pruning-shears; secateurs.
seccotine [sekɔ'tin], *n.f.* (*reg. trade mark*) Seccotine.
sécession [sese'sjɔ̃], *n.f.* secession.
séchage [se'ʃa:ʒ], *n.m.* drying.
sèchement [seʃ'mɑ̃], *adv.* dryly; curtly.
sécher [se'ʃe], *v.t.* (*conjug. like* CÉDER) to dry; to dry up; to cure.—*v.i.* to dry; to wither; to pine away. **se sécher**, *v.r.* to dry oneself; to dry (*of a thing*).
sécheresse [se'ʃrɛs], *n.f.* dryness; drought; (*fig.*) sharpness.
séchoir [se'ʃwa:r], *n.m.* drying room; clothes-horse; clothes airer; hair dryer.
second [sə'gɔ̃, zgɔ̃], *a.* second.—*n.m.* (*fem.* **-e**) second, assistant.—*n.m.* second floor.—*n.f.* (**-e**) second class; (*Sch.*) fifth grade; second (*of time*).
secondaire [səgɔ̃'dɛ:r], *a.* secondary; accessory.
secondairement [səgɔ̃dɛr'mɑ̃], *adv.* secondarily.
secondement [səgɔ̃d'mɑ̃], *adv.* secondly.
seconder [səgɔ̃'de], *v.t.* to second, to assist; to back (up), to support; to promote.
secouement [səku'mɑ̃], **secouage** [sə'kwa:ʒ], *n.m.* shaking, jogging, jolting.
secouer [sə'kwe], *v.t.* to shake, to jolt; to shake off; to shock; to rouse. **se secouer**, *v.r.* to shake oneself, to bestir oneself.
secourable [səku'rabl], *a.* helpful, helping; relievable.
secourir [səku'ri:r], *v.t. irr.* (*conjug. like* COURIR) to succor, to assist, to help, to relieve.
secourisme [səku'rism], *n.m.* first aid.
secouriste [səku'rist], *n.* qualified first-aider.
secours [sə'ku:r], *n.m.* help, assistance, aid; rescue; *appeler police secours*, to call police emergency; *au secours !* help!
secousse [sə'kus], *n.f.* shake, shock; blow, concussion; jerk, jolt.
secret [sə'krɛ], *a.* (*fem.* **-ète**) secret, private, hidden; reserved.—*n.m.* secret; secrecy, privacy, mystery.
secrétaire [sakre'tɛ:r], *n.* secretary.—*n.m.* writing desk.
secrétariat [səkreta'rja], *n.m.* secretaryship; secretary's office; secretariat.
secrètement [səkrɛt'mɑ̃], *adv.* secretly, in secret, inwardly.
sécréter [sekre'te], *v.t.* (*conjug. like* CÉDER) to secrete (*of glands etc.*).
sécréteur [sekre'tœːr], *a.* (*fem.* **-euse** or **-trice**) secretory.
sécrétion [sekre'sjɔ̃], *n.f.* secretion.
sectaire [sɛk'tɛ:r], *a.* sectarian.—*n.* sectary.
sectateur [sɛkta'tœːr], *n.m.* (*fem.* **-trice**) follower, votary.
secte [sɛkt], *n.f.* sect.
secteur [sɛk'tœːr], *n.m.* sector, section; district.
section [sɛk'sjɔ̃], *n.f.* section; division.
sectionnement [sɛksjɔn'mɑ̃], *n.m.* division into parts.
sectionner [sɛksjɔ'ne], *v.t.* to divide into sections; to cut off.
séculaire [seky'lɛ:r], *a.* secular, coming once in a century; ancient; time-honored.

séculier [seky'lje], *a.* (*fem.* **-ière**) secular, lay; temporal, worldly.—*n.m.* layman.
secundo [səgɔ̃'do], *adv.* secondly.
sécurité [sekyri'te], *n.f.* security, safety.
sédatif [seda'tif], *a.* (*fem.* **-tive**) and *n.m.* sedative.
sédentaire [sedɑ̃'tɛːr], *a.* sedentary; settled, stationary.
sédiment [sedi'mɑ̃], *n.m.* sediment.
sédimentaire [sedimɑ̃'tɛːr], *a.* sedimentary.
séditieusement [sedisjøz'mɑ̃], *adv.* seditiously.
séditieux [sedi'sjø], *a.* (*fem.* **-euse**) seditious; mutinous.—*n.m.* rebel, mutineer.
sédition [sedi'sjɔ̃], *n.f.* sedition, mutiny, riot.
séducteur [sedyk'tœːr], *a.* (*fem.* **-trice**) seductive; enticing, alluring.—*n.m.* (*fem.* **-trice**) seducer, enticer.
séduction [sedyk'sjɔ̃], *n.f.* seduction; allurement; bribing.
séduire [se'dɥiːr], *v.t. irr.* (*conjug. like* CONDUIRE) to seduce; to beguile; to charm; to fascinate; to bribe.
séduisant [sedɥi'zɑ̃], *a.* seductive, alluring; fascinating; tempting.
segment [sɛg'mɑ̃], *n.m.* segment.
ségrégation [segrega'sjɔ̃], *n.f.* segregation.
seigle [sɛgl], *n.m.* rye.
seigneur [sɛ'nœːr], *n.m.* lord; lord of the manor, squire; nobleman; **le Seigneur**, the Lord.
seigneurial [sɛɲœ'rjal], *a.* (*m. pl.* **-aux**) manorial; lordly.
seigneurie [sɛɲœ'ri], *n.f.* lordship; manor.
sein [sɛ̃], *n.m.* breast, bosom; (*fig.*) heart, midst; womb.
seine [sɛːn], *n.f.* seine, (fishing-) net.
séisme [se'ism], *n.m.* earthquake.
seize [sɛːz], *a.* and *n.m.* sixteen, sixteenth.
seizième [sɛ'zjɛm], *a.* and *n.* sixteenth.
séjour [se'ʒuːr], *n.m.* stay, abode, sojourn; place where one sojourns.
séjourner [seʒur'ne], *v.i.* to stay, to sojourn.
sel [sɛl], *n.m.* salt; (*fig.*) wit, pungency; (*pl.*) smelling salts.
sélecteur [selɛk'tœːr], *a.* (*fem.* **-trice**) selecting; selective.
sélection [selɛk'sjɔ̃], *n.f.* selection.
sélectivité [selɛktivi'te], *n.f.* selectivity.
sellage [sɛ'laːʒ], *n.m.* saddling.
selle [sɛl], *n.f.* saddle; bowel movement.
seller [sɛ'le], *v.t.* to saddle.
sellerie [sɛl'ri], *n.f.* saddlery; harness room.
sellette [sɛ'lɛt], *n.f.* stool of repentance; shoeblack's box; (*Naut.*) slung cradle.
sellier [sɛ'lje], *n.m.* saddler.
selon [sə'lɔ̃], *prep.* according to; **c'est selon**, that depends; **selon moi**, in my opinion; **selon que**, according as.
semailles [sə'maːj], *n.f. pl.* seeds; sowing; sowing time.
semaine [sə'mɛn], *n.f.* week; week's work; week's money.
semainier [səmɛ'nje], *n.m.* (*fem.* **-ière**) person on duty for the week.—*n.m.* (*Ind.*) time-sheet; weekly output.
sémaphore [sema'fɔːr], *n.m.* semaphore, signal post.
semblable [sɑ̃'blabl], *a.* like, similar, alike.—*n.* like; fellow, match, equal.—*n.m.* fellow creature.

semblablement [sɑ̃blablə'mɑ̃], *adv.* likewise, also.
semblant [sɑ̃'blɑ̃], *n.m.* appearance, semblance, look; pretence; **faire semblant**, to pretend.
sembler [sɑ̃'ble], *v.i.* to seem, to appear.
semé [sə'me], *a.* sowed, sown; strewn (**de**).
semelle [sə'mɛl], *n.f.* sole (*of boots, shoes etc.*); foot (*of stockings*); length of a foot.
semence [sə'mɑ̃ːs], *n.f.* seed; semen; (*fig.*) cause.
semer [sə'me], *v.t.* (*conjug. like* AMENER) to sow; to scatter, to strew, to sprinkle.
semestre [sə'mɛstr], *n.m.* half-year, six months.
semestriel [səmɛstri'ɛl], *a.* (*fem.* **-elle**) half-yearly.
semeur [sə'mœːr], *n.m.* (*fem.* **-euse**) sower; (*fig.*) disseminator.
semi-circulaire [səmisirky'lɛːr], *a.* semi-circular.
sémillance [semi'jɑ̃ːs], *n.f.* sprightliness, liveliness.
sémillant [semi'jɑ̃], *a.* brisk, lively, sprightly.
semi-mensuel [səmimɑ̃'sɥɛl], *a.* (*fem.* **-elle**) fortnightly.
séminaire [semi'nɛːr], *n.m.* seminary, theological college; specialized course.
semis [sə'mi], *n.m.* sowing; seed bed; seedlings.
sémitique [semi'tik], *a.* Semitic.
sémitisme [semi'tism], *n.m.* Semitism.
semi-ton [səmi'tɔ̃], *n.m.* (*pl.* **-tons**) semitone.
semoir [sə'mwaːr], *n.m.* seed bag; seed drill.
semonce [sə'mɔ̃ːs], *n.f.* rebuke, reprimand, lecture.
semoncer [səmɔ̃'se], *v.t.* (*conjug. like* COMMENCER) to reprimand, to lecture.
semoule [sə'mul], *n.f.* semolina.
sempiternel [sɛ̃pitɛr'nɛl], *a.* (*fem.* **-elle**) sempiternal, everlasting.
sénat [se'na], *n.m.* senate; senate building.
sénateur [sena'tœːr], *n.m.* senator.
sénatorial [senato'rjal], *a.* (*m. pl.* **-aux**) senatorial.
séné [se'ne], *n.m.* senna.
seneçon [sən'sɔ̃], *n.m.* groundsel.
Sénégal [sene'gal], **le**, *m.* Senegal.
sénégalais [senega'le], *a.* Senegalese.—*n.m.* (**Sénégalais**, *fem.* **-aise**) Senegalese (*person*).
Sénèque [se'nɛk], *m.* Seneca.
*****sénestre** [sə'nɛstr], **senestre** [sə'nɛstr], *a.* left, (*Her.*) sinister.
sénile [se'nil], *a.* senile.
sénilité [senili'te], *n.f.* senility, old age.
senne [sɛn], [SEINE].
sens [sɑ̃ːs], *n.m. inv.* sense; senses, feelings; intelligence; consciousness; meaning; opinion; way, direction; **à contre-sens**, in a wrong sense; **à double sens**, with double meaning; **sens dessus dessous**, upside down; **sens interdit**, no entry.
sensation [sɑ̃sa'sjɔ̃], *n.f.* sensation, feeling.
sensationnel [sɑ̃sasjo'nɛl], *a.* (*fem.* **-elle**) sensational.
sensé [sɑ̃'se], *a.* sensible, intelligent.
sensément [sɑ̃se'mɑ̃], *adv.* sensibly, judiciously.
sensibilité [sɑ̃sibili'te], *n.f.* sensibility, sensitiveness, feeling; compassion.

serrage

sensible [sɑ̃'sibl], *a.* sensitive, susceptible, sympathetic; tender, sore (*skin etc.*); perceptible, noticeable, tangible.

sensiblement [sɑ̃siblə'mɑ̃], *adv.* appreciably; feelingly, deeply; obviously; considerably.

sensiblerie [sɑ̃siblə'ri], *n.f.* sentimentality; (*fam.*) sob stuff.

sensitif [sɑ̃si'tif], *a.* (*fem.* **-tive**) sensitive; sensory.—*n.f.* (**-tive**) sensitive plant.

sensitivité [sɑ̃sitivi'te], *n.f.* sensitivity.

sensualiste [sɑ̃sɥa'list], *a.* sensual.—*n.* sensualist.

sensualité [sɑ̃sɥali'te], *n.f.* sensuality.

sensuel [sɑ̃'sɥɛl], *a.* (*fem.* **-elle**) sensual.—*n.m.* (*fem.* **-elle**) sensualist.

sensuellement [sɑ̃sɥɛl'mɑ̃], *adv.* sensually.

sentence [sɑ̃'tɑ̃:s], *n.f.* maxim; sentence, judgment, verdict.

sentencieusement [sɑ̃tɑ̃sjøz'mɑ̃], *adv.* sententiously.

sentencieux [sɑ̃tɑ̃'sjø], *a.* (*fem.* **-euse**) sententious.

senteur [sɑ̃'tœ:r], *n.f.* smell; scent, perfume; *pois de senteur,* sweet pea.

senti [sɑ̃'ti], *a.* felt, experienced.

sentier [sɑ̃'tje], *n.m.* path, footpath; *sentier battu,* beaten track.

sentiment [sɑ̃ti'mɑ̃], *n.m.* feeling; sensation; sentiment; affection, *esp.* love; perception, sense; opinion.

sentimental [sɑ̃timɑ̃'tal], *a.* (*m. pl.* **-aux**) sentimental.

sentimentalement [sɑ̃timɑ̃tal'mɑ̃], *adv.* sentimentally.

sentimentaliste [sɑ̃timɑ̃ta'list], *n.* sentimentalist.

sentimentalité [sɑ̃timɑ̃tali'te], *n.f.* sentimentality.

sentinelle [sɑ̃ti'nɛl], *n.f.* sentinel, sentry.

sentir [sɑ̃'ti:r], *v.t. irr.* to feel; to guess; to perceive; to smell; to savor of; to seem.—*v.i.* to smell. **se sentir,** *v.r.* to feel oneself, to feel; to be conscious; to feel the effects (*de*); to be perceived, felt etc.

seoir (1) [swa:r], *v.i. irr.* (*only used in pres. p.* **séant** *and p.p.* **sis**) to sit, to be sitting.

seoir (2) [swa:r], *v.i. irr.* (*pres. p.* **seyant**, *no p.p.*) to suit, to become.

Séoudite [seu'dit], [ARABIE].

séparable [sepa'rabl], *a.* separable.

séparation [separa'sjɔ̃], *n.f.* separation, parting.

séparé [sepa're], *a.* separate; distinct.

séparément [separe'mɑ̃], *adv.* separately, apart.

séparer [sepa're], *v.t.* to separate, to part; to sever. **se séparer,** *v.r.* to separate, to part; to divide.

sépia [se'pja], *n.f.* sepia.

sept [sɛt], *a. and n.m. inv.* seven; seventh.

septembre [sɛp'tɑ̃:br], *n.m.* September.

septénaire [sɛpte'nɛ:r], *a. and n.m.* septenary.

septennal [sɛptɛ'nal], *a.* (*m. pl.* **-aux**) septennial.

septentrion [sɛptɑ̃tri'ɔ̃], *n.m.* north.

septentrional [sɛptɑ̃triɔ'nal], *a.* (*m. pl.* **-aux**) north, northern.

septicémie [sɛptise'mi], *n.f.* (*Med.*) septicemia, blood poisoning.

septième [sɛ'tjɛm], *a. and n.* seventh.

septique [sɛp'tik], *a.* septic.

septuagénaire [sɛptɥaʒe'nɛ:r], *a. and n.* septuagenarian.

sépulcral [sepyl'kral], *a.* (*m. pl.* **-aux**) sepulchral.

sépulcre [se'pylkr], *n.m.* sepulcher.

sépulture [sepyl'ty:r], *n.f.* burial, interment; burial place, tomb.

séquelle [se'kɛl], *n.f.* (*pl.*) after-effects (*of illness*).

séquence [se'kɑ̃:s], *n.f.* sequence.

séquestration [sekɛstra'sjɔ̃], *n.f.* sequestration.

séquestre [se'kɛstr], *n.m.* sequestration; sequestrator; depository.

séquestrer [sekɛs'tre], *v.t.* to sequester, to sequestrate; to shut up illegally. **se séquestrer,** *v.r.* to sequester oneself.

sequin [sə'kɛ̃], *n.m.* sequin (*gold coin*).

sérail [se'ra:j], *n.m.* seraglio.

séraphin [sera'fɛ̃], *n.m.* seraph.

séraphique [sera'fik], *a.* seraphic.

serbe [sɛrb], *a.* Serbian.—*n.* (**Serbe**) Serb.

Serbie [sɛr'bi], **la,** *f.* Serbia.

serein [sə'rɛ̃], *a.* serene, placid, calm.—*n.m.* (*poet.*) night dew.

sérénade [sere'nad], *n.f.* serenade.

sérénité [sereni'te], *n.f.* serenity, calmness; equanimity.

séreux [se'rø], *a.* (*fem.* **-euse**) serous, watery.

serf [sɛrf], *a.* (*fem.* **serve**) in bondage, servile.—*n.m.* (*fem.* **serve**) serf, bondsman, bondswoman.

serge [sɛrʒ], *n.f.* serge.

sergent [sɛr'ʒɑ̃], *n.m.* sergeant; *sergent de ville,* police constable.

séricicole [serisi'kɔl], *a.* silk-producing.

sériciculteur [serisikyl'tœ:r], *n.m.* silk grower.

sériciculture [serisikyl'ty:r], *n.f.* silk culture.

série [se'ri], *n.f.* series; succession; run; (*Spt.*) heat; *fabrication en série,* mass production.

sérieusement [serjøz'mɑ̃], *adv.* seriously, gravely.

sérieux [se'rjø], *a.* (*fem.* **-euse**) serious, grave; earnest; real, true.—*n.m.* seriousness, importance, gravity.

serin [sə'rɛ̃], *n.m.* canary; (*fig.*) duffer, fool.

seriner [səri'ne], *v.t.* to din (*something*) into someone.

seringue [sə'rɛ̃:g], *n.f.* syringe, squirt.

seringuer [sərɛ̃'ge], *v.t.* to syringe, to squirt; to inject.

serment [sɛr'mɑ̃], *n.m.* oath, promise, solemn declaration; (*pl.*) swearing.

sermon [sɛr'mɔ̃], *n.m.* sermon; lecture.

sermonner [sɛrmɔ'ne], *v.t., v.i.* to sermonize, to lecture, to reprimand.

sermonneur [sɛrmɔ'nœ:r], *n.m.* (*fem.* **-euse**) sermonizer, preacher, fault-finder.

sérosité [serozi'te], *n.f.* serosity, wateriness.

serpe [sɛrp], *n.f.* bill-hook.

serpent [sɛr'pɑ̃], *n.m.* serpent, snake; *serpent à sonnettes,* rattlesnake.

serpenter [sɛrpɑ̃'te], *v.i.* to meander, to wind.

serpentin [sɛrpɑ̃'tɛ̃], *a.* serpentine.—*n.m.* paper streamer.

serpette [sɛr'pɛt], *n.f.* pruning knife.

serpolet [sɛrpɔ'le], *n.m.* wild thyme.

serrage [sɛ'ra:ʒ], *n.m.* tightening, pressing.

serre [sɛːr], *n.f.* squeeze, pressure; talon, claw (*of birds*); clip; hot-house, greenhouse, conservatory.

serré [sɛ're], *a.* close; compact; tight; clenched; (*fam.*) close-fisted.

serre-frein(s) [sɛr'frɛ̃], *n.m. inv.* (*Rail.*) brakeman.

serre-livres [sɛːr'livr], *n.m. inv.* book ends.

serrement [sɛr'mã], *n.m.* pressing, squeezing; **serrement de cœur**, pang (*of grief*); **serrement de main**, handshake.

serre-papiers [sɛrpa'pje], *n.m. inv.* paper clip; file (*for papers*); set of pigeon-holes (*for papers*).

serrer [sɛ're], *v.t.* to press, to squeeze; to fasten, to lock; to grip; to condense, to put close together; to press; to close (*the ranks*); to clench (*one's fist, teeth etc.*). **se serrer**, *v.r.* to press each other close; to sit, lie *or* stand close together; to stint oneself.

serre-tête [sɛr'tɛːt], *n.m. inv.* headband; crash helmet.

serrure [sɛ'ryːr], *n.f.* lock.

serrurier [sɛry'rje], *n.m.* locksmith.

sérum [se'rɔm], *n.m.* serum.

servage [sɛr'vaːʒ], *n.m.* servitude, bondage.

servant [sɛr'vã], *a.m.* serving; in waiting.—*n.m.* (*Artill.*) gunner.

servante [sɛr'vãːt], *n.f.* maid-servant; servant-girl; dinner wagon.

serveur [sɛr'vœːr], *n.m.* (*fem.* **-euse**) (*Ten.*) server; waiter, barman; (*Cards*) dealer.

serviable [sɛr'vjabl], *a.* willing, obliging.

service [sɛr'vis], *n.m.* service; attendance; duty; function; divine service.

serviette [sɛr'vjɛt], *n.f.* napkin, serviette; towel; briefcase.

servile [sɛr'vil], *a.* servile, menial; slavish.

servilement [sɛrvil'mã], *adv.* servilely, slavishly.

servir [sɛr'viːr], *v.t. irr.* (*conjug. like* SENTIR) to serve, to attend; to serve up; to be of service to; to assist.—*v.i.* to serve, to be of use; to serve up a meal. **se servir**, *v.r.* to serve oneself; to be served up (*of dishes*); **servez-vous**, help yourself.

serviteur [sɛrvi'tœːr], *n.m.* servant, man-servant.

servitude [sɛrvi'tyd], *n.f.* servitude, slavery.

ses [sɛ], [SON].

session [sɛ'sjɔ̃], *n.f.* session, sitting; term (*of law courts etc.*).

seuil [sœːj], *n.m.* threshold; door-step; shelf (*of ocean bed*).

seul [sœl], *a.* alone; single, only, sole; mere, bare.—*n.m.* one only, the only one.

seulement [sœl'mã], *adv.* only; but; solely, merely.

sève [sɛːv], *n.f.* sap; (*fig.*) pith, vigor, strength.

sévère [se'vɛːr], *a.* severe, stern, austere; strict.

sévèrement [sever'mã], *adv.* severely, sternly; strictly.

sévérité [severi'te], *n.f.* severity; strictness; purity.

séveux [se'vø], *a.* (*fem.* **-euse**) (*Bot.*) sappy; (*fig.*) vigorous.

sévices [se'vis], *n.m. pl.* (*Law*) cruelty, ill-treatment.

sévir [se'viːr], *v.i.* to deal severely (*contre*); to rage (*of war etc.*).

sevrage [sə'vraːʒ], *n.m.* weaning.

sevrer [sə'vre], *v.t.* (*conjug. like* AMENER) to wean; (*fig.*) to deprive (**de**).

sexagénaire [sɛkzaʒe'nɛːr], *a.* and *n.* sexagenarian.

sexe [sɛks], *n.m.* sex.

sextant [sɛks'tã], *n.m.* sextant.

sextuple [sɛks'typl], *a.* and *n.m.* sextuple, six-fold.

sexualité [sɛksɥali'te], *n.f.* sexuality.

sexuel [sɛk'sɥɛl], *a.* (*fem.* **-elle**) sexual.

shampooing [ʃã'pwɛ̃], *n.m.* shampoo, hair-wash.

shérif [ʃe'rif], *n.m.* sheriff.

short [ʃɔrt], *n.m.* (*Cost.*) shorts.

shunt [ʃœt], *n.m.* (*Elec.*) shunt.

shunter [ʃœ'te], *v.t.* to shunt.

si (1) [si], *conj.* if; whether; supposing, what if.

si (2) [si], *adv.* so, so much, however much; yes.

si (3) [si], *n.m. inv.* (*Mus.*) si; the note B.

Siam [sjam], **le**, *m.* Thailand, Siam.

siamois [sja'mwa], *a.* Siamese.—*n.m.* Siamese (*language*); (**Siamois**, *fem.* **-oise**) Siamese (*person*).

Sibérie [sibe'ri], **la**, *f.* Siberia.

sibérien [sibe'rjɛ̃], *a.* (*fem.* **-enne**) Siberian. —*n.m.* (**Sibérien**, *fem.* **-enne**) Siberian (*person*).

sibilant [sibi'lã], *a.* sibilant, hissing.

siccatif [sika'tif], *a.* (*fem.* **-tive**) siccative, drying.

Sicile [si'sil], **la**, *f.* Sicily.

sicilien [sisi'ljɛ̃], *a.* (*fem.* **-enne**) Sicilian.—*n.m.* (**Sicilien**, *fem.* **-enne**) Sicilian (*person*).

sidérurgie [sideryr'ʒi], *n.f.* iron and steel industry.

siècle [sjɛkl], *n.m.* century; age, period.

siège [sjɛːʒ], *n.m.* seat; bench (*of a court of justice*); headquarters (*of society etc.*); (*Eccles.*) see; siege.

siéger [sje'ʒe], *v.i.* (*conjug. like* ASSIÉGER) to sit (*of assemblies, courts etc.*); to hold one's see (*of bishops*); to be seated; (*fig.*) to lie (*of a thing*); to have one's headquarters (*of business, society*).

sien [sjɛ̃], *pron. poss. 3rd pers. sing.* (*fem.* **sienne**) his, hers, its, one's.—*n.m.* one's own (*property, work etc.*).

Sienne [sjɛn], *f.* Sienna.

Sierra-Leone [sjerale'ɔn], **le**, *m.* Sierra Leone.

sieste [sjɛst], *n.f.* siesta.

sifflant [si'flã], *a.* hissing; whistling; wheezing.

sifflement [siflə'mã], *n.m.* hissing, hiss; whistling, whistle; whizzing; wheezing.

siffler [si'fle], *v.t.* to whistle; to hiss.—*v.i.* to hiss; to whistle; to whizz; to wheeze.

sifflet [si'flɛ], *n.m.* whistle (*instrument and sound*); catcall; hiss; (*colloq.*) windpipe.

siffleur [si'flœːr], *a.* (*fem.* **-euse**) whistling, piping (*of birds*); wheezing (*of horses*).—*n.m.* (*fem.* **-euse**) whistler; hisser.

sigle [sigl], *n.m.* initial letter; group of initial letters used as abbreviation of phrase (*U.N. etc.*).

signal [si'nal], *n.m.* (*pl.* **-aux**) signal.

signalé [siɲa'le], *a.* signal, remarkable, conspicuous.

signalement [siɲal'mã], *n.m.* description (*of a man etc.*), particulars.

signaler [siɲa′le], *v.t.* to signal; to give the description of; to point out, to mark out; to signalize. **se signaler**, *v.r.* to signalize *or* distinguish oneself.

signaleur [siɲa′lœːr], *n.m.* signalman; (*Mil.*) signaller.

signalisateur [siɲaliza′tœːr], *n.m.*(*Motor.*) directional signal.

signataire [siɲa′tɛːr], *n.* signer, subscriber, signatory.

signature [siɲa′tyːr], *n.f.* signature; signing.

signe [siɲ], *n.m.* sign; mark, indication; badge; omen; *faire signe de la main*, to beckon; *signe de la tête*, nod.

signer [si′ɲe], *v.t.*, *v.i.* to sign, to subscribe. **se signer**, *v.r.* to cross oneself.

signet [si′ɲɛ], *n.m.* signet; book mark; signet ring.

significatif [siɲifika′tif], *a.* (*fem.* **-tive**) significant.

signification [siɲifika′sjɔ̃], *n.f.* signification, meaning; (*Law*) legal notice.

significativement [siɲifikativ′mɑ̃], *adv.* significantly.

signifier [siɲi′fje], *v.t.* to signify, to mean; to notify, to intimate; (*Law*) to serve.

silence [si′lɑ̃ːs], *n.m.* silence; stillness; secrecy; (*Mus.*) rest.

silencieusement [silɑ̃sjøz′mɑ̃], *adv.* silently.

silencieux [silɑ̃′sjø], *a.* (*fem.* **-euse**) silent; still.—*n.m.* (*Motor.*) muffler.

silex [si′lɛks], *n.m.* silex, flint.

silhouette [si′lwɛt], *n.f.* silhouette; outline, profile.

silice [si′lis], *n.f.* (*Chem.*) silica, flint.

sillage [si′jaːʒ], *n.m.* wake, wash; slip-stream.

sillon [si′jɔ̃], *n.m.* furrow made by plow; seed drill; (*fig.*) track, wake (*of a ship etc.*); wrinkle.

sillonner [sijɔ′ne], *v.t.* to furrow; to streak.

silo [si′lo], *n.m.* silo (*pit or tower for preserving fodder*).

silotage [silɔ′taːʒ], *n.m.* silage.

simagrée [sima′gre], *n.f.* pretence, affectation; (*pl.*) fuss.

simiesque [si′mjɛsk], *a.* ape-like, apish (*face*).

similaire [simi′lɛːr], *a.* similar.

similarité [similari′te], *n.f.* similarity, likeness.

similitude [simili′tyd], *n.f.* similitude, resemblance; simile.

simoun [si′muːn], *n.m.* simoom, simoon.

simple [sɛ̃ːpl], *a.* simple, single; easy; only, mere; common, plain; private (*soldier*); simple-minded, silly; natural.—*n.m.* that which is simple; (*Ten.*) singles; *simple dames*, women's singles.

simplement [sɛ̃plə′mɑ̃], *adv.* simply.

simplet [sɛ̃′plɛ], *a.* (*fem.* **-ette**) naïve, simple; (*fam.*) a bit off; (*Am.*) green.—*n.m.* (*fem.* **-ette**) simpleton, silly.

simplicité [sɛ̃plisi′te], *n.f.* simplicity; artlessness; silliness.

simplification [sɛ̃plifika′sjɔ̃], *n.f.* simplification.

simplifier [sɛ̃pli′fje], *v.t.* to simplify.

simulacre [simy′lakr], *n.m.* image; phantom; semblance, sham.

simulé [simy′le], *a.* feigned, sham.

simuler [simy′le], *v.t.* to feign, to sham.

simultané [simylta′ne], *a.* simultaneous.

simultanément [simyltane′mɑ̃], *adv.* simultaneously.

sincère [sɛ̃′sɛːr], *a.* sincere, frank; honest.

sincèrement [sɛ̃sɛr′mɑ̃], *adv.* sincerely, honestly.

sincérité [sɛ̃seri′te], *n.f.* sincerity.

sinécure [sine′kyːr], *n.f.* sinecure.

Singapour [sɛ̃ga′puːr], *m.* Singapore.

singe [sɛ̃ːʒ], *n.m.* ape, monkey; hoist; (*Mil. slang*) bully beef.

singer [sɛ̃′ʒe], *v.t.* (*conjug. like* MANGER) to ape, to mimic.

singerie [sɛ̃′ʒri], *n.f.* monkey house; grimace; antic; mimicry.

singeur [sɛ̃′ʒœːr], *a.* (*fem.* **-euse**) aping, mimicking.—*n.m.* (*fem.* **-euse**) ape, mimic.

singulariser [sɛ̃gylari′ze], *v.t.* to singularize; to make conspicuous. **se singulariser**, *v.r.* to make oneself conspicuous.

singularité [sɛ̃gylari′te], *n.f.* singularity; peculiarity.

singulier [sɛ̃gy′lje], *a.* (*fem.* **-ière**) singular; peculiar; odd.—*n.m.* (*Gram.*) singular.

singulièrement [sɛ̃gyljɛr′mɑ̃], *adv.* singularly, oddly.

sinistre [si′nistr], *a.* sinister; dismal; evil.—*n.m.* disaster, calamity.

sinistré [sinis′tre], *a.* affected by disaster (*shipwreck, fire etc.*).—*n.m.* (*fem.* **-ée**) victim of disaster; casualty.

sinon [si′nɔ̃], *conj.* otherwise, if not, else; except, unless; *sinon que*, except that.

sinueux [si′nɥø], *a.* (*fem.* **-euse**) sinuous, winding.

sinuosité [sinɥozi′te], *n.f.* sinuosity, winding.

sinus [si′nyːs], *n.m. inv.* sine; (*Anat.*) sinus.

sinusite [siny′zit], *n.f.* sinusitis.

siphon [si′fɔ̃], *n.m.* siphon; (*Naut.*) waterspout.

sire [siːr], *n.m.* sire (*title of kings and emperors*).

sirène [si′rɛn], *n.f.* siren, mermaid; horn, fog-horn.

sirocco [sirɔ′ko], *n.m.* sirocco.

sirop [si′ro], *n.m.* syrup.

siroter [sirɔ′te], *v.t.* to sip; (*pop.*) to tipple.

sirupeux [siry′pø], *a.* (*fem.* **-euse**) syrupy.

sis [si], *a.* seated, situated [SEOIR (I)].

Sisyphe [si′zif], *m.* Sisyphus.

site [sit], *n.m.* site (*situation with regard to scenery etc.*); *un beau site*, a beauty spot.

sitôt [si′to], *adv.* so soon, as soon; *sitôt dit, sitôt fait*, no sooner said than done; *sitôt que*, as soon as.

situation [sitɥa′sjɔ̃], *n.f.* situation, site, position; state of affairs, predicament.

situé [si′tɥe], *a.* situated, lying.

situer [si′tɥe], *v.t.* to place.

six [sis *before a consonant,* siz *before a vowel* sis *at the end of a sentence*], *a.* six; sixth.—[sis], *n.m.* six; sixth; sixth day.

sixième [si′zjɛm], *a. and n.* sixth.—*n.m.* sixth (part); sixth floor.—*n.f.* (*in France*) sixth class, (*in England*) first form (*of upper school*).

ski [ski], *n.m.* ski; *faire du ski*, to go in for skiing; *ski nautique*, water-skiing.

slave [slav], *a.* Slav, Slavonic.—*n.* (**Slave**) Slav (*person*).

slip [slip], *n.m.* (*Cost.*) trunks, briefs; *slip de bain*, (swimming) trunks.

slovène

slovène [slɔ'vɛn], *a.* Slovenian.—*n.* (**Slovène**) Slovene.

smoking [smɔ'kiŋ], *n.m.* dinner jacket.

snob [snɔb], *a.* (*fam.*) swanky.—*n.m.* person who tries to be always in the swim.

snobisme [snɔ'bism], *n.m.* affected up-to-dateness.

sobre [sɔbr], *a.* (*of persons*) abstemious, temperate, moderate; (*of colors, style etc.*) sober, quiet, unadorned.

sobrement [sɔbrə'mã], *adv.* soberly, moderately.

sobriété [sɔbrie'te], *n.f.* sobriety; abstemiousness (*in food and drink*).

sobriquet [sɔbri'kɛ], *n.m.* nickname.

soc [sɔk], *n.m.* ploughshare.

sociabilité [sɔsjabili'te], *n.f.* sociability, good fellowship.

sociable [sɔ'sjabl], *a.* sociable, companionable.

sociablement [sɔsjablə'mã], *adv.* sociably.

social [sɔ'sjal], *a.* (*m. pl.* **-aux**) social; **siège social**, registered office; head office.

socialement [sɔsjal'mã], *adv.* socially.

socialisme [sɔsja'lism], *n.m.* socialism.

socialiste [sɔsja'list], *a.* and *n.* socialist.

sociétaire [sɔsje'tɛːr], *n.* associate, member; partner; shareholder.

société [sɔsje'te], *n.f.* society, association; community, firm; partnership; **société anonyme**, incorporated company.

sociologie [sɔsjɔlɔ'ʒi], *n.f.* sociology.

sociologiste [sɔsjɔlɔ'ʒist], **sociologue** [sɔsjɔ'lɔg], *n.* sociologist.

socle [sɔkl], *n.m.* socle, pedestal, stand, base.

socque [sɔk], *n.m.* clog, patten.

Socrate [sɔ'krat], *m.* Socrates.

sœur [sœːr], *n.f.* sister; nun.

sœurette [sœ'rɛt], *n.f.* (*colloq.*) little sister, sis(s).

sofa [sɔ'fa], *n.m.* sofa, settee.

soi [swa], **soi-même** [swa'mɛm], *impers. pron. 3rd pers. sing.* oneself, itself; self.

soi-disant [swadi'zã], *a. inv.* self-styled, would-be, so-called.

soie [swa], *n.f.* silk; silken hair; bristle (*of hogs*); **papier de soie**, tissue paper.

soierie [swa'ri], *n.f.* silks, silk goods; silk-trade; silk-factory.

soif [swaf], *n.f.* thirst; **avoir soif**, to be thirsty.

soigné [swa'ɲe], *a.* carefully done; neat, smart; (*colloq.*) first-rate.

soigner [swa'ɲe], *v.t.* to take care of, to look after; to nurse. **se soigner**, *v.r.* to take care of oneself.

soigneusement [swaɲøz'mã], *adv.* carefully.

soigneux [swa'ɲø], *a.* (*fem.* **-euse**) careful; solicitous.

soi-même [swa'mɛm], *see* soi.

soin [swɛ̃], *n.m.* care; attendance; (*pl.*) attentions, pains, trouble.

soir [swaːr], *n.m.* evening; night.

soirée [swa're], *n.f.* evening (*duration*); evening party.

soit [swat, swa], *adv.* be it so, well and good, granted; let us say.—*conj.* either, or; whether.

soixantaine [swasã'tɛn], *n.f.* about sixty.

soixante [swa'sãːt], *a.* and *n.m.* sixty.

soixantième [swasã'tjɛːm], *a.* and *n.* sixtieth.

---

sol [sɔl], *n.m.* ground; soil; earth.

solaire [sɔ'lɛːr], *a.* solar.

soldat [sɔl'da], *n.m.* soldier; **simple soldat**, private; **les simples soldats**, the rank and file.

soldatesque [sɔlda'tɛsk], *n.f.* (*usu. pej.*) soldiery.

solde (1) [sɔld], *n.f.* (*Mil.*) pay.

solde (2) [sɔld], *n.m.* balance (*between debit and credit*); clearance sale; (*pl.*) sale bargains, reductions.

solder (1) [sɔl'de], *v.t.* to pay (*soldiers*); to have in one's pay.

solder (2) [sɔl'de], *v.t.* to settle (*an account*); to sell off, to clear.

sole [sɔl], *n.f.* sole (*of animal's foot*); sole (*fish*).

solécisme [sɔle'sism], *n.m.* solecism.

soleil [sɔ'lɛːj], *n.m.* sun; sunshine; (*fig.*) star; catherine wheel (*firework*); sunflower.

solennel [sɔla'nɛl], *a.* (*fem.* **-elle**) solemn.

solennellement [sɔlanɛl'mã], *adv.* solemnly.

solenniser [sɔlani'ze], *v.t.* to solemnize.

solennité [sɔlani'te], *n.f.* solemnity.

solénoïde [sɔlenɔ'id], *n.m.* solenoid.

solidaire [sɔli'dɛːr], *a.* jointly and separately liable.

solidairement [sɔlidɛr'mã], *adv.* jointly and severally.

solidariser [sɔlidari'ze], *v.t.* to render jointly liable.

solidarité [sɔlidari'te], *n.f.* joint and separate liability; solidarity, fellowship.

solide [sɔ'lid], *a.* solid; strong; substantial, sound; reliable.—*n.m.* solid, solid body.

solidement [sɔlid'mã], *adv.* solidly; firmly; soundly.

solidification [sɔlidifika'sjɔ̃], *n.f.* solidification.

solidifier [sɔlidi'fje], *v.t.* and **se solidifier**, *v.r.* to solidify.

solidité [sɔlidi'te], *n.f.* solidity; strength; stability; soundness.

soliloque [sɔli'lɔk], *n.m.* soliloquy.

soliste [sɔ'list], *a.* solo.—*n.* soloist.

solitaire [sɔli'tɛːr], *a.* solitary, single, alone; lonely, desert.—*n.m.* lonely person, recluse; solitaire (*diamond* or *game*).

solitairement [sɔlitɛr'mã], *adv.* solitarily, alone.

solitude [sɔli'tyd], *n.f.* solitude, loneliness; desert.

solive [sɔ'liːv], *n.f.* joist.

soliveau [sɔli'vo], *n.m.* (*pl.* **-eaux**) small joist.

sollicitation [sɔlisita'sjɔ̃], *n.f.* solicitation; pull (*of magnet*).

solliciter [sɔlisi'te], *v.t.* to incite; to solicit, to entreat; to call into action; to attract (*of magnet*).

sollicitude [sɔlisi'tyd], *n.f.* solicitude, care; concern.

solo [sɔ'lo], *a. inv.* solo.—*n.m.* (*pl.* **solos** or **soli**) solo.

solstice [sɔls'tis], *n.m.* solstice.

solubilité [sɔlybili'te], *n.f.* solubility.

soluble [sɔ'lybl], *a.* soluble.

solution [sɔly'sjɔ̃], *n.f.* solution; resolution; (*Law*) discharge; **solution de continuité**, interruption, break, fault.

solvabilité [sɔlvabili'te], *n.f.* solvency.

solvable [sɔl'vabl], *a.* solvent.

solvant [sɔl'vã], *n.m.* solvent.

somali [sɔmaˈli], *a.* Somali *(language).*—*n.* (**Somali**) Somali *(person)*; **Côte Française des Somalis**, French Somaliland.

Somalie [sɔmaˈli], **la**, *f.* Somalia, Somaliland.

sombre [sɔ̃:br], *a.* dark, somber, gloomy; dim; overcast; melancholy.

sombrer [sɔ̃ˈbre], *v.i.* (*Naut.*) to founder.

sombrero [sɔ̃breˈro], *n.m.* sombrero.

sommaire [sɔˈmɛːr], *a.* summary, concise; scanty.—*n.m.* summary, abstract.

sommairement [sɔmɛrˈmã], *adv.* summarily; hastily.

sommation [sɔmaˈsjɔ̃], *n.f.* summons, demand; (*Mil.*) challenge.

somme [sɔm], *n.f.* sum, total; amount; summary; burden.—*n.m.* nap; **faire un somme**, to have forty winks.

sommeil [sɔˈmɛːj], *n.m.* sleep; **avoir sommeil**, to be sleepy.

sommeiller [sɔmɛˈje], *v.i.* to slumber; to doze.

sommelier [sɔmǝˈlje], *n.m.* butler, cellarman, wine waiter.

sommellerie [sɔmɛlˈri], *n.f.* butler's pantry.

sommer [sɔˈme], *v.t.* to summon, to call upon; to sum up.

sommet [sɔˈmɛ], *n.m.* top, summit; acme; crown *(of the head etc.).*

sommier (1) [sɔˈmje], *n.m.* pack horse; box mattress; wind chest *(of organ)*; (*Arch.*) cross-beam.

sommier (2) [sɔˈmje], *n.m.* cash book, register.

sommité [sɔmiˈte], *n.f.* summit, top; head, principal; chief point; prominent person.

somnambule [sɔmnãˈbyl], *a.* somnambulistic.—*n.* sleepwalker.

somnambulisme [sɔmnãbyˈlism], *n.m.* somnambulism, sleep-walking.

somnolence [sɔmnɔˈlãːs], *n.f.* somnolence.

somnolent [sɔmnɔˈlã], *a.* somnolent, sleepy.

somptuaire [sɔ̃pˈtɥɛːr], *a.* sumptuary.

somptueusement [sɔ̃ptɥøzˈmã], *adv.* sumptuously.

somptueux [sɔ̃pˈtɥø], *a.* (*fem.* **-euse**) sumptuous; magnificent.

somptuosité [sɔ̃ptɥoziˈte], *n.f.* sumptuousness.

son (1) [sɔ̃], *a.* (*fem.* **sa**, *pl.* **ses**) his, her, its; one's.

son (2) [sɔ̃], *n.m.* sound.

son (3) [sɔ̃], *n.m.* bran; **tache de son**, freckle.

sonate [sɔˈnat], *n.f.* sonata.

sondage [sɔ̃ˈdaːʒ], *n.m.* sounding; (*Mining*) boring.

sonde [sɔ̃:d], *n.f.* sounding-line, lead; (*Surg. etc.*) probe; (*Mining*) drill, boring machine.

sonder [sɔ̃ˈde], *v.t.* to sound; to taste; to search, to fathom, to investigate.

sondeur [sɔ̃ˈdœːr], *n.m.* (*Naut.*) leadsman; (*Mining*) driller, borer.

songe [sɔ̃:ʒ], *n.m.* dream; dreaming.

songe-creux [sɔ̃ʒˈkrø], *n.m. inv.* dreamer, visionary.

songer [sɔ̃ˈʒe], *v.t.* (*conjug. like* MANGER) to dream; (*fig.*) to imagine; to think of.—*v.i.* to dream; (*fig.*) to day-dream; to think; to mean, to intend, to propose.

songerie [sɔ̃ˈʒri], *n.f.* dreaming; musing; day-dreaming.

songeur [sɔ̃ˈʒœːr], *a.* (*fem.* **-euse**) thoughtful, dreamy.—*n.m.* (*fem.* **-euse**) dreamer.

sonique [sɔˈnik], *a.* sonic.

sonnant [sɔˈnã], *a.* sounding; sonorous.

sonner [sɔˈne], *v.t., v.i.* to sound; to ring, to toll, to strike *(of clocks etc.).*

sonnerie [sɔnˈri], *n.f.* ring, ringing *(of bells)*; bells, chimes; striking part *(of a clock etc.)*; (*Mil.*) bugle call.

sonnet [sɔˈnɛ], *n.m.* sonnet.

sonnette [sɔˈnɛt], *n.f.* small bell; hand bell.

sonneur [sɔˈnœːr], *n.m.* bell ringer.

sonore [sɔˈnɔːr], *a.* resonant; clear; **ondes sonores**, sound waves.

sonorité [sɔnɔriˈte], *n.f.* resonance.

sophisme [sɔˈfism], *n.m.* sophism, fallacy.

sophiste [sɔˈfist], *a.* sophistical.—*n.* sophist.

sophistiqué [sɔfistiˈke], *a.* sophisticated; affected.

soporifique [sɔpɔriˈfik], *a.* soporific; (*fig.*) tedious.—*n.m.* soporific.

soprano [sɔpraˈno], *n.* (*pl.* **soprani** or **sopranos**) soprano, treble.

sorbet [sɔrˈbɛ], *n.m.* sherbet.

sorbier [sɔrˈbje], *n.m.* mountain ash, rowan tree.

sorcellerie [sɔrsɛlˈri], *n.f.* sorcery, witchcraft.

sorcier [sɔrˈsje], *n.m.* (*fem.* **-ière**) sorcerer, wizard, sorceress, witch.

sordide [sɔrˈdid], *a.* sordid, filthy; mean, vile.

sordidement [sɔrdidˈmã], *adv.* sordidly.

Sorlingues [sɔrˈlɛ̃:g], **les**, *f. pl.* the Scilly Isles.

sornette [sɔrˈnɛt], *n.f.* (*usu. in pl.*) idle talk, small talk.

sort [sɔ:r], *n.m.* fate, destiny; lot; condition; fortune; chance; spell, charm; **au sort**, by lot; **le sort en est jeté**, the die is cast; **tirer au sort**, to draw lots; to toss.

sortable [sɔrˈtabl], *a.* suitable.

sortablement [sɔrtablǝˈmã], *adv.* suitably.

sortant [sɔrˈtã], *a.* outgoing, retiring, leaving *(office etc.)*; drawn *(of numbers in lotteries).*—*n.m.* person going out; person leaving office etc.; **les entrants et les sortants**, the incomers and outgoers.

sorte [sɔrt], *n.f.* sort, kind, species; manner, way; **de la sorte**, thus, in that way; **de sorte que** or **en sorte que**, so that.

sortie [sɔrˈti], *n.f.* going or coming out; exit, way out; outing, trip; exportation; sortie; (*colloq.*) outburst, attack; **droit de sortie**, export duty; **jour de sortie**, day off, holiday.

sortilège [sɔrtiˈlɛːʒ], *n.m.* sorcery, magic; spell, charm.

sortir [sɔrˈtiːr], *v.t. irr.* (*conjug. like* SENTIR *with aux.* AVOIR) to bring out, to take out; to pull out, to extricate.—*v.i.* (*with aux.* ÊTRE) to go out, to come out, to come forth, to emerge; to make one's exit; to leave, to depart; to swerve; to wander *(from a subject)*; to proceed, to result; to spring, to come up; to sally forth; to burst forth; to escape; (*Paint. etc.*) to stand out; to be in relief.—*n.m.* going out, leaving; rising.

sosie [sɔˈzi], *n.m.* double, counterpart.

sot [so], *a.* (*fem.* **sotte**) stupid, silly, foolish; (*fig.*) embarrassed, sheepish.—*n.m.* (*fem.* **sotte**) fool, ass, idiot.

sottement [sɔtˈmã], *adv.* stupidly; foolishly.

299

sottise [sɔ'ti:z], *n.f.* silliness, folly; foolish trick, nonsense; insult; (*pl.*) abusive language.

sou [su], *n.m.* sou (*copper coin worth 5 centimes*); copper, penny.

soubresaut [subrə'so], *n.m.* sudden leap *or* bound; plunge (*of a horse*); start; jolt.

soubresauter [subrə'sote], *v.i.* to start, to jump, to plunge.

soubrette [su'brɛt], *n.f.* lady's maid, waiting-woman.

souche [suʃ], *n.f.* stump, stock, stub, stem; (*fig.*) blockhead; founder (*of a family etc.*); origin; chimney-stack; counterfoil; tally; *faire souche*, to found a family.

souci (1) [su'si], *n.m.* care, anxiety.

souci (2) [su'si], *n.m.* (*Bot.*) marigold.

soucier (se) [səsu'sje], *v.r.* to care, to mind, to be concerned, to be anxious (*de*).

soucieux [su'sjø], *a.* (*fem.* **-euse**) anxious, full of care; pensive, thoughtful.

soucoupe [su'kup], *n.f.* saucer.

soudage [su'da:ʒ], *n.m.* soldering, welding; (*fig.*) reconciliation.

soudain [su'dɛ̃], *a.* sudden, unexpected.—*adv.* suddenly.

soudainement [sudɛn'mã], *adv.* suddenly, all of a sudden.

soudaineté [sudɛn'te], *n.f.* suddenness.

Soudan [su'dã], **le**, *n.m.* the Sudan.

soudanais [suda'nɛ], *a.* Sudanese.—*n.m.* (**Soudanais**, *fem.* **-aise**) Sudanese (*person*).

soude [sud], *n.f.* soda.

souder [su'de], *v.t.* to solder, to braze, to weld; (*fig.*) to unite. **se souder**, *v.r.* to be soldered *or* welded; to knit (*of bones*).

soudeur [su'dœ:r], *n.m.* welder.

soudoyer [sudwa'je], *v.t.* (*conjug. like* EMPLOYER) to keep in one's pay; to hire; to bribe.

soudure [su'dy:r], *n.f.* solder; soldering, welding; *soudure autogène*, oxyacetylene welding.

soue [su], *n.f.* pigsty.

soufflage [su'fla:ʒ], *n.m.* glass-blowing.

soufflant [su'flã], *a.* blowing.

souffle [sufl], *n.m.* breath, breathing; puff (*of wind etc.*); (*fig.*) inspiration, influence.

soufflé [su'fle], *a.* soufflé (*of pastry etc.*); exaggerated (*reputation*).—*n.m.* soufflé (*light dish*).

soufflement [suflə'mã], *n.m.* blowing.

souffler [su'fle], *v.t.* to blow, to blow out; to inflate; to whisper; (*Theat.*) to prompt; to huff (*at checkers*); (*Naut.*) to sheathe.—*v.i.* to blow, to breathe; to pant, to puff; (*fig.*) to breathe a word etc.; *souffler aux oreilles de quelqu'un*, to whisper in someone's ear.

soufflerie [suflə'ri], *n.f.* bellows (*of an organ*).

soufflet [su'flɛ], *n.m.* pair of bellows; box on the ear, slap in the face; affront.

souffleter [sufla'te], *v.t.* (*conjug. like* APPELER) to slap in the face, to box the ears of; (*fig.*) to insult.

souffleur [su'flœ:r], *a.* (*fem.* **-euse**) blowing, puffing.—*n.m.* (*fem.* **-euse**) blower; (*Theat.*) prompter.—(*C*) *n.f.* (**-euse**) snow blower.

souffrance [su'frã:s], *n.f.* suffering, pain; suspense; (*Law*) sufferance; *en souffrance*, awaiting delivery; in abeyance.

souffrant [su'frã], *a.* suffering; unwell; long-suffering.

souffre-douleur [sufrədu'lœ:r], *n.m. inv.* drudge; butt, laughing-stock.

souffreteux [sufrə'tø], *a.* (*fem.* **-euse**) needy; poorly, sickly, weakly.

souffrir [su'fri:r], *v.t. irr.* (*conjug. like* OUVRIR) to suffer; to bear, to endure, to undergo, to sustain; to stand, to tolerate; to admit of; *faire souffrir*, to pain, to grieve.—*v.i.* to suffer, to be in pain; to be pained; to be injured.

soufre [sufr], *n.m.* sulphur, brimstone.

souhait [swɛ], *n.m.* wish, desire; *à souhait*, to one's heart's content, as one would have it.

souhaitable [swɛ'tabl], *a.* desirable.

souhaiter [swɛ'te], *v.t.* to desire, to wish for.

souiller [su'je], *v.t.* to soil, to dirty; to stain, to blemish, to sully; to defile. **se souiller**, *v.r.* to soil oneself, to get dirty; to tarnish one's good name.

souillon [su'jõ], *n.* sloven, slut; scullion.

souillure [su'jy:r], *n.f.* spot, stain; blot, blemish; contamination.

soûl *or* **saoul** [su], *a.* glutted, surfeited (*de*); drunk; satiated, heartily sick (*de*).—*n.m.* fill, bellyful; *tout son soûl*, to one's heart's content.

soulagement [sulaʒ'mã], *n.m.* relief, alleviation; solace, help.

soulager [sula'ʒe], *v.t.* (*conjug. like* MANGER) to relieve, to ease; to alleviate, to allay; to soothe, to comfort. **se soulager**, *v.r.* to relieve oneself; to help each other.

soûlard [su'la:r], *a.* drunken.—*n.m.* (*fem.* **-e**) drunkard, sot.

soûler [su'le], *v.t.* to fill, to glut; to make drunk. **se soûler**, *v.r.* to gorge; to get drunk.

soûlerie [sul'ri], *n.f.* drinking bout, 'binge'.

soulèvement [sulɛv'mã], *n.m.* heaving; swelling (*of sea waves etc.*); rising (*of the stomach*); (*fig.*) insurrection, revolt.

soulever [sul've], *v.t.* (*conjug. like* AMENER) to raise, to lift up; to heave; to take up; (*fig.*) to excite, to stir up; to sicken; to rouse the indignation of. **se soulever**, *v.r.* to raise oneself, to rise; to heave, to swell; to rise in insurrection.

soulier [su'lje], *n.m.* shoe; *être dans ses petits souliers*, to be ill at ease; *souliers ferrés*, hobnailed boots.

soulignement [sulin'mã], *n.m.* underlining.

souligner [suli'ne], *v.t.* to underline; (*fig.*) to emphasize.

soumettre [su'mɛtr], *v.t. irr.* (*conjug. like* METTRE) to subdue, to subject; to submit, to refer; to subordinate. **se soumettre**, *v.r.* to submit, to yield; to comply, to assent (*à*).

soumis [su'mi], *a.* submissive.

soumission [sumi'sjõ], *n.f.* submission, compliance, obedience; subjection; mark of respect; bid for a contract etc.

soumissionner [sumisjɔ'ne], *v.t.* to bid for.

soupape [su'pap], *n.f.* valve; *soupape de sûreté*, safety-valve.

soupçon [sup'sõ], *n.m.* suspicion; surmise, conjecture; (*fig.*) slight taste, dash, touch.

soupçonner [supsɔ'ne], *v.t.* to suspect; to surmise.

soupçonneux [supsɔ'nø], *a.* (*fem.* **-euse**) suspicious.

soupe [sup], *n.f.* soup; sop; *c'est une soupe au lait*, he has a quick temper; *trempé comme une soupe*, drenched to the skin.

soupente [su'pɑ̃:t], *n.f.* straps (*of a horse*); loft, garret.

souper [su'pe], *v.i.* to sup, to have supper. —*n.m.* supper.

soupeser [supə'ze], *v.t.* (*conjug. like* AMENER) to weigh in one's hand, to try the weight of.

soupière [su'pjɛ:r], *n.f.* soup tureen.

soupir [su'pi:r], *n.m.* sigh; breath, gasp; (*Mus.*) quarter rest.

soupirail [supi'ra:j], *n.m.* (*pl.* **-aux**) air-hole, ventilator.

soupirant [supi'rɑ̃], *a.* sighing.—*n.m.* wooer, lover.

soupirer [supi're], *v.t.* to breathe forth, to sigh out.—*v.i.* to sigh; to gasp; to long.

souple [supl], *a.* supple, pliant, flexible, yielding; docile.

souplesse [su'plɛs], *n.f.* suppleness, flexibility; compliance, pliancy; versatility; toughness.

souquenille [suk'ni:j], *n.f.* smock frock; (shabby) old garment.

source [surs], *n.f.* spring, source, fountain.

sourcier [sur'sje], *n.m.* (*fem.* **-ière**) water diviner.

sourcil [sur'si], *n.m.* eyebrow, brow; *froncer le sourcil*, to frown.

sourciller [sursi'je], *v.i.* to knit one's brows, to frown; to wince.

sourcilleux [sursi'jø], *a.* (*fem.* **-euse**) haughty, proud, supercilious; frowning; uneasy.

sourd [su:r], *a.* deaf; (*fig.*) dull; insensible; hollow, muffled (*of sound*); underhand.—*n.m.* (*fem.* **-e**) deaf person.

sourdement [surdə'mɑ̃], *adv.* indistinctly; with a hollow voice; in an underhand manner.

sourdine [sur'din], *n.f.* mute (*of a musical instrument*); damper (*of a piano etc.*); *en sourdine*, secretly, on the sly.

sourd-muet [sur'mɥɛ], *a.* and *n.m.* (*fem.* **sourde-muette**) deaf-and-dumb (person), deaf-mute.

sourdre [surdr], *v.i.* to spring, to gush, to well; (*fig.*) to result.

souriant [su'rjɑ̃], *a.* smiling.

souricière [suri'sjɛ:r], *n.f.* mouse-trap.

sourire [su'ri:r], *v.i. irr.* (*conjug. like* RIRE) to smile; to be agreeable, to delight, to please; to be propitious.—*n.m.* smile; *large sourire*, grin; *sourire affecté*, smirk.

souris [su'ri], *a. inv.* mouse-colored.— *n.f.* mouse; mouse-color; knuckle (*of a leg of mutton*).

sournois [sur'nwa], *a.* artful, cunning, sly.— *n.m.* (*fem.* **-e**) sneak.

sournoisement [surnwaz'mɑ̃], *adv.* cunningly, slyly.

sournoiserie [surnwaz'ri], *n.f.* slyness, cunning; underhand trick.

sous [su], *prep.* under, beneath, below; on, upon; with; in; by; *affirmer sous serment*, to swear under oath; *sous dix jours*, within ten days; *sous peu*, in a short time.

sous-alimentation [suzalimɑ̃ta'sjɔ̃], *n.f.* mal-nutrition.

sous-alimenté [suzalimɑ̃'te], *a.* underfed.

sous-chef [su'ʃɛf], *n.m.* deputy head-clerk; assistant manager.

souscripteur [suskrip'tœ:r], *n.m.* subscriber; (*Comm.*) underwriter.

souscription [suskrip'sjɔ̃], *n.f.* subscription; signature.

souscrire [sus'kri:r], *v.t. irr.* (*conjug. like* ÉCRIRE) to subscribe, to sign.—*v.i.* to consent, to agree (*à*).

sous-développé [sudevlɔ'pe], *a.* under-developed (*country*).

sous-dit [su'di], *a.* undermentioned.

sous-entendre [suzɑ̃'tɑ̃:dr], *v.t.* not to express fully, to hint, to imply.

sous-entendu [suzɑ̃tɑ̃'dy], *n.m.* thing understood, implication.

sous-entente [suzɑ̃'tɑ̃:t], *n.f.* mental reservation.

sous-lieutenant [suljøt'nɑ̃], *n.m.* second-lieutenant; *sous-lieutenant aviateur*, pilot officer.

sous-louer [su'lwe], *v.t.* to sub-let.

sous-main [su'mɛ̃], *n.m. inv.* writing pad; *en sous-main*, behind the scenes.

sous-marin [suma'rɛ̃], *a.* and *n.m.* sub-marine.

sous-off [su'zɔf], *abbr. fam. of* **sous-officier** [suzɔfi'sje], *n.m.* non-commissioned officer, N.C.O.

sous-ordre [su'zɔrdr], *n.m. inv.* subordinate.

sous-préfet [supre'fɛ], *n.m.* subprefect, under-sheriff.

sous-produit [suprɔ'dɥi], *n.m.* by-product.

sous-secrétaire [susəkre'tɛ:r], *n.* under-secretary.

soussigné [susi'ɲe], *a.* undersigned; *nous soussignés certifions*, we, the undersigned, certify.

sous-sol [su'sɔl], *n.m.* subsoil; basement.

sous-titre [su'titr], *n.m.* sub-title.

soustraction [sustrak'sjɔ̃], *n.f.* taking away, subtraction.

soustraire [sus'trɛ:r], *v.t. irr.* (*conjug. like* TRAIRE) to take away, to withdraw, to screen; (*Arith.*) to subtract. **se soustraire**, *v.r.* to escape, to flee, to avoid; to withdraw oneself; to be subtracted.

sous-traitant [sutrɛ'tɑ̃], *n.m.* subcontractor.

soutache [su'taʃ], *n.f.* braid.

soutane [su'tan], *n.f.* cassock; (*fig.*) the cloth.

soute [sut], *n.f.* (*Naut.*) store-room; (*Av.*) luggage bay, bomb bay.

soutenable [sut'nabl], *a.* sustainable; tenable.

soutènement [sutɛn'mɑ̃], *n.m.* (*Arch.*) support.

soutenir [sut'ni:r], *v.t. irr.* (*conjug. like* TENIR) to hold up, to support, to sustain, to keep up, to prop up; (*fig.*) to maintain, to uphold; to countenance; to afford (*an expense*); to endure. **se soutenir**, *v.r.* to support oneself; to hold oneself up; to bear up, to hold out; to stand firm; to succeed; to continue; to sustain one another.

soutenu [sut'ny], *a.* sustained; unremitting, unceasing, constant; lofty, elevated.

souterrain [sutɛ'rɛ̃], *a.* underground; (*fig.*) underhand.—*n.m.* underground vault, cavern; (*Rail.*) tunnel; underground passage.

soutien

soutien [su'tjɛ̃], *n.m.* support, prop, stay, staff.

soutien-gorge [sutjɛ̃'gɔrʒ], *n.m. inv.* brassiere.

soutirer [suti're], *v.t.* to draw off, to rack (*liquors*); (*fig.*) to worm out (*à*), to extract (*money, information*).

souvenir [suv'ni:r], *n.m.* recollection; reminder, souvenir, keepsake.—*v. impers. irr.* (*conjug. like* TENIR *but with aux.* ÊTRE) to occur to the mind; *il m'en souvient,* I remember it. **se souvenir,** *v.r.* to remember, to call to mind, to recollect.

souvent [su'vɑ̃], *adv.* often, frequently.

souverain [su'vrɛ̃], *a.* sovereign, supreme; highest, extreme; infallible.—*n.m.* (*fem.* **-e**) sovereign (*monarch*).—*n.m.* sovereign (*coin*).

souverainement [suvrɛn'mɑ̃], *adv.* in the extreme; supremely.

souveraineté [suvrɛn'te], *n.f.* sovereignty, dominion.

soviet [sɔ'vjɛt], *n.m.* soviet.

soviétique [sɔvje'tik], *a.* *l'Union des Républiques socialistes soviétiques* (*U.R.S.S.*), the Union of Soviet Socialist Republics (*U.S.S.R.*).—*n.* (**Soviétique**) Soviet citizen.

soyeux [swa'jø], *a.* (*fem.* **-euse**) silky, silken.

spacieusement [spasjøz'mɑ̃], *adv.* spaciously.

spacieux [spa'sjø], *a.* (*fem.* **-euse**) spacious, wide, roomy.

spahi [spa'i], *n.m.* spahi (*Algerian native trooper*).

sparadrap [spara'dra], *n.m.* sticking plaster.

Sparte [spart], **la**, *f.* Sparta.

spartiate [spar'sjat], *a.* Spartan.—*n.* (**Spartiate**) Spartan (*person*).

spasme [spasm], *n.m.* spasm.

spasmodique [spasmɔ'dik], *a.* spasmodic.

spasmodiquement [spasmɔdik'mɑ̃], *adv.* spasmodically.

spatule [spa'tyl], *n.f.* spatula.

speaker [spi'kœːr], *n.m.* (*fem.* **speakerine**) (*Rad.*) announcer.

spécial [spe'sjal], *a.* (*m. pl.* **-aux**) special, especial, particular; professional.

spécialement [spesjal'mɑ̃], *adv.* especially, particularly.

spécialisation [spesjaliza'sjɔ̃], *n.f.* specialization.

spécialiser [spesjali'ze], *v.t.* to specialize.

spécialiste [spesja'list], *n.* specialist, expert.

spécialité [spesjali'te], *n.f.* peculiarity, specialty; patent medicine.

spécieux [spe'sjø], *a.* (*fem.* **-euse**) specious, plausible.

spécification [spesifika'sjɔ̃], *n.f.* specification.

spécifier [spesi'fje], *v.t.* to specify.

spécifique [spesi'fik], *a.* and *n.m.* specific.

spécifiquement [spesifik'mɑ̃], *adv.* specifically.

spécimen [spesi'mɛn], *n.m.* specimen.

spectacle [spɛk'takl], *n.m.* spectacle, scene, sight; theatre; play, performance; show; *se donner en spectacle,* to make an exhibition of oneself.

spectaculaire [spɛktaky'lɛːr], *a.* spectacular.

spectateur [spɛkta'tœːr], *n.m.* (*fem.* **-trice**) spectator, looker-on.

spectral [spɛk'tral], *a.* (*m. pl.* **-aux**) spectral.

spectre [spɛktr], *n.m.* specter, ghost; spectrum.

spéculateur [spekyla'tœːr], *n.m.* (*fem.* **-trice**) speculator.

spéculatif [spekyla'tif], *a.* (*fem.* **-tive**) speculative.

spéculation [spekylɑ'sjɔ̃], *n.f.* speculation.

spéculativement [spekylativ'mɑ̃], *adv.* in a speculative manner.

spéculer [speky'le], *v.i.* to speculate.

sperme [spɛrm], *n.m.* sperm, seed.

sphaigne [sfɛːɲ], *n.f.* sphagnum moss.

sphère [sfɛːr], *n.f.* sphere, orb, globe; (*fig.*) circle.

sphérique [sfe'rik], *a.* spherical.

sphinx [sfɛ̃ks], *n.m.* sphinx.

spinal [spi'nal], *a.* (*m. pl.* **-aux**) spinal.

spiral [spi'ral], *a.* (*m. pl.* **-aux**) spiral.—*n.m.* hair-spring (*of watch*).

spirale [spi'ral], *n.f.* spiral.

spirite [spi'rit], *a.* spiritualistic.—*n.* spiritualist.

spiritisme [spiri'tism], *n.m.* spiritualism.

spiritualisme [spiritɥa'lism], *n.m.* spiritualism.

spiritualiste [spiritɥa'list], *a.* and *n.* spiritualist.

spirituel [spiri'tɥɛl], *a.* (*fem.* **-elle**) spiritual; intellectual; witty, shrewd, lively, intelligent.

spirituellement [spiritɥɛl'mɑ̃], *adv.* spiritually, wittily, cleverly.

spiritueux [spiri'tɥø], *a.* (*fem.* **-euse**) spirituous.—*n.m.* spirit, spirituous liquor.

spleen [splin], *n.m.* spleen; (*fam.*) *avoir le spleen,* to be in the dumps.

splendeur [splɑ̃'dœːr], *n.f.* splendor, brilliance; magnificence.

splendide [splɑ̃'did], *a.* sumptuous, magnificent.

splendidement [splɑ̃did'mɑ̃], *adv.* splendidly.

spoliateur [spɔlja'tœːr], *a.* (*fem.* **-trice**) despoiling.—*n.m.* (*fem.* **-trice**) spoiler, despoiler.

spoliation [spɔlja'sjɔ̃], *n.f.* spoliation.

spolier [spɔ'lje], *v.t.* to despoil, to plunder.

spongieux [spɔ̃'ʒjø], *a.* (*fem.* **-euse**) spongy.

spontané [spɔ̃ta'ne], *a.* spontaneous.

spontanéité [spɔ̃tanei'te], *n.f.* spontaneity.

spontanément [spɔ̃tane'mɑ̃], *adv.* spontaneously.

sporadique [spɔra'dik], *a.* sporadic.

spore [spɔːr], *n.f.* spore.

sport [spɔːr], *n.m.* games, outdoor games; *faire du sport,* to play games.

sportif [spɔr'tif], *a.* (*fem.* **-tive**) sporting; *réunion sportive,* athletics meeting.—*n.m.* (*fem.* **-tive**) athlete; devotee of out-door games; sportsman, sportswoman.

spumeux [spy'mø], *a.* (*fem.* **-euse**) spumy.

square [skwaːr], *n.m.* residential square with enclosed garden.

squelette [skə'lɛt], *n.m.* skeleton; carcass, frame (*of a ship*).

squelettique [skəle'tik], *a.* lanky.

stabilisateur [stabiliza'tœːr], *a.* (*fem.* **-trice**) stabilizing.—*n.m.* (*Av.*, *Naut.*) stabilizer.

stabiliser [stabili'ze], *v.t.* to stabilize.

stabilité [stabili'te], *n.f.* stability, durability.

stable [stabl], *a.* stable, firm; durable, lasting, permanent.

stade [stad], *n.m.* sports ground, stadium; (*fig.*) stage, period.

stage [staːʒ], *n.m.* term of probation, study, residence etc.; training course; (*fig.*) probation.

stagiaire [staˈʒjɛːr], *n.* probationer, trainee.

stagnant [stagˈnɑ̃], *a.* stagnant, at a standstill.

stagnation [stagnɑˈsjɔ̃], *n.f.* stagnation.

stagner [stagˈne], *v.i.* to stagnate.

stalactite [stalakˈtit], *n.f.* stalactite.

stalagmite [stalagˈmit], *n.f.* stalagmite.

stalle [stal], *n.f.* stall; box (*for horses*) (*Theat.*) stall, seat.

stance [stɑ̃ːs], *n.f.* stanza.

stand [stɑ̃ːd], *n.m.* rifle range; shooting gallery; stall, stand (*at exhibitions etc.*).

standard [stɑ̃ˈdaːr], *n.m.* (*in house* or *office*) switchboard; standard (*of living*).

standardiser [stɑ̃dardiˈze], *v.t.* to standardize.

standardiste [stɑ̃darˈdist], *n.* switchboard operator.

star [staːr], *n.f.* (*Cine.*) star.

starlette [starˈlɛt], *n.f.* starlet.

starter [starˈtɛːr], *n.m.* (*Motor.*) choke; (*Racing*) starter.

station [stɑˈsjɔ̃], *n.f.* station, standing; stop (*of bus etc.*); taxi stand; resort.

stationnaire [stasjɔˈnɛːr], *a.* stationary.

stationnement [stasjɔnˈmɑ̃], *n.m.* stationing, standing; parking; *stationnement interdit*, no parking, no standing.

stationner [stasjɔˈne], *v.i.* to stop, to stand, to park (*of cars*).

statique [staˈtik], *a.* static.—*n.f.* statics.

statisticien [statistiˈsjɛ̃], *n.m.* statistician.

statistique [statisˈtik], *a.* statistical.—*n.f.* statistics.

statuaire [staˈtɥɛːr], *a.* statuary.—*n.* sculptor. —*n.f.* statuary (*art*).

statue [staˈty], *n.f.* statue.

statuer [staˈtɥe], *v.t.* to decree, to resolve, to ordain.—*v.i.* to give a ruling.

statuette [staˈtɥɛt], *n.f.* statuette.

stature [staˈtyːr], *n.f.* stature, height.

statut [staˈty], *n.m.* statute, ordinance, bylaw; status.

statutaire [statyˈtɛːr], *a.* statutory.

stellaire [stɛlˈlɛːr], *a.* stellar, starry.

stencil [stɛnˈsil], *n.m.* stencil.

sténo [steˈno], *abbr. of* **sténographe** or **sténographie**.

sténo-dactylo(graphe) [stenodaktiˈlo(ˈgraf)], *n.* shorthand typist.

sténographe [stenɔˈgraf], *n.* stenographer, shorthand writer.

sténographie [stenɔgraˈfi], *n.f.* stenography, shorthand.

sténographier [stenɔgraˈfje], *v.t.* to take down in shorthand.

stentor [stɑ̃ˈtɔːr], *n.m.* stentor; *d'une voix de stentor*, in a stentorian voice.

steppe [stɛp], *n.f.* steppe.

stéréoscope [stereɔsˈkɔp], *n.m.* stereoscope.

stéréotypé [stereɔtiˈpe], *a.* stereotyped, hackneyed.

stérile [steˈril], *a.* sterile, barren; (*fig.*) fruitless, vain.

stérilisant [steriliˈzɑ̃], *a.* sterilizing.—*n.m.* sterilizing agent.

stérilisation [sterilizaˈsjɔ̃], *n.f.* sterilization.

stériliser [steriliˈze], *v.t.* to sterilize.

stérilité [steriliˈte], *n.f.* sterility, barrenness.

sterling [stɛrˈliŋ], *a. inv.* and *n.m.* sterling.

stéthoscope [stetɔsˈkɔp], *n.m.* stethoscope.

stigmate [stigˈmat], *n.m.* scar, stigma, stain; brand.

stigmatiser [stigmatiˈze], *v.t.* to stigmatize, to brand.

stimulant [stimyˈlɑ̃], *a.* stimulating.—*n.m.* stimulant; stimulus; incentive.

stimulation [stimylaˈsjɔ̃], *n.f.* stimulation.

stimuler [stimyˈle], *v.t.* to stimulate; to excite, to rouse.

stipendiaire [stipɑ̃ˈdjɛːr], *a.* and *n.m.* stipendiary, mercenary.

stipendié [stipɑ̃ˈdje], *a.* hired.—*n.m.* stipendiary, hireling.

stipendier [stipɑ̃ˈdje], *v.t.* to hire, to keep on the payroll.

stipulation [stipylaˈsjɔ̃], *n.f.* stipulation.

stipuler [stipyˈle], *v.t.* to stipulate; to contract.

stock [stɔk], *n.m.* (*Comm.*) stock.

stocker [stɔˈke], *v.t.* to stock; to stockpile.

stockiste [stɔˈkist], *n.m.* warehouseman; dealer; agent (*for a certain make of car*); service station (*with spare parts*).

stoïcien [stɔiˈsjɛ̃], *a.* stoic, stoical.—*n.m.* (*fem.* **-enne**) stoic.

stoïcisme [stɔiˈsism], *n.m.* stoicism.

stoïque [stɔˈik], *a.* stoic, stoical.—*n.* stoic.

stoïquement [stɔikˈmɑ̃], *adv.* stoically.

stop [stɔp], *int.* stop!—*n.m.* (*Motor.*) stop-light.

stoppage [stɔˈpaːʒ], *n.m.* invisible mending; stoppage (*of motion, current*).

stopper [stɔˈpe], *v.t.* to mend invisibly; to stop.—*v.i.* to stop (*of a train, steamboat etc.*).

store [stɔːr], *n.m.* (*spring-roller*) blind.

strabisme [straˈbism], *n.m.* squinting.

strangulation [strɑ̃gylaˈsjɔ̃], *n.f.* strangulation.

strapontin [strapɔ̃ˈtɛ̃], *n.m.* folding seat, tip-up seat.

strass or **stras** [stras], *n.m.* strass, paste jewels.

stratagème [strataˈʒɛm], *n.m.* stratagem.

strate [strat], *n.f.* stratum.

stratégie [strateˈʒi], *n.f.* strategy.

stratégique [strateˈʒik], *a.* strategic.

stratégiquement [strateʒikˈmɑ̃], *adv.* strategically.

stratégiste [strateˈʒist], *n.m.* strategist.

stratosphère [stratɔsˈfɛːr], *n.f.* stratosphere.

strict [strikt], *a.* strict, precise; severe.

strictement [striktəˈmɑ̃], *adv.* strictly; severely.

strident [striˈdɑ̃], *a.* strident, jarring.

strié [striˈe], *a.* striate, streaked; corrugated; scored.

strontium [strɔ̃ˈsjɔm], *n.m.* strontium.

strophe [strɔf], *n.f.* strophe; stanza.

structural [stryktyˈral], *a.* (*m. pl.* **-aux**) structural.

structure [strykˈtyːr], *n.f.* structure; form, make.

strychnine [strikˈnin], *n.f.* strychnin(e).

stuc [styk], *n.m.* stucco.

stucage [styˈkaːʒ], *n.m.* stucco-work.

studieusement [stydjøzˈmɑ̃], *adv.* studiously.

studieux [styˈdjø], *a.* (*fem.* **-euse**) studious.

studio [styˈdjo], *n.m.* (*Cine.*) film studio; (*Rad., Tel.*) broadcasting studio; one-room flat.

stupéfaction [stypefak′sjɔ̃], *n.f.* stupefaction, amazement.
stupéfait [stype′fɛ], *a.* amazed, dumbfounded.
stupéfiant [stype′fjã], *a.* stupefactive; amazing, astounding.—*n.m.* narcotic.
stupéfier [stype′fje], *v.t.* to stupefy, to astound, to dumbfound.
stupeur [sty′pœ:r], *n.f.* stupor; amazement.
stupide [sty′pid], *a.* stunned; stupid, foolish, dull.
stupidement [stypid′mã], *adv.* stupidly.
stupidité [stypidi′te], *n.f.* stupidity.
style (1) [stil], *n.m.* style.
style (2) [stil], *n.m.* stylus.
stylé [sti′le], *a.* stylate; (*colloq.*) trained, taught, clever.
styler [sti′le], *v.t.* to train, to form, to school.
stylet [sti′lɛ], *n.m.* stiletto; (*Surg.*) probe.
stylo [sti′lo], *abbr. of* **stylographe** [stilɔ′graf], *n.m.* fountain pen; *stylo à bille*, ball-point pen.
stylomine [stilo′min], *n.m.* mechanical pencil.
styptique [stip′tik], *a.* and *n.m.* styptic.
su (1) [sy], *n.m.* knowledge; *au vu et au su de tout le monde*, as everybody knows.
su (2) [sy], *p.p.* [SAVOIR].
suaire [sɥɛ:r], *n.m.* winding sheet, shroud.
suant [sɥã], *a.* sweating, in a sweat.
suave [sɥa:v], *a.* sweet, agreeable; suave, bland; soft.
suavement [sɥav′mã], *adv.* suavely; sweetly.
suavité [sɥavi′te], *n.f.* suavity; sweetness.
subalterne [sybal′tɛrn], *a.* and *n.* subaltern, subordinate; inferior.
subdiviser [sybdivi′ze], *v.t.* to subdivide. **se subdiviser**, *v.r.* to be subdivided.
subdivision [sybdivi′zjɔ̃], *n.f.* subdivision.
subir [sy′bi:r], *v.t.* to support; to go through, to undergo, to suffer; to submit to.
subit [sy′bit], *a.* sudden, unexpected.
subitement [sybit′mã], *adv.* suddenly, all of a sudden.
subjectif [sybʒɛk′tif], *a.* (*fem.* **-tive**) subjective.
subjection [sybʒɛk′sjɔ̃], *n.f.* subjection.
subjectivement [sybʒɛktiv′mã], *adv.* subjectively.
subjonctif [sybʒɔ̃k′tif], *a.* (*fem.* **-tive**) and *n.m.* subjunctive.
subjugation [sybʒyga′sjɔ̃], *n.f.* subjugation.
subjuguer [sybʒy′ge], *v.t.* to subjugate, to subdue.
sublimation [syblima′sjɔ̃], *n.f.* sublimation.
sublime [sy′blim], *a.* lofty, sublime, splendid. —*n.m.* the sublime.
sublimement [syblim′mã], *adv.* sublimely.
submerger [sybmɛr′ʒe], *v.t.* (*conjug. like* MANGER) to submerge, to swamp, to flood; (*fig.*) to overwhelm.
submersible [sybmɛr′sibl], *a.* submersible. —*n.m.* submarine (*boat*).
submersion [sybmɛr′sjɔ̃], *n.f.* submersion.
subordination [sybɔrdina′sjɔ̃], *n.f.* subordination.
subordonné [sybɔrdɔ′ne], *a.* and *n.m.* (*fem.* **-ée**) subordinate, dependent.
subordonner [sybɔrdɔ′ne], *v.t.* to subordinate.
suborner [sybɔr′ne], *v.t.* to suborn, to bribe.
suborneur [sybɔr′nœ:r], *a.* (*fem.* **-euse**)

suborning, bribing.—*n.m.* (*fem.* **-euse**) suborner, briber.
subreptice [sybrɛp′tis], *a.* surreptitious.
subrepticement [sybrɛptis′mã], *adv.* surreptitiously.
subséquemment [sybseka′mã], *adv.* subsequently.
subséquent [sybse′kã], *a.* subsequent.
subside [syb′sid], *n.m.* subsidy; (*colloq.*) aid.
subsidiaire [sybsi′djɛ:r], *a.* subsidiary, auxiliary.
subsidiairement [sybsidjɛr′mã], *adv.* further, also, additionally.
subsistance [sybzis′tã:s], *n.f.* subsistence, sustenance, maintenance; (*pl.*) provisions.
subsistant [sybzis′tã], *a.* subsisting, existing.
subsister [sybzis′te], *v.i.* to subsist, to stand; to hold good; to exist, to live.
substance [sybs′tã:s], *n.f.* substance.
substantiel [sybstã′sjɛl], *a.* (*fem.* **-elle**) substantial.
substantiellement [sybstãsjɛl′mã], *adv.* substantially.
substantif [sybstã′tif], *a.* (*fem.* **-tive**) substantive.—*n.m.* (*Gram.*) noun.
substituer [sybsti′tɥe], *v.t.* to substitute; (*Law*) to entail.
substitut [sybsti′ty], *n.m.* substitute, deputy (*to someone*).
substitution [sybstity′sjɔ̃], *n.f.* substitution; (*Law*) entail.
subterfuge [sybtɛr′fy:ʒ], *n.m.* subterfuge, evasion, shift.
subtil [syb′til], *a.* subtile, tenuous; penetrating; acute, keen, sharp; cunning; fine-spun, subtle.
subtilement [sybtil′mã], *adv.* subtly, craftily.
subtiliser [sybtili′ze], *v.t.* to subtilize, to refine; (*colloq.*) to sneak, to steal.
subtilité [sybtili′te], *n.f.* subtlety, fineness; acuteness; shrewdness.
suburbain [sybyr′bɛ̃], *a.* suburban.
subvenir [sybvə′ni:r], *v.i. irr.* (*conjug. like* TENIR) to be helpful; to supply, to provide.
subvention [sybvã′sjɔ̃], *n.f.* subsidy, aid.
subventionner [sybvãsjɔ′ne], *v.t.* to subsidize, to make a grant to.
subversif [sybvɛr′sif], *a.* (*fem.* **-sive**) subversive.
subversion [sybvɛr′sjɔ̃], *n.f.* subversion, overthrow.
suc [syk], *n.m.* juice; (*fig.*) essence, quintessence.
succéder [sykse′de], *v.i.* (*conjug. like* CÉDER) to succeed, to follow after (*à*). **se succéder**, *v.r.* to succeed each other.
succès [syk′sɛ], *n.m.* success.
successeur [syksɛ′sœ:r], *n.m.* successor.
successif [syksɛ′sif], *a.* (*fem.* **-ive**) successive, in succession.
succession [syksɛ′sjɔ̃], *n.f.* succession; inheritance; heritage, estate.
successivement [syksɛsiv′mã], *adv.* successively, in succession.
succinct [syk′sɛ̃], *a.* succinct, concise.
succinctement [syksɛt′mã], *adv.* succinctly, briefly.
succion [syk′sjɔ̃], *n.f.* suction.
succomber [sykɔ̃′be], *v.i.* to sink, to faint; to yield, to succumb; to fail; to die.
succulence [syky′lã:s], *n.f.* succulence.
succulent [syky′lã], *a.* succulent, juicy; rich.

succursale [sykyr'sal], *n.f.* branch (*of a bank etc.*).

sucement [sys'mā], *n.m.* sucking, suck.

sucer [sy'se], *v.t.* (*conjug. like* COMMENCER) to suck, to suck in; to imbibe.

sucette [sy'sɛt], *n.f.* lollipop;   pacifier (*for baby*).

suceur [sy'sœ:r], *a.* (*fem.* **-euse**) sucking.— *n.m.* sucker; nozzle (*of a vacuum cleaner*).

suçoir [sy'swa:r], *n.m.* sucker.

sucre [sykr], *n.m.* sugar; *sucre cristallisé,* granulated sugar; *sucre d'orge,* barley-sugar; *sucre en poudre,* powdered sugar.

sucré [sy'kre], *a.* sugared, sweet, sugary; (*fig.*) demure, prim.

sucrer [sy'kre], *v.t.* to sugar, to sweeten.

sucrerie [sykrə'ri], *n.f.* sugar refinery; (*pl.*) sweets.

sucrier [sykri'e], *n.m.* sugar bowl; sugar maker.

sud [syd], *a. inv.* south, southerly (*of the wind*).—*n.m.* south; south wind.

sud-est [sy'dɛst], *a. inv.* and *n.m.* south-east.

Sudètes [sy'dɛt], **les**, *m. pl.* Sudetenland.

sud-ouest [sy'dwɛst], *a. inv.* and *n.m.* south-west.

Suède [sɥɛd], **la**, *f.* Sweden.

suède [sɥɛd], *n.m.* suede (*glove leather*).

suédois [sɥe'dwa], *a.* Swedish.—*n.m.* Swedish (*language*); (**Suédois**, *fem.* **-oise**) Swede.

suée [sɥe], *n.f.* sweating.

suer [sɥe], *v.t.* to sweat.—*v.i.* to sweat, to perspire; (*fig.*) to toil, to drudge; to ooze (*of walls*).

sueur [sɥœ:r], *n.f.* sweat, perspiration; (*pl.*) labor, toil.

suffire [sy'fi:r], *v.i. irr.* to suffice, to be sufficient; to be adequate; *cela suffit,* that's enough. **se suffire,** *v.r.* to provide for oneself.

suffisamment [syfiza'mā], *adv.* sufficiently.

suffisance [syfi'zā:s], *n.f.* sufficiency, adequacy; conceit, self-sufficiency.

suffisant [syfi'zā], *a.* sufficient; conceited.— *n.m.* (*fem.* **-e**) conceited person.

suffixe [sy'fiks], *n.m.* suffix.

suffocant [syfo'kā], *a.* suffocating, choking.

suffocation [syfoka'sjō], *n.f.* suffocation.

suffoquer [syfo'ke], *v.t.* to suffocate, to choke. —*v.i.* to choke.

suffrage [sy'fra:3], *n.m.* suffrage, vote; approbation, commendation.

suggérer [syg3e're], *v.t.* (*conjug. like* CÉDER) to suggest.

suggestif [syg3ɛs'tif], *a.* (*fem.* **-tive**) suggestive; erotic.

suggestion [syg3ɛs'tjō], *n.f.* suggestion, hint, instigation.

suicide [sɥi'sid], *n.m.* suicide.

suicidé [sɥisi'de], *a.m.* (*fem.* **-ée**) suicide.

suicider (se) [səsɥisi'de], *v.r.* to commit suicide.

suie [sɥi], *n.f.* soot.

suif [sɥif], *n.m.* tallow.

suintement [sɥɛ̃t'mā], *n.m.* oozing, sweating.

suinter [sɥɛ̃'te], *v.i.* to ooze, to sweat (*of walls etc.*); to leak, to run (*of vessels*).

Suisse [sɥis], **la**, *f.* Switzerland.

suisse [sɥis], *a.* Swiss.—*n.m.* porter (*of a mansion*); church officer; (**Suisse**, *fem.* **Suissesse**) Swiss (*person*).

suite [sɥit], *n.f.* the rest; retinue, attendants; sequel, continuation; series; set; connection; result; *à la suite,* after, behind; *de suite,* consecutively; *et ainsi de suite,* and so on; *tout de suite,* immediately.

suivant [sɥi'vā], *prep.* according to; in the direction of; *suivant que,* as, according as. —*a.* next, following, subsequent.—*n.m.* (*fem.* **-e**) follower, attendant.—*n.f.* (**-e**) lady's maid.

suivi [sɥi'vi], *a.* followed; connected; consistent; popular.

suivre [sɥi:vr], *v.t. irr.* to follow; to be next to; to attend; to observe; to pursue; to practise (*a profession etc.*).—*v.i.* to follow; to come after; to result, to ensue; *à faire suivre,* to be forwarded; *à suivre,* to be continued. **se suivre,** *v.r.* to follow each other, to be continuous.

sujet [sy'3ɛ], *a.* (*fem.* **-ette**) subject, subjected, liable, exposed; apt, addicted, inclined (*à*).—*n.m.* subject; topic; cause.

sujétion [sy3e'sjō], *n.f.* subjection, servitude; constraint.

sulfate [syl'fat], *n.m.* sulphate.

sulfureux [sylfy'rø], *a.* (*fem.* **-euse**) sulphurous, sulphureous.

sulfurique [sylfy'rik], *a.* sulphuric (*acid*).

sultan [syl'tā], *n.m.* sultan.

sultane [syl'tan], *n.f.* sultana, sultaness.

sumac [sy'mak], *n.m.* sumac.

superbe [sy'pɛrb], *a.* proud, arrogant; superb; stately; lofty; vainglorious.—*n.* proud person.—*n.f.* arrogance; vainglory.

superbement [sypɛrbə'mā], *adv.* haughtily, superbly.

supercarburant [sypɛrkarby'rā], *n.m.* high-octane gasolene.

supercherie [sypɛrʃə'ri], *n.f.* deceit, fraud.

superficie [sypɛrfi'si], *n.f.* area, surface; (*fig.*) superficiality.

superficiel [sypɛrfi'sjɛl], *a.* (*fem.* **-elle**) superficial; shallow.

superficiellement [sypɛrfisjɛl'mā], *adv.* superficially.

superfin [sypɛr'fɛ̃], *a.* superfine, of superior quality.

superflu [sypɛr'fly], *a.* superfluous; unnecessary.—*n.m.* superfluity, excess.

superfluité [sypɛrflɥi'te], *n.f.* superfluity.

supérieur [sype'rjœ:r], *a.* superior; upper, higher.—*n.m.* (*fem.* **-e**) superior.

supérieurement [syperjœr'mā], *adv.* in a superior manner; superlatively.

supériorité [syperjori'te], *n.f.* superiority.

superlatif [sypɛrla'tif], *a.* (*fem.* **-tive**) superlative.—*n.m.* (*Gram.*) superlative.

superlativement [sypɛrlativ'mā], *adv.* superlatively.

superposer [sypɛrpo'ze], *v.t.* to superpose; to superimpose.

superposition [sypɛrpozi'sjō], *n.f.* superposition; superimposition.

supersonique [sypɛrso'nik], *a.* supersonic.

superstitieusement [sypɛrstisjøz'mā], *adv.* superstitiously.

superstitieux [sypɛrsti'sjø], *a.* (*fem.* **-euse**) superstitious.

superstition [sypɛrsti'sjō], *n.f.* superstition.

superstructure [sypɛrstryk'ty:r], *n.f.* superstructure; right of way (*of railway*).

supin [sy'pɛ̃], *n.m.* (*Gram.*) supine.

supplantation

supplantation [syplɑ̃tɑ'sjɔ̃], *n.f.* supplantation; supersession.

supplanter [syplɑ̃'te], *v.t.* to supplant, to oust, to supersede.

suppléance [syple'ɑ̃:s], *n.f.* substitution, deputyship.

suppléant [syple'ɑ̃], *a.* and *n.m.* (*fem.* -e) substitute, assistant, deputy, understudy.

suppléer [syple'e], *v.t.* to supply, to fill up; to take the place of.—*v.i.* to make up the deficiency, to compensate for (*à*).

supplément [syple'mɑ̃], *n.m.* supplement; additional price, excess fare.

supplémentaire [syplemɑ̃'tɛ:r], *a.* supplementary, supplemental, additional, extra.

suppliant [sypli'ɑ̃], *a.* suppliant, beseeching. —*n.m.* (*fem.* -e) suppliant, supplicant, petitioner.

supplication [syplika'sjɔ̃], *n.f.* supplication, entreaty.

supplice [sy'plis], *n.m.* corporal punishment; torture; (*fig.*) torment, ordeal; *être au supplice*, to be upon the rack.

supplicié [sypli'sje], *n.m.* (*fem.* -ée) executed criminal.

supplicier [sypli'sje], *v.t.* to put to death, to execute.

supplier [sypli'e], *v.t.* to beseech, to entreat, to beg.

supplique [sy'plik], *n.f.* petition, entreaty.

support [sy'pɔ:r], *n.m.* support, prop; rest, stand, bracket.

supportable [sypɔr'tabl], *a.* supportable, bearable, tolerable.

supportablement [sypɔrtablə'mɑ̃], *adv.* tolerably.

supporter (1) [sypɔr'tœ:r], *n.m.* (*Spt.*) supporter, partisan.

supporter (2) [sypɔr'te], *v.t.* to support, to uphold; to endure, to suffer; to stand. **se supporter**, *v.r.* to be borne; to bear with each other.

supposable [sypo'zabl], *a.* supposable.

supposé [sypo'ze], *a.* pretended, forged, assumed; reputed.

supposer [sypo'ze], *v.t.* to suppose; to admit, to imply; to conjecture; to forge (*a will*).

supposition [sypozi'sjɔ̃], *n.f.* supposition; substitution; forgery.

suppôt [sy'po], *n.m.* agent, tool, abettor.

suppressif [sypre'sif], *a.* (*fem.* -ive) suppressive.

suppression [sypre'sjɔ̃], *n.f.* suppression; cancelling (*of passage*); concealment.

supprimer [sypri'me], *v.t.* to suppress; to omit; to abolish, to cancel.

suppuration [sypyra'sjɔ̃], *n.f.* suppuration.

suppurer [sypy're], *v.i.* to suppurate, to run.

supputation [sypyta'sjɔ̃], *n.f.* computation, calculation.

supputer [sypy'te], *v.t.* to calculate, to compute, to reckon.

suprématie [syprema'si], *n.f.* supremacy.

suprême [sy'prɛ:m], *a.* supreme, highest; last.

suprêmement [syprɛmə'mɑ̃], *adv.* supremely.

sur (1) [syr], *prep.* on, upon; over; in; towards; about; concerning; out of.

sur (2) [sy:r], *a.* sour, tart.

sûr [sy:r], *a.* sure, certain; safe, secure; firm, steady; trustworthy; *à coup sûr*, for certain; *en lieu sûr*, in a place of safety; *je* *suis sûr de vous*, I can depend on you; *sûr et certain*, positive.

surabondamment [syrabɔ̃da'mɑ̃], *adv.* superabundantly.

surabondance [syrabɔ̃'dɑ̃:s], *n.f.* superabundance; glut.

surabondant [syrabɔ̃'dɑ̃], *a.* superabundant.

surabonder [syrabɔ̃'de], *v.i.* to superabound; to be glutted (*de*).

suraigu [syre'gy], *a.* (*fem.* -ë) overshrill; very acute (*inflammation*).

suralimenté [syralimɑ̃'te], *a.* overfed.

suralimenter [syralimɑ̃'te], *v.t.* to overfeed, to feed up; (*Motor.*) to supercharge.

suranné [syra'ne], *a.* expired; superannuated, antiquated.

surcharge [syr'ʃarʒ], *n.f.* overloading; (*stamp*) surcharge; excess.

surcharger [syrʃar'ʒe], *v.t.* (*conjug. like* MANGER) to overload, to overtax; (*fig.*) to overwhelm; to oppress; *surcharger d'impôts*, to overtax.

surchauffer [syrʃo'fe], *v.t.* to overheat.

surclasser [syrklɑ'se], *v.t.* to outclass.

surcompresseur [syrkɔ̃prɛ'sœ:r], *n.m.* supercharger.

surcompression [syrkɔ̃prɛ'sjɔ̃], *n.f.* supercharging.

surcomprimé [syrkɔ̃pri'me], *a.* supercharged.

surcroît [syr'krwa], *n.m.* addition, increase; surplus, excess.

surcuit [syr'kɥi], *a.* overdone.

surdité [syrdi'te], *n.f.* deafness.

sureau [sy'ro], *n.m.* (*pl.* -eaux) elder (tree).

surélever [syrel've], *v.t.* (*conjug. like* AMENER) to raise higher; (*Golf*) to tee.

sûrement [syr'mɑ̃], *adv.* surely, certainly, to be sure; safely.

surenchère [syrɑ̃'ʃɛ:r], *n.f.* higher bid, outbidding.

surenchérir [syrɑ̃ʃe'ri:r], *v.i.* to overbid, to bid higher.

surestimation [syrɛstima'sjɔ̃], *n.f.* overestimate, overvaluation.

surestimer [syrɛsti'me], *v.t.* to overestimate; to overrate.

sûreté [syr'te], *n.f.* safety, security; warranty; *la Sûreté*, Criminal Investigation Department.

surexcitation [syrɛksita'sjɔ̃], *n.f.* excitement, overexcitement.

surexciter [syrɛksi'te], *v.t.* to overexcite.

surexposer [syrɛkspo'ze], *v.t.* (*Phot.*) to overexpose.

surexposition [syrɛkspozi'sjɔ̃], *n.f.* (*Phot.*) overexposure.

surface [syr'fas], *n.f.* surface; outside.

surfaire [syr'fɛ:r], *v.t. irr.* (*conjug. like* FAIRE) to ask too much for; to overrate, to overpraise.

surfin [syr'fɛ̃], *a.* (*Comm.*) superfine.

surgir [syr'ʒi:r], *v.i.* to rise, to surge; to loom up.

surgissement [syrʒis'mɑ̃], *n.m.* upheaval.

surhomme [sy'rɔm], *n.m.* superman.

surhumain [syry'mɛ̃], *a.* superhuman.

surintendant [syrɛ̃tɑ̃'dɑ̃], *n.m.* superintendent, overseer; steward (*of large estate*).

surintendante [syrɛ̃tɑ̃'dɑ̃:t], *n.f.* woman superintendent; superintendent's wife.

surir [sy'ri:r], *v.i.* to turn sour.

sur-le-champ [syrlə'ʃɑ̃], *adv.* at once.

surlendemain [syrlãd'mɛ̃], *n.m.* two days after.

surmenage [syrmə'na:ʒ], *n.m.* excess fatigue; overworking.

surmener [syrmə'ne], *v.t.* (*conjug. like* AMENER) to overwork, to overtire. **se surmener**, *v.r.* to overwork.

surmontable [syrmɔ̃'tabl], *a.* surmountable, superable.

surmonter [syrmɔ̃'te], *v.t.* to surmount; to overcome; to surpass.

surmultiplication [syrmyltiplika'sjɔ̃], *n.f.* (*Motor.*) overdrive.

surnager [syrna'ʒe], *v.i.* (*conjug. like* MANGER) to float on the surface; (*fig.*) to survive.

surnaturel [syrnaty'rɛl], *a.* (*fem.* **-elle**) supernatural.—*n.m.* supernatural.

surnaturellement [syrnatyrɛl'mã], *adv.* supernaturally.

surnom [syr'nɔ̃], *n.m.* nickname.

surnommer [syrnɔ'me], *v.t.* to nickname.

surnuméraire [syrnyme'rɛ:r], *a.* and *n.m.* supernumerary.

surpasser [syrpa'se], *v.t.* to surpass, to excel, to outdo, to exceed.

surpeuplé [syrpœ'ple], *a.* overpopulated.

surpeuplement [syrpœplə'mã], *n.m.* overpopulation, overcrowding.

surplis [syr'pli], *n.m. inv.* surplice.

surplomb [syr'plɔ̃], *n.m.* overhang (*of buildings*); **en surplomb**, overhanging.

surplomber [syrplɔ̃'be], *v.t., v.i.* to overhang.

surplus [syr'ply], *n.m. inv.* surplus, remainder, excess.

surpoids [syr'pwa], *n.m.* overweight, excess weight.

surprenant [syrprə'nã], *a.* surprising, astonishing.

surprendre [syr'prã:dr], *v.t. irr.* (*conjug. like* PRENDRE) to surprise, to catch; to overhear; to entrap; to intercept. **se surprendre**, *v.r.* to surprise oneself; to catch oneself (*napping etc.*).

surprise [syr'pri:z], *n.f.* surprise; amazement.

surproduction [syrprɔdyk'sjɔ̃], *n.f.* overproduction.

surréalisme [syrrea'lism], *n.m.* surrealism.

surréaliste [syrrea'list], *a.* and *n.* surrealist.

sursaut [syr'so], *n.m.* start, jump.

sursauter [syrso'te], *v.i.* to start up; *faire sursauter* (*quelqu'un*), to startle (someone).

surseoir [syr'swa:r], *v.t., v.i. irr.* to suspend, to delay, to postpone.

sursis [syr'si], *n.m.* delay, respite, reprieve.

surtaxe [syr'taks], *n.f.* surtax; surcharge.

surtaxer [syrtak'se], *v.t.* to overtax.

surtout [syr'tu], *adv.* above all, chiefly.—*n.m.* overcoat; centrepiece (*for table*).

surveillance [syrvɛ'jã:s], *n.f.* supervision; surveillance.

surveillant [syrvɛ'jã], *n.m.* (*fem.* **-e**) inspector, superintendent; supervisor.

surveiller [syrvɛ'je], *v.t.* to superintend, to inspect; to watch, to supervise.

survenir [syrvə'ni:r], *v.i. irr.* (*conjug. like* TENIR, *but with aux.* ÊTRE) to arrive or happen unexpectedly; to drop in.

survêtement [syrvɛt'mã], *n.m.* (*Spt.*) track suit.

survivant [syrvi'vã], *a.* surviving.—*n.m.* (*fem.* **-e**) survivor.

survivre [syr'vi:vr], *v.i. irr.* (*conjug. like* VIVRE) to survive, to outlive someone (*à*). **se survivre**, *v.r.* to live or exist again.

survoler [syrvɔ'le], *v.t.* to fly over (*of aircraft*).

sus [sys], *prep.* upon; *en sus*, over and above. —*int.* courage! come on!

susceptibilité [sysɛptibili'te], *n.f.* susceptibility; irritability.

susceptible [sysɛp'tibl], *a.* susceptible, capable; likely to; touchy; irascible.

susciter [sysi'te], *v.t.* to raise up, to set up; to create; to arouse, to instigate.

suscription [syskrip'sjɔ̃], *n.f.* superscription, address.

susdit [sys'di], *a.* and *n.m.* (*fem.* **-e**) aforesaid.

suspect [sys'pɛkt, sys'pɛ], *a.* suspected, suspicious, suspect, doubtful.—*n.m.* suspect.

suspecter [syspɛk'te], *v.t.* to suspect.

suspendre [sys'pã:dr], *v.t.* to suspend, to hang up; to delay, to defer.

suspendu [syspã'dy], *a.* suspended, hung up; in suspense.

suspens [sys'pã], *adv. phr.* **en suspens**, in suspense; (*person*) in doubt; (*thing*) in abeyance.

suspension [syspã'sjɔ̃], *n.f.* suspension, interruption; hanging lamp.

suspicion [syspi'sjɔ̃], *n.f.* suspicion.

susurration [sysyra'sjɔ̃], *n.f.*, **susurrement** [sysyr'mã], *n.m.* susurration, whispering, murmur; rustling.

suttée [sy'te], **suttie** [sy'ti], *n.f.* suttee.

suture [sy'ty:r], *n.f.* suture; joint; stitching.

Suzanne [sy'zan], *f.* Susan.

suzerain [syz'rɛ̃], *a.* paramount, suzerain.—*n.m.* (*fem.* **-e**) suzerain, lord or lady paramount.

suzeraineté [syzrɛn'te], *n.f.* suzerainty.

svastika [zvasti'ka], *n.m.* swastika.

svelte [zvɛlt], *a.* slender, slim.

sveltesse [zvɛl'tɛs], *n.f.* slenderness, slimness.

sybarite [siba'rit], *a.* sybaritic.—*n.* sybarite, voluptuary.

sycomore [sikɔ'mɔ:r], *n.m.* sycamore.

sycophante [sikɔ'fã:t], *a.* sycophantic.—*n.m.* informer; hypocrite, impostor; sycophant, (*fam.*) toady.

syllabe [sil'lab], *n.f.* syllable.

syllabique [silla'bik], *a.* syllabic.

syllogisme [sillɔ'ʒism], *n.m.* syllogism.

sylphe [silf], *n.m.*, **sylphide** [sil'fid], *n.f.* sylph.

sylvain [sil'vɛ̃], *n.m.* sylvan.

sylvestre [sil'vɛstr], *a.* sylvan, growing in woods.

Sylvie [sil'vi], *f.* Sylvia.

symbole [sɛ̃'bɔl], *n.m.* symbol, sign, emblem; creed.

symbolique [sɛ̃bɔ'lik], *a.* symbolic, symbolical.

symboliser [sɛ̃bɔli'ze], *v.t.* to symbolize.

symbolisme [sɛ̃bɔ'lism], *n.m.* symbolism.

symétrie [sime'tri], *n.f.* symmetry.

symétrique [sime'trik], *a.* symmetrical.

symétriquement [simetrik'mã], *adv.* symmetrically.

sympathie [sɛ̃pa'ti], *n.f.* liking, fellow feeling.

sympathique [sɛ̃pa'tik], *a.* congenial, likeable.

sympathisant

sympathisant [sɛpati'zɑ̃], *a.* sympathizing.—*n.m. (Pol.)* fellow traveller.
sympathiser [sɛpati'ze], *v.i.* to get on well together.
symphonie [sɛ̃fɔ'ni], *n.f.* symphony.
symptomatique [sɛ̃ptɔma'tik], *a.* symptomatic.
symptôme [sɛ̃p'to:m], *n.m.* symptom; indication, sign; token.
synagogue [sina'gɔg], *n.f.* synagogue.
synchronisation [sɛ̃krɔniza'sjɔ̃], *n.f.* synchronization.
synchroniser [sɛ̃krɔni'ze], *v.t.* to synchronize.
syncope [sɛ̃'kɔp], *n.f.* syncope, swoon, fainting fit; *(Mus.)* syncopation.
syndic [sɛ̃'dik], *n.m.* syndic, trustee; assignee *(in bankruptcy).*
syndicalisme [sɛ̃dika'lism], *n.m.* **syndicalisme ouvrier,** trade-unionism.
syndicaliste [sɛ̃dika'list], *a.* and *n.* trade-unionist.
syndicat [sɛ̃di'ka], *n.m.* syndicate, trusteeship; **syndicat d'initiative,** tourists' information bureau; **syndicat ouvrier,** trade union.
synonyme [sinɔ'nim], *a.* synonymous.—*n.m.* synonym.
syntaxe [sɛ̃'taks], *n.f.* syntax.
synthétique [sɛ̃te'tik], *a.* synthetic.
syriaque [si'rjak], *a.* Syriac.—*n.m.* Syriac *(language).*
Syrie [si'ri], **la,** *f.* Syria.
syrien [si'rjɛ̃], *a.* Syrian.—*n.m.* Syrian *(language);* (**Syrien,** *fem.* **-enne**) Syrian *(person).*
systématique [sistema'tik], *a.* systematic(al).
systématiquement [sistematik'mɑ̃], *adv.* systematically.
système [sis'tɛm], *n.m.* system, scheme, plan; device.

T

T, t [te], *n.m.* the twentieth letter of the alphabet.
t' [t], *elision* [TE].
ta [ta], [TON (I)].
tabac [ta'ba], *n.m.* tobacco; snuff.
tabatière [taba'tjɛ:r], *n.f.* snuff box.
tabernacle [tabɛr'nakl], *n.m.* tent; tabernacle.
table [tabl], *n.f.* table; board *(food, fare);* mess *(of officers etc.);* slab; face *(of anvil etc.);* table of contents etc.; **faire table rase,** to make a clean sweep; **mettre** or **dresser la table,** to lay the table.
tableau [ta'blo], *n.m. (pl.* **-eaux**) picture, painting, tableau; scene; description; list; blackboard.
tablée [ta'ble], *n.f.* company at table.
tablette [ta'blɛt], *n.f.* shelf; tablet; slab, bar *(of chocolate);* (*Pharm.*) lozenge; note-book.
tablier [ta'blje], *n.m.* apron *(in all senses);* chess *or* checker board.
tabou [ta'bu], *a.* and *n.m.* taboo.

tabouret [tabu'rɛ], *n.m.* stool, foot-stool.
tabourin [tabu'rɛ̃], *n.m.* chimney cowl.
tabulateur [tabyla'tœ:r], *n.m.* tabulator; *(Teleph.)* dial.
tachant [ta'ʃɑ̃], *a.* easily soiled.
tache [taʃ], *n.f.* spot, stain; *(fig.)* blot.
tâche [tɑ:ʃ], *n.f.* task, job.
tacher [ta'ʃe], *v.t.* to stain, to spot; *(fig.)* to taint.
tâcher [tɑ'ʃe], *v.i.* to try, to endeavor, to strive.
tacheter [taʃ'te], *v.t. (conjug. like* APPELER) to fleck, to speckle, to mottle.
tacite [ta'sit], *a.* tacit, implied.
tacitement [tasit'mɑ̃], *adv.* tacitly.
taciturne [tasi'tyrn], *a.* taciturn.
taciturnité [tasityrni'te], *n.f.* taciturnity.
tact [takt], *n.m.* feeling, touch; tact.
tacticien [takti'sjɛ̃], *n.m.* tactician.
tactile [tak'til], *a.* tactile.
tactilité [taktili'te], *n.f.* tactility.
tactique [tak'tik], *a.* tactical.—*n.f.* tactics; *(fig.)* stratagem, move.
taffetas [taf'ta], *n.m.* taffeta.
taie (I) [tɛ], *n.f.* **taie d'oreiller,** pillow-case.
taie (2) [tɛ], *n.f.* film, speck *(in the eye).*
taillade [tɑ'jad], *n.f.* slash, gash, cut.
taillader [tɑja'de], *v.t.* to slash, to cut, to gash.
taillant [tɑ'jɑ̃], *n.m.* edge *(of a knife etc.).*
taille [tɑ:j], *n.f.* cutting, cut, fashion; edge *(of a sword);* height, stature; waist, figure; *(Hort.)* pruning; **de taille à,** quite capable of.
taillé [tɑ'je], *a.* cut, carved; well-built *(person).*
taille-crayon [tɑjkrɛ'jɔ̃], *n.m. (pl.* **-crayons**) pencil sharpener.
taille-ongles [tɑj'ɔ̃:gl], *n.m. inv.* nail clippers.
tailler [tɑ'je], *v.t.* to cut, to cut out; to carve; to hew; to prune; to sharpen; to shape; to deal *(cards).*
tailleur [tɑ'jœ:r], *n.m.* tailor; cutter; hewer; *(woman's two-piece)* suit.
tailleuse [tɑ'jø:z], *n.f.* tailoress.
taillis [tɑ'ji], *n.m. inv.* copse; brushwood.
tain [tɛ̃], *n.m.* foil; silvering *(for mirrors).*
taire [tɛ:r], *v.t. irr.* to say nothing of, to pass over in silence, to suppress, to keep dark. **se taire,** *v.r.* to be silent; to remain unsaid.
talc [talk], *n.m.* talc, talcum powder.
talent [ta'lɑ̃], *n.m.* talent; *(fig.)* ability.
talion [ta'ljɔ̃], *n.m.* talion, retaliation.
talisman [talis'mɑ̃], *n.m.* talisman.
taloche [ta'lɔʃ], *n.f.* cuff, thump, buffet.
talocher [talɔ'ʃe], *v.t.* to cuff, to box *(someone's)* ears.
talon [ta'lɔ̃], *n.m.* heel; counterfoil, stub.
talonner [talɔ'ne], *v.t.* to be close on the heels of; to press hard, to spur.—*v.i. (Naut.)* to ground; *(Ftb.)* to heel out *(of the scrum).*
talonneur [talɔ'nœ:r], *n.m. (Ftb.)* hooker.
talus [ta'ly], *n.m.* slope, ramp; embankment.
talutage [taly'ta:ʒ], *n.m.* sloping, embanking.
tamarin [tama'rɛ̃], *n.m.* tamarind.
tamaris [tama'ris], **tamarisc** [tama'risk], *n.m.* tamarisk.
tambour [tɑ̃'bu:r], *n.m.* drum; drummer; embroidery frame; *(Anat.)* tympanum; **tambour de ville,** town crier.
tambourin [tɑ̃bu'rɛ̃], *n.m.* Provençal tabor.
tambourinage [tɑ̃buri'na:ʒ], *n.m.* drumming.
tambouriner [tɑ̃buri'ne], *v.t.* to advertise.—*v.i.* to drum, to tattoo.

tambour-major [tāburma'ʒɔ:r], *n.m.* (*pl.* **tambours-majors**) drum major.
tamis [ta'mi], *n.m. inv.* sieve, sifter, strainer.
tamisage [tami'za:ʒ], *n.m.* sifting, straining.
Tamise [ta'mi:z], **la**, *f.* the Thames.
tamiser [tami'ze], *v.t.* to sift, to strain; to filter.
tamiseur [tami'zœ:r], *n.m.* (*fem.* **-euse**) sifter.
tampon [tā'pɔ̃], *n.m.* stopper; plug; bung; buffer; pad (*used in engraving etc.*).
tamponnement [tāpɔn'mā], *n.m.* plugging, stopping; (*Rail.*) head-on collision.
tamponner [tāpɔ'ne], *v.t.* to plug, to stop up; to run into (*another train etc.*). **se tamponner**, *v.r.* to collide.
tan [tā], *a. inv.* tan(-colored). —*n.m.* tan; tanner's bark.
tancer [tā'se], *v.t.* (*conjug. like* COMMENCER) to rate, to lecture, to scold.
tanche [tā:ʃ], *n.f.* tench.
tandem [tā'dɛm], *n.m.* tandem.
tandis [tā'di] **que**, *conj. phr.* while; whereas.
tangage [tā'ga:ʒ], *n.m.* pitching (*of ship, airplane*).
tangent [tā'ʒā], *a.* tangential.—*n.f.* (**-e**) tangent.
tangible [tā'ʒibl], *a.* tangible.
tangiblement [tāʒiblə'mā], *adv.* tangibly.
tangue [tā:g], *n.f.* slimy sand (*used as manure*).
tanguer [tā'ge], *v.i.* (*Naut.*) to pitch.
tanière [ta'njɛ:r], *n.f.* den, hole, lair (*of beasts*).
tank [tāk], *n.m.* (*Mil.*) tank.
tannage [ta'na:ʒ], *n.m.* tanning.
tannant [ta'nā], *a.* tanning; (*pop.*) tiresome, annoying.
tanné [ta'ne], *a.* tanned, sunburnt (*skin*); tawny.—*n.m.* tan (*color*).
tanner [ta'ne], *v.t.* to tan; (*pop.*) to tease; to beat.
tannerie [tan'ri], *n.f.* tan-yard, tannery.
tanneur [ta'nœ:r], *n.m.* tanner.
tant [tā], *adv.* so much, such; so many; as much, as many; to such a degree, so; so far; so long, as long; **tant bien que mal**, somehow or other, after a fashion; **tant pis**, too bad, never mind.
tantaliser [tātali'ze], *v.t.* to tantalize.
tante [tā:t], *n.f.* aunt; (*pop.*) pawnbroker, 'uncle'.
tantôt [tā'to], *adv.* presently, by and by, anon; soon; a little while ago, just now; sometimes.
Tanzanie [tāza'ni], **la**, *f.* Tanzania.
taon [tā], *n.m.* botfly, gadfly, cleg.
tapage [ta'pa:ʒ], *n.m.* noise, uproar, row; (*colloq.*) show.
tapageur [tapa'ʒœ:r], *a.* (*fem.* **-euse**) rackety, boisterous, noisy; flashy.—*n.m.* (*fem.* **-euse**) noisy person, blusterer.
tape [tap], *n.f.* rap, slap, tap, thump.
taper [ta'pe], *v.t.* to hit, to slap; to smack, to tap.—*v.i.* to hit, to stamp; to strum; to beat down (*of sun*).
tapinois [tapi'nwa], *only in* **en tapinois**, *adv. phr.* stealthily, slyly.
tapioca [tapjɔ'ka], *n.m.* tapioca.
tapir [ta'pi:r], *n.m.* tapir (*animal*).
tapir (**se**) [səta'pi:r], *v.r.* to squat, to crouch, to cower, to lurk.

tapis [ta'pi], *n.m.* carpet, rug; cover cloth (*for tables etc.*).
tapis-brosse [tapi'brɔs], *n.m.* (*pl.* **-brosses**) door-mat.
tapisser [tapi'se], *v.t.* to hang with tapestry; to cover; to deck, to adorn; to paper; to carpet.
tapisserie [tapis'ri], *n.f.* tapestry, hangings; wallpaper; upholstery.
tapissier [tapi'sje], *n.m.* (*fem.* **-ière**) upholsterer; tapestry worker.
tapoter [tapɔ'te], *v.t.* to pat, to tap; to strum.
taquin [ta'kɛ̃], *a.* teasing.—*n.m.* (*fem.* **-e**) tease, teasing person.
taquiner [taki'ne], *v.t.* to tease, to plague.
taquinerie [takin'ri], *n.f.* teasing; teasing disposition.
tard [ta:r], *adv.* late.—*n.m.* late hour.
tarder [tar'de], *v.i.* to delay; to tarry, to loiter; to be long; (*impers.*) to long (*de*).
tardif [tar'dif], *a.* (*fem.* **-dive**) tardy, late; slow, belated; backward.
tardivement [tardiv'mā], *adv.* tardily, slowly, belatedly.
tare [ta:r], *n.f.* tare; (*Comm.*) waste, damage; (*fig.*) blemish, defect.
taré [ta're], *a.* damaged, spoiled; disreputable.
tarentule [tarā'tyl], *n.f.* tarantula.
tarer [ta're], *v.t.* to injure, to damage, to spoil; (*Comm.*) to tare. **se tarer**, *v.r.* to spoil, to deteriorate.
targuer (**se**) [sətar'ge], *v.r.* to boast, to brag.
tarif [ta'rif], *n.m.* tariff, rate, scale of prices.
tarifer [tari'fe], *v.t.* to tariff, to price, to rate.
tarir [ta'ri:r], *v.t.* to dry up; to exhaust.—*v.i.* to dry up; to be exhausted; to cease. **se tarir**, *v.r.* to dry up.
tarissable [tari'sabl], *a.* exhaustible.
tarissement [taris'mā], *n.m.* exhausting, drying up.
tartan [tar'tā], *n.m.* tartan, plaid.
tarte [tart], *n.f.* tart; flan.
tartelette [tar'tlɛt], *n.f.* tartlet.
tartine [tar'tin], *n.f.* slice of bread (*with butter, jam etc.*).
tartufe [tar'tyf], *n.m.* hypocrite.
tas [tɑ], *n.m. inv.* heap, pile; (*fig.*) lot, set (*of persons etc.*).
Tasmanie [tasma'ni], **la**, *f.* Tasmania.
tasmanien [tasma'njɛ̃], *a.* Tasmanian.—*n.m.* (**Tasmanien**, *fem.* **-enne**) Tasmanian (*person*).
tasse [tɑ:s], *n.f.* cup.
tassement [tas'mā], *n.m.* settling, sinking, subsidence.
tasser [tɑ'se], *v.t.* to heap *or* pile up; to compress, to squeeze, to cram.—*v.i.* to grow thick. **se tasser**, *v.r.* to sink, to settle, to subside; to huddle together (*of persons*).
tâter [tɑ'te], *v.t.* to feel; to try, to taste; to sound, to test.—*v.i.* to taste, to try (*de or à*). **se tâter**, *v.r.* to examine oneself.
tatillon [tati'jɔ̃], *a.* (*fem.* **-onne**) niggling, finical.
tâtonnement [tatɔn'mā], *n.m.* groping.
tâtonner [tatɔ'ne], *v.i.* to feel one's way, to grope.
tâtons (**à**) [atɑ'tɔ̃], *adv. phr.* gropingly.
tatouage [ta'twa:ʒ], *n.m.* tattooing.
tatouer [ta'twe], *v.t.* to tattoo.
taudis [to'di], *n.m.* hovel, slum, hole.
taupe [to:p], *n.f.* mole; moleskin.

taupier [to'pje], *n.m.* mole catcher.
taupière [to'pjɛːr], *n.f.* mole trap.
taupinière [topi'njɛːr], **taupinée** [topi'ne], *n.f.* mole-hill; hillock, knoll.
taure [toːr], *n.f.* heifer.
taureau [tɔ'ro], *n.m.* (*pl.* **-eaux**) bull; (*Astron.*) Taurus.
taux [to], *n.m. inv.* price, rate; rate of interest.
taverne [ta'vɛrn], *n.f.* tavern, café, restaurant.
tavernier [tavɛr'nje], *n.m.* (*fem.* **-ière**) innkeeper.
taxation [taksɑ'sjɔ̃], *n.f.* taxation; fixing of prices.
taxe [taks], *n.f.* tax; duty, rate; fixing of prices; controlled price.
taxer [tak'se], *v.t.* to tax; to rate, to fix the price of; to accuse (*de*).
taxi [tak'si], *n.m.* taxi (-cab).
taxiphone [taksi'fɔn], *n.m.* public telephone booth.
Tchécoslovaquie [tʃekɔslɔva'ki], **la**, *f.* Czechoslovakia.
t'chèque [tʃɛk], *a.* Czech.—*n.m.* Czech (*language*).—*n.* (**Tchèque**) Czech (*person*).
te [tə, t], *pron. obj.* *thee, you.
technicien [tɛkni'sjɛ̃], *n.m.* (*fem.* **-enne**) technician.
technique [tɛk'nik], *a.* technical.—*n.f.* technique.
techniquement [tɛknik'mɑ̃], *adv.* technically.
technologie [tɛknɔlɔ'ʒi], *n.f.* technology.
technologique [tɛknɔlɔ'ʒik], *a.* technological.
technologue [tɛknɔ'lɔg], *n.* technologist.
teck or **tek** [tɛk], *n.m.* teak, teak-wood.
teigne [tɛɲ], *n.f.* tinea (*moth*); tinea (*skin disease, such as ringworm*).
teigneux [tɛ'ɲø], *a.* (*fem.* **-euse**) scurvy.—*n.m.* (*fem.* **-euse**) scurfy person.
teindre [tɛ̃:dr], *v.t. irr.* (*conjug. like* CRAINDRE) to dye, to stain.
teint [tɛ̃], *n.m.* dye, color; complexion; hue.
teinte [tɛ̃:t], *n.f.* tint, color, shade, hue; (*fig.*) smack, touch.
teinter [tɛ̃'te], *v.t.* to tint; to give a color to.
teinture [tɛ̃'ty:r], *n.f.* dye; dyeing; color, hue; (*Pharm.*) tincture.
teinturerie [tɛ̃ty'ri], *n.f.* dyeing; dye works; dry cleaning.
teinturier [tɛ̃ty'rje], *n.m.* (*fem.* **-ière**) dyer; dry cleaner.
tek [TECK].
tel [tɛl], *a.* (*fem.* **telle**) such; like, similar.—*pron. indef.* such a one; **M. un tel**, Mr. So-and-so.
télécommande [telekɔ'mɑ̃:d], *n.f.* remote control.
télécommunications [telekɔmynikɑ'sjɔ̃], *n.f. pl.* telecommunications.
télégramme [tele'gram], *n.m.* telegram.
télégraphe [tele'graf], *n.m.* telegraph.
télégraphie [telegra'fi], *n.f.* telegraphy; **télégraphie sans fil**, wireless telegraphy.
télégraphier [telegra'fje], *v.t., v.i.* to telegraph; to wire, to cable.
télégraphique [telegra'fik], *a.* telegraphic.
télégraphiste [telegra'fist], *n.* telegraphist.
téléguidé [telegi'de], *a.* guided; **engin téléguidé**, guided missile.
téléimprimeur [teleɛ̃pri'mœːr], **télescripteur** [teleskrip'tœːr], *n.m.* teleprinter.
télémètre [tele'mɛtr], *n.m.* rangefinder.

télépathie [telepa'ti], *n.f.* telepathy.
télépathique [telepa'tik], *a.* telepathic.
téléphérique [telefe'rik], *a.* and *n.m.* teleferic.
téléphone [tele'fɔn], *n.m.* telephone; **un coup de téléphone**, a telephone call.
téléphoner [telefɔ'ne], *v.t., v.i.* to telephone, to ring up.
téléphonique [telefɔ'nik], *a.* **cabine téléphonique**, telephone booth.
téléphoniste [telefɔ'nist], *n.* telephone operator.
télescope [telɛs'kɔp], *n.m.* telescope.
télescopique [telɛskɔ'pik], *a.* telescopic.
téléscripteur [teleskrip'tœːr], [TÉLÉIMPRIMEUR].
téléspectateur [telespɛktɑ'tœːr], *n.m.* (*fem.* **-trice**) televiewer.
téléviser [televi'ze], *v.t.* to televise.
téléviseur [televi'zœːr], *n.m.* television (receiving-)set.
télévision [televi'zjɔ̃], *n.f.* television.
tellement [tɛl'mɑ̃], *adv.* so, in such a manner; so much, so far.
téméraire [teme'rɛːr], *a.* rash, reckless.—*n.* reckless person, daredevil.
témérairement [temerɛr'mɑ̃], *adv.* rashly, recklessly.
témérité [temeri'te], *n.f.* temerity.
témoignage [temwa'naːʒ], *n.m.* testimony, evidence, witness; testimonial; (*fig.*) token, mark, proof.
témoigner [temwa'ne], *v.t.* to testify; to show, to prove, to be the sign of.—*v.i.* to testify, to give evidence (*de*).
témoin [te'mwɛ̃], *n.m.* witness, evidence, proof, mark; second (*in duels*).
tempe [tɑ̃:p], *n.f.* (*Anat.*) temple.
tempérament [tɑ̃pera'mɑ̃], *n.m.* constitution, temperament; temper; (*fig.*) moderation, compromise; **à tempérament**, by instalments.
tempérance [tɑ̃pe'rɑ̃:s], *n.f.* temperance.
température [tɑ̃pera'ty:r], *n.f.* temperature.
tempéré [tɑ̃pe're], *a.* temperate (*of climate*); limited, constitutional (*of governments*); restrained, sober (*of style*).
tempérer [tɑ̃pe're], *v.t.* (*conjug. like* CÉDER) to temper, to moderate, to allay; to assuage, to check. **se tempérer**, *v.r.* to become mild (*of the weather*).
tempête [tɑ̃'pɛːt], *n.f.* storm, tempest.
tempêter [tɑ̃pe'te], *v.i.* to storm, to bluster, to fume.
tempétueusement [tɑ̃petɥøz'mɑ̃], *adv.* tempestuously, violently.
tempétueux [tɑ̃pe'tɥø], *a.* (*fem.* **-euse**) tempestuous, boisterous, stormy.
temple [tɑ̃:pl], *n.m.* temple; French Protestant church.
templier [tɑ̃pli'e], *n.m.* Knight Templar.
temporaire [tɑ̃pɔ'rɛːr], *a.* temporary.
temporairement [tɑ̃pɔrɛr'mɑ̃], *adv.* temporarily, provisionally.
temporel [tɑ̃pɔ'rɛl], *a.* (*fem.* **-elle**) temporal.
temporisateur [tɑ̃pɔriza'tœːr], *a.* (*fem.* **-trice**) procrastinating, temporizing.—*n.m.* (*fem.* **-trice**) temporizer, procrastinator.
temporisation [tɑ̃pɔriza'sjɔ̃], *n.f.* temporizing, procrastination.
temporiser [tɑ̃pɔri'ze], *v.i.* to temporize, to delay.

temps [tā], *n.m. inv.* time, while, period, term; occasion; season; weather; (*Gram.*) tense; *à temps*, in time; *avec le temps*, in course of time; *dans le temps*, formerly; *en temps et lieu*, in proper time and place.

tenable [tə'nabl], *a.* tenable; bearable.

tenace [tə'nas], *a.* tenacious, adhesive, sticky.

ténacité [tenasi'te], *n.f.* tenacity, toughness; retentiveness (*of memory*).

tenaille [tə'naːj], *n.f.* (*usu. in pl.*) pincers, nippers, pliers.

tenailler [tənɑ'je], *v.t.* to torture with red-hot pincers; (*fig.*) to torture.

tenant [tə'nɑ̃], *a.* *séance tenante*, during the sitting; forthwith, then and there.—*n.m.* titlist (*at a tournament*); (*fig.*) champion, defender.

tendance [tɑ̃'dɑ̃ːs], *n.f.* tendency; leaning, bent, inclination.

tendancieux [tɑ̃dɑ̃'sjø], *a.* (*fem.* **-euse**) tendentious; insinuating, suggestive.

tendeur [tɑ̃'dœːr], *n.m.* (*fem* **-euse**) spreader, layer, setter (*of snares*); wire-stretcher.

tendoir [tɑ̃'dwaːr], *n.m.* clothes-line.

tendon [tɑ̃'dɔ̃], *n.m.* tendon, sinew.

tendre (1) [tɑ̃ːdr], *a.* tender, soft; delicate, sensitive; affectionate; moving; early, young, new.

tendre (2) [tɑ̃:dr], *v.t.* to stretch, to strain; to bend (*a bow etc.*); to spread, to lay, to set; to hold out; to pitch (*tents*); to hang (*tapestry etc.*).—*v.i.* to lead; to tend, to conduce.

tendrement [tɑ̃drə'mɑ̃], *adv.* tenderly, affectionately.

tendresse [tɑ̃'drɛs], *n.f.* tenderness, fondness; (*pl.*) endearments.

tendron [tɑ̃'drɔ̃], *n.m.* shoot (*of plants*).

tendu [tɑ̃'dy], *a.* stretched, held out; tight, tense; strained.

ténèbres [te'nɛ:br], *n.f.* (*used only in pl.*) darkness, night, gloom.

ténébreusement [tenebrøz'mɑ̃], *adv.* darkly, gloomily; secretly.

ténébreux [tene'brø], *a.* (*fem.* **-euse**) dark, gloomy, overcast; obscure, mysterious.

teneur (1) [tə'nœːr], *n.f.* tenor, terms, text; purport.

teneur (2) [tə'nœːr], *n.m.* (*fem.* **-euse**) holder; *teneur de livres*, book-keeper.

ténia [te'nja], *n.m.* tapeworm.

tenir [tə'niːr], *v.t. irr.* to hold, to have hold of; to have, to possess; to seize; to occupy; to keep, to follow; to retain; to perform; to consider.—*v.i.* to hold; to adhere, to stick; to hold together; to cling; to prize (*à*); to be attached *or* related (*à*); to be contiguous; to depend, to result (*de*); to be held (*of fairs, markets, assemblies etc.*); to take after; to savor; to persist; to resist; to be anxious (*à*). **se tenir**, *v.r.* to hold fast, to remain; to adhere; to consider oneself; to contain oneself, to refrain.

tennis [te'nis], *n.m.* lawn tennis.

tenon [tə'nɔ̃], *n.m.* tenon; bolt (*of fire-arms*).

ténor [te'nɔːr], *n.m.* (*Mus.*) tenor.

tension [tɑ̃'sjɔ̃], *n.f.* tension, strain; tenseness; (*Elec.*) voltage.

tentacule [tɑ̃ta'kyl], *n.m.* tentacle, feeler.

tentant [tɑ̃'tɑ̃], *a.* tempting.

tentateur [tɑ̃ta'tœːr], *a.* (*fem.* **-trice**) tempting.—*n.m.* (*fem.* **-trice**) tempter, temptress.

tentation [tɑ̃ta'sjɔ̃], *n.f.* temptation.

tentative [tɑ̃ta'tiːv], *n.f.* attempt, trial, endeavor.

tente [tɑ̃:t], *n.f.* tent, pavilion; (*Naut.*) awning.

tenter [tɑ̃'te], *v.t.* to attempt, to try; to tempt.

tenture [tɑ̃'tyːr], *n.f.* hangings, tapestry; wall-paper; paper-hanging.

ténu [te'ny], *a.* tenuous, thin, slender.

tenue [tə'ny], *n.f.* holding (*of assemblies etc.*); session; attitude (*of a person*); behavior, bearing; dress; keeping (*of books*); *grande tenue*, (*Mil.*) full dress; *petite tenue*, undress.

ténuité [tenui'te], *n.f.* tenuity, thinness; (*fig.*) insignificance.

tenure [tə'nyːr], *n.f.* tenure.

ter [tɛːr], *adv.* thrice; for the third time.

térébenthine [terebɑ̃'tin], *n.f.* turpentine.

térébinthe [tere'bɛ̃:t], *n.m.* turpentine tree, terebinth.

tergiversation [tɛrʒivɛrsɑ'sjɔ̃], *n.f.* tergiversation, evasion.

tergiverser [tɛrʒivɛr'se], *v.i.* to waver, to beat about the bush.

terme [tɛrm], *n.m.* term; termination, end; limit, boundary; time; three months; quarter's rent; expression; (*pl.*) state, conditions, terms; *avant terme*, prematurely.

terminaison [tɛrmine'zɔ̃], *n.f.* termination, ending.

terminer [tɛrmi'ne], *v.t.* to bound, to limit; to terminate, to conclude. **se terminer**, *v.r.* to terminate; to be bounded.

terminus [tɛrmi'nys], *n.m.* terminus (*of railway*).

terne [tɛrn], *a.* dull, dim; wan; spiritless.

ternir [tɛr'niːr], *v.t.* to dull, to deaden; to tarnish. **se ternir**, *v.r.* to tarnish, to grow dull; to fade (*of colors*).

ternissure [tɛrni'syːr], *n.f.* tarnishing, fading; stain.

terrain [tɛ'rɛ̃], *n.m.* piece of ground; soil, earth; site; field, course.

terrassant [tɛra'sɑ̃], *a.* crushing (*news etc.*).

terrasse [tɛ'ras], *n.f.* terrace; flat roof, balcony.

terrassement [tɛras'mɑ̃], *n.m.* earthwork, embankment; ballasting.

terrasser [tɛra'se], *v.t.* to embank; to throw to the ground; to beat; to confound, to dismay.

terrassier [tɛra'sje], *n.m.* digger, excavator, laborer; earthwork contractor.

terre [tɛːr], *n.f.* earth; land; ground, soil; dominion, territory; grounds, estate, property; (*C*) farm.

terreau [tɛ'ro], *n.m.* (*pl.* **-eaux**) compost.

Terre-Neuve [tɛr'nœ:v], *f.* Newfoundland.

terre-neuve [tɛr'nœ:v], *n.m. inv.* Newfoundland (*dog*).

terrer [tɛ're], *v.t.* to earth up (*a tree etc.*). *v.i.* to burrow. **se terrer**, *v.r.* to dig oneself in.

terrestre [tɛ'rɛstr], *a.* terrestrial, earthly.

terreur [tɛ'rœːr], *n.f.* terror; awe, dread.

terreux [tɛ'rø], *a.* (*fem.* **-euse**) terreous, earthy; dirty; dull (*of colors*); ashen (*of the face*).

terrible [tɛ'ribl], *a.* terrible, dreadful; unmanageable (*of children*).

terriblement [tɛriblə'mã], *adv.* terribly; (*colloq.*) with a vengeance.
terrier [tɛ'rje], *n.m.* burrow, hole; earth (*of fox*); terrier (*dog*).
terrifier [tɛri'fje], *v.t.* to terrify, to dismay.
terrine [tɛ'rin], *n.f.* earthen pan, dish; potted meat.
territoire [tɛri'twa:r], *n.m.* territory, district
territorial [tɛrito'rjal], *a.* (*m. pl.* **-aux**) territorial.
terroir [tɛ'rwa:r], *n.m.* soil, ground; *goût de terroir*, raciness (*of style*); native tang (*of wine*).
terroriser [tɛrɔri'ze], *v.t.* to terrorize.
terrorisme [tɛrɔ'rism], *n.m.* terrorism.
terroriste [tɛrɔ'rist], *n.m.* terrorist.
tertiaire [tɛr'sjɛ:r], *a.* tertiary.
tertre [tɛrtr], *n.m.*, knoll, hillock.
tes [te], [TON (1).]
tesson [tɛ'sɔ̃], *n.m.* potsherd, fragment of broken glass etc.
test [tɛst], *n.m.* shell; trial, test.
testacé [tɛsta'se], *a.* testaceous.—*n.m.* testacean.
testament [tɛsta'mã], *n.m.* will.
tester [tɛs'te], *v.t.* to test.—*v.i.* to make one's will.
testimonial [tɛstimɔ'njal], *a.* (*m. pl.* **-aux**) testifying, testimonial.
tétanos [teta'nɔs], *n.m.* tetanus, lock-jaw.
têtard [te'ta:r], *n.m.* tadpole.
tête [tɛ:t], *n.f.* head; head-piece; face; beginning; top; van, vanguard; (*fig.*) brains, sense, judgment; presence of mind; *en tête*, in one's head; in front, ahead; *mal de tête*, headache; *tête de mort*, skull.
tête-à-tête [tɛta'tɛ:t], *n.m. inv.* tête-à-tête, private interview or conversation; settee (*for two*).
téter [te'te], *v.t.* (*conjug. like* CÉDER) to suck.
têtière [tɛ'tjɛ:r], *n.f.* infant's cap; head-stall (*of a bridle*); antimacassar.
tétin [te'tɛ̃], *n.m.* nipple, teat; breast.
téton [te'tɔ̃], *n.m.* teat; (*fam.*) breast.
tétrarque [te'trark], *n.m.* tetrarch.
tétras [te'trɑ], *n.m. inv.* (*Orn.*) grouse.
têtu [te'ty], *a.* headstrong, stubborn, obstinate.
teutonique [tøtɔ'nik], *a.* teutonic.
texte [tɛkst], *n.m.* text; theme, matter, subject; passage (*of Scripture*).
textile [tɛks'til], *a.* and *n.m.* textile.
textuel [tɛks'tɥɛl], *a.* (*fem.* **-elle**) textual, word for word.
textuellement [tɛkstɥɛl'mã], *adv.* textually.
texture [tɛks'ty:r], *n.f.* texture; disposition.
thaïlandais [tailã'dɛ], *a.* Thai.—*n.m.* Thai (*language*); (**Thaïlandais**, *fem.* **-aise**) Thai (*person*).
Thaïlande [tai'lã:d], **la**, *f.* Thailand, Siam.
thé [te], *n.m.* tea; tea party.
théâtral [teɑ'tral], *a.* (*m. pl.* **-aux**) theatrical.
théâtre [te'ɑ:tr], *n.m.* theatre, playhouse; stage; plays (*collection*), scene; *coup de théâtre*, striking event.
théerie [te'ri], *n.f.* tea plantation.
théière [te'jɛ:r], *n.f.* teapot.
théisme [te'ism], *n.m.* theism.
thème [tɛ:m], *n.m.* topic, subject, theme; (*sch.*) prose, composition.
théodolite [teɔdɔ'lit], *n.m.* theodolite.
théologie [teɔlɔ'ʒi], *n.f.* theology; divinity.

théologien [teɔlɔ'ʒjɛ̃], *n.m.* theologian.
théorème [teɔ'rɛm], *n.m.* theorem.
théorie [teɔ'ri], *n.f.* theory, speculation.
théorique [teɔ'rik], *a.* theoretical.
théoriquement [teɔrik'mã], *adv.* theoretically.
théoriser [teɔri'ze], *v.t., v.i.* to theorize.
théoriste [teɔ'rist], *n.* theorist.
thérapie [tera'pi], *n.f.* therapy.
Thérèse [te'rɛ:z], *f.* Theresa.
thermal [tɛr'mal], *a.* (*m. pl.* **-aux**) thermal; *eaux thermales*, hot springs.
thermomètre [tɛrmɔ'mɛtr], *n.m.* thermometer.
thermos [tɛr'mɔs], *n.m.* thermos (flask).
thermostat [tɛrmɔ'sta], *n.m.* thermostat.
thésauriser [tezɔri'ze], *v.t.* to treasure.—*v.i.* to hoard treasure.
thèse [tɛ:z], *n.f.* thesis, proposition.
thibaude [ti'bo:d], *n.f.* hair-cloth, coarse drugget.
Thomas [tɔ'mɑ], *m.* Thomas.
thon [tɔ̃], *n.m.* tunny-fish.
thoracique [tɔra'sik], *a.* thoracic.
thorax [tɔ'raks], *n.m.* thorax, chest.
thrombose [trɔ̃'bo:z], *n.f.* thrombosis.
thym [tɛ̃], *n.m.* thyme.
thyroïde [tirɔ'id], *a.* thyroid.
tiare [tja:r], *n.f.* tiara.
Tibet [ti'bɛ], **le** *m.* Tibet.
tibétain [tibe'tɛ̃], *a.* Tibetan.—*n.m.* Tibetan (*language*); (**Tibétain**, *fem.* **-aine**) Tibetan (*person*).
tibia [ti'bja], *n.m.* (*Anat.*) tibia, shin-bone.
tic [tik], *n.m.* tic, twitching; bad habit.
ticket [ti'kɛ], *n.m.* ticket (*for bus, underground etc., but not railways*).
tiède [tjɛd], *a.* lukewarm, tepid, mild; (*fig.*) indifferent.
tièdement [tjɛd'mã], *adv.* with indifference.
tiédeur [tje'dœ:r], *n.f.* lukewarmness; (*fig.*) indifference.
tiédir [tje'di:r], *v.t.* to take the chill off, to tepefy.—*v.i.* to cool, to grow lukewarm.
tien [tjɛ̃], *pron. poss. m.* (*fem.* **tienne**) *thine, yours.—*n.* (*pl.*) **les tiens**, your relations and friends.
tiens! [tjɛ̃], *2nd sing. imper.* [TENIR], *int.* well hello! look here! here! really? you don't say so!
tierce (1) [tjɛrs], *n.f.* a third (*of time*); tierce (*at cards etc.*).
tiers [tjɛ:r], *a.* (*fem.* **tierce** (2)) third.—*n.m.* third person, third party; (*fig.*) stranger; third part.
tige [ti:ʒ], *n.f.* stem, stalk; trunk (*of tree*); straw (*of grain*); shank (*of a key, anchor etc.*); stock (*of a family*).
tignasse [ti'ɲas], *n.f.* old wig; (*pop.*) mop, shock (*of hair*).
tigre [tigr], *n.m.* (*fem.* **-esse**) tiger, tigress.
tigrer [ti'gre], *v.t.* to stripe, to spot, to speckle.
tillac [ti'jak], *n.m.* deck.
tilleul [ti'jœl], *n.m.* lime tree, linden tree.
timbale [tɛ̃'bal], *n.f.* kettledrum, timbal; metal cup *or* mug; kitchen mold.
timbre [tɛ̃:br], *n.m.* bell, clock chime; sound, tone; stamp; stamp duty; postmark.
timbré [tɛ̃'bre], *a.* stamped; (*fam.*) cracked.
timbre-poste [tɛ̃brə'pɔst], *n.m.* (*pl.* **timbres-poste**) postage stamp.

timbrer [tɛ̃'bre], *v.t.* to stamp; to stick a stamp on (*a letter*).
timide [ti'mid], *a.* shy, bashful, self-conscious; timid.
timidement [timid'mɑ̃], *adv.* shyly; timidly.
timidité [timidi'te], *n.f.* shyness, bashfulness; timidity.
timon [ti'mɔ̃], *n.m.* pole (*of a carriage, cart etc.*); shaft; beam (*of a plough*); (*Naut.*) helm, tiller; (*fig.*) direction, government.
timonerie [timɔn'ri], *n.f.* steerage, steering.
timonier [timɔ'nje], *n.m.* steersman, helmsman; wheel horse.
timoré [timɔ're], *a.* timorous, fearful.
Timothée [timɔ'te], *m.* Timothy.
tine [tin], *n.f.* tub, water cask.
tintamarre [tɛ̃ta'ma:r], *n.m.* hubbub, uproar, hurly-burly, din.
tintement [tɛ̃t'mɑ̃], *n.m.* ringing sound, tinkling; tolling; singing *or* buzzing (*in the ears etc.*).
tinter [tɛ̃'te], *v.t.* to ring, to toll; to sound (*a knell etc.*); (*Naut.*) to prop, to support.—*v.i.* to ring, to toll; to tinkle, to jingle; to tingle.
tintouin [tɛ̃'twɛ̃], *n.m.* (*fam.*) anxiety, trouble.
tique [tik], *n.f.* cattle tick, dog tick.
tiquer [ti'ke], *v.i.* to have a tic, to twitch.
tiqueté [tik'te], *a.* speckled, spotted.
tiqueture [tik'ty:r], *n.f.* mottling, speckles.
tir [ti:r], *n.m.* shooting; firing, fire; shooting gallery, rifle range.
tirade [ti'rad], *n.f.* passage (*of prose or verse*); tirade.
tirage [ti'ra:ʒ], *n.m.* drawing, hauling, towing; tow-path; (*fig.*) difficulties; working off; printing, circulation (*of newspaper*); drawing (*of a lottery*); focal length (*of camera*).
tiraillement [tirɑj'mɑ̃], *n.m.* pulling, hauling about; twinge, pain; (*fig.*) jarring, wrangling, vexation.
tirailler [tirɑ'je], *v.t.* to pull about; to tease, to pester.—*v.i.* to shoot wildly; to skirmish. **se tirailler**, *v.r.* to pull each other about.
tirailleur [tirɑ'jœ:r], *n.m.* sharpshooter; skirmisher.
tirant [ti'rɑ̃], *n.m.* purse-string; boot-strap; (*Carp. etc.*) tie-beam; brace (*of a drum*); **tirant d'eau**, ship's draft.
tire [ti:r], *n.f.* pull.
tiré [ti're], *a.* drawn; fatigued.—*n.m.* (*Comm.*) drawee (*of a bill*).
tire-bouchon [tirbu'ʃɔ̃], *n.m.* (*pl.* **-bouchons**) corkscrew; ringlet (*of hair*).
tire-bouton [tirbu'tɔ̃], *n.m.* (*pl.* **-boutons**) button-hook.
tire-d'aile (**à**) [atir'dɛl], *adv. phr.* at full speed (*of a bird flying*).
tire-larigot (**à**) [atirlari'go], *adv. phr.* (*fam.*) to one's heart's content.
tirelire [tir'li:r], *n.f.* money box.
tirer [ti're], *v.t.* to draw, to pull; to take out, to extract; to tap (*liquors*); to stretch, to tighten; to receive, to reap; to infer; to put on; to get; to shoot, to fire; (*Print.*) to print.—*v.i.* to draw, to pull; to fire; to tend, to border, to verge (*sur*). **se tirer**, *v.r.* to extricate oneself; to get out; to recover (*from illness*).
tiret [ti're], *n.m.* hyphen, dash.
tiretaine [tir'tɛ:n], *n.f.* linsey-woolsey.

tireur [ti'rœ:r], *n.m.* (*fem.* **-euse**) one who draws; marksman, sharpshooter.
tiroir [ti'rwa:r], *n.m.* drawer (*in a table etc.*); slide, slide-valve (*steam engine*).
tisane [ti'zan], *n.f.* infusion of herbs etc.
tison [ti'zɔ̃], *n.m.* brand, fire-brand; (*fig.*) embers.
tisonner [tizɔ'ne], *v.t.*, *v.i.* to poke (*the fire*).
tisonnier [tizɔ'nje], *n.m.* poker, fire iron.
tissage [ti'sa:ʒ], *n.m.* weaving; cloth mill.
tisser [ti'se], *v.t.* to weave; **métier à tisser** weaving-loom.
tisserand [tis'rɑ̃], *n.m.* (*fem.* **-e**) weaver.
tissu [ti'sy], *a.* woven.—*n.m.* material, fabric; tissue.
tissure [ti'sy:r], *n.f.* tissue, texture.
titan [ti'tɑ̃], *n.m.* Titan, titan.
titanesque [tita'nɛsk], **titanique** [tita'nik], *a.* titanic, Titanic.
titillant [titil'lɑ̃], *a.* titillating, tickling.
titillation [titilla'sjɔ̃], *n.f.* titillation, tickling.
titiller [titil'le], *v.t.*, *v.i.* to titillate, to tickle.
titre [titr], *n.m.* title, style, denomination; title page; head, heading; right, claim, reason; voucher; title deed; **titre de circulation**, (railway) ticket *or* pass; **à bon titre** *or* **à juste titre**, deservedly, justly.
titrer [ti'tre], *v.t.* to give a title to.
titubant [tity'bɑ̃], *a.* staggering.
titubation [tityba'sjɔ̃], *n.f.* reeling, staggering.
tituber [tity'be], *v.i.* to stagger, to reel.
titulaire [tity'lɛ:r], *a.* titular.—*n.* titular incumbent, holder, chief.
toast [tost], *n.m.* toast, health; toast(ed bread); **porter un toast** (*à quelqu'un*), to toast (*someone*).
toboggan [tɔbɔ'gɑ̃], *n.m.* toboggan.
toc [tɔk], *int.* tap, rap.—*n.m.* rap, knock (*at a door etc.*).
tocsin [tɔk'sɛ̃], *n.m.* tocsin, alarm bell.
toge [tɔ:ʒ], *n.f.* toga; (*fig.*) robe, gown (*of a judge etc.*).
Togo [tɔ'go], **le**, *m.* Togo.
togolais [tɔgɔ'lɛ], *a.* of Togo.—*n.m.* (**Togolais**, *fem.* **-aise**) native of Togo.
tohu-bohu [tɔybɔ'y], *n.m.* chaos; (*fig.*) confusion; jumble, hubbub.
toi [twa], *pron. pers.* *thou, *thee, you.
toile [twal], *n.f.* linen, cloth; canvas; sail; painting, picture; web; **toile cirée**, oilcloth; **toile d'araignée**, cobweb, spider's web.
toilette [twa'lɛt], *n.f.* doily; toilet set; dressing table, wash-stand; dress, attire; **cabinet de toilette**, dressing room; **grande toilette**, full dress; **les toilettes**, toilets.
toise [twa:z], *n.f.* fathom; fathom measure; (*fig.*) measure, standard.
toiser [twa'ze], *v.t.* to measure; to survey; (*fig.*) to eye from head to foot.
toiseur [twa'zœ:r], *n.m.* measurer; quantity surveyor.
toison [twa'zɔ̃], *n.f.* fleece; (*fig.*) mop, thick head of hair.
toit [twa], *n.m.* roof, house-top; top, roof (*of a mine*); (*fig.*) house, home; **toit à cochons** pigsty.
toiture [twa'ty:r], *n.f.* roofing, roof.
tôle [to:l], *n.f.* sheet iron; plate of steel; **tôle ondulée**, corrugated iron.

313

tolérable [tɔle'rabl], *a.* tolerable, bearable; middling.

tolérablement [tɔlerablə'mã], *adv.* tolerably.

tolérance [tɔle'rã:s], *n.f.* tolerance, toleration; endurance, forbearance; indulgence; tolerance (*in coins*).

tolérant [tɔle'rã], *a.* tolerant.

tolérer [tɔle're], *v.t.* (*conjug. like* CÉDER) to tolerate, to allow; to endure, to bear; to wink at.

tomate [tɔ'mat], *n.f.* tomato.

tombal [tɔ̃'bal], *a.* (*m. pl.* **-aux**) pertaining to a tomb; *pierre tombale*, tombstone.

tombe [tɔ̃:b], *n.f.* tomb, grave; tombstone.

tombeau [tɔ̃'bo], *n.m.* (*pl.* **-eaux**) tomb, grave; (*fig.*) sepulcher, death.

tombée [tɔ̃'be], *n.f.* fall (*of night etc.*).

tomber [tɔ̃'be], *v.i.* (*with aux.* ÊTRE) to fall, to fall down; to sink; to decay, to droop; to abate; to sag; to fall into; to meet, to light (upon) (*sur*); *laisser tomber*, to drop; *tomber amoureux* (*de*), to fall in love (with); *tomber bien* or *mal*, to come at the right *or* wrong moment; *tomber d'accord*, to agree; *tomber malade*, to fall ill.

tombereau [tɔ̃'bro], *n.m.* (*pl.* **-eaux**) tip-cart.

tombola [tɔ̃bɔ'la], *n.f.* tombola; raffle.

tome [to:m], *n.m.* volume, tome.

ton (1) [tɔ̃], *a. poss. m.* (*fem.* **ta**, *pl.* **tes**) *thy, your.

ton (2) [tɔ̃], *n.m.* tone; intonation, accent; tint; (*fig.*) manner, style; breeding; (*Mus.*) pitch, key.

tondaison [TONTE].

tondeur [tɔ̃'dœ:r], *n.m.* (*fem.* **-euse**) shearer, clipper.—*n.f.* (**-euse**) shearing machine, clipper; *tondeuse* (*de gazon*), lawn-mower.

tondre [tɔ̃:dr], *v.t.* to shear, to clip, to crop; to cut, to mow, to trim.

tondu [tɔ̃'dy], *a.* shorn.

tonique [tɔ'nik], *a.* tonic; stressed.—*n.m.* (*Med.*) tonic.—*n.f.* (*Mus.*) keynote.

tonnage [tɔ'na:ʒ], *n.m.* tonnage; displacement.

tonne [tɔn], *n.f.* tun (*wooden vessel*); ton (*20 cwt., approx. 1000 kil.*).

tonneau [tɔ'no], *n.m.* (*pl.* **-eaux**) tun (*cask*); tun (*measure*); ton [TONNE]; (*colloq.*) drunkard; *mettre un tonneau en perce*, to broach a cask; *tonneau percé*, (*fig.*) spendthrift.

tonnelier [tɔnə'lje], *n.m.* cooper.

tonnelle [tɔ'nɛl], *n.f.* arbor, bower.

tonnellerie [tɔnɛl'ri], *n.f.* cooperage.

tonner [tɔ'ne], *v.i.* to thunder; (*fig.*) to inveigh.

tonnerre [tɔ'nɛ:r], *n.m.* thunder, thunderbolt; *coup* or *éclat de tonnerre*, clap of thunder.

tonsure [tɔ̃'sy:r], *n.f.* tonsure.

tonsuré [tɔ̃sy're], *a.m.* tonsured, shaven.—*n.m.* cleric, priest.

tonte [tɔ̃:t], **tondaison** [tɔ̃dɛ'zɔ̃], *n.f.* sheep-shearing, clipping.

tonture [tɔ̃'ty:r], *n.f.* shearings, clippings; flock (*of cloth*); (*Naut.*) sheer.

top [tɔp], *n.m.* time signal; *les tops*, the pips.

topaze [tɔ'pɑ:z], *n.f.* topaz.

toper [tɔ'pe], *v.i.* to agree; *tope là !* done! agreed!

topinambour [tɔpinã'bu:r], *n.m.* Jerusalem artichoke.

topographe [tɔpɔ'graf], *n.m.* topographer.

topographie [tɔpɔgra'fi], *n.f.* topography.

topographique [tɔpɔgra'fik], *a.* topographical.

toquade or **tocade** [tɔ'kad], *n.f.* (*colloq.*) infatuation, whim, fad, craze.

toque [tɔk], *n.f.* toque; jockey's cap; magistrate's cap.

toqué [tɔ'ke], *a.* (*fam.*) cracked, touched; infatuated.

torche [tɔrʃ], *n.f.* torch; twist (*of straw etc.*); pad (*on head*).

torcher [tɔr'ʃe], *v.t.* to wipe, to clean; (*fig.*) to polish off. **se torcher**, *v.r.* to wipe oneself.

torchère [tɔr'ʃɛ:r], *n.f.* torch-holder, tall candelabrum, hall lamp.

torchis [tɔr'ʃi], *n.m.* loam; *mur de torchis*, mud wall.

torchon [tɔr'ʃɔ̃], *n.m.* duster, house-cloth, dish-cloth.

tordage [tɔr'da:ʒ], *n.m.* twisting, twist.

tordeur [tɔr'dœ:r], *n.m.* (*fem.* **-euse**) twister (*of wool etc.*); throwster (*of silk*).

tordoir [tɔr'dwa:r], *n.m.* mangle, wringer.

tordre [tɔrdr], *v.t.* to twist, to wring; to contort, to disfigure. **se tordre**, *v.r.* to twist; to writhe.

tordu [tɔr'dy], *a.* twisted, distorted.

toréador [tɔrea'dɔ:r], *n.m.* toreador, bullfighter.

tornade [tɔr'nad], *n.f.* tornado.

torpédo [tɔrpe'do], *n.f.* (*Motor.*) touring car.

torpeur [tɔr'pœ:r], *n.f.* torpor.

torpide [tɔr'pid], *a.* torpid.

torpille [tɔr'pi:j], *n.f.* torpedo (*numb-fish*) (*Navy, Av.*) torpedo.

torpiller [tɔrpi'je], *v.t.* to torpedo.

torpilleur [tɔrpi'jœ:r], *n.m.* torpedo boat.

torréfier [tɔre'fje], *v.t.* to torrefy, to roast (*coffee*).

torrent [tɔ'rã], *n.m.* torrent, stream; flood (*of tears etc.*); flow (*of words etc.*).

torrentiel [tɔrã'sjɛl], **torrentueux** [tɔrã'tɥø], *a.* (*fem.* **-elle**, **-euse**) torrential; impetuous.

torride [tɔ'rid], *a.* torrid.

tors [tɔr], *a.* (*fem.* **torse** (1) or **torte**) twisted, wreathed, contorted; wry, crooked.—*n.m.* twisting (*of ropes etc.*); torsion.

torsade [tɔr'sad], *n.f.* twisted fringe *or* cord; bullion (*on epaulets etc.*).

torse (2) [tɔrs], *n.m.* torso, trunk, bust.

torsion [tɔr'sjɔ̃], *n.f.* torsion, twisting.

tort [tɔ:r], *n.m.* wrong, injustice; harm, injury, mischief, offence; prejudice, detriment; *à tort ou à raison*, rightly or wrongly; *avoir tort*, to be wrong.

torticolis [tɔrtikɔ'li], *n.m.* wryneck, stiff neck; crick (*in the neck*).

tortiller [tɔrti'je], *v.t.* to twist.—*v.i.* to wriggle, to shuffle; to prevaricate. **se tortiller**, *v.r.* to wriggle, to writhe.

tortionnaire [tɔrsjɔ'nɛ:r], *n.m.* executioner, torturer.

tortu [tɔr'ty], *a.* crooked, tortuous; *jambes tortues*, bandy legs.

tortue [tɔr'ty], *n.f.* tortoise; *tortue de mer*, turtle.

tortueux [tɔr'tɥø], *a.* (*fem.* **-euse**) tortuous, winding, crooked; (*fig.*) artful, crafty.

torture [tɔr'ty:r], *n.f.* torture; the rack.

torturer [tɔrty're], *v.t.* to torture, to put on the rack.

tôt [to], *adv.* soon, quickly; early; *au plus tôt* or *le plus tôt possible*, as soon as possible; *tôt ou tard*, sooner or later.

total [tɔ'tal], *a.* (*m. pl.* **-aux**) total, whole, entire; utter.—*n.m.* whole, total, sum total.

totalement [tɔtal'mã], *adv.* totally, wholly; utterly, completely.

totalisateur [tɔtaliza'tœ:r], *n.m.* calculating-machine; totalisator.

totaliser [tɔtali'ze], *v.t.* to tot up, to total up.

totalitaire [tɔtali'tɛ:r], *a.* totalitarian.

totalitarisme [tɔtalita'rism], *n.m.* totalitarianism.

totalité [tɔtali'te], *n.f.* totality, whole.

touage [twa:ʒ], *n.m.* towage, towing, warping.

toucan [tu'kã], *n.m.* toucan.

touchant [tu'ʃã], *a.* touching, moving, affecting.—*n.m.* the moving, affecting *or* impressive part.—*prep.* concerning, with regard to.

touche [tuʃ], *n.f.* touch; assay, trial; (*Paint. etc.*) manner, style; key (*of piano, typewriter etc.*); stop (*of organ*); (*Fishing*) nibble, bite; (*Fenc. etc.*) hit; drove of cattle; *pierre de touche*, touchstone.

touche-à-tout [tuʃa'tu], *a. inv.* meddling.—*n. inv.* meddler; jack-of-all-trades.

toucher [tu'ʃe], *v.t.* to touch; to handle, to feel, to finger; to assay, to try (*precious metals etc.*); to receive (*money*); to hit; to offend; to move, to affect; to whip, to drive (*animals*); to play on (*a musical instrument*); to express, to describe; to allude to; to concern, to regard; *toucher un chèque*, to cash a check. —*v.i.* to touch, to meddle (*à*); to reach; to play (*on a musical instrument*); to draw near, to be related, to be like; to concern; (*Naut.*) to go aground. **se toucher**, *v.r.* to touch, to touch each other; to be adjoining.—*n.m.* touch, feeling.

toue [tu], *n.f.* barge.

touée [tu'e], *n.f.* towing, warping; towline.

touer [tu'e], *v.t.* to tow, to warp.

toueur [tu'œ:r], *n.m.* towboat, tug.

touffe [tuf], *n.f.* tuft, clump, bunch, wisp.

touffer [tu'fe], *v.t.* to arrange in tufts.—*v.i.* to grow in a tuft *or* tufts.

touffu [tu'fy], *a.* tufted, bushy; leafy; full, thick; labored (*of style*).

toujours [tu'ʒu:r], *adv.* always, ever, for ever; still; all the same, nevertheless, at least; *toujours est-il que* . . ., still, the fact remains that . . . .

toupet [tu'pɛ], *n.m.* tuft of hair; forelock; front, foretop (*on a horse*); (*colloq.*) effrontery, cheek, impudence.

toupie [tu'pi], *n.f.* top, spinning-top.

toupiller [tupi'je], *v.i.* to spin, to whirl round and round.

tour (1) [tu:r], *n.f.* tower; (*Chess*) rook, castle.

tour (2) [tu:r], *n.m.* turn, winding; revolution; circumference, circuit; twist, strain; tour, trip; trick; feat; *à tour de rôle*, in turn; *tour de force*, feat of strength; *tour de reins*, sprain in the back.

tour (3) [tu:r], *n.m.* lathe.

tourangeau [turã'ʒo], *a.* (*fem.* **-elle**, *m. pl.* **-eaux**) of Touraine.—*n.m.* (**Tourangeau**, *fem.* **-elle**) native of Touraine.

tourbe [turb], *n.f.* mob, rabble; peat, turf.

tourbeux [tur'bø], *a.* (*fem.* **-euse**) peaty.

tourbillon [turbi'jõ], *n.m.* whirlwind; whirlpool, eddy; (*fig.*) hurly-burly, bustle.

tourbillonner [turbijo'ne], *v.i.* to whirl, to eddy; to swirl.

tourelle [tu'rɛl], *n.f.* turret; gun turret; *tourelle de veille*, conning tower.

touret [tu'rɛ], *n.m.* wheel (*of a lathe etc.*); angler's reel.

tourie [tu'ri], *n.f.* carboy.

tourillon [turi'jõ], *n.m.* axle; axle-tree, arbor; spindle, pivot.

tourisme [tu'rism], *n.m.* touring, tourism.

touriste [tu'rist], *n.* tourist.

tourment [tur'mã], *n.m.* torment, torture; anguish, pain; agony of mind.

tourmente [tur'mã:t], *n.f.* tempest, storm; (*fig.*) disturbance, turmoil.

tourmenter [turmã'te], *v.t.* to torment, to torture, to rack; to distress, to harass; to worry; to jolt; to toss. **se tourmenter**, *v.r.* to be uneasy, to fret; to warp (*of wood*); to labor hard (*of a ship*).

tourmenteur [turmã'tœ:r], *a.* (*fem.* **-euse**) torturing, tormenting.—*n.m.* (*fem.* **-euse**) torturer, tormentor.

tournailler [turna'je], *v.i.* (*colloq.*) to prowl round.

tournant [tur'nã], *a.* turning, winding; *plaque tournante*, turn-table; *pont tournant*, swing-bridge.—*n.m.* turn, turning, bend; street corner; (*fig.*) indirect means; turning-point.

tourné [tur'ne], *a.* turned, shaped; expressed; sour, spoilt; *avoir l'esprit mal tourné*, to be cross-grained.

tournebroche [turnə'brɔʃ], *n.m.* roasting-jack; turnspit.

tourne-disques [turnə'disk], *n.m. inv.* record player.

tournedos [turnə'do], *n.m. inv.* filet mignon.

tournée [tur'ne], *n.f.* round, turn, visit, journey; circuit.

tournemain (en un) [ãnœturnə'mɛ], *adv. phr.* in a trice.

tourner [tur'ne], *v.t.* to turn; to turn round, to revolve, to twirl; to wind; (*Ciné.*) to shoot (*a film*); to convert; to interpret; to shape.—*v.i.* to turn, to turn round, to revolve; to turn out; to change; to ripen; to spoil, to curdle (*of liquids*). **se tourner**, *v.r.* to turn round; to turn; to change.

tournesol [turnə'sɔl], *n.m.* turnsole, sunflower; (*Chem.*) litmus.

tourneur [tur'nœ:r], *n.m.* turner.

tournevent [turnə'vã], *n.m.* cowl (*for chimney*).

tournevis [turnə'vis], *n.m.* screwdriver.

tourniole [tur'njɔl], *n.f.* whitlow.

tourniquet [turni'kɛ], *n.m.* turnstile; swivel; (*Surg.*) tourniquet.

tournoi [tur'nwa], *n.m.* tournament.

tournoiement [turnwa'mã], *n.m.* turning round, whirling, swirling; dizziness.

tournoyer [turnwa'je], *v.i.* (*conjug. like* EMPLOYER) to turn round and round, to wind; to eddy; (*fig.*) to beat about the bush, to shilly-shally.

tournure [tur′ny:r], *n.f.* turn, direction, course; figure, shape; (*fig.*) cast (*of mind, style etc.*); phrase, construction (*of language*); *les choses commencent à prendre une mauvaise tournure,* things are beginning to look bad.

tourte [turt], *n.f.* covered pie; round loaf.

tourtereau [turtə′ro], *n.m.* (*pl.* **-eaux**) young turtle-dove; (*pl.*) (*fam.*) lovers.

tourterelle [turtə′rɛl], *n.f.* turtle-dove.

Toussaint [tu′sɛ̃], **la**, *f.* All Saints' Day.

tousser [tu′se], *v.i.* to cough.

tout [tu; *liaison-form,* tut], *a.* (*m. pl.* **tous**) all; whole, the whole of; every; each; any; *tous les jours,* every day; *toutes les fois que,* as often as, every time that; *tout le monde,* all the world, everybody.—*pron. indef.* (*m. pl. pronounced* tu:s) all, everything; (*pl.*) all men; *à tout prendre,* on the whole; *comme tout,* exceedingly, extremely; *du tout,* not at all; *en tout,* in all, on the whole.—*n.m.* whole, the whole; the chief point, only thing.—*adv.* wholly, entirely, quite, thoroughly; all, altogether; although, however, for all; *parler tout haut,* to speak aloud; *tout à coup,* suddenly; *tout à fait,* quite, entirely; *tout à l'heure,* just now; presently; *tout à vous,* sincerely yours; *tout beau* or *tout doux,* softly, gently, not so fast; *tout de bon,* in earnest; *tout de suite,* immediately; *tout nu,* stark naked.

toutefois [tut′fwa], *adv.* yet, nevertheless, however, still.

toute-puissance [tutpɥi′sɑ̃:s], *n.f.* omnipotence, almighty power.

tout-puissant [tupɥi′sɑ̃], *a.* (*fem.* **toute-puissante**) almighty.—*n.m.* (**Tout-Puissant**) the Almighty.

toux [tu], *n.f. inv.* cough.

toxémie [tɔkse′mi], *n.f.* (*Med.*) toxemia, blood poisoning.

toxique [tɔk′sik], *a.* toxic, poisonous.—*n.m.* poison.

tracas [tra′kɑ], *n.m.* bustle, turmoil, disturbance; worry, annoyance.

tracassement [trakas′mɑ̃], *n.m.* worrying.

tracasser [traka′se], *v.t.* to worry, to pester. **se tracasser,** *v.r.* to worry.

tracasserie [trakas′ri], *n.f.* worry, pestering, annoyance, vexation; (*pl.*) bickering.

tracassier [traka′sje], *a.* (*fem.* **-ière**) pestering, worrying, annoying; fussy; mischief-making.—*n.m.* (*fem.* **-ière**) pesterer, busybody; troublesome person, mischief-maker.

trace [tras], *n.f.* trace, track, footprint; spoor, trail; mark, impression, vestige; outline, sketch.

tracé [tra′se], *n.m.* outline, sketch (*of figure*); marking out; laying out (*of grounds etc.*); direction.

tracement [tras′mɑ̃], *n.m.* tracing, laying out (*of grounds, roads etc.*).

tracer [tra′se], *v.t.* (*conjug. like* COMMENCER) to trace, to draw, to trace out; to sketch; to portray; to lay out (*grounds, roads etc.*); (*fig.*) to set forth, to mark out.—*v.i.* to spread roots (*of trees*); to burrow (*of moles*).

trachée [tra′ʃe], *n.f.* trachea, air vessel.

trachée-artère [traʃear′tɛ:r], *n.f.* (*pl.* **trachées-artères**) trachea, windpipe.

tract [trakt], *n.m.* tract, leaflet (*for propaganda*).

tracteur [trak′tœ:r], *n.m.* tractor, traction engine.

traction [trak′sjɔ̃], *n.f.* traction; pulling; draft. t; *traction avant,* front-wheel drive.

tradition [tradi′sjɔ̃], *n.f.* tradition; (*Law*) delivery.

traditionnel [tradisjɔ′nɛl], *a.* (*fem.* **-elle**) traditional.

traducteur [tradyk′tœ:r], *n.m.* (*fem.* **-trice**) translator.

traduction [tradyk′sjɔ̃], *n.f.* translation, (*sch.*) crib, pony.

traduire [tra′dɥi:r], *v.t. irr.* (*conjug. like* CONDUIRE) to translate; to interpret, to construe; to convey, to express; to indicate, to denote.

traduisible [tradɥi′zibl], *a.* translatable.

trafic [tra′fik], *n.m.* traffic; trading, trade; dealings.

trafiquant [trafi′kɑ̃], *n.m.* (*fem.* **-e**) trafficker.

trafiquer [trafi′ke], *v.i.* to traffic, to trade, to deal (*de*).

tragédie [traʒe′di], *n.f.* tragedy.

tragédien [traʒe′djɛ̃], *n.m.* (*fem.* **-enne**) tragedian.

tragique [tra′ʒik], *a.* tragic, tragical.—*n.m.* tragedy, tragic art; tragic writer.

trahir [tra′i:r], *v.t.* to betray; to deceive; to divulge, to reveal. **se trahir,** *v.r.* to betray oneself; to betray each other.

trahison [trai′zɔ̃], *n.f.* treachery, treason, perfidy; breach of faith.

train [trɛ̃], *n.m.* pace, rate; train, suite, attendants; way, manner; noise, clatter, dust; carriage; quarters (*of a horse etc.*); (*Rail.*) train; *à fond de train,* at full speed; *être en train de faire quelque chose,* to be (in the act of) doing something; *train de maison,* style of living; *train de marchandises,* freight train; *train omnibus,* slow or local train.

traînage [trɛ′na:ʒ], *n.m.* dragging, drawing; sledging, sleighing.

traînant [trɛ′nɑ̃], *a.* dragging, trailing (*dress*); drawling (*voice*); shuffling (*gait*).

traînard [trɛ′na:r], *n.m.* straggler, laggard; slow-coach.

traîne [trɛ:n], *n.f.* dragging, being dragged or drawn; train (*of a dress etc.*).

traîneau [trɛ′no], *n.m.* (*pl.* **-eaux**) sledge, sleigh; drag-net.

traînée [trɛ′ne], *n.f.* train (*of gunpowder etc.*); trail, track.

traîner [trɛ′ne], *v.t.* to drag, to draw; to track; to spin out, to drag out, to protract; to drawl; to put off.—*v.i.* to trail, to draggle, to lag; to droop; to languish, to flag; to lie about; to loiter, to linger, to be protracted. **se traîner,** *v.r.* to crawl along, to creep; to lag, to drag oneself along.

train-train [trɛ̃′trɛ̃], *n.m.* (*colloq.*) routine, regular course.

traire [trɛ:r], *v.t. irr.* to milk; to draw (*milk*).

trait [trɛ], *n.m.* arrow, dart, bolt, shaft; thunderbolt; stroke, hit; trace (*of harness*); leash (*for dogs*); turn (*of the scale*); draft; gulp; dash (*of the pen etc.*); flash (*of light*); stroke, touch; trait, feature, lineament; act, deed; prime move (*at chess, draughts etc.*); **avoir trait à**, to have reference to; **boire à longs traits**, to drink long draughts of; **d'un seul trait**, at one gulp; **trait de génie**, stroke of genius, (*fam.*) brain-wave; **trait d'union**, hyphen.

traite [trɛt], *n.f.* stage, journey, stretch; milking; (*Comm.*) draft, bill; **traite des noirs**, slave trade.

traité [trɛ'te], *n.m.* treatise, tract, dissertation; treaty; agreement.

traitement [trɛt'mã], *n.m.* treatment; (*Ind.*) processing; reception; salary, pay.

traiter [trɛ'te], *v.t.* to treat; (*Ind.*) to process; to entertain; to use, to behave to; to discuss, to handle; to call, to style; to negotiate; to execute, to do.—*v.i.* to treat, to negotiate.

traiteur [trɛ'tœːr], *n.m.* restaurant keeper; caterer.

traître [trɛːtr], *a.* (*fem.* **-esse**) treacherous, perfidious.—*n.m.* (*fem.* **-esse**) treacherous person, traitor, traitress.

traîtreusement [trɛtrœz'mã], *adv.* treacherously.

traîtrise [trɛ'triːz], *n.f.* treachery.

trajectoire [traʒɛk'twaːr], *a.* and *n.f.* trajectory.

trajet [tra'ʒɛ], *n.m.* passage, journey, crossing, voyage; (*Med.*) course.

trame [tram], *n.f.* weft, woof; plot, conspiracy; course, progress, thread.

tramer [tra'me], *v.t.* to weave; (*fig.*) to plot, to contrive, to hatch.

tramontane [tramɔ̃'tan], *n.f.* tramontane, north wind; north; North Star.

tramway [tra'mwe], *n.m.* trolley car.

tranchant [trã'ʃã], *a.* sharp, cutting; (*fig.*) trenchant, decisive; salient, prominent.—*n.m.* edge.

tranche [trãːʃ], *n.f.* slice, chop; slab; edge (*of a book*); **doré sur tranche**, gilt-edged (*of a book*); **tranche de lard**, rasher of bacon.

tranchée [trã'ʃe], *n.f.* trench, cutting; (*pl.*) colic.

trancher [trã'ʃe], *v.t.* to cut; to cut off; to slice; to decide, to determine, to settle.—*v.i.* to cut; to decide; to set up for; to affect; to be glaring (*of colors*).

tranchoir [trã'ʃwaːr], *n.m.* trencher, cuttingboard.

tranquille [trã'kil], *a.* quiet, calm, tranquil, placid, peaceful; undisturbed (*in mind etc.*); **soyez tranquille**, set your mind at ease.

tranquillement [trãkil'mã], *adv.* peacefully, quietly.

tranquillisant [trãkili'zã], *a.* tranquillizing. —*n.m.* tranquillizer.

tranquilliser [trãkili'ze], *v.t.* to tranquillize, to make easy, to soothe. **se tranquilliser**, *v.r.* to become tranquil, to calm down.

tranquillité [trãkili'te], *n.f.* tranquillity, quiet, peace.

transaction [trãzak'sjɔ̃], *n.f.* transaction, arrangement.

transalpin [trãzal'pɛ̃], *a.* transalpine.

transatlantique [trãzatlã'tik], *a.* transatlantic.—*n.m.* liner; deck chair.

transborder [trãsbɔr'de], *v.t.* to tranship.

transbordeur [trãsbɔr'dœːr], *n.m.* transporter; **pont transbordeur**, transporter bridge.

transcendant [trãsã'dã], *a.* transcendent.

transcription [trãskrip'sjɔ̃], *n.f.* transcription, transcript, copy.

transcrire [trã'skriːr], *v.t. irr.* (*conjug. like* ÉCRIRE) to transcribe, to copy out.

transe [trãːs], *n.f.* fright, apprehension; trance.

transférable [trãsfe'rabl], *a.* transferable.

transférer [trãsfe're], *v.t.* (*conjug. like* CÉDER) to transfer, to transport, to convey, to move.

transfert [trãs'fɛːr], *n.m.* transfer.

transfiguration [trãsfigyra'sjɔ̃], *n.f.* transfiguration.

transfigurer [trãsfigy're], *v.t.* to transfigure. **se transfigurer**, *v.r.* to be transfigured.

transformateur [trãsfɔrma'tœːr], *n.m.* (*Elec.*) transformer.

transformation [trãsfɔrma'sjɔ̃], *n.f.* transformation.

transformer [trãsfɔr'me], *v.t.* to transform; to change, to convert. **se transformer**, *v.r.* to be transformed.

transfuge [trãs'fyːʒ], *n.m.* deserter; fugitive; turncoat.

transgresser [trãsgrɛ'se], *v.t.* to transgress, to infringe, to contravene.

transgression [trãsgrɛ'sjɔ̃], *n.f.* transgression.

transhumance [trãzy'mãːs], *n.f.* transhumance.

transi [trã'zi], *à.* chilled, benumbed.

transiger [trãzi'ʒe], *v.i.* (*conjug. like* MANGER) to compound, to compromise, to come to terms (*avec*).

transir [trã'ziːr], *v.t.* to chill, to benumb; to paralyse.—*v.i.* to be chilled; to be paralyzed (*with fear etc.*).

transissement [trãzis'mã], *n.m.* chill, numbness; shivering (*with terror etc.*).

transistor [trãzis'tor], *n.m.* transistor.

transit [trã'zit], *n.m.* transit.

transitaire [trãzi'tɛːr], *a.* pertaining to the transit of goods.

transitif [trãzi'tif], *a.* (*fem.* **-tive**) transitive.

transition [trãzi'sjɔ̃], *n.f.* transition.

transitoire [trãzi'twaːr], *a.* transitory.

translation [trãsla'sjɔ̃], *n.f.* transfer(ring), relaying.

translucide [trãsly'sid], *a.* translucent.

translucidité [trãslysidi'te], *n.f.* translucence.

transmarin [trãsma'rɛ̃], *a.* transmarine, oversea.

transmetteur [trãsmɛ'tœːr], *n.m.* (*Rad.*) transmitter.

transmettre [trãs'mɛtr], *v.t. irr.* (*conjug. like* METTRE) to transmit, to convey, to send on; to transfer.

transmigration [trãsmigra'sjɔ̃], *n.f.* transmigration.

transmigrer [trãsmi'gre], *v.i.* to transmigrate.

transparence [trãspa'rãːs], *n.f.* transparency.

transparent [trãspa'rã], *a.* transparent.—*n.m.* paper ruled with black lines; transparency.

transpercer [trãspɛr'se], *v.t.* (*conjug. like* COMMENCER) to pierce through; to run through (*with a sword etc.*), to transfix.

transpiration [trãspira'sjɔ̃], *n.f.* perspiration, perspiring.

transpirer [trãspi're], *v.i.* to perspire; to ooze out; to transpire.

transplanter

transplanter [trãsplã′te], *v.t.* to transplant.

transport [trãs′pɔ:r], *n.m.* carriage, conveyance; transport, removal; transfer; assignment; (*fig.*) rapture, ecstasy; transport ship; **transport au cerveau**, stroke, fit of delirium.

transportation [trãsporta′sjõ], *n.f.* transportation.

transporté [trãspɔr′te], *n.m.* (*fem.* **-ée**) deported person, convict.

transporter [trãspɔr′te], *v.t.* to convey, to transport; to transfer; to banish; to enrapture. **se transporter**, *v.r.* to transport oneself, to go.

transporteur [trãspɔr′tœ:r], *n.m.* carrier, conveyor.

transposer [trãspo′ze], *v.t.* to transpose.

transposition [trãspozi′sjõ], *n.f.* transposition.

transrhénan [trãsre′nã], *a.* from beyond the Rhine.

transsubstantiation [trãssybstãsja′sjõ], *n.f.* transubstantiation.

transvaser [trãsva′ze], *v.t.* to decant.

transversal [trãzvɛr′sal], *a.* (*m.pl.* **-aux**) transversal, transverse.

trapèze [tra′pɛ:z], *n.m.* trapezium; trapeze.

trappe [trap], *n.f.* trap door; trap, pitfall; curtain, register (*of chimney*).

trappeur [tra′pœ:r], *n.m.* trapper.

trappiste [tra′pist], *a.* and *n.m.* Trappist.

trapu [tra′py], *a.* squat, dumpy, thick-set, stocky.

traquer [tra′ke], *v.t.* (*Hunt.*) to beat for game; to enclose, to encircle; to track down.

travail [tra′va:j], *n.m.* (*pl.* **-aux**) labor, work; toil; travail; piece of work; workmanship; occupation; study; **cabinet de travail**, study (*room*); **travaux forcés**, hard labor.

travaillé [trava′je], *a.* worked, wrought; labored, elaborate; laboring (*under*).

travailler [trava′je], *v.t.* to work, to work at; to do with care; to fashion; to till (*the ground*).—*v.i.* to labor, to work; to study; to strive; to ferment (*of wines*); to warp (*of wood*). **se travailler**, *v.r.* to torment oneself; to be overwrought.

travailleur [trava′jœ:r], *a.* (*fem.* **-euse**) industrious, hard-working; painstaking.—*n.m.* (*fem.* **-euse**) workman, laborer; hard-working person.

travailliste [trava′jist], *a.* Labour, Socialist.—*n.* member of the Labour Party.

travée [tra′ve], *n.f.* (*Arch.*) bay; truss (*of bridges*); (*Av.*) rib (*of wing*).

travers [tra′vɛ:r], *n.m.* breadth; fault, failing; oddity; (*Naut.*) side, broadside; **à travers**, across; **au travers de**, through; **de travers**, obliquely, awry, askew; **en travers**, across, crosswise; **à tort et à travers**, at random.

traverse [tra′vɛrs], *n.f.* cross-bar, cross-piece; cross-road, short cut; (*Rail.*) tie; (*pl.*) (*fig.*) setbacks.

traversée [travɛr′se], *n.f.* passage, crossing.

traverser [travɛr′se], *v.t.* to cross, to go over or through, to traverse, to get through or across; to run through (*with a sword etc.*); to lie across, to span; to intersect; to penetrate; to thwart.

traversier [travɛr′sje], *a.* (*fem.* **-ière**) cross-; that plies across.

traversin [travɛr′sɛ̃], *n.m.* bolster; (*Carp. etc.*) cross-beam; (*Naut.*) stretcher (*in boats*).

travesti [travɛs′ti], *a.* disguised; travestied, parodied.

travestir [travɛs′ti:r], *v.t.* to disguise, to travesty; (*fig.*) to misrepresent.

travestissement [travɛstis′mã], *n.m.* disguise; travesty.

trébuchant [treby′ʃã], *a.* of full weight (*of coins*); stumbling.

trébucher [treby′ʃe], *v.i.* to stumble, to slip; to err; (*fig.*) to turn the scale.

trébuchet [treby′ʃɛ], *n.m.* bird trap; assay-balance.

tréfiler [trefi′le], *v.t.* to wire-draw.

trèfle [trefl], *n.m.* trefoil, clover; (*Cards*) clubs; **trèfle blanc**, shamrock.

tréfonds [tre′fõ], *n.m.* subsoil; (*fig.*) bottom, heart.

treillage [trɛ′ja:ʒ], *n.m.* trellis(-work), lattice-work.

treille [trɛ:j], *n.f.* vine trellis; shrimp net.

treillis [trɛ′ji], *n.m.* trellis, lattice; coarse canvas etc., sackcloth.

treizaine [trɛ′zɛn], *n.f.* baker's dozen.

treize [trɛ:z], *a.* and *n.m.* thirteen; thirteenth.

treizième [trɛ′zjɛm], *a.* and *n.* thirteenth (part).

tréma [tre′ma], *n.m.* dieresis.

tremblant [trã′blã], *a.* trembling, quivering; flickering (*of light etc.*).

tremble [trã:bl], *n.m.* aspen.

tremblé [trã′ble], *a.* wavy (*of lines*); shaky (*of writing*).

tremblement [trãblə′mã], *n.m.* trembling, shaking, quaking, trepidation, tremor; flickering (*of light*); (*Mus.*) tremolo; **tremblement de terre**, earthquake.

trembler [trã′ble], *v.i.* to tremble, to shake, to shiver; to quake, to fear; to flutter (*of wings*).

tremblotant [trãblɔ′tã], *a.* trembling, tremulous (*of sound etc.*); shivering, quivering, fluttering.

tremblotement [trãblɔt′mã], *n.m.* trembling, shivering.

trembloter [trãblɔ′te], *v.i.* to tremble (*of sound*); to quiver, to shiver; to flutter (*of wings*); to flicker (*of light*).

trémousser [tremu′se], *v.t.* to bestir, to move about, to flutter.—*v.i.* to shake, to stir. **se trémousser**, *v.r.* to flutter or frisk about; to bestir oneself.

trempage [trã′pa:ʒ], *n.m.* steeping, soaking; (*Print.*) wetting.

trempe [trã:p], *n.f.* temper (*of steel etc.*); (*fig.*) character, stamp, quality.

tremper [trã′pe], *v.t.* to soak, to steep, to wet, to drench; to temper (*iron, steel etc.*); to dilute (*wine etc.*).—*v.i.* to soak, to be steeped; to be implicated (*in a crime*).

tremplin [trã′plɛ̃], *n.m.* spring-board, diving board; trampoline.

trentaine [trã′tɛn], *n.f.* about thirty; age of thirty.

trente [trã:t], *a.* and *n.m.* thirty; thirtieth.

trentième [trã′tjɛm], *a.* and *n.* thirtieth (part).

trépan [tre'pɑ̃], *n.m.* trepan (*instrument*); trepanning.

trépaner [trepa'ne], *v.t.* to trepan.

trépas [tre'pɑ], *n.m. inv.* (*poet.*) decease, death.

trépassé [trepa'se], *n.m.* (*fem.* **-ée**) dead person.

trépasser [trepa'se], *v.i.* to depart this life, to pass away.

trépidant [trepi'dɑ̃], *a.* vibrating; (*fig.*) agitated, hectic.

trépidation [trepidɑ'sjɔ̃], *n.f.* trepidation, trembling; agitation.

trépied [tre'pje], *n.m.* trivet; tripod.

trépignement [trepiɲ'mɑ̃], *n.m.* stamping (*of feet*).

trépigner [trepi'ne], *v.i.* to stamp, to stamp one's foot.

très [trɛ], *adv.* very; most; very much.

trésor [tre'zɔːr], *n.m.* treasure; treasury; exchequer; thesaurus.

trésorerie [trezɔr'ri], *n.f.* treasury; treasurer-ship.

trésorier [trezɔ'rje], *n.m.* treasurer; (*Mil.*) paymaster.

tressage [trɛ'saːʒ], *n.m.* plaiting, braiding.

tressaillement [tresaj'mɑ̃], *n.m.* start, bound, thrill, shudder; flutter.

tressaillir [tresa'jir], *v.i. irr.* (*conjug. like* ASSAILLIR) to start, to thrill; to quake, to tremble, to shudder.

tresse [trɛs], *n.f.* tress, plait (*of hair*); braid.

tresser [trɛ'se], *v.t.* to weave, to plait, to braid; to wreathe.

tréteau [tre'to], *n.m.* (*pl.* **-eaux**) trestle; (*pl.*) stage.

treuil [trœːj], *n.m.* windlass; winch.

trêve [trɛːv], *n.f.* truce.

tri [tri], *n.m.* sorting (*of letters etc.*).

triage [tri'jaːʒ], *n.m.* picking, sorting; choice, selection.

triangle [tri'jɑ̃ːgl], *n.m.* triangle.

triangulaire [trijɑ̃gy'lɛːr], *a.* triangular.

tribord [tri'bɔːr], *n.m.* (*Naut.*) starboard.

tribu [tri'by], *n.f.* tribe.

tribulation [tribylɑ'sjɔ̃], *n.f.* tribulation.

tribun [tri'bœ̃], *n.m.* tribune; (*fig.*) demo-cratic leader.

tribunal [triby'nal], *n.m.* (*pl.* **-aux**) tribunal, bench; court of justice.

tribune [tri'byn], *n.f.* tribune (*rostrum*); hustings; gallery.

tribut [tri'by], *n.m.* tribute; grant, contribu-tion; *duty; (*fig.*) debt.

tributaire [triby'tɛːr], *a.* dependent (*upon*).— *n.m.* tributary.

tricher [tri'ʃe], *v.t., v.i.* to cheat, to trick.

tricherie [triʃ'ri], *n.f.* cheating, trick, trickery.

tricheur [tri'ʃœːr], *n.m.* (*fem.* **-euse**) cheat, trickster.

tricolore [trikɔ'lɔːr], *a.* tricolored.

tricorne [tri'kɔrn], *a.* three-cornered.—*n.m.* three-cornered hat.

tricot [tri'ko], *n.m.* knitting; jersey, jumper, (*fam.*) woolly; *tricot de corps*, vest.

tricotage [trikɔ'taːʒ], *n.m.* knitting.

tricoter [trikɔ'te], *v.t., v.i.* to knit.

trictrac [trik'trak], *n.m.* tric-trac (*form of* backgammon).

tricycle [tri'sikl], *n.m.* three-wheeled vehicle; tricycle.

trident [tri'dɑ̃], *n.m.* trident.

triennal [triɛ'nal], *a.* (*m. pl.* **-aux**) triennial.

trier [tri'je], *v.t.* to pick, to choose, to sort, to select; to route (freight cars).

trieur [tri'jœːr], *n.m.* (*fem.* **-euse**) sorter, picker.

trigonométrie [trigɔnɔme'tri], *n.f.* trigono-metry.

trille [triːj], *n.m.* quaver, trill.

triller [tri'je], *v.t.* to trill, to quaver.

trillion [tri'ljɔ̃], *n.m.* (*since 1948 = 1 followed by 18 ciphers*) trillion, one million billion(s); (*Am.*) quintillion.

trilogie [trilɔ'ʒi], *n.f.* trilogy.

trimbaler [trɛ̃ba'le], *v.t.* (*fam.*) to drag *or* lug about (*parcels*); to trail (*children*) about. **se trimbaler**, *v.r.* (*pop.*) to traipse round.

trimer [tri'me], *v.i.* (*pop.*) to drudge, to wear oneself out.

trimestre [tri'mɛstr], *n.m.* quarter (*three months*); quarter's pay; (*Sch.*) term.

trimestriel [trimɛstri'ɛl], *a.* (*fem.* **-elle**) quarterly.

tringle [trɛ̃ːgl], *n.f.* rod.

Trinité [trini'te], *n.f.* Trinity; *la Trinité*, Trinity Sunday; (*'île de*) *la Trinité*, Trinidad.

trinquer [trɛ̃'ke], *v.i.* to clink glasses (*before drinking*); to drink to one another's health; (*pop.*) to suffer, to be hurt.

trio [tri'o], *n.m.* trio.

triomphal [triɔ̃'fal], *a.* (*m. pl.* **-aux**) trium-phal.

triomphalement [triɔ̃fal'mɑ̃], *adv.* trium-phantly.

triomphant [triɔ̃'fɑ̃], *a.* triumphant.

triomphe [tri'ɔ̃ːf], *n.m.* triumph.

triompher [triɔ̃'fe], *v.i.* to triumph; to overcome; to exult; to excel.

triparti [tripar'ti], **tripartite** [tripar'tit], *a.* tripartite.

tripe [trip], *n.f.* tripe; imitation velvet, velveteen (*also called tripe de velours*).

triperie [trip'ri], *n.f.* tripe shop.

triple [tripl], *a.* and *n.m.* treble, triple, three-fold.

tripler [tri'ple], *v.t., v.i.* to treble, to triple.

triplicata [triplika'ta], *n.m. inv.* triplicate.

tripode [tri'pɔd], *a.* and *n.m.* tripod.

tripot [tri'po], *n.m.* gambling den; house of ill fame.

tripotage [tripɔ'taːʒ], *n.m.* mess; underhand dealing; chore.

tripoter [tripɔ'te], *v.t.* to meddle with; to speculate in.—*v.i.* to make mischief, to mess about; to act in an underhand way.

tripoteur [tripɔ'tœːr], *n.m.* (*fem.* **-euse**) mischief-maker, shady speculator.

trique [trik], *n.f.* (*fam.*) cudgel, stick, bludgeon.

trisaïeul [triza'jœl], *n.m.* (*pl.* **-aïeuls**) great-great-grandfather.

trisaïeule [triza'jœl], *n.f.* great-great-grand-mother.

triste [trist], *a.* sorrowful, mournful, sad, melancholy, dejected; dull, dreary, dismal; poor, sorry (*of persons*); mean, paltry.

tristement [triste'mɑ̃], *adv.* sadly.

tristesse [tris'tɛs], *n.f.* sadness; melancholy; dreariness.

triton [tri'tɔ̃], *n.m.* triton, newt.

trivial [tri'vjal], *a.* (*m. pl.* **-aux**) vulgar, trifling; trite, hackneyed.—*n.m.* vulgarity.

trivialité [trivjali'te], *n.f.* vulgarity; triteness.
troc [trɔk], *n.m.* trade, barter, swap.
troène [trɔ'ɛn], *n.m.* privet.
troglodyte [trɔglɔ'dit], *n.m.* troglodyte.
trogne [trɔɲ], *n.f.* reddish *or* bloated face.
trognon [trɔ'ɲɔ̃], *n.m.* core (*of a pear or apple*); stump (*of a cabbage*).
Troie [trwa], *f.* Troy.
trois [trwa], *a.* and *n.m. inv.* three; third.
troisième [trwa'zjɛm], *a.* third.—*n.* third.—*n.m.* third floor.
troisièmement [trwazjɛm'mã], *adv.* thirdly.
trombe [trɔ̃:b], *n.f.* waterspout.
tromblon [trɔ̃'blɔ̃], *n.m.* blunderbuss.
trombone [trɔ̃'bɔn], *n.m.* trombone; paper clip (*of wire*).
trompe [trɔ̃:p], *n.f.* *trump, horn; proboscis, trunk (*of elephants*).
tromper [trɔ̃'pe], *v.t.* to deceive, to impose upon; to delude; to cheat, to take in; to betray, to be unfaithful to (*wife, husband*). **se tromper**, *v.r.* to be mistaken, to make a mistake, to deceive oneself.
tromperie [trɔ̃'pri], *n.f.* cheat, fraud; illusion, delusion.
trompeter [trɔ̃pə'te], *v.t.* (*conjug. like* APPELER) to trumpet abroad.
trompette [trɔ̃'pɛt], *n.f.* trumpet.—*n.m.* trumpeter.
trompeur [trɔ̃'pœːr], *a.* (*fem.* **-euse**) deceitful; false, misleading.—*n.m.* (*fem.* **-euse**) deceiver, cheat, impostor; betrayer.
trompeusement [trɔ̃pøz'mã], *adv.* deceitfully, deceptively.
tronc [trɔ̃], *n.m.* trunk, bole (*of tree*); stock; poor box.
tronçon [trɔ̃'sɔ̃], *n.m.* broken piece, fragment, stump.
tronçonner [trɔ̃sɔ'ne], *v.t.* to cut into pieces.
trône [tro:n], *n.m.* throne.
trôner [tro'ne], *v.i.* to sit on a throne; (*fig.*) to lord it.
tronquer [trɔ̃'ke], *v.t.* to mutilate, to truncate; (*fig.*) to garble, to mangle.
trop [tro], *adv.* too much, too, over, too many; **de trop**, too much, too many; **être de trop**, to be in the way, not to be wanted; **par trop**, excessively.—*n.m.* excess, superfluity.
trophée [trɔ'fe], *n.m.* trophy.
tropical [trɔpi'kal], *a.* (*m. pl.* **-aux**) tropical.
tropique [trɔ'pik], *n.m.* tropic.
trop-plein [trɔ'plɛ̃], *n.m.* (*pl.* **-pleins**) overflow, waste; surplus, excess.
troquer [trɔ'ke], *v.t.* to trade, to barter, to exchange.
trot [tro], *n.m.* trot.
trotte-menu [trɔtmə'ny] *a. inv.* running with little steps, pitter-pattering.
trotter [trɔ'te], *v.i.* to trot; to run about, to toddle (*children*).
trotteur [trɔ'tœːr], *n.m.* (*fem.* **-euse**) trotter.—*n.f.* (**-euse**) second hand (*of watch*).
trottin [trɔ'tɛ̃], *n.m.* errand girl.
trottiner [trɔti'ne], *v.i.* to go at a jog-trot; to toddle along.
trottinette [trɔti'nɛt], *n.f.* (*child's*) scooter.
trottoir [trɔ'twaːr], *n.m.* foot-path, pavement, (*Am.*) sidewalk; **le bord du trottoir**, the curb.
trou [tru], *n.m.* hole; gap; orifice, mouth; **boucher un trou**, to stop a gap, to pay a

debt; **trou d'air**, air pocket; **trou de la serrure**, keyhole; **trou du souffleur**, (*Theat.*) prompter's box.
troubadour [truba'duːr], *n.m.* troubadour.
troublant [tru'blã], *a.* disturbing, troubling.
trouble [trubl], *a.* thick, muddy, turbid, cloudy; dull.—*adv.* dimly, confusedly.—*n.m.* confusion, disorder, disturbance; perplexity, uneasiness; dispute, quarrel; (*pl.*) disturbances, dissensions.
trouble-fête [trublə'fɛːt], *n.m. inv.* kill-joy.
troubler [tru'ble], *v.t.* to disturb, to make thick, to make muddy; to muddle, to turn; to confuse, to agitate; to perplex, to disconcert; to trouble; to interrupt; to ruffle, to annoy; to dim, to dull. **se troubler**, *v.r.* to grow thick, to become muddy; to be confused, to be disconcerted; to become cloudy; to become confused.
trouée [tru'e], *n.f.* opening, gap, breach; pass.
trouer [tru'e], *v.t.* to bore, to make a hole in. **se trouer**, *v.r.* to get holes in it.
trouille [truːj], *n.f.* (*vulg.*) fear.
troupe [trup], *n.f.* troop, band; crew, gang, set; company (*of actors*); flock, crowd; (*pl.*) troops, forces.
troupeau [tru'po], *n.m.* (*pl.* **-eaux**) flock, herd, drove.
troupier [tru'pje], *n.m.* soldier.
trousse [truːs], *n.f.* bundle, truss; (*Surg.*) case of instruments; case for razors, toilet articles etc; **je suis à ses trousses**, I am after him.
troussé [tru'se], *a.* tucked up; **bien troussé**, well set up, neat, dapper.
trousseau [tru'so], *n.m.* (*pl.* **-eaux**) bunch (*of keys*); trousseau; outfit, kit.
trousser [tru'se], *v.t.* to tuck up, to turn up, to pin up; to truss; to dispatch (*business etc.*). **se trousser**, *v.r.* to tuck up one's clothes.
trouvaille [tru'vaːj], *n.f.* godsend, windfall; find.
trouvé [tru've], *a.* found; **bien trouvé**, felicitous; **enfant trouvé**, foundling.
trouver [tru've], *v.t.* to find, to discover, to meet with, to hit upon; to detect; to find out; to deem, to judge; **trouver à dire** or **à redire à**, to find fault with; **trouver bon**, to think fit; **trouver mauvais**, to blame, to be displeased with; **vous trouvez?** you think so, do you? **se trouver**, *v.r.* to find oneself; to be, to exist; to feel; to prove, to turn out; **se trouver mal**, to faint.
truand [try'ã], *a.* vagrant.—*n.m.* (*fem.* **-e**) vagrant, beggar, tramp; crook.
truc (1) [tryk], *n.m.* knack, dodge, trick; (*Theat.*) machinery; (*pop.*) thing, thingumajig, gadget.
truc (2) or **truck** [tryk], *n.m.* (*Rail.*) flat-car.
trucheman or **truchement** [tryʃ'mã], *n.m.* interpreter; go-between.
truculent [tryky'lã], *a.* truculent.
truelle [try'ɛl], *n.f.* trowel; **truelle à poisson**, slice of fish.
truffe [tryf], *n.f.* truffle.
truie [trɥi], *n.f.* sow.
truite [trɥit], *n.f.* trout.
truité [trɥi'te], *a.* spotted, speckled.
trumeau [try'mo], *n.m.* (*pl.* **-eaux**) pier; pier glass; leg of beef.

tsar [tsa:r], *n.m.* Tsar.
tsigane [TZIGANE].
tu [ty], *pron.* *thou, you.
tuant [tyⁿɑ̃], *a.* killing, tiresome, laborious.
tube [tyb], *n.m.* tube, pipe; (*Anat.*) duct.
tuberculeux [tybɛrkylø], *a.* (*fem.* **-euse**) tuberculous.
tuberculose [tybɛrkylo:z], *n.f.* tuberculosis.
tubulaire [tybylɛ:r], *a.* tubular.
tuer [tɥe], *v.t.* to kill, to slay; to slaughter, to butcher; to tire to death; to while away. **se tuer**, *v.r.* to kill oneself, to be killed; (*fig.*) to wear oneself out.
tuerie [tyri], *n.f.* slaughter, butchery; slaughter-house.
tue-tête (à) [atytɛ:t], *adv. phr.* at the top of one's voice.
tueur [tɥœ:r], *n.m.* (*fem.* **-euse**) killer, thug.
tuile [tɥil], *n.f.* tile.
tuilerie [tɥilri], *n.f.* tile-works; *les Tuileries*, the Tuileries (*before 1871 a Royal palace, now a garden in Paris*).
tulipe [tylip], *n.f.* tulip.
tulle [tyl], *n.m.* tulle, net.
tumeur [tymœ:r], *n.f.* tumor, swelling.
tumulte [tymylt], *n.m.* tumult, uproar; hubbub.
tumultueux [tymyltɥø], *a.* (*fem.* **-euse**) tumultuous, riotous.
tunique [tynik], *n.f.* tunic; envelope, film.
Tunisie [tynizi], **la**, *f.* Tunisia.
tunisien [tynizjɛ̃], *a.* Tunisian.—*n.m.* (**Tunisien**, *fem.* **-enne**) Tunisian (*person*).
tunnel [tynɛl], *n.m.* tunnel.
turban [tyrbɑ̃], *n.m.* turban.
turbine [tyrbin], *n.f.* turbine.
turbopropulseur [tyrbopropylsœ:r], *n.m.* turbo-prop.
turboréacteur [tyrboreaktœ:r], *n.m.* jet engine; turbo-jet.
turbot [tyrbo], *n.m.* turbot.
turbulence [tyrbylɑ̃:s], *n.f.* turbulence.
turbulent [tyrbylɑ̃], *a.* turbulent, boisterous; rowdy.
turc [tyrk], *a.* (*fem.* **turque**) Turkish.—*n.m.* Turkish (*language*); (**Turc**, *fem.* **Turque**) Turk.
turelure [tyrly:r], *n.f.* fol-de-rol (*burden of a song*).
turf [tyrf], *n.m.* the turf, horse racing.
turpitude [tyrpityd], *n.f.* turpitude, baseness, ignominy.
turque [TURC].
Turquie [tyrki], **la**, *f.* Turkey.
turquoise [tyrkwa:z], *a.* and *n.f.* turquoise.
tussor [tyso:r], *n.m.* tussore (*silk*).
tutelle [tytɛl], *n.f.* tutelage, guardianship; (*Polit.*) trusteeship.
tuteur [tytœ:r], *n.m.* (*fem.* **tutrice**) guardian, trustee, protector.—*n.m.* (*Hort.*) stake.
tutoiement or **tutoîment** [tytwamɑ̃], *n.m.* addressing a person as 'tu', 'theeing and thouing'.
tutoyer [tytwaje], *v.t.* (*conjug. like* EMPLOYER) to be on intimate terms with. **se tutoyer**, *v.r.* to be on familiar terms.
tutrice [tytris], [TUTEUR].
tuyau [tɥijo], *n.m.* (*pl.* **-aux**) pipe; tube; (chimney-)flue; shaft, funnel; stalk (*of grain*); nozzle (*of bellows etc.*); stem (*of a tobacco pipe*); *tuyau d'arrosage*, garden

hose; *tuyau d'incendie*, fire hose; *tuyau de poêle*, stove-pipe.
tuyautage [tɥijota:ʒ], *n.m.* frilling, fluting; tubing.
tuyauter [tɥijote], *v.t.* to goffer, to frill.
tuyauterie [tɥijotri], *n.f.* system of pipes; plumbing; pipe trade.
tympan [tɛ̃pɑ̃], *n.m.* ear-drum, tympanum; tympan; spandrel.
type [tip], *n.m.* type; model, pattern; symbol, emblem; standard; (*Astron.*) plan, drawing; (*colloq.*) guy, chap, fellow.
typhoïde [tifoid], *a.* typhoid.
typhon [tifɔ̃], *n.m.* typhoon.
typhus [tify:s], *n.m.* typhus.
typique [tipik], *a.* typical; characteristic.
typographe [tipograf], *n.m.* typographer.
typographie [tipografi], *n.f.* typography.
tyran [tirɑ̃], *n.m.* tyrant.
tyrannie [tirani], *n.f.* tyranny.
tyrannique [tiranik], *a.* tyrannical.
tyranniser [tiranize], *v.t.* to tyrannize, to oppress.
tzar [TSAR].
tzigane or **tsigane** [tsigan], *a.* and *n.* gipsy.

U

U, u [y], *n.m.* the twenty-first letter of the alphabet.
ubiquité [ybikɥite], *n.f.* ubiquity.
Ukraine [ykrɛn], **l'**, *f.* the Ukraine.
ukrainien [ykrɛnjɛ̃], *a.* Ukrainian.—*n.m.* (**Ukrainien**, *fem.* **-enne**) Ukrainian (*person*).
ulcère [ylsɛ:r], *n.m.* ulcer.
ulcéré [ylse're], *a.* ulcerated; (*fig.*) embittered.
ulcérer [ylse're], *v.t.* (*conjug. like* CÉDER) to ulcerate; (*fig.*) to embitter, to incense.
ultérieur [ylterjœ:r], *a.* ulterior, further, later, subsequent.
ultérieurement [ylterjœrmɑ̃], *adv.* later on.
ultimatum [ultimatɔm], *n.m.* ultimatum.
ultime [yltim], *a.* last, final, ultimate.
ultra-sonore [yltrasɔnɔ:r], *a.* supersonic.
ultra-violet [yltraviɔlɛ], *a.* (*fem.* **-ette**) ultra-violet.
ululer [ylyle], *v.i.* to ululate, to hoot.
Ulysse [ylis], *m.* Ulysses.
umbre [ɔ̃:br], **omble** [ɔ̃:bl], **ombre** [ɔ̃:br], *n.m.* grayling (*fish*).
un [œ̃], *a.* and *art. indef.* (*fem.* **une**) one, the first; single; a, an; any, a certain.—*pron. indef.* one thing; one; *c'est tout un*, it is all one; *les uns disent oui, les autres disent non*, some say yes, others say no; *les uns et les autres*, all, all together; *l'un et l'autre*, both; *l'un ou l'autre*, the one or the other; *l'un vaut l'autre*, one is as good as the other; *un à un*, one by one.—*n.m.* one.
unanime [ynanim], *a.* unanimous.
unanimement [ynanimmɑ̃], *adv.* unanimously.
unanimité [ynanimite], *n.f.* unanimity.

uni [y′ni], *a.* united; smooth, even, level; uniform; plain, unaffected.
unicorne [yni′kɔrn], *n.m.* unicorn.
unième [y′njɛm], *a.* (*in compounds only*) first; *vingt et unième*, 21st.
unification [ynifika′sjɔ̃], *n.f.* unification.
unifier [yni′fje], *v.t.* to unify, to unite; to amalgamate.
uniforme [yni′fɔrm], *a.* uniform.—*n.m.* uniform, regimentals.
uniformément [ynifɔrme′mã], *adv.* uniformly.
uniformité [ynifɔrmi′te], *n.f.* uniformity.
unilatéral [ynilate′ral], *a.* (*m. pl.* **-aux**) unilateral.
uniment [yni′mã], *adv.* evenly, smoothly; plainly.
union [y′njɔ̃], *n.f.* union; concord, agreement; mixture; marriage.
unique [y′nik], *a.* only, sole; single, unique, unparalleled; odd, singular; *fils unique*, only son; *sens unique*, one way (*street*).
uniquement [ynik′mã], *adv.* solely.
unir [y′niːr], *v.t.* to unite, to join; to smooth, to level; to pair. **s'unir**, *v.r.* to unite, to join together.
unisson [yni′sɔ̃], *n.m.* unison; (*fig.*) harmony, concert.
unité [yni′te], *n.f.* unity; unit; (*fig.*) concord, agreement.
univers [yni′vɛːr], *n.m. inv.* universe.
universalité [yniversali′te], *n.f.* universality; sum total, whole.
universel [yniver′sɛl], *a.* (*fem.* **-elle**) universal; residuary (*of legacies*).
universellement [yniversɛl′mã], *adv.* universally.
universitaire [yniversi′tɛːr], *a.* of the university, academic.—*n.* teacher, professor.
université [yniversi′te], *n.f.* university.
uranium [yra′njɔm], *n.m.* uranium.
urbain [yr′bɛ̃], *a.* urban.
urbanisme [yrba′nism], *n.m.* town-planning.
urbaniste [yrba′nist], *n.m.* town-planner.
urbanité [yrbani′te], *n.f.* urbanity.
urgence [yr′ʒãːs], *n.f.* urgency; emergency; *d'urgence*, urgently; immediately.
urgent [yr′ʒã], *a.* urgent, pressing.
urinaire [yri′nɛːr], *a.* urinary.
urine [y′rin], *n.f.* urine.
uriner [yri′ne], *v.i.* to urinate, to make water.
urinoir [yri′nwaːr], *n.m.* (public) urinal.
urne [yrn], *n.f.* urn; *urne électorale*, ballot box.
Ursule [yr′syl], *f.* Ursula.
urticaire [yrti′kɛːr], *n.f.* nettle rash; urticaria.
Uruguay [yry′gɛ], *l'*, *m.* Uruguay.
uruguayen [yrygɛ′jɛ̃], *a.* Uruguayan.—*n.m.* (**Uruguayen**, *fem.* **-enne**) Uruguayan (*person*).
us [ys, yz], *n.m. pl.* **les us et coutumes**, the ways and customs.
usage [y′zaːʒ], *n.m.* custom, practice, usage; use; wear (*of clothes etc.*); *avoir de l'usage*, to have breeding; *hors d'usage*, out of use; *faire de l'usage* or *faire un bon usage*, to last or wear a long time.
usagé [yza′ʒe], *a.* used, worn, second-hand.
usager [yza′ʒe], *n.m.* user; *les usagers de la route*, road-users.

usé [y′ze], *a.* worn-out, threadbare; stale, trite, hackneyed.
user [y′ze], *v.t.* to use up, to consume; to wear out; to spend, to waste.—*v.i.* to make use of. **s'user**, *v.r.* to wear oneself out; to wear away.
usine [y′zin], *n.f.* works, mills, factory.
usinier [yzi′nje], *n.m.* manufacturer, mill owner.
usité [yzi′te], *a.* used, usual, in common use.
ustensile [ystã′sil], *n.m.* utensil; tool, implement.
usuel [y′zɥɛl], *a.* (*fem.* **-elle**) usual, customary, ordinary.
usuellement [ysɥɛl′mã], *adv.* habitually, ordinarily.
usure [y′zyːr], *n.f.* usury, excessive interest; wear and tear.
usurier [yzy′rje], *a.* (*fem.* **-ière**) usurious.—*n.m.* (*fem.* **-ière**) usurer.
usurpateur [yzyrpa′tœːr], *a.* (*fem.* **-trice**) usurping.—*n.m.* (*fem.* **-trice**) usurper.
usurpation [yzyrpa′sjɔ̃], *n.f.* usurpation; encroachment.
usurper [yzyr′pe], *v.t.* to usurp; to encroach upon.
ut [yt], *n.m.* (*Mus.*) ut, do, the note C.
utérus [yte′rys], *n.m.* uterus, womb.
utile [y′til], *a.* useful, serviceable; advantageous, expedient, beneficial; *en temps utile*, in due or good time.—*n.m.* utility, usefulness.
utilement [ytil′mã], *adv.* usefully.
utilisation [ytiliza′sjɔ̃], *n.f.* use, utilization.
utiliser [ytili′ze], *v.t.* to use, to find use for, to employ.
utilité [ytili′te], *n.f.* utility, usefulness; benefit, profit, service, avail.
utopie [ytɔ′pi], *n.f.* utopia.
utopique [ytɔ′pik], *a.* utopian.

V

V, v [ve], *n.m.* the twenty-second letter of the alphabet.
vacance [va′kãːs], *n.f.* vacancy; (*pl.*) vacation, holiday; recess (*of parliament etc.*).
vacant [va′kã], *a.* vacant; unoccupied, empty.
vacarme [va′karm], *n.m.* hubbub, uproar, fuss.
vacation [vaka′sjɔ̃], *n.f.* attendance, sitting (*of public officers etc.*); day's sale (*at auctions*); vacation (*of courts*).
vaccin [vak′sɛ̃], *n.m.* vaccine.
vaccination [vaksina′sjɔ̃], *n.f.* inoculation, vaccination.
vacciner [vaksi′ne], *v.t.* to inoculate, to vaccinate; to immunize.
vache [vaʃ], *n.f.* cow; cow-hide.
vacher [va′ʃe], *n.m.* (*fem.* **-ère**) cow-herd.
vacherie [va′ʃri], *n.f.* cow-house, byre.
vacillant [vasi′jã], *a.* vacillating, wavering, flickering; shaky, uncertain, unsteady.
vacillation [vasija′sjɔ̃], *n.f.* wobbling, flickering.

vaciller [vasi'je], *v.i.* to vacillate; to waver, to stagger; to flicker (*of light etc.*).

vacuité [vakųi'te], *n.f.* vacuity, emptiness.

vacuum [va'kɥɔm], *n.m.* vacuum.

va-et-vient [vae'vjɛ̃], *n.m. inv.* reciprocating motion, swing, see-saw motion, oscillation; (*fig.*) coming and going.

vagabond [vaga'bɔ̃], *a.* and *n.m.* (*fem.* **-e**) vagabond, vagrant.

vagabondage [vagabɔ̃'da:ʒ], *n.m.* vagrancy.

vagabonder [vagabɔ̃'de], *v.i.* to be a vagabond; to roam; (*fig.*) to flit from one thing to another.

vagin [va'ʒɛ̃], *n.m.* (*Anat.*) vagina.

vagir [va'ʒiːr], *v.i.* to wail, to pule (*of infants*).

vague (1) [vag], *n.f.* wave, billow.

vague (2) [vag], *a.* vague, indeterminate, uncertain; faint, indistinct, hazy; empty, vacant; *terres vagues*, waste-land; *terrain vague*, vacant site, piece of waste ground. —*n.m.* vagueness, looseness, uncertainty; empty space.

vaguement [vag'mɑ̃], *adv.* vaguely, dimly.

vaguer [va'ge], *v.i.* to ramble, to wander, to stray.

vaillamment [vaja'mɑ̃], *adv.* valiantly.

vaillance [va'jɑ̃:s], *n.f.* valor, bravery.

vaillant [va'jɑ̃], *a.* valiant, brave, gallant; stout (*heart*); *n'avoir pas un sou vaillant*, to be penniless.

vain [vɛ̃], *a.* vain, fruitless, ineffectual; empty, hollow; trifling; vainglorious; conceited; *en vain*, vainly, in vain.

vaincre [vɛ̃:kr], *v.t. irr.* to vanquish, to conquer, to overcome, to defeat; to outdo, to surpass; *se laisser vaincre*, to give way to, to yield.

vaincu [vɛ̃'ky], *a.* conquered, vanquished.—*n.m.* (*fem.* **-e**) conquered person, loser.

vainement [vɛn'mɑ̃], *adv.* vainly, in vain.

vainqueur [vɛ̃'kœːr], *a.* conquering, victorious.—*n.m.* vanquisher, conqueror, victor; prize winner.

vairon [vɛ'rɔ̃], *n.m.* minnow.

vaisseau [vɛ'so], *n.m.* (*pl.* **-eaux**) vessel, receptacle; ship; large covered space (*of a building*); (*Anat., Bot.*) vessel, tube, duct; (*pl.*) shipping.

vaisselle [vɛ'sɛl], *n.f.* plates and dishes; plate (*of gold* or *silver*); *faire la vaisselle*, to wash up.

val [val], *n.m.* (*pl.* **vals** or **vaux**) narrow valley, vale, dale.

valable [va'labl], *a.* valid, good.

valet [va'lɛ], *n.m.* footman, valet, man-servant; jack (*at cards*); door weight; holdfast; *valet de chambre*, valet; *valet de chiens*, whipper-in; *valet de ferme*, farm worker.

valeter [val'te], *v.i.* (*conjug. like* APPELER) to cringe, to dance attendance.

valétudinaire [valetydi'nɛːr], *a.* valetudinary.—*n.* valetudinarian, invalid.

valeur [va'lœːr], *n.f.* value, worth, price; consideration; import, meaning; valor, bravery; (*pl.*) bills, paper, stocks, shares, securities.

valeureusement [valœrøz'mɑ̃], *adv.* bravely, courageously.

valeureux [valœ'rø], *a.* (*fem.* **-euse**) brave, courageous, gallant.

valide [va'lid], *a.* valid, good; healthy, able-bodied.—*n.* person in good health.

valider [vali'de], *v.t.* to make valid; to ratify, to validate.

validité [validi'te], *n.f.* validity; availability (*of a ticket*).

valise [va'liːz], *n.f.* suit-case; valise, portmanteau.

vallée [va'le], *n.f.* valley.

vallon [va'lɔ̃], *n.m.* small valley, vale, dale.

valoir [va'lwaːr], *v.t. irr.* to yield, to bring in; to procure, to furnish.—*v.i.* to be worth, to be as good as, to be equal to; to deserve, to merit; *autant vaut*, to all intents and purposes; *à valoir*, on account; *faire valoir son droit*, to assert one's right; *se faire valoir*, to boast; *vaille que vaille*, for better or worse; *valoir mieux*, to be better.

valse [vals], *n.f.* waltz.

valser [val'se], *v.i.* to waltz.

valve [valv], *n.f.* valve; electron tube.

vampire [vɑ̃'piːr], *n.m.* vampire.

van [vɑ̃], *n.m.* (*Agric.*) winnowing basket.

vandale [vɑ̃'dal], *n.* vandal.

vandalisme [vɑ̃da'lism], *n.m.* vandalism.

vanille [va'niːj], *n.f.* vanilla.

vanité [vani'te], *n.f.* vanity, conceit.

vaniteux [vani'tø], *a.* (*fem.* **-euse**) vainglorious, vain.

vannage [va'na:ʒ], *n.m.* winnowing.

vanne [van], *n.f.* sluice, sluice gate.

vanneau [va'no], *n.m.* (*pl.* **-eaux**) lapwing, peewit.

vanner [va'ne], *v.t.* to winnow, to fan, to sift; (*pop.*) to tire out.

vannerie [van'ri], *n.f.* basket-making, basket trade.

vanneur [va'nœːr], *a.* (*fem.* **-euse**) winnowing.—*n.m.* (*fem.* **-euse**) winnower.—*n.f.* (**-euse**) winnowing machine.

vannier [va'nje], *n.m.* (*fem.* **-iere**) basket-maker.

vannure [va'nyːr], *n.f.* chaff.

vantard [vɑ̃'taːr], *a.* boasting, boastful, bragging.—*n.m.* (*fem.* **-e**) boaster, braggart.

vantardise [vɑ̃tar'diːz], *n.f.* boasting, bragging.

vanter [vɑ̃'te], *v.t.* to praise, to commend, to extol. **se vanter**, *v.r.* to boast, to pride oneself on (*de*).

vanterie [vɑ̃'tri], *n.f.* boasting, bragging.

va-nu-pieds [vany'pje], *n. inv.* ragamuffin.

vapeur [va'pœːr], *n.f.* vapor; steam; haze, mist; *à la vapeur* or *à toute vapeur*, at full speed.—*n.m.* steamer, steamship.

vaporeux [vapo'rø], *a.* (*fem.* **-euse**) vaporous; steamy, hazy.

vaquer [va'ke], *v.i.* to be vacant; to attend, to devote oneself (*à*).

varech or **varec** [va'rɛk], *n.m* sea-wrack, sea-weed.

variabilité [varjabili'te], *n.f.* variability, changeableness.

variable [va'rjabl], *a.* variable, fickle, unsettled.—*n.f.* (*Math.*) variable.

variant [va'rjɑ̃], *a.* variable, fickle.—*n.f.* (**-e**) variant (*reading* or *interpretation*).

variation [varja'sjɔ̃], *n.f.* variation.

varice [va'ris], *n.f.* varix, varicose vein.

varier [va'rje], *v.t.* to vary, to change; to variegate.—*v.i.* to vary, to be changeable; to disagree.

variété [varje'te], *n.f.* variety, diversity, change; (*pl.*) miscellanea.
variole [va'rjɔl], *n.f.* smallpox.
Varsovie [varsɔ'vi], *f.* Warsaw.
vase (1) [vɑːz], *n.m.* vase, vessel.
vase (2) [vɑːz], *n.f.* slime, mud, mire, ooze.
vaseline [vaz'lin], *n.f.* petroleum jelly, Vaseline (*reg. trade mark*).
vaseux [va'zø], *a.* (*fem.* **-euse**) slimy, muddy, miry.
vasistas [vazis'tɑːs], *n.m. inv.* transom, fanlight (*over a door or a window*).
vassal [va'sal], *n.m.* (*fem.* **-e**, *m. pl.* **-aux**) vassal.
vaste [vast], *a.* vast, wide, spacious.
vastement [vastə'mɑ̃], *adv.* vastly, widely.
Vatican [vati'kɑ̃], **le**, *m.* the Vatican.
va-tout [va'tu], *n.m. inv.* one's all (*at cards*); *jouer son va-tout*, to stake one's all.
vaudeville [vod'vil], *n.m.* vaudeville; light form of comedy.
vau-l'eau (**à**) [avo'lo], *adv. phr.* with the current, down-stream; to rack and ruin.
vaurien [vo'rjɛ̃], *n.m.* (*fem.* **-enne**) good-for-nothing, scamp; rogue.
vautour [vo'tuːr], *n.m.* vulture.
vautre [voːtr], *n.m.* boar-hound.
vautrer (**se**) [səvo'tre], *v.r.* to wallow; to sprawl.
veau [vo], *n.m.* (*pl.* **veaux**) calf; (*Cook.*) veal; calf-skin, calf leather; (*fig.*) slow-witted fellow; *veau marin*, seal, seal-skin.
vedette [və'dɛt], *n.f.* vedette, mounted sentinel; scout; observation post, watch-tower; (*Theat.*) star.
végétal [veʒe'tal], *a.* (*m. pl.* **-aux**) vegetable. —*n.m.* (*pl.* **-aux**) vegetable, plant.
végétarien [veʒeta'rjɛ̃], *a. and n.m.* (*fem.* **-enne**) vegetarian.
végétation [veʒetɑ'sjɔ̃], *n.f.* vegetation; (*pl.*) adenoids.
végéter [veʒe'te], *v.i.* (*conjug. like* CÉDER) to vegetate.
véhémence [vee'mɑ̃ːs], *n.f.* vehemence.
véhément [vee'mɑ̃], *a.* vehement, impetuous, hot, passionate.
véhiculaire [veiky'lɛːr], *a.* vehicular.
véhicule [vei'kyl], *n.m.* vehicle; medium.
veille [vɛːj], *n.f.* sleeplessness, watching; being awake, vigil; eve, day before; point, verge; (*pl.*) midnight work; *être à la veille de*, to be on the point of; *la veille de Noël*, Christmas Eve.
veillée [ve'je], *n.f.* time from supper to bed-time, evening (*in company*); sitting up to work etc. in company; night attendance (*upon a sick person*).
veiller [ve'je], *v.t.* to watch by, to nurse, to look after, to sit up with.—*v.i.* to sit up, to watch; to attend, to take care, to have an eye (**à**).
veilleur [vɛ'jœːr], *n.m.* (*fem.* **-euse**) watcher; *veilleur de nuit*, night watchman.—*n.f.* (**-euse**) night-light.
veinard [vɛ'naːr], *a. and n.m.* (*fem.* **-e**) (*pop.*) lucky (person), lucky dog.
veine [vɛːn], *n.f.* vein; (*Geol. etc.*) seam; (*pop.*) good luck; *avoir de la veine*, to be in luck; *en veine de*, in the mood for; *un coup de veine*, a fluke.
veiné [vɛ'ne], *a.* veined, veiny.

veineux [vɛ'nø], *a.* (*fem.* **-euse**) veined, veiny; venous (*system, blood*).
vélin [ve'lɛ̃], *n.m.* vellum.
velléité [velei'te], *n.f.* passing fancy, wish, whim.
vélo [ve'lo], *n.m.* (*fam.*) bike.
vélocité [velɔsi'te], *n.f.* velocity.
vélodrome [velɔ'drɔm], *n.m.* cycle-racing track.
vélomoteur [velɔmɔ'tœːr], *n.m.* motorbike.
velours [və'luːr], *n.m.* velvet; *velours à côtes*, corduroy; *velours de coton*, velveteen.
velouté [vəlu'te], *a.* velvet, velvety, velvet-like; soft and smooth to the palate (*of wines*).—*n.m.* velvet pile; softness; bloom (*of fruit*); smooth rich soup *or* sauce; *velouté de laine*, velours.
velu [və'ly], *a.* hairy, shaggy, rough.—*n.m.* shagginess.
vélum [ve'lɔm], *n.m.* awning.
venaison [vənɛ'zɔ̃], *n.f.* venison.
vénal [ve'nal], *a.* (*m. pl.* **-aux**) venal, mercenary.
vénalité [venali'te], *n.f.* venality.
venant [və'nɑ̃], *a.* coming, thriving.—*n.m.* comer; *tout-venant*, unsorted (*of produce*).
vendable [vɑ̃'dabl], *a.* saleable, marketable.
vendange [vɑ̃'dɑ̃ːʒ], *n.f.* vintage, grape gathering.
vendanger [vɑ̃dɑ̃'ʒe], *v.t.* (*conjug. like* MANGER) to gather in the grapes from; (*fig.*) to ravage, to spoil.—*v.i.* to pick (*the grapes*); (*fig.*) to make illicit profits.
vendangeur [vɑ̃dɑ̃'ʒœːr], *n.m.* (*fem.* **-euse**) vintager, grape gatherer.
vendéen [vɑ̃de'ɛ̃], *a.* (*fem.* **-éenne**) Vendean.
vendetta [vɛ̃de'ta], *n.f.* vendetta.
vendeur [vɑ̃'dœːr], *n.m.* (*fem.* **-euse**) vendor, seller, dealer; salesman, shop assistant.
vendre [vɑ̃ːdr], *v.t.* to sell; (*fig.*) to betray; *à vendre*, for sale. **se vendre**, *v.r.* to sell oneself; to be sold; to go off (*well etc.*).
vendredi [vɑ̃drə'di], *n.m.* Friday; *le Vendredi saint*, Good Friday.
vené [və'ne], *a.* high (*of meat*).
vénéneux [vene'nø], *a.* (*fem.* **-euse**) poisonous (*when eaten*).
vénérable [vene'rabl], *a.* venerable.
vénération [venerɑ'sjɔ̃], *n.f.* veneration.
vénérer [vene're], *v.t.* (*conjug. like* CÉDER) to venerate, to hold in reverence.
vénerie [ven'ri], *n.f.* venery, hunting.
veneur [və'nœːr], *n.m.* huntsman.
Vénézuéla [venezɥe'la], **le**, *m.* Venezuela.
vénézuélien [venezɥe'ljɛ̃], *a.* (*fem.* **-enne**) Venezuelan.—*n.m.* (**Vénézuélien**, *fem.* **-enne**) Venezuelan (*person*).
vengeance [vɑ̃'ʒɑ̃ːs], *n.f.* vengeance, revenge.
venger [vɑ̃'ʒe], *v.t.* (*conjug. like* MANGER) to revenge, to avenge. **se venger**, *v.r.* *se venger de quelqu'un*, to revenge oneself on someone.
vengeur [vɑ̃'ʒœːr], *a.* (*fem.* **-eresse**) revengeful, avenging.—*n.m.* (*fem.* **-eresse**) avenger, revenger.
véniel [ve'njɛl], *a.* (*fem.* **-elle**) venial.
venimeux [vəni'mø], *a.* (*fem.* **-euse**) communicating poison (*from outside*), venomous (*snake etc.*); (*fig.*) malignant, harmful.

venin [və'nɛ̃], *n.m.* venom, poison; (*fig.*) spite, malice.

venir [və'ni:r], *v.i. irr.* (*conjug. like* TENIR, *but with aux.* ÊTRE) to come, to be coming; to arrive; to reach; to occur, to happen; to grow, to grow up; to thrive; to issue, to arise; to be descended; *d'où vient cela?* what is the cause of that? *en venir aux mains*, to come to blows; *faire venir le médecin*, to send for the doctor; *il va et vient*, he goes in and out; *je ne ferai qu'aller et venir*, I will not stay, I shall come straight back; *le voilà qui vient*, here he comes; *où voulez-vous en venir?* what are you getting at? *s'en venir*, to come away; *si ma lettre venait à se perdre*, if my letter should happen to go astray; *venir à bout de*, to master; *venir de*, to come from, (*followed by an infinitive*, to have just—*je viens de le voir*, I have just seen him; *je venais de le quitter*, I had just left him).

Venise [və'ni:z], *f.* Venice.

vent [vã], *n.m.* wind; breeze; breath, breathing; (*Med.*) (*pl.*) flatulence; (*Hunt.*) scent; (*fig.*) vanity, emptiness; *autant en emporte le vent*, all that is idle talk; *avoir vent de*, to get wind of; *coup de vent*, gust of wind; (*colloq.*) *dans le vent*, 'with it'; *en plein vent*, in the open air; *il fait du vent*, it is windy.

vente [vã:t], *n.f.* sale; selling, auction; felling *or* cutting (*of timber*); *en vente*, for sale, on sale; *vente aux enchères*, sale at auction.

venter [vã'te], *v.i.* (*usu. impers.*) to blow, to be windy.

venteux [vã'tø], *a.* (*fem.* **-euse**) windy, gusty.

ventilateur [vãtila'tœ:r], *n.m.* ventilator, fan, blower.

ventilation [vãtila'sjɔ̃], *n.f.* ventilation, airing.

ventiler [vãti'le], *v.t.* to ventilate, to air; (*fig.*) to discuss.

ventosité [vãtozi'te], *n.f.* flatulence.

ventouse [vã'tu:z], *n.f.* cupping-glass; vent, air-hole; sucker (*of leech*); nozzle (*of vacuum cleaner*).

ventre [vã:tr], *n.m.* belly, abdomen; stomach; womb; bowels, one's inside; bulge; *à plat ventre*, flat on one's face; *ventre à terre*, at full speed; *j'ai mal au ventre*, I have a stomach ache.

ventrière [vãtri'ɛ:r], *n.f.* abdominal belt; sling, brace; girth (*of horse*).

ventriloque [vãtri'lɔk], *n.* ventriloquist.

ventriloquie [vãtrilo'ki], *n.f.* ventriloquy.

ventru [vã'try], *a.* big-bellied, corpulent; bulging.—*n.m.* (*fem.* **-e**) pot-bellied person.

venu [və'ny], *a.* come; done; come up, grown; *bien venu* [BIENVENU]; *enfant bien venu*, well-grown child; *mal venu*, unwelcome; open to censure.—*n.m.* (*fem.* **-e**) *le dernier venu*, the last arrival; *le premier venu* or *la première venue*, the first comer, anyone.—*n.f.* (**-e**) coming, arrival, advent; growth.

Vénus [ve'nys], *f.* Venus.

vêpres [vɛ:pr], *n.f. pl.* vespers.

ver [vɛ:r], *n.m.* worm; maggot, mite; moth; *mangé* or *rongé des vers*, worm-eaten; *nu comme un ver*, stark naked; *ver* *blanc*, grub; *ver à soie*, silkworm; *ver luisant*, glow-worm; *ver solitaire*, tapeworm.

véracité [verasi'te], *n.f.* veracity.

véranda [verã'da], *n.f.* veranda.

verbal [vɛr'bal], *a.* (*m. pl.* **-aux**) verbal.

verbalement [vɛrbal'mã], *adv.* verbally; (*colloq.*) by word of mouth.

verbaliser [vɛrbali'ze], *v.i.* to draw up a written statement.

verbe [vɛrb], *n.m.* verb; (*Theol.*) *le Verbe*, the Word.

verbeux [vɛr'bø], *a.* (*fem.* **-euse**) verbose.

verbiage [vɛr'bja:ʒ], *n.m.* verbiage.

verbosité [vɛrbozi'te], *n.f.* verbosity.

verdâtre [vɛr'dɑ:tr], *a.* greenish.

verdelet [vɛr'dlɛ], *a.* (*fem.* **-ette**) greenish; tart (*of wine*); hale (*of old people*).

verdeur [vɛr'dœ:r], *n.f.* greenness, sap (*of wood*); tartness, harshness (*of wine*); vigor; spryness (*of old people*); (*fig.*) crudeness (*of language*).

verdict [vɛr'dikt], *n.m.* verdict, finding.

verdier [vɛr'dje], *n.m.* greenfinch; verderer, ranger.

verdir [vɛr'di:r], *v.t.* to make *or* paint green. —*v.i.* to turn green.

verdoyant [vɛrdwa'jã], *a.* verdant, green.

verdoyer [vɛrdwa'je], *v.i.* (*conjug. like* EMPLOYER) to become green.

verdure [vɛr'dy:r], *n.f.* verdure; greenery; pot-herbs.

verdurier [vɛrdy'rje], *n.m.* (*fem.* **-ière**) greengrocer, fruit and vegetable grocer.

véreux [ve'rø], *a.* (*fem.* **-euse**) worm-eaten, maggoty; rotten; (*fig.*) suspect; insecure (*of bills etc.*).

verge [vɛ:rʒ], *n.f.* rod, wand; shaft, pin; shank (*of an anchor etc.*); (C) yard (*measure*).

verger [vɛr'ʒe], *n.m.* orchard.

vergeté [vɛrʒə'te], *a.* streaky.

vergette [vɛr'ʒɛt], *n.f.* clothes brush; bundle of rods, switch.

verglacé [vɛrgla'se], *a.* covered with glazed frost; icy.

verglas [vɛr'glɑ], *n.m.* thin coating of ice, frost after a thaw or rain; glazed frost.

vergne [vɛrɲ], **verne** [vɛrn], *n.m.* alder(tree).

vergogne [vɛr'gɔɲ], *n.f.* shame; *sans vergogne*, shameless(ly).

vergue [vɛrg], *n.f.* yard (*for sail*).

véridicité [veridisi'te], *n.f.* veracity, truthfulness.

véridique [veri'dik], *a.* veracious, truthful.

vérificateur [verifika'tœ:r], *n.m.* verifier, examiner, inspector; (*Eng.*) calipers, gauge; *vérificateur des comptes*, auditor.

vérification [verifika'sjɔ̃], *n.f.* verification, auditing, probate.

vérifier [veri'fje], *v.t.* to verify, to inspect, to examine, to audit; to prove.

vérin [ve'rɛ̃], *n.m.* (*Eng.*) jack.

véritable [veri'tabl], *a.* true, genuine, real; staunch, downright, thorough.

véritablement [veritablə'mã], *adv.* truly, in reality, indeed.

vérité [veri'te], *n.f.* truth, verity, truthfulness; *à la vérité*, indeed, it is true, I admit; *dire la vérité*, to speak the truth; *en vérité*, indeed, truly.

verjus [vɛr'ʒy], *n.m.* verjuice; sour grapes.

verjuté [vɛrʒy'te], *a.* sharp, tart, acid.

vermeil [vɛrˈmɛːj], *a.* (*fem.* **-eille**) vermilion, ruddy, rosy.—*n.m.* vermeil, silver-gilt.

vermicelle [vɛrmiˈsɛl], *n.m.* vermicelli.

vermiculaire [vɛrmikyˈlɛːr], *a.* vermicular, worm-shaped.

vermillon [vɛrmiˈjɔ̃], *a. inv.* and *n.m.* vermilion.

vermine [vɛrˈmin], *n.f.* vermin (*only insects such as fleas, lice etc.*); (*fig.*) rabble.

vermoulu [vɛrmuˈly], *a.* worm-eaten.

vermoulure [vɛrmuˈlyːr], *n.f.* worm hole, rottenness caused by worms (*in wood*).

vermout(h) [vɛrˈmut], *n.m.* vermouth.

vernaculaire [vɛrnakyˈlɛːr], *a.* and *n.m.* vernacular.

vernal [vɛrˈnal], *a.* (*m. pl.* **-aux**) vernal, spring-like.

vernier [vɛrˈnje], *n.m.* vernier, sliding scale.

vernir [vɛrˈniːr], *v.t.* to varnish; to glaze, to polish.

vernis [vɛrˈni], *n.m.* varnish, polish, glaze.

vernissage [vɛrniˈsaːʒ], *n.m.* varnishing; private view (*of art exhibition*).

vernisser [vɛrniˈse], *v.t.* to glaze (*pottery etc.*).

vérole [veˈrɔl], *n.f.* **petite vérole**, smallpox; **petite vérole volante**, chicken pox.

véronal [veroˈnal], *n.m.* (*Chem.*) veronal, barbitone.

Véronique [veroˈnik], *f.* Veronica.

véronique [veroˈnik], *n.f.* veronica, speedwell.

verrat [vɛˈra], *n.m.* boar.

verre [vɛːr], *n.m.* glass; **verre à eau** or **verre gobelet**, tumbler; **verre à vin**, wine glass; **verre de vin**, glass of wine.

verrerie [vɛrˈri], *n.f.* glass-works; glass-ware.

verrier [vɛˈrje], *n.m.* glass-maker.

verrière [vɛˈrjɛːr], *n.f.* stained-glass window.

verroterie [vɛroˈtri], *n.f.* small glass-ware, glass beads.

verrou [vɛˈru], *n.m.* bolt, bar.

verrouiller [veruˈje], *v.t.* to bolt. **se verrouiller**, *v.r.* to bolt oneself in.

verrue [vɛˈry], *n.f.* wart; **verrue plantaire**, verruca.

vers (1) [vɛːr], *n.m. inv.* verse, line (*of poetry*).

vers (2) [vɛːr], *prep.* towards, to; about; **vers (les) quatre heures**, about four o'clock.

versable [vɛrˈsabl], *a.* apt to overturn, liable to upset.

versage [vɛrˈsaːʒ], *n.m.* emptying, tipping; (*Agric.*) first ploughing (*of fallow land*).

versant (1) [vɛrˈsɑ̃], *a.* liable to be overturned.

versant (2) [vɛrˈsɑ̃], *n.m.* declivity, side, slope; watershed.

versatile [vɛrsaˈtil], *a.* inconstant, changeable.

versatilité [vɛrsatiliˈte], *n.f.* inconstancy.

verse (à) [aˈvɛrs], *adv.* abundantly; **il pleut à verse**, it is pouring down rain.

versé [vɛrˈse], *a.* spilt; well versed, conversant.

versement [vɛrsaˈmɑ̃], *n.m.* payment; deposit.

verser [vɛrˈse], *v.t.* to pour, to pour out; to discharge, to empty; to shed, to spill; to pay in, to deposit; to overturn, to upset; to lay (*grain*).—*v.i.* to overturn, to upset (*of vehicles*); to be laid flat (*of standing grain*).

verset [vɛrˈsɛ], *n.m.* (*Bibl. etc.*) verse.

versificateur [vɛrsifikaˈtœːr], *n.m.* (*fem.* **-trice**) versifier.

versification [vɛrsifikaˈsjɔ̃], *n.f.* versification.

versifier [vɛrsiˈfje], *v.t.*, *v.i.* to versify.

version [vɛrˈsjɔ̃], *n.f.* version; (*Sch.*) translation.

verso [vɛrˈso], *n.m.* verso, back, left-hand page.

vert [vɛːr], *a.* green: sharp, harsh (*of things*); tart (*of wine*); raw; sour; (*fig.*) vigorous, robust; spicy (*of stories*).—*n.m.* green, green color; green food; sharpness (*of wine etc.*); (*Golf*) (putting-)green.

vert-de-gris [vɛrdəˈgri], *n.m.* verdigris.

vertèbre [vɛrˈtɛːbr], *n.f.* vertebra.

vertébré [vɛrteˈbre], *a.* and *n.m.* vertebrate.

vertement [vɛrtaˈmɑ̃], *adv.* sharply; harshly, severely.

vertical [vɛrtiˈkal], *a.* (*m. pl.* **-aux**) vertical.

verticalement [vɛrtikalˈmɑ̃], *adv.* vertically.

vertige [vɛrˈtiːʒ], *n.m.* dizziness, giddiness, vertigo; (*fig.*) madness, intoxication.

vertigineux [vɛrtiʒiˈnø], *a.* (*fem.* **-euse**) dizzy, giddy; (*fig.*) breath-taking.

vertigo [vɛrtiˈgo], *n.m.* staggers; (*fig.*) whim.

vertu [vɛrˈty], *n.f.* virtue, chastity; property, faculty, quality; efficacy, force.

vertueusement [vɛrtɥøzˈmɑ̃], *adv.* virtuously.

vertueux [vɛrˈtɥø], *a.* (*fem.* **-euse**) virtuous, chaste.

verve [vɛrv], *n.f.* warmth, animation, verve, spirit, zest.

verveine [vɛrˈvɛːn], *n.f.* vervain, verbena.

vésicule [veziˈkyl], *n.f.* vesicle, bladder; **vésicule biliaire**, gall bladder.

vespasienne [vɛspaˈzjɛn], *n.f.* public urinal; public convenience.

vessie [vɛˈsi], *n.f.* bladder.

veste [vɛst], *n.f.* jacket.

vestiaire [vɛsˈtjɛːr], *n.m.* cloakroom; changing room; robing room (*for judges*); hat-and-coat rack.

vestibule [vɛstiˈbyl], *n.m.* vestibule, lobby, hall.

vestige [vɛsˈtiːʒ], *n.m.* footprint, vestige, sign, mark; trace, remains.

veston [vɛsˈtɔ̃], *n.m.* jacket, coat; **complet veston**, business suit.

Vésuve [veˈzyːv], *le*, *m.* Vesuvius.

vêtement [vɛtˈmɑ̃], *n.m.* garment; (*pl.*) dress, clothes; (*poet.*) raiment; **vêtements de dessous**, underwear.

vétéran [veteˈrɑ̃], *n.m.* veteran; (*Sch.*) boy who stays in a grade a second year.

vétérinaire [veteriˈnɛːr], *a.* veterinary.—*n.m.* veterinary surgeon.

vétille [veˈtiːj], *n.f.* trifle, bagatelle.

vétiller [vetiˈje], *v.i.* to trifle; to split hairs.

vétilleux [vetiˈjø], *a.* (*fem.* **-euse**) particular, finicky.

vêtir [vɛˈtiːr], *v.t. irr.* to clothe; to array, to dress; to put on. **se vêtir**, *v.r.* to dress oneself.

véto [veˈto], *n.m.* veto.

vêtu [vɛˈty], *a.* dressed, clothed, arrayed.

vétuste [veˈtyst], *a.* old, antiquated; dilapidated, worn out.

vétusté [vetysˈte], *n.f.* antiquity, old age, decay.

vilement

veuf [vœf], *a.* (*fem.* **veuve**) widowed.—*n.m.* widower.—*n.f.* (**veuve**) widow.

veule [vœ:l], *a.* feckless, weak, feeble.

veuvage [vœ'va:ʒ], *n.m.* widowhood, widowerhood.

vexant [vɛk'sɑ̃], *a.* vexing, provoking.

vexer [vɛk'se], *v.t.* to vex, to plague, to annoy.

viable [vjabl], *a.* likely to live, viable; fit for traffic.

viaduc [vja'dyk], *n.m.* viaduct.

viager [vja'ʒe], *a.* (*fem.* **-ère**) for life, during life; *rente viagère*, life annuity.

viande [vjɑ̃:d], *n.f.* meat; *menue viande*, fowl and game; *grosse viande*, butcher's meat.

vibrant [vi'brɑ̃], *a.* vibrating; vibrant, resonant.

vibration [vibrɑ'sjɔ̃], *n.f.* vibration.

vibrer [vi'bre], *v.i.* to vibrate.

vicaire [vi'kɛ:r], *n.m.* curate (*of a parish*).

vicariat [vika'rja], *n.m.*, **vicairie** [vikɛ'ri], *n.f.* curacy; vicariate.

vice [vis], *n.m.* fault, defect, flaw, blemish; vice, viciousness.

vice-amiral [visami'ral], *n.m.* (*pl.* **-aux**) vice admiral; second ship of a fleet.

vice-roi [vis'rwa], *n.m.* (*pl.* **vice-rois**) viceroy.

vicié [vi'sje], *a.* vitiated, depraved, corrupted; foul (*of air etc.*).

vicier [vi'sje], *v.t.* to vitiate, to taint, to corrupt.

vicieusement [visjøz'mɑ̃], *adv.* viciously.

vicieux [vi'sjø], *a.* (*fem.* **-euse**) vicious; faulty, defective.

vicinal [visi'nal], *a.* (*m. pl.* **-aux**) local, connecting (*of roads*); *chemin vicinal*, by-road.

vicissitude [visisi'tyd], *n.f.* vicissitude, change.

vicomte [vi'kɔ̃:t], *n.m.* viscount.

vicomtesse [vikɔ̃'tɛs], *n.f.* viscountess.

victime [vik'tim], *n.f.* victim; sufferer; casualty.

Victoire [vik'twa:r], **Victoria** [viktɔ'rja], *f.* Victoria.

victoire [vik'twa:r], *n.f.* victory.

victorieux [viktɔ'rjø], *a.* (*fem.* **-euse**) victorious.

victuaille [vik'tɥa:j], *n.f.* (*colloq.*) provisions.

vidange [vi'dɑ̃:ʒ], *n.f.* emptying; draining off; night soil; *tonneau en vidange*, broached cask.

vidanger [vidɑ̃'ʒe], *v.t.* (*conjug. like* MANGER) to empty, to clean out, to drain, to blow off.

vidangeur [vidɑ̃'ʒœ:r], *n.m.* scavenger.

vide [vid], *a.* empty; void, vacant, blank; destitute.—*n.m.* empty space, blank; vacuum; gap, hole; emptiness.—*adv. phr.* *à vide*, empty.

vidé [vi'de], *a.* emptied, exhausted.

vider [vi'de], *v.t.* to empty; to drain; to hollow out; to draw (*poultry*); to gut (*fish*); to vacate; to decide, to settle.

vie [vi], *n.f.* life; lifetime; existence, days; vitality: livelihood, living; food, subsistence; spirit, animation; noise; *être en vie*, to be alive; *le coût de la vie*, the cost of living; *niveau de vie*, standard of living.

vieil [vjɛj], [VIEUX].

vieillard [vjɛ'ja:r], *n.m.* old man.

vieille [vjɛj], [VIEUX].

vieillerie [vjɛj'ri], *n.f.* (*usu. pl.*) old things, old clothes, old lumber, rubbish; obsolete ideas.

vieillesse [vjɛ'jɛs], *n.f.* old age; oldness.

vieillir [vjɛ'ji:r], *v.t.* to make old; to make look old.—*v.i.* to grow old; to become obsolete.

vieillissant [vjɛji'sɑ̃], *a.* growing old.

vieillot [vjɛ'jo], *a.* (*fem.* **-otte**) oldish.

vielle [vjɛl], *n.f.* *hurdy-gurdy.

Vienne [vjɛn], *f.* Vienna.

viennois [vjɛ'nwa], *a.* Viennese.—*n.m.* (**Viennois**, *fem.* **-oise**) Viennese (*person*).

vierge [vjɛrʒ], *a.* virgin, virginal, maiden; pure, untrodden; unwrought; free (*from*).—*n.f.* virgin, maid; (*Astron.*) Virgo.

Viet-Nam [vjɛt'nam], **le**, *m.* Vietnam.

vietnamien [vjɛtna'mjɛ̃], *a.* (*fem.* **-enne**) Vietnamese.—*n.m.* Vietnamese (*language*); (**Vietnamien**, *fem.* **-enne**) Vietnamese (*person*).

vieux [vjø], *a.* (*before a vowel or* h *mute*, **vieil**, *fem.* **vieille**) old, aged, advanced in years; ancient, venerable; *vieux jeu*, old-fashioned.—*n.m.* (*fem.* **vieille**) old man, old woman; *la retraite des vieux*, old-age pension; *mon vieux*, (a term of endearment) old friend, old chap.

vif [vif], *a.* (*fem.* **vive**) alive, live, living; quick; lively, brisk, sprightly, animated, fiery, mettlesome, ardent, eager; hasty; keen; sharp, violent (*of pain etc.*); bracing (*of air etc.*); vivid, bright (*of colors*).—*n.m.* the quick (*live flesh*); living person; *être pris sur le vif*, to be very lifelike; *piquer au vif*, to sting to the quick.

vif-argent [vifar'ʒɑ̃], *n.m.* quicksilver.

vigie [vi'ʒi], *n.f.* look-out man; look-out (*station* or *ship*); (*Rail.*) seat on the top of trainmen's car.

vigilance [viʒi'lɑ̃:s], *n.f.* vigilance.

vigilant [viʒi'lɑ̃], *a.* vigilant, watchful.

vigile [vi'ʒil], *n.f.* vigil, eve.

vigne [viɲ], *n.f.* vine; vineyard; *vigne vierge*, wild grape; Virginia creeper.

vigneron [viɲə'rɔ̃], *n.m.* (*fem.* **-onne**) vine dresser, wine grower.

vignette [vi'nɛt], *n.f.* vignette; (*pop.*) meadow-sweet.

vignoble [vi'nɔbl], *n.m.* vineyard.

vigoureusement [vigurøz'mɑ̃], *adv.* vigorously, energetically.

vigoureux [vigu'rø], *a.* (*fem.* **-euse**) vigorous, energetic; stout, stalwart.

vigueur [vi'gœ:r], *n.f.* vigor, strength; force, power, energy; *entrer en vigueur*, to come into force (*of laws etc.*).

vil [vil], *a.* vile, base, mean; abject, low; worthless; *à vil prix*, dirt cheap.

vilain [vi'lɛ̃], *a.* ugly; unsightly; pitiful; nasty; sordid, wretched; naughty (*of a child*); *un vilain tour*, a dirty trick; *vilain temps*, vile weather.—*n.m.* (*fem.* **-e**) *villein (*bondman*); nasty fellow; (*childish*) naughty boy *or* girl.

vilainement [vilɛn'mɑ̃], *adv.* uglily; basely, shamefully, deplorably.

vilebrequin [vilbrə'kɛ̃], *n.m.* brace, wimble; (*Mech.*) crankshaft.

vilement [vil'mɑ̃], *adv.* vilely, basely.

327

vilenie [vil′ni], *n.f.* nastiness, foulness; vile action; stinginess, meanness; (*pl.*) offensive words.

vileté [vil′te], *n.f.* cheapness, low price; vileness; mean action.

vilipender [vilipɑ̃′de], *v.t.* to vilify; to disparage.

villa [vil′la], *n.f.* villa.

village [vi′la:ʒ], *n.m.* village.

villageois [vila′ʒwa], *a.* rustic.—*n.m.* (*fem.* **-e**) villager.

ville [vil], *n.f.* town, city; *être en ville*, to be out (*not at home*); *hôtel de ville*, town hall; *ville d'eaux*, spa.

villégiature [vileʒia′ty:r], *n.f.* sojourn in the country; *en villégiature*, staying in the country.

vin [vɛ̃], *n.m.* wine; *à bon vin point d'enseigne*, good wine needs no bush; *vin de Bordeaux rouge*, claret; *vin de marque*, vintage wine; *vin mousseux*, sparkling wine; *vin ordinaire*, dinner wine.

vinaigre [vi′nɛ:gr], *n.m.* vinegar.

vinaigrer [vinɛ′gre], *v.t.* to season with vinegar.

vindicatif [vɛ̃dika′tif], *a.* (*fem.* **-tive**) vindictive, revengeful.

vingt [vɛ̃], *a.* and *n.m. inv.* twenty, score; twentieth.

vingtaine [vɛ̃′tɛ:n], *n.f.* a score, about twenty.

vingt-et-un [vɛ̃te′œ̃], *n.m.* twenty-one (*card game*).

vingtième [vɛ̃′tjɛ:m], *a.* and *n.* twentieth.

vinicole [vini′kɔl], *a.* wine-growing, wine-producing.

viol [vjɔl], *n.m.* rape (*Law*).

violateur [vjɔla′tœ:r], *a.* (*fem.* **-trice**) violating, transgressing, infringing.—*n.m.* (*fem.* **-trice**) violator, infringer, breaker.

violation [vjɔla′sjɔ̃], *n.f.* violation, breach, infringement.

violâtre [vjɔ′lɑ:tr], *a.* purplish.

viole [vjɔl], *n.f.* viol.

violemment [vjɔla′mã], *adv.* violently.

violence [vjɔ′lã:s], *n.f.* violence; (*Law*) duress; (*fig.*) stress, fury.

violent [vjɔ′lã], *a.* violent; strong (*of suspicion etc.*); (*colloq.*) excessive; *c'est par trop violent*, it really is too bad.

violenter [vjɔlã′te], *v.t.* to offer *or* do violence to, to force; to constrain; to violate.

violer [vjɔ′le], *v.t.* to violate; to outrage, to transgress.

violet [vjɔ′lɛ], *a.* (*fem.* **-ette**) violet-colored, purple.—*n.m.* violet(color).—*n.f.* (**-ette**) (*Bot.*) violet.

violier [vjɔ′lje], *n.m.* wallflower, gillyflower.

violon [vjɔ′lɔ̃], *n.m.* violin, fiddle; violinist, fiddler; (*pop.*) lock-up, cells (*prison*).

violoncelle [vjɔlɔ̃′sɛl], *n.m.* violoncello, cello.

violoncelliste [vjɔlɔ̃sɛ′list], *n.* violoncellist, cellist.

violoniste [vjɔlɔ′nist], *n.* violinist.

viorne [vjɔrn], *n.f.* viburnum.

vipère [vi′pɛ:r], *n.f.* viper, adder.

virage [vi′ra:ʒ], *n.m.* turning, cornering; turn, bend, corner; (*Naut.*) tacking; *virage incliné*, bank; *virage en épingle à cheveux*, hair-pin bend.

virago [vira′go], *n.f.* virago, termagant.

virée [vi′re], *n.f.* turning; winding.

virement [vir′mã], *n.m.* turning; (*Naut.*) veering about, tacking; (*Book-keeping*) clearing, transfer; *banque de virement*, clearing-bank.

virer [vi′re], *v.t.* to transfer, to clear (*a sum o money*).—*v.i.* to turn, to turn about; (*Naut.*) to tack, to veer about.

vireux [vi′rø], *a.* (*fem.* **-euse**) poisonous, noxious, nauseous.

virginal [virʒi′nal], *a.* (*m. pl.* **-aux**) virginal, maidenly.

Virginie [virʒi′ni], *f.* Virginia; (*Geog.*) *La Virginie*, Virginia.

virginité [virʒini′te], *n.f.* virginity, maidenhood.

virgule [vir′gyl], *n.m.* comma; *point et virgule*, semi-colon.

viril [vi′ril], *a.* virile, male; manly.

virilement [viril′mã], *adv.* like a man; in a manly way.

virilité [virili′te], *n.f.* virility; manhood.

virole [vi′rɔl], *n.f.* ferrule.

virtuel [vir′tɥɛl], *a.* (*fem.* **-elle**) virtual.

virtuellement [virtɥɛl′mã], *adv.* virtually; potentially.

virtuose [vir′tɥo:z], *n.* virtuoso.

virtuosité [virtɥozi′te], *n.f.* virtuosity.

virulence [viry′lã:s], *n.f.* virulence.

virulent [viry′lã], *a.* virulent.

virus [vi′ry:s], *n.m.* virus.

vis [vis], *n.f. inv.* screw; *escalier à vis*, spiral staircase.

visa [vi′za], *n.m.* visa, signature, endorsement (*on passports etc.*).

visage [vi′za:ʒ], *n.m.* face, visage, countenance; aspect, look, air; *à deux visages*, double-faced; *à visage découvert*, openly, barefacedly; *avoir bon visage*, to look well.

vis-à-vis [viza′vi], *prep. phr.* opposite, over against; towards, in relation to; *vis-à-vis de l'église*, opposite the church.—*adv. phr.* opposite.—*n.m. inv.* vis-à-vis (*in dancing etc.*); person opposite (*at table etc.*).

viscère [vi′sɛ:r], *n.m.* any of the viscera or vital organs.

viscosité [viskozi′te], *n.f.* viscosity, viscidity stickiness.

visée [vi′ze], *n.f.* aim, end; design, plan.

viser [vi′ze], *v.t.* to aim at; to allude to; to pursue; to endorse.—*v.i.* to aim, to take aim; to aspire (*à*).

viseur [vi′zœ:r], *n.m.* (*Phot.*) view finder.

visibilité [vizibili′te], *n.f.* visibility.

visible [vi′zibl], *a.* visible; evident, manifest, obvious.

visiblement [vizibla′mã], *adv.* visibly, obviously.

visière [vi′zjɛ:r], *n.f.* visor (*of a helme*); peak (*of caps etc.*), eye shade; sight (*on fire-arms*).

vision [vi′zjɔ̃], *n.f.* vision, sight; dream, phantom, fancy.

visionnaire [vizjɔ′nɛ:r], *a.* visionary, fanciful.—*n.* seer; dreamer, visionary.

visite [vi′zit], *n.f.* visit; call; visitation (*of a bishop etc.*); examination, inspection; search; *droit de visite*, right of search; *faire la visite des bagages*, to examine luggage; *faire une visite* or *rendre visite*, to pay a visit.

visiter [vizi'te], v.t. to visit (patients, clients etc.); to visit (cathedral etc.); to search, to examine, to inspect.

visiteur [vizi'tœ:r], n.m. (fem. **-euse**) visitor, caller; inspector, searcher.

vison [vi'zɔ̃], n.m. mink (animal).

visqueux [vis'køø], a. (fem. **-euse**) viscous, sticky; slimy; clammy.

visser [vi'se], v.t. to screw, to screw on, up or down. **se visser**, v.r. to fix or attach oneself firmly.

visserie [vi'sri], n.f. screws, nuts and bolts.

Vistule [vis'tyl], **la**, f. the Vistula.

visuel [vi'zɥɛl], a. (fem. **-elle**) visual.

vital [vi'tal], a. (m. pl. **-aux**) vital; (fig.) essential.

vitalement [vital'mɑ̃], adv. vitally.

vitalité [vitali'te], n.f. vitality.

vitamine [vita'min], n.f. vitamin.

vite [vit], a. swift, quick, speedy, rapid.— adv. quick, quickly, fast, rapidly, expeditiously; **vite !** quick! look sharp!

vitesse [vi'tɛs], n.f. quickness, rapidity, celerity, swiftness, speed; (Motor.) gear; **à grande** or **à toute vitesse**, at full speed; **boîte de vitesse**, gear box; **changement de vitesse**, change of gear; **gagner (quelqu'un) de vitesse**, to outrun (someone).

Viti [vi'ti], **les Îles**, f.pl. the Fiji Islands.

viticole [viti'kɔl], a. pertaining to vine culture, viticultural.

viticulture [vitikyl'ty:r], n.f. vine-growing.

vitrage [vi'tra:ʒ], n.m. glazing; glass windows.

vitrail [vi'tra:j], n.m. (pl. **-aux**) stained-glass window.

vitre [vitr], n.f. pane of glass; window.

vitré [vi'tre], a. glazed, of glass; (Anat. etc.) vitreous; **porte vitrée**, glass door.

vitrer [vi'tre], v.t. to furnish with glass windows, to glaze.

vitreux [vi'trø], a. (fem. **-euse**) vitreous, glassy.

vitrier [vitri'e], n.m. glass-maker; glazier.

vitrine [vi'trin], n.f. shop window; showcase.

vitriol [vitri'ɔl], n.m. vitriol.

vitupération [vitypera'sjɔ̃], n.f. vituperation.

vitupérer [vitype're], v.t. (conjug. like CÉDER) to vituperate, to reprimand.

vivace [vi'vas], a. long-lived, perennial (of plants); inveterate, deep-rooted.

vivacité [vivasi'te], n.f. vivacity, liveliness, sprightliness; spirit, life, ardor.

vivant [vi'vɑ̃], a. living, alive; lively, animated; **langue vivante**, modern language; **portrait vivant**, lifelike portrait.—n.m. life, lifetime; **de son vivant**, in his lifetime. —n.m. (fem. **-e**) living person.

vivat [vi'vat], int. and n.m. hurrah! huzza!

vivement [viv'mɑ̃], adv. quickly, briskly, sharply, vigorously; eagerly; keenly, acutely; smartly, angrily; spiritedly.

viveur [vi'vœ:r], n.m. (fem. **-euse**) rake, gay dog, person who leads a fast life.

vivier [vi'vje], n.m. fish pond.

vivifiant [vivi'fjɑ̃], a. vivifying, quickening; refreshing, invigorating.

vivifier [vivi'fje], v.t. to vivify, to quicken, to give life to; to enliven, to revive.

vivisection [vivisɛk'sjɔ̃], n.f. vivisection.

(C) **vivoir** [vi'vwa:r], n.m. living room.

vivoter [vivɔ'te], v.i. to live poorly, to scrape along.

vivre [vi:vr], v.i. irr. to live, to be alive; to subsist, to live on, to be maintained; to board, to take one's meals; to behave; to last; **vive la France !** long live France! **qui vive?** who goes there? **il ne sait pas vivre**, he has no manners.—n.m. living, board, food; (pl.) provisions, victuals, rations.

vocable [vɔ'kabl], n.m. vocable, word, name.

vocabulaire [vɔkaby'lɛ:r], n.m. vocabulary.

vocal [vɔ'kal], a. (m. pl. **-aux**) vocal.

vocation [vɔka'sjɔ̃], n.f. vocation, calling, call; inclination; bent, talent.

vociférant [vɔsife'rɑ̃], a. vociferous.

vociférer [vɔsife're], v.t. (conjug. like CÉDER) to vociferate, to bawl.

vœu [vø], n.m. (pl. **vœux**) vow; prayer, wish, desire; vote, suffrage.

vogue [vɔg], n.f. vogue, fashion; credit, craze; **avoir de la vogue**, to be in fashion.

voguer [vɔ'ge], v.i. to move forward by rowing (of a galley etc.); to sail, to float, to move along.

voici [vwa'si], prep. see here, behold; here is, here are, this is, these are; ago, past; **le voilà, me voici**, there he is, here I am; **monsieur que voici**, this gentleman; **voici trois mois que je suis à l'hôpital**, I have been in hospital for the past three months.

voie [vwa], n.f. way, road; line, path, track; (fig.) organ, medium, channel, course; conveyance; gauge, breadth (between the wheels of carriages); load; (Chem.) process; **être en voie de**, to be in a fair way to; **voie d'eau**, (Naut.) leak; **voie ferrée**, railway track; **voie libre**, line clear.

voilà [vwa'la], prep. there, behold, there now, there is, there are, that is; **ah ! vous voilà,** oh! there you are! **voilà une heure qu'il parle**, he has been speaking for an hour.

voile (1) [vwal], n.m. veil; (fig.) cover, mask, disguise, show, pretence.

voile (2) [vwal], n.f. sail; canvas; (fig.) ship; **faire voile**, to sail, to set sail.

voilé [vwa'le], a. rigged; veiled; clouded, dull, dim; (wheel) buckled, out of true.

voiler [vwa'le], v.t. to veil; to cover, to cloak, to blind, to disguise, to conceal; to buckle (wheel).—v.i. and **se voiler**, v.r. to wear a veil; to cloud over (of the sky); to buckle (of a wheel).

voilier [vwa'lje], n.m. sail maker; sailing ship.

voir [vwa:r], v.t. irr. to see; to behold; to witness; to look at, to observe, to view; to inspect, to superintend; to overlook; to visit; to frequent; **faire voir**, to show, to let see; **voyons !** let us see! now then!—v.i. to see, to look, to watch; to have one's sight; **voir à** or **voir à ce que**, to see to it that. **se voir**, v.r. to see oneself; to see each other; to visit each other; to be obvious.

voire [vwa:r], adv. and even, and indeed.

voirie [vwa'ri], n.f. roads, system of roads; commission of public streets and highways; refuse dump.

voisin [vwa'zɛ̃], a. bordering, adjacent, next; next door, neighboring. —n.m. (fem. **-e**) neighbor.

voisinage [vwazi′na:ʒ], *n.m.* neighborhood; vicinity, proximity, nearness; neighbors.

voiturage [vwaty′ra:ʒ], *n.m.* carriage, cartage (*of goods etc.*).

voiture [vwa′ty:r], *n.f.* vehicle, conveyance; carriage; coach; cart, car; cart-load; *descendre de voiture*, to alight from a carriage; *en voiture!* all aboard! *se promener en voiture* or *aller en voiture*, to drive; *voiture d'enfant*, perambulator, baby carriage, (*fam.*) pram.

voiturer [vwaty′re], *v.t.* to carry, to convey, to cart.

voiturier [vwaty′rje], *n.m.* carrier, carter.

voix [vwa], *n.f. inv.* voice; tone, sound; vote; suffrage; opinion, judgment; singer; *à demi-voix*, in a low voice; *à haute voix*, in a loud voice; *de vive voix*, by word of mouth.

vol (1) [vɔl], *n.m.* flying, soaring; flight; flock (*of birds*); spread (*of wings*); *au vol*, on the wing; *à vol d'oiseau*, as the crow flies.

vol (2) [vɔl], *n.m.* theft, robbery, stealing, larceny; stolen goods; *vol à l'étalage*, shoplifting; *vol avec effraction*, burglary.

volage [vɔ′la:ʒ], *a.* fickle, inconstant, flighty.

volaille [vɔ′la:j], *n.f.* poultry, fowls; *marchand de volaille*, poultry dealer.

volant [vɔ′lɑ̃], *a.* flying; loose, floating; movable, portable.—*n.m.* shuttlecock; flounce (*of a dress*); flywheel (*of machinery*); steering wheel (*of a car*); sail (*of a windmill*).

volatil [vɔla′til], *a.* (*Chem.*) volatile; (*fig.*) volatile (*of temperament*).

volatile [vɔla′til], *a.* winged.—*n.m.* winged creature, bird.

vol-au-vent [vɔlo′vɑ̃], *n.m. inv.* vol-au-vent, puff-pie.

volcan [vɔl′kɑ̃], *n.m.* volcano.

volcanique [vɔlka′nik], *a.* volcanic, fiery.

volée [vɔ′le], *n.f.* flight (*of birds etc.*); flock, covey; brood; bevy; volley (*of guns*); shower (*of blows*); thrashing; peal (*of bells*); *à la volée*, flying, as it flies, in the air; (*fig.*) rashly, at random; *sonner à toute volée*, to ring a full peal; *volée d'escalier*, flight of stairs.

voler (1) [vɔ′le], *v.i.* to fly; to take wing, to soar; *entendre voler une mouche*, to hear a pin drop.

voler (2) [vɔ′le], *v.t.* to steal, to rob; to fleece, to plunder; (*fig.*) to embezzle, to usurp.—*v.i.* to steal.

volerie [vɔl′ri], *n.f.* robbery; pilfering.

volet [vɔ′lɛ], *n.m.* (window-)shutter; dovecot; (*Av.*) flap.

voleter [vɔl′te], *v.i.* (*conjug. like* APPELER) to flutter.

voleur [vɔ′lœ:r], *n.m.* (*fem.* **-euse**) thief, robber; plunderer, extortioner; stealer; *au voleur!* stop thief!

volière [vɔ′ljɛ:r], *n.f.* aviary, large bird cage.

volontaire [vɔlɔ̃′tɛ:r], *a.* voluntary, willing; intended, intentional; spontaneous; obstinate, wilful.—*n.* volunteer.

volontairement [vɔlɔ̃tɛr′mɑ̃], *adv.* voluntarily; wilfully.

volonté [vɔlɔ̃′te], *n.f.* will; (*pl.*) whims, caprices; *avoir de la bonne volonté*, to be willing; *à volonté*, at pleasure, at will; *dernières volontés*, last will and testament; *faire ses quatre volontés*, (*colloq.*)

to do as one pleases; *mauvaise volonté*, illwill; unwillingness.

volontiers [vɔlɔ̃′tje], *adv.* willingly, gladly, with pleasure.

volt [vɔlt], *n.m.* (*Elec.*) volt.

voltage [vɔl′ta:ʒ], *n.m.* voltage.

volte-face [vɔlt′fas], *n.f. inv.* turning round; *faire volte-face*, to face about; (*fig.*) to reverse one's opinions completely.

voltige [vɔl′ti:ʒ], *n.f.* slack-rope gymnastics, flying-trapeze exercises.

voltigeant [vɔlti′ʒɑ̃], *a.* fluttering, hovering.

voltigement [vɔltiʒ′mɑ̃], *n.m.* tumbling; fluttering.

voltiger [vɔlti′ʒe], *v.i.* (*conjug. like* MANGER) to flutter, to fly about, to hover.

voltigeur [vɔlti′ʒœ:r], *n.m.* vaulter; light-infantry soldier, rifleman.

voltmètre [vɔlt′mɛtr], *n.m.* voltmeter.

volubilis [vɔlybi′lis], *n.m.* convolvulus.

volubilité [vɔlybili′te], *n.f.* volubility, fluency, glibness.

volume [vɔ′lym], *n.m.* volume; bulk, size, mass.

volumineux [vɔlymi′nø], *a.* (*fem.* **-euse**) voluminous, bulky.

volupté [vɔlyp′te], *n.f.* voluptuousness, sensual pleasure.

voluptueux [vɔlyp′tɥø], *a.* (*fem.* **-euse**) voluptuous, sensual.—*n.m.* (*fem.* **-euse**) voluptuary.

volute [vɔ′ly:t], *n.f.* volute; scroll.

vomir [vɔ′mi:r], *v.t.* to vomit, to throw up, (*fig.*) to belch forth.—*v.i.* to vomit, to be sick.

vomissement [vɔmis′mɑ̃], *n.m.* vomit(ing).

vorace [vɔ′ras], *a.* voracious, ravenous.

voracité [vɔrasi′te], *n.f.* voracity.

vos [vo], [VOTRE].

votant [vɔ′tɑ̃], *n.m.* (*fem.* **-e**) voter.

vote [vɔt], *n.m.* vote; division, voting, poll.

voter [vɔ′te], *v.t., v.i.* to vote; to pass (*a bill*).

votif [vɔ′tif], *a.* (*fem.* **-tive**) votive.

votre [vɔtr], *a. poss.* (*pl.* **vos**) your.

vôtre [vo:tr], *pron.poss.* (*m. sing.* **le vôtre**, *fem. sing.* **la vôtre**, *pl.* **les vôtres**) yours.—*n.* your own, your own property; (*pl.*) your relations, friends etc.; your pranks, tricks.

vouer [vwe], *v.t.* to devote, to dedicate; to vow, to swear. **se vouer**, *v.r.* to devote oneself.

vouloir [vu′lwa:r], *v.t. irr.* to want; to desire, to wish, to require; to consent; to please; to choose; to determine; to try, to attempt; to admit, to grant; to mean; *en vouloir à quelqu'un*, to bear someone a grudge; *oui, je (le) veux bien*, yes, I am willing; *que veut dire cela?* what does that mean? *que voulez-vous?* what do you want? what can I do for you? what can you expect? *veuillez me dire*, please tell me.—*n.m.* will; *bon vouloir*, goodwill, *mauvais vouloir*, illwill.

voulu [vu′ly], *a.* wished, desired, required, requisite; due, received; deliberate, studied.

vous [vu], *pron. pers.* you; to you.

voûte [vut], *n.f.* arch, vault. (*fig.*) roof, canopy; *clef de voûte*, keystone.

voûté [vu′te], *a.* vaulted, curved.

voûter [vu′te], *v.t.* to vault, to arch over; to bend. **se voûter**, *v.r.* to arch, to vault; to be bent, to stoop.

vouvoyer [vuvwa′je], *v.t.* (*conjug. like* EM-PLOYER) to say *vous* instead of *tu* when addressing somebody.

voyage [vwa′ja:ʒ], *n.m.* travel; journey, voyage, trip; visit; (*pl.*) travels; *bon voyage !* pleasant journey to you! *être en voyage*, to be travelling.

voyager [vwaja′ʒe], *v.i.* (*conjug. like* MANGER) to travel, to journey.

voyageur [vwaja′ʒœːr], *a.* (*fem.* **-euse**) travelling; migrating; *commis voyageur*, commercial traveller; *oiseau voyageur*, migratory bird; *pigeon voyageur*, carrier pigeon.—*n.m.* (*fem.* **-euse**) traveller; passenger.

voyant [vwa′jɑ̃], *a.* gaudy, showy (*of colors*). —*n.m.* (*fem.* **-e**) seer, clairvoyant.

voyelle [vwa′jɛl], *n.f.* vowel.

voyou [vwa′ju], *n.m.* (*fam.*) guttersnipe, hooligan; loafer.

vrac (en) [ɑ̃′vrak], *adv. phr.* in bulk, loose, pell-mell.

vrai [vrɛ], *a.* true, real, genuine; right, proper, fit; downright, arrant.—*int.* truly, really, in truth!—*n.m.* truth; *à vrai dire*, to tell the truth, as a matter of fact.

vraiment [vrɛ′mɑ̃], *adv.* truly, in truth; indeed, really!

vraisemblable [vrɛsɑ̃′blabl], *a.* likely, probable.—*n.m.* probability, likelihood.

vraisemblance [vrɛsɑ̃′blɑ̃:s], *n.f.* probability, likelihood, verisimilitude.

vrille [vri:j], *n.f.* gimlet, borer, piercer; (*Bot.*) tendril; (*Av.*) tail-spin.

vriller [vri′je], *v.t.* to bore.—*v.i.* to ascend spirally.

vrillette [vri′jɛt], *n.f.* death-watch beetle.

vrombir [vrɔ̃′biːr], *v.i.* to buzz, to hum, to whirr, to purr, to throb.

vu [vy], *a.* considered, regarded; seen, observed.—*prep.* considering, in view of.—*n.m.* sight, examination, inspection; (*Law*) preamble.—*conj. phr.* *vu que*, seeing that, whereas.

vue [vy], *n.f.* sight, eyesight; eyes; view, survey, inspection; prospect; appearance; light, window; design; *à perte de vue*, as far as the eye can reach, out of sight; *à vue d'œil*, visibly.

Vulcain [vyl′kɛ̃], *m.* Vulcan.

vulcaniser [vylkani′ze], *v.t.* to vulcanize.

vulgaire [vyl′gɛːr], *a.* vulgar, common.—*n.m.* the common herd.

vulgairement [vylgɛr′mɑ̃], *adv.* vulgarly, commonly.

vulgariser [vylgari′ze], *v.t.* to popularize.

vulgarité [vylgari′te], *n.f.* vulgarity.

vulnérabilité [vylnerabili′te], *n.f.* vulnerability.

vulnérable [vylne′rabl], *a.* vulnerable.

W

W, w [dublə′ve], *n.m.* this twenty-third letter of the alphabet is used only in borrowed words.

wagon [va′gɔ̃], *n.m.* (*Rail.*) car, coach; freight car.

wagon-lit [vagɔ̃′li], *n.m.* (*pl.* **wagons-lits**) sleeping-car, sleeper.

wagonnet [vagɔ′nɛ], *n.m.* tip-truck.

wallon [wa′lɔ̃], *a.* (*fem.* **-onne**) Walloon.—*n.m.* Walloon (*language*); (**Wallon,** *fem.* **-onne**) Walloon (*person*).

warrant [va′rɑ̃], *n.m.* warrant.

warranter [varɑ̃′te], *v.t.* to warrant, to guarantee, to certify.

water [wa′tɛr], **les W.C.** [ɛve′se], *n.m. pl.* water closet, lavatory, toilet.

watt [wat], *n.m.* (*Elec.*) watt.

wattman [wat′man], *n.m.* (*pl.*-men) motor-man.

week-end [wik′ɛnd], *n.m.* (*pl.* **week-ends**) week-end.

whisky [wis′ki], *n.m.* whisky.

whist [wist], *n.m.* whist.

wigwam [wig′wam], *n.m.* wigwam.

wolfram [vɔl′fram], *n.m.* wolfram (*tungsten ore*).

X

X, x [iks], *n.m.* the twenty-fourth letter of the alphabet; *rayons X*, X-rays.

xénophobe [ksenɔ′fɔb], *a.* and *n.* xenophobe.

xérès [kse′rɛs], *n.m.* sherry (*wine*).

xylophone [ksilɔ′fɔn], *n.m.* (*Mus.*) xylophone.

Y

Y, y [i grɛk], *n.m.* the twenty-fifth letter of the alphabet.

y [i], *adv.* there; thither; within, at home; *ça y est !* that's it! *il y a*, there is, there are; *je l'y ai vu*, I saw him there; *j'y suis*, I follow you, I get you; *y compris*, included.—*pron.* by, for, in, at *or* to him, her, it *or* them.

yacht [jɔt, jak], *n.m.* yacht.

Yémen [je′mɛn], **le**, *m.* Yemen.

yéménite [jema′nit], *a.* Yemeni.—*n.* (**Yéménite**) Yemeni (*person*).

yeuse [jøːz], *n.f.* ilex, holm oak.

yeux [jøː], [ŒIL].

yodler [jɔ′dle], *v.i.* (*Mus.*) to yodel.

yogi or **yogui** [jɔ′gi], *n.m.* yogi.

yole [jɔl], *n.f.* yawl, gig.

yougoslave [jugɔs′lav], *a.* Yugoslav.—*n.m.* Yugoslav (*language*).—*n.* (**Yougoslave**) Yugoslav (*person*).

Yougoslavie [jugɔsla′vi], **la**, *f.* Yugoslavia.

youyou [ju′ju], *n.m.* dinghy.

Z

Z, z [zed], *n.m.* the twenty-sixth letter of the alphabet.

Zambie [zɑ̃'bi], **la**, *f.* Zambia.

zèbre [zɛbr], *n.m.* zebra.

zébré [ze'bre], *a.* striped like the zebra.

zèle [zɛ:l], *n.m.* zeal, warmth, ardor, enthusiasm.

zélé [ze'le], *a.* zealous.

zélote [ze'lɔt], *n.m.* zealot.

zénith [ze'nit], *n.m.* zenith.

zéphire, zéphyr or **zéphyre** [ze'fi:r], *n.m.* zephyr, gentle breeze.

zéro [ze'ro], *n.m.* nought; zero (*of the thermometer*); (*fig.*) a mere cipher, nonentity.

zeste [zɛst], *n.m.* woody skin dividing sections of a walnut; peel (*of orange, lemon etc.*), rind; (*fig.*) straw, fig, nothing.

zézaiement or **zézayement** [zeze(j)'mɑ̃] *n.m.* -lisping, lisp (*incorrect pronunciation of* [z] *instead of* [ʒ]).

zézayer [zeze'je], *v.i.* (*conjug. like* PAYER) to lisp.

zibeline [zi'blin], *n.f.* sable.

zigzag [zig'zag], *n.m.* zigzag; *éclair en zig-zag,* forked lightning.

zinc [zɛ̃:g], *n.m.* zinc; (*slang*) bar or counter of a bistro.

zingaro [zɛ̃ga'ro], *n.m.* (*pl.* **zingari**) gipsy.

zinguer [zɛ̃'ge], *v.t.* to cover with zinc; to zinc.

zizanie [ziza'ni], *n.f.* tare, *darnel; (*fig.*) discord, bickering.

zodiaque [zɔ'djak], *n.m.* zodiac.

zone [zo:n], *n.f.* zone, belt, area.

zoo [zo'o], *n.m.* (*fam.*) zoo.

zoologie [zɔɔlɔ'ʒi], *n.f.* zoology.

zoologique [zɔɔlɔ'ʒik], *a.* zoological.

zoologiste [zɔɔlɔ'ʒist], *n.* zoologist.

zouave [zwa:v], *n.m.* Zouave (*soldier*).

zut! [zyt], *int.* (*fam.*) (*to convey anger, scorn, disappointment, flat refusal*); *zut! zut alors! non, zut!* be blowed! no go! never! bother!

A, a (1) [ei]. première lettre de l'alphabet; (*Mus.*) la, *m.*; *a.m.*, du matin.

a (2) [ei, ə], **an** [æn, ən] (*before vowel*), *indef. art.* un, *m.*, une, *f.*; *a shilling a pound*, un shilling la livre; *three a day*, trois par jour.

aback [ə'bæk], *adv.* en arrière; (*fig.*) à l'improviste, au dépourvu.

abacus ['æbəkəs], *n.* (*pl.* **abaci** ['æbəkai]) (*Arch., Math.*) abaque, *m.*

abaft [ə'bɑːft], *adv.* sur l'arrière, en arrière.— *prep.* en arrière de, à l'arrière de.

abandon [ə'bændən], *v.t.* abandonner; délaisser, quitter; renoncer à, se désister de. —*n.* abandon, *m.*; désinvolture, *f.*

abandoned [ə'bændənd], *a.* abandonné; dépravé.

abandonment [ə'bændənmənt], *n.* abandonnement; délaissement; abandon, *m.*

abase [ə'beis], *v.t.* abaisser; ravaler.

abasement [ə'beismənt], *n.* abaissement; ravalement, *m.*; humiliation, *f.*

abash [ə'bæʃ], *v.t.* déconcerter, décontenancer; interdire, confondre.

abate [ə'beit], *v.t.* diminuer; rabattre; affaiblir, atténuer; amortir; calmer, apaiser. —*v.i.* diminuer; s'affaiblir; se calmer, s'apaiser (*temps etc.*); tomber, baisser, s'abattre (*vent etc.*).

abatement [ə'beitmənt], *n.* diminution, réduction, *f.*, rabais; affaiblissement, adoucissement; apaisement, *m.*

abbacy ['æbəsi], *n.* dignité d'abbé, *f.*

abbess ['æbes], *n.* abbesse, *f.*

abbey ['æbi], *n.* abbaye, *f.*

abbot ['æbət], *n.* abbé, supérieur (*d'abbaye*), *m.*

abbreviate [ə'briːvieit], *v.t.* abréger; raccourcir.

abbreviation [əbriːvi'eiʃən], *n.* abréviation, *f.*

abdicate ['æbdikeit], *v.t.*, *v.i.* abdiquer.

abdication [æbdi'keiʃən], *n.* abdication, *f.*

abdomen [æb'doumən, 'æbdəmən], *n.* abdomen, bas-ventre, *m.*

abdominal [æb'dɔminəl], *a.* abdominal.

abduct [æb'dʌkt], *v.t.* détourner, enlever (*clandestinement* ou *par force*).

abduction [æb'dʌkʃən], *n.* abduction, *f.*, enlèvement (*de mineur etc.*), détournement, *m.*

abductor [æb'dʌktə], *n.* (*Anat.*) abducteur; (*Law*) ravisseur, *m.*

abed [ə'bed], *adv.* au lit, couché.

aberration [æbə'reiʃən], *n.* aberration, *f.*; éloignement, écart, égarement, *m.*; erreur (*de jugement*), *f.*

abet [ə'bet], *v.t.* soutenir, encourager (*à un crime*); *to aid and abet*, être le complice.

abetment [ə'betmənt], **abetting** [ə'betiŋ], *n.* encouragement (*à un crime*), *m.*

abettor [ə'betə], *n.* instigateur (*d'un crime*), *m.*; complice, *m., f.*

abeyance [ə'beiəns], *n.* vacance; suspension, *f.*; *in abeyance*, en suspens; *to fall into abeyance*, tomber en désuétude.

abhor [əb'hɔː], *v.t.* abhorrer, détester.

abhorrence [əb'hɔrəns], *n.* horreur, *f.*

abhorrent [əb'hɔrənt], *a.* odieux, répugnant (à).

abide [ə'baid], *v.t. irr.* attendre; supporter; subir, souffrir.—*v.i.* demeurer, rester; séjourner; durer; *to abide by* (*a decision etc.*), rester fidèle à; *to abide by* (*the laws etc.*), se conformer à.

abiding [ə'baidiŋ], *a.* constant, immuable.

ability [ə'biliti], *n.* capacité, *f.*; pouvoir; talent, *m.*; habileté, *f.*

abject ['æbdʒekt], *a.* abject, bas, vil.

abjection [æb'dʒekʃən], **abjectness** ['æbdʒektnis], *n.* abjection, misère, *f.*

abjectly ['æbdʒektli], *adv.* d'une manière abjecte.

abjure [æb'dʒuə], *v.t.* abjurer; renoncer à, renier.

ablative ['æblativ], *a.* and *n.* (*Gram.*) ablatif, *m.*

ablaze [ə'bleiz], *a.* en feu, en flammes; (*fig.*) enflammé.

able [eibl], *a.* capable (*de*), à même (*de*); habile; *to be able to*, pouvoir.

able-bodied ['eiblbɔdid], *a.* fort, robuste, vigoureux.

ablution [ə'bluːʃən], *n.* ablution, *f.*

ably ['eibli], *adv.* habilement, avec talent.

abnegation [æbni'geiʃən], *n.* abnégation, renonciation, *f.*; désaveu, *m.*

abnormal [æb'nɔːməl], *a.* anormal.

abnormality [æbnɔː'mæliti], *n.* anomalie, difformité, *f.*

abnormally [æb'nɔːməli], *adv.* anormalement.

aboard [ə'bɔːd], *adv.* à bord (*de*).

abode (1) [ə'boud], *n.* demeure, habitation, *f.*; séjour, *m.*

abode (2) [ə'boud], *past and p.p.* [ABIDE].

abolish [ə'bɔliʃ], *v.t.* abolir; supprimer.

abolishment [ə'bɔliʃmənt], **abolition** [æbə'liʃən], *n.* abolition, suppression, *f.*; abolissement, *m.*

abominable [ə'bɔminəbl], *a.* abominable, infâme, détestable.

abominably [ə'bɔminəbli], *adv.* abominablement.

abominate [ə'bɔmineit], *v.t.* abominer, détester.

abomination [əbɔmi'neiʃən], *n.* abomination, horreur, *f.*

aboriginal [æbə'ridʒinəl], *a.* aborigène, primitif.—*n.* aborigène, *m., f.*

aborigine [æbə'ridʒini], *n.* aborigène, *m., f.*

abortion [ə'bɔːʃən], *n.* avortement (*acte*); avorton (*embryon*), *m.*

abortive [ə'bɔːtiv], *a.* abortif, manqué; avorté.

abortively [ə'bɔːtivli], *adv.* avant terme; (*fig.*) sans résultat, sans succès.

abortiveness [ə'bɔːtivnis], *n.* (*fig.*) insuccès, *m.*

abound [ə'baund], *v.i.* abonder (*de* ou *en*), regorger (*de*).

abounding [ə'baundiŋ], *a.* abondant.

about [ə'baut], *prep.* autour de; auprès de; sur; vers; environ; touchant, au sujet de, à l'égard de; à peu près; sur le point de; dans, par; *about that*, là-dessus, à ce sujet; *about two o'clock*, vers (les) deux heures; *what is it all about?* de quoi s'agit-il ?—*adv.* tout autour, à l'entour, à la ronde; çà et là; *to be about to*, être sur le point de.

above [ə'bʌv], *prep.* au-dessus de, par-dessus; en amont de; plus de; au delà de; *above all*, surtout, par-dessus tout; *above board*, ouvertement, franchement.—*adv.* en haut; là-haut; au-dessus; ci-dessus.

abrasion [ə'breiʒən], *n.* abrasion, écorchure, *f.*

abrasive [ə'breisiv], *a.* and *n.* abrasif, *m.*

abreast [ə'brest], *adv.* de front, à côté l'un de l'autre; (*fig.*) de pair avec.

abridge [ə'bridʒ], *v.t.* abréger, raccourcir; restreindre, priver; *abridged edition* (*of book*), édition réduite, *f.*

abridgment [ə'bridʒmənt], *n.* abrégé, précis, *m.*; réduction, diminution, *f.*

abroad [ə'brɔːd], *adv.* à l'étranger; au loin, de tous côtés; *to get abroad*, se répandre (*nouvelles*).

abrogate ['æbrogeit], *v.t.* abroger.

abrogation [æbro'geiʃən], *n.* abrogation, *f.*

abrupt [ə'brʌpt], *a.* brusque; brisé, saccadé; précipité, soudain; abrupt, escarpé, à pic.

abruptly [ə'brʌptli], *adv.* brusquement, tout à coup.

abruptness [ə'brʌptnis], *n.* précipitation; (*fig.*) brusquerie, rudesse, *f.*; escarpement, *m.*

abscess ['æbses], *n.* abcès, dépôt, *m.*

abscond [əb'skɔnd], *v.i.* se soustraire (*furtivement*) aux poursuites de la justice; disparaître; (*fam.*) décamper.

absconder [əb'skɔndə], *n.* fugitif, *m.*; (*Law*) contumace, *m.*, *f.*

absence ['æbsəns], *n.* absence, *f.*; éloignement, *m.*; absence d'esprit, distraction, *f.*; manque, *m.*

absent ['æbsənt], *a.* absent.—[æb'sent], *v.r. to absent oneself*, s'absenter.

absentee [æbsən'tiː], *n.* absent, manquant, *m.*

absenteeism [æbsən'tiːizm], *n.* absentéisme, *m.*

absent-minded ['æbsənt'maindid], *a.* distrait.

absinthe ['æbsinθ], *n.* absinthe, *f.*

absolute ['æbsəluːt], *a.* absolu, illimité; irrévocable (*décret*); véritable.

absolutely [æbsə'luːtli], *adv.* absolument.

absolution [æbsə'luːʃən], *n.* absolution; (*R.-C. Ch.*) absoute, *f.*

absolve [əb'zɔlv], *v.t.* absoudre (*de*); délier, décharger, dégager, affranchir.

absorb [əb'sɔːb], *v.t.* absorber; amortir (*un choc*).

absorbent [əb'sɔːbənt], *a.* and *n.* absorbant, *m.*

absorption [əb'sɔːpʃən], *n.* absorption, *f.*; absorbement, amortissement, *m.*

abstain [əb'stein], *v.i.* s'abstenir (*de*).

abstainer [əb'steinə], *n.* buveur d'eau, *m.*, abstème, *m.*, *f.*; *total abstainer*, personne qui ne boit jamais d'alcool, *f.*

abstemious [əb'stiːmiəs], *a.* tempérant, sobre.

abstemiously [əb'stiːmiəsli], *adv.* sobrement, avec modération.

abstemiousness [əb'stiːmiəsnis], *n.* abstinence; modération, sobriété, *f.*

abstention [əb'stenʃən], *n.* abstention, *f.*

abstinence ['æbstinəns], *n.* abstinence, *f.*

abstinent ['æbstinənt], *a.* abstinent, sobre.

abstract (1) [æb'strækt], *v.t.* soustraire dérober, détourner; faire abstraction de; résumer, abréger.

abstract (2) ['æbstrækt], *a.* abstrait.—*n.* abrégé, résumé, précis, *m.*; analyse, *f.*; (*Comm.*) relevé, *m.*

abstracted [æb'stræktid], *a.* séparé; distrait, rêveur, pensif; soustrait, dérobé.

abstractedness [æb'stræktidnis], *n.* caractère abstrait, *m.*; préoccupation, *f.*

abstraction [æb'strækʃən], *n.* soustraction, distraction; abstraction; préoccupation, *f.*

abstractly ['æbstræktli], *adv.* abstractivement, d'une manière abstraite.

abstruse [æb'struːs], *a.* caché; abstrus, obscur.

absurd [əb'səːd], *a.* absurde.

absurdity [əb'səːditi], *n.* absurdité, *f.*

absurdly [əb'səːdli], *adv.* absurdement.

abundance [ə'bʌndəns], *n.* abondance, grande quantité, *f.*; grand nombre, *m.*; (*fig.*) prospérité, *f.*

abundant [ə'bʌndənt], *a.* abondant.

abundantly [ə'bʌndəntli], *adv.* abondamment, en abondance, à foison.

abuse (1) [ə'bjuːz], *v.t.* abuser de; maltraiter; médire de; injurier, dire des injures à; séduire.

abuse (2) [ə'bjuːs], *n.* abus, *m.*; insultes, injures, *f. pl.*

abuser [ə'bjuːzə], *n.* détracteur; séducteur; trompeur, *m.*

abusive [ə'bjuːsiv], *a.* abusif; injurieux.

abusively [ə'bjuːsivli], *adv.* abusivement; injurieusement.

abusiveness [ə'bjuːsivnis], *n.* langage injurieux *ou* grossier, *m.*

abut [ə'bʌt], *v.i.* aboutir (*à*); (*Build.*) s'appuyer (*contre*).

abysmal [ə'bizməl], *a.* sans fond; (*ignorance*) profonde.

abyss [ə'bis], *n.* abîme, gouffre, *m.*

Abyssinia [æbi'sinjə]. l'Abyssinie, l'Éthiopie, *f.*

Abyssinian [æbi'sinjən], *a.* abyssinien.—*n.* Abyssinien (*personne*), *m.*

acacia [ə'keiʃə], *n.* acacia, *m.*

academic [ækə'demik], **academical** [ækə'demikəl], *a.* académique, universitaire, classique, scolaire.

academician [əkædə'miʃən], *n.* académicien, *m.*

academy [ə'kædəmi], *n.* académie (*société savante*); école libre, *f.*, pensionnat, *m.*, institution, *f.*

acanthus [ə'kænθəs], *n.* acanthe, *f.*

accede [æk'siːd], *v.i.* accéder, consentir (*à*); monter (*sur le trône*).

accelerate [æk'seləreit], *v.t.* accélérer; hâter.—*v.i.* s'accélérer.

acceleration [æksælə'reiʃən], *n.* accélération, *f.*

accelerator [æk'seləreitə], *n.* accélérateur, *m.*

accent (1) [æk'sent], *v.t.* accentuer.

accent (2) ['æksənt], *n.* accent, *m.*

accentuate [æk'sentjueit], *v.t.* accentuer.

accept [ək sept], *v.t.* accepter, agréer, admettre.

acceptability [əkseptə'biliti], **acceptableness** [ək'septəblnis], *n.* acceptabilité, *f.*; droit au bon accueil, *m.*

acceptable [ək'septəbl], *a.* acceptable; agréable.

acceptance [ək'septəns], *n.* acceptation, *f.*; accueil favorable, *m.*

acceptation [æksep'teiʃən], *n.* acception, *f.*, sens (*d'un mot*), *m.*

access ['ækses], *n.* accès, abord, *m.*; entrée, admission, *f.*

accessible [æk'sesibl], *a.* accessible, abordable.

accession [æk'seʃən], *n.* acquisition; augmentation, addition, *f.*, accroissement; avènement (*au trône etc.*), *m.*

accessory [æk'sesəri], *a.* accessoire.—*n.* accessoire (*chose*), *m.*; complice (*personne*), *m.*, *f.*

accidence ['æksidəns], *n.* morphologie, *f.*; rudiments (*de grammaire*), *m. pl.*

accident ['æksidənt], *n.* accident, *m.*, avarie, *f.*, hasard; incident; malheur, *m.*

accidental [æksi'dentəl], *a.* accidentel, fortuit.

accidentally [æksi'dentəli], *adv.* accidentellement; par hasard.

acclaim [ə'kleim], *v.t.* acclamer, applaudir à; proclamer.—*n.* acclamation, *f.*

acclamation [æklə'meiʃən], *n.* acclamation, *f.*

acclimatation [əklaimə'teiʃən], **acclimation** [æklai'meiʃən], *n.* acclimatement, *m.*; acclimatation, *f.*

acclimatization [əklaimətai'zeiʃən], *n.* acclimatation, *f.*

acclimatize [ə'klaimətaiz], *v.t.* acclimater; **to become acclimatized**, s'acclimater; s'accoutumer.

acclivity [ə'kliviti], *n.* montée, côte, rampe, *f.*

accolade [æko'leid], *n.* accolade, *f.*

accommodate [ə'kɔmədeit], *v.t.* accommoder, ajuster; loger, recevoir; fournir; obliger (*par*), servir (*de*).

accommodating [ə'kɔmədeitiŋ], *a.* accommodant, obligeant; complaisant.

accommodation [əkɔmə'deiʃən], *n.* ajustement, accommodement, *m.*; complaisance; convenance, *f.*; logement, *m.*; facilités, *f.pl.*

accompaniment [ə'kʌmpnimənt], *n.* accompagnement, *m.*

accompanist [ə'kʌmpənist], *n.* (*Mus.*) accompagnateur, *m.*, accompagnatrice, *f.*

accompany [ə'kʌmpəni], *v.t.* accompagner; reconduire (*à sa voiture etc.*).

accomplice [ə'kʌmplis], *n.* complice, *m.*, *f.*, compère, *m.*

accomplish [ə'kʌmpliʃ], *v.t.* accomplir, achever; effectuer; réaliser (*une prédiction etc.*).

accomplished [ə'kʌmpliʃt], *a.* accompli, achevé; parfait.

accomplishment [ə'kʌmpliʃmənt], *n.* accomplissement, *m.*; exécution, *f.*; (*usu. pl.*) arts d'agrément, talents, *m.pl.*

accord [ə'kɔ:d], *v.t.* accorder, concéder.—*v.i.* s'accorder, être d'accord.—*n.* accord, consentement, *m.*; **of one's own accord**, de son propre gré, spontanément; **with one accord**, d'un commun accord.

accordance [ə'kɔ:dəns], *n.* accord, rapport, *m.*; conformité, *f.*

according [ə'kɔ:diŋ], *a.* conforme (*à*); **according as**, selon que, suivant que; **according to**, selon, suivant, conformément à, d'après.

accordingly [ə'kɔ:diŋli], *adv.* en conséquence; donc, aussi.

accordion [ə'kɔ:diən], *n.* accordéon, *m.*

accost [ə'kɔst], *v.t.* accoster, aborder.

account [ə'kaunt], *n.* compte; mémoire, rapport, exposé, compte rendu, *m.*; relation, *f.*, récit, *m.*; raison; cause; (*fig.*) considération, valeur, *f.*; cas, poids, *m.*; **by all accounts**, au dire de tout le monde; **current account**, compte courant; **on account of**, à cause de; **to keep accounts**, tenir les livres.—*v.t.* compter; estimer (*de*), regarder (*comme*), tenir (*pour*).—*v.i.* **to account for**, rendre compte de, expliquer; répondre de, rendre raison de.

accountable [ə'kauntəbl], *a.* responsable; comptable.

accountancy [ə'kauntənsi], *n.* comptabilité, *f.*

accountant [ə'kauntənt], *n.* comptable, agent comptable, *m.*; **chartered accountant**, expert comptable, *m.*

account book [ə'kauntbuk], *n.* livre de comptes, *m.*

accouter [ə'ku:tə], *v.t.* habiller, équiper; accoutrer (*un chevalier etc.*).

accouterment [ə'ku:təmənt], *n.* harnachement; équipement (*du soldat*), *m.*

accredit [ə'kredit], *v.t.* accréditer.

accretion [ə'kri:ʃən], *n.* accroissement, *m.*

accrue [ə'kru:], *v.i.* provenir, résulter (*de*); s'accumuler.

accumulate [ə'kju:mjuleit], *v.t.* accumuler, entasser; amonceler.—*v.i.* s'accumuler, s'amonceler.

accumulation [əkju:mju'leiʃən], *n.* accumulation, *f.*; amoncellement, amas, entassement, *m.*

accumulative [ə'kju:mjulətiv], *a.* (*chose*) qui s'accumule; (*personne*) qui accumule, thésauriseur.

accumulator [ə'kju:mjuleitə], *n.* accumulateur, *m.*

accuracy ['ækjurisi], **accurateness** ['ækju ritnis], *n.* exactitude, justesse; précision, *f.*; soin, *m.*

accurate ['ækjurit], *a.* exact, juste, correct, précis.

accurately ['ækjuritli], *adv.* exactement, avec justesse.

accurateness [ACCURACY].

accursed [ə'kə:sid], *a.* maudit; détestable, exécrable.

accusation [ækju'zeiʃən], *n.* accusation, *f.*

accusative [ə'kju:zətiv], *a. and n.* (*Gram.*), accusatif, *m.*

accusatory [ə'kju:zətri], *a.* accusateur.

accuse [ə'kju:z], *v.t.* accuser.

accuser [ə'kju:zə], *n.* accusateur, *m.*

accustom [ə'kʌstəm], *v.t.* accoutumer, habituer.

ace [eis], *n.* as; (*fig.*) point, iota, *m.*; **within an ace of**, à deux doigts de.

acerb [ə'sə:b], *a.* acerbe, aigre.

acerbity [ə'sə:biti], *n.* acerbité, aigreur; (*fig.*) âpreté, sévérité, *f.*

acetic [ə'si:tik, ə'setik], *a.* acétique.

acetylene [əˈsetiliːn], *n.* acétylène, *m.*
ache [eik], *n.* mal, *m.*; douleur, *f.*; *headache*, mal de tête; *toothache*, mal de dents.—*v.i.* faire mal; (*fig.*) souffrir (*de*); *my head aches*, j'ai mal à la tête.
achieve [əˈtʃiːv], *v.t.* exécuter, accomplir; remporter (*une victoire*); atteindre (à).
achievement [əˈtʃiːvmənt], *n.* exploit, fait d'armes; accomplissement, succès, *m.*; réalisation, *f.*
aching [ˈeikiŋ], *a.* endolori, douloureux; *an aching heart*, un cœur dolent.
acid [ˈæsid], *a.* and *n.* acide, *m.*; *acid drops*, bonbons acidulés, *m.pl.*
acidity [əˈsiditi], *n.* acidité, *f.*
acknowledge [ækˈnɔlidʒ], *v.t.* reconnaître; avouer, confesser; accuser réception de (*lettre*); répondre à.
acknowledgment [ækˈnɔlidʒmənt], *n.* reconnaissance, *f.*; aveu; accusé de réception, *m.*; remerciements, *m.pl.*
acme [ˈækmi], *n.* comble, faîte; apogée, *m.*
acolyte [ˈækolait], *n.* acolyte, *m.*
aconite [ˈækonait], *n.* (*Bot.*) aconit, *m.*
acorn [ˈeikɔːn], *n.* gland, *m.*
acoustic [əˈkuːstik], *a.* acoustique.—*n.* (*pl.*) acoustique, *f.*
acquaint [əˈkweint], *v.t.* informer (*de*); faire savoir à, faire part à; *to be acquainted with*, connaître, savoir.
acquaintance [əˈkweintəns], *n.* connaissance (*de*); personne de ma (sa *etc.*) connaissance, *f.*
acquainted [əˈkweintid], *a.* connu; instruit (*de*), familier (*avec*).
acquiesce [ækwiˈes], *v.i.* acquiescer (à); accéder (à).
acquiescence [ækwiˈesəns], *n.* acquiescement; consentement, *m.*
acquiescent [ækwiˈesənt], *a.* résigné, soumis; consentant.
acquire [əˈkwaiə], *v.t.* acquérir, obtenir, gagner.
acquirement [əˈkwaiəmənt], *n.* acquisition; connaissance, *f.*
acquisition [ækwiˈziʃən], *n.* acquisition, *f.*
acquisitive [əˈkwizitiv], *a.* âpre au gain.
acquit [əˈkwit], *v.t.* régler (*une dette*); absoudre, acquitter (*un accusé*); s'acquitter (*d'un devoir*); *to acquit oneself well*, faire son devoir.
acquittal [əˈkwitəl], *n.* acquittement, *m.*
acre [ˈeikə], *n.* arpent, *m.*, acre, *f.*
acreage [ˈeikəridʒ], *n.* superficie, *f.*
acrid [ˈækrid], *a.* âcre; (*fig.*) acerbe.
acridity [æˈkriditi], *n.* âcreté, *f.*
acrimonious [ækriˈmouniəs], *a.* acrimonieux.
acrimoniously [ækriˈmouniəsli], *adv.* avec aigreur, avec acrimonie.
acrimony [ˈækriməni], *n.* acrimonie, aigreur, *f.*
acrobat [ˈækrəbæt], *n.* acrobate, *m.*, *f.*
acrobatic [ækroˈbætik], *a.* acrobatique.—*n.* (*pl.*) acrobatie, *f.*
acropolis [əˈkrɔpəlis], *n.* acropole, *f.*
across [əˈkrɔs, əˈkrɔːs], *prep.* à travers, sur; *to come across*, rencontrer.—*adv.* à travers, en travers; de l'autre côté; *across the street*, de l'autre côté de la rue.
acrostic [əˈkrɔstik], *n.* acrostiche, *m.*
act [ækt], *n.* acte, *m.*, loi; action, *f.*; *in the act*, sur le fait; *in the act of doing it*, en train de le faire; *in the very act*, en flagrant délit.—*v.t.* jouer, représenter; feindre, contrefaire.—*v.i.* agir (*en, sur etc.*); se conduire; se comporter; opérer.
acting [ˈæktiŋ], *a.* qui agit; suppléant; (*Comm.*) gérant; *acting manager*, directeur gérant, *m.*—*n.* (*Theat.*) jeu, *m.*; (*fig.*) feinte, *f.*
action [ˈækʃən], *n.* action, *f.*, fait; (*Law*) procès, *m.*; bataille, *f.*
actionable [ˈækʃənəbl], *a.* actionnable, sujet à procès.
activate [ˈæktiveit], *v.t.* activer; rendre radioactif.
active [ˈæktiv], *a.* actif, agile, alerte.
actively [ˈæktivli], *adv.* activement.
activity [ækˈtiviti], *n.* activité, *f.*
actor [ˈæktə], *n.* acteur, comédien, *m.*
actress [ˈæktris], *n.* actrice, comédienne, *f.*
actual [ˈæktjuəl], *a.* réel, véritable, effectif.
actuality [æktjuˈæliti], *n.* réalité, *f.*
actually [ˈæktjuəli], *adv.* réellement, en effet, positivement, véritablement; à vrai dire.
actuarial [æktjuˈɛəriəl], *a.* actuariel.
actuary [ˈæktjuəri], *n.* actuaire, *m.*
actuate [ˈæktjueit], *v.t.* mettre en action; pousser, animer.
acuity [əˈkjuiti], *n.* acuité, *f.*
acumen [əˈkjuːmen], *n.* finesse, pénétration, *f.*
acute [əˈkjuːt], *a.* aigu, pointu, fin; (*fig.*) violent, poignant; perçant, pénétrant.
acutely [əˈkjuːtli], *adv.* vivement; avec finesse.
acuteness [əˈkjuːtnis], *n.* acuité; intensité; finesse, pénétration, *f.*
adage [ˈædidʒ], *n.* adage, proverbe, *m.*
adamant [ˈædəmənt], *a.* inflexible, intransigeant.—*n.* diamant, *m.*
adamantine [ædəˈmæntain], *a.* adamantin, inflexible.
adapt [əˈdæpt], *v.t.* adapter, approprier, ajuster (à).
adaptability [ədæptəˈbiliti], *n.* faculté d'adaptation, souplesse, *f.*
adaptable [əˈdæptəbl], *a.* adaptable, qui peut s'adapter.
adapter [əˈdæptə], *n.* (*Elec.*) raccord, *m.*
add [æd], *v.t.* ajouter, joindre; additionner.
adder [ˈædə], *n.* vipère, *f.*
addict [ˈædikt], *n.* personne adonnée à (*stupéfiants etc.*), *f.*—[əˈdikt], *v.i.* s'adonner, se livrer (à).
addictedness [əˈdiktidnis], **addiction** [əˈdikʃən], *n.* attachement, goût (*pour*), penchant (à), *m.*
addition [əˈdiʃən], *n.* addition, *f.*; surcroît, supplément, accroissement, *m.*
additional [əˈdiʃənəl], *a.* additionnel, supplémentaire, de plus.
additionally [əˈdiʃənəli], *adv.* par addition, en sus, de plus, en outre.
addle [ædl], *v.t.* rendre couvi, corrompre; (*fig.*) brouiller (*le cerveau*).—*a.* or **addled** [ædld], couvi (*œuf*); pourri; (*fig.*) stérile.
addle-headed [ˈædlˈhedid], *a.* à cerveau vide, écervelé, à l'esprit brouillon.
address [əˈdres], *n.* adresse; habileté, dextérité; allocution, *f.*, discours; (*fig.*) abord, *m.*—*v.t.* adresser (*une lettre*); adresser la parole à, aborder (*quelqu'un*); (*Golf*) *to address the ball*, viser la balle.
addressee [ædreˈsiː], *n.* destinataire, *m.*, *f.*

adduce [ə'dju:s], v.t. alléguer; apporter, avancer, produire.
Adela ['ædilə]. Adèle, f.
Adelaide ['ædəleid]. Adélaïde, f.
adenoid ['ædinɔid], a. adénoïde.—n. (pl.) adénite, f.; végétations, f. pl.
adept [æ'dept], a. adepte, habile, versé (dans).—n. adepte, m., f.
adequacy ['ædikwəsi], **adequateness** ['ædi kwitnis], n. juste proportion, suffisance, f.
adequate ['ædikwit], a. proportionné, suffisant (à), compétent.
adequately ['ædikwitli], adv. en juste proportion, suffisamment, convenablement.
adequateness [ADEQUACY].
adhere [əd'hiə], v.i. adhérer, s'attacher, s'en tenir (à).
adherence [əd'hiərəns], n. adhérence, f., attachement, m.
adherent [əd'hiərənt], n. adhérent, m.
adhesion [əd'hi:ʒən], n. adhésion, f.
adhesive [əd'hi:siv], a. adhésif, tenace; gommé, agglutinant.
adieu [ə'dju:], adv. and n. adieu, m.; **to bid someone adieu**, faire ses adieux à quelqu'un.
adipose ['ædipous], a. adipeux.
adjacency [ə'dʒeisənsi], n. contiguïté, f., voisinage, m.
adjacent [ə'dʒeisənt], a. adjacent, contigu (à), avoisinant.
adjectival [ædʒək'taivəl], a. comme adjectif.
adjectivally [ædʒək'taivəli], adv. adjective-ment.
adjective ['ædʒəktiv], a. and n. adjectif, m.
adjoin [ə'dʒɔin], v.t. adjoindre, joindre; toucher, se joindre à.—v.i. se toucher, être contigu.
adjoining [ə'dʒɔiniŋ], a. adjacent, avoisinant, contigu (à).
adjourn [ə'dʒə:n], v.t. ajourner, différer, remettre.—v.i. s'ajourner, lever la séance.
adjournment [ə'dʒə:nmənt], n. ajourne-ment, m; remise, f.
adjudge [ə'dʒʌdʒ], v.t. adjuger; juger, con-damner; (fig.) estimer.
adjudicate [ə'dʒu:dikeit], v.t. adjuger; pro-noncer.
adjudication [ədʒu:di'keiʃən], n. jugement, m.; décision, f., arrêt, m.
adjudicator [ə'dʒu:dikeitə], n. juge, arbitre, m., f.
adjunct ['ædʒʌŋkt], a. adjoint, accessoire.—n. accessoire; adjoint, m.
adjure [ə'dʒuə], v.t. adjurer.
adjust [ə'dʒʌst], v.t. ajuster, régler, arranger.
adjustable [ə'dʒʌstəbl], a. réglable.
adjustment [ə'dʒʌstmənt], n. ajustement, arrangement, accord, m.; mise au point, f., réglage, m.
adjutant ['ædʒutənt], n. capitaine adjudant major; major de la garnison, m.
administer [əd'ministə], v.t. administrer, gérer, régir; faire prêter (un serment).
administrate [əd'ministreit], v.t. adminis-trer; régir.
administration [ədminis'treiʃən], n. administra-tion, f., gouvernement, m.
administrative [əd'ministrətiv], a. administra-tif.
administrator [əd'ministreitə], n. adminis-trateur; (Law) curateur, m.

admirable ['ædmərəbl], a. admirable.
admirably ['ædmərəbli], adv. admirable-ment, à ravir, à merveille.
admiral ['ædmərəl], n. amiral, m.; **rear admiral**, contre-amiral, m.; **vice admiral**, vice-amiral, m.
admiralty ['ædmərəlti], n. amirauté, f.; Ministère de la Marine (en France), m.; **Board of Admiralty**, conseil d'amirauté, m.; **First Lord of the Admiralty**, ministre de la marine, m.
admiration [ædmə'reiʃən], n. admiration, f.; étonnement, m.
admire [əd'maiə], v.t. admirer; aimer; s'étonner de.—v.i. s'étonner.
admirer [əd'maiərə], n. admirateur, m., admiratrice, f.
admissible [əd'misibl], a. admissible.
admission [əd'miʃən], n. admission, entrée, f.; accès; aveu, m., concession, f.
admit [əd'mit], v.t. admettre, laisser entrer; avouer, reconnaître; tolérer.—v.i. **to admit of**, comporter, permettre; souffrir.
admittance [əd'mitəns], n. accès, m.; admis-sion, entrée, f.; **no admittance**, défense d'entrer.
admittedly [əd'mitidli], adv. de l'aveu général; il est vrai que.
admixture [əd'mikstʃə], n. mélange, m.
admonish [əd'mɔniʃ], v.t. avertir, exhorter; reprendre, réprimander.
admonition [ædmɔ'niʃən], n. admonition, f., avertissement, m.; remontrance, répri-mande, f.
ado [ə'du:], n. bruit, fracas, m., façons, céré-monies, f.pl., embarras, m., peine, diffi-culté, f.; **much ado about nothing**, beau-coup de bruit pour rien; **without any more ado**, sans plus de façons.
adolescence [ædo'lesəns], n. adolescence, f.
adolescent [ædo'lesənt], a. and n. adolescent, m.
Adolphus [ə'dɔlfəs]. Adolphe, m.
adopt [ə'dɔpt], v.t. adopter.
adopted [ə'dɔptid], **adoptive** [ə'dɔptiv], a. adoptif, adopté, d'adoption.
adoption [ə'dɔpʃən], n. adoption, f.
adoptive [ADOPTED].
adorable [ə'dɔ:rəbl], a. adorable.
adorably [ə'dɔ:rəbli], adv. d'une manière adorable, adorablement.
adoration [ædo'reiʃən], n. adoration, f.
adore [ə'dɔ:], v.t. adorer.
adorer [ə'dɔ:rə], n. adorateur, m.
adoringly [ə'dɔ:riŋli], adv. avec adoration.
adorn [ə'dɔ:n], v.t. orner; parer, embellir; (fig.) faire l'ornement de.
adornment [ə'dɔ:nmənt], n. ornement, m., parure; ornementation, f.
Adrian ['eidriən]. Adrien, m.
Adriatic Sea [eidri'ætik'si:]. la mer Adria-tique, l'Adriatique, f.
adrift [ə'drift], adv. en ou à la dérive; à l'abandon.
adroit [ə'drɔit], a. adroit, habile.
adroitly [ə'drɔitli], adv. adroitement.
adroitness [ə'drɔitnis], n. adresse, dextérité, f.
adulate ['ædjuleit], v.t. aduler.
adulation [ædju'leiʃən], n. adulation, f.
adulatory ['ædjuleitəri], a. adulateur.
adult [ə'dʌlt, 'ædʌlt], a. and n. adulte, m., f.

337

adulterate

adulterate [ə'dʌltəreit], *v.t.* adultérer, fre-later, falsifier, sophistiquer; (*fig.*) corrompre.
adulteration [ədʌltə'reiʃən], *n.* falsification, sophistication, *f.*, frelatage, *m.*
adulterator [ə'dʌltəreitə], *n.* frelateur, falsificateur, *m.*
adulterer [ə'dʌltərə], *n.* adultère, *m.*
adulteress [ə'dʌltəris], *n.* (femme) adultère, *f.*
adulterous [ə'dʌltərəs], *a.* adultère; (*fig.*) altéré, faux.
adultery [ə'dʌltəri], *n.* adultère, *m.*
advance [əd'vɑːns], *v.t.* avancer, faire avancer; élever, hausser, augmenter.—*v.i.* avancer, s'avancer, se porter en avant.—*n.* mouvement en avant, *m.*; avance (*de fonds*), *f.*; avancement, progrès, *m.*; **in advance**, d'avance.
advance guard [əd'vɑːnsgɑːd], *n.* avant-garde, *f.*
advancement [əd'vɑːnsmənt], *n.* avancement, progrès, *m.*; (*Comm.*) avance, *f.*
advantage [əd'vɑːntidʒ], *n.* avantage; profit, intérêt, *m.*; **to have the advantage**, avoir le dessus; **to take advantage of**, profiter de; **to take advantage of someone's kindness**, abuser de la bonté de quelqu'un.
advantageous [ædvən'teidʒəs], *a.* avantageux (*à* ou *de*).
advantageously [ædvən'teidʒəsli], *adv.* avantageusement.
Advent ['ædvənt]. (*Eccles.*) l'Avent, *m.*
advent ['ædvənt], *n.* venue, *f.*
adventitious [ædven'tiʃəs], *a.* adventice, fortuit.
adventure [əd'ventʃə], *n.* aventure, entreprise hasardeuse, *f.*—*v.t.* aventurer, hasarder.—*v.i.* s'aventurer, se hasarder.
adventurer [əd'ventʃərə], *n.* aventurier, *m.*
adventuress [əd'ventʃəris], *n.* aventurière, *f.*
adventurous [əd'ventʃərəs], *a.* aventureux, hardi.
adventurously [əd'ventʃərəsli], *adv.* aventureusement.
adverb ['ædvəːb], *n.* adverbe, *m.*
adverbial [əd'vəːbjəl], *a.* adverbial.
adverbially [əd'vəːbjəli], *adv.* adverbialement.
adversary ['ædvəsəri], *n.* adversaire, *m.*, *f.*
adverse ['ædvəːs], *a.* adverse, contraire (*à*); défavorable.
adversely ['ædvəːsli], *adv.* d'une manière hostile, malheureusement.
adversity [əd'vəːsiti], *n.* adversité, *f.*
advert [əd'vəːt], *v.i.* faire allusion (*à*); parler (*de*).
advertise ['ædvətaiz], *v.t.* annoncer, faire annoncer, afficher, faire de la publicité pour.
advertisement [əd'vəːtizmənt], *n.* annonce (*journal*), publicité, réclame, *f.*; avis, *m.*; **classified advertisements**, petites annonces, *f.pl.*
advertiser ['ædvətaizə], *n.* personne qui fait des annonces, *f.*; journal d'annonces, *m.*
advertising ['ædvətaiziŋ], *n.* publicité, réclame, *f.*; **advertising agency**, agence de publicité, *f.*
advice [əd'vais], *n.* avis, conseil, *m.*; **if you take my advice**, si vous m'en croyez; **to take advice**, prendre conseil (*de*), consulter (*un médecin etc.*).

advisable [əd'vaizəbl], *a.* judicieux, convenable (*pour* ou *de*); opportun.
advisability [ədvaizə'biliti], *n.* convenance, utilité, opportunité, *f.*
advise [əd'vaiz], *v.t.* conseiller; donner avis (*de*); prévenir (*de*); annoncer.—*v.i.* délibérer, prendre conseil, consulter.
advisedly [əd'vaizidli], *adv.* avec réflexion, de propos délibéré.
adviser [əd'vaizə], *n.* conseiller, *m.*
advisory [əd'vaizəri], *a.* copsultatif.
advocacy ['ædvəkəsi], *n.* profession d'avocat; défense, *f.*, plaidoyer, *m.*
advocate ['ædvəkit], *n.* avocat, défenseur; intercesseur, *m.*—['ædvəkeit], *v.t.* défendre, plaider; soutenir, appuyer, préconiser.
adze [ædz], *n.* herminette, doloire; aissette, *f.*—*v.t.* entailler à l'herminette, doler.
Aegean Sea [iː'dʒiːənsiː]. la mer Égée, *f.*
aegis ['iːdʒis], *n.* égide, *f.*
Aeneas [iː'niːəs]. Énée, *m.*
Aeneid [iː'niːid]. l'Énéide, *f.*
aeon ['iːən], *n.* éternité, *f.*, éon, *m.*
aerate ['ɛəreit], *v.t.* aérer; gazéifier.
aeration [ɛə'reiʃən], *n.* aération, *f.*
aerial ['ɛəriəl], *a.* aérien.—*n.* antenne, *f.*
aerie, aery, eyrie, eyry ['ɛəri, 'iəri], *n.* aire, *f.*
aerobatics [ɛəro'bætiks], *n.pl.* acrobaties aériennes, *f.pl.*
aerodrome ['ɛərodroum], *n.* aérodrome, *m.*
aerodynamic ['ɛərodai'næmik], *a.* aérodynamique.—*n.* (*pl.*) aérodynamique, *f.*
aerolite ['ɛərolait], **aerolith** ['ɛəroliθ], *n.* aérolithe, bolide, *m.*
aeronaut ['ɛərɔnɔːt], *n.* aéronaute, *m.*, *f.*
aeronautic [ɛəro'nɔːtik], *a.* aéronautique.
aeroplane ['ɛəroplein], *n.* aéroplane, avion, *m.*
aerostat ['ɛərostæt], *n.* aérostat, *m.*
Aeschylus ['iːskiləs]. Eschyle, *m.*
Aesop ['iːsɔp]. Ésope, *m.*
aesthete ['iːsθiːt], *n.* esthète, *m.*, *f.*
aesthetic [iːs'θetik], **aesthetical** [iːs'θetikəl], *a.* esthétique.
aesthetically [iːs'θetikəli], *adv.* esthétiquement.
aestival [iːs'taivəl], *a.* estival.
aether [ETHER].
afar [ə'fɑː], *adv.* loin, de loin, au loin.
affability [æfə'biliti], **affableness** ['æfəblnis], *n.* affabilité, *f.*
affable ['æfəbl], *a.* affable, doux, gracieux.
affably ['æfəbli], *adv.* affablement, avec affabilité.
affair [ə'fɛə], *n.* affaire, *f.*
affect [ə'fekt], *v.t.* affecter; intéresser, toucher, émouvoir.
affectation [æfek'teiʃən], **affectedness** [ə'fektidnis], *n.* affectation, *f.*
affected [ə'fektid], *a.* disposé (*pour etc.*); affecté, précieux; maniéré, prétentieux (*style*).
affecting [ə'fektiŋ], *a.* touchant, émouvant, attendrissant.
affection [ə'fekʃən], *n.* affection, *f.*, amour; goût, attachement, penchant, *m.*; maladie, *f.*
affectionate [ə'fekʃənit], *a.* affectueux, affectionné.
affectionately [ə'fekʃənitli], *adv.* affectueusement.
affiance [ə'faiəns], *v.t.* fiancer.—*n.* fiançailles, *f.pl.*

affianced [ə'faiənst], *a.* fiancé.

affidavit [æfi'deivit], *n.* déclaration par écrit sous serment, attestation, *f.*

affiliate [ə'filieit], *v.t.* affilier; attribuer, rattacher (*à*).

affiliation [əfili'eiʃən], *n.* affiliation, *f.*

affinity [ə'finiti], *n.* affinité, *f.*

affirm [ə'fə:m], *v.t.* affirmer.

affirmation [æfə'meiʃən], *n.* affirmation, *f.*

affirmative [ə'fə:mətiv], *a.* affirmatif.—*n.* affirmative, *f.*

affirmatively [ə'fə:mətivli], *adv.* affirmativement.

affix [ə'fiks], *v.t.* apposer, attacher (*à*).

afflatus [ə'fleitəs], *n.* souffle, *m.*, inspiration, *f.*

afflict [ə'flikt], *v.t.* affliger (*de*); tourmenter.

afflicting [ə'fliktiŋ], *a.* affligeant.

affliction [ə'flikʃən], *n.* affliction; calamité, *f.*, malheur, *m.*

affluence ['æfluəns], *n.* opulence, affluence; abondance, *f.*, concours (*de personnes*), *m.*

affluent ['æfluənt], *a.* opulent, riche; affluent.

afford [ə'fɔ:d], *v.t.* donner, fournir, accorder; avoir les moyens de, pouvoir.

afforestation [əfɔris'teiʃən], *n.* boisement; reboisement, *m.*

affranchise [ə'fræntʃaiz], *v.t.* affranchir.

affray [ə'frei], *n.* bagarre, échauffourée, *f.*

affright [ə'frait], *v.t.* effrayer.

affront [ə'frʌnt], *n.* affront, *m.*, insulte, injure, *f.*, outrage, *m.*—*v.t.* affronter, offenser, insulter.

afield [ə'fi:ld], *adv.* aux champs, à la campagne; *to go far afield*, aller très loin.

afire [ə'faiə], *adv.* en feu.

aflame [ə'fleim], *adv.* en flammes.

afloat [ə'flout], *adv.* à flot; (*fig.*) en circulation.

afoot [ə'fut], *adv.* à pied; en marche, en route; (*fig.*) sur pied; en train.

afore [ə'fɔ:], *adv.* précédemment, auparavant; par devant.

aforementioned [ə'fɔ:menʃənd], *a.* mentionné plus haut, susdit, précité.

aforesaid [ə'fɔ:sed], *a.* susdit, ledit, susnommé.

aforethought [ə'fɔ:θɔ:t], *a. with malice aforethought*, avec intention criminelle.

afraid [ə'freid], *a.* effrayé, pris de peur; *I am afraid not*, je crains que non; *I am afraid she's gone*, je crains bien qu'elle ne soit partie; *to be afraid of*, avoir peur de.

afresh [ə'freʃ], *adv.* de nouveau, de plus belle.

Africa ['æfrikə]. l'Afrique, *f.*

African ['æfrikən], *a.* africain.—*n.* Africain (*personne*), *m.*

aft [ɑ:ft], *a.* arrière, de l'arrière.—*adv.* (*Naut.*) à l'arrière.

after ['ɑ:ftə], *a.* subséquent, ultérieur, futur; arrière.—*prep.* après; sur, à la suite de; selon, d'après, d'après.—*adv.* après, d'après, ensuite.—*conj.* après que.

aftercrop ['ɑ:ftəkrɔp], *n.* seconde récolte, *f.*; regain, *m.*

aftereffects ['ɑ:ftərifekts], *n. pl.* suites, *f. pl.*, répercussion, *f.*

afterlife ['ɑ:ftəlaif], *n.* suite de la vie, *f.*; au-delà, *m.*

aftermath ['ɑ:ftəmæθ], *n.* regain, *m.*; (*fig.*) suites, *f. pl.*

afternoon [ɑ:ftə'nu:n], *n.* après-midi, *m.* ou *f.*

afterthought ['ɑ:ftəθɔ:t], *n.* réflexion après coup, *f.*

afterward ['ɑ:ftəwəd], **afterwards** ['ɑ:ftəwədz], *adv.* après, ensuite, plus tard.

again [ə'gein], *adv.* encore; encore une fois, de nouveau; *again and again*, à plusieurs reprises; *as much again*, encore autant; *never again*, jamais plus.

against [ə'geinst], *prep.* contre; vis-à-vis; vers; pour.

agape [ə'geip], *adv.* bouche bée.

agate ['ægeit], *n.* agate, *f.*

Agatha ['ægəθə]. Agathe, *f.*

age [eidʒ], *n.* âge, *m.*; époque, *f.*; *of age*, majeur; *under age*, mineur; *Middle Ages*, moyen âge.—*v.t., v.i.* vieillir.

aged ['eidʒid, (*after prefix*) eidʒd], *a.* vieux, âgé; *middle-aged*, entre deux âges.

ageless ['eidʒlis], *a.* toujours jeune.

agency ['eidʒənsi], *n.* action, entremise; (*Comm.*) agence, *f.*

agenda [ə'dʒendə], *n.* ordre du jour; programme, *m.*

agent ['eidʒənt], *n.* représentant, agent, mandataire, *m.*

agglomerate [ə'glɔməreit], *v.t.* agglomérer.—*v.i.* s'agglomérer.—*a.* aggloméré.

agglomeration [əglɔmə'reiʃən], *n.* agglomération, *f.*

aggrandize [ə'grændaiz], *v.t.* agrandir.

aggrandizement [ə'grændizmənt], *n.* agrandissement, *m.*

aggravate ['ægrəveit], *v.t.* aggraver; exagérer; (*colloq.*) agacer, pousser à bout, exaspérer.

aggravation [ægrə'veiʃən], *n.* aggravation; circonstance aggravante, *f.*; agacement, *m.*

aggregate ['ægrigit], *a.* collectif, global, réuni.—*n.* masse, *f.*; ensemble, *m.*, somme totale, *f.*—['ægrigeit], *v.t.* rassembler.

aggregation [ægri'geiʃən], *n.* agrégation, *f.*, assemblage, *m.*

aggression [ə'greʃən], *n.* agression, *f.*

aggressive [ə'gresiv], *a.* agressif.

aggressiveness [ə'gresivnis], *n.* caractère agressif, *m.*

aggressor [ə'gresə], *n.* agresseur, *m.*

aggrieve [ə'gri:v], *v.t.* chagriner, affliger; blesser, léser.

aghast [ə'gɑ:st], *a.* consterné, ébahi, médusé, tout pantois.

agile ['ædʒail], *a.* agile, leste.

agility [ə'dʒiliti], *n.* agilité, *f.*

agio ['ædʒiou], *n.* prix du change, agio, *m.*

agiotage ['ædʒiotidʒ], *n.* agiotage, *m.*

agitate ['ædʒiteit], *v.t.* agiter, exciter; remuer, troubler.

agitation [ædʒi'teiʃən], *n.* agitation; discussion, *f.*, examen, *m.*

agitator ['ædʒiteitə], *n.* agitateur; meneur, *m.*

aglow [ə'glou], *a.* enflammé, resplendissant.

agnostic [æg'nɔstik], *a. and n.* agnosticiste, agnostique, *n.*

agnosticism [æg'nɔstisizm], *n.* agnosticisme, *m.*

ago [ə'gou], *adv.* passé, il y a; *two days ago*, il y a deux jours.

agog [ə'gɔg], *adv.* excité, impatient, empressé; en train, en l'air; *to be all agog*, avoir la tête montée.

agonize ['ægənaiz], *v.t.* torturer, mettre au supplice.—*v.i.* souffrir l'agonie, être au supplice.

agonizing ['ægənaiziŋ], *a.* atroce, déchirant.

agony ['ægəni], *n.* douleur, angoisse, *f.*, paroxysme, *m.*

agrarian [ə'grɛəriən], *a.* agraire.

agree [ə'gri:], *v.i.* s'accorder (*à* ou *avec*); être d'accord; consentir (*à*); convenir (*de*); être conforme (*à*).

agreeable [ə'gri:əbl], *a.* agréable, aimable; conforme (*à*); consentant.

agreeably [ə'gri:əbli], *adv.* agréablement; conformément (*à*).

agreed [ə'gri:d], *a.* convenu, d'accord; *it's agreed,* c'est entendu.

agreement [ə'gri:mənt], *n.* accord, *m.*; convention, *f.*, contrat, pacte, marché, *m.*; conformité, *f.*

agricultural [ægri'kʌltʃərəl], *a.* agricole, d'agriculture.

agriculture ['ægrikʌltʃə], *n.* agriculture, *f.*

agriculturist [ægri'kʌltʃərist], *n.* agriculteur, agronome, *m.*

aground [ə'graund], *adv.* échoué; à terre.

ague ['eigju:], *n.* fièvre intermittente, *f.*

ahead [ə'hed], *adv.* en avant; (*fig.*) en tête; *go ahead!* en avant! vas-y! *straight ahead,* tout droit; *ahead of time,* en avance.

aid [eid], *v.t.* aider, assister; secourir; *to aid each other,* s'entr'aider.—*n.* aide, assistance, *f.*; secours, concours, subside, *m.*; *with the aid of,* à l'aide de.

aide-de-camp [eiddə'kɑ̄], *n.* aide de camp, *m.*

aigrette ['eigret], *n.* aigrette *f.*

ail [eil], *v.t.* faire mal à; chagriner; *what ails him?* qu'est-ce qu'il a?—*v.i.* être souffrant.

aileron ['eilerɔn], *n.* aileron, *m.*

ailing ['eiliŋ], *a.* souffrant, indisposé, mal portant.

ailment ['eilmənt], *n.* mal, malaise, *m.*, indisposition, *f.*

aim [eim], *v.t.* viser; diriger, lancer (*un coup etc.*).—*v.i.* viser (*à*); aspirer (*à*); avoir pour but (*de*).—*n.* point de mire, but, objet, dessein, *m.*; visée, *f.*; *to take aim at,* viser, coucher en joue.

aimless ['eimlis], *a.* sans but, sans objet.

air [ɛə], *n.* air; vent, *m.*, brise; (*fig.*) mine, expression, *f.*; *in the air,* en l'air; *in the open air,* en plein air.—*v.t.* aérer, donner de l'air à, mettre à l'air; sécher.

air-[ɛə], see also **aero-**.

airborne ['ɛəbɔːn], *a.* (*Av.*) aéroporté.

air-conditioned ['ɛəkəndiʃənd], *a.* climatisé.

air conditioning ['ɛəkəndiʃəniŋ], *n.* climatisation, *f.*

air cooling ['ɛəku:liŋ], *n.* refroidissement par air, *m.*

aircraft ['ɛəkrɑ:ft], *n.* avion, *m.*; les avions, *m.pl.*

aircrew ['ɛəkru:], *n.* équipage (d'avion), *m.*

airfield ['ɛəfi:ld], *n.* terrain d'aviation, *m.*

air hostess ['ɛəhoustis], *n.* hôtesse de l'air, *f.*

airily ['ɛərili], *adv.* allègrement, légèrement.

airiness ['ɛərinis], *n.* situation aérée; (*fig.*) légèreté, vivacité, désinvolture, *f.*

airing ['ɛəriŋ], *n.* aérage, *m.*, exposition à l'air, *f.*, éventage, *m.*; promenade, *f.*

airlift ['ɛəlift], *n.* pont aérien, *m.*

airline ['ɛəlain], *n.* ligne aérienne, *f.*

airliner ['ɛəlainə], *n.* avion de ligne, *m.*

air mail ['ɛəmeil], *n.* poste aérienne, *f.*

airman ['ɛəmən], *n.* aviateur, *m.*

air mattress ['ɛəmætris], *n.* matelas à air, *m.*

air pocket ['ɛəpɔkit], *n.* (*Av.*) trou d'air, *m.*

airport ['ɛəpɔːt], *n.* aéroport, *m.*

airship ['ɛəʃip], *n.* dirigeable, *m.*

airsickness ['ɛəsiknis], *n.* mal de l'air, *m.*

airstrip ['ɛəstrip], *n.* piste d'atterrissage, *f.*

airtight ['ɛətait], *a.* imperméable à l'air, hermétique.

airworthy ['ɛəwɔːði], *a.* navigable.

airy ['ɛəri], *a.* ouvert à l'air; aérien, aéré; (*fig.*) léger, dégagé, gai, enjoué, insouciant; *airy words,* paroles en l'air, *f.pl.*

aisle [ail], *n.* bas-côté, passage, *m.*

ajar [ə'dʒɑ:], *a.* entr'ouvert, entrebâillé.

akimbo [ə'kimbou], *adv.* appuyé sur la hanche; *with one's arms akimbo,* les poings sur les hanches.

akin [ə'kin], *a.* allié (*à*); parent (*de*); (*fig.*) qui a rapport (*avec*).

alabaster ['æləbɑ:stə], *a.* d'albâtre.—*n.* albâtre, *m.*

alacrity [ə'lækriti], *n.* alacrité, *f.*, empressement, *m.*, promptitude, *f.*

Alan, Allan, Allen ['ælən]. Alain, *m.*

alarm [ə'lɑ:m], *n.* alarme, alerte, *f.*; réveil (*réveille-matin*), *m.*—*v.t.* alarmer; effrayer, faire peur à.

alarm bell [ə'lɑ:mbel], *n.* cloche d'alarme, *f.*, tocsin, *m.*

alarm clock [ə'lɑ:mklɔk], *n.* réveille-matin, *m.*

alarming [ə'lɑ:miŋ], *a.* alarmant.

alarmingly [ə'lɑ:miŋli], *adv.* d'une manière alarmante.

alarmist [ə'lɑ:mist], *n.* alarmiste, *m.*, *f.*

alas! [ə'læs], *int.* hélas!

Albania [æl'beinjə]. l'Albanie, *f.*

Albanian [æl'beinjən], *a.* albanais.—*n.* Albanais (*personne*), *m.*

albatross ['ælbətrɔs], *n.* albatros, *m.*

albeit [ɔːl'bi:it], *conj.* quoique, bien que (*with subj.*).

albino [æl'bi:nou], *a.* and *n.* albinos, *m.*, *f.*

album ['ælbəm], *n.* album, *m.*

albumen [æl'bju:min], *n.* albumen; blanc d'œuf, *m.*; albumine, *f.*

albuminous [æl'bju:minəs], *a.* albumineux.

alburnum [æl'bə:nəm], *n.* aubier, *m.*

alchemic [æl'kemik], **alchemical** [æl'kemikəl], *a.* alchimique.

alchemist ['ælkimist], *n.* alchimiste, *m.*

alchemistic [ælki'mistik], **alchemistical** [ælki'mistikəl], *a.* d'alchimie, alchimique.

alchemy ['ælkimi], *n.* alchimie, *f.*

alcohol ['ælkəhɔl], *n.* alcool, *m.* [see **spirit**]

alcoholic [ælkə'hɔlik], *a.* and *n.* alcoolique, *m.*, *f.*

alcoholism ['ælkəhɔlizm], *n.* alcoolisme, *m.*

Alcoran [ælkɔ'rɑ:n]. le Coran, le Koran.

alcove ['ælkouv], *n.* alcôve; niche, *f.*, enfoncement, *m.*

alder ['ɔːldə], *n.* aune, vergne, *m.*

alder grove ['ɔːldəgrouv], *n.* aunaie, *f.*

alderman ['ɔːldəmən], *n.* (*pl.* **-men** [men]) conseiller municipal, alderman, échevin, *m.*

ale [eil], *n.* ale, bière, *f.*

alehouse ['eilhaus], *n.* taverne, *f.*

alembic [ə'lembik], *n.* alambic, *m.*

alert [ə'lə:t], *a.* alerte, vigilant, éveillé.—*n.* alerte, *f.*; *on the alert,* sur le qui-vive.

alertness [ə'lə:tnis], *n.* vigilance, promptitude, prestesse, *f.*

Alexander [ælig'za:ndə]. Alexandre, *m.*

alexandrine [ælig'za:ndrin], *n.* (*Pros.*) alexandrin, *m.*

alfresco [æl'freskou], *adv.* en plein air.

algebra ['ældʒəbrə], *n.* algèbre, *f.*

algebraic [ældʒə'breiik], **algebraical** [ældʒə'breiikəl], *a.* algébrique.

Algeria [æl'dʒiəriə]. l'Algérie, *f.*

Algerian [æl'dʒiəriən], *a.* algérien.—*n.* Algérien (*personne*), *m.*

Algiers [æl'dʒiəz]. Alger, *m.*

alias ['eiliəs], *n.* nom d'emprunt *ou* de rechange, *m.*—*adv.* dit, autrement nommé, alias.

alibi ['ælibai], *n.* alibi, *m.*

alien ['eiljən], *a.* étranger (*à*); éloigné (*de*).— *n.* étranger, *m.*

alienate ['eiljəneit], *v.t.* aliéner (*de*).

alienation [eiljə'neiʃən], *n.* aliénation, *f.*

alienist ['eiljənist], *n.* aliéniste, *m., f.*

alight [ə'lait], *a.* allumé, embrasé.—*v.i.* descendre; mettre pied à terre; s'abattre (*oiseau etc.*); atterrir (*aviateur*), amerrir (*sur l'eau*).

align [ALINE].

alike [ə'laik], *adv.* également; de même, de la même manière; à la fois.—*a.* semblable, pareil; *to be alike*, se ressembler.

aliment ['ælimənt], *n.* aliment, *f.*

alimentary [æli'mentəri], *a.* alimentaire.

alimony ['æliməni], *n.* pension alimentaire, *f.*

aline, align [ə'lain], *v.t.* aligner; dresser.— *v.i.* s'aligner.

alinement, alignment [ə'lainmənt], *n.* alignement, *m.*

alive [ə'laiv], *a.* en vie, vivant; vif, éveillé; au monde; animé, sensible (*à*); *dead or alive*, mort ou vif; *to be alive with*, grouiller de, fourmiller de; *alive to*, sensible à; *while alive*, de son vivant.

alkali ['ælkəlai], *n.* alcali, *m.*

Alkoran [ALCORAN].

all [ɔ:l], *a.* tout, tous; *all of you*, vous tous; *for all that*, malgré cela; *it is all the same to me*, cela m'est égal; *with all speed*, au plus vite, à toute vitesse.—*adv.* tout, entièrement; *all at once*, tout à coup, tout d'un coup; *all the better*, tant mieux; *not at all*, point du tout.—*n.* and *pron.* tout, *m.*; *above all*, surtout; *all but*, presque; *all aboard!* en voiture!

allay [ə'lei], *v.t.* apaiser, adoucir, calmer.

allegation [ælə'geiʃən], *n.* allégation, *f.*

allege [ə'ledʒ], *v.t.* alléguer, prétendre (*that, que*).

allegiance [ə'li:dʒəns], *n.* fidélité; obéissance, *f.*

allegorical [ælə'gɔrikəl], *a.* allégorique.

allegorically [ælə'gɔrikəli], *adv.* allégoriquement.

allegory ['æləgəri], *n.* allégorie, *f.*

allelujah [æli'lu:jə], *n.* and *int.* alléluia, *m.*

allergic [ə'lə:dʒik], *a.* (*Med.*) allergique.

allergy ['ælədʒi], *n.* allergie, *f.*

alleviate [ə'li:vieit], *v.t.* alléger, soulager, adoucir.

alleviation [əli:vi'eiʃən], *n.* allégement, adoucissement, soulagement, *m.*

alley ['æli], *n.* ruelle (*d'une ville*); allée (*jardin*),

f.; *blind alley*, impasse, *f.*, cul de sac; *m.*

All Fools' Day [ɔ:l'fu:lzdei]. le Ier avril.

alliance [ə'laiəns], *n.* alliance, *f.*

allied ['ælaid, ə'laid], *a.* allié; parent, voisin (*de*).

alligator ['æligeitə], *n.* alligator, caïman, *m.*

alliteration [əlitə'reiʃən], *n.* allitération, *f.*

alliterative [ə'litərətiv], *a.* allitératif.

allocate ['ælokeit], *v.t.* allouer, assigner.

allocation [ælo'keiʃən], *n.* allocation, *f.*

allot [ə'lɔt], *v.t.* assigner, donner en partage; répartir.

allotment [ə'lɔtmənt], *n.* partage, lot, lotissement, *m.*, portion; distribution, *f.*; lopin de terre, jardin ouvrier, *m.*

allow [ə'lau], *v.t.* permettre, autoriser; accorder, allouer; admettre, reconnaître; *to allow someone to do something*, permettre à quelqu'un de faire quelque chose.

allowable [ə'lauəbl], *a.* permis, admissible, légitime.

allowance [ə'lauəns], *n.* pension, rente; allocation; ration; remise, réduction; indulgence, indemnité, *f.*; *to make allowance for*, tenir compte de; *to put on short allowance*, rationner.

alloy [ə'lɔi], *n.* alliage, mélange, *m.*—*v.t.* allier; (*fig.*) altérer, diminuer, corrompre.

All Saints' Day [ɔ:l'seintsdei]. la Toussaint, *f.*

All Souls' Day [ɔ:l'soulzdei]. Jour des Morts, *m.*

allude [ə'lju:d], *v.i.* faire allusion (*à*).

allure [ə'ljuə], *v.t.* amorcer, attirer, séduire, inviter (*à*).

allurement [ə'ljuəmənt], *n.* amorce, *f.*, appât, charme, attrait, *m.*

alluring [ə'ljuəriŋ], *a.* attrayant, séduisant.

alluringly [ə'ljuəriŋli], *adv.* d'une manière séduisante.

allusion [ə'lju:ʒən], *n.* allusion, *f.*

allusive [ə'lju:siv], *a.* allusif, plein d'allusions.

allusively [ə'lju:sivli], *adv.* par allusion.

alluvia [ə'lju:viə], *n.pl.* terres d'alluvion, *f.pl.*, alluvion, *f.*

alluvial [ə'lju:viəl], *a.* alluvial, d'alluvion.

alluvium [ə'lju:viəm], *n.* alluvion, *f.*

ally [ə'ai], *v.t.* allier.—*v.i.* s'allier (*à* ou *avec*). —['ælai, ə'ai], *n.* allié, confédéré, *m.*

almanac ['ɔ:lmənæk], *n.* almanach, *m.*

almighty [ɔ:l'maiti], *a.* tout-puissant; *the Almighty*, le Tout-Puissant.

almond ['a:mənd], *n.* amande, *f.*; *burnt almond*, praline, *f.*

almond-tree ['a:məndtri:], *n.* amandier, *m.*

almost ['ɔ:lmoust], *adv.* presque, à peu près; *I almost fell*, j'ai failli tomber.

alms [a:mz], *n.* aumône, *f.*; *to give alms*, faire l'aumône.

almshouse ['a:mzhaus], *n.* maison de retraite, *f.*, asile, *m.*

aloe ['ælou], *n.* aloès, *m.*; *bitter aloes*, amer d'aloès, *m.*

aloft [ə'lɔft], *adv.* en haut, en l'air; (*Naut.*) dans la mâture.

alone [ə'loun], *a.* seul, solitaire; *leave me alone*, laissez-moi tranquille.

along [ə'lɔŋ], *adv.* and *prep.* le long de; *all along* (*time*), tout le temps; (*place*) tout le long du chemin; *along with*, avec; *come along*, venez donc; *get along with you*, allez-vous en, allez-vous promener.

341

alongside [ə'lɔŋsaid], *adv.* bord à bord; bord à quai.—*prep.* à côté de.

aloof [ə'lu:f], *a.* distant.—*adv.* au loin, (*Naut.*) au large; éloigné, à l'écart; *to keep aloof*, se tenir à l'écart.

aloofness [ə'lu:fnis], *n.* attitude distante, *f.*

aloud [ə'laud], *adv.* à haute voix, haut.

alpaca [æl'pækə], *n.* alpaga (*tissu*); alpaca (*animal*), *m.*

alphabet ['ælfəbet], *n.* alphabet; abécédaire (*livre d'enfant*), *m.*

alphabetic [ælfə'betik], **alphabetical** [ælfə'betikəl], *a.* alphabétique.

alphabetically [ælfə'betikəli], *adv.* alphabétiquement.

alpine ['ælpain], *a.* alpin; des Alpes, alpestre.

alpinist ['ælpinist], *n.* alpiniste, *m.*, *f.*

Alps [ælps]. les Alpes, *f. pl.*

already [ɔ:l'redi], *adv.* déjà.

Alsatian [æl'seiʃən], *a.* alsacien.—*n.* (*chien*) chien-loup; (*personne*) Alsacien, *m.*

also ['ɔ:lsou], *adv.* aussi, également.

altar ['ɔ:ltə], *n.* autel, *m.*; **high altar**, maître-autel, *m.*

altar cloth ['ɔ:ltəklɔθ], *n.* nappe d'autel, *f.*

altar screen ['ɔ:ltəskri:n], *n.* retable, *m.*

alter ['ɔ:ltə], *v.t.* changer, modifier; retoucher, corriger.—*v.i.* changer, se changer.

alteration [ɔ:ltə'reiʃən], *n.* changement, *m.*, modification, *f.*

altercation [ɔ:ltə'keiʃən], *n.* altercation, dispute, *f.*

alternate ['ɔ:ltəneit], *v.t.* alterner, faire alternativement.—*v.i.* alterner; se succéder; **alternating current**, courant alternatif, *m.*— ['ɔ:ltənit], *a.* alternatif; alternant; **alternate rhymes**, rimes croisées, *f.pl.*

alternately [ɔ:l'tə:nitli], *adv.* alternativement, tour à tour.

alternative [ɔ:l'tə:nətiv], *a.* alternatif.—*n.* alternative; autre solution, *f.*

alternatively [ɔ:l'tə:nətivli], *adv.* alternativement, tour à tour.

alternator ['ɔ:ltəneitə], *n.* (*Elec.*) alternateur, *m.*

although [ɔ:l'ðou], *conj.* quoique, bien que (*with subj.*).

altimeter [ælti'mi:tə], *n.* altimètre, *m.*

altitude ['ældtitju:d], *n.* altitude, élévation, hauteur, *f.*

alto ['æltou], *n.* alto, *m.*

altogether [ɔ:ltə'geðə], *adv.* tout à fait, entièrement.

altruistic [æltru'istik], *a.* altruiste.

alum ['æləm], *n.* alun, *m.*

aluminum [æ'lu:minəm], *n.* aluminium, *m.*

always ['ɔ:lweiz], *adv.* toujours.

*****amain** [ə'mein], *adv.* avec force, de toutes ses forces.

amalgam [ə'mælgəm], *n.* amalgame, *m.*

amalgamate [ə'mælgəmeit], *v.t.* amalgamer; (*Comm.*) fusionner.—*v.i.* s'amalgamer; (*Comm.*) fusionner.

amalgamation [əmælgə'meiʃən], *n.* amalgamation, *f.*; (*fig.*) amalgame, fusionnement, *m.*

amanuensis [əmænju'ensis], *n.* (*pl.* **amanuenses** [əmænju'ensi:z]) secrétaire, *m.*, *f.*

amaranth ['æmərænθ], *n.* amarante, *f.*

amass [ə'mæs], *v.t.* amasser.

amateur ['æmətə:, 'æmətjuə], *n.* amateur, *m.*

amateurish [æmə'tə:riʃ, 'æmətjuəriʃ], *a.* d'amateur.

amateurism ['æmətə:rizm, 'æmətjuərizm], *n.* (*Spt.*) amateurisme, *m.*

amatory ['æmətəri], *a.* d'amour, amoureux.

amaze [ə'meiz], *v.t.* étonner, confondre, stupéfier; *to be amazed*, s'étonner.

amazement [ə'meizmənt], **amazedness** [ə'meizidnis], *n.* étonnement, *m.*, stupeur, stupéfaction, *f.*

amazing [ə'meizin], *a.* étonnant.

Amazon ['æməzən], **the.** l'Amazone, *m.*

amazon ['æməzən], *n.* amazone, *f.*

ambassador [æm'bæsədə], *n.* ambassadeur, *m.*

ambassadress [æm'bæsədris], *n.* ambassadrice, *f.*

amber ['æmbə], *a.* d'ambre; *amber light* (*traffic*), feu orange, *m.*—*n.* ambre, *m.*

amber-colored [æm'bəkʌləd], *a.* ambré.

ambergris ['æmbəgris], *n.* ambre gris, *m.*

ambidexter [æmbi'dekstə], *a.* and *n.* ambidextre, *m.*, *f.*

ambidextrous [æmbi'dekstrəs], *a.* ambidextre.

ambient ['æmbiənt], *a.* ambiant.

ambiguity [æmbi'gju:iti], **ambiguousness** [æm'bigjuəsnis], *n.* ambiguïté; équivoque, *f.*

ambiguous [æm'bigjuəs], *a.* ambigu; équivoque; douteux.

ambiguously [æm'bigjuəsli], *adv.* ambigument, d'une manière équivoque.

ambit ['æmbit], *n.* tour, circuit, *m.*; (*fig.*) étendue, portée, *f.*

ambition [æm'biʃən], *n.* ambition, *f.*

ambitious [æm'biʃəs], *a.* ambitieux.

ambitiously [æm'biʃəsli], *adv.* ambitieusement.

amble [æmbl], *v.i.* aller (à) l'amble (*cheval*); (*fig.*) trottiner, aller son chemin, déambuler. —*n.* amble, *m.*

Ambrose ['æmbrouz]. Ambroise, *m.*

ambrosia [æm'brouziə], *n.* ambroisie, *f.*

ambulance ['æmbjuləns], *n.* ambulance, *f.*; hôpital militaire, *m.*

ambulant ['æmbjulənt], *a.* ambulant.

ambulatory ['æmbjulətri], *a.* ambulatoire.

ambuscade [æmbəs'keid], *n.* embuscade, *f.*; *to lay an ambuscade for*, dresser une embuscade à.—*v.t.* embusquer; mettre en embuscade.

ambush ['æmbuʃ], *n.* embuscade, *f.*, guet-apens, *m.*—*v.t.* embusquer.

Amelia [ə'mi:liə]. Amélie, *f.*

ameliorate [ə'mi:ljəreit], *v.t.* améliorer.— *v.i.* s'améliorer.

amelioration [əmi:ljə'reiʃən], *n.* amélioration, *f.*

amen [ɑ:'men], *int.* amen, ainsi soit-il.

amenable [ə'mi:nəbl], *a.* responsable, comptable; docile, soumis, sujet (*à*).

amend [ə'mend], *v.t.* amender, corriger; réformer.—*v.i.* s'amender, se corriger.

amendment [ə'mendmənt], *n.* modification, *f.*, amendement, *m.*, amélioration, *f.*

amends [ə'mendz], *n.pl.* dédommagement, *m.*, compensation, réparation, *f.*; *to make amends for*, dédommager de, faire réparation de.

amenity [ə'mi:niti, ə'meniti], *n.* aménité, *f.* agrément, *m.*

America [ə'merikə]. l'Amérique, *f.*

American [ə'merikən], _a._ américain.—_n._ Américain (_personne_), _m._

amethyst ['æməθist], _n._ améthyste, _f._

amiability [eimjə'biliti], **amiableness** ['eimjəblnis], _n._ amabilité, _f._

amiable ['eimjəbl], _a._ aimable.

amiably ['eimjəbli], _adv._ aimablement, avec amabilité.

amicable ['æmikəbl], _a._ amical; _amicable settlement_, arrangement à l'amiable, _m._

amicably ['æmikəbli], _adv._ amicalement; à l'amiable.

amid [ə'mid], _prep._ au milieu de; parmi.

amidships [ə'midʃips], _adv._ (_Naut._) par le travers.

amidst [ə'midst], [AMID].

amiss [ə'mis], _adv._ mal, en mauvaise part; (_unseasonably_) mal à propos.

amity ['æmiti], _n._ amitié, _f._

ammeter ['æmitə], _n._ ampèremètre, _m._

ammonia [ə'mouniə], _n._ ammoniaque, _f._

ammunition [æmju'niʃən], _n._ munitions de guerre; cartouches, _f.pl._

amnesia [æm'ni:ziə], _n._ amnésie, _f._

amnesty ['æmnəsti], _n._ amnistie, _f._—_v.t._ amnistier.

amoeba [ə'mi:bə], _n._ (_pl._ **amoebae** [ə'mi:bai], **amoebas** [ə'mi:bəz]) amibe, _f._

amok [AMUCK].

among [ə'mʌŋ], **amongst** [ə'mʌŋst], _prep._ entre, parmi; au milieu de, chez, avec; _among other things_, entre autres choses; _from among_, d'entre.

amorous ['æmərəs], _a._ amoureux; porté à l'amour.

amorously ['æmərəsli], _adv._ amoureusement.

amorousness ['æmərəsnis], _n._ tempérament amoureux, _m._, tendance à l'amour, _f._

amorphous [ə'mɔ:fəs], _a._ amorphe.

amount [ə'maunt], _n._ montant, total, _m._, somme; quantité; (_fig._) valeur, _f._, résultat, _m._; _to the amount of_, jusqu'à concurrence de.—_v.i._ s'élever, se monter (_à_); revenir (_à_), se réduire (_à_); _that amounts to the same thing_, cela revient au même.

amour [ə'muə], _n._ intrigue amoureuse, _f._

ampere ['æmpɛə], _n._ (_Elec._) ampère, _m._

amphibian [æm'fibiən], _n._ amphibie, _m._

amphibious [æm'fibiəs], _a._ amphibie.

amphitheater [æmfi'θiətə], _n._ amphithéâtre, _m._

amphitheatrical [æmfiθi'ætrikəl], _a._ amphithéâtral, d'amphithéâtre.

amphora ['æmfərə], _n._ amphore, _f._

ample [æmpl], _a._ ample, large, abondant, copieux; très suffisant.

ampleness ['æmplnis], _n._ ampleur; grandeur, _f._

amplification [æmplifi'keiʃən], _n._ amplification, _f._

amplifier ['æmplifaiə], _n._ (_Rad._, _Tel._) amplificateur, _m._

amplify ['æmplifai], _v.t._ amplifier; exagérer.

amplitude ['æmplitju:d], _n._ amplitude, étendue, largeur, _f._

amply ['æmpli], _adv._ amplement.

amputate ['æmpjuteit], _v.t._ amputer.

amputation [æmpju'teiʃən], _n._ amputation, _f._

amuck [ə'mʌk], **amock**, **amok** [ə'mɔk], _adv._ _to run amuck_, devenir fou furieux.

amulet ['æmjulit], _n._ amulette, _f._

amuse [ə'mju:z], _v.t._ amuser, divertir; _to be amused at_, s'amuser _ou_ se divertir de.

amusement [ə'mju:zmənt], _n._ amusement, divertissement, _m._

amusing [ə'mju:ziŋ], _a._ amusant, divertissant.

amusingly [ə'mju:ziŋli], _adv._ d'une manière amusante.

Amy ['eimi]. Aimée, _f._

an [A (2)].

anachronism [ə'nækrənizm], _n._ anachronisme, _m._

anachronistic [ænækrə'nistik], _a._ anachronique.

anaconda [ænə'kɔndə], _n._ anaconda, eunecte, _m._

anaemia [ə'ni:miə], _n._ anémie, _f._

anaemic [ə'ni:mik], _a._ anémique.

anaesthesia [ænəs'θi:ziə], _n._ anesthésie, _f._

anaesthetic [ænəs'θetik], _a._ and _n._ anesthésique, _m._

anaesthetist [ə'ni:sθətist], _n._ anesthésiste, _m._, _f._

anaesthetize [ə'ni:sθətaiz], _v.t._ anesthésier.

anagram ['ænəgræm], _n._ anagramme, _f._

analgesia [ænæl'dʒi:ziə], _n._ analgésie, analgie, _f._

analgical [ænə'lɔdʒikəl], _a._ analogique.

analogism [ə'nælədʒizm], _n._ (_Phil._) analogisme, _m._

analogous [ə'næləgəs], _a._ analogue.

analogy [ə'nælədʒi], _n._ analogie, _f._

analysis [ə'nælisis], _n._ analyse, _f._

analyst ['ænəlist], _n._ analyste, _m._, _f._

analytic [ænə'litik], **analytical** [ænə'litikəl], _a._ analytique.

analytically [ænə'litikəli], _adv._ analytiquement.

analyze ['ænəlaiz], _v.t._ analyser, faire l'analyse de.

anarchism ['ænəkizm], _n._ anarchisme, _m._

anarchist ['ænəkist], _a._ and _n._ anarchiste, _m._, _f._

anarchy ['ænəki], _n._ anarchie, _f._

anathema [ə'næθimə], _n._ anathème, _m._

anathematize [ə'næθimataiz], _v.t._ anathématiser, frapper d'anathème; maudire.

anatomical [ænə'tɔmikəl], _a._ anatomique.

anatomically [ænə'tɔmikəli], _adv._ anatomiquement.

anatomist [ə'nætəmist], _n._ anatomiste, _m._, _f._

anatomize [ə'nætəmaiz], _v.t._ anatomiser.

anatomy [ə'nætəmi], _n._ anatomie, _f._

ancestor ['ænsəstə], _n._ aïeul, _m._

ancestors ['ænsəstəz], _n.pl._ ancêtres, pères, aïeux, _m.pl._

ancestral [æn'sestrəl], _a._ ancestral, d'ancêtres, de ses ancêtres; héréditaire.

ancestry ['ænsəstri], _n._ ancêtres, _m.pl._; race, origine, naissance, _f._; lignage, _m._

anchor ['æŋkə], _n._ ancre, _f._; _sheet anchor_, maîtresse ancre, (_fig._) ancre de miséricorde; _to ride at anchor_, être à l'ancre; _to weigh anchor_, lever l'ancre.—_v.t._ mouiller, ancrer.—_v.i._ ancrer, s'ancrer, jeter l'ancre, mouiller; (_fig._) se fixer.

anchorage ['æŋkəridʒ], _n._ mouillage, ancrage, _m._; retraite (_d'anachorète_), .

anchoret ['æŋkəret], **anchorite** ['æŋkərait], _n._ anachorète, ermite, _m._, _f._

anchovy [æn'tʃouvi, 'æntʃəvi], _n._ anchois, _m._

ancient ['einʃənt], *a.* ancien; antique.—*n.* ancien, *m.*; *the Ancient of Days*, l'Éternel, *m.*

anciently ['einʃəntli], *adv.* anciennement.

ancillary [æn'siləri], *a.* ancillaire, subordonné, auxiliare.

and [ænd], *conj.* et; *and so on*, et ainsi de suite; *better and better*, de mieux en mieux; *carriage and pair*, voiture à deux chevaux, *f.*; *go and see*, allez voir.

Andes ['ændi:z], the. les Andes, *f.pl.*

andiron ['ændaiən], *n.* landier; chenet, *m.*

Andrew ['ændru:]. André, *m.*

anecdote ['ænikdout], *n.* anecdote, *f.*

anecdotal [ænik'doutl], *a.* anecdotique.

anemone [ə'neməni], *n.* anémone, *f.*

***anent** [ə'nent], *prep.* touchant.

aneroid ['ænərɔid], *a.* and *n.* anéroïde, *m.*

anes-. see **anaes-.**

aneurism ['ænjurizm], *n.* anévrisme, *m.*

anew [ə'nju:], *adv.* de nouveau.

angel ['eindʒəl], *n.* ange, *m.*

Angela ['ændʒələ]. Angèle, *f.*

angelic [æn'dʒelik], **angelical** [æn'dʒelikəl], *a.* angélique.

angelica [æn'dʒelikə], *n.* angélique, *f.*

angelus ['ændʒələs], *n.* angélus, *m.*

anger ['æŋgə], *n.* colère, *f.*; emportement; courroux, *m.*—*v.t.* fâcher, irriter, mettre en colère.

angina [æn'dʒainə], *n.* (*Path.*) angine, *f.*

angle (1) [æŋgl], *n.* angle; coin, *m.*

angle (2) [æŋgl], *v.i.* pêcher à la ligne.

angled [æŋgld], *a.* à angles; *right-angled*, rectangulaire.

angler ['æŋglə], *n.* pêcheur à la ligne, *m.*; (*Ichth.*) baudroie, *f.*; crapaud de mer, *m.*

Anglican ['æŋglikən], *a.* anglican.—*n.* Anglican, *m.*

Anglicism ['æŋglisizm], *n.* anglicisme, *m.*

Anglicize ['æŋglisaiz], *v.t.* angliciser.

angling ['æŋgliŋ], *n.* pêche à la ligne, *f.*

Anglophil(e) ['æŋgləf(a)il], *n.* anglophile, *m.,f.*

Anglo-Saxon ['æŋglo'sæksən], *a.* anglo-saxon.—*n.* Anglo-Saxon, *m.*

angrily ['æŋgrili], *adv.* en colère, avec colère.

angry ['æŋgri], *a.* en colère, fâché, irrité (*contre* ou *de*), courroucé; *to be angry with*, être en colère contre, en vouloir à.

anguish ['æŋgwiʃ], *n.* angoisse, douleur, *f.*—*v.t.* angoisser, navrer de douleur.

angular ['æŋgjulə], *a.* angulaire, angulé; anguleux; maigre, décharné.

angularity [æŋgju'læriti], *n.* angularité, *f.*

angularly ['æŋgjuləli], *adv.* angulairement.

anile ['einail], *a.* de vieille femme, débile.

aniline ['ænilain], *n.* (*Chem.*) aniline, *f.*

anility [ə'niliti], *n.* seconde enfance, *f.*, radotage, *m.*

animadversion [æniməd'və:ʃən], *n.* animadversion, censure, critique, *f.*

animadvert [ænimæd'və:t], *v.i.* *to animadvert upon*, critiquer, censurer.

animal ['æniməl], *a.* and *n.* animal, *m.*

animalism ['æniməlizm], *n.* animalité, *m.*

animality [æni'mæliti], *n.* animalité, *f.*

animalize ['æniməlaiz], *v.t.* animaliser.

animate ['ænimeit], *v.t.* animer (*de*).—['ænimit], *a.* animé.

animated ['ænimeitid], *a.* animé, vif.

animatedly ['ænimeitidli], *adv.* vivement.

animating ['ænimeitiŋ], *a.* qui anime, qui ranime.

animation [æni'meiʃən], *n.* animation, vivacité, vie, *f.*

animator ['ænimeitə], *n.* animateur, *m.*

animosity [æni'mɔsiti], *n.* animosité, *f.*

animus ['æniməs], *n.* animosité, hostilité, *f.*; esprit (*de*), *m.*

anise ['ænis], *n.* anis, *m.*

aniseed ['ænisi:d], *n.* graine d'anis, *f.*

ankle [æŋkl], *n.* cheville du pied, *f.*

ankle bone ['æŋklboun], *n.* astragale, *m.*

ankle deep ['æŋkldi:p], *adv.* jusqu'aux chevilles.

Anna ['ænə]. Anne, *f.*

annalist ['ænəlist], *n.* annaliste, *m.,f.*

annals ['ænəlz], *n.pl.* annales, *f.pl.*

Ann(e) [æn]. Anne, *f.*

anneal [ə'ni:l], *v.t.* détremper; adoucir (*acier etc.*), recuire (*verre*).

annealing [ə'ni:liŋ], *n.* recuite, *f.*

annex [ə'neks], *v.t.* annexer, joindre (*à*).—['æneks], *n.* annexe, *f.*

annexation [ænek'seiʃən], *n.* annexation, *f.*

annexed [ə'nekst], *a.* ci-joint, annexé.

annihilate [ə'naiileit], *v.t.* anéantir, annihiler.

annihilation [ənaii'leiʃən], *n.* anéantissement, *m.*, annihilation, *f.*

annihilator [ə'naiileitə], *n.* annihilateur, *m.*

anniversary [æni'və:səri], *a.* and *n.* anniversaire, *m.*

Anno Domini ['ænou'dɔminai], (*abbr.* **A.D.** [ei'di:]). l'an du Seigneur; l'an de grâce; ap. J.-C.

annotate ['ænoteit], *v.t.* annoter.

annotation [æno'teiʃən], *n.* annotation, *f.*

annotator ['ænoteitə], *n.* annotateur, *m.*

announce [ə'nauns], *v.t.* annoncer, proclamer.

announcement [ə'naunsmənt], *n.* annonce, *f.*, avis, *m.*; lettre de faire-part, *f.*

announcer [ə'naunsə], *n.* annonciateur; (*Theat.*) compère, *m.*, commère, *f.*; (*Rad., Tel.*) speaker, *m.*, speakerine, *f.*

annoy [ə'nɔi], *v.t.* gêner; incommoder, ennuyer, importuner; contrarier, tracasser.

annoyance [ə'nɔiəns], *n.* ennui, désagrément, chagrin, *m.*; contrariété, *f.*

annoying [ə'nɔiiŋ], *a.* ennuyeux, contrariant, vexant.

annoyingly [ə'nɔiiŋli], *adv.* ennuyeusement.

annual ['ænjuəl], *a.* annuel.—*n.* annuaire, *m.*

annually ['ænjuəli], *adv.* annuellement, tous les ans.

annuitant [ə'nju:itənt], *n.* bénéficiaire d'une pension *ou* d'une rente viagère, *m., f.*

annuity [ə'nju:iti], *n.* annuité, rente annuelle, pension, *f.*; *life annuity*, rente viagère, *f.*

annul [ə'nʌl], *v.t.* annuler.

annular ['ænjulə], *a.* annulaire.

annulet ['ænjulit], *n.* annelet, filet, *m.*

annulment [ə'nʌlmənt], *n.* annulation, *f.*; *decree of annulment*, décret abolitif, *m.*

Annunciation [ənʌnsi'eiʃən], **the.** (*Eccles.*) l'Annonciation, *f.*

annunciation [ənʌnsi'eiʃən], *n.* annonce, proclamation, *f.*, avis, *m.*

anode ['ænoud], *n.* (*Elec.*) anode, *f.*

anodyne ['ænədain], *a.* anodin, calmant.—*n.* anodin (*remède*), *m.*

anoint [ə'nɔint], *v.t.* oindre.

anointed [ə'nɔintid], *a.* oint; *the Lord's Anointed*, l'Oint du Seigneur, *m.*

anomalous [ə'nɔmələs], *a.* anomal, irrégulier.

anomaly [ə'nɔməli], *n.* anomalie, *f.*

anon [ə'nɔn], *adv.* tout à l'heure, bientôt; à l'instant.

anonymity [æno'nimiti], *n.* anonymat, *m.*

anonymous [ə'nɔniməs], *a.* anonyme.

anonymously [ə'nɔniməsli], *adv.* anonymement.

another [ə'nʌðə], *a.* and *pron.* autre, un autre; encore un; *one another*, l'un l'autre, les uns les autres.

answer ['a:nsə], *v.t.* répondre; répondre à; satisfaire, suffire à.—*v.i.* faire réponse; répondre (*de* ou *pour*); raisonner; réussir.—*n.* réponse; solution (*d'un problème*), *f.*

answerable ['a:nsərəbl], *a.* susceptible de réponse; responsable (*for, de*).

ant [ænt], *n.* fourmi, *f.*

antagonism [æn'tægənizm], *n.* antagonisme, *m.*, opposition, *f.*

antagonist [æn'tægənist], *n.* antagoniste, *m.*,*f.*

antagonistic [æntægə'nistik], *a.* opposé (*à*); antagonique.

antagonize [æn'tægənaiz], *v.t.* eveiller l'antagonisme (*de*).

Antarctic [ænt'a:ktik], *a.* antarctique.—*n.* Antarctique, *f.*

ant-eater ['ænti:tə], *n.* fourmilier, *m.*

antecedence [ænti'si:dəns], *n.* antériorité, *f.*

antecedent [ænti'si:dənt], *a.* and *n.* antécédent, *m.*

ante-chamber ['æntitʃeimbə], *n.* antichambre, *f.*

antediluvian [æntidi'lu:viən], *a.* and *n.* antédiluvien, *m.*

antelope ['æntiloup], *n.* antilope, *f.*

ante-meridiem [æntimə'ridiəm], (*abbr.* **a.m.** [ei'em]), *adv.* avant midi; *at* **11** *a.m.*, à onze heures du matin.

ante-natal ['ænti'neitəl], *a.* prénatal.

antenna [æn'tenə], *n.* (*pl.* **antennae** [æn'teni:]) antenne, *f.*

antepenult [æntipi'nʌlt], **antepenultimate** [æntipi'nʌltimit], *a.* and *n.* antépénultième, *f.*

anterior [æn'tiəriə], *a.* antérieur.

anteroom ['æntiru:m], *n.* antichambre, *f.*

anthem ['ænθəm], *n.* hymne (national), *m.*; antienne, *f.*

ant-hill ['ænthil], *n.* fourmilière, *f.*

anthology [æn'θɔlədʒi], *n.* anthologie, chrestomathie, *f.*

Anthony ['æntəni]. Antoine, *m.*

anthracite ['ænθrəsait], *n.* anthracite, *m.*

anthrax ['ænθræks], *n.* (*Med.*) anthrax, *m.*

anthropoid ['ænθrəpɔid], *a.* and *n.* anthropoide, *m.*

anthropological [ænθrəpə'lɔdʒikəl], *a.* anthropologique.

anthropologist [ænθrə'pɔlədʒist], *n.* anthropologiste, anthropologue, *m.*,*f.*

anthropology [ænθrə'pɔlədʒi], *n.* anthropologie, *f.*

anti-aircraft [ænti'ɛəkra:ft], *a.* contre-avion, antiaérien.

antibiotic ['æntibai'ɔtik], *a.* and *n.* antibiotique, *m.*

antic ['æntik], *n.* bouffonnerie, farce, *f.*

Antichrist ['æntikraist], *n.* antéchrist, *m.*

antichristian ['ænti'kristjən], *a.* and *n.* antichrétien, *m.*

anticipate [æn'tisipeit], *v.t.* anticiper; prévenir, devancer; s'attendre à, prévoir, envisager; jouir d'avance de; se promettre.

anticipation [æntisi'peiʃən], *n.* anticipation, *f.*; avant-goût, *m.*; attente, *f.*

anticipatory [æn'tisipətri], *a.* par anticipation.

anticlerical [ænti'klerikəl], *a.* and *n.* anticlérical, *m.*

anticlericalism [ænti'klerikəlizm], *n.* anticléricalisme, *m.*

anti-climax [ænti'klaimæks], *n.* anticlimax, *m.*

anti-clockwise [COUNTER-CLOCKWISE].

anticyclone [ænti'saikloun], *n.* anticyclone, *m.*

anti-dazzle ['ænti'dæzl], *a.* anti-aveuglant; (*Motor*) *anti-dazzle head lights*, pharescode, *m.pl.*

antidote ['æntidout], *n.* antidote, contre-poison, *m.*

anti-freeze ['æntifri:z], *n.* anti-gel, *m.*

Antilles [æn'tili:z], **the.** les Antilles, *f.pl.*

antimacassar [æntimə'kæsə], *n.* têtière, *f.*

antimony ['æntiməni], *n.* antimoine, *m.*

antinomy [æn'tinəmi], *n.* antinomie, *f.*

antipathetic [æntipə'θetik], **antipathetical** [æntipə'θetikəl], *a.* antipathique.

antipathy [æn'tipəθi], *n.* antipathie, aversion, *f.*

antiphony [æn'tifəni], *n.* contre-chant, *m.*

antiphrasis [æn'tifrəsis], *n.* antiphrase, *f.*

antipodal [æn'tipədəl], *a.* antipodal.

antipodes [æn'tipədi:z], *n. pl.* antipodes, *m.pl.*

anti-pope ['æntipoup], *n.* antipape *m.*

antiquarian [ænti'kwɛəriən], *a.* d'antiquaire; archéologique.—*n.* antiquaire, *m.*

antiquary ['æntikwəri], *n.* archéologue; antiquaire, *m.*

antiquated ['æntikweitid], *a.* vieilli, vétuste; suranné, démodé.

antique [æn'ti:k], *a.* antique, ancien.—*n. the antique*, l'antique, *m.*; *an antique*, un objet antique, une antiquité.

antiquity [æn'tikwiti], *n.* antiquité; ancienneté, *f.*

antirrhinum [ænti'rainəm], *n.* antirrhine, *f.*

anti-Semitism [ænti'semitizm], *n.* antisémitisme, *m.*

antiseptic [ænti'septik], *a.* and *n.* antiseptique, *m.*

anti-tank [ænti'tæŋk], *a.* anti-chars.

antithesis [æn'tiθisis], *n.* antithèse, *f.*

antithetic [ænti'θetik], **antithetical** [ænti'θetikəl], *a.* antithétique.

antler ['æntlə], *n.* andouiller, bois (*de cerf*), *m.*

Antony ['æntəni]. Antoine, *m.*

Antwerp ['æntwə:p]. Anvers, *m.*

anvil ['ænvil], *n.* enclume, *f.*; (*fig.*) *on the anvil*, sur le métier, en préparation.

anxiety [æŋ'zaiəti], *n.* anxiété, inquiétude, sollicitude, *f.*; désir, *m.*

anxious ['æŋkʃəs], *a.* inquiet, soucieux, plein de sollicitude (*pour*); désireux (*de*); *to be anxious to*, désirer vivement (*de*), tenir à.

anxiously ['æŋkʃəsli], *adv.* anxieusement, avec anxiété, avec inquiétude.

any ['eni], *a.* and *pron.* du, de la, etc.; en; aucun; quelque; n'importe lequel; *any man*, tout homme; *any others*, d'autres; *at any rate*, en tout cas; *I haven't any*, je n'en ai pas; *scarcely any*, presque pas.

anybody ['enibɔdi], **anyone** ['eniwʌn], *pron.* quelqu'un, chacun, qui que ce soit, n'importe qui, tout le monde; *I didn't see anybody*, je n'ai vu personne.

anyhow ['enihau], **anyway** ['eniwei], *adv.* de toute façon, de quelque manière que ce soit, en tout cas, quand même.

anyone [ANYBODY].

anything ['eniθiŋ], *pron.* quelque chose, *m.*, quoi que ce soit, n'importe quoi; *not to say anything*, ne rien dire.

anyway [ANYHOW].

anywhere ['eniwɛə], *adv.* quelque part, dans quelque endroit que ce soit, n'importe où; *not anywhere*, nulle part.

apace [ə'peis], *adv.* vite, à grands pas.

apanage, appanage ['æpənidʒ], *n.* apanage, *m.*

apart [ə'pɑːt], *adv.* à part; de côté, séparément.

apartheid [ə'pɑːtheit], *n.* (*en Afrique du Sud*) ségrégation, *f.*

apartment [ə'pɑːtmənt], *n.* chambre; pièce (*d'un appartement*), *f.*; logement; (*Am.*) appartement; (*pl.*) appartement, *m.*

apathetic [æpə'θetik], *a.* apathique.

apathy ['æpəθi], *n.* apathie, *f.*

ape [eip], *n.* singe, *m.*, guenon, *f.*—*v.t.* singer.

aperient [ə'piəriənt], **aperitive** [ə'peritiv], *a.* and *n.* laxatif, *m.*

aperture ['æpətjuə], *n.* ouverture, *f.*; orifice, *m.*

apex ['eipeks], *n.* (*pl.* **apices** ['eipisiːz], **apexes** ['eipeksiz]) sommet, *m.*, pointe, *f.*

aphorism ['æfərizm], *n.* aphorisme, *m.*

apiary ['eipiəri], *n.* rucher, *f.*

apiece [ə'piːs], *adv.* la pièce; par tête, par personne, chacun.

apish ['eipiʃ], *a.* de singe, simiesque; *apish trick*, singerie, *f.*

apocalypse [ə'pɔkəlips], *n.* apocalypse, *f.*

apocalyptic [əpɔkə'liptik], **apocalyptical** [əpɔkə'liptikəl], *a.* apocalyptique.

Apocrypha [ə'pɔkrifə], *n.pl.* les Apocryphes, *m.pl.*

apocryphal [ə'pɔkrifəl], *a.* apocryphe.

apogee ['æpədʒiː], *n.* apogée, *m.*

apologetic [əpɔlə'dʒetik], **apologetical** [əpɔlə'dʒetikəl], *a.* qui s'excuse, qui regrette; *he was quite apologetic about it*, il s'en excusa vivement.

apologetically [əpɔlə'dʒetikəli], *adv.* pour s'excuser, en s'excusant.

apologia [æpə'loudʒiə], *n.* apologie; justification, *f.*

apologist [ə'pɔlədʒist], *n.* apologiste, *m.*, *f.*

apologize [ə'pɔlədʒaiz], *v.i.* s'excuser, faire des excuses (*de* ou *auprès de*).

apologue ['æpəlɔg], *n.* apologue, *m.*

apology [ə'pɔlədʒi], *n.* excuses, *f.pl.*, apologie, *f.*

apoplectic [æpə'plektik], *a.* apoplectique; *apoplectic stroke*, coup de sang, *m.*

apoplexy ['æpəpleksi], *n.* apoplexie, *f.*; *a fit of apoplexy*, congestion cérébrale, *f.*

apostasy [ə'pɔstəsi], *n.* apostasie, *f.*

apostate [ə'pɔsteit], *a.* and *n.* apostat, *m.*

apostle [ə'pɔsl], *n.* apôtre, *m.*; *the Acts of the Apostles*, les Actes des Apôtres, *m.pl.*

apostolic [æpəs'tɔlik], **apostolical** [æpəs'tɔlikəl], *a.* apostolique.

apostrophe [ə'pɔstrəfi], *n.* apostrophe, *f.*

apostrophize [ə'pɔstrəfaiz], *v.t.* apostropher.

apothecary [ə'pɔθikəri], *n.* apothicaire; pharmacien, *m.*

apotheosis [əpɔθi'ousis], *n.* apothéose, *f.*

appal [ə'pɔːl], *v.t.* épouvanter, consterner.

appalling [ə'pɔːliŋ], *a.* épouvantable, effrayant.

appallingly [ə'pɔːliŋli], *adv.* épouvantablement.

appanage [APANAGE].

apparatus [æpə'reitəs], *n.* appareil, dispositif, *m.*

apparel [ə'pærəl], *v.t.* vêtir; parer.—*n.* habillement, vêtement, *m.*

apparent [ə'pærənt], *a.* évident, manifeste, apparent; *heir apparent*, héritier présomptif, *m.*

apparently [ə'pærəntli], *adv.* en apparence, apparemment.

apparition [æpə'riʃən], *n.* apparition, *f.*

appeal [ə'piːl], *v.i.* appeler, en appeler (*de*); faire appel (*à*); (*Law*) se pourvoir en cassation, réclamer (*contre* ou *à*); (*fig.*) attirer, séduire.—*n.* appel, attrait, *m.*; *Court of Appeal*, cour de cassation, *f.*

appealing [ə'piːliŋ], *a.* suppliant, attrayant, séduisant.

appear [ə'piə], *v.i.* paraître, apparaître; se montrer, se présenter (*à*).

appearance [ə'piərəns], *n.* apparition; apparence, figure, mine, *f.*, air, aspect, *m.*; (*Law*) comparution, *f.*; *at first appearance*, au premier abord, au premier coup d'œil.

appeasable [ə'piːzəbl], *a.* qu'on peut apaiser.

appease [ə'piːz], *v.t.* apaiser, pacifier.

appeasement [ə'piːzmənt], *n.* apaisement, adoucissement, *m.*; conciliation, *f.*

appellant [ə'pelənt], *a.* and *n.* (*Law*) appelant, *m.*

appellation [æpə'leiʃən], *n.* nom, *m.*, appellation, dénomination, *f.*

append [ə'pend], *v.t.* apposer, attacher (*à*).

appendage [ə'pendidʒ], *n.* accessoire, apanage, *m.*

appendant [ə'pendənt], *a.* accessoire, attaché, annexé (*à*).

appendicitis [əpendi'saitis], *n.* appendicite, *f.*

appendix [ə'pendiks], *n.* (*pl.* **appendixes** [ə'pendiksiz], **appendices** [ə'pendisiːz]) appendice, *m.*

appertain [æpə'tein], *v.i.* appartenir (*à*).

appetite ['æpitait], *n.* appétit; (*fig.*) désir, *m.*, soif, *f.*

appetize ['æpitaiz], *v.t.* mettre en appétit.

appetizer ['æpitaizə], *n.* apéritif, *m.*

appetizing ['æpitaiziŋ], *a.* appétissant.

applaud [ə'plɔːd], *v.t.*, *v.i.* applaudir (*à*).

applause [ə'plɔːz], *n.* applaudissements, *m.pl.*

apple [æpl], *n.* pomme, *f.*; *apple of the eye*, prunelle, *f.*

apple pie ['æpl'pai], *n.* tourte aux pommes, *f.*

apple-sauce ['æpl'sɔːs], *n.* compote de pommes, *f.*

apple tart ['æpl'tɑːt], *n.* tarte aux pommes, *f.*

apple tree ['æpltriː], *n.* pommier, *m.*

appliance [ə'plaiəns], *n.* instrument, appareil, dispositif, *m.*

applicability [æplikə'biliti], **applicableness** ['æplikəblnis], *n.* applicabilité, *f.*

applicable ['æplikəbl], *a.* applicable.

applicant ['æplikənt], *n.* postulant, candidat; (*Law*) demandeur, *m.*

application [æpli'keiʃən], *n.* application; sollicitation, demande, *f.*; usage, *m.*; **for external application**, usage externe; **on application**, sur demande; **to make application to**, s'adresser à, faire une demande à.

apply [ə'plai], *v.t.* appliquer (à); **to apply the brake**, freiner; serrer le frein.—*v.i.* s'adresser (à); s'appliquer, être applicable; **to apply for** (*a job*), faire une demande (d'emploi); **to apply to**, s'adresser à *ou* chez.

appoint [ə'point], *v.t.* appointer, désigner, fixer; nommer; installer, équiper; **at the appointed hour**, à l'heure convenue; **a well-appointed house**, une maison bien installée.

appointment [ə'pointmənt], *n.* nomination, *f.*; décret, arrêt; établissement; emploi; rendez-vous, *m.*; convocation, *f.*

apportion [ə'pɔ:ʃən], *v.t.* partager, répartir, assigner.

apportionment [ə'pɔ:ʃənmənt], *n.* répartition, *f.*, partage, *m.*

apposite ['æpəzait], *a.* juste; à propos; approprié, convenable (à).

appositely ['æpəzaitli], *adv.* convenablement, justement, à propos.

appositeness ['æpəzaitnis], *n.* à-propos, *m.*, opportunité, *f.*

appraisal [APPRAISEMENT].

appraise [ə'preiz], *v.t.* priser, évaluer, estimer.

appraisement [ə'preizmənt], **appraisal** [ə'preizəl], *n.* évaluation, estimation; expertise, *f.*

appraiser [ə'preizə], *n.* commissaire-priseur, expert, *m.*

appreciable [ə'pri:ʃəbl], *a.* appréciable, sensible.

appreciably [ə'pri:ʃəbli], *adv.* sensiblement.

appreciate [ə'pri:ʃieit], *v.t.* apprécier, estimer.—*v.i.* (*Comm. etc.*) augmenter de valeur.

appreciation [əpri:ʃi'eiʃən], *n.* appréciation; hausse de valeur, *f.*

appreciative [ə'pri:ʃjətiv], *a.* appréciateur.

apprehend [æpri'hend], *v.t.* comprendre; prendre, saisir, arrêter, appréhender; craindre.

apprehension [æpri'henʃən], *n.* appréhension; arrestation, prise de corps; crainte, inquiétude, *f.*

apprehensive [æpri'hensiv], *a.* intelligent, prompt à saisir; appréhensif, inquiet.

apprentice [ə'prentis], *n.* apprenti, *m.*—*v.t.* mettre en apprentissage.

apprenticeship [ə'prentisʃip], *n.* apprentissage, *m.*

apprise [ə'praiz], *v.t.* prévenir; informer, instruire.

approach [ə'proutʃ], *n.* approche, *f.*; abord, accès; rapprochement, *m.*; (*Math.*) approximation, *f.*—*v.t.* approcher de, s'approcher de, aborder; (*fig.*) pressentir, tâter (*quelqu'un*).—*v.i.* approcher, s'approcher.

approachable [ə'proutʃəbl], *a.* abordable, accessible.

approbation [æpro'beiʃən], *n.* approbation, *f.*; **on approbation**, à condition, à l'essai.

appropriate [ə'prouprieit], *v.t.* approprier, affecter (à); s'approprier; s'emparer de.—[ə'proupriət], *a.* approprié; propre, convenable (à).

appropriately [ə'proupriətli], *adv.* à juste titre; convenablement.

appropriateness [ə'proupriətnis], *n.* convenance, *f.*, à-propos, *m.*, justesse, *f.*

appropriation [əproupri'eiʃən], *n.* application, destination, appropriation, *f.*; crédit (*budgétaire*), *m.*

approval [ə'pru:vəl], *n.* approbation, *f.*; **on approval**, à condition.

approve [ə'pru:v], *v.t.* approuver; trouver bon (*que, with subj.*).

approver [ə'pru:və], *n.* approbateur, *m.*

approving [ə'pru:viŋ], *a.* approbateur, approbatif.

approvingly [ə'pru:viŋli], *adv.* avec approbation, d'un air approbateur.

approximate [ə'prɔksimeit], *v.t.* rapprocher.—*v.i.* se rapprocher (de).—[ə'prɔksimit], *a.* approximatif.

approximately [ə'prɔksimitli], *adv.* approximativement, à peu près.

approximation [əprɔksi'meiʃən], *n.* approximation, *f.*; rapprochement, *m.*

appulse [ə'pʌls], *n.* choc, *m.*

appurtenance [ə'pə:tinəns], *n.* appartenance, dépendance, *f.*; (*pl.*) accessoires, *m.pl.*

appurtenant [ə'pə:tinənt], *a.* appartenant (à), dépendant (de).

apricot ['eiprikɔt], *n.* abricot, *m.*

apricot tree ['eiprikɔttri:], *n.* abricotier, *m.*

April ['eipril]. avril, *m.*; **to make an April fool of**, donner un poisson d'avril à.

apron ['eiprən], *n.* tablier, *m.*; (*Av.*) aire de manœuvre *ou* d'atterrissage, *f.*

apron⟨stage⟩['eiprənsteidʒ], *n.* avant-scène, *f.*

apse [æps], **apsis** ['æpsis], *n.* (*pl.* **apses** ['æpsi:z], **apsides** [æp'saidi:z]) abside; (*Astron.*) apside, *f.*

apt [æpt], *a.* sujet, enclin, porté (à); propre, convenable (à); capable; juste (*mot*).

aptitude ['æptitju:d], **aptness** ['æptnis], *n.* aptitude, disposition, *f.*

aptly ['æptli], *adv.* à propos; convenablement.

aqua fortis [ækwə'fɔ:tis], *n.* eau-forte, *f.*

aquamarine [ækwəmə'ri:n], *n.* aigue-marine, *f.*

aqua regia [ækwə'ri:dʒiə], *n.* eau régale, *f.*

aquarium [ə'kweəriəm], *n.* aquarium, *m.*

aquatic [ə'kwɔtik, ə'kwætik], *a.* aquatique.

aquatics [ə'kwætiks], **aquatic sports** [ə'kwætiksnɔ:ts], *n.pl.* sports nautiques, *m.pl.*

aqua vitae [ækwə'vaiti:], *n.* eau de vie, *f.*

aqueduct ['ækwidʌkt], *n.* aqueduc, *m.*

aqueous ['eikwiəs], *a.* aqueux.

aquiline ['ækwilain], *a.* aquilin, d'aigle.

Arab ['ærəb], *a.* arabe.—*n.* Arabe. *m.,f.*

arabesque [ærə'besk], *a.* and *n.* arabesque, *f.*

Arabia [ə'reibjə]. l'Arabie, *f.*; **Saudi Arabia**, l'Arabie Séoudite.

Arabian [ə'reibiən], *a.* arabe.

Arabic ['ærəbik], *a.* arabe, arabique; *Arabic figures,* chiffres arabes, *m.pl.*—*n.* arabe (*langue*), *m.*
arable ['ærəbl], *a.* arable, labourable.
arbalest ['ɑ:bəlest], *n.* arbalète, *f.*
arbiter ['ɑ:bitə], *n.* arbitre, *m.*, *f.*
arbitrament [ɑ:'bitrəmənt], *n.* arbitrage, *m.*, arbitration, *f.*; jugement, *m.*
arbitrarily ['ɑ:bitrərəli], *adv.* arbitrairement.
arbitrary ['ɑ:bitrəri], *a.* arbitraire.
arbitrate ['ɑ:bitreit], *v.t.*, *v.i.* arbitrer, décider.
arbitration [ɑ:bi'treiʃən], *n.* arbitrage, *m.*
arbitrator ['ɑ:bitreitə], *n.* arbitre, *m.*, *f.*
arbor ['ɑ:bə], *n.* berceau, *m.*, tonnelle, *f.*
arbutus [ɑ:'bju:təs], *n.* arbousier, *m.*
arc [ɑ:k], *n.* arc, *m.*
arcade [ɑ:'keid], *n.* arcade, *f.*; passage, *m.*
arch [ɑ:tʃ], *a.* moqueur, malin, espiègle; grand, maître, archi-, insigne, fieffé.—*n.* arche, *f.*; arc, cintre, *m.*, voûte, *f.*; *pointed arch,* ogive, *f.*; *triumphal arch,* arc de triomphe.—*v.t.* voûter, cintrer, arquer.
archaeological [ɑ:kiə'lɔdʒikəl], *a.* archéologique.
archaeologist [ɑ:ki'ɔlədʒist], *n.* archéologue, *m.*, *f.*
archaeology [ɑ:ki'ɔlədʒi], *n.* archéologie, *f.*
archaic [ɑ:'keiik], *a.* archaïque.
archaism ['ɑ:keiizm], *n.* archaïsme, *m.*
archangel ['ɑ:keindʒəl], *n.* archange, *m.*
archbishop [ɑ:tʃ'biʃəp], *n.* archevêque, *m.*
archbishopric [ɑ:tʃ'biʃəprik], *n.* archevêché, *m.*
archdeacon [ɑ:tʃ'di:kən], *n.* archidiacre, *m.*
archduchess [ɑ:tʃ'dʌtʃis], *n.* archiduchesse, *f.*
archduchy [ɑ:tʃ'dʌtʃi], *n.* archiduché, *m.*
archduke [ɑ:tʃ'dju:k], *n.* archiduc, *m.*
archer ['ɑ:tʃə], *n.* archer, *m.*; (*Astron.*) *the Archer,* Sagittaire, *m.*
archery ['ɑ:tʃəri], *n.* tir à l'arc, *m.*
archetype ['ɑ:kitaip], *n.* archétype; étalon (*mesure*), *m.*
archiepiscopal [ɑ:kiə'piskəpəl], *a.* archiépiscopal.
archipelago [ɑ:ki'peləgou], *n.* archipel, *m.*
architect ['ɑ:kitekt], *n.* architecte; (*fig.*) artisan, *m.*
architectural [ɑ:ki'tektʃərəl], *a.* architectural.
architecture ['ɑ:kitektʃə], *n.* architecture, *f.*
archives ['ɑ:kaivz], *n. pl.* archives, *f.pl.*
archivist ['ɑ:kivist], *n.* archiviste, *m.*, *f.*
archly ['ɑ:tʃli], *adv.* avec espièglerie, d'un air malin.
archness ['ɑ:tʃnis], *n.* malice, espièglerie, *f.*
arc light ['ɑ:klæmp], *n.* lampe à arc, *f.*
Arctic ['ɑ:ktik], *a.* arctique.
ardent ['ɑ:dənt], *a.* ardent; *ardent spirits,* spiritueux, *m.pl.*
ardently ['ɑ:dəntli], *adv.* ardemment, avec ardeur.
ardor ['ɑ:də], *n.* ardeur, *f.*
arduous ['ɑ:djuəs], *a.* ardu, rude, pénible, difficile.
arduously ['ɑ:djuəsli], *adv.* difficilement, péniblement.
arduousness ['ɑ:djuəsnis], *n.* difficulté, *f.*
area ['ɛəriə], *n.* étendue; aire, surface, superficie; région, zone; courette d'entrée (*devant la maison*), *f.*; *area steps,* escalier de service, *m.*; *postal area,* zone postale, *f.*

arena [ə'ri:nə], *n.* arène, *f.*
argent ['ɑ:dʒənt], *a.* argenté.—*n.* (*Her.*) argent, *m.*
Argentina [ɑ:dʒən'ti:nə], l'Argentine, la République Argentine, *f.*
Argentine ['ɑ:dʒəntain], *a.* argentin.—*n.* Argentin, *m.*; *the Argentine* [ARGENTINA].
Argentinian [ɑ:dʒən'tinjən], *a.* argentin.—*n.* Argentin (*personne*), *m.*
argil ['ɑ:dʒil], *n.* argile, *f.*
argonaut ['ɑ:gənɔ:t], *n.* argonaute, *m.*
argosy ['ɑ:gəsi], *n.* caraque, *f.*
argue ['ɑ:gju:], *v.t.* discuter; soutenir; (*fig.*) dénoter, indiquer, accuser.—*v.i.* argumenter (*contre*), raisonner (*sur*), discuter (*avec*); (*Law*) plaider.
argument ['ɑ:gjumənt], *n.* argument, raisonnement, *m.*; discussion, dispute; thèse, *f.*; *for argument's sake,* à titre d'exemple.
argumentative [ɑ:gju'mentətiv], *a.* raisonneur; disposé à argumenter.
aria ['ɑ:riə], *n.* aria, *f.*
arid ['ærid], *a.* aride.
aridity [ə'riditi], **aridness** ['æridnis], *n.* aridité, *f.*
aright [ə'rait], *adv.* correctement; bien.
arise [ə'raiz], *v.i. irr.* (*conjug. like* RISE) se lever; s'élever; survenir, se présenter; provenir, résulter (*de*); *if the question arises,* le cas échéant.
aristocracy [æris'tɔkrəsi], *n.* aristocratie, *f.*
aristocrat ['æristəkræt], *n.* aristocrate, *m.*, *f.*
aristocratic [æristə'krætik], *a.* aristocratique.
arithmetic [ə'riθmətik], *n.* arithmétique, *f.*, calcul, *m.*
arithmetical [æriθ'metikəl], *a.* arithmétique.
arithmetically [æriθ'metikəli], *adv.* arithmétiquement.
arithmetician [æriθmə'tiʃən], *n.* arithméticien, *m.*
ark [ɑ:k], *n.* arche, *f.*; *Noah's ark,* l'arche de Noé.
arm [ɑ:m], *n.* bras, *m.*; arme (*à feu*), *f.*; (*pl.*) (*Her.*) armes, armoiries, *f.pl.*; *arm in arm,* bras dessus bras dessous; *with arms folded,* les bras croisés; *with open arms,* à bras ouverts.—*v.t.* armer; donner des armes à.—*v.i.* armer; s'armer (*de*); prendre les armes.
armada [ɑ:'mɑ:də], *n.* armada, *f.*
armadillo [ɑ:mə'dilou], *n.* tatou, *m.*
armament ['ɑ:məmənt], *n.* armement, *m.*, armée, flotte, *f.*; *armaments race,* course aux armements, *f.*
armature ['ɑ:mətjuə], *n.* armature, *f.*, induit, *m.*
arm band ['ɑ:mbænd], *n.* brassard, *m.*
arm-chair ['ɑ:mtʃɛə], *n.* fauteuil, *m.*
Armenia [ɑ:'mi:nə], *n.* l'Arménie, *f.*
Armenian [ɑ:'mi:niən], *a.* arménien.—*n.* arménien (*langue*); Arménien (*personne*), *m.*
armful ['ɑ:mful], *n.* brassée, *f.*
arm-hole ['ɑ:mhoul], *n.* emmanchure, entournure, *f.*
armistice ['ɑ:mistis], *n.* armistice, *m.*
armless ['ɑ:mlis], *a.* sans bras.
armlet ['ɑ:mlit], *n.* brassard; bracelet; petit bras (*de mer*), *m.*
armor ['ɑ:mə], *n.* armure, *f.*; blindés, *m.pl.*—*v.t.* cuirasser, blinder.
armored ['ɑ:məd], *a.* cuirassé, blindé.
armorer ['ɑ:mərəl], *n.* armurier, *m.*

armorial [ɑː'mɔːriəl], *a.* armorial; ***armorial bearings***, armoiries, *f.pl.*

armor plate ['ɑːmə'pleit], *n.* plaque de blindage, *f.*

armor-plated ['ɑːmə'pleitid], *a.* cuirassé, blindé.

armory ['ɑːməri], *n.* arsenal, *m.*; salle d'armes; armurerie, *f.*

armpit ['ɑːmpit], *n.* aisselle, *f.*

army ['ɑːmi], *n.* armée; (*fig.*) foule, multitude, *f.*; ***the Salvation Army***, l'Armée du Salut.

Arnold ['ɑːnəld]. Arnaud, *m.*

aroma [ə'roumə], *n.* arome *ou* arôme; bouquet (*de vin*), *m.*

aromatic [ærə'mætik], *a.* aromatique.

around [ə'raund], *prep.* autour de; (*colloq.*) environ, vers, à peu près.—*adv.* autour, à l'entour, aux alentours.

arouse [ə'rauz], *v.t.* réveiller, éveiller; exciter, provoquer.

arraign [ə'rein], *v.t.* accuser, poursuivre en justice, attaquer.

arraignment [ə'reinmənt], *n.* mise en accusation, *f.*

arrange [ə'reindʒ], *v.t.* arranger, régler, disposer, distribuer; organiser.

arrangement [ə'reindʒmənt], *n.* arrangement, *m.*, disposition, organisation, *f.*, dispositif, *m.*

arrant ['ærənt], *a.* insigne, achevé, fieffé.

arrantly ['ærəntli], *adv.* notoirement, impudemment.

array [ə'rei], *v.t.* ranger, déployer; revêtir, parer.—*n.* ordre, rang; étalage; appareil, *m.*

arrear [ə'riə], *n.* arriéré, *m.*; (*pl.*) arrérages, *m.pl.*; ***to be in arrears***, être en retard, avoir de l'arriéré.

arrest [ə'rest], *v.t.* arrêter; fixer; suspendre. —*n.* arrestation, prise de corps, *f.*; arrêt, *m.*, suspension, *f.*

arresting [ə'restiŋ], *a.* frappant, qui arrête l'attention.

arrival [ə'raivəl], *n.* arrivée, *f.*; arrivage (*de marchandises etc.*), *m.*; ***arrival platform***, quai d'arrivée, débarcadère, *m.*

arrive [ə'raiv], *v.i.* arriver (*à*); parvenir (*à*).

arrogance ['ærəgəns], *n.* arrogance, *f.*

arrogant ['ærəgənt], *a.* arrogant.

arrogantly ['ærəgəntli], *adv.* arrogamment.

arrogate ['ærogeit], *v.t.* attribuer injustement; ***to arrogate to oneself***, s'arroger.

arrogation [æro'geiʃən], *n.* prétention, usurpation, *f.*

arrow ['ærou], *n.* flèche, *f.*; (*fig.*) trait, *m.*— *v.t.* indiquer par des flèches.

arrow-root ['ærouruːt], *n.* arrow-root, *m.*

arsenal ['ɑːsənəl], *n.* arsenal, *m.*

arsenic ['ɑːsenik], *a.* arsénique.—['ɑːsənik], *n.* arsenic, *m.*

arson ['ɑːsən], *n.* incendie volontaire, *m.*

art [ɑːt], *n.* art, *m.*; adresse, habileté, *f.*; ***faculty of arts***, faculté des lettres, *f.*; ***fine arts***, beaux-arts, *m.pl.*; ***school of art***, école de dessin, académie, *f.*

arterial [ɑː'tiəriəl], *a.* artériel; ***arterial road***, route à grande circulation, *f.*

artery ['ɑːtəri], *n.* artère, *f.*

artesian [ɑː'tiːʒən], *a.* artésien.

artful ['ɑːtful], *a.* rusé, fin, artificieux.

artfully ['ɑːtfuli], *adv.* avec artifice, artificieusement, adroitement.

artfulness ['ɑːtfulnis], *n.* ruse, finesse, *f.*, artifice, *m.*

arthritic [ɑː'θritik], *a.* arthritique.

arthritis [ɑː'θraitis], *n.* arthrite, *f.*

artichoke ['ɑːtitʃouk], *n.* ***Chinese artichoke***, crosne (du Japon), *m.*; ***globe artichoke***, artichaut, *m.*; ***Jerusalem artichoke***, topinambour, *m.*

article ['ɑːtikl], *n.* article; objet; statut, *m.*— *v.t.* engager par contrat; placer (*chez un avoué*) comme clerc; ***articled clerk***, clerc d'avoué, *m.*

articulate [ɑː'tikjuleit], *v.t.*, *v.i.* articuler; énoncer, parler distinctement.—[ɑː'tikjulit], *a.* articulé.

artifice ['ɑːtifis], *n.* artifice, *m.*, ruse, finesse, *f.*

artificer [ɑː'tifisə], *n.* artisan, ouvrier; mécanicien, *m.*

artificial [ɑːti'fiʃəl], *a.* artificiel; factice.

artificiality [ɑːtifiʃi'æliti], *n.* nature artificielle, *f.*

artificially [ɑːti'fiʃəli], *adv.* artificiellement.

artillery [ɑː'tiləri], *n.* artillerie, *f.*

artilleryman [ɑː'tilərimən], *n.* (*pl.* **-men** [men]) artilleur, *m.*

artisan [ɑːti'zæn], *n.* artisan, ouvrier, *m.*

artist ['ɑːtist], *n.* artiste, *m.*, *f.*

artistic [ɑː'tistik], *a.* artistique.

artistically [ɑː'tistikli], *adv.* artistement, avec art.

artless ['ɑːtlis], *a.* ingénu, naïf; sans art, naturel.

artlessly ['ɑːtlisli], *adv.* ingénument, naïvement; sans art.

artlessness ['ɑːtlisnis], *n.* naïveté; simplicité, *f.*

as [æz], *conj.* comme; tel que; à titre de; aussi . . . que; à mesure que; en, pour; parce que; ***as big as***, aussi gros que; ***as cold as charity***, froid comme le marbre; ***as for***, quant à, pour; ***as he advanced***, à mesure qu'il avançait; ***as he was walking***, comme il marchait; ***as if***, comme si; ***as it were***, pour ainsi dire; ***as much as***, autant que, tant que; ***as yet***, jusqu'à présent, encore; ***as you were***, (*Mil.*) au temps! ***be that as it may***, quoi qu'il en soit; ***do as you wish***, faites comme vous voudrez; ***rich as she is***, toute riche qu'elle est; ***she was dressed as a page***, elle était habillée en page; ***that's as may be***, c'est selon; ***to act as***, agir en.

asbestos [æz'bestɔs], *n.* asbeste, amiante, *m.*

ascend [ə'send], *v.t.* monter; gravir, faire l'ascension de; remonter (*un fleuve*).—*v.i.* monter (*à* ou *sur*); remonter; s'élever (*montagne etc.*).

ascendancy [ə'sendənsi], *n.* ascendant, *m.*; supériorité, influence, *f.*

ascendant [ə'sendənt], *a.* ascendant; supérieur.—*n.* ascendant, *m.*; supériorité, *f.*, dessus, *m.*

Ascension [ə'senʃən], *n.* (*Eccles.*) Ascension, *f.*; ***Ascension Day***, jour de l'Ascension, *m.*

ascent [ə'sent], *n.* ascension; élévation, montée, pente, *f.*

ascertain [æsə'tein], *v.t.* s'assurer, s'informer de, constater, vérifier.

ascetic [ə'setik], *a.* ascétique.—*n.* ascète, ascétique, *m.*, *f.*

asceticism [ə'setisizm], *n.* ascétisme, *m.*

ascribable [ə'skraibəbl], *a.* attribuable, imputable.

ascribe [ə'skraib], *v.t.* attribuer, imputer (*à*).

aseptic [æ'septik], *a.* and *n.* aseptique, *m.*

asexual [æ'seksjuəl], *a.* asexué, asexuel.

ash (1) [æʃ], *a.* de frêne.—*n.* frêne (*arbre*); bâton, *m.*; **mountain ash**, sorbier, *m.*

ash (2) [æʃ], *n.* cendre, *f.*; cendres, *f.pl.*

ashamed [ə'ʃeimd], *a.* honteux, confus; **to be ashamed of**, avoir honte de.

ash bin, **pit** ['æʃbin, -pit], *n.* cendrier, *m.*

ashcan ['æʃkæn], *n.* (*Am.*) boîte à ordures, *f.*

ashen (1) [æʃn], *a.* de frêne.

ashen (2) [æʃn], *a.* cendré; gris pâle.

ashore [ə'ʃɔː], *adv.* à terre; échoué (*navire*); **to go ashore**, débarquer.

ash pit [ASH BIN].

ashtray ['æʃtrei], *n.* cendrier, *m.*

Ash Wednesday [æʃ'wenzdi]. mercredi des Cendres, *m.*

ashy ['æʃi], *a.* cendré; gris pâle.

Asia ['eiʃə]. l'Asie, *f.*

Asia Minor ['eiʃə'mainə]. l'Asie-Mineure, *f.*

Asiatic [eiʃi'ætik], **Asian** ['eiʃən], *a.* asiatique. —*n.* Asiatique (*personne*), *m.,f.*

aside [ə'said], *adv.* de côté; (*Theat.*) à part; à l'écart.—*n.* (*Theat.*) aparté, *m.*

asinine ['æsinain], *a.* d'âne; sot.

ask [ɑːsk], *v.t.* demander, prier (*de*); inviter (*à*); s'informer, se renseigner; poser (*une question*); **to ask in**, prier d'entrer; **to ask someone to do something**, demander à quelqu'un de faire quelque chose; **to ask to see**, demander à voir.

askance [ə'skɑːns], *adv.* de travers, obliquement.

askew [ə'skjuː], *adv.* de côté, de biais.

aslant [ə'slɑːnt], *adv.* obliquement, de biais, de côté, en travers.

asleep [ə'sliːp], *a.* endormi; **to be asleep**, dormir; **to fall asleep**, s'endormir.

asp (1) [æsp], **aspic** ['æspik], *n.* aspic, *m.*

asp (2) [æsp], **aspen** ['æspən], *n.* tremble, *m.*

asparagus [əs'pærəgəs], *n.* asperges, *f.pl.*

aspect ['æspekt], *n.* aspect, *m.*; exposition, *f.*; **to have a southern aspect**, être exposé au midi.

aspen ['æspən], *a.* de tremble.—*n.* [ASP (2)].

asperity [æs'periti], *n.* aspérité, âpreté, rudesse, *f.*

aspersion [æs'pɔːʃən], *n.* calomnie, *f.*; **to cast aspersions on**, répandre des calomnies sur.

asphalt ['æsfælt], *a.* d'asphalte.—*n.* asphalte, *m.*

asphyxia [æs'fiksiə], *n.* asphyxie, *f.*

asphyxiate [æs'fiksieit], *v.t.* asphyxier.

aspic [ASP (1)].

aspirant [ə'spaiərənt], *n.* aspirant, candidat, *m.*

aspirate ['æspireit], *v.t.* aspirer.—['æspirit], *a.* aspiré.

aspiration [æspi'reiʃən], *n.* aspiration, *f.*

aspire [ə'spaiə], *v.i.* aspirer (*à*), ambitionner.

aspirin ['æspirin], *n.* aspirine, *f.*

asquint [ə'skwint], *adv.* de travers, en louchant.

ass [æs], *n.* âne, *m.*; **he is a silly ass**, il est bête à manger du foin; **she-ass**, ânesse, *f.*; **to make an ass of oneself**, agir sottement; **young ass**, ânon, *m.*

assail [ə'seil], *v.t.* assaillir, attaquer.

assailant [ə'seilənt], *n.* assaillant, *m.*

assassin [ə'sæsin], *n.* assassin (*politique*), *m.*

assassinate [ə'sæsineit], *v.t.* assassiner.

assassination [əsæsi'neiʃən], *n.* assassinat, *m.*

assault [ə'sɔːlt], *n.* assaut, *m.*, attaque brusquée; (*Law*) tentative de voie de fait, *f.*; **assault and battery**, voies de fait, *f.pl.*; **indecent assault**, outrage aux mœurs, *m.* —*v.t.* assaillir, attaquer.

assay [ə'sei], *n.* épreuve, vérification, *f.*; essai, *m.*—*v.t.* essayer.

assemble [ə'sembl], *v.t.* assembler, réunir.— *v.i.* s'assembler, se réunir.

assembly [ə'sembli], *n.* assemblée, réunion, *f.*; assemblage (*d'une machine*), *m.*; **assembly line**, chaîne de montage, *f.*

assent [ə'sent], *v.i.* donner son assentiment (*à*), admettre.—*n.* assentiment, consentement, *m.*

assert [ə'sɔːt], *v.t.* affirmer, prétendre, soutenir; revendiquer, faire valoir (*ses droits etc.*).

assertion [ə'sɔːʃən], *n.* assertion, revendication, *f.*

assertive [ə'sɔːtiv], *a.* assertif.

assertively [ə'sɔːtivli], *adv.* d'un ton péremptoire.

assess [ə'ses], *v.t.* répartir, fixer; imposer; évaluer.

assessment [ə'sesmənt], *n.* imposition, répartition, assiette; évaluation, *f.*

assessor [ə'sesə], *n.* assesseur; répartiteur, *m.*

asset ['æset], *n.* avoir; avantage, *m.*

assets ['æsets], *n.pl.* actif, *m*; **assets and liabilities**, actif et passif, *m.*; **personal assets**, biens meubles, *m.pl.*; **real assets**, biens immobiliers, *m.pl.*

asseverate [ə'sevəreit], *v.t.* affirmer solennellement.

assiduity [æsi'djuːiti], *n.* assiduité, *f.*

assiduous [ə'sidjuəs], *a.* assidu.

assiduously [ə'sidjuəsli], *adv.* assidûment.

assign [ə'sain], *v.t.* assigner, attribuer; transférer (*à*).—*n.* (*Law*) ayant droit, *m.*

assignation [æsig'neiʃən], *n.* attribution, assignation, cession, *f.*; rendez-vous, *m.*

assignee [æsi'niː], *n.* cessionnaire, *m.,f.*; syndic (*de faillite*), *m.*

assimilate [ə'simileit], *v.t.* assimiler.—*v.i.* s'assimiler.

assimilation [əsimi'leiʃən], *n.* assimilation, *f.*

assist [ə'sist], *v.t.* aider; **to assist each other**, s'entr'aider.

assistance [ə'sistəns], *n.* assistance, aide, *f.*; secours, concours, *m.*

assistant [ə'sistənt], *a.* qui aide, auxiliaire.— *n.* aide; adjoint; commis (*dans une boutique*), *m.*; **assistant examiner**, examinateur adjoint, *m.*; **assistant manager**, sous-directeur, *m.*

assizes [ə'saiziz], *n. pl.* assises, *f.pl.*

associate [ə'souʃieit], *v.t.* associer (*avec* ou *à*). —*v.i.* s'associer (*avec* ou *à*); **to associate with**, fréquenter.—[ə'souʃiit], *a.* associé.— *n.* associé, *m.*; complice, *m.,f.*

association [əsousi'eiʃən], *n.* association, *f.*; souvenir, *m.*

assort [ə'sɔːt], *v.t.* assortir.

assorted [ə'sɔːtid], *a.* assorti.

assortment [ə'sɔːtmənt], *n.* assortiment, *m.*; classification, *f.*

assuage [ə'sweidʒ], *v.t.* adoucir, apaiser, calmer, soulager.—*v.i.* s'apaiser, se calmer.

assume [ə'sju:m], *v.t.* prendre sur soi, s'arroger, s'attribuer; assumer (*une responsabilité*); supposer, présumer; se donner; affecter.

assuming [ə'sju:miŋ], *a.* arrogant, présomptueux, prétentieux; *assuming that*, en supposant que.

assumption [ə'sʌmpʃən], *n.* supposition; prétention, *f.*; (*Eccles.*) *the Assumption*, l'Assomption (*de la Sainte Vierge*), *f.*

assurance [ə'ʃuərəns], *n.* assurance, *f.*

assure [ə'ʃuə], *v.t.* assurer.

assuredly [ə'ʃuəridli], *adv.* assurément, à coup sûr.

Assyria [ə'siriə]. l'Assyrie, *f.*

Assyrian [ə'siriən], *a.* assyrien.—*n.* assyrien (*langue*); Assyrien (*personne*), *m.*

aster ['æstə], *n.* (*Bot., Biol.*) aster, *m.*

asterisk ['æstərisk], *n.* astérisque, *m.*

astern [ə'stə:n], *adv.* (*Naut.*) à l'arrière, sur l'arrière; *to go astern*, culer.

asteroid ['æstərɔid], *n.* astéroïde, *m.*

asthma ['æsθmə], *n.* asthme, *m.*

asthmatic [æsθ'mætik], *a.* asthmatique.

astigmatism [ə'stigmətizm], *n.* astigmatisme, *m.*

astir [ə'stə:], *a.* en mouvement, agité, en émoi; debout.

astonish [ə'stɔniʃ], *v.t.* étonner.

astonishing [ə'stɔniʃiŋ], *a.* étonnant.

astonishment [ə'stɔniʃmənt], *n.* étonnement, *m.*

astound [ə'staund], *v.t.* étonner, ébahir, étourdir.

astounding [ə'staundiŋ], *a.* renversant, abasourdissant.

astray [ə'strei], *adv.* égaré, (*fig.*) dévoyé; *to go astray*, s'égarer.

astride [ə'straid], *adv.* à califourchon; *astride upon*, à cheval sur.

astringent [ə'strindʒənt], *a.* and *n.* astringent, *m.*

astrologer [ə'strɔlədʒə], *n.* astrologue, *m.,f.*

astrology [ə'strɔlədʒi], *n.* astrologie, *f.*

astronaut ['æstrənɔ:t], *n.* astronaute, *m.,f.*

astronomer [ə'strɔnəmə], *n.* astronome, *m.,f.*

astronomic [æstrə'nɔmik], **astronomical** [æstrə'nɔmikəl], *a.* astronomique.

astronomy [ə'strɔnəmi], *n.* astronomie, *f.*

astute [ə'stju:t], *a.* fin, avisé; rusé, astucieux.

astuteness [ə'stju:tnis], *n.* astuce, sagacité, *f.*

asunder [ə'sʌndə], *adv.* en deux.

asylum [ə'sailəm], *n.* asile, refuge; hospice, *m.*

at [æt], *prep.* à, en, dans; après; *at first*, d'abord; *at hand*, sous la main; *at home*, chez soi; *at last*, enfin; *at least*, (*quantity*) au moins; (*fig.*) du moins; *at once*, tout de suite; à la fois; *at school*, à l'école; *at the same time*, en même temps; *at work*, à l'ouvrage.

atheism ['eiθiizm], *n.* athéisme, *m.*

atheist ['eiθiist], *n.* athée, *m., f.*

atheistic [eiθi'istik], *a.* athée, athéistique.

Athens ['æθənz]. Athènes, *f.*

athirst [ə'θə:st], *a.* altéré, assoiffé.

athlete ['æθli:t], *n.* athlète, *m., f.*

athletic [æθ'letik], *a.* athlétique.

athletics [æθ'letiks], *n. pl.* l'athlétisme, *m.*

Atlantic [ət'læntik], *a.* atlantique.—*n.* l'(Océan) Atlantique, *m.*

atlas ['ætləs], *n.* atlas, *m.*

atmosphere ['ætməsfiə], *n.* atmosphère, *f.*

atmospheric [ætməs'ferik], **atmospherical** [ætməs'ferikəl], *a.* atmosphérique.

atmospherics [ætməs'feriks], *n.pl.* (*Rad.*) parasites, *m.pl.*

atoll ['ætɔl], *n.* atoll, attoll, *m.*

atom ['ætəm], *n.* atome, *m.*; *atom bomb*, bombe atomique, *f.*

atomic [ə'tɔmik], *a.* atomique.

atomize ['ætəmaiz], *v.t.* pulvériser, vaporiser.

atomizer ['ætəmaizə], *n.* pulvérisateur, *m.*

atone [ə'toun], *v.t., v.i.* expier; racheter.

atonement [ə'tounmənt], *n.* expiation, *f.*

atop [ə'tɔp], *adv.* au sommet, en haut.

atrocious [ə'trouʃəs], *a.* atroce.

atrociously [ə'trouʃəsli], *adv.* atrocement.

atrocity [ə'trɔsiti], *n.* atrocité, *f.*

atrophy ['ætrəfi], *n.* atrophie, *f.*—*v.t.* atrophier.—*v.i.* s'atrophier.

attach [ə'tætʃ], *v.t.* attacher, lier (*à*).

attachable [ə'tætʃəbl], *a.* qu'on peut attacher.

attaché case [ə'tæʃikeis], *n.* mallette, *f.*

attachment [ə'tætʃmənt], *n.* attachement, *m.*

attack [ə'tæk], *v.t.* attaquer.—*n.* attaque, *f.*, accès, assaut, *m.*

attacker [ə'tækə], *n.* agresseur, *m.*

attain [ə'tein], *v.t.* atteindre, parvenir à.

attainable [ə'teinəbl], *a.* qu'on peut atteindre.

attainment [ə'teinmənt], *n.* acquisition, *f.*; talent, *m.*; (*pl.*) connaissances, *f.pl.*

attaint [ə'teint], *v.t.* accuser; condamner; flétrir, dégrader.

attempt [ə'tempt], *v.t.* tenter, essayer, tâcher (*de*).—*n.* tentative, *f.*, essai, effort; attentat, *m.*

attend [ə'tend], *v.t.* s'occuper de; soigner (*un malade*); servir; assister (*à*).—*v.i.* faire attention, écouter; assister (*à*); servir; s'appliquer (*à*).

attendance [ə'tendəns], *n.* service, *m.*; assistance (*à une réunion*); présence; fréquentation (*scolaire*), *f.*; soins (*pour un malade*), *m.pl.*

attendant [ə'tendənt], *a.* qui suit.—*n.* assistant, aide; serviteur, *m.*

attention [ə'tenʃən], *n.* attention, *f.*; (*pl.*) soins, *m.pl.*

attentive [ə'tentiv], *a.* attentif (*à*), assidu (*auprès de*).

attentively [ə'tentivli], *adv.* attentivement.

attest [ə'test], *v.t.* attester.

attic ['ætik], *n.* mansarde, *f.*; grenier, *m.*

attire [ə'taiə], *v.t.* vêtir, parer.—*n.* vêtements *m.pl.*, costume, *m.*; parure, *f.*, atours, *m.pl.*

attitude ['ætitju:d], *n.* attitude, pose, *f.*

attorney [ə'tə:ni], *n.* (*Am.*) avoué; mandataire, *m.*; *power of attorney*, procuration, *f.* [see **prosecutor**]

attorney general [ə'tə:ni'dʒenərəl], *n.* procureur-général, *m.*

attract [ə'trækt], *v.t.* attirer.

attraction [ə'trækʃən], *n.* attraction, *f.*; (*pl.*) attraits, appas, *m.pl.*

attractive [ə'træktiv], *a.* attrayant, séduisant; attractif (*de l'aimant etc.*).

attractiveness [ə'træktivnis], *n.* attrait, charme, *m.*

attributable [ə'tribjutəbl], *a.* attribuable.

attribute [ə'tribju:t], *v.t.* attribuer, imputer (*à*).—['ætribju:t], *n.* attribut, *m.*, qualité, *f.*

attrition [ə'triʃən], *n.* attrition, *f.*; *war of attrition*, guerre d'usure, *f.*

attune [ə'tju:n], *v.t.* accorder.

auburn ['ɔ:bən], *a.* châtain roux.

auction ['ɔ:kʃən], *n.* enchère, *f.*—*v.t.* vendre aux enchères.

auctioneer [ɔ:kʃə'niə], *n.* commissaire-priseur, *m.*

auction-room ['ɔ:kʃənru:m], *n.* salle des ventes, *f.*

audacious [ɔ:'deiʃəs], *a.* audacieux.

audaciously [ɔ:'deiʃəsli], *adv.* audacieusement.

audacity [ɔ:'dæsiti], *n.* audace, *f.*

audible ['ɔ:dibl], *a.* qu'on peut entendre, audible; distinct, intelligible.

audibly ['ɔ:dibli], *adv.* de manière à être entendu.

audience ['ɔ:djəns], *n.* auditoire, *m.*, assistance, audience, *f.*

audio-visual ['ɔ:djo'vizjuəl], *a.* audio-visuel.

audit ['ɔ:dit], *v.t.* apurer, vérifier (*des comptes*).—*n.* apurement, *m.*, vérification de comptes, *f.*; *audit office*, cour des comptes, *f.*

audition [ɔ:'diʃən], *n.* audition, *f.*—*v.t.* (*fam.*) auditionner.

auditor ['ɔ:ditə], *n.* vérificateur; expert comptable, *m.*

auger ['ɔ:gə], *n.* tarière, *f.*

aught [ɔ:t], *n.* quelque chose; quoi que ce soit, *m.*; *for aught I know*, pour autant que je sache.

augment [ɔ:g'ment], *v.t.* augmenter, accroître.

augur ['ɔ:gə], *v.t.*, *v.i.* augurer, présager.—*n.* augure, *m.*

augury ['ɔ:gjuri], *n.* augure, *m.*

August ['ɔ:gəst]. août, *m.*; *in August*, en août.

august [ɔ:'gʌst], *a.* auguste, imposant.

auk [ɔ:k], *n.* (*Orn.*) pingouin, *m.*

aunt [ɑ:nt], *n.* tante, *f.*

auntie ['ɑ:nti], *n.* (*colloq.*) tata, *f.*

aura ['ɔ:rə], *n.* exhalaison, *f.*, effluve, *m.*

aural ['ɔ:rəl], *a.* de l'oreille.

Aurora [ɔ:'rɔ:rə], *n.* aurore, *f.*; *Aurora Borealis*, aurore boréale.

auspice ['ɔ:spis], *n.* (*usu. in pl.*) auspice, *m.*

auspicious [ɔ:'spiʃəs], *a.* de bon augure, propice.

auspiciously [ɔ:'spiʃəsli], *adv.* sous d'heureux auspices.

austere [ɔ:s'tiə], *a.* austère; âpre.

austerity [ɔ:s'teriti], *n.* austérité, *f.*

Australasia [ɔstrə'leiʃiə]. l'Australasie, *f.*

Australia [ɔs'treiliə]. l'Australie, *f.*

Australian [ɔs'treiliən], *a.* australien.—*n.* Australien (*personne*), *m.*

Austria ['ɔstriə]. l'Autriche, *f.*

Austrian ['ɔstriən], *a.* autrichien.—*n.* Autrichien (*personne*), *m.*

authentic [ɔ:'θentik], *a.* authentique.

authentically [ɔ:'θentikli], *adv.* authentiquement.

authenticate [ɔ:'θentikeit], *v.t.* authentiquer, constater.

authenticated [ɔ:'θentikeitid], *a.* authentique, avéré.

authenticity [ɔ:θen'tisiti], *n.* authenticité, *f.*

author ['ɔ:θə], *n.* auteur, *m.*

authoress ['ɔ:θəris], *n.* femme auteur, femme écrivain, *f.*

authoritative [ɔ:'θɔritətiv], *a.* d'autorité; autorisé; autoritaire, impérieux.

authority [ɔ:'θɔriti], *n.* autorité; autorisation, *f.*, mandat, *m.*

authorization [ɔ:θərai'zeiʃən], *n.* autorisation, *f.*

authorize ['ɔ:θəraiz], *v.t.* autoriser.

authorship ['ɔ:θəʃip], *n.* qualité d'auteur; (*colloq.*) paternité, *f.*

autobiographer [ɔ:təbai'ɔgrəfə], *n.* autobiographe, *m.*, *f.*

autobiography [ɔ:təbai'ɔgrəfi], *n.* autobiographie, *f.*

autocracy [ɔ:'tɔkrəsi], *n.* autocratie, *f.*

autocrat ['ɔ:təkræt], *n.* autocrate, *m.*, *f.*

auto-cycle ['ɔ:tosaikl], *n.* cyclomoteur, *m.*

autograph ['ɔ:təgra:f], *n.* autographe, *m.*—*v.t.* signer, autographier.

autogyro [ɔ:tə'dʒairou], *n.* autogyre, *m.*

automatic [ɔ:tə'mætik], *a.* automatique.

automatically [ɔ:tə'mætikli], *adv.* automatiquement; machinalement.

automation [ɔ:tə'meiʃən], *n.* automation, *f.*

automaton [ɔ:'təmətən], *n.* (*pl.* **automata** [ɔ:'təmətə]) automate, *m.*

automobile ['ɔ:təməbi:l], *n.* (*Am.*) automobile, auto, voiture, *f.*

autonomous [ɔ:'tɔnəməs], *a.* autonome.

autonomy [ɔ:'tɔnəmi], *n.* autonomie, *f.*

autopsy ['ɔ:tɔpsi, ɔ:'tɔpsi], *n.* autopsie, *f.*

autumn ['ɔ:təm], *n.* automne, *m.* ou *f.*

autumnal [ɔ:'tʌmnəl], *a.* automnal, d'automne.

auxiliary [ɔ:g'ziljəri], *a.* and *n.* auxiliaire, *m.*

avail [ə'veil], *v.t.*, *v.i.* profiter, servir; *to avail oneself of*, se servir de.—*n.* service, avantage, *m.*, utilité, *f.*; *of what avail is it?* à quoi bon?

available [ə'veiləbl], *a.* disponible; valable.

avalanche [ævəla:nʃ], *n.* avalanche, *f.*

avarice ['ævəris], *n.* avarice, *f.*

avaricious [ævə'riʃəs], *a.* avare, avaricieux.

avenge [ə'vendʒ], *v.t.* venger; *to avenge oneself*, se venger (*de* ou *sur*).

avenger [ə'vendʒə], *n.* vengeur, *m.*

avenging [ə'vendʒiŋ], *a.* vengeur.—*n.* vengeance, *f.*

avenue ['ævənju:], *n.* avenue, *f.*

aver [ə'və:], *v.t.* affirmer.

average ['ævəridʒ], *a.* commun, moyen.—*n.* moyenne, *f.*, prix moyen, terme moyen, *m.*; (*Naut.*) avarie, *f.*; *on an average*, en moyenne.—*v.t.* établir la moyenne de; atteindre une moyenne de.

averse [ə'və:s], *a.* opposé (*à*), ennemi (*de*).

aversely [ə'və:sli], *adv.* à contre-cœur.

aversion [ə'və:ʃən], *n.* répugnance, aversion, *f.*; *it is his pet aversion*, c'est sa bête noire.

avert [ə'və:t], *v.t.* détourner, écarter.

aviary ['eiviəri], *n.* volière, *f.*

aviation [eivi'eiʃən], *n.* aviation, *f.*

aviator ['eivieitə], *n.* aviateur, *m.*

avid ['ævid], *a.* avide.

avidly ['ævidli], *adv.* avec avidité, avidement.

avoid [ə'void], *v.t.* éviter.

avoidable [ə'voidəbl], *a.* évitable.

avoidance [ə'voidəns], *n.* action d'éviter, *f.*

avoirdupois [ævədə'pɔiz], *n.* poids du commerce, *m.*

avow [ə'vau], *v.t.* avouer, confesser, déclarer.

avowal [ə'vauəl], *n.* aveu, *m.*
avowedly [ə'vauidli], *adv.* de son propre aveu.
await [ə'weit], *v.t.* attendre.
awake [ə'weik], *v.t. irr.* éveiller, réveiller.— *v.i.* s'éveiller, se réveiller.—*a.* éveillé; attentif.
awaken [ə'weikən], *v.t.* éveiller, réveiller.
awakening [ə'weikniŋ], *n.* réveil, *m.*
award [ə'wɔ:d], *v.t.* décerner, adjuger.—*n.* décision, *f.*, jugement, *m.*, sentence; (*Sch.*) récompense, *f.*
aware [ə'wɛə], *a.* qui sait; instruit; *to be aware of*, savoir, avoir connaissance de; *not to be aware of*, ignorer.
awareness [ə'wɛənis], *n.* conscience, *f.*
away [ə'wei], *adv.* absent; loin, au loin; *away with you!* allez-vous en! *far away*, au loin; *right away*, immédiatement.
awe [ɔ:], *n.* crainte, terreur, *f.*, respect, *m.*
awe-inspiring ['ɔ:inspaiəriŋ], *a.* terrifiant.
awestruck ['ɔ:strʌk], *a.* frappé de terreur.
awful ['ɔ:ful], *a.* terrible, redoutable, effroyable; solennel; *what awful weather!* quel temps affreux!
awfully ['ɔ:fuli], *adv.* horriblement, terriblement; (*fam.*) diablement.
awhile [ə'wail], *adv.* un instant, un peu.
awkward ['ɔ:kwəd], *a.* gauche, maladroit; embarrassant.
awkwardly ['ɔ:kwədli], *adv.* gauchement, maladroitement.
awkwardness ['ɔ:kwədnis], *n.* gaucherie, maladresse, *f.*
awl [ɔ:l], *n.* alène, *f.*; poinçon, *m.*
awning ['ɔ:niŋ], *n.* tente, banne, bâche, *f.*
awry [ə'rai], *a.* and *adv.* de travers.
axe [æks], *n.* hache, cognée, *f.*
axiom ['æksiəm], *n.* axiome, *m.*
axiomatic [æksiə'mætik], *a.* axiomatique.
axis ['æksis], *n.* (*pl.* **axes** ['æksi:z]) axe, *m.*
axle [æksl], *n.* arbre, essieu, *m.*; (*Motor.*) *rear axle*, pont arrière, *m.*
ay, aye [ai], *adv.* oui, c'est vrai; *aye, aye!* (*Naut.*) bon quart!—*n.* **ayes and noes**, voix pour et contre, *f.pl.*
azalea [ə'zeiliə], *n.* (*Bot.*) azalée, *f.*
Azores [ə'zɔ:z], *the.* les Açores, *f.pl.*
azote [ə'zout], *n.* (*Chem.*) azote, *m.*
azure ['æʒuə, 'eiʒə], *a.* d'azur.—*n.* azur, *m.*

B

B, b [bi:]. deuxième lettre de l'alphabet; (*Mus.*) si, *m.*
baa [bɑ:], *v.i.* bêler.—*n.* bêlement, *m.*
babble [bæbl], *v.i.* babiller; gazouiller, jaser; (*fig.*) murmurer (*ruisseau*).—*n.* babil, caquet; (*fig.*) murmure, *m.*, jaserie, *f.*
babbler ['bæblə], *n.* babillard, *m.*
babbling ['bæbliŋ], *a.* babillard, bavard.
babe [beib], *n.* enfant nouveau-né, petit enfant, *m.*
Babel ['beibəl]. Babel, *f.*

baboon [bə'bu:n], *n.* babouin, *m.*
baby ['beibi], *n.* bébé, *m.*; *baby grand (piano)*, piano à demi-queue, *m.*; *baby linen*, layette, *f.* [**carriage**, see **pram**]
babyhood ['beibihud], *n.* première enfance, *f.*
babyish ['beibiiʃ], *a.* enfantin.
bacchanalia [bækə'neiliə], *n.pl.* bacchanales, *f.pl.*
bacchanalian [bækə'neiliən], *a.* bachique.—*n.* ivrogne, *m.*
bachelor ['bætʃələ], *n.* célibataire, vieux garçon; bachelier (*ès lettres*), *m.*
back [bæk], *a.* arrière, de derrière; *a back street*, une petite rue.—*n.* dos, *m.*, reins, *m.pl.*; envers (*d'un tissu*); verso (*d'une page etc.*); fond (*d'une salle etc.*); (*Ftb.*) arrière; revers (*d'une colline etc.*); derrière (*d'une maison etc.*); dossier (*d'une chaise*), *m.*; *at the back of*, derrière; *back to back*, dos à dos; *on the back of* (*a letter etc.*), au verso.—*adv.* en arrière; de retour, rentré; *a few years back*, il y a quelques années; *to be back*, être de retour; *to call back*, rappeler; *to come back*, revenir.—*v.t.* soutenir; (*Betting*) jouer (*un cheval*); faire reculer.—*v.i.* reculer.
backbite ['bækbait], *v.t.* médire de, calomnier.
backbiting ['bækbaitiŋ], *n.* médisance, *f.*
backbone ['bækboun], *n.* épine dorsale, *f.*
back door ['bæk'dɔ:], *n.* porte de derrière, *f.*
backer ['bækə], *n.* partisan, second; parieur pour, *m.*
back-fire [bæk'faiə], *v.i.* (*Motor.*) pétarader.
backgammon [bæk'gæmən], *n.* trictrac, *m.*
back garden ['bæk'gɑ:dn], *n.* jardin de derrière, *m.*
background ['bækgraund], *n.* arrière-plan, fond, *m.*
back room ['bæk'ru:m], *n.* chambre de derrière, *f.*
backside ['bæk'said], *n.* (*pop.*) derrière, *m.*
backslide ['bæk'slaid], *v.i.* retomber dans le vice *ou* le péché.
backstage ['bæk'steidʒ], *adv.* derrière la scène; dans les coulisses.
backstairs [bæk'stɛəz], *n.* escalier de service, *m.*
backward ['bækwəd], *a.* arriéré; en retard; en arrière; lent, tardif.
backward(s) ['bækwəd(z)], *adv.* à reculons; en arrière; à la renverse.
backwoodsman ['bækwudzmən], *n.* (*pl.* **-men** [men]) défricheur de forêts, *m.*
back-yard ['bæk'jɑ:d], *n.* cour de derrière, *f.*
bacon ['beikən], *n.* lard, *m.*
bacterium [bæk'tiəriəm], *n.* (*pl.* **bacteria** [bæk'tiəriə]) bactérie, *f.*
bad [bæd], *a.* mauvais; méchant (*enfant etc.*); gâté (*aliment etc.*); malade; *that is too bad*, c'est trop fort.
badge [bædʒ], *n.* insigne, *m.*; plaque, *f.*; (*Mil.*) écusson; brassard, *m.*
badger ['bædʒə], *n.* blaireau, *m.*—*v.t.* harceler.
badly ['bædli], *adv.* mal; grièvement, fort, beaucoup.
badness ['bædnis], *n.* méchanceté, *f.*; mauvais état, *m.*
baffle [bæfl], *v.t.* déjouer; confondre.

bag [bæg], *n.* sac; cornet (*papier*), *m.*; **game bag**, gibecière, *f.*; **with bag and baggage**, avec armes et bagages.—*v.t.* mettre en sac; abattre (*du gibier*); (*colloq.*) s'emparer de; (*slang*) chiper.—*v.i.* bouffer (*pantalon*).
baggage ['bægidʒ], *n.* (*chiefly Am.*) bagages, *m.pl.*
bagpipes ['bægpaips], *n. pl.* cornemuse, *f.*
bail (1) [beil], *n.* caution, *m.*; **on bail**, sous caution.
bail (2) [beil], *v.t.* vider l'eau d' (un bateau), écoper. —*v.i.* **to bail out**, (*Av.*) sauter en parachute.
bailiff ['beilif], *n.* huissier, *m.*; **farm bailiff**, régisseur, *m.*
bait [beit], *v.t.* amorcer (*un hameçon*); (*fig.*) harceler, tourmenter.—*n.* amorce, *f.*; appât, leurre, *m.*
baize [beiz], *n.* serge, *f.*; **green baize**, tapis vert, *m.*
bake [beik], *v.t., v.i.* cuire au four.
bakehouse ['beikhaus], *n.* fournil, *m.*, boulangerie, *f.*
Bakelite ['beikəlait], *n.* bakélite (*reg. trade mark*), *f.*
baker ['beikə], *n.* boulanger, *m.*
bakery ['beikəri], *n.* boulangerie, *f.*
baking ['beikiŋ], *n.* cuisson; fournée, *f.*
balance ['bæləns], *n.* balance, *f.*; équilibre; balancier (*d'une pendule*), *m.*—*v.t.* équilibrer, balancer; **to balance up**, arrêter.
balance-sheet ['bælənsʃi:t], *n.* bilan, *m.*
balance-weight ['bælənsweit], *n.* contre-poids, *m.*
balcony ['bælkəni], *n.* balcon, *m.*
bald [bɔːld], *a.* chauve; (*fig.*) plat, sec (*style*).
baldly ['bɔːldli], *adv.* pauvrement, platement, sèchement.
baldness ['bɔːldnis], *n.* calvitie; (*fig.*) platitude, *f.*
bale (2) [beil], *n.* balle, *f.*, ballot, *m.*—*v.t.* emballer.
baleful ['beilful], *a.* sinistre, funeste.
balefully ['beilfuli], *adv.* d'une manière funeste.
balk, baulk [bɔːk], *n.* poutre, bille; (*Billiards*) ligne de départ, *f.*—*v.t.* frustrer, contrarier, déjouer.
Balkan ['bɔːlkən], *a.* balkanique.
Balkans ['bɔːlkənz], **the.** les Balkans, les États Balkaniques, *m.pl.*
ball (1) [bɔːl], *n.* balle; boule (*de neige*); pelote, *f.*, peloton (*de laine, de ficelle*); boulet (*de canon*), *m.*; (*Billiards*) bille; (*Cook.*) boulette, *f.*; ballon (*plein d'air*), *m.*; prunelle (*d'œil*), *f.*; **ball-point pen**, stylo à bille, *m.*
ball (2) [bɔːl], *n.* bal, *m.*; **fancy-dress ball**, bal masqué.
ballad ['bæləd], *n.* (*Mus.*) romance; ballade, *f.*
ballast ['bæləst], *n.* lest, *m.*; (*Rail.*) ballast, *m.*; **in ballast**, sur lest.—*v.t.* lester; (*Rail.*) ensabler.
ballerina [bælə'riːnə], *n.* ballerine, *f.*
ballet ['bælei], *n.* ballet, *m.*
balloon [bə'luːn], *n.* ballon, aérostat, *m.*—*v.i.* se ballonner.
ballot ['bælət], *n.* boule, *f.*; bulletin, scrutin, *m.*; **by ballot**, au scrutin.—*v.i.* voter au scrutin.
ballot box ['bælətbɔks], *n.* urne électorale, *f.*
ballot (paper) ['bælətpeipə], *n.* bulletin de vote, *m.*

balm [bɑːm], *n.* baume, *m.*; mélisse, *f.*—*v.t.* parfumer.
balmy ['bɑːmi], *a.* embaumé, parfumé.
balsam ['bɔːlsəm], *n.* baume, *m.*
Baltic ['bɔːltik], **the.** la Baltique, *f.*
balustrade [bæləs'treid], *n.* balustrade, *f.*
bamboo [bæm'buː], *n.* bambou, *m.*
bamboozle [bæm'buːzl], *v.t.* (*colloq.*) tromper, duper, enjôler.
ban [bæn], *n.* ban, *m.*; interdiction, *f.*; (*Eccles.*) interdit, *m.*—*v.t.* interdire, proscrire.
banal [bə'næl, 'beinəl], *a.* banal.
banality [bə'næliti], *n.* banalité, *f.*
banana [bə'nɑːnə], *n.* banane, *f.*
banana tree [bə'nɑːnətriː], *n.* bananier, *m.*
band (1) [bænd], *n.* bande, *f.*, lien; ruban, *m.*; raie, *f.*—*v.t.* bander.
band (2) [bænd], *n.* bande, troupe; (*Mil.*) musique, *f.*; orchestre, *m.*; **brass band**, fanfare, *f.*—*v.t.* liguer, réunir en troupe.—*v.i.* se liguer.
bandage ['bændidʒ], *n.* bandeau; (*Surg.*) bandage, pansement, *m.*
bandbox ['bændbɔks], *n.* carton (*de modiste*), *m.*
bandit ['bændit], *n.* bandit, *m.*
bandmaster ['bændmɑːstə], *n.* chef de musique, *m.*
bandoleer, bandolier [bændə'liə], *n.* bandoulière, *f.*
bandsman ['bændzmən], *n.* (*pl.* **-men** [men]) musicien, *m.*
bandstand ['bændstænd], *n.* kiosque à musique, *m.*
bandy ['bændi], *v.t.* renvoyer; échanger; se renvoyer; **to bandy words**, se renvoyer des paroles.—*v.i.* se disputer.
bandy-legged ['bændilegd], *a.* bancal.
bane [bein], *n.* poison; (*fig.*) fléau, *m.*
baneful ['beinful], *a.* pernicieux, funeste, nuisible.
bang [bæŋ], *n.* coup, grand bruit, *m.*, détonation, *f.*—*v.t.* frapper violemment, taper; **to bang a door**, claquer une porte.—*int.* pan! paf! boum!
bangle [bæŋgl], *n.* porte-bonheur, bracelet, *m.*
banish ['bæniʃ], *v.t.* bannir, exiler.
banishment ['bæniʃmənt], *n.* bannissement, exil, *m.*
bank (1) [bæŋk], *n.* rivage, bord, *m.*; berge, rive; terrasse, *f.*, remblai, talus; banc (*de sable, de gazon etc.*), *m.*; digue, *f.*; carreau (*de mine*), *m.*—*v.t.* terrasser, remblayer.
bank (2) [bæŋk], *n.* (*Comm.*) banque, *f.*; **savings bank**, caisse d'épargne, *f.*—*v.t.* encaisser (*de l'argent*).
banker ['bæŋkə], *n.* banquier, *m.*
banking ['bæŋkiŋ], *n.* banque, *f.*
bank note ['bæŋknout], *n.* billet de banque, *m.*
bankrupt ['bæŋkrʌpt], *a.* failli, en faillite; (*fig.*) ruiné.—*v.t.* mettre en faillite, ruiner.—*n.* banqueroutier, failli, *m.*; **to go bankrupt**, faire faillite.
bankruptcy ['bæŋkrʌptsi], *n.* banqueroute, faillite, *f.*
banner ['bænə], *n.* bannière, *f.*
bannock ['bænək], *n.* (*grosse*) galette d'avoine, *f.*
banns [bænz], *n.pl.* **banns of marriage**, bans de mariage, *m.pl.*

banquet ['bæŋkwit], *n.* banquet; *festin, *m.*
banter ['bæntə], *v.t.* railler, badiner.—*n.* badinage, *m.*, raillerie, *f.*
baptism ['bæptizm], *n.* baptême, *m.*
baptismal [bæp'tizməl], *a.* baptismal.
baptist ['bæptist], *n.* baptiste, *m.*, *f.*
baptize [bæp'taiz], *v.t.* baptiser.
bar (1) [ba:], *n.* barre, *f.*; (*Law etc.*) barreau, parquet, *m.*; (*fig.*) barrière; buvette, *f.*, comptoir, bar (*de café, hôtel etc.*); (*Law*) banc des accusés, *m.*; (*Mus.*) mesure; tablette (*de chocolat*), *f.*; **to be admitted to the bar**, être reçu avocat.—*v.t.* barrer, empêcher; exclure.
bar (2) [BARRING].
barb [ba:b], *n.* barbillon, dardillon (*hameçon*), *m.*; pointe (*flèche*); barbe, arête (*blé*), *f.*
Barbados [ba:'beidəs], la Barbade, *f.*
barbarian [ba:'bɛəriən], *a.* and *n.* barbare, *m.*, *f.*
barbaric [ba:'bærik], *a.* barbare.
barbarism ['ba:bərizm], *n.* barbarie, *f.*; (*Gram.*) barbarisme, *m.*
barbarity [ba:'bæriti], *n.* barbarie, cruauté, *f.*
barbarous ['ba:bərəs], *a.* barbare.
barbecue ['ba:bəkju:], *n.* grand gril; grand pique-nique (en plein air), *m.*—*v.t.* rôtir à la broche.
barbed [ba:bd], *a.* barbelé; (*fig.*) acéré; **barbed wire**, fil de fer barbelé, *m.*
barbel ['ba:bəl], *n.* (*Ichth.*) barbeau, *m.*
barber ['ba:bə], *n.* coiffeur, *m.*
Barcelona [ba:sə'lounə], Barcelone, *f.*
bard [ba:d], *n.* barde, trouvère, *m.*
bare [bɛə], *a.* nu, découvert; (*fig.*) seul, simple; pauvre.—*v.t.* découvrir, dépouiller; mettre à nu.
bareback ['bɛəbæk], *adv.* à dos nu.
barefaced ['bɛəfeist], *a.* à visage découvert; éhonté, sans déguisement.
barefoot ['bɛəfut], *a.* nu-pieds, les pieds nus.
bareheaded ['bɛə'hedid], *a.* nu-tête, la tête nue.
barely ['bɛəli], *adv.* à peine; tout juste, simplement, seulement; pauvrement.
bareness ['bɛənis], *n.* nudité; misère, *f.*
bargain ['ba:gin], *n.* marché, *m.*, affaire; occasion, *f.*; **into the bargain**, par-dessus le marché; **it is a bargain**, c'est convenu; **to strike a bargain**, conclure un marché. —*v.i.* marchander, faire marché.
barge [ba:dʒ], *n.* chaland, *m.*; péniche, *f.*— *v.i.* **to barge into**, se heurter contre, bousculer.
bargee [ba:'dʒi:], **bargeman** ['ba:dʒmən] (*pl.* **-men** [men]), *n.* batelier, *m.*
baritone ['bæritoun], *a.* de baryton.—*n.* baryton, *m.*
bark (1) [ba:k], *n.* écorce, *f.*; tan, *m.*
bark (2) [ba:k], *n.* aboiement, *m.*—*v.i.* aboyer.
bark (3), **barque** [ba:k], *n.* trois-mâts, *m.*
barking ['ba:kiŋ], *n.* aboiement, *m.*
barley ['ba:li], *n.* orge, *f.*
barmaid ['ba:meid], *n.* barmaid, *f.*
barman ['ba:mən], *n.* (*pl.* **-men** [men]) barman, *m.*
barmy ['ba:mi], *a.* (*colloq.*) fou, toqué.
barn [ba:n], *n.* grange, *f.*; (*Am.*) étable, *f.*
barnacle ['ba:nəkl], *n.* barnache (*oie*), *f.*; balane, anatife (*crustacé*), *m.*
barometer [bə'rɔmitə], *n.* baromètre, *m.*

barometric [bærə'metrik], *a.* barométrique.
baron ['bærən], *n.* baron, *m.*; **baron of beef**, double aloyau, *m.*
baroness ['bærənis], *n.* baronne, *f.*
baronet ['bærənet], *n.* baronnet, *m.*
baronial [bə'rouniəl], *a.* baronnial, seigneurial.
barony ['bærəni], *n.* baronnie, *f.*
barouche [bə'ru:ʃ], *n.* calèche, *f.*
barque [BARK (3)].
barrack ['bærək], *n.* (*usu. in pl.*) caserne, *f.*; quartier (*pour la cavalerie*), *m.*
barrage ['bærid3, 'bærɑ:3], *n.* barrage, *m.*
barrel ['bærəl], *n.* baril, *m.*; gonne, caque (*de poissons etc.*), *f.*; corps (*de pompe*); cylindre, tambour (*de machine*); canon (*de fusil*), *m.* —*v.t.* embariller, entonner, mettre en baril, encaquer.
barrel organ ['bærələ:gən], *n.* orgue de Barbarie, *m.*
barren ['bærən], *a.* stérile; infertile (*terre*).
barrenness ['bærənis], *n.* stérilité, *f.*
barricade [bæri'keid], *n.* barricade, *f.*—*v.t.* barricader.
barrier ['bæriə], *n.* barrière, *f.*
barring ['ba:riŋ], **bar** (2) [ba:], *prep.* excepté, hormis, sauf.
barrister ['bæristə], *n.* avocat, *m.*
barrow ['bærou], *n.* brouette, *f.*
barrow-boy ['bærouboi], *n.* (*fam.*) marchand des quatre saisons, *m.*
barter ['ba:tə], *n.* échange, troc; trafic, *m.*— *v.t.* troquer, échanger.—*v.i.* échanger, faire échange.
basalt [bə'sɔ:lt], *n.* basalte, *m.*
base (1) [beis], *a.* bas, vil, indigne, méprisable; illégitime (*enfant*); de mauvais aloi; non précieux, faux (*monnaie*).
base (2) [beis], *n.* base, *f.*, fondement; fond, *m.*—*v.t.* fonder (*sur*); asseoir (*l'impôt*).
baseball ['beisbɔ:l], *n.* (*Spt.*) base-ball, *m.*
baseless ['beislis], *a.* sans fondement.
basely ['beisli], *adv.* bassement, lâchement.
basement ['beismənt], *n.* sous-sol, *m.*
baseness ['beisnis], *n.* bassesse, lâcheté, *f.*
bashful ['bæʃful], *a.* timide, intimidé.
bashfully ['bæʃfuli], *adv.* timidement, en rougissant.
bashfulness ['bæʃfulnis], *n.* timidité, fausse honte, *f.*
basic ['beisik], *a.* (*Chem.*) basique; de base.
basilica [bə'zilikə], *n.* basilique, *f.*
basilisk ['bæzilisk], *n.* basilic, *m.*
basin ['beisən], *n.* bassin; bol, *m.*; cuvette, *f.*
basis ['beisis], *n.* (*pl.* **bases** ['beisi:z]) base, *f.* fondement, *m.*
bask [ba:sk], *v.i.* se chauffer.
basket ['ba:skit], *n.* panier, *m.*, corbeille, *f.*
basketball ['ba:skitbɔ:l], *n.* (*Spt.*) basketball, (*fam.*) basket, *m.*
Basle [ba:l]. Bâle, *f.*
bas-relief [ba:rə'li:f], *n.* bas-relief, *m.*
bass (1) [beis], *n.* (*Mus.*) basse; basse-taille, *f.*; **double bass**, contre-basse, *f.*
bass (2) [bæs], *n.* (*Ichth.*) bar, *m.*; perche, *f.*
bassinet [bæsi'net], *n.* bercelonnette, *f.*, moïse, *m.*
bassoon [bə'su:n], *n.* basson, *m.*
bastard ['bæstəd], *a.* bâtard; (*fig.*) faux.—*n.* bâtard, *m.*, bâtarde, *f.*; (*pop.*) salaud, *m.*
baste [beist], *v.t.* arroser (*viande*); (*fig.*) bâtonner; (*Needlework*) bâtir.

355

bastion ['bæstiən], *n.* bastion, *m.*

bat (1) [bæt], *n.* (*Cricket*) batte, *f.*; *off his own bat*, de sa propre initiative.—*v.i.* être au guichet.

bat (2) [bæt], *n.* (*Zool.*) chauve-souris, *f.*

Batavian [bə'teiviən], *a.* batave.—*n.* Batave (*personne*), *m.*, *f.*

batch [bætʃ], *n.* fournée (*pain*); (*fig.*) troupe, bande, *f.*; tas; lot, *m.*

bate [beit], *v.t.* rabattre, rabaisser.

bath [bɑːθ], *n.* bain, *m.*; baignoire, *f.*; *shower bath*, douche, *f.*—*v.t.* donner un bain à, baigner.—*v.i.* prendre un bain.

bathe [beið], *v.t.* baigner; tremper, mouiller. —*v.i.* se baigner.—*n.* baignade, *f.*

bather ['beiðə], *n.* baigneur, *m.*, baigneuse, *f.*

bathing ['beiðiŋ], *n.* baignade, *f.*; bains, *m.pl.*

bathing suit ['beiðiŋsjuːt], *n.* costume de bain, maillot, *m.*

bathos ['beiθɔs], *n.* pathos, *m.*, enflure, *f.*

bathroom ['bɑːθrum], *n.* salle de bain(s), *f.*

batman ['bætmən], *n.* (*pl.* **-men** [men]) ordonnance, brosseur, *m.*

baton ['bætən], *n.* bâton, *m.*; baguette, *f.*

batsman ['bætsmən], *n.* (*Cricket*) batteur, *m.*

battalion [bə'tæliən], *n.* bataillon, *m.*

batten ['bætən], *n.* volige, latte, *f.*—*v.t.* fermer; (*Carp.*) voliger.—*v.i.* s'engraisser.

batter ['bætə], *v.t.* battre en brèche; battre; délabrer, ébranler, démolir.—*n.* pâte, *f.*

battered ['bætəd], *a.* délabré.

battering-ram ['bætəriŋræm], *n.* bélier, *m.*

battery ['bætəri], *n.* batterie (*Elec.*) pile, batterie, *f.*, accumulateur, *m.*; action de battre en brèche, *f.*; (*Law*) voies de fait, *f.pl.*

battle [bætl], *n.* bataille, *f.*, combat, *m.*; *pitched battle*, bataille rangée; *to give battle*, livrer bataille.—*v.i.* lutter, combattre; (*colloq.*) batailler.

battle-axe ['bætlæks], *n.* hache d'armes, *f.*

battledore ['bætldɔ:], *n.* raquette, *f.*

battle dress ['bætldres], *n.* tenue de campagne, *f.*

battle-field ['bætlfiːld], *n.* champ de bataille, *m.*

battlement ['bætlmənt], *n.* créneau, *m.*

battleship ['bætlʃip], *n.* cuirassé, *m.*

bauble [bɔːbl], *n.* bibiole, fanfreluche, *f.*; *fool's bauble*, marotte, *f.*

baulk [BALK].

bauxite ['bɔːksait, 'bouzait], *n.* bauxite, *f.*

Bavaria [bə'veəriə], la Bavière, *f.*

Bavarian [bə'veəriən], *a.* bavarois.—*n.* Bavarois (*personne*).

bawdy ['bɔːdi], *a.* obscène, paillard.

bawl [bɔːl], *v.i.* crier, brailler.

bay (1) [bei], *a.* bai (*cheval*).

bay (2) [bei], *n.* baie, *f.*, golfe *m.*; (*Arch.*) baie, *f.*

bay (3) [bei], *n.* (*Bot.*) baie, *f.*; laurier, *m.*

bay (4) [bei], *n.* abois, *m.pl.*; *at bay*, aux abois.—*v.i.* aboyer.

bayonet ['beiənit], *n.* baïonnette, *f.*—*v.t.* tuer *ou* percer à coups de baïonnette.

bay window ['beiwindou], *n.* fenêtre en saillie *ou* à baie, *f.*

bazaar [bə'zɑː], *n.* bazar, *m.*; vente de charité, *f.*

bazooka [bə'zuːkə], *n.* bazooka, *m.*

be [biː], *v.i. irr.* être; exister; subsister; y avoir, se trouver; avoir; faire; devoir, falloir; *be it so*, soit; *be that as it may*, quoi qu'il en soit; *how is it that . . .?* comment se fait-il que . . .? *I was to*, je devais; *to be better*, valoir mieux; se porter mieux; *to be mistaken*, se tromper; *to be right*, avoir raison.

beach [biːtʃ], *n.* plage, grève, *f.*, rivage, *m.*—*v.t.* échouer.

beacon ['biːkən], *n.* phare, fanal, *m.*; balise, *f.* —*v.t.* baliser, éclairer.

bead [biːd], *n.* grain (*de chapelet, de bracelet, de collier*); globule, *m.*; *string of beads*, collier, chapelet, *m.*; *to tell one's beads*, égrener son chapelet.

beadle [biːdl], *n.* bedeau; appariteur, *m.*

beagle [biːgl], *n.* chien briquet, bigle, *m.*

beak [biːk], *n.* bec, *m.*; bigorne (*enclume*), *f.*; (*Naut.*) éperon, *m.*

beaker ['biːkə], *n.* gobelet, *m.*, coupe, *f.*

beakful ['biːkful], *n.* becquée, *f.*

beam [biːm], *n.* poutre, *f.*; timon (*charrue, voiture etc.*); rayon (*lumière*); large sourire (*de joie etc.*), *m.*—*v.t.* lancer, darder (*des rayons*).—*v.i.* rayonner.

beaming ['biːmiŋ], *a.* rayonnant, radieux.—*n.* rayonnement, *m.*

bean [biːn], *n.* fève, *f.*; haricot; grain (*de café*), *m.*; *French beans*, haricots verts; *kidney beans*, haricots, soissons.

bear (1) [beə], *n.* ours; (*St. Exch.*) joueur à la baisse, baissier, *m.*; *polar bear*, ours blanc.

bear (2) [beə], *v.t. irr.* porter, soutenir; endurer, supporter, souffrir, subir; avoir, produire (*fruits etc.*); enfanter; donner naissance à; y tenir; remporter.—*v.i.* endurer, souffrir; porter, peser; avoir rapport (*à*); appuyer; porter (*sur*); rapporter.

bearable ['beərəbl], *a.* supportable.

beard [biəd], *n.* barbe, *f.*—*v.t.* braver, défier.

bearded ['biədid], *a.* barbu.

beardless ['biədlis], *a.* imberbe.

bearer ['beərə], *n.* porteur; (*Arch.*) support, *m.*

bearing ['beəriŋ], *n.* rapport; maintien, port, *m.*, conduite, relation, *f.*, aspect, *m.*, portée; face, *f.*; (*Arch.*) support; (*Mech.*) coussinet, *m.*; *ball bearings*, roulement à billes, *m.*; *to take one's bearings*, s'orienter.

bearskin ['beəskin], *n.* (*Mil.*) bonnet d'oursin, *m.*

beast [biːst], *n.* bête, *f.*; (*fig.*) animal, cochon, *m.*

beastliness ['biːstlinis], *n.* saleté, saloperie, *f.*

beastly ['biːstli], *a.* bestial; sale, malpropre, dégoûtant.

beat [biːt], *v.t. irr.* battre; frapper; piler, broyer; l'emporter sur; fouetter (*pluie, neige etc.*); se frapper (*la poitrine etc.*); *beat it!* fiche-moi le camp! *that beats all*, cela dépasse tout; *to beat a retreat*, battre en retraite.—*v.i.* battre; être agité.—*n.* coup, battement; son; itinéraire, *m.*; ronde (*d'un agent de police*), *f.*, parcours (*facteurs etc.*), *m.*; (*Hunt.*) battue; (*Mus.*) mesure, *f.*, temps, *m.*; *beat of the drum*, batterie de tambour, *f.* [*see* whisk]

beaten [biːtn], *a.* battu.

beater ['biːtə], *n.* batteur; (*Spt.*) rabatteur, *m.*; batte (*instrument*), *f.* [*see* whisk]

beating ['biːtiŋ], *n.* battement, *m.*; rossée, *f.*; coups, *m.pl.*; batterie, *f.*; roulement (*tambour etc.*), *m.*

beau [bou], *n.* (*pl.* **beaux** [bouz]) petit-maître; prétendant (*amant*), *m.*
beauteous ['bju:tiəs], *a.* (*Poet.*) beau.
beauteously ['bju:tiəsli], *adv.* avec beauté.
beautiful ['bju:tiful], *a.* très beau; (*colloq.*) magnifique.
beautifully ['bju:tifuli], *adv.* admirablement.
beautify ['bju:tifai], *v.t.* embellir, orner.—*v.i.* s'embellir.
beauty ['bju:ti], *n.* beauté (*personne et qualité*), *f.*
beauty spot ['bju:tispɔt], *n.* mouche, *f.*, grain de beauté; site pittoresque, *m.*
beaver ['bi:və], *n.* castor; chapeau de castor, *m.*

becalm [bi'kɑ:m], *v.t.* *apaiser, calmer; abriter (*navire*).
because [bi'kɔz], *conj.* parce que; **because of**, à cause de.
beck (1) [bek], *n.* signe (*du doigt etc.*), *m.*—*v.i.* faire signe (*du doigt etc.*).
beck (2) [bek], *n.* ruisseau, *m.*
beckon ['bekən], *v.t.* faire signe à, appeler.—*v.i.* faire signe (à).
become [bi'kʌm], *v.t.* *irr.* (*conjug. like* COME) aller bien à, convenir à, être propre à.—*v.i.* devenir, commencer à être.
becoming [bi'kʌmiŋ], *a.* bienséant, convenable, qui va bien, attrayant.
becomingly [bi'kʌmiŋli], *adv.* avec bienséance.
bed [bed], *n.* lit, *m.*; couche; (*Geol.*) assise, *f.*; encaissement (*rue*); parterre, *m.*, plate-bande (*fleurs*), *f.*; carré, *m.*—*v.t.* coucher, mettre au lit; loger, fixer, enfoncer; parquer (*huîtres*).—*v.i.* coucher, se coucher.
bedaub [bi'dɔ:b], *v.t.* barbouiller.
bedazzle [bi'dæzl], *v.t.* éblouir.
*****bed-chamber** [BEDROOM].
bedclothes ['bedklouðz], *n.pl.* les draps et les couvertures, *m.pl.*
bedding ['bediŋ], *n.* literie; litière (*pour animaux*), *f.*
bedeck [bi'dek], *v.t.* parer (*de*).
bedfellow ['bedfelou], *n.* camarade de lit, *m.*
*****bedizen** [bi'daizn], *v.t.* attifer, parer.
bedraggle [bi'drægl], *v.t.* crotter, traîner dans la boue.
bedridden ['bedridn], *a.* alité.
bedroom ['bedru:m], *****bed-chamber** [bed tʃeimbə], *n.* chambre (à coucher), *f.*
bedside ['bedsaid], *n.* ruelle, *f.*, chevet, bord du lit, *m.*
bed-spread ['bedspred], *n.* couvrelit, dessus de lit, *m.*
bedstead ['bedsted], *n.* lit, bois de lit, *m.*; couchette, *f.*
bee [bi:], *n.* abeille, *f.*; **to have a bee in one's bonnet**, avoir une araignée dans le plafond.
beech [bi:tʃ], *n.* hêtre, *m.*
beef [bi:f], *n.* bœuf (*viande*); (*pl.* **beeves** [bi:vz]) bœuf (*animal*), *m.*
beef-steak ['bi:f'steik], *n.* bifteck, *m.*
beehive ['bi:haiv], *n.* ruche, *f.*
bee-line ['bi:lain], *n.* ligne droite, *f.*; **in a bee-line**, à vol d'oiseau; **to make a bee-line for**, se diriger tout droit vers.
Beelzebub [bi'elzəbʌb], Belzébuth, *m.*
beer [biə], *n.* bière, *f.*; **glass of beer**, bock, *m.*
beet [bi:t], *n.* betterave, *f.*
beetle (1) [bi:tl], *n.* coléoptère, scarabée, escarbot, *m.*

beetle (2) [bi:tl], *n.* maillet, *m.*, mailloche; batte, *f.*, battoir (*de laveuse*), *m.*; hie, demoiselle (*d'un paveur*), *f.*; mouton (*à enfoncer les pieux*), *m.*
beetle (3) [bi:tl], *v.i.* surplomber.—*a.* en surplomb.
beets ['bi:tz], *n.* betterave rouge, *f.*
beet-sugar [bi:t'ʃugə], *n.* sucre de betterave, *m.*
befall [bi'fɔ:l], *v.t.*, *v.i. irr.* (*conjug. like* FALL) arriver, survenir (à).
befit [bi'fit], *v.t.* convenir à.
befitting [bi'fitiŋ], *a.* convenable à.
before [bi'fɔ:], *adv.* avant (*temps, ordre etc.*); auparavant, en avant; plus haut; jusqu'alors, naguère, jusqu'ici.—*prep.* devant (*endroit*); avant (*temps etc.*); **before going there**, avant d'y aller.—*conj.* avant que (*with subj.*).
beforehand [bi'fɔ:hænd], *adv.* à l'avance, d'avance.
befriend [bi'frend], *v.t.* seconder, aider, secourir; devenir l'ami de (*quelqu'un*).
beg [beg], *v.t.* mendier (*demander l'aumône*); demander, prier (*de*).—*v.i.* mendier.
beget [bi'get], *v.t. irr.* engendrer; (*fig.*) produire, causer.
beggar ['begə], *n.* mendiant, *m.*, mendiante, *f.*; gueux, *m.*, gueuse, *f.*—*v.t.* appauvrir, ruiner; (*fig.*) épuiser.
beggarly ['begəli], *a.* chétif, pauvre, misérable.
beggary ['begəri], *n.* mendicité, misère, *f.*
begging ['begiŋ], *n.* mendicité, *f.*
begin [bi'gin], *v.t. irr.* commencer; entamer, débuter; se mettre à.—*v.i.* commencer (**by**, **with**, *par*); **begin afresh**, recommencez.
beginner [bi'ginə], *n.* commençant; débutant, *m.*
beginning [bi'giniŋ], *n.* commencement, début, *m.*, origine, *f.*
begone! [bi'gɔn], *int.* va-t'en! allez-vous-en!
begonia [bi'gounjə], *n.* (*Bot.*) bégonia, *m.*
begrudge [bi'grʌdʒ], *v.t.* envier; refuser (à).
begrudgingly [bi'grʌdʒiŋli], *adv.* à contre-cœur.
beguile [bi'gail], *v.t.* tromper, séduire; (*fig.*) passer (*le temps*).
behalf [bi'hɑ:f], *n.* faveur, part, *f.*; **on behalf of**, au nom de.
behave [bi'heiv], *v.i.* se comporter, se conduire; **well-behaved**, sage.
behavior [bi'heivjə], *n.* conduite, tenue, *f.*; comportement, *m.*; manières, *f.pl.*
behead [bi'hed], *v.t.* décapiter.
behest [bi'hest], *n.* commandement, ordre, *m.*
behind [bi'haind], *adv.* derrière, par derrière, en arrière.—*prep.* derrière, en arrière de; après, en retard de.—*n.* (*colloq.*) derrière, *m.*
behindhand [bi'haindhænd], *a.* and *adv.* en arrière, en retard.
behold [bi'hould], *v.t. irr.* (*conjug. like* HOLD) voir, regarder.—*int.* voyez! voici! voilà!
beholden [bi'houldən], *a.* redevable (à).
behoove [bi'houv], *v.i.impers.* incomber à; **it behooves**, il faut, il convient.
beige [beiʒ], *a.* and *n.* beige, *m.*
being [bi:iŋ], *n.* être, *m.*; existence, *f.*; **in being**, existant, vivant.—*pres.p.* [BE] étant; **for the time being**, pour le moment.
Beirut [bei'ru:t], Beyrouth, *m.*
belated [bi'leitid], *a.* attardé; tardif.

357

belch [beltʃ], v.t., v.i. roter, éructer; *to belch forth*, vomir; *to belch out flames*, vomir des flammes.—n. rot, m., éructation, f.

beleaguer [bi'li:gə], v.t. assiéger, investir.

belfry ['belfri], n. clocher, beffroi, m.

Belgian ['beldʒən], a. belge.—n. Belge (*personne*), m., f.

Belgium ['beldʒəm], la Belgique, f.

belie [bi'lai], v.t. démentir.

belief [bi'li:f], n. croyance, f.; credo, m.

believable [bi'li:vəbl], a. croyable.

believe [bi'li:v], v.t. croire.—v.i. croire (*en ou à*); *I believe not*, je crois que non, je ne le crois pas; *I believe so*, je crois que oui, je le crois.

believer [bi'li:və], n. croyant, m.

bell [bel], n. cloche, clochette, f.; grelot (*de chevaux etc.*), m.; sonnette (*de maison*), f.; timbre (*horloge, bicyclette*); (*Arch.*) vase, m.

belle [bel], n. belle, beauté, f.

bellicose ['belikous], a. belliqueux.

belligerent [bi'lidʒərənt], a. and n. belligérant, m.

bellow ['belou], v.i. beugler; mugir (*mer*); gronder (*tonnerre*).—n. beuglement, m.

bellows ['belouz], n.pl. soufflet, m.

bell ringer ['belriŋə], n. sonneur, m.

bell rope ['belroup], n. corde de cloche, f.

bell tower ['beltauə], n. campanile, f.; clocher, m.

belly ['beli], n. ventre, m.—v.i. bomber, s'enfler, se gonfler.

belong [bi'lɔŋ], v.i. appartenir, être (à).

belongings [bi'lɔŋiŋz], n.pl. effets, m.pl., affaires, f.pl.

beloved [bi'lʌvd, bi'lʌvid], a. cher, chéri, bien-aimé.

below [bi'lou], prep. sous, au-dessous de; en aval de.—adv. au-dessous, dessous, en bas; *here below*, ici-bas.

belt [belt], n. ceinture, f.; ceinturon; baudrier, m.; (*Mach.*) courroie, f.; *green belt*, zone verte, f.—v.t. ceindre, entourer.

bemoan [bi'moun], v.t. pleurer, déplorer.—v.i. gémir (*sur*).

bemuse [bi'mju:z], v.t. stupéfier.

bench [bentʃ], n. banc; gradin, m.; banquette, f.; établi (*de menuisier*); siège, tribunal, m.

bend [bend], v.t. irr. plier; courber, faire plier; incliner, tendre (*un arc*); fléchir (*le genou*); (*fig.*) appliquer.—v.i. plier, ployer; se courber, se pencher, s'incliner; s'appliquer (à); tourner; fléchir.—n. courbure, f.; coude, (*Motor.*) tournant, virage, m.

beneath [bi'ni:θ], prep. sous, au-dessous de.—adv. au-dessous, en bas.

Benedict ['benidikt], Benoît, m.

benediction [beni'dikʃən], n. bénédiction, f.

benefaction [beni'fækʃən], n. bienfait, m.

benefactor ['benifæktə], n. bienfaiteur, m.

benefactress ['benifæktris], n. bienfaitrice, f.

benefice ['benifis], n. bénéfice, m.

beneficence [bə'nefisəns], n. bienfaisance, f.

beneficial [beni'fiʃəl], a. salutaire, avantageux.

beneficiary [beni'fiʃəri], a. and n. bénéficiaire, m., f.

benefit ['benifit], n. bienfait, profit; bénéfice, m.; indemnité (*de chômage etc.*), f.—v.t. faire du bien à.—v.i. profiter.

Benelux ['benilʌks], Bénélux, m.

benevolence [bə'nevələns], n. bienveillance, f.

benevolent [bə'nevələnt], a. bienveillant, bienfaisant.

benighted [bi'naitid], a. anuité, surpris par la nuit; (*fig.*) ignorant.

benign [bi'nain], a. bénin, m., bénigne (*maladie, médecine etc.*), f.; bienfaisant (*personne*); doux, affable.

benignant [bi'nignənt], a. bon, bienveillant.

bent (1) [bent], past and p.p. [BEND].

bent (2) [bent], a. courbé, plié; *bent on*, résolu à.—n. penchant, m., disposition, tendance, f.

benumb [bi'nʌm], v.t. engourdir.

benzene ['benzi:n], n. benzène, m.

benzine ['benzi:n], n.pl. benzine, f.

bequeath [bi'kwi:ð], v.t. léguer.

bequest [bi'kwest], n. legs, m.

bereave [bi'ri:v], v.t. irr. priver (*de*).

bereavement [bi'ri:vmənt], n. privation, perte, f.; deuil, m.

beret ['berei], n. béret, m.

Bermuda(s) [bə:'mju:də(z)], (**the**) les (Îles) Bermudes, f.pl.

berry ['beri], n. baie, f.; grain, m.

berth [bə:θ], n. mouillage; lit, m., couchette, f.; poste, m., place, f., emploi, m.—v.t. amarrer à quai.—v.i. mouiller.

Bertha ['bə:θə]. Berthe, f.

beseech [bi'si:tʃ], v.t. irr. supplier, implorer.

beset [bi'set], v.t. irr. (*conjug. like* SET) obséder, entourer, assaillir.

besetting [bi'setiŋ], a. habituel, obsesseur.

beside [bi'said], prep. à côté de, auprès de; hors, hormis, excepté.

besides [bi'saidz], prep. outre, hors, hormis, excepté.—adv. d'ailleurs, du reste, en outre, de plus.

besiege [bi'si:dʒ], v.t. assiéger.

besmear [bi'smiə], v.t. barbouiller; souiller.

besmirch [bi'smə:tʃ], v.t. tacher, salir.

besom ['bi:zəm], n. balai, m.

bespatter [bi'spætə], v.t. éclabousser, couvrir de boue.

bespeak [bi'spi:k], v.t. irr. (*conjug. like* SPEAK) commander; retenir; annoncer, dénoter, accuser.

best [best], a. and n. le meilleur, la meilleure, le mieux; *at best*, au mieux, tout au plus; *best man* (*at weddings*), garçon d'honneur, m.; *to do one's best*, faire de son mieux; *to have the best of it*, avoir le dessus; *to make the best of it*, tirer le meilleur parti; *to the best of my belief*, autant que je sache.—adv. le mieux.

bestial ['bestial], a. bestial, de bête.

bestir [bi'stə:], v.t. remuer, mettre en mouvement.

bestow [bi'stou], v.t. donner, accorder.

bestrew [bi'stru:], v.t. irr. (*conjug. like* STREW) joncher (*de*), parsemer (*de*).

bestride [bi'straid], v.t. irr. (*conjug. like* STRIDE) enjamber, enfourcher (*un cheval*); être à cheval sur.

bet [bet], n. pari, m., gageure, f.—v.t., v.i. parier.

betake [bi'teik], v.r. irr. (*conjug. like* TAKE) *to betake oneself to*, se mettre à, s'en aller à, avoir recours à.

bethink [bi'θiŋk], v.t. irr. (*conjug. like* THINK) s'aviser (*de*); *to bethink oneself of*, se rappeler.

Bethlehem ['beθlihem, 'beθliəm]. Bethléem, *m.*

betide [bi'taid], *v.t.* irr. *woe betide you*, malheur à vous.—*v.i.* arriver, advenir.

betimes [bi'taimz], *adv.* de bonne heure.

betoken [bi'toukn], *v.t.* annoncer, présager.

betray [bi'trei], *v.t.* trahir; tromper; révéler; faire tomber, entraîner.

betrayal [bi'treiəl], *n.* trahison, perfidie, *f.*

betrayer [bi'treiə], *n.* traître, *m.*

betroth [bi'trouð], *v.t.* fiancer.

betrothal [bi'trouðəl], *n.* fiançailles, *f.pl.*

betrothed [bi'trouðd], *a.* and *n.* fiancé, *m.* fiancée, *f.*

better ['betə], *a.* meilleur; *to get the better of*, l'emporter sur.—*adv.* mieux; *better late than never*, mieux vaut tard que jamais; *better and better*, de mieux en mieux; *for better for worse*, vaille que vaille; *I had better*, je ferais mieux; *so much the better!* tant mieux!—*n.* meilleur; supérieur, *m.*—*v.t.* améliorer, avancer.

betterment ['betəmənt], *n.* amélioration, *f.*

betting ['betiŋ], *n.* paris, *m.pl.*

Betty ['beti]. Babette, *f.*

between [bi'twi:n], *prep.* entre.

*betwixt [bi'twikst], *prep.* entre; *betwixt and between*, entre les deux.

bevel ['bevəl], *a.* de biais, en biseau.—*n.* fausse équerre (*outil*), *f.*—*v.t.* tailler en biseau.—*v.i.* biaiser.

beverage ['bevəridʒ], *n.* boisson, *f.*; *breuvage, *m.*

bevy ['bevi], *n.* volée; troupe, compagnie, *f.*

bewail [bi'weil], *v.t.* pleurer, lamenter.

bewailing [bi'weiliŋ], *n.* lamentation, *f.*

beware [bi'wɛə], *v.i.* se garder (*de*); prendre garde (*à*); se méfier (*de*).

bewilder [bi'wildə], *v.t.* égarer, embarrasser.

bewildering [bi'wildəriŋ], *a.* déroutant, ahurissant.

bewilderment [bi'wildəmənt], *n.* égarement, *m.*

bewitch [bi'witʃ], *v.t.* ensorceler.

bewitching [bi'witʃiŋ], *a.* enchanteur, séduisant.

beyond [bi'jɔnd], *prep.* par delà, au delà de; au-dessus de; outre, hors de.—*adv.* là-bas. —*n.* au-delà, *m.*

bias ['baiəs], *a.* and *adv.* de biais, de travers.— *n.* biais, *m.*, pente, *f.*; penchant, parti pris, préjugé, *m.*—*v.t.* décentrer (*boule*); faire pencher; prévenir; influencer.

biased ['baiəst], *a.* décentré; partial, prédisposé.

bib (1) [bib], *n.* bavette, *f.*

bib (2) [bib], *n.* tacaud (*poisson*), *m.*

Bible [baibl], *n.* Bible, *f.*

biblical ['biblikəl], *a.* biblique.

biceps ['baiseps], *n.* (*Anat.*) biceps, *m.*

bicker ['bikə], *v.i.* se quereller, se chamailler.

bickering ['bikəriŋ], *n.* bisbille, *f.*, querelles, *f.pl.*

bicycle ['baisikl], *n.* bicyclette, *f.*; (*pop.*) vélo, *m.*, bécane, *f.*

bid [bid], *v.t.* irr. ordonner, dire, commander (*de*); inviter (*à*); offrir, enchérir; *to bid good-bye to*, dire adieu à.—*n.* enchère, *f.*

bidder ['bidə], *n.* enchérisseur, acheteur, *m.*

bidding ['bidiŋ], *n.* commandement, ordre, *m.*; invitation, prière, *f.*; enchères, *f.pl.*

bide [baid], *v.t.* irr. *archaic except in* to bide one's time, attendre le bon moment.

biennial [bai'eniəl], *a.* biennal; (*Bot.*) bisannuel.

biennially [bai'eniəli], *adv.* tous les deux ans.

bier [biə], *n.* civière, *f.*, corbillard, *m.*

big [big], *a.* gros; grand, vaste; enceinte, grosse (*d'enfant*), pleine (*bête*); (*fig.*) fier, hautain.

bigamist ['bigəmist], *n.* bigame, *m.*, *f.*

bigamy ['bigəmi], *n.* bigamie, *f.*

bigness ['bignis], *n.* grosseur, grandeur, *f.*

bigot ['bigət], *n.* bigot, cagot, *m.*, fanatique, *m.*, *f.*

bigoted ['bigətid], *a.* bigot.

bigotry ['bigətri], *n.* bigoterie, *f.*, sectarisme, fanatisme, *m.*

bigwig ['bigwig], *n.* (*fam.*) gros bonnet, *m.*

bike [baik], *n.* (*colloq.*) vélo, *m.*, bécane, *f.*

bikini [bi'ki:ni], *n.* (*Cost.*) bikini, *m.*

bile [bail], *n.* bile, *f.*

bilge [bildʒ], *n.* (*Naut.*) sentine, *f.*; (*colloq.*) bêtises, *f.pl.*

bilge water ['bildʒwɔ:tə], *n.* eau de la cale, *f.*

bilingual [bai'liŋwəl], *a.* bilingue.

bilious ['biljəs], *a.* bilieux.

bill (1) [bil], *n.* bec (*d'oiseau*), *m.*

bill (2) [bil], *n.* hallebarde, *f.*

bill (3) [bil], *n.* mémoire, compte, *m.*; facture (*invoice*), note (*hôtels etc.*), addition (*restaurants*); (*Comm.*) note, *f.*; billet, effet, *m.*; (*Banking*) lettre de change, *f.*; (*Parl.*) projet de loi, *m.*; affiche, *f.*, placard, *m.*; *bill of fare*, menu, *m.*, carte, *f.*; *bill of health*, patente de santé, *f.*; *post no bills!* défense d'afficher!

billet ['bilit], *n.* bûche, *f.*; (*Mil.*) billet de logement, *m.*—*v.t.*, *v.i.* loger chez l'habitant.

bill-hook ['bilhuk], *n.* serpe, *f.*, vouge, *m.*

billiard ['biljəd], *a.* de billard.

billiard ball ['biljədbɔ:l], *n.* bille, *f.*

billiards ['biljədz], *n.pl.* billard, *m.*; *to play a game of billiards*, faire une partie de billard.

billiard table ['biljədteibl], *n.* billard, *m.*

billion ['biljən], *n.* (*since 1948*) billion; (*Am.*) milliard, *m.*

billow ['bilou], *n.* grande vague, lame, *f.*— *v.i.* s'élever en vagues, rouler.

billowy ['biloui], *a.* houleux.

bill-sticker ['bilstikə], *n.* afficheur, colleur d'affiches, *m.*

billy goat ['biligout], *n.* bouc, *m.*

bin [bin], *n.* huche, *f.*, bac; coffre, *m.*

binary ['bainəri], *a.* binaire.

bind [baind], *v.t.* irr. lier; obliger; resserrer; border (*chaussures etc.*); garrotter; serrer; rendre constipé; relier (*livres*); *to be bound to*, être tenu de.—*n.* (*pop.*) *that's a bind*, quelle scie!

binder ['baində], *n.* lieur; relieur, *m.*; bande, attache, *f.*

binding ['baindiŋ], *a.* obligatoire; (*Med.*) astringent.—*n.* reliure, *f.*; bandeau, galon, *m.*, bordure, *f.*

bindweed ['baindwi:d], *n.* liseron, *m.*

binge [bindʒ], *n.* (*pop.*) bombe, *f.*; *to be on a binge*, faire la bombe.

binoculars [bi'nɔkjuləz], *n.pl.* jumelles, *f.pl.*

binomial [bai'noumiəl], *a.* (*Alg.*) binôme, *f.*

biochemist [baio'kemist], *n.* biochimiste, *m.*

biochemistry [baio'kemistri], *n.* biochimie, *f.*

biographer [bai'ɔgrəfə], *n.* biographe, *m.*
biography [bai'ɔgrəfi], *n.* biographie, *f.*
biologist [bai'ɔlədʒist], *n.* biologiste, biologue, *m.*
biology [bai'ɔlədʒi], *n.* biologie, *f.*
biped ['baiped], *n.* bipède, *m.*
birch [bəːtʃ], *n.* bouleau, *m.*; verges, *f.pl.*; **silver birch**, bouleau blanc.—*v.t.* fouetter.
bird [bəːd], *n.* oiseau; (*pop.*) type, *m.*; *little bird*, oiselet, *m.*
bird cage ['bəːdkeidʒ], *n.* cage d'oiseau, *f.*
bird-lime ['bəːdlaim], *n.* glu, *f.*
bird's-eye view ['bəːdzai'vjuː], *n.* vue à vol d'oiseau, *f.*
bird's nest ['bəːdznest], *n.* nid d'oiseau, *m.*
birth [bəːθ], *n.* naissance, *f.*; enfantement, *m.*; (*fig.*) origine, source, *f.*
birth control ['bəːθkəntroul], *n.* limitation des naissances, *f.*
birthday ['bəːθdei], *n.* anniversaire, *m.*
birthplace ['bəːθpleis], *n.* lieu de naissance, pays natal, *m.*
birth rate ['bəːθreit], *n.* natalité, *f.*
birthright ['bəːθrait], *n.* droit d'aînesse, *m.*
Biscay ['biskei]. la Biscaye, *f.*; *the Bay of Biscay*, le Golfe de Gascogne, *m.*
biscuit ['biskit], *n.* biscuit, *m.*
bisect [bai'sekt], *v.t.* couper en deux.
bishop ['biʃəp], *n.* évêque; (*Chess*) fou, *m.*
bishopric ['biʃəprik], *n.* évêché, *m.*
bit (1) [bit], *n.* morceau, *m.*; pièce (*de monnaie*), *f.*; (*colloq.*) brin, bout, peu, *m.*; mèche (*outil*); (*Naut.*) bitte, *f.*; mors (*de bride*), *m.*
bit (2) [bit], *past* [BITE].
bitch [bitʃ], *n.* chienne; femelle (*in compounds*), *f.*
bite [bait], *n.* morsure; piqûre, *f.*; coup de dent, *m.*, bouchée; (*Fishing*) touche, *f.*—*v.t. irr.* mordre; piquer; ronger; (*fig.*) attraper, pincer, couper (*vent*).—*v.i.* mordre.
biting ['baitiŋ], *a.* mordant, piquant; coupant (*vent*).
bitter ['bitə], *a.* amer, acerbe; (*fig.*) acharné, mordant, aigre.—*n.* amer, *m.*
bitterly ['bitəli], *adv.* avec amertume; amèrement.
bittern ['bitəːn], *n.* butor, *m.*
bitterness ['bitənis], *n.* amertume, aigreur, âpreté, *f.*
bitumen [bi'tjuːmən], *n.* bitume, *m.*
bivouac ['bivuæk], *n.* bivouac, *m.*—*v.i.* bivouaquer.
blab [blæb], *v.i.* jaser, bavarder.—*n.* bavard, *m.*
black [blæk], *a.* noir; (*fig.*) obscur, sombre, triste.—*v.t.* noircir; cirer (*chaussures*).—*n.* noir, *m.*
black-ball ['blækbɔːl], *n.* boule noire, *f.*—*v.t.* rejeter au scrutin.
black beetle ['blæk'biːtl], *n.* cafard, *m.*, blatte, *f.*
blackberry ['blækbəri], *n.* mûre (sauvage), *f.*
blackbird ['blækbəːd], *n.* merle, *m.*
blackboard ['blækbɔːd], *n.* tableau noir, *m.*
black currant ['blæk'karənt], *n.* cassis, *m.*
blacken ['blækən], *v.t., v.i.* noircir.
blackguard ['blægaːd], *n.* polisson, gredin, vaurien, *m.*
blacking ['blækiŋ], *n.* cirage (*chaussures*); noircissement, *m.*
blackish ['blækiʃ], *a.* noirâtre.
black lead [blæk'led], *n.* mine de plomb, *f.*

blackleg ['blækleg], *n.* (*Gambling*) escroc; (*Strikes*) renard, jaune, *m.*
blackmail ['blækmeil], *n.* chantage, *m.*—*v.t.* faire chanter.
blackmailer ['blækmeilə], *n.* maître-chanteur, *m.*
black market [blæk'maːkit], *n.* marché noir, *m.*
blackness ['blæknis], *n.* noirceur, *f.*
black-out ['blækaut], *n.* extinction des lumières, *f.*; black-out, *m.*
blacksmith ['blæksmiθ], *n.* forgeron, *m.*
bladder ['blædə], *n.* vessie; (*Bot.*) vésicule, *f.*
blade [bleid], *n.* lame (*de couteau etc.*), *f.*; brin (*d'herbe*), *m.*; pelle (*d'un aviron*), pale (*d'hélice*), *f.*; (*fig.*) gaillard (*personne*), *m.*
blain [blein], *n.* pustule, *f.*
blame [bleim], *n.* blâme, *m.*; faute, *f.*—*v.t.* blâmer, s'en prendre à; censurer, reprocher.
blameless ['bleimlis], *a.* innocent, sans tache.
blanch [blaːntʃ], *v.t.* blanchir; pâlir; faire pâlir; monder (*amandes*).—*v.i.* blanchir; pâlir.
blancmange [blə'mɔnʒ], *n.* blanc-manger, *m.*
bland [blænd], *a.* doux, aimable, affable.
blandish ['blændiʃ], *v.t.* caresser, flatter, cajoler.
blandishment ['blændiʃmənt], *n.* flatterie, *f.*
blank [blæŋk], *a.* blanc, en blanc; (*fig.*) vide, confus, déconcerté.—*n.* blanc; (*Lotteries*) billet blanc; (*fig.*) vide, *m.*, lacune, *f.*
blanket ['blæŋkit], *n.* couverture, *f.*
blare [bleə], *v.t.* faire retentir.—*v.i.* sonner (*comme une trompette*), cuivrer.—*n.* sonnerie, *f.*
blaspheme [blæs'fiːm], *v.t., v.i.* blasphémer.
blasphemer [blæs'fiːmə], *n.* blasphémateur, *m.*
blasphemous ['blæsfəməs], *a.* blasphématoire.
blasphemy ['blæsfəmi], *n.* blasphème, *m.*
blast [blaːst], *n.* vent, coup de vent; son (*d'un instrument à vent*), *m.*; explosion, *f.*—*v.t.* flétrir, brûler; détruire, ruiner; faire sauter.—*int.* sacrebleu!
blast furnace ['blaːstfəːnis], *n.* haut fourneau, *m.*
blasting ['blaːstiŋ], *a.* destructeur.—*n.* coup de mine, *m.*, explosion, *f.*
blatant ['bleitənt], *a.* bruyant, criard.
blatantly ['bleitəntli], *adv.* avec une vulgarité criarde.
blaze (1) [bleiz], *n.* flamme; flambée, *f.*; feu; (*fig.*) éclat, *m.*; étoile (*de cheval*), *f.*—*v.t. to blaze a trail*, se frayer un chemin.—*v.i.* être en flammes; flamber, brûler.
blaze (2) [bleiz], **blazon** (1) ['bleizən], *v.t.* proclamer; *to blaze abroad*, répandre, crier par-dessus les toits.
blazing ['bleiziŋ], *a.* flambant; enflammé, embrasé; (*fig.*) brillant.
blazon (2) ['bleizən], *n.* blason, *m.*—*v.t.* blasonner.
bleach [bliːtʃ], *v.t., v.i.* blanchir; (*Hairdressing*) oxygéner.—*n.* agent de blanchiment, *m.*, eau de javel; (*Hairdressing*) oxygénée, *f.*
bleak [bliːk], *a.* ouvert, sans abri; froid; désert; triste, morne.
bleakness ['bliːknis], *n.* exposition découverte, *f.*; froid, *m.*; tristesse, *f.*; aspect morne, *m.*
blear [bliə], **bleary** ['bliəri], *a.* larmoyant.
bleat [bliːt], *v.i.* bêler.—*n.* bêlement, *m.*

bleed [bli:d], *v.t. irr.* saigner; *(colloq.)* débourser.—*v.i.* saigner; pleurer *(vignes etc.)*.
bleeding ['bli:diŋ], *a.* saignant.—*n.* saignement, *m.*; *(Surg.)* saignée, *f.*
blemish ['blemiʃ], *v.t.* tacher, flétrir.—*n.* tache, flétrissure, *f.*, défaut, *m.*
blend [blend], *v.t.* mêler, mélanger; fondre.—*v.i.* se fondre; se marier *(à* ou *avec)*.—*n.* mélange, *m.*
bless [bles], *v.t.* bénir; rendre heureux, réjouir.
blessed [blest, 'blesid], *a.* béni, saint; bienheureux.
blessedness ['blesidnis], *n.* béatitude, félicité, *f.*, bonheur, *m.*
blessing ['blesiŋ], *n.* bénédiction, *f.*; bonheur, bien, *m.*
blight [blait], *v.t.* flétrir; brouir *(soleil)*; *(fig.)* frustrer, détruire.—*n.* brouissure *(des fleurs et des fruits)*; rouille *(du blé etc.)*; *(fig.)* flétrissure, *f.*
blind [blaind], *a.* aveugle; obscur; **blind alley**, impasse, *f.*; **blind in one eye**, borgne; **blind side**, côté faible, *m.*—*n.* store *(fenêtre)*; abat-jour, *m.*; banne *(de boutique)*; persienne *(à l'extérieur)*, *f.*; *(fig.)* voile, *m.*; **Venetian blind**, jalousie, *f.*—*v.t.* aveugler; *(fig.)* éblouir.
blindfold ['blaindfould], *v.t.* bander les yeux à.—*a.* les yeux bandés.
blindly ['blaindli], *adv.* aveuglément.
blind-man's buff ['blaind:mænz'bʌf], *n.* colin-maillard, *m.*
blindness ['blaindnis], *n.* cécité, *f.*; aveuglement, *m.*
blink [bliŋk], *v.i.* clignoter, cligner des yeux; vaciller *(lumière)*.—*n.* clignotement, *m.*
blinker ['bliŋkə], *n.* œillère *(de cheval)*, *f.*
bliss [blis], *n.* félicité, béatitude, *f.*
blissful ['blisful], *a.* bienheureux.
blister ['blistə], *n.* ampoule, bulle; cloque *(peinture)*, *f.*—*v.t.* faire venir des ampoules à.—*v.i.* se couvrir d'ampoules; se cloquer *(peinture)*.
blithe [blaið], *a.* gai, joyeux.
blithesome ['blaiðsəm], *a.* gai, joyeux.
blitz [blits], *n.* bombardement aérien *(2me guerre mondiale)*, *m.*
blizzard ['blizəd], *n.* tempête de neige, *f.*
bloat [blout], *v.t.* gonfler, bouffir, enfler.
bloater ['bloutə], *n.* hareng saur, *m.*
blob [blɔb], *n.* goutte *(d'eau)*, *f.*; pâté *(d'encre)*, *m.*
block [blɔk], *n.* bloc, *m.*, bille, *f.*; billot; *(fig.)* obstacle, *m.*; **block of houses**, pâté de maisons, *m.*; **block of flats**, immeuble, *m.*—*v.t.* bloquer; **to block up**, fermer, boucher.
blockade [blɔ'keid], *n.* blocus, *m.*—*v.t.* bloquer.
blockhead ['blɔkhed], *n.* imbécile, sot, *m.*
bloke [blouk], *n.* *(pop.)* type, *m.*
blond(e) [blɔnd], *a.* and *n.* blond, *m.*
blood [blʌd], *n.* sang, *m.*; *(fig.)* parenté, *f.*; tempérament, *m.*; race *(de cheval)*, *f.*
blood group ['blʌdgru:p], *n.* groupe sanguin, *m.*
bloodhound ['blʌdhaund], *n.* limier, *m.*
bloodless ['blʌdlis], *a.* exsangue; pâle.
bloodshed ['blʌdʃed], *n.* effusion de sang, *f.*
bloodshot ['blʌdʃɔt], *a.* injecté de sang.

bloodthirsty ['blʌdθə:sti], *a.* sanguinaire.
bloody ['blʌdi], *a.* sanglant, ensanglanté, sanguinaire.
bloom [blu:m], *n.* fleur, *f.*; duvet, velouté *(de fruit)*, *m.*; *(Metal.)* loupe, *f.*—*v.i.* fleurir; *(fig.)* être éclatant.
blooming ['blu:miŋ], *a.* fleurissant; *(pop.)* sacré, satané.—*n.* floraison, *f.*
blossom ['blɔsəm], *n.* fleur, *f.*—*v.i.* fleurir; être en fleur; **to blossom out**, s'épanouir.
blossoming ['blɔsəmiŋ], *n.* floraison, *f.*
blot [blɔt], *n.* tache, *f.*; pâté *(d'encre)*, *m.*—*v.t.* tacher, salir; faire un pâté sur; sécher *(avec papier buvard)*; **to blot out**, rayer, effacer.—*v.i.* boire *(papier)*.
blotch [blɔtʃ], *n.* pustule, tache, *f.*
blotchy ['blɔtʃi], *a.* tacheté.
blotting paper ['blɔtiŋpeipə], *n.* papier buvard, *m.*
blouse [blauz], *n.* blouse; chemisette, *f.*; corsage, chemisier, *m.*
blow (1) [blou], *n.* coup, *m.*; **to come to blows**, en venir aux mains.
blow (2) [blou], *v.t. irr.* souffler; sonner *(un instrument à vent)*; faire sauter *(plomb)*; **to blow away**, chasser; **to blow out**, éteindre *(une lumière)*; faire sauter *(la cervelle)*; **to blow up**, faire sauter, gonfler *(un pneu)*.—*v.i.* souffler; faire du vent; sauter *(plomb)*; claquer *(ampoule électrique)*; **to blow up**, sauter, éclater.
blow (3) [blou], *v.i.* s'épanouir *(fleurs)*.
blower ['blouə], *n.* souffleur; rideau de cheminée, *m.*
blow-lamp ['bloulæmp], *n.* lampe à souder, *f.*
blubber ['blʌbə], *n.* graisse de baleine, *f.*
bludgeon ['blʌdʒən], *n.* gourdin, *m.*; trique, *f.*
blue [blu:], *a.* bleu.—*n.* bleu; azur, *m.*—*v.t.* bleuir.
blue-bell ['blu:bel], *n.* jacinthe des prés, *f.*
blueness ['blu:nis], *n.* couleur bleue, *f.*
blue-print ['blu:print], *n.* dessin négatif; *(fam.)* bleu, projet, *m.*
bluestocking ['blu:stɔkiŋ], *n.* bas bleu, *m.*
bluff (1) [blʌf], *a.* escarpé, accore; brusque *(personne)*.—*n.* à-pic, *m.*, falaise, *f.*, escarpement, *m.*
bluff (2) [blʌf], *n.* bluff *(feinte)*, *m.*—*v.t.* bluffer.
bluffness ['blʌfnis], *n.* rudesse, brusquerie, *f.*
bluish ['blu:iʃ], *a.* bleuâtre.
blunder ['blʌndə], *n.* bévue, étourderie, balourdise, *f.*—*v.t.* embrouiller.—*v.i.* faire une bévue.
blunderbuss ['blʌndəbʌs], *n.* tromblon, *m.*
blunderer ['blʌndərə], *n.* maladroit, étourdi, *m.*
blundering ['blʌndəriŋ], *a.* maladroit.
blunt [blʌnt], *a.* émoussé; *(fig.)* brusque, bourru.—*v.t.* émousser; épointer; *(fig.)* amortir.
bluntly ['blʌntli], *adv.* brusquement, carrément.
bluntness ['blʌntnis], *n.* état émoussé, *m.*; brusquerie, *f.*
blur [blə:], *v.t.* tacher, barbouiller; *(fig.)* brouiller.
blurt [blə:t], *v.t.* **to blurt out**, laisser échapper.
blush [blʌʃ], *v.i.* rougir.—*n.* rougeur, *f.*; **at the first blush**, au premier abord.
blushing ['blʌʃiŋ], *a.* rougissant.

bluster ['blʌstə], *v.i.* tempêter, crier (*contre*), fanfaronner.—*n.* fracas, tapage, *m.*, fanfaronnade, fureur (*d'une tempête*), *f.*
blusterer ['blʌstərə], *n.* fanfaron, *m.*, bravache, *m.*, *f.*
blustering ['blʌstəriŋ], *a.* orageux; bruyant; bravache.
boa ['bouə], *n.* boa, *m.*
boar [bɔ:], *n.* verrat, *m.*; *wild boar*, sanglier, *m.*
board [bɔ:d], *n.* planche, *f.*; écriteau, *m.*; table, pension, *f.*; conseil, *m.*, administration, *f.*; (*Bookb.*) carton; (*Tailors*) établi; (*Naut.*) bord; (*Chess*) échiquier, *m.*; *Board of Trade*, ministère du commerce, *m.*; *on board*, à bord.—*v.t.* planchéier; nourrir; (*Naut.*) aborder; *to board out*, mettre en pension.—*v.i.* se mettre en pension.
boarder ['bɔ:də], *n.* pensionnaire; interne, *m.*, *f.*
boarding ['bɔ:diŋ], *n.* planchéiage, plancher, *m.*; table, pension, *f.*; (*Naut.*) abordage, *m.*
boarding house ['bɔ:diŋhaus], *n.* pension de famille, *f.*
boarding school ['bɔ:diŋsku:l], *n.* pensionnat, internat, *m.*
boast [boust], *v.i.* se vanter, se glorifier.—*n.* vanterie, *f.*
boaster ['boustə], *n.* vantard, *m.*
boastful ['boustful], *a.* vantard.
boat [bout], *n.* bateau, canot, *m.*, barque, *f.*
boating ['boutiŋ], *n.* canotage, *m.*
boatman ['boutmən], *n.* batelier, *m.*
boatswain, **bosun** [bousn], *n.* maître d'équipage, *m.*
bob [bɔb], *n.* (*Hairdressing*) perruque ronde; lentille (*d'un pendule*); secousse, *f.*; coup, *m.*, tape; petite révérence, *f.*—*v.t.* écourter (*la queue*); secouer, ballotter, balancer.—*v.i.* pendiller, osciller, s'agiter; *to bob up*, revenir à la surface.
bobbin ['bɔbin], *n.* bobine, *f.*
bode [boud], *v.t.*, *v.i.* présager; *to bode well* (*ill*), être de bon (mauvais) augure.
bodice ['bɔdis], *n.* corsage, *m.*
bodiless ['bɔdilis], *a.* sans corps.
bodily ['bɔdili], *a.* corporel, matériel.—*adv.* corporellement; entièrement, en masse.
boding ['boudiŋ], *n.* présage, pressentiment, *m.*
bodkin ['bɔdkin], *n.* poinçon; passe-lacet, *m.*
body ['bɔdi], *n.* corps; fond; cœur, centre; gros (*d'une armée*), *m.*; bande, troupe; nef (*d'une église*); personne; sève (*de vin*), carrosserie (*d'un véhicule*), *f.*; corsage (*d'une robe*), *m.*
body-guard ['bɔdiga:d], *n.* garde du corps, *m.*
body-work ['bɔdiwə:k], *n.* carrosserie, *f.*
boffin ['bɔfin], *n.* (*fam.*) savant, inventeur, *m.*
bog [bɔg], *n.* marécage, *m.*, fondrière, *f.*; *to get bogged down*, s'embourber.
boggle [bɔgl], *v.i.* hésiter (*à*); reculer (*devant*).
boggy ['bɔgi], *a.* marécageux.
bogie ['bougi], *n.* (*Rail.*) bogie, *m.*
bogus ['bougəs], *a.* faux, simulé.
boil (1) [bɔil], *v.t.* faire bouillir; faire cuire à l'eau.—*v.i.* bouillir; bouillonner; *to boil over*, déborder.
boil (2) [bɔil], *n.* (*Med.*) furoncle, clou, *m.*

boiled [bɔild], *a.* bouilli, cuit à l'eau; *a boiled egg*, un œuf à la coque.
boiler ['bɔilə], *n.* chaudière, *f.*; réservoir à eau chaude, *m.*
boiler house ['bɔiləhaus], *n.* salle des chaudières, *f.*
boiler maker ['bɔiləmeikə], *n.* chaudronnier, *m.*
boiler suit ['bɔiləsju:t], *n.* bleus, *m.pl.*
boiling ['bɔiliŋ], *a.* en ébullition.—*n.* bouillonnement, *m.*
boisterous ['bɔistərəs], *a.* orageux, violent; bruyant, turbulent.
boisterously ['bɔistərəsli], *adv.* impétueusement; violemment; bruyamment.
boisterousness ['bɔistərəsnis], *n.* impétuosité, turbulence; violence, *f.*
bold [bould], *a.* hardi; audacieux, téméraire; impudent, effronté; saillant, net.
bold-faced ['bouldfeist], *a.* impudent, effronté.
boldly ['bouldli], *adv.* hardiment, intrépidement; impudemment.
boldness ['bouldnis], *n.* hardiesse, audace; assurance, effronterie, *f.*
bole [boul], *n.* tronc, fût (*d'un arbre*), *m.*
Bolivia [bə'liviə]. la Bolivie, *f.*
Bolivian [bə'liviən], *a.* bolivien.—*n.* Bolivien (*personne*), *m.*
bollard ['bɔləd], *n.* (*Naut.*) pieu d'amarrage, *m.*
Bolshevik ['bɔlʃivik], *a.* bolchevik.—*n.* Bolchevik, *m.*
Bolshevism ['bɔlʃivizm], *n.* bolchevisme, *m.*
bolster ['boulstə], *n.* traversin; coussin, *m.*—*v.t.* mettre un traversin sous; (*fig.*) appuyer, soutenir.
bolt [boult], *n.* verrou; pêne; (*Tech.*) boulon, *m.*, cheville, *f.*; (*fig.*) trait, *m.*, flèche; fuite, *f.*; *thunder-bolt*, éclair, *m.*—*v.t.* verrouiller; fermer au verrou; gober, avaler (*to swallow*).—*v.i.* décamper, filer; s'emporter, s'emballer (*cheval*).
bomb [bɔm], *n.* bombe, *f.*—*v.t.* bombarder.
bombard [bɔm'ba:d], *v.t.* bombarder.
bombardier [bɔmbə'diə], *n.* bombardier, *m.*
bombardment [bɔm'ba:dmənt], *n.* bombardement, *m.*
bombast ['bɔmbæst], *n.* emphase, enflure, *f.*, boursouflage, *m.*
bombastic [bɔm'bæstik], *a.* enflé, ampoulé.
bomber ['bɔmə], *n.* avion de bombardement, *m.*
bombing ['bɔmiŋ], *n.* bombardement, *m.*
bona fide [bounə'faidi], *a.* sérieux, de bonne foi.
bond [bɔnd], *n.* lien, *m.*; liaison, *f.*; engagement, *m.*; obligation, *f.*; (*Fin.*) bon, *m.*; *in bonds*, dans les fers.—*v.t.* entreposer; *bonded goods*, marchandises entreposées, *f.pl.*
bondage ['bɔndidʒ], *n.* esclavage, *m.*, servitude, *f.*
bond-holder ['bɔndhouldə], *n.* obligataire, *m.*, *f.*, porteur d'obligation, *m.*
bondman ['bɔndmən], **bondsman** ['bɔndzmən], *n.* (*pl.* **-men** [men]) serf, esclave, *m.*
bondwoman ['bɔndwumən], **bondswoman** ['bɔndzwumən], *n.* (*pl.* **-women** [wimin]) esclave, *f.*
bone [boun], *n.* os, *m.*; arête (*de poisson*), baleine (*whale bone*); ivoire (*des dents*), *f.*; (*pl.*) ossements, *m.pl.*; *bone of contention*, pomme de discorde, *f.*—*v.t.* désosser.

bower

bonfire ['bɔnfaiə], *n.* feu de joie *ou* de jardin, *m.*

bonnet ['bɔnit], *n.* chapeau (*de femme*); bonnet (*d'un Écossais*).

bonny ['bɔni], *a.* gentil, joli, joyeux, gai.

bonus ['bounəs], *n.* boni, *m.*; prime, *f.*

bony ['bouni], *a.* osseux; plein d'arêtes (*poisson*).

boo [bu:], *v.t., v.i.* huer.—*n.* huée, *f.*—*int.* hou!

booby ['bu:bi], *n.* nigaud, benêt, *m.*

booby trap ['bu:bitræp], *n.* attrape-nigaud, *m.*; (*Mil.*) mine-piège, *f.*

book [buk], *n.* livre, livret; registre; bouquin (*vieux livre*), *m.*; **exercise book**, cahier, *m.*—*v.t.* retenir, réserver; enregistrer, inscrire.

bookbinder ['bukbaində], *n.* relieur, *m.*

bookbinding ['bukbaindiŋ], *n.* reliure, *f.*

book-case ['bukkeis], *n.* bibliothèque, *f.*

booking office ['bukiŋɔfis], *n.* bureau d'enregistrement; guichet (*de gare etc.*), *m.*

bookish ['bukiʃ], *a.* studieux; livresque (*style*).

book-keeper ['bukki:pə], *n.* teneur de livres, *m.*

book-keeping ['bukki:piŋ], *n.* comptabilité, *f.*

book lover ['buklʌvə], *n.* bibliophile, *m., f.*

bookseller ['buksələ], *n.* libraire, *m., f.*

bookshelf ['bukʃelf], *n.* rayon (*de bibliothèque*), *m.*

book-shop ['bukʃɔp], (*Am.*) **bookstore** ['bukstɔ:], *n.* librairie, *f.*

book-stall ['bukstɔ:l], *n.* (*Rail.*) bibliothèque, *f.*, étalage de livres, *m.*

boom [bu:m], *n.* (*Naut.*) bout-dehors, *m.*; chaîne (*des ports etc.*); (*Cine.*) perche, *f.*; grondement, retentissement, *m.*; (*fig., Comm.*) grande (et rapide) hausse, *f.*—*v.i.* gronder, retentir; (*Comm.*) être en hausse, prospérer.

boomerang ['bu:məraŋ], *n.* boumerang, *m.*

boon (1) [bu:n], *n.* bienfait, *m.*, faveur, *f.*; bien, avantage, *m.*

boon (2) [bu:n], *a.* gai, joyeux.

boor [buə], *n.* rustre, *m.*

boorish ['buəriʃ], *a.* rustre, grossier.

boost [bu:st], *v.t.* (*Am.*) pousser (*par derrière*); lancer; (*Elec.*) survolter.

boot (1) [bu:t], *n.* chaussure, bottine, botte, *f.*

boot (2) [bu:t], *n.* (*used only in*) **to boot**, en sus, par-dessus le marché.

booth [bu:ð], *n.* baraque, tente; cabine, *f.*

booty ['bu:ti], *n.* butin, *m.*

borax ['bɔ:ræks], *n.* borax, *m.*

border ['bɔ:də], *n.* bord, *m.*; bordure (*de vêtement etc.*); frontière (*d'un pays*), *f.*; (*Gard.*) parterre, *m.*, platebande, *f.*—*v.t.* border.—*v.i.* aboutir, toucher (*à*); avoisiner.

bordering ['bɔ:dəriŋ], *a.* contigu, voisin.

border-line ['bɔ:dəlain], *a.* indéterminé.—*n.* ligne de démarcation, *f.*

bore (1) [bɔ:], *v.t.* percer, forer; sonder, creuser; (*fig.*) ennuyer, embêter.—*v.i.* percer.—*n.* trou; calibre; (*fig.*) fâcheux (*personne*); ennui (*chose*); mascaret (*d'un fleuve*), *m.*

bore (2) [bɔ:], *past* [BEAR].

boredom ['bɔ:dəm], *n.* ennui, *m.*

born [bɔ:n], *a.* né; **to be born**, naître.

borough ['bʌrə], *n.* bourg, *m.*, ville, *f.*

borrow ['bɔrou], *v.t.* emprunter (*à*).

borrower ['bɔrouə], *n.* emprunteur, *m.*

bosh [bɔʃ], *n.* blague, farce, *f.*, bêtises, *f.pl.* galimatias, *m.*

bosom ['buzəm], *n.* sein; (*fig.*) cœur, *m.*

boss (1) [bɔs], *n.* bosse, *f.*; moyeu (*d'une roue*), *m.*

boss (2) [bɔs], *n.* patron, chef, contremaître, *m.*—*v.t.* diriger, contrôler; régenter.

bosun [BOATSWAIN].

botanic [bɔ'tænik], **botanical** [bɔ'tænikəl], *a.* botanique.

botanist ['bɔtənist], *n.* botaniste, *m., f.*

botany ['bɔtəni], *n.* botanique, *f.*

botch [bɔtʃ], *n.* pustule, *f.*; (*fig.*) ravaudage, replâtrage, travail mal fait, *m.*—*v.t.* ravauder, replâtrer, saboter.

both [bouθ], *a.* and *pron.* tous les deux, tous deux, l'un et l'autre.—*conj.* tant, à la fois.

bother ['bɔðə], *v.t.* ennuyer, tracasser; (*colloq.*) embêter.—*n.* ennui, tracas, embêtement, *m.*

bottle [bɔtl], *n.* bouteille, *f.*; flacon; biberon (*d'enfant*), *m.*; botte (*de foin*), *f.*; **hot water bottle**, bouillotte, *f.*—*v.t.* mettre en bouteille.

bottle-neck ['bɔtlnek], *n.* goulot; embouteillage (*de circulation routière*), *m.*

bottling ['bɔtliŋ], *n.* mise en bouteilles, *f.*

bottom ['bɔtəm], *n.* fond; bas; dessous, pied; derrière, *m.*; base; (*Naut.*) carène, *f.*

bottomless ['bɔtəmlis], *a.* sans fond.

boudoir ['bu:dwa:], *n.* boudoir, *m.*

bough [bau], *n.* branche, *f.*, rameau, *m.*

boulder ['bouldə], *n.* grosse pierre, *f.* bloc, *m.*

bounce [bauns], *v.i.* sauter, (re)bondir.—*n.* saut, (re)bond, *m.*

bouncer ['baunsə], *n.* (*pop.*) expulseur, videur, *m.*

bound (1) [baund], *n.* bond, saut *m.*—*v.i.* bondir, sauter.

bound (2) [baund], *n.* borne, limite, *f.*—*v.t.* borner, limiter.

bound (3) [baund], *a.* (*Naut.*) allant (*à*), en partance (*pour*).

bound (4) [baund], *past* and *p.p.* [BIND].

boundary ['baundri], *n.* limite, borne, frontière, *f.*

bounden ['baundən], *a.* obligatoire, impérieux.

boundless ['baundlis], *a.* sans bornes; illimité.

bounteous ['bauntiəs], **bountiful** ['bauntiful], *a.* libéral, généreux; abondant.

bounty ['baunti], *n.* bonté, générosité, libéralité, *f.*; don, *m.*

bouquet [bu'kei], *n.* bouquet, *m.*

bourne, bourn [bɔ:n], *n.* borne, frontière, limite, *f.*; terme, but, *m.*

bout [baut], *n.* tour, *m.*, partie, *f.*; accès, *m.*, crise, *f.*

bovine ['bouvain], *a.* bovin.

bow (1) [bau], *v.t.* courber, plier, fléchir, incliner.—*v.i.* se courber, s'incliner; saluer; se soumettre (*à*).—*n.* salut, *m.*, révérence, *f.*

bow (2) [bau], *n.* (*Naut.*) avant, bossoir, *m.*

bow (3) [bou], *n.* arc; archet (*de violon*); nœud (*rubans*), *m.*

bowels ['bauəlz], *n.pl.* entrailles, *f.pl.*, intestins, boyaux, *m.pl.*; (*fig.*) compassion, *f.*

bower ['bauə], *n.* berceau de verdure, *m.*, tonnelle, *f.*

363

bowl

bowl [boul], *n.* bol, vase, *m.*, coupe; jatte, *f.*; fourneau (*d'une pipe*), *m.*; boule (*sphère*), *f.*; (*pl.*) boules, *f.pl.*; **to play** (*at*) **bowls**, jouer aux boules.—*v.t.* rouler, faire rouler; (*Cricket*) lancer, bôler.

bow-legged ['bouleg(i)d], *a.* à jambes arquées, bancal.

bowler(-hat) ['boulə(hæt)], *n.* chapeau melon, *m.*

bowsprit ['bousprit], *n.* (*Naut.*) beaupré, *m.*

bow tie ['bou'tai], *n.* nœud carré, *m.*

bow window ['bou'windou], *n.* fenêtre en saillie, *f.*

box (1) [bɔks], *n.* boîte, *f.*; coffret (*petit*); coffre (*grand*), *m.*, caisse; malle; (*Theat.*) loge, *f.*; buis (*arbre*), *m.*—*v.t.* enfermer dans une boîte, emboîter, encaisser.

box (2) [bɔks], *v.t.* souffleter, gifler.—*v.i.* boxer.—*n.* soufflet, *m.*, gifle, *f.*

boxer ['bɔksə], *n.* boxeur, pugiliste, *m.*

boxing ['bɔksiŋ], *n.* la boxe, *f.*

box office ['bɔksɔfis], *n.* (*Theat.*) bureau de location, *m.*

boy [bɔi], *n.* garçon, petit garçon; fils, *m.*

boycott ['bɔikɔt], *v.t.* boycotter.

boycotting ['bɔikɔtiŋ], *n.* boycottage, *m.*

boyhood ['bɔihud], *n.* enfance, adolescence, *f.*

boyish ['bɔiiʃ], *a.* puéril; d'enfant, enfantin.

boy scout ['bɔi'skaut], *n.* (jeune) éclaireur, scout, *m.*

bra [bra:], (*pop.*) [BRASSIÈRE].

brace [breis], *n.* couple (*gibier*); paire (*pistolets*), *f.*; vilebrequin (*outil*), *m.*; (*pl.*) bretelles, *f.pl.*—*v.t.* lier, serrer, attacher; (*fig.*) fortifier.

bracelet ['breislit], *n.* bracelet, *m.*

bracing ['breisiŋ], *a.* fortifiant, tonifiant.

bracken ['brækən], *n.* fougère, *f.*

bracket ['brækit], *n.* console, applique, *f.*, tasseau, *m.*; accolade, *f.*; bras (*pour une lampe etc.*), *m.*; (*Print.*) parenthèse, *f.*

brackish ['brækiʃ], *a.* saumâtre.

bradawl ['brædɔ:l], *n.* poinçon, *m.*

brag [bræg], *v.i.* se vanter.—*n.* fanfaronnade, vanterie, *f.*

braggart ['brægət], *n.* fanfaron, *m.*

braid [breid], *n.* tresse; soutache, ganse, *f.*; lacet, galon, *m.*—*v.t.* tresser, natter, soutacher.

braille [breil], *n.* braille, *m.*

brain [brein], *n.* cerveau (*organe*), *m.*; cervelle (*substance*), *f.*; (*fig.*) jugement, esprit, *m.*; tête, *f.*

brainless ['breinlis], *a.* sans cervelle; stupide.

brainy ['breini], *a.* intelligent.

braise [breiz], *v.t.* braiser.

brake (1) [breik], *n.* fourré, hallier, *m.*, fougère (*thicket*), *f.*

brake (2) [breik], *n.* frein; *m.*; **to put on the brake,** serrer le frein.—*v.t.*, *v.i.* freiner.

braking ['breikiŋ], *n.* freinage, *m.*

bramble ['bræmbl], *n.* ronce, *f.*

bran [bræn], *n.* son, *m.*

branch [bra:ntʃ], *n.* branche, *f.*, rameau, *m.*; succursale (*d'une banque etc.*), *f.*—*v.i.* **to branch off,** s'embrancher, bifurquer; **to branch out,** se ramifier.

brand [brænd], *n.* brandon, tison; fer chaud, stigmate, *m.*; flétrissure (*d'infamie*); (*Comm.*) marque, *f.*—*v.t.* marquer au fer chaud; flétrir; (*fig.*) stigmatiser (*de*).

brandish ['brændiʃ], *v.t.* brandir.

brand-new ['brænd'nju:], *a.* tout (flambant) neuf.

brandy ['brændi], *n.* eau-de-vie, *f.*, cognac, *m.*

brash [bræʃ], *a.* effronté, présomptueux.

brass [bra:s], *n.* cuivre jaune, laiton; (*fig.*) toupet, *m.*, effronterie, *f.*

brassière ['bræsjɛə], *n.* soutien-gorge, *m.*

brat [bræt], *n.* marmot, bambin, *m.*

bravado [brə'va:dou], *n.* bravade, *f.*

brave [breiv], *a.* courageux, brave, vaillant; (*fig.*) fameux, excellent.—*v.t.* braver, défier.

bravely ['breivli], *adv.* courageusement, bravement.

bravery ['breivəri], *n.* bravoure, *f.*, courage, *m.*

brawl [brɔ:l], *n.* dispute, rixe, querelle, *f.*; bruit, tapage, *m.*—*v.i.* brailler, disputer.

brawler ['brɔ:lə], *n.* tapageur; braillard, querelleur, *m.*

brawn [brɔ:n], *n.* pâté de cochon, fromage de tête, *m.*; (*fig.*) muscles, *m.pl.*

brawny ['brɔ:ni], *a.* charnu, musculeux.

bray (1) [brei], *v.t.* broyer, piler.

bray (2) [brei], *v.i.* braire (*ânes etc.*); (*fig.*) résonner.—*n.* braiment, *m.*

brazen ['breizən], *a.* d'airain; (*fig.*) effronté, impudent.—*v.t.* **to brazen it out,** payer d'effronterie.

brazen-faced ['breizənfeist], *a.* à front d'airain; effronté.

brazier ['breiziə], *n.* chaudronnier, *m.*

Brazil [brə'zil]. le Brésil, *m.*

Brazilian [brə'ziljən], *a.* brésilien.—*n.* Brésilien (*personne*), *m.*

Brazil nut [brə'zilnʌt], *n.* noix du Brésil, *f.*

breach [bri:tʃ], *n.* brèche, rupture; (*fig.*) violation, infraction, *f.*—*v.t.* battre en brèche.

bread [bred], *n.* pain, *m.*; **brown bread,** pain bis; **stale bread,** pain rassis.

breadcrumb ['bredkrʌm], *n.* miette, *f.*; (*pl.*) (*Cook.*) chapelure, *f.*, gratin, *m.*

breadth [bredθ], *n.* largeur, *f.*

bread-winner ['bredwinə], *n.* soutien de famille, *m.*

break [breik], *v.t. irr.* casser; briser; rompre; violer, enfreindre; ruiner; défricher (*terrain inculte*); (*fig.*) faire part de, communiquer (*une nouvelle*); amortir (*un choc*); **to break through the sound barrier,** franchir le mur du son.—*v.i.* se casser, se briser, se rompre, casser, rompre; éclater (*tempête etc.*); (*Comm.*) faire faillite; poindre (*jour*); changer (*temps*); **to break away,** se détacher; (*Mil.*) rompre les rangs; (*Box.*) cesser le corps-à-corps; **to break down,** s'abattre, se délabrer, s'effondrer, s'écrouler; (*Motor.*) tomber en panne; défaillir, s'altérer (*santé*); fondre en larmes; **to break in,** pénétrer dans; (*Motor.*) roder; **to break into,** entamer; éclater en; **to break loose,** s'échapper, s'évader, (*fig.*) s'émanciper; **to break off,** rompre, s'arrêter; **to break out,** éclater, se déclarer (*maladie*); jaillir, paraître, s'échapper; **to break up,** se disperser; entrer en vacances; **to break with,** rompre avec.—*n.* rupture, brisure, fracture; trouée, fente; (*fig.*) interruption, *f.*; changement (*de temps*); arrêt (*dans un voyage*), *m.*; (*Sch.*) récréation, *f.*; **break of day,** point du jour, *m.*

breakage ['breikidʒ], n. rupture, cassure; (Comm.) casse, f.
breakdown ['breikdaun], n. (Motor., Mech.) panne; (fig.) débâcle, f.; **nervous breakdown**, dépression nerveuse, f.
breaker ['breikə], n. infracteur, briseur; violateur; brisant (mer), m.
breakfast ['brekfəst], n. petit déjeuner, m.— v.i. prendre le petit déjeuner.
breakwater ['breikwɔ:tə], n. brise-lames, m., digue, jetée, f.
bream [bri:m], n. (Ichth.) brème, f.
breast [brest], n. sein, m., poitrine, f.; (fig.) cœur, m., âme, conscience, f.; poitrail (d'un cheval), m.
breastplate ['brestpleit], n. cuirasse, f.
breath [breθ], n. haleine, respiration, f., souffle, m.; (fig.) vie, existence, f.; **to be out of breath**, être hors d'haleine ou tout essoufflé.
breathe [bri:ð], v.t. respirer, souffler; **to breathe in**, aspirer; **to breathe one's last**, rendre le dernier soupir; **to breathe out**, exhaler.—v.i. respirer; souffler, reprendre haleine.
breathing-space ['bri:ðiŋ'speis], n. temps de respirer, relâche, répit, m.
breathless ['breθlis], a. hors d'haleine, essoufflé, haletant.
breech [bri:tʃ], n. culasse (fusil), f.—v.t. culotter.
breeches ['britʃiz], n.pl. culotte, f.
breed [bri:d], v.t. irr. élever; faire naître.— v.i. multiplier, se reproduire.—n. race, f.
breeder ['bri:də], n. éleveur, m.
breeding ['bri:diŋ], n. élevage (de bestiaux etc.), m.; reproduction; éducation, f.; **good breeding**, politesse, f., savoir-vivre, m.
breeze [bri:z], n. (forte) brise, f., vent assez fort, m.
breezy ['bri:zi], a. frais; jovial.
brevity ['breviti], n. brièveté, concision, f.
brew [bru:], v.t. brasser; faire une infusion; (fig.) tramer, machiner.—v.i. faire de la bière; (fig.) se préparer, se tramer, couver.
brewer ['bru:ə], n. brasseur, m.
brewery ['bru:əri], n. brasserie, f.
bribe [braib], n. présent (dans le but de corrompre); pot-de-vin, m.—v.t. gagner, corrompre, acheter.
bribery ['braibəri], n. corruption, f.
brick [brik], a. de briques, en briques.—n. brique, f.; (fig.) brave garçon, bon enfant, m.
brickbat ['brikbæt], n. briqueton, m.
brick kiln ['brikkiln], n. four à briques, m.
bricklayer ['brikleiə], n. maçon, m.
bridal ['braidl], a. nuptial, de noces.—n. fête nuptiale, noce, f.
bride [braid], n. nouvelle mariée, mariée, f.
bridegroom ['braidgru:m], n. nouveau marié, m.
bridesmaid ['braidzmeid], n. demoiselle d'honneur, f.
bridge [bridʒ], n. pont, m.; passerelle (de navire etc.), f.; chevalet (d'instrument à cordes); dos (du nez); (Cards) bridge, m.— v.t. jeter un pont sur; (fig.) combler (une lacune).
bridge-head ['bridʒhed], n. tête de pont, f., point d'appui, m.
Bridget ['bridʒit]. Brigitte, f.

bridle [braidl], n. bride, f.; (fig.) frein, m.— v.t. brider; (fig.) mettre un frein à.—v.i. redresser la tête, se rebiffer.
brief [bri:f], a. bref, court; (fig.) concis.—n. abrégé; dossier, m.—v.t. confier une cause à; donner des instructions à.
brief-case ['bri:fkeis], n. serviette, f.
briefly ['bri:fli], adv. brièvement, en peu de mots.
brier ['braiə], n. bruyère, f.; églantier, m.; (pl.) ronces, f.pl.
brig [brig], n. (Naut.) brick, m.
brigade [bri'geid], n. brigade, f.
brigadier [brigə'diə], n. général de brigade, m.
brigand ['brigənd], n. brigand, m.
brigantine ['brigənti:n], n. brigantin, m.
bright [brait], a. brillant; poli; clair, lumineux; éclatant, vif; (fig.) joyeux, intelligent.
brighten [braitn], v.t. faire briller; éclaircir, égayer; polir; (fig.) illustrer, embellir; dégourdir.—v.i. s'éclaircir; briller, étinceler.
brightly ['braitli], adv. brillamment, avec éclat.
brightness ['braitnis], n. brillant, m.; clarté, f.; éclat, m.; (fig.) joie, vivacité; intelligence, f.
brill [bril], n. (Ichth.) barbue, f.
brilliance ['briljəns], **brilliancy** ['briljənsi], n. lustre, éclat, m.
brilliant ['briljənt], a. brillant, éclatant.—n. brillant (diamant), m.
brilliantly ['briljəntli], adv. brillamment, avec éclat.
brim [brim], n. bord, m.—v.i. être plein jusqu'au bord; **brimming over**, débordant.
brimful ['brimful], a. rempli jusqu'au bord, tout plein.
brimstone ['brimstən], n. soufre, m.
brindle(d) [brindl(d)], a. tacheté, bringé.
brine [brain], n. saumure, f.
bring [briŋ], v.t. irr. apporter (choses); amener (personnes et animaux); conduire; porter (to carry); transporter; réduire (to reduce); (fig.) mettre; **to bring about**, amener, causer, opérer, provoquer; **to bring down**, descendre, abattre; **to bring forth**, produire, mettre au monde, mettre bas; **to bring forward**, amener, avancer; **to bring in**, faire entrer, rapporter; **to bring into play**, mettre en œuvre; **to bring off**, tirer d'affaire, sauver; conduire à bien, réussir; **to bring on**, amener, occasionner; **to bring to again**, faire reprendre connaissance à; **to bring together**, réunir, assembler, réconcilier; **to bring up**, nourrir, élever.
brink [briŋk], n. bord, m.
briny ['braini], a. saumâtre, salé; (fig.) amer.
brisk [brisk], a. vif; (fig.) animé, actif, gai, frais, dispos.
briskly ['briskli], adv. vivement.
briskness ['brisknis], n. vivacité; activité, f.
bristle [brisl], n. soie, f.; poil raide, m.—v.i. se hérisser (de); se raidir (contre).
bristling ['brisliŋ], **bristly** ['brisli], a. hérissé (de); (Bot.) poilu.
Britain ['britən]. la Grande-Bretagne, f.
Britannic [bri'tænik], a. (rare) britannique.
British ['britiʃ], a. britannique; **the British**, les Anglais, les Britanniques, m.pl.

365

Brittany ['britəni]. la Bretagne, f.
brittle [britl], a. fragile, cassant.
brittleness ['britlnis], n. fragilité, f.
broach [brout∫], n. broche, f.—v.t. embrocher; mettre (un tonneau) en perce; introduire, entamer (un sujet).
broad [brɔ:d], a. large, grand, gros, vaste; (fig.) libre, grossier, hardi; peu voilé (allusion); prononcé (accent).
broadcast ['brɔ:dka:st], a. à la volée; radiodiffusé.—v.t. irr. semer (du grain) à la volée; répandre (une nouvelle); radiodiffuser.—n. émission, f.
broadcaster ['brɔ:dka:stə], n. speaker, m.
broadcasting ['brɔ:dka:stiŋ], n. radiodiffusion, f.; **broadcasting station**, poste émetteur, m.
broaden [brɔ:dn], v.t. élargir.—v.i. s'élargir, s'étendre.
broadly ['brɔ:dli], adv. largement.
broad-minded ['brɔ:d'maindid], a. tolérant, à l'esprit large.
broadness ['brɔ:dnis], n. largeur; (fig.) grossièreté, f.
broadside ['brɔ:dsaid], n. (Naut.) côté, flanc, m.; bordée, f.
brocade [bro'keid], n. brocart, m.
brogue (1) [broug], n. accent irlandais, m.
brogue (2) [broug], n. brogue (chaussure), f.
broil (1) [brɔil], n. querelle, f., tumulte, m.
broil (2) [brɔil], v.t. griller.—v.i. se griller.
broken ['broukən], a. cassé, brisé, rompu; (fig.) navré; entrecoupé, décousu (discours etc.); accidenté (terrain); interrompu (sommeil); délabré (santé).
broker ['broukə], n. courtier; brocanteur (articles d'occasion), m.; **ship broker**, courtier maritime; **stockbroker**, agent de change, m.
brokerage ['broukəridʒ], n. courtage, m.
bromide ['broumaid], n. bromure, m.
bromine ['broumi:n, 'broumain], n. brome, m.
bronchia ['brɔŋkiə], n.pl. bronches, f.pl.
bronchial ['brɔŋkiəl], a. bronchial.
bronchitis [brɔŋ'kaitis], n. bronchite, f.
bronze [brɔnz], n. bronze, m.
bronzed [brɔnzd], a. bronzé, basané.
brooch [brout∫], n. broche, f.
brood [bru:d], v.i. couver; **to brood over**, rêver à, ruminer.—n. couvée, f.
broody ['bru:di], a. couveuse (poule); distrait (personne).
brook (1) [bruk], n. ruisseau, m.
brook (2) [bruk], v.t. (always neg.) souffrir; avaler, digérer.
broom [bru:m], n. balai; genêt (plante), m.
broth [brɔθ], n. bouillon, potage, m.
brother ['brʌðə], n. (pl. **brothers** ['brʌðəz], rhet. **brethren** ['breðrin]) frère, m.; **brother in arms**, frère d'armes; **foster brother**, frère de lait.
brotherhood ['brʌðəhud], n. fraternité; confrérie, confraternité, f.
brother-in-law ['brʌðərinlɔ:], n. beau-frère, m.
brotherly ['brʌðəli], a. fraternel.
brow [brau], n. front; sourcil; (fig.) sommet, m.
browbeat ['braubi:t], v.t. irr. (conjug. like BEAT) intimider, rudoyer.
brown [braun], a. brun; sombre, rembruni; châtain (chevelure); (Cook.) rissolé; **brown bread**, pain bis, m.; **brown study**, rêverie, f.; **brown sugar**, sucre brut, m.—

n. brun, m.—v.t. brunir; (Cook.) rissoler, faire dorer.
brownie ['brauni], n. jeannette, f.
brownish ['brauni∫], a. brunâtre.
browse [brauz], v.i. brouter.
bruise [bru:z], v.t. meurtrir, contusionner; écraser, froisser.—n. meurtrissure, contusion, f.
brunette [bru:'net], a. and n. brune, f.
brunt [brʌnt], n. choc, m., violence, fureur, f.; **to bear the brunt of**, faire tous les frais de.
brush [brʌ∫], n. brosse, f.; balai; pinceau, m.; (fig.) escarmouche; queue (d'un renard), f.—v.t. brosser; balayer; (fig.) effleurer, raser.
brush-maker ['brʌ∫meikə], n. brossier, m.
brushwood ['brʌ∫wud], n. broussailles, f.pl., fourré, m.
brusque [brusk], a. brusque.
Brussels [brʌslz]. Bruxelles, f; **Brussels sprouts**, choux de Bruxelles, m.pl.
brutal [bru:tl], a. brutal, cruel, inhumain.
brutality [bru:'tæliti], n. brutalité, cruauté, f.
brutally ['bru:təli], adv. brutalement.
brute [bru:t], a. brut, insensible; sauvage; brutal (animaux).—n. animal, m., brute, bête, f., brutal, m.
bubble [bʌbl], n. bulle; (fig.) chimère, illusion; duperie, f.—v.i. bouillonner; pétiller (vin).
bubonic [bju:'bɔnik], a. bubonique.
buccaneer [bʌkə'niə], n. boucanier, flibustier, m.
buck [bʌk], n. daim; chevreuil; mâle (lièvre ou lapin); (fig.) gaillard, beau, élégant, m.
bucket ['bʌkit], n. seau; baquet, m.
buckle [bʌkl], n. boucle, agrafe, f.—v.t. boucler, agrafer.—v.i. se boucler; se courber.
buckler ['bʌklə], n. bouclier, m.
buckram ['bʌkrəm], n. bougran, m.
buckwheat ['bʌkwi:t], n. sarrasin, blé noir, m.
bucolic [bju:'kɔlik], a. bucolique.—n. poème bucolique, m.
bud [bʌd], n. bourgeon, bouton; (fig.) germe, m.—v.t. écussonner.—v.i. bourgeonner.
Buddha ['budə]. Bouddha, m.
Buddhism ['budizm], n. bouddhisme, m.
Buddhist ['budist], n. bouddhiste, m., f.
budge [bʌdʒ], v.t. bouger.—v.i. bouger, se remuer.
budgerigar [bʌdʒəri'gɑ:], n. (Orn.) perruche inséparable, f.
budget ['bʌdʒit], n. sac; (Fin.) budget, m.
buff [bʌf], a. de couleur chamois.—n. buffle, m., peau de buffle; couleur chamois, f.—v.t. polir au buffle.
buffalo ['bʌfəlou], n. buffle, m.
buffer ['bʌfə], n. tampon, amortisseur, m.
buffet (1) [bu'fei], n. buffet (sideboard); buffet (meal), m.
buffet (2) ['bʌfit], v.t. frapper à coups de poing, souffleter.—v.i. se battre à coups de poing.—n. soufflet, coup de poing, m.
buffoon [bʌ'fu:n], n. bouffon, m.
buffoonery [bʌ'fu:nəri], n. bouffonnerie, f.
bug [bʌg], n. punaise, f., insecte, m.
bugle [bju:gl], n. cor de chasse; (Mil.) clairon, m.
bugler ['bju:glə], n. clairon, m.
build [bild], v.t. irr. bâtir, faire bâtir, construire; (fig.) édifier, fonder, baser.—n. construction; forme, carrure, taille, f.

builder ['bildə], n. constructeur, entrepreneur de maçonnerie, m.
building ['bildiŋ], n. construction, f.; édifice, bâtiment, m.; **building and loan association**, société immobilière, f.
bulb [bʌlb], n. bulbe, oignon, m.; cuvette (de thermomètre); poire (en caoutchouc); (Elec.) ampoule, lampe, f.
bulbous ['bʌlbəs], a. bulbeux.
Bulgaria [bʌl'gɛəriə]. la Bulgarie, f.
Bulgarian [bʌl'gɛəriən], a. bulgare.—n. bulgare (langue), m.; Bulgare (personne), m., f.
bulge [bʌldʒ], n. bombement, m., bosse, f.—v.t., v.i. faire saillie, bomber.
bulging ['bʌldʒiŋ], a. bombé.
bulk [bʌlk], n. volume, m., grosseur; masse, f., gros, m.; (Naut.) charge, f.; **in bulk**, en bloc, en gros.
bulkhead ['bʌlkhed], n. cloison étanche, f.
bulky ['bʌlki], a. gros, encombrant.
bull (1) [bul], n. taureau; (St. Exch.) haussier, m.
bull (2) [bul], n. bulle (du Pape), f.
bulldog ['buldɔg], n. bouledogue, m.
bulldozer ['buldouzə], n. bulldozer, m.
bullet ['bulit], n. balle, f.
bulletin ['bulətin], n. bulletin, communiqué, m. [**bulletin board**, see **notice-board**]
bullet-proof ['bulitpru:f], a. à l'épreuve des balles.
bullfinch ['bulfintʃ], n. (Orn.) bouvreuil, m.
bullion ['buljən], n. or ou argent en lingots, m.
bullock ['bulək], n. bœuf, bouvillon, m.
bull's-eye ['bulzai], n. centre, noir (d'une cible); œil-de-bœuf (fenêtre), m.
bully ['buli], n. matamore, bravache, m.; brute, f.—v.t. malmener, intimider.—v.i. faire le matamore.
bulrush ['bulrʌʃ], n. (Bot.) jonc, m.
bulwark ['bulwək], n. rempart; (Naut.) pavois, m.
bumble-bee ['bʌmblbi:], n. bourdon, m.
bump [bʌmp], n. bosse, f.; heurt, cahot, coup, choc, m.—v.t. frapper, cogner.—v.i. se cogner, se heurter.
bumper ['bʌmpə], n. rasade, f., rouge-bord; (Motor.) pare-choc, m.
bumpkin ['bʌmpkin], n. rustre, lourdaud, m.
bumpy ['bʌmpi], a. cahoteux (route).
bun [bʌn], n. petit pain rond (au lait); chignon (coiffure), m.
bunch [bʌntʃ], n. botte, f.; bouquet, m., gerbe (de fleurs); grappe (de raisins), f.; régime (de bananes); trousseau (de clefs), m.
bundle [bʌndl], n. paquet; ballot; faisceau, fagot (de bois etc.), m.; liasse (de papiers), f.—v.t. empaqueter.
bung [bʌŋ], n. bondon, tampon, m.—v.t. boucher.
bungalow ['bʌŋgəlou], n. maison sans étage, f.
bung-hole ['bʌŋhoul], n. bonde, f.
bungle [bʌŋgl], v.t. bousiller, gâcher, rater.—v.i. s'y prendre gauchement, faire de la mauvaise besogne.—n. bousillage; gâchis, m.
bungler ['bʌŋglə], n. maladroit, savetier, bousilleur, m.
bungling ['bʌŋgliŋ], a. maladroit, gauche.
bunion ['bʌnjən], n. oignon (de pied), m.
bunk [bʌŋk], n. (Naut.) couchette, f.

bunker ['bʌŋkə], n. soute (à charbon); (Golf) banquette, f.
bunting ['bʌntiŋ], n. étamine, f.; (Orn.) bruant, m.; (fig.) drapeaux, pavillons, m.pl.
buoy [bɔi], n. bouée, f.; **life buoy**, bouée de sauvetage; **mooring buoy**, coffre d'amarrage, m.—v.t. **to buoy up**, soutenir sur l'eau; (fig.) encourager.
buoyancy ['bɔiənsi], n. légèreté, f.; élan, m.; vivacité, animation, f.
buoyant ['bɔiənt], a. léger, flottant; animé, vif.
burble [bə:bl], v.i. murmurer, bafouiller.—n. murmure, m.
burden [bə:dn], n. fardeau, m.; charge, f.; poids; refrain (d'une chanson), m.—v.t. charger.
burdensome ['bə:dnsəm], a. pesant, lourd; ennuyeux.
bureau [bjuə'rou], n. bureau, m.
bureaucracy [bjuə'rɔkrəsi], n. bureaucratie, f.
bureaucrat ['bjuərokræt], n. bureaucrate, m., f.
bureaucratic [bjuəro'krætik], a. bureaucratique.
burgess ['bə:dʒis], n. bourgeois, citoyen, électeur, m.
burgh ['bʌrə], n. (Sc.) bourg, m.
burglar ['bə:glə], n. cambrioleur, m.
burglary ['bə:gləri], n. vol avec effraction; cambriolage, m.
burgle [bə:gl], v.t., v.i. cambrioler.
burgomaster ['bə:gomɑ:stə], n. bourgmestre, m.
burial ['beriəl], n. enterrement, m., obsèques, f.pl.; inhumation, f.
burlesque [bə:'lesk], a. and n. burlesque, m.—v.t. parodier, travestir.
burliness ['bə:linis], n. grosseur, corpulence, f.
burly ['bə:li], a. de forte carrure.
Burma(h) ['bə:mə]. la Birmanie, f.
Burmese [bə:'mi:z], a. birman.—n. birman (langue); Birman (personne), m.
burn [bə:n], v.t. irr. brûler; cuire (briques etc.); incendier.—v.i. brûler; (fig.) brûler, être impatient de.—n. brûlure, f.
burner ['bə:nə], n. brûleur; bec (de gaz etc.), m.
burning ['bə:niŋ], a. en feu; brûlant, ardent.—n. brûlure, f.; incendie, m.
burnish ['bə:niʃ], v.t. brunir, polir.
burrow ['bʌrou], n. terrier, trou, m.—v.t. creuser.—v.i. se terrer; (fig.) se cacher.
bursar ['bə:sə], n. économe, intendant, trésorier; boursier, m.
bursary ['bə:səri], n. bourse (d'études), f.
burst [bə:st], v.t. irr. crever; faire éclater; fendre; rompre.—v.i. crever, éclater; sauter; jaillir; s'élancer; éclore (bourgeon); **to burst into tears**, fondre en larmes; **to burst out laughing**, éclater de rire.—n. éclat, éclatement, m., explosion; rupture, hernie, f.
bury ['beri], v.t. enterrer, ensevelir; (fig.) enfoncer; cacher.
bus [bʌs], n. autobus, m.
bus conductor ['bʌskəndʌktə], n. receveur (d'autobus), m.
bush [buʃ], n. buisson, fourré, m.
bushel [buʃl], n. boisseau, m.
bushy ['buʃi], a. buissonneux; touffu.

busily ['bizili], *adv.* activement; avec empressement.

business ['biznis], *n.* affaire, occupation, *f.*, devoir; état, métier, *m.*; affaires, *f.pl.*, commerce, *m.*; *what business is that of yours ?* est-ce que cela vous regarde ? *you have no business here*, vous n'avez que faire ici; *business suit*, complet veston, *m.*

businesslike ['biznislaik], *a.* pratique, régulier, méthodique; franc, droit, sérieux.

buskin ['bʌskin], *n.* brodequin; (*fig.*) cothurne, *m.*

bust [bʌst], *n.* (*Sculp.*) buste, *m.*; gorge (*de femme*); (*Art*) bosse, *f.*

bustard ['bʌstəd], *n.* (*Orn.*) outarde, *f.*

bustle [bʌsl], *n.* mouvement; bruit, *m.*, confusion, activité, agitation, *f.*—*v.i.* se remuer, s'empresser.

bustling ['bʌsliŋ], *a.* empressé, affairé, remuant; bruyant.

busy ['bizi], *a.* affairé, occupé, empressé, diligent.—*v.r.* *to busy oneself*, s'occuper.

busybody ['bizibodi], *n.* officieux, *m.*

but [bʌt], *conj.* mais, que; sauf que; qui ne; *but that*, sans que.—*adv.* ne . . . que; seulement; *all but*, presque.—*prep.* sans, excepté, à part.

butcher ['butʃə], *n.* boucher, *m.*; *butcher's shop*, boucherie, *f.*—*v.t.* égorger, massacrer.

butchery ['butʃəri], *n.* boucherie; tuerie, *f.*, massacre, carnage, *m.*

butler ['bʌtlə], *n.* maître d'hôtel, *m.*

butt (1) [bʌt], *n.* bout, *m.*; crosse (*d'un fusil*); masse (*d'une queue de billard*), *f.*

butt (2) [bʌt], *n.* cible, *f.*; (*fig.*) point de mire; plastron (*personne*), *m.*

butt (3) [bʌt], *n.* coup de tête, *m.*—*v.t.* cosser, frapper de la tête (*animal*).

butt (4) [bʌt], *n.* barrique, *f.*

butter ['bʌtə], *n.* beurre, *m.*—*v.t.* beurrer.

buttercup ['bʌtəkʌp], *n.* bouton d'or, *m.*

butter dish ['bʌtədiʃ], *n.* beurrier, *m.*

butterfly ['bʌtəflai], *n.* papillon, *m.*

buttermilk ['bʌtəmilk], *n.* petit-lait, *m.*

buttery ['bʌtəri], *a.* de beurre, graisseux.—*n.* dépense, *f.*

buttock ['bʌtək], *n.* fesse; croupe (*de cheval*); culotte (*de bœuf*), *f.*

button [bʌtn], *n.* bouton, *m.*—*v.t.* boutonner. —*v.i.* se boutonner.

buttonhole ['bʌtnhoul], *n.* boutonnière, *f.*—*v.t.* accrocher (*quelqu'un*).

button-hook ['bʌtnhuk], *n.* tire-bouton, *m.*

buttress ['bʌtris], *n.* contrefort, éperon, *m.*; *flying buttress*, arc-boutant, *m.*—*v.t.* arc-bouter.

buxom ['bʌksəm], *a.* plein de santé et d'entrain; rondelette et fraîche (*femme*).

buy [bai], *v.t. irr.* acheter; prendre (*billet*); corrompre, acheter (*quelqu'un*); *to buy up*, accaparer.

buyer ['baiə], *n.* acheteur, acquéreur, *m.*

buying ['baiiŋ], *n.* achat, *m.*

buzz [bʌz], *v.i.* bourdonner.—*n.* bourdonnement; brouhaha (*de conversation*), *m.*

buzzard ['bʌzəd], *n.* (*Orn.*) buse, *f.*

buzzer ['bʌzə], *n.* trompe, *f.*; vibreur, appel vibré, *m.*

by [bai], *prep.* par; de; à; sur; près de, auprès de, à côté de; en (*with participles*); *by far*, de beaucoup; *by no means*, nullement; *by sight*, de vue.—*adv.* près; passé.

by-election ['baiilekʃən], *n.* élection partielle, *f.*

bygone ['baigon], *a.* passé, d'autrefois.

by-pass ['baipɑːs], *n.* route d'évitement, déviation, *f.*—*v.t.* contourner, éviter (*une ville*).

by-play ['baiplei], *n.* jeu de scène, jeu muet, *m.*

by-product ['baiprodʌkt], *n.* sous-produit, *m.*

byre ['baiə], *n.* étable à vaches, *f.*

bystander ['baistændə], *n.* spectateur, assistant, *m.*

byword ['baiwəːd], *n.* dicton, proverbe, *m.*; (*fig.*) risée, *f.*

C

C, c [siː]. troisième lettre de l'alphabet; (*Mus.*) ut, do, *m.*

cab [kæb], *n.* fiacre, taxi, *m.*

cabal [kə'bæl], *n.* cabale, *f.*—*v.i.* cabaler.

cabbage ['kæbidʒ], *n.* chou, *m.*

cabin ['kæbin], *n.* cabine, chambre (*pour officiers etc.*); (*Av.*) carlingue; cabane, case, hutte, *f.*

cabin boy ['kæbinbɔi], *n.* mousse, *m.*

cabinet ['kæbinit], *n.* meuble à tiroirs; classeur; cabinet; ministère, *m.*

cabinet-maker ['kæbiñit'meikə], *n.* ébéniste, *m.*, *f.*

cable [keibl], *n.* câble; câblogramme, *m.*—*v.t.* câbler, télégraphier.

cablegram ['keiblgræm], *n.* câblogramme, *m.*

caboose [kə'buːs], *n.* (*Naut.*) cuisine, cambuse, *f.*

cackle [kækl], *n.* caquet, *m.*—*v.i.* caqueter; (*fig.*) ricaner, glousser; cacarder (*oie*).

cackling ['kækliŋ], *n.* caquetage, *m.*

cactus ['kæktəs], *n.* cactus, *m.*

cad [kæd], *n.* goujat, *m.*; canaille, *f.*

cadaverous [kə'dævərəs], *a.* cadavéreux.

caddie ['kædi], *n.* (*Golf*) cadet, *m.*—*v.i.* servir de cadet.

caddy ['kædi], *n.* boîte à thé, *f.*

cadet [kə'det], *n.* cadet; élève-officier (*d'une école militaire ou d'une école navale*), *m.*

cadge [kædʒ], *v.t.*, *v.i.* colporter; quémander; écornifler.

cage [keidʒ], *n.* cage, *f.*—*v.t.* mettre en cage.

Cairo ['kaiərou]. le Caire, *m.*

cajole [kə'dʒoul], *v.t.* cajoler, enjôler.

cake [keik], *n.* gâteau, *m.*; masse, croûte (*matière solidifiée*), *f.*; *cake of soap*, savonnette, *f.*—*v.i.* se cailler, se prendre, se coller.

calamitous [kə'læmitəs], *a.* calamiteux, désastreux, funeste.

calamity [kə'læmiti], *n.* calamité, *f.*, désastre, malheur, *m.*

calculate ['kælkjuleit], *v.t.* calculer; compter; évaluer.

calculation [kælkju'leiʃən], *n.* calcul, compte, *m.*

calculus ['kælkjuləs], *n.* (*Med.*) calcul; (*Math.*) calcul infinitésimal, *m.*
Caledonia [kæli'dounjə]. la Calédonie, *f.*
calendar ['kæləndə], *n.* calendrier, *m.*; (*Law*) liste, *f.*
calender ['kæləndə], *n.* calandre, *f.*
calends ['kæləndz], *n.pl.* calendes, *f.pl.*
calf [kɑːf], *n.* (*pl.* **calves** [kɑːvz]) veau; mollet (*de la jambe*), *m.*
calibre ['kælibə], *n.* calibre; (*Tech.*) compas, *m.*
calibrate ['kælibreit], *v.t.* calibrer, graduer.
calico ['kælikou], *n.* indienne, *f.*
California [kæli'fɔːnjə]. la Californie, *f.*
caliph ['keilif], *n.* calife, *m.*
calk [kɔːk], *v.t.* ferrer à glace (*cheval etc.*).
call [kɔːl], *n.* appel, cri, *m.*; voix, *f.*; (*Naut.*) sifflet, *m.*; (*fig.*) obligation, *f.*, devoir, *m.*; demande, invitation; visite, *f.*; coup de téléphone, *m.*; *within call*, à portée de voix.—*v.t.* appeler; nommer, qualifier (*de*); convoquer; rappeler; *to be called Peter*, s'appeler Pierre; *to call for*, demander, exiger; aller chercher; *to call in*, faire rentrer; *to call in a doctor*, faire venir un médecin; *to call off*, rappeler, rompre, décommander; *to call out*, appeler, crier; *to call to mind*, se rappeler; *to call up*, faire monter; réveiller; appeler sous les drapeaux, mobiliser.—*v.i.* appeler, crier; venir *ou* aller (*chez*), rendre visite (*à*); (*Naut.*) toucher (*à*); *to call at*, passer par, s'arrêter à; *to call on*, inviter, prier, rendre visite à; *to call upon*, faire appel (*à quelqu'un*).
call-box ['kɔːlbɒks], *n.* cabine téléphonique, *f.*
call-boy ['kɔːlbɔi], *n.* (*Theat.*) avertisseur, *m.*
caller ['kɔːlə], *n.* visiteur, *m.*; (*Teleph.*) celui *ou* celle qui appelle, *m.*, *f.*
calling ['kɔːliŋ], *n.* appel, *m.*; profession, vocation, *f.*, métier, état, *m.*
callipers ['kælipəz], *n.* compas de calibre, *m.*
callous ['kæləs], *a.* calleux, endurci; insensible.
callously ['kæləsli], *adv.* durement, impitoyablement.
callousness ['kæləsnis], *n.* insensibilité, *f.*, endurcissement, *m.*
callow ['kælou], *a.* sans plume; (*fig.*) jeune, novice.
call-up ['kɔːlʌp], *n.* (*Mil.*) appel sous les drapeaux, *m.*
calm [kɑːm], *a.* and *n.* calme, *m.*—*v.t.* calmer, apaiser.
calmly ['kɑːmli], *adv.* avec calme, tranquillement.
calorie ['kæləri], *n.* calorie, *f.*
calumniate [kə'lʌmnieit], *v.t.* calomnier.
calumnious [kə'lʌmniəs], *a.* calomnieux.
calumny ['kæləmni], *n.* calomnie, *f.*
calvary ['kælvəri], *n.* calvaire; chemin de la croix, *m.*
calve [kɑːv], *v.i.* vêler.
calves [CALF].
calyx ['keiliks, 'kæliks], *n.* calice, *m.*
cam [kæm], *n.* (*Mech.*) came, *f.*
camber ['kæmbə], *n.* cambrure, *f.*
Cambodia [kæm'boudiə]. le Cambodge, *m.*
Cambodian [kæm'boudiən], *a.* cambodgien. —*n.* cambodgien (*langue*); Cambodgien (*personne*), *m.*
cambric ['keimbrik], *n.* batiste, *f.*

camel ['kæməl], *n.* chameau, *m.*
camellia [kə'miːljə], *n.* camélia, *m.*
camel hair ['kæməlhɛə], *n.* poil de chameau, *m.*
cameo ['kæmiou], *n.* camée, *m.*
camera ['kæmərə], *n.* appareil (photographique), *m.*; *movie camera*, (ciné)caméra, *f.*
cameraman ['kæmərəmæn], *n.* (*pl.* **cameramen** ['kæmərəmen]) photographe (*de presse*); (*Cine., Tel.*) opérateur, cameraman, *m.*
camouflage ['kæmuflɑːʒ], *n.* camouflage, *m.* —*v.t.* camoufler.
camp [kæmp], *n.* camp, *m.*; *to break up a camp*, lever un camp; *to pitch a camp*, établir un camp.—*v.i.* camper.
campaign [kæm'pein], *n.* campagne, *f.*—*v.i.* faire campagne.
campaigner [kæm'peinə], *n.* vieux soldat, *m.*
campanile [kæmpə'niːli], *n.* campanile, *m.*
campanula [kæm'pænjulə], *n.* (*Bot.*) campanule, *f.*
camp bed ['kæmpbed], *n.* lit de camp, *m.*
camper ['kæmpə], *n.* campeur, *m.*
camphor ['kæmfə], *n.* camphre, *m.*
camping ['kæmpiŋ], *n.* (*Mil.*) campement; camping, *m.*; *to go camping*, faire du camping.
can (1) [kæn], *n.* pot, broc, bidon, *m.*; boîte en fer blanc, *f.*—*v.t.* mettre en boîte.
can (2) [kæn], *v.* aux. *irr.* (*inf.* **to be able**) pouvoir (*to be able*); savoir (*to know how to*); *he can read*, il sait lire; *I can do it*, je peux *ou* je sais le faire.
Canada ['kænədə]. le Canada, *m.*
Canadian [kə'neidiən], *a.* canadien.—*n.* Canadien (*personne*), *m.*
canal [kə'næl], *n.* canal, *m.*
canary [kə'nɛəri], *n.* (*Orn.*) serin, *m.*
cancel ['kænsəl], *v.t.* annuler; effacer, biffer, rayer; oblitérer (*un timbre*); décommander; (*Comm.*) résilier.
cancellation [kænsə'leiʃən], *n.* annulation; résiliation, oblitération, *f.*
cancer ['kænsə], *n.* cancer, *m.*
cancerous ['kænsərəs], *a.* cancéreux.
candelabrum [kændi'lɑːbrəm], **candelabra** [kændi'lɑːbrə], *n.* candélabre, *m.*
candid ['kændid], *a.* sincère, franc.
candidate ['kændidit], *n.* aspirant, candidat, *m.*
candidature ['kændiditʃə], *n.* candidature, *f.*
candidly ['kændidli], *adv.* franchement, de bonne foi.
candle [kændl], *n.* chandelle; bougie; (*fig.*) lumière, *f.*; (*Ch.*) cierge, *m.*
Candlemas ['kændlməs]. la Chandeleur, *f.*
candlestick ['kændlstik], *n.* chandelier; bougeoir, *m.*
candle wax ['kændlwæks], *n.* suif, *m.*
candor ['kændə], *n.* franchise, sincérité, bonne foi, *f.*
candy ['kændi], *n.* candi, *m.*; (*Am.*) bonbons, *m.pl.*
cane [kein], *n.* canne, *f.*
canine ['kænain, 'keinain], *a.* canin, de chien.
caning ['keiniŋ], *n.* coups de canne, *m.pl.*, râclée, *f.*

canister ['kænistə], *n.* boîte en fer blanc; boîte à thé, *f.*

canker ['kæŋkə], *n.* chancre; (*fig.*) ver rongeur; fléau, *m.*—*v.t.* ronger; (*fig.*) corrompre, empoisonner.—*v.i.* se ronger; (*fig.*) se gangrener, se corrompre.

canned [kænd], *a.* (*Am.*) conservé en boîtes (*fruits etc.*); (*fam.*) enregistré (*musique*).

cannibal ['kænibəl], *n.* cannibale, anthropophage, *m., f.*

cannibalism ['kænibəlizm], *n.* cannibalisme, *m.*

cannon ['kænən], *n.* canon; (*Billiards*) carambolage, *m.*—*v.i.* caramboler.

cannonade [kænə'neid], *n.* cannonade, *f.*

cannon ball ['kænənbɔ:l], *n.* boulet de canon, *m.*

canoe [kə'nu:], *n.* canoë, *m.*; périssoire; pirogue, *f.*

canoeist [kə'nu:ist], *n.* canoëiste, *m., f.*

canon ['kænən], *n.* chanoine; canon (*règle*), *m.*

canonical [kə'nɔnikl], *a.* canonique.

canonization [kænənai'zeiʃən], *n.* canonisation, *f.*

canonize ['kænənaiz], *v.t.* canoniser.

can opener ['kænoupənə], *n.* (*Am.*) ouvre-boîte, *m.*

canopy ['kænəpi], *n.* dais; (*Arch.*) baldaquin, *m.*; voûte (*du ciel*), *f.*

cant (1) [kænt], *n.* cant, langage hypocrite, *m.*; afféterie; hypocrisie, *f.*—*v.i.* parler avec afféterie *ou* avec affectation.

cant (2) [kænt], *n.* (*Arch.*) pan coupé, *m.*—*v.t.* pousser, jeter de côté, incliner.

cantankerous [kæn'tæŋkərəs], *a.* acariâtre, revêche, bourru.

cantankerousness [kæn'tæŋkərəsnis], *n.* humeur acariâtre, *f.*

cantata [kæn'tɑ:tə], *n.* cantate, *f.*

canteen [kæn'ti:n], *n.* cantine, *f.*, restaurant; bidon (*boîte*), *m.*; **canteen of cutlery**, ménagère, *f.*

canter ['kæntə], *n.* petit galop, *m.*—*v.i.* aller au petit galop.

canticle ['kæntikl], *n.* cantique, *m.*

cantilever ['kæntiliːvə], *n.* (*Arch.*) encorbellement, modillon, *m.*

canto ['kæntou], *n.* chant, *m.*

canton ['kæntən], *n.* canton, *m.*

cantonment [kæn'tu:nmənt], *n.* cantonnement, *m.*

canvas ['kænvəs], *n.* toile, *f.*; tableau, *m.*, peinture; voile, toile à voiles, *f.*; **under canvas**, sous la tente.

canvass ['kænvəs], *n.* débat, *m.*, discussion; sollicitation de suffrages, *f.*—*v.t.* agiter, discuter; solliciter.—*v.i.* solliciter des suffrages; faire la place.

canvasser ['kænvəsə], *n.* agent électoral; (*Comm.*) représentant, *m.*

canvassing ['kænvəsiŋ], *n.* propagande électorale; (*Comm.*) prospection, *f.*

canyon ['kænjən], *n.* gorge, *f.*, défilé, *m.*

cap [kæp], *n.* bonnet (*de femme*), *m.*; casquette (*d'homme*); barrette (*d'un cardinal*); capsule, amorce (*d'armes à feu*), *f.*; (*Phot.*) chapeau (*d'un objectif etc.*); capuchon (*d'un stylo*), *m.* —*v.t.* coiffer, couvrir; (*fig.*) couronner, surpasser.

capability [keipə'biliti], *n.* capacité, *f.*

capable ['keipəbl], *a.* capable; susceptible (*de*); compétent.

capacious [kə'peiʃəs], *a.* ample, vaste, spacieux.

capaciousness [kə'peiʃəsnis], *n.* capacité, étendue, *f.*

capacitate [kə'pæsiteit], *v.t.* rendre capable de.

capacity [kə'pæsiti], *n.* capacité, *f.*; **in the capacity of**, en qualité de.

cap-à-pie [kæpə'pi:], *adv.* de pied en cap.

caparison [kə'pærizn], *n.* caparaçon, *m.*—*v.t.* caparaçonner.

cape (1) [keip], *n.* cap, promontoire, *m.*

cape (2) [keip], *n.* pèlerine, cape (*manteau*), *f.*

caper (1) ['keipə], *n.* bond, entrechat, *m.*—*v.i.* cabrioler; bondir, sauter.

caper (2) ['keipə], *n.* (*Bot.*) câpre, *f.*

capillary [kə'piləri], *a.* capillaire.

capital ['kæpitl], *a.* capital; (*colloq.*) excellent; (*Print.*) majuscule.—*n.* capital, *m.*, capitaux, *m.pl.*; capitale (*ville*), *f.*; (*Comm.*) fonds; (*Arch.*) chapiteau, *m.*; (*Print.*) majuscule, *f.*

capitalism ['kæpitəlizm], *n.* capitalisme, *m.*

capitalist ['kæpitəlist], *n.* capitaliste, *m., f.*

capitalize ['kæpitəlaiz], *v.t.* capitaliser.

capitally ['kæpitəli], *adv.* principalement; admirablement, à merveille.

capitulate [kə'pitjuleit], *v.i.* capituler.

capitulation [kəpitju'leiʃən], *n.* capitulation, *f.*

capon ['keipən], *n.* chapon, *m.*

caprice [kə'pri:s], *n.* caprice, *m.*

capricious [kə'priʃəs], *a.* capricieux.

capriciously [kə'priʃəsli], *adv.* capricieusement.

capsize [kæp'saiz], *v.t.* faire chavirer.—*v.i.* chavirer (*bateau*).

capstan ['kæpstən], *n.* cabestan, *m.*

capsule ['kæpsjuːl], *n.* capsule, *f.*

captain ['kæptin], *n.* capitaine, *m.*

caption ['kæpʃən], *n.* arrestation; saisie (*choses*), *f.*; en-tête (*d'un chapitre etc.*), *m.*, légende (*d'une photographie etc.*), *f.*; (*Cine.*) sous-titre, *m.*

captious ['kæpʃəs], *a.* insidieux, chicaneur.

captiousness ['kæpʃəsnis], *n.* esprit de chicane; sophisme, *m.*

captivate ['kæptiveit], *v.t.* captiver; charmer, séduire.

captivating ['kæptiveitiŋ], *a.* enchanteur, séduisant.

captive ['kæptiv], *a.* captif.—*n.* captif, prisonnier, *m.*

captivity [kæp'tiviti], *n.* captivité, *f.*

capture ['kæptʃə], *n.* capture; prise, arrestation, *f.*—*v.t.* capturer, prendre, arrêter.

car [kɑ:], *n.* (*Motor.*) auto, voiture, *f.*; (*Rail.*) wagon; (*Lit.*) char, chariot, *m.*; nacelle (*d'un ballon*), *f.*; **dining car**, wagon-restaurant, *m.*; **sleeping car**, wagon-lit, *m.* **[freight car**, see **van**]

caramel ['kærəmel], *n.* caramel, *m.*

carat ['kærət], *n.* carat, *m.*

caravan [kærə'væn, 'kærəvæn], *n.* caravane; roulotte, *f.*

caravanserai [kærə'vænsərai], *n.* caravansérail, *m.*

caraway ['kærəwei], *n.* (*Bot.*) carvi, cumin des prés, *m.*

carbide ['kɑ:baid], *n.* carbure, *m.*

carbine ['kɑ:bain], *n.* carabine, *f.*

carbohydrate [kɑ:bou'haidreit], *n.* hydrate de carbone, *m.*

carbolic [kɑːˈbɔlik], *a.* phénique.
carbon [ˈkɑːbən], *n.* (*Chem.*) carbone; (*Elec.*) charbon, *m.*
carbonic [kɑːˈbɔnik], *a.* carbonique.
carboniferous [kɑːbəˈnifərəs], *a.* carbonifère.
carboy [ˈkɑːbɔi], *n.* tourie, bonbonne, *f.*
carbuncle [ˈkɑːbaŋkl], *n.* escarboucle, *f.*; (*Med.*) charbon, furoncle, *m.*
carburation [kɑːbjuˈreiʃən], *n.* carburation, *f.*
carburetor [kɑːbjuˈretə], *n.* carburateur, *m.*
carcase, carcass [ˈkɑːkəs], *n.* carcasse, *f.*; cadavre, *m.*
card [kɑːd], *n.* carte à jouer; fiche, carte; (*Manuf.*) carde, *f.*—*v.t.* carder.
cardboard [ˈkɑːdbɔːd], *n.* carton, *m.*
cardiac [ˈkɑːdiæk], *a.* cardiaque.
cardigan [ˈkɑːdigən], *n.* gilet de tricot, *m.*
cardinal [ˈkɑːdinl], *a.* cardinal, fondamental. —*n.* cardinal, *m.*
card index [ˈkɑːdindeks], *n.* fichier, *m.*—*v.t.* encarter.
cardiograph [ˈkɑːdiogrɑːf, -grɑːf], *n.* cardiographe, *m.*
card-sharper [ˈkɑːdʃɑːpə], *n.* grec, fileur de cartes, *m.*
card table [ˈkɑːdteibl], *n.* table de jeu, *f.*
care [kɛə], *n.* soin; souci, *m.*, sollicitude; précaution, attention, *f.*; *care of* (*abbr.* c/o), aux bons soins de, chez; *to take care of,* avoir soin de, s'occuper de.—*v.i.* se soucier, s'inquiéter (*de*); *I dont care!* cela m'est égal! je m'en moque!
career [kəˈriə], *n.* carrière, course, *f.*—*v.i.* courir rapidement.
carefree [ˈkɛəfriː], *a.* libre de soucis; insouciant.
careful [ˈkɛəful], *a.* soigneux, attentif; prudent, économe; soucieux.
carefully [ˈkɛəfuli], *adv.* soigneusement, avec soin.
carefulness [ˈkɛəfulnis], *n.* attention, *f.*; soin, *m.*
careless [ˈkɛəlis], *a.* insouciant, nonchalant; négligent (*de*).
carelessly [ˈkɛəlisli], *adv.* nonchalamment, négligemment.
carelessness [ˈkɛəlisnis], *n.* insouciance, nonchalance; négligence, *f.*
caress [kəˈres], *n.* caresse, *f.*—*v.t.* caresser.
caretaker [ˈkɛəteikə], *n.* gardien, *m.*, concierge, *m., f.*
cargo [ˈkɑːgou], *n.* cargaison, *f.*, chargement, *m.*
cargo boat [ˈkɑːgoubout], *n.* cargo, *m.*
Caribbean [kæriˈbiːən], *a.* antillais; *Caribbean Sea,* la mer des Antilles, *f.*—*n. the Caribbean,* les Antilles, *f.pl.*
caribou [kæriˈbuː], *n.* caribou, *m.*
caricature [ˈkærikəˈtjuə], *n.* caricature, charge, *f.*—*v.t.* caricaturer, faire la charge de.
carking [ˈkɑːkiŋ], *a.* cuisant (*souci*); rongeur.
carmine [ˈkɑːmain], *a.* and *n.* carmin, *m.*
carnage [ˈkɑːnidʒ], *n.* carnage, *m.*
carnal [ˈkɑːnl], *a.* charnel.
carnally [ˈkɑːnəli], *adv.* charnellement.
carnation [kɑːˈneiʃən], *n.* (*Bot.*) œillet, incarnat, *m.*; carnation (*couleur*), *f.*
carnival [ˈkɑːnivl], *n.* carnaval, *m.*

carnivorous [kɑːˈnivərəs], *a.* carnivore, carnassier.
carol [ˈkærəl], *n.* chanson, *f.*, chant, *m.*; *Christmas carol,* noël, *m.*—*v.i.* chanter.
carousal [kəˈrauzəl], *n.* orgie, débauche, ripaille, *f.*; festin, *m.*
carouse [kəˈrauz], *v.i.* boire, faire la fête.
carp (1) [kɑːp], *n.* (*Ichth.*) carpe, *f.*
carp (2) [kɑːp], *v.i.* critiquer, chicaner (*sur*).
car-park [ˈkɑːpɑːk], *n.* parc de stationnement, *m.*
carpenter [ˈkɑːpintə], *n.* menuisier, charpentier, *m.*
carpentry [ˈkɑːpintri], *n.* grosse menuiserie, charpenterie, *f.*
carpet [ˈkɑːpit], *n.* tapis. *m.*; *fitted carpet,* moquette, *f.*—*v.t.* garnir de tapis, tapisser.
carpet sweeper [ˈkɑːpitswiːpə], *n.* balai mécanique, *m.*
carping [ˈkɑːpiŋ], *a.* chicanier, pointilleux.
carpingly [ˈkɑːpiŋli], *adv.* en glosant; malignement.
carriage [ˈkæridʒ], *n.* voiture, *f.*; équipage; (*Rail.*) wagon, *m.*, voiture, *f.*; port, factage (*de paquets etc.*); affût (*de canon*), *m.*; (*Comm.*) frais de transport, *m.pl.*; (*fig.*) maintien, *m.*, tenue, démarche, *f.*
carriageway [ˈkæridʒwei], *n. dual carriageway,* route à double circulation, *f.*
carrier [ˈkæriə], *n.* camionneur; porteur, messager; (*Cycl.*) porte-bagages, *m.*; *aircraft carrier,* porte-avions, *m.inv.*; *carrier pigeon,* pigeon voyageur, *m.*
carrion [ˈkæriən], *n.* charogne, *f.*
carrion crow [ˈkæriənˈkrou], *n.* corbeau, *m.*, corbine, *f.*
carrot [ˈkærət], *n.* carotte, *f.*
carry [ˈkæri], *v.t.* porter; emporter; rapporter (*chien*); mener, conduire, entraîner; faire voter, adopter; (*Arith.*) retenir; *to carry away,* emporter, enlever, emmener; *to carry off,* emporter, enlever, remporter; *to carry on,* poursuivre, continuer; *to carry out,* porter dehors; mettre à exécution; *to carry through,* mener à bonne fin. —*v.i.* porter (*sons*).
cart [kɑːt], *n.* charrette, *f.*; (*Mil.*) fourgon, *m.*; carriole (*de paysan*), *f.*—*v.t.* charrier, transporter, voiturer.
cartage [ˈkɑːtidʒ], *n.* charriage, transport, *m.*
carte [kɑːt], *n.* carte, *f.*; menu, *m.*
carter [ˈkɑːtə], *n.* charretier, roulier, voiturier, *m.*
cart horse [ˈkɑːthɔːs], *n.* cheval de trait, *m.*
cartilage [ˈkɑːtilidʒ], *n.* cartilage, *m.*
cart-load [ˈkɑːtloud], *n.* charretée, *f.*
carton [ˈkɑːtən], *n.* carton, *m.*; petite boîte en carton, *f.*
cartoon [kɑːˈtuːn], *n.* carton, *m.*; (*Polit.*) caricature, *f.*; dessin humoristique; (*Cine.*) dessin animé, *m.*
cartoonist [kɑːˈtuːnist], *n.* caricaturiste, *m., f.*
cartridge [ˈkɑːtridʒ], *n.* cartouche, *f.*
cartridge paper [ˈkɑːtridʒpeipə], *n.* (*Ind.*) papier à cartouche, *m.*
cartridge pouch [ˈkɑːtridʒpautʃ], *n.* cartouchière, giberne, *f.*
cart shed [ˈkɑːtʃed], *n.* hangar, *m.*
cartwright [ˈkɑːtrait], *n.* charron, *m.*
carve [kɑːv], *v.t.* sculpter, tailler; graver, ciseler; découper (*viande etc.*).

carver ['kɑːvə], *n.* découpeur; (*Art.*) sculpteur, graveur, ciseleur, *m.*

carving ['kɑːviŋ], *n.* découpage (*de viande*), *m.*; (*Art*) sculpture, gravure, ciselure, *f.*

cascade [kæsˈkeid], *n.* cascade, *f.*—*v.i.* tomber en cascade, cascader.

case (1) [keis], *n.* cas, état, *m.*; question; (*Law*) cause, affaire, *f.*; (*Med.*) malade, blessé, *m.*; **in any case**, en tout cas; **in case**, dans le cas où.

case (2) [keis], *n.* étui, fourreau, *m.*; caisse (*d'emballage*), *f.*; écrin (*à bijoux*), *m.*—*v.t.* enfermer; emballer; encaisser.

casemate ['keismeit], *n.* casemate, *f.*—*v.t.* casemater.

casement ['keismənt], *n.* châssis de fenêtre, *m.*

cash [kæʃ], *n.* argent, numéraire, *m.*; espèces (*argent*), *f.pl.*; **cash down**, argent comptant; **cash on delivery**, contre remboursement; **to pay cash**, payer en espèces; **to sell for cash**, vendre au comptant.—*v.t.* toucher, encaisser (*chèque, mandat-poste*); changer (*billet*); **to cash in on**, tirer profit de, tirer parti de.

cash-book ['kæʃbuk], *n.* livre de caisse, *m.*

cash box ['kæʃbɔks], *n.* caisse, *f.*

cash-desk ['kæʃdesk], *n.* caisse, *f.*

cashier (1) [kæˈʃiə], *n.* caissier, *m.*

cashier (2) [kæˈʃiə], *v.t.* (*Mil.*) casser, dégrader.

cashmere ['kæʃmiə], *n.* cachemire, *m.*

cash register ['kæʃredʒistə], *n.* caisse enregistreuse, *f.*

cask [kɑːsk], *n.* fût, baril, *m.*, barrique, *f.*, tonneau, *m.*

casket ['kɑːskit], *n.* écrin, *m.*, cassette, *f.*

Caspian (Sea) ['kæspiən(siː)], **the.** la mer Caspienne, *f.*

cassock ['kæsək], *n.* soutane, *f.*

cast [kɑːst], *v.t. irr.* jeter; se dépouiller de (*arbre, animal*); (*Metal.*) couler, fondre; (*Theat.*) distribuer les rôles; **to cast a glance at**, jeter un regard sur; **to cast aside**, mettre de côté, rejeter; **to cast down**, jeter par terre, abattre, décourager; **to cast its slough**, faire peau neuve; **to cast off**, rejeter, repousser, abandonner.—*v.i.* se jeter; se déjeter (*arbre*).—*a.* fondu.—*n.* coup, jet; moule, *m.*; (*Metal.*) fonte; (*Theat.*) distribution des rôles, *f.*; rôles, acteurs, *m.pl.*; (*fig.*) nuance, tournure, *f.*, air, caractère, *m.*; (*Sculp.*) statuette, figure, *f.*, plâtre, *m.*

castanet [kæstəˈnet], *n.* castagnette, *f.*

castaway ['kɑːstəwei], *a.* rejeté.—*n.* naufragé, *m.*

caste [kɑːst], *n.* caste, *f.*

castigate ['kæstigeit], *v.t.* châtier, punir; critiquer sévèrement.

castigation [kæstiˈgeiʃən], *n.* châtiment, *m.*, correction, discipline, *f.*

casting ['kɑːstiŋ], *n.* (*Metal.*) coulée, fonte, *f.*, moulage, *m.*; (*Theat.*) distribution des rôles, *f.*

cast-iron ['kɑːstˈaiən], *a.* en fonte; (*fig.*) de fer, rigide.—*n.* fonte, *f.*

castle [kɑːsl], *n.* château, château fort, *m.*; (*Chess*) tour, *f.*; **castles in the air**, châteaux en Espagne.

castor ['kɑːstə], *n.* roulette (*de meuble*); poivrière, *f.*; (**pair of**) **castors**, huilier, *m.*

castor oil ['kɑːstərˈɔil], *n.* huile de ricin, *f.*

castrate [kæsˈtreit], *v.t.* châtrer.

casual ['kæʒjuəl], *a.* fortuit, accidentel, casuel, de passage; insouciant.

casually ['kæʒjuəli], *adv.* fortuitement, par hasard; négligemment.

casualty ['kæʒjuəlti], *n.* accident; accidenté (*personne*), *m.*; (*pl.*) (*Mil.*) pertes, *f.pl.*

cat [kæt], *n.* chat; (*Mil., Navy*) fouet, martinet (*à neuf queues*), *m.*; **tom-cat**, matou, *m.*

catacombs ['kætəkuːmz], *n.pl.* catacombes, *f.pl.*

catalepsy ['kætəlepsi], *n.* catalepsie, *f.*

catalogue ['kætəlɔg], *n.* catalogue, *m.*, liste, *f.*

catamaran [kætəməˈræn], *n.* catamaran, *m.*

catapult ['kætəpult], *n.* catapulte, *f.*; lance-pierre (*jouet*), *m.*

cataract ['kætərækt], *n.* cataracte, *f.*

catarrh [kəˈtɑː], *n.* catarrhe, *m.*

catastrophe [kəˈtæstrəfi], *n.* catastrophe, *f.*; désastre, *m.*

catch [kætʃ], *v.t. irr.* attraper, prendre, saisir; (*colloq.*) pincer; frapper (*l'œil etc.*); **to catch a cold**, s'enrhumer; **to catch on**, avoir du succès, réussir; **to catch up**, atteindre, rattraper.—*v.i.* s'accrocher (*à*), se prendre (*à*).—*n.* prise; attrape; (*fig.*) aubaine, belle affaire, *f.*; cliquet (*d'une roue*); crampon (*d'une porte*); mentonnet (*d'un loquet*), *m.*

catching ['kætʃiŋ], *a.* contagieux; communicatif (*rire*); facile à retenir (*air*).—*n.* prise, capture, *f.*

catechism ['kætikizm], *n.* catéchisme, *m.*

categorical [kætəˈgɔrikəl], *a.* catégorique.

categorically [kætəˈgɔrikəli], *adv.* catégoriquement.

category ['kætəgəri], *n.* catégorie, *f.*

cater ['keitə], *v.i.* pourvoir (*à*).

caterer ['keitərə], *n.* pourvoyeur, fournisseur, *m.*

caterpillar ['kætəpilə], *n.* chenille, *f.*; **caterpillar tractor**, tracteur à chenilles, *m.*

cathedral [kəˈθiːdrəl], *n.* cathédrale, *f.*

catholic ['kæθəlik], *a.* universel; éclectique; catholique.

catkin ['kætkin], *n.* (*Bot.*) chaton, *m.*

cattiness ['kætinis], **cattishness** ['kætiʃnis], *n.* méchanceté, sournoiserie, *f.*

cattish ['kætiʃ], **catty** ['kæti], *a.* méchant, sournois, rosse.

cattle [kætl], *n.* bétail, *m.*, bestiaux, *m.pl.*

Caucasus ['kɔːkəsəs], **the.** le Caucase, *m.*

cauldron ['kɔːldrən], *n.* chaudron, *m.*, chaudière, *f.*

cauliflower ['kɔliflauə], *n.* chou-fleur, *m.*

caulk [kɔːk], *v.t.* calfater (*navire*).

cause [kɔːz], *n.* raison, cause, *f.*, motif, sujet, *m.*—*v.t.* causer, être cause de; occasionner, provoquer (*un accident*).

causeway ['kɔːzwei], *n.* chaussée, *f.*

caustic ['kɔːstik], *a.* caustique, corrosif; (*fig.*) mordant.

cauterize ['kɔːtəraiz], *v.t.* cautériser.

cautery ['kɔːtəri], *n.* cautère, *f.*

caution ['kɔːʃən], *n.* avis (*avertissement*), *m.*; précaution, prévoyance, prudence; caution, garantie, *f.*—*v.t.* avertir, aviser (*de*); réprimander.

cautious ['kɔːʃəs], *a.* circonspect, prudent, en garde.

cautiously ['kɔːʃəsli], *adv.* avec précaution, prudemment.
cavalcade ['kævəl'keid], *n.* cavalcade, *f.*
cavalier [kævə'liə], *a.* cavalier, désinvolte.—*n.* cavalier, *m.*
cavalry ['kævəlri], *n.* cavalerie, *f.*
cave [keiv], *n.* caverne, *f.*, antre, souterrain, *m.* —*v.t.* creuser.—*v.i.* **to cave in,** céder, s'affaisser, s'effondrer (*édifice*).
cavern ['kævən], *n.* caverne, *f.*
cavernous ['kævənəs], *a.* caverneux.
caviare [kævi'aː], *n.* caviar, *m.*
cavil ['kævil], *v.i.* chicaner (*sur*).
cavilling ['kæviliŋ], *a.* chicaneur.—*n.* chicanerie, *f.*
cavity ['kæviti], *n.* cavité, *f.*
cavort [kə'vɔːt], *v.i.* cabrioler.
caw [kɔː], *v.i.* croasser.
cawing ['kɔːiŋ], *n.* croassement, *m.*
cease [siːs], *v.t.* cesser; faire cesser.—*v.i.* cesser, discontinuer.
ceaseless ['siːslis], *a.* incessant, continuel.
ceaselessly ['siːslisli], *adv.* sans cesse.
Cecilia [sə'siliə] Cécile, *f.*
cedar ['siːdə], *n.* cèdre, *m.*
cede [siːd], *v.t., v.i.* (*Law*) céder.
cedilla [sə'dilə], *n.* (*Gram.*) cédille, *f.*
ceiling ['siːliŋ], *n.* plafond, *m.*
celebrate ['selibreit], *v.t.* célébrer, fêter.
celebrated ['selibreitid], *a.* célèbre, fameux.
celebration [seli'breiʃən], *n.* célébration, *f.*
celebrity [sə'lebriti], *n.* célébrité, *f.*
celerity [sə'leriti], *n.* célérité, vitesse, *f.*
celery ['seləri], *n.* céleri, *m.*
celestial [sə'lestjəl], *a.* céleste.
celibacy ['selibəsi], *n.* célibat, *m.*
celibate ['selibit], *a. and n.* célibataire, *m., f.*
cell [sel], *n.* cellule, case; alvéole (*d'abeilles*), *f.*; compartiment; cachot; (*Elec.*) élément, *m.*, pile, *f.*
cellar ['selə], *n.* cave, *f.*; cellier, caveau, *m.*
cello ['tʃelou], *n.* (*abbr. of* **violoncello**) violoncelle, *m.*
cellophane ['seləfein], *n.* cellophane, *f.*
celluloid ['seljulɔid], *n.* celluloïd, celluloïde, *m.*
Celt [kelt, selt], *n.* Celte, *m., f.*
Celtic ['keltik, 'seltik], *a.* celtique.
cement [si'ment], *n.* ciment, *m.*—*v.t.* cimenter; (*fig.*) consolider, fortifier.
cement mixer [si'mentmiksə], *n.* bétonnière, *f.*
cemetery ['semətri], *n.* cimetière, *m.*
cenotaph ['senotæf, -taːf], *n.* cénotaphe, *m.*
censer ['sensə], *n.* encensoir, *m.*
censor ['sensə], *n.* censeur, *m.*—*v.t.* soumettre à des coupures; censurer.
censorious [sen'sɔːriəs], *a.* critique, hargneux.
censorship ['sensəʃip], *n.* censure, *f.*; fonctions de censeur, *f.pl.*
censure ['senʃə], *n.* censure, critique, *f.*, blâme, *m.*—*v.t.* censurer, critiquer, blâmer.
census ['sensəs], *n.* recensement, *m.*
cent [sent], *n.* cent; sou (*pièce de monnaie*), *m.*; **ten per cent,** dix pour cent.
centaur ['sentɔː], *n.* centaure, *m.*
centenarian [senti'nɛəriən], *n.* centenaire, *m., f.*
centenary [sen'tiːnəri], *a. and n.* centenaire, *m.*
centennial [sen'teniəl], *a.* de cent ans, séculaire.

center ['sentə], *n.* centre; milieu; (*fig.*) foyer, *m.*—*v.t.* placer au centre; concentrer.—*v.i.* se concentrer.
centesimal [sen'tesiməl], *a.* centésimal.—*n.* centième, *m.*
centigrade ['sentigreid], *a.* centigrade.
centipede ['sentipiːd], *n.* scolopendre, *f.*, mille-pattes, *m.*
central ['sentrəl], *a.* central; **central heating,** chauffage central, *m.*
centralization [sentrəlai'zeiʃən], *n.* centralisation, *f.*
centralize ['sentrəlaiz], *v.t.* centraliser.
centrifugal [sen'trifjugəl], *a.* centrifuge.
centripetal [sen'tripitl], *a.* centripète.
centuple ['sentjupl], *a. and n.* centuple, *m.*—*v.t.* centupler.
centurion [sen'tjuəriən], *n.* centurion, (*Bibl.*) centenier, *m.*
century ['sentʃuri], *n.* siècle, *m.*
ceramic [sə'ræmik], *a.* céramique.
ceramics [sə'ræmiks], *n.pl.* céramique, *f.*
cereal ['siəriəl], *a. and n.* céréale, *f.*
cerebral ['serəbrəl], *a.* cérébral.
ceremonial [seri'mouniəl], *a.* de cérémonie. —*n.* cérémonie, étiquette, *f.*, cérémonial, *m.*
ceremonially [seri'mouniəli], *adv.* rituellement.
ceremonious [seri'mouniəs], *a.* cérémonieux.
ceremoniously [seri'mouniəsli], *adv.* cérémonieusement.
ceremony ['seriməni], *n.* cérémonie, solennité, *f.*; **without ceremony,** sans façon.
cerise [sə'riːs], *a. and n.* cerise (*couleur*), *m.*
certain ['səːtin], *a.* certain, sûr; **he is certain to do it,** il le fera certainement; **to make certain of something,** s'assurer de quelque chose.
certainly ['səːtinli], *adv.* certainement.
certainty ['səːtinti], *n.* certitude; chose certaine, *f.*
certificate [sə'tifikit], *n.* certificat; diplôme, brevet; concordat (*de faillite*); acte (*de naissance, de mariage ou de mort*), *m.*
certify ['səːtifai], *v.t.* certifier; notifier, donner avis à.
certitude ['səːtitjuːd], *n.* certitude, *f.*
cessation [se'seiʃən], *n.* cessation, suspension, *f.*
cession ['seʃən], *n.* cession, *f.*
cesspit ['sespit], **cesspool** ['sespuːl], *n.* puisard, *m.*, fosse d'aisances; (*fig.*) sentine, *f.*
Ceylon [si'lɔn], le Ceylan, *m.*
Ceylonese [silə'niːz], *a.* cingalais.—*n.* Cingalais (*personne*), *m.*
chafe [tʃeif], *v.t.* échauffer, irriter; érailler (*un câble*).—*v.i.* frotter; s'user, s'érailler (*un câble*); s'irriter; s'enflammer.
chafer (1) ['tʃeifə], *n.* hanneton (*insecte*), *m.*
chafer (2) [tʃeifə], *n.* réchaud (*plat*), *m.*
chafing dish ['tʃeifiŋdiʃ], *n.* réchaud (*de table*), *m.*
chaff [tʃaːf], *n.* menue paille; (*colloq.*) plaisanterie, raillerie, blague, *f.*—*v.t.* blaguer, taquiner, se moquer de.
chaffinch ['tʃæfintʃ], *n.* (*Orn.*) pinson, *m.*
chagrin [ʃæ'griːn], *n.* chagrin; dépit, *m.*— *v.t.* chagriner, vexer.
chain [tʃein], *n.* chaîne; chaînée, *f.*—*v.t.* enchaîner. [**chain store,** see **multiple**]

chair [tʃɛə], n. chaise, f.; siège, m.; chaire (à l'université), f.; fauteuil (d'un président), m.; **arm-chair**, fauteuil; **deck chair**, chaise longue, transat(lantique), m.; **rocking chair**, fauteuil à bascule; **wheel chair**, fauteuil roulant; **to be in the chair**, présider.

chairman ['tʃɛəmən], n. président, m.

chalice ['tʃælis], n. calice, m., coupe, f.

chalk [tʃɔ:k], n. craie, f., calcaire; crayon (pour dessiner), m.—v.t. blanchir avec de la craie; marquer ou écrire à la craie.

chalk pit ['tʃɔ:kpit], n. carrière de craie, f.

chalky ['tʃɔ:ki], a. crayeux, crétacé, calcaire.

challenge ['tʃælindʒ], n. défi, cartel, m.; (fig.) provocation, demande; (Law) récusation, f.; (Mil.) qui-vive; (Spt.) challenge, m.—v.t. défier; contester; (Law) récuser.

challenger ['tʃælindʒə], n. auteur d'un cartel; provocateur, agresseur, champion; (Spt.) challenger, m.

chamber ['tʃeimbə], n. chambre; salle, pièce, f., cabinet, m.; (Artill.) âme, f.; (pl.) bureaux, m.pl., étude, f.

chamberlain ['tʃeimbəlin], n. chambellan; camérier (du Pape), m.

chamber-maid ['tʃeimbəmeid], n. femme de chambre, f.

chamber music ['tʃeimbəmju:zik], n. musique de chambre, f.

chameleon [kə'mi:ljən], n. caméléon, m.

chamfer ['tʃæmfə], n. chanfrein, m.—v.t. chanfreiner, biseauter.

chamois ['tʃæmwɑ:], n. chamois, m.

chamois leather ['ʃæmi'leðə], n. chamois, m., peau de chamois, f.

champ [tʃæmp], v.t. ronger, mâcher.—v.i. ronger son frein.

champagne [ʃæm'pein], n. champagne, vin de Champagne, m.

champion ['tʃæmpiən], n. champion, m.—v.t. soutenir, défendre.

championship ['tʃæmpiənʃip], n. championnat, m.

chance [tʃɑ:ns], a. accidentel, de hasard.—n. chance, f., hasard, sort, m.; **by chance**, par hasard; **to stand a chance of**, avoir des chances de.—v.t. risquer.—v.i. arriver par hasard, venir à.

chancel ['tʃɑ:nsəl], n. sanctuaire, chœur, m.

chancellery ['tʃɑ:nsələri], n. chancellerie, f.

chancellor ['tʃɑ:nsələ], n. chancelier, m.

chancery ['tʃɑ:nsəri], n. cour de la chancellerie, f.

chandelier [ʃændi'liə], n. lustre, m.

chandler ['tʃɑ:ndlə], n. marchand ou fabricant de chandelles, m.; **corn-chandler**, marchand de blé; **ship chandler**, approvisionneur de navires, m.

change [tʃeindʒ], n. changement, m.; phase (de la lune); monnaie (espèces), f.; **change of life**, retour d'âge, m.; **changes of life**, vicissitudes, f.pl.; **for a change**, pour changer.—v.t. changer; modifier; donner la monnaie (de).—v.i. changer (de); se renouveler (la lune); **to change for the better**, s'améliorer.

changeable ['tʃeindʒəbl], a. changeant, variable, inconstant.

changer ['tʃeindʒə], n. changeur, m.

channel [tʃænl], n. canal; lit (de rivière), m.; passe (de port), f.; (Naut.) détroit, m.; (fig.) voie, f., moyen, m., entremise, f.; **the Channel Islands**, les îles Anglo-normandes, f.pl.; **the English Channel**, la Manche, f.—v.t. creuser.

chant [tʃɑ:nt], n. chant, plain-chant, m.—v.t., v.i. chanter.

chaos ['keiɔs], n. chaos, m.

chaotic [kei'ɔtik], a. chaotique.

chap (1) [tʃæp], v.t. gercer.—v.i. gercer, se gercer.—n. gerçure, crevasse (dans la peau etc.), f.

chap (2) [tʃæp], n. garçon, gaillard, type, m.; **old chap**, (colloq.) mon vieux.

chap (3) [tʃæp], **chop** (1) [tʃɔp], n. mâchoire, bouche; bajoue (de cochon), f.

chapel [tʃæpl], n. chapelle, f.

chaperon ['ʃæpərəun], n. chaperon, m.—v.t. chaperonner.

chap-fallen ['tʃæpfɔ:lən], a. (fam.) penaud, abattu, consterné.

chaplain ['tʃæplin], n. aumônier, m.

chaplet ['tʃæplit], n. chapelet, m., guirlande, f.

chapter ['tʃæptə], n. chapitre, m.

chapter house ['tʃæptəhaus], n. chapitre, m.

char (1) [tʃɑ:], v.t. carboniser.—v.i. se carboniser.

char (2) [tʃɑ:], v.i. faire des ménages.—n. (pop. abbr. of CHARWOMAN) femme de ménage, f.

character ['kæriktə], n. caractère; (Theat.) rôle, personnage; genre, m., nature, qualité, réputation, f.; certificat (de mœurs); (fig.) personnage, type, m.; **a bad character**, un mauvais sujet; **he is quite a character**, c'est un vrai original; **out of character**, déplacé.

characteristic [kæriktə'ristik], a. caractéristique.—n. trait caractéristique, m.

charade [ʃə'rɑ:d], n. charade, f.

charcoal ['tʃɑ:koul], n. charbon de bois, m.

charge [tʃɑ:dʒ], v.t. charger, accuser (de); faire payer; (fig.) adjurer; ordonner à.—v.i. (Mil.) charger.—n. charge, f.; prix, m.; garde, f.; soin; ordre, commandement, (Law) acte d'accusation, m., accusation, f.; mandement (d'un évêque); résumé (d'un juge), m.; (pl.) frais, dépens, m.pl.; **free of charge**, gratis; **the officer in charge**, l'officier commandant, m.; **to take charge of**, se charger de.

chargeable ['tʃɑ:dʒəbl], a. à charge (à); accusable (de).

charger ['tʃɑ:dʒə], n. grand plat; cheval de bataille; (Elec.) chargeur, m.

charily ['tʃɛərili], adv. avec précaution; frugalement.

chariot ['tʃæriət], n. char, chariot, m.

charioteer [tʃæriə'tiə], n. conducteur de chariot, m.

charitable ['tʃæritəbl], a. de charité; charitable.

charitably ['tʃæritəbli], adv. charitablement.

charity ['tʃæriti], n. charité, bienveillance; aumône, f.

charlatan ['ʃɑ:lətən], n. charlatan, m.

charm [tʃɑ:m], n. charme, m.; breloque (trinket), f., porte-bonheur, m. inv.; (pl.) attraits, m.pl.—v.t. charmer, enchanter.

charmer ['tʃɑ:mə], n. enchanteur, charmeur, m.

charming ['tʃɑ:miŋ], a. enchanteur, charmant; ravissant.

charnel ['tʃɑːnəl], *a.* de charnier.
charnel house ['tʃɑːnəlhaus], *n.* charnier, ossuaire, *m.*
chart [tʃɑːt], *n.* carte marine, *f.*—*v.t.* porter sur une carte.
charter ['tʃɑːtə], *n.* charte, *f.*, acte, *m.*; **on charter**, loué, affrété.—*v.t.* établir par un acte; (*Comm.*) fréter, affréter; **chartered accountant**, expert comptable, *m.*; **chartered plane**, avion-taxi, *m.*
charwoman ['tʃɑːwumən], *n.* (*pl.* **-women** [wimin]) femme de journée, femme de ménage, *f.*
chary ['tʃɛəri], *a.* prudent, économe.
chase (1) [tʃeis], *n.* chasse; poursuite, *f.*—*v.t.* chasser, poursuivre; **to chase away**, chasser.
chase (2) [tʃeis], *v.t.* (*Metal.*) ciseler.
chasm [kæzm], *n.* abîme; chasme; vide énorme, *m.*, brèche, fissure, *f.*
chassis ['ʃæsi], *n.* (*Motor.*) châssis, *m.*
chaste [tʃeist], *a.* chaste, pudique; pur (*langage*); de bon goût.
chasten [tʃeisn], *v.t.* châtier; purifier.
chastise [tʃæs'taiz], *v.t.* châtier.
chastisement ['tʃæstizmənt], *n.* châtiment, *m.*
chastity ['tʃæstiti], *n.* chasteté, pureté, *f.*
chasuble ['tʃæzjubl], *n.* chasuble, *f.*
chat [tʃæt], *n.* causerie, (*colloq.*) causette, *f.*, entretien, *m.*—*v.i.* causer, bavarder; (*colloq.*) faire la causette.
chattel [tʃætl], *n.* bien meuble, *m.*; **goods and chattels**, biens et effets, *m.pl.*
chatter ['tʃætə], *v.i.* jaser, bavarder; jacasser (*singes etc.*); babiller; claquer (*dents*).—*n.* caquetage, *m.*, jaserie, *f.*
chatterbox ['tʃætəbɔks], *n.* moulin à paroles, jaseur, babillard. *m.*
chattering ['tʃætəriŋ], *n.* jaserie, *f.*; claquement (*des dents*), *m.*
chatty ['tʃæti], *a.* causeur, bavard.
chauffeur ['ʃoufə, ʃou'fə:], *n.* chauffeur, *m.*
cheap [tʃiːp], *a.* (à) bon marché; peu coûteux, de peu de valeur; **dirt cheap**, pour rien, à vil prix.
cheapen ['tʃiːpən], *v.t.* faire baisser le prix de; **to cheapen oneself**, se déprécier.
cheaper ['tʃiːpə], *a.* (à) meilleur marché.
cheaply ['tʃiːpli], *adv.* à bon marché, à bon compte.
cheapness ['tʃiːpnis], *n.* bon marché, bas prix, *m.*
cheat [tʃiːt], *n.* fourberie, tromperie, *f.*; trompeur; (*Cards etc.*) tricheur, *m.*—*v.t.* tromper; (*Cards etc.*) tricher.
cheating ['tʃiːtiŋ], *n.* tromperie, (*Cards etc.*) tricherie, *f.*
check [tʃek], *v.t.* réprimer; arrêter; contenir; (*Comm.*) vérifier; enregistrer (*bagages etc.*); contrôler (*comptes*); (*Chess*) faire échec à.—*n.* échec, obstacle; (*Comm.*) bon; (*Am.*) [CHEQUE] carreau, damier (*dessin*); (*Chess*) échec, *m.* **[checkroom, see luggage]**
checking ['tʃekiŋ], *n.* répression, *f.*, contrôle, *m.*
checkmate ['tʃekmeit], *n.* échec et mat, *m.*—*v.t.* mettre échec et mat, mater.
cheek [tʃiːk], *n.* joue; bajoue (*cochon*); (*fig.*) impudence, *f.*, front, toupet, *m.*; **cheek by jowl**, côte à côte.—*v.t.* narguer.
cheek-bone ['tʃiːkboun], *n.* pommette, *f.*
cheeky ['tʃiːki], *a.* impudent, effronté.

cheep [tʃiːp], *n.* piaulement, *m.*—*v.i.* piauler.
cheer [tʃiə], *n.* chère (*aliment etc.*); gaieté, *f.*, courage, *m.*; acclamation, *f.*, applaudissement, hourra, vivat, *m.*—*v.t.* égayer, réjouir, animer; applaudir, acclamer.—*v.i.* se réjouir; applaudir.
cheerful ['tʃiəful], *a.* joyeux, gai; riant (*paysage etc.*).
cheerfully ['tʃiəfuli], *adv.* gaiement, joyeusement.
cheerfulness ['tʃiəfulnis], *n.* gaieté, allégresse, bonne humeur, *f.*
cheerily ['tʃiərili], *adv.* gaiement.
cheering ['tʃiəriŋ], *a.* consolant, encourageant.—*n.* applaudissements, *m.pl.*
cheerio! ['tʃiəriou], *int.* (*fam.*) (*good-bye*) à bientôt! (*when drinking*) à votre santé!
cheerless ['tʃiəlis], *a.* triste, morne.
cheery ['tʃiəri], *a.* gai, joyeux, réjoui.
cheese [tʃiːz], *n.* fromage, *m.*
cheese-paring ['tʃiːzpɛəriŋ], *n.* (*fig.*) économie de bouts de chandelle, *f.*
cheetah, chetah ['tʃiːtə], *n.* guépard, *m.*
chef [ʃef], *n.* chef (*cuisinier*), *m.*
chemical ['kemikəl], *a.* chimique.
chemically ['kemikli], *adv.* chimiquement.
chemicals ['kemikəlz], *n.pl.* produits chimiques, *m.pl.*
chemise [ʃi'miːz], *n.* chemise de femme, *f.*
chemist ['kemist], *n.* (*scientist*) chimiste, *m.*, *f.*; (*druggist*) pharmacien, *m.*; **chemist's shop**, pharmacie, *f.*
chemistry ['kemistri], *n.* chimie, *f.*
cheque [tʃek], *n.* chèque, *m.*; **traveller's cheque**, chèque de voyage, *m.*
cheque-book ['tʃekbuk], *n.* carnet de chèques, *m.*
cherish ['tʃeriʃ], *v.t.* chérir; soigner; nourrir, entretenir (*de l'espoir etc.*).
cherry ['tʃeri], *n.* cerise, *f.*
cherry tree ['tʃeritriː], *n.* cerisier, *m.*
cherub ['tʃerəb], *n.* (*pl.* **cherubs** ['tʃerəbz], **cherubim** ['tʃerəbim]) chérubin, *m.*
cherubic [tʃə'ruːbik], *a.* de chérubin, angélique.
chess [tʃes], *n.* échecs, *m.pl.*
chess-board ['tʃesbɔːd], *n.* échiquier, *m.*
chessman ['tʃesmən], *n.* (*pl.* **chessmen** ['tʃesmen]) pièce, *f.*; **a set of chessmen**, un jeu d'échecs.
chest [tʃest], *n.* coffre, *m.*, caisse; (*Anat.*) poitrine, *f.*; poitrail (*de cheval*), *m.*; **chest of drawers**, commode, *f.*
chestnut ['tʃesnʌt], *a.* châtain, marron (*couleur*); alezan (*cheval*).—*n.* marron, *m.*; châtaigne, *f.*
chestnut tree ['tʃesnʌttriː], *n.* châtaignier (*Spanish chestnut*); marronnier (d'Inde) (*horse chestnut*), *m.*
chevalier [ʃevə'liə], *n.* chevalier, *m.*
chevron ['ʃevrən], *n.* chevron, *m.*
chew [tʃuː], *v.t.* mâcher; (*fig.*) **to chew over**, ruminer.
chick [tʃik], *n.* poussin; (*fig.*) poulet, *m.*
chicken ['tʃikin], *n.* poussin, poulet, *m.*
chicken-hearted ['tʃikin'hɑːtid], *a.* peureux, poltron.
chicken pox ['tʃikinpɔks], *n.* varicelle, *f.*
chickweed ['tʃikwiːd], *n.* mouron des oiseaux, *m.*

chicory

chicory ['tʃikəri], n. chicorée (assaisonnement ou pour remplacer le café); endive (légume), f.
chide [tʃaid], v.t. gronder, blâmer.
chief [tʃiːf], a. principal.—n. chef, m.; partie principale, f.; (fam.) the chief, le patron, m.
chiefly ['tʃiːfli], adv. surtout, principalement.
chieftain ['tʃiːftən], n. chef de clan, m.
chiffon ['ʃifɔn], n. chiffon, m.
chiffonier [ʃifə'niə], n. chiffonnier, m.
chilblain ['tʃilblein], n. engelure, f.
child [tʃaild], n. (pl. children ['tʃildrən]) enfant, m.,f.; with child, enceinte.
child-bed ['tʃaildbed], n. couches, f.pl.
child-birth ['tʃaildbəːθ], n. enfantement, m.
childhood ['tʃaildhud], n. enfance, f.
childish ['tʃaildiʃ], a. enfantin; puéril.
childishness ['tʃaildiʃnis], n. puérilité, f.; enfantillage, m.
Chile ['tʃili]. le Chili, m.
Chilean ['tʃiliən], a. chilien.—n. Chilien (personne), m.
chill [tʃil], a. froid; glacé.—n. froid; refroidissement, frisson, m.; to catch a chill, prendre froid.—v.t. refroidir; (fig.) glacer; décourager.
chilli ['tʃili], n. piment, m.
chilliness ['tʃilinis], n. froid, frisson, m.; froideur, f.
chilly ['tʃili], a. un peu froid (chose); frileux (personne ou temps).
chime [tʃaim], n. carillon, m.—v.t., v.i. carillonner.
chimera [kai'miərə], n. chimère, f.
chimney ['tʃimni], n. cheminée, f.
chimney corner ['tʃimni'kɔːnə], n. coin du feu, m.
chimney piece ['tʃimnipiːs], n. chambranle ou manteau de cheminée, m.; (colloq.) cheminée, f.
chimney pot ['tʃimnipɔt], n. tuyau de cheminée, m.
chimney sweep ['tʃimniswiːp], n. ramoneur, m.
chimpanzee [tʃimpæn'ziː], n. chimpanzé, m.
chin [tʃin], n. menton, m.
China ['tʃainə]. la Chine, f.
china ['tʃainə], n. porcelaine, f.
Chinese [tʃai'niːz], a. chinois, de Chine.—n. chinois (langue); Chinois (personne), m.
chink [tʃink], n. crevasse, fente, lézarde, f.; son, tintement; (slang) argent, m.—v.t. crevasser; faire sonner.—v.i. se fendiller; sonner.
chintz [tʃints], n. (Tex.) indienne, f.
chip [tʃip], n. copeau, fragment, éclat (de bois); (Cards) jeton, m.; (pl., Cook.) (pommes de terre) frites, f.pl.—v.t. tailler; railler.—v.i. s'écorner; s'écailler (porcelaine etc.).
chiropodist [ki'rɔpədist], n. pédicure, m.,f.
chirp [tʃəːp], v.i. pépier, gazouiller; crier (insectes).—n. gazouillement, pépiement; cri (insectes), m.
chirpy ['tʃəːpi], a. (colloq.) gai, réjoui.
chirrup ['tʃirəp], [CHIRP].
chisel ['tʃizl], n. ciseau, m.—v.t. ciseler.
chit [tʃit], n. marmot, bambin; billet (lettre), m.
chitchat ['tʃittʃæt], n. caquet, babillage, m.
chivalrous ['ʃivalrəs], a. chevaleresque.
chivalry ['ʃivalri], n. chevalerie, f.
chives [tʃaivz], n.pl. ciboulette, f.
chlorate ['klɔːreit], n. (Chem.) chlorate, m.

chlorinate ['klɔːrineit], v.t. verduniser (eau potable).
chlorine ['klɔːriːn], n. chlore, m.
chloroform ['klɔrəfɔːm], n. chloroforme, m.—v.t. chloroformer.
chlorophyll ['klɔrəfil], n. chlorophylle, f.
choc-ice ['tʃɔkais], n. chocolat glacé, m.
chock-full [tʃɔk'ful], (fam.) chock-a-block ['tʃɔkə'blɔk], a. plein comme un œuf, comble.
chocolate ['tʃɔkəlit], n. chocolat, m.
choice [tʃɔis], a. choisi; de choix; recherché; fin (vin).—n. choix, m.; élite, f.; assortiment, m.
choir ['kwaiə], n. chœur, m.
choke [tʃouk], v.t. étouffer, suffoquer; engorger.—v.i. s'engorger.—n. étranglement (de voix); (Motor.) starter, m.
choking ['tʃoukiŋ], a. étouffant.—n. étouffement, m., suffocation, f.
choky ['tʃouki], a. étouffant, suffoquant.
choler ['kɔlə], n. colère, bile, f.
cholera ['kɔlərə], n. choléra, m.
choleric ['kɔlərik], a. colérique, irascible.
choose [tʃuːz], v.t. irr. choisir; élire; préférer; vouloir.
chop (1) [CHAP].
chop (2) [tʃɔp], v.t. couper en morceaux, hacher; trafiquer; troquer; to chop down, abattre.—v.i. trafiquer, troquer; (Naut.) tourner (vent); clapoter (mer); chopping block, hachoir, billot, m.—n. tranche; côtelette (de mouton); (colloq., pl.) gueule, f.
chopper ['tʃɔpə], n. couperet, m.
chopping ['tʃɔpiŋ], n. coupe, action de couper, f.
choppy ['tʃɔpi], a. crevassé, haché; clapoteux (mer).
choral ['kɔːrəl], a. choral, en ou de chœur.
chord [kɔːd], n. corde, f.; (Mus.) accord, m.
chores [tʃɔːz], n.pl. corvées domestiques, f.pl.
chorister ['kɔristə], n. choriste, m.; enfant de chœur, m.,f.
chorus ['kɔːrəs], n. chœur; refrain, m.
Christ [kraist]. le Christ, m.
christen [krisn], v.t. baptiser.
Christendom ['krisndəm], n. chrétienté, f.
christening ['krisniŋ], n. baptême, m.
Christian ['kristjən], a. and n. chrétien, m.; Christian name, prénom, m.
Christianity [kristi'æniti], n. christianisme, m.
Christmas ['krisməs]. Noël, m., la fête de Noël, f.; Christmas carol, chant de Noël, m.; Christmas Eve, la veille de Noël, f.
Christmas box ['krisməsbɔks], n. étrennes, f.pl.
Christopher ['kristəfə]. Christophe, m.
chrome [kroum], n. bichromate de potasse, m.; chrome leather, cuir chromé, m.
chromium ['kroumiəm], n. chrome, m.
chronic ['krɔnik], a. chronique.
chronicle ['krɔnikl], n. chronique, f.
chronicler ['krɔniklə], n. chroniqueur, m.
chronological [krɔnə'lɔdʒikəl], a. chronologique.
chrysalis ['krisəlis], n. chrysalide, f.
chrysanthemum [kri'sænθəmʌm], n. chrysanthème, m.
chub [tʃʌb], n. (Ichth.) chabot, chevesne, m.
chubby ['tʃʌbi], a. joufflu; potelé (mains).

376

chuck (1) [tʃʌk], *n.* gloussement, *m.*—*v.i.* glousser.

chuck (2) [tʃʌk], *n.* petite tape sous le menton, *f.*

chuckle [tʃʌkl], *v.i.* rire tout bas, rire sous cape (*de*).—*n.* rire étouffé, gloussement, *m.*

chum [tʃʌm], *n.* copain, *m.*

chummy [tʃʌmi], *a.* intime.

chump [tʃʌmp], *n.* tronçon (*de bois*); (*colloq.*) idiot, *m.*; *chump chop*, côtelette de gigot, *f.*

chunk [tʃʌŋk], *n.* gros morceau, *m.*

church [tʃəːtʃ], *n.* église, *f.*; (*Protestant*) temple, *m.*

churchwarden [tʃəːtʃwɔːdn], *n.* marguillier, *m.*

churchyard [tʃəːtʃjɑːd], *n.* cimetière, *m.*

churl [tʃəːl], *n.* rustre, manant, ladre, *m.*

churlish [tʃəːliʃ], *a.* grossier, rude, ladre.

churlishly [tʃəːliʃli], *adv.* grossièrement.

churlishness [tʃəːliʃnis], *n.* grossièreté, *f.*

churn [tʃəːn], *n.* baratte, *f.*; *milk churn*, bidon à lait, *m.*—*v.i.* baratter.

chute [ʃuːt], *n.* chute (*d'eau*); glissière, piste (*de luges*), *f.*

Cicero [sisərou], *n.* Cicéron, *m.*

cider [saidə], *n.* cidre, *m.*

cigar [siɡɑː], *n.* cigare, *m.*

cigarette [siɡəret], *n.* cigarette, *f.*

cinder [sində], *n.* cendre, *f.*; (*pl.*) escarbilles (*de charbon*), *f.pl.*

Cinderella [sindərelə], Cendrillon, *f.*

cine-camera [sinikæmərə], *n.* (ciné)caméra, *f.*

cinema [sinimə], *n.* cinéma, *m.*

cinnamon [sinəmən], *n.* cannelle, *f.*

cipher [saifə], *n.* zéro; chiffre, *m.*—*v.t., v.i.* chiffrer; calculer.

circle [səːkl], *n.* cercle, *m.*; (*fig.*) coterie, *f.*—*v.t.* entourer (*de*).—*v.i.* tournoyer.

circlet [səːklit], *n.* petit cercle, anneau, *m.*

circuit [səːkit], *n.* rotation, révolution, *f.*, tour; circuit, *m.*, circonférence; tournée (*de juge etc.*), *f.*

circuitous [səːkjuitəs], *a.* détourné, sinueux.

circular [səːkjulə], *a.* circulaire.—*n.* circulaire, *f.*, bulletin, *m.*

circulate [səːkjuleit], *v.t.* mettre en circulation, faire circuler, répandre.—*v.i.* circuler.

circulating [səːkjuleitiŋ], *a.* circulant.

circulation [səːkjuleiʃən], *n.* circulation, *f.*; tirage (*d'un journal etc.*), *m.*

circumference [səːkʌmfərəns], *n.* circonférence, périphérie, *f.*

circumflex [səːkəmfleks], *a.* (*Gram.*) circonflexe.

circumlocution [səːkəmləkjuːʃən], *n.* circonlocution, *f.*

circumscribe [səːkəmskraib], *v.t.* circonscrire.

circumspect [səːkəmspekt], *a.* circonspect.

circumstance [səːkəmstæns], *n.* circonstance, *f.*; état, *m.*; (*pl.*) moyens, *m.pl.*; *in straitened circumstances*, dans la gêne; *in easy circumstances*, dans l'aisance; *under no circumstances*, en aucun cas.

circumstantial [səːkəmstænʃəl], *a.* circonstancié, minutieux; indirect (*témoignage*).

circumvent [səːkəmvent], *v.t.* circonvenir.

circumvention [səːkəmvenʃən], *n.* circonvention, *f.*

circus [səːkəs], *n.* cirque; rond-point (*de rues*), *m.*

cistern [sistən], *n.* citerne, *f.*, réservoir, *m.*

citadel [sitədl], *n.* citadelle, *f.*

citation [saiteiʃən], *n.* citation, *f.*

cite [sait], *v.t.* citer; sommer (*de*).

citizen [sitizn], *n.* citoyen, bourgeois; habitant, *m.*

citron [sitrən], *n.* cédrat, *m.*

city [siti], *n.* ville; cité, *f.* [see **town** etc.]

civet [sivit], *n.* civette, *f.*

civic [sivik], *a.* civique.

civil [sivl], *a.* civil; municipal; honnête, poli; *civil servant*, fonctionnaire, *m.*; *in the Civil Service*, dans l'administration.

civilian [siviljən], *n.* bourgeois, civil, *m.*

civility [siviliti], *n.* civilité, politesse, *f.*

civilization [sivilaizeiʃən], *n.* civilisation, *f.*

civilize [sivilaiz], *v.t.* civiliser.

claim [kleim], *v.t.* demander, prétendre (*à*), réclamer, revendiquer.—*n.* demande, *f.*; titre, droit, *m.*

claimant [kleimənt], *n.* réclamateur, prétendant, *m.*

clam [klæm], *n.* peigne (*bivalve*), *m.*, palourde, *f.*

clamber [klæmbə], *v.i.* grimper (*sur* ou *à*).

clammy [klæmi], *a.* visqueux, pâteux; moite (*mains*).

clamor [klæmə], *n.* clameur, *f.*, bruit, *m.*—*v.i.* crier, vociférer.

clamorous [klæmərəs], *a.* bruyant, criard.

clamp [klæmp], *n.* crampon; (*Carp.*) serre-joints, *m.*—*v.t.* cramponner; serrer; entasser.

clan [klæn], *n.* clan, *m.*; clique, tribu, *f.*

clandestine [klændestin], *a.* clandestin.

clang [klæŋ], clank [klæŋk], *n.* cliquetis, son métallique, *m.*—*v.t.* faire résonner.—*v.i.* résonner.

clap [klæp], *n.* coup, *m.*; claque, *f.*; battement de mains; coup (*de tonnerre*), *m.*—*v.t.* claquer, frapper, battre (*mains, ailes etc.*); applaudir.—*v.i.* claquer *ou* battre des mains; applaudir.

clapper [klæpə], *n.* applaudisseur; battant (*d'une cloche*); claquet (*d'un moulin*), *m.*

clapping [klæpiŋ], *n.* battement des mains, *m.*, applaudissements, *m.pl.*

Clara [klɛərə], Clare [klɛə], Claire, *f.*

claret [klærət], *n.* vin de Bordeaux rouge, *m.*

clarify [klærifai], *v.t.* clarifier.—*v.i.* se clarifier.

clarinet [klærinet], *n.* clarinette, *f.*

clarion [klæriən], *n.* clairon, *m.*

clarity [klæriti], *n.* clarté, *f.*

clash [klæʃ], *v.t.* faire résonner (*en frappant*); choquer, heurter.—*v.i.* résonner, se heurter; (*fig.*) être aux prises (*avec*), s'opposer.—*n.* fracas, choc, conflit; cliquetis (*d'armes etc.*), *m.*

clasp [klɑːsp], *n.* fermoir, *m.*; agrafe, *f.*; (*fig.*) embrassement, *m.*, étreinte, *f.*—*v.t.* agrafer; serrer, presser.

clasp knife [klɑːspnaif], *n.* couteau de poche, *m.*

class [klɑːs], *n.* classe, *f.*; (*Sch.*) cours; genre, *m.*, catégorie, *f.*—*v.t.* classer.

classic [klæsik], *a.* and *n.* classique, *m*; *to study classics*, faire ses humanités *f.pl.*

classical [klæsikl], *a.* classique.

classification [klæsifikeiʃən], *n.* classification, *f.*

classify

classify [ˈklæsifai], *v.t.* classifier.
classroom [ˈklɑːsruːm], *n.* salle de classe, classe, *f.*
clatter [ˈklætə], *n.* bruit, tapage, fracas (*de ferraille etc.*), tintamarre, *m.*—*v.i.* faire du bruit, claquer.
clause [klɔːz], *n.* clause; proposition, *f.*
clavicle [ˈklævikl], *n.* (*Anat.*) clavicule, *f.*
claw [klɔː], *n.* griffe; (*Zool.*) serre; pince (*de crabes*), *f.*—*v.t.* griffer; déchirer; égratigner; (*fig.*) railler, gronder.
clay [klei], *n.* argile, terre glaise, glaise, *f.*—*v.t.* (*Agric.*) glaiser; terrer (*sucre*).
clayey [ˈkleii], *a.* argileux.
clean [kliːn], *a.* propre; blanc (*linge*); ciré (*chaussures*); (*fig.*) net, droit.—*adv.* entièrement, tout à fait, droit, raide.—*v.t.* nettoyer; décrotter, cirer (*chaussures*); écurer (*égouts, canaux etc.*).
cleaner [ˈkliːnə], *n.* nettoyeur (*personne*), *m.*
cleaning [ˈkliːniŋ], *n.* nettoyage, nettoiement, *m.*; **dry cleaning**, nettoyage à sec.
cleanliness [ˈklenlinis], **cleanness** [ˈkliːnnis], *n.* propreté; netteté, *f.*
cleanly [ˈklenli], *a.* propre; (*fig.*) pur.— [ˈkliːnli], *adv.* proprement, nettement.
cleanness [CLEANLINESS].
cleanse [klenz], *v.t.* nettoyer; curer (*égouts etc.*); (*fig.*) purifier.
cleansing [ˈklenziŋ], *n.* nettoiement, nettoyage, *m.*; (*fig.*) purification, *f.*
clear [kliə], *a.* clair; net, évident; sûr; innocent, sans tache.—*adv.* clair.—*v.t.* éclaircir; clarifier (*liquides*); faire évacuer (*salle etc.*); déblayer (*débris etc.*); gagner (*profit etc.*); (*Agric.*) défricher; (*fig.*) acquitter; (*Customs*) passer.—*v.i.* s'éclaircir; **to clear off**, s'en aller, filer; **to clear out**, se retirer; **to clear up**, élucider (*problème, mystère*); s'éclaircir, se rasséréner (*temps*).
clearance [ˈkliərəns], *n.* dégagement; déblaiement (*débris*), *m.*; levée (*du courrier*), *f.*; (*Naut.*) congé; (*Customs*) dédouanement, *m.*; **clearance sale**, solde, *m.*; liquidation, *f.*
clear-cut [ˈkliəkʌt], *a.* net, d'une grande netteté.
clear-headed [ˈkliəˈhedid], *a.* à l'esprit clair.
clearing [ˈkliəriŋ], *n.* éclaircissement; débrouillement; acquittement; (*Customs*) dédouanement; défrichement (*de terrain*), *m.*; éclaircie (*de forêt*), *f.*; déblaiement (*débris*), *m.*
clearing-house [ˈkliərinhaus], *n.* (*Rail.*) bureau de liquidation, *m.*; (*Banking*) banque de virement, *f.*
clearly [ˈkliəli], *adv.* nettement, clairement, évidemment.
clearness [ˈkliənis], *n.* clarté, netteté, pureté, *f.*
cleavage [ˈkliːvidʒ], *n.* clivage, *m.*; fissure, scission, *f.*
cleave [kliːv], *v.t. irr.* fendre, se fendre; **in a cleft stick**, (*fig.*) dans une impasse.
clef [klef], *n.* (*Mus.*) clef, *f.*
cleft [kleft], *n.* fente, fissure, crevasse, *f.*
clemency [ˈklemənsi], *n.* clémence; douceur (*du temps*), *f.*
clement [ˈklemənt], *a.* doux, clément.
clench [klentʃ], *v.t.* river (*clous etc.*); serrer (*poing*).
Cleopatra [kliəˈpætrə]. Cléopâtre, *f.*
clergy [ˈkləːdʒi], *n.* clergé, *m.*

clergyman [ˈkləːdʒimən], *n.* (*pl.* **-men** [men]) ecclésiastique; (*R.-C. Ch.*) prêtre, abbé, curé; (*Protestant*) ministre, pasteur, *m.*
cleric [ˈklerik], *n.* ecclésiastique, prêtre, *m.*
clerical [ˈklerikəl], *a.* clérical; **clerical error**, faute de copiste, *f.*
clerk [klɑːk], *n.* (*Law*) clerc; (*Eccles.*) ecclésiastique; (*Comm.*) commis; (*Civil Service*) employé, *m.* [see **shop-assistant**]
clerkship [ˈklɑːkʃip], *n.* place de clerc, place de commis, *f.*
clever [ˈklevə], *a.* adroit, habile, (*colloq.*) malin; intelligent; bien fait; **to be clever at**, être fort en.
cleverly [ˈklevəli], *adv.* habilement, adroitement, avec adresse.
cleverness [ˈklevənis], *n.* habileté, dextérité, adresse; intelligence, *f.*
click [klik], *v.i.* faire tic-tac, cliqueter.—*n.* bruit sec, clic; cliquetis; déclic, *m.*
client [ˈklaiənt], *n.* client, *m.*
clientele [kliːɑ̃ˈtel], *n.* clientèle, *f.*
cliff [klif], *n.* falaise, *f.*; rocher escarpé, *m.*
climate [ˈklaimit], *n.* climat, *m.*
climatic [klaiˈmætik], *a.* climatique.
climax [ˈklaimæks], *n.* gradation, *f.*; (*fig.*) comble, apogée, *m.*
climb [klaim], *v.t.* escalader, gravir, monter.—*v.i.* grimper; monter (*sur*); (*fig.*) s'élever.—*n.* ascension, montée, *f.*
climber [ˈklaimə], *n.* grimpeur, *m.*; alpiniste, *m.*, *f.*; **social climber**, arriviste, *m.*, *f.*
clime [klaim], *n.* (*poet.*) climat; pays, *m.*
clinch [klintʃ], *v.t.* river (*clous*); **to clinch an argument**, confirmer un argument.—*n.* (*Box.*) corps à corps, *m.*
cling [kliŋ], *v.i. irr.* se cramponner, s'attacher, s'accrocher (*à*); coller (*à*) (*robe*).
clinic [ˈklinik], *n.* and *a.* clinique, *f.*
clinical [ˈklinikəl], *a.* clinique.
clink [kliŋk], *n.* tintement, cliquetis, *m.*—*v.t.* faire tinter.—*v.i.* tinter.
clinker [ˈkliŋkə], *n.* mâchefer, *m.*
clip [klip], *v.t.* couper (*à ciseaux*); tondre (*chiens, chevaux*); écorcher, estropier (*paroles*); contrôler (*billets*).—*n.* tonte, *f.*; pince-notes, *m.*
clipper [ˈklipə], *n.* rogneur; (*Naut.*) fin voilier, *m.*
clippers [ˈklipəz], *n.pl.* tondeuse, *f.*
clique [kliːk], *n.* coterie, *f.*
cloak [klouk], *n.* manteau; (*fig.*) voile, masque, prétexte, *m.*—*v.t.* couvrir d'un manteau, (*fig.*) masquer, voiler, cacher.
cloak-room [ˈkloukruːm], *n.* (*Rail.*) consigne, *f.*, (*Theat.*) vestiaire, *m.*
clock [klɔk], *n.* horloge (*grand*); pendule (*petit*), *f.*; réveille-matin, *m.*—*v.i.* (*Ind.*) **to clock in** or **out**, pointer à l'arrivée *ou* au départ.
clock-maker [ˈklɔkmeikə], *n.* horloger, *m.*
clockwise [ˈklɔkwaiz], *adv.* dans le sens des aiguilles d'une montre.
clockwork [ˈklɔkwəːk], *a.* mécanique.—*n.* mouvement, mécanisme d'horlogerie; (*fig.*) travail régulier, *m.*
clod [klɔd], *n.* motte de terre, *f.*
clodhopper [ˈklɔdhɔpə], *n.* rustre; manant, *m.*
clog [klɔg], *n.* sabot, *m.*—*v.t.* obstruer.—*v.i.* se boucher, s'obstruer.

cloister ['klɔistə], n. cloître, m.
close (1) [klouz], v.t. fermer; clore, terminer. —v.i. se fermer; clore, se terminer, conclure, finir.—n. fin, conclusion, clôture, f.
close (2) [klous], a. clos, bien fermé; serré; lourd (temps); (fig.) mystérieux.—adv. près; de près; **close by**, tout près; **close to**, près de.
close-fisted ['klous'fistid], a. avare.
closely ['klousli], adv. de près; étroitement; secrètement.
closeness ['klousnis], n. proximité; exactitude; lourdeur (temps); intimité, f.
closet ['klɔzit], n. cabinet; boudoir, m.; garde-robe, armoire, f.—v.t. **to be closeted with**, être en tête-à-tête avec.
close-up ['klousʌp], n. (Cine.) gros plan, m.
closing ['klouziŋ], a. dernier, final.—n. clôture, fermeture (de magasin) fin, conclusion, f.
closure ['klouʒə], n. clôture, fermeture, f.
clot [klɔt], n. grumeau, caillot, m.—v.i. se cailler, se figer.
cloth [klɔ:θ], n. drap (de laine ou tissu d'or ou d'argent), m.; toile (de lin), f.; **table-cloth**, nappe, f.; tapis (de laine), m.
clothe [klouð], v.t. habiller, (re)vêtir.
clothes [klouðz], n.pl. habits, vêtements, m.pl.; hardes, f.pl.; **bed-clothes**, draps et couvertures, m.pl.
clothing ['klouðiŋ], n. vêtement, habillement, m.; vêtements, m.pl.
cloud [klaud], n. nuage, m.; (poet.) nue; (fig.) nuée, f.; **every cloud has a silver lining**, après la pluie le beau temps; **to be under a cloud**, être mal vu du monde.—v.t. couvrir de nuages; obscurcir; (fig.) assombrir.—v.i. se couvrir (de nuages).
cloudburst ['klaudbə:st], n. trombe, rafale de pluie, f.
cloudless ['klaudlis], a. sans nuage.
cloudy ['klaudi], a. nuageux, couvert; trouble (liquides); (fig.) ténébreux.
clout [klaut], n. torchon, linge, m.; gifle, tape, f.—v.t. rapetasser; taper, souffleter.
clove [klouv], n. clou de girofle, m.; **clove of garlic**, gousse d'ail, f.
cloven [klouvn], a. fendu; fourchu; **to show the cloven foot**, laisser voir le bout de l'oreille.
clover ['klouvə], n. trèfle, m.
clown [klaun], n. rustre, manant; (Theat.) bouffon, clown, m.
cloy [klɔi], v.t. écœurer, rassasier.
club [klʌb], n. massue, f.; (Golf) club (instrument), m.; crosse, f.; cercle, club, m., association, f.; (Cards) trèfle, m.—v.t. frapper avec une massue.—v.i. se cotiser, s'associer.
club-foot ['klʌbfut], n. pied bot, m.
club-house ['klʌbhaus], n. cercle; pavillon (de golf etc.), m.
cluck [klʌk], v.i. glousser.
clucking ['klʌkiŋ], n. gloussement, m.
clue [klu:], n. fil, indice, signe, m.; idée, f.
clueless ['klu:lis], a. (fam.) **to be clueless**, ne savoir rien de rien.
clump [klʌmp], n. masse, f., gros bloc; (fig.) groupe, m.; **clump of trees**, bouquet d'arbres, m.
clumsily ['klʌmzili], adv. gauchement, maladroitement.

clumsiness ['klʌmzinis], n. gaucherie, maladresse, f.
clumsy ['klʌmzi], a. gauche, maladroit; mal fait (chose).
cluster ['klʌstə], n. grappe (de raisin), f.; bouquet (de fleurs); régime (de bananes); nœud (de diamants), m.—v.i. se former en grappes; se grouper.
clutch [klʌtʃ], v.t. saisir, empoigner.—n. griffe, serre, étreinte, f.; (Motor.) embrayage, m.; couvée (d'œufs), f.
clutter ['klʌtə], n. fracas, vacarme; encombrement, désordre, m.—v.t. **to clutter up**, encombrer.
coach [koutʃ], n. voiture, f., carrosse, m.; (Rail.) voiture, f., wagon; autocar, car; (Sch.) répétiteur; (Spt.) entraîneur, m.—v.t. entraîner; préparer aux examens.
coaching ['koutʃiŋ], n. (Spt.) entraînement (d'équipe), m.; (Sch.) répétitions, f.pl.
coachman ['koutʃmən], n. (pl. -men [men]) cocher, m.
coachwork ['koutʃwə:k], n. carrosserie, f.
coagulate [kou'ægjuleit], v.t. coaguler.—v.i. se coaguler.
coal [koul], n. charbon, m.; houille, f.; **live coal**, charbon ardent.—v.t. charbonner.—v.i. s'approvisionner de charbon (navire).
coal cellar ['koulselə], n. cave à charbon, f.
coalesce [kouə'les], v.i. s'unir, se fondre, fusionner.
coal-field ['koulfi:ld], n. bassin houiller, m.
coalition [kouə'liʃən], n. coalition, f.
coal mine ['koulmain], n. mine de charbon, houillère, f.
coal miner ['koulmainə], n. mineur, m.
coal scuttle ['koulskʌtl], n. seau à charbon, m.
coarse [kɔ:s], a. gros, grossier.
coarseness ['kɔ:snis], n. grossièreté, f.
coast [koust], n. côte, plage, f., rivage, littoral, m.—v.t. côtoyer.—v.i. côtoyer, suivre la côte; caboter; planer (oiseau); (Motor.) rouler au débrayé.
coastal ['koustəl], a. côtier.
coaster ['koustə], n. caboteur, m.
coast guard ['koustgɑ:d], n. garde-côte, m.
coast-line ['koustlain], n. littoral, m.
coat [kout], n. habit; enduit (de goudron etc.), m.; robe (de certains animaux); (Paint.) tunique; (Mil.) couche, f.; **coat of mail**, cotte de mailles, f.; **double breasted coat**, veston croisé, m.—v.t. revêtir; enduire (de).
coat hanger ['kouthæŋə], n. cintre, m.; porte-vêtements, m. inv.
coax [kouks], v.t. amadouer, cajoler, flatter.
co-axial [kou'æksiəl], a. coaxial.
coaxing ['kouksiŋ], n. cajolerie, f., enjôlement, m.
cob [kɔb], n. bidet, goussant (cheval); épi (de mais), m.
cobalt ['koubɔ:lt], n. cobalt, m.
cobble [kɔbl], v.t. saveter, raccommoder; paver en cailloutis.—n. galet rond, pavé m.
cobbler ['kɔblə], n. cordonnier, m.
cobnut ['kɔbnʌt], n. aveline, f.
cobra ['koubrə], n. cobra, m.
cobweb ['kɔbweb], n. toile d'araignée, f.
cocaine [ko'kein], n. cocaïne, f.
cochineal ['kɔtʃini:l], n. cochenille, f.

cock

cock [kɔk], *n.* coq; mâle (*de petits oiseaux*); robinet (*tap*); chien (*de fusil*); tas, meulon (*de foin*), *m.*; **black-cock**, coq de bruyère; **cock-and-bull story**, coq-à-l'âne, *m.*— *v.t.* relever; retrousser; armer (*fusil*); **cocked hat**, chapeau à cornes, *m.*

cockade [kɔˈkeid], *n.* cocarde, *f.*

cock-a-doodle-doo [ˈkɔkədu:dlˈdu:], *n.* coquerico, cocorico, *m.*

cockatoo [kɔkəˈtu:], *n.* kakatoès, cacatois, *m.*

cockatrice [ˈkɔkətri:s], *n.* basilic, *m.*

cockchafer [ˈkɔktʃeifə], *n.* hanneton, *m.*

cock-crow [ˈkɔkkrou], *n.* chant du coq; (*fig.*) point du jour, *m.*

cockerel [ˈkɔkərəl], *n.* jeune coq, *m.*

cock-eyed [ˈkɔkaid], *a.* de biais, de travers.

cockle [ˈkɔkl], *n.* bucarde, *f.*

cock-pit [ˈkɔkpit], *n.* arène des combats de coqs; (*Av.*) carlingue, *f.*

cockroach [ˈkɔkroutʃ], *n.* blatte, *f.*

cockscomb [ˈkɔkskoum], *n.* crête de coq, *f.*; [COXCOMB].

cocksure [ˈkɔkˈʃuə], *a.* sûr et certain, outre-cuidant.

cocktail [ˈkɔkteil], *n.* cocktail, *m.*; **cocktail party**, cocktail.

cocky [ˈkɔki], *a.* effronté, suffisant.

coco [ˈkoukou], *n.* coco, *m.*

cocoa [ˈkoukou], *n.* cacao, *m.*

coconut, cocoa-nut [ˈkoukənʌt], *n.* coco, *m.*, noix de coco, *f.*

cocoon [kəˈku:n], *n.* cocon, *m.*

cod [kɔd], *n.* morue, *f.*; cabillaud (*morue fraîche*), *m.*

coddle [ˈkɔdl], *v.t.* mitonner; dorloter, choyer.

code [koud], *n.* code, *m.*—*v.t.* coder; chiffrer.

codicil [ˈkɔdisil], *n.* codicille, *m.*

codify [ˈkoudifai], *v.t.* codifier.

cod-liver oil [ˈkɔdlivərˈɔil], *n.* huile de foie de morue, *f.*

co-education [ˈkouedjuˈkeiʃən], *n.* enseignement mixte, *m.*

co-educational [ˈkouedjuˈkeiʃənəl], *a.* (*Sch.*) mixte.

coefficient [kouiˈfiʃənt], *n.* coefficient, *m.*

coerce [kouˈə:s], *v.t.* forcer, contraindre.

coercion [kouˈə:ʃən], *n.* coercition, contrainte, *f.*

coexist [kouigˈzist], *v.i.* coexister.

coexistence [kouigˈzistəns], *n.* coexistence, *f.*

coffee [ˈkɔfi], *n.* café, *m.*; **white coffee**, café au lait.

coffee bean [ˈkɔfibi:n], *n.* grain de café, *m.*

coffee house [ˈkɔfihaus], *n.* café, *m.*

coffee mill [ˈkɔfimil], **coffee grinder** [ˈkɔfi graində], *n.* moulin à café, *m.*

coffee-pot [ˈkɔfipɔt], *n.* cafetière, *f.*

coffer [ˈkɔfə], *n.* coffre; caisson; sas, *m.*

coffin [ˈkɔfin], *n.* cercueil, *m.*, bière, *f.*

cog [kɔg], *n.* dent, *f.*

cogency [ˈkoudʒənsi], *n.* force, puissance, *f.*

cogent [ˈkoudʒənt], *a.* puissant, fort.

cogged [kɔgd], *a.* denté, à dents.

cogitate [ˈkɔdʒiteit], *v.t.* penser (à.)—*v.i.* méditer, penser.

cogitation [kɔdʒiˈteiʃən], *n.* réflexion, pensée, méditation, *f.*

cognate [ˈkɔgneit], *a.* de la même famille; analogue.

cognizance [ˈkɔgnizəns], *n.* connaissance, *f.*; (*Her.*) insigne, *m.*

cognomen [kɔgˈnoumən], *n.* surnom; nom de guerre, sobriquet, *m.*

cog-wheel [ˈkɔgwi:l], *n.* roue d'engrenage, *f.*

cohabit [kouˈhæbit], *v.i.* cohabiter.

cohabitation [kouhæbiˈteiʃən], *n.* cohabitation, *f.*

coherence [kouˈhiərəns], *n.* cohésion, cohérence, *f.*

coherent [kouˈhiərənt], *a.* cohérent; conséquent.

coherently [kouˈhiərəntli], *adv.* d'une manière cohérente.

cohesion [kouˈhi:ʒən], *n.* cohésion, *f.*

cohesive [kouˈhi:siv], *a.* cohésif.

cohort [ˈkouhɔ:t], *n.* cohorte, *f.*

coil [kɔil], *n.* rouleau (*de cheveux etc.*); repli (*de serpents*), *m.*; (*Elec.*) bobine, *f.*—*v.t.* replier, enrouler.—*v.i.* se replier, s'enrouler.

coin [kɔin], *n.* pièce de monnaie, *f.*—*v.t.* monnayer; forger, fabriquer, inventer.

coinage [ˈkɔinidʒ], *n.* monnayage, *m.*, monnaie; (*fig.*) fabrication, *f.*

coincide [kouinˈsaid], *v.i.* s'accorder, coïncider (*avec*).

coincidence [kouˈinsidəns], *n.* coïncidence, *f.*

coincidental [kouinsiˈdentl], *a.* de coïncidence.

coiner [ˈkɔinə], *n.* monnayeur; faux monnayeur, *m.*

coition [kouˈiʃən], *n.* coït, *m.*

coke [kouk], *n.* coke, *m.*

colander [ˈkʌləndə], *n.* passoire, *f.*

cold [kould], *a.* froid; **it is cold**, il fait froid; **to be cold** (*of people*), avoir froid.—*n.* froid; rhume (*maladie*), refroidissement; frisson (*sensation*), *m.*; **to catch cold**, s'enrhumer.

coldly [ˈkouldli], *adv.* froidement.

cole [koul], *n.* chou marin, *m.*

colic [ˈkɔlik], *n.* colique, *f.*

collaborate [kəˈlæbəreit], *v.i.* collaborer.

collaboration [kəlæbəˈreiʃən], *n.* collaboration, *f.*

collaborator [kəˈlæbəreitə] *n.* collaborateur, *m.*

collapse [kəˈlæps], *v.i.* s'affaisser, s'écrouler, s'effondrer.—*n.* affaissement, *m.*, débâcle, *f.*

collapsible [kəˈlæpsibl], *a.* pliant, démontable.

collar [ˈkɔlə], *n.* collier (*de chien, de cheval, de décoration*); col (*de chemise*); collet (*de pardessus*), *m.*; collerette (*de dames*), *f.*— *v.t.* colleter, prendre au collet.

collar-bone [ˈkɔləboun], *n.* clavicule, *f.*

collar stud [ˈkɔləstʌd], *n.* bouton de col, *m.*

collate [kəˈleit], *v.t.* collationner, comparer.

collateral [kɔˈlætərəl], *a.* collatéral.

collation [kəˈleiʃən], *n.* collation, *f.*; don, présent; repas froid, *m.*

colleague [ˈkɔli:g], *n.* collègue, confrère, *m.*

collect (1) [kəˈlekt], *v.t.* recueillir; ramasser; collectionner; percevoir, encaisser (*impôts*); recouvrer (*dettes*); quêter; faire la levée (*du courrier*).—*v.i.* s'amasser.

collect (2) [ˈkɔlikt], *n.* collecte; (courte) prière, *f.*

collected [kəˈlektid], *a.* rassemblé; (*fig.*) recueilli, calme, tranquille.

collection [kəˈlekʃən], *n.* collection, *f.*; assemblage, rassemblement, *m.*; collecte, quête; levée (*du courrier*), *f.*

collective [kəˈlektiv], *a.* collectif.

collector [kə'lektə], *n.* collecteur; collectionneur; percepteur (*impôts*); quêteur (*aumône*); receveur (*douane*), *m.*
college ['kɔlidʒ], *n.* collège (d'Université), *m.*; école, *f.*
collide [kə'laid], *v.i.* se heurter.
collier ['kɔliə], *n.* mineur; (*Naut.*) (bateau) charbonnier, *m.*
colliery ['kɔljəri], *n.* houillère, mine de charbon, *f.*
collision [kə'liʒən], *n.* collision, *f.*, choc, *m.*
colloquial [kə'loukwiəl], *a.* de la conversation, familier; **colloquial French**, français parlé, *m.*
colloquialism [kə'loukwiəlizm], *n.* expression familière, *f.*
colloquy ['kɔləkwi], *n.* colloque, entretien, *m.*
collusion [kə'lu:ʒən], *n.* collusion, connivence, *f.*
Colombia [kə'lʌmbiə]. la Colombie, *f.*
colon (1) ['koulən], *n.* (*Anat.*) colon, *m.*
colon (2) ['koulən], *n.* (*Gram.*) deux points, *m.pl.*
colonel [kə:nl], *n.* colonel, *m.*
colonial [kə'lounjəl], *a.* colonial.
colonist ['kɔlənist], *n.* colon, *m.*
colonization [kɔlənai'zeiʃən], *n.* colonisation, *f.*
colonize ['kɔlənaiz], *v.t.* coloniser.
colony ['kɔləni], *n.* colonie, *f.*
color ['kʌlə], *n.* couleur, *f.*; (*fig.*) prétexte, *m.*, apparence, *f.*; (*pl.*) (*Mil.*) drapeau; (*Navy*) pavillon, *m.*; **to be off color**, être pâle, n'être pas bien en train; **with the colors**, sous les drapeaux.—*v.t.* colorer; colorier, enluminer (*gravure etc.*).—*v.i.* rougir (*personne*); se colorer (*chose*).
Colorado-beetle ['kɔlərɑ:dou'bi:tl], *n.* doryphore, *m.*
color-blind ['kʌləblaind], *a.* daltonien.
color-blindness ['kʌləblaindnis], *n.* daltonisme, *m.*
colored ['kʌləd], *a.* coloré; colorié; de couleur.
colorful ['kʌləful], *a.* coloré, pittoresque.
coloring ['kʌlərin], *n.* coloris, *m.*; couleur, *f.*
colorless ['kʌləlis], *a* sans couleur.
colossal [kə'lɔsl], *a.* colossal.
Colosseum [kɔlə'si:əm]. Colisée, *m.*
colossus [kə'lɔsəs], *n.* (*pl.* **colossi** [kə'lɔsai], **colossuses** [kə'lɔsəsiz]) colosse, *m.*
colt [koult], *n.* poulain, *f.*; (*fig.*) novice, *m.*
Columbus [kə'lʌmbəs]. Colomb, *m.*
column ['kɔləm], *n.* colonne, *f.*
coma ['koumə], *n.* coma; assoupissement, *m.*
comb [koum], *n.* peigne, *m.*; étrille (*chevaux*); crête (*coq*), *f.*; rayon (*miel*) *m.*—*v.t.* peigner; étriller (*cheval*).
combat ['kɔmbæt], *n.* combat, *m.*—*v.t., v.i.* combattre.
combatant ['kɔmbətənt], *n.* combattant, *m.*
combination [kɔmbi'neiʃən], *n.* combinaison; association, coalition, *f.*; concours (*de circonstances*), *m.*
combine [kəm'bain], *v.t.* combiner; réunir; allier.—*v.i.* se combiner; se coaliser (*avec*); s'unir (*à*); se syndiquer.—['kɔmbain], (*Comm.*) cartel, *m.*
combine-harvester ['kɔmbain'hɑ:vistə], *n.* moissonneuse-batteuse, *f.*
combustion [kəm'bʌstʃən], *n.* combustion, *f.*

come [kʌm], *v.i. irr.* venir; arriver, parvenir; se présenter, advenir, se faire; devenir; **come in!** entrez! **come on!** allons! **to come back**, revenir; **to come down**, descendre; **to come for**, venir chercher; **to come forward**, s'avancer; **to come home**, rentrer; **to come in**, entrer; **to come off**, se détacher; **to come out**, sortir; **to come up**, monter.
comedian [kə'mi:diən], *n.* comédien, *m.*
comedy ['kɔmidi], *n.* comédie, *f.*
comeliness ['kʌmlinis], *n.* aspect gracieux, *m.*; agréments, *m.pl.*
comely ['kʌmli], *a.* avenant.
comer ['kʌmə], *n.* venant; venu, *m.*; **first comer**, premier venu; **newcomer**, nouveau venu.
comet ['kɔmit], *n.* comète, *f.*
comfort ['kʌmfət], *n.* réconfort; bien-être, agrément, confort, *m.*; aise(s); aisance, *f.*; **to take comfort**, se consoler.—*v.t.* réconforter, soulager; consoler.
comfortable ['kʌmfətəbl], *a.* à son aise; agréable, confortable.
comfortably ['kʌmfətəbli], *adv.* à son aise, confortablement.
comforter ['kʌmfətə], *n.* consolateur (*le Saint Esprit*); cache-nez (*foulard*), *m.*; couvre-pieds (*inv.*) piqué, *m.*
comfortless ['kʌmfətlis], *a.* sans consolation; désolé, triste.
comic ['kɔmik], **comical** ['kɔmikəl], *a.* comique, drôle.
comically ['kɔmikli], *adv.* comiquement.
coming ['kʌmin], *n.* venue; arrivée; approche, *f.*
comma ['kɔmə], *n.* virgule, *f.*; **inverted commas**, guillemets, *m.pl.*
command [kə'mɑ:nd], *n.* ordre, commandement; pouvoir, *m.*; autorité, *f.*—*v.t.* commander; posséder; inspirer (*respect*).
commandant ['kɔməndænt], *n.* commandant, *m.*
commandeer [kɔmən'diə], *v.t.* réquisitionner.
commander [kə'mɑ:ndə], *n.* commandant; commandeur (*décoration*); (*Navy*) capitaine (*de frégate etc.*), *m.*
commander-in-chief [kəmɑ:ndərin'tʃi:f], *n.* généralissime, commandant en chef, *m.*
commanding [kə'mɑ:ndin], *a.* commandant; imposant (*important*); qui domine (*surplombant*); impérieux (*de commandement*).
commandment [kə'mɑ:ndmənt], *n.* commandement (*de Dieu*), *m.*
commando [kə'mɑ:ndou], *n.* (*Mil.*) corps franc, commando, *m.*
commemorate [kə'meməreit], *v.t.* célébrer, solenniser; commémorer.
commemoration [kəmemə'reiʃən], *n.* célébration, commémoration, *f.*; souvenir, *m.*
commence [kə'mens], *v.t., v.i.* commencer.
commencement [kə'mensmənt], *n.* commencement, début, *m.*
commend [kə'mend], *v.t.* confier (*à*); recommander; louer.
commendable [kə'mendəbl], *a.* louable.
commendation [kɔmen'deiʃən], *n.* éloge, *m.*, louange, *f.*
comment ['kɔment], *n.* commentaire, *m.*—*v.i.* commenter.

commentary ['kɔməntəri], *n.* commentaire, *m.*; **running commentary**, radio-reportage (*d'un match*), *m.*

commerce ['kɔmə:s], *n.* commerce, *m.*

commercial [kə'mə:ʃəl], *a.* commercial, de commerce; commerçant (*ville etc.*); **commercial traveller**, commis voyageur, *m.*— *n.* (*Tel.*) film publicitaire, *m.*

commingle [kə'miŋgl], *v.t.* mêler ensemble, mêler.—*v.i.* se mêler ensemble *ou* avec; se fondre (*dans* ou *en*).

commissariat [kɔmi'sɛəriət], *n.* commissariat, *m.*, intendance, *f.*

commission [kə'miʃən], *n.* commission, *f.*; (*Mil.*) brevet; (*Law*) mandat, *m.*—*v.t.* charger, commissionner.

commissionaire [kəmiʃə'nɛə], *n.* portier (de *magasin*); chasseur (*d'hôtel*); commissionnaire, *m.*

commissioner [kə'miʃənə], *n.* commissaire, *m.*

commit [kə'mit], *v.t.* commettre; confier, livrer, consigner; engager.

committee [kə'miti], *n.* comité, *m.*; (*Parl.*) commission, *f.*

commode [kə'moud], *n.* commode, *f.*

commodious [kə'moudjəs], *a.* spacieux.

commodity [kə'mɔditi], *n.* marchandise, denrée, *f.*, produit, *m.*

commodore ['kɔmədɔ:], *n.* (*Navy*) chef de division, *m.*; **air-commodore**, général de brigade, *m.*

common ['kɔmən], *a.* commun; ordinaire; vulgaire; (*fig.*) trivial; (*Mil.*) simple.—*n.* commune, *f.*; communal, *m.*; bruyère, lande, *f.*; **House of Commons**, Chambre des Communes, *f.*

commoner ['kɔmənə], *n.* bourgeois, roturier, *m.*

commonly ['kɔmənli], *adv.* ordinairement.

commonplace ['kɔmənpleis], *a.* banal, commun, trivial.—*n.* lieu commun, *m.*, banalité, *f.*

commonweal ['kɔmən'wi:l], *n.* le bien public, *m.*

commonwealth ['kɔmənwelθ], *n.* la chose publique, *f.*, l'État, *m.*; **the (British) Commonwealth**, le Commonwealth (britannique).

commotion [kə'mouʃən], *n.* secousse, agitation, *f.*, tumulte, *m.*

communal ['kɔmjunəl], *a.* communal.

commune (1) [kə'mju:n], *v.i.* parler, converser, s'entretenir (*avec*).

commune (2) ['kɔmju:n], *n.* commune, *f.*

communicate [kə'mju:nikeit], *v.t.* communiquer.—*v.i.* se communiquer.

communication [kəmju:ni'keiʃən], *n.* communication, *f.*

communion [kə'mju:njən], *n.* (*Eccles.*) communion, *f.*; commerce, *m.*

communiqué [kə'mju:nikei], *n.* communiqué, *m.*

Communism ['kɔmjunizm], *n.* communisme, *m.*

Communist ['kɔmjunist], *a.* and *n.* communiste, *m.*, *f.*

community [kə'mju:niti], *n.* communauté, société, *f.*

commutator ['kɔmjuteitə], *n.* commutateur, *m.*

compact (1) ['kɔmpækt], *n.* pacte, contrat; poudrier (de *dame*), *m.*

compact (2) [kəm'pækt], *a.* compact, serré, bien lié; concis.—*v.t.* rendre compact, unir.

companion [kəm'pænjən], *n.* compagnon, *m.*, compagne; dame *ou* demoiselle de compagnie (*to a lady*), *f.*; pendant (*mobilier*), *m.*

companionship [kəm'pænjənʃip], *n.* camaraderie; compagnie, *f.*

company ['kʌmpəni], *n.* compagnie; société, corporation; troupe (*acteurs*), *f.*; (*Naut.*) équipage, *m.*; **we have company today**, nous avons du monde aujourd'hui.

comparable ['kɔmpərəbl], *a.* comparable.

comparative [kəm'pærətiv], *a.* comparatif.

comparatively [kəm'pærətivli], *adv.* relativement, comparativement.

compare [kəm'pɛə], *v.t.* comparer.—*v.i.* être comparable à, rivaliser.

comparison [kəm'pærisən], *n.* comparaison, *f.*

compartment [kəm'pɑ:tmənt], *n.* compartiment, *m.*

compass ['kʌmpəs], *n.* compas; circuit, cercle, *m.*; boussole; portée (*atteinte*); étendue (de la *voix*), *f.*; **a pair of compasses**, un compas.—*v.t.* faire le tour de, entourer; accomplir; **to compass about**, environner.

compassion [kəm'pæʃən], *n.* compassion, pitié, *f.*

compassionate [kəm'pæʃənit], *a.* compatissant.

compatible [kəm'pætəbl], *a.* compatible (*avec*).

compatriot [kəm'pætriət], *n.* compatriote, *m.*, *f.*

compel [kəm'pel], *v.t.* contraindre, forcer (de), obliger (à ou de).

compelling [kəm'peliŋ], *a.* compulsif, irrésistible.

compensate ['kɔmpənseit], *v.t.* dédommager (de); compenser.—*v.i.* **to compensate for**, remplacer, racheter.

compensation [kɔmpən'seiʃən], *n.* dédommagement, *m.*; compensation, *f.*

compete [kəm'pi:t], *v.i.* concourir (*pour*), faire concurrence (à); disputer, rivaliser.

competence ['kɔmpitəns], *n.* capacité, aptitude; (*fig.*) aisance (*fortune*), *f.*

competent ['kɔmpitənt], *a.* compétent (*pour*), capable (de).

competently ['kɔmpitəntli], *adv.* avec compétence; suffisamment.

competition [kɔmpi'tiʃən], *n.* (*Comm.*) concurrence, *f.*; concours, *m.*

competitive [kəm'petitiv], *a.* compétitif, de concurrence; **competitive examination**, concours, *m.*

competitor [kəm'petitə], *n.* compétiteur; (*Comm.*) concurrent, *m.*

compile [kəm'pail], *v.t.* compiler, composer.

complacent [kəm'pleisənt], *a.* suffisant, de suffisance.

complacently [kəm'pleisəntli], *adv.* avec un air *ou* ton suffisant.

complain [kəm'plein], *v.i.* se plaindre (de).

complaint [kəm'pleint], *n.* plainte; maladie, *f.*, mal (*illness*), *m.*; réclamation, *f.*; **to lodge a complaint**, porter plainte.

complaisance [kəm'pleisəns], *n.* complaisance, *f.*

complement ['kɔmplimənt], *n.* complément, *m.*

complementary [kɔmpli'mentəri], _a._ complémentaire.

complete [kəm'pli:t], _a._ complet, entier; achevé.—_v.t._ compléter, achever; (_fig._) accomplir; remplir (_une fiche_).

completely [kəm'pli:tli], _adv._ complètement.

completion [kəm'pli:ʃən], _n._ achèvement, accomplissement, _m._, perfection, _f._

complex ['kɔmpleks], _a._ and _n._ complexe, _m._

complexion [kəm'plekʃən], _n._ teint, _m._, couleur, _f._; caractère, _m._; **to put a different complexion on**, présenter sous un autre jour.

complexity [kəm'pleksiti], _n._ complexité, _f._

compliance [kəm'plaiəns], _n._ acquiescement, _m._; obéissance, _f._; **in compliance with**, conformément à.

complicate ['kɔmplikeit], _v.t._ compliquer; embrouiller.

complicated ['kɔmplikeitid], _a._ compliqué.

complication [kɔmpli'keiʃən], _n._ complication, _f._

compliment ['kɔmplimənt], _n._ compliment, _m._; (_pl._) salutations, _f.pl._, hommages (_à une dame_), _m.pl._—[kɔmpli'ment], _v.t._ complimenter, féliciter.

complimentary [kɔmpli'mentəri], _a._ flatteur; en hommage; **complimentary ticket**, billet de faveur, _m._

comply [kəm'plai], _v.i._ se soumettre, se conformer; accéder (_à_).

component [kəm'pounənt], _a._ constituant, composant.—_n._ (_Mech._) composant, _m._

compose [kəm'pouz], _v.t._ composer; écrire; rédiger, arranger; calmer.

composed [kəm'pouzd], _a._ composé; calme.

composer [kəm'pouzə], _n._ auteur, _m._; (_Mus._) compositeur, _m._

composite ['kɔmpəzit] _a._ composé; (_Arch._) composite.

composition [kɔmpə'ziʃən], _n._ composition; (_Sch._) rédaction, _f._; **French composition**, thème français, _m._

compositor [kəm'pɔzitə], _n._ (_Print._) compositeur, _m._

compost ['kɔmpɔst], _n._ compost, terreau, _m._

composure [kəm'pouʒə], _n._ calme, _m._

compound ['kɔmpaund], _a._ and _n._ composé, _m._; **compound interest**, intérêts composés, _m.pl._—[kəm'paund], _v.t._ composer; mêler, combiner; (_Comm._) atermoyer.—_v.i._ s'arranger.

comprehend [kɔmpri'hend], _v.t._ comprendre.

comprehensible [kɔmpri'hensibl], _a._ compréhensible.

comprehension [kɔmpri'henʃən], _n._ compréhension, _f._

comprehensive [kɔmpri'hensiv], _a._ étendu, compréhensif; **comprehensive study**, étude d'ensemble, _f._

compress ['kɔmpres], _n._ compresse, _f._—[kəm'pres], _v.t._ comprimer; (_fig._) resserrer.

comprise [kəm'praiz], _v.t._ contenir, renfermer, comporter.

compromise ['kɔmprəmaiz], _n._ compromis, arrangement, _m._—_v.t._ compromettre.—_v.i._ transiger.

compromising ['kɔmprəmaiziŋ], _a._ compromettant.

compulsion [kəm'pʌlʃən], _n._ contrainte, _f._

compulsorily [kəm'pʌlsərili], _adv._ par force, forcément.

compulsory [kəm'pʌlsəri], _a._ forcé, obligatoire.

compute [kəm'pju:t], _v.t._ calculer, supputer.

computer [kəm'pju:tə], _n._ machine à calculer, _f._; ordinateur, _m._

comrade ['kɔmrid], _n._ camarade, compagnon, _m._

comradeship ['kɔmridʃip], _n._ camaraderie, _f._

concave ['kɔnkeiv], _a._ concave, creux.

conceal [kən'si:l], _v.t._ cacher; (_fig._) dissimuler; celer _ou_ céler (_à_).

concealment [kən'si:lmənt], _n._ dissimulation, _f._; secret, mystère, _m._; retraite, cachette, _f._

concede [kən'si:d], _v.t._ concéder, accorder, admettre.—_v.i._ faire des concessions.

conceit [kən'si:t], _n._ suffisance, vanité, _f._

conceited [kən'si:tid], _a._ suffisant, vaniteux.

conceivable [kən'si:vəbl], _a._ concevable, imaginable.

conceive [kən'si:v], _v.t._ concevoir; imaginer.—_v.i._ concevoir, devenir enceinte (_femme_).

concentrate ['kɔnsəntreit], _v.t._ concentrer.—_v.i._ se concentrer.

concentration [kɔnsən'treiʃən], _n._ concentration, _f._

conception [kən'sepʃən], _n._ conception, idée, _f._

concern [kən'sə:n], _n._ intérêt; soin, souci, _m._, anxiété; (_Comm._) entreprise; (_fig._) affaire, _f._—_v.t._ concerner, regarder; intéresser; inquiéter.

concerning [kən'sə:niŋ], _prep._ touchant, concernant, en ce qui concerne, à l'égard de.

concert [kən'sə:t], _v.t._ concerter.—_v.i._ se concerter.—['kɔnsət], _n._ concert; accord, _m._

concerto [kən'tʃə:tou], _n._ (_Mus._) concerto, _m._

concession [kən'seʃən], _n._ concession, _f._

concessionary [kən'seʃənəri], _a._ concessionnaire.

conch [kɔŋk], _n._ conque, _f._

conciliate [kən'silieit], _v.t._ concilier.

conciliation [kənsili'eiʃən], _n._ conciliation, _f._

conciliator [kən'silieitə], _n._ conciliateur, _m._

conciliatory [kən'siljətri], _a._ conciliant, conciliatoire.

concise [kən'sais], _a._ concis.

concisely [kən'saisli], _adv._ succinctement.

conclude [kən'klu:d], _v.t._ conclure; terminer, achever; estimer.

concluding [kən'klu:diŋ], _a._ final, dernier.

conclusion [kən'klu:ʒən], _n._ conclusion, fin; décision, _f._

conclusive [kən'klu:siv], _a._ concluant; conclusif.

concoct [kən'kɔkt], _v.t._ confectionner; inventer, préparer; machiner (_un plan_), tramer.

concoction [kən'kɔkʃən], _n._ confection (_d'un plat_); potion; (_fig._) machination (_complot_), _f._

concord ['kɔŋkɔ:d], _n._ concorde, harmonie, _f._; (_Mus._) accord, _m._

concourse ['kɔŋkɔ:s], _n._ concours, _m._, affluence, foule; réunion, _f._

concrete ['kɔŋkri:t], _a._ concret.—_n._ béton; bétonnage, _m._; **reinforced concrete**, béton armé.—_v.t._ bétonner.

concubine ['kɔŋkjubain], _n._ concubine, _f._

concur [kən'kə:], _v.i._ s'accorder, être d'accord (_avec_).

concurrence [kən'kʌrəns], _n._ assentiment; concours, _m._

concurrent [kən'kʌrənt], *a.* qui concourt, qui s'accorde, concourant.
concurrently [kən'kʌrəntli], *adv.* concurremment.
concussion [kən'kʌʃən], *n.* secousse, *f.*; choc, *m.*; (*Med.*) commotion, *f.*
condemn [kən'dem], *v.t.* condamner (*à*); déclarer coupable; blâmer.
condemnation [kɔndem'neiʃən], *n.* condamnation, censure, *f.*, blâme, *m.*
condensation [kɔnden'seiʃən], *n.* condensation, *f.*
condense [kən'dens], *v.t.* condenser; (*fig.*) resserrer, abréger.
condenser [kən'densə], *n.* condenseur; (*Phys.*) condensateur, *m.*
condescend [kɔndə'send], *v.i.* condescendre, daigner (*à*).
condescension [kɔndə'senʃən], *n.* condescendance, *f.*; acte de condescendance, *m.*
condiment ['kɔndimənt], *n.* assaisonnement, condiment, *m.*
condition [kən'diʃən], *n.* condition, *f.*, état, *m.*—*v.t.* conditionner.
conditional [kən'diʃənəl], *a.* conditionnel.
conditionally [kən'diʃənəli], *adv.* conditionnellement.
condole [kən'doul], *v.i.* prendre part à la douleur (*de*), exprimer ses condoléances.
condolence [kən'douləns], *n.* condoléance, *f.*
condone [kən'doun], *v.t.* excuser, pardonner.
condor ['kɔndə], *n.* condor, *m.*
conduce [kən'dju:s], *v.i.* contribuer (*à*).
conducive [kən'dju:siv], *a.* qui contribue (*à*).
conduct ['kɔndəkt], *n.* conduite; direction, *f.*; *safe conduct*, sauf-conduit, *m.*—[kən'dʌkt], *v.t.* conduire (*à*); diriger, mener.
conductor [kən'dʌktə], *n.* receveur (d'autobus); (*Am.*) (*Rail.*) chef de train; (*Mus.*) chef d'orchestre; (*Phys.*) conducteur, *m.*; *lightning-conductor*, paratonnerre, *m.*
conductress [kən'dʌktris], *n.* receveuse (d'autobus), *f.*
conduit ['kʌndit, 'kɔndit], *n.* conduit; tuyau, *m.*
cone [koun], *n.* cône; (*Bot.*) strobile, *m.*, pomme de pin, *f.*; *ice-cream cone*, cornet de glace, *m.*
confection [kən'fekʃən], *n.* bonbon, *m.*, friandise, *f.*
confectioner [kən'fekʃənə], *n.* confiseur, *m.*
confectionery [kən'fekʃənəri], *n.* confiserie, *f.*, bonbons, *m.pl.*
confederacy [kən'fedərəsi], *n.* confédération (*d'États*); ligue (*de conspirateurs*), *f.*
confederate [kən'fedərit], *a.* confédéré.—*n.* confédéré, *m.*, complice, *m.*; *f.*
confederation [kɔnfedə'reiʃən], *n.* confédération, *f.*
confer [kən'fə:], *v.t.* conférer, accorder.—*v.i.* conférer (*de*).
conference ['kɔnfərəns], *n.* conférence, *f.*, congrès, *m.*
confess [kən'fes], *v.t.* confesser, avouer.—*v.i.* se confesser.
confessed [kən'fest], *a.* reconnu, confessé, avoué.
confessedly [kən'fesidli], *adv.* de son propre aveu.
confession [kən'feʃən], *n.* confession, *f.*, aveu, *m.*
confessor [kən'fesə], *n.* confesseur, *m.*

confidant ['kɔnfidænt], *n.* confident, *m.*
confide [kən'faid], *v.t.* confier (*à*).—*v.i.* se confier, se fier (*à*).
confidence ['kɔnfidəns], *n.* confiance; hardiesse; assurance; confidence (*secret*), *f.*
confident ['kɔnfidənt], *a.* confiant, certain, sûr; assuré.
confidential [kɔnfi'denʃəl], *a.* de confiance (*personne*); confidentiel (*chose*).
confidentially [kɔnfi'denʃəli], *adv.* de confiance; confidentiellement.
confidently ['kɔnfidəntli], *adv.* avec confiance.
confine [kən'fain], *v.t.* confiner, enfermer; retenir; limiter; *to be confined* (*of woman*), faire ses couches, accoucher.—['kɔnfain], *n.* (*usu. in pl.*) confins, *m.pl.*; (*fig.*) limite, borne, *f.*
confinement [kən'fainmənt], *n.* emprisonnement, *m.*; (*Mil.*) arrêts, *m.pl.*; accouchement, *m.*, couches (*de femme*), *f.pl.*
confirm [kən'fə:m], *v.t.* confirmer; affermir.
confirmation [kɔnfə'meiʃən], *n.* confirmation, *f.*, affermissement, *m.*
confirmed [kən'fə:md], *a.* invétéré, fieffé, incorrigible.
confiscate ['kɔnfiskeit], *v.t.* confisquer.
confiscation [kɔnfis'keiʃən], *n.* confiscation, *f.*
conflagration [kɔnflə'greiʃən], *n.* conflagration, *f.*, incendie, *m.*
conflict ['kɔnflikt], *n.* conflit, *m.*; (*fig.*) lutte, contradiction, *f.*—[kən'flikt], *v.i.* s'entrechoquer, lutter (*contre*); être en conflit (*avec*).
conflicting [kən'fliktiŋ], *a.* en conflit, contradictoire.
confluence ['kɔnfluəns], *n.* confluent; concours, *m.*; (*Path.*) confluence, *f.*
conform [kən'fɔ:m], *v.t.* conformer.—*v.i.* se conformer.
conformity [kən'fɔ:miti], *n.* conformité, *f.*; *in conformity with*, conformément à.
confound [kən'faund], *v.t.* confondre; (*fig.*) bouleverser; embarrasser; *confound it!* zut!
confounded [kən'faundid], *a.* maudit, sacré.
confoundedly [kən'faundidli], *adv.* terriblement, furieusement, diablement.
confront [kən'frʌnt], *v.t.* confronter; affronter, faire face à.
confuse [kən'fju:z], *v.t.* rendre confus, embrouiller; (*fig.*) déconcerter.
confused [kən'fju:zd], *a.* confus; embrouillé.
confusedly [kən'fju:zidli], *adv.* confusément.
confusion [kən'fju:ʒən], *n.* confusion, *f.*, désordre; (*fig.*) embarras, *m.*
confute [kən'fju:t], *v.t.* réfuter.
congeal [kən'dʒi:l], *v.t.* congeler, glacer, geler, figer.—*v.i.* se congeler, se geler, se figer.
congenial [kən'dʒi:niəl], *a.* de la même nature; sympathique (*à ou avec*); qui convient (*à*); *a congenial task*, une tâche agréable.
conger ['kɔŋgə], *n.* (*Ichth.*) congre, *m.*, anguille de mer, *f.*
congest [kən'dʒest], *v.t.* entasser; engorger; *to become congested*, se congestionner; s'embouteiller (*rues*).
congestion [kən'dʒestʃən], *n.* amoncellement, *m.*; (*Path.*) congestion, *f.*; encombrement (*des rues*), *m.*

conglomerate [kən'glɔməreit], *v.t.* conglomérer.—*v.i.* se conglomérer.—[kən'glɔmərit], *n.* (*Geol.*) conglomérat, *m.*
conglomeration [kɔnglɔmə'reiʃən], *n.* conglomération, *f.*
Congo ['kɔŋgou]. le Congo, *m.*
Congolese [kɔŋgo'li:z], *a.* congolais.—*n.* Congolais (*personne*).
congratulate [kən'grætjuleit], *v.t.* féliciter.
congratulation [kəngrætju'leiʃən], *n.* félicitation, *f.*
congregate ['kɔngrigeit], *v.t.* rassembler.—*v.i.* se rassembler.
congregation [kɔngri'geiʃən], *n.* (*Eccles.*) congrégation, *f.*, fidèles, *m.pl.*; assemblée, *f.*, auditoire, *m.*; assistance, *f.*
congress ['kɔngres], *n.* congrès, *m.*
congressional [kən'greʃənl], *a.* congressionnel.
congressman ['kɔngresmən], *n.* (*pl.* -men [men]) (*U.S.*) membre du Congrès, *m.*
conic ['kɔnik], **conical** ['kɔnikəl], *a.* conique.
conifer ['kounifə], *n.* conifère, *m.*
coniferous [ko'nifərəs], *a.* conifère.
conjecture [kən'dʒektʃə], *v.t.*, *v.i.* conjecturer.—*n.* conjecture, *f.*
conjugal ['kɔndʒugəl], *a.* conjugal.
conjugate ['kɔndʒugeit], *v.t.* conjuguer.
conjugation [kɔndʒu'geiʃən], *n.* conjugaison, *f.*
conjunction [kən'dʒʌŋkʃən], *n.* conjonction, *f.*
conjure ['kʌndʒə], *v.t.* ensorceler; escamoter; **to conjure up**, évoquer.
conjurer, conjuror ['kʌndʒərə], *n.* escamoteur, prestidigitateur, illusionniste, *m.*
conjuring ['kʌndʒəriŋ], *n.* prestidigitation, *f.*, escamotage, *m.*
connect [kə'nekt], *v.t.* lier, joindre, rattacher, unir (*à*); accoupler.—*v.i.* se lier; faire correspondance (*trains*).
connected [kə'nektid], *a.* joint, uni, lié; cohérent; en relations.
connection (**connexion**) [kə'nekʃən], *n.* connexion, liaison, suite, *f.*; rapport, *m.*; (*Rail.*) correspondance, *f.*; (*Elec.*) contact, *m.*; (*Comm.*) clientèle, *f.*; (*pl.*) parents, *m.pl.*; **in connection with**, à propos de.
connivance [kə'naivəns], *n.* connivence, *f.*
connive [kə'naiv], *v.i.* **to connive at**, fermer les yeux sur, être de connivence dans.
connoisseur [kɔnə'sə:], *n.* connaisseur, *m.*
connubial [kə'nju:biəl], *a.* conjugal.
conquer ['kɔŋkə], *v.t.* vaincre, dompter; conquérir.—*v.i.* vaincre, remporter la victoire.
conqueror ['kɔŋkərə], *n.* vainqueur, conquérant, *m.*
conquest ['kɔŋkwest], *n.* conquête, *f.*
conscience ['kɔnʃəns], *n.* conscience, *f.*; **conscience money**, restitution anonyme, *f.*
conscientious [kɔnʃi'enʃəs], *a.* consciencieux; de conscience; **conscientious objector**, objecteur de conscience, *m.*
conscientiously [kɔnʃi'enʃəsli], *adv.* consciencieusement.
conscious ['kɔnʃəs], *a.* conscient; **to be conscious**, avoir sa connaissance; **to be conscious of**, avoir conscience de.
consciously ['kɔnʃəsli], *adv.* sciemment, en connaissance de cause.

consciousness ['kɔnʃəsnis], *n.* conscience; connaissance, *f.*
conscript ['kɔnskript], *a.* and *n.* conscrit, *m.*—[kən'skript], *v.t.* enrôler (par la conscription).
conscription [kən'skripʃən], *n.* conscription, *f.*
consecrate ['kɔnsikreit], *v.t.* consacrer (*une église*); bénir (*pain*); sacrer (*évêque, roi*); **consecrated ground**, terre sainte, *f.*
consecration [kɔnsi'kreiʃən], *n.* consécration; canonisation, *f.*; sacre (*d'évêque, de roi etc.*), *m.*
consecutive [kən'sekjutiv], *a.* consécutif.
consent [kən'sent], *v.i.* consentir (*à*).—*n.* consentement; accord, *m.*
consequence ['kɔnsikwəns], *n.* conséquence, suite, *f.*, effet, *m.*; importance, *f.*
consequent ['kɔnsikwənt], *a.* résultant; (*Log.*) conséquent.—*n.* conséquent, *m.*
consequential [kɔnsi'kwenʃəl], *a.* conséquent, logique; (*fig.*) suffisant, important.
consequently ['kɔnsikwəntli], *adv.* and *conj.* par conséquent.
conservative [kən'sə:vətiv], *a.* and *n.* conservateur, *m.*
conservatory [kən'sə:vətri], *n.* conservatoire (*théâtre, musique*), *m.*; (*Hort.*) serre, *f.*
consider [kən'sidə], *v.t.* considérer, examiner; estimer.—*v.i.* considérer, réfléchir (*à*).
considerable [kən'sidərəbl], *a.* considérable, grand, important.
considerably [kən'sidərəbli], *adv.* considérablement.
considerate [kən'sidərit], *a.* modéré, indulgent; attentif, plein d'égards; prévenant.
consideration [kənsidə'reiʃən], *n.* considération, *f.*, examen, *m.*; égards, *m.pl.*; récompense, *f.*, dédommagement, *m.*; **to take into consideration**, tenir compte de.
considering [kən'sidəriŋ], *prep.* eu égard à, étant donné, vu.—*conj.* vu que, attendu que, étant donné que.
consign [kən'sain], *v.t.* consigner, livrer, confier (*à*); (*Comm.*) expédier.
consignment [kən'sainmənt], *n.* expédition, *f.*, envoi, *m.*
consist [kən'sist], *v.i.* consister (*en*); **to consist of**, se composer (*de*).
consistency [kən'sistənsi], *n.* consistance, suite, *f.*, esprit de suite; accord, *m.*, harmonie; stabilité, *f.*
consistent [kən'sistənt], *a.* consistant; compatible (*avec*), conséquent.
consistently [kən'sistəntli], *adv.* d'une manière conséquente, conséquemment.
consolation [kɔnsə'leiʃən], *n.* consolation, *f.*
console [kən'soul], *v.t.* consoler (*de*).
consolidate [kən'sɔlideit], *v.t.* consolider.—*v.i.* se consolider; **consolidated annuities**, (*abbr.*) **consols**, consolidés, *m.pl.*
consolidation [kənsɔli'deiʃən], *n.* consolidation, *f.*
consoling [kən'souliŋ], *a.* consolant, consolateur.
consonant ['kɔnsənənt], *a.* consonant, conforme (*à*).—*n.* (*Phon.*) consonne, *f.*
consort ['kɔnsɔ:t], *n.* compagnon, *m.*, compagne, *f.*; époux, *m.*, épouse, *f.*—[kən'sɔ:t], *v.i.* s'associer (*à*); **to consort with**, fréquenter.

conspicuous [kən'spikjuəs], *a.* bien visible, en évidence; remarquable, éminent.

conspicuously [kən'spikjuəsli], *adv.* visiblement, manifestement, éminemment.

conspiracy [kən'spirəsi], *n.* conspiration, conjuration, *f.*

conspirator [kən'spirətə], *n.* conspirateur; conjuré, *m.*

conspire [kən'spaiə], *v.i.* conspirer, comploter (*contre*); (*fig.*) se réunir (*pour*).

constable ['kʌnstəbl], *n.* gouverneur (*de château*); agent de police, *m.*; **chief constable**, commissaire de police, *m.*

constabulary [kən'stæbjuləri], *n.* police; gendarmerie, *f.*

constancy ['kɔnstənsi], *n.* constance, fermeté, fidélité; régularité, *f.*

constant ['kɔnstənt], *a.* stable, constant, fidèle; continu.

constantly ['kɔnstəntli], *adv.* constamment, invariablement.

constellation [kɔnstə'leiʃən], *n.* constellation, *f.*

consternation [kɔnstə'neiʃən], *n.* consternation, *f.*, atterrement, *m.*

constipation [kɔnsti'peiʃən], *n.* constipation, *f.*

constituency [kən'stitjuənsi], *n.* circonscription électorale, *f.*, électeurs, *m.pl.*

constituent [kən'stitjuənt], *a.* constituant.— *n.* constituant; (*Polit.*) commettant, électeur, *m.*

constitute ['kɔnstitju:t], *v.t.* constituer, faire.

constitution [kɔnsti'tju:ʃən], *n.* constitution, *f.*, tempérament, *m.*

constitutional [kɔnsti'tju:ʃənəl], *a.* constitutionnel.—*n.* promenade de santé, *f.*

constrain [kən'strein], *v.t.* contraindre, forcer; retenir; gêner.

constraint [kən'streint], *n.* contrainte, gêne, *f.*

constrict [kən'strikt], *v.t.* resserrer, étrangler; brider.

construct [kən'strʌkt], *v.t.* construire, bâtir.

construction [kən'strʌkʃən], *n.* construction, *f.*; bâtiment, *m.*; (*fig.*) interprétation, *f.*, sens, *m.*

constructive [kən'strʌktiv], *a.* constructif; implicite.

construe [kən'stru:], *v.t.* traduire mot-à-mot; (*fig.*) expliquer, interpréter.

consul ['kɔnsəl], *n.* consul, *m.*

consular ['kɔnsjulə], *a.* consulaire.

consulate ['kɔnsjulit], **consulship** ['kɔnsəlʃip], *n.* consulat, *m.*

consult [kən'sʌlt], *v.t.* consulter.—*v.i.* délibérer.

consultation [kɔnsəl'teiʃən], *n.* consultation, délibération, *f.*

consume [kən'sju:m], *v.t.* consumer, dissiper, dévorer; gaspiller; consommer (*to use*).

consumer [kən'sju:mə], *n.* consommateur; abonné (*de gaz etc.*), *m.*; **consumer goods**, biens de consommation, *m.pl.*

consummate ['kɔnsəmeit], *v.t.* consommer, achever, accomplir.—[kən'sʌmit], *a.* consommé, complet, achevé, fieffé.

consummation [kɔnsə'meiʃən], *n.* consommation, fin, *f.*; (*fig.*) comble, *m.*

consumption [kən'sʌmpʃən], *n.* consommation; phtisie, consomption (*maladie*), *f.*

consumptive [kən'sʌmptiv], *a.* poitrinaire, phtisique, tuberculeux.

contact ['kɔntækt], *n.* contact, rapport, *m.*— *v.t.* contacter, se mettre en relation avec, entrer en contact avec.

contagion [kən'teidʒən], *n.* contagion, *f.*

contagious [kən'teidʒəs], *a.* contagieux.

contain [kən'tein], *v.t.* contenir; retenir, renfermer.

container [kən'teinə], *n.* récipient, réservoir, *m.*; (*Comm.*) boîte, *f.*

contaminate [kən'tæmineit], *v.t.* souiller, contaminer.

contamination [kəntæmi'neiʃən], *n.* souillure, contamination, *f.*

contemplate ['kɔntəmpleit], *v.t.* contempler; méditer, projeter.—*v.i.* songer, méditer.

contemplation [kɔntəm'pleiʃən], *n.* contemplation; méditation, *f.*; projet, *m.*

contemplative [kən'templətiv], *a.* contemplatif; pensif.

contemporaneous [kəntempə'reinjəs], *a.* contemporain.

contemporary [kən'tempərəri], *a.* and *n.* contemporain, *m.*

contempt [kən'tempt], *n.* mépris, dédain, *m.*

contemptible [kən'temptəbl], *a.* méprisable, à dédaigner.

contemptuous [kən'temptjuəs], *a.* méprisant, dédaigneux.

contend [kən'tend], *v.i.* lutter, combattre; contester; prétendre (*que*).

contender [kən'tendə], *n.* compétiteur, concurrent, *m.*

content (1) [kən'tent], *a.* content, satisfait; **to be content with**, se contenter de.—*n.* contentement, *m.*—*v.t.* contenter, satisfaire.

content (2) ['kɔntent], *n.* contenu, *m.*; **table of contents**, table des matières, *f.*

contented [kən'tentid], *a.* satisfait, content (*de*).

contentedly [kən'tentidli], *adv.* avec contentement.

contention [kən'tenʃən], *n.* dispute, lutte, *f.*, débat, *m.*; prétention, *f.*; **bone of contention**, pomme de discorde, *f.*

contentious [kən'tenʃəs], *a.* contentieux, litigieux, querelleur.

contentiousness [kən'tenʃəsnis], *n.* humeur querelleuse, *f.*

contentment [kən'tentmənt], *n.* contentement, *m.*

conterminous [kən'tə:minəs], *a.* limitrophe, voisin (*de*); attenant (*à*).

contest ['kɔntest], *n.* lutte, *f.*, combat; concours, *m.*—[kən'test], *v.t.*, *v.i.* contester, disputer.

contestant [kən'testənt], *n.* contestant, concurrent, *m.*

context ['kɔntekst], *n.* contexte, *m.*; **in this context**, à ce sujet.

contiguity [kɔnti'gju:iti], *n.* contiguïté, *f.*

contiguous [kən'tigjuəs], *a.* contigu, attenant (*à*).

continence ['kɔntinəns], *n.* continence, chasteté; (*fig.*) retenue, *f.*

continent (1) ['kɔntinənt], *a.* continent, chaste; (*fig.*) modéré, retenu.

continent (2) ['kɔntinənt], *n.* continent, *m.*

continental [kɔnti'nentl], *a.* and *n.* continental, *m.*

contingence [kən'tindʒəns], **contingency** [kən'tindʒənsi], *n.* éventualité, *f.*, cas imprévu, *m.*

contingent [kən'tindʒənt], *a.* contingent, fortuit, imprévu.—*n.* (*Mil.*) contingent, *m.*
contingently [kən'tindʒəntli], *adv.* éventuellement, fortuitement.
continual [kən'tinjuəl], *a.* continuel.
continually [kən'tinjuəli], *adv.* continuellement.
continuance [kən'tinjuəns], *n.* continuation; durée, *f.*
continuation [kəntinju'eiʃən], *n.* continuation, durée, *f.*
continue [kən'tinju:], *v.t.* continuer; prolonger; reprendre; perpétuer.—*v.i.* continuer; demeurer; durer.
continued [kən'tinju:d], *a.* continu, suivi; à suivre (*feuilleton*); **to be continued**, à suivre.
continuity [kɔnti'nju:iti], *n.* continuité, *f.*
continuous [kən'tinjuəs], *a.* continu.
continuously [kən'tinjuəsli], *adv.* continûment, sans interruption.
contort [kən'tɔ:t], *v.t.* tordre, contourner, défigurer.
contorted [kən'tɔ:tid], *a.* tordu, contourné, défiguré.
contortion [kən'tɔ:ʃən], *n.* contorsion; (*Anat.*) luxation, *f.*
contortionist [kən'tɔ:ʃənist], *n.* contorsionniste, *m., f.*
contour ['kɔntuə], *n.* contour, tracé (*de niveau*), *m.*
contra ['kɔntrə], *prep.* contre; (*Comm.*) d'autre part.
contraband ['kɔntrəbænd], *a.* de contrebande.—*n.* contrebande, *f.*
contraception [kɔntrə'sepʃən], *n.* procédés anticonceptionnels, *m.pl.*
contraceptive [kɔntrə'septiv], *a.* anticonceptionnel.—*n.* procédé *ou* appareil anticonceptionnel, *m.*
contract [kən'trækt], *v.t.* contracter (*dans tous les sens*); abréger; (*fig.*) resserrer; rider, froncer (*les sourcils etc.*); prendre (*habitude*).—*v.i.* se contracter, se resserrer, se rétrécir; (*Comm.*) traiter (*pour*), contracter, entreprendre, soumissionner; **to contract out of something**, renoncer à *ou* se dégager de quelquechose par contrat.—['kɔntrækt], *n.* contrat; pacte, *m.*, convention; adjudication, *f.*
contractible [kən'træktəbl], *a.* contractile.
contraction [kən'trækʃən], *n.* contraction, *f.*, rétrécissement; raccourcissement; retrait (*métaux*), *m.*; (*Math.*) abréviation, *f.*
contractor [kən'træktə], *n.* contractant; entrepreneur (*constructeur*); fournisseur (*aux forces armées*); adjudicataire (*concesseur*), *m.*
contradict [kɔntrə'dikt], *v.t.* contredire, démentir.
contradiction [kɔntrə'dikʃən], *n.* contradiction, incompatibilité, *f.*, démenti (*négation*), *m.*
contradictory [kɔntrə'diktəri], *a.* contradictoire.
contralto [kən'træltou], *n.* (*Mus.*) contralto, contralte, *m.*
contrariety [kɔntrə'raiəti], *n.* contrariété, opposition, *f.*
contrarily ['kɔntrərili], *adv.* contrairement, en sens contraire.

contrary ['kɔntrəri], *a.* contraire, opposé; (*fam.*) [kɔn'treəri], contrariant (*personne*).—*n.* contraire, *m.*; **on the contrary**, au contraire.—*adv.* contrairement (*à*); à l'encontre (*de*).
contrast ['kɔntra:st], *n.* contraste, *m.*—[kɔn'tra:st], *v.t.* faire contraster; mettre en contraste.—*v.i.* contraster, faire contraste.
contravene [kɔntrə'vi:n], *v.t.* contrevenir à, enfreindre.
contravention [kɔntrə'venʃən], *n.* contravention, infraction, *f.*
contribute [kən'tribju:t], *v.t.* contribuer, payer.—*v.i.* contribuer (*à*).
contribution [kɔntri'bju:ʃən], *n.* contribution, *f.*
contributor [kən'tribjutə], *n.* contribuant; (*Journ.*) collaborateur, *m.*
contributory [kən'tribjutəri], *a.* contribuant.
contrite ['kɔntrait], *a.* contrit, pénitent.
contritely ['kɔntraitli], *adv.* avec contrition.
contriteness ['kɔntraitnis], **contrition** [kən'triʃən], *n.* contrition, pénitence, *f.*
contrivance [kən'traivəns], *n.* invention, combinaison, idée, *f.*; artifice, *m.*
contrive [kən'traiv], *v.t.* inventer, imaginer; pratiquer, ménager.—*v.i.* s'arranger (*pour*), trouver moyen (*de*); parvenir (*à*).
contriver [kən'traivə], *n.* inventeur, *m.*, inventrice, *f.*
contriving [kən'traiviŋ], *a.* ingénieux.
control [kən'troul], *n.* autorité (*supérieure*); surveillance; (*Tech.*) commande, *f.*; **out of control**, désemparé; **remote control**, télécommande, *f.*—*v.t.* diriger, régler; gouverner, commander; **to control oneself**, se dominer, se retenir.
controller [kən'troulə], *n.* contrôleur, *m.*
controversial [kɔntrə'və:ʃəl], *a.* sujet à controverse, polémique.
controversy ['kɔntrəvə:si], *n.* controverse, polémique, *f.*; différend, *m.*
controvert ['kɔntrəvə:t], *v.t.* controverser, disputer.
contumacious [kɔntju'meiʃəs], *a.* obstiné, récalcitrant, opiniâtre; (*Law*) contumace.
contumaciousness [kɔntju'meiʃəsnis], **contumacy** ['kɔntjuməsi], *n.* obstination, opiniâtreté; (*Law*) contumace, *f.*
contumelious [kɔntju'mi:liəs], *a.* injurieux, outrageant.
contumely ['kɔntjuməli], *n.* injure, *f.*, outrage, *m.*, honte, *f.*
contuse [kən'tju:z], *v.t.* contusionner.
contusion [kən'tju:ʃən], *n.* contusion, meurtrissure, *f.*
conundrum [kə'nʌndrəm], *n.* énigme, devinette, *f.*
convalesce [kɔnvə'les], *v.i.* être en convalescence.
convalescence [kɔnvə'lesəns], *n.* convalescence, *f.*
convalescent [kɔnvə'lesənt], *a. and n.* convalescent, *m.*, convalescente, *f.*
convection [kən'vekʃən], *n.* convection, *f.*
convene [kən'vi:n], *v.t.* convoquer, réunir, assembler.—*v.i.* s'assembler, se réunir.
convenience [kən'vi:niəns], *n.* commodité, convenance, *f.*
convenient [kən'vi:niənt], *a.* commode, convenable.

conveniently [kən'viːniəntli], *adv.* commodément, convenablement, sans inconvénient.

convent ['kɔnvənt], *n.* couvent, *m.*

conventicle [kən'ventikl], *n.* conventicule, *m.*

convention [kən'venʃən], *n.* convention; assemblée, *f.*; (*pl.*) convenances *f.pl.*

conventional [kən'venʃənəl], *a.* conventionnel, de convention.

conventual [kən'ventjuəl], *a.* conventuel.—*n.* conventuel, religieux, *m.*, religieuse, *f.*

converge [kən'vəːdʒ], *v.i.* converger.

conversant [kən'vəːsənt], *a.* versé (*dans*); familier (*avec*), au courant de.

conversation [kɔnvə'seiʃən], *n.* conversation, *f.*, entretien, *m.*

conversational [kɔnvə'seiʃənəl], *a.* de conversation.

conversationalist [kɔnvə'seiʃənəlist], *n.* causeur, *m.*

converse [kən'vəːs], *v.i.* causer, converser, s'entretenir.—['kɔnvəːs], *n.* entretien, *m.*, conversation; (*Math.*) réciproque, *f.*

conversely ['kɔnvəːsli], *adv.* réciproquement.

conversion [kən'vəːʃən], *n.* conversion, *f.*

convert [kən'vəːt], *v.t.* convertir, transformer; faire servir.—['kɔnvəːt], *n.* converti, *m.*, convertie, *f.*

converter [kən'vəːtə], *n.* convertisseur, *m.*

convertible [kən'vəːtibl], *a.* convertible (*chose*); convertissable (*personne*); (*Motor.*) décapotable.

convex ['kɔnveks], *a.* convexe.

convey [kən'vei], *v.t.* transporter (*marchandises etc.*); porter, conduire, amener; transmettre (*son etc.*); présenter (*remerciements etc.*); donner (*idée etc.*); communiquer (*nouvelle etc.*); céder (*propriété etc.*).

conveyable [kən'veiəbl], *a.* transportable; exprimable.

conveyance [kən'veiəns], *n.* transport, *m.*; transmission, *f.*; véhicule, *m.*; (*Law*) cession, *f.*

conveyor [kən'veiə], *n.* porteur, voiturier; (appareil) transporteur; conducteur (électrique), *m.*; **conveyor belt**, chaîne de montage, *f.*

convict [kən'vikt], *v.t.* condamner, déclarer coupable; convaincre (*quelqu'un de son erreur etc.*).—['kɔnvikt], *n.* forçat, *m.*

conviction [kən'vikʃən], *n.* conviction, persuasion; (*Law*) condamnation, *f.*

convince [kən'vins], *v.t.* convaincre, persuader.

convincing [kən'vinsiŋ], *a.* convaincant; persuasif.

convincingly [kən'vinsiŋli], *adv.* d'une manière convaincante.

convivial [kən'viviəl], *a.* joyeux, jovial.

conviviality [kənvivi'æliti], *n.* franche gaieté, *f.*; (*pl.*) joyeux repas, *m.pl.*

convocation [kɔnvə'keiʃən], *n.* convocation; (*Eccles.*) assemblée, *f.*, synode, *m.*

convoke [kən'vouk], *v.t.* convoquer, assembler.

convolvulus [kən'vɔlvjuləs], *n.* (*pl.* **convolvuli** [kən'vɔlvjulai]) volubilis, liseron, *m.*, belle-de-jour, *f.*

convoy ['kɔnvɔi], *n.* convoi, *m.*, escorte, *f.*

convulse [kən'vʌls], *v.t.* convulser; (*fig.*) ébranler, bouleverser.

convulsion [kən'vʌlʃən], *n.* convulsion; (*fig.*) commotion, *f.*

convulsive [kən'vʌlsiv], *a.* convulsif.

cony, coney ['kouni], *n.* lapin, *m.*

coo [kuː], *v.i.* roucouler.

cooing ['kuːiŋ], *n.* roucoulement, *m.*

cook [kuk], *n.* cuisinier, *m.*, cuisinière, *f.*; (*Naut.*) coq, *m.*; **head cook**, chef, *m.*—*v.t.* cuire, faire cuire.—*v.i.* cuire; faire la cuisine, cuisiner.

cooker ['kukə], *n.* cuisinière (*appareil*), *f.*; fruit à cuire, *m.*; **pressure cooker**, cocotte-minute, *f.*

cookery ['kukəri], *n.* cuisine (*art*), *f.*

cooking ['kukiŋ], *n.* cuisine; cuisson, *f.*

cool [kuːl], *a.* frais, (*fig.*) calme, tranquille; peu gêné.—*n.* frais, *m.*, fraîcheur, *f.*—*v.t.* rafraîchir; refroidir; (*fig.*) calmer.—*v.i.* se refroidir; refroidir; **to cool down**, se calmer, s'apaiser.

cooling ['kuːliŋ], *a.* rafraîchissant, calmant; **cooler**, refroidisseur, *m.*

coolly ['kuːlli], *adv.* fraîchement; (*fig.*) de sangfroid, tranquillement.

coolness ['kuːlnis], *n.* fraîcheur, *f.*, frais, *m.*; (*fig.*) froideur (*indifférence*), *f.*; sang-froid; sans-gêne (*insolence*), *m.*

coop [kuːp], *n.* cage à poules, mue, *f.*—*v.t.* mettre en mue; **to coop up**, enfermer étroitement, claquemurer.

cooper ['kuːpə], *n.* tonnelier, *m.*

co-operate [kou'ɔpəreit], *v.i.* coopérer, concourir (*à*).

co-operation [kouɔpə'reiʃən], *n.* coopération, *f.*; concours, *m.*

co-operative [kou'ɔpərətiv], *a.* coopérant, coopératif.

co-opt [kou'ɔpt], *v.t.* coopter.

co-ordinate [kou'ɔːdineit], *v.t.* coordonner.—[kou'ɔːdinit], *a.* du même rang, égal; (*Math.*) coordonné.

coot [kuːt], *n.* (*Orn.*) foulque, *f.*

cop [kɔp], *n.* cime, *f.*, sommet, *m.*; huppe, aigrette (*d'oiseau*), *f.*; (*slang*) flic (*agent de police*), *m.*

copartner [kou'pɑːtnə], *n.* associé, *m.*

copartnership [kou'pɑːtnəʃip], *n.* société en nom collectif, *f.*

cope (1) [koup], *n.* chaperon, *m.*, chape (*vêtement sacerdotal*), *f.*—*v.t.* couvrir, chaperonner.

cope (2) [koup], *v.i.* se débrouiller; **to cope with**, tenir tête à; venir à bout de.

Copenhagen [koupən'heigən]. Copenhague, *f.*

copier ['kɔpiə], **copyist** ['kɔpiist], *n.* copiste, *m.*, *f.*; (*fig.*) imitateur, *m.*

coping ['koupiŋ], *n.* faîte (*d'un édifice*); couronnement (*d'un mur*), *m.*

copious ['koupiəs], *a.* abondant, copieux.

copiously ['koupiəsli], *adv.* copieusement, abondamment.

copiousness ['koupiəsnis], *n.* abondance, *f.*

copper ['kɔpə], *a.* de cuivre, en cuivre.—*n.* cuivre (rouge), *m.*; chaudière (*boiler*), *f.*; (*slang*) flic (*agent de police*), *m.*; (*pl.*) petite monnaie, *f.*—*v.t.* cuivrer; (*Naut.*) doubler en cuivre.

copper-beech ['kɔpə'biːtʃ], *n.* hêtre rouge, *m.*

copper-smith ['kɔpəsmiθ], *n.* chaudronnier, *m.*

coppice ['kɔpis], **copse** [kɔps], *n.* taillis, *m.*

copy ['kɔpi], *n.* copie, *f.*; exemple (*d'écriture*); exemplaire (*livre*); numéro (*journal*); modèle (*de dessin*), *m.*; *rough copy*, brouillon, *m.*—*v.t.* copier; imiter. [**copy editor**, see **sub-editor**]

copy-book ['kɔpibuk], *n.* cahier d'écriture, *m.*

copyist [COPIER].

copyright ['kɔpirait], *n.* droits d'auteur, *m.pl.*; propriété littéraire, *f.*

coquet [kɔ'ket], *v.i.* faire des coquetteries (*à*); faire la coquette (*avec*).

coquette [kɔ'ket], *n.* coquette, *f.*

coquetry ['koukətri], *n.* coquetterie, *f.*

coquettish [kɔ'ketiʃ], *a.* coquet, en coquette; provocant (*sourire*).

coquettishly [kɔ'ketiʃli], *adv.* d'un air provocant.

coral ['kɔrəl], *a.* de corail.—*n.* corail, *m.*

cord [kɔːd], *n.* corde, *f.*, cordon; cordage, *m.*, ganse, *f.*; (*fig.*) lien, *m.*—*v.t.* corder.

cordial ['kɔːdiəl], *a.* cordial.—*n.* cordial, *m.*, liqueur, *f.*

cordiality [kɔːdi'æliti], *n.* cordialité, *f.*

cordially ['kɔːdiəli], *adv.* cordialement.

cordon ['kɔːdən], *n.* cordon, *m.*—*v.t.* *to cordon off*, isoler par un cordon (*de police*).

corduroy ['kɔːdjurɔi], *n.* velours à côtes, *m.*

core [kɔː], *n.* cœur; noyau (*d'un moule*); (*fig.*) milieu, centre, *m.*; (*Naut.*) âme (*de corde*), *f.*; trognon (*de pomme*), *m.*—*v.t.* vider (*une pomme*); creuser, évider (*un moule*).

co-respondent [kouris'pɔndənt], *n.* complice, *m.*, *f.*, co-défendeur (*en adultère*), *m.*

corgi, corgy ['kɔːgi], *n.* basset gallois, *m.*

cork [kɔːk], *n.* liège; bouchon (*à bouteille etc.*), *m.*—*v.t.* boucher.

corkscrew ['kɔːkskru], *n.* tire-bouchon, *m.*; *corkscrew staircase*, escalier en colimaçon, *m.*

cork-tipped ['kɔːk'tipt], *a.* à bouts de liège (*cigarettes*).

corm [kɔːm], *n.* (*Bot.*) bulbe, *m.*

cormorant ['kɔːmərənt], *n.* cormoran; (*fig.*) rapace, affameur, *m.*

corn (1) [kɔːn], *n.* grain, *m.*; céréales, *f.pl.*; blé, *m.*; (*Am.*) **corn**, maïs, *m.*—*v.t.* saler (*bœuf*).

corn (2) [kɔːn], *n.* cor (au pied), *m.*

corn-chandler ['kɔːntʃɑːndlə], *n.* blatier, marchand de blé, *m.*

corn-crake ['kɔːnkreik], *n.* râle de genêt, *m.*

cornea ['kɔːniə], *n.* (*Anat.*) cornée, *f.*

corned beef ['kɔːnd'biːf], *n.* bœuf salé, bœuf de conserve, *m.*

corner ['kɔːnə], *n.* coin, angle, *m.*; encoignure, *f.*; (*fig.*) monopole, accaparement, *m.*; *blind corner*, tournant (*ou* virage) masqué, *m.*—*v.t.* (*Comm.*) accaparer; (*fig.*) pousser dans un coin, acculer.—*v.i.* prendre un virage, virer.

corner-stone ['kɔːnəstoun], *n.* pierre angulaire, *f.*

cornet ['kɔːnit], *n.* cornet (*à pistons*), *m.*

cornfield ['kɔːnfiːld], *n.* champ de maïs, *m.*

cornflakes ['kɔːnfleiks], *n.pl.* paillettes de maïs, *f.pl.*

corn-flower ['kɔːnflauə], *n.* bluet, *m.*

cornice ['kɔːnis], *n.* corniche, *f.*

corn-poppy ['kɔːnpɔpi], *n.* coquelicot, *m.*

cornstarch ['kɔːnstɑːtʃ], *n.* farine de maïs, *f.*

corollary [kɔ'rɔləri], *n.* corollaire, *m.*

coronation [kɔrə'neiʃən], *n.* couronnement, sacre, *m.*

coroner ['kɔrənə], *n.* coroner, *m.*

coronet ['kɔrənit], *n.* (petite) couronne, *f.*

corporal ['kɔːpərəl], *a.* corporel.—*n.* caporal (*infanterie*); brigadier (*cavalerie*), *m.*

corporate ['kɔːpərit], *a.* érigé en corporation; de corporation.

corporately ['kɔːpəritli], *adv.* collectivement.

corporation [kɔːpə'reiʃən], *n.* corporation, *f.*; conseil municipal, *m.*, municipalité (*d'une ville*), *f.*

corporeal [kɔː'pɔːriəl], *a.* corporel, matériel.

corps [kɔː], *n.inv.* corps, *m.*, formation, *f.*

corpse [kɔːps], *n.* cadavre, *m.*

corpulence ['kɔːpjuləns], **corpulency** ['kɔːpjulənsi], *n.* corpulence, *f.*, embonpoint, *m.*

corpulent ['kɔːpjulənt], *a.* corpulent, gros, gras.

corpuscle ['kɔːpʌsl], *n.* corpuscule, globule, *m.*

correct [kɔ'rekt], *a.* correct, exact, juste; (*fig.*) convenable, en règle; pur, bon (*style*); bien élevé (*personne*); comme il faut.—*v.t.* corriger, rectifier, reprendre; punir.

correction [kɔ'rekʃən], *n.* correction; punition, *f.*

correctly [kɔ'rektli], *adv.* correctement, exactement, justement.

correctness [kɔ'rektnis], *n.* exactitude, justesse; pureté (*de style*), *f.*

correlate ['kɔrileit], *v.t.* mettre en corrélation. —*v.i.* correspondre.

correlation [kɔri'leiʃən], *n.* corrélation, *f.*

correspond [kɔris'pɔnd], *v.i.* correspondre (*à* ou *avec*); répondre (*à*); s'accorder (*avec*); être conforme (*à*).

correspondence [kɔris'pɔndəns], *n.* correspondance, *f.*, rapport, *m.*

correspondent [kɔris'pɔndənt], *a.* conforme, qui se rapporte (*à*).—*n.* correspondant, *m.*

corridor ['kɔridɔː], *n.* corridor; couloir, *m.*

corroborate [kɔ'rɔbəreit], *v.t.* corroborer, confirmer.

corroboration [kɔrɔbə'reiʃən], *n.* corroboration, confirmation, *f.*; *in corroboration of*, à l'appui de.

corrode [kɔ'roud], *v.t.* corroder, ronger; (*fig.*) détruire.—*v.i.* se corroder.

corrosion [kɔ'rouʒən], *n.* corrosion; (*fig.*) destruction, *f.*

corrosive [kɔ'rouziv], *a.* corrosif; (*fig.*) rongeur.—*n.* corrosif, *m.*

corrugate ['kɔrugeit], *v.t.* rider, plisser, froncer; onduler; *corrugated iron*, tôle ondulée, *f.*—*v.i.* se plisser, se froncer.

corrupt [kɔ'rʌpt], *v.t.* corrompre.—*v.i.* se corrompre.—*a.* corrompu, dépravé, vicié.

corruption [kɔ'rʌpʃən], *n.* corruption; (*fig.*) altération (*d'un texte etc.*), *f.*

corruptive [kɔ'rʌptiv], *a.* corruptif.

corruptly [kɔ'rʌptli], *adv.* par corruption.

corsair ['kɔːsɛə], *n.* corsaire, *m.*

corset ['kɔːsit], *n.* corset, *m.*

corset-maker ['kɔːsitmeikə], *n.* corsetier, *m.* corsetière, *f.*

Corsica ['kɔːsikə]. la Corse, *f.*

Corsican ['kɔːsikən], *a.* corse.—*n.* Corse (*personne*), *m.*, *f.*

corslet ['kɔːslit], *n.* corselet. *m.*

cortège [kɔːˈteiʒ], *n.* cortège (*funèbre*), *m.*, procession; suite, *f.*

cortisone ['kɔːtizoun], *n.* cortisone, *f.*

coruscate ['kɔrəskeit], *v.i.* scintiller, briller.

corvette [kɔːˈvet], *n.* (*Naut.*) corvette, *f.*

cosh [kɔʃ], *n.* matraque, *f.*—*v.t.* matraquer.

cosily ['kouzili], *adv.* à l'aise, bien au chaud, douillettement.

cosmetic [kɔzˈmetik], *a.* and *n.* cosmétique, *m.*

cosmic ['kɔzmik], **cosmical** ['kɔzmikəl], *a.* cosmique.

cosmopolitan [kɔzmoˈpɔlitən], *a.* and *n.* cosmopolite, *m.*, *f.*

cosmos ['kɔzmɔs], *n.* cosmos, *m.*

cosset ['kɔsit], *v.t.* dorloter, choyer.

cost [kɔst], *n.* prix; frais, *m.*, dépense, *f.*; (*Comm.*) cout, *m.*; (*Law, pl.*) dépens, *m.pl.*; *at any cost, at all costs,* à tout prix; *cost of living,* coût de la vie.—*v.i. irr.* coûter; *cost what it may,* coûte que coûte.

coster ['kɔstə], **costermonger** ['kɔstəmʌŋgə], *n.* marchand des quatre saisons, *m.*

costive ['kɔstiv], *a.* constipé.

costliness ['kɔstlinis], *n.* haut prix, prix élevé, *m.*

costly ['kɔstli], *a.* coûteux, de prix; somptueux.

costume ['kɔstjuːm], *n.* costume, *m.*

cosy ['kouzi], *a.* chaud, confortable, douillet; commode et petit (*appartement*).—*n.* (**tea**) *cosy,* couvre-théière, *m.*

cot [kɔt], *n.* cabane, chaumière, *f.*; bercail, parc (*à moutons*); petit lit, lit d'enfant, *m.*

coterie ['koutəri], *n.* coterie, clique, *f.*

cottage ['kɔtidʒ], *n.* chaumière; villa, *f.*

cotter pin, see **split pin.**

cotton [kɔtn], *n.* coton, *m.*

cotton mill ['kɔtnmil], *n.* filature de coton, *f.*

cotton plant ['kɔtnplɑːnt], **cotton bush** ['kɔtnbuʃ], *n.* cotonnier, *m.*

cotton-spinning ['kɔtnspiniŋ], *n.* filage du coton, *m.*

cotton-wool ['kɔtnˈwul], *n.* ouate, *f.*

couch [kautʃ], *n.* canapé, divan, *m.*—*v.t.* coucher; (*fig.*) rédiger, exprimer.—*v.i.* se coucher; se tapir.

cougar ['kuːgə], *n.* couguar, puma, *m.*

cough [kɔf], *n.* toux, *f.*; *whooping cough,* coqueluche, *f.*—*v.i.* tousser.

coughing ['kɔfiŋ], *n.* toux, *f.*; *fit of coughing,* quinte de toux, *f.*

council ['kaunsil], *n.* conseil; (*Eccles.*) concile, *m.*

councilor ['kaunsilə], *n.* conseiller, *m.*

counsel ['kaunsəl], *n.* conseil, avis; dessein; avocat, *m.*—*v.t.* conseiller.

counsellor ['kaunsələ], *n.* conseiller; avocat, *m.*

count (1) [kaunt], *n.* comte (*titre*), *m.*

count (2) [kaunt], *n.* calcul, compte, total, *m.*—*v.t.* compter; (*fig.*) regarder, considérer; *to count on* or *upon,* compter sur.

countenance ['kauntinəns], *n.* figure, mine, *f.*, air, *m.*; (*fig.*) approbation, *f.*, appui, *m.*; *to give countenance to,* favoriser, encourager; *to keep one's countenance,* garder son sérieux; *to put out of countenance,* décontenancer.—*v.t.* appuyer, encourager, favoriser; être en faveur de.

counter ['kauntə], *n.* calculateur; compteur (*instrument*); (*Cards etc.*) jeton; comptoir (*de magasin*), *m.*—*adv.* contre, contrairement (*à*), à l'encontre (*de*).—*v.t.*, *v.i.* parer; contrer.

counteract [kauntəˈrækt], *v.t.* contrecarrer, contre-balancer, neutraliser.

counteraction [kauntəˈrækʃən], *n.* action contraire, opposition, résistance, *f.*

counter-clockwise ['kauntəˈklɔkwaiz], **anti-clockwise** ['æntiˈklɔkwaiz], *adv.* dans le sens contraire des aiguilles d'une montre.

counter-espionage ['kauntərˈespiənɑːʒ], *n.* contre-espionnage, *m.*

counterfeit ['kauntəfiːt], *a.* contrefait, imité; faux.—*n.* contrefaçon; fausse pièce, fausse monnaie; imitation, *f.*—*v.t.* contrefaire, imiter; feindre.—*v.i.* feindre.

counterfoil ['kauntəfɔil], *n.* talon (*de registre*), *m.*, souche, *f.*

countermand [kauntəˈmɑːnd], *v.t.* contremander.—*n.* contremandement, *m.*

counterpane ['kauntəpein], *n.* couvre-pied, couvre-lit, *m.*

counterpart ['kauntəpɑːt], *n.* contre-partie, *f.*; pendant, *m.*

countess ['kauntis], *n.* comtesse, *f.*

counting ['kauntiŋ], *n.* compte; dépouillement (*élections*), *m.*

counting house ['kauntiŋhaus], *n.* bureau, comptoir, *m.*, caisse, *f.*

countless ['kauntlis], *a.* innombrable, sans nombre.

countrified ['kʌntrifaid], *a.* (devenu) campagnard *ou* provincial.

country ['kʌntri], *n.* pays, *m.*; contrée; région; campagne (*opposée à la ville*); province (*opposée à la capitale*); patrie (*fatherland*), *f.*; *across country,* à travers champs; *in open country,* en rase campagne; *in the country,* à la campagne.

countryman ['kʌntrimən], *n.* (*pl.* **-men** [men]) paysan, campagnard, *m.*; *fellow countryman,* compatriote, *m.*

countryside ['kʌntrisaid], *n.* campagne, *f.*; paysage, *m.*

country-woman ['kʌntriwumən], *n.* (*pl.* **-women** [wimin]) paysanne, *f.*

county ['kaunti], *n.* comté, *m.*; *county council,* conseil général, *m.*; *county seat,* chef-lieu *m.*

couple [kʌpl], *n.* couple, *f.*; couple (*mâle et femelle*), *m.*—*v.t.* coupler, accoupler; atteler; joindre.—*v.i.* s'accoupler.

couplet ['kʌplit], *n.* couplet, distique, *m.*

coupling ['kʌpliŋ], *n.* accouplement, *m.*

coupon ['kuːpɔn], *n.* coupon; bon, *m.*

courage ['kʌridʒ], *n.* courage, *m.*

courageous [kəˈreidʒəs], *a.* courageux.

courageously [kəˈreidʒəsli], *adv.* courageusement.

courier ['kuriə], *n.* courrier, *m.*

course [kɔːs], *n.* cours, *m.*; carrière, voie, suite, *f.*; lit (*d'une rivière*); genre (*de vie*); service (*de repas*); courant (*durée*); (*Racing*) terrain de course; hippodrome, *m.*; (*Naut.*) route, *f.*; (*Med., pl.*) règles, *f.pl.*; *in due course,* en temps voulu; *of course,* naturellement, bien entendu.—*v.t.* courir; faire courir; chasser (*le lièvre*).—*v.i.* courir; circuler (*sang*).

courser ['kɔːsə], *n.* coureur, coursier, *m.*

court [kɔːt], *n.* cour, *f.*; tribunal, *m.*; impasse, *f.*, passage (*petite rue*); (*Ten.*) court, *m.*—*v.t.* faire sa cour à, courtiser; rechercher; briguer.

courteous [ˈkɔːtiəs], *a.* courtois, poli.

courteously [ˈkɔːtiəsli], *adv.* courtoisement, poliment.

courtesan [kɔːtiˈzæn], *n.* courtisane, *f.*

courtesy [ˈkɔːtəsi], *n.* courtoisie, politesse, *f.*

court-house [ˈkɔːthaus], *n.* palais de justice, *m.*

courtier [ˈkɔːtiə], *n.* courtisan, homme de cour, *m.*

courtliness [ˈkɔːtlinis] *n.* élégance, politesse, *f.*

courtly [ˈkɔːtli], *a.* poli, élégant, courtois.

court-martial [ˈkɔːtˈmɑːʃəl], *n.* conseil de guerre, *m.*—*v.t.* faire passer en conseil de guerre.

courtship [ˈkɔːtʃip], *n.* cour, *f.*

courtyard [ˈkɔːtjɑːd], *n.* cour (*de maison*), *f.*

cousin [kʌzn], *n.* cousin, *m.*

cove [kouv], *n.* anse, crique, *f.*

covenant [ˈkʌvənənt], *n.* convention, *f.*, pacte, contrat, *m.*—*v.t.* stipuler par contrat. —*v.i.* convenir (*de*), s'engager (*à*).

Coventry [ˈkʌvəntri, ˈkʌvəntri]. (*colloq.*) **to send to Coventry**, mettre en quarantaine.

cover [ˈkʌvə], *v.t.* couvrir; voiler, déguiser; cacher.—*n.* couverture; cloche (*d'un plat etc.*); enveloppe (*d'une lettre etc.*); housse (*d'une chaise*), *f.*; couvercle (*d'une casserole etc.*); couvert (*gibier*); (*fig.*) voile, abri, *m.*; **under cover of**, sous la protection de, à la faveur de.

covering [ˈkʌvəriŋ], *n.* couverture; enveloppe; housse (*de chaise*), *f.*; habits (*vêtements*), *m.pl.*; **covering letter**, lettre d'envoi, *f.*

coverlet [ˈkʌvəlit], *n.* couvre-pied, couvre-lit, *m.*

covert [ˈkʌvəːt], *a.* couvert, caché, secret.—*n.* couvert, abri; gîte, *m.*, tanière, *f.*

covertly [ˈkʌvəːtli], *adv.* secrètement, en cachette.

covet [ˈkʌvit], *v.t.* convoiter, désirer ardemment.

covetous [ˈkʌvitəs], *a.* avide, avaricieux, cupide.

covetously [ˈkʌvitəsli], *adv.* avec convoitise, avidement.

covetousness [ˈkʌvitəsnis], *n.* convoitise, cupidité, *f.*

covey [ˈkʌvi], *n.* compagnie (*de perdrix*), *f.*

cow (1) [kau], *n.* vache, *f.*

cow (2) [kau], *v.t.* intimider, dompter.

coward [ˈkauəd], *n.* lâche, poltron, *m.*, poltronne, *f.*

cowardice [ˈkauədis], **cowardliness** [ˈkauəd linis], *n.* couardise, poltronnerie, lâcheté, *f.*

cowardly [ˈkauədli], *a.* couard, lâche, poltron. —*adv.* lâchement.

cowboy [ˈkauboi], *n.* jeune vacher; (*Am.*) cowboy, *m.*

cower [ˈkauə], *v.i.* s'accroupir, se blottir, se tapir.

cowherd [ˈkauhəːd], *n.* vacher, *m.*

cowhide [ˈkauhaid], *n.* peau de vache, *f.*

cowl [kaul], *n.* capuchon; (*Naut., Av.*) capot; tabourin (*de cheminée*), *m.*

cow-shed [ˈkauʃed], *n.* vacherie, étable à vaches, *f.*

cowslip [ˈkauslip], *n.* primevère, *f.*, coucou, *m.*

coxcomb, cockscomb [ˈkɔkskoum], *n.* petit-maître, freluquet, fat, *m.*

coxswain [ˈkɔksn], *n.* patron de chaloupe; (*Row.*) barreur, *m.*

coy [kɔi], *a.* timide, réservé.

coyly [ˈkɔili], *adv.* timidement, avec réserve.

coyness [ˈkɔinis], *n.* timidité, réserve, *f.*

coyote [kɔiˈjouti], *n.* loup de prairie, coyote, *m.*

cozen [kʌzn], *v.t.* duper, tromper.

crab [kræb], *n.* crabe, cancre; (*Astron.*) cancer, *m.*

crab apple [ˈkræbæpl], *n.* pomme sauvage, *f.*

crabbed [kræbd], *a.* acariâtre, revêche, bourru.

crab tree [ˈkræbtriː], *n.* pommier sauvage, *m.*

crabwise [ˈkræbwaiz], *adv.* comme un crabe, de biais.

crack [kræk], *v.t.* fendre; fêler (*porcelaine etc.*); gercer (*la peau etc.*); casser (*noix etc.*); faire claquer (*fouet*); faire sauter (*bouteille de vin*); faire, lâcher (*plaisanterie*); (*fig.*) rompre, briser.—*v.i.* se fendre, se lézarder; se gercer (*la peau etc.*); claquer (*fouet*); se fêler (*verre etc.*); muer (*la voix*).—*a.* fameux, d'élite; **to be a crack shot**, être un fin tireur.—*n.* fente, crevasse, fissure; détonation (*de fusil*); lézarde, fêlure (*verre*), *f.*; craquement (*bruit*); claquement (*d'un fouet*), *m.*; mue (*de la voix*); hâblerie (*boast*), *f.*

crack-brained [ˈkrækbreind], *a.* (*fam.*) timbré, fou.

cracked [krækd], *a.* fendu, fêlé; (*fig.*) timbré.

cracker [ˈkrækə], *n.* vantard; pétard (*feu d'artifice*); (*Am.*) biscuit, *m.*; **nut-crackers**, casse-noix, *m.inv.*

crackle [krækl], *v.i.* pétiller, craqueter, crépiter.

crackling [ˈkræklíŋ], *n.* pétillement, crépitement; (*fig.*) rissolé (*de rôti de porc*), *m.*

cracknel [ˈkræknəl], *n.* craquelin, *m.*, croquignole, *f.*

cradle [kreidl], *n.* berceau; (*Naut.*) ber, *m.*—*v.t.* bercer; endormir (*en berçant*).

cradle-song [ˈkreidlsɔŋ], *n.* berceuse, *f.*

craft [krɑːft], *n.* métier (*trade*), *m.*; ruse, astuce (*cunning*); (*Naut.*) embarcation, *f.*, bâtiment, *m.*

craftily [ˈkrɑːftili], *adv.* sournoisement, avec ruse.

craftiness [ˈkrɑːftinis], *n.* artifice, *m.*, ruse, astuce, *f.*

craftsman [ˈkrɑːftsmən], *n.* (*pl.* -**men** [men]) artisan; artiste dans son métier, *m.*

craftsmanship [ˈkrɑːftsmənʃip], *n.* habileté technique, exécution, *f.*

crafty [ˈkrɑːfti], *a.* rusé, astucieux.

crag [kræg], *n.* rocher escarpé, rocher à pic, *m.*

craggy [ˈkrægi], *a.* rocailleux, escarpé, abrupt.

crake [kreik], *n.* (*Orn.*) râle, *m.*

cram [kræm], *v.t.* fourrer, remplir, bourrer; préparer, chauffer (*étudiants*).—*v.i.* se bourrer, s'empiffrer; (*fig.*) piocher, bûcher.

crammer [ˈkræmə], *n.* préparateur; (*colloq.*) colleur, *m.*

cramp [kræmp], *n.* crampe, *f.*; (*Tech.*) crampon, *m.*; (*fig.*) gêne, entrave, *f.*—*v.t.* cramponner; resserrer; (*fig.*) gêner, entraver, restreindre.

cramped [kræmpt], *a.* gêné; **to be cramped** (*for space*), être très à l'étroit.

cranberry ['krænbəri], *n.* (*Bot.*) canneberge, *f.*

crane [krein], *n.* (*Orn.*, *Tech.*) grue, *f.*—*v.t.* allonger, tendre (*le cou*).

cranial ['kreiniəl], *a.* crânien.

cranium ['kreiniəm], *n.* crâne, *m.*

crank [krænk], *n.* manivelle, *f.*; coude, *m.*; (*fig.*) maniaque, excentrique, *m.*, *f.*, original (*personne*), *m.*

crankshaft ['krænkʃɑ:ft], *n.* arbre de manivelle; (*Motor.*) vilebrequin, *m.*

cranky ['krænki], *a.* capricieux, fantasque; impatient.

crannied ['krænid], *a.* crevassé, lézardé.

cranny ['kræni], *n.* crevasse, fente, lézarde, fissure, *f.*

crape [kreip], *n.* crêpe, *m.*

crash [kræʃ], *v.t.* fracasser, briser.—*v.i.* éclater, retentir; se tamponner (*deux autos etc.*).—*n.* fracas, grand bruit, *m.*; (*Motor.*) collision; (*fig.*) débâcle, ruine; faillite, *f.*

crash helmet ['kræʃhelmit], *n.* casque, *m.*

crash landing ['kræʃ'lændiŋ], *n.* (*Av.*) atterrissage brutal; crash, *m.*

crass [kræs], *a.* crasse, grossier, stupide.

crate [kreit], *n.* caisse à claire-voie, *f.*—*v.t.* emballer.

crater ['kreitə], *n.* cratère, *m.*

cravat [krə'væt], *n.* cravate, *f.*

crave [kreiv], *v.t.* implorer, solliciter; (*fig.*) soupirer après.

craven [kreivn], *a.* and *n.* lâche, poltron, *m.*

craving ['kreiviŋ], *n.* désir ardent.

crawfish [CRAYFISH].

crawl [krɔ:l], *v.i.* ramper, se traîner; to crawl with, grouiller de.—*n.* mouvement traînant; (*Swim.*) crawl, *m.*

crawling ['krɔ:liŋ], *a.* rampant; grouillant, fourmillant (*de*).

crayfish ['kreifiʃ], **crawfish** ['krɔ:fiʃ], *n.* écrevisse (*d'eau douce*), *f.*; sea crayfish, langouste, *f.*

crayon ['kreiən], *n.* crayon, pastel, fusain, *m.*—*v.t.* crayonner, dessiner au pastel.

craze [kreiz], *v.t.* craqueler (*porcelaine*); frapper de folie, rendre fou.—*n.* folie; (*fig.*) passion folle; toquade, *f.*

crazed [kreizd], *a.* craquelé (*porcelaine*); fou, dément.

crazily ['kreizili], *adv.* follement.

craziness ['kreizinis], *n.* délabrement, *m.*; démence, folie, *f.*

crazy ['kreizi], *a.* délabré; (*fam.*) fou, toqué.

creak [kri:k], *v.i.* crier, craquer, grincer.—*n.* cri, grincement, *m.*

creaking ['kri:kiŋ], *a.* qui crie, qui craque.—*n.* cri, grincement, *m.*

cream [kri:m], *n.* crème, *f.*—*v.i.* crémer, mousser.

cream-color(ed) ['kri:mkʌlə(d)], *a.* crème.

creamery ['kri:məri], *n.* crémerie, *f.*

cream pitcher['kri:mpitʃə], *n.* pot à crème, *m.*

creamy ['kri:mi], *a.* crémeux; de crème.

crease [kri:s], *n.* pli, faux pli, *m.*—*v.t.* faire des plis à, plisser, chiffonner, friper.—*v.i.* se plisser; se friper.

create [kri:'eit], *v.t.* créer, faire naître; produire, engendrer, occasionner; faire.

creation [kri:'eiʃən], *n.* création; nature, *f.*, univers, *m.*; dernière mode, *f.*

creative [kri:'eitiv], *a.* créateur.

creator [kri:'eitə], *n.* créateur, *m.*

creature ['kri:tʃə], *n.* créature, personne, *f.*, être; animal, *m.*

crèche [kreiʃ], *n.* crèche, *f.*

credence ['kri:dəns], *n.* créance, croyance, foi, *f.*; to give credence to, ajouter foi à.

credentials [kri'denʃəlz], *n.pl.* lettres de créance, *f.pl.*

credibility [kredi'biliti], *n.* crédibilité, *f.*

credible ['kredibl], *a.* croyable, digne de foi.

credibly ['kredibli], *adv.* d'une manière digne de foi; to be credibly informed, tenir de bonne source.

credit ['kredit], *n.* croyance, foi; (*fig.*) influence; réputation, *f.*; mérite, honneur; (*Comm.*) crédit, *m.*; on credit, à crédit; to do credit to, faire honneur à.—*v.t.* ajouter foi à, croire à; faire honneur à; (*Comm.*) faire crédit à.

creditable ['kreditəbl], *a.* honorable, estimable.

creditably ['kreditəbli], *adv.* honorablement.

creditor ['kreditə], *n.* créancier; (*Bookkeeping*) créditeur, avoir, *m.*

credulity [kre'dju:liti], **credulousness** ['kredjuləsnis], *n.* crédulité, *f.*

credulous ['kredjuləs], *a.* crédule.

creed [kri:d], *n.* credo, *m.*; (*fig.*) profession de foi; croyance, foi, *f.*

creek [kri:k], *n.* ruisseau, *m.*

creel [kri:l], *n.* panier de pêche, *m.*

creep [kri:p], *v.i. irr.* se traîner, ramper, se glisser.

creeper ['kri:pə], *n.* reptile, *m.*; plante grimpante, *f.*; tree creeper, (*Orn.*) grimpereau, *m.*

creeping ['kri:piŋ], *a.* rampant, grimpant; qui fait frissonner.—*n.* fourmillement (*sensation*), *m.*

creepy ['kri:pi], *a.* horrifique, qui donne la chair de poule; rampant.

cremate [kri'meit], *v.t.* incinérer.

cremation [kri'meiʃən], *n.* crémation, incinération, *f.*

crematorium [kremə'tɔ:riəm], *n.* crématorium, *m.*

Creole ['kri:oul], *a.* créole.—*n.* Créole, *m.*, *f.*

creosote ['kri:əsout], *n.* créosote, *f.*

crêpe [kreip], *n.* crêpe blanc (*ou* clair), *m.*

crescent ['kresənt], *a.* croissant.—*n.* croissant, *m.*, demi-lune; rue en demi-cercle, *f.*

cress [kres], *n.* cresson, *m.*

crest [krest], *n.* cimier, *m.*; crête (*d'un coq ou d'une montagne*), huppe (*d'un oiseau*); aigrette (*de paon*), *f.*; (*Her.*) écusson, *m.*; armoiries, *f.pl.*

crestfallen ['krestfɔ:lən], *a.* abattu, découragé, l'oreille basse.

Cretan ['kri:tən], *a.* crétois.—*n.* Crétois, *m.*

Crete [kri:t]. la Crète, la Candie, *f.*

crevasse [krə'væs], *n.* crevasse (*d'un glacier*), *f.*—*v.i.* se crevasser.

crevice ['krevis], *n.* crevasse, lézarde, fente (*mur*); fissure (*rocher*), *f.*—*v.t.* crevasser, lézarder, fissurer.

crew (1) [kru:], *n.* bande, troupe, *f.*; (*Naut.*) équipage, *m.*

crew (2) [kru:], *past* [CROW (2)].

crib [krib], *n.* lit d'enfant, *m.*; crèche, mangeoire, *f.*; (*colloq.*) livre de corrigés, *m.*—*v.t.* chiper; copier (*sur*).

crick [krik], *n.* crampe, *f.*, effort, torticolis, *m.* —*v.t.* **to crick one's neck**, se donner le torticolis.

cricket (1) ['krikit], *n.* (*Ent.*) grillon, *m.*

cricket (2) ['krikit], *n.* cricket (*jeu*), *m.*; (*colloq.*) **that's not cricket**, ça ne se fait pas, ce n'est pas loyal.

crier ['kraiə], *n.* crieur; huissier (*d'une cour*), *m.*

crime [kraim], *n.* crime, *m.*

Crimea [krai'miːə], la Crimée, *f.*

criminal ['kriminl], *a.* and *n.* criminel, *m.*

criminologist [krimi'nɔlədʒist], *n.* criminaliste, *m.f.*

criminology [krimi'nɔlədʒi], *n.* criminologie, *f.*

crimp [krimp], *v.t.* gaufrer; friser, boucler (*les cheveux*).

crimson [krimzn], *a.* and *n.* cramoisi; pourpre, *m.*—*v.t.* teindre en cramoisi.—*v.i.* devenir cramoisi.

cringe [krindʒ], *v.i.* faire des courbettes; s'humilier, ramper.

cringing ['krindʒiŋ], *a.* craintif; obséquieux. —*n.* basse servilité, *f.*

crinkle [kriŋkl], *v.t.* froisser; former en zigzag.—*v.i.* serpenter, aller en zigzag.—*n.* sinuosité, *f.*; pli, *m.*; fronce, *f.*

crinkly ['kriŋkli], *a.* ratatiné.

cripple [kripl], *n.* boiteux; estropié, *m.*—*v.t.* estropier; (*fig.*) paralyser.

crisis ['kraisis], *n.* (*pl.* **crises** ['kraisiːz]) crise, *f.*; dénouement, *m.*

crisp [krisp], *a.* croquant, croustillant (*pâtisserie etc.*); crépu, frisé (*cheveux*).—*v.t.* friser (*cheveux etc.*); crêper (*tissu*).—*v.i.* se crêper.

crispness ['krispnis], *n.* qualité de ce qui est croquant *ou* cassant; frisure; netteté (*style etc.*), *f.*

criss-cross ['kriskrɔs], *a.* entrecroisé, croisé, en croix.—*n.* entrecroisement, *m.*—*v.t.* entrecroiser.—*v.i.* s'entrecroiser.

criterion [krai'tiəriən], *n.* critérium, *m.*

critic ['kritik], *n.* critique; censeur, *m.*; **dramatic critic**, critique de théâtre.

critical ['kritikl], *a.* critique, (*fig.*) difficile, délicat.

critically ['kritikli], *adv.* d'une manière critique; avec soin; **critically ill**, dangereusement malade.

criticism ['kritisizm], *n.* critique, appréciation, censure, *f.*

criticize ['kritisaiz], *v.t.* critiquer, faire la critique de, censurer.—*v.i.* faire de la critique.

croak [krouk], *v.i.* coasser (*grenouille*); croasser (*freux*); (*fig.*) gronder, grogner.—*n.* coassement (*grenouille*); croassement (*freux*); (*fig.*) grognement, *m.*

croaker ['kroukə], *n.* grognon, *m.*; (*fig.*) pessimiste, *m.*, *f.*

croaky ['krouki] *a.* enroué, rauque.

crochet ['krouʃei], *n.* ouvrage au crochet, *m.* —*v.t.*, *v.i.* broder au crochet.

crock [krɔk], *n.* cruche, *f.*; pot de terre, *m.*; (*fam.*) **old crock**, vieux clou, tacot (*bicyclette, auto etc.*); vieux débris, croulant (*personne*), *m.*

crockery ['krɔkəri], *n.* faïence, vaisselle, *f.*

crocodile ['krɔkədail], *n.* crocodile, *m.*; (*fig.*) procession, *f.*

crocus ['kroukəs], *n.* safran, crocus, *m.*

croft [krɔft], *n.* petit clos, *m.*, petite ferme, *f.*

crofter ['krɔftə], *n.* petit cultivateur, *m.*

crone [kroun], *n.* vieille femme, vieille, *f.*

crony ['krouni], *n.* vieux camarade; copain, compère, *m.*

crook [kruk], *n.* courbure; houlette (*de berger*); crosse (*d'évêque*), *f.*; (*fig.*) escroc (*personne*), *m.*; **by hook or by crook**, coûte que coûte, par un moyen ou par un autre.—*v.t.* courber; (*fig.*) pervertir.—*v.i.* se courber.

crook-backed ['krukbækt], *a.* bossu, voûté.

crooked ['krukid], *a.* courbé, crochu, tortueux; tortu; (*fig.*) malhonnête.

crookedly ['krukidli], *adv.* tortueusement, de travers.

crookedness ['krukidnis], *n.* nature tortueuse; difformité, *f.*; (*fig.*) travers, *m.*, perversité, *f.*

croon [kruːn], *v.i.* chantonner, fredonner.

crooner ['kruːnə], *n.* fredonneur, chanteur de charme, *m.*

crop [krɔp], *n.* récolte, moisson; cueillette (*de fruits*), *f.*; jabot (*d'un oiseau*), *m.*; coupe (*cheveux*), *f.*; **hunting crop**, fouet (*de chasse*), *m.*; **second crop**, regain, *m.*—*v.t.* tondre; couper; écourter (*chevaux*); brouter (*l'herbe*).

crosier, crozier ['krouziə], *n.* crosse (*d'évêque*), *f.*

cross [krɔs], *a.* en travers de travers; fâcheux, contraire; maussade, de mauvaise humeur, fâché.—*n.* croix, *f.*; (*fig.*) malheur, *m.*, traverse, *f.*; croisement (*dans la reproduction*), *m.*; **criss-cross**, croisé, en croix.—*v.t.* croiser; marquer d'une croix, barrer (*un chèque*); (*fig.*) franchir; contrarier; **to cross off** or **out**, effacer, rayer, biffer; **to cross oneself**, faire le signe de la croix.—*v.i.* être mis en travers; faire la traversée; se croiser (*lettres*).

crossbow ['krɔsbou], *n.* arbalète, *f.*

cross-breed ['krɔsbriːd], *n.* race croisée, *f.*; métis, *m.*—*v.t.* croiser.

cross-country ['krɔs'kʌntri], *a.* à travers champs; (*Racing*) **cross-country running**, cross, *m.*

cross-examination ['krɔsigzæmi'neiʃən], *n.* contre-interrogatoire, *m.*

cross-examine ['krɔsig'zæmin], *v.t.* interroger; (*Law*) contre-interroger.

crossing ['krɔsiŋ], *n.* traversée (*de la mer*), *f.*; passage; carrefour, croisement (*de routes*); croisement (*animaux*), *m.*; **pedestrian crossing**, passage clouté.

crossly ['krɔsli], *adv.* de travers; avec mauvaise humeur.

crossness ['krɔsnis], *n.* mauvaise humeur, méchanceté, *f.*

cross-roads ['krɔsroudz], *n.pl.* carrefour, *m.*

crossword ['krɔswəːd], *n.* **crossword** (**puzzle**), mots croisés, *m.pl.*

crotchet ['krɔtʃit], *n.* lubie, *f.*, caprice, *m.*, marotte; (*Mus.*) noire, *f.*

crotchety ['krɔtʃiti], *a.* capricieux, d'humeur difficile.

crouch [krautʃ], *v.i.* se tapir, se blottir.

crouching ['krautʃiŋ], *a.* accroupi, tapi.

croup [kruːp], *n.* croupe (*animaux*), *f.*; croupion (*oiseaux*); (*Path.*) croup, *m.*

crow (1) [krou], *n.* corneille, *f.*; *as the crow flies*, à vol d'oiseau; *crow's nest*, (*Naut.*) hune, *f.*

crow (2) [krou], *v.i. irr.* chanter (*coq*).—*n.* chant du coq, *m.*

crow-bar ['krouba:], *n.* pince, *f.*; levier, *m.*

crowd [kraud], *n.* foule, cohue, *f.*—*v.t.* serrer, encombrer; presser.—*v.i.* se presser en foule, se serrer.

crown [kraun], *n.* couronne; crête, *f.*, sommet; écu (*pièce de monnaie*); fond (*d'un chapeau*), *m.*—*v.t.* couronner; combler.

crozier [CROSIER].

crucial ['kru:ʃəl], *a.* crucial; (*fig.*) définitif, décisif.

crucible ['kru:sibl], *n.* creuset, *m.*

crucifix ['kru:sifiks], *n.* crucifix, *m.*

crucifixion [kru:si'fikʃən], *n.* crucifiement, *m.*, crucifixion, *f.*

crucify ['kru:sifai], *v.t.* crucifier.

crude [kru:d], *a.* cru; (*fig.*) informe, indigeste; grossier; brut.

crudely ['kru:dli], *adv.* crûment.

crudeness ['kru:dnis], **crudity** ['kru:diti], *n.* crudité, nature informe, *f.*

cruel ['kru:əl], *a.* cruel.

cruelly ['kru:əli], *adv.* cruellement.

cruelty ['kru:əlti], *n.* cruauté, inhumanité, *f.*

cruet ['kru:it], *n.* burette, *f.*

cruet stand ['kru:itstænd], *n.* huilier, *m.*

cruise ['kru:z], *n.* croisière, course, *f.*—*v.i.* croiser, faire la course; marauder (*taxi*).

cruiser ['kru:zə], *n.* croiseur, *m.*

crumb [krʌm], *n.* mie; miette, *f.*—*v.t.* émietter.

crumble [krʌmbl], *v.t.* émietter; (*fig.*) pulvériser, broyer.—*v.i.* s'émietter; tomber en poussière; *to crumble down*, tomber en ruine, s'écrouler.

crump [krʌmp], *n.* coup violent, *m.*; chute, *f.*

crumpet ['krʌmpit], *n.* sorte de petite crêpe, crêpe bretonne (*pour le thé*), *f.*

crumple [krʌmpl], *v.t.* chiffonner, froisser.—*v.i.* se rider, se chiffonner.

crunch [krʌntʃ], *v.t.* croquer; broyer, écraser.—*v.i.* crisser, s'écraser.—*n.* coup de dent; grincement, crissement, *m.*

crupper ['krʌpə], *n.* croupe; croupière, *f.*

crusade [kru:'seid], *n.* croisade, *f.*

crusader [kru:'seidə], *n.* croisé, *m.*

crush [krʌʃ], *n.* écrasement, choc, *m.*; foule, cohue, *f.*—*v.t.* écraser, broyer; froisser (*une robe*); (*fig.*) accabler, anéantir.—*v.i.* s'écraser.

crushing ['krʌʃiŋ], *a.* écrasant; (*fig.*) foudroyant.—*n.* broiement, écrasement, *m.*

crust [krʌst], *n.* croûte, *f.*, croûton, *m.*—*v.i.* s'encroûter.

crustily ['krʌstili], *adv.* d'une manière morose.

crusty ['krʌsti], *a.* couvert d'une croûte; (*fig.*) bourru, hargneux.

crutch [krʌtʃ], *n.* béquille, *f.*

crux [krʌks], *n.* nœud (*d'une question*), *m.*; crise, *f.*

cry [krai], *n.* cri, *m.*—*v.t.* crier.—*v.i.* pleurer; crier; s'écrier.

crying ['kraiiŋ], *n.* larmes, *f.pl.*, pleurs, *m.pl.*; cri, *m.*, cris, *m.pl.*

crypt [kript], *n.* crypte, *f.*

cryptic ['kriptik], *a.* secret; énigmatique.

crystal [kristl], *a.* de cristal.—*n.* cristal, *m.*

crystallize ['kristəlaiz], *v.t.* cristalliser.—*v.i.* se cristalliser; *crystallized fruits*, fruits glacés, *m.pl.*

cub [kʌb], *n.* petit (*d'une bête sauvage*); ourson (*ours*); lionceau (*lion*); louveteau (*loup*); renardeau (*renard*), *m.*

Cuba ['kju:bə]. le Cuba, *m.*

Cuban ['kju:bən], *a.* cubain.—*n.* Cubain, *m.*

cubby-hole ['kʌbihoul], *n.* retraite, *f.*; placard, *m.*; niche, *f.*

cube [kju:b], *n.* cube, *m.*

cubicle ['kju:bikl], *n.* compartiment, *m.* cabine, *f.*

cubit ['kju:bit], *n.* coudée, *f.*

cuckoo ['kuku:], *n.* coucou, *m.*

cucumber ['kju:kʌmbə], *n.* concombre, *m.*

cud [kʌd], *n.* bol alimentaire, *m.*; *to chew the cud*, ruminer.

cuddle [kʌdl], *v.t.* serrer (tendrement) dans ses bras; étreindre.—*v.i.* s'étreindre (amoureusement); se blottir; se peloter.

cudgel ['kʌdʒəl], *n.* bâton, gourdin, *m.*—*v.t.* bâtonner.

cue [kju:], *n.* queue de billard; (*Theat.*) réplique, *f.*; (*fig.*) avis, mot, indice, *m.*

cuff (1) [kʌf], *v.t.* souffleter, calotter, battre.—*n.* calotte, taloche, *f.*

cuff (2) [kʌf], *n.* manchette (*d'une manche*), *f.*; parement (*d'un pardessus*); poignet (*d'une robe*), *m.*

cuff link ['kʌfliŋk], *n.* bouton de manchette, *m.*

cuirass [kwi'ræs], *n.* cuirasse, *f.*

cuirassier [kwi'ræsiə], *n.* cuirassier, *m.*

culinary ['kʌlinəri], *a.* de cuisine, culinaire.

cull [kʌl], *v.t.* recueillir, cueillir; (*fig.*) choisir.

culminate ['kʌlmineit], *v.i.* se terminer (*en*), finir (*par*); (*Astron.*) culminer.

culmination [kʌlmi'neiʃən], *n.* point culminant, apogée, *m.*; (*Astron.*) culmination, *f.*

culpable ['kʌlpəbl], *a.* coupable.

culprit ['kʌlprit], *n.* accusé; inculpé, *m.*; coupable, *m., f.*

cult [kʌlt], *n.* culte, *m.*

cultivate ['kʌltiveit], *v.t.* cultiver.

cultivation [kʌlti'veiʃən], *n.* culture, *f.*

cultivator ['kʌltiveitə], *n.* cultivateur, *m.*

cultural ['kʌltʃərəl], *a.* agricole, cultural; culturel.

culture ['kʌltʃə], *n.* culture; (*fig.*) instruction éducation, *f.*

cultured ['kʌltʃəd], *a.* cultivé.

culvert ['kʌlvə:t], *n.* ponceau, petit aqueduc, *m.*

cumber ['kʌmbə], *v.t.* embarrasser, encombrer (*de*).—*n.* embarras, obstacle, *m.*

cumbersome ['kʌmbəsəm], **cumbrous** ['kʌmbrəs], *a.* embarrassant, gênant.

cumulate ['kju:mjuleit], *v.t.* accumuler, cumuler.

cunning ['kʌniŋ], *a.* fin, rusé, adroit, astucieux.—*n.* finesse, ruse, astuce, *f.*

cunningly ['kʌniŋli], *adv.* avec finesse, adroitement; par ruse.

cup [kʌp], *n.* tasse, coupe, *f.*; gobelet; (*Bot. etc.*) calice, *m.*; (*Med.*) ventouse, *f.*—*v.t.* (*Med.*) appliquer des ventouses à.

cupbearer ['kʌpbeərə], *n.* échanson, *m.*

cupboard ['kʌbəd], *n.* armoire (*pour vêtements etc.*), *f.*; placard (*dans un mur*), *m.*

cupidity [kju:'piditi], *n.* cupidité, *f.*

cupola ['kju:pələ], *n.* coupole, *f.*

cur [kə:], *n.* chien bâtard; roquet; (*fig.*) malotru, *m.*, vilaine bête, *f.*
curable [ˈkjuərəbl], *a.* guérissable.
curate [ˈkjuərit], *n.* vicaire, desservant, *m.*
curator [kjuəˈreitə], *n.* administrateur; conservateur (*de musée*), *m.*
curb [kə:b], *n.* gourmette, *f.*; (*fig.*) frein, *m.*; [KERB].—*v.t.* gourmer; (*fig.*) réprimer, contenir, brider; freiner.
curd [kə:d], *n.* caillé, lait caillé, *m.*—*v.t.* cailler, figer.
curdle [ˈkə:dl], *v.t.* cailler, figer.—*v.i.* se cailler, se figer.
cure [kjuə], *n.* guérison, *f.*; remède, *m.*; (*Eccles.*) cure, *f.*—*v.t.* guérir; sécher (*foin etc.*); mariner (*poisson etc.*); saler (*viande etc.*); (*fig.*) corriger.
curfew [ˈkə:fju:], *n.* couvre-feu, *m.*
curio [ˈkjuəriou], *n.* curiosité, *f.*; bibelot, *m.*
curiosity [kjuəriˈɔsiti], *n.* curiosité, *f.*
curious [ˈkjuəriəs], *a.* curieux; (*fig.*) remarquable, singulier.
curiously [ˈkjuəriəsli], *adv.* curieusement.
curl [kə:l], *n.* boucle (*de cheveux*); moue (*de lèvres*); spirale (*de fumée*); ondulation, *f.*—*v.t.* boucler, friser, (*fig.*) faire onduler,—*v.i.* friser; se replier (*serpent etc.*); s'entrelacer (*vignes etc.*); tourbillonner (*fumée*); onduler (*vagues*); **to curl up**, s'enrouler, se pelotonner (*chat*).
curled [kə:ld], *a.* frisé.
curlew [ˈkə:lju:], *n.* (*Orn.*) courlis, *m.*
curly [ˈkə:li], *a.* frisé, bouclé.
curmudgeon [kə:ˈmʌdʒən], *n.* ladre, pingre; bourru, *m.*
currant [ˈkʌrənt], *n.* groseille (*à grappes*), *f.*; **black currant**, cassis, *m.*; (**dried**) **currants**, raisins de Corinthe, *m.pl.*
currant bush [ˈkʌrəntbuʃ], *n.* groseillier, *m.*
currency [ˈkʌrənsi], *n.* circulation (*d'argent etc.*); monnaie, *f.*; cours; crédit, *m.*, vogue, *f.*
current [ˈkʌrənt], *a.* courant; actuel; admis, reçu; **current events**, actualités, *f.pl.*—*n.* courant; cours d'eau, *m.*
currently [ˈkʌrəntli], *adv.* couramment; généralement.
curriculum [kəˈrikjuləm], *n.* (*Sch.*) programme, plan d'études, *m.*
currier [ˈkʌriə], *n.* corroyeur, *m.*
curry (1) [ˈkʌri], *v.t.* corroyer (*cuir*); étriller (*un cheval*); (*fig.*) rosser.
curry (2) [ˈkʌri], *v.t.* (*Cook.*) apprêter au cari. —*n.* cari, *m.*
curry-comb [ˈkʌrikoum], *n.* étrille, *f.*
curse [kə:s], *n.* malédiction, *f.*; (*fig.*) fléau, malheur, *m.*—*v.t.* maudire; (*fig.*) affliger.—*v.i.* jurer; (*colloq.*) sacrer.
cursed [ˈkə:sid], *a.* maudit, exécrable.
cursorily [ˈkə:sərili], *adv.* rapidement, superficiellement.
cursory [ˈkə:səri], *a.* rapide, superficiel; général.
curt [kə:t], *a.* brusque, bref, sec.
curtail [kə:ˈteil], *v.t.* retrancher, raccourcir, abréger.
curtailment [kə:ˈteilmənt], *n.* raccourcissement, *m.*, réduction, *f.*
curtain [ˈkə:tn], *n.* rideau, *m.*; toile, *f.*—*v.t.* garnir de rideaux; (*fig.*) voiler.
curtly [ˈkə:tli], *adv.* brusquement, sèchement.

curtsy, or **curtsey** [ˈkə:tsi], *n.* révérence, *f.*—*v.i.* faire la révérence.
curve [kə:v], *n.* courbe, *f.*—*v.t.* courber; cintrer.—*v.i.* se courber.
curvet [kə:ˈvet], *v.i.* faire des courbettes; sauter, gambader.—*n.* courbette, *f.*
cushion [ˈkuʃən], *n.* coussin, *m.*; (*Billiards*) bande, *f.*—*v.t.* garnir de coussins; amortir.
custard [ˈkʌstəd], *n.* crème (au lait), *f.*; flan, *m.*
custodian [kʌsˈtoudiən], *n.* gardien; conservateur, *m.*
custody [ˈkʌstədi], *n.* garde; prison, détention, *f.*
custom [ˈkʌstəm], *n.* coutume, habitude, *f.*, usage, *m.*; pratique (*d'une boutique*), *f.*; achalandage (*d'un magasin*), *m.*; (*pl.*) douane, *f.*; droits (*taxes*), *m.pl.*
customarily [ˈkʌstəmərili], *adv.* ordinairement, d'habitude.
customary [ˈkʌstəməri], *a.* ordinaire, d'usage.
customer [ˈkʌstəmə], *n.* chaland, client, *m.*; pratique, *f.*; (*colloq.*) individu, *m.*
customs officer [ˈkʌstəmzɔfisə], *n.* douanier, *m.*
cut [kʌt], *n.* coup, *m.*; coupure (*place cut open*); coupe (*de vêtements, cheveux, cartes à jouer*); taille (*forme*), façon, tournure (*silhouette*); (*Engr.*) gravure, planche, *f.*; chemin de traverse (*raccourci*); (*Ten. etc.*) coup tranchant, *m.*—*v.t. irr.* couper, trancher; fendre; rogner; se rogner (*les ongles*); piquer, percer; faire (*une dent*); **to cut down**, abattre; réduire; **to cut out**, tailler, découper; **to cut short**, abréger; interrompre, couper la parole à; **to be cut up**, être blessé; avoir de la peine.—*v.i.* couper; se couper; percer (*dent*).
cute [kju:t], *a.* rusé, fin; (*Am.*) attirant (*enfant, fille*); amusant (*chose, truc*).
cuticle [ˈkju:tikl], *n.* cuticule, *f.*
cutler [ˈkʌtlə], *n.* coutelier, *m.*
cutlery [ˈkʌtləri], *n.* coutellerie, *f.*
cutlet [ˈkʌtlit], *n.* côtelette; escalope, *f.*
cut-price [ˈkʌtprais], *n.* prix réduit, *m.*
cutter [ˈkʌtə], *n.* coupeur; coupoir (*outil*); (*Naut.*) cutter, cotre, *m.*
cutting [ˈkʌtiŋ], *a.* incisif; (*fig.*) piquant, tranchant, mordant.—*n.* incision; rognure (*morceau*); coupe (*bois, cartes, cheveux etc.*); (*Hort.*) bouture, *f.*
cyanide [ˈsaiənaid], *n.* cyanure, *m.*
cycle [saikl], *n.* cycle, *m.*; bicyclette, *f.*, vélo, *m.*—*v.i.* aller à bicyclette.
cyclone [ˈsaikloun], *n.* cyclone, *m.*
cygnet [ˈsignit], *n.* jeune cygne, *m.*
cylinder [ˈsilində], *n.* cylindre, *m.*
cymbal [ˈsimbəl], *n.* cymbale, *f.*
cynic [ˈsinik], *n.* cynique; sceptique, *m.*, *f.*
cynical [ˈsinikl], *a.* cynique.
cynically [ˈsinikli], *adv.* cyniquement.
cynicism [ˈsinisizm], *n.* cynisme, *m.*
cynosure [ˈsainəʃuə], *n.* (*fig.*) point de mire, *m.*
cypress [ˈsaiprəs], *n.* cyprès, *m.*
Cyprian [ˈsiprian], *a.* cypriote.—*n.* Cypriote, *m.*, *f.*
Cypriot [ˈsipriət], *n.* Cypriote, *m.*, *f.*
Cyprus [ˈsaiprəs]. la Chypre, *f.*
cyst [sist], *n.* (*Anat. etc.*) kyste, *m.*
czar [TSAR].

Czech

Czech [tʃek], *a.* tchèque.—*n.* tchèque (*langue*), *m.*; Tchèque (*personne*), *m.*, *f.*
Chechoslovak [tʃeko'slouvæk], *a.* tchécoslovaque.—*n.* tchécoslovaque (*langue*), *m.*; Tchécoslovaque (*personne*), *m.*, *f.*
Czechoslovakia [tʃekoslo'vækiə]. la Tchécoslovaquie, *f.*

D

D, d [di:]. quatrième lettre de l'alphabet; (*Mus.*) ré, *m.*
dab [dæb], *n.* coup léger, *m.*, tape; éclaboussure, tache, *f.*; (*slang*) adepte, *m.*; (*Ichth.*) limande, *f.*—*v.t.* toucher légèrement; éponger à petits coups.
dabble [dæbl], *v.t.* humecter; éclabousser.—*v.i.* barboter, patauger; *to dabble in*, se mêler de.
dace [deis], *n.* (*Ichth.*) vandoise, *f.*, dard, *m.*
dachshund ['dækshund], *n.* basset allemand, *m.*
dad [dæd], **daddy** ['dædi], *n.* papa, *m.*
dado ['deidou], *n.* lambris (*de mur*), *m.*
daffodil ['dæfədil], *n.* jonquille, *f.*, narcisse des prés, *m.*
daft [dɑ:ft], *a.* niais, sot, à moitié fou.
dagger ['dægə], *n.* poignard, *m.*, dague, *f.*
dahlia ['deiliə], *n.* (*Bot.*) dahlia, *m.*
daily ['deili], *a.* journalier, quotidien.—*n.* (journal) quotidien, *m.*; femme de ménage, *f.*—*adv.* journellement, tous les jours.
daintily ['deintili], *adv.* délicatement; avec délicatesse.
daintiness ['deintinis], *n.* délicatesse, *f.*, goût difficile, *m.*
dainty ['deinti], *a.* friand; délicat, difficile.—*n.* friandise, *f.*
dairy ['dɛəri], *n.* laiterie, *f.*
dairy farm ['dɛərifɑːm], *n.* ferme laitière, *f.*
dairy-man ['dɛərimən], *n.* (*pl.* **-men** [men]) nourrisseur; crémier, *m.*
dais [deis, 'deiis], *n.* estrade, *f.*
daisy ['deizi], *n.* marguerite, pâquerette, *f.*
dale [deil], *n.* vallon, *m.*; vallée, *f.*
dalliance ['dæliəns], *n.* folâtrerie, *f.*; badinage, *m.*; caresses, *f.pl.*
dally ['dæli], *v.i.* folâtrer, perdre son temps; tarder; (*fig.*) badiner (*avec*).
dam (1) [dæm], *n.* mère (*animaux*), *f.*
dam (2) [dæm], *n.* digue (*d'un canal*), *f.*; barrage (*d'une rivière*), *m.*—*v.t.* diguer, barrer.
damage ['dæmidʒ], *n.* dommage; tort, dégât; (*fig.*) préjudice, détriment, *m.*; (*pl.*) (*Law*) dommages-intérêts, *m.pl.*—*v.t.* endommager; avarier (*en transportant*); (*fig.*) faire tort à, nuire à.—*v.i.* s'endommager.
damask ['dæməsk], *n.* damas; damassé, *m.*
dame [deim], *n.* (*poet.*) dame, *f.*
damn [dæm], *v.t.* damner; (*fig.*) condamner, désapprouver.
damnation [dæm'neiʃən], *n.* damnation, *f.*
damnatory ['dæmnətəri], *a.* condamnatoire.
damned [dæmd], *a.* damné, maudit, exécrable.

damning ['dæmiŋ], *a.* écrasant (*témoignage*).
damp [dæmp], *a.* humide; moite; (*fig.*) triste, abattu.—*n.* or **dampness** ['dæmpnis], humidité; (*fig.*) tristesse, *f.*—*v.t.* rendre humide; (*fig.*) décourager.
damper ['dæmpə], *n.* éteignoir; (*Piano*) étouffoir; (*fig.*) rabat-joie, *m.*
*damsel ['dæmzəl], *n.* jeune fille, demoiselle, *f.*
damson ['dæmzən], *n.* prune de Damas, *f.*
dance [dɑːns], *n.* danse, *f.*; bal, *m.*—*v.t.* danser; faire danser.—*v.i.* danser.
dancer ['dɑːnsə], *n.* danseur, *m.*, danseuse, *f.*
dandelion ['dændilaiən], *n.* (*Bot.*) pissenlit, *m.*
dandle [dændl], *v.t.* dorloter, bercer.
dandruff ['dændrʌf], *n.* pellicules, *f.pl.*
dandy ['dændi], *n.* dandy, élégant, petit-maître, *m.*
Dane [dein], *n.* Danois (*personne*), *m.*
danger ['deindʒə], *n.* danger, péril, *m.*
dangerous ['deindʒərəs], *a.* dangereux.
dangerously ['deindʒərəsli], *adv.* dangereusement.
dangle [dæŋgl], *v.t.* laisser pendre, balancer.—*v.i.* pendiller, baller.
Danish ['deiniʃ], *a.* danois.—*n.* danois (*langue*), *m.*
dank [dæŋk], *a.* humide et froid.
Danube ['dænjuːb], **the**. le Danube, *m.*
dapper ['dæpə], *a.* petit et vif, pimpant; soigné (*homme*).
dapple [dæpl], *v.t.* tacheter, pommeler.—*v.i.* se pommeler, se tacheter.—*a.* or **dappled** [dæpld], pommelé, truité, miroité.
dare [dɛə], *v.t.* défier, braver; provoquer.—*v.i.* oser; *I dare say!* sans doute; je le crois bien.
dare-devil ['dɛədevəl], *a.* and *n.* cassecou, *m.*
daring ['dɛəriŋ], *a.* audacieux, hardi, casse-cou.—*n.* hardiesse, audace, *f.*
dark [dɑːk], *a.* obscur, sombre, noir; foncé (*couleur*); brun, basané (*teint*); (*fig.*) secret, mystérieux.—*n.* ténèbres, *f.pl.*, obscurité, *f.*; *after dark*, à la nuit close.
darken ['dɑːkən], *v.t.* obscurcir; brunir (*teint*); (*Paint.*) assombrir (*couleurs*).—*v.i.* s'obscurcir; s'assombrir.
darkening ['dɑːkniŋ], *n.* obscurcissement, assombrissement, *m.*
darkness ['dɑːknis], *n.* obscurité, *f.*, ténèbres, *f.pl.*, teint brun (*du visage*), *m.*
darling ['dɑːliŋ], *a.* and *n.* chéri, mignon, bien-aimé, *m.*; *my darling*, (*colloq.*) mon ange, mon chou, *m.*, ma chérie, *f.*
darn [dɑːn], *n.* reprise, *f.*—*v.t.* repriser.
darning ['dɑːniŋ], *n.* reprise, *f.*
dart [dɑːt], *n.* dard, trait, *m.*; fléchette, *f.*; élan soudain, *m.*—*v.t.* darder, lancer (*contre*).—*v.i.* se lancer, s'élancer (*sur*).
dash [dæʃ], *n.* choc, coup, *m.*; impétuosité, *f.*, entrain, cran; élan soudain; tiret; trait (*de plume*); (*fig.*) soupçon (*petite quantité*), *m.*—*v.t.* jeter; heurter, briser; abattre.—*v.i.* se briser; se précipiter.—*int.* zut!
dash-board ['dæʃbɔːd], *n.* (*Motor.*) tableau de bord, *m.*
dashing ['dæʃiŋ], *a.* fougueux, brillant; pimpant, élégant.
dastard ['dæstəd], *n.* lâche ignoble, *m.*
dastardly ['dæstədli] *a.* lâche.

date (1) [deit], *n.* date, échéance, *f.*, millésime (*de pièce de monnaie*); (*Am. pop.*) rendez-vous, *m.*; *up to date*, à la page, à jour.—*v.t.* dater.—*v.i.* dater (*de*).

date (2) [deit], *n.* datte (*fruit*), *f.*

date palm ['deitpɑ:m], *n.* dattier, *m.*

dative ['deitiv], *a.* and *n.* datif, *m.*

datum ['deitəm], *n.* (*pl.* **data** ['deitə]) donnée, *f.*

daub [dɔ:b], *v.t.* barbouiller, enduire; (*fig.*) déguiser (*de*).—*n.* barbouillage, *m.*; (*Paint.*) croûte, *f.*

daughter ['dɔ:tə], *n.* fille, *f.*

daughter-in-law ['dɔ:tərinlɔ:], *n.* belle-fille, bru, *f.*

daunt [dɔ:nt], *v.t.* effrayer, intimider, décourager.

dauntless ['dɔ:ntlis], *a.* intrépide.

dauphin ['dɔ:fin], *n.* dauphin, *m.*

David ['deivid]. David, *m.*

davit ['dævit], *n.* (*Naut.*) bossoir, *m.*

dawdle [dɔ:dl], *v.i.* flâner, muser.

dawdler ['dɔ:dlə], *n.* flâneur, musard, *m.*

dawn [dɔ:n], *v.i.* poindre, paraître; (*fig.*) naître, percer.—*n.* aube, *f.*, point du jour, *m.*; aurore, *f.*

day [dei], *n.* jour, *m.*; journée (*de travail etc.*); (*fig.*) bataille, victoire, *f.*; *at the present day*, de nos jours; *every day*, tous les jours; *the day after*, le lendemain; *the day before*, la veille; *today*, aujourd'hui.

day boarder ['deibɔ:də], *n.* demi-pensionnaire, *m.*, *f.*

day-book ['deibuk], *n.* journal, *m.*

day boy ['deibɔi], **day girl** ['deigə:l], *n.* externe, *m.*, *f.*

day-break ['deibreik], *n.* [DAWN].

daylight ['deilait], *n.* lumière du jour, *f.*

daze [deiz], *v.t.* éblouir; hébéter.—*n.* stupéfaction, *f.*; *in a daze*, hébété.

dazzle [dæzl], *v.t.* éblouir, aveugler.

dazzling ['dæzliŋ], *a.* éblouissant.

deacon ['di:kən], *n.* diacre, *m.*

dead [ded], *a.* mort; inanimé; inerte, insensible; éventé (*boisson alcoolique*); mat (*couleur*); au rebut (*lettres*); *dead drunk*, ivre-mort; *dead loss*, perte sèche, *f.*; (*fig.*) crétin (*personne*), *m.*; *dead march*, marche funèbre, *f.*; *dead stop*, halte subite, *f.*; *dead weight*, poids mort, *m.*; *for a dead certainty*, à coup sûr.—*n.* cœur (*de l'hiver*), fort, *m.*; *at dead of night*, au plus profond de la nuit.

dead-beat ['ded'bi:t], *a.* éreinté, épuisé.

deaden [dedn], *v.t.* amortir; émousser (*les sens*); éventer (*boisson alcoolique*); assourdir (*son*).

dead-end ['ded'end], *n.* cul-de-sac, *m.*; impasse, *f.*

deadlock ['dedlɔk], *n.* situation sans issue; impasse, *f.*

deadly ['dedli], *a.* mortel, à mort; meurtrier.—*adv.* mortellement.

deadness ['dednis], *n.* mort, *f.*; (*fig.*) engourdissement, *m.*, froideur, *f.*

deaf [def], *a.* sourd; (*fig.*) insensible.

deafen [defn], *v.t.* rendre sourd, assourdir.

deafening ['defniŋ], *a.* assourdissant.

deaf-mute ['def'mju:t], *n.* sourd-muet, *m.*

deafness ['defnis], *n.* surdité, *f.*

deal (1) [di:l], *n.* quantité; (*Cards*) donne; affaire, *f.*, marché, *m.*; *a great* or *good*

deal, beaucoup (*de*); *by a good deal*, à beaucoup près.—*v.t. irr.* distribuer; répartir; (*Cards*) donner; porter, asséner (*coups*).—*v.i.* agir, traiter, en user (*avec*).

deal (2) [di:l], *n.* bois blanc, bois (*de sapin*), *m.*

dealer ['di:lə], *n.* marchand; (*Cards*) donneur, *m.*

dealing ['di:liŋ], *n.* conduite, *f.*; procédé, *m.*, affaire, *f.*; (*pl.*) relations, *f.pl.*, rapports, *m.pl.*

dean [di:n], *n.* doyen, *m.*

dear [diə], *a.* cher; précieux; (*fig.*) joli, gentil, charmant.—*adv.* cher; chèrement, beaucoup.—*n.* cher; cher ami, *m.*—*int.* **oh dear!** mon Dieu!

dearth [də:θ], *n.* disette, *f.*

death [deθ], *n.* mort, *f.*; (*poet.*) trépas; (*Law*) décès, *m.*

death duties ['deθdju:tiz], *n.pl.* droits de succession, *m.pl.*

death rate ['deθreit], *n.* taux de mortalité, *m.*

death rattle ['deθrætl], *n.* râle, *m.*

death throes ['deθθrouz], *n.* agonie, *f.*

debar [di'bɑ:], *v.t.* exclure, priver (*de*).

debase [di'beis], *v.t.* avilir, abaisser; abâtardir; (*Chem.*) adultérer; (*Coin.*) altérer.

debasement [di'beismənt], *n.* abaissement, avilissement, *m.*; (*Coin.*) altération, dépréciation, *f.*

debasing [di'beisiŋ], *a.* avilissant.

debatable [di'beitəbl], *a.* contestable.

debate [di'beit], *n.* débat, *m.*; discussion, *f.*—*v.t.* débattre, discuter, disputer.—*v.i.* délibérer (*sur*); contester (*avec*).

debauch [di'bɔ:tʃ], *n.* débauche, *f.*—*v.t.* débaucher, corrompre, pervertir.

debauchery [di'bɔ:tʃəri], *n.* débauche, *f.*

debenture [di'bentʃə], *n.* obligation, *f.*

debilitate [di'biliteit], *v.t.* débiliter, affaiblir, anémier.

debilitation [dibili'teiʃən], *n.* débilitation, *f.*, affaiblissement, *m.*

debility [di'biliti], *n.* débilité, faiblesse, *f.*

debit ['debit], *n.* débit, *m.*—*v.t.* débiter (*de*).

debonair [debə'nɛə], *a.* jovial; de caractère enjoué; élégant.

debouch [di'bu:ʃ], *v.i.* déboucher.

débris, debris ['debri:], *n.* débris, *m.pl.*

debt [det], *n.* dette, *f.*; dettes, *f.pl.*; créance, *f.*

debtor ['detə], *n.* débiteur, *m.*

debutante ['deibjutɑ:t], *n.* débutante (*à la cour*), *f.*

decade ['dekeid], *n.* décade, décennie, *f.*

decadence ['dekədəns], *n.* décadence, *f.*

decadent ['dekədənt], *a.* décadent.

decamp [di'kæmp], *v.i.* décamper; lever le camp.

decant [di'kænt], *v.t.* décanter, verser.

decanter [di'kæntə], *n.* carafe, *f.*

decapitate [di'kæpiteit], *v.t.* décapiter.

decapitation [dikæpi'teiʃən], *n.* décapitation, *f.*

decay [di'kei], *n.* décadence; pourriture; ruine; carie (*de dent*), *f.*—*v.i.* tomber en décadence; dépérir (*plante*); se carier (*dent*).

decease [di'si:s], *n.* (*Law*) décès, *m.*—*v.i.* décéder.

deceased [di'si:st], *a.* décédé, feu.—*n.* défunt, *m.*

deceit [di'si:t], *n.* supercherie, fourberie, tromperie, ruse, *f.*

397

deceitful [di'si:tful], *a.* trompeur; décevant (*choses*).

deceive [di'si:v], *v.t.* tromper, abuser.

deceiver [di'si:və], *n.* imposteur, trompeur, *m.*

decelerate [di:'seləreit], *v.t.*, *v.i.* ralentir.

December [di'sembə]. décembre, *m.*

decency ['di:sənsi], *n.* bienséance, *f.*, convenances, *f.pl.*; décence (*modestie*), *f.*

decennial [di'senjəl], *a.* décennal.

decent ['di:sənt], *a.* bienséant, décent; propre, convenable; gentil.

decently ['di:səntli], *adv.* décemment; convenablement.

decentralization ['di:sentrəlai'zeiʃən], *n.* décentralisation, *f.*, régionalisme, *m.*

decentralize [di:'sentrəlaiz], *v.t.* décentraliser.

deception [di'sepʃən], *n.* tromperie, fraude, duperie, *f.*

deceptive [di'septiv], *a.* trompeur.

decibel ['desibel], *n.* décibel, *m.*

decide [di'said], *v.t.* décider; décider de.—*v.i.* se décider.

decided [di'saidid], *a.* décidé, prononcé; positif; résolu.

decidedly [di'saididli], *adv.* décidément; positivement.

decimal ['desiməl], *a.* décimal; **decimal point**, virgule, *f.*—*n.* (fraction) décimale, *f.*

decimate ['desimeit], *v.t.* décimer.

decipher [di'saifə], *v.t.* déchiffrer.

decision [di'siʒən], *n.* décision, *f.*; (*fig.*) résolution, fermeté, *f.*

decisive [di'saisiv], *a.* décisif; concluant.

decisively [di'saisivli], *adv.* décisivement.

deck [dek], *n.* (*Naut.*) pont; tillac (*navire marchand*); plan (*avion*), *m.*—*v.t.* parer (*de*); orner.

deck chair ['dek'tʃɛə], *n.* transat(lantique), *m.*

declaim [di'kleim], *v.t.*, *v.i.* déclamer (*contre*).

declamatory [di'klæmətəri], *a.* déclamatoire.

declaration [deklə'reiʃən], *n.* déclaration; proclamation, *f.*

declare [di'klɛə], *v.t.* déclarer; (*fig.*) annoncer, affirmer.—*v.i.* se déclarer; se prononcer (*pour*).

decline [di'klain], *v.t.* pencher, incliner; refuser.—*v.i.* pencher; décliner; baisser (*prix*).—*n.* déclin, *m.*, décadence; (*Path.*) maladie de langueur, *f.*

declutch [di:'klʌtʃ], *v.i.* débrayer.

decode [di:'koud], *v.t.* déchiffrer.

decompose [di:kəm'pouz], *v.t.* décomposer. —*v.i.* se décomposer.

decompression [di:kəm'preʃən], *n.* décompression, *f.*

decontaminate [di:kən'tæmineit], *v.t.* désinfecter.

decontrol [di:kən'troul], *v.t.* rendre libre de nouveau, libérer (*prix, loyers etc.*).—*n.* libération (*prix, loyers etc.*), *f.*

decorate ['dekəreit], *v.t.* décorer, orner.

decoration [dekə'reiʃən], *n.* décoration, *f.*; ornement, *m.*

decorator ['dekəreitə], *n.* décorateur, *m.*

decorous ['dekərəs, di'kɔ:rəs], *a.* bienséant, convenable.

decorously ['dekərəsli, di'kɔ:rəsli], *adv.* convenablement.

decorum [di'kɔ:rəm], *n.* bienséance, *f.*, décorum, *m.*

decoy [di'kɔi], *v.t.* leurrer, amorcer.—*n.* leurre; piège, *m.*

decrease ['di:kri:s], *n.* décroissement, *m.*; diminution; décrue (*eau*), *f.*—[di'kri:s], *v.t.* faire décroître.—*v.i.* diminuer; décroître.

decree [di'kri:], *n.* décret; (*Law*) arrêt, *m.*—*v.t.* arrêter, décréter.

decrepit [di'krepit], *a.* décrépit, caduc.

decry [di'krai], *v.t.* décrier, dénigrer.

dedicate ['dedikeit], *v.t.* dédier (*à*); consacrer (*à*).

dedication [dedi'keiʃən], *n.* dédicace, *f.*

deduce [di'dju:s], *v.t.* déduire, inférer (*de*).

deduct [di'dʌkt], *v.t.* déduire, rabattre.

deduction [di'dʌkʃən], *n.* déduction, *f.*

deed [di:d], *n.* action, *f.*; fait, exploit; (*Law*) titre, *m.*

deem [di:m], *v.t.* juger; penser, estimer.

deep [di:p], *a.* profond, extrême; foncé (*couleur*); grave (*son*); (*fig.*) rusé.—*n.* (*poet.*) océan, *m.*

deepen ['di:pən], *v.t.* approfondir; assombrir. —*v.i.* devenir plus profond *ou* plus foncé.

deep-freeze ['di:p'fri:z], *n.* réfrigérateur à basse température, *m.*

deeply ['di:pli], *adv.* profondément; extrêmement.

deep-rooted ['di:p'ru:tid], **deep-seated** ['di:p'si:tid], *a.* profond, enraciné.

deer [diə], *n.* cervidé, *m.*; **fallow deer**, daim, *m.*, daine, *f.*; **red deer**, cerf, *m.*

deface [di'feis], *v.t.* défigurer; mutiler.

defamation [defə'meiʃən], *n.* diffamation, *f.*

defame [di'feim], *v.t.* diffamer.

default [di'fɔ:lt], *n.* défaut, manque, *m.*; (*Law*) contumace, *f.*

defaulter [di'fɔ:ltə], *n.* délinquant; (*Mil.*) réfractaire; (*Law*) défaillant, *m.*

defeat [di'fi:t], *n.* défaite, déroute, *f.*—*v.t.* battre, vaincre; (*fig.*) annuler, déjouer.

defeatism [di'fi:tizm], *n.* défaitisme, *m.*

defeatist [di'fi:tist], *a. and n.* défaitiste, *m.*, *f.*

defect [di'fekt], *n.* défaut, *m.*; imperfection, *f.*

defective [di'fektiv], *a.* défectueux, imparfait.

defend [di'fend], *v.t.* défendre (*de*), protéger (*contre*).

defender [di'fendə], *n.* défenseur, *m.*

defense [di'fens], *n.* défense, *f.* [see **war-office**]

defensible [di'fensəbl], *a.* défendable; (*fig.*) soutenable.

defensive [di'fensiv], *a.* défensif.—*n.* défensive, *f.*

defer [di'fə:], *v.t.* différer, remettre.—*v.i.* différer; déférer (*à*).

deference ['defərəns], *n.* déférence, *f.*

deferential [defə'renʃəl] *a.* de déférence, respectueux.

deferment [di'fə:mənt], *n.* (*Mil.*) sursis, *m.*

defiance [di'faiəns], *n.* défi, *m.*

defiant [di'faiənt], *a.* défiant.

deficiency [di'fiʃənsi], *n.* défaut, *m.*; insuffisance, *f.*

deficient [di'fiʃənt], *a.* défectueux; insuffisant.

deficit ['defisit], *n.* déficit, *m.*

defile (1) [di:'fail], *n.* défilé, *m.*

defile (2) [di'fail], *v.t.* souiller; déshonorer.

define [di'fain], *v.t.* déterminer.

definite ['definit], *a.* déterminé; (*Gram.*) défini.

definitely ['definitli], *adv.* absolument, nettement, d'une manière déterminée.

definition [defi'niʃən], *n.* définition, *f.*

deflate [di'fleit], *v.t.* dégonfler.

deflation [di'fleiʃən], *n.* dégonflement, *m.*; déflation monétaire, *f.*

deflect [di'flekt], *v.t.* faire dévier, détourner. —*v.i.* dévier.

deforestation [di:fɔris'teiʃən], *n.* déboisement, *m.*

deform [di'fɔ:m], *v.t.* déformer, défigurer.

deformation [di:fɔ:'meiʃən], *n.* déformation, *f.*

deformed [di'fɔ:md], *a.* difforme.

deformity [di'fɔ:miti], *n.* difformité; laideur, *f.*

defraud [di'frɔ:d], *v.t.* frauder.

defray [di'frei], *v.t.* défrayer; payer.

deft [deft], *a.* adroit, habile.

deftly ['deftli], *adv.* adroitement, lestement.

defunct [di'fʌŋkt], *a.* défunt, trépassé, décédé.—*n.* défunt, *m.*

defy [di'fai], *v.t.* défier, braver.

degeneracy [di'dʒenərəsi], **degeneration** [didʒenə'reiʃən], *n.* dégénérescence, *f.*

degenerate [di'dʒenərit], *a.* and *n.* dégénéré, *m.*—[di'dʒenəreit], *v.i.* dégénérer, s'abâtardir (*dans* ou *en*).

degradation [degrə'deiʃən], *n.* dégradation, *f.*; (*fig.*) avilissement, *m.*

degrade [di'greid], *v.t.* dégrader; (*fig.*) avilir.

degrading [di'greidiŋ], *a.* dégradant, avilissant.

degree [di'gri:], *n.* degré; rang, ordre, *m.*; qualité, *f.*; *university degree*, grade universitaire, *m.*

de-ice [di:'ais], *v.t., v.i.* dégivrer.

deify ['di:ifai], *v.t.* déifier.

deign [dein], *v.t., v.i.* daigner.

deity ['di:iti], *n.* divinité, *f.*; (*Myth.*) déité, *f.*

dejected [di'dʒektid], *a.* abattu, triste.

dejection [di'dʒekʃən], *n.* abattement, *m.*

delay [di'lei], *n.* délai, retard, *m.*—*v.t.* différer; remettre.—*v.i.* tarder.

delegacy ['deligəsi], *n.* délégation, *f.*

delegate [deligit], *n.* délégué, *m.*—['deligeit], *v.t.* déléguer.

delegation [deli'geiʃən], *n.* délégation, *f.*

delete [di'li:t], *v.t.* effacer, rayer, biffer.

deletion [di'li:ʃən], *n.* rature, *f.*, grattage, *m.*

deliberate [di'libərit], *a.* délibéré, prémédité; réfléchi.—[di'libəreit], *v.i.* délibérer.

deliberately [di'libəritli], *adv.* à dessein; lentement.

deliberation [dilibə'reiʃən], *n.* délibération, *f.*

delicacy ['delikəsi], *n.* délicatesse; friandise (*a titbit*), *f.*

delicate ['delikit], *a.* délicat.

delicious [di'liʃəs], *a.* délicieux.

deliciously [di'liʃəsli], *adv.* délicieusement.

delight [di'lait], *n.* délices, *f.pl.*, plaisir, *m.*—*v.t.* plaire à, réjouir, enchanter; *to be delighted to*, être enchanté de.—*v.i.* se plaire à.

delightful [di'laitful], *a.* délicieux; charmant (*personne*).

delineate [di'linieit], *v.t.* esquisser, dessiner; (*fig.*) décrire.

delinquency [di'liŋkwənsi], *n.* délit, *m.*; *juvenile delinquency*, délinquance juvénile, *f.*

delinquent [di'liŋkwənt], *n.* délinquant, *m.*; *juvenile delinquent*, jeune délinquant.

delirious [di'liriəs], *a.* en délire; délirant.

delirium [di'liriəm], *n.* délire; (*fig.*) transport de joie, *m.*

deliver [di'livə], *v.t.* délivrer, sauver; distribuer (*lettres etc.*); remettre (*lettre, paquet etc.*); livrer (*marchandises*), prononcer (*un discours*); (faire) accoucher (*femme*).

deliverance [di'livərəns], *n.* délivrance, *f.*

deliverer [di'livərə], *n.* libérateur, sauveur, *m.*

delivery [di'livəri], *n.* délivrance, remise, *f.*; débit, *m.*, diction (*d'un discours*); livraison (*de marchandises*); distribution (*du courrier*), *f.*; (*Med.*) accouchement, *m.*; *payment on delivery*, livraison contre remboursement.

delivery van [də'livərivæn], *n.* camion de livraison, *m.*; camionnette, *f.*

dell [del], *n.* vallon, *m.*

delta ['deltə], *n.* delta, *m.*

delude [di'lju:d], *v.t.* tromper, abuser.

deluge ['delju:dʒ], *n.* déluge, *m.*—*v.t.* inonder.

delusion [di'lju:ʒən], *n.* illusion, erreur, *f.*

delve [delv], *v.t., v.i.* bêcher, creuser; (*fig.*) sonder.

demagnetize [di:'mægnitaiz], *v.t.* démagnétiser.

demagogue ['deməgɔg], *n.* démagogue, *m.*, *f.*

demand [di'mɑ:nd], *n.* exigence; réclamation; demande, requête, *f.*; *in great demand*, très demandé, très recherché; *on demand*, sur demande; *supply and demand*, l'offre et la demande, *f.*—*v.t.* exiger; réclamer; demander.

demarcation [di:mɑ:'keiʃən], *n.* démarcation, *f.*; *line of demarcation*, ligne de démarcation, *f.*

demean [di'mi:n], *v.i.* se comporter, se conduire; (*colloq.*) s'abaisser, se dégrader.

demeanor [di'mi:nə], *n.* conduite, *f.*, maintien, *m.*; tenue, *f.*

demented [di'mentid], *a.* fou, dément.

demi ['demi], *prep.* demi, à demi.

demigod ['demigɔd], *n.* demi-dieu, *m.*

demise [di'maiz], *n.* décès, *m.*, mort, *f.*—*v.t.* léguer; céder à bail.

demi-semiquaver ['demi'semikweivə], *n.* (*Mus.*) triple croche, *f.*

demister [di:'mistə], *n.* (*Motor.*) appareil antibuée, *m.*

demobilization [di:moubilai'zeiʃən], *n.* démobilisation, *f.*

demobilize [di:'moubilaiz], *v.t.* démobiliser.

democracy [di'mɔkrəsi], *n.* démocratie, *f.*

democrat ['deməkræt], *n.* démocrate, *m.*, *f.*

democratic [demə'krætik], *a.* démocratique.

democratically [demə'krætikəli], *adv.* démocratiquement.

demolish [di'mɔliʃ], *v.t.* démolir.

demolition [demə'liʃən], *n.* démolition, *f.*

demon ['di:mən], *n.* démon, diable, *m.*

demonstrate ['demənstreit], *v.t.* démontrer. —*v.i.* (*Polit.*) manifester.

demonstration [demən'streiʃən], *n.* démonstration; (*Polit.*) manifestation, *f.*

demonstrative [di'mɔnstrətiv], *a.* démonstratif.

demoralize [di:'mɔrəlaiz], *v.t.* démoraliser.

demote [di'mout], *v.t.* (*Mil.*) réduire à un grade inférieur, rétrograder.

demur [di'mə:], *n.* hésitation, objection, *f.*— *v.i.* hésiter, temporiser.

demure [di'mjuə], *a.* réservé, posé; d'une modestie affectée.

demurely [di'mjuəli], *adv.* d'un air posé; avec une modestie affectée.

den [den], *n.* antre; repaire (*de voleurs etc.*), *m.*; loge (*de ménagerie*), *f.*; (*fig.*) bouge, taudis; (*colloq.*) cabinet de travail, *m.*

denationalize [di:'næʃnəlaiz], *v.t.* dénationaliser.

denial [di'naiəl], *n.* déni, *m.*, dénégation, *f.*

denier ['deniə], *n.* (*Hosiery*) denier, *m.*; *a 15-denier stocking*, un bas 15 deniers.

denigrate ['denigreit], *v.t.* noircir, dénigrer.

Denis [DENNIS].

denizen ['denizn], *n.* citoyen, habitant, *m.*

Denmark ['denmɑ:k], le Danemark, *m.*

Dennis ['denis], Denis, *m.*

denomination [dinɔmi'neiʃən], *n.* dénomination, *f.*; culte, *m.*, secte, *f.*

denominational [dinɔmi'neiʃənl], *a.* confessionnel (*école*).

denote [di'nout], *v.t.* dénoter, marquer, indiquer; signifier.

denounce [di'nauns], *v.t.* dénoncer.

dense [dens], *a.* dense, épais; compact; stupide.

densely ['densli], *adv.* en masse.

density ['densiti], *n.* densité, épaisseur, *f.*

dent [dent], *n.* renfoncement, *m.*, bosselure; coche, *f.*—*v.t.* bosseler, cabosser.

dental [dentl], *a.* dentaire; (*Phon.*) dental; *dental surgeon*, chirurgien dentiste, *m.*

dentifrice ['dentifris], *n.* dentifrice, *m.*

dentist ['dentist], *n.* dentiste, *m.*, *f.*

dentistry ['dentistri], *n.* dentisterie, *f.*

denture ['dentʃə], *n.* dentier; (*fam.*) râtelier, *m.*

denude [di'nju:d], *v.t.* dénuder; (*fig.*) dénuer.

denunciation [dinʌnsi'eiʃən], *n.* dénonciation, *f.*

deny [di'nai], *v.t.* nier, démentir; (*Law*) dénier, renier; refuser.

deodorant [di:'oudərənt], **deodorizer** [di:'oudəraizə], *n.* désinfectant, désinfecteur, désodorisant, *m.*

depart [di'pɑ:t], *v.i.* quitter.—*v.i.* partir, s'en aller, se retirer, s'éloigner; (*fig.*) mourir.

departed [di'pɑ:tid], *a.* mort, défunt; passé, évanoui.—*n. the departed*, le défunt, *m.*, les trépassés, *m.pl.*

department [di'pɑ:tmənt], *n.* département, service; (*Polit.*) bureau; comptoir, rayon (*de boutique*), *m.*; *department store*, grand magasin, *m.*

departmental [di:pɑ:t'mentl], *a.* départemental.

departure [di'pɑ:tʃə], *n.* départ; éloignement, *m.*; déviation; (*fig.*) mort, *f.*

depend [di'pend], *v.i.* dépendre (*de*); compter (*sur*), se reposer (*sur*).

dependable [di'pendəbl], *a.* digne de confiance; sûr.

dependent [di'pendənt], *a.* dépendant; (*Law*) à la charge de; (*Gram.*) subordonné; *dependent relatives*, parents à charge, *m.pl.*

depict [di'pikt], *v.t.* peindre, dépeindre.

deplete [di'pli:t], *v.t.* amoindrir, épuiser.

deplorable [di'plɔ:rəbl], *a.* déplorable; pitoyable (*lamentable*).

deplore [di'plɔ:], *v.t.* déplorer.

deploy [di'plɔi], *v.t.* (*Mil.*) déployer.—*v.i.* déployer.

depopulate [di:'pɔpjuleit], *v.t.* dépeupler.—*v.i.* se dépeupler.

deport [di'pɔ:t], *v.t.* déporter, expulser; *to deport oneself*, se comporter.

deportment [di'pɔ:tmənt], *n.* tenue, conduite, *f.*, manières, *f.pl.*

depose [di'pouz], *v.t.*, *v.i.* déposer (*de*).

deposit [di'pɔzit], *n.* dépôt; (*Banking*) versement; gage, nantissement, *m.*, arrhes, *f.pl.*, caution, *f.*; (*Geol.*) gisement, gîte, *m.*; *deposit account*, compte de dépôt, *m.*—*v.t.* déposer; verser.

deposition [depə'ziʃən, di:pə'ziʃən], *n.* déposition, *f.*; dépôt, *m.*

depositor [di'pɔzitə], *n.* (*Comm.*) déposant, *m.*

depository [di'pɔzitri], *n.* dépôt; garde-meubles, *m.*

depot [depou], *n.* dépôt, *m.*; (*Am.*) ['di:pou], gare, *f.*

deprave [di'preiv], *v.t.* dépraver, corrompre.

depraved [di'preivd], *a.* dépravé, corrompu.

depravity [di'præviti], *n.* dépravation, *f.*

deprecate ['deprikeit], *v.t.* désapprouver, désavouer, s'opposer à.

deprecatingly ['deprikeitiŋli], *adv.* avec désapprobation.

deprecative ['deprikeitiv], **deprecatory** ['deprikeitəri], *a.* de déprécation.

depreciate [di'pri:ʃieit], *v.t.* déprécier.—*v.i.* se déprécier.

depreciation [dipri:ʃi'eiʃən], *n.* dépréciation, *f.*

depress [di'pres], *v.t.* baisser, abaisser; abattre; accabler, décourager.

depressed [di'prest], *a.* abattu; bas.

depression [di'preʃən], *n.* abaissement, *m.*; dépression; (*Comm.*) crise, *f.*

deprivation [depri'veiʃən], *n.* privation, perte, *f.*

deprive [di'praiv], *v.t.* priver (*de*); déposséder.

depth [depθ], *n.* profondeur, *f.*; enfoncement (*recoin*); fort (*des saisons*), *m.*; *in the depth of winter*, au cœur *ou* au plus fort de l'hiver, *m.*; *to get out of one's depth*, perdre pied.

depth charge ['depθtʃɑ:dʒ], *n.* grenade sous-marine, *f.*

deputation [depju'teiʃən], *n.* députation, délégation, *f.*

depute [di'pju:t], *v.t.* députer, déléguer.

deputize ['depjutaiz], *v.i.* remplacer quelqu'un.

deputy ['depjuti], *n.* député, délégué; adjoint, *m.*

derail [di:'reil], *v.t.* (*Rail.*) dérailler.

derailment [di:'reilmənt], *n.* déraillement, *m.*

derange [di'reindʒ], *v.t.* déranger.

derangement [di'reindʒmənt], *n.* dérangement, *m.*

derelict ['derilikt], *a.* délaissé, abandonné.

deride [di'raid], *v.t.* tourner en dérision, se moquer de.

derision [di'riʒən], *n.* dérision, moquerie, *f.*

derisive [di'raisiv], *a.* dérisoire.

derivation [deri'veiʃən], *n.* dérivation; origine, *f.*

derivative [di'rivətiv], *n.* (*Gram.*) dérivé, *m.*

derive [di'raiv], *v.t.* dériver.—*v.i.* venir, dériver (*de*).

derogatory [di'rɔgətəri], *a.* péjoratif, dérogatoire, dérogeant (*à*).
derrick ['derik], *n.* grue, *f.*; derrick, *m.*
dervish ['dəːviʃ], *n.* derviche, *m.*
descend [di'send], *v.i.* descendre, tomber;
s'abaisser; **to be descended from**,
descendre de; **to descend upon**, tomber
sur.
descendant [di'sendənt], *n.* descendant, *m.*
descendent [di'sendənt], *a.* descendant, qui
descend, provenant (*de*).
descent [di'sent], *n.* descente; chute, pente;
descendance, naissance, origine (*lignée*), *f.*
describe [dis'kraib], *v.t.* décrire, dépeindre,
peindre.
description [dis'kripʃən], *n.* description;
désignation (*d'une personne*), *f.*; (*Law*)
signalement, *m.*; (*colloq.*) qualité, sorte,
espèce, *f.*
descriptive [dis'kriptiv], *a.* descriptif.
descry [dis'krai], *v.t.* découvrir, apercevoir;
aviser; reconnaître.
desecrate ['desəkreit], *v.t.* profaner.
desecration [desə'kreiʃən], *n.* profanation, *f.*
desert (1) [di'zəːt], *n.* mérite, *m.*; mérites,
m.pl.
desert (2) ['dezət], *a.* désert; solitaire.—*n.*
désert, *m.*; solitude, *f.*
desert (3) [di'zəːt], *v.t.* abandonner, déserter.
deserted [di'zəːtid], *a.* abandonné, désert.
deserter [di'zəːtə], *n.* déserteur, *m.*
desertion [di'zəːʃən], *n.* désertion, *f.*, abandon, *m.*
deserve [di'zəːv], *v.t.* mériter, être digne de.
deservedly [di'zəːvidli], *adv.* à bon droit,
justement.
deserving [di'zəːviŋ], *a.* de mérite, méritoire.
desiccated ['desikeitid], *a.* desséché.
design [di'zain], *n.* dessein, projet; dessin
(*drawing*); (*Manuf.*) modèle, *m.*; **by design**,
à dessein.—*v.t.* projeter, se proposer de;
dessiner.
designedly [di'zainidli], *adv.* à dessein.
designer [di'zainə], *n.* inventeur; auteur;
architecte; dessinateur (*draftsman*), *m.*
designing [di'zainiŋ], *a.* artificieux, intrigant.
designate ['dezigneit], *v.t.* désigner, nommer.—['dezignit], *a.* désigné, nommé.
desirable [di'zaiərəbl], *a.* désirable, à souhaiter.
desire [di'zaiə], *n.* désir, *m.*; prière, demande,
f.—*v.t.* désirer, souhaiter; prier.
desirous [di'zaiərəs], *a.* désireux (*de*), empressé (*à*); **to be desirous of**, avoir envie
de.
desist [di'zist], *v.i.* se désister, cesser (*de*).
desk [desk], *n.* pupitre (*école*); bureau
(*meuble*), *m.*; caisse (*boutique*); chaire (*de
professeur*), *f.*
desolate ['desəlit], *a.* désolé, inhabité, solitaire, dévasté.
desolation [desə'leiʃən], *n.* désolation, *f.*
despair [dis'pɛə], *n.* désespoir, *m.*—*v.i.*
désespérer (*de*).
despatch [DISPATCH].
desperado [despə'reidou, despə'raːdou], *n.*
désespéré, *m.*
desperate ['despərit], *a.* désespéré; furieux,
forcené; acharné, terrible.
desperately ['despəritli], *adv.* désespérément; (*fig.*) excessivement.

desperation [despə'reiʃən], *n.* désespoir, *m.*;
fureur, *f.*, acharnement, *m.*
despicable ['dispikəbl], *a.* méprisable.
despise [dis'paiz], *v.t.* mépriser, dédaigner.
despite [dis'pait], *n.* (*Lit.*) dépit, *m.*—*prep.* en
dépit de, malgré.
despoil [dis'pɔil], *v.t.* dépouiller.
despondency [dis'pɔndənsi], *n.* abattement,
désespoir, *m.*
despondent [dis'pɔndənt], *a.* découragé,
abattu.
despot ['despɔt], *n.* despote, *m.*, *f.*
despotic [des'pɔtik], *a.* despotique.
despotism ['despətizm], *n.* despotisme, *m.*
dessert [di'zəːt], *n.* dessert, *m.*
destination [desti'neiʃən], *n.* destination, *f.*
destine ['destin], *v.t.* destiner, désigner.
destiny ['destini], *n.* destin, *m.*, destinée, *f.*
destitute ['destitjuːt], *a.* dépourvu, destitué;
indigent.
destitution [desti'tjuːʃən], *n.* dénuement,
abandon, *m.*, indigence, *f.*
destroy [dis'trɔi], *v.t.* détruire, ruiner.
destroyer [dis'trɔiə], *n.* (*Naut.*) contre-
torpilleur, *m.*
destroying [dis'trɔiiŋ], *a.* destructeur, destructif.
destruction [dis'trʌkʃən], *n.* destruction, *f.*,
anéantissement, *m.*; ruine, *f.*
destructive [dis'trʌktiv], *a.* destructeur;
funeste, fatal (*à*).
desultorily ['desəltərili], *adv.* à bâtons
rompus, sans suite.
desultory ['desəltəri], *a.* à bâtons rompus,
décousu, sans suite.
detach [di'tætʃ], *v.t.* détacher (*de*); isoler; **to
become detached**, se détacher.
detachable [di'tætʃəbl], *a.* démontable,
détachable.
detached [di'tætʃt], *a.* détaché, isolé.
detachment [di'tætʃmənt], *n.* détachement,
m.
detail ['diːteil], *n.* détail, *m.*—[di'teil], *v.t.*
détailler; (*Mil.*) désigner (*pour*).
detain [di'tein], *v.t.* retenir; détenir; (*Law*)
empêcher.
detect [di'tekt], *v.t.* découvrir; détecter.
detection [di'tekʃən], *n.* découverte, *f.*
detective [di'tektiv], *n.* agent de la (police de)
sûreté, policier, détective, *m.*; **a detective
story**, un roman policier.
detention [di'tenʃən], *n.* action de retenir;
(*Law*) détention; (*Sch.*) consigne, *f.*
deter [di'təː], *v.t.* détourner, empêcher (*de*);
dissuader (*de*).
detergent [di'təːdʒənt], *a.* and *n.* détersif,
détergent, *m.*
deteriorate [di'tiəriəreit], *v.i.* se détériorer.
deterioration [ditiəriə'reiʃən], *n.* détérioration, *f.*; dépérissement, *m.*
determination [ditəːmi'neiʃən], *n.* détermination, décision, *f.*
determine [di'təːmin], *v.t.* déterminer,
décider.—*v.i.* se déterminer, se décider,
résoudre.
determined [di'təːmind], *a.* résolu, obstiné.
deterrent [di'terənt], *a.* préventif.—*n.* arme
préventive, *f.*
detest [di'test], *v.t.* détester.
detestable [di'testəbl], *a.* détestable; (*fig.*)
odieux.
detestation [diːtes'teiʃən], *n.* détestation, *f.*

dethrone [di'θroun], *v.t.* détrôner.
detonation [detə'neiʃən], *n.* détonation, *f.*
detonator ['detəneitə], *n.* détonateur, *m.*
detour [di'tuə], *n.* déviation, *f.*
detract [di'trækt], *v.t.* enlever, ôter (à); dénigrer.—*v.i.* déroger (à).
detriment ['detrimənt], *n.* détriment, préjudice, *m.*
detrimental [detri'mentl], *a.* préjudiciable, nuisible (à).
deuce [dju:s], *n.* (*Cards*) deux; (*Ten.*) à deux; à égalité; (*colloq.*) diable, diantre, *m.*
Deuteronomy [dju:tə'ronəmi]. Deutéronome, *m.*
devaluation [di:vælju'eiʃən], *n.* dévaluation, *f.*
devalue [di:'vælju], **devaluate** [di:'væljueit], *v.t.* dévaluer, déprécier.
devastate ['devəsteit], *v.t.* dévaster.
devastation [devəs'teiʃən], *n.* dévastation, *f.*
develop [di'veləp], *v.t.* développer.
developer [di'veləpə], *n.* (*Phot.*) révélateur, *m.*
development [di'veləpmənt], *n.* développement, *m.*
deviate ['di:vieit], *v.i.* dévier, se dévier; s'écarter (*de*).
deviation [di:vi'eiʃən], *n.* déviation, *f.*, écart, *m.*
device [di'vais], *n.* dessein, moyen, stratagème; dispositif, mécanisme, *m.*; devise (*motto*), *f.*
devil [devl], *n.* diable, démon, *m.*; **daredevil**, téméraire, *m.f.*—*v.t.* griller et poivrer; **devil-may-care**, étourdi, *m.*
devilish ['deviliʃ], *a.* maudit, diabolique.
devilment ['devilmənt], **deviltry** ['deviltri], *n.* diablerie, *f.*
devious ['di:viəs], *a.* détourné, écarté; (*fig.*) errant.
devise [di'vaiz], *v.t.* imaginer, inventer; tramer, machiner.
devitalize [di:'vaitəlaiz], *v.t.* dévitaliser.
devoid [di'vɔid], *a.* exempt, dénué (*de*).
devote [di'vout], *v.t.* dévouer, consacrer (à).
devoted [di'voutid], *a.* dévoué, consacré.
devotee [devo'ti:], *n.* dévot; passionné, *m.*, fanatique, *m.*
devotion [di'vouʃən], *n.* dévotion, *f.*; dévouement, *m.*
devour [di'vauə], *v.t.* dévorer.
devout [di'vaut], *a.* dévot, pieux, fervent.
devoutly [di'vautli], *adv.* dévotement.
dew [dju:], *n.* rosée, *f.*
dewdrop ['dju:drɔp], *n.* goutte de rosée, *f.*
dewlap ['dju:læp], *n.* fanon, *m.*
dewy ['dju:i], *a.* (couvert) de rosée.
dexterity [deks'teriti], *n.* dextérité, adresse, *f.*
dexterous ['dekstrəs], *a.* adroit; habile.
diabetes [daiə'bi:ti:z], *n.* diabète, *m.*
diabetic [daiə'betik], *a.* and *n.* diabétique, *m.f.*
diabolic [daiə'bɔlik], **diabolical** [daiə'bɔlikl], *a.* diabolique.
diadem ['daiədem], *n.* diadème, *m.*
diæresis [dai'iərəsis], *n.* (*pl.* **diæreses** [dai'iərəsi:z]) tréma, *m.*
diagnose [daiəg'nouz], *v.t.* diagnostiquer.
diagnosis [daiəg'nousis], *n.* diagnose, *f.*; diagnostic, *m.*
diagonal [dai'ægənəl], *a.* diagonal.—*n.* diagonale, *f.*

diagram ['daiəgræm], *n.* diagramme, schéma, *m.*, épure, *f.*
diagrammatic [daiəgrə'mætik], *a.* schématique.
dial ['daiəl], *n.* cadran, *m.*; **sun-dial**, cadran solaire.—*v.t.* (*Teleph.*) composer (*un numéro*).
dialect ['daiəlekt], *n.* dialecte, patois; (*fig.*) langage, *m.*
dialogue ['daiəlɔg], *n.* dialogue; entretien, *m.*
diameter [dai'æmitə], *n.* diamètre, *m.*
diamond ['daiəmənd], *n.* diamant; (*Cards*) carreau, *m.*
diamond cutter ['daiəməndkʌtə], *n.* lapidaire, *m.*
diamond-shaped ['daiəməndʃeipt], *a.* en losange.
Diana [dai'ænə]. (*Myth.*) Diane, *f.*
diaper ['daiəpə], *n.* linge ouvré, *m.*; (*Am.*) serviette hygiénique, couche (*d'enfant*), *f.*
diarrhoea [daiə'ri:ə], *n.* diarrhée, *f.*
diary ['daiəri], *n.* journal (particulier); agenda, *m.*
diatribe ['daiətraib], *n.* diatribe, *f.*
dice [dais], *n.pl.* dés, *m.pl.*—*v.i.* jouer aux dés.
dicky ['diki], *n.* faux plastron (de chemise), *m.*
dictate [dik'teit], *v.t.* dicter.—*v.i.* commander (à).—['dikteit], *n.* précepte, ordre, *m.*
dictation [dik'teiʃən], *n.* dictée, *f.*
dictator [dik'teitə], *n.* dictateur, *m.*
dictatorial [diktə'tɔ:riəl], *a.* dictatorial; impérieux.
dictatorship [dik'teitəʃip], *n.* dictature, *f.*
diction ['dikʃən], *n.* diction, *f.*; débit, *m.*
dictionary ['dikʃənri], *n.* dictionnaire, *m.*
dictum ['diktəm], *n.* (*pl.* **dicta** ['diktə]) dicton, *m.*
diddle [didl], *v.t.* (*colloq.*) duper, rouler.
die (1) [dai], *n.* (*pl.* **dies** [daiz]) coin (*pour estamper*).
die (2) [dai], *n.* (*pl.* **dice** [dais]) dé (à jouer), *m.*; (*fig.*) chance, *f.*
die (3) [dai], *v.i.* mourir; (*fig.*) s'éteindre; **to die down**, s'apaiser, se calmer; **to die of**, mourir de; **to die out**, s'éteindre, disparaître, s'oublier.
die-hard ['daiha:d], *n.* intransigeant, *m.*
diet ['daiət], *n.* diète, *f.*, régime, *m.*; diète (*assemblée*), *f.*—*v.t.* mettre à la diète, mettre au régime.—*v.i.* faire diète, être au régime.
dietetics [daiə'tetiks], *n.pl.* diététique, *f.*
differ ['difə], *v.i.* différer (*de*); se quereller (*avec*).
difference ['difrəns], *n.* différence; dispute, *f.*; différend (*de valeur*), *m.*; **to split the difference**, partager le différend.
different ['difrənt], *a.* différent.
differentiate [difə'renʃieit], *v.t.* différencier, distinguer.
differently ['difrəntli], *adv.* différemment, autrement.
difficult ['difikəlt], *a.* difficile; malaisé.
difficulty ['difikəlti], *n.* difficulté; peine, *f.*, embarras; (*pl.*) embarras pécuniaire, *m.*
diffidence ['difidəns], *n.* défiance (*de soi*), modestie, timidité, *f.*
diffident ['difidənt], *a.* timide, hésitant.
diffidently ['difidəntli], *adv.* avec hésitation, timidement.
diffuse [di'fju:s], *a.* répandu, étendu; diffus, verbeux (*style*).—[di'fju:z], *v.t.* répandre.
diffusely [di'fju:sli], *adv.* diffusément.

dig [dig], *v.t. irr.* creuser; bêcher; piocher.—
v.i. bêcher, piocher; faire des fouilles.—*n.*
coup *(de coude)*; *(colloq.)* coup de patte, *m.*

digest [di′dʒest], *v.t.* digérer *(aliment etc.)*;
résumer.—*v.i.* digérer.—[′daidʒest], *n.* sommaire, abrégé, *m.*

digestion [di′dʒestʃən], *n.* digestion, *f.*

digestive [di′dʒestiv], *a.* and *n.* digestif, *m.*

digger [′digə], *n.* terrassier; mineur; fouil-
leur *(archéologue)*; *(pop.)* Australien, *m.*

digging [′digin], *n.* fouille, *f.*, creusement, *m.*;
(pl.) (pop.) (abbr. **digs** [digz]) logement, *m.*

dignified [′dignifaid], *a.* plein de dignité,
digne; noble.

dignify [′dignifai], *v.t.* honorer, élever,
illustrer.

dignitary [′dignitri], *n.* dignitaire, *m., f.*

dignity [′digniti], *n.* dignité, *f.*

digress [dai′gres], *v.i.* faire une digression;
s'écarter *(de).*

digression [dai′greʃən], *n.* digression, *f.*

dike or **dyke** [daik], *n.* digue, *f.*, fossé, *m.*

dilapidated [di′læpideitid], *a.* délabré.

dilapidation [dilæpi′deiʃən], *n.* délabrement,
m.

dilate [dai′leit], *v.t.* dilater, élargir, étendre.—
v.i. se dilater.

dilatory [′dilətəri], *a.* négligent, lent.

dilemma [di′lemə, dai′lemə], *n.* dilemme;
(fig.) embarras, *m.*; **on the horns of a
dilemma**, enfermé dans un dilemme.

diligence [′dilidʒəns], *n.* diligence, assiduité,
f.

diligent [′dilidʒənt], *a.* diligent, appliqué.

dilute [dai′lju:t, di′lju:t], *v.t.* délayer; diluer;
couper *(vin)*; *(fig.)* affaiblir.—*a.* dilué,
mitigé.

dilution [dai′lju:ʃən, di′lju:ʃən], *n.* dilution
(liquides), *f.*; délayement; *(fig.)* affaiblissement, *m.*

dim [dim], *a.* obscur, trouble; blafard; terne
(lumière); indécis.—*v.t.* obscurcir; ternir.

dimension [di′menʃən, dai′menʃən], *n.*
dimension, étendue, *f.*

dimensional [di′menʃənəl, dai′menʃənəl], *a.*
dimensionnel; *(Cine.)* **three-dimensional
(3-D) film**, film en relief, *m.*

diminish [di′miniʃ], *v.t.* diminuer; abaisser.
—*v.i.* diminuer.

diminutive [di′minjutiv], *a.* diminutif,
minuscule.

dimly [′dimli], *adv.* obscurément, indistinctement, faiblement, à peine; sans éclat.

dimness [′dimnis], *n.* obscurcissement, *m.*;
obscurité; faiblesse *(de vue)*, *f.*

dimple [dimpl], *n.* fossette, *f.*—*v.i. (fig.)* se
rider *(eau etc.).*

din [din], *n.* vacarme, tapage, fracas; cliquetis
(d'armes etc.), *m.*

dine [dain], *v.i.* dîner *(de).*

diner [′dainə], *n.* dîneur, *m.*

dinghy [′dingi], *n. (Naut.)* youyou, canot, *m.*

dinginess [′dindʒinis], *n.* couleur terne, *f.*;
aspect sale, *m.*

dingy [′dindʒi], *a.* terne; sale; défraîchi.

dining car [′daininka:], *n.* wagon-restaurant,
m.

dining room [′daininrum], *n.* salle à manger,
f.

dinner [′dinə], *n.* dîner, *m.*

dinner jacket [′dinədʒækit], *n.* smoking, *m.*

dint (1) [dint], *n.* force, *f.*, pouvoir, *m.*; **by
dint of**, à force de.

dint (2) [dint], [DENT].

diocese [′daiəsis], *n.* diocèse, *m.*

dioxide [dai′oksaid], *n. (Chem.)* bioxyde, *m.*

dip [dip], *v.t.* plonger *(dans)*; tremper, mouiller; *(Motor.)* mettre en code *(phares).*—*v.i.*
plonger; **to dip into**, s'engager dans,
feuilleter *(un livre).*—*n.* plongeon, *m.*, baignade, *f.*

diphtheria [dif′θiəriə], *n.* diphtérie, *f.*

diphthong [′difθɔn], *n.* diphtongue, *f.*

diploma [di′ploumə], *n.* diplôme, *m.*

diplomacy [di′ploumǝsi], *n.* diplomatie, *f.*

diplomat [′diploumæt], **diplomatist** [di′plou
mǝtist], *n.* diplomate, *m., f.*

diplomatic [diplo′mætik], *a.* diplomatique.

dip-stick [′dipstik], *n. (Motor.)* réglette-
jauge, *f.*

dire [′daiə], *a.* terrible, affreux, cruel.

direct [di′rekt, dai′rekt], *a.* direct, droit;
exprès, clair.—*adv. (colloq.)* directement.—
v.t. diriger; ordonner, charger *(de)*; indiquer, donner des renseignements à;
(Theat.) mettre en scène.

direction [di′rekʃən], *n.* direction, *f.*; ordre,
m., instruction, *f.*; sens, côté, *m.*; adresse
(d'une lettre), *f.*

directional signal [di′rekʃənəl ′signəl],
n. (Motor.) clignotant, *m.*

directly [di′rektli], *adv.* directement.

director [di′rektə], *n.* directeur, administrateur, gérant; *(Cine.)* réalisateur, *m.*

directory [di′rektəri], *n.* directoire; *(Postal,
Teleph.)* annuaire, *m.*

direful [′daiəful], *a.* terrible, affreux.

dirge [də:dʒ], *n.* chant funèbre, *m.*

dirt [də:t], *n.* saleté; crasse; boue, fange;
ordure, *f.*

dirtily [′də:tili], *adv.* salement; *(fig.)* vilainement.

dirtiness [′də:tinis], *n.* saleté; *(fig.)* bassesse, *f.*

dirty [′də:ti], *a.* sale, malpropre, crasseux;
(fig.) bas, vilain.—*v.t.* salir, crotter; *(fig.)*
souiller.

disability [disə′biliti], *n.* incapacité, *f.*

disable [dis′eibl], *v.t.* rendre incapable,
mettre hors d'état *(de).*

disabled [dis′eibld], *a.* hors de service; *(Mil.)*
hors de combat; **disabled ex-service
men**, mutilés de guerre, *m.pl.*

disadvantage [disəd′va:ntidʒ], *n.* désavantage, inconvénient, *m.*; perte, *f.*

disagree [disə′gri:], *v.i.* différer, ne pas s'accorder; **my dinner disagreed with me**,
mon dîner m'a fait mal.

disagreeable [disə′gri:əbl], *a.* désagréable;
fâcheux.

disagreeableness [disə′gri:əblnis], *n.* désagrément, *m.*, nature désagréable, *f.*

disagreeably [disə′gri:əbli], *adv.* désagréablement.

disagreement [disə′gri:mənt], *n.* différence,
f., désaccord; différend, *m.*; brouille, *f.*

disallow [disə′lau], *v.t.* désapprouver; refuser,
défendre.

disappear [disə′piə], *v.i.* disparaître.

disappearance [disə′piərəns], *n.* disparition,
f.

disappoint [disə′pɔint], *v.t.* désappointer,
décevoir.

disappointing [disə′pɔintin], *a.* décevant.

403

disappointment [disə'pɔintmənt], n. désappointement, m.; déception, f.; contretemps, m.

disapprobation [disæpro'beiʃən], **disapproval** [disə'pruːvəl], n. désapprobation, f.

disapprove [disə'pruːv], v.t. désapprouver.—v.i. **to disapprove of**, désapprouver.

disarm [dis'ɑːm], v.t. désarmer.

disarmament [dis'ɑːməmənt], n. désarmement, m.

disarrange [disə'reindʒ], v.t. déranger.

disarray [disə'rei], v.i. mettre en désarroi ou en désordre.—n. désarroi, désordre, m.

disaster [di'zɑːstə], n. désastre, malheur, m.

disastrous [di'zɑːstrəs], a. désastreux.

disavow [disə'vau], v.t. désavouer.

disband [dis'bænd], v.t. licencier, congédier; disperser.—v.i. se disperser.

disbelief [disbi'liːf], n. incrédulité, f.

disbelieve [disbi'liːv], v.t. ne pas croire, refuser de croire.

disbeliever [disbi'liːvə], n. incrédule, m., f.

disc [DISK].

discard [dis'kɑːd], v.t. mettre de côté; congédier; écarter; éliminer; (Cards) faire son écart.—['diskɑːd], n. (Cards) écart, m.

discern [di'səːn, di'zəːn], v.t. discerner, distinguer.

discerning [di'səːniŋ, di'zəːniŋ], a. judicieux, éclairé, attentif.

discernment [di'səːnmənt, di'zəːnmənt], n. discernement, jugement, m.

discharge [dis'tʃɑːdʒ], n. déchargement, m.; décharge (arme à feu etc.); mise en liberté (d'un prisonnier), f.; accomplissement (d'un devoir), m.; réhabilitation (d'un failli); quittance (récépissé), f.; congé (d'employé); (Mil.) congé définitif; (Med.) écoulement, m.—v.t. décharger; congédier (employé); libérer (de prison); acquitter (dette); décharger (arme à feu); remplir (devoir); (Mil., Navy) congédier; (Law) quitter.—v.i. suppurer (blessure etc.).

disciple [di'saipl], n. disciple, m.

disciplinarian [disipli'nɛəriən], a. disciplinaire.—n. personne rigide pour la discipline, f.

disciplinary ['disiplinəri], a. disciplinaire.

discipline ['disiplin], n. discipline, f.—v.t. discipliner.

disclaim [dis'kleim], v.t. désavouer, renier, nier.

disclose [dis'klouz], v.t. découvrir, révéler.

disclosure [dis'klouʒə], n. révélation, découverte, f.

discolor [dis'kʌlə], v.t. décolorer.

discomfort [dis'kʌmfət], n. incommodité, f., inconfort, malaise, m.; gêne, f.

discompose [diskəm'pouz], v.t. déranger, troubler.

discomposure [diskəm'pouʒə], n. trouble, désordre, m., agitation, f.

disconcert [diskən'səːt], v.t. déconcerter.

disconnect [diskə'nekt], v.t. désunir, séparer; (Elec.) débrancher; (Mach.) désembrayer.

disconnected [diskə'nektid], a. débrayé; déconnecté; (fig.) décousu.

disconsolate [dis'kɔnsəlit], a. inconsolable, désolé.

discontent [diskən'tent], n. mécontentement, m.

discontented [diskən'tentid], a. mécontent (de).

discontinue [diskən'tinjuː], v.t., v.i. discontinuer; cesser de.

discord ['diskɔːd], n. discorde; (Mus.) dissonance, f.

discordant [dis'kɔːdənt], a. discordant; (fig.) en désaccord.

discount ['diskauntl, n. escompte; rabais, m. **at a discount**, au rabais, en baisse.—[dis'kaunt], v.t. escompter; (fig.) décompter, rabattre.—v.i. faire l'escompte.

discourage [dis'kʌridʒ], v.t. décourager, détourner.

discouragement [dis'kʌridʒmənt], n. découragement, m.

discouraging [dis'kʌridʒiŋ], a. décourageant.

discourse (1) ['diskɔːs], n. discours, entretien; (fig.) langage, propos, m.—[dis'kɔːs], v.i. discourir, s'entretenir, traiter (de).

discourteous [dis'kəːtiəs], a. impoli.

discourtesy [dis'kəːtisi], n. impolitesse, f.

discover [dis'kʌvə], v.t. découvrir; révéler, montrer.

discovery [dis'kʌvəri], n. découverte, f.

discredit [dis'kredit], n. discrédit, m.; honte, f.—v.t. ne pas croire; déshonorer.

discreditable [dis'kreditəbl], a. peu honorable; honteux.

discreet [dis'kriːt], a. discret, prudent, circonspect, sage.

discreetly [dis'kriːtli], adv. discrètement, sagement, prudemment.

discrepancy [dis'krepənsi], n. désaccord, m.

discretion [dis'kreʃən], n. discrétion, prudence, sagesse, f.; jugement, discernement, m.

discriminate [dis'krimineit], v.t. discriminer, distinguer.—v.i. faire des distinctions.

discriminating [dis'krimineitiŋ], a. discriminatoire, distinctif.

discrimination [diskrimi'neiʃən], n. discrimination, f., discernement, m.

discuss [dis'kʌs], v.t. discuter, débattre.

discussion [dis'kʌʃən], n. discussion, f., débat, m.

disdain [dis'dein], n. dédain, mépris, m.—v.t. dédaigner, mépriser.

disdainful [dis'deinful], a. dédaigneux, méprisant.

disease [di'ziːz], n. maladie, f., mal; (fig.) vice, m.

diseased [di'ziːzd], a. malade; (fig.) dérangé.

disembark [disim'bɑːk], v.t., v.i. débarquer.

disembarkation [disembɑː'keiʃən], n. débarquement, m.

disembodied [disim'bɔdid], a. désincarné.

disembowel [disim'bauəl], v.t. éventrer.

disengage [disin'geidʒ], v.t. dégager; (Tech.) débrayer.—v.i. se dégager.

disengaged [disin'geidʒd], a. dégagé; libre.

disentangle [disin'tæŋgl], v.t. démêler, débrouiller.

disentanglement [disin'tæŋglmənt], n. débrouillement, m.

disestablish [disis'tæbliʃ], v.t. séparer (l'Église de l'État).

disestablishment [disis'tæbliʃmənt], n. séparation de l'Église et de l'État, f.

disfavor [dis'feivə], n. défaveur, f.

disfigure [dis'figə], v.t. défigurer, enlaidir.

dispirited

disfigurement [dis'figəmənt], *n.* action de défigurer; difformité, *f.*

disfranchisement [dis'fræntʃizmənt], *n.* privation *ou* perte des privilèges électoraux, *f.*

disgorge [dis'gɔːdʒ], *v.t.* dégorger, rendre, vomir.—*v.i.* rendre gorge.

disgrace [dis'greis], *n.* disgrâce, honte, *f.*, déshonneur, *m.*—*v.t.* disgracier; déshonorer.

disgraceful [dis'greisful], *a.* honteux; déshonorant, ignoble.

disgracefully [dis'greisfuli], *adv.* honteusement.

disgruntled [dis'grʌntld], *a.* mécontent; de mauvaise humeur.

disguise [dis'gaiz], *n.* déguisement, travestissement; (*fig.*) masque, voile, *m.*—*v.t.* déguiser; (*fig.*) cacher, voiler.

disguised [dis'gaizd], *a.* déguisé.

disgust [dis'gʌst], *n.* dégoût, *m.*, aversion, *f.*; ennui, *m.*—*v.t.* dégoûter (*de*); écœurer.

disgusting [dis'gʌstiŋ], *a.* dégoûtant.

dish [diʃ], *n.* (*pl.* **dishes** ['diʃiz]) plat (*vaisselle*); mets (*aliment*), *m.*; (*pl.*) vaisselle, *f.*—*v.t.* dresser, servir, apprêter; (*colloq.*) enfoncer.

dish-cloth ['diʃklɔθ], *n.* torchon, *m.*

dishearten [dis'hɑːtn], *v.t.* décourager.

disheartening [dis'hɑːtniŋ], *a.* décourageant.

dishevel [di'ʃevəl], *v.t.* ébouriffer.

dishevelled [di'ʃevəld], *a.* dépeigné, ébouriffé.

dishonest [dis'ɔnist], *a.* malhonnête.

dishonestly [dis'ɔnistli], *adv.* malhonnêtement.

dishonesty [dis'ɔnisti], *n.* improbité, malhonnêteté, *f.*

dishonor [dis'ɔnə], *n.* déshonneur, *m.*—*v.t.* déshonorer; avilir; (*Comm.*) **dishonored check**, chèque impayé, *m.*

dishonorable [dis'ɔnərəbl], *a.* sans honneur; honteux (*chose*).

dishonorably [dis'ɔnərəbli], *adv.* malhonnêtement.

disillusion [disi'ljuːʒən], *v.t.* désillusionner.—*n.*, *also* **disillusionment** [disi'ljuːʒənmənt], désillusionnement, *m.*

disinclination [disinkli'neiʃən], *n.* éloignement, *m.*; aversion, *f.*

disinclined [disin'klaind], *a.* peu disposé.

disinfect [disin'fekt], *v.t.* désinfecter.

disinfectant [disin'fektənt], *n.* désinfectant, *m.*

disingenuous [disin'dʒenjuəs], *a.* sans franchise, de mauvaise foi, dissimulé.

disingenuously [disin'dʒenjuəsli], *adv.* de mauvaise foi.

disingenuousness [disin'dʒenjuəsnis], *n.* dissimulation, mauvaise foi, fausseté, *f.*

disinherit [disin'herit], *v.t.* déshériter.

disinheritance [disin'heritəns], *n.* déshéritement, *m.*

disintegrate [dis'intigreit], *v.t.* désagréger; désintégrer.—*v.i.* se désagréger, se désintégrer.

disintegration [disinti'greiʃən], *n.* désagrégation; désintégration, *f.*

disinter [disin'təː], *v.t.* déterrer, exhumer.

disinterested [dis'intrəstid], *a.* désintéressé.

disjointed [dis'dʒɔintid], *a.* désarticulé, disloqué; (*fig.*) décousu, sans suite (*style etc.*).

disjointedly [dis'dʒɔintidli], *adv.* d'une manière décousue *ou* incohérente.

disk [disk], *n.* disque, *m.*; (*Med.*) **slipped disk**, hernie discale, *f.*

dislike [dis'laik], *v.t.* ne pas aimer; avoir du dégoût pour.—*n.* aversion, *f.*; dégoût, *m.*

dislocate ['dislokeit], *v.t.* disloquer, démettre; déboîter (*os etc.*).

dislodge [dis'lɔdʒ], *v.t.* déloger; déplacer.

disloyal [dis'lɔiəl], *a.* perfide, déloyal.

disloyalty [dis'lɔiəlti], *n.* défection (*de*), déloyauté, perfidie, *f.*

dismal ['dizməl], *a.* sombre, morne, triste.

dismally ['dizməli], *adv.* lugubrement, tristement.

dismantle [dis'mæntl], *v.t.* dévêtir; démonter (*machine*).

dismay [dis'mei], *n.* effroi, *m.*, terreur épouvante, *f.*—*v.t.* effarer, épouvanter, consterner.

dismiss [dis'mis], *v.t.* renvoyer (*de*); congédier; quitter (*sujet etc.*); rejeter (*appel etc.*); chasser (*pensées etc.*).

dismissal [dis'misəl], *n.* renvoi; congé; (*Law*) acquittement, *m.*

dismount [dis'maunt], *v.t.* démonter.—*v.i.* descendre de cheval.

disobedience [diso'biːdiəns], *n.* désobéissance, *f.*

disobedient [diso'biːdiənt], *a.* désobéissant.

disobey [diso'bei], *v.t.* désobéir à.

disobliging [diso'blaidʒiŋ], *a.* désobligeant.

disorder [dis'ɔːdə], *n.* désordre, dérèglement, *m.*; maladie (*Med.*), *f.*—*v.t.* déranger, troubler.

disordered [dis'ɔːdəd], *a.* en désordre, dérangé; malade.

disorderly [dis'ɔːdəli], *a.* en désordre, déréglé; vicieux; tumultueux.

disorganization [disɔːgəni'zeiʃən], *n.* désorganisation, *f.*

disorganize [dis'ɔːgənaiz], *v.t.* désorganiser.

disown [dis'oun], *v.t.* désavouer, nier.

disparage [dis'pæridʒ], *v.t.* déprécier, ravaler, dénigrer.

disparagement [dis'pæridʒmənt], *n.* dénigrement, déshonneur, reproche, *m.*; honte, *f.*, tort, *m.*

disparaging [dis'pæridʒiŋ], *a.* dénigrant, injurieux.

disparagingly [dis'pæridʒiŋli], *adv.* avec mépris.

dispassionate [dis'pæʃənit], *a.* calme; impartial.

dispatch, despatch [dis'pætʃ], *v.t.* dépêcher, expédier; achever.—*n.* dépêche, *f.*, envoi, *m.*; promptitude, *f.*; **mentioned in dispatches**, cité à l'ordre du jour.

dispel [dis'pel], *v.t.* dissiper, chasser.

dispensary [dis'pensəri], *n.* dispensaire, *m.*; pharmacie, *f.*

dispensation [dispən'seiʃən], *n.* dispensation, *f.*; (*fig.*) bienfait, don, *m.*

dispense [dis'pens], *v.t.* distribuer, dispenser, administrer; (*Pharm.*) préparer (*médecine*); **to dispense with**, se passer de.

dispenser [dis'pensə], *n.* dispensateur, pharmacien, *m.*

dispersal [dis'pəːsəl], *n.* dispersion, *f.*

disperse [dis'pəːs], *v.t.* disperser; dissiper.—*v.i.* se disperser.

dispirited [dis'piritid], *a.* découragé, abattu.

405

displace

displace [dis'pleis], *v.t.* déplacer; destituer (*d'un emploi*).

displacement [dis'pleismənt], *n.* déplacement, *m.*

display [dis'plei], *n.* exposition, parade, *f.*; (*fig.*) étalage, *m.*—*v.t.* montrer, exposer, étaler.

displease [dis'pli:z], *v.t.* déplaire à; fâcher.

displeased [dis'pli:zd], *a.* mécontent, offensé (*de*).

displeasing [dis'pli:ziŋ], *a.* désagréable.

displeasure [dis'pleʒə], *n.* déplaisir; courroux, *m.*

disport [dis'pɔːt], *v.t.* to disport oneself, s'amuser, se divertir.

disposal [dis'pouzəl], *n.* disposition; vente, cession (*sale*), *f.*

dispose [dis'pouz], *v.t.* disposer; porter (*à croire*); to dispose of, céder, vendre, se défaire de, se débarrasser de.

disposition [dispə'ziʃən], *n.* disposition, *f.*; caractère, naturel, *m.*

dispossess [dispə'zes], *v.t.* déposséder (*de*).

disproportionate [dispro'pɔːʃənit], *a.* disproportionné.

disprove [dis'pruːv], *v.t.* réfuter.

dispute [dis'pjuːt], *n.* différend; conflit, *m.*; beyond dispute, sans contredit.—*v.t.* disputer, discuter.

disqualification [diskwɔlifi'keiʃən], *n.* incapacité, *f.*

disqualify [dis'kwɔlifai], *v.t.* rendre incapable (*de*).

disquiet [dis'kwaiət], *n.* inquiétude, *f.*

disregard [disri'gɑːd], *n.* insouciance, indifférence, *f.*—*v.t.* négliger, faire peu de cas de.

disrepair [disri'pɛə], *n.* délabrement, *m.*

disreputable [dis'repjutəbl], *a.* de mauvaise réputation; compromettant, déshonorant (*chose*).

disrepute [disri'pjuːt], *n.* discrédit, déshonneur, *m.*; mauvaise réputation, *f.*

disrespect [disris'pekt], *n.* manque de respect, irrespect, *m.*

disrespectful [disris'pektful], *a.* irrespectueux.

disrobe [dis'roub], *v.t.* déshabiller, dévêtir.—*v.i.* se déshabiller.

disrupt [dis'rʌpt], *v.t.* rompre.

dissatisfaction [dissætis'fækʃən], *n.* mécontentement, *m.*

dissatisfied [dis'sætisfaid], *a.* mécontent (*de*).

dissect [di'sekt], *v.t.* disséquer.

dissection [di'sekʃən], *n.* dissection, *f.*

dissemble [di'sembl], *v.t.* dissimuler, déguiser, cacher.—*v.i.* dissimuler, feindre.

disseminate [di'semineit], *v.t.* disséminer, répandre, propager.

dissension [di'senʃən], *n.* dissension, *f.*; to sow dissension, semer la zizanie.

dissent [di'sent], *n.* dissentiment, *m.*; (*Relig.*) dissidence, *f.*—*v.i.* différer (*de*); différer de sentiment (*avec*).

dissenter [di'sentə], *n.* dissident, *m.*, nonconformiste, *m.*, *f.*

disservice [dis'sə:vis], *n.* mauvais service, *m.*

dissever [di'sevə], *v.t.* séparer (*de*).

dissimilar [di'similə], *a.* dissemblable (*à*); différent (*de*).

dissimulate [di'simjuleit], *v.t.* dissimuler.

dissipate ['disipeit], *v.t.* dissiper.—*v.i.* se dissiper.

dissociate [di'souʃieit], *v.t.* désassocier, dissocier.

dissolute ['disəluːt], *a.* dissolu.

dissolve [di'zɔlv], *v.t.* dissoudre; désunir; supprimer; résoudre (*doute etc.*).—*v.i.* se dissoudre.

dissonance ['disənəns], *n.* dissonance; discordance, *f.*

dissuade [di'sweid], *v.t.* dissuader (*de*).

distaff ['distɑːf], *n.* quenouille, *f.*; the distaff side, le côté maternel.

distance ['distəns], *n.* distance, *f.*; éloignement, lointain, *m.*; (*fig.*) réserve, *f.*

distant ['distənt], *a.* éloigné, lointain; (*fig.*) réservé, froid.

distaste [dis'teist], *n.* dégoût, *m.*, aversion (*pour*), *f.*

distasteful [dis'teistful], *a.* désagréable, offensant.

distemper [dis'tempə], *n.* maladie (*de chien*); (*Paint.*) détrempe, *f.*—*v.t.* peindre en détrempe.

distend [dis'tend], *v.t.* étendre; dilater, enfler. —*v.i.* se détendre.

distil [dis'til], *v.t.*, *v.i.* distiller.

distillation [disti'leiʃən], *n.* distillation, *f.*

distiller [dis'tilə], *n.* distillateur, *m.*

distillery [dis'tiləri], *n.* distillerie, *f.*

distinct [dis'tiŋkt], *a.* distinct; exprès, clair, net.

distinction [dis'tiŋkʃən], *n.* distinction; (*Sch.*) mention, *f.*

distinctive [dis'tiŋktiv], *a.* distinctif.

distinctly [dis'tiŋktli], *adv.* distinctement, clairement; (*fig.*) indéniablement.

distinguish [dis'tiŋgwiʃ], *v.t.* distinguer (*de*).

distinguished [dis'tiŋgwiʃt], *a.* distingué; a distinguished man, un homme éminent.

distort [dis'tɔːt], *v.t.* tordre, contourner; décomposer (*les traits*); (*fig.*) torturer, défigurer.

distorted [dis'tɔːtid], *a.* tordu, décomposé; (*fig.*) torturé.

distortion [dis'tɔːʃən], *n.* contorsion, déformation, *f.*

distract [dis'trækt], *v.t.* distraire, détourner (*de*); tourmenter.

distracted [dis'træktid], *a.* bouleversé, fou, hors de soi.

distracting [dis'træktiŋ], *a.* atroce, déchirant, affolant.

distraction [dis'trækʃən], *n.* distraction, *f.*, trouble, *m.*, confusion; démence, folie, *f.*; to drive to distraction, mettre hors de soi.

distraught [dis'trɔːt], *a.* affolé, éperdu.

distress [dis'tres], *n.* détresse, affliction, peine, *f.*, chagrin, *m.*; misère (*pauvreté*), *f.*— *v.t.* affliger, désoler.

distressed [dis'trest], *a.* affligé, malheureux; dans la misère (*pauvre*).

distressing [dis'tresiŋ], *a.* affligeant, désolant; pénible.

distribute [dis'tribjuːt], *v.t.* distribuer.

distribution [distri'bjuːʃən], *n.* distribution, répartition, *f.*

district ['distrikt], *n.* contrée, région, *f.*, arrondissement, district; quartier (*de ville*); (*Postal*) secteur, *m.*

distrust [dis'trʌst], *n.* méfiance, *f.*—*v.t.* se méfier de.

distrustful [dis'trʌstful], *a.* défiant; méfiant, soupçonneux.

disturb [dis'tə:b], *v.t.* troubler; déranger.

disturbance [dis'tə:bəns], *n.* trouble, *m.*; confusion, émeute, *f.*; bruit, tapage; désordre, *m.*

disuse [dis'ju:s], *n.* désuétude, *f.*

disused [dis'ju:zd], *a.* hors d'usage.

ditch [ditʃ], *n.* fossé, *m.*—*v.t.* (*pop.*) abandonner.—*v.i.* creuser un fossé.

dither ['diðə], *n.* **to be all of a dither**, être tout agité.—*v.i.* trembler, trembloter, hésiter.

ditto ['ditou], *adv.* idem; (*Comm.*) dito.

ditty ['diti], *n.* chanson, chansonnette, *f.*

diurnal [dai'ə:nəl], *a.* journalier, du jour; (*Med.*) quotidien.

divan [di'væn], *n.* divan, *m.*

dive [daiv], *v.i.* plonger.—*n.* plongeon, *m.*; (*pop.*) boîte de nuit, *f.*

diver ['daivə], *n.* plongeur; plongeon (*oiseau*), *m.*

diverge [dai'və:dʒ], *v.i.* diverger (*de*).

divergent [dai'və:dʒənt], *a.* divergent.

diverse [dai'və:s], *a.* divers, varié.

diversify [dai'və:sifai], *v.t.* diversifier; varier (*couleurs*).

diversion [dai'və:ʃən], *n.* divertissement, amusement, *m.*; diversion, distraction, *f.*

diversity [dai'və:siti], *n.* diversité, variété, *f.*

divert [dai'və:t], *v.t.* divertir, réjouir; distraire; dévier, détourner (*de*).

diverting [dai'və:tiŋ], *a.* divertissant, amusant.

divest [di'vest, dai'vest], *v.t.* dépouiller (*de*).

divide [di'vaid], *v.t.* diviser; partager.—*v.i.* se diviser.

dividend ['dividend], *n.* dividende, *m.*

dividers [di'vaidəz], *n. pl.* compas à pointes sèches, *m.*

divine [di'vain], *a.* divin; (*fam.*) adorable.—*n.* théologien, ecclésiastique, *m.*—*v.t.* deviner, pressentir.

diving ['daiviŋ], *n.* plongement, plongeon, *m.*

diving board ['daiviŋbɔ:d], *n.* plongeoir, *m.*

divinity [di'viniti], *n.* divinité; théologie, *f.*

divisible [di'vizibl], *a.* divisible.

division [di'viʒən], *n.* division, *f.*, partage, *m.*; scission, *f.*; vote, *m.*

divorce [di'vɔ:s], *n.* divorce, *m.*; séparation, *f.*—*v.t.* séparer, divorcer avec.—*v.i.* se séparer (*de*).

divorcee [divɔː'si:], *n.* divorcé, *m.*, divorcée, *f.*

divulge [dai'vʌldʒ, di'vʌldʒ]. *v.t.* divulguer, publier.

dizziness ['dizinis], *n.* vertige, étourdissement, *m.*

dizzy ['dizi], *a.* étourdi; vertigineux (*élévation*).

do [du:], *v.t. irr.* faire; rendre (*service, justice etc.*); finir (*achever*); (*Cook.*) cuire; (*colloq.*) duper; **done!** c'est entendu! **done to a turn**, cuit à point; **he is done for**, c'en est fait de lui; **it can't be done**, pas moyen; **overdone**, trop cuit (*viande*); **to be doing well**, faire de bonnes affaires, réussir; **to do over**, enduire (*de*), couvrir (*de*); **to do up**, empaqueter, emballer, remettre en état, remettre à neuf; **underdone**, saignant (*viande*); **well done!** bravo! **what is to be done?** que faire?—*v.i.* se porter, se conduire; aller, convenir (*faire l'affaire*); suffire (*répondre à un besoin*); finir (*terminer*); **how do you do?** comment allez-vous ? **to do away with**, supprimer, se défaire de, faire disparaître; **to do by**, agir envers; **to do without**, se passer de.—*n.* duperie; soirée, réception, *f.*

docile ['dousail], *a.* docile.

docility [dou'siliti], *n.* docilité, *f.*

dock [dɔk], *v.t.* écourter; rogner (*comptes etc.*); (*Naut.*) mettre dans le bassin.—*v.i.* entrer aux docks.—*n.* bassin, dock, *m.*; (*Bot.*) patience, *f.*; (*Law*) banc des accusés, *m.*

docker ['dɔkə], *n.* déchargeur, docker, *m.*

docket ['dɔkit], *n.* étiquette, fiche, *f.*—*v.t.* étiqueter; enregistrer.

doctor ['dɔktə], *n.* docteur, médecin, *m.*—*v.t.* soigner, droguer; (*fig.*) altérer; frelater (*vin*).

doctrinaire [dɔktri'nɛə], *a.* doctrinaire.

doctrinal [dɔk'trainəl], *a.* doctrinal.

doctrine ['dɔktrin], *n.* doctrine, *f.*

document ['dɔkjumənt], *n.* document, titre, *m.*—*v.t.* munir de documents.

documentary [dɔkju'mentəri], *a.* justificatif, authentique.—*n.* (*Cine.*) documentaire, *m.*

documentation [dɔkjumen'teiʃən], *n.* documentation, *f.*

dodge [dɔdʒ], *v.t.* éviter; esquiver.—*v.i.* s'esquiver; (*fig.*) ruser, faire des détours.—*n.* tour, détour, *m.*; (*fig.*) ruse, ficelle, *f.*

dodger ['dɔdʒə], *n.* rusé, malin, finaud, *m.*

doe [dou], *n.* daine, *f.*

doer ['du:ə], *n.* faiseur; auteur, *m.*

doff [dɔf], *v.t.* tirer, enlever, ôter.

dog [dɔg], *n.* chien, (*facet.*) coquin, gaillard, *m.*; **lucky dog!** quel veinard!—*v.t.* suivre à la piste; harceler, épier.

dog days ['dɔgdeiz], *n.pl.* canicule, *f.*

dogged ['dɔgid], *a.* obstiné; acharné.

doggedly ['dɔgidli], *adv.* avec acharnement.

doggedness ['dɔgidnis], *n.* obstination, *f.* acharnement, *m.*

doggerel ['dɔgərəl], *n.* vers burlesques, vers de mirliton, *m.pl.*

doggie ['dɔgi], *n.* (*Childish*) tou-tou, *m.*

doggo ['dɔgou], *adv.* **to lie doggo**, se tenir coi.

dogma ['dɔgmə], *n.* dogme, *m.*

dogmatic [dɔg'mætik], *a.* dogmatique.

dogmatism ['dɔgmətizm], *n.* dogmatisme, *m.*

doily ['dɔili], *n.* serviette de dessert, *f.*, napperon, *m.*

doing ['du:iŋ], *n.* (*usu. in pl.*) faits, *m.pl.*; actions, *f.pl.*, exploits, *m.pl.*

dole [doul], *n.* aumône, *f.*, partage, *m.*; allocation de chômage, *f.*—*v.t.* **to dole out**, distribuer, répartir avec parcimonie.

doleful ['doulful], *a.* plaintif, lugubre.

doll [dɔl], *n.* poupée, *f.*—*v.r.* **to doll oneself up**, se pomponner.

dollar ['dɔlə], *n.* dollar, *m.*

dolphin ['dɔlfin], *n.* dauphin, *m.*

dolt [doult], *n.* lourdaud, sot, butor, *m.*

domain [do'mein], *n.* domaine, *m.*

dome [doum], *n.* dôme, *m.*

domestic [də'mestik], *a.* de famille; domestique (*animaux*).—*n.* domestique, *m.,f.*, servante, *f.*

domesticate [də'mestikeit], *v.t.* domestiquer, apprivoiser; (*fig.*) rendre casanier.

domesticated [də'mestikeited], _a._ casanier (_personnes_); apprivoisé (_animaux_).
domicile ['dɔmisail, 'dɔmisil], _n._ domicile, _m._
dominance ['dɔminəns], _n._ dominance, _f._
dominant ['dɔminənt], _a._ dominant.
dominate ['dɔmineit], _v.t._ dominer sur.—_v.i._ dominer; prévaloir, prédominer.
domination [dɔmi'neiʃən], _n._ domination, _f._
domineer [dɔmi'niə], _v.i._ dominer (_sur_).
domineering [dɔmi'niəriŋ], _a._ impérieux, autoritaire.
Dominican [do'minikən], _a._ dominicain.—_n._ Dominicain (_personne_), _m.;_ _Dominican nun_, Dominicaine, _f._
dominie ['dɔmini], _n._ (_Sc._) maître d'école, _m._
dominion [do'miniən], _n._ domination, autorité, _f.;_ empire, _m.;_ (_pl._) états, _m.pl._
domino ['dɔminou], _n._ domino (_capuchon, jeu_), _m._
don [dɔn], _n._ don (_titre_); (_fig._) grand seigneur; (_Univ._) professeur d'université, _m._—_v.t._ mettre, endosser.
donate [do'neit], _v.t._ faire un don de.
donation [do'neiʃən], _n._ donation, _f.,_ don, _m._
donkey ['dɔŋki], _n._ âne, baudet, _m._
donor ['dounə], _n._ donateur, _m._
doodle [du:dl], _v.i._ griffonner.—_n._ griffonnage, _m._
doom [du:m], _v.t._ condamner (à); (_fig._) destiner (à).—_n._ jugement; destin funeste, _m.;_ perte, ruine, _f._
doomsday ['du:mzdei], _n._ jour du jugement dernier, _m._
door [dɔː], _n._ porte; portière (_d'une voiture_), _f.;_ _folding doors_, porte à deux battants; _next door_, à côté; _indoors_, à la maison; _out of doors_, dehors; _behind closed doors_, à huis clos.
door-bell ['dɔːbel], _n._ sonnette, _f._
door-keeper ['dɔːkiːpə], _n._ concierge, portier (_d'une maison_); gardien (_des monuments publics_), _m._
doorman ['dɔːmən], _n._ portier, _m._
door mat ['dɔːmæt], _n._ paillasson, _m._
door-step ['dɔːstep], _n._ seuil de la porte, pas de (la) porte, _m._
door-way ['dɔːwei], _n._ entrée, porte, _f._
dope [doup], _n._ drogue, _f._, narcotique, _m._—_v.t._ droguer.
dormant ['dɔːmənt], _a._ dormant; assoupi.
dormer window ['dɔːməwindou], _n._ lucarne, _f._
dormitory ['dɔːmitri], _n._ dortoir, _m._
dormouse ['dɔːmaus], _n._ (_pl._ **dormice** ['dɔːmais]) loir, _m._
Dorothy ['dɔrəθi], Dorothée, _f._
dose [dous], _n._ dose, _f._—_v.t._ médicamenter; doser.
dossier ['dɔsjei], _n._ dossier, _m._
dot [dɔt], _n._ point, _m._—_v.t._ marquer d'un point, marquer avec des points; (_Paint._) pointiller.
dotage ['doutidʒ], _n._ seconde enfance, _f._, radotage, _m._
dote [dout], _v.t._ radoter; raffoler (_de_).
double ['dʌbl], _a._ double, en deux; _bent double_, voûté.—_n._ double, pendant, sosie; (_Mil._) pas de course, _m._—_adv._ au double; _to fold double_, plier en deux.—_v.t._ doubler; serrer (_poings_).—_v.i._ doubler;

user de ruse; _to double back_, revenir sur ses pas.
double bed ['dʌbl'bed], _n._ lit à deux places, _m._
double-breasted ['dʌblbrestid], _a._ croisé.
double-cross ['dʌbl'krɔs], _v.t._ duper, tromper.
double-dealing ['dʌbl'diːliŋ], _n._ duplicité, _f._
double decker ['dʌbl'dekə], _n._ autobus à impériale, _m._
double-room ['dʌbl'ruːm], _n._ chambre pour deux personnes, _f._
doubt [daut], _n._ doute, _m._; hésitation, _f._; _beyond a doubt_, sans aucun doute.—_v.t._ douter de.—_v.i._ douter; soupçonner.
doubtful ['dautful], _a._ douteux, incertain.
doubtless ['dautlis], _adv._ sans doute.
dough [dou], _n._ pâte, _f._
dough-nut ['dounʌt], _n._ pet-de-nonne, _m._
doughty ['dauti], _a._ vaillant, preux.
dour ['duə], _a._ (_Sc._) austère et froid.
douse [daus], _v.t._ plonger dans l'eau; éteindre.
dove [dʌv], _n._ colombe, _f._; pigeon, _m._
dove-cot(e) ['dʌvkɔt, 'dʌvkout], _n._ colombier, _m._
Dover ['douvə]. Douvres, _m._; _the Straits of Dover_, le Pas-de-Calais, _m._
dowager ['dauədʒə], _n._ douairière, _f._
dowdy ['daudi], _a.f._ gauche et mal mise, mal fagotée.
dowel ['dauəl], _n._ (_Carp._) goujon, _m._
down (1) [daun], _n._ duvet (_poil follet_), _m._; dune (_colline_), _f._
down (2) [daun], _adv._ en bas; à bas; bas, à terre; tombé, apaisé (_vent_); couché (_soleil_); à plat (_pneu_); en baisse (_prix_); (_fig._) sur le déclin; _to go down_, descendre.—_prep._ en bas de; vers le bas de.
downcast ['daunkɑːst], _a._ abattu.
downfall ['daunfɔːl], _n._ chute, _f._; (_fig._) débâcle, _f._
downhill ['daunhil], _a._ incliné; en pente.— [daun'hil], _adv._ en descendant.
downpour ['daunpɔː], _n._ averse, _f._
downright ['daunrait], _a._ direct; franc.— _adv._ net, tout à fait.
downstairs [daun'stɛəz], _adv._ en bas (de l'escalier).
downtrodden ['dauntrɔdn], _a._ opprimé.
downward ['daunwəd], _a._ de haut en bas, qui descend, descendant.—_adv._ (_also_ **downwards** ['daunwədz]) en bas, en descendant; en aval.
downy ['dauni] _a._ de duvet, duveteux.
dowry ['dauri], _n._ dot, _f._
doze [douz], _v.i._ s'assoupir, sommeiller, être assoupi.—_n._ petit somme, _m._
dozen [dʌzn], _n._ douzaine, _f._
drab [dræb], _a._ gris sale, brun terne; (_fig._) terne, décoloré.—_n._ (_fig._) traînée (_femme_), _f._
draft [drɑːft], _v.t._ dessiner, rédiger; (_Mil._) détacher.—_n._ dessin (_esquisse_); brouillon (_projet_), _m._; (_Comm._) traite, _f._; (_Mil._) détachement, _m._
draft [drɑːft], _n._ tirage, _f._; courant d'air; coup (_boisson_); dessin (_esquisse_); coup de filet (_de pêcheur_); tirant (_d'un navire_), _m._; (_Med._) potion, _f._; (_pl._) jeu de dames, _m._
draft-board ['drɑːftbɔːd], _n._ damier, _m._
draft-horse ['drɑːfthɔːs], _n._ cheval de trait, _m._
draftsman ['drɑːftsmən], _n._ (_pl._ **-men** [men]) dessinateur, _m._
drafty ['drɑːfti], _a._ plein de courants

d'air.

drag [dræg], *v.t.* traîner, tirer; (*Naut.*) draguer; **to drag away from**, entraîner, arracher de; **to drag on**, entraîner; (*fig.*) traîner en longueur; **to drag out**, faire sortir de force.—*v.i.* se traîner; traîner; chasser (*ancre*).

draggle [drægl], *v.t.* traîner dans la boue.

drag-net ['drægnet], *n.* seine, *f.*, chalut, *m.*

dragoman ['drægomən], *n.* drogman, *m.*

dragon ['drægən], *n.* dragon, *m.*

dragon-fly ['drægənflai], *n.* demoiselle, libellule, *f.*, agrion, *m.*

dragoon [drə'gu:n], *n.* (*Mil.*) dragon, *m.*—*v.t.* (*fig.*) forcer par des mesures violentes.

drain [drein], *v.t.* faire écouler; dessécher; drainer; (*fig.*) épuiser; vider (*verre etc.*).—*v.i.* s'écouler.—*n.* tranchée, *f.*, égout, *m.*

drainage ['dreinidʒ], **draining** ['dreiniŋ] *n.* écoulement; (*Agric.*) drainage, *m.*

draining-board ['dreiniŋbɔ:d], *n.* égouttoir, *m.*

drake [dreik], *n.* canard, *m.*

dram [dræm], *n.* (*Pharm.*) drachme, *f.*

drama ['drɑ:mə], *n.* drame; (*fig.*) théâtre, *m.*

dramatic [drə'mætik], **dramatical** [drə'mætikəl], *a.* dramatique.

dramatist ['drɑ:mətist, 'dræmətist], *n.* auteur dramatique, *m.*, dramaturge, *m.*, *f.*

dramatize ['drɑ:mətaiz, 'dræmətaiz], *v.t.* dramatiser.

drape [dreip], *v.t.* draper, tendre (*de*).—*n.* (*Am.*) rideau, *m.*

draper ['dreipə], *n.* drapier; marchand de drap, *m.*

drapery ['dreipəri], *n.* draperie, *f.*

drastic ['dræstik], *a.* énergique, radical, brutal.

draw [drɔ:], *v.t. irr.* tirer; traîner; dessiner (*tableau etc.*); toucher (*rations, appointements etc.*); arracher (*dent*); puiser (*eau etc.*); (*fig.*) attirer (*à ou sur*); **to draw lots for**, tirer au sort.—*v.i.* tirer; dégainer; dessiner (*au crayon*); (*Spt.*) faire partie nulle *ou* match nul.—*n.* tirage (*au sort*), *m.*; attraction; (*Spt.*) partie nulle, *f.*

drawback ['drɔ:bæk], *n.* mécompte, désavantage, inconvénient, *m.*

drawbridge ['drɔ:bridʒ], *n.* pont-levis, *m.*

drawer ['drɔ:ə], *n.* tireur (*d'un chèque*); puiseur (*d'eau*); tiroir (*meuble*); (*pl.*) caleçon (*vêtement*), *m.*; **chest of drawers**, commode, *f.*

drawing ['drɔ:iŋ], *n.* tirage; dessin (*croquis*), *m.*

drawing board ['drɔ:iŋbɔ:d], *n.* planche à dessin, *f.*

drawing-pin ['drɔ:iŋpin], *n.* punaise (*pour le dessin*), *f.*

drawing room ['drɔ:iŋru:m], *n.* salon, *m.*; (*Court*) réception, *f.*

drawl [drɔ:l], *v.i.* parler d'une voix traînante.—*n.* voix traînante *f.*

drawling ['drɔ:liŋ], *a.* traînant.

drawn [drɔ:n], *a.* indécis, égal (*bataille etc.*); tiré, nu (*épée*); **drawn game**, partie nulle, *f.*

dray [drei], *n.* camion, haquet, *m.*

dread [dred], *a.* redoutable, terrible; auguste.—*n.* terreur, crainte, *f.*—*v.t.* craindre, redouter.

dreadful ['dredful], *a.* affreux, terrible, épouvantable.

dreadfully ['dredfuli], *adv.* terriblement, affreusement.

dream [dri:m], *n.* songe, rêve, *m.*; **daydream**, rêverie, *f.*—*v.t. irr.* rêver.—*v.i.* rêver; (*fig.*) s'imaginer.

dreamer ['dri:mə], *n.* rêveur, *m.*; (*fig.*) visionnaire, *m.*, *f.*

dreamy ['dri:mi], *a.* rêveur; chimérique, visionnaire.

drear [driə], **dreary** ['driəri], *a.* triste, morne, lugubre.

drearily ['driərili], *adv.* tristement, lugubrement.

dreariness ['driərinis], *n.* tristesse, *f.*, aspect morne, *m.*

dredge (1) [dredʒ], *n.* drague, *f.*—*v.t.*, *v.i.* draguer.

dredge (2) [dredʒ], *v.t.* saupoudrer (*de farine etc.*).

dredger (1) ['dredʒə], *n.* dragueur (*bateau*), *m.*

dredger (2) ['dredʒə], *n.* saupoudreuse, *f.*

dregs [dregz], *n.pl.* lie, *f.*

drench [drentʃ], *v.t.* tremper, mouiller (*de*); noyer (*de*).

dress [dres], *v.t.* habiller, vêtir, parer, orner; panser (*blessure etc.*); apprêter (*aliments etc.*); (*Mil.*) aligner; (*Navy*) pavoiser.—*v.i.* s'habiller; faire sa toilette; (*Mil.*) s'aligner.—*n.* habillement, *m.*; robe (*de femme*); mise, toilette; (*Mil.*) tenue, *f.*; **dress rehearsal**, répétition générale, *f.*; **evening dress**, tenue de soirée, *f.*

dress circle ['dres'sə:kl], *n.* (*Theat.*) fauteuils de balcon, *m.pl.*

dresser ['dresə], *n.* habilleur (*personne*); dressoir (*de cuisine*), *m.*

dressing ['dresiŋ], *n.* toilette, *f.*, habillement; pansement (*de blessure etc.*); (*Cook.*) assaisonnement, *m.*; (*Agric.*) fumure, *f.*, engrais, *m.*

dressing case ['dresiŋkeis], *n.* mallette de toilette, *f.*

dressing gown ['dresiŋgaun], *n.* robe de chambre, *f.*, peignoir, *m.*

dressing room ['dresiŋru:m], *n.* cabinet de toilette, *m.*

dressing table ['dresiŋteibl], *n.* coiffeuse, table de toilette, *f.*

dressmaker ['dresmeikə], *n.* couturière, *f.*

dressmaking ['dresmeikiŋ], *n.* confections pour dames, *f.pl.*, couture, *f.*

dressy ['dresi], *a.* élégant, chic, coquet (*personne*); habillé (*robe*).

dribble [dribl], *v.t.* laisser dégoutter, laisser tomber goutte à goutte; (*Ftb.*) dribbler.—*v.i.* tomber goutte à goutte, dégoutter; baver; (*Ftb.*) dribbler.

drier ['draiə], *comp. a.* [DRY].—*n.* [DRYER].

drift [drift], *n.* monceau; tourbillon, *m.*, rafale, *f.*; objet flottant, *m.*; (*fig.*) tendance; (*Naut.*) dérive, *f.*—*v.t.* chasser, pousser; amonceler.—*v.i.* dériver, aller à la dérive, flotter; s'amonceler, s'amasser.

drifter ['driftə], *n.* (*Naut.*) chalutier, *m.*

drill [dril], *n.* foret, *m.*, mèche, *f.*; (*Agric.*) sillon; (*Mil.*) exercice, *m.*, manœuvre, *f.*—*v.t.* forer, percer; (*Mil.*) exercer.—*v.i.* (*Mil.*) faire l'exercice.

409

drilling ['drilin], *n.* forage; (*Dent.*) fraisage; (*Mil.*) exercice, *m.*

drink [drink], *n.* boisson; (*fig.*) ivresse (*drunkenness*), *f.*—*v.t., v.i.* irr. boire.

drinker ['drinkə], *n.* buveur; ivrogne, *m.*

drinking ['drinkin], *a.* potable; à boire.—*n:* boire, *m.*; ivrognerie, *f.*, alcoolisme, *m.*

drinking fountain ['drinkinfauntin], *n.* fontaine publique, *f.*

drip [drip], *v.t.* faire dégoutter.—*v.i.* dégoutter, tomber goutte à goutte.—*n.* goutte, *f.*; égout, *m.*

dripping ['dripin], *n.* graisse de rôti, *f.*; (*pl.*) gouttes, *f.pl.*

drive [draiv], *v.t.* irr. pousser; chasser; enfoncer (*clou etc.*); mener, conduire (*voiture, cheval etc.*); forcer, réduire (*à*); **to drive away**, chasser, éloigner; **to drive back**, repousser; **to drive in**, faire entrer, enfoncer; **to drive out**, faire sortir, chasser.—*v.i.* conduire; aller en voiture; **to drive at**, tendre à, vouloir en venir à; **to drive up**, arriver (en voiture).—*n.* promenade *ou* course en voiture; grande avenue *ou* allée, *f.*

drivel [drivl], *n.* bave, *f.*—*v.i.* baver; (*fig.*) radoter.

driver ['draivə], *n.* cocher (*d'un carrosse*); voiturier (*d'une charrette*); (*Rail.*) mécanicien; (*Motor. etc.*) chauffeur, conducteur, *m.*

driving ['draivin], *n.* action de conduire, *f.*; percement (*d'un tunnel*), *m.*

driving license ['draivinlaisəns], *n.* permis de conduire *m.*

driving test ['draivintest], *n.* examen pour permis de conduire, *m.*

drizzle [drizl], *v.i.* bruiner.—*n.* bruine, pluie fine, *f.*

droll [droul], *a.* plaisant, drôle.

drollery ['drouləri], *n.* plaisanterie, drôlerie, farce, *f.*

dromedary ['drʌmədəri, 'drɔmədəri], *n.* dromadaire, *m.*

drone [droun], *n.* (*Ent., Mus.*) faux-bourdon; (*fig.*) frelon; fainéant (*personne*); bourdonnement (*son*), *m.*—*v.i.* bourdonner.

droning ['drounin], *a.* bourdonnant.—*n.* bourdonnement, *m.*

droop [dru:p], *v.t.* laisser tomber, laisser pendre.—*v.i.* languir, se pencher, tomber, pencher; (*fig.*) s'affaiblir.

drooping ['dru:pin], *a.* languissant, abattu, penché.—*n.* abattement, *m.*, langueur, *f.*

drop [drɔp], *n.* goutte; chute (*descente*), *f.*; pendant (*bijou*), *m.*—*v.t.* laisser tomber; jeter (*l'ancre*); sauter (*une maille*); déposer (*quelqu'un*) quelque part; laisser échapper (*prononcer*); abandonner (*lâcher*).—*v.i.* tomber goutte à goutte; dégoutter (*de*); échapper (*glisser*); **to drop behind**, se laisser dépasser, rester en arrière; **to drop in**, entrer en passant; **to drop out**, se retirer.

dropsy ['drɔpsi], *n.* hydropisie, *f.*

dross [drɔs], *n.* scorie, crasse, *f.*; (*fig.*) rebut, *m.*

drought [draut], *n.* sécheresse, *f.*

drove (1) [drouv]. *n.* troupeau (*en marche*), *m.*; (*fig.*) foule (*en marche*), *f.*

drove (2) [drouv], *past* [DRIVE].

drover ['drouvə], *n.* conducteur de bestiaux, bouvier, *m.*

drown [draun], *v.t.* noyer; (*fig.*) submerger; étouffer (*bruit*).—*v.i.* se noyer.

drowsily ['drauzili], *adv.* comme endormi; (*fig.*) avec indolence.

drowsiness ['drauzinis], *n.* assoupissement, *m.*

drowsy ['drauzi], *a.* assoupi; somnolent; lourd, stupide.

drub [drʌb], *v.t.* rosser, battre.

drubbing ['drʌbin], *n.* volée (de coups), *f.*

drudge [drʌdʒ], *n.* homme (*ou* femme) de peine, souffre-douleur, *m.*, *f.*—*v.i.* travailler sans relâche, peiner.

drudgery ['drʌdʒəri], *n.* travail pénible, *m.*; corvée, vile besogne, *f.*

drug [drʌg], *n.* drogue, *f.*—*v.t.* droguer; (*fig.*) empoisonner.

drug addict ['drʌgædikt], *n.* toxicomane, *m.*, *f.*

druggist ['drʌgist], *n.* (*Am.*) pharmacien, *m.*

drug store ['drʌgstɔ:], *n.* (*Am.*) pharmacie, *f.*

druid ['dru:id], *n.* druide, *m.*

drum [drʌm], *n.* tambour; caisse, *f.*; tympan (*de l'oreille*), *m.*—*v.t.* (*Mil.*) **to drum out**, dégrader.—*v.i.* battre du tambour (*sur*); (*fig.*) tinter.

drum major ['drʌmmeidʒə], *n.* tambour-major, *m.*

drummer ['drʌmə], *n.* tambour (*homme*), *m.*

drum-stick ['drʌmstik], *n.* baguette de tambour, *f.*

drunk [drʌŋk], *a.* ivre, gris, soûl.

drunkard ['drʌŋkəd], *n.* ivrogne, *m.*

drunkenness ['drʌŋkənnis], *n.* ivresse; ivrognerie, *f.*

dry [drai], *a.* sec, desséché; aride; altéré; (*fig.*) caustique; ennuyeux.—*v.t.* sécher; dessécher.—*v.i.* sécher; **to dry up**, tarir; se taire.

dry-dock ['draidɔk], *n.* bassin de radoub, *m.*, cale sèche, *f.*

dryer, drier ['draiə], *n.* (*Ind. etc.*) séchoir; (*Paint.*) siccatif, dessiccatif, *m.*

dryness ['drainis], *n.* sécheresse, aridité, *f.*

dry-shod ['draiʃɔd], *a.* and *adv.* à pied sec.

dual ['dju:əl], *a.* double; **dual carriageway**, route à double circulation, *f.*—*n.* duel, *m.*

dub [dʌb], *v.t.* armer chevalier; (*colloq.*) qualifier, baptiser; (*Cine.*) doubler (*film*).

dubiety [dju'baiəti], **dubiousness** ['dju:biəsnis], *n.* doute, *m.*, incertitude, *f.*

dubious ['dju:biəs], *a.* douteux, incertain.

dubiously ['dju:biəsli], *adv.* douteusement.

duchess ['dʌtʃis], *n.* duchesse, *f.*

duchy ['dʌtʃi], *n.* duché, *m.*

duck (1) [dʌk], *n.* cane, *f.*; canard; (*colloq.*) chou (*mot tendre*), *m.*

duck (2) [dʌk], *n.* (*Box.*) esquive, *f.*—*v.t.* plonger dans l'eau.—*v.i.* plonger; baisser la tête subitement; (*Box.*) esquiver.

duck (3) [dʌk], *n.* toile à voile, *f.*; (*pl.*) pantalon blanc, *m.*

ducking ['dʌkin], *n.* plongeon; (*Naut.*) baptême de la ligne, *m.*

duckling ['dʌklin], *n.* caneton, *m.*

duck-weed ['dʌkwi:d], *n.* lentille d'eau, *f.*

duct [dʌkt], *n.* conduit, *m.*; (*Anat.*) canal, *m.*

dudgeon ['dʌdʒən], *n.* colère, *f.*; **in high dudgeon**, fort en colère.

due [dju:], *a.* dû; convenable, propre, juste; (*Comm.*) échu; (*fig.*) requis, voulu; **to fall due**, échoir.—*n.* dû; (*pl.*) droit, impôt, *m.*, redevance, *f.*—*adv.* droit, directement.
duel ['dju:əl], *n.* duel, *m.*, (*fig.*) lutte, *f.*
duellist ['dju:əlist], *n.* duelliste, *m.*
duenna [dju:'enə], *n.* duègne, *f.*
duet [dju:'et], *n.* duo, *m.*
duke [dju:k], *n.* duc, *m.*
dukedom ['dju:kdəm], *n.* duché, *m.*; dignité de duc, *f.*
dull [dʌl], *a.* lourd, hébété, stupide (*personne*); lourd, gris, sombre (*temps*); sourd (*son*); triste (*morne*); émoussé (*moins aigu*); terne (*couleur*); ennuyeux.—*v.t.* hébéter; émousser (*rendre moins aigu*); ternir (*ôter l'éclat de*); engourdir (*de froid*).—*v.i.* s'hébéter; s'engourdir; s'émousser.
dullard ['dʌləd], *n.* âne, lourdaud (*personne*), *m.*
dullness ['dʌlnis], *n.* lenteur, *f.*; assoupissement, ennui; manque d'éclat, *m.*, faiblesse (*de son*), *f.*
dully ['dʌlli], *adv.* lourdement, tristement.
duly ['dju:li], *adv.* dûment, justement.
dumb [dʌm], *a.* muet, réduit au silence; (*Am.*) stupide.
dumb-bells ['dʌmbelz], *n.pl.* haltères, *m.pl.*
dumbfound [dʌm'faund], *v.t.* confondre, abasourdir, interdire.
dumbly ['dʌmli], *adv.* en silence.
dumbness ['dʌmnis], *n.* mutisme; (*fig.*) silence, *m.*
dumb show ['dʌmʃou], *n.* pantomime, *f.*, jeu muet, *m.*
dummy ['dʌmi], *n.* muet, *m.*, muette, *f.*; mannequin, objet imité; (*fig.*) homme de paille; (*Cards*) mort, *m.*
dump [dʌmp], *v.t.* déposer, décharger, déverser.—*n.* tas; dépotoir, *m.*
dumpling ['dʌmpliŋ], *n.* pâte cuite, *f.*
dumpy ['dʌmpi], *a.* trapu, gros et court.
dun (1) [dʌn], *a.* brun foncé; bai (*cheval*).
dun (2) [dʌn], *n.* créancier importun, *m.*—*v.t.* importuner.
dunce [dʌns], *n.* ignorant, âne, sot, *m.*
dune [dju:n], *n.* dune, *f.*
dung [dʌŋ], *n.* crotte, *f.*; crottin; (*Agric.*) fumier, *m.*
dung cart ['dʌŋka:t], *n.* tombereau à fumier, *m.*
dungeon ['dʌndʒən], *n.* cachot, *m.*
dunghill ['dʌŋhil], *n.* fumier, *m.*
duodenal [dju:o'di:nl], *a.* (*Anat.*) duodénal; **duodenal ulcer**, ulcère au duodénum, *m.*
dupe [dju:p], *n.* dupe, *f.*—*v.t.* duper, tromper.
duplicate ['dju:plikit], *a.* double.—*n.* double, duplicata, *m.*—['dju:plikeit], *v.t.* doubler, copier.
duplicity [dju:'plisiti], *n.* duplicité, mauvaise foi, *f.*
durability [djuərə'biliti], **durableness** ['djuərəblnis], *n.* solidité, durabilité, *f.*
durable ['djuərəbl], *a.* durable.
duration [djuə'reiʃən], *n.* durée, *f.*
during ['djuəriŋ], *prep.* pendant, durant.
dusk [dʌsk], *n.* crépuscule, *m.*; obscurité, *f.*
duskiness ['dʌskinis], *n.* obscurité, teinte sombre, *f.*
dusky ['dʌski], *a.* foncé, sombre; noiraud, noirâtre.
dust [dʌst], *n.* poussière; poudre, *f.*; (*fig.*)

cendres (des morts), *f.pl.*; **sawdust**, sciure, *f.*—*v.t.* épousseter.
dust-bin ['dʌstbin], *n.* boîte à ordures, poubelle, *f.*
dust-cart ['dʌstka:t], *n.* tombereau, *m.*
duster ['dʌstə], *n.* torchon, chiffon, *m.*
dustman ['dʌstmən], *n.* (*pl.* **-men** [men]) boueur, *m.*
dusty ['dʌsti], *a.* poussiéreux, couvert de poussière; poudreux.
Dutch [dʌtʃ], *a.* hollandais, de Hollande.—*n.* hollandais (*langue*), *m.*; **the Dutch**, les Hollandais, *m.pl.*
Dutchman ['dʌtʃmən], *n.* (*pl.* **-men** [men]) Hollandais, *m.*
Dutchwoman ['dʌtʃwumən], *n.* (*pl.* **-women** [wimin]) Hollandaise, *f.*
duteous ['dju:tiəs], **dutiful** ['dju:tiful], *a.* obéissant, soumis.
dutifully ['dju:tifuli], *adv.* avec soumission, respectueusement.
duty ['dju:ti], *n.* (*pl.* **duties** ['dju:tiz]) devoir; (*Customs*) droit; (*Mil. etc.*) service, *m.*; **on duty**, de service, de garde, en faction.
dwarf [dwɔ:f], *a.* and *n.* nain, *m.*, naine, *f.*—*v.t.* rapetisser; (*Hort.*) rabougrir.
dwell [dwel], *v.i. irr.* demeurer, habiter; rester; **to dwell on**, insister sur.
dweller ['dwelə], *n.* habitant, *m.*, habitante, *f.*
dwelling ['dweliŋ], *n.* habitation, demeure, *f.*
dwindle [dwindl], *v.i.* diminuer, s'amoindrir; dépérir.
dye [dai], *v.t.* teindre.—*v.i.* teindre, se teindre.—*n.* teinture, teinte; couleur, nuance, *f.*; (*fig.*) caractère, *m.*
dyeing ['daiiŋ], *n.* teinture, *f.*
dyer ['daiə], *n.* teinturier, *m.*, teinturière, *f.*
dye-works ['daiwə:ks], *n.pl.* teinturerie, *f.*
dying ['daiiŋ], *a.* mourant, moribond; suprême, dernier.
dyke [DIKE].
dynamic [dai'næmik], **dynamical** [dai'næmikəl], *a.* dynamique.
dynamics [dai'næmiks], *n.pl.* dynamique, *f.*
dynamite ['dainəmait], *n.* dynamite, *f.*—*v.t.* dynamiter.
dynamo ['dainəmou], *n.* dynamo, *f.*
dynasty ['dinəsti], *n.* dynastie, *f.*
dysentery ['disəntri], *n.* dysenterie, *f.*
dyspepsia [dis'pepsiə], *n.* dyspepsie, *f.*
dyspeptic [dis'peptik], *a.* dyspepsique, dyspeptique.

E

E, e [i:]. cinquième lettre de l'alphabet; (*Mus.*) mi, *m.*
e-, see also **ae-**.
each [i:tʃ], *a.* à chaque.—*pron.* chacun, *m.*, chacune, *f.*; **each other**, l'un l'autre, les uns les autres.
eager ['i:gə], *a.* vif, ardent (à); impatient (de); désireux; empressé (à ou de).
eagerly ['i:gəli], *adv.* ardemment; impatiemment.

411

eagerness

eagerness ['i:gənis], *n.* ardeur, *f.*; empressement, *m.*

eagle [i:gl], *n.* aigle, *m.*, *f.*

eaglet ['i:glit], *n.* aiglon, *m.*

ear [iə], *n.* oreille, *f.*; épi (*de blé*), *m.*—*v.i.* monter en épi.

ear-ache ['iəreik], *n.* mal d'oreille, *m.*

ear-drum ['iədrʌm], *n.* tympan, tambour de l'oreille, *m.*

earl [ə:l], *n.* comte, *m.*

earldom ['ə:ldəm], *n.* comté, *m.*

earliness ['ə:linis], *n.* heure peu avancée; précocité (*de fruits*), *f.*

early ['ə:li], *a.* matinal; matineux (*personne*); ancien; précoce, hâtif (*fruit etc.*).—*adv.* de bonne heure, de bon matin, de grand matin; tôt.

ear-mark ['iəmɑ:k], *v.t.* (*fig.*) réserver, mettre de côté.

earn [ə:n], *v.t.* gagner, acquérir; (*fig.*) mériter.

earnest (1) ['ə:nist], *a.* sérieux, empressé, sincère.

earnest (2) ['ə:nist], *n.* gage, *m.*, garantie, *f.*, arrhes, *f.pl.*

earnestly ['ə:nistli], *adv.* sérieusement, avec empressement.

earnestness ['ə:nistnis], *n.* ardeur, *f.*, empressement, sérieux, *m.*

earnings ['ə:niŋz], *n.pl.* gain, *m.*; gages, *m.pl.*

ear-phones ['iəfounz], *n.pl.* casque, *m.*

ear-ring ['iəriŋ], *n.* boucle d'oreille, *f.*

earth [ə:θ], *n.* terre, *f.*; terrier (*de renard etc.*), *m.*—*v.t.* enterrer, enfouir, couvrir de terre; (*Elec.*) joindre à la terre.

earthen ['ə:θən], *a.* de terre.

earthenware ['ə:θənwɛə], *n.* poterie, vaisselle de terre, faïence, *f.*

earthly ['ə:θli], *a.* terrestre.

earthquake ['ə:θkweik], *n.* tremblement de terre, *m.*

earthy ['ə:θi], *a.* de terre, terreux.

earwig ['iəwig], *n.* perce-oreille, *m.*

ease [i:z], *n.* aisance, aise; facilité; tranquillité, *f.*, repos; (*fig.*) abandon; soulagement (*de douleur*), *m.*—*v.t.* soulager, mettre à l'aise; (*fig.*) tranquilliser, calmer.

easel [i:zl], *n.* chevalet, *m.*

easily ['i:zili], *adv.* facilement, sans peine; aisément.

east [i:st], *a.* d'est, d'orient; oriental.—*n.* est, orient; levant, *m.*

Easter ['i:stə]. Pâques, *m.*

easterly ['i:stəli], *a.* d'est.—*adv.* vers l'orient, vers l'est.

eastern ['i:stən], *a.* d'est, d'orient, oriental.

eastward ['i:stwəd], *adv.* vers l'est, vers l'orient.

easy ['i:zi], *a.* facile; aisé; confortable; tranquille; naturel (*style*); à l'aise; *easy chair*, fauteuil, *m.*—*adv.* doucement.

easy-going ['i:zigouiŋ], *a.* accommodant, peu exigeant.

eat [i:t], *v.t.*, *v.i. irr.* manger; ronger (*corroder*); *to eat away*, consumer, ronger; *to eat up*, manger, achever de manger.

eatable ['i:təbl], *a.* mangeable, comestible.—*n.* comestible, *m.*; (*pl.*) vivres, *m.pl.*

eating ['i:tiŋ], *n.* action de manger, *f.*; manger, *m.*

eaves [i:vz], *n.* avance du toit, *f.*; gouttières, *f.pl.*

eavesdrop ['i:vzdrɔp], *v.i.* écouter aux portes.

eavesdropper ['i:vzdrɔpə], *n.* écouteur aux portes, *m.*

ebb [eb], *v.i.* baisser; décliner, refluer, se retirer.—*n.* reflux; (*fig.*) déclin, *m.*, décadence, *f.*

ebb tide ['ebtaid], *n.* jusant, *m.*

ebony ['ebəni], *a.* d'ébène.—*n.* ébène, *f.*, bois d'ébène, *m.*

ebony tree ['ebənitri:], *n.* ébénier, *m.*

ebullience [i'bʌliəns], **ebulliency** [i'bʌliənsi], *n.* ébullition, effervescence, *f.*

ebullient [i'bʌliənt], *a.* en ébullition, bouillonnant; (*fig.*) exubérant, pétulant.

ebullition [ebə'liʃən], *n.* ébullition; (*fig.*) effervescence, *f.*, transport, *m.*

eccentric [ek'sentrik], *a.* excentrique; désaxé; (*fig.*) singulier.

eccentricity [eksen'trisiti], *n.* excentricité, *f.*

ecclesiastic [ikli:zi'æstik], *a. and n.* ecclésiastique, *m.*

echo ['ekou], *n.* écho, *m.*—*v.t.* répercuter; (*fig.*) répéter.—*v.i.* faire écho; retentir, résonner (*de*).

eclipse [i'klips], *n.* éclipse, *f.*—*v.t.* éclipser; (*fig.*) surpasser.—*v.i.* s'éclipser.

economic [i:kə'nɔmik], **economical** [i:kə'nɔmikəl], *a.* économique (*chose*); économe, ménager (*personne*).

economically [i:kə'nɔmikəli], *adv.* économiquement.

economics [i:kə'nɔmiks], *n.pl.* économie politique, *f.*

economist [i'kɔnəmist], *n.* économiste, *m.*, *f.*

economize [i'kɔnəmaiz], *v.t.* économiser.—*v.i.* user d'économie.

economy [i'kɔnəmi], *n.* économie, *f.*; système, *m.*; *planned economy*, économie planifiée.

ecstasy ['ekstəsi], *n.* extase, *f.*, transport, *m.*

ecstatic [eks'tætik], **ecstatical** [eks'tætikəl], *a.* extatique, d'extase.

Ecuador [ekwə'dɔ:]. (la République de) l'Équateur, *f.*

Ecuadorean [ekwə'dɔ:riən], *a.* équatorien.—*n.* Équatorien (*personne*), *m.*

eczema ['eksimə], *n.* eczéma, *m.*

eddy ['edi], *n.* remous (*eau*); tourbillon (*vent*), *m.*—*v.i.* tourbillonner.

Eden ['i:dən]. Éden, *m.*

edge [edʒ], *n.* bord (*marge*); fil, tranchant (*de couteau etc.*), *m.*; lisière (*d'une forêt etc.*), *f.*; cordon (*d'une pièce de monnaie*), *m.*; tranche (*d'un livre*), *f.*—*v.t.* affiler, aiguiser; border (*entourer*).—*v.i. to edge away*, s'éloigner graduellement.

edged [edʒd], *a.* tranchant; bordé.

edgeways ['edʒweiz], **edgewise** ['edʒwaiz], *adv.* de côté, de champ.

edging ['edʒiŋ], *n.* bordure, *f.*

edible ['edibl], *a.* comestible, bon à manger.

edict ['i:dikt], *n.* édit, *m.*

edifice ['edifis], *n.* édifice, *m.*

edify ['edifai], *v.t.* édifier.

Edinburgh ['edinbrə]. Édimbourg, *m.*

edit ['edit], *v.t.* éditer, rédiger.

edition [i'diʃən], *n.* édition, *f.*

editor ['editə], *n.* compilateur, annotateur; (*Journ.*) rédacteur en chef, directeur, *m.*

editorial [edi'tɔ:riəl], *a.* de rédacteur.—*n.* article de fond, éditorial, *m.*

Edmund ['edmənd]. Edmond, *m.*
educate ['edjukeit], *v.t.* élever; instruire.
education [edju'keiʃən], *n.* éducation, *f.*; enseignement, *m.*; instruction, *f.*
Edward ['edwəd]. Édouard, *m.*
eel [i:l], *n.* anguille, *f.*
eerie ['iəri], *a.* étrange, mystérieux.
eeriness ['iərinis], *n.* étrangeté surnaturelle, *f.*
efface [i'feis], *v.t.* effacer.
effect [i'fekt], *n.* effet, *m.*; (*pl.*) effets, biens, *m.pl.*; **in effect**, en effet; **to carry into effect**, accomplir, exécuter, mettre à effet; **to no effect**, en vain, sans résultat; **to take effect**, faire son effet, opérer; (*Law*) entrer en vigueur.—*v.t.* effectuer, exécuter, accomplir.
effective [i'fektiv], *a.* effectif; efficace.
effectively [i'fektivli], *adv.* effectivement; efficacement.
effeminacy [i'feminəsi], *n.* mollesse, nature efféminée, *f.*
effeminate [i'feminit], *a.* efféminé.
effervesce [efə'ves], *v.i.* être en effervescence; mousser (*boisson*).
effervescence [efə'vesəns], *n.* effervescence, *f.*
effervescent [efə'vesənt], **effervescing** [efə'vesiŋ], *a.* effervescent; mousseux; gazeux (*eau minérale*).
effete [i'fi:t], *a.* usé; stérile, épuisé, caduc.
efficacious [efi'keiʃəs], *a.* efficace.
efficacy ['efikəsi], *n.* efficacité, *f.*
efficiency [i'fiʃənsi], *n.* efficacité; bonne condition, *f.*; (*Mach.*) rendement, *m.*
efficient [i'fiʃənt], *a.* efficace (*remède*); capable, compétent (*personne*).
efficiently [i'fiʃəntli], *adv.* efficacement.
effigy ['efidʒi], *n.* effigie, *f.*
effloresce [eflə'res], *v.i.* s'effleurir.
efflorescence [eflə'resəns], *n.* efflorescence; (*Bot.*) floraison, *f.*
efflorescent [eflə'resənt], *a.* efflorescent; (*Bot.*) fleurissant.
effluvium [i'fl u:viəm], *n.* (*pl.* **effluvia** [i'flu:viə]) exhalaison, *f.*, effluve, *m.*
effort ['efət], *n.* effort, *m.*
effortless ['efətlis], *a.* sans effort.
effrontery [i'frʌntəri], *n.* effronterie, *f.*
effulgence [i'fʌldʒəns], *n.* splendeur, *f.*, éclat, *m.*
effulgent [i'fʌldʒənt], *a.* resplendissant, éclatant.
effusion [i'fju:ʒən], *n.* effusion, *f.*, épanchement, *m.*
effusive [i'fju:siv], *a.* expansif; (*fig.*) excessif, exubérant.
egg [eg], *n.* œuf, *m.*; **boiled egg**, œuf à la coque; **fried egg**, œuf sur le plat; **hard-boiled egg**, œuf dur; **new-laid egg**, œuf frais.—*v.t.* pousser (*à*).
egg cup ['egkʌp], *n.* coquetier, *m.*
egg-shell ['egʃel], *n.* coquille d'œuf, *f.*
eglantine ['egləntain], *n.* églantier, *m.*; églantine (*fleur*), *f.*
egoism ['egouizm], *n.* égoïsme, *m.*
egoist ['egouist], *n.* égoïste, *m.*, *f.*
egotism ['egətizm], *n.* égotisme, culte du moi, *m.*
egotist ['egətist], *n.* égotiste, *m.*, *f.*
egregious [i'gri:dʒəs], *a.* insigne, énorme; fameux.

egress ['i:gres], *n.* sortie, issue, *f.*
Egypt ['i:dʒipt]. l'Égypte, *f.*
Egyptian [i'dʒipʃən], *a.* égyptien.—*n.* Egyptien (*personne*), *m.*
eider ['aidə], **eider duck** ['aidədʌk], *n.* eider, *m.*
eiderdown ['aidədaun], *n.* édredon, *m.*
eight [eit], *a.* huit.
eighteen ['eiti:n], *a.* dix-huit.
eighteenth ['eiti:nθ], *a.* dix-huitième; dix-huit (*roi etc.*).—*n.* dix-huitième (*fraction*), *m.*
eighth [eitθ], *a.* huitième; huit (*roi etc.*).—*n.* huitième (*fraction*), *m.*; (*Mus.*) octave, *f.*
eightieth ['eitiiθ], *a.* quatre-vingtième.—*n.* quatre-vingtième (*fraction*), *m.*
eighty ['eiti], *a.* quatre-vingts.
Eire ['ɛərə]. l'Irlande, *f.*
either ['aiðə, 'i:ðə], *pron.* l'un ou l'autre, *m.*, l'une ou l'autre, *f.*; l'un d'eux, *m.*, l'une d'elles, *f.*; (*used negatively*) ni l'un ni l'autre, *m.*, ni l'une ni l'autre, *f.*—*conj.* ou, soit.—*adv.* non plus.
ejaculate [i'dʒækjuleit], *v.t.* pousser (*un cri*).—*v.i.* s'écrier; éjaculer.
ejaculation [idʒækju'leiʃən], *n.* cri, *m.* exclamation; éjaculation, *f.*
eject [i'dʒekt], *v.t.* rejeter; émettre (*flammes*); chasser, expulser.
ejection [i'dʒekʃən], **ejectment** [i'dʒektmənt], *n.* expulsion, éjection; (*Law*) éviction, *f.*
eke [i:k], *v.t.* **to eke out**, allonger; suppléer à, augmenter; ménager; **to eke out a living**, se faire une maigre pitance.
elaborate [i'læbərit], *a.* élaboré, soigné, compliqué.—[i'læbəreit], *v.t.* élaborer.
elaboration [ilæbə'reiʃən], *n.* élaboration, *f.*
elapse [i'læps], *v.i.* s'écouler.
elastic [i'læstik], *a.* and *n.* élastique, *m.*
elasticity [elæs'tisiti], *n.* élasticité, *f.*
elate [i'leit], *v.t.* élever, exalter, transporter.
elation [i'leiʃən], *n.* transport de joie, *m.*, exaltation, ivresse, *f.*
elbow ['elbou], *n.* coude, *m.*—*v.t.* coudoyer, pousser du coude.
elder (1) ['eldə], *n.* sureau (*arbre*), *m.*
elder (2) ['eldə], *a.* aîné, plus âgé; plus ancien.—*n.* aîné; ancien, *m.*
elderly ['eldəli], *a.* d'un certain âge.
eldest ['eldist], *a.* le plus âgé, l'aîné.
Eleanor ['elinə]. Éléonore, *f.*
elect [i'lekt], *a.* élu, choisi, nommé.—*n.* élu, *m.*—*v.t.* élire, nommer, choisir; (*fig.*) se décider à.
election [i'lekʃən], *n.* élection, *f.*
electioneer [ilekʃə'niə], *v.i.* solliciter des votes, travailler les électeurs.
electioneering [ilekʃə'niəriŋ], *n.* manœuvres électorales, *f.pl.*
elective [i'lektiv], *a.* électif; électoral.
elector [i'lektə], *n.* électeur, votant, *m.*
electric [i'lektrik], **electrical** [i'lektrikəl], *a.* électrique; **electric shock**, secousse électrique, *f.*
electrician [elek'triʃən, ilek'triʃən], *n.* électricien, *m.*
electricity [elek'trisiti, ilek'trisiti], *n.* électricité, *f.*
electrify [i'lektrifai], *v.t.* électriser; électrifier.
electrocute [i'lektrokju:t], *v.t.* électrocuter.
electron [i'lektrɔn] *n.* électron, *m.*

413

electronic

electronic [elek'trɔnik, ilek'trɔnik], *a.* électronique.

electronics [elek'trɔniks, ilek'trɔniks], *n.* électronique, *f.*

electro-plate [i'lektroupleit], *n.* argenture électrique, *f.*—*v.t.* plaquer, argenter.

elegance ['eligəns], *n.* élégance, *f.*

elegant ['eligənt], *a.* élégant, chic.—*n.* élégant, beau, *m.*

elegantly ['eligəntli], *adv.* élégamment.

elegiac [eli'dʒaiək], *a.* élégiaque.—*n.* vers élégiaque, *m.*

elegist ['elidʒist], *n.* poète élégiaque, *m.*

elegy ['elidʒi], *n.* élégie, *f.*

element ['elimənt], *n.* élément, *m.*; (*pl.*) rudiments, *m.pl.*

elemental [eli'mentl], **elementary** [eli'mentri], *a.* élémentaire.

elephant ['elifənt], *n.* éléphant, *m.*

elephantine [eli'fæntain], *a.* éléphantin.

elevate ['eliveit], *v.t.* élever; hausser, exalter, exciter.

elevation [eli'veiʃən], *n.* élévation; hauteur, altitude, *f.*

elevator [eli'veitə], *n.* (*Anat. etc.*) élévateur; (*Am.*) [LIFT].

eleven [i'levn], *a.* onze; **the eleven**, les apôtres, *m.pl.*; (*Spt.*) le onze, *m.*

eleventh [i'levnθ], *a.* onzième; onze (*roi etc.*). —*n.* onzième (*fraction*), *m.*

elf [elf], *n.* (*pl.* **elves** [elvz]) esprit follet, lutin, elfe, *m.*

elfin ['elfin], *a.* des lutins, des elfes.—*n.* gamin, bambin, *m.*

elicit [i'lisit], *v.t.* faire sortir, tirer (*de*); déduire, découvrir, faire avouer (*à*).

elide [i'laid], *v.t.* (*Gram.*) élider.—*v.i.* s'élider.

eligible ['elidʒibl], *a.* éligible; convenable (*pour*); acceptable.

eliminate [i'limineit], *v.t.* éliminer, supprimer.

eliminating [i'limineitiŋ], *a.* éliminateur, éliminatoire.

elimination [ilimi'neiʃən], *n.* élimination, *f.*

elision [i'liʒən], *n.* élision, *f.*

elixir [i'liksə], *n.* élixir, *m.*

Elizabeth [i'lizəbəθ]. Élisabeth, *f.*

elk [elk], *n.* (*Zool.*) élan, *m.*

ell [el], *n.* aune, *f.*

Ellen ['elin]. Hélène, *f.*

ellipse [i'lips], *n.* ellipse, *f.*

elliptic [i'liptik], **elliptical** [i'liptikəl], *a.* elliptique.

elm [elm], *n.* orme, *m.*

elocution [elo'kju:ʃən], *n.* élocution, diction, *f.*

elocutionist [elo'kju:ʃənist], *n.* déclamateur, *m.*

elongate ['i:lɔŋgeit], *v.t.* allonger, prolonger.

elongation [i:lɔŋ'geiʃən], *n.* allongement, prolongement, *m.*; (*Surg.*) élongation, *f.*

elope [i'loup], *v.i.* s'enfuir (*avec un amant*).

elopement [i'loupmənt], *n.* fuite, *f.*, enlèvement, *m.*

eloquence ['eləkwəns], *n.* éloquence, *f.*

eloquent ['eləkwənt], *a.* éloquent.

eloquently ['eləkwəntli], *adv.* éloquemment.

else [els], *adv.* autrement, ou bien, ailleurs.— *a.* autre; **anywhere else**, n'importe où ailleurs; **everything else**, tout le reste; **nobody else**, personne d'autre; **nothing else**, rien d'autre; **someone** (**somebody**) **else**, quelqu'un d'autre.

elsewhere ['elswɛə], *adv.* ailleurs, autre part.

Elsie ['elsi]. Élise, *f.*

elucidate [i'lju:sideit], *v.t.* expliquer, éclaircir, élucider.

elucidation [ilju:si'deiʃən], *n.* éclaircissement, *m.*, élucidation, explication, *f.*

elude [i'lju:d], *v.t.* éluder, éviter, échapper à.

elusion [i'lju:ʒən], *n.* subterfuge, *m.*, réponse évasive, *f.*

elusive [i'lju:siv], *a.* artificieux (*réponse*); fuyant, insaisissable (*personne*).

elves [ELF].

emaciate [i'meiʃieit], *v.t.* amaigrir.—*v.i.* maigrir, s'amaigrir.

emaciated [i'meiʃieitid], *a.* amaigri, maigre, décharné.

emaciation [imeiʃi'eiʃən], *n.* amaigrissement, *m.*, maigreur, *f.*

emanate ['eməneit], *v.i.* émaner.

emancipate [i'mænsipeit], *v.t.* affranchir, émanciper (*de*).

emancipation [imænsi'peiʃən], *n.* affranchissement, *m.*, émancipation, *f.*

emasculate [i'mæskjuleit], *v.t.* châtrer; (*fig.*) affaiblir, efféminer.

embalm [im'ba:m], *v.t.* embaumer.

embalmer [im'ba:mə], *n.* embaumeur, *m.*

embalming [im'ba:miŋ], *n.* embaumement, *m.*

embank [im'bæŋk], *v.t.* endiguer, remblayer; encaisser (*canal etc.*).

embankment [im'bæŋkmənt], *n.* levée, *f.*; terrassement, talus, (*Rail.*) remblai; quai (*rivière, canal*), *m.*

embarcation [EMBARKATION].

embargo [im'ba:gou], *n.* embargo, *m.*—*v.t.* mettre l'embargo sur; défendre, interdire.

embark [im'ba:k], *v.t.* embarquer.—*v.i.* s'embarquer (*sur*); (*fig.*) s'engager (*dans*).

embarkation or **embarcation** [emba:'keiʃən], *n.* embarquement, *m.*

embarrass [im'bærəs], *v.t.* embarrasser; gêner.

embarrassment [im'bærəsmənt], *n.* embarras, *m.*; (*fig.*) perplexité; gêne (*manque d'argent*), *f.*

embassy ['embəsi], *n.* ambassade, *f.*

embellish [im'beliʃ], *v.t.* embellir, orner (*avec*).

embellishment [im'beliʃmənt], *n.* embellissement, ornement, *m.*

ember ['embə], *n.* braise, cendre ardente, *f.*

embezzle [im'bezl], *v.t.* détourner; s'approprier frauduleusement (*des fonds*).

embezzlement [im'bezlmənt], *n.* détournement, *m.*

embezzler [im'bezlə], *n.* détourneur (*de fonds*), *m.*

embitter [im'bitə], *v.t.* rendre amer; (*fig.*) empoisonner; aigrir.

emblazon [im'bleizn], *v.t.* blasonner (*de*); (*fig.*) publier, proclamer.

emblem ['embləm], *n.* emblème, *m.*; (*Her.*) devise, *f.*

embodiment [im'bɔdimənt], *n.* incarnation; personnification; (*Mil.*) incorporation, *f.*

embody [im'bɔdi], *v.t.* incarner; (*Mil. etc.*) incorporer (*dans*); (*fig.*) personnifier.

embolden [im'bouldn], *v.t.* enhardir.

emboss [im'bɔs], *v.t.* bosseler, relever en bosse; gaufrer (*papier*).

embossing [im'bɔsiŋ], *n.* bosselage; gaufrage, *m.*

embrace [im'breis], *n.* embrassement, *m.*, étreinte, *f.*—*v.t.* embrasser, étreindre; (*fig.*) accepter; comprendre.

embrocation [embrə'keiʃən], *n.* embrocation, *f.*

embroider [im'brɔidə], *v.t.* broder.

embroidery [im'brɔidəri], *n.* broderie, *f.*

embroil [im'brɔil], *v.t.* brouiller, embrouiller.

embryo ['embriou], *n.* embryon, germe, *m.*

emend [i'mend], *v.t.* corriger; (*Law*) émender.

emendation [i:men'deiʃən], *n.* correction, émendation, *f.*

emerald ['emərəld], *n.* émeraude, *f.*

emerge [i'mə:dʒ], *v.i.* surgir; sortir (*de*); ressortir.

emergency [i'mə:dʒənsi], *n.* circonstance critique; crise, *f.*, cas imprévu, *m.*; *in case of emergency*, en cas d'urgence; *emergency exit*, sortie de secours, *f.*

emery ['eməri], *n.* émeri, *m.*; *emery cloth*, toile d'émeri, *f.*

emetic [i'metik], *n.* émétique, *m.*

emigrant ['emigrənt], *n.* émigrant; (*Fr. Hist.*) émigré, *m.*

emigrate ['emigreit], *v.i.* émigrer.

emigration [emi'greiʃən], *n.* émigration, *f.*

Emily ['emili], Émilie, *f.*

eminence ['eminəns], *n.* éminence, colline; (*fig.*) grandeur, distinction, *f.*

eminent ['eminənt], *a.* éminent; distingué, illustre.

eminently ['eminəntli], *adv.* éminemment, par excellence.

emissary ['emisəri], *n.* émissaire, messager, *m.*

emission [i'miʃən], *n.* émission, *f.*

emit [i'mit], *v.t.* jeter; exhaler, dégager; (*Fin.*) émettre.

emolument [i'mɔljumənt], *n.* (*usu. pl.*) émoluments, *m.pl.*, rémunération, *f.*; (*fig.*) profit, *m.*

emotion [i'mouʃən], *n.* émotion, *f.*

emotional [i'mouʃənəl], *a.* porté à l'émotion, émotif, *m.*

emperor ['empərə], *n.* empereur. *m.*

emphasis ['emfəsis], *n.* (*pl.* **emphases** ['emfəsi:z]) force, énergie, emphase, *f.*; accent, *m.*

emphasize ['emfəsaiz], *v.t.* appuyer sur; accentuer, souligner.

emphatic [im'fætik], *a.* fort, énergique; expressif; accentué, emphatique; (*fig.*) positif.

emphatically [im'fætikəli], *adv.* avec force, énergiquement; positivement.

empire ['empaiə], *n.* empire, *m.*

empiric [em'pirik], *n.* empirique; charlatan, *m.*—*a.* (*also* **empirical** [em'pirikəl]) empirique, guidé par l'expérience.

employ [im'plɔi], *v.t.* employer; se servir de. —*n.* emploi, *m.*; occupation, *f.*

employee [im'plɔii:], *n.* employé, *m.*

employer [im'plɔiə], *n.* patron; employeur, *m.*

employment [im'plɔimənt], *n.* emploi, *m.*, occupation, *f.*

emporium [em'pɔ:riəm], *n.* entrepôt; (*fam.*) grand magasin, *m.*

empower [em'pauə], *v.t.* autoriser (*à*), mettre à même (*de*).

empress ['empris], *n.* impératrice, *f.*

emptiness ['emptinis], *n.* vide, *m.*; (*fig.*) vanité, *f.*, néant, *m.*

empty ['empti], *a.* vide, à vide; désert (*rues etc.*); (*fig.*) vain, stérile.—*v.t.* vider, décharger.—*v.i.* se vider.

emu ['i:mju:], *n.* (*Orn.*) émeu, *m.*

emulate ['emjuleit], *v.t.* rivaliser avec; imiter.

emulation [emju'leiʃən], *n.* émulation, rivalité, *f.*

emulsion [i'mʌlʃən], *n.* émulsion, *f.*

enable [i'neibl], *v.t.* mettre à même (*de*); mettre en état (*de*); permettre (*de*).

enact [i'nækt], *v.t.* ordonner, arrêter; rendre (*loi*); jouer, faire (*un rôle*).

enactment [i'næktmənt], *n.* loi, ordonnance, *f.*, décret, *m.*

enamel [i'næml], *n.* émail, *m.*—*v.t.* émailler (*de*).—*v.i.* peindre en émail.

enamelling [i'næməliŋ], *n.* émaillure, *f.*; émaillage, *m.*

enamor [i'næmə], *v.t.* (*used now only in p.p.*) *to be enamored of,* être épris de.

encamp [in'kæmp], *v.t.*, *v.i.* camper.

encase [in'keis], *v.t.* encaisser, enfermer.

enchain [in'tʃein], *v.t.* enchaîner.

enchant [in'tʃa:nt], *v.t.* enchanter; (*fig.*) charmer, ravir (*de*).

enchanter [in'tʃa:ntə], *n.* enchanteur, *m.*

enchanting [in'tʃa:ntiŋ], *a.* enchanteur, ravissant, charmant.

enchantment [in'tʃa:ntmənt], *n.* enchantement, charme, *m.*; fascination, *f.*

enchantress [in'tʃa:ntris], *n.* enchanteresse, *f.*

encircle [in'sə:kl], *v.t.* ceindre, entourer (*de*), encercler.

enclose [in'klouz], *v.t.* enclore; entourer, environner; envoyer sous le même pli (*lettre etc.*).

enclosed [in'klouzd], *a.* entouré, environné; inclus, ci-inclus, sous ce pli (*paquet, lettre etc.*).

enclosure [in'klouʒə], *n.* clôture, enceinte (*espace clos*), *f.*; contenu (*objet renfermé*), *m.*

encomium [en'koumjəm], *n.* éloge, *m.*, louange, *f.*

encompass [in'kʌmpəs], *v.t.* entourer, environner; renfermer.

encore [ɔŋ'kɔ:], *n. and int.* bis.—*v.t.* bisser.

encounter [in'kauntə], *n.* rencontre, *f.*; combat, *m.*, lutte, *f.*—*v.t.* rencontrer, aborder; (*fig.*) éprouver, essuyer.

encourage [in'kʌridʒ], *v.t.* encourager.

encouragement [in'kʌridʒmənt], *n.* encouragement, *m.*

encroach [in'kroutʃ], *v.i.* empiéter (*sur*); abuser (*de*).

encroachment [in'kroutʃmənt], *n.* empiétement, *m.*, usurpation, *f.*

encumber [in'kʌmbə], *v.t.* encombrer, accabler, embarrasser (*de*); grever (*un héritage*).

encumbrance [in'kʌmbrəns], *n.* encombrement, embarras, *m.*; (*Law*) hypothèque, *f.*

encyclopaedia [insaiklə'pi:diə], *n.* encyclopédie, *f.*

encyclopaedic [insaiklə'pi:dik], *a.* encyclopédique.

end [end], *n.* fin; extrémité, *f.*, bout; but, objet; (*fig.*) dessein, *m.*, issue, *f.*; *at an end*, fini, terminé; *big end*, (*Motor.*) tête de bielle, *f.*; *from end to end*, d'un bout à l'autre; *in the end*, à la fin; *three days on end*, trois jours de suite; *to be at a loose end*, être désœuvré, se trouver sans avoir rien à faire; *to draw to an end*, tirer *ou* toucher à sa fin; *to make an end of*, en finir avec; *to make both ends meet*, joindre les deux bouts.—*v.t.* finir, terminer, achever.—*v.i.* finir, se terminer (*en*); cesser (*de*); aboutir (*à*).

endanger [in'deindʒə], *v.t.* mettre en danger, compromettre, risquer.

endear [in'diə], *v.t.* rendre cher (*à*).

endearing [in'diəriŋ], *a.* tendre, affectueux.

endearment [in'diəmənt], *n.* charme, *m.*; (*pl.*) caresses, *f.pl.*

endeavor [in'devə], *n.* effort, *m.*, tentative, *f.* —*v.i.* tâcher, essayer, tenter (*de*), chercher (*à*).

ending ['endiŋ], *n.* fin, conclusion; (*Gram.*) terminaison, *f.*

endive ['endiv], *n.* chicorée; escarole, *f.*

endless ['endlis], *a.* sans fin; éternel, perpétuel, interminable.

endlessly ['endlisli], *adv.* à l'infini, sans cesse.

endorse [in'dɔ:s], *v.t.* endosser; viser (*passeport*); (*fig.*) sanctionner, approuver.

endorsement [in'dɔ:smənt], *n.* suscription, *f.*; (*Comm.*) endossement (*signature au dos*); visa (*de passeport*), *m.*; (*fig.*) sanction, *f.*

endow [in'dau], *v.t.* doter (*de*); (*fig.*) douer (*de*).

endowment [in'daumənt], *n.* dotation, *f.*

endurable [in'djuərəbl], *a.* supportable, endurable.

endurance [in'djuərəns], *n.* endurance; souffrance, patience, *f.*

endure [in'djuə], *v.t.* supporter, souffrir, endurer.—*v.i.* durer; endurer, souffrir.

enduring [in'djuəriŋ], *a.* endurant, qui endure, patient; durable, qui dure (*permanent*).

endways ['endweiz], **endwise** ['endwaiz], *adv.* debout, de champ; bout à bout (*horizontalement*).

enema ['enimə, i'ni:mə], *n.* lavement, *m.*

enemy ['enəmi], *n.* ennemi, *m.*

energetic [enə'dʒetik], *a.* énergique.

energy ['enədʒi], *n.* énergie, *f.*

enervate ['enəveit], *v.t.* affaiblir, énerver.

enfeeble [in'fi:bl], *v.t.* affaiblir.

enfold [in'fould], *v.t.* envelopper.

enforce [in'fɔ:s], *v.t.* donner de la force à; faire respecter; faire exécuter; forcer.

enforcement [in'fɔ:smənt], *n.* mise en vigueur, exécution, *f.*

enfranchise [in'fræntʃaiz], *v.t.* affranchir (*un esclave*); donner le droit de vote à.

enfranchisement [in'fræntʃizmənt], *n.* affranchissement, *m.*; admission au suffrage, *f.*

engage [in'geidʒ], *v.t.* engager; retenir, prendre (*réserver*); louer (*prendre à louage*); arrêter (*un marché*); occuper (*attention etc.*); (*fig.*) en venir aux mains avec.—*v.i.* s'engager (*à*); livrer combat.

engaged [in'geidʒd], *a.* fiancé (*futur époux*);

occupé (*pris par le travail*); pas libre (*téléphone, cabinets*); aux prises (*combat*).

engagement [in'geidʒmənt], *n.* engagement, *m.*; occupation, *f.*; fiançailles, *f.pl.*; combat, *m.*

engaging [in'geidʒiŋ], *a.* engageant, attrayant.

engender [in'dʒendə], *v.t.* engendrer, faire naître, causer.

engine [in'dʒin], *n.* machine, *f.*, moteur, *m.*; (*Rail.*) locomotive, *f.*; *fire engine*, pompe à incendie, *f.*; *steam engine*, machine à vapeur.

engine-driver ['endʒindraivə], *n.* (*Rail.*) mécanicien, *m.*

engineer [endʒi'niə], *n.* ingénieur; (*Manuf.*) constructeur-mécanicien; (*Mil.*) soldat du génie; (*pl.*) le génie, *m.*

engineering [endʒi'niəriŋ], *n.* art de l'ingénieur, *m.*; *civil engineering*, génie civil, *m.*; *electrical engineering*, technique électrique, *f.*

England ['iŋglənd]. l'Angleterre, *f.*

English ['iŋgliʃ], *a.* anglais; de l'Angleterre; *the English Channel*, la Manche, *f.*—*n.* anglais (*langue*), *m.*; *the English*, les Anglais, *m.pl.*

Englishman ['iŋgliʃmən], *n.* (*pl.* **-men** [men]) Anglais, *m.*

Englishwoman ['iŋgliʃwumən], *n.* (*pl.* **-women** [wimin]) Anglaise, *f.*

engrave [in'greiv], *v.t.* graver.

engraver [in'greivə], *n.* graveur, *m.*

engraving [in'greiviŋ], *n.* gravure; *copper-plate engraving*, taille-douce, *f.*

engross [in'grous], *v.t.* grossoyer (*copier*); accaparer (*monopoliser*); absorber, occuper (*l'esprit*).

engulf [in'gʌlf], *v.t.* engouffrer; (*fig.*) engloutir.

enhance [in'ha:ns], *v.t.* enchérir, renchérir; (*fig.*) rehausser.

enhancement [in'ha:nsmənt], *n.* hausse, *f.*; (*fig.*) rehaussement, *m.*

enigma [i'nigmə], *n.* énigme, *f.*

enigmatic [enig'mætik], **enigmatical** [enig'mætikəl], *a.* énigmatique, obscur.

enjoin [in'dʒɔin], *v.t.* enjoindre; prescrire (*à*).

enjoy [in'dʒɔi], *v.t.* jouir de, posséder; goûter; *to enjoy oneself*, s'amuser.

enjoyable [in'dʒɔiəbl], *a.* agréable.

enjoyment [in'dʒɔimənt], *n.* jouissance (*de*) *f.*; plaisir, *m.*

enkindle [in'kindl], *v.t.* enflammer; (*fig.*) exciter.

enlace [in'leis], *v.t.* enlacer.

enlarge [in'la:dʒ], *v.t.* agrandir, étendre, dilater.—*v.i.* grandir, s'agrandir.

enlargement [in'la:dʒmənt], *n.* agrandissement (*also Phot.*), *m.*; augmentation, *f.*

enlighten [in'laitn], *v.t.* éclairer; (*fig.*) éclaircir.

enlightenment [in'laitnmənt], *n.* éclaircissement, *m.*; lumières, *f.pl.*

enlist [in'list], *v.t.* enrôler, engager.—*v.i.* s'engager.

enlistment [in'listmənt], *n.* engagement, enrôlement, *m.*

enliven [in'laivn], *v.t.* égayer, animer.

enmity ['enmiti], *n.* inimitié; animosité, haine, hostilité, *f.*

ennoble [i'noubl], *v.t.* anoblir; (*fig.*) ennoblir.

ennoblement [i'noublmənt], *n.* anoblissement; (*fig.*) ennoblissement, *m.*

enormity [i'nɔ:miti], **enormousness** [i'nɔ:məsnis], *n.* énormité, *f.*

enormous [i'nɔ:məs], *a.* énorme; (*fig.*) atroce, monstrueux.

enormously [i'nɔ:məsli], *adv.* énormément.

enough [i'nʌf], *a.* and *adv.* assez; *large enough*, assez grand; *more than enough*, plus qu'il n'en faut.

enquire [INQUIRE].

enrage [in'reidʒ], *v.t.* faire enrager; exaspérer.

enrapture [in'ræptʃə], *v.t.* transporter, ravir.

enrich [in'ritʃ], *v.t.* enrichir.

enrichment [in'ritʃmənt], *n.* enrichissement, *m.*

enroll [in'roul], *v.t.* enrôler, enregistrer, inscrire.—*v.i.* s'enrôler, se faire inscrire.

enrollment [in'roulmənt], *n.* enrôlement, *m.*, inscription, *f.*

ensconce [in'skɔns], *v.t.* cacher; *to ensconce oneself*, se cacher (*dans*), se blottir.

enshrine [in'ʃrain], *v.t.* enchâsser (*dans*).

enshroud [in'ʃraud], *v.t.* mettre dans un linceul; (*fig.*) couvrir.

ensign ['ensain, (*R. Navy*) 'ensin], *n.* enseigne, *f.*, drapeau, *m.*; (*Mil.*) porte-drapeau (*personne*), *m.*

enslave [in'sleiv], *v.t.* asservir; (*fig.*) captiver.

ensnare [in'snɛə], *v.t.* prendre au piège; (*fig.*) attraper séduire.

ensue [in'sju:], *v.i.* s'ensuivre.

ensuing [in'sju:iŋ], *a.* suivant; prochain.

ensure [in'ʃuə], *v.t.* assurer; garantir.

entail [en'teil], *v.t.* substituer (*à*); (*fig.*) entraîner; impliquer.

entangle [in'tæŋgl], *v.t.* emmêler; enchevêtrer; empêtrer (*les pieds*); (*fig.*) embrouiller.

entanglement [in'tæŋglmənt], *n.* embrouillement, embarras, *m.*

enter ['entə], *v.t.* entrer dans, pénétrer; inscrire (*nom etc.*); enregistrer (*paquet*).—*v.i.* entrer; s'engager (*dans*).

enteritis [entə'raitis], *n.* entérite, *f.*

enterprise ['entəpraiz], *n.* entreprise, hardiesse, *f.*; esprit d'entreprise, *m.*

entertain [entə'tein], *v.t.* recevoir (*des invités*); divertir, amuser (*distraire*); concevoir (*idée etc.*); accepter (*proposition*).—*v.i.* recevoir (*invités*).

entertainer [entə'teinə], *n.* (*Theat. etc.*) diseur, *m.*, diseuse, *f.*, comique, *m.*, *f.*; hôte, *m.*, hôtesse, *f.*

entertainment [entə'teinmənt], *n.* hospitalité, *f.*; accueil (*reception*); festin, *m.*, fête, *f.*; divertissement, spectacle (*amusement*), *m.*

enthrall [in'θrɔ:l], *v.t.* asservir, assujettir; (*fig.*) ravir.

enthuse [in'θju:z], *v.i.* s'enthousiasmer de *ou* pour.

enthusiasm [in'θju:ziæzm], *n.* enthousiasme, *m.*

enthusiast [in'θju:ziæst], *n.* enthousiaste, *m.*, *f.*

enthusiastic [inθju:zi'æstik], *a.* enthousiaste, *m.*, *f.*

entice [in'tais], *v.t.* attirer; entraîner (*dans*); séduire (*à*).

enticement [in'taismənt], *n.* appât, charme, *m.*; tentation, *f.*

enticer [in'taisə], *n.* tentateur, séducteur, *m.*

enticing [in'taisiŋ], *a.* séduisant, attrayant, tentant.

entire [in'taiə], *a.* entier, complet.

entirely [in'taiəli], *adv.* entièrement, complètement, tout entier.

entirety [in'taiəti], *n.* totalité; intégrité, *f.*

entitle [in'taitl], *v.t.* intituler, appeler; donner droit à.

entity ['entiti], *n.* entité, *f.*, être de raison, *m.*

entomb [in'tu:m], *v.t.* ensevelir.

entrails ['entreilz], *n.pl.* entrailles, *f.pl.*

entrance (1) ['entrəns], *n.* entrée, *f.*; commencement, début (*de carrière*), *m.*; (*fig.*) initiation, *f.*

entrance (2) [in'trɑ:ns], *v.t.* extasier, ravir.

entrancing [in'trɑ:nsiŋ], *a.* prenant; ravissant.

entrant ['entrənt], *n.* inscrit (*de concours*), *m.*; inscrite, *f.*; débutant (*dans une profession nouvelle*), *m.*, débutante, *f.*

entrap [in'træp], *v.t.* prendre au piège, attraper (*dans*).

entreat [in'tri:t], *v.t.* supplier, prier instamment (*de*).

entreaty [in'tri:ti], *n.* prière; supplication; (*pl.*) sollicitation, *f.*, instances, *f.pl.*

entrust [in'trʌst], *v.t.* charger (*de*).

entry ['entri], *n.* entrée; inscription (*enregistrement*); (*Book-keeping*) écriture, *f.*, article, *m.*; (*Customs*) déclaration d'entrée, *f.*; *no entry*, sens interdit, passage interdit.

entwine [in'twain], *v.t.* enlacer, entortiller.—*v.i.* s'enlacer, s'entortiller.

enumerate [i'nju:məreit], *v.t.* énumérer, dénombrer.

enunciate [i'nʌnsieit], *v.t.* énoncer; prononcer.—*v.i.* articuler.

envelop [in'veləp], *v.t.* envelopper (*de* ou *dans*).

envelope ['enviloup, 'ɔnviloup], *n.* enveloppe, *f.*

envenom [in'venəm], *v.t.* envenimer; exaspérer (*aigrir*).

envious ['enviəs], *a.* envieux (*de*).

environ [in'vaiərən], *v.t.* environner (*de*).

environment [in'vaiərənmənt], *n.* milieu, entourage, environnement, *m.*

environs [in'vaiərənz], *n.pl.* environs, *m.pl.*

envisage [in'vizidʒ], *v.t.* envisager.

envoy ['envɔi], *n.* envoyé, *m.*

envy ['envi], *n.* envie, *f.*—*v.t.* envier, porter envie à.

epaulet(te) ['epɔ:let], *n.* épaulette, *f.*

ephemeral [i'femərəl], *a.* éphémère.

epic ['epik], *a.* épique; (*fig.*) légendaire.—*n.* épopée, *f.*, poème épique, *m.*

epicure ['epikjuə], *n.* gourmet, *m.*, gastronome, *m.*, *f.*

epidemic [epi'demik], *a.* épidémique.—*n.* épidémie, *f.*

epigram ['epigræm], *n.* épigramme, *f.*

epilepsy ['epilepsi], *n.* épilepsie, *f.*

epileptic [epi'leptik], *a.* and *n.* épileptique, *m.*, *f.*

epilogue ['epilɔg], *n.* épilogue, *m.*

episcopacy [i'piskəpəsi], *n.* épiscopat, *m.*

episcopal [i'piskəpəl], *a.* épiscopal.

episode ['episoud], *n.* épisode, *m.*

epistle [i'pisl], *n.* épître, *f.*

epitaph ['epitɑ:f], *n.* épitaphe, *f.*

epithet ['epiθet], *n.* épithète, *f.*

epitome [i'pitəmi], *n.* épitomé, abrégé, précis, *m.*
epitomize [i'pitəmaiz], *v.t.* faire un abrégé de; être une image en petit de.
epoch ['i:pɔk], *n.* époque, *f.*
equable ['ekwəbl], *a.* uniforme, égal.
equal ['i:kwəl], *a.* égal; (*fig.*) impartial, juste; *equal to*, de force à, à la hauteur de.—*n.* égal, *m.*, égale, *f.*; (*pl.*) pareils, égaux, *m.pl.* —*v.t.* égaler, être égal à.
equality [i'kwɔliti], *n.* égalité, *f.*
equalize ['i:kwəlaiz], *v.t.* égaliser; compenser.
equally ['i:kwəli], *adv.* également, pareillement.
equanimity [i:kwə'nimiti], *n.* égalité d'âme, équanimité, *f.*
equation [i'kweiʃən], *n.* équation, *f.*
equator [i'kweitə], *n.* équateur, *m.*
equatorial [ekwə'tɔ:riəl], *a.* équatorial, de l'équateur.
equerry ['ekwəri], *n.* écuyer, *m.*
equestrian [i'kwestriən], *a.* équestre.—*n.* cavalier; (*Circus*) écuyer, *m.*
equilibrium [i:kwi'libriəm], *n.* équilibre, *m.*
equine ['i:kwain, 'ekwain], *a.* du cheval, équin.
equinox ['i:kwinɔks], *n.* équinoxe, *m.*
equip [i'kwip], *v.t.* équiper; (*Tech.*) outiller.
equipment [i'kwipmənt], *n.* équipement, matériel, outillage, *m.*
equitable ['ekwitəbl], *a.* équitable, juste.
equity ['ekwiti], *n.* équité, justice, *f.*
equivalent [i'kwivələnt], *a.* équivalent (*à*); *to be equivalent to*, être équivalent à, équivaloir à.—*n.* équivalent, *m.*
equivocal [i'kwivəkl], *a.* équivoque, ambigu.
equivocate [i'kwivəkeit], *v.i.* user d'équivoque, équivoquer.
era ['iərə], *n.* ère, *f.*
eradicate [i'rædikeit], *v.t.* déraciner; (*fig.*) exterminer.
erase [i'reiz], *v.t.* raturer, effacer, rayer.
eraser [i'reizə], *n.* grattoir, *m.*, gomme à effacer, *f.*
erasure [i'reiʒə], *n.* grattage, *m.*, rature, *f.*
***ere** [ɛə], *conj.* avant que; plutôt que.—*prep.* avant.
erect [i'rekt], *a.* debout, droit, élevé.—*v.t.* ériger, dresser; (*fig.*) établir.
erection [i'rekʃən], *n.* construction, érection, élévation; (*fig.*) fondation, *f.*
ermine ['ə:min], *a.* d'hermine.—*n.* hermine, *f.*
erode [i'roud], *v.t.* éroder, ronger.
erosion [i'rouʒən], *n.* érosion, *f.*
erotic [i'rɔtik], *a.* érotique.
err [ə:], *v.i.* s'écarter, s'égarer (*de*); (*fig.*) se tromper.
errand ['erənd], *n.* message, *m.*, commission, course, *f.*
errand boy ['erəndbɔi], *n.* petit commissionnaire; saute-ruisseau (*de bureau*), chasseur (*dans un restaurant*), *m.*
erratic [i'rætik], *a.* erratique, errant, excentrique; irrégulier, inégal.
erroneous [i'rouniəs], *a.* erroné, faux.
erroneously [i'rouniəsli], *adv.* à faux, à tort.
error ['erə], *n.* erreur, faute, *f.*, écart, *m.*
erudite ['erudait], *a.* érudit, savant.
erudition [eru'diʃən], *n.* érudition, *f.*
erupt [i'rʌpt], *v.i.* faire éruption (*volcan*); percer (*dent*).

eruption [i'rʌpʃən], *n.* éruption, *f.*
erysipelas [eri'sipiləs], *n.* érysipèle, *m.*
escalade [eskə'leid], *n.* escalade, *f.*—*v.t.* escalader.
escalate ['eskəleit], *v.i.* escalader.
escalation [eskə'leiʃən], *n.* escalade, *f.*
escalator ['eskəleitə], *n.* escalier roulant, *m.*
escapade [eskə'peid], *n.* escapade, *f.*
escape [is'keip], *n.* évasion; fuite (*gaz*); (*fig.*) délivrance, *f.*; *fire escape*, échelle de sauvetage, *f.*; *to have a narrow escape*, l'échapper belle.—*v.t.* échapper à; éviter.—*v.i.* (s')échapper; s'évader (*de prison*).
escarpment [is'kɑ:pmənt], *n.* escarpement, talus, *m.*
eschew [is'tʃu:], *v.t.* éviter; renoncer à.
escort [is'kɔ:t], *v.t.* escorter.—['eskɔ:t], *n.* escorte, *f.*; cavalier, *m.*
escutcheon [is'kʌtʃən], *n.* écusson, *m.*
Eskimo ['eskimou], *a.* esquimau.—*n.* Esquimau (*personne*), *m.*
especial [is'peʃəl], *a.* spécial, particulier.
especially [is'peʃəli], *adv.* spécialement, surtout.
esplanade [esplə'neid], *n.* esplanade, promenade, *f.*
espouse [is'pauz], *v.t.* épouser; (*fig.*) adopter.
espy [is'pai], *v.t.* apercevoir, aviser, épier.
essay ['esei], *n.* essai; effort, *m.*; (*Sch.*) composition, dissertation, *f.*—[e'sei], *v.t.* essayer (*de*).
essence ['esəns], *n.* essence, *f.*
essential [i'senʃəl], *a.* essentiel.—*n.* (*also pl.*) essentiel, *m.*
essentially [i'senʃəli], *adv.* essentiellement, *f.*
establish [is'tæbliʃ], *v.t.* établir, fonder; (*fig.*) confirmer; prouver.
establishment [is'tæbliʃmənt], *n.* établissement, *m.*; maison; (*fig.*) confirmation, *f.*
estate [is'teit], *n.* état, rang (*condition*), *m.*; propriété, *f.*, bien (*immeuble*), *m.*
estate agent [is'teiteidʒənt], *n.* agent immobilier, *m.*
estate duty [is'teitdju:ti], *n.* droits de succession, *m.pl.*
esteem [is'ti:m], *n.* estime, considération, *f.* —*v.t.* estimer, regarder comme.
estimate ['estimit], *n.* évaluation, *f.*, calcul, devis, *m.*; (*fig.*) appréciation, *f.*—['estimeit] *v.t.* estimer, apprécier; évaluer, calculer.
Estonia [es'touniə]. l'Esthonie, *f.*
Estonian [es'touniən], *a.* esthonien.—*n.* esthonien (*langue*); Esthonien (*personne*), *m.*
estrange [is'treindʒ], *v.t.* aliéner, éloigner (*de*).
estrangement [is'treindʒmənt], *n.* aliénation, *f.*, éloignement, *m.*, brouille, *f.*
estuary ['estjuəri], *n.* estuaire, *m.*
etching ['etʃiŋ], *n.* gravure à l'eau-forte, *f.*
eternal [i'tə:nl], *a.* and *n.* éternel, *m.*
eternity [i'tə:niti], *n.* éternité, *f.*
ether ['i:θə], *n.* éther, *m.*
ethereal [i'θiəriəl], *a.* éthéré; céleste.
ethic ['eθik], **ethical** ['eθikəl], *a.* éthique; moral.
ethics ['eθiks], *n.pl.* morale, éthique, *f.*
Ethiopia [i:θi'oupiə]. l'Éthiopie, *f.*
Ethiopian [i:θi'oupiən], *a.* éthiopien.—*n.* Éthiopien (*personne*), *m.*
etiquette ['etiket], *n.* étiquette, *f.*, convenances, *f.pl.*
Etruria [i'truəriə]. l'Étrurie, *f.*

Etruscan [i'trʌskən], *a.* étrusque.—*n.* étrusque (*langue*); Étrusque (*personne*), *m.*, *f.*

etymology [eti'mɔlədʒi], *n.* étymologie, *f.*

eucharist ['ju:kərist], *n.* eucharistie, *f.*

eulogium [ju:'loudʒiəm], eulogy ['ju:lədʒi], *n.* éloge, panégyrique, *m.*

eulogize ['ju:lədʒaiz], *v.t.* louer, faire l'éloge de.

eunuch ['ju:nək], *n.* eunuque, *m.*

euphemism ['ju:fimizm], *n.* euphémisme, *m.*

euphony ['ju:fəni], *n.* euphonie, *f.*

Eurasian [juə'reiʃən], *a.* eurasien.—*n.* Eurasien (*personne*), *m.*

Europe ['juərəp]. l'Europe, *f.*

European [juərə'piən], *a.* européen.—*n.* Européen (*personne*), *m.*

euthanasia [ju:θə'neiziə], *n.* euthanasie, *f.*

evacuate [i'vækjueit], *v.t.* évacuer.

evacuation [ivækju'eiʃən], *n.* évacuation, *f.*

evade [i'veid], *v.t.* éluder, esquiver, éviter, se soustraire à; échapper à, déjouer (*la loi*).

evaluate [i'væljueit], *v.t.* évaluer.

evaporate [i'væpəreit], *v.t.* faire évaporer.—*v.i.* s'évaporer.

evaporation [ivæpə'reiʃən], *n.* évaporation, *f.*

evasion [i'veiʒən], *n.* subterfuge, *m.*; échappatoire, défaite, *f.*

eve [i:v], *n.* veille, *f.*; on the eve of, à la veille de.

even (1) [i:vn], *n.* (*Poet.*) soir, *m.*

even (2) [i:vn], *a.* égal; régulier (*respiration, pouls*); uni (*lisse*); de niveau (*avec*); pair (*numéro*).—*adv.* même, aussi bien; précisément.—*v.t.* égaler, égaliser; niveler.

evening ['i:vniŋ], *a.* du soir; evening dress, tenue de soirée, *f.*—*n.* soir, *m.*; soirée, *f.*; (*fig.*) déclin, *m.*

evenly ['i:vnli], *adv.* également; de niveau; (*fig.*) impartialement.

evenness ['i:vnnis], *n.* égalité; régularité; sérénité, *f.*

evensong ['i:vnsɔŋ], *n.* chant du soir, *m.*, vêpres, *m.pl.*

event [i'vent], *n.* événement, *m.*; issue, *f.*; at all events, en tout cas, dans tous les cas; in the event of, au cas où.

even-tempered ['i:vntempəd], *a.* calme, placide, égal.

eventful [i'ventful], *a.* mouvementé.

eventual [i'ventjuəl], *a.* éventuel, aléatoire; final, définitif.

eventually [i'ventjuəli], *adv.* finalement, à la fin, par la suite.

ever ['evə], *adv.* toujours; jamais; ever since, depuis; for ever, à jamais.

evergreen ['evəgri:n], *a.* toujours vert.—*n.* arbre toujours vert, *m.*

everlasting [evə'la:stiŋ], *a.* éternel, perpétuel.—*n.* éternité, *f.*; éternel, *m.*

everlastingly [evə'la:stiŋli], *adv.* éternellement.

evermore ['evəmɔ:], *adv.* toujours; éternellement.

every ['evri], *a.* chaque, tout, tous les; every one, chacun, *m.*, chacune, *f.*, tous, *pl.*

everybody [EVERYONE].

everyday ['evridei], *a.* quotidien; ordinaire; de tous les jours.

everyone ['evriwʌn], everybody ['evribɔdi], *n.* tout le monde, *m.*

everything ['evriθiŋ], *n.* tout, *m.*

everywhere ['evriwɛə], *adv.* partout.

evict [i'vikt], *v.t.* évincer, expulser.

eviction [i'vikʃən], *n.* éviction, expulsion, *f.*

evidence ['evidəns], *n.* évidence; preuve, *f.*, témoignage; témoin (*personne*), *m.*—*v.t.* montrer, prouver, démontrer.

evident ['evidənt], *a.* évident, visible.

evidently ['evidəntli], *adv.* évidemment.

evil [i:vl], *a.* mauvais; malheureux, malfaisant, méchant (*esprit etc.*).—*n.* mal; malheur, *m.*, calamité, *f.*—*adv.* mal.

evil-doer ['i:vldu:ə], *n.* malfaiteur, méchant, *m.*

evil-speaking ['i:vl'spi:kiŋ], *n.* médisance, *f.*

evince [i'vins], *v.t.* montrer, manifester, démontrer.

evoke [i'vouk], *v.t.* évoquer; susciter.

evolution [i:və'lu:ʃən], *n.* évolution, *f.*

evolve [i'vɔlv], *v.t.* dérouler; développer.—*v.i.* se dérouler; se développer.

ewe [ju:], *n.* brebis, *f.*

ewer ['juə], *n.* aiguière, *f.*, broc, *m.*

exact [ig'zækt], *v.t.* exiger, extorquer.—*a.* exact, précis.

exaction [ig'zækʃən], *n.* exaction, *f.*

exactitude [ig'zæktitju:d], exactness [ig'zæktnis], *n.* exactitude, *f.*

exactly [ig'zæktli], *adv.* exactement, précisément, au juste; juste.

exaggerate [ig'zædʒəreit], *v.t.* exagérer.

exaggeration [igzædʒə'reiʃən], *n.* exagération, *f.*

exalt [ig'zɔ:lt], *v.t.* exalter, élever; (*fig.*) louer.

exaltation [egzɔ:l'teiʃən], *n.* exaltation, élévation, *f.*

examination [igzæmi'neiʃən], *n.* examen, *m.*; inspection, vérification, *f.*; (*Law*) interrogatoire (*de prisonniers*), *m.*; audition (*de témoins*), *f.*; to pass an examination, réussir à un examen; to sit (for) an examination, passer un examen.

examine [ig'zæmin], *v.t.* examiner; visiter; (*Law*) interroger.

examiner [ig'zæminə], *n.* examinateur; (*Law*) juge d'instruction, *m.*

example [ig'za:mpl], *n.* exemple, *m.*; for example, par exemple.

exasperate [ig'za:spəreit], *v.t.* exaspérer; irriter, aigrir.

exasperation [igza:spə'reiʃən], *n.* exaspération, irritation, *f.*

excavate ['ekskəveit], *v.t.* creuser, excaver.

excavation [ekskə'veiʃən], *n.* excavation, *f.*; fouilles, *f.pl.*

excavator ['ekskəveitə], *n.* piocheuse-défonceuse, *f.*

exceed [ik'si:d], *v.t.* excéder, dépasser; (*fig.*) surpasser.

exceeding [ik'si:diŋ], *a.* grand, extrême.

exceedingly [ik'si:diŋli], *adv.* très, fort, extrêmement.

excel [ik'sel], *v.t.* surpasser, l'emporter sur.—*v.i.* exceller, se distinguer (*à*).

excellence ['eksələns], *n.* excellence, supériorité, *f.*

excellent ['eksələnt], *a.* excellent.

excellently ['eksələntli], *adv.* excellemment, parfaitement.

except [ik'sept], *v.t.* excepter; exclure (*de*).—*prep.* excepté, à l'exception de, hors, sauf.—*conj.* à moins que, à moins de.

excepting [ik'septiŋ], *prep.* excepté, hormis.

exception [ik'sepʃən], *n.* exception; objection, *f.*; *to take exception to*, se formaliser de.
exceptionable [ik'sepʃənəbl], *a.* blâmable, à critiquer.
exceptional [ik'sepʃənəl], *a.* exceptionnel.
exceptionally [ik'sepʃənəli], *adv.* exceptionnellement.
excerpt ['eksə:pt], *n.* extrait, *m.*, citation, *f.*
excess [ik'ses], *n.* excès; excédent (*poids*), *m.*
excessive [ik'sesiv], *a.* excessif, extrême; immodéré.
excessively [ik'sesivli], *adv.* excessivement, à l'excès.
exchange [iks'tʃeindʒ], *n.* échange; (*Comm.*) change, *m.*; Bourse (*édifice*), *f.*; *bill of exchange*, lettre de change, *f.*; *rate of exchange*, taux du change, *m.*; *telephone exchange*, central téléphonique, *m.—v.t.* échanger, changer (*contre* ou *pour*).
exchequer [iks'tʃekə], *n.* trésor; Ministère des Finances, *m.*
excisable [ek'saizəbl], *a.* imposable; sujet aux droits de l'accise.
excise ['eksaiz], *n.* (*England*) excise, *f.*; (*France*) contributions indirectes, *f.pl.*, régie, *f.*
excise-man ['eksaizmən], *n.* (*pl.* -men [men]) préposé *ou* employé de la régie, *m.*
excitable [ik'saitəbl], *a.* excitable, impressionnable.
excite [ik'sait], *v.t.* exciter; irriter; émouvoir; (*fig.*) provoquer.
excitement [ik'saitmənt], *n.* émoi, *m.*, surexcitation; émotion, agitation, *f.*
exciting [ik'saitiŋ], *a.* émouvant, passionnant, palpitant.
exclaim [iks'kleim], *v.i.* s'écrier, se récrier, s'exclamer.
exclamation [eksklə'meiʃən], *n.* exclamation, *f.*, cri, *m.*
exclude [iks'klu:d], *v.t.* exclure (*de*); proscrire.
excluding [iks'klu:diŋ], *prep.* sans compter.
exclusion [iks'klu:ʒən], *n.* exclusion, *f.*
exclusive [iks'klu:siv], *a.* exclusif.
excommunicate [ekskə'mju:nikeit], *v.t.* excommunier.
excrement ['ekskrimənt], *n.* excrément, *m.*
excrescence [iks'kresəns], *n.* excroissance, *f.*
excruciate [iks'kru:ʃieit], *v.t.* tourmenter, torturer.
excruciating [iks'kru:ʃieitiŋ], *a.* atroce, affreux, horrible.
exculpate ['ekskʌlpeit], *v.t.* disculper, justifier.
excursion [iks'kə:ʃən], *n.* excursion, randonnée; (*fig.*) digression, *f.*
excusable [iks'kju:zəbl], *a.* excusable.
excuse [iks'kju:s], *n.* excuse, *f.*; prétexte, *m.*; *to find an excuse*, chercher des excuses; *to make excuses*, s'excuser.—[eks'kju:z], *v.t.* excuser, pardonner; *excuse me !* pardon! *to be excused from duty*, être exempt de service.
execrable ['eksikrəbl], *a.* exécrable.
execrate ['eksikreit], *v.t.* exécrer, maudire.
execute ['eksikju:t], *v.t.* exécuter, accomplir; remplir (*un ordre*); *to execute a deed*, signer un contrat.
execution [eksi'kju:ʃən], *n.* exécution, *f.*; accomplissement supplice, *m.*

executioner [eksi'kju:ʃənə], *n.* bourreau, *m.*
executive [ig'zekjutiv], *a.* exécutif.—*n.* pouvoir exécutif; (*Comm.*) directeur, *m.*
executor [ig'zekjutə], *n.* exécuteur testamentaire, *m.*
exemplar [ig'zemplə], *n.* modèle, exemplaire, *m.*
exemplary [ig'zempləri], *a.* exemplaire; modèle.
exemplify [ig'zemplifai], *v.t.* démontrer par des exemples, illustrer; donner un exemple de.
exempt [ig'zempt, eg'zemt], *v.t.* exempter (*de*).—*a.* exempt.
exemption [ig'zempʃən], *n.* exemption, *f.*
exercise ['eksəsaiz], *n.* exercice; (*Sch.*) thème, devoir, *m.—v.t.* exercer; promener (*un chien*).—*v.i.* s'exercer; (*Mil.*) faire l'exercice.
exercise book ['eksəsaizbuk], *n.* cahier (*de devoirs*), *m.*
exert [ig'zə:t], *v.t.* déployer; mettre en œuvre; exercer (*influence, pression etc.*); *to exert oneself*, faire des efforts (*pour*).
exertion [ig'zə:ʃən], *n.* effort, *m.*
exhale [eks'heil], *v.t.* exhaler, émettre.
exhaust [ig'zɔ:st], *v.t.* épuiser.—*n.* échappement, *m.*
exhausted [ig'zɔ:stid], *a.* épuisé.
exhaustion [ig'zɔ:stʃən], *n.* épuisement, *m.*
exhaustive [ig'zɔ:stiv], *a.* qui épuise; (*fig.*) complet.
exhaust pipe [ig'zɔ:stpaip], *n.* (*Motor.*) tuyau d'échappement, *m.*
exhibit [ig'zibit], *v.t.* montrer; exposer; (*fig.*) exhiber.—*n.* objet exposé, *m.*
exhibition [eksi'biʃən], *n.* exposition; représentation, *f.*, spectacle, *m.*; (*Univ.*) bourse, *f.*
exhibitioner [eksi'biʃənə], *n.* (*Univ.*) boursier, *m.*
exhibitor [ig'zibitə], *n.* exposant, *m.*
exhilarate [ig'zilareit], *v.t.* réjouir, égayer.
exhilarating [ig'zilareitiŋ], *a.* qui égaye, réjouissant.
exhilaration [igzilə'reiʃən], *n.* réjouissance, gaieté, joie de vivre, *f.*
exhort [ig'zɔ:t], *v.t.* exhorter (*à*).
exhortation [egzɔ:'teiʃən], *n.* exhortation, *f.*
exhume [eks'hju:m], *v.t.* exhumer, déterrer.
exile ['eksail], *n.* exil; exilé (*personne*), *m.—v.t.* exiler.
exist [ig'zist], *v.i.* exister.
existence [ig'zistəns], *n.* existence, *f.*; être, *m.*
exit ['eksit], *n.* sortie, *f.—v.i.* (*Theat.*) il (elle) sort.
exodus ['eksədəs], *n.* exode, *m.*
exonerate [ig'zonəreit], *v.t.* décharger, exempter, exonérer, justifier.
exorbitant [ig'zɔ:bitənt], *a.* exorbitant, excessif, exagéré.
exotic [eg'zɔtik], *a.* exotique.
expand [iks'pænd], *v.t.* étendre, faire épanouir; amplifier; dilater (*gaz*).—*v.i.* se dilater; s'épanouir; se développer.
expanse [iks'pæns], *n.* étendue, *f.*
expansion [iks'pænʃən], *n.* expansion, *f.*
expatiate [eks'peiʃieit], *v.i.* s'étendre (*sur*).
expatriate [eks'peitrieit], *v.t.* expatrier, bannir.
expect [iks'pekt], *v.t.* attendre; s'attendre à, compter sur (*choses*); espérer; *she is expecting*, elle attend un bébé; *to know what to expect*, savoir à quoi s'en tenir.

expectant [iks'pektənt], *a.* expectant.
expectation [ekspek'teiʃən], *n.* attente, espérance; expectative; probabilité, *f.*
expedience [iks'pi:diəns], **expediency** [iks'pi:diənsi], *n.* convenance, utilité, opportunité, *f.*
expedient [iks'pi:diənt], *a.* convenable, à propos, utile, opportun.—*n.* expédient, *m.*
expedite ['ekspədait], *v.t.* expédier, hâter, accélerer.
expedition [ekspə'diʃən], *n.* expédition; promptitude, *f.*
expeditious [ekspi'diʃəs], *a.* expéditif, prompt.
expel [iks'pel], *v.t.* expulser, chasser; (*Sch.*) renvoyer.
expend [iks'pend], *v.t.* dépenser; (*fig.*) employer.
expenditure [iks'penditʃə], *n.* dépense, *f.,* dépenses, *f.pl.*; (*fig.*) sacrifice, *m.*
expense [iks'pens], *n.* dépense, *f.*; dépens, frais, *m.pl.*; **at any expense**, à tout prix; **incidental expenses**, faux frais; **to clear one's expenses**, faire ses frais.
expensive [iks'pensiv], *a.* coûteux, cher (*chose*); dépensier (*personne*).
expensively [iks'pensivli], *adv.* à grands frais.
experience [iks'piəriəns], *n.* expérience, *f.*; sentiment, *m.*—*v.t.* éprouver, faire l'expérience de.
experienced [iks'piəriənst], *a.* éprouvé, expérimenté.
experiment [eks'perimənt], *n.* expérience, *f.* —*v.i.* expérimenter.
experimental [eksperi'mentl], *a.* expérimental.
expert ['ekspə:t], *a.* expert, habile.—*n.* expert, *m.*
expiate ['ekspieit], *v.t.* expier.
expiation [ekspi'eiʃən], *n.* expiation, *f.*
expiration [ekspi'reiʃən], **expiry** [iks'paiəri], *n.* expiration; fin, *f.*, terme, *m.*
expire [iks'paiə], *v.i.* expirer, mourir.
explain [iks'plein], *v.t.* expliquer.—*v.i.* s'expliquer.
explanation [eksplə'neiʃən], *n.* explication, *f.*
explanatory [iks'plænətri], *a.* explicatif.
explicit [iks'plisit], *a.* explicite, formel; franc.
explode [iks'ploud], *v.t.* faire éclater; faire sauter (*mine*); (*fig.*) discréditer; **exploded theory**, théorie abandonnée, *f.*—*v.i.* éclater, sauter, faire explosion.
exploit ['eksplɔit], *n.* exploit, haut fait, *m.* —[iks'plɔit], *v.t.* exploiter.
exploitation [eksplɔi'teiʃən], *n.* exploitation, *f.*
exploration [eksplɔ:'reiʃən], *n.* exploration, *f.*; (*fig.*) examen, *m.*
explore [iks'plɔ:], *v.t.* explorer; (*fig.*) examiner.
explorer [iks'plɔ:rə], *n.* explorateur, *m.*
explosion [iks'plouʒən], *n.* explosion, *f.*
explosive [iks'plousiv], *a.* and *n.* explosif, *m.*
exponent [eks'pounənt], *n.* (*Math.*) exposant, *f.* (*fig.*) représentant, *m.*
export ['ekspɔ:t], *n.* exportation; marchandise exportée, *f.*—[eks'pɔ:t], *v.t.* exporter, *f.*
expose [iks'pouz], *v.t.* exposer; (*fig.*) révéler, découvrir, démasquer.
expostulate [iks'pɔstjuleit], *v.i.* faire des remontrances (à).
exposure [iks'pouʒə], *n.* exposition (*aux*

intempéries, à un danger), *f.*; étalage (*de marchandises*); esclandre, *m.*; (*Phot.*) pose, *f.*; **to die of exposure**, mourir de froid.
expound [iks'paund], *v.t.* expliquer, exposer.
express [iks'pres], *a.* exprès; formel, explicite; **by express delivery**, par exprès.—*n.* exprès (*messager*); train express, *m.*—*v.t.* exprimer.
expression [iks'preʃən], *n.* expression, *f.*
expressive [iks'presiv], *a.* expressif.
expressly [iks'presli], *adv.* expressément, formellement.
expropriate [eks'prouprieit], *v.t.* exproprier.
expulsion [iks'pʌlʃən], *n.* expulsion, *f.*
expurgate ['ekspə:geit], *v.t.* corriger, expurger (*livre*).
exquisite ['ekskwizit], *a.* exquis; vif, extrême (*douleur*); raffiné, délicat.
exquisitely ['ekskwizitli], *adv.* d'une manière exquise; parfaitement.
ex-service man [eks'sə:vismən], *n.* (*pl.* **-men** [men]) ancien combattant, *m.*
extant [ek'stænt], *a.* qui existe encore.
extempore [eks'tempəri], *a.* improvisé.—*adv.* impromptu, sans préparation.
extemporize [eks'tempəraiz], *v.t.* improviser.
extend [iks'tend], *v.t.* étendre; prolonger; tendre (*la main*); **to extend a welcome**, souhaiter la bienvenue.—*v.i.* s'étendre; se prolonger (*temps*).
extension [iks'tenʃən], *n.* extension; étendue, prolongation (*de temps*), *f.*; (*Teleph.*) poste, *m.*; (*Elec.*) [FLEX].
extensive [iks'tensiv], *a.* étendu, vaste; ample.
extensively [iks'tensivli], *adv.* d'une manière étendue; bien, très, au loin.
extent [iks'tent], *n.* étendue, *f.*; (*fig.*) degré, point, *m.*; **to a certain extent**, jusqu'à un certain point; **to the extent of**, jusqu'à.
extenuate [eks'tenjueit], *v.t.* atténuer, amoindrir.
extenuating [eks'tenjueitiŋ], *a.* (*Law*) atténuant.
exterior [eks'tiəriə], *a.* extérieur, en dehors.—*n.* extérieur, *m.*
exterminate [iks'tə:mineit], *v.t.* exterminer; extirper.
extermination [ikstə:mi'neiʃən], *n.* extermination, *f.*
external [eks'tə:nl], *a.* extérieur; externe (*étudiant etc.*).
extinct [iks'tiŋkt], *a.* éteint; qui n'existe plus (*espèce etc.*); aboli.
extinguish [iks'tiŋgwiʃ], *v.t.* éteindre; (*fig.*) éclipser.
extinguisher [iks'tiŋgwiʃə], *n.* extincteur (*appareil*), *m.*
extirpate ['ekstə:peit], *v.t.* extirper.
extol [iks'toul], *v.t.* exalter, vanter.
extort [iks'tɔ:t], *v.t.* extorquer, arracher.
extortion [iks'tɔ:ʃən], *n.* extorsion, *f.*
extortionate [iks'tɔ:ʃənit], *a.* extorsionnaire, exorbitant.
extra ['ekstrə], *a.* en sus; supplémentaire. **extra charge**, prix en sus, supplément, *m.* —*n.* supplément; (*Cine.*) figurant, *m.*—*adv.* en sus, de plus; **extra strong**, extra-solide.
extract [eks'trækt], *n.* extrait; concentré (*de viande etc.*), *m.*—[iks'trækt], *v.t.* extraire, tirer (*de*); arracher (*dent*) à.

extraction [iks'trækʃən], *n.* extraction; origine, *f.*

extraneous [eks'treinjəs], *a.* étranger (*à*); non-essentiel.

extraordinarily [iks'trɔːdnrili], *a.* extraordinairement.

extraordinary [iks'trɔːdnri], *a.* extraordinaire, rare.

extravagance [iks'trævəgəns], *n.* extravagance; prodigalité, *f.*, gaspillage, *m.*

extravagant [iks'trævəgənt], *a.* extravagant (*immodéré*); prodigue, dépensier; exorbitant (*prix*).

extravagantly [iks'trævəgəntli], *adv.* d'une manière extravagante.

extreme [iks'triːm], *a.* extrême.—*n.* extrémité, *f.*; extrême, *m.*

extremely [iks'triːmli], *adv.* extrêmement, au dernier degré.

extremist [iks'triːmist], *n.* extrémiste, *m.*, *f.*; ultra, *m.*

extremity [iks'tremiti], *n.* extrémité, *f.*, extrême; bout, comble, *m.*

extricate ['ekstrikeit], *v.t.* débarrasser, dégager; **to extricate oneself,** se tirer d'affaire.

extrovert ['ekstrəvəːt], *n.* extroverti, *m.*

exuberance [ig'zjuːbərəns], *n.* exubérance, surabondance, *f.*

exuberant [ig'zjuːbərənt], *a.* exubérant, surabondant.

exude [ek'sjuːd], *v.t.* faire exsuder.—*v.i.* exsuder.

exult [ig'zʌlt], *v.i.* se réjouir, exulter (*de*).

exultant [ig'zʌltənt], *a.* joyeux, triomphant.

exultation [egzʌl'teiʃən], *n.* triomphe, *m.*, exultation, *f.*

eye [ai], *n.* œil; trou (*d'une aiguille*); (*Bot.*) œil, bouton, *m.*; (*Needlework*) porte; (*fig.*) vue, *f.*; **black eye,** œil poché; **blind in one eye,** borgne; **in the twinkling of an eye,** en un clin d'œil; **to keep an eye on,** surveiller.—*v.t.* regarder; lorgner.

eyeball ['aibɔːl], *n.* bulbe de l'œil, *m.*

eyebrow ['aibrau], *n.* sourcil, *m.*

eyed [aid], *a.* **a blue-eyed,** aux yeux bleus.

eyeglass ['aiglɑːs], *n.* monocle (*un seul verre*); lorgnon, pince-nez (*double*), *m.*

eye-hole ['aihoul], *n.* orbite; petit judas, *m.*

eyelash ['ailæʃ], *n.* cil, *m.*

eyelet ['ailit], *n.* œillet, *m.*

eyelid ['ailid], *n.* paupière, *f.*

eyesight ['aisait], *n.* vue, *f.*

eyesore ['aisɔː], *n.* chose qui blesse l'œil, *f.*, objet d'aversion, *m.*

eye-witness ['aiwitnis], *n.* témoin oculaire, *m.*

eyrie, eyry [AERIE].

F

F, f [ef]. sixième lettre de l'alphabet; (*Mus.*) fa, *m.*

fable [feibl], *n.* fable, *f.*, conte, *m.*

fabric ['fæbrik], *n.* construction, *f.*; édifice, ouvrage, *m.*; étoffe, *f.*; (*fig.*) système, *m.*

fabricate ['fæbrikeit], *v.t.* fabriquer, inventer, contrefaire.

fabrication [fæbri'keiʃən], *n.* fabrication, *f.*

fabulous ['fæbjuləs], *a.* fabuleux.

face [feis], *n.* figure, *f.*; visage, *m.*; face, surface (*des choses*); (*fig.*) apparence, *f.*, état, *m.*; mine, physionomie, *f.*; front (*insolence*), *m.*; façade, *f.*, devant (*front*), *m.*; facette (*d'un diamant*), *f.*; cadran (*de pendule*), *m.*; **face to face,** vis-à-vis; **to make faces at,** faire des grimaces à.—*v.t.* faire face à, affronter; mettre un revers à, parer (*vêtements*); revêtir (*mur etc.*); donner sur (*maison etc.*).—*v.i.* prendre un faux dehors; (*Mil.*) faire front; **face about!** volte-face!

facet ['fæsit], *n.* facette, *f.*—*v.t.* facetter.

facetious [fə'siːʃəs], *a.* facétieux.

facetiously [fə'siːʃəsli], *adv.* facétieusement.

facetiousness [fə'siːʃəsnis], *n.* plaisanterie, *f.*

facial ['feiʃəl], *a.* facial.

facile ['fæsail], *a.* facile; complaisant.

facility [fə'siliti], *n.* facilité, *f.*

facilitate [fə'siliteit], *v.t.* faciliter.

facing ['feisiŋ], *n.* parement (*de vêtements*); revers, *m.*

facsimile [fæk'simili], *n.* fac-similé, *m.*

fact [fækt], *n.* fait, *m.*; **as a matter of fact, in fact,** en effet; **in point of fact,** au fait; **matter-of-fact man,** homme positif, *m.*

faction ['fækʃən], *n.* faction; (*fig.*) discorde, dissension, *f.*

factor ['fæktə], *n.* agent; facteur, *m.*

factory ['fæktri], *n.* usine, fabrique, *f.*; (*obs.*), comptoir (*d'outre-mer*) *m.*

faculty ['fækəlti], *n.* faculté, *f.*, pouvoir, talent, *m.*

fad [fæd], *n.* marotte, manie, *f.*

fade [feid], *v.t.* faire flétrir, faire flétrir.—*v.i.* se faner, se flétrir; disparaître, périr.

fag [fæg], *v.t.* forcer à piocher; fatiguer, éreinter; **fagged out,** éreinté.—*v.i.* travailler dur, piocher (*à*).—*n.* fatigue, peine, corvée, *f.*; (*pop.*) cigarette, *f.*

fag end ['fægend], *n.* (*pop.*) mégot (*de cigarette*), *m.*

faggot ['fægət], *n.* fagot, *m.*

fail [feil], *v.t.* manquer à, abandonner.—*v.i.* faillir; manquer (*to miss*); échouer (*ne pas réussir*); (*Comm.*) faire faillite.—*n.* manque, insuccès, *m.*

failing ['feiliŋ], *n.* défaut, *m.*, faute, (*Comm.*) faillite, *f.*—*prep.* à défaut de.

failure ['feiljə], *n.* manque, défaut (*want*); échec; insuccès, *m.*, affaire manquée, *f.*, fiasco, *m.*; chute (*d'une pièce etc.*); (*Comm.*) faillite, *f.*; **he is a failure,** c'est un raté.

*fain [fein], *adv.* avec plaisir, volontiers.

faint [feint], *a.* faible; affaibli; languissant; découragé; timide.—*v.i.* s'évanouir, défaillir.—*n.* évanouissement, *m.*

faint-hearted ['feinthɑːtid], *a.* timide, sans courage, découragé.

fainting ['feintiŋ], *n.* évanouissement, *m.*, défaillance, *f.*

faintly ['feintli], *adv.* faiblement; mollement.

faintness ['feintnis], *n.* faiblesse, *f.*

fair [feə], *a.* beau; favorable (*vent*); clair (*teint*); blond (*cheveux etc.*); juste, équitable;

(*fig.*) assez bon, passable; *fair play*, franc jeu, *m.*; *fair price*, juste prix, *m.*; *that is not fair* (*at games*), cela n'est pas de jeu.—*adv.* bien; de bonne foi, honorablement.—*n.* foire (*marché*), *f.*

fairly ['fɛəli], *adv.* bien; loyalement; doucement; avec justesse; de bonne foi; passablement, assez.

fairness ['fɛənis], *n.* beauté; couleur blonde (*des cheveux*); blancheur (*du teint*); équité, impartialité, *f.*

fairy ['fɛəri], *a.* des fées, féerique.—*n.* fée, *f.*

fairy tale ['fɛəriteil], *n.* conte de fées, *m.*

faith [feiθ], *n.* foi, croyance; (*fig.*) fidélité *f.*—*int.* ma foi! en vérité!

faithful ['feiθful], *a.* fidèle.

faithfully ['feiθfuli], *adv.* fidèlement; *yours faithfully* (*lettre d'affaires*), veuillez agréer mes salutations distinguées.

faithfulness ['feiθfulnis], *n.* fidélité, *f.*

faithless ['feiθlis], *a.* sans foi. infidèle.

faithlessness ['feiθlisnis], *n.* infidélité; déloyauté, *f.*

fake [feik], *v.t.*, *v.i.* truquer, maquiller.

falcon ['fɔːlkən], *n.* faucon, *m.*

fall [fɔːl]. *v.i.* irr. tomber; s'abaisser; baisser, diminuer; *to fall away from*, abandonner, quitter; *to fall back* tomber en arrière; (*Mil.*) reculer; *to fall down*, tomber par terre; *to fall for*, tomber amoureux de; *to fall for it*, s'y laisser prendre; *to fall in*, s'écrouler; (*Mil.*) se mettre en rangs, s'aligner; *to fall off*, tomber; diminuer; *to fall out*, tomber; se brouiller; (*Mil.*) *fall out!* rompez vos rangs! to fall through, échouer; *to fall to*, se mettre à; to fall under, être compris sous; tomber sous; *to fall upon*, tomber sur, attaquer; incomber à.—*n.* chute, *f.*; (*Am.*) automne, *m.* ou *f.*; tombée (*de la nuit*), *f.*; baisse (*de prix*), *f.*; éboulement (*de terre*), *m.*; chute, cascade (*de rivières etc.*); décrue (*des eaux*); diminution (*de quantité*), *f.*

fallacy ['fæləsi], *n.* erreur, fausseté, illusion, *f.*

fallible ['fæləbl], *a.* faillible.

fall-out ['fɔːlaut], *n.* retombées radioactives, *f.pl.*

fallow ['fælou], *a.* en jachère; (*fig.*) inculte; fauve (*daim etc.*).—*n.* jachère, friche, *f.*

false [fɔːls], *a.* faux, perfide, déloyal; infidèle; prétendu; illégal (*détention*).

falsehood ['fɔːlshud], *n.* mensonge, *f.*

falsely ['fɔːlsli], *adv.* faussement.

falseness ['fɔːlsnis], *n.* fausseté; perfidie, *f.*

falsetto [fɔːl'setou], *n.* (*Mus.*) voix de fausset, *f.*

falsify ['fɔːlsifai], *v.t.* falsifier; fausser.

falter ['fɔːltə], *v.i.* hésiter; bégayer; chanceler.

faltering ['fɔːltəriŋ], *n.* hésitation, *f.*

fame [feim], *n.* gloire, renommée, *f.*

famed [feimd], *a.* renommé.

familiar [fə'miljə], *a.* familier, intime; de la famille; *to be familiar with*, être familier avec, connaître.—*n.* ami intime; esprit familier, *m.*

familiarity [fəmili'æriti], *n.* familiarité, *f.*

familiarly [fə'miliəli], *adv.* familièrement, sans cérémonie.

family ['fæmili], *a.* de famille, de la famille.—*n.* famille, *f.*

famine ['fæmin], *n.* famine, disette, *f.*

famished ['fæmiʃt], *a.* affamé.

famous ['feiməs], *a.* fameux, célèbre.

famously ['feiməsli], *adv.* fameusement; (*fig.*) prodigieusement.

fan [fæn], *n.* éventail; ventilateur; (*colloq.*) admirateur enthousiaste (*d'un artiste ou d'un sport*), *m.*—*v.t.* éventer; souffler (*feu*); (*Agric.*) vanner; (*fig.*) exciter, activer.

fanatic [fə'nætik], *a.* and *n.* fanatique, *m.*, *f.*

fanatical [fə'nætikəl], *a.* fanatique.

fanaticism [fə'nætisizm], *n.* fanatisme, *m.*

fancied ['fænsid], *a.* imaginaire, imaginé; (*Turf*) favori.

fancier ['fænsiə], *n.* amateur (*de*), *m.*

fanciful ['fænsiful], *a.* fantasque, capricieux.

fancy ['fænsi], *a.* de fantaisie.—*n.* fantaisie, imagination; idée, *f.*, caprice, goût (*pour*), *m.*, envie (*de*), *f.*—*v.t.* s'imaginer, se figurer; avoir du goût pour.—*v.i.* s'imaginer, se figurer; *just fancy!* figurez-vous!

fancy dress ['fænsidres], *n.* travesti, *m.*; *fancy-dress ball*, bal costumé, *m.*

fane [fein], *n.* temple, édifice sacré, *m.*

fanfare ['fænfeə], *n.* fanfare, *f.*

fang [fæŋ], *n.* croc (*de chien*), *m.*; racine (*d'une dent*); défense (*de sanglier*); (*fig.*) griffe, *f.*

fantastic [fæn'tæstik], *a.* fantastique; fantasque (*personne*).

fantasy ['fæntəsi], *n.* fantaisie, *f.*

far [fɑː], *a.* (*comp.* **farther**, **further**; *superl.* **farthest**, **furthest**) lointain, éloigné, reculé; *the Far East*, l'extrême Orient, *m.*—*adv.* loin, au loin; bien, fort, beaucoup; *as far as*, aussi loin que, jusqu'à; *by far*, de beaucoup; *far and wide*, de tous côtés; *how far?* jusqu'où ?

far-away ['fɑːrəwei], *a.* rêveur (*regard*); lointain.

farce [fɑːs], *n.* farce, *f.*

farcical ['fɑːsikl], *a.* burlesque; (*fig.*) drôle.

fare [fɛə], *v.i.* aller; se porter; se nourrir, vivre.—*n.* prix de la course; place (*personne*), *m.*, voyageur (*personne*), *m.*; chère (*aliment*), *f.*; *bill of fare*, menu, *m.*, carte du jour, *f.*; *return fare*, aller et retour, *m.*; *single fare*, billet simple, *m.*

farewell ['fɛəwel, fɛə'wel], *a.* d'adieu.—*n.* adieu, *m.*

far-fetched [fɑː'fetʃt], *a.* recherché; tiré par les cheveux.

farm [fɑːm], *n.* ferme, *f.*—*v.t.* affermer, prendre à ferme; exploiter.

farmer ['fɑːmə], *n.* fermier, métayer; cultivateur, *m.*

farm-house ['fɑːmhaus], *n.* ferme, *f.*

farming ['fɑːmiŋ], *n.* agriculture, exploitation agricole, *f.*

farm-yard ['fɑːmjɑːd], *n.* basse-cour, *f.*

Faroe ['fɛərou] **Islands**. les îles Féroé, *f.pl.*

far-reaching ['fɑːriːtʃiŋ], *a.* d'une grande portée.

farrier ['færiə] *n.* maréchal ferrant, *m.*

farther [FURTHER].

farthest [FURTHERMOST].

fascinate ['fæsineit], *v.t.* fasciner; charmer, séduire.

fascinating ['fæsineitiŋ], *a.* fascinateur, enchanteur, séduisant.

fascination [fæsi'neiʃən], *n.* fascination, *f.*, charme, *m.*

fascism ['fæʃizm], *n.* fascisme, *m.*

fascist ['fæʃist], *a.* and *n.* fasciste, *m.*, *f.*

fashion [ˈfæʃən], *n.* façon, forme; mode, *f.*; le grand monde, *m.*; *after a fashion,* tant bien que mal; *in fashion,* à la mode; *to set the fashion,* donner le ton.—*v.t.* façonner, former.

fashionable [ˈfæʃnəbl], *a.* à la mode, élégant, de bon ton, (*fam.*) chic.

fashionably [ˈfæʃnəbli], *adv.* à la mode, élégamment.

fast (1) [fɑːst], *n.* jeûne, *m.*—*v.i.* jeûner.

fast (2) [fɑːst], *a.* ferme, fixe (*solide*); fidèle (*constant*); bon teint (*couleur*); serré (*nœud*); (*Naut.*) amarré (*fixé*); bien fermé (*porte*); vite, rapide; en avance (*horloge etc.*); (*fig.*) dissolu; *to make fast,* assujettir, fermer (*porte, fenêtre*); (*Naut.*) amarrer.—*adv.* ferme (*stable*); vite, rapidement (*avec célérité*); fort (*pluie*); *to hold fast,* tenir bon; *to stand fast,* ne pas broncher.

fasten [fɑːsn], *v.t.* attacher, fixer; lier; fermer (*fenêtre, porte etc.*).—*v.i.* s'attacher (*à*); se fermer.

fastener [ˈfɑːsnə], **fastening** [ˈfɑːsniŋ], *n.* attache; agrafe (*de robe*); fermeture, *f.*

fastidious [fæsˈtidiəs], *a.* difficile; dédaigneux; délicat; exigeant.

fastness [ˈfɑːstnis], *n.* fermeté; vitesse; place forte (*forteresse*); légèreté de conduite, *f.*

fat [fæt], *a.* gras; gros (*personne*); (*fig.*) riche, fertile.—*n.* gras, *m.*; graisse; (*fig.*) substance, *f.*; (*pl.*) matières grasses, *f.pl.*

fatal [feitl], *a.* fatal, funeste; mortel.

fatality [fəˈtæliti], *n.* fatalité, *f.*; accident mortel, *m.*

fatally [ˈfeitəli], *adv.* fatalement, mortellement.

fate [feit], *n.* destin, sort, *m.*

fated [ˈfeitid], *a.* destiné.

fateful [ˈfeitful], *a.* fatal; décisif.

fat-head [ˈfæthed], *n.* (*colloq.*) nigaud, *m.*

father [ˈfɑːðə], *n.* père, *m.*; (*pl.*) pères, ancêtres, aïeux, *m.pl.*; *godfather,* parrain, *m.*; *grandfather,* grand-père, *m.*; *stepfather,* beau-père, *m.*

father-in-law [ˈfɑːðərinlɔː], *n.* beau-père, *m.*

fatherland [ˈfɑːðəlænd], *n.* pays natal, *m.*, patrie, *f.*

fatherly [ˈfɑːðəli], *a.* paternel, de père.

fathom [ˈfæðəm], *n.* toise; (*Naut.*) brasse (= 6 pieds = 1 m. 829); (*fig.*) portée, profondeur, *f.*—*v.t.* sonder; (*fig.*) approfondir.

fatigue [fəˈtiːg], *n.* fatigue; (*Mil.*) corvée, *f.*—*v.t.* fatiguer, lasser.

fatiguing [fəˈtiːgiŋ], *a.* fatigant.—*pres.p.* fatiguant.

fatten [fætn], *v.t.* engraisser; (*fig.*) enrichir.

fattening [ˈfætniŋ], *a.* engraissant.—*n.* engraissement, *m.*

fatty [ˈfæti], *a.* graisseux.

fatuous [ˈfætjuəs], *a.* sot; béat.

fatuousness [ˈfætjuəsnis], *n.* fatuité, *f.*

fault [fɔːlt], *n.* faute, *f.*; défaut, vice, *m.*; (*Geol.*) faille, *f.*

faultless [ˈfɔːltlis], *a.* sans défaut, sans faute, impeccable.

faultlessly [ˈfɔːltlisli], *adv.* irréprochablement.

faultlessness [ˈfɔːltlisnis], *n.* perfection, *f.*

faulty [ˈfɔːlti], *a.* fautif, blâmable, défectueux.

favor [ˈfeivə], *n.* faveur, *f.*, bonnes grâces, *f.pl.*; bienfait, *m.*; grâce (*permission*), *f.*; couleurs, faveurs (*rubans*), *f.pl.*; (*Comm.*) honorée, *f.*—*v.t.* favoriser, honorer (*de*).

favorable [ˈfeivərəbl], *a.* favorable.

favorably [ˈfeivərəbli], *adv.* favorablement.

favorite [ˈfeivərit], *a.* favori, préféré.—*n.* favori, *m.*

fawn [fɔːn], *n.* faon, *m.*—*v.i.* *to fawn upon,* caresser, flatter.

fawning [ˈfɔːniŋ], *a.* flatteur, servile.—*n.* caresse, flatterie, *f.*

fear [fiə], *n.* crainte, peur; inquiétude, *f.*; *for fear of,* de peur de.—*v.t.* craindre, redouter, avoir peur de.—*v.i.* craindre, avoir peur.

fearful [ˈfiəful], *a.* craintif, timide; terrible, affreux, effrayant.

fearless [ˈfiəlis], *a.* sans peur, intrépide.

fearlessly [ˈfiəlisli], *adv.* sans crainte, avec intrépidité.

feasible [ˈfiːzəbl], *a.* faisable, praticable.

feast [fiːst], *n.* festin, *m.*; fête, *f.*; régal, *m.*—*v.t.* fêter, régaler.—*v.i.* faire festin, se régaler.

feat [fiːt], *n.* exploit, fait, haut fait, *m.*

feather [ˈfeðə], *n.* plume; penne (*aile et queue d'oiseau*), *f.*; (*Mil.*) plumet, *m.*—*v.t.* orner d'une plume; *to feather one's nest,* faire sa pelote.

feature [ˈfiːtʃə], *n.* trait, *m.*; (*pl.*) visage, *m.* figure; (*fig.*) spécialité, *f.*

February [ˈfebruəri]. février, *m.*

feckless [ˈfeklis], *a.* faible, veule.

fecundity [fəˈkʌnditi], *n.* fécondité, *f.*

federal [ˈfedərəl], *a.* fédéral.

federate [ˈfedərit], *a.* fédéré.—[ˈfedəreit], *v.t.* fédérer.—*v.i.* se fédérer.

federation [fedəˈreiʃən], *n.* fédération, *f.*

fee [fiː], *n.* honoraires, *m.pl.*; cachet, salaire; (*Eccles. etc.*) droit, *m.*

feeble [fiːbl], *a.* faible; débile.

feebleness [ˈfiːblnis], *n.* faiblesse, *f.*

feebly [ˈfiːbli], *adv.* faiblement.

feed [fiːd], *n.* nourriture; pâture, *f.*, pâturage (*pour bestiaux*), *m.*—*v.t. irr.* nourrir; donner à manger à; paître, faire paître (*bestiaux*); (*pop.*) *to be fed up,* en avoir marre.—*v.i.* se nourrir; paître (*animaux*).

feed-back [ˈfiːdbæk], *n.* (*Rad.*) rétro-action, *f.*

feeding [ˈfiːdiŋ], *n.* nourriture; pâture (*pour bestiaux*), *f.*

feeding bottle [ˈfiːdiŋbɔtl], *n.* biberon, *m.*

feel [fiːl], *v.t. irr.* tâter, toucher, sentir; éprouver; *to feel one's way,* avancer à tâtons.—*v.i.* sentir, se sentir; se trouver; *to feel cold,* avoir froid; *to feel like doing something,* avoir envie de faire quelque chose.—*n.* toucher; attouchement; tact, *m.*

feeler [ˈfiːlə], *n.* antenne (*d'insecte*), *f.*; (*fig.*) ballon d'essai, *m.*

feeling [ˈfiːliŋ], *a.* tendre, touchant.—*n.* toucher; sentiment, *m.*, sensibilité, émotion, *f.*

feet [FOOT].

feign [fein], *v.t.* feindre, simuler.—*v.i.* feindre, faire semblant (*de*).

feigned [feind], *a.* feint, simulé.

feint [feint], *n.* feinte, *f.*—*v.i.* feinter.

felicitate [fiˈlisiteit], *v.t.* féliciter.

felicitation [filisiˈteiʃən], *n.* félicitation, *f.*

felicity [fiˈlisiti], *n.* félicité, *f.*, bonheur, *m.*

fell (1) [fel], *v.t.* abattre, assommer, terrasser.

fell (2) [fel], *past* [FALL].

fellow ['felou], *n.* compagnon, camarade, confrère; associé, membre; pendant, pareil (*choses*); (*colloq.*) garçon; individu, type, *m.*; **good fellow**, brave type.

fellow citizen ['felou'sitizn], *n.* concitoyen, *m.*

fellow countryman ['felou'kʌntrimən], *n.* (*pl.* **-men** [men]) compatriote, *m.*

fellow feeling ['felou'fi:liŋ], *n.* sympathie, *f.*

fellowship ['felouʃip], *n.* société, association; camaraderie, *f.*

fellow traveller ['felou'trævlə], *n.* compagnon de voyage; (*Polit.*) sympathisant communiste, communisant, *m.*

felon ['felən], *a.* félon, traître.—*n.* criminel, *m.*

felony ['feləni], *n.* crime, *m.*

felt (1) [felt], *n.* feutre, chapeau de feutre, *m.*; **roofing felt**, carton bitumé, *m.*

felt (2) [felt], *past* [FEEL].

female ['fi:meil], *a.* féminin, de femme; femelle (*animaux*); **a female friend**, une amie.—*n.* femme; jeune personne; femelle (*animaux*), *f.*

feminine ['feminin], *a.* féminin.

fen [fen], *n.* marais, marécage, *m.*

fence [fens], *n.* clôture, enceinte; palissade, barrière; (*Turf*) haie; (*Spt.*) escrime (*à l'épée*); (*fig.*) défense, *f.*; (*slang*) receleur (*d'objets volés*), *m.*; **to sit on the fence**, (*fig.*) ne pas s'engager, ménager la chèvre et le chou.—*v.t.* enclore, mettre une clôture à, palissader; (*fig.*) protéger.—*v.i.* faire des armes.

fencing ['fensiŋ], *n.* (*Spt.*) escrime; enceinte, clôture, *f.*

fencing master ['fensiŋma:stə], *n.* maître d'armes, *m.*

fend [fend], *v.t.* **to fend off**, parer.—*v.i.* **to fend for oneself**, se débrouiller, veiller à ses intérêts.

fender ['fendə], *n.* garde-feu, *m.*; (*Naut.*) défense, *f.*; (*Am. Motor.*) pare-boue, *m.*

ferment ['fə:mənt], *n.* ferment, *m.*; fermentation, *f.*—[fə:'ment], *v.t.* faire fermenter.—*v.i.* fermenter.

fermentation [fə:mən'teiʃən], *n.* fermentation, *f.*

fern [fə:n], *n.* fougère, *f.*

ferocious [fə'rouʃəs], *a.* féroce.

ferociously [fə'rouʃəsli], *adv.* avec férocité.

ferocity [fə'rɔsiti], *n.* férocité, *f.*

ferret ['ferit], *n.* furet, *m.*—*v.t.* fureter; **to ferret out**, dépister, dénicher.

ferrule ['feru:l], *n.* virole (*anneau*), *f.*

ferry ['feri], *v.t.* passer en bac.—*n.* bac, passage, *m.*; **air ferry**, avion transbordeur, *m.*

ferry-boat ['feribout], *n.* bac, bateau transbordeur de trains, *m.*

fertile ['fə:tail], *a.* fertile, fécond.

fertility [fə'tiliti], *n.* fertilité, fécondité, *f.*

fertilize ['fə:tilaiz], *v.t.* fertiliser.

fertilizer ['fə:tilaizə], *n.* fertilisant, engrais, *m.*

fervent ['fə:vənt], *a.* ardent, fervent, vif.

fervently ['fə:vəntli], *adv.* ardemment, avec ferveur.

fester ['festə], *v.i.* s'ulcérer; (*fig.*) se corrompre.—*n.* abcès, *m.*, pustule, *f.*

festival ['festivl], *a.* de fête, joyeux.—*n.* fête, *f.*; (*Mus., Theat.*) festival, *m.*

festive ['festiv], *a.* de fête, joyeux.

festivity [fes'tiviti], *n.* fête, *f.*; réjouissances, *f.pl.*

festoon [fes'tu:n], *n.* feston, *m.*—*v.t.* festonner (*de*).

fetch [fetʃ], *v.t.* chercher, aller chercher; apporter (*choses*); amener (*personnes etc.*); rapporter (*prix*).—*n.* ruse, *f.*; tour, *m.*

fête [feit], *n.* fête, *f.*—*v.t.* fêter.

fetlock ['fetlɔk], *n.* fanon (de cheval), *m.*

fetter ['fetə], *v.t.* entraver, enchaîner.

fetters ['fetəz], *n.pl.* (*fig.*) fers, *m.pl.*, chaînes; entraves (*de cheval*), *f.pl.*

fettle [fetl], *v.t.* arranger, préparer.—*n.* bon état, *m.*

feud [fju:d], *n.* querelle; vendetta, *f.*

feudal ['fju:dl], *a.* féodal.

feudalism ['fju:dlizm], *n.* féodalité, *f.*

fever ['fi:və], *n.* fièvre, *f.*

feverish ['fi:vəriʃ], *a.* fiévreux; (*fig.*) fébrile.

few [fju:], *a.* peu de; **a few**, quelques.—*n.* peu de gens, *m.pl.*; **a few**, quelques-uns, *m.pl.*, quelques-unes, *f.pl.*

fewer ['fju:ə], *a.* moins (*de*); moins nombreux.

fiasco [fi'æskou], *n.* fiasco, four, *m.*

fib [fib], *n.* petit mensonge, *m.*—*v.i.* mentir.

fibber ['fibə], *n.* menteur, *m.*

fibre ['faibə], *n.* fibre, *f.*

fibrositis [faibrə'saitis], *n.* (*Med.*) cellulite, *f.*

fibrous ['faibrəs], *a.* fibreux.

fickle [fikl], *a.* volage, inconstant.

fickleness ['fiklnis], *n.* inconstance, légèreté, *f.*

fiction ['fikʃən], *n.* fiction, *f.*; **works of fiction**, romans, *m.pl.*

fictitious [fik'tiʃəs], *a.* fictif, imaginaire; (*fig.*) faux, factice.

fiddle [fidl], *n.* violon; (*pej.*) crincrin, *m.*; (*pop.*) resquille, combine, *f.*—*v.i.* jouer du violon; (*fig.*) niaiser (*baguenauder*); (*pop.*) resquiller.

fiddler ['fidlə], *n.* joueur de violon; ménétrier, *m.*

fiddlesticks! ['fidlstiks], *int.* bah! quelle blague!

fidelity [fi'deliti], *n.* fidélité, *f.*

fidget ['fidʒit], *n.* agitation, *f.*; être remuant (*personne*), *m.*—*v.i.* se remuer, s'agiter.

fidgety ['fidʒiti], *a.* remuant, agité; ennuyeux (*gênant*).

field [fi:ld], *n.* champ; pré, *m.*, prairie; (*Mil.*) campagne, *f.*; champ de bataille, *m.*; (*Turf etc.*) courants, *m.pl.*; **in the scientific field**, dans le domaine des sciences.—*v.t.* (*Cricket*) arrêter (*une balle*); réunir (*équipe*).—*v.i.* (*Cricket*) tenir le champ.

field day ['fi:lddei], *n.* (*Mil.*) jour de manœuvres; (*fig.*) jour de grand succès, *m.*

field marshal ['fi:ldma:ʃl], *n.* maréchal, *m.*

fiend [fi:nd], *n.* démon, *m.*

fiendish ['fi:ndiʃ], *a.* diabolique, infernal.

fierce [fiəs], *a.* féroce, farouche, furieux.

fiercely ['fiəsli], *adv.* férocement, furieusement.

fierceness ['fiəsnis], *n.* violence, fureur, brutalité, *f.*; (*fig.*) acharnement, *m.*

fieriness ['faiərinis], *n.* fougue, ardeur, *f.*

fiery ['faiəri], *a.* de feu; (*fig.*) ardent, fougueux.

fife [faif], *n.* fifre, *m.*

fifteen [fif'ti:n], *a.* and *n.* quinze, *m.*

fifteenth [fif'ti:nθ], *a.* quinze (*jour du mois, roi etc.*).—*n.* quinzième (*fraction*), *m.*

fifth [fifθ], *a.* cinquième; cinq (*jour du mois, roi etc.*); ***Charles the Fifth***, Charles-Quint.—*n.* cinquième (*fraction*), *m.*; (*Mus.*) quinte, *f.*

fiftieth ['fiftiəθ], *a.* cinquantième.—*n.* cinquantième (*fraction*), *m.*

fifty ['fifti], *a.* and *n.* cinquante, *m.*; ***about fifty***, une cinquantaine.

fig [fig], *n.* figue, *f.*; figuier (*arbre*), *m.*

fight [fait], *v.t. irr.* se battre avec, combattre; livrer (*une bataille*).—*v.i.* se battre; combattre (*avec*).—*n.* combat, *m.*, bataille; (*fig.*) lutte, *f.*

fighter ['faitə], *n.* combattant; (*pej.*) batailleur; (*Av.*) chasseur, *m.*

fighting ['faitiŋ], *n.* combat, *m.*; lutte, *f.*

figment ['figmənt], *n.* fiction, invention, *f.*

figurative ['figjuərətiv], *a.* figuré; figuratif.

figuratively ['figjuərətivli], *adv.* au figuré; figurativement.

figure ['figə], *n.* figure; taille, tournure (*d'une personne*), *f.*; dessin (*sur un tissu*); (*Arith.*) chiffre, *m.*; ***figure of speech***, figure de rhétorique, métaphore; (*fam.*) façon de parler, *f.*; ***to cut a figure***, faire figure.—*v.t.* figurer, former; façonner; (*fig.*) imaginer; ***to figure out***, calculer.—*v.i.* figurer.

figure-head ['figəhed], *n.* (*Naut.*) figure de proue, *f.*; (*fig.*) homme de paille; prête-nom, *m.*

Fiji ['fi:dʒi:], **the Fiji Islands**, les îles Fidji *ou* Viti, *f.pl.*

filament ['filəmənt], *n.* filament, *m.*

filbert ['filbət], *n.* aveline, grosse noisette, *f.*

filch [filtʃ], *v.t.* escamoter, filouter, chiper.

file [fail], *n.* lime (*outil*); liasse, *f.*, dossier, classeur (*de papiers*), *m.*; liste; collection (*de journaux*); (*Mil.*) file; (*Theat. etc.*) queue, *f.*; ***card-index file***, fichier, *m.*—*v.t.* limer, affiler; mettre en liasse; (*Law*) déposer (*une requête etc.*); ***to file away***, classer.—*v.i.* (*Mil.*) marcher à la file; ***to file off*** or ***past***, défiler.

filial ['filiəl], *a.* filial.

filibuster ['filibʌstə], *n.* flibustier, *m.*

filing ['failiŋ], *n.* limage, *m.*; mise en liasse, *f.*, classement, *m.*; (*pl.*) limaille, *f.*

filing cabinet ['failiŋkæbinit], *n.* cartonnier, classeur, *m.*

fill [fil], *v.t.* emplir, remplir; combler (*jusqu'au bord*); occuper; rassasier; ***to fill a tooth***, plomber une dent.—*v.i.* se remplir, s'emplir. —*n.* suffisance, *f.*; (*colloq.*) ***one's fill***, tout son soûl.

fillet ['filit], *n.* bandeau; filet (*de poisson*), *m.*

filling ['filiŋ], *a.* rassasiant.—*n.* plombage, *m.*

filling station ['filiŋ'steiʃən], *n.* poste d'essence, *m.*

filly ['fili], *n.* pouliche, *f.*

film [film], *n.* taie (*devant les yeux*), pellicule; (*Anat.*) tunique, *f.*; (*fig.*) nuage, voile, *m.*; (*Phot.*) pellicule, couche sensible, *f.*; (*Cine.*) film, *m.*; ***film script***, scénario, script, *m.*; ***film star***, vedette de cinéma, *f.*—*v.t.* couvrir d'une tunique, d'une pellicule etc.; filmer, mettre à l'écran.—*v.i.* tourner un film.

film-strip ['filmstrip], *n.* film fixe, *m.*

filter ['filtə], *n.* filtre, *m.*—*v.t.* filtrer.

filter top ['filtə'tip], *n.* bout filtrant, *m.*

filth [filθ], *n.* ordure, saleté; (*fig.*) corruption, *f.*

filthy ['filθi], *a.* sale, immonde; (*fig.*) obscène, infect.

fin [fin], *n.* nageoire, *f.*; aileron (*de requin*), *m.*; (*Naut., Av.*) dérive; (*Motor.*) ailette (*de radiateur*), *f.*

final [fainl], *a.* final, dernier; décisif.—*n.* (*Spt.*) finale, *f.*

finally ['fainəli], *adv.* enfin, finalement; définitivement.

finance [fi'næns, fai'næns], *n.* finance, *f.*

financial [fi'nænʃəl], *a.* financier.

financier [fi'nænsiə], *n.* financier, *m.*

finch [fintʃ], *n.* (*Orn.*) pinson, *m.*

find [faind], *v.t. irr.* trouver; estimer; (*Law*) déclarer (*coupable*); prononcer (*un verdict*); (*fig.*) pourvoir; ***to find out***, trouver, découvrir, inventer, résoudre; démasquer; ***to find out about***, se renseigner sur; découvrir la vérité de.—*n.* découverte, trouvaille, *f.*

finding ['faindiŋ], *n.* (*Law*) verdict, *m.*

fine (1) [fain], *n.* amende, *f.*—*v.t.* mettre à l'amende.

fine (2) [fain], *a.* fin; raffiné; subtil; beau (*à voir*); (*fig.*) bon, accompli; (*colloq.*) fameux; ***it is fine***, il fait beau (*temps*).

fine arts [fain'a:ts], *n.pl.* beaux arts, *m.pl.*

finely ['fainli], *adv.* fin, délicatement; élégamment; (*colloq.*) bien; (*iron.*) joliment.

fineness ['fainnis], *n.* finesse, délicatesse, *f.*

finery ['fainəri], *n.* parure, *f.*, beaux habits, *m.pl.*

finesse [fi'nes], *n.* finesse, *f.*

finger ['fiŋgə], *n.* doigt, *m.*; (*fig.*) main, *f.*—*v.t.* toucher, manier.—*v.i.* (*Mus.*) doigter.

fingering ['fiŋgəriŋ], *n.* maniement; (*Mus.*) doigté, *m.*

finger-nail ['fiŋgəneil], *n.* ongle de la main, *m.*

finger-print ['fiŋgəprint], *n.* empreinte digitale, *f.*

finger-stall ['fiŋgəstɔ:l], *n.* doigtier, *m.*

finical ['finikl], **finicking** ['finikiŋ], (*colloq.*) **finicky** ['finiki], *a.* précieux, méticuleux, vétilleux.

finish ['finiʃ], *v.t.* finir, terminer; achever; (*Tech.*) usiner.—*v.i.* cesser, finir, prendre fin.—*n.* fini, *m.*; (*fig.*) fin; (*Spt.*) arrivée, *f.*

finished ['finiʃt], *a.* fini; (*fig.*) parfait.

finishing ['finiʃiŋ], *a.* dernier; (*Spt.*) ***finishing line***, ligne d'arrivée, *f.*

finite ['fainait], *a.* fini, borné.

Finland ['finlənd], la Finlande, *f.*

Finn [fin], *n.* Finlandais, Finnois, *m.*

Finnish ['finiʃ], *a.* finlandais.—*n.* finnois (*langue*), *m.*

fir [fə:], *n.* sapin; bois de sapin, *m.*

fir cone ['fə:koun], *n.* pomme de pin, *f.*

fire [faiə], *n.* feu; incendie (*accidentel*), *m.*; (*fig.*) ardeur, *f.*; ***fire!*** au feu! ***to be on fire***, être en feu; ***to catch fire***, prendre feu; ***to hang fire***, faire long feu; ***to miss fire***, rater; ***to set on fire***, ***to set fire to***, mettre le feu à.—*v.t.* mettre le feu à; embraser, incendier; tirer (*fusil*); (*pop.*) renvoyer.—*v.i.* prendre feu; tirer; (*Motor.*) donner; ***fire !*** (*Mil.*) feu!

fire alarm ['faiərəla:m], *n.* avertisseur d'incendie, *m.*

fire-arms ['faiəra:mz], *n.pl.* armes à feu, *f.pl.*

fire brigade ['faiəbrigeid], · *n.* (corps de) sapeurs pompiers, *m.*

fire engine ['faiərendʒin], *n.* pompe à incendie, *f.*

fire escape ['faiəriskeip], *n.* échelle de sauvetage, *f.*

fire extinguisher ['faiərikstingwiʃə], *n.* extincteur, *m.*

fire-fly ['faiəflai], *n.* luciole, *f.*

fire-guard ['faiəga:d], *n.* garde-feu, *m.*

fireman ['faiəmən], *n.* (*pl.* **-men** [men]) pompier, *m.*

fireplace ['faiəpleis], *n.* cheminée, *f.*, foyer, âtre, *m.*

fireproof ['faiəpru:f], *a.* incombustible, ignifuge.

fireside ['faiəsaid], *n.* coin du feu; (*fig.*) foyer domestique, *m.*

fire station ['faiəsteiʃən], *n.* caserne de pompiers, *f.*

fireworks ['faiəwə:ks], *n.pl.* feu d'artifice, *m.*

firing ['faiəriŋ], *n.* action d'incendier, *f.*; chauffage (*heating*), *m.*; cuisson (*de poterie etc.*), *f.*; combustible (*fuel*); (*Mil.*) feu, tir, *m.*, fusillade, *f.*

firm [fə:m], *a.* ferme, solide; constant.—*n.* maison de commerce, raison sociale, firme, *f.*

firmament ['fə:məmənt], *n.* firmament, *m.*

firmly ['fə:mli], *adv.* fermement, solidement.

firmness ['fə:mnis], *n.* fermeté, solidité, *f.*

first [fə:st], *a.* premier; (*in compounds*) unième; **twenty-first**, vingt et unième.—*n.* (le) premier, *m.*, (la) première, *f.*—*adv.* premièrement; **at first**, d'abord.

first aid ['fə:st'eid], *n.* premiers secours, *m.pl.*; **first-aid post**, poste de secours, *m.*

first-born ['fə:stbɔ:n], *a.* premier-né, aîné.

first-class ['fə:st'kla:s], **first-rate** ['fə:st'reit], *a.* de premier ordre; de premier choix; (*colloq.*) de première force; **first-class compartment**, compartiment de première classe, *m.*

firth [fə:θ], *n.* (*Sc.*) estuaire, *m.*

fiscal ['fiskəl], *a.* fiscal.

fiscally ['fiskəli], *adv.* fiscalement.

fish [fiʃ], *n.* poisson, *m.*; **a pretty kettle of fish**, un beau gâchis; **a queer fish**, un drôle de type.—*v.t.* pêcher.—*v.i.* pêcher; **to fish for**, pêcher; (*fig.*) rechercher, quêter.

fish bone ['fiʃboun], *n.* arête, *f.*

fisher ['fiʃə], **fisherman** ['fiʃəmən] (*pl.* **-men** [men]), *n.* pêcheur, *m.*

fishery ['fiʃəri], *n.* pêche; pêcherie, *f.*

fish-hook ['fiʃhuk], *n.* hameçon.

fishing ['fiʃiŋ], *n.* pêche, *f.*; **to go fishing**, aller à la pêche.

fishing boat ['fiʃiŋbout], *n.* bateau de pêche, *m.*

fishing rod ['fiʃiŋrɔd], *n.* canne à pêche, *f.*

fish knife ['fiʃnaif], *n.* couteau à poisson, *m.*

fishmonger ['fiʃmʌŋgə], *n.* marchand de poisson, *m.*

fish-slice ['fiʃslais], *n.* truelle à poisson, *f.*

fishy ['fiʃi], *a.* de poisson, poissonneux; qui sent le poisson; (*slang*) louche, véreux.

fission ['fiʃən], *n.* (*Biol.*) fissiparité, *f.*; (*Phys.*) fission, désintégration, *f.*; **nuclear fission**, fission nucléaire.

fissure ['fiʃə], *n.* fissure, fente, *f.*

fist [fist], *n.* poing, *m.*

fisted ['fistid], *a.* **close-fisted**, avare, dur à la détente.

fisticuffs ['fistikʌfs], *n.pl.* coups de poing, *m.pl.*

fit (1) [fit], *n.* accès (*de colère etc.*), *m.*; attaque (*de maladie*); convulsion, *f.*; **by fits and starts**, à bâtons rompus, par accès.

fit (2) [fit], *a.* propre, bon, convenable (*à*); juste, à propos; capable (*de*); en bonne santé, en forme; **to think fit**, juger convenable, juger bon.—*n.* ajustement (*de vêtements*), *m.*; (*fig.*) coupe, forme, *f.*—*v.t.* convenir à; aller à (*vêtements*); habiller; adapter, ajuster (*un navire*).—*v.i.* convenir; s'adapter (*à*), aller bien (*vêtements*); **to fit in with**, s'accorder avec.

fitful ['fitful], *a.* agité; capricieux; irrégulier.

fitfully ['fitfuli], *adv.* par boutades; irrégulièrement.

fitly ['fitli], *adv.* à propos, convenablement.

fitness ['fitnis], *n.* convenance, *f.*; à-propos, *m.*; **physical fitness**, bonne forme, *f.*

fitter ['fitə], *n.* ajusteur, *m.*; (*Dress.*) essayeur, *m.*

fitting ['fitiŋ], *a.* convenable, à propos, juste. —*n.* ajustement, essayage, *m.*, (*pl.*) garniture, *f.*

five [faiv], *a.* and *n.* cinq, *m.*

fix [fiks], *v.t.* fixer, attacher, arrêter, établir; (*colloq.*) réparer.—*v.i.* se fixer.—*n.* difficulté, impasse, *f.*, embarras, *m.*

fixation [fik'seiʃən], *n.* fixation, *f.*

fixed [fikst], *a.* fixe, fixé.

fixedly ['fiksidli], *adv.* fixement.

fixture ['fikstʃə], *n.* meuble à demeure, *m.*, agencements fixes, *m.pl.*; match, engagement (*prévu, annoncé*), *m.*

fizzy ['fizi], *a.* gazeux (*limonade etc.*), mousseux (*vin*).

flabby ['flæbi], *a.* flasque; mollasse (*personne*).

flag (1) [flæg], *v.i.* pendre mollement; se relâcher, faiblir; s'affaisser.

flag (2) [flæg], *n.* drapeau; (*Naut.*) pavillon, iris (*plante*); carreau, *m.*, dalle (*pierre*), *f.*—*v.t.* pavoiser; daller; pavoiser.

flag day ['flægdei], *n.* jour de quête, *m.*

flag officer ['flægɔfisə], *n.* chef d'escadre, *m.*

flagon ['flægən], *n.* flacon, *m.*; burette (*d'église*), *f.*

flagrancy ['fleigrənsi], *n.* énormité, notoriété, *f.*

flagrant ['fleigrənt], *a.* flagrant, notoire, énorme.

flag-ship ['flægʃip], *n.* vaisseau amiral, *m.*

flagstaff ['flægsta:f], *n.* mât de pavillon, *m.*

flagstone ['flægstoun], *n.* dalle, *f.*

flail [fleil], *n.* fléau, *m.*

flair [fleə], *n.* perspicacité, *f.*, flair, *m.*; aptitude (*à*), *f.*

flake [fleik], *n.* flocon, *m.*; écaille; étincelle, *f.*—*v.t.* former en flocons, écailler.—*v.i.* s'écailler.

flaky ['fleiki], *a.* floconneux; écaillé; feuilleté (*pâtisserie*).

flame [fleim], *n.* flamme, *f.*; feu, *m.*—*v.i.* flamber.

flaming ['fleimiŋ], *a.* flamboyant, flambant; (*fig.*) violent, ardent; (*pop.*) sacré.

flamingo [flə'miŋgou], *n.* (*Orn.*) flamant, *m.*

flan [flæn], *n.* flan, *m.*

Flanders ['fla:ndəz], la Flandre, *f.*

flange

flange [flændʒ], *n.* bride, *f.*, rebord (*d'un tube etc.*); (*Tech.*) boudin (*de roue*), *m.*; (*Motor.*) ailette, collerette, *f.*

flank [flæŋk], *n.* flanc; côté, *m.*—*v.t.* flanquer (*de*); (*Mil.*) prendre en flanc.—*v.i.* border.

flannel [flænl], *a.* de flanelle.—*n.* flanelle, *f.*; (*pl.*) pantalon de flanelle, *m.*

flap [flæp], *v.t.* frapper légèrement; battre, agiter.—*v.i.* battre légèrement; (*fig., pop.*) s'affoler.—*n.* battement (*d'aile*); claquement (*de voile*); petit coup (*de la main*), *m.*, tape, *f.*; battant (*d'une table etc.*), *m.*; patte (*d'une poche*), *f.*, pan (*d'un habit*); rabat (*d'une enveloppe*); (*fig., pop.*) affolement, *m.*

flare [flɛə], *v.i.* flamboyer; s'évaser (*jupe*); **to flare up,** flamber; (*fig.*) se mettre en colère.—*n.* flamme, *f.*; (*Av.*) brûlot, *m.*

flash [flæʃ], *n.* éclair, éclat, jet de lumière; (*fig.*) trait; (*Mil.*) écusson, *m.*—*v.t.* faire jaillir, lancer.—*v.i.* luire, éclater, étinceler.

flashy [flæʃi], *a.* voyant, clinquant; superficiel.

flask [flɑːsk], *n.* flacon, *m.*, gourde, *f.*

flat [flæt], *a.* plat; étendu (*à terre*); éventé (*vin etc.*); (*Comm.*) languissant; (*Mus.*) bémol; grave (*son*); (*fig.*) net, clair; fade, insipide (*goût*).—*n.* surface plane, *f.*; étage (*d'une maison*), appartement; (*Mus.*) bémol; (*Theat.*) châssis, *m.*

flat-iron [flætaiən], *n.* fer à repasser, *m.*

flatly [flætli], *adv.* à plat; (*fig.*) nettement, clairement.

flatten [flætn], *v.t.* aplatir, aplanir; éventer (*boisson alcoolique*); (*fig.*) abattre, attrister; (*Mus.*) rendre grave.—*v.i.* s'aplatir; s'éventer (*boisson alcoolique*).

flatter [flætə], *v.t.* flatter.

flatterer [flætərə], *n.* flatteur, *m.*

flattering [flætəriŋ], *a.* flatteur.

flattery [flætəri], *n.* flatterie, *f.*

flatulence [flætjuləns], *n.* flatuosité; flatulence, *f.*

flatulent [flætjulənt], *a.* flatueux.

flaunt [flɔːnt], *v.t.* faire parade de, étaler, déployer.—*v.i.* se pavaner, parader, flotter.—*n.* étalage, *m.*, parade, *f.*

flavor [fleivə], *n.* saveur, *f.*; goût, fumet (*de viande*); arome (*de thé, café etc.*); bouquet (*de vin*), *m.*—*v.t.* donner du goût, un arome etc. à, assaisonner (*de*).

flavoring [fleivəriŋ], *n.* assaisonnement, *m.*

flaw [flɔː], *n.* défaut, *m.*; fêlure, brèche, fente; paille (*de pierres précieuses*), *f.*

flawless [flɔːlis], *a.* parfait, sans défaut.

flax [flæks], *a.* de lin.—*n.* lin, *m.*

flaxen [flæksən], *a.* de lin; blond filasse (*cheveux*).

flay [flei], *v.t.* écorcher.

flaying [fleiiŋ], *n.* écorchement, *m.*

flea [fliː], *n.* puce, *f.*

fleck [flek], *n.* tache, moucheture, marque, *f.*—*v.t.* moucheter, tacheter (*de*).

fledg(e)ling [fledʒliŋ], *n.* oisillon, *m.*

flee [fliː], *v.t. irr.* fuir, éviter.—*v.i.* s'enfuir, se réfugier.

fleece [fliːs], *n.* toison, *f.*—*v.t.* tondre; (*fig.*) écorcher, plumer.

fleecy [fliːsi], *a.* laineux, (*fig.*) floconneux.

fleet (1) [fliːt], *n.* flotte, *f.*; **the Home Fleet,** la flotte métropolitaine.

fleet (2) [fliːt], *a.* vite, rapide, leste.

fleeting [fliːtiŋ], *a.* fugitif, passager.

Fleming [flemiŋ], *n.* Flamand, *m.*

Flemish [flemiʃ], *a.* flammand.—*n.* flamand (*langue*), *m.*

flesh [fleʃ], *n.* chair; viande (*meat*), *f.*; **in the flesh,** en chair et en os; **to put on flesh,** s'empâter, prendre de l'embonpoint.—*v.t.* (*Hunt.*) acharner; écharner (*peaux*).

fleshy [fleʃi], *a.* charnu.

flex (1) [fleks], *n.* fil électrique, *m.*

flex (2) [fleks], *v.t.* fléchir.

flexibility [fleksi'biliti], *n.* flexibilité, souplesse, *f.*

flexible [fleksibl], *a.* flexible, souple.

flick [flik], *n.* petit coup (*de fouet, de torchon*), *m.*; chiquenaude, *f.*; (*pl.*) (*pop.*) ciné, *m.*—*v.t.* effleurer; donner une chiquenaude à.

flicker [flikə], *v.i.* trembloter, vaciller (*lumière*); ciller (*paupières*).

flickering [flikəriŋ], *a.* vacillant, clignotant.—*n.* trémoussement; clignement, *m.*; vacillation, *f.*

flight [flait], *n.* vol, *m.*, volée (*d'oiseaux etc.*); fuite, *f.*; (*fig.*) élan, *m.*; (*Av.*) escadrille, *f.*; **flight of stairs,** escalier, *m.*; **flight of steps,** perron, *m.*; **in flight,** en déroute.

flightiness [flaitinis], *n.* légèreté, étourderie, *f.*

flighty [flaiti], *a.* étourdi, léger; volage.

flimsiness [flimzinis], *n.* légèreté; (*fig.*) mesquinerie, *f.*

flimsy [flimzi], *a.* mollasse, léger, sans consistance.

flinch [flintʃ], *v.i.* reculer, céder.

fling [fliŋ], *v.t. irr.* jeter, lancer.—*n.* coup (*lancé*), *m.*; ruade (*de cheval*), *f.*; pas seul (*danse écossaise*); (*fig.*) essai; trait, coup de patte, *m.*, raillerie, *f.*

flint [flint], *n.* silex, *m.*, pierre à briquet; (*fig.*) roche, dureté, *f.*

flip [flip], *n.* petit coup, *m.*, chiquenaude, *f.*; flip (*boisson*), *m.*

flippancy [flipənsi], *n.* ton léger; bavardage, *m.*

flippant [flipənt], *a.* léger; désinvolte; cavalier (*manières, mine*).

flipper [flipə], *n.* nageoire, *f.*

flirt [fləːt], *v.i.* faire la coquette, flirter (*femme*); conter fleurette (*homme*).—*n.* coquette, *f.*

flirtation [fləː'teiʃən], *n.* coquetterie, *f.*; flirt, *m.*

flit [flit], *v.i.* fuir, voltiger; (*Sc.*) déménager.—*n.* **to do a moonlight flit,** déménager à la cloche de bois.

float [flout], *v.t.* faire flotter, (*fig.*) lancer.—*v.i.* flotter, surnager; **to float on one's back,** faire la planche.—*n.* train (*bois*); flotteur; char (*carnaval*), *m.*

floating [floutiŋ], *a.* flottant; **floating capital,** fonds de roulement, *m.*; **floating dock,** bassin à flot, *m.*

flock [flɔk], *n.* troupeau, *m.*; bande, troupe, *f.*; ouailles (*paroissiens*), *f.pl.*; flocon, *m.*, bourre (*de laine etc.*), *f.*—*v.i.* s'attrouper, s'assembler.

floe [flou], *n.* nappe de glaçons flottants; banquise, *f.*

flog [flɔg], *v.t.* fouetter, flageller; (*pop.*) bazarder.

flogging [flɔgiŋ], *n.* fouet, *m.*; flagellation, *f.*

flood [flʌd], *n.* déluge, *m.*; inondation, crue, *f.*; (*fig.*) cours d'eau, torrent, *m.*; marée, *f.*—*v.t.* inonder, submerger, noyer.

flood-light ['flʌdlait], *n.* projecteur, *m.*—*v.t.* illuminer (*un monument*) avec des projecteurs.

flood tide ['flʌdtaid], *n.* marée montante, *f.*

floor [flɔ:], *n.* plancher; carreau, parquet (*pavage*), étage (*storey*), *m.*—*v.t.* planchéier, parqueter; (*fig.*) terrasser, réduire au silence.

flooring ['flɔ:riŋ], *n.* plancher, parquet, *m.*

floorwalker, see **shop-walker**.

flop [flɔp], *int.* plouf!—*n.* (*Theat.*) four, *m.*

floral ['flɔrəl, 'flɔ:rəl], *a.* floral; **floral games**, jeux floraux, *m.pl.*

Florence ['flɔrəns], Florence, *f.*

florid ['flɔrid], *a.* fleuri.

Florida ['flɔridə], la Floride, *f.*

florist ['flɔrist], *n.* fleuriste, *m., f.*

floss [flɔs], *n.* bourre (*de soie*), *f.*; (*Metal.*) floss; (*Bot.*) duvet, *m.*

flotilla [flo'tilə], *n.* flottille, *f.*

flounder (1) ['flaundə], *n.* (*Ichth.*) flet, pétit flétan, *m.*

flounder (2) ['flaundə], *v.i.* se débattre; patauger.

flour ['flauə], *n.* farine; fécule (*des pommes de terre etc.*), *f.*

flourish ['flʌriʃ], *n.* éclat, *m.*; fleur de rhétorique, *f.*; panache (*manières, geste*), moulinet, tour, *m.*; (*Mus.*) fioriture; fanfare (*trompettes*), *f.*—*v.t.* fleurir; parafer; brandir (*épée etc.*).—*v.i.* fleurir; venir bien (*plantes*); prospérer.

flourishing ['flʌriʃiŋ], *a.* florissant.

flout [flaut], *v.t.* railler; se moquer de.—*n.* moquerie, raillerie, *f.*

flow [flou], *v.i.* s'écouler, couler; monter (*marée*); (*fig.*) découler (*de*).—*n.* écoulement; flux; (*fig.*) épanchement, *m.*

flower ['flauə], *n.* fleur; (*fig.*) élite, *f.*—*v.i.* fleurir, être en fleur.

flower-bed ['flauəbed], *n.* plate-bande, *f.*, parterre, *m.*

flowered ['flauədl, *a.* figuré: fleuri.

flower garden ['flauəga:dn], *n.* jardin d'agrément, *m.*

flower-pot ['flauəpɔt], *n.* pot à fleurs, *m.*

flowing ['flouiŋ], *a.* coulant; (*fig.*) naturel.—*n.* cours, écoulement, *m.*

flown [floun], *a.* envolé; **high-flown**, gonflé, outré (*style*).

flu [flu:], (*colloq.*) [INFLUENZA].

fluctuate ['flʌktjueit], *v.i.* balancer, flotter, varier.

fluctuating ['flʌktjueitiŋ], *a.* flottant; incertain; variable.

fluctuation [flʌktju'eiʃən], *n.* fluctuation, *f.*; (*fig.*) balancement, doute, *m.*

flue [flu:], *n.* tuyau de cheminée; carneau (*d'un fourneau*), *m.*

fluency ['flu:ənsi], *n.* facilité (*de parole*), *f.*

fluent ['flu:ənt], *a.* coulant, courant; facile.

fluently ['flu:əntli], *adv.* couramment, avec facilité.

fluff [flʌf], *n.* duvet, *m.*, peluches, *f.pl.*

fluid ['flu:id], *a.* and *n.* fluide, liquide, *m.*

fluke [flu:k], *n.* patte (*d'ancre*), *f.*; carrelet (*poisson*); (*fig.*) coup de raccroc, *m.*

flunkey ['flʌŋki], *n.* laquais; (*colloq.*) sycophante, *m.*

flurry ['flʌri], *n.* agitation, *f.*, désordre, émoi, *m.*—*v.t.* agiter, ahurir.

flush [flʌʃ], *a.* frais, plein de vigueur; à fleur, au ras (*de niveau*); **flush with the ground**, à ras de terre.—*n.* rougeur, *f.*; transport, *m.*; chasse d'eau, *f.*; (*Cards*), flush, *m.*—*v.t.* faire rougir; laver à grande eau; (*Hunt.*) lever; (*fig.*) animer.—*v.i.* rougir; partir tout à coup.

fluster ['flʌstə], *v.t.* déconcerter, agiter, ahurir.—*n.* agitation, *f.*

flute [flu:t], *n.* flûte, *f.*

fluted ['flu:tid], *a.* cannelé.

flutter ['flʌtə], *n.* trémoussement, émoi, *m.*; agitation, *f.*; battement d'ailes, *m.*—*v.t.* mettre en désordre, agiter, ahurir.—*v.i.* battre des ailes; s'agiter; palpiter.

flux [flʌks], *n.* flux, courant; (*Metal.*) fondant, *m.*

fly (1) [flai], *n.* (*pl.* **flies** [flaiz]) (*Ent.*) mouche, *f.*

fly (2) [flai], *v.t. irr.* faire voler; fuir, éviter.—*v.i.* voler, s'envoler, se sauver, prendre la fuite, fuir s'enfuir; **to fly into a passion**, s'emporter, se mettre en colère; **to fly over**, survoler.—*a.* (*pop.*) malin.

flyer ['flaiə], *n.* aviateur, *m.*

flying ['flaiiŋ], *a.* volant; **flying squad**, brigade mobile, *f.*

flying boat ['flaiiŋbout], *n.* hydravion, *m.*

flying buttress ['flaiiŋ'bʌtris], *n.* arc-boutant, *m.*

fly-over ['flaiouvə], *n.* enjambement, *m.*

fly-paper ['flaipeipə], *n.* papier tue-mouches, *m.*

fly-past ['flaipɑ:st], *n.* défilé aérien, *m.*

foal [foul], *n.* poulain, *m.*, pouliche, *f.*—*v.i.* pouliner, mettre bas.

foam [foum], *n.* écume; bave; mousse, *f.*—*v.i.* écumer; moutonner (*mer*); baver (*animaux*).

foaming ['foumiŋ], *a.* écumant.

fob [fɔb], *n.* gousset (*de pantalon*), *m.*—*v.t.* (*fam.*) **to fob someone off with something**, refiler quelque chose à quelqu'un.

fo'c'sle [fouksl], [FORECASTLE].

focus ['foukəs], *n.* (*pl.* **foci** ['fousai], **focuses** ['foukəsiz]) foyer, *m.*—*v.t.* mettre au point.

fodder ['fɔdə], *n.* fourrage, *m.*, pâture, *f.*; **cannon fodder**, chair à canon, *f.*

foe [fou], *n.* ennemi, adversaire, *m.*

fog [fɔg], *n.* brouillard, *m.*; (*fig.*) perplexité, *f.*; **sea fog**, brume, *f.*

fog-bound ['fɔgbaund], *a.* enveloppé de brouillard; arrêté par le brouillard.

foggy ['fɔgi], *a.* brumeux; (*fig.*) sombre; **it is foggy**, il fait du brouillard.

fogy, fogey ['fougi], *n.* ganache, vieille perruque, *f.*

foil [fɔil], *n.* feuille de métal, *f.*; tain (*de miroir*), *m.*; défaite, *f.*, échec (*check*); contraste, repoussoir (*set off*); (*Fenc.*) fleuret, *m.* —*v.t.* déjouer, faire échouer; frustrer.

fold (1) [fould], *v.t.* plier, ployer; envelopper; serrer; **to fold one's arms**, croiser les bras. —*n.* pli, repli, *m.*; **threefold**, triple; **twofold**, double.

fold (2) [fould], *n.* parc (*à moutons*), *m.*, bergerie, *f.*—*v.t.* **to fold sheep**, parquer des moutons.

folder ['fouldə], *n.* chemise (*à documents*), *f.*; dépliant, prospectus, *m.*

folding ['fouldiŋ], *a.* pliant; brisé, à deux battants (*porte*).
foliage ['fouliidʒ], *n.* feuillage, *m.*
folio ['fouliou], *n.* in-folio, *m.*; page, *f.*, folio, *m.*
folk(s) [fouk(s)], *n.* (*pl.*) gens, *m.pl.*, *f.pl.*, personnes, *f.pl.*
folklore ['fouklɔː], *n.* folklore, *m.*, légendes, traditions populaires, *f.pl.*
folk song ['fouksɔŋ], *n.* chanson populaire, *f.*
follow ['fɔlou], *v.t.* suivre; poursuivre; observer, imiter; exercer (*une profession*).— *v.i.* s'ensuivre, résulter; *as follows*, comme suit.
follower ['fɔlouə], *n.* suivant; partisan; compagnon; (*colloq.*) amoureux, *m.*
following ['fɔlouiŋ], *a.* suivant.—*n.* suite, *f.*, parti, *m.*
folly ['fɔli], *n.* folie, sottise, bêtise, *f.*
foment [fo'ment], *v.t.* fomenter.
fond [fɔnd], *a.* passionné (*pour*); fou (*de*); indulgent (*pour*); doux, cher (*espoir*); vain, sot; *to be* (*passionately*) *fond of*, aimer (à la folie).
fondle [fɔndl], *v.t.* câliner, caresser.
fondly ['fɔndli], *adv.* tendrement.
fondness ['fɔndnis], *n.* tendresse; affection, *f.*; penchant, goût, *m.*
font [fɔnt], *n.* fonts baptismaux, *m.pl.*
food [fuːd], *n.* nourriture, *f.*, aliment. *m.*; vivres, *m.pl.*; denrées, *f.pl.*; pâture (*pour animaux*), *f.*
food-stuffs ['fuːdstʌfs], *n.pl.* comestibles, *m.pl.*
fool [fuːl], *n.* sot; insensé, imbécile, niais, *m.*; dupe, *f.*, fou (*bouffon*), *m.*; *to make a fool of*, se moquer de; *to make a fool of one-self*, se rendre ridicule, se faire moquer de soi.—*v.t.* duper; (*colloq.*) se moquer de.— *v.i.* faire la bête; *you are fooling*, vous plaisantez; vous blaguez.
foolery ['fuːləri], *n.* folie, sottise; niaiserie, *f.*
foolhardy ['fuːlhɑːdi], *a.* téméraire.
foolish ['fuːliʃ], *a.* sot, insensé, bête, ridicule.
foolishly ['fuːliʃli], *adv.* follement, sottement.
foolishness ['fuːliʃnis], *n.* folie, sottise, *f.*
foolproof ['fuːlpruːf], *a.* indéréglable.
foot [fut], *n.* (*pl.* **feet** [fiːt]) pied, *m.*; patte (*d'insectes etc.*); base (*de colonne*), *f.*; bas (*d'une page*), *m.*; (*Mil.*) infanterie, *f.*; *on foot*, à pied.
football ['futbɔːl], *n.* ballon; football (*jeu*), *m.*
foot-bridge ['futbridʒ], *n.* passerelle, *f.*
footfall ['futfɔːl], *n.* pas, bruit de pas, *m.*
foothold ['futhould], *n.* prise pour le pied, *f.*; (*fig.*) point d'appui, *m.*
footing ['futiŋ], *n.* pied, point d'appui; établissement. *m.*; position, *f.*; *on an equal footing*, sur un pied d'égalité.
footlights ['futlaits], *n.pl.* (*Theat.*) rampe, *f.*
footman ['futmən], *n.* (*pl.* **-men** [men]) laquais, valet de pied, *m.*
footnote ['futnout], *n.* note au bas de la page, apostille, *f.*
foot-path ['futpɑːθ], *n.* sentier; trottoir (*de rue*), *m.*
foot-print ['futprint] *n.* empreinte du pied, *f.*
foot soldier ['futsouldʒə], *n.* fantassin, *m.*
footstep ['futstep], *n.* pas, *m.*; trace, *f.*; vestige, *m.*
footstool ['futstuːl], *n.* tabouret, *m.*
footwear ['futwɛə], *n.* chaussures, *f.pl.*

fop [fɔp], *n.* fat, *m.*
foppery ['fɔpəri], *n.* affectation, fatuité, *f.*
foppish ['fɔpiʃ], *a.* affecté sot, fat.
for [fɔː], *prep.* pour, par; de, à, vers, pendant; depuis; en place de, en lieu de; en faveur de; à cause de, pour le compte de; malgré; pour avoir; pour que (*with subj.*).—*conj.* car.
forage ['fɔridʒ], *n.* fourrage, *m.*—*v.i.* fourrager.
***forasmuch** [fɔrəz'mʌtʃ], *conj.* *forasmuch as*, d'autant que, vu que.
foray ['fɔrei], *n.* incursion, razzia, *f.*, raid, *m.*
forbear (1) [FOREBEAR].
forbear (2) [fɔː'bɛə], *v.t. irr.* cesser; épargner, supporter.—*v.i.* s'abstenir, se garder (*de*).
forbearance [fɔː'bɛərəns], *n.* patience; indulgence, *f.*
forbid [fə'bid], *v.t. irr.* défendre, interdire (*de*); empêcher (*de*); *God forbid!* à Dieu ne plaise!
forbidding [fə'bidiŋ], *a.* rebutant, repoussant.
force [fɔːs], *n.* force; violence; efficacité; valeur, *f.*; (*Mil., pl.*) forces, *f.pl.*, armée, *f.*; *in force*, (*Law*) en vigueur.—*v.t.* forcer, contraindre (*à* ou *de*); violenter.
forced [fɔːst], *a.* forcé, contraint; guindé (*style*).
forcedly ['fɔːsidli], *adv.* de force.
forceps ['fɔːseps], *n.pl.* (*Surg.*) pince, *f.*, forceps, *m.*
forcible ['fɔːsibl], **forceful** ['fɔːsful], *a.* fort; énergique.
forcibly ['fɔːsibli], *adv.* par force; fortement.
ford [fɔːd], *n.* gué, *m.*—*v.t.* passer à gué, guéer.
fore! (1) [fɔː], *int.* (*Golf*) gare devant!
fore (2) [fɔː], *a.* antérieur, de devant; (*Naut.*) de misaine; *fore and aft*, (*Naut.*) de l'avant à l'arrière.—*adv.* d'avance; (*Naut.*) de l'avant.
forearm (1) [fɔːr'ɑːm], *v.t.* prémunir.
forearm (2) ['fɔːrɑːm], *n.* avant-bras, *m.*
forebear ['fɔːbɛə], *n.* aïeul, ancêtre, *m.*
forebode [fɔː'boud], *v.t.* présager, prédire, pressentir.
foreboding [fɔː'boudiŋ], *n.* présage, pressentiment, *m.*
forecast [fɔː'kɑːst], *n.* prévoyance, prévision, *f.*; pronostic, *m.*; *weather forecast*, prévisions météorologiques, *f.pl.*—*v.t.* prévoir; pronostiquer.
forecastle [fouksl, 'fɔːkɑːsl], *n.* gaillard d'avant, *m.*
fore-court ['fɔːkɔːt], *n.* avant-cour, *f.*
forefather ['fɔːfɑːðə], *n.* aïeul, ancêtre, *m.*
forefinger ['fɔːfiŋgə], *n.* index, *m.*
forego [fɔː'gou], *v.t.* précéder, aller devant.
foregone [fɔː'gɔːn], *a.* prévu, résolu, décidé d'avance.
foreground ['fɔːgraund], *n.* premier plan, *m.*
forehead ['fɔrid], *n.* front, *m.*
foreign ['fɔrin], *a.* étranger; *Foreign Office*, Ministère des Affaires Étrangères, *m.*
foreigner ['fɔrinə], *n.* étranger, *m.*
foreland ['fɔːlənd], *n.* promontoire, cap, *m.*
foreleg ['fɔːleg], *n.* patte de devant, *f.*
forelock ['fɔːlɔk], *n.* goupille, *f.*; toupet, *m.*
foreman ['fɔːmən], *n.* (*pl.* **-men** [men]) chef (*d'un jury*); contremaître; chef d'atelier *ou* d'équipe; brigadier, *m.*
foremast ['fɔːmɑːst], *n.* mât de misaine, *m.*

foremost ['fɔ:moust], *a.* premier; en tête, au premier rang; *first and foremost*, tout d'abord.

forenoon ['fɔ:nu:n], *n.* matin, *m.*, matinée, *f.*

forensic [fɔ'rensik], *a.* *forensic medicine*, médecine légale, *f.*

forerunner ['fɔ:rʌnə], *n.* précurseur, *m.*

foresee [fɔ'si:], *v.t. irr.* (*conjug. like* SEE) prévoir.

foreseeable [fɔ'si:əbl], *a.* prévisible.

foreshore ['fɔ:ʃɔ:], *n.* plage, *f.*

foreshorten [fɔ'ʃɔ:tn], *v.t.* (*Paint.*) dessiner en raccourci.

foreshortening [fɔ'ʃɔ:tniŋ], *n.* raccourci, *m.*

foresight ['fɔ:sait], *n.* prévoyance, *f.*; guidon (*d'arme à feu*), *m.*; *lack of foresight*, imprévoyance, *f.*

forest ['fɔrist], *a.* de forêt, forestier.—*n.* forêt, *f.*

forestall [fɔ:'stɔ:l], *v.t.* anticiper, devancer.

forester ['fɔristə], *n.* garde forestier; habitant d'une forêt, *m.*

forestry ['fɔristri], *n.* sylviculture, *f.*

foretaste ['fɔ:teist], *n.* avant-goût, *m.*; anticipation, *f.*

foretell [fɔ:'tel], *v.t. irr.* (*conjug. like* TELL) prédire.

forethought ['fɔ:θɔ:t], *n.* prévoyance, prescience, *f.*

forewarn [fɔ:'wɔ:n], *v.t.* prévenir, avertir.

foreword ['fɔ:wə:d], *n.* préface, *f.*; avant-propos, *m.*

forfeit ['fɔ:fit], *a.* confisqué; (*fig.*) perdu.—*n.* amende (*à payer*); forfaiture, confiscation, *f.*; (*Games*) gage, *m.*—*v.t.* forfaire (*à*); confisquer; perdre.

forfeiture ['fɔ:fitʃə], *n.* forfaiture, confiscation; perte, déchéance, *f.*

forgather [fɔ:'gæðə], *v.i.* s'assembler, se réunir.

forge [fɔ:dʒ], *n.* forge, *f.*—*v.t.* forger; contrefaire (*monnaie etc.*), fabriquer (*document etc.*).—*v.i.* commettre un faux; *to forge ahead*, pousser de l'avant.

forger ['fɔ:dʒə], *n.* faussaire; faux-monnayeur, *m.*

forgery ['fɔ:dʒəri], *n.* falsification; contrefaçon, *f.*; faux, *m.*

forget [fə'get], *v.t., v.i. irr.* oublier.

forgetful [fə'getful], *a.* oublieux.

forgetfulness [fə'getfulnis], *n.* oubli, manque de mémoire, *m.*; négligence, *f.*

forget-me-not [fə'getminɔt], *n.* myosotis, *m.*

forgive [fə'giv], *v.t. irr.* (*conjug. like* GIVE) pardonner, faire grâce de; pardonner à.

forgiveness [fə'givnis], *n.* pardon, *m.*; clémence, grâce, *f.*

forgiving [fə'giviŋ], *a.* clément, miséricordieux.

forgo [fɔ:'gou], *v.t. irr.* (*conjug. like* GO) renoncer à, s'abstenir de, se refuser à.

fork [fɔ:k], *n.* fourchette; fourche; bifurcation (*de rues*); pointe (*d'une flèche etc.*), *f.*; zigzag (*d'éclair*), *m.*—*v.t.* enlever avec une fourche.—*v.i.* fourcher; bifurquer.

forked [fɔ:kt], *a.* fourchu; (*Bot.*) bifurqué.

forlorn [fə'lɔ:n], *a.* abandonné, désespéré, délaissé.

forlornness [fə'lɔ:nnis], *n.* délaissement, abandon; état désespéré, *m.*

form [fɔ:m], *n.* forme, figure; formalité, *f.*; banc (*siège*), *m.*; (*Sch.*) classe, *f.*; gîte (*de lièvre*);

imprimé (*fiche*), *m.*—*v.t.* former, faire; façonner.—*v.i.* se former; se gîter (*lièvres*).

formal ['fɔ:məl], *a.* formel; pointilleux; affecté, cérémonieux, formaliste.

formality [fɔ:'mæliti], *n.* formalité, cérémonie, *f.*

formally ['fɔ:məli], *adv.* avec formalité, en forme, formellement.

formation [fɔ:'meiʃən], *n.* formation, *f.*; ordre, *m.*

formative ['fɔ:mətiv], *a.* formatif, formateur, plastique.

former ['fɔ:mə], *a.* précédent, passé; ancien; premier (*de deux*).—*pron.* celui-là, celle-là.—*n.* moule, *m.*

formerly ['fɔ:məli], *adv.* autrefois, auparavant; jadis.

formidable ['fɔ:midəbl], *a.* formidable, redoutable.

formless ['fɔ:mlis], *a.* informe, sans forme.

Formosa [fɔ:'mouzə]. Formose, *f.*

formula ['fɔ:mjulə], *n.* (*pl.* **formulæ** ['fɔ:mjul(a)i]) formule, *f.*

forsake [fə'seik], *v.t. irr.* délaisser, abandonner.

forsaking [fə'seikiŋ], *n.* délaissement, abandon, *m.*

*forsooth [fə'su:θ], *adv.* en vérité ma foi.

forswear [fɔ:'swɛə], *v.t. irr.* (*conjug. like* SWEAR) abjurer, répudier.—*v.i.* se parjurer.

fort [fɔ:t], *n.* fort, *m.*, forteresse, *f.*

forth [fɔ:θ], *adv.* en avant; au dehors; *and so forth*, et ainsi de suite.

forthcoming [fɔ:θ'kʌmiŋ], *a.* tout prêt, prêt à paraître; prochain, à venir.

forthright ['fɔ:θrait], *a.* franc, carré, brutal.

forthwith [fɔ:θ'wið], *adv.* incontinent, aussitôt, sur-le-champ, tout de suite.

fortieth ['fɔ:tiəθ], *a.* quarantième.—*n.* quarantième (*fraction*), *m.*

fortification [fɔ:tifi'keiʃən], *n.* fortification, *f.*

fortify ['fɔ:tifai], *v.t.* fortifier; munir (*de*).

fortifying ['fɔ:tifaiiŋ], *a.* (*fig.*) réconfortant, fortifiant.

fortitude ['fɔ:titju:d], *n.* force d'âme, *f.* courage, *m.*

fortnight ['fɔ:tnait], *n.* quinze jours, *m.pl.*, quinzaine, *f.*

fortnightly ['fɔ:tnaitli], *a.* bimensuel.—*adv.* tous les quinze jours.

fortress ['fɔ:tris], *n.* forteresse, place forte, *f.*

fortuitous [fɔ:'tju:itəs], *a.* fortuit.

fortuitously [fɔ:'tju:itəsli], *adv.* fortuitement, par hasard.

fortunate ['fɔ:tʃənit, 'fɔ:tjunit], *a.* heureux, fortuné.

fortunately ['fɔ:tʃənitli], *adv.* heureusement.

fortune ['fɔ:tʃən], *n.* fortune, *f.*, sort (*lot*), destin, *m.*; *by good fortune*, par bonheur.

fortune hunter ['fɔ:tʃənhʌntə], *n.* aventurier, coureur de dots, *m.*

fortune-teller ['fɔ:tʃəntelə], *n.* diseur de bonne aventure, *m.*

forty ['fɔ:ti], *a.* quarante; *she must be nearly forty*, elle doit friser la quarantaine.

forward ['fɔ:wəd], *a.* avancé; (*fig.*) empressé (*de*), ardent (*à*); précoce (*fruits etc.*); présomptueux.—*n.* (*Ftb.*) avant, *m.*—*adv.* en avant; en évidence.—*v.t.* avancer, hâter; (*Comm.*) envoyer, expédier; faire suivre (*lettre*).

forwardness ['fɔːwədnis], *n.* empressement; progrès, *m.*; précocité (*fruits etc.*); hardiesse; effronterie, *f.*

fossil ['fɔsil], *a.* and *n.* fossile, *m.*

foster ['fɔstə], *v.t.* élever, nourrir; (*fig.*) encourager.

foster brother ['fɔstəbrʌðə], *n.* frère de lait, *m.*

foster child ['fɔstətʃaild], *n.* nourrisson, *m.*

foster father ['fɔstəfɑːðə], *n.* père nourricier, *m.*

foster mother ['fɔstəmʌðə], *n.* mère nourricière, *f.*

foster sister ['fɔstəsistə], *n.* sœur de lait, *f.*

foul [faul], *a.* sale, malpropre, immonde, trouble, bourbeux (*eau*); grossier (*langage*); **by fair means or foul**, de gré ou de force; **foul air**, air vicié, *m.*; **foul play**, trahison, *f.*—*n.* (*Spt.*) coup-bas, *m.*—*v.t.* salir, souiller, troubler; encrasser (*arme à feu*); (*Naut.*) aborder; s'engager (*cordes*).

foully ['faulli], *adv.* salement, honteusement.

foul-mouthed ['faulmauðd], *a.* grossier.

foulness ['faulnis], *n.* saleté, impureté; turpitude, noirceur, *f.*

found (1) [faund], *past* and *p.p.* [FIND].

found (2) [faund], *v.t.* fonder, établir; fondre (*to cast*).

foundation [faun'deiʃən], *n.* fondement, *m.*, fondation, *f.*; (*fig.*) base, source, *f.*

founder (1) ['faundə], *n.* fondateur, auteur; (*Metal.*) fondeur, *m.*

founder (2) ['faundə], *v.t.* surmener (*un cheval*).—*v.i.* (*Naut.*) sombrer, couler bas; broncher (*un cheval*); (*fig.*) échouer.

foundered ['faundəd], *a.* courbatu (*cheval*); sombré (*navire*).

foundling ['faundliŋ], *n.* enfant trouvé, *m.*

foundry ['faundri], *n.* fonderie, *f.*

fount [faunt], *n.* fontaine, (*fig.*) cause, source, *f.*

fountain ['fauntin], *n.* fontaine, source, *f.*; jet d'eau, *m.*

fountain-head ['fauntinhed], *n.* source, origine, *f.*

fountain pen ['fauntinpen], *n.* stylo, *m.*

four [fɔː], *a.* and *n.* quatre, *m.*; **carriage and four**, voiture à quatre chevaux, *f.*; **on all fours**, à quatre pattes.

four-engined ['fɔːrendʒind], *a.* (*Av.*) quadrimoteur.

four-fold ['fɔːfould], *a.* quatre fois, quatre fois autant, quadruple.

four-footed ['fɔːfutid], *a.* quadrupède, à quatre pieds.

fourteen ['fɔːtiːn], *a.* and *n.* quatorze, *m.*

fourteenth ['fɔːtiːnθ], *a.* quatorzième; quatorze (*date; rois etc.*).—*n.* quatorzième (*fraction*), *m.*

fourth [fɔːθ], *a.* quatrième; quatre (*date, roi etc.*).—*n.* quart (*fraction*), *m.*; (*Mus.*) quarte, *f.*

fowl [faul], *n.* oiseau, *m.*, poule (*hen*); (*Cook.*) volaille, *f.*

fowler ['faulə], *n.* oiseleur, *m.*

fowl-house ['faulhaus], *n.* poulailler, *m.*

fowling piece ['fauliŋpiːs], *n.* fusil de chasse, *m.*

fox [fɔks], *n.* (*pl.* **foxes** ['fɔksiz]) renard; (*fig.*) rusé, *m.*

foxglove ['fɔksglʌv], *n.* digitale, *f.*

foxy ['fɔksi], *a.* de renard, rusé; roux (*red*).

fraction ['frækʃən], *n.* fraction, *f.*

fractious ['frækʃəs], *a.* revêche, maussade, hargneux, de mauvaise humeur.

fracture ['fræktʃə], *n.* fracture, cassure, *f.*—*v.t.* casser, rompre; (*Surg.*) fracturer.

fragile ['frædʒail], *a.* fragile.

fragility [frə'dʒiliti], *n.* fragilité, *f.*

fragment ['frægmənt], *n.* fragment, éclat, *m.*

fragrance ['freigrəns], *n.* odeur suave, *f.*, parfum, *m.*

fragrant ['freigrənt], *a.* odoriférant, parfumé.

frail [freil], *a.* frêle, fragile, faible.—*n.* cabas, panier d'emballage, *m.*

frailty ['freilti], *n.* faiblesse, fragilité, *f.*

frame [freim], *n.* charpente, *f.*; châssis (*de fenêtre etc.*), chambranle (*de porte*), *m.*; (*fig.*) forme, *f.*; cadre (*de tableau etc.*), *m.*; disposition (*d'esprit*), *f.*—*v.t.* former, construire; encadrer; inventer.

framer ['freimə], *n.* encadreur, *m.*; (*fig.*) auteur (*d'un projet*), *m.*

France [frɑːns]. la France, *f.*

Frances ['frɑːnsis]. Françoise, *f.*

franchise ['fræntʃaiz], *n.* franchise, *f.*, droit de vote, *m.*

Francis ['frɑːnsis]. François, Francis, *m.*

Franciscan [fræn'siskən], *a.* and *n.* Franciscain, *m.*

frank [fræŋk], *a.* franc, sincère, libéral; libre.—*v.t.* affranchir.

frankincense ['fræŋkinsens], *n.* encens, *m.*

frankly ['fræŋkli], *adv.* franchement.

frankness ['fræŋknis], *n.* franchise, sincérité, *f.*

frantic ['fræntik], *a.* frénétique, forcené, furieux.

frantically ['fræntikəli], *adv.* follement, avec frénésie.

fraternal [frə'təːnəl], *a.* fraternel.

fraternity [frə'təːniti], *n.* fraternité, confrérie, *f.*

fraud [frɔːd], *n.* imposteur (*personne*), *m.*; (*also* **fraudulence** ['frɔːdjuləns]) fraude, supercherie, *f.*, dol, *m.*

fraudulent ['frɔːdjulənt], *a.* frauduleux, de mauvaise foi.

fraught [frɔːt], *a.* rempli, plein (*de*); riche, fertile (*en*).

fray (1) [frei], *n.* échauffourée, mêlée, bagarre, *f.*

fray (2) [frei], *v.t.* érailler, effilocher.—*v.i.* s'érailler.

fraying ['freiiŋ], *n.* éraillure, *f.*

freak [friːk], *n.* caprice, *m.*; bizarrerie, *f.*; monstre, *m.*; bigarrure, *f.*—*v.t.* bigarrer, tacheter (*de*).

freakish ['friːkiʃ], *a.* bizarre, fantasque, capricieux.

freckle [frekl], *n.* tache de rousseur, tache de son, *f.*—*v.t.* tacheter.

Frederick ['fredrik]. Frédéric, *m.*

free [friː], *a.* libre; exempt; sincère, franc; gratuit; aisé, dégagé; **delivered free**, rendu franco à domicile; **free and easy**, sans façon.—*adv.* gratis.—*v.t.* délivrer, libérer.

freebooter ['friːbuːtə], *n.* maraudeur; flibustier, *m.*

freedman ['friːdmən], *n.* (*pl.* **-men** [men]) affranchi, *m.*

freedom ['friːdəm], *n.* liberté; indépendance; aisance; bourgeoisie (*d'une ville*), *f.*

freehold ['fri:hould], *n.* propriété foncière libre, *f.*

free-holder ['fri:houldə], *n.* propriétaire foncier, *m.*

freely ['fri:li], *adv.* librement, sans contrainte, gratuitement; libéralement.

freeman ['fri:mən], *n.* (*pl.* **-men** [men]) citoyen, homme libre, *m.*

freemason ['fri:meisn], *n.* franc-maçon, *m.*

freemasonry ['fri:meisnri], *n.* franc-maçonnerie, *f.*

freestone ['fri:stoun], *n.* pierre de taille, *f.*

freestyle ['fri:stail], *n.* nage libre, *f.*

freethinker ['fri:'θiŋkə], *n.* esprit fort, libre penseur, *m.*

free trade ['fri:'treid], *n.* libre-échange, *m.*; **free-trade area**, zone de libre-échange, *f.*

free-trader ['fri:'treidə], *n.* libre-échangiste, *m.*, *f.*

freeze [fri:z], *v.t. irr.* geler; (*Fin.*) bloquer (*prix, salaires*).—*v.i.* se geler, se glacer.

freezing ['fri:ziŋ], *a.* glacial.—*n.* congélation, *f.*; (*Fin.*) blocage, *m.*

freight [freit], *n.* cargaison, *f.*, chargement; fret (*cost*), *m.*—*v.t.* fréter.

French [frentʃ], *a.* français; **French window**, porte-fenêtre, *f.*—*n.* français (*langue*), *m.*; **the French**, les Français, *m.pl.*

Frenchman ['frentʃmən], *n.* (*pl.* **-men** [men]) Français, *m.*

Frenchwoman ['frentʃwumən], *n.* (*pl.* **-women** [wimin]) Française, *f.*

frenzy ['frenzi], *n.* frénésie, *f.*; délire, *m.*

frequence ['fri:kwəns], **frequency** ['fri:kwənsi], *n.* fréquence; répétition fréquente, *f.*; **V.H.F.**, modulation de fréquence, *f.*

frequent ['fri:kwənt], *a.* fréquent, très répandu; rapide (*pouls*).—[fri'kwent], *v.t.* fréquenter; hanter.

frequently ['fri:kwəntli], *adv.* fréquemment, souvent.

fresco ['freskou], *n.* fresque, *f.*

fresh [freʃ], *a.* frais; récent, nouveau; (*fig.*) vigoureux, novice, vert; **fresh water**, eau douce, *f.*

freshen ['freʃən], *v.t.* rafraîchir.—*v.i.* se rafraîchir.

freshly ['freʃli], *adv.* fraîchement; récemment, depuis peu.

freshman ['freʃmən], *n.* (*pl.* **-men** [men]) étudiant de première année, bizuth, *m.*

freshness ['freʃnis], *n.* fraîcheur, *f.*; (*fig.*) nouveauté, *f.*

freshwater ['freʃwɔ:tə], *a.* d'eau douce *ou* de rivière.

fret [fret], *n.* fermentation; (*fig.*) agitation de l'âme, *f.*—*v.t.* frotter (*contre*); ronger, écorcher (*excorier*); chagriner, irriter; découper.—*v.i.* se chagriner, s'inquiéter; s'user, s'érailler.

fretful ['fretful], *a.* chagrin, maussade; agité, inquiet.

fretfulness ['fretfulnis], *n.* mauvaise humeur, irritation, *f.*

fretsaw ['fretsɔ:], *n.* scie à découper, *f.*

fretwork ['fretwə:k], *n.* ouvrage à claire-voie; découpage, *m.*

friable ['fraiəbl], *a.* friable.

friar ['fraiə], *n.* moine, *m.*

friction ['frikʃən], *n.* frottement, *m.*; (*Med.*) friction, *f.*

Friday ['fraid(e)i], *n.* vendredi, *m.*; **Good Friday**, vendredi saint.

friend [frend], *n.* ami, *m.*, amie, *f.*

friendless ['frendlis], *a.* sans ami, délaissé.

friendliness ['frendlinis], *n.* bienveillance, *f.*

friendly ['frendli], *a.* d'ami, amical; bienveillant (*pour*).

friendship ['frendʃip], *n.* amitié, *f.*

frieze [fri:z], *a.* de frise.—*n.* frise, *f.*

frigate ['frigit], *n.* frégate, *f.*

fright [frait], *n.* effroi, *m.*, épouvante, frayeur, *f.*

frighten [fraitn], *v.t.* épouvanter, effrayer, faire peur à.

frightful ['fraitful], *a.* épouvantable, effroyable, affreux.

frightfulness ['fraitfulnis], *n.* horreur, frayeur, *f.*

frigid ['fridʒid], *a.* froid, glacial.

frigidity [fri'dʒiditi], **frigidness** ['fridʒidnis], *n.* frigidité, froideur, *f.*

frill [fril], *n.* volant, *m.*, ruche, *f.*, jabot (*de chemise*), *m.*; **without frills**, sans façons.—*v.t.* plisser, froncer; rucher.

fringe [frindʒ], *n.* frange; crépine, *f.*; bord, *m.*; bordure, *f.*; effilé, *m.*—*v.t.* franger, border.

frippery ['fripəri], *n.* parure sans valeur, *f.*; clinquant, *m.*

frisk [frisk], *n.* gambade, *f.*—*v.i.* sautiller, gambader, frétiller.

friskiness ['friskinis], *n.* folâtrerie, gaieté, vivacité, *f.*

frisky ['friski], *a.* vif, enjoué, folâtre; fringant (*cheval*).

fritter ['fritə], *n.* (*Cook.*) beignet, *m.*—*v.t.* couper en morceaux, morceler; **to fritter away** (*one's time ou money*), gaspiller *ou* dissiper (son temps *ou* son argent).

frivolity [fri'vəliti], *n.* frivolité, *f.*

frivolous ['frivələs], *a.* frivole.

frivolousness ['frivələsnis], *n.* frivolité, *f.*

frizz [friz], **frizzle** [frizl], *v.t.* friser, crêper.—*v.i.* frisotter (*cheveux*).—*n.* frisure, *f.*

frizzy ['frizi], *a.* frisottant, crêpé.

fro [frou], *adv.* en s'éloignant; **to go to and fro**, aller et venir.

frock [frok], *n.* robe d'enfant, robe, *f.*; froc (*de moine*), *m.*

frock coat ['frokkout], *n.* redingote, *f.*

frog [frog], *n.* grenouille, *f.*

frogman ['frogmən], *n.* (*pl.* **-men** [men]) homme-grenouille, *m.*

frolic ['frolik], *n.* espièglerie, *f.*, ébats, *m.pl.*, gambades, *f.pl.*—*v.i.* folâtrer, gambader.

frolicsome ['froliksəm], *a.* folâtre, espiègle.

from [from], *prep.* de; depuis, dès, à partir de; par (*à cause de*); d'après (*selon*); par suite de, en conséquence de (*en raison de*); de la part de (*comme représentant de*); **as from**, à partir de (*telle ou telle date*); **from above**, d'en haut; **from afar**, de loin; **from behind**, de derrière; **from hence**, d'ici; **from thence**, de là; **from . . . till**, depuis . . . jusqu'à; **from you**, de votre part.

front [frʌnt], *n.* devant, *m.*; face, façade (*d'un édifice*); audace, *f.*, front, *m.*—*v.t.* faire face à; s'opposer à; donner sur.

frontage ['frʌntidʒ], *n.* façade, devanture (*de magasin*), *f.*

front door ['frʌnt'dɔ:], *n.* porte d'entrée, *f.*

433

frontier ['frʌntiə], *a.* and *n.* frontière, *f.*

frontispiece ['frʌntispi:s], *n.* frontispice, *m.*

frost [frɔst], *n.* gelée, *f.*, gel, *m.*; *glazed frost*, verglas, *m.*; *ground frost*, gelée blanche; *hoar-frost*, givre, *m.*—*v.t.* glacer; damasquiner.

frost-bite ['frɔstbait], *n.* gelure, froidure, *f.*

frosted ['frɔstid], *a.* givré; dépoli (*verre*).

frosty ['frɔsti], *a.* de gelée; glacé; (*fig.*) froid.

froth [frɔθ], *n.* écume; mousse (*de boisson*), *f.* —*v.i.* écumer; mousser.

frothy ['frɔθi], *a.* écumeux; écumant; mousseux; (*fig.*) vain, frivole.

frown [fraun], *n.* froncement de sourcil, *m.*— *v.i.* froncer les sourcils; être contraire (*à*); (*fig.*) *to frown upon*, désapprouver.

frowning ['frauniŋ], *a.* rechigné, renfrogné; (*fig.*) menaçant.

frowzy ['frauzi], *a.* sale, malpropre.

frozen ['frouzn], *a.* glacé, gelé; (*Fin.*) bloqué. —*v.i.* fructifier.

fructify ['frʌktifai], *v.t.* fertiliser, féconder.— *v.i.* fructifier.

frugal ['fru:gl], *a.* frugal, économe, ménager.

frugality [fru:'gæliti], *n.* économie, frugalité, *f.*

fruit [fru:t], *a.* à fruit, fruitier.—*n.* fruit, *m.*; fruits, *m.pl.*; (*fig.*) avantage, profit, *m.*; *first fruits*, prémices, *f.pl.*

fruiterer ['fru:tərə], *n.* fruitier, *m.*

fruitful ['fru:tful], *a.* fertile; (*fig.*) fécond.

fruitfully ['fru:tfuli], *adv.* fertilement, abondamment.

fruitfulness ['fru:tfulnis], *n.* fertilité; (*fig.*) fécondité, *f.*

fruition [fru:'iʃən], *n.* jouissance, réalisation, *f.*

fruitless ['fru:tlis], *a.* stérile; (*fig.*) infructueux, inutile.

frump [frʌmp], *n.* femme désagréable et mal habillée, *f.*

frustrate [frʌs'treit], *v.t.* frustrer, rendre inutile, déjouer.

frustration [frʌs'treiʃən], *n.* frustration, *f.*, insuccès, *m.*

fry (1) [frai], *n.* fretin, frai (*petits poissons*), *m.*

fry (2) [frai], *n.* (*Cook.*) friture, *f.*—*v.t.* frire, faire frire, sauter; *fried eggs*, œufs au plat, *m.pl.*—*v.i.* frire.

frying pan ['fraiiŋpæn], *n.* poêle à frire, *f.*

fuchsia ['fju:ʃə], *n.* fuchsia, *m.*

fuddle [fʌdl], *v.t.* griser; hébéter.—*v.i.* se griser.

fudge [fʌdʒ], *int.* bah!—*n.* blague, faribole, *f.*; fondant américain (*bonbon*), *m.*

fuel ['fjuəl], *n.* combustible; (*fig.*) aliment, *m.*

fuel-oil ['fjuəlɔil], *n.* mazout, *m.*

fugitive ['fju:dʒitiv], *a.* fugitif; fuyard, passager.—*n.* fugitif, transfuge, déserteur; (*Mil.*) fuyard, *m.*

fugue [fju:g], *n.* (*Mus.*) fugue, *f.*

fulcrum ['fʌlkrəm], *n.* (*pl.* **fulcra** ['fʌlkrə]) point d'appui, *m.*

fulfil [ful'fil], *v.t.* accomplir, réaliser; satisfaire.

fulfilment [ful'filmənt], *n.* exécution, *f.*, accomplissement, *m.*

full [ful], *a.* plein, rempli; comble, replet, gras; entier, complet; ample; (*fig.*) repu; (*Gram.*) *full stop*, point, *m.*; *full up!* (*autobus etc.*) complet!—*adv.* tout à fait, entièrement; parfaitement.—*n.* plein; comble, *m.*, satiété, *f.*; soûl, *m.*

full-back ['fulbæk], *n.* (*Ftb.*) arrière, *m.*

full-blown ['fulbloun], *a.* épanoui; (*fig.*) dans tout son éclat.

full-bodied ['fulbɔdid], *a.* gros, replet; corsé (*vin*).

fuller ['fulə], *n.* foulon, *m.*

full-faced ['ful'feist], *a.* au visage plein.

full-length ['ful'leŋθ], *a.* en pied (*portrait*).

fullness ['fulnis], *n.* plénitude, abondance; ampleur, *f.*

fully ['fuli], *adv.* pleinement, entièrement, tout à fait; parfaitement.

fulmar ['fulmə], *n.* (*Orn.*) fulmar, *m.*

fulminate ['fʌlmineit], *v.t.*, *v.i.* fulminer.

fulsome ['fulsəm], *a.* excessif, écœurant, servile; gonflé (*style*).

fumble [fʌmbl], *v.t.* manier maladroitement. —*v.i.* farfouiller; tâtonner.

fumbler ['fʌmblə], *n.* maladroit, *m.*

fume [fju:m], *n.* fumée, vapeur; (*fig.*) colère, *f.*—*v.t.* fumer.—*v.i.* fumer, s'exhaler; (*fig.*) être en colère.

fumigate ['fju:migeit], *v.t.* fumiger; désinfecter.

fun [fʌn], *n.* amusement, *m.*, plaisanterie, drôlerie, *f.*

function ['fʌŋkʃən], *n.* fonction, *f.*, métier, *m.*; cérémonie, réception, *f.*—*v.i.* fonctionner, marcher.

fund [fʌnd], *n.* fonds, *m.*; caisse, *f.*

fundamental [fʌndə'mentl], *a.* fondamental. —*n.* (*pl.*) principe fondamental, *m.*

funeral ['fju:nərəl], *a.* funèbre, funéraire.— *n.* enterrement, convoi funèbre, *m.*; funérailles, obsèques, *f.pl.*

funereal [fju:'niəriəl], *a.* funèbre; lugubre.

fungus ['fʌŋgəs], *n.* (*pl.* **fungi** ['fʌndʒai]) champignon; (*Med.*) fongus, *m.*

funk [fʌŋk], *n.* peur, *f.*—*v.t.* éviter, avoir peur de.

funnel [fʌnl], *n.* entonnoir; tuyau, *m.*; cheminée (*de bateau à vapeur*), *f.*

funny ['fʌni], *a.* amusant, drôle, comique; bizarre.

fur [fə:], *n.* fourrure, *f.*; gibier à poil; (*fig.*) dépôt, *m.*, incrustation, *f.*—*v.t.* fourrer, garnir de fourrure.—*v.i.* s'incruster, s'encrasser (*la langue*).

furbish ['fə:biʃ], *v.t.* fourbir.

furious ['fjuəriəs], *a.* furieux, acharné.

furiously ['fjuəriəsli], *adv.* avec fureur, avec acharnement.

furl [fə:l], *v.t.* (*Naut.*) ferler, serrer.

furlong ['fə:lɔŋ], *n.* furlong (*le huitième d'un mille anglais, 201 mètres*), *m.*

furlough ['fə:lou], *n.* (*Mil.*) congé, *m.*

furnace ['fə:nis], *n.* fournaise, *f.*; fourneau (*d'une forge*); foyer (*de locomotive*), *m.*; *blast furnace*, haut fourneau, *m.*

furnish ['fə:niʃ], *v.t.* fournir, garnir, pourvoir (*de*); meubler.

furnisher ['fə:niʃə], *n.* fournisseur, marchand de meubles, *m.*

furnishing ['fə:niʃiŋ], *n.* ameublement, *m.*, garniture, *f.*

furniture ['fə:nitʃə], *n.* meubles, *m.pl.* mobilier, ameublement; équipage, *m.*; *a piece of furniture*, un meuble, *m.*

furrier ['fʌriə], *n.* fourreur, pelletier, *m.*

furrow ['fʌrou], *n.* sillon, *m.*; ride, rainure, *f.* —*v.t.* sillonner, rider (*la figure*).

furry ['fə:ri], *a.* fourré.

further ['fə:ðə], *v.t.* avancer; faciliter, favoriser, seconder.—*a.* (*also* **farther** ['fɑ:ðə]) plus éloigné, ultérieur; autre, nouveau; *further end*, extrémité, *f.*—*adv.* (*also* **farther** ['fɑ:ðə]) plus loin; de plus, en outre, davantage, encore; ultérieurement; au delà.

furtherance ['fə:ðərəns], *n.* avancement; progrès, *m.*

furthermore ['fə:ðəmɔː], *adv.* de plus, en outre, d'ailleurs.

furthermost ['fə:ðəmoust], **furthest** ['fə:ðist], **farthest** ['fɑ:ðist], *a.* le plus éloigné; le plus reculé.—*adv.* and *n.* le plus loin.

furtive ['fə:tiv], *a.* furtif.

furtively ['fə:tivli], *adv.* furtivement, à la dérobée.

fury ['fjuəri], *n.* furie, fureur, *f.*; acharnement, *m.*

furze [fə:z], *n.* ajonc, genêt épineux, *m.*

fuse [fju:z], *v.t.* fondre, liquéfier.—*v.i.* se fondre.—*n.* mèche, fusée, *f.*; (*Elec.*) fusible, plomb, *m.*; *the fuse has gone*, le plomb a sauté.

fuselage ['fju:zilɑ:ʒ, 'fju:zilidʒ], *n.* fuselage, *m.*

fuse wire ['fju:zwaiə], *n.* fil fusible, *m.*

fusible ['fju:zibl], *a.* fusible.

fusilier [fju:zi'liə], *n.* fusilier, *m.*

fusillade [fju:zi'leid], *n.* fusillade, *f.*

fusion ['fju:ʒən], *n.* fusion, *f.*

fuss [fʌs], *n.* fracas, embarras, *m.*, façons, *f.pl.*

fussily ['fʌsili], *adv.* avec embarras.

fussy ['fʌsi], *a.* qui fait des embarras; affairé.

fustian ['fʌstjən], *n.* futaine, *f.*; (*fig.*) galimatias, *m.*

fusty ['fʌsti], *a.* qui sent le renfermé *ou* le moisi.

futile ['fju:tail], *a.* futile, vain, frivole.

futility [fju:'tiliti], *n.* futilité, *f.*

future ['fju:tʃə], *a.* futur, à venir.—*n.* avenir; (*Gram.*) futur, *m.*

fuzz [fʌz], *n.* bourre, *f.*, duvet (*de couverture*); flou (*de photographie*), *m.*

fuzzy ['fʌzi], *a.* duveteux, floconneux; bouffant, moutonné (*cheveux*); flou (*photographie*).

G

G, g [dʒi:]. septième lettre de l'alphabet; (*Mus.*) sol, *m.*

gab [gæb], *n.* faconde, *f.*, bagout, *m.*; *to have the gift of the gab*, (*colloq.*) avoir la langue bien pendue.

gabardine [GABERDINE].

gabble [gæbl], *v.i.* parler très vite, bredouiller; caqueter, jacasser.—*n.* bredouillement; caquet, *m.*

gaberdine, gabardine [gæbə'di:n], *n.* gabardine, *f.*

gable [geibl], *n.* pignon, gable, *m.*

gadfly ['gædflai], *n.* taon, *m.*

gadget ['gædʒit], *n.* instrument, accessoire; truc, machin, *m.*

gaff [gæf], *n.* gaffe, *f.*—*v.t.* gaffer (*poisson*).

gag [gæg], *n.* bâillon, *m.*; (*Theat.*) plaisanterie, *f.*; (*Cine.*) gag, *m.*—*v.t.* bâillonner.

gage [geidʒ], *n.* gage, *m.*, assurance, *f.*

gaggle [gægl], *n.* troupeau d'oies, *m.*

gaiety ['geiəti], *n.* gaieté, *f.*; éclat, *m.*

gaily ['geili], *adv.* gaiement, joyeusement.

gain [gein], *n.* gain, profit, avantage, *m.*—*v.t.* gagner, acquérir; remporter (*victoire*); atteindre.—*v.i.* avancer (*montre etc.*).

gainings ['geiniŋz], *n.pl.* gains, profits, *m.pl.*

gainsay ['geinsei, gein'sei], *v.t.* contredire.

gait [geit], *n.* démarche, allure, *f.*

gaiter ['geitə], *n.* guêtre, *f.*

gala ['geilə, 'gɑ:lə], *n.* gala, *m.*; fête, *f.*

galaxy ['gæləksi], *n.* voie lactée, galaxie, *f.*; (*fig.*) assemblage brillant, *m.*

gale [geil], *n.* coup de vent, *m.*, tempête, *f.*

Galilee ['gʌlili:]. la Galilée, *f.*

gall [gɔ:l], *n.* fiel, *m.*; écorchure (*plaie*); noix de galle, galle (*d'arbres etc.*); (*fig.*) rancune, *f.*, chagrin, *m.*—*v.t.* écorcher; (*fig.*) fâcher.

gallant ['gælənt], *a.* brave, intrépide; [gə'lænt] galant.—*n.* brave; preux; [gə'lænt] galant; amant, *m.*

gallantry ['gæləntri], *n.* vaillance; galanterie, *f.*

gall bladder ['gɔ:lblædə], *n.* vésicule bilaire, *f.*

galleon ['gæliən], *n.* galion, *m.*

gallery ['gæləri], *n.* galerie, *f.*; (*Theat.*) balcon, *m.*; (*Parl.*) tribune publique, *f.*

galley ['gæli], *n.* galère; (*Naut.*) cuisine, *f.*

galley slave ['gælisleiv], *n.* galérien, *m.*

Gallic ['gælik], *a.* gaulois.

galling ['gɔ:liŋ], *a.* irritant, vexant.

gallon ['gælən], *n.* gallon (*quatre litres et demi*), *m.*

gallop ['gæləp], *n.* galop, *m.*—*v.i.* galoper, aller au galop.

gallows ['gælouz], *n.* potence, *f.*

galvanize ['gælvənaiz], *v.t.* galvaniser.

Gambia ['gæmbiə]. la Gambie, *f.*

gamble [gæmbl], *v.i.* jouer de l'argent.

gambler ['gæmblə], *n.* joueur, *m.*

gambling ['gæmbliŋ], *n.* jeu, *m.*

gambol [gæmbl], *n.* gambade, *f.*; ébats, *m.pl.*—*v.i.* gambader, folâtrer.

game (1) [geim], *a.* estropié (*jambe, bras etc.*).

game (2) [geim], *a.* courageux.—*n.* jeu, *m.*, partie, *f.*; *drawn game*, partie nulle; *to make game of*, se moquer de.—*v.i.* jouer de l'argent.

game (3) [geim], *n.* gibier, *m.*

game bag ['geimbæg], *n.* carnassière, *f.*

game-keeper ['geimki:pə], *n.* garde-chasse, *m.*

gamester ['geimstə], *n.* joueur, *m.*

gammon ['gæmən], *n.* quartier de lard fumé, *m.*—*v.t.* saler et fumer (*jambon*).

gamut ['gæmət], *n.* (*Mus.*) gamme, *f.*

gander ['gændə], *n.* jars, *m.*

gang [gæŋ], *n.* bande, troupe, brigade, équipe (*d'ouvriers*), *f.*

ganger ['gæŋə], *n.* chef d'équipe; cantonnier, *m.*

Ganges ['gændʒi:z]. le Gange, *m.*

gangrene ['gæŋgri:n], *n.* gangrène, *f.*

gangster ['gæŋstə], *n.* (*Am.*) bandit, gangster, *m.*

gangway ['gæŋwei], *n.* passage, *m.*; (*Naut.*) passerelle (*pour débarquer*), coupée, *f.*

gannet ['gænit], *n.* (*Orn.*) fou, *m.*

gaol [JAIL].

gap [gæp], *n.* brèche, ouverture, *f.*, trou, *m.*; *(fig.)* lacune; trouée *(dans une forêt)*, *f.*

gape [geip], *v.i.* bâiller; s'entr'ouvrir *(porte etc.)*; *(fig.)* bayer; **to gape at,** regarder bouche bée.—*n.* bâillement, *m.*

gaping ['geipiŋ], *a.* béant.—*n.* bâillement, *m.*

garage ['gæra:ʒ], *n.* garage, *m.*—*v.t.* garer.

garb [ga:b], *n.* costume, habit, habillement, *m.*

garbage ['ga:bidʒ], *n.* entrailles, issues; *(Am.)* ordures, *f.pl.* [see also **dust-bin** etc.]

garble [ga:bl], *v.t.* mutiler, tronquer *(citation etc.)*, altérer.

garden [ga:dn], *n.* jardin, *m.*—*v.i.* jardiner.

garden-city ['ga:dn'siti], *n.* cité-jardin, *f.*

gardener ['ga:dnə], *n.* jardinier, *m.*

gardenia [ga:'di:njə], *n.* gardenia, *m.*

gardening ['ga:dniŋ], *n.* jardinage, *m.*

gargle [ga:gl], *v.i.* se gargariser.—*n.* gargarisme, *m.*

gargoyle ['ga:gɔil], *n.* gargouille, *f.*

garish ['gɛəriʃ], *a.* éclatant, voyant.

garland ['ga:lənd], *n.* guirlande, *f.*—*v.t.* enguirlander.

garlic ['ga:lik], *n.* ail, *m.*

garment ['ga:mənt], *n.* vêtement, *m.*

garner ['ga:nə], *n.* grenier, *m.*—*v.t.* mettre en grenier, engranger; *(fig.)* amasser.

garnet ['ga:nit], *n.* grenat, *m.*

garnish ['ga:niʃ], *v.t.* garnir, orner de.—*n.* garniture, *f.*

garret ['gærət], *n.* galetas, *m.*, mansarde, soupente, *f.*

garrison ['gærisən], *n.* garnison, *f.*—*v.t.* mettre garnison dans; mettre en garnison.

garrotte [gə'rɔt], *n.* garrotte, *f.*—*v.t.* garrotter.

garrulity [gə'ru:liti], *n.* garrulité, loquacité, *f.*

garrulous ['gæruləs], *a.* babillard, loquace.

garter ['ga:tə], *n.* jarretière, *f.*; *(Am.)* support-chaussette, *m.*

gas [gæs], *n.* (*pl.* **gases** ['gæsiz]) gaz, *m.*; **laughing gas,** gaz hilarant.—*v.t.* gazer; intoxiquer par un gaz. [see **petrol**]

gas cooker ['gæs'kukə], *n.* réchaud à gaz, four à gaz, *m.*

gaseous ['geisiəs], *a.* gazeux.

gash [gæʃ], *n.* balafre, estafilade, entaille, *f.*—*v.t.* balafrer, taillader.

gas-holder ['gæshouldə], **gasometer** [gæ'sɔmitə], *n.* gazomètre, *m.*

gas mask ['gæsma:sk], *n.* masque à gaz, *m.*

gasometer [GAS-HOLDER].

gasp [ga:sp], *v.i.* respirer avec peine.—*n.* respiration haletante, *f.*; sursaut *(de surprise)*, soupir convulsif, *m.*

gasping ['ga:spiŋ], *a.* haletant.—*n.* respiration haletante, *f.*

gas stove ['gæsstouv], *n.* fourneau à gaz, *m.*

gastric ['gæstrik], *a.* gastrique.

gastronomy [gæs'trɔnəmi], *n.* gastronomie, *f.*

gate [geit], *n.* porte; barrière *(de péage)*; grille *(en fer forgé)*, *f.*

gate-keeper ['geitki:pə], *n.* portier; *(Rail.)* garde-barrière, *f.*

gate-post ['geitpoust], *n.* montant de porte, *m.*

gateway ['geitwei], *n.* porte, porte cochère, *f.*; portail *(grand)*; guichet *(petit)*, *m.*

gather ['gæðə], *v.t.* ramasser; assembler; recueillir *(réunir)*; cueillir *(fruits etc.)*; *(fig.)*

gatherer ['gæðərə], *n.* cueilleur; percepteur *(des contributions directes)*; vendangeur *(de raisins)*, *m.*

gathering ['gæðəriŋ], *n.* rassemblement, *m.*; assemblée, réunion; perception *(des contributions directes)*; récolte *(de fruits etc.)*, *f.*: *(Dress.)* froncis; *(Med.)* abcès, *m.*

gaudiness ['gɔ:dinis], *n.* faste, faux brillant, *m.*

gaudy ['gɔ:di], *a.* éclatant; criard, fastueux, de mauvais goût.

gauge [geidʒ], *v.t.* jauger, mesurer; *(fig.)* juger.—*n.* jauge, mesure, *f.*; calibre, *m.*; *(Rail.)* voie, *f.*

Gaul [gɔ:l], la Gaule, *f.*

Gauls [gɔ:lz], **the.** les Gaulois, *m.pl.*

gaunt [gɔ:nt], *a.* maigre, décharné.

gauntlet ['gɔ:ntlit], *n.* gantelet, *m.*

gauze [gɔ:z], *n.* gaze, *f.*

gawk [gɔ:k], *n.* sot, maladroit, *m.*

gawky ['gɔ:ki], *a.* dégingandé.

gay [gei], *a.* gai, réjoui, joyeux; pimpant.

gayety [GAIETY].

gayly [GAILY].

gaze [geiz], *v.i.* regarder fixement.—*n.* regard fixe *ou* attentif, *m.*

gazelle [gə'zel], *n.* gazelle, *f.*

gazette [gə'zet], *n.* gazette, *f.*; bulletin officiel, *m.*—*v.t.* publier *ou* annoncer dans le journal officiel.

gazetteer [gæzi'tiə], *n.* dictionnaire géographique; gazetier, *m.*

gear [giə], *n.* appareil, attirail; harnais *(d'un cheval)*, *m.*; *(colloq.)* vêtements; *(Naut.)* apparaux, *m.pl.*; *(Mach.)* engrenage, *m.*; *(Motor.)* vitesse, *f.*; *(Motor.)* **bottom, first** or **low gear,** première, *f.*; **neutral gear,** point mort, *m.*; **in top gear,** en prise.

gear-box ['giəbɔks], *n.* boîte de changement de vitesse, *f.*

geese [GOOSE].

gelatine ['dʒeləti:n], *n.* gélatine, *f.*

gelatinous [dʒe'lætinəs], *a.* gélatineux.

gelding ['geldiŋ], *n.* cheval hongre, *m.*

gem [dʒem], *n.* pierre précieuse, *f.*, joyau, *m.*

gender ['dʒendə], *n.* genre, *m.*

genealogical [dʒi:niə'lɔdʒikl], *a.* généalogique.

genealogist [dʒi:ni'ælədʒist], *n.* généalogiste, *m.*, *f.*

genealogy [dʒi:ni'ælədʒi], *n.* généalogie, *f.*

general ['dʒenərəl], *a.* général, commun.—*n.* général, *m.*

generalize ['dʒenrəlaiz], *v.t.* généraliser.

generally ['dʒenrəli], *adv.* en général, ordinairement, généralement.

generate ['dʒenəreit], *v.t.* produire, engendrer.

generation [dʒenə'reiʃən], *n.* génération, famille; production, *f.*; âge, *m.*

generator ['dʒenəreitə], *n.* générateur, *m.*; **electricity generator,** génératrice, *f.*

generic [dʒə'nerik], **generical** [dʒe'nerikəl], *a.* générique.

generosity [dʒenə'rɔsiti], *n.* générosité, magnanimité, libéralité, *f.*

generous ['dʒenərəs], *a.* généreux; *(fig.)* abondant, riche *(en)*.

generously ['dʒenərəsli], *adv.* généreuse-ment.

genesis ['dʒenəsis], *n.* genèse, *f.*

genetics [dʒə'netiks], *n.* génétique, *f.*

Geneva [dʒə'niːvə]. Genève, *f.*

genial ['dʒiːniəl], *a.* bon; affable; cordial, joyeux.

geniality [dʒiːni'æliti], *n.* bonne humeur, nature sympathique, gaieté, *f.*, entrain, *m.*

genially ['dʒiːniəli], *adv.* avec bonté, d'un air affable.

genie ['dʒiːni], *n.* (*Myth.*) génie, djinn, *m.*

genitive ['dʒenitiv], *n.* (*Gram.*) génitif, *m.*

genius ['dʒiːniəs], *n.* génie, *m.*

Genoa ['dʒenouə]. Gênes, *f.*

genteel [dʒen'tiːl], *a.* (*now often iron.*) de bon ton, comme il faut, distingué.

gentility [dʒen'tiliti], *n.* bon ton, *m.*, distinction, *f.*

gentle [dʒentl], *a.* doux, aimable; paisible; modéré (*pente etc.*).

gentlefolk ['dʒentlfouk], *n.pl.* personnes de bon ton, *f.pl.*, gens comme il faut, *m.pl.*

gentleman ['dʒentlmən], *n.* (*pl.* **gentlemen** [-men]) monsieur; homme comme il faut, galant homme, homme bien né, *m.*

gentlemanly ['dʒentlmənli], *a.* distingué, de bon ton, comme il faut.

gentleness ['dʒentlnis], *n.* douceur, bonté, *f.*

gentlewoman ['dʒentlwumən], *n.* (*pl.* **-women** [wimin]) dame *ou* jeune fille de bonne famille, *f.*

gently ['dʒentli], *adv.* doucement.

genuine ['dʒenjuin], *a.* pur, vrai, véritable, authentique, naturel; sincère.

genuinely ['dʒenjuinli], *adv.* purement, sincèrement, authentiquement.

genuineness ['dʒenjuinnis], *n.* authenticité; sincérité, *f.*

genus ['dʒiːnəs], *n.* (*pl.* **genera** ['dʒenərə]) genre, *m.*

Geoffrey ['dʒefri]. Geoffroi, *m.*

geographer [dʒi'ɔgrəfə], *n.* géographe, *m.*, *f.*

geographical [dʒiə'græfikl], *a.* géographique.

geography [dʒi'ɔgrəfi], *n.* géographie, *f.*

geology [dʒi'ɔlədʒi], *n.* géologie, *f.*

geometry [dʒi'ɔmitri], *n.* géométrie, *f.*

George [dʒɔːdʒ]. Georges, *m.*

geranium [dʒə'reiniəm], *n.* (*Bot.*) géranium, *m.*

germ [dʒəːm], *n.* germe, *m.*

German ['dʒəːmən], *a.* allemand.—*n.* allemand (*langue*); Allemand (*personne*), *m.*

Germany ['dʒəːməni]. l'Allemagne, *f.*

germinate ['dʒəːmineit], *v.t.* germer; pousser.

gesticulate [dʒes'tikjuleit], *v.i.* gesticuler.

gesticulation [dʒestikju'leiʃən], *n.* gesticulation, *f.*

gesture ['dʒestʃə], *n.* geste, *m.*, action, *f.*—*v.i.* gesticuler.

get [get], *v.t. irr.* (se) procurer, acquérir, obtenir; recevoir; remporter (*to gain*); gagner (*to earn*); avoir; acheter (*to buy*); arriver à, atteindre (*to reach*); aller chercher (*to fetch*); trouver (*to find*); faire, se faire (*to induce, make, cause etc.*); attraper, s'attirer (*to catch etc.*); **to get hold of**, s'emparer de, saisir, obtenir.—*v.i.* se mettre (*en*); devenir, se faire (*to become*); aller (*to go*); se faire, sortir, prendre de l'exercice; **to get at**, arriver à; attaquer; atteindre; **to get away**, s'en aller, se

sauver, échapper (*à*); **to get back**, revenir, regagner; recouvrer; **to get in**, entrer, faire entrer, rentrer; **to get off**, s'en tirer, s'échapper; descendre; ôter, enlever; **to get on**, avancer, réussir, faire des progrès; monter sur; **to get out**, sortir, s'en tirer, faire sortir; **to get over**, passer, surmonter, vaincre; se consoler de; **to get rid of**, se débarrasser de; **to get through**, passer par, parcourir; réussir (*à un examen*); **to get up**, se lever, monter, faire monter, lever; préparer.

gewgaw ['gjuːgɔː], *n.* babiole, bagatelle, *f.*, colifichet, *m.*

geyser ['giːzə], *n.* chauffe-bain; (*Geol.*) geyser, *m.*

Ghana ['gɑːnə]. le Ghana, *m.*

Ghanaian [gɑː'neiən], *a.* du Ghana.—*n.* citoyen(ne) du Ghana, *m.*, *f.*

ghastliness ['gɑːstlinis], *n.* pâleur, *f.*; aspect effrayant, *m.*

ghastly ['gɑːstli], *a.* pâle, pâle comme la mort; horrible, affreux.

gherkin ['gəːkin], *n.* cornichon, *m.*

ghetto ['getou], *n.* ghetto, *m.*

ghost [goust], *n.* revenant, fantôme, spectre, *m.*; ombre, *f.*; **the Holy Ghost**, le Saint-Esprit.

ghostly ['goustli], *a.* spirituel; de spectre.

ghoul [guːl], *n.* goule, *f.*

ghoulish ['guːliʃ], *a.* de goule.

ghyll [GILL (2)].

giant ['dʒaiənt], *a.* de géant.—*n.* géant, *m.*

gibber ['dʒibə], *v.i.* baragouiner.

gibberish ['dʒibəriʃ], *n.* baragouin, charabia, *m.*

gibbet ['dʒibit], *n.* potence, *f.*, gibet, *m.*

gibe [dʒaib], *v.t.*, *v.i.* railler, se moquer (*de*).—*n.* sarcasme, *m.*; raillerie, moquerie, *f.*

giblets ['dʒiblits], *n.pl.* abatis, *m.pl.*

giddily ['gidili], *adv.* étourdiment, à l'étourdie.

giddiness ['gidinis], *n.* vertige, *m.*; (*fig.*) étourderie, *f.*

giddy ['gidi], *a.* étourdi; (*fig.*) volage; vertigineux; **I feel giddy**, la tête me tourne; **that makes me feel giddy**, cela me donne le vertige.

gift [gift], *n.* don, présent, cadeau; (*fig.*) talent, *m.*; **Christmas gifts**, étrennes, *f.pl.*—*v.t.* douer, doter (*de*).

gifted ['giftid], *a.* doué, de talent.

gigantic [dʒai'gæntik], *a.* gigantesque, de géant.

giggle [gigl], *v.i.* rire nerveusement, rire un peu bêtement.—*n.* ricanement, petit rire bête, *m.*

gild [gild], *v.t. irr.* dorer; (*fig.*) embellir.

gilding ['gildiŋ], *n.* dorure, *f.*

Giles [dʒailz]. Gilles, *m.*

gill (1) [gil], *n.* (*usu. pl.*) ouïe (*de poisson*), *f.*

gill (2), **ghyll** [gil], *n.* ravin boisé; ruisseau (*du ravin*), *m.*

gill (3) [dʒil], *n.* treize centilitres, *m.pl.*

gillyflower ['dʒiliflauə], *n.* giroflée, *f.*

gilt [gilt], *a.* doré.—*n.* dorure, *f.*

gilt-edged ['giltedʒd], *a.* **gilt-edged securities**, valeurs de tout repos, *f.pl.*

gimcrack ['dʒimkræk], *n.* pacotille, camelote, *f.*

gimlet ['gimlit], *n.* vrille, *f.*

gimmick ['gimik], *n.* machin; tour (*artifice*), *m.*

gin

gin (1) [dʒin], *n.* trébuchet, piège, *m.*
gin (2) [dʒin], *n.* genièvre, gin (*liquor*), *m.*
ginger ['dʒindʒə], *n.* gingembre; (*fam.*) poil de carotte (*personne aux cheveux roux*), *m.*
gingerbread ['dʒindʒəbred], *n.* pain d'épice, *m.*
gingerly ['dʒindʒəli], *adv.* tout doucement, délicatement.
gipsy, gypsy ['dʒipsi], *n.* bohémien, tzigane, *m.*, bohémienne, *f.*
giraffe [dʒi'rɑːf], *n.* girafe, *f.*
gird [gəːd], *v.t. irr.* ceindre (*de*); entourer (*de*).
girder ['gəːdə], *n.* poutre, solive, traverse, *f.*
girdle [gəːdl], *n.* ceinture, *f.*; ceinturon, *m.*; gaine, *f.*—*v.t.* ceinturer.
girl [gəːl], *n.* fille, jeune fille; jeune personne, *f.*
girlish ['gəːliʃ], *a.* de jeune fille.
girl scout [gəː'skaut], *n.* éclaireuse, *f.*
girth [gəːθ], *n.* sangle, *f.*; tour, *m.*, circonférence, *f.*
gist [dʒist], *n.* fond, fin mot; point principal, *m.*, substance (*d'un discours*), *f.*
give [giv], *v.t. irr.* donner; livrer, rendre, accorder; faire (*réponse, crédit, compliment, amitiés etc.*); remettre; porter (*un coup etc.*); pousser (*un gémissement etc.*); émettre (*un son*); **to give away**, donner; trahir; **to give up**, abandonner, renoncer à.—*v.i.* ceder; plier (*se courber*); prêter (*s'allonger*); **give and take**, donnant donnant; **to give in**, céder; **to give oneself up**, se rendre; **to give way**, céder, se relâcher.
given [givn], *a.* adonné, porté (*à*); donné; **given these difficulties**, étant donné ces difficultés.
giver ['givə], *n.* donneur, *m.*
gizzard ['gizəd], *n.* gésier, *m.*
glacial ['gleiʃəl], *a.* glacial, glaciaire.
glacier ['glæsiə], *n.* glacier, *m.*
glad [glæd], *a.* content, aise, bien aise; heureux (*de*).
gladden [glædn], *v.t.* réjouir.
glade [gleid], *n.* clairière, percée, *f.*
gladiator ['glædieitə], *n.* gladiateur, *m.*
gladiolus [glædi'ouləs], *n.* (*pl.* **gladioli** [glædi'oulai]) glaïeul, *m.*
gladly ['glædli], *adv.* volontiers, avec plaisir.
glamorous ['glæmərəs], *a.* charmeur, ensorcelant.
glamour ['glæmə], *n.* charme, prestige, éclat, *m.*
glance [glɑːns], *n.* ricochet, coup en biais; regard, coup d'œil, *m.*—*v.i.* jeter un coup d'œil (*sur*); étinceler; **to glance off**, ricocher.
gland [glænd], *n.* (*Anat.*) glande, *f.*
glare [glɛə], *n.* éclat, *m.*, lueur, *f.*; regard irrité *ou* farouche, *m.*—*v.i.* éblouir; luire; regarder d'un air furieux.
glaring ['glɛəriŋ], *a.* voyant, éblouissant, choquant; manifeste.
glass [glɑːs], *a.* de verre.—*n.* (*pl.* **glasses** ['glɑːsiz]) verre, *m.*; vitre (*de fenêtre*), *f.*; (*pl.*) lunettes, *f. pl.*; **cut glass**, cristal taillé, *m.*; **field glasses**, jumelles, *f.pl.*; **looking glass**, miroir, *m.*; **magnifying glass**, loupe, *f.*; **stained glass**, vitraux, *m.pl.*; (**weather-)glass**, baromètre, *m.*
glass-maker ['glɑːsmeikə], *n.* verrier, *m.*

glass-ware ['glɑːswɛə], *n.* verrerie, *f.*
glassy ['glɑːsi], *a.* vitreux, transparent.
glaze [gleiz], *v.t.* vitrer; vernir.
glazier ['gleiziə], *n.* vitrier, *m.*
glazing ['gleiziŋ], *n.* vitrage (*de fenêtres*); vernissage (*de peintures*), *m.*
gleam [gliːm], *n.* rayon, *m.*, lueur, *f.*—*v.i.* briller, luire (*de*).
gleaming ['gliːmiŋ], *a.* miroitant, luisant.
glean [gliːn], *v.t.* glaner.
gleaner ['gliːnə], *n.* glaneur, *m.*
glebe [gliːb], *n.* glèbe, terre, *f.*, sol, *m.*
glee [gliː], *n.* joie, gaieté, *f.*
gleeful ['gliːful], *a.* joyeux, gai.
glen [glen], *n.* vallon, ravin, *m.*
glib [glib], *a.* coulant, délié, volubile.
glibly ['glibli], *adv.* avec volubilité; douceureusement.
glide [glaid], *v.i.* couler, glisser; se glisser (*dans*).—*n.* glissade, *f.*; (*Av.*) vol plané, *m.*
glider ['glaidə], *n.* (*Av.*) planeur, *m.*
glimmer ['glimə], *n.* lueur, *f.*, faible rayon, *m.*—*v.i.* entre-luire, luire faiblement; poindre (*l'aube*).
glimpse [glimps], *n.* coup d'œil, *m.*, vue rapide, *f.*; **to catch a glimpse of**, entrevoir.
glint [glint], *n.* trait de lumière, *m.*, lueur, *f.*—*v.i.* luire par moments.
glisten [glisn], **glister** ['glistə], **glitter** ['glitə], *v.i.* reluire, scintiller, chatoyer.—*n.* éclat, lustre, *m.*
gloaming ['gloumiŋ], *n.* crépuscule, *m.*
gloat [glout], *v.i.* dévorer *ou* couver des yeux; (*fig.*) se régaler de.
global ['gloubl], *a.* global; **global war**, conflit mondial, *m.*
globe [gloub], *n.* globe, *m.*
globule ['globjuːl], *n.* globule, *m.*
gloom [gluːm], **gloominess** ['gluːminis], *n.* obscurité, *f.*, ténèbres, *f.pl.*; (*fig.*) tristesse, *f.*
gloomily ['gluːmili], *adv.* obscurément; d'un air triste, lugubrement.
gloomy ['gluːmi], *a.* sombre, obscur; morne, triste.
glorify ['gloːrifai], *v.t.* glorifier.
glorious ['gloːriəs], *a.* glorieux; illustre, superbe.
glory ['gloːri], *n.* gloire; (*Paint.*) auréole, *f.*—*v.i.* se glorifier (*de*).
gloss [glɔs], *n.* lustre; apprêt, *m.*; (*fig.*) glose, *f.*, commentaire, *m.*—*v.i.* gloser, interpréter; lustrer; **to gloss over**, glisser sur.
glossary ['glɔsəri], *n.* glossaire, *m.*
glossiness ['glɔsinis], *n.* lustre, brillant, glacé, *m.*
glossy ['glɔsi], *a.* lustré, brillant, luisant.
glove [glʌv], *n.* gant, *m.*
glover ['glʌvə], *n.* gantier, *m.*
glow [glou], *v.i.* brûler (*de*); briller; (*fig.*) s'échauffer.—*n.* lueur rouge, *f.*; (*fig.*) feu, éclat, *m.*, splendeur, *f.*
glowing ['glouiŋ], *a.* embrasé; ardent, chaleureux.
glow-worm ['glouwəːm], *n.* ver luisant, *m.*
glue [gluː], *n.* colle-forte, *f.*—*v.t.* coller.
glum [glʌm], *a.* maussade, de mauvaise humeur, morne.
glut [glʌt], *v.t.* gorger, rassasier; engorger (*le marché*).—*n.* surabondance, *f.*, excès, *m.*
glutton [glʌtn], *n.* gourmand, goinfre, *m.*

438

gluttonous ['glʌtənəs], *a.* gourmand, glouton, vorace.

gluttony ['glʌtəni], *n.* gloutonnerie, *f.*

glycerine ['glisəri:n], *n.* glycérine, *f.*

gnarled [nɑ:ld], *a.* noueux.

gnash [næʃ], *v.t.* grincer.—*v.i.* grincer des dents.

gnashing ['næʃiŋ], *n.* grincement, *m.*

gnat [næt], *n.* cousin, moucheron, *m.*

gnaw [nɔ:], *v.t.* ronger.

gnawing ['nɔ:iŋ], *a.* rongeant, rongeur.—*n.* rongement, *m.*

gnome [noum], *n.* gnome, *m.*

gnu [nu:], *n.* gnou, *m.*

go [gou], *v.i. irr.* aller, se rendre; marcher, passer; s'en aller, partir (*to leave*); disparaître; devenir (*to become*); **to go astray**, s'égarer; **to go away**, s'en aller, partir; **to go back**, retourner, s'en retourner, reculer; **to go backward**, aller à reculons, reculer; **to go down**, descendre; se coucher (*soleil*); tomber; **to go off**, partir (*fusil*); s'en aller; **to go on**, aller, avancer, continuer; se passer; **to go through**, passer par, traverser; subir, souffrir; **to go to sleep**, s'endormir; **to go without**, se passer de; **to let go**, lâcher prise.—*n.* mode, vogue, *f.*; (*fig.*) entrain, coup, essai, *m.*

goad [goud], *n.* aiguillon, *m.*—*v.t.* aiguillonner; (*fig.*) stimuler.

goal [goul], *n.* but; terme, *m.*

goal-keeper ['goulki:pə], *n.* (*Ftb.*) gardien de but, *m.*

goat [gout], *n.* chèvre, *f.*; **he-goat**, bouc, *m.*

gobble [gɔbl], *v.t.* gober, avaler.—*v.i.* glouglouter (*dindon*).

goblet ['gɔblit], *n.* gobelet, *m.*

goblin ['gɔblin], *n.* lutin, *m.*

God [gɔd]. Dieu, *m.*

god [gɔd], *n.* dieu, *m.*

godchild ['gɔdtʃaild], *n.* filleul, *m.*, filleule, *f.*

goddaughter ['gɔddɔ:tə], *n.* filleule, *f.*

goddess ['gɔdis], *n.* déesse, *f.*

godfather ['gɔdfɑ:ðə], *n.* parrain, *m.*

Godfrey ['gɔdfri]. Godefroi, *m.*

godless ['gɔdlis], *a.* athée, impie.

godliness ['gɔdlinis], *n.* piété, *f.*

godly ['gɔdli], *a.* pieux, dévot.

godmother ['gɔdmʌðə], *n.* marraine, *f.*

godsend ['gɔdsend], *n.* aubaine, trouvaille, *f.*

godson ['gɔdsʌn], *n.* filleul, *m.*

godspeed ['gɔd'spi:d], *n.* succès, *m.*

goffer ['gɔfə], *v.t.* gaufrer.

goggle [gɔgl], *v.i.* rouler de gros yeux; **goggle eyes**, des yeux en boules de loto, *m.pl.*

goggles [gɔglz], *n.pl.* lunettes (protectrices), *f.pl.*

going ['gouiŋ], *n.* marche, démarche, allée, *f.*, départ, *m.*

goitre ['gɔitə], *n.* (*Med.*) goitre, *m.*

gold [gould], *a.* d'or, en or.—*n.* or, *m.*

golden [gouldn], *a.* d'or.

goldfinch ['gouldfintʃ], *n.* chardonneret, *m.*

goldfish ['gouldfiʃ], *n.* poisson rouge, *m.*

goldsmith ['gouldsmiθ], *n.* orfèvre, *m.*

golf [gɔlf, gɔf], *n.* golf, *m.*

golf club ['gɔlfklʌb], *n.* club de golf (*société ou instrument*), *m.*

golf course ['gɔlfkɔ:s], *n.* terrain de golf, *m.*

gondola ['gɔndələ], *n.* gondole; nacelle (*de ballon*), *f.*

gondolier [gɔndə'liə], *n.* gondolier, *m.*

gone [gɔ:n, gɔn], *a.* allé, parti; perdu, disparu; passé, écoulé; adjugé (*aux enchères*).

gong [gɔŋ], *n.* gong; timbre (*d'une horloge*), *m.*

good [gud], *a.* bon; de bien, honnête; convenable, avantageux; valide, solide; (*colloq.*) sage; **good luck**, bonheur, *m.*, bonne chance, *f.*; **to make good**, exécuter; compenser, indemniser; assurer.—*n.* bien, bon, avantage, profit, *m.*; **for good (and all)**, pour (tout) de bon; **what's the good of?** à quoi bon? (*pl.*) effets, biens, *m.pl.*, marchandises, *f.pl.*—*adv.* bien.—*int.* bon! bien! c'est très bien!

good-bye! [gud'bai], *int.* adieu! **good-bye for the present**, au revoir.

good-for-nothing [gudfə'nʌθiŋ], *n.* vaurien, *m.*

Good Friday [gud'fraid(e)i]. vendredi saint, *m.*

good-humored ['gud'hju:məd], *a.* de bonne humeur, enjoué, gai.

good-natured ['gud'neitʃəd], *a.* d'un bon naturel, bon, bienveillant.

goodness ['gudnis], *n.* bonté; probité, *f.*; **thank goodness!** Dieu merci!

goodwill [gud'wil], *n.* bienveillance, bonne volonté, bonté; (*Comm.*) clientèle, *f.*

goose [gu:s], *n.* (*pl.* **geese** [gi:s]) oie, *f.*; (*fig.*) imbécile, nigaud, *m.*

gooseberry ['guzbri], *n.* groseille à maquereau, *f.*

gooseberry bush ['guzbribuʃ], *n.* groseillier, *m.*

goose flesh ['gu:sfleʃ], *n.* chair de poule, *f.*

gore [gɔ:], *n.* sang, sang caillé, *m.*—*v.t.* donner un coup de corne à.

gorge [gɔ:dʒ], *n.* gorge, *f.*; gosier, *m.*—*v.t.* gorger, avaler, rassasier.—*v.i.* se gorger (*de*).

gorgeous ['gɔ:dʒəs], *a.* magnifique, splendide, fastueux.

gorilla [gə'rilə], *n.* gorille, *m.*

gorse [gɔ:s], *n.* ajonc, *m.*

gory ['gɔ:ri], *a.* sanglant, couvert de sang.

gosling ['gɔzliŋ], *n.* oison, *m.*

gospel ['gɔspəl], *n.* évangile, *m.*

gossamer ['gɔsəmə], *n.* fil de la Vierge, *m.*

gossip ['gɔsip], *n.* commère, *f.*; causeur (*personne*), *m.*; causerie, *f.*, commérage, *m.*—*v.i.* bavarder, faire des commérages.

gossip writer ['gɔsipraitə], *n.* (*Journ.*) échotier, *m.*

Goth [gɔθ], *n.* Goth; (*fig.*) barbare, *m.*

Gothic ['gɔθik], *a.* gothique, ogival.

gouge [gaudʒ], *n.* gouge, *f.*—*v.t.* gouger; **to gouge out**, arracher (*l'œil etc.*).

gourd [guəd], *n.* gourde, calebasse, *f.*

gout [gaut], *n.* goutte, *f.*

gouty ['gauti], *a.* goutteux.

govern ['gʌvən], *v.t.* gouverner, régir, diriger.

governess ['gʌvənis], *n.* institutrice, gouvernante, *f.*

government ['gʌvənmənt], *n.* gouvernement, *m.*, administration, *f.*, régime, *m.*

governor ['gʌvənə], *n.* gouverneur, gouvernant; directeur (*d'une institution*); (*Mech.*) régulateur, *m.*

gown [gaun], *n.* robe, *f.*; **dressing gown**, peignoir, *m.*, robe de chambre, *f.*; **nightgown**, chemise de nuit, *f.*

grab [græb], *v.t.* empoigner, saisir (d'un geste brusque).

grace [greis], *n.* grâce; faveur, *f.*; pardon; (*Mus.*) agrément; bénédicité (*avant le repas*), *m.*; grâces (*après le repas*), *f.pl.*—*v.t.* orner, embellir; illustrer, honorer (*de*).
graceful ['greisful], *a.* gracieux, bien fait, élégant.
gracefully ['greisfuli], *adv.* gracieusement, élégamment.
gracefulness ['greisfulnis], *n.* grâce, *f.*
graceless ['greislis], *a.* sans grâce; dépravé.
gracious ['greiʃəs], *a.* gracieux, clément, bon, favorable, bénin.
graciously ['greiʃəsli], *adv.* gracieusement, avec bonté, favorablement.
graciousness ['greiʃəsnis], *n.* bonté, grâce, *f.*
grade [greid], *n.* grade; degré, rang, *m.*—*v.t.* classer; calibrer; graduer.
grading ['greidiŋ], *n.* classement; calibrage, *m.*; graduation, *f.*
gradient ['greidiənt], *n.* (*Rail.*) rampe, inclinaison, *f.*
gradual ['grædjuəl], *a.* graduel, par degrés, gradué.
gradually ['grædjuəli], *adv.* graduellement, par degrés, peu à peu.
graduate ['grædjueit], *v.t.* graduer.—*v.i.* être reçu à un examen d'enseignement supérieur.—['grædjuit], *n.* gradué, *m.*
graduation [grædju'eiʃən], *n.* graduation; (*Univ.*) remise d'un diplôme, *f.*
graft (1) [grɑːft], *v.t.* greffer, enter (*sur*).—*n.* greffe, *f.*
graft (2) [grɑːft], *n.* (*colloq.*) corruption, *f.*
grafting ['grɑːftiŋ], *n.* greffe, *f.*
grafting knife ['grɑːftiŋnaif], *n.* greffoir, *m.*
grain [grein], *n.* grain, *m.*; céréales; fibres (*de bois*), *f.pl.*; **against the grain**, contre le fil, (*fig.*) à contre-cœur, à rebrousse-poil.
gram, gramme [græm], *n.* gramme, *m.*
grammar ['græmə], *n.* grammaire, *f.*
grammar school ['græməskuːl], *n.* école primaire, *f.*
grammatical [grə'mætikəl], *a.* grammatical; de grammaire.
gramophone ['græməfoun], *n.* gramophone; phonographe, *m.*
grampus ['græmpəs], *n.* épaulard, *m.*
granary ['grænəri], *n.* grenier, *m.*
grand [grænd], *a.* grand, magnifique, sublime, grandiose; **grand (piano)**, piano à queue, *m.*
grandchild ['græntʃaild], *n.* (*pl.* **grandchildren** ['græntʃildrən]) petit-fils, *m.*, petite-fille, *f.*
granddaughter ['grændɔːtə], *n.* petite-fille, *f.*
grandee [græn'diː], *n.* grand d'Espagne, *m.*
grandeur ['grændjə], *n.* grandeur, *f.*, éclat, *m.*
grandfather ['grænfɑːðə], *n.* grand-père, *m.*
grandiloquence [græn'diləkwəns], *n.* langage pompeux, *m.*; emphase, grandiloquence, *f.*
grandiloquent [græn'diləkwənt], *a.* pompeux, enflé, grandiloquent.
grandly ['grændli], *adv.* grandement, avec éclat.
grandmother ['grænmʌðə], *n.* grand-mère, *f.*
grandson ['grænsʌn], *n.* petit-fils, *m.*
grandstand ['grændstænd], *n.* tribune, *f.*
grange [greindʒ], *n.* manoir (avec ferme), *m.*
granite ['grænit], *n.* granit, *m.*
grant [grɑːnt], *v.t.* accorder, concéder; convenir, avouer, admettre.—*n.* aide, bourse; concession, *f.*

granulate ['grænjuleit], *v.t.* grener, granuler.—*v.i.* se granuler.
granule ['grænjuːl], *n.* granule, *m.*
grape [greip], *n.* grain de raisin, *m.*; (*pl.*) raisins, *m.pl.*; **a bunch of grapes**, une grappe de raisin.
grape-fruit ['greipfruːt], *n.* pamplemousse, *m.*
grape-shot ['greipʃɔt], *n.* mitraille, *f.*
graph [grɑːf], *n.* (*Math.*) courbe, *f.*; graphique, *m.*—*v.t.* graphiquer.
graphic ['græfik], *a.* graphique, pittoresque.
graph paper ['grɑːfpeipə], *n.* papier quadrillé, *m.*
graphite ['græfait], *n.* graphite, *m.*
grapnel ['græpnəl], *n.* grappin, *m.*
grapple [græpl], *n.* grappin, *m.*; lutte, *f.*—*v.t.* accrocher; grappiner.—*v.i.* en venir aux prises; lutter (*contre*).
grasp [grɑːsp], *v.t.* empoigner, saisir, serrer; embrasser; vouloir se saisir de.—*n.* prise, étreinte, poignée; (*fig.*) portée; compréhension, *f.*; **within one's grasp**, à la portée de la main.
grasping ['grɑːspiŋ], *a.* avide, cupide, avare.
grass [grɑːs], *n.* herbe, *f.*; gazon, herbage, *m.*
grasshopper ['grɑːshɔpə], *n.* sauterelle, *f.*
grassy ['grɑːsi], *a.* herbeux, couvert de gazon, verdoyant.
grate [greit], *n.* grille, *f.*; foyer (*âtre*), *m.*—*v.t.* râper; frotter.—*v.i.* crisser (*sur ou contre*).
grateful ['greitful], *a.* reconnaissant; (*fig.*) agréable.
gratefully ['greitfuli], *adv.* avec reconnaissance; (*fig.*) agréablement.
grater ['greitə], *n.* râpe, *f.*
gratification [grætifi'keiʃən], *n.* satisfaction, *f.*; plaisir, *m.*; gratification, récompense, *f.*
gratify ['grætifai], *v.t.* satisfaire, faire plaisir à; récompenser.
gratifying ['grætifaiiŋ], *a.* agréable; (*fig.*) flatteur.
grating ['greitiŋ], *a.* grinçant, discordant, choquant, désagréable.—*n.* grille, *f.*, grillage; grincement (*bruit*), *m.*
gratis ['greitis], *adv.* gratuitement, gratis, pour rien.
gratitude ['grætitjuːd], *n.* gratitude, reconnaissance, *f.*
gratuitous [grə'tjuːitəs], *a.* gratuit; (*fig.*) volontaire; bénévole.
gratuitously [grə'tjuːitəsli], *adv.* gratuitement; (*fig.*) sans motif.
gratuity [grə'tjuːiti], *n.* don, présent, *m.* gratification, *f.*; pourboire, *m.*
grave (1) [greiv], *n.* tombe, fosse, *f.*; tombeau, *m.*
grave (2) [greiv], *a.* grave, sérieux.
grave (3) [greiv], *v.t.* graver, tailler, ciseler.
grave-digger ['greivdigə], *n.* fossoyeur, *m.*
gravel [grævl], *n.* gravier, sable, *m.*—*v.t.* sabler.
gravely ['greivli], *adv.* gravement, sérieusement.
graven [greivn], *a.* gravé, taillé, ciselé.
graver ['greivə], *n.* graveur; burin (*instrument*), *m.*
gravity ['græviti], *n.* gravité, *f.*, air sérieux, *m.*; pesanteur, *f.*
gravy ['greivi], *n.* jus (*de viande*), *m.*; sauce, *f.*
gravy boat, see **sauce boat**.

gray (*Am.*) [GREY].

graze [greiz], *v.t.* effleurer, raser, frôler; érafler, écorcher (*la peau*).—*v.i.* paître, brouter.—*n.* écorchure, éraflure, *f.*

grease [gri:s], *n.* graisse, *f.*—*v.t.* graisser.

greasiness ['gri:sinis, 'gri:zinis], *n.* état graisseux, *m.*; (*fig.*) onctuosité, *f.*

greasy ['gri:si, 'gri:zi], *a.* gras, graisseux; (*fig.*) onctueux.

great [greit], *a.* grand; considérable; important, principal; gros (*de*); **a great deal** (*of*), **a great many** (*of*), beaucoup (de).

great-coat ['greitkout], *n.* pardessus, *m.*; (*Mil.*) capote, *f.*

great-grandparents ['greitgrændpɛərənts], *n.pl.* arrière-grands-parents, *m.pl.*

greatly ['greitli], *adv.* grandement, fort, beaucoup, de beaucoup.

greatness ['greitnis], *n.* grandeur; sublimité; force, *f.*

Grecian ['gri:ʃən], *a.* grec, de Grèce.—*n.* Helléniste, *m.*, *f.*

Greece [gri:s]. la Grèce, *f.*

greed [gri:d], **greediness** ['gri:dinis], *n.* cupidité, avidité; gourmandise, *f.*

greedily ['gri:dili], *adv.* avidement.

greedy ['gri:di], *a.* cupide, avide; glouton.

Greek [gri:k], *a.* grec, de Grèce.—*n.* grec (*langue*); Grec (*personne*), *m.*

green [gri:n], *a.* vert; (*fig.*) frais, nouveau; novice.—*n.* vert, *m.*; verdure, *f.*; gazon, *m.*; (*pl.*) légumes verts, *m.pl.*

greenfinch ['gri:nfintʃ], *n.* verdier, *m.*

greengage ['gri:ngeidʒ], *n.* reine-claude, *f.*

greengrocer ['gri:ngrousə], *n.* fruitier, marchand de légumes, *m.*

greenhorn ['gri:nhɔ:n], *n.* blanc-bec, niais, *m.*

greenhouse ['gri:nhaus], *n.* serre, *f.*

greenish ['gri:niʃ], *a.* verdâtre.

Greenland ['gri:nlənd]. le Groenland, *m.*

greet [gri:t], *v.t.* saluer, accueillir.

greeting ['gri:tiŋ], *n.* salutation, *f.*, salut, *m.*; (*pl.*) compliments, *m.pl.*

gregarious [gri'gɛəriəs], *a.* grégaire.

Gregory ['gregəri]. Grégoire, *m.*

grenade [grə'neid], *n.* grenade, *f.*

grenadier [grenə'diə], *n.* grenadier, *m.*

grey [grei], *a.* gris.

greyhound ['greihaund], *n.* lévrier, *m.*

greyish ['greiiʃ], *a.* grisâtre.

grid [grid], **gridiron** ['gridaiən], *n.* gril, *m.*

grief [gri:f], *n.* douleur, tristesse, peine, *f.*; chagrin, *m.*

grievance ['gri:vəns], *n.* grief, *m.*; injustice, *f.*

grieve [gri:v], *v.t.* chagriner, attrister, faire de la peine à.—*v.i.* se chagriner, s'affliger.

grievous ['gri:vəs], *a.* lourd, douloureux, grave, affligeant; atroce.

grievously ['gri:vəsli], *adv.* grièvement, cruellement.

grill [gril], *v.t.* griller, faire griller.—*n.* gril, *m.*; grillade (*viande grillée*), *f.*

grim [grim], *a.* farouche, féroce; lugubre, effrayant; sinistre.

grimace [gri'meis], *n.* grimace; (*pl.*) grimacerie, *f.*—*v.i.* grimacer.

grime [graim], *n.* saleté, noirceur, *f.*

grimly ['grimli], *adv.* d'un air farouche *ou* sinistre.

grimness ['grimnis], *n.* air renfrogné, air farouche, *m.*

grimy ['graimi], *a.* sale, noirci, encrassé.

grin [grin], *n.* grimace, *f.*, ricanement, *m.*—*v.i.* ricaner, grimacer.

grind [graind], *v.t.* *irr.* moudre; broyer; aiguiser, repasser (*couteau etc.*); grincer (*dents*); (*fig.*) opprimer.

grinder ['graində], *n.* repasseur, émouleur; broyeur, *m.*; dent molaire, *f.*

grinding ['graindiŋ], *n.* broiement, grincement (*des dents etc.*); repassage (*de couteaux*), *m.*; (*fig.*) oppression, *f.*

grindstone ['graindstoun], *n.* meule, *f.*

grip [grip], *n.* prise, étreinte, *f.*, serrement, *m.*—*v.t.* empoigner, saisir, serrer.

gripe [graip], *v.t.* saisir; opprimer; donner la colique à.—*v.i.* avoir la colique.—*n.* saisine; (*pl.*) colique, *f.*

griping ['graipiŋ], *a.* (*fig.*) cuisant, affreux; avare (*pingre*).—*n.* colique, *f.*

grisly ['grizli], *a.* hideux, affreux, horrible.

grist [grist], *n.* blé à moudre, *m.*, mouture, *f.*; (*fig.*) gain, profit, *m.*

gristle ['grisl], *n.* cartilage, *m.*

grit [grit], *n.* grès, sable; (*fig.*) courage, *m.*

gritty ['griti], *a.* graveleux.

grizzled ['grizld], *a.* grison, grisâtre.

grizzly ['grizli], *a.* grisâtre; **grizzly bear**, ours gris d'Amérique, *m.*

groan [groun], *n.* gémissement, grognement, *m.*—*v.i.* gémir, grogner.

grocer ['grousə], *n.* épicier, *m.*

grocery ['grousəri], *n.* épicerie, *f.*

groggy ['grɔgi], *a.* gris, pochard; titubant; aux jambes faibles (*cheval*).

groin [grɔin], *n.* aine; (*Arch.*) arête, *f.*

groom [gru:m], *n.* palefrenier, valet d'écurie, *m.*—*v.t.* panser; **well-groomed**, bien soigné, *m.*

groove [gru:v], *n.* rainure, rayure, cannelure; (*fig.*) ornière (*rut*), *f.*—*v.t.* creuser, canneler.

grope [group], *v.i.* tâtonner.

gropingly ['groupiŋli], *adv.* à tâtons.

gross [grous], *a.* gros; grossier, rude; (*Comm.*) brut; (*fig.*) flagrant, énorme.—*n.* gros, *m.*, grosse; masse, *f.*

grossly ['grousli], *adv.* grossièrement; d'une manière flagrante.

grossness ['grousnis], *n.* grossièreté; énormité, *f.*

grotto ['grɔtou], *n.* grotte, *f.*

grotesque [gro'tesk], *a.* grotesque.

ground (1) [graund], *past* and *p.p.* [GRIND] and *a.* broyé, moulu; aiguisé (*affilé*).

ground (2) [graund], *n.* terre, *f.*; terrain (*plot*); sol (*soil*), *m.*; fond (*de tableau, de dessin textile etc.*); (*fig.*) fondement, sujet, motif, *m.*, cause, *f.*; (*pl.*) terrains, *m.pl.*, sédiment, marc de café, *m.*—*v.t.* fonder, baser, établir, appuyer (*sur*).—*v.i.* échouer.

grounded ['graundid], *a.* fondé, établi; **well-grounded**, bien fondé.

ground floor ['graund'flɔ:], *n.* rez-de-chaussée, *m.*

groundless ['graundlis], *a.* sans fondement.

groundlessly ['graundlisli], *adv.* sans fondement.

group [gru:p], *n.* groupe, peloton, *m.*—*v.t.* grouper.

grouping ['gru:piŋ], *n.* groupement, *m.*

grouse (1) [graus], *n.* (*Orn.*) tétras; coq de bruyère, *m.*

grouse (2) [graus], *v.i.* grogner, grincher.

grove [grouv], *n.* bocage, bosquet, *m.*

grovel [grɔvl], *v.i.* ramper, se vautrer.

grovelling ['grɔvliŋ], *a.* rampant, abject, vil. —*n.* bassesse, *f.*

grow [grou], *v.t. irr.* cultiver.—*v.i.* croître, pousser; s'accroître; devenir, se faire (*to become*); **to grow up**, croître, grandir, arriver à maturité.

grower ['grouə], *n.* cultivateur, producteur, *m.*

growing ['grouiŋ], *a.* croissant.—*n.* croissance; culture, *f.*

growl [graul], *v.i.* grogner, gronder.—*n.* grognement, grondement, *m.*

grown-up ['grounʌp], *a.* fait, grand.—*n.* adulte, *m., f.*

growth [grouθ], *n.* croissance, *f.*; produit, cru, *m.*, récolte (*produce*), *f.*; (*fig.*) progrès, *m.*

grub [grʌb], *n.* larve, *f.*, ver blanc, *m.*—*v.t.* défricher, fouiller.—*v.i.* bêcher, creuser.

grubby ['grʌbi], *a.* véreux; (*fig.*) sale.

grudge [grʌdʒ], *n.* rancune, animosité, *f.*; **to bear a grudge against**, en vouloir à.— *v.t.* donner à contre-cœur.

grudgingly ['grʌdʒiŋli], *adv.* à contre-cœur; de mauvaise grâce.

gruel ['gru:əl], *n.* gruau, *m.*

gruesome ['gru:səm], *a.* macabre, horrible, lugubre.

gruff [grʌf], *a.* bourru, rude, rébarbatif.

grumble [grʌmbl], *v.i.* se plaindre, grogner, grommeler (*contre* ou *de*).

grumbler ['grʌmblə], *n.* grondeur, grogneur, *m.*

grumbling ['grʌmbliŋ], *n.* grognement, *m.*

grunt [grʌnt], *v.i.* grogner.—*n.* grognement, *m.*

guarantee [gærən'ti:], *n.* garant, *m.*, caution, garantie, *f.*—*v.t.* garantir.

guard [ga:d], *n.* garde; défense, protection, *f.*; garde (*personne*); (*Rail.*) conducteur, chef de train, *m.*—*v.t.* garder, défendre, protéger, veiller sur.—*v.i.* se garder, se prémunir (*contre*).

guarded ['ga:did], *a.* prudent, circonspect; réservé.

guardedly ['ga:didli], *adv.* avec circonspection, avec réserve.

guardian ['ga:djən], *a.* gardien, tutélaire.—*n.* gardien; tuteur (*de jeunes*), *m.*

guardianship ['ga:djənʃip], *n.* tutelle, protection, *f.*

guard-room ['ga:drum], *n.* corps de garde, *m.*, salle de police, *f.*

Guatemala [gwætə'ma:lə], le Guatemala, *m.*

gudgeon ['gʌdʒən], *n.* goujon; (*Mech.*) tourillon, *m.*; (*fig.*) dupe, *f.*

guess [ges], *v.t., v.i.* deviner, conjecturer.— *n.* conjecture, *f.*

guest [gest], *n.* invité, *m.*, convive, *m., f.*; hôte, *m.*

guffaw [gə'fɔ:], *n.* gros rire, *m.*—*v.i.* pouffer de rire.

guidance ['gaidəns], *n.* conduite, direction, *f.*

guide [gaid], *n.* guide, conducteur, *m.*; *Girl Guide*, éclaireuse, *f.*—*v.t.* conduire, guider, diriger; *guided missile*, (*Mil.*) engin téléguidé, *m.*

guild [gild], *n.* corporation, guilde, *f.*

guildhall ['gildhɔ:l], *n.* hôtel de ville, *m.*

guile [gail], *n.* astuce, *f.*, artifice, *m.*

guilt [gilt], *n.* culpabilité, *f.*

guiltily ['giltili], *adv.* criminellement.

guiltless ['giltlis], *a.* innocent.

guilty ['gilti], *a.* coupable; *the guilty party*, le coupable; *to find guilty*, (*Law*) déclarer coupable; *to plead guilty*, s'avouer coupable.

Guinea ['gini]. la Guinée, *f.*

guinea ['gini], *n.* guinée, *f.*

guinea fowl ['ginifaul], *n.* pintade, *f.*

guinea pig ['ginipig], *n.* cochon d'Inde, *m.*

guise [gaiz], *n.* guise, façon, apparence, *f.*; costume, *m.*, dehors, *m.pl.*

guitar [gi'ta:], *n.* guitare, *f.*

gulf [gʌlf], *n.* golfe; (*fig.*) gouffre, *m.*

gull [gʌl], *n.* mouette, *f.*, goéland; (*fig.*) jobard, *m.*—*v.t.* duper, flouer.

gullet ['gʌlit], *n.* gosier, *m.*

gullible ['gʌlibl], *a.* crédule.

gully ['gʌli], *n.* ravin, *m.*

gulp [gʌlp], *v.t.* avaler, gober.—*n.* goulée, gorgée, *f.*, trait, *m.*; *at a gulp*, d'un trait.

gum [gʌm], *n.* gomme; (*Anat.*) gencive, *f.*

gumboil ['gʌmbɔil], *n.* abcès aux gencives, *m.*

gumption ['gʌmpʃən], *n.* (*colloq.*) sens pratique, *m.*, jugeotte, *f.*

gum tree ['gʌmtri:], *n.* gommier, *m.*; (*fig.*) *up a gum tree*, dans le pétrin.

gun [gʌn], *n.* canon, *m.*; pièce d'artillerie, bouche à feu, *f.*; fusil (non rayé); (*Am.*) revolver, *m.*; *machine gun*, mitrailleuse *f.*

gunboat ['gʌnbout], *n.* canonnière, *f.*

guncarriage ['gʌnkæridʒ], *n.* affût (de canon), *m.*

gunnel [GUNWALE].

gunner ['gʌnə], *n.* canonnier, servant, artilleur, *m.*

gunnery ['gʌnəri], *n.* artillerie, *f.*; tir au canon, *m.*

gunpowder ['gʌnpaudə], *n.* poudre à canon, *f.*

gunshot ['gʌnʃɔt], *n.* portée de fusil (*distance*), *f.*; coup de canon (*décharge*); coup de feu (*blessure*), *m.*

gunwale [gʌnl], *n.* (*Naut.*) plat-bord, *m.*

gurgle [gə:gl], *v.i.* faire glouglou; gargouiller.

gush [gʌʃ], *n.* jaillissement, *m.*; effusion, *f.*, jet; débordement (*de sentiments*), *m.*—*v.i.* jaillir; (*fig.*) être sentimental à l'excès.

gusher ['gʌʃə], *n.* (*Min.*) puits jaillissant, *m.*

gushing ['gʌʃiŋ], *a.* jaillissant; bouillonnant; (*fig.*) expansif, empressé.

gusset ['gʌsit], *n.* gousset, *m.*

gust [gʌst], *n.* coup de vent, *m.*, bouffée, rafale, *f.*

gusty ['gʌsti], *a.* orageux, venteux.

gut [gʌt], *n.* boyau, intestin, *m.*; corde à boyau (*fabriqué*), *f.*; (*pl.*) (*fam.*) intestins, *m.pl.*, ventre; courage, cran, *m.*—*v.t.* éventrer, vider; (*fig.*) détruire.

gutter ['gʌtə], *n.* gouttière (*d'une maison*), *f.*; ruisseau, caniveau (*dans la rue*), *m.*—*v.i.* couler.

guttersnipe ['gʌtəsnaip], *n.* gamin, voyou, *m.*

guttural ['gʌtərəl], *a.* guttural.

guy [gai], *n.* épouvantail, *m.*; (*Naut.*) corde soutien, *f.*; (*Am.*) type, individu, *m.*

Guyana [gi'a:nə, gai'a:nə]. la Guyane, *f.*

guzzle [gʌzl], *v.t., v.i.* bouffer (*aliment*), lamper (*boisson*).

gym [dʒim], [GYMNASIUM].

gymkhana [dʒim'ka:nə], *n.* gymkhana, *m.*

gymnasium [dʒim'neiziəm], *n.* gymnase, *m.*

hand

gymnast ['dʒimnæst], *n.* gymnaste, *m.*, *f.*
gymnastic [dʒim'næstik], *a.* gymnastique.—
n.(pl.) gymnastique, *f.*
gypsum ['dʒipsəm], *n.* gypse, *m.*
gypsy [GIPSY].
gyrate [dʒai'reit], *v.i.* tournoyer.
gyration [dʒai'reiʃən], *n.* mouvement giratoire, *m.*

H

H, h [eitʃ]. huitième lettre de l'alphabet, *m.*
ou *f.*; *H-bomb*, [HYDROGEN].
haberdasher ['hæbədæʃə], *n.* confectionneur
et chemisier, *m.*
haberdashery ['hæbədæʃəri], *n.* confection
pour hommes, *f.*
habit ['hæbit], *n.* habitude, coutume, *f.*; *(pl.)*
mœurs, *f.pl.*; *riding habit*, amazone, *f.*;
to be in the habit of, avoir coutume de.—
v.t. vêtir.
habitable ['hæbitəbl], *a.* habitable.
habitation [hæbi'teiʃən], *n.* habitation, demeure, *f.*
habitual [hə'bitjuəl], *a.* habituel.
habitually [hə'bitjuəli], *adv.* habituellement,
d'habitude.
habituate [hə'bitjueit], *v.t.* habituer, accoutumer.
hack (1) [hæk], *v.t.* hacher, couper; ébrécher;
(fig.) massacrer, écorcher.
hack (2) [hæk], *n.* cheval de louage, *m.*; rosse
(cheval sans force), *f.*; *(fig.)* écrivassier à
gages, *m.*
hackney ['hækni], *n.* *hackney carriage*,
fiacre, *m.*
hackneyed ['hæknid], *a.* banal, rebattu;
hackneyed phrase, cliché, *m.*
haddock ['hædək], *n.* *(Ichth.)* aiglefin, *m.*
Hades ['heidi:z]. les Enfers, *m.pl.*
haemoglobin [hi:mə'gloubin], *n.* hémoglobine, *f.*
haemorrhage ['heməridʒ], *n.* hémorragie, *f.*
haft [hɑ:ft], *n.* manche, *m.*, poignée, *f.*
hag [hæg], *n.* vieille sorcière; *(pop.)* vieille
fée, *f.*
haggard ['hægəd], *a.* hagard, farouche, égaré.
haggle [hægl], *v.i.* marchander.
Hague [heig], **The**. La Haye, *f.*
hail (1) [heil], *n.* grêle, *f.*—*v.i.* grêler.
hail (2) [heil], *n.* salut, appel, *m.*—*int.* salut!
—*v.t.* saluer; *(Naut.)* héler; *to hail a
taxi*, héler *ou* appeler un taxi; *to hail
from*, venir de.
hailstone ['heilstoun], *n.* grêlon, *m.*
hailstorm ['heilstɔ:m], *n.* tempête de grêle, *f.*
hair [hɛə], *n.* cheveu *(a single hair)*, *m.*;
cheveux, *m.pl.*, chevelure *(head of hair)*, *f.*;
poil *(on the body, on animals etc.)*, crin
(horsehair), *m.*; soies *(bristles)*, *f.pl.*; *to do
one's hair*, se coiffer; *to split hairs*,
chicaner sur les mots.
hair-brush ['hɛəbrʌʃ], *n.* brosse à cheveux, *f.*
hair-cut ['hɛəkʌt], *n.* coupe de cheveux, *f.*
hairdresser ['hɛədresə], *n.* coiffeur, *m.*
hairless ['hɛəlis], *a.* chauve, sans cheveux;
sans poil *(animal)*.

hair net ['hɛənet], *n.* résille, *f.*
hairy ['hɛəri], *a.* velu, chevelu, poilu.
Haiti [hai'i:ti]. Haïti, *m.* ou *f.*
Haitian [hai'i:ʃən], *a.* haïtien.—*n.* Haïtien
(personne), *m.*
hake [heik], *n.* *(Ichth.)* merluche, *f.*, *(fam.)*
colin, *m.*
halberd ['hælbəd], *n.* hallebarde, *f.*
hale [heil], *a.* robuste, sain, bien portant; *to
be hale and hearty*, avoir bon pied, bon
œil.
half [hɑ:f], *a.* demi.—*n.* *(pl. halves* [hɑ:vz])
moitié, *f.*, demi, *m.*, *half an hour*, une
demi-heure, *f.*; *(pop.)* *not half!* tu parles!
—*adv.* à demi, à moitié.
half-back ['hɑ:fbæk], *n.* *(Ftb.)* demi, *m.*
half brother ['hɑ:fbrʌðə], *n.* demi-frère,
frère utérin, frère consanguin, *m.*
half-caste ['hɑ:fkɑ:st], *n.* métis, *m.*
half fare ['hɑ:f'fɛə], *n.* demi-place, *f.*, demitarif, *m.*
half holiday ['hɑ:f'hɔlidi], *n.* demi-congé, *m.*
half pay ['hɑ:f'pei], *n.* demi-solde, *f.*
half time ['hɑ:f'taim], *n.* *(Spt.)* la mi-temps, *f.*
half-way ['hɑ:f'wei], *adv.* à mi-chemin; *halfway up the hill*, à mi-côte.
half-witted ['hɑ:f'witid], *a.* niais, sot, idiot.
half year ['hɑ:f'jiə], *n.* semestre, *m.*
halibut ['hælibət], *n.* *(Ichth.)* flétan, *m.*
hall [hɔ:l], *n.* salle, *f.*; vestibule *(entrancehall)*; château, manoir *(seat)*; réfectoire
(dining hall); hôtel de ville *(town hall)*, *m.*;
hall porter, concierge, *m.*
hall-mark ['hɔ:lmɑ:k], *n.* poinçon de contrôle, *m.*—*v.t.* contrôler.
hallo! [hɔ:'lou], *int.* holà! hé!
hallow ['hælou], *v.t.* sanctifier, consacrer.
hallucinate [hə'lju:sineit], *v.t.* halluciner.
hallucination [həlju:si'neiʃən], *n.* hallucination; *(fig.)* déception, illusion, *f.*
halo ['heilou], *n.* *(Astron.)* halo, *m.*; *(Paint.
etc.)* auréole, *f.*
halt (1) [hɔ:lt], *n.* halte, *f.*; arrêt; clochement,
m.—*v.i.* faire halte.—*int.* halte-là!
***halt** (2) [hɔ:lt], *a.* boiteux, estropié.
halter ['hɔ:ltə], *n.* licou, *m.*, longe *(à cheval)*;
corde *(du gibet)*, *f.*
halve [hɑ:v], *v.t.* diviser en deux.
ham [hæm], *n.* jambon; jarret *(humain)*, *m.*
hamlet ['hæmlit], *n.* hameau, *m.*
hammer ['hæmə], *n.* marteau; chien *(de
fusil)*, *m.*; *to bring under the hammer*,
mettre aux enchères.—*v.t.* marteler, forger.
—*v.i.* marteler.
hammock ['hæmək], *n.* hamac, *m.*
hamper (1) ['hæmpə], *n.* panier, *m.*, manne, *f.*
hamper (2) ['hæmpə], *v.t.* empêtrer, embarrasser, gêner.
hamstring ['hæmstriŋ], *n.* tendon du jarret,
m.—*v.t. irr. (conjug. like* STRING) couper le
jarret à; *(fig.)* couper les moyens à.
hand [hænd], *n.* main; palme *(mesure de 4
pouces)*; signature; écriture *(calligraphie)*, *f.*;
(Cards) jeu, *m.*; aiguille *(d'une montre etc.)*,
f.; ouvrier, employé, *m.*; *at hand*, sous la
main; *off-hand*, sur-le-champ; *secondhand*, d'occasion.—*v.t.* passer, donner,
remettre; donner la main à; conduire,
guider; *to hand about ou round*, faire
passer de main en main, faire circuler; *to
hand down*, transmettre; *to hand over*,
remettre, céder.

443

handbag ['hændbæg], *n.* sac à main, *m.*
hand bell ['hændbel], *n.* sonnette, clochette, *f.*
handbook ['hændbuk], *n.* manuel; guide, *m.*
handcuff ['hændkʌf], *n.* menotte, *f.—v.t.* mettre les menottes à.
handful ['hændful], *n.* poignée, *f.*; (*fig.*) petit nombre, peu, *m.*
handicap ['hændikæp], *n.* handicap, *m.—v.t.* handicaper.
handicraft ['hændikrɑ:ft], *n.* métier, travail manuel, *m.*
handiwork ['hændiwə:k], *n.* ouvrage, travail manuel, *m.*
handkerchief ['hæŋkətʃif], *n.* mouchoir, *m.*
handle [hændl], *n.* manche, *m.*; poignée (*d'une epée etc.*), *f.*; bouton (*d'une porte*), *m.*; anse (*d'une cruche*); queue (*d'une poêle*), *f.*; **starting handle,** (*Motor.*) manivelle (de mise en marche), *f.—v.t.* manier; toucher à, manipuler.
handle-bar ['hændlbɑ:], *n.* guidon (*de bicyclette*), *m.*
handling ['hændliŋ], *n.* maniement, traitement, *m.*
handmaid ['hændmeid], *n.* servante, *f.*
handrail ['hændreil], *n.* garde-fou, *m.*, rampe, main courante, *f.*
handshake ['hændʃeik], *n.* poignée de main, *f.*, serrement de main, *m.*
handsome ['hænsəm], *a.* beau, élégant; (*fig.*) gracieux.
handsomely ['hænsəmli], *adv.* joliment, élégamment; généreusement.
handwriting ['hændraitiŋ], *n.* écriture, *f.*
handy ['hændi], *a.* adroit (*personne*); commode; à portée de la main.
hang [hæŋ], *v.t. irr.* pendre, suspendre; accrocher (*à*); tendre, tapisser (*de*); laisser pendre, pencher, baisser (*la tête etc.*); poser (*portes etc.*); **hang it!** fichtre! **go and be hanged,** va-t-en au diable! **to hang fire,** faire long feu; (*fig.*) vaciller.—*v.i.* pendre, être suspendu; s'accrocher, se pendre; baisser, se pencher (*à*); **to hang about,** rôder autour de; **to hang over,** être suspendu sur, surplomber.
hangar ['hæŋə], *n.* (*Av.*) hangar, *m.*
hang-dog ['hæŋdɔg], *n.* **hang-dog look,** mine patibulaire, *f.*
hanger-on ['hæŋə'rɔn], *n.* dépendant, parasite, *m.*
hanging ['hæŋiŋ], *a.* suspendu.—*n.* suspension, pendaison; pose (*papier de tenture*), *f.*; collage, *m.*; (*pl.*) tapisserie, tenture, *f.*
hangman ['hæŋmən], *n.* (*pl.* **-men** [men]) bourreau, *m.*
hank [hæŋk], *n.* poignée, *f.*, écheveau, *m.*
hanker ['hæŋkə], *v.i.* **to hanker after,** désirer ardemment.
hankering ['hæŋkəriŋ], *n.* grande envie, *f.*, vif désir, *m.*
haphazard [hæp'hæzəd], *a.* au petit bonheur, fortuit.—*n.* hasard, sort, *m.*
haply ['hæpli], *adv.* par hasard; peut-être.
happen [hæpn], *v.i.* arriver, advenir, se passer; se trouver par hasard.
happily ['hæpili], *adv.* heureusement, par bonheur.
happiness ['hæpinis], *n.* bonheur, *m.*
happy ['hæpi], *a.* heureux, content.
harass ['hærəs], *v.t.* harasser, harceler.

harbinger ['hɑ:bindʒə], *n.* avant-coureur, précurseur, *m.*
harbor ['hɑ:bə], *n.* port, havre; (*fig.*) refuge, asile, gîte, *m.—v.t.* héberger, recéler, donner asile à; (*fig.*) entretenir, nourrir.—*v.i.* se réfugier.
hard [hɑ:d], *a.* dur, ferme; (*fig.*) malaisé, difficile; pénible, rude, rigoureux; dur à la détente (*pingre*); **hard frost,** forte gelée, *f.*; **hard labor,** travaux forcés, *m.pl.*; **hard up,** à court (d'argent).—*adv.* dur, rudement, péniblement; fort, ferme.
harden [hɑ:dn], *v.t.* durcir; (*fig.*) endurcir (*à*).—*v.i.* s'endurcir, devenir dur.
hardening ['hɑ:dniŋ], *n.* durcissement; (*fig.*) endurcissement, *m.*; trempe (*d'acier*), *f.*
hardihood ['hɑ:dihud], *n.* hardiesse, audace, intrépidité, *f.*
hardily ['hɑ:dili], *adv.* durement, hardiment.
hardiness ['hɑ:dinis], *n.* hardiesse, *f.*; tempérament robuste, *m.*; (*fig.*) effronterie, assurance, *f.*
hardly ['hɑ:dli], *adv.* durement, rudement, mal; à peine, guère (*presque pas*); **hardly ever,** presque jamais.
hardness ['hɑ:dnis], *n.* dureté, solidité; difficulté; crudité (*d'eau*), *f.*
hardship ['hɑ:dʃip], *n.* fatigue, peine, privation, *f.*; (*pl.*) épreuves, souffrances, *f.pl.*
hardware ['hɑ:dwɛə], *n.* quincaillerie, *f.*
hardy ['hɑ:di], *a.* hardi, courageux; fort; de pleine terre (*plantes*).
hare [hɛə], *n.* lièvre, *m.*
hare-brained ['hɛəbreind], *a.* écervelé, étourdi.
hare-lip ['hɛəlip], *n.* bec-de-lièvre, *m.*
hark [hɑ:k], *v.i.* écouter, prêter l'oreille.—*int.* écoutez!
harlequin ['hɑ:likwin], *n.* arlequin, *m.*
harm [hɑ:m], *n.* tort, dommage, mal, *m.—v.t.* nuire à, faire du mal à.
harmful ['hɑ:mful], *a.* nuisible, malfaisant, nocif.
harmless ['hɑ:mlis], *a.* innocent, inoffensif.
harmonic [hɑ:'mɔnik], *a.* harmonique; harmonieux.—*n.*(*pl.*) harmonique, *f.*
harmonious [hɑ:'mouniəs], *a.* harmonieux; mélodieux.
harmonize ['hɑ:mənaiz], *v.t.* rendre harmonieux, accorder, harmoniser.—*v.i.* s'harmoniser; (*fig.*) s'accorder.
harmony ['hɑ:məni], *n.* harmonie, *f.*; accord, *m.*
harness ['hɑ:nis], *n.* harnais, harnachement, *m.—v.t.* harnacher; atteler (*à une voiture*).
harp [hɑ:p], *n.* harpe, *f.*; **jew's harp,** guimbarde, *f.—v.i.* jouer de la harpe; **to harp on one string,** rabâcher toujours la même chose.
harpist ['hɑ:pist], *n.* harpiste, *m.*, *f.*
harpoon [hɑ:'puːn], *n.* harpon, *m.—v.t.* harponner.
harpsichord ['hɑ:psikɔːd], *n.* clavecin, *m.*
harridan ['hæridən], *n.* chipie, mégère, *f.*
harrow ['hærou], *n.* herse, *f.—v.t.* herser; (*fig.*) torturer.
harrowing ['hærouiŋ], *a.* navrant.—*n.* hersage; (*fig.*) déchirement, *m.*
Harry ['hæri], Henri, *m.*
harry ['hæri], *v.t.* harceler; piller.
harsh [hɑ:ʃ], *a.* âpre, rude, dur; discordant.
harshly ['hɑ:ʃli], *adv.* durement, sévèrement.

harshness ['hɑːʃnis], *n.* âpreté; discordance, *f.*

harum-scarum ['hɛərəm'skɛərəm], *a.* écervelé, étourdi.

harvest ['hɑːvist], *n.* moisson (*de blé*); récolte (*de fruits etc.*); vendange (*de raisins*), *f.*—*v.t.* moissonner; récolter; vendanger.

harvester. see **combine-harvester.**

hash [hæʃ], *n.* hachis, *m.*—*v.t.* hacher, hacher menu; (*fig.*) plagier.

hasp [hæsp, hɑːsp], *n.* loquet, *m.*

hassock ['hæsək], *n.* coussin (*pour les genoux ou les pieds*), *m.*

haste [heist], *n.* hâte, précipitation, *f.*, emportement, *m.*; diligence, *f.*; *in haste*, à la hâte; *to make haste*, se hâter, se dépêcher. —*v.i.* or **hasten** [heisn], se hâter, se dépêcher, s'empresser.

hasten [heisn], *v.t.* hâter, dépêcher.

hastily ['heistili], *adv.* à la hâte; brusquement.

hastiness ['heistinis], *n.* hâte, précipitation, *f.*; emportement, *m.*

hasty ['heisti], *a.* rapide, précipité; inconsidéré, emporté.

hat [hæt], *n.* chapeau, *m.*; *bowler-hat*, chapeau melon; *felt hat*, feutre, *m.*; *soft felt hat*, chapeau mou; *straw hat*, chapeau de paille; *top hat*, chapeau haut de forme.

hatch (1) [hætʃ], *n.* (*pl.* **hatches** ['hætʃiz]) couvée (*de poulets*); éclosion (*d'œufs*); porte coupée (*dans le mur*); (*Naut.*) écoutille, *f.*; (*pl.*) panneaux des écoutilles, *m.pl.*—*v.t.* couver (*incuber*); faire éclore; (*fig.*) tramer, produire.—*v.i.* éclore.

hatch (2) [hætʃ], *v.t.* hacher (*un dessin*).

hatchet ['hætʃit], *n.* cognée, hachette, hache, *f.*

hate [heit], *n.* haine, *f.*—*v.t.* haïr, détester.

hateful ['heitful], *a.* odieux, détestable.

hatred ['heitrid], *n.* haine, *f.*

hat stand ['hætstænd], *n.* porte-chapeaux, *m. inv.*

hatter ['hætə], *n.* chapelier, *m.*

haughtily ['hɔːtili], *adv.* hautainement, avec arrogance.

haughtiness ['hɔːtinis], *n.* arrogance, *f.*

haughty ['hɔːti], *a.* hautain, arrogant.

haul [hɔːl], *n.* tirage, remorquage; coup de filet, *m.*—*v.t.* tirer, remorquer, haler; charrier, transporter.

haulage ['hɔːlidʒ], *n.* camionnage, roulage; remorquage, *m.*

hauler ['hɔːlə], *n.* camionneur, *m.*

haunch [hɔːntʃ], *n.* hanche (*d'un animal*), *f.*, cuissot (*de venaison*), *m.*

haunt [hɔːnt], *n.* retraite, *f.*; repaire (*de voleurs etc.*), *m.*—*v.t.* hanter, fréquenter; (*fig.*) obséder.

Havana [hə'vænə]. la Havane, *f.*

have [hæv], *v.t.* and *aux. irr.* avoir; tenir, posséder; contenir; prendre; faire; *I had rather*, j'aimerais mieux; *I have it*, j'y suis; *to have to*, devoir, falloir, avoir à.

haven [heivn], *n.* havre, port; (*fig.*) asile, *m.*

haversack ['hævəsæk], *n.* (*Mil.*) musette, *f.*; havresac, *m.*

havoc ['hævək], *n.* dégât, ravage, *m.*

hawk [hɔːk], *n.* faucon, *m.*—*v.t.* chasser au faucon; colporter (*vendre*).

hawker ['hɔːkə], *n.* colporteur, *m.*

hawser ['hɔːzə], *n.* haussière, *f.*, grelin, *m.*

hawthorn ['hɔːθɔːn], *n.* aubépine, *f.*

hay [hei], *n.* foin, *m.*

hay fever ['hei'fiːvə], *n.* rhume des foins, *m.*

hay-making ['heimeikiŋ], *n.* fenaison, *f.*

hayrick ['heirik], **haystack** ['heistæk], *n.* meule de foin, *f.*

hazard ['hæzəd], *n.* hasard, danger, risque, *m.* —*v.t.* hasarder, risquer.—*v.i.* se hasarder, s'aventurer.

hazardous ['hæzədəs], *a.* hasardeux, risqué, dangereux.

haze [heiz], *n.* petite brume; (*fig.*) obscurité, *f.*

hazel [heizl], *a.* noisette.—*n.* noisetier, coudrier, *m.*

hazel-nut ['heizlnʌt], *n.* noisette, *f.*

hazily ['heizili], *adv.* indistinctement.

hazy ['heizi], *a.* brumeux; *to have hazy notions*, avoir des idées vagues.

he [hiː], *pron.* il, celui, lui; *he and I*, lui et moi; *he that* or *he who*, celui qui.

he- [hiː], *pref.* mâle.

head [hed], *a.* premier, principal, en chef.— *n.* tête, *f.*; chef, avant, *m.*; proue (*de navire*), *f.*; haut bout (*d'une table*), *m.*; chevet (*d'un lit*), *m.*; chute (*d'eau*), *f.*; pièces (*de gibier*), *f.pl.*; source (*d'une rivière*), *f.*; (*fig.*) sujet, chapitre, *m.*—*v.t.* conduire, diriger.—*v.i. to head for*, (*Naut.*) mettre le cap sur; se diriger vers, s'avancer vers.

headache ['hedeik], *n.* mal de tête, *m.*, migraine, *f.*

head-dress ['heddres], *n.* coiffure, *f.*

heading ['hediŋ], *n.* titre, en-tête, *m.*

headland ['hedlənd], *n.* cap, promontoire, *m.*

head-light ['hedlait], *n.* (*Motor.*) phare, *m.*

headline ['hedlain], *n.* (*Journ.*) titre, soustitre, *m.*

headlong ['hedlɔŋ], *adv.* la tête la première; (*fig.*) tête baissée.—*a.* précipité, irréfléchi.

headmaster ['hed'mɑːstə], *n.* principal, directeur, proviseur, *m.*

head-mistress ['hed'mistris], *n.* directrice, *f.*

head-phone ['hedfoun], *n.* (*Teleph.*) écouteur, *m.*

head-quarters ['hed'kwɔːtəz], *n.pl.* quartier général, *m.*

headstone ['hedstoun], *n.* pierre tombale, *f.*

headstrong ['hedstrɔŋ], *a.* opiniâtre, obstiné, entêté.

headway ['hedwei], *n.* progrès, *m.*; *to make headway*, avancer, progresser.

heady ['hedi], *a.* capiteux (*boisson*).

heal [hiːl], *v.t.* guérir; (*fig.*) apaiser.—*v.i.* guérir, se guérir; se cicatriser.

healing ['hiːliŋ], *a.* curatif; (*fig.*) salutaire.— *n.* guérison, *f.*

health [helθ], *n.* santé, *f.*; toast, *m.*; *National Health Service*, sécurité sociale, *f.*; *bill of health*, patente de santé, *f.*

healthily ['helθili], *adv.* en santé; sainement.

healthy ['helθi], *a.* bien portant, en bonne santé; sain, salubre.

heap [hiːp], *n.* tas, monceau, amas, *m.*—*v.t.* entasser, amonceler.

hear [hiə], *v.t. irr.* entendre; entendre dire; écouter (*faire attention à*); (*fig.*) apprendre; *to hear it said*, entendre dire.—*v.i.* entendre; entendre parler; écouter; recevoir des nouvelles, avoir des nouvelles (*de*); *hear! hear!* très bien! bravo!

445

hearing ['hiəriŋ], *n.* ouïe (*sens auditif*); audition (*de témoins*), *f.*; ***hard of hearing***, dur d'oreille; ***within hearing***, à portée de la voix.

hearken ['hɑːkn], *v.i.* écouter.

hearsay ['hiəsei], *n.* ouï-dire, *m.*

hearse [həːs], *n.* corbillard, *m.*

heart [hɑːt], *n.* cœur, *m.*; (*fig.*) courage; centre, *m.*

heart attack ['hɑːtətæk], *n.* crise cardiaque, *f.*

heart-breaking ['hɑːtbreikiŋ], *a.* qui fend le cœur, navrant.

heart-broken ['hɑːtbroukən], *a.* qui a le cœur brisé.

heartburn ['hɑːtbəːn], *n.* brûlures d'estomac, aigreurs, *f.pl.*

hearten [hɑːtn], *v.t.* encourager, animer.

heart failure ['hɑːtfeiljə], *n.* arrêt du cœur, *m.*

heartfelt ['hɑːtfelt], *a.* qui vient du cœur.

hearth [hɑːθ], *n.* âtre, foyer, *m.*

heartily ['hɑːtili], *adv.* cordialement, de bon cœur; de bon appétit (*manger*).

heartiness ['hɑːtinis], *n.* cordialité; vigueur (*de l'appétit*), *f.*

heartless ['hɑːtlis], *a.* sans cœur, sans pitié.

hearty ['hɑːti], *a.* sincère, cordial; abondant, bon (*repas*).

heat [hiːt], *n.* chaleur; (*fig.*) ardeur; colère (*courroux*); (*Racing*) épreuve, *f.*—*v.t.* chauffer, échauffer.—*v.i.* s'échauffer.

heated ['hiːtid], *a.* chaud; échauffé; animé.

heath [hiːθ], *n.* bruyère, lande; brande (*plante*), *f.*

heathen ['hiːðn], *a.* and *n.* païen, *m.*

heather ['heðə], *n.* bruyère, brande, *f.*

heating ['hiːtiŋ], *n.* chauffage, *m.*

heave [hiːv], *n.* effort (*pour soulever*), *m.*, secousse, *f.*; soulèvement, *m.*—*v.t. irr.* lever; élever; soulever; pousser (*un soupir*).—*v.i.* se soulever; palpiter, battre (*sein, cœur etc.*).

heaven [hevn], *n.* ciel, *m.*, cieux, *m.pl.*

heavenly ['hevnli], *a.* céleste, divin.

heavily ['hevili], *adv.* pesamment, lourdement; fortement.

heaviness ['hevinis], *n.* pesanteur, lourdeur; (*fig.*) tristesse, *f.*

heavy ['hevi], *a.* lourd, pesant; (*fig.*) gros; triste.

Hebrew ['hiːbruː], *a.* hébreu, *m.*; hébraïque, *f.*—*n.* hébreu (*langue*); Hébreu, Juif (*personne*), *m.*

heckle [hekl], *v.t.* embarrasser de questions, harasser (*en public*).

hectic ['hektik], *a.* hectique; agité, fiévreux.

hedge [hedʒ], *n.* haie, *f.*—*v.t.* entourer d'une haie.—*v.i.* (*fig.*) éviter de se compromettre.

hedgehog ['hedʒhɔg], *n.* hérisson, *m.*

hedge sparrow ['hedʒspærou], *n.* mouchet, *m.*, fauvette d'hiver, *f.*

heed [hiːd], *n.* attention, *f.*, soin, *m.*—*v.t.* faire attention à, prendre garde à, écouter.

heedless ['hiːdlis], *a.* étourdi, inattentif, insouciant.

heedlessly ['hiːdlisli], *adv.* négligemment; étourdiment.

heel [hiːl], *n.* talon, *m.*; ***to be down at heel***, traîner la savate; ***to cool one's heels***, faire antichambre.—*v.i.* ***to heel over***, (*Naut.*) donner de la bande.

hefty ['hefti], *a.* (*fam.*) solide, costaud.

heifer ['hefə], *n.* génisse, *f.*

height [hait], *n.* hauteur, élévation; taille, *f.*; (*fig.*) comble, faîte, *m.*; ***the height of summer***, le cœur ou le fort de l'été.

heighten [haitn], *v.t.* rehausser, relever.

heinous ['heinəs], *a.* atroce.

heir [ɛə], *n.* héritier, *m.*

heiress ['ɛəris], *n.* héritière, *f.*

heirloom ['ɛəluːm], *n.* meuble ou bijou (de famille), *m.*

Helen ['helin]. (*Myth.*) Hélène, *f.*

helicopter ['helikɔptə], *n.* hélicoptère, *m.*

helium ['hiːliəm], *n.* (*Chem.*) hélium, *m.*

hell [hel], *n.* enfer, *m.*

hellish ['heliʃ], *a.* infernal, d'enfer.

hello! [he'lou], **hullo!** [hʌ'lou], *int.* holà! allô! (*au téléphone*); tiens! (*surprise*).

helm (1) [helm], *n.* (*Naut.*) gouvernail, timon, *m.*, barre, *f.*

helm (2) [helm], *n.* (*poet.*) heaume (*casque*), *m.*

helmet ['helmit], *n.* casque, *m.*

helmsman ['helmzmən], *n.* (*pl.* **-men** [men]) timonier, *m.*

help [help], *n.* secours, *m.*; aide, assistance, *f.*; remède (*recours*), *m.*; ***help !*** au secours!— *v.t.* aider, secourir, assister; servir (*à table*); empêcher (*prevent*); éviter (*avoid*); ***help yourself*** (*at table*), servez-vous; ***how can I help it?*** que voulez-vous que j'y fasse? ***how can it be helped?*** qu'y faire? ***I can't help it***, je n'y puis rien; ***I cannot help saying***, je ne puis m'empêcher de dire.— *v.i.* aider, servir, contribuer.

helper ['helpə], *n.* aide, *m.*, *f.*

helpful ['helpful], *a.* utile; secourable.

helpless ['helplis], *a.* faible, impuissant; sans appui.

helplessly ['helplisli], *adv.* faiblement; sans ressource.

helter-skelter ['heltə'skeltə], *adv.* pêle-mêle; en pagaille.

helve [helv], *n.* manche, *m.*

hem [hem], *n.* ourlet, bord, *m.*—*v.t.* ourler, border; ***to hem in***, entourer.

hemisphere ['hemisfiə], *n.* hémisphère, *m.*

hemlock ['hemlɔk], *n.* ciguë, *f.*

hemorrhage [HAEMORRHAGE].

hemp [hemp], *n.* (*Bot.*) chanvre, *m.*; (*fig.*) corde, *f.*

hen [hen], *n.* poule; femelle (*d'oiseau*), *f.*

hence [hens], *adv.* d'ici; de là, ainsi (*pour cela*); désormais (*temps*).

henceforth ['hensfɔːθ], **henceforward** [hens'fɔːwəd], *adv.* désormais, dorénavant, à l'avenir.

henchman ['hentʃmən], *n.* (*pl.* **-men** [men]) écuyer, valet; (*fig.*) partisan, *m.*

hen house ['henhaus], *n.* poulailler, *m.*

hen-pecked ['henpekt], *a.* gouverné par sa femme.

Henry ['henri]. Henri, *m.*

her [həː], *pers. pron.* elle, la, lui.—*poss. a.* son, sa, ses.—*dem. pron.* celle, *f.*

herald ['herəld], *n.* héraut; (*fig.*) avant-coureur, précurseur, *m.*—*v.i.* annoncer.

heraldry ['herəldri], *n.* science héraldique, *f.*, blason, *m.*

herb [həːb], *n.* herbe, *f.*; ***pot-herbs***, herbes potagères, *f.pl.*; ***sweet herbs***, fines herbes, *f.pl.*

herbaceous [həː'beiʃəs], *a.* herbacé.

herbage ['həːbidʒ], *n.* herbage, *m.*

herbalist ['hə:bəlist], *n.* herboriste, *m.*, *f.*
Hercules ['hə:kjuli:z]. Hercule, *m.*
herd [hə:d], *n.* troupeau, *m.*, troupe, *f.*—*v.t.* garder.—*v.i.* vivre en troupeau.
herdsman ['hə:dzmən], *n.* (*pl.* **-men** [men]) bouvier, *m.*
here [hiə], *adv.* ici; voici, que voici; *here!* présent! *here and there*, çà et là; *here they are*, les voici; *I am here*, me voici; *this one here*, celui-ci.
hereafter [hiər'ɑːftə], *adv.* désormais; dans la vie à venir.—*n.* l'au-delà, *m.*
hereby [hiə'bai], *adv.* par ce moyen, par là.
hereditary [hi'reditəri], *a.* héréditaire.
heredity [hi'rediti], *n.* hérédité, *f.*
heresy ['herisi], *n.* hérésie, *f.*
heretic ['heritik], *n.* hérétique, *m.*, *f.*
heretical [hi'retikəl], *a.* hérétique.
heretofore ['hiətufɔː], *adv.* jadis, jusqu'ici.
hereupon [hiərə'pɔn], *adv.* là-dessus.
herewith [hiə'wið], *adv.* ci-joint.
heritage ['heritidʒ], *n.* héritage, *m.*
hermetic [hə:'metik], *a.* hermétique.
hermetically [hə:'metikli], *adv.* hermétiquement.
hermit ['hə:mit], *n.* ermite, *m.*
hero ['hiərou], *n.* (*pl.* **heroes** ['hiərouz]) héros, *m.*
heroic [hi'rouik], **heroical** [-əl], *a.* héroïque.
heroine ['herouin], *n.* héroïne, *f.*
heroism ['herouizm], *n.* héroïsme, *m.*
heron ['herən], *n.* héron, *m.*
herring ['heriŋ], *n.* hareng, *m.*; *red herring*, hareng saur; (*fig.*) diversion, *f.*
hers [hə:z], *pron.* le sien, *m.*, la sienne, *f.*, les siens, *m.pl.*, les siennes, *f.pl.*; *a friend of hers*, une de ses amies, *f.*
herself [hə:'self], *pron.* elle-même, elle; (*reflexive*) se; *by herself*, toute seule.
hesitant ['hezitənt], *a.* hésitant.
hesitate ['heziteit], *v.i.* hésiter.
hesitation [hezi'teiʃən], *n.* hésitation, *f.*
heterodox ['hetərədɔks], *a.* hétérodoxe.
heterogeneous [hetərə'dʒiːniəs], *a.* hétérogène.
hew [hju:], *v.t. irr.* tailler, couper.
hewer ['hjuə], *n.* tailleur (*de pierre*); piqueur (*de charbon*); fendeur (*de bois*), *m.*
hexagon ['heksəgən], *n.* hexagone, *m.*
heyday ['heidei], *n.* beaux jours, *m.pl.*
hiatus [hai'eitəs], *n.* hiatus, *m.*; (*fig.*) lacune, *f.*
hibernate ['haibəneit], *v.i.* hiverner, hiberner, *m.*
hiccough, hiccup ['hikʌp], *n.* hoquet, *m.*—*v.i.* avoir le hoquet.
hidden [hidn], *a.* caché, secret; (*fig.*) occulte.
hide (1) [haid], *n.* peau, *f.*, cuir, *m.*
hide (2) [haid], *v.t. irr.* cacher; enfouir (*en terre*); *hide-and-seek*, cache-cache, *m.*—*v.i.* se cacher, se tenir caché.
hideous ['hidiəs], *a.* hideux, affreux.
hiding (1) ['haidiŋ], *n.* (*colloq.*) rossée, raclée, *f.*; *to give someone a good hiding*, tanner le cuir à quelqu'un.
hiding (2) ['haidiŋ], *n. in hiding*, caché; *hiding place*, cachette, *f.*
hie [hai], *v.i.* se hâter, se rendre (à).
hierarchy ['haiərɑːki], *n.* hiérarchie, *f.*
high [hai], *a.* haut, élevé; (*fig.*) grand; sublime; fier, altier; faisandé (*gibier*); avancé (*viande*); *from on high*, d'en haut; *high road*, grand-route, *f.*; *high street*, grand-

rue, *f.*; *it is high time*, il est grand temps.—*adv.* haut, hautement; grandement; fort; *to run high*, s'échauffer (*sentiments*).
highbrow ['haibrau], *a.* and *n.* (*fam.*) intellectuel, *m.*
higher ['haiə], *comp. a.* plus haut, plus élevé; supérieur.
highest ['haiist], *superl. a.* le plus haut, le plus élevé; *at the highest*, au comble.
high-flown ['haifloun], *a.* enflé; ampoulé (*style*).
high-handed ['hai'hændid], *a.* arbitraire, tyrannique.
Highland ['hailənd], *a.* de la Haute Écosse.
highland ['hailənd], *a.* des montagnes.
Highlander ['hailəndə], *n.* montagnard de l'Écosse, *m.*
Highlands ['hailəndz], **the.** les hautes terres d'Écosse, *f.pl.*, la haute Écosse, *f.*
highlands ['hailəndz], *n.pl.* pays montagneux, *m.*
highlight ['hailait], *n.* point culminant, (*fam.*) clou, *m.*
highly ['haili], *adv.* hautement; fortement.
Highness ['hainis], *n.* Altesse (*titre*), *f.*
highness ['hainis], *n.* hauteur, *f.*
high-pitched ['haipitʃt], *a.* aigu (*son*).
high-sounding ['haisaundiŋ], *a.* pompeux; ronflant (*style*).
high-spirited ['haispiritid], *a.* fougueux, plein de cœur.
highway ['haiwei], *n.* grand chemin, *m.*, grand-route, *f.*
highwayman ['haiweimən], *n.* (*pl.* **-men** [men]) voleur de grand chemin, *m.*
hike [haik], *n.* excursion à pied, *f.*—*v.i.* aller à pied, vagabonder; faire des excursions à pied.
hiker ['haikə], *n.* touriste à pied, *m.*, *f.*
hilarious [hi'lɛəriəs], *a.* gai, joyeux.
hilarity [hi'læriti], *n.* hilarité, *f.*
hill [hil], *n.* colline, montagne, *f.*, coteau, *m.*, butte; côte, *f.*
hillock ['hilək], *n.* monticule, *m.*, butte, *f.*
hilly ['hili], *a.* montagneux, accidenté.
hilt [hilt], *n.* poignée, garde, *f.*
him [him], *pers. pron.* le, lui.—*dem. pron.* celui.
himself [him'self], *pron.* lui-même, lui; (*reflexive*) se; *by himself*, tout seul.
hind (1) [haind], *n.* (*Zool.*) biche, *f.*
hind (2) [haind], *a.* de derrière, postérieur, arrière.
hinder ['hində], *v.t.* empêcher; gêner, embarrasser, retarder.
hindrance ['hindrəns], *n.* empêchement, obstacle, *m.*
Hindu [hin'du:], *a.* hindou.—*n.* Hindou, *m.*
hinge [hindʒ], *n.* gond, *m.*; paumelle; charnière (*butt hinge*), *f.*; (*fig.*) pivot, *m.*
hint [hint], *n.* insinuation, allusion, *f.*; (*fig.*) soupçon, *m.*; conseils, *m.pl.*; *broad hint*, allusion évidente; *to take the hint*, comprendre à demi-mot.—*v.i.* donner à entendre (à), insinuer, suggérer.
hip [hip], *n.* hanche, *f.*
hippopotamus [hipə'pɔtəməs], *n.* (*pl.* **hippopotami** [hipə'pɔtəmai], **hippopotamuses** [hipə'pɔtəməsəz]) hippopotame, *m.*
hire ['haiə], *n.* louage, prix de louage; salaire, *m.*, gages, *m.pl.*; *for hire*, à louer, libre (*taxi*).—*v.t.* louer; engager, employer.
hireling ['haiəliŋ], *a.* and *n.* mercenaire, *m.*

447

hire-purchase [′haiə′pəːtʃəs], *n.* vente à tempérament, location-vente, *f.*

hirsute [′həːsjuːt], *a.* velu, hirsute.

his [hiz], *a.* son, sa, ses.—*pron.* le sien, *m.*, la sienne, *f.*, les siens, *m.pl.*, les siennes, *f.pl.*; *a friend of his*, un de ses amis; *it is his*, c'est à lui.

hiss [his], *v.t., v.i.* siffler.—*n.* sifflement; sifflet, *m.*

hissing [′hisiŋ], *a.* sifflant.—*n.* sifflement, *m.*

historian [his′tɔːriən], *n.* historien, *m.*

historic [his′tɔrik], **historical** [his′tɔrikəl], *a.* historique.

history [′histəri], *n.* histoire, *f.*

hit [hit], *v.t. irr.* frapper, heurter; atteindre (*le but*); donner (*un coup*); toucher.—*v.i.* frapper, heurter (*contre*).—*n.* coup, *m.*; chance, trouvaille; (*fig.*) invention, *f.*; (*Theat.*) succès, *m.*

hitch [hitʃ], *v.t.* accrocher, attacher; (*Naut.*) nouer, amarrer.—*n.* accroc, *m.*; entrave, *f.*; empêchement; (*Naut.*) nœud, *m.*

hitch-hike [′hitʃhaik], *v.i.* faire de l'auto-stop.

hither [′hiðə], *adv.* ici; *hither and thither*, çà et là.

hitherto [hiðə′tuː], *adv.* jusqu'ici.

hive [haiv], *n.* ruche, *f.*; (*fig.*) essaim (*swarm*), *m.*

hoard [hɔːd], *n.* monceau, amas (*secret*); trésor, *m.*—*v.t.* amasser, accumuler.—*v.i.* thésauriser.

hoarding [′hɔːdiŋ], *n.* accumulation, *f.*; panneau-réclame, *m.*

hoar-frost [′hɔːfrɔst], *n.* gelée blanche, *f.*, givre, *m.*

hoarse [hɔːs], *a.* enroué, rauque.

hoary [′hɔːri], *a.* blanc; aux cheveux gris *ou* blancs.

hoax [houks], *n.* mystification, *f.*; mauvais tour (*brimade*); canard (*fausse nouvelle*), *m.* —*v.t.* mystifier; attraper.

hob [hɔb], *n.* plaque (*de l'âtre*), *f.*

hobble [hɔbl], *v.t.* entraver.—*v.i.* clocher, clopiner; aller clopin clopant.—*n.* clochement, *m.*, difficulté, *f.*; embarras, entrave, *f.*

hobby [′hɔbi], *n.* marotte (*manie*), distraction, *f.*, passe-temps, *m.*

hobby-horse [′hɔbihɔːs], *n.* cheval de bois, dada, *m.*

hobgoblin [hɔb′gɔblin], *n.* lutin, *m.*

hobnob [′hɔb′nɔb], *v.i.* trinquer ensemble.

hobo [′houbou], *n.* (*Am.*) chemineau, *m.*

hock [hɔk], *n.* jarret (*d'un cheval*); vin du Rhin, *m.*

hockey [′hɔki], *n.* hockey, *m.*

hockey stick [′hɔkistik], *n.* crosse de hockey, *f.*

hoe [hou], *n.* houe, binette, *f.*; *Dutch hoe*, sarcloir, *m.*—*v.t., v.i.* biner; sarcler.

hog [hɔg], *n.* cochon; goret, *m.*; (*Comm.*) porc, pourceau; (*fam.*) glouton, *m.*

hogshead [′hɔgzhed], *n.* muid, *m.*; barrique de 240 litres (*tonneau*), *f.*

hoist [hɔist], *v.t.* hisser; guinder (*avec un treuil*); lever; arborer (*un drapeau*).—*n.* grue, *f.*, palan, *m.*

hold [hould], *n.* prise, *f.*; soutien (*appui*), *m.*; garde (*custody*); place forte (*forteresse*); (*Naut.*) cale, *f.*; *to take hold of*, prendre, saisir; *to let go one's hold*, lâcher prise.— *v.t. irr.* tenir, retenir; arrêter; garder, maintenir; occuper, avoir; contenir (*to contain*);

regarder comme; célébrer; *to hold back*, retenir, cacher; *to hold fast*, tenir ferme, tenir bon; *to hold off*, tenir à distance; *to hold over*, remettre, ajourner; *to hold up*, lever, soulever, soutenir; arrêter, retarder. —*v.i.* tenir; se maintenir, durer; supporter; adhérer (*à*); rester; s'arrêter; être vrai; *hold on*, arrêtez! (*Teleph.*) ne quittez pas! *hold tight!* ne lâchez pas! *to hold back*, se tenir en arrière, hésiter; *to hold fast*, tenir ferme; *to hold forth*, haranguer, pérorer; *to hold on*, s'accrocher à; persévérer, poursuivre.

hold-all [′houldɔːl], *n.* enveloppe de voyage, *f.*

holder [′houldə], *n.* personne qui tient, *f.*; (*Spt.*) tenant, locataire, *m.*; poignée, anse, *f.*, manche, *m.*, (*in compound words*) porte-; (*Fin.*) titulaire, *m.*

holding [′houldiŋ], *n.* possession, tenure; ferme, *f.*

hold-up [′houldʌp], *n.* arrêt de la circulation, *m.*; panne, *f.*; hold-up, *m.*

hole [houl], *n.* trou; antre, *m.*, caverne, *f.*; orifice, *m.*, ouverture, *f.*

holiday [′hɔlidei], *a.* de fête, de congé; de vacances.—*n.* fête, *f.*, jour de fête, jour férié, (*Sch. etc.*) congé, *m.*, (*pl.*) vacances, *f.pl.*; *bank holiday*, fête légale; *on holiday*, en vacance(s).

holiness [′houlinis], *n.* sainteté, *f.*

Holland [′hɔlənd]. la Hollande, *f.*

hollow [′hɔlou], *a.* creux; vide; sourd (*son*). —*n.* creux, *m.*, cavité, *f.*; bas-fond, *m.*—*v.t.* creuser, évider.

holly [′hɔli], *n.* houx, *m.*

hollyhock [′hɔlihɔk], *n.* rose trémière, *f.*

holster [′houlstə], *n.* fonte (*de selle*), *f.*; étui (*de revolver*), *m.*

holy [′houli], *a.* saint, sacré; bénit; *Holy Ghost*, le Saint-Esprit; *Holy Land*, la Terre Sainte; *holy water*, eau bénite, *f.*; *Holy Week*, la semaine sainte, *f.*

homage [′hɔmidʒ], *n.* hommage, *m.*

home [houm], *a.* de la maison, domestique; (*fig.*) qui porte (*coup*).—*n.* foyer domestique, chez-soi; logis, *m.*, maison, *f.*, intérieur, *m.*; (*fig.*) demeure, *f.*; pays, *m.*, patrie (*pays natal*), *f.*; *at home*, chez soi, à la maison; *Home Office*, Ministère de l'Intérieur, *m.*; *to make oneself at home*, faire comme chez soi.—*adv.* chez soi, au logis, à la maison; dans son pays; (*fig.*) directement; *to bring home to*, faire admettre à; *homing pigeon*, pigeon voyageur, *m.*

home-coming [′houmkʌmiŋ], *n.* retour au foyer, *m.*

homeland [′houmlænd], *n.* patrie, *f.*; pays natal, *m.*

homeliness [′houmlinis], *n.* caractère domestique, *m.*; simplicité; rusticité, *f.*

homely [′houmli], *a.* du ménage; simple, sans façon; (*Am.*) laid.

Homer [′houmə]. Homère, *m.*

home-sick [′houmsik], *a.* qui a le mal du pays, nostalgique.

home-sickness [′houmsiknis], *n.* mal du pays, *m.*, nostalgie, *f.*

homestead [′houmsted], *n.* manoir, *m.*, ferme, *f.*

homeward(s) [′houmwəd(z)], *adv.* vers la maison; vers son pays.

homework ['houmwə:k], *n.* devoirs, *m.pl.*
homicide ['hɔmisaid], *n.* homicide, *m.*
homogeneous [hɔmə'dʒi:niəs], *a.* homogène.
homosexual [houmo'seksjuəl], *a.* and *n.* homosexuel, *m.*
Honduran [hɔn'djuərən], *a.* hondurien.—*n.* Hondurien (*personne*), *m.*
Honduras [hɔn'djuərəs]. l'Honduras, *m.*
hone [houn], *n.* pierre à aiguiser. *f.*—*v.t.* aiguiser.
honest ['ɔnist], *a.* honnête, loyal, probe, de bonne foi, sincère; **honest man**, homme de bien, honnête homme, *m.*
honestly ['ɔnistli], *adv.* honnêtement, sincèrement.
honesty ['ɔnisti], *n.* honnêteté, probité, bonne foi, sincérité, *f.*
honey ['hʌni], *n.* miel, *m.*; (*fig.*) (*Am.*) chérie, *f.*, ange, *m.*
honeycomb ['hʌnikoum], *n.* rayon de miel, *m.*
honeymoon ['hʌnimu:n], *n.* lune de miel, *f.*
honeysuckle ['hʌnisʌkl], *n.* chèvrefeuille, *m.*
honorary ['ɔnərəri], *a.* honoraire.
honor ['ɔnə], *n.* honneur, *m.*; (*fig.*) dignité, estime, *f.*—*v.t.* honorer (*de*); faire honneur à, faire bon accueil à (*une facture*).
honorable ['ɔnərəbl], *a.* honorable, d'honneur.
hood [hud], *n.* capuchon, *m.*; coiffe; capote (*de voiture*), *f.*; (*Am. Motor.*) [BONNET].
hoodwink ['hudwiŋk], *v.t.* bander les yeux à; (*fig.*) tromper.
hoof [hu:f, huf], *n.* (*pl.* **hooves** [hu:vz]) sabot, *m.*
hook [huk], *n.* crochet, croc; hameçon (*pour pêcher*), *m.*; faucille (*sickle*), *f.*; **hook and eye**, agrafe et porte, *f.*—*v.t.* accrocher; agrafer; attraper.
hooked [hukt], *a.* crochu, recourbé; aquilin (*nez*).
hooligan ['hu:ligən], *n.* voyou, *m.*
hooliganism ['hu:ligənizm], *n.* voyouterie, *f.*
hoop [hu:p], *n.* cercle; cerceau, *m.*; huppe (*d'oiseau*); jante (*de roue*), *f.*; panier (*de robe*); (*Croquet*) arceau, *m.*—*v.t.* cercler; (*fig.*) entourer.
hoot [hu:t], *v.t.*, *v.i.* hululer (*hibou*); huer; (*Motor.*) klaxonner.
hooter ['hu:tə], *n.* (*colloq.*) sirène d'usine, *f.* klaxon, *m.*
hop (1) [hɔp], *n.* saut, sautillement; bal populaire, *m.*—*v.i.* sauter, sautiller; (*pop.*) **to hop it**, ficher le camp.
hop (2) [hɔp], *n.* (*Bot.*) houblon, *m.*
hop-field ['hɔpfi:ld], *n.* houblonnière, *f.*
hopscotch ['hɔpskɔtʃ], *n.* marelle, *f.*
hope [houp], *n.* espérance, *f.*, espoir, *m.*, attente, *f.*—*v.t.* espérer, s'attendre à.—*v.i.* espérer.
hopeful ['houpful], *a.* plein d'espérance; qui promet beaucoup; encourageant.
hopefully ['houpfuli], *adv.* avec espoir, avec confiance; si tout va bien.
hopeless ['houplis], *a.* vain (*effort*); non valable (*excuse*); inextricable (*difficulté*); inconsolable (*douleur*); irrémédiable (*mal*); inutile (*négociation*); incorrigible (*personne*); désespéré (*situation*).
hopelessly ['houplisli], *adv.* sans espoir.
hopper ['hɔpə], *n.* trémie (*d'un moulin*), *f.*; (*Agric.*) semoir, *m.*

horizon [hə'raizən], *n.* horizon, *m.*
horizontal [hɔri'zɔntl], *a.* horizontal.
hormone ['hɔ:moun], *n.* hormone, *f.*
horn [hɔ:n], *a.* de corne.—*n.* corne, *f.*; bois (*de cerf*), *m.*; coupe (*à boire*); (*Ent.*) antenne *f.*; (*Mus.*) cor, cornet, *m.*; (*Motor.*) klaxon, *m.*
hornet ['hɔ:nit], *n.* frelon, *m.*
horrible ['hɔribl], *a.* horrible, affreux.
horribly ['hɔribli], *adv.* horriblement, affreusement.
horrid ['hɔrid], *a.* affreux, horrible.
horrific [hə'rifik], *a.* horrifique.
horrify ['hɔrifai], *v.t.* horrifier.
horror ['hɔrə], *n.* horreur, *f.*
horse [hɔ:s], *n.* cheval, *m.*, chevaux, *m.pl.*; (*Mil.*) cavalerie, *f.*; chevalet (*pour scier*), séchoir (*pour le linge*), *m.*
horseback ['hɔ:sbæk], *n.* dos de cheval, *m.*; **on horseback**, à cheval.
horseblock ['hɔ:sblɔk], *n.* montoir, *m.*
horse chestnut ['hɔ:s'tʃesnʌt], *n.* marron d'Inde; marronnier d'Inde (*arbre*), *m.*
horse dealer ['hɔ:sdi:lə], *n.* maquignon, *m.*
horse doctor ['hɔ:sdɔktə], *n.* vétérinaire, *m.*
horse-fly ['hɔ:sflai], *n.* taon, *m.*
horseman ['hɔ:smən], *n.* (*pl.* **-men** [men]) cavalier; écuyer, *m.*
horsemanship ['hɔ:smənʃip], *n.* équitation, *f.*; manège, *m.*
horse-play ['hɔ:splei], *n.* jeu de mains, *m.*
horse-power ['hɔ:spauə], *n.* cheval-vapeur, *m.*
horseshoe ['hɔ:ʃʃu:], *a.* en fer à cheval.—*n.* fer de cheval; fer à cheval, *m.*
horsewhip ['hɔ:swip], *n.* cravache, *f.*—*v.t.* cravacher.
horticulture ['hɔ:tikʌltʃə], *n.* horticulture, *f.*
hose [houz], *n.* bas, *m.pl.*; tuyau d'arrosage, boyau, *m.*
hosiery ['houʒəri], *n.* bonneterie, *f.*
hospitable ['hɔspitəbl], *a.* hospitalier.
hospital ['hɔspitl], *n.* hôpital, *m.*, infirmerie, *f.*; hospice, *m.*
hospitality [hɔspi'tæliti], *n.* hospitalité, *f.*
host [houst], *n.* hôte; hôtelier, aubergiste, *m.*; armée, foule; (*R.-C. Ch.*) hostie, *f.*
hostage ['hɔstidʒ], *n.* otage, *m.*
hostel ['hɔstəl], *n.* hôtel *ou* foyer pour les étudiants etc., *m.*; **youth hostel**, auberge de la jeunesse, *f.*
hostess ['houstis, 'houstes], *n.* hôtesse, *f.*
hostile ['hɔstail], *a.* hostile, ennemi; (*fig.*) opposé (*à*).
hostility [hɔs'tiliti], *n.* hostilité, *f.*
hot [hɔt], *a.* chaud, ardent; brûlant, piquant, épicé (*plat, sauce*); (*fig.*) vif, violent, échauffé; **boiling hot**, tout bouillant; **to be hot**, avoir chaud (*personne*), faire chaud (*temps*), être chaud (*chose*).
hotbed ['hɔtbed], *n.* couche, *f.*
hotel [ho'tel], *n.* hôtel, *m.*
hot-headed ['hɔt'hedid], *a.* violent, fougueux.
hot-house ['hɔthaus], *n.* serre, *f.*
hotly ['hɔtli], *adv.* avec chaleur, avec acharnement.
hotness ['hɔtnis], *n.* chaleur; (*fig.*) passion, violence, *f.*
hot-water bottle [hɔt'wɔ:təbɔtl], *n.* bouillotte, *f.*
hough [hɔk], *n.* jarret (*d'animal*), *m.*
hound [haund], *n.* chien de chasse, *m.*—*v.t.* chasser; (*fig.*) traquer; exciter.

hour [ˈauə], *n.* heure, *f.*; *an hour ago*, il y a une heure; *an hour and a half*, une heure et demie; *a quarter of an hour*, un quart d'heure; *half an hour*, une demi-heure.

hourly [ˈauəli], *a.* continuel, d'heure en heure, à l'heure.—*adv.* d'heure en heure.

house [haus], *n.* maison, *f.*, logis, *m.*, demeure, habitation, *f.*; ménage (*household*), *m.*; famille; (*Parl.*) chambre; (*Theat.*) salle, *f.*; *a country house*, une maison de campagne; *a nobleman's house*, un hôtel; *house full*, (*Theat.*) salle comble; *public house*, café, *m.*, brasserie, *f.*—[hauz], *v.t.* loger, héberger; garer (*une voiture*); rentrer (*blé etc.*); faire rentrer (*bestiaux etc.*).

house agent [ˈhauseidʒənt], *n.* agent de location, agent immobilier, *m.*

house-breaker [ˈhausbreikə], *n.* cambrioleur (*voleur*); démolisseur (*ouvrier*), *m.*

house-breaking [ˈhausbreikiŋ], *n.* vol avec effraction, *m.*

household [ˈhaushould], *a.* de ménage, domestique.—*n.* maison, *f.*, ménage, *m.*, famille, *f.*

householder [ˈhaushouldə], *n.* chef de famille, chef de maison, *m.*

housekeeper [ˈhauskiːpə], *n.* femme de charge, ménagère, *f.*; concierge, *m.*, *f.*

housekeeping [ˈhauskiːpiŋ], *n.* ménage, *m.*

housemaid [ˈhausmeid], *n.* bonne à tout faire, *f.*

house surgeon [ˈhaussəːdʒən], *n.* interne (en chirurgie), *m.*

housewife [ˈhauswaif], *n.* ménagère, *f.*

housework [ˈhauswəːk], *n.* travaux ménagers, *m.pl.*; *to do the housework*, faire le ménage.

housing [ˈhauziŋ], *n.* logement, *m.*; rentrée, *f.*, rentrage, *m.*; (*Tech.*) enchâssure, *f.*

hovel [ˈhɔvl], *n.* appentis, *m.*, bicoque, *f.*, taudis, *m.*, masure, *f.*

hover [ˈhɔvə], *v.i.* planer; hésiter.

how [hau], *adv.* comment, de quelle façon; combien; comme, que; *how are you?* comment allez-vous? *how far*, jusqu'où; *how many*, *how much*, combien de; *how old are you?* quel âge avez-vous?

however [hauˈevə], *conj.* cependant, pourtant, du reste, d'ailleurs, toutefois.—*adv.* de quelque manière que; quelque . . . que; *however rich he may be*, quelque riche qu'il soit, tout riche qu'il est; *however that may be*, quoi qu'il en soit.

howl [haul], *n.* hurlement, cri; mugissement, *m.*—*v.i.* hurler, crier; mugir.

howler [ˈhaulə], *n.* faute grossière, bévue, *f.*

howling [ˈhauliŋ], *a.* hurlant; *a howling success*, un succès fou.—*n.* hurlement, *m.*

hoyden [ˈhɔidn], *n.* garçon manqué (*se dit d'une jeune fille*), *m.*

hub [hʌb], *n.* moyeu, *m.*; (*fig.*) centre, *m.*

hubbub [ˈhʌbʌb], *n.* vacarme, brouhaha, tintamarre, *m.*

hub cap [ˈhʌbkæp], *n.* (*Motor.*) enjoliveur, *m.*

huddle [hʌdl], *v.t.* entasser pêle-mêle, (*fig.*) brouiller, confondre ensemble.—*v.i.* se mêler, se presser les uns contre les autres; (*fig.*) se confondre.—*n.* tas confus, fouillis, méli-mélo, ramassis, *m.*

hue [hjuː], *n.* couleur, teinte, nuance; huée, clameur, *f.*; *to raise a hue and cry after*, crier haro sur, élever un tollé contre.

huff [hʌf], *n.* emportement, accès de colère, *m.* —*v.t.* froisser; (*checkers*) souffler.—*v.i.* se gonfler, se mettre en colère.

hug [hʌg], *v.t.* embrasser, étreindre; étouffer (*en serrant*).—*n.* embrassement, *m.*, étreinte, *f.*

huge [hjuːdʒ], *a.* vaste, immense, énorme.

hulk [hʌlk], *n.* carcasse (*d'un navire*), *f.*, ponton; (*pl.*) bagne, *m.*

hulking [ˈhʌlkiŋ], *a.* gros, lourd.

hull [hʌl], *n.* coque (*d'un navire*); cosse, gousse (*de pois, fèves etc.*); écale (*de noix*), *f.*—*v.t.* écaler (*noix*); écosser (*fèves*).

hullo [HELLO].

hum [hʌm], *v.t.*, *v.i.* fredonner (*personne*), bourdonner (*abeilles*); *to hum and ha(w)*, bredouiller.—*n.* bourdonnement; brouhaha (*de conversation*), *m.*

human [ˈhjuːmən], *a.* humain.

humane [hjuːˈmein], *a.* humain, compatissant.

humanist [ˈhjuːmənist], *n.* humaniste, *m.*, *f.*

humanity [hjuːˈmæniti], *n.* humanité, *f.*

humanly [ˈhjuːmənli], *adv.* humainement.

humble [hʌmbl], *a.* humble; modeste.—*v.t.* humilier, abaisser, mortifier.

humble-bee [ˈhʌmblbiː], *n.* bourdon, *m.*

humbly [ˈhʌmbli], *adv.* humblement, avec humilité; modestement.

humbug [ˈhʌmbʌg], *n.* blague, farce, *f.*, charlatanisme; blagueur, farceur, charlatan, *m.*

humdrum [ˈhʌmdrʌm], *a.* monotone, assommant.

humid [ˈhjuːmid], *a.* humide.

humidity [hjuːˈmiditi], *n.* humidité, *f.*

humiliate [hjuːˈmilieit], *v.t.* humilier, abaisser.

humiliating [hjuːˈmilieitiŋ], *a.* humiliant.

humiliation [hjuːmiliˈeiʃən], *n.* humiliation, *f.*

humility [hjuːˈmiliti], *n.* humilité, *f.*

humming [ˈhʌmiŋ], *n.* bourdonnement, fredonnement; (*fig.*) murmure, *m.*

humming-bird [ˈhʌmiŋbəːd], *n.* oiseau-mouche, colibri, *m.*

humor [ˈhjuːmə], *n.* humeur, disposition, *f.*; humour. *m*—*v.t.* complaire à, laisser faire.

humorist [ˈhjuːmərist], *n.* humoriste, *m.*, *f.*, personne spirituelle, *f.*

humorous [ˈhjuːmərəs], *a.* humoristique; plaisant, drôle, comique.

hump [hʌmp], *n.* bosse, *f.*; *to have the hump*, (*slang*) être maussade.

humpbacked [ˈhʌmpbækt], *a.* bossu.

hunch [hʌntʃ], *n.* gros morceau (*de pain, de fromage*), *m.*; bosse (*du dos*); (*fig.*, *fam.*) idée, *f.*, soupçon, *m.*; *to have a hunch that*, soupçonner que.

hunchback [ˈhʌntʃbæk], *n.* bossu, *m.*

hundred [ˈhʌndrəd], *a.* cent.—*n.* cent, *m.*, centaine, *f.*; canton, district, *m.*

hundredth [ˈhʌndrətθ], *a.* centième.—*n.* centième (*fraction*), *m.*

hundredweight [ˈhʌndrədweit], *n.* quintal, *m.*

Hungarian [hʌŋˈgɛəriən], *a.* hongrois.—*n.* hongrois (*langue*); Hongrois (*personne*), *m.*

Hungary [ˈhʌŋgəri]. la Hongrie, *f.*

hunger [ˈhʌŋgə], *n.* faim, *f.*—*v.i.* avoir faim; être affamé (*de*).

hungrily [ˈhʌŋgrili], *adv.* avidement.

hungry ['hʌŋgri], *a.* affamé, «qui a faim; maigre (*terre etc.*); **to be hungry**, avoir faim.

hunk [hʌŋk], *n.* gros morceau (*de gâteau, de fromage*), *m.*

hunt [hʌnt], *v.t.* chasser à courre; (*fig.*) poursuivre, chercher.—*v.i.* chasser, aller à la chasse.—*n.* chasse à courre, *f.*

hunter ['hʌntə], *n.* chasseur; cheval de chasse, *m.*

hunting ['hʌntiŋ], *n.* chasse; (*fig.*) recherche, *f.*

huntress ['hʌntris], *n.* chasseuse; (*poet.*) chasseresse, *f.*

huntsman ['hʌntsmən], *n.* (*pl.* -**men** [men]) veneur, piqueur, *m.*

hurdle [hə:dl], *n.* claie, *f.*; (*Spt.*) obstacle, *m.*, haie, *f.*; **hurdle race**, course de haies, *f.*

hurdy-gurdy ['hə:di'gə:di], *n.* vielle, *f.*

hurl [hə:l], *v.t.* lancer (avec force), précipiter, jeter.

hurly-burly ['hə:li'bə:li], *n.* tintamarre, brouhaha, tohu-bohu, *m.*

hurrah [hu'rɑ:], **hurray** [hu'rei], *n.* hourra, *m.*

hurricane ['hʌrikən], *n.* ouragan, *m.*

hurried ['hʌrid], *a.* précipité, pressé; fait à la hâte.

hurriedly ['hʌridli], *adv.* précipitamment, à la hâte.

hurry ['hʌri], *n.* hâte, précipitation, *f.*; (*fig.*) tumulte, *m.*, confusion, *f.*; **to be in a hurry**; être pressé.—*v.t.* hâter, presser, précipiter.—*v.i.* se hâter, se dépêcher, se presser.

hurt [hə:t], *n.* mal, *m.*, blessure, *f.*; (*fig.*) tort, *m.*—*v.t. irr.* faire mal à, (*fig.*) nuire à, offenser, blesser; **to hurt oneself**, se faire du mal.—*v.i.* faire du mal; faire mal.

hurtful ['hə:tful], *a.* nuisible (*à*).

hurtle [hə:tl], *v.t.* lancer.—*v.i.* se précipiter; se heurter.

husband ['hʌzbənd], *n.* mari, époux, *m.*—*v.t.* ménager, économiser.

husbandman ['hʌzbəndmən], *n.* (*pl.* -**men** [men]) laboureur, cultivateur, *m.*

husbandry ['hʌzbəndri], *n.* agriculture, industrie agricole; économie, *f.*

hush [hʌʃ], *n.* silence, calme, *m.*—*int.* chut! paix!—*v.t.* taire, faire taire; (*fig.*) calmer.—*v.i.* se taire, faire silence.

husk [hʌsk], *n.* cosse, gousse (*de pois etc.*), *f.*; brou, *m.*, écale (*de noix*); balle, pellicule (*de grain*), *f.*

huskiness ['hʌskinis], *n.* enrouement (*de la voix*), *m.*

husky ['hʌski], *a.* cossu; rauque, enroué (*voix*); (*colloq.*) costaud, fort.—*n.* chien esquimau, *m.*

hussar [hu'za:], *n.* hussard, *m.*

hussy ['hʌsi], *n.* friponne, coquine, *f.*

hustle [hʌsl], *v.t.* bousculer, presser, pousser.—*v.i.* se presser, se dépêcher.

hut [hʌt], *n.* hutte, cabane; (*Mil.*) baraque, *f.*

hutch [hʌtʃ], *n.* huche, *f.*; clapier (*de lapin*), *m.*

hyacinth ['haiəsinθ], *n.* (*Bot.*) jacinthe, *f.*

hybrid ['haibrid], *a.* and *n.* hybride, *m.*

hydrangea [hai'drændʒə, hai'dreindʒə], *n.* (*Bot.*) hortensia, *m.*

hydrant ['haidrənt], *n.* prise d'eau, *f.*; **fire hydrant**, bouche d'incendie, *f.*

hydraulic [hai'drɔ:lik], *a.* hydraulique.

hydrochloric [haidrə'klɔrik], *a.* (*acide*) chlorhydrique.

hydrogen ['haidridʒən], *n.* hydrogène, *m.*; **hydrogen bomb** or (*fam.*) **H-bomb**, bombe à hydrogène, bombe H, *f.*

hydrophobia [haidro'foubiə], *n.* hydrophobie, rage, *f.*

hyena [hai'i:nə], *n.* hyène, *f.*

hygiene ['haidʒi:n], *n.* hygiène, *f.*

hygienic [hai'dʒi:nik], *a.* hygiénique.

hymn [him], *n.* (*Eccles.*) hymne, *m.* ou *f.*, cantique, *m.*

hymn book ['himbuk], **hymnal** [himnl], *n.* hymnaire, *m.*

hyperbola [hai'pə:bələ], *n.* (*Geom.*) hyperbole, *f.*

hyperbole [hai'pə:bəli], *n.* (*Gram.*) hyperbole, *f.*

hyphen ['haifən], *n.* trait d'union, *m.*

hypnosis [hip'nousis], *n.* hypnose, *f.*

hypnotism ['hipnətizm], *n.* hypnotisme, *m.*

hypnotist ['hipnətist], *n.* hypnotiste, *m.*, *f.*

hypocrisy [hi'pɔkrisi], *n.* hypocrisie, *f.*

hypocrite ['hipəkrit], *n.* hypocrite, *m.*, *f.*

hypocritical [hipə'kritikl], *a.* hypocrite.

hypothesis [hai'pɔθisis], *n.* (*pl.* **hypotheses** [hai'pɔθisi:z]) hypothèse, *f.*

hysteria [his'tiəriə], *n.*, **hysterics** [his'teriks], *n.pl.* crise de nerfs, attaque de nerfs, *f.*

hysterical [his'terikəl], *a.* hystérique.

I

I (1), **i** [ai]. neuvième lettre de l'alphabet, *m.*

I (2) [ai], *pron.* je; moi.

ibex ['aibeks], *n.* bouquetin, *m.*

ibis ['aibis], *n.* (*Orn.*) ibis, *m.*

ice [ais], *n.* glace, *f.*—*v.t.* glacer (*gâteau*); frapper (*vin*).—*v.i.* (*Av.*) **to ice up**, givrer.

ice axe ['aisæks], *n.* piolet, *m.*

iceberg ['aisbə:g], *n.* iceberg, *m.*

ice-bound ['aisbaund], *a.* pris dans *ou* bloqué par les glaces.

ice-box ['aisbɔks], *n.* glacière, *f.*

ice-breaker ['aisbreikə], *n.* brise-glace, *m.*

ice cream ['ais'kri:m], *n.* glace, *f.*

iced [aist], *a.* glacé; frappé (*vin etc.*); **iced lollypop**, sucette, *f.*

ice-floe ['aisflou], *n.* banc de glace, *m.*

Iceland ['aislənd] l'Islande, *f.*

Icelander ['aisləndə], *n.* Islandais, *m.*

Icelandic [ais'lændik], *a.* islandais, d'Islande.

ice pack, see **pack-ice**.

icicle ['aisikl], *n.* petit glaçon, *m.*

icing ['aisiŋ], *n.* glacé; frappage (*de vin*), *m.*

icon ['aikɔn], *n.* icone, *f.*

icy ['aisi], *a.* glacé, glacial; **icy road**, route verglacée, *f.*

idea [ai'diə], *n.* idée, *f.*

ideal [ai'diəl], *a.* and *n.* idéal, *m.*

idealism [ai'diəlizm], *n.* idéalisme, *m.*

idealist [ai'diəlist], *n.* idéaliste, *m.*, *f.*

ideally [ai'diəli], *adv.* idéalement.

identical [ai'dentikl], *a.* identique.

identification [aidentifi'keiʃən], *n.* identification, *f.*

identify [ai′dentifai], *v.t.* identifier (*avec*); reconnaître.
identity [ai′dentiti], *n.* identité, *f.*
idiocy [′idiəsi], *n.* idiotie, *f.*
idiom [′idiəm], *n.* idiome; idiotisme, *m.*
idiomatic [idiə′mætik], *a.* idiomatique.
idiot [′idiət], *n.* idiot, *m.*; imbécile, *m.*, *f.*
idiotic [idi′ɔtik], *a.* idiot, d'imbécile.
idle [aidl], *a.* oisif, paresseux (*indolent*); désœuvré (*inactif*); en chômage (*personne sans travail*), en repos (*machine*); (*fig.*) inutile, frivole; **idle fellow**, fainéant, paresseux, *m.*; **idle talk**, balivernes, *f.pl.*— *v.t.* **to idle away**, perdre, gaspiller.— *v.i.* ne̅ rien faire, faire le paresseux, fainéanter; (*Motor.*) tourner au ralenti.
idleness [′aidlnis], *n.* paresse; oisiveté; (*fig.*) inutilité, *f.*; désœuvrement, *m.*
idler [′aidlə], *n.* oisif, fainéant, paresseux, *m.*
idly [′aidli], *adv.* dans l'oisiveté, en paresseux; inutilement.
idol [aidl], *n.* idole, *f.*
idolater [ai′dɔlətə], **idolatress** [ai′dɔlətris], *n.* idolâtre, *m.*, *f.*
idolatry [ai′dɔlətri], *n.* idolâtrie, *f.*
idolize [′aidəlaiz], *v.t.* idolâtrer.
idyllic [ai′dilik, i′dilik], *a.* idyllique.
if [if], *conj.* si, quand, quand même; **even if**, même si, quand même; **if necessary**, s'il le faut, au besoin; **if not**, sinon, si ce n'est.
igloo [′iglu:], *n.* hutte de neige, *f.*; igloo (*des Esquimaux*), *m.*
ignite [ig′nait], *v.t.* allumer.—*v.i.* prendre feu.
ignition [ig′niʃən], *n.* ignition, *f.*; (*Motor.*) allumage, *m.*; **ignition key**, clé de contact, *f.*
ignoble [ig′noubl], *a.* roturier; ignoble.
ignominious [ignə′miniəs], *a.* ignominieux.
ignominy [′ignəmini], *n.* ignominie, *f.*
ignoramus [ignə′reiməs], *n.* ignorant, (*fam.*) âne bâté, *m.*
ignorance [′ignərəns], *n.* ignorance, *f.*
ignorant [′ignərənt], *a.* ignorant.
ignore [ig′nɔ:], *v.t.* feindre d'ignorer; ne tenir point compte de.
ill [il], *a.*; malade (*santé*); mauvais, méchant.— *n.* mal, *m.*; mal; peu; **it ill becomes you**, il vous sied mal.
ill-bred [′il′bred], *a.* mal élevé.
illegal [i′li:gəl], *a.* illégal; illicite.
illegible [i′ledʒibl], *a.* illisible.
illegitimate [ilə′dʒitimit], *a.* illégitime; naturel (*enfant*).
ill-fated [′il′feitid], *a.* infortuné, malheureux.
ill-feeling [′il′fi:liŋ], *n.* ressentiment, *m.*
ill-gotten [′il′gɔtn], *a.* mal acquis.
ill-health [′il′helθ], *n.* mauvaise santé, *f.*
illicit [i′lisit], *a.* illicite.
ill-informed [′ilin′fɔ:md], *a.* mal renseigné.
illiteracy [i′litərəsi], *n.* analphabétisme, *m.*
illiterate [i′litərit], *a.* and *n.* illettré, *m.*
ill-mannered [′il′mænəd], *a.* malappris.
illness [′ilnis], *n.* maladie, indisposition, *f.*
illogical [i′lɔdʒikl], *a.* illogique, peu logique.
ill-tempered [′il′tempəd], *a.* maussade, de mauvaise humeur.
ill-treat [′il′tri:t], *v.t.* maltraiter.
illuminate [i′lju:mineit], *v.t.* illuminer, éclairer; enluminer (*un livre*).
illumination [ilju:mi′neiʃən], *n.* illumination; enluminure (*de livres etc.*), *f.*

illusion [i′lu:ʒən, i′lju:ʒən], *n.* illusion, *f.*
illustrate [′iləstreit], *v.t.* illustrer; (*fig.*) expliquer; orner, embellir.
illustration [iləs′treiʃən], *n.* illustration; explication, *f.*; éclaircissement, *m.*
illustrative [i′lʌstrətiv], *a.* explicatif.
illustrious [i′lʌstriəs], *a.* illustre, célèbre.
ill-will [′il′wil], *n.* mauvais vouloir, *m.*; rancune, *f.*
I'm [aim] (=**I am**) [BE].
image [′imidʒ], *n.* image, *f.*; (*fig.*) portrait, *m.*
imagery [′imidʒri], *n.* images, *f.pl.*; langage figuré, *m.*
imaginable [i′mædʒinəbl], *a.* imaginable.
imaginary [i′mædʒinəri], *a.* imaginaire.
imagination [imædʒi′neiʃən], *n.* imagination; conception, idée, *f.*
imagine [i′mædʒin], *v.t.* imaginer; s'imaginer, se figurer.
imbecile [′imbisi:l], *a.* and *n.* faible d'esprit, *m.*, *f.*
imbecility [imbi′siliti], *n.* faiblesse d'esprit, *f.*
imbibe [im′baib], *v.t.* imbiber, absorber; (*fig.*) puiser.
imbue [im′bju:], *v.t.* imprégner, teindre; (*fig.*) pénétrer, douer (*de*).
imbued [im′bju:d], *a.* imbu, pénétré (*de*).
imitate [′imiteit], *v.t.* imiter.
imitation [imi′teiʃən], *n.* imitation; (*Comm.*) contrefaçon, *f.*
imitative [′imitətiv], *a.* imitatif, imitateur.
immaculate [i′mækjulit], *a.* sans tache, immaculé.
immaterial [imə′tiəriəl], *a.* immatériel; peu important.
immature [imə′tjuə], *a.* pas mûr; prématuré.
immeasurable [i′meʒərəbl], *a.* infini; incommensurable.
immeasurably [i′meʒərəbli], *adv.* outre mesure, infiniment.
immediate [i′mi:djit], *a.* immédiat; urgent, très pressé (*sur enveloppe*).
immediately [i′mi:djitli], *adv.* immédiatement, tout de suite, sur-le-champ.—*conj.* aussitôt que, dès que.
immense [i′mens], *a.* immense.
immensely [i′mensli], *adv.* immensément.
immensity [i′mensiti], *n.* immensité, *f.*
immerse [i′mə:s], *v.t.* plonger, immerger.
immigrant [′imigrənt], *a.* and *n.* immigrant, *m.*
immigrate [′imigreit], *v.i.* immigrer.
immigration [imi′greiʃən], *n.* immigration, *f.*
imminent [′iminənt], *a.* imminent.
immobilize [i′moubilaiz], *v.t.* immobiliser.
immodest [i′mɔdist], *a.* immodeste, peu modeste, impudique.
immoral [i′mɔrl], *a.* immoral; dissolu.
immorality [imə′ræliti], *n.* immoralité, *f.*
immortal [i′mɔ:tll], *a.* immortel.
immortality [imɔ:′tæliti], *n.* immortalité, *f.*
immortalize [i′mɔ:tələaiz], *v.t.* immortaliser, rendre immortel.
immovable [i′mu:vəbl], *a.* fixe, immuable, inébranlable.
immutable [i′mju:təbl], *a.* immuable.
imp [imp], *n.* diablotin, petit démon; petit diable (*gamin*), *m.*
impact [′impækt], *n.* choc, impact, *m.*— [im′pækt], *v.t.* serrer, encastrer.
impair [im′pɛə], *v.t.* altérer, affaiblir.

impale [im'peil], v.t. empaler.
impalpable [im'pælpəbl], a. impalpable; intangible.
impart [im'pɑːt], v.t. accorder, donner; communiquer.
impartial [im'pɑːʃl], a. impartial, désintéressé.
impartially [im'pɑːʃəli], adv. impartialement.
impassable [im'pɑːsəbl], a. impraticable, infranchissable.
impassioned [im'pæʃənd], a. passionné.
impassive [im'pæsiv], a. impassible, insensible.
impatience [im'peiʃəns], n. impatience, f.
impatient [im'peiʃənt], a. impatient; (fig.) emporté.
impatiently [im'peiʃəntli], adv. impatiemment.
impeach [im'piːtʃ], v.t. accuser; attaquer.
impeachment [im'piːtʃmənt], n. mise en accusation; accusation, f.
impeccable [im'pekəbl], a. impeccable.
impecunious [impi'kjuːniəs], a. besogneux.
impede [im'piːd], v.t. empêcher; retarder, gêner.
impediment [im'pedimənt], n. empêchement, obstacle, m.; (fig.) difficulté, f.
impel [im'pel], v.t. pousser (à); forcer (de).
impelling [im'pelin], a. impulsif, moteur.
impend [im'pend], v.i. être suspendu sur, menacer; être imminent.
impending [im'pendin], a. imminent, menaçant.
impenetrable [im'penitrəbl], a. impénétrable; (fig.) insensible.
impenitent [im'penitənt], a. impénitent.
imperative [im'perətiv], a. impératif; (fig.) obligatoire.—n. (Gram.) impératif, m.
imperceptible [impə'septibl], a. imperceptible, insensible.
imperceptibly [impə'septibli], adv. imperceptiblement.
imperfect [im'pəːfikt], a. imparfait; incomplet; (Gram.) imparfait.—n. (Gram.) imparfait, m.
imperfection [impə'fekʃən], n. imperfection, f.
imperfectly [im'pəːfiktli], adv. imparfaitement.
imperial [im'piəriəl], a. impérial; (fig.) princier.
imperil [im'peril], v.t. mettre en danger, hasarder.
imperious [im'piəriəs], a. impérieux.
imperishable [im'periʃəbl], a. impérissable.
impersonal [im'pəːsənəl], a. impersonnel.
impersonate [im'pəːsəneit], v.t. personnifier; (Theat.) représenter, jouer le rôle de.
impertinence [im'pəːtinəns], n. impertinence, insolence, f.
impertinent [im'pəːtinənt], a. impertinent, insolent; hors de propos.
impertinently [im'pəːtinəntli], adv. d'un ton insolent; mal à propos.
imperturbable [impəːtə'bəbl], a. imperturbable.
impervious [im'pəːviəs], a. imperméable, impénétrable; (fig.) inaccessible.
impetuous [im'petjuəs], a. impétueux.
impetus ['impitəs], n. impulsion, f.; élan, essor, m.

impinge [im'pindʒ], v.i. se heurter (à ou contre); empiéter (sur).
impious ['impiəs], a. impie.
impiously ['impiəsli], adv. en impie, avec impiété.
impish ['impiʃ], a. espiègle, malicieux.
implacable [im'plækəbl], a. implacable, acharné.
implant [im'plɑːnt], v.t. implanter; (fig.) imprimer, inculquer.
implement ['implimənt], n. outil; instrument; ustensile, m.—['impliment], v.t. exécuter; accomplir.
implicate ['implikeit], v.t. impliquer.
implication [impli'keiʃən], n. implication, f.; by implication, implicitement.
implicit [im'plisit], a. implicite; (fig.) aveugle.
implied [im'plaid], a. implicite, tacite.
implore [im'plɔː], v.t. implorer, conjurer, supplier (de).
imply [im'plai], v.t. impliquer, signifier, vouloir dire; donner à entendre (suggérer).
impolite [impə'lait], a. impoli.
impoliteness [impə'laitnis], n. impolitesse, f.
import [im'pɔːt], n. portée, signification, f., sens, m.; importance; (Comm.) importation, f.—[im'pɔːt], v.t. importer; introduire; signifier.
importance [im'pɔːtəns], n. importance, f.
important [im'pɔːtənt], a. important.
importer [im'pɔːtə], n. importateur, m.
importunate [im'pɔːtjunit], a. importun; pressant.
importune [impɔː'tjuːn], v.t. importuner.
impose [im'pouz], v.t. imposer.—v.i. en imposer (à).
imposing [im'pouzin], a. imposant.
imposition [impə'ziʃən], n. impôt (taxe), m.; imposture (tromperie), f.; (Sch.) pensum, m.
impossibility [impɔsi'biliti], n. impossibilité, f.
impossible [im'pɔsibl], a. impossible.
impostor [im'pɔstə], n. imposteur, m.
imposture [im'pɔstʃə], n. imposture, tromperie, f.
impotence ['impotəns], impotency ['impotənsi], n. impuissance, f.
impotent ['impotənt], a. impuissant, faible.
impound [im'paund], v.t. mettre en fourrière; (fig.) enfermer, confisquer.
impoverish [im'pɔvəriʃ], v.t. appauvrir.
impracticable [im'præktikəbl], a. impossible, impraticable; intraitable (personne).
imprecation [imprə'keiʃən], n. imprécation, f.
impregnable [im'pregnəbl], a. imprenable; (fig.) inébranlable.
impregnate [im'pregneit], v.t. imprégner (de); féconder.
impress [im'pres], v.t. imprimer (à); faire bien comprendre (quelque chose à quelqu'un); pénétrer (de); impressionner.
impression [im'preʃən], n. impression, empreinte; (fig.) idée, f.
impressive [im'presiv], a. impressionnant, frappant, touchant, émouvant.
impressiveness [im'presivnis], n. force, puissance, grandeur, f.
imprint [im'print], v.t. imprimer, empreindre.—['imprint], n. empreinte, f.

453

imprison

imprison [im'prizn], *v.t.* emprisonner, enfermer.
imprisonment [im'priznmənt], *n.* emprisonnement, *m.*, détention, *f.*
improbability [improbə'biliti], *n.* improbabilité; invraisemblance, *f.*
improbable [im'probəbl], *a.* improbable, invraisemblable.
impromptu [im'promptju:], *a.* impromptu, improvisé.—*adv.* par improvisation, impromptu.
improper [im'propə], *a.* inconvenant; peu propre (à), impropre (*langage*).
improperly [im'propəli], *adv.* d'une manière peu convenable; à tort, mal à propos.
impropriety [imprə'praiəti], *n.* inconvenance (*de conduite*); impropriété (*de langage*), *f.*
improve [im'pru:v], *v.t.* améliorer, perfectionner (*invention etc.*); faire avancer; utiliser; bonifier (*terre etc.*); embellir (*rendre plus beau*); exploiter (*cultiver*).—*v.i.* s'améliorer; se perfectionner; se bonifier (*vin etc.*); faire des progrès; (*Comm.*) hausser; augmenter de prix; *to improve upon*, améliorer, perfectionner, surpasser.
improvement [im'pru:vmənt], *n.* amélioration, *f.*; perfectionnement; progrès, avancement (*en connaissances*), *m.*
improvident [im'providənt], *a.* imprévoyant.
improvisation [improvai'zeiʃən], *n.* improvisation, *f.*
improvise ['improvaiz], *v.t.* improviser.
imprudence [im'pru:dəns], *n.* imprudence, *f.*
imprudent [im'pru:dənt], *a.* imprudent.
imprudently [im'pru:dəntli], *adv.* imprudemment.
impudence ['impjudəns], *n.* impudence, effronterie, *f.*
impudent ['impjudənt], *a.* impudent, effronté.
impudently ['impjudəntli], *adv.* impudemment, effrontément.
impugn [im'pju:n], *v.t.* attaquer, contester; (*fig.*) mettre en doute.
impulse ['impʌls], **impulsion** [im'pʌlʃən], *n.* impulsion, *f.*, mouvement; (*fig.*) élan, *m.*; *sudden impulse*, coup de tête, *m.*
impulsive [im'pʌlsiv], *a.* impulsif, primesautier.
impulsively [im'pʌlsivli], *adv.* par impulsion, par un mouvement involontaire.
impunity [im'pju:niti], *n.* impunité, *f.*; *with impunity*, impunément.
impure [im'pjuə], *a.* impur; impudique.
impurity [im'pjuəriti], *n.* impureté; impudicité, *f.*
imputation [impju'teiʃən], *n.* imputation, accusation, *f.*
impute [im'pju:t], *v.t.* imputer, attribuer (à).
in [in], *prep.* en, dans; à; par; pour; sur; avec; chez, parmi (*en compagnie de*); *he will do it in one hour*, il fera cela en une heure; *he will start in one hour*, il partira dans une heure; *in bed*, au lit; *in England*, en Angleterre; *in Japan*, au Japon; *in Paris*, à Paris; *in spite of*, malgré; *in spring*, au printemps; *in summer* (*autumn, winter*), en été (automne, hiver); *in the morning*, le matin; *in the U.S.A.*, aux États-Unis; *one in ten*, un sur dix; *to be clothed in*, être vêtu de.—*adv.* dedans, au dedans, rentré; chez soi, à la maison, y (*at*

home); élu (*vainqueur aux élections*); au pouvoir (*parti politique*); *all in*, las, fatigué.
—*n. to know all the ins and outs of a matter*, connaître les tenants et les aboutissants d'une affaire.
inability [inə'biliti], *n.* impuissance, incapacité, *f.*
inaccessible [inæk'sesibl], *a.* inaccessible; inabordable (à).
inaccuracy [in'ækjurəsi], *n.* inexactitude, *f.*
inaccurate [in'ækjurit], *a.* inexact.
inaction [in'ækʃən], *n.* inaction, inertie, *f.*
inactive [in'æktiv], *a.* inactif; inerte (*choses*).
inactivity [inæk'tiviti], *n.* inactivité, *f.*
inadequacy [in'ædikwəsi], *n.* insuffisance, imperfection, *f.*
inadequate [in'ædikwit], *a.* insuffisant; imparfait, défectueux, incomplet.
inadequately [in'ædikwitli], *adv.* insuffisamment.
inadmissible [inəd'misibl], *a.* inadmissible.
inadvertence [inəd'və:təns], **inadvertency** [inəd'və:tənsi], *n.* inadvertance, *f.*
inadvertent [inəd'və:tənt], *a.* négligent, inattentif.
inadvertently [inəd'və:təntli], *adv.* par inadvertance.
inalienable [in'eiliənəbl], *a.* inaliénable; inséparable.
inane [i'nein], *a.* vide; (*fig.*) inepte, absurde.
inanimate [in'ænimit], *a.* inanimé; mort.
inanition [inə'niʃən], *n.* inanition, *f.*
inanity [i'næniti], *n.* inanité, *f.*
inapplicable [in'æplikəbl], *a.* inapplicable.
inappreciable [inə'pri:ʃiəbl], *a.* inappréciable, insensible.
inappropriate [inə'proupriit], *a.* peu propre, qui ne convient pas.
inapt [in'æpt], *a.* inapte, impropre, peu propre (à).
inarticulate [ina:'tikjulit], *a.* inarticulé, qui s'exprime peu clairement.
inartistic [ina:'tistik], *a.* peu artistique.
inasmuch [inəz'mʌtʃ], *adv.* vu que, attendu que, d'autant que.
inattention [inə'tenʃən], *n.* inattention; distraction, *f.*
inattentive [inə'tentiv], *a.* inattentif, distrait; négligent.
inattentively [inə'tentivli], *adv.* sans attention, négligemment.
inaudible [in'o:dibl], *a.* imperceptible, qu'on ne peut entendre.
inaudibly [in'o:dibli], *adv.* à ne pouvoir être entendu.
inaugural [in'o:gjurəl], *a.* inaugural.
inaugurate [in'o:gjureit], *v.t.* inaugurer.
inauspicious [ino:'spiʃəs], *a.* malheureux, peu propice.
inauspiciously [ino:'spiʃəsli], *adv.* sous de mauvais auspices.
inborn ['inbo:n], **inbred** ['inbred], *a.* inné, naturel.
incalculable [in'kælkjuləbl], *a.* incalculable.
incapable [in'keipəbl], *a.* incapable (*de*).
incapacitate [inkə'pæsiteit], *v.i.* rendre incapable (*de*).
incarcerate [in'ka:səreit], *v.t.* incarcérer, mettre en prison.
incarnate [in'ka:nit], *a.* incarné.
incautious [in'ko:ʃəs], *a.* inconsidéré, imprudent.

454

incendiarism [in'sendjərizm], *n.* crime d'incendie, *m.*

incendiary [in'sendjəri], *a.* and *n.* incendiaire, *m.*, *f.*

incense ['insens], *n.* encens, *m.*—[in'sens], *v.t.* irriter, exaspérer (*contre*).

incentive [in'sentiv], *a.* excitant, stimulant.— *n.* motif, stimulant, encouragement, *m.*

inception [in'sepʃən], *n.* commencement, *m.*

incessant [in'sesənt], *a.* incessant; continuel.

incest ['insest], *n.* inceste, *m.*

inch [intʃ], *n.* pouce (*2,539 centimètres*), *m.*

incident ['insidənt], *a.* qui arrive; particulier. —*n.* incident, événement, *m.*

incidental [insi'dentl], *a.* fortuit, accidentel; accessoire; *incidental expenses*, faux frais, *m.pl.*

incidentally [insi'dentli], *adv.* fortuitement, par hasard; soit dit en passant.

incinerate [in'sinəreit], *v.t.* incinérer.

incipient [in'sipiənt], *a.* naissant, qui commence.

incise [in'saiz], *v.t.* inciser, graver.

incision [in'siʒən], *n.* incision, *f.*

incisive [in'saisiv], *a.* incisif.

incite [in'sait], *v.t.* inciter, stimuler; encourager (*à*).

incitement [in'saitmənt], *n.* encouragement, motif, stimulant, *m.*

incivility [insi'viliti], *n.* incivilité, impolitesse, *f.*

inclemency [in'klemənsi], *n.* inclémence, *f.*; intempéries, *f.pl.*, rigueur (*du temps etc.*), *f.*

inclement [in'klemənt], *a.* inclément; rigoureux.

inclination [inkli'neiʃən], *n.* inclinaison, pente; inclination (*de la tête* ou *du corps*), *f.*; penchant, goût (*disposition*), *m.*

incline ['inklain], *n.* pente; (*Rail.*) rampe, *f.* —[in'klain], *v.t.* incliner, (faire) pencher; (*fig.*) porter, disposer (*à*).—*v.i.* incliner, s'incliner, pencher; (*fig.*) être porté (*à*).

inclined [in'klaind], *a.* incliné; enclin (*à*); porté, disposé (*à*).

include [in'klu:d], *v.t.* comprendre, renfermer.

included [in'klu:did], *a.* compris, y compris.

including [in'klu:diŋ], *prep.* comprenant, y compris.

inclusion [in'klu:ʒən], *n.* inclusion, *f.*

inclusive [in'klu:siv], *a.* inclusif; qui renferme, qui comprend; *inclusive of*, y compris.

incoherence [inko'hiərəns], *n.* incohérence, *f.*

incoherent [inko'hiərənt], *a.* incohérent.

incombustible [inkəm'bʌstibl], *a.* incombustible.

income ['inkəm], *n.* revenu, *m.*; *private income*, rente, *f.*, rentes, *f.pl.*

income tax ['inkəmtæks], *n.* impôt sur le revenu, *m.*

incommode [inkə'moud], *v.t.* incommoder, gêner, déranger.

incommodious [inkə'moudjəs], *a.* incommode.

incomparable [in'kɔmprəbl], *a.* incomparable.

incompatible [inkəm'pætibl], *a.* incompatible.

incompetence [in'kɔmpitəns], *n.* incompétence, insuffisance; incapacité, *f.*

incompetent [in'kɔmpitənt], *a.* incompétent, incapable.

incompetently [in'kɔmpitəntli], *adv.* avec incompétence.

incomplete [inkəm'pli:t], *a.* imparfait, inachevé, incomplet.

incompletely [inkəm'pli:tli], *adv.* incomplètement, imparfaitement.

incomprehensibility [inkɔmprihensi'biliti], *n.* incompréhensibilité, *f.*

incomprehensible [inkɔmpri'hensibl], *a.* incompréhensible.

inconceivable [inkən'si:vəbl], *a.* inconcevable.

inconclusive [inkən'klu:siv], *a.* qui n'est pas concluant.

incongruity [inkɔŋ'gru:iti], *n.* désaccord, *m.*, incongruité; inconvenance, *f.*

incongruous [in'kɔŋgruəs], *a.* incongru, inconvenant, (*fig.*) disparate.

inconsequence [in'kɔnsikwəns], *n.* inconséquence; fausse déduction, *f.*

inconsequent [in'kɔnsikwənt], *a.* inconséquent.

inconsiderable [inkən'sidərəbl], *a.* petit, insignifiant; de peu d'importance.

inconsiderate [inkən'sidərit], *a.* inconsidéré, irréfléchi; sans égards pour les autres.

inconsistency [inkən'sistənsi], *n.* inconséquence; contradiction, *f.*

inconsistent [inkən'sistənt], *a.* incompatible (*avec*), contradictoire (*à*); inconséquent.

inconsistently [inkən'sistəntli], *adv.* avec un manque de continuité.

inconspicuous [inkən'spikjuəs], *a.* peu apparent, peu remarquable; discret.

inconstancy [in'kɔnstənsi], *n.* inconstance, *f.*; caractère changeant, *m.*

inconstant [in'kɔnstənt], *a.* inconstant, volage, changeant.

incontestable [inkən'testəbl], *a.* incontestable, irrécusable.

incontrovertible [inkɔntrə'və:tibl], *a.* incontestable, indisputable.

inconvenience [inkən'vi:niəns], *n.* inconvénient; embarras, dérangement, *m.*—*v.t.* déranger, incommoder, gêner.

inconvenient [inkən'vi:niənt], *a.* incommode, gênant.

inconveniently [inkən'vi:niəntli], *adv.* incommodément, mal.

incorporate [in'kɔ:pəreit], *v.t.* incorporer, former en société.—*v.i.* s'incorporer.

incorporated, see **joint-stock**.

incorrect [inkə'rekt], *a.* incorrect, inexact.

incorrectly [inkə'rektli], *adv.* incorrectement; inexactement.

incorrectness [inkə'rektnis], *n.* incorrection; inexactitude, *f.*

incorrigible [in'kɔridʒibl], *a.* incorrigible.

incorrupt [inkə'rʌpt], *a.* incorrompu, pur.

incorruptible [inkə'rʌptibl], *a.* incorruptible.

increase [in'kri:s], *v.t.* augmenter, agrandir, accroître.—*v.i.* croître, s'accroître; augmenter.—['inkri:s], *n.* augmentation (*de prix*), *f.*, accroissement (*de vitesse*); (*fig.*) produit, *m.*; crue (*de rivière*), *f.*

increasing [in'kri:siŋ], *a.* croissant.

increasingly [in'kri:siŋli], *adv.* de plus en plus.

incredible [in'kredibl], *a.* incroyable.

455

incredibly [in'kredibli], *adv.* incroyablement, d'une manière incroyable.
incredulity [inkrə'dju:liti], *n.* incrédulité, *f.*
incredulous [in'kredjuləs], *a.* incrédule.
increment ['inkrimənt], *n.* augmentation, *f.*; produit, *m.*
incriminate [in'krimineit], *v.t.* incriminer.
incubate ['inkjubeit], *v.t.* couver.
incubation [inkju'beiʃən], *n.* incubation, *f.*
incubator ['inkjubeitə], *n.* couveuse artificielle, *f.*
incubus ['inkjubəs], *n.* incube, cauchemar, (*fig.*) grand poids, *m.*
inculcate ['inkʌlkeit], *v.t.* inculquer (*à*).
incumbent [in'kʌmbənt], *a.* couché (*sur*); imposé, obligatoire; **to be incumbent on,** incomber à; **to feel it incumbent on one to do,** se faire un devoir de.—*n.* titulaire, bénéficier, *m.*
incur [in'kə:], *v.t.* encourir (*blâme*), s'attirer (*colère*); faire (*dettes*).
incurable [in'kjuərəbl], *a.* incurable, inguérissable.—*n.* incurable, *m., f.*
incursion [in'kə:ʃən], *n.* incursion, irruption, *f.*
indebted [in'detid], *a.* endetté; redevable (*de*).
indebtedness [in'detidnis], *n.* dette, obligation, *f.*
indecency [in'di:sənsi], *n.* indécence, *f.*
indecent [in'di:sənt], *a.* indécent.
indecently [in'di:səntli], *adv.* indécemment.
indecision [indi'siʒən], *n.* irrésolution, *f.*
indecisive [indi'saisiv], *a.* peu décisif, indécis.
indecorous [in'dekərəs], *a.* inconvenant.
indecorousness [in'dekərəsnis], **indecorum** [indi'kɔ:rəm], *n.* manque de décorum, *m.*, inconvenance, *f.*
indeed [in'di:d], *adv.* en effet, en vérité; vraiment; à dire vrai, à la vérité.—*int.* vraiment! allons donc!
indefatigable [indi'fætigəbl], *a.* infatigable.
indefensible [indi'fensibl], *a.* indéfendable, inexcusable.
indefinable [indi'fainəbl], *a.* indéfinissable.
indefinite [in'definit], *a.* indéfini, vague.
indefinitely [in'definitli], *adv.* indéfiniment, vaguement.
indelible [in'delibl], *a.* indélébile, ineffaçable.
indelibly [in'delibli], *adv.* d'une manière indélébile, ineffaçablement.
indelicacy [in'delikəsi], *n.* indélicatesse, grossièreté, inconvenance, *f.*
indelicate [in'delikit], *a.* indélicat, grossier, inconvenant.
indemnify [in'demnifai], *v.t.* dédommager, indemniser (*de*).
indemnity [in'demniti], *n.* dédommagement, *m.*; indemnité, *f.*
indent [in'dent], *v.t.* denteler; ébrécher, échancrer.—*v.i.* **to indent for,** réquisitionner.—*n.* dentelure, bosselure, *f.*
indented [in'dentid], *a.* dentelé; échancré.
indenture [in'dentʃə], *n.* titre; (*esp. pl.*) contrat d'apprentissage, *m.*—*v.t.* mettre en apprentissage.
independence [indi'pendəns], **independency** [indi'pendənsi], *n.* indépendance, *f.*
independent [indi'pendənt], *a.* indépendant; libre.
independently [indi'pendəntli], *adv.* indépendamment; dans l'indépendance.
indescribable [indi'skraibəbl], *a.* indicible, indescriptible.

indestructible [indi'strʌktibl], *a.* indestructible.
index ['indeks], *n.* (*pl.* **indexes** ['indeksiz], **indices** ['indisi:z]) indice, signe, indicateur; index (*d'un livre*), *m.*; aiguille (*d'une montre etc.*), *f.*; (*Anat.*) index, doigt indicateur; (*Math.*) exposant, *m.*
India ['indjə]. l'Inde, *f.*
Indian ['indjən], *a.* indien; des Indiens; de l'Inde, des Indes; **Indian corn,** maïs, *m.*—*n.* Indien (*personne*), *m.*; **Red Indian,** Peau-Rouge, *m., f.*
India rubber ['indjə'rʌbə], *n.* caoutchouc, *m.*
indicate ['indikeit], *v.t.* indiquer.
indication [indi'keiʃən], *n.* indication, *f.*, signe, indice, *m.*
indicative [in'dikətiv], *a.* and *n.* indicatif, *m.*
indicator ['indikeitə], *n.* indicateur, *m.*
indict [in'dait], *v.t.* inculper, mettre en accusation.
indictment [in'daitmənt], *n.* accusation; mise en accusation, *f.*
Indies ['indiz], **the.** les Indes, *f.pl.*; **the West Indies,** les Antilles, *f.pl.*
indifference [in'difrəns], *n.* indifférence, apathie, *f.*
indifferent [in'difrənt], *a.* indifférent; impartial; passable, médiocre.
indifferently [in'difrəntli], *adv.* indifféremment; médiocrement.
indigence ['indidʒəns], *n.* indigence, *f.*
indigent ['indidʒənt], *a.* nécessiteux, indigent.
indigenous [in'didʒinəs], *a.* du pays, indigène.
indigestible [indi'dʒestibl], *a.* indigeste.
indigestion [indi'dʒestʃən], *n.* indigestion, dyspepsie, *f.*
indignant [in'dignənt], *a.* indigné (*de*); plein d'indignation.
indignantly [in'dignəntli], *adv.* avec indignation.
indignation [indig'neiʃən], *n.* indignation, *f.*
indignity [in'digniti], *n.* indignité, *f.*; outrage, affront, *m.*
indigo ['indigou], *n.* indigo, *m.*
indirect [indi'rekt], *a.* indirect; (*fig.*) oblique, insidieux.
indiscreet [indis'kri:t], *a.* indiscret, irréfléchi, imprudent.
indiscreetly [indis'kri:tli], *adv.* indiscrètement.
indiscretion [indis'kreʃən], *n.* indiscrétion, imprudence, *f.*
indiscriminate [indis'kriminit], *a.* confus, sans distinction; aveugle.
indiscriminately [indis'kriminitli], *adv.* sans distinction, à tort et à travers, aveuglément.
indispensable [indis'pensəbl], *a.* indispensable, nécessaire.
indispose [indis'pouz], *v.t.* indisposer (*contre*), déranger, détourner (*de*).
indisposed [indis'pouzd], *a.* souffrant.
indisposition [indispə'ziʃən], *n.* indisposition, *f.*; malaise, *m.*
indisputable [indis'pju:təbl], *a.* incontestable, indiscutable.
indisputably [indis'pju:təbli], *adv.* incontestablement.
indissoluble [indi'sɔljubl], *a.* indissoluble.
indistinct [indis'tiŋkt], *a.* indistinct, confus, imprécis, vague.

indistinctly [indis'tiŋktli], adv. indistinctement, confusément, vaguement.
indistinguishable [indis'tiŋgwiʃəbl], a. indistinct, imperceptible.
indite [in'dait], v.t. rédiger.
individual [indi'vidjuəl], a. individuel; seul,
unique.—n. individu, particulier, m.
individuality [individju'æliti], n. individualité, personnalité, f.
individually [indi'viduəli], adv. individuellement.
indivisible [indi'vizibl], a. indivisible.
indoctrinate [in'dɔktrineit], v.t. instruire;
endoctriner.
indolence ['indələns], n. indolence, paresse, f.
indolent ['indələnt], a. indolent, paresseux.
indolently ['indələntli], adv. indolemment,
nonchalamment.
indomitable [in'dɔmitəbl], a. indomptable.
Indonesia [indo'ni:ziə]. l'Indonésie, f.
Indonesian [indo'ni:ziən], a. indonésien.—n.
indonésien (langue); Indonésien (personne),
m.
indoors [in'dɔ:z], adv. à la maison, au dedans.
indubitable [in'dju:bitəbl], a. indubitable,
incontestable.
induce [in'dju:s], v.t. porter, persuader,
induire, pousser (à); amener, causer, produire.
inducement [in'dju:smənt], n. raison, tentation, f., motif, mobile, m.
induction [in'dʌkʃən], n. installation; induction, f.
indulge [in'dʌldʒ], v.t. satisfaire; avoir trop
d'indulgence pour; (fig.) flatter, caresser (une
espérance etc.).—v.i. se laisser aller, se livrer
à, s'abandonner (à).
indulgence [in'dʌldʒəns], n. faveur, f.,
plaisir, agrément, m.; (R.-C. Ch.) indulgence, f.
indulgent [in'dʌldʒənt], a. indulgent, facile,
complaisant.
industrial [in'dʌstriəl], a. industriel, de
l'industrie.
industrialist [in'dʌstriəlist], n. industriel, m.
industrious [in'dʌstriəs], a. travailleur; diligent, laborieux.
industriously [in'dʌstriəsli], adv. assidûment,
diligemment.
industry ['indəstri], n. travail, m., diligence,
assiduité, f.; (fig.) empressement, m.;
industrie (production), f.
inebriate [i'ni:brieit], v.t. enivrer.—[i'ni:
briit], a. enivré.—n. ivrogne, m., f.
inebriation [ini:bri'eiʃən], **inebriety** [ini
'braiəti], n. ivresse, ébriété, f.
inedible [in'edibl], a. immangeable; non
comestible.
ineffable [in'efəbl], a. ineffable.
ineffaceable [ini'feisəbl], a. ineffaçable, indélébile.
ineffective [ini'fektiv], a. inefficace, sans
effet.
ineffectual [ini'fektjuəl], a. inefficace, inutile,
vain; incapable.
ineffectually [ini'fektjuəli], adv. inutilement,
sans effet.
inefficacious [inefi'keiʃəs], a. inefficace.
inefficiency [ini'fiʃənsi], n. inefficacité, incapacité, incompétence, f.
inefficient [ini'fiʃənt], a. inefficace; incapable.

ineligible [in'elidʒibl], a. inéligible; peu
propre (à).
inept [in'ept], a. inepte, sot, absurde, peu
propre (à).
inequality [ini'kwɔliti], n. inégalité, disparité, f.
inert [i'nə:t], a. inerte.
inertia [i'nə:ʃə], n. inertie, inactivité, f.
inestimable [in'estiməbl], a. inestimable;
incalculable.
inevitable [in'evitəbl], a. inévitable; fatal.
inevitably [in'evitəbli], adv. inévitablement.
inexact [inig'zækt], a. inexact.
inexcusable [iniks'kju:zəbl], a. inexcusable,
sans excuse.
inexhaustible [inig'zɔ:stibl], a. inépuisable.
inexorable [in'eksərəbl], a. inexorable,
inflexible.
inexpedient [iniks'pi:djənt], a. inopportun,
mal à propos.
inexpensive [iniks'pensiv], a. peu coûteux,
bon marché.
inexperience [iniks'piəriəns], n. inexpérience,
f.
inexperienced [iniks'piəriənst], a. inexpérimenté, sans expérience.
inexplicable [in'eksplikəbl], a. inexplicable.
inexpressible [iniks'presibl], a. inexprimable,
indicible.
inextricable [in'ekstrikəbl], a. inextricable.
infallible [in'fælibl], a. infaillible, immanquable.
infamous ['infəməs], a. infâme.
infamy ['infəmi], n. infamie, f.
infancy ['infənsi], n. première enfance, f.,
bas âge, m.
infant ['infənt], a. en bas âge, dans l'enfance,
petit; (fig.) naissant, qui commence.—n.
enfant en bas âge, nourrisson, bébé; (Law)
mineur, m.
infantile ['infəntail], a. enfantin, d'enfant.
infantry ['infəntri], n. infanterie, f.
infant-school ['infənt'sku:l], n. école maternelle, f.
infatuate [in'fætjueit], v.t. infatuer, entêter,
affoler; **to become infatuated with**,
s'engouer de, s'amouracher de.
infatuation [infætju'eiʃən], n. engouement,
m.; infatuation; (fam.) toquade, f.
infect [in'fekt], v.t. infecter (de).
infection [in'fekʃən], n. infection, contagion,
f.
infectious [in'fekʃəs], a. infect; contagieux,
infectieux.
infectiousness [in'fekʃəsnis], n. nature con-
tagieuse, contagion, f.
infer [in'fə:], v.t. inférer; (fig.) supposer.
inference ['infərəns], n. conséquence, conclusion, déduction, f.
inferior [in'fiəriə], a. inférieur; subordonné.
—n. inférieur, m.
inferiority [infiəri'ɔriti], n. infériorité, f.
infernal [in'fə:nəl], a. infernal, d'enfer;
(fig.) diabolique.
inferno [in'fə:nou], n. enfer; brasier, m.
infest [in'fest], v.t. infester.
infidel ['infidəl], a. and n. infidèle; incrédule,
m., f.
infidelity [infi'deliti], n. infidélité; déloyauté
(d'un serviteur), f.
infiltrate ['infiltreit], v.i. s'infiltrer (dans);
pénétrer.

457

infinite [′infinit], *a.* and *n.* infini, *m.*
infinitely [′infinitli], *adv.* infiniment, à l'infini; fort.
infinitive [in′finitiv], *a.* and *n.* infinitif, *m.*
infinity [in′finiti], *n.* infinité; immensité, *f.*
infirm [in′fə:m], *a.* infirme, faible; (*fig.*) inconstant, irrésolu.
infirmary [in′fə:məri], *n.* hôpital, *m.*, infirmerie, *f.*
infirmity [in′fə:miti], *n.* infirmité, faiblesse, *f.*
inflame [in′fleim], *v.t.* enflammer; (*fig.*) exciter.—*v.i.* s'enflammer.
inflammable [in′flæməbl], *a.* inflammable.
inflammation [inflə′meiʃən], *n.* inflammation, fluxion, *f.*
inflammatory [in′flæmətri], *a.* inflammatoire; (*fig.*) incendiaire.
inflate [in′fleit], *v.t.* enfler, gonfler.
inflated [in′fleitid], *a.* enflé, gonflé; exagéré; boursouflé (*style*).
inflation [in′fleiʃən], *n.* enflure, *f.*, gonflement, *m.*; inflation (monétaire), *f.*
inflect [in′flekt], *v.t.* fléchir; varier, moduler (*la voix*).
inflection [in′flekʃən], *n.* inflexion, modulation, *f.*
inflexible [in′fleksibl], *a.* inflexible.
inflict [in′flikt], *v.t.* infliger, faire (*une peine*).
infliction [in′flikʃən], *n.* infliction; (*fig.*) peine, *f.*
influence [′influəns], *n.* influence (*sur*), *f.*, empire, *m.*—*v.t.* influencer; influer (*sur*).
influential [influ′enʃəl], *a.* influent, qui a de l'influence.
influenza [influ′enzə], *n.* influenza, grippe, *f.*
influx [′inflʌks], *n.* affluence, *f.*; invasion; embouchure, *f.*
inform [in′fɔ:m], *v.t.* informer, instruire, renseigner, avertir; faire savoir à; *to inform against*, dénoncer.
informal [in′fɔ:məl], *a.* sans cérémonie, simple.
informality [infɔ:′mæliti], *n.* manque de cérémonie, *m.*; simplicité, *f.*
informally [in′fɔ:məli], *adv.* sans cérémonie; sans façon.
informant [in′fɔ:mənt], *n.* correspondant; informateur, *m.*
information [infə′meiʃən], *n.* renseignements, *m.pl.*; *piece of information*, renseignement, avis, *m.*, nouvelle, *f.*; savoir, *m.*; (*Law*) dénonciation, *f.*
informative [in′fɔ:mətiv], *a.* instructif; éducatif.
informer [in′fɔ:mə], *n.* délateur, dénonciateur, *m.*
infraction [in′frækʃən], *n.* infraction, contravention, *f.*
infra-red [infrə′red], *a.* infra-rouge.
infrequent [in′fri:kwənt], *a.* rare.
infringe [in′frindʒ], *v.t.* enfreindre, violer, transgresser.
infringement [in′frindʒmənt], *n.* infraction, violation; contrefaçon (*d'un brevet*), *f.*
infuriate [in′fjuərieit], *v.t.* rendre furieux.
infuriated [in′fjuərieitid], *a.* furieux, en fureur.
infuse [in′fju:z], *v.t.* infuser; faire infuser; macérer; (*fig.*) inspirer (*à*).
infusion [in′fju:ʒən], *n.* infusion, *f.*
ingenious [in′dʒi:niəs], *a.* ingénieux, habile.

ingeniously [in′dʒi:niəsli], *adv.* ingénieusement; spirituellement.
ingeniousness [in′dʒi:niəsnis], **ingenuity** [indʒi′nju:iti], *n.* ingéniosité, habileté, *f.*
ingenuous [in′dʒenjuəs], *a.* ingénu; naïf; candide.
ingenuously [in′dʒenjuəsli], *adv.* ingénument, naïvement.
ingenuousness [in′dʒenjuəsnis], *n.* ingénuité, naïveté, *f.*
inglorious [in′glɔ:riəs], *a.* obscur; inconnu; honteux.
ingloriously [in′glɔ:riəsli], *adv.* sans gloire; honteusement.
ingoing [′ingouiŋ], *a.* entrant, nouveau.—*n.* entrée, *f.*
ingot [′ingət], *n.* lingot, *m.*
ingrained [in′greind], *a.* encrassé; (*fig.*) enraciné, invétéré.
ingratiate [in′greiʃieit], *v.t.* insinuer (*dans*); *to ingratiate oneself with*, s'insinuer dans les bonnes grâces de.
ingratitude [in′grætitju:d], *n.* ingratitude, *f.*
ingredient [in′gri:diənt], *n.* ingrédient; élément, *m.*
ingrowing [′ingrouiŋ], *a.* incarné (*ongle*).
inhabit [in′hæbit], *v.t.* habiter; habiter (*dans*).
inhabitable [in′hæbitəbl], *a.* habitable.
inhabitant [in′hæbitənt], *n.* habitant, *m.*
inhabited [in′hæbitid], *a.* habité.
inhalation [inhə′leiʃən], *n.* inhalation; inspiration, *f.*
inhale [in′heil], *v.t.* aspirer; respirer, humer.
inherent [in′hiərənt], *a.* inhérent, naturel (*à*).
inherit [in′herit], *v.t.* hériter (*de*).—*v.i.* hériter.
inheritance [in′heritəns], *n.* héritage, patrimoine, *m.*
inheritance tax, see **death-duties**.
inhibit [in′hibit], *v.t.* arrêter, empêcher interdire.
inhibition [inhi′biʃən], *n.* interdiction; (*Psych.*) inhibition, *f.*
inhospitable [in′hɔspitəbl], *a.* inhospitalier.
inhuman [in′hju:mən], *a.* inhumain; dénaturé; cruel.
inhumanity [inhju′mæniti], *n.* inhumanité; brutalité, *f.*
inhumation [inhju′meiʃən], *n.* inhumation, *f.*, enterrement, *m.*
inimical [i′nimikl], *a.* hostile, ennemi; contraire (*à*).
inimitable [i′nimitəbl], *a.* inimitable.
iniquitous [i′nikwitəs], *a.* inique, injuste.
iniquity [i′nikwiti], *n.* iniquité, *f.*
initial [i′niʃəl], *a.* initial; premier.—*n.* initiale, *f.*—*v.t.* mettre ses initiales à.
initially [i′niʃəli], *adv.* au commencement.
initiate [i′niʃieit], *v.t.* initier (*à* ou *dans*); amorcer, commencer.
initiation [iniʃi′eiʃən], *n.* initiation, *f.*
initiative [i′niʃiətiv], *n.* initiative, *f.*
inject [in′dʒekt], *v.t.* injecter; faire une piqûre.
injection [in′dʒekʃən], *n.* injection; (*Med.*) piqûre, *f.*
injudicious [indʒu′diʃəs], *a.* peu judicieux, malavisé, imprudent.
injudiciously [indʒu′diʃəsli], *adv.* peu judicieusement, imprudemment.
injunction [in′dʒʌŋkʃən], *n.* injonction; recommandation, *f.*

injure ['indʒə], v.t. nuire à, faire tort à, léser; endommager (to damage); faire mal à, blesser.

injured ['indʒəd], a. offensé; blessé; *the injured*, les blessés, les accidentés, m.pl.

injurious [in'dʒuəriəs], a. nuisible, préjudiciable (à).

injuriously [in'dʒuəriəsli], adv. à tort.

injury ['indʒəri], n. tort, mal; dégât, dommage (à des marchandises), m.; (Med.) lésion, blessure, f.

injustice [in'dʒʌstis], n. injustice, f.

ink [iŋk], n. encre, f.; *India ink*, encre de Chine.—v.t. tacher ou barbouiller d'encre.

inkling ['iŋkliŋ], n. soupçon, vent (d'une affaire), m.

inkstand ['iŋkstænd], n. encrier de bureau, m.

ink-well ['iŋkwel], n. encrier, m.

inky ['iŋki], a. d'encre; taché d'encre.

inlaid [in'leid], a. incrusté, marqueté.

inland ['inlənd], a. intérieur, de l'intérieur.—n. intérieur (d'un pays), m.

inlay ['inlei], n. marqueterie, incrustation, f.—[in'lei], v.t. irr. (conjug. like LAY) marqueter, incruster.

inlet ['inlit], n. entrée, f., passage, m., voie, f.; petit bras de mer, m.

inmate ['inmeit], n. habitant, m., locataire (dans une maison); interne, pensionnaire (dans une maison de santé), m., f.

inmost ['inmoust], a. le plus profond, le plus secret.

inn [in], n. auberge, f.; hôtel, m.; hôtellerie, f.; *to put up at an inn*, descendre à une auberge.

innate [i'neit], a. inné; foncier.

innavigable [i'nævigəbl], a. innavigable.

inner ['inə], a. intérieur, de l'intérieur; (fig.) interne, secret.

innermost ['inəmoust], a. le plus intérieur, le plus reculé.

innkeeper ['inki:pə], n. aubergiste, m., f., hôtelier, m.

innocence ['inəsəns], n. innocence, f.

innocent ['inəsənt], a. innocent; permis, légitime.

innocently ['inəsəntli], adv. innocemment.

innocuous [i'nɔkjuəs], a. innocent, inoffensif.

innovate ['inoveit], v.i. innover.

innovation [ino'veiʃən], n. innovation, f., changement, m.

innuendo [inju'endou], n. insinuation, allusion malveillante, f.

innumerable [i'nju:mərəbl], a. innombrable, sans nombre.

inoculate [i'nɔkjuleit], v.t. inoculer, vacciner.

inoculation [inɔkju'leiʃən], n. inoculation, f., vaccin, m.

inodorous [in'oudərəs], a. inodore.

inoffensive [ino'fensiv], a. inoffensif.

inopportune [in'ɔpətju:n], a. inopportun, intempestif, mal à propos.

inopportunely [in'ɔpətju:nli], adv. inopportunément, mal à propos.

inordinate [i'nɔ:dinit], a. démesuré, immodéré.

inordinately [i'nɔ:dinitli], adv. démesurément, immodérément.

inorganic [inɔ:'gænik], a. inorganique.

inquest ['inkwest], n. enquête (après une mort subite), f.

inquire [in'kwaiə], v.t. demander.—v.i. s'enquérir, s'informer (de); s'adresser (à ou chez).

inquiring [in'kwaiəriŋ], a. investigateur, curieux.

inquiry [in'kwaiəri], n. demande, investigation, recherche, f.; (pl.) informations, f.pl. renseignements, m.pl., (Law) enquête, f.

inquisition [inkwi'ziʃən], n. recherche, investigation; (R.-C. Ch.) inquisition, f.

inquisitive [in'kwizitiv], a. curieux.

inroad ['inroud], n. incursion, invasion, f.; (fig.) empiétement (sur), m.

insalubrious [insə'lju:briəs], a. insalubre.

insane [in'sein], a. fou, aliéné; dérangé; (fig.) insensé.

insanitary [in'sænitəri], a. insalubre, malsain.

insanity [in'sæniti], n. folie, démence, f.

insatiable [in'seiʃəbl], a. insatiable.

insatiate [in'seiʃiit], a. insatiable; inassouvi.

inscribe [in'skraib], v.t. inscrire; dédier (à).

inscription [in'skripʃən], n. inscription, f.; titre (title), m.; dédicace (dedication), f.

inscrutable [in'skru:təbl], a. inscrutable, impénétrable.

insect ['insekt], n. insecte, m.

insecticidal [in'sektisaidl], a. insecticide.

insecticide [in'sektisaid], n. insecticide, m.

insecure [insi'kjuə], a. en danger; chanceux, hasardeux; peu sûr, mal assuré.

insecurely [insi'kjuəli], adv. sans sûreté, en danger.

insecurity [insi'kjuəriti], n. manque de sûreté; danger, péril, m.; incertitude, f.

insensible [in'sensibl], a. imperceptible; insignifiant; inconscient (unconscious); sans connaissance.

insensibly [in'sensibli], adv. insensiblement, peu à peu.

insensitive [in'sensitiv], a. insensible.

inseparable [in'sepərəbl], a. inséparable.

insert [in'sə:t], v.t. insérer, faire insérer (dans).

insertion [in'sə:ʃən], n. insertion; interpolation, f.

inshore [in'ʃɔ:], a. and adv. près du rivage.

inside ['insaid], a. intérieur, d'intérieur.—n. dedans, intérieur, m.; *inside out*, à l'envers; [in'said] entrailles, f.pl.—[in'said], adv. à l'intérieur, en dedans.—[in'said], prep. en, dans, à l'intérieur de.

insidious [in'sidiəs], a. insidieux, captieux, perfide.

insight ['insait], n. perspicacité, pénétration, f.

insignia [in'signiə], n.pl. insignes, m.pl.

insignificance [insig'nifikəns], n. insignifiance, f., peu d'importance, m.

insignificant [insig'nifikənt], a. insignifiant.

insincere [insin'siə], a. peu sincère, faux, hypocrite.

insincerely [insin'siəli], adv. de mauvaise foi, hypocritement.

insincerity [insin'seriti], n. manque de sincérité, m., fausseté, f.

insinuate [in'sinjueit], v.t. insinuer, glisser (dans); donner à entendre.—v.i. s'insinuer, se glisser (dans).

insinuation [insinju'eiʃən], n. insinuation, f.

insipid [in'sipid], a. insipide, fade.

insipidity [insi'piditi], n. insipidité, fadeur, f.

insist [in'sist], v.i. insister (sur ou à); persister; vouloir absolument.

insistence [in'sistəns], n. insistance, f.

459

insistent

insistent [in'sistənt], *a.* insistant.
insobriety [insə'braiəti], *n.* intempérance, *f.*
insolence ['insələns], *n.* insolence; effronterie, *f.*
insolent ['insələnt], *a.* insolent.
insolently ['insələntli], *adv.* insolemment.
insoluble [in'sɔljubl], *a.* insoluble.
insolvency [in'sɔlvənsi], *n.* insolvabilité, faillite, *f.*
insolvent [in'sɔlvənt], *a.* insolvable, en faillite.
insomnia [in'sɔmniə], *n.* insomnie, *f.*
insomuch [inso'mʌtʃ], *adv.* au point (*que*), à un tel point (*que*), tellement (*que*).
inspect [in'spekt], *v.t.* inspecter, examiner, visiter.
inspection [in'spekʃən], *n.* inspection, revue, *f.*, contrôle, examen, *m.*; surveillance, *f.*
inspector [in'spektə], *n.* inspecteur, *m.*
inspiration [inspi'reiʃən], *n.* inspiration, *f.*; encouragement, *m.*
inspire [in'spaiə], *v.t.* inspirer, souffler (*dans*); animer (*de*).—*v.i.* aspirer.
inspiring [in'spaiəriŋ], *a.* inspirateur; qui donne du courage; qui élève l'esprit.
instability [instə'biliti], *n.* instabilité, *f.*
install [in'stɔ:l], *v.t.* installer; monter (*appareil, machine*).
installation [instə'leiʃən], *n.* installation, *f.*; montage (*de machine, équipement*), *m.*
installment [in'stɔ:lmənt], *n.* installation, *f.*; (*Comm.*) accompte, versement (*partiel*); épisode (*de feuilleton*), *m.*
installment plan, see **hire-purchase**.
instance ['instəns], *n.* requête, demande, *f.*; exemple, *m.*, occasion, *f.*, cas, *m.*; *for instance*, par exemple; *in the first instance*, en premier lieu.—*v.t.* citer comme exemple.
instant ['instənt], *a.* instant, pressant, immédiat; courant (*mois*).—*n.* instant, moment, *m.*
instantaneous [instən'teiniəs], *a.* instantané.
instantaneously [instən'teiniəsli], *adv.* instantanément.
instantly ['instəntli], *adv.* à l'instant; tout de suite; sur-le-champ.
instead [in'sted], *adv.* à la place; *instead of*, au lieu de.
instep ['instep], *n.* cou-de-pied, *m.*
instigate ['instigeit], *v.t.* exciter, inciter, pousser (*à*).
instigation [insti'geiʃən], *n.* instigation, *f.*
instill [in'stil], *v.t.* instiller; (*fig.*) inspirer (*à*).
instillation [insti'leiʃən], *n.* instillation, *f.* (*fig.*) inspiration, *f.*
instinct ['instiŋkt], *n.* instinct, *m.*
instinctive [in'stiŋktiv], *a.* instinctif; (*fig.*) spontané.
instinctively [in'stiŋktivli], *adv.* d'instinct, instinctivement.
institute ['institju:t], *n.* institut, *m.*—*v.t.* instituer, établir; intenter (*un procès*).
institution [insti'tju:ʃən], *n.* institution, *f.*, établissement, *m.*
instruct [in'strʌkt], *v.t.* instruire, enseigner; charger (*de*).
instruction [in'strʌkʃən], *n.* instruction, *f.*, enseignement, *m.*
instructive [in'strʌktiv], *a.* instructif.
instructor [in'strʌktə], *n.* (*Mil.*) instructeur; précepteur, *m.*

instructress [in'strʌktris], *n.* préceptrice, monitrice, *f.*
instrument ['instrumənt], *n.* instrument; (*fig.*) agent, *m.*
instrumental [instru'mentl], *a.* instrumental; *to be instrumental in*, contribuer à.
insubordinate [insə'bɔ:dinit], *a.* insubordonné; indocile.
insubordination [insəbɔ:di'neiʃən], *n.* insubordination; insoumission, *f.*
insufferable [in'sʌfərəbl], *a.* insupportable, intolérable.
insufficiency [insə'fiʃənsi], *n.* insuffisance, *f.*
insufficient [insə'fiʃənt], *a.* insuffisant.
insufficiently [insə'fiʃəntli], *adv.* insuffisamment.
insular ['insjulə], *a.* insulaire; (*fig.*) borné, rétréci.
insularity [insju'læriti], *n.* insularité, *f.*
insulate ['insjuleit], *v.t.* isoler; calorifuger.
insulation [insju'leiʃən], *n.* isolement, *m.*; (*Phys.*) isolation, *f.*
insulator ['insjuleitə], *n.* isolateur, isoloir, *m.*
insulin ['insjulin], *n.* insuline, *f.*
insult [in'sʌlt], *v.t.* insulter, faire insulte à, injurier.—['insʌlt], *n.* insulte, injure, *f.*, affront, *m.*
insulting [in'sʌltiŋ], *a.* insultant, outrageux, injurieux.
insultingly [in'sʌltiŋli], *adv.* insolemment, injurieusement.
insuperable [in'sju:pərəbl], *a.* insurmontable, invincible.
insupportable [insə'pɔ:təbl], *a.* insupportable, intolérable.
insuppressible [insə'presibl], *a.* irrépressible, irrésistible, inextinguible (*rire*).
insurance [in'ʃuərəns], *n.* assurance, *f.*; *fire insurance*, assurance contre l'incendie; *life insurance*, assurance sur la vie.
insure [in'ʃuə], *v.t.* assurer, faire assurer; (*fig.*) garantir.
insurgent [in'sə:dʒənt], *a.* and *n.* insurgé, *m.*
insurmountable [insə'mauntəbl], *a.* insurmontable, infranchissable.
insurrection [insə'rekʃən], *n.* insurrection, *f.* soulèvement, *m.*
intact [in'tækt], *a.* intact, indemne.
intangible [in'tændʒibl], *a.* intangible.
integer ['intədʒə], *n.* nombre entier, *m.*
integral ['intəgrəl], *a.* intégral; *an integral part*, une partie intégrante.—*n.* totalité, *f.*, tout, *m.*
integrate ['intigreit], *v.t.* compléter, rendre entier.
integrity [in'tegriti], *n.* intégrité, probité, *f.*
intellect ['intilekt], *n.* intelligence, *f.*, esprit, *m.*
intellectual [inti'lektjuəl], *a.* intellectuel; intelligent.—*n.* intellectuel, *m.*
intellectually [inti'lektjuəli], *adv.* intellectuellement.
intelligence [in'telidʒəns], *n.* intelligence, *f.*, esprit; renseignement, avis, *m.*; nouvelle, *f.*
intelligent [in'telidʒənt], *a.* intelligent.
intelligently [in'telidʒəntli], *adv.* intelligemment, avec intelligence.
intelligibility [intelidʒi'biliti], *n.* intelligibilité, clarté, *f.*
intelligible [in'telidʒibl], *a.* intelligible.

intemperance [in'tempərəns], *n.* intempérance, *f.*

intemperate [in'tempərit], *a.* démesuré, immodéré; intempérant; violent, emporté (*langage*).

intend [in'tend], *v.t.* se proposer de, avoir l'intention de, compter, vouloir; destiner (à); vouloir dire.

intended [in'tendid], *a.* projeté; intentionnel; **to be intended for**, être destiné à.

intense [in'tens], *a.* intense, véhément; (*fig.*) opiniâtre, très sérieux; vif, fort, aigu (*douleur etc.*).

intensely [in'tensli], *adv.* avec intensité, vivement, fortement.

intenseness [in'tensnis], **intensity** [in'tensiti], *n.* intensité; force, violence, *f.*

intensify [in'tensifai], *v.t.* rendre plus vif, intensifier.

intensive [in'tensiv], *a.* intensif.

intent [in'tent], *a.* attentif, absorbé (*par*); déterminé (à); fixe (*regard*).—*n.* dessein, but; sens, *m.*; intention, portée, *f.*; **to all intents and purposes**, à tous égards.

intention [in'tenʃən], *n.* intention, *f.*; dessein, but, *m.*

intentional [in'tenʃənəl], *a.* intentionnel, fait à dessein.

intentionally [in'tenʃənəli], *adv.* avec intention, à dessein, exprès.

intently [in'tentli], *adv.* attentivement.

intentness [in'tentnis], *n.* attention, force d'application, *f.*

inter [in'tə:], *v.t.* enterrer, inhumer, ensevelir.

intercede [intə'si:d], *v.t.* intercéder (*auprès de*).

intercept [intə'sept], *v.t.* intercepter; arrêter; (*fig.*) surprendre.

interchange [intə'tʃeindʒ], *v.t.* échanger.—['intətʃeindʒ], *n.* échange, *m.*, succession; (*fig.*) variété, *f.*

intercourse ['intəkɔ:s], *n.* commerce, *m.*, relations, *f.pl.*, rapports, *m.pl.*

interdict [intə'dikt], *v.t.* interdire, interdire à, défendre à.—['intədikt], *n.* or **interdiction** [intə'dikʃən], interdit, *m.*, défense, interdiction, *f.*

interest ['intrəst], *v.t.* intéresser; **to be interested in**, s'intéresser à.—*n.* intérêt, *m.*; protection, *f.*, crédit, *m.*

interested ['intrəstid], *a.* intéressé.

interesting ['intrəstiŋ], *a.* intéressant.

interfere [intə'fiə], *v.i.* intervenir, se mêler (*de*); **to interfere with**, se mêler de, gêner, contrarier, déranger.

interference [intə'fiərəns], *n.* intervention, *f.*; (*Rad.*) brouillage, *m.*

interim ['intərim], *a.* provisoire.—*n.* intérim, intervalle, *m.*; **in the interim**, en attendant.

interior [in'tiəriə], *a.* and *n.* intérieur, *m.*; **interior angle**, angle interne, *m.*

interject [intə'dʒekt], *v.t.* interjecter; s'écrier (*en conversation*).

interjection [intə'dʒekʃən], *n.* interjection, *f.*

interlace [intə'leis], *v.t.* entrelacer.

interlacing [intə'leisiŋ], *n.* entrelacement, *m.*

interleave [intə'li:v], *v.t.* interfolier (*de*).

interloper ['intəloupə], *n.* intrus, *m.*

interlude ['intəlu:d], *n.* intermède, *m.*

intermediary [intə'mi:diəri], *a.* and *n.* intermédiaire, *m.*

intermediate [intə'mi:djit], *a.* intermédiaire, moyen.

interment [in'tə:mənt], *n.* enterrement, *m.*, inhumation, *f.*

interminable [in'tə:minəbl], *a.* interminable.

intermingle [intə'miŋgl], *v.t.* entremêler.—*v.i.* s'entremêler.

intermission [intə'miʃən], *n.* interruption momentanée, *f.*; relâche, intervalle;(*Theat.*) entr'acte, *m.*

intermittent [intə'mitənt], *a.* intermittent.

intermittently [intə'mitəntli], *adv.* par intervalles.

intern [in'tə:n], *v.t.* interner.

intern ['intə:n], *n.* (*Med.*) interne, *m., f.*

internal [in'tə:nl], *a.* interne, intérieur.

international [intə'næʃənl], *a.* international.—*n.* (joueur) international, *m.*

internecine [intə'ni:sain], *a.* meurtrier.

internee [intə:'ni:], *n.* interné, *m.*

internment [in'tə:nmənt], *n.* internement, *m.*; **internment camp**, camp de concentration, camp de prisonniers, *m.*

interplanetary [intə'plænətəri], *a.* interplanétaire.

interpolate [in'tə:poleit], *v.t.* interpoler; intercaler.

interpose [intə'pouz], *v.t.* interposer.—*v.i.* s'interposer, intervenir.

interpret [in'tə:prit], *v.t.* interpréter; expliquer.

interpretation [intə:pri'teiʃən], *n.* interprétation, *f.*

interpreter [in'tə:pritə], *n.* interprète, *m., f.*

interracial [intə'reiʃəl], *a.* interracial.

interrogate [in'terəgeit], *v.t.* interroger, questionner.

interrogation [interə'geiʃən], *n.* interrogation, question, *f.*

interrogative [intə'rɔgətiv], *a.* interrogatif, interrogateur.

interrupt [intə'rʌpt], *v.t.* interrompre.

interruption [intə'rʌpʃən], *n.* interruption, *f.*; (*fig.*) obstacle, *m.*

intersect [intə'sekt], *v.t.* entrecouper; (*Geom.*) couper.—*v.i.* (*Geom.*) se couper, se croiser.

intersection [intə'sekʃən], *n.* intersection, *f.*

intersperse [intə'spə:s], *v.t.* entremêler (*de*); parsemer (*de*).

interstice [in'tə:stis], *n.* interstice; intervalle, *m.*

intertwine [intə'twain], *v.t.* entrelacer.—*v.i.* s'entrelacer.

interval ['intəvəl], *n.* intervalle, *m.*

intervene [intə'vi:n], *v.i.* intervenir, s'interposer; survenir, arriver (*événements*); s'écouler (*temps*).

intervening [intə'vi:niŋ], *a.* intervenant (*personnes*); intermédiaire (*espace, endroits, temps etc.*).

intervention [intə'venʃən], *n.* intervention, *f.*

interview ['intəvju:], *n.* entrevue; (*Journ.*) interview, *f.*—*v.t.* avoir une entrevue avec; (*Journ.*) interviewer.

interviewer ['intəvju:ə], *n.* interviewer, *m.*

interweave [intə'wi:v], *v.t. irr.* (*conjug. like* WEAVE) entrelacer; entremêler.

intestate [in'testit], *a.* intestat.

intestine [in'testin], *a.* and *n.* intestin, *m.*

intimacy ['intiməsi], *n.* intimité, *f.*

intimate ['intimit], *a.* intime, lié.—['intimeit], *v.t.* donner à entendre; intimer (à).

intimately

intimately ['intimitli], *adv.* intimement.
intimation [inti'meiʃən], *n.* avis, *m.*, indication, *f.*
intimidate [in'timideit], *v.t.* intimider.
intimidation [intimi'deiʃən], *n.* intimidation, *f.*
into ['intu], *prep.* dans, en, à, entre.
intolerable [in'tɔlərəbl], *a.* intolérable, insupportable.
intolerance [in'tɔlərəns], *n.* intolérance, *f.*
intolerant [in'tɔlərənt], *a.* intolérant.
intonation [into'neiʃən], *n.* intonation, *f.*
intone [in'toun], *v.t.*, *v.i.* psalmodier; entonner.
intoxicant [in'tɔksikənt], *n.* boisson alcoolique, *f.*
intoxicate [in'tɔksikeit], *v.t.* enivrer (*de*).
intoxicated [in'tɔksikeitid], *a.* ivre; (*fig.*) enivré (*de*).
intoxicating [in'tɔksikeitiŋ], *a.* enivrant.
intoxication [intɔksi'keiʃən], *n.* ivresse, *f.*; (*fig.*) enivrement, *m.*
intractability [intræktə'biliti], *n.* naturel intraitable, *m.*, indocilité, *f.*
intractable [in'træktəbl], *a.* intraitable, indocile.
intransigence [in'trænsidʒəns, in'trɑːnsidʒəns], *n.* intransigeance, *f.*
intransigent [in'trænsidʒənt, in'trɑːnsidʒənt], *a.* intransigeant.
intransitive [in'trænsitiv, in'trɑːnsitiv], *a.* intransitif.
intrepid [in'trepid], *a.* intrépide.
intricacy ['intrikəsi], *n.* embrouillement, *m.*; complication, *f.*, dédale, *m.*
intricate [in'trikit], *a.* embrouillé; embarrassé; obscur; compliqué.
intrigue [in'triːg], *n.* intrigue, *f.*—*v.t.* intriguer.—*v.i.* intriguer, s'intriguer.
intriguing [in'triːgiŋ], *a.* intrigant, qui excite la curiosité.
intrinsic [in'trinsik], **intrinsical** [in'trinsikəl], *a.* intrinsèque.
introduce [intrə'djuːs], *v.t.* introduire, faire entrer; présenter (*personnes*), faire connaître (*à*).
introduction [intrə'dʌkʃən], *n.* introduction; présentation; recommandation (*par lettre*), *f.*; avant-propos (*de livre*), *m.*
introductory [intrə'dʌktəri], *a.* introductoire, préliminaire.
introspection [intro'spekʃən], *n.* introspection, *f.*
introspective [intro'spektiv], *a.* introspectif; qui s'analyse.
introvert ['introvəːt], *n.* introverti, *m.*
intrude [in'truːd], *v.i.* s'introduire, se faufiler, se fourrer; **to intrude on**, importuner, déranger.
intruder [in'truːdə], *n.* intrus, *m.*
intrusion [in'truːʒən], *n.* intrusion, importunité; (*fig.*) usurpation, *f.*, empiètement, *m.*
intuition [intju'iʃən], *n.* intuition, *f.*
intuitive [in'tjuːitiv], *a.* intuitif, d'intuition.
inundate ['inʌndeit], *v.t.* inonder (*de*).
inundation [inʌn'deiʃən], *n.* inondation, *f.*, débordement, *m.*
inure [i'njuə], *v.t.* habituer, endurcir, rompre.
invade [in'veid], *v.t.* envahir.
invader [in'veidə], *n.* envahisseur, *m.*
invading [in'veidiŋ], *a.* envahissant; d'invasion.

invalid ['invəliːd], *a.* malade, infirme; [in'vælid], (*Law*) invalide, de nul effet.—*n.* malade, *m.*, *f.*, personne malade, *f.*—*v.t.* **invalid out** (*of the army*), réformer.
invalidate [in'vælideit], *v.t.* invalider, casser.
invaluable [in'væljuəbl], *a.* inestimable, sans prix.
invariable [in'vɛəriəbl], *a.* invariable, constant, uniforme.
invariably [in'vɛəriəbli], *adv.* invariablement; constamment.
invasion [in'veiʒən], *n.* invasion, *f.*, envahissement, *m.*; (*fig.*) violation, *f.*
invective [in'vektiv], *n.* invective, *f.*
inveigh [in'vei], *v.i.* invectiver (*contre*).
inveigle [in'viːgl, in'veigl], *v.t.* séduire, attirer, entraîner.
invent [in'vent], *v.t.* inventer.
invention [in'venʃən], *n.* invention, *f.*
inventive [in'ventiv], *a.* inventif.
inventor [in'ventə], *n.* inventeur, *m.*
inventory ['inventri], *n.* inventaire, *m.*
inverse [in'vəːs], *a.* inverse.
inversely [in'vəːsli], *adv.* en sens inverse, inversement.
inversion [in'vəːʃən], *n.* inversion, *f.*
invert [in'vəːt], *v.t.* tourner sens dessus dessous, renverser.
invertebrate [in'vəːtibrit], *a.* and *n.* invertébré, *m.*
invest [in'vest], *v.t.* vêtir, revêtir (*de*); (*Mil.*) investir, bloquer; placer (*argent*).
investigate [in'vestigeit], *v.t.* rechercher, examiner; enquêter sur.
investigation [investi'geiʃən], *n.* investigation, recherche, enquête, *f.*
investigator [in'vestigeitə], *n.* investigateur, *m.*; **private investigator**, détective privé, *m.*
investment [in'vestmənt], *n.* placement (*d'argent*); (*Mil.*) investissement, *m.*
investor [in'vestə], *n.* actionnaire, *m.*, *f.*, personne qui place ses fonds, *f.*
inveterate [in'vetərit], *a.* invétéré, enraciné; acharné.
invidious [in'vidiəs], *a.* odieux; désagréable, ingrat (*tâche*).
invigorate [in'vigəreit], *v.t.* fortifier; donner de la vigueur à.
invigorating [in'vigəreitiŋ], *a.* fortifiant, vivifiant, tonifiant.
invincible [in'vinsibl], *a.* invincible.
inviolable [in'vaiələbl], *a.* inviolable.
inviolate [in'vaiəlit], *a.* inviolé, pur, intact.
invisible [in'vizibl], *a.* invisible.
invitation [invi'teiʃən], *n.* invitation, *f.*
invite [in'vait], *v.t.* inviter, engager (*à*); (*fig.*) appeler, provoquer.
inviting [in'vaitiŋ], *a.* attrayant, appétissant, tentant.
invoice ['invɔis], *n.* facture, *f.*—*v.t.* facturer.
invoke [in'vouk], *v.t.* invoquer.
involuntarily [in'vɔləntərili], *adv.* involontairement.
involuntary [in'vɔləntəri], *a.* involontaire.
involve [in'vɔlv], *v.t.* envelopper (*to envelop*); compromettre, impliquer, entraîner (*to entail*); comprendre, renfermer (*to comprise*); embarrasser, entortiller (*to entangle*).
involved [in'vɔlvd], *a.* embrouillé, entortillé, compliqué.
invulnerable [in'vʌlnərəbl], *a.* invulnérable.

Italian

inward ['inwəd], a. intérieur, interne.—adv. (also inwards ['inwədz]) en dedans, intérieurement.

inwardly ['inwədli], adv. intérieurement, intimement.

iodine ['aiədi:n, 'aiədain], n. iode, m.

ion ['aiən], n. ion, m.

ionosphere [ai'ɔnəsfiə], n. ionosphère, f.

iota [ai'outə], n. iota; rien, m.

Iran [i'rɑ:n]. l'Iran, m.

Iranian [i'reiniən, ai'reiniən], a. iranien, m.—n. Iranien (personne), m.

Iraq, Irak [i'rɑ:k]. l'Irak, m.

Iraqi [i'rɑ:ki], a. irakien.—n. Irakien (personne), m.

irascible [i'ræsibl], a. irascible.

irate [ai'reit], a. courroucé, irrité.

ire ['aiə], n. colère, f.; courroux, m.

Ireland ['aiələnd]. l'Irlande, f.

Irene [ai'ri:ni, ai'ri:n]. Irène, f.

iridescent [iri'desənt], a. iridescent, irisé; chatoyant.

iris ['aiəris], n. (pl. irises ['aiərisiz]) iris, m.

Irish ['aiəriʃ], a. irlandais.—n. irlandais (langue), m.; the Irish, les Irlandais, m.pl.

Irishman ['aiəriʃmən], n. (pl. -men [men]) Irlandais, m.

Irishwoman ['aiəriʃwumən], n. (pl. -women [wimin]) Irlandaise, f.

irk [ə:k], v.t. peiner, affliger; ennuyer.

irksome ['ə:ksəm], a. ingrat, ennuyeux.

iron ['aiən], n. fer à repasser, m.

iron ['aiən], a. de fer, en fer.—n. fer, m.; cast iron, fonte, f.; corrugated iron, tôle ondulée, f.; sheet iron, tôle, f.; wrought iron, fer forgé.—v.t. repasser (linge etc.).

ironic [aiə'rɔnik], ironical [aiə'rɔnikəl], a. ironique.

ironing ['aiəniŋ], a. à repasser.—n. repassage, m.

ironing board ['aiəniŋbɔ:d], n. planche à repasser, f.

ironmonger ['aiənmʌŋgə], n. quincaillier, m.

ironmongery ['aiənmʌŋgəri], n. quincaillerie, f.

iron ore ['aiən'ɔ:], n. minerai de fer, m.

iron-works ['aiənwə:ks], n.pl. forges, f.pl.; usine métallurgique, f.

irony ['aiərəni], n. ironie, f.

irradiate [i'reidieit], v.t. rayonner sur; éclairer.—v.i. rayonner.

irrational [i'ræʃənl], a. irraisonnable, déraisonnable; (Math.) irrationnel.

irreclaimable [iri'kleiməbl], a. incorrigible, invétéré.

irreconcilable [irekən'sailəbl], a. irréconciliable (avec); incompatible (avec); implacable.

irrecoverable [iri'kʌvərəbl], a. irrécouvrable; irréparable.

irredeemable [iri'di:məbl], a. irrachetable; irrémédiable.

irreducible [iri'dju:sibl], a. irréductible.

irreformable [iri'fɔ:məbl], a. inaltérable, irréformable.

irrefutable [i'refjutəbl], a. irréfutable.

irregular [i'regjulə], a. irrégulier, anormal; déréglé.

irregularity [iregju'læriti], n. irrégularité, f., déréglement, m.

irregularly [i'regjuləli], adv. irrégulièrement.

irrelevant [i'reləvənt], a. hors de propos, non pertinent; inapplicable (à).

irreligious [iri'lidʒəs], a. irréligieux.

irremediable [iri'mi:diəbl], a. irrémédiable, sans remède.

irremovable [iri'mu:vəbl], a. inébranlable, immuable; inamovible.

irreparable [i'repərəbl], a. irréparable.

irreplaceable [iri'pleisəbl], a. irremplaçable.

irrepressible [iri'presibl], a. irrépressible; inextinguible (rire).

irreproachable [iri'proutʃəbl], a. irréprochable, sans tache.

irresistible [iri'zistibl], a. irrésistible.

irresolute [i'rezolju:t], a. irrésolu, indécis.

irresolutely [i'rezolju:tli], adv. irrésolument, avec hésitation.

irresolution [irezo'lju:ʃən], irresoluteness [i'rezolju:tnis], n. irrésolution, indécision, f.

irrespective [iris'pektiv], a. indépendant (de), sans égard (pour); irrespective of, indépendamment de.

irrespectively [iris'pektivli], adv. indépendamment (de), sans égard (pour).

irresponsibility [irisponsi'biliti], n. irresponsabilité, étourderie, f.

irresponsible [iris'ponsibl], a. irresponsable; irréfléchi, étourdi.

irretrievable [iri'tri:vəbl], a. irréparable, irrémédiable.

irreverence [i'revərəns], n. irrévérence, f., manque de respect, m.

irreverent [i'revərənt], a. irrévérencieux.

irrevocable [i'revəkəbl], a. irrévocable.

irrigate ['irigeit], v.t. arroser, irriguer.

irrigation [iri'geiʃən], n. arrosement, m.; irrigation, f.

irritability [iritə'biliti], n. irritabilité, f.

irritable ['iritəbl], a. irritable.

irritate ['iriteit], v.t. irriter; to be irritated, s'irriter.

irritation [iri'teiʃən], n. irritation, f.

irruption [i'rʌpʃən], n. irruption, f.

Isabel ['izəbəl], Isabella [izə'belə]. Isabelle, f.

island ['ailənd], n. île, f.; refuge (au centre de la rue), m.

islander ['ailəndə], n. insulaire, m., f.

isle [ail], n. île, f.

islet ['ailit], n. îlot, m.

isobar ['aisobɑ:], n. isobare, f.

isolate ['aisəleit], v.t. isoler.

isolated ['aisəleitid], a. isolé, seul.

isolation [aisə'leiʃən], n. isolement, m.

isosceles [ai'sɔsəli:z], a. isocèle, isoscèle.

Israel ['izreil]. l'Israel, m.

Israeli [iz'reili], a. israélien.—n. Israélien (personne), m.

issue ['isju:, 'iʃju:], n. issue, sortie (egress), f.; écoulement (d'eau etc.), m.; distribution (envoi); émission (de billets de banque, timbres-poste); publication (de livres etc.), f.; résultat (conséquence), m.; enfants, m.pl.; (Law) question, f.; at issue, en question.—v.t. publier; expédier, distribuer; émettre (billets de banque).—v.i. sortir, jaillir (de); (fig.) provenir.

isthmus ['ismas], n. isthme, m.

it [it], pron. il, m., elle, f.; (accusatif) le, m., la, f.; (datif) lui; (impersonnel) il, ce, cela.

Italian [i'tæliən], a. italien.—n. italien (langue); Italien (personne), m.

italic

italic [i'tælik], *a.* italique.—*n.* (*pl.*) italiques, *m.pl.*

italicize [i'tælisaiz], *v.t.* mettre *ou* imprimer en italiques.

Italy ['itəli]. l'Italie, *f.*

itch [itʃ], *n.* démangeaison; gale (*maladie*), *f.*—*v.i.* démanger.

item ['aitəm], *n.* article; détail, *m.*, rubrique, *f.*; **item of news**, nouvelle, *f.*—*adv.* item, de plus.

itinerant [i'tinərənt], *a.* ambulant.

itinerary [i'tinərəri], *n.* itinéraire, *m.*

its [its], *poss. a.* son, *m.*, sa, *f.*; ses, *m.pl.*

itself [it'self], *pron.* lui, *m.*, elle, *f.*, soi, lui-même, *m.*, elle-même, *f.*, soi-même, *m.*; (*reflexive*) se.

ivory ['aivəri], *a.* d'ivoire.—*n.* ivoire, *m.*

ivy ['aivi], *n.* lierre, *m.*

J

J, j [dʒei]. dixième lettre de l'alphabet, *m.*

jabber ['dʒæbə], *v.i.* jaboter, baragouiner.—*n.* bavardage, baragouinage, *m.*

jack [dʒæk], *n.* chevalet (*de scieur*); cric (*pour auto*); (*Cards*) valet; (*Bowls*) cochonnet, *m.*—*v.t.* **to jack up**, soulever avec un cric.

jackal ['dʒækɔːl], *n.* chacal, *m.*

jackanapes ['dʒækəneips], *n.* singe; fat, *m.*

jackass ['dʒækæs], *n.* âne, baudet, bourriquet; (*fig.*) idiot, *m.*

jackdaw ['dʒækdɔː], *n.* choucas, *m.*

jacket ['dʒækit], *n.* veste, *f.*; veston, *m.*; (*Tech.*) chemise, enveloppe, jaquette, *f.*

jack-in-the-box ['dʒækinðəbɔks], *n.* boîte à surprise, *f.*

jack-tar ['dʒæk'tɑː], *n.* marin, *m.*

jade (1) [dʒeid], *n.* rosse; haridelle; (*fig.*) coquine (*femme*), *f.*—*v.t.* surmener, harasser, éreinter.

jade (2) [dʒeid], *n.* (*Min.*) jade, *m.*

jaded ['dʒeidid], *a.* surmené, éreinté.

jagged ['dʒægid], **jaggy** ['dʒægi], *a.* dentelé, ébréché.

jaguar ['dʒægjuə], *n.* jaguar, *m.*

jail [dʒeil], *n.* prison, geôle, *f.*

jailer ['dʒeilə], *n.* geôlier, *m.*

jam [dʒæm], *n.* confitures, *f.pl.*; encombrement, embouteillage (*de circulation*), *m.*—*v.t.* serrer, presser, bloquer; (*Rad.*) brouiller.—*v.i.* se coincer.

jamming ['dʒæmiŋ], *n.* coincement; (*Rad.*) brouillage, *m.*

Jamaica [dʒə'meikə]. la Jamaïque, *f.*

Jamaican [dʒə'meikən], *a.* jamaïquain.—*n.* Jamaïquain (*personne*), *m.*

James [dʒeimz]. Jacques, *m.*

Jane [dʒein]. Jeanne, *f.*

jangle ['dʒæŋgl], *v.t.* choquer avec bruit; (*fig.*) agacer (*nerfs*).—*v.i.* faire un bruit de ferraille.

janitor ['dʒænitə], *n.* portier, concierge, *m.*

January ['dʒænjuəri]. janvier, *m.*

Japan [dʒə'pæn]. le Japon, *m.*

japan [dʒə'pæn], *n.* laque, vernis, *m.*—*v.* laquer; vernir.

Japanese [dʒæpə'niːz], *a.* japonais.—*n.* japonais (*langue*); Japonais (*personne*), *m.*

jar (1) [dʒɑː], *v.t.* remuer, secouer; ébranler.—*v.i.* être discordant (*instrument de musique*); heurter, s'entrechoquer (*être en conflit*); jurer (*couleurs*); (*fig.*) se disputer.—*n.* son discordant, choc, *m.*; querelle, *f.*

jar (2) [dʒɑː], *n.* jarre, cruche (*faience*), *f.*, bocal (*verre*), *m.*

jargon ['dʒɑːgən], *n.* jargon, *m.*

jarring ['dʒɑːriŋ], *a.* discordant; en conflit.—*n.* son discordant, *m.*; querelles, *f.pl.*

jasmine ['dʒæzmin], *n.* jasmin, *m.*

jasper ['dʒæspə], *n.* jaspe, *m.*

jaundice ['dʒɔːndis], *n.* jaunisse, *f.*

jaundiced ['dʒɔːndist], *a.* qui a la jaunisse; (*fig.*) prévenu (*contre*).

jaunt [dʒɔːnt], *n.* petite promenade *ou* excursion, *f.*—*v.i.* faire une petite promenade *ou* excursion.

jauntily ['dʒɔːntili], *adv.* avec insouciance, légèrement.

jauntiness ['dʒɔːntinis], *n.* légèreté, *f.*, enjouement, *m.*

jaunty ['dʒɔːnti], *a.* léger, enjoué, sémillant.

javelin ['dʒævəlin], *n.* javeline, *f.*, javelot, *m.*

jaw [dʒɔː], *n.* mâchoire, *f.*; (*fig., pl.*) portes, *f.pl.*; bras, *m.pl.*, étreintes, *f.pl.*

jawbone ['dʒɔːboun], *n.* mâchoire, *f.*

jay [dʒei], *n.* geai, *m.*

jay-walker ['dʒeiwɔːkə], *n.* piéton distrait, *m.*

jazz [dʒæz], *n.* jazz, *m.*

jealous ['dʒeləs], *a.* jaloux.

jealously ['dʒeləsli], *adv.* jalousement; par jalousie.

jealousy ['dʒeləsi], *n.* jalousie, *f.*

jean [dʒiːn], *n.* coutil, treillis; (*pl.*) pantalon (de coutil), *m.*

jeep [dʒiːp], *n.* jeep, *f.*

jeer [dʒiə], *n.* raillerie, moquerie, *f.*—*v.t.* railler, huer, se moquer de.—*v.i.* railler, se moquer, goguenarder.

jeering ['dʒiəriŋ], *a.* railleur, moqueur, goguenard.—*n.* raillerie, moquerie, *f.*

jeeringly ['dʒiəriŋli], *adv.* en raillant, d'un ton moqueur.

jelly ['dʒeli], *n.* gelée, *f.*

jelly-fish ['dʒelifiʃ], *n.* méduse, *f.*

jennet ['dʒenit], *n.* genet (*d'Espagne*), *m.*

jeopardize ['dʒepədaiz], *v.t.* hasarder, risquer, mettre en danger.

jeopardy ['dʒepədi], *n.* danger, hasard, *m.*

jerk [dʒəːk], *n.* saccade, secousse, *f.*—*v.t.* donner une poussée à; jeter.

jerkily ['dʒəːkili], *adv.* par saccades.

jerkin ['dʒəːkin], *n.* pourpoint; paletot (de cuir), *m.*

jerky ['dʒəːki], *a.* saccadé; irrégulier.

jersey ['dʒəːzi], *n.* vareuse de laine, *f.*, maillot, tricot, *m.*

jest [dʒest], *n.* plaisanterie, facétie, *f.*, bon mot, *m.*; risée (*objet de rire*), *f.*—*v.i.* plaisanter (*de ou avec*), badiner (*sur*).

jester ['dʒestə], *n.* plaisant, railleur; bouffon, fou, *m.*

jesting ['dʒestiŋ], *a.* pour rire, badin.—*n.* raillerie, plaisanterie, *f.*, badinage, *m.*

jestingly ['dʒestiŋli], *adv.* en plaisantant, pour rire.

Jesuit ['dʒezjuit], *n.* Jésuite, *m.*

Jesus ['dʒi:zəs]. Jésus, *m.*

jet [dʒet], *n.* jet, jet d'eau; (*Min.*) jais, *m.*; **jet engine**, turbo-réacteur, *m.*; **jet plane**, avion à réaction, *m.*—*v.i.* s'élancer; gicler.

jet-black ['dʒet'blæk], *a.* noir comme du jais.

jetsam ['dʒetsəm], *n.* marchandise jetée à la mer, *f.*, épaves, *f.pl.*

jettison ['dʒetisən], *n.* jet à la mer, *m.*—*v.t.* jeter par-dessus bord.

jetty ['dʒeti], *n.* jetée, *f.*

Jew [dʒu:], *n.* Juif, *m.*

jewel ['dʒu:əl], *n.* joyau, bijou, *m.*, pierre précieuse, *f.*; (*pl.*) pierreries, *f.pl.*; rubis (*de montre*), *m.pl.*—*v.t.* orner de bijoux.

jeweler ['dʒu:ələ], *n.* joaillier, bijoutier, *m.*

jewelry ['dʒu:əlri], *n.* joaillerie, bijouterie, *f.*

Jewess ['dʒu:is], *n.* Juive, *f.*

Jewish ['dʒu:iʃ], *a.* juif, des Juifs.

Jewry ['dʒu:ri], *n.* Juiverie, *f.*

jib [dʒib], *n.* (*Naut.*) foc, *m.*—*v.i.* reculer; regimber.

jiffy ['dʒifi], *n.* **in a jiffy**, en un clin d'œil.

jig [dʒig], *n.* gigue (*danse*), *f.*, gabarit, *m.*—*v.i.* danser la gigue.

jilt [dʒilt], *n.* coquette, *f.*—*v.t.* planter là; abandonner, (*fam.*) plaquer (*un amoureux*).

jingle ['dʒiŋgl], *n.* tintement (*de cloches*); cliquetis (*de verres, métaux etc.*), *m.*—*v.t.* faire tinter, faire cliqueter.—*v.i.* tinter (*grelots etc.*); s'entrechoquer (*verres etc.*).

jingo ['dʒiŋgou], *n.* chauvin, *m.*; **by jingo !** par exemple!

jingoism ['dʒiŋgouizm], *n.* chauvinisme, *m.*

jinx [dʒiŋks], *n.* porte-guigne, *m.*

Joan [dʒoun]. Jeanne, *f.*; **Joan of Arc**, Jeanne d'Arc.

job [dʒɔb], *n.* travail, ouvrage, *m.*; tâche, pièce; besogne, affaire, *f.*; emploi, *m.*; **job lot**, solde, *m.*, occasion, *f.*; **that's just the job**, cela fait juste l'affaire.—*v.t.* louer; tripoter.—*v.i.* travailler à la tâche; (*Comm.*) agioter, spéculer.

jobber ['dʒɔbə], *n.* ouvrier à la tâche; (*Comm.*) agioteur, coulissier; exploiteur, *m.*

jobbing ['dʒɔbiŋ], *a.* **jobbing gardener**, jardinier à la journée, *m.*—*n.* ouvrage à la tâche; (*Comm.*) agiotage; tripotage, *m.*

jockey ['dʒɔki], *n.* jockey, *m.*

jocose [dʒɔ'kous], *a.* plaisant, jovial.

jocular ['dʒɔkjulə], *a.* plaisant, facétieux.

jocularly ['dʒɔkjuləli], *adv.* facétieusement.

jocund ['dʒɔkənd], *a.* joyeux, enjoué, gai.

jog [dʒɔg], *v.t.* pousser d'un coup de coude; secouer, cahoter; (*fig.*) rafraîchir (*la mémoire*).—*v.i.* se mouvoir; marcher lentement; **to jog along**, aller doucement.—*n.* secousse légère, *f.*, cahot; coup de coude, *m.*; **jog trot**, petit trot, *m.*

John [dʒɔn]. Jean, *m.*; **Johnnie**, (*colloq.*) Jeannot, *m.*

join [dʒɔin], *v.t.* joindre, unir; associer (*à*); rejoindre (*rattraper*); relier (*rues etc.*); **will you join us?** voulez-vous être des nôtres ? —*v.i.* se joindre, s'unir; s'inscrire; s'associer; prendre part (*à*).

joiner ['dʒɔinə], *n.* menuisier, *m.*

joinery ['dʒɔinəri], *n.* menuiserie, *f.*

joint [dʒɔint], *a.* commun, ensemble, réuni.— *n.* jointure, *f.*, joint, *m.*; pièce, *f.*; rôti (*de viande*), *m.*; phalange (*du doigt*); charnière (*de porte*); soudure, (*Anat.*) articulation, *f.*; (*Bot.*) nœud, *m.*; (*slang*) boîte, *f.*; **out of joint**, disloqué, (*fig.*) dérangé; **to put one's arm out of joint**, se démettre le bras.— *v.t.* couper aux jointures; joindre.

jointed ['dʒɔintid], *a.* articulé, jointé; séparé.

jointly ['dʒɔintli], *adv.* conjointement.

joint stock ['dʒɔintstɔk], *n.* capital, fonds commun, *m.*; **joint-stock bank**, banque par actions, *f.*; **joint-stock company**, société anonyme, *f.*

joist [dʒɔist], *n.* solive, poutre, poutrelle, *f.*

joke [dʒouk], *n.* bon mot, mot pour rire, *m.*, plaisanterie, (*fam.*) blague, *f.*; **a practical joke**, une farce, un mauvais tour; **to crack a joke**, dire un bon mot.—*v.t.* plaisanter sur, railler de.—*v.i.* plaisanter, badiner; rire de.

joker ['dʒoukə], *n.* plaisant, farceur; (*Cards*) joker, *m.*

joking ['dʒoukiŋ], *n.* plaisanterie, farce, *f.*

jokingly ['dʒoukiŋli], *adv.* en plaisantant, pour rire.

jollification [dʒɔlifi'keiʃən], *n.* partie de plaisir, *f.*

jollity ['dʒɔliti], *n.* joie, gaieté, *f.*

jolly ['dʒɔli], *a.* gai, joyeux, gaillard, réjoui.

jolt [dʒoult], *n.* cahot, choc, *m.*—*v.t.* cahoter. —*v.i.* faire des cahots.

Jonah ['dʒounə]. Jonas, *m.*—*n.* porte-malheur, *m.*

jonquil ['dʒɔŋkwil], *n.* (*Bot.*) jonquille, *f.*

Jordan ['dʒɔ:dən]. le Jourdain (*rivière*), *m.*; la Jordanie (*pays*), *f.*

Jordanian [dʒɔ:'deiniən], *a.* jordanien.—*n.* Jordanien (*personne*), *m.*

jostle [dʒɔsl], *v.t.* pousser, bousculer; (*Spt.*) gêner (*un concurrent*).—*v.i.* jouer des coudes.

jot [dʒɔt], *n.* iota, brin, *m.*—*v.t.* **to jot down**, noter, prendre note de.

journal ['dʒə:nəl], *n.* journal, *m.*; revue, *f.*

journalism ['dʒə:nəlizm], *n.* journalisme, *m.*

journalist ['dʒə:nəlist], *n.* journaliste, *m.*, *f.*

journey ['dʒə:ni], *n.* voyage; trajet (*distance*), *m.*; **a pleasant journey to you!** bon voyage! **on the journey**, en route; **to go on a journey**, faire un voyage.—*v.i.* voyager.

journeyman ['dʒə:nimən], *n.* (*pl.* **-men** [men]) garçon, ouvrier, *m.*

joust [dʒaust, dʒu:st], *n.* joute, *f.*—*v.t.* jouter.

Jove [dʒouv]. Jupiter, *m.*; **by Jove !** bigre! mâtin!

jovial ['dʒouviəl], *a.* joyeux, gai.

joviality [dʒouvi'æliti], *n.* humeur joviale, jovialité, *f.*

jowl [dʒaul], *n.* joue; hure (*de saumon*), *f.*; **cheek by jowl**, côte à côte.

joy [dʒɔi], *n.* joie, *f.*; **to wish someone joy**, féliciter quelqu'un.—*v.i.* se réjouir (*de ou avec*).

joyful ['dʒɔiful], *a.* joyeux.

joyfully ['dʒɔifuli], *adv.* joyeusement.

joyfulness ['dʒɔifulnis], *n.* allégresse, joie, *f.*

joyous ['dʒɔiəs], *a.* joyeux.

jubilant ['dʒu:bilənt], *a.* réjoui; jubilant.

jubilation [dʒu:bi'leiʃən], *n.* réjouissances de triomphe, *f.pl.*, jubilation, *f.*

jubilee ['dʒu:bili:], *n.* jubilé, *m.*

Judaea [dʒu:'diə]. la Judée, *f.*

Judaism ['dʒu:deiizm], *n.* judaïsme, *m.*

judge [dʒʌdʒ], *n.* juge; (*fig.*) connaisseur, *m.*; *to be a judge of*, se connaître à *ou* en.—*v.t.* juger; discerner, considérer.

judgment ['dʒʌdʒmənt], *n.* jugement; arrêt, *m.*, sentence, *f.*; (*fig.*) avis, sens, *m.*, opinion, *f.*

judicature ['dʒu:dikətʃə], *n.* judicature, justice; cour de justice, *f.*

judicial [dʒu:'diʃl], *a.* judiciaire, juridique.

judicious [dʒu:'diʃəs], *a.* judicieux, prudent.

judiciously [dʒu:'diʃəsli], *adv.* judicieusement.

judo ['dʒu:dou], *n.* jiu-jitsu, (*fam.*) judo, *m.*

jug [dʒʌg], *n.* broc, *m.*; cruche, *f.*; *water jug*, pot à eau, *m.*—*v.t.* faire un civet de (*lièvre*); *jugged hare*, civet de lièvre, *m.*

juggle [dʒʌgl], *v.t.* jouer, duper, escamoter.—*v.i.* faire des tours de passe-passe; (*fig.*) escamoter.—*n.* jonglerie, *f.*; escamotage, tour de passe-passe, *m.*

juggler ['dʒʌglə], *n.* jongleur; escamoteur; (*fig.*) charlatan, *m.*

juggling ['dʒʌgliŋ], *n.* jonglerie, *f.*, escamotage, *m.*

jugular ['dʒʌgjulə], *a. and n.* jugulaire, *f.*

juice [dʒu:s], *n.* jus; suc, *m.*

juicy ['dʒu:si], *a.* juteux; succulent.

ju-jitsu [dʒu:'dʒitsu], *n.* jiu-jitsu, *m.*

jukebox ['dʒu:kbɔks], *n.* phonographe à sous, jukebox, *m.*

Julian ['dʒu:liən]. Julien, *m.*

Juliet ['dʒu:liət]. Juliette, *f.*

July [dʒu'lai]. juillet, *m.*

jumble [dʒʌmbl], *v.t.* jeter pêle-mêle, mêler ensemble, confondre.—*n.* pêle-mêle, méli-mélo, *m.*, confusion, *f.*; *jumble sale*, vente de charité, *f.*

jump [dʒʌmp], *n.* saut, bond; sursaut; obstacle (à sauter), *m.*; *high jump*, saut en hauteur; *broad jump*, saut en longueur.—*v.t* sauter, franchir d'un bond; sauter de; faire sauter; (*fam.*) *to jump the queue*, resquiller (dans une queue).—*v.i.* sauter; se jeter, se précipiter (*sur*); *to jump at*, accepter avec empressement.

jumper (1) ['dʒʌmpə], *n.* sauteur, *m.*

jumper (2) ['dʒʌmpə], *n.* chandail, jersey, jumper, *m.*

jumpy ['dʒʌmpi], *a.* nerveux.

junction ['dʒʌŋkʃən], *n.* jonction, *f.*; (*Rail.*) embranchement, *m.*

juncture ['dʒʌŋktʃə], *n.* jointure, *f.*; moment critique, *m.*

June [dʒu:n]. juin, *m.*

jungle [dʒʌŋgl], *n.* jungle, *f.*; fourré, *m.*

junior ['dʒu:niə], *a.* jeune, cadet.—*n.* cadet, inférieur en âge, *m.*

juniper ['dʒu:nipə], *n.* genièvre, *m.*

junk (1) [dʒʌŋk], *n.* jonque (*navire*), *f.*

junk (2) [dʒʌŋk], *n.* objets de rebut, *m.pl.*

junket ['dʒʌŋkit], *n.* lait caillé, *m.*; jonchée (*fromage*), talmouse (*gâteau*), *f.*—*v.t.* régaler.—*v.i.* se régaler.

jurisdiction [dʒuəris'dikʃən], *n.* juridiction, *f.*

jurisprudence [dʒuəris'pru:dəns], *n.* jurisprudence, *f.*

jurist ['dʒuərist], *n.* juriste, *m.*, *f.*

juror ['dʒuərə], *n.* juré, *m.*

jury ['dʒuəri], *n.* jury, *m.*

juryman ['dʒuərimən], *n.* (*pl.* **-men** [men]) juré, *m.*

just [dʒʌst], *a.* juste, équitable.—*adv.* juste, justement, précisément; tout, tout juste, seulement, un peu; *he has just gone out*, il vient de sortir; *just now*, à l'instant, tout à l'heure; *just so*, précisément.

justice ['dʒʌstis], *n.* justice, *f.*; juge (*magistrat*), *m.*; *Justice of the Peace*, juge de paix; *to do justice to*, (*fig.*) faire honneur à (*un repas etc.*).

justifiable [dʒʌsti'faiəbl], *a.* justifiable, légitime.

justification [dʒʌstifi'keiʃən], *n.* justification, *f.*

justify ['dʒʌstifai], *v.t.* justifier, autoriser, permettre; *to feel justified in*, se croire autorisé à, croire devoir.

justly ['dʒʌstli], *adv.* exactement, justement; à bon droit.

jut [dʒʌt], *v.i.* avancer, faire saillie.

jutting ['dʒʌtiŋ], *a.* en saillie, saillant.

jute [dʒu:t], *n.* jute, *m.*

juvenile ['dʒu:vənail], *a.* jeune; juvénile, de jeunesse; *juvenile delinquent*, jeune délinquant, *m.*—*n.* jeune, *m.*, *f.*; adolescent, *m.*

juxtaposition [dʒʌkstəpə'ziʃən], *n.* juxtaposition, *f.*; *in juxtaposition*, juxtaposé.

K

K, k [kei]. onzième lettre de l'alphabet, *m.*

kale, kail [keil], *n.* (*Sc.*) chou, *m.*; *sea kale*, chou marin.

kaleidoscope [kə'laidəskoup], *n.* kaléidoscope, *m.*

kangaroo [kæŋgə'ru:], *n.* kangourou, *m.*

Katharine, Katherine ['kæθərin]. Catherine, *f.*

keel [ki:l], *n.* quille; carène, *f.*

keen [ki:n], *a.* affilé, aigu, aiguisé; (*fig.*) vif, ardent; amer, mordant (*acerbe*); pénétrant, perçant (*brisant la surface de*); dévorant (*appétit*).

keenly ['ki:nli], *adv.* vivement, ardemment, âprement.

keenness ['ki:nnis], *n.* finesse (*de tranchant*); (*fig.*) subtilité; vivacité, ardeur, *f.*, empressement; mordant (*de troupes*), *m.*, âpreté (*du froid*), *f.*

keep [ki:p], *v.t. irr.* tenir, retenir, garder; maintenir, conserver (*ne pas perdre*); avoir (*volaille etc.*); entretenir (*subvenir aux besoins de*); nourrir (*avoir en pension*); avoir à son service; (*fig.*) observer; célébrer, fêter; garantir, protéger; remplir; continuer; *keep it up!* continuez! *to keep away*, éloigner, tenir éloigné; *to keep back*, retenir, garder, tenir en réserve; retarder; *to keep from*, préserver de, empêcher de; *to keep in*, tenir enfermé, retenir; *to keep on*, continuer; *to keep out*, ne pas admettre, écarter, éloigner; *to keep to*, s'en tenir à; *to keep up*, tenir levé, soutenir; continuer; entretenir.—*v.i.* se tenir, rester, demeurer (*ne pas cesser d'être*); se garder, se

knife

conserver (*durer*); (*fig.*) se garder, s'abstenir; **to keep away**, se tenir éloigné; **to keep back**, se tenir en arrière; **to keep** (*doing, saying, telling etc.*), ne pas cesser de; **to keep silent**, se taire; **to keep up with**, aller de pair avec.—*n.* donjon, réduit (*forteresse*), *m.*; nourriture, *f.*, entretien (*subsistance*), *m.*

keeper ['kiːpə], *n.* garde; gardien; surveillant, *m.*

keeping ['kiːpiŋ], *n.* garde, surveillance; conservation; (*fig.*) harmonie, *f.*

keepsake ['kiːpseik], *n.* souvenir, *m.*

keg [keg], *n.* caque (*de hareng*), *f.*, petit baril, *m.*

ken [ken], *n.* vue; portée, *f.*

kennel [kenl], *n.* chenil, *m.*; niche, *f.*

Kenya ['kenjə], le Kénya, *m.*

kept [kept], *a.* entretenu.—*p.p.* [KEEP].

kerb [kəːb], *n.* bordure (*de trottoir*), margelle (*de puits*), *f.* (*Am.* **curb**)

kerb-stone ['kəːbstoun], *n.* bordure (*de trottoir*), *f.*, pavement, *m.*

***kerchief** ['kəːtʃif], *n.* fichu, *m.*

kernel [kəːnl], *n.* graine, amande, *f.*, pignon (*de pomme de pin*); noyau (*de drupe*); (*fig.*) fond, essentiel, *m.*

kerosene ['kerosiːn], *n.* kérosène; pétrole lampant, *m.*

kestrel ['kestrəl], *n.* crécerelle, *f.*

ketch [ketʃ], *n.* (*Naut.*) quaiche, *f.*, ketch, *m.*

kettle [ketl], *n.* bouilloire, *f.*; chaudron (*bassine à confitures*), *m.*; **a pretty kettle of fish**, un beau gâchis.

kettledrum ['ketldrʌm], *n.* timbale, *f.*

key [kiː], *n.* clef, clé, *f.*; (*Arith. etc.*) corrigé; (*Mus.*) ton, *m.*; touche (*sur le piano etc.*), *f.*; **under lock and key**, sous clef.

key-board ['kiːbɔːd], *n.* clavier, *m.*

keyhole ['kiːhoul], *n.* trou de la serrure, *m.*

key-note ['kiːnout], *n.* tonique; (*fig.*) idée maîtresse, *f.*

key-stone ['kiːstoun], *n.* clef de voûte, *f.*

khaki ['kaːki], *n.* kaki, *m.*

khan [kaːn], *n.* kan, khan, *m.*

kick [kik], *n.* coup de pied; recul (*d'un fusil*), *m.*; ruade (*d'animal*), *f.*; (*Ftb.*) **free kick**, coup franc, *m.*—*v.t.* donner un coup de pied à; frapper *ou* pousser du pied; (*Ftb.*) botter; **to kick out**, chasser à coups de pied; **to kick up a row**, faire du tapage.—*v.i.* donner des coups de pied; ruer, regimber (*animal*); reculer (*fusil*).

kick-off ['kikɔf], *n.* (*Ftb.*) coup d'envoi, *m.*

kid [kid], *a.* de chevreau; **kid gloves**, gants de chevreau, *m.pl.*—*n.* chevreau; (*colloq.*) enfant, gosse, *m.*—*v.t.* (*fam.*) en conter à; **no kidding!** sans blague!

kidnap ['kidnæp], *v.t.* enlever.

kidney ['kidni], *n.* rein; rognon (*d'animal*), *m.*

kidney bean ['kidni'biːn], *n.* haricot, *m.*

kill [kil], *v.t.* tuer; faire mourir; abattre (*assassiner*).

killer ['kilə], *n.* tueur, *m.*

killing ['kiliŋ], *a.* mortel; assommant (*travail*).—*n.* tuerie, boucherie, *f.*, massacre, *m.*

kiln [kiln], *n.* four, *m.*

kilogram ['kiləgræm], *n.* kilogramme, *m.*

kilometer ['kiləmiːtə], *n.* kilomètre, *m.*

kilowatt ['kilowɔt], *n.* kilowatt, *m.*

kin [kin], *n.* parenté, *f.*; parent, allié, *m.*; **next of kin**, le plus proche parent.

kind [kaind], *a.* bon, bienveillant, bienfaisant; obligeant, complaisant (*accommodant*); **my kind regards to him**, faites-lui toutes mes amitiés; **will you be so kind as to**, voulez-vous avoir la bonté de.—*n.* genre, *m.*, sorte, espèce, *f.*; **in kind**, en nature.

kindergarten ['kindəgaːtn], *n.* école maternelle, *f.*

kindhearted ['kaind'haːtid], *a.* bon, bienveillant.

kindle [kindl], *v.t.* allumer, enflammer; (*fig.*) éveiller, exciter.—*v.i.* s'allumer, s'enflammer.

kindliness ['kaindlinis], *n.* bienveillance, bonté, *f.*

kindly ['kaindli], *a.* bon, bienveillant, favorable.—*adv.* avec bienveillance.

kindness ['kaindnis], *n.* bienveillance, bonté, *f.*; bienfait, *m.*

kindred ['kindrid], *a.* de même nature.—*n.* parenté, *f.*; parents, *m.pl.*

kinema ['kinimə], [CINEMA].

king [kiŋ], *n.* roi, *m.*; (*checkers*) dame, *f.*

kingdom ['kiŋdəm], *n.* royaume; (*fig.*) empire; (*Nat. Hist.*) règne, *m.*; **the United Kingdom**, le Royaume-Uni.

kingfisher ['kiŋfiʃə], *n.* (*Orn.*) martin-pêcheur, *m.*

kingly ['kiŋli], *a.* de roi, royal.

kink [kiŋk], *n.* nœud; (*colloq.*) point faible, défaut, *m.*

kinsman ['kinzmən], *n.* (*pl.* **-men** [men]) parent, allié, *m.*

kiosk ['kiɔsk], *n.* kiosque, *m.*; **telephone kiosk**, cabine téléphonique, *f.*

kirk [kəːk], *n.* église d'Écosse, *f.*

kiss [kis], *n.* baiser, *m.*—*v.t.*, *v.i.* embrasser; **to kiss (each other)**, s'embrasser.

kit [kit], *n.* petit équipement, *m.*, effets, *m.pl.*; trousse, *f.*; outils (*d'un ouvrier*), *m.pl.*

kit bag ['kitbæg], *n.* sac, *m.*

kitchen ['kitʃin], *n.* cuisine, *f.*

kitchen garden ['kitʃingaːdn], *n.* jardin potager, *m.*

kitchen utensils ['kitʃinjuːtenslz], *n.pl.* batterie de cuisine, *f.*

kite [kait], *n.* milan (*oiseau*); cerf-volant (*jouet*), *m.*

kith [kiθ], *n.* **kith and kin**, parents et amis, *m.pl.*

kitten [kitn], *n.* chaton, petit chat, *m.*

knack [næk], *n.* adresse, *f.*, tour de main, *m.*

knapsack ['næpsæk], *n.* havresac, *m.*

knave [neiv], *n.* fripon, coquin; (*Cards*) valet, *m.*

knavery ['neivəri], *n.* friponnerie, coquinerie, *f.*

knavish ['neiviʃ], *a.* fripon; malin.

knead [niːd], *v.t.* pétrir.

knee [niː], *n.* genou, *m.*

knee breeches ['niːbritʃiz], *n.pl.* culotte courte, *f.*

knee-cap ['niːkæp], *n.* genouillère; (*Anat.*) rotule, *f.*

kneel [niːl], *v.i. irr.* s'agenouiller.

knell [nel], *n.* glas, *m.*

knickers ['nikəz], *n.* culotte (*de femme*), *f.*

knick-knack ['niknæk], *n.* brimborion, *m.*, babiole, *f.*; colifichet, bibelot, *m.*

knife [naif], *n.* (*pl.* **knives** [naivz]) couteau; (*Tech.*) coupoir; (*Surg.*) scalpel, bistouri, *m.*; **carving knife**, couteau à découper, *m.*; **pen-knife**, canif, *m.*—*v.t.* poignarder.

knife-grinder ['naifgraində], *n*. rémouleur, *m.*

knight [nait], *n.* chevalier; (*Chess*) cavalier, *m.*—*v.t.* créer chevalier.

knighthood ['naithud], *n.* chevalerie, *f.*

knightly ['naitli], *a.* chevaleresque, de chevalier.

knit [nit], *v.t.* tricoter; froncer (*les sourcils*); (*fig.*) joindre, attacher, lier.

knitting ['nitiŋ], *n.* tricot, *m.*

knitting needle ['nitiŋni:dl], *n.* aiguille à tricoter, *f.*

knives [KNIFE].

knob [nɔb], *n.* bosse, *f.*; bouton (*de porte*), *m.*

knock [nɔk], *v.t.* frapper, heurter, cogner; *to knock about*, bousculer, malmener; *to knock down*, renverser, assommer; adjuger (*aux enchères*).—*v.i. to knock about*, rouler sa bosse, aller de par le monde; *to knock off*, cesser le travail.—*n.* coup, choc; cognement, *m.*

knocker ['nɔkə], *n.* marteau (*de porte*), *m.*

knocking ['nɔkiŋ], *n.* coups, *m.pl.*

knoll [noul], *n.* monticule, tertre, *m.*, butte, *f.*

knot [nɔt], *n.* nœud; groupe (*de personnes etc.*), *m.*; (*fig.*) difficulté, *f.*, embarras, *m.*—*v.t.* nouer; lier; (*fig.*) embrouiller.—*v.i.* faire des nœuds; se nouer.

knotted ['nɔtid], *a.* noueux.

knotty ['nɔti], *a.* noueux; (*fig.*) dur (*difficile*); embrouillé, compliqué.

know [nou], *v.t. irr.* savoir, apprendre (*to learn*); connaître (*to be acquainted with*); reconnaître (*to recognize*); *to know by heart*, savoir par cœur; *to know by sight*, connaître de vue; *to know someone*, connaître quelqu'un; *to know something*, savoir quelque chose.—*n. to be in the know*, être dans le secret.

know-how ['nouhau], *n.* savoir-faire, *m.*

knowing ['nouiŋ], *a.* intelligent, instruit; fin, malin.

knowingly ['nouiŋli], *adv.* sciemment; avec ruse.

knowledge ['nɔlidʒ], *n.* connaissance, science, *f.*; savoir, *m.*; *not to my knowledge*, pas que je sache; *without my knowledge*, à mon insu.

knowledgeable ['nɔlidʒəbl], *a.* bien informé.

knuckle [nʌkl], *n.* jointure, articulation du doigt, *f.*; jarret (*de viande*), *m.*—*v.i. to knuckle under*, se soumettre, mettre les pouces.

knuckle-bone ['nʌklboun], *n.* osselet, *m.*

Korea [kə'ri:ə], la Corée, *f.*

Korean [kə'ri:ən], *a.* coréen.—*n.* coréen (*langue*); Coréen (*personne*), *m.*

Kuwait [ku'weit], le Koweit, *m.*

L

L, 1 [el]. douzième lettre de l'alphabet, *m.*

la [lɑ:], *n.* (*Mus.*) la, *m.*

lab [læb], *n.* (*fam.*) labo, *m.*

label [leibl], *n.* étiquette, *f.*; (*Ind.*) label, *m.*—*v.t.* étiqueter; (*fig.*) désigner sous le nom de.

labor ['leibə], *n.* travail, labeur, *m.*, peine, *f.*; ouvrage (*piece of work*); travail d'enfant (*accouchement*), *m.*; *hard labor*, travaux forcés, *m.pl.*; *manual labor*, main-d'œuvre, *f.*; *the Labor Party*, le parti travailliste.—*v.t.* travailler; (*fig.*) élaborer.—*v.i.* travailler; souffrir, peiner; chercher (*à*), s'efforcer (*de*); *to labor under a delusion*, être dans l'erreur.

laboratory [lə'bɔrətəri, 'læbrətəri], *n.* laboratoire, *m.*

laborer ['leibərə], *n.* manœuvre, homme de peine, *m.*

labor-exchange ['leibəriks'tʃeindʒ], *n.* bureau de placement (*municipal* ou *d'état*), *m.*

laborious [lə'bɔ:riəs], *a.* laborieux, pénible.

laboriously [lə'bɔ:riəsli], *adv.* laborieusement, péniblement.

labor-saving ['leibəseiviŋ], *a. labor-saving device*, économiseur de travail, *m.*

Labrador ['læbrədɔ:]. le Labrador, *m.*

labrador ['læbrədɔ:], *n.* chien de Labrador, *m.*

laburnum [lə'bə:nəm], *n.* faux ébénier; cytise, *m.*

labyrinth ['læbirinθ], *n.* labyrinthe, *m.*

lace [leis], *n.* dentelle, *f.*; point, galon; lacet (*cordon*); ruban (*bande*), *m.*; *shoelace*, lacet de bottine.—*v.t.* lacer (*ses souliers*); garnir de dentelle, galonner (*orner de dentelle*); (*fig.*) orner.

lacerate ['læsəreit], *v.t.* déchirer, lacérer.

laceration [læsə'reiʃən], *n.* déchirure, lacération, *f.*

lachrymose ['lækrimous], *a.* larmoyant.

lacing ['leisiŋ], *n.* lacement, *m.*

lack [læk], *n.* manque, besoin, défaut, *m.*; *for lack of*, faute de.—*v.t.* manquer de.—*v.i.* manquer.

lackey ['læki], *n.* laquais, *m.*

lacking ['lækiŋ], *a.* manquant (*de*), dépourvu (*de*).

laconic [lə'kɔnik], *a.* laconique.

lacquer ['lækə], *n.* laque, *m.*

lad [læd], *n.* garçon, jeune homme; gaillard, *m.*

ladder ['lædə], *n.* échelle, *f.*; démaillage (*d'un bas*) *m.*; *ladder-proof*, indémaillable (*bas*).—*v.t.* démailler (*un bas*).

lade [kid], *v.t.* (*Naut.*) charger.

laden [leidn], *a.* chargé.

lading ['leidiŋ], *n.* chargement, *m.*; *bill of lading*, connaissement, *m.*

ladle [leidl], *n.* louche, cuiller à pot, *f.*

lady ['leidi], *n.* (*pl.* **ladies** ['leidiz]) dame, *f.*; *young lady*, demoiselle, *f.*

lady-bird ['leidibə:d], *n.* coccinelle, bête à bon Dieu, *f.*

lady-killer ['leidikilə], *n.* bourreau des cœurs, *m.*

lady-like ['leidilaik], *a.* de dame, comme il faut, qui a l'air distingué.

lag [læg], *v.i.* se traîner; traîner (*choses*).—*n.* retard, *m.*

laggard ['lægəd], *n.* traînard, lambin, *m.*

lager ['lɑ:gə], *n.* bière blonde (*allemande*), *f.*

lagoon [lə'gu:n], *n.* lagune, *f.*

lair [lɛə], *n.* repaire, antre, *m.*

laird [lɛəd], *n.* (*Sc.*) propriétaire, châtelain, *m.*

laity ['leiiti], *n.* laïques, *m.pl.*

lake [leik], *n.* lac, *m.*; laque (*couleur*), *f.*
lamb [læm], *n.* agneau, *m.*—*v.i.* agneler.
lambkin ['læmkin], *n.* agnelet, petit agneau, *m.*
lame [leim], *a.* boiteux, estropié (*infirme*); (*fig.*) défectueux, imparfait; *a lame excuse*, une piètre excuse; *a lame man*, un boiteux.—*v.t.* estropier.
lamely ['leimli], *adv.* en boitant; (*fig.*) imparfaitement, mal.
lameness ['leimnis], *n.* claudication, *f.*; clochement, boitement, *m.*; (*fig.*) faiblesse (*d'une excuse*), *f.*
lament [lə'ment], *v.t.* se lamenter sur, pleurer; s'affliger de.—*v.i.* se lamenter, pleurer.—*n.* lamentation, complainte, plainte, *f.*
lamentable ['læməntəbl], *a.* lamentable, pitoyable.
lamentation [læmən'teiʃən], *n.* lamentation, plainte, jérémiade, *f.*
lamented [lə'mentid], *a.* regretté (*feu*).
lamp [læmp], *n.* lampe; lanterne (*carrosse etc.*); (*fig.*) lumière, *f.*; *street lamp*, réverbère, *m.*
lampoon [læm'pu:n], *n.* satire, *f.*, libelle, *m.*
lamp-post ['læmppoust], *n.* lampadaire, *m.*
lamp shade ['læmpʃeid], *n.* abat-jour, *m.*
lance [lɑ:ns], *n.* lance, *f.*—*v.t.* percer d'un coup de lance; (*Surg.*) donner un coup de lancette à, percer.
lance corporal ['lɑ:ns'kɔ:pərəl], *n.* soldat de première classe, *m.*
lancer ['lɑ:nsə], *n.* lancier, *m.*
lancet ['lɑ:nsit], *n.* lancette; (*Arch.*) ogive, *f.*
land [lænd], *n.* terre, *f.*; pays (*territoire*); (*Law*) bien-fonds, *m.*; *Holy Land*, la Terre Sainte.—*v.t.* mettre à terre, prendre (*poisson*); débarquer.—*v.i.* débarquer (*à ou sur*), aborder; (*fig.*) arriver; (*Av.*) atterrir.
landed ['lændid], *a.* foncier; territorial.
landing ['lændiŋ], *n.* palier (*d'escalier*); (*Naut.*) débarquement; (*Av.*) atterrissage, *m.*
landing ground ['lændiŋgraund], *n.* terrain d'atterrissage, *m.*
landing stage ['lændiŋsteidʒ], *n.* débarcadère, *m.*
landing strip ['lændiŋstrip], *n.* piste d'atterrissage, *f.*
landlady ['lænleidi], *n.* propriétaire (*d'une maison*), logeuse (*d'un meuble*); aubergiste, hôtesse (*d'une auberge*), *f.*
landlord ['lænlɔ:d], *n.* propriétaire; hôte, hôtelier, aubergiste (*d'une auberge*), *m.*
landlubber ['lændlʌbə], *n.* marin d'eau douce, *m.*
landmark ['lændmɑ:k], *n.* borne, limite, *f.*; point de repère, *m.*
landowner ['lændounə], *n.* propriétaire foncier, *m.*
landscape ['lændskeip], *n.* paysage, *m.*; vue, *f.*
landscape garden ['lændskeip'gɑ:dən], *n.* jardin paysager, *m.*
land tax ['lændtæks], *n.* impôt foncier, *m.*
lane [lein], *n.* ruelle, *f.*, passage, *m.*; voie (*d'autoroute*), *f.*; chemin vicinal (*de campagne*), *m.*
language ['læŋgwidʒ], *n.* langage, *m.*, langue, expression, *f.*; *modern languages*, langues vivantes, *f.pl.*
languid ['læŋgwid], *a.* languissant.

languish ['læŋgwiʃ], *v.i.* languir.
languishing ['læŋgwiʃiŋ], *a.* languissant, langoureux.
languor ['læŋgə], *n.* langueur, *f.*
laniard [LANYARD].
lank [læŋk], *a.* efflanqué; maigre; décharné; fluet, grêle.
lanky ['læŋki], *a.* grand et maigre; *lanky fellow*, grand flandrin, *m.*
lantern ['læntən], *n.* lanterne, *f.*; (*Mil.*) falot; (*Naut.*) fanal, phare, *m.*; *Chinese lantern*, lanterne vénitienne; *dark lantern*, lanterne sourde; *lantern jaws*, joues creuses, *f.pl.*
lanyard ['lænjəd], *n.* (*Naut.*) ride, *f.*; (*Artill.*) (cordon) tire-feu, *m.*
Laos [laus]. le Laos, *m.*
Laotian ['lauʃən], *a.* laotien.—*n.* laotien (*langue*); Laotien (*personne*), *m.*
lap (1) [læp], *n.* pan (*de manteau etc.*); giron, *m.*; (*fig.*) genou, *m.*; (*Racing*) tour de piste, *m.*; *in the lap of*, au sein de.—*v.i.* se replier.
lap (2) [læp], *v.t.* (*Racing*) prendre un tour (*à*).
lap (3) [læp], *v.t.* laper (*boire*).—*v.i.* laper; clapoter (*vagues*).
lap dog ['læpdɔg], *n.* bichon, petit chien, *m.*
lapel [lə'pel], *n.* revers (*d'habit*), *m.*
lapidary ['læpidəri], *a.* and *n.* lapidaire, *m.*—*v.t.* lapider.
lapidation [læpi'deiʃən], *n.* lapidation, *f.*
Lapland ['læplənd]. la Laponie, *f.*
Laplander ['læpləndə], *n.* Lapon, *m.*
Lapp [læp], *a.* lapon.—*n.* lapon (*langue*); Lapon (*personne*), *m.*
lapse [læps], *n.* cours, laps (*temps*), *m.*; faute, erreur, *f.*; manquement, écart, manque (*divergence*), *m.*—*v.i.* s'écouler; tomber, faillir, manquer (*à*).
lapsed [læpst], *a.* périmé; caduc (*contrat, testament*).
lapwing ['læpwiŋ], *n.* vanneau, *m.*
larceny ['lɑ:səni], *n.* larcin, vol, *m.*
larch [lɑ:tʃ], *n.* (*Bot.*) mélèze, *m.*
lard [lɑ:d], *n.* saindoux, *m.*—*v.t.* larder (*de*).
larder ['lɑ:də], *n.* garde-manger, *m.*
large [lɑ:dʒ], *a.* grand, gros; étendu, considérable; fort; *as large as life*, grandeur nature; *at large*, en liberté, libre; en général.
largely ['lɑ:dʒli], *adv.* amplement, largement; au long, en grande partie.
largeness ['lɑ:dʒnis], *n.* grandeur, étendue, ampleur, *f.*
largess(e) ['lɑ:dʒes], *n.* largesse, libéralité, *f.*
lark [lɑ:k], *n.* alouette, *f.*; (*fig.*) escapade, *f.*
larkspur ['lɑ:kspə:], *n.* pied-d'alouette, *m.*
larva ['lɑ:və], *n.* (*pl.* **larvae** ['lɑ:vi:]) larve, *f.*
laryngitis [lærin'dʒaitis], *n.* laryngite, *f.*
larynx ['læriŋks], *n.* (*pl.* **larynges** ['lærindʒi:z]) larynx, *m.*
lascar ['læskə], *n.* matelot indien, *m.*
lascivious [lə'siviəs], *a.* lascif.
lash [læʃ], *n.* coup de fouet; (*fig.*) coup, trait, *m.*; *eyelash* [EYE].—*v.t.* cingler, fouetter; châtier; lier, attacher (*to tie*).
lashing ['læʃiŋ], *n.* coup de fouet, fouettant.—*n.* coups de fouet, *m.pl.*; (*Naut.*) ligne d'amarrage, *f.*
lass [læs], *n.* (*Sc.*) jeune fille, *f.*
lassitude ['læsitju:d], *n.* lassitude, *f.*

last (I) [lɑːst], *a.* dernier, passé; *last but one*, avant-dernier; *last night*, hier soir; *last week*, la semaine dernière; *the last time*, la dernière fois; *this day vaut week*, il y a aujourd'hui huit jours.—*n.* bout, *m.*, fin, *f.*; *at last*, à la fin, enfin; *to the last*, jusqu'au bout, jusqu'à la fin.—*v.i.* durer.

last (2) [lɑːst], *n.* forme (*pour chaussures*), *f.*

lasting ['lɑːstiŋ], *a.* durable, permanent.

lastly ['lɑːstli], *adv.* en dernier lieu, enfin.

latch [lætʃ], *n.* loquet, *m.*—*v.t.* fermer au loquet.

latchkey ['lætʃkiː], *n.* passe-partout, *m.*, clef de la maison, *f.*

late [leit], *a.* tard; en retard; tardif (*fruits, légumes etc.*); avancé (*heure*); ancien, ex-(*autrefois*); feu (*décédé*); récent, dernier (*depuis peu*); *the late king*, feu le roi; *to be late*, être en retard.—*adv.* tard; sur la fin; récemment, depuis peu; *at latest*, au plus tard; *better late than never*, mieux vaut tard que jamais; *of late*, récemment; *to be getting late*, (*impers.*) se faire tard.

lately ['leitli], *adv.* dernièrement, récemment.

lateness ['leitnis], *n.* retard, *m.*; heure avancée, *f.*, temps avancé, *m.*; tardiveté, *f.*

latent ['leitənt], *a.* caché, secret, latent.

later ['leitə], *a.* postérieur, ultérieur.—*adv.* plus tard.

lateral ['lætərəl], *a.* de côté, latéral.

latest ['leitist], *a.* dernier; *at the latest*, au plus tard.

lath [lɑːθ], *n.* latte, *f.*

lathe [leið], *n.* tour, *m.*

lather ['læðə, lɑːðə], *n.* mousse, *f.* (*fig.*) écume, *f.*—*v.t.* savonner; (*colloq.*) rosser.

Latin ['lætin], *a.* latin.—*n.* latin (*langue*), *m.*

Latin-American ['lætinəmerikən], *a.* latino-américain.—*n.* Latino-Américain (*personne*), *m.*

latish ['leitiʃ], *a.* un peu tard, un peu en retard.—*adv.* un peu tard.

latitude ['lætitjuːd], *n.* latitude, *f.*; étendue (*breadth*), *f.*

latter ['lætə], *a.* dernier; moderne, récent; *the latter*, ce dernier, celui-ci, *m.*

lattice ['lætis], *n.* trellis, treillage, *m.*

Latvia ['lætviə], la Lettonie, *f.*

Latvian ['lætviən], *a.* lette, letton.—*n.* lette, letton (*langue*), *m.*; Lette, *m.*, *f.*, Letton, *m.* (*personne*).

laud [lɔːd], *v.t.* louer, célébrer.

laudable ['lɔːdəbl], *a.* louable, digne de louanges.

laugh [lɑːf], *n.* rire, *m.*, risée (*moquerie*), *f.*; *loud laugh*, gros rire, éclat de rire, *m.*—*v.i.* rire; *to burst out laughing*, éclater de rire; *to laugh at*, se moquer de.

laughable ['lɑːfəbl], *a.* risible.

laughing ['lɑːfiŋ], *a.* rieur, enjoué; *it is no laughing matter*, il n'y a pas de quoi rire.

laughing-stock ['lɑːfiŋstɔk], *n.* risée, *f.*

laughingly ['lɑːfiŋli], *adv.* en riant.

laughter ['lɑːftə], *n.* rire, *m.*, rires, *m.pl.*; risée, moquerie, *f.*; *burst of laughter*, éclat de rire, *m.*

launch [lɔːntʃ], *v.t.* lancer; mettre à la mer.—*v.i.* se lancer, se jeter.—*n.* lancement, *m.*; chaloupe (*bateau*), vedette, *f.*

launching ['lɔːntʃiŋ], *n.* (*Naut.*) mise à l'eau,

f., lancement, *m.*; *launching pad*, piste de lancement, *f.*

launder ['lɔːndə], *v.t.* blanchir; lessiver (*linge*).

launderette [lɔːndə'ret], *n.* laverie automatique, *f.*

laundress ['lɔːndris], *n.* blanchisseuse, *f.*

laundromat ['lɔːndrəmæt], (*Am.*) [LAUNDERETTE].

laundry ['lɔːndri], *n.* buanderie; blanchisserie, *f.*; linge à blanchir, *m.*

laurel ['lɔrəl], *n.* laurier, *m.*

lava ['lɑːvə], *n.* lave, *f.*

lavatory ['lævət(ə)ri], *n.* water-closet, *m.*, les lavabos, les water, *m.pl.*

lavender ['lævində], *n.* lavande, *f.*

lavish ['læviʃ], *a.* prodigue.—*v.t.* prodiguer.

lavishly ['læviʃli], *adv.* prodigalement.

lavishness ['læviʃnis], *n.* prodigalité, *f.*

law [lɔː], *n.* loi, *f.*; droit, *m.*; *Law Courts*, Palais de Justice, *m.*

lawful ['lɔːful], *a.* légitime, licite, permis.

lawfully ['lɔːfuli], *adv.* légitimement.

lawless ['lɔːlis], *a.* sans loi; (*fig.*) sans frein, déréglé.

lawlessness ['lɔːlisnis], *n.* désordre, *m.* licence, *f.*

lawn (I) [lɔːn], *n.* pelouse, *f.*

lawn (2) [lɔːn], *n.* linon (*tissu*), *m.*

lawn mower ['lɔːnmouə], *n.* tondeuse de gazon, *f.*

lawsuit ['lɔːsjuːt], *n.* procès, *m.*

lawyer ['lɔːjə], *n.* homme de loi; avocat; avoué (*solicitor*); notaire (*notary*), *m.*

lax [læks], *a.* lâche, mou, flasque; (*fig.*) relâché, négligent.

laxative ['læksətiv], *a.* and *n.* laxatif, *m.*

laxity ['læksiti], **laxness** ['læksnis], *n.* relâchement, *m.*; flaccidité, *f.*; manque d'exactitude, *m.*

lay (I) [lei], *past* [LIE (2).]

lay (2) [lei], *v.t. irr.* placer, mettre, poser; coucher, étendre (*de tout son long*); faire; parier (*pari*); pondre (*œuf*); tendre, dresser (*piège*); abattre (*poussière*); calmer, apaiser (*rendre tranquille*); *to lay aside*, mettre de côté; *to lay claim to*, prétendre à; *to lay down*, mettre bas, poser (*principe*); *to lay down one's life for*, donner sa vie pour; *to lay hold of*, s'emparer de; *to lay in*, faire provision de; *to lay on*, appliquer, (*fam.*) arranger; *to lay out*, arranger; ensevelir (*cadavre*); disposer (*jardin etc.*); *to lay siege to*, assiéger; *to lay up*, mettre de côté, faire garder la chambre à; *to lay waste*, dévaster.—*v.i.* pondre (*œufs*).

lay (3) [lei], *n.* lai, *m.*, chanson, *f.*, chant, *m.*

lay (4) [lei], *a.* lai, laïque.

layer ['leiə], *n.* couche, *f.*, lit (*strate*), *m.*; (*Geol.*) assise; (*Hort.*) marcotte, *f.*; provin (*de vigne*), *m.*; pondeuse (*poule*), *f.*

laying ['leiiŋ], *n.* mise, pose; ponte (*d'œufs*), *f.*

layman ['leimən], *n.* (*pl.* **-men** [men]) laïque, profane, séculier, *m.*

lay-out ['leiaut], *n.* dessin, tracé, *m.*; disposition, *f.*

Lazarus ['læzərəs]. Lazare, *m.*

laze [leiz], *v.i. to laze about*, baguenauder.

lazily ['leizili], *adv.* lentement; en paresseux.

laziness ['leizinis], *n.* paresse, oisiveté, *f.*

lazy ['leizi], *a.* paresseux, indolent; *lazy fellow*, fainéant, *m.*

lea [li:], n. (poet.) prairie, f.
lead (1) [led], n. plomb (métal), m.; (Naut.) sonde; (Print.) interligne; mine de plomb (pour des crayons), f.; **black lead**, mine de plomb.
lead (2) [li:d], v.t. irr. mener, guider, conduire; porter, faire, induire (à); entraîner (à ou dans); **to lead astray**, égarer; **to lead back**, ramener, reconduire; **to lead in**, introduire; **to lead out**, emmener; **to lead someone to believe**, faire croire à quelqu'un; **to lead up to**, amener.—v.i. conduire, mener; (Spt.) jouer le premier. —n. conduite, direction, f., commandement, m.; laisse (chien), f.; (Spt.) début; (Theat.) premier rôle, m., vedette, f.; (Elec.) conducteur, m.
leader ['li:də], n. conducteur, guide, chef, meneur; (Journ.) article de fond, éditorial; (Polit.) chef de parti, leader, m.
leadership ['li:dəʃip], n. conduite, direction, f.; qualités de chef, f.pl.
leading ['li:diŋ], a. premier, principal; **leading article**, article de fond, m.—n. conduite, direction, f.
leaf [li:f], n. (pl. **leaves** [li:vz]) feuille, f.; feuillet (livre etc.); battant (porte), m.; rallonge (table), f.; **to turn over a new leaf**, (fig.) changer de conduite; **to turn over the leaves**, feuilleter.
leaflet ['li:flit], n. feuillet, imprimé, prospectus, m.
leafy ['li:fi], a. feuillu, couvert de feuilles.
league [li:g], n. ligue; lieue (3 miles), f.
leak [li:k], n. fuite, perte d'eau; (Naut.) voie d'eau, f.; **to spring a leak**, (Naut.) faire eau.—v.i. fuir, couler, faire eau; prendre l'eau (chaussures); **to leak out**, s'éventer.
leakage ['li:kidʒ], n. coulage, m.; fuite, f.
leaky ['li:ki], a. qui coule; (Naut.) qui fait eau.
lean (1) [li:n], a. and n. maigre, m.
lean (2) [li:n], v.t. irr. appuyer, faire pencher, incliner.—v.i. s'appuyer, s'incliner, se pencher; **to lean against**, s'adosser à; **to lean out**, se pencher au dehors.
leaning ['li:niŋ], a. penché.—n. penchant, m.; (fig.) tendance, f.
leanness ['li:nnis], n. maigreur, f.
lean-to ['li:ntu:], n. appentis, m.
leap [li:p], n. saut, bond, m.—v.t. irr. sauter, franchir.—v.i. sauter, bondir; s'élancer, se précipiter.
leap-frog ['li:pfrɔg], n. saute-mouton, m.
leap year ['li:pjiə], n. année bissextile, f.
learn [lə:n], v.t. irr. apprendre.—v.i. apprendre, s'instruire.
learned ['lə:nid], a. savant, instruit, érudit; **learned man**, savant, m.; **learned profession**, profession libérale, f.
learner ['lə:nə], n. élève, commençant, apprenti, m.; **learner driver**, élève chauffeur.
learning ['lə:niŋ], n. science, instruction, f., savoir, m., connaissances, f.pl.; érudition, f.
lease [li:s], n. bail, m.—v.t. louer, donner à bail; prendre à bail.
leasehold ['li:should], a. à bail.—n. tenure par bail, f.
leash [li:ʃ], n. laisse, f.—v.t. mener en laisse, attacher.
least [li:st], a. le moindre, le plus petit.—adv. le moins; **at least**, au moins, du moins; **not in the least**, point du tout, nullement.

leather ['leðə], a. de cuir.—n. cuir, m.; **upper leather**, empeigne, f.—v.t. (colloq.) étriller, rosser.
leave [li:v], n. permission, f., congé; adieu, m.; **on leave**, en congé (un mois ou plus), en permission (moins d'un mois); **with your leave**, avec votre permission.—v.t. irr. laisser; quitter, partir de (s'en aller de); cesser (de); **he left the house**, il quitta la maison, il partit de la maison; **he left the pen on the table**, il laissa le stylo sur la table; **to be left**, rester; **to leave about**, laisser traîner; **to leave alone**, laisser tranquille; **to leave off**, cesser (de); **to leave out**, supprimer, omettre; oublier. —v.i. partir, quitter; cesser.
leaven [levn], n. levain, f.—v.t. faire lever.
leaves [LEAF].
leave-taking ['li:vteikiŋ], n. adieux, m.pl.
leavings ['li:viŋz], n.pl. restes, m.pl.
Lebanese ['lebəni:z], a. libanais.—n. Libanais (personne), m.
Lebanon ['lebənən]. le Liban, m.
lecherous ['letʃərəs], a. lascif, libertin, lubrique.
lecherousness ['letʃərəsnis], **lechery** ['letʃəri], n. lasciveté, f.
lectern ['lektə:n], n. lutrin, m.
lecture ['lektʃə], n. conférence (sur), leçon (de), f.; (fig.) sermon, m., semonce, f.—v.t. faire un cours à; (fig.) sermonner, semoncer. —v.i. faire un cours (de), faire une conférence (sur).
lecturer ['lektʃərə], n. conférencier; maître de conférences, m.
lecture room ['lektʃəru:m], n. salle de conférences, f.
ledge [ledʒ], n. rebord, bord, m.; (Arch.) saillie, f.
ledger ['ledʒə], n. grand livre, m.
lee [li:], a. sous le vent.—n. (Naut.) côté sous le vent, m.
leech [li:tʃ], n. sangsue, f.
leek [li:k], n. poireau, m.
leer [liə], n. œillade, f.; regard de côté, m.— v.i. lorgner.
lees [li:z], n.pl. lie, f.
leeward ['lu:əd], a. and adv. (Naut.) sous le vent.
lee-way ['li:wei], n. dérive, f.; (fig.) marge, f.
left (1) [left], past and p.p. [LEAVE].
left (2) [left], a. and n. gauche, f.; **on the left**, à gauche.
left-handed ['left'hændid], a. gaucher; à gauche (vis); (fig.) gauche.
left-overs ['leftouvəz], n.pl. restes (d'un repas), m.pl.
leg [leg], n. jambe; patte (d'oiseau, d'insecte etc.); tige (bottines); cuisse (volaille), f.; pied (meuble); gigot (mouton), m.; trumeau (bœuf), m.; branche (compas), f.; **to pull someone's leg**, se moquer de quelqu'un.
legacy ['legəsi], n. legs, m.
legal ['li:gl], a. légal, judiciaire, juridique.
legality [li'gæliti], n. légalité, f.
legalize ['li:gəlaiz], v.t. légaliser, (fig.) autoriser.
legally ['li:gəli], adv. légalement.
legation [li'geiʃən], n. légation, f.
legend ['ledʒənd], n. légende, f.
legendary ['ledʒəndri], a. légendaire, fabuleux.
legged [legd, 'legid], a. à jambes, à pieds;

four-legged, à quatre pattes; **two-legged**, à deux jambes, bipède.

leggings ['leginz], *n.pl.* jambières, guêtres, *f.pl.*

legibility [ledʒi'biliti], *n.* lisibilité, netteté d'écriture, *f.*

legible ['ledʒibl], *a.* lisible.

legion ['li:dʒən], *n.* légion, *f.*; **the Foreign Legion**, la Légion (étrangère).

legislate ['ledʒisleit], *v.t.* légiférer, faire des lois.

legislation [ledʒis'leiʃən], *n.* législation, *f.*

legislative ['ledʒislətiv], *a.* législatif.

legitimate [lə'dʒitimit], *a.* légitime; juste, correct.

leisure ['leʒə], *n.* loisir, *m.*; **at leisure**, de loisir; **at one's leisure**, à loisir; **you are at leisure to come or not**, il vous est loisible de venir ou non.

leisurely ['leʒəli], *a.* sans hâte, mesuré.—*adv.* à loisir.

lemon ['lemən], *n.* citron, limon, *m.*

lemonade [lemə'neid], *n.* citron pressé, *m.*

lemon squash ['lemən'skwɔʃ], *n.* citronnade, *f.*

lemon-squeezer ['lemən'skwi:zə], *n.* presse-citrons, *m.inv.*

lemon tree ['leməntri:], *n.* citronnier, *m.*

lend [lend], *v.t. irr.* prêter; (*fig.*) donner.

lender ['lendə], *n.* prêteur, *m.*

lending ['lendiŋ], *n.* prêt, *m.*; **lending library**, bibliothèque de prêt, *f.*

length [leŋθ], *n.* longueur; étendue, *f.*; degré, point (*extrémité*), *m.*; durée (*temps*), *f.*; **at full length**, tout au long (*non abrégé*); en toutes lettres (*mots*); de tout son; long (*personnes*); **at great length**, longuement; **at length**, enfin; **full length**, de grandeur nature; **two feet in length**, deux pieds de longueur *ou* de long.

lengthen [leŋθn], *v.t.* allonger, étendre; prolonger (*temps*).—*v.i.* s'allonger, s'étendre; se prolonger (*temps*); (*colloq.*) rallonger (*journées etc.*).

lengthening ['leŋθniŋ], *n.* allongement, *m.*; prolongation (*de temps*), *f.*; accroissement (*des journées*).

lengthways ['leŋθweiz], **lengthwise** ['leŋθwaiz], *adv.* en longueur, en long.

lengthy ['leŋθi], *a.* un peu long, ennuyeux.

leniency ['li:niənsi], *n.* douceur, clémence, indulgence (*pour*), *f.*

lenient ['li:niənt], *a.* doux, indulgent (à, envers ou pour).

leniently ['li:niəntli], *adv.* avec douceur, avec indulgence.

lens [lenz], *n.* (*pl.* **lenses** ['lenziz]) (*Opt.*) lentille, loupe, *f.*

Lent [lent], *n.* le carême, *m.*

lentil ['lentil], *n.* lentille, *f.*

leonine ['li:ənain], *a.* de lion, léonin.

leopard ['lepəd], *n.* léopard, *m.*

leper ['lepə], *n.* lépreux, *m.*

leprosy ['leprəsi], *n.* lèpre, *f.*

leprous ['leprəs], *a.* lépreux.

less [les], *a.* moindre, plus petit, inférieur; **to grow less**, diminuer.—*adv.* moins; **less and less**, de moins en moins; **no less**, rien moins, pas moins; **so much the less**, d'autant moins; **the less . . . the more . . .**, moins . . . plus. . . .—*n.* moins; moindre, *m.*

lessee [le'si:], *n.* locataire à bail, *m.*, *f.*

lessen [lesn], *v.t.* diminuer, amoindrir, rapetisser, rabaisser (*to lower*); ralentir (*la vitesse*).—*v.i.* diminuer, s'amoindrir.

lesser ['lesə], *a.* moindre, plus petit.

lesson [lesn], *n.* leçon, *f.*

lest [lest], *conj.* de peur que, de crainte que (*followed by* ne *with subj.*).

let (1) [let], *v.t. irr.* laisser, permettre à (*donner la permission à*); souffrir que (*with subjunctive*); faire (*causer*); louer (*maison*); **let him come**, qu'il vienne; **let me see**, voyons; **let us go**, allons; **let me alone**, laisser tranquille; **to let down**, descendre, faire descendre, baisser, rabattre; **to let fall**, laisser tomber; **to let go**, lâcher; **to let in**, faire entrer; **to let know**, faire savoir à; **to let off**, laisser échapper; tirer (*arme à feu*); **to let out**, faire sortir, laisser sortir; élargir (*vêtements*).

let (2) [let], *n.* empêchement; obstacle, délai, *m.*; (*Tennis*) (balle) à remettre.

lethal ['li:θl], *a.* mortel, fatal.

lethargic [lə'θɑ:dʒik], *a.* léthargique.

lethargy ['leθədʒi], *n.* léthargie, *f.*

letter ['letə], *n.* lettre, *f.*; (*pl.*, *fig.*) belles-lettres, *f.pl.*; **registered letter**, lettre recommandée.

letter box ['letəbɔks], *n.* boîte aux lettres, *f.*

letter-card ['letəkɑ:d], *n.* carte-lettre, *f.*

lettered ['letəd], *a.* lettré, savant.

lettering ['letəriŋ], *n.* titre, *m.*

letting ['letiŋ], *n.* louage, *m.*; **letting out**, location, *f.*; agrandissement (*de vêtement*), *m.*

lettuce ['letis], *n.* laitue, *f.*

let-up ['letʌp], *n.* diminution, *f.*

Levant [lə'vænt], **the**. le Levant, *m.*

Levantine [li'væntain], *a.* du Levant, levantin.—*n.* Levantin (*personne*), *m.*; levantine (*soie*), *f.*

level [levl], *a.* de niveau (*avec*), au niveau (*de*); uni (*surface*); égal (à); **level crossing**, passage à niveau, *m.*—*n.* niveau, *m.*, surface unie, *f.*; **at ministerial level**, à l'échelon ministériel.—*v.t.* aplanir, niveler, mettre de niveau; braquer, pointer (*arme à feu*); porter (*coup*).—*v.i.* viser, mettre en joue, pointer.

level-headed ['levlhedid], *a.* équilibré, de sens rassis.

levelling ['levliŋ], *n.* nivellement; pointage (*de fusil*), *m.*

lever ['li:və], *n.* levier, *m.*; **hand lever** manette, *f.*

leveret ['levərit], *n.* levraut, *m.*

levity ['leviti], *n.* légèreté, *f.*; manque de sérieux, *m.*

levy ['levi], *n.* levée; perception (*d'impôts*), *f.*—*v.t.* lever; imposer (*amende etc.*).

lewd [lju:d], *a.* impudique, lascif.

lexicon ['leksikn], *n.* lexique, dictionnaire, *m.*

liability [laiə'biliti], *n.* responsabilité; tendance, *f.*; danger, *m.*; (*Comm.*) (*pl.*) engagements, *m.pl.*, passif, *m.*; **assets and liabilities**, actif et passif, *m.*

liable ['laiəbl], *a.* sujet (à), exposé (à), responsable (de).

liar ['laiə], *n.* menteur, *m.*

libel [laibl], *n.* libelle, écrit diffamatoire, *m.*—*v.t.* diffamer.

libelous ['laibələs], *a.* diffamatoire.

liberal ['libərəl], *a.* libéral, généreux; prodigue, abondant.—*n.* (*Polit.*) Libéral, *m.*

liberality [libə'ræliti], *n.* libéralité, *f.*

liberate ['libəreit], *v.t.* libérer, rendre libre; délivrer (*de*).

liberation [libə'reiʃən], *n.* mise en liberté, *f.*, élargissement (*de prisonniers*); affranchissement, *m.*; libération, délivrance, *f.*

liberator ['libəreitə], *n.* libérateur, *m.*

Liberia [lai'biəriə]. le Libéria, *m.*

Liberian [lai'biəriən], *a.* libérien.—*n.* Libérien (*personne*), *m.*

liberty ['libəti], *n.* liberté, *f.*; privilèges, *m.pl.*, franchises, *f.pl.*

librarian [lai'breəriən], *n.* bibliothécaire, *m.,f.*

library ['laibrəri], *n.* bibliothèque, *f.*; *film library*, cinémathèque, *f.*; *record library*, discothèque, *f.*

Libya ['libiə]. la Lybie, *f.*

Libyan ['libiən], *a.* libyen.—*n.* Libyen (*personne*), *m.*

lice [LOUSE].

license ['laisəns], *n.* licence, liberté; permission, *f.*, permis; certificat; (*fig.*) dérèglement, *m.*; autorisation (*de prédicateur*), *f.*; brevet (*de libraire*), *m.*; (*Comm.*) patente, *f.*; *driving license*, permis de conduire; *gun license*, permis de port d'armes; permis de chasse; *marriage license*, dispense de bans, *f.* [see **number-plate**]

license ['laisəns], *v.t.* autoriser, accorder un permis à.

licensed ['laisənst], *a.* autorisé; breveté; (*Comm.*) patenté.

licentious [lai'senʃəs], *a.* licencieux.

lichen ['laikən], *n.* lichen, *m.*

lick [lik], *v.t.* lécher; laper (*boire*); (*slang*) rosser (*battre*).—*n.* coup de langue, *m.*

licking ['likiŋ], *n.* (*slang*) coups, *m.pl.*, raclée, *f.*

licorice [LIQUORICE].

lid [lid], *n.* couvercle, *m.*; paupière (*d'œil*), *f.*

lie (1) [lai], *n.* mensonge; démenti, *m.*; *to give the lie to*, donner un démenti à; *white lie*, mensonge pieux.—*v.i.* mentir.

lie (2) [lai], *v.i. irr.* être couché, se coucher; reposer, être, être situé, se trouver; s'appuyer (*se soutenir*); rester (*to remain*); consister; *here lies*, ci-gît; *lie down!* (*à un chien*) couché! *to lie about* (*objets*), traîner çà et là; *to lie down*, se coucher, se reposer.—*n.* gisement, *m.*, position, situation, *f.*

lieutenant [lef'tenənt], *n.* lieutenant, *m.*

life [laif], *n.* (*pl.* **lives** [laivz]) vie, *f.*; homme vivant, *m.*; personne; (*fig.*) vie, âme, vivacité, *f.*, entrain; mouvement; (*Paint. etc.*) naturel, *m.*; *a double life*, une vie double; *for life*, à vie, à perpétuité; *from life*, d'après nature; *high life*, le grand monde, *m.*; *never in my life*, jamais de ma vie; *pension for life*, pension viagère, *f.*; *prime of life*, fleur de l'âge, *f.*; *single life*, célibat, *m.*; *to come to life*, s'animer.

life belt ['laifbelt], *n.* ceinture de sauvetage, *f.*

life boat ['laifbout], *n.* canot de sauvetage, *m.*

life buoy ['laifbɔi], *n.* bouée de sauvetage, *f.*

lifeguard ['laifgɑːd], *n.* garde du corps, *m.*; (*pl.*) les Gardes du corps, *m.pl.*; sauveteur, *m.*

life-insurance ['laifinʃuərəns], *n.* assurance sur la vie, *f.*

lifeless ['laiflis], *a.* sans vie, inanimé.

lifelike ['laiflaik], *a.* comme un être vivant, d'après nature, vivant.

lifelong ['laiflɔŋ], *a.* de toute la vie.

life-size ['laifsaiz], *a.* de grandeur nature.

lifetime ['laiftaim], *n.* vie, *f.*, vivant, *m.*; *in his* or *her lifetime*, de son vivant.

lift [lift], *n.* action de lever, élévation, *f.*, effort; coup de main (*aide*), monte-charge (*machine*); ascenseur, *m.*—*v.t.* lever, soulever, hausser, soupeser (*évaluer le poids de*); (*fig.*) élever, relever.

lift man ['liftmən], *n.* (*pl.* **men** [men]) liftier, *m.*

light (1) [lait], *n.* lumière, *f.*, jour (*du soleil*); clair (*de la lune etc.*), *m.*; clarté (*de l'œil etc.*); lueur, *f.*; (*fig.*) aspect; point de vue, *m.*; *electric light*, éclairage à l'électricité, *m.*; *it is light*, il fait jour; *light and shade*, clair-obscur, *m.*; *traffic lights*, feux de circulation, *m.pl.*; *will you give me a light?* voulez-vous me donner du feu?—*v.t. irr.* allumer; illuminer, éclairer (*fenêtres etc.*).—*v.i. to light up*, briller, s'enflammer.

light (2) [lait], *v.i. to light upon*, descendre *ou* tomber sur.

light (3) [lait], *a.* léger; (*fig.*) gai, frivole; clair (*couleur etc.*); blond (*teint*).

lighten (1) [laitn], *v.t.* éclairer, illuminer.—*v.i* éclairer; faire des éclairs.

lighten (2) [laitn], *v.t.* soulager, alléger (*adoucir*).

lightening ['laitniŋ], *n.* éclaircissement; allègement; soulagement, *m.*

lighter ['laitə], *n.* allumeur; briquet (*pour cigarettes*), *m.*; (*Naut.*) allège, gabare, *f.*, chaland, *m.*

light-hearted [lait'hɑːtid], *a.* gai, réjoui.

light-heartedness [lait'hɑːtidnis], *n.* enjouement, *m.*, gaieté, *f.*

lighthouse ['laithaus], *n.* phare, *m.*

lighting ['laitiŋ], *n.* éclairage, *m.*; *lighting-up time*, heure d'éclairage, *f.*

lightly ['laitli], *adv.* légèrement, à la légère; lestement, facilement, aisément; gaiement.

lightness ['laitnis], *n.* légèreté, *f.*

lightning ['laitniŋ], *n.* éclair, *m.*, les éclairs, *m.pl.*; foudre, *f.*; *flash of lightning*, éclair.

lightning rod ['laitniŋrɔd], *n.* paratonnerre, *m.*

lights [laits], *n.pl.* mou (*d'animal*), *m.*

lightship ['laitʃip], *n.* bateau-feu, *m.*

like (1) [laik], *a.* semblable, tel, pareil; même, égal, *vraisemblable; *as like as not*, probablement; *that is something like!* à la bonne heure! *to be like*, ressembler à; *to feel like doing something*, avoir envie de faire quelque chose; *what is he like?* comment est-il?—*prep.* comme, semblable à, pareil à.—*n.* chose pareille, *f.*, pareil, *m.*; même chose, *f.*; *the likes of you*, les gens de votre sorte, *m.pl.*, *f.pl.*

like (2) [laik], *v.t.* aimer, aimer bien, trouver bon, trouver bien; vouloir (bien), désirer, être bien aise (*de*); *as you like*, comme il vous plaira, comme vous voudrez.—*n.* goût, *m.*; préférence, *f.*; *everyone has his likes and dislikes*, chacun son goût.

likeable ['laikəbl], *a.* sympathique, aimable.

likelihood ['laiklihud], *n.* probabilité, vraisemblance, *f.*

likely ['laikli], *a.* probable, vraisemblable.—*adv.* probablement, vraisemblablement.

liken [laikn], *v.t.* comparer (*à* ou *avec*).
likeness ['laiknis], *n.* ressemblance, *f.*; portrait, *m.*
likewise ['laikwaiz], *adv.* également, pareillement, de même, aussi.
liking ['laikiŋ], *n.* gré, goût, penchant, *m.*, inclination; amitié, *f.*
lilac ['lailək], *n.* lilas, *m.*
lily ['lili], *n.* lis, *m.*; *lily of the valley*, muguet, *m.*
limb [lim], *n.* membre (*du corps*); (*colloq.*) enfant terrible, *m.*; grosse branche (*d'arbre*), *f.*
limber (1) ['limbə], *a.* souple, flexible; (*fig.*) agile.—*v.i.* *to limber up*, se chauffer les muscles.
limber (2) ['limbə], *n.* avant-train, *m.*
limbo ['limbou], *n.* limbes, *m.pl.*
lime (1) [laim], *n.* (*Bot.*) lime, limette, *f.*; *lime juice*, jus de limette, *m.*; *lime tree*, tilleul (*linden*); limettier, *m.*
lime (2) [laim], *n.* chaux; glu (*pour prendre des oiseaux*), *f.*
limelight ['laimlait], *n.* (*Theat.*) les feux de la lampe, *m.pl.*; *to be in the limelight*, être en évidence.
limestone ['laimstoun], *n.* pierre à chaux, *f.*; (*Geol.*) calcaire, *m.*
limit ['limit], *n.* limite, borne, *f.*; (*fam.*) *that's the limit!* ça c'est le comble!—*v.t.* limiter, borner, restreindre.
limitation [limi'teiʃən], *n.* limitation, restriction, *f.*
limited ['limitid], *a.* limité, borné; (*Comm.*) anonyme.
limitless ['limitlis], *a.* sans limite.
limp [limp], *a.* mou, flasque, sans consistance.—*v.i.* boiter.
limpet ['limpit], *n.* lépas, *m.*, patelle, *f.*
limpid ['limpid], *a.* limpide.
linden [lindn], *n.* (*Bot.*) tilleul, *m.*
line (1) [lain], *n.* ligne; corde, *f.*, cordeau (*ficelle*), *m.*; file, *f.*, alignement (*rang*); trait (*écrit*), *m.*; raie (*bande*), *f.*; contour (*profil*), *m.*; ride (*pli du visage*) (*Rail.*) voie; lignée, race (*descendance*), *f.*; (*fig.*) genre (*d'affaires etc.*); (*Pros.*) vers; mot, petit mot (*lettre brève*), *m.*; limite (*de territoire*), *f.*; *air-line*, ligne aérienne; (*Teleph.*) *hold the line!* ne quittez pas! *it is hard lines*, c'est dur; *not in my line*, pas de mon ressort.—*v.t.* ligner, régler; to *line up*, aligner. **[queue]**
line (2) [lain], *v.t.* doubler (*vêtement*); garnir (*de*); border (*de*).
lineage ['liniədʒ], *n.* lignée, race, famille, *f.*
lineal ['liniəl], *a.* linéaire.
lineally ['liniəli], *adv.* en ligne directe.
linear ['liniə], *a.* linéaire.
linen ['linin], *a.* de toile.—*n.* toile, toile de lin, *f.*, lin; linge (*habits*), *m.*
liner ['lainə], *n.* (*Naut.*) paquebot de ligne, transatlantique, *m.*
linesman ['lainzmən], *n.* (*pl.* **-men** [men]) (*Ftb.*) arbitre de touche, *m.*
linger ['liŋgə], *v.i.* traîner, tarder; hésiter.
lingering ['liŋgəriŋ], *a.* qui traîne, lent; languissant.—*n.* retard, *m.*, lenteur; hésitation, *f.*
lingo ['liŋgou], *n.* (*slang*) jargon, *m.*; langue, *f.*
linguist ['liŋgwist], *n.* linguiste, *m.*, *f.*
liniment ['linimənt], *n.* liniment, *m.*
lining ['lainiŋ], *n.* doublure; garniture (*de*

vêtement); coiffe (*de chapeau*), *f.*; (*Build.*) revêtement, *m.*
link [liŋk], *n.* chaînon, anneau; (*fig.*) lien; trait d'union, *m.*; *cuff links*, boutons de manchettes, *m.pl.*—*v.t.* lier, relier (*avec.*); enchaîner (*dans*); unir.—*v.i.* s'allier (*à*).
links [liŋks], *n.pl.* *golf links*, terrain de golf, *m.*
linnet ['linit], *n.* linotte, *f.*
linoleum [li'nouljəm], *n.* linoléum, *m.*
linotype ['lainotaip], *n.* linotype, *f.*
linseed ['linsi:d], *n.* graine de lin, *f.*; *linseed oil*, huile de lin, *f.*
lint [lint], *n.* charpie, *f.*
lintel [lintl], *n.* linteau, *m.*
lion ['laiən], *n.* lion, *m.*; (*fig.*) célébrité, *f.*; *lion's cub*, lionceau, *m.*
lioness ['laiənes], *n.* lionne, *f.*
lion tamer ['laiənteimə], *n.* dompteur de lions, *m.*
lip [lip], *n.* lèvre; babine (*de certains animaux*), *f.*; bord (*de choses*), *m.*; (*fig.*) impertinence, *f.*
lipstick ['lipstik], *n.* bâton de rouge, *m.*
liquefy ['likwifai], *v.t.* liquéfier.—*v.i.* se liquéfier.
liqueur [li'kjuə], *n.* liqueur, *f.*
liquid ['likwid], *a.* liquide; doux, coulant.—*n.* liquide, *m.*
liquidate ['likwideit], *v.t.* liquider.
liquidation [likwi'deiʃən], *n.* liquidation, *f.*, acquittement (*d'une dette*), *m.*
liquor ['likə], *n.* (*Chem.*) liqueur, solution; (*Am.*) boisson alcoolique, *f.*; (*Am.*) *hard liquor*, alcool, *m.*
liquorice ['likəris], *n.* réglisse, *f.*
Lisbon ['lizbən]. Lisbonne, *f.*
lisp [lisp], *v.t.*, *v.i.* dire (θ, ð) au lieu de (s, z); (*colloq.*) susurrer, zozoter.
lissom [lism], *a.* souple, leste.
list (1) [list], *n.* liste, *f.*, rôle, *m.*; *Army List*, annuaire de l'armée, *m.*—*v.t.* enrôler, enregistrer.
list (2) [list], *v.i.* (*Naut.*) donner de la bande. —*n.* (*Naut.*) bande, *f.*
listen [lisn], *v.i.* écouter.
listener ['lisnə], *n.* auditeur, *m.*
listless ['listlis], *a.* apathique.
listlessness ['listlisnis], *n.* apathie, *f.*
lists [lists], *n. pl.* lice, arène (*arena*), *f.*
litany ['litəni], *n.* litanie, *f.*
literal ['litərəl], *a.* littéral.
literally ['litərəli], *adv.* littéralement, à la lettre.
literary ['litərəri], *a.* littéraire; lettré (*personne*).
literature ['litəritʃə], *n.* littérature, *f.*
lithe [laið], *a.* pliant, flexible, souple.
lithograph ['liθogra:f], *n.* lithographie, *f.*
lithographer [li'θografə], *n.* lithographe, *m.*, *f.*
Lithuania [liθju'einiə]. la Lituanie, la Lithuanie, *f.*
Lithuanian [liθju'einiən], *a.* lituanien, lithuanien.—*n.* lituanien, lithuanien (*langue*); Lituanien, Lithuanien (*personne*), *m.*
litigant ['litigənt], *n.* plaideur, *m.*
litigate ['litigeit], *v.t.* plaider, disputer.—*v.i.* être en procès.
litigation [liti'geiʃən], *n.* litige; procès, *m.*
litre ['li:tə], *n.* litre, *m.*
litter ['litə], *n.* litière, civière (*véhicule*), *f.*; ordures, *f.pl.*, détritus, *m.pl.*; (*fig.*) fouillis, désordre, *m.*; portée (*d'animal*), *f.*—*v.t.*

joncher; jeter çà et là; (*fig.*) mettre en désordre; mettre bas (*animal*); salir; *to litter down* (*of horse*), faire la litière à.

litter bin ['litəbin], *n.* boîte à ordures, *f.*

little [litl], *a.* petit; minime, exigu; mesquin; *little one*, enfant, *m.*, *f.*, petit, *m.*—*n.* peu, *m.*; *to think little of*, faire peu de cas de.— *adv.* peu, un peu, pas beaucoup, peu de chose, peu de; *a little*, un peu; *as little as possible*, le moins possible; *little by little*, petit à petit, peu à peu; *little or none*, peu ou point.

littleness ['litlnis], *n.* petitesse, *f.*

liturgy ['litədʒi], *n.* liturgie, *f.*

live (1) [liv], *v.t.* mener (une vie).—*v.i.* vivre; résider, demeurer, habiter; *long live the Queen!* vive la Reine! *to live by*, vivre de; *to live down a scandal*, faire oublier un scandale avec le temps; *to live on*, se nourrir de.

live (2) [laiv], *a.* en vie, vivant; ardent, vif (*charbons*); *live rail*, rail conducteur, *m.*; *livestock*, bétail, *m.*; *live wire*, fil sous tension, *m.*

lived [livd], *a.* de vie; *long-lived*, qui vit longtemps, de longue vie.

livelihood ['laivlihud], *n.* vie, subsistance, *f.*; gagne-pain, *m.*

liveliness ['laivlinis], *n.* vivacité, gaieté, *f.*

livelong ['livlɔŋ], *a.* durable, long, sans fin; *the livelong day*, toute la sainte journée.

lively ['laivli], *a.* vif, gai, enjoué, animé; vivant (*endroit*).

liven [laivn], *v.t.* *to liven up*, animer.

liver (1) ['livə], *n.* *fast liver*, viveur, noceur, *m.*

liver (2) ['livə], *n.* (*Anat.*) foie, *m.*

livery ['livəri], *n.* livrée; pension (*de chevaux*), *f.*

lives [LIFE].

livestock ['laivstɔk], [LIVE (2)].

livid ['livid], *a.* livide, blême.

living ['liviŋ], *a.* en vie, vivant; vif.—*n.* vie, subsistance, existence, *f.*; genre de vie, *m.*, chère, *f.*; (*Eccles.*) bénéfice, *m.*, cure, *f.*

living room ['liviŋrum], *n.* salle de séjour, *f.*

lizard ['lizəd], *n.* lézard, *m.*

llama ['lɑːmə], *n.* lama, *m.*

lo! [lou], *int.* voici! voilà! voyez! regardez!

load [loud], *n.* charge, *f.*, fardeau, *m.*; (*fig.*) chargement, *m.*; charretée (*cartful*), *f.*—*v.t.* charger; (*fig.*) combler, accabler (*de*).

loaf [louf], *n.* (*pl.* **loaves** [louvz]) pain (*long*), *m.*; miche (*rond*), *f.*—*v.i.* flâner, fainéanter; *to loaf about town*, battre le pavé.

loafer ['loufə], *n.* fainéant, batteur de pavé, *m.*

loam [loum], *n.* terre grasse, *f.*

loamy ['loumi], *a.* glaiseux.

loan [loun], *n.* emprunt; prêt, *m.*; *to raise a loan*, faire un emprunt.—*v.t.* prêter.

loath [louθ], *a.* fâché, peiné; *to be loath to*, faire à contre-cœur.

loathe [louð], *v.t.* détester.

loathing ['louðiŋ], *n.* dégoût, *m.*, aversion, *f.*

loathsome ['louðsəm], *a.* dégoûtant, odieux.

loaves [LOAF].

lobby ['lɔbi], *n.* couloir, *m.*; salle d'attente (*vestibule*); (*Theat.*) entrée, *f.*—*v.t.*, *v.i.* (*Polit.*) faire les couloirs.

lobe [loub], *n.* lobe, *m.*

lobelia [loˈbiːliə], *n.* lobélie, *f.*

lobster ['lɔbstə], *n.* homard, *m.*

local ['loukəl], *a.* local; topographique.

locality [loˈkæliti], *n.* localité, *f.*

localize ['loukəlaiz], *v.t.* localiser.

locally ['loukəli], *adv.* localement.

locate [loˈkeit], *v.t.* placer, localiser; repérer.

location [loˈkeiʃən], *n.* situation, *f.*, emplacement, *m.*; location, *f.*; (*Cine.*) extérieurs, *m.pl.*

loch [lɔx], *n.* (*Sc.*) lac, *m.*

lock [lɔk], *n.* serrure; écluse (*de canal*); platine (*de fusil*); mèche, boucle (*de cheveux*), *f.*; flocon (*de laine*), *m.*; (*pl.*) cheveux, *m.pl.*; *dead-lock*, impasse, *f.*; *padlock*, cadenas, *m.*—*v.t.* fermer à clef; accrocher (*roues etc.*); *to lock in*, enfermer; *to lock up*, serrer, enfermer, mettre en prison.—*v.i.* fermer à clef.

locker ['lɔkə], *n.* armoire, *f.*; coffre, *m.*

locket ['lɔkit], *n.* médaillon, *m.*

lock-jaw ['lɔkdʒɔː], *n.* trisme, tétanos, *m.*

locksmith ['lɔksmiθ], *n.* serrurier, *m.*

locomotion [loukəˈmouʃən], *n.* locomotion, *f.*

locomotive ['loukəmoutiv], *a.* locomotif.—*n.* locomotive, *f.*

locust (1) ['loukəst], *n.* sauterelle d'Orient, *f.*, criquet, *m.*

locust (2) ['loukəst], *n.* caroubier (*plante*), *m.*; *locust tree*, caroubier, *m.*

lodge [lɔdʒ], *n.* loge (*de concierge*), *f.*; pavillon, *m.*; maisonnette (*de garde*), *f.*—*v.t.* loger; abriter; enfoncer (*mettre dans*); déposer (*placer*); implanter (*dans le cœur*); interjeter (*appel*); *to lodge a complaint*, porter plainte.—*v.i.* loger, se loger; s'arrêter, se fixer.

lodger ['lɔdʒə], *n.* locataire; pensionnaire, *m.*, *f.*

lodging ['lɔdʒiŋ], *n.* logement; appartement, *m.*; *to live in furnished lodgings*, loger en garni *ou* en meublé.

lodging house ['lɔdʒiŋhaus], *n.* hôtel garni, hôtel meublé, *m.*

loft [lɔft], *n.* grenier, *m.*; tribune, *f.*; pigeonnier, *m.*

loftily ['lɔftili], *adv.* haut, avec hauteur, pompeusement.

loftiness ['lɔftinis], *n.* élévation; hauteur, fierté, pompe; sublimité, *f.*

lofty ['lɔfti], *a.* haut, élevé; altier; sublime (*style*).

log [lɔg], *n.* bûche, *f.*; (*Naut.*) loch, *m.*; *to sleep like a log*, dormir comme une souche.

loganberry ['lougənberi], *n.* ronce-framboise, *f.*

logarithm ['lɔgəriðm], *n.* logarithme, *m.*

log-book ['lɔgbuk], *n.* journal *ou* livre de bord; (*Motor.*) carnet de route, *m.*

loggerhead ['lɔgəhed], *n.* lourdaud, *m.*; *to be at loggerheads*, être aux prises *ou* à couteaux tirés.

logic ['lɔdʒik], *n.* logique, *f.*

logical ['lɔdʒikəl], *a.* logique, de la logique.

loin [lɔin], *n.* longe (*de veau*), *f.*; filet (*de mouton*), *m.*; (*pl.*) reins, lombes, *m.pl.*

loiter ['lɔitə], *v.t.* perdre, gaspiller.—*v.i.* flâner, traîner, s'amuser en chemin.

loiterer ['lɔitərə], *n.* musard, flâneur, *m.*

loitering ['lɔitəriŋ], *n.* flânerie, *f.*

loll [lɔl], *v.t.* laisser pendre (*la langue*).—*v.i.* s'étaler, se pencher; pendre (*la langue*).

lolling ['lɔliŋ], *a.* étendu, étalé.
lollipop ['lɔlipɔp], *n.* sucre d'orge, *m.*, sucette, *f.*
lolly ['lɔli], *n.* (*fam.*) sucette; (*slang*) galette (*argent*), *f.*
London ['lʌndən]. Londres, *m.* ou *f.*
Londoner ['lʌndənə], *n.* Londonien, *m.*
lone [loun], *a.* isolé, solitaire; délaissé.
loneliness ['lounlinis], *n.* solitude, *f.*; isolement, *m.*
lonely ['lounli], *a.* isolé; délaissé.
long (1) [lɔŋ], *v.i.* avoir bien envie, brûler (*de*); (*impers.*) tarder (*de*).
long (2) [lɔŋ], *a.* long; étendu, prolongé, allongé; *a long time*, longtemps, depuis longtemps, pendant longtemps; *in the long run*, à la longue; *to be three feet long*, avoir trois pieds de long, être long de trois pieds.—*n.* *the long and the short of*, le fort et le faible de.—*adv.* fort; longtemps, longuement; depuis longtemps; pendant longtemps; durant; *all night long*, tout le long de la nuit; *before long*, bientôt, avant peu, sous peu; *how long have you been here?* combien de temps y a-t-il que vous êtes ici? *long ago*, il y a longtemps, depuis longtemps; *long after*, peu de temps après; *so long as*, tant que.
longer ['lɔŋɡə], *a.* plus long.—*adv.* plus longtemps; de plus.
longing ['lɔŋiŋ], *n.* désir ardent, *m.*, envie, *f.*
longitude ['lɔndʒitju:d], *n.* longitude, *f.*
long-sighted ['lɔŋsaitid], *a.* presbyte; (*fig.*) clairvoyant; *I am long-sighted*, j'ai la vue longue.
look [luk], *v.i.* regarder (*d'une fenêtre*); sembler, avoir l'air, paraître; donner sur (*maison etc.*); *look out!* attention! gare! *to look after*, soigner, s'occuper de; *to look away*, détourner ses regards; *to look back*, regarder en arrière; *to look down upon*, mépriser; *to look for*, chercher; *to look forward to*, attendre avec impatience; *to look in*, faire une petite visite, dire un petit bonjour à; *to look into*, examiner; *to look like*, ressembler à; *to look on*, regarder, considérer; *to look over*, jeter un coup d'œil sur, examiner.—*n.* regard, air, *m.*, apparence, mine, *f.*; coup d'œil, *m.*
looker-on ['lukərɔn], *n.* spectateur, *m.*
looking ['lukiŋ], *a.* à l'air...; à la mine...; *good-looking*, beau.
looking glass ['lukiŋɡlɑ:s], *n.* miroir, *m.*, glace, *f.*
look-out ['lukaut], *n.* guet, *m.*, vigilance, vue, *f.*; (*Mil.*) guetteur, *m.*; (*Naut.*) vigie, *f.*; *to keep a look-out*, avoir l'œil au guet.
loom [lu:m], *n.* métier à tisser, *m.*—*v.i.* apparaître indistinctement, surgir.
looming ['lu:miŋ], *a.* vague, estompé.
loop [lu:p], *n.* boucle; bride (*pour bouton*), *f.*; (*Av.*) looping, *m.*
loop-hole ['lu:phoul], *n.* meurtrière (*pour bouton*); (*fig.*) échappatoire, *f.*, faux-fuyant, *m.*
loose [lu:s], *a.* délié, défait; branlant; (*fig.*) relâché, lâche (*mœurs*); vague; licencieux; libre; *loose cash*, menue monnaie, *f.*—*n.* *on the loose*, dissolu, dissipé.—*v.t.* délier, lâcher, (*fig.*) déchaîner.
loosely ['lu:sli], *adv.* librement, négligemment; licencieusement.

loosen [lu:sn], *v.t.* délier, détacher, défaire; desserrer; ébranler.—*v.i.* se délier, se défaire; se desserrer.
looseness ['lu:snis], *n.* état desserré, relâchement; caractère vague, *m.*
loot [lu:t], *n.* butin; pillage, *m.*—*v.t.* piller.
looter ['lu:tə], *n.* pillard, *m.*
lop [lɔp], *v.t.* élaguer, ébrancher.
lopsided ['lɔpsaidid], *a.* qui penche trop d'un côté, déjeté.
loquacious [lo'kweiʃəs], *a.* loquace.
lord [lɔ:d], *n.* seigneur; (*fig.*) maître; lord (*titre anglais*); Monseigneur (*à un prince, noble, évêque etc.*), *m.*; *Our Lord*, notre Seigneur; *the Lord's Prayer*, l'oraison dominicale, *f.*; *the year of our Lord*, l'an de grâce, *m.*—*v.t.* *to lord it over*, dominer, faire le maître.
lordliness ['lɔ:dlinis], *n.* hauteur, *f.*, orgueil, *m.*
lordling ['lɔ:dliŋ], *n.* petit seigneur; hobereau, *m.*
lordly ['lɔ:dli], *a.* de seigneur, noble; hautain, fier.
lore [lɔ:], *n.* savoir, *m.*; science, *f.*
lorry ['lɔri], *n.* camion, *m.*
lose [lu:z], *v.t. irr.* perdre; égarer; *to lose one's temper*, s'emporter; *to lose one's way*, s'égarer; *to lose sight of*, perdre de vue.—*v.i.* perdre (*de valeur*); retarder (*horloge etc.*).
loss [lɔs], *n.* perte, *f.*; (*Hunt.*) défaut, *m.*; extinction (*de voix*), *f.*; *at a loss*, dans l'embarras; *dead loss*, perte sèche.
lost [lɔst], *a.* perdu; égaré (*fourvoyé*); abîmé (*endommagé*).
lot [lɔt], *n.* sort, destin, *m.*, part; quantité, *f.*; tas (*de personnes*); lot (*à une vente*), *m.*; *a lot of*, beaucoup de; *to draw* or *cast lots*, tirer au sort. [see **plot**]
lotion ['louʃən], *n.* lotion, *f.*
lottery ['lɔtəri], *n.* loterie, *f.*
loud [laud], *a.* haut; fort, grand; bruyant, retentissant; tapageur (*tumultueux*); criard (*couleurs*).
loudly ['laudli], *adv.* haut, fort, à haute voix; avec grand bruit, à grands cris.
loudness ['laudnis], *n.* force, *f.*, grand bruit, éclat, *m.*
loud-speaker [laud'spi:kə], *n.* (*Rad.*) haut-parleur, *m.*
Louisa [lu'i:zə], **Louise** [lu'i:z]. Louise, *f.*
lounge [laundʒ], *v.i.* flâner; être couché *ou* étendu *ou* appuyé paresseusement (*sur*).—*n.* promenoir; sofa (*canapé*); petit salon; hall (*d'hôtel*), *m.*; *lounge jacket*, veston, *m.*; *lounge suit*, complet veston, *m.*
lounger ['laundʒə], *n.* flâneur, *m.*
lour, lower (1) ['lauə], *v.i.* froncer les sourcils; s'assombrir, s'obscurcir (*du temps*); *the sky lours*, le temps se couvre.
louring, lowering (1) ['lauəriŋ], *a.* couvert, sombre; (*fig.*) menaçant.
louse [laus], *n.* (*pl.* **lice** [lais]) pou, *m.*
lousy ['lauzi], *a.* pouilleux; (*fig.*) bas, vil, sale.
lout [laut], *n.* rustre, butor, *m.*
loutish ['lautiʃ], *a.* rustre.
lovable ['lʌvəbl], *a.* digne d'être aimé; aimable.
love [lʌv], *v.t.* aimer, adorer.—*n.* amour, *m.*, affection; amitié, *f.*; ami (*mot tendre*), *m.*; (*Ten.*) zéro, rien, *m.*; *my love to all*, mes

amitiés à tous; **to be in love with**, être amoureux de.

love affair ['lʌvəfɛə], n. amourette, f.

love letter ['lʌvletə], n. billet doux, m.

loveliness ['lʌvlinis], n. amabilité; beauté, f., charme, m.

lovely ['lʌvli], a. charmant, ravissant, séduisant, gracieux.

lover ['lʌvə], n. amant, amoureux; amateur (de), m.

lovesick ['lʌvsik], a. en mal d'amour.

loving ['lʌviŋ], a. aimant, affectueux, affectionné, tendre; d'amour (choses); **loving kindness**, bonté, miséricorde, f.

low (1) [lou], a. bas; petit; peu élevé, vulgaire; profond (révérence); (fig.) lent (fièvre); abattu (humeur); **at low water**, à marée basse; **in a low voice**, d'une voix basse.—adv. bas, en bas; à voix basse; profondément (révérence).

low (2) [lou], v.i. beugler.

low-brow ['loubrau], a. peu intellectuel.—n. philistin, m.

lower (1) [LOUR].

lower (2) ['louə], a. plus bas, inférieur; bas.— v.t. baisser, abaisser; descendre; rabaisser, humilier; diminuer, affaiblir.

lower class ['louəkla:s], n. peuple, m.

lowering (1) [LOURING].

lowering (2) ['louəriŋ], n. abaissement, m., diminution, f.

lowest ['louist], a. le plus bas, le dernier.

lowing ['louiŋ], n. mugissement, beuglement, m.

lowliness ['loulinis], n. humilité, f.

lowly ['louli], a. humble.—adv. humblement.

lowness ['lounis], n. situation basse, petitesse; faiblesse (santé); dépression (prix), f.; abaissement (température); abattement (humeur), découragement, m.; vulgarité, f.

loyal ['loiəl], a. fidèle, loyal.

loyalty ['loiəlti], n. fidélité, f.

lozenge ['lozindʒ], n. pastille, f.; (Geom., Her. etc.) losange, m.

lubber ['lʌbə], n. lourdaud, m.; **land-lubber**, marin d'eau douce, m.

lubricant ['lu:brikənt], n. lubrifiant, m.

lubricate ['lu:brikeit], v.t. lubrifier.

lubrication [lu:bri'keiʃən], n. lubrication, f.

lucid ['lu:sid], a. lucide; limpide, transparent.

lucidity [lu:'siditi], **lucidness** ['lu:sidnis], n. transparence, limpidité, lucidité, f.

luck [lʌk], n. chance, fortune, f., bonheur, m.; **by good luck**, par bonheur; **by ill luck**, par malheur; **good luck**, bonne chance.

luckily ['lʌkili], adv. heureusement, par bonheur.

lucky ['lʌki], a. heureux; **to be lucky**, avoir de la chance; porter bonheur (chose).

lucrative ['lu:krətiv], a. lucratif.

lucre ['lu:kə], n. lucre, m.

Lucy ['lu:si]. Lucie, f.

ludicrous ['lu:dikrəs], a. risible, comique, ridicule.

luggage ['lʌgidʒ], n. bagage, m., bagages, m.pl.; **left-luggage office**, consigne, f.

lugubrious [lu'gju:briəs], a. lugubre.

lukewarm ['lu:kwo:m], a. tiède; (fig.) peu zélé.

lull [lʌl], v.t. bercer, endormir; calmer.—v.i. se calmer, s'apaiser.—n. moment de calme, m.; (Naut.) accalmie, f.

lullaby ['lʌləbai], n. berceuse, f.

lumbago [lʌm'beigou], n. lumbago, m.

lumber ['lʌmbə], n. vieilleries, f.pl.; (Am.) bois de charpente, m.—v.t. entasser sans ordre; remplir de fatras.—v.i. se traîner lourdement.

lumbering ['lʌmbəriŋ], a. lourd, encombrant.

lumberjack ['lʌmbədʒæk], n. bûcheron, m.

luminous ['lju:minəs], a. lumineux.

lump [lʌmp], n. masse, f.; morceau, bloc (piece), m.—v.t. prendre en bloc; réunir ensemble.

lumpish ['lʌmpiʃ], a. gros, lourd, pesant.

lumpy ['lʌmpi], a. grumeleux.

lunacy ['lu:nəsi], n. aliénation mentale, f.

lunar ['lu:nə], a. lunaire.

lunatic ['lu:nətik], a. de fou,' d'aliéné.—n. aliéné; fou, m., folle, f.

lunatic asylum ['lu:nətikəsailəm], n. asile d'aliénés, m.

lunch [lʌntʃ], n. déjeuner (vers midi), m.—v.i. déjeuner.

lung [lʌŋ], n. (usu. in pl.) poumon; mou (de veau), m.; **iron lung**, poumon d'acier.

lunge [lʌndʒ], n. (Fenc.) botte, f., coup droit, m.—v.i. porter une botte.

lupin ['lju:pin], n. (Bot.) lupin, m.

lurch [lə:tʃ], n. embardée, f., cahot; (fig.) embarras, m.; **to leave in the lurch**, planter là.—v.i. faire une embardée (navire).

lure [ljuə], n. leurre, appât, piège; (fig.) attrait, m.—v.t. leurrer, attirer, séduire.

lurid ['ljuərid], a. sombre, blafard; sensationnel.

lurk [lə:k], v.i. être aux aguets; se tenir caché.

luscious ['lʌʃəs], a. délicieux, savoureux; liquoreux (vin).

lusciousness ['lʌʃəsnis], n. nature succulente, douceur extrême; volupté, f.

lush [lʌʃ], a. luxuriant.

lust [lʌst], n. luxure, f.; désir lascif, m.; (fig.) convoitise, f.—v.i. désirer immodérément; **to lust after**, convoiter.

luster ['lʌstə], n. brillant, lustre; (fig.) éclat, m., splendeur, f.

lustily ['lʌstili], adv. vigoureusement.

lustrous ['lʌstrəs], a. brillant, lustré.

lusty ['lʌsti], a. vigoureux, robuste, fort.

lute [lju:t], n. luth, m.

Luxembourg ['lʌksəmbə:g]. le Luxembourg (Duché), m.

luxuriance [lʌg'zjuəriəns], n. exubérance, surabondance, luxuriance, f.

luxuriant [lʌg'zjuəriənt], a. exubérant, surabondant, luxuriant.

luxurious [lʌg'zjuəriəs], a. de luxe, somptueux, luxueux.

luxuriously [lʌg'zjuəriəsli], adv. avec luxe, somptueusement.

luxuriousness [lʌg'zjuəriəsnis], n. somptuosité, f.

luxury ['lʌkʃəri], n. luxe, m., exubérance, f.; fin morceau; objet de luxe, m.

lying ['laiiŋ], a. menteur; mensonger (choses). —n. mensonge, m.

lymph [limf], n. lymphe, f.; vaccin, m.

lynch [lintʃ], v.t. lyncher (exécuter sommairement).

lynx [liŋks], n. lynx, m.

lyre ['laiə], *n.* lyre, *f.*
lyric ['lirik], *a.* lyrique.—*n.* poème lyrique, *m.*; (*pl.*) paroles (*d'une chanson*), *f.pl.*
lyrical ['lirikəl], *a.* lyrique.

M

M, m [em]. treizième lettre de l'alphabet, *m.*
macadam [mə'kædəm], *n.* macadam, *m.*
macaroni [mækə'rouni], *n.* macaroni, *m.*
macaroon [mækə'ru:n], *n.* macaron, *m.*
mace [meis], *n.* masse (*de cérémonie*), *f.*
mace-bearer ['meisbɛərə], *n.* massier, *m.*
Macedonia [mæsə'douniə]. la Macédoine, *f.*
Macedonian [mæsə'douniən], *a.* macédonien. —*n.* Macédonien (*personne*), *m.*
macerate ['mæsəreit], *v.t.* macérer.
machine [mə'ʃi:n], *n.* machine, *f.*; (*fig.*) instrument; appareil (*avion*), *m.*
machine gun [mə'ʃi:ngʌn], *n.* mitrailleuse, *f.*
machinery [mə'ʃi:nəri], *n.* mécanique, *f.*, mécanisme, *m.*; machines, *f.pl.*
machine tool [mə'ʃi:ntu:l], *n.* machine-outil, *f.*
mackerel ['mækərəl], *n.* maquereau, *m.*
mackintosh ['mækintɔʃ], *n.* imperméable, *m.*
mad [mæd], *a.* fou, aliéné, insensé; affolé; furieux (*déchaîné*); enragé (*animal*).
Madagascan [mædə'gæskən], *a.* malgache.— *n.* Malgache (*personne*), *m.*, *f.*
Madagascar [mædə'gæskə]. Madagascar, *m.*
madam ['mædəm], *n.* madame, *f.*
madcap ['mædkæp], *a.* étourdi, fou.—*n.* fou, *m.*
madden [mædn], *v.t.* rendre fou; faire enrager.
maddening ['mædniŋ], *a.* à rendre fou, enrageant.
madder ['mædə], *n.* garance, *f.*
made [meid], *a.* fait, confectionné; *self-made man*, fils de ses œuvres, *m.*; *made up*, inventé (*histoire*); maquillé (*visage*).
Madeira [mə'diərə]. Madère, *f.*—*n.* madère (*vin*), *m.*
madly ['mædli], *adv.* follement, furieusement.
madman ['mædmən], *n.* (*pl.* **-men** [men]) aliéné, fou, *m.*
madness ['mædnis], *n.* démence, fureur, folie; rage (*d'animal*), *f.*
Madonna [mə'dɔnə]. la Madone, *f.*
maelstrom ['meilstroum, 'meilstrəm], *n.* (*Geog.*) malstrom; (*fig.*) tourbillon, *m.*
magazine [mægə'zi:n], *n.* magasin (*boutique*; *aussi chargeur d'arme à feu*); magazine, *m.*, revue (*périodique*), *f.*
magenta [mə'dʒentə], *a.* and *n.* magenta (*couleur*), *m.*
maggot ['mægət], *n.* larve, *f.*, ver, asticot, *m.*
magic ['mædʒik], *a.* magique.— *n.* magie, *f.*
magical ['mædʒikəl], *a.* magique.
magician [mə'dʒiʃən], *n.* magicien, *m.*
magisterial [mædʒis'tiəriəl], *a.* de maître; magistral.
magistrate ['mædʒistreit], *n.* magistrat, *m.*; *examining magistrate*, juge d'instruc-

tion, *m.*; *police court magistrate*, juge de paix, *m.*
magnanimity [mægnə'nimiti], *n.* magnanimité, *f.*
magnanimous [mæg'næniməs], *a.* magnanime.
magnate ['mægneit], *n.* magnat; grand; (*colloq.*) gros bonnet, *m.*
magnesia [mæg'ni:ʃə], *n.* magnésie, *f.*
magnesium [mæg'ni:ziəm], *n.* magnésium, *m.*
magnet ['mægnit], *n.* aimant, *m.*
magnetic [mæg'netik], *a.* aimanté; magnétique; (*fig.*) attirant.
magnetism ['mægnitizm], *n.* magnétisme, *m.*; (*Elec.*) aimantation, *f.*
magnetize ['mægnitaiz], *v.t.* aimanter; (*fig.*) magnétiser.
magneto [mæg'ni:tou], *n.* magnéto, *f.*
magnificence [mæg'nifisəns], *n.* magnificence, *f.*
magnificent [mæg'nifisənt], *a.* magnifique, superbe.
magnify ['mægnifai], *v.t.* magnifier, augmenter, grossir; (*fig.*) exalter.
magnifying ['mægnifaiiŋ], *a.* qui grossit; *magnifying glass*, loupe, *f.*
magnitude ['mægnitju:d], *n.* grandeur, importance, *f.*
magnolia [mæg'nouliə], *n.* (*Bot.*) magnolia, magnolier, *m.*
magpie ['mægpai], *n.* pie, *f.*
mahogany [mə'hɔgəni], *n.* acajou, bois d'acajou, *m.*
maid [meid], *n.* fille, jeune fille; vierge (*virgin*); bonne, servante, domestique, *f.*; *chambermaid*, fille de chambre; *kitchen maid*, fille de cuisine; *maid of all work*, bonne à tout faire; *maid of honor*, demoiselle d'honneur, *f.*
maiden [meidn], *a.* de fille, de jeune fille; virginal; (*fig.*) pur, neuf; *maiden aunt*, tante non mariée, *f.*; *maiden name*, nom de jeune fille, *m.*; *maiden speech*, premier discours (*d'un nouveau membre du Parlement*), *m.*; *maiden voyage*, premier voyage, *m.*—*n.* jeune fille, fille, *f.*
maidenly ['meidnli], *a.* de jeune fille; modeste, chaste.
mail (1) [meil], *n.* mailles (*armure*), *f.pl.*
mail (2) [meil], *n.* courrier, *m.*, dépêches (*lettres*), *f.pl.*—*v.t.* (*Am.*) mettre à la poste.
mail-bag ['meilbæg], *n.* sac postal, *m.*
mail train ['meiltrein], *n.* train-postal, *m.*
maim [meim], *v.t.* mutiler, estropier.
main (1) [mein], *a.* principal, premier; grand; important, essentiel.—*n.* gros, *m.*, plus grande partie, *f.*; principal océan, *m.*; *in the main*, pour la plupart, en général.
main (2) [mein], *n.* force, *f.*
main deck ['meindek], *n.* premier pont, *m.*
mainland ['meinlənd], *n.* continent, *m.*
mainly ['meinli], *adv.* principalement, surtout.
mainmast ['meinmɑ:st], *n.* grand mât, *m.*
mainstay ['meinstei], *n.* soutien, *m.*
maintain [mein'tein], *v.t.* maintenir; soutenir, alléguer; conserver; entretenir, nourrir (*subvenir aux besoins de*).
maintenance ['meintənəns], *n.* maintien, soutien; entretien, *m.*
maize [meiz], *n.* maïs, *m.*

majestic [mə'dʒestik], a. majestueux.
majesty ['mædʒəsti], n. majesté, f.; *His* or *Her Majesty*, Sa Majesté.
major ['meidʒə], a. plus grand, majeur.—n. commandant, m.; (*Law*) personne majeure, f.; *drum major*, tambour-major, m.; *sergeant major*, adjudant, m.
Majorca [mə'jɔ:kə]. Majorque, f.
majority [mə'dʒɔriti], n. majorité, f.
make [meik], v.t. *irr.* faire; créer, façonner, fabriquer, confectionner; rendre (*faire devenir*); forcer, contraindre (*obliger*); amasser, gagner (*argent*); *to make a mistake*, se tromper; *to make a noise*, faire du bruit; *to make believe*, faire accroire à; *to make fun of*, se moquer de; *to make good*, soutenir; réparer; dédommager de; *to make it up*, se raccommoder; *to make known*, faire connaître, faire savoir à; *to make out*, comprendre, déchiffrer, distinguer; *to make over to*, céder à; *to make sure of*, s'assurer de; *to make up*, compléter, inventer (*histoire*); arranger (*querelle*); régler (*comptes*); *to make up for*, suppléer à; rattraper (*temps*); *to make up one's mind*, se décider.—v.i. se diriger (*vers*); contribuer (à); faire (*comme si*); *to make believe*, faire semblant; *to make of*, comprendre; *to make off*, se sauver; *to make up*, se maquiller; *to make up for*, suppléer à; dédommager de, compenser.—n. façon, forme, tournure; fabrication, f.
make-believe ['meikbili:v], n. feinte, f., semblant, m.
maker ['meikə], n. créateur, auteur; faiseur; (*Comm.*) fabricant, m.
makeshift ['meikʃift], n. pis aller, expédient, m.
make-up ['meikʌp], n. contexture, f.; maquillage (*du visage*), m.
make-weight ['meikweit], n. supplément; (*fig.*) remplissage, m.
making ['meikiŋ], n. création; façon, fabrication, construction; confection (*de vêtements*), f.
maladjusted [mælə'dʒʌstid], a. inadapté.
maladjustment [mælə'dʒʌstmənt], n. inadaptation, f.
maladministration [mælədminis'treiʃən], n. mauvaise administration, f.
malady ['mælədi], n. maladie, f.
malaria [mə'lɛəriə], n. malaria, f., paludisme, m.
Malay [mə'lei], a. malais.—n. malais (*langue*); Malais (*personne*), m.
Malaysia [mə'leiziə]. la Malaisie, f.
Malaysian [mə'leiziən], a. malais.—n. Malais (*personne*), m.
malcontent ['mælkəntent], a. and n. mécontent, m.
male [meil], a. mâle; masculin.—n. mâle, m.
malediction [mæli'dikʃən], n. malédiction, f.
malefactor ['mælifæktə], n. malfaiteur, m.
malevolence [mə'levələns], n. malveillance, f.
malevolent [mə'levələnt], a. malveillant.
Mali ['mɑ:li]. le Mali, m.
malice ['mælis], n. malice; malveillance, méchanceté; rancune, f.; *to bear malice*, vouloir du mal à, garder rancune à.
malicious [mə'liʃəs], a. malicieux, méchant.
maliciously [mə'liʃəsli], adv. méchamment.

maliciousness [mə'liʃəsnis], n. malice, malveillance, f.
malign [mə'lain], a. malin; méchant.—v.t. diffamer, noircir.
malignant [mə'lignənt], a. malin, méchant.
malignantly [mə'lignəntli], adv. malignement, méchamment.
malignity [mə'ligniti], n. malignité, malveillance, f.
malinger [mə'liŋgə], v.i. (*Mil.*) faire le malade; tirer au flanc.
mall (1) [mɔ:l], n. gros maillet, m.
mall (2) [mæl], n. mail (*rue*), m.
mallard ['mæləd], n. (*Orn.*) canard sauvage, m.
malleability [mæliə'biliti], n. malléabilité, f.
malleable ['mæliəbl], a. malléable.
mallet ['mælit], n. maillet, m.; tapette, f.
mallow ['mælou], n. (*Bot.*) mauve, f.
malmsey ['mɑ:mzi], n. malvoisie, f.
malnutrition [mælnju'triʃən], n. sous-alimentation, f.
malpractice [mæl'præktis], n. malversation, f., méfait, m.
malt [mɔ:lt], n. malt, m.—v.t. malter.
Malta ['mɔ:ltə]. Malte, f.
Maltese [mɔ:l'ti:z], a. maltais.—n. Maltais (*personne*), m.
maltreat [mæl'tri:t], v.t. maltraiter.
maltreatment [mæl'tri:tmənt], n. mauvais traitement, m.
mammal ['mæməl], n. mammifère, m.
mammoth ['mæməθ], n. mammouth, m.
man [mæn], n. (*pl.* **men** [men]) homme; domestique, valet (*servant*), m.; (*Chess*) pièce, f.; (*Draughts*) pion, m.; *the man in the street*, l'homme de la rue, le grand public. —v.t. garnir d'hommes; armer (*pompe, bateau*).
manacle ['mænəkl], v.t. mettre les menottes à.—n. (*pl.*) menottes, f.pl.
manage ['mænidʒ], v.t. diriger, mener, conduire; arranger (*choses*); gouverner, administrer, gérer; ménager (*habilement*); manier, dompter (*cheval*).—v.i. s'arranger (*pour*); parvenir à; venir à bout (*de*).
manageable ['mænidʒəbl], a. traitable, maniable.
management ['mænidʒmənt], n. conduite, administration; (*Comm.*) gestion (*direction*), f.; artifice, savoir-faire (*manège*), m.
manager ['mænidʒə], n. directeur, administrateur; (*Comm.*) gérant; (*Theat.*) régisseur; (*Spt.*) manager, m.
manageress [mænidʒə'res], n. directrice, gérante, f.
Manchuria [mæn'tʃuəriə]. la Mandchourie, f.
Manchu(rian) [mæn'tʃu(əriən)], a. mandchou.—n. mandchou (*langue*); Mandchou (*personne*), m.
mandarin ['mændərin], n. mandarin, m.; mandarine (*orange*), f.
mandate ['mændeit], n. commandement, mandat; ordre, m.
mandatory ['mændətəri], a. and n. mandataire, m.
mandolin ['mændəlin], n. mandoline, f.
mane [mein], n. crinière, f.
maneuver, see manœuvre.
manfully ['mænfuli], adv. en homme, virilement, vaillamment.
manganese ['mæŋgəni:z], n. manganèse, m.

mange [meindʒ], *n.* gale (*d'animaux*), *f.*
manger [ˈmeindʒə], *n.* mangeoire, crèche, *f.*
mangle [mæŋgl], *v.t.* déchirer, mutiler; calandrer (*linge*).—*n.* calandre, *f.*
mango [ˈmæŋgou], *n.* (*Bot.*) mangue, *f.*; manguier (*arbre*), *m.*
mangrove [ˈmæŋgrouv], *n.* (*Bot.*) mangle, *f.*; manglier, manguier (*arbre*), *m.*
mangy [ˈmeindʒi], *a.* galeux.
man-handle [ˈmænhændl], *v.t.* manutentionner; (*fig.*) maltraiter.
man-hole [ˈmænhoul], *n.* bouche d'égout, *f.*
manhood [ˈmænhud], *n.* virilité, *f.*; âge viril, *m.*; nature humaine, *f.*
mania [ˈmeiniə], *n.* folie, rage, manie, *f.*
maniac [ˈmeiniæk], *a.* furieux, fou.—*n.* fou furieux, fou, *m.*; (*fig.*) maniaque, *m.*, *f.*
maniacal [məˈnaiəkl], *a.* furieux, fou.
manicure [ˈmænikjuə], *n.* soin des ongles, *m.* —*v.t.* soigner les ongles.
manicurist [ˈmænikjuərist], *n.* manucure, *m.*, *f.*
manifest [ˈmænifest], *v.t.* manifester, témoigner, montrer; **to manifest a cargo**, déclarer une cargaison.—*a.* manifeste, évident.—*n.* manifeste, *m.*
manifestation [mænifesˈteiʃən], *n.* manifestation, *f.*
manifesto [mæniˈfestou], *n.* manifeste, *m.*
manifold [ˈmænifould], *a.* divers, multiple; varié.
manikin [ˈmænikin], *n.* bout d'homme, mannequin, homuncule, *m.*
Manila [məˈnilə], Manille, *f.*
manipulate [məˈnipjuleit], *v.t.* manipuler.
mankind [mænˈkaind], *n.* genre humain, *m.*, l'humanité, *f.*
manlike [ˈmænlaik], *a.* d'homme, viril; mâle; hommasse (*femme*).
manliness [ˈmænlinis], *n.* caractère viril, *m.*
manly [ˈmænli], *a.* d'homme, viril, mâle.
manna [ˈmænə], *n.* manne, *f.*
mannequin [ˈmænikin], *n.* (*Dress.*) mannequin, *m.*; **mannequin parade**, défilé de mannequins, *m.*
manner [ˈmænə], *n.* manière, *f.*, air; genre, *m.*, sorte, façon, espèce; coutume, habitude, *f.*; (*pl.*) mœurs, *f.*, politesse, *f.*; **after the manner of**, à la manière de, d'après; **all manner of things**, toutes sortes de choses, *f.pl.*; **in the same manner as**, de même que.
mannerism [ˈmænərizm], *n.* air maniéré, maniérisme; tic, *m.*
mannerly [ˈmænəli], *a.* poli.
manning [ˈmæniŋ], *n.* armement, équipement, *m.*
mannish [ˈmæniʃ], *a.* hommasse.
manœuvre [məˈnuːvə], *n.* manœuvre, *f.*— *v.t.*, *v.i.* manœuvrer.
manor [ˈmænə], *n.* seigneurie, *f.*; manoir, château seigneurial, *m.*
manorial [məˈnɔːriəl], *a.* seigneurial.
man-power [ˈmænpauə], *n.* main d'œuvre, *f.*
manse [mæns], *n.* presbytère, *m.*
mansion [ˈmænʃən], *n.* château (*à la campagne*); hôtel particulier (*en ville*), *m.*
manslaughter [ˈmænslɔːtə], *n.* (*Law*) homicide involontaire, *m.*
mantel [mæntl], **mantelpiece** [ˈmæntlpiːs], *n.* manteau *ou* dessus de cheminée, *m.*, cheminée, *f.*

mantilla [mænˈtilə], *n.* mantille, *f.*
mantis [ˈmæntis], *n.* (*Ent.*) mante, *f.*; **praying mantis**, mante religieuse.
mantle [mæntl], *n.* manteau, *m.*—*v.t.* couvrir, voiler.
manual [ˈmænjuel], *a.* manuel, de la main.— *n.* manuel (*livre*); (*Organ*) clavier, *m.*
manufacture [mænjuˈfæktʃə], *n.* manufacture, confection, fabrication, *f.*; (*pl.*) produits manufacturés, *m.pl.*—*v.t.* manufacturer, fabriquer.
manufacturer [mænjuˈfæktʃərə], *n.* fabricant, industriel, *m.*
manure [məˈnjuə], *n.* engrais, fumier, *m.*— *v.t.* engraisser, fumer.
manuscript [ˈmænjuskript], *a.* and *n.* manuscrit, *m.*
Manx [mæŋks], *a.* de l'île de Man, mannois (*f.*); **Manx cat**, chat sans queue, *m.*
many [ˈmeni], *a.* beaucoup (*de*), bien (*des*); nombreux; plusieurs, maint; **as many as**, autant que, jusqu'à (*devant un numéro*); **how many?** combien? **many a time**, maintes fois; **so many**, tant, tant de; **too many**, trop, trop de.—*n.* **the many**, la multitude, la foule, *f.*
many-colored [ˈmenikʌləd], *a.* multicolore.
many-sided [ˈmenisaidid], *a.* polygone; (*fig.*) complexe.
map [mæp], *n.* carte, carte géographique, *f.*; **map of a town**, plan d'une ville, *m.*; **map of the world**, mappemonde, *f.*—*v.t.* faire une carte *ou* un plan de, tracer.
maple [meipl], *n.* érable, *m.*
mar [mɑː], *v.t.* gâter, défigurer; (*fig.*) troubler.
marathon [ˈmærəθɔn], *n.* marathon, *m.*
marauder [məˈrɔːdə], *n.* maraudeur, malandrin, *m.*
marauding [məˈrɔːdiŋ], *n.* maraude, *f.* maraudage, *m.*
marble [mɑːbl], *a.* de marbre.—*n.* marbre, *m.*; bille (*jouet*), *f.*
marbled [mɑːbld], *a.* marbré.
marbling [ˈmɑːbliŋ], *n.* marbrure, *f.*
March [mɑːtʃ], *n.* mars (*mois*), *m.*
march (1) [mɑːtʃ], *n.* (*Mil.*) marche, *f.*; (*fig.*) progrès, *m.*; **march past**, défilé, *m.*—*v.t.* mettre en marche; emmener.—*v.i.* marcher, se mettre en marche; (*fig.*) avancer; **to march past**, défiler devant.
march (2) [mɑːtʃ], *n.* frontière, *f.*
marching [ˈmɑːtʃiŋ], *a.* de marche.—*n.* marche, *f.*
marchioness [mɑːʃəˈnes], *n.* marquise, *f.*
mare [mɛə], *n.* jument, *f.*
Margaret [ˈmɑːgərit], Marguerite, *f.*
margarine [ˈmɑːgəriːn, ˈmɑːdʒəriːn], *n.* margarine, *f.*
margin [ˈmɑːdʒin], *n.* marge (*de papier etc.*), *f.*; bord (*de rivière, de lac*), *m.*—*v.t.* border.
marginal [ˈmɑːdʒinəl], *a.* en marge; marginal.
marigold [ˈmærigould], *n.* (*Bot.*) souci, *m.*
marine [məˈriːn], *a.* marin, de mer; naval.— *n.* fusilier marin, *m.*; **tell that to the marines**, allez conter cela à d'autres.
mariner [ˈmærinə], *n.* marin, *m.*
maritime [ˈmæritaim], *a.* maritime.
Mark [mɑːk], Marc, *m.*
mark (1) [mɑːk], *n.* marque, *f.*, signe, *m.*; em-

preinte; (*fig.*) distinction, importance, *f.*; témoignage (*d'estime*), *m.*; (*Sch.*) note, *f.*, point, *m.*; cible (*but*); croix (*signature*), *f.* —*v.t.* marquer, remarquer; (*Sch.*) noter; (*fig.*) observer, faire attention à.

mark (2) [ma:k], *n.* marc (*pièce de monnaie*), *m.*

marked [ma:kt], *a.* marqué, évident; prononcé (*accent*).

marker ['ma:kə], *n.* marqueur; jeton (*au jeu*); signet (*de livre*), *m.*

market ['ma:kit], *n.* marché, *m.*; halle, *f.*; débit (*vente*); cours (*prix*); (*Comm.*) débouché, *m.*—*v.t.* acheter au marché, vendre au marché.

market garden ['ma:kit'ga:dn], *n.* jardin maraîcher, *m.*

market gardener ['ma:kit'ga:dnə], *n.* maraîcher, *m.*

marking ['ma:kiŋ], *n.* marquage, *m.*

marking ink ['ma:kiŋiŋk], *n.* encre à marquer, *f.*

marksman ['ma:ksmən], *n.* (*pl.* **-men** [men]) bon tireur, *m.*

marksmanship ['ma:ksmənʃip], *n.* adresse au tir, *f.*

marl [ma:l], *n.* marne, *f.*—*v.t.* marner.

marline-spike ['ma:linspaik], *n.* épissoir, *m.*

marmalade ['ma:məleid], *n.* confiture d'oranges, *f.*

marmoset ['ma:məzet], *n.* ouistiti, *m.*

marmot ['ma:mət], *n.* marmotte, *f.*

maroon (1) [mə'ru:n], *n.* noir marron, *m.*—*v.t.* abandonner dans une île déserte.

maroon (2) [mə'ru:n], *a.* and *n.* marron pourpré (*couleur*), *m.*

marquee [ma:'ki:], *n.* grande tente, *f.*

marquess, marquis ['ma:kwis], *n.* marquis, *m.*

marquetry ['ma:kətri], *n.* marqueterie, *f.*

marquis [MARQUESS].

marriage ['mæridʒ], *n.* mariage, *m.*; noces (*fêtes*), *f.pl.*

marriageable ['mæridʒəbl], *a.* mariable, nubile.

married ['mærid], *a.* marié; conjugal.

marrow ['mærou], *n.* moelle; (*fig.*) essence, *f.*; *vegetable marrow*, courgette, *f.*

marry ['mæri], *v.t.* marier (*donner* ou *unir en mariage*); se marier avec, épouser (*prendre pour époux*).—*v.i.* se marier.

Marseilles [ma:'seilz]. Marseille, *f.*

marsh [ma:ʃ], *n.* marais, *m.*

marshal [ma:ʃl], *n.* maréchal.—*v.t.* ranger; mettre en ordre; classer.

marsh-mallow ['ma:ʃ'mælou], *n.* (*Bot.*) guimauve, *f.*; bonbon à la guimauve, *m.*

marshy ['ma:ʃi], *a.* marécageux.

mart [ma:t], *n.* marché, entrepôt, *m.*

marten [ma:tn], *n.* martre, *f.*; *beech marten*, fouine, *f.*

Martha ['ma:θə]. Marthe, *f.*

martial [ma:ʃl], *a.* martial; de guerre, de bataille; guerrier, belliqueux.

martin ['ma:tin], *n.* martin, martinet, *m.*

martinet [ma:ti'net], *n.* officier strict sur la discipline, *m.*

Martinmas ['ma:tinmæs]. la Saint-Martin, *f.*

martyr ['ma:tə], *n.* martyr, *m.*—*v.t.* martyriser.

martyrdom ['ma:tədəm], *n.* martyre, *m.*

martyrize ['ma:təraiz], *v.t.* (*fam.*) faire souffrir, martyriser.

marvel [ma:vl], *n.* merveille, *f.*—*v.i.* s'émerveiller, s'étonner.

marvellous ['ma:v(i)ləs], *a.* merveilleux, étonnant.

marvellously ['ma:v(i)ləsli], *adv.* à merveille.

Marxism ['ma:ksizm], *n.* Marxisme, *m.*

Marxist ['ma:ksist], *a.* marxiste.—*n.* Marxiste, *m.*, *f.*

Mary ['mɛəri]. Marie, *f.*

marzipan [ma:zi'pæn], *n.* massepain, *m.*

mascot ['mæskət], *n.* mascotte, *f.*

masculine ['mæskjulin], *a.* mâle, d'homme; (*Gram.*) masculin; hommasse (*femme*).—*n.* masculin, *m.*

mash [mæʃ], *n.* mélange, *m.*, pâte, bouillie; mâche (*pour bestiaux*); pâtée (*pour chien, volaille*), *f.*—*v.t.* broyer; mélanger; (*Brewing*) brasser; *mashed potatoes*, purée de pommes de terre, *f.*

mask [ma:sk], *n.* masque; loup (*de soie, de velours*), *m.*—*v.t.* masquer; déguiser.—*v.i.* se masquer.

mason [meisn], *n.* maçon, *m.*; *freemason*, franc-maçon, *m.*

masonic [mə'sɔnik], *a.* maçonnique.

masonry ['meisənri], *n.* maçonnerie, *f.*; *freemasonry*, franc-maçonnerie, *f.*

masquerade [mæskə'reid], *n.* mascarade *f.* —*v.i.* se masquer; *to masquerade as*, se faire passer pour.

mass (1) [mæs], *n.* masse, *f.*; amas, gros, *m.*; multitude, foule (*de gens*), *f.*—*v.i.* se masser; s'amonceler (*nuages*).

mass (2) [mæs, ma:s], *n.* (R.-C. Ch.) messe, *f.*

massacre ['mæsəkə], *n.* massacre, *m.*—*v.t.* massacrer.

massive ['mæsiv], *a.* massif.

mass meeting ['mæs'mi:tiŋ], *n.* assemblée en masse, *f.*, grand meeting, *m.*

mast [ma:st], *n.* mât, *m.*; (*pl.*) mâts, *m.pl.*, mâture, *f.*; *half-mast*, à mi-mât, en berne.

master ['ma:stə], *n.* maître, directeur, chef; (*Naut.*) patron, maître (*d'un navire*); patron (*d'ouvriers*); (*Sch. etc.*) maître d'école, professeur; (*fig.*) possesseur, *m.*—*v.t.* maîtriser, surmonter, dompter, vaincre; se rendre maître de; l'emporter sur.

masterful ['ma:stəful], *a.* de maître, impérieux, dominateur.

master key ['ma:stəki:], *n.* passe-partout, *m.*

masterly ['ma:stəli], *a.* de maître; magistral.

master-mind ['ma:stəmaind], *n.* esprit supérieur, *m.*

masterpiece ['ma:stəpi:s], *n.* chef-d'œuvre, *m.*

master-stroke ['ma:stəstrouk], **master-touch** ['ma:stətʌtʃ], *n.* coup de maître, *m.*

mastery ['ma:stəri], *n.* empire, pouvoir, *m.*; supériorité, maîtrise, *f.*

masticate ['mæstikeit], *v.t.* mâcher.

mastication [mæsti'keiʃən], *n.* mastication, *f.*

mastiff ['mæstif], *n.* mâtin, *m.*

mastitis [mæs'taitis], *n.* mastite, *f.*

mastodon ['mæstədɔn], *n.* mastodonte, *m.*

mastoid ['mæstɔid], *a.* mastoïde.

mat [mæt], *n.* natte, *f.*; dessous de lampe, *m.*; *door mat*, paillasson, *m.*; *table mat*, dessous de plat, *m.*—*v.t.* natter, tresser.

match

match (1) [mætʃ], *n.* pareil, pendant, égal (*semblable*); mariage; parti (*futur époux*), *m.*; lutte (*concours*), *f.*; (*Spt.*) match, *m.*, partie; course, *f.*; **to be a bad match**, aller mal ensemble (*choses*); **to be more than a match for**, être trop fort pour; **to make a good match**, faire un bon mariage.—*v.t.* assortir, appareiller, égaler, apparier (*deux choses*); se mesurer avec (*opposer*).—*v.i.* s'assortir, être pareil.

match (2) [mætʃ], *n.* allumette, *f.*

match-box ['mætʃbɔks], *n.* boîte d'allumettes *ou* à allumettes, *f.*

matchless ['mætʃlis], *a.* incomparable, sans pareil.

match-maker (1) ['mætʃmeikə], *n.* marieur, *m.*

match-maker (2) ['mætʃmeikə], *n.* fabricant d'allumettes, *m.*

mate (1) [meit], *n.* camarade, compagnon, *m.*, compagne, *f.*; second (*de marine marchande*), *m.*—*v.t.* égaler, assortir, apparier; tenir compagnie avec; accoupler (*oiseaux*).—*v.i.* s'accoupler (*animaux*).

mate (2) [meit], *n.* (*Chess*) mat, *m.*—*v.t.* mater.

material [mə'tiəriəl], *a.* matériel; important. —*n.* matière; étoffe, *f.*, tissu (*textile*); matériel (*réserves*), *m.*; (*pl.*) matériaux, *m.pl.*; **raw material**, matière première.

materialism [mə'tiəriəlizm], *n.* matérialisme, *m.*

materialist [mə'tiəriəlist], *n.* matérialiste, *m.*, *f.*

materialistic [mətiəriə'listik], *a.* matérialiste.

materialize [mə'tiəriəlaiz], *v.t.* matérialiser. —*v.i.* se réaliser; se concrétiser.

materially [mə'tiəriəli], *adv.* matériellement; essentiellement.

maternal [mə'tə:nl], *a.* maternel.

maternity [mə'tə:niti], *n.* maternité, *f.*

mathematics [mæθə'mætiks], *n.pl.* mathématiques, *f.pl.*

Matilda [mə'tildə]. Mathilde, *f.*

matins ['mætinz], *n.pl.* matines, *f.pl.*

matriarch ['meitriɑ:k], *n.* matriarche, *f.*

matricide ['mætrisaid], *n.* matricide (*crime*), *m.*; matricide (*criminel*), *m.*, *f.*

matrimonial [mætri'mouniəl], *a.* conjugal.

matrimony ['mætriməni], *n.* mariage, *m.*, vie conjugale, *f.*

matron ['meitrən], *n.* matrone, mère de famille; infirmière en chef, *f.*

matronly ['meitrənli], *a.* de matrone; d'un certain âge; respectable.

matt [mæt], *a.* mat.

matter ['mætə], *n.* matière; chose, affaire, *f.*; fond; sujet; (*Med.*) pus, *m.*; (*fig.*) importance, *f.*; **as a matter of fact**, le fait est que; **what is the matter? Nothing**, qu'y a-t-il? Il n'y a rien; **what is the matter with you? Nothing**, qu'avez-vous? Je n'ai rien.—*v.imp.* importer; **it doesn't matter**, n'importe; **it doesn't matter very much**, ce n'est pas grand'chose; **it matters little**, peu importe; **what matter?** qu'importe?

matter-of-fact ['mætərəvfækt], *a.* pratique, positif.

Matthew ['mæθju]. Mathieu, *m.*

mattock ['mætək], *n.* pioche, *f.*

mattress ['mætris], *n.* matelas, *m.*

mature [mə'tjuə], *a.* mûr, mûri.—*v.t.* mûrir, faire mûrir.—*v.i.* mûrir; (*Comm.*) échoir.

maturity [mə'tjuəriti], *n.* maturité; (*Comm.*) échéance, *f.*

matutinal [mætju'tainl], *a.* matutinal, du matin.

Maud [mɔ:d]. Madelon, *f.*

maudlin ['mɔ:dlin], *a.* pleurard, pleurnichard.

maul [mɔ:l], *n.* maillet, *m.*—*v.t.* rosser, rouer de coups.

maul-stick ['mɔ:lstik], *n.* (*Paint.*) appui-main, *m.*

Mauritania [mɔri'teiniə]. la Mauritanie, *f.*

Mauritanian [mɔri'teiniən], *a.* mauritanien. —*n.* Mauritanien (*personne*), *m.*

Mauritian [mə'riʃən], *a.* mauritien.—*n.* Mauritien (*personne*), *m.*

Mauritius [mə'riʃəs]. l'Île Maurice, *f.*

mausoleum [mɔ:sə'li:əm], *n.* mausolée, *m.*

mauve [mouv], *a.* mauve.

maw [mɔ:], *n.* jabot (*d'oiseau*), *m.*; caillette (*de ruminant*), *f.*

mawkish ['mɔ:kiʃ], *a.* fade, insipide; sottement sentimental.

maxim ['mæksim], *n.* maxime, *f.*

maximum ['mæksiməm], *n.* (*pl.* **maxima** ['mæksimə]) maximum, *m.*

May [mei]. mai (*mois*), *m.*

may [mei], *v.aux. irr.* pouvoir, être autorisé à; **he may go**, il peut sortir; **it may be that**, il se peut que (*with subj.*); **it might be**, cela se pourrait; **maybe**, peut-être; **may I?** puis-je? **one might as well**, autant vaudrait; **that may be**, cela se peut; **that might be**, cela pourrait être; **you might have gone there**, vous auriez pu y aller.

may-blossom ['meiblɔsəm], *n.* aubépine, *f.*

May Day ['meidei], *n.* premier mai, *m.*

mayor [mɛə], *n.* maire, *m.*

maze [meiz], *n.* labyrinthe, dédale; (*fig.*) embarras, *m.*

mazy ['meizi], *a.* sinueux; (*fig.*) compliqué.

mazurka [mə'zə:kə], *n.* mazurka, *f.*

me [mi:], *pron.* me, moi.

mead [mi:d], *n.* hydromel; (*poet.*) pré (*champ*), *m.*

meadow ['medou], *n.* pré, *m.*, prairie, *f.*

meager ['mi:gə], *a.* maigre; pauvre.

meagerness ['mi:gənis], *n.* maigreur; pauvreté, *f.*

meal (1) [mi:l], *n.* repas, *m.*

meal (2) [mi:l], *n.* farine, *f.*

mealy ['mi:li], *a.* farineux, poudreux.

mealy-mouthed ['mi:limauðd], *a.* doucereux.

mean (1) [mi:n], *a.* bas, méprisable, vil, abject; médiocre (*de peu de valeur*); mesquin; pauvre, humble; sordide; avare; **a mean trick**, un vilain tour.

mean (2) [mi:n], *a.* moyen.—*n.* milieu, moyen terme, *m.*; (*Math.*) moyenne, *f.*; **golden mean**, le juste milieu.

mean (3) [mi:n], *v.t. irr.* signifier, vouloir dire, entendre; se proposer de, avoir l'intention de, vouloir (*to intend*); destiner (*pour ou de*); **do you mean it?** êtes-vous sérieux? **what does that word mean?** que veut dire ce mot? **what do you mean?** que voulez-vous dire?—*v.i.* vouloir, entendre; **to mean well**, avoir de bonnes intentions.

482

melt

meander [mi'ændə], n. détour, méandre, m.,
sinuosité, f.—v.i. serpenter.
meandering [mi'ændəriŋ], a. onduleux,
sinueux, tortueux.
meaning ['ni:niŋ], a. significatif; à intentions; **well-meaning**, bien intentionné.—
n. signification, f., sens, m.; intention, f.,
dessein, m.; pensée (idée), f.; **double
meaning**, double sens.
meaningless ['mi:niŋlis], a. qui n'a pas de
sens, dénué de sens.
meanly ['mi:nli], adv. bassement; vilement;
abjectement; pauvrement; médiocrement.
meanness ['mi:nnis], n. bassesse; pauvreté,
mesquinerie; médiocrité, f.
means [mi:nz], n. moyen, m., voie, f.; moyens,
m.pl., fortune, f., ressources, f.pl.
meantime ['mi:ntaim], meanwhile ['mi:n
wail], n. and adv. **in the meantime**, dans
l'intervalle, en attendant, cependant, sur ces
entrefaites.
measles [mi:zlz], n.pl. rougeole, f.; **German
measles**, rubéole, f.
measurable ['meʒərəbl], a. mesurable.
measure ['meʒə], n. mesure; (fig.) capacité,
portée, f.; (Parl.) projet de loi, m.; assise (de
charbon), f.—v.t. mesurer; arpenter (terre);
prendre mesure à (une personne pour vêtements); (fig.) considérer, toiser, métrer; **this
measures ten feet**, ceci a dix pieds de
longueur.
measured ['meʒəd], a. mesuré; égal, cadencé.
measurement ['meʒəmənt], n. mesurage;
arpentage (de terre), m.; mesure, dimension,
f.
meat [mi:t], n. viande; nourriture, f., aliment
(manger), m.
meat-safe ['mi:tseif], n. garde-manger, m.
meaty ['mi:ti], a. charnu; (fig.) bien rempli.
Mecca ['mekə]. la Mecque, f.
mechanic [mi'kænik], n. artisan, ouvrier
mécanicien, m.; **garage mechanic**,
garagiste, m.
mechanical [mi'kænikəl], a. mécanique;
d'ouvrier; machinal (fait sans intelligence).
mechanically [mi'kænikli], adv. mécaniquement; machinalement (sans intelligence).
mechanics [mi'kæniks], n.pl. mécanique, f.
mechanism ['mekənizm], n. mécanisme, m.
mechanization [mekənai'zeiʃən], n. mécanisation, f.
mechanize ['mekənaiz], v.t. mécaniser;
mechanized farming, motoculture, f.;
mechanized army, armée motorisée, f.
medal [medl], n. médaille, f.
medallion [mi'dæljən], n. médaillon, m.
medallist ['medlist], n. médaillé (honoré), m.
meddle [medl], v.i. se mêler (de), toucher (à),
s'immiscer (dans).
meddler ['medlə], n. intrigant; officieux, m.
meddlesome ['medlsəm], meddling
['medliŋ], a. intrigant; officieux.
mediaeval [medi'i:vəl], a. du moyen âge.
medial ['mi:diəl], a. moyen; (Gram.) médial.
mediate ['mi:dieit], v.i. s'entremettre; s'interposer (dans).
mediation [mi:di'eiʃən], n. médiation, entremise, f.
mediator ['mi:dieitə], n. médiateur, m.
medical ['medikəl], a. médical; de médecine
(école); en médecine (étudiant); **medical

officer**, officier sanitaire, m.; **to take
medical advice**, consulter un médecin.
medicament [me'dikəmənt], n. médicament,
m.
medicinal [mə'disinl], a. médicinal.
medicine ['medsin], n. médecine, f., médicament; (fig.) remède, m.
medicine chest ['medsintʃest], n. pharmacie, f.
medicine man ['medsinmæn], n. sorcier, m.
mediocre ['mi:dioukə], a. médiocre.
mediocrity [mi:di'ɔkriti], n. médiocrité, f.
meditate ['mediteit], v.t. se proposer de,
projeter.—v.i. méditer (sur.).
meditation [medi'teiʃən], n. méditation, f.
Mediterranean [medito'reiniən], a. méditerrané; méditerranéen.—n. la Méditerranée, f.
medium ['mi:djəm], a. moyen.—n. (pl.
media ['mi:diə], **mediums** ['mi:djəmz])
milieu, moyen, m.; voie, entremise; (Math.)
moyenne proportionnelle, f.; agent intermédiaire; (Spiritualism) médium, m.
medlar ['medlə], n. nèfle (fruit), f.; néflier
(arbre), m.
medley ['medli], a. mêlé, hétéroclite.—n.
mélange, m.; confusion, f.; (Mus.) pot
pourri, m.
medulla [mi'dʌlə], n. médulle, moelle, f.
meed [mi:d], n. récompense; part (portion), f.
meek [mi:k], a. doux, humble, soumis.
meekly ['mi:kli], adv. avec douceur; humblement.
meekness ['mi:knis], n. douceur; humilité, f.
meet (1) [mi:t], v.t. irr. rencontrer, aller à la
rencontre de; trouver, recevoir (atteindre);
faire la connaissance de; faire face à, affronter (braver); se présenter devant (paraître
devant); faire honneur à (dette); (fig.) satisfaire, remplir (demande).—v.i. se rencontrer; se voir; se réunir, s'assembler; se
joindre (s'unir); **to meet half-way**, se
faire des concessions mutuelles.—n. rendez-
vous de chasse, m.
meet (2) [mi:t], a. propre, convenable.
meeting ['mi:tiŋ], n. rencontre; entrevue;
assemblée, réunion, f.; meeting, m.; séance
(session), f.; confluent (rivières), m.; jonction
(routes), f.
megaton ['megətɔn], n. mégatonne, f.
melancholy ['melənkəli], a. mélancolique,
triste, affligeant.—n. mélancolie, tristesse, f.
mellifluous [mə'lifluəs], a. mielleux, doucereux.
mellow ['melou], a. mûr, fondant (fruit);
moelleux, doux; gris (à moitié ivre); meuble
(terre).—v.t. mûrir, faire mûrir; ameublir
(terre); (fig.) adoucir.—v.i. mûrir; devenir
meuble (terre); (fig.) s'adoucir.
mellowness ['melounis], n. maturité, f.;
moelleux, m.; (fig.) douceur, f.
melodious [mə'loudiəs], a. mélodieux.
melodiously [mə'loudiəsli], adv. mélodieusement.
melodrama ['melədra:mə], n. mélodrame,
m.
melodramatic [melədrə'mætik], a. mélodramatique.
melody ['melədi], n. mélodie, f., air, m.
melon ['melən], n. melon, m.
melt [melt], v.t. fondre, faire fondre; (fig.)
attendrir.—v.i. fondre, se fondre; (fig.)
s'attendrir.

483

melting

melting ['meltiŋ], *a.* qui fond; fondant (*glace*); (*fig.*) attendrissant.—*n.* fusion, fonte, *f.*; attendrissement, *m.*

melting pot ['meltiŋpɔt], *n.* creuset, *m.*

member ['membə], *n.* membre; (*Parl.*) député, *m.*

membered ['membəd], *a.* membré; qui a des membres; *large-membered*, membru.

membership ['membəʃip], *n.* les membres d'une société etc., *m.pl.*

membrane ['membrein], *n.* membrane, *f.*

memento [mə'mentou], *n.* souvenir, mémento, *m.*

memoir ['memwɑ:], *n.* mémoire, *m.*

memorable ['memərəbl], *a.* mémorable.

memorandum [memə'rændəm], *n.* (*pl.* **memoranda** [memə'rændə]) note, *f.*, mémorandum; (*Comm.*) bordereau, *m.*

memorial [mi'mɔ:riəl], *a.* commémoratif.— *n.* souvenir, mémoire; monument commémoratif, *m.*; requête, pétition, *f.*

memorize ['meməraiz], *v.t.* apprendre par cœur.

memory ['meməri], *n.* mémoire, *f.*; (*colloq.*) souvenir, *m.*; *in memory of*, en souvenir de; *to the best of my memory*, autant qu'il m'en souvient.

men [MAN].

menace ['menəs], *n.* menace, *f.*—*v.t.* menacer.

menagerie [mə'nædʒəri], *n.* ménagerie, *f.*

mend [mend], *v.t.* raccommoder, réparer; corriger, améliorer; *to mend one's ways*, rentrer dans le bon chemin.—*v.i.* s'améliorer, se corriger; se rétablir (*santé*); se remettre au beau (*temps*).

mendacious [men'deiʃəs], *a.* mensonger.

mendacity [men'dæsiti], *n.* mensonge, *m.*; duplicité, *f.*

mendicant ['mendikənt], *a. and n.* mendiant, *m.*

mendicity [men'disiti], *n.* mendicité, *f.*

mending ['mendiŋ], *n.* raccommodage; reprisage (*des bas*), *m.*; réparation, *f.*

menial ['mi:niəl], *a.* de domestique; (*fig.*) servile.—*n.* domestique, *m.*, *f.*; (*fig.*) valet, laquais, *m.*

meningitis [menin'dʒaitis], *n.* méningite, *f.*

mental [mentl], *a.* mental; *a mental case*, un aliéné.

mentality [men'tæliti], *n.* mentalité, *f.*; esprit, *m.*

mention ['menʃən], *n.* mention, indication, *f.* —*v.t.* dire, faire mention de, mentionner, parler de; citer; *don't mention it!* il n'y a pas de quoi! *not to mention*, sans compter.

menu ['menju], *n.* menu, *m.*, carte, *f.*

mercantile ['mə:kəntail], *a.* marchand, de commerce, commerçant; *mercantile marine*, marine marchande, *f.*

mercenary ['mə:sənri], *a.* mercenaire, vénal. —*n.* mercenaire, *f.*

merchandise ['mə:tʃəndaiz], *n.* marchandise, *f.*

merchant ['mə:tʃənt], *a.* marchand; commercial.—*n.* négociant, commerçant; marchand en gros, *m.*

merchantman ['mə:tʃəntmən] (*pl.* **-men** [men]), **merchant ship** ['mə:tʃəntʃip], *n.* navire marchand, *m.*

merchant marine ['mə:tʃənt mə'ri:n], *n.* marine marchande, *f.*

merciful ['mə:siful], *a.* miséricordieux.

merciless ['mə:silis], *a.* sans pitié, impitoyable.

mercurial [mə:'kjuəriəl], *a.* de Mercure; de mercure; (*fig.*) mercuriel, vif.

mercury ['mə:kjuəri], *n.* mercure, *m.*

mercy ['mə:si], *n.* miséricorde; pitié; grâce, indulgence (*pardon*), *f.*; *for mercy's sake*, par grâce; *recommendation to mercy*, recours en grâce, *m.*; *sisters of mercy*, sœurs de charité, *f.pl.*

mere (1) [miə], *n.* lac, étang, *m.*

mere (2) [miə], *a.* pur, simple, seul, rien que.

merely ['miəli], *adv.* simplement, seulement, rien que.

meretricious [meri'triʃəs], *a.* d'un éclat factice (*style*).

merge [mə:dʒ], *v.t.* fondre, amalgamer, absorber.—*v.i.* se perdre (*dans*).

merger ['mə:dʒə], *n.* fusion, *f.*

meridian [mə'ridiən], *a.* méridien; de midi. —*n.* méridien; (*fig.*) apogée, *m.*

merino [mə'ri:nou], *n.* mérinos, *m.*

merit ['merit], *n.* mérite, *m.*—*v.t.* mériter.

meritorious [meri'tɔ:riəs], *a.* méritoire (*choses*); méritant (*personnes*).

meritoriously [meri'tɔ:riəsli], *adv.* d'une manière méritoire.

mermaid ['mə:meid], *n.* sirène, *f.*

merrily ['merili], *adv.* joyeusement, gaiement.

merriment ['merimənt], *n.* gaieté, réjouissance, *f.*

merry ['meri], *a.* joyeux, gai, plaisant; un peu gris; *to make merry*, se réjouir, se divertir.

merry-go-round ['merigouraund], *n.* chevaux de bois, *m.pl.*; manège, *m.*

merry-making ['merimeikiŋ], *n.* réjouissance, fête, *f.*, divertissement, *m.*

mesh [meʃ], *n.* maille, *f.*; engrenage, *m.*

mesmerism ['mezmərizm], *n.* mesmérisme, magnétisme animal, *m.*

mesmerize ['mezməraiz], *v.t.* magnétiser; hypnotiser.

mess (1) [mes], *n.* gâchis, *m.*; saleté, *f.*; *to be in a fine mess*, être dans de beaux draps; *what a mess!* quel gâchis!—*v.t.* salir.— *v.i.* faire du gâchis.

mess (2) [mes], *n.* mets, plat; (*Mil.*) mess, *m.*; *mess tin*, gamelle (individuelle), *f.*—*v.t.* donner à manger à.—*v.i.* manger; manger ensemble.

message ['mesidʒ], *n.* message, *m.*, commission, *f.*

messenger ['mesəndʒə], *n.* messager; commissionnaire; coursier (*dans un bureau*); (*fig.*) avant-coureur, *m.*

Messiah [mə'saiə], *n.* Messie, *m.*

messmate ['mesmeit], *n.* camarade de table, *m.*

messy ['mesi], *a.* sale; graisseux, salissant.

metabolism [mə'tæbolizm], *n.* métabolisme, *m.*

metal [metl], *n.* métal; cailloutis, empierrement (*pour routes*), *m.*

metalled [metld], *a.* empierré.

metallic [mə'tælik], *a.* métallique.

metallurgy [me'tælədʒi], *n.* métallurgie, *f.*

metamorphosis [metə'mɔ:fəsis], *n.* métamorphose, *f.*

metaphor ['metəfə], *n.* métaphore, *f.*

metaphysical [metə'fizikl], *a.* métaphysique.

metaphysics [metə'fiziks], *n.pl.* métaphysique, *f.*

mete [mi:t], *v.t.* mesurer; *to mete out*, distribuer, décerner (*prix*); assigner (*punitions*).

meteor ['mi:tiə], *n.* météore, *m.*

meteoric [mi:ti'orik], *a.* météorique.

meteorite ['mi:tiərait], *n.* météorite, *m.* ou *f.*

meteorological [mi:tiərə'lodʒikl], *a.* météorologique.

meteorologist [mi:tiə'rolədʒist], *n.* météorologiste, *m., f.*

meteorology [mi:tiə'rolədʒi], *n.* météorologie, *f.*

meter ['mi:tə], *n.* mesureur; compteur (*de gaz*), *m.*

method ['meθəd], *n.* méthode, *f.*; procédé, *m.*; modalité; (*fig.*) manière, *f.*, ordre, *m.*

methodical [mə'θodikəl], *a.* méthodique.

methylate ['meθileit], *v.t.* méthyler; *methylated spirit*, alcool à brûler, *m.*

meticulous [mə'tikjuləs], *a.* méticuleux.

meticulousness [mə'tikjuləsnis], *n.* méticulosité, *f.*

metre ['mi:tə], *n.* mètre, *m.*; (*Pros.*) vers, *m.,* mesure, *f.*

metric ['metrik], *a.* métrique.

metrical ['metrikl], *a.* métrique; en vers.

metropolis [mə'trɔpəlis], *n.* capitale, métropole, *f.*

metropolitan [metrə'politən], *a.* de la capitale, métropolitain.

mettle [metl], *n.* courage, cœur, *m.*; fougue, ardeur, vivacité, *f.*; caractère, *m.*; *to put someone on his mettle*, piquer quelqu'un d'honneur.

mettled [metld], **mettlesome** ['metlsəm], *a.* fougueux, ardent, vif.

mew (1) [mju:], *n.* mue, cage, *f.*; (*pl.*) écuries, *f.pl.*; impasse, ruelle (*derrière les grandes maisons de ville*), *f.*—*v.t.* enfermer (*emprisonner*).

mew (2) [mju:], *v.i.* miauler (*chat*).

mew (3) [mju:], *n.* (*Orn.*) mouette, *f.*

mewing ['mju:iŋ], *n.* miaulement (*de chat*), *m.*

Mexican ['meksikn], *a.* mexicain.—*n.* Mexicain (*personne*), *m.*

Mexico ['meksikou], le Mexique (*pays*); *Mexico City*, Mexico, *m.*

miasma [mi'æzmə], *n.* (*pl.* **miasmata** [mi'æzmətə]) miasme, *m.*

mica ['maikə], *n.* mica, *m.*

mice [MOUSE].

Michael [maikl], Michel, *m.*

Michaelmas ['miklməs], la Saint-Michel, *f.*

microbe ['maikroub], *n.* microbe, *m.*

microphone ['maikrəfoun], *n.* microphone, *m.*

microscope ['maikrəskoup], *n.* microscope, *m.*

microscopic [maikrə'skɔpik], *a.* microscopique.

mid [mid], *a.* du milieu, moyen.—*prep.* au milieu de.

mid-air [mid'ɛə], *n.* milieu de l'air, haut des airs, *m.*; *in mid-air*, entre ciel et terre.

midday ['middei], *a.* de midi.—*n.* midi, *m.*

middle [midl], *a.* du milieu, moyen, central; *Middle Ages*, Moyen Âge, *m.*; *middle class*, bourgeoisie, *f.*; *middle course*, moyen terme, *m.*—*n.* milieu, centre, *m.*; ceinture, *f.*

middle-aged ['midleidʒd], *a.* entre deux âges.

middle-man ['midlmæn], *n.* (*pl.* **-men** [men]) intermédiaire, tiers, *m.*

middling ['midliŋ], *a.* médiocre, passable, assez bien (*santé*); (*Comm.*) bon, ordinaire.

midget ['midʒit], *n.* nain, nabot, *m.*

midland ['midlənd], *a.* de l'intérieur, du centre.

Mid-Lent ['mid'lent], mi-carême, *f.*

midnight ['midnait], *a.* de minuit.—*n.* minuit, *m.*

midriff ['midrif], *n.* diaphragme, *m.*

midshipman ['midʃipmən], *n.* (*pl.* **-men** [men]) aspirant de marine, *m.*

midships ['midʃips], [AMIDSHIPS].

midst [midst], *n.* milieu; (*fig.*) fort, sein, cœur, *m.*—*prep.* au milieu de, parmi.

midstream ['midstri:m], *n.* milieu du courant; milieu du fleuve, *m.*

midsummer ['midsʌmə], *n.* milieu de l'été, cœur de l'été, *m.*; *Midsummer Day*, la Saint-Jean, *f.*

midway ['midwei], *a.* and *adv.* à mi-chemin; à mi-côte (*d'une colline*).

midwife ['midwaif], *n.* (*pl.* **midwives** ['midwaivz]) sage-femme, accoucheuse, *f.*

midwifery ['midwifri], *n.* obstétrique, *f.*

midwinter ['midwintə], *n.* fort de l'hiver, *m.*

mien [mi:n], *n.* mine, *f.*, air, *m.*

might (1) [mait], *past* [MAY].

might (2) [mait], *n.* force, puissance, *f.*

mightily ['maitili], *adv.* fortement, vigoureusement; extrêmement.

mighty ['maiti], *a.* fort, puissant; grand, important.—*adv.* fort, très, extrêmement.

mignonette [minjə'net], *n.* réséda, *m.*

migraine ['mi:grein], *n.* (*Med.*) migraine, *f.*

migrate [mai'greit], *v.i.* émigrer.

migration [mai'greiʃən], *n.* migration, *f.*

migratory ['maigrətəri], *a.* migratoire; migrateur.

milch [miltʃ], *a.* à lait, laitière.

mild [maild], *a.* doux; léger (*boisson, tabac etc.*); bénin.

mildew ['mildju:], *n.* rouille, moisissure, *f.*, taches d'humidité, *f.pl.*—*v.t.* gâter par l'humidité; souiller, tacher.

mildly ['maildli], *adv.* doucement, avec douceur; modérément.

mildness ['maildnis], *n.* douceur, *f.*

mile [mail], *n.* mille, *m.*

mileage ['mailidʒ], *n.* distance en milles, *f.*; prix par mille, *m.*

milestone ['mailstoun], *n.* borne milliaire, borne kilométrique, *f.*

militant ['militənt], *a.* militant.—*n.* activiste, *m., f.*

militarism ['militərizm], *n.* militarisme, *m.*

military ['militəri], *a.* militaire.—*n. the military*, les militaires, *m.pl.*, la troupe, *f.*

militate ['militeit], *v.i.* militer (*contre*).

militia [mi'liʃə], *n.* milice, *f.*

milk [milk], *n.* lait, *m.*; *milk and water*, lait coupé; (*fig.*) fade, insipide, sans caractère; *skim milk*, lait écrémé; *to come home with the milk*, rentrer à la première heure.—*v.t.* traire.

milk can ['milkkæn], *n.* pot au lait, *m.*

milkiness ['milkinis], *n.* nature laiteuse; (*fig.*) douceur, *f.*

milkmaid ['milkmeid], *n.* laitière, *f.*

milkman ['milkmən], *n.* (*pl.* **-men** [men]) laitier, *m.*

milk pail ['milkpeil], *n.* seau à lait, *m.*

milksop ['milksɔp], *n.* (*colloq.*) poule mouillée, *f.*

milky ['milki], *a.* laiteux; **Milky Way**, voie lactée, *f.*

mill [mil], *n.* moulin, *m.*; filature, fabrique (*usine*), *f.*—*v.t.* moudre; (*Coin.*) estamper.—*v.i.* fourmiller (*foule*).

millenary ['milənəri], *a.* millénaire.

millennium [mi'leniəm], *n.* millénaire, *m.*, mille ans; les temps messianiques, *m.pl.*

miller ['milə], *n.* meunier, *m.*

millet ['milit], *n.* millet, mil, *m.*

millimetre ['milimi:tə], *n.* millimètre, *m.*

milliner ['milinə], *n.* marchande de modes; modiste, *f.*

millinery ['milinri], *n.* modes, *f.pl.*

million ['miljən], *n.* million, *m.*

millionaire [miljə'nɛə], *n.* millionnaire, *m.*, *f.*

millstone ['milstoun], *n.* meule de moulin, *f.*

mime [maim], *n.* mime, *m.*—*v.t.* mimer (*une scène*).—*v.i.* jouer par gestes.

mimic ['mimik], *a.* imitateur, mimique; imitatif (*animaux*).—*n.* mime, imitateur, *m.* —*v.t.* contrefaire, imiter.

mimicry ['mimikri], *n.* mimique, imitation, *f.*

minatory ['minətəri], *a.* menaçant.

mince [mins], *v.t.* hacher menu.—*v.i.* marcher à petits pas; minauder (*parler d'une façon affectée*).—*n.* hachis, haché, *m.*

mincemeat ['minsmi:t], *n.* pâte d'épices, *f.*, mincemeat, *m.*

mince pie ['mins'pai], *n.* tartelette au mincemeat, *f.*

mincing ['minsiŋ], *a.* affecté, minaudier.

mind [maind], *n.* esprit, *m.*, intelligence; envie, *f.*, désir (*inclination*), *m.*; pensée, *f.*, avis (*opinion*); souvenir (*mémoire*), *m.*—*v.t.* songer à, faire attention à; regarder à (*s'occuper de*); se défier de (*se douter de*); obéir à, écouter (*se soumettre à*); soigner, garder (*veiller sur*); surveiller, observer (*étudier*); **mind your own business**, mêlez-vous de ce qui vous regarde; **never mind**, n'importe, tant pis.

minded ['maindid], *a.* disposé, enclin.

mindful ['maindful], *a.* attentif (*à*), soigneux (*de*); qui se souvient (*de*).

mindfulness ['maindfulnis], *n.* attention, *f.*

mindless ['maindlis], *a.* inattentif (*à*); sans esprit.

mine (1) [main], *pron.poss.* le mien, *m.*, la mienne, *f.*; les miens, *m.pl.*, les miennes, *f.pl.*—*a.* à moi; **a friend of mine**, un de mes amis.

mine (2) [main], *n.* mine, *f.*—*v.t.* miner, saper.

mine-layer ['mainleiə], *n.* (*Navy*) mouilleur de mines, *m.*

miner ['mainə], *n.* mineur, *m.*

mineral ['minərəl], *a.* and *n.* minéral, *m.*

mineralogy [minə'rælədʒi], *n.* minéralogie, *f.*

mine-sweeper ['mainswi:pə], *n.* (*Navy*) dragueur de mines, *m.*

mingle [miŋgl], *v.t.* mélanger, mêler.—*v.i.* se mêler, se mélanger (*avec, dans* ou *en*).

mingling ['miŋgliŋ], *n.* mélange, *m.*

miniature ['mini(ə)tʃə], *a.* en miniature.—*n.* miniature, *f.*

minim ['minim], *n.* goutte, *f.*; (*Mus.*) blanche, *f.*

minimum ['miniməm], *n.* (*pl.* **minima** ['minimə]) minimum, *m.*

mining ['mainiŋ], *a.* des mines; de mineur, minier.—*n.* travail dans les mines, *m.*

minion ['minjən], *n.* favori, *m.*, favorite, *f.*

minister ['ministə], *n.* ministre; (*Eccles.*) pasteur, *m.*—*v.t.* administrer; fournir.—*v.i.* servir (*à*); (*Eccles.*) officier à.

ministerial [minis'tiəriəl], *a.* de ministère, ministériel.

ministration [minis'treiʃən], *n.* ministère; service, *m.*

ministry ['ministri], *n.* ministère, département, *m.*

mink [miŋk], *n.* vison, *m.*

minnow ['minou], *n.* vairon, *m.*

minor ['mainə], *a.* moindre; secondaire; (*Mus., Geog. etc.*) mineur.—*n.* mineur, *m.*

Minorca [mi'nɔ:kə], Minorque, *f.*

minority [mai'nɔriti], *n.* minorité, *f.*

minster ['minstə], *n.* cathédrale, église abbatiale, *f.*

minstrel ['minstrəl], *n.* ménestrel; (*fam.*) poète, musicien, chanteur, *m.*

mint (1) [mint], *n.* menthe, *f.*; **peppermint**, menthe poivrée.

mint (2) [mint], *n.* **The Mint**, la Monnaie, *f.* —*v.t.* monnayer, frapper; (*fig.*) forger.

mintage ['mintidʒ], *n.* objet monnayé, *m.*

minting ['mintiŋ], *n.* monnayage, *m.*

minuet [minju'et], *n.* menuet, *m.*

minus ['mainəs], *prep.* moins; sans (*n'ayant pas de*).—*n.* moins, *m.*

minute (1) [mai'nju:t], *a.* menu, minuscule, très petit; minutieux.

minute (2) ['minit], *n.* minute, *f.*; instant; moment, *m.*; note, *f.*; (*pl.*) procès-verbal, compte-rendu (*d'une réunion*), *m.*—*v.t.* minuter, prendre note de.

minute-book ['minitbuk], *n.* journal, *m.*

minute hand ['minithænd], *n.* grande aiguille, *f.*

minutely [mai'nju:tli], *adv.* minutieusement; exactement; en détail.

minuteness [mai'nju:tnis], *n.* petitesse; exactitude, *f.*; détails minutieux, *m.pl.*

minx [miŋks], *n.* coquine, friponne, *f.*

miracle ['mirəkl], *n.* miracle, *m.*

miraculous [mi'rækjuləs], *a.* miraculeux.

mirage ['mira:ʒ], *n.* mirage, *m.*

mire ['maiə], *n.* boue, bourbe, fange, vase, *f.*

miry ['maiəri], *a.* fangeux, bourbeux.

mirror ['mirə], *n.* miroir, *m.*, glace, *f.*; **rearview mirror**, rétroviseur, *m.* —*v.t.* refléter.

mirth [mə:θ], *n.* gaieté, hilarité, *f.*, rire, *m.*

mirthful ['mə:θful], *a.* gai, joyeux.

misadventure [misəd'ventʃə], *n.* mésaventure, *f.*, contretemps, *m.*

misanthropist [mi'sænθrəpist], *n.* misanthrope, *m.*, *f.*

misanthropy [mi'sænθrəpi], *n.* misanthropie, *f.*

misapplication [misæpli'keiʃən], *n.* mauvaise application, *f.*

misapply [misə'plai], *v.t.* mal appliquer, détourner (*fonds etc.*).

misapprehend [misæpri'hend], *v.t.* comprendre mal.

misapprehension [misæpri'henʃən], *n.* malentendu, *m.*, méprise, *f.*

misappropriate [misə'prouprieit], *v.t.* détourner.

misappropriation [misəproupri'eiʃən], *n.* détournement, mauvais emploi, *m.*

misbehave [misbi'heiv], *v.i.* se conduire mal.

misbehavior [misbi'heivjə], *n.* mauvaise conduite, *f.*

miscalculate [mis'kælkjuleit], *v.t.* calculer mal.

miscalculation [miskælkju'leiʃən], *n.* calcul erroné; mécompte, *m.*

miscarriage [mis'kæridʒ], *n.* insuccès, coup manqué, *m.*; fausse couche (*de femme*), *f.*

miscarry [mis'kæri], *v.i.* manquer, échouer; faire une fausse couche (*femme*).

miscellaneous [misi'leinjəs], *a.* varié, divers; général; *miscellaneous news*, faits divers, *m.pl.*

miscellany [mi'seləni], *n.* (*pl.* **miscellanies** [mi'seləniz]) mélange, *m.*; mélanges (*livre*), *m.pl.*

mischance [mis'tʃɑːns], *n.* malheur, accident, *m.*, mésaventure, infortune, *f.*

mischief ['mistʃif], *n.* mal, dommage, dégât, tort, *m.*

mischief-maker ['mistʃifmeikə], *n.* brouillon, *m.*

mischievous ['mistʃivəs], *a.* méchant, malicieux; malfaisant, mauvais, nuisible (*chose*); espiègle (*enfant*).

mischievously ['mistʃivəsli], *adv.* méchamment.

mischievousness ['mistʃivəsnis], *n.* méchanceté; espièglerie (*d'enfant*), *f.*

misconceive [miskən'siːv], *v.t.*, *v.i.* mal concevoir, juger mal.

misconception [miskən'sepʃən], *n.* malentendu, *m.*

misconduct [mis'kɔndʌkt], *n.* mauvaise conduite, *f.*—[miskən'dʌkt], *v.t.* conduire mal; *to misconduct oneself*, se conduire mal.

misconstruction [miskən'strʌkʃən], *n.* fausse interprétation, *f.*, contresens, *m.*

misconstrue [miskən'struː], *v.t.* mal interpréter.

miscount [mis'kaunt], *v.t.* compter mal.—*v.i.* faire une erreur de compte.—*n.* mécompte, *m.*

miscreant ['miskriənt], *n.* mécréant, *m*; (*fig.*) misérable, *m.*, *f.*

misdeal [mis'diːl], *v.t.* maldonner.—*n.* maldonne, *f.*

misdeed [mis'diːd], *n.* méfait, *m.*

misdemean [misdə'miːn], *v.r.* *to misdemean oneself*, se comporter mal.

misdemeanor [misdə'miːnə], *n.* délit, crime, *m.*, offense, *f.*

misdirect [misdi'rekt], *v.t.* mal diriger, renseigner mal; mettre une fausse adresse à (*lettre*).

misdoing [mis'duːiŋ], *n.* méfait, *m.*

miser ['maizə], *n.* avare, *m.*, *f.*

miserable ['mizərəbl], *a.* misérable, pitoyable, malheureux; mesquin (*piètre*).

miserliness ['maizəlinis], *n.* avarice, *f.*

miserly ['maizəli], *a.* d'avare, avare, sordide.

misery ['mizəri], *n.* misère, *f.*; (*fig.*) tourment; supplice, *m.*; *to put out of misery*, mettre fin aux souffrances (*de*).

misfire [mis'faiə], *v.i.* rater; (*Motor.*) avoir des ratés.—*n.* raté d'allumage, *m.*

misfit ['misfit], *n.* vêtement manqué; inadapté (*personne*), *m.*

misfortune [mis'fɔːtʃən], *n.* malheur, *m.*, infortune, *f.*

misgiving [mis'giviŋ], *n.* pressentiment, soupçon, doute, *m.*; inquiétude, *f.*

misgovern [mis'gʌvən], *v.t.* gouverner mal.

misgovernment [mis'gʌvənmənt], *n.* mauvais gouvernement, *m.*

misguided [mis'gaidid], *a.* malencontreux; peu judicieux; dévoyé.

mishandle [mis'hændl], *v.t.* manier mal, malmener.

mishap [mis'hæp], *n.* contretemps, malheur, *m.*, mésaventure, *f.*

misinform [misin'fɔːm], *v.t.* mal renseigner.

misinterpret [misin'təːprit], *v.t.* interpréter mal.

misjudge [mis'dʒʌdʒ], *v.t.* juger mal, méjuger.

mislay [mis'lei], *v.t. irr.* (*conjug. like* LAY) égarer.

mislead [mis'liːd], *v.t. irr.* (*conjug. like* LEAD) égarer; induire en erreur, fourvoyer; tromper.

misleading [mis'liːdiŋ], *a.* trompeur.

mismanage [mis'mænidʒ], *v.t.* diriger mal. —*v.i.* s'y prendre mal, s'arranger mal (*pour*).

mismanagement [mis'mænidʒmənt], *n.* mauvaise administration, *f.*

misnomer [mis'noumə], *n.* faux nom, *m.*

misogynist [mi'sɔdʒinist], *n.* misogyne, *m.*

misogyny [mi'sɔdʒini], *n.* misogynie, *f.*

misplace [mis'pleis], *v.t.* mal placer; déplacer.

misprint ['misprint], *n.* faute d'impression, *f.* —[mis'print], *v.t.* imprimer incorrectement.

mispronounce [misprə'nauns], *v.t.* prononcer mal.

mispronunciation [misprʌnʌnsi'eiʃən], *n.* prononciation incorrecte, *f.*

misquote [mis'kwout], *v.t.* citer à faux.

misread [mis'riːd], *v.t. irr.* (*conjug. like* READ) mal lire, mal interpréter.

misrepresent [misrepri'zent], *v.t.* représenter mal, dénaturer.

misrepresentation [misreprizen'teiʃən], *n.* faux rapport, *m.*

misrule [mis'ruːl], *n.* désordre; mauvais gouvernement, *m.*

miss (1) [mis], *n.* mademoiselle, demoiselle, *f.*

miss (2) [mis], *n.* manque, *m.*; perte (*privation*); erreur (*méprise*), *f.*; coup manqué, *m.* —*v.t.* manquer; omettre; s'apercevoir de l'absence de, regretter vivement, ne plus trouver; *I miss my friend very much*, mon ami me manque beaucoup.—*v.i.* manquer; ne pas réussir, échouer, se tromper; *to be missing*, être absent, manquer.

missal [misl], *n.* missel, *m.*

misshapen [mis'ʃeipən], *a.* difforme.

missile ['misail], *a.* de jet, de trait.—*n.* projectile, *m.*; *guided missile*, engin téléguidé, *m.*

missing ['misiŋ], *a.* absent, perdu, disparu.

mission ['miʃən], *n.* mission, *f.*

missionary ['miʃənəri], *a.* des missions.—*n.* missionnaire, *m.*, *f.*

missive ['misiv], *a.* missive.—*n.* missive, lettre, *f.*

misspell [mis'spel], *v.t. irr.* (*conjug. like* SPELL) épeler mal.

misspelling [mis'spelin], *n.* faute d'orthographe, *f.*

misspend [mis'spend], *v.t. irr. (conjug. like* SPEND) employer mal; gaspiller.

misstate [mis'steit], *v.t.* rapporter incorrectement.

misstatement [mis'steitmənt], *n.* rapport erroné, *m.*

mist [mist], *n.* brume; buée (*sur une glace*), *f.*; **Scotch mist**, bruine, *f.—v.t.* couvrir (*une glace*) de buée.—*v.i.* se couvrir de buée.

mistake [mis'teik], *v.t. irr. (conjug. like* TAKE) se tromper de *ou* sur, se méprendre à *ou* sur; tromper.—*v.i.* se tromper, se méprendre, s'abuser.—*n.* erreur, méprise, faute; bévue (*erreur grossière*), *f.*; **to make a mistake**, se tromper.

mistaken [mis'teikən] *a.* qui se trompe; faux, erroné (*chose*).

mistimed [mis'taimd], *a.* inopportun.

mistletoe [misltou], *n.* gui, *m.*

mistress [mistris], *n.* maîtresse; patronne; institutrice (*d'école primaire*), *f.*; **head-mistress**, directrice, *f.*

mistrust [mis'trʌst], *n.* méfiance, *f.*, soupçon, *m.—v.t.* se méfier de, soupçonner.

mistrustful [mis'trʌstful], *a.* méfiant.

misty [misti], *a.* brumeux; vaporeux (*lumière*); (*fig.*) confus.

misunderstand [misʌndə'stænd], *v.t. irr. (conjug. like* STAND) mal comprendre, entendre mal, se méprendre sur.

misunderstanding [misʌndə'stændiŋ], *n.* malentendu (*manque de compréhension*), *m.*; mésintelligence (*querelle*), *f.*

misuse [mis'ju:s], *n.* abus, *m.*—[mis'ju:z], *v.t.* mésuser de; maltraiter (*faire du mal à*).

mite (1) [mait], *n.* (*Zool.*) mite, *f.*

mite (2) [mait], *n.* denier (*argent*); (*fig.*) rien, *m.*, obole, *f.*; (*fam.*) petit gosse, *m.*

miter ['maitə], *n.* mitre, *f.*

mitigate ['mitigeit], *v.t.* mitiger, adoucir, modérer.

mitigating ['mitigeitiŋ], *a.* adoucissant, atténuant.

mitigation [miti'geiʃən], *n.* mitigation, *f.*, adoucissement, *m.*

mitten [mitn], *n.* mitaine, *f.*

mix [miks], *v.t.* mêler, mélanger; couper (*boissons*); **to mix up**, mêler, embrouiller, confondre.—*v.i.* se mélanger, se mêler (*de*); s'associer (*à*).

mixed [mikst], *a.* mélangé, mêlé (*de*); mixte.

mixture ['mikstʃə], *n.* mélange, *m.*; (*Pharm.*) potion, mixture, *f.*

mix-up ['miksʌp], *n.* confusion, *f.*, embrouillement, *m.*; (*pop.*) pagaïe, *f.*

mizzen [mizn], *n.* artimon, *m.*

mizzen-mast ['miznmɑ:st], *n.* mât d'artimon, *m.*

moan [moun], *n.* gémissement *m.*, plainte; (*fig.*) lamentation, *f.—v.t.* gémir de *ou* sur; se lamenter sur.—*v.i.* gémir; (*fig.*) se lamenter; (*pop.*) grognonner.

moat [mout], *n.* fossé, *m.*, douve, *f.*

mob [mɔb], *n.* foule; populace, canaille, *f.—v.t.* houspiller, malmener; assiéger.

mobile ['moubail], *a.* mobile.

mobility [mou'biliti], *n.* mobilité; légèreté (*inconstance*), *f.*

mobilization [moubilai'zeiʃən], *n.* mobilisation, *f.*

mobilize ['moubilaiz], *v.t.* mobiliser.

mock [mɔk], *v.t.* se moquer de; narguer.—*v.i.* railler.—*a.* dérisoire; faux, simulé.

mocker ['mɔkə], *n.* moqueur, *m.*

mockery ['mɔkəri], *n.* moquerie, *f.*

mocking-bird ['mɔkiŋbə:d], *n.* oiseau moqueur, *m.*

mode [moud], *n.* mode, façon, manière, *f.*

model [mɔdl], *n.* modèle, mannequin, *m.—v.t.* modeler; (*Cloth.*) présenter des vêtements (*défilé de mannequins*).

moderate ['mɔdərit], *a.* modéré; modique, ordinaire, passable, médiocre.—['mɔdəreit], *v.t.* modérer, adoucir, tempérer.—*v.i.* se modérer.

moderately ['mɔdəritli], *adv.* modérément, passablement.

moderation [mɔdə'reiʃən], *n.* modération, *f.*

moderator ['mɔdəreitə], *n.* modérateur, *m.*

modern ['mɔdən], *a.* and *n.* moderne, *m.*, *f.*; **modern languages**, langues vivantes, *f.pl.*

modernize ['mɔdənaiz], *v.t.* moderniser.

modest ['mɔdist], *a.* modeste; pudique; modéré (*demandes etc.*).

modesty ['mɔdisti], *n.* modestie, *f.*

modicum ['mɔdikəm], *n.* petite portion, *f.*

modification [mɔdifi'keiʃən], *n.* modification, *f.*

modify ['mɔdifai], *v.t.* modifier.

modulate ['mɔdjuleit], *v.t.* moduler.

modulation [mɔdju'leiʃən], *n.* modulation, *f.*

mohair ['mouhɛə], *n.* poil de chèvre angora, mohair, *m.*

Mohammed [mo'hæməd]. Mahomet, *m.*

Mohammedan [mo'hæmədən], *a.* mahométan.—*n.* Mahométan, *m.*

Mohammedanism [mo'hæmədənizm], *n.* mahométisme, *m.*

moist [mɔist], *a.* moite, humide.

moisten [mɔisn], *v.t.* humecter; mouiller.

moisture ['mɔistʃə], **moistness** ['mɔistnis], *n.* moiteur, humidité, *f.*

mol-, see **moul-**.

molasses [mo'læsiz], *n.pl.* mélasse, *f.*

mole (1) [moul], *n.* taupe (*animal*), *f.*

mole (2) [moul], *n.* tache, *f.*, grain de beauté (*sur la peau*), *m.*

mole (3) [moul], *n.* môle (*jetée*), *m.*

molecular [mo'lekjulə], *a.* moléculaire.

molecule ['mɔlikju:l], *n.* molécule *f.*

mole-hill ['moulhil], *n.* taupinière, *f.*

moleskin ['moulskin], *n.* peau de taupe, molesquine, *f.*, velours de coton, *m.*

molest [mo'lest], *v.t.* molester; vexer.

mollify ['mɔlifai], *v.t.* amollir; adoucir.

molten ['moultən], *a.* fondu.

moment ['moumənt], *n.* moment, instant, *m.*; (*fig.*) importance, *f.*; **at the present moment**, actuellement; **at this moment**, en ce moment; **not for a moment**, pour rien au monde; **of no moment**, d'aucune importance; **the moment that**, dès que, aussitôt que.

momentarily ['moumentərili], *adv.* momentanément.

momentary ['moumentəri], *a.* momentané.

momentous [mo'mentəs], *a.* important, d'une importance capitale.

momentum [mo'mentəm], *n.* (*Phys.*) force vive; vitesse acquise, *f.*; élan, *m.*

monarch ['mɔnək], *n.* monarque, *m.*

mortar

monarchy ['mɔnəki], *n.* monarchie, *f.*
monastery ['mɔnəstri], *n.* monastère, *m.*
monastic [mə'næstik], *a.* monastique.
monasticism [mə'næstisizm], *n.* monachisme, *m.*
Monday ['mʌndi], lundi, *m.*
monetary ['mʌnətəri], *a.* monétaire.
money ['mʌni], *n.* argent, *m.*; monnaie, *f.*, espèces (*pièces*), *f.pl.*; *made of money*, cousu d'or; *ready money*, argent comptant; *to make money*, gagner de l'argent.
money box ['mʌnibɔks], *n.* tirelire, *f.*
money-changer ['mʌnitʃeindʒə], *n.* changeur, *m.*
moneyed ['mʌnid], *a.* riche.
money grubber ['mʌnigrʌbə], *n.* grippe-sou, *m.*
money-lender ['mʌnilendə], *n.* prêteur d'argent, *m.*
money market ['mʌniməːkit], *n.* bourse, *f.*
money order ['mʌniɔːdə], *n.* mandat, *m.*
Mongol ['mɔŋgɔl], *a.* mongol.—*n.* Mongol (*personne*), *m.*
Mongolia [mɔŋ'gouliə], la Mongolie, *f.*
Mongolian [mɔŋ'gouliən], *a.* mongol.—*n.* mongol (*langue*); Mongol (*personne*), *m.*
mongrel ['mʌŋgrəl], *a.* métis.—*n.* métis, *m.*, métisse, *f.*
monitor ['mɔnitə], *n.* moniteur, *m.*
monk [mʌŋk], *n.* moine, *m.*
monkey ['mʌŋki], *n.* singe, *m.*; guenon, *f.*
monkey wrench ['mʌŋkirentʃ], *n.* clé anglaise, *f.*
monocle ['mɔnəkl], *n.* monocle, *m.*
monogram ['mɔnəgræm], *n.* monogramme, *m.*
monologue ['mɔnəlɔg], *n.* monologue, *m.*
monoplane ['mɔnəplein], *n.* monoplan, *m.*
monopoly [mə'nɔpəli], *n.* monopole, accaparement, *m.*
monorail ['mɔnəreil], *n.* monorail, *m.*
monotonous [mə'nɔtənəs], *a.* monotone.
monotonously [mə'nɔtənəsli], *adv.* avec monotonie.
monotony [mə'nɔtəni], *n.* monotonie, *f.*
monsoon [mɔn'suːn], *n.* mousson, *f.*
monster ['mɔnstə], *n.* monstre, *m.*
monstrosity [mɔn'strɔsiti], *n.* monstruosité, *f.*
monstrous ['mɔnstrəs], *a.* monstrueux; prodigieux.
month [mʌnθ], *n.* mois, *m.*; *calendar month*, mois civil; *the day of the month*, le quantième du mois, *m.*
monthly ['mʌnθli], *a.* mensuel, de tous les mois.—*n.* (*fam.*) revue mensuelle, *f.*—*adv.* tous les mois, par mois.
monument ['mɔnjumənt], *n.* monument, *m.*
monumental [mɔnju'mentl], *a.* monumental.
moo [muː], *v.i.* meugler, beugler.—*n.* meuglement, *m.*
mood [muːd], *n.* humeur, *f.*; (*Gram. etc.*) mode, *m.*
moody ['muːdi], *a.* de mauvaise humeur, triste.
moon [muːn], *n.* lune, *f.*; *by the light of the moon*, au clair de la lune.—*v.i.* muser; *to moon about*, flâner.
moonbeam ['muːnbiːm], *n.* rayon de lune, *m.*
moonlight ['muːnlait], *n.* clair de lune, *m.*
moonlit ['muːnlit], *a.* éclairé par la lune.

moonshine ['muːnʃain], *n.* clair de lune, *m.*; (*fig.*) chimères, *f.pl.*
moonstrike ['muːnstraik], *n.* alunissage, *m.*
moonstruck ['muːnstrʌk], *a.* lunatique.
Moor [muə], *n.* Maure, *m.*, *f.*
moor (1) [muə], *n.* lande, bruyère, *f.*; marais, *m.*
moor (2) [muə], *v.t.* amarrer.—*v.i.* s'amarrer.
moor hen ['muəhen], *n.* poule d'eau, *f.*
moorings ['muərinʒ], *n.* amarres, *f.pl.*, mouillage, *m.*
moorland ['muələnd], *n.* lande, bruyère, *f.*, marais, *m.*
moose [muːs], *n.* élan du Canada, *m.*
moot [muːt], *v.t.* discuter, débattre, controverser.—*a.* *moot point*, question discutable, *f.*
mop [mɔp], *n.* balai à laver, *m.*—*v.t.* nettoyer avec un balai, éponger; *to mop one's face*, s'éponger la figure.
mope [moup], *v.i.* s'ennuyer; être hébété.
moping ['moupiŋ], *a.* triste, hébété.
moral ['mɔrəl], *a.* moral.—*n.* morale; moralité, *f.*; (*pl.*) mœurs, *f.pl.*
morale [mɔ'raːl], *n.* moral (*de militaires etc.*), *m.*
morality [mə'ræliti], *n.* morale; moralité, *f.*
moralize ['mɔrəlaiz], *v.i.* moraliser.
morally ['mɔrəli], *adv.* moralement.
morass [mə'ræs], *n.* marais, *m.*, fondrière, *f.*
morbid ['mɔːbid], *a.* maladif, malsain, morbide.
morbidly ['mɔːbidli], *adv.* morbidement.
morbidity [mɔː'biditi], **morbidness** ['mɔːbidnis], *n.* état maladif, état morbide, *m.*
more [mɔː], *a.* and *adv.* plus; plus de; plus nombreux; encore; davantage; *more and more*, de plus en plus; *more than*, plus que, plus de (*suivi d'un nombre*); *no more*, pas davantage; *no more of that!* arrêtez cela! *once more*, encore une fois; *some more*, encore un peu, davantage.
moreover [mɔː'rouvə], *adv.* de plus, d'ailleurs, en outre.
moribund ['mɔribʌnd], *a.* moribond.
Mormon ['mɔːmən], *a.* mormon.—*n.* Mormon (*personne*), *m.*
morn [mɔːn], *n.* (*poet.*) matin, *m.*; aurore, *f.*
morning ['mɔːniŋ], *a.* du matin.—*n.* matin, *m.*, matinée, *f.*; *good morning*, bonjour; *in the morning*, le matin; *the next morning*, le lendemain matin.
Moroccan [mə'rɔkən], *a.* marocain.—*n.* Marocain (*personne*), *m.*
Morocco [mə'rɔkou], le Maroc, *m.*
morocco leather [mə'rɔkou'leðə], *n.* maroquin, *m.*
moron ['mɔːrɔn], *n.* crétin, idiot, *m.*
morose [mə'rous], *a.* morose.
morphia ['mɔːfiə], **morphine** ['mɔːfiːn], *n.* morphine, *f.*
morrow ['mɔrou], *n.* (*poet.*) demain, lendemain, *m.*; *tomorrow*, demain.
morsel [mɔːsl], *n.* morceau, *m.*
mortal [mɔːtl], *a.* mortel, funeste (*fatal*); des mortels, humain (*terrestre*); à outrance, à mort (*combat*); *any mortal thing*, n'importe quoi.—*n.* mortel, *m.*
mortality [mɔː'tæliti], *n.* mortalité; humanité, *f.*
mortally ['mɔːtəli], *adv.* mortellement, à mort.
mortar ['mɔːtə], *n.* mortier, *m.*

489

mortgage ['mɔːgidʒ], *n.* hypothèque, *f.*—*v.t.* hypothéquer.

mortician [mɔːˈtiʃən], *n.* (*Am.*) entrepreneur de pompes funèbres, *m.*

mortification [mɔːtifiˈkeiʃən], *n.* mortification; (*Path.*) gangrène, *f.*

mortify ['mɔːtifai], *v.t.* mortifier; (*Path.*) faire gangrener.—*v.i.* se gangrener.

mortise ['mɔːtis], *n.* mortaise, *f.*—*v.t.* mortaiser.

mortuary ['mɔːtjuəri], *a.* mortuaire.—*n.* morgue, *f.*, dépôt mortuaire, *m.*

mosaic [moˈzeiik], *a.* and *n.* mosaïque, *f.*

Moscow ['mɔskou]. Moscou, *m.*

Moses ['mouziz]. Moïse, *m.*

Moslem ['mʌzlim, 'mɔzləm], *a.* musulman.—*n.* Musulman (*personne*), *m.*

mosque [mɔsk], *n.* mosquée, *f.*

mosquito [mɔsˈkiːtou], *n.* moustique, *m.*

mosquito net [mɔsˈkiːtounet], *n.* moustiquaire, *f.*

moss ['mɔs], *n.* mousse, *f.*; marais, *m.*; tourbière (bog), *f.*

moss-grown ['mɔsgroun], **mossy** ['mɔsi], *a.* couvert de mousse, moussu.

moss rose ['mɔsrouz], *n.* rose moussue, *f.*

most [moust], *a.* le plus; le plus grand; *most men*, la plupart des hommes; *the most part*, la plus grande partie.—*adv.* le plus, plus; très, fort; *a most valuable book*, un livre de plus précieux; *most likely*, très probablement.—*n.* la plupart, *f.*; le plus grand nombre, *m.*

mostly ['moustli], *adv.* pour la plupart; le plus souvent; principalement.

mote [mout], *n.* grain de poussière, *m.*; paille (*dans l'œil*), *f.*

motel ['moutel], *n.* motel, *m.*

motet [mouˈtet], *n.* (*Mus.*) motet, *m.*

moth [mɔθ], *n.* (*Ent.*) lépidoptère; papillon de nuit, *m.*; phalène; mite (*de vêtements*), *f.*

moth-eaten ['mɔθiːtn], *a.* mité.

mother ['mʌðə], *n.* mère; maternel; métropolitain (*église*); *mother tongue*, langue maternelle, *f.*—*n.* mère; bonne mère, bonne femme (*terme familier*), *f.*; *stepmother*, belle-mère, *f.*—*v.t.* servir de mère à; adopter; enfanter (*quelque chose*).

mother country ['mʌðəkʌntri], *n.* mère patrie, *f.*

mother-in-law ['mʌðərinlɔ:], *n.* belle-mère, *f.*

motherly ['mʌðəli], *a.* maternel, de mère.—*adv.* maternellement, en mère.

mother-of-pearl [mʌðərəvˈpəːl], *n.* nacre, *f.*

motion ['mouʃən], *n.* mouvement; signe (*signal*), *m.*; motion, proposition (*à une réunion*); (*Med.*) selle, *f.*—*v.t.* faire signe (*à*).

motionless ['mouʃənlis], *a.* immobile.

motivate ['moutiveit], *v.t.* motiver (*une action*).

motive ['moutiv], *a.* moteur, qui fait mouvoir; *motive power*, force motrice, *f.*—*n.* motif, mobile, *m.*

motley ['mɔtli], *a.* bigarré, mélangé.

motor ['moutə], *n.* moteur, *m.*—*v.i.* aller *ou* voyager en auto.

motor-boat ['moutəbout], *n.* canot automobile, *m.*

motor car ['moutəkaː], *n.* automobile, auto, voiture, *f.*

motor-cycle ['moutəsaikl], *n.* motocyclette, *f.*

motoring ['moutəriŋ], *n.* automobilisme, *m.*

motorist ['moutərist], *n.* automobiliste, *m.*, *f.*

motorway ['moutəwei], *n.* autoroute, *f.*

mottle [mɔtl], *v.t.* madrer; marbrer.

motto ['mɔtou], *n.* (*pl.* **mottoes** ['mɔtouz]) devise, *f.*

mould (1) [mould], *n.* moisi (*mousse*); terreau (*humus*), *m.*—*v.i.* se moisir.

mould (2) [mould], *n.* moule, *m.*, forme, *f.*—*v.t.* mouler; (*fig.*) petrir.

moulder ['mouldə], *v.i.* se réduire en poudre *ou* en poussière.

mouldiness ['mouldinis], *n.* moisissure, *f.*

moulding ['mouldiŋ], *n.* moulure, *f.*

mouldy ['mouldi], *a.* moisi.

moult [moult], *v.i.* muer.

moulting ['moultiŋ], *n.* mue, *f.*

mound [maund], *n.* butte, *f.*, tertre, *m.*; (*Fort.*) remparts, *m.pl.*

mount [maunt], *n.* mont, *m.*, montagne; monture (*cheval*); (*Turf*) monte, *f.*; (*Phot.*) carton, *m.*—*v.t.* monter, monter sur.—*v.i.* monter, s'élever; monter à cheval.

mountain ['mauntin], *a.* de montagne, des montagnes, montagnard, montagneux (*paysage*).—*n.* montagne, *f.*

mountaineer [maunti'niə], *n.* montagnard, *m.*; alpiniste, *m.*, *f.*

mountaineering [maunti'niəriŋ], *n.* alpinisme, *m.*

mountainous ['mauntinəs], *a.* montagneux, de montagnes; (*fig.*) énorme.

mountebank ['mauntibæŋk], *n.* charlatan, *m.*

mounted ['mauntid], *a.* monté, à cheval; (*Phot.*) collé.

mounting ['mauntiŋ], *n.* montage, *m.*, monture, *f.*; (*Phot.*) collage, *m.*

mourn [mɔːn], *v.t.* pleurer, déplorer.—*v.i.* pleurer, se lamenter.

mourner ['mɔːnə], *n.* personne affligée, *f.*; pleureur (*professionnel*), *m.*, personne qui suit le convoi, *f.*

mournful ['mɔːnful], *a.* triste, lugubre.

mourning ['mɔːniŋ], *a.* affligé, triste; de deuil.—*n.* affliction, lamentation, *f.*; deuil (*vêtements*), *m.*

mouse [maus], *n.* (*pl.* **mice** [mais]) souris, *f.*; *field mouse*, mulot, *m.*

mouse-trap ['maustræp], *n.* souricière, *f.*

moustache [mə'staːʃ], *n.* moustache, *f.*

mousy ['mausi], *a.* gris (*couleur*); timide.

mouth [mauθ], *n.* (*pl.* **mouths** [mauðz]) bouche; gueule (*de bête sauvage*); embouchure (*de rivière*); ouverture, entrée, *f.*, orifice (*donnant accès*); goulot (*d'une bouteille*), *m.*; *by word of mouth*, de vive voix. —[mauð], *v.t.*, *v.i.* crier.

mouthed [mauðd], *a.* *foul-mouthed*, mal embouché; *mealy-mouthed*, doucereux.

mouthful ['mauθful], *n.* bouchée; gorgée (*de vin*), *f.*

mouthpiece ['mauθpiːs], *n.* embouchure, *f.*; (*fig.*) interprète, porte-parole, *m.*

movable ['muːvəbl], *a.* mobile.—*n.* meuble, *m.*

move [muːv], *v.t.* remuer; déplacer; mouvoir, faire mouvoir, mettre en mouvement, faire marcher, faire aller; transporter (*marchandises etc.*); (*fig.*) émouvoir, toucher; exciter, pousser (*à*); proposer (*que*); (*Chess*) jouer; *to move forward*, avancer; *to move out*, déloger, sortir.—*v.i.* bouger, se remuer, se mouvoir, se déplacer; se mettre en mouvement, aller, partir, marcher, s'avancer; s'ébranler (*armée*); déménager (*changer de résidence*); (*Chess*) jouer; *move on!* circulez! *to move aside*, s'écarter; *to move away*, s'éloigner; *to move back*, reculer, se reculer; *to move in*, emménager; *to move off*, s'éloigner, s'en aller; *to move on*, avancer; *to move out*, sortir, déménager.—*n.* mouvement; coup; (*Chess*) trait, *m.*; *masterly move*, coup de maître; *to be on the move*, être en mouvement, se remuer; *to get a move on*, se presser.

movement ['mu:vmənt], *n.* mouvement, *m.*

mover ['mu:və], *n.* moteur; mobile, *m.*; force motrice, *f.*; déménageur, *m.*

movie ['mu:vi], *n.* (*Am.*) film, *m.*; *the movies*, le cinéma, *m.*

moving ['mu:viŋ], *a.* mouvant, mobile; (*fig.*) émouvant.—*n.* mouvement; déménagement (*de mobilier*); déplacement (*changement de place*), *m.*

movingly ['mu:viŋli], *adv.* d'une manière émouvante.

mow [mou], *v.t. irr.* faucher; tondre.

mower ['mouə], *n.* faucheur (*personne*), *m.*; faucheuse, tondeuse (*machine*), *f.*

Mr. ['mistə]. Monsieur (*abbr.* M.).

Mrs. ['misiz]. Madame (*abbr.* Mme.).

much [mʌtʃ], *adv.* beaucoup, bien, fort, très; *as much*, autant; *how much?* combien (de)? *much more*, bien plus; *nothing much*, pas grand'chose; *pretty much*, à peu près; *so much*, tant; *so much more*, d'autant plus; *so much the better*, tant mieux; *to make much of*, faire grand cas de; *too much*, trop (*de*).

muck [mʌk], *n.* fumier (*engrais*), *m.*; fange (*boue*), *f.*; (*fig.*) saleté, *f.*—*v.t.* fumer; salir.

muckiness ['mʌkinis], *n.* saleté, ordure, *f.*

mucky ['mʌki], *a.* sale, malpropre.

mucous ['mju:kəs], *a.* muqueux; *mucous membrane*, muqueuse, *f.*

mucus ['mju:kəs], *n.* mucus, *m.*; mucosité, *f.*

mud [mʌd], *n.* boue, bourbe, vase, *f.*; limon, *m.*

mudguard ['mʌdgɑ:d], *n.* garde-boue, *m.*

muddle [mʌdl], *v.t.* brouiller; troubler; gâcher.—*v.i.* faire du gâchis.—*n.* confusion, *f.*, désordre, gâchis, *m.*

muddled [mʌdld], *a.* troublé; hébété.

muddler ['mʌdlə], *n.* brouillon, *m.*

muddy ['mʌdi], *a.* boueux, bourbeux; crotté.

muff [mʌf], *n.* manchon, *m.*—*v.t.* gâcher.

muffle [mʌfl], *v.t.* emmitoufler, affubler; assourdir (*cloche*); voiler (*tambour*).—*n.* moufle,*f.*

muffler ['mʌflə], *n.* cache-nez, *m.*; (*Motor.*) pot d'échappement, *m.*

mug [mʌg], *n.* pot, *m.*, tasse; (*slang*) gueule, binette, *f.*; (*colloq.*) imbécile, *m.*, *f.*

muggy ['mʌgi], *a.* humide, lourd.

mulberry ['mʌlbəri], *n.* mûre, *f.*; *mulberry bush*, mûrier, *m.*

mulch [mʌltʃ], *n.* paillis, *m.*—*v.t.* pailler, fumer.

mule [mju:l], *n.* mulet, *m.*, mule, *f.*

mulish ['mju:liʃ], *a.* de mulet; (*fig.*) têtu.

mull [mʌl], *v.i.* réfléchir.—*v.t.* faire chauffer et épicer; *mulled wine*, vin chaud épicé.

multicolored ['mʌltikʌləd], *a.* multicolore.

multifarious [mʌlti'fɛəriəs], *a.* varié, divers, multiplié.

multi-millionaire ['mʌltimiljə'nɛə], *n.* milliardaire, *m.*, *f.*

multiple ['mʌltipl], *a.* and *n.* multiple, *m.*; *multiple store*, maison à succursales, *f.*

multiplication [mʌltipli'keiʃən], *n.* multiplication, *f.*

multiplicity [mʌlti'plisiti], *n.* multiplicité, *f.*

multiply ['mʌltiplai], *v.t.* multiplier.—*v.i.* multiplier, se multiplier.

multitude ['mʌltitju:d], *n.* multitude, *f.*

multitudinous [mʌlti'tju:dinəs], *a.* très nombreux, innombrable.

mum (1) [mʌm], *a.* muet.—*int.* bouche close! chut!

mum (2) [mʌm], *n.* (*fam.*) maman, *f.*

mumble [mʌmbl], *v.i.* marmotter.

mumbler ['mʌmblə], *n.* marmotteur, *m.*

mummer ['mʌmə], *n.* mime (*acteur*), *m.*

mummify ['mʌmifai], *v.t.* momifier.

mummy (1) ['mʌmi], *n.* momie, *f.*

mummy (2), **mummie** ['mʌmi], *n.* (*fam.*) maman, *f.*

mumps [mʌmps], *n.pl.* (*Med.*) oreillons, *m.pl.*

munch [mʌntʃ], *v.t.*, *v.i.* mâcher, croquer.

mundane ['mʌndein], *a.* mondain.

municipal [mju'nisipl], *a.* municipal.

municipality [mjunisi'pæliti], *n.* municipalité, *f.*

munificence [mju'nifisəns], *n.* munificence, *f.*

munificent [mju'nifisənt], *a.* libéral, généreux.

munition [mju'niʃən], *n.* munitions (*de guerre*), *f.pl.*—*v.t.* approvisionner.

mural ['mjuərəl], *a.* mural.—*n.* peinture murale, *f.*

murder ['mə:də], *n.* meurtre, homicide, *m.*; *wilful murder*, meurtre avec préméditation, assassinat, *m.*—*v.t.* assassiner, tuer; (*fig.*) écorcher (*une langue etc.*).

murderer ['mə:dərə], *n.* meurtrier, assassin, *m.*

murderess ['mə:dəris], *n.* meurtrière, *f.*

murdering ['mə:dəriŋ], **murderous** ['mə:dərəs], *a.* meurtrier, assassin.

murkiness ['mə:kinis], *n.* obscurité, *f.*

murky ['mə:ki], *a.* sombre, obscur, ténébreux.

murmur ['mə:mə], *n.* murmure, *m.*—*v.i.* murmurer.

murmuring ['mə:məriŋ], *a.* murmurant, murmurateur.—*n.* murmure, *m.*, murmures, *m.pl.*

muscle [mʌsl], *n.* muscle, *m.*

muscular ['mʌskjulə], *a.* musculaire (*force*); musculeux (*membres*).

Muse [mju:z], *n.* muse, *f.*

muse [mju:z], *v.i.* méditer (*sur*) rêver (*à*).—*n.* muse, rêverie, méditation, *f.*

museum [mju'zi:əm], *n.* musée, *m.*

mushroom ['mʌʃrum], *n.* champignon, *m.*

music ['mju:zik], *n.* musique, *f.*

musical ['mju:zikəl], *a.* musical; (*fig.*) harmonieux, mélodieux; qui aime la musique.

musician [mju'ziʃən], *n.* musicien, *m.*

music stand ['mju:zikstænd], *n.* pupitre à musique, *m.*

music stool ['mju:zikstu:l], *n.* tabouret de piano, *m.*

musing ['mju:ziŋ], *n.* méditation; (*pl.*) rêverie, *f.*

musk [mʌsk], *n.* musc, *m.*
musket [ˈmʌskit], *n.* fusil, mousquet, *m.*
musketeer [mʌskiˈtiə], *n.* mousquetaire, *m.*
musketry [ˈmʌskitri], *n.* mousqueterie, *f.*, tir, *m.*
musky [ˈmʌski], *a.* musqué, parfumé de musc.
Muslim [ˈmʌzlim], [MOSLEM].
muslin [ˈmʌzlin], *a.* de mousseline.—*n.* mousseline, *f.*
mussel [mʌsl], *n.* moule, *f.*
must (1) [mʌst], *v. aux.* falloir; devoir; *I must do it*, il faut que je le fasse; *you must know*, vous devez savoir.
must (2) [mʌst], *n.* moût (*de vin*), *m.*
mustard [ˈmʌstəd], *n.* moutarde, *f.*
muster [ˈmʌstə], *n.* appel, *m.*, revue, *f.*; rassemblement, *m.*; troupe, bande, *f.*; contrôles (*liste*), *m.pl.*—*v.t.* faire l'appel de; passer en revue; réunir, rassembler; se procurer; *to muster up courage*, prendre son courage à deux mains.—*v.i.* s'assembler, se réunir.
mustiness [ˈmʌstinis], *n.* moisi, *m.*
musty [ˈmʌsti], *a.* moisi; qui sent le renfermé.
mutability [mjuːtəˈbiliti], *n.* mutabilité, *f.*
mutation [mjuːˈteiʃən], *n.* mutation, *f.*
mute [mjuːt], *a.* and *n.* muet, *m.*—*v.t.* amortir (*les cordes d'un violon etc.*).
mutely [ˈmjuːtli], *adv.* en silence.
mutilate [ˈmjuːtileit], *v.t.* mutiler, estropier.
mutilated [ˈmjuːtileitid], *a.* mutilé.
mutilation [mjuːtiˈleiʃən], *n.* mutilation, *f.*
mutineer [mjuːtiˈniə], *n.* révolté, rebelle, mutin, *m.*
mutinous [ˈmjuːtinəs], *a.* rebelle, mutiné, mutin.
mutinously [ˈmjuːtinəsli], *adv.* séditieusement.
mutiny [ˈmjuːtini], *n.* mutinerie, sédition, révolte, *f.*—*v.i.* se mutiner, s'insurger.
mutter [ˈmʌtə], *v.t.*, *v.i.* marmotter.—*n.* marmottement, *m.*
muttering [ˈmʌtəriŋ], *a.* marmotteur, murmurant.—*n.* murmure, marmottement, marmottage, *m.*
mutton [mʌtn], *n.* mouton (*viande*), *m.*; *leg of mutton*, gigot, *m.*
mutton chop [ˈmʌtnˈtʃɔp], *n.* côtelette de mouton, *f.*
mutual [ˈmjuːtjuəl], *a.* mutuel, réciproque; *mutual friend*, ami commun, *m.*
mutually [ˈmjuːtjuəli], *adv.* mutuellement.
muzzle [mʌzl], *n.* museau (*d'animal*), *m.*; bouche, gueule (*de canon*), *f.*; bout (*de fusil etc.*), *m.*; muselière (*pour chien*), *f.*—*v.t.* museler.
muzzy [ˈmʌzi], *a.* brouillé, confus.
my [mai], *poss. a.* mon, *m.*, ma, *f.*, mes, *pl.*
myopic [maiˈɔpik], *a.* myope.
myriad [ˈmiriəd], *a.* (*poet.*) innombrable.—*n.* myriade, *f.*
myrrh [məː], *n.* myrrhe, *f.*
myrtle [məːtl], *n.* myrte, *m.*
myself [maiˈself], *pron.* me; moi-même; moi; *I consider myself*, je me crois.
mysterious [misˈtiəriəs], *a.* mystérieux.
mysteriously [misˈtiəriəsli], *adv.* mystérieusement.
mystery [ˈmistəri], *n.* mystère, *m.*
mystic [ˈmistik], *a.* and *n.* (*Theol.*) mystique, *m.*, *f.*

mysticism [ˈmistisizm], *n.* mysticisme, *m.*
mystify [ˈmistifai], *v.t.* envelopper de mystère, mystifier.
mystique [misˈtiːk], *n.* mystique, *f.*
myth [miθ], *n.* mythe, *m.*
mythical [ˈmiθikl], *a.* mythique.
mythology [miˈθɔlədʒi], *n.* mythologie, *f.*

N

N, n [en]. quatorzième lettre de l'alphabet, *m.* ou *f.*
nab [næb], *v.t.* happer, saisir, pincer.
nag (1) [næg], *n.* bidet, petit cheval, *m.*
nag (2) [næg], *v.t.*, *v.i.* gronder, chamailler, criailler.
nagging [ˈnægiŋ], *a.* querelleur (*personne*); agaçant (*sensation*).
nail [neil], *n.* clou; ongle (*de griffes, de doigts*), *m.*—*v.t.* clouer; clouter.
nail brush [ˈneilbrʌʃ], *n.* brosse à ongles, *f.*
naïve [naiˈiːv], *a.* naïf, ingénu.
naked [ˈneikid], *a.* nu, à nu; à découvert, ouvert (*sans protection*); dégarni (*sans meubles*); *stark naked*, tout nu.
nakedness [ˈneikidnis], *n.* nudité, *f.*
name [neim], *n.* nom; (*fig.*) renom, *m.*, renommée, réputation, *f.*; *Christian name*, nom de baptême, prénom, *m.*; *maiden name*, nom de jeune fille; *what is your name?* comment vous appelez-vous?—*v.t.* nommer, appeler; désigner; *to be named*, s'appeler, se nommer.
named [neimd], *a.* nommé, désigné.
nameless [ˈneimlis], *a.* sans nom, anonyme; inconnu.
namely [ˈneimli], *adv.* à savoir, c'est-à-dire.
namesake [ˈneimseik], *n.* homonyme, *m.*
nanny [ˈnæni], *n.* bonne d'enfant; (*childish*) nounou, *f.*
nap (1) [næp], *n.* somme (*sommeil*), *m.*; *afternoon nap*, sieste, *f.*; *to take a nap*, faire un somme; *to catch napping*, prendre au dépourvu.
nap (2) [næp], *n.* poil (*de tissu etc.*), *m.*
nap (3) [næp], *n.* napoléon (*jeu*); tuyau certain (*courses de chevaux*), *m.*
nape [neip], *n.* nuque, *f.*
napkin [ˈnæpkin], *n.* serviette; couche (*de bébé*), *f.*
Napoleon [nəˈpouljən]. Napoléon, *m.*
narcissus [naːˈsisəs], *n.* narcisse, *m.*
narcotic [naːˈkɔtik], *a.* and *n.* narcotique, *m.*
narrate [næˈreit], *v.t.* raconter, narrer.
narration [nəˈreiʃən], *n.* narration, *f.*, récit, *m.*
narrative [ˈnærətiv], *a.* narratif.—*n.* récit, narré, *m.*
narrator [nəˈreitə], *n.* narrateur, *m.*
narrow [ˈnærou], *a.* étroit, resserré; à l'étroit, gêné; rétréci, limité, borné (*esprit*); *to have a narrow escape*, l'échapper belle.—*n.* (*pl.*) détroit, pas, *m.*—*v.t.* rétrécir, resserrer, limiter, borner.—*v.i.* se rétrécir, se resserrer.
narrowly [ˈnærouli], *adv.* étroitement, à l'étroit; de près.

narrow-minded ['nærou'maindid], *a.* à l'esprit étroit.

narrowness ['nærounis], *n.* étroitesse, *f.*

nasal [neizl], *a.* nasal, du nez.

nascent ['næsənt], *a.* naissant.

nastily ['na:stili], *adv.* salement, malproprement.

nastiness ['na:stinis], *n.* saleté; grossièreté, *f.*

nasturtium [nəs'tə:ʃəm], *n.* capucine, *f.*

nasty ['na:sti], *a.* sale, malpropre; (*fig.*) méchant, vilain; dégoûtant.

natal [neitl], *a.* natal, de naissance.

nation ['neiʃən], *n.* nation, *f.*

national ['næʃənl], *a.* national; **national anthem**, hymne national, *m.*; **national debt**, dette publique, *f.*; **national insurance**, assurances sociales, *f.pl.*

nationalism ['næʃnəlizm], *n.* nationalisme, *m.*

nationality [næʃə'næliti], *n.* nationalité, *f.*

nationalization [næʃnəlai'zeiʃən], *n.* nationalisation (*d'une industrie*); (*Am.*) naturalisation (*d'une personne*), *f.*

nationalize ['næʃnəlaiz], *v.t.* nationaliser.

native ['neitiv], *a.* natif, naturel; indigène (*personne ou plante*); maternel (*langue etc.*); **native land**, patrie, *f.*—*n.* natif (*d'une ville*); habitant (*d'une île*); naturel (*de tribu sauvage*); indigène (*des pays d'outremer*), *m.*; **a native of England**, Anglais de naissance, *m.*; **a native of Paris**, natif de Paris.

nativity [nə'tiviti], *n.* nativité; naissance, *f.*

natty ['næti], *a.* pimpant, propret, coquet.

natural ['nætʃərəl], *a.* naturel; réel; naïf, simple; (*Mus.*) bécarre.

naturalist ['nætʃərəlist], *n.* naturaliste, *m.*, *f.*

naturalization [nætʃərəlai'zeiʃən], *n.* naturalisation, *f.*

naturally ['nætʃərəli], *adv.* naturellement.

nature ['neitʃə], *n.* nature, *f.*; naturel (*disposition*), *m.*

naught [nɔ:t], *n.* néant, rien, *m.*; (*Arith.*) zéro, *m.*; **to come to naught**, échouer.

naughtily ['nɔ:tili], *adv.* par méchanceté.

naughtiness ['nɔ:tinis], *n.* méchanceté, *f.*

naughty ['nɔ:ti], *a.* méchant, vilain.

nausea ['nɔ:ziə], *n.* nausée, *f.*

nauseating ['nɔ:zieitiŋ], *a.* nauséabond, dégoûtant, écœurant.

nautical ['nɔ:tikl], *a.* nautique; marin (*milles etc.*).

naval [neivl], *a.* naval; maritime; de la marine (*de guerre*); **naval officer**, officier de marine, *m.*

nave (1) [neiv], *n.* nef (*d'église*), *f.*

nave (2) [neiv], *n.* moyeu (*de roue*), *m.*

navel [neivl], *n.* nombril, *m.*

navigable ['nævigəbl], *a.* navigable.

navigate ['nævigeit], *v.t.* gouverner.—*v.i.* naviguer.

navigation [nævi'geiʃən], *n.* navigation, *f.*

navigator ['nævigeitə], *n.* navigateur, *m.*

navvy ['nævi], *n.* terrassier, *m.*

navy ['neivi], *n.* marine de guerre, *f.*; **Merchant Navy**, marine marchande.

navy blue ['neivi'blu:], *a.* and *n.* bleu marine, *m.inv.*

*****nay** [nei], *adv.* non; bien plus; et même, qui plus est; **to say nay**, refuser.

Neapolitan [niə'pɔlitən], *a.* napolitain, de Naples.—*n.* Napolitain (*personne*), *m.*

neap tide ['ni:p'taid], *n.* marée de morte eau, *f.*

near [niə], *a.* proche, rapproché; chiche (*parcimonieux*); cher (*bien-aimé*); fidèle (*intime*); de gauche (*left*).—*adv.* près, de, de près; presque.—*prep.* près de, auprès de.—*v.t.*, *v.i.* s'approcher de.

nearby ['niəbai], *a.*, [niə'bai], *adv.* tout près, tout proche.

nearly ['niəli], *adv.* de près; à peu près; presque; **he was nearly drowned**, il faillit se noyer.

nearness ['niənis], *n.* proximité; parcimonie (*avarice*), *f.*

neat [ni:t], *a.* propre, soigné, net; simple et élégant; pur, sec (*sans mélange*).

neatly ['ni:tli], *adv.* proprement; nettement; adroitement (*habilement*).

neatness ['ni:tnis], *n.* propreté, netteté, *f.*

nebula ['nebjulə], *n.* (*Astron.*) nébuleuse, *f.*

nebulous ['nebjuləs], *a.* nébuleux.

necessaries ['nesəsəriz], *n.pl.* nécessaire, *m.*

necessarily ['nesəsərili], *adv.* nécessairement, forcément.

necessary ['nesəsəri], *a.* nécessaire.

necessitate [ni'sesiteit], *v.t.* nécessiter.

necessitous [ni'sesitəs], *a.* nécessiteux, dans le besoin.

necessity [ni'sesiti], *n.* nécessité, *f.*; besoin (*indigence*), *m.*; **of necessity**, nécessairement, forcément.

neck [nek], *n.* cou; goulot (*de bouteille etc.*); manche (*de violon*); collet (*de viande*), *m.*; encolure (*d'une robe*), langue (*de terre*), *f.*; **stiff neck**, torticolis, *m.*

neckerchief ['nekətʃif], *n.* foulard (*d'homme*), fichu (*de femme*), *m.*

necklace ['neklis], *n.* collier, *m.*

neck-tie ['nektai], *n.* cravate, *f.*

necromancy ['nekrəmænsi], *n.* nécromancie, *f.*

necropolis [ni'krɔpəlis], *n.* nécropole, *f.*

nectar ['nektə], *n.* nectar, *m.*

nectarine ['nektərin], *n.* brugnon, *m.*

need [ni:d], *n.* besoin, *m.*; nécessité; indigence, *f.*; **if need be**, le cas échéant; **in case of need**, au besoin; **to be in need**, être dans la misère; **to be in need of** or **to have need of**, avoir besoin de.—*v.t.* avoir besoin de; exiger.—*v.i.* avoir besoin; devoir, avoir (à); (*impers.*) falloir, être nécessaire.

needful ['ni:dful], *a.* nécessaire; **the needful**, le nécessaire, *m.*

needle [ni:dl], *n.* aiguille, *f.*

needless ['ni:dlis], *a.* inutile.

needlework ['ni:dlwə:k], *n.* ouvrage à l'aiguille, *m.*; (*Sch.*) couture, *f.*

*****needs** [ni:dz], *adv.* (*used only with* must) nécessairement, absolument; **I must needs**, il faut absolument que je (*with subj.*).

needy ['ni:di], *a.* indigent, nécessiteux.

ne'er [nɛə], (*poet.*) [NEVER].

nefarious [ni'fɛəriəs], *a.* abominable, infâme.

negation [ni'geiʃən], *n.* négation, *f.*

negative ['negətiv], *a.* négatif.—*n.* négative, *f.*; (*Phot.*) cliché, négatif, *m.*—*v.t.* rejeter.

neglect [ni'glekt], *n.* négligence, *f.*; oubli, *m.* —*v.t.* négliger.

neglected [ni'glektid], *a.* négligé.

neglectful [ni'glektful], *a.* négligent.

negligence ['neglidʒəns], *n.* négligence, *f.*

negligent ['neglidʒənt], *a.* négligent.

negligible ['neglidʒibl], a. négligeable.
negotiable [ni'gouʃiəbl], a. négociable.
negotiate [ni'gouʃieit], v.t., v.i. négocier.
negotiation [nigouʃi'eiʃən], n. négociation, f.
negotiator [ni'gouʃieitə], n. négociateur, m.
Negress ['ni:gres], n. (pej.) noire, f.
Negro ['ni:grou], n. noir, m., noire, f.
neigh [nei], v.i. hennir.—n. hennissement, m.
neighbor ['neibə], n. voisin, m.; (Bibl.) prochain, m.
neighborhood ['neibəhud], n. voisinage, m.; alentours, environs, m.pl.; quartier, m.
neighboring ['neibəriŋ], a. voisin.
neighborly ['neibəli], a. de voisin, de bon voisin.
neighing ['neiiŋ], n. hennissement, m.
neither ['naiðə, 'ni:ðə], a. and pron. ni l'un ni l'autre, m.—conj. ni; non plus; **neither . . . nor**, ni . . . ni.—adv. du reste, d'ailleurs.
nemesis ['nemisis]. némésis, f.
neolithic [ni:ə'liθik], a. néolithique.
neon ['ni:ɔn], a. **neon light**, lampe au néon, f.—n. (Chem.) néon, m.
Nepal [nə'pɔ:l]. le Népal, m.
Nepalese [nepə'li:z], a. népalais.—n. Népalais (personne), m.
nephew ['nefju, 'nevju], n. neveu, m.
nepotism ['nepətizm], n. népotisme, m.
Nero ['niərou]. Néron, m.
nerve [nə:v], n. nerf; (fig.) courage, m.; audace, f.; (pop.) toupet, m.
nerve cell ['nə:vsel], n. cellule nerveuse, f.
nerveless ['nə:vlis], a. sans nerf; (fig.) sans vigueur.
nerve-racking ['nə:vrækiŋ], a. horripilant, énervant.
nervous ['nə:vəs], a. nerveux (physiquement); timide, craintif (moralement); **nervous breakdown**, dépression nerveuse, f.
nervousness ['nə:vəsnis], n. inquiétude, timidité; nervosité, f.
nest [nest], n. nid, m.; nichée (couvée d'oiseaux), f.; (fig.) repaire, m.; **nest of tables**, table gigogne, f.—v.i. nicher, faire un nid.
nestle [nesl], v.i. nicher, se nicher.
nestling ['nesliŋ], n. petit oiseau encore au nid, béjaune m.
net [net], a. net; pur.—n. filet, rets, m.; résille (à cheveux), f.; tulle (tissu), m.—v.t. prendre dans un filet; (Comm.) rapporter net.
nether ['neðə], a. bas, inférieur.
Netherlands ['neðələndz], **the**. les Pays-Bas, m.pl.
nethermost ['neðəmoust], a. le plus bas.
netting ['netiŋ], n. filet, réseau; grillage (de fil de fer), m.
nettle [netl], n. ortie, f.—v.t. piquer, agacer, irriter.
nettlerash ['netlræʃ], n. urticaire, f.
network ['netwə:k], n. réseau, enchevêtrement, m.
neuralgia [nju'rældʒə] n. névralgie, f.
neuritis [nju'raitis], n. névrite, f.
neurosis [nju'rousis], n. névrose, f.
neurotic [nju'rɔtik], a. and n. névrosé, m., neurotique, m., f.
neuter ['nju:tə], a. and n. neutre, m.
neutral ['nju:trəl], a. neutre; indifférent.—n. (Motor.) point-mort, m.
neutrality [nju'træliti], n. neutralité; indifférence, f.

neutralize ['nju:trəlaiz], v.t. neutraliser.
neutron ['nju:trɔn], n. neutron, m.
never ['nevə], adv. jamais; ne . . . jamais; **never mind!** peu importe!
nevermore [nevə'mɔ:], adv. ne . . . jamais plus, ne . . . plus jamais.
nevertheless [nevəðə'les], conj. néanmoins, cependant, pourtant.
new [nju:], a. neuf (qui n'a pas servi); nouveau (récemment acquis, différent); frais, récent (arrivé depuis peu); **brand-new**, flambant neuf, tout battant neuf; **New Year's Day**, le jour de l'an, m.
new-born ['nju:bɔ:n], a. nouveau-né; **new-born daughters**, filles nouveau-nées, f.pl.
new-comer ['nju:kʌmə], n. nouveau venu, m.
Newfoundland ['nju:fəndlænd, nju:'faund lənd]. la Terre-Neuve, f.—n. terre-neuve (chien), m.
New Guinea [nju:'gini]. la Nouvelle-Guinée, f.
new-laid ['nju:leid], a. frais (œuf).
newly ['nju:li], adv. nouvellement, fraîchement, récemment, de nouveau.
newness ['nju:nis], n. nouveauté, f.
New Orleans [nju:'ɔ:liənz]. la Nouvelle-Orléans, f.
news [nju:z], n. nouvelle, f.; nouvelles, f.pl.; (Rad., Tel.) bulletin d'informations, m.
news-agent ['nju:zeidʒənt], n. marchand de journaux, m.
newspaper ['nju:speipə], n. journal, m.
newt [nju:t], n. triton, m., salamandre, f.
New Zealand [nju:'zi:lənd]. la Nouvelle-Zélande, f.—a. néo-zélandais.
New Zealander [nju:'zi:ləndə], n. Néo-Zélandais, m.
next [nekst], a. voisin, le plus voisin; le plus près; de côté; prochain (dans l'avenir); suivant (dans le passé); premier (à la suite de).—adv. après, ensuite, puis; **what next?** et après? ensuite?—prep. **next to**, à côté de.
nib [nib], n. bec (de stylo), m.; pointe (d'outil), f.
nibble [nibl], v.t. mordiller, grignoter; mordre à (l'hameçon); brouter (l'herbe etc.).—n. grignotement, m.; touche (du poisson), f.
Nicaragua [nikə'rægjuə]. le Nicaragua, m.
Nicaraguan [nikə'rægjuən], a. nicaraguayen.—n. Nicaraguayen (personne), m.
nice [nais], a. bon, agréable, friand; (colloq.) délicat, gentil, aimable, charmant, propre; exact, difficile, exigeant (délicat); **a nice child**, un enfant gentil, m.
nicely ['naisli], adv. bien, agréablement; délicatement; gentiment, aimablement; joliment; d'une manière recherchée.
nicety ['naisəti], n. (pl. niceties ['naisətiz]) délicatesse, finesse, f.; soin scrupuleux, m.; précision; exactitude, f.; (pl.) subtilités, finesses, f.
niche [nitʃ], n. niche, f.
Nicholas ['nikələs]. Nicolas, m.
nick [nik], n. moment précis, m.; encoche, entaille (coupure), f.; (Print.) cran, m.; **in the nick of time**, fort à propos, à point nommé.
nickel [nikl], n. nickel, m.; (Am.) pièce de cinq cents, f.
nickname ['nikneim], n. sobriquet, surnom, m.—v.t. donner un sobriquet à.
nicotine ['nikəti:n], n. nicotine, f.

niece [niːs], *n.* nièce, *f.*
nifty ['nifti], *a.* (*fam.*) pimpant.
Niger ['naidʒə], **the.** le Niger, *m.*
Nigeria [nai'dʒiəriə]. le Nigéria, *m.*
Nigerian [nai'dʒiəriən], *a.* nigérien.—*n.* Nigérien (*personne*), *m.*
niggard ['nigəd], *a.* and *n.* avare, ladre, *m.*
niggardliness ['nigədlinis], *n.* mesquinerie, ladrerie, *f.*
niggardly ['nigədli], *a.* mesquin, ladre, chiche.—*adv.* avec avarice, en avare.
niggle [nigl], *v.i.* tatillonner; fignoler.
nigh [nai], *adv.* près; presque; *to draw nigh*, approcher, s'approcher (*de*).
night [nait], *n.* nuit, *f.*; soir, *m.*; *first night*, première, *f.*
night-club ['naitklʌb], *n.* boîte de nuit, *f.*
night-dress ['naitdres], *n.* chemise de nuit, *f.*
night-fall ['naitfɔːl], *n.* tombée de la nuit, *f.*
nightie ['naiti], *colloq. abbr.* [NIGHT-DRESS].
nightingale ['naitiŋgeil], *n.* rossignol, *m.*
night-light ['naitlait], *n.* veilleuse, *f.*
nightly ['naitli], *a.* nocturne, de nuit.—*adv.* chaque nuit, toutes les nuits; tous les soirs.
nightmare ['naitmɛə], *n.* cauchemar, *m.*
night-time ['naittaim], *n.* nuit, *f.*; *in the night-time*, pendant la nuit.
night-watchman ['nait'wɔtʃmən], *n.* (*pl.* **-men** [men]) veilleur de nuit, *m.*
nihilism ['naiilizm], *n.* nihilisme, *m.*
nil [nil], *n.* rien, néant, zéro, *m.*
Nile [nail], **the.** le Nil, *m.*
nimble [nimbl], *a.* agile, léger, leste.
nimbly ['nimbli], *adv.* agilement, lestement.
nine [nain], *a.* and *n.* neuf, *m.*
ninefold ['nainfould], *a.* neuf fois autant.
ninepins ['nainpinz], *n.pl.* quilles, *f.pl.*; jeu de quilles, *m.*
nineteen [nain'tiːn], *a.* and *n.* dix-neuf, *m.*
nineteenth [nain'tiːnθ], *a.* dix-neuvième; dix-neuf (*du mois* ou *souverains*).—*n.* dix-neuvième (*fraction*), *m.*
ninetieth ['naintiiθ], *a.* quatre-vingt-dixième. —*n.* quatre-vingt-dixième (*fraction*), *m.*
ninety ['nainti], *a.* and *n.* quatre-vingt-dix, *m.*
ninny ['nini], *n.* nigaud, niais, *m.*
ninth [nainθ], *a.* neuvième; neuf (*du mois* ou *souverains*).—*n.* neuvième (*fraction*), *m.*
nip [nip], *n.* pincement, *m.*, pince, *f.*; serrement, *m.*; morsure; (*Hort.*) brûlure (*par le froid*), *f.*—*v.t.* pincer; mordre; (*Hort.*) brûler (par le froid); *to nip off*, couper, enlever le bout de.
nipper ['nipə], *n.* pince, *f.*; (*colloq.*) gamin, gosse, *m.*; (*pl.*) pincettes, pinces, *f.pl.*
nipple [nipl], *n.* mamelon, bout de sein, *m.*
nippy ['nipi], *a.* preste, rapide; perçant (*froid*).
nit [nit], *n.* lente, *f.*
nitrate ['naitreit], *n.* nitrate, *m.*
nitre ['naitə], *n.* nitre, *m.*
nitric ['naitrik], *a.* nitrique, azotique.
nitrogen ['naitrədʒən], *n.* azote, *m.*
nitwit ['nitwit], *n.* imbécile, *m.*, *f.*
no [nou], *a.* and *adv.* non, pas, ne . . . pas de, ne . . . point de; pas un, nul, aucun.—*n.* non, *m.*
Noah ['nouə]. Noé, *m.*
nob [nɔb], *n.* (*colloq.*) caboche, *f.*; gros bonnet, *m.*
nobility [no'biliti], *n.* noblesse, *f.*
noble [noubl], *a.* noble; illustre, grand; généreux.—*n.* noble, *m.*

nobleman ['noublmən], *n.* (*pl.* **-men** [men]) noble, gentilhomme, *m.*
nobly ['noubli], *adv.* noblement; superbement.
nobody ['noubədi], *pron.* personne, *m.*; *I know nobody*, je ne connais personne; *nobody else*, personne d'autre.—*n.* zéro, inconnu, *m.*
nocturnal [nɔk'təːnl], *a.* nocturne, de nuit.
nod [nɔd], *n.* signe de tête, *m.*; inclination de tête, *f.*—*v.i.* faire un signe de tête; s'incliner; sommeiller (*s'assoupir*).
noggin ['nɔgin], *n.* petit pot (*en étain*), *m.*
noise [nɔiz], *n.* bruit; tapage, fracas, vacarme; tintement (*de cloche*), bourdonnement (*d'insectes etc.*); (*fig.*) éclat, *m.*—*v.t.* ébruiter, publier, répandre.
noiseless ['nɔizlis], *a.* sans bruit; silencieux.
noiselessly ['nɔizlisli], *adv.* sans bruit.
noisily ['nɔizili], *adv.* bruyamment.
noisome ['nɔisəm], *a.* malsain, infect, nuisible.
noisy ['nɔizi], *a.* bruyant; turbulent (*enfants*).
nomad ['noumæd], *n.* nomade, *m.*
nomadic [no'mædik], *a.* nomade.
nominal ['nɔminl], *a.* nominal; de nom; *nominal roll*, état nominatif, *m.*
nominally ['nɔminəli], *adv.* de nom; nominalement.
nominate ['nɔmineit], *v.t.* nommer; désigner; présenter, proposer (*un candidat etc.*).
nomination [nɔmi'neiʃən], *n.* nomination; présentation, *f.*
nominative ['nɔminətiv], *a.* au nominatif, nominatif.—*n.* (*Gram.*) nominatif, *m.*
nominee [nɔmi'niː], *n.* personne nommée, *f.*
nonagenarian [nounədʒi'nɛəriən], *a.* and *n.* nonagénaire, *m.*, *f.*
non-aggression [nɔnə'greʃən], *n.* non-agression, *f.*
non-alcoholic [nɔnælkə'hɔlik], *a.* non-alcoolique.
non-attendance [nɔnə'tendəns], *n.* absence, *f.*
nonchalance ['nɔnʃələns], *n.* nonchalance, *f.*
non-combatant [nɔn'kʌmbətənt, nɔn'kɔmbətənt], *a.* and *n.* non-combattant, *m.*
non-commissioned [nɔnkə'miʃənd], *a.* sans brevet; *non-commissioned officer*, sous-officier, *m.*
non-committal [nɔnkə'mitl], *a.* qui n'engage à rien, diplomatique.
nonconformist [nɔnkən'fɔːmist], *a.* and *n.* dissident, nonconformiste, *m.*, *f.*
nondescript ['nɔndiskript], *a.* indéfinissable, quelconque.—*n.* chose sans nom, chose indéfinissable, *f.*
none [nʌn], *a.* and *pron.* nul, *m.*, nulle, *f.*, aucun, *m.*, aucune, *f.*, pas un, *m.*, pas une, *f.*, personne, *m.*—*adv.* pas, point; néant (*sur des bordereaux*).
nonentity [nɔ'nentiti], *n.* néant, *m.*; (*fig.*) nullité, *f.*, zéro, *m.*
nonesuch ['nʌnsʌtʃ], *a.* sans pareil, nonpareil.
non-existent ['nɔnig'zistənt], *a.* qui n'existe pas.
non-intervention ['nɔnintə'venʃən], *n.* non-intervention, *f.*
non-observance ['nɔnəb'zəːvəns], *n.* inobservation, *f.*
non-payment ['nɔn'peimənt], *n.* non-payement, *m.*

nonplussed ['nɔn'plʌst], *a.* embarrassé, dérouté.

nonsense ['nɔnsəns], *n.* non-sens, *m.*; sottise, absurdité, *f.*; **nonsense!** allons donc! quelle sottise!

nonsensical [nɔn'sensikl], *a.* vide de sens, absurde.

non-skid ['nɔn'skid], *a.* antidérapant.

non-stop ['nɔn'stɔp], *a.* and *adv.* sans arrêt.

noodle [nu:dl], *n.* nigaud, benêt, sot, *m.*; (*pl.*) (*Cook.*) nouilles, *f.pl.*

nook [nuk], *n.* recoin, réduit, *m.*

noon [nu:n], *n.* midi, *m.*

noonday ['nu:ndei], *a.* de midi.—*n.* midi, *m.*

noontide ['nu:ntaid], *n.* heure de midi, *f.*, midi, *m.*

noose [nu:s], *n.* nœud coulant, lacet, *m.*

nor [nɔ:], *conj.* ni; ni . . . ne.

norm [nɔ:m], *n.* norme, *f.*

normal [nɔ:ml], *a.* normal.

normally ['nɔ:məli], *adv.* normalement.

Norman ['nɔ:mən], *a.* normand.—*n.* Normand (*personne*), *m.*

Normandy ['nɔ:məndi]. la Normandie, *f.*

north [nɔ:θ], *a.* du nord, septentrional.—*n.* nord, septentrion, *m.*—*adv.* au nord.

north-east [nɔ:θ'i:st], *n.* nord-est, *m.*

northerly ['nɔ:ðəli], *a.* septentrional, du nord. —*adv.* au nord, vers le nord.

northern ['nɔ:ðən], *a.* du nord; **northern lights,** aurore boréale, *f.*

northerner ['nɔ:ðənə], *n.* habitant du nord, *m.*

north-west [nɔ:θ'west], *n.* nord-ouest, *m.*

Norway ['nɔ:wei]. la Norvège, *f.*

Norwegian [nɔ:'wi:dʒən], *a.* norvégien.—*n.* norvégien (*langue*); Norvégien (*personne*), *m.*

nose [nouz], *n.* nez; museau (*d'animal*); odorat (*flair*), *m.*; **Roman nose,** nez aquilin; **to blow one's nose,** se moucher; **to put someone's nose out of joint,** supplanter quelqu'un; **to turn up one's nose at,** faire fi de; **turned-up nose,** nez retroussé.—*v.t.* flairer.—*v.i.* **to nose about,** fureter.

nose-bag ['nouzbæg], *n.* musette (*de cheval etc.*), *f.*

nose-dive ['nouzdaiv], *v.i.* (*Av.*) piquer du nez.—*n.* piqué, *m.*

nosegay ['nouzgei], *n.* bouquet, *m.*

nostalgia [nɔs'tældʒiə], *n.* nostalgie, *f.*, mal du pays, *m.*

nostril ['nɔstril], *n.* narine, *f.*; naseau (*de cheval etc.*), *m.*

nosy ['nouzi], *a.* (*pop.*) fouinard.

not [nɔt], *adv.* non; ne . . . pas, ne . . . point, pas, non pas; **not at all,** point du tout; **why not?** pourquoi pas?

notability [noutə'biliti], *n.* notabilité, *f.*

notable ['noutəbl], *a.* notable, insigne; remarquable.—*n.* notable, *m.*, *f.*

notably ['noutəbli], *adv.* notamment (*particulièrement*).

notary ['noutəri], *n.* notaire, *m.*

notation [no'teiʃən], *n.* notation, *f.*

notch [nɔtʃ], *n.* encoche, entaille, brèche, *f.*— *v.t.* entailler, ébrécher.

note [nout], *n.* note, marque, *f.*, signe, *m.*; lettre, *f.*, billet, *m.*; marque (*distinction*), *f.*; **bank note,** billet de banque, *m.*; **to take a note of,** prendre note de.—*v.t.* noter; remarquer.

notebook ['noutbuk], *n.* carnet, *m.*

noted ['noutid], *a.* distingué (*personne*); célèbre (*chose*).

notepaper ['noutpeipə], *n.* papier à lettres, *m.*

noteworthy ['noutwə:ði], *a.* remarquable.

nothing ['nʌθiŋ], *n.* rien, néant, *m.*; **a mere nothing,** (*fig.*) un zéro.—*pron.* (ne) . . . rien; **good-for-nothing,** bon à rien, *m.*; **nothing at all,** rien du tout; **to do nothing but,** ne faire que.—*adv.* en rien, nullement, aucunement.

nothingness ['nʌθiŋnis], *n.* néant, rien, *m.*

notice ['noutis], *n.* connaissance; attention, *f.*; préavis, *m.*; notice (*article dans un journal*); (*Law*) notification; annonce (*dans un journal*); affiche (*avis placardé*), *f.*; **a week's notice,** un préavis de huit jours; **at short notice,** à court délai; **to give notice,** avertir, donner congé; **to take notice of,** faire attention à, remarquer; **until further notice,** jusqu'à nouvel ordre.—*v.t.* prendre connaissance de, remarquer, s'apercevoir de.

noticeable ['noutisəbl], *a.* perceptible.

noticeably ['noutisəbli], *adv.* perceptiblement, sensiblement.

notice-board ['noutisbɔ:d], *n.* écriteau, *m.*

notification [noutifi'keiʃən], *n.* notification, *f.*, avis, avertissement, *m.*

notify ['noutifai], *v.t.* faire savoir, notifier.

notion ['nouʃən], *n.* notion, idée, *f.*

notoriety [noutə'raiəti], *n.* notoriété, *f.*

notorious [no'tɔ:riəs], *a.* notoire.

notwithstanding [nɔtwið'stændiŋ], *prep.* malgré, nonobstant.—*adv.* néanmoins.

noun [naun], *n.* nom, substantif, *m.*

nourish ['nʌriʃ], *v.t.* nourrir; (*fig.*) entretenir.

nourishing ['nʌriʃiŋ], *a.* nourrissant, nutritif.

nourishment ['nʌriʃmənt], *n.* nourriture, alimentation, *f.*

Nova Scotia ['nouvə'skouʃə]. la Nouvelle-Écosse, *f.*

novel [nɔvl], *a.* nouveau, original.—*n.* roman, *m.*

novelist ['nɔvəlist], *n.* romancier, *m.*

novelty ['nɔvəlti], *n.* nouveauté, *f.*

November [no'vembə], *n.* novembre, *m.*

novercal [no'və:kl], *a.* de marâtre.

novice ['nɔvis], *n.* novice, *m.*, *f.*

novitiate [nə'viʃiit], *n.* noviciat, *m.*

now [nau], *adv.* maintenant, à présent, actuellement; alors, or, donc (*raisonnement*); **now and then,** de temps en temps; **now . . . now,** tantôt . . . tantôt; **now then!** eh bien!

nowadays ['nauədeiz], *adv.* aujourd'hui, de nos jours.

nowhere ['nouwɛə], *adv.* nulle part.

nowise ['nouwaiz], *adv.* en aucune manière.

noxious ['nɔkʃəs], *a.* nuisible.

nozzle [nɔzl], *n.* nez; bec, bout; (*Motor. etc.*) ajutage, *m.*; lance (*de tuyau*), *f.*

nuclear ['nju:kliə], *a.* nucléaire; **nuclear fission,** fission de l'atome, *f.*; **nuclear war,** guerre atomique, *f.*

nucleus ['nju:kliəs], *n.* noyau, *m.*

nude [nju:d], *a.* and *a.* nu, nu, *m.*

nudge [nʌdʒ], *n.* coup de coude, *m.*—*v.t.* donner un coup de coude à, pousser du coude.

nugget ['nʌgit], *n.* pépite (*d'or*), *f.*

nuisance ['nju:səns], *n.* peste, plaie, *f.*, fléau, *m.*; (*Law*) dommage, *m.*

null [nʌl], *a.* nul; *null and void,* nul et non avenu.
nullify ['nʌlifai], *v.t.* annuler.
nullity ['nʌliti], *n.* nullité, *f.*
numb [nʌm], *a.* engourdi, transi.—*v.t.* engourdir (*par*).
number ['nʌmbə], *n.* nombre; chiffre (*de o à* 9); numéro (*d'une série*), *m.*; livraison (*de publications*), *f.*; (*fig., pl.*) nombres, *m.pl.*; *a number of,* plusieurs, une foule de (*gens*); *cardinal, ordinal, odd,* or *even number,* nombre cardinal, ordinal, impair *ou* pair.—*v.t.* compter; numéroter (*en série*).
numberless ['nʌmbəlis], *a.* innombrable.
number-plate ['nʌmbəpleit], *n.* (*Motor.*) plaque d'immatriculation, *f.*
numbness ['nʌmnis], *n.* engourdissement, *m.*
numeral ['nju:mərəl], *a.* numéral.—*n.* lettre numérale, *f.*, chiffre, *m.*
numerical [nju'merikl], *a.* numérique.
numerous ['nju:mərəs], *a.* nombreux.
numskull ['nʌmskʌl], *n.* benêt, idiot, *m.*
nun [nʌn], *n.* religieuse, (*fam.*) nonne, *f.*
nunnery ['nʌnəri], *n.* couvent (de religieuses), *m.*
nuptial ['nʌpʃəl], *a.* nuptial, de noces.
nuptials ['nʌpʃəlz], *n.pl.* noces, *f.pl.*
nurse [nə:s], *n.* bonne d'enfant, *f.*; garde-malade, *m., f.*; infirmier, *m.*, infirmière, *f.* (*à l'hôpital*); *wet nurse,* nourrice, *f.*—*v.t.* nourrir, élever; soigner, garder (*les malades*), *f.*
nurse-maid ['nə:smeid], *n.* bonne d'enfant, *f.*
nursery ['nə:səri], *n.* chambre d'enfants; (*Hort.*) pépinière, *f.*; *nursery rhyme,* chanson d'enfants, *f.*
nursery-man ['nə:sərimən], *n.* (*pl.* **-men** [men]) pépiniériste, *m.*
nursery school ['nə:sərisku:l], *n.* école maternelle, *f.*
nursing home ['nə:siŋhoum], *n.* clinique, maison de santé, *f.*
nurture ['nə:tʃə], *n.* nourriture; éducation, *f.*—*v.t.* nourrir; élever.
nut [nʌt], *n.* noix (*du noyer etc.*); noisette (*du noisetier*), *f.*; (*Tech.*) écrou, *m.*
nut-brown ['nʌtbraun], *a.* châtain.
nut-cracker ['nʌtkrækə], *n.* casse-noix (*oiseau*), *m.*; (*pl.*) casse-noisettes, *m.pl.*
nutmeg ['nʌtmeg], *n.* muscade, *f.*
nutrient ['nju:triənt], *a.* nourrissant.
nutrition [nju'triʃən], *n.* nutrition; alimentation, *f.*
nutritious [nju'triʃəs], *a.* nourrissant, nutritif.
nutshell ['nʌtʃel], *n.* coquille de noix, *f.*
nut tree ['nʌttri:], *n.* noisetier, *m.*
nutty ['nʌti], *a.* qui a un goût de noisette; (*pop.*) fêlé, toqué.
nylon ['nailən], *n.* nylon, *m.*
nymph [nimf], *n.* nymphe, *f.*

O

O, o [ou]. quinzième lettre de l'alphabet, *m.*
oaf [ouf], *n.* idiot, *m.*
oafish ['oufiʃ], *a.* stupide, idiot.

oak [ouk], *n.* chêne; bois de chêne, *m.*
oak apple ['oukæpl], *n.* pomme de chêne, *f.*
oak tree ['ouktri:], *n.* chêne, *m.*
oar [ɔ:], *n.* aviron, *m.*, rame, *f.*
oarlock, see **rowlock.**
oarsman ['ɔ:zmən], *n.* (*pl.* **-men** [men]) rameur, *m.*
oasis [ou'eisis], *n.* (*pl.* **oases** [ou'eisi:z]) oasis, *f.*
oatcake ['outkeik], *n.* galette d'avoine, *f.*
oaten [outn], *a.* d'avoine.
oath [ouθ], *n.* serment; juron, *m.*; *on oath,* sous serment; *to take an oath,* prêter serment.
oatmeal ['outmi:l], *n.* farine d'avoine, *f.*
oats [outs], *n.pl.* avoine, *f.*
obduracy ['ɔbdjurəsi], *n.* endurcissement, entêtement, *m.*
obdurate ['ɔbdjurit], *a.* endurci; obstiné, opiniâtre; impénitent.
obedience [o'bi:djəns], *n.* obéissance, soumission, *f.*
obedient [o'bi:djənt], *a.* obéissant, soumis.
obediently [o'bi:djəntli], *adv.* avec obéissance.
obeisance [o'beisəns], *n.* révérence, *f.*
obelisk ['ɔbəlisk], *n.* obélisque, *m.*
obese [o'bi:s], *a.* obèse.
obesity [o'bi:siti], *n.* obésité, *f.*
obey [o'bei], *v.t.* obéir à.—*v.i.* obéir.
obfuscate ['ɔbfʌskeit], *v.t.* offusquer, obscurcir.
obituary [o'bitjuəri], *a.* obituaire; nécrologique.—*n.* nécrologie, *f.*
object (1) ['ɔbdʒikt], *n.* objet; but (*fin*), *m.*; considération, *f.*; (*Gram.*) régime, *m.*
object (2) [əb'dʒekt], *v.t.* objecter.—*v.i.* s'opposer (à).
objection [əb'dʒekʃən], *n.* objection, *f.*; obstacle, *m.*; (*Racing*) contestation, *f.*
objectionable [əb'dʒekʃənəbl], *a.* déplaisant; inadmissible.
objective [əb'dʒektiv], *a.* objectif.—*n.* objectif, but, *m.*
objectively [əb'dʒektivli], *adv.* objectivement.
oblation [o'bleiʃən], *n.* oblation, offrande, *f.*
obligation [əbli'geiʃən], *n.* obligation, *f.*; engagement, *m.*
obligatory [ə'bligətəri], *a.* obligatoire.
oblige [ə'blaidʒ], *v.t.* obliger; faire plaisir à.
obliging [ə'blaidʒiŋ], *a.* obligeant.
oblique [ə'bli:k], *a.* oblique; indirect.
obliterate [ə'blitəreit], *v.t.* effacer, oblitérer.
obliteration [əblitə'reiʃən], *n.* oblitération, *f.*
oblivion [ə'bliviən], *n.* oubli, *m.*; *act of oblivion,* loi d'amnistie, *f.*
oblivious [ə'bliviəs], *a.* oublieux (*de*).
oblong ['ɔblɔŋ], *a.* oblong.—*n.* rectangle, *m.*
obnoxious [ɔb'nɔkʃəs], *a.* odieux, désagréable, déplaisant.
oboe ['oubou], *n.* hautbois, *m.*
obscene [əb'si:n], *a.* obscène, sale.
obscenity [əb'seniti], *n.* obscénité, *f.*
obscure [əb'skjuə], *a.* obscur; (*fig.*) caché.—*v.t.* obscurcir; voiler (*lumière*).
obscurely [əb'skjuəli], *adv.* obscurément.
obscurity [əb'skjuəriti], *n.* obscurité, *f.*
obsequies ['ɔbsikwiz], *n.pl.* obsèques, *f.pl.*
obsequious [əb'si:kwiəs], *a.* obséquieux.
obsequiousness [əb'si:kwiəsnis], *n.* soumission obséquieuse, *f.*

observance [əb'zə:vəns], *n.* observance; pratique, observation, *f.*
observant [əb'zə:vənt], *a.* observateur.
observation [ɔbzə'veiʃən], *n.* observation, *f.*
observatory [əb'zə:vətri], *n.* observatoire, *m.*
observe [əb'zə:v], *v.t.* observer; remarquer; faire remarquer.
observer [əb'zə:və], *n.* observateur, *m.*
obsess [əb'ses], *v.t.* obséder.
obsessed [əb'sest], *a.* obsédé.
obsession [əb'seʃən], *n.* obsession, *f.*
obsolete ['ɔbsəli:t], *a.* vieilli, suranné; tombé en désuétude.
obstacle ['ɔbstəkl], *n.* obstacle, *m.*
obstetrics [əb'stetriks], *n.pl.* obstétrique, *f.*
obstinacy ['ɔbstinəsi], *n.* obstination, opiniâtreté, *f.*; entêtement (*de caractère*), *m.*
obstinate ['ɔbstinit], *a.* obstiné, opiniâtre, entêté; têtu (*enfant*).
obstinately ['ɔbstinitli], *adv.* obstinément.
obstreperous [əb'strepərəs], *a.* turbulent, tapageur; récalcitrant.
obstruct [əb'strʌkt], *v.t.* empêcher, retarder; obstruer, encombrer, boucher.
obstruction [əb'strʌkʃən], *n.* empêchement, obstacle, *m.*; (*Med., Polit.*) obstruction, *f.*; encombrement (*circulation*), *m.*
obstructive [əb'strʌktiv], *a.* qui empêche; (*Med.*) obstructif.
obtain [əb'tein], *v.t.* obtenir, gagner; se procurer.—*v.i.* prévaloir.
obtainable [əb'teinəbl], *a.* qu'on peut obtenir, procurable.
obtrude [əb'tru:d], *v.t.* imposer.—*v.i.* s'introduire de force; être importun.
obtrusive [əb'tru:siv], *a.* importun.
obtuse [əb'tju:s], *a.* obtus; émoussé; stupide.
obtuseness [əb'tju:snis], *n.* (*fig.*) stupidité, *f.*
obverse ['ɔbvə:s], *n.* face, *f.*, avers, obvers (*de médaille etc.*), *m.*
obviate ['ɔbvieit], *v.t.* éviter, obvier à.
obvious ['ɔbviəs], *a.* évident, clair.
obviously ['ɔbviəsli], *adv.* évidemment.
occasion [ə'keiʒən], *n.* occasion, rencontre; raison, cause, *f.*; besoin (*nécessité*), *m.*—*v.t.* occasionner, causer.
occasional [ə'keiʒənəl], *a.* occasionnel, fortuit.
occasionally [ə'keiʒənəli], *adv.* quelquefois, de temps en temps.
occident ['ɔksidənt], *n.* occident, *m.*
occidental [ɔksi'dentl], *a.* occidental.
occult [ə'kʌlt], *a.* occulte.
occupant ['ɔkjupənt], *n.* occupant, *m.*; locataire (*de chambre louée*); titulaire (*d'un poste*), *m., f.*
occupation [ɔkju'peiʃən], *n.* occupation, *f.*; emploi, métier, *m.*; possession, *f.*
occupier ['ɔkjupaiə], *n.* occupant, *m.*; locataire (*de chambre louée*), *m., f.*, habitant, *m.*
occupy ['ɔkjupai], *v.t.* occuper; employer; habiter (*une maison*).
occur [ə'kə:], *v.i.* arriver, avoir lieu, se produire; venir à l'esprit; *it occurred to me that*, l'idée m'est venue que.
occurrence [ə'kʌrəns], *n.* occurrence, rencontre, *f.*, événement, *m.*
ocean ['ouʃən], *n.* océan, *m.*
oceanic [ousi'ænik], *a.* océanique.
ochre ['oukə], *n.* ocre, *f.*
o'clock [ə'klɔk], [CLOCK].
octagon ['ɔktəgən], *n.* octogone, *m.*

octagonal [ɔk'tægənəl], *a.* octogone, octogonal.
octane ['ɔktein], *n.* octane, *m.*; *high-octane fuel,* supercarburant, *m.*
octave ['ɔktiv], *n.* (*Mus., Eccles.*) octave, *f.*
octavo [ɔk'teivou], *n.* in-octavo, *m.*
octet(te) [ɔk'tet], *n.* (*Mus.*) octuor, *m.*
October [ɔk'toubə]. octobre, *m.*
octogenarian [ɔktoudʒi'nɛəriən], *a.* and *n.* octogénaire, *m., f.*
octopus ['ɔktəpəs], *n.* pieuvre, *f.*
ocular ['ɔkjulə], *a.* oculaire.
oculist ['ɔkjulist], *n.* oculiste, *m.*
odd [ɔd], *a.* impair; de surplus; d'appoint (*argent*); dépareillé (*article isolé d'une collection*); étrange, singulier, bizarre; *odd moments,* moments perdus, *m.pl.*; *odd number,* nombre impair, *m.*
oddity ['ɔditi], *n.* bizarrerie, *f.*; original (*personne*), *m.*
odd-looking ['ɔdlukiŋ], *a.* à la mine bizarre.
oddly ['ɔdli], *adv.* étrangement; bizarrement.
oddments ['ɔdmənts], *n.pl.* bric-à-brac, *m.*, fins de séries, *f.pl.*
odds [ɔdz], *n.pl.* inégalité, *f.*; (*fig.*) avantage, *m.*, supériorité, *f.*; chances, *f.pl.*; *it makes no odds,* cela ne fait rien; *odds and ends,* petits bouts, *m.pl.*; *to be at odds with,* être mal avec.
ode [oud], *n.* ode, *f.*
odious ['oudiəs], *a.* odieux.
odium ['oudiəm], *n.* détestation, *f.*
odor ['oudə], *n.* odeur, *f.*, parfum, *m.*; *in bad odor,* en mauvaise odeur.
odorless ['oudəlis], *a.* sans odeur.
odorous ['oudərəs], *a.* odorant.
o'er ['ɔ:ə], (*poet.*) [OVER].
of [ɔv], *prep.* de; d'entre.
off [ɔf, ɔ:f], *adv.* au loin, à distance; d'ici; rompu, enlevé; fini; fermé (*électricité etc.*); qui n'est plus frais (*aliments*); *day off,* jour de congé, *m.*; *fifty yards off,* à cinquante pas; *I am off,* je m'en vais; *off and on,* de temps à autre; *time off,* temps libre, *m.*; *to be well off,* être dans l'aisance.—*a. off day,* jour de congé, *m.*; *off side,* côté droit, hors montoir; (*Ftb.*) hors-jeu; *off white,* blanc teinté.—*prep.* de, de dessus; éloigné de (*Naut.*) au large de.
offal ['ɔfl], *n.* issues, *f.pl.*; abats, *m.pl.*; rebut, *m.*
offence [ə'fens], *n.* agression; offense; injure; violation (*d'une loi etc.*), *f.*, délit, crime, *m.*
offend [ə'fend], *v.t.* offenser, outrager, blesser; violer (*transgresser*).—*v.i.* déplaire (à); commettre une offense.
offender [ə'fendə], *n.* offenseur; (*Law*) délinquant, *m.*
offensive [ə'fensiv], *a.* offensant, désagréable; choquant; offensif (*attaquant*).—*n.* offensive, *f.*
offensively [ə'fensivli], *adv.* d'une manière offensante; offensivement.
offensiveness [ə'fensivnis], *n.* nature offensante, *f.*
offer ['ɔfə], *v.t.* offrir, présenter, proposer à.—*v.i.* s'offrir, se présenter à; essayer de.—*n.* offre, *f.*
offering ['ɔfəriŋ], *n.* offrande, *f.*; sacrifice, *m.*
off-hand ['ɔf'hænd], *adv.* au premier abord; sans réflexion, sur-le-champ; cavalière-

ment.—*a.* brusque, cavalier; impromptu, improvisé.

off-handed ['ɔf'hændid], *a.* sans façon, sans gêne.

off-handedness ['ɔf'hændidnis], *n.* sans-façon, sans-gêne, *m.*

office ['ɔfis], *n.* bureau (*immeuble*), *m.*, agence, *f.*; cabinet (*du directeur*), *m.*; étude (*d'avoué etc.*), *f.*; office, emploi; ministère, *m.*, charge, *f.*, fonctions, *f.pl.*; (*pl.*) devoirs (*services*), *m.pl.*; place, *f.*; cabinet (of physician, dentist, lawyer), *m.*

officer ['ɔfisə], *n.* officier; fonctionnaire (*du gouvernement*) agent (*de police*), *m.*; **non-commissioned officer**, sous-officier, *m.*—*v.t.* fournir des officiers à; encadrer.

official [ə'fiʃəl], *a.* officiel.—*n.* fonctionnaire, employé, *m.*

officialdom [ə'fiʃəldəm], *n.* bureaucratie, *f.*

officially [ə'fiʃəli], *adv.* officiellement.

officiate [ə'fiʃieit], *v.i.* officier, desservir.

officious [ə'fiʃəs], *a.* officieux; importun.

officiousness [ə'fiʃəsnis], *n.* zèle officieux, *m.*

offing ['ɔfiŋ], *n.* (*Naut.*) **in the offing**, au large; (*fig.*) en perspective.

offset ['ɔfset], *v.t.* (*Comm.*) compenser; (*Tech.*) désaxer, décaler.

offshoot ['ɔfʃuːt], *n.* rejeton, *m.*

offspring ['ɔfspriŋ], *n.* enfants, descendants, *m.pl.*; (*fig.*) fruit, produit, *m.*

often ['ɔfn], ***oft** [ɔft], ***oftentimes** ['ɔfn taimz], ***oft-times** ['ɔfttaimz], *adv.* souvent, maintes fois.

ogle [ougl], *v.t.* lorgner; lancer des œillades à. —*n.* œillade, *f.*

ogler ['ouglə], *n.* lorgneur, *m.*

ogling ['ougliŋ], *n.* lorgnerie, *f.*, œillades, *f.pl.*

ogre ['ougə], *n.* ogre, *m.*

ogress ['ougris], *n.* ogresse, *f.*

oh! [ou], *int.* oh! hélas!

ohm [oum], *n.* (*Elec.*) ohm, *m.*

oil [ɔil], *n.* huile, *f.*; (*crude*) **oil**, pétrole (brut), *m.*; **fuel oil**, mazout, *m.*; **coal oil**, pétrole (lampant), *m.*—*v.t.* huiler; graisser; (*fig.*) délier (*la langue*).

oilcake ['ɔilkeik], *n.* tourteau, *m.*

oil-can ['ɔilkæn], *n.* burette, *f.*

oil-cloth ['ɔilklɔθ], *n.* toile cirée, *f.*

oil field ['ɔilfiːld], *n.* gisement pétrolifère, *m.*

oiliness ['ɔilinis], *n.* onctuosité, nature huileuse, *f.*

oil lamp ['ɔillæmp], *n.* lampe à huile *ou* à pétrole, *f.*

oil painting ['ɔilpeintiŋ], *n.* peinture à l'huile, *f.*

oilskin ['ɔilskin], *n.* toile cirée vernie, *f.*

oil stove ['ɔilstouv], *n.* réchaud à pétrole, *m.*

oil tanker ['ɔiltæŋkə], *n.* (*Naut.*) pétrolier; (*Motor.*) camion-citerne, *m.*

oil well ['ɔilwel], *n.* puits de pétrole, *m.*

oily ['ɔili], *a.* huileux; (*fig.*) oléagineux, onctueux.

ointment ['ɔintmənt], *n.* onguent, *m.*, pommade, *f.*

old [ould], *a.* vieux; âgé; ancien, antique; **how old are you?** quel âge avez-vous? **old man** (*chap, boy*), mon vieux, mon brave; **to grow old**, vieillir.

olden ['ouldən], *a.* vieux, ancien; **in olden times**, au temps jadis.

old-fashioned [ould'fæʃənd] *a.* démodé, suranné.

oldish ['ouldiʃ], *a.* un peu vieux, vieillot.

old maid ['ouldmeid], *n.* vieille fille, *f.*

oleaginous [ouli'ædʒinəs], *a.* oléagineux.

oleander [ouli'ændə], *n.* (*Bot.*) laurier-rose, oléandre, *m.*

oligarchy ['ɔligɑːki], *n.* oligarchie, *f.*

olive ['ɔliv], *n.* olive, *f.*, olivier (*arbre*), *m.*

Oliver ['ɔlivə]. Olivier, *m.*

Olympian [o'limpiən], *a.* olympien.

Olympic [o'limpik], *a.* olympique; **the Olympic Games**, les jeux olympiques, *m.pl.*

Olympus [o'limpəs]. Olympe, *m.*

omega ['oumigə], *n.* oméga, *m.*

omelet(te) ['ɔməlit], *n.* omelette, *f.*

omen ['oumən], *n.* augure, *m.*

ominous ['ɔminəs], *a.* de mauvais augure, sinistre; menaçant.

ominously ['ɔminəsli], *adv.* de mauvais augure.

omission [o'miʃən], *n.* omission, *f.*

omit [o'mit], *v.t.* omettre; oublier.

omnipotence [ɔm'nipətəns], *n.* omnipotence, toute-puissance, *f.*

omnipotent [ɔm'nipətənt], *a.* tout-puissant, omnipotent.

omniscient [ɔm'nisiənt], *a.* omniscient.

omnivorous [ɔm'nivərəs], *a.* omnivore.

on [ɔn], *prep.* sur, dessus; à; de; en, dans; lors de, après; **on foot**, à pied; **on Monday**, lundi; **on purpose**, à dessein, exprès; **on the whole**, en somme.—*adv.* dessus; en avant, avant, avancé; toujours (*continuation*); de suite (*succession*); **and so on**, et ainsi de suite; **on and on**, sans cesse, interminablement; **play on**, continuez de jouer; **read on**, lisez toujours.

once [wʌns], *adv.* une fois, une seule fois; autrefois, jadis (*anciennement*); **at once**, sur-le-champ, tout de suite; **once upon a time there was**, il était une fois.

one [wʌn], *a.* un; seul, unique; un certain.— *n.* un, *m.*, une, *f.*—*pron.* on; l'on; vous (*accusatif*); celui, *m.*, celle, *f.*; quelqu'un; un homme, *m.*, une femme, *f.*

one-armed ['wʌnɑːmd], *a.* manchot.

one-eyed ['wʌnaid], *a.* borgne.

onerous ['ɔnərəs], *a.* onéreux.

onerousness ['ɔnərəsnis], *n.* poids, *m.*, charge, *f.*

oneself [wʌn'self], *pron.* soi, soi-même; (*reflexive*) se.

one-sided ['wʌn'saidid], *a.* à un côté, à une face; (*fig.*) partial, unilatéral.

one-sidedness ['wʌn'saididnis], *n.* partialité, *f.*

one-way ['wʌnwei], *a.* **one-way street**, rue à sens unique, *f.*; **one-way ticket**, billet simple, *m.*

onion ['ʌnjən], *n.* oignon, *m.*; **spring onion**, ciboule, *f.*

onion bed ['ʌnjənbed], *n.* oignonnière, *f.*

onlooker ['ɔnlukə], *n.* spectateur, *m.*

only ['ounli], *a.* seul; unique; **only child**, enfant unique, *m., f.*—*adv.* seulement; rien que; uniquement; ne . . . que.—*conj.* mais.

onset ['ɔnset], *n.* assaut, *m.*, attaque, charge, *f.*

onslaught ['ɔnslɔːt], *n.* attaque, *f.*; assaut, *m.*

onus ['ounəs], *n.* charge, responsabilité, obligation, *f.*

onward ['ɔnwəd], *a.* en avant; avancé, progressif.—*adv.* or **onwards** ['ɔnwədz], en avant.

onyx ['ɔniks], *n.* onyx, *m.*

ooze [u:z], *n.* limon, *m.*—*v.i.* suinter, filtrer; (*fig.*) s'ébruiter.

oozing ['u:ziŋ], *n.* suintement; (*fig.*) ébruitement, *m.*

oozy ['u:zi], *a.* vaseux, limoneux.

opal [oupl], *n.* opale, *f.*

opaque [o'peik], ı. opaque; (*fig.*) épais.

opaqueness [o'peiknis], *n.* opacité, *f.*

open ['oupən], *v.t.* ouvrir; déboucher (*une bouteille*); (*fig.*) expliquer; commencer, entamer; révéler; décacheter (*une lettre*); défaire (*un colis*); inaugurer.—*v.i.* s'ouvrir; commencer.—*a.* ouvert, découvert, à découvert, nu, à nu; franc, sincère; libre; (*fig.*) clair; **in the open (*air*)**, en plein air; **on the open sea**, en pleine mer.

opener ['oupnə], *n.* ouvreur, *m.*; **tin-opener**, ouvre-boîte, *m.*

open-handed ['oupən'hændid], *a.* libéral, généreux.

open-hearted ['oupən'hɑ:tid], *a.* franc.

opening ['oupniŋ], *a.* qui commence, d'inauguration; **the opening chapter**, le premier chapitre.—*n.* ouverture, embrasure, *f.*; commencement, début, *m.*; chance; éclaircie (*dans une forêt etc.*), *f.*

openly ['oupənli], *adv.* ouvertement; franchement.

open-minded ['oupən'maindid], *a.* sans parti pris, libéral, à l'esprit ouvert.

open-mouthed ['oupən'mauðd], *a.* bouche béante, bouche bée.

openness ['oupənnis], *n.* franchise, sincérité, candeur, *f.*

opera ['ɔpərə], *n.* opéra, *m.*

opera glass ['ɔprəglɑ:s], *n.* lorgnette, *f.*; (*pl.*) jumelles, *f.pl.*

opera hat ['ɔprəhæt], *n.* claque, *m.*

opera house ['ɔprəhaus], *n.* opéra, *m.*

operate ['ɔpəreit], *v.t.* opérer, effectuer.—*v.i.* opérer, agir; (*Fin.*) spéculer; **to operate on someone for appendicitis**, opérer quelqu'un de l'appendicite.

operatic [ɔpə'rætik], *a.* d'opéra.

operation [ɔpə'reiʃən], *n.* opération, action, *f.*

operative ['ɔpərətiv], *a.* actif, efficace; des ouvriers.—*n.* artisan, ouvrier, *m.*

operator ['ɔpəreitə], *n.* opérateur, *m.* **telephone operator** téléphoniste, *m., f.*; **radio operator**, radio, *m.*

operetta [ɔpə'retə], *n.* opérette, *f.*

opiate ['oupiit], *a.* opiacé.—*n.* opiat, *m.*

opinion [ə'pinjən], *n.* opinion, *f.*, avis, sentiment, *m.*; idée, pensée; (*Law*) consultation, *f.*; **in my opinion**, à mon avis.

opinionated [ə'pinjəneitid], *a.* opiniâtre; têtu, imbu de ses opinions.

opium ['oupjəm], *n.* opium, *m.*

opossum [o'pɔsəm], *n.* opossum, *m.*; sarigue, *f.*

opponent [ə'pounənt], *n.* opposant, *m.*, adversaire, *m., f.*

opportune ['ɔpətju:n], *a.* opportun, à propos.

opportunely [ɔpə'tju:nli], *adv.* à propos.

opportunity [ɔpə'tju:niti], *n.* occasion, *f.*

oppose [ə'pouz], *v.t.* opposer; s'opposer à.

opposite ['ɔpəzit], *a.* opposé; vis-à-vis, contraire (*à*), en face.—*n.* opposé, contre-pied,

m.—*adv.* vis-à-vis, en face.—*prep.* en face de, vis-à-vis de.

opposition [ɔpə'ziʃən], *n.* opposition, résistance; concurrence (*rivalité*), *f.*; obstacle, *m.*

oppress [ə'pres], *v.t.* opprimer; accabler.

oppression [ə'preʃən], *n.* oppression, *f.*

oppressive [ə'presiv], *a.* accablant, oppressif; lourd.

oppressiveness [ə'presivnis], *n.* caractère oppressif, *m.*, lourdeur, *f.*

oppressor [ə'presə], *n.* oppresseur, *m.*

opprobrious [ə'proubriəs], *a.* infamant; injurieux.

opprobrium [ə'proubriəm], *n.* opprobre, *m.*

opt [ɔpt], *v.i.* opter.

optic ['ɔptik], **optical** ['ɔptikəl], *a.* optique; d'optique.

optician [ɔp'tiʃən], *n.* opticien, *m.*

optimism ['ɔptimizm], *n.* optimisme, *m.*

optimist ['ɔptimist], *n.* optimiste, *m., f.*

optimistic [ɔpti'mistik], *a.* optimiste.

option ['ɔpʃən], *n.* option, *f.*, choix, *m.*

optional ['ɔpʃənəl], *a.* facultatif.

opulence ['ɔpjuləns], *n.* opulence, *f.*

opulent ['ɔpjulənt], *a.* opulent.

or [ɔ:], *conj.* ou; (*negatively*) ni; **or else**, ou bien, autrement.

oracle ['ɔrəkl], *n.* oracle, *m.*

oracular [ɔ'rækjulə], *a.* d'oracle; (*fig.*) dogmatique.

oral ['ɔ:rəl], *a.* oral.

orally ['ɔ:rəli], *adv.* oralement; par la bouche.

orange ['ɔrindʒ], *n.* orange; couleur orange, *m.*

orangery ['ɔrindʒəri], *n.* orangerie, *f.*

orange-tree ['ɔrindʒtri:], *n.* oranger, *m.*

orang-outang [o'ræŋu'tæŋ], *n.* orang-outang, *m.*

oration [o'reiʃən], *n.* allocution, *f.*, discours, *m.*; **funeral oration**, oraison funèbre, *f.*

orator ['ɔrətə], *n.* orateur, *m.*

oratorical [ɔrə'tɔrikəl], *a.* oratoire.

oratorio [ɔrə'tɔːriou], *n.* oratorio, *m.*

oratory ['ɔrətri], *n.* art oratoire, *m.*, éloquence, *f.*; oratoire (*chapelle*), *m.*

orb [ɔ:b], *n.* globe; corps sphérique; orbe, *m.*

orbit ['ɔ:bit], *n.* orbe, *m.*; (*Anat., Astron.*) orbite, *f.*

orchard ['ɔ:tʃəd], *n.* verger, *m.*

orchestra ['ɔ:kistrə], *n.* orchestre, *m.* [see **stall**]

orchestral [ɔ:'kestrəl], *a.* d'orchestre, orchestral.

orchid ['ɔ:kid], *n.* orchidée, *f.*

ordain [ɔ:'dein], *v.t.* ordonner, décréter.

ordeal [ɔ:'di:əl], *n.* dure épreuve, *f.*

order [ɔ:də], *n.* ordre; règlement, *m.*; décoration (*insigne*); (*Mil.*) consigne, classe, *f.*, rang, *m.*; commande (*de marchandises*), *f.*; mandat (*de payer*), *m.*; **in order that**, afin que; **in order to**, afin de; **money order**, mandat-poste, *m.*—*v.t.* ordonner; régler; diriger (*administrer*); commander; prescrire (*médecine*).

ordering ['ɔ:dəriŋ], *n.* disposition, *f.*, arrangement, *m.*

orderliness ['ɔ:dəlinis], *n.* bon ordre, *m.*, méthode, *f.*

orderly ['ɔ:dəli], *a.* en bon ordre, méthodique, rangé.—*n.* (*Mil.*) planton, *m.*

ordinal ['ɔ:dinl], *a.* ordinal.

ordinance ['ɔ:dinəns], *n.* ordonnance, *f.*

ordinarily ['ɔːdinrili], *adv.* ordinairement, d'ordinaire.
ordinary ['ɔːdinri], *a.* ordinaire; moyen.— *n.* ordinaire, *m.*; table d'hôte, *f.*
ordination [ɔːdi'neiʃən], *n.* ordination, *f.*
ordnance ['ɔːdnəns], *n.* artillerie, *f.*; **ord- nance map**, carte d'état major, *f.*
ore [ɔː], *n.* minerai, *m.*
organ ['ɔːgən], *n.* (*Anat. etc.*) organe; (*Mus.*) orgue, *m.*
organic [ɔː'gænik], *a.* organique; des organes.
organism ['ɔːgənizm], *n.* organisme, *m.*
organist ['ɔːgənist], *n.* organiste, *m.*, *f.*
organization [ɔːgənai'zeiʃən], *n.* organisa- tion; œuvre, *f.*
organize ['ɔːgənaiz], *v.t.* organiser; aménager.
organizer ['ɔːgənaizə], *n.* organisateur, *m.*
orgy ['ɔːdʒi], *n.* orgie, *f.*
orient ['ɔːriənt], *n.* orient, *m.*
Oriental [ɔːri'entl], *a.* oriental, d'Orient.—*n.* natif de l'Orient, oriental, *m.*
orifice ['ɔrifis], *n.* orifice, *m.*, ouverture, *f.*
origin ['ɔridʒin], *n.* origine, source; pro- venance, *f.*
original [ə'ridʒinl], *a.* original, inédit (*nouveau*); primitif (*sens des mots etc.*).—*n.* original, *m.*
originality [əridʒi'næliti], *n.* originalité, *f.*
originally [ə'ridʒinəli], *adv.* originairement; originalement.
originate [ə'ridʒineit], *v.t.* faire naître, pro- duire; (*fig.*) inventer.—*v.i.* tirer son origine (*de*), provenir de.
originator [ə'ridʒineitə], *n.* initiateur, auteur, *m.*
oriole ['ɔːrioul], *n.* (*Orn.*) loriot, *m.*
orison ['ɔrizn], *n.* oraison, prière, *f.*
Orkneys ['ɔːkniz], **the.** les Orcades, *f.pl.*
ornament ['ɔːnəmənt], *n.* ornement, *m.*— *v.t.* orner, décorer (*de*).
ornamental [ɔːnə'mentl], *a.* ornemental, d'ornement; d'agrément.
ornate [ɔː'neit], *a.* orné, élégant, paré.
ornately [ɔː'neitli], *adv.* avec ornement.
ornithologist [ɔːni'θɔlədʒist], *n.* ornitho- logiste, ornithologue, *m.*, *f.*
ornithology [ɔːni'θɔlədʒi], *n.* ornithologie, *f.*
orphan ['ɔːfən], *a.* and *n.* orphelin, *m.*
orphanage ['ɔːfənidʒ], *n.* état d'orphelin; orphelinat, *m.*
orthodox ['ɔːθədɔks], *a.* orthodoxe.
orthodoxy ['ɔːθədɔksi], *n.* orthodoxie, *f.*
orthographic [ɔːθə'græfik], *a.* orthographi- que.
orthography [ɔː'θɔgrəfi], *n.* orthographe, orthographie, *f.*
orthop(a)edic [ɔːθə'piːdik], *a.* orthopédique.
orthop(a)edist [ɔːθə'piːdist], *n.* orthopédiste, *m.*
orthop(a)edy ['ɔːθəpiːdi], *n.* orthopédie, *f.*
oscillate ['ɔsileit], *v.i.* osciller; (*fig.*) balancer, vaciller.
oscillation [ɔsi'leiʃən], *n.* oscillation, *f.*
oscillatory ['ɔsileitəri], *a.* oscillatoire.
osier ['ouʒiə], *n.* osier, *m.*
osier bed ['ouʒiəbed], *n.* oseraie, *f.*
osprey ['ɔsprei], *n.* (*Orn.*) orfraie, *f.*
osseous ['ɔsiəs], *a.* osseux.
ossicle ['ɔsikl], *n.* ossicule, osselet, *m.*
ossification [ɔsifi'keiʃən], *n.* ossification, *f.*
ossify ['ɔsifai], *v.t.* ossifier.—*v.i.* s'ossifier.
ostensible [ɔs'tensibl], *a.* prétendu.

ostensibly [ɔs'tensibli], *adv.* en apparence.
ostentation [ɔsten'teiʃən], *n.* ostentation, *f.*, faste, *m.*
ostentatious [ɔsten'teiʃəs], *a.* pompeux, fastueux.
osteopath ['ɔstiopæθ], *n.* ostéopathe, *m.*
ostler ['ɔslə], *n.* garçon d'écurie, *m.*
ostracism ['ɔstrəsizm], *n.* ostracisme, *m.*
ostracize ['ɔstrəsaiz], *v.t.* frapper d'ostra- cisme, exiler.
ostrich ['ɔstritʃ], *n.* autruche, *f.*
other ['ʌðə], *a.* autre; **every other day**, tous les deux jours; **other people**, d'autres, autrui.—*pron.* autre; autrui; **all the others**, tous les autres.
otherwise ['ʌðəwaiz], *adv.* autrement; sans quoi.
otter ['ɔtə], *n.* loutre, *f.*
ought [ɔːt], *v.aux.* devoir; falloir; **you ought to do it**, vous devriez le faire; **you ought to have seen**, il aurait fallu voir.
ounce (1) [auns], *n.* once (*poids*), *f.*
ounce (2) [auns], *n.* (*Zool.*) once, *f.*
our ['auə], *a.poss.* notre, *sing.*, nos, *pl.*
ours ['auəz], *pron.* le nôtre, *m.*, la nôtre, *f.*, les nôtres, *pl.*; à nous.
ourselves [auə'selvz], *pron.* nous-mêmes; nous.
oust [aust], *v.t.* évincer, déloger.
out [aut], *adv.* hors, dehors; sorti (*pas. chez soi*); découvert, exposé (*dévoilé*); éteint (*feu etc.*); épuisé, fini (*tout vendu* ou *tout consumé*), jusqu'au bout; haut, à haute voix (*parler*); dans l'erreur (*pas exact*); publié, paru (*livre*); épanoui (*fleur*).—*a.* externe.
outbid [aut'bid], *v.t. irr.* (*conjug. like* BID) enchérir sur, surenchérir.
outboard ['autbɔːd], *a.* **outboard motor- boat**, hors-bord, *m.*
outbreak ['autbreik], *n.* éruption, explo- sion; épidémie, *f.*
outburst ['autbəːst], *n.* explosion, *f.*, trans- port, éclat, *m.*
outcast ['autkɑːst], *a.* expulsé, proscrit, rejeté.—*n.* proscrit, banni, paria, *m.*
outcome ['autkʌm], *n.* résultat, *m.*
outcry ['autkrai], *n.* clameur, *f.*, tollé, *m.*
outdated [aut'deitid], *a.* démodé.
outdo [aut'du], *v.t. irr.* (*conjug. like* DO) sur- passer, exceller.
outdoor ['autdɔː], *a.* en plein air; externe.
outdoors [aut'dɔːz], *adv.* en plein air; hors de la maison.
outer ['autə], *a.* extérieur, du dehors, externe.
outermost ['autəmoust], *a.* le plus extérieur.
outfit ['autfit], *n.* attirail, équipement; trousseau, *m.*
outfitter ['autfitə], *n.* confectionneur et chemisier, *m.*
outflank [aut'flæŋk], *v.t.* déborder, tourner.
outgoing ['autgouiŋ], *a.* sortant, qui sort.— *n.* (*pl.*) dépenses, *f.pl.*
outgrow [aut'grou], *v.t. irr.* (*conjug. like* GROW) dépasser, surpasser.
outgrowth ['autgrouθ], *n.* excroissance; con- séquence, *f.*
outhouse ['authaus], *n.* hangar, *m.*; dépen- dance, *f.*
outing ['autiŋ], *n.* excursion, promenade, *f.*
outlandish [aut'lændiʃ], *a.* étranger; bizarre; retiré.
outlast [aut'lɑːst], *v.t.* survivre à.

501

outlaw ['autlɔ:], *n.* proscrit, *m.*—*v.t.* mettre hors la loi, proscrire.

outlay ['autlei], *n.* dépense, *f.*, débours, *m.pl.*

outlet ['autlit], *n.* issue, sortie, *f.*; (*Comm.*) débouché, *m.*

outline ['autlain], *n.* contour; profil, *m.*, ébauche, *f.*—*v.t.* esquisser.

outlive [aut'liv], *v.t.* survivre à.

outlook ['autluk], *n.* vue, perspective, *f.*

outlying ['autlaiiŋ], *a.* éloigné, détaché.

outnumber [aut'nʌmbə], *v.t.* surpasser en nombre.

out-of-date [autəv'deit], *a.* démodé, dépassé.

outpost ['autpoust], *n.* avant-poste, *m.*

outpour [aut'pɔ:], *v.t.* épancher, verser à flots.

outpouring ['autpɔ:riŋ], *n.* effusion, *f.*, épanchement, *m.*

outrage ['autreidʒ], *n.* outrage, *m.*—*v.t.* outrager.

outrageous [aut'reidʒəs], *a.* outrageux, outrageant.

outrageousness [aut'reidʒəsnis], *n.* nature outrageante, énormité, *f.*

outright ['autrait], *adv.* complètement; carrément (*à cœur ouvert*).

outrun [aut'rʌn], *v.t. irr.* (*conjug. like* RUN) dépasser à la course, gagner de vitesse.

outset ['autset], *n.* début, commencement, *m.*; *at the very outset*, dès l'origine.

outshine [aut'ʃain], *v.t. irr.* (*conjug. like* SHINE) surpasser en éclat, éclipser.

outside ['autsaid], *a.* extérieur, externe, du dehors.—*n.* dehors, extérieur, *m.*—[aut 'said], *adv.* en dehors, à l'extérieur.—[aut'said], *prep.* hors de, à l'extérieur de.

outsider [aut'saidə], *n.* étranger; (*Racing*) outsider, *m.*

outsize ['autsaiz], *a.* de grande taille, hors série.

outskirts ['autskə:ts], *n.pl.* bords, *m.pl.*; lisière (*d'un bois*), banlieue, *f.*, faubourg (*d'une ville*), *m.*

outspoken [aut'spoukən], *a.* franc, clair, carré.

outstanding [aut'stændiŋ], *a.* saillant, remarquable, excellent; non payé; en suspens (*affaires*).

outstretched [aut'stretʃt], *a.* étendu, déployé, tendu.

outstrip [aut'strip], *v.t.* devancer, distancer.

outward ['autwəd], *a.* extérieur, du dehors, externe; superficiel.—*adv.* or **outwards** ['autwədz], à l'extérieur; au dehors, extérieurement; *outward bound*, en partance.

outwardly ['autwədli], *adv.* extérieurement, à l'extérieur; (*fig.*) en apparence.

outweigh [aut'wei], *v.t.* peser plus que; l'emporter sur.

outwit [aut'wit], *v.t.* surpasser en finesse, duper.

oval [ouvl], *a. and n.* ovale, *m.*

ovary ['ouvəri], *n.* ovaire, *m.*

ovation [o'veiʃən], *n.* ovation, *f.*

oven [ʌvn], *n.* four, *m.*

over ['ouvə], *prep.* sur; par-dessus; au-dessus de; de l'autre côté de (*en face*); pendant (*au cours de*); *over there*, là-bas. —*adv.* d'un côté à l'autre; par-dessus, au-dessus; trop (*à l'excès*); plus de (*excédant*); de reste (*surplus inemployé*); fini, terminé, fait; passé.

overact [ouvər'ækt], *v.t.* outrer, exagérer.

overall ['ouvərɔ:l], *a.* total.—*n.* blouse, *f.*; tablier, *m.*; (*pl.*) salopette, combinaison, *f.*

overawe [ouvər'ɔ:], *v.t.* intimider, imposer à.

overbalance [ouvə'bæləns], *v.t.* l'emporter sur.—*v.i.* perdre l'équilibre.

overbearing [ouvə'bɛəriŋ], *a.* impérieux, autoritaire.

overboard ['ouvəbɔ:d], *adv.* par-dessus bord.

overburden [ouvə'bə:dn], *v.t.* surcharger; accabler (*de*).

overcast [ouvə'ka:st], *a.* couvert, nuageux.

overcharge [ouvə'tʃa:dʒ], *v.t.* surcharger; faire payer trop cher.—*n.* prix excessif, *m.*

overcoat ['ouvəkout], *n.* pardessus, *m.*

overcome [ouvə'kʌm], *v.t. irr.* (*conjug. like* COME) surmonter, vaincre, accabler.—*v.i.* l'emporter.

over-confident ['ouvə'kɔnfidənt], *a.* trop confiant; présomptueux, téméraire.

overcrowd [ouvə'kraud], *v.t.* encombrer à l'excès, trop remplir.

overcrowding [ouvə'kraudiŋ], *n.* surpeuplement, *m.*

overdo [ouvə'du:], *v.t. irr.* (*conjug. like* DO) exagérer, outrer; faire trop cuire; harasser.

overdone [ouvə'dʌn], *a.* trop cuit; (*fig.*) exagéré.

overdose ['ouvədous], *n.* dose trop forte, *f.*

overdraw [ouvə'drɔ:], *v.t. irr.* (*conjug. like* DRAW) excéder; *to overdraw one's account*, tirer à découvert; tirer un chèque sans provision.

overdue [ouvə'dju:], *a.* en retard.

overestimate [ouvər'estimeit], *v.t.* évaluer trop haut.

overflow [ouvə'flou], *v.t.* inonder.—*v.i.* déborder, se déborder.—['ouvəflou], *n.* inondation, *f.*, débordement, *m.*

overflowing [ouvə'flouiŋ], *a.* qui déborde, trop plein.—*n.* débordement, *m.*

overgrown [ouvə'groun], *a.* couvert (*d'herbes, ronces*); trop grand, énorme.

overhang ['ouvəhæŋ], *n.* surplomb, *m.*— [ouvə'hæŋ], *v.t. irr.* (*conjug. like* HANG) pencher sur, surplomber; faire saillie.

overhanging ['ouvəhæŋiŋ], *a.* en surplomb.

overhaul [ouvə'hɔ:l], *v.t.* examiner, revoir; réviser, vérifier, démonter.—['ouvəhɔ:l], *n.* examen détaillé, *m.*

overhead [ouvə'hed], *adv.* par-dessus la tête, en haut.—*a.* aérien (*fil etc.*).—['ouvə hedz], *n.* (*pl.*) (*Comm.*) frais généraux, *m.pl.*

overhear [ouvə'hiə], *v.t. irr.* (*conjug. like* HEAR) entendre par hasard.

overheat [ouvə'hi:t], *v.t.* surchauffer.

overjoyed [ouvə'dʒɔid], *a.* transporté de joie, ravi.

overland ['ouvəlænd], *a. and adv.* par voie de terre.

overlap [ouvə'læp], *v.t.* recouvrir.—['ouvə læp], *n.* recouvrement, *m.*

overlapping [ouvə'læpiŋ], *n.* recouvrement, chevauchement, *m.*

overload [ouvə'loud], *v.t.* surcharger, surmener.

overlook [ouvə'luk], *v.t.* donner sur, dominer; surveiller (*diriger*); fermer les yeux sur (*passer sur*); oublier, négliger.

overlooking [ouvə'lukiŋ], *a.* donnant (*sur*).
overmuch ['ouvəmʌtʃ], *a.* excessif.—*n.* trop, *m.*—*adv.* par trop, excessivement.
overnight [ouvə'nait], *adv.* durant la nuit; hier soir; du jour au lendemain.
overpay [ouvə'pei], *v.t. irr.* (*conjug. like* PAY) payer trop.
overpower [ouvə'pauə], *v.t.* vaincre; accabler (*de*).
overpowering [ouvə'pauəriŋ], *a.* accablant, écrasant.
overproduction [ouvəprə'dʌkʃən], *n.* surproduction, *f.*
overrate [ouvə'reit], *v.t.* estimer trop haut.
overreach [ouvə'ri:tʃ], *v.t.* tromper.—*v.i.* forger (*chevaux*); **to overreach oneself,** trop présumer de ses forces.
override [ouvə'raid], *v.t. irr.* (*conjug. like* RIDE) surmener, outrepasser.
overrule [ouvə'ru:l], *v.t.* dominer; (*Law*) rejeter.
overrun [ouvə'rʌn], *v.t. irr.* (*conjug. like* RUN) envahir, faire une irruption dans; infester (*de*).—*v.i.* déborder.
oversea ['ouvəsi:], **overseas** ['ouvəsi:z, ouvə'si:z], *a.* and *adv.* d'outre-mer.
oversee [ouvə'si:], *v.t. irr.* (*conjug. like* SEE) surveiller.
overseer ['ouvəsiə], *n.* surveillant; contremaître (*d'usine etc.*), *m.*
overshadow [ouvə'ʃædou], *v.t.* ombrager; éclipser.
overshoes ['ouvəʃu:z], *n.pl.* caoutchoucs, *m.pl.*
overshoot [ouvə'ʃu:t], *v.t. irr.* (*conjug. like* SHOOT) dépasser.
oversight ['ouvəsait], *n.* inadvertance, *f.*, oubli, *m.*
oversleep [ouvə'sli:p], *v.i. irr.* (*conjug. like* SLEEP) dormir au delà de son heure.
overstate [ouvə'steit], *v.t.* exagérer.
overstatement [ouvə'steitmənt], *n.* exagération, *f.*
overstep [ouvə'step], *v.t.* dépasser.
overt ['ouvə:t], *a.* ouvert, manifeste.
overtake [ouvə'teik], *v.t. irr.* (*conjug. like* TAKE) rattraper; doubler, dépasser.
overtax [ouvə'tæks], *v.t.* surtaxer, surcharger.
overthrow [ouvə'θrou], *v.t. irr.* (*conjug. like* THROW) renverser; défaire, détruire.—['ouvəθrou], *n.* renversement, *m.*, défaite, destruction, *f.*
overtime ['ouvətaim], *n.* heures supplémentaires, *f.pl.*
overtop [ouvə'tɔp], *v.t.* s'élever au-dessus de, dépasser.
overture ['ouvətjuə], *n.* ouverture; offre, *f.*
overturn [ouvə'tə:n], *v.t.* renverser; bouleverser.—*v.i.* verser.
overweening [ouvə'wi:niŋ], *a.* présomptueux, outrecuidant.
overweight ['ouvəweit], *n.* excédent, *m.*
overwhelm [ouvə'welm], *v.t.* accabler (*de*); combler (*de*) (*bontés etc.*).
overwhelming [ouvə'welmiŋ], *a.* accablant, écrasant.
overwork [ouvə'wə:k], *v.t.* surcharger de travail, surmener.—*n.* travail excessif; surmenage, *m.*
ovoid ['ouvɔid], *a.* ovoïde.
owe [ou], *v.t.* devoir; être redevable à . . . de.

owing ['ouiŋ], *a.* dû (*à*); **owing to,** à cause de, grâce à.
owl [aul], *n.* hibou, *m.*; chouette, *f.*
owlet ['aulit], *n.* jeune hibou, *m.*
own (1) [oun], *a.* propre (*à soi*); **my own money,** mon propre argent; **to hold one's own,** se maintenir.—*v.t.* posséder, être propriétaire de (*avoir*).
own (2) [oun], *v.t.* avouer, confesser.
owner ['ounə], *n.* possesseur, *m.*, propriétaire, *m.*, *f.*
ownership ['ounəʃip], *n.* propriété, *f.*
ox [ɔks], *n.* (*pl.* **oxen** [ɔksən]) bœuf, *m.*
oxalic [ɔk'sælik], *a.* oxalique.
ox-fly ['ɔksflai], *n.* taon, *m.*
oxide ['ɔksaid], *n.* oxyde, *m.*
oxidization [ɔksidai'zeiʃən], *n.* oxydation, calcination, *f.*
oxidize ['ɔksidaiz], *v.t.* oxyder; calciner.
oxyacetylene [ɔksiə'setili:n], *a.* oxyacétylénique.
oxygen ['ɔksidʒən], *n.* oxygène, *m.*
oxygenate ['ɔksidʒəneit], *v.t.* oxygéner.
oxygenous [ɔk'sidʒənəs], *a.* d'oxygène.
oyster ['ɔistə], *n.* huître, *f.*
oyster bed ['ɔistəbed], *n.* banc d'huîtres, *m.*
ozone [ou'zoun], *n.* ozone, *m.*

P

P, p [pi:]. seizième lettre de l'alphabet, *m.*
pabulum ['pæbjuləm], *n.* aliment, *m.*, nourriture, *f.*
pace [peis], *n.* pas, *m.*; allure (*de cheval*), *f.*; train, *m.*; vitesse, *f.*; **to put someone through his paces,** mettre quelqu'un à l'épreuve.—*v.t.* arpenter; (*Spt.*) entraîner.—*v.i.* aller au pas, marcher.
pacific [pə'sifik], *a.* pacifique, paisible.—*n.* **the Pacific** (*Ocean*), le Pacifique, l'océan Pacifique, *m.*
pacification [pæsifi'keiʃən], *n.* pacification, *f.*
pacifier ['pæsifaiə], *n.* pacificateur, *m.*
pacifism ['pæsifizm], *n.* pacifisme, *m.*
pacifist ['pæsifist], *n.* pacifiste, *m.*, *f.*
pacify ['pæsifai], *v.t.* pacifier, apaiser.
pack [pæk], *n.* paquet, ballot, *m.*; meute (*chiens de chasse*), *f.*; jeu (*de cartes*), *m.*—*v.t.* emballer, empaqueter.—*v.i.* s'assembler; se grouper; faire sa malle.
package ['pækidʒ], *n.* colis, paquet, *m.*
packer ['pækə], *n.* emballeur, *m.*
packet ['pækit], *n.* paquet; paquebot (*bateau*), *m.*
pack horse ['pækhɔ:s], *n.* cheval de bât, *m.*
pack-ice ['pækais], *n.* glace de banquise, *f.*, pack, *m.*
packing ['pækiŋ], *n.* emballage, *m.*
pact [pækt], *n.* pacte, *m.*
pad [pæd], *n.* tampon; coussinet, *m.*; **writing pad,** sous-main, bloc de papier, *m.*—*v.t.* ouater; rembourrer.—*v.i.* aller à pied.
padding ['pædiŋ], *n.* ouate, bourre, *f.*

paddle

paddle [pædl], *n.* pagaie; aube (*de roue*), *f.* —*v.t.* pagayer.—*v.i.* patauger.
paddle boat ['pædlbout], *n.* bateau à aubes, *m.*
paddock ['pædək], *n.* enclos, pré, pâturage, *m.*
padlock ['pædlɔk], *n.* cadenas, *m.*—*v.t.* cadenasser, fermer au cadenas.
paean ['pi:ən], *n.* péan, *m.*
pagan ['peigən], *a.* and *n.* païen, *m.*
paganism ['peigənizm], *n.* paganisme, *m.*
page (1) [peidʒ], *n.* page (*garçon*), *m.*
page (2) [peidʒ], *n.* page (*de livre*), *f.*
pageant ['pædʒənt], *n.* spectacle pompeux, cortège *ou* spectacle historique, *m.*
pageantry ['pædʒəntri], *n.* pompe, *f.*, faste, apparat, *m.*
pagoda [pə'goudə], *n.* pagode, *f.*
paid [peid], *a.* payé, acquitté; affranchi (*lettres*).
pail [peil], *n.* seau, *m.*
pailful ['peilful], *n.* (plein) seau, *m.*
pain [pein], *n.* douleur; peine (*effort*), *f.*; **on pain of**, sous peine de; **to take pains**, se donner de la peine.—*v.t.* faire mal à; (*fig.*) faire de la peine à; affliger.
painful ['peinful], *a.* douloureux, pénible.
painless ['peinlis], *a.* sans douleur, indolore.
painstaking ['peinzteikiŋ], *a.* soigneux, assidu.
paint [peint], *n.* couleur; peinture, *f.*; fard (*pour le visage*), *m.*—*v.t.* peindre; farder (*le visage*).—*v.i.* peindre; se farder.
painter (1) ['peintə], *n.* peintre, *m.*
painter (2) ['peintə], *n.* (*Naut.*) amarre, *f.*
painting ['peintiŋ], *n.* peinture, *f.*; tableau (*picture*), *m.*
pair [pɛə], *n.* paire, *f.*; couple (*époux etc.*), *m.* —*v.t.* accoupler.—*v.i.* s'accoupler.
pajamas [pi'dʒa:məz], *n.pl.* pyjama, *m.*
Pakistan [pa:ki'sta:n]. le Pakistan, *m.*
Pakistani [pa:ki'sta:ni], *a.* pakistanais.—*n.* Pakistanais (*personne*), *m.*
pal [pæl], *n.* (*colloq.*) camarade, copain, *m.*
palace ['pælis], *n.* palais, *m.*; **archbishop's palace**, archevêché, *m.*; **bishop's palace**, évêché, *m.*
palatable ['pælətəbl], *a.* agréable au goût.
palate ['pælit], *n.* palais (*fig.*) goût, *m.*
palatial [pə'leiʃl], *a.* du palais, palatial; grandiose.
palaver [pə'la:və], *n.* palabre (*chez certains peuples primitifs*), *f.*; verbiage, *m.*; flagornerie, *f.*—*v.i.* palabrer, faire des phrases.
pale (1) [peil], *a.* pâle, blême; (*fig.*) blafard (*lumière*).—*v.i.* pâlir; (*fig.*) s'éclipser.
pale (2) [peil], *n.* pieu, palis, *m.*; limites (*bornes*), *f.pl.*; **beyond the pale**, au ban de la société.
pale-faced ['peilfeist], *a.* au teint pâle.
paleness ['peilnis], *n.* pâleur, *f.*
Palestine ['pælistain]. la Palestine, *f.*
Palestinian [pælis'tiniən], *a.* palestinien.
palette ['pælit], *n.* palette, *f.*
palfrey ['pɔ:lfri], *n.* palefroi, *m.*
paling ['peiliŋ], *n.* palissade, *f.*
palisade [pæli'seid], *n.* palissade, *f.*—*v.t.* palissader.
palish ['peiliʃ], *a.* un peu pâle, pâlot.
pall [pɔ:l], *n.* poêle *m.* (*fig.*) drap mortuaire;

voile (*de fumée etc.*), *m.*—*v.i.* devenir fade, s'affadir.
pallet ['pælit], *n.* grabat, *m.*, paillasse, *f.*
palliate ['pælieit], *v.t.* pallier.
palliation [pæli'eiʃən], *n.* palliation, *f.*
palliative ['pæliətiv], *a.* and *n.* palliatif, *m.*
pallid ['pælid], *a.* pâle, blême, blafard.
pallor ['pælə], *n.* pâleur, *f.*
palm (1) [pa:m], *n.* paume (*de main*), *f.*—*v.t.* **to palm off** (*something on someone*), passer, refiler (*quelque chose à quelqu'un*).
palm (2) [pa:m], *n.* palmier (*arbre*), *m.*; palme (*rameau*), *f.*; **Palm Sunday**, dimanche des Rameaux, *m.*
palmist ['pa:mist], *n.* chiromancien, *m.*
palmistry ['pa:mistri], *n.* chiromancie, *f.*
palmy ['pa:mi], *a.* beau, glorieux, heureux.
palpable ['pælpəbl], *a.* palpable; manifeste.
palpitate ['pælpiteit], *v.i.* palpiter.
palpitation [pælpi'teiʃən], *n.* palpitation, *f.*
palsied ['pɔ:lzid], *a.* frappé de paralysie, paralytique.
palsy ['pɔ:lzi], *n.* paralysie, *f.*
palter ['pɔ:ltə], *v.i.* tergiverser, biaiser.
paltriness ['pɔ:ltrinis], *n.* mesquinerie, *f.*
paltry ['pɔ:ltri], *a.* mesquin, misérable.
pamper ['pæmpə], *v.t.* choyer, dorloter.
pamphlet ['pæmflit], *n.* brochure, *f.*; (*pej.*) pamphlet, *m.*
pamphleteer [pæmfli'tiə], *n.* auteur de brochures, *m.*; (*pej.*) pamphlétaire, *m.*, *f.*
pan [pæn], *n.* casserole, *f.*; poêlon, *m.*; **frying pan**, poêle, *f.*
panacea [pænə'si:ə], *n.* panacée, *f.*
Panama ['pænəma:]. le Panama, *m.*
Panamanian [pænə'meiniən], *a.* panamanien. —*n.* Panamanien (*personne*), *m.*
pancake ['pænkeik], *n.* crêpe, *f.*
pancreas ['pænkriəs], *n.* (*Anat.*) pancréas, *m.*
pandemonium [pændi'mouniəm], *n.* pandémonium, *m.*
pander ['pændə], *v.i.* se prêter à, se faire complaisant pour.
pane [pein], *n.* carreau, *m.*, vitre, *f.*
panegyric [pæni'dʒirik], *a.* de panégyrique.— *n.* panégyrique, *m.*
panegyrist [pæni'dʒirist], *n.* panégyriste, *m.*, *f.*
panel [pænl], *n.* panneau, *m.*; liste (*de juré etc.*), *f.*; **instrument panel**, tableau de manœuvre, *m.*—*v.t.* diviser en panneaux; lambrisser.
panelling ['pænliŋ], *n.* panneaux, *m.pl.*, lambrissage, *m.*
pang [pæŋ], *n.* angoisse, vive douleur, *f.*, serrement de cœur, *m.*
panic ['pænik], *a.* panique.—*n.* panique; terreur panique, *f.*—*v.i.* s'affoler.
pannier ['pæniə], *n.* panier, *m.*, hotte, *f.*
panoply ['pænəpli], *n.* panoplie, armure complète, *f.*
panorama [pænə'ra:mə], *n.* panorama, *m.*
panoramic [pænə'ræmik], *a.* panoramique.
pansy ['pænzi], *n.* (*Bot.*) pensée, *f.*
pant [pænt], *n.* palpitation, *f.*, halètement, *m.* —*v.i.* haleter, palpiter, panteler.
pantechnicon [pæn'teknikn], *n.* garde-meuble, *m.*; voiture de déménagement, *m.*
pantheism ['pænθiizm], *n.* panthéisme, *m.*
pantheist ['pænθiist], *n.* panthéiste, *m.*, *f.*
pantheistic [pænθi'istik], *a.* panthéistique.
panther ['pænθə], *n.* panthère, *f.*

pantile ['pæntail], *n.* tuile faîtière *ou* flamande, *f.*
pantomime ['pæntəmaim], *n.* pantomime, *f.*
pantomimic [pæntə'mimik], *a.* pantomime.
pantry ['pæntri], *n.* office, *f.*, garde-manger, *m.*
pants [pænts], *n.pl.* (*colloq.*) caleçon; (*Am.*) pantalon, *m.* [**panties**, see **knickers**]
pap [pæp], *n.* mamelle; bouillie (*aliment*), *f.*
papacy ['peipəsi], *n.* papauté, *f.*
papal ['peipəl], *a.* papal, du pape.
paper ['peipə], *a.* de papier.—*n.* papier, *m.*; feuille de papier, *f.*; journal; papier-monnaie, *m.*; billets, *m.pl.*; mémoire, *m.*, étude (*article*); composition (*d'examen*), *f.*; (*pl.*) papiers, *m.pl.*; dossier, *m.*; *blotting paper*, papier buvard; *kraft paper*, papier gris.—*v.t.* tapisser (de papier).
paper-back ['peipəbæk], *n.* livre broché, *m.*
paper clip ['peipəklip], *n.* attache, *f.*, trombone (*de fil*), *m.*
paper-hanger ['peipəhæŋə], *n.* colleur de papier, *m.*
paper-knife ['peipənaif], *n.* coupe-papier, *m.*
paper maker ['peipəmeikə], *n.* fabricant de papier, *m.*
paper mill ['peipəmil], *n.* papeterie, *f.*
paper trade ['peipətreid], *n.* papeterie, *f.*
papism ['peipizm], *n.* papisme, *m.*
papist ['peipist], *n.* papiste, *m.*, *f.*
Papua [pə'puə]. la Papouasie, *f.*
Papuan [pə'puən], *a.* papou.—*n.* Papou (*personne*), *m.*
papyrus [pə'paiərəs], *n.* (*pl.* **papyri** [pə'paiərai]) papyrus, *m.*
par [pɑ:], *n.* pair, *m.*, égalité, (*Golf*) normale, *f.*; *at par*, au pair.
parable ['pærəbl], *n.* parabole, *f.*
parabola [pə'ræbələ], *n.* (*Math.*) parabole, *f.*
parachute [pærə'ʃu:t], *n.* parachute, *m.*—*v.t.*, *v.i.* parachuter.
parachutist [pærə'ʃu:tist], *n.* parachutiste, *m.*, *f.*
parade [pə'reid], *n.* parade, *f.*; étalage, *m.*; esplanade, *f.*; (*Mil.*) rassemblement, *m.*; procession, *f.*—*v.t.* faire parade de.—*v.i.* faire de la parade; (*Mil.*) parader.
paradise ['pærədais], *n.* paradis, *m.*
paradox ['pærədɔks], *n.* paradoxe, *m.*
paradoxical [pærə'dɔksikl], *a.* paradoxal.
paraffin ['pærəfin], *n.* (*Chem.*) paraffine, *f.*; *paraffin* (*oil*), pétrole (lampant), *m.*
paragon ['pærəgən], *n.* parangon; modèle, *m.*
paragraph ['pærəgrɑ:f], *n.* paragraphe; alinéa, *m.*—*v.t.* diviser en paragraphes.
Paraguay ['pærəgwai]. le Paraguay, *m.*
Paraguayan [pærə'gwaiən], *a.* paraguayen.—*n.* Paraguayen (*personne*), *m.*
parakeet ['pærəki:t], *n.* (*Orn.*) perruche, *f.*
parallel ['pærəlel], *a.* parallèle; (*fig.*) semblable, pareil.—*n.* ligne parallèle, *f.*, parallèle, *m.*; (*fig.*) comparaison, *f.*—*v.t.* mettre en parallèle; (*fig.*) comparer (*à*); être pareil (*à*).
parallelism ['pærəlelizm], *n.* parallélisme, *m.*; (*fig.*) comparaison, *f.*
parallelogram [pærə'leləgræm], *n.* parallélogramme, *m.*
paralysis [pə'rælisis], *n.* paralysie, *f.*
paralytic [pærə'litik], *a.* and *n.* paralytique, *m.*, *f.*
paralyze ['pærəlaiz], *v.t.* paralyser.

paramount ['pærəmaunt], *a.* souverain, suprême; *of paramount importance*, d'une importance capitale.—*n.* souverain, seigneur, *m.*
paramour ['pærəmuə], *n.* amant, *m.*, maîtresse, *f.*
parapet ['pærəpit], *n.* (*Fort.*) parapet; garde-fou (*sur un pont etc.*), *m.*
paraphernalia [pærəfə'neiliə], *n.pl.* (*Law*) biens paraphernaux, *m.pl.*; équipage, attirail, *m.*
paraphrase ['pærəfreiz], *n.* paraphrase, *f.*—*v.t.* paraphraser.
parasite ['pærəsait], *n.* parasite, *m.*
parasitic [pærə'sitik], **parasitical** [pærə'sitikəl], *a.* parasite, parasitique.
parasol [pærə'sɔl], *n.* ombrelle, *f.*, parasol, *m.*
paratrooper ['pærətru:pə], *n.* (soldat) parachutiste, *m.*
parcel [pɑ:sl], *n.* colis, paquet; lot, *m.*—*v.t.* morceler, diviser, partager; empaqueter.
parch [pɑ:tʃ], *v.t.* brûler, dessécher (*par la chaleur*).—*v.i.* se brûler; se dessécher.
parchment ['pɑ:tʃmənt], *n.* parchemin, *m.*
pardon [pɑ:dn], *n.* pardon, *m.*; (*Law*) grâce, *f.*; *I beg your pardon?* plaît-il? pardon? comment?—*v.t.* pardonner (*quelque chose à quelqu'un*); *pardon me!* pardon! permettez!
pardonable [pɑ:'dnəbl], *a.* excusable, pardonnable (*acte*); digne de pardon (*personne*).
pare [peə], *v.t.* peler (*fruits etc.*); éplucher; rogner (*ongles etc.*).
parent ['pɛərənt], *a.* mère.—*n.* père, *m.*, mère, *f.*; (*pl.*) parents, les père et mère, *m.pl.*
parentage ['pɛərəntidʒ], *n.* parentage, *m.*; extraction, *f.*
parental [pə'rentl], *a.* des parents, du père, de la mère; paternel, maternel.
parenthesis [pə'renθisis], *n.* (*pl.* **parentheses** [pə'renθisi:z]) parenthèse, *f.*
parenthetic [pærən'θetik], **parenthetical** [pærən'θetikəl], *a.* entre parenthèses.
pariah ['pæriə], *n.* paria, *m.*
paring ['pɛəriŋ], *n.* rognage; épluchage, *m.*
paring knife ['pɛəriŋnaif], *n.* tranchet, *m.*
parish ['pæriʃ], *a.* de la commune; communal, vicinal (*routes, impôts etc.*); (*Eccles.*) de la paroisse, paroissial.—*n.* (*Eccles.*) paroisse; (*civil*) commune, *f.*
parishioner [pə'riʃənə], *n.* paroissien, *m.*
Parisian [pə'riziən], *a.* de Paris, parisien.—*n.* Parisien (*personne*), *m.*
parity ['pæriti], *n.* parité; égalité (*de rang etc.*), *f.*
park [pɑ:k], *n.* parc, *m.*—*v.t.* parquer, garer.—*v.i.* stationner.
parking ['pɑ:kiŋ], *n.* stationnement, parcage, *m.* [see **car-park**]
parlance ['pɑ:ləns], *n.* parler, langage, *m.*; *in common parlance*, dans le langage ordinaire.
parley ['pɑ:li], *n.* pourparlers, *m.pl.*—*v.i.* être *ou* entrer en pourparlers (*avec*); (*Mil.*) parlementer.
parliament ['pɑ:ləmənt], *n.* parlement, *m.*; (*France*) les Chambres, *f.pl.*
parliamentary [pɑ:lə'mentəri], *a.* parlementaire, du parlement.
parlor ['pɑ:lə], *n.* petit salon; parloir (*de couvent* ou *école*), *m.*
parlous ['pɑ:ləs], *a.* alarmant, précaire.

505

parochial [pə'roukiəl], *a.* communal; (*Eccles.*) paroissial.
parody ['pærədi], *n.* parodie, *f.*—*v.t.* parodier.
parole [pə'roul], *n.* parole (d'honneur), *f.*
paroxysm ['pærəksizm], *n.* paroxysme, accès, *m.*
parquet ['pɑːkei, pɑː'ket], *n.* parquet, *m.*—*v.t.* parqueter.
parquetry ['pɑːkitri], *n.* parqueterie, *f.*
parricidal [pæri'saidl], *a.* parricide.
parricide ['pærisaid], *n.* parricide (*crime*), *m.*; parricide (*personne*), *m.*, *f.*
parrot ['pærət], *n.* (*Orn.*) perroquet, *m.*
parry ['pæri], *v.t.* parer, détourner; (*fig.*) éviter.
parse [pɑːz], *v.t.* analyser (grammaticalement).
parsimonious [pɑːsi'mouniəs], *a.* parcimonieux; pingre.
parsimony ['pɑːsiməni], *n.* parcimonie, épargne, *f.*
parsley ['pɑːsli], *n.* (*Bot.*) persil, *m.*
parsnip ['pɑːsnip], *n.* (*Bot.*) panais, *m.*
parson [pɑːsn], *n.* curé; (*Protestant*) pasteur, *m.*
parsonage ['pɑːsnidʒ], *n.* presbytère, *m.*, cure, *f.*
part [pɑːt], *n.* partie; part, portion, *f.*; (*Theat.*) rôle; parti (*dans une dispute etc.*), *m.*; région (*de ville, pays etc.*), *f.*; quartier (*de ville*); (*pl.*) talent, *m.*; **spare parts**, pièces de rechange, *f.pl.*—*v.t.* partager; séparer (*de*).—*v.i.* se séparer (*de*); se quitter; se rompre (*câble*).
partake [pɑː'teik], *v.t.*, *v.i. irr.* (*conjug. like* TAKE) prendre part à, participer à.
partaker [pɑː'teikə], *n.* participant, *m.*
partial [pɑːʃl], *a.* partial (*prévenu*), injuste; partiel (*en partie*).
partiality [pɑːʃi'æliti], *n.* partialité (*favoritisme*), *f.*; (*fig.*) goût, *m.*
partially ['pɑːʃəli], *adv.* partialement (*injustement*); en partie.
participant [pɑː'tisipənt], *a.* and *n.* participant, *m.*
participate [pɑː'tisipeit], *v.i.* participer (*à*).
participation [pɑːtisi'peiʃən], *n.* participation, *f.*
participle ['pɑːtisipl], *n.* participe, *m.*
particle ['pɑːtikl], *n.* particule, molécule, parcelle, *f.*; atome, *m.*
particular [pə'tikjulə], *a.* particulier, spécial; méticuleux, pointilleux; exigeant (*difficile*).—*n.* particularité, *f.*, détail, *m.*; (*pl.*) renseignements, *m.pl.*; signalement, *m.*
particularity [pətikju'læriti], *n.* particularité, *f.*; détail, *m.*
particularize [pə'tikjuləraiz], *v.t.* particulariser.—*v.i.* préciser.
particularly [pə'tikjuləli], *adv.* particulièrement; principalement, surtout.
parting ['pɑːtiŋ], *a.* de séparation; d'adieu; dernier.—*n.* séparation; raie (*cheveux*), *f.*
partisan [pɑːti'zæn], *n.* partisan, *m.*
partition [pɑː'tiʃən], *n.* partage (*division*), *m.*; cloison (*dans une pièce etc.*), *f.*—*v.t.* partager, diviser.
partitive ['pɑːtitiv], *a.* and *n.* partitif, *m.*
partly ['pɑːtli], *adv.* en partie, partiellement.
partner ['pɑːtnə], *n.* (*Comm.*) associé; (*Dancing*) danseur, cavalier, *m.*; (*Cards, Spt.*) partenaire, *m.*, *f.*—*v.t.* s'associer à;

(*Spt.*) être le partenaire de.
partnership ['pɑːtnəʃip], *n.* association, *f.*
partridge ['pɑːtridʒ], *n.* (*Orn.*) perdrix, *f.*; **young partridge**, perdreau, *m.*
part-time ['pɑːttaim], *a.* and *n.* (emploi) à temps partiel, *m.*; **to be on part-time**, être en chômage partiel.
party ['pɑːti], *n.* parti (*politique*), *m.*; partie (*de plaisir*), *f.*; (*fig.*) réunion; réception, *f.*, groupe, *m.*; **to give a party**, recevoir du monde, donner une soirée.
party wall ['pɑːtiwɔːl], *n.* mur mitoyen, *m.*
pasha ['pɑːʃə], *n.* pacha, *m.*
pass [pɑːs], *v.t.* (*Motor.*) doubler.
pass [pɑːs], *v.t.* passer; passer par, passer devant; dépasser; devancer; faire passer; prononcer (*sur*); voter (*un projet de loi etc.*); **to pass an examination**, être reçu *ou* réussir à un examen.—*v.i.* passer, se passer, s'écouler (*temps*); mourir; (*Exam.*) être reçu; (*Ftb.*) faire une passe; (*fig.*) arriver; **to pass away**, disparaître, mourir; **to pass out**, sortir; (*fig.*) s'évanouir.—*n.* passage, défilé, *m.*; gorge, *f.*, col; permis; laissez-passer, *m.*, permission; (*Ftb.*) passe, *f.*; (*fig.*) point, état, *m.*, extrémité, *f.*
passable ['pɑːsəbl], *a.* praticable; navigable (*fleuve etc.*); passable.
passage ['pæsidʒ], *n.* passage, *m.*, traversée, *f.*; (*Arch.*) couloir, corridor, *m.*
pass-book ['pɑːsbuk], *n.* livre de compte, carnet de banque, *m.*
passenger ['pæsindʒə], *n.* voyageur; passager (*par mer ou avion*), *m.*
passer-by ['pɑːsə'bai], *n.* (*pl.* **passers-by** ['pɑːsəz'bai]) passant, *m.*
passing ['pɑːsiŋ], *a.* passager, éphémère, fugitif.—*adv.* extrêmement, éminemment.—*n.* passage; écoulement (*de temps*); (*fig.*) trépas (*mort*), *m.*
passion ['pæʃən], *n.* passion; colère, *f.*, emportement, *m.*
passionate ['pæʃənit], *a.* passionné, ardent; irascible.
passionately ['pæʃənitli], *adv.* à la passion; à la folie, passionnément.
passion-flower ['pæʃənflauə], *n.* passiflore, fleur de la passion, *f.*
passion play ['pæʃənplei], *n.* mystère (de la Passion), *m.*
Passion Week ['pæʃənwiːk], semaine de la Passion, *f.*
passive ['pæsiv], *a.* and *n.* passif, *m.*
passiveness ['pæsivnis], *n.* passivité, inertie, *f.*
pass-key ['pɑːski], *n.* passe-partout, *m.*
Passover ['pɑːsouvə], *n.* la Pâque, *f.*
passport ['pɑːspɔːt], *n.* passeport, *m.*
password ['pɑːswɔːd], *n.* mot de passe; mot d'ordre, *m.*
past [pɑːst], *a.* passé; ancien; dernier (*récent*).—*prep.* au-delà de; près de; sans, hors de; plus de (*âge*); **past three o'clock**, trois heures passées.—*n.* passé, *m.*
paste [peist], *n.* colle (*glu*); pâte (*pour pâtisseries*), *f.*; stras (*faux diamant*), *m.*—*v.t.* coller; **to paste up**, afficher.
pastel ['pæstəl], *n.* pastel, *m.*
pastern ['pæstəːn], *n.* paturon, *m.*
pasteurize ['pæstjuəraiz], *v.t.* pasteuriser (*lait*).
pastille [pæs'tiːl], *n.* pastille, *f.*

pastime ['pɑːstaim], *n.* passe-temps, amusement, *m.*, distraction, *f.*
pastor ['pɑːstə], *n.* (*literal and fig.*) pasteur; (*literal*) berger, *m.*
pastoral ['pɑːstərəl], *a.* pastoral.—*n.* pastorale, églogue, *f.*
pastry ['peistri], *n.* pâtisserie, *f.*
pastry cook ['peistrikuk], *n.* pâtissier, *m.*
pasture ['pɑːstʃə], *n.* pâture, *f.*, herbage; pâturage (*champ etc.*), *m.*—*v.t.* faire paître. —*v.i.* paître.
pasty ['peisti], *n.* pâteux.—['pɑːsti], *n.* pâté, *m.*
pat [pæt], *a. and adv.* à propos, tout juste.—*n.* petite tape; caresse, *f.*; rond de beurre, *m.*— *v.t.* taper, tapoter, caresser.
patch [pætʃ], *n.* pièce; mouche (*pour le visage*), *f.*; morceau (*de terre*); pan (*de ciel*), *m.*; tache (*de couleur*), *f.*—*v.t.* rapiécer, raccommoder; arranger.
patching ['pætʃiŋ], *n.* rapiéçage, ravaudage, *m.*
patchwork ['pætʃwəːk], *n.* mélange, *m.*, mosaïque, *f.*
patchy ['pætʃi], *a.* inégal.
pate [peit], *n.* (*colloq.*) caboche, tête, *f.*
patent ['peitənt, 'pætənt], *a.* breveté; (*fig.*) patent, apparent, évident.—*n.* lettres patentes, *f.pl.*, brevet d'invention, *m.*—*v.t.* breveter.
patentee [peitən'tiː], *n.* breveté, *m.*
paternal [pə'təːnl], *a.* paternel.
paternally [pə'təːnəli], *adv.* paternellement.
paternity [pə'təːniti], *n.* paternité, *f.*
paternoster ['pætə'nɔstə], *n.* patenôtre, *f.*, pater, *m.*
path [pɑːθ], *n.* sentier, chemin, *m.*; allée (*dans un jardin*), *f.*
pathless ['pɑːθlis], *a.* sans chemin frayé; (*fig.*) inconnu.
pathetic [pə'θetik], *a. and n.* pathétique, *m.*
pathfinder ['pɑːθfaində], *n.* pionnier, éclaireur, *m.*
pathological [pæθə'lɔdʒikl], *a.* pathologique.
pathologist [pə'θɔlədʒist], *n.* pathologiste, *m.*, *f.*
pathology [pə'θɔlədʒi], *n.* pathologie, *f.*
pathos ['peiθɔs], *n.* pathétique, *m.*
pathway ['pɑːθwei], *n.* sentier; trottoir (*de rue*); accotement (*de route*), *m.*
patience ['peiʃəns], *n.* patience; (*Cards*) réussite, *f.*
patient ['peiʃənt], *a.* patient, endurant.—*n.* malade, *m.,f.*; patient; client (*de médecin*), *m.*
patiently ['peiʃəntli], *adv.* patiemment.
patriarch ['peitriɑːk], *n.* patriarche, *m.*
patriarchal [peitri'ɑːkl], *a.* patriarcal.
Patrick ['pætrik], Patrice, *m.*
patrimony ['pætriməni], *n.* patrimoine, *m.*
patriot ['peitriət, 'pætriət], *n.* patriote, *m.,f.*
patriotic [peitri'ɔtik], *a.* patriotique (*chose*); patriote (*personne*).
patriotism ['peitriətizm], *n.* patriotisme, *m.*
patrol [pə'troul], *n.* patrouille, ronde, *f.*—*v.t.* faire la patrouille dans.—*v.i.* patrouiller; faire une ronde. [see **prison-van**]
patron ['peitrən], *n.* patron; protecteur; (*Comm.*) client, *m.*; pratique, *f.*
patronage ['pætrənidʒ], *n.* patronage, *m.*, protection, *f.*
patroness ['peitrənes], *n.* patronne, protec-

trice; dame patronnesse (*d'œuvre de bienfaisance*), *f.*
patronize ['pætrənaiz], *v.t.* protéger, patronner; fréquenter (*un magasin*); traiter avec condescendance.
patronizing ['pætrənaiziŋ], *a.* protecteur; ***patronizing tone***, ton de condescendance, *m.*
patronymic [pætrə'nimik], *a.* patronymique. —*n.* nom patronymique, *m.*
patten ['pætən], *n.* patin, socque; (*Arch.*) soubassement, *m.*
patter ['pætə], *v.i.* frapper à petits coups, crépiter; trottiner.
pattering ['pætəriŋ], *n.* grésillement; bruit de petits coups, *m.*
pattern ['pætən], *n.* modèle (*pour*); patron (*à couper*); échantillon (*morceau de tissu etc.*); dessin (*de décoration*); exemple, *m.*
patty ['pæti], *n.* petit pâté, *m.*; bouchée (*à la reine*), *f.*
paucity ['pɔːsiti], *n.* petit nombre, *m.*, disette (*de*), *f.*
Paul [pɔːl]. Paul, *m.*
Paula ['pɔːlə]. Paule, *f.*
paunch [pɔːntʃ], *n.* panse, *f.*, ventre, *m.*
paunchy ['pɔːntʃi], *a.* pansu.
pauper ['pɔːpə], *n.* indigent, *m.*
pauperism ['pɔːpərizm], *n.* paupérisme, *m.*
pauperize ['pɔːpəraiz], *v.t.* réduire à l'indigence.
pause [pɔːz], *n.* pause, *f.*; moment de silence; intervalle, *m.*—*v.i.* faire une pause, s'arrêter.
pave [peiv], *v.t.* paver (*de*); ***to pave the way for***, frayer le chemin à *ou* pour.
pavement ['peivmənt], *n.* trottoir (*bord de rue*); dallage; pavé (*de marbre etc.*), *m.*
paver ['peivə], **pavior** ['peivjə], *n.* paveur, *m.*
pavilion [pə'viliən], *n.* pavillon, *m.*, tente, *f.*
paving ['peiviŋ], *n.* pavage, *m.*
paw [pɔː], *n.* patte; (*facet.*) main, *f.*—*v.t.* manier, tripoter (*manier*); ***to paw the ground***, piaffer.
pawn (1) [pɔːn], *n.* (*Chess*) pion, *m.*
pawn (2) [pɔːn], *v.t.* engager, mettre en gage. —*n.* gage, *m.*
pawnbroker ['pɔːnbroukə], *n.* prêteur sur gage, *m.*
pawnshop ['pɔːnʃɔp], *n.* mont-de-piété, *m.*
pay [pei], *n.* paie, *f.*, salaire (*ouvrier*), traitement (*fonctionnaire*), *m.*; gages (*domestique*), *m.pl.*; (*Mil.*) solde (*officier*), *m.*; prêt (*soldat*), *m.*—*v.t. irr.* payer, acquitter, s'acquitter de; faire (*compliments etc.*); rendre (*honneur*); ***carriage paid***, port payé; ***to pay a visit to***, faire une visite à.—*v.i.* payer; rapporter.
payable ['peiəbl], *a.* payable; ***payable to bearer***, au porteur; ***payable to order***, à l'ordre de.
payee [pei'iː], *n.* porteur, *m.*, bénéficiaire, *m.,f.*
payer ['peiə], *n.* payeur, *m.*
pay-load ['peiloud], *n.* (*Av.*) poids utile, *m.*
paymaster ['peimɑːstə], *n.* payeur; trésorier, *m.*
payment ['peimənt], *n.* payement, paiement, versement, *m.*
pea [piː], *n.* pois, *m.*; ***green peas***, petits pois, *m.pl.*; ***sweet pea***, pois de senteur, *m.*
peace [piːs], *n.* paix, *f.*

peaceable ['pi:səbl], *a.* pacifique.
peaceably ['pi:səbli], *adv.* en paix; avec calme.
peaceful ['pi:sful], *a.* paisible; tranquille, calme.
peacefully ['pi:sfuli], *adv.* paisiblement, tranquillement.
peacefulness ['pi:sfulnis], *n.* tranquillité, *f.*, calme, *m.*
peaceless ['pi:slis], *a.* sans paix, agité.
peacemaker ['pi:smeikə], *n.* pacificateur, *m.*
peach [pi:tʃ], *n.* pêche, *f.*
peach tree ['pi:tʃtri:], *n.* pêcher, *m.*
peacock ['pi:kɔk], *n.* paon, *m.*
pea-green ['pi:gri:n], *a. and n.* vert pois.
pea-hen ['pi:hen], *n.* paonne, *f.*
peak [pi:k] *n.* cime (*de montagne*), *f.*; pic, sommet, *m.*; visière (*d'une casquette*), *f.*
peaked [pi:kt], *a.* à pic, à pointe; à visière.
peal [pi:l], *n.* carillon (*de cloches*); coup, bruit, grondement (*de tonnerre etc.*); éclat (*de rire*), *m.*—*v.i.* carillonner; retentir, résonner; gronder.
peanut ['pi:nʌt], *n.* arachide, cacahuète, *f.*
pea pod ['pi:pɔd], *n.* cosse de pois, *f.*
pear [peə], *n.* poire, *f.*
pearl [pə:l], *n.* perle, *f.*; **mother-of-pearl**, nacre, *f.*—*v.t.*, *v.i.* perler.
pearl oyster ['pə:l'ɔistə], *n.* huître perlière, *f.*
pearly ['pə:li], *a.* de perle, perlé.
pear tree ['peətri:], *n.* poirier, *m.*
peasant ['pezənt], *n.* paysan, *m.*
peasantry ['pezəntri], *n.* paysans, *m.pl.*
pea soup ['pi:'su:p], *n.* purée de pois, *f.*
peat [pi:t], *n.* tourbe, *f.*
peat bog ['pi:tbɔg], *n.* tourbière, *f.*
pebble [pebl], *n.* caillou, galet (*de plage*), *m.*
pebbly ['pebli], *a.* caillouteux.
peccadillo [pekə'dilou], *n.* peccadille, *f.*
peck (1) [pek], *n.* picotin (*d'avoine etc.*), *m.*
peck (2) [pek], *n.* coup de bec (*d'oiseau*), *m.*—*v.t.* becqueter; **a hen-pecked husband**, un mari mené par sa femme.
pectoral ['pektərəl], *a. and n.* pectoral, *m.*
peculation [pekju'leiʃən], *n.* péculat, *m.*
peculator ['pekjuleitə], *n.* concussionnaire, *m.*, *f.*
peculiar [pi'kju:liə], *a.* particulier, propre; singulier, bizarre.
peculiarity [pikjuli'æriti], *n.* singularité, particularité, *f.*
peculiarly [pi'kju:liəli], *adv.* particulièrement, singulièrement.
pecuniary [pi'kju:niəri], *a.* pécuniaire.
pedagogic(al) [pedə'gɔdʒik(l)], *a.* pédagogique.
pedagogue ['pedəgɔg], *n.* pédagogue, *m.*, *f.*
pedal [pedl], *n.* pédale, *f.*—*v.i.* pédaler.
pedant ['pedənt], *n.* pédant, *m.*
pedantic [pi'dæntik], *a.* pédant (*personne*), pédantesque (*choses*).
pedantry ['pedəntri], *n.* pédantisme, *m.*, pédanterie, *f.*
peddle [pedl], *v.t.* colporter.—*v.i.* faire le colportage.
peddler [PEDLAR].
pedestal ['pedistl], *n.* piédestal, socle, *m.*
pedestrian [pə'destriən], *a.* à pied, pédestre; (*fig.*) prosaïque.—*n.* piéton, marcheur, *m.*
pedigree ['pedigri:], *n.* généalogie; origine, *f.*; arbre généalogique, *m.*
pediment ['pedimənt], *n.* (*Arch.*) fronton, *m.*

508

pedlar ['pedlə], *n.* colporteur, *m.*
pedometer [pə'dɔmitə], *n.* podomètre, *m.*
peel [pi:l], *n.* pelure; écorce (*d'orange etc.*), *f.*—*v.t.* peler; éplucher.—*v.i.* se peler; s'écailler.
peep [pi:p], *n.* coup d'œil furtif, *m.*; pointe (*du jour*), *f.*—*v.i.* regarder à la dérobée; paraître, poindre.
peeper ['pi:pə], *n.* curieux, *m.*
peep-hole ['pi:phoul], *n.* judas, *m.*
peeping-Tom ['pi:piŋ'tɔm], *n.* voyeur, *m.*
peer (1) [piə], *v.i.* scruter du regard.
peer (2) [piə], *n.* pair; (*fig.*) égal, pareil, *m.*
peerage ['piəridʒ], *n.* pairie, *f.*; les pairs, *m.pl.*
peeress ['piəris], *n.* pairesse, *f.*
peerless ['piəlis], *a.* incomparable; sans pareil.
peerlessly ['piəlisli], *adv.* incomparablement.
peerlessness ['piəlisnis], *n.* supériorité incomparable, *f.*
peevish ['pi:viʃ], *a.* irritable, maussade.
peevishly ['pi:viʃli], *adv.* maussadement, avec mauvaise humeur.
peevishness ['pi:viʃnis], *n.* maussaderie, humeur acariâtre, *f.*
peewit [PEWIT].
peg [peg], *n.* cheville; patère (*à chapeau etc.*), *f.*; fausset (*de tonneaux*), piquet (*de tente*), *m.*—*v.t.*, *v.i.* cheviller.
pejorative [pə'dʒɔrətiv, 'pi:dʒərətiv], *a.* péjoratif.
Pekinese [pi:ki'ni:z], *a.* pékinois.—*n.* (*épagneul*) pékinois; Pékinois (*personne*), *m.*
Peking [pi:'kiŋ], Pékin, *m.*
Pekingese [pi:kin'i:z], [PEKINESE].
pelican ['pelikən], *n.* pélican, *m.*
pellet ['pelit], *n.* boulette, *f.*; grain de plomb, *m.*
pellicle ['pelikl], *n.* pellicule, *f.*
pell-mell ['pel'mel], *adv.* pêle-mêle.
pellucid [pə'lju:sid], *a.* transparent, clair, pellucide.
pelmet ['pelmit], *n.* lambrequin, *m.*
pelt (1) [pelt], *v.t.* assaillir, battre.
pelt (2) [pelt], *n.* peau, *f.*—*v.t.* écorcher.
pelting ['peltiŋ], *a.* battant (*pluie*).—*n.* attaque, *f.*, assaut, *m.*; grêle (*de pierres*), *f.*
pelvic ['pelvik], *a.* pelvien.
pelvis ['pelvis], *n.* bassin, *m.*
pemmican ['pemikən], *n.* conserve de viande, *f.*; pemmican, *m.*
pen [pen], *n.* plume, *f.*; parc, enclos (*bestiaux etc.*); poulailler (*pour volaille*), *m.*; **fountain pen**, stylo, *m.*—*v.t.* écrire; rédiger; parquer, enfermer (*bétail*).
penal [pi:nl], *a.* pénal, passible d'une amende; **penal servitude**, travaux forcés, *m.pl.*
penalize ['pi:nəlaiz], *v.t.* infliger une peine à (*quelqu'un*); (*Spt.*) pénaliser.
penalty ['penəlti], *n.* peine; pénalité, amende, *f.*; (*Ftb.*) penalty, *m.*
penance ['penəns], *n.* pénitence, *f.*
pence [PENNY].
pencil [pensl], *n.* crayon, *m.*—*v.t.* dessiner *ou* écrire au crayon.
pencil case ['penslkeis], *n.* porte-crayon, *m.*
pencil sharpener ['pensl'ʃɑ:pnə], *n.* taille-crayon, *m.*
pendant ['pendənt], *n.* pendant, *m.*; pendeloque, *f.*; pendentif, *m.*

pendent ['pendənt], *a.* pendant; suspendu.
pending ['pendiŋ], *a.* pendant, non décidé; en cours.—*prep.* en attendant.
pendulum ['pendjuləm], *n.* pendule, balancier, *m.*
penetrable ['penitrəbl], *a.* pénétrable, sensible.
penetrate ['penitreit], *v.t., v.i.* pénétrer (*dans*).
penetrating ['penitreitiŋ], *a.* pénétrant, perçant; clairvoyant, perspicace.
penetration [peni'treiʃən], *n.* pénétration, *f.*
penguin ['peŋgwin], *n.* manchot, *m.*
pen-holder ['penhouldə], *n.* porte-plume, *m.*
penicillin [peni'silin], *n.* pénicilline, *f.*
peninsula [pi'ninsjulə], *n.* péninsule, presqu'île, *f.*
peninsular [pi'ninsjulə], *a.* péninsulaire.
penitence ['penitəns], *n.* pénitence, *f.*, repentir, *m.*
penitent ['penitənt], *a.* pénitent, repentant.
penitentiary [peni'tenʃəri], *a.* pénitentiaire. —*n.* pénitencier, *m.*; (*Am.*) prison, *f.*
penknife ['pennaif], *n.* canif, *m.*
pennant ['penənt], *n.* (*Naut.*) flamme, *f.*
penniless ['penilis], *a.* sans le sou, sans ressources.
penny ['peni], *n.* (*pl.* **pence** [pens], *of a sum*, or **pennies** ['peniz], *of a number of coins*) penny, *m.*
pension ['penʃən], *n.* pension; pension de retraite, retraite (*d'officiers etc.*), *f.*—*v.t.* **to pension off**, mettre à la retraite.
pensioner ['penʃənə], *n.* pensionnaire, *m., f.*; (*Mil.*) invalide, *m.*
pensive ['pensiv], *a.* pensif, préoccupé, rêveur.
pensively ['pensivli], *adv.* d'un air pensif.
pensiveness ['pensivnis], *n.* air pensif, air préoccupé, *m.*
pent [pent], *a.* **pent up**, enfermé, (*fig.*) étouffé, refoulé.
pentagon ['pentəgən], *n.* pentagone, *m.*
Pentecost ['pentikɔst]. Pentecôte, *f.*
penthouse ['penthaus], *n.* appartement sur toit; appentis, *m.*
penultimate [pe'nʌltimit], *a.* pénultième, avant-dernier.
penurious [pi'njuəriəs], *a.* avare; ladre; pauvre (*choses*).
penury ['penjuəri], *n.* pénurie, *f.*
peony ['pi:əni], *n.* pivoine, *f.*
people [pi:pl], *n.* peuple, *m.*, nation, *f.*, gens, *m.pl.*; on, monde, *m.*, personnes (*en général*), *f.pl.*—*v.t.* peupler (*de*).
pepper ['pepə], *n.* poivre, *m.*—*v.t.* poivrer; (*fig.*) cribler de coups.
pepper caster ['pepə'ka:stə], *n.* poivrière, *f.*
peppercorn ['pepəkɔ:n], *n.* grain de poivre, *m.*
peppermint ['pepəmint], *n.* menthe poivrée, *f.*
peppery ['pepəri], *a.* poivré; (*fig.*) irritable.
per [pə:], *prep.* par; le, *m.*, la, *f.*, les, *pl.*; **three francs per pound**, trois francs la livre.
perambulate [pə'ræmbjuleit], *v.t.* parcourir.
perambulation [pəræmbju'leiʃən], *n.* parcours, *m.*; promenade, *f.*
perambulator [pə'ræmbjuleitə], *n.* voiture d'enfant, *f.*
perceive [pə'si:v], *v.t.* apercevoir (*visuellement*), s'apercevoir de (*se rendre compte de*).

percentage [pə'sentidʒ], *n.* pourcentage, *m.*
perceptibility [pəsepti'biliti], *n.* perceptibilité, *f.*
perceptible [pə'septibl], *a.* perceptible, sensible.
perceptibly [pə'septibli], *adv.* perceptiblement, sensiblement.
perception [pə'sepʃən], *n.* perception, sensibilité; découverte, *f.*
perceptive [pə'septiv], *a.* perceptif.
perch (1) [pə:tʃ], *n.* perche (*poisson*), *f.*
perch (2) [pə:tʃ], *n.* perchoir (*à poules etc.*) *m.* —*v.t., v.i.* percher.
percolate ['pə:kəleit], *v.t., v.i.* filtrer, passer.
percolation [pə:kə'leiʃən], *n.* filtration, infiltration, *f.*
percolator ['pə:kəleitə], filtre (à café), *m.*
percussion [pə'kʌʃən], *n.* percussion, *f.*
percussion cap [pə'kʌʃənkæp], *n.* capsule, *f.*
perdition [pə'diʃən], *n.* perdition, ruine, *f.*
peregrinate ['perigrineit], *v.i.* voyager.
peregrination [perigri'neiʃən], *n.* pérégrination, *f.*, voyage à l'étranger, *m.*
peremptorily [pə'remptərili], *adv.* péremptoirement, absolument, formellement.
peremptory [pə'remptəri], *a.* péremptoire, absolu.
perennial [pə'reniəl], *a.* vivace (*plantes*); (*fig.*) éternel.—*n.* plante vivace, *f.*
perfect (1) ['pə:fikt], *a.* parfait; achevé.— [pə'fekt], *v.t.* rendre parfait, perfectionner; achever.
perfect (2) ['pə:fikt], *n.* (*Gram.*) parfait, *m.*
perfection [pə'fekʃən], *n.* perfection, *f.*
perfectly ['pə:fiktli], *adv.* parfaitement.
perfidious [pə'fidiəs], *a.* perfide.
perfidiousness [pə'fidiəsnis], **perfidy** ['pə:fidi], *n.* perfidie, *f.*
perforate ['pə:fəreit], *v.t.* perforer, percer.
perforation [pə:fə'reiʃən], *n.* percement, *m.*, perforation; dentelure (*de timbre-poste*), *f.*
perforce [pə'fɔ:s], *adv.* forcément, de force.
perform [pə'fɔ:m], *v.t.* exécuter, accomplir; (*Theat.*) jouer.—*v.i.* jouer un rôle.
performance [pə'fɔ:məns], *n.* accomplissement; ouvrage, *m.*, œuvre (*chose achevée*), *f.*; (*Mach.*) fonctionnement, *m.*; (*Theat.*) représentation; (*Mus.*) exécution; (*Spt.*) performance, *f.*
performer [pə'fɔ:mə], *n.* (*Theat.*) acteur, *m.*, actrice, *f.*; (*Mus.*) artiste, *m., f.*
perfume ['pə:fjum], *n.* parfum, *m.*—[pə'fju:m], *v.t.* parfumer (*de*).
perfumery [pə'fju:məri], *n.* parfumerie, *f.*
perfunctorily [pə'fʌŋktərili], *adv.* par manière d'acquit; tant bien que mal.
perfunctory [pə'fʌŋktəri], *a.* de pure forme; négligent.
perhaps [pə'hæps], *adv.* peut-être; **perhaps not**, peut-être que non; **perhaps so**, peut-être que oui.
peril ['peril], *n.* péril, danger, *m.*
perilous ['periləs], *a.* périlleux, dangereux.
perilously ['periləsli], *adv.* périlleusement.
perimeter [pə'rimitə], *n.* périmètre, *m.*
period ['piəriəd], *n.* période, *f.*, temps, *m.*, durée; époque; fin, *f.*, terme (*conclusion*); (*Am.*) point (*ponctuation*), *m.*; (*Rhet. etc.*) phrase, *f.*; (*Physiol.*) règles, *f.pl.*
periodic [piəri'ɔdik], *a.* périodique.
periodical [piəri'ɔdikl], *a.* and *n.* périodique, *m.*

509

periodically [piəri'ɔdikli], adv. périodiquement.
peripatetic [peripə'tetik], a. péripatéticien.
periphery [pə'rifəri], n. périphérie, f.
periphrasis [pə'rifrəsis], n. (pl. **periphrases** [pə'rifrəsi:z]) périphrase, f.
periscope ['periskoup], n. périscope, m.
perish ['periʃ], v.i. périr (de), mourir; dépérir.
perishable ['periʃəbl], a. périssable.
peritonitis [perita'naitis], n. péritonite, f.
***periwig** ['periwig], n. perruque, f.
periwinkle ['periwiŋkl], n. (Bot.) pervenche, f.; bigorneau (mollusque), m.
perjure ['pə:dʒə], v.t. **to perjure oneself**, se parjurer.
perjurer ['pə:dʒərə], n. parjure, m., f.
perjury ['pə:dʒəri], n. parjure; (Law) faux témoignage, faux serment, m.; **wilful perjury**, parjure prémédité.
perk [pə:k], v.i. **to perk up**, se ranimer, se raviver.—n. (pl.) (fam.) [PERQUISITE].
perky ['pə:ki], a. déluré; outrecuidant.
permanency ['pə:mənənsi], **permanence** ['pə:mənəns], n. permanence, f.
permanent ['pə:mənənt], a. permanent; en permanence.
permanently ['pə:mənəntli], adv. en permanence.
permeable ['pə:miəbl], a. perméable.
permeate ['pə:mieit], v.t. pénétrer.
permissible [pə'misibl], a. permis.
permission [pə'miʃən], n. permission, f., permis, m.
permissive [pə'misiv], a. qui permet; toléré.
permit [pə'mit], v.t. permettre (à quelqu'un de . . .).—['pə:mit], n. permis, m.
permutation [pə:mju'teiʃən], n. permutation, f.
pernicious [pə'niʃəs], a. pernicieux.
perniciously [pə'niʃəsli], adv. pernicieusement.
peroration [perə'reiʃən], n. péroraison, f.
peroxide [pə'rɔksaid], n. peroxyde, m.—v.t. oxygéner (cheveux).
perpendicular [pə:pən'dikjulə], a. and n. perpendiculaire, f.
perpendicularly [pə:pən'dikjuləli], adv. perpendiculairement.
perpetrate ['pə:pitreit], v.t. commettre; (Law) perpétrer.
perpetration [pə:pi'treiʃən], n. exécution; (Law) perpétration, f.
perpetrator ['pə:pitreitə], n. auteur (d'un crime), m.
perpetual [pə'petjuəl], a. perpétuel.
perpetually [pə'petjuali], adv. perpétuellement.
perpetuate [pə'petjueit], v.t. perpétuer.
perpetuation [pəpetju'eiʃən], n. perpétuation, f.
perpetuity [pə:pi'tju:iti], n. perpétuité, f.
perplex [pə'pleks], v.t. embarrasser.
perplexed [pə'plekst], a. perplexe, embarrassé.
perplexing [pə'pleksiŋ], a. embarrassant.
perplexity [pə'pleksiti], n. perplexité, f.
perquisite ['pə:kwizit], n. émolument casuel, m.
perry ['peri], n. poiré, m.
persecute ['pə:sikju:t], v.t. persécuter.
persecuting ['pə:sikju:tiŋ], a. persécuteur.
persecution [pə:si'kju:ʃən], n. persécution, f.

persecutor ['pə:sikjutə], n. persécuteur, m.
perseverance [pə:si'viərəns], n. persévérance, f.
persevere [pə:si'viə], v.i. persévérer (à ou dans).
persevering [pə:si'viəriŋ], a. persévérant.
perseveringly [pə:si'viəriŋli], adv. avec persévérance.
Persia ['pə:ʃə]. la Perse, f.
Persian ['pə:ʃən], a. de Perse, persan.—n. perse (langue); Persan (personne), m.; **the Persian Gulf**, le Golfe Persique.
persist [pə'sist], v.i. persister (dans ou à); continuer.
persistence [pə'sistəns], n. persistance, f.
persistent [pə'sistənt], a. persistant; opiniâtre.
person ['pə:sən], n. personne, f.; personnage, caractère, m.; (pl.) personnes, f.pl., gens, m.pl., f.pl.; **young persons**, les jeunes gens.
personage ['pə:sənidʒ], n. personnage, m.
personal ['pə:sənl], a. personnel.
personality [pə:sə'næliti], n. personnalité, f.
personally ['pə:sənli], adv. personnellement.
personate ['pə:səneit], v.t. se faire passer pour; représenter, contrefaire.
personification [pəsɔnifi'keiʃən], n. personnification, f.
personify [pə'sɔnifai], v.t. personnifier.
personnel [pə:sə'nel], n. personnel, m.
perspective [pə'spektiv], a. perspectif.—n. perspective, f.
perspicacious [pə:spi'keiʃəs], a. pénétrant, perspicace; perçant (la vision), f.
perspicacity [pə:spi'kæsiti], n. perspicacité, f.
perspicuity [pə:spi'kju:iti], n. clarté, f.
perspicuous [pə'spikjuəs], a. clair, net.
perspiration [pə:spi'reiʃən], n. transpiration, sueur, f.
perspire [pə'spaiə], v.i. transpirer, suer.
persuade [pə'sweid], v.t. persuader; **to persuade from**, dissuader de.
persuasion [pə'sweiʒən], n. persuasion, f.
persuasive [pə'sweisiv], a. persuasif.
persuasiveness [pə'sweisivnis], n. force persuasive, f.
pert [pə:t], a. mutin, hardi; impertinent, insolent (effronté).
pertain [pə'tein], v.i. appartenir.
pertinacious [pə:ti'neiʃəs], a. obstiné, opiniâtre.
pertinacity [pə:ti'næsiti], n. obstination, f.
pertinence ['pə:tinəns], n. convenance, f.
pertinent ['pə:tinənt], a. pertinent, convenable.
pertly ['pə:tli], adv. impertinemment, insolemment.
pertness ['pə:tnis], n. impertinence, f.
perturb [pə'tə:b], v.t. agiter, troubler.
perturbation [pə:tə'beiʃən], n. agitation, f.
perturbed [pə'tə:bd], a. troublé, inquiet.
Peru [pə'ru:]. le Pérou, m.
perusal [pə'ru:zl], n. lecture, f.
peruse [pə'ru:z], v.t. lire attentivement.
Peruvian [pə'ru:viən], a. péruvien, du Pérou.—n. Péruvien (personne), m.
pervade [pə'veid], v.t. pénétrer dans; se répandre dans, remplir.
pervading [pə'veidiŋ], a. **all-pervading**, dominant.
perverse [pə'və:s], a. pervers.

perversely [pə'və:sli], *adv.* avec perversité.
perverseness [pə'və:snis], **perversity** [pə'və:siti], *n.* perversité, *f.*
perversion [pə'və:ʃən], *n.* perversion, *f.*
pervert [pə'və:t], *v.t.* pervertir; fausser, dénaturer.—['pə:və:t], *n.* perverti, *m.*
perverted [pə'və:tid], *a.* perverti.
pervious ['pə:viəs], *a.* perméable, pénétrable.
pessimism ['pesimizm], *n.* pessimisme, *m.*
pessimist ['pesimist], *n.* pessimiste, *m.*, *f.*
pessimistic [pesi'mistik], *a.* pessimiste.
pest [pest], *n.* peste, *f.*
pester ['pestə], *v.t.* tourmenter, ennuyer.
pestilence ['pestiləns], *n.* peste, pestilence, *f.*
pestilent ['pestilənt], *a.* pestilentiel, contagieux.
pestilential [pesti'lenʃl], *a.* pestilentiel.
pet (1) [pet], *a.* favori; *pet aversion*, bête noire, *f.*—*n.* chéri, *m.*, chérie, *f.*, favori, *m.*, favorite, *f.*; animal familier; enfant gâté, *m.* —*v.t.* choyer, dorloter; (*Am.*) caresser.
pet (2) [pet], *n.* accès d'humeur, *m.*
petal [petl], *n.* pétale, *m.*
Peter ['pi:tə]. Pierre, *m.*
peter out [pi:tə'raut], *v.i.* (*colloq.*) s'épuiser; tomber à l'eau (*projet*), flancher (*machine*).
petition [pi'tiʃən], *n.* pétition, *f.*—*v.t.* pétitionner.
petitioner [pi'tiʃənə], *n.* (*Law*) requérant, *m.*; pétitionnaire, *m.*, *f.*
petrel ['petrəl], *n.* (*Orn.*) pétrel, *m.*
petrifaction [petri'fækʃən], *n.* pétrification, *f.*
petrify ['petrifai], *v.t.* pétrifier.—*v.i.* se pétrifier.
petrol ['petrəl], *n.* essence, *f.*; *petrol station*, poste d'essence, *m.*
petrol can ['petrəlkæn], *n.* bidon d'essence, *m.*
petroleum [pi'trouliəm], *n.* pétrole, *m.*, huile de pétrole, *f.*
petticoat ['petikout], *n.* jupon, *m.*
pettifogging ['petifogin], *a.* avocassier, chicaneur; chicanier (*méthodes etc.*).
pettiness ['petinis], *n.* petitesse, mesquinerie, *f.*
petty ['peti], *a.* petit; mesquin, chétif; (*Law*) inférieur.
petty officer ['peti'ofisə], *n.* (*Navy*) officier marinier, *m.*
petulance ['petjuləns], *n.* irritabilité, *f.*
petulant ['petjulənt], *a.* irritable.
pew [pju:], *n.* banc d'église, *m.*
pewit ['pi:wit], *n.* (*Orn.*) vanneau, *m.*
pewter ['pju:tə], *n.* étain, potin, *m.*; vaisselle d'étain, *f.*
phalanx ['fælæŋks], *n.* (*pl.* **phalanges** [fə'lændʒi:z]) phalange, *f.*
phantom ['fæntəm], *n.* fantôme, *m.*
Pharaoh ['fɛərou], *n.* Pharaon, *m.*
Pharisee ['færisi:], *n.* Pharisien, *m.*
pharmaceutical [fa:mə'sju:tikəl], *a.* pharmaceutique.
pharmacy ['fa:məsi], *n.* pharmacie, *f.*
phase [feiz], *n.* phase, *f.*
pheasant ['fezənt], *n.* faisan, *m.*
phenomenal [fi'nəmənəl], *a.* phénoménal.
phenomenon [fi'nəmənən], *n.* (*pl.* **phenomena** [fi'nəmənə]) phénomène, *m.*
phew! [fju:], *int.* pouf!
phial [faiəl], *n.* fiole, *f.*
philanthropic [filən'θrɔpik], *a.* philanthropique.

philanthropist [fi'lænθrəpist], *n.* philanthrope, *m.*, *f.*
philanthropy [fi'lænθrəpi], *n.* philanthropie, *f.*
philatelist [fi'lætəlist], *n.* philatéliste, *m.*, *f.*
philharmonic [filha:'mɔnik], *a.* philharmonique.
Philip ['filip]. Philippe, *m.*
Philippine ['filipi:n], *a.* philippine.
Philippines ['filipi:nz], **the**, les Philippines, *f.pl.*
Philistine ['filistain], *a.* philistin.—*n.* Philistin (*personne*), *m.*
philologist [fi'lɔlədʒist], *n.* philologue, *m.*, *f.*
philology [fi'lɔlədʒi], *n.* philologie, *f.*
philosopher [fi'lɔsəfə], *n.* philosophe, *m.*, *f.*
philosophical [filə'sɔfikl], *a.* philosophique; philosophe (*personnes*).
philosophize [fi'lɔsəfaiz], *v.i.* philosopher.
philosophy [fi'lɔsəfi], *n.* philosophie, *f.*; *natural philosophy*, la physique, *f.*
philter, philtre ['filtə], *n.* philtre, *m.*
phlegm [flem], *n.* flegme, *m.*
phlegmatic [fleg'mætik], *a.* flegmatique.
phobia ['foubiə], *n.* phobie, *f.*
Phoebe ['fi:bi]. Phébé, *f.*
Phoenician [fi'ni:ʃən], *a.* phénicien.—*n.* Phénicien (*personne*), *m.*
phoenix ['fi:niks], *n.* phénix, *m.*
phone [foun], *n.* (*colloq.*) [TELEPHONE].
phonetic [fə'netik], *a.* phonétique.
phonetics [fə'netiks], *n.pl.* phonétique, *f.*
phoney ['founi], *a.* (*colloq.*) faux, factice.—*n.* charlatan, *m.*
phonograph, see **gramophone**.
phosphate ['fɔsfeit], *n.* phosphate, *m.*
phosphor ['fɔsfə], *n.* phosphore, *m.*
phosphoric [fɔs'fɔrik], *a.* phosphorique.
phosphorus ['fɔsfərəs], *n.* phosphore, *m.*
photo ['foutou], *n.* (*colloq.*) [PHOTOGRAPH].
photogenic [foutə'dʒenik], *a.* photogénique.
photograph ['foutəgra:f, 'foutəgræf], *n.* photographie, (*colloq.*) photo, *f.*—*v.t.* photographier.
photographer [fə'tɔgrəfə], *n.* photographe, *m.*, *f.*
photographic [foutə'græfik], *a.* photographique.
photography [fə'tɔgrəfi], *n.* photographie, *f.*
photostat ['foutəstæt], *n.* appareil photostat, *m.*
phrase [freiz], *n.* phrase, locution, *f.*—*v.t.* exprimer, nommer; (*Mus.*) phraser.
phraseology [freizi'ɔlədʒi], *n.* phraséologie, *f.*
phrenetic [fre'netik], *a.* fou, frénétique.
phrenologist [fre'nɔlədʒist], *n.* phrénologiste, phrénologue, *m.*, *f.*
phrenology [fre'nɔlədʒi], *n.* phrénologie, *f.*
physic ['fizik], *n.* médecine, *f.*—*v.t.* médicamenter; purger.
physical ['fizikəl], *a.* physique; *physical training*, éducation physique, *f.*
physically ['fizikəli], *adv.* physiquement.
physician [fi'ziʃən], *n.* médecin, *m.*
physicist ['fizisist], *n.* physicien, *m.*
physics ['fiziks], *n.pl.* physique, *f.*
physiognomy [fizi'ɔnəmi, fizi'ɔgnəmi], *n.* physionomie, *f.*
physiological [fiziə'lɔdʒikl], *a.* physiologique.
physiology [fizi'ɔlədʒi], *n.* physiologie, *f.*

physiotherapy [fizio'θerəpi], *n.* physiothérapie, *f.*

physique [fi'zi:k], *n.* physique, *m.*

pianist ['piənist], *n.* pianiste, *m.*, *f.*

piano ['pjænou, 'pjɑ:nou], **pianoforte** [-'fɔ:ti], *n.* piano, *m*; ***grand piano***, piano à queue; ***to play (on) the piano***, jouer du piano. [see **music-stool**]

pick [pik], *n.* pic, *m.*, pioche (*outil*), *f.*; choix, *m.*—*v.t.* piquer; cueillir; choisir, trier; ronger (*un os*); chercher (*querelle*); voler à la tire (*dans une poche*); crocheter (*une serrure*); ***to pick up***, ramasser, relever.

pickaback ['pikəbæk], *adv.* sur le dos.

pickaxe ['pikæks], *n.* pioche, *f.*

picked [pikt], *a.* d'élite, choisi.

picker ['pikə], *n.* cueilleur, *m.*

picket ['pikit], *n.* piquet, jalon; petit poste, *m.*—*v.t.* former en piquet; guetter (*grévistes etc.*).

pickle [pikl], *n.* saumure, marinade, *f.*; (*pl.*) conserves au vinaigre, *f.pl.*—*v.t.* conserver au vinaigre, mariner; saler.

pickled [pikld], *a.* mariné, conservé au vinaigre; (*pop.*) ivre.

pickpocket ['pikpɔkit], *n.* voleur à la tire, *m.*

pick-up ['pikʌp], *n.* ramassage, *m.*; reprise (*de machine, des affaires*), *f.*; pick-up (*tourne-disque*), *m.*

picnic ['piknik], *n.* pique-nique, *m.*—*v.i.* faire un pique-nique.

pictorial [pik'tɔ:riəl], *a.* illustré; de peintre.

pictorially [pik'tɔ:riəli], *adv.* avec illustrations.

picture ['piktʃə], *n.* tableau, *m.*; peinture, (*fig.*) image, *f.*; (*pl.*) ***the pictures***, le cinéma.—*v.t.* peindre; (*fig.*) dépeindre, représenter.

picturesque [piktʃə'resk], *a.* pittoresque.

pie [pai], *n.* pâté (*de viande*), *m.*; tourte (*de fruit*), *f.*; (*colloq.*) ***as easy as pie***, simple comme bonjour; ***to eat humble pie***, avaler des couleuvres.

piebald ['paibɔ:ld], *a.* pie (*cheval*).

piece [pi:s], *n.* pièce (*grand*), *f.*; morceau (*petit*); fragment, bout, *m.*; ***a piece of furniture***, un meuble; ***a piece of news***, une nouvelle; ***to break to pieces***, mettre en pièces; ***to take to pieces***, démonter.—*v.t.* rapiécer.

piecemeal ['pi:smi:l], *adv.* par morceaux, peu à peu.

pied [paid], *a.* bariolé, bigarré; pie (*cheval*).

pie dish ['paidiʃ], *n.* tourtière, terrine, *f.*

pier [piə], *n.* jetée, *f.*; ponton (*de rivière*), *m.*; pile (*d'un pont*), *f.*

pierce [piəs], *v.t.* percer, pénétrer.

pierced [piəst], *a.* à jour (*ouvrage*), *m.*

piercing ['piəsiŋ], *a.* perçant; pénétrant.

pier glass ['piəglɑ:s], *n.* trumeau, *m.*

piety ['paiəti], *n.* piété, *f.*

pig [pig], *n.* cochon, porc, pourceau, *m.*; ***to buy a pig in a poke***, acheter chat en poche.

pigeon ['pidʒin], *a.* timide, craintif.—*n.* pigeon, *m.*; ***carrier pigeon***, pigeon voyageur.

pigeon-hole ['pidʒinhoul], *n.* boulin, *m.*; case (*à papiers etc.*), *f.*; ***set of pigeon-holes***, casier, *m.*—*v.t.* classer.

piggery ['pigəri], *n.* étable à cochons, *f.*

piggy ['pigi], **piglet** ['piglit], *n.* porcelet, goret, *m.*

pigheaded ['pighedid], *a.* têtu, stupide.

pig iron ['pigaiən], *n.* gueuse, *f.*

pigment ['pigmənt], *n.* couleur, *f.*, pigment *m.*

pigmy [PYGMY].

pigsty ['pigstai], *n.* porcherie, *f.*

pigtail ['pigteil], *n.* queue (*de cheveux*), *f.*

pigtailed ['pigteild], *a.* à queue.

pike [paik], *n.* pique (*arme*), *f.*; brochet (*poisson*), *m.*

pilchard ['piltʃəd], *n.* (*Ichth.*) pilchard, *m.*

pile [pail], *n.* tas, monceau; (*fig.*) (*Build.*) édifice, bâtiment; pieu (*poteau*); poil (*de tissu*), *m.*; ***atomic pile***, pile atomique, *f.*; ***funeral pile***, bûcher, *m.*—*v.t.* entasser, empiler, amonceler.—*v.i.* ***to pile up***, s'empiler, s'entasser.

piles [pailz], *n.pl.* (*Path.*) hémorroïdes, *f.pl.*

pilfer ['pilfə], *v.t.* dérober, chiper.—*v.i.* dérober.

pilferer ['pilfərə], *n.* chapardeur, chipeur, *m.*

pilfering ['pilfəriŋ], *n.* petit vol, larcin, *m.*

pilgrim ['pilgrim], *n.* pèlerin, *m.*

pilgrimage ['pilgrimidʒ], *n.* pèlerinage, *m.*

pill [pil], *n.* pilule, *f.*

pillage ['pilidʒ], *n.* pillage, saccagement, *m.*—*v.t.* saccager, piller.

pillar ['pilə], *n.* pilier, *m.*, colonne, *f.*; (*fig.*) soutien, *m.*

pillar-box ['piləbɔks], *n.* boîte aux lettres, *f.*

pillion ['piljən], *n.* coussinet (*de cheval*), *m.*; siège, *m.* (*ou* selle, *f.*) arrière (*de motocyclette*); ***to ride pillion***, monter en croupe, monter derrière.

pillory ['piləri], *n.* pilori, *m.*—*v.t.* pilorier, mettre au pilori.

pillow ['pilou], *n.* oreiller, *m.*—*v.t.* reposer, coucher.

pillow-case ['piloukeis], **pillow slip** ['pilou slip], *n.* taie d'oreiller, *f.*

pilot ['pailət], *n.* pilote, *m.*; ***test pilot***, pilote d'essais.—*v.t.* piloter, servir de pilote à.

pilotage ['pailətidʒ], *n.* pilotage, *m.*

pimpernel ['pimpənel], *n.* pimprenelle, *f.*, mouron, *m.*

pimple [pimpl], *n.* bouton, *m.*

pimply ['pimpli], *a.* bourgeonné, pustuleux.

pin [pin], *n.* épingle; cheville (*de bois*), *f.*; (*fig.*) rien, *m.*—*v.t.* épingler, attacher; cheviller.

pinafore ['pinəfɔ:], *n.* tablier (d'enfant), *m.*

pincers ['pinsəz], *n.pl.* pince, *f.*, tenailles, *f.pl.*

pinch [pintʃ], *n.* pincée (*de sel etc.*); prise (*de tabac*), *f.*; (*fig.*) embarras, *m.*; ***at a pinch***, à la rigueur, au besoin.—*v.t.* pincer, serrer, gêner (*habits*); (*pop.*) chiper (*voler*); pincer (*arrêter*).—*v.i.* pincer; se gêner.

pinching ['pintʃiŋ], *a.* pressant, piquant (*froid*).—*n.* pincement, *m.*

pin-cushion ['pinkuʃən], *n.* pelote, *f.*

pine (1) [pain], *n.* pin (*arbre*); bois de pin, *m.*

pine (2) [pain], *v.i.* languir; ***to pine after***, soupirer après.

pineapple ['painæpl], *n.* ananas, *m.*

ping [piŋ], *n.* sifflement (*de balle de fusil*), *m.*—*v.i.* siffler.

ping-pong ['piŋpɔŋ], *n.* ping-pong, *m.*

pinion ['pinjən], *n.* aileron, bout d'aile, *m.*—*v.t.* couper le bout de l'aile à; lier.

pink (1) [piŋk], *a.* couleur de rose, rose.—*n.* œillet (*fleur*); rose (*couleur*), *m.*; ***in the pink of condition***, en excellente condition;

(colloq.) **to be in the pink**, se porter à merveille.
pink (2) [piŋk], *v.i.* cliqueter *(moteur)*.
pinnace ['pinəs], *n.* pinasse, *f.*
pinnacle ['pinəkl], *n.* pinacle, *m.*
pin-point ['pinpɔint], *v.t.* indiquer exactement.
pin pricks ['pinpriks], *n.pl.* coups d'épingles, *m.pl.*
pint [paint], *n.* pinte *(un demi-litre)*, *f.*
pintail ['pinteil], *n.* *(Orn.)* pilet, *m.*
pioneer [paiə'niə], *n.* pionnier, *m.*
pious ['paiəs], *a.* pieux.
piously ['paiəsli], *adv.* pieusement.
pip [pip], *n.* pépin *(de fruit)*; *(Rad.)* top, *m.—v.i.* piauler *(oiseaux)*.
pipe [paip], *n.* tuyau, conduit, *m.*; pipe *(à fumer, à vin etc.)*, *f.*; *(Mus.)* pipeau, chalumeau, *m.—v.i.* jouer du chalumeau, siffler; *(pop.)* **pipe down!** boucle-la!
pipe-line ['paiplain], *n.* canalisation, *f.*, oléoduc, pipe-line, *m.*
piper ['paipə], *n.* joueur de flûte etc., *m.*
piping ['paipiŋ], *a.* qui joue du chalumeau, sifflant; flûté *(la voix).—n.* tubulure, *f.*, tuyautage, *m.*
pipit ['pipit], *n.* *(Orn.)* pipit, *m.*
pippin ['pipin], *n.* reinette, *f.*
piquancy ['pi:kənsi], *n.* goût piquant, *m.*
piquant ['pi:kənt], *a.* piquant.
pique [pi:k], *n.* pique, brouillerie, *f.*
piquet [pi'ket], *n.* *(Cards)* piquet, *m.*
piracy ['pairəsi], *n.* piraterie; *(fig.)* contrefaçon, *f.*, plagiat, *m.*
pirate ['pairit], *n.* pirate; *(fig.)* contrefacteur, *m.*
piratical [pai'rætikl], *a.* de pirate; *(fig.)* de contrefaçon.
pirouette [piru'et], *n.* pirouette, *f.*
pish! [piʃ], *int.* bah!
piss [pis], *v.i.* *(vulg.)* pisser.—*n.* urine, *f.*
pistol [pistl], *n.* pistolet, *m.*
piston ['pistən], *n.* piston, *m.*
piston ring ['pistənriŋ], *n.* segment de piston, *m.*
piston rod ['pistənrɔd], *n.* tige de piston, *f.*
pit [pit], *n.* fosse; *(fig.)* cavité, *f.*; *(Theat.)* parterre; *(Mining)* puits; creux *(de l'estomac)*, *m.*; aisselle *(du bras)*, *f.—v.t.* creuser; marquer de petits creux.
pitch (1) [pitʃ], *n.* jet, lancement *(de caillou, balle)*; *(Naut.)* tangage; point, degré, *m.*; pente *(de toit etc.)*, *f.*; *(Mus.)* ton, diapason, *m.*; **to play pitch-and-toss**, jouer à pile ou face.—*v.t.* jeter, lancer; établir *(fixer)*; dresser *(une tente).—v.i.* *(Naut.)* tanguer, plonger; tomber, se jeter.
pitch (2) [pitʃ], *n.* poix, *f.*; **pitch dark**, noir comme dans un four.
pitched [pitʃt], *a.* rangé; **pitched battle**, bataille rangée, *f.*
pitcher ['pitʃə], *n.* cruche, *f.*
pitchfork ['pitʃfɔ:k], *n.* fourche, *f.*
pitching ['pitʃiŋ], *n.* plongement *(de véhicules)*; *(Naut.)* tangage, *m.*
pitch pine ['pitʃpain], *n.* pin à trochets, pitchpin, *m.*
piteous ['pitiəs], *a.* piteux; pitoyable *(digne de pitié)*.
piteously ['pitiəsli], *adv.* piteusement.
piteousness ['pitiəsnis], *n.* état piteux, *m.*; tristesse, *f.*

pitfall ['pitfɔ:l], *n.* trappe, *f.*, piège, *m.*
pith [piθ], *n.* moelle; vigueur, énergie, *f.*; essentiel, *m.*
pithily ['piθili], *adv.* fortement, vigoureusement.
pithy ['piθi], *a.* plein de moelle; *(fig.)* substantiel, concis.
pitiable ['pitiəbl], *a.* pitoyable, à faire pitié.
pitiful ['pitiful], *a.* pitoyable.
pitifully ['pitifuli], *adv.* pitoyablement.
pitiless ['pitilis], *a.* impitoyable, sans pitié.
pitilessly ['pitilisli], *adv.* impitoyablement, sans pitié.
pitman ['pitmən], *n.* *(pl.* **-men** [men]) mineur, *m.*
pittance ['pitəns], *n.* pitance, *f.*
pitted ['pitid], *a.* grêlé *(de petite vérole)*.
pity ['piti], *n.* pitié, *f.*; dommage *(regret)*, *m.*; **what a pity!** quel dommage!—*v.t.* avoir pitié de, plaindre.
pityingly ['pitiiŋli], *adv.* avec pitié.
pivot ['pivət], *n.* pivot, *m.*
placable ['plækəbl], *a.* facile à apaiser.
placard ['plækɑ:d], *n.* placard, *m.*, affiche, pancarte, *f.—v.t.* afficher, placarder *(de)*.
placate [plə'keit], *v.t.* apaiser.
place [pleis], *n.* lieu, endroit, *m.*, localité; place *(siège etc.)*; position, *f.*, rang *(classe)*, *m.*; demeure, résidence *(chez soi)*, *f.*; emploi *(profession)*, *m.*; **come to my place**, venez chez moi; **to take place**, avoir lieu; **out of place**, déplacé, inopportun.—*v.t.* placer, mettre.
placid ['plæsid], *a.* placide, tranquille, calme.
plagiarism ['pleidʒiərizm], *n.* plagiat, *m.*
plagiarist ['pleidʒiərist], *n.* plagiaire, *m.*, *f.*
plagiarize ['pleidʒiəraiz], *v.t.* plagier.
plague [pleig], *n.* peste; *(fig.)* plaie, *f.*, fléau, *m.—v.t.* *(fig.)* tourmenter.
plaice [pleis], *n.* carrelet, *m.*; plie franche, *f.*
plaid [plæd], *n.* *(Sc.)* plaid; tartan, *m.*
plain [plein], *a.* uni, plat; simple, sans façon; ordinaire; sans attraits *(mine)*; évident *(qui saute aux yeux)*; franc *(sincère)*; **in plain clothes**, en civil; **plain cooking**, cuisine bourgeoise *ou* au naturel, *f.—n.* plaine, *f.—adv.* simplement; franchement.
plainly ['pleinli], *adv.* bonnement; distinctement; franchement.
plainness ['pleinnis], *n.* simplicité; clarté; sincérité, *f.*
plain speaking ['plein'spi:kiŋ], *n.* franchise, *f.*
plain-spoken ['plein'spoukn], *a.* franc, clair, explicite.
plaint [pleint], *n.* plainte, *f.*
plaintiff ['pleintif], *n.* plaignant, *m.*
plaintive ['pleintiv], *a.* plaintif.
plaintively ['pleintivli], *adv.* d'une voix plaintive.
plaintiveness ['pleintivnis], *n.* ton plaintif, *m.*
plait [plæt], *n.* natte, tresse *(de cheveux)*, *f.*; pli, *m.—v.t.* tresser, natter *(cheveux)*; plisser.
plaited ['plætid], *a.* tressé *(cheveux)*; plissé.
plan [plæn], *n.* plan; dessein, projet; système, *m.—v.t.* tracer un plan de; *(fig.)* projeter.
plane (1) [plein], *n.* *(Geom.)* plan; *(Carp.)* rabot; *(colloq.)* avion, *m.—v.t.* raboter, aplanir.
plane (2) [plein], **plane tree** ['pleintri:], *n.* platane, *m.*
planet ['plænit], *n.* planète, *f.*

513

planetarium [plæni'tɛəriəm], *n.* planéta-
rium, *m.*
planetary ['plænitəri], *a.* planétaire.
planing ['pleiniŋ], *n.* rabotage, *m.*
plank [plæŋk], *n.* planche, *f.*, madrier; (*Naut.*)
bordage, *m.*—*v.t.* planchéier; (*Naut.*)
border.
plankton ['plæŋktən], *n.* plancton, *m.*
planner ['plænə], *n.* auteur d'un plan, *m.*;
town planner, urbaniste, *m.*
planning ['plæniŋ], *n.* tracé d'un plan, *m.*;
planification; (*fig.*) invention, *f.*; *town
planning*, urbanisme, *m.*
plant [plɑ:nt], *n.* plante, *f.*; (*Tech.*) matériel,
m.—*v.t.* planter; (*fig.*) poser.
plantain ['plæntin], *n.* plantain, *m.*
plantation [plɑ:n'teiʃən], *n.* plantation, *f.*
planter ['plɑ:ntə], *n.* planteur, colon, *m.*
planting ['plɑ:ntiŋ], *n.* plantage, *m.*, plantation, *f.*
plasma ['plæzmə], *n.* plasma (du sang), *m.*
plaster ['plɑ:stə], *n.* plâtre, *f.*; (*Pharm.*) emplâtre, *m.*; *sticking plaster*, sparadrap, *m.*
—*v.t.* plâtrer.
plasterer ['plɑ:stərə], *n.* plâtrier, *m.*
plastering ['plɑ:stəriŋ], *n.* plâtrage, *m.*
plastic ['plæstik], *a.* plastique.—*n.* (*pl.*) plas-
tiques, *m.pl.*
plat [PLAIT].
Plate [pleit], **the River.** le Rio de la Plata, *m.*
plate [pleit], *n.* assiette; (*Metal., Phot.*)
plaque, *f.*—*v.t.* plaquer (*de*); laminer;
étamer (*une glace*).
plateau ['plætou, plə'tou], *n.* plateau, *m.*
plated ['pleitid], *a.* plaqué.
plateful ['pleitful], *n.* assiettée, *f.*
plate glass ['pleitglɑ:s], *n.* glace sans tain, *f.*
plate-layer ['pleitleiə], *n.* (*Rail.*) poseur de
rails, *m.*
plate rack ['pleitræk], *n.* porte-assiettes, *m.*
platform ['plætfɔ:m], *n.* plateforme; estrade,
f.; (*Rail.*) quai, *m.*
plating ['pleitiŋ], *n.* placage, *m.*; *armor-
plating*, blindage, *m.*
platinum ['plætinəm], *n.* platine, *m.*
platitude ['plætitju:d], *n.* platitude, *f.*
Plato ['pleitou]. Platon, *m.*
platoon [plə'tu:n], *n.* (*Mil.*) section, *f.*
platter ['plætə], *n.* écuelle, *f.*; (*Am.*) plat, *m.*
platypus ['plætipəs], *n.* ornithor(h)ynque, *m.*
plaudit ['plɔ:dit], *n.* applaudissement, *m.*
plausible ['plɔ:zibl], *a.* plausible; spécieux.
play [plei], *n.* jeu, *m.*; récréation (*d'enfants*),
f.; essor (*champ libre*); badinage, *m.*; (*Mus.*)
exécution; (*Theat.*) comédie, pièce, *f.*; *fair
play*, franc jeu.—*v.t.* jouer, jouer à; faire
jouer (*une machine etc.*); représenter, faire
(*une pièce, un rôle etc.*); (*Mus.*) jouer de.—
v.i. jouer; folâtrer (*s'amuser*).
play-bill ['pleibil], *n.* affiche de théâtre, *f.*
player ['pleiə], *n.* joueur; (*Theat.*) acteur, *m.*,
actrice, *f.*; artiste, *m., f.*
playfellow ['pleifelou], **playmate** ['plei
meit], *n.* camarade de jeu, *m., f.*
playful ['pleiful], *a.* folâtre, badin.
playfully ['pleifuli], *adv.* en badinant.
playfulness ['pleifulnis], *n.* badinage, enjouement, *m.*
playground ['pleigraund], *n.* cour de récréation, *f.*
playhouse ['pleihaus], *n.* théâtre, *m.*
plaything ['pleiθiŋ], *n.* jouet, joujou, *m.*

playtime ['pleitaim], *n.* récréation, *f.*
playwright ['pleirait], *n.* auteur dramatique,
m., dramaturge, *m., f.*
plea [pli:], *n.* procès, *m.*, cause, *f.*; prétexte,
m., excuse, *f.*
plead [pli:d], *v.t., v.i.* plaider.
pleasant ['plezənt], *a.* agréable, charmant.
pleasantly ['plezəntli], *adv.* agréablement.
pleasantness ['plezəntnis], *n.* agrément,
charme, *m.*
pleasantry ['plezəntri], *n.* plaisanterie, *f.*
please [pli:z], *v.t.* plaire à; *to be pleased*,
être content.—*v.i.* plaire (*à*); (*impers.*) il
plaît; *as you please*, comme vous voudrez;
if I please, si cela me plaît; (*if you*)
please, s'il vous plaît.
pleased [pli:zd], *a.* charmé, content (*de*);
satisfait (*de choses*).
pleasing ['pli:ziŋ], *a.* agréable, charmant.
pleasurable ['pleʒərəbl], *a.* agréable.
pleasure ['pleʒə], *n.* plaisir; gré (*will*), *m.*
pleasure ground ['pleʒəgraund], *n.* parc,
jardin d'agrément, *m.*
pleat [pli:t], *n.* plissé, *m.*—*v.t.* plisser.
plebeian [plə'bi:ən], *a.* and *n.* plébéien, *m.*
pledge [pledʒ], *n.* gage; nantissement, *m.*;
(*Law*) caution, *f.*—*v.t.* engager; garantir.
plenary ['pli:nəri], *a.* plein, complet, entier.
plenipotentiary [plenipo'tenʃəri], *a.* and *n.*
plénipotentiaire, *m.*
plenitude ['plenitju:d], *n.* plénitude, *f.*
plenteous ['plentiəs], *a.* abondant.
plenteously ['plentiəsli], *adv.* abondamment.
plentiful ['plentiful], *a.* abondant.
plenty ['plenti], *n.* abondance, *f.*; *plenty
of*, beaucoup de.
plethora ['pleθərə], *n.* pléthore, *f.*
pleurisy ['pluərəsi], *n.* pleurésie, *f.*
pliable ['plaiəbl], *a.* pliable, flexible.
pliancy ['plaiənsi], *n.* flexibilité, *f.*
pliant ['plaiənt], *a.* pliant, flexible.
pliers ['plaiəz], *n.pl.* pinces, *f.pl.*
plight [plait], *n.* état, *m.*, condition; situation
difficile, *f.*—*v.t.* engager.
plinth [plinθ], *n.* plinthe, *f.*
plod [plɔd], *v.i.* marcher péniblement; (*fig.*)
peiner, travailler assidûment.
plodder ['plɔdə], *n.* piocheur, *m.*
plodding ['plɔdiŋ], *a.* laborieux, piocheur.—
n. travail pénible, *m.*
plop [plɔp], *adv., n., int.* plouf, flac, pouf, *m.*
plot [plɔt], *n.* complot; petit terrain, *m.*;
intrigue (*d'une pièce etc.*), *f.*; *building-
plot*, lotissement, *m.*—*v.t.* comploter;
(*Surv.*) faire le plan de.—*v.i.* comploter.
plotter ['plɔtə], *n.* conspirateur, comploteur,
m.
plotting ['plɔtiŋ], *n.* complots, *m.pl.*; (*Surv.*)
action de rapporter, *f.*
plough [plau], *n.* charrue, *f.*; *the Plough*, le
Chariot, *m.*, la Grande-Ourse, *f.*—*v.t.*
labourer; (*fig.*) sillonner.—*v.i.* labourer.
ploughing ['plauiŋ], *n.* labourage, *m.*
ploughman ['plaumən], *n.* (*pl.* -**men** [men])
laboureur, *m.*
ploughshare ['plauʃɛə], *n.* soc de charrue, *m.*
plover ['plʌvə], *n.* (*Orn.*) pluvier, vanneau, *m.*
plow, see **plough.**
pluck [plʌk], *v.t.* cueillir (*fleurs, fruits etc.*);
plumer (*volaille*); épiler (*sourcils*).—*n.* cœur,
courage, *m.*
pluckily ['plʌkili], *adv.* courageusement.

plucky ['plʌki], *a.* courageux.
plug [plʌg], *n.* tampon, bouchon, *m.*; bonde (*de tonneau*); (*Elec.*) prise de courant; (*Teleph.*) fiche, *f.*; **spark plug**, bougie (d'allumage), *f.*—*v.t.* tamponner, boucher.
plum [plʌm], *n.* prune, *f.*
plumage ['plu:midʒ], *n.* plumage, *m.*
plumb [plʌm], *a.* droit, vertical.—*adv.* à plomb; (*Am.*, *colloq.*) complètement.—*v.t.* plomber; (*Naut.*) sonder.—*n.* plomb, *m.*
plumber ['plʌmə], *n.* plombier, *m.*
plumbing ['plʌmiŋ], *n.* plomberie; tuyauterie, *f.*
plumb line ['plʌmlain], *n.* fil à plomb, *m.*
plume [plu:m], *n.* plume, *f.*; plumet, *m.*—*v.t.* plumer.
plummet ['plʌmit], *n.* plomb, *m.*
plump (1) [plʌmp], *a.* dodu, potelé, gras.
plump (2) [plʌmp], *adv.* tout d'un coup; droit.—*v.i.* **to plump for**, donner tous ses votes pour.
plumpness ['plʌmpnis], *n.* embonpoint, *m.*, rondeur, *f.*
plum tree ['plʌmtri:], *n.* prunier, *m.*
plunder ['plʌndə], *v.t.* piller, dépouiller.—*n.* butin (*chose pillée*); pillage (*acte de piller*), *m.*
plunderer ['plʌndərə], *n.* pillard, *m.*
plunge [plʌndʒ], *v.t.* plonger, précipiter.—*v.i.* plonger; se précipiter.—*n.* plongeon, *m.*
plural ['pluərəl], *a.* and *n.* pluriel, *m.*
plus [plʌs], *prep.* (*Math.*) plus.—*a.* positif.—*n.* plus, *m.*—*adv.* et davantage.
plush [plʌʃ], *n.* peluche, *f.*
plutocrat ['plu:tokræt], *n.* ploutocrate, *m.*, *f.*
plutocratic [plu:to'krætik], *a.* ploutocratique.
plutonium [plu'tounjəm], *n.* plutonium, *m.*
pluvial ['plu:viəl], *a.* pluvial.
ply (1) [plai], *v.t.* manier (*fortement*); exercer, employer; presser (*quelqu'un de prendre quelque chose*).—*v.i.* travailler; faire le service.
ply (2) [plai], *n.* pli (*de tissu*); fil (*de laine*); toron (*de corde*), *m.*
plywood ['plaiwud], *n.* contre-plaqué, *m.*
pneumatic [nju'mætik], *a.* pneumatique.
pneumonia [nju'mouniə], *n.* pneumonie, *f.*
poach (1) [poutʃ], *v.t.* braconner, voler.—*v.i.* braconner.
poach (2) [poutʃ], *v.t.* pocher (*œufs*).
poacher ['poutʃə], *n.* braconnier, *m.*
poaching ['poutʃiŋ], *n.* braconnage, *m.*
pock [pɔk], *n.* pustule (*de petite vérole*), *f.*
pocket ['pɔkit], *n.* poche, *f.*; gousset (*du gilet*), *m.*; blouse (*de billard*), *f.*—*v.t.* empocher, mettre en poche.
pocket-book ['pɔkitbuk], *n.* portefeuille (*pour l'argent*); livre de poche; calepin (*carnet*), *m.*
pocketful ['pɔkitful], *n.* pleine poche, *f.*
pocket-knife ['pɔkitnaif], *n.* couteau de poche, canif, *m.*
pocket money ['pɔkitmʌni], *n.* argent de poche, *m.*
pod [pɔd], *n.* cosse, gousse, *f.*—*v.t.* écosser.
podgy ['pɔdʒi], *a.* gras, potelé.
poem ['pouim], *n.* poème, *m.*
*poesy ['pouizi], *n.* poésie, *f.*
poet ['pouit], *n.* poète, *m.*
poetaster [poui'tæstə], *n.* rimailleur, *m.*
poetess [poui'tes], *n.* poétesse, *f.*
poetic [pou'etik], **poetical** [pou'etikəl], *a.* poétique.

poetry ['pouitri], *n.* poésie, *f.*
poignancy ['pɔinjənsi], *n.* piquant, *m.*; nature poignante, *f.*
poignant ['pɔinjənt], *a.* piquant, vif, poignant.
poignantly ['pɔinjəntli], *adv.* d'une manière piquante.
point [pɔint], *n.* point (*endroit*), *m.*; pointe (*bout aiguisé etc.*), *f.*; (*Compass*) quart de vent; (*Spt.*) point; (*fig.*) but; (*pl.*) (*Rail.*) aiguillage, *m.*; **decimal point**, virgule, *f.*; **in point of fact**, en effet; **not to the point**, hors de propos; **that is not the point**, ce n'est pas là la question; **to make a point of**, se faire un devoir de; **to the point**, à propos.—*v.t.* aiguiser, tailler (*affiler*); indiquer; pointer (*fusils etc.*); (*Build.*) jointoyer; **to point out**, signaler; faire remarquer.—*v.i.* se tourner (*vers*); tomber en arrêt (*chiens*); **to point at**, montrer du doigt, indiquer.
point-blank ['pɔint'blæŋk], *adv.* à bout portant; à brûle-pourpoint, carrément.
pointed ['pɔintid], *a.* pointu; (*fig.*) mordant.
pointedly ['pɔintidli], *adv.* d'une manière piquante.
pointer ['pɔintə], *n.* index; chien d'arrêt, *m.*
pointing ['pɔintiŋ], *n.* (*Build.*) jointoiement, *m.*
pointless ['pɔintlis], *a.* sans pointe; (*fig.*) inutile, plat.
pointsman ['pɔintsmən], *n.* (*pl.* **-men** [men]) (*Rail.*) aiguilleur, *m.*
poise [pɔiz], *n.* poids, équilibre, *m.*—*v.t.* balancer, tenir en équilibre.
poison [pɔizn], *n.* poison, *m.*—*v.t.* empoisonner.
poisoner ['pɔiznə], *n.* empoisonneur, *m.*
poisoning ['pɔizniŋ], *n.* empoisonnement, *m.*
poisonous ['pɔiznəs], *a.* vénéneux (*plante*); venimeux (*serpent etc.*); toxique (*gaz*).
poke (1) [pouk], *n.* coup de coude *ou* de poing, *m.*—*v.t.* fourrer; pousser (*des doigts*); remuer, fourgonner (*le feu*); **to poke fun at**, se moquer de.—*v.i.* **to poke about**, tâtonner.
poke (2) [pouk], *n.* *sac, *m.*; poche, *f.*
poker ['poukə], *n.* tisonnier; (*Cards*) poker, *m.*
poky ['pouki], *a.* (*colloq.*) petit, mesquin.
Poland ['poulənd], la Pologne, *f.*
polar ['poulə], *a.* polaire.
Pole [poul], *n.* Polonais (*personne*), *m.*
pole (1) [poul], *n.* perche, *f.*; bâton (*de rideau*); timon (*d'une voiture*); échalas (*de vignes etc.*); mât (*de drapeau etc.*); poteau (*télégraphique*), *m.*
pole (2) [poul], *n.* (*Astron.*, *Geog.*) pôle, *m.*
poleaxe ['poulæks], *n.* hache d'armes, *f.*; assommoir, merlin, *m.*—*v.t.* assommer.
polecat ['poulkæt], *n.* putois, *m.*
polemics [pə'lemiks], *n.pl.* polémique, *f.*
pole-star ['poulsta:], *n.* étoile polaire, *f.*
pole vault ['poulvɔ:lt], *n.* saut à la perche, *m.*
police [pə'li:s], *n.* police, *f.*; **county police**, gendarmerie, *f.*; **police court**, tribunal de simple police, *m.*; **police station**, commissariat *ou* poste de police, *m.*—*v.t.* policer.
policeman [pə'li:smən], *n.* (*pl.* **-men** [men]) agent de police, gardien de la paix, *m.*
policewoman [pə'li:swumən], *n.* (*pl.* **-women** [wimin]) femme agent, *f.*
policy ['pɔlisi], *n.* politique, *f.*; plan, *m.*; **insurance policy**, police d'assurance, *f.*

515

poliomyelitis

poliomyelitis [ˈpouliomaiəˈlaitis], (*fam.*) **polio** [ˈpouliou], *n.* poliomyélite, *f.*
Polish [ˈpouliʃ], *a.* polonais.—*n.* polonais (*langue*), *m.*
polish [ˈpɔliʃ], *v.t.* polir; vernir (*meubles*); cirer (*chaussures*).—*v.i.* se polir.—*n.* poli, *m.*; (*fig.*) élégance, *f.*; **floor polish**, cire à parquet, *f.* **shoe polish**, cirage, *m.*
polished [ˈpɔliʃt], *a.* poli.
polisher [ˈpɔliʃə], *n.* polisseur; polissoir (*outil*), *m.*; **floor polisher**, cireur de parquet, *m.*
polite [pəˈlait], *a.* poli, élégant, complaisant (*pour*).
politely [pəˈlaitli], *adv.* poliment.
politeness [pəˈlaitnis], *n.* politesse, *f.*
politic [ˈpɔlitik], *a.* politique.
political [pəˈlitikl], *a.* politique.
politically [pəˈlitikli], *adv.* politiquement.
politician [pɔliˈtiʃən], *n.* homme politique; (*pej.*) politicien, *m.*
politics [ˈpɔlitiks], *n.pl.* politique, *f.*
poll [poul], *n.* (*Anat.*) *tête; liste électorale; élection, *f.*, scrutin; sondage (*de l'opinion publique*), *m.*—*v.t.* étêter (*arbres*); voter; obtenir (*un certain nombre de votes*).
pollen [ˈpɔlən], *n.* pollen, *m.*
pollination [pɔliˈneiʃən], *n.* pollination, *f.*
polling [ˈpoulin], *n.* élection, *f.*; **polling booth**, bureau de scrutin, *m.*
pollute [pəˈljuːt], *v.t.* polluer, souiller (*de*).
pollution [pəˈljuːʃən], *n.* pollution, souillure, *f.*
polo [ˈpoulou], *n.* polo, *m.*
polygamist [pɔˈligəmist], *n.* polygame, *m.*, *f.*
polygamy [pɔˈligəmi], *n.* polygamie, *f.*
polyglot [ˈpɔliglɔt], *a.* and *n.* polyglotte, *m.*, *f.*
polygon [ˈpɔligən], *n.* polygone, *m.*
Polynesia [pɔliˈniːziə]. la Polynésie, *f.*
polypus [ˈpɔlipəs], *n.* polype, *m.*
polytechnic [pɔliˈteknik], *a.* polytechnique.—*n.* école d'arts et métiers, *f.*
pomade [pəˈmeid], *n.* pommade, *f.*
pomegranate [ˈpɔmgrænit], *n.* grenade, *f.*; **pomegranate tree**, grenadier, *m.*
pommel [pʌml], *v.t.* battre, rosser.—*n.* pommeau (*d'une selle, d'une épée etc.*), *m.*
pomp [pɔmp], *n.* pompe, *f.*, éclat, faste, *m.*
Pompey [ˈpɔmpi]. Pompée, *m.*
pompon [ˈpɔmpɔn], *n.* pompon, *m.*
pomposity [pɔmˈpɔsiti], *n.* pompe, *f.*
pompous [ˈpɔmpəs], *a.* pompeux, fastueux.
pompously [ˈpɔmpəsli], *adv.* pompeusement.
pond [pɔnd], *n.* étang, vivier, *m.*; mare (*pool*), *f.*
ponder [ˈpɔndə], *v.t.* peser, considérer, réfléchir à.—*v.i.* méditer.
ponderous [ˈpɔndərəs], *a.* lourd, pesant.
ponderously [ˈpɔndərəsli], *adv.* pesamment.
pontiff [ˈpɔntif], *n.* pontife, *m.*
pontificate [pɔnˈtifikeit], *n.* pontificat, *m.*—*v.i.* pontifier.
Pontius Pilate [ˈpɔntʃəsˈpailət]. Ponce Pilate, *m.*
pontoon [pɔnˈtuːn], *n.* ponton, *m.*; (*Cards*) vingt-et-un, *m.*
pony [ˈpouni], *n.* poney, petit cheval, *m.*
poodle [puːdl], *n.* caniche, *m.*
pooh! [puː], *int.* bah! allons donc!
pooh-pooh [ˈpuːˈpuː], *v.t.* tourner en ridicule.
pool [puːl], *n.* étang, *m.*, mare; piscine (*pour nager*); (*Cards, Billiards etc.*) poule; mise en commun, *f.*—*v.t.* mettre en commun.
poop [puːp], *n.* dunette, poupe, *f.*
poor [puə], *a.* pauvre, indigent; malheureux (*sans joie*); triste (*de pauvre qualité*); mauvais (*pas bon*).
poor-box [ˈpuəbɔks], *n.* tronc des pauvres, *m.*
poor-house [ˈpuəhaus], *n.* asile des indigents, *m.*
*poor-law [ˈpuəlɔː], *n.* loi sur l'assistance publique, *f.*
poorly [ˈpuəli], *a.* indisposé, souffrant.—*adv.* pauvrement, mal, tristement.
poorness [ˈpuənis], *n.* pauvreté; médiocrité, *f.*
pop (1) [pɔp], *n.* petit bruit vif et sec, *m.*; (*colloq.*) boisson pétillante, *f.*—*v.t.* pousser, fourrer *ou* mettre subitement.—*v.i.* entrer *ou* sortir subitement.—*int.* crac! pan!
pop (2) [pɔp], *n.* (*Am.colloq.*) papa, *m.*
pop (3) [pɔp], *a.* and *n.* (*colloq.*) (musique) populaire, *f.*; **the pops**, les chansons en vogue, *f.pl.*
Pope [Poup], *n.* Pape, *m.*
popedom [ˈpoupdəm], *n.* papauté, *f.*
popery [ˈpoupəri], *n.* papisme, *m.*
popish [ˈpoupiʃ], *a.* papiste; de papiste (*choses*).
poplar [ˈpɔplə], *n.* (*Bot.*) peuplier, *m.*
poplin [ˈpɔplin], *n.* popeline, *f.*
poppet [ˈpɔpit], *n.* poupée, marionnette, *f.*
poppy [ˈpɔpi], *n.* pavot (*cultivé*); coquelicot (*sauvage*), *m.*
populace [ˈpɔpjuləs], *n.* populace, *f.*
popular [ˈpɔpjulə], *a.* populaire; en vogue.
popularity [pɔpjuˈlæriti], *n.* popularité, *f.*
popularize [ˈpɔpjuləraiz], *v.t.* populariser.
popularly [ˈpɔpjuləli], *adv.* populairement.
populate [ˈpɔpjuleit], *v.t.* peupler.
population [pɔpjuˈleiʃən], *n.* population, *f.*
populous [ˈpɔpjuləs], *a.* populeux.
porcelain [ˈpɔːslin], *n.* porcelaine, *f.*
porch [pɔːtʃ], *n.* porche, *m.*
porcupine [ˈpɔːkjupain], *n.* porc-épic, *m.*
pore (1) [pɔː], *n.* pore, *m.*
pore (2) [pɔː], *v.i.* regarder avec grande attention; **to pore over**, dévorer (*un livre*).
pork [pɔːk], *n.* porc, *m.*
pork-butcher [ˈpɔːkbutʃə], *n.* charcutier, *m.*; **pork-butcher's shop**, charcuterie, *f.*
porker [ˈpɔːkə], *n.* porc d'engrais, cochon, *m.*
pork pie [ˈpɔːkˈpai], *n.* pâté de porc, *m.*
pornography [pɔːˈnɔgrəfi], *n.* pornographie, *f.*
porous [ˈpɔːrəs], *a.* poreux.
porphyry [ˈpɔːfiri], *n.* porphyre, *m.*
porpoise [ˈpɔːpəs], *n.* marsouin, *m.*
porridge [ˈpɔridʒ], *n.* bouillie, *f.*
porringer [ˈpɔrindʒə], *n.* bol à bouillie, *m.*
port (1) [pɔːt], *n.* port (*ville maritime*), *m.*
port (2) [pɔːt], *n.* (*Naut.*) bâbord, *m.*
port (3) [pɔːt], *n.* porto (*vin*), *m.*
portable [ˈpɔːtəbl], *a.* portatif, transportable.
portal [pɔːtl], *n.* portail, *m.*
portcullis [pɔːtˈkʌlis], *n.* herse, *f.*
portend [pɔːˈtend], *v.t.* présager, augurer.
portent [ˈpɔːtənt], *n.* mauvais augure, *m.*
portentous [pɔːˈtentəs], *a.* de mauvais augure.
porter [ˈpɔːtə], *n.* commissionnaire; concierge (*de maison*); porteur (*de rue*); (*Rail.*) porteur, *m.*
porterage [ˈpɔːtəridʒ], *n.* port; factage, *m.*

portfolio [pɔːˈfouliou], n. carton, m.; serviette, f.; (Polit.) portefeuille, m.
port-hole [ˈpɔːthoul], n. sabord, m.
portico [ˈpɔːtikou], n. portique, m.
portion [ˈpɔːʃən], n. partie, part; dot (de mariage), f.—v.t. partager; doter (pour le mariage).
portliness [ˈpɔːtlinis], n. corpulence, f.
portly [ˈpɔːtli], a. d'un port majestueux; corpulent.
portmanteau [pɔːtˈmæntou], n. valise, f.
portrait [ˈpɔːtrit], n. portrait, m.
portray [pɔːˈtrei], v.t. peindre; (fig.) dépeindre, décrire.
Portugal [ˈpɔːtʃug(ə)l]. le Portugal, m.
Portuguese [pɔːtʃuˈgiːz], a. portugais.—n. portugais (langue); Portugais (personne), m.
pose [pouz], v.t. embarrasser, confondre; poser (une question).—v.i. poser (avec affectation).—n. pose, f.
poser [ˈpouzə], n. question embarrassante, f.
poseur [pouˈzəː], n. poseur, m.
position [pəˈziʃən], n. situation, position, f.
positive [ˈpɔzitiv], a. positif; absolu, sûr; décisif.—n. positif, m.
positively [ˈpɔzitivli], adv. positivement; absolument.
positiveness [ˈpɔzitivnis], n. nature positive, f.
posse [ˈpɔsi], n. détachement (d'agents de police), m.
possess [pəˈzes], v.t. posséder; avoir; jouir de.
possession [pəˈzeʃən], n. possession, f.
possessive [pəˈzesiv], a. possessif.
possessor [pəˈzesə], n. possesseur, m.
***posset** [ˈpɔsit], n. lait caillé au vin, m.
possibility [pɔsiˈbiliti], n. possibilité, f.; moyen (façon), m.
possible [ˈpɔsibl], a. possible.
possibly [ˈpɔsibli], adv. peut-être.
post (1) [poust], n. emploi; (Mil.) poste; courrier (livraison de lettres), m.; (Post office) poste, f.—v.t. mettre à la poste; (Mil. etc.) poster, affecter.
post (2) [poust], n. poteau (en bois); montant (de porte), m.—v.t. afficher.
postage [ˈpoustidʒ], n. port de lettre, port, affranchissement, m.
postage stamp [ˈpoustidʒstæmp], n. timbre-poste, m.
postal [ˈpoustəl], a. postal; **postal order**, mandat-poste, m.
postcard [ˈpoustkaːd], n. carte postale, f.
postdate [poustˈdeit], v.t. postdater.
poster [ˈpoustə], n. affiche, f., placard, m.
posterior [pɔsˈtiəriə], a. postérieur.
posterity [pɔsˈteriti], n. postérité, f.
postern [ˈpoustəːn], a. de derrière.—n. poterne, f.
post-haste [ˈpoustˈheist], adv. en grande hâte.
posthumous [ˈpɔstjuməs], a. posthume.
posthumously [ˈpɔstjuməsli], adv. après décès.
postillion [pɔsˈtiljən], n. postillon, m.
postman [ˈpoustmən], n. (pl. -men [men]) facteur, m.
postmark [ˈpoustmaːk], n. cachet de la poste, m.
postmaster [ˈpoustmaːstə], n. receveur des postes, m.
post meridiem [ˈpoustməˈridiəm], (abbr.

p.m. [ˈpiːˈem]) adv. de l'après-midi, du soir.
post-mortem [poustˈmɔːtəm], adv. après décès.—n. autopsie, f.
post office [ˈpoustɔfis], n. bureau de poste, m., poste, f.
postpone [poustˈpoun], v.t. ajourner, différer, remettre.
postponement [poustˈpounmənt], n. ajournement, m., remise, f.
postscript [ˈpoustskript], (abbr. **P.S.** [ˈpiːˈes]) n. post-scriptum, m.
postulate [ˈpɔstjuleit], v.t. postuler.
posture [ˈpɔstʃə], n. posture, pose, f.
post-war [poustˈwɔː], a. d'après guerre.
posy [ˈpouzi], n. petit bouquet, m.
pot [pɔt], n. pot, m.; marmite, f.; **pots and pans**, batterie de cuisine, f.—v.t. empoter, mettre en pot.
potable [ˈpoutəbl], a. potable.
potash [ˈpɔtæʃ], n. potasse, f.
potassium [pəˈtæsiəm], n. potassium, m.
potato [pəˈteitou], n. (pl. **potatoes** [pəˈteitouz]) pomme de terre, f.
pot-bellied [ˈpɔtbelid], a. pansu, ventru.
potency [ˈpoutənsi], n. puissance, force, f.
potent [ˈpoutənt], a. puissant, fort; (fig.) efficace.
potentate [ˈpoutənteit], n. potentat, m.
potential [pəˈtenʃəl], a. potentiel, latent.—n. (Elec. etc.) potentiel, m.
potful [ˈpɔtful], n. potée, f.
***pother** [ˈpɔðə], n. tumulte; bruit, m.
pot-hole [ˈpɔthoul], n. (Geol.) marmite torrentielle; (Motor.) flache, f.
pot-holer [ˈpɔthoulə], n. spéléologue, m., f.
pot-holing [ˈpɔthoulin], n. spéléologie, f.
pothook [ˈpɔthuk], n. crémaillère, f.
potion [ˈpouʃən], n. potion, f.; breuvage, m.
pot-luck [ˈpɔtˈlʌk], n. fortune du pot, f.
pot shot [ˈpɔtʃɔt], n. coup tiré au petit bonheur, m.
***pottage** [ˈpɔtidʒ], n. potage (épais), m.
potted [ˈpɔtid], a. en pot, en terrine; **potted meat**, conserve de viande, f.
potter [ˈpɔtə], n. potier, m.—v.i. **to potter about**, s'amuser à des riens.
pottery [ˈpɔtəri], n. poterie, f.
potting [ˈpɔtin], a. **potting shed**, serre, resserre, f.—n. (Hort.) mise en pot, f.
pouch [pautʃ], n. poche, f., petit sac, m.; blague (à tabac), f.
poulterer [ˈpoultərə], n. marchand de volailles, m.
poultice [ˈpoultis], n. cataplasme, m.—v.t. mettre un cataplasme à.
poultry [ˈpoultri], n. volaille, f.
pounce [pauns], v.i. fondre (sur).
pound [paund], n. livre; livre sterling; fourrière (clôture), f.—v.t. broyer; (Metal.) bocarder.
poundage [ˈpaundidʒ], n. commission de tant par livre, f.
pounding [ˈpaundin], n. broiement; (Metal.) bocardage, m.
pour [pɔː], v.t. verser.—v.i. couler; pleuvoir à verse (pluie).
pouring [ˈpɔːrin], a. torrentiel (pluie).
pout [paut], v.i. bouder, faire la moue.—n. bouderie, moue, f.
pouting [ˈpautin], a. qui fait la moue; boudeur.

517

poverty ['pɔvəti], *n.* pauvreté, misère, indigence, *f.*
poverty-stricken ['pɔvətistrikn], *a.* réduit à la misère, indigent.
powder ['paudə], *n.* poudre, *f.*; *face powder*, poudre de riz; *gunpowder*, poudre à canon; *tooth powder*, poudre dentifrice.—*v.t.* réduire en poudre; poudrer (*les cheveux*); (*Cook.*) saupoudrer; *to powder one's face*, se poudrer.
powder compact ['paudəkɔmpækt], *n.* poudrier (*de dame*), *m.*
powdered ['paudəd], *a.* pulvérisé; poudré (*cheveux*).
powder puff ['paudəpʌf], *n.* houppe, *f.*, pompon, *m.*
powdery ['paudəri], *a.* poudreux; friable.
power ['pauə], *n.* pouvoir, *m.*; force (*physique*); autorité, puissance (*morale*), *f.*; *the Great Powers*, les grandes puissances, *f.pl.*; *to be in power*, être au pouvoir.
powerful ['pauəful], *a.* puissant, fort.
powerfully ['pauəfuli], *adv.* puissamment, fortement.
powerless ['pauəlis], *a.* impuissant, faible.
power station ['pauəsteiʃən], *n.* usine génératrice, centrale électrique, *f.*
pox [pɔks], *n.* vérole, *f.*; *chicken pox*, varicelle, *f.*; *small-pox*, petite vérole, variole, *f.*
practicability [præktikə'biliti], *n.* possibilité, praticabilité, *f.*
practicable ['præktikəbl], *a.* praticable.
practical ['præktikl], *a.* pratique; *practical joke*, mauvaise farce, *f.*
practically ['præktikli], *adv.* en pratique; à peu près.
practice ['præktis], *n.* pratique, habitude, *f.*, usage, exercice, *m.*; clientèle (*de médecin, d'avocat etc.*); intrigue, *f.*
practice ['præktis], *v.t.* pratiquer, mettre en pratique; exercer, pratiquer (*une profession etc.*); (*Mus.*) étudier.—*v.i.* (*Mus.*) étudier; s'exercer (*à*); exercer, faire de la clientèle (*médecin*).
practised ['præktist], *a.* exercé (*à*); versé (*dans*); habile.
practising ['præktisiŋ], *a.* praticien, exerçant.
practitioner [præk'tiʃənə], *n.* praticien, *m.*; *general practitioner*, médecin ordinaire, *m.*; *medical practitioner*, médecin, *m.*
pragmatic [præg'mætik], **pragmatical** [præg'mætikəl], *a.* pragmatique; officieux; infatué de soi.
pragmatism ['prægmətizm], *n.* pragmatisme, *m.*
prairie ['prɛəri], *n.* prairie, savane, *f.*
praise [preiz], *n.* louange, *f.*, éloge, *m.*—*v.t.* louer, faire l'éloge de; vanter.
praiseworthy ['preizwə:ði], *a.* louable, digne d'éloges.
pram [præm], *n.* voiture d'enfant, *f.*
prance [prɑːns], *v.i.* fringuer (*cheval*).
prancing ['prɑːnsiŋ], *a.* fringant.
prank [præŋk], *n.* escapade, niche, *f.*, tour, *m.*
prate [preit], *v.i.* jaser, babiller, bavarder (*de*).
prating ['preitiŋ], *a.* bavard, babillard.
pratingly ['preitiŋli], *adv.* en bavard, en babillard.
prattle [prætl], *v.i.* babiller, jaser, caqueter.—*n.* babil, caquetage, bavardage, *m.*

prattler ['prætlə], *n.* bavard, babillard, *m.*
prattling ['prætliŋ], *n.* bavardage, caquet, *m.*
prawn [prɔːn], *n.* crevette rouge; salicoque, *f.*
pray [prei], *v.t.* prier, supplier.—*v.i.* prier.
prayer [prɛə], *n.* prière, supplication; (*Law*) demande, *f.*; *the Lord's Prayer*, l'oraison dominicale, *f.*
prayer book ['prɛəbuk], *n.* livre de prières, *m.*; liturgie, *f.*
preach [priːtʃ], *v.t., v.i.* prêcher.
preacher ['priːtʃə], *n.* prédicateur, *m.*
preaching ['priːtʃiŋ], *n.* prédication, *f.*
preamble [priːˈæmbl], *n.* préambule, *m.*
prearrange [priːəˈreindʒ], *v.t.* arranger d'avance.
prebendary ['prebəndəri], *n.* chanoine, prébendier, *m.*
precarious [pri'kɛəriəs], *a.* précaire.
precariously [pri'kɛəriəsli], *adv.* précairement.
precariousness [pri'kɛəriəsnis], *n.* nature précaire; incertitude, *f.*
precaution [pri'kɔːʃən], *n.* précaution, *f.*
precautionary [pri'kɔːʃənri], *a.* de précaution.
precede [pri'siːd], *v.t.* précéder.
precedence [pri'siːdəns], *n.* préséance, *f.*; *to have* or *take precedence over*, avoir le pas sur.
precedent (1) [pri'siːdənt], **preceding** [pri'siːdiŋ], *a.* précédent.
precedent (2) ['presidənt], *n.* précédent, *m.*
precept ['priːsept], *n.* précepte, *m.*
precinct ['priːsiŋkt], *n.* limite, borne, enceinte, *f.*
precious ['preʃəs], *a.* précieux; affecté; (*fam.*) fameux, fichu.
preciously ['preʃəsli], *adv.* précieusement; (*fam.*) fameusement, diablement.
preciousness ['preʃəsnis], *n.* haute valeur, *f.*
precipice ['presipis], *n.* précipice, *m.*
precipitate (1) [pri'sipitit], *a.* précipité.—*n.* (*Chem.*) précipité, *m.*
precipitate (2) [pri'sipiteit], *v.t.* précipiter.—*v.i.* se précipiter.
precipitation [prisipi'teiʃən], *n.* précipitation, *f.*
precipitous [pri'sipitəs], *a.* escarpé, abrupt.
precipitously [pri'sipitəsli], *adv.* à pic, en précipice; (*fig.*) précipitamment.
precise [pri'sais], *a.* précis, exact; formaliste, pointilleux, scrupuleux.
precisely [pri'saisli], *adv.* précisément.
precision [pri'siʒən], *n.* précision, exactitude, *f.*
preclude [pri'kluːd], *v.t.* exclure; empêcher (*mettre obstacle à*).
preclusion [pri'kluːʒən], *n.* exclusion, *f.*
precocious [pri'kouʃəs], *a.* précoce.
precociousness [pri'kouʃəsnis], *n.* précocité, *f.*
preconceived ['priːkənˈsiːvd], *a.* formé d'avance; *preconceived idea*, idée préconçue, *f.*
precursor [pri'kəːsə], *n.* précurseur, avant-coureur, *m.*
predatory ['predətəri], *a.* de rapine, de proie, pillard, rapace.
predecease ['priːdiˈsiːs], *v.t.* prédécéder.
predestinate [pri'destineit], **predestine** [pri'destin], *v.t.* prédestiner.

predestination [pri:ɪ:esti'neiʃən], n. prédestination, f.
predetermine [pri:di'tə:min], v.t. prédéterminer, arrêter d'avance.
predicament [pri'dikəmənt], n. état, m., position difficile, situation fâcheuse; catégorie, f., ordre, m.
predicate ['predikit], n. prédicat, attribut, m.
predict [pri'dikt], v.t. prédire.
prediction [pri'dikʃən], n. prédiction, prévision, f.
predilection [pri:di'lekʃən], n. prédilection, f.
predispose [pri:dis'pouz], v.t. prédisposer.
predisposition [pri:dispə'ziʃən], n. prédisposition, f.
predominance [pri'dominəns], n. prédominance, f., ascendant, m.
predominant [pri'dominənt], a. prédominant.
predominantly [pri'dominəntli], adv. d'une manière prédominante.
predominate [pri'domineit], v.i. prédominer, prévaloir.
pre-eminence [pri:'eminəns], n. prééminence, supériorité, f.
pre-eminent [pri:'eminənt], a. prééminent.
pre-eminently [pri:'eminəntli], adv. par excellence.
preen [pri:n], v.t lisser, nettoyer (ses plumes); *to preen oneself*, se piquer.
pre-engage [pri:in'geidʒ], v.t. engager d'avance.
pre-exist [pri:ig'zist], v.i. préexister.
pre-existence [pri:ig'zistəns], n. préexistence, f.
prefabricate [pri:'fæbrikeit], v.t. préfabriquer.
preface ['prefis], n. préface, f.; avant-propos, m.—v.t. faire une préface à.
prefect ['pri:fekt], n. préfet; (Sch.) surveillant, m.
prefer [pri'fə:], v.t. préférer, aimer mieux; avancer, élever (aux honneurs); porter (une accusation).
preferable ['prefərəbl], a. préférable (à).
preferably ['prefərəbli], adv. préférablement, de préférence.
preference ['prefərəns], n. préférence, f.
preferential [prefə'renʃl], a. préférentiel.
preferment [pri'fə:mənt], n. avancement, m., promotion, f.
prefix ['pri:fiks], n. (Gram.) préfixe, m.
pregnancy ['pregnənsi], n. grossesse, f.
pregnant ['pregnənt], a. enceinte, grosse; (fig.) gros, plein (de); fertile, fécond (en).
prehensile [pri'hensàil], a. préhensile.
prehistoric [pri:his'tɔrik], a. préhistorique.
prejudge [pri:'dʒʌdʒ], v.t. juger d'avance.
prejudice ['predʒudis], v.t. prévenir, nuire à (faire du tort à).—n. prévention, f., préjugé; préjudice, tort (détriment), m.
prejudiced ['predʒudist], a. prévenu.
prejudicial [predʒu'diʃl], a. préjudiciable, nuisible (à).
prelate ['prelit], n. prélat, m.
preliminary [pri'liminəri], a. and n. préliminaire, m.
prelude ['prelju:d], n. prélude, m.
premature ['premətjuə], a. prématuré.

prematurely [premə'tjuəli], adv. prématurément.
premeditate [pri'mediteit], v.t. préméditer.
premeditated [pri'mediteitid], a. prémédité.
premeditation [primedi'teiʃən], n. préméditation, f.
premier ['pri:miə, 'premiə], a. premier (de rang).—n. premier ministre, m.
premise ['premis], n. (Log.) prémisse, f.
premises ['premisiz], n.pl. lieux, m.pl.; établissement, local, m.
premium ['pri:miəm], n. prime, f.; prix, m.
premonition [pri:mə'niʃən], n. avertissement; pressentiment, m.
prenatal [pri:'neitl], a. prénatal.
preoccupied [pri:'ɔkjupaid], a. préoccupé.
preordain [pri:ɔ:'dein], v.t. ordonner ou arranger d'avance.
prep [prep], a. (Sch. fam. abbr. **preparatory**) préparatoire.
prepaid [pri:'peid], a. affranchi, franc de port.—adv. franco.
preparation [prepə'reiʃən], n. préparation, f.; préparatifs, apprêts (de voyage etc.), m.pl.
preparatory [pri'pærətri], a. préparatoire.
prepare [pri'pɛə], v.t. préparer.—v.i. se préparer, s'apprêter (à).
preparedness [pri'pɛə(ri)dnis], n. état de préparation, m.
prepay [pri:'pei], v.t. irr (conjug. like PAY) payer d'avance; affranchir (lettres).
prepayment [pri:'peimənt], n. payement d'avance; affranchissement (de lettres), m.
preponderance [pri'pondərəns], n. prépondérance, f.
preponderant [pri'pondərənt], a. prépondérant.
preponderate [pri'pondəreit], v.i. avoir la prépondérance, l'emporter (sur).
preposition [prepə'ziʃən], n. préposition, f.
prepossessing [pri:pə'zesiŋ], a. prévenant, engageant.
preposterous [pri'postərəs], a. absurde, déraisonnable.
preposterously [pri'postərəsli], adv. absurdement, déraisonnablement.
prerogative [pri'rogətiv], n. prérogative, f.
Presbyterian [prezbi'tiəriən], a. and n. presbytérien, m.
Presbyterianism [prezbi'tiəriənizm], n. presbytérianisme, m.
presbytery ['prezbitəri], n. presbytère, m.
prescience ['preʃəns], n. prescience, f.
prescribe [pri'skraib], v.t. prescrire; (Med.) ordonner.—v.i. (Med.) faire une ordonnance.
prescription [pri'skripʃən], n. (Law) prescription; (Med.) ordonnance, f.
presence ['prezəns], n. présence, f.; air, maintien, m., mine (aspect), f.; personnage supérieur, m.; *presence of mind*, présence d'esprit.
present ['prezənt], a. présent; actuel; *at the present moment*, à présent, actuellement; *to be present at*, assister à.—n. présent; cadeau, don, m.; *for the present*, pour le moment.—[pri'zent], v.t. présenter, offrir (à).
presentable [pri'zentəbl], a. présentable.
presentation [prezən'teiʃən], n. présentation, f.; don, m.

519

presentiment [pri'zentimənt], n. pressentiment, m.

presently ['prezəntli], adv. tout à l'heure, bientôt; à présent, actuellement.

preservation [prezə'veiʃən], n. salut, m., conservation; préservation (de), f.

preservative [pri'zə:vətiv], a. and n. préservateur, préservatif, m.

preserve [pri'zə:v], n. confiture, f., conserves, f.pl.; réserve, chasse réservée, f.—v.t. préserver (de); conserver; confire (fruits etc.); **preserved fruits**, fruits confits, m.pl.; **preserved meat**, conserves de viande, f.pl.

preserver [pri'zə:və], n. sauveur; conservateur, m.; **life preserver**, see **life-belt**.

preside [pri'zaid], v.i. présider (à).

presidency ['prezidənsi], n. présidence, f.

president ['prezidənt], n. président, m.; **vice president**, vice-président, m.

presidential [prezi'denʃəl], a. présidentiel; de président.

presiding [pri'zaidiŋ], a. président.

press (1) [pres], v.t. presser; serrer, étreindre; satiner (papier); pressurer (fruits); repasser (vêtements); (fig.) insister sur.—v.i. presser, pousser; avancer, se presser.—n. presse, pression, f.; pressoir (à fruits etc.), m.; armoire à linge, f.; **the press**, la presse.

press (2) [pres], v.t. enrôler (marins) de force.

press agency ['preseidʒənsi], n. agence de presse, f.

press clipping ['presklipiŋ], n. coupure de journal, f.

pressed [prest], a. satiné; **hard pressed**, serré de près; aux abois; **pressed for time**, très pressé.

*press gang ['presgæŋ], n. (Naut.) presse, f.

pressing ['presiŋ], a. urgent, pressant.

pressman ['presmən], n. (pl. **-men** [men]) journaliste, reporter, m.

pressure ['preʃə], n. pression; tension; urgence, f.; poids (lourdeur), m.; **blood pressure**, tension artérielle.

pressure cooker ['preʃəkukə], n. autoclave; auto-cuiseur, m., cocotte-minute, f.

pressure gauge ['preʃəgeidʒ], n. manomètre, m.

pressurize ['preʃəraiz], v.t. pressuriser.

prestige [pres'ti:ʒ], n. prestige, m.

presumably [pri'zju:məbli], adv. probablement.

presume [pri'zju:m], v.t. présumer; supposer.—v.i. présumer se permettre, avoir l'audace (de), prendre la liberté (de); **to presume upon**, présumer trop de.

presuming [pri'zju:miŋ], a. présomptueux, indiscret.

presumption [pri'zʌmpʃən], n. présomption, f.

presumptive [pri'zʌmptiv], a. présumé; (Law) présomptif.

presumptuous [pri'zʌmptjuəs], a. présomptueux.

presumptuousness [pri'zʌmptjuəsnis], n. présomption, f.

presuppose [pri:sə'pouz], v.t. présupposer.

pretend [pri'tend], v.t. prétexter; feindre.— v.i. prétendre (à); feindre (de), faire semblant (de).

pretended [pri'tendid], a. prétendu, soi-disant.

pretender [pri'tendə], n. prétendant, m.

pretense [pri'tens], n. prétexte, m., simulation; prétention, f.; **to make a pretense of**, faire semblant de; **under false pretenses**, par des moyens frauduleux.

pretension [pri'tenʃən], n. prétention, f.

pretentious [pri'tenʃəs], a. prétentieux, ambitieux.

pretentiousness [pri'tenʃəsnis], n. air prétentieux, m., prétention, f.

preternatural [pri:tə'nætʃərəl], a. surnaturel, contre nature.

pretext ['pri:tekst], n. prétexte, faux semblant, m.; **under the pretext of**, sous prétexte de.

prettily ['pritili], adv. joliment, gentiment.

prettiness ['pritinis], n. gentillesse, f., agrément, m.

pretty ['priti], a. joli, gentil.—adv. assez; passablement; **pretty much**, presque, à peu près.

prevail [pri'veil], v.i. prévaloir, l'emporter (sur); réussir (avoir du succès); dominer.

prevailing [pri'veiliŋ], a. dominant, régnant; général.

prevalence ['prevələns], n. influence, prédominance; fréquence, durée (de temps, maladie etc.), f.

prevalent ['prevələnt], a. régnant, dominant; général.

prevaricate [pri'værikeit], v.i. équivoquer; tergiverser, mentir.

prevarication [priværi'keiʃən], n. tergiversation, f.

prevaricator [pri'værikeitə], n. chicaneur, menteur, m.

prevent [pri'vent], v.t. empêcher, détourner (de); prévenir.

preventable [pri'ventəbl], a. évitable.

prevention [pri'venʃən], n. empêchement, m.

preventive [pri'ventiv], a. préventif.—n. préservatif, m.

preview ['pri:vju:], n. avant-première, f.

previous ['pri:viəs], a. antérieur, préalable.

previously ['pri:viəsli], adv. antérieurement, auparavant.

previousness ['pri:viəsnis], n. antériorité, priorité; (colloq.) anticipation, f.

prey [prei], n. proie, f.; **to be a prey to**, être en proie à.—v.i. **to prey on**, faire sa proie de; tourmenter, obséder (l'esprit).

price [prais], n. prix, m.; **at any price**, à tout prix; **cost price**, prix coûtant; **market price**, prix courant.—v.t. tarifer, mettre un prix à.

priceless ['praislis], a. sans prix, inappréciable; impayable (plaisanterie etc.).

price list ['praislist], n. tarif, m.

prick [prik], n. piqûre; pointe, f.; (fig.) aiguillon (stimulant); remords, m.—v.t. piquer; dresser (les oreilles); aiguillonner (stimuler); (fig.) exciter, tourmenter de remords.

pricker ['prikə], n. poinçon, m., pointe, f.

pricking ['prikiŋ], a. qui pique, piquant.—n. piqûre, f.; picotement (sensation), m.

prickle ['prikl], n. aiguillon, piquant, m.; épine, f.—v.t. piquer.

prickly ['prikli], a. piquant, épineux, hérissé.

pride [praid], n. orgueil, m., fierté; bande (de lions), f.—v.r. **to pride oneself on**, se piquer de, s'enorgueillir de.

prier ['praiə], n. curieux, m.

priest [pri:st], *n.* prêtre, *m.*
priestess ['pri:stes], *n.* prêtresse, *f.*
priesthood ['pri:sthu:d], *n.* prêtrise, *f.*, sacerdoce, clergé, *m.*
priestly ['pri:stli], *a.* de prêtre, sacerdotal.
prig [prig], *n.* faquin, fat; pédant, *m.*
priggish ['prigiʃ], *a.* suffisant, pédant.
priggishly ['prigiʃli], *adv.* avec suffisance.
prim [prim], *a.* affecté, précieux, collet monté.
primacy ['praiməsi], *n.* primauté, *f.*
primal ['praiməl], *a.* primitif; principal.
primarily ['praimərili], *adv.* dans le principe.
primary ['praiməri], *a.* primitif, premier; principal; (*Sch.*) primaire, élémentaire.
primate ['praimit], *n.* primat, *m.*
prime [praim], *a.* premier, principal; de premier rang, de première qualité; *prime minister*, premier ministre, *m.—n.* aube, *f.*; commencement; printemps, *m.*; fleur, élite, *f.*, choix (*mieux*), *m.*; première jeunesse, *f.*; *prime of life*, fleur de l'âge, *f.* *—v.t.* amorcer (*fusils*); (*Paint.*) imprimer.
primer [['primə], *n.* premier livre (*de lecture etc.*); (*R.-C. Ch.*) livre d'heures, *m.*
primeval [prai'mi:vəl], *a.* primitif, primordial.
priming ['praimiŋ], *n.* amorçage, *m.*; amorce (*d'un fusil*); (*Paint.*) impression, *f.*
primitive ['primitiv], *a.* and *n.* primitif, *m.*
primitiveness ['primitivnis], *n.* caractère primitif, *m.*
primly ['primli], *adv.* d'un air collet monté.
primness ['primnis], *n.* afféterie, *f.*
primogeniture [praimou'dʒenitjuə], *n.* primogéniture, *f.*
primordial [prai'mɔ:diəl], *a.* primordial.
primrose ['primrouz], *n.* primevère, *f.*
prince [prins], *n.* prince, *m.*
princeliness ['prinslinis], *n.* caractère de prince, *m.*
princely ['prinsli], *a.* de prince, princier; magnifique.*—adv.* en prince, en princesse, magnifiquement.
princess [prin'ses], *n.* princesse, *f.*
principal ['prinsipl], *a.* principal, premier, en chef.*—n.* partie principale, *f.*, chef; directeur, patron; proviseur (*d'un lycée*), *m.*; directrice, *f.*
principality [prinsi'pæliti], *n.* principauté, *f.*
principally ['prinsipli], *adv.* principalement, surtout.
principle ['prinsipl], *n.* principe, *m.*
principled ['prinsipld], *a.* qui a des principes.
print [print], *v.t.* imprimer; faire une empreinte sur; (*Phot. etc.*) tirer; *printed matter*, imprimé(s), *m.* (*pl.*).*—n.* empreinte (*de pas etc.*), impression; estampe, gravure; indienne (*tissu*); (*Phot.*) épreuve, *f.*; (*Print.*) caractère, *m.*
printer ['printə], *n.* imprimeur, typographe, *m.*
printing ['printiŋ], *n.* impression (*tirage*); imprimerie (*art etc.*), *f.*
printing machine ['printiŋmə'ʃi:n], *n.* presse mécanique, *f.*
printing press ['printiŋpres], *n.* presse à imprimer, *f.*
prior ['praiə], *a.* antérieur.*—adv.* antérieurement (*à*), avant.*—n.* prieur, *m.*
prioress ['praiəris], *n.* prieure, *f.*
priority [prai'ɔriti], *n.* priorité, *f.*

priory ['praiəri], *n.* prieuré, *m.*
prise [praiz], *n.* levier, *m.—v.t. to prise open*, ouvrir avec un levier.
prism [prizm], *n.* prisme, *m.*
prismatic [priz'mætik], **prismatical** [priz 'mætikəl], *a.* prismatique.
prison [prizn], *n.* prison, *f.*
prisoner ['priznə], *n.* prisonnier, *m.*; (*Law*) *prisoner* (*at the bar*), accusé, prévenu, *m.*
prison-van ['priznvæn], *n.* voiture cellulaire, *f.*
pristine ['pristain], *a.* primitif, premier.
privacy ['praivəsi, 'privəsi], *n.* retraite, solitude, intimité, *f.*
private ['praivit], *a.* particulier, personnel, privé; confidentiel, secret; (*Law*) à huis clos.*—n.* (*Mil.*) simple soldat, *m.*
privateer [praivə'tiə], *n.* corsaire, *m.*
privately ['praivitli], *adv.* en particulier; en secret; (*Law*) à huis clos.
privation [prai'veiʃən], *n.* privation, *f.*
privet ['privit], *n.* (*Bot.*) troène, *m.*
privilege ['privilidʒ], *n.* privilège, *m.*, (*Law*) immunité, *f.—v.t.* privilégier.
privileged ['privilidʒd], *a.* privilégié.
privily ['privili], *adv.* secrètement, en secret.
privy ['privi], *a.* privé, secret; caché; *Privy Council*, conseil privé, *m.*
prize [praiz], *n.* prise (*ce qu'on prend*), *f.*; prix (*récompense*); lot (*dans une loterie*), *m.—v.t.* priser, estimer.
prize-giving ['praizgiviŋ], *n.* distribution des prix, *f.*
prize-winner ['praizwinə], *n.* lauréat, gagnant, *m.*
pro [prou], *prep.* pour; *pros and cons*, le pour et le contre.
probability [prɔbə'biliti], *n.* probabilité, vraisemblance, *f.*
probable ['prɔbəbl], *a.* probable; vraisemblable.
probably ['prɔbəbli], *adv.* probablement.
probate ['proubeit], *n.* vérification (*d'un testament*), *f.*
probation [prə'beiʃən], *n.* probation, épreuve, *f.*; (*Univ. etc.*) examen, stage, *m.*; *on probation*, (*Law*) sous surveillance de la police.
probationary [prə'beiʃənəri], *a.* d'épreuve; de probation.
probationer [prə'beiʃənə], *n.* aspirant, *m.*, stagiaire; novice, *m., f.*
probe [proub], *n.* sonde, *f.*, stylet, *m.—v.t.* sonder; (*fig.*) examiner à fond.
probing ['proubiŋ], *a.* pénétrant (*question*).
probity ['proubiti], *n.* probité, *f.*
problem ['prɔbləm], *n.* problème, *m.*
problematic [prɔbli'mætik], **problematical** [prɔbli'mætikəl], *a.* problématique.
proboscis [prə'bɔsis], *n.* (*pl.* **probosces** [prə'bɔsi:z]) trompe, *f.*, (*facet.*) nez, *m.*
procedure [prə'si:dʒə], *n.* procédé, *m.*, procédure, *f.*
proceed [prə'si:d], *v.i.* procéder, avancer, continuer son chemin; provenir (*de*); se mettre (*à*).
proceeding [prə'si:diŋ], *n.* procédé, *m.*; manière d'agir, *f.*; (*pl.*) démarches, *f.pl.*, faits, actes, *m.pl.*
proceeds ['prousi:dz], *n.pl.* produit, montant, *m.*

process ['prouses], n. procédé; processus; cours, m., marche, suite (du temps), f.—v.t. (Ind.) traiter.

procession [prə'seʃən], n. procession, f., cortège, m.

processional [prə'seʃənəl], a. processionnel. —n. hymne processionnel, m.

proclaim [prə'kleim], v.t. proclamer, déclarer, publier.

proclamation [prɔklə'meiʃən], n. proclamation, publication, déclaration; ordonnance, f.

proclivity [prə'kliviti], n. penchant, m., inclination (à), f.

procrastinate [pro'kræstineit], v.t. remettre. —v.i. retarder.

procrastination [prokræsti'neiʃən], n. retardement, délai, m.

procrastinator [pro'kræstineitə], n. temporiseur, m.

procreate ['proukrieit], v.t. procréer.

procreation [proukri'eiʃən], n. procréation, f.

procreative ['proukrieitiv], a. procréateur, productif.

proctor ['proktə], n. (Univ.) censeur; (Law) procureur, m.

procurable [prə'kjuərəbl], a. qu'on peut se procurer.

procuration [prɔkju'reiʃən], n. gestion des affaires d'autrui; (Law) procuration, f.

procurator ['prɔkjureitə], n. agent d'affaires; (Law) procurateur, m.

procure [prə'kjuə], v.t. procurer, faire avoir, se procurer.

prod [prɔd], v.t. pousser du doigt ou du bout d'un bâton; piquer; (fig.) aiguillonner.—n. coup de pointe, m.

prodigal ['prɔdigl], a. and n. prodigue, m., f.

prodigality [prɔdi'gæliti], n. prodigalité, f.

prodigious [prə'didʒəs], a. prodigieux.

prodigy ['prɔdidʒi], n. prodige, m., f.

produce ['prɔdju:s], n. produit, m.—[prə'dju:s], v.t. produire; exhiber, montrer; (Geom.) prolonger.

producer [prə'dju:sə], n. producteur; (Theat.) producteur, m.

producible [prə'dju:sibl], a. productible.

product ['prɔdʌkt], n. produit, m.; by-product, sous-produit, m.

production [prə'dʌkʃən], n. production, f.; (Chem. etc.) produit, m.; (Theat.) mise en scène, f.

productive [prə'dʌktiv], a. productif; fécond.

productivity [prɔdʌk'tiviti], n. productivité, f.

profanation [prɔfə'neiʃən], n. profanation, f.

profane [prə'fein], a. profane.—v.t. profaner.

profanely [prə'feinli], adv. d'une manière profane.

profaner [prə'feinə], n. profanateur, m.

profanity [prə'fæniti], n. conduite profane, impiété, f.; langage profane, m.

profess [prə'fes], v.t. professer, faire profession de, déclarer.

professed [prə'fest], a. déclaré, de profession.

professedly [prə'fesidli], adv. ouvertement; de profession.

profession [prə'feʃən], n. profession, f.; état, métier (emploi), m.

professional [prə'feʃənəl], a. de sa profession, professionnel; **professional man**, homme qui exerce une carrière libérale, m.—n. homme du métier, homme de l'art; (Spt.) professionnel, m.

professionalism [prə'feʃənəlizm], n. caractère professionnel; (Spt.) professionnalisme, m.

professionally [prə'feʃənəli], adv. par profession; en homme du métier.

professor [prə'fesə], n. professeur (d'université), m.

professorial [profe'sɔ:riəl], a. de professeur, professoral.

professorship [prə'fesəʃip], n. professorat, m., chaire, f.

proffer ['prɔfə], n. offre, f.—v.t. offrir, proposer.

proficiency [prə'fiʃənsi], n. capacité, f.; talent, m., compétence, f.

proficient [prə'fiʃənt], a. versé, fort, compétent.

profile ['proufail], n. profil, m.; **in profile**, de profil.

profit ['prɔfit], n. profit, bénéfice, rapport; (fig.) avantage, m.—v.t. profiter à, faire du bien à; avantager.—v.i. profiter (de).

profitable ['prɔfitəbl], a. profitable, avantageux.

profitably ['prɔfitəbli], adv. avantageusement, avec profit.

profiteer [prɔfi'tiə], n. profiteur, m.—v.i. faire des bénéfices excessifs.

profitless ['prɔfitlis], a. sans profit, inutile.

profligacy ['prɔfligəsi], n. dérèglement, m., dissolution, f., libertinage, m.

profligate ['prɔfligit], a. débauché, dissolu, libertin.—n. libertin, mauvais sujet, m.

profound [prə'faund], a. profond; approfondi.

profoundly [prə'faundli], adv. profondément.

profundity [prə'fʌnditi], n. profondeur, f.

profuse [prə'fju:s], a. prodigue, abondant, excessif (choses).

profusely [prə'fju:sli], adv. profusément, à profusion.

profuseness [prə'fju:snis], **profusion** [prə'fju:ʒən], n. profusion, prodigalité, abondance, f.

progenitor [prou'dʒenitə], n. aïeul, ancêtre, m.

progeny ['prɔdʒəni], n. postérité, f., descendants, m.pl.

prognostic [prɔg'nɔstik], a. pronostique.—n. pronostic, m.

prognosticate [prɔg'nɔstikeit], v.t. pronostiquer.

prognostication [prɔgnɔsti'keiʃən], n. pronostic, m.

program ['prougræm], n. programme, m.

progress ['prougres], n. progrès, avancement, cours, m.; marche, f.; voyage (de cérémonie), m.—[prə'gres], v.i. s'avancer, faire des progrès, avancer.

progression [prə'greʃən], n. progression, f.

progressive [prə'gresiv], a. and n. progressif, m.; (Polit.) progressiste, m., f.

progressiveness [prə'gresivnis], n. marche progressive, f.

prohibit [prə'hibit], v.t. prohiber, défendre, interdire; **smoking prohibited**, défense de fumer.

prohibition [prouhi'biʃən], n. prohibition, défense, f.

prohibitive [prə'hibitiv], **prohibitory** [prə'hibitri], a. prohibitif (mœurs); **prohibitive price**, prix exorbitant, m.

project ['prɔdʒekt], n. projet, dessein, m.— [prə'dʒekt], v.t. projeter.—v.i. avancer, faire saillie.

projectile [prə'dʒektail], n. projectile, m.

projecting [prə'dʒektiŋ], a. saillant, en saillie.

projection [prə'dʒekʃən], n. projection, saillie, f.; (Arch.) ressaut, m.

projector [prə'dʒektə], n. homme à projets, projeteur; projecteur (lumière); (Cine.) appareil de projection, m.

proletarian [prouli'tɛəriən], a. and n. prolétaire, m., f.

proletariat [prouli'tɛəriət], n. prolétariat, m.

prolific [prə'lifik], a. prolifique; fécond, fertile.

prolix ['prouliks], a. prolixe.

prolixity [prə'liksiti], **prolixness** ['prouliks nis], n. prolixité, f.

prologue ['proulɔg], n. prologue, m.

prolong [prə'lɔŋ], v.t. prolonger; retarder, différer (remettre); **to be prolonged**, se prolonger.

prolongation [proulɔŋ'geiʃən], n. prolongement, m.; prolongation (du temps etc.), f.

promenade [promə'na:d], n. promenade; esplanade (au bord de la mer), f.—v.i. se promener, se faire voir.

promenader [promə'na:də], n. promeneur, m.

prominence ['prominəns], n. proéminence; (fig.) distinction, f.

prominent ['prominənt], a. proéminent, saillant; prononcé (remarquable); (fig.) éminent, distingué.

prominently ['prominəntli], adv. en saillie; d'une manière frappante.

promiscuity [promis'kju:iti], **promiscuousness** [prə'miskjuəsnis], n. mélange confus, m.; promiscuité, f.

promiscuous [prə'miskjuəs], a. sans distinction de sexe, promiscu; mêlé, confus, sans ordre.

promiscuously [prə'miskjuəsli], adv. confusément; en commun, en promiscuité.

promise ['promis], n. promesse; (fig.) espérance, f.—v.t., v.i. promettre.

promising ['promisiŋ], a. prometteur, qui promet; qui donne des espérances.

promissory ['promisəri], a. qui contient une promesse; **promissory note**, billet à ordre, m.

promontory ['promontri], n. promontoire, m.

promote [prə'mout], v.t. servir, avancer; promouvoir; encourager; **to promote a company**, lancer une société anonyme.

promoter [prə'moutə], n. promoteur, protecteur, instigateur; (Comm.) lanceur d'affaires, m.

promotion [prə'mouʃən], n. promotion, f., avancement, m.

prompt [prompt], v.t. exciter, porter, pousser; inspirer, suggérer; (Theat.) souffler.—a. prompt, empressé.

prompter ['promptə], n. souffleur, m.; **prompter's box**, trou du souffleur, m.

promptitude, ['promptitju:d], **promptness** ['promptnis], n. promptitude, f., empressement, m.

promptly ['promptli], adv. promptement, avec empressement.

promptness [PROMPTITUDE].

promulgate ['promǝlgeit], v.t. promulguer.

promulgation [promǝl'geiʃǝn], n. promulgation, f.

promulgator ['promǝlgeitǝ], n. promulgateur, m.

prone [proun], a. penché, incliné; couché, étendu; (fig.) disposé, porté (à).

proneness ['prounnis], n. disposition, inclination, f., penchant, m.

prong [proŋ], n. fourchon, m., dent, f.

pronged [proŋd], a. à fourchons, à dents.

pronoun ['prounaun], n. pronom, m.

pronounce [prə'nauns], v.t. prononcer; déclarer, annoncer, dire.

pronounceable [prə'naunsəbl], a. prononçable.

pronouncement [prə'naunsmənt], n. prononcement, m., déclaration, f.

pronunciation [prənʌnsi'eiʃən], n. prononciation, f., accent, m.

proof [pru:f], a. **proof against**, résistant à, à l'épreuve de; **waterproof**, imperméable. —n. preuve; épreuve, f.

proofless ['pru:flis], a. sans preuve.

proof sheet ['pru:fʃi:t], n. (Print.) épreuve, f.

prop [prop], n. étai, étançon; (Hort.) tuteur, échalas; (fig.) appui, soutien; (Theat.) (fam.) accessoire, m.—v.t. étayer; appuyer, soutenir; (Hort.) échalasser.

propaganda [propə'gændə], n. propagande, f.

propagandist [propə'gændist], n. propagandiste, m., f.

propagate ['propəgeit], v.t. propager; (fig.) répandre; créer, enfanter (des êtres).—v.i. se propager.

propagation [propə'geiʃən], n. propagation, f.

propagator ['propəgeitə], n. propagateur, m.

propel [prə'pel], v.t. pousser en avant, faire marcher, propulser.

propeller [prə'pelə], n. hélice, f.; propulseur, moteur, m.

propelling [prə'peliŋ], a. propulseur, moteur; **propelling force**, force motrice, f.

propensity [prə'pensiti], n. penchant, m., tendance, f.

proper ['propə], a. propre, particulier; convenable, à propos (comme il faut); juste, exact (correct).

properly ['propəli], adv. proprement, comme il faut.

property ['propəti], n. propriété, f.; bien, m., biens, m.pl.; qualité, f.; (Theat., Cine.) accessoire, m.

property tax ['propətitæks], n. impôt foncier, m.

prophecy ['profəsi], n. prophétie, f.

prophesy ['profəsai], v.t. prophétiser, prédire.

prophet ['profit], n. prophète, m.

prophetess ['profites], n. prophétesse, f.

prophetic [prə'fetik], **prophetical** [prə'fetikəl], a. prophétique.

propinquity [prə'piŋkwiti], n. proximité; parenté (de personnes), f.

propitiate [prə'piʃieit], v.t. rendre propice.

propitiation [prəpiʃi'eiʃən], n. propitiation, f.

propitiator [prə'piʃieitə], n. propitiateur, m.

propitiatory [prə'piʃiətri], a. and n. propitiatoire, m.

propitious [prə'piʃəs], a. propice, favorable.

523

propitiousness

propitiousness [prə'piʃəsnis], *n.* nature propice, *f.*
proportion [prə'pɔːʃən], *n.* proportion; partie; portion, *f.*; *in proportion as*, à mesure que.—*v.t.* proportionner.
proportional [prə'pɔːʃənəl], *a.* en proportion; proportionnel.
proportionate [prə'pɔːʃənit], *a.* proportionné.
proposal [prə'pouzl], *n.* proposition; demande en mariage, *f.*
propose [prə'pouz], *v.t.* proposer; offrir; *to propose a toast*, porter un toast.—*v.i.* se proposer; faire une demande en mariage.
proposer [prə'pouzə], *n.* auteur d'une proposition, *m.*
proposition [prɔpə'ziʃən], *n.* proposition; affaire, *f.*
propound [prə'paund], *v.t.* proposer, exposer, mettre en avant.
proprietary [prə'praiətri], *a.* de propriété.—*n.* actionnaires, *m.pl.*
proprietor [prə'praiətə], *n.* propriétaire, *m.*
proprietress [prə'praiətris], *n.* propriétaire, maîtresse, *f.*
propriety [prə'praiəti], *n.* convenance, propriété, *f.*
propulsion [prə'pʌlʃən], *n.* propulsion, *f.*; *jet propulsion*, propulsion à réaction.
prorogation [prourə'geiʃən], *n.* prorogation, *f.*
prorogue [prə'roug], *v.t.* proroger.
prosaic [pro'zeiik], *a.* prosaïque.
proscenium [prə'siːniəm], *n.* proscenium, *m.*, avant-scène, *f.*
proscribe [pro'skraib], *v.t.* proscrire.
proscription [pro'skripʃən], *n.* proscription, *f.*
prose [prouz], *n.* prose, *f.*
prosecute ['prɔsikjuːt], *v.t.* poursuivre; revendiquer (*ses droits etc.*).
prosecution [prɔsi'kjuːʃən], *n.* poursuite, *f.*, procès criminel, *m.*; *witness for the prosecution*, témoin à charge, *m.*
prosecutor ['prɔsikjuːtə], *n.* poursuivant, plaignant, *m.*; *public prosecutor*, procureur de la république, *m.*
prosecutrix ['prɔsikjuːtriks], *n.* poursuivante, plaignante, *f.*
proselyte ['prɔsəlait], *n.* prosélyte, *m.*
proselytism ['prɔsəlitizm], *n.* prosélytisme, *m.*
proselytize ['prɔsəlitaiz], *v.t.* convertir.—*v.i.* faire des prosélytes.
prose writer ['prouzraitə], *n.* prosateur, *m.*
prosily ['prouzili], *adv.* prosaïquement, ennuyeusement.
prosiness ['prouzinis], *n.* prosaïsme, *m.*; verbosité, *f.*
prosody ['prɔsədi], *n.* prosodie, *f.*
prospect ['prɔspekt], *n.* vue; perspective, *f.*; (*fig.*) espoir; avenir, *m.*—[prə'spekt], *v.t.* faire des recherches (*minerai, pétrole etc.*), prospecter.
prospective [prə'spektiv], *a.* en perspective; à venir.
prospectively [prə'spektivli], *adv.* pour l'avenir.
prospector [prə'spektə], *n.* explorateur; *orpailleur, *m.*
prospectus [prə'spektəs], *n.* prospectus, *m.*

prosper ['prɔspə], *v.t.* faire prospérer, favoriser.—*v.i.* prospérer, réussir.
prosperity [prɔs'periti], *n.* prospérité, *f.*
prosperous ['prɔspərəs], *a.* prospère; florissant (*affaires*); (*fig.*) heureux; favorable.
prostitute ['prɔstitjuːt], *n.* prostituée, *f.*—*v.t.* prostituer.
prostitution [prɔsti'tjuːʃən], *n.* prostitution, *f.*
prostrate ['prɔstreit], *v.t.* coucher, prosterner; (*fig.*) renverser; *to prostrate oneself before*, se prosterner devant.—*a.* prosterné; (*fig.*) abattu.
prostration [prɔs'treiʃən], *n.* prosternation, *f.*; (*fig.*) abattement, *m.*
prosy ['prouzi], *a.* ennuyeux, fastidieux.
protagonist [prou'tægənist], *n.* protagoniste, *m.*
protect [prə'tekt], *v.t.* protéger, défendre; garantir, abriter (*contre le temps etc.*); sauvegarder (*intérêts*).
protection [prə'tekʃən], *n.* protection, défense; garantie, *f.*, abri (*contre le temps etc.*), *m.*; (*Law*) sauvegarde, *f.*
protectionism [prə'tekʃənizm], *n.* protectionnisme, *m.*
protectionist [prə'tekʃənist], *a.* and *n.* protectionniste, *m.*, *f.*
protective [prə'tektiv], *a.* protecteur.
protector [prə'tektə], *n.* protecteur, *m.*
protectorate [prə'tektərit], *n.* protectorat, *m.*
protectress [prə'tektris], *n.* protectrice, *f.*
protein ['proutiːn], *n.* protéine, *f.*
protest ['proutest], *n.* protestation, *f.*; (*Comm.*) protêt, *m.*—[prə'test], *v.t.*, *v.i.* protester.
Protestant ['prɔtistənt], *a.* and *n.* protestant, *m.*
Protestantism ['prɔtistəntizm], *n.* protestantisme, *m.*
protestation [prɔtes'teiʃən], *n.* protestation, *f.*
protester [prə'testə], *n.* personne qui fait faire un protêt, *m.*
protocol ['proutəkɔl], *n.* protocole, *m.*
proton ['prouton], *n.* proton, *m.*
prototype ['proutətaip], *n.* prototype, *m.*
protract [prə'trækt], *v.t.* prolonger, traîner en longueur.
protraction [prə'trækʃən], *n.* prolongation, *f.*
protractor [prə'træktə], *n.* rapporteur (*instrument*), *m.*
protrude [prə'truːd], *v.t.* pousser en avant, faire sortir.—*v.i.* s'avancer, faire saillie.
protruding [prə'truːdiŋ], *a.* en saillie, saillant.
protrusion [prə'truːʒən], *n.* saillie, *f.*
protuberance [prə'tjuːbərəns], *n.* protubérance, *f.*
protuberant [prə'tjuːbərənt], *a.* protubérant.
proud [praud], *a.* fier (*de*); orgueilleux.
proudly ['praudli], *adv.* fièrement, orgueilleusement.
provable ['pruːvəbl], *a.* prouvable, démontrable.
prove [pruːv], *v.t.* prouver, démontrer; mettre à l'épreuve, éprouver (*la qualité de*); vérifier (*testament etc.*).—*v.i.* se montrer, se révéler.
proved [pruːvd], *a.* prouvé, démontré, reconnu.
provender ['prɔvəndə], *n.* fourrage, *m.*, nourriture (*d'animaux*), *f.*

524

proverb ['prɔvə:b], *n.* proverbe, *m.*
proverbial [prə'və:biəl], *a.* proverbial.
provide [prə'vaid], *v.t.* pourvoir, fournir, munir; préparer (*à*); stipuler —*v.i.* pourvoir.
provided [prə'vaidid], *a.* pourvu.—*conj.* **provided that**, pourvu que (*with subj.*).
providence ['prɔvidəns], *n.* providence (*divine*); prévoyance (*humaine*), *f.*
provident ['prɔvidənt], *a.* prévoyant; économe.
providential [prɔvi'denʃəl], *a.* providentiel, de la providence.
providently ['prɔvidəntli], *adv.* avec prévoyance.
provider [prə'vaidə], *n.* pourvoyeur, fournisseur, *m.*
province ['prɔvins], *n.* province, *f.*; (*fig.*) département, ressort, *m.*
provincial [prə'vinʃəl], *a.* provincial, de province.—*n.* provincial, *m.*
provincialism [prə'vinʃəlizm], *n.* provincialisme, *m.*
proving ['pru:viŋ], *n.* vérification, mise à l'épreuve, *f.*
provision [prə'viʒən], *n.* action de pourvoir; stipulation; (*Law*) disposition (*d'un projet de loi etc.*), *f.*; (*pl.*) vivres, comestibles, *m.pl.*—*v.t.* approvisionner.
provisional [prə'viʒənəl], *a.* provisoire.
provision dealer [prə'viʒəndi:lə], *n.* marchand de comestibles, *m.*
proviso [prə'vaizou], *n.* condition, clause conditionnelle, *f.*
provisory [prə'vaizəri], *a.* provisoire, conditionnel.
provocation [prɔvə'keiʃən], *n.* provocation, *f.*
provocative [prə'vɔkətiv], *a.* provocant, provocateur.
provoke [prə'vouk], *v.t.* provoquer; inciter; fâcher, irriter.
provoker [prə'voukə], *n.* provocateur, *m.*
provoking [prə'voukiŋ], *a.* provocant; ennuyeux, fâcheux, agaçant.
provokingly [prə'voukiŋli], *adv.* d'une manière provocante *ou* contrariante.
provost ['prɔvəst], *n.* prévôt; (*Univ.*) principal; (*Sc.*) maire, *m.*
prow [prau], *n.* proue, *f.*
prowess ['prauis], *n.* bravoure, prouesse, *f.*
prowl [praul], *n.* action de rôder, *f.*—*v.i.* rôder.
prowler ['praulə], *n.* rôdeur, *m.*
proximate ['prɔksimit], *a.* proche, immédiat.
proximity [prɔk'simiti], *n.* proximité, *f.*
proximo ['prɔksimou], *adv.* du mois prochain.
proxy ['prɔksi], *n.* mandataire, *m.*, *f.*, délégué, *m.*; procuration (*chose*), *f.*; **by proxy**, par procuration.
prude [pru:d], *n.* prude, mijaurée, *f.*
prudence ['pru:dəns], *n.* prudence, *f.*
prudent ['pru:dənt], *a.* prudent, sage.
prudential [pru'denʃəl], *a.* de prudence, dicté par la prudence.
prudently ['pru:dəntli], *adv.* prudemment, sagement.
prudery ['pru:dəri], *n.* pruderie, *f.*
prudish ['pru:diʃ], *a.* prude, de prude.
prudishly ['pru:diʃli], *adv.* avec pruderie.
prune [pru:n], *n.* pruneau, *m.*—*v.t.* élaguer, tailler, émonder.
prunella [pru'nelə], *n.* prunelle, *f.*

pruning ['pru:niŋ], *n.* taille, *f.*, élagage, *m.*
pruning shears ['pru:niŋʃiəz], *n.pl.* sécateur, *m.*, cisailles, *f.pl.*
prurience ['pruəriəns], **pruriency** ['pruəriənsi], *n.* démangeaison, *f.*
prurient ['pruəriənt], *a.* qui démange.
Prussia ['prʌʃə], la Prusse, *f.*
Prussian ['prʌʃən], *a.* prussien.—*n.* Prussien (*personne*), *m.*
prussic ['prʌsik], *a.* prussique.
pry [prai], *v.t.* soulever avec un levier.—*v.i.* fureter; fouiller (*dans*); **to pry into**, se mêler de.—*n.* regard scrutateur, regard indiscret, *m.*
prying ['praiiŋ], *a.* scrutateur, curieux.—*n.* curiosité, *f.*
psalm [sɑ:m], *n.* psaume, *m.*
psalmist ['sɑ:mist], *n.* psalmiste, *m.*
psalmody ['sɑ:mədi], *n.* psalmodie, *f.*
psalter ['sɔ:ltə], *n.* psautier, *m.*
pseudonym ['sju:dənim], *n.* pseudonyme, *m.*
pshaw! [pʃɔ:], *int.* bah! fi donc!
psychiatric [saiki'ætrik], *a.* psychiatrique.
psychiatrist [sai'kaiətrist], *n.* psychiatre, *m.*, *f.*
psychiatry [sai'kaiətri], *n.* psychiatrie, *f.*
psychic(al) ['saikik(l)], *a.* psychique.
psycho-analysis [saikouə'næləsis], *n.* psychanalyse, *f.*
psycho-analyst [saikou'ænəlist], *n.* psychanalyste, *m.*, *f.*
psycho-analyze [saikou'ænəlaiz], *v.t.* psychanalyser.
psychological [saikə'lɔdʒikl], *a.* psychologique.
psychologist [sai'kɔlədʒist], *n.* psychologiste, psychologue, *m.*
psychology [sai'kɔlədʒi], *n.* psychologie, *f.*
psychopath ['saikopæθ], *n.* psychopathe, *m.*, *f.*
psychosis [sai'kousis], *n.* psychose, *f.*
ptarmigan ['tɑ:migən], *n.* lagopède, *m.*
ptomaine ['toumein], *n.* ptomaïne, *f.*; **ptomaine poisoning**, intoxication alimentaire, *f.*
puberty ['pju:bəti], *n.* puberté, *f.*
pubescence [pju'besəns], *n.* pubescence, *f.*
pubescent [pju'besənt], *a.* pubescent.
public ['pʌblik], *a.* and *n.* public, *m.*
publican ['pʌblikən], *n.* cafetier, patron de bistro(t); (*Bibl.*) publicain, *m.*
publication [pʌbli'keiʃən], *n.* publication, *f.*
public-house ['pʌblik'haus], *n.* café, *m.*, brasserie, *f.*, bistro(t), *m.*
publicist ['pʌblisist], *n.* publiciste, journaliste; publicitaire, *m.*, *f.*
publicity [pʌb'lisiti], *n.* publicité; réclame, *f.*
publicize ['pʌblisaiz], *v.t.* faire connaître au public.
publicly ['pʌblikli], *adv.* publiquement; en public.
publish ['pʌbliʃ], *v.t.* publier; éditer.
publisher ['pʌbliʃə], *n.* éditeur, *m.*; **bookseller and publisher**, libraire-éditeur, *m.*
puce [pju:s], *a.* puce.
puck (1) [pʌk], *n.* lutin, *m.*
puck (2) [pʌk], *n.* (*Spt.*) palet de hockey (sur glace), *m.*
pucker ['pʌkə], *v.t.* rider, plisser; (*Dress.*) faire goder.—*v.i.* goder.—*n.* ride; (*Dress.*) poche, *f.*; mauvais pli, *m.*
puckering ['pʌkəriŋ], *n.* froncement, *m.*
puckish ['pʌkiʃ], *a.* malicieux; de lutin.

pudding ['pudiŋ], n. pudding, pouding, m.;
puddle [pʌdl], n. flaque (d'eau), mare, f.—
v.t. troubler, rendre bourbeux.
puerile ['pjuərail], a. puéril.
puerility [pjuəˈriliti], n. puérilité, f.
puff [pʌf], n. souffle (d'haleine), m.; bouffée (de vent, fumée etc.), f.; feuilleté (pâtisserie), m.; houppe à poudrer (de dames), f.; bouillon (de robes); puff, m., réclame tapageuse, f.—v.t. souffler, bouffir (les joues), gonfler; (fig.) faire mousser (publicité).—v.i. souffler, boursoufler, bouffir, bouffer, se gonfler; haleter.
puffin ['pʌfin], n. (Orn.) macareux, m.
puffiness ['pʌfinis], n. boursouflure, enflure, f.
puff pastry ['pʌfpeistri], n. pâte feuilletée, f.
puffy ['pʌfi], a. bouffi, gonflé.
pug [pʌg], n. carlin (chien), m.
pugilism ['pjuːdʒilizm], n. pugilat, m., boxe, f.
pugilist ['pjuːdʒilist], n. boxeur, pugiliste, m.
pugilistic [pjudʒiˈlistik], a. de pugilat.
pugnacious [pʌgˈneiʃəs], a. querelleur; batailleur.
pugnaciously [pʌgˈneiʃəsli], adv. d'un air batailleur.
pugnacity [pʌgˈnæsiti], n. pugnacité, f.
pug nose ['pʌgnouz], n. nez épaté, m.
puke [pjuːk], v.i. vomir.
pule [pjuːl], v.i. piauler.
puling ['pjuːliŋ], n. cri; piaulement, m.
pull [pul], v.t. tirer; arracher; presser (la détente); **to pull a wry face**, faire la grimace; **to pull down**, abattre, démolir; **to pull off**, arracher, enlever; **to pull up**, hisser; déraciner; arrêter.—v.i. ramer (tirer la rame); **to pull in**, s'arrêter; **to pull round**, se remettre; **to pull through**, guérir, s'en tirer; **to pull up**, s'arrêter.—n. action de tirer, traction, f.; coup (d'aviron), effort, m.; secousse, f.; (fig.) avantage, m.; **hard pull**, rude effort.
pullet ['pulit], n. poulette, f.
pulley ['puli], n. poulie, f.
pullover ['pulouvə], n. pull-over, m.
pulmonary ['pʌlmənəri], a. pulmonaire.
pulp [pʌlp], n. pulpe; pâte (papier), f.—v.t. réduire en pâte.
pulpiness ['pʌlpinis], n. nature pulpeuse, f.
pulpit ['pulpit], n. chaire, f.
pulpous ['pʌlpəs], **pulpy** ['pʌlpi], a. pulpeux.
pulsate [pʌlˈseit], v.i. battre; palpiter.
pulsation [pʌlˈseiʃən], n. pulsation, f.
pulsatory ['pʌlsətri], a. pulsatoire.
pulse [pʌls], n. pouls, m.; pulsation, f.; plantes légumineuses, f.pl.
pulverization [pʌlvəraiˈzeiʃən], n. pulvérisation, f.
pulverize ['pʌlvəraiz], v.t. pulvériser.
puma ['pjuːmə], n. puma, couguar, m.
pumice ['pʌmis], n. pierre ponce, f.
pump [pʌmp], n. pompe, f.; escarpin (chaussure), m.—v.t. pomper; (fig.) sonder; **to pump up**, gonfler (pneu).—v.i. pomper.
pumpkin ['pʌmpkin], n. citrouille, courge, f., potiron, m.
pump room ['pʌmpruːm], n. buvette, f.
pun [pʌn], n. calembour, jeu de mots, m.—v.i. faire des calembours.
punch (1) [pʌntʃ], n. emporte-pièce; (Print.) poinçon, m.—v.t. percer, poinçonner.

punch (2) [pʌntʃ], n. coup de poing, m.—v.t. donner un coup de poing à.
punch (3) [pʌntʃ], n. punch (boisson), m.
punch bowl ['pʌntʃboul], n. bol à punch, m.
puncheon ['pʌntʃən], n. poinçon, m., pièce (de vin), f.
punctilio [pʌŋkˈtiliou], n. exactitude scrupuleuse, f., point d'étiquette, m.
punctilious [pʌŋkˈtiliəs], a. pointilleux.
punctiliousness [pʌŋkˈtiliəsnis], n. exactitude scrupuleuse, pointillerie, f.
punctual ['pʌŋktjuəl], a. ponctuel, exact.
punctuality [pʌŋktjuˈæliti], n. ponctualité, exactitude, f.
punctually ['pʌŋktjuəli], adv. ponctuellement, exactement.
punctuate ['pʌŋktjueit], v.t. ponctuer.
punctuation [pʌŋktjuˈeiʃən], n. ponctuation, f.
puncture ['pʌŋktʃə], n. piqûre; crevaison (d'un pneu), f.—v.t. piquer; crever (pneu).
pundit ['pʌndit], n. pandit, m.
pungency ['pʌndʒənsi], n. âcreté; aigreur, f.
pungent ['pʌndʒənt], a. âcre; piquant, mordant.
pungently ['pʌndʒəntli], adv. avec causticité.
puniness ['pjuːninis], n. petitesse, nature chétive, f.
punish ['pʌniʃ], v.t. punir, corriger; malmener.
punishable ['pʌniʃəbl], a. punissable.
punishment ['pʌniʃmənt], n. punition; peine, f., châtiment, m.; **capital punishment**, peine capitale.
punitive ['pjuːnitiv], a. punitif.
punt [pʌnt], n. bachot, m.—v.i. conduire un bachot (à la perche).
puny ['pjuːni], a. petit, chétif.
pup [pʌp], n. petit chien, petit; (pej.) freluquet, fat, m.
pupil (1) ['pjuːpil], n. élève, m., f.
pupil (2) ['pjuːpil], n. pupille (de l'œil), f.
pupilary ['pjuːpiləri], a. pupillaire.
puppet ['pʌpit], n. marionnette, f.; **glove puppet**, marionnette à gaine; **puppet government**, gouvernement fantoche, m.
puppet show ['pʌpitʃou], n. (spectacle de) marionnettes, f.pl.
puppy ['pʌpi], n. petit chien; (fig.) fat, freluquet, m.
purblind ['pəːblaind], a. myope.
purchase ['pəːtʃis], n. achat, m., acquisition, emplette; (Mech.) prise, f.—v.t. acheter, acquérir.
purchase deed ['pəːtʃisdiːd], n. contrat d'achat, m.
purchaser ['pəːtʃisə], n. acquéreur, acheteur, m.
purchasing ['pəːtʃisiŋ], n. achat, m.; **purchasing power**, pouvoir d'achat, m.
pure [pjuə], a. pur; **pure-bred**, de race.
purely ['pjuəli], adv. purement.
pureness ['pjuənis], n. pureté, f.
purgation [pəːˈgeiʃən], n. purgation, f.
purgative ['pəːgətiv], a. and n. purgatif, m.
purgatorial [pəːgəˈtɔːriəl], a. du purgatoire.
purgatory ['pəːgətəri], n. purgatoire, m.
purge [pəːdʒ], v.t. purger; purifier, épurer.—n. purgation, purge, f.; (Polit.) nettoyage, m.

purification [pjuərifi'keiʃən], *n.* purification; épuration, *f.*

purifier ['pjuərifaiə], *n.* purificateur, *m.*

purify ['pjuərifai], *v.t.* purifier.—*v.i.* se purifier.

purist ['pjuərist], *n.* puriste, *m., f.*

puritan ['pjuəritən], *n.* puritain, *m.*

puritan ['pjuəritən], *a.* puritain.

puritanical [pjuəri'tænikl], *a.* de puritain, puritain.

puritanism ['pjuəritənizm], *n.* puritanisme, *m.*

purity ['pjuəriti], *n.* pureté, *f.*

purl [pə:l], *v.t.* engrêler (*dentelle*).—*v.i.* murmurer, gazouiller.—*n.* engrêlure (*de dentelle*), *f.*; doux murmure; gazouillement, *m.*

purlieu ['pə:lju:], *n.* alentours, environs, *m.pl.*

purloin [pə'lɔin], *v.t.* dérober, voler.

purple [pə:pl], *a.* violet, mauve; pourpre.—*n.* pourpre, mauve (*couleur*), *m.*; pourpre (*teinture etc.*), *f.*—*v.t.* teindre en pourpre, empourprer, rougir.

purport ['pə:pət], *n.* sens, *m.*, teneur, portée, *f.*—[pə'pɔ:t], *v.t.* tendre à montrer, signifier, vouloir dire.

purpose ['pə:pəs], *n.* but, objet, *m.*, fin, *f.*, dessein, *m.*, intention, *f.*; **on purpose**, exprès, à dessein; **to answer one's purpose**, faire son affaire.—*v.t., v.i.* se proposer, avoir l'intention (de).

purposely ['pə:pəsli], *adv.* à dessein, exprès.

purr [pə:], *v.i.* ronronner.

purring ['pə:riŋ], *a.* qui fait ronron.—*n.* ronron, *m.*

purse [pə:s], *n.* porte-monnaie, *m.*; bourse, *f.*; (*Am.*) sac à main, *m.*—*v.t.* plisser, froncer (*les sourcils etc.*).

purser ['pə:sə], *n.* commissaire (*de navire*); (*Mining*) agent comptable, *m.*

pursuance [pə'sju:əns], *n.* poursuite, conséquence, *f.*; **in pursuance of**, conformément à.

pursuant [pə'sju:ənt], *a.* en conséquence (de), conforme (à).

pursue [pə'sju:ə], *v.t.* poursuivre; suivre, chercher.

pursuer [pə'sju:ə], *n.* poursuivant, *m.*

pursuit [pə'sju:t], *n.* poursuite, recherche, occupation, *f.*; (*pl.*) travaux, *m.pl.*

purulence ['pjuəruləns], **purulency** ['pjuərulənsi], *n.* purulence, *f.*

purulent ['pjuərulənt], *a.* purulent.

purvey [pə'vei], *v.t.* fournir, approvisionner; procurer.

purveyor [pə'veiə], *n.* pourvoyeur, fournisseur, *m.*

pus [pʌs], *n.* pus, *m.*

push [puʃ], *v.t.* pousser; (*fig.*) presser, importuner; **to push back**, repousser, faire reculer; **to push down**, faire tomber, renverser.—*v.i.* pousser; faire un effort; **to push off**, pousser au large; **to push on**, pousser en avant.—*n.* impulsion, poussée, *f.*; effort, *m.*; extrémité, *f.*

pushing ['puʃiŋ], *a.* entreprenant.

pusillanimity [pju:silə'nimiti], *n.* pusillanimité, *f.*

pusillanimous [pju:si'læniməs], *a.* pusillanime.

puss [pus], *n.* (*colloq.*) minet, *m.*, minette, *f.*

pustule ['pʌstju:l], *n.* pustule, *f.*

put [put], *v.t. irr.* mettre, poser, placer; proposer (*solution etc.*); lancer (*poids etc.*); **to put about**, gêner; **to put aside**, mettre de côté; **to put back**, replacer, remettre; **to put by**, mettre de côté; **to put forward**, mettre en avant; **to put off**, ôter; remettre; **to put on**, mettre (*vêtements*); **to put on the light**, allumer; **to put out**, mettre dehors; éteindre (*feu etc.*); **to put up**, installer; loger, caser (*dans un hôtel etc.*).—*v.i.* aller; germer, pousser; (*Naut.*) se mettre; **to put in**, entrer au port; **to put up**, loger (à ou chez), descendre (à); **to put up with**, supporter.

putrefaction [pju:tri'fækʃən], *n.* putréfaction, *f.*

putrefy ['pju:trifai], *v.t.* putréfier.—*v.i.* se putréfier.

putrid ['pju:trid], *a.* putride.

putridity [pju:'triditi], *n.* putridité, *f.*

putt [pʌt], *v.t.* (*Golf*) poter.

putter ['pʌtə], *n.* (*Golf*) poteur, *m.*

putting ['putiŋ], *n.* action du mettre, mise, *f.*

putty ['pʌti], *n.* mastic, *m.*

puzzle [pʌzl], *n.* (*fig.*) énigme, *f.*; jeu de patience, casse-tête (*jouet*), *m.*; **crossword puzzle**, mots croisés, *m.pl.*—*v.t.* intriguer, embarrasser; **to puzzle one's brains**, se creuser la tête.

pygmean [pig'miən], *a.* de pygmée.

pygmy ['pigmi], *n.* pygmée, *m., f.*

pyjamas [pi'dʒɑ:məz], *n.pl.* pyjama, *m.*

pylon ['pailən], *n.* pylône, *m.*

pyramid ['pirəmid], *n.* pyramide, *f.*

pyramidal [pi'ræmidl], *a.* pyramidal.

pyre ['paiə], *n.* bûcher, *m.*

Pyrenees [pirə'ni:z], **the**. les Pyrénées, *f.pl.*

pyrethrum [pai'ri:θrəm], *n.* (*Bot.*) pyrèthre, *m.*

pyrotechnic [paiərou'teknik], **pyrotechnical** [paiərou'teknikəl], *a.* pyrotechnique, pyrique.

pyrotechnics [paiərou'tekniks], *n.pl.* pyrotechnie, *f.*

pyrotechnist [paiərou'teknist], *n.* artificier, *m.*

python ['paiθən], *n.* python, *m.*

pyx [piks], *n.* ciboire, *m.*

Q

Q, q [kju:]. dix-septième lettre de l'alphabet, *m.*

quack [kwæk], *a.* de charlatan.—*n.* charlatan; couac, cri du canard, *m.*—*v.i.* crier (comme les canards *etc.*).

quackery ['kwækəri], *n.* charlatanisme, *m.*

Quadragesima [kwɔdrə'dʒesimə]. Quadragésime, *f.*

quadrangle ['kwɔdræŋgl], *n.* quadrilatère carré, *m.*; (*Univ.*) cour d'honneur, *f.*

quadrant ['kwɔdrənt], *n.* quart de cercle, *m.*

quadratic [kwɔd'rætik], *a.* du second degré.

quadrennial [kwɔd'reniəl], *a.* quadriennal.

quadrennially [kwɔd'reniəli], *adv.* tous les quatre ans.

quadrilateral

quadrilateral [kwɔdri'lætərəl], *a.* quadri-
latéral.—*n.* quadrilatère, *m.*
quadrille [kwə'dril], *n.* quadrille, *m.*; contredanse, *f.*
quadroon [kwə'druːn], *n.* quarteron, *m.*
quadruped ['kwɔdruped], *n.* quadrupède, *m.*
quadruple ['kwɔdrupl], *a. and n.* quadruple,
m.—v.t. quadrupler.
quadruplet ['kwɔdruplit], *n.* quadruplette, *f.*;
(*pl.*) (*colloq.*) **quads** [kwɔdz], quadruplés,
m.pl.
quaff [kwæf], *v.t.* boire à grands traits.
quaffer ['kwæfə], *n.* buveur, *m.*
quagmire ['kwægmaiə], *n.* fondrière, *f.*
quail (1) [kweil], *v.i.* perdre courage, fléchir.
quail (2) [kweil], *n.* (*Orn.*) caille, *f.*
quaint [kweint], *a.* singulier, bizarre; pittoresque.
quaintly ['kweintli], *adv.* singulièrement,
bizarrement.
quaintness ['kweintnis], *n.* bizarrerie, originalité, *f.*
quake [kweik], *v.i.* trembler; branler.—*n.*
tremblement, *m.*
Quaker ['kweikə], *n.* Quaker, *m.*
Quakerism ['kweikərizm], *n.* Quakerisme,
m.
quaking ['kweikiŋ], *a.* tremblant.—*n.* tremblement, *m.*; terreur, *f.*
qualifiable ['kwɔlifaiəbl], *a.* qualifiable.
qualification [kwɔlifi'keiʃən], *n.* qualification, qualité, *f.*; aptitude, *f.*, talent, *m.*; réserve,
restriction, *f.*; (*pl.*) qualités, *f.pl.*, titres,
m.pl.
qualified ['kwɔlifaid], *a.* qui a les qualités
requises (*pour*), propre (*à*); **qualified
teacher**, professeur diplômé, *m.*
qualify ['kwɔlifai], *v.t.* rendre capable (*de*);
autoriser (*à*); modérer.—*v.i.* se préparer (*à*).
qualifying ['kwɔlifaiiŋ], *a.* qualificatif.
quality ['kwɔliti], *n.* qualité, *f.*; (*colloq.*)
talent, *m.*
qualm [kwɑːm], *n.* nausée, *f.*; (*fig.*) scrupule,
m.
qualmish ['kwɑːmiʃ], *a.* qui a mal au cœur.
quandary ['kwɔndəri], *n.* embarras, *m.*,
impasse, *f.*
quantitative ['kwɔntitətiv], *a.* quantitatif.
quantity ['kwɔntiti], *n.* quantité, *f.*; grand
nombre, *m.*
quantum ['kwɔntəm], *n.* montant, quantum,
m.
quarantine ['kwɔrəntiːn], *n.* quarantaine, *f.*
—*v.t.* mettre en quarantaine.
quarrel ['kwɔrəl], *n.* querelle, dispute,
brouille, *f.—v.i.* se quereller, se brouiller.
quarreller ['kwɔrələ], *n.* querelleur, *m.*
quarrelling ['kwɔrəliŋ], *n.* querelle; dispute,
f.
quarrelsome ['kwɔrəlsəm], *a.* querelleur.
quarrelsomeness ['kwɔrəlsəmnis], *n.* humeur
querelleuse, *f.*
quarry (1) ['kwɔri], *n.* carrière, *f.—v.t.* tirer
d'une carrière.
quarry (2) ['kwɔri], *n.* (*Hunt.*) curée; proie,
f.
quarrying ['kwɔriiŋ], *n.* extraction d'une
carrière, *f.*
quarryman ['kwɔrimən], *n.* (*pl.* **-men** [men])
carrier, *m.*
quart [kwɔːt], *n.* quart de gallon (*1,14 litre*), *m.*
quarter ['kwɔːtə], *n.* quart; quart de quintal

(*12,70 kg.*); quartier (*de ville, de la lune, de
mouton etc.*), *m.*; partie, région (*d'un pays*),
f.; côté (*direction*); trimestre (*de l'année*), *m.*;
hanche (*de navire*), *f.*; (*pl.*) logement; (*Mil.*)
quartier, *m.*; **to come to close quarters**
en venir aux mains.—*v.t.* diviser en quatre;
(*Mil.*) caserner; loger (*dans une maison*);
(*Her.*) écarteler.
quarter day ['kwɔːtədei], *n.* jour du terme, *m.*
quarter-deck ['kwɔːtədek], *n.* gaillard d'arrière, *m.*
quartering ['kwɔːtəriŋ], *n.* division en quatre
parties, *f.*; (*Mil.*) logement; (*Her.*) écartèlement, *m.*
quarterly ['kwɔːtəli], *a.* trimestriel.—*adv.*
par trimestre, tous les trois mois.
quartermaster ['kwɔːtəmɑːstə], *n.* (*Navy*)
maître timonier; (*Mil.*) officier d'approvisionnement, *m.*
quartet [kwɔː'tet], *n.* quatuor, *m.*
quarto ['kwɔːtou], *a. and n.* in-quarto, *m.*
quartz [kwɔːts], *n.* quartz, *m.*
quash [kwɔʃ], *v.t.* écraser; (*fig.*) dompter;
(*Law*) annuler, casser.
quasi ['kweisai], *adv.* quasi.
quatrain ['kwɔtrein], *n.* quatrain, *m.*
quaver ['kweivə], *n.* tremblement de la voix,
trille, *m.*; (*Mus.*) croche, *f.—v.i.* trembler;
(*Mus.*) faire des trilles.
quavering ['kweivəriŋ], *a.* tremblant, chevrotant.—*n.* trille, tremolo; tremblement de
voix, *m.*
quay [kiː], *n.* quai, *m.*
quayage ['kiːidʒ], *n.* quayage, *m.*
queen [kwiːn], *n.* reine; (*Cards etc.*) dame, *f.*
queen bee ['kwiːnbiː], *n.* reine-abeille, *f.*
queen like ['kwiːnlaik], **queenly** ['kwiːnli],
adv. de reine, digne d'une reine.
queen-mother [kwiːn'mʌðə], *n.* reine-
mère, *f.*
queer [kwiə], *a.* bizarre, étrange, drôle.
queerly ['kwiəli], *adv.* étrangement, bizarrement.
queerness ['kwiənis], *n.* étrangeté, bizarrerie,
f.; malaise, *m.*
quell [kwel], *v.t.* réprimer, dompter.
quench [kwentʃ], *v.t.* éteindre; étancher;
étouffer (*élan etc.*); **to quench one's
thirst**, étancher sa soif, se désaltérer.
quenchable ['kwentʃəbl], *a.* extinguible.
quenchless ['kwentʃlis], *a.* inextinguible.
querulous ['kweruləs], *a.* plaintif, maussade.
querulousness ['kweruləsnis], *n.* humeur
chagrine, *f.*
query ['kwiəri], *n.* question, *f.*; point d'interrogation, *m.—v.t.* mettre en doute.—*v.i.*
questionner.
quest [kwest], *n.* enquête; recherche, *f.*; **in
quest of**, à la recherche de.
question ['kwestʃən], *n.* question, interrogation, demande, *f.*; sujet (*problème*), *m.*;
(*Parl.*) interpellation, *f.*; **out of the question**, absolument impossible; **that is not
the question**, il ne s'agit pas de cela; **to
ask a question**, poser une question.—*v.t.*
questionner, interroger; mettre en doute.—
v.i. se demander (*si*).
questionable ['kwestʃənəbl], *a.* contestable,
douteux, incertain; suspect, équivoque.
questioner ['kwestʃənə], *n.* questionneur, *m.*
questioning ['kwestʃəniŋ], *n.* questions, *f.pl.*,
interrogation, *f.*

question master [ˈkwestʃənmɑːstə], n. (*Rad.*, *Tel.*) meneur de débats, m.
questionnaire [kwestʃəˈnɛə], n. questionnaire, m.
queue [kjuː], n. queue, f.—*v.i.* faire la queue.
quibble [kwibl], n. argutie, chicane, f.—*v.i.* ergoter, chicaner.
quibbler [ˈkwiblə], n. ergoteur, chicaneur, m.
quick [kwik], a. vite, rapide, prompt; agile, leste; vif (*vivant*); (*fig.*) fin.—*adv.* vite, promptement, lestement.—n. vif, m.; chair vive, f.; **stung to the quick**, piqué au vif; (*collect.*) **the quick**, les vivants, m.pl.
quicken [ˈkwikən], v.t. animer, vivifier; raviver, accélérer, hâter.—*v.i.* prendre vie, s'animer.
quickening [ˈkwikəniŋ], a. vivifiant, qui ranime.
quicklime [ˈkwiklaim], n. chaux vive, f.
quickly [ˈkwikli], adv. vite; promptement; bientôt.
quickness [ˈkwiknis], n. vitesse; promptitude; activité; pénétration; fréquence (*du pouls*), f.
quicksand [ˈkwiksænd], n. sable mouvant, m.
quickset [ˈkwikset], a. vive; **quickset hedge**, haie vive, f.—n. plante vive, f.
quicksilver [ˈkwiksilvə], n. vif-argent, mercure, m.
quicksilvered [ˈkwiksilvəd], a. étamé.
quicksilvering [ˈkwiksilvəriŋ], n. étamage, m.
quick-tempered [ˈkwikˈtempəd], a. emporté, vif, colérique.
quick-witted [ˈkwikˈwitid], a. à l'esprit vif.
quid [kwid], n. chique; (*slang*) livre sterling, f.
quidnunc [ˈkwidnʌŋk], n. curieux, colporteur de nouvelles, m.
quiescence [kwiˈesəns], n. quiétude, tranquillité, f., repos, m.
quiescent [kwiˈesənt], a. paisible, en repos, tranquille.
quiet [ˈkwaiət], a. tranquille, calme; paisible, silencieux; (*fig.*) modeste; **be quiet!** silence! taisez-vous! **to keep quiet**, se tenir tranquille, rester tranquille.—n. tranquillité, quiétude, f.; repos, calme, m.—*v.t.* (*also* **quieten** [ˈkwaiətn]) tranquilliser, apaiser, calmer.—*v.i.* **to quiet(en) down**, s'apaiser, se calmer.
quieten, v.t., v.i. [QUIET].
quieting [ˈkwaiətiŋ], a. calmant, tranquillisant.
quietly [ˈkwaiətli], adv. tranquillement; doucement; en silence, sans bruit, discrètement, sans éclat.
quietness [ˈkwaiətnis], n. tranquillité, f.; calme, repos, m.
quietude [ˈkwaiitjuːd], n. quiétude, tranquillité, f.
quietus [kwaiˈiːtəs], n. repos, m.; mort, f.; (*fig.*) coup de grâce, m.; décharge, quittance, f.
quill [kwil], n. (tuyau de) plume; plume d'oie (*pour écrire*), f.; piquant (*de porc-épic*), m.—*v.t.* tuyauter, rucher.
quilling [ˈkwiliŋ], n. tuyautage, m., ruche, f.
quilt [kwilt], n. édredon, m., courtepointe, f.—*v.t.* piquer.
quilting [ˈkwiltiŋ], n. piqué; piquage, m.
quince [kwins], n. coing; cognassier (*arbre*), m.
quinine [ˈkwainain], n. quinine, f.

Quinquagesima [kwiŋkwəˈdʒesimə]. Quinquagésime, f.
quinquennial [kwiŋˈkweniəl], a. quinquennial.
quinquina [kiŋˈkiːnə], n. quinquina, m.
quinsy [ˈkwinzi], n. angine, f.
quint [kwint], n. quinte, f.
quintal [kwintl], n. quintal, m.
quintessence [kwinˈtesəns], n. quintessence, f.
quintet [kwinˈtet], n. quintette, m.
quintuple [ˈkwintjupl], a. quintuple.—*v.t.* quintupler.
quintuplets [ˈkwintjuplits], (*colloq.*) **quins** [kwinz], n.pl. quintuplés, m.pl.
quip [kwip], n. mot piquant, sarcasme, m.—*v.t.* railler.
quire [ˈkwaiə], n. main (*de papier*), f.
quirk [kwəːk], n. sarcasme, m., pointe; subtilité (*chicane*), f.
quit [kwit], v.t. irr. quitter, abandonner; **notice to quit**, congé, m.—a. quitte; **to get quit of**, se débarrasser de.
quite [kwait], adv. tout à fait, entièrement, tout; bien, parfaitement; assez.
quits [kwits], a. quitte.
quiver [ˈkwivə], n. carquois, m.—*v.i.* trembler, frissonner; palpiter (*la chair*); frémir.
quivering [ˈkwivəriŋ], n. tremblement, frissonnement; battement des paupières, m.
Quixote [ˈkwiksət], **Don.** Don Quichotte, m.
quixotic [kwikˈsotik], a. de Don Quichotte; extravagant, exalté.
quiz [kwiz], n. plaisanterie; devinette, f.; examen oral, m., colle, f.; **radio quiz**, jeu radiophonique, m.—*v.t.* questionner, interroger; [see **question master**]
quizzical [ˈkwizikəl], a. douteur.
quodlibet [ˈkwɔdlibet], n. quolibet, m.; subtilité, f.
quoin [kɔin], n. coin, m.
quoit [kɔit], n. palet, m.
quondam [ˈkwɔndəm], a. ci-devant, ancien.
quorum [ˈkwɔːrəm], n. nombre suffisant, quorum, m.
quota [ˈkwoutə], n. quote-part, f.
quotable [ˈkwoutəbl], a. citable.
quotation [kwoˈteiʃən], n. citation; (*Comm.*) cote, f.; (*St. Exch.*) cours, m.[see **comma**]
quote [kwout], v.t. citer; alléguer; (*Comm.*) coter.
quotidian [kwoˈtidiən], a. quotidien, journalier.
quotient [ˈkwouʃənt], n. quotient, m.

R

R, r [ɑː]. dix-huitième lettre de l'alphabet, m.
rabbet [ˈræbət], n. feuillure, rainure, f.—*v.t.* faire une rainure à.
rabbet-plane [ˈræbətplein], n. guillaume, m.

rabbi ['ræbai], *n.* rabbin, *m.*; *chief rabbi*, grand rabbin.

rabbit ['ræbit], *n.* lapin, *m.*; *young rabbit*, lapereau, *m.*

rabble [ræbl], *n.* foule; populace, canaille, *f.*

rabid ['ræbid], *a.* féroce, furieux; enragé (*chien*).

rabies ['reibi:z], *n.* rage, hydrophobie, *f.*

raccoon [rə'ku:n], *n.* raton laveur, *m.*

race (1) [reis], *n.* (*Biol.*) race, *f.*

race (2) [reis], *n.* (*Spt.*) course, *f.*; raz, raz de marée (*courant*), *m.*—*v.i.* courir vite, courir, lutter de vitesse; *to go to the races*, aller aux courses.

race-course ['reiskɔ:s], *n.* champ de courses, hippodrome, *m.*

race-horse ['reishɔ:s], *n.* cheval de course, *m.*

racer ['reisə], *n.* coureur; cheval de course, *m.*

race-track ['reistræk], *n.* piste, *f.*

racial ['reiʃəl], *a.* de (la) race, ethnique.

raciness ['reisinis], *n.* piquant, *m.*, verve, *f.*

racing ['reisiŋ], *a.* de course.—*n.* les courses, *f.pl.*

racing car ['reisiŋka:], *n.* automobile de course, *f.*

racism ['reisizm], *n.* racisme, *m.*

rack [ræk], *n.* râtelier (*dans une écurie etc.*); chevalet (*instrument de tension*), *m.*; roue (*instrument de supplice*) (*Tech.*) crémaillère, *f.*; *luggage rack*, (*Rail.*) filet, *m.*—*v.t.* mettre à la torture; (*fig.*) tourmenter; *to rack one's brains*, se creuser la cervelle.

racket ['rækit], *n.* fracas, tapage, tintamarre, caquet, *m.*; (*Ten.*) raquette; escroquerie, supercherie, combine, *f.*

rackety ['rækiti], *a.* tapageur.

racking ['rækiŋ], *a.* de torture; atroce (*douleur*).

racy ['reisi], *a.* (*fig.*) vif, piquant, plein de verve (*style etc.*).

radar ['reidɑ:], *n.* radar, *m.*

radiance ['reidiəns], **radiancy** ['reidiənsi], *n.* rayonnement, éclat, *m.*, splendeur, *f.*

radiant ['reidiənt], *a.* rayonnant (*de*); radieux, éclatant.

radiantly ['reidiəntli], *adv.* en rayonnant, splendidement.

radiate ['reidieit], *v.t.* émettre comme des rayons.—*v.i.* rayonner (*de*).

radiation [reidi'eiʃən], *n.* rayonnement, *m.*, radiation, *f.*

radiator ['reidieitə], *n.* radiateur, *m.*

radical ['rædikəl], *a.* radical; fondamental.—*n.* radical, *m.*

radicalism ['rædikəlizm], *n.* radicalisme, *m.*

radically ['rædikəli], *adv.* radicalement, essentiellement.

radio ['reidiou], *n.* radio, la T.S.F., *f.* [see **wireless**]

radioactive [reidiou'æktiv], *a.* radio-actif.

radioactivity ['reidiouæk'tiviti], *n.* radio-activité, *f.*

radio control ['reidioukən'troul], *n.* télé-guidage, *m.*—*v.t.* téléguider.

radiogram ['reidiougræm], *n.* radio-gramme, *m.*

radiography [reidi'ɔgrəfi], *n.* radiographie, *f.*

radish ['rædiʃ], *n.* radis, *m.*; *horse-radish*, raifort, *m.*

radium ['reidiəm], *n.* radium, *m.*

radius ['reidiəs], *n.* rayon, *m.*

radix ['reidiks], *n.* (*pl.* **radices** ['reidisi:z]) racine; base, *f.*

raffle [ræfl], *n.* loterie, tombola, *f.*—*v.t.* mettre en tombola.

raft [rɑ:ft], *n.* radeau; train de bois, *m.*

rafter ['rɑ:ftə], *n.* chevron, *m.*

raftered ['rɑ:ftəd], *a.* à chevrons.

rafting ['rɑ:ftiŋ], *n.* flottage en train, *m.*

raftsman ['rɑ:ftsmən], *n.* flotteur, *m.*

rag [ræg], *n.* chiffon (*nettoyage etc.*); haillon, *m.*, guenille, loque (*de vêtement*), *f.*; (*Sch.*) chahut, *m.*; brimade, *f.*—*v.t.* (*Sch.*) chahuter.

ragamuffin ['rægəmʌfin], *n.* gueux, polisson, va-nu-pieds, *m.*

rage [reidʒ], *n.* rage, fureur, emportement, *m.*; furie, manie, *f.*; *it's all the rage*, cela fait fureur.—*v.i.* être furieux, être en fureur, s'emporter; (*fig.*) sévir.

ragged ['rægid], *a.* en haillons, déguenillé (*personnes*); en lambeaux, déchiré (*choses*).

raggedness ['rægidnis], *n.* délabrement, déguenillement, *m.*; guenilles, *f.pl.*

raging ['reidʒiŋ], *a.* furieux, en fureur; déchaîné, acharné, violent (*tempête, guerre etc.*).—*n.* fureur, violence, *f.*

ragman ['rægmən], *n.* (*pl.* **-men** [men]) chiffonnier, *m.*

rag-time ['rægtaim], *n.* (*Mus.*) musique syncopée, *f.*

raid [reid], *n.* incursion, *f.*; raid, coup de main, *m.*; *air raid*, raid aérien.—*v.t.* faire une incursion dans; piller; bombarder.

raider ['reidə], *n.* maraudeur; commando, *m.*

rail (1) [reil], *n.* barre, *f.*, barreau (*bois, métal etc.*), *m.*; rampe (*d'escalier*), *f.*; parapet (*de pont etc.*); (*Rail.*) rail, *m.*—*v.t.* enclore, griller.

rail (2) [reil], *v.i.* *to rail at*, criailler, invectiver.

railer ['reilə], *n.* criailleur, médisant, *m.*

railing (1) ['reiliŋ], *n.* grille, *f.*, garde-fou, *m.*

railing (2) ['reiliŋ], *n.* injures, invectives, *f.pl.*

raillery ['reiləri], *n.* raillerie, *f.*

railway ['reilwei], *n.* chemin de fer, *m.*, voie ferrée, *f.*

railwayman ['reilweimən], *n.* (*pl.* **-men** [men]) employé des chemins de fer, cheminot, *m.*

raiment ['reimənt], *n.* vêtement, *m.*

rain [rein], *n.* pluie, *f.*—*v.t.* faire pleuvoir.—*v.i.* pleuvoir; *it is pouring with rain*, il pleut à verse.

rainbow ['reinbou], *n.* arc-en-ciel, *m.*

raincoat ['reinkout], *n.* imperméable, *m.*

rainfall ['reinfɔ:l], *n.* pluie annuelle, pluie tombée, *f.*

rain gauge ['reingeidʒ], *n.* pluviomètre, *m.*

rainy ['reini], *a.* pluvieux.

raise [reiz], *v.t.* lever; élever; hausser (*prix etc.*); soulever (*élever à une petite hauteur etc.*); cultiver (*légumes*); augmenter, accroître (*ajouter à*); faire naître (*soupçons*); pousser (*un cri*); faire lever (*pâte*); se procurer (*argent*); faire (*un emprunt etc.*).—*n.* augmentation (*de gages*), *f.*

raised [reizd], *a.* levé; en relief.

raisin [reizn], *n.* raisin sec, *m.*

raising ['reiziŋ], *n.* augmentation, *f.*, accroissement, *m.*; levée (*d'impôts, de troupes, de sièges etc.*), *f.*; élevage (*de bestiaux*), *m.*; culture (*de plantes etc.*), *f.*

rake (1) [reik], *n.* (*Hort.*) râteau.—*v.t.* (*Agric.*) râteler; (*Hort.*) ratisser; ramasser (*rassembler*); (*Mil.*) enfiler.

rake (2) [reik], *n.* roué (*libertin*), *m.*

raking ['reikiŋ], *a.* d'enfilade.—*n.* (*Hort.*) ratissage; (*Agric.*) râtelage, *m.*

rakish ['reikiʃ], *a.* dissolu; élancé (*navire*).

rakishness ['reikiʃnis], *n.* libertinage; air crâne, *m.*

rally ['ræli], *v.t.* rallier, rassembler.—*v.i.* rallier, se rassembler; (*fig.*) se remettre.—*n.* ralliement, *m.*

Ralph [reif, rælf]. Raoul, *m.*

ram [ræm], *n.* bélier; mouton, *m.*—*v.t.* enfoncer; pilonner, tasser (*terre etc.*); bourrer (*dans un canon*).

ramble [ræmbl], *n.* excursion à pied, grande promenade; (*fig.*) divagation, *f.*—*v.i.* errer, se promener; errer çà et là; (*fig.*) divaguer.

rambler ['ræmblə], *n.* excursionniste (à pied), *m., f.*; (*Hort.*) rosier grimpant, *m.*

rambling ['ræmbliŋ], *a.* errant, vagabond; (*fig.*) décousu, incohérent.—*n.* excursions, promenades à l'aventure; (*fig.*) divagations, *f.pl.*

ramification [ræmifi'keiʃən], *n.* ramification, *f.*

ramify ['ræmifai], *v.i.* se ramifier.

rammer ['ræmə], *n.* pilon, *m.*

ramp [ræmp], *n.* rampe, montée; (*fam.*) escroquerie, *f.*

rampant ['ræmpənt], *a.* dominant, violent; effréné; (*Her.*) rampant.

rampart ['ræmpɑ:t], *n.* rempart, *m.*

ramrod ['ræmrɔd], *n.* baguette (*de fusil*), *f.*; écouvillon (*de canon*), *m.*; *stiff as a ramrod*, droit comme un piquet.

ramshackle ['ræmʃækl], *a.* qui tombe en ruines, délabré.

rancid ['rænsid], *a.* rance.

rancidity [ræn'siditi], **rancidness** ['rænsidnis], *n.* rancidité, *f.*

rancor ['ræŋkə], *n.* haine, rancune, *f.*

rancorous ['ræŋkərəs], *a.* rancunier, haineux.

Randolph ['rændɔlf]. Rodolphe, *m.*

random ['rændəm], *a.* fait au hasard.—*n.* hasard, *m.*; *at random*, au hasard.

range [reindʒ], *n.* rangée, *f.*, rang (*file*), *m.*; chaîne (*de montagnes etc.*); étendue, portée, *f.*, fourneau; tir (*armes à feu*), *m.*; gamme (*de couleurs*), *f.*—*v.t.* ranger, arranger; aligner (*avec*); parcourir.—*v.i.* s'aligner; être rangé.

range finder ['reindʒfaində], *n.* télémètre, *m.*

ranger ['reindʒə], *n.* garde-forestier, *m.*

rank (1) [ræŋk], *n.* rang, ordre, *m.*, classe, *f.*; (*Mil.*) grade; (*fig.*) haut rang, *m.*; station de taxis, *f.*—*v.t.* ranger, classer.—*v.i.* se ranger, être classé; occuper un rang.

rank (2) [ræŋk], *a.* luxuriant; (*fig.*) rude; extrême; fétide (*odeur*).

rankle [ræŋkl], *v.i.* s'envenimer, s'enflammer.

rankness ['ræŋknis], *n.* surabondance; grossièreté, *f.*; rancidité, *f.*

ransack ['rænsæk], *v.t.* saccager, piller; fouiller.

ransacking ['rænsækiŋ], *n.* pillage, *m.*

ransom ['rænsəm], *n.* rançon, *f.*—*v.t.* rançonner.

rant [rænt], *n.* déclamation extravagante, *f.*—*v.i.* extravaguer; tempêter.

ranter ['ræntə], *n.* déclamateur, énergumène, *m.*

ranting ['ræntiŋ], *a.* d'énergumène, extravagant.

ranunculus [rə'nʌŋkjuləs], *n.* (*Bot.*) renoncule, *f.*

rap [ræp], *n.* tape, *f.*, petit coup sec, *m.*—*v.t. v.i.* frapper.

rapacious [rə'peiʃəs], *a.* rapace.

rapaciously [rə'peiʃəsli], *adv.* avec rapacité.

rapaciousness [rə'peiʃəsnis], **rapacity** [rə'pæsiti], *n.* rapacité, *f.*

rape (1) [reip], *n.* (*Poet.*) rapt, enlèvement; (*Law*) viol, *m.*—*v.t.* enlever de force; violer.

rape (2) [reip], *n.* (*Agric.*) colza, *m.*, navette, *f.*

rapid ['ræpid], *a.* and *n.* rapide, *m.*

rapidity [rə'piditi], **rapidness** ['ræpidnis], *n.* rapidité, *f.*

rapidly ['ræpidli], *adv.* rapidement.

rapier ['reipiə], *n.* rapière, *f.*

rapine ['ræpain], *n.* rapine, *f.*

rapt [ræpt], *a.* ravi, extasié; profond (*attention*).

rapture ['ræptʃə], *n.* ravissement, transport, *m.*, extase, *f.*

rapturous ['ræptʃərəs], *a.* ravissant; joyeux.

rapturously ['ræptʃərəsli], *adv.* avec transport.

rare [rɛə], *a.* rare; clairsemé; à moitié cru (*viande*).

rarefaction [rɛəri'fækʃən], *n.* raréfaction, *f.*

rarefy ['rɛərifai], *v.t.* raréfier.—*v.i.* se raréfier.

rarely ['rɛəli], *adv.* rarement.

rareness ['rɛənis], **rarity** ['rɛəriti], *n.* rareté, *f.*

rascal [rɑːskl], *n.* coquin, fripon, gredin, *m.*

rascality [rɑːs'kæliti], *n.* friponnerie, gredinerie, coquinerie, *f.*

rascally ['rɑːskəli], *a.* coquin, fripon.

rase [RAZE].

rash (1) [ræʃ], *a.* téméraire; irréfléchi, imprudent.

rash (2) [ræʃ], *n.* éruption, *f.*

rasher ['ræʃə], *n.* tranche, *f.*

rashly ['ræʃli], *adv.* témérairement; imprudemment.

rashness ['ræʃnis], *n.* témérité; précipitation, imprudence, *f.*

rasp [rɑːsp], *n.* râpe, *f.*—*v.t.* râper; râcler, écorcher (*surface, peau*).—*v.i.* grincer, crisser.

raspberry ['rɑːzbəri], *n.* framboise, *f.*

raspberry bush ['rɑːzbəribuʃ], *n.* framboisier, *m.*

rasping ['rɑːspiŋ], *a.* grinçant, âpre, rauque (*voix*).—*n.* râpage; crissement, *m.*

rat [ræt], *n.* rat, *m.*; *to smell a rat*, se douter de quelque chose.

ratchet ['rætʃit], *n.* cliquet, *m.*, dent d'engrenage, *f.*

ratchet-brace ['rætʃitbreis], **ratchet-jack** ['rætʃitdʒæk], *n.* vilbrequin à cliquet, *m.*

rate (1) [reit], *n.* prix, *m.*; raison, proportion, *f.*; taux (*argent, population*); cours (*de change*); degré, rang, ordre, *m.*; vitesse; taxe, *f.*, impôt (*taxe municipale*), *m.*; *at any rate*, en tout cas; *first-rate*, de première classe.—*v.t.* évaluer; classer; taxer; faire une estimation; regarder (*comme*).—*v.i.* *to rate as*, être classé comme.

rate (2) [reit], *v.t.* gronder.

rateable ['reitəbl], *a.* imposable; *rateable value*, valeur locative imposable (*d'un immeuble*), *f.*
rate-payer ['reitpeiə], *n.* contribuable, *m., f.*
rather ['rɑːðə], *adv.* plutôt; un peu, quelque peu (*légèrement*); assez, passablement (*suffisamment*).
ratification [rætifi'keiʃən], *n.* ratification, *f.*
ratify ['rætifai], *v.t.* ratifier, approuver.
ratifying ['rætifaiiŋ], *a.* ratificatif.
rating (1) ['reitiŋ], *n.* estimation, évaluation; répartition d'impôt, *f.*; (*Navy*) matelot, *m.*
rating (2) ['reitiŋ], *n.* gronderie, *f.*
ratio ['reiʃiou], *n.* proportion, raison, *f.*, rapport, *m.*
ration ['ræʃən], *n.* ration, *f.*—*v.t.* rationner.
ration book ['ræʃənbuk], *n.* carte d'alimentation, *f.*
rationing ['ræʃəniŋ], *n.* rationnement, *m.*
rational ['ræʃənl], *a.* raisonnable, rationnel.
rationalism ['ræʃnəlizm], *n.* rationalisme, *m.*
rationalist ['ræʃnəlist], *n.* rationaliste, *m., f.*
rationalize ['ræʃnəlaiz], *v.t.* rationaliser.
rationally ['ræʃnəli], *adv.* raisonnablement, rationnellement.
rattan [rə'tæn], *n.* rotin, *m.*
ratten [rætn], *v.t.* intimider; saboter.
rattle [rætl], *v.t.* faire claquer, faire sonner; secouer (*chaînes etc.*).—*v.i.* faire un bruit sec, cliqueter, crépiter.—*n.* bruit; cliquetis (*de métaux*); râle (*à la gorge*); hochet (*jouet*), *m.*; crécelle, *f.*
rattlesnake ['rætlsneik], *n.* serpent à sonnettes, crotale, *m.*
rattling ['rætliŋ], *a.* bruyant; (*fig.*) excellent.—*n.* bruit, cliquetis, *m.*
rat-trap ['rættræp], *n.* ratière, *f.*
raucous ['rɔːkəs], *a.* rauque.
ravage ['rævidʒ], *n.* ravage, *m.*—*v.t.* ravager.
ravager ['rævidʒə], *n.* ravageur, dévastateur, *m.*
rave [reiv], *v.i.* être en délire; (*fig.*) extravaguer.
ravel [rævl], *v.t.* embrouiller, entortiller.—*v.i.* s'embrouiller, s'entortiller.
raven (1) [reivn], *n.* (*Orn.*) corbeau, *m.*
raven (2) [rævn], *v.t.* dévorer.
ravenous ['rævənəs], *a.* dévorant, vorace.
ravenously ['rævənəsli], *adv.* avec voracité.
ravenousness ['rævənəsnis], *n.* voracité, rapacité, *f.*
ravine [rə'viːn], *n.* ravin, *m.*
raving ['reiviŋ], *a.* en délire, délirant; furieux, fou.—*n.* délire, *m.*
ravish ['ræviʃ], *v.t.* ravir; enlever; (*fig.*) transporter.
ravisher ['ræviʃə], *n.* ravisseur, *m.*
ravishing ['ræviʃiŋ], *a.* ravissant.
raw [rɔː], *a.* cru, vif, écorché (*égratigné etc.*); (*fig.*) sans expérience, novice; pur (*alcool*); brut (*cuir etc.*); froid et humide (*temps*); *raw materials*, matières premières, *f.pl.*
raw-boned ['rɔːbound], *a.* maigre, décharné.
rawness ['rɔːnis], *n.* crudité, *f.*; froid humide (*du temps*), *m.*; (*fig.*) inexpérience, *f.*
ray (1) [rei], *n.* rayon, *m.*
ray (2) [rei], *n.* (*Ichth.*) raie, *f.*
rayless ['reilis], *a.* sans rayon, sans lumière.
Raymond ['reimənd], Raymond, *m.*
rayon ['reiən], *n.* rayonne, *f.*
raze [reiz], *v.t.* raser, effleurer; rayer, effacer (*supprimer*); abattre, détruire (*édifice*).

razor ['reizə], *n.* rasoir, *m.*; *safety razor*, rasoir de sûreté.
re [riː, rei], *prep.* au sujet de, à propos de.
reach [riːtʃ], *n.* portée, atteinte; étendue (*capacité*), *f.*; bief (*de canal*), *m.*—*v.t.* atteindre, toucher; passer, donner (*rendre*); arriver à, parvenir à (*accomplir*).—*v.i.* s'étendre de . . . à.
reachable ['riːtʃəbl], *a.* qu'on peut atteindre.
react [riː'ækt], *v.i.* réagir (*sur*).
reaction [riː'ækʃən], *n.* réaction, *f.*
reactionary [riː'ækʃənəri], *a. and n.* réactionnaire, *m., f.*
reactor [riː'æktə], *n.* réacteur, *m.*
read [riːd], *v.t. irr.* lire; faire la lecture de; (*fig.*) étudier.—*v.i.* lire; faire la lecture; se lire.
readable ['riːdəbl], *a.* lisible; qui se lit avec plaisir.
readableness ['riːdəblnis], *n.* lisibilité, *f.*
readdress [riːə'dres], *v.t.* faire suivre (*lettre*).
reader ['riːdə], *n.* lecteur; (*Print.*) correcteur; liseur (*amateur de lecture*); (*Sch.*) livre de lecture, *m.*
readily ['redili], *adv.* tout de suite, promptement; volontiers (*de bon gré*), avec plaisir.
readiness ['redinis], *n.* empressement, *m.*; promptitude; facilité; bonne volonté (*complaisance*), *f.*
reading ['riːdiŋ], *n.* lecture; variante (*textuelle*), leçon; hauteur (*de baromètre*), *f.*
reading book ['riːdiŋbuk], *n.* livre de lecture, *m.*
reading desk ['riːdiŋdesk], *n.* pupitre, *m.*
reading lamp ['riːdiŋlæmp], *n.* lampe de travail, *f.*
reading room ['riːdiŋruːm], *n.* salle de lecture, *f.*
readjust [riːə'dʒʌst], *v.t.* rajuster, rectifier.
readjustment [riːə'dʒʌstmənt], *n.* rajustement, *m.*
ready ['redi], *a.* prêt, prompt; facile; vif (*qui comprend vite*); *ready money*, argent comptant, *m.*
ready-made ['redimeid], *a.* tout fait, confectionné.
ready-reckoner ['redi'rekənə], *n.* barème, *m.*
ready-witted ['redi'witid], *a.* à l'esprit vif.
reaffirm [riːə'fəːm], *v.t.* réaffirmer.
reafforestation [riːəfɔris'teiʃən], *n.* reboisement, *m.*
real ['riːəl], *a.* réel; vrai, véritable; effectif; (*Law*) immeuble, immobilier. [see **realty**; **estate-agent**; **house-agent**]
realism ['riːəlizm], *n.* réalisme, *m.*
realist ['riːəlist], *n.* réaliste, *m., f.*
realistic [riːə'listik], *a.* réaliste.
reality [riː'æliti], *n.* réalité, *f.*; réel, *m.*
realizable ['riːəlaizəbl], *a.* réalisable.
realization [riːəlai'zeiʃən], *n.* réalisation; conception nette, *f.*
realize ['riːəlaiz], *v.t.* réaliser; effectuer; se rendre compte de, bien comprendre; se figurer; rapporter (*somme*).
really ['riːəli], *adv.* réellement, en effet, effectivement; vraiment.—*int.* en vérité! à vrai dire!
realm [relm], *n.* royaume, *f.*; domaine, *m.*
realty ['riːəlti], *n.* biens immeubles, *m.pl.*
ream [riːm], *n.* rame (*de papier*), *f.*

reap [ri:p], *v.t., v.i.* moissonner; (*fig.*) recueillir.

reaper ['ri:pə], *n.* moissonneur, *m.*

reaping ['ri:piŋ], *n.* moisson, *f.*

reaping machine ['ri:piŋməʃi:n], *n.* moissonneuse, *f.*

reappear [ri:ə'piə], *v.i.* reparaître, réapparaître.

reappearance [ri:ə'piərəns], *n.* réapparition; rentrée (*d'acteur*), *f.*

reappoint [ri:ə'pɔint], *v.t.* réintégrer; renommer.

reappointment [ri:ə'pɔintmənt], *n.* réintégration, *f.*

rear (1) [riə], *a.* situé à l'arrière; postérieur; *rear wheel*, roue arrière, *f.—n.* dernier rang, *m.*; arrière-garde, *f.*; derrière (*d'édifice etc.*), *m.*; *to bring up the rear*, fermer la marche.

rear (2) [riə], *v.t.* élever.—*v.i.* se cabrer.

rear admiral ['riərædmərəl], *n.* contre-amiral, *m.*

re-arm [ri:'ɑ:m], *v.t., v.i.* réarmer.

re-armament [ri:'ɑ:məmənt], *n.* réarmement, *m.*

rearwards ['riəwədz], *adv.* à l'arrière.

reascend [ri:ə'send], *v.t., v.i.* remonter.

reason [ri:zn], *n.* raison, *f.*; raisonnement, *m.*; *the reason why*, la raison pour laquelle; *that stands to reason*, cela va sans dire; *to have reason to believe*, avoir lieu de croire.—*v.t., v.i.* raisonner.

reasonable ['ri:znəbl], *a.* raisonnable; modéré.

reasonableness ['ri:znəblnis], *n.* raison, modération, *f.*

reasonably ['ri:znəbli], *adv.* raisonnablement.

reasoner ['ri:zənə], *n.* raisonneur, logicien, *m.*

reasoning ['ri:zəniŋ], *n.* raisonnement, *m.*

reassemble [ri:ə'sembl], *v.t.* rassembler.—*v.i.* se rassembler.

reassert [ri:ə'sə:t], *v.t.* affirmer de nouveau.

reassess [ri:ə'ses], *v.t.* réévaluer.

reassessment [ri:ə'sesmənt], *n.* réimposition; réévaluation, *f.*

reassign [ri:ə'sain], *v.t.* réassigner.

reassignment [ri:ə'sainmənt], *n.* réassignation, *f.*

reassume [ri:ə'sju:m], *v.t.* réassumer; reprendre (*position*).

reassurance [ri:ə'ʃuərəns], *n.* action de rassurer; (*Comm.*) réassurance, *f.*

reassure [ri:ə'ʃuə], *v.t.* rassurer; (*Comm.*) réassurer.

rebate ['ri:beit], *n.* rabais, *m.*, remise, *f.—* [ri'beit], *v.t.* diminuer, rabattre.

rebel [rebl], *n.* rebelle, *m., f.*, révolté, *m.—* [ri'bel], *v.i.* se révolter, se soulever (*contre*).

rebellion [ri'beljən], *n.* rébellion, *f.*

rebellious [ri'beljəs], *a.* rebelle.

rebelliously [ri'beljəsli], *adv.* en rebelle.

rebelliousness [ri'beljəsnis], *n.* rébellion, *f.*

rebirth [ri:'bə:θ], *n.* renaissance, *f.*

reborn [ri:'bɔ:n], *a.* né de nouveau; réincarné.

rebound ['ri:baund], *n.* rebondissement, contre-coup, *m.—*[ri'baund], *v.i.* rebondir.

rebuff [ri'bʌf], *n.* rebuffade, *f.*, échec, *m.—v.t.* rebuter, repousser.

rebuild [ri:'bild], *v.t. irr.* (*conjug. like* BUILD) rebâtir, reconstruire.

rebuke [ri'bju:k], *n.* réprimande, *f.*, reproche, *m.—v.t.* réprimander, reprendre, censurer.

rebus ['ri:bəs], *n.* rébus, *m.*

rebut [ri'bʌt], *v.t.* rebuter, repousser, réfuter.

recalcitrant [ri'kælsitrənt], *a.* récalcitrant, insoumis, réfractaire.

recall [ri'kɔ:l], *n.* rappel, *m.*; révocation, *f.*; *beyond recall*, irrévocablement.—*v.t.* rappeler; se rappeler (*se souvenir de*).

recant [ri'kænt], *v.t.* rétracter, désavouer, abjurer.—*v.i.* se rétracter.

recantation [ri:kæn'teiʃən], *n.* rétractation, palinodie, *f.*

recapitulate [ri:kə'pitjuleit], *v.t.* récapituler.

recapitulation [ri:kəpitju'leiʃən], *n.* récapitulation, *f.*

recapture [ri:'kæptʃə], *n.* reprise, *f.—v.t.* reprendre.

recast [ri:'kɑ:st], *v.t. irr.* (*conjug. like* CAST) refondre; (*Theat.*) faire une nouvelle distribution des rôles.

recede [ri'si:d], *v.i.* se retirer (*de*); s'éloigner.

receding [ri'si:diŋ], *a.* fuyant (*le front*), effacé (*menton*).

receipt [ri'si:t], *n.* reçu, *m.*, quittance, *f.*, acquit, *m.*; réception (*le fait de recevoir*); (*pl.*) recette, *f.*, recettes, *f.pl.*; récépissé, *m.* —*v.t.* acquitter.

receive [ri'si:v], *v.t.* recevoir, accepter; accueillir; receler (*biens volés*).

receiver [ri'si:və], *n.* receveur, receleur (*d'objets volés*); liquidateur (*faillite*); (*Teleph.*) récepteur, *m.*

receiving [ri'si:viŋ], *n.* réception, *f.*; recel (*d'objets volés*), *m.*

recent ['ri:sənt], *a.* récent, frais, nouveau.

recently ['ri:səntli], *adv.* récemment, depuis peu.

receptacle [ri'septekl], *n.* réceptacle; récipient, *m.*

reception [ri'sepʃən], *n.* réception, *f.*; accueil, *m.*

receptionist [ri'sepʃənist], *n.* réceptionniste, *m., f.*

receptive [ri'septiv], *a.* réceptif (*esprit*).

recess [ri'ses], *n.* enfoncement, *m.*, niche, *f.*; recoin, *m.*; vacances, *f.pl.*

recession [ri'seʃən], *n.* retraite, *f.*; désistement (*d'une revendication*), *m.*; (*St. Exch.*) baisse, *f.*

recidivist [ri'sidivist], *n.* récidiviste, *m., f.*

recipe ['resipi], *n.* (*Cook.*) recette, *f.*

recipient [ri'sipiənt], *n.* personne qui reçoit, *f.*, destinataire (*de lettre*), *m., f.*; (*Chem.*) récipient, *m.*

reciprocal [ri'siprəkl], *a.* réciproque.

reciprocate [ri'siprəkeit], *v.t.* échanger; répondre à.—*v.i.* alterner, se succéder.

reciprocation [risiprə'keiʃən], **reciprocity** [resi'prositi], *n.* réciprocité, *f.*

recital [ri'saitl], *n.* récit, *m.*; narration, énumération, *f.*; (*Mus.*) récital, *m.*

recitation [resi'teiʃən], *n.* récitation, *f.*

recitative [resitə'ti:v], *n.* récitatif, *m.*

recite [ri'sait], *v.t.* réciter, faire le récit de; raconter.

reciter [ri'saitə], *n.* récitateur; diseur, narrateur, *m.*

reck [rek], *v.i.* se soucier de.

reckless ['reklis], *a.* insouciant (*de*); téméraire, insensé.

recklessly

recklessly ['reklisli], *adv.* témérairement, avec insouciance.

recklessness ['reklisnis], *n.* insouciance, témérité, *f.*

reckon [rekn], *v.t.* compter, calculer; regarder, évaluer (*comme*).—*v.i.* compter; *to reckon on*, compter sur; *to reckon with*, tenir compte de.

reckoner ['reknə], *n.* calculateur, chiffreur, *m.*; *ready-reckoner*, barême, *m.*

reckoning ['reknɪŋ], *n.* compte, calcul; écot, *m.*, note (*dans un hôtel*); addition (*dans un restaurant*); (*Naut.*) estime, *f.*

reclaim [ri:'kleim], *v.t.* réformer, corriger; ramener (*de*); réclamer, revendiquer (*ses droits*); défricher (*terre*).

reclaimable [ri:'kleiməbl], *a.* corrigible; cultivable, défrichable (*terre*).

reclaiming [ri:'kleimiŋ], **reclamation** [reklə 'meiʃən], *n.* défrichement (*de terre*), *m.*; réforme, correction (*de criminels*), *f.*

recline [ri'klain], *v.i.* s'appuyer, se reposer, se coucher.

reclining [ri'klainiŋ], *a.* incliné, appuyé, couché.

reclothe [ri:'klouð], *v.t.* rhabiller.

recluse [ri'klu:s], *a.* reclus; solitaire, retiré.— *n.* reclus, *m.*

reclusion [ri'klu:ʒən], *n.* réclusion, *f.*

recognition [rekəg'niʃən], *n.* reconnaissance, *f.*

recognizable [rekəg'naizəbl], *a.* reconnaissable.

recognizance [ri'kɔgnizəns], *n.* reconnaissance; (*Law*) obligation contractée, *f.*

recognize ['rekəgnaiz], *v.t.* reconnaître.

recoil [ri'kɔil], *n.* recul; contre-coup, *m.*; (*fig.*) répugnance, *f.*—*v.i.* reculer; retomber.

recollect [rekə'lekt], *v.t.* se souvenir de, se rappeler.

recollection [rekə'lekʃən], *n.* souvenir, *m.*; mémoire, *f.*

recommence [ri:kə'mens], *v.t.*, *v.i.* recommencer.

recommend [rekə'mend], *v.t.* recommander.

recommendation [rekəmen'deiʃən], *n.* recommandation; apostille (*d'une pétition*), *f.*

recompense ['rekəmpens], *n.* récompense, *f.*; dédommagement, *m.*—*v.t.* récompenser (*de*); dédommager (*de*); compenser, réparer.

reconcilable [rekən'sailəbl], *a.* réconciliable; conciliable (*avec*).(*choses*).

reconcile ['rekənsail], *v.t.* réconcilier (*avec*); habituer, accoutumer (*familiariser*); *to reconcile oneself to*, se résigner à.

reconciliation [rekənsili'eiʃən], *n.* réconciliation; conciliation (*de choses*); (*Bibl.*) expiation, *f.*

recondite [ri'kɔndait, 'rekəndait], *a.* secret, abstrus, profond, mystérieux.

recondition [ri:kən'diʃən], *v.t.* remettre à neuf, refaire.

reconnaissance [ri'kɔnisəns], *n.* reconnaissance, *f.*

reconnoiter [rekə'nɔitə], *v.t.* reconnaître.— *v.i.* faire une reconnaissance.

reconsider [ri:kən'sidə], *v.t.* considérer de nouveau; revenir sur (*une décision*).

reconsideration [ri:kənsidə'reiʃən], *n.* reconsidération, *f.*

reconstitute [ri:'kɔnstitju:t], *v.t.* reconstituer.

reconstruct [ri:kən'strʌkt], *v.t.* reconstruire.

reconstruction [ri:kən'strʌkʃən], *n.* reconstruction, *f.*

record ['rekɔ:d], *n.* registre, *m.*, archives, *f.pl.* disque (*de phonographe*); (*Spt.*) record dossier, *m.*; *keeper of the records*, archiviste, *m.*, *f.*; *long-playing record*, disque longue durée, *m*; *public records*, archives, *f.pl.*; *record library*, discothèque, *f.*; greffe, *m.*—[ri'kɔ:d], *v.t.* enregistrer; graver, imprimer (*dans l'esprit etc.*); mentionner (*fait historique*).

recorder [ri'kɔ:də], *n.* enregistreur, archiviste; greffier; (*Law*) officier judiciaire d'une ville; (*Mus.*) flageolet, *m.*; *tape recorder*, magnétophone, *m.*

recording [ri'kɔ:diŋ], *n.* enregistrement, *m.*

recount (1) [ri'kaunt], *v.t.* raconter.

recount (2) [ri:'kaunt], *v.t.* recompter.— ['ri:kaunt], *n.* nouvelle addition des voix (*aux élections*), *f.*

recoup [ri'ku:p], *v.t.* rembourser, dédommager (*de*).

recourse [ri'kɔ:s], *n.* recours, *m.*

recover (1) [ri'kʌvə], *v.t.* recouvrer, retrouver; réparer (*perte*).—*v.i.* se rétablir, guérir; se remettre (*d'une maladie*); se relever (*d'une perte*).

recover (2) [ri:'kʌvə], *v.t.* recouvrir; regarnir.

recovery [ri'kʌvəri], *n.* recouvrement, *m.*; guérison, *f.*; rétablissement, *m.*; (*Écon.*) reprise, *f.*; *past recovery*, incurable, sans remède.

recreant ['rekriənt], *a.* and *n.* lâche, infidèle, *m.*, *f.*, apostat, *m.*

re-create [ri:kri'eit], *v.t.* recréer.

recreation [rekri'eiʃən], *n.* récréation, *f.*, divertissement, *m.*

recriminate [ri'krimineit], *v.i.* récriminer (*contre*).

recrimination [rikrimi'neiʃən], *n.* récrimination, *f.*

recriminatory [ri'kriminətri], *a.* récriminatoire.

recrudescence [ri:kru'desəns], *n.* recrudescence, *f.*

recruit [ri'kru:t], *n.* recrue, *f.*, conscrit, *m.*— *v.t.* rétablir, réparer (*restaurer*); (*Mil.*) recruter.—*v.i.* se recruter, se remettre.

recruiting [ri'kru:tiŋ], **recruitment** [ri'kru:t mənt], *n.* recrutement, *m.*; *recruiting officer*, officier de recrutement, *m.*

rectangle ['rektæŋgl], *n.* rectangle, *m.*

rectangular [rek'tæŋgjulə], *a.* rectangulaire, rectangle, à angle droit.

rectifiable ['rektifaiəbl], *a.* rectifiable.

rectification [rektifi'keiʃən], *n.* rectification, *f.*

rectifier ['rektifaiə], *n.* rectificateur; (*Elec.*) redresseur, *m.*

rectify ['rektifai], *v.t.* rectifier; redresser.

rectilineal [rekti'liniəl], *a.* rectiligne.

rectitude ['rektitju:d], *n.* rectitude, droiture, *f.*

rector ['rektə], *n.* (*Ch. of England*) prêtre; (*R.-C.*) curé; (*Univ. etc.*) recteur, principal, *m.*

rectorial [rek'tɔ:riəl], *a.* rectoral.

rectorship ['rektəʃip], *n.* rectorat, *f.*

rectory ['rektəri], *n.* cure, *f.*, presbytère, *m.*

recumbent [ri'kʌmbənt], *a.* couché, étendu; appuyé (*sur*).

recuperate [ri'ku:pəreit], v.t. recouvrer, récupérer.—v.i. se rétablir, se remettre, reprendre ses forces.

recuperation [riku:pə'reiʃən], n. recouvrement; rétablissement (personne), m.

recur [ri'kə:], v.i. revenir; se reproduire.

recurrence [ri'kʌrəns], n. retour, m.

recurrent [ri'kʌrənt], **recurring** [ri'kə:riŋ], a. périodique; (Anat. etc.) récurrent.

red [red], a. rouge; roux (cheveux); vermeil (lèvres etc.); **red lead**, minium, m.; **red-letter day**, jour de fête, m.—n. rouge, m.

redbreast ['redbrest], n. rouge-gorge, m.

redden [redn], v.t., v.i. rougir.

reddish ['rediʃ], a. rougeâtre, roussâtre.

redeem [ri'di:m], v.t. racheter; (Fin.) rembourser, amortir; retirer (objets mis en gage); (fig.) réparer.

redeemable [ri'di:məbl], a. rachetable.

redeemer [ri'di:mə], n. rédempteur, m.

redeeming [ri'di:miŋ], a. qui rachète.

redemption [ri'dempʃən], n. rédemption, f.; (Fin.) amortissement; rachat (de billets), m.

red-hot ['redhɔt], a. tout rouge, chauffé au rouge, ardent (charbon).

redirect [ri:di'rekt], v.t. faire suivre (lettre).

rediscover [ri:dis'kʌvə], v.t. redécouvrir.

redistribution [ri:distri'bju:ʃən], n. nouvelle distribution, répartition, f.

redness ['rednis], n. rougeur; rousseur (de cheveux), f.

redolence ['redoləns], n. parfum, m.; senteur, f.

redolent ['redolənt], a. qui a un parfum de; **redolent of . . .**, qui sent le . . .

redouble [ri:'dʌbl], v.t., v.i. redoubler.

redoubt [ri'daut], n. redoute, f.

redoubtable [ri'dautəbl], a. redoutable.

redound [ri'daund], v.i. contribuer (à, en), résulter (pour), rejaillir (sur).

redpole, redpoll ['redpoul], n. (pop.) linotte, f.

redraft [ri:'drɑ:ft], n. nouveau dessin, m.; (Comm.) retraite, f.—v.t. rédiger de nouveau.

redress [ri'dres], v.t. redresser, corriger, réparer.—n. redressement, m., réparation, f.; remède, m.

redshank [redʃæŋk], n. (Orn.) chevalier, m., gambette, f.

redskin ['redskin], n. Peau-Rouge, m., f.

red tape ['red'teip], n. bolduc, m.; (fig.) routine administrative, f.

reduce [ri'dju:s], v.t. réduire (à ou en); maigrir (chair); dégrader (abaisser); **a person in reduced circumstances**, une personne tombée dans la gêne.—v.i. maigrir.

reduction [ri'dʌkʃən], n. réduction, f.; **a reduction in prices**, une baisse des prix, f.; **reduction to the ranks**, cassation, f.

redundance [ri'dʌndəns], **redundancy** [ri'dʌndənsi], n. redondance, f.

redundant [ri'dʌndənt], a. redondant, superflu.

re-echo [ri:'ekou], v.t. répéter.—v.i. retentir.—n. écho répété, m.

reed [ri:d], n. roseau; chalumeau, m.; (Mus.) anche, f.

reed pipe ['ri:dpaip], n. chalumeau, pipeau, m.

reedy ['ri:di], a. couvert de roseaux; flûtée (voix).

reef (1) [ri:f], n. récif, écueil, m.

reef (2) [ri:f], n. ris (de voile), m.—v.t. prendre un ris dans.

reef knot ['ri:fnɔt], n. nœud plat, m.

reek [ri:k], n. fumée, f., relent, m.—v.i. fumer; exhaler; **reeking with**, tout fumant de; **to reek of**, puer, empester.

reel (1) [ri:l], n. dévidoir, m.; bobine (de coton), f.; (Angling) moulinet, m.; (Cine.) bobine, bande, f.; **newsreel**, les actualités, f.pl.—v.t. **to reel off**, dévider, débiter.—v.i. tournoyer, chanceler, trébucher.

reel (2) [ri:l], n. branle écossais (danse), m.

re-elect [ri:i'lekt], v.t. réélire.

re-election [ri:i'lekʃən], n. réélection, f.

re-embark [ri:əm'bɑ:k], v.t. rembarquer.—v.i. se rembarquer.

re-embarkation [ri:embɑ:'keiʃən], n. rembarquement, m.

re-embody [ri:əm'bɔdi], v.t. réincorporer.

re-enact [ri:i'nækt], v.t. remettre en vigueur (une loi); reconstituer (un crime).

re-enactment [ri:i'næktmənt], n. remise en vigueur; reconstitution, f.

re-engage [ri:in'geidʒ], v.t. rengager.

re-enlist [ri:in'list], v.t., v.i. (se) rengager.

re-enter [ri:'entə], v.t., v.i. rentrer.

re-entrant [ri:'entrənt], a. and n. rentrant, m.

re-establish [[ri:is'tæbliʃ], v.t. rétablir.

re-establishment [ri:is'tæbliʃmənt], n. rétablissement, m.

re-examine [ri:ig'zæmin], v.t. examiner de nouveau, revoir.

re-export [ri:iks'pɔ:t], v.t. réexporter.

refashion [ri:'fæʃən], v.t. refaçonner.

refasten [ri:'fɑ:sn], v.t. rattacher; ragrafer.

refection [ri'fekʃən], n. repas, m., collation, f.

refectory [ri'fektəri], n. réfectoire, m.

refer [ri'fə:], v.t. renvoyer, rapporter; adresser (à); remettre à la décision de.—v.i. se référer, se rapporter, avoir rapport (à); s'en rapporter, se référer (personnes); s'adresser (à).

referee [refə'ri:], n. arbitre, m., f.—v.t., v.i. (Spt.) arbitrer.

reference ['refərəns], n. renvoi; rapport (respect), m.; allusion, f.; renseignements, m.pl., références (de bonne vie et mœurs), f.pl.; (Comm.) référence, f.; **book of reference**, ouvrage à consulter, m.; **with reference to**, au sujet de; **to make reference to**, faire allusion à.

referendum [refə'rendəm], n. référendum, m.

refill [ri:'fil], v.t. remplir.—v.i. (Motor.) faire le plein (d'essence).—['ri:fil], n. objet (feuilles, pile, ampoule) de rechange; (Motor.) plein (d'essence), m.

refine [ri'fain], v.t. épurer (liquides); (Metal.) affiner; raffiner (sucre etc.); (fig.) purifier.

refined [ri'faind], a. raffiné; pur, délicat (goût).

refinement [ri'fainmənt], n. raffinage (de sucre); (Metal.) affinage, m.; épuration (de liquides); (fig.) délicatesse, f.

refinery [ri'fainəri], n. raffinerie (de sucre); (Metal.) affinerie, f.

refit [ri:'fit], v.t. réparer; (Naut.) radouber.—['ri:fit], n. réparation (Naut.), refonte, f.

reflect [ri'flekt], v.t. réfléchir; faire rejaillir sur; refléter.—v.i. réfléchir; **to reflect upon**, réfléchir à, méditer sur.

reflected [ri'flektid], a. réfléchi.

reflection

reflection [REFLEXION].

reflective [ri'flektiv], *a.* réfléchissant; méditatif.

reflector [ri'flektə], *n.* réflecteur; (*Cycl., Motor.*) catadioptre, *m.*

reflex ['ri:fleks], *a.* réfléchi; (*Paint.*) reflété; (*Physiol. etc.*) réflexe.—*n.* (*Paint.*) reflet; (*Physiol.*) réflexe, *m.*

reflexion [ri'flekʃən], *n.* réflexion, *f.*; reflet (*lumière etc.*), *m.*; censure, *f.*; blâme, *m.*

reflexive [ri'fleksiv], *a.* réfléchi.

reform [ri'fɔ:m], *n.* réforme, *f.*—*v.t.* réformer; corriger.—*v.i.* se réformer, se corriger.

re-form [ri:'fɔ:m], *v.t.* reformer.—*v.i.* se reformer.

reformation [refɔ:'meiʃən], *n.* réformation; réforme, *f.*; **the Reformation**, (*Hist.*) la Réforme.

re-formation [ri:fɔ:'meiʃən], *n.* formation nouvelle, *f.*

reformer [ri'fɔ:mə], *n.* réformateur, *m.*

refract [ri'frækt], *v.t.* réfracter.

refraction [ri'frækʃən], *n.* réfraction, *f.*

refractive [ri'fræktiv], *a.* réfractif; réfringent.

refractory [ri'fræktri], *a.* indocile, récalcitrant, intraitable, rebelle; (*Chem. etc.*) réfractaire; rétif (*cheval*).

refrain [ri'frein], *v.i.* se retenir, s'abstenir (*de*).—*n.* refrain, *m.*

refresh [ri'freʃ], *v.t.* rafraîchir; délasser, restaurer; **to refresh oneself**, se rafraîchir.

refreshing [ri'freʃiŋ], *a.* rafraîchissant; réparateur, qui repose.

refreshment [ri'freʃmənt], *n.* rafraîchissement, *m.*; **refreshment bar**, buvette, *f.*; **refreshment car**, wagon-restaurant, *m.*; **refreshment room**, buffet, *m.*

refrigerate [ri'fridʒəreit], *v.t.* réfrigérer, frigorifier.

refrigeration [rifridʒə'reiʃən], *n.* réfrigération, *f.*

refrigerator [ri'fridʒəreitə], *n.* réfrigérateur; (*fam.*) Frigidaire (*marque déposée*), *m.*

refuel [ri:'fjuəl], *v.i.* (*Av.*) faire le plein (d'essence).

refuge ['refju:dʒ], *n.* refuge (*contre*), *m.*; **to take refuge**, se réfugier.

refugee [refju'dʒi:], *n.* réfugié, *m.*

refulgence [ri'fʌldʒəns], *n.* éclat, *m.*, splendeur, *f.*

refulgent [ri'fʌldʒənt], *a.* éclatant.

refund [ri'fʌnd], *v.t.* rembourser, rendre.—['ri:fʌnd], *n.* remboursement, *m.*

refurnish [ri:'fɔ:niʃ], *v.t.* remeubler.

refusal [ri'fju:zl], *n.* refus, *m.*

refuse ['refju:s], *n.* rebut, *m.*, ordures (*ménagères, de marché*), *f.pl.*; **refuse dump**, voirie, *f.*—[ri'fju:z], *v.t.* refuser; rejeter.—*v.i.* refuser.

refute [ri'fju:t], *v.t.* réfuter.

regain [ri'gein], *v.t.* regagner, reprendre.

regal [ri:gl], *a.* royal.

regale [ri'geil], *v.t.* régaler.—*v.i.* se régaler.

regally ['ri:gəli], *adv.* royalement, en roi.

regard [ri'gɑ:d], *n.* égard, *m.*; considération, *f.*; respect (*estime*), *m.*; (*pl.*) amitiés, *f.pl.*, compliments, *m.pl.*; **out of regard for**, par égard pour; **with regard to**, quant à.—*v.t.* regarder; considérer; **as regards**, quant à.

regarding [ri'gɑ:diŋ], *prep.* quant à, concernant.

regardless [ri'gɑ:dlis], *a.* peu soigneux (*de*); sans égard (*pour*); **regardless of**, sans se soucier de.

regatta [ri'gætə], *n.* régate(s), *f.(pl.)*.

regency ['ri:dʒənsi], *n.* régence, *f.*

regenerate [ri'dʒenərət], *a.* régénéré.—[ri:'dʒenəreit], *v.t.* régénérer.

regenerating [ri'dʒenəreitiŋ], *a.* régénérateur.

regeneration [ri:dʒenə'reiʃən], *n.* régénération, *f.*

regent ['ri:dʒənt], *n.* régent, *m.*

regicide ['redʒisaid], *n.* régicide (*crime*), *m.*; régicide (*personne*), *m.*, *f.*

régime [rei'ʒi:m], *n.* (*Polit.*) régime, *m.*

regimen ['redʒimən], *n.* (*Gram., Med.*) régime, *m.*

regiment ['redʒimənt], *n.* régiment, *m.*

regimental [redʒi'mentl], *a.* du régiment, de régiment.

regimentation [redʒimen'teiʃən], *n.* en-régimentation, *f.*

Reginald ['redʒinəld]. Renaud, *m.*

region ['ri:dʒən], *n.* région, *f.*

regional ['ri:dʒənl], *a.* régional.

register ['redʒistə], *n.* registre, *m.*; liste électorale (*de votants*), *f.*—*v.t.* enregistrer; recommander (*lettre, paquet*); déclarer (*naissance*); immatriculer (*voiture*); déposer (*marque de fabrique etc.*).

registrar ['redʒistra:], *n.* (*Law*) greffier; (*Univ.*) secrétaire et archiviste; officier de l'état civil (*de naissances etc.*), *m.*

registration [redʒis'treiʃən], *n.* enregistrement; chargement (*de lettres*); dépôt (*d'une marque de fabrique etc.*), *m.*; immatriculation (*de véhicule*); inscription (*des bagages*), *f.*; **registration number**, (*Motor.*) numéro minéralogique, *m.*

registry ['redʒistri], *n.* enregistrement; (*Law*) greffe, *m.*

registry office ['redʒistri'ɔfis], *n.* bureau de l'état civil, *m.*

regret [ri'gret], *n.* regret, *m.*—*v.t.* regretter (*de*), avoir du regret (*à*).

regretful [ri'gretful], *a.* plein de regrets; regrettable.

regretfully [ri'gretfuli], *adv.* avec regret, à regret.

regrettable [ri'gretəbl], *a.* fâcheux, regrettable.

regular ['regjulə], *a.* régulier; réglé; en règle; ordinaire (*normal*); (*fig.*) franc, fieffé.

regularity [regju'læriti], *n.* régularité, *f.*

regularly ['regjuləli], *adv.* régulièrement.

regulate ['regjuleit], *v.t.* régler; diriger.

regulation [regju'leiʃən], *a.* réglementaire.—*n.* règlement, *m.*

regulator ['regjuleitə], *n.* régulateur, *m.*

rehabilitate [ri:hə'biliteit], *v.t.* réhabiliter.

rehabilitation [ri:həbili'teiʃən], *n.* réhabilitation, *f.*

rehearsal [ri'hə:sl], *n.* récit, *m.*; (*Theat.*) répétition, *f.*; **dress rehearsal**, répétition générale.

rehearse [ri'hə:s], *v.t.* (*Theat.*) répéter; (*fig.*) raconter (*narrer*).

rehouse [ri:'hauz], *v.t.* reloger.

reign [rein], *n.* règne, *m.*—*v.i.* régner.

reigning ['reiniŋ], *a.* régnant; *(fig.)* dominant (*prevailing*).
reimburse [ri:im'bə:s], *v.t.* rembourser.
reimbursement [ri:im'bə:smənt], *n.* remboursement, *m.*
rein [rein], *n.* rêne, *f.*—*v.t.* conduire à la bride, gouverner, brider; contenir.
reincarnation [ri:inka:'neiʃən], *n.* réincarnation, *f.*
reindeer ['reindiə], *n.* renne, *m.*
reinforce [ri:in'fɔ:s], *v.t.* renforcer; **reinforced concrete**, béton armé, *m.*
reinforcement [ri:in'fɔ:smənt], *n.* renforcement; *(Mil.)* renfort, *m.*
reinstall [ri:in'stɔ:l], *v.t.* réinstaller.
reinstate [ri:in'steit], *v.t.* rétablir.
reinstatement [ri:in'steitmənt], *n.* rétablissement, *m.*
reintroduce [ri:intrə'dju:s], *v.t.* introduire de nouveau, réintroduire.
reinvest [ri:in'vest], *v.t.* replacer.
reinvigorate [ri:in'vigəreit], *v.t.* ranimer.
reissue [ri:'isju:], *v.t.* émettre de nouveau; rééditer (*livre*).—*n.* nouvelle émission; nouvelle édition, *f.*
reiterate [ri:'itəreit], *v.t.* réitérer.
reiteration [ri:itə'reiʃən], *n.* réitération, *f.*
reiterative [ri:'itərətiv], *a.* réitératif.
reject [ri'dʒekt], *v.t.* rejeter.—['ri:dʒekt], *n.* pièce de rebut, *f.*
rejection [ri'dʒekʃən], *n.* rejet, *m.*
rejoice [ri'dʒɔis], *v.t.* réjouir.—*v.i.* se réjouir (*de*).
rejoicing [ri'dʒɔisiŋ], *n.* réjouissance, joie, *f.*
rejoin [ri:'dʒɔin], *v.t.* rejoindre.—[ri'dʒɔin], *v.i.* répliquer, répondre.
rejoinder [ri'dʒɔində], *n.* repartie; (*Law*) réplique, *f.*
rejuvenate [ri'dʒu:vəneit], *v.t.* rajeunir.
rejuvenation [ridʒu:və'neiʃən], *n.* rajeunissement, *m.*
rekindle [ri:'kindl], *v.t.* rallumer.
relapse [ri'læps], *n.* rechute, *f.*—*v.i.* retomber (*dans*); récidiver (*criminel*).
relate [ri'leit], *v.t.* raconter; rapporter.—*v.i.* se rapporter, avoir rapport (*à*).
related [ri'leitid], *a.* ayant rapport; parent (*de*); allié (*à*) (*par mariage etc.*).
relating [ri'leitiŋ], *a.* relatif, qui se rapporte (*à*).
relation [ri'leiʃən], *n.* relation, *f.*, rapport; récit (*narration*); parent (*de la famille*); allié (*par mariage*), *m.*; (*pl.*) relations, *f.pl.*, rapports (*contact*), *m.pl.*
relationship [ri'leiʃənʃip], *n.* parenté, *f.*; rapport, *m.*
relative ['relətiv], *a.* relatif (*à*).—*n.* parent; (*Gram.*) relatif, *m.*
relatively ['relətivli], *adv.* relativement.
relativity [relə'tiviti], *n.* relativité, *f.*
relax [ri'læks], *v.t.* relâcher, détendre.—*v.i.* se relâcher; se détendre; se délasser.
relaxation [ri:læk'seiʃən], *n.* relâchement, relâche, *m.*, détente, *f.*; (*Med.*) repos, *m.*
relaxing [ri'læksiŋ], *a.* relâchant; énervant, débilitant (*climat*).
relay ['ri:lei], *n.* relais, *m.*—*v.t.* relayer.
re-lay [ri:'lei], *v.t.* poser de nouveau.
release [ri'li:s], *v.t.* relâcher, élargir (*un prisonnier*); décharger (*de*); déclencher.—*n.* élargissement, *m.*; délivrance; décharge

(*d'une obligation*); *(Cine.)* sortie (*d'un film*), *f.*; déclenchement (*de ressort etc.*), *m.*
relegate ['reləgeit], *v.t.* reléguer.
relegation [relə'geiʃən], *n.* relégation, *f.*
relent [ri'lent], *v.i.* s'amollir, s'attendrir; se repentir (*regretter*).
relenting [ri'lentiŋ], *n.* attendrissement, *m.*
relentless [ri'lentlis], *a.* inflexible, impitoyable.
relentlessly [ri'lentlisli], *adv.* impitoyablement.
relentlessness [ri'lentlisnis], *n.* rigueur, dureté, *f.*
relevance ['reləvəns], **relevancy** ['reləvənsi], *n.* relation, *f.*, rapport, *m.*; pertinence, convenance, *f.*, à-propos, *m.*
relevant ['reləvənt], *a.* relatif, applicable (*à*); à propos, pertinent.
reliable [ri'laiəbl], *a.* digne de confiance; sûr, exact, bien fondé (*renseignement*).
reliability [ri'laiə'biliti], *n.* crédibilité, véracité; sûreté, *f.*
reliance [ri'laiəns], *n.* confiance, *f.*
relic ['relik], *n.* relique (*de saint* ou *martyr*), *f.*; (*pl.*) restes (*d'un être*); vestiges (*du passé*), *m.pl.*
relief [ri'li:f], *n.* soulagement (*de douleur etc.*); secours (*aide*), *m.*; (*Mil.*) relève, *f.*; (*Sculp. etc.*) relief, *m.*; **relief train**, train supplémentaire, *m.*
relieve [ri'li:v], *v.t.* soulager, adoucir; délivrer (*de*); secourir, aider (*assister*); (*Mil.*) relever (*sentinelle*).
religion [ri'lidʒən], *n.* religion, *f.*
religious [ri'lidʒəs], *a.* religieux; de religion.
religiously [ri'lidʒəsli], *adv.* religieusement.
relinquish [ri'liŋkwiʃ], *v.t.* abandonner; renoncer à.
relinquishment [ri'liŋkwiʃmənt], *n.* abandon, *m.*; renonciation, *f.*
reliquary ['relikwəri], *n.* reliquaire, *m.*
relish ['reliʃ], *n.* goût, *m.*, saveur, *f.*; *(Cook.)* assaisonnement, *m.*; *(fig.)* charme; appétit, *m.*—*v.t.* goûter, savourer; relever le goût de.
relive [ri:'liv], *v.t.* revivre.
reload [ri:'loud], *v.t.* recharger.
reluctance [ri'lʌktəns], *n.* répugnance, *f.*
reluctant [ri'lʌktənt], *a.* qui a de la répugnance à, qui agit à contre-cœur; peu disposé (*à*).
reluctantly [ri'lʌktəntli], *adv.* à contre-cœur.
rely [ri'lai], *v.i.* compter (*sur*), avoir confiance (*en*).
remain [ri'mein], *v.i.* rester, demeurer.
remainder [ri'meində], *n.* reste, *m.*
remaining [ri'meiniŋ], *a.* de reste, restant.
remains [ri'meinz], *n.pl.* restes; débris, *m.pl.*; **mortal remains**, dépouille mortelle, *f.*
remake [ri:'meik], *v.t. irr.* (*conjug. like* MAKE) refaire.
remand [ri'ma:nd], *v.t.* renvoyer à une autre audience.—*n.* renvoi à une autre audience, *m.*
remark [ri'ma:k], *n.* remarque, *f.*—*v.t.* remarquer, observer; faire remarquer, faire observer (*à une personne*).
remarkable [ri'ma:kəbl], *a.* remarquable.
remarkably [ri'ma:kəbli], *adv.* remarquablement.
remarriage [ri:'mærədʒ], *n.* remariage, *m.*
remarry [ri:'mæri], *v.t.* épouser de nouveau. —*v.i.* se remarier.

remedial [ri'mi:djəl], *a.* réparateur; (*Med.*) curatif.

remedy ['remədi], *n.* remède; (*Law*) recours, *m.*—*v.t.* remédier à, porter remède à.

remember [ri'membə], *v.t.* se souvenir de, se rappeler; reconnaître (*de vue*).

remembrance [ri'membrəns], *n.* souvenir, *m.*, mémoire, *f.*

remind [ri'maind], *v.t.* rappeler à, faire souvenir (*à . . . de*), faire penser à.

reminder [ri'maində], *n.* mémento, *m.*

reminisce [remi'nis], *v.i.* raconter ses souvenirs.

reminiscence [remi'nisəns], *n.* réminiscence, *f.*

reminiscent [remi'nisənt], *a.* qui rappelle.

remiss [ri'mis], *a.* négligent.

remission [ri'miʃən], *n.* rémission, *f.*, pardon; relâchement (*détente*), *m.*; remise (*de dette, peine*), *f.*

remit [ri'mit], *v.t.* relâcher (*détendre*); remettre (*amende etc.*).—*v.i.* se relâcher; se calmer; diminuer.

remittance [ri'mitəns], *n.* remise, *f.*; envoi de fonds, *m.*

remittent [ri'mitənt], *a.* (*Path.*) rémittent.

remnant ['remnənt], *n.* reste; coupon, bout (*de tissu*), *m.*; (*pl.*) restes, débris, *m.pl.*

remodel [ri:'mɔdl], *v.t.* remodeler.

remould [ri:'mould], *v.t.* mouler de nouveau.

remonstrance [ri'mɔnstrəns], *n.* remontrance, *f.*

remonstrate ['remənstreit], *v.i.* remontrer.

remorse [ri'mɔ:s], *n.* remords, *m.*

remorseful [ri'mɔ:sful], *a.* rempli de remords.

remorseless [ri'mɔ:slis], *a.* sans remords, impitoyable.

remorselessness [ri'mɔ:slisnis], *n.* cruauté, inhumanité, *f.*

remote [ri'mout], *a.* éloigné, lointain; reculé (*époque*); distant (*personne*).

remotely [ri'moutli], *adv.* de loin; faiblement.

remoteness [ri'moutnis], *n.* éloignement, *m.*; réserve (*attitude*), *f.*

remount [ri:'maunt], *v.t., v.i.* remonter.—*n.* remonte, *f.*

removable [ri'mu:vəbl], *a.* transportable; (*fig.*) amovible (*fonctionnaire etc.*).

removal [ri'mu:vl], *n.* éloignement, départ; transport; déménagement (*de meubles*); déplacement, *m.*; révocation (*de ses fonctions*), *f.*

remove [ri'mu:v], *n.* degré (*parenté*), *m.*; distance, *f.*—*v.t.* éloigner; déplacer (*bouger*); transporter; déménager (*meubles*); ôter, enlever (*emporter*); renvoyer (*de ses fonctions*).—*v.i.* s'éloigner, se déplacer; déménager (*changer de domicile*).

removed [ri'mu:vd], *a.* éloigné; **first cousin once removed**, cousin issu de germains, *m.*

remover [ri'mu:və], *n.* déménageur, *m.*; **nail polish remover**, dissolvant (pour ongles), *m.*

remunerate [ri'mju:nəreit], *v.t.* rémunérer.

remuneration [rimju:nə'reiʃən], *n.* rétribution, rémunération, *f.*

remunerative [ri'mju:nərətiv], *a.* rémunérateur; (*Law*) rémunératoire.

rename [ri:'neim], *v.t.* renommer.

rend [rend], *v.t. irr.* déchirer; (*fig.*) fendre.

render ['rendə], *v.t.* rendre; interpréter, traduire; (*Cook.*) fondre (*graisse etc.*).

rendering ['rendəriŋ], *n.* traduction, interprétation, *f.*

renegade ['renigeid], *n.* renégat, *m.*

renew [ri'nju:], *v.t.* renouveler; renouer (*connaissance*).

renewal [ri'nju:əl], *n.* renouvellement, *m.*; **renewal of subscription**, réabonnement, *m.*

renounce [ri'nauns], *v.t.* renoncer (*à*); renier.

renouncement [ri'naunsmənt], *n.* renoncement, *m.*, renonciation, *f.*

renovate ['renəveit], *v.t.* renouveler; rajeunir.

renovation [renə'veiʃən], *n.* rénovation, *f.*

renovator ['renəveitə], *n.* rénovateur, *m.*

renown [ri'naun], *n.* renommée, *f.*, renom, *m.*

renowned [ri'naund], *a.* renommé.

rent (1) [rent], *n.* déchirure, fente, *f.*; accroc (*de vêtements*), *m.*

rent (2) [rent], *n.* loyer (*de maison ou d'appartement*); fermage (*de ferme*), *m.*; (*pl.*) rentes, *f.pl.*, revenu, *m.*; **ground rent**, rente foncière, *f.*—*v.t.* louer, prendre à ferme, donner à ferme.—*v.i.* se louer.

rent (3) [rent], *past and p.p.* [REND].

rental [rentl], *n.* valeur locative, *f.*

rent-free ['rentfri:], *a.* exempt de loyer.

renunciation [rinʌnsi'eiʃən], *n.* renonciation, *f.*, renoncement, *m.*

reoccupation [ri:ɔkju'peiʃən], *n.* réoccupation, *f.*

reoccupy [ri:'ɔkjupai], *v.t.* réoccuper.

reopen [ri:'oupən], *v.t.* rouvrir.—*v.i.* rentrer (*écoles, tribunaux etc.*).

reopening [ri:'oupniŋ], *n.* réouverture; rentrée (*d'écoles etc.*), *f.*

reorganization [ri:ɔ:gənai'zeiʃən], *n.* réorganisation, *f.*

reorganize [ri:'ɔ:gənaiz], *v.t.* réorganiser.

rep (1) [rep], *a.* de reps.—*n.* reps (*tissu*), *m.*

rep (2) [rep], [REPERTORY].

rep (3) [rep], [REPRESENTATIVE].

repaint [ri:'peint], *v.t.* repeindre.

repair (1) [ri'pɛə], *v.t.* réparer; raccommoder (*vêtements etc.*); (*fig.*) rétablir.—*n.* réparation, *f.*; raccommodage (*de vêtements etc.*); **to keep in repair**, entretenir.

repair (2) [ri'pɛə], *n.* séjour (*retraite*), *m.*—*v.i.* aller; se rendre (*à*).

repairer [ri'pɛərer], *n.* réparateur; raccommodeur (*de vêtements*), *m.*

reparable ['repərəbl], *a.* réparable.

reparation [repə'reiʃən], *n.* réparation (*d'une offense*), *f.*

repartee [repɑ:'ti:], *n.* repartie, riposte, *f.*

repast [ri'pɑ:st], *n.* repas, *m.*

repatriate [ri:'pætrieit], *v.t.* rapatrier.

repay [ri'pei], *v.t. irr.* (*conjug. like* PAY) rembourser; (*fig.*) valoir la peine (*de*).

repayment [ri:'peimənt], *n.* remboursement, *m.*

repeal [ri'pi:l], *v.t.* révoquer; abroger (*loi etc.*).—*n.* révocation; abrogation (*de loi*), *f.*

repeat [ri'pi:t], *v.t.* répéter, réitérer; réciter (*par cœur*); bis (*après vers de chanson etc.*).—*n.* répétition; (*Mus.*) reprise, *f.*

repeated [ri'pi:tid], *a.* répété, réitéré.

repeatedly [ri'pi:tidli], *adv.* à plusieurs reprises; souvent, bien des fois.

repeating [ri'pi:tiŋ], *a.* qui répète; à répétition.

repel [ri'pel], *v.t.* repousser; combattre.
repellent [ri'pelənt], *a.* répulsif, répugnant.—*n.* répulsif; (*Med.*) révulsif, *m.*
repent [ri'pent], *v.t.* se repentir de.—*v.i.* se repentir.
repentance [ri'pentəns], *n.* repentir, *m.*
repentant [ri'pentənt], *a.* repentant.
repercussion [ri:pə'kʌʃən], *n.* répercussion, *f.*
repertory ['repətri], *n.* répertoire, *m.*; *repertory theatre*, (*fam.*) *rep*, troupe à demeure, *f.*
repetition [repi'tiʃən], *n.* répétition; (*Mus.*) reprise, *f.*
repetitive [ri'petitiv], *a.* qui se répète.
repine [ri'pain], *v.i.* murmurer (*contre*); se plaindre (*de*).
repining [ri'painiŋ], *a.* disposé à se plaindre, mécontent.—*n.* plainte, *f.*, regret, *m.*
replace [ri:'pleis], *v.t.* replacer; remplacer (*substituer*).
replacement [ri:'pleismənt], *n.* remplacement, *m.*
replant [ri:'plɑ:nt], *v.t.* replanter.
replay ['ri:plei], *n.* match rejoué, *m.*—[ri:'plei], *v.t.*, *v.i.* rejouer.
replenish [ri'pleniʃ], *v.t.* remplir (*de*).—*v.i.* se remplir.
replenishment [ri'pleniʃmənt], *n.* remplissage, *m.*
replete [ri'pli:t], *a.* plein, rempli (*de*).
repletion [ri'pli:ʃən], *n.* plénitude; (*Med.*) réplétion, *f.*
replica ['replikə], *n.* double, *m.*, copie, *f.*
reply [ri'plai], *n.* réponse; (*Law*) réplique, *f.* —*v.t.*, *v.i.* répondre, répliquer.
repopulate [ri:'pɔpjuleit], *v.t.* repeupler.
report [ri'pɔ:t], *v.t.* rapporter, raconter, dire; rendre compte de; signaler; dénoncer (*à la police*); *to report oneself*, se présenter à.— *n.* rapport; bruit, ouï-dire (*rumeur*); compte rendu, procès-verbal (*de réunion etc.*); (*Sch.*) bulletin; coup (*de fusil*), *m.*; réputation (*renom*), *f.*
reporter [ri'pɔ:tə], *n.* rapporteur; reporter (*journaliste*), *m.*
reporting [ri'pɔ:tiŋ], *n.* reportage, *m.*
repose [ri'pouz], *v.t.* reposer.—*v.i.* se reposer. —*n.* repos, *m.*
repository [ri'pɔzitri], *n.* dépôt, *m.*
repossess [ri:pə'zes], *v.t.* rentrer en possession de.
reprehend [repri'hend], *v.t.* réprimander, censurer, blâmer (*de*).
reprehensible [repri'hensibl], *a.* répréhensible, blâmable.
represent [repri'zent], *v.t.* représenter.
representation [reprizen'teiʃən], *n.* représentation, *f.*
representative [repri'zentətiv], *a.* représentatif, qui représente.—*n.* représentant; (*Comm.*) (*fam. abbr.* **rep**) agent, *m.*
repress [ri'pres], *v.t.* réprimer.
repression [ri'preʃən], *n.* répression, *f.*
repressive [ri'presiv], *a.* répressif.
reprieve [ri'pri:v], *n.* sursis; répit, *m.*—*v.t.* accorder un sursis à; commuer (*une peine*), gracier.
reprimand ['reprimɑ:nd], *n.* réprimande, *f.* — *v.t.* réprimander.
reprint ['ri:print], *n.* réimpression, *f.*— [ri:'print], *v.t.* réimprimer.
reprisal [ri'praizl], *n.* représailles, *f.pl.*

reproach [ri'proutʃ], *n.* reproche; opprobre (*honte*), *m.*; *above reproach*, irréprochable. —*v.t.* reprocher.
reprobate ['reprəbit], *n.* vaurien, *m.*
reprobation [reprə'beiʃən], *n.* réprobation, *f.*
reproduce [ri:prə'dju:s], *v.t.* reproduire.— *v.i.* se reproduire.
reproduction [ri:prə'dʌkʃən], *n.* reproduction, *f.*
reproductive [ri:prə'dʌktiv], *a.* reproducteur.
reproof [ri'pru:f], *n.* reproche, *m.*, réprimande, *f.*
reprove [ri'pru:v], *v.t.* blâmer; censurer.
reproving [ri'pru:viŋ], *a.* réprobateur.
reprovingly [ri'pru:viŋli], *adv.* d'un air *ou* ton réprobateur.
reptile ['reptail], *a.* reptile; (*fig.*) rampant, vil.—*n.* reptile, *m.*
reptilian [rep'tiliən], *a.* reptilien.
republic [ri'pʌblik], *n.* république, *f.*
republican [ri'pʌblikən], *a.* and *n.* républicain, *m.*
republication [ri:pʌbli'keiʃən], *n.* nouvelle édition, réimpression (*de livre*), *f.*
republish [ri:'pʌbliʃ], *v.t.* republier, rééditer.
repudiate [ri'pju:dieit], *v.t.* répudier.
repudiation [ripju:di'eiʃən], *n.* répudiation, *f.*
repugnance [ri'pʌgnəns], *n.* répugnance, *f.*
repugnant [ri'pʌgnənt], *a.* répugnant.
repulse [ri'pʌls], *v.t.* repousser, rebuter.—*n.* échec, refus, *m.*, rebuffade, *f.*; *to meet with a repulse*, essuyer un échec.
repulsion [ri'pʌlʃən], *n.* répulsion, *f.*
repulsive [ri'pʌlsiv], *a.* rebutant; repoussant (*forbidding*).
repulsiveness [ri'pʌlsivnis], *n.* caractère repoussant, *m.*
repurchase [ri:'pə:tʃis], *v.t.* racheter.—*n.* rachat; (*Law*) réméré, *m.*
reputable ['repjutəbl], *a.* honorable, de bonne réputation, considéré.
reputably ['repjutəbli], *adv.* honorablement.
reputation [repju'teiʃən], *n.* réputation, *f.*
repute [ri'pju:t], *v.t.* (*usu. pass.*) réputer, estimer.—*n.* réputation, *f.*, renom, *m.*
reputed [ri'pju:tid], *a.* réputé, censé, qui passe pour.
request [ri'kwest], *n.* demande, prière; (*Law*) requête, *f.*; *request stop*, arrêt facultatif (*autobus*), *m.*—*v.t.* demander; prier.
requiem ['rekwiem], *n.* requiem, *m.*
require [ri'kwaiə], *v.t.* exiger, requérir; avoir besoin de (*manquer de*); (*impers.*) falloir.
requirement [ri'kwaiəmənt], *n.* exigence, nécessité, *f.*, besoin, *m.*; condition requise, *f.*
requisite ['rekwizit], *a.* requis, exigé, nécessaire.—*n.* qualité *ou* condition requise; chose requise, *f.*
requisition [rekwi'ziʃən], *n.* réquisition, *f.*— *v.t.* réquisitionner.
requital [ri'kwaitl], *n.* récompense, *f.*
requite [ri'kwait], *v.t.* récompenser; rendre la pareille à; payer de retour.
reredos ['riədɔs], *n.* retable, *m.*
rescind [ri'sind], *v.t.* rescinder, annuler.
rescue ['reskju:], *n.* délivrance, *f.*; sauvetage, *m.*; *to the rescue*, au secours!—*v.t.* sauver, délivrer (*de*).
rescuer ['reskjuə], *n.* sauveteur, libérateur, *m.*
research [ri'sə:tʃ], *n.* recherche, *f.*—*v.i.* faire des recherches.

reseat [riːˈsiːt], *v.t.* rasseoir.
resemblance [riˈzembləns], *n.* ressemblance, *f.*; (*fig.*) rapport, *m.*
resemble [riˈzembl], *v.t.* ressembler (*à*); *to resemble each other*, se ressembler.
resent [riˈzent], *v.t.* ressentir, se ressentir de; s'offenser de; prendre en mauvaise part.
resentful [riˈzentful], *a.* rancunier.
resentfully [riˈzentfuli], *adv.* avec ressentiment.
resentment [riˈzentmənt], *n.* ressentiment, *m.*, rancœur, *f.*
reservation [rezəˈveiʃən], *n.* réserve, restriction, arrière-pensée, *f.*; (*Am.*) terrain réservé, *m.*; réservation, location (*place assise*), *f.*
reserve [riˈzəːv], *n.* réserve; retenue, prudence; arrière-pensée, *f.*—*v.t.* réserver.
reserved [riˈzəːvd], *a.* réservé.
reservedly [riˈzəːvidli], *adv.* avec réserve.
reservist [riˈzəːvist], *n.* réserviste, *m.*, *f.*
reservoir [ˈrezəvwɑː], *n.* réservoir, *m.*
reset [riːˈset], *v.t. irr.* (*conjug. like* SET) poser *ou* fixer de nouveau; (*Print.*) composer de nouveau; (*Surg.*) remettre.
resetting [riːˈsetiŋ], *n.* remontage (*de pierre précieuse*), *m.*; (*Print.*) recomposition, *f.*
resettle [riːˈsetl], *v.t.* rétablir.—*v.i.* s'établir de nouveau.
resettlement [riːˈsetlmənt], *n.* rétablissement, *m.*
reshape [riːˈʃeip], *v.t.* reformer; remanier.
reside [riˈzaid], *v.i.* résider, demeurer.
residence [ˈrezidəns], *n.* résidence, demeure, *f.*; *board (and) residence*, la table et le logement.
resident [ˈrezidənt], *a.* résidant; interne (*de la maison*).—*n.* habitant; résident, *m.*
residential [reziˈdenʃl], *a.* résidentiel.
residual [riˈzidjuəl], *a.* résiduel.
residuary [riˈzidjuəri], *a.* de résidu, de reste; universel (*légataire*).
residue [ˈrezidjuː], *n.* reste, (*Chem.*) résidu; reliquat (*de dette*), *m.*
resign [riˈzain], *v.t.* donner sa démission à; renoncer à; *to be resigned to* or *resign oneself to*, se résigner à.—*v.i.* donner sa démission, démissionner (*de*).
resignation [rezigˈneiʃən], *n.* résignation; cession; démission (*de ses fonctions*), *f.*
resigned [riˈzaind], *a.* résigné; démissionnaire (*d'un poste*).
resilience [riˈziliəns], **resiliency** [riˈziliənsi], *n.* rebondissement, *m.*; élasticité, *f.*
resilient [riˈziliənt], *a.* rebondissant.
resin [ˈrezin], *n.* résine; colophane (*pour violons*), *f.*
resist [riˈzist], *v.t.* résister à.—*v.i.* résister.
resistance [riˈzistəns], *n.* résistance, *f.*
resistant [riˈzistənt], *a.* résistant.
re-sole [riːˈsoul], *v.t.* ressemeler.
resolute [ˈrezəljuːt], *a.* déterminé, résolu.
resolutely [ˈrezəljuːtli], *adv.* résolument.
resoluteness [ˈrezəljuːtnis], *n.* résolution, fermeté, *f.*
resolution [rezəˈljuːʃən], *n.* résolution; décision (*d'assemblée*), *f.*
resolve [riˈzɔlv], *n.* résolution, *f.*—*v.t.* résoudre; fondre (*liquéfier*); éclaircir, dissiper (*doutes etc.*); déterminer, décider (*assemblée*).—*v.i.* se résoudre, se décider; se fondre (*se dissoudre*).

resolved [riˈzɔlvd], *a.* résolu.
resolvent [riˈzɔlvənt], *n.* (*Med.*) résolvant, *m.*
resonance [ˈrezənəns], *n.* résonance, *f.*
resonant [ˈrezənənt], *a.* résonnant, sonore.
resort [riˈzɔːt], *n.* ressource, *f.*, recours; séjour, rendezvous (*endroit*); (*Law*) ressort, *m.*; *seaside resort*, station balnéaire, plage, *f.*—*v.i.* recourir, avoir recours (*à*); se rendre, aller (*à*).
resound [riˈzaund], *v.i.* résonner, retentir.
resounding [riˈzaundiŋ], *a.* retentissant.—*n.* retentissement, *m.*
resource [riˈsɔːs], *n.* ressource, *f.*
resourceful [riˈsɔːsful], *a.* plein de ressources.
respect [riˈspekt], *n.* respect, *m.*, estime, *f.*; égard, *m.*; (*pl.*) respects, hommages, *m.pl.*; *in every respect*, sous tous les rapports; *in respect to*, à l'égard de.—*v.t.* respecter, considérer, avoir égard à.
respectability [rispektəˈbiliti], *n.* honorabilité, *f.*; convenances, *f.pl.*; bienséance, *f.*
respectable [riˈspektəbl], *a.* respectable, honorable; comme il faut, convenable.
respectably [riˈspektəbli], *adv.* comme il faut, très bien.
respectful [riˈspektful], *a.* respectueux.
respectfully [riˈspektfuli], *adv.* avec respect; *yours respectfully* (*à un supérieur hiérarchique*), veuillez agréer, Monsieur, l'assurance de mes sentiments respectueux.
respecting [riˈspektiŋ], *prep.* à l'égard de, quant à, touchant.
respective [riˈspektiv], *a.* respectif, relatif.
respectively [riˈspektivli], *adv.* respectivement.
respiration [respiˈreiʃən], *n.* respiration, *f.*
respirator [ˈrespireitə], *n.* respirateur, *m.*
respiratory [ˈrespirətri], *a.* respiratoire.
respire [riˈspaiə], *v.t.*, *v.i.* respirer.
respite [ˈrespit], *n.* répit, relâche; (*Law*) sursis, *m.*
resplendence [riˈsplendəns], *n.* éclat, *m.*, splendeur, *f.*
resplendent [riˈsplendənt], *a.* resplendissant (*de*).
respond [riˈspɔnd], *v.i.* répondre (*à*).
respondent [riˈspɔndənt], *n.* répondant; (*Law*) défendeur, *m.*
response [riˈspɔns], *n.* réponse, *f.*; (*fig.*) écho; (*Eccles.*) répons, *m.*
responsibility [risponsiˈbiliti], *n.* responsabilité, *f.*
responsible [riˈsponsibl], *a.* chargé (*de*), responsable (*de*); digne de confiance.
responsive [riˈsponsiv], *a.* sensible, facile à émouvoir.
rest (1) [rest], *n.* repos, *m.*; (*Mus.*) pause, *f.*; appui (*soutien*), *m.*; *at rest*, en repos.—*v.t.* reposer; faire reposer; (*fig.*) fonder.—*v.i.* se reposer; s'appuyer; *it rests with me to . . .*, c'est à moi de . . .; *to rest assured*, être assuré.
rest (2) [rest], *n.* reste, restant, *m.*; les autres, *m.pl.*—*v.i.* demeurer, rester.
restart [riːˈstɑːt], *v.t.*, *v.i.* recommencer.
restaurant [ˈrestərɑ̃], *n.* restaurant, *m.*
restful [ˈrestful], *a.* qui donne du repos, paisible.
resting [ˈrestiŋ], *a.* couché, se reposant; appuyé, s'appuyant.—*n.* repos, *m.*
resting place [ˈrestiŋpleis], *n.* lieu de repos, gîte, *m.*

restitution [resti'tju:ʃən], n. restitution, f.
restive ['restiv], a. rétif; inquiet.
restiveness ['restivnis], n. naturel rétif, m.; nervosité, f.
restless ['restlis], a. sans repos; inquiet; agité.
restlessly ['restlisli], adv. sans repos.
restlessness ['restlisnis], n. agitation; insomnie, f.
restock [ri:'stɔk], v.t. repeupler (chasse réservée); regarnir (boutique), réassortir.
restoration [restə'reiʃən], n. restauration, f.; rétablissement, m.; restitution (après une perte injuste), f.
restorative [ri'stɔ:rətiv], a. and n. fortifiant, m.
restore [ri'stɔ:], v.t. restituer, rendre (redonner); ramener (personne); restaurer (bâtiment etc.); remettre (replacer); rétablir.
restorer [ri'stɔ:rə], n. restaurateur, m.
restrain [ri'strein], v.t. retenir, contenir; to restrain from, empêcher de; to restrain oneself, se contraindre, se contenir.
restraining [ri'streiniŋ], a. qui restreint, restrictif.
restraint [ri'streint], n. contrainte; gêne, f.
restrict [ri'strikt], v.t. restreindre.
restriction [ri'strikʃən], n. restriction, f.
restrictive [ri'striktiv], a. restrictif.
result [ri'zʌlt], n. résultat, m.; as a result of, par suite de.—v.i. résulter; to result in, aboutir à.
resultant [ri'zʌltənt], a. résultant.—n. résultante, f.
resume [ri'zju:m], v.t. reprendre, renouer, continuer.
resumption [ri'zʌmpʃən], n. reprise, f.
resurface [ri:'sə:fis], v.t. remettre en état (route).—v.i. remonter à la surface.
resurgence [ri:'sə:dʒəns], n. résurrection, f.
resurrect [rezə'rekt], v.t. ranimer, ressusciter.
resurrection [rezə'rekʃən], n. résurrection, f.
resuscitate [ri'sʌsiteit], v.t. ressusciter.
resuscitation [risʌsi'teiʃən], n. résurrection; renaissance (des arts etc.); (Med.) ressuscitation, f.
retail ['ri:teil], a. en détail; retail price, prix de détail m.—n. détail, m., vente au détail, f. —[ri'teil], v.t. vendre en détail, détailler; (fig.) débiter; colporter (nouvelles).
retailer [ri'teilə], n. détaillant; colporteur (de nouvelles), m.
retain [ri'tein], v.t. retenir; engager (en payant des arrhes).
retainer [ri'teinə], n. serviteur, dépendant, m.; honoraires donnés d'avance (acompte), m.pl.
retaining [ri'teiniŋ], a. qui retient; retaining wall, mur de soutènement, m.
retake [ri:'teik], v.t. irr. (conjug. like TAKE) reprendre; (Cine.) retourner (un plan).
retaking [ri:'teikiŋ], n. reprise, f.
retaliate [ri'tælieit], v.i. rendre la pareille à.
retaliation [ritæli'eiʃən], n. représailles, f.pl.
retaliatory [ri'tæliətəri], a. de représailles.
retard [ri'ta:d], v.t. retarder.
retch [ri:tʃ], v.i. avoir des haut-le-cœur.
retching ['ri:tʃiŋ], n. haut-le-cœur, m.
retell [ri:'tel], v.t. irr. (conjug. like TELL) redire, répéter.
retention [ri'tenʃən], n. conservation; (Med.) rétention, f.

retentive [ri'tentiv], a. qui retient; tenace, fidèle (la mémoire).
retentiveness [ri'tentivnis], n. pouvoir de rétention, m.; fidélité (de la mémoire), f.
reticence ['retisəns], n. réticence, f.
reticent ['retisənt], a. réservé, taciturne.
reticular [re'tikjulə], a. réticulaire.
reticulate [re'tikjulit], a. réticulé.
retina ['retinə], n. rétine, f.
retinue ['retinju:], n. suite, f.; cortège, m.
retire [ri'taiə], v.t. retirer.—v.i. se retirer, prendre sa retraite.
retired [ri'taiəd], a. retiré, retraité (qui a pris sa retraite); ancien (qui n'exerce plus cette profession); on the retired list, en retraite.
retirement [ri'taiəmənt], n. retraite; (fig.) solitude, f.
retiring [ri'taiəriŋ], a. réservé, timide, modeste; sortant (d'un emploi).
retort (1) [ri'tɔ:t], n. réplique, riposte, f.— v.i. riposter, répliquer.
retort (2) [ri'tɔ:t], n. (Chem.) cornue, f.
retouch [ri:'tʌtʃ], v.t. retoucher.
retrace [ri'treis], v.t. (Paint.) retracer; to retrace one's steps, revenir sur ses pas, rebrousser chemin.
retract [ri'trækt], v.t. rétracter.—v.i. se rétracter, se dédire.
retractable [ri'træktebl], a. (Av.) escamotable.
retransmit [ri:trɑ:ns'mit], v.t. retransmettre.
retread [ri:'tred], v.t. (Motor.) rechaper (pneu).—[ri:'tred], n. pneu rechapé, m.
retreat [ri'tri:t], n. retraite, f.—v.i. se retirer (à ou dans); (Mil.) battre en retraite.
retreating [ri'tri:tiŋ], a. qui bat en retraite; fuyant (le front).
retrench [ri'trentʃ], v.t. retrancher.—v.i. se retrancher.
retrenchment [ri'trentʃmənt], n. retranchement, m.
retribution [retri'bju:ʃən], n. récompense, rétribution, f.; (fig.) châtiment, m., vengeance, f.
retrievable [ri'tri:vəbl], a. recouvrable (argent); réparable (perte).
retrieve [ri'tri:v], v.t. rétablir; réparer (chose brisée); recouvrer (chose perdue); rapporter (chien).
retriever [ri'tri:və], n. chien rapporteur, m.
retroaction [ri:trou'ækʃən], n. rétroaction, f.
retroactive [ri:trou'æktiv], a. rétroactif.
retrograde ['retrougreid], a. rétrograde.
retrogression [retro'greʃən], n. rétrogression, rétrogradation, f.
retrogressive [retro'gresiv], a. rétrogressif.
retrospect ['retrospekt], n. regard jeté en arrière, m.; revue, f.; in retrospect, en rétrospective.
retrospective [retro'spektiv], a. rétrospectif; (Law) rétroactif.
retrospectively [retro'spektivli], adv. rétrospectivement; (Law) rétroactivement.
retroversion [retro'və:ʃən], n. renversement, m.
retrovert [retro'və:t], v.t. renverser.
return [ri'tə:n], v.t. rendre; renvoyer; rembourser (argent etc.); rapporter (intérêt); (Comm.) rendre compte; élire (candidat); he was returned, il fut élu.—v.i. revenir; retourner; rentrer.—n. retour, m., rentrée, f.; renvoi, m.; remise en place (chose déplacée) f.; profit, m.; restitution, f.; remboursement,

m.; élection, *f.*; rapport, relevé, état (*impôts etc.*); bilan (*de banque*); (*pl.*) produit, *m.*; *by return mail*, par retour du courrier; *in return for*, en retour de; *nil return*, état néant; *on sale or return*, en dépôt; *return journey*, retour; *return match*, revanche, *f.*; *return ticket*, billet d'aller et retour, *m.*

returnable [ri'tə:nəbl], *a.* restituable.

reunion [ri:'ju:niən], *n.* réunion, *f.*

reunite [ri:ju'nait], *v.t.* réunir.—*v.i.* se réunir.

rev [rev], *n.* (*colloq.*, *Motor.*) tour, *m.*—*v.t. to rev the engine*, faire s'emballer le moteur. —*v.i.* s'emballer.

reveal [ri'vi:l], *v.t.* révéler.

reveille [ri'væli], *n.* réveil, *m.*

revel [revl], *n.* (*pl.*) divertissements, *m.pl.*— *v.i.* se réjouir, se divertir; *to revel in*, se délecter à.

revelation [revə'leifən], *n.* révélation, *f.*; *Book of Revelation*, Apocalypse, *f.*

reveller ['revələ], *n.* joyeux convive, *m.*

revelry ['revəlri], *n.* réjouissances, *f.pl.*, joyeux ébats, *m.pl.*

revenge [ri'vend3], *n.* vengeance; (*Spt.*) revanche, *f.*—*v.t.* venger; se venger de; *to revenge oneself on*, se venger de.

revengeful [ri'vend3ful], *a.* vindicatif.

revengefully [ri'vend3fuli], *adv.* par vengeance.

revenue ['revənju:], *n.* revenu; (*State*) fisc, trésor, *m.*; *revenue officer*, officier de la douane, *m.*

reverberate [ri'və:bəreit], *v.t.* réverbérer; renvoyer (*son*, *chaleur etc.*).—*v.i.* se répercuter.

reverberation [rivə:bə'reifən], *n.* réverbération (*de chaleur*); répercussion, *f.*

revere [ri'viə], *v.t.* révérer, vénérer.

reverence ['revərəns], *n.* révérence, *f.*

reverend ['revərənd], *a.* révérend (*titre ecclésiastique*).

reverent ['revərənt], *a.* révérencieux.

reverently ['revərəntli], *adv.* avec révérence.

reverie ['revəri], *n.* rêverie, *f.*

reversal [ri'və:sl], *n.* annulation; cassation, *f.*

reverse [ri'və:s], *a.* contraire, opposé.—*n.* revers, *m.*; défaite, *f.*; *quite the reverse*, tout le contraire (*de*); *the reverse way*, en sens inverse.—*v.t.* renverser; appliquer en sens inverse; (*Law*) infirmer, casser.—*v.i.* (*Motor.*) faire marche *ou* machine en arrière.

reversed [ri'və:st], *a.* renversé; inverse.

reversible [ri'və:sibl], *a.* révocable, réversible, à double face (*tissu*).

reversion [ri'və:ʃən], *n.* réversion, *f.*

revert [ri'və:t], *v.i.* revenir (*sur*).

revertible [ri'və:tibl], *a.* réversible.

revetment [ri'vetmənt], *n.* revêtement, *m.*

revictual [ri:'vitl], *v.t.* ravitailler.

revictualling [ri:'vitliŋ], *n.* ravitaillement, *m.*

review [ri'vju:], *n.* revue, revision; critique; revue, *f.*, périodique, *m.*—*v.t.* revoir, reviser; passer en revue; analyser, critiquer (*livre etc.*).

reviewer [ri'vju:ə], *n.* critique, *m.*, *f.*

revile [ri'vail], *v.t.* injurier, insulter, outrager.

revilement [ri'vailmənt], *n.* injure, insulte, *f.*

reviling [ri'vailiŋ], *a.* diffamatoire, outrageant. —*n.* insultes, injures, *f.pl*

revisal [ri'vaizl], *n.* revision, *f.*

revise [ri'vaiz], *v.t.* revoir, reviser, réviser.

reviser [ri'vaizə], *n.* personne qui revoit, *f.*, reviseur, *m.*

revision [ri'vi3ən], *n.* revision, révision, *f.*

revisit [ri:'vizit], *v.t.* revisiter, retourner voir.

revitalize [ri:'vaitəlaiz], *v.t.* revivifier.

revival [ri'vaivl], *n.* rétablissement, *m.*; renaissance (*des arts*); reprise (*d'une pièce*), *f.*; réveil (*religieux*), *m.*

revive [ri'vaiv], *v.t.* ressusciter; raviver.—*v.i.* se ranimer; renaître (*arts etc.*).

revivify [ri'vivifai], *v.t.* revivifier.

revocable ['revəkəbl], *a.* révocable.

revocation [revə'keifən], *n.* révocation, *f.*

revoke [ri'vouk], *v.t.* révoquer.—*v.i.* (*Cards*) renoncer.—*n.* (*Cards*) renonce, *f.*

revolt [ri'voult], *n.* révolte, *f.*—*v.i.* se révolter, se soulever.

revolting [ri'voultiŋ], *a.* révoltant.

revolution [revə'lju:ʃən], *n.* révolution, *f.*; tour (*de roue*), *m.*

revolutionary [revə'lju:ʃənəri], *a.* and *n.* révolutionnaire, *m.*, *f.*

revolve [ri'volv], *v.t.* tourner; retourner; repasser, rouler (*dans l'esprit*).—*v.i.* tourner; (*fig.*) retourner, revenir.

revolver [ri'volvə], *n.* revolver, *m.*

revolving [ri'volviŋ], *a.* tournant.

revue [ri'vju:], *n.* (*Theat.*) revue, *f.*

revulsion [ri'vʌlʃən], *n.* révulsion, *f.*

reward [ri'wo:d], *n.* récompense, *f.*; prix, *m.* —*v.t.* récompenser (*de*).

rewind [ri:'waind], *v.t. irr.* (*conjug. like* WIND) rebobiner (*soie etc.*); remonter (*montre*, *horloge*); rembobiner (*film*).

rewrite [ri:'rait], *v.t. irr.* (*conjug. like* WRITE) récrire.

rhapsody ['ræpsədi], *n.* rapsodie, *f.*

Rheims [ri:mz], Reims, *m.*

Rhenish ['reniʃ], *a.* du Rhin.—*n.* vin du Rhin, *m.*

rheostat ['ri:ostæt], *n.* rhéostat, *m.*

rhesus ['ri:səs], *a.* (*Med.*) rhésus.

rhetoric ['retərik], *n.* rhétorique, *f.*

rhetorical [ri'tərikl], *a.* de rhétorique; *rhetorical question*, question de pure forme, *f.*

rheum [ru:m], *n.* rhume, catarrhe, *m.*

rheumatic [ru:'mætik], *a.* rhumatismal; *rheumatic fever*, rhumatisme articulaire aigu, *m.*

rheumatism ['ru:mətizm], *n.* rhumatisme, *m.*

rheumatoid ['ru:mətɔid], *a.* rhumatoïde; *rheumatoid arthritis*, rhumatisme articulaire, *m.*

Rhine [rain], **the.** le Rhin, *m.*

Rhineland ['rainlænd], la Rhénanie, *f.*

Rhinelander ['rainlændə], *n.* Rhénan, *m.*

rhinoceros [rai'nosərəs], *n.* rhinocéros, *m.*

Rhodesia [rou'di:ziə], la Rhodésie, *f.*

Rhodesian [rou'di:ziən], *a.* rhodésien.—*n.* Rhodésien (*personne*), *m.*

rhododendron [roudə'dendrən], *n.* rhododendron, *m.*

rhombus ['rombəs], *n.* losange, *m.*

Rhone [roun], le Rhône, *m.*

rhubarb ['ru:ba:b], *n.* rhubarbe, *f.*

rhyme [raim], *n.* rime, *f.*; (*pl.*) vers, *m.pl.*— *v.t.*, *v.i.* rimer; rimailler.

rhythm [riðm], *n.* rythme, *m.*; cadence, *f.*

rhythmical ['riðmikl], *a.* rythmique.

rhythmically ['riðmikli], *adv.* avec rythme.

rib [rib], *n.* côte; baleine (*de parapluie*), *f.*

ribald ['ribəld], *a.* grossier, obscène.

ribaldry ['ribəldri], *n.* obscénités, *f.pl.*

ribbed [ribd], *a.* à côtes.

ribbon ['ribən], *n.* ruban; cordon (*de médaille*); lambeau (*morceau de tissu déchiré*), *m.*

rice [rais], *n.* riz, *m.*; *rice field*, rizière, *f.*

rich [ritʃ], *a.* riche; fertile, fécond (*terre*); de haut goût (*fort assaisonné*); voyant (*couleur*); (*fig.*) délicieux, généreux (*vin*); *the rich*, les riches, *m.pl.*; *to grow rich*, s'enrichir.

riches ['ritʃiz], *n.pl.* richesse, *f.*

richly ['ritʃli], *adv.* richement; grandement; (*fam.*) joliment.

richness ['ritʃnis], *n.* richesse; fécondité, *f.*; haut goût, *m.*

rick [rik], *n.* meule, *f.*

rickets ['rikits], *n.pl.* rachitis, rachitisme, *m.*

rickety ['rikiti], *a.* (*fig.*) boiteux (*meuble*).

rickshaw ['rikʃɔ:], *n.* pousse-pousse, *m.*

ricochet ['rikəʃei], *n.* ricochet, *m.—v.i.* ricocher.

rid [rid], *v.t. irr.* délivrer, débarrasser; *to get rid of*, se débarrasser de.

riddance ['ridəns], *n.* débarras, *m.*

riddle (1) [ridl], *n.* énigme, *f.*

riddle (2) [ridl], *v.t.* cribler.—*n.* crible, *m.*

ride [raid], *v.t. irr.* monter, être monté sur; mener, conduire; faire (*une distance précise*). *—v.i.* monter (*à cheval, à bicyclette etc.*), aller, venir, être *ou* se promener (*à cheval, à bicyclette, en voiture etc.*); être monté (*sur*); flotter, voguer (*sur*); être (à l'ancre); *to ride away*, partir, s'en aller; *to ride back*, revenir, s'en retourner.—*n.* promenade, course (*à cheval, en voiture, à bicyclette etc.*), *f.*; trajet, *m.*; allée cavalière (*sentier dans un bois etc.*), *f.*

rider ['raidə], *n.* cavalier, *m.*, cavalière, *f.*; écuyer, *m.*, écuyère (*de cirque*), *f.*; jockey; codicille (*document*), *m.*

riderless ['raidəlis], *a.* sans cavalier.

ridge [ridʒ], *n.* sommet (*pic*), *m.*, cime; chaîne (*de montagnes*), arête, crête (*d'une montagne*) *f.*; faîte (*de toit*), *m.*; (*Agric.*) sillon, billon, *m.—v.t.* sillonner.

ridicule ['ridikju:l], *n.* ridicule, *m.—v.t.* tourner en ridicule, ridiculiser.

ridiculous [ri'dikjuləs], *a.* ridicule.

ridiculously [ri'dikjuləsli], *adv.* ridiculement.

riding (1) ['raidiŋ], *n.* promenade à cheval, *f.*, exercice à cheval, *m.*, équitation, *f.*; (*Naut.*) mouillage, *m.*

riding (2) ['raidiŋ], *n.* (*Yorkshire*) arrondissement, *m.*

riding habit ['raidiŋhæbit], *n.* amazone, *f.*

riding hood ['raidiŋhud], *n.* capuchon, *m.*; *Little Red Riding Hood*, le petit Chaperon rouge.

rife [raif], *a.* abondant, répandu; *to be rife*, régner (*tumulte etc.*), courir (*bruit*).

riff-raff ['rifræf], *n.* racaille, canaille, *f.*

rifle (1) [raifl], *v.t.* piller, dévaliser.

rifle (2) [raifl], *v.t.* rayer (*armes à feu*).—*n.* fusil (rayé), *m.*, carabine, *f.*; *rifle gallery* or *range*, tir, *m.*; *rifle practice* or *shooting*, tir au fusil, tir à la carabine, *m.*; *rifle shot*, coup de fusil, *m.*

rifleman ['raiflmən], *n.* (*pl.* **-men** [men]) carabinier, *m.*

rifling (1) ['raifliŋ], *n.* pillage.

rifling (2) ['raifliŋ], *n.* rayage (*de fusils*), *m.*

rift [rift], *n.* fente; éclaircie (*aux nuages*), *f.*

rig [rig], *n.* gréement; accoutrement (*vêtements*), *m.—v.t.* équiper, gréer; (*fig.*) accoutrer, attifer.

rigged [rigd], *a.* gréé.

rigging ['rigiŋ], *n.* gréement, *m.*, agrès, *m.pl.*

right [rait], *a.* droit; direct, en ligne droite; vrai, véritable; bon, propre, convenable; juste, correct; en règle; *all right!* c'est bien! *that is right*, c'est cela; *the right man*, l'homme qu'il faut; *the right road*, le bon chemin; *to be right*, avoir raison; être juste (*compte*); *to put right*, mettre en bon ordre, arranger.—*adv.* droit, tout droit; justement (*avec justice*); comme il faut, bien (*correctement*); tout à fait (*entièrement*); fort (*beaucoup*); très.—*n.* droit, *m.*, justice, raison, *f.*; côté droit, *m.*, droite, *f.*; *on* or *to the right*, à droite; *right of way*, droit de passage; *to put* or *set to rights*, arranger, mettre en ordre.—*v.t.* redresser, corriger (*choses*).—*v.i.* se redresser, se relever.

righteous ['raitʃəs], *a.* juste, droit.

righteously ['raitʃəsli], *adv.* justement.

righteousness ['raitʃəsnis], *n.* droiture, vertu, *f.*

rightful ['raitful], *a.* légitime, véritable.

right-handed ['raithændid], *a.* droitier.

rightly ['raitli], *adv.* bien; à juste titre; comme il faut (*convenablement*); juste (*exactement*).

rightness ['raitnis], *n.* rectitude; droiture; justesse, *f.*

rigid ['ridʒid], *a.* rigide, raide.

rigidity [ri'dʒiditi], *n.* rigidité; raideur, *f.*

rigidly ['ridʒidli], *adv.* rigidement; avec raideur.

rigmarole ['rigməroul], *n.* galimatias, *m.*

rigor ['rigə, 'raigə], *n.* (*Path.*) rigidité, *f.*

rigor ['rigə], *n.* rigueur, *f.*

rigorous ['rigərəs], *a.* rigoureux.

rigorously ['rigərəsli], *adv.* rigoureusement, avec rigueur, à la rigueur.

rile [rail], *v.t.* (*colloq.*) faire enrager, agacer.

rill [ril], *n.* petit ruisseau, *m.*

rim [rim], *n.* bord, rebord, *m.*; jante (*de roue*), *f.*

rime [raim], *n.* givre, *m.*; gelée blanche, *f.*

rimless ['rimlis], *a.* sans monture (*lunettes*).

rind [raind], *n.* écorce, peau, pelure; croûte (*de fromage*); couenne (*de lard*), *f.*

ring (1) [riŋ], *n.* anneau, *m.*, bague (*pour le doigt etc.*), *f.*; cercle, rond, *m.*; arène (*pour se battre*), *f.*; ring (*pour la boxe*), *m.*; (*fig.*) bande, clique, *f.*; (*Comm.*) syndicat, *m.— v.t.* mettre un anneau à; entourer.

ring (2) [riŋ], *v.t. irr.* sonner, faire sonner; *to ring someone up*, téléphoner à quelqu'un. *—v.i.* sonner; retentir (*de*); tinter (*aux oreilles*).—*n.* son, tintement, coup de sonnette, *m.*; sonnerie, *f.*; *there's a ring at the door*, on sonne.

ring-dove ['riŋdʌv], *n.* pigeon ramier, *m.*

ringer ['riŋə], *n.* sonneur, *m.*

ringing ['riŋiŋ], *n.* son (*de cloche*), *m.*; sonnerie, *f.*, tintement, retentissement, *m.*

ringleader ['riŋli:də], *n.* meneur, chef de bande, *m.*

ringlet ['riŋlit], *n.* boucle (*de cheveux*), *f.*

ring-road ['riŋroud], *n.* route de ceinture, *f.*

ringworm ['riŋwə:m], *n.* herpès tonsurant, *m.*

rink [riŋk], *n.* patinoire (*de glace*), *f.*; skating (*pour patinage à roulettes*), *m.*

rinse [rins], *v.t.* rincer.

riot [ˈraiət], *n.* émeute, *f.*; vacarme, tumulte (*bruit*), *m.*; (*fig.*) festins, *m.pl.*—*v.i.* faire une émeute.

rioter [ˈraiətə], *n.* émeutier; tapageur, *m.*

riotous [ˈraiətəs], *a.* séditieux, tumultueux.

rip (1) [rip], *v.t.* fendre, déchirer; **to rip open,** ouvrir.—*n.* déchirure, *f.*

rip (2) [rip], *n.* (*slang*) vaurien, polisson, *m.*

ripe [raip], *a.* mûr.

ripen [ˈraipən], *v.t.* mûrir, faire mûrir.—*v.i.* mûrir, venir à maturité.

ripeness [ˈraipnis], *n.* maturité, *f.*

ripening [ˈraipniŋ], *n.* maturation, *f.*

ripple [ripl], *v.t.* rider.—*v.i.* se rider; onduler. —*n.* ride (*d'eau*), *f.*

rippling [ˈripliŋ], *n.* clapotis, murmure, *m.*

rip-roaring [ˈriproːriŋ], *a.* tumultueux; robuste; épatant.

rise [raiz], *v.i. irr.* se lever, se relever (*après une chute, un malheur etc.*); s'élever, monter; se dresser (*montagne etc.*); s'augmenter, hausser (*prix*); aller en montant (*rue*); se soulever (*rébellion*); ressusciter (*les morts*); prendre sa source (*en ou dans*).—*n.* lever, *m.*; montée (*de colline etc.*); crue (*des eaux*); hausse (*de prix*), augmentation; source, origine, *f.*

riser [ˈraizə], *n.* marche (*d'escalier*), *f.*; **early riser,** personne matinale, *f.*

risible [ˈrizibl], *a.* rieur.

rising [ˈraiziŋ], *a.* levant; montant (*marée*); (*fig.*) naissant; qui a de l'avenir (*qui promet*). —*n.* lever (*du lit, du soleil*), *m.*; montée (*de colline*); crue (*des eaux*); clôture (*d'assemblée*); résurrection, *f.*; soulèvement, *m.*, insurrection, *f.*

risk [risk], *n.* risque, *m.*—*v.t.* risquer.

risky [ˈriski], *a.* risqué, hasardeux.

rite [rait], *n.* rite, *m.*, cérémonie, *f.*

ritual [ˈritjuəl], *a.* du rite.—*n.* rituel, *m.*

rival [raivl], *a.* et *n.* rival, *m.*—*v.t.* rivaliser avec.

rivalry [ˈraivlri], *n.* rivalité, *f.*

rive [raiv], *v.t. irr.* fendre.—*v.i.* se fendre.

river [ˈrivə], *a.* de rivière, fluvial.—*n.* fleuve (*qui débouche dans la mer*), *m.*; (*autrement*) rivière, *f.*; **down the river,** en aval; **up the river,** en amont.

riverside [ˈrivəsaid], *a.* au bord de l'eau.—*n.* bord de l'eau, *m.*

rivet [ˈrivit], *n.* rivet, *m.*; attache (*de porcelaine*), *f.*—*v.t.* river, riveter; (*fig.*) fixer.

riveting [ˈrivitiŋ], *n.* rivetage, *m.*

rivulet [ˈrivjulit], *n.* ruisseau, *m.*

roach [routʃ], *n.* (*Ichth.*) gardon, *m.*

road [roud], *n.* route, *f.*, chemin, *m.*; chaussée; rue (*en ville*); (*Naut.*) rade, *f.*; **by-road,** chemin détourné; **carriage road,** route carrossable; **cross-roads,** carrefour, *m.*; **high road,** grand-route, *f.*; **roads and bridges,** ponts et chaussées, *m.pl.*

road hog [ˈroudhɔg], *n.* (*Motor.*) chauffard, *m.*

road-house [ˈroudhaus], *n.* auberge, hôtellerie, *f.*

road map [ˈroudmæp], *n.* carte routière, *f.*

road mender [ˈroudmendə], *n.* cantonnier, *m.*

road metal [ˈroudmetl], *n.* cailloutis, empierrement, *m.*

roadside [ˈroudsaid], *n.* bord de la route, *m.*; **by the roadside,** au bord de la route.

roadstead [ˈroudsted], *n.* rade, *f.*

roadway [ˈroudwei], *n.* chaussée; voie (*de pont*), *f.*

roadworthy [ˈroudwəːði], *a.* (*Motor.*) en état de marche.

roam [roum], *v.t.* rôder dans *ou* parmi.—*v.i.* errer, rôder.

roan [roun], *a.* rouan.

roar [rɔː], *n.* rugissement (*de lion etc.*); mugissement (*de la mer etc.*); éclat (*de rire*); grondement (*de tonnerre etc.*), *m.*—*v.i.* rugir (*lion etc.*); mugir (*mer etc.*); gronder (*tonnerre, canon etc.*); (*colloq.*) vociférer; **to roar with laughter,** rire aux éclats.

roaring [ˈrɔːriŋ], *a.* rugissant, mugissant; **to do a roaring trade,** faire des affaires d'or.

roast [roust], *v.t.* rôtir; faire rôtir; torréfier (*café*); (*Metal.*) griller.—*v.i.* rôtir; griller. —*a.* rôti; **roast beef,** rosbif, *m.*; **roast pork,** rôti de porc, *m.*

roaster [ˈroustə], *n.* rôtisseur (*personne*), *m.*; rôtissoire (*chose*), *f.*

roasting [ˈroustiŋ], *a.* brûlant.—*n.* (*Metal.*) grillage, *m.*; torréfaction (*de café*), *f.*

rob [rɔb], *v.t.* voler; piller; priver (*de*).

robber [ˈrɔbə], *n.* voleur, *m.*

robbery [ˈrɔbəri], *n.* vol, *m.*

robe [roub], *n.* robe, *f.*—*v.t.* vêtir (*d'une robe*); revêtir (*de*).

robin [ˈrɔbin], **robin redbreast** [rɔbinˈred brest], *n.* (*Orn.*) rouge-gorge, *m.*

robot [ˈroubɔt], *n.* automate, robot, *m.*

robust [roˈbʌst], *a.* robuste, vigoureux.

robustness [roˈbʌstnis], *n.* robustesse, vigueur, *f.*

rock (1) [rɔk], *n.* rocher, roc, *m.*; (*Geol.*) roche, *f.*; sucre d'orge (*bonbon*), *m.*

rock (2) [rɔk], *v.t.* balancer; bercer, remuer.— *v.i.* se balancer; branler, trembler.

rockery [ˈrɔkəri], *n.* jardin de rocaille, *m.*

rocket [ˈrɔkit], *n.* fusée, *f.*; **rocket launcher,** lance-fusée, *m.*—*v.i.* monter en flèche (*prix*).

rockiness [ˈrɔkinis], *n.* nature rocailleuse, *f.*

rocking [ˈrɔkiŋ], *n.* balancement; bercement, *m.*

rocking chair [ˈrɔkiŋtʃeə], *n.* chaise à bascule, *f.*

rocking horse [ˈrɔkiŋhɔːs], *n.* cheval à bascule, *m.*

rock salt [ˈrɔksɔːlt], *n.* sel gemme, *m.*

rocky [ˈrɔki], *a.* rocailleux, rocheux.

rod [rɔd], *n.* verge; baguette; tringle (*à rideaux etc.*); canne à pêche; perche (= *5,091 metres*); bielle (*de piston*), *f.*

rodent [ˈroudənt], *n.* (*Zool.*) rongeur, *m.*

rodeo [roˈdeiou], *n.* rodéo, *m.*

roe (1) [rou], *n.* œufs (*de poisson*), *m.pl.*

roe (2) [rou], *n.* chevreuil, *m.*, chevrette, *f.*

roebuck [ˈroubʌk], *n.* chevreuil, *m.*

Roger [ˈrɔdʒə]. Roger, *m.*

rogue [roug], *n.* coquin, fripon, fourbe, *m.*

roguery [ˈrougəri], *n.* coquinerie, friponnerie, fourberie, *f.*

roguish [ˈrougiʃ], *a.* coquin, fripon; (*facet.*) espiègle.

roguishly [ˈrougiʃli], *adv.* en fripon, en fourbe; (*facet.*) avec espièglerie.

roister ['rɔistə], *v.i.* faire du tapage.
roisterer ['rɔistərə], *n.* tapageur, *m.*
roistering ['rɔistəriŋ], *a.* tapageur, bruyant.
—*n.* tapage, *m.*
role [roul], *n.* rôle, *m.*
roll [roul], *n.* rouleau; roulement (*acte de rouler quelque chose*); roulis (*de navire*); petit pain; roulement (*de tambour*); rôle (*liste*), *m.*; (*pl.*) rôles, *m.pl.*; annales, archives, *f.pl.*—*v.t.* rouler; passer au rouleau (*gazon, gravier etc.*); (*Metal.*) laminer.—*v.i.* rouler, se rouler; tourner; (*Naut.*) avoir du roulis.
roll call ['roulkɔ:l], *n.* appel, *m.*
roller ['roulə], *n.* rouleau; cylindre, *m.*
roller skate ['roul5skeit], *n.* patin à roulettes, *m.*
rollicking ['rɔlikiŋ], *a.* folâtre, joyeux.
rolling ['rouliŋ], *n.* roulement; roulis (*de navire*); (*Metal.*) laminage, *m.*; **rolling stock**, matériel roulant, *m.*
rolling pin ['rouliŋpin], *n.* rouleau, *m.*
Roman ['roumən], *a.* romain; aquilin (*nez*).—*n.* Romain (*personne*), *m.*
Romance [ro'mæns], *a.* roman; **Romance languages**, langues romanes, *f.pl.*
romance [ro'mæns], *n.* roman de chevalerie, *m.*; histoire romanesque; (*Mus.*) romance; (*fam.*) amourette, aventure, *f.*—*v.i.* inventer à plaisir, exagérer, broder.
romanesque [roumə'nesk], *a.* (*Arch.*) roman.
Romania [ro'meiniə], [RUMANIA].
romantic [ro'mæntik], *a.* romanesque; romantique (*paysage, style etc.*).
romanticism [ro'mæntisizm], *n.* romantisme, *m.*
romanticist [ro'mæntisist], *n.* romantique, *m., f.*
Rome [roum]. Rome, *f.*
romp [rɔmp], *n.* gamine, garçonnière (*jeune fille*), *f.*; jeu violent, tapage, *m.*—*v.i.* jouer rudement, folâtrer.
rompers ['rɔmpəz], *n.pl.* barboteuse, *f.*
romping ['rɔmpiŋ], *n.* jeux rudes, *m.pl.*
roof [ru:f], *n.* toit; palais (*de la bouche*), *m.*—*v.t.* couvrir d'un toit; couvrir.
roofing ['ru:fiŋ], *n.* toiture, *f.*
roof rack ['ru:fræk], *n.* (*Motor.*) galerie, *f.*
rook (1) [ruk], *n.* freux, *m.*, (*pop.*) corneille, *f.*; (*slang*) tricheur, *m.*—*v.t.*, *v.i.* (*slang*) friponner, filouter.
rook (2) [ruk], *n.* (*Chess*) tour, *f.*
rookery ['rukəri], *n.* colonie de freux, *f.*
rookie ['ruki], *n.* (*slang*) bleu, *m.*
room [ru:m], *n.* place, *f.*, espace, *m.*; chambre, salle, pièce(*d'appartement*),*f.*[see **residence**]
roomful ['ru:mful], *n.* chambrée, *f.*
roominess ['ru:minis], *n.* nature spacieuse, grandeur, *f.*
roomy ['ru:mi], *a.* spacieux, vaste.
roost [ru:st], *n.* juchoir, perchoir, *m.*—*v.i.* se jucher.
rooster ['ru:stə], *n.* coq, *m.*
root [ru:t], *n.* racine; (*fig.*) source, *f.*—*v.t.* **to root out**, déraciner, extirper.
rooted ['ru:tid], *a.* enraciné; (*fig.*) invétéré.
rooting ['ru:tiŋ], *n.* enracinement, *m.*; **rooting out**, arrachement, *m.*, extirpation, *f.*
rope [roup], *n.* corde, *f.*; (*Naut.*) cordage, *m.*; (*Mount.*) cordée, *f.*; **a piece of rope**, un bout de filin.—*v.t.* attacher avec une corde; lier.—*v.i.* filer (*vin etc.*); (*Mount.*) s'encorder.
rope-walker ['roupwɔ:kə], *n.* funambule, *m., f.*
ropiness ['roupinis], *n.* viscosité, *f.*
ropy ['roupi], *a.* qui file, filant, visqueux.
rosary ['rouzəri], *n.* chapelet, *m.*
rose (1) [rouz], *n.* rose; (*Tech.*) pomme d'arrosoir; (*Arch.*) rosace, *f.*
rose (2) [rouz], *past* [RISE].
roseate ['rouziit], *a.* rosé.
rose bed ['rouzbed], *n.* massif de rosiers, *m.*
rosebud ['rouzbʌd], *n.* bouton de rose, *m.*
rose-bush ['rouzbuʃ], *n.* rosier, *m.*
rose garden ['rouzga:dn], *n.* roseraie, *f.*
rosemary ['rouzməri], *n.* romarin, *m.*
rosette [ro'zet], *n.* rosette, *f.*
rose window ['rouzwindou], *n.* rosace, *f.*
rosin ['rɔzin], *n.* colophane, *f.*
rosiness ['rouzinis], *n.* couleur rose, *f.*
rostrum ['rɔstrəm], *n.* (*Rom. Hist.*) rostres, *m.pl.*; tribune (*estrade*), *f.*
rosy ['rouzi], *a.* de rose, rose, rosé, vermeil.
rot [rɔt], *n.* pourriture; (*colloq.*) blague, *f.*—*v.t.* pourrir, faire pourrir; carier (*dent*).—*v.i.* pourrir, se pourrir; se carier (*dent*).
rota ['routə], *n.* **by rota**, à tour de rôle.
rotary ['routəri], *a.* rotatif, rotatoire.
rotate [ro'teit], *v.t.*, *v.i.* tourner.
rotation [ro'teiʃən], *n.* rotation, succession, *f.*; **rotation of crops**, assolement, *m.*
rote [rout], *n.* routine, *f.*; **by rote**, par cœur.
rotten [rɔtn], *a.* pourri; carié (*dent*); gâté (*œuf*).
rottenness ['rɔtnnis], *n.* pourriture; carie (*des dents*), *f.*
rotter ['rɔtə], *n.* (*fam.*) sale type, *m.*
rotting ['rɔtiŋ], *a.* qui pourrit; qui se carie.—*n.* putréfaction, *f.*
rotund [ro'tʌnd], *a.* rond, arrondi.
rotundity [ro'tʌnditi], *n.* rondeur, rotondité, *f.*
rouble [ru:bl], *n.* rouble, *m.*
rouge [ru:ʒ], *n.* rouge, fard, *m.*
rough [rʌf], *a.* rude; hérissé; raboteux (*chemin*); grosse, houleuse (*mer*); orageux (*temps*); âpre (*goût*); dépoli (*verre*); grossier (*manières*); approximatif (*pas exact*); **rough-and-ready**, fait à la va-vite; **rough copy** or **draft**, brouillon, *m.*; **rough estimate**, appréciation en gros, *f.*—*adv.* brutalement, rudement.—*n.* voyou, polisson, *m.*; **rough-and-tumble**, mêlée, bousculade, *f.*
roughcast ['rʌfka:st], *v.t.* ébaucher; (*Build.*) crépir.—*n.* ébauche, *f.*; (*Build.*) crépi, *m.*
roughen [rʌfn], *v.t.* rendre rude.
rough-hewn ['rʌfhju:n], *a.* ébauché.
rough-house ['rʌfhaus], *n.* (*fam.*) chahut, *m.*
roughly ['rʌfli], *adv.* rudement, grossièrement; à peu près.
roughness ['rʌfnis], *n.* aspérité, rudesse; apreté (*au goût*); agitation (*de la mer*); grossiéreté (*de manières*), *f.*; mauvais état (*de rue*), *m.*
round [raund], *a.* rond; circulaire; en rond.—*adv.* en rond; à la ronde; tout autour, à l'entour; **to go round**, faire le tour de.—*prep.* autour de.—*n.* tour (*petite promenade*), *m.*; rouelle (*de bœuf etc.*); salve (*d'applaudissements*), *f.*; (*Artill.*) coup de canon, *m.*; ronde (*de veilleurs, police etc.*); (*Golf*) tournée, *f.*; (*Box.*) round, *m.*; **round**

545

of ammunition, cartouche, *f.—v.t.* arrondir; entourer, faire le tour de *(faire un cercle)*; doubler *(cap)*; **to round off**, arrondir, finir, compléter; **to round up**, rassembler *(bestiaux etc.)*; faire une rafle.—*v.i.* s'arrondir.

roundabout ['raundəbaut], *a.* détourné; indirect.—*n.* manège; *(Motor.)* rondpoint, *m.*

rounded ['raundid], *a.* arrondi.

***roundelay** ['raundəlei], *n.* rondeau, *m.*

rounders ['raundəz], *n.pl.* balle au camp, *f.*

roundish ['raundiʃ], *a.* arrondi; rondelet *(personne)*.

roundly ['raundli], *adv.* en rond; *(fig.)* rondement.

roundness ['raundnis], *n.* rondeur; *(fig.)* franchise, *f.*

round trip, see return.

round-up ['raundʌp], *n.* rassemblement *(de bétail)*, *m.*; rafle *(de criminels)*, *f.*

roup [ru:p], *n.* pépie *(maladie de volaille)*, *f.*

rouse [rauz], *v.t.* éveiller, *(fig.)* réveiller, exciter.

rout [raut], *n.* cohue; déroute *(d'une armée)*, *f.* —*v.t.* mettre en déroute.

route [ru:t], *n.* itinéraire, parcours, *m.—v.t.* router *(circulation, colis etc.)*.

route map ['ru:tmæp], *n.* carte routière, *f.*

routine [ru:'ti:n], *n.* routine, *f.*

rove [rouv], *v.i.* rôder, courir.

rover ['rouvə], *n.* rôdeur, vagabond; pirate; *(Scouting)* éclaireur chevalier, *m.*

roving ['rouviŋ], *a.* errant, vagabond.

row (1) [rau], *n.* tapage, vacarme, *m.*; querelle, scène, *f.*

row (2) [rou], *n.* rang, *m.*, rangée, file; colonne *(de chiffres)*, *f.*

row (3) [rou], *n.* promenade en bateau, *f.—v.t.* *(Naut.)* faire aller à la rame.—*v.i.* ramer; *(Naut.)* nager.

rowan ['rauən], *n.* *(Sc.)* sorbier des oiseaux, *m.*

rowdy ['raudi], *a.* tapageur.—*n.* voyou, gredin, *m.*

rowdyism ['raudiizm], *n.* tapage, *m.*

rowdiness ['raudinis], *n.* tapage, *m.*

rower ['rouə], *n.* rameur; *(Naut.)* nageur, *m.*

rowing ['rouiŋ], *n.* canotage, *m.*

rowing-boat ['rouiŋbout], *n.* bateau à rames, *m.*

rowlock ['rʌlək], *n.* tolet, *m.*, dame, *f.*

royal ['rɔiəl], *a.* royal, de roi.

royalist ['rɔiəlist], *a.* and *n.* royaliste, *m.*, *f.*

royally ['rɔiəli], *adv.* royalement, en roi.

royalty ['rɔiəlti], *n.* royauté, *f.*; *(usu. pl.)* commission, *f.*, droit d'auteur, *m.*

rub [rʌb], *v.t.*, *v.i.* frotter; *(Med.)* frictionner. —*n.* frottement; coup de brosse, *m.*; *(fig.)* difficulté, *f.*, obstacle, *m.*

rubber (1) ['rʌbə], *n.* frotteur; frottoir *(chose)*, *m.*; *(pl.)* *(Am.)* caoutchoucs *(chaussures)*, *m.pl.*; **India rubber**, caoutchouc, *m.*, gomme (à effacer), *f.*

rubber (2) ['rʌbə], *n.* *(Cards)* rob, *m.*

rubber-stamp ['rʌbəstæmp], *n.* tampon; *(fig.)* béni-oui-oui, *m.—v.t.* ratifier.

rubbing ['rʌbiŋ], *n.* frottement; frottage, *m.*; *(Med.)* friction, *f.*

rubbish ['rʌbiʃ], *n.* débris, *m.pl.*; ordures, *f.pl.*; fatras *(sottises)*, *m.*

rubbish bin ['rʌbiʃbin], *n.* poubelle, *f.*

rubbish cart ['rʌbiʃka:t], *n.* tombereau, *m.*

rubbish dump ['rʌbiʃdʌmp], *n.* dépotoir, *m.*

rubbishy ['rʌbiʃi], *a.* de rebut, sans valeur.

rubble [rʌbl], *n.* blocaille, *f.*, moellons; décombres, *m.pl.*

rubicund ['ru:bikənd], *a.* rubicond.

rubric ['ru:brik], *n.* rubrique, *f.*

ruby ['ru:bi], *a.* de rubis, vermeil.—*n.* rubis, *m.*; teinte rouge, *f.*, incarnat, *m.*

ruck [rʌk], *n.* peloton *(de coureurs, cyclistes)*, *m.*

rucksack ['rʌksæk], *n.* sac à dos, *m.*

ruction ['rʌkʃən], *n.* *(colloq.)* bagarre, dispute, *f.*

rudder ['rʌdə], *n.* gouvernail, *m.*

ruddiness ['rʌdinis], *n.* rougeur, *f.*

ruddy ['rʌdi], *a.* rouge, au teint vermeil.

rude [ru:d], *a.* grossier, impoli; *(fig.)* rude, violent.

rudely ['ru:dli], *adv.* grossièrement; rudement.

rudeness ['ru:dnis], *n.* rudesse; grossièreté; insolence; violence, *f.*

rudiment ['ru:dimənt], *n.* rudiment, *m.*

rudimentary [ru:di'mentri], *a.* rudimentaire.

rue [ru:], *v.t.* se repentir de, regretter.

rueful ['ru:ful], *a.* triste; lamentable.

ruefully ['ru:fuli], *adv.* tristement, déplorablement.

ruff [rʌf], *n.* fraise, collerette, *f.*

ruffian ['rʌfiən], *n.* bandit, *m.*; brute, *f.*

ruffianism ['rʌfiənizm], *n.* brutalité, *f.*

ruffianly ['rʌfiənli], *a.* de brigand, brutal.

ruffle [rʌfl], *n.* manchette, ruche, *f.—v.t.* froncer *(le front etc.)*; froisser *(sentiments)*; ébouriffer *(les cheveux)*.

rug [rʌg], *n.* couverture, *f.*; tapis, *m.*

rugby ['rʌgbi], *n.* *(Spt.)* rugby, *m.*

rugged ['rʌgid], *a.* rude; raboteux; âpre; bourru *(personne)*.

ruggedness ['rʌgidnis], *n.* rudesse, âpreté, *f.*

ruin ['ru:in], *n.* ruine; perte, *f.—v.t.* ruiner.

ruination [ru:i'neiʃən], *n.* perte, *f.*

ruinous ['ru:inəs], *a.* ruineux; en ruine.

ruinously ['ru:inəsli], *adv.* ruineusement.

rule [ru:l], *n.* règle, *f.*; règlement; gouvernement, empire *(domination)*, *m.*; *(Law)* ordonnance, *f.*; **as a rule**, en général, d'ordinaire.—*v.t.* régler, diriger; gouverner, régir; *(Law)* décider.—*v.i.* gouverner; *(Law)* décider; **to rule over**, régner sur.

ruler ['ru:lə], *n.* gouvernant, souverain, *m.*; règle *(instrument)*, *f.*

ruling ['ru:liŋ], *a.* dominant, régnant, dirigeant.—*n.* *(Law)* ordonnance de juge, décision, *f.*

rum (1) [rʌm], *a.* drôle; *(colloq.)* cocasse.

rum (2) [rʌm], *n.* rhum, *m.*

Rumania [ru:'meinjə], la Roumanie, *f.*

Rumanian [ru:'meinjən], *a.* roumain.—*n.* roumain *(langue)*; Roumain *(personne)*, *m.*

rumba ['rʌmbə], *n.* rumba, *f.*

rumble [rʌmbl], *v.i.* gronder, gargouiller.

rumbling ['rʌmbliŋ], *a.* qui gronde; qui gargouille.—*n.* grondement; gargouillement, *m.*

rumbustious [rʌm'bʌstʃəs], *a.* *(fam.)* turbulent, tapageur.

ruminant ['ru:minənt], *a.* and *n.* ruminant, *m.*

ruminate ['ru:mineit], *v.i.* ruminer.

rumination [ru:mi'neiʃən], *n.* rumination, *f.*

rummage ['rʌmidʒ], *v.t., v.i.* fouiller.—*n.* remue-ménage, *m.*

rummage sale ['rʌmidʒseil], *n.* vente d'objets usagés, *f.*

rumor ['ru:mə], *n.* rumeur, *f.*; bruit, *m.*—*v.t.* faire courir le bruit de.

rump [rʌmp], *n.* croupe; culotte (*de viande*), *f.*; croupion (*de volaille*), *m.*

rumple [rʌmpl], *v.t.* chiffonner, froisser.—*n.* pli, *m.*, froissure, *f.*

rumpus ['rʌmpəs], *n.* (*colloq.*) tapage, *m.*

run [rʌn] (*stocking*), see **ladder**.

run [rʌn], *v.t. irr.* courir; encourir; faire courir, faire marcher, conduire (*machines*); pousser, enfoncer, diriger, exploiter, tenir; *to run down*, dénigrer (*décrier*); (*Hunt.*) forcer; *to run for*, courir chercher; *to run in*, enfoncer; arrêter, coffrer; (*Motor.*) roder; *to run out*, faire sortir; épuiser; *to run over*, (*Motor.*) écraser (*personne, animal*); *to run up*, monter en courant.—*v.i.* courir; accourir (*s'approcher*); se sauver (*s'échapper*); s'étendre; fuir (*bateau*); couler (*liquide*); se fondre (*couleurs*); fondre (*se dissoudre*); être (*exister*); courir, circuler; faire le service (*autobus etc.*); marcher, être en marche (*mécanisme*); s'écouler (*temps*); pleurer (*les yeux*); rouler (*avancer en tournant*); devenir; filer (*navire etc.*); suppurer (*ulcère etc.*); monter (*somme*); (*Am.*) se présenter (*aux élections*); *to run about*, courir çà et là; *to run after*, chercher; *to run against*, courir contre; *to run aground*, échouer; *to run at*, attaquer; *to run away*, se sauver, s'emballer (*cheval*); s'écouler (*liquide etc.*); *to run down*, descendre en courant, aller, venir, couler (*liquide*); s'arrêter (*mécanisme*); *to run from*, s'enfuir de; *to run for office*, see **stand**; *to run out*, courir dehors; couler; fuir; se terminer, expirer, tirer à sa fin; descendre (*marée*); *to run over*, déborder (*liquide etc.*); *to run through*, passer à travers de, parcourir; gaspiller; *to run up*, courir en haut, monter; *to run up to*, s'élever à, monter à.—*n.* course (*action de courir*), *f.*; cours (*série*); trajet, voyage, *m.*; durée, *f.*, succès (*vogue*), *m.*; irruption (*dans une banque etc.*), *f.*; commun (*généralité*), *m.*; *in the long run*, à la fin, à la fin.

runaway ['rʌnəwei], *a.* emballé (*cheval*).—*n.* fuyard; fugitif, déserteur, *m.*

rung (1) [rʌŋ], *n.* échelon (*d'échelle*); bâton (*de chaise etc.*), *m.*

rung (2) [rʌŋ], *p.p.* [RING (2)].

runner ['rʌnə], *n.* coureur; messager, courrier; (*Bot.*) rejeton, *m.*; *scarlet runner*, haricot d'Espagne, *m.*

running ['rʌniŋ], *a.* courant; de suite (*consécutivement*).—*n.* course, *f.*; écoulement (*d'eau*), *m.*

runt [rʌnt], *n.* bétail petit *ou* chétif; (*fig.*) avorton, nain, *m.*

runway ['rʌnwei], *n.* (*Av.*) piste d'envol, *f.*

rupee [ru:'pi:], *n.* roupie, *f.*

rupture ['rʌptʃə], *n.* rupture; (*Med.*) hernie, *f.*—*v.t.* rompre.—*v.i.* se rompre.

rural ['ruərəl], *a.* champêtre, rural, rustique.

ruse [ru:z], *n.* ruse, *f.*, stratagème, *m.*

rush (1) [rʌʃ], *n.* (*Bot.*) jonc, *m.*

rush (2) [rʌʃ], *n.* ruée, *f.*, mouvement précipité, *m.*; foule, presse (*gens*), *f.*—*v.t.* en-

traîner brusquement; dépêcher; envahir.—*v.i.* se jeter, se ruer, se précipiter (*sur*).

rushing ['rʌʃiŋ], *a.* impétueux.—*n.* élan, *m.*, précipitation, *f.*

rusk [rʌsk], *n.* biscotte, *f.*

russet ['rʌsit], *a.* roussâtre.—*n.* roux, *m.*; reinette grise (*pomme*), *f.*

Russia ['rʌʃə]. la Russie, *f.*

Russian ['rʌʃən], *a.* russe, de Russie.—*n.* russe (*langue*), *m.*; Russe (*personne*), *m., f.*

rust [rʌst], *n.* rouille, *f.*—*v.i.* se rouiller.

rustic ['rʌstik], *a.* rustique, champêtre.—*n.* rustre, paysan, *m.*

rusticate ['rʌstikeit], *v.t.* reléguer à la campagne; (*Univ.*) renvoyer temporairement.—*v.i.* se retirer à *ou* habiter la campagne.

rustication [rʌsti'keiʃən], *n.* villégiature, *f.*; (*Univ.*) renvoi temporaire, *m.*

rusticity [rʌs'tisiti], *n.* simplicité, rusticité, *f.*

rustiness ['rʌstinis], *n.* rouille, *f.*

rustle [rʌsl], *v.t.* (*Am.*) voler (*du bétail*).—*v.i.* bruire, frémir; faire frou-frou (*robe*); *to rustle against*, frôler.—*n.* frôlement; bruissement; frou-frou (*de robe*), *m.*

rustler ['rʌslə], *n.* (*Am.*) voleur de bétail, *m.*

rustless ['rʌstlis], *a.* inoxydable.

rustling ['rʌsliŋ], *a.* qui fait frou-frou, frémissant.—*n.* (*Am.*) vol de bétail, *m.*

rusty ['rʌsti], *a.* rouillé; roux (*couleur*).

rut [rʌt], *n.* ornière (*de route*), *f.*—*v.t.* sillonner d'ornières.

ruthless ['ru:θlis], *a.* impitoyable, insensible.

ruthlessly ['ru:θlisli], *adv.* sans pitié, sans merci.

ruthlessness ['ru:θlisnis], *n.* cruauté, inhumanité, *f.*

Rwanda ['rwʌndə]. le Rwanda, le Ruanda, *m.*

rye [rai], *n.* seigle, *m.*

rye grass ['raigra:s], *n.* ivraie, *f.*, ray-grass, *m.*

S

S, s [es]. dix-neuvième lettre de l'alphabet, *m.*

Saar [sɑ:]. la Sarre, *f.*

Sabbath ['sæbəθ], *n.* (*Jews*) sabbat; dimanche; (*fig.*) repos, *m.*

sabbatic [sə'bætik], **sabbatical** [sə'bætikəl], *a.* sabbatique, du sabbat.

saber ['seibə], *n.* sabre, *m.*—*v.t.* sabrer.

sable [seibl], *a.* de zibeline, de martre; (*Her.*) de sable.—*n.* martre, zibeline, *f.*; (*Her.*) sable, *m.*

sabot ['sæbou], *n.* sabot, *m.*

sabotage ['sæbətɑ:ʒ], *n.* sabotage, *m.*—*v.t.* saboter.

saboteur [sæbə'tə:], *n.* saboteur, *m.*

sac [sæk], *n.* (*Anat.*) sac, *m.*; bourse, *f.*

saccharine ['sækərin], *n.* saccharine, *f.*

sacerdotal [sæsə'doutl], *a.* sacerdotal.

sack (1) [sæk], *n.* sac, *m.*; *to get the sack*, (*colloq.*) être renvoyé; *to give the sack to*, renvoyer, congédier.—*v.t.* (*colloq.*) congédier.

sack (2) [sæk], *n.* sac, saccagement (*d'une ville*), *m.*—*v.t.* saccager, mettre à sac.

sackcloth

sackcloth ['sækkləθ], *n.* toile à sac, *f.*
sackful ['sækful], *n.* sac plein, *m.*, sachée, *f.*
sacking (1) ['sækiŋ], *n.* toile à sac, *f.*
sacking (2) ['sækiŋ], *n.* sac, saccagement (*de ville*), *m.*
sacrament ['sækrəmənt], *n.* sacrement, *m.*
sacramental [sækrə'mentl], *a.* sacramentel.
sacred ['seikrid], *a.* sacré; saint (*histoire etc.*); (*fig.*) inviolable.
sacredly ['seikridli], *adv.* saintement; religieusement.
sacredness ['seikridnis], *n.* sainteté, *f.*, caractère sacré, *m.*
sacrifice ['sækrifais], *v.t.*, *v.i.* sacrifier.—*n.* sacrifice, *m.*; victime, *f.*
sacrificer ['sækrifaisə], *n.* sacrificateur, *m.*
sacrificial [sækri'fiʃl], *a.* des sacrifices, sacrificatoire.
sacrilege ['sækrilidʒ], *n.* sacrilège, *m.*
sacrilegious [sækri'lidʒəs], *a.* sacrilège.
sacrilegiously [sækri'lidʒəsli], *adv.* d'une manière sacrilège.
sacrilegiousness [sækri'lidʒəsnis], *n.* caractère sacrilège, *m.*
sacristy ['sækristi], *n.* sacristie, *f.*
sacrosanct ['sækrosæŋkt], *a.* sacro-saint.
sad [sæd], *a.* triste; pitoyable; déplorable; cruel (*perte*)
sadden [sædn], *v.t.* attrister.—*v.i.* s'attrister.
saddle [sædl], *n.* selle, *f.*; *pack-saddle*, bât, *m.*; *side-saddle*, selle d'amazone.—*v.t.* seller; charger, accabler.
saddle-bag ['sædlbæg], *n.* sacoche, *f.*
saddle-bow ['sædlbou], *n.* arçon, *m.*
saddler ['sædlə], *n.* sellier, *m.*
saddle room ['sædlru:m], *n.* sellerie, *f.*
saddlery ['sædləri], *n.* sellerie, *f.*
sadism ['seidizm], *n.* sadisme, *m.*
sadist ['seidist], *n.* sadique, *m.*, *f.*
sadistic [sə'distik], *a.* sadique.
sadly ['sædli], *adv.* tristement; mal, beaucoup, grandement.
sadness ['sædnis], *n.* tristesse, *f.*
safe [seif], *a.* sauf, en sûreté; à l'abri (*de*); sûr; *safe and sound*, sain et sauf.—*n.* coffrefort (*pour l'argent*); garde-manger (*pour aliments*), *m.*
safe-conduct ['seif'kɔndʌkt], *n.* sauf-conduit, *m.*
safeguard ['seifgɑ:d], *n.* sauvegarde, *f.*—*v.t.* sauvegarder.
safe-keeping ['seif'ki:piŋ], *n.* bonne garde, sûreté, *f.*
safely ['seifli], *adv.* sain et sauf; en sûreté.
safety ['seifti], *a.* de sûreté.—*n.* sûreté, *f.*, salut, *m.*
safety catch ['seiftikætʃ], *n.* cran de sûreté, cran d'arrêt, *m.*
safety lamp ['seiftilæmp], *n.* lampe de sûreté, *f.*
safety match ['seiftimætʃ], *n.* allumette suédoise, *f.*
safety pin ['seiftipin], *n.* épingle de sûreté, *f.*
safety valve ['seiftivælv], *n.* soupape de sûreté, *f.*
saffron ['sæfrən], *a.* couleur safran; de safran. —*n.* safran, *m.*
saffrony ['sæfrəni], *a.* safrané.
sag [sæg], *v.i.* plier, ployer, s'affaisser; se relâcher (*câble*).
saga ['sɑ:gə], *n.* saga, *f.*

sagacious [sə'geiʃəs], *a.* sagace; intelligent (*animal*).
sagaciously [sə'geiʃəsli], *adv.* avec sagacité.
sagaciousness [sə'geiʃəsnis], **sagacity** [sə'gæsiti], *n.* sagacité, *f.*
sage (1) [seidʒ], *a.* sage, prudent.—*n.* sage, *m.*
sage (2) [seidʒ], *n.* sauge (*herbes*), *f.*
sagely ['seidʒli], *adv.* sagement, prudemment.
sagging ['sægiŋ], *a.* affaissé, fléchi, ployé.— *n.* courbure, *f.*, affaissement, *m.*; baisse (*de prix*), *f.*
sago ['seigou], *n.* sagou; sagouier, sagoutier (*arbre*), *m.*
sagy ['seidʒi], *a.* qui a un goût de sauge.
Sahara [sə'hɑ:rə], **the.** le Sahara, *m.*
said [sed], *a.* dit, susdit [SAY].
sail [seil], *n.* voile, *f.*; (*collect.*) voiles, *f.pl.*, voilure, *f.*; aile (*de moulin à vent*); course *ou* promenade à la voile (*sur l'eau*), *f.*—*v.t.* naviguer (*sur*), voguer (*sur ou dans*).—*v.i.* faire voile; cingler, naviguer; mettre à la voile, appareiller.
sailable ['seiləbl], *a.* navigable.
sail-cloth ['seilkləθ], *n.* toile à voiles, *f.*
sailing ['seiliŋ], *a.* à voiles.—*n.* navigation, *f.*; appareillage, *m.*; partance (*départ*), *f.*
sailing boat ['seiliŋbout], *n.* bateau à voiles, *m.*
sailing ship ['seiliŋʃip], *n.* bâtiment à voiles voilier, *m.*
sail-maker ['seilmeikə], *n.* voilier, *m.*
sailor ['seilə], *n.* marin, matelot, *m.*
saint [seint] *strong form*, [sənt] *weak form*, *n.* saint, *m.*, sainte, *f.*; *All Saints' Day*, la Toussaint, *f.*
saintliness ['seintlinis], *n.* sainteté, *f.*
saintly ['seintli], *a.* saint; de saint, vénérable.
sake [seik], *n.* (*used only with* FOR); *art for art's sake*, l'art pour l'art; *for God's sake*, pour l'amour de Dieu; *for the sake of appearances*, pour sauver les apparences; *for the sake of health*, pour cause de santé; *for your sake*, par égard pour vous.
sal [sæl], *n.* sel, *m.*
salaam [sə'lɑ:m], *n.* salamalec, *m.*
salad ['sæləd], *n.* salade, *f.*
salad bowl ['sælədboul], *n.* saladier, *m.*
salad oil ['sælədɔil], *n.* huile de table, *f.*
salamander ['sæləmændə], *n.* salamandre, *f.*
salaried ['sælərid], *a.* qui touche des appointements.
salary ['sæləri], *n.* appointements, *m.pl.*; traitement (*de fonctionnaire*), *m.*
sale [seil], *n.* vente; mise en vente, *f.*; *for sale*, à vendre; *on sale*, en vente; *private sale*, vente à l'amiable; *sale by auction*, vente aux enchères; *to put up for sale*, mettre en vente.
saleable ['seiləbl], *a.* vendable; de bonne vente.
sale-room ['seilru:m], *n.* salle des ventes, *f.*
salesman ['seilzmən], *n.* (*pl.* **-men** [men]) vendeur, marchand; courtier de commerce, *m.*
Salic ['sælik], *a.* salique.
salient ['seiliənt], *a.* and *n.* saillant, *m.*
saliently ['seiliəntli], *adv.* d'une manière saillante.
salify ['sælifai], *v.t.* salifier.
saline ['seilain], *a.* salin.
saliva [sə'laivə], *n.* salive, *f.*

salivate ['sæliveit], *v.t.* faire saliver.
sallow ['sælou], *a.* jaunâtre, jaune, blême.
sallowness ['sælounis], *n.* teint blême, *m.*
sally ['sæli], *n.* sortie; (*fig.*) excursion; saillie (*d'esprit*), *f.*—*v.i.* sortir, faire une sortie.
salmon ['sæmən], *n.* saumon, *m.*
salmon trout ['sæməntraut], *n.* truite saumonée, *f.*
saloon [sə'lu:n], *n.* (grand) salon, *m.*, salle; (*Am.*) buvette, *f.*, bar, *m.*; conduite-intérieure (*voiture*), *f.*
salsify ['sælsifi], *n.* (*Bot.*) salsifis, *m.*
salt [so:lt], *a.* salé; de sel.—*n.* sel, *m.*; *Epsom salts*, sels anglais, *m.pl.*—*v.t.* saler.
salt-cellar ['so:ltselə], *n.* salière, *f.*
salted ['so:ltid], *a.* salé; (*fig.*) aguerri.
salter ['so:ltə], *n.* saunier; saleur, *m.*
salting ['so:ltiŋ], *n.* salaison, *f.*, salage, *m.*
saltish ['so:ltiʃ], *a.* un peu salé, saumâtre.
saltless ['so:ltlis], *a.* sans sel; (*fig.*) insipide.
salt marsh ['so:ltma:ʃ], *n.* marais salant, *m.*
salt mine ['so:ltmain], *n.* mine de sel, *f.*
saltness ['so:ltnis], *n.* salure, *f.*
saltpeter [so:lt'pi:tə], *n.* salpêtre, *m.*
saltpeter-works [so:lt'pi:təwə:ks], *n.pl.* salpêtrière, *f.*
saltpetrous [so:lt'petrəs], *a.* salpêtreux.
salt water [so:lt'wo:tə], *n.* eau de mer, *f.*
salty ['so:lti], *a.* salé; qui a un goût de sel.
salubrious [sə'lju:briəs], *a.* salubre, sain.
salubriously [sə'lju:briəsli], *adv.* d'une manière salubre.
salubrity [sə'lju:briti], *n.* salubrité, *f.*
salutary ['sæljutəri], *a.* salutaire.
salutation [sælju'teiʃən], *n.* salut, *m.*, salutation, *f.*
salute [sə'lju:t], *n.* salut, *m.*, salutation, salve (*de fusils*), *f.*—*v.t.* saluer.
Salvador ['sælvədo:], El. le Salvador, *m.*
Salvadorean [sælvə'do:riən], *a.* salvadorègne.—*n.* Salvadorègne (*personne*), *m.*, *f.*
salvage ['sælvidʒ], *n.* sauvetage, *m.*, objets sauvés, *m.pl.*; (*Ind.*) récupération, *f.*—*v.t.* récupérer; relever (*navire*).
salvage money ['sælvidʒmʌni], *n.* prix *ou* droit de sauvetage, *m.*
salvage vessel ['sælvidʒvesl], *n.* navire de relevage, *m.*
salvation [sæl'veiʃən], *n.* salut, *m.*; *Salvation Army*, Armée du Salut, *f.*
salve [sælv, sa:v], *n.* onguent; (*fig.*) remède, baume, *m.*—[sælv], *v.t.* remédier à; (*Naut.*) sauver, sauveter.
salver ['sælvə], *n.* plateau, *m.*
salvo ['sælvou], *n.* réserve, restriction; salve (*d'artillerie*), *f.*
Samaritan [sə'mæritən], *a.* samaritain.—*n.* Samaritain (*personne*), *m.*, *f.*
same [seim], *a.* même.—*n.* le même, *m.*, la même; même chose, *f.*; ledit, *m.*, ladite, *f.*, lesdits, *m.pl.*, lesdites, *f.pl.*; *all the same*, néanmoins, quand même; *it is all the same*, c'est égal; *just the same*, tout de même; *much about the same*, à peu près de même; *the same to you*, et vous de même.
sameness ['seimnis], *n.* identité; uniformité, *f.*
sample [sa:mpl], *n.* échantillon, *m.*—*v.t.* échantillonner; déguster (*vin*).
sampler ['sa:mplə], *n.* modèle; (*Needlework*) canevas, *m.*

sampling ['sa:mpliŋ], *n.* échantillonnage, *m.*; gustation (*des mets*), *f.*
sanatorium [sænə'to:riəm], *n.* sanatorium, *m.*
sanctification [sæŋktifi'keiʃən], *n.* sanctification, *f.*
sanctified ['sæŋktifaid], *a.* sanctifié, saint.
sanctify ['sæŋktifai], *v.t.* sanctifier.
sanctimonious [sæŋkti'mouniəs], *a.* papelard, béat, hypocrite.
sanctimoniously [sæŋkti'mouniəsli], *adv.* d'un air béat.
sanctimoniousness [sæŋkti'mouniəsnis], *n.* dévotion affectée; cagoterie, *f.*
sanction ['sæŋkʃən], *n.* sanction, autorité, *f.*—*v.t.* sanctionner, autoriser.
sanctity ['sæŋktiti], *n.* sainteté, *f.*
sanctuary ['sæŋktjuəri], *n.* sanctuaire, asile, refuge, *m.*
sanctum ['sæŋktəm], *n.* sanctuaire; (*colloq.*) cabinet de travail, *m.*, retraite, *f.*
sand [sænd], *n.* sable; sablon (*sable fin*), *m.*; (*pl.*) plage, *f.*, bord de la mer, *m.*—*v.t.* sabler.
sandal [sændl], *n.* sandale, *f.*; santal, *m.*
sandbag ['sændbæg], *n.* sac de terre, *m.*
sand bank ['sændbæŋk], *n.* banc de sable, *m.*
sand drift ['sænddrift], *n.* amas de sable, *m.*
sand eel ['sændi:l], *n.* lançon, *m.*, équille, *f.*
sand glass ['sændgla:s], *n.* sablier, *m.*
sand martin ['sændma:tin], *n.* hirondelle de rivage, *f.*
sand-paper ['sændpeipə], *n.* papier de verre, *m.*—*v.t.* passer au papier de verre.
sand pit ['sændpit], *n.* sablière, sablonnière, *f.*
sand shoes ['sændʃu:z], *n.pl.* espadrilles, *f.pl.*
sandstone ['sændstoun], *n.* grès, *m.*
sand-storm ['sændsto:m], *n.* ouragan de sable, *m.*
sandwich ['sændwitʃ], *n.* sandwich, *m.*
sandwich man ['sændwitʃmən], *n.* (*pl.* **men** [men]) homme-sandwich, homme-affiche, *m.*
sandy ['sændi], *a.* sablonneux, de sable; d'un blond ardent, roux (*couleur*).
sane [sein], *a.* sain, sain d'esprit.
sanguinary ['sæŋgwinəri], *a.* sanguinaire.
sanguine ['sæŋgwin], *a.* sanguin; plein de confiance, confiant.
sanguineness ['sæŋgwinnis], *n.* confiance, assurance, *f.*
sanitary ['sænitəri], *a.* sanitaire, hygiénique; *sanitary napkin*, serviette hygiénique, *f.*
sanitation [sæni'teiʃən], *n.* assainissement, *m.*
sanity ['sæniti], *n.* état sain, jugement sain, *m.*
Sanskrit ['sænskrit], *a.* and *n.* sanscrit, *m.*
Santa Claus ['sæntə'klo:z]. Père Noël, *m.*
sap (1) [sæp], *n.* sève, *f.*
sap (2) [sæp], *n.* (*Mil.*) sape, *f.*—*v.t.* saper.
sapience ['seipiəns], *n.* sagesse, *f.*
sapient ['seipiənt], *a.* sage.
sapless ['sæplis], *a.* sans sève; sec, desséché.
sapling ['sæpliŋ], *n.* jeune arbre, baliveau, *m.*
saponaceous [sæpə'neiʃəs], *a.* saponacé.
saponify [sə'pɔnifai], *v.t.* saponifier.—*v.i.* se saponifier.
sapper ['sæpə], *n.* sapeur, *m.*
sapphic ['sæfik], *a.* and *n.* (*Pros.*) saphique, *m.*
sapphire ['sæfaiə], *n.* saphir, *m.*
sappiness ['sæpinis], *n.* abondance de sève, *f.*
sappy ['sæpi], *a.* plein de sève.
saraband ['særəbænd], *n.* sarabande, *f.*

Saracen ['særəsn], *a.* sarrasin.—*n.* Sarrasin, *m.*
sarcasm ['sɑːkæzm], *n.* sarcasme, *m.*
sarcastic [sɑːˈkæstik], *a.* sarcastique.
sarcastically [sɑːˈkæstikəli], *adv.* d'une manière *ou* d'un ton sarcastique.
sarcophagus [sɑːˈkɔfəgəs], *n.* sarcophage, *m.*
sardine [sɑːˈdiːn], *n.* sardine, *f.*
Sardinia [sɑːˈdinjə], la Sardaigne, *f.*
Sardinian [sɑːˈdinjən], *a.* sarde.—*n.* Sarde (*personne*), *m., f.*
sardonic [sɑːˈdɔnik], *a.* sardonique.
sarong [səˈrɔŋ], *n.* pagne, *m.*, jupe (*malaisien*), *f.*
sarsaparilla [sɑːsəpəˈrilə], *n.* salsepareille, *f.*
sash (1) [sæʃ], *n.* ceinture; écharpe (*décoration*), *f.*
sash (2) [sæʃ], *n.* châssis (*de fenêtre*), *m.*
sash window ['sæʃwindou], *n.* fenêtre à guillotine, *f.*
sassafras ['sæsəfræs], *n.* (*Bot.*) sassafras, *m.*
Satan ['seitən], Satan, *m.*
satanic [səˈtænik], **satanical** [səˈtænikəl], *a.* satanique.
satchel [sætʃl], *n.* sacoche, *f.*; sac d'écolier, cartable, *m.*
sate [seit], *v.t.* rassasier (*de*), assouvir.
satellite ['sætəlait], *n.* satellite, *m.*
satiate ['seiʃieit], *v.t.* rassasier (*de*).
satiated ['seiʃieitid], *a.* rassasié (*de*); gorgé.
satiety [səˈtaiəti], *n.* satiété, *f.*
satin ['sætin], *a.* de satin.—*n.* satin, *m.*
satin-wood ['sætinwuːd], *n.* bois de citronnier, *m.*
satire ['sætaiə], *n.* satire, *f.*
satiric [səˈtirik], **satirical** [səˈtirikəl], *a.* satirique.
satirist ['sætirist], *n.* satirique, *m., f.*
satirize ['sætiraiz], *v.t.* satiriser.
satisfaction [sætisˈfækʃən], *n.* satisfaction; réparation (*récompense*), *f.*
satisfactorily [sætisˈfæktərili], *adv.* d'une manière satisfaisante.
satisfactory [sætisˈfæktri], *a.* satisfaisant.
satisfy ['sætisfai], *v.t.* satisfaire; satisfaire à; acquitter (*dette*); assouvir (*passion*); rassasier (*de*) (*appétit*); **to be satisfied that**, être persuadé, être convaincu que; **to be satisfied with**, être satisfait de, être content de.—*v.i.* satisfaire, donner satisfaction.
satisfying ['sætisfaiiŋ], *a.* satisfaisant; nourrissant (*nourriture*).
saturate ['sætʃureit], *v.t.* saturer.
saturation [sætʃuˈreiʃən], *n.* saturation, *f.*
Saturday ['sætədei], samedi, *m.*
Saturn ['sætən], Saturne, *m.*
Saturnalia [sætəˈneiliə], saturnales, *f.pl.*
saturnine ['sætənain], *a.* sombre, taciturne.
satyr ['sætə], *n.* satyre, *m.*
sauce [sɔːs], *n.* sauce; (*fig.*) insolence, impertinence, *f.*—*v.t.* assaisonner; flatter (*le goût*); (*fig.*) dire des impertinences à.
sauce boat ['sɔːsbout], *n.* saucière, *f.*
saucer ['sɔːsə], *n.* soucoupe, *f.*; **flying saucer**, soucoupe volante.
saucepan ['sɔːspən], *n.* casserole, *f.*
saucily ['sɔːsili], *adv.* insolemment.
sauciness ['sɔːsinis], *n.* insolence, impertinence, *f.*
saucy ['sɔːsi], *a.* insolent, impertinent.
Saudi Arabia ['saudiəˈreibiə], l'Arabie Séoudite, *f.*
sauerkraut ['sauəkraut], *n.* choucroute, *f.*

saunter ['sɔːntə], *v.i.* flâner.—*n.* flânerie, *f.*
saunterer ['sɔːntərə], *n.* flâneur, *m.*
sauntering ['sɔːntəriŋ], *a.* de flâneur.—*n.* flânerie, *f.*
sausage ['sɔsidʒ], *n.* saucisse (*à cuire*), *f.*; saucisson (*salami etc.*), *m.*
sausage meat ['sɔsidʒmiːt], *n.* chair à saucisse, *f.*
sausage-roll ['sɔsidʒˈroul], *n.* friand, *m.*
savage ['sævidʒ], *a.* sauvage; féroce.—*n.* sauvage, *m., f.*—*v.t.* attaquer, mordre (*bête*).
savagely ['sævidʒli], *adv.* sauvagement, en sauvage; d'une manière féroce.
savageness ['sævidʒnis], *n.* férocité, brutalité; sauvagerie, *f.*
savagery ['sævidʒəri], *n.* férocité, barbarie, *f.*
savannah [səˈvænə], *n.* savane, prairie, *f.*
save [seiv], *v.t.* sauver (*de*); épargner (*argent etc.*); mettre de côté, économiser.—*v.i.* économiser, faire des économies.—*n.* (*Spt.*) arrêt, *m.*—*prep.* hormis, excepté, sauf.
saver ['seivə], *n.* sauveur, libérateur, *m.*; économe (*ménager*), *m., f.*
saving ['seiviŋ], *a.* économe, ménager.—*n.* épargne; économie, *f.*; salut, *m.*
savings bank ['seiviŋzbæŋk], *n.* caisse d'épargne, *f.*
savior ['seivjə], *n.* sauveur, *m.*
savor ['seivə], *n.* saveur, *f.*; goût, *m.*, odeur, *f.*—*v.t.* goûter, savourer.—*v.i.* avoir du goût; sentir.
savoriness ['seivərinis], *n.* goût agréable, *m.*, saveur, *f.*
savory ['seivəri], *a.* savoureux, appétissant.—*n.* plat épicé, *m.*
saw (1) [sɔː], *past* [SEE].
saw (2) [sɔː], *n.* scie, *f.*—*v.t., v.i. irr.* scier.
saw (3) [sɔː], *n.* adage, dicton (*proverbe*), *m.*
sawdust ['sɔːdʌst], *n.* sciure (de bois), *f.*
saw-mill ['sɔːmil], *n.* scierie, *f.*
sawyer ['sɔːjə], *n.* scieur, scieur de long, *m.*
saxifrage ['sæksifreidʒ], *n.* (*Bot.*) saxifrage, *f.*
Saxon ['sæksən], *a.* saxon, de Saxe.—*n.* saxon (*langue*); Saxon (*personne*), *m.*
saxophone ['sæksəfoun], *n.* saxophone, *m.*
say [sei], *v.t. irr.* dire; parler, répéter, réciter; **I say!** dites donc! **that is to say**, c'est-à-dire; **they say**, on dit.—*n.* dire, mot, ce qu'on a à dire, *m.*
saying ['seiiŋ], *n.* mot, proverbe, dicton, *m.*; sentence, maxime, *f.*
scab [skæb], *n.* croûte (*sur blessure etc.*); gale (*de mouton etc.*), *f.* [see **blackleg**]
scabbard ['skæbəd], *n.* fourreau, *m.*
scabbiness ['skæbinis], *n.* état galeux, *m.*
scabby ['skæbi], *a.* couvert de croûtes; galeux.
scabious ['skeibiəs], *a.* scabieux.—*n.* scabieuse (*plante*), *f.*
scaffold ['skæfəld], *n.* échafaud, *m.*—*v.t.* échafauder.
scaffolding ['skæfəldiŋ], *n.* échafaudage, *m.*
scald [skɔːld], *n.* brûlure, *f.*—*v.t.* échauder, ébouillanter.
scalding ['skɔːldiŋ], *n.* échaudage, *m.*
scalding-hot ['skɔːldiŋ'hɔt], *a.* tout bouillant.
scale (1) [skeil], *n.* échelle; (*Mus.*) gamme, *f.*—*v.t.* escalader.
scale (2) [skeil], *n.* écaille (*de poisson*), *f.*
scale (3) [skeil], *n.* bassin, plateau (*balance*), *m.*; **scales** or **pair of scales**, balance, *f.*

scale-maker ['skeilmeikə], *n.* balancier, *m.*
scalene ['skeili:n], *a.* scalène.
scaliness ['skeilinis], *n.* nature écailleuse, *f.*
scaling (1) ['skeiliŋ], *n.* escalade (*montagnes*), *f.*
scaling (2) ['skeiliŋ], *n.* écaillage (*peintures*), *m.*
scallop ['skɔləp], *n.* coquille Saint-Jacques; coquille; dentelure, *f.*, feston, *m.*—*v.t.* denteler; (*Needlework*) festonner.
scalp [skælp], *n.* cuir chevelu, *m.*, chevelure, *f.*, scalpe; (*fig.*) front, *m.*, tête, *f.*—*v.t.* scalper.
scalpel ['skælpəl], *n.* (*Surg.*) scalpel, *m.*
scaly ['skeili], *a.* écaillé; (*Bot.*) écailleux.
scamp [skæmp], *n.* chenapan, vaurien, *m.*; *young scamp*, petit polisson, *m.*—*v.t.* bâcler.
scamper ['skæmpə], *v.i.* courir, s'enfuir.—*n.* course rapide, *f.*
scampi ['skæmpi], *n.pl.* langoustine, *f.*
scan [skæn], *v.t.* scruter; (*Pros.*) scander; (*Rad.*) balayer.
scandal [skændl], *n.* scandale, *m.*; honte; médisance, *f.*
scandalize ['skændəlaiz], *v.t.* scandaliser, choquer; calomnier.
scandal-monger ['skændlmʌŋgə], *n.* médisant, *m.*
scandalous ['skændələs], *a.* scandaleux; honteux.
Scandinavia [skændi'neivjə], la Scandinavie, *f.*
Scandinavian [skændi'neivjən], *a.* scandinave.—*n.* Scandinave (*personne*), *m.*, *f.*
scanner ['skænə], *n.* scrutateur, *m.*; *radar scanner*, déchiffreur de radar, *m.*
scanning ['skæniŋ], *n.* examen minutieux, *m.*; (*Pros.*) scansion, *f.*; (*Rad.*) balayage, *m.*
scansion ['skænʃən], *n.* scansion, *f.*
scant [skænt], *a.* rare; rétréci; faible; peu de.
scantily ['skæntili], *adv.* faiblement, d'une manière insuffisante.
scantiness ['skæntinis], *n.* insuffisance (*de vivres etc.*); faiblesse (*de poids*), *f.*
scantling ['skæntliŋ], *n.* échantillon, *m.*; (*Carp.*) volige, *f.*, équarrissage, *m.*
scanty ['skænti], *a.* rétréci, faible, peu abondant, insuffisant; clairsemé (*cheveux*).
scapegoat ['skeipgout], *n.* bouc émissaire; (*fig.*) souffre-douleur, *m.*
scapegrace ['skeipgreis], *n.* vaurien, mauvais sujet, *m.*
scapement ['skeipmənt], *n.* échappement, *m.*
scapula ['skæpjulə], *n.* (*Anat.*) omoplate, *f.*
scapular ['skæpjulə], *a.* scapulaire.
scapulary ['skæpjuləri], *n.* (*R.-C. Ch.*) scapulaire, *m.*
scar [skɑː], *n.* cicatrice, balafre, *f.*—*v.t.* cicatriser; balafrer.
scarab ['skærəb], **scarabaeus** [skærə'bi:əs], *n.* scarabée, *m.*
scaramouch ['skærəmu:ʃ], *n.* scaramouche, *m.*
scarce [skeəs], *a.* rare; *to make oneself scarce*, disparaître, décamper, filer.
scarcely ['skeəsli], *adv.* à peine, presque pas, guère.
scarcity ['skeəsiti], *n.* rareté; disette (*famine*), *f.*
scare [skeə], *n.* panique, frayeur subite, *f.*—*v.t.* effrayer, épouvanter, effaroucher.

scarecrow ['skeəkrou], *n.* épouvantail, *m.*
scarf [skɑːf], *n.* (*pl.* **scarfs** [skɑːfs], **scarves** [skɑːvz]) écharpe, *f.*; cache-nez, *m.inv.*; foulard, *m.*
scarifier ['skærifaiə], *n.* scarificateur, *m.*
scarify ['skærifai], *v.t.* scarifier (*peau*), ameublir (*terre*).
scarlatina [skɑːlə'ti:nə], *n.* (fièvre) scarlatine, *f.*
scarlet ['skɑːlit], *a.* and *n.* écarlate, *f.*; *scarlet fever*, fièvre scarlatine, *f.*; *scarlet runner*, haricot d'Espagne, *m.*
scarp [skɑːp], *n.* (*Fort.*) escarpe, *f.*—*v.t.* escarper.
scarves [SCARF].
scatheless ['skeiðlis], *a.* sans dommage, sain et sauf.
scathing ['skeiðiŋ], *a.* acerbe, cinglant, cassant.
scatter ['skætə], *v.t.* disperser, dissiper; répandre, éparpiller.—*v.i.* se disperser, se répandre.
scattered ['skætəd], *a.* dispersé, éparpillé, épars.
scattering ['skætəriŋ], *n.* éparpillement; petit nombre, *m.*
scavenge ['skævindʒ], *v.t.* ébouer, balayer.
scavenger ['skævindʒə], *n.* boueur; balayeur, *m.*
scavenging ['skævindʒiŋ], *n.* ébouage, balayage, *m.*
scene [si:n], *n.* scène (*Theat.*) scène, décoration, *f.*; décor (*fig.*) théâtre, *m.*; *behind the scenes*, dans la coulisse; *scene shifter*, machiniste, *m.*,
scenery ['si:nəri], *n.* scène; (*fig.*) vue, perspective, *f.*, paysage, *m.*; (*Theat.*) décors, *m.pl.*
scenic ['si:nik], *a.* scénique.
scent [sent], *n.* odeur, senteur, *f.*, parfum; odorat; flair, nez (*de chien*), *m.*; voie (*de cerf*); (*fig.*) piste (*traces*), *f.*—*v.t.* parfumer (*de*); sentir, flairer (*animal*).
scent bottle ['sentbɔtl], *n.* flacon de parfum, *m.*
scentless ['sentlis], *a.* sans odeur, inodore.
scent spray ['sentsprei], *n.* vaporisateur, *m.*
sceptic ['skeptik], *n.* sceptique, *m.*, *f.*
sceptical ['skeptikl], *a.* sceptique.
scepticism ['skeptisizm], *n.* scepticisme, *m.*
sceptre ['septə], *n.* sceptre, *m.*
sceptred ['septəd], *a.* portant le sceptre.
schedule ['ʃedjuːl, (*Am.*) 'skedjuːl], *n.* liste, *f.*, inventaire; (*Comm.*) bilan; (*Law*) bordereau, *m.*—*v.t.* enregistrer, inventorier.
scheme [ski:m], *n.* arrangement, *m.*, combinaison, *f.*; projet, système, *m.*—*v.t.* projeter, combiner.—*v.i.* faire des projets; (*fig.*) intriguer.
schemer ['ski:mə], *n.* faiseur de projets; (*fig.*) intrigant, *m.*
scheming ['ski:miŋ], *a.* à projets; intrigant.—*n.* projets *m.pl.*, intrigues, *f.pl.*
schism [sizm], *n.* schisme, *m.*
schismatic [siz'mætik], *n.* schismatique, *m.*, *f.*
schizophrenia [skitso'fri:niə], *n.* (*Med.*) schizophrénie, *f.*
schizophrenic [skitso'fri:nik], *a.* and *n.* schizophrène, *f.*
scholar ['skɔlə], *n.* écolier; érudit, savant (*learned person*), *m.*; *day scholar*, externe, *m.*, *f.*

scholarly [ˈskɔləli], *a.* d'érudit, savant.
scholarship [ˈskɔləʃip], *n.* érudition, *f.*, savoir, *m.*; (*Univ. etc.*) bourse, *f.*
scholastic [skoˈlæstik], *a.* and *n.* scolastique, *m.*, *f.*
scholasticism [skoˈlæstisizm], *n.* scolastique, *f.*
school [skuːl], *n.* école; bande, troupe (*de baleines etc.*), *f.*; **at school**, en classe, à l'école; **boarding school**, pension, *f.*, pensionnat, *m.*; **primary school**, école primaire; **grammar school**, collège, lycée, *m.*; **nursery school**, école maternelle.—*v.t.* instruire, enseigner; réprimander.
schooled [skuːld], *a.* formé, entraîné, dressé.
schooling [ˈskuːliŋ], *n.* instruction; réprimande, *f.*
schoolmaster [ˈskuːlmɑːstə], *n.* instituteur, professeur, *m.*
schoolmistress [ˈskuːlmistris], *n.* maîtresse d'école, institutrice, *f.*
schooner [ˈskuːnə], *n.* (*Naut.*) goélette, *f.*
sciatic [saiˈætik], *a.* sciatique.
sciatica [saiˈætikə], *n.* sciatique, *f.*
science [ˈsaiəns], *n.* science, *f.*
scientific [saiənˈtifik], *a.* scientifique.
scientist [ˈsaiəntist], *n.* homme de science, savant, *m.*
Scilly Isles [ˈsiliailz], **the**, les Sorlingues, *f.pl.*
scimitar [ˈsimitə], *n.* cimeterre, *m.*
scintillant [ˈsintilənt], *a.* scintillant.
scintillate [ˈsintileit], *v.i.* scintiller.
scintillation [sintiˈleiʃən], *n.* scintillation, *f.*, scintillement, *m.*
scion [ˈsaiən], *n.* (*Bot.*) scion; (*fig.*) rejeton, *m.*
scission [ˈsiʃən], *n.* scission, *f.*
scissors [ˈsizəz], *n.pl.* ciseaux, *m.pl.*
scoff [skɔf], *n.* moquerie, *f.*, sarcasme, *m.*—*v.t.* se moquer de, bafouer.—*v.i.* railler.
scoffer [ˈskɔfə], *n.* moqueur, railleur, *m.*
scoffing [ˈskɔfiŋ], *a.* moqueur.—*n.* moquerie, dérision, *f.*
scoffingly [ˈskɔfiŋli], *adv.* par moquerie, en dérision.
scold [skould], *v.t.* gronder, criailler (*après*).—*v.i.* gronder.
scolding [ˈskouldiŋ], *a.* bougon.—*n.* semonce, *f.*
sconce [skɔns], *n.* candélabre (*fixé au mur*), *m.*; bobèche (*de bougeoir*), *f.*
scone [skɔn, skoun], *n.* petite galette (ronde), *f.*
scoop [skuːp], *n.* grande cuiller; (*Naut.*) écope; (*Journ. slang*) nouvelle à sensation, *f.*—*v.t.* vider, creuser; (*Naut.*) écoper.
scooter [ˈskuːtə], *n.* patinette, *f.*; scooter, *m.*
scope [skoup], *n.* portée, étendue; visée; liberté, *f.*
scorch [skɔːtʃ], *v.t.* brûler, roussir, griller.—*v.i.* se brûler.
scorching [ˈskɔːtʃiŋ], *a.* brûlant, très chaud.
score [skɔː], *n.* entaille, coche, *f.*; compte; vingt, *m.*, vingtaine, *f.*; (*Games*) nombre de points; (*fig.*) motif, *m.*, raison, cause; (*Mus.*) partition, *f.*; **on what score?** à quel titre ?—*v.t.* entailler, marquer; rayer; (*Mus.*) orchestrer; **to score out**, rayer, biffer (*texte*).—*v.i.* marquer des points.
scorer [ˈskɔːrə], *n.* marqueur, *m.*
scoring [ˈskɔːriŋ], *n.* (*Games etc.*) marque; (*Mus.*) orchestration, *f.*
scorn [skɔːn], *v.t.* mépriser; dédaigner.—*v.i.* mépriser; dédaigner (*de*); **to scorn to fly**,

dédaigner de fuir.—*n.* mépris, dédain, *m.* dérision, *f.*
scornful [ˈskɔːnful], *a.* méprisant, dédaigneux.
scornfully [ˈskɔːnfuli], *adv.* dédaigneusement, avec dédain.
scornfulness [ˈskɔːnfulnis], *n.* caractère dédaigneux, *m.*
scorpion [ˈskɔːpjən], *n.* scorpion, *m.*
Scot [skɔt], *n.* Écossais, *m.* ·
Scotch [skɔtʃ], *a.* écossais (*but used* ONLY *in certain fixed expressions, which include the following*) **Scotch terrier**, terrier griffon, *m.*; **Scotch** (**whisky**), whisky écossais, *m.*; [SCOTS].
scotch [skɔtʃ], *v.t.* entailler; enrayer (*roue*); (*fig.*) annuler.
scot-free [skɔtˈfriː], *a.* sans frais; (*fig.*) sain et sauf, indemne.
Scotland [ˈskɔtlənd], l'Écosse, *f.*
Scots [skɔts], **Scottish** [ˈskɔtiʃ], *a.* écossais; **Scots Law**, droit écossais, *m.*
Scotsman [ˈskɔtsmən], *n.* (*pl.* **-men** [men]) Écossais, *m.*
Scotswoman [ˈskɔtswumən], *n.* (*pl.* **-women** [wimin]) Écossaise, *f.*
Scottish [SCOTS].
scoundrel [ˈskaundrəl], *n.* gredin, coquin, scélérat, *m.*
scour (1) [ˈskauə], *v.t.* nettoyer, récurer, purger, écurer.—*v.i.* écurer; nettoyer.
scour (2) [ˈskauə], *v.t.* parcourir.—*v.i.* courir.
scourer [ˈskauərə], *n.* récureur, nettoyeur, *m.*
scourge [skəːdʒ], *n.* fouet; (*fig.*) fléau, *m.*—*v.t.* fouetter, flageller; (*fig.*) châtier.
scourger [ˈskəːdʒə], *n.* châtieur; (*Eccles. Hist.*) flagellant, *m.*
scourging [ˈskəːdʒiŋ], *n.* flagellation, *f.*
scouring [ˈskauəriŋ], *n.* récurage; nettoyage, *m.*
scout [skaut], *n.* éclaireur; scout, *m.*; (*Naut.*) vedette, *f.*; (*Av.*) avion de chasse, *m.*—*v.t.* repousser avec mépris.—*v.i.* aller en éclaireur.
scowl [skaul], *v.i.* se re(n)frogner, froncer le sourcil.—*n.* re(n)frognement, froncement de sourcil, *m.*
scowling [ˈskauliŋ], *a.* re(n)frogné, menaçant.
scrag [skræg], *n.* corps décharné, squelette, *m.*; **scrag-end**, bout saigneux (*de viande*), *m.*
scragginess [ˈskræginis], *n.* état raboteux, *m.*; maigreur, *f.*
scraggy [ˈskrægi], *a.* noueux, rugueux; rabougri.
scramble [skræmbl], *v.t.* (*Teleg.*) brouiller (*message*); **scrambled eggs**, œufs brouillés, *m.pl.*—*v.i.* grimper; se battre, se disputer.—*n.* mêlée, lutte, *f.*
scrap (1) [skræp], *n.* morceau, fragment, bout, *m.*; (*pl.*) bribes, *f.pl.*; restes, *m.pl.*—*v.t.* mettre au rebut.
scrap (2) [skræp], *n.* (*slang*) bagarre, rixe, *f.*
scrap-book [ˈskræpbuk], *n.* album, *m.*
scrape [skreip], *v.t.* gratter, érafler, râcler; décrotter (*bottes etc.*); (*Cook.*) ratisser; **to scrape together**, amasser petit à petit.—*v.i.* gratter; (*fam.*) râcler (*jouer du violon*); **to scrape through**, passer de justesse; **to bow and scrape**, faire des salamalecs.—*n.* grattage, *m.*; (*fig.*) difficulté, mauvaise affaire, *f.*

scraper ['skreipə], *n.* grattoir; râcloir, *m.*; (*Agric.*) ratissoire, *f.*; décrottoir (*pour chaussures*), *m.*

scrap heap ['skræphi:p], *n.* tas de ferraille, *m.*

scraping ['skreipiŋ], *n.* grattage, *m.*; ratissure (*de légumes*), *f.*; **with much bowing and scraping,** avec force révérences.

scrap iron ['skræpaiən], *n.* ferraille, *f.*

scratch [skrætʃ], *n.* égratignure, *f.*; coup de griffe *ou* d'ongle, *m.*; raie, rayure (*sur une surface polie*), *f.*—*v.t.* gratter; rayer (*surface polie*).—*v.i.* gratter; (*Spt.*) renoncer à concourir.

scratcher ['skrætʃə], *n.* égratigneur; grattoir (*instrument*), *m.*

scratching ['skrætʃiŋ], *n.* grattage, *m.*; égratignure; rayure, *f.*

scrawl [skrɔ:l], *n.* griffonnage, *m.*, pattes de mouche, *f.pl.*—*v.t.*, *v.i.* griffonner.

scrawler ['skrɔ:lə], *n.* griffonneur, *m.*

scrawny ['skrɔ:ni], *a.* décharné, émacié.

scream [skri:m], *n.* cri perçant, *m.*—*v.i.* crier, pousser des cris.

screamer ['skri:mə], *n.* crieur, *m.*

screaming ['skri:miŋ], *a.* perçant; qui crie.—*n.* cris, *m.pl.*

screech [skri:tʃ], *n.* cri perçant, *m.*—*v.i.* crier.

screech owl ['skri:tʃaul], *n.* effraie, chouette, *f.*

screen [skri:n], *n.* écran; paravent (*pliant*); rideau (*d'arbres etc.*), *m.*; (*fig.*) voile, *f.*, abri, *m.*; défense, *f.*—*v.t.* mettre à couvert; abriter (*contre*).

screw [skru:], *a.* à hélice.—*n.* vis; hélice (*de navire etc.*), *f.*—*v.t.* visser; (*fig.*) serrer (*presser*); pressurer (*opprimer*).—*v.i.* se visser.

screw bolt ['skru:boult], *n.* boulon à vis, *m.*

screw cap ['skru:kæp], *n.* couvercle à vis, *m.*

screw-driver ['skru:draivə], *n.* tournevis, *m.*

screw nail ['skru:neil], *n.* vis à bois, *f.*

screw nut ['skru:nʌt], *n.* écrou, *m.*

screw-wrench ['skru:rentʃ], *n.* clef anglaise, *f.*

scribble [skribl], *n.* griffonnage; barbouillage, *m.*—*v.t.*, *v.i.* griffonner.

scribbler ['skriblə], *n.* griffonneur; grattepapier, *m.*

scribe [skraib], *n.* scribe; écrivain, *m.*—*v.t.* (*Carp.*) tracer.

scrimmage ['skrimidʒ], *n.* lutte, rixe; (*Ftb.*) mêlée, *f.*

scrip [skrip], *n.* petit sac; (*Comm.*) titre *ou* certificat provisoire, *m.*

script [skript], *n.* manuscrit; (*Cine.*) scénario, *m.*

scriptural ['skriptʃuərəl], *a.* de l'Écriture Sainte, biblique, scriptural.

Scripture ['skriptʃə], *n.* l'Écriture Sainte, *f.*

script-writer ['skriptraitə], *n.* (*Cine.*) scénariste, *m.*, *f.*

scrofula ['skrɔfjulə], *n.* scrofule, *f.*

scrofulous ['skrɔfjuləs], *a.* scrofuleux.

scroll [skroul], *n.* rouleau, *m.*

scrounge [skraundʒ], *v.t.*, *v.i.* (*slang*) chiper, chaparder, grapiller; **to scrounge on someone,** vivre aux crochets de quelqu'un.

scrounger ['skraundʒə], *n.* chapardeur, *m.*

scrub [skrʌb], *v.t.*, *v.i.* frotter fort; laver, récurer.—*n.* broussailles, *f.pl.*; maquis, *m.*

scrubbing ['skrʌbiŋ], *n.* frottage, récurage, *m.*

scrubbing brush ['skrʌbiŋbrʌʃ], *n.* brosse de cuisine, *f.*

scrubby ['skrʌbi], *a.* rabougri, chétif, mal rasé.

scruff [skrʌf], *n.* nuque, *f.*

scruple [skru:pl], *n.* scrupule, *m.*—*v.i.* se faire scrupule (*de*), hésiter (*à*).

scrupulous ['skru:pjuləs], *a.* scrupuleux.

scrupulously ['skru:pjuləsli], *adv.* scrupuleusement.

scrupulousness ['skru:pjuləsnis], *n.* scrupule, doute, *m.*

scrutator [skru:'teitə], *n.* scrutateur, *m.*

scrutineer [skru:ti'niə], *n.* pointeur (*de votes*); scrutateur, *m.*

scrutinize ['skru:tinaiz], *v.t.* scruter, examiner à fond.

scrutinizing ['skru:tinaiziŋ], *a.* scrutateur, inquisiteur.

scrutiny ['skru:tini], *n.* enquête rigoureuse, vérification, *f.*

scud [skʌd], *n.* léger nuage, *m.*; course rapide, *f.*—*v.i.* s'enfuir; courir (*nuages*).

scuffle [skʌfl], *n.* bagarre, rixe, mêlée, *f.*—*v.i.* se battre; traîner les pieds.

scull [skʌl], *n.* rame; godille, *f.*—*v.i.* ramer.

scullery ['skʌləri], *n.* arrière-cuisine, laverie, *f.*; **scullery maid,** laveuse de vaisselle, *f.*

sculptor ['skʌlptə], *n.* sculpteur, *m.*

sculpture ['skʌlptʃə], *n.* sculpture, *f.*—*v.t.* sculpter.

scum [skʌm], *n.* écume, *f.*; (*fig.*) rebut (*ordures*), *m.*; lie, *f.*—*v.t.* écumer.

scupper ['skʌpə], *n.* (*Naut.*) dalot, *m.*—*v.t.* saborder.

scurf [ska:f], *n.* pellicules (*des cheveux*), *f.pl.*

scurfy ['ska:fi], *a.* pelliculeux (*cheveux*).

scurrility [skʌ'riliti], **scurrilousness** ['skʌriləsnis], *n.* grossièreté, *f.*

scurrilous ['skʌriləs], *a.* grossier, ordurier.

scurry ['skʌri], *n.* débandade, *f.*; tourbillon (*de poussière, de neige etc.*), *m.*—*v.i.* se hâter.

scurvily ['ska:vili], *adv.* bassement, vilement.

scurviness ['ska:vinis], *n.* état scorbutique, *m.*; (*fig.*) bassesse; mesquinerie (*avarice*), *f.*

scurvy ['ska:vi], *a.* scorbutique; (*fig.*) vil, vilain.—*n.* scorbut, *m.*

scut [skʌt], *n.* couette (*de lièvre etc.*), *f.*

scutcheon ['skʌtʃən], [ESCUTCHEON].

scuttle (1) [skʌtl], *n.* panier; seau à charbon, *m.*

scuttle (2) [skʌtl], *n.* (*Naut.*) hublot, *m.*; écoutille, *f.*—*v.t.* saborder.

scuttle (3) [skʌtl], *v.i.* aller à pas précipités.

scuttling ['skʌtliŋ], *a.* en fuite, qui détale.—*n.* sabordage, *m.*

scythe [saið], *n.* faux, *f.*—*v.t.* faucher.

sea [si:], *a.* de mer, marin, maritime.—*n.* mer; lame; (*fig.*) multitude, *f.*, déluge, *m.*; **at sea,** en mer; **heavy sea,** mer houleuse; **in the open sea,** en pleine mer, au grand large.

seaboard ['si:bɔ:d], *n.* littoral, rivage, *m.*, côte, *f.*

sea-borne ['si:bɔ:n], *a.* transporté par mer.

sea calf ['si:ka:f], *n.* veau marin, *m.*

sea cow ['si:kau], *n.* lamantin, *m.*

sea dog ['si:dɔg], *n.* loup de mer (*marin*), *m.*

seafarer ['si:fɛərə], *n.* homme de mer, marin, *m.*

seafaring ['si:fɛəriŋ], *a.* marin; **seafaring man,** marin, *m.*

sea-front ['si:frʌnt], *n.* esplanade, *f.*, bord de mer, *m.*

553

sea-gauge ['siːgeidʒ], *n.* tirant d'eau, *m.*
sea-going ['siːgouiŋ], *a.* de haute mer.
sea gull ['siːɡʌl], *n.* mouette, *f.*, goéland, *m.*
sea horse ['siːhɔːs], *n.* morse, *m.*
sea kale ['siːkeil], *n.* chou marin, *m.*
seal (1) [siːl], *n.* cachet; sceau (*officiel*), *m.*; (*Law*) scellés, *m.pl.*; **Privy Seal**, petit sceau.—*v.t.* cacheter; (*Law*) sceller; (*Customs*) plomber.
seal (2) [siːl], *n.* phoque, *m.*
sea legs ['siːlegz], *n.pl.* pied marin, *m.*
sea level ['siːlevəl], *n.* niveau de la mer, *m.*
sealing ['siːliŋ], *n.* action de sceller, *f.*
sealing wax ['siːliŋwæks], *n.* cire à cacheter, *f.*
sea lion ['siːlaiən], *n.* lion de mer, *m.*, otarie, *f.*
seam [siːm], *n.* (*Dress.*) couture; (*Mining*) couche; (*Geol.*) veine, *f.*—*v.t.* coudre; couturer.
seaman ['siːmən], *n.* (*pl.* **-men** [men]) marin, matelot, homme de mer, *m.*
seamanship ['siːmənʃip], *n.* matelotage, *m.*
seamless ['siːmlis], *a.* sans couture.
seamstress ['siːmstris], [SEMPSTRESS].
seamy ['siːmi], *a.* plein de coutures; **the seamy side of life**, les dessous de la vie, *m.pl.*
sea nymph ['siːnimf], *n.* néréide, *f.*
seaplane ['siːplein], *n.* hydravion, *m.*
seaport ['siːpɔːt], *n.* port de mer, *m.*
sear [siə], *a.* séché, fané, flétri.—*v.t.* brûler; cautériser; faner.
search [səːtʃ], *n.* recherche; (*Law*) perquisition; (*Customs*) visite, *f.*—*v.t.* chercher, examiner; fouiller; (*Law*) faire une perquisition chez; (*Customs*) visiter.—*v.i.* fouiller.
searcher ['səːtʃə], *n.* chercheur, *m.*
searching ['səːtʃiŋ], *a.* scrutateur, pénétrant; vif, perçant (*vent*).
searchingly ['səːtʃiŋli], *adv.* minutieusement.
searchlight ['səːtʃlait], *n.* projecteur, *m.*
search party ['səːtʃpɑːti], *n.* expédition de secours, *f.*
search warrant ['səːtʃwɔrənt], *n.* mandat de perquisition, *m.*
sea route ['siːruːt], *n.* voie de mer, *f.*
seascape ['siːskeip], *n.* (*Paint.*) marine, *f.*
Sea Scout ['siːskaut], *n.* (*boy-*)scout marin, *m.*
sea-shell ['siːʃel], *n.* coquillage, *m.*
seashore ['siːʃɔː], *n.* bord de la mer, rivage, *m.*, côte, *f.*
sea-sick ['siːsik], *a.* qui a le mal de mer.
sea-sickness ['siːsiknis], *n.* mal de mer, *m.*
seaside ['siːsaid], *n.* bord de la mer, *m.*
season [siːzn], *n.* saison, *f.*; (*fig.*) temps, moment opportun, *m.*—*v.t.* assaisonner (*de*); sécher (*bois*); (*fig.*) accoutumer (*à*).—*v.i.* s'acclimater; se sécher (*bois*).
seasonable ['siːznəbl], *a.* de saison; (*fig.*) à propos, opportun, convenable.
seasonably ['siːznəbli], *adv.* à propos.
seasonal ['siːzənəl], *a.* des saisons; saisonnier.
seasoned [siːznd], *a.* assaisonné (*viande*); (*fig.*) endurci, aguerri, acclimaté.
seasoning ['siːzniŋ], *n.* assaisonnement; séchage (*du bois*), *m.*
season ticket ['siːznˈtikit], *n.* carte d'abonnement, *f.*
seat [siːt], *n.* siège; banc, *m.*; banquette (*dans un véhicule*); (*fig.*) place; demeure (*château*), *f.*; théâtre (*de guerre*); fond (*de pantalon*), *m.*;

take your seats, please! en voiture!—*v.t.* asseoir; faire asseoir; placer.
seated ['siːtid], *a.* assis, placé.
sea wall ['siːwɔːl], *n.* digue, chaussée, *f.*
seaward ['siːwəd], *a.* tourné vers la mer.—*adv.* vers la mer.
seaweed ['siːwiːd], *n.* algue, *f.*, goémon, varech, *m.*
seaworthiness ['siːwəːðinis], *n.* navigabilité (*navire*), *f.*
seaworthy ['siːwəːði], *a.* en bon état (de navigation).
secant ['siːkənt], *a.* sécant.—*n.* sécante, *f.*
secede [siˈsiːd], *v.i.* se séparer (*de*).
seceder [siˈsiːdə], *n.* scissionnaire, *m.*, *f.*; dissident, *m.*
secession [siˈseʃən], *n.* sécession, séparation, *f.*
seclude [siˈkluːd], *v.t.* séparer; éloigner.
secluded [siˈkluːdid], *a.* retiré, isolé, solitaire.
seclusion [siˈkluːʒən], *n.* retraite, solitude, *f.*
second ['sekənd], *a.* second, deuxième; deux (*du mois*); inférieur; **on second thoughts**, à la réflexion.—*n.* témoin, second (*dans un duel*), *m.*; seconde (*temps*), *f.*—*v.t.* seconder, aider; appuyer (*une motion*); [siˈkɔnd] détacher (*fonctionnaire*).
secondary ['sekəndri], *a.* secondaire; accessoire.
seconder ['sekəndə], *n.* personne qui appuie, *f.*
second-hand ['sekəndˈhænd], *a.* and *adv.* d'occasion.
secondly ['sekəndli], *adv.* secondement; en second lieu.
second-rate ['sekəndreit], *a.* de second ordre.
secrecy ['siːkrəsi], *n.* secret, *m.*; discrétion, *f.*
secret ['siːkrit], *a.* secret; retiré (*maison etc.*). —*n.* secret, *m.*
secretarial [sekrəˈtɛəriəl], *a.* de secrétaire.
secretariat [sekrəˈtɛəriæt], *n.* secrétariat, *m.*
secretary ['sekrətri], *n.* secrétaire, *m.*, *f.*
secretaryship ['sekrətriʃip], *n.* secrétariat, *m.*
secrete [siˈkriːt], *v.t.* cacher; (*Physiol.*) sécréter.
secretion [siˈkriːʃən], *n.* sécrétion, *f.*
secretive ['siːkrətiv], *a.* réservé, dissimulé.
secretiveness ['siːkrətivnis], *n.* caractère cachottier, *m.*
secretly ['siːkrətli], *adv.* en secret; intérieurement.
sect [sekt], *n.* secte, *f.*
sectarian [sekˈtɛəriən], *a.* de sectaire.—*n.* sectaire, *m.*, *f.*
sectarianism [sekˈtɛəriənizm], *n.* esprit de secte, sectarisme, *m.*
section ['sekʃən], *n.* section; coupe, *f.*, profil; (*Mil.*) groupe de combat, *m.*
sectional ['sekʃənəl], *a.* en coupe; en sections.
sector ['sektə], *n.* secteur, *m.*
secular ['sekjulə], *a.* temporel; laïque; séculaire (*année*).
secularity [sekjuˈlæriti], **secularness** ['sekjulənis], *n.* sécularité, mondanité, *f.*
secularization [sekjuləraiˈzeiʃən], *n.* sécularisation, *f.*
secularize ['sekjuləraiz], *v.t.* séculariser.
secure [siˈkjuə], *a.* dans la sécurité, en sûreté; sûr, assuré (*chose*); bien fermé.— *v.t.* mettre en sûreté; assurer (*garantir*); s'assurer de; fermer; barrer (*attacher fortement*); (*fig.*) affermir.
securely [siˈkjuəli], *adv.* en sûreté; sûrement; fortement.

self-preservation

secureness [si'kjuənis], *n.* sécurité, *f.*
security [si'kjuəriti], *n.* sécurité, sûreté; garantie, *f.*; (*pl.*) titres, *m.pl.*, valeurs, *f.pl.*; (*Law*) caution, *f.*
sedan [si'dæn] (*Motor.*), see **saloon.**
sedate [si'deit], *a.* posé, calme, rassis.
sedately [si'deitli], *adv.* posément, avec calme.
sedateness [si'deitnis], *n.* calme, *m.*
sedative ['sedətiv], *a.* and *n.* sédatif, *m.*
sedentary ['sedntri], *a.* sédentaire; inactif.
sedge [sedʒ], *n.* laîche, *f.*, jonc, *m.*
sediment ['sedimənt], *n.* sédiment, dépôt, *m.*
sedition [si'diʃən], *n.* sédition, *f.*
seditious [si'diʃəs], *a.* séditieux.
seditiousness [si'diʃəsnis], *n.* esprit séditieux, *m.*
seduce [si'dju:s], *v.t.* séduire.
seducer [si'dju:sə], *n.* séducteur, *m.*
seducing [si'dju:siŋ], *a.* séduisant.
seduction [si'dʌkʃən], *n.* séduction, *f.*
seductive [si'dʌktiv], *a.* séducteur, séduisant.
sedulity [si'dju:liti], **sedulousness** ['sedjuləsnis], *n.* assiduité, diligence, *f.*
sedulous ['sedjuləs], *a.* assidu, diligent, zélé.
sedulously ['sedjuləsli], *adv.* assidûment, diligemment, avec application.
sedulousness [SEDULITY].
see (1) [si:], *n.* siège épiscopal, évêché; archevêché (*d'un archevêque*), *m.*; **the Holy See,** le Saint-Siège, *m.*
see (2) [si:], *v.t. irr.* voir; comprendre; accompagner, conduire.—*v.i.* voir; s'occuper (*de*); *I will see to it,* j'y veillerai.
seed [si:d], *n.* semence; graine (*de légumes*); (*fig.*) race, *f.*; **to run to seed,** monter en graine.—*v.t.* ensemencer; (*Spt.*) trier.—*v.i.* grener.
seed bed ['si:dbed], *n.* semis, *m.*
seed cake ['si:dkeik], *n.* gâteau à l'anis, *m.*
seedling ['si:dliŋ], *n.* semis, sauvageon, *m.*
seedsman ['si:dzmən], *n.* (*pl.* **-men** [men]) grainetier, *m.*
seed-time ['si:dtaim], *n.* semailles, *f.pl.*
seedy ['si:di], *a.* râpé, usé (*vêtement*); souffrant; miteux.
seeing ['si:iŋ], *n.* vue; vision, *f.*—*conj. phr.* **seeing that,** vu que, puisque.
seek [si:k], *v.t. irr.* chercher; poursuivre, en vouloir à (*la vie etc.*).—*v.i.* chercher.
seeker ['si:kə], *n.* chercheur, *m.*
seeking ['si:kiŋ], *n.* recherche, poursuite, *f.*
seem [si:m], *v.i.* sembler, paraître, avoir l'air (*de*).
seeming ['si:miŋ], *a.* apparent, spécieux.—*n.* semblant, *m.*, apparence, *f.*, dehors, *m.*
seemingly ['si:miŋli], *adv.* en apparence, apparemment.
seemliness ['si:mlinis], *n.* bienséance; convenance, *f.*
seemly ['si:mli], *a.* bienséant, convenable, joli.—*adv.* convenablement.
seep [si:p], *v.i.* s'infiltrer, suinter.
seer ['si:ə], *n.* prophète, voyant, *m.*
seesaw ['si:so:], *n.* bascule, balançoire, *f.*, va-et-vient, *m.*—*v.i.* faire la bascule.
seethe [si:ð], *v.t.* faire bouillir.—*v.i.* bouillir, bouillonner.
segment ['segmənt], *n.* segment, *m.*
segregate ['segrigeit], *v.t.* séparer.—*v.i.* se diviser.

segregation [segri'geiʃən], *n.* séparation, ségrégation, *f.*
seize [si:z], *v.t.* saisir; se saisir de, s'emparer de; (*Naut.*) amarrer.—*v.i.* (*Mech.*) gripper, caler; se coincer.
seizure ['si:ʒə], *n.* saisie, prise de possession; (*Path.*) attaque, *f.*
seldom ['seldəm], *adv.* rarement.
select [si'lekt], *a.* choisi; d'élite.—*v.t.* choisir.
selection [si'lekʃən], *n.* choix, *m.*
selectness [si'lektnis], *n.* excellence, *f.*
self [self], *pron.* (*pl.* **selves** [selvz]) même, soi-même; (*reflexively*) se.—*n.* le moi, individu, *m.*, personne, *f.*
self-assertion ['selfə'sə:ʃən], *n.* caractère impérieux, *m.*, outrecuidance, *f.*
self-assertive ['selfə'sə:tiv], *a.* autoritaire, outrecuidant.
self-centered['self'sentəd], *a.* égocentrique.
self-confidence ['self'kɔnfidəns], *n.* confiance en soi-même, assurance, *f.*
self-confident ['self'kɔnfidənt], *a.* sûr de soi-même.
self-conscious ['self'kɔnʃəs], *a.* embarrassé, intimidé; gêné.
self-consciousness ['self'kɔnʃəsnis], *n.* embarras, *m.*, gêne, *f.*
self-contained ['selfkən'teind], *a.* indépendant; avec entrée particulière (*appartement*).
self-control ['selfkən'troul], *n.* sang-froid, *m.*; maîtrise de soi, *f.*
self-defense ['selfdi'fens], *n.* défense personnelle; légitime défense, *f.*
self-denial ['selfdi'naiəl], *n.* abnégation, *f.*; désintéressement, *m.*
self-denying ['selfdi'naiiŋ], *a.* qui fait abnégation de soi.
self-educated ['self'edjukeitid], *a.* autodidacte.
self-esteem ['selfi'sti:m], *n.* amour-propre, *m.*
self-evident ['self'evidənt], *a.* évident en soi, qui saute aux yeux.
self-governed ['self'gʌvənd], *a.* indépendant, autonome.
self-government ['self'gʌvənmənt], *n.* autonomie, *f.*
self-help ['self'help], *n.* efforts personnels, *m.pl.*
self-importance ['selfim'pɔ:təns], *n.* suffisance, vanité, *f.*
self-important ['selfim'pɔ:tənt], *a.* plein de soi, suffisant.
self-inflicted ['selfin'fliktid], *a.* volontaire.
selfish ['selfiʃ], *a.* égoïste.
selfishly ['selfiʃli], *adv.* en égoïste, d'une manière égoïste.
selfishness ['selfiʃnis], *n.* égoïsme, *m.*
selfless ['selflis], *a.* désintéressé.
self-made ['self'meid], *a.* qui s'est fait ce qu'il est; **he is a self-made man,** il est fils de ses œuvres.
self-opinioned ['selfə'pinjənd], **self-opinionated** ['selfə'pinjəneitid], *a.* entêté.
self-possessed ['selfpə'zest], *a.* calme; maître de soi.
self-possession ['selfpə'zeʃən], *n.* sang-froid, aplomb, *m.*
self-praise ['self'preiz], *n.* éloge de soi-même, *m.*
self-preservation ['selfprezə'veiʃən], *n.* conservation de soi-même, *f.*

self-propelled [ˈselfprəˈpeld], *a.* autopropulsé.
self-registering [ˈselfˈredʒistriŋ], *a.* à registre, enregistreur.
self-reliance [ˈselfriˈlaiəns], *n.* confiance en soi, indépendance, *f.*
self-respect [ˈselfrisˈpekt], *n.* respect de soi-même, amour-propre, *m.*; dignité, *f.*
self-righteous [ˈselfˈraitʃəs], *a.* pharisaïque.
self-sacrifice [ˈselfˈsækrifais], *n.* sacrifice de soi-même, *m.*, abnégation, *f.*
self-same [ˈselfseim], *a.* absolument le même.
self-satisfied [ˈselfˈsætisfaid], *a.* content de soi.
self-seeking [ˈselfˈsiːkiŋ], *a.* égoïste.
self-service [ˈselfˈsəːvis], *n.* libre service, self-service, *m.*
self-starter [ˈselfˈstɑːtə], *n.* démarreur automatique, *m.*
self-styled [ˈselfˈstaild], *a.* soi-disant, prétendu.
self-sufficiency [ˈselfsəˈfiʃənsi], *n.* suffisance; indépendance, *f.*
self-sufficient [ˈselfsəˈfiʃənt], *a.* suffisant; indépendant.
self-supporting [ˈselfsəˈpɔːtiŋ], *a.* qui subsiste par ses propres moyens.
self-taught [ˈselfˈtɔːt], *a.* autodidacte.
self-will [ˈselfˈwil], *n.* obstination, opiniâtreté, *f.*
self-willed [ˈselfˈwild], *a.* obstiné, opiniâtre.
sell [sel], *v.t. irr.* vendre.—*v.i.* se vendre; **to be sold out of an article**, avoir tout vendu, ne plus avoir d'un article.—*n.* attrape, *f.*
seller [ˈselə], *n.* vendeur, *m.*, vendeuse, *f.*
selling [ˈseliŋ], *n.* vente, *f.*; **selling off**, liquidation, *f.*
seltzer [ˈseltsə], **seltzer water** [ˈseltsəˈwɔːtə], *n.* eau de Seltz, *f.*
selvedge [ˈselvidʒ], *n.* lisière, *f.*
selves [SELF].
semaphore [ˈseməfɔː], *n.* sémaphore, *m.*
semblance [ˈsembləns], *n.* semblant, *m.*, apparence, *f.*
semi [ˈsemi], *pref.* semi, demi, à demi, à moitié.
semibreve [ˈsemibriːv], *n.* (*Mus.*) ronde, *f.*
semi-circle [ˈsemisəːkl], *n.* demi-cercle, *m.*
semicolon [ˈsemiˈkoulən], *n.* point-virgule, *m.*
semi-detached [ˈsemidiˈtætʃt], *a.* **semi-detached houses**, maisons jumelles, *f.pl.*
semi-final [ˈsemifainl], *n.* demi-finale, *f.*
seminary [ˈseminəri], *n.* séminaire, *m.*; institution (*école*), *f.*
semi-official [ˈsemiəˈfiʃl], *a.* demi-officiel, officieux.
semiquaver [ˈsemikweivə], *n.* (*Mus.*) double croche, *f.*
semitone [ˈsemitoun], *n.* (*Mus.*) demi-ton, semi-ton, *m.*
semolina [seməˈliːnə], *n.* semoule, *f.*
sempstress [ˈsempstris, ˈsemstris], *n.* couturière, *f.*
senate [ˈsenit], *n.* sénat, *m.*
senator [ˈsenitə], *n.* sénateur, *m.*
senatorial [seniˈtɔːriəl], *a.* sénatorial.
send [send], *v.t. irr.* envoyer, faire parvenir; expédier (*marchandises*); **to send away**, renvoyer, congédier; **to send back**, renvoyer; **to send for**, envoyer chercher, faire venir; **to send forth**, lancer, émettre; **to**

send in, faire entrer; **to send on**, faire suivre (*lettres etc.*).—*v.i.* envoyer.
sender [ˈsendə], *n.* envoyeur; (*Comm.*) expéditeur, *m.*
Senegal [ˈsenigɔːl]. le Sénégal, *m.*
Senegalese [senigəˈliːz], *a.* sénégalais.—*n.* Sénégalais (*personne*), *m.*
senile [ˈsiːnail], *a.* de vieillard, sénile.
senility [səˈniliti], *n.* sénilité, *f.*
senior [ˈsiːnjə], *a.* aîné; ancien; plus ancien, supérieur.—*n.* aîné; ancien; doyen, *m.*
seniority [siːniˈɔriti], *n.* priorité d'âge; ancienneté, *f.*
senna [ˈsenə], *n.* séné, *m.*
sensation [senˈseiʃən], *n.* sensation, *f.*
sensational [senˈseiʃənl], *a.* à sensation, à effet.
sensationalism [senˈseiʃənlizm], *n.* recherche du sensationnel, *f.*
sense [sens], *n.* sens; bon sens, sens commun; sentiment, *m.*; signification, *f.*
senseless [ˈsenslis], *a.* sans connaissance, insensible; insensé, absurde (*pas raisonnable*).
senselessly [ˈsenslisli], *adv.* d'une manière insensée; sottement.
senselessness [ˈsenslisnis], *n.* sottise, absurdité, *f.*
sensibility [sensiˈbiliti], *n.* sensibilité, *f.*; sentiment, *m.*
sensible [ˈsensibl], *a.* sensé, raisonnable (*intelligent*); sensible (*de*); en pleine connaissance.
sensibly [ˈsensibli], *adv.* sensiblement; sensément, sagement (*avec intelligence*).
sensitive [ˈsensitiv], *a.* sensible (*à*); sensitif, impressionnable; susceptible (*ombrageux*).
sensitiveness [ˈsensitivnis], **sensitivity** [sensiˈtiviti], *n.* sensibilité; susceptibilité (*facilité à se vexer etc.*), *f.*
sensitized [ˈsensitaizd], *a.* (*Phot.*) sensible (*papier*).
sensory [ˈsensəri], *a.* sensoriel, des sens.
sensual [ˈsensjuəl], *a.* sensuel; des sens.
sensualist [ˈsensjuəlist], *n.* sensualiste, *m.*, *f.*, sensuel, *m.*
sensuality [sensjuˈæliti], *n.* sensualité, *f.*
sentence [ˈsentəns], *n.* phrase; maxime, *f.*; jugement, arrêt, *m.*, sentence, *f.*—*v.t.* prononcer une sentence *ou* un jugement (*contre*), condamner.
sententious [senˈtenʃəs], *a.* sentencieux.
sententiousness [senˈtenʃəsnis], *n.* caractère sentencieux, *m.*
sentient [ˈsenʃənt], *a.* sensible.
sentiment [ˈsentimənt], *n.* sentiment; avis, *m.*, pensée, *f.*
sentimental [sentiˈmentl], *a.* sentimental.
sentimentality [sentimenˈtæliti], *n.* sensiblerie, sentimentalité, *f.*
sentinel [ˈsentinl], **sentry** [ˈsentri], *n.* sentinelle, *f.*, factionnaire, *m.*
sentry box [ˈsentribɔks], *n.* guérite, *f.*
separable [ˈsepərəbl], *a.* séparable, divisible.
separate [ˈsepərit], *a.* séparé; disjoint, désuni.—[ˈsepəreit], *v.t.* séparer; disjoindre, désunir.—*v.i.* se séparer; se disjoindre.
separately [ˈsepəritli], *adv.* séparément, à part.
separation [sepəˈreiʃən], *n.* séparation; désunion, *f.*
sepia [ˈsiːpjə], *n.* sépia (*couleur*); seiche (*poisson*), *f.*

556

sepoy ['si:pɔi], n. cipaye, m.
September [sep'tembə]. septembre, m.
septennial [sep'teniəl], a. septennal.
septennially [sep'teniəli], adv. tous les sept ans.
septic ['septik], a. septique; infecté (blessure).
septuagenarian [septjuədʒə'nɛəriən], a. and n. septuagénaire, m., f.
Septuagesima [septjuə'dʒesimə]. Septuagésime, f.
sepulchral [si'pʌlkrəl], a. sépulcral.
sepulchre ['sepəlkə], n. sépulcre, m.
sepulture ['sepəltʃə], n. sépulture; inhumation, f.
sequel ['si:kwəl], n. suite, conséquence, f.
sequence ['si:kwəns], n. suite, série; succession; (Cine.) séquence, f.
sequester [si'kwestə], v.t. séquestrer.
sequestered [si'kwestəd], a. retiré, écarté; (Law) en séquestre.
sequestrate ['si:kwəstreit, si'kwestreit], v.t. séquestrer.
sequestration [si:kwəs'treiʃən], n. séquestre, m.; retraite, f., isolement (personne), m.
sequestrator ['si:kwəstreitə], n. (Law) séquestre, m.
sequin ['si:kwin], n. sequin, m.
seraglio [se'rɑ:ljou], n. sérail, m.
seraph ['serəf], n. (pl. seraphim ['serəfim]) séraphin, m.
seraphic [sə'ræfik], a. séraphique.
Serbia ['sə:biə]. la Serbie, f.
Serbian ['sə:biən], a. serbe.—n. serbe (langue), m.; Serbe (personne), m., f.
sere [SEAR].
serenade [serə'neid], n. sérénade, f.—v.t. donner une sérénade à.
serene [si'ri:n], a. serein, calme; sérénissime (titre).
serenely [si'ri:nli], adv. avec sérénité.
sereneness [si'ri:nnis], serenity [si'reniti], n. sérénité, f., calme, m.
serf [sə:f], n. serf, m.
serfdom ['sə:fdəm], n. servage, m.
serge [sə:dʒ], n. serge, f.
sergeant, serjeant ['sɑ:dʒənt], n. sergent (infanterie); maréchal des logis (cavalerie, artillerie); brigadier (police), m.
sergeant major ['sɑ:dʒənt'meidʒə], n. adjudant, m.
serial ['siəriəl], a. paraissant par numéros ou par livraisons; serial (story), (roman-) feuilleton, m.
serially ['siəriəli], adv. par numéros.
seriatim [siəri'eitim], adv. par série; successivement.
series ['siəri:z], n. série, suite, succession, f.
serious ['siəriəs], a. sérieux; grave.
seriously ['siəriəsli], adv. sérieusement; gravement.
seriousness ['siəriəsnis], n. sérieux, m.; gravité, f.
serjeant [SERGEANT].
sermon ['sə:mən], n. sermon, m.
sermonize ['sə:mənaiz], v.t. prêcher; sermonner.
sermonizer ['sə:mənaizə], n. sermonneur, m.
serpent ['sə:pənt], n. serpent, m.
serpentine ['sə:pəntain], a. serpentin, sinueux.—n. (Min.) serpentine, f.
serrate ['sereit], a. en scie, dentelé; serraté.

serration [se'reiʃən], n. dentelure, f.
serried ['serid], a. compact, serré.
serum ['siərəm], n. sérum, m.
servant ['sə:vənt], n. serviteur, m., servante, f.; employé (de compagnies etc.), m.; domestique, m.; ordonnance (d'officier), m., f.; civil servant, fonctionnaire, m., f.
serve [sə:v], v.t. servir; servir à, être bon à; faire (apprentissage); desservir (localité); signifier (une assignation); it serves him right, c'est bien fait.—v.i. servir; être au service; suffire.—n. (fam.) (Ten.) service, m.
server ['sə:və], n. servant; (Ten.) serveur; (Eccles.) acolyte, m.
service ['sə:vis], n. service; (fig.) avantage, m.; utilité; signification (d'assignation); (Mil.) arme, f.—v.t. (Motor.) entretenir, réparer.
serviceable ['sə:visəbl], a. utile (à), avantageux, de bon usage.
serviceableness ['sə:visəblnis], n. utilité, f.
service station ['sə:vissteiʃən], n. station-service, f.
serviette [sə:vi'et], n. serviette de table, f.
servile ['sə:vail], a. servile; asservi.
servility [sə:'viliti], n. servilité, bassesse, f.
serving ['sə:vin], a. servant, qui sert.
servitude ['sə:vitju:d], n. servitude, f., asservissement, m.; penal servitude, travaux forcés, m.pl.
sesame ['sesəmi], n. sésame, m.
session ['seʃən], n. session, séance, f.; (pl.) assises, f.pl.
set [set], v.t. irr. poser, opposer (sceau, signature), mettre, placer, poster; planter (fleurs); fixer; ajuster, arranger (régler); affûter (outil); donner (exemple); (Mus.) mettre en musique; remettre (os); sertir (pierre précieuse); dresser, tendre (piège); déployer (voiles); (Print.) composer; to set aside, mettre de côté; to set at ease, mettre à l'aise; to set back, reculer; to set forth, énoncer; to set forward, avancer; to set off, faire ressortir (faire valoir); to set up, ériger, établir (fonder).—v.i. se fixer; diriger, porter (vers ou à); se coucher (soleil); prendre (confitures etc.); to set about, commencer, se mettre à; to set out, partir, se mettre en route; to set up (dans un commerce etc.), s'établir.—a. mis, posé, placé; serti (pierre précieuse); prêt, arrêté, fixe; réglé; d'apparat, préparé (discours); all set? ça y est?—n. collection, f., ensemble, assortiment, m., série, f., jeu; service (de porcelaine etc.), m.; parure (de pierres précieuses); mise en plis (cheveux), f.; (Theat.) décor; groupe, m.
set-back ['setbæk], n. recul, échec, m.
set-square ['setskweə], n. équerre, f.
settee [se'ti:], n. canapé, m., causeuse, f.
setter ['setə], n. chien d'arrêt, m.; bone-setter, rebouteur, rebouteux, m.
setting ['setin], n. mise, pose, f.; coucher (du soleil etc.); décor (naturel ou de théâtre), m. (Mus.) mise en musique, f.; remboîtement (d'os), m.; monture (de pierre précieuse), f.
settle (I) [setl], v.t. fixer; établir; décider, arrêter; assigner (des biens à); coloniser (un pays); accommoder; payer, régler (dettes).—v.i. s'établir, se fixer; se marier; se calmer (devenir tranquille); se poser (oiseau); s'ar-

ranger (*avec*); **to settle down**, se fixer, s'établir; **to settle down to**, s'appliquer à.
settle (2) [setl], *n.* banc (à dossier), *m.*
settled [setld], *a.* établi; calme, tranquille.
settlement ['setlmənt], **settling** ['setliŋ], *n.* établissement, arrangement; dépôt (*au fond des liquides*); accord, contrat, *m.*; colonisation; colonie, *f.*; règlement, solde (*des comptes*); (*Build.*) tassement, *m.*
settler ['setlə], *n.* colon, immigrant, *m.*
set-up ['setʌp], *n.* organisation, *f.*
seven ['sevən], *a.* and *n.* sept, *m.*
sevenfold ['sevənfould], *a.* septuple.—*adv.* sept fois.
seventeen [sevən'ti:n], *a.* and *n.* dix-sept, *m.*
seventeenth ['sevənti:nθ], *a.* dix-septième; dix-sept (*des rois etc.*).—*n.* dix-septième (*fraction*), *m.*
seventh ['sevənθ], *a.* septième; sept (*des rois etc.*).—*n.* septième (*fraction*), *m.*; (*Mus.*) septième, *f.*
seventieth ['sevəntiiθ], *a.* soixante-dixième.—*n.* soixante-dixième (*fraction*), *m.*
seventy ['sevənti], *a.* and *n.* soixante-dix, *m.*
sever ['sevə], *v.t.* séparer, diviser (*de*); disjoindre; couper.—*v.i.* se séparer (*de*).
several ['sevrəl], *a.* plusieurs, divers; distinct, respectif.
severally ['sevrəli], *adv.* séparément, individuellement.
severance ['sevərəns], *n.* séparation, disjonction; rupture, *f.*
severe [si'viə], *a.* sévère; rigoureux, rude (*temps etc.*); violent, aigu, vif (*douleur etc.*).
severity [si'veriti], *n.* sévérité; rigueur, *f.*
sew [sou], *v.t. irr.* coudre; brocher (*livre*).
sewage ['sju:idʒ], *n.* eaux d'égout, *f.pl.*
sewer (1) ['souə], *n.* couseur, *m.*
sewer (2) ['sju:ə], *n.* égout, *m.*
sewerage ['sju:əridʒ], *n.* système d'égouts, *m.*, égouts, *m.pl.*
sewing ['souiŋ], *n.* couture, *f.*; **sewing machine**, machine à coudre, *f.*
sex [seks], *n.* sexe, *m.*
sexagenarian [seksədʒə'neəriən], *a.* and *n.* sexagénaire, *m.*, *f.*
Sexagesima [seksə'dʒesimə], Sexagésime, *f.*
sexennial [sek'seniəl], *a.* sexennal.
sexennially [sek'seniəli], *adv.* tous les six ans.
sextant ['sekstənt], *n.* sextant, *m.*
sextet [seks'tet], *n.* (*Mus.*) sextuor, *m.*
sexton ['sekstən], *n.* sacristain; fossoyeur, *m.*
sextuple ['sekstjupl], *a.* and *n.* sextuple, *m.*
sexual ['seksjuəl], *a.* sexuel.
sexuality [seksju'æliti], *n.* sexualité, *f.*
shabbily ['ʃæbili], *adv.* mal, pauvrement (*mis* ou *vêtu*); (*fig.*) mesquinement.
shabbiness ['ʃæbinis], *n.* état râpé (*de vêtements*), *m.*; (*fig.*) mesquinerie, *f.*
shabby ['ʃæbi], *a.* râpé; mal vêtu, mal mis; (*fig.*) mesquin, ignoble.
shackle [ʃækl], *v.t.* enchaîner; (*fig.*) entraver.
shackles [ʃæklz], *n.pl.* fers, *m.pl.*, chaînes; (*fig.*) entraves, *f.pl.*
shad [ʃæd], *n.* alose (*poisson*), *f.*
shade [ʃeid], *n.* ombre, *f.*; ombrage (*d'arbre etc.*); abat-jour (*de lampe etc.*); garde-vue (*pour les yeux*), *m.*; nuance (*couleur*), *f.*; (*pl.*) enfers (*où vivent les immortels*), *m.pl.*; **in the shade**, à l'ombre.—*v.t.* ombrager (*de*); obscurcir; abriter (*protéger*); (*Paint.*) ombrer, nuancer; hachurer (*une carte*).

shaded ['ʃeidid], *a.* à l'ombre; ombragé (*de*); (*Paint.*) ombré.
shadiness ['ʃeidinis], *n.* ombrage, *m.*, ombre; (*fig.*) nature suspecte, *f.*
shading ['ʃeidiŋ], *n.* ombres, nuances; hachures, *f.pl.*
shadow ['ʃædou], *n.* ombre, *f.*—*v.t.* ombrager; filer, espionner (*suivre de près*).
shadowing ['ʃædouiŋ], *n.* espionnage, *m.*, filature, *f.*
shadowy ['ʃædoui], *a.* ombragé; sombre (*morne*); vague, chimérique (*irréel*).
shady ['ʃeidi], *a.* ombragé, ombreux; sombre (*noir*); (*colloq.*) louche (*malhonnête*).
shaft [ʃɑ:ft], *n.* flèche, *f.*, dard, trait; brancard (*de charette*); manche (*d'outil, d'arme*); puits (*de mine*); (*Mach.*) arbre, *m.*
shag [ʃæg], *n.* poil rude; caporal (*tabac*); cormoran huppé (*oiseau*), *m.*
shagginess ['ʃæginis], *n.* état poilu, état hérissé, *m.*
shaggy ['ʃægi], *a.* poilu, velu; raboteux (*pays*).
shagreen [ʃə'gri:n], *a.* de peau de chagrin.—*n.* peau de chagrin, *f.*
shah [ʃɑ:], *n.* shah, *m.*
shake [ʃeik], *n.* secousse, *f.*; serrement, *m.*; poignée (*de main*), *f.*; hochement (*de tête*), *m.*—*v.t. irr.* secouer, branler, agiter; ébranler, faire trembler; **to shake hands with**, serrer la main à.—*v.i.* trembler (*de*); s'agiter, branler; chanceler (*sur ses jambes*).
shakedown ['ʃeikdaun], *n.* lit improvisé, *m.*
shakily ['ʃeikili], *adv.* en branlant; à pas chancelants.
shaking ['ʃeikiŋ], *n.* secousse, *f.*, ébranlement, tremblement; ballottement (*à cheval*), *m.*
shako ['ʃækou], *n.* shako, *m.*
shaky ['ʃeiki], *a.* branlant; (*fig.*) peu solide; faible, chancelant (*personne*).
shale [ʃeil], *n.* argile schisteuse, *f.*
shall [ʃæl], *v.aux. irr.* (*used as sign of the future*) **I shall go**, j'irai; devoir; vouloir; **shall I go?** dois-je aller? voulez-vous que j'aille? **but he shall**, mais je l'y forcerai; **but I shall not**, mais je n'en ferai rien.
shallop ['ʃæləp], *n.* chaloupe, péniche, pinasse, *f.*
shallot [ʃə'lɔt], *n.* échalote, *f.*
shallow ['ʃælou], *a.* peu profond; (*fig.*) superficiel, léger, borné.
shallowness ['ʃælounis], *n.* peu de profondeur; esprit borné, *m.*
sham [ʃæm], *a.* feint, simulé; faux, factice.—*n.* feinte, *f.*, prétexte, *m.*; imposture, frime, *f.*—*v.t.* feindre, simuler; faire le, la ou les.—*v.i.* feindre, faire semblant; jouer la comédie.
shamble [ʃæmbl], *v.i.* marcher en traînant les pieds.
shambles [ʃæmblz], *n.pl.* abattoir, *m.*; (*fig.*) scène de carnage; une belle pagaille, *f.*
shambling ['ʃæmbliŋ], *a.* traînant.
shame [ʃeim], *n.* honte; ignominie (*déshonneur*), *f.*; opprobre, *m.*; **what a shame!** quel dommage! *f.* faire honte à.
shamefaced ['ʃeimfeist], *a.* honteux, confus.
shamefacedly ['ʃeim'feisidli], *adv.* d'un air penaud.
shamefacedness ['ʃeimfeistnis], *n.* mauvaise honte; timidité, *f.*
shameful ['ʃeimful], *a.* honteux; déshonnête.

shamefulness ['ʃeimfulnis], *n.* honte, ignominie, *f.*

shameless ['ʃeimlis], *a.* éhonté, effronté, impudent.

shamelessly ['ʃeimlisli], *adv.* sans honte, effrontément.

shamelessness ['ʃeimlisnis], *n.* effronterie, impudence, *f.*

shammer ['ʃæmə], *n.* simulateur, *m.*

shampoo [ʃæm'pu:], *v.t.* frictionner; nettoyer (*la tête*).—*n.* shampooing, *m.*

shamrock ['ʃæmrɔk], *n.* trèfle (d'Irlande), *m.*

shank [ʃæŋk], *n.* jambe, *f.*

shanty ['ʃænti], *n.* cabane, bicoque, hutte, *f.*

shanty-town ['ʃæntitaun], *n.* bidonville, *m.*

shape [ʃeip], *n.* forme, figure; tournure, taille (*de personne*); façon, coupe (*de vêtement*), *f.* —*v.t.* former, façonner; modeler (*sur*).

shapeless ['ʃeiplis], *a.* informe, sans forme.

shapelessness ['ʃeiplisnis], *n.* absence de forme, difformité, *f.*

shapeliness ['ʃeiplinis], *n.* beauté de forme, *f.*, galbe, *m.*

shapely ['ʃeipli], *a.* bien fait, beau.

share (1) [ʃɛə], *n.* soc (*de charrue*), *m.*

share (2) [ʃɛə], *n.* part, portion; (*St. Exch.*) action, *f.*; **preferred share**, action privilégiée.—*v.t., v.i.* partager; prendre part à; avoir part à.

shareholder ['ʃɛəhouldə], *n.* actionnaire, *m., f.*

sharer ['ʃɛərə], *n.* participant; (*Law*) partageant, *m.*

sharing ['ʃɛəriŋ], *n.* partage, *m.*

shark [ʃɑ:k], *n.* requin; (*fig.*) escroc, filou (*personne*), *m.*

sharp [ʃɑ:p], *a.* tranchant, affilé, qui coupe bien; pointu, aigu; saillant (*angle*); (*fig.*) vif, intelligent, pénétrant, perçant; anguleux (*traits*); piquant, aigre (*goût etc.*); rusé (*astucieux*); (*Mus.*) dièse; **sharp practice**, filouterie, rouerie, *f.*—*adv.* précise (*l'heure*); **at four o'clock sharp**, à quatre heures précises; **look sharp!** faites vite!—*n.* (*Mus.*) dièse, *m.*

sharpen ['ʃɑ:pən], *v.t.* affiler, aiguiser; tailler en pointe, tailler (*crayon etc.*); (*fig.*) rendre vif.

sharper ['ʃɑ:pə], *n.* aigrefin, escroc, chevalier d'industrie, *m.*

sharply ['ʃɑ:pli], *adv.* rudement, vivement; nettement.

sharpness ['ʃɑ:pnis], *n.* tranchant (*d'une lame*), *m.*; pointe (*acuité*); acidité (*de fruit*); violence (*de douleur etc.*); âpreté (*de langage etc.*); netteté (*de contour etc.*), *f.*; esprit éveillé (*d'enfants etc.*), *m.*

sharp-sighted ['ʃɑ:p'saitid], *a.* à la vue perçante.

sharp-witted ['ʃɑ:p'witid], *a.* à l'esprit délié.

shatter ['ʃætə], *v.t.* fracasser, briser en pièces. —*v.i.* se briser, se fracasser.

shave [ʃeiv], *v.t.* raser; faire la barbe à; effleurer (*friser*); (*Tech.*) planer.—*v.i.* se raser, se faire la barbe; **to have a close shave**, l'échapper belle; **to have a shave**, se raser, se faire raser.

shaving ['ʃeiviŋ], *n.* action de raser, *f.*; copeau (*de bois*), *m.*

shaving brush ['ʃeiviŋbrʌʃ], *n.* blaireau, *m.*

shaving cream ['ʃeiviŋkri:m], *n.* crème à raser, *f.*

shaving soap ['ʃeiviŋsoup], *n.* savon pour la barbe, *m.*

shawl [ʃɔ:l], *n.* châle, *m.*

she [ʃi:], *pron.* elle; femelle (*de certains animaux*), *f.*

sheaf [ʃi:f], *n.* (*pl.* **sheaves** [ʃi:vz]) gerbe, *f.*; faisceau (*de flèches*), *m.*—*v.t.* engerber, mettre en gerbe.

shear [ʃiə], *v.t. irr.* tondre.

shearer ['ʃiərə], *n.* tondeur, *m.*; tondeuse (*machine*), *f.*

shearing ['ʃiəriŋ], *n.* tonte, tondaison, *f.*

shears [ʃiəz], *n.pl.* grands ciseaux, *m.pl.*; cisailles (*pour haie, pour métal*), *f.pl.*

she-ass ['ʃi:æs], *n.* ânesse, *f.*

sheath [ʃi:θ], *n.* (*pl.* **sheaths** [ʃi:ðz]) gaine, *f.*; fourreau (*à épée*); étui (*à ciseaux etc.*); (*Ent.*) élytre, *m.*

sheathe [ʃi:ð], *v.t.* mettre dans le fourreau, rengainer; envelopper; revêtir (*de*).

sheaves [ʃi:vz] [SHEAF].

she-cat ['ʃi:kæt], *n.* chatte, *f.*

shed (1) [ʃed], *n.* hangar; (*Build.*) atelier, *m.*; **cow-shed**, étable (à vaches), *f.*; **lean-to shed**, appentis, *m.*

shed (2) [ʃed], *v.t. irr.* répandre, verser; se dépouiller de, perdre (*feuilles etc.*); jeter (*animal*).

shedding ['ʃediŋ], *n.* effusion (*de sang*); perte (*feuilles etc.*), *f.*

sheen [ʃi:n], *n.* éclat, lustre, brillant, *m.*

sheep [ʃi:p], *n.inv.* mouton, *m.*; (*fig.*) brebis, *f.*; **black sheep**, brebis galeuse; **lost sheep**, brebis égarée.

sheep dip ['ʃi:pdip], *n.* bain parasiticide, *m.*

sheep dog ['ʃi:pdɔg], *n.* chien de berger, *m.*

sheep-fold ['ʃi:pfould], *n.* bergerie, *f.*, bercail, *m.*

sheepish ['ʃi:piʃ], *a.* penaud, bête, niais.

sheepishly ['ʃi:piʃli], *adv.* d'un air penaud.

sheep pen ['ʃi:ppen], *n.* parc à moutons, *m.*

sheep-shearing ['ʃi:pʃiəriŋ], *n.* tonte, *f.*

sheepskin ['ʃi:pskin], *n.* peau de mouton; basane (*cuir*), *f.*

sheer (1) [ʃiə], *a.* pur; escarpé, à pic (*rocher*); **sheer force**, pure force, *f.*; **sheer nonsense**, pure sottise, *f.*—*adv.* tout droit; tout à fait.

sheer (2) [ʃiə], *n.* (*Naut.*) tonture; embardée, *f.*—*v.i.* faire des embardées; **to sheer off**, pousser au large, s'esquiver.

sheet [ʃi:t], *n.* drap, *m.*; feuille (*de papier ou métal*); nappe (*d'eau etc.*); (*Naut.*) écoute (*corde*), *f.*; **winding sheet**, linceul, *m.*

sheet anchor ['ʃi:tæŋkə], *n.* ancre de miséricorde; (*fig.*) ancre de salut, *f.*

sheet iron ['ʃi:taiən], *n.* tôle, *f.*

sheet lightning ['ʃi:t'laitniŋ], *n.* éclair en nappe, *m.*

sheikh [ʃeik], *n.* cheik, *m.*

shelf [ʃelf], *n.* (*pl.* **shelves** [ʃelvz]) planche, *f.*; rayon (*de bibliothèque*), *m.*; tablette, *f.*; écueil (*dans la mer*), *m.*; **set of shelves**, étagères, *f.pl.*

shell [ʃel], *n.* coque (*d'œuf, fruits etc.*); coquille (*œuf vide*); cosse (*de petits pois etc.*); écaille (*d'huître, de tortue*); carapace (*de homard*), *f.*; (*Artill.*) obus; (*fig.*) extérieur, *m.* —*v.t.* écaler (*noisette etc.*); écosser (*petits pois etc.*); égrener (*graine*); (*Mil.*) bombarder.

shell-fish ['ʃelfiʃ], *n.* coquillage, mollusque, *m.*, crustacés, *m.pl.*

shelling ['ʃeliŋ], n. écossage; égrenage; (*Mil.*) bombardement, *m.*
shell-proof ['ʃelpruːf], a. blindé.
shelter ['ʃeltə], n. abri, couvert; (*fig.*) asile, *m.*; **to take shelter**, s'abriter.—*v.t.* abriter; protéger.—*v.i.* s'abriter.
sheltered ['ʃeltəd], a. abrité.
shelve [ʃelv], *v.t.* mettre sur un rayon; (*fig.*) enterrer.—*v.i.* aller en pente.
shelves [SHELF].
shelving ['ʃelviŋ], a. en pente, incliné.
shepherd ['ʃepəd], n. berger, pâtre; (*fig.*) pasteur, *m.*—*v.t.* piloter, guider.
shepherdess ['ʃepədes], n. bergère, *f.*
sherbet ['ʃəːbət], n. sorbet, *m.*
sheriff ['ʃerif], n. shérif; (*Am.*) chef de police (*d'un comté*), *m.*
sherry ['ʃeri], n. vin de Xérès, *m.*
shield [ʃiːld], n. bouclier; écran protecteur; (*Her.*) écu, écusson, *m.*—*v.t.* défendre de, protéger contre.
shift [ʃift], n. changement; expédient, *m.*, ressource, *f.*; détour, faux-fuyant (*artifice*), *m.*; *chemise de femme; équipe, journée (*d'ouvriers*), *f.*—*v.t.*, *v.i.* changer; changer de place; (*fig.*) trouver des expédients; **to shift for oneself**, se débrouiller.
shiftiness ['ʃiftinis], n. manque de franchise, *m.*
shifting ['ʃiftiŋ], a. changeant; **shifting sand**, sable mouvant, *m.*—*n.* changement; déplacement (*de cargaison etc.*), *m.*
shiftless ['ʃiftlis], a. sans initiative; sans énergie; paresseux.
shifty ['ʃifti], a. plein d'expédients; **he is a shifty customer**, c'est un roublard.
shilling ['ʃiliŋ], n. shilling, *m.*
shilly-shally ['ʃili'ʃæli], n. irrésolution, *f.*—*v.i.* hésiter, être irrésolu.
shimmer ['ʃimə], n. lueur, *f.*—*v.i.* miroiter.
shin [ʃin], n. devant de la jambe; jarret (*de bœuf*), *m.*
shin-bone ['ʃinboun], n. tibia, *m.*
shindy ['ʃindi], n. tapage, *m.*
shine [ʃain], *v.i. irr.* luire; reluire; briller.—*n.* brillant, éclat, lustre, *m.*
shingle (1) [ʃiŋgl], n. bardeau (*pour toiture*), *m.*; coiffure à la garçonne, *f.*
shingle (2) [ʃiŋgl], n. galets, cailloux (*au bord de la mer*), *m.*
shingles [ʃiŋglz], n.pl. (*Med.*) zona, *m.*
shingly ['ʃiŋgli], a. couvert de galets.
shining ['ʃainiŋ], a. luisant, brillant.
shiny ['ʃaini], a. luisant, reluisant.
ship [ʃip], n. navire; vaisseau, bâtiment, *m.*—*v.t.* embarquer; expédier (*marchandises*); armer (*avirons*).—*v.i.* s'embarquer.
shipboard ['ʃipbɔːd], n. bord de navire, *m.*
shipbuilder ['ʃipbildə], n. constructeur de navires, *m.*
shipbuilding ['ʃipbildiŋ], n. construction navale, *f.*
ship chandler ['ʃip'tʃɑːndlə], n. fournisseur de navires, *m.*
shipmate ['ʃipmeit], n. camarade de bord, *m.*
shipment ['ʃipmənt], n. chargement, *m.*
shipowner ['ʃipounə], n. armateur, *m.*
shipper ['ʃipə], n. expéditeur, *m.*
shipping ['ʃipiŋ], a. maritime.—*n.* vaisseaux, navires, *m.pl.*; navigation; marine marchande; mise à bord (*chargement*), *f.*
ship's boat ['ʃips'bout], n. chaloupe, *f.*

ship's carpenter ['ʃips'kɑːpintə], n. charpentier du bord, *m.*
shipshape ['ʃipʃeip], a. en ordre, bien arrangé.
shipwreck ['ʃiprek], n. naufrage, *m.*—*v.t.* faire faire naufrage à; **to be shipwrecked**, faire naufrage.
shipwrecked ['ʃiprekt], a. naufragé.
shipwright ['ʃiprait], n. constructeur de navires, *m.*
shipyard ['ʃipjɑːd], n. chantier naval, *m.*
shire ['ʃaiə], n. comté, *f.*
shirk [ʃəːk], *v.t.* éviter, éluder.—*v.i.* finasser; tirer au flanc.
shirker ['ʃəːkə], n. carottier; flanchard, *m.*
shirt [ʃəːt], n. chemise (*d'homme*), *f.*; **shirt collar**, col de chemise, *m.*; **shirt front**, devant de chemise, plastron, *m.*
shiver (1) ['ʃivə], *v.t.* briser en morceaux, fracasser.—*v.i.* se briser en morceaux.—*n.* fragment, morceau, éclat, *m.*
shiver (2) ['ʃivə], *v.i.* grelotter (*de froid*); frissonner (*de peur*).—*n.* frisson, tremblement, *m.*
shivering ['ʃivəriŋ], a. frissonnant.—*n.* frissonnement, frisson, *m.*
shoal [ʃoul], n. banc (*de poissons*), *m.*; (*fig.*) foule, *f.*; bas-fond, haut-fond (*de la mer*), *m.*; **in shoals**, en foule.
shock (1) [ʃɔk], n. choc, *m.*; (*Elec.*) secousse, *f.*—*v.t.* choquer, heurter; scandaliser.
shock (2) [ʃɔk], n. moyette (*de blé*); tignasse (*de cheveux*), *f.*
shock absorber ['ʃɔkəbsɔːbə], n. (*Motor.*) amortisseur, *m.*
shocking ['ʃɔkiŋ], a. choquant, affreux, dégoûtant.
shockingly ['ʃɔkiŋli], adv. affreusement.
shod [ʃɔd], a. ferré (*cheval*); chaussé (*personne*).
shoddy ['ʃɔdi], a. d'effilochage; de pacotille. —*n.* drap de laine d'effilochage, *m.*
shoe [ʃuː], n. soulier, *m.*; chaussure, *f.*; fer (*à cheval*); sabot (*en bois*), *m.*—*v.t. irr.* chausser; ferrer (*cheval etc.*).
shoe-black ['ʃuːblæk], n. cireur, *m.*
shoe-horn ['ʃuːhɔːn], n. chausse-pied, *m.*
shoeing ['ʃuːiŋ], n. ferrage, *m.*
shoeing-smith ['ʃuːiŋsmiθ], n. maréchal ferrant, *m.*
shoe-lace ['ʃuːleis], n. lacet de chaussure, *m.*
shoemaker ['ʃuːmeikə], n. cordonnier, *m.*
shoe-making ['ʃuːmeikiŋ], n. cordonnerie, *f.*
shoe polish ['ʃuːpɔliʃ], n. cirage, *m.*
shoot [ʃuːt], *v.t. irr.* tirer, lancer, darder; décharger, tirer un coup (*de fusil etc.*); atteindre (*une cible*); tuer (*faire mourir*); fusiller; descendre (*rapides etc.*); **to shoot a film**, tourner un film; **to shoot oneself**, se tuer.—*v.i.* tirer; chasser (*gibier*); (*fig.*) s'élancer; filer (*étoile etc.*); pousser (*plante etc.*).—*n.* rejeton, *m.*, pousse (*plante*), *f.*; sarment (*de vigne*); dépôt de décombres (*ordures*), *m.*
shooter ['ʃuːtə], n. tireur, *m.*
shooting ['ʃuːtiŋ], a. lancinant (*douleur*); **shooting star**, étoile filante, *f.*—*n.* tir (*de fusil*), *m.*; chasse au fusil, *f.*; élancement (*de douleur*), *m.*; pousse (*de plante*); décharge (*des ordures*), *f.*; (*Cine.*) tournage (*de film*), *m.*
shooting-brake ['ʃuːtiŋbreik], n. (*Motor.*) canadienne, *f.*

shooting gallery [ˈʃuːtiŋgæləri], *n.* tir, stand, *m.*

shop [ʃɔp], *n.* boutique (*petit*), *f.*, magasin (*grand*); atelier (*de fabrication*), *m.*—*v.i.* faire des emplettes; **to go shopping,** aller faire des courses.

shop-assistant [ˈʃɔpəsistənt], *n.* vendeur, *m.*, vendeuse, commise, *f.*

shopkeeper [ˈʃɔpkiːpə], *n.* marchand, *m.*

shoplifter [ˈʃɔpliftə], *n.* voleur à l'étalage, *m.*

shoplifting [ˈʃɔpliftiŋ], *n.* vol à l'étalage, *m.*

shopper [ˈʃɔpə], *n.* acheteur, client, *m.*

shopping center [ˈʃɔpiŋsentə], *n.* quartier commerçant, *m.*

shop steward [ˈʃɔpstjuəd], *n.* responsable syndical, délégué ouvrier, *m.*

shop-walker [ˈʃɔpwɔːkə], *n.* chef de rayon; inspecteur de magasin, *m.*

shop window [ˈʃɔpˈwindou], *n.* devanture, vitrine, *f.*, étalage, *m.*

shopworn [ˈʃɔpwɔːn], *a.* défraîchi.

shore [ʃɔː], *n.* rivage, bord, *m.*, plage, côte, *f.* —*v.t.* étayer, étançonner.

short [ʃɔːt], *a.* court; bref; passager (*temps*); petit (*taille*); insuffisant; croquant (*pâte*); brusque (*bourru*); **short circuit,** court-circuit, *m.*; **short story,** conte, *m.*, nouvelle, *f.*; **to cut the matter short,** pour en finir. —*adv.* court, vivement, brusquement; **it falls far short of it,** il s'en faut de beaucoup.

shortbread [ˈʃɔːtbred], *n.* (gâteau) sablé, *m.*

short-circuit [ˈʃɔːtˈsəːkit], *v.t.* mettre en court-circuit.

shortcoming [ˈʃɔːtkʌmiŋ], *n.* défaut, *m.*, insuffisance, *f.*

shorten [ʃɔːtn], *v.t.* raccourcir; abréger.— *v.i.* (se) raccourcir.

shortening [ˈʃɔːtniŋ], *n.* raccourcissement, *m.*

shorthand [ˈʃɔːthænd], *n.* sténographie, *f.*

short-handed [ˈʃɔːtˈhændid], *a.* à court de personnel.

shorthand-typist [ˈʃɔːthændˈtaipist], *n.* sténodactylographe, (*fam.*) sténodactylo, *f.*

short-lived [ˈʃɔːtˈlivd], *a.* qui vit peu de temps, éphémère.

shortly [ˈʃɔːtli], *adv.* bientôt, sous peu; brièvement.

shortness [ˈʃɔːtnis], *n.* courte durée, *f.*; peu d'étendue, *m.*; petitesse (*de taille*), *f.*

shorts [ˈʃɔːts], *n.pl.* culotte courte, *f.*, caleçon court, slip; short, *m.*

short-sighted [ˈʃɔːtˈsaitid], *a.* myope; (*fig.*) peu prévoyant.

short-sightedness [ˈʃɔːtˈsaitidnis], *n.* myopie, *f.*; (*fig.*) manque de prévoyance, *m.*

short-tempered [ˈʃɔːtˈtempəd], *a.* vif, pétulant, brusque.

short-winded [ˈʃɔːtˈwindid], *a.* à l'haleine courte; poussif (*cheval*).

shot (1) [ʃɔt], *past and p.p.* [SHOOT].

shot (2) [ʃɔt], *a.* chatoyant; **shot silk,** soie gorge-de-pigeon, *f.*—*n.* coup de fusil, coup; trait (*d'arc*), *m.*; balle (*de fusil*), *f.*, boulet (*de canon*); plomb (*de fusil de chasse*), *m.*; (*Artill.*) charge; portée (*étendue*), *f.*; tireur (*personne*); (*Ftb.*) coup au but, *m.*; (*Med.*) injection; (*Cine.*) prise, *f.*; **at a shot,** d'un seul coup; **like a shot,** comme un trait; **to be a good shot,** être bon tireur; **to fire a shot,** tirer un coup de feu. [see **shy**]

shot-gun [ˈʃɔtgʌn], *n.* fusil de chasse, *m.*

should [ʃud], *v.aux.* (*past of* **shall,** *used as sign of the conditional*) **I should speak,** je parlerais; (=**ought to,** *conditional tense of* **devoir**) **you should see it,** vous devriez le voir.

shoulder [ˈʃouldə], *n.* épaule; (*Tech.*) languette, *f.*; **round shoulders,** dos rond, *m.*—*v.t.* charger sur les épaules; se charger de; porter (*armes*).

shoulder blade [ˈʃouldəbleid], *n.* omoplate, *f.*

shout [ʃaut], *v.t.*, *v.i.* crier, huer, pousser des cris; vociférer.—*n.* cri, *m.*; acclamations, *f.pl.*; éclat (*de rire*), *m.*

shouting [ˈʃautiŋ], *n.* acclamation, *f.*, cris, *m.pl.*

shove [ʃʌv], *v.t.* pousser; **to shove away,** repousser, éloigner.—*v.i.* pousser.—*n.* coup, *m.*, poussée, *f.*

shovel [ʃʌvl], *n.* pelle, *f.*—*v.t.* ramasser avec la pelle, pelleter.

shovelful [ˈʃʌvlful], *n.* pelletée, *f.*

show [ʃou], *v.t.* irr. montrer, faire voir, exposer à la vue; manifester, témoigner, démontrer; indiquer; expliquer; **to show in,** faire entrer; **to show off,** faire valoir.— *v.i.* paraître; se montrer; se faire remarquer; **to show off,** poser, se donner des airs.— *n.* apparence, *f.*; étalage, *m.*, parade, *f.*; spectacle, concours, *m.*; exposition, *f.*

show-case [ˈʃoukeis], *n.* montre, vitrine, *f.*

shower [ˈʃauə], *n.* ondée (*légère*); averse (*grosse*); pluie, grêle (*de coups, pierres etc.*); douche, *f.*—*v.t.* inonder (*de pluie*); (*fig.*) verser.

shower bath [ˈʃauəbɑːθ], *n.* douche, *f.*, bain-douche, *m.*

showery [ˈʃauəri], *a.* pluvieux.

show-ring [ˈʃouriŋ], *n.* arène de vente, *f.*

show room [ˈʃouruːm], *n.* salle d'exposition, *f.*

showy [ˈʃoui], *a.* voyant, prétentieux, criard.

shrapnel [ˈʃræpnəl], *n.* éclats d'obus, *m.pl.*

shred [ʃred], *n.* lambeau, bout, brin, *m.*; **to tear to shreds,** déchirer en lambeaux.— *v.t.* déchiqueter; râper grossièrement.

shrew [ʃruː], *n.* mégère, femme acariâtre, *f.*

shrewd [ʃruːd], *a.* sagace, fin, perspicace.

shrewdly [ˈʃruːdli], *adv.* avec sagacité, avec pénétration, finement.

shrewdness [ˈʃruːdnis], *n.* sagacité, pénétration, finesse, *f.*

shrewish [ˈʃruːiʃ], *a.* acariâtre.

shrewishly [ˈʃruːiʃli], *adv.* en mégère.

shrewishness [ˈʃruːiʃnis], *n.* humeur acariâtre, *f.*

shriek [ʃriːk], *n.* cri perçant, *m.*—*v.t.* crier.— *v.i.* jeter un cri aigu.

shrieking [ˈʃriːkiŋ], *n.* cris stridents, *m.pl.*

shrift [ʃrift], *n.* confession, *f.*; (*fig.*) **short shrift,** très court délai, *m.*

shrill [ʃril], *a.* aigu, perçant; aigre (*voix*).

shrillness [ˈʃrilnis], *n.* son aigu, ton aigu, *m.*

shrilly [ˈʃrili], *adv.* d'un ton aigu.

shrimp [ʃrimp], *n.* crevette (*grise*), *f.*

shrine [ʃrain], *n.* châsse, *f.*; tombeau, *m.*; chapelle (*d'un saint*), *f.*

shrink [ʃriŋk], *v.t.* irr. rétrécir, faire rétrécir. —*v.i.* rétrécir; se rétrécir; se retirer; reculer; se ratatiner; se tasser (*en vieillissant*).

shrinkage [ˈʃriŋkidʒ], *n.* rétrécissement, *m.*, contraction, *f.*

561

shrinking [ˈʃriŋkiŋ], n. rétrécissement, m.; action de reculer, f.

*shrive [ʃraiv], v.t. irr. confesser.

shrivel [ˈʃrivl], v.t. faire ratatiner, faire recroqueviller, rider, racornir.—v.i. se ratatiner, se recroqueviller.

shroud [ʃraud], n. linceul, suaire, m.; (Naut., pl.) haubans, m.pl.—v.t. (fig.) abriter, couvrir.

Shrovetide [ˈʃrouvtaid]. les jours gras, m.pl.; **Shrove Tuesday**, mardi-gras, m.

shrub [ʃrʌb], n. arbuste, arbrisseau, m.

shrubbery [ˈʃrʌbəri], n. plantation d'arbrisseaux, f.

shrubby [ˈʃrʌbi], a. plein d'arbrisseaux, touffu.

shrug [ʃrʌg], n. haussement d'épaules, m.—v.t. hausser; **to shrug one's shoulders**, hausser les épaules.

shudder [ˈʃʌdə], v.i. frissonner, frémir (de).—n. frissonnement, frémissement, m.

shuffle [ˈʃʌfl], v.t. mêler; (Cards) battre.—v.i. traîner les pieds; battre les cartes; tergiverser (équivoquer).

shuffling [ˈʃʌfliŋ], a. chicaneur, biaiseur; traînant (allure).—n. marche traînante, f.; (Cards) battement des cartes, m.; (fig.) chicane, f.

shun [ʃʌn], v.t. éviter, fuir.

shunt [ʃʌnt], v.t. garer (train); détourner.

shunting [ˈʃʌntiŋ], n. changement de voie, garage, m.

shut [ʃʌt], v.t. irr. fermer; enfermer; **to shut off**, intercepter, couper (vapeur etc.); **to shut out**, exclure; **to shut up**, fermer, enfermer; condamner (porte etc.); faire taire.—v.i. fermer, se fermer; **shut up!** taisez-vous!

shutter [ˈʃʌtə], n. volet, contrevent (à l'extérieur de la fenêtre), m.

shuttle [ʃʌtl], n. navette; vanne, f.

shuttle-cock [ˈʃʌtlkɔk], n. volant, m.

shuttle service [ˈʃʌtləːvis], n. navette, f.

shy (1) [ʃai], a. réservé, timide, honteux.—v.i. être ombrageux, faire un écart (cheval).

shy (2) [ʃai], v.t. jeter, lancer.—n. coup (de pierre etc.); essai, m.; **to have a shy at**, s'essayer à (faire quelque chose).

shyly [ˈʃaili], adv. timidement, avec réserve.

shyness [ˈʃainis], n. timidité, retenue, réserve; fausse honte, f.

Siam [saiˈæm]. le Siam, m.

Siamese [saiəˈmiːz], a. siamois.—n. siamois (langue); Siamois (personne), m.

Siberia [saiˈbiəriə]. la Sibérie, f.

Siberian [saiˈbiəriən], a. sibérien.—n. Sibérien (personne), m.

sibilant [ˈsibilənt], a. sifflant.—n. lettre sifflante, f.

siccative [ˈsikətiv], a. and n. siccatif, m.

Sicilian [siˈsiliən], a. sicilien.—n. Sicilien (personne), m.

Sicily [ˈsisili]. la Sicile, f.

sick [sik], a. malade; qui a des nausées, qui a mal au cœur; **sick headache**, migraine, f.; **sick man** or **woman**, malade, m., f.; **sick of**, dégoûté de; **to be sea-sick**, avoir le mal de mer; **to be sick**, vomir.

sick-bed [ˈsikbed], n. lit de douleur, m.

sicken [sikn], v.t. rendre malade; (fig.) lasser, dégoûter.—v.i. tomber malade.

sickening [ˈsikniŋ], a. écœurant; (fig.) dégoûtant.

sickle [sikl], n. faucille, f.

sick leave [ˈsikliːv], n. congé de convalescence, m.

sickliness [ˈsiklinis], n. mauvaise santé, f.

sick list [ˈsiklist], n. rôle des malades, m.

sickly [ˈsikli], a. maladif; affadissant, affadi (goût etc.).

sickness [ˈsiknis], n. maladie, f.; nausées, f.pl.

sick-nurse [ˈsiknəːs], n. garde-malade, f.

sick-room [ˈsikruːm], n. chambre de malade, f.

side [said], a. de côté; latéral; indirect.—n. côté; flanc; bord; versant (de montagne); parti; (Spt.) camp, m.; **by his side**, à côté de lui; **side by side**, côte à côte; **this side up** (caisses), dessus; **to take sides**, prendre parti; **wrong side out**, à l'envers.—v.i. **to side with**, se ranger du côté de.

sideboard [ˈsaidbɔːd], n. buffet, m.

sided [ˈsaidid], a. à côtés, à faces; **two-sided**, à deux faces.

side door [ˈsaiddɔː], n. porte latérale, f.

side-line [ˈsaidlain], n. occupation secondaire, f.

sidelong [ˈsaidlɔŋ], a. and adv. de côté.

side show [ˈsaidʃou], n. spectacle forain, m.

sidesman [ˈsaidzmən], n. (pl. -men [men]) (Eccles.) marguillier, m.

side-track [ˈsaidtræk], v.t. garer (train); (fig.) semer (quelqu'un).

sidewalk [ˈsaidwɔːk], n. (Am.) trottoir (de rue), m.

sideways [ˈsaidweiz], adv. de côté; obliquement.

siding [ˈsaidiŋ], n. voie d'évitement, voie de garage, f.

sidle [saidl], v.i. marcher de côté; s'insinuer.

siege [siːdʒ], n. siège, m.; **to lay siege to**, mettre le siège devant, faire le siège de, assiéger.

Sienna [siˈenə]. Sienne, f.

sierra [siˈɛərə], n. sierra, f.

Sierra Leone [siˈɛərəliˈoun]. le Sierra-Leone, m.

siesta [siˈestə], n. sieste, f.

sieve [siv], n. tamis (fin); crible (grand), m.

sift [sift], v.t. tamiser; cribler; sasser (farine); (fig.) examiner.

sifting [ˈsiftiŋ], n. tamisage, m.; (fig.) examen minutieux, m.

sigh [sai], n. soupir, m.—v.i. soupirer; **to sigh after**, soupirer après; **to sigh over**, gémir sur.

sighing [ˈsaiiŋ], n. soupirs, m.pl.

sight [sait], n. vue, vision, f.; regard, m., yeux, m.pl.; guidon, m., hausse (armes à feu), f.; spectacle, m.; **a sight better**, beaucoup mieux; **at first sight**, à première vue; **by sight**, de vue; **in sight**, en vue; **out of sight**, hors de vue; **second sight**, clairvoyance, f.; **to catch sight of**, apercevoir; **to come in sight**, apparaître.—v.t. apercevoir.

sighted [ˈsaitid], a. en vue; qui voit, voyant; **long-sighted**, presbyte; **short-sighted**, myope; (fig.) peu clairvoyant.

sightless [ˈsaitlinis], n. beauté, f.

sight-reading [ˈsaitriːdiŋ], n. (Mus.) déchiffrement, m.

sight-seeing ['saitsi:iŋ], *n.* *to go sight-seeing*, aller voir les curiosités.

sight-seer ['saitsi:ə], *n.* touriste, *m.*, *f.*, visiteur (*d'une ville*), *m.*

sign [sain], *n.* signe; indice, *m.*; enseigne (*panneau*), *f.*—*v.t.*, *v.i.* signer.

signal ['signəl], *a.* signalé, insigne.—*n.* signal; signe; (*Rail.*) sémaphore, *m.*; (*pl.*) (*Mil.*) les transmissions, *f.pl.*—*v.t.* signaler, faire signe à.—*v.i.* signaler; donner un signal.

signal-box ['signəlbɔks], *n.* poste à signaux, *m.*

signalman ['signəlmən], *n.* (*pl.* -men [men]) (*Rail.*) signaleur, *m.*

signaller ['signələ], *n.* signaleur, *m.*

signally ['signəli], *adv.* remarquablement.

signatory ['signətəri], *a.* and *n.* signataire, *m.*, *f.*

signature ['signətʃə], *n.* signature, *f.*

sign-board ['sainbɔːd], *n.* enseigne, *f.*

signet ['signit], *n.* sceau; cachet, *m.*

signet ring ['signitriŋ], *n.* chevalière, *f.*

significance [sig'nifikəns], *n.* signification, *f.*, sens, *m.*; importance, *f.*

significant [sig'nifikənt], *a.* significatif.

signification [signifi'keiʃən], *n.* signification, *f.*

signify ['signifai], *v.t.* vouloir dire, signifier; faire connaître; importer.

sign-post ['sainpoust], *n.* poteau indicateur, *m.*

silence ['sailəns], *n.* silence, *m.*; *silence!* (*notice*), défense de parler.—*v.t.* réduire au silence, faire taire.

silent ['sailənt], *a.* silencieux; peu loquace (*qui ne parle pas beaucoup*); muet (*lettre, film*).

silently ['sailəntli], *adv.* silencieusement, en silence; sans bruit.

silent partner ['sailənt'pɑːtnə], *n.* associé commanditaire, *m.*

Silesia [sai'liːʃə, sai'liːsiə], la Silésie, *f.*

silex ['saileks], *n.* silex, *m.*

silhouette [silu'et], *n.* silhouette, *f.*

silica ['silikə], *n.* silice, *f.*

silicon ['silikən], *n.* silicium, *m.*

silicosis [sili'kousis], *n.* (*Med.*) silicose, *f.*

silk [silk], *a.* de soie, en soie.—*n.* soie, *f.*; (*pl.*) soieries, *f.pl.*

silken ['silkən], *a.* de soie; soyeux.

silkiness ['silkinis], *n.* nature soyeuse, *f.*

silkworm ['silkwəːm], *n.* ver à soie, *m.*

silky ['silki], *a.* de soie, soyeux.

sill [sil], *n.* seuil (*d'une porte*); rebord (*d'une fenêtre*), *m.*

silliness ['silinis], *n.* sottise, niaiserie, *f.*

silly ['sili], *a.* and *n.* sot, nigaud, niais, *m.*; *silly ass*, imbécile, *m.*; *silly thing*, sottise, *f.*; nigaud (*personne*).

silt [silt], *v.t.* envaser.—*v.i.* s'envaser.—*n.* vase, *f.*, limon, *m.*

silting ['siltiŋ], *n.* envasement, *m.*

silver ['silvə], *a.* d'argent; argenté (*couleur*); argentin (*son*).—*n.* argent, *m.*; monnaie d'argent; argenterie (*vaisselle*), *f.*—*v.t.* argenter; étamer (*miroir*).

silvering ['silvəriŋ], *n.* argenture, *f.*; étamage (*de miroirs*), *m.*

silver-plated ['silvə'pleitid], *a.* argenté, en plaqué.

silversmith ['silvəsmiθ], *n.* orfèvre, *m.*

silvery ['silvəri], *a.* d'argent; argenté (*couleur*); argentin (*son*).

similar ['similə], *a.* semblable, pareil; similaire (*de nature*).

similarity [simi'læriti], *n.* ressemblance, similitude; similarité (*de nature*), *f.*

similarly ['similəli], *adv.* pareillement, d'une manière semblable.

simile ['simili], *n.* comparaison, *f.*

similitude [si'militjuːd], *n.* similitude, *f.*

simmer ['simə], *v.i.* bouillir lentement, mijoter.

simmering ['siməriŋ], *n.* mijotement, *m.*

simnel ['simnəl], *n.* gâteau de Pâques *ou* de la mi-carême, *m.*

simper ['simpə], *n.* sourire niais, *m.*—*v.i.* sourire niaisement, minauder.

simpering ['simpəriŋ], *a.* minaudier.—*n.* minauderie, *f.*

simperingly ['simpəriŋli], *adv.* en minaudant.

simple [simpl], *a.* simple; *as simple as ABC*, simple comme bonjour.—*n.* simple, *m.*

simple-hearted ['simpl'hɑːtid], **simple-minded** ['simplmaindid], *a.* simple, ingénu, naïf.

simpleness ['simplnis], *n.* simplicité, *f.*

simpleton ['simpltən], *n.* niais, nigaud, *m.*

simplicity [sim'plisiti], *n.* simplicité, *f.*

simplification ['simplifi'keiʃən], *n.* simplification, *f.*

simplify ['simplifai], *v.t.* simplifier.

simply ['simpli], *adv.* simplement (*sans complexité*); tout bonnement (*et rien de plus*).

simulate ['simjuleit], *v.t.* feindre, simuler.

simulation [simju'leiʃən], *n.* simulation, *f.*

simulator ['simjuleitə], *n.* simulateur, *m.*

simultaneous [siməl'teinjəs], *a.* simultané.

simultaneously [siməl'teinjəsli], *adv.* simultanément.

sin [sin], *n.* péché, *m.*; (*fig.*) offense, *f.*—*v.i.* pécher.

since [sins], *conj.* puisque (*parce que*); depuis que (*temps*).—*prep.* depuis; *since then*, depuis lors.—*adv.* depuis; *ever since*, depuis ce temps-là; *long since*, il y a longtemps.

sincere [sin'siə], *a.* sincère.

sincerely [sin'siəli], *adv.* sincèrement; *yours sincerely* (*lettre amicale mais sans cérémonie*), veuillez croire, cher Monsieur, à mes sentiments les meilleurs.

sincerity [sin'seriti], *n.* sincérité, bonne foi, *f.*

sine [sain], *n.* (*Trig.*) sinus, *m.*

sinecure ['sainəkjuə], *n.* sinécure, *f.*

sinew ['sinjuː], *n.* tendon, (*colloq.*) nerf, *m.*

sinewy ['sinjui], *a.* tendineux; (*fig.*) nerveux, vigoureux.

sinful ['sinful], *a.* pécheur, coupable.

sinfully ['sinfuli], *adv.* d'une manière coupable, en pécheur.

sinfulness ['sinfulnis], *n.* culpabilité, iniquité, *f.*

sing [siŋ], *v.t.*, *v.i. irr.* chanter; célébrer (*louer*); siffler (*vent*); *to make someone sing small*, rabattre le caquet à quelqu'un.

Singapore [siŋə'pɔː]. Singapour, *m.*

singe [sindʒ], *v.t.* flamber; roussir (*vêtements etc.*); (*Tech.*) griller.—*n.* légère brûlure, *f.*

singeing ['sindʒiŋ], *n.* flambage; (*Tech.*) grillage, *m.*

singer ['siŋə], *n.* chanteur, *m.*; cantatrice (*professionnelle*), *f.*

singing ['siɲiɲ], *a.* qui chante; chanteur (*oiseau*).—*n.* chant; bourdonnement (*dans les oreilles*), *m.*

single [siɲgl], *a.* seul, simple, unique; particulier (*individuel*); singulier (*combat*); non marié, célibataire; **single bedroom**, chambre à un lit, *f.*; **single man**, célibataire, garçon, *m.*; **single** (*ticket*), billet simple, *m.*; **single woman**, femme non mariée, fille, *f.*—*n.* (*pl.*) (*Ten.*) partie simple, *f.*—*v.t.* choisir; **to single out**, choisir, distinguer de la foule.

single-handed ['siɲgl'hændid], *adv.* tout seul, sans aide.

single-hearted ['siɲgl'hɑːtid], *a.* sincère, honnête.

singleness ['siɲglnis], *n.* sincérité, simplicité, *f.*

singlet ['siɲglit], *n.* maillot fin, *m.*

single-track ['siɲgltræk], *a.* (*Rail.*) à voie unique; (*Cine.*) à simple piste.

singly ['siɲgli], *adv.* seulement; séparément; individuellement, un à un.

singsong ['siɲsɔɲ], *n.* chant monotone, *m.*

singular ['siɲgjulə], *a.* singulier; étrange (*bizarre*); simple (*pas complexe*), (*Gram.*)—*n.* singulier, *m.*

singularity [siɲgju'læriti], *n.* singularité, *f.*

singularly ['siɲgjuləli], *adv.* singulièrement.

sinister ['sinistə], *a.* sinistre; (*Her.*) sénestre.

sink [siɲk], *n.* évier (*de cuisine*); égout (*conduit*), *m.*; **a sink of iniquity**, un cloaque d'iniquité.—*v.t. irr.* faire tomber au fond, enfoncer; couler (*navire*); creuser (*puits etc.*); placer (*argent*) à fonds perdu; amortir (*dette*).—*v.i.* aller au fond, tomber au fond; s'enfoncer; sombrer, couler (*navire*); décliner, s'affaiblir (*santé etc.*); baisser (*prix etc.*); être abattu (*âme, cœur etc.*); descendre, se coucher (*soleil etc.*); dégénérer (*en*).

sinker ['siɲkə], *n.* plomb (*de ligne de pêche*), *m.*

sinking ['siɲkiɲ], *a.* qui coule (*navire*).—*n.* foncement (*de puits etc.*); tassement (*de fondements*); affaissement (*santé*); placement à fonds perdu (*d'argent*); amortissement (*d'une dette*); engloutissement (*de navire*), *m.*

sinking fund ['siɲkiɲfʌnd], *n.* fonds, *m.*, ou caisse d'amortissement (*d'une dette etc.*), *f.*

sinless ['sinlis], *a.* sans péché, innocent; pur.

sinner ['sinə], *n.* pécheur, *m.*, pécheresse, *f.*

sinuous ['sinjuəs], *a.* sinueux.

sinus ['sainəs], *n.* (*Anat.*) sinus, *m.*

sip [sip], *n.* petit coup, *m.*, petite gorgée, *f.*—*v.t., v.i.* boire à petit coups, siroter.

siphon ['saifən], *n.* siphon, *m.*—*v.t.* siphonner.

sir [sə:], *n.* monsieur, *m.*

sire ['saiə], *n.* père; sire (*à un roi*), *m.*; (*pl.*) pères, aïeux, *m.pl.*; **grand-sire**, grand-père, *m.*

siren ['saiərən], *n.* sirène, *f.*

Sirius ['siriəs]. (*Astron.*) Sirius, *m.*

sirloin [sə:'lɔin], *n.* aloyau; faux-filet, *m.*

sirocco [si'rɔkou], *n.* siroco, *m.*

siskin ['siskin], *n.* (*Orn.*) tarin, *m.*

sissy ['sisi], *n.* (*colloq.*) poule mouillée, *f.*

sister ['sistə], *a.* sœur; du même gabarit (*navire*).—*n.* sœur; (*Med.*) infirmière-major, *f.*

sisterhood ['sistəhud], *n.* communauté de sœurs, *f.*, sœurs, *f.pl.*

sister-in-law ['sistərinlɔ:], *n.* belle-sœur, *f.*

sisterly ['sistəli], *a.* de sœur, en sœur.

sit [sit], *v.t. irr.* asseoir; se tenir sur (*cheval*).—*v.i.* s'asseoir (*acte*); être assis (*attitude*); siéger, tenir séance, se réunir (*assemblée, cour, juge etc.*); couver (*poule etc.*), percher (*oiseau*); poser (*pour un portrait*); **to sit down**, s'asseoir; **to sit up**, se tenir droit; veiller (*s'abstenir du sommeil*).

sit-down strike ['sitdaunstraik], *n.* grève sur le tas, *f.*

site [sait], *n.* situation, *f.*, emplacement (*de bâtiment*); site (*paysage*), *m.*—*v.t.* placer.

sitfast ['sitfɑːst], *n.* (*Vet.*) cor, durillon, *m.*

sitter ['sitə], *n.* personne assise, *f.*; (*Paint.*) modèle, *m.*

sitting ['sitiɲ], *a.* assis; en séance (*cour etc.*); perché (*oiseau*); qui couve (*poule*).—*n.* séance; audience (*d'un cour*); couvaison (*des œufs*); place (*réservée*); (*Paint.*) séance, *f.*

sitting room ['sitiɲru:m], *n.* petit salon, *m.*

situate (1) ['sitjueit], *v.t.* situer.

situate (2) ['sitjuit], **situated** ['sitjueitid], *a.* situé; (*Law*) sis.

situation [sitju'eiʃən], *n.* situation, position, *f.*, état, *m.*; place, *f.*, emploi, *m.*

six [siks], *a.* and *n.* six, *m.*

sixteen ['siks'ti:n], *a.* and *n.* seize, *m.*

sixteenth [siks'ti:nθ], *a.* seizième; seize (*rois etc.*).—*n.* seizième (*fraction*), *m.*

sixth [siksθ], *a.* sixième; six (*rois etc.*).—*n.* sixième (*fraction*), *m.*; (*Mus.*) sixte, *f.*

sixthly ['siksθli], *adv.* sixièmement.

sixtieth ['sikstiiθ], *a.* soixantième.—*n.* soixantième (*fraction*), *m.*

sixty ['siksti], *a.* and *n.* soixante, *m.*; **about sixty**, une soixantaine (*de*), *f.*

sizable ['saizəbl], *a.* d'une bonne grosseur.

size (1) [saiz], *n.* grandeur, dimension, taille (*physique*), grosseur, *f.*, volume (*espace occupé*); calibre (*de cartouche*); format (*de livre* ou *de papier*), *m.*; encolure (*de chemise*); pointure (*de gant, de chaussure etc.*), *f.*; effectif (*d'école, de classe etc.*); (*Comm.*) numéro, *m.*—*v.t.* classer, ranger (*par grosseur, par taille*); **to size up**, juger.

size (2) [saiz], *n.* colle, *f.*, encollage, *m.*—*v.t.* coller, encoller.

sized [saizd], *a.* de grosseur; de taille.

sizzle [sizl], *n.* grésillement, *m.*—*v.i.* grésiller.

skate (1) [skeit], *n.* (*Ichth.*) raie, *f.*

skate (2) [skeit], *n.* patin, *m.*; **roller skate**, patin à roulettes.—*v.i.* patiner.

skater ['skeitə], *n.* patineur, *m.*

skating ['skeitiɲ], *n.* patinage, *m.*

skating rink ['skeitiɲriɲk], *n.* patinoire, *f.*

skein [skein], *n.* écheveau, *m.*

skeleton ['skelətən], *n.* squelette, *m.*; (*Tech.*) charpente, carcasse, *f.*

skeleton key ['skelətən'ki:], *n.* passe-partout, *m.inv.*, crochet, *m.*

sketch [sketʃ], *n.* esquisse, *f.*, croquis, *m.*, ébauche; (*Theat.*) saynète, *f.*; (*fig.*) aperçu, *m.*—*v.t.* esquisser, ébaucher.

sketch-book ['sketʃbuk], *n.* cahier de croquis, *m.*

sketchily ['sketʃili], *adv.* incomplètement.

sketchy ['sketʃi], *a.* d'esquisse, ébauché; rudimentaire.

skew [skju:], *a.* oblique, en biais.

skewer ['skju:ə], *n.* brochette, *f.*—*v.t.* embrocher.

ski [ski:], *n.* ski, *m.*—*v.i.* faire du ski.

skid [skid], *n.* (*Motor.*) dérapage (*de*), *m.*, embardée, *f.*; (*Av.*) patin, *m.*—*v.i.* déraper (*bicyclette* ou *véhicule*).

skier ['ski:ə], *n.* skieur, *m.*

skiff [skif], *n.* esquif, *m.*

ski-ing ['ski:iŋ], *n.* le ski, *m.*

ski-lift ['ski:lift], *n.* remonte-pentes, *m.inv.*

skill [skil], *n.* habileté, dextérité, adresse, *f.*

skilled [skild], *a.* habile, adroit; **skilled labor**, main-d'œuvre spécialisée, *f.*; **skilled workman**, ouvrier qualifié, *m.*

skillful ['skilful], *a.* adroit, habile.

skillfully ['skilfuli], *adv.* adroitement, habilement.

skim [skim], *v.t.* écumer; écrémer (*lait*); (*fig.*) raser, effleurer.

skimp [skimp], *v.t.* lésiner; bâcler (*travail*).

skimpy ['skimpi], *a.* mesquin, chiche; étriqué.

skin [skin], *n.* peau, *f.*; **banana skin**, pelure de banane, *f.*; **to escape by the skin of one's teeth**, l'échapper belle; **wet to the skin**, trempé jusqu'aux os.—*v.t.* écorcher (*personne* ou *animal*); peler, éplucher (*fruits etc.*); (*fig.*) écorcher, plumer.

skin-deep ['skindi:p], *a.* superficiel, peu profond.

skinflint ['skinflint], *n.* pince-maille, grigou, ladre, *m.*

skinless ['skinlis], *a.* sans peau.

skinner ['skinə], *n.* écorcheur; pelletier (*marchand*), *m.*

skinny ['skini], *a.* maigre, décharné.

skip [skip], *n.* saut, bond, *m.*—*v.t.* sauter; passer (*en lisant*).—*v.i.* sauter, sautiller, gambader.

skipper ['skipə], *n.* patron (*de navire marchand*); (*Spt.*) chef d'équipe, *m.*

skipping ['skipiŋ], *n.* action de sauter, *f.*; saut à la corde, *m.*

skipping-rope ['skipiŋroup], *n.* corde à sauter, *f.*

skirmish ['skə:miʃ], *n.* escarmouche, *f.*—*v.i.* escarmoucher.

skirmisher ['skə:miʃə], *n.* tirailleur, *m.*

skirmishing ['skə:miʃiŋ], *n.* escarmouches, *f.pl.*

skirt [skə:t], *n.* pan (*d'un habit*), *m.*; jupe (*de robe*); (*pl.*) lisière, extrémité, *f.*, bord (*de forêt etc.*), *m.*; **outskirts**, bords, faubourgs, *m.pl.*—*v.t.* border; longer (*rivière etc.*).

skirting ['skə:tiŋ], **skirting-board** ['skə:tiŋ bɔ:d], *n.* bord, *m.*, bordure; (*Arch.*) plinthe, *f.*

skit [skit], *n.* parodie, *f.*

skittish ['skitiʃ], *a.* capricieux, volage.

skittishly ['skitiʃli], *adv.* capricieusement.

skittishness ['skitiʃnis], *n.* légèreté, inconstance, *f.*

skittle [skitl], *n.* quille, *f.*

skittle alley ['skitl'æli], *n.* jeu de quilles, *m.*

skulk [skʌlk], *v.i.* se cacher; rôder (*autour de*).

skull [skʌl], *n.* crâne, *m.*

skull-cap ['skʌlkæp], *n.* calotte, *f.*

skunk [skʌŋk], *n.* putois d'Amérique, *m.*

sky [skai], *n.* ciel, *m.*

sky-blue ['skaiblu:], *a.* bleu ciel, azuré.

sky-high ['skai'hai], *a.* qui touche aux cieux; **to blow up sky-high**, faire sauter jusqu'aux cieux; (*fig.*) tancer vertement.

skylark ['skaila:k], *n.* alouette (des champs), *f.*—*v.i.* (*fig.*) faire des farces.

skylarking ['skaila:kiŋ], *n.* farces, *f.pl.*

skylight ['skailait], *n.* châssis vitré, *m.*, lucarne faîtière, *f.*

sky-line ['skailain], *n.* horizon, *m.*

sky-scraper ['skaiskreipə], *n.* gratte-ciel, *m.*

slab [slæb], *n.* dalle, plaque, table; tablette (*de chocolat*); dosse, *f.*

slack [slæk], *a.* lâche; faible, mou; détendu (*corde*); négligent; **business is slack**, les affaires ne vont pas; **the slack season**, la morte-saison, *f.*—*n.* menu charbon; mou (*de corde*); (*Eng.*) jeu; (*pl.*) pantalon, *m.*

slacken ['slækən], *v.t.* relâcher, détendre; affaiblir (*la rigueur*); ralentir (*vitesse*).—*v.i.* se relâcher, se détendre; se ralentir; diminuer; tomber.

slackening ['slækniŋ], *n.* relâchement, *m.*

slacker ['slækə], *n.* paresseux, *m.*

slacking ['slækiŋ], *n.* paresse, *f.*

slackly ['slækli], *adv.* mollement, lâchement; négligemment.

slackness ['slæknis], *n.* relâchement, *m.*; négligence, nonchalance (*morale*), *f.*

slag [slæg], *n.* scorie, *f.*; mâchefer, *m.*

slag-heap ['slæghi:p], *n.* crassier, *m.*

slake [sleik], *v.t.* éteindre (*chaux*); **to slake one's thirst**, se désaltérer.

slam [slæm], *v.t.* fermer avec violence, claquer.—*v.i.* se fermer avec bruit.—*n.* (*Cards*) vole, *f.*, chelem, *m.*

slander ['slɑ:ndə], *n.* calomnie; (*Law*) diffamation, *f.*—*v.t.* calomnier; (*Law*) diffamer.

slanderer ['slɑ:ndərə], *n.* calomniateur; (*Law*) diffamateur, *m.*

slanderous ['slɑ:ndərəs], *a.* calomnieux; (*Law*) diffamatoire.

slang [slæŋ], *n.* argot, *m.*, langue verte, *f.*

slangy ['slæŋi], *a.* d'argot, argotique.

slant [slɑ:nt], *v.t.* incliner.—*v.i.* incliner; être de biais, biaiser.—*n.* inclinaison, pente, *f.*; **on the slant**, en écharpe, en biais.

slanting ['slɑ:ntiŋ], *a.* oblique; en écharpe (*coup d'épée etc.*).

slantingly ['slɑ:ntiŋli], **slantwise** ['slɑ:nt waiz], *adv.* obliquement, en biais.

slap [slæp], *n.* tape, *f.*; soufflet (*sur la figure*), *m.*—*v.t.* souffleter, donner une fessée à (*un enfant*).—*adv.* tout droit, en plein.

slapdash ['slæpdæʃ], *adv.* à la six-quatre-deux, n'importe comment.—*a.* fait à la hâte.

slap-happy ['slæp'hæpi], *a.* toqué.

slapstick ['slæpstik], *n.* (*Theat., Cine.*) **slapstick comedy** (*fam.*), tarte à la crème, *f.*

slash [slæʃ], *n.* taillade; balafre (*sur la figure*), *f.*—*v.t.* taillader; balafrer (*la figure*).—*v.i.* frapper.

slashing ['slæʃiŋ], *a.* mordant, cinglant.

slate [sleit], *n.* ardoise, *f.*—*v.t.* couvrir d'ardoises; (*colloq.*) tancer.

slate-colored ['sleitkʌləd], *a.* ardoisé, gris d'ardoise.

slate pencil ['sleitpensl], *n.* crayon d'ardoise, *m.*

slater ['sleitə], *n.* couvreur en ardoise, *m.*

slating ['sleitiŋ], *n.* toiture en ardoise, *m.*; (*colloq.*) semonce, *f.*

slattern ['slætən], *n.* femme malpropre, souillon, *f.*

slatternly ['slætənli], *a.* négligent, malpropre, mal soigné.

slaty ['sleiti], *a.* schisteux, d'ardoise; ardoisé (*couleur*).

slaughter ['slɔ:tə], *n.* tuerie, boucherie, *f.*, massacre; abattage (*des animaux*), *m.*—*v.t.* massacrer; abattre (*animaux*).

slaughterer ['slɔ:tərə], *n.* abatteur, *m.*

slaughter-house ['slɔ:təhaus], *n.* abattoir, *m.*

Slav [slɑ:v], *a.* slave.—*n.* Slave (*personne*), *m.*, *f.*

slave [sleiv], *n.* esclave, *m.*, *f.*—*v.i.* travailler comme un esclave, peiner.

slave driver ['sleivdraivə], *n.* (*fig.*) maître sévère et cruel, *m.*

slaver (1) ['sleivə], *n.* négrier, bâtiment négrier, *m.*

slaver (2) ['slævə], *v.i.* baver (*sur*).—*n.* bave, salive, *f.*

slavery ['sleivəri], *n.* esclavage, *m.*

slave trade ['sleivtreid], *n.* traite des noirs, *f.*

slavish ['sleiviʃ], *a.* d'esclave; servile (*imitation etc.*).

slavishly ['sleiviʃli], *adv.* en esclave; servilement.

slavishness ['sleiviʃnis], *n.* servilité, *f.*

Slavonic [slə'vɔnik], *a.* slave.—*n.* slave (*langues*), *m.*

slay [slei], *v.t. irr.* tuer.

slayer ['sleiə], *n.* tueur (*de*), meurtrier, *m.*

slaying ['sleiiŋ], *n.* tuerie, *f.*

sledge [sledʒ], *n.* traîneau, *m.*—*v.i.* (*also to go sledging*) se promener en traîneau.

sledge hammer ['sledʒhæmə], *n.* marteau à deux mains, *m.*

sleek [sli:k], *a.* lisse, luisant, poli; (*fig.*) doucereux, onctueux.

sleekness ['sli:knis], *n.* luisant, *m.*; (*fig.*) douceur, onctuosité, *f.*

sleep [sli:p], *n.* sommeil, *m.*; *beauty sleep*, sommeil avant minuit; *sound sleep*, profond sommeil; *to go to sleep*, s'endormir; *to put a dog to sleep*, tuer un chien.—*v.t. irr.* dormir.—*v.i.* dormir, coucher (*à, chez* ou *dans*).

sleeper ['sli:pə], *n.* dormeur, *m.*; (*Rail.*) traverse, *f.*; (*colloq.*) wagon-lit, *m.*

sleepily ['sli:pili], *adv.* d'un air endormi.

sleepiness ['sli:pinis], *n.* assoupissement, *m.*

sleeping ['sli:piŋ], *a.* endormi; dormant.—*n.* sommeil, repos, *m.*; *sleeping pills* or *tablets*, somnifère, *m.*

sleeping bag ['sli:piŋbæg], *n.* sac de couchage, *m.*

sleeping berth ['sli:piŋbə:θ], *n.* couchette, *f.*

sleeping car ['sli:piŋkɑ:], *n.* wagon-lit, *m.*

sleeping draft ['sli:piŋdrɑ:ft], *n.* somnifère, *m.*

sleeping partner ['sli:piŋ'pɑ:tnə], *n.* associé commanditaire, *m.*

sleepless ['sli:plis], *a.* sans sommeil.

sleeplessness ['sli:plisnis], *n.* insomnie, *f.*

sleep-walker ['sli:pwɔ:kə], *n.* somnambule, *m.*, *f.*

sleepy ['sli:pi], *a.* qui a envie de dormir; soporifique (*somnifère*); *to feel sleepy*, avoir sommeil.

sleepy-head ['sli:pihed], *n.* paresseux, *m.*

sleet [sli:t], *n.* neige fondue, *f.*; grésil, *m.*

sleeve [sli:v], *n.* manche, *f.*

sleeveless ['sli:vlis], *a.* sans manches.

sleigh [slei], *n.* traîneau, *m.*

sleight [slait], *n.* habileté, *f.*, escamotage, *m.*; *sleight of hand*, tour de passe-passe, *m.*

slender ['slendə], *a.* mince; élancé; svelte (*taille*); (*fig.*) léger; chétif, maigre.

slenderness ['slendənis], *n.* minceur, légèreté; modicité, *f.*

sleuth(-hound) ['slu:θ(haund)], *n.* (chien) limier; (*fig.*) détective, *m.*

slice [slais], *n.* tranche; écumoire (*ustensile*), *f.*; *fish-slice*, truelle, *f.*; *slice of bread and jam*, tartine de confiture, *f.*—*v.t.* couper en tranches.

slick [slik], *a.* adroit.

slickness ['sliknis], *n.* adresse, habileté, *f.*

slide [slaid], *n.* glissoire, glissade, *f.*; *lantern slide*, diapositive, vue fixe, *f.*—*v.t. irr.* glisser; tirer (*de*).—*v.i.* glisser; couler.

slide rule ['slaidru:l], *n.* règle à calcul, *f.*

sliding ['slaidiŋ], *a.* glissant; à coulisse.—*n.* glissade, *f.*, glissement, *m.*

sliding door ['slaidiŋ'dɔ:], *n.* porte à coulisse, *f.*

sliding scale ['slaidiŋ'skeil], *n.* (*Econ.*) échelle mobile, *f.*

slight [slait], *a.* mince, léger; insignifiant; *not in the slightest*, pas le moins du monde.—*n.* manque d'égards; affront, *m.*, insulte, *f.*—*v.t.* traiter sans égards; mépriser.

slightingly ['slaitiŋli], *adv.* avec mépris, avec dédain.

slightly ['slaitli], *adv.* légèrement, un peu.

slightness ['slaitnis], *n.* minceur; légèreté, *f.*

slim [slim], *a.* svelte, mince; (*colloq.*) rusé.—*v.i.* s'amincir.

slime [slaim], *n.* vase, *f.*, limon, *m.*, bave (*de colimaçon*), *f.*

sliminess ['slaiminis], *n.* viscosité, *f.*

slimness ['slimnis], *n.* sveltesse, taille mince, *f.*

slimy ['slaimi], *a.* vaseux, limoneux; visqueux, gluant; (*fam.*) obséquieux.

sling [sliŋ], *n.* fronde; bretelle (*de fusil*); écharpe (*pour un membre cassé*), *f.*—*v.t. irr.* lancer (*avec une fronde*); suspendre (*fusil etc.*).

slinger ['sliŋə], *n.* frondeur, *m.*

slink [sliŋk], *v.i. irr.* s'esquiver, se dérober.

slip [slip], *v.t.* glisser, couler; perdre; lâcher; filer (*câble*); pousser (*verrou*); *to slip in*, introduire; *to slip off*, enlever, ôter; *to slip on*, passer, mettre.—*v.i.* glisser, couler (*nœud*); patiner (*roues*); (*fig.*) faire un faux pas; *to slip away*, s'esquiver; *to slip down*, tomber; *to slip in*, se faufiler, entrer furtivement; *to slip up*, (*fam.*) se tromper.—*n.* glissade; combinaison (*sous-vêtement*); laisse (*à chien*), *f.*; engobe (*céramique*); (*Hort.*) scion, *m.*; cale (*de port etc.*); faute d'étourderie, *f.*, lapsus, *m.*; *pillow slip*, taie d'oreiller, *f.*; *slip of paper*, bout de papier, *m.*; *slip of the pen*, erreur de plume, *f.*; *to give someone the slip*, planter quelqu'un là; *to make a slip*, faire un faux pas.

slip-knot ['slipnɔt], *n.* nœud coulant, *m.*

slipper ['slipə], *n.* pantoufle, *f.*

slippered ['slipəd], *a.* en pantoufles.

slipperiness ['slipərinis], *n.* nature glissante; volubilité (*de la langue*), *f.*

slippery ['slipəri], *a.* glissant; incertain, peu sûr; peu stable; matois, rusé; *slippery customer*, rusé compère, *m.*

slipshod ['slipʃɔd], *a.* (*fig.*) négligé; décousu (*style*).

slipstream ['slipstri:m], *n.* sillage, *m.*
slipway ['slipwei], *n.* cale, *f.*
slit [slit], *v.t. irr.* fendre.—*v.i.* se fendre.—*n.* fente, fissure, *f.*
slither ['sliðə], *v.i.* glisser; ramper (*reptile*).
sliver ['slivə, 'slaivə], *n.* éclat, *m.*, tranche, *f.*, ruban, *m.*
slobber ['slɔbə], *v.i.* baver.
sloe [slou], *n.* (*Bot.*) prunelle, *f.*
sloe tree ['sloutri:], *n.* prunellier, *m.*
slogan ['slougən], *n.* mot d'ordre, *m.*, devise, *f.*, slogan, *m.*
sloop [slu:p], *n.* sloop, aviso, *m.*
slop [slɔp], *n.* (*usu. in pl.*) rinçures, *f.pl.*—*v.t.* répandre, renverser.
slop basin ['slɔpbeisn], **slop bowl** ['slɔp boul], *n.* bol à rinçures (*de thé*), *m.*
slope [sloup], *n.* pente, *f.*; talus, versant, *m.*—*v.t.* couper en biais; taluter.—*v.i.* pencher, aller en pente, incliner.
sloping ['sloupiŋ], *a.* de biais, en pente.
sloppiness ['slɔpinis], *n.* état détrempé, *m.*; mollesse (*personne*), *f.*
sloppy ['slɔpi], *a.* bourbeux, humide; (*fig.*) mou.
slot [slɔt], *n.* rainure, mortaise, fente; barre de bois, *f.*
sloth (1) [slouθ], *n.* paresse, fainéantise, *f.*
sloth (2) [slouθ], *n.* (*Zool.*) paresseux, aï, *m.*
slothful ['slouθful], *a.* paresseux, fainéant.
slot machine ['slɔtməʃi:n], *n.* distributeur automatique, *m.*
slouch [slautʃ], *n.* démarche molle *ou* lourde, *f.*; lourdaud (*personne*), *m.*—*v.i.* marcher lourdement; **to slouch along,** marcher d'un pas traînant.
slouching ['slautʃiŋ], *a.* lourd et gauche.
slough [slau], *n.* bourbier, *m.*, fondrière; dépouille (*de serpent*), *f.*
Slovak ['slouvæk], *a.* slovaque.—*n.* Slovaque (*personne*), *m.*, *f.*
sloven [slʌvn], *n.* sans-soin, mal-soigné, *m.*
Slovene ['slouvi:n], *n.* Slovène (*personne*), *m.*, *f.*
Slovenian [slo'vi:niən], *a.* slovène.
slovenliness ['slʌvnlinis], *n.* malpropreté, saleté, négligence, *f.*
slovenly ['slʌvnli], *a.* mal soigné, mal peigné, débraillé.
slow [slou], *a.* lent, tardif; lourd (*pesant*); en retard (*montre etc.*).—*adv.* lentement.—*v.t.* ralentir.—*v.i.* se ralentir.
slowly ['slouli], *adv.* lentement, tardivement.
slowness ['slounis], *n.* lenteur; paresse; lourdeur (*pesanteur*), *f.*; retard (*de montre etc.*), *m.*
slow-worm ['slouwə:m], *n.* orvet, *m.*
sludge [slʌdʒ], *n.* boue, vase, *f.*; cambouis, *m.*
slug [slʌg], *n.* limace, *f.*; lingot (*de fusil*), *m.*
sluggard ['slʌgəd], *n.* paresseux, *m.*
sluggish ['slʌgiʃ], *a.* paresseux, indolent, lourd; lent (*ruisseau*).
sluggishly ['slʌgiʃli], *adv.* paresseusement, lourdement.
sluggishness ['slʌgiʃnis], *n.* paresse; lenteur (*de ruisseau*), *f.*
sluice [slu:s], *n.* écluse; bonde (*dans un étang*), *f.*—*v.t.* lâcher par une écluse; inonder d'eau.
sluice-gate ['slu:sgeit], *n.* vanne, *f.*
slum [slʌm], *n.* taudis, *m.*, (*pl.*) bas quartiers, *m.pl.*; **slum clearance,** lutte contre les taudis, *f.*

slumber ['slʌmbə], *n.* sommeil, *m.*—*v.i.* sommeiller, dormir.
slumberer ['slʌmbərə], *n.* dormeur, *m.*
slumbering ['slʌmbəriŋ], *a.* endormi, assoupi.—*n.* sommeil, assoupissement, *m.*
slump [slʌmp], *v.i.* s'enfoncer soudainement.—*n.* baisse subite; crise, *f.*
slur [slə:], *n.* tache; (*Mus.*) liaison, *f.*; **to cast a slur upon,** flétrir, dénigrer.—*v.t.* tacher, salir; (*Mus.*) lier; **to slur over,** glisser sur.
slurred [slə:d], *a.* (*Mus.*) coulé; brouillé (*paroles*).
slurring ['slə:riŋ], *n.* (*Mus.*) liaison, *f.*
slush [slʌʃ], *n.* boue, fange; neige à moitié fondue, *f.*
slut [slʌt], *n.* saligaude, souillon, *f.*
sly [slai], *a.* sournois, rusé; **on the sly,** en sourdine; **sly dog,** fin matois, *m.*
slyly ['slaili], *adv.* avec ruse, sournoisement.
slyness ['slainis], *n.* ruse, finesse, nature sournoise, *f.*
smack (1) [smæk], *n.* claquement (*de fouet*), *m.*; claque (*de la main*); gifle (*sur la figure*), *f.*; gros baiser, *m.*—*adv.* **smack in the middle,** en plein milieu.—*v.t.* faire claquer (*fouet, les lèvres*); donner une claque à.
smack (2) [smæk], *n.* (*fig.*) saveur, *f.*—*v.i.* **to smack of** (*matière*), sentir (*le, la etc.*).
smack (3) [smæk], *n.* bateau de pêche, *m.*
smacking ['smækiŋ], *n.* claquement, *m.*; fessée, *f.*
small [smɔ:l], *a.* petit; fin, menu; (*fig.*) chétif, mince, pauvre; modeste, peu considérable; **small arms,** armes portatives, *f.pl.*; **small fry,** menu fretin, *m.*; **small letters,** minuscules, *f.pl.*—*n.* partie mince, *f.*; **small of the back,** chute des reins, *f.*
smallish ['smɔ:liʃ], *a.* un peu petit, un peu menu.
smallness ['smɔ:lnis], *n.* petitesse, *f.*; peu d'importance, *m.*
smallpox ['smɔ:lpɔks], *n.* petite vérole, *f.*
smarmy ['smɑ:mi], *a.* (*pop.*) mielleux.
smart [smɑ:t], *a.* piquant, cuisant, vif; vigoureux, rude; intelligent, éveillé; beau, élégant, pimpant, chic; **look smart!** dépêchez-vous! **smart Aleck,** finaud, *m.*—*n.* douleur aiguë, vive douleur, cuisson, *f.*—*v.i.* cuire, éprouver une vive douleur.
smarten [smɑ:tn] (**up**), *v.t.* animer; **to smarten oneself up,** se faire beau, s'attifer.
smarting ['smɑ:tiŋ], *a.* cuisant, poignant.—*n.* douleur cuisante, *f.*
smartly ['smɑ:tli], *adv.* lestement, vivement; habilement; vigoureusement, rudement; élégamment.
smartness ['smɑ:tnis], *n.* force, vigueur, élégance, *f.*, éclat (*de vêtements*), *m.*; finesse (*astuce*), *f.*
smash [smæʃ], *v.t.* briser, écraser; (*fig.*) ruiner.—*v.i.* se briser.—*n.* fracas, *m.*; (*Fin.*) déconfiture, faillite, banqueroute; (*Rail.*) catastrophe, *f.*—*adv.* **to go smash,** faire faillite.
smashing ['smæʃiŋ], *a.* (*pop.*) formidable, épatant.
smattering ['smætəriŋ], *n.* connaissances superficielles, *f.pl.*
smear [smiə], *v.t.* enduire; (*fig.*) salir.—*n.* tache, *f.*; (*fig.*) calomnie, atteinte à la réputation, *f.*

567

smell [smel], *n.* odeur, *f.*; odorat (*sens*); flair (*de chien*), *m.—v.t., v.i. irr.* sentir; flairer (*chien*).
smelly ['smeli], *a.* malodorant.
smelt (1) [smelt], *n.* (*Ichth.*) éperlan, *m.*
smelt (2) [smelt], *v.t.* fondre.
smelting ['smeltiŋ], *n.* fonte, *f.*
smile [smail], *n.* sourire, *m.—v.i.* sourire.
smiling ['smailiŋ], *a.* souriant; riant (*paysage etc.*).
smilingly ['smailiŋli], *adv.* en souriant.
smirch [smə:tʃ], *v.t.* souiller, salir.—*n.* tache, *f.*
smirk [smə:k], *v.i.* minauder.—*n.* sourire affecté, *m.*
smirking ['smə:kiŋ], *a.* affecté, minaudier.
smite [smait], *v.t. irr.* frapper; détruire; châtier; (*fig.*) charmer.
smith [smiθ], *n.* forgeron, *m.*
smithereens [smiðə'ri:nz], *n.pl.* **to smash to smithereens,** mettre en miettes.
smithy ['smiði], *n.* forge, *f.*
smock [smɔk], *n.* blouse, *f.*
smog [smɔg], *n.* brouillard épais et enfumé, *m.*
smoke [smouk], *n.* fumée, *f.—v.t., v.i.* fumer.
smokeless ['smouklis], *a.* sans fumée.
smoker ['smoukə], *n.* fumeur (*personne*), *m.*
smoke-stack ['smoukstæk], *n.* cheminée, *f.*
smokiness ['smoukinis], *n.* état enfumé, *m.*
smoking ['smoukiŋ], *a.* fumant.—*n.* habitude de fumer, *f.*; **no smoking,** défense de fumer.
smoky ['smouki], *a.* qui fume, plein de fumée.
smooth [smu:ð], *a.* uni; égal (*régulier*); doux (*non âpre*); poli, lisse (*verni*); plat (*mer*); doucereux (*personne*).—*v.t.* polir; adoucir; aplanir, unir; dérider (*le front*); lisser (*les cheveux*).
smooth-faced ['smu:ðfeist], *a.* imberbe.
smoothing-iron ['smu:ðiŋaiən], *n.* fer à repasser, *m.*
smoothly ['smu:ðli], *adv.* uniment; sans difficulté; doucement.
smoothness ['smu:ðnis], *n.* égalité; douceur, *f.*; calme (*de la mer*), *m.*
smooth-tongued ['smu:ð'tʌŋd], *a.* mielleux, doucereux.
smother ['smʌðə], *v.t.* suffoquer, étouffer.
smothering ['smʌðəriŋ], *a.* étouffant, suffocant.—*n.* étouffement, *m.*
smoulder ['smouldə], *v.i.* brûler sans fumée ni flamme; (*fig.*) couver.
smouldering ['smouldəriŋ], *a.* qui couve.
smudge [smʌdʒ], *v.t.* barbouiller, noircir.—*n.* barbouillage, *m.*, tache, *f.*
smudgy ['smʌdʒi], *a.* barbouillé; taché.
smug [smʌg], *a.* suffisant, content de soi.
smuggle [smʌgl], *v.t.* passer en contrebande.—*v.i.* faire la contrebande.
smuggled [smʌgld], *a.* de contrebande.
smuggler ['smʌglə], *n.* contrebandier, *m.*
smuggling ['smʌgliŋ], *n.* contrebande, fraude, *f.*
smugness ['smʌgnis], *n.* suffisance, *f.*
smut [smʌt], *n.* tache de suie; (*fig.*) saleté (*grivoiserie*), *f.—v.t.* noircir.
smuttiness ['smʌtinis], *n.* noirceur; (*fig.*) saleté, *f.*
smutty ['smʌti], *a.* noir; (*fig.*) obscène, grivois.
snack [snæk], *n.* morceau; casse-croûte, *m.*

snack-bar ['snækbɑ:], *n.* snack-bar, *m.*
snaffle [snæfl], *n.* mors de bridon, filet, *m.*—
snag [snæg], *n.* (*fig.*) obstacle caché, *m.*
snail [sneil], *n.* escargot, limaçon, colimaçon, *m.*
snail's pace ['sneilzpeis], *n.* pas de tortue, *m.*
snake [sneik], *n.* serpent, *m.—v.i.* (*Naut.*) serpenter.
snap [snæp], *v.t.* saisir, happer; casser, rompre, éclater; faire claquer (*fouet etc.*); fermer avec un bruit sec; dire d'un ton sec.—*v.i.* tâcher de mordre *ou* de happer; se casser, se rompre; craquer; **to snap at,** (*fam.*) brusquer.—*a.* imprévu.—*n.* coup de dent, *m.*; cassure, *f.*; claquement (*de fouet etc.*); bruit sec; fermoir (*de sac à main*); biscuit craquant, *m.*; vivacité, *f.*
snapdragon ['snæpdrægn], *n.* muflier, *m.*
snappy ['snæpi], *a.* vif; **make it snappy!** dépêchez-vous!
snapshot ['snæpʃɔt], *n.* (*colloq.* **snap** [snæp]) instantané, *m.*
snare [snɛə], *n.* lacet, collet; (*fig.*) piège, *m.*—*v.t.* prendre (au piège).
snarl [snɑ:l], *v.i.* grogner; montrer les dents.—*n.* grognement, *m.*
snarling ['snɑ:liŋ], *a.* hargneux.—*n.* grognement, *m.*
snatch [snætʃ], *v.t.* saisir; **to snatch at,** chercher à saisir; **to snatch from,** arracher à; **to snatch up,** empoigner.—*n.* **by snatches,** à bâtons rompus; **snatches of conversation,** des bribes de conversation, *f.pl.*
sneak [sni:k], *v.t.* chiper.—*v.i.* s'en aller furtivement; (*Sch.*) cafarder, moucharder.—*n.* pleutre, pied-plat; cafard, *m.*
sneaking ['sni:kiŋ], *a.* rampant, servile; furtif, inavoué.
sneer [sniə], *n.* rire *ou* sourire moqueur, sarcasme, ricanement, *m.—v.i.* ricaner, se moquer (*de*).
sneering ['sniəriŋ], *a.* ricaneur, moqueur.—*n.* ricanement, *m.*
sneeringly ['sniəriŋli], *adv.* en ricanant.
sneeze [sni:z], *n.* éternuement, *m.—v.i.* éternuer.
sneezing ['sni:ziŋ], *n.* éternuement, *m.*
sniff [snif], *v.t.* flairer.—*v.i.* renifler.—*n.* reniflement, *m.*
snigger ['snigə], *v.i.* rire du bout des lèvres, ricaner.—*n.* rire en dessous, *m.*
snip [snip], *n.* coup de ciseaux, *m.*; (*pop.*) certitude, *f.—v.t.* couper (*d'un coup de ciseaux*).
snipe [snaip], *n.* bécassine, *f.—v.i.* (*Shooting*) canarder.
sniper ['snaipə], *n.* tireur embusqué, franc-tireur, *m.*
snippet ['snipit], *n.* petit morceau, *m.*
snivel [snivl], *v.i.* être morveux; (*fig.*) pleurnicher.
sniveller ['snivlə], *n.* pleurnicheur, *m.*
snivelling ['snivliŋ], *a.* morveux; (*fig.*) pleurnicheur.—*n.* pleurnicherie, *f.*
snob [snɔb], *n.* poseur; fat, snob, *m.*
snobbery ['snɔbəri], *n.* snobisme, *m.*
snobbish ['snɔbiʃ], *a.* affecté, poseur, prétentieux.
snobbishness ['snɔbiʃnis], *n.* snobisme, *m.*
snoop [snu:p], *v.i.* fureter.
snooper ['snu:pə], *n.* fureteur, *m.*

snooze [snu:z], *n.* somme, *m.—v.i.* sommeiller.

snore [snɔː], *v.i.* ronfler.—*n.* ronflement, *m.*

snorkel [ˈsnɔːrkl], *n.* schnorkel, *m.*

snort [snɔːt], *v.i.* renâcler, s'ébrouer (*cheval*); ronfler.

snorting [ˈsnɔːtiŋ], *n.* ronflement, *m.*

snot [snɔt], *n.* (*vulg.*) morve, *f.*

snotty [ˈsnɔti], *a.* (*vulg.*) morveux.

snout [snaut], *n.* museau; mufle (*de taureau*); groin (*de cochon*), *m.*

snow [snou], *n.* neige, *f.—v.i.* neiger, tomber de la neige.

snowball [ˈsnoubɔːl], *n.* boule de neige, *f.*

snow-capped [ˈsnoukæpt], *a.* couronné de neige.

snow-drift [ˈsnoudrift], *n.* congère, *f.*, amas de neige, *m.*

snowdrop [ˈsnoudrɔp], *n.* perce-neige, *m.*

snowflake [ˈsnoufleik], *n.* flocon de neige, *m.*

snow-man [ˈsnoumæn], *n.* (*pl.* **-men** [men]) bonhomme de neige, *m.*

snowplow [ˈsnouplau], *n.* chasse-neige, *m.*

snow-shoe [ˈsnouʃuː], *n.* raquette, *f.*

snow-storm [ˈsnoustɔːm], *n.* tempête de neige, *f.*

Snow White [ˈsnouˈwait]. Blanche-Neige, *f.*

snow-white [ˈsnouwait], *a.* blanc comme la neige.

snowy [ˈsnoui], *a.* de neige; neigeux.

snub [snʌb], *n.* rebuffade, *f.*; affront, *m.—v.t.* rabrouer, rembarrer.

snub-nosed [ˈsnʌbnouzd], *a.* au nez camus.

snuff (1) [snʌf], *n.* tabac (à priser), *m.*; **pinch of snuff**, prise de tabac, *f.*

snuff (2) [snʌf], *n.* lumignon (*de mèche*), *m.—v.t.* moucher (*chandelle*).

snuff-box [ˈsnʌfbɔks], *n.* tabatière, *f.*

snuffle [snʌfl], *n.* reniflement, *m.—v.i.* nasiller, renifler.

snuffling [ˈsnʌfliŋ], *a.* nasillard.—*n.* nasillement, *m.*

snug [snʌg], *a.* confortable, commode et agréable, où l'on est bien; gentil; serré, compact; **we are very snug here**, nous sommes on ne peut mieux ici.

snuggery [ˈsnʌgəri], *n.* endroit petit et commode (*où l'on se sent chez soi*), *m.*

snuggle [snʌgl], *v.t.* serrer.—*v.i.* se serrer.

snugly [ˈsnʌgli], *adv.* commodément, à son aise.

snugness [ˈsnʌgnis], *n.* confort, bien-être, *m.*

so [sou], *adv.* and *conj.* ainsi, de cette manière, comme cela, comme ça (*de cette façon*); de même, de la même manière, tel (*pareillement*); si, tellement, tant (*à tel point*); aussi, donc (*alors*); **and so on**, et ainsi de suite; **be it so**, soit! **how so?** comment cela? **is that so?** vraiment? **just so!** parfaitement! *Mr.* **So-and-So,** Monsieur un tel; **or so,** environ, à peu près; **so as to,** de manière à; **so that,** de sorte que.

soak [souk], *v.t.* tremper; (*colloq.*) estamper. —*v.i.* tremper, s'infiltrer.

soaking [ˈsoukin], *a.* qui trempe.—*n.* trempée (*de pluie*), *f.*

soap [soup], *n.* savon, *m.—v.t.* savonner.

soap bubble [ˈsoupbʌbl], *n.* bulle de savon, *f.*

soap flakes [ˈsoupfleiks], *n.pl.* savon en paillettes, *m.*

soap-suds [ˈsoupsʌdz], *n.pl.* eau de savon, *f.*

soar [sɔː], *v.i.* prendre l'essor, s'élever; **to soar over,** planer sur.

soaring [ˈsɔːriŋ], *a.* qui s'élève; (*fig.*) élevé.— *n.* essor, élan, *m.*

sob [sɔb], *v.i.* sangloter.—*n.* sanglot, *m.*

sobbing [ˈsɔbiŋ], *n.* sanglots, *m.pl.*

sober [ˈsoubə], *a.* qui n'a pas bu, qui n'est pas ivre; sobre, tempéré; grave, sérieux; sensé; calme, posé, rassis.—*v.t.* dégriser; (*fig.*) calmer.—*v.i.* **to sober up,** se désenivrer.

soberly [ˈsoubəli], *adv.* sobrement; raisonnablement.

soberness [ˈsoubənis], **sobriety** [səˈbraiəti], *n.* sobriété, tempérance; gravité, *f.*

so-called [ˈsoukɔːld], *a.* soi-disant, prétendu.

soccer [ˈsɔkə], *n.* (*fam.*) football, *m.*

sociability [souʃəˈbiliti], *n.* sociabilité, *f.*

sociable [ˈsouʃəbl], *a.* sociable.

social [ˈsouʃəl], *a.* social.

socialism [ˈsouʃəlizm], *n.* socialisme, *m.*

socialist [ˈsouʃəlist], *a.* and *n.* socialiste, *m., f.*

socially [ˈsouʃəli], *adv.* socialement.

society [səˈsaiəti], *n.* société; la société, *f.*; le monde, *m.*

sociology [sousiˈɔlədʒi], *n.* sociologie, *f.*

sock [sɔk], *n.* chaussette; semelle (*intérieure*), *f.*

socket [ˈsɔkit], *n.* emboîture; orbite (*de l'œil*), *f.*; trou, *m.*, cavité; douille (*d'outil etc.*), *f.*

Socrates [ˈsɔkrətiːz]. Socrate, *m.*

sod [sɔd], *n.* gazon, *m.*; motte de gazon, *f.*

soda [ˈsoudə], *n.* soude, *f.*; **baking soda,** bicarbonate de soude, *m.*

soda water [ˈsoudəwɔːtə], *n.* eau de Seltz, *f.*, soda, *m.*

sodden [sɔdn], *a.* imprégné d'eau, détrempé; pâteux (*pain*); abruti (*d'alcool*).

sodium [ˈsoudiəm], *n.* (*Chem.*) sodium, *m.*

sodomy [ˈsɔdəmi], *n.* sodomie, *f.*

sofa [ˈsoufə], *n.* canapé, *m.*

soft [sɔft], *a.* mou, mol, mollet; délicat, doux, facile, pas résistant; tendre; efféminé; faible; sot, niais; (*Gram.*) doux; **soft fruits,** fruits rouges, *m.pl.—adv.* mollement, doucement.—*int.* doucement! tout doux!

soften [sɔfn], *v.t.* amollir, ramollir; adoucir, apaiser; affaiblir; attendrir (*cœur*).—*v.i.* s'amollir, se ramollir; s'affaiblir; s'attendrir (*cœur*).

softener [ˈsɔfnə], *n.* chose qui amollit, *f.*

softening [ˈsɔfniŋ], *n.* amollissement; affaiblissement; attendrissement (*du cœur*), *m.*

soft-headed [ˈsɔftˈhedid], *a.* niais; sot.

soft-hearted [ˈsɔftˈhɑːtid], *a.* tendre, compatissant.

softly [ˈsɔftli], *adv.* mollement; doucement; tendrement.

softness [ˈsɔftnis], *n.* mollesse; faiblesse; niaiserie; douceur, *f.*

soggy [ˈsɔgi], *a.* détrempé; pâteux (*pain*).

soil (1) [sɔil], *n.* sol, terrain, terroir, *m.*, terre, *f.*

soil (2) [sɔil], *n.* tache, souillure, *f.—v.t.* salir, souiller.

sojourn [ˈsɔdʒən], *n.* séjour, *m.—v.i.* séjourner.

sojourning [ˈsɔdʒəniŋ], *n.* séjour, *m.*

solace [ˈsɔlis], *n.* consolation, *f.*, soulagement, *m.—v.t.* consoler (*de*).

solar [ˈsoulə], *a.* solaire, du soleil.

solder [ˈsɔ(l)də], *n.* soudure, *f.—v.t.* souder.

soldering [ˈsɔ(l)dəriŋ], *n.* soudure, *f.*; soudage (*action*), *m.*; **soldering iron,** fer à souder, *m.*

569

soldier ['sould͡ʒə], n. soldat, militaire, m.; *foot soldier*, fantassin, m.; *private soldier*, simple soldat.—*v.i.* servir comme soldat.

soldierly ['sould͡ʒəli], a. de soldat, militaire, martial.

soldiery ['sould͡ʒəri], n. troupes, f.pl., soldats, m.pl.

sole (1) [soul], a. seul, unique.

sole (2) [soul], n. plante (*du pied*); semelle (*de soulier, d'outil etc.*), f.—*v.t.* ressemeler.

sole (3) [soul], n. (*Ichth.*) sole, f.

solecism ['sɔlisizm], n. solécisme, m.

solely ['soulli], adv. seulement, uniquement.

solemn ['sɔləm], a. solennel.

solemnity [sə'lemniti], n. solennité, f.

solemnization [sɔləmnai'zeiʃən], n. solennisation; célébration solennelle, f.

solemnize ['sɔləmnaiz], v.t. solenniser, célébrer.

solemnly ['sɔləmli], adv. solennellement.

solenoid ['sɔlinɔid], n. (*Elec.*) solénoïde, m.

solicit [sə'lisit], v.t. solliciter.

solicitation [səlisi'teiʃən], n. sollicitation, f.

solicitous [sə'lisitəs], a. désireux; *solicitous about*, soigneux, attentif à.

solicitude [sə'lisitjuːd], n. sollicitude, f.

solid ['sɔlid], a. solide, massif.—n. solide, m.

solidarity [sɔli'dæriti], n. solidarité, f.

solidification [səlidifi'keiʃən], n. solidification, f.

solidify [sə'lidifai], v.t. solidifier.—v.i. se solidifier.

solidity [sə'liditi], **solidness** ['sɔlidnis], n. solidité, f.

solidly ['sɔlidli], adv. solidement.

soliloquize [sə'liləkwaiz], v.i. faire un soliloque.

soliloquy [sə'liləkwi], n. soliloque, m.

soling ['soulin], n. ressemelage, m.

solitary ['sɔlitəri], a. solitaire, retiré, isolé; seul.

solitude ['sɔlitjuːd], n. solitude, f.

solo ['soulou], n. solo, m.

soloist ['soulouist], n. soliste, m., f.

Solomon ['sɔləmən]. Salomon, m.

solstice ['sɔlstis], n. solstice, m.

solubility [sɔlju'biliti], n. solubilité, f.

soluble ['sɔljubl], a. soluble.

solution [sə'ljuːʃən], n. solution, f.

solvable ['sɔlvəbl], a. soluble.

solve [sɔlv], v.t. résoudre, expliquer, éclaircir.

solvency ['sɔlvənsi], n. (*Fin.*) solvabilité, f.

solvent ['sɔlvənt], a. dissolvant; (*Comm.*) solvable.—n. dissolvant, m.

Somali [so'maːli], a. somali.—n. somali (*langue*); Somali (*personne*), m.

Somalia [so'maːliə]. la Somalie, f.

Somaliland [so'maːlilænd]. la Somalie, f.

somber ['sɔmbə], a. sombre.

somberly ['sɔmbəli], adv. sombrement.

some [sʌm], a. quelque, m., f., quelques, pl.; un certain, m., certains, m.pl., plusieurs, pl.; du, m., de la, f., de l', m., f., des, pl., de; quelconque; un certain nombre de, un peu de, une partie de.—adv. à peu près, environ, quelque.—pron. quelques-uns, m.pl., quelques-unes, f.pl.; les uns, m.pl., les unes, f.pl., . . . les autres, pl.; en.

somebody ['sʌmbədi], **someone** ['sʌmwʌn], pron. quelqu'un, m., quelqu'une, f., on; *somebody else*, quelqu'un d'autre, quelque autre, un autre.

somehow ['sʌmhau], adv. d'une manière ou d'une autre, de façon ou d'autre.

someone [SOMEBODY].

somersault ['sʌməsɔːlt], n. saut périlleux, m., culbute, f.

something ['sʌmθin], n. and pron. quelque chose (*de*), m.; *something else*, autre chose, f.—adv. un peu, quelque peu, tant soit peu.

sometime ['sʌmtaim], adv. autrefois, jadis; *sometime or other*, tôt ou tard.—a. ancien.

sometimes ['sʌmtaimz], adv. quelquefois, parfois; tantôt.

somewhat ['sʌmwɔt], adv. quelque peu, un peu; assez.—n. un peu, quelque peu, tant soit peu, m.

somewhere ['sʌmwɛə], adv. quelque part; *somewhere else*, ailleurs.

somnambulist [sɔm'næmbjulist], n. somnambule, m., f.

somniferous [sɔm'nifərəs], a. somnifère.

somnolence ['sɔmnələns], n. somnolence, f.

somnolent ['sɔmnələnt], a. somnolent.

son [sʌn], n. fils, m.; (*fig.*) descendant, m.

sonata [sə'naːtə], n. sonate, f.

song [sɔn], n. chanson, f.; chant, m.; (*fig.*) ballade, f.; *a mere song*, un rien, m., une bagatelle, f.

songster ['sɔnstə], n. chanteur; oiseau chanteur, m.

songstress ['sɔnstris], n. chanteuse, f.

song thrush ['sɔnθrʌʃ], n. grive chanteuse, f.

song-writer ['sɔnraitə], n. chansonnier, m.

son-in-law ['sʌninlɔː], n. gendre, m.

sonnet ['sɔnit], n. sonnet, m.

sonorous ['sɔnərəs], a. sonore.

soon [suːn], adv. bientôt; tôt (*de bonne heure*); *as soon as*, aussitôt que, dès que; *how soon?* quand? *see you soon!* à bientôt; *so soon*, si tôt; *too soon*, trop tôt.

sooner ['suːnə], adv. plus tôt (*de meilleure heure*); plutôt (*mieux*); *no sooner said than done*, aussitôt dit, aussitôt fait; *sooner or later*, tôt ou tard; *sooner than*, plutôt que.

soonest ['suːnist], adv. le plus tôt.

soot [sut], n. suie, f.

soothe [suːð], v.t. apaiser, calmer; (*fig.*) charmer.

soothing ['suːðin], a. calmant, consolant; flatteur.

soothingly ['suːðinli], adv. d'un ton doux.

soothsay ['suːθsei], v.i. prophétiser, prédire.

soothsayer ['suːθseiə], n. devin, m., devineresse, f.; prophète, m.

sooty ['suti], a. de suie, fuligineux; plein ou couvert de suie.

sop [sɔp], n. morceau (de pain) trempé; (*fig.*) pot-de-vin (*pourboire*), m.—v.t. tremper.

Sophia [sə'faiə]. Sophie, f.

sophism ['sɔfizm], n. sophisme, m.

sophist ['sɔfist], n. sophiste, m., f.

sophisticate [sə'fistikeit], v.t. sophistiquer, falsifier.

sophisticated [sə'fistikeitid], *a.* falsifié; blasé (*personne*).

sophistication [səfisti'keiʃən], *n.* sophistication, falsification, *f.*

sophistry ['sɔfistri], *n.* sophismes, *m.pl.*

Sophocles ['sɔfəkli:z]. Sophocle, *m.*

soporific [sɔpə'rifik], *a.* and *n.* soporifique, *m.*

sopping ['sɔpiŋ] (**wet**), *a.* trempé.

soprano [sə'prɑ:nou], *n.* soprano, *m.*, *f.*

sorcerer ['sɔ:sərə], *n.* sorcier, magicien, *m.*

sorceress ['sɔ:səris], *n.* sorcière, magicienne, *f.*

sorcery ['sɔ:səri], *n.* sorcellerie, magie, *f.*

sordid ['sɔ:did], *a.* sordide, sale; bas, vil.

sordidly ['sɔ:didli], *adv.* sordidement.

sordidness ['sɔ:didnis], *n.* sordidité, *f.*

sore [sɔ:], *a.* douloureux, endolori, sensible; (*fig.*) rude; fâché; **sore throat**, mal à la gorge, *m.*—*n.* plaie, *f.*

sorely ['sɔ:li], *adv.* gravement, fortement, cruellement, rudement.

soreness ['sɔ:nis], *n.* douleur; sensation pénible, *f.*

sorrel ['sɔrəl], *a.* saure; alezan.—*n.* oseille, *f.*; alezan (*cheval*), *m.*

sorrily ['sɔrili], *adv.* misérablement, pauvrement.

sorrow ['sɔrou], *n.* chagrin, *m.*, douleur; peine, tristesse, *f.*—*v.i.* être affligé.

sorrowful ['sɔrɔful], *a.* triste, affligé.

sorrowfully ['sɔrɔfuli], *adv.* tristement.

sorrowing ['sɔrouiŋ], *a.* affligé.

sorry ['sɔri], *a.* fâché, désolé (*de*); triste, pauvre, méchant, pitoyable; **I am sorry for you**, je vous plains; **I am sorry to say that . . .**, je regrette d'avoir à dire que . . .; **sorry!** pardon!

sort (1) [sɔ:t], *n.* sorte, *f.*, genre, *m.*, espèce; manière, façon, *f.*; **nothing of the sort**, pas du tout.

sort (2) [sɔ:t], *v.t.* assortir, classer, distribuer; trier (*lettres etc.*).

sorted ['sɔ:tid], *a.* assorti; trié, arrangé, séparé.

sorter ['sɔ:tə], *n.* trieur, *m.*

sortie ['sɔ:ti], *n.* (*Mil.*) sortie, *f.*; (*Av.*) vol, *m.*

sorting ['sɔ:tiŋ], *n.* triage, tri; assortiment (*classement*), *m.*

so-so ['sou'sou], *a.* comme ci comme ça, (*fam.*) couci-couça.

sot [sɔt], *n.* ivrogne, *m.*, *f.*

sottish ['sɔtiʃ], *a.* hébété, abruti.

sough [sau, sʌf], *v.i.* murmurer, soupirer (*vent*).

soughing ['sauiŋ], *n.* bruissement, murmure, *m.*

soul [soul], *n.* âme, *f.*; (*fig.*) être; principe (*essence*), *m.*; **All Souls' Day**, le jour des morts, *m.*

soulful ['soulful], *a.* sentimental.

soulfully ['soulfuli], *adv.* avec expression; avec sentiment.

soulless ['soullis], *a.* sans âme; abrutissant.

sound (1) [saund], *n.* détroit (*goulet*), *m.*; (*Surg.*) sonde, *f.*—*v.t.* sonder (*les profondeurs etc.*); (*Surg.*) ausculter.

sound (2) [saund], *a.* en bon état, sain; (*fig.*) solide; profond (*sommeil*); valide, bien fondé; **safe and sound**, sain et sauf.

sound (3) [saund], *v.t.* faire sonner; proclamer.—*v.i.* sonner; retentir, résonner (*de*); sembler.—*n.* son, bruit, *m.*; **to break the**

sound barrier, (*Av.*) franchir le mur du son.

sounding (1) ['saundiŋ], *n.* sondage, *m.*; (*Surg.*) auscultation, *f.*

sounding (2) ['saundiŋ], *a.* résonnant, retentissant; (*fig.*) pompeux.—*n.* retentissement, résonnement, *m.*

sounding balloon ['saundiŋbə'lu:n], *n.* (*Meteor.*) ballon sonde, *m.*

sounding-lead ['saundiŋled], *n.* plomb de sonde, *m.*

sounding line ['saundiŋlain], *n.* ligne de sonde, *f.*

soundless ['saundlis], *a.* sans bruit, muet.

soundly ['saundli], *adv.* vigoureusement, rudement, ferme, bien; sainement, solidement; profondément (*sommeil*).

soundness ['saundnis], *n.* bon état, *m.*; force, vigueur (*physique*); droiture (*morale*), *f.*

sound-proof ['saundpru:f], *a.* insonore.

sound track ['saundtræk], *n.* (*Cine.*) piste sonore, *f.*

sound wave ['saundweiv], *n.* onde sonore, *f.*

soup [su:p], *n.* potage, *m.*, soupe, *f.*; (*colloq.*) **to be in the soup**, être dans le pétrin.

soup ladle ['su:pleidl], *n.* louche, *f.*

soup tureen ['su:ptju'ri:n], *n.* soupière, *f.*

sour ['sauə], *a.* aigre, acide; tourné (*lait*); (*fig.*) âpre.—*v.t.* aigrir; (*fig.*) empoisonner. —*v.i.* s'aigrir.

source [sɔ:s], *n.* source, *f.*

souring ['sauəriŋ], *n.* aigrissement, *m.*

sourish ['sauəriʃ], *a.* suret, aigrelet.

sourly ['sauəli], *adv.* avec aigreur; (*fig.*) aigrement, âprement.

sourness ['sauənis], *n.* aigreur, acidité; (*fig.*) âpreté, *f.*

souse [saus], *v.t.* tremper; faire mariner.—*n.* marinade, *f.*

south [sauθ], *a.* sud, du sud, du midi, méridional.—*n.* sud, midi, *m.*—*adv.* vers le midi, vers le sud, au sud; **South Africa**, l'Afrique du Sud, *f.*; **South America**, l'Amérique du Sud, *f.*

south-east ['sauθ'i:st], *a.* sud-est, du sud-est.—*n.* sud-est, *m.*—*adv.* vers le sud-est.

south-easter ['sauθ'i:stə], *n.* vent du sud-est, *m.*

south-easterly ['sauθ'i:stəli], **south-eastern** ['sauθ'i:stn], *a.* du sud-est.

southerly ['sʌðəli], **southern** ['sʌðən], *a.* du sud, du midi, méridional.

southerner ['sʌðənə], *n.* méridional, *m.*; (*Am.*) sudiste, *m.*

southernmost ['sʌðənmost], *a.* à l'extrême sud.

southward ['sauθwəd], *adv.* vers le sud, au sud.

south-west ['sauθ'west], *a.* sud-ouest, du sud-ouest.—*n.* sud-ouest, *m.*—*adv.* vers le sud-ouest.

southwester [sau'westə], [SOU'WESTER].

south-westerly ['sauθ'westəli], **south-western** ['sauθ'westən], *a.* du sud-ouest, sud-ouest.

souvenir ['su:vəniə], *n.* souvenir, *m.*

sou'wester, southwester [sau'westə], *n.* vent du sud-ouest; suroît (*coiffure*), *m.*

sovereign ['sɔvrin], *a.* and *n.* souverain, *m.*

sovereignty ['sɔvrinti], *n.* souveraineté, *f.*

Soviet ['souviet], *n.* Soviet, *m.*; **the Soviet Union**, l'Union Soviétique, *f.*

sow (1) [sau], *n.* truie; gueuse (*de fer*), *f.*
sow (2) [sou], *v.t. irr.* semer.—*v.i.* semer, faire les semailles.
sower ['souə], *n.* semeur, *m.*
sowing ['souiŋ], *n.* semailles, *f.pl.*, ensemencement, *m.*
soya-bean ['sɔiə'bi:n], *n.* soya, soja, *m.*
spa [spɑ:], *n.* source minérale; ville d'eaux, *f.*
space [speis], *n.* espace, *m.*, étendue; place, *f.*; intervalle, *m.*—*v.t.* (*Print.*) espacer.
space ship ['speisʃip], *n.* astronef, *m.*
space suit ['speissju:t], *n.* combinaison spatiale, *f.*
space travel ['speistrævl], *n.* astronautique, *f.*, voyages interplanétaires, *m.pl.*
space traveller ['speistrævlə], *n.* astronaute, cosmonaute, *m.*, *f.*
spacing ['speisiŋ], *n.* espacement; (*Print.*) interligne, *m.*
spacious ['speiʃəs], *a.* spacieux, vaste.
spaciously ['speiʃəsli], *adv.* spacieusement; amplement.
spaciousness ['speiʃəsnis], *n.* vaste étendue, *f.*
spade [speid], *n.* bêche, pelle (*d'enfant*), *f.*; (*Cards*) pique, *m.*
spadeful ['speidful], *n.* pelletée, *f.*
Spain [spein]. l'Espagne, *f.*
span [spæn], *n.* empan, *m.*; envergure (*d'ailes*), *f.*; moment, instant, *m.*—*v.t.* mesurer; embrasser; traverser.
spangle [spæŋgl], *n.* paillette, *f.*—*v.t.* pailleter (*de*).
Spaniard ['spænjəd], *n.* Espagnol, *m.*
spaniel ['spænjəl], *n.* épagneul, *m.*
Spanish ['spæniʃ], *a.* espagnol, d'Espagne.—*n.* espagnol (*langue*), *m.*
spank [spæŋk], *v.t.* fesser.—*n.* (*also* spanking (1) ['spæŋkiŋ]) fessée, *f.*
spanking (2) ['spæŋkiŋ], *a.* vigoureux; rapide (*pas*).
spanner ['spænə], *n.* clef à écrous, *f.*; *adjustable spanner*, clef anglaise, *f.*
spar [spɑ:], *n.* perche, *f.*, poteau; (*Naut.*) espar; (*Box.*) combat d'entraînement, *m.*—*v.i.* faire un assaut amical (*de boxe* ou *de paroles*); se disputer.
spare [spɛə], *v.t.* épargner; ménager, économiser (*dépenser avec précaution*); se passer de (*se priver de*); donner, céder; prêter.—*a.* disponible, de reste (*superflu*); libre (*temps*); (*Motor. etc.*) de rechange; modique, faible, pauvre; maigre, sec (*taille*).
spareness ['spɛənis], *n.* maigreur, *f.*
spare-rib ['spɛə'rib], *n.* côte de porc, *f.*
sparing ['spɛəriŋ], *a.* économe, ménager, frugal, sobre (*de*); parcimonieux.
sparingly ['spɛəriŋli], *adv.* frugalement, avec parcimonie; économiquement.
sparingness ['spɛəriŋnis], *n.* frugalité, épargne, parcimonie, *f.*
spark [spɑ:k], *n.* étincelle; (*fig.*) lueur, *f.*—*v.i.* produire des étincelles.
spark plug [spɑ:'kiŋplʌg], *n.* (*Motor.*) bougie (d'allumage), *f.*
sparkle [spɑ:kl], *n.* étincellement, éclat, *m.*; vivacité (*d'esprit*), *f.*—*v.i.* étinceler, scintiller; pétiller (*boisson*).
sparkling ['spɑ:kliŋ], *a.* étincelant; mousseux (*boisson*).
sparling ['spɑ:liŋ], *n.* (*Ichth.*) éperlan, *m.*
sparrow ['spærou], *n.* moineau, passereau, *m.*
sparrow hawk ['spærouhɔ:k], *n.* épervier, *m.*

sparse [spɑ:s], *a.* épars; éparpillé, clairsemé.
sparsely ['spɑ:sli], *adv.* d'une manière éparse, de loin en loin.
sparseness ['spɑ:snis], *n.* rareté, *f.*; éparpillement, *m.*
Sparta ['spɑ:tə]. Sparte, *f.*
Spartan ['spɑ:tən], *a.* spartiate.—*n.* Spartiate (*personne*), *m.*, *f.*
spasm [spæzm], *n.* spasme, accès, *m.*
spasmodic [spæz'mɔdik], spasmodical [spæz'mɔdikəl], *a.* spasmodique.
spasmodically [spæz'mɔdikəli], *adv.* par à-coups.
spastic ['spæstik], *a.* spasmodique.—*n.* paraplégique, *m.*, *f.*
spat (1) [spæt], *past* and *p.p.* [SPIT].
spat (2) [spæt], *n.* guêtre de ville, *f.*
spate [speit], *n.* crue (*de rivière*); (*fig.*) affluence, *f.*
spatter ['spætə], *v.t.* éclabousser (*de*).
spatula ['spætjulə], *n.* spatule, *f.*
spavin ['spævin], *n.* éparvin, *m.*
spawn [spɔ:n], *n.* frai, *m.*; (*fig.*) race, engeance, *f.*—*v.t.* (*fig.*) engendrer.—*v.i.* frayer; (*fig.*) naître.
spawning ground ['spɔ:niŋgraund], *n.* frayère, *f.*
speak [spi:k], *v.t. irr.* parler; dire; (*Naut.*) héler; *to speak one's mind*, dire sa pensée.—*v.i.* parler; causer (*avec*); faire un discours (*en public*); dire; *so to speak*, pour ainsi dire; *to speak out*, parler à haute voix; *to speak up*, parler plus fort.
speaker ['spi:kə], *n.* personne qui parle, *f.*; orateur; (*Parl.*) président; (*Rad.* = *loudspeaker*) haut-parleur, *m.*
speaking ['spi:kiŋ], *a.* parlant, qui parle.—*n.* parole, *f.*, langage, discours, *m.*
speaking-tube ['spi:kiŋtju:b], *n.* tuyau *ou* tube acoustique, *m.*
spear [spiə], *n.* lance, *f.*—*v.t.* percer d'un coup de lance; harponner (*poisson etc.*).
spear-head ['spiəhed], *n.* fer de lance, *m.*; (*Mil.*) avancée, pointe, *f.*
spearman ['spiəmən], *n.* (*pl.* -men [men]) lancier, *m.*
spearmint ['spiəmint], *n.* menthe verte, *f.*
special [speʃl], *a.* spécial, exprès; extraordinaire. [special delivery, see express]
specialist ['speʃəlist], *n.* spécialiste, *m.*, *f.*
speciality [speʃi'æliti], specialty ['speʃəlti], *n.* spécialité, *f.*
specialization [speʃəlai'zeiʃən], *n.* spécialisation, *f.*
specialize ['speʃəlaiz], *v.i.* se spécialiser.
specially ['speʃəli], *adv.* particulièrement, surtout.
specie ['spi:ʃi:], *n.* espèces, *f.pl.*, numéraire, *m.*
species ['spi:ʃi:z], *n.* espèce, *f.*; (*fig.*) genre, *m.*, sorte, *f.*
specific [spi'sifik], *a.* spécifique; précis.
specification [spesifi'keiʃən], *n.* spécification; description précise (*de brevet d'invention*), *f.*
specify ['spesifai], *v.t.* spécifier, déterminer; fixer d'avance (*une heure*).
specimen ['spesimən], *n.* spécimen, modèle, échantillon, *m.*
specious ['spi:ʃəs], *a.* spécieux, captieux.
speciousness ['spi:ʃəsnis], *n.* spéciosité, apparence plausible, *f.*

speck [spek], *n.* petite tache, marque, *f.*, point; grain (*de poussière*), *m.*—*v.t.* tacher, marquer.

speckle [spekl], *v.t.* tacheter, marqueter, moucheter (*de*).—*n.* moucheture (*peau d'animal*), *f.*

speckled [spekld], *a.* tacheté, marqueté, moucheté.

spectacle ['spektəkl], *n.* spectacle, *m.*; (*pl.*) lunettes, *f.pl.*

spectacle case ['spektəklkeis], *n.* étui à lunettes, *m.*

spectacle maker ['spektəklmeikə], *n.* lunetier, *m.*

spectacular [spek'tækjulə], *a.* théâtral, impressionnant.

spectator [spek'teitə], *n.* spectateur, *m.*; (*pl.*) assistants, *m.pl.*

specter ['spektə], *n.* spectre, fantôme, *m.*

spectral ['spektrəl], *a.* de spectre, spectral.

spectroscope ['spektrəskoup], *n.* spectroscope, *m.*

spectrum ['spektrəm], *n.* (*pl.* **spectra** ['spektrə]) spectre, *m.*

speculate ['spekjuleit], *v.i.* spéculer (*sur*), méditer (*sur*).

speculation [spekju'leiʃən], *n.* spéculation, méditation, *f.*

speculative ['spekjulətiv], *a.* spéculatif, contemplatif; (*Comm.*) spéculateur.

speculatively ['spekjulətivli], *adv.* en théorie.

speculator ['spekjuleitə], *n.* spéculateur, *m.*

speech [spi:tʃ], *n.* parole, *f.*; discours, *m.*, allocution (*public*); langue (*parler*), *f.*; ***extempore speech***, improvisation, *f.*; (*Parl.*) ***maiden speech***, discours de début.

speech-day ['spi:tʃdei], *n.* (*Sch.*) distribution des prix, *f.*

speechless ['spi:tʃlis], *a.* sans voix; muet, interdit.

speechlessness ['spi:tʃlisnis], *n.* mutisme, *m.*

speed [spi:d], *n.* vitesse, rapidité, célérité; hâte, diligence, vitesse, *f.*; (*fig.*) succès, *m.*; ***God-speed!*** bon succès! bonne chance!—*v.t. irr.* expédier, hâter; faire réussir (*faciliter*).—*v.i.* se hâter, se dépêcher.

speed-boat ['spi:dbout], *n.* motoglisseur, *m.*; hors-bord, *m.inv.*

speedily ['spi:dili], *adv.* vite, en toute hâte.

speediness ['spi:dinis], *n.* célérité, hâte, *f.*

speed limit ['spi:dlimit], *n.* limitation de vitesse, *f.*

speedometer [spi:'dɔmitə], *n.* indicateur de vitesse, tachymètre, *m.*

speedwell ['spi:dwel], *n.* (*Bot.*) véronique, *f.*

speedy ['spi:di], *a.* rapide, vite, prompt.

spell (1) [spel], *n.* temps, *m.*, période, *f.*; tour (*de service*), *m.*

spell (2) [spel], *n.* charme, *m.*—*v.t., v.i. irr.* épeler (*nommer les lettres*); orthographier (*écrire correctement*); signifier.

spell-bound ['spelbaund], *a.* charmé, fasciné.

speller ['spelə], *n.* personne qui orthographie *ou* qui épèle, *f.*

spelling ['spelin], *n.* orthographe; épellation, *f.*

spelling bee ['spelinbi:], *n.* concours orthographique, *m.*

spelling book ['spelinbuk], *n.* abécédaire, syllabaire, *m.*

spelter ['speltə], *n.* zinc, *m.*

spend [spend], *v.t. irr.* dépenser; gaspiller,

perdre (*prodiguer*); passer (*temps*).—*v.i.* dépenser; se perdre (*se dissiper*); se consumer.

spending ['spendin], *n.* action de dépenser, dépense, *f.*

spendthrift ['spendθrift], *n.* prodigue, *m.*, *f.*, dissipateur, *m.*

spent [spent], *a.* épuisé; mort (*balle etc.*).

sperm [spə:m], *n.* sperme; frai (*poisson etc.*); blanc de baleine, *m.*

spew [spju:], *v.t., v.i.* vomir.

spewing ['spju:in], *n.* vomissement, *m.*

sphere ['sfiə], *n.* sphère, *f.*

spherical ['sferikl], *a.* sphérique.

spherics ['sferiks], *n.pl.* théorie de la sphère, *f.*

spheroid ['sfiərɔid], *n.* sphéroïde, *m.*

sphinx [sfinks], *n.* (*pl.* **sphinxes** ['sfinksiz]) sphinx, *m.*

spice [spais], *n.* épice, *f.*—*v.t.* épicer (*de*).

spiciness ['spaisinis], *n.* goût épicé, *m.*

spick-and-span ['spikənd'spæn], *a.* tiré à quatre épingles; bien astiqué.

spicy ['spaisi], *a.* épicé, aromatique, parfumé.

spider ['spaidə], *n.* araignée, *f.*

spigot ['spigət], *n.* fausset; (*Am., Sc.*) robinet, *m.*

spike [spaik], *n.* pointe, *f.*; clou à grosse tête (*de métal*), *m.*; cheville (*de bois*), *f.*; ***marline-spike***, épissoir, *m.*—*v.t.* clouer; hérisser. [*see* **stiletto heels**]

spiked [spaikt], *a.* à pointes, barbelé.

spikenard ['spaiknɑ:d], *n.* nard indien, *m.*

spiky ['spaiki], *a.* à pointe aiguë; armé de pointes.

spill (1) [spil], *v.t. irr.* répandre, verser; renverser.—*v.i.* se verser, se répandre.—*n.* culbute (*renversement*), *f.*

spill (2) [spil], *n.* allumette de papier, allumette en copeau, *f.*

spin [spin], *v.t. irr.* filer; faire tourner.—*v.i.* filer (*aller vite*); tourner.—*n.* tournoiement, *m.*; (*Av.*) vrille, *f.*; (*Motor.*) tour, *m.*; promenade, *f.*

spinach ['spinidʒ], *n.* épinards, *m.pl.*

spinal [spainl], *a.* spinal; ***spinal column***, colonne vertébrale, *f.*

spindle [spindl], *n.* fuseau; pivot; (*Mach.*) essieu; (*Tech.*) axe, *m.*

spindleful ['spindlful], *n.* fusée, *f.*

spindle-legs ['spindllegz], **spindle-shanks** ['spindlʃæŋks], *n.pl.* jambes de fuseau, *f.pl.*

spindrift ['spindrift], *n.* embrun, *m.*

spine [spain], *n.* épine dorsale; (*Bot.*) épine, *f.*

spineless ['spainlis], *a.* sans épines; (*fig.*) mou, flasque, invertébré.

spinet ['spinit, spi'net], *n.* épinette, *f.*

spinner ['spinə], *n.* fileur, *m.*

spinney ['spini], *n.* petit bois, bosquet, *m.*

spinning ['spinin], *a.* tournoyant, tournant.—*n.* filage (*processus*), *m.*; filature (*art*), *f.*; tournoiement, *m.*

spinning machine ['spininmə'shi:n], *n.* machine à filer, *f.*

spinning mill ['spininmil], *n.* filature, *f.*

spinning top ['spinintɔp], *n.* toupie, *f.*

spinning wheel ['spininwi:l], *n.* rouet, *m.*

spinous ['spainəs], *a.* épineux.

spinster ['spinstə], *n.* fille non mariée, célibataire, *f.*

spinsterhood ['spinstəhud], *n.* célibat, *m.*

spiny ['spaini], *a.* épineux, couvert d'épines; (*fig.*) difficile.

spiraea [spai'ri:ə], *n.* (*Bot.*) spirée, *f.*
spiral ['spaiərəl], *a.* spiral; en colimaçon (*escalier*).—*n.* spirale, *f.*—*v.i.* monter en spirale.
spirally ['spaiərəli], *adv.* en spirale.
spire ['spaiə], *n.* aiguille, flèche, *f.*
spirit (1) ['spirit], *n.* esprit, *m.*, âme, *f.*, fantôme, spectre (*apparition*), *m.*—*v.t.* **to spirit away**, faire disparaître.
spirit (2) ['spirit], **spiritedness** ['spiritidnis], *n.* (*fig.*) ardeur, force, vigueur, *f.*, feu, élan, entrain, *m.*; fougue (*d'un cheval*); verve, bonne humeur, *f.*, entrain, courage, *m.*—*v.t.* animer, encourager.
spirit (3) ['spirit], *n.* (*sing.* or *pl.*) spiritueux, *m. inv.*; liqueur spiritueuse *ou* alcoolique, *f.*; esprit (*de vin etc.*), *m.*; **methylated spirit**, alcool à brûler, *m.*
spirited ['spiritid], *a.* animé, plein de cœur, plein de vivacité; vif, plein de verve; fougueux (*cheval*).
spiritedly ['spiritidli], *adv.* avec ardeur, chaleureusement, avec force, avec entrain.
spiritedness [SPIRIT (2)].
spirit lamp ['spiritlæmp], *n.* lampe à alcool, *f.*
spiritless ['spiritlis], *a.* sans vigueur, mou, énervé; sans courage; abattu (*découragé*).
spirit level ['spiritlevl], *n.* niveau à bulle d'air, *m.*
spiritual ['spiritjuəl], *a.* spirituel.—*n.* chant religieux (*des Noirs*), *m.*
spiritualism ['spiritjuəlizm], *n.* spiritisme (*communication avec les esprits*), *m.*
spiritualist ['spiritjuəlist], *n.* spirite (*adepte du spiritisme*), *m.*, *f.*
spiritualize ['spiritjuəlaiz], *v.t.* spiritualiser.
spirituous ['spiritjuəs], *a.* spiritueux.
spiry ['spaiəri], *a.* en flèche, élancé.
spit (1) [spit], *n.* broche; profondeur de bêche (*plongée dans la terre*), *f.*—*v.t.* embrocher, mettre à la broche.
spit (2) [spit], *n.* crachat, *m.*, salive, *f.*—*v.t. irr.* cracher.—*v.i.* cracher (*sur* ou *à*).
spite [spait], **spitefulness** ['spaitfulnis], *n.* dépit, *m.*; rancune, malveillance, *f.*; **in spite of**, en dépit de, malgré; **out of spite**, par dépit; **to have a spite against**, en vouloir à.—*v.t.* vexer, blesser, contrarier.
spiteful ['spaitful], *a.* rancunier, malveillant, vindicatif.
spitefully ['spaitfuli], *adv.* par dépit, par rancune.
spitefulness [SPITE].
spitfire ['spitfaiə], *n.* rageur, *m.*
spitter ['spitə], *n.* cracheur, *m.*
spitting ['spitiŋ], *n.* crachement, *m.*
spittle [spitl], *n.* salive, *f.*; (*colloq.*) crachat, *m.*
splash [splæʃ], *v.t.* éclabousser.—*v.i.* éclabousser; clapoter (*vagues*); patauger.—*n.* éclaboussure, *f.*; clapotement, clapotis (*des vagues*); flac (*bruit*), *m.*
splashing ['splæʃiŋ], *n.* éclaboussement (*acte*), *m.*; éclaboussure (*ce qui rejaillit*), *f.*
splashy ['splæʃi], *a.* éclaboussé, bourbeux.
splay [splei], *v.t.* évaser; (*Arch.*) ébraser; épauler (*cheval*).—*n.* écartement; (*Arch.*) ébrasement, *m.*
splay-footed ['spleifutid], *a.* aux pieds plats et tournés en dehors.
spleen [spli:n], *n.* rate, *f.*; (*fig.*) fiel, *m.*, animosité, *f.*; spleen, *m.*, mélancolie, *f.*

splendid ['splendid], *a.* resplendissant, sompteux, magnifique.
splendidly ['splendidli], *adv.* avec éclat, magnifiquement.
splendor ['splendə], *n.* splendeur, *f.*, éclat, *m.*
splenetic [splə'netik], *a.* splénétique, atrabilaire.
splice [splais], *n.* épissure, *f.*, raccordement, *m.*—*v.t.* épisser (*Carp.*) joindre.
splint [splint], *n.* éclisse, attelle, *f.*—*v.t.* éclisser.
splinter ['splintə], *n.* éclat, éclat de bois, *m.*—*v.t.* briser en éclats.—*v.i.* voler en éclats.
splintery ['splintəri], *a.* plein d'éclats, esquilleux.
split [split], *a.* fendu; **split personality**, dédoublement de la personnalité, *m.*; **split pin**, goupille, *f.*—*n.* fente; (*fig.*) scission, *f.*—*v.t. irr.* fendre; diviser, partager.—*v.i.* se fendre; se quereller.
split-second ['splitsekənd], *a.* ultra-rapide.
splitting ['splitiŋ], *n.* fendage, *m.*; **splitting of the atom**, fission de l'atome, *f.*
splotch [splotʃ], *n.* grosse tache, *f.*, barbouillage, *m.*
splutter ['splʌtə], *v.i.* bredouiller, cracher (*plume* ou *graisse*).—*n.* or **spluttering** ['splʌtəriŋ], bredouillement, crachage, *m.*
spoil [spoil], *v.t. irr.* gâter, abîmer; dépouiller (*de*); ravager (*piller*).—*v.i.* se gâter, s'abîmer.—*n.* butin, *m.*, dépouille, *f.*, pillage, *m.*
spoiled [spoild], *a.* gâté.
spoiler ['spoilə], *n.* personne qui gâte, *f.*; spoliateur (*pilleur*), *m.*
spoiling ['spoiliŋ], *n.* action de gâter; avarie, *f.*
spoil-sport ['spoilspo:t], *n.* trouble-fête, *m.*
spoke [spouk], *n.* rais, rayon, *m.*
spoke-shave ['spoukʃeiv], *n.* (*Carp.*) plane, *f.*
spokesman ['spouksmən] (*pl.* **-men** [men]), **spokeswoman** ['spoukswumən] (*pl.* **-women** [wimin]), *n.* porte-parole, *m.inv.*
spoliate ['spoulieit], *v.t.* spolier, piller.
spoliation [spouli'eiʃən], *n.* spoliation, *f.*
sponge [spʌndʒ], *n.* éponge, *f.*; (*Artill.*) écouvillon, *m.*—*v.t.* éponger; (*Artill.*) écouvillonner.—*v.i.* **to sponge on**, vivre aux dépens de.
sponge cake ['spʌndʒkeik], *n.* gâteau de Savoie, *m.*
sponger ['spʌndʒə], *n.* pique-assiette, parasite, *m.*
sponginess ['spʌndʒinis], *n.* nature spongieuse, *f.*
sponging ['spʌndʒiŋ], *n.* épongement, *m.*; (*fig.*) écorniflerie, *f.*
spongy ['spʌndʒi], *a.* spongieux.
sponsor ['spɔnsə], *n.* parrain, *m.*, marraine, *f.*; garant (*qui cautionne*), *m.*—*v.t.* répondre pour; parrainer.
sponsorship ['spɔnsəʃip], *n.* parrainage, *m.*
spontaneity [spɔntə'ni:iti], *n.* spontanéité, *f.*
spontaneous [spɔn'teiniəs], *a.* spontané.
spontaneously [spɔn'teiniəsli], *adv.* spontanément.
spool [spu:l], *n.* bobine, *f.*
spoon [spu:n], *n.* cuiller, cuillère, *f.*
spoonbill ['spu:nbil], *n.* (*Orn.*) palette, *f.*
spoonful ['spu:nful], *n.* cuillerée, *f.*
spoor [spuə], *n.* trace, *f.*, empreintes, *f.pl.*
sporadic [spə'rædik], *a.* sporadique.
spore [spo:], *n.* spore, *f.*

sport [spɔ:t], *n.* jeu, divertissement, amusement, *m.*; moquerie, raillerie, *f.*; jouet; sport, *m.*—*v.t.* faire parade de.—*v.i.* se divertir, s'amuser.

sporting ['spɔ:tiŋ], *a.* de sport; sportif.

sportive ['spɔ:tiv], *a.* badin, folâtre.

sportively ['spɔ:tivli], *adv.* en badinant.

sportiveness ['spɔ:tivnis], *n.* folâtrerie, *f.*

sportsman ['spɔ:tsmən], *n.* (*pl.* **-men** [men]) sportif, sportsman, *m.*

sportsmanship ['spɔ:tsmənʃip], *n.* sportivité, *f.*

spot [spɔt], *n.* tache, *f.*; endroit, lieu, *m.*; **on the spot**, sur place, sur-le-champ.—*v.t.* tacheter, moucheter; tacher; (*fam.*) repérer; (*colloq.*) observer.

spot-check ['spɔt'tʃek], *n.* contrôle-surprise, *m.*

spotless ['spɔtlis], *a.* sans tache; (*fig.*) immaculé, pur, irréprochable.

spotlessness ['spɔtlisnis], *n.* pureté, *f.*

spotted ['spɔtid], *a.* tacheté, moucheté; truité.

spotter ['spɔtə], *n.* (*Mil. Av.*) observateur, *m.*

spotty ['spɔti], *a.* couvert de taches, moucheté, tacheté.

spouse [spauz], *n.* époux, *m.*, épouse, *f.*; mari, *m.*, femme, *f.*

spout [spaut], *n.* tuyau, *m.*; gouttière (*de maison*), *f.*; bec (*de cruche etc.*), *m.*—*v.i.* jaillir; (*fam.*) déclamer.

spouter ['spautə], *n.* (*fam.*) déclamateur, *m.*

spouting ['spautiŋ], *n.* jaillissement, *m.*; déclamation, *f.*

sprain [sprein], *n.* entorse, foulure, *f.*—*v.t.* fouler; se faire une entorse à.

sprat [spræt], *n.* esprot, sprat, *m.*

sprawl [sprɔ:l], *v.i.* s'étendre, s'étaler.

spray [sprei], *n.* branche, ramille (*d'arbrisseau etc.*), *f.*; embrun, *m.*; poussière (*d'eau*), *f.*; vaporisateur, *m.*—*v.t.* pulvériser, vaporiser, asperger.

spread [spred], *v.t. irr.* étendre, déployer; répandre; couvrir (*table*); mettre (*nappe*); tendre (*voiles etc.*).—*v.i.* s'étendre, se déployer; se répandre, se propager.—*n.* étendue; envergure (*ailes*), *f.*; (*fam.*) festin (*banquet*), *m.*

spreading ['sprediŋ], *a.* étendu, qui se répand.

spree [spri:], *n.* (*colloq.*) bamboche, bombe, *f.*

sprig [sprig], *n.* brin, *m.*, brindille; pointe (*clou*), *f.*

sprightliness ['spraitlinis], *n.* vivacité, *f.*, entrain, *m.*

sprightly ['spraitli], *a.* enjoué, vif, animé, gai.

spring [spriŋ], *v.t. irr.* (*Naut.*) **to spring a leak**, faire une voie d'eau; **to spring upon**, présenter à l'improviste . . . à.—*v.i.* bondir, s'élancer; jaillir (*sourdre*); pousser, naître (*se développer*); paraître, poindre (*jour*); provenir, découler, descendre (*avoir pour ancêtres*).—*n.* saut, bond, élan; ressort (*élasticité*), *m.*; source; cause, origine, *f.*; printemps, *m.*; (*pl.*) suspension (*de voiture*), *f.*

spring-board ['spriŋbɔ:d], *n.* tremplin, *m.*

springiness ['spriŋinis], *n.* élasticité, *f.*

springlike ['spriŋlaik], *a.* printanier.

spring tide ['spriŋtaid], *n.* grande marée, *f.*

springy ['spriŋi], *a.* élastique.

sprinkle [spriŋkl], *v.t.* répandre; arroser (*de*), asperger (*de*) (*eau bénite*); saupoudrer (*de*).

sprinkler ['spriŋklə], *n.* (*Eccles.*) aspersoir, *m.*; (*Hort.*) arroseuse à jet tournant, *f.*

sprinkling ['spriŋkliŋ], *n.* arrosage, *m.*; (*Eccles.*) aspersion, *f.*; (*fig.*) petit nombre, *m.*

sprint [sprint], *n.* sprint, *m.*—*v.i.* courir à toute vitesse.

sprinter ['sprintə], *n.* coureur de vitesse, sprinter, *m.*

sprite [sprait], *n.* esprit follet, lutin, *m.*

sprout [spraut], *n.* pousse, *f.*, jet, rejeton, *m.*; **Brussels sprouts**, choux de Bruxelles, *m.pl.*—*v.i.* pousser, bourgeonner (*plantes*).

sprouting ['sprautiŋ], *n.* germination, *f.*

spruce (1) [spru:s], *a.* paré, bien mis, pimpant.—*v.t.* attifer.

spruce (2) [spru:s], *n.* sapin (*arbre*), *m.*

spry [sprai], *a.* alerte, plein d'entrain.

spunk [spʌŋk], *n.* amadou; (*colloq.*) cœur, courage, *m.*

spur [spə:], *n.* éperon; ergot (*de coq etc.*); (*fig.*) aiguillon, stimulant, *m.*—*v.t.* éperonner; stimuler.

spurious ['spjuəriəs], *a.* faux, falsifié.

spuriousness ['spjuəriəsnis], *n.* fausseté, *f.*

spurn [spə:n], *v.t.* repousser, écarter (*du pied*); mépriser.—*n.* mépris, dédain, *m.*

spurred [spə:d], *a.* éperonné.

spurt [spə:t], *v.t.* faire jaillir.—*v.i.* s'élancer; (*Spt.*) démarrer.—*n.* jaillissement; (*fig.*) effort soudain; (*Spt.*) démarrage, *m.*

sputnik ['spʌtnik, 'sputnik], *n.* spoutnik, *m.*

sputter ['spʌtə], *v.i.* cracher; bredouiller.—*n.* salive, *f.*

sputtering ['spʌtəriŋ], *n.* bredouillement, *m.*

sputum ['spju:təm], *n.* crachat, *m.*

spy [spai], *n.* espion, *m.*—*v.t.* scruter; apercevoir.—*v.i.* épier, espionner.

spy-glass ['spaigla:s], *n.* longue-vue, *f.*

spying ['spaiiŋ], *n.* espionnage, *m.*

spy ring ['spairiŋ], **spy system** ['spaisistəm], *n.* espionnage, *m.*

squabble ['skwɔbl], *n.* dispute, querelle, *f.*—*v.i.* se chamailler.

squabbler ['skwɔblə], *n.* querelleur, *m.*

squad [skwɔd], *n.* (*Mil.*) peloton, *m.*; (*Rail.*) brigade; équipe (*de sauvetage etc.*), *f.*

squadron ['skwɔdrən], *n.* (*Mil.*) escadron, *m.*; (*Av.*) escadrille; (*Naut.*) escadre, *f.*

squadron leader ['skwɔdrənli:də], *n.* (*Av.*) commandant, *m.*

squalid ['skwɔlid], *a.* malpropre, sale.

squalidness [SQUALOR].

squall [skwɔ:l], *n.* cri; coup de vent, *m.*, bourrasque, rafale (*de vent*), *f.*—*v.i.* crier, brailler.

squalling ['skwɔ:liŋ], *a.* criard, braillard.—*n.* criaillerie, *f.*

squally ['skwɔ:li], *a.* à grains, à rafales.

squalor ['skwɔlə], **squalidness** ['skwɔlidnis], *n.* malpropreté, *f.*

squamous ['skweiməs], *a.* squameux; écailleux.

squander ['skwɔndə], *v.t.* dissiper, gaspiller.

squanderer ['skwɔndərə], *n.* gaspilleur, *m.*, prodigue, *m., f.*

squandering ['skwɔndəriŋ], *n.* gaspillage, *m.*

square [skwɛə], *a.* carré; soldé (*comptes etc.*); (*fig.*) équitable, juste; de superficie (*mesure*).—*n.* carré; carreau (*de verre etc.*), *m.*; case (*d'échiquier*); place (*dans une ville*); place d'armes (*de ville de garnison*), *f.*, parvis (*devant une église*), *m.*—*v.t.* carrer; (*Carp.*)

équarrir; balancer (*comptes*); (*fig.*) régler, ajuster.—*v.i.* cadrer, s'accorder (*avec*).

square-built ['skwɛəbilt], *a.* aux épaules carrées.

squarely ['skwɛəli], *adv.* carrément; (*fig.*) justement.

squareness ['skwɛənis], *n.* forme carrée, *f.*

squaring ['skwɛəriŋ], *n.* équarrissage, *m.*; *squaring of the circle*, quadrature du cercle, *f.*

squarish ['skwɛəriʃ], *a.* à peu près carré.

squash [skwɔʃ], *v.t.* écraser, aplatir; (*fig.*) rembarrer (*personne*).—*n.* écrasement (*aplatissement*), *m.*; foule serrée (*de gens*), *f.*; *lemon squash*, citronnade, *f.*

squashy ['skwɔʃi], *a.* mou et humide.

squat [skwɔt], *a.* accroupi, blotti; trapu, ramassé (*courtaud*).—*v.i.* s'accroupir; se blottir; (*Am.*) s'établir (*sans droit*).

squatter ['skwɔtə], *n.* personne accroupie, *f.*; colon (*sans droit*), *m.*

squatting ['skwɔtiŋ], *n.* accroupissement, *m.*

squaw [skwɔ:], *n.* femme peau-rouge, *f.*

squawk [skwɔ:k], *n.* cri rauque; couac, *m.*—*v.i.* pousser des cris rauques.

squeak [skwi:k], *n.* petit cri aigu, *m.*—*v.i.* pousser des cris aigus; jurer (*instrument de musique*).

squeaking ['skwi:kiŋ], *a.* criard; qui jure (*instrument de musique*).

squeal [skwi:l], *v.i.* pousser des cris perçants.—*n.* cri perçant, *m.*

squeamish ['skwi:miʃ], *a.* qui se soulève (*l'estomac*); trop délicat, difficile (*scrupuleux*).

squeamishly ['skwi:miʃli], *adv.* avec dégoût.

squeamishness ['skwi:miʃnis], *n.* délicatesse exagérée, *f.*, goût difficile, *m.*

squeeze [skwi:z], *n.* compression; cohue, *f.*—*v.t.* serrer, presser; *to squeeze money out of*, extorquer de l'argent à; *to squeeze out*, exprimer; *to squeeze through*, forcer à travers.—*v.i.* *to squeeze through*, se forcer à travers.

squeezing ['skwi:ziŋ], *n.* étreinte, compression, *f.*; serrement (*de la main*), *m.*

squelch [skweltʃ], *v.t.* écraser, aplatir.

squib [skwib], *n.* pétard, *m.*; (*fig.*) satire, *f.*

squill [skwil], *n.* scille (*plante*), *f.*

squint [skwint], *a.* louche.—*n.* regard louche, *m.*—*v.i.* loucher.

squinting ['skwintiŋ], *a.* louche.—*n.* action de loucher, *f.*, strabisme, *m.*

squire ['skwaiə], *n.* écuyer; châtelain; cavalier servant (*d'une dame*), *m.*—*v.t.* escorter (*une dame*).

squireen [skwaiə'ri:n], *n.* hobereau, *m.*

squirm [skwə:m], *v.i.* se tortiller, se tordre (*de douleur* ou *d'embarras*).

squirrel ['skwirəl], *n.* écureuil, *m.*

squirt [skwə:t], *n.* seringue, *f.*—*v.t.* seringuer, faire jaillir.—*v.i.* jaillir.

stab [stæb], *n.* coup de poignard, de couteau etc., *m.*—*v.t.* poignarder.

stabbing ['stæbiŋ], *a.* lancinant.—*n.* coup de poignard, *m.*

stability [stə'biliti], *n.* stabilité, solidité; (*fig.*) fermeté, *f.*

stabilization [steibilai'zeiʃən], *n.* stabilisation, *f.* [see **tail-plane**]

stabilize ['steibilaiz], *v.t.* stabiliser.

stable (1) [steibl], *a.* stable, fixe, solide; (*fig.*) constant.

stable (2) [steibl], *n.* écurie, *f.*—*v.t.* loger (*chevaux*); établer (*bétail*).

stable-boy ['steiblbɔi], **stableman** ['steiblmən] (*pl.* **-men** [men]), *n.* garçon d'écurie, *m.*

stabling ['steibliŋ], *n.* écuries (*pour chevaux*) étables (*pour bétail*), *f.pl.*

staccato [stə'kɑːtou], *a.* saccadé.—*adv.* en staccato.

stack [stæk], *n.* souche (*d'une cheminée*); pile, *f.*, tas (*de charbon, de bois*), *m.*; meule (*de foin etc.*), *f.*—*v.t.* empiler (*bois*); emmeuler (*foin etc.*).

stacking ['stækiŋ], *n.* emmeulage, empilage, entassement, *m.*

stack-yard ['stækjɑːd], *n.* cour de ferme, *f.*

stadium ['steidiəm], *n.* stade, *m.*

staff [stɑːf], *n.* (*pl.* **staves** [steivz]) bâton, bourdon (*de pèlerin*), *m.*; hampe (*à drapeau*), *f.*; (*pl.* **staffs**) corps, personnel; (*Mil.*) état-major, *m.*; *to be on the staff*, être attaché à, faire partie du personnel de.—*v.t.* fournir le personnel de.

staff officer ['stɑːfɔfisə], *n.* officier d'état-major, *m.*

stag [stæg], *n.* cerf, *m.*

stag beetle ['stægbiːtl], *n.* (*Ent.*) cerf-volant, lucane, *m.*

stage [steidʒ], *n.* estrade (*dans une salle*); (*Theat.*) scène, *f.*; (*fig.*) théâtre, *m.*; étape (*voyage*), *f.*; (*fig.*) degré, *m.*, phase, période, *f.*—*v.t.* *to stage a play*, monter une pièce.

stage-coach ['steidʒkoutʃ], *n.* diligence, *f.*

stage door ['steidʒ'dɔː], *n.* entrée des artistes, *f.*

stage effect ['steidʒifekt], *n.* effet scénique, *m.*

stage-hand ['steidʒhænd], *n.* machiniste, *m.*

stage manager ['steidʒ'mænidʒə], *n.* régisseur, *m.*

stage properties ['steidʒ'prɔpətiz], *n.pl.* accessoires de théâtre, *m.pl.*

stage set ['steidʒset], *n.* décor, *m.*

stagger ['stægə], *v.t.* faire chanceler; (*fig.*) étonner; échelonner (*heures, vacances etc.*).—*v.i.* chanceler.

staggering ['stægəriŋ], *a.* chancelant; incertain.—*n.* chancellement; échelonnage, *m.*

stagnancy ['stægnənsi], **stagnation** [stæg neiʃən], *n.* stagnation, *f.*

stagnant ['stægnənt], *a.* stagnant; (*fig.*) inactif, mort.

stagnate [stæg'neit], *v.i.* être stagnant.

stagnation [stæg (STAGNANCY).

staid [steid], *a.* posé, sérieux, grave.

staidness ['steidnis], *n.* gravité, *f.*

stain [stein], *n.* tache (*Paint.*) teinte; (*fig.*) honte, *f.*, opprobre (*disgrâce*), *m.*—*v.t.* tacher (*de*); (*fig.*) souiller; (*Dyeing*) teindre.—*v.i.* se tacher.

stained [steind], *a.* taché; (*fig.*) souillé; (*Dyeing*) teint; *stained glass*, vitrail, *m.*

stainer ['steinə], *n.* teinturier, *m.*

staining ['steiniŋ], *n.* teinture, *f.*

stainless ['steinlis], *a.* sans tache; inoxydable (*acier*).

stair [stɛə], *n.* marche, *f.*; degré; (*pl.*) escalier, *m.*

staircase ['stɛəkeis], *n.* escalier, *m.*; cage d'escalier, *f.*; *back staircase*, escalier de service; *moving staircase*, escalier roulant.

stair-rod ['stɛərɔd], *n.* tringle (de tapis) d'escalier, *f.*

stake [steik], *n.* pieu, poteau, bûcher (*de martyre*); (*Cards etc.*) enjeu, *m.*, mise, *f.* —*v.t.* parier, gager; hasarder (*risquer*); **to stake out**, jalonner.

stalactite ['stæləktait], *n.* stalactite, *f.*

stalagmite ['stæləgmait], *n.* stalagmite, *f.*

stale [steil], *a.* vieux, rassis (*pain*); (*fig.*) suranné, passé, usé.

stalemate ['steilmeit], *v.t.* (*Chess*) faire pat.— *n.* pat, *m.*; (*fig.*) impasse, *f.*

staleness ['steilnis], *n.* vieillesse, *f.*; état rassis (*pain*), *m.*; banalité, *f.*

stalk [stɔːk], *n.* tige; queue (*de fleur*), *f.* trognon (*de chou*), *m.*; démarche fière (*allure*), *f.*—*v.t.* chasser à l'affût.—*v.i.* marcher fièrement.

stalker ['stɔːkə], *n.* chasseur à l'affût, *m.*

stalking ['stɔːkiŋ], *n.* (*Hunt.*) chasse à l'affût, *f.*

stall (1) [stɔːl], *n.* stalle (*d'église* ou *d'écurie*), étable (*à bétail*); écurie (*à chevaux*); échoppe, boutique, *f.*, étalage; (*Theat.*) fauteuil d'orchestre, *m.*

stall (2) [stɔːl], *v.t.*, *v.i.* caler (*machine*).

stallion ['stæljən], *n.* étalon, *m.*

stalwart ['stɔːlwət], *a.* vigoureux, robuste; vaillant.

stamen ['steimen], *n.* (*Bot.*) étamine, *f.*

stamina ['stæminə], *n.* vigueur, résistance, *f.*

stammer ['stæmə], *v.t.*, *v.i.* bégayer, balbutier.—*n.* bégaiement, *m.*

stammerer ['stæmərə], *n.* bègue, *m.*, *f.*

stammering ['stæməriŋ], *a.* bègue.—*n.* bégaiement, *m.*

stamp [stæmp], *v.t.* frapper du pied; piétiner; empreindre, imprimer; contrôler (*garantir*); estamper (*pièce de monnaie*); timbrer (*documents, lettres etc.*); (*Metal.*) bocarder; estampiller (*marchandises*); affranchir (*payer d'avance*); poinçonner (*billet*).—*v.i.* trépigner, frapper du pied.—*n.* estampe (*outil*), *f.*; coin, poinçon, *m.*; empreinte, marque (*impression*), *f.*; poinçon de contrôle (*sur l'or*); timbre (*sur documents*); (*Metal.*) bocard, *m.*; (*Comm.*) estampille (*sur marchandises*), *f.*; (*fig.*) caractère, *m.*, trempe, *f.*; coup de pied, trépignement; timbre-poste, *m.*; **rubber stamp**, tampon, *m.*

stamp collecting ['stæmpkəlektiŋ], *n.* philatélie, *f.*

stamp collector ['stæmpkə'lektə], *n.* philatéliste, *m.*, *f.*

stamp duty ['stæmp'djuːti], *n.* droit de timbre, *m.*

stampede [stæm'piːd], *n.* débandade, panique, *f.*—*v.i.* fuir en désordre.

stamping ['stæmpiŋ], *n.* contrôlage (*garantie*); timbrage; (*Metal.*) bocardage; piétinement, trépignement (*des pieds*), *m.*

stamp machine ['stæmpmə'ʃiːn], *n.* distributeur automatique de timbres-poste, *m.*

stanch [stɑːntʃ], **staunch** [stɔːntʃ], *a.* solide, ferme; (*fig.*) sûr, dévoué.—*v.t.* étancher.

stanchion ['stɑːnʃən], *n.* étançon, étai, *m.*

stanchness ['stɑːntʃnis], **staunchness** ['stɔːntʃnis], *n.* fermeté; constance, dévotion, *f.*

stand [stænd], *v.t. irr.* mettre debout, placer, poser; endurer, souffrir, supporter, soutenir; subir; résister à; payer (*à boire*).—*v.i.* se tenir; rester debout; se soutenir (*difficilement*); se placer, se mettre (*prendre place*); être debout; se trouver, être (*bâtiment*); se maintenir (*ne pas lâcher pied*); se présenter (*comme candidat*); **stand by!** attention! **to stand aside**, se tenir à l'écart; **to stand by**, assister à (*être présent*); défendre, s'en tenir à (*un avis etc.*); se tenir prêt; **to stand down**, se retirer; **to stand firm**, tenir ferme, tenir bon; **to stand for**, soutenir; signifier; **to stand in for someone**, remplacer quelqu'un; **to stand out**, se dessiner (*être en relief*); résister; **to stand still**, s'arrêter, se tenir tranquille; **to stand up**, se lever.—*n.* arrêt, *m.*, halte, pause, *f.*; stand, étalage (*exposition etc.*); socle (*à vases etc.*), *m.*; (*fig.*) cessation, résistance, *f.*

standard ['stændəd], *a.* type, standard, normal; étalon; sur titre (*argent*); classique (*livre*); (*Hort.*) en plein vent (*arbre*), sur tige (*roses*); régulateur (*prix*).—*n.* étendard, (*Naut.*) pavillon; étalon (*de poids et mesures*); titre (*d'or et d'argent*); (*fig.*) type, modèle; (*Hort.*) arbre en plein vent, *m.*

standard-bearer ['stændədbɛərə], *n.* porte-étendard, *m.*

standardization [stændədai'zeiʃən], *n.* étalonnage, *m.*; (*Comm.*) standardisation, *f.*

standardize ['stændədaiz], *v.t.* étalonner, standardiser.

stand-by ['stændbai], *n.* appui, soutien, *m.*, ressource, *f.*

stand-in ['stændin], *n.* remplaçant, *m.*

standing ['stændiŋ], *a.* stagnant; fixe; debout, sur pied (*non abattu*); (*fig.*) invariable.—*n.* position, *f.*; rang, *m.*; durée, date, *f.*, service, *m.*

stand-offish ['stænd'ɔfiʃ], *a.* réservé, distant.

stand-point ['stændpɔint], *n.* point de vue, *m.*

standstill ['stændstil], *n.* arrêt, *m.*

stand-to ['stænd'tuː], *n.* (*Mil.*) alerte, *f.*

stanza ['stænzə], *n.* stance, strophe, *f.*

staple (1) [steipl], *a.* établi; principal.—*n.* denrée principale (*marchandises*), *f.*; (*fig.*) fond, *m.*

staple (2) [steipl], *n.* agrafe; gâche (*de serrure*), *f.*—*v.t.* agrafer.

stapler ['steiplə], *n.* agrafeuse (*machine*), *f.*

star [stɑː], *n.* étoile, *f.*, astre, *m.*; (*Theat., Cine.*) vedette, *f.*—*v.t.* étoiler, parsemer d'étoiles; avoir comme vedettes.—*v.i.* tenir le premier rôle.

starboard ['stɑːbəd], *n.* tribord, *m.*

starch [stɑːtʃ], *n.* amidon, *m.*; fécule (*aliment*); (*fig.*) raideur, *f.*—*v.t.* empeser.

starchiness ['stɑːtʃinis], *n.* raideur, *f.*

starchy ['stɑːtʃi], *a.* féculent; empesé; (*fig.*) guindé.

stare [stɛə], *v.t.* dévisager.—*v.i.* regarder fixement; ouvrir de grands yeux (*être ébahi*).— *n.* regard fixe; regard ébahi, *m.*

starfish ['stɑːfiʃ], *n.* étoile de mer, *f.*

star-gazer ['stɑːgeizə], *n.* astrologue, *m.*, *f.*; rêveur, *m.*

staring ['stɛəriŋ], *a.* voyant, tranchant (*couleur etc.*).

stark [stɑːk], *adv.* tout, tout à fait.—*a.* raide; stérile (*paysage*).

starless ['stɑːlis], *a.* sans étoiles.

starling ['stɑːliŋ], *n.* étourneau, sansonnet, *m.*

starlit ['stɑːlit], *a.* étoilé.

starry ['stɑːri], *a.* étoilé; (*fig.*) étincelant; **starry-eyed**, peu pratique.

start [stɑ:t], *v.t.* commencer; faire lever (*gibier*); faire partir; mettre en marche (*machine*).—*v.i.* tressaillir (*de* ou *à*); partir (*s'en aller*); commencer, débuter; sursauter (*faire un bond*).—*n.* tressaillement; saut, bond; commencement, début; départ, *m.*; *to wake with a start*, se réveiller en sursaut.

starter [ˈstɑ:tə], *n.* starter (*de course*); (*Motor.*) démarreur, *m.*

starting [ˈstɑ:tiŋ], *n.* tressaillement; départ; commencement, début, *m.*; mise en marche (*de moteur etc.*), *f.*

starting-handle [ˈstɑ:tiŋhændl], *n.* (*Motor.*) manivelle, *f.*

starting point [ˈstɑ:tiŋpɔint], *n.* point de départ, *m.*

starting post [ˈstɑ:tiŋpoust], *n.* poteau de départ, *m.*

startle [stɑ:tl], *v.t.* faire tressaillir, effrayer.

startling [ˈstɑ:tliŋ], *a.* étonnant, saisissant.

starvation [stɑ:ˈveiʃən], *n.* inanition, faim, *f.*

starve [stɑ:v], *v.t.* faire mourir de faim; affamer.—*v.i.* mourir de faim.

starveling [ˈstɑ:vliŋ], *n.* affamé, meurt-de-faim, *m.*

starving [ˈstɑ:viŋ], *a.* affamé, mourant de faim.

state [steit], *n.* état, *m.*, condition, *f.*; état (*organisme politique*); pompe, *f.*, apparat (*pompe*), *m.*; *the United States*, les États-Unis, *m.pl.*—*v.t.* énoncer, déclarer.

state-controlled [ˈsteitkənˈtrould], *a.* étatisé.

statecraft [ˈsteitkrɑ:ft], *n.* politique, *f.*

stated [ˈsteitid], *a.* réglé, fixe.

stateless [ˈsteitlis], *a.* *stateless person*, apatride, *m.*, *f.*

stateliness [ˈsteitlinis], *n.* majesté, grandeur, *f.*

stately [ˈsteitli], *a.* imposant, majestueux, noble.—*adv.* majestueusement, avec dignité.

statement [ˈsteitmənt], *n.* exposé, énoncé, rapport, *m.*; déclaration, *f.*

statesman [ˈsteitsmən], *n.* (*pl.* **-men** [men]) homme d'État, *m.*

statesmanlike [ˈsteitsmənlaik], *a.* d'homme d'État.

statesmanship [ˈsteitsmənʃip], *n.* science du gouvernement, politique, *f.*

static [ˈstætik], **statical** [ˈstætikəl], *a.* statique.

station [ˈsteiʃən], *n.* station, *f.*; rang (*classe*), *m.*; position; (*Rail.*) gare, *f.*; (*Mil.*) poste, *m.*, garnison, *f.*—*v.t.* placer; (*Mil.*) poster.

stationary [ˈsteiʃənəri], *a.* stationnaire; fixe.

stationer [ˈsteiʃənə], *n.* papetier, *m.*

stationery [ˈsteiʃənəri], *n.* papeterie, *f.*

station wagon [ˈsteiʃənwægən], *n.* (*Motor.*) canadienne, *f.*

statistic [stəˈtistik], **statistical** [stəˈtistikəl], *a.* statistique.

statistician [stætisˈtiʃən], *n.* statisticien, *m.*

statistics [stəˈtistiks], *n.pl.* statistique, *f.*

statuary [ˈstætjuəri], *n.* statuaire, *f.*

statue [ˈstætju:], *n.* statue, *f.*

statuesque [stætjuːˈesk], *a.* plastique.

stature [ˈstætʃə], *n.* stature, taille, *f.*

status [ˈsteitəs], *n.* statut légal, *m.*; condition, *f.*, rang, *m.*

statute [ˈstætjuːt], *n.* statut, *m.*, loi, *f.*

statutory [ˈstætjutəri], *a.* réglementaire, statutaire.

staunch [STANCH].

stave [steiv], *n.* douve (*de baril*); (*Mus.*) portée, *f.*; verset (*de psaume*), *m.*—*v.t. irr.* crever; défoncer (*baril*); *to stave off*, chasser, repousser, éloigner, écarter, prévenir (*danger*).

staves [STAFF].

stay [stei], *v.t.* arrêter; apaiser (*sa faim*); étayer, accoter (*appuyer*).—*v.i.* rester; demeurer (*séjourner*); descendre; attendre. —*n.* séjour; (*Law*) sursis; soutien, appui (*aide*), *m.*

stay-at-home [ˈsteiəthoum], *a.* and *n.* casanier, *m.*

stead [sted], *n.* lieu, *m.*, place, *f.*

steadfast [ˈstedfəst], *a.* ferme, constant, stable.

steadfastly [ˈstedfəstli], *adv.* fermement, avec constance.

steadfastness [ˈstedfəstnis], *n.* fermeté, constance, *f.*

steadily [ˈstedili], *adv.* fermement, avec persistance.

steadiness [ˈstedinis], *n.* fermeté; assurance, *f.*

steady [ˈstedi], *a.* ferme, assuré; posé (*sérieux*); régulier.—*adv.* doucement.—*v.t.* affermir; assujettir (*fixer*); calmer.

steak [steik], *n.* tranche (*de viande*), *f.*; entre-côte, *m.*; *fillet steak*, bifteck dans le filet, *m.*

steal [sti:l], *v.t. irr.* voler, dérober.—*v.i.* se dérober, se glisser furtivement, aller *ou* venir à la dérobée.

stealer [ˈsti:lə], *n.* voleur, *m.*

stealing [ˈsti:liŋ], *n.* vol, *m.*

stealth [stelθ], *n.* *by stealth*, à la dérobée, furtivement.

stealthily [ˈstelθili], *adv.* à la dérobée, furtivement, à pas de loup.

stealthy [ˈstelθi], *a.* dérobé, furtif.

steam [sti:m], *n.* vapeur, *f.*—*v.t.* (*Cook.*) cuire à la vapeur.—*v.i.* jeter de la vapeur; fumer.

steamboat [ˈsti:mbout], *n.* bateau à vapeur, *m.*

steam engine [ˈsti:mendʒin], *n.* machine à vapeur, *f.*

steamer [ˈsti:mə], *n.* vapeur, steamer, *m.*

steam gauge [ˈsti:mgeidʒ], *n.* manomètre, *m.*

steaming [ˈsti:miŋ], *a.* fumant.

steam pipe [ˈsti:mpaip], *n.* tuyau de vapeur, *m.*

steam-roller [ˈsti:mroulə], *n.* rouleau compresseur, *m.*—*v.t.* (*fig.*) écraser.

steamship [ˈsti:mʃip], *n.* vapeur, *m.*

steam whistle [ˈsti:mwisl], *n.* sifflet à vapeur, *m.*

steamy [ˈsti:mi], *a.* humide.

steed [sti:d], *n.* (*poet*) coursier, *m.*

steel [sti:l], *a.* d'acier, en acier.—*n.* acier; fusil (*pour aiguiser un couteau*); (*fig.*) fer, *m.*—*v.t.* acérer, garnir d'acier; (*fig.*) fortifier.

steel-clad [ˈsti:lklæd], *a.* revêtu d'acier, bardé de fer.

steeliness [ˈsti:linis], *n.* dureté d'acier; (*fig.*) dureté, *f.*

steel-plated [ˈsti:lpleitid], *a.* cuirassé.

steel-works [ˈsti:lwə:ks], *n.pl.* aciérie, *f.*

steely [ˈsti:li], *a.* d'acier; (*fig.*) dur, de fer.

steelyard ['sti:lja:d], *n.* romaine, *f.*
steep (1) [sti:p], *a.* escarpé, à pic; raide (*escalier*).—*n.* pente rapide, *f.*; escarpement, *m.*
steep (2) [sti:p], *v.t.* tremper; (*fig.*) saturer (*de*).
steeping ['sti:piŋ], *n.* trempage, *m.*
steeple [sti:pl], *n.* clocher, *m.*
steeplechase [sti:pltʃeis], *n.* course au clocher, *f.*, steeplechase, *m.*
steepled [sti:pld], *a.* à clocher.
steeple-jack ['sti:pldʒæk], *n.* réparateur de clochers *ou* de cheminées, *m.*
steeply ['sti:pli], *adv.* en pente rapide.
steepness ['sti:pnis], *n.* raideur, pente rapide, *f.*
steer [stiə], *n.* bouvillon, jeune bœuf, *m.*—*v.t.* gouverner; diriger; (*Motor. etc.*) conduire. —*v.i.* se diriger.
steerage ['stiəridʒ], *n.* timonerie, *f.*; l'avant; logement des passagers de troisième classe, *m.*
steering ['stiəriŋ], *n.* direction; (*Motor.*) conduite, *f.*
steering wheel ['stiəriŋwi:l], *n.* volant, *m.*
steersman ['stiəzmən], *n.* (*pl.* -men [men]) timonier, *m.*
stellar ['stelə], *a.* stellaire.
stem [stem], *n.* tige; queue (*d'une fleur etc.*); (*fig.*) souche (*d'une famille*), *f.*—*v.t.* refouler (*courant*); (*fig.*) résister à.—*v.i.* **to stem from**, être issu de.
stench [stentʃ], *n.* puanteur, *f.*
stencil ['stensil], *n.* patron, pochoir, stencil, *m.*—*v.t.* tracer au patron, tirer au stencil.
sten gun ['stengʌn], *n.* fusil mitrailleur, *m.*
stenographer [ste'nɔgrəfə], *n.* sténographe, *m.*, *f.*
stenography [ste'nɔgrəfi], *n.* sténographie, *f.*
stentorian [sten'tɔ:riən], *a.* de stentor.
step [step], *v.t.* mesurer en comptant les pas, arpenter.—*v.i.* faire un pas, marcher pas à pas; marcher, aller; monter (*dans*); descendre (*de*); **to step aside**, s'écarter; **to step back**, reculer; **to step forward**, s'avancer; **to step on**, fouler; **to step over**, enjamber.—*n.* pas; degré, *m.*, marche (*d'escalier*), *f.*; échelon (*d'échelle*); marchepied (*de voiture ou de bicyclette*), *m.*; (*fig.*) démarche; (*pl.*) échelle, *f.*
stepbrother ['stepbrʌðə], *n.* beau-frère, *m.*
stepchild ['steptʃaild], *n.* beau-fils, *m.*, belle-fille, *f.*
stepfather ['stepfɑ:ðə], *n.* beau-père, *m.*
Stephen [sti:vn]. Étienne, *m.*
stepmother ['stepmʌðə], *n.* belle-mère; marâtre, *f.*
steppe [step], *n.* steppe (*plaine*), *f.*
stepping ['stepiŋ], *n.* marche, allure, *f.*
stepping-stone ['stepiŋstoun], *n.* (*pl.*) pierres de gué, *f.pl.*; (*fig.*) introduction, *f.*
stepsister ['stepsistə], *n.* belle-sœur, *f.*
stereoscopic [stiəriə'skɔpik], *a.* stéréoscopique.
stereotype ['stiəriətaip], *n.* stéréotypé; cliché. —*n.* stéréotypage; (*fig.*) cliché, *m.*—*v.t.* clicher; stéréotyper.
stereotyped ['stiəriətaipt], *a.* (*usu. fig.*) stéréotypé.
sterile ['sterail], *a.* stérile.
sterility [stə'riliti], *n.* stérilité, *f.*

sterilization [sterilai'zeiʃən], *n.* stérilisation, *f.*
sterilize ['sterilaiz], *v.t.* stériliser.
sterling ['stə:liŋ], *a.* sterling; (*fig.*) vrai, de bon aloi.
stern (1) [stə:n], *a.* sévère, dur; rigoureux.
stern (2) [stə:n], *n.* (*Naut.*) arrière, *m.*
sternly ['stə:nli], *adv.* sévèrement, durement.
sternmost ['stə:nmoust], *a.* le dernier.
sternness [stə:nnis], *n.* sévérité, austérité, *f.*
stethoscope ['steθəskoup], *n.* stéthoscope, *m.*
stevedore ['sti:vədɔ:], *n.* arrimeur; déchargeur, *m.*
stew [stju:], *n.* étuvée, *f.*, ragoût (*de viande*); (*fig.*) embarras, *m.*, confusion, *f.*; **Irish stew**, ragoût de mouton.—*v.t.* étuver; mettre en ragoût, faire un ragoût de.—*v.i.* cuire à l'étuvée; (*fig.*) cuire dans sa peau.
steward ['stju:əd], *n.* intendant, régisseur (*d'une propriété*); économe (*de collège*); commissaire (*de bal etc.*); (*Naut.*) steward, *m.*; **steward's room**, cambuse, *f.*
stewardess ['stju:ədis], *n.* femme de chambre (*de bord*), stewardesse, *f.*
stewardship ['stju:ədʃip], *n.* intendance; (*fig.*) administration, *f.*
stewed [stju:d], *a.* étuvé, en ragoût; en compote.
stew-pan ['stju:pæn], *n.* casserole, *f.*
stew-pot ['stju:pɔt], *n.* cocotte, *f.*, faitout, *m.*
stick (1) [stik], *n.* bâton, *m.*; canne (*pour marcher*), *f.*; (*Av.*) manche; chapelet (*de bombes*), *m.*
stick (2) [stik], *v.t. irr.* percer, piquer; enfoncer; coller; **stick no bills**, défense d'afficher.—*v.i.* se coller, s'attacher; rester (*demeurer*); **to stick close**, ne pas quitter; **to stick out**, faire saillie; persister; **to stick to**, s'en tenir à; **to stick up**, se dresser.
stickiness ['stikinis], *n.* viscosité, *f.*
sticking plaster ['stikiŋ'plɑ:stə], *n.* taffetas d'Angleterre, *m.*
stickle [stikl], *v.i.* tenir beaucoup (*à*); se disputer.
stickleback ['stiklbæk], *n.* épinoche, *f.*
stickler ['stiklə], *n.* partisan, *m.*; rigoriste, *m.*, *f.*
sticky ['stiki], *a.* gluant, collant; (*fig.*) difficile (*personne*).
stiff [stif], *a.* raide, rigide, tenace; dur, ferme (*non fluide*); opiniâtre (*entêté*); gêné (*contraint*); courbatu (*muscles*); affecté, guindé (*style*).
stiffen [stifn], *v.t.* raidir; (*fig.*) endurcir.—*v.i.* se raidir; (*fig.*) s'endurcir.
stiffening ['stifniŋ], *n.* raidissement; soutien (*appui*), *m.*
stiffly ['stifli], *adv.* avec raideur; obstinément.
stiff neck ['stifnek], *n.* torticolis, *m.*
stiff-necked ['stifnekt], *a.* opiniâtre, entêté.
stiffness ['stifnis], *n.* raideur; gêne (*contrainte*); opiniâtreté (*entêtement*), *f.*; (*fig.*) air guindé, *m.*
stifle [staifl], *v.t., v.i.* étouffer, suffoquer.—*n.* (*Vet.*) grasset, *m.*
stifling ['staifliŋ], *a.* étouffant, suffocant. —*n.* suffocation, *f.*
stigma ['stigmə], *n.* stigmate, *m.*, flétrissure, *f.*
stigmatize ['stigmətaiz], *v.t.* stigmatiser, flétrir.

579

stile [stail], *n.* échallier, échalis, *m.*
stiletto [sti'letou], *n.* stylet, *m.*; ***stiletto heels***, talons aiguille, *m.pl.*
still (1) [stil], *a.* silencieux; tranquille, calme, paisible, en repos; immobile; non mousseux (*vin*).—*adv.* encore, toujours; cependant, néanmoins (*malgré tout*).—*v.t.* calmer, apaiser.
still (2) [stil], *n.* alambic, *m.*
still-born ['stilbɔːn], *a.* mort-né.
stillness ['stilnis], *n.* tranquillité, *f.*, calme, *m.*
still room ['stilruːm], *n.* distillerie, *f.*, laboratoire, *m.*
stilt [stilt], *n.* échasse, *f.*; pilotis, pieu (*de pont etc.*), *m.*
stilted ['stiltid], *a.* guindé, pompeux.
stimulant ['stimjulənt], *n.* stimulant, *m.*
stimulate ['stimjuleit], *v.t.* stimuler; (*fig.*) exciter.
stimulating ['stimjuleitiŋ], *a.* stimulant.
stimulation [stimju'leiʃən], *n.* stimulation, *f.*
stimulus ['stimjuləs], *n.* stimulant, aiguillon, stimulus, *m.*
sting [stiŋ], *n.* aiguillon; dard (*d'ortie etc.*), *m.*; piqûre; (*fig.*) pointe, *f.*—*v.t. irr.* piquer; (*fig.*) irriter.
stingily ['stindʒili], *adv.* chichement, mesquinement.
stinginess ['stindʒinis], *n.* mesquinerie, ladrerie, *f.*
stinging ['stiŋiŋ], *a.* piquant; cinglant.—*n.* piqûre, *f.*
stingy ['stindʒi], *a.* avare, mesquin, ladre, chiche.
stink [stiŋk], *n.* puanteur, mauvaise odeur, *f.*—*v.i. irr.* puer; sentir mauvais.
stinking ['stiŋkiŋ], *a.* puant.
stint [stint], *v.t.* limiter, restreindre; ***to stint oneself***, se priver (*de*).—*n.* limite, borne; portion; besogne, *f.*
stipend ['staipend], *n.* traitement (*d'ecclésiastique ou de magistrat*), *m.*
stipendiary [sti'pendiəri], *a.* appointé.
stipple [stipl], *v.t.* pointiller.
stippling ['stipliŋ], *n.* pointillage (*processus*); pointillé (*résultat*), *m.*
stipulate ['stipjuleit], *v.i.* stipuler (*de ou que*).
stipulation [stipju'leiʃən], *n.* stipulation, condition, *f.*
stipulator ['stipjuleitə], *n.* partie stipulante, *f.*
stir [stəː], *v.t.* remuer; (*fig.*) agiter; ***to stir the fire***, attiser le feu.—*v.i.* remuer, se remuer, bouger.—*n.* remuement, bruit, *m.*; agitation, *f.*
stirring ['stəːriŋ], *a.* remuant; émouvant (*histoire etc.*).—*n.* agitation, *f.*
stirrup ['stirəp], *n.* étrier, *m.*
stirrup cup ['stirəpkʌp], *n.* coup de l'étrier, *m.*
stirrup leather ['stirəp'leðə], *n.* étrivière, *f.*
stitch [stitʃ], *n.* point, *m.*; maille (*en tricot*), *f.*; (*Med.*) point de suture, *m.*; ***a stitch in time saves nine***, un point à temps en épargne cent.—*v.t.* piquer, coudre; brocher (*livres*); (*Med.*) suturer.
stitched [stitʃt], *a.* piqué, broché (*livre*).
stitching ['stitʃiŋ], *n.* couture, *f.*; brochage (*de livre*), *m.*; (*Med.*) suture, *f.*
stoat [stout], *n.* hermine d'été, *f.*
stock (1) [stɔk], *a.* courant, habituel.—*n.* souche (*d'arbre, famille etc.*), *f.*; cep (*de vigne*); bloc (*de bois etc.*), *m.*; monture (*de

fusil); (*Hort.*) ente (*pour greffer*), *f.*; (*Cook.*) consommé, *m.*; (*fig.*) race, famille, *f.*; approvisionnement, stock (*réserve*), assortiment (*sélection*), *m.*; (*pl.*) fonds, fonds publics, *m.pl.*, rentes, actions, *f.pl.*; (*Shipbuilding*) chantier, *m.*, cale de construction, *f.*; ceps (*punition*), *m.pl.*; ***rolling stock***, matériel roulant, *m.*; ***to take stock of***, faire l'inventaire de.—*v.t.* pourvoir (*de*); stocker (*magasin*); meubler (*ferme*); empoissonner (*vivier*).
stock (2) [stɔk], *n.* (*St. Exch.*), see **share** (2).
stockade [stɔ'keid], *n.* palissade, *f.*—*v.t.* palissader.
stock book ['stɔkbuk], *n.* livre de magasin, magasinier, *m.*
stock-breeder ['stɔkbriːdə], *n.* éleveur, *m.*
stock-breeding ['stɔkbriːdiŋ], *n.* élevage, *m.*
stockbroker ['stɔkbroukə], *n.* agent de change, *m.*
stock exchange ['stɔkikstʃeindʒ], *n.* bourse; compagnie des agents de change, *f.*
stockholder ['stɔkhouldə], *n.* actionnaire, *m.*, *f.*, rentier, *m.*
stocking ['stɔkiŋ], *n.* bas, *m.*
stockpile ['stɔkpail], *n.* stocks de réserve, *m.pl.*—*v.t.*, *v.i.* stocker.
stock-still ['stɔk'stil], *a.* immobile.—*adv.* sans bouger.
stock-taking ['stɔkteikiŋ], *n.* inventaire, *m.*
stocky ['stɔki], *a.* trapu.
stodgy ['stɔdʒi], *a.* pâteux, lourd.
stoic ['stouik], *n.* stoïcien, *m.*
stoic ['stouik], **stoical** ['stouikəl], *a.* stoïcien; (*fig.*) stoïque.
stoicism ['stouisizm], *n.* stoïcisme, *m.*
stoke [stouk], *v.t.* chauffer; tisonner (*le feu*).
stoker ['stoukə], *n.* chauffeur, *m.*
stoking ['stoukiŋ], *n.* chauffage, *m.*, chauffe, *f.*
stole (1) [stoul], *n.* étole; (*Cost.*) écharpe, *f.*
stole (2) [stoul], *past* STEAL.
stolen ['stoulən], *a.* volé, dérobé.
stolid ['stɔlid], *a.* lourd, impassible.
stolidity [stɔ'liditi], **stolidness** ['stɔlidnis], *n.* flegme, *m.*
stomach ['stʌmək], *n.* estomac; (*euph.*) ventre; appétit, *m.*—*v.t.* avaler; endurer.
stomach ache ['stʌməkeik], *n.* mal à l'estomac, *m.*, colique, *f.*
stone [stoun], *a.* de pierre, en pierre; de grès (*céramique*).—*n.* pierre, *f.*; caillou (*galet*); noyau (*de fruits*); pépin (*de raisins*); (*Path.*) calcul; (*Weight*) stone (*kg. 6,348*), *m.*—*v.t.* lapider; ôter les noyaux de (*fruits*).
stone-blind ['stounblaind], *a.* complètement aveugle.
stone-cold ['stounkould], *a.* complètement froid.—*adv.* complètement.
stone-dead ['stoun'ded], *a.* raide mort.
stone-deaf ['stoundef], *a.* complètement sourd.
stone fruit ['stounfruːt], *n.* fruit à noyau, *m.*
stone-mason ['stounmeisən], *n.* maçon, marbrier (*pour tombes*), *m.*
stone's throw ['stounzθrou], *n.* jet de pierre, *m.*
stoneware ['stounwɛə], *n.* grès, *m.*, poterie de grès, *f.*
stonework ['stounwəːk], *n.* maçonnerie, *f.*
stoniness ['stouninis], *n.* nature pierreuse; (*fig.*) dureté, *f.*
stoning ['stouniŋ], *n.* lapidation, *f.*

stony ['stouni], *a.* de pierre; pierreux (*plein de pierres*); (*fig.*) insensible; **stony-hearted**, au cœur de pierre.

stook [stu:k], *n.* tas de gerbes, *m.*—*v.t.* mettre en gerbes.

stool [stu:l], *n.* tabouret; escabeau, *m.*

stoop [stu:p], *v.i.* se pencher, se baisser; se voûter; (*fig.*) s'abaisser.—*n.* inclination, *f.*; (*fig.*) abaissement, *m.*

stooping ['stu:piŋ], *a.* penché, courbé.

stop [stɔp], *n.* halte; pause, *f.*; obstacle; (*Organ*) jeu, registre; arrêt (*de trains etc.*), *m.*; (*Gram.*) **full stop**, point, *m.*—*v.t.* arrêter, empêcher; couper (*le souffle*); suspendre (*paiement etc.*); retenir (*la paye*); (*Mus.*) presser; (*Gram.*) ponctuer; boucher (*trou etc.*); stopper (*machine*); plomber (*dent*).—*v.i.* s'arrêter; stopper.

stopcock ['stɔpkɔk], *n.* robinet d'arrêt, *m.*

stop-gap ['stɔpgæp], *n.* bouche-trou, *m.*

stoppage ['stɔpidʒ], *n.* interruption, halte, *f.*; arrêt (*d'un train etc.*), *m.*; obstruction; retenue (*de salaire*), *f.*; chômage (*arrêt de travail*); plombage (*de dent*), *m.*

stopper ['stɔpə], *n.* bouchon (*en verre*), *m.*—*v.t.* boucher.

stopping ['stɔpiŋ], *n.* arrêt; plombage (*de dent*), *m.*; matière à plomber, *f.*

stop-watch ['stɔpwɔtʃ], *n.* chronomètre, *m.*

storage ['stɔ:ridʒ], *n.* emmagasinage, *m.*, accumulation, *f.*

store [stɔ:], *n.* provision, *f.*; approvisionnement, *m.*, réserve, *f.*; magasin, *m.*, boutique, *f.*; (*fig.*) fonds, trésor, *m.*; **in store**, en réserve; **to lay in a store of**, faire une provision de.—*v.t.* pourvoir, munir, approvisionner (*de*); enrichir (*l'esprit*).

store-house ['stɔ:haus], *n.* magasin, entrepôt, dépôt, *m.*

store-keeper ['stɔ:ki:pə], *n.* garde-magasin; marchand (*boutiquier*), *m.*

store-room ['stɔ:ru:m], *n.* dépôt, office, *m.*; réserve, *f.*

storey, story (1) ['stɔ:ri], *n.* étage, *m.*

storied (1) ['stɔ:rid], *a.* à étage.

storied (2) ['stɔ:rid], *a.* historié.

stork [stɔ:k], *n.* cigogne, *f.*

storm [stɔ:m], *n.* orage, *m.*, tempête, *f.*—*v.t.* donner l'assaut à, prendre d'assaut.—*v.i.* faire de l'orage; (*fig.*) tempêter, s'emporter.

storm bell ['stɔ:mbel], *n.* tocsin, *m.*

storm cloud ['stɔ:mklaud], *n.* nuée, *f.*

storminess ['stɔ:minis], *n.* état orageux, *m.*

storming ['stɔ:miŋ], *n.* assaut, *m.*, prise d'assaut; (*fig.*) rage, *f.*

stormy ['stɔ:mi], *a.* orageux, à l'orage; **stormy petrel**, pétrel, *m.*

story (1) [STOREY].

story (2) ['stɔ:ri], *n.* histoire, *f.*, récit; conte (*littéraire*); mensonge (*tromperie*), *m.*

story-book ['stɔ:ribuk], *n.* livre de contes, *m.*

story-teller ['stɔ:ritelə], *n.* conteur (*narrateur*); menteur (*trompeur*), *m.*

stout [staut], *a.* fort; gros, corpulent; (*fig.*) brave, courageux.—*n.* stout, *m.*, bière brune forte (*boisson*), *f.*

stoutly ['stautli], *adv.* vigoureusement, fort et ferme.

stoutness ['stautnis], *n.* embonpoint, *m.*, corpulence; (*fig.*) fermeté, *f.*

stove (1) [stouv], *past and p.p.* [STAVE].

stove (2) [stouv], *n.* poêle; fourneau (*de cuisine*), *m.*

stow [stou], *v.t.* mettre en place; (*Naut.*) arrimer; **to stow away**, emmagasiner.

stowage ['stouidʒ], *n.* mise en place, *f.*, (*Naut.*) arrimage, *m.*

stowaway ['stouəwei], *n.* passager clandestin, *m.*—*v.i.* s'embarquer clandestinement.

straddle ['strædl], *v.t.* enfourcher.—*v.i.* écarter les jambes, marcher les jambes écartées.

strafe [strɑ:f], *v.t.* mitrailler, bombarder.

straggle ['strægl], *v.i.* s'écarter; marcher à la débandade.

straggler ['stræglə], *n.* rôdeur; (*Mil.*) traînard, *m.*

straggling ['strægliŋ], *a.* séparé; éparpillé (*disséminé*).

straight [streit], *a.* droit; (*fig.*) équitable, juste.—*adv.* droit, tout droit, directement; **straight away**, sur-le-champ, tout de suite.

straight-edge ['streitedʒ], *n.* règle à araser, *f.*

straighten [streitn], *v.t.* rendre droit, redresser; ajuster (*habits*); mettre en ordre (*affaires, maison*).

straight-faced ['streit'feisd], *a.* imperturbable.

straightforward [streit'fɔ:wəd], *a.* droit, direct; (*fig.*) franc; simple (*problème*).

straightforwardly [streit'fɔ:wədli], *adv.* avec droiture; (*colloq.*) carrément.

straightforwardness [streit'fɔ:wədnis], *n.* droiture, franchise, *f.*

straightness ['streitnis], *n.* ligne directe; droiture, *f.*

straightway ['streitwei], *adv.* sur-le-champ, à l'instant.

strain (1) [strein], *v.t.* tendre; forcer (*contraindre*); se fouler (*muscles*); filtrer, passer (*liquide*).—*v.i.* s'efforcer; se filtrer (*liquide*).—*n.* grand effort, *m.*, tension; entorse, foulure (*de muscles*), *f.*; ton; chant, *m.*

strain (2) [strein], *n.* race, lignée, *f.*

strained [streind], *a.* forcé, pas naturel (*langage etc.*); tendu.

strainer ['streinə], *n.* passoire, *f.*

straining ['streiniŋ], *n.* tension, *f.*, grand effort, *m.*, exagération, *f.*; filtrage (*d'un liquide*), *m.*

strait [streit], *a.* étroit, serré; strict.—*n.* (*usu. pl.*) (*Geog.*) détroit, *m.*; (*pl.*) gêne, difficulté, *f.*, embarras, *m.*

straiten [streitn], *v.t.* rétrécir (*resserrer*); (*fig.*) gêner.

strait-laced ['streitleist], *a.* lacé étroitement; (*fig.*) sévère, prude.

straitness ['streitnis], *n.* étroitesse, *f.*

strait-waistcoat ['streitweiskout], **strait-jacket** ['streitdʒækit], *n.* camisole de force, *f.*

strand (1) [strænd], *n.* plage, grève, *f.*—*v.t.* jeter à la côte, échouer.—*v.i.* échouer.

strand (2) [strænd], *n.* cordon (*de corde*), *m.*

stranded ['strændid], *a.* échoué; (*fig.*) dans l'embarras.

stranding ['strændiŋ], *n.* échouement, échouage, *m.*

strange [streindʒ], *a.* étrange, singulier, bizarre.

strangely ['streindʒli], *adv.* étrangement, singulièrement.

strangeness ['streindʒnis], *n.* étrangeté, bizarrerie, *f.*
stranger ['streindʒə], *n.* étranger, inconnu, *m.*
strangle [stræŋgl], *v.t.* étrangler.
strangler ['stræŋglə], *n.* étrangleur, *m.*
strangling ['stræŋgliŋ], *n.* étranglement, *m.*
strangulation [stræŋgju'leiʃən], *n.* strangulation, *f.*
strap [stræp], *n.* courroie, *f.*; lien, *m.*, bande (*de fer*), *f.*—*v.t.* attacher avec une courroie; lier.
strapper ['stræpə], *n.* grand gaillard, *m.*
strapping ['stræpiŋ], *a.* bien découplé, bien bâti.
stratagem ['strætədʒəm], *n.* stratagème, *m.*
strategic [strə'ti:dʒik], **strategical** [strə'ti:dʒikəl], *a.* stratégique.
strategist ['strætədʒist], *n.* stratégiste, *m.*, *f.*
strategy ['strætədʒi], *n.* stratégie, *f.*
stratify ['strætifai], *v.t.* stratifier.
stratocruiser ['stræto'kru:zə], *n.* avion stratosphérique.
stratosphere ['strætəsfiə], *n.* stratosphère, *f.*
stratum ['stra:təm], *n.* (*pl.* **strata** ['stra:tə]) couche, *f.*
straw [strɔ:], *a.* de paille.—*n.* paille, *f.*; **it's the last straw**, c'est le comble.—*v.t.* rempailler (*chaise*).
strawberry ['strɔ:bəri], *n.* fraise, *f.*; fraisier (*plante*), *m.*
straw-colored ['strɔ:kʌləd], *a.* jaune-paille.
straw mat ['strɔ:'mæt], *n.* paillasson, *m.*
stray [strei], *v.i.* s'égarer, errer, vaguer; s'écarter (*de*).—*a.* égaré; (*fig.*) fortuit.—*n.* épave, *f.*; **waifs and strays**, des épaves, *f.pl.*
straying ['streiiŋ], *n.* égarement, *m.*
streak [stri:k], *n.* raie, bande, *f.*; **streak of lightning**, éclair, *m.*—*v.t.* rayer, strier; barioler, bigarrer.—*v.i.* filer.
streaked [stri:kt], *a.* rayé (*de*); bariolé, bigarré.
streaky ['stri:ki], *a.* rayé; veiné (*marbre*); entrelardé (*viande*).
stream [stri:m], *n.* courant; cours d'eau, *m.*, rivière, *f.*; ruisseau; (*fig.*) cours; jet (*de lumière etc.*); torrent (*de paroles etc.*), *m.*; **to go down stream**, aller en aval; **to go up stream**, aller en amont.—*v.i.* couler; ruisseler (*sang etc.*); rayonner (*lumière*).
streamer ['stri:mə], *n.* banderole; (*Naut.*) flamme, *f.*; (*pl.*) serpentins (*de papier*), *m.pl.*
streamlet ['stri:mlit], *n.* petit ruisseau; ru, *m.*
stream-line ['stri:mlain], *n.* fil de l'eau, *m.* —*v.t.* caréner; (*fig.*) moderniser.
stream-lined ['stri:mlaind], *a.* **stream-lined body**, carrosserie carénée, *f.*; **stream-lined car**, voiture aérodynamique, *f.*
street [stri:t], *n.* rue, *f.*
street door ['stri:t'dɔ:], *n.* porte sur la rue, *f.*
street lamp ['stri:tlæmp], *n.* réverbère, *m.*
street sweeper ['stri:tswi:pə], *n.* balayeur de rue (*personne*), *m.*; balayeuse (*machine*), *f.*
strength [streŋθ], *n.* force, *f.*, forces, *f.pl.*; (*Build.*) solidité, *f.*; (*Mil.*) effectif, *m.*
strengthen [streŋθn], *v.t.* fortifier, affermir, raffermir; (*Mil.*) renforcer.—*v.i.* se fortifier, s'affermir, se raffermir.
strengthener ['streŋθnə], *n.* (*Med.*) fortifiant, *m.*
strengthening ['streŋθniŋ], *a.* fortifiant.

strenuous ['strenjuəs], *a.* énergique, vif, ardent, vigoureux.
strenuously ['strenjuəsli], *adv.* avec zèle, ardemment; vigoureusement.
strenuousness ['strenjuəsnis], *n.* zèle, *m.*, ardeur; vigueur, *f.*
streptococcus [strepto'kɔkəs], *n.* streptocoque, *m.*
streptomycin [strepto'maisin], *n.* streptomycine, *f.*
stress [stres], *n.* force, emphase, *f.*, poids; (*Gram.*) accent, *m.*; violence (*du temps*); (*Mech.*) tension, *f.*—*v.t.* appuyer sur, accentuer.
stretch [stretʃ], *v.t.* tendre (*un élastique*); étendre; déployer (*ailes*); élargir; forcer (*faire violence à*); (*fig.*) exagérer.—*v.i.* s'étendre; s'étirer; se déployer; s'élargir; prêter (*gants, tissu*).—*n.* étendue, tension, extension; section (*de route*), *f.*; (*fig.*) effort, *m.*; **at a stretch**, d'un trait.
stretcher ['stretʃə], *n.* brancard, *m.*, civière, *f.*; baguette (*à gants*), *f.*, tendeur (*à chaussures*), *m.*
stretcher-bearer ['stretʃəbɛərə], *n.* brancardier, *m.*
stretching ['stretʃiŋ], *n.* élargissement, *m.*; tension, *f.*
strew [stru:], *v.t. irr.* répandre, parsemer, semer.
strewing ['stru:iŋ], *n.* jonchée, *f.*
striate ['straiit], **striated** [strai'eitid], *a.* strié.
striation [strai'eiʃən], *n.* striure, *f.*
stricken [strikn], *p.p.* [STRIKE].—*a.* affligé; (*Med.*) atteint (*de*).
strict [strikt], *a.* exact, strict, précis; rigide; sévère.
strictly ['striktli], *adv.* strictement, formellement; **strictly speaking**, rigoureusement parlant.
strictness ['striktnis], *n.* exactitude, rigueur; sévérité, *f.*
stricture ['striktʃə], *n.* censure, critique, *f.*; (*Med.*) étranglement, *m.*
stride [straid], *n.* grand pas, *m.*, enjambée, *f.* —*v.i. irr.* marcher à grands pas *ou* à grandes enjambées.
strident ['straidənt], *a.* strident.
strife [straif], *n.* lutte, querelle, dispute, *f.*
strike [straik], *v.t. irr.* frapper; battre, cogner; asséner, porter (*un coup*); sonner (*l'heure*); rendre (*muet etc.*); établir (*l'équilibre*); allumer (*allumette*); faire (*marché etc.*); amener (*drapeau*); plier (*tente*); **to strike down**, abattre; **to strike off**, retrancher, effacer.—*v.i.* frapper; toucher; échouer (*heurter un écueil etc.*); heurter, donner (*contre*); sonner (*pendule etc.*); (*Hort.*) prendre racine; faire grève, se mettre en grève (*ouvriers*); **to strike out**, se lancer; (*Mus.*) **to strike up**, commencer à jouer.— *n.* grève (*d'ouvriers*), *f.*; **sit-down strike**, débrayage, *m.*; **stay-in-strike**, grève sur le tas.
striker ['straikə], *n.* frappeur, *m.*; gréviste (*ouvrier en grève*), *m.*, *f.*; percuteur (*de fusil*), *m.*
striking ['straikiŋ], *a.* frappant, saisissant; remarquable.—*n.* frappement, *m.*; frappe; sonnerie (*de pendule*), *f.*
strikingly ['straikiŋli], *adv.* d'une manière frappante.

string [striŋ], *n.* ficelle, corde, *f.*; fil; cordon, lacet (*de chaussures etc.*); chapelet (*d'oignons etc.*), *m.*; corde (*de violon*); bride (*de bonnet etc.*); (*fig.*) suite, série, *f.*; *the strings*, les instruments à cordes (*d'un orchestre*), *m.pl.*—*v.t. irr.* garnir de cordes; enfiler (*grains etc.*); (*Mus.*) accorder.
stringed [striŋd], *a.* à cordes (*instrument de musique*).
stringency ['strindʒənsi], *n.* rigueur, *f.*
stringent ['strindʒənt], *a.* rigoureux, strict.
stringy ['striŋi], *a.* fibreux; filandreux (*viande*).
strip [strip], *n.* bande, *f.*, ruban; lambeau, *m.*, langue (*de terre*), *f.*—*v.t.* dépouiller (*de*); dévaliser (*voler*); déshabiller (*dévêtir*); *to strip off*, se dépouiller de.—*v.i.* se déshabiller.
stripe [straip], *n.* raie; barre, bande; marque (*cicatrice*), *f.*; (*Mil.*) chevron, galon, *m.*—*v.t.* rayer, barrer.
striped [straipt], **stripy** ['straipi], *a.* rayé, à raies, zébré.
stripling ['stripliŋ], *n.* adolescent, *m.*
strive [straiv], *v.i. irr.* s'efforcer (*de*), faire des efforts (*pour*), se débattre; se disputer (*rivaliser*).
striving ['straiviŋ], *n.* lutte, *f.*, efforts, *m.pl.*
stroke [strouk], *n.* coup; trait; trait de plume; coup d'aviron, *m.*; brassée (*de la nage*), course (*de piston*), *f.*; (*Med.*) coup de sang, *m.*, attaque, *f.*; chef de nage (*de bateau à rames*), *m.*; *at a stroke*, d'un coup, d'un trait.—*v.t.* caresser.
stroking ['stroukiŋ], *n.* caresses, *f.pl.*
stroll [stroul], *n.* (courte) promenade, *f.*, tour, *m.*, flânerie, *f.*—*v.i.* errer, flâner.
stroller ['stroulə], *n.* flâneur, *m.*
strong [strɔŋ], *a.* fort, solide; (*fig.*) vigoureux, résolu; *strong light*, vive lumière, *f.*
strong-box ['strɔŋbɔks], *n.* coffre-fort, *m.*
stronghold ['strɔŋhould], *n.* forteresse, *f.*, fort, *m.*
strongly ['strɔŋli], *adv.* fortement, fermement.
strong-room ['strɔŋru:m], *n.* cave aux coffres-forts, *f.*
strontium ['strɔnʃiəm], *n.* strontium, *m.*
strop [strɔp], *n.* cuir à rasoir, *m.*—*v.t.* repasser, affiler.
strophe ['stroufi, 'strofi], *n.* stance, strophe, *f.*
structural ['strʌktʃərəl], *a.* de structure, structural.
structure ['strʌktʃə], *n.* construction, structure, *f.*; édifice, *m.*; facture (*de pièce, de poème*), *f.*
struggle ['strʌgl], *n.* lutte, *f.*, effort, *m.*—*v.i.* lutter, se débattre.
struggling ['strʌgliŋ], *n.* lutte, *f.*; effort, *m.*
strum [strʌm], *v.i.* tapoter, taper (*sur*).
strumming ['strʌmiŋ], *n.* tapotage, *m.*
strut [strʌt], *n.* démarche fière, *f.*; (*Carp. etc*) étai, *m.*—*v.i.* se pavaner, se carrer.
strychnine ['strikni:n], *n.* strychnine, *f.*
stub [stʌb], *n.* souche, *f.*; bout, *m.*
stubble [stʌbl], *n.* chaume, *m.*
stubborn ['stʌbən], *a.* obstiné, opiniâtre.
stubbornness ['stʌbənnis], *n.* opiniâtreté, *f.*
stubby ['stʌbi], *a.* trapu (*taille*).
stucco ['stʌkou], *n.* stuc, *m.*
stud (1) [stʌd], *n.* bouton de chemise; clou, *m.* —*v.t.* clouter; parsemer (*de*).

stud (2) [stʌd], *n.* écurie, *f.*; *stud farm*, haras, *m.*
student ['stju:dənt], *n.* étudiant, *m.*, élève, *m.,f.*
studied ['stʌdid], *a.* étudié (*style etc.*); prémédité (*calculé*).
studio ['stju:diou], *n.* atelier; (*Cine., Rad.*) studio, *m.*
studious ['stju:diəs], *a.* studieux; diligent.
studiously ['stju:diəsli], *adv.* studieusement.
studiousness ['stju:diəsnis], *n.* application, *f.*
study ['stʌdi], *n.* étude, *f.*; soin, *m.*, application (*attention*), *f.*; cabinet d'étude (*pièce*), *m.*; *to be in a brown study*, être dans la lune.—*v.t.* étudier, s'occuper de.—*v.i.* étudier, travailler.
stuff [stʌf], *n.* étoffe, *f.*, tissu, *m.*; (*fig.*) matière, *f.*; fatras (*bêtises*), *m.*—*v.t.* rembourrer; bourrer (*remplir*); boucher (*trou*); (*Taxidermy*) empailler; (*Cook.*) farcir.—*v.i.* se bourrer, se gorger.
stuffing ['stʌfiŋ], *n.* bourre (*substances*), *f.*; rembourrage (*opération*), *m.*; (*Cook.*) farce, *f.*; (*Taxidermy*) empaillage, *m.*
stuffy ['stʌfi], *a.* privé d'air, renfermé; *to be stuffy*, sentir le renfermé; (*fig.*) avoir des préjugés.
stultify ['stʌltifai], *v.t.* rendre nul; contredire (*démentir*); *to stultify oneself*, se rendre ridicule.
stumble [stʌmbl], *v.i.* trébucher, broncher; (*fig.*) faire un faux pas, faillir.—*n.* faux pas, *m.*
stumbling ['stʌmbliŋ], *a.* trébuchant.—*n.* trébuchement, *m.*
stumbling block ['stʌmbliŋblɔk], *n.* pierre d'achoppement, *f.*
stump [stʌmp], *n.* tronçon, *m.*, souche, *f.*; chicot (*de dent*); trognon (*de chou*); moignon (*de membre*), *m.*; (*Drawing*) estompe, *f.*
stumpy ['stʌmpi], *a.* trapu (*personne*).
stun [stʌn], *v.t.* étourdir.
stunning ['stʌniŋ], *a.* étourdissant; (*slang*) épatant.
stunt (1) [stʌnt], *v.t.* rabougrir.
stunt (2) [stʌnt], *n.* tour de force, *m.*; réclame, *f.*
stunted ['stʌntid], *a.* rabougri.
stupefaction [stju:pi'fækʃən], *n.* stupéfaction, *f.*
stupefy ['stju:pifai], *v.t.* hébéter, abrutir; stupéfier.
stupefying ['stju:pifaiiŋ], *a.* stupéfiant.
stupendous [stju'pendəs], *a.* prodigieux, foudroyant.
stupid ['stju:pid], *a.* stupide, sot, bête.
stupidity [stju'piditi], *n.* stupidité, bêtise, *f.*
stupidly ['stju:pidli], *adv.* stupidement.
stupor ['stju:pə], *n.* stupeur, *f.*
sturdy ['stə:di], *a.* vigoureux, fort, robuste; hardi.
sturgeon ['stə:dʒən], *n.* esturgeon, *m.*
stutter ['stʌtə], *v.t., v.i.* bégayer.
stutterer ['stʌtərə], *n.* bègue, *m., f.*
stuttering ['stʌtəriŋ], *n.* bégaiement, *m.*
sty (1) [stai], *n.* étable (à cochons), *f.*
sty (2), **stye** [stai], *n.* orgelet (à l'œil), *m.*
Stygian ['stidʒiən], *a.* stygien.
style [stail], *n.* style; (*fig.*) genre, *m.*, manière, *f.*; titre, *m.*; raison sociale (*d'une compagnie*), *f.*; *to live in style*, avoir un train de maison.—*v.t.* appeler, qualifier de.

stylish ['stailiʃ], *a.* élégant, de bon ton.
stylus ['stailəs], *n.* style, *m.*
styptic ['stiptik], *a.* and *n.* (*Med.*) styptique, *m.*
suave [swɑ:v], *a.* suave.
suavity ['swɑ:viti], *n.* suavité, *f.*
subaltern ['sʌbəltən], *a.* subalterne.—*n.* (sous-)lieutenant, *m.*
subconscious [sʌb'kɔnʃəs], *a.* and *n.* (*Psych.*) subconscient, *m.*
subconsciously [sʌb'kɔnʃəsli], *adv.* inconsciemment.
subdivide [sʌbdi'vaid], *v.t.* subdiviser.
subdue [səb'dju:], *v.t.* subjuguer; dompter, étouffer; *subdued light*, demi-jour, *m.*
sub-editor [sʌb'editə], *n.* secrétaire de la rédaction, *m.*, *f.*
subject ['sʌbdʒikt], *a.* assujetti, soumis; sujet (*à*), exposé (*à*).—*n.* sujet, *m.*; (*Sch.*) matière, *f.*; particulier, *m.*, personne, *f.*—[səb'dʒekt], *v.t.* assujettir, soumettre; rendre sujet (*à*), exposer (*à*).
subjection [səb'dʒekʃən], *n.* sujétion, *f.*
subjective [səb'dʒektiv], *a.* subjectif.
subjectively [səb'dʒektivli], *adv.* subjectivement.
subject matter ['sʌbdʒiktmætə], *n.* sujet, *m.* matière, *f.*
subjugate ['sʌbdʒugeit], *v.t.* subjuguer.
subjunctive [səb'dʒʌŋktiv], *a.* and *n.* (*Gram.*) subjonctif, *m.*
sublet [sʌb'let], *v.t.* irr. (*conjug. like* LET) sous-louer.
sub-lieutenant [sʌblef'tenənt], *n.* (*Navy*) enseigne, *m.*
sublimate ['sʌblimeit], *v.t.* sublimer.
sublime [sə'blaim], *a.* and *n.* sublime, *m.*
sublimeness [sə'blaimnis], *n.* sublimité, *f.*; sublime, *m.*
sub-machine gun [sʌbmə'ʃi:ngʌn], *n.* mitraillette, *f.*
submarine ['sʌbməri:n], *a.* and *n.* sous-marin, *m.*
submerge [səb'mə:dʒ], *v.t.* submerger.—*v.i.* plonger.
submission [səb'miʃən], *n.* soumission; résignation, déférence, *f.*
submissive [səb'misiv], *a.* soumis (*à*); docile.
submit [səb'mit], *v.t.* soumettre (*à*).—*v.i.* se soumettre (*à*).
subnormal [sʌb'nɔ:ml], *a.* sous-normal.
subordinate [sə'bɔ:dinit], *a.* subordonné (*à*).—*n.* subordonné, *m.*—[sə'bɔ:dineit], *v.t.* subordonner (*à*).
subordination [səbɔ:di'neiʃən], *n.* subordination, *f.*; rang inférieur, *m.*
suborn [sə'bɔ:n], *v.t.* suborner.
subpoena [sʌb'pi:nə], *n.* (*Law*) citation, assignation, *f.*—*v.t.* citer, assigner.
subscribe [səb'skraib], *v.t.* souscrire.—*v.i.* souscrire (*à ou pour*); s'abonner (*à un journal*).
subscriber [səb'skraibə], *n.* abonné (*à un journal*), *m.*
subscription [səb'skripʃən], *n.* souscription, *f.*; abonnement (*à un journal etc.*), *m.*
subsection ['sʌbsekʃən], *n.* subdivision, *f.*
subsequent ['sʌbsikwənt], *a.* subséquent, postérieur.
subsequently ['sʌbsikwəntli], *adv.* ensuite, après.

subservient [səb'sə:vjənt], *a.* subordonné (*à*); qui contribue à; obséquieux.
subserviently [səb'sə:viəntli], *adv.* en sous-ordre, utilement; servilement.
subside [səb'said], *v.i.* s'affaisser (*être accablé*); baisser, s'abaisser, se calmer, s'apaiser (*s'adoucir*); se taire (*personne*); *to subside into*, se changer en.
subsidence ['sʌbsidəns, səb'saidəns], *n.* affaissement, *m.*; (*fig.*) baisse (*rivière*), *f.*
subsidiary [səb'sidjəri], *a.* subsidiaire (*à*).—*n.* auxiliaire, *m.*; filiale (*compagnie*), *f.*
subsidize ['sʌbsidaiz], *v.t.* subventionner.
subsidy ['sʌbsidi], *n.* subvention, *f.*
subsist [səb'sist], *v.i.* subsister, exister.
subsistence [səb'sistəns], *n.* subsistance, *f.*; entretien, *m.*; existence, *f.*
subsistent [səb'sistənt], *a.* existant, qui existe.
subsoil ['sʌbsɔil], *n.* sous-sol, *m.*
sub-species ['sʌbspi:ʃi:z], *n.* sous-espèce, *f.*
substance ['sʌbstəns], *n.* substance, *f.*; fond (*l'essentiel*), *m.*; biens (*richesses*), *m.pl.*
substantial [səb'stænʃl], *a.* substantiel, réel, solide; aisé (*riche*).
substantially [səb'stænʃəli], *adv.* solidement, fortement, considérablement.
substantiate [səb'stænʃieit], *v.t.* établir, confirmer.
substantive ['sʌbstəntiv], *a.* indépendant; (*Gram.*) substantif.—*n.* (*Gram.*) substantif, *m.*
substitute ['sʌbstitju:t], *v.t.* substituer (*à*).—*n.* substitut, remplaçant, *m.*
substitution [sʌbsti'tju:ʃən], *n.* substitution, *f.*
substratum [sʌb'strɑ:təm], *n.* (*pl.* **substrata** [sʌb'strɑ:tə]) substratum, substrat, *m.*, couche inférieure, *f.*; (*Agric.*) sous-sol, *m.*
subtenant ['sʌbtenənt], *n.* sous-locataire, *m.*, *f.*
subterfuge ['sʌbtəfju:dʒ], *n.* subterfuge, faux-fuyant, *m.*
subterranean [sʌbtə'reiniən], *a.* souterrain.
sub-title ['sʌbtaitl], *n.* sous-titre, *m.*
subtle [sʌtl], *a.* subtil, rusé; fin.
subtlety ['sʌtlti], *n.* subtilité, finesse, *f.*
subtly ['sʌtli], *adv.* subtilement.
subtract [səb'trækt], *v.t.* défalquer; (*Arith.*) soustraire.
subtraction [səb'trækʃən], *n.* (*Arith.*) soustraction, *f.*
suburb ['sʌbə:b], *n.* faubourg, *m.*, (*pl.*) alentours, environs, *m.pl.*, banlieue, *f.*; *garden suburb*, cité-jardin, *f.*
suburban [sə'bə:bən], *a.* de la banlieue, suburbain.
subvention [səb'venʃən], *n.* subvention, *f.*
subversive [sʌb'və:siv], *a.* subversif.
subway ['sʌbwei], *n.* passage souterrain; (*Am.*) métro, *m.*
succeed [sək'si:d], *v.t.* succéder à; suivre; *to succeed each other*, se succéder.—*v.i.* succéder (*à*); hériter (*une propriété*); parvenir (*à*), réussir (*avoir du succès*).
succeeding [sək'si:diŋ], *a.* suivant (*dans le passé*); à venir, futur (*à l'avenir*); successif (*consécutif*).
success [sək'ses], *n.* succès, *m.*; *I wish you success!* bonne chance!
successful [sək'sesful], *a.* heureux; couronné de succès, réussi, victorieux; *to be successful*, réussir.

successfully [sək'sesfuli], *adv.* heureusement, avec succès.
succession [sək'seʃən], *n.* succession, suite, *f.*; avènement (*au trône etc.*), *m.*; postérité (*descendance*), *f.*; **in succession**, successivement, de suite.
successive [sək'sesiv], *a.* successif, consécutif.
successor [sək'sesə], *n.* successeur, *m.*
succinct [sək'siŋkt], *a.* succinct, concis.
succinctly [sək'siŋktli], *adv.* avec concision.
succinctness [sək'siŋktnis], *n.* concision, brièveté, *f.*
succor ['sʌkə], *v.t.* secourir, aider.—*n.* secours, *m.*, aide, *f.*
succulent ['sʌkjulənt], *a.* succulent, plein de jus.
succumb [sə'kʌm], *v.i.* succomber (*à*).
such [sʌtʃ], *a.* tel, pareil, semblable; **he is such a bore**, il est si ennuyeux; **such a one**, un tel, *m.*, une telle, *f.*; **such a one as**, tel que; **such as it is**, tel quel, *m.*; **such quelle**, *f.*; **such as you**, tel que vous.
suchlike ['sʌtʃlaik], *a.* semblable, pareil; de ce genre.
suck [sʌk], *v.t.*, *v.i.* sucer; têter (*à la mamelle*); aspirer.
sucker ['sʌkə], *n.* suceur; (*fig.*) gobeur, *m.*
sucking ['sʌkiŋ], *a.* qui suce, aspirant.—*n.* sucement, *m.*, succion, *f.*
sucking pig ['sʌkiŋpig], *n.* cochon de lait, *m.*
suckle ['sʌkl], *v.t.* allaiter, nourrir.
suction ['sʌkʃən], *n.* succion, aspiration, *f.*
Sudan [su'dæn, su'dɑ:n]. le Soudan, *m.*
Sudanese [sudə'ni:z], *a.* soudanais.—*n.* Soudanais (*personne*), *m.*
sudden [sʌdn], *a.* subit, soudain; (*fam.*) **all of a sudden**, tout à coup.
suddenly ['sʌdnli], *adv.* subitement, soudain, tout à coup.
suddenness ['sʌdnnis], *n.* soudaineté, *f.*
Sudetenland [su'deitnlænd]. les Sudètes, *m.pl.*
suds [sʌdz], **soap-suds** ['soupsʌdz], *n.pl.* eau de savon, lessive, *f.*
sue [sju:], *v.t.* poursuivre (en justice).—*v.i.* implorer.
suède [sweid], *n.* daim (*chaussures*); suède (*gants*), *m.*
suet ['sju:it], *n.* graisse de bœuf, *f.*
suffer ['sʌfə], *v.t.* souffrir; supporter, endurer, subir (*éprouver*); laisser, permettre (*autoriser*).—*v.i.* souffrir (*de*); **to suffer for**, porter la peine de.
sufferable ['sʌfərəbl], *a.* supportable, tolérable.
sufferance ['sʌfərəns], *n.* tolérance, *f.*
sufferer ['sʌfərə], *n.* victime (*de*), *f.*; patient, *m.*
suffering ['sʌfəriŋ], *a.* souffrant.—*n.* souffrance, douleur, *f.*
suffice [sə'fais], *v.t.* suffire à, satisfaire.—*v.i.* suffire.
sufficiency [sə'fiʃənsi], *n.* suffisance; aisance (*financière*), *f.*
sufficient [sə'fiʃənt], *a.* suffisant, assez.
sufficiently [sə'fiʃəntli], *adv.* suffisamment, assez.
suffix ['sʌfiks], *n.* suffixe, *m.*
suffocate ['sʌfəkeit], *v.t.*, *v.i.* suffoquer, étouffer, asphyxier.
suffocating ['sʌfəkeitiŋ], *a.* suffocant, étouffant, asphyxiant.

suffocation [sʌfə'keiʃən], *n.* suffocation, asphyxie, *f.*
suffrage ['sʌfridʒ], *n.* suffrage, *m.*
suffuse [sə'fju:z], *v.t.* répandre, couvrir (*de*); répandre sur; se répandre sur.
suffusion [sə'fju:ʒən], *n.* épanchement, *m.*, suffusion, *f.*
sugar ['ʃugə], *n.* sucre, *m.*; **barley sugar**, sucre d'orge; **brown(unrefined)sugar**, cassonade, *f.*; **powdered sugar**, sucre en poudre; **granulated sugar**, sucre cristallisé; **lump sugar**, sucre cassé.—*v.t.* sucrer; (*fig.*) adoucir.
sugar beet ['ʃugəbi:t], *n.* betterave à sucre, *f.*
sugar bowl ['ʃugəboul], *n.* sucrier, *m.*
sugar cane ['ʃugəkein], *n.* canne à sucre, *f.*
sugared ['ʃugəd], *a.* sucré; (*fig.*) doux.
sugar loaf ['ʃugəlouf], *n.* pain de sucre, *m.*
sugar refinery ['ʃugəri'fainəri], *n.* raffinerie de sucre, *f.*
sugary ['ʃugəri], *a.* sucré; trop sucré.
suggest [sə'dʒest], *v.t.* suggérer; inspirer.
suggestion [sə'dʒestʃən], *n.* suggestion; proposition, idée; nuance, *f.*
suggestive [sə'dʒestiv], *a.* suggestif.
suicidal [sju:i'saidl], *a.* de suicide; fatal.
suicide ['sju:isaid], *n.* suicide (*acte*); suicidé (*personne*), *m.*; **to commit suicide**, se suicider.
suit [sju:t], *n.* suite, collection complète, *f.*, assortiment, *m.*; (*Cards*) couleur; sollicitation, prière; recherche en mariage; (*Law*) instance, *f.*, procès, *m.*; **suit (of clothes)**, complet (*d'homme*), tailleur (*de femme*), *m.*—*v.t.* adapter; convenir à, aller à; plaire à—*v.i.* s'accorder (*à*).
suitability [sju:tə'biliti], *n.* convenance, *f.*
suitable ['sju:təbl], *a.* convenable (*à*); à propos.
suitably ['sju:təbli], *adv.* convenablement.
suite [swi:t], *n.* suite, *f.*, ensemble, *m.*; **suite of rooms**, appartement, *m.*; **suite of furniture**, ameublement complet, *m.*
suitor ['sju:tə], *n.* prétendant (*amoureux*); (*Law*) plaideur, *m.*
sulk [sʌlk], *v.i.* bouder, faire la mine.
sulkily ['sʌlkili], *adv.* en boudant, en faisant la mine.
sulkiness ['sʌlkinis], **sulking** ['sʌlkiŋ], *n.* bouderie, *f.*
sulks [sʌlks], *n.pl.* mauvaise humeur, bouderie, *f.*
sulky ['sʌlki], *a.* boudeur.
sullen ['sʌlən], *a.* maussade, morose, renfrogné.
sullenly ['sʌlənli], *adv.* maussadement, d'un air renfrogné.
sullenness ['sʌlənnis], *n.* air maussade, *m.*
sully ['sʌli], *v.t.* souiller, ternir (*de*).
sulphate ['sʌlfeit], *n.* sulfate, *m.*
sulphide ['sʌlfaid], *n.* sulfure, *m.*
sulphite ['sʌlfait], *n.* sulfite, *m.*
sulphonamide [sʌl'founəmaid], *n.* sulfamide, *f.*
sulphur ['sʌlfə], *n.* soufre, *m.*
sulphuric [sʌl'fjuərik], *a.* sulfurique.
sulphurous ['sʌlfjurəs], *a.* sulfureux.
sultan ['sʌltən], *n.* sultan, *m.*
sultana [sʌl'tɑ:nə], *n.* sultane, *f.*; (*pl.*) raisins de Smyrne, *m.pl.*
sultriness ['sʌltrinis], *n.* chaleur étouffante, *f.*

sultry ['sʌltri], *a.* d'une chaleur étouffante, étouffant, suffocant; (*fam.*) épicé, salé (*histoire etc.*); *it is very sultry*, il fait très lourd.

sum [sʌm], *n.* somme (*d'argent*), *f.*; (*Arith.*) problème, calcul, *m.*; *the four sums*, les quatre opérations, *f.pl.*—*v.t.* *to sum up*, additionner, faire l'addition de; (*fig.*) récapituler.

summarily ['sʌmərili], *adv.* sommairement.
summarize ['sʌməraiz], *v.t.* résumer sommairement.
summary ['sʌməri], *a.* sommaire, prompt.—*n.* sommaire, résumé, *m.*
summer ['sʌmə], *a.* d'été, estival—*n.* été, *m.*; *in summer*, en été.
summer-house ['sʌməhaus], *n.* pavillon, *m.*
summing-up ['sʌmiŋ'ʌp], *n.* résumé, *m.*
summit ['sʌmit], *n.* sommet, *m.*, cime, *f.*; (*fig.*) comble, *m.*
summon ['sʌmən], *v.t.* convoquer (*un rassemblement etc.*); sommer (*ordonner*); (*Law*) citer en justice; assigner (*témoins*).
summons ['sʌmənz], *n.* sommation (*commandement*); convocation, *f.*; appel (*invitation*), *m.*; (*Law*) citation, *f.*, mandat de comparution, *m.*—*v.t.* assigner, citer (en justice), appeler à comparaître.
sump [sʌmp], *n.* (*Mining*) puisard; (fond de) carter (*de voiture*), *m.*
sumptuous ['sʌmptjuəs], *a.* somptueux.
sumptuously ['sʌmptjuəsli], *adv.* somptueusement.
sun [sʌn], *n.* soleil, *m.*—*v.t.* exposer au soleil.
sun bath ['sʌnbɑ:θ], *n.* bain de soleil, *m.*
sun-bathe ['sʌnbeið], *v.i.* prendre des bains de soleil.
sunbeam ['sʌnbi:m], *n.* rayon de soleil, *m.*
sun-blind ['sʌnblaind], *n.* store, *m.*
sunburn ['sʌnbə:n], *n.* hâle; coup de soleil, *m.*
sunburnt ['sʌnbə:nt], *a.* hâlé; basané.
Sunday ['sʌndi], *n.* dimanche, *m.*
sunder ['sʌndə], *v.t.* séparer; couper en deux.
sundial ['sʌndaiəl], *n.* cadran solaire, *m.*
sundries ['sʌndriz], *n.pl.* choses diverses, *f.pl.*
sundry ['sʌndri], *a.* divers.
sun-flower ['sʌnflauə], *n.* tournesol, *m.*
sunken ['sʌŋkən], *a.* enfoncé; cave (*joues*); creux (*yeux*).
sunless ['sʌnlis], *a.* sans soleil.
sunlight ['sʌnlait], *n.* lumière du soleil, *f.*
sunlit ['sʌnlit], *a.* ensoleillé.
sunny ['sʌni], *a.* ensoleillé; (*fig.*) heureux; *it is sunny*, il fait du soleil.
sunrise ['sʌnraiz], *n.* lever du soleil, *m.*
sunset ['sʌnset], *n.* coucher du soleil, *m.*
sunshade ['sʌnʃeid], *n.* parasol, *m.*, ombrelle, *f.*
sunshine ['sʌnʃain], *n.* soleil, *m.*, clarté du soleil, *f.*
sunstroke ['sʌnstrouk], *n.* coup de soleil, *m.*, insolation, *f.*
sup [sʌp], *n.* (*Sc.*) petit coup, *m.*, gorgée, *f.*—*v.t.* boire à petits coups.—*v.i.* souper.
super ['sju:pə], *a.* (*slang*) *it is super*, c'est sensass (sensationnel).
superable ['sju:pərəbl], *a.* surmontable.
superabundance [sju:pərə'bʌndəns], *n.* surabondance, *f.*
superannuate [sju:pər'ænjueit], *v.t.* mettre à la retraite.

superannuated [sju:pər'ænjueitid], *a.* mis à la retraite, en retraite (*personne*); démodé.
superannuation [sju:pərænju'eiʃən], *n.* mise à la retraite, retraite, *f.*; *superannuation fund*, caisse de retraites, *f.*
superb [sju:'pə:b], *a.* superbe.
superbly [sju:'pə:bli], *adv.* superbement.
supercilious [sju:pə'siliəs], *a.* hautain, arrogant.
superciliously [sju:pə'siliəsli], *adv.* avec hauteur.
superciliousness [sju:pə'siliəsnis], *n.* hauteur; arrogance, *f.*
superficial [sju:pə'fiʃl], *a.* superficiel; de superficie (*mesure*).
superficiality [sju:pəfiʃi'æliti], *n.* caractère superficiel, *m.*
superficially [sju:pə'fiʃəli], *adv.* superficiellement.
superfine ['sju:pəfain], *a.* superfin; (*Comm.*) surfin.
superfluity [sju:pə'flu:iti], *n.* superfluité, *f.*; superflu, *m.*
superfluous [sju'pə:fluəs], *a.* superflu, inutile.
superhuman [sju:pə'hju:mən], *a.* surhumain.
superimpose [sju:pərim'pouz], *v.t.* superposer, surimposer.
superintend [sju:pərin'tend], *v.t.* surveiller.
superintendent [sju:pərin'tendənt], *n.* chef; directeur, inspecteur, surintendant; commissaire de police, *m.*
superior [sju'piəriə], *a.* and *n.* supérieur, *m.*
superiority [sjupiəri'oriti], *n.* supériorité, *f.*
superlative [sju'pə:lətiv], *a.* suprême; (*Gram.*) superlatif.—*n.* (*Gram.*) superlatif, *m.*
superman ['sju:pəmæn], *n.* (*pl.* **-men** [men]) surhomme, *m.*
supernatural [sju:pə'nætʃərəl], *a.* and *n.* surnaturel, *m.*
supernumerary [sju:pə'nju:mərəri], *a.* surnuméraire.—*n.* surnuméraire; (*Theat.*) figurant, *m.*
superscribe [sju:pə'skraib], *v.t.* mettre une adresse, une suscription *ou* une inscription à.
superscription [sju:pə'skripʃən], *n.* suscription; inscription; (*Coin.*) légende, *f.*; entête (*de lettre*), *m.*
supersede [sju:pə'si:d], *v.t.* remplacer.
superseded [sju:pə'si:did], *a.* démodé, périmé.
supersonic [sju:pə'sɔnik], *a.* (*onde*) ultra-sonore; (*Av.*) supersonique.
superstition [sju:pə'stiʃən], *n.* superstition, *f.*
superstitious [sju:pə'stiʃəs], *a.* superstitieux.
superstructure ['sju:pəstrʌktʃə], *n.* superstructure, *f.*
super-tax ['sju:pətæks], *n.* surtaxe, *f.*
supervene [sju:pə'vi:n], *v.i.* survenir.
supervention [sju:pə'venʃən], *n.* survenance, *f.*
supervise ['sju:pəvaiz], *v.t.* surveiller.
supervision [sju:pə'viʒən], *n.* surveillance; inspection, *f.*
supervisor ['sju:pəvaizə], *n.* surveillant, *m.*
supine [sju'pain], *a.* couché sur le dos; (*fig.*) nonchalant.—['sju:pain], *n.* (*Gram.*) supin, *m.*
supper ['sʌpə], *n.* souper, *m.*; *supper time*, heure du souper, *f.*
supplant [sə'plɑ:nt], *v.t.* supplanter.

supple [sʌpl], *a.* souple, flexible.
supplement [sʌpli'ment], *v.t.* suppléer à; compléter.—['sʌplimənt], *n.* supplément, *m.*
supplementary [sʌpli'mentəri], *a.* supplémentaire.
suppleness ['sʌplnis], *n.* souplesse, *f.*
suppliant ['sʌpliənt], *a.* and *n.* suppliant, *m.*
supplicate ['sʌplikeit], *v.t.* supplier, implorer.
supplication [sʌpli'keiʃən], *n.* supplication, prière, *f.*
supplier [sə'plaiə], *n.* pourvoyeur; fournisseur, *m.*
supply [sə'plai], *n.* fourniture; provision, *f.*, approvisionnement (*réserve*), *m.*; (*Elec.*) alimentation, *f.*; (*Mil., pl.*) vivres (*ravitaillement*); (*Parl.*) subsides, *m.pl.*—*v.t.* fournir; pourvoir à, subvenir à (*besoins*), ravitailler.
support [sə'pɔ:t], *v.t.* soutenir, supporter; entretenir (*faire vivre*); appuyer (*aider*).—*n.* appui, soutien; support (*physique*); entretien (*des dépendants*), *m.*
supportable [sə'pɔ:təbl], *a.* supportable.
supporter [sə'pɔ:tə], *n.* adhérent, partisan; appui, soutien; (*Spt.*) supporter; (*Her.*) support, *m.*
suppose [sə'pouz], *v.t.* supposer, s'imaginer; *to be supposed to* (*know*), être censé (*savoir*); *suppose we go*, si nous y allions.
supposed [sə'pouzd], *a.* présumé; prétendu; soi-disant; censé.
supposedly [sə'pouzidli], *adv.* censément.
supposing [sə'pouziŋ], *conj.* supposons, supposé (*que*).
supposition [sʌpə'ziʃən], *n.* supposition, *f.*
suppress [sə'pres], *v.t.* supprimer; réprimer (*révolte etc.*); étouffer; *a suppressed laugh*, un rire étouffé.
suppression [sə'preʃən], *n.* suppression; répression; dissimulation (*de la vérité*), *f.*
suppressor [sə'presə], *n.* (*Rad., Tel.*) dispositif anti-parasites, *m.*
suppurate ['sʌpjureit], *v.i.* suppurer.
suppuration [sʌpju'reiʃən], *n.* suppuration, *f.*
supremacy [sju'preməsi], *n.* suprématie, *f.*
supreme [sju'pri:m], *a.* suprême.
supremely [sju'pri:mli], *adv.* suprêmement.
surcharge ['sə:tʃɑ:dʒ], *n.* surcharge, surtaxe, *f.*
sure [ʃuə], *a.* sûr, certain; assuré; *to be sure!* certainement! bien sûr! *to be sure to*, ne pas manquer de.—*adv.* sûrement, à coup sûr.
sure-footed [ʃuə'futid], *a.* au pied sûr.
surely ['ʃuəli], *adv.* sûrement, assurément, à coup sûr.
sureness ['ʃuənis], *n.* certitude, sûreté, *f.*
surety ['ʃuəti], *n.* certitude (*véracité*); sûreté, sécurité (*garantie*), *f.*; (*Law*) garant, *m.*
surf [sə:f], *n.* ressac, *m.*, brisants sur la plage, *m.pl.*
surface ['sə:fis], *n.* surface, *f.*
surfeit ['sə:fit], *n.* rassasiement, *m.*; *to have a surfeit of*, être rassasié de.
surf-riding ['sə:fraidiŋ], *n.* sport de l'aquaplane, planking, surf, *m.*
surge [sə:dʒ], *n.* houle, lame de fond, *f.*—*v.i.* s'enfler, s'élever.
surgeon ['sə:dʒən], *n.* chirurgien, *m.*
surgery ['sə:dʒəri], *n.* chirurgie (*art*), *f.*
surgical ['sə:dʒikl], *a.* chirurgical.
surliness ['sə:linis], *n.* morosité, *f.*

surly ['sə:li], *a.* morose; hargneux (*chien*).
surmise ['sə:maiz], *n.* soupçon, *m.*, conjecture, *f.*—[sə'maiz], *v.t.* soupçonner, conjecturer.
surmount [sə'maunt], *v.t.* surmonter.
surmountable [sə'mauntəbl], *a.* surmontable.
surname ['sə:neim], *n.* nom de famille, *m.*
surpass [sə'pɑ:s], *v.t.* surpasser, l'emporter sur.
surpassable [sə'pɑ:səbl], *a.* qu'on peut surpasser.
surpassing [sə'pɑ:siŋ], *a.* éminent, supérieur, rare.
surplice ['sə:plis], *n.* surplis, *m.*
surplus ['sə:pləs], *a.* de surplus.—*n.* surplus, *m.*; *surplus stock*, solde, *m.*
surprise [sə'praiz], *n.* surprise, *f.*; étonnement, *m.*—*v.t.* surprendre, étonner.
surprising [sə'praiziŋ], *a.* surprenant, étonnant.
surrealism [sə'ri:əlizm], *n.* surréalisme, *m.*
surrender [sə'rendə], *n.* reddition, capitulation, *f.*; abandon (*d'un titre, d'un droit*), *m.*; (*Law*) cession, *f.*—*v.t.* rendre; (*fig.*) abandonner, livrer (*personne etc.*); (*Law*) céder. —*v.i.* se rendre.
surreptitious [sʌrəp'tiʃəs], *a.* subreptice, clandestin; frauduleux.
surreptitiously [sʌrəp'tiʃəsli], *adv.* subrepticement.
surround [sə'raund], *v.t.* entourer, environner (*de*), (*Mil.*) cerner.
surrounding [sə'raundiŋ], *a.* environnant, d'alentour.—*n.* (*pl.*) alentours, environs, *m.pl.*, entourage, milieu, *m.*
surtax ['sə:tæks], *n.* surtaxe, *f.*
survey ['sə:vei], *n.* vue, *f.*, coup d'œil, *m.*; inspection (*examen*); expertise (*évaluation*), *f.*; arpentage (*de terrain etc.*); (*Ordnance*) levé topographique, *m*; *aerial survey*, levé aérophotogrammétrique, *m.*—[sə'vei], *v.t.* arpenter (*terrain*); (*Ordnance*) lever le plan de; (*fig.*) examiner, contempler.
surveying [sə'veiiŋ], *n.* arpentage, levé de plans, *m.*
surveyor [sə'veiə], *n.* inspecteur; arpenteur (*de terrain*); agent voyer (*ponts et chaussées*), *m.*
survival [sə'vaivl], *n.* survivance; survie, *f.*
survive [sə'vaiv], *v.t.* survivre à.—*v.i.* survivre.
surviving [sə'vaiviŋ], *a.* survivant.
survivor [sə'vaivə], *n.* survivant, *m.*
Susan [su:zn]. Suzanne, *f.*
susceptibility [səsepti'biliti], *n.* susceptibilité; sensibilité, *f.*
susceptible [sə'septibl], *a.* susceptible (*de*).
suspect ['sʌspekt], *a.* and *n.* suspect, *m.*—[sə'spekt], *v.t.*, *v.i.* soupçonner.
suspend [sə'spend], *v.t.* suspendre; cesser (*payements*).
suspender [sə'spendə], *n.* (*pl.*) jarretelles (*pour bas*); (*Am.*) bretelles (*pour pantalon*), *f.pl.*
suspense [sə'spens], *n.* suspens, doute, *m.*
suspension [sə'spenʃən], *n.* suspension, *f.*
suspicion [sə'spiʃən], *n.* soupçon, *m.*
suspicious [sə'spiʃəs], *a.* soupçonneux; suspect, louche (*équivoque*).
suspiciously [sə'spiʃəsli], *adv.* avec méfiance; d'une manière suspecte.

suspiciousness [sə'spiʃəsnis], *n.* caractère soupçonneux, *m.*, défiance, méfiance, *f.*

sustain [sə'stein], *v.t.* soutenir, supporter; éprouver, essuyer (*perte*).

sustaining [sə'steiniŋ], *a.* fortifiant, nourrissant.

sustenance ['sʌstinəns], *n.* nourriture, *f.*, aliments, *m.pl.*; entretien, *m.*, subsistance, *f.*

suzerain ['sju:zərein], *a.* and *n.* suzerain, *m.*

suzerainty ['sju:zəreinti], *n.* suzeraineté, *f.*

swab [swɔb], *n.* torchon; (*Naut.*) faubert; tampon (*de coton hydrophile*), *m.*—*v.t.* fauberter; nettoyer.

swaddle [swɔdl], *v.t.* emmailloter.

swaddling ['swɔdliŋ], *n.* emmaillotement, *m.*; **swaddling clothes**, maillot, *m.*

swag [swæg], *n.* (*slang*) butin; (*Australia*) baluchon, *m.*

swagger ['swægə], *v.i.* faire le rodomont; se donner des airs, se vanter.

swaggerer ['swægərə], *n.* fanfaron, *m.*

swaggering ['swægəriŋ], *a.* de fanfaron.—*n.* fanfaronnade, *f.*

swagman ['swægmən], *n.* (*pl.* **-men** [men]) (*Australia*) chemineau, *m.*

swain [swein], *n.* (*poet.*) berger, jeune paysan, *m.*

swallow (1) ['swɔlou], *v.t.* avaler; engloutir (*faire disparaître*); consumer; (*fig.*) gober.—*n.* (*pop.*) avaloir, gosier (*gorge*), *m.*; gorgée (*ce qu'on avale*), *f.*

swallow (2) ['swɔlou], *n.* hirondelle (*oiseau*), *f.*

swallow dive ['swɔloudaiv], *n.* (*Swim.*) saut de l'ange, *m.*

swallower ['swɔlouə], *n.* avaleur, *m.*

swallow-tail ['swɔlouteil], *a.* en queue d'aronde.—*n.* habit à queue de morue, *m.*

swamp [swɔmp], *n.* marais, marécage, *m.*—*v.t.* submerger; faire couler (*bateau*).

swampy ['swɔmpi], *a.* marécageux.

swan [swɔn], *n.* cygne, *m.* [see **swallow dive**]

swank [swæŋk], *n.* pose; (*pop.*) épate, *f.*—*v.i.* (*pop.*) crâner, poser; faire du chiqué.

swanky ['swæŋki], *a.* chic, rupin.

swap [swɔp], *v.t.* (*colloq.*) échanger, troquer.—*n.* troc, échange, *m.*

sward [swɔ:d], *n.* (*poet.*) gazon, *m.*, pelouse, *f.*

swarm [swɔ:m], *n.* essaim (*d'abeilles*), *m.*—*v.i.* essaimer; (*fig.*) accourir en foule.

swarming ['swɔ:miŋ], *n.* essaimage, *m.*

swarthiness ['swɔ:ðinis], *n.* teint basané, *m.*

swarthy ['swɔ:ði], *a.* basané, hâlé.

swashbuckler ['swɔʃbʌklə], *n.* fanfaron, matamore, *m.*

swastika ['swɔstikə], *n.* croix gammée, *f.*

swat [swɔt], *v.t.* écraser, tuer (*mouche*).

swath [swɔ:θ], *n.* andain, *m.*, fauchée, *f.*

swathe [sweið], *v.t.* emmailloter.

sway [swei], *v.t.* manier, porter; balancer (*agiter*); diriger (*gouverner*); influencer (*l'opinion*).—*v.i.* se balancer.—*n.* empire, *m.*; domination (*règne*), *f.*

swaying ['sweiiŋ], *n.* balancement, *m.*; oscillation, *f.*

swear [swɛə], *v.t. irr.* faire prêter serment à (*témoins etc.*); prêter (*serment*); **to swear at**, injurier.—*v.i.* jurer; prêter serment.

swearer ['swɛərə], *n.* jureur, *m.*

swearing ['swɛəriŋ], *n.* serments; jurons (*gros mots*), *m.pl.*; **swearing in**, prestation de serment, assermentation (*de juges etc.*), *f.*

swear-word ['swɛəwə:d], *n.* juron, gros mot, *m.*

sweat [swet], *n.* sueur, transpiration, *f.*—*v.t.* faire suer.—*v.i.* suer, transpirer.

sweater ['swetə], *n.* chandail, tricot, pullover (*vêtement*), *m.*

sweatiness ['swetinis], *n.* sueur, *f.*, état de sueur, *m.*

sweating ['swetiŋ], *a.* en sueur; tout en sueur.—*n.* moiteur; fatigue, *f.*

sweaty ['sweti], *a.* en sueur.

Swede [swi:d], *n.* Suédois (*personne*), *m.*

swede [swi:d], *n.* (*Bot.*) rutabaga, *m.*

Sweden [swi:dn], la Suède, *f.*

Swedish ['swi:diʃ], *a.* suédois, de Suède,—*n.* suédois (*langue*), *m.*

sweep [swi:p], *v.t. irr.* balayer; ramoner (*cheminée*); draguer (*rivière*).—*v.i.* passer rapidement.—*n.* coup de balai; ramoneur (*de cheminées*), *m.*; étendue, portée (*distance*), courbe, *f.*; (*fig.*) sweepstake, *m.*; **to make a clean sweep of**, faire table rase de.

sweeper ['swi:pə], *n.* balayeur; ramoneur (*de cheminées*), *m.*

sweeping ['swi:piŋ], *a.* rapide, irrésistible; (*fig.*) général.—*n.* balayage; ramonage (*de cheminées*), *m.*; (*pl.*) balayures, ordures, *f.pl.*

sweepstake ['swi:psteik], *n.* poule, *f.*; sweepstake, *m.*

sweet [swi:t], *a.* doux, sucré; parfumé (*odeur*); (*Mus.*) suave, mélodieux; frais (*poisson etc.*); (*fig.*) joli, charmant.—*n.* chose douce, *f.*; (*pl.*) entremets, sucreries, *f.pl.*; chéri, *m.*

sweetbread ['swi:tbred], *n.* ris de veau *ou* d'agneau, *m.*

sweeten [swi:tn], *v.t.* sucrer; purifier (*salle, l'air etc.*); (*fig.*) adoucir.

sweetener ['swi:tnə], *n.* adoucissant, *m.*

sweetening ['swi:tniŋ], *n.* adoucissement, *m.*

sweetheart ['swi:thɑ:t], *n.* amoureux; amant; bon ami, *m.*

sweetly ['swi:tli], *adv.* doucement, gentiment; mélodieusement.

sweetmeat ['swi:tmi:t], *n.* sucrerie, *f.*, bonbon, *m.*

sweetness ['swi:tnis], *n.* douceur; fraîcheur; mélodie, *f.*; (*fig.*) charme, *m.*

sweet pea ['swi:t'pi:], *n.* pois de senteur, *m.*

sweet shop ['swi:tʃɔp], *n.* confiserie, *f.*

sweet william ['swi:t'wiljəm], *n.* œillet de poète, *m.*

swell [swel], *v.t. irr.* enfler, gonfler; aggraver; augmenter (*ajouter à*).—*v.i.* enfler, s'enfler, se gonfler; grossir, croître (*multiplier*); (*fig.*) bouffir (*d'orgueil, de colère etc.*).—*a.* (*colloq.*) à la mode, chic; épatant.—*n.* élévation, montée, *f.*; renflement (*de son*), *m.*; houle (*de mer*), *f.*; (*colloq.*) rupin, élégant, *m.*

swelling ['sweliŋ], *a.* grandissant (*qui augmente*).—*n.* enflure; bouffissure (*pathologique*), *f.*; gonflement (*protubérance*), *m.*, crue (*de rivière*), *f.*; soulèvement (*des vagues*); (*fig.*) mouvement, transport (*de colère etc.*), *m.*

swelter ['sweltə], *v.i.* étouffer de chaleur; **it is sweltering hot**, il fait une chaleur étouffante.

swerve [swə:v], *v.i.* s'écarter, se détourner, faire un écart (*cheval*), faire une embardée (*voiture*).

swerving ['swə:viŋ], *n.* écart, *m.*, déviation, embardée (*de voiture*), *f.*

swift [swift], *a.* vite; rapide, prompt.—*n.* (*Orn.*) martinet, *m.*
swift-footed ['swift'futid], *a.* rapide à la course; au pied léger.
swiftly ['swiftli], *adv.* vite, rapidement.
swiftness ['swiftnis], *n.* rapidité, vitesse, *f.*
swig [swig], *v.t., v.i.* (*pop.*) boire à longs traits. —*n.* long trait (*d'alcool*), *m.*
swill [swil], *v.t.* laver, rincer; boire avidement.—*v.i.* boire; (*colloq.*) s'enivrer.—*n.* lavure de vaisselle, lavure, *f.*; grand coup (*d'alcool*), *m.*
swim [swim], *v.t. irr.* traverser à la nage.— *v.i.* nager; flotter, surnager; (*fam.*) tourner (*la tête*); être inondé (de) (*être submergé*).— *n.* nage, *f.*; **in the swim**, à la page.
swimmer ['swimə], *n.* nageur, *m.*
swimming ['swimiŋ], *n.* natation (*sport*); nage (*action*), *f.*; (*fam.*) étourdissement (*de tête*), *m.*; **by swimming**, à la nage.
swimming baths ['swimiŋbɑ:θz], **swimming pool** ['swimiŋpu:l], *n.* piscine, *f.*
swimmingly ['swimiŋli], *adv.* à merveille.
swim-suit ['swimsju:t], *n.* maillot de bain, *m.*
swindle [swindl], *v.t.* escroquer.—*n.* escroquerie, *f.*
swindler ['swindlə], *n.* escroc, filou, *m.*
swindling ['swindliŋ], *n.* escroquerie, *f.*
swine [swain], *n.inv.* cochon, pourceau, porc; (*pop.*) salaud, *m.*
swing [swiŋ], *v.t. irr.* balancer; brandir (*une arme etc.*).—*v.i.* se balancer; osciller; pendiller, être suspendu.—*n.* oscillation (*mouvement*), *f.*; balancement, *m.*; balançoire (*siège*), *f.*; (*Mus.*) swing, *m.*; **in full swing**, en pleine activité.
swing-door ['swiŋ'dɔ:], *n.* porte battante, *f.*
swinging ['swiŋiŋ], *n.* balancement, *m.*, oscillation, *f.*
swipe [swaip], *n.* taloche, *f.*—*v.t.* donner une taloche à; (*fam.*) chiper.
swirl [swə:l], *v.i.* tourbillonner.—*n.* remous, *m.*
swish [swiʃ], *v.t.* cingler, fouetter.—*v.i.* siffler, bruire.
Swiss [swis], *a.* helvétique, suisse.—*n.* Suisse (*personne*), *m.*, Suissesse, *f.*
switch [switʃ], *n.* badine, houssine, gaule; (*Rail.*) aiguille, *f.*; (*Elec.*) commutateur, interrupteur, *m.*—*v.t.* houspiller, cingler; (*Rail.*) aiguiller; changer (*de*); **to switch off**, couper; **to switch on**, ouvrir.—*v.i.* **to switch off**, couper le courant; **to switch on**, mettre le courant; [see **pointsman**]
switchboard ['switʃbɔ:d], *n.* standard (*téléphonique*), *m.*; **switchboard operator**, standardiste, *m.*, *f.*
Switzerland ['switsələnd]. la Suisse, *f.*
swivel [swivl], *n.* émerillon; pivot, *m.*—*v.i.* pivoter.
swoon [swu:n], *v.i.* s'évanouir.—*n.* evanouissement, *m.*
swoop [swu:p], *v.i.* fondre (*sur*).—*n.* **at one (fell) swoop**, d'un seul coup (*fatal*).
sword [sɔ:d], *n.* épée, *f.*
sword bearer ['sɔ:dbɛərə], *n.* porte-épée, *m.*
sword-fish ['sɔ:dfiʃ], *n.* espadon, *m.*
swordsman ['sɔ:dzmən], *n.* (*pl.* **-men** [men]) tireur, homme d'épée, *m.*

swordstick ['sɔ:dstik], *n.* canne à épée, *f.*
sworn [swɔ:n], *a.* juré; (*Law*) assermenté; acharné (*ennemi*).
swot [swɔt], *v.i.* (*Sch. slang*) piocher, bûcher.— *n.* bûcheur, *m.*
sycamore ['sikəmɔ:], *n.* sycomore, *m.*
sycophancy ['sikəfənsi], *n.* adulation, *f.*
sycophant ['sikəfənt], *n.* adulateur, *m.*
sycophantic [sikə'fæntik], *a.* adulateur.
syllabic [si'læbik], *a.* syllabique.
syllable ['siləbl], *n.* syllabe, *f.*
syllabus ['siləbəs], *n.* résumé; sommaire, programme (*surtout d'études scolaires*), *m.*
syllogism ['siləd3izm], *n.* syllogisme, *m.*
sylph [silf], *n.* sylphe, *m.*
sylvan ['silvən], *a.* sylvestre, des bois, champêtre, agreste.
symbol [simbl], *n.* symbole, *m.*
symbolic [sim'bɔlik], **symbolical** [sim'bɔlikl], *a.* symbolique.
symbolism ['simbəlizm], *n.* symbolisme, *m.*
symbolize ['simbəlaiz], *v.t., v.i.* symboliser.
symmetrical [si'metrikl], *a.* symétrique.
symmetry ['simitri], *n.* symétrie, *f.*
sympathetic [simpə'θetik], *a.* sympathique (*nerf*); compatissant.
sympathize ['simpəθaiz], *v.i.* sympathiser (*avec*); compatir (*à*).
sympathizer ['simpəθaizə], *n.* sympathisant, *m.*
sympathy ['simpəθi], *n.* sympathie; compréhension, *f.*; condoléances, *f.pl.*
symphony ['simfəni], *n.* symphonie, *f.*
symposium [sim'pouzjəm], *n.* (*fig.*) recueil d'articles (*sur un seul sujet*), *m.*
symptom ['simptəm], *n.* symptôme, *m.*
symptomatic [simptə'mætik], *a.* symptomatique.
synagogue ['sinəgɔg], *n.* synagogue, *f.*
synchromesh ['siŋkromeʃ], *a.* and *n.* synchromesh, *m.*
synchronize ['siŋkrənaiz], *v.i.* synchroniser (*avec*).
syncopate ['siŋkəpeit], *v.t.* syncoper.
syndic ['sindik], *n.* syndic, *m.*
syndicate ['sindikit], *n.* syndicat, *m.*—['sindikeit], *v.t.* syndiquer.—*v.i.* se syndiquer.
synod ['sinəd], *n.* synode, *m.*
synonym ['sinənim], *n.* synonyme, *m.*
synonymous [si'nɔniməs], *a.* synonyme.
synopsis [si'nɔpsis], *n.* (*pl.* **synopses** [si'nɔpsi:z]) sommaire, *m.*
syntax ['sintæks], *n.* syntaxe, *f.*
synthesis ['sinθisis], *n.* (*pl.* **syntheses** ['sinθisi:z]) synthèse, *f.*
synthesize ['sinθisaiz], *v.t.* synthétiser.
synthetic [sin'θetik], *a.* synthétique.
synthetically [sin'θetikli], *adv.* synthétiquement.
Syria ['siriə]. la Syrie, *f.*
Syriac ['siriæk], *a.* syriaque.—*n.* syriaque (*langue*), *m.*
Syrian ['siriən], *a.* syrien.—*n.* syrien (*langue*); Syrien (*personne*), *m.*
syringe ['sirind3], *n.* seringue, *f.*—*v.t.* seringuer.
syrup ['sirəp], *n.* sirop, *m.*
syrupy ['sirəpi], *a.* sirupeux.
system ['sistəm], *n.* système, régime; réseau (*ferroviaire*), *m.*

systematic

systematic [sistə′mætik], *a.* systématique.
systematically [sistə′mætikli], *adv.* systématiquement.
systematize [′sistəmətaiz], *v.t.* systématiser.

T

T, t [ti:]. vingtième lettre de l'alphabet, *m.*; **T-square**, té à dessin, *m.*
tab [tæb], *n.* étiquette; patte, *f.*, écusson, *m.*
tabby [′tæbi], *a.* tacheté, moucheté.—*n.* chat moucheté, rayé *ou* tigré, *m.*
tabernacle [′tæbənækl], *n.* tabernacle, *m.*
table [teibl], *n.* table, *f.*; *to be seated at table*, être attablé; *to clear the table*, desservir; *to lay the table*, mettre le couvert; *to sit down to table*, se mettre à table.—*v.t.* déposer (*un projet de loi*).
table-cloth [′teiblklɔθ], *n.* nappe, *f.*
table linen [′teibllinin], *n.* linge de table, *m.*
tablespoon [′teiblspu:n], *n.* cuiller à soupe, *f.*
tablespoonful [′teiblspu:nful], *n.* grande cuillerée, *f.*
tablet [′tæblit], *n.* tablette, *f.*; (*Med.*) comprimé, *m.*
taboo [tə′bu:], *a.* and *n.* tabou, *m.*
tabulate [′tæbjuleit], *v.t.* cataloguer.
tacit [′tæsit], *a.* tacite, implicite.
tacitly [′tæsitli], *a.* tacitement, implicitement.
taciturn [′tæsitə:n], *a.* taciturne.
Tacitus [′tæsitəs]. (*L. Lit.*) Tacite, *m.*
tack [tæk], *n.* petit clou, *m.*, broquette; (*Naut.*) amure, *f.*—*v.t.* clouer; (*Needlework*) bâtir, faufiler.—*v.i.* (*Naut.*) virer vent devant.
tackiness [′tækinis], *n.* viscosité, *f.*
tacking [′tækiŋ], *n.* cloutage, *m.*; (*Needlework*) faufilure, *f.*; (*Naut.*) virement de bord, louvoyage, *m.*
tackle [tækl], *n.* attirail; (*Naut.*) palan; (*Spt.*) plaquage, *m.*; (*fig.*) ustensiles, *m.pl.*; *fishing tackle*, articles de pêche, *m.pl.*—*v.t.* empoigner; (*Ftb.*) plaquer; (*fig.*) attaquer (*travail etc.*).
tacky [′tæki], *a.* collant, visqueux, gluant.
tact [tækt], *n.* toucher; (*fig.*) tact, savoir-faire, *m.*
tactful [′tæktful], *a.* plein de tact.
tactical [′tæktikl], *a.* tactique.
tactician [tæk′tiʃən], *n.* tacticien, *m.*
tactics [′tæktiks], *n.pl.* tactique, *f.*
tactile [′tæktail], *a.* tactile.
tactless [′tæktlis], *a.* sans tact, sans savoir-faire.
tadpole [′tædpoul], *n.* têtard, *m.*
taffeta [′tæfitə], *n.* taffetas, *m.*
taffrail [′tæfreil], *n.* couronnement (*de la poupe*), *m.*
tag [tæg], *n.* ferret, fer, bout ferré, *m.*; étiquette (*fiche*), *f.*; dicton, *m.*—*v.t.* ferrer (*cordon*); (*fig.*) coudre (*à*).
tail [teil], *n.* queue; (*fig.*) extrémité, *f.*; bout; pan (*d'habit*), *m.*; pile (*de pièce de monnaie*), *f.*; empennage (*d'avion*), *m.*—*v.t.* couper la queue (*d'un animal*); ôter les queues (*de fruits*); (*fam.*) filer (*criminels etc.*).
tail coat [′teilkout], *n.* habit, *m.*
tailed [teild], *a.* à queue.
tailless [′teillis], *a.* sans queue, anoure.
tail-light [′teillait], *n.* feu arrière, *m.*
tailor [′teilə], *n.* tailleur, *m.*
tailor-made [′teilə′meid], *a.* and *n.* tailleur, *m.*
tail-plane [′teilplein], *n.* (*Av.*) stabilisateur, *m.*
taint [teint], *v.t.* corrompre, gâter.—*v.i.* se corrompre; se gâter (*viande*).—*n.* souillure, corruption; tache (*du péché*), *f.*
take [teik], *v.t. irr.* prendre; mener (*quelqu'un*); conduire (*personne en voiture*); porter (*chose*); emmener (*quelqu'un*); enlever (*voler*); soustraire (*retrancher*); saisir; accepter; (*fig.*) supposer; profiter de (*une occasion*); contenir (*avoir de la place pour*); faire (*une promenade etc.*); avoir (*vengeance etc.*); retenir (*chambre etc.*); suivre (*une route etc.*); mettre (*temps*); *to take advantage of*, profiter de; *to take away*, emmener (*personne*); emporter (*choses*), ôter (*retirer*); desservir (*le couvert etc.*); dérober (*voler*); *to take back*, reprendre, remporter; *to take down*, descendre; rabattre (*humilier*); démolir (*maison*); prendre note de (*inscrire*); *to take heed*, prendre garde (*à*); *to take in*, faire entrer; comprendre (*consister en*); recevoir, recevoir chez soi (*loger*); tromper, duper; faire sa provision de (*vivres etc.*); *to take off*, enlever, ôter, retirer (*vêtement*); caricaturer (*imiter*); *to take out*, faire sortir, sortir (*chose*); promener (*personne*); arracher (*dents*); ôter, enlever (*taches etc.*); *to take over*, se charger de, prendre la succession de (*affaires*); *to take up*, monter, faire monter, soulever (*lever*); ramasser (*relever*); commencer, entamer, aborder (*des études etc.*); occuper (*temps*).—*v.i.* réussir (*avoir du succès*); prendre (*feu etc.*); *to take after*, ressembler à; (*Av.*) *to take off*, décoller; (*fam.*) *to take on*, se lamenter, s'affliger; *to take up with*, s'associer à.—*n.* prise, pêche, quantité (*de poissons*); (*Cine.*) prise de vue, *f.*
take-in [′teikin], *n.* duperie, attrape, *f.*
take-off [′teikɔ:f], *n.* caricature, charge, *f.*; (*Av.*) décollage, *m.*
take-over [′teikouvə], *n.* (*Fin.*) rachat (*d'entreprise*), *m.*; *take-over bid*, offre de rachat, *f.*
taking [′teikiŋ], *a.* attrayant, séduisant; (*colloq.*) contagieux (*maladie*).—*n.* prise; arrestation, *f.*; (*pl.*) recettes (*argent*), *f.pl.*
talc [tælk], *n.* talc, *m.*
talcum powder [′tælkəm′paudə], *n.* talc, *m.*
tale [teil], *n.* conte, récit, *m.*; histoire, *f.*
talent [′tælənt], *n.* talent, *m.*
talented [′tæləntid], *a.* de talent, habile, bien doué.
talisman [′tælizmən], *n.* talisman, *m.*
talk [tɔ:k], *v.t.* parler, dire; *to talk over*, cajoler (*quelqu'un*); discuter (*quelque chose*).—*v.i.* parler (*de*); converser, causer; bavarder, jaser (*babiller*); *to talk at*, haranguer.—*n.* entretien, *m.*, propos, *m.pl.*, conversation; causerie (*intime*), *f.*; bavardage, bruit (*racontar*), *m.*; *small talk*, banalités, *f.pl.*
talkative [′tɔ:kətiv], *a.* causeur, bavard.

talker ['tɔ:kə], *n.* causeur, parleur, *m.*
talking ['tɔ:kiŋ], *a.* causeur, bavard.—*n.* conversation, causerie, *f.*
tall [tɔ:l], *a.* grand (*personne*); haut (*chose*).
tallboy ['tɔ:lbɔi], *n.* chiffonnier, *m.*; (haute) commode-secrétaire, *f.*
tallness ['tɔ:lnis], *n.* grande taille, hauteur, *f.*
tallow ['tælou], *n.* suif, *m.*
tallow-candle ['tælou'kændl], *n.* chandelle, *f.*
tally ['tæli], *n.* taille; entaille, marque; étiquette (*à bagages*), *f.*—*v.i.* s'accorder; **to tally with**, s'accorder avec, correspondre à.
tally-ho! [tæli'hou], *int.* (*Hunt.*) taïaut!
Talmud ['tælmʌd], *n.* talmud, *m.*
talon ['tælən], *n.* serre, griffe, *f.*
tambourine [tæmbə'ri:n], *n.* tambour de basque, *m.*
tame [teim], *a.* apprivoisé; domestique; (*fig.*) insipide.—*v.t.* apprivoiser; dompter (*dominer*).
tamely ['teimli], *adv.* avec soumission; sans cœur.
tameness ['teimnis], *n.* apprivoisement, *m.*, domesticité; soumission; (*fig.*) faiblesse (*de style etc.*), *f.*
tamer ['teimə], *n.* dompteur (*de bête sauvage*) *m.*
taming ['teimiŋ], *n.* apprivoisement, *m.*
tamp [tæmp], *v.t.* bourrer, tamponner.
tamper ['tæmpə], *v.i.* **to tamper with**, se mêler (*de*); expérimenter (*avec*); jouer avec; fausser (*serrure etc.*).
tampering ['tæmpəriŋ], *n.* menées secrètes, *f.pl.*
tan [tæn], *n.* tan; tanné (*couleur*); hâle (*de la peau*), *m.*—*v.t.* tanner; bronzer (*la peau*).
tandem ['tændəm], *n.* tandem (*bicyclette*), *m.*
tang [tæŋ], *n.* goût, *m.*, saveur, *f.*
tangent ['tændʒənt], *n.* tangente, *f.*
tangerine [tændʒə'ri:n], *n.* mandarine, *f.*
tangible ['tændʒibl], *a.* tangible, palpable.
Tangier(s) [tæn'dʒiə(z)]. Tanger, *m.*
tangle [tæŋgl], *n.* enchevêtrement, *m.*—*v.t.* embrouiller, enchevêtrer.
tangled [tæŋgld], *a.* embrouillé.
tango ['tæŋgou], *n.* tango, *m.*
tank [tæŋk], *n.* réservoir, *m.*; (*Mil.*) char (d'assaut), *m.*
tankard ['tæŋkəd], *n.* chope, *f.*
tanker ['tæŋkə], *n.* bateau citerne, *m.*
tanner ['tænə], *n.* tanneur, *m.*
tannery ['tænəri], *n.* tannerie, *f.*
tanning ['tæniŋ], *n.* tannage, *m.*; (*fam.*) rossée, *f.*
tantalize ['tæntəlaiz], *v.t.* tantaliser, tourmenter.
tantalizing ['tæntəlaiziŋ], *a.* tentant, torturant.
tantamount ['tæntəmaunt], *a.* équivalent (*à*).
tantrum ['tæntrəm], *n.* mauvaise humeur, *f.*
Tanzania [tænzə'ni.ə]. la Tanzanie, *f.*
tap (1) [tæp], *n.* robinet (*bain*); comptoir (*bar*), *m.*; cannelle (*de baril*), *f.*; taraud (*outil*), *m.*; **on tap**, en perce.—*v.t.* tirer (*liquide*); mettre en perce (*baril*); inciser (*arbre*); tarauder (*vis etc.*); (*Surg.*) faire la ponction à.
tap (2) [tæp], *n.* tape, *f.*, petit coup (*à la porte etc.*), *m.*—*v.t.* taper, frapper doucement.—*v.i.* taper, frapper.
tape [teip], *n.* ruban (*de fil*), *m.*; ganse (*sur habit*); bande (*magnétique*), *f.*; **red tape**, (*fig.*) routine administrative, *f.*

tape measure ['teipmeʒə], *n.* mètre ruban, *m.*
taper ['teipə], *n.* bougie effilée, *f.*; (*Eccles.*) cierge, *m.*
tape recorder ['teiprikɔ:də], *n.* magnétophone, *m.*
tape recording ['teiprikɔ:diŋ], *n.* enregistrement magnétique, *m.*
tapering ['teipəriŋ], *a.* effilé.
tapestry ['tæpistri], *n.* tapisserie, *f.*
tape-worm ['teipwə:m], *n.* ver solitaire, *m.*
tapioca [tæpi'oukə], *n.* tapioca, *m.*
tapir ['teipiə], *n.* tapir, *m.*
tappet ['tæpit], *n.* taquet (*de soupape*), *m.*
tapping (1) ['tæpiŋ], *n.* taraudage (*de vis*), *m.*; mise en perce (*de baril*); incision (*d'arbre*); (*Surg.*) ponction, *f.*
tapping (2) ['tæpiŋ], *n.* tapotement, *m.*
tar [ta:], *n.* goudron; loup de mer (*matelot*), *m.*—*v.t.* goudronner.
tarantella [tærən'telə], *n.* tarentelle (*danse*), *f.*
tarantula [tə'ræntjulə], *n.* tarentule, *f.*
tardily ['ta:dili], *adv.* tardivement, lentement.
tardiness ['ta:dinis], *n.* lenteur; tardiveté (*de fruit*), *f.*
tardy ['ta:di], *a.* lent; en retard, tardif.
tare (1) [tɛə], *n.* tare (*poids*), *f.*
tare (2) [tɛə], *n.* (*Script.*) ivraie; (*pl.*) (*Agric.*) vesce, *f.*
target ['ta:git], *n.* cible, *f.*; but, objectif, *m.*
tariff ['tærif], *n.* tarif, *m.*
tarmac ['ta:mæk], *n.* macadam, *m.*; (*Av.*) piste d'envol, *f.*—*v.t.* goudronner.
tarn [ta:n], *n.* petit lac (*de montagne*), *m.*
tarnish ['ta:niʃ], *v.t.* ternir; (*fig.*) souiller, flétrir.—*v.i.* se ternir.
tarpaulin [ta:'pɔ:lin], *n.* (*Naut.*) prélart, *m.*, bâche, toile goudronnée, *f.*
tarry (1) ['ta:ri], *a.* goudronneux, bitumeux.
tarry (2) ['tæri], *v.i.* rester, tarder.
tart (1) [ta:t], *n.* tarte, tourte, *f.*
tart (2) [ta:t], *a.* acide, âcre; (*fig.*) aigre.
tartan ['ta:tən], *n.* tartan, *m.*
tartar ['ta:tə], *n.* (*Chem.*) tartre, *m.*
tartaric [ta:'tærik], *a.* tartrique.
tartish ['ta:tiʃ], *a.* aigrelet.
tartly ['ta:tli], *adv.* avec aigreur; (*fig.*) vertement, sévèrement.
tartness ['ta:tnis], *n.* acidité; (*fig.*) aigreur, *m.*
task [ta:sk], *n.* tâche, *f.*; devoir (*leçon*); pensum (*punition*), *m.*; **to take to task**, réprimander, semoncer.
taskmaster ['ta:skma:stə], *n.* chef de corvée, *m.*
Tasmania [tæz'meinjə]. la Tasmanie, *f.*
Tasmanian [tæz'meinjən], *a.* tasmanien.—*n.* Tasmanien (*personne*), *m.*
tassel [tæsl], *n.* gland, *m.*
taste [teist], *v.t.* goûter; (*fig.*) savourer, éprouver.—*v.i.* goûter (*de*); avoir un goût (*de*).—*n.* goût; soupçon (*trace*), *m.*
tasteful ['teistful], *a.* de bon goût.
tastefully ['teistfuli], *adv.* avec goût.
tasteless ['teistlis], *a.* fade, insipide.
tastelessly ['teistlisli], *adv.* insipidement, fadement.
taster ['teistə], *n.* dégustateur, *m.*
tasting ['teistiŋ], *n.* dégustation, *f.*
tasty ['teisti], *a.* (*colloq.*) de bon goût; savoureux.

tatter

tatter ['tætə], *n.* haillon, lambeau, *m.*, guenille, *f.*

tattered ['tætəd], *a.* déguenillé, en haillons (*personne*); en lambeaux, tout déchiré (*vêtements etc.*).

tatting ['tætiŋ], *n.* frivolité (*dentelle*), *f.*

tattle [tætl], *n.* babil, caquet, *m.—v.i.* bavarder.

tattler ['tætlə], *n.* babillard, bavard, *m.*

tattling ['tætliŋ], *a.* babillard, bavard.

tattoo [tə'tu:], *v.t.* tatouer.—*n.* tatouage, *m.*; (*Mil.*) fête militaire, *f.*

taunt [[tɔ:nt], *n.* injure, *f.*, reproche amer, *m.* —*v.t.* tancer, reprocher à, injurier.

tauntingly ['tɔ:ntiŋli], *adv.* injurieusement.

Taurus ['tɔ:rəs], (*Astron.*) le Taureau, *m.*

taut [tɔ:t], *a.* raide, tendu; enflé (*voile*).

tautology [tɔ:'tɔlədʒi], *n.* tautologie, *f.*

tavern ['tævən], *n.* taverne, *f.*; cabaret, *m.*

tawdry ['tɔ:dri], *a.* criard, de mauvais goût, prétentieux.

tawny ['tɔ:ni], *a.* fauve.

tawse [tɔ:z], *n.* martinet, *m.*

tax [tæks], *n.* impôt, *m.*, taxe; (*fig.*) contribution, *f.*; *income tax*, impôt sur le revenu; *purchase tax*, taxe de luxe; *tax evasion*, fraude fiscale, *f.*; *surtax*, surtaxe, *f.—v.t.* imposer, taxer; (*fig.*) accuser (*de*).

taxable ['tæksəbl], *a.* imposable.

taxation [tæk'seiʃən], *n.* taxation, *f.*

tax-free ['tæks'fri:], *a.* exempt d'impôts.

taxi ['tæksi], *n.* taxi, *m.*

tax-payer ['tækspeiə], *n.* contribuable, *m.*, *f.*

tea [ti:], *n.* thé, *m.*; tisane (*infusion*), *f.*; goûter (*repas*), *m.*

tea caddy ['ti:kædi], *n.* boîte à thé, *f.*

tea cake ['ti:keik], *n.* brioche, *f.*

teach [ti:tʃ], *v.t.* irr. enseigner, instruire; apprendre (*à*).—*v.i.* enseigner, professer.

teachable ['ti:tʃəbl], *a.* disposé à apprendre, docile; enseignable (*chose*).

teacher ['ti:tʃə], *n.* maître, instituteur; professeur (*de lycée*), *m.*

tea chest ['ti:tʃest], *n.* caisse à thé, *f.*

teaching ['ti:tʃiŋ], *n.* enseignement, *m.*

tea-cup ['ti:kʌp], *n.* tasse à thé, *f.*

teak [ti:k], *n.* (*Bot.*) teck, tek, *m.*

teal [ti:l], *n.* (*Orn.*) sarcelle, *f.*

team [ti:m], *n.* attelage, *m.*, (*Spt.*) équipe, *f.*

teapot ['ti:pɔt], *n.* théière, *f.*

tear (1) [tiə], *n.* larme, *f.*, pleur, *m.*

tear (2) [tɛə], *v.t.* irr. déchirer; (*fig.*) arracher; *to tear asunder*, déchirer en deux.—*v.i.* se déchirer.—*n.* déchirure, *f.*; *wear and tear*, usure, *f.*

tear-drop ['tiədrɔp], *n.* larme, *f.*

tearful ['tiəful], *a.* tout en larmes.

tearfully ['tiəfuli], *adv.* les larmes aux yeux.

tearing ['tɛəriŋ], *n.* déchirement, *m.*

tease [ti:z], *v.t.* taquiner, tourmenter; carder (*laine*).—*n.* taquin, *m.*

tea service ['ti:sə:vis], *n.* service à thé, *m.*

teasing ['ti:ziŋ], *a.* taquin.—*n.* taquinerie, *f.*

teaspoon ['ti:spu:n], *n.* cuiller à thé, *f.*

teaspoonful ['ti:spu:nful] *n.* petite cuillerée, *f.*

tea strainer ['ti:streinə], *n.* passe-thé, *m.*

teat [ti:t], *n.* mamelon, tétin, *m.*; tette, *f.*

tea table ['ti:teibl], *n.* table à thé, *f.*

tea time ['ti:taim], *n.* l'heure du thé, *f.*

tea tray ['ti:trei], *n.* plateau à thé, *m.*

tea urn ['ti:ə:n], *n.* fontaine à thé, *f.*

technical ['teknikl], *a.* technique, de l'art; *technical school*, école professionnelle, *f.*

technicality [tekni'kæliti], *n.* caractère technique; terme technique (*mot*), *m.*; (*fig.*) formalité, *f.*

technically ['teknikli], *adv.* techniquement.

technician [tek'niʃən], *n.* technicien, *m.*

technique [tek'ni:k], *n.* technique, *f.*

technologist [tek'nɔlədʒist], *n.* technologue, *m.*, *f.*

technology [tek'nɔlədʒi], *n.* technologie, *f.*

teddy ['tedi], *n.* *teddy bear*, ours en peluche, *m.*

tedious ['ti:diəs], *a.* ennuyeux, fatigant.

tedium ['ti:diəm], *n.* ennui, *m.*

tee [ti:], *n.* dé (*au golf*), *m.*

teem [ti:m], *v.i.* être fécond (*en*); *to teem with*, abonder en.

teeming ['ti:miŋ], *a.* fécond, fertile, surabondant (*de*).

teenager ['ti:neidʒə], *n.* adolescent, *m.*

teens [ti:nz], *n.pl.* l'âge de treize à dix-neuf ans, *m.*; *to be in one's teens*, n'avoir pas vingt ans.

teeth [TOOTH].

teethe [ti:ð], *v.i.* faire ses dents.

teething ['ti:ðiŋ], *n.* dentition, *f.*

teetotal [ti:'toutl], *a.* de tempérance.

teetotal(l)er [ti:'toutlə], *n.* buveur d'eau, *m.*

teetotalism [ti:'toutəlizm], *n.* abstinence de boissons alcooliques, *f.*

telegram ['teligræm], *n.* télégramme, *m.*, dépêche, *f.*

telegraph ['teligrɑ:f, -græf], *n.* télégraphe, *m.*; *telegraph office*, bureau télégraphique, *m.—v.t., v.i.* télégraphier.

telegraphic [teli'græfik], *a.* télégraphique.

telegraphist [ti'legrəfist], *n.* télégraphiste, *m.*, *f.*

telegraph post ['teligrɑ:fpoust], **telegraph pole** ['teligrɑ:fpoul], *n.* poteau télégraphique, *m.*

telegraph wire ['teligrɑ:fwaiə], *n.* fil télégraphique, *m.*

telegraphy [ti'legrəfi], *n.* télégraphie, *f.*; *wireless telegraphy*, télégraphie sans fil.

telepathy [ti'lepəθi], *n.* télépathie, *f.*

telephone ['telifoun], *n.* téléphone, *m.*; *telephone exchange*, central téléphonique, *m.*; *telephone booth*, cabine téléphonique, *f.*; *telephone operator*, téléphoniste, *m.*, *f.* —*v.t., v.i.* téléphoner.

telephonic [teli'fɔnik], *a.* téléphonique.

teleprinter ['teliprintə], *n.* téléimprimeur, télétype, *m.*

telescope ['teliskoup], *n.* (*Astron.*) télescope, *m.*; longue vue, *f.*

telescopic [teli'skɔpik], *a.* télescopique.

televiewer ['telivju:ə], *n.* téléspectateur, *m.*

televise ['telivaiz], *v.t.* téléviser.

television [teli'viʒən], *n.* télévision, *f.*; *television set*, téléviseur, appareil de télévision, *m.*

tell [tel], *v.t.* irr. dire; faire part de; raconter (*réciter*); montrer, indiquer (*expliquer*); révéler, dévoiler; énumérer (*compter*); avouer (*confesser*); reconnaître (*à*); savoir (*deviner*).—*v.i.* dire; faire son effet, porter (*influer*); juger (*interpréter*).

teller ['telə], *n.* diseur; raconteur; (*Am., Sc.*) caissier (*de banque*); (*Parl.*) scrutateur, *m.*

592

telling ['teliŋ], *a.* qui porte; expressif.—*n.* récit, *m.*, narration, *f.*

tell-tale ['telteil], *a.* rapporteur; (*fig.*) révélateur.—*n.* rapporteur, *m.*

temerity [ti'meriti], *n.* témérité, *f.*

temper ['tempə], *n.* tempérament, *m.*, disposition; humeur; colère (*rage*), *f.*; sangfroid (*équanimité*), *m.*; trempe (*d'acier etc.*), *f.*; **to lose one's temper**, se mettre en colère.—*v.t.* tempérer (*de*); détremper (*couleurs*); tremper (*acier etc.*); (*fig.*) adoucir.

temperament ['tempərəmənt], *n.* tempérament, *m.*

temperamental [tempərə'mentl], *a.* capricieux, instable.

temperance ['tempərəns], *n.* tempérance, *f.*

temperate ['tempərit], *a.* modéré; tempéré (*climat*).

temperature ['tempritʃə], *n.* température, *f.*

tempest ['tempist], *n.* tempête, *f.*

tempestuous [tem'pestjuəs], *a.* orageux, tempétueux.

templar ['templə], *n.* templier, *m.*

temple [templ], *n.* temple, *m.*; (*Anat.*) tempe, *f.*

templet ['templit], *n.* patron, gabarit, *m.*

temporal ['tempərəl], *a.* temporel; (*Anat.*) temporal.

temporarily ['tempərərili], *adv.* temporairement.

temporary ['tempərəri], *a.* temporaire, provisoire.

temporization [tempərai'zeiʃən], *n.* temporisation, *f.*

temporize ['tempəraiz], *v.i.* temporiser.

tempt [tempt], *v.t.* tenter (*de*); pousser (*à*).

temptation [temp'teiʃən], *n.* tentation, *f.*

tempter ['temptə], *n.* tentateur, *m.*

tempting ['temptiŋ], *a.* tentant, séduisant, attrayant; appétissant (*nourriture*).

temptress ['temptris], *n.* tentatrice, *f.*

ten [ten], *a.* dix.—*n.* dix, *m.*; une dizaine (*dix environ*), *f.*

tenable ['tenəbl], *a.* soutenable.

tenacious [ti'neiʃəs], *a.* tenace.

tenaciously [ti'neiʃəsli], *adv.* d'une manière tenace, obstinément.

tenacity [ti'næsiti], *n.* ténacité, *f.*

tenancy ['tenənsi], *n.* location, *f.*

tenant ['tenənt], *n.* locataire, *m.*, *f.*

tench [tentʃ], *n.* (*Ichth.*) tanche, *f.*

tend [tend], *v.t.* garder, soigner.—*v.i.* tendre (*à*); se diriger vers.

tendency ['tendənsi], *n.* tendance, disposition, *f.*

tender (1) ['tendə], *n.* offre (*proposition*); (*Comm.*) soumission, *f.*; **legal tender**, monnaie légale, *f.*—*v.t.* offrir.—*v.i.* **to tender for**, soumissionner pour.

tender (2) ['tendə], *n.* (*Naut.*) allège, *f.*; (*Rail.*) tender, *m.*

tender (3) ['tendə], *a.* tendre; sensible (*vulnérable*).

tender-hearted ['tendə'ha:tid], *a.* sensible, au cœur tendre.

tenderly ['tendəli], *adv.* tendrement.

tenderness ['tendənis], *n.* tendresse; sensibilité (*vulnérabilité*); sollicitude, *f.*

tendon ['tendən], *n.* tendon, *m.*

tendril ['tendril], *n.* (*Bot.*) vrille, *f.*

tenement ['tenimənt], *n.* habitation, maison,

tenet ['ti:nit, 'tenit], *n.* principe, *m.*

tenfold ['tenfould], *a.* décuple.—*adv.* dix fois.

tennis ['tenis], *n.* tennis; *jeu de paume, *m.*

tennis court ['teniskɔ:t], *n.* court de tennis, tennis; *jeu de paume, *m.*

tennis racket ['tenisrækit], *n.* raquette de tennis, *f.*

tenor ['tenə], *n.* (*Mus.*) ténor, *m.*

tense (1) [tens], *n.* (*Gram.*) temps, *m.*

tense (2) [tens], *a.* tendu, raide.

tensile ['tensail], *a.* ductile (*métal*).

tension ['tenʃən], *n.* tension, *f.*

tent [tent], *n.* tente, *f.*; **bell tent**, tente conique.

tentacle ['tentəkl], *n.* tentacule, *m.*

tentative ['tentətiv], *a.* tentatif, d'essai.

tentatively ['tentətivli], *adv.* en guise d'essai.

tenter-hook ['tentəhuk], *n.* clou à crochet, *m.*; **to be on tenter-hooks**, être sur des épines.

tenth [tenθ], *a.* dixième; dix (*du mois, roi etc.*).—*n.* dixième (*fraction*), *m.*; (*Eccles.*) dîme, *f.*

tenuous ['tenjuəs], *a.* délié, mince, ténu.

tenure ['tenjuə], *n.* tenure, *f.*

tepid ['tepid], *a.* tiède.

tercentenary [tə:sen'ti:nəri], *a.* de trois siècles.—*n.* tricentenaire, *m.*

term [tə:m], *n.* terme, *m.*; limite; (*Law*) session, *f.*; (*Sch.*) trimestre, *m.*; (*pl.*) conditions, *f.pl.*; prix, *m.*—*v.t.* nommer, appeler.

termagant ['tə:məgənt], *n.* mégère, *f.*

terminable ['tə:minəbl], *a.* terminable.

terminal ['tə:minl], *a.* terminal.—*n.* (*Elec.*) borne, *f.*; **air terminal**, gare aérienne, aérogare, *f.*

terminate ['tə:mineit], *v.t.* terminer, finir.

termination [tə:mi'neiʃən], *n.* fin, terminaison, *f.*

terminology [tə:mi'nɔlədʒi], *n.* terminologie, *f.*

terminus ['tə:minəs], *n.* terminus (*gare*), *m.*; tête de ligne, *f.*

tern [tə:n], *n.* sterne, *m.*, hirondelle de mer, *f.*

ternary ['tə:nəri], *a.* ternaire.

terrace ['teris], *n.* terrasse, *f.*

terraced ['terist], *a.* étagé en terrasse.

terra cotta ['terə'kɔtə], *n.* terre cuite, *f.*

terra firma ['terə'fə:mə], *n.* terre ferme, *f.*

terrestrial [tə'restriəl], *a.* terrestre.

terrible ['teribl], *a.* terrible.

terribly ['teribli], *adv.* terriblement; (*colloq.*) diablement.

terrier ['teriə], *n.* terrier, chien terrier, *m.*

terrific [tə'rifik], *a.* terrible, épouvantable; (*fam.*) formidable.

terrify ['terifai], *v.t.* terrifier.

territorial [teri'tɔ:riəl], *a.* territorial.

territory ['teritəri], *n.* territoire, *m.*

terror ['terə], *n.* terreur, *f.*; effroi, *m.*

terrorism ['terərizm], *n.* terrorisme, *m.*

terrorist ['terərist], *n.* terroriste, *m.*, *f.*

terrorize ['terəraiz], *v.t.* terroriser.

terse [tə:s], *a.* net, concis; bien tourné, élégant.

tersely ['tə:sli], *adv.* nettement; d'une manière concise.

terseness ['tə:snis], *n.* netteté, *f.*

tertian ['tə:ʃən], *a.* tierce.

tertiary ['tə:ʃəri], *a.* tertiaire.

tessellated [tesə'leitid], *a.* tessellé.

test [test], *n.* épreuve, *f.*; test; essai, *m.*; pierre de touche, *f.*—*v.t.* éprouver, mettre à l'épreuve, tester; (*Metal.*) coupeller.

testament ['testəmənt], *n.* testament, *m.*

testator [tes'teitə], *n.* testateur, *m.*

testicle ['testikl], *n.* testicule, *m.*

testify ['testifai], *v.t.* témoigner; (*Law*) déposer (*de*).—*v.i.* (*Law*) déposer.

testimonial [testi'mouniəl], *n.* témoignage; certificat, témoignage d'estime, *m.*

testimony ['testiməni], *n.* témoignage, *m.*

testiness ['testinis], *n.* humeur, irritabilité, *f.*

testing ['testiŋ], *n.* épreuve, *f.*, essai, *m.*

test tube ['testtju:b], *n.* éprouvette, *f.*

testy ['testi], *a.* irritable, susceptible.

tetanus ['tetənəs], *n.* tétanos, *m.*

tether ['teðə], *n.* longe, *f.*; *to be at the end of one's tether*, être à bout de forces.—*v.t.* mettre à l'attache, attacher (*à*).

tetrahedron [tetrə'hi:drən], *n.* tétraèdre, *m.*

tetrarch ['tetra:k], *n.* tétrarque, *m.*

Teuton ['tju:tən], *a.* teuton.—*n.* Teuton (*personne*), *m.*

Teutonic [tju:'tonik], *a.* teutonique.

text [tekst], *n.* texte, *m.*

text-book ['tekstbuk], *n.* manuel, livre de classe, *m.*

textile ['tekstail], *a.* textile.—*n.* tissu, textile, *m.*, étoffe, *f.*

textual ['tekstjuəl], *a.* textuel.

texture ['tekstʃə], *n.* tissu, *m.*; contexture (*d'écrits etc.*), *f.*

Thai [tai], *a.* thaïlandais.—*n.* thaïlandais (*langue*); Thaïlandais (*personne*), *m.*

Thailand ['tailænd]. la Thaïlande, *f.*, le Siam, *m.*

Thames [temz], **the.** la Tamise, *f.*

than [ðæn], *conj.* que; de (*between* more *or* less *and a number*); que de (*before an infinitive*).

thank [θæŋk], *v.t.* remercier (*de*); rendre grâces à.

thankful ['θæŋkful], *a.* reconnaissant (*de*).

thankfully ['θæŋkfuli], *adv.* avec reconnaissance.

thankfulness ['θæŋkfulnis], *n.* reconnaissance, *f.*

thankless ['θæŋklis], *a.* ingrat; oublié (*non reconnu*).

thanklessness ['θæŋklisnis], *n.* ingratitude, *f.*

thank offering ['θæŋkɔfəriŋ], *n.* sacrifice d'actions de grâces, *m.*

thanks [θæŋks], *n.pl.* remercîments, remercîments, *m.pl.*, grâces, *f.pl.*—*int.* merci.

thanksgiving ['θæŋksgiviŋ], *n.* actions de grâces, *f.pl.*

that [ðæt], *dem.a.* (*pl.* **those** [ðouz]) ce, cet, *m.*, cette, *f.*; (*emphatically*) ce . . . -là, cet . . . -là, *m.*, cette . . . -là, *f.*—*dem.pron.* celui-là, *m.*, celle-là (*that one*), *f.*; cela, (*colloq.*) ça, *m.*—*rel.pron.* qui, que, lequel, *m.*, laquelle, *f.*, lesquels, *m.pl.*, lesquelles, *f.pl.*—*conj.* que.

thatch [θætʃ], *n.* chaume, *m.*—*v.t.* couvrir de chaume.

thatcher ['θætʃə], *n.* couvreur en chaume, *m.*

thaw [θɔ:], *n.* dégel, *m.*—*v.t.* dégeler; (*fig.*) fondre, attendrir.—*v.i.* dégeler, se dégeler; (*fig.*) fondre, s'attendrir.

the [ðə], *before vowel* **thee** [ði], *def. art.* le, l', *m.*, la, l', *f.*, les, *pl.*

theater ['θiətə], *n.* théâtre, *m.*

theatrical [θi:'ætrikl], *a.* de théâtre, théâtral.

theatricals [θi:'ætriklz], *n.pl.* spectacle, *m.*

*thee [ði:], *pron.* (*also Poet.*) toi; te.

theft [θeft], *n.* vol, *m.*; *petty theft*, larcin, *m.*

their [ðɛə], *poss.a.* leur, leurs, *pl.*

theirs [ðɛəz], *poss.pron.* le leur, *m.*, la leur, *f.*, les leurs, *pl.*, à eux, *m.pl.*, à elles, *f.pl.*

theism ['θi:izm], *n.* théisme, *m.*

theist ['θi:ist], *n.* théiste, *m.*, *f.*

theistic [θi:'istik], *a.* théiste.

them [ðem], *pron.* eux, *m.pl.*, elles, *f.pl.*; (*obj.*) les; (*dat.*) leur, *pl.*

theme [θi:m], *n.* thème, sujet, *m.*

theme song ['θi:msɔŋ], *n.* chanson leit-motif, *f.*

themselves [ðem'selvz], *pron.* eux-mêmes, *m.pl.*, elles-mêmes, *f.pl.*; (*reflexive*) se, *pl.*

then [ðen], *adv.* alors; ensuite, puis (*après*); dans ce cas (*puisqu'il en est ainsi*); donc; *but then*, par contre; *by then*, alors, déjà; *now and then*, de temps en temps.—*conj.* donc.

thence [ðens], *adv.* de là, en; dès lors.

thenceforth [ðens'fɔ:θ], **thenceforward** [ðens'fɔ:wəd], *adv.* dès lors, depuis lors, à partir de ce moment-là.

theocracy [θi:'ɔkrəsi], *n.* théocratie, *f.*

theocratic [θi:ə'krætik], *a.* théocratique.

theodolite [θi:'ɔdəlait], *n.* théodolite, *m.*

theologian [θi:ə'loudʒiən], *n.* théologien, *m.*

theological [θi:ə'lɔdʒikl], *a.* théologique.

theology [θi:'ɔlədʒi], *n.* théologie, *f.*

theorem ['θi:ərəm], *n.* théorème, *m.*

theoretic [θi:ə'retik], **theoretical** [θi:ə'reti kəl], *a.* théorique.

theorist ['θi:ərist], **theorizer** ['θi:əraizə], *n.* théoricien, *m.*

theorize ['θi:əraiz], *v.i.* théoriser.

theory ['θi:əri], *n.* théorie, *f.*

therapeutic [θerə'pju:tik], *a.* thérapeutique.

therapeutics [θerə'pju:tiks], *n.pl.* thérapeutique, *f.*

therapist ['θerəpist], *n.* praticien, *m.*

therapy ['θerəpi], *n.* thérapie, *f.*

there [ðɛə], *adv.* là, y; (*impers.*) il; en cela; voilà; *here and there*, çà et là; *over there*, là-bas; *there and then*, séance tenante; *there he comes!* le voilà qui vient! *there is* or *there are*, il y a.

thereabout [ðɛərə'baut], **thereabouts** [ðɛərə 'bauts], *adv.* par là, près de là; à peu près, environ (*plus ou moins*).

thereafter [ðɛər'a:ftə], *adv.* après, d'après cela, ensuite.

thereat [ðɛər'æt], *adv.* par là, à cet endroit; (*fig.*) là-dessus, à cela.

thereby [ðɛə'bai], *adv.* par là, par ce moyen.

therefore ['ðɛəfɔ:], *adv.* donc, par conséquent.

therefrom [ðɛə'frɔm], *adv.* de là, en.

therein [ðɛər'in], *adv.* là-dedans, en cela; y.

thereof [ðɛər'ɔv], *adv.* en, de cela.

thereon [ðɛər'ɔn], *adv.* là-dessus.

Theresa [tə'ri:zə]. Thérèse, *f.*

thereto [ðɛə'tu:], **thereunto** [ðɛər'ʌntu], *adv.* y, à cela; à quoi.

thereupon [ðɛərə'pɔn], *adv.* là-dessus, sur cela, sur ce.

therewith [ðɛə'wið], *adv.* avec cela, de cela, en.

therm [θə:m], *n.* thermie, *f.*

thermal ['θə:məl], *a.* thermal.

thermometer [θə'mɔmitə], *n.* thermomètre, *m.*

thermometrical [θə:mo'metrikl], *a.* thermo-métrique.

thermonuclear [θə:mo'nju:kliə], *a.* thermo-nucléaire.

thermos ['θə:mɔs], *a.* (*reg. trade mark*) **thermos flask**, bouteille Thermos *ou* isolante, *f.*

thermostat ['θə:məstæt], *n.* thermostat, *m.*

these [ði:z], *a.* ces, ces . . . -ci, *pl.*—*pron.* ceux-ci, *m.pl.*, celles-ci, *f.pl.*

thesis ['θi:sis], *n.* thèse, *f.*

Thespian ['θespiən], *a.* tragique, de la tragédie.

thew [θju:], *n.* tendon, muscle, nerf, *m.*

they [ðei], *pron.* ils, eux, *m.pl.*, elles, *f.pl.*; (*followed by a relative*) ceux, *m.pl.*, celles, *f.pl.*; (*impers.*) on (*les gens*); **they say**, on dit.

thick [θik], *a.* épais; gros (*tuyau*); fort, solide (*porte etc.*); trouble (*boisson*); dru, serré (*touffu*); indistinct (*prononciation*); (*fam.*) intime.—*n.* fort, *m.*; **in the thick of**, au (plus) fort de.—*adv.* (*also* **thickly** ['θikli]) épais; dru (*vite*); en foule (*l'un après l'autre*).

thicken [θikn], *v.t.* épaissir; lier (*sauce*).—*v.i.* s'épaissir; augmenter; se lier (*sauce*).

thickening ['θikniŋ], *n.* épaississement, *m.*; liaison (*d'une sauce*), *f.*

thicket ['θikit], *n.* fourré, hallier, taillis, *m.*

thick-headed ['θik'hedid], *a.* sot, bête, stupide.

thickly [THICK].

thickness ['θiknis], *n.* épaisseur; consistance (*composition*), *f.*

thick-set ['θikset], *a.* touffu; trapu (*personne*).

thick-skinned ['θik'skind], *a.* (*fig.*) peu sensible.

thief [θi:f], *n.* (*pl.* **thieves** [θi:vz]) voleur; larron, *m.*

thieve [θi:v], *v.i.* voler.

thieving ['θi:viŋ], *n.* vol, larcin, *m.*, rapine, *f.*

thievish ['θi:viʃ], *a.* adonné au vol; voleur.

thievishly ['θi:viʃli], *adv.* en voleur; par le vol.

thievishness ['θi:viʃnis], *n.* penchant au vol, *m.*, habitude du vol, *f.*

thigh [θai], *n.* cuisse, *f.*

thigh-bone ['θaiboun], *n.* fémur, *m.*

thimble [θimbl], *n.* dé, *m.*

thimbleful ['θimblful], *n.* un plein dé, *m.*

thin [θin], *a.* mince; maigre (*décharné*); élancé, délié (*svelte*); peu nombreux (*gens*); clair; clairsemé, rare (*arbres etc.*); grêle, faible (*son etc.*).—*adv.* d'une manière éparse, clair.—*v.t.* amincir, allonger (*sauce etc.*); éclaircir; raréfier.

*thine [ðain], *pron.* le tien, *m.*, la tienne, *f.*, les tiens, *m.pl.*, les tiennes, *f.pl.*; à toi.

thing [θiŋ], *n.* chose, *f.*, objet, *m.*, affaire, *f.*; être, *m.*; (*pl.*) affaires, *f.pl.*, effets, *m.pl.*

think [θiŋk], *v.t. irr.* penser; croire (*tenir pour vrai*); imaginer, songer (*avoir l'idée*); trouver, juger (*considérer*).—*v.i.* penser; croire; s'imaginer; songer (*à*); s'aviser (*de*); avoir une idée *ou* opinion (*de*); **to think over**, réfléchir à; **to think up**, inventer.

thinker ['θiŋkə], *n.* penseur, *m.*

thinking ['θiŋkiŋ], *a.* pensant, qui pense, réfléchi.—*n.* pensée, *f.*; jugement, avis, *m.*

thinly ['θinli], *adv.* légèrement (*vêtu*); clairsemé, de loin en loin (*répandu*).

thinness ['θinnis], *n.* ténuité; fluidité; rareté,

f., petit nombre (*quantité*), *m.*; maigreur (*du corps*), *f.*

thin-skinned ['θin'skind], *a.* à la peau mince; (*fig.*) irritable, chatouilleux, susceptible.

third [θə:d], *a.* troisième; trois (*mois, roi etc.*). —*n.* tiers (*fraction*), *m.*; (*Mus.*) tierce, *f.*

thirdly ['θə:dli], *adv.* troisièmement.

thirst [θə:st], *n.* soif, *f.*; **to quench one's thirst**, se désaltérer.—*v.i.* avoir soif (*de*).

thirstily ['θə:stili], *adv.* avidement.

thirstiness ['θə:stinis], *n.* soif, *f.*

thirsty ['θə:sti], *a.* qui a soif; altéré.

thirteen [θə:'ti:n], *a.* and *n.* treize, *m.*

thirteenth [θə:'ti:nθ], *a.* treizième; treize (*rois etc.*).—*n.* treizième (*fraction*), *m.*

thirtieth ['θə:tiiθ], *a.* trentième; trente (*du mois*).—*n.* trentième (*fraction*), *m.*

thirty ['θə:ti], *a.* and *n.* trente, *m.*

this [ðis], *a.* (*pl.* **these** [ði:z]) ce, cet, *m.*, cette, *f.*; ce . . . -ci, cet . . . -ci, *m.*; cette . . . -ci, *f.*—*pron.* celui-ci, *m.*, celle-ci (*this one*), *f.*; ceci, *m.*

thistle [θisl], *n.* (*Bot.*) chardon, *m.*

thistly ['θisli], *a.* plein de chardons.

thither ['ðiðə], *adv.* là, y; **hither and thither**, çà et là.

thong [θɔŋ], *n.* courroie, lanière, sangle, *f.*

thoracic [θɔ'ræsik], *a.* thoracique.

thorax ['θɔ:ræks], *n.* thorax, *m.*

thorn [θɔ:n], *n.* épine, *f.*

thorn bush ['θɔ:nbuʃ], *n.* buisson épineux, *m.*

thorny ['θɔ:ni], *a.* épineux.

thorough ['θʌrə], *a.* entier, complet; achevé, parfait; vrai (*véritable*).

thoroughbred ['θʌrəbred], *a.* pur sang (*cheval*); (*colloq.*) consommé.

thoroughfare ['θʌrəfɛə], *n.* voie de passage, *f.*, passage, *m.*; artère, *f.*; **no thoroughfare**, passage interdit.

thoroughgoing ['θʌrəgouiŋ], *a.* résolu; achevé, consommé.

thoroughly ['θʌrəli], *adv.* tout à fait, entièrement; à fond.

thoroughness ['θʌrənis], *n.* caractère achevé, *m.*, perfection, *f.*

thorough-paced ['θʌrəpeist], *a.* achevé, franc, fieffé.

those [ðouz], *a.* ces; ces . . . -là, *pl.*—*pron.* ceux-là, *m.pl.*, celles-là, *f.pl.*

*thou [ðau], *pron.* tu; **than thou**, que toi.

though [ðou], *conj.* quoique, bien que (*with subj.*); quand même (*même si*).—*adv.* cependant, pourtant.

thought (1) [θɔ:t], *past and p.p.* [THINK].

thought (2) [θɔ:t], *n.* pensée; idée, *f.*; sentiment (*opinion*), *m.*

thoughtful ['θɔ:tful], *a.* pensif, réfléchi; rêveur, méditatif; inquiet (*troublé*); attentif, soucieux (*prévenant*).

thoughtfully ['θɔ:tfuli], *adv.* pensivement, avec attention.

thoughtfulness ['θɔ:tfulnis], *n.* méditation, *f.*, recueillement, *m.*; sollicitude, prévenance (*attentions*), *f.*

thoughtless ['θɔ:tlis], *a.* irréfléchi, insouciant.

thoughtlessly ['θɔ:tlisli], *a.* avec insouciance; sans réflexion.

thoughtlessness ['θɔ:tlisnis], *n.* insouciance, négligence, *f.*

thousand ['θauzənd], *a.* mille; mil (*dates*).—*n.* mille; millier, *m.*, (*pl.*) milliers, *m.pl.*

thousandth

thousandth [ˈθauzəndθ], *a.* millième.—*n.* millième (*fraction*), *m.*

thraldom [ˈθrɔːldəm], *n.* esclavage, asservissement, *m.*

thrall [θrɔːl], *n.* esclave, *m.*, *f.*; esclavage, *m.*

thrash [θræʃ], *v.t.* battre, rosser (*quelqu'un*); [THRESH].

thrasher [ˈθræʃə], [THRESHER].

thrashing [ˈθræʃiŋ], *n.* rossée, *f.*; [THRESHING].

thrashing machine [THRESHING MACHINE].

thread [θred], *n.* fil; filet (*de vis*), *m.*—*v.t.* enfiler; traverser (*faire son chemin à travers*).

threadbare [ˈθredbeə], *a.* râpé; (*fig.*) rebattu.

threat [θret], *n.* menace, *f.*

threaten [θretn], *v.t.* menacer (*de*).

threatening [ˈθretniŋ], *a.* menaçant; de menaces.—*n.* menaces, *f.pl.*

threateningly [ˈθretniŋli], *adv.* avec menaces; d'un air menaçant.

three [θriː], *a.* and *n.* trois, *m.*

three-cornered [ˈθriːkɔːnəd], *a.* à trois cornes; **three-cornered hat,** tricorne, *m.*

threefold [ˈθriːfould], *a.* triple.

three-master [ˈθriːmɑːstə], *n.* trois-mâts, *m.*

three-ply [ˈθriːplai], *a.* à trois épaisseurs; **three-ply wood,** contreplaqué, *m.*

threescore [ˈθriːskɔː], *a.* soixante.—*n.* soixantaine, *f.*

thresh [θreʃ], *v.t.* (*Agric.*) battre (*en grange*).

thresher [ˈθreʃə], *n.* batteur en grange, *m.*

threshing [ˈθreʃiŋ], *n.* (*Agric.*) battage, *m.*

threshing machine [ˈθreʃiŋməˈʃiːn], *n.* batteuse, *f.*

threshold [ˈθreʃould], *n.* seuil; (*fig.*) début, *m.*

thrift [θrift], **thriftiness** [ˈθriftinis], *n.* épargne, économie, *f.*

thriftily [ˈθriftili], *adv.* avec économie.

thriftiness [THRIFT].

thriftless [ˈθriftlis], *a.* dépensier, prodigue.

thriftlessly [ˈθriftlisli], *adv.* en prodigue, follement.

thriftlessness [ˈθriftlisnis], *n.* prodigalité, *f.*, gaspillage, *m.*

thrifty [ˈθrifti], *a.* ménager, économe, frugal.

thrill [θril], *v.t.* faire frissonner, faire tressaillir (*de*).—*v.i.* frémir, tressaillir (*de*). tressaillement, frisson, *m.*

thriller [ˈθrilə], *n.* (*fam.*) roman *ou* film à sensation, *m.*

thrilling [ˈθriliŋ], *a.* saisissant, poignant, palpitant.

thrive [θraiv], *v.i. irr.* prospérer; réussir.

thriving [ˈθraiviŋ], *a.* florissant, vigoureux.

throat [θrout], *n.* gorge, *f.*; gosier, *m.*

throaty [ˈθrouti], *a.* guttural (*voix*).

throb [θrɔb], *v.i.* battre; palpiter.—*n.* battement, *m.*

throbbing [ˈθrɔbiŋ], *a.* palpitant, vibrant; lancinant (*douleur*).—*n.* battement; ronflement (*de moteur*), *m.*

throes [θrouz], *n. pl.* douleurs, angoisses, *f.pl.*

thrombosis [θrɔmˈbousis], *n.* thrombose, *f.*

throne [θroun], *n.* trône, *m.*

throng [θrɔŋ], *n.* foule, multitude, *f.*—*v.t.* remplir.—*v.i.* accourir en foule, se presser.

thronged [θrɔŋd], *a.* serré (*personnes*); comble (*salle*).

throstle [θrɔsl], *n.* (*Orn.*) grive chanteuse, *f.*

throttle [θrɔtl], *v.t.* étrangler; étouffer.—*n.* gosier; (*Motor. etc.*) papillon, *m.*

through [θruː], *prep.* à travers; au travers de;

par; dans; par suite de (*à cause de*).—*a.* direct (*train, billet etc.*).—*adv.* directement, droit (*sans s'arrêter*); de part en part; d'un bout à l'autre (*dans toute sa longueur*); jusqu'à la fin, jusqu'au bout; complètement; **to be wet through,** être trempé jusqu'aux os; **to fall through,** manquer, échouer (*projet*); **to go through with (something),** **to see (something) through,** mener (quelque chose) à bonne fin.

throughout [θruːˈaut], *prep.* dans tout, par tout.—*adv.* d'un bout à l'autre; entièrement.

throw [θrou], *v.t. irr.* jeter; lancer; renverser; tordre (*soie*); démonter, désarçonner (*cavalier*); **to throw aside,** jeter de côté; **to throw away,** jeter, rejeter; gaspiller; **to throw off,** se défaire de, ôter (*vêtements*). —*n.* jet, coup; (*fig.*) élan, *m.*

thrower [ˈθrouə], *n.* jeteur, lanceur, *m.*

thrush [θrʌʃ], *n.* (*Orn.*) grive, *f.*

thrust [θrʌst], *v.t. irr.* pousser, enfoncer, fourrer; presser.—*v.i.* porter une botte *ou* un coup (*à*); se fourrer.—*n.* coup, *m.*; (*Fenc.*) botte; (*Arch. etc.*) poussée, *f.*

thud [θʌd], *n.* bruit sourd; son mat, *m.*—*v.i.* faire un bruit sourd.

thug [θʌg], *n.* bandit, *m.*

thumb [θʌm], *n.* pouce, *m.*—*v.t.* manier gauchement; feuilleter; salir (avec les pouces).

thumbnail [ˈθʌmneil], *a.* en raccourci, minuscule.

thumb-screw [ˈθʌmskruː], *n.* vis à ailettes, *f.*; poucettes (*supplice*), *f.pl.*

thumbstall [ˈθʌmstɔːl], *n.* poucier, doigtier, *m.*

thump [θʌmp], *v.t.* frapper du poing, cogner. —*n.* coup, *m.*, bourrade, *f.*

thunder [ˈθʌndə], *n.* tonnerre, *m.*; (*fig.*) foudre, *f.*—*v.i.* tonner; (*fig.*) fulminer.

thunderbolt [ˈθʌndəboult], *n.* foudre, *f.*

thunder-clap [ˈθʌndəklæp], *n.* coup de tonnerre, *m.*

thundering [ˈθʌndəriŋ], *a.* tonnant, foudroyant; (*colloq.*) énorme.

thunderous [ˈθʌndərəs], *a.* orageux; à tout rompre (*applaudissements*).

thunderstorm [ˈθʌndəstɔːm], *n.* orage (accompagné de tonnerre), *m.*

thunderstruck [ˈθʌndəstrʌk], *a.* foudroyé; (*fig.*) atterré.

thundery [ˈθʌndəri], *a.* orageux.

Thursday [ˈθəːzd(e)i], jeudi, *m.*

thus [ðʌs], *adv.* ainsi; **thus far,** jusqu'ici.

thwack [θwæk], *n.* coup, *m.*—*v.t.* frapper, rosser, battre.

thwacking [ˈθwækiŋ], *n.* roulée de coups, raclée, *f.*

thwart [θwɔːt], *v.t.* traverser; (*fig.*) contrarier.—*adv.* en travers.—*n.* banc de rameurs, *m.*

*thy [ðai], *poss.a.* (*also poet.*) ton, *m.*, ta, *f.*, tes, *pl.*

thyme [taim], *n.* thym, *m.*

thyroid [ˈθairɔid], *a.* thyroïde.

*thyself [ðaiˈself], *pron.* (*also poet.*) toi-même, toi; (*reflexive*) te.

tiara [tiˈɑːrə], *n.* tiare, *f.*

Tibet [tiˈbet], le Tibet, *m.*

Tibetan [tiˈbetn], *a.* tibétain.—*n.* tibétain (*langue*); Tibétain (*personne*), *m.*

tibia ['tibiə], *n.* (*Anat.*) tibia (*os de la jambe*), *m.*

tic [tik], *n.* tic, *m.*

tick (1) [tik], *n.* tic-tac (*bruit*), *m.*; marque, *f.*
—*v.t.* marquer; **to tick off**, pointer.—*v.i.*
faire tic-tac, battre (*horloges etc.*).

tick (2) [tik], *n.* coutil (*de matelas*), *m.*

ticket ['tikit], *n.* billet; ticket, *m.*; étiquette,
f.; **return ticket**, billet d'aller et retour;
season ticket, carte d'abonnement, *f.*;
single ticket, billet simple.—*v.t.* étiqueter,
numéroter.

ticket collector ['tikitkəlektə], *n.* contrôleur,
m.

ticket office ['tikitɔfis], *n.* bureau des billets,
guichet, *m.*

ticking (1) ['tikiŋ], *n.* tic-tac, battement (*de
montre etc.*), *m.*

ticking (2) ['tikiŋ], *n.* coutil *m.*, toile à matelas,
f.

tickle [tikl], *v.t., v.i.* chatouiller.

tickling ['tikliŋ], *n.* chatouillement, *m.*

ticklish ['tikliʃ], *a.* chatouilleux; critique,
délicat.

tidal [taidl], *a.* de marée; **tidal harbor**, port
à marée, *m.*; **tidal wave**, raz de marée, *m.*

tide [taid], *n.* marée, *f.*; courant (*flot*), *m.*;
(*fig.*) époque, *f.*

tidily ['taidili], *adv.* proprement, en bon
ordre.

tidiness ['taidinis], *n.* propreté, netteté, *f.*,
bon ordre, *m.*

tidings ['taidiŋz], *n.pl.* nouvelles, *f.pl.*

tidy ['taidi], *a.* rangé, bien arrangé, en ordre,
propre, net.—*v.t.* mettre en ordre; ranger;
arranger (*papiers etc.*).

tie [tai], *v.t.* lier, attacher; nouer, faire (*un
nœud*).—*v.i.* se lier, se nouer; être à égalité.
—*n.* lien; nœud (*knot*); cordon (*de chaussure*), *m.*; cravate; (*Mus.*) liaison; (*Games*)
partie nulle, *f.*

tier [tiə], *n.* rang, *m.*; rangée, *f.*

tierce [tiəs], *n.* (*Cards*) tierce, *f.*

tiff [tif], *n.* petite querelle, pique, *f.*

tiffany ['tifəni], *n.* gaze de soie (*tissu*), *f.*

tiger ['taigə], *n.* tigre, *m.*

tiger lily ['taigəlili], *n.* (*Bot.*) lis tigré, *m.*

tiger moth ['taigəmɔθ], *n.* arctie, *f.*

tight [tait], *a.* serré; raide, tendu (*corde*); trop
étroit (*vêtements*); imperméable; **air-tight**
or **water-tight**, imperméable à l'air *ou* à
l'eau.

tighten [taitn], *v.t.* serrer; tendre (*contraindre*); (*fig.*) resserrer.

tight-fisted ['tait'fistid], *a.* serré, ladre.

tightly ['taitli], *adv.* ferme, fortement; étroitement serré.

tightness ['taitnis], *n.* raideur; étroitesse (*des
vêtements*), *f.*

tight-rope ['taitroup], *n.* corde raide, *f.*;
tight-rope walker, funambule, danseur
de corde, *m.*

tights [taits], *n.pl.* collant, maillot, *m.*

tigress ['taigris], *n.* tigresse, *f.*

tile [tail], *n.* tuile, *f.*; carreau (*for flooring*), *m.*
—*v.t.* couvrir de tuiles; carreler (*une pièce*).

tiler ['tailə], *n.* couvreur (en tuiles), *m.*

tile works ['tailwə:ks], *n.* tuilerie, *f.*

till (1) [til], *prep.* jusqu'à.—*conj.* jusqu'à ce
que (*with subj.*).

till (2) [til], *n.* caisse, *f.*

till (3) [til], *v.t.* labourer, cultiver.

tillable ['tiləbl], *a.* labourable.

tillage ['tilidʒ], *n.* labourage, *m.*

tiller (1) ['tilə], *n.* laboureur, *m.*

tiller (2) ['tilə], *n.* (*Naut.*) barre du gouvernail, *f.*

tilt (1) [tilt], *n.* bâche, banne (*toile*), *f.*

tilt (2) [tilt], *n.* joute; inclinaison, *f.*—*v.t.*
incliner, faire pencher.—*v.i.* jouter; incliner,
pencher.

tilth [tilθ], *n.* labourage, *m.*, culture, *f.*

timber ['timbə], *n.* bois de construction, *m.*—
v.t. boiser.

timbering ['timbəriŋ], *n.* boisage, *m.*

timber-work ['timbəwə:k], *n.* charpente, *f.*

timbrel ['timbrəl], *n.* tambour de basque,
tambourin, *m.*

time [taim], *n.* temps, *m.*; saison, époque, *f.*;
terme (*période*), *m.*; heure (*de la journée*), *f.*;
moment, *m.*; occasion; fois (*répétition*);
époque, *f.*, siècle (*d'histoire*), *m.*; mesure, *f.*;
(*Drilling*) pas, *m.*; **at times**, parfois, de
temps à autre; **in no time**, en un clin d'œil;
in time, à temps; (*Mus.*) en mesure.—*v.t.*
faire à propos; fixer l'heure de; (*Spt.*)
chronométrer; **ill-timed**, inopportun;
well-timed, opportun, à propos.

time bomb ['taimbɔm], *n.* bombe à retardement, *f.*

time fuse ['taimfju:z], *n.* fusée à temps, *f.*

time-honored ['taimɔnəd], *a.* vénérable;
séculaire.

time-keeper ['taimki:pə], *n.* surveillant, contrôleur, *m.*

time lag ['taimlæ:g], *n.* décalage, retard, *m.*

timeliness ['taimlinis], *n.* opportunité, *f.*, à-
propos, *m.*

timely ['taimli], *a.* opportun, à propos.

time-piece ['taimpi:s], *n.* pendule, *f.*

time sheet ['taimʃi:t], *n.* feuille de présence,
f.

timetable ['taimteibl], *n.* indicateur, horaire;
(*Sch.*) emploi du temps, *m.*

time-worn ['taimwɔ:n], *a.* usé par le temps.

timid ['timid], *a.* timide, craintif, peureux.

timidity [ti'miditi], *n.* timidité, *f.*

timing ['taimiŋ], *n.* ajustement, règlement;
réglage (*de montre etc.*), *m.*

timorous ['timərəs], *a.* timoré, timide.

timorously ['timərəsli], *adv.* craintivement.

timorousness ['timərəsnis], *n.* timidité, *f.*

tin [tin], *n.* étain, *m.*; boîte (*de conserve*), *f.*—
v.t. étamer.

tincture ['tiŋktʃə], *n.* teinture, *f.*, extrait, *m.*;
(*fig.*) nuance, *f.*—*v.t.* teindre (*de*).

tinder ['tində], *n.* amadou, *m.*

tinder-box ['tindəbɔks], *n.* boîte à amadou,
f., briquet à silex, *m.*

tinfoil ['tinfɔil], *n.* feuille d'étain, *f.*

tinge [tindʒ], *n.* teinte, nuance, *f.*; soupçon
(*goût*), *m.*—*v.t.* teindre.

tingle [tiŋgl], *v.i.* tinter; picoter, cuire
(*douleur*).

tingling ['tiŋgliŋ], *n.* tintement (*son*); picotement, *m.*

tinker ['tiŋkə], *n.* rétameur, *m.*—*v.t.* rétamer;
raccommoder.

tinkle [tiŋkl], *v.t.* faire tinter.—*v.i.* tinter.—*n.*
tintement, *m.*

tinkling ['tiŋkliŋ], *n.* tintement, *m.*

tinny ['tini], *a.* qui abonde en étain; grêle
(*son*).

tin plate ['tinpleit], *n.* fer-blanc, *m.*

tinsel ['tinsəl], *a.* de clinquant; (*fig.*) faux.—*n.* clinquant; (*fig.*) faux éclat, *m.*
tinsmith ['tinsmiθ], *n.* ferblantier, *m.*
tint [tint], *n.* teinte, nuance, *f.*—*v.t.* teinter, nuancer (*de*).
tin-tack ['tintæk], *n.* semence étamée, *f.*
tinware ['tinwɛə], *n.* ferblanterie, *f.*
tiny ['taini], *a.* tout petit, minuscule.
tip (1) [tip], *n.* bout, *m.*; extrémité, pointe, *f.*—*v.t.* garnir le bout.
tip (2) [tip], *n.* tape (*coup léger*), *f.*; pourboire (*gratuity*); dépotoir (*débris*); (*Spt.*) tuyau, *m.*—*v.t.* donner un pourboire à; décharger (*véhicule*); (*Spt.*) tuyauter.
tippet ['tipit], *n.* pèlerine, palatine (*fourrure*), *f.*
tipple [tipl], *v.i.* boire, pinter.—*n.* boisson, *f.*
tippler ['tiplə], *n.* buveur, *m.*
tippling ['tipliŋ], *n.* ivrognerie, *f.*
tipstaff ['tipstɑ:f], *n.* huissier, *m.*
tipster ['tipstə], *n.* (*Spt.*) tuyauteur, *m.*
tipsy ['tipsi], *a.* gris, ivre.
tiptoe ['tiptou], *n.* pointe du pied, *f.*; **on tip-toe**, sur la pointe des pieds.
tip-top ['tiptɔp], *a.* (*colloq.*) excellent.—*n.* comble, sommet, *m.*
tirade [ti'reid, tai'reid], *n.* tirade, diatribe, *f.*
tire (1) ['taiə], *n.* pneu (*de roue*), *m.*
tire (2) ['taiə], *v.t.* lasser, fatiguer; ennuyer (*moralement*).—*v.i.* se fatiguer, se lasser.
tired ['taiəd], *a.* las, fatigué; ennuyé.
tiredness ['taiədnis], *n.* fatigue, lassitude, *f.*
tiresome ['taiəsəm], *a.* fatigant; ennuyeux (*assommant*).
tiresomeness ['taiəsəmnis], *n.* nature fatigante, *f.*; ennui, *m.*
tissue ['tiʃju:, 'tisju:], *n.* tissu, *m.*—*v.t.* tisser, broder.
tissue paper ['tiʃju:peipə], *n.* papier de soie, *m.*
tit (1) [tit], *n.* mésange (*oiseau*), *f.*
tit (2) [tit], *n.* **tit for tat**, un prêté pour un rendu.
titanic [tai'tænik], *a.* titanique, titanesque.
titbit ['titbit], *n.* morceau friand, *m.*
tithe [taið], *n.* dîme, *f.*, dixième, *m.*—*v.t.* dîmer.
titillate ['titileit], *v.t.*, *v.i.* chatouiller, titiller.
titillation [titi'leiʃən], *n.* titillation, *f.*, chatouillement, *m.*
titlark ['titlɑ:k], *n.* alouette des prés, *f.*
title [taitl], *n.* titre; (*fig.*) droit, document, *m.*—*v.t.* titrer, qualifier (*de*).
titled [taitld], *a.* titré.
title deed ['taitldi:d], *n.* titre (de propriété), *m.*
title page ['taitlpeidʒ], *n.* titre, *m.*
titmouse ['titmaus], *n.* (*pl.* **titmice** ['titmais]) mésange, *f.*
titter ['titə], *v.i.* rire tout bas.—*n.* petit rire étouffé, *m.*
tittle [titl], *n.* point, iota, *m.*
tittle-tattle ['titltætl], *n.* caquetage, bavardage, *m.*—*v.i.* jaser, bavarder.
titular ['titjulə], *a.* titulaire.
titulary ['titjuləri], *a.* de titre.—*n.* titulaire, *m.*, *f.*
to [tu], *prep.* à, de (*before infinitive*); pour, afin de (*dans le but de*); à (*un endroit*); en (*before names of countries of the feminine gender and those of the masculine gender beginning with a vowel*); dans (*followed by* le, la, etc.); vers (*un endroit*); contre (*pari*); près de (*cour royale etc.*); outre, en addition à (*en plus de*);

pour (*faire quelque chose*); en comparaison de, auprès de (*à côté de*); jusqu'à (*telle ou telle limite*); envers (*à l'égard de*).
toad [toud], *n.* crapaud, *m.*
toadish ['toudiʃ], *a.* de crapaud.
toadstool ['toudstu:l], *n.* champignon vénéneux, *m.*
toady ['toudi], *n.* flagorneur, *m.*—*v.t.* flagorner, aduler.
toadyism ['toudiizm], *n.* flagornerie, servilité, *f.*
toast [toust], *n.* rôtie, tranche de pain grillée, *f.*; toast (*bu à la santé de quelqu'un*), *m.*—*v.t.* rôtir, griller; porter un toast à.
toaster ['toustə], *n.* grille-pain, *m.inv.*
toasting fork ['toustiŋfɔ:k], *n.* fourchette à rôties, *f.*
toast-master ['toustmɑ:stə], *n.* préposé aux toasts, *m.*
toast rack ['toustræk], *n.* porte-rôties, porte-toasts, *m.inv.*
tobacco [tə'bækou], *n.* tabac, *m.*
tobacco box [tə'bækoubɔks], *n.* boîte à tabac, *f.*
tobacco jar [tə'bækoudʒɑ:], *n.* pot à tabac, *m.*
tobacconist [tə'bækənist], *n.* marchand de tabac, *m.*; **tobacconist's shop**, bureau de tabac, *m.*
tobacco pouch [tə'bækoupautʃ], *n.* blague à tabac, *f.*
toboggan [tə'bɔgən], *n.* toboggan, *m.*; luge, *f.*—*v.i.* luger.
tocsin ['tɔksin], *n.* tocsin, *m.*
today [tə'dei], *adv.* aujourd'hui.
toddle [tɔdl], *v.i.* trottiner.
toddler ['tɔdlə], *n.* tout petit enfant, *m.*
to-do [tə'du:], *n.* tapage, éclat, *m.*, (*fam.*) histoire, *f.*
toe [tou], *n.* orteil, doigt de pied; devant du sabot, *m.*, pince (*de cheval*), *f.*; bout (*de bas*), *m.*
toe-nail ['touneil], *n.* ongle de pied, *m.*
toffee, toffy ['tɔfi], *n.* caramel au beurre, *m.*
toga ['tougə], *n.* toge, *f.*
together [tə'geðə], *adv.* ensemble, à la fois, en même temps (*simultanément*); de concert (*entre eux*); de suite (*consécutivement*).
Togo ['tougou]. le Togo, *m.*
Togolese [tougo'li:z], *a.* togolais.—*n.* Togolais (*personne*), *m.*
toil [tɔil], *n.* travail dur, labeur, *m.*; peine, *f.*; (*pl.*) piège, *m.*—*v.i.* travailler fort, se fatiguer.
toiler ['tɔilə], *n.* travailleur, *m.*
toilet ['tɔilit], *n.* toilette, *f.*; les toilettes (*dans les hôtels etc.*), *f.pl.*, cabinet d'aisances, *m.*
toiling ['tɔiliŋ], *n.* travail, labeur, *m.*, peine, *f.*
toilsome ['tɔilsəm], *a.* pénible, laborieux, fatigant.
toilsomeness ['tɔilsəmnis], *n.* difficulté, *f.*
token ['toukən], *n.* marque, *f.*; gage (*témoignage*); jeton (*jeux de cartes, téléphone etc.*), *m.*; **book token**, bon de livre, *m.*; **token strike**, grève d'avertissement, *f.*
tolerable ['tɔlərəbl], *a.* tolérable, passable (*assez bon*).
tolerably ['tɔlərəbli], *adv.* passablement, assez.
tolerance ['tɔlərəns], *n.* tolérance, *f.*
tolerant ['tɔlərənt], *a.* tolérant.

total

tolerate ['toləreit], *v.t.* tolérer; supporter.
toleration [tolə'reiʃən], *n.* tolérance, *f.*
toll (1) [toul], *n.* péage; droit; octroi (*impôt municipal*), *m.*
toll (2) [toul], *n.* tintement, glas (*de cloche*), *m.* —*v.t., v.i.* sonner, tinter (*cloche*).
toll-bar ['toulbɑ:], **toll-gate** ['toulgeit], *n.* barrière de péage, *f.*
toll bridge ['toulbridʒ], *n.* pont à péage, *m.*
toll call, see **trunk-call**.
toll-house ['toulhaus], *n.* bureau de péage, *m.*
tolling ['touliŋ], *n.* tintement, *m.*
tomahawk ['toməhɔ:k], *n.* tomahawk, *m.*; hache de guerre, *f.*
tomato [tə'mɑ:tou], *n.* tomate, *f.*
tomb [tu:m], *n.* tombeau, *m.*; tombe, *f.*
tomboy ['tombɔi], *n.* garçon manqué, *m.*
tombstone ['tu:mstoun], *n.* pierre tombale, *f.*
tom-cat ['tomkæt], *n.* matou, *m.*
tome [toum], *n.* tome, volume, *m.*
tomfool [tom'fu:l], *n.* sot, bête, niais, *m.*
tomfoolery [tom'fu:ləri], *n.* sottise, bêtise, niaiserie, *f.*
Tommy gun ['tomigʌn], *n.* mitraillette, *f.*
tomorrow [tə'mɔrou], *adv.* demain.
tomtit ['tomtit], *n.* (*Orn.*) mésange bleue, *f.*
tom-tom ['tomtom], *n.* tam-tam, *m.*
ton [tʌn], *n.* tonne (*1016,04 kg.* (*U.K.*), *907 kg.* (*U.S.*), *f.*
tone [toun], *n.* ton; accent, timbre (*de voix*), *m.*—*v.t.* donner le ton à, régler; (*Mus.*) accorder; (*Phot.*) virer; **to tone down**, adoucir, pallier.
toneless ['tounlis], *a.* sans éclat, sans chaleur (*voix*).
tongs [toŋz], *n.pl.* pincettes; (*Tech.*) tenailles, pinces, *f.pl.*
tongue [tʌŋ], *n.* langue, *f.*; **to hold one's tongue**, se taire.
tongued [tʌŋd], *a.* à langue.
tongue-tied ['tʌŋtaid], *a.* qui a la langue liée; (*fig.*) réduit au silence, muet.
tonic ['tonik], *a.* and *n.* (*Med.*) tonique, fortifiant, *m.*
tonight [tə'nait], *n.* cette nuit, *f.*, ce soir, *m.*
tonnage ['tʌnidʒ], *n.* tonnage, *m.*
tonsil [tonsl], *n.* (*Anat.*) amygdale, *f.*
tonsil(l)itis [tonsi'laitis], *n.* amygdalite, *f.*
tonsure ['tonʃə], *n.* tonsure, *f.*—*v.t.* tonsurer.
too [tu:], *adv.* trop, par trop; aussi, de même, également (*pareillement*); d'ailleurs, de plus; **too much** or **too many**, trop.
tool [tu:l], *n.* outil, instrument; (*fig.*) agent, *m.*
tool chest ['tu:ltʃest], *n.* boîte à outils, *f.*
tooth [tu:θ], *n.* (*pl.* **teeth** [ti:θ]) dent, *f.*; **set of teeth**, râtelier, *m.*; **wisdom tooth**, dent de sagesse.—*v.t.* denteler.
toothache ['tu:θeik], *n.* mal de dents, *m.*
toothbrush ['tu:θbrʌʃ], *n.* brosse à dents, *f.*
toothed ['tu:θt], *a.* à dents; (*Tech.*) denté.
toothless ['tu:θlis], *a.* sans dents, édenté.
tooth-paste ['tu:θpeist], *n.* pâte dentifrice, *f.*, dentifrice, *m.*
tooth-pick ['tu:θpik], *n.* cure-dents, *m.inv.*
tooth-powder ['tu:θpaudə], *n.* poudre dentifrice, *f.*
toothsome ['tu:θsəm], *a.* agréable au goût, savoureux, friand.
toothsomeness ['tu:θsəmnis], *n.* goût agréable, *m.*
top (1) [top], *a.* premier, principal, extrême.—*n.* haut, sommet, *m.*; cime (*de montagne etc.*),

f.; faîte (*d'édifice*), *m.*; (*Naut.*) hune, *f.*; dessus (*de table*), *m.*—*v.t.* couronner, surmonter (*de*).
top (2) [top], *n.* toupie (*jouet*), *f.*
topaz ['toupæz], *n.* topaze, *f.*
top boots ['topbu:ts], *n.pl.* bottes à revers, *f.pl.*
top-coat ['topkout], *n.* pardessus, *m.*
tope (1) [toup], *v.i.* (*colloq.*) pinter, boire.
tope (2) [toup], *n.* chien de mer, *m.*
toper ['toupə], *n.* ivrogne, *m.*, *f.*
top hat ['top'hæt], *n.* chapeau haut de forme, *m.*
topic ['topik], *n.* matière, *f.*, sujet, *m.*
topical ['topikl], *a.* d'actualité; (*Med.*) topique.
topmast ['topmɑ:st], *n.* mât de hune, *m.*
topmost ['topmoust], *a.* le plus haut, le plus élevé.
top-sail [topsl], *n.* hunier, *m.*
topographer [tə'pogrəfə], *n.* topographe, *m.*
topographic [topə'græfik], **topographical** [topə'græfikəl], *a.* topographique.
topography [tə'pogrəfi], *n.* topographie, *f.*
topple [topl], *v.i.* tomber, dégringoler.
topsy-turvy ['topsi'tə:vi], *adv.* sens dessus dessous.
torch [tɔ:tʃ], *n.* torche, *f.*, flambeau, *m.*, lampe de poche, *f.*
torch-bearer ['tɔ:tʃbɛərə], *n.* porte-flambeau, *m.*
toreador [toriə'dɔ:], *n.* toréador, *m.*
torment (1) ['tɔ:ment], *n.* tourment, *m.*, torture, *f.*; supplice, *m.*
torment (2) [tɔ:'ment], *v.t.* tourmenter, torturer.
tormentor [tɔ:'mentə], *n.* tourmenteur, bourreau, *m.*
tornado [tɔ:'neidou], *n.* tornade, *f.*, ouragan, cyclone, *m.*
torpedo [tɔ:'pi:dou], *n.* torpille, *f.*—*v.t.* torpiller.
torpedo boat [tɔ:'pi:doubout], *n.* torpilleur, *m.*
torpid ['tɔ:pid], *a.* engourdi, torpide, inerte.
torpor ['tɔ:pə], *n.* torpeur, apathie, *f.*
torrefaction [tori'fækʃən], *n.* torréfaction, *f.*
torrefy ['tɔrifai], *v.t.* torréfier.
torrent ['tɔrənt], *n.* torrent, *m.*
torrential [tɔ'renʃl], *a.* torrentiel.
torrid ['tɔrid], *a.* brûlant, torride.
torridness ['tɔridnis], **torridity** [tɔ'riditi], *n.* chaleur brûlante, *f.*
torsion ['tɔ:ʃən], *n.* torsion, *f.*
torso ['tɔ:sou], *n.* torse, *m.*
tortoise ['tɔ:təs], *n.* tortue, *f.*
tortoise-shell ['tɔ:təsʃel], *a.* d'écaille.—*n.* écaille de tortue, écaille, *f.*
tortuous ['tɔ:tjuəs], *a.* tortueux, sinueux.
tortuousness ['tɔ:tjuəsnis], *n.* tortuosité, *f.*
torture ['tɔ:tʃə], *n.* torture, *f.*; supplice, *m.*—*v.t.* torturer; (*fig.*) faire souffrir.
torturer ['tɔ:tʃərə], *n.* bourreau, *m.*
toss [tɔs], *n.* jet, lancement, *m.*; **to win the toss**, gagner (à pile ou face).—*v.t.* lancer ou jeter (*en l'air*); ballotter; secouer.—*v.i.* s'agiter.
tossing ['tɔsiŋ], *n.* secousse, *f.*; ballottement, hochement, *m.*
toss-up ['tɔsʌp], *n.* coup de pile ou face, *m.*
total [toutl], *a.* total, complet, entier.—*n.* total, montant, *m.*, somme, *f.*—*v.t.* se monter à.

599

totalitarian [toutæli'tɛəriən], *a.* (*Polit.*) totalitaire.

totalitarianism [toutæli'tɛəriənizm], *n.* totalitarisme, *m.*

totality [tou'tæliti], *n.* totalité, *f.*, montant, tout, *m.*

totalizator ['toutəlaizeitə], *n.* totalisateur, *m.*

totally ['toutəli], *adv.* totalement, tout à fait, entièrement.

totem ['toutəm], *n.* totem, *m.*

totter ['tɔtə], *v.i.* chanceler; (*fig.*) vaciller, trembler.

tottering ['tɔtəriŋ], *a.* chancelant, tremblant. —*n.* chancellement, *m.*

tottery ['tɔtəri], *a.* chancelant.

touch [tʌtʃ], *v.t.* toucher; toucher à (*s'ingérer dans*); émouvoir (*attendrir*); **to touch up**, retoucher.—*v.i.* toucher; se toucher; **to touch at**, aborder à (*navire*); **to touch upon**, effleurer, (*fig.*) faire allusion à.—*n.* le toucher (*sens tactile*); attouchement (*contact*), *m.*; légère attaque (*d'une maladie*), *f.*; (*fig.*) soupçon (*trace*), *m.*; **it was touch and go**, il s'en est fallu de bien peu; **to get in touch with**, se mettre en rapports, entrer en contact avec; **to keep in touch with**, garder le contact avec.

touchiness ['tʌtʃinis], *n.* irascibilité, *f.*

touching ['tʌtʃiŋ], *a.* touchant, émouvant.—*prep.* concernant, au sujet de.

touch-line ['tʌtʃlain], *n.* (*Ftb.*) ligne de touche, *f.*

touchstone ['tʌtʃstoun], *n.* pierre de touche, *f.*

touch-wood ['tʌtʃwud], *n.* amadou, *m.*

touchy ['tʌtʃi], *a.* irritable, susceptible.

tough [tʌf], *a.* dur, raide, résistant; coriace (*viande*); fort (*solide*); difficile.

toughen [tʌfn], *v.t.* durcir.—*v.i.* s'endurcir.

toughish ['tʌfiʃ], *a.* un peu dur.

toughly ['tʌfli], *adv.* durement; vigoureusement.

toughness ['tʌfnis], *n.* raideur; dureté, nature coriace (*viande etc.*); (*fig.*) difficulté, *f.*

tour ['tuə], *n.* tour, voyage, *m.*; randonnée, tournée, *f.*—*v.t.*, *v.i.* visiter (*un pays*); voyager dans (*un pays*); excursionner.

tourism ['tuərizm], *n.* tourisme, *m.*

tourist ['tuərist], *n.* touriste, *m.*, *f.*, voyageur, *m.*; **tourist agency**, bureau de tourisme, *m.*

tournament ['tuənəmənt], *n.* tournoi; concours, *m.*

tourniquet ['tuənikei], *n.* garrot, *m.*

tousle [tauzl], *v.t.* tirailler, chiffonner; **tousled hair**, cheveux ébouriffés, *m.pl.*

tout [taut], *v.i.* racoler.—*n.* racoleur, *m.*

touting ['tautiŋ], *n.* racolage, *m.*

tow [tou], *n.* filasse, étoupe (*chanvre*); remorque, *f.*; **in tow**, à la remorque.—*v.t.* remorquer, touer, haler.

towage ['touidʒ], *n.* remorquage, touage, halage, *m.*

toward, towards [tu'wɔ:d(z)], *prep.* vers, envers; du côté de; à l'égard de (*par respect pour*); sur, environ, vers (*l'heure*).

tow-boat ['toubout], *n.* remorqueur, *m.*

towel ['tauəl], *n.* essuie-mains, *m.inv.*, serviette, *f.*

towelling ['tauəliŋ], *n.* toile pour serviettes, *f.*; tissu-éponge, *m.*

tower ['tauə], *n.* tour, *f.*—*v.i.* s'élever (*au-dessus de*), dominer.

towering ['tauəriŋ], *a.* élevé; dominant; violent.

towing ['touiŋ], *n.* remorque, *f.*; halage (*sur canal*), *m.*

towing-boat ['touiŋbout], [TOW-BOAT].

tow(ing)-line ['tou(iŋ)lain], **tow(ing)-rope** ['tou(iŋ)roup], *n.* cable de remorque, *m.*, remorque, *f.*

tow(ing)-path ['tou(iŋ)pɑ:θ], *n.* chemin de halage, *m.*

town [taun], *n.* ville, *f.*

town clerk ['taun'klɑ:k], *n.* secrétaire de, mairie, *m.*

town council ['taun'kaunsl], *n.* conseil municipal, *m.*

town councilor ['taun'kaunsilə], *n.* conseiller municipal, *m.*

town hall ['taun'hɔ:l], *n.* hôtel de ville, *m.*, mairie, *f.*

town planning ['taun plæniŋ], *n.* urbanisme, *m.*

townsfolk [TOWNSPEOPLE].

township ['taunʃip], *n.* commune, *f.*

townsman ['taunzmən], *n.* (*pl.* **-men** [men]) habitant de la ville, bourgeois, *m.*

townspeople ['taunzpi:pl], **townsfolk** ['taunz fouk], *n.* habitants (de la ville), citadins, *m.pl.*

tow-rope [TOW(ING)-LINE].

toxic ['tɔksik], *a.* toxique.

toxicology [tɔksi'kɔlədʒi], *n.* toxicologie, *f.*

toy [tɔi], *n.* jouet, joujou, *m.*—*v.i.* jouer; folâtrer, s'amuser (*avec*).

trace (1) [treis], *n.* trace, *f.*; tracé (*calque*), *m.*—*v.t.* tracer; calquer (*dessin*); suivre la trace de (*to track*); (*fig.*) remonter à l'origine de.

trace (2) [treis], *n.* (*usu. pl.*) traits (*harnais*), *m.pl.*

traceable ['treisəbl], *a.* que l'on peut tracer.

tracer ['treisə], *n.* traceur; traçoir (*instrument*), *m.*

tracery ['treisəri], *n.* (*Arch.*) réseau, *m.*

trachea [trə'ki:ə], *n.* (*Anat.*) trachée-artère, *f.*

tracing ['treisiŋ], *n.* tracé, tracement; calque, *m.*; **tracing paper**, papier à calquer, *m.*

track [træk], *n.* (*Spt.*) piste, *f.*, chemin (*route*), *m.*; (*Hunt.*) piste; (*Rail.*) voie; (*Astron.*) orbite, *f.*, sillage (*de bateau*), *m.*; **beaten track**, sentier battu, *m.*; (*Cine.*) **sound track**, bande sonore, *f.*—*v.t.* suivre à la piste; haler, remorquer.

tracker ['trækə], *n.* traqueur, *m.*

tracking ['trækiŋ], *n.* action de suivre à la trace, *f.*

trackless ['træklis], *a.* sans trace; sans chemins.

tract [trækt], *n.* étendue; contrée; brochure (*petit livre*), *f.*

tractable ['træktəbl], *a.* traitable, maniable.

tractile ['træktail], *a.* ductile.

traction ['trækʃən], *n.* traction, tension, *f.*

traction engine ['trækʃənendʒin], *n.* locomotive routière, *f.*

tractor ['træktə], *n.* tracteur, *m.*

trade [treid], *n.* commerce, trafic, négoce; métier, *m.*, profession (*vocation*), *f.*; **Board of Trade**, Ministère du Commerce, *m.*; **free trade**, libre-échange, *m.*; (*Comm.*) **trade name**, marque déposée, *f.*—*v.i.* trafiquer, faire le commerce (*de*).

trade-mark ['treidmɑ:k], n. marque de fabrique, f.
trader ['treidə], n. négociant, m.
tradesman ['treidzmən], n. (pl. -men [men]) marchand, boutiquier (détaillant); fournisseur, m.
trade union ['treid 'ju:njən], n. syndicat ouvrier, m.
trade unionism ['treid'ju:njənizm], n. syndicalisme, m.
trade unionist ['treid'ju:njənist], n. syndicaliste, m., f.
trade winds ['treidwindz], n.pl. vents alizés, m.pl.
trading ['treidiŋ], a. marchand, de commerce.—n. négoce, commerce, m.
tradition [trə'diʃən], n. tradition, f.
traditional [trə'diʃənəl], a. traditionnel.
traduce [trə'dju:s], v.t. diffamer, calomnier.
traducer [trə'dju:sə], n. calomniateur, m.
traffic ['træfik], n. trafic; commerce, négoce, m.; circulation (de voitures), f.; (Rail.) mouvement, m.; **traffic jam**, embouteillage; **traffic light**, feu de signalisation. m.—v.i. trafiquer, commercer.
trafficker ['træfikə], n. trafiquant, m.
tragedian [trə'dʒi:diən], n. auteur tragique; tragédien, m.
tragedy ['trædʒədi], n. tragédie, f.
tragic ['trædʒik], **tragical** ['trædʒikəl], a. tragique.
tragi-comedy ['trædʒi'kɔmidi], n. tragi-comédie, f.
tragi-comical ['trædʒi'kɔmikəl], a. tragi-comique.
trail [treil], n. traînée; (Hunt.) piste, f.—v.t. suivre à la piste; traîner (tirer après soi).—v.i. traîner.
trailer ['treilə], n. remorque (bicyclette, camion etc.); (Am.) roulotte, caravane; (Cine.) bande de lancement, f.
train [trein], n. (Rail.) train, m.; suite, f. cortège (personnel), m.; série, f., enchaînement (succession), m.; traînée (de poudre à canon); queue, traîne (de robe), f.; **breakdown train**, train de secours; **freight train**, train de marchandises, m.—v.t. exercer, instruire; dresser, entraîner (cheval etc.); former.—v.i. s'entraîner.
train bearer ['treinbɛərə], n. porte-queue, m.
trainee [trei'ni:], n. stagiaire, m., f.
trainer ['treinə], n. dresseur; entraîneur, m.
training ['treiniŋ], n. éducation, instruction, f.; dressage (de cheval); entraînement (de cheval de course), m.
training ship ['treiniŋʃip], n. vaisseau-école, m.
trait [trei, treit], n. trait, m.
traitor ['treitə], n. traître, m.
traitorous ['treitərəs], a. traître, perfide.
traitorously ['treitərəsli], adv. en traître, perfidement.
traitress ['treitris], n. traîtresse, f.
trajectory [trə'dʒektəri], n. trajectoire, f.
tram(-car) ['træm(kɑ:)], n. tramway, m.
trammel ['træml], n. tramail (filet), m.; entrave (de cheval), f.—v.t. entraver, empêtrer (de).
tramp [træmp], v.t. faire à pied, faire.—v.i. aller à pied, marcher lourdement.—n. randonnée (à pied), f.; bruit de pas (marche pesante); vagabond, m.

trample [træmpl], v.t. fouler (aux pieds).
trampling ['træmpliŋ], n. piétinement, bruit de pas, m.
trance [trɑ:ns], n. extase; (Path.) catalepsie, f.
tranquil ['træŋkwil], a. tranquille.
tranquillity [træŋ'kwiliti], n. tranquillité, f., calme, m.
tranquillize ['træŋkwilaiz], v.t. tranquilliser, calmer.
tranquillizer ['træŋkwilaizə], n. calmant, m.
transact [træn'zækt], v.t. traiter, expédier.
transaction [træn'zækʃən], n. transaction, affaire, f.
transactor [træn'zæktə], n. négociateur, m.
transalpine [træn'zælpain], a. transalpin.
transatlantic [trænzət'læntik], a. transatlantique.
transcend [træn'send], v.t. dépasser, surpasser.
transcendence [træn'sendəns], **transcendency** [træn'sendənsi], n. excellence, transcendance, f.
transcendent [træn'sendənt], a. transcendant.
transcendental [trænsen'dentl], a. transcendantal.
transcribe [træn'skraib], v.t. transcrire, copier.
transcriber [træn'skraibə], n. copiste, m., f., transcripteur, m.
transcript ['trænskript], n. copie, f.
transcription [træn'skripʃən], n. transcription, f.
transept ['trænsept], n. transept, m.
transfer [træns'fə:], v.t. transporter; (Law) transférer.—['trænsfə:], n. copie, f.; (Law) transfert, m.
transferable ['trænsfərəbl], a. transférable, transmissible.
transference ['trænsfərəns], n. transfert, m.
transfiguration [trænsfigju'reiʃən], n. transfiguration, transformation, f.
transfigure [træns'figə], v.t. transfigurer.
transfix [træns'fiks], v.t. transpercer.
transform [træns'fɔ:m], v.t. transformer, changer (en).—v.i. se transformer (en).
transformation [trænsfə'meiʃən], n. transformation, f., changement, m.; **transformation scene**, changement à vue, m.
transformer [træns'fɔ:mə], n. transformateur, m.
transfuse [træns'fju:z], v.t. transfuser.
transfusion [træns'fju:ʒən], n. transfusion, f.
transgress [træns'gres, trænz'gres], v.t. transgresser, enfreindre.—v.i. transgresser, pécher.
transgression [træns'greʃən], n. transgression, infraction, f.
transgressor [træns'gresə], n. pécheur, m., pécheresse, f.
tranship [træn'ʃip], v.t. transborder.
transience ['trænziəns], n. nature transitoire, courte durée, f.
transient ['trænziənt], a. passager, transitoire.
transistor [træn'zistə], n. transistor, transistron, m.
transit ['trænzit], n. passage, m.; **in transit**, en transit.
transition [træn'ziʃən], n. transition, f.
transitional [træn'ziʃənəl], a. de transition.
transitive ['trænzitiv], a. qui passe; (Gram.) transitif.

transitoriness

transitoriness ['trænzitərinis], *n.* nature transitoire, courte durée, *f.*
transitory ['trænzitəri], *a.* transitoire, passager.
translatable [træns'leitəbl], *a.* traduisible.
translate [træns'leit], *v.t.* traduire; transférer (*évêque*).
translation [træns'leiʃən], *n.* traduction; translation (*d'un évêque*), *f.*
translator [træns'leitə], *n.* traducteur, *m.*
translucent [trænz'lju:sənt], *a.* translucide.
transmarine [trænzmə'ri:n], *a.* d'outremer.
transmigrate ['trænzmaigreit], *v.i.* passer d'un corps dans un autre; émigrer.
transmigration [trænzmai'greiʃən], *n.* transmigration; métempsyc(h)ose (*des âmes*), *f.*
transmissible [trænz'misibl], *a.* transmissible.
transmission [trænz'miʃən], *n.* transmission, *f.* [(*Motor.*) see **gear-box**]
transmit [trænz'mit], *v.t.* transmettre, envoyer; (*Rad.*) émettre.
transmitter [trænz'mitə], *n.* (*Rad.*) émetteur, *m.*
transmutable [trænz'mju:təbl], *a.* transmuable.
transmutation [trænzmju'teiʃən], *n.* transmutation, *f.*; changement (*de couleur*), *m.*
transmute [trænz'mju:t], *v.t.* transmuer, convertir.
transom ['trænsəm], *n.* traverse (*de fenêtre*), imposte, *f.*
transparency [træns'pɛərənsi], *n.* transparence; (*Phot.*) diapositive, *f.*
transparent [træns'pɛərənt], *a.* transparent.
transparently [træns'pɛərəntli], *adv.* avec transparence; évidemment.
transpire [træns'paiə, trænz'paiə], *v.i.* transpirer; (*fig.*) avoir lieu, arriver.
transplant [træns'plɑ:nt, trænz'plɑ:nt], *v.t.* transplanter; (*fig.*) déplacer.
transplanting [træns'plɑ:ntiŋ, trænz'plɑ:ntiŋ], *n.* transplantation, *f.*
transport ['trænspɔ:t], *n.* transport, *m.*—[træns'pɔ:t], *v.t.* transporter; déporter (*forçat*).
transportation [trænspɔ:'teiʃən], *n.* transport, *m.*; déportation (*des forçats*), *f.*
transporter [træns'pɔ:tə], *n.* entrepreneur de transports; (*pont*) transbordeur, *m.*
transporting [træns'pɔ:tiŋ], *a.* ravissant, transportant.
transposal [træns'pouzl], *n.* transposition, *f.*
transpose [træns'pouz], *v.t.* transposer.
transubstantiation [trænsəbstænʃi'eiʃən], *n.* transsubstantiation, *f.*
Transvaal ['trænzvɑ:l], *the.* le Transvaal, *m.*
transversal [trænz'və:sl], *a.* transversal.
transversely [trænz'və:sli], *adv.* en travers.
transverse [trænz'və:s], *a.* transverse, transversal.
trap [træp], *n.* trappe, *f.*, piège, *m.*; carriole (*véhicule*), *f.*—*v.t.* prendre au piège, attraper.
trap door ['træpdɔ:], *n.* trappe, *f.*
trapeze [trə'pi:z], *n.* trapèze, *m.*
trapper ['træpə], *n.* trappeur, *m.*
trappings ['træpiŋz], *n.pl.* harnais, *m.*; (*fig.*) parure, *f.*, atours, *m.pl.*
traps [træps], *n.pl.* bagages, *m.pl.*
trash [træʃ], *n.* rebut, *m.*; camelote, *f.*; fatras (*écrits*), *m.*

trashy ['træʃi], *a.* de rebut, sans valeur.
travel [trævl], *v.t.* parcourir; faire (*distance etc.*).—*v.i.* voyager, être en voyage.—*n.* voyage, *m.*
traveller ['trævlə], *n.* voyageur; (*Comm.*) commis voyageur, *m.*; **traveller's check**, chèque de voyage, *m.*
travelling ['trævliŋ], *a.* voyageur, de voyage; ambulant (*itinérant*); **travelling expenses**, frais de déplacement, *m.pl.*; **travelling-case**, nécessaire de voyage, *m.*—*n.* voyage, *m.*, voyages, *m.pl.*
travelogue ['trævləg], *n.* film de tourisme, *m.*
traverse ['trævəs], *a.* oblique.—*n.* traverse, *f.*—*v.t.* traverser; (*Law*) nier.
travesty ['trævəsti], *n.* travestissement, *m.*; parodie, *f.*—*v.t.* travestir, parodier.
trawl [trɔ:l], *n.* chalut (*filet*), *m.*—*v.i.* pêcher au chalut.
trawler ['trɔ:lə], *n.* chalutier, *m.*
trawling ['trɔ:liŋ], *n.* pêche au chalut, *f.*
tray [trei], *n.* plateau, *m.*
treacherous ['tretʃərəs], *a.* traître, perfide.
treacherously ['tretʃərəsli], *adv.* en traître.
treachery ['tretʃəri], *n.* trahison, perfidie, *f.*
treacle [tri:kl], *n.* mélasse, *f.*
tread [tred], *v.t. irr.* fouler, écraser.—*v.i.* mettre le pied, marcher (*sur*); se poser (*pieds*).—*n.* pas, *m.*; marche (*d'escalier*); chape (*d'un pneu*), *f.*
treading ['trediŋ], *n.* pas, *m.*; marche, *f.*; foulage (*de raisins etc.*), *m.*
treadle [tredl], *n.* marche; pédale, *f.*
treadmill ['tredmil], *n.* trépigneuse, *f.*
treason [tri:zn], *n.* trahison, *f.*; **high treason**, lèse-majesté, *f.*
treasonable ['tri:znəbl], *a.* de trahison.
treasonably ['tri:znəbli], *adv.* par trahison, traîtreusement.
treasure ['treʒə], *n.* trésor, *m.*—*v.t.* garder, priser.
treasurer ['treʒərə], *n.* trésorier, *m.*
treasure-trove ['treʒətrouv], *n.* trésor trouvé, *m.*
treasury ['treʒəri], *n.* trésor, trésor public, *m.*, finances, *f.pl.*, trésorerie, *f.*
treat [tri:t], *n.* régal, festin, (*fig.*) plaisir, *m.*—*v.t.* traiter; régaler (*de*).—*v.i.* traiter (*de*); négocier.
treatise ['tri:tis], *n.* traité (*de ou sur*), *m.*
treatment ['tri:tmənt], *n.* traitement, *m.*
treaty ['tri:ti], *n.* traité, *m.*
treble [trebl], *a.* triple; (*Mus.*) de dessus, soprano.—*n.* triple; (*Mus.*) dessus, soprano, *m.*—*v.t.*, *v.i.* tripler.
trebling ['trebliŋ], *n.* triplement, *m.*
trebly ['trebli], *adv.* triplement, trois fois.
tree [tri:], *n.* arbre; embauchoir (*pour botte*), *m.*; (*fig.*) croix, *f.*
trefoil ['tri:foil], *n.* trèfle, *m.*
trellis ['trelis], *n.* treillis, treillage, *m.*
trellised ['trelist], *a.* treillissé.
tremble [trembl], *v.i.* trembler.
trembling ['trembliŋ], *a.* tremblant, tremblotant.—*n.* tremblement, *m.*
tremendous [tri'mendəs], *a.* terrible, épouvantable.
tremendously [tri'mendəsli], *adv.* terriblement.
tremor ['tremə], *n.* tremblement, *m.*; secousse, *f.*

tremulous ['tremjuləs], *a.* tremblant, (*fig.*) craintif.
tremulously ['tremjuləsli], *adv.* en tremblant, en tremblotant.
tremulousness ['tremjuləsnis], *n.* tremblotement, *m.*
trench [trentʃ], *n.* fossé, *m.*, tranchée; rigole (*entre sillons etc.*), *f.*—*v.t.* creuser.
trenchancy ['trentʃənsi], *n.* causticité, *f.*
trenchant ['trentʃənt], *a.* tranchant, caustique.
trencher ['trentʃə], *n.* tranchoir, tailloir, *m.*
trencherman ['trentʃəmən], *n.* (*pl.* **-men** [men]) gros mangeur, *m.*
trend [trend], *n.* direction, tendance, *f.*—*v.i.* se diriger, tendre (*vers*).
trepan [trə'pæn], *n.* (*Surg.*) trépan, *m.*—*v.t.* trépaner.
trepanning [trə'pæniŋ], *n.* trépanation, *f.*
trepidation [trepi'deiʃən], *n.* trépidation, *f.*
trespass ['trespəs], *n.* violation de propriété, *f.*, délit, *m.*; (*Scripture*) offense, *f.*—*v.i.* violer la propriété; empiéter (*sur*); (*Scripture*) pécher; transgresser.
trespasser ['trespəsə], *n.* violateur du droit de propriété, *m.*; (*Scripture*) pécheur, *m.*, pécheresse, *f.*
tress [tres], *n.* tresse, boucle, *f.*
trestle [tresl], *n.* tréteau, *m.*
trestle bed ['treslbed], *n.* lit de sangle, *m.*
triad ['traiæd], *n.* triade, *f.*
trial ['traiəl], *a.* d'essai.—*n.* expérience, épreuve, *f.*, essai; (*Law*) procès, *m.*
triangle ['traiæŋgl], *n.* triangle, *m.*
triangular [trai'æŋgjulə], *a.* triangulaire.
tribal [traibl], *a.* tribal.
tribe [traib], *n.* tribu, peuplade; (*fig.*) race, *f.*
tribulation [tribju'leiʃən], *n.* tribulation, *f.*
tribunal [trai'bju:nl], *n.* tribunal, *m.*
tribune ['tribju:n], *n.* (*Rom. Hist.*) tribun, *m.*; tribune (*estrade*), *f.*
tributary ['tribjutəri], *a.* tributaire.—*n.* tributaire; affluent (*rivière*), *m.*
tribute ['tribju:t], *n.* tribut; (*fig.*) hommage, *m.*
trice (1) [trais], *n.* **in a trice**, en un clin d'œil.
trice (2) [trais], *v.t.* (*Naut.*) hisser.
trick [trik], *n.* tour, artifice, *m.*; (*Cards*) levée; ruse, finesse, *f.*; tic (*habitude*), *m.*; **nasty trick**, vilain tour; **to play someone a trick**, faire une niche *ou* jouer un tour à quelqu'un.—*v.t.* duper; tricher (*en jouant*); **to trick out**, parer, orner.
trickery ['trikəri], *n.* tromperie, fourberie, tricherie, *f.*
trickish ['trikiʃ], *a.* trompeur, fourbe, fin.
trickle [trikl], *v.i.* suinter, dégoutter.
trickling ['trikliŋ], *n.* écoulement, *m.*
trickster ['trikstə], *n.* fourbe, escroc, *m.*
tricky ['triki], *a.* fourbe, rusé; (*fig.*) compliqué; délicat (*à manier*).
tricolor ['traikʌlə], *n.* drapeau tricolore, *m.*
tricolored ['traikʌləd], *a.* tricolore.
tricycle ['traisikl], *n.* tricycle, *m.*
trident ['traidənt], *n.* trident, *m.*
tried [traid], *a.* éprouvé.
triennial [trai'eniəl], *a.* triennal.—*n.* (*Bot.*) plante triennale, *f.*
triennially [trai'eniəli], *adv.* tous les trois ans.
trier ['traiə], *n.* (*Law*) juge; arbitre, *m.*; (*fig.*) épreuve, pierre de touche, *f.*

trifle [traifl], *n.* bagatelle; (*Cook.*) sorte de charlotte russe, *f.*—*v.i.* badiner; **to trifle with**, plaisanter avec, se moquer de.
trifler ['traiflə], *n.* personne frivole, *f.*
trifling ['traifliŋ], *a.* de rien, insignifiant, frivole.—*n.* frivolité, *f.*, badinage, *m.*
trigamy ['trigəmi], *n.* trigamie, *f.*
trigger ['trigə], *n.* détente, *f.*
trigonometry [trigə'nɔmətri], *n.* trigonométrie, *f.*
trilateral [trai'lætərəl], *a.* trilatéral.
trill [tril], *n.* trille, *m.*—*v.i.* triller.
trillion ['triljən], *n.* (*since* 1948) trillion; (*before* 1948) quintillion, *m.*
trilogy ['trilədʒi], *n.* trilogie, *f.*
trim [trim], *a.* soigné, coquet, bien mis, bien arrangé.—*n.* bon ordre, *m.*; assiette (*de bateau*), *f.*; orientement (*des voiles*); arrimage (*de cale*), *m.*—*v.t.* arranger, mettre en ordre; garnir, parer (*de*); émonder, tailler (*couper*); (*Naut.*) arrimer (*cargaison*); orienter (*voiles*). —*v.i.* (*Polit. slang*) balancer entre deux partis.
trimly ['trimli], *adv.* bien, gentiment, proprement.
trimmer ['trimə], *n.* (*Polit.*) opportuniste, *m.*, *f.*; (*Naut.*) soutier, *m.*
trimming ['trimiŋ], *n.* garniture; semonce; (*pl.*) parure (*de viande*), *f.*
trimness ['trimnis], *n.* air soigné, bon ordre, *m.*
Trinidad ['trinidæd]. (Île de la) Trinité, *f.*
Trinity ['triniti], *n.* Trinité, *f.*
trinket ['triŋkit], *n.* petit bijou, *m.*, breloque. *f.*
trinomial [trai'noumiəl], *a.* and *n.* trinôme, *m.*
trio ['tri:ou], *n.* trio, *m.*
trip [trip], *v.t.* renverser, faire tomber.—*v.i.* trébucher, faire un faux pas; fourcher (*la langue*); courir légèrement.—*n.* croc-en-jambe, faux pas, *m.*; excursion, *f.*, tour, voyage, *m.*
tripe [traip], *n.* tripes, *f.pl.*
triple [tripl], *a.* triple.—*v.t.* tripler.
triplet ['triplit], *n.* (*Pros.*) tercet; (*Mus.*) triolet, *m.*; (*pl.*) triplés, *m.pl.*
triplicate ['triplikit], *a.* triplé.—*n.* triplicata (*copie*), *m.*
tripod ['traipɔd], *n.* trépied, *m.*
tripper ['tripə], *n.* (*colloq.*) excursionniste, *m.*, *f.*
tripping ['tripiŋ], *a.* agile, léger.—*n.* croc en jambe, faux pas, *m.*; erreur, *f.*; pas léger, *m.*
trireme ['trairi:m], *n.* trirème, *f.*
trisect [trai'sekt], *v.t.* couper en trois.
trisyllabic [traisi'læbik], *a.* trissyllabe.
trisyllable [trai'siləbl], *n.* trissyllabe, *m.*
trite [trait], *a.* usé, banal, rebattu.
triteness ['traitnis], *n.* nature banale, trivialité, *f.*
Triton ['traitən]. Triton, *m.*
triumph ['traiəmf], *n.* triomphe, *m.*—*v.i.* triompher.
triumphal [trai'ʌmfl], *a.* triomphal.
triumphant [trai'ʌmfənt], *a.* triomphant.
triumphantly [trai'ʌmfəntli], *adv.* en triomphe.
triumvir [trai'ʌmvə], *n.* triumvir, *m.*
triumvirate [trai'ʌmvərit], *n.* triumvirat, *m.*
trivet ['trivit], *n.* trépied, *m.*

trivial

trivial ['triviəl], *a.* banal, insignifiant, sans importance.
triviality [trivi'æliti], *n.* insignifiance; banalité, *f.*
troat [trout], *n.* bramement, *m.*—*v.t.* bramer, raire (*cerf*).
trochaic [tro'keiik], *a.* trochaïque.
trochee ['trouki], *n.* trochée, *m.*
Trojan ['troud3ən], *a.* troyen.—*n.* Troyen, *m.*
troll [troul], *v.t.* rouler, tourner.
trolley, trolly ['troli], *n.* fardier, chariot; (*Elec.*) trolley, *m.*; **dinner trolley**, table roulante, *f.* [see **tram(-car)**]
trolley bus ['trolibʌs], *n.* trolleybus, *m.*
trollop ['trolop], *n.* souillon, *f.*
trombone [trom'boun], *n.* trombone, *m.*
troop [tru:p], *n.* troupe, bande, *f.*—*v.i.* s'attrouper, s'assembler.
trooper ['tru:pə], *n.* (*Mil.*) soldat à cheval, cavalier, *m.*
trophy ['troufi], *n.* trophée, *m.*
tropic ['tropik], *n.* tropique, *m.*
tropical ['tropikəl], *a.* tropical, des tropiques.
trot [trot], *n.* trot, *m.*—*v.i.* trotter, aller au trot; trottiner (*enfant*).
troth [trouθ], *n.* foi, *f.*; **by my troth !** ma foi!
trotter ['trotə], *n.* cheval de trot, trotteur, *m.*; (*pl.*) pieds de mouton, pieds de cochon, *m.pl.*
trotting ['trotiŋ], *a.* trotteur.—*n.* trot, *m.*
troubadour ['tru:bəduə], *n.* troubadour, *m.*
trouble [trʌbl], *v.t.* agiter; troubler, déranger (*gêner*); tourmenter, affliger (*faire souffrir*); inquiéter (*préoccuper*).—*v.i.* s'inquiéter, se donner la peine (*de*).—*n.* trouble, *m.*; peine (*effort*), affliction, *f.*, souci, chagrin (*tristesse*); ennui (*difficulté*), *m.*; **it is not worth the trouble**, ce n'est pas la peine.
troubled [trʌbld], *a.* inquiet, agité; trouble (*eau etc.*).
troublesome ['trʌblsəm], *a.* ennuyeux, incommode; fatigant, fâcheux.
troublesomeness ['trʌblsəmnis], *n.* ennui, embarras, *m.*, gêne, *f.*
***troublous** ['trʌbləs], *a.* troublé, agité, orageux.
trough [trof], *n.* auge, huche, *f.*; (*Cook.*) pétrin; auget, abreuvoir (*pour boire*), *m.*
trounce [trauns], *v.t.* rosser, étriller.
trouncing ['traunsiŋ], *n.* raclée, *f.*, étrillage, *m.*
trouser-press ['trauzəpres], *n.* presse-pantalon, *m.*
trousers ['trauzəz], *n.pl.* pantalon, *m.*
trousseau ['tru:sou], *n.* trousseau, *m.*
trout [traut], *n.* truite, *f.*
trowel ['trauəl], *n.* truelle, *f.*
Troy [troi], Troie, *f.*
troy weight ['troiweit], *n.* troy (*poids de douze onces à la livre*), *m.*
truant ['tru:ənt], *n.* fainéant, vagabond, *m.*; **to play truant**, faire l'école buissonnière.
truce [tru:s], *n.* trêve, *f.*
truck [trʌk], *n.* fardier, chariot (*charrette*); (*Am.*) camion; (*Rail.*) wagon, *m.*—*v.i.* troquer.
truckle [trʌkl], *n.* roulette, *f.*—*v.i.* ramper, s'abaisser (*devant*).
truckle bed ['trʌklbed], *n.* grabat, *m.*.
truckling ['trʌkliŋ], *n.* soumission, *f.*, abaissement, *m.*

truculence ['trʌkjuləns], *n.* férocité, truculence, *f.*
truculent ['trʌkjulənt], *a.* brutal, féroce, farouche.
trudge [trʌdʒ], *n.* marche pénible, *f.*—*v.i.* clopiner, marcher péniblement.
true [tru:], *a.* vrai, véritable; fidèle (*véridique*); exact (*juste*); loyal (*honnête*); droit (*vertueux*); **to come true**, se réaliser.—*int.* c'est vrai! c'est juste!—*adv.* juste (*précisément*).—*v.t.* ajuster.
true-bred ['tru:bred], *a.* de bonne race, pur sang; (*fig.*) accompli.
true-hearted ['tru:'ha:tid], *a.* au cœur sincère.
trueness ['tru:nis], *n.* fidélité; justesse, *f.*
truffle [trʌfl], *n.* truffe, *f.*; **to stuff with truffles**, truffer.
truism ['tru:izm], *n.* truisme, *m.*
truly ['tru:li], *adv.* vraiment, véritablement.
trump [trʌmp], *n.* trompe, trompette, *f.*; (*Cards.*) atout, *m.*—*v.t.* jouer atout, couper.
trumpery ['trʌmpəri], *a.* sans valeur, mesquin.—*n.* rebut, *m.*, blague, *f.*
trumpet ['trʌmpit], *n.* trompette, *f.*—*v.t.* proclamer.—*v.t.* jouer atout, couper.
trumpet call ['trʌmpitkɔ:l], *n.* coup de trompette, *m.*
trumpeter ['trʌmpitə], *n.* trompette, *m.*
truncate [trʌŋ'keit], *v.t.* tronquer.
truncheon ['trʌntʃən], *n.* bâton, *m.*; matraque, *f.*
trundle [trʌndl], *v.t.* rouler.
trunk [trʌŋk], *n.* tronc, *m.*; malle (*boîte*); trompe (*d'éléphant*), *f.*; coffre (*d'auto*), *m.*
trunk call ['trʌŋkkɔ:l], *n.* (*Teleph.*) appel interurbain, *m.*
trunk road ['trʌŋkroud], *n.* route à grande circulation, *f.*
trunnion ['trʌnjən], *n.* tourillon, *m.*
truss [trʌs], *n.* botte (*de foin etc.*), *f.*; paquet; (*Surg.*) bandage herniaire, *m.*—*v.t.* trousser (*une poule*); lier (*foin*).
trust [trʌst], *n.* confiance (*en*), *f.*; dépôt, *m.*; garde (*charge*), *f.*; crédit; (*Law*) fidéicommis; (*Comm.*) trust, syndicat, *m.*—*v.t.* se fier à, se confier à; faire crédit à (*en matière d'argent*).—*v.i.* avoir confiance (*en* ou *dans*); s'attendre (*à*).
trust deed ['trʌstdi:d], *n.* acte fiduciaire, *m.*
trusted ['trʌstid], *a.* de confiance.
trustee [trʌs'ti:], *n.* gardien, *m.*, dépositaire; (*Law*) fidéicommissaire, *m.*, *f.*
trusteeship [trʌs'ti:ʃip], *n.* administration; tutelle, *f.*, (*Law*) fidéicommis, *m.*
trustiness ['trʌstinis], *n.* fidélité, loyauté, *f.*
trusting ['trʌstiŋ], *a.* plein de confiance.
trustworthiness ['trʌstwə:ðinis], *n.* fidélité (*personne*); exactitude (*des nouvelles etc.*), *f.*
trustworthy ['trʌstwə:ði], *a.* digne de confiance; exact (*nouvelles*).
trusty ['trʌsti], *a.* sûr, fidèle, loyal.
truth [tru:θ], *n.* vérité, *f.*, vrai, *m.*; **to tell the truth . . .**, à vrai dire . . . .
truthful ['tru:θful], *a.* véridique, vrai.
truthfully ['tru:θfuli], *adv.* véridiquement, avec vérité.
truthfulness ['tru:θfulnis], *n.* véracité, *f.*
try [trai], *v.t.* essayer, mettre à l'épreuve; tenter (*se prêter à*); (*Law*) juger.—*v.i.* essayer, tâcher (*de*).—*n.* essai, *m.*

604

trying ['traiiŋ], *a.* difficile, pénible.

*tryst [traist], *n.* rendez-vous, *m.*

Tsar [zɑ:], *n.* Tsar, *m.*

Tsarina [zɑ:'ri:nə], *n.* Tsarine, *f.*

tsetse ['tsetsi], *n.* mouche tsé-tsé, *f.*

tub [tʌb], *n.* cuve, *f.*, baquet; bain (*moderne*), *m.*—*v.t.* encuver; (*Gard.*) encaisser.

tuba ['tju:bə], *n.* tuba, *m.*; contrebasse à vent, *f.*

tubby ['tʌbi], *a.* gros, obèse.

tube [tju:b], *n.* tube; (*Anat.*) conduit, canal; (*Rail.*) métro, *m.*; **inner tube**, chambre à air, *f.*; (*Rad.*) lampe, *f.*

tuber ['tju:bə], *n.* tubercule, *m.*

tubercular [tju'bə:kjulə], *a.* tuberculeux.

tuberculosis [tjubə:kju'lousis], *n.* tuberculose, *f.*

tuberose ['tju:bərous], *a.* tubéreux.—*n.* tubéreuse, *f.*

tuberous ['tju:bərəs], *a.* tubéreux.

tubular ['tju:bjulə], *a.* tubulaire.

tuck [tʌk], *n.* pli, *m.*—*v.t.* plisser; serrer; retrousser.

tucker ['tʌkə], *n.* chemisette, collerette, *f.*

Tuesday ['tju:zd(e)i]. mardi, *m.*; *Shrove Tuesday*, mardi gras.

tuft [tʌft], *n.* touffe (*d'herbe* ou *de cheveux*); huppe (*d'oiseau*), *f.*

tufted ['tʌftid], *a.* touffu; huppé (*oiseau*).

tug [tʌg], *v.t.* tirer avec effort; remorquer (*to tow*).—*n.* tiraillement; remorqueur (*bateau*), *m.*

tuition [tju'iʃən], *n.* instruction, *f.*, enseignement, *m.*; frais d'inscription, *m.*

tulip ['tju:lip], *n.* tulipe, *f.*

tulle [tju:l], *n.* tulle, *m.*

tumble [tʌmbl], *n.* culbute, chute, *f.*—*v.i.* culbuter.—*v.i.* tomber; rouler (*descendre en roulant*); dégringoler (*se tourner*).

tumbledown ['tʌmbldaun], *a.* croulant, délabré.

tumbler ['tʌmblə], *n.* verre sans pied; gobelet; culbutant (*pigeon*), *m.*

tumblerful ['tʌmbləful], *n.* plein un grand verre, *m.*

tumbril ['tʌmbril], **tumbrel** ['tʌmbrəl], *n.* tombereau, *f.*

tumefaction [tju:mi'fækʃən], *n.* tuméfaction, *f.*

tumefy ['tju:mifai], *v.t.* tuméfier.—*v.i.* se tuméfier.

tumid ['tju:mid], *a.* enflé, gonflé; (*fig.*) boursouflé.

tumidity [tju'miditi], **tumidness** ['tju:mid nis], *n.* enflure; (*fig.*) turgescence, *f.*

tumor ['tju:mə], *n.* tumeur, *f.*

tumular ['tju:mjulə], *a.* en monticule.

tumult ['tju:mʌlt], *n.* tumulte; trouble, *m.*

tumultuous [tju'mʌltjuəs], *a.* tumultueux, turbulent, agité.

tumultuousness [tju'mʌltjuəsnis], *n.* turbulence, *f.*

tun [tʌn], *n.* tonneau, fût, *m.*; cuve, *f.*

tunable ['tju:nəbl], *a.* accordable.

tundra ['tundrə], *n.* toundra, *f.*

tune [tju:n], *n.* air; accord, *m.*; (*fig.*) harmonie, humeur, *f.*; **in tune**, d'accord; **out of tune**, faux.—*v.t.* accorder, mettre d'accord.—*v.i.* (*Rad.*) **to tune in**, accrocher (*un poste*).

tuneful ['tju:nful], *a.* harmonieux, mélodieux.

tuneless ['tju:nlis], *a.* discordant.

tuner ['tju:nə], *n.* accordeur, *m.*

tungsten ['tʌŋstən], *n.* tungstène, *m.*

tunic ['tju:nik], *n.* tunique, *f.*

tuning ['tju:niŋ], *n.* accord, *m.*, action d'accorder, *f.*

tuning fork ['tju:niŋfɔ:k], *n.* diapason, *m.*

tuning hammer ['tju:niŋhæmə], *n.* accordoir, *m.*

Tunisia [tju'niziə]. la Tunisie, *f.*

Tunisian [tju'niziən], *a.* tunisien.—*n.* Tunisien (*personne*), *m.*

tunnel [tʌnl], *n.* tunnel, passage souterrain, *m.*—*v.t.* percer un tunnel dans.

tunnelling ['tʌnəliŋ], *n.* construction de tunnels, *f.*

tunny ['tʌni], *n.* (*Ichth.*) thon, *m.*

turban ['tə:bən], *n.* turban, *m.*

turbid ['tə:bid], *a.* trouble, bourbeux.

turbidity [tə:'biditi], **turbidness** ['tə:bidnis], *n.* état bourbeux, état trouble, *m.*

turbine ['tə:bin, 'tə:bain], *n.* turbine, *f.*

turbo-prop ['tə:bɔprɔp], *a.* (*Av.*) à turbopropulseur.

turbot ['tə:bət], *n.* turbot, *m.*

turbulence ['tə:bjuləns], **turbulency** ['tə:bjulənsi], *n.* turbulence, *f.*, tumulte, *m.*

turbulent ['tə:bjulənt], *a.* tumultueux, turbulent.

turbulently ['tə:bjuləntli], *adv.* tumultueusement.

tureen [tju'ri:n], *n.* soupière, *f.*

turf [tə:f], *n.* gazon, *m.*; motte de gazon; tourbe (*combustible*), *f.*; (*fig.*) turf, *m.*—*v.t.* gazonner.

turfing ['tə:fiŋ], *n.* gazonnement, *m.*

turf-moss ['tə:fmɔs], **turf-pit** ['tə:fpit], *n.* tourbière, *f.*

turfy ['tə:fi], *a.* gazonné; tourbeux.

turgid ['tə:dʒid], *a.* gonflé; boursouflé.

turgidity [tə'dʒiditi], **turgidness** ['tə:dʒid nis], *n.* turgescence; (*fig.*) emphase (*de style*), *f.*

Turk [tə:k], *n.* Turc (*personne*), *m.*

Turkey ['tə:ki]. la Turquie, *f.*

turkey ['tə:ki], *n.* dindon, *m.*; **hen turkey**, dinde, *f.*

Turkish ['tə:kiʃ], *a.* de Turquie, turc.—*n.* turc (*langue*), *m.*

turmoil ['tə:mɔil], *n.* tumulte, *m.*, agitation, *f.*

turn [tə:n], *v.t.* tourner, faire tourner; faire pencher (*la balance*); retourner (*vêtement etc.*); changer, convertir (*transformer*); traduire (*en une autre langue*); soulever (*l'estomac*); émousser (*le tranchant*); (*fig.*) rouler (*dans la tête*); **to turn aside**, détourner, écarter (*de*); **to turn away**, renvoyer, congédier; **to turn back**, faire retourner; **to turn down**, rabattre (*un col*); refuser; **to turn in**, tourner en dedans; **to turn into**, changer en; **to turn off**, couper (*vapeur*), fermer (*robinet*); **to turn on**, donner (*vapeur*), ouvrir (*robinet*); **to turn out**, mettre dehors; éteindre (*lumière*); **to turn over**, retourner, feuilleter (*pages d'un livre*); **to turn tail**, prendre la fuite; **to turn up**, retrousser.—*v.i.* tourner, se tourner; se retourner (*vers*); se détourner (*s'écarter*); se changer (*en*); devenir, se faire; **to turn back**, rebrousser chemin; **to turn from**, s'éloigner de; **to turn in**, se coucher (*aller au lit*); **to turn round**, tourner, se turncoat

tourner, se retourner; *to turn to*, s'adresser
à; *to turn up*, se retrousser; arriver *(se
passer)*.—*n.* tour; coude, détour *(tournant)*;
service; changement, *m.*; occasion; tournure
(d'esprit), *f.*; trait *(de balance)*, *m.*; *a bad
turn*, un mauvais tour; *a good turn*, un
service; *by turns*, *in turns*, à tour de
rôle.
turncoat ['tə:nkout], *n.* renégat, *m.*
turn-cock ['tə:nkɔk], *n.* fontainier, *m.*
turner ['tə:nə], *n.* tourneur, *m.*
turnery ['tə:nəri], *n.* art du tourneur, *m.*
turning ['tə:niŋ], *n.* tournant *(de route etc.)*;
(Carp.) tournage, *m.*
turning-lathe ['tə:niŋleið], *n.* tour, *m.*
turning point ['tə:niŋpoint], *n.* point décisif,
moment critique, *m.*
turnip ['tə:nip], *n.* navet, *m.*
turnkey ['tə:nki:], *n.* guichetier, porte-clefs,
m.
turn-out ['tə:naut], *n.* équipage, *m.*; tenue, *f.*
turn-over ['tə:nouvə], *n.* chiffre d'affaires;
chausson *(pâte)*, *m.*
turnpike ['tə:npaik], *n.* barrière de péage, *f.*;
autoroute, *f.*
turnspit ['tə:nspit], *n.* tournebroche, *m.*
turnstile ['tə:nstail], *n.* tourniquet, *m.*
turn-table ['tə:nteibl], *n.* plaque tournante;
platine, *f.*
turn-up ['tə:nʌp], *n.* revers *(de pantalon)*, *m.*
turpentine ['tə:pəntain], *n.* térébenthine, *f.*
turpitude ['tə:pitju:d], *n.* turpitude, *f.*
turquoise ['tə:kwɔiz], *n.* turquoise, *f.*
turret ['tʌrit], *n.* tourelle, *f.*
turreted ['tʌritid], *a.* garni de tourelles.
turtle [tə:tl], *n.* tortue de mer, *f.*; *to turn
turtle*, chavirer *(bateau)*, capoter *(voiture)*.
turtle-dove ['tə:tldʌv], *n.* tourterelle, *f.*
Tuscan ['tʌskən], *a.* toscan.—*n.* Toscan
(personne), *m.*
Tuscany ['tʌskəni], la Toscane, *f.*
tush! [tʌʃ], *int.* bah! fi donc!
tusk [tʌsk], *n.* défense *(d'éléphant)*, *f.*; croc
(dent), *m.*
tussle [tʌsl], *n.* lutte, bagarre, *f.*
tut! [tʌt], *int.* bah! allons donc!
tutelage ['tju:tilidʒ], *n.* tutelle, *f.*
tutor ['tju:tə], *n.* précepteur *(dans une
famille)*; *(Univ.)* maître-assistant, *m.*—*v.t.*
instruire, enseigner.
tutorial [tju:'tɔ:riəl], *a.* de précepteur.
tutoring ['tju:təriŋ], *n.* instruction, *f.*
tutorship ['tju:təʃip], *n.* préceptorat, *m.*
twaddle [twɔdl], *n.* bavardage, caquetage, *m.*
***twain** [twein], *a.* and *n.* deux, *m.*
twang [twæŋ], *n.* son sec *(d'une corde qui
vibre)*; accent nasillard *(voix)*, *m.*—*v.t.* faire
résonner, faire vibrer.—*v.i.* résonner,
nasiller.
tweak [twi:k], *v.t.* pincer *(en tordant)*.
tweezers ['twi:zəz], *n.pl.* pinces à épiler *(pour
poils)*, *f.pl.*
twelfth [twelfθ], *a.* douzième; douze *(du mois,
des rois etc.)*, *m.*; *Twelfth Night*, jour des
Rois, *m.*—*n.* douzième *(fraction)*, *m.*
twelve [twelv], *a.* and *n.* douze, *m.*; *twelve
o'clock*, midi *(noon)*, minuit *(midnight)*, *m.*
twelvemonth ['twelvmʌnθ], *n.* an, *m.*, année,
f.
twentieth ['twentiəθ], *a.* vingtième; vingt
(du mois etc.).—*n.* vingtième *(fraction)*, *m.*

twenty ['twenti], *a.* and *n.* vingt, *m.*
twenty-first ['twenti'fə:st], *a.* vingt et unième,
vingt et un *(du mois etc.)*.
twice [twais], *adv.* deux fois.
twig [twig], *n.* brindille, ramille, *f.*
twilight ['twailait], *a.* crépusculaire.—*n.*
crépuscule, *m.*
twill [twil], *n.* étoffe croisée, *f.*
twin [twin], *a.* jumeau; jumelé; *(Bot.)* double,
géminé.—*n.* jumeau, mi., jumelle, *f.*
twine [twain], *n.* ficelle, *f.*—*v.t.* retordre;
enlacer.—*v.i.* s'entrelacer, s'enrouler.
twinge [twindʒ], *n.* élancement; remords *(de
conscience)*, *m.*—*v.i.* élancer; *(fig.)* torturer.
twinkle [twiŋkl], *v.i.* étinceler.
twinkling ['twiŋkliŋ], *a.* étincelant, scintillant.
—*n.* scintillement, clignotement *(des yeux)*,
m.; *in the twinkling of an eye*, en un
clin d'œil.
twirl [twə:l], *v.t.* faire tournoyer; friser
(favoris).—*v.i.* tournoyer, tourner rapidement.—*n.* tournoiement, *m.*; pirouette, *f.*
twist [twist], *v.t.* tordre; tortiller, retordre;
cercler, entourer; enlacer *(entortiller)*; *(fig.)*
pervertir *(dénaturer)*.—*v.i.* se tordre, s'entrelacer, s'enlacer, s'enrouler.—*n.* cordon, *m.*,
corde, *f.*; tortillon *(de papier)*, *m.*; carotte
(de tabac), *f.*
twisted ['twistid], *a.* tordu; *(fig.)* perverti,
défiguré, dénaturé.
twisting ['twistiŋ], *a.* tortueux.—*n.* tordage;
tortillement, *m.*
twitch [twitʃ], *n.* saccade, *f.*; tic *(contraction
spasmodique)*; tiraillement *(de douleur)*, *m.*—
v.t. tirer brusquement; crisper.—*v.i.* se
contracter nerveusement.
twitching ['twitʃiŋ], *n.* saccade, crispation
(des muscles etc.), *f.*; tiraillement *(de douleur)*,
m.
twitter ['twitə], *v.t.*, *v.i.* gazouiller.—*n.* gazouillement, *m.*
two [tu:], *a.* and *n.* deux, *m.*
two-edged ['tu:edʒd], *a.* à deux tranchants.
twofold ['tu:fould], *a.* double.—*adv.* doublement, deux fois.
two-stroke ['tu:strouk], *a.* à deux temps.
tycoon [tai'ku:n], *n.* taicoun; *(fam.)* brasseur
d'affaires, manitou, *m.*
type [taip], *n.* type; *(Print.)* caractère; *(pop.)*
type, *m.*—*v.t.* [TYPEWRITE].
typewrite ['taiprait], *v.t.* écrire à la machine,
dactylographier, taper.
typewriter ['taipraitə], *n.* machine à écrire, *f.*
typewritten ['taipritn], *a.* tapé à la machine.
typhoid ['taifɔid], *a.* typhoïde.
typhoon [tai'fu:n], *n.* typhon, *m.*, trombe, *f.*
typhus ['taifəs], *n.* typhus, *m.*
typical ['tipikl], *a.* typique.
typically ['tipikli], *adv.* d'une manière
typique.
typify ['tipifai], *v.t.* symboliser.
typing ['taipiŋ], *n.* dactylographie, *(fam.)*
dactylo, *f.*
typist ['taipist], *n.* dactylographe, *(fam.)*
dactylo, *m.*, *f.*
typography [tai'pɔgrəfi], *n.* typographie, *f.*
tyrannical [ti'rænikl], *a.* tyrannique.
tyrannically [ti'rænikli], *adv.* tyrannique-
ment.
tyrannize ['tirənaiz], *v.i.* faire le tyran; *to
tyrannize over*, tyranniser.

606

tyranny ['tirəni], *n.* tyrannie, *f.*
tyrant ['taiərənt], *n.* tyran, *m.*
tyre ['taiə], *n.* pneu (*de roue*), *m.*
tyro ['taiərou], *n.* novice, débutant, *m.*
Tzar [TSAR].

U

U, u [ju:]. vingt et unième lettre de l'alphabet, *m.*
ubiquitous [ju'bikwitəs], *a.* omniprésent.
ubiquity [ju'bikwiti], *n.* ubiquité, *f.*
udder ['Adə], *n.* mamelle, *f.*, pis, *m.*
ugh! [u:x, u:h, ʌx, uf], *int.* pouah!
ugliness ['ʌglinis], *n.* laideur, *f.*
ugly ['ʌgli], *a.* laid, vilain.
Ukraine [ju'krein], **the.** l'Ukraine, *f.*
Ukrainian [ju'kreiniən], *a.* ukrainien.—*n.* Ukrainien (*personne*), *m.*
ukulele [ju:kə'leili], *n.* ukulélé, *m.*
ulcer ['ʌlsə], *n.* ulcère, *m.*
ulcerate ['ʌlsəreit], *v.t.* ulcérer.—*v.i.* s'ulcérer.
ulcerated ['ʌlsəreitid], *a.* ulcéré.
ulceration [ʌlsə'reiʃən], *n.* ulcération, *f.*
ulcerous ['ʌlsərəs], *a.* ulcéreux.
ullage ['ʌlidʒ], *n.* vidange, *f.*
ulterior [ʌl'tiəriə], *a.* ultérieur; *without ulterior motive*, sans arrière-pensée.
ultimate ['ʌltimit], *a.* dernier; extrême.
ultimately ['ʌltimitli], *adv.* finalement, à la fin.
ultimatum [ʌlti'meitəm], *n.* (*pl.* **ultimata** [ʌlti'meitə]) ultimatum, *m.*
ultimo ['ʌltimou], *adv.* (*abbr.* **ult.** [ʌlt]) du mois dernier.
ultra ['ʌltrə], *n.* ultra, *m.*
ultramarine [ʌltrəmə'ri:n], *a.* d'outremer.—*n.* outremer, *m.*
ululate ['ju:ljuleit], *v.i.* ululer.
Ulysses [ju'lisi:z]. Ulysse, *m.*
umber ['ʌmbə], *n.* (*Paint.*) terre d'ombre, *f.*
umbilical [ʌm'bilikl], *a.* ombilical.
umbrage ['ʌmbridʒ], *n.* ombrage, *m.*
umbrella [ʌm'brelə], *n.* parapluie, *m.*; *umbrella stand*, porte-parapluies, *m.inv.*
umpire ['ʌmpaiə], *n.* arbitre, *m.*—*v.t.*, *v.i.* arbitrer.
unabashed [ʌnə'bæʃt], *a.* sans être confus.
unabated [ʌnə'beitid], *a.* sans diminution.
unable [ʌn'eibl], *a.* incapable (*de*); *to be unable to*, ne pas pouvoir.
unabridged [ʌnə'bridʒd], *a.* non abrégé; en entier.
unacceptable [ʌnək'septəbl], *a.* inacceptable.
unaccommodating [ʌnə'kɔmədeitiŋ], *a.* peu accommodant.
unaccompanied [ʌnə'kʌmpənid], *a.* seul, sans suite.
unaccountable [ʌnə'kauntəbl], *a.* inexplicable, inconcevable.
unaccountably [ʌnə'kauntəbli], *adv.* inconcevablement.
unaccustomed [ʌnə'kʌstəmd], *a.* inaccoutumé (*à*); peu habitué.

unacknowledged [ʌnək'nɔlidʒd], *a.* non reconnu; sans réponse (*lettre*).
unacquainted [ʌnə'kweintid], *a.* étranger (*à*); peu familier (*avec*).
unadopted [ʌnə'dɔptid], *a.* non adopté.
unadorned [ʌnə'dɔ:nd], *a.* sans ornement.
unadulterated [ʌnə'dʌltəreitid], *a.* pur, non frelaté.
unadvisable [ʌnəd'vaizəbl], *a.* peu sage, inopportun.
unadvised [ʌnəd'vaizd], *a.* malavisé; imprudent (*rash*).
unadvisedly [ʌnəd'vaizidli], *adv.* inconsidérément.
unaffected [ʌnə'fektid], *a.* sans affectation; insensible (*peu ému*).
unaffectedly [ʌnə'fektidli], *adv.* sans affectation.
unafraid [ʌnə'freid], *a.* sans peur.
unaided [ʌn'eidid], *a.* seul, sans aide.
unallayed [ʌnə'leid], *a.* non apaisé.
unallowable [ʌnə'lauəbl], *a.* non permis; inadmissible.
unalloyed [ʌnə'lɔid], *a.* pur, sans alliage, sans mélange.
unalterable [ʌn'ɔ:ltərəbl], *a.* inaltérable, invariable.
unalterably [ʌn'ɔ:ltərəbli], *adv.* immuablement.
unambitious [ʌnæm'biʃəs], *a.* sans ambition.
unanimity [ju:nə'nimiti], *n.* unanimité, *f.*
unanimous [ju'næniməs], *a.* unanime.
unanimously [ju'næniməsli], *adv.* unanimement, à l'unanimité.
unanswerable [ʌn'ɑ:nsərəbl], *a.* incontestable.
unanswered [ʌn'ɑ:nsəd], *a.* sans réponse.
unappeasable [ʌnə'pi:zəbl], *a.* implacable.
unappetizing [ʌn'æpitaiziŋ], *a.* peu appétissant.
unappreciated [ʌnə'pri:ʃieitid], *a.* inapprécié.
unapproachable [ʌnə'proutʃəbl], *a.* inaccessible, inabordable.
unarmed [ʌn'ɑ:md], *a.* sans armes.
unascertainable [ʌnæsə'teinəbl], *a.* qu'on ne peut constater.
unashamed [ʌnə'ʃeimd], *a.* sans honte.
unasked [ʌn'ɑ:skt], *a.* sans être invité; spontané.—*adv.* spontanément.
unaspiring [ʌnə'spaiəriŋ], *a.* sans ambition.
unassailable [ʌnə'seiləbl], *a.* hors d'atteinte; inattaquable, irréfutable.
unassisted [ʌnə'sistid], *a.* sans aide.
unassuming [ʌnə'sju:miŋ], *a.* sans prétention, modeste.
unattached [ʌnə'tætʃt], *a.* sans être attaché (*à*); en disponibilité.
unattainable [ʌnə'teinəbl], *a.* inaccessible.
unattended [ʌnə'tendid], *a.* seul, sans suite.
unattested [ʌnə'testid], *a.* non attesté.
unattractive [ʌnə'træktiv], *a.* peu attrayant, sans attrait.
unauthenticated [ʌnɔ:'θentikeitid], *a.* dont l'authenticité n'est pas prouvée.
unauthorized [ʌn'ɔ:θəraizd], *a.* sans autorisation; illicite, illégal (*chose*).
unavailable [ʌnə'veiləbl], *a.* non valable; inutilisable (*billet*); indisponible (*fonds, personne*); qu'on ne peut se procurer (*chose*).
unavailing [ʌnə'veiliŋ], *a.* inutile, inefficace.
unavenged [ʌnə'vendʒd], *a.* impuni, non vengé.

unavoidable

unavoidable [ʌnə'vɔidebl], *a.* inévitable.
unavoidably [ʌnə'vɔidəbli], *adv.* inévitablement.
unaware [ʌnə'wɛə], *a.* ignorant; *to be unaware of*, ignorer.
unawares [ʌnə'wɛəz], *adv.* à l'improviste; à son insu (*sans s'en rendre compte*); *to be taken unawares*, être pris au dépourvu.
unbalanced [ʌn'bælənst], *a.* mal équilibré.
unbearable [ʌn'bɛərəbl], *a.* insupportable, intolérable.
unbearably [ʌn'bɛərəbli], *adv.* insupportablement.
unbeatable [ʌn'bi:təbl], *a.* invincible.
unbeaten [ʌn'bi:tn], *a.* invaincu.
unbecoming [ʌnbi'kʌmiŋ], *a.* peu convenable, malséant; qui ne va pas bien (*vêtement*).
unbecomingly [ʌnbi'kʌmiŋli], *adv.* d'une manière peu séante.
unbefitting [ʌnbi'fitiŋ], *a.* qui ne convient pas, peu propre.
unbeknown [ʌnbi'noun], *a.* inconnu; *unbeknown to me*, à mon insu.
unbelief [ʌnbi'li:f], *n.* incrédulité, incroyance, *f.*
unbelievable [ʌnbi'li:vəbl], *a.* incroyable.
unbeliever [ʌnbi'li:və], *n.* incrédule; sceptique, *m., f.*
unbelieving [ʌnbi'li:viŋ], *a.* incrédule; sceptique.
unbend [ʌn'bend], *v.t. irr.* (*conjug. like* BEND) détendre, relâcher; débander (*l'arc*); (*fig.*) délasser (*l'esprit*).—*v.i.* se détendre.
unbending [ʌn'bendiŋ], *a.* inflexible.
unbiased [ʌn'baiəst], *a.* sans prévention, impartial.
unbidden [ʌn'bidn], *a.* sans être invité.
unbind [ʌn'baind], *v.t. irr.* (*conjug. like* BIND) délier, détacher.
unbleached [ʌn'bli:tʃt], *a.* écru.
unblemished [ʌn'blemiʃt], *a.* sans tache.
unblushing [ʌn'blʌʃiŋ], *a.* qui ne rougit point, éhonté, sans vergogne.
unblushingly [ʌn'blʌʃiŋli], *adv.* sans rougir.
unbolt [ʌn'boult], *v.t.* tirer les verrous de, ouvrir.
unborn [ʌn'bɔ:n], *a.* encore à naître; futur, à venir (*chose*).
unbosom [ʌn'buzm], *v.t. to unbosom oneself*, ouvrir son cœur.
unbound [ʌn'baund], *a.* délié; non relié (*livre*).
unbounded [ʌn'baundid], *a.* illimité, infini.
unbreakable [ʌn'breikəbl], *a.* incassable.
unbridled [ʌn'braidld], *a.* débridé; (*fig.*) effréné.
unbroken [ʌn'broukn], *a.* non rompu; continu (*ininterrompu*); indompté (*non vaincu*); intact (*non violé*); non dressé (*animal*).
unbrotherly [ʌn'brʌðəli], *a.* peu fraternel.
unbuckle [ʌn'bʌkl], *v.t.* déboucler.
unburden [ʌn'bə:dn], *v.t.* décharger; *to unburden oneself*, ouvrir son cœur.
unburied [ʌn'berid], *a.* sans sépulture.
unbusinesslike [ʌn'biznislaik], *a.* peu pratique.
unbutton [ʌn'bʌtn], *v.t.* déboutonner.
uncalled [ʌn'kɔ:ld], *a.* sans être appelé; *uncalled for*, sans être demandé; gratuit (*superflu*); peu convenable (*mal élevé*); non mérité (*injuste*).

uncanny [ʌn'kæni], *a.* mystérieux, surnaturel.
uncared-for [ʌn'kɛədfɔ:], *a.* négligé.
unceasing [ʌn'si:siŋ], *a.* incessant, sans cesse.
unceasingly [ʌn'si:siŋli], *adv.* continuellement, sans cesse.
uncensored [ʌn'sensəd], *a.* non expurgé.
unceremonious [ʌnseri'mouniəs], *a.* peu cérémonieux; sans façon.
unceremoniously [ʌnseri'mouniəsli], *adv.* sans cérémonie, sans façon.
uncertain [ʌn'sə:tin], *a.* incertain, peu sûr.
uncertainty [ʌn'sə:tinti], *n.* incertitude, *f.*
uncertificated [ʌnsə'tifikətid], *a.* non diplômé (*instituteur*).
unchain [ʌn'tʃein], *v.t.* déchaîner.
unchallenged [ʌn'tʃælindʒd], *a.* indisputé.
unchangeable [ʌn'tʃeindʒəbl], *a.* inaltérable, immuable.
unchanged [ʌn'tʃeindʒd], *a.* inchangé, toujours le même.
unchanging [ʌn'tʃeindʒiŋ], *a.* invariable, constant.
uncharitable [ʌn'tʃæritəbl], *a.* peu charitable.
uncharitableness [ʌn'tʃæritəblnis], *n.* manque de charité, *m.*
uncharitably [ʌn'tʃæritəbli], *adv.* sans charité.
uncharted [ʌn'tʃɑ:tid], *a.* inexploré.
unchaste [ʌn'tʃeist], *a.* incontinent, impudique.
unchecked [ʌn'tʃekt], *a.* non réprimé, sans frein; non vérifié.
unchivalrous [ʌn'ʃivlrəs], *a.* peu chevaleresque.
unchristian [ʌn'kristiən], *a.* peu chrétien.
uncircumcised [ʌn'sə:kəmsaizd], *a.* incirconcis.
uncivil [ʌn'sivil], *a.* malhonnête, impoli.
uncivilized [ʌn'sivilaizd], *a.* peu civilisé, barbare.
uncivilly [ʌn'sivili], *adv.* malhonnêtement, impoliment.
unclaimed [ʌn'kleimd], *a.* non réclamé.
unclasp [ʌn'klɑ:sp], *v.t.* dégrafer, défaire.
unclassified [ʌn'klæsifaid], *a.* non classé.
uncle [ʌŋkl], *n.* oncle, *m.*; (*slang*) *at uncle's*, chez ma tante (*le prêteur sur gage*).
unclean [ʌn'kli:n], *a.* malpropre, sale; impudique (*obscène*); impur.
uncleanliness [ʌn'klenlinis], **uncleanness** [ʌn'kli:nnis], *n.* saleté; (*fig.*) impureté, *f.*
unclench [ʌn'klentʃ], *v.t.* ouvrir, desserrer.
uncloak [ʌn'klouk], *v.t.* dévoiler.
unclose [ʌn'klouz], *v.t.* ouvrir.
unclosed [ʌn'klouzd], *a.* non fermé, ouvert.
unclothe [ʌn'klouð], *v.t.* déshabiller.
unclothed [ʌn'klouðd], *a.* déshabillé, nu.
unclouded [ʌn'klaudid], *a.* sans nuage, serein.
uncock [ʌn'kɔk], *v.t.* désarmer (*fusil etc.*).
uncoil [ʌn'kɔil], *v.t.* dérouler.—*v.i.* se dérouler.
uncombed [ʌn'koumd], *a.* mal peigné, ébouriffé.
uncomfortable [ʌn'kʌmftəbl], *a.* peu confortable, incommode (*personne*).
uncomfortably [ʌn'kʌmftəbli], *adv.* peu confortablement; mal à l'aise.
uncommitted [ʌnkə'mitid], *a.* non commis; non engagé, libre.

uncommon [ʌnˈkɔmən], *a.* peu commun; rare.

uncommonly [ʌnˈkɔmənli], *adv.* rarement; infiniment *(singulièrement)*.

uncommunicative [ʌnkəˈmjuːnikətiv], *a.* peu communicatif, réservé.

uncomplaining [ʌnkəmˈpleiniŋ], *a.* sans plainte, résigné.

uncomplainingly [ʌnkəmˈpleininli], *adv.* sans se plaindre, sans plainte.

uncompleted [ʌnkəmˈpliːtid], *a.* inachevé, incomplet.

uncomplimentary [ʌnkɔmpliˈmentəri], *a.* peu flatteur.

uncompromising [ʌnˈkɔmprəmaiziŋ], *a.* peu accommodant, intransigeant.

unconcern [ʌnkənˈsəːn], *n.* insouciance, indifférence, *f.*

unconcerned [ʌnkənˈsəːnd], *a.* indifférent, insouciant.

unconcernedly [ʌnkənˈsəːnidli], *adv.* avec indifférence.

unconditional [ʌnkənˈdiʃənl], *a.* sans conditions, absolu.

unconditionally [ʌnkənˈdiʃənəli], *adv.* sans condition.

unconfined [ʌnkənˈfaind], *a.* libre; illimité.

unconfinedly [ʌnkənˈfainidli], *adv.* sans limite.

unconfirmed [ʌnkənˈfəːmd], *a.* non confirmé.

uncongenial [ʌnkənˈdʒiːniəl], *a.* désagréable; peu sympathique.

unconnected [ʌnkəˈnektid], *a.* détaché, sans rapport *(avec)*; décousu *(style)*.

unconquerable [ʌnˈkɔŋkərəbl], *a.* invincible.

unconquered [ʌnˈkɔŋkəd], *a.* insoumis.

unconscionable [ʌnˈkɔnʃənəbl], *a.* déraisonnable.

unconscionably [ʌnˈkɔnʃənəbli], *adv.* déraisonnablement.

unconscious [ʌnˈkɔnʃəs], *a.* ignorant *(de)*; sans connaissance, insensible.—*n.* inconscient, *m.*

unconsciously [ʌnˈkɔnʃəsli], *adv.* à son insu.

unconsciousness [ʌnˈkɔnʃəsnis], *n.* inconscience, *f.*; évanouissement, *m.*

unconsecrated [ʌnˈkɔnsikreitid], *a.* non consacré.

unconsidered [ʌnkənˈsidəd], *a.* inconsidéré.

unconstitutional [ʌnkɔnstiˈtjuːʃənl], *a.* inconstitutionnel.

unconstrained [ʌnkənˈstreind], *a.* sans contrainte; aisé *(style)*.

unconstraint [ʌnkənˈstreint], *n.* aisance, *f.*

uncontaminated [ʌnkənˈtæmineitid], *a.* sans souillure.

uncontested [ʌnkənˈtestid], *a.* incontesté.

uncontrollable [ʌnkənˈtrouləbl], *a.* irrésistible; fou *(rire)*.

uncontrollably [ʌnkənˈtrouləbli], *adv.* irrésistiblement.

uncontrolled [ʌnkənˈtrould], *a.* irrésistible.

unconventional [ʌnkənˈvenʃənl], *a.* peu conventionnel.

unconverted [ʌnkənˈvəːtid], *a.* inconverti.

unconvinced [ʌnkənˈvinst], *a.* non convaincu.

unconvincing [ʌnkənˈvinsiŋ], *a.* peu convaincant.

uncooked [ʌnˈkukt], *a.* non cuit, cru.

uncork [ʌnˈkɔːk], *v.t.* déboucher.

uncorrupted [ʌnkəˈrʌptid], *a.* non corrompu *(par)*; intègre.

uncouple [ʌnˈkʌpl], *v.t.* découpler; débrayer.

uncouth [ʌnˈkuːθ], *a.* bizarre; grossier; gauche.

uncouthly [ʌnˈkuːθli], *adv.* rudement; gauchement.

uncover [ʌnˈkʌvə], *v.t.* découvrir.

uncovered [ʌnˈkʌvəd], *a.* découvert.

uncreasable [ʌnˈkriːsəbl], *a.* infroissable.

uncritical [ʌnˈkritikl], *a.* sans discernement.

uncrowned [ʌnˈkraund], *a.* non couronné.

unction [ˈʌŋkʃən], *n.* onction, *f.*

unctuous [ˈʌŋktjuəs], *a.* onctueux.

unctuously [ˈʌŋktjuəsli], *adv.* onctueusement.

uncultivated [ʌnˈkʌltiveitid], *a.* inculte.

uncultured [ʌnˈkʌltʃəd], *a.* sans culture.

uncurl [ʌnˈkəːl], *v.t.* dérouler; défriser *(cheveux)*.—*v.i.* se dérouler; se défriser *(cheveux)*.

uncustomary [ʌnˈkʌstəməri], *a.* inaccoutumé.

uncut [ʌnˈkʌt], *a.* non coupé; entier; non entamé *(pain etc.)*.

undamaged [ʌnˈdæmidʒd], *a.* non endommagé; intact *(réputation)*.

undated [ʌnˈdeitid], *a.* sans date.

undaunted [ʌnˈdɔːntid], *a.* intrépide.

undeceive [ʌndiˈsiːv], *v.t.* désabuser, détromper.

undecided [ʌndiˈsaidid], *a.* indécis.

undecipherable [ʌndiˈsaifərəbl], *a.* indéchiffrable.

undefeated [ʌndiˈfiːtid], *a.* invaincu.

undefended [ʌndiˈfendid], *a.* sans défense, non défendu; sans défenseur *(accusé)*.

undefiled [ʌndiˈfaild], *a.* sans tache, immaculé.

undefinable [ʌndiˈfainəbl], *a.* indéfinissable.

undefined [ʌndiˈfaind], *a.* indéfini.

undelivered [ʌndiˈlivəd], *a.* non délivré.

undemonstrative [ʌndiˈmɔnstrətiv], *a.* peu démonstratif, réservé.

undeniable [ʌndiˈnaiəbl], *a.* incontestable.

undenominational [ʌndinɔmiˈneiʃənl], *a.* laïque *(école)*.

under [ˈʌndə], *a.* de dessous, inférieur; sous, subalterne, subordonné *(rang)*.—*prep.* sous; au-dessous de *(inférieur à etc.)*; dans, en *(en état de)*; avec, à *(ayant)*; **to be under obligations to**, avoir des obligations à; **to be under way** *(ship)*, être en marche; **under age**, mineur; **under consideration**, à l'examen; **under cover of**, sous prétexte de; **under discussion**, en discussion; **under the breath**, à demi-voix; **under these circumstances**, dans ces circonstances.—*adv.* dessous, au-dessous; **see under**, voyez ci-dessous.

under-carriage [ˈʌndəkæridʒ], *n. (Av.)* train d'atterrissage, *m.*

underclothes [ˈʌndəklouðz], *n.pl.* sous-vêtements, *m.pl.*

undercurrent [ˈʌndəkʌrənt], *n.* courant inférieur, *m.*

undercut (1) [ˈʌndəkʌt], *n.* filet *(de bœuf)*, *m.*

undercut (2) [ʌndəˈkʌt], *v.t. irr. (conjug. like CUT)* vendre meilleur marché.

under-developed [ʌndədiˈveləpt], *a.* sous-développé.

under-dog [ˈʌndədɔg], *n.* opprimé, *m.*

underdone [ʌndəˈdʌn], *a.* peu cuit, saignant.

under-estimate

under-estimate [ʌndər'estimeit], *v.t.* sous-estimer.
under-exposed [ʌndəriks'pouzd], *a.* (*Phot.*) sous-exposé.
underfelt ['ʌndəfelt], *n.* thibaude, *f.*
underfoot [ʌndə'fut], *adv.* sous les pieds.
undergo [ʌndə'gou], *v.t. irr.* (*conjug. like* GO) subir; supporter, endurer.
undergraduate [ʌndə'grædjuət], *n.* étudiant, *m.*
underground ['ʌndəgraund], *a.* souterrain; clandestin.—*n.* (*Rail.*) métro, *m.*—[ʌndə'graund], *adv.* sous terre.
undergrowth ['ʌndəgrouθ], *n.* broussailles, *f.pl.*
underhand ['ʌndəhænd], *a.* clandestin; sournois (*personne*).—[ʌndə'hænd], *adv.* sous main; en cachette.
underline [ʌndə'lain], *v.t.* souligner.
underling ['ʌndəliŋ], *n.* subalterne, *m.*, *f.*
underlying [ʌndə'laiiŋ], *a.* fondamental.
under-manned [ʌndə'mænd], *a.* à court de personnel.
undermentioned [ʌndə'menʃənd], *a.* ci-dessous.
undermine [ʌndə'main], *v.t.* miner; (*fig.*) détruire.
undermost ['ʌndəmoust], *a.* le plus bas.
underneath [ʌndə'ni:θ], *prep.* sous, au-dessous de.—*adv.* dessous, au-dessous, par-dessous, en dessous.
under-nourished [ʌndə'nʌriʃt], *a.* sous-alimenté.
underpaid [ʌndə'peid], *a.* mal payé.
underpants ['ʌndəpænts], *n.pl.* caleçons, *m.pl.*
under-privileged [ʌndə'privilidʒd], *a.* non privilégié.
under-production [ʌndəprə'dʌkʃən], *n.* sous-production, *f.*
underrate [ʌndə'reit], *v.t.* sous-estimer, déprécier.
under-ripe [ʌndə'raip], *a.* pas assez mûr, vert.
under-secretary ['ʌndəsekrətəri], *n.* sous-secrétaire, *m.*, *f.*
under-side ['ʌndəsaid], *n.* dessous, *m.*
undersigned ['ʌndəsaind], *a.* and *n.* sous-signé, *m.*
undersized [ʌndə'saizd], *a.* au-dessous de la moyenne.
understand [ʌndə'stænd], *v.t. irr.* (*conjug. like* STAND) entendre, comprendre; apprendre, entendre dire (*être informé de*); s'entendre (*à* ou *en*) (*savoir faire*).—*v.i.* comprendre.
understandable [ʌndə'stændəbl], *a.* intelligible; compréhensible.
understanding [ʌndə'stændiŋ], *n.* entendement, *m.*, intelligence; compréhension; entente (*accord*), *f.*
understudy ['ʌndəstʌdi], *n.* doublure, *f.*
undertake [ʌndə'teik], *v.t. irr.* (*conjug. like* TAKE) entreprendre, se charger (*de*); s'engager (*à*); promettre (*de*).
undertaker [ʌndə'teikə], *n.* entrepreneur des pompes funèbres, *m.*
undertaking [ʌndə'teikiŋ], *n.* entreprise, *f.*
undertone ['ʌndətoun], *n.* ton bas, *m.*; *in an undertone*, à voix basse.
underwear ['ʌndəweə], *n.* sous-vêtements, *m.pl.*

underworld ['ʌndəwə:ld], *n.* enfer, *m.*; (*fig.*) bas-fonds (*des criminels*), *m.pl.*
underwrite [ʌndə'rait], *v.t. irr.* (*conjug. like* WRITE) souscrire; (*Insurance*) assurer.
underwriter ['ʌndəraitə], *n.* assureur, *m.*
undeserved [ʌndi'zə:vd], *a.* immérité, non mérité.
undeservedly [ʌndi'zə:vidli], *adv.* à tort, injustement.
undesirable [ʌndi'zaiərəbl], *a.* peu désirable.
undetected [ʌndi'tektid], *a.* non découvert, inaperçu.
undetermined [ʌndi'tə:mind], *a.* indéterminé, indéfini.
undeterred [ʌndi'tə:d], *a.* sans être découragé.
undeveloped [ʌndi'veləpt], *a.* non développé.
undies ['ʌndiz], *n.pl.* (*fam.*) lingerie, *f.*
undigested [ʌndi'dʒestid], *a.* non digéré.
undignified [ʌn'dignifaid], *a.* sans dignité.
undiluted [ʌndai'lju:tid], *a.* non dilué.
undiminished [ʌndi'miniʃt], *a.* non diminué.
undiplomatic [ʌndiplo'mætik], *a.* peu diplomatique.
undisciplined [ʌn'disiplind], *a.* indiscipliné.
undisclosed [ʌndis'klouzd], *a.* non révélé, caché.
undiscovered [ʌndis'kʌvəd], *a.* non découvert.
undisguised [ʌndis'gaizd], *a.* sans déguisement.
undismayed [ʌndis'meid], *a.* sans peur, sans terreur.
undisputed [ʌndis'pju:tid], *a.* incontesté.
undistinguished [ʌndis'tiŋgwiʃt], *a.* (*fig.*) sans distinction.
undisturbed [ʌndis'tə:bd], *a.* tranquille, calme.
undivided [ʌndi'vaidid], *a.* sans partage, tout entier.
undo [ʌn'du:], *v.t. irr.* (*conjug. like* DO) défaire; délier, détacher (*dénouer*); ruiner, perdre (*détruire*).
undoing [ʌn'du:iŋ], *n.* ruine, perte, *f.*
undone [ʌn'dʌn], *a.* ruiné, perdu; défait, délié.
undoubted [ʌn'dautid], *a.* incontestable, certain.
undoubtedly [ʌn'dautidli], *adv.* sans aucun doute.
undress [ʌn'dres], *v.t.* déshabiller.—*v.i.* se déshabiller.—*n.* (*Mil.*) petite tenue, *f.*
undressed [ʌn'drest], *a.* déshabillé.
undrinkable [ʌn'driŋkəbl], *a.* imbuvable, non potable.
undue [ʌn'dju:], *a.* non dû; excessif.
undulate ['ʌndjuleit], *v.i.* onduler, ondoyer.
undulating ['ʌndjuleitiŋ], *a.* accidenté (*terrain*).
undulation [ʌndju'leiʃən], *n.* ondulation, *f.*
unduly [ʌn'dju:li], *adv.* indûment; à tort; trop.
undying [ʌn'daiiŋ], *a.* impérissable, immortel.
unearned [ʌn'ə:nd], *a.* qu'on n'a pas gagné; immérité; *unearned income*, rentes, *f.pl.*
unearth [ʌn'ə:θ], *v.t.* déterrer.
unearthly [ʌn'ə:θli], *a.* surnaturel; (*colloq.*) infernal.
uneasily [ʌn'i:zili], *adv.* mal à son aise; difficilement, péniblement, avec gêne.

uneasiness [ʌn'i:zinis], *n.* malaise, *m.*, peine; inquiétude (*d'esprit*), *f.*
uneasy [ʌn'i:zi], *a.* inquiet, gêné.
uneatable [ʌn'i:təbl], *a.* immangeable.
uneconomical [ʌni:kə'nɔmikl], *a.* non économique.
uneducated [ʌn'edjukeitid], *a.* sans éducation.
unemotional [ʌni'mouʃənl], *a.* peu impressionnable; peu émotif.
unemployed [ʌnim'plɔid], *a.* sans travail, inoccupé; (*fig.*) inactif, oisif.—*n.pl.* the **unemployed**, les sans-travail, les chômeurs, *m.pl.*
unemployment [ʌnim'plɔimənt], *n.* manque de travail, chômage, *m.*
unencumbered [ʌnin'kʌmbəd], *a.* non embarrassé (*de*); non hypothéqué (*biens*).
unending [ʌn'endiŋ], *a.* interminable.
unendurable [ʌnin'djuərəbl], *a.* insupportable, intolérable.
un-English [ʌn'iŋgliʃ], *a.* non anglais; indigne d'un Anglais.
unenlightened [ʌnin'laitnd], *a.* peu éclairé.
unenterprising [ʌn'entəpraiziŋ], *a.* peu entreprenant.
unenthusiastic [ʌninθju:zi'æstik], *a.* peu enthousiaste.
unenviable [ʌn'enviəbl], *a.* peu enviable.
unequal [ʌn'i:kwəl], *a.* inégal; au-dessous (*de*); **unequal to the task**, pas à la hauteur de la tâche.
unequalled [ʌn'i:kwəld], *a.* sans égal, sans pareil.
unequivocal [ʌni'kwivəkl], *a.* non équivoque.
unequivocally [ʌni'kwivəkli], *adv.* sans équivoque.
unerring [ʌn'ə:riŋ], *a.* infaillible, sûr.
uneven [ʌn'i:vn], *a.* inégal; raboteux (*terrain*).
unevenly [ʌn'i:vinli], *adv.* inégalement.
unevenness [ʌn'i:vinnis], *n.* inégalité, *f.*
uneventful [ʌni'ventful], *a.* sans incidents, monotone.
unexaggerated [ʌnig'zædʒəreitid], *a.* nullement exagéré.
unexciting [ʌnik'saitiŋ], *a.* peu intéressant.
unexpected [ʌniks'pektid], *a.* inopiné, inattendu; imprévu.
unexpectedly [ʌniks'pektidli], *adv.* à l'improviste.
unexpired [ʌniks'paiəd], *a.* non expiré.
unexplained [ʌniks'pleind], *a.* sans explication, inexpliqué.
unexploded [ʌniks'ploudid], *a.* non éclaté.
unexplored [ʌniks'plɔ:d], *a.* inexploré.
unexposed [ʌniks'pouzd], *a.* non exposé.
unextinguished [ʌniks'tiŋgwiʃt], *a.* non éteint.
unfading [ʌn'feidiŋ], *a.* (*fig.*) impérissable, immortel.
unfailing [ʌn'feiliŋ], *a.* inépuisable; infaillible (*certain*).
unfair [ʌn'fɛə], *a.* injuste; (*Spt.*) pas de jeu.
unfairly [ʌn'fɛəli], *adv.* injustement.
unfairness [ʌn'fɛənis], *n.* injustice, *f.*
unfaithful [ʌn'feiθful], *a.* infidèle.
unfaithfulness [ʌn'feiθfulnis], *n.* infidélité, *f.*
unfaltering [ʌn'fɔ:ltəriŋ], *a.* ferme, assuré; résolu (*actions etc.*).
unfamiliar [ʌnfə'miljə], *a.* peu familier (*avec*); peu connu.
unfashionable [ʌn'fæʃənəbl], *a.* démodé.

unfasten [ʌn'fɑ:sn], *v.t.* ouvrir, détacher, défaire.
unfathomable [ʌn'fæðəməbl], *a.* insondable.
unfavorable [ʌn'feivərəbl], *a.* peu favorable.
unfed [ʌn'fed], *a.* mal nourri.
unfeeling [ʌn'fi:liŋ], *a.* insensible, dur, cruel.
unfeigned [ʌn'feind], *a.* vrai, sincère.
unfeignedly [ʌn'feinidli], *adv.* sincèrement.
unfelt [ʌn'felt], *a.* qu'on ne sent pas.
unfenced [ʌn'fenst], *a.* sans clôture.
unfetter [ʌn'fetə], *v.t.* ôter les fers à; (*fig.*) délivrer.
unfettered [ʌn'fetəd], *a.* libre, sans entraves.
unfilial [ʌn'filiəl], *a.* peu filial.
unfinished [ʌn'finiʃt], *a.* inachevé.
unfit [ʌn'fit], *a.* peu propre; impropre (*à*); incapable (*de*); en mauvaise santé.
unfitting [ʌn'fitiŋ], *a.* inconvenant.
unfix [ʌn'fiks], *v.t.* détacher.
unfixed [ʌn'fikst], *a.* mobile; indécis.
unflagging [ʌn'flægiŋ], *a.* infatigable.
unfledged [ʌn'fledʒd], *a.* sans plumes; (*fig.*) novice.
unflinching [ʌn'flintʃiŋ], *a.* ferme, déterminé.
unfold [ʌn'fould], *v.t.* déplier, déployer; révéler.—*v.i.* se déployer, se dévoiler.
unforeseen [ʌnfɔ:'si:n], *a.* imprévu.
unforgettable [ʌnfə'getəbl], *a.* inoubliable.
unforgiving [ʌnfə'giviŋ], *a.* implacable.
unforgotten [ʌnfə'gɔtn], *a.* pas oublié.
unfortified [ʌn'fɔ:tifaid], *a.* non fortifié, ouvert.
unfortunate [ʌn'fɔ:tʃənit], *a.* infortuné, malheureux.
unfortunately [ʌn'fɔ:tʃənitli], *adv.* malheureusement.
unfounded [ʌn'faundid], *a.* sans fondement.
unframed [ʌn'freimd], *a.* sans cadre.
unfrequented [ʌnfri'kwentid], *a.* peu fréquenté, solitaire.
unfriendliness [ʌn'frendlinis], *n.* disposition peu amicale, *f.*
unfriendly [ʌn'frendli], *a.* peu amical (*personne*); malveillant (*chose*).
unfrock [ʌn'frɔk], *v.t.* défroquer.
unfruitful [ʌn'fru:tful], *a.* infertile, stérile.
unfulfilled [ʌnful'fild], *a.* non accompli.
unfurl [ʌn'fə:l], *v.t.* déferler, déployer.
unfurnished [ʌn'fə:niʃt], *a.* non meublé.
ungainly [ʌn'geinli], *a.* maladroit.
ungenerous [ʌn'dʒenərəs], *a.* peu généreux.
ungentlemanliness [ʌn'dʒentlmənlinis], *n.* impolitesse, *f.*
ungentlemanly [ʌn'dʒentlmənli], *a.* de mauvais ton.
ungodliness [ʌn'gɔdlinis], *n.* impiété, *f.*
ungodly [ʌn'gɔdli], *a.* impie.
ungovernable [ʌn'gʌvənəbl], *a.* ingouvernable; effréné.
ungraceful [ʌn'greisful], *a.* peu gracieux.
ungracious [ʌn'greiʃəs], *a.* peu gracieux, déplaisant.
ungrammatical [ʌngrə'mætikl], *a.* incorrect.
ungrateful [ʌn'greitful], *a.* ingrat (*envers*).
ungratefully [ʌn'greitfuli], *adv.* avec ingratitude.
ungrudging [ʌn'grʌdʒiŋ], *a.* de bon cœur.
ungrudgingly [ʌn'grʌdʒiŋli], *adv.* volontiers, de bon cœur.
unguarded [ʌn'gɑ:did], *a.* sans défense; imprudent, irréfléchi (*inconsidéré*).

unguardedly [ʌn'gɑ:didli], *adv.* imprudement.

unguent ['ʌŋgwənt], *n.* onguent, *m.*

unhallowed [ʌn'hæloud], *a.* non sanctifié.

unhampered [ʌn'hæmpəd], *a.* non embarrassé (*par*).

***unhand** [ʌn'hænd], *v.t.* lâcher.

unhappily [ʌn'hæpili], *adv.* malheureusement.

unhappiness [ʌn'hæpinis], *n.* malheur, *m.*

unhappy [ʌn'hæpi], *a.* malheureux.

unharmed [ʌn'hɑ:md], *a.* sain et sauf.

unharness [ʌn'hɑ:nis], *v.t.* déharnacher; dételer (*d'une charrette*).

unhatched [ʌn'hætʃt], *a.* non éclos.

unhealthy [ʌn'helθi], *a.* insalubre, malsain; maladif (*personne*).

unheard [ʌn'hə:d], *a.* sans être entendu; *unheard of*, inconnu, inouï (*extraordinaire*).

unheeded [ʌn'hi:did], *a.* inaperçu, négligé.

unheedful [ʌn'hi:dful], **unheeding** [ʌn'hi:diŋ], *a.* insouciant; inattentif.

unhesitating [ʌn'heziteitiŋ], *a.* sans hésitation; résolu.

unhesitatingly [ʌn'heziteitiŋli], *adv.* sans hésiter.

unhewn [ʌn'hju:n], *a.* brut; non taillé.

unhinge [ʌn'hindʒ], *v.t.* démonter.

unhitch [ʌn'hitʃ], *v.t.* décrocher; dételer (*cheval*).

unholy [ʌn'houli], *a.* profane, impie.

unhook [ʌn'huk], *v.t.* décrocher; dégrafer (*vêtements*).

unhoped [ʌn'houpt], *a.* inattendu; *unhoped for*, inespéré.

unhorse [ʌn'hɔ:s], *v.t.* désarçonner, démonter.

unhurried [ʌn'hʌrid], *a.* lent, sans précipitation.

unhurt [ʌn'hə:t], *a.* sain et sauf, sans blessures.

unhygienic [ʌnhai'dʒi:nik], *a.* peu hygiénique.

unicorn ['ju:nikɔ:n], *n.* licorne, *f.*

unidentified [ʌnai'dentifaid], *a.* non identifié.

unification [ju:nifi'keiʃən], *n.* unification, *f.*

uniform ['ju:nifɔ:m], *a.* and *n.* uniforme, *m.*

uniformity [ju:ni'fɔ:miti], *n.* uniformité, *f.*

uniformly ['ju:nifɔ:mli], *adv.* uniformément.

unify ['ju:nifai], *v.t.* unifier.

unilateral [ju:ni'lætərəl], *a.* unilatéral.

unimaginable [ʌni'mædʒinəbl], *a.* inimaginable, inconcevable.

unimaginative [ʌni'mædʒinətiv], *a.* peu imaginatif.

unimpaired [ʌnim'pɛəd], *a.* inaltéré, intact.

unimpeachable [ʌnim'pi:tʃəbl], *a.* irréprochable.

unimpeded [ʌnim'pi:did], *a.* sans empêchement.

unimportance [ʌnim'pɔ:təns], *n.* peu d'importance, *m.*, insignifiance, *f.*

unimportant [ʌnim'pɔ:tənt], *a.* sans importance, insignifiant.

unimpressed [ʌnim'prest], *a.* sans être ému.

unimpressive [ʌnim'presiv], *a.* peu frappant.

uninformed [ʌnin'fɔ:md], *a.* non informé; ignorant.

uninhabitable [ʌnin'hæbitəbl], *a.* inhabitable.

uninhabited [ʌnin'hæbitid], *a.* inhabité.

uninitiated [ʌni'niʃieitid], *a.* non initié.

uninjured [ʌn'indʒəd], *a.* sain et sauf, sans blessures.

uninspired [ʌnin'spaiəd], *a.* non inspiré, terne.

uninspiring [ʌnin'spaiəriŋ], *a.* banal.

unintelligible [ʌnin'telidʒibl], *a.* inintelligible.

unintentional [ʌnin'tenʃənl], *a.* sans intention, involontaire.

unintentionally [ʌnin'tenʃənli], *adv.* fait sans le vouloir, sans intention.

uninterested [ʌn'intristid], *a.* non intéressé, indifférent.

uninteresting [ʌn'intristiŋ], *a.* peu intéressant.

uninterrupted [ʌnintə'rʌptid], *a.* ininterrompu.

uninvited [ʌnin'vaitid], *a.* sans invitation.

uninviting [ʌnin'vaitiŋ], *a.* peu attrayant; peu appétissant (*nourriture*).

union ['ju:niən], *n.* union, *f.*; *trade union*, syndicat ouvrier, syndicat (corporatif), *m.*

unique [ju'ni:k], *a.* unique.

uniquely [ju'ni:kli], *adv.* d'une manière unique.

unison ['ju:nizn], *n.* unisson, *m.*; *in unison*, à l'unisson.

unit ['ju:nit], *n.* unité, *f.*, bloc, élément, *m.*

unite [ju'nait], *v.t.* unir (*à* ou *avec*); joindre, réunir (*efforts etc.*).—*v.i.* s'unir, se réunir; se joindre (*à* ou *avec*).

united [ju'naitid], *a.* uni; réuni; joint; *the United Kingdom*, le Royaume-Uni, *m.*; *the United States*, les États-Unis, *m.pl.*

unity ['ju:niti], *n.* unité; union, *f.*

universal [ju:ni'və:sl], *a.* universel.

universally [ju:ni'və:səli], *adv.* universellement.

universe ['ju:nivə:s], *n.* univers, *m.*

university [ju:ni'və:siti], *n.* université, *f.*; *university degree*, grade universitaire, *m.*

unjust [ʌn'dʒʌst], *a.* injuste, inique.

unjustly [ʌn'dʒʌstli], *adv.* injustement.

unjustifiable [ʌn'dʒʌstifaiəbl], *a.* injustifiable.

unjustified [ʌn'dʒʌstifaid], *a.* sans justification.

unkind [ʌn'kaind], *a.* désobligeant; peu aimable; cruel.

unkindliness [ʌn'kaindlinis], *n.* désobligeance; malveillance, *f.*

unkindly [ʌn'kaindli], *a.* peu propice, défavorable.—*adv.* sans bienveillance; cruellement, mal.

unkindness [ʌn'kaindnis], *n.* manque d'amabilité, *m.*, désobligeance; cruauté, dureté, *f.*

unknowingly [ʌn'nouiŋli], *adv.* sans le savoir, à son insu.

unknown [ʌn'noun], *a.* inconnu; *unknown to me* (*without my knowledge*), à mon insu.

unlace [ʌn'leis], *v.t.* délacer, détacher.

unladylike [ʌn'leidilaik], *a.* peu digne d'une dame, de mauvais ton.

unlatch [ʌn'lætʃ], *v.t.* lever le loquet de, ouvrir.

unlawful [ʌn'lɔ:ful], *a.* illégal; illicite.

unlawfully [ʌn'lɔ:fuli], *adv.* illégalement; illicitement.

unleash [ʌn'li:ʃ], *v.t.* lâcher (*chien*).

unleavened [ʌn'levənd], *a.* sans levain; (*Scripture*) azyme.

unless [ʌn'les], *conj.* à moins que . . . ne (*with subjunctive*); à moins de (*followed by infinitive*); si . . . ne . . . pas (*followed by indicative*); si ce n'est, excepté que.

unlicensed [ʌn'laisənst], *a.* non autorisé; (*Comm.*) non patenté.

unlike [ʌn'laik], *a.* différent (*de*); qui ne ressemble pas (*à*).

unlikelihood [ʌn'laiklihud], *n.* invraisemblance, improbabilité, *f.*

unlikely [ʌn'laikli], *a.* improbable, invraisemblable, peu sûr.

unlimited [ʌn'limitid], *a.* illimité.

unlined [ʌn'laind], *a.* non doublé.

unlink [ʌn'liŋk], *v.t.* défaire, détacher.

unload [ʌn'loud], *v.t.* décharger; désarmer (*fusil*).

unlock [ʌn'lɔk], *v.t.* ouvrir.

unlooked-for [ʌn'luktfɔ:], *a.* inattendu, imprévu.

unloose [ʌn'lu:s], *v.t.* délier, détacher.

unloved [ʌn'lʌvd], *a.* pas aimé.

unluckily [ʌn'lʌkili], *adv.* malheureusement, par malheur.

unlucky [ʌn'lʌki], *a.* malheureux, infortuné; sinistre, de mauvais augure, de mauvais présagé.

unmade [ʌn'meid], *a.* défait; pas fait (*lit*); non empierré (*route*).

unmanageable [ʌn'mænidʒəbl], *a.* ingouvernable; rebelle.

unmanliness [ʌn'mænlinis], *n.* conduite indigne d'un homme, lâcheté, *f.*

unmanly [ʌn'mænli], *a.* indigne d'un homme, lâche; mou, efféminé.

unmannerliness [ʌn'mænəlinis], *n.* grossièreté, impolitesse, *f.*

unmannerly [ʌn'mænəli], *a.* grossier, mal appris, impoli.

unmarked [ʌn'mɑ:kt], *a.* non marqué (*de*); inaperçu.

unmarketable [ʌn'mɑ:kitəbl], *a.* invendable.

unmarried [ʌn'mærid], *a.* célibataire; **unmarried man**, célibataire, *m.*; **unmarried woman**, demoiselle; vieille fille, *f.*

unmask [ʌn'mɑ:sk], *v.t.* démasquer; (*fig.*) dévoiler.

unmastered [ʌn'mɑ:stəd], *a.* indompté.

unmatched [ʌn'mætʃt], *a.* dépareillé; (*fig.*) sans pareil.

unmentionable [ʌn'menʃənəbl], *a.* dont on ne parle pas.

unmerciful [ʌn'mə:siful], *a.* impitoyable, cruel.

unmercifully [ʌn'mə:sifuli], *adv.* impitoyablement, sans pitié.

unmerited [ʌn'meritid], *a.* immérité.

unmindful [ʌn'maindful], *a.* peu soucieux (*de*).

unmistakable [ʌnmis'teikəbl], *a.* évident, clair.

unmistakably [ʌnmis'teikəbli], *adv.* évidemment, clairement.

unmitigated [ʌn'mitigeitid], *a.* non adouci; (*colloq.*) fieffé (*gredin etc.*).

unmolested [ʌnmə'lestid], *a.* sans être molesté.

unmotherly [ʌn'mʌðəli], *a.* peu maternel.

unmounted [ʌn'mauntid], *a.* à pied (*sans cheval*); non collé (*photographie etc.*).

unmourned [ʌn'mɔ:nd], *a.* sans être pleuré.

unmoved [ʌn'mu:vd], *a.* immobile; (*fig.*) non ému.

unmusical [ʌn'mju:zikl], *a.* peu harmonieux; pas musicien (*personne*).

unmuzzle [ʌn'mʌzl], *v.t.* démuseler.

unnamed [ʌn'neimd], *a.* innommé; anonyme.

unnatural [ʌn'nætʃrəl], *a.* contre nature; dénaturé (*personne*).

unnavigable [ʌn'nævigəbl], *a.* innavigable.

unnecessarily [ʌn'nesəsərili], *adv.* sans nécessité, inutilement; par trop.

unnecessary [ʌn'nesəsəri], *a.* peu nécessaire, inutile.

unneighborly [ʌn'neibəli], *a.* peu obligeant; de mauvais voisin.

unnerve [ʌn'nə:v], *v.t.* énerver; (*fig.*) décourager.

unnoticed [ʌn'noutist], *a.* inaperçu, inobservé.

unnumbered [ʌn'nʌmbəd], *a.* innombrable.

unobjectionable [ʌnəb'dʒekʃənəbl], *a.* irrécusable.

unobliging [ʌnə'blaidʒiŋ], *a.* désobligeant.

unobservant [ʌnəb'zə:vənt], *a.* peu observateur.

unobserved [ʌnəb'zə:vd], *a.* inaperçu.

unobtainable [ʌnəb'teinəbl], *a.* impossible à obtenir.

unobtrusive [ʌnəb'tru:siv], *a.* réservé, discret.

unobtrusively [ʌnəb'tru:sivli], *adv.* sans importunité, avec modestie.

unoccupied [ʌn'ɔkjupaid], *a.* inoccupé; libre, disponible (*temps etc.*); inhabité (*maison*).

unofficial [ʌnə'fiʃl], *a.* non officiel.

unofficially [ʌnə'fiʃəli], *adv.* non officiellement.

unopened [ʌn'oupənd], *a.* fermé; non décacheté (*lettre etc.*).

unopposed [ʌnə'pouzd], *a.* sans opposition.

unorganized [ʌn'ɔ:gənaizd], *a.* non organisé.

unoriginal [ʌnə'ridʒinəl], *a.* peu original.

unorthodox [ʌn'ɔ:θədɔks], *a.* peu orthodoxe.

unostentatious [ʌnɔsten'teiʃəs], *a.* sans faste; modeste.

unostentatiously [ʌnɔsten'teiʃəsli], *adv.* sans ostentation.

unpack [ʌn'pæk], *v.t.* déballer (*marchandises*); dépaqueter (*paquets*).

unpacking [ʌn'pækiŋ], *n.* déballage; dépaquetage (*de petits paquets*), *m.*

unpaid [ʌn'peid], *a.* non payé, sans paye.

unpalatable [ʌn'pælətəbl], *a.* désagréable (au goût).

unparalleled [ʌn'pærəleld], *a.* sans pareil; sans précédent.

unpardonable [ʌn'pɑ:dnəbl], *a.* impardonnable.

unparliamentary [ʌnpɑ:li'mentəri], *a.* peu parlementaire.

unpatriotic [ʌnpætri'ɔtik], *a.* peu patriotique (*sentiment*); peu patriote (*personne*).

unpaved [ʌn'peivd], *a.* non pavé. [see **unmade**]

unperturbed [ʌnpə'tə:bd], *a.* peu ému, impassible.

unphilosophical [ʌnfilə'sɔfikl], *a.* peu philosophique.

unpick [ʌn'pik], *v.t.* découdre.

unpicked [ʌn'pikt], *a.* non cueilli; décousu (*couture*).

unpin

unpin [ʌn'pin], *v.t.* défaire.
unpitied [ʌn'pitid], *a.* qu'on ne plaint pas.
unpitying [ʌn'pitiiŋ], *a.* sans pitié, impitoyable.
unplayable [ʌn'pleiəbl], *a.* injouable.
unpleasant [ʌn'plezənt], *a.* déplaisant, fâcheux.
unpleasantly [ʌn'plezəntli], *adv.* désagréablement.
unpleasantness [ʌn'plezəntnis], *n.* désagrément, *m.*
unplowed [ʌn'plaud], *a.* non labouré.
unpoetical [ʌnpo'etikl], *a.* peu poétique.
unpolished [ʌn'pɔliʃt], *a.* non poli; mat (*or etc.*); non ciré (*chaussures*); dépoli (*verre*); (*fig.*) grossier.
unpolluted [ʌnpə'lju:tid], *a.* non souillé; pur.
unpopular [ʌn'pɔpjulə], *a.* impopulaire.
unpopularity [ʌnpɔpju'læriti], *n.* impopularité, *f.*
unpractical [ʌn'præktikl], *a.* peu pratique.
unpractised [ʌn'præktist], *a.* inexpérimenté.
unprecedented [ʌn'presidəntid], *a.* sans précédent.
unprejudiced [ʌn'predʒudist], *a.* sans préjugés, impartial.
unpremeditated [ʌnpri'mediteitid], *a.* inopiné, improvisé, sans préméditation.
unprepared [ʌnpri'pɛəd], *a.* non préparé; *to be unprepared for,* ne pas s'attendre à.
unpreparedness [ʌnpri'pɛəridnis], *n.* manque de préparation, *m.*
unprepossessing [ʌnpri:pə'zesiŋ], *a.* peu engageant.
unprincipled [ʌn'prinsipld], *a.* sans principes, sans mœurs.
unproductive [ʌnprə'dʌktiv], *a.* improductif; stérile (*terre*).
unproductiveness [ʌnprə'dʌktivnis], *n.* stérilité, *f.*
unprofessional [ʌnprə'feʃənəl], *a.* contraire aux règles d'une profession.
unprofitable [ʌn'prɔfitəbl], *a.* peu lucratif, sans profit; inutile.
unprofitably [ʌn'prɔfitəbli], *adv.* inutilement, sans profit.
unpronounceable [ʌnprə'naunsəbl], *a.* imprononçable.
unpropitious [ʌnprə'piʃəs], *a.* peu propice (à).
unprotected [ʌnprə'tektid], *a.* sans protection, sans défense; à découvert.
unprovided [ʌnprə'vaidid], *a.* dépourvu, dénué (*de*); *we were unprovided for that,* nous ne nous attendions pas à cela.
unprovoked [ʌnprə'voukt], *a.* sans provocation; *an unprovoked insult,* une insulte gratuite.
unpublished [ʌn'pʌbliʃt], *a.* inédit.
unpunished [ʌn'pʌniʃt], *a.* impuni.
unqualified [ʌn'kwɔlifaid], *a.* incapable (*de*), incompétent; (*fig.*) sans réserve; (*Law*) inhabile (à); non autorisé (*médecins etc.*).
unquenchable [ʌn'kwentʃəbl], *a.* inextinguible.
unquestionable [ʌn'kwestʃənəbl], *a.* incontestable, indubitable.
unquestionably [ʌn'kwestʃənəbli], *adv.* incontestablement; sans contredit.
unravel [ʌn'rævl], *v.t.* démêler, débrouiller.
—*v.i.* se démêler, se débrouiller, s'effiler.
unreadable [ʌn'ri:dəbl], *a.* illisible.

unreadily [ʌn'redili], *adv.* lentement, à contre-cœur.
unreadiness [ʌn'redinis], *n.* manque de préparation *ou* de bonne volonté, *m.*
unready [ʌn'redi], *a.* mal préparé; lent.
unreal [ʌn'ri:əl], *a.* irréel; chimérique, imaginaire.
unrealistic [ʌnri:ə'listik], *a.* peu réaliste.
unreality [ʌnri'æliti], *n.* défaut de réalité, *m.*
unrealizable [ʌn'ri:əlaizəbl], *a.* irréalisable.
unreasonable [ʌn'ri:znəbl], *a.* déraisonnable; exorbitant.
unreasonableness [ʌn'ri:znəblnis], *n.* déraison; absurdité, extravagance (*de demande*), *f.*
unreasonably [ʌn'ri:znəbli], *adv.* sans raison, à l'excès.
unrecognizable [ʌn'rekəgnaizəbl], *a.* méconnaissable.
unrecognized [ʌn'rekəgnaizd], *a.* sans être reconnu; (*fig.*) méconnu (*non apprécié*).
unrecompensed [ʌn'rekəmpenst], *a.* sans récompense.
unreconciled [ʌn'rekənsaild], *a.* irréconcilié.
unrecorded [ʌnri'kɔ:did], *a.* non enregistré.
unredeemable [ʌnri'di:məbl], *a.* irrachetable.
unredeemed [ʌnri'di:md], *a.* non racheté.
unrefined [ʌnri'faind], *a.* non raffiné, brut; (*fig.*) grossier.
unregistered [ʌn'redʒistəd], *a.* non enregistré; non recommandé (*lettre etc.*).
unrelated [ʌnri'leitid], *a.* sans rapport (*avec*); *who is unrelated to,* qui n'est pas parent de.
unrelenting [ʌnri'lentiŋ], *a.* inflexible, implacable.
unreliable [ʌnri'laiəbl], *a.* peu sûr; sur qui *ou* sur quoi l'on ne peut compter.
unrelieved [ʌnri'li:vd], *a.* non soulagé; sans relief.
unremitting [ʌnri'mitiŋ], *a.* incessant, infatigable.
unremunerative [ʌnri'mju:nərətiv], *a.* peu rémunérateur, peu lucratif.
unrepentant [ʌnri'pentənt], *a.* impénitent.
unrepresented [ʌnrepri'zentid], *a.* non représenté.
unrequited [ʌnri'kwaitid], *a.* sans être récompensé; qui n'est pas payé de retour (*amour*).
unreserved [ʌnri'zə:vd], *a.* sans réserve; absolu (*total*).
unreservedly [ʌnri'zə:vidli], *adv.* sans réserve.
unresisting [ʌnri'zistiŋ], *a.* qui ne résiste pas, soumis.
unresolved [ʌnri'zɔlvd], *a.* non résolu; irrésolu, indécis (*personne*).
unresponsive [ʌnris'pɔnsiv], *a.* peu sensible; froid.
unrest [ʌn'rest], *n.* inquiétude, agitation, *f.*
unrestrained [ʌnri'streind], *a.* non restreint; non réprimé; effréné, déréglé.
unrestricted [ʌnri'striktid], *a.* sans restriction.
unretentive [ʌnri'tentiv], *a.* peu tenace; peu fidèle (*la mémoire*).
unrevenged [ʌnri'vendʒd], *a.* non vengé.
unrevised [ʌnri'vaizd], *a.* non revu, non revisé.
unrewarded [ʌnri'wɔ:did], *a.* sans récompense.

unrewarding [ʌnri'wɔ:diŋ], *a.* peu rémunérateur.

unrig [ʌn'rig], *v.t.* dégréer.

unrighteous [ʌn'raitʃəs], *a.* injuste, inique.

unrighteousness [ʌn'raitʃəsnis], *n.* injustice, iniquité, *f.*

unripe [ʌn'raip], *a.* pas mûr, vert; (*fig.*) prématuré.

unrivaled [ʌn'raivəld], *a.* sans rival, sans égal.

unroll [ʌn'roul], *v.t.* dérouler, déployer.— *v.i.* se dérouler, se déployer.

unruffled [ʌn'rʌfld], *a.* tranquille, calme.

unruly [ʌn'ru:li], *a.* indiscipliné, insoumis, turbulent.

unsaddle [ʌn'sædl], *v.t.* desseller; débâter (*âne*); désarçonner (*cavalier*).

unsafe [ʌn'seif], *a.* peu sûr, dangereux, hasardeux.

unsaleable [ʌn'seiləbl], *a.* invendable.

unsalted [ʌn'sɔ:ltid], *a.* non salé, sans sel.

unsanctified [ʌn'sæŋktifaid], *a.* non consacré, profane.

unsatisfactorily [ʌnsætis'fæktərili], *adv.* d'une manière peu satisfaisante.

unsatisfactory [ʌnsætis'fæktəri], *a.* peu satisfaisant.

unsatisfied [ʌn'sætisfaid], *a.* peu satisfait.

unsavoriness [ʌn'seivərinis], *n.* insipidité, fadeur, *f.*; mauvais goût, *m.*

unsavory [ʌn'seivəri], *a.* sans saveur, insipide; repoussant (*désagréable*).

unscarred [ʌn'ska:d], *a.* sans cicatrices.

unscathed [ʌn'skeiðd], *a.* sans blessures, sain et sauf.

unscholarly [ʌn'skɔləli], *a.* illettré, ignorant.

unscientific [ʌnsaiən'tifik], *a.* peu scientifique.

unscientifically [ʌnsaiən'tifikli], *adv.* peu scientifiquement.

unscrew [ʌn'skru:], *v.t.* dévisser.

unscrupulous [ʌn'skru:pjuləs], *a.* peu scrupuleux.

unscrupulously [ʌn'skru:pjuləsli], *adv.* sans scrupule.

unscrupulousness [ʌn'skru:pjuləsnis], *n.* manque de scrupule, *m.*

unseal [ʌn'si:l], *v.t.* décacheter; desceller.

unsealed [ʌn'si:ld], *a.* décacheté, ouvert.

unseasonable [ʌn'si:znəbl], *a.* mal à propos; indu (*heure*); pas de saison (*temps*).

unseat [ʌn'si:t], *v.t.* renverser; désarçonner (*d'un cheval*); (*Polit.*) invalider.

unseaworthy [ʌn'si:wə:ði], *a.* incapable de tenir la mer, innavigable.

unsecured [ʌnsi'kjuəd], *a.* sans garantie; mal fermé (*porte*).

unseeing [ʌn'si:iŋ], *a.* aveugle.

unseemliness [ʌn'si:mlinis], *n.* inconvenance, *f.*

unseemly [ʌn'si:mli], *a.* inconvenant; indécent.

unseen [ʌn'si:n], *a.* sans être vu, invisible.

unselfish [ʌn'selfiʃ], *a.* désintéressé.

unserviceable [ʌn'sə:visəbl], *a.* inutile, bon à rien.

unsettle [ʌn'setl], *v.t.* déranger; (*fig.*) troubler.

unsettled [ʌn'setld], *a.* mal fixé, mal établi; incertain (*temps etc.*); irrésolu (*personne*); dérangé, troublé (*esprit*); variable, changeant (*inconstant*).

unshackled [ʌn'ʃækld], *a.* sans entraves, libre.

unshaken [ʌn'ʃeikn], *a.* inébranlable, ferme.

unshapely [ʌn'ʃeipli], *a.* difforme, informe.

unshaved [ʌn'ʃeivd], **unshaven** [ʌn'ʃeivn], *a.* non rasé.

unsheathe [ʌn'ʃi:ð], *v.t.* dégainer.

unship [ʌn'ʃip], *v.t.* débarquer; démonter (*gouvernail etc.*); désarmer (*avirons*).

unshod [ʌn'ʃɔd], *a.* sans chaussures; déferré (*cheval*).

unshorn [ʌn'ʃɔ:n], *a.* non tondu.

unshrinkable [ʌn'ʃriŋkəbl], *a.* irrétrécissable.

unsightliness [ʌn'saitlinis], *n.* laideur, *f.*

unsightly [ʌn'saitli], *a.* laid, déplaisant.

unsigned [ʌn'saind], *a.* non signé.

unsisterly [ʌn'sistəli], *a.* peu digne d'une sœur.

unskilled [ʌn'skild], *a.* inexpérimenté (*dans*); non qualifié; **unskilled labor**, travail de manœuvre, *m.*; main-d'œuvre non spécialisée, *f.*

unskillful [ʌn'skilful], *a.* inhabile, maladroit.

unsociable [ʌn'souʃəbl], *a.* insociable.

unsoiled [ʌn'sɔild], *a.* sans tache.

unsold [ʌn'sould], *a.* invendu.

unsoldierly [ʌn'souldʒəli], *a.* indigne d'un soldat.

unsolicited [ʌnsə'lisitid], *a.* sans être sollicité.

unsolved [ʌn'sɔlvd], *a.* non résolu.

unsophisticated [ʌnsə'fistikeitid], *a.* qui n'est pas frelaté; pur, vrai.

unsought [ʌn'sɔ:t], *a.* non recherché; spontané.

unsound [ʌn'saund], *a.* défectueux, malsain; faux, erroné; mal établi (*crédit*); vicieux, pas sain (*cheval*); **of unsound mind**, non sain d'esprit.

unsparing [ʌn'spɛəriŋ], *a.* libéral, prodigue; impitoyable (*sans pitié*).

unsparingly [ʌn'spɛəriŋli], *adv.* avec prodigalité; impitoyablement.

unspeakable [ʌn'spi:kəbl], *a.* inexprimable; indicible; ignoble, sans nom.

unspecified [ʌn'spesifaid], *a.* non spécifié.

unspoiled [ʌn'spɔild], *a.* non corrompu; bien élevé (*enfant*).

unspoken [ʌn'spoukn], *a.* non prononcé; tacite.

unsportsmanlike [ʌn'spɔ:tsmənlaik], *a.* indigne d'un chasseur *ou* d'un sportsman.

unspotted [ʌn'spɔtid], *a.* sans tache.

unstable [ʌn'steibl], *a.* irrésolu; inconstant; (*Mech.*) instable.

unstained [ʌn'steind], *a.* sans tache.

unstamped [ʌn'stæmpt], *a.* non timbré, sans timbre.

unsteadily [ʌn'stedili], *adv.* en chancelant; d'une manière irrégulière.

unsteadiness [ʌn'stedinis], *n.* instabilité, irrésolution, *f.*

unsteady [ʌn'stedi], *a.* chancelant; mal assuré, irrésolu, inconstant, irrégulier (*conduite*).

unstinted [ʌn'stintid], *a.* non restreint, abondant.

unstop [ʌn'stɔp], *v.t.* déboucher, ouvrir.

unstrengthened [ʌn'streŋθənd], *a.* non renforcé.

unstressed [ʌn'strest], *a.* inaccentué, atone.

unsubdued [ʌnsəb'dju:d], *a.* indompté.

unsubmissive [ʌnsəb'misiv], *a.* insoumis.

unsubmissiveness [ʌnsəb'misivnis], *n.* insoumission, *f.*
unsubstantial [ʌnsəb'stænʃl], *a.* peu substantiel; peu solide; (*fig.*) immatériel; chimérique.
unsuccessful [ʌnsək'sesful], *a.* qui n'a pas réussi, sans succès.
unsuccessfully [ʌnsək'sesfuli] *adv.* sans succès.
unsuitable [ʌn'sjuːtəbl], *a.* peu convenable, peu propre (*à*).
unsuited [ʌn'sjuːtid], *a.* peu fait (*pour*), peu convenable (*à*).
unsullied [ʌn'sʌlid], *a.* sans souillure, sans tache.
unsung [ʌn'sʌŋ], *a.* non célébré.
unsupervised [ʌn'sjuːpəvaizd], *a.* non surveillé.
unsupported [ʌnsə'pɔːtid], *a.* non soutenu; (*fig.*) sans appui.
unsuppressed [ʌnsə'prest], *a.* mal contenu.
unsure [ʌn'ʃuə], *a.* peu sûr.
unsurpassed [ʌnsə'pɑːst], *a.* non surpassé, sans égal.
unsuspected [ʌnsə'spektid], *a.* insoupçonné; non suspect.
unsuspecting [ʌnsə'spektiŋ], sans soupçon, confiant.
unsuspicious [ʌnsə'spiʃəs], *a.* sans méfiance, confiant.
unsustained [ʌnsə'steind], *a.* non soutenu.
unswayed [ʌn'sweid], *a.* qui ne se laisse pas influencer.
unswerving [ʌn'swəːviŋ], *a.* qui ne s'écarte pas, inébranlable.
unsymmetrical [ʌnsi'metrikl], *a.* asymétrique.
unsympathetic [ʌnsimpə'θetik], *a.* froid, peu compatissant.
unsystematic [ʌnsisti'mætik], *a.* peu systématique.
untainted [ʌn'teintid], *a.* non corrompu; frais (*viande*).
untamable [ʌn'teiməbl], *a.* indomptable.
untamed [ʌn'teimd], *a.* indompté, non apprivoisé.
untapped [ʌn'tæpt], *a.* inexploité (*ressources*).
untarnished [ʌn'tɑːniʃt], *a.* non terni.
untaught [ʌn'tɔːt], *a.* ignorant, illettré.
untaxed [ʌn'tækst], *a.* exempt d'impôts.
unteachable [ʌn'tiːtʃəbl], *a.* incapable d'apprendre.
untearable [ʌn'tɛərəbl], *a.* indéchirable.
untempered [ʌn'tempəd], *a.* non trempé (*métal*).
untenable [ʌn'tenəbl], *a.* insoutenable.
untended [ʌn'tendid], *a.* non gardé.
untested [ʌn'testid], *a.* inessayé.
unthanked [ʌn'θæŋkt], *a.* sans être remercié.
unthinking [ʌn'θiŋkiŋ], *a.* inconsidéré, étourdi.
unthinkingly [ʌn'θiŋkiŋli], *adv.* sans y penser.
untidily [ʌn'taidili], *adv.* sans ordre, sans soin.
untidiness [ʌn'taidinis], *n.* désordre, *m.*
untidy [ʌn'taidi], *a.* en désordre; négligé.
untie [ʌn'tai], *v.t.* délier, dénouer; défaire (*nœud*).
until [ən'til], *prep.* jusqu'à; avant.—*conj.* jusqu'à ce que, avant que.
untilled [ʌn'tild], *a.* inculte, en friche.
untimeliness [ʌn'taimlinis], *n.* inopportunité, *f.*

616

untimely [ʌn'taimli], *a.* prématuré, inopportun.—*adv.* avant terme, prématurément.
untiring [ʌn'taiəriŋ], *a.* infatigable.
untiringly [ʌn'taiəriŋli], *adv.* sans relâche.
***unto** ['ʌntu], *prep.* [TO].
untold [ʌn'tould], *a.* non raconté, non exprimé; sans nombre; inouï.
untouchable [ʌn'tʌtʃəbl], *a.* and *n.* hors caste, paria, intouchable, *m., f.*
untouched [ʌn'tʌtʃt], *a.* non touché; (*fig.*) non ému (*de*).
untoward [ʌn'tɔːd, ʌn'touəd], *a.* insoumis, indocile (*rebelle*); fâcheux.
untraceable [ʌn'treisəbl], *a.* introuvable.
untrained [ʌn'treind], *a.* inexpérimenté (*inexpert*); indiscipliné; non dressé (*animal*).
untrammelled [ʌn'træməld], *a.* sans entraves.
untranslatable [ʌntrɑːns'leitəbl], *a.* intraduisible.
untravelled [ʌn'trævld], *a.* peu connu (*terre*); qui n'a pas voyagé (*personne*).
untried [ʌn'traid], *a.* non essayé; qui n'a pas encore été jugé.
untrimmed [ʌn'trimd], *a.* sans garniture; non émondé (*arbre*).
untrodden [ʌn'trɔdn], *a.* non frayé; immaculé (*neige*).
untroubled [ʌn'trʌbld], *a.* calme, tranquille.
untrue [ʌn'truː], *a.* faux; inexact (*nouvelle etc.*); déloyal (*à*).
untrustworthiness [ʌn'trʌstwəːðinis], *n.* inexactitude, fausseté, *f.*
untrustworthy [ʌn'trʌstwəːði], *a.* indigne de confiance; inexact, mensonger (*nouvelle etc.*).
untruth [ʌn'truːθ], *n.* contre-vérité, fausseté, *f.*
untruthful [ʌn'truːθful], *a.* menteur; mensonger (*nouvelle etc.*); perfide, faux, déloyal (*traître*).
untruthfulness [ʌn'truːθfulnis], *n.* fausseté, *f.*
untutored [ʌn'tjuːtəd], *a.* peu instruit, ignorant.
untwine [ʌn'twain], *v.t.* détordre; dérouler.
untwist [ʌn'twist], *v.t.* détordre, détortiller, défaire.
unused (1) [ʌn'juːzd], *a.* non employé, inutilisé; inusité (*mot*).
unused (2) [ʌn'juːst], *a.* inaccoutumé; **unused to**, inaccoutumé à.
unusual [ʌn'juːʒuəl], *a.* peu commun, rare.
unusually [ʌn'juːʒuəli], *adv.* rarement, extraordinairement.
unutterable [ʌn'ʌtərəbl], *a.* inexprimable, indicible.
unuttered [ʌn'ʌtəd], *a.* non prononcé.
unvanquished [ʌn'væŋkwiʃt], *a.* indompté.
unvaried [ʌn'vɛərid], *a.* uniforme.
unvarnished [ʌn'vɑːniʃt], *a.* non verni; (*fig.*) simple, naturel.
unvarying [ʌn'vɛəriiŋ], *a.* invariable, uniforme.
unveil [ʌn'veil], *v.t.* dévoiler; découvrir.
unventilated [ʌn'ventileitid], *a.* mal aéré.
unversed [ʌn'vəːst], *a.* peu versé (*dans*).
unvisited [ʌn'vizitid], *a.* non visité, peu fréquenté.
unwarily [ʌn'wɛərili], *adv.* sans précaution, imprudemment.

unwariness [ʌn'wɛərinis], *n.* imprévoyance, imprudence, *f.*

unwarlike [ʌn'wɔ:laik], *a.* pacifique, peu belliqueux.

unwarrantable [ʌn'wɔrəntəbl], *a.* injustifiable.

unwarrantably [ʌn'wɔrəntəbli], *adv.* inexcusablement.

unwarranted [ʌn'wɔrəntid], *a.* non garanti; *an unwarranted insult*, une insulte gratuite.

unwary [ʌn'wɛəri], *a.* inconsidéré, imprudent.

unwashed [ʌn'wɔʃt], *a.* non lavé, sale, malpropre.

unwavering [ʌn'weivəriŋ], *a.* résolu, inébranlable.

unwearable [ʌn'wɛərəbl], *a.* qu'on ne peut plus porter.

unwearied [ʌn'wiərid], *a.* non lassé, infatigable.

unwelcome [ʌn'welkəm], *a.* importun; fâcheux.

unwell [ʌn'wel], *a.* indisposé, souffrant, mal portant.

unwept [ʌn'wept], *a.* non pleuré, non regretté.

unwholesome [ʌn'houlsəm], *a.* malsain, insalubre.

unwieldy [ʌn'wi:ldi], *a.* lourd, pesant, difficile à manier.

unwilling [ʌn'wiliŋ], *a.* peu disposé, mal disposé; *to be unwilling to*, n'être pas disposé à.

unwillingly [ʌn'wiliŋli], *adv.* à contre-cœur, sans le vouloir.

unwillingness [ʌn'wiliŋnis], *n.* mauvaise volonté, *f.*

unwind [ʌn'waind], *v.t. irr.* (*conjug. like* WIND) dévider; dérouler; (*fig.*) débrouiller.
—*v.i.* se dévider.

unwise [ʌn'waiz], *a.* peu sage, malavisé, insensé.

unwisely [ʌn'waizli], *adv.* peu sagement, imprudemment.

unwished (for) [ʌn'wiʃt(fɔ:)], *a.* non souhaité.

unwitnessed [ʌn'witnist], *a.* sans témoin, non certifié.

unwitting [ʌn'witiŋ], *a.* inconscient.

unwittingly [ʌn'witiŋli], *adv.* sans le savoir, inconsciemment.

unwomanly [ʌn'wumənli], *a.* indigne d'une femme.

unwonted [ʌn'wountid], *a.* inaccoutumé, rare.

unworkable [ʌn'wə:kəbl], *a.* impraticable.

unworked [ʌn'wə:kt], *a.* inexploité (*mine etc.*).

unworn [ʌn'wɔ:n], *a.* non usé, non usagé.

unworthily [ʌn'wə:ðili], *adv.* indignement, sans le mériter.

unworthiness [ʌn'wə:ðinis], *n.* indignité, *f.*

unworthy [ʌn'wə:ði], *a.* indigne (*de*), sans mérite.

unwrap [ʌn'ræp], *v.t.* défaire, désenvelopper.

unwrinkle [ʌn'riŋkl], *v.t.* dérider.

unwrinkled [ʌn'riŋkld], *a.* sans rides, uni.

unwritten [ʌn'ritn], *a.* non écrit; (*fig.*) oral, traditionnel.

unyielding [ʌn'ji:ldiŋ], *a.* qui ne cède pas, inflexible.

unyoke [ʌn'jouk], *v.t.* ôter le joug à, dételer.

up [ʌp], *adv.* au haut, en haut, haut; en l'air; levé, sur pied (*pas au lit*); sur l'horizon; debout (*pas assis*); en révolte, en insurrection; fini (*expiré*); élevé (*prix*); en hausse (*valeurs de Bourse*); excité; en révolte, en insurrection; fini (*expiré*); élevé (*prix*); en hausse (*valeurs de Bourse*); *it is up to us to do it*, c'est à nous de le faire; *road up*, rue barrée; *to be up to*, être au courant de; *to make up to*, faire des avances à; *up and down*, en haut et en bas, çà et là, de long en large, de haut en bas; *up there*, là-haut; *up to*, jusqu'à la hauteur de; *up to date*, à la dernière mode; à jour; *up to now*, jusqu'ici; *up to then*, jusque-là; *what's up?* (*colloq.*) qu'est-ce qu'il y a donc?—*prep.* en haut de, au haut de; en montant; *up hill* or *up stream*, en amont. —*n.* haut, *m.*; *the ups and downs*, les hauts et les bas, *m.pl.*

upbraid [ʌp'breid], *v.t.* reprocher à; réprouver.

upbraiding [ʌp'breidiŋ], *n.* reproche, *m.*

upcast ['ʌpka:st], *n.* jet; coup, *m.*

upheaval [ʌp'hi:vl], *n.* soulèvement, *m.*

uphill ['ʌphil], *a.* qui monte; (*fig.*) ardu, pénible.—[ʌp'hil], *adv.* en côte, en montant.

uphold [ʌp'hould], *v.t. irr.* (*conjug. like* HOLD) soutenir, maintenir.

upholster [ʌp'houlstə], *v.t.* tapisser.

upholsterer [ʌp'houlstərə], *n.* tapissier, *m.*

upholstery [ʌp'houlstəri], *n.* tapisserie, *f.*

upkeep ['ʌpki:p], *n.* entretien, *m.*

upland ['ʌplənd], *a.* élevé, des hautes terres.

uplands ['ʌpləndz], *n.pl.* terrain élevé, haut pays, *m.*, hautes terres, *f.pl.*

uplift [ʌp'lift], *v.t.* lever, élever, soulever. —['ʌplift], *n.* (*fig.*) inspiration, *f.*

uplifting [ʌp'liftiŋ], *n.* soulèvement, *m.*

upon [ə'pɔn], *prep.* sur; *upon pain of*, sous peine de.

upper ['ʌpə], *a.* supérieur, d'en haut, de dessus, au-dessus; haut; *the Upper House* la Chambre Haute; *upper circle*, troisièmes loges, *f.pl.*; *upper deck*, pont supérieur, *m.*; *upper hand*, dessus, *m.*, supériorité, *f.*

uppermost ['ʌpəmoust], *a.* le plus élevé; (*fig.*) le plus fort.

uppers ['ʌpəz], *n.pl.* empeignes (*de chaussures*), *f.pl.*; (*fam.*) *to be on one's uppers*, être dans la débine.

Upper Volta ['ʌpə'vɔltə]. la Haute Volta, *f.*

uppish ['ʌpiʃ], *a.* fier, arrogant.

uppishness ['ʌpiʃnis], *n.* fierté, arrogance, *f.*

upraise [ʌp'reiz], *v.t.* soulever, élever.

upright ['ʌprait], *a.* droit, debout; d'aplomb, vertical; (*fig.*) honnête (*intègre*).—*adv.* tout droit.—*n.* montant, *m.*

uprightness ['ʌpraitnis], *n.* droiture, intégrité, *f.*

uprising [ʌp'raiziŋ], *n.* lever; soulèvement, *m.*

uproar ['ʌprɔ:], *n.* tumulte, désordre; tapage, *m.*

uproarious [ʌp'rɔ:riəs], *a.* bruyant; tumultueux.

uproariously [ʌp'rɔ:riəsli], *adv.* avec un grand vacarme.

uproot [ʌp'ru:t], *v.t.* déraciner, extirper.

uprooting [ʌp'ru:tiŋ], *n.* déracinement, *m.*

upset [ʌp'set], *v.t. irr.* (*conjug. like* SET) renverser; (*fig.*) bouleverser.—*v.i.* se renverser;

verser (*véhicules*).—['ʌpset], *n.* bouleversement, *m.*

upshot ['ʌpʃɔt], *n.* résultat, *m.*, fin, *f.*, fin mot, *m.*

upside-down ['ʌpsaid'daun], *adv.* sens dessus dessous.

upstairs ['ʌpstɛəz], *a.* d'en haut.—[ʌp'stɛəz], *adv.* en haut.

upstanding [ʌp'stændiŋ], *a.* droit, debout.

upstart ['ʌpstɑːt], *n.* parvenu, nouveau riche, *m.*

upsurge [ʌp'sɔːdʒ], *n.* poussée, *f.*

upward ['ʌpwəd], *a.* dirigé en haut; ascendant.—*adv.* or **upwards** ['ʌpwədz], en haut; en montant; *upwards of*, plus de.

Ural ['juərəl] **Mountains**. les Monts Ourals, *m.pl.*

uranium [ju'reiniəm], *n.* uranium, *m.*

urban ['ə:bən], *a.* urbain.

urbane [ə:'bein], *a.* qui a de l'urbanité, poli.

urbanely [ə:'beinli], *adv.* avec urbanité.

urbanity [ə:'bæniti], *n.* urbanité, *f.*

urbanize ['ə:bənaiz], *v.t.* urbaniser.

urchin ['ə:tʃin], *n.* gamin, polisson; (*colloq.*) mioche, gosse, *m.*; *sea urchin*, oursin, *m.*

urge [ə:dʒ], *v.t.* presser; pousser, exciter, porter (*à*); alléguer (*insister sur*); *to urge on*, pousser en avant.—*n.* impulsion; poussée, *f.*

urgency ['ə:dʒənsi], *n.* urgence, *f.*

urgent ['ə:dʒənt], *a.* urgent, instant.

urgently ['ə:dʒəntli], *adv.* avec urgence, instamment.

urging ['ə:dʒiŋ], *n.* sollicitation, *f.*

uric ['juərik], *a.* urique.

urinal ['juərinl], *n.* urinoir; (*Med.*) urinal, *m.*; vespasienne (*urinoir public*), *f.*

urinate ['juərineit], *v.i.* uriner.

urine ['juərin], *n.* urine, *f.*

urn [ə:n], *n.* urne; fontaine (*à thé, à café etc.*), *f.*

Ursula ['ə:sjulə]. Ursule, *f.*

Uruguay ['juərugwai]. l'Uruguay, *m.*

Uruguayan [juəru'gwaiən], *a.* uruguayen.— *n.* Uruguayen (*personne*), *m.*

us [ʌs], *pron.* nous; *for us Frenchmen*, pour nous autres Français.

usable ['ju:zəbl], *a.* utilisable, employable.

usage ['ju:zidʒ], *n.* usage, *m.*

use [ju:s], *n.* usage, emploi, *m.*; utilité, *f.*, avantage, profit, *m.*; habitude, *f.*; (*Law*) usufruit, *m.*; *it is of no use*, cela ne sert à rien; *of use*, utile; *to make use of*, se servir de; *what is the use of that?* à quoi sert cela?—[ju:z], *v.t.* user de, faire usage de, employer, se servir de; utiliser; consommer.

used [ju:zd], *a.* usité (*mot etc.*), d'occasion (*voiture*); *very little used*, qui a peu servi, presque neuf (*vêtement etc.*).—[ju:st] *to be* or *get used to*, s'accoutumer à, s'habituer à.—[ju:st], *v. aux. in the expression* **used to** (*followed by inf.*) *usu. translated by the Imp. Tense in French*; *he used to admire*, il admirait.

useful ['ju:sful], *a.* utile.

usefully ['ju:sfuli], *adv.* utilement, avec profit.

usefulness ['ju:sfulnis], *n.* utilité, *f.*

useless ['ju:slis], *a.* inutile; vain.

uselessly ['ju:slisli], *adv.* inutilement.

uselessness ['ju:slisnis], *n.* inutilité, *f.*

usher ['ʌʃə], *n.* huissier (*de cour de justice*);

sous-maître, *m.*—*v.t.* faire entrer, introduire (*dans*); (*fig.*) annoncer.

usherette [ʌʃə'ret], *n.* (*Cine.*) ouvreuse, *f.*

usual ['ju:ʒuəl], *a.* usuel, ordinaire, habituel, accoutumé; d'usage; *as usual*, comme d'habitude.

usually ['ju:ʒuəli], *adv.* ordinairement, d'ordinaire, d'habitude.

usurer ['ju:ʒərə], *n.* usurier, *m.*

usurious [ju:'zjuəriəs], *a.* usuraire.

usurp [ju'zə:p], *v.t.* usurper.

usurpation [ju:zə'peiʃən], *n.* usurpation, *f.*

usurper [ju'zə:pə], *n.* usurpateur, *m.*

usury ['ju:ʒəri], *n.* usure, *f.*

utensil [ju'tensil], *n.* ustensile, *m.*

uterine ['ju:tərain], *a.* utérin.

uterus ['ju:tərəs], *n.* utérus, *m.*

utilitarian [ju:tili'tɛəriən], *a.* utilitaire.

utilitarianism [ju:tili'tɛəriənizm], *n.* utilitarisme, *m.*

utility [ju:'tiliti], *n.* utilité, *f.*

utilizable ['ju:tilaizəbl], *a.* utilisable.

utilization [ju:tilai'zeiʃən], *n.* utilisation, *f.*

utilize ['ju:tilaiz], *v.t.* utiliser.

utmost ['ʌtmoust], *a.* extrême, le dernier, le plus haut, le plus grand; le plus élevé (*prix etc.*).—*n.* extrême, comble, *m.*; *to do one's utmost*, faire tout son possible (*pour*).

Utopia [ju:'toupiə]. Utopie, *f.*

Utopian [ju:'toupiən], *a.* d'utopie, utopique.

utter (1) ['ʌtə], *a.* entier, complet; absolu; le plus profond (*extrême*); vrai; fieffé (*véritable*).

utter (2) ['ʌtə], *v.t.* pousser, proférer, prononcer; dire; émettre (*fausse monnaie*).

utterable ['ʌtərəbl], *a.* exprimable.

utterance ['ʌtərəns], *n.* énonciation, prononciation, parole, expression, *f.*

utterer ['ʌtərə], *n.* personne qui prononce, *f.*; émetteur (*de fausse monnaie*), *m.*

utterly ['ʌtəli], *adv.* tout à fait, entièrement.

uttermost ['ʌtəmoust], *a.* extrême; le plus reculé.

uvula ['ju:vjulə], *n.* (*Anat.*) luette, uvule, *f.*

uvular ['ju:vjulə], *a.* uvulaire.

uxorious [ʌk'sɔ:riəs], *a.* uxorieux, esclave de sa femme.

uxoriousness [ʌk'sɔ:riəsnis], *n.* complaisance excessive pour sa femme, *f.*

V

V, v [vi:]. vingt-deuxième lettre de l'alphabet, *m.*

vacancy ['veikənsi], *n.* vacance, place vacante, *f.*; vide, *m.*; lacune (*trou*), *f.*

vacant ['veikənt], *a.* vacant, vide; libre (*inoccupé*); vide d'expression (*regard perdu*).

vacate [və'keit], *v.t.* laisser vacant, quitter.

vacation [və'keiʃən], *n.* vacation, *f.*, vacances, *f.pl.*

vaccinate ['væksineit], *v.t.* vacciner.

vaccination [væksi'neiʃən], *n.* vaccination, vaccine, *f.*

vaccine ['væksi:n], *a.* de vache.—*n.* vaccin, *m.*

vacillate ['væsileit], *v.i.* vaciller; (*fig.*) hésiter.
vacillating ['væsileitiŋ], *a.* vacillant, indécis.
vacillation [væsi'leiʃən], *n.* vacillation, indécision, *f.*
vacuity [və'kju:iti], *n.* vide, *m.*; vacuité, *f.*
vacuous ['vækjuəs], *a.* vide; (*fig.*) bête.
vacuum ['vækjuəm], *n.* vide, *m.*
vacuum cleaner ['vækjuəm'kli:nə], *n.* aspirateur, *m.*
vade-mecum ['veidi'mi:kəm], *n.* vade-mecum, *m.*
vagabond ['vægəbɔnd], *a.* errant, vagabond. —*n.* vagabond, *m.*
vagary ['veigəri], *n.* caprice, *m.*, lubie, boutade, *f.*
vagina [və'dʒainə], *n.* (*Anat.*) vagin, *m.*
vagrancy ['veigrənsi], *n.* vagabondage, *m.*
vagrant ['veigrənt], *a.* vagabond, errant.—*n.* vagabond, mendiant, *m.*
vague [veig], *a.* vague.
vaguely ['veigli], *adv.* vaguement.
vagueness ['veignis], *n.* vague, *m.*
vain [vein], *a.* vain; faux (*creux*); vaniteux, glorieux (*fier*); *in vain*, en vain.
vainglorious [vein'glɔ:riəs], *a.* vain, vaniteux.
vainglory [vein'glɔ:ri], *n.* vaine gloire, gloriole, *f.*
vainly ['veinli], *adv.* en vain, vainement.
vainness ['veinnis], *n.* vanité, *f.*
valance ['væləns], *n.* frange de lit, *f.*
vale [veil], *n.* (*poet.*) vallon, *m.*, vallée, *f.*
valedictory [væli'diktəri], *a.* d'adieu.—*n.* discours d'adieu, *m.*
valet ['vælit], *n.* valet de chambre, *m.*
valetudinarian [vælitju:di'nɛəriən], *a.* and *n.* valétudinaire, *m.*, *f.*
valiant ['væliənt], *a.* vaillant, valeureux.
valiantly ['væliəntli], *adv.* vaillamment.
valid ['vælid], *a.* valide, valable.
validate ['vælideit], *v.t.* valider, rendre valable.
validity [və'liditi], **validness** ['vælidnis], *n.* validité, *f.*
validly ['vælidli], *adv.* validement.
validness [VALIDITY].
valise [və'li:z], *n.* valise, *f.*; sac de voyage, *m.*
valley ['væli], *n.* vallée, *f.*, vallon, *m.*
valor ['vælə], *n.* valeur, vaillance, *f.*
valorous ['vælərəs], *a.* valeureux.
valuable ['væljuəbl], *a.* précieux.
valuation [vælju'eiʃən], *n.* évaluation, *f.*
valuator ['væljueitə], *n.* estimateur, *m.*
value ['vælju:], *n.* valeur, *f.*; prix, *m.*—*v.t.* évaluer, estimer.
valued ['vælju:d], *a.* estimé, apprécié.
valueless ['væljulis], *a.* sans valeur.
valuer ['væljuə], *n.* estimateur, commissaire-priseur, *m.*
valve [vælv], *n.* soupape; valve; (*Rad.*) lampe, *f.*
valved [vælvd], *a.* à soupape; (*Bot.*) valvé, à valves.
valvular ['vælvjulə], *a.* (*Med.*) valvulaire.
vamp [væmp], *n.* empeigne; enjôleuse, femme fatale, *f.*—*v.t.* (*fig.*) raccommoder, rapiécer; (*Mus.*) improviser.
vampire ['væmpaiə], *n.* vampire, *m.*
van [væn], *n.* camionnette, voiture (*de déménagement*), *f.*; (*Rail. etc.*) fourgon, *m.*; avant-garde (*précurseur*), *f.*

vandal [vændl], *n.* vandale, *m.*, *f.*
vandalism ['vændəlizm], *n.* vandalisme, *m.*
vane [vein], *n.* girouette, *f.*
vanguard ['vænga:d], *n.* avant-garde, *f.*
vanilla [və'nilə], *n.* vanille, *f.*
vanish ['væniʃ], *v.i.* s'évanouir, disparaître.
vanishing point ['væniʃiŋpɔint], *n.* point de fuite, *m.*
vanity ['væniti], *n.* vanité, *f.*
vanquish ['vænkwiʃ], *v.t.* vaincre.
vanquisher ['vænkwiʃə], *n.* vainqueur, *m.*
vantage ['va:ntidʒ], *n.* avantage, *m.*, supériorité, *f.*
vapid ['væpid], *a.* fade, insipide; éventé (*boisson alcoolique*).
vapidity [væ'piditi], **vapidness** ['væpidnis], *n.* fadeur, insipidité, *f.*
vapor ['veipə], *n.* vapeur; (*fig.*) fumée, *f.*
vaporish ['veipəriʃ], **vapory** ['veipəri], *a.* vaporeux.
vaporization [veipərai'zeiʃən], *n.* vaporisation, *f.*
vaporize ['veipəraiz], *v.t.* vaporiser.—*v.i.* se vaporiser.
vaporous ['veipərəs], *a.* vaporeux.
variability [vɛəriə'biliti], **variableness** ['vɛəriəblnis], *n.* variabilité; inconstance, *f.*
variable ['vɛəriəbl], *a.* variable; inconstant.
variance ['vɛəriəns], *n.* désaccord, *m.*
variation [vɛəri'eiʃən], *n.* variation, *f.*, changement, *m.*
varicose ['værikous], *a.* variqueux; *varicose vein*, varice, *f.*
varied ['vɛərid], *a.* varié, divers.
variegate ['vɛərigeit], *v.t.* varier; nuancer.
variegated ['vɛərigeitid], *a.* varié, bigarré; (*Bot.*) panaché.
variegation [vɛəri'geiʃən], *n.* bigarrure, *f.*
variety [və'raiəti], *n.* variété, diversité, *f.*
various ['vɛəriəs], *a.* divers, différent.
variously ['vɛəriəsli], *adv.* diversement.
varnish ['va:niʃ], *n.* vernis, *m.*—*v.t.* vernir; vernisser (*poterie etc.*).
varnisher ['va:niʃə], *n.* vernisseur, *m.*
varnishing ['va:niʃiŋ], *n.* vernissure, *f.*; vernissage, *m.*
vary ['vɛəri], *v.t.* varier; diversifier.—*v.i.* varier, changer.
varying ['vɛəriiŋ], *a.* changeant, qui varie, divers.
vascular ['væskjulə], *a.* vasculaire.
vase [va:z], *n.* vase, *m.*
vaseline ['væsəli:n], *n.* (*reg. trade mark*) vaseline, *f.*
vassal [væsl], *n.* vassal, *m.*
vassalage ['væsəlidʒ], *n.* vasselage, *m.*; (*fig.*) servitude, *f.*
vast [va:st], *a.* vaste, immense.—*n.* immensité, *f.*
vastly ['va:stli], *adv.* immensément, excessivement.
vastness ['va:stnis], *n.* vaste étendue, grandeur, *f.*
vat [væt], *n.* cuve, *f.*
vatful ['vætful], *n.* cuvée, *f.*
Vatican ['vætikən], le Vatican, *m.*
vaudeville ['voudəvil], *n.* vaudeville, *m.*
vault [vɔ:lt], *n.* voûte, cave, *f.*; caveau (*lieu de sépulture*); saut (*bond*), *m.*—*v.t.* voûter.—*v.i.* sauter.
vaulted ['vɔ:ltid], *a.* voûté, en voûte.

vaulter

vaulter ['vɔːltə], *n.* voltigeur, sauteur, *m.*, acrobate, *m.*, *f.*
vaulting ['vɔːltiŋ], *n.* construction de voûtes, *f.*; voûtes, *f.pl.*; voltige (*acrobatie*), *f.*
vaunt [vɔːnt], *n.* vanterie, *f.*—*v.t.* vanter, élever jusqu'aux nues.
vaunter ['vɔːntə], *n.* vantard, *m.*
vaunting ['vɔːntiŋ], *a.* plein de jactance.
vauntingly ['vɔːntiŋli], *adv.* avec jactance.
veal [viːl], *n.* veau, *m.*
vedette [ve'det], *n.* vedette, *f.*
veer [viə], *v.t.* virer (*bateau*).—*v.i.* tourner, changer de direction; virer (*bateau*).
vegetable ['vedʒitəbl], *a.* végétal.—*n.* végétal, légume, *m.*
vegetal ['vedʒitl], *a.* végétal.
vegetarian [vedʒi'teəriən], *a.* and *n.* végétarien, *m.*
vegetate ['vedʒiteit], *v.i.* végéter.
vegetation [vedʒi'teiʃən], *n.* végétation, *f.*
vegetative ['vedʒitətiv], *a.* végétatif, végétant.
vehemence ['viːiməns], *n.* véhémence; (*fig.*) ardeur, *f.*
vehement ['viːimənt], *a.* véhément, impétueux.
vehemently ['viːiməntli], *adv.* avec véhémence, impétueusement.
vehicle ['viːikl], *n.* véhicule, *m.*, voiture, *f.*
veil [veil], *n.* voile, *m.*; voilette (*de dame*), *f.*— *v.t.* voiler; (*fig.*) déguiser.
vein [vein], *n.* veine; (*fig.*) humeur, *f.*—*v.t.* veiner.
veined [veind], *veiny* ['veini], *a.* veiné.
vellum ['veləm], *n.* vélin, *m.*
velocity [və'lɔsiti], *n.* vélocité, vitesse, rapidité, *f.*
velvet ['velvit], *a.* de velours; (*Bot.*) velouté. —*n.* velours, *m.*
velveteen [velvə'tiːn], *n.* velours de coton, *m.*
velvety ['velviti], *a.* velouté.
venal [viːnl], *a.* vénal.
venality [viː'næliti], *n.* vénalité, *f.*
vend [vend], *v.t.* vendre (*petits articles*).
vending machine, see **slot-machine**.
vendetta [ven'detə], *n.* vendetta, *f.*
vendible ['vendibl], *a.* vendable.
vendor ['vendə], *n.* vendeur, *m.*
veneer [və'niə], *n.* feuille (*de bois etc.*); plaque, *f.*; (*fig.*) vernis, *m.*—*v.t.* plaquer (*de*).
veneering [və'niəriŋ], *n.* placage, *m.*
venerable ['venərəbl], *a.* vénérable.
venerableness ['venərəblnis], *n.* caractère vénérable, *m.*
venerate ['venəreit], *v.t.* vénérer.
veneration [venə'reiʃən], *n.* vénération, *f.*
venerator ['venəreitə], *n.* vénérateur, *m.*
venery ['venəri], *n.* chasse, vénerie, *f.*
Venetian [və'niːʃən], *a.* vénitien, de Venise; *Venetian blind*, jalousie, *f.*; *Venetian shutter*, persienne, *f.*—*n.* Vénitien (*personne*), *m.*
Venezuela [venə'zweilə], le Vénézuéla, *m.*
Venezuelan [venə'zweilən], *a.* vénézuélien.— *n.* Vénézuélien (*personne*), *m.*
vengeance ['vendʒəns], *n.* vengeance, *f.*; *with a vengeance*, furieusement, à outrance.
vengeful ['vendʒful], *a.* vindicatif.
venial ['viːniəl], *a.* véniel, pardonnable.
veniality [viːni'æliti], *n.* vénialité, *f.*

Venice ['venis]. Venise, *f.*
venison ['venizn], *n.* venaison, *f.*
venom ['venəm], *n.* venin, *m.*
venomous ['venəməs], *a.* venimeux (*animal*); vénéneux (*plante*); (*fig.*) méchant.
venous ['viːnəs], *a.* veineux.
vent [vent], *v.t.* donner issue à, exhaler, décharger.—*n.* issue, *f.*, passage, cours; trou de fausse (*de baril*); soupirail (*pour l'air*), *m.*; *to give vent to*, donner libre cours à.
ventilate ['ventileit], *v.t.* ventiler; aérer, (*fig.*) discuter.
ventilation [venti'leiʃən], *n.* ventilation, *f.*; *ventilation shaft*, puits d'aérage, *m.*
ventilator ['ventileitə], *n.* ventilateur, *m.*
ventral ['ventrəl], *a.* ventral.
ventricle ['ventrikl], *n.* ventricule, *m.*
ventriloquism [ven'triləkwizm], *n.* ventriloquie, *f.*
ventriloquist [ven'triləkwist], *n.* ventriloque, *m.*, *f.*
venture ['ventʃə], *n.* aventure, entreprise, *f.* —*v.t.* aventurer, risquer.—*v.i.* oser, se hasarder, s'aventurer; s'aviser de (*se permettre*).
venturer ['ventʃərə], *n.* personne aventureuse, *f.*
venturesome ['ventʃəsəm], *a.* aventureux, audacieux.
venue ['venjuː], *n.* juridiction, *f.*; lieu de réunion, *m.*
Venus ['viːnəs]. Vénus, *f.*
veracious [və'reiʃəs], *a.* véridique.
veracity [və'ræsiti], *n.* véracité, *f.*
veranda, verandah [və'rændə], *n.* véranda, *f.*
verb [vəːb], *n.* verbe, *m.*
verbal ['vəːbəl], *a.* verbal, littéral.
verbally ['vəːbəli], *adv.* verbalement, mot à mot.
verbatim [vəː'beitim], *adv.* mot pour mot.
verbena [vəː'biːnə], *n.* verveine, *f.*
verbiage ['vəːbiidʒ], *n.* verbiage, *m.*
verbose [vəː'bous], *a.* verbeux, diffus, prolixe.
verbosity [vəː'bɔsiti], *n.* verbosité, *f.*
verdant ['vəːdənt], *a.* verdoyant, vert.
verdict ['vəːdikt], *n.* verdict; (*fig.*) arrêt, *m.*
verdigris ['vəːdigriːs], *n.* vert-de-gris, *m.*
verdure ['vəːdjə], *n.* verdure, *f.*
verge (1) [vəːdʒ], *n.* bord, *m.*, bordure; lisière (*de forêt etc.*); verge (*baguette*), *f.*; *on the verge of setting out*, à la veille de partir. —*v.i.* pencher (*vers*); *to verge on*, toucher à.
verger ['vəːdʒə], *n.* bedeau, huissier à verge, *m.*
verification [verifi'keiʃən], *n.* vérification, *f.*
verifier ['verifaiə], *n.* vérificateur, *m.*
verify ['verifai], *v.t.* vérifier.
***verily** ['verili], *adv.* en vérité, vraiment.
verisimilar [veri'similə], *a.* vraisemblable.
verisimilitude [verisi'militjuːd], *n.* vraisemblance, *f.*
veritable ['veritəbl], *a.* véritable.
verity ['veriti], *n.* vérité, *f.*
vermicelli [vəːmi'seli], *n.* vermicelle, *m.*
vermicule ['vəːmikjuːl], *n.* vermisseau, *m.*
vermilion [və'miljən], *a.* vermeil.—*n.* vermillon, *m.*
vermin ['vəːmin], *n.* vermine, *f.*
verminous ['vəːminəs], *a.* vermineux.

620

vernacular [vəˈnækjulə], *a.* du pays, indigène.
—*n.* langue vernaculaire, *f.*
vernal [ˈvəːnəl], *a.* printanier.
veronica [vəˈrɔnikə], *n.* véroniquɛ, *f.*
versatile [ˈvəːsətail], *a.* qui a ʿes connaissances variées; qui se plie à tout.
versatility [vəːsəˈtiliti], *n.* souplesse, faculté
d'adaptation, *f.*
verse [vəːs], *n.* vers, *m.*, poésie; strophe
(*stance*), *f.*
versed [vəːst], *a.* versé (*dans*).
versification [vəːsifiˈkeiʃən], *n.* versification,
f.
versifier [ˈvəːsifaiə], *n.* versificateur, rimailleur, *m.*
versify [ˈvəːsifai], *v.t.* mettre en vers.—*v.i.*
versifier.
version [ˈvəːʃən], *n.* version, *f.*
versus [ˈvəːsəs], *prep.* contre.
vertebra [ˈvəːtibrə], *n.* (*pl.* **vertebræ** [ˈvəːti
briː]) vertèbre, *f.*
vertebral [ˈvəːtibrəl], *a.* vertébral.
vertebrate [ˈvəːtibrit], *a.* and *n.* vertébré, *m.*
vertex [ˈvəːteks], *n.* (*pl.* **vertices** [ˈvəːtisiːz])
sommet, zénith, *m.*
vertical [ˈvəːtikl], *a.* vertical.
vertically [ˈvəːtikli], *adv.* verticalement.
vertiginous [vəːˈtidʒinəs], *a.* vertigineux.
vertigo [ˈvəːtigou], *n.* vertige, *m.*
verve [vəːv], *n.* verve, *f.*
very [ˈveri], *a.* vrai, même, véritable.—*adv.*
fort, bien, très.
vesper [ˈvespə], *n.* étoile du soir, *f.*; soir
m.; (*pl.*) vêpres, *f.pl.*
vessel [vesl], *n.* vase; vaisseau, bâtiment,
navire, *m.*
vest [vest], *n.* tricot de corps; (*Am.*) gilet, *m.*—
v.t. vêtir, revêtir; investir (*de*).—*v.i.* échoir
(à).
vestal [vestl], *a.* vestale, de Vesta; (*fig.*)
chaste.—*n.* vestale, *f.*
vestibule [ˈvestibjuːl], *n.* vestibule, *m.*
vestige [ˈvestidʒ], *n.* vestige, *m.*, trace, *f.*
vestment [ˈvestmənt], *n.* vêtement (de cérémonie), *m.*; chasuble, *f.*
vestry [ˈvestri], *n.* sacristie, *f.*
vesture [ˈvestʃə], *n.* vêtements, *m.pl.*
Vesuvius [viˈsuːvjəs], le Vésuve, *m.*
vetch [vetʃ], *n.* vesce, *f.*
veteran [ˈvetərən], *a.* vieux, ancien, expérimenté.—*n.* vétéran, *m.*
veterinary [ˈvetərinri], *a.* vétérinaire;
veterinary surgeon, vétérinaire, *m.*, *f.*
veto [ˈviːtou], *n.* veto, *m.*—*v.t.* mettre son veto
à, interdire.
vex [veks], *v.t.* fâcher, vexer, contrarier.
vexation [vekˈseiʃən], *n.* vexation, contrariété,
f., chagrin, *m.*
vexatious [vekˈseiʃəs], *a.* vexatoire; irritant,
fâcheux, ennuyeux.
vexatiousness [vekˈseiʃəsnis], *n.* caractère
vexatoire, *m.*
vexed [vekst], *a.* vexé, fâché; (*fig.*) épineux
(*question*).
vexing [ˈveksiŋ], *a.* contrariant, vexant, ennuyeux.
via [ˈvaiə], *prep.* par, par voie de, via.
viability [vaiəˈbiliti], *n.* viabilité, *f.*
viable [ˈvaiəbl], *a.* viable.
viaduct [ˈvaiədʌkt], *n.* viaduc, *m.*
vial [ˈvaiəl], *n.* fiole, *f.*

viands [ˈvaiəndz], *n. pl.* aliments, *m.pl.*; mets,
m.
viaticum [vaiˈætikəm], *n.* viatique, *m.*
vibrate [vaiˈbreit], *v.t.* faire vibrer.—*v.i.*
vibrer, osciller.
vibration [vaiˈbreiʃən], *n.* vibration, oscillation, *f.*
vibrating [vaiˈbreitiŋ], **vibratory** [ˈvaibrə
təri], *a.* vibrant, vibratoire.
vicar [ˈvikə], *n.* (*Engl. Ch.*) pasteur; (*R.-C.
Ch.*) curé (*de paroisse*), *m.*; *vicar general*,
vicaire, *m.*
vicarage [ˈvikəridʒ], *n.* cure, *f.*, presbytère, *m.*
vicarial [viˈkɛəriəl], *a.* de la cure, du curé.
vicarious [viˈkɛəriəs], *a.* vicarial, de vicaire;
(*fig.*) de substitution.
vicariously [viˈkɛəriəsli], *adv.* par délégation, par substitution.
vice (1) [vais], *n.* vice, défaut, *m.*; *vice squad*,
brigade de mœurs, *f.*
vice (2) [vais], *n.* (*Tech.*) étau, *m.*
vice admiral [ˈvaisædmirəl], *n.* vice-amiral,
m.
vice chancellor [ˈvaistʃɑːnsələ], *n.* vice-
chancelier; (*Univ.*) recteur, *m.*
vice president [ˈvaisprezidənt], *n.* vice-
président, *m.*
viceroy [ˈvaisrɔi], *n.* vice-roi, *m.*
vicinity [viˈsiniti], *n.* voisinage, *m.*, proximité,
f., alentours, *m.pl.*
vicious [ˈviʃəs], *a.* vicieux; haineux.
viciously [ˈviʃəsli], *adv.* vicieusement;
rageusement.
viciousness [ˈviʃəsnis], *n.* nature vicieuse, *f.*,
vice, *m.*
vicissitude [viˈsisitjuːd], *n.* vicissitude, *f.*
victim [ˈviktim], *n.* victime, *f.*
victimization [viktimaiˈzeiʃən], *n.* tyrannisa-
tion, *f.*
victimize [ˈviktimaiz], *v.t.* exercer des
représailles contre, tromper.
victor [ˈviktə], *n.* vainqueur, *m.*
victorious [vikˈtɔːriəs], *a.* victorieux, de
victoire.
victoriously [vikˈtɔːriəsli], *adv.* victorieuse-
ment, en vainqueur.
victory [ˈviktəri], *n.* victoire, *f.*
victual [vitl], *v.t.* approvisionner, ravitailler.
victualler [ˈvitlə], *n.* pourvoyeur, fournisseur
(de vivres), *m.*; *licensed victualler*,
débitant de boissons, *m.*
victualling [ˈvitliŋ], *n.* ravitaillement, *m.*
victuals [vitlz], *n.pl.* vivres, *m.pl.*, provisions,
f.pl.
vie [vai], *v.i.* rivaliser, lutter (*de*); le disputer
(à).
Vienna [viˈenə]. Vienne, *f.*
Viennese [viːəˈniːz], *a.* viennois.—*n.* Viennois
(*personne*), *m.*
Vietnam [vjetˈnæm]. le Vietnam, *m.*
Vietnamese [vjetnəˈmiːz], *a.* vietnamien.—*n.*
Vietnamien (*personne*), *m.*
view [vjuː], *n.* vue, perspective, scène, *f.*;
regard (*coup d'œil*); aperçu, examen (*exposé*),
m.; intention, *f.*, dessein, *m.*; opinion,
pensée, *f.*; *in view of*, en considération de;
on view, ouvert au public; *with a view
to*, en vue de.—*v.t.* regarder; considérer;
examiner, inspecter; explorer.
viewer [ˈvjuə], *n.* spectateur; téléspectateur,
m.
viewing [ˈvjuːiŋ], *n.* examen, *m.*, inspection, *f.*

view-point ['vju:pɔint], *n.* point de vue, *m.*
vigil ['vidʒil], *n.* veille, veillée, (*Eccles.*) vigile, *f.*
vigilance ['vidʒiləns], *n.* vigilance, *f.*
vigilant ['vidʒilənt], *a.* vigilant, éveillé.
vigilantly ['vidʒiləntli], *adv.* avec vigilance.
vigorous ['vigərəs], *a.* vigoureux.
vigorously ['vigərəsli], *adv.* vigoureusement.
vigorousness ['vigərəsnis], **vigor** ['vigə], *n.* vigueur, *f.*
vile [vail], *a.* vil, abject, bas; détestable.
vileness ['vailnis], *n.* bassesse, *f.*
vilification [vilifi'keiʃən], *n.* diffamation, *f.*
vilifier ['vilifaiə], *n.* diffamateur, *m.*
vilify ['vilifai], *v.t.* vilipender, dénigrer.
villa ['vilə], *n.* villa, maison de campagne, *f.*
village ['vilidʒ], *n.* village, *m.*
villager ['vilidʒə], *n.* villageois, *m.*
villain ['vilən], *n.* scélérat, gredin; (*Theat.*) traître, *m.*
villainous ['vilənəs], *a.* vil, infâme.
villainy ['viləni], *n.* scélératesse, vilenie, *f.*
vindicate ['vindikeit], *v.t.* soutenir, défendre, justifier; venger.
vindication [vindi'keiʃən], *n.* défense, justification, *f.*
vindicator ['vindikeitə], *n.* défenseur, *m.*
vindictive [vin'diktiv], *a.* vindicatif.
vindictively [vin'diktivli], *adv.* d'une manière vindicative.
vindictiveness [vin'diktivnis], *n.* esprit de vengeance, *m.*
vine [vain], *n.* vigne, *f.*
vine-dresser ['vaindresə], *n.* vigneron, *m.*
vinegar ['vinigə], *n.* vinaigre, *m.*
vine grower ['vaingrouə], *n.* viticulteur, *m.*
vine-growing ['vaingrouiŋ], *n.* viticulture, *f.*
vine harvest ['vainhɑ:vist], *n.* vendange, *f.*
vine prop ['vainprɔp], *n.* échalas, *m.*
vinery ['vainəri], *n.* serre à vignes, *f.*
vineyard ['vinjəd], *n.* vigne, *f.*; vignoble, *m.*
vinicultural [vini'kʌltʃərəl], *a.* vinicole.
viniculture ['vinikʌltʃə], *n.* viniculture, *f.*
vinous ['vainəs], *a.* vineux.
vintage ['vintidʒ], *n.* vendange; vinée, récolte de vin (*cueillette*), *f.*; vendanges (*temps de la récolte*), *f.pl.*; *a vintage wine*, un vin de marque, *m.*
vintager ['vintidʒə], *n.* vendangeur, *m.*
vintner ['vintnə], *n.* négociant en vins, *m.*
viny ['vaini], *a.* de vigne, de raisin; de vignoble.
viola (1) [vi'oulə], *n.* (*Mus.*) alto, *m.*; *viola player*, altiste, *m., f.*
viola (2) ['vaiələ], *n.* (*Bot.*) violette, *f.*
violate ['vaiəleit], *v.t.* violer, faire violence à; outrager.
violation [vaiə'leiʃən], *n.* violation, infraction, *f.*, viol (*d'une femme*), *m.*
violator ['vaiəleitə], *n.* violateur, *m.*
violence ['vaiələns], *n.* violence, *f.*; *with violence* (*of robbery*), à main armée.
violent ['vaiələnt], *a.* violent; atroce (*douleur*).
violently ['vaiələntli], *adv.* violemment, avec violence.
violet ['vaiəlit], *n.* violette (*plante*), *f.*; violet (*couleur*), *m.*
violin [vaiə'lin], *n.* violon, *m.*
violinist [vaiə'linist], *n.* violoniste, *m., f.*
violist [vi'oulist], *n.* altiste, violiste, *m., f.*

violoncellist [vaiələn'tʃelist], *n.* violoncelliste, *m., f.*
violoncello [vaiələn'tʃelou], *n.* violoncelle, *m.*
viper ['vaipə], *n.* vipère, *f.*
viperish ['vaipəriʃ], **viperous** ['vaipərəs], *a.* de vipère; (*fig.*) venimeux.
virago [vi'rɑ:gou], *n.* virago, mégère, *f.*
virgin ['və:dʒin], *a.* vierge; virginal, de vierge.—*n.* vierge, *f.*
virginal ['və:dʒinəl], *a.* virginal, de vierge.
Virginia creeper [və'dʒinjə'kri:pə], *n.* vigne vierge, *f.*
virginity [və'dʒiniti], *n.* virginité, *f.*
viridity [vi'riditi], *n.* verdeur, fraîcheur, *f.*
virile ['virail], *a.* viril, mâle.
virility [vi'riliti], *n.* virilité, nature virile, *f.*
virtual ['və:tjuəl], *a.* virtuel; de fait.
virtually ['və:tjuəli], *adv.* virtuellement, de fait.
virtue ['və:tju:], *n.* vertu; (*fig.*) valeur, *f.*, mérite, *m.*
virtuosity [və:tju'ɔsiti], *n.* virtuosité, *f.*
virtuoso [və:tju'ousou], *n.* (*pl.* **virtuosi** [və:tju'ousi:]) virtuose, *m., f.*
virtuous ['və:tjuəs], *a.* vertueux.
virtuously ['və:tjuəsli], *adv.* vertueusement.
virtuousness ['və:tjuəsnis], *n.* vertu, *f.*
virulence ['viruləns], *n.* virulence, *f.*
virulent ['virulənt], *a.* virulent.
virus ['vaiərəs], *n.* virus, *m.*
visa ['vi:zə], *n.* visa, *m.*—*v.t.* viser.
visage ['vizidʒ], *n.* visage, *m.*, figure, *f.*
viscera ['visərə], *n.pl.* viscères, *m.pl.*
viscid ['visid], *a.* visqueux.
viscosity [vis'kɔsiti], *n.* viscosité, *f.*
viscount ['vaikaunt], *n.* vicomte, *m.*
viscountess ['vaikauntis], *n.* vicomtesse, *f.*
viscountship ['vaikauntʃip], *n.* vicomté, *f.*
viscous ['viskəs], *a.* visqueux, glutineux.
vise [vais], *n.* (*Tech.*) étau, *m.*
visibility [vizi'biliti], *n.* visibilité, *f.*
visible ['vizibl], *a.* visible; clair.
visibly ['vizibli], *adv.* visiblement, à vue d'œil.
vision ['viʒən], *n.* vision, vue, *f.*
visionary ['viʒənəri], *a. and n.* visionnaire, *m., f.*
visit ['vizit], *n.* visite, *f.*; séjour (*a stay*), *m.*—*v.t.* visiter, aller, rendre visite à; *I visit the theatre twice a week*, je vais au théâtre deux fois par semaine.—*v.i.* faire des visites.
visitant ['vizitənt], *n.* visiteur, *m.*
visitation [vizi'teiʃən], *n.* inspection; épreuve, *f.*
visiting ['vizitiŋ], *a.* en visite, de visite.—*n.* visites, *f.pl.*
visitor ['vizitə], *n.* visiteur; (*official*) inspecteur, *m.*; *she has visitors*, elle a du monde.
visor ['vaizə], *n.* visière, *f.*
vista ['vistə], *n.* vue, perspective, *f.*
Vistula ['vistjulə], **the.** la Vistule, *f.*
visual ['viʒjuəl], *a.* visuel.
visualize ['viʒjuəlaiz], *v.t.* se représenter.
vital [vaitl], *a.* vital, de vie; (*fig.*) essentiel.
vitality [vai'tæliti], *n.* vitalité, *f.*
vitalize ['vaitəlaiz], *v.t.* vivifier; (*fig.*) animer.
vitally ['vaitəli], *adv.* vitalement.
vitals [vaitlz], *n.pl.* parties vitales, *f.pl.*
vitamin ['vitəmin], *n.* vitamine, *f.*

vitiate ['viʃieit], *v.t.* vicier; (*fig.*) corrompre.
vitiation [viʃi'eiʃən], *n.* viciation; (*fig.*) corruption, *f.*
vitreous ['vitriəs], *a.* vitreux; (*Anat.*) vitré.
vitrify ['vitrifai], *v.t.* vitrifier.—*v.i.* se vitrifier.
vitriol ['vitriəl], *n.* vitriol, *m.*
vitriolic [vitri'ɔlik], *a.* vitriolique.
vituperate [vi'tju:pəreit], *v.t.* vilipender, injurier.
vituperation [vitju:pə'reiʃən], *n.* reproches, *m.pl.*, invectives, *f.pl.*
vituperative [vi'tju:pərətiv], *a.* injurieux, hargneux.
vivacious [vi'veiʃəs], *a.* vif, vivace, animé.
vivaciously [vi'veiʃəsli], *adv.* vivement, avec vivacité.
vivaciousness [vi'veiʃəsnis], **vivacity** [vi'væsiti], *n.* vivacité, *f.*
vivary ['vivəri], *n.* vivier, *m.*
vivid ['vivid], *a.* vif, frappant.
vividly ['vividli], *adv.* d'une manière frappante, avec éclat.
vividness ['vividnis], *n.* vivacité, *f.*, éclat, *m.*
vivification [vivifi'keiʃən], *n.* vivification, *f.*
vivify ['vivifai], *v.t.* vivifier.
vivifying ['vivifaiiŋ], *a.* vivifiant.
viviparous [vi'vipərəs], *a.* vivipare.
vivisection [vivi'sekʃən], *n.* vivisection, *f.*
vivisector [vivi'sektə], *n.* vivisecteur, *m.*
vixen ['viksən], *n.* renarde (*bête*); mégère (*femme*), *f.*
vixenish ['viksəniʃ], *a.* de mégère, méchante.
viz. [viz] (*usu. read* namely), *adv.* à savoir.
vizier [vi'ziə], *n.* vizir, *m.*
vocabulary [vo'kæbjuləri], *n.* vocabulaire, *m.*
vocal [voukl], *a.* vocal, de la voix.
vocalist ['voukəlist], *n.* chanteur, *m.*, chanteuse, *f.*
vocalize ['voukəlaiz], *v.t.*, *v.i.* vocaliser.
vocally ['voukəli], *adv.* par la voix, vocalement.
vocation [vo'keiʃən], *n.* vocation; profession, *f.*
vocational [vo'keiʃənəl], *a.* professionnel.
vocative ['vɔkətiv], *n.* vocatif, *m.*
vociferate [və'sifəreit], *v.t.*, *v.i.* vociférer.
vociferation [vəsifə'reiʃən], *n.* vocifération, *f.*
vociferous [və'sifərəs], *a.* qui vocifère, bruyant.
vociferously [və'sifərəsli], *adv.* en vociférant.
vodka ['vɔdkə], *n.* vodka, *f.*
vogue [voug], *n.* vogue, *f.*
voice [vɔis], *n.* voix, *f.*; *at the top of one's voice*, à tue-tête.—*v.t.* publier; exprimer.
void [vɔid], *a.* vide, vacant; (*Law*) nul, de nul effet.—*n.* vide, espace vide, *m.*—*v.t.* vider; (*Law*) annuler.
voidable ['vɔidəbl], *a.* annulable.
volatile ['vɔlətail], *a.* volatil; qui vole, volant; inconstant (*volage*).
volatility [vɔlə'tiliti], *n.* volatilité, *f.*
volcanic [vɔl'kænik], *a.* volcanique.
volcano [vɔl'keinou], *n.* volcan, *m.*
vole [voul], *n.* campagnol, *m.*
volition [və'liʃən], *n.* volition, volonté, *f.*
volley ['vɔli], *n.* décharge, salve (*de mousqueterie*); volée (*de canon*), *f.*—*v.t.* (*Ten.*) renvoyer (*la balle*) de volée.
volt [voult], *n.* (*Elec.*) volt, *m.*

voltage ['voultidʒ], *n.* voltage, *m.*
volte-face ['vɔltfɑ:s], *n.* volte-face, *f.*
volubility [vɔlju'biliti], *n.* volubilité, *f.*
voluble ['vɔljubl], *a.* délié (*langue*); facile (*débit*).
volubly ['vɔljubli], *adv.* avec volubilité.
volume ['vɔljum], *n.* volume; tome (*livre*), *m.*
voluminous [və'lju:minəs], *a.* volumineux.
voluminously [və'lju:minəsli], *adv.* d'une manière volumineuse.
voluminousness [və'lju:minəsnis], *n.* grosseur, *f.*
voluntarily ['vɔləntərili], *adv.* volontairement, spontanément.
voluntariness ['vɔləntərinis], *n.* spontanéité, *f.*
voluntary ['vɔləntəri], *a.* volontaire, spontané; libre; intentionnel.—*n.* (*Mus.*) improvisation, *f.*
volunteer [vɔlən'tiə], *n.* volontaire, *m.*, *f.*—*v.t.* offrir volontairement.—*v.i.* offrir ses services; s'engager comme volontaire.
voluptuary [və'lʌptjuəri], *n.* voluptueux, épicurien, *m.*
voluptuous [və'lʌptjuəs], *a.* voluptueux.
voluptuously [və'lʌptjuəsli], *adv.* voluptueusement.
voluptuousness [və'lʌptjuəsnis], *n.* volupté, *f.*
volute [və'lju:t], *n.* volute, *f.*
voluted [və'lju:tid], *a.* voluté.
volution [və'lju:ʃən], *n.* spirale, *f.*
vomit ['vɔmit], *v.t.*, *v.i.* vomir.—*n.* vomissement, *m.*
voodoo ['vu:du:], *n.* vaudou, *m.*
voracious [və'reiʃəs], *a.* vorace.
voraciously [və'reiʃəsli], *adv.* avec voracité.
voraciousness [və'reiʃəsnis], **voracity** [və'ræsiti], *n.* voracité, *f.*
vortex ['vɔ:teks], *n.* (*pl.* **vortices** ['vɔ:tisi:z]) tourbillon, *m.*
vortical ['vɔ:tikl], *a.* tourbillonnant, en tourbillon.
votaress ['voutəris], *n.* adoratrice, *f.*
votary ['voutəri], *n.* adorateur; (*fig.*) admirateur, *m.*
vote [vout], *n.* vote, *m.*; voix, *f.*—*v.t.*, *v.i.* voter.
voter ['voutə], *n.* votant, *m.*
voting ['voutiŋ], *n.* vote, *m.*; *voting-paper*, bulletin de vote, *m.*
votive ['voutiv], *a.* votif, voué.
vouch [vautʃ], *v.t.* attester; affirmer.—*v.i.* témoigner (*de*); répondre (*de*).
voucher ['vautʃə], *n.* garant, *m.*, garantie, pièce justificative, *f.*; *luncheon voucher*, bon de repas, *m.*
vouchsafe [vautʃ'seif], *v.t.* daigner, accorder.
vow [vau], *n.* vœu, *m.*—*v.t.* vouer.—*v.i.* faire un vœu; jurer.
vowel ['vauəl], *n.* voyelle, *f.*
voyage ['vɔiidʒ], *n.* voyage (*par mer*), *m.*
voyager ['vɔiidʒə], *n.* voyageur, passager, *m.*
vulcanite ['vʌlkənait], *n.* caoutchouc vulcanisé, *m.*, ébonite, *f.*
vulcanize ['vʌlkənaiz], *v.t.* vulcaniser.
vulgar ['vʌlgə], *a.* vulgaire, commun.
vulgarism ['vʌlgərizm], *n.* expression vulgaire, *f.*
vulgarity [vʌl'gæriti], *n.* vulgarité, grossièreté, *f.*; mauvais goût, *m.*
vulgarize ['vʌlgəraiz], *v.t.* vulgariser.

vulnerability [vʌlnərəˈbiliti], n. vulnérabilité, f.
vulnerable [ˈvʌlnərəbl], a. vulnérable.
vulpine [ˈvʌlpain], a. de renard; (fig.) rusé.
vulture [ˈvʌltʃə], n. vautour, m.

W

W, w [ˈdʌbəlju:]. vingt-troisième lettre de l'alphabet, m.
wad [wɔd], n. bourre (armes à feu etc.), f.; tampon, paquet (faisceau), m.—v.t. bourrer (armes à feu etc.); ouater (vêtement etc.).
wadded [ˈwɔdid], a. ouaté (de).
wadding [ˈwɔdiŋ], n. bourre (armes à feu); ouate (rembourrage), f.
waddle [ˈwɔdl], v.i. se dandiner.
waddling [ˈwɔdliŋ], n. dandinement, m.
wade [weid], v.t. traverser à gué.—v.i. marcher (dans l'eau ou dans la vase).
wafer [ˈweifə], n. pain à cacheter, m.; gaufrette; (R.-C. Ch.) hostie, f.
waffle [wɔfl], n. gaufre, f.
waffle iron [ˈwɔflaiən], n. gaufrier, m.
waft [wɔft], v.t. porter, transporter; faire flotter.
wag [wæg], n. badin, plaisant, farceur, m.—v.t. remuer, agiter.—v.i. s'agiter, remuer, se mouvoir.
wage [weidʒ], v.t. faire.—n. [WAGES].
wager [ˈweidʒə], n. gageure, f., pari, m.—v.t. gager, parier.
wages [ˈweidʒiz], n.pl. gages (de serviteur), m.pl.; salaire, m., paye (d'ouvrier), f.
waggery [ˈwægəri], n. espièglerie, plaisanterie, f.
waggish [ˈwægiʃ], a. badin, malin, facétieux.
waggishness [ˈwægiʃnis], n. badinage, m., espièglerie, f.
waggle [wægl], v.t. remuer.—v.i. frétiller.
wagon [ˈwægən], n. charrette, f., chariot; (Mil.) caisson, fourgon; (Rail.) wagon, m.
wagtail [ˈwægteil], n. hochequeue, m.
waif [weif], n. épave, f.
wail [weil], v.t. pleurer, lamenter.—v.i. pleurer, gémir, se lamenter.—n. (also **wailing** [ˈweiliŋ]) cri, m., lamentation, plainte, f.
wain [wein], n. charrette, f.
wainscot [ˈweinzkət], n. lambris, m., boiserie, f.
waist [weist], n. ceinture, taille, f.
waistband [ˈweistbænd], n. ceinture (de pantalon etc.), f.
waistcoat [ˈweis(t)kout], n. gilet, m.
wait [weit], v.t. attendre.—v.i. attendre; servir (à table etc.).—n. embuscade, f., guet-apens, m.; attente, f.
waiter [ˈweitə], n. garçon, m.
waiting [ˈweitiŋ], n. attente, f.; service (attentions), m.; **no waiting**, stationnement interdit, m.
waiting-maid [ˈweitiŋmeid], **waiting-woman** [ˈweitiŋwumən] (pl. **-women**

[wimin]), n. femme de chambre; camériste (de princesse etc.), f.
waiting room [ˈweitiŋru:m], n. salle d'attente, f..
waitress [ˈweitris], n. servante, fille de service, f.
waits [weits], n.pl. chanteurs de noëls, m.pl.
waive [weiv], v.t. écarter, mettre de côté; abandonner, renoncer.
wake (1) [weik], v.t. irr. éveiller, réveiller.—v.i. veiller (ne pas se coucher); se réveiller (de sommeil).—n. fête de village, f.
wake (2) [weik], n. sillage (de navire), m.; (fig.) suite, f.
wakeful [ˈweikful], a. éveillé; vigilant.
wakefulness [ˈweikfulnis], n. insomnie, f.
waken [ˈweikən], v.t. éveiller, réveiller.—v.i. s'éveiller, se réveiller.
waking [ˈweikiŋ], **wakening** [ˈweikniŋ], a. éveillé.—n. réveil, m.
wale [weil], n. marque (de fouet); côte (de tissu); (pl.) (Naut.) préceinte, f.
Wales [weilz]. le Pays de Galles, m.
walk [wɔ:k], v.t. parcourir, traverser à pied; faire à pied (distance etc.); (cheval).—v.i. marcher; aller à pied; se promener (pour le plaisir); aller au pas (cheval); **to walk over**, traverser ou parcourir à pied.—n. marche; promenade, f., tour, m.; allée (sentier); démarche, allure, f.; pas (de cheval), m.; (fig.) sphère, f., chemin, m.; **at a walk**, au pas.
walker [ˈwɔ:kə], n. promeneur, marcheur; piéton, m.
walkie-talkie [ˈwɔ:kiˈtɔ:ki], n. (fam.) émetteur-récepteur portatif, m.
walking [ˈwɔ:kiŋ], a. ambulant; de marche.—n. la marche; promenade à pied, f.
walking stick [ˈwɔ:kiŋstik], n. canne, f.
walk-over [ˈwɔ:kouvə], n. (Spt.) **to have a walk-over**, remporter une victoire facile, gagner sans concurrent.
wall [wɔ:l], n. muraille, f., mur, m., paroi, f., espalier (à fruits), m.—v.t. entourer de murailles; **to wall up**, murer.
wallet [ˈwɔlit], n. portefeuille, m.
wall-eye [ˈwɔ:lai], n. œil vairon, m.
wallflower [ˈwɔ:lflauə], n. giroflée jaune, ravenelle, f.
wall fruit [ˈwɔ:lfru:t], n. fruit d'espalier, m.
walling [ˈwɔ:liŋ], n. muraillement, m.; murs, m.pl.
wallop [ˈwɔləp], v.t. rosser.
walloping [ˈwɔləpiŋ], n. rossée, volée de coups, roulée, f.
wallow [ˈwɔlou], v.i. se vautrer, se rouler.
wall-paper [ˈwɔ:lpeipə], n. papier peint, m.
walnut [ˈwɔ:lnʌt], n. noix, f.; noyer (bois), m.
walnut tree [ˈwɔ:lnʌttri:], n. noyer, m.
walrus [ˈwɔ:lrəs], n. morse, cheval marin, m.
Walter [ˈwɔ:ltə]. Gauthier, m.
waltz [wɔ:l(t)s], n. valse, f.—v.i. valser.
waltzer [ˈwɔ:l(t)sə], n. valseur, m.
waltzing [ˈwɔ:l(t)siŋ], n. valse, f.
wan [wɔn], a. blême, pâle, pâlot.
wand [wɔnd], n. baguette, f.
wander [ˈwɔndə], v.i. errer; divaguer (l'esprit); délirer.
wanderer [ˈwɔndərə], n. vagabond, m.
wandering [ˈwɔndəriŋ], a. errant, vagabond; nomade (tribu etc.); (fig.) distrait.—n. course errante, divagation, f.; délire, m.

wanderlust ['wɔndəlʌst], *n.* manie des voyages, *f.*

wane [wein], *n.* déclin, *m.*; (*fig.*) décadence, *f.* —*v.i.* décroître (*lune*); (*fig.*) décliner.

wanly ['wɔnli], *adv.* avec pâleur.

wanness ['wɔnnis], *n.* pâleur, *f.*

want [wɔnt], *n.* besoin; manque, défaut (*absence*), *m.*; indigence, misère (*pauvreté*), *f.*; **for want of,** faute de.—*v.t.* avoir besoin de; manquer de; vouloir, désirer (*avoir envie de*); demander (*réclamer*).—*v.i.* manquer (*de*).

wanting ['wɔntiŋ], *a.* qui manque, manquant.

wanton ['wɔntən], *a.* folâtre (*capricieux*); licencieux, libertin (*impudique*); gratuit (*sans cause*).—*n.* débauchée, *f.*—*v.i.* folâtrer.

wantonly ['wɔntənli], *adv.* en folâtrant; gratuitement.

wantonness ['wɔntənnis], *n.* légèreté, *f.*; libertinage, *m.*

war [wɔ:], *n.* guerre, *f.*—*v.i.* faire la guerre (*à*), lutter (*contre*).

warble [wɔ:bl], *v.t.*, *v.i.* gazouiller; (*fig.*) chanter.

warbler ['wɔ:blə], *n.* oiseau chanteur, *m.*; fauvette (*oiseau*), *f.*

warbling ['wɔ:bliŋ], *a.* mélodieux.—*n.* gazouillement, *m.*

ward [wɔ:d], *n.* pupille, *m.*, *f.*; tutelle (*protection*); garde (*de serrure*); salle (*d'hôpital*), *f.*; arrondissement (*de ville*), *m.*—*v.i.* **to ward off,** parer, détourner.

warden [wɔ:dn], *n.* gardien; gouverneur, recteur (*d'université*); directeur (*de collège*), conservateur (*de jardin public*), *m.*

warder ['wɔ:də], *n.* gardien de prison, *m.*

wardress ['wɔ:dris], *n.* gardienne de prison, *f.*

wardrobe ['wɔ:droub], *n.* garde-robe; armoire (*meuble*), *f.*

ward-room ['wɔ:dru:m], *n.* (*Naut.*) carré des officiers, *m.*

ware [wɛə], *n.* (*collect.*) articles fabriqués, *m.pl.*; (*pl.*) marchandises, *f.pl.*

warehouse ['wɛəhaus], *n.* magasin; entrepôt, *m.*—*v.t.* emmagasiner.

warehousing ['wɛəhauziŋ], *n.* emmagasinage, *m.*

warfare ['wɔ:fɛə], *n.* la guerre, *f.*; les opérations, *f.pl.*

warily ['wɛərili], *adv.* prudemment, avec circonspection.

wariness ['wɛərinis], *n.* prudence, circonspection, *f.*

warlike ['wɔ:laik], *a.* guerrier, martial, belliqueux.

warlock ['wɔ:lɔk], *n.* sorcier, *m.*

warm [wɔ:m], *a.* chaud; (*fig.*) zélé, ardent; chaleureux (*accueil*).—*v.t.* chauffer; réchauffer (*ce qui s'était refroidi*); (*fig.*) échauffer.—*v.i.* chauffer, se chauffer, (*fig.*) s'animer.

warming ['wɔ:miŋ], *n.* chauffage, *m.*

warming pan ['wɔ:miŋpæn], *n.* bassinoire, *f.*

warmly ['wɔ:mli], *adv.* chaudement; (*fig.*) vivement.

war-monger ['wɔ:mʌŋgə], *n.* belliciste, *m.*

warmth [wɔ:mθ], *n.* chaleur; (*fig.*) ardeur, *f.*

war-office ['wɔ:rɔfis], *n.* ministère de la guerre, *m.*

warn [wɔ:n], *v.t.* avertir, prévenir (*de*); **to warn against,** mettre en garde contre.

warning ['wɔ:niŋ], *n.* avertissement, avis, *m.*

warp [wɔ:p], *n.* chaîne (*tissage*), *f.*—*v.t.* ourdir (*tissage*); faire déjeter (*bois*); (*Naut.*) touer; (*fig.*) fausser, pervertir.—*v.i.* se déjeter, se déformer; gauchir; (*fig.*) dévier (*de*).

warping ['wɔ:piŋ], *n.* ourdissage (*tissage*); déjettement, gauchissement (*de bois*), *m.*

warrant ['wɔrənt], *n.* autorisation, garantie, *f.*; ordre, mandat; mandat d'amener, *m.*; (*fig.*) justification, *f.*—*v.t.* garantir, autoriser.

warrant officer ['wɔrəntɔfisə], *n.* (*Mil.*) adjudant; (*Naut.*) premier maître, *m.*

warrantor ['wɔrəntə], *n.* (*Law*) garant, *m.*

warranty ['wɔrənti], *n.* garantie, *f.*

warren ['wɔrən], *n.* garenne, *f.*

warrior ['wɔriə], *n.* guerrier, soldat, *m.*

Warsaw ['wɔ:sɔ:]. Varsovie, *f.*

wart [wɔ:t], *n.* verrue, *f.*, poireau, *m.*

warted ['wɔ:tid], **warty** ['wɔ:ti], *a.* couvert de verrues; (*Bot.*) verruqueux.

wary ['wɛəri], *a.* avisé, prudent; défiant.

wash [wɔʃ], *n.* blanchissage, *m.*, lessive (*de linge*), *f.*; (*Paint.*) lavis; sillage (*de navire*), *m.*—*v.t.* blanchir (*linge*); (*fig.*) mouiller, laver.—*v.i.* se laver; faire la lessive (*blanchisseuse etc.*); **to wash up,** faire la vaisselle.

washable ['wɔʃəbl], *a.* lavable.

washbasin ['wɔʃbeisn], *n.* lavabo, *m.*, cuvette, *f.*

washer ['wɔʃə], *n.* laveur, *m.*; machine à laver; (*Tech.*) rondelle, *f.*

washer-woman ['wɔʃəwumən], *n.* (*pl.* **-women** [wimin]) blanchisseuse, *f.*

wash-house ['wɔʃhaus], *n.* lavoir, *m.*, buanderie, *f.*

washing ['wɔʃiŋ], *n.* lavage; blanchissage (*du linge*), *m.*

washing machine ['wɔʃiŋməʃi:n], *n.* machine à laver, *f.*

wash-leather ['wɔʃleðə], *n.* peau de chamois, *f.*

wash-stand ['wɔʃstænd], *n.* toilette, *f.*; lavabo (*petit*), *m.*

wash-tub ['wɔʃtʌb], *n.* baquet, *m.*

washy ['wɔʃi], *a.* humide, mouillé; (*fig.*) fade.

wasp [wɔsp], *n.* guêpe, *f.*; **wasps' nest,** guêpier, *m.*

waspish ['wɔspiʃ], *a.* irascible, irritable.

waspishness ['wɔspiʃnis], *n.* humeur irascible, *f.*

wastage ['weistidʒ], *n.* gaspillage, *m.*

waste [weist], *a.* de rebut; sans valeur; perdu (*inemployé*); inculte (*terre*).—*n.* perte (*mauvais emploi*), *f.*; déchet (*à nettoyer*); gaspillage; rebut, *m.*; terre inculte, *f.*—*v.t.* gaspiller; perdre (*employer mal*); gâcher (*faire sans soin*); ravager, dévaster (*piller*).—*v.i.* s'user, s'épuiser; **to waste away,** dépérir, maigrir.

waste-book ['weistbuk], *n.* brouillard, *m.*

wasteful ['weistful], *a.* dissipateur, prodigue.

wastefulness ['weistfulnis], *n.* prodigalité, perte, *f.*, gaspillage, *m.*

waste paper ['weist'peipə], *n.* papier de rebut, *m.*

waste-paper basket ['weistpeipə'ba:skit], *n.* corbeille à papier, *f.*

waste-pipe ['weistpaip], *n.* tuyau de dégagement; écoulement, *m.*

waster ['weistə], **wastrel** ['weistril], *n.* prodigue, *m.*, *f.*, gaspilleur, *m.*

wasting ['weistiŋ], *a.* qui épuise.—*n.* dépérissement, *m.*, consumption (*du corps*), *f.*

watch [wɔtʃ], *n.* montre; veille (*nocturne*); vigilance (*attention*); garde, *f.*; (*Naut.*) quart, *m.*—*v.t.* veiller sur, surveiller, regarder, épier.—*v.i.* veiller (*ne pas dormir*); prendre, garde (*faire attention*); monter la garde; (*Naut.*) faire le quart.

watch-dog ['wɔtʃdɔg], *n.* chien de garde, *m.*

watcher ['wɔtʃə], *n.* surveillant, veilleur, *m.*

watch fire ['wɔtʃfaiə], *n.* feu de bivouac, *m.*

watchful ['wɔtʃful], *a.* vigilant, attentif.

watchfulness ['wɔtʃfulnis], *n.* vigilance, *f.*

watching ['wɔtʃiŋ], *n.* surveillance, *f.*

watch-maker ['wɔtʃmeikə], *n.* horloger, *m.*

watch-making ['wɔtʃmeikiŋ], *n.* horlogerie, *f.*

watchman ['wɔtʃmən], *n.* (*pl.* -men [men]) gardien; veilleur de nuit, *m.*

watch-tower ['wɔtʃtauə], *n.* tour de guet, *f.*

watchword ['wɔtʃwə:d], *n.* mot d'ordre, *m.*

water ['wɔ:tə], *a.* d'eau, à eau; aquatique. —*n.* eau; marée (*flux*), *f.*, (*fig.*) ordre, rang, *m.*; **drinking water**, eau potable; **fresh water**, eau douce (*pas salée*).—*v.t.* arroser; donner à boire à, abreuver (*animal*); mettre de l'eau dans, couper (*diluer*); moirer (*étoffe*).

water bottle ['wɔ:təbɔtl], *n.* carafe, *f.*; (*Mil. etc.*) bidon, *m.*; bouillotte (*pour chauffer le lit*), *f.*

water carrier ['wɔ:təkæriə], *n.* porteur d'eau; broc (*à eau*), *m.*

water cart ['wɔ:təka:t], *n.* voiture d'arrosage, *f.*

water closet ['wɔ:təklɔzit], *n.* toilettes, *f.pl.*, cabinet d'aisances, *m.*

water color ['wɔ:təkʌlə], *n.* aquarelle, *f.*

watercress ['wɔ:təkres], *n.* cresson, cresson de fontaine, *m.*

water cure ['wɔ:təkjuə], *n.* hydrothérapie, *f.*

watered ['wɔ:təd], *a.* arrosé; moiré (*étoffe*).

waterfall ['wɔ:təfɔ:l], *n.* cascade; chute d'eau, *f.*

water-fowl ['wɔ:təfaul], *n.* oiseau aquatique, *m.*

waterfront ['wɔ:təfrʌnt], *n.* les· quais, *m.pl.*, port, *m.*

water hen ['wɔ:təhen], *n.* poule d'eau, *f.*

wateriness ['wɔ:tərinis], *n.* aquosité, *f.*

watering ['wɔ:təriŋ], *n.* arrosage (*plantes*), *m.*; irrigation (*terre*), *f.*; abreuvage (*animaux*); moirage (*étoffe*), *m.*

watering can ['wɔ:təriŋkæn], *n.* arrosoir, *m.*

watering place ['wɔ:təriŋpleis], *n.* ville d'eaux, station thermale, *f.*; abreuvoir (*pour animaux*), *m.*

water jug ['wɔ:tədʒʌg], *n.* pot à eau, *m.*

water level ['wɔ:təlevl], *n.* niveau d'eau, *m.*

water lily ['wɔ:təlili], *n.* nénuphar, *m.*

water line ['wɔ:təlain], *n.* ligne de flottaison, *f.*

water-logged ['wɔ:təlɔgd], *a.* envahi par les eaux.

watermark ['wɔ:təma:k], *n.* étiage (*de rivière*); filigrane (*sur papier*), *m.*

water-melon ['wɔ:təmelən], *n.* melon d'eau, *m.*, pastèque, *f.*

water mill ['wɔ:təmil], *n.* moulin à eau, *m.*

water pipe ['wɔ:təpaip], *n.* tuyau d'eau, *m.*

water plant ['wɔ:təpla:nt], *n.* plante aquatique, *f.*

water polo ['wɔ:təpoulou], *n.* polo nautique, *m.*

water-power ['wɔ:təpauə], *n.* force hydraulique, *f.*

water pressure ['wɔ:təpreʃə], *n.* pression d'eau, *f.*

waterproof ['wɔ:təpru:f], *a.* and *n.* imperméable, *m.*—*v.t.* rendre imperméable, cirer (*un tissu*).

water rat ['wɔ:təræt], *n.* rat d'eau, *m.*

water-rate ['wɔ:təreit], *n.* taux d'abonnement aux eaux de la ville, *m.*

watershed ['wɔ:təʃed], *n.* versant, *m.*

waterspout ['wɔ:təspaut], *n.* trombe, *f.*; tuyau de descente, *m.*

water tank ['wɔ:tətæŋk], *n.* réservoir à eau, *m.*, citerne, *f.*

water-tight ['wɔ:tətait], *a.* étanche.

water-works ['wɔ:təwə:ks], *n.pl.* établissement pour la distribution des eaux, *m.*, machine hydraulique, *f.*

watery ['wɔ:təri], *a.* aqueux; mouillé, plein d'eau; (*poet.*) humide.

watt [wɔt], *n.* (*Elec.*) watt, *m.*

wattage ['wɔtidʒ], *n.* (*Elec.*) wattage, *m.*

wattle [wɔtl], *n.* claie (*d'osier etc.*), *f.*—*v.t.* clayonner.

wave [weiv], *n.* vague, *f.*, flot, *m.*, lame, ondulation; (*poet.*) onde, *f.*; signe (*de la main*), *m.*; **permanent wave**, permanente, indéfrisable, *f.*; **long waves**, (*Rad.*) grandes ondes, *f.*; **short waves**, petites ondes, ondes courtes, *f.pl.*—*v.t.* agiter, faire signe de (*la main*); onduler (*cheveux*).—*v.i.* ondoyer, onduler, flotter; faire signe (*à*).

waved [weivd], *a.* ondulé.

wave-length ['weivleŋθ], *n.* longueur d'onde, *f.*

waver ['weivə], *v.i.* hésiter, vaciller, balancer.

waverer ['weivərə], *n.* personne indécise, *f.*, esprit vacillant, *m.*

wavering ['weivəriŋ], *a.* indécis, vacillant, irrésolu.—*n.* hésitation, indécision, *f.*

waving ['weiviŋ], *n.* ondoiement, *m.*, ondulation (*blé etc.*), *f.*; geste (*de la main*), *m.*

wavy ['weivi], *a.* ondoyant, onduleux.

wax [wæks], *n.* cire; poix (*de cordonnier*); (*colloq.*) colère, *f.*—*v.t.* cirer, enduire de cire. —*v.i.* croître (*lune*), s'accroître; devenir.

wax candle ['wæks'kændl], *n.* bougie, *f.*

waxen ['wæksn], *a.* de cire; cireux.

wax taper ['wæks'teipə], *n.* rat de cave; (*Eccles.*) cierge, *m.*

waxwing ['wækswiŋ], *n.* (*Orn.*) jaseur, *m.*

waxwork ['wækswə:k], *n.* ouvrage de cire, *m.*; (*pl.*) figures de cire, *f.*, *pl.*

waxy ['wæksi], *a.* cireux.

way [wei], *n.* chemin, *m.*, route, voie, *f.*; passage; côté, sens, *m.*, direction; manière, façon, mode, *f.*; moyen, *m.*, méthode, *f.*; état (*condition*), *m.*; **a long way off**, loin, très loin; **by a long way** (*by far*), de beaucoup; **by the way**, à propos.

way-bill ['weibil], *n.* feuille de route, *f.*

wayfarer ['weifeərə], *n.* voyageur, *m.*

wayfaring ['weifeəriŋ], *a.* qui voyage.

waylay [wei'lei], *v.t.* guetter, guetter au passage.

wayside ['weisaid], *a.* au bord de la route.—*n.* bord de la route, *m.*

wayward ['weiwəd], *a.* capricieux, entêté.

waywardness ['weiwədnis], *n.* humeur capricieuse, *f.*

we [wi:], *pron.* nous; (*indef.*) on; *we Frenchmen,* nous autres Français.

weak [wi:k], *a.* faible, infirme, débile.

weaken ['wi:kn], *v.t.* affaiblir; atténuer.—*v.i.* s'affaiblir.

weakening ['wi:kniŋ], *n.* affaiblissement, *m.*

weakling ['wi:kliŋ], *n.* être faible, faiblard, *m.*

weakly ['wi:kli], *a.* faible; infirme, débile.— *adv.* faiblement, sans force.

weak-minded ['wi:k'maindid], *a.* d'esprit faible.

weakness ['wi:knis], *n.* faiblesse; débilité, *f.*; (*fig.*) faible, *m.*

weak-spirited ['wi:k'spiritid], *a.* mou, sans courage.

weal [wi:l], *n.* bien, bien-être, bonheur, *m.*; marque (*sur la peau*), *f.*

wealth [welθ], *n.* richesse, *f.*, richesses, *f.pl.*; profusion, *f.*

wealthy ['welθi], *a.* riche, opulent.

wean [wi:n], *v.t.* sevrer; (*fig.*) détacher.

weaning ['wi:niŋ], *n.* sevrage, *m.*

weanling ['wi:nliŋ], *n.* enfant *ou* animal en sevrage, *m.*

weapon [wepn], *n.* arme, *f.*

wear [wɛə], *v.t. irr.* porter (*habits*); mettre (*enfiler*); *to wear out,* user, (*fig.*) épuiser, lasser.—*v.i.* s'user (*s'élimer*); se porter (*habits*); (*fig.*) se conserver.—*n.* usage (*port*), *m.*; usure (*élimage*), *f.*

wearable ['wɛərəbl], *a.* mettable.

wearied ['wiərid], *a.* fatigué, las; (*fig.*) ennuyé.

wearily ['wiərili], *adv.* péniblement, d'un air las.

weariness ['wiərinis], *n.* fatigue, lassitude, *f.*; (*fig.*) ennui, *m.*

wearisome ['wiərisəm], *a.* ennuyeux; lassant.

wearisomeness ['wiərisəmnis], *n.* nature ennuyeuse, *f.*

weary ['wiəri], *a.* fatigué, las, ennuyé; ennuyeux (*chose*).—*v.t.* lasser, fatiguer; ennuyer.

weasel [wi:zl], *n.* belette, *f.*

weather ['weðə], *a.* du côté du vent.—*n.* temps, *m.*; (*fig.*) tempête, *f.*—*v.t.* résister à (*tempête etc.*); (*fig.*) tenir tête à.

weather-beaten ['weðəbi:tn], *a.* battu par la tempête; (*fig.*) fatigué; hâlé.

weathercock ['weðəkɔk], *n.* girouette, *f.*

weather-glass ['weðəgla:s], *n.* baromètre, *m.*

weather-proof ['weðəpru:f], *a.* à l'épreuve du (*mauvais*) temps, imperméable.

weather report ['weðəripɔ:t], *n.* bulletin météorologique, *m.*

weather ship ['weðəʃip], *n.* navire météorologique, *m.*

weave [wi:v], *n.* (*Tex.*) tissage, *m.*—*v.t., v.i. irr.* tisser; tresser (*entrelacer*).

weaver ['wi:və], *n.* tisserand, *m.*

weaving ['wi:viŋ], *n.* tissage, *m.*

web [web], *n.* tissu, *m.*; sangle (*pour selle*); toile (*d'araignée*), *f.*

webbed [webd], **webby** ['webi], *a.* palmé.

webbing ['webiŋ], *n.* sangles (*de chaise, lit etc.*), *f.pl.*

web-footed ['webfutid], *a.* palmipède.

wed [wed], *v.t.* épouser, se marier avec.—*v.i.* se marier.

wedded ['wedid], *a.* marié (*à*); conjugal.

wedding ['wediŋ], *a.* de noces, de mariage.— *n.* noce, *f.*, noces, *f.pl.*, mariage, *m.*

wedding ring ['wediŋriŋ], *n.* alliance, *f.*

wedge [wedʒ], *n.* coin, *m.*; cale (*pour tenir immobile*), *f.*—*v.t.* serrer; caler; coincer.

wedge-shaped ['wedʒʃeipt], *a.* en forme de coin, cunéiforme.

wedlock ['wedlɔk], *n.* mariage, *m.*

Wednesday ['wenzd(e)i]. mercredi, *m.*; *Ash Wednesday,* mercredi des Cendres.

weed [wi:d], *n.* mauvaise herbe, *f.*; *widow's weeds,* vêtements de deuil, *m.pl.*—*v.t.* sarcler; (*fig.*) nettoyer; *to weed out,* extirper.

weeder ['wi:də], *n.* sarcleur (*personne*); sarcloir (*outil*), *m.*

weeding ['wi:diŋ], *n.* sarclage, *m.*

weed killer ['wi:dkilə], *n.* herbicide, *m.*

weedy ['wi:di], *a.* plein de mauvaises herbes.

week [wi:k], *n.* semaine, *f.*; *this day week,* d'aujourd'hui en huit (*avenir*); il y a huit jours (*passé*).

weekday ['wi:kdei], *n.* jour ouvrable, jour de semaine, *m.*

week-end ['wi:k'end], *n.* fin de la semaine, *f.*, week-end, *m.*

weekly ['wi:kli], *a.* de la semaine; hebdomadaire (*revue*).—*n.* hebdomadaire, *m.*—*adv.* par semaine, tous les huit jours.

weep [wi:p], *v.t., v.i. irr.* pleurer; *to weep bitterly,* pleurer à chaudes larmes.

weeping ['wi:piŋ], *a.* qui pleure, éploré; (*Bot.*) pleureur; *weeping willow,* saule pleureur, *m.*—*n.* pleurs, *m.pl.*, larmes, *f.pl.*

weever ['wi:və], *n.* (*Ichth.*) vive, *f.*

weevil ['wi:vl], *n.* charançon, *m.*

weft [weft], *n.* trame, *f.*

weigh [wei], *v.t.* peser; (*fig.*) juger; (*Naut.*) lever (*l'ancre*).—*v.i.* peser.

weigh-bridge ['weibridʒ], *n.* pont à bascule, *m.*

weighing ['weiiŋ], *n.* pesage, *m.*; *weighing machine,* bascule, *f.*

weight [weit], *n.* poids, *m.*; *atomic weight,* masse atomique, *f.*

weighted ['weitid], *a.* chargé (*de*).

weightily ['weitili], *adv.* pesamment.

weightless ['weitlis], *a.* sans poids.

weightlessness ['weitlisnis], *n.* apesanteur, *f.*

weighty ['weiti], *a.* pesant, lourd; (*fig.*) important.

weir [wiə], *n.* barrage, déversoir, *m.*

weird [wiəd], *a.* fantastique, étrange.

weirdness ['wiədnis], *n.* étrangeté, magie, *f.*

welcome ['welkəm], *a.* bienvenu, agréable (*chose*); libre (*à profiter de quelque chose*).— *n.* bienvenue, *f.*, accueil, *m.*; *to bid (someone) welcome,* souhaiter la bienvenue à (quelqu'un).—*int.* soyez le bienvenu.—*v.t.* souhaiter la bienvenue à.   bien accueilli. *you are welcome,* see **mention**.

weld [weld], *v.t.* souder; (*fig.*) unir.—*n.* soudure, *f.*

welder ['weldə], *n.* soudeur, *m.*

welding ['weldiŋ], *n.* soudure, *f.*

welfare ['welfɛə], *n.* bien-être, bien, *m.*; *Welfare State,* état providence, *m.*

well (1) [wel], *n.* puits, *m.*; (*Tech.*) source, *f.*; *ink-well,* encrier, *m.*—*v.i.* jaillir (*de*).

well (2) [wel], *a.* bien, en bonne santé; bon, heureux (*fortuné*); utile, profitable; *to get well,* se rétablir; *well off,* aisé (*riche*).—

627

adv. bien; très, fort; comme il faut; *well!* eh bien! *well done!* très bien! bravo! *well, I never!* pas possible!

well-being ['wel'bi:iŋ], *n.* bien-être, *m.*

well-informed ['welin'fɔ:md], *a.* instruit; bien renseigné.

wellingtons ['weliŋtənz], *n.pl.* demi-bottes, *f.pl.*

well-known ['welnoun], *a.* bien connu, célèbre.

well-meaning ['wel'mi:niŋ], *a.* bien intentionné.

well-meant ['wel'ment], *a.* fait à bonne intention.

well-nigh ['welnai], *adv.* presque.

well-timed ['wel'taimd], *a.* à propos, fait à propos.

well-to-do ['weltə'du:], *a.* très aisé, cossu.

well-wisher ['welwiʃə], *n.* ami, partisan, *m.*

Welsh [welʃ], *a.* gallois, du pays de Galles.— *n.* gallois (*langue*), *m.*; *the Welsh*, les Gallois, *m.pl.*

Welshman ['welʃmən], *n.* (*pl.* **-men** [men]) Gallois, *m.*

welt [welt], *n.* bordure (*de gant*); trépointe (*de semelle*), *f.*

welter ['weltə], *n.* confusion, *f.*—*v.i.* se vautrer, se rouler.

wen [wen], *n.* loupe, *f.*; goitre, *m.*

wench [wentʃ], *n.* donzelle; (*pej.*) souillon, *f.*

wend [wend], *v.t., v.i.* aller; *to wend one's way,* se diriger (*vers*).

wer(e)wolf ['wə:wulf], *n.* loup-garou, *m.*

west [west], *a.* de l'ouest, occidental.—*n.* ouest, occident, couchant, *m.*—*adv.* à l'ouest.

westerly ['westəli], *a.* d'ouest.—*adv.* vers l'ouest.

western ['westən], *a.* de l'ouest, occidental, ouest, d'occident; à l'ouest (*vue*).—*n.* (*Cine.*) western, *m.*

westward ['westwəd], *adv.* à l'ouest.

wet [wet], *a.* mouillé, humide; pluvieux (*temps*); *it is wet,* il pleut; *to get wet,* se mouiller; *wet through,* mouillé jusqu'aux os, trempé.—*n.* humidité; pluie, *f.* —*v.t. irr.* mouiller, humecter; arroser.

wetness ['wetnis], *n.* humidité, *f.*; état pluvieux, *m.*

wetting ['wetiŋ], *n.* trempage, *m.*

whack [hwæk], *n.* grand coup, *m.*; (*fam.*) part, *f.*—*v.t.* frapper, battre.

whale [hweil], *n.* baleine, *f.*

whalebone ['hweilboun], *n.* baleine, *f.*

whale oil ['hweilɔil], *n.* huile de baleine, *f.*

whaler ['hweilə], *n.* baleinier, *m.*

wharf [hwɔ:f], *n.* (*pl.* **wharfs** [hwɔ:fs], **wharves** [hwɔ:vz]) quai, embarcadère, débarcadère; entrepôt (*pour marchandises*), *m.*

what [hwɔt], *a.* quel, *m.*, quelle, *f.*, quels, *m.pl.*, quelles, *f.pl.*—*pron.rel.* ce qui, ce que; qui, que; quoi.—*inter. pron.* qu'est-ce qui? que? qu'est-ce que? quoi? *what!* comment!

whatever [hwɔt'evə], **whatsoever** [hwɔtsou 'evə], *pron.* and *a.* quoi que ce soit; quelque ... que; tout ce qui, tout ce que (*all that*).

whatnot ['hwɔtnɔt], *n.* étagère, *f.*

whatsoever [WHATEVER].

wheat [hwi:t], *n.* blé, froment, *m.*

wheaten ['hwi:tn], *a.* de froment.

wheedle ['hwi:dl], *v.t.* cajoler, câliner.

wheedling ['hwi:dliŋ], *a.* cajoleur, câlin.—*n.* cajolerie, câlinerie, *f.*

wheel [hwi:l], *n.* roue, *f.*; volant (*pour conduire*); rouet (*pour filer*), *m.*; révolution, *f.*, tour, cercle (*rotation*); soleil (*feu d'artifice*), *m.*; *driving wheel,* roue motrice, *f.*; *flywheel,* volant, *m.*—*v.t.* rouler, faire tourner; brouetter; voiturer.—*v.i.* rouler (*sur des roues*); tourner, se tourner (*en cercle*); tournoyer (*pirouetter*); (*Mil.*) faire une conversion; *to wheel round,* faire volte-face.

wheel-barrow ['hwi:lbærou], *n.* brouette, *f.*

wheel-chair ['hwi:ltʃɛə], *n.* voiture de malade, *f.*, fauteuil roulant, *m.*

wheeled [hwi:ld], *a.* à roues.

wheeling ['hwi:liŋ], *n.* (*Mil.*) conversion, *f.*; tournoiement (*d'oiseau*), *m.*

wheelwright ['hwi:lrait], *n.* charron, *m.*

wheeze [hwi:z], *v.i.* siffler en respirant.

wheezing ['hwi:ziŋ], *n.* sifflement, *m.*

wheezy ['hwi:zi], *a.* poussif, asthmatique.

whelk [hwelk], *n.* buccin, *m.*

whelp [hwelp], *n.* petit (d'un fauve), *m.*—*v.i.* mettre bas.

when [hwen], *conj.* quand, lorsque; que, où; *the day when I saw him,* le jour où je l'ai vu.—*inter. adv.* quand est-ce que? quand?

whence [hwens], *adv.* d'où.

whenever [hwen'evə], **whensoever** [hwen sou'evə], *adv.* toutes les fois que, quand, à n'importe quel moment que.

where [hwɛə], *adv.* où; là où.

whereabouts ['hwɛərəbauts], *adv.* où à peu près.—*n.* to know someone's *whereabouts,* savoir où est quelqu'un.

whereas [hwɛər'æz], *adv.* au lieu que, tandis que; (*Law*) vu que.

whereat [hwɛər'æt], *adv.* à quoi, de quoi; sur quoi.

whereby [hwɛə'bai], *adv.* par lequel, par où.

wherefore ['hwɛəfɔ:], *adv.* pourquoi, c'est pourquoi.

wherein [hwɛər'in], *adv.* en quoi, dans lequel, où.

whereof [hwɛər'ɔv], *adv.* dont, de quoi, duquel.

whereon [hwɛər'ɔn], **whereupon** ['hwɛərə 'pɔn], *adv.* sur quoi, sur lequel; là-dessus.

wheresoever [hwɛəsou'evə], [WHEREVER].

wherever [hwɛər'evə], *adv.* partout où, n'importe où.

wherewith [hwɛə'wið], *adv.* avec quoi; de quoi.

wherewithal [hwɛəwið'ɔ:l], *n. to find the wherewithal to . . .,* trouver les moyens de . . . *ou* l'argent pour . . . .

wherry ['hweri], *n.* bachot, *m.*

whet [hwet], *v.t.* aiguiser, affiler; (*fig.*) stimuler.—*n.* aiguisement, repassage; (*fig.*) stimulant, *m.*

whether ['hweðə], *conj.* soit que; si, que; *whether . . . or,* soit . . . soit; si . . . ou, que . . . ou.

whetstone ['hwetstoun], *n.* pierre à aiguiser, *f.*

whey [hwei], *n.* petit lait, *m.*

which [hwitʃ], *a.* quel, *m.*, quelle, *f.*, quels, *m.pl.*, quelles, *f.pl.*; lequel, *m.*, laquelle, *f.*, lesquels, *m.pl.*, lesquelles, *f.pl.*—*rel. pron.*

qui, que, lequel, *m.*, laquelle, *f.*, lesquels, *m.pl.*, lesquelles, *f.pl.*; ce qui, ce que (*that which*), *m.*

whichever [hwitʃ'evə], *pron.* lequel, *m.*, laquelle, *f.*, lesquels, *m.pl.*, lesquelles, *f.pl.*; quelque . . . que; *whichever you buy,* n'importe lequel que vous achetiez.

whiff [hwif], *n.* bouffée, haleine, *f.*—*v.t.* lancer en bouffées.

while [hwail], *n.* temps, *m.*; *a little while ago,* il y a peu de temps; *it is not worth while,* cela n'en vaut pas la peine.—*v.t.* passer, faire passer; *to while away the time,* tuer le temps.—(*also* **whilst** [hwailst]) *conj.* pendant que (*au cours de*); tandis que (*par contraste*); tant que (*tout le temps que*); en, tout en (*suivi d'un participe présent*).

whilst [WHILE].

whim [hwim], *n.* caprice, *m.*

whimper ['hwimpə], *v.i.* pleurnicher.

whimpering ['hwimpəriŋ], *a.* pleurnicheur, geignard.—*n.* pleurnichement, *m.*

whimsical ['hwimzikl], *a.* fantasque; capricieux.

whimsically ['hwimzikli], *adv.* capricieusement, fantasquement.

whin [hwin], *n.* ajonc, genêt épineux, *m.*

whine [hwain], *v.i.* se plaindre, geindre, pleurnicher.—*n.* pleurnichement, *m.*

whining ['hwainiŋ], *a.* plaintif, dolent.—*n.* gémissement, geignement, *m.*; (*fig.*) plaintes, *f.pl.*

whinny ['hwini], *v.i.* hennir.—*n.* hennissement, *m.*

whip [hwip], *n.* fouet, *m.*; cravache (*de cavalier*), *f.*; (*Parl.*) secrétaire d'un parti, appel fait aux membres d'un parti, *m.*—*v.t.* fouetter; (*fig.*) battre.

whip-cord ['hwipkɔːd], *n.* fouet; (*Tex.*) fil à fouet, *m.*

whip hand ['hwiphænd], *n.* dessus, avantage, *m.*

whip-lash ['hwiplæʃ], *n.* mèche (de fouet), *f.*

whipper-in ['hwipər'in], *n.* piqueur, *m.*

whipper-snapper ['hwipəsnæpə], *n.* petit bout d'homme, *m.*

whippet ['hwipit], *n.* lévrier (de course), *m.*

whipping ['hwipiŋ], *n.* coups de fouet, *m.pl.*

whipping-top ['hwipiŋtɔp], *n.* sabot, *m.*

whir [hwəː], *v.i.* tourner avec bruit; vrombir.—(*also* **whirring** ['hwəːriŋ]), *n.* bruissement, ronronnement, *m.*

whirl [hwəːl], *v.t.* faire tourner, faire tournoyer.—*v.i.* tournoyer, tourbillonner; pirouetter.—*n.* tournoiement; tourbillon (*de poussière etc.*), *m.*

whirligig ['hwəːligig], *n.* tourniquet, *m.*; pirouette, *f.*

whirlpool ['hwəːlpuːl], *n.* tourbillon (d'eau),*m.*

whirlwind ['hwəːlwind], *n.* tourbillon, cyclone, *m.*

whirring [WHIR].

whisk [hwisk], *n.* vergette, époussette, verge (à œufs etc.), *f.*—*v.t.* épousseter; fouetter (*crème*); battre (*œufs*).—*v.i.* passer rapidement.

whiskered ['hwiskəd], *a.* à favoris; à moustaches (*animal*).

whiskers ['hwiskəz], *n.* favoris, *m.pl.*; moustache (*de chat etc.*), *f.*

whisky, whiskey ['hwiski], *n.* whisky, *m.*

whisper ['hwispə], *n.* chuchotement, *m.*—*v.t.* chuchoter, dire à l'oreille.—*v.i.* chuchoter, parler tout bas.

whispering ['hwispəriŋ], *n.* chuchotement, *m.*

whist [hwist], *n.* whist, *m.*

whistle [hwisl], *n.* sifflet; coup de sifflet; sifflement (*du vent*); (*colloq.*) gosier, bec (*gorge*), *m.*—*v.t.*, *v.i.* siffler.

whistler ['hwislə], *n.* siffleur, *m.*

whistling ['hwisliŋ], *a.* sifflant.—*n.* sifflement, coup de sifflet, *m.*

whit [hwit], *n.* iota, point, atome, brin, *m.*

white [hwait], *a.* blanc; (*fig.*) sans tache, pur.—*n.* blanc; aubier (*de bois*), *m.*

whitebait ['hwaitbeit], *n.* blanchaille, *f.*

whiten [hwaitn], *v.t.* blanchir; (*Build.*) badigeonner.—*v.i.* blanchir.

whiteness ['hwaitnis], *n.* blancheur; pâleur, *f.*

whitening ['hwaitniŋ], *n.* action de blanchir, *f.*; [WHITING (1)].

whitewash ['hwaitwɔʃ], *n.* blanc de chaux, *m.*—*v.t.* blanchir à la chaux; badigeonner.

whither ['hwiðə], *adv.* où, par où.

whithersoever [hwiðəsou'evə], *adv.* n'importe où.

whiting (1) ['hwaitiŋ], **whitening** ['hwaitniŋ], *n.* blanc d'Espagne, *m.*

whiting (2) ['hwaitiŋ], *n.* (*Ichth.*) merlan, *m.*

whitish ['hwaitiʃ], *a.* blanchâtre.

whitlow ['hwitlou], *n.* panaris, *m.*

Whitsun ['hwitsən], *a.* de la Pentecôte; *Whitsunday,* le dimanche de la Pentecôte.

Whitsuntide ['hwitsəntaid]. Pentecôte, *f.*

whiz(z) [hwiz], *v.t.* siffler.

whizzing ['hwiziŋ], *n.* sifflement, *m.*

who [huː], *pron.* (*rel.*) qui; lequel; (*inter.*) qui ? qui est-ce qui ?

whodunit [huː'dʌnit], *n.* (*colloq.*) roman policier, *m.*

whoever [huː'evə], *pron.* qui, quiconque; qui que ce soit; celui qui.

whole [houl], *a.* tout, entier, tout entier, complet; intégral; bien portant; en grains (*non moulu*).—*n.* tout, ensemble; total, montant, *m.*; somme, totalité, *f.*; *on the whole,* en somme, dans l'ensemble.

whole-hearted [houl'haːtid], *a.* sincère.

whole-heartedly [houl'haːtidli], *adv.* sincèrement.

wholesale ['houlseil], *a.* en gros.—*n.* vente en gros, *f.*

wholesome ['houlsəm], *a.* sain, salubre; salutaire; utile.

wholesomeness ['houlsəmnis], *n.* salubrité, nature salutaire, *f.*

wholly ['houlli], *adv.* entièrement, complètement, tout à fait.

whom [huːm], *pron.* (*rel.*) que, lequel; (*inter.*) qui ? qui est-ce que ?

whomsoever [huːmsou'evə], *pron.* qui que ce soit que.

whoop [huːp], *n.* huée, *f.*; cri (*de guerre*), *m.*—*v.t.*, *v.i.* huer, crier.

whooping ['huːpiŋ], *n.* huées, *f.pl.*

whooping cough ['huːpiŋkɔf], *n.* coqueluche, *f.*

whopper ['hwɔpə], *n.* (*slang*) chose énorme, *f.*; mensonge énorme, *m.*; bourde, *f.*

whose [huːz], *pron.* (*rel.*) dont, de qui; duquel, *m.*, de laquelle, *f.*, desquels, *m.pl.*, desquelles, *f.pl.*; (*inter.*) à qui ?

whosoever [hu:sou′evə], *pron.* qui que ce soit qui.
why [hwai], *adv.* pourquoi ?—*int.* eh bien, mais ! tiens !
wick [wik], *n.* mèche, *f.*
wicked [′wikid], *a.* méchant, malin.
wickedly [′wikidli], *adv.* méchamment.
wickedness [′wikidnis], *n.* méchanceté, perversité, *f.*
wicker [′wikə], *a.* d'osier, en osier.—*n.* osier, *m.*
wicker-work [′wikəwə:k], *n.* clayonnage, *m.*; vannerie, *f.*
wicket [′wikit], *n.* guichet, *m.*
wide [waid], *a.* large, grand, ample, vaste, immense (*d'étendue*); *three feet wide*, large de trois pieds; *to open wide*, ouvrir tout grand.—*adv.* loin, au loin, largement; *far and wide*, partout; *wide apart*, écarté, espacé.
wide-awake [′waidə′weik], *a.* bien éveillé.
widely [′waidli], *adv.* au loin, loin; grandement; largement; *widely known*, bien connu.
widen [waidn], *v.t.* élargir, étendre.—*v.i.* s'élargir, s'étendre.
wideness [′waidnis], *n.* largeur, étendue, *f.*
widening [′waidniŋ], *n.* élargissement, *m.*
wide-spread [′waidspred], *a.* répandu; général, universel.
widow [′widou], *n.* veuve, *f.*
widowed [′widoud], *a.* veuf, veuve; (*fig.*) privé (*de*).
widower [′widouə], *n.* veuf, *m.*
widowhood [′widouhud], *n.* veuvage, *m.*
width [widθ], *n.* largeur, étendue, *f.*
wield [wi:ld], *v.t.* manier, tenir.
wife [waif], *n.* (*pl.* **wives** [waivz]) femme, épouse, *f.*
wifely [′waifli], **wife-like** [′waiflaik], *a.* de femme, d'épouse, conjugal.
wig [wig], *n.* perruque, *f.*
wig-maker [′wigmeikə], *n.* perruquier, *m.*
wigged [wigd], *a.* à perruque, portant perruque.
wigging [′wigiŋ], *n.* (*colloq.*) savon, *m.*, semonce, *f.*
wiggle [wigl], *v.t.* agiter.—*v.i.* se dandiner.
wild [waild], *a.* sauvage; farouche (*non apprivoisé*); effaré, déréglé (*désordonné*); furieux (*de rage*); insensé, extravagant (*fou*); étrange, bizarre (*baroque*); *wild beast*, fauve, *m.*; *wild boar*, sanglier, *m.*;*wildcat*, chat sauvage, *m.*—*n.*(*pl.*) désert, lieu sauvage, *m.*
wilderness [′wildənis], *n.* lieu désert, *m.*
wildfire [′waildfaiə], *n.* feu grégeois, *m.*; *like wildfire*, comme l'éclair.
wildly [′waildli], *adv.* d'une manière farouche, d'un air effaré; étourdiment, follement; à tort et à travers.
wildness [′waildnis], *n.* état sauvage; dérèglement, désordre, *m.*, turbulence, licence, *f.*
wile [wail], *n.* (*usu. pl.*) artifice, *m.*, ruse, *f.*
wilful [′wilful], *a.* opiniâtre; obstiné, volontaire, prémédité.
wilfully [′wilfuli], *adv.* opiniâtrement; à dessein.
wilfulness [′wilfulnis], *n.* obstination, opiniâtreté, *f.*
will [wil], *n.* volonté, *f.*; vouloir; bon plaisir, gré (*inclination*); (*Law*) testament, *m.*—

v.t. vouloir, ordonner; léguer (*par testament*).—*v. aux. irr.*, *when used to indicate the future it is not translated*; *he will come*, il viendra; *when used emphatically it is translated by* ***vouloir***; *I will not do it*, je ne veux pas le faire.
William [′wiljəm]. Guillaume, *m.*
willing [′wiliŋ], *a.* bien disposé; de bonne volonté; *to be willing*, vouloir bien, être disposé (*à*).
willingly [′wiliŋli], *adv.* volontiers.
willingness [′wiliŋnis], *n.* bonne volonté, *f.*, bon vouloir, *m.*; complaisance, *f.*
will-o′-the-wisp [wiləðə′wisp], *n.* feu follet, *m.*
willow [′wilou], *n.* saule, *m.*
willy-nilly [′wili′nili], *adv.* bon gré mal gré.
wily [′waili], *a.* rusé, fin, astucieux.
win [win], *v.t. irr.* gagner (*bataille, argent etc.*); remporter (*prix, victoire etc.*).—*v.i.* gagner; remporter la victoire, triompher.
wince [wins], *v.i.* sourciller, tressaillir (de douleur).—*n.* tressaillement, *m.*
winch [wintʃ], *n.* manivelle, *f.*, treuil (*cabestan*), *m.*
wind (1) [wind], *n.* vent; souffle, *m.*, respiration, haleine (*breath*), *f.*; (*Med.*) vents, *m.pl.* flatuosité, *f.*—*v.t.* faire perdre haleine à essouffler (*cheval*).
wind (2) [waind], *v.t. irr.* enrouler (*en peloton*); dévider (*soie etc.*); *to wind up*, remonter (*pendule etc.*); terminer (*négociations*); (*Comm.*) liquider.—*v.i.* tourner; se rouler, s'enrouler, s'enlacer; faire un détour; serpenter (*route, rivière*).
wind-bag [′windbæg], *n.* (*fig.*) moulin à paroles, *m.*
winded [′windid], *a.* hors d'haleine, essoufflé; *long-winded*, de longue haleine.
winder [′waində], *n.* dévidoir (*appareil*); remontoir (*de montre*), *m.*
windfall [′windfɔ:l], *n.* (*fig.*) bonne aubaine, *f.*
wind gauge [′windgeidʒ], *n.* anémomètre, *m.*
winding [′waindiŋ], *a.* sinueux, tortueux; en spirale (*escalier*).—*n.* sinuosité, *f.*; (*Elec.*) enroulement, *m.*
winding sheet [′waindiŋʃi:t], *n.* linceul, *m.*
wind-jammer [′winddʒæmə], *n.* (*Naut.*) voilier, *m.*
windlass [′windləs], *n.* treuil (*Naut.*) guindeau, cabestan, *m.*
windmill [′windmil], *n.* moulin à vent, *m.*
window [′windou], *n.* fenêtre; glace (*de train, voiture etc.*); montre, vitrine, *f.*, étalage (*de magasin*), *m.*; (*pl.*) vitraux (*d'église*), *m.pl.*
window box [′windouboks], *n.* jardinière, *f.*
window cleaner [′windoukli:nə], *n.* laveur de carreaux, *m.*
window-dresser [′windoudresə], *n.* étalagiste, *m.*, *f.*
window-dressing [′windoudresiŋ], *n.* art de l'étalage; (*fam.*) trompe-l'œil, *m.*
window frame [′windoufreim], *n.* châssis de fenêtre, *m.*
window pane [′windoupein], *n.* carreau, *m.*
window-shopping [′windouʃopiŋ], *n.* lèche-vitrine, *m.*
window shutter [′windouʃʌtə], *n.* volet; contrevent, *m.*
window sill [′windousil], *n.* rebord *ou* appui de fenêtre, *m.*
windpipe [′windpaip], *n.* trachée-artère, *m.*

windshield ['windʃi:ld], *n.* (*Motor.*) pare-brise, *m.*

wind-sock ['windsɔk], *n.* (*Av.*) manche à air, *f.*

wind tunnel ['windtʌnl], *n.* (*Av.*) tunnel aérodynamique, *m.*

windward ['windwəd], *adv.* au vent.—*n.* côté du vent, *m.*

windy ['windi], *a.* du vent; venteux; *it is windy*, il fait du vent.

wine [wain], *n.* vin, *m.*—*v.t.* *to wine and dine*, fêter.

wine-bibber ['wainbibə], *n.* buveur, *m.*, ivrogne, *m.*, *f.*

wine bin ['wainbin], *n.* porte-bouteilles, *m.*

wine cellar ['wainselə], *n.* cave, *f.*

wineglass ['waingla:s], *n.* verre à vin, *m.*

wine-growing ['waingrouiŋ], *a.* viticole.—*n.* viticulture, *f.*

wine merchant ['wainmə:tʃənt], *n.* négociant en vins, *m.*

wine-press ['wainpres], *n.* pressoir, *m.*

wine-tasting ['wainteistiŋ], *n.* dégustation de vins, *f.*

wine waiter ['wainweitə], *n.* sommelier, *m.*

wing [wiŋ], *n.* aile; (*Av.*) escadre; (*Theat.*) (*pl.*) coulisse, *f.*; *on the wing*, au vol.—*v.t.* blesser à l'aile.

winged [wiŋd], *a.* ailé; (*fig.*) rapide; blessé à l'aile.

winger ['wiŋə], *n.* (*Ftb.*) ailier, *m.*

wing span ['wiŋspæn], *n.* envergure, *f.*

wink [wiŋk], *n.* clin d'œil, *m.*, œillade, *f.*—*v.i.* cligner de l'œil; clignoter (*lumière*).

winking ['wiŋkiŋ], *a.* clignotant.—*n.* clignotement; clignement d'œil, *m.*

winkle [wiŋkl], *n.* (*Ichth.*) bigorneau, *m.*

winner ['winə], *n.* gagnant; vainqueur (*d'une course etc.*), *m.*

winning ['winiŋ], *a.* gagnant; (*fig.*) attrayant, séduisant.—*n.* (*pl.*) gain, *m.*

winning post ['winiŋpoust], *n.* poteau d'arrivée, but, *m.*

winnow ['winou], *v.t.* vanner.

winter ['wintə], *a.* d'hiver.—*n.* hiver, *m.*; *in winter*, en hiver.—*v.i.* hiverner, passer l'hiver (*à*).

wintry ['wintri], *a.* d'hiver, hivernal; (*fig.*) glacial.

wipe [waip], *v.t.* essuyer; *to wipe off*, effacer; *to wipe up*, nettoyer.

wiper ['waipə], *n.* *windshield wiper*, essuie-glace, *m.*

wire ['waiə], *n.* fil métallique, fil de fer, *m.*; dépêche (*télégramme*), *f.*; *barbed wire*, fil de fer barbelé.—*v.t.* attacher *ou* lier avec du fil de métal; griller; (*fig.*) télégraphier.

wire cutters ['waiəkʌtəz], *n.pl.* cisailles coupe-fil, *f.pl.*

wire-haired ['waiəhɛəd], *a.* à poil dur (*chien*).

wireless ['waiəlis], *a.* sans fil.—*n.* radio, T.S.F., *f.*; *wireless set*, poste de T.S.F., *m.*, radio, *f.*

wire netting ['waiə'netiŋ], *n.* grillage, treillis métallique, *m.*

wire rope ['waiə'roup], *n.* câble métallique, *m.*

wiring ['waiəriŋ], *n.* (*Elec.*) canalisation, *f.*; câblage, *m.*

wiry ['waiəri], *a.* (*fig.*) nerveux, souple.

wisdom ['wizdəm], *n.* sagesse; prudence, *f.*

wise [waiz], *a.* sage; discret, prudent.—*n.* manière, façon, sorte, guise, *f.*

wise-crack ['waizkræk], *n.* bon mot, *m.*

wisely ['waizli], *adv.* sagement; prudemment.

wish [wiʃ], *n.* souhait, désir, *m.*, envie, *f.*—*v.t.*, *v.i.* souhaiter, désirer, vouloir; *I wish I could*, je voudrais pouvoir; *I wish I were . . .*, je voudrais être . . .; *to wish well to*, vouloir du bien à.

wish-bone ['wiʃboun], *n.* lunette, fourchette, *f.*

wishful ['wiʃful], *a.* désireux (*de*).

wishy-washy ['wiʃi'wɔʃi], *a.* faible, pauvre.

wisp [wisp], *n.* bouchon de paille etc., *m.*; mèche (*de cheveux*), *f.*

wisteria [wis'tɛəriə], *n.* glycine, *f.*

wistful ['wistful], *a.* désireux; d'envie, de regret, pensif (*air, regard, sourire*).

wistfully ['wistfuli], *adv.* d'un air de vague regret.

wit [wit], *n.* esprit; entendement, jugement; (*fig.*) bel esprit; (*pl.*) esprit, *m.*, raison, tête, *f.*, sens, bon sens, *m.*; *to be at one's wits' end*, ne savoir que faire.—*v.t.* savoir; *to wit*, c'est-à-dire.

witch [witʃ], *n.* sorcière, magicienne, *f.*

witchcraft ['witʃkra:ft], *n.* sorcellerie, magie noire, *f.*

witch hazel ['witʃheizl], *n.* (*Bot.*) hamamélis, *m.*

with [wið], *prep.* avec; de, par (*au moyen de*); à, au, à la, aux (*in descriptive phrases*); chez, parmi (*en compagnie de*); auprès de (*de l'avis de*); malgré (*en dépit de*); *angry with*, fâché contre.

withal [wið'ɔ:l], *adv.* avec tout cela, en outre.

withdraw [wið'drɔ:], *v.t. irr.* (*conjug. like* DRAW) retirer; rappeler; éloigner (*de*).—*v.i.* se retirer, s'éloigner (*de*).

withdrawal [wið'drɔ:əl] *n.* retraite (*des vaincus*), *f.*; retrait (*enlèvement*), *m.*

wither ['wiðə], *v.i.* se flétrir, se faner.

withering ['wiðəriŋ], *a.* écrasant (*sarcastique*).

withers ['wiðəz], *n.pl.* garrot (*de cheval*), *m.*

withhold [wið'hould], *v.t. irr.* (*conjug. like* HOLD) retenir; refuser.

within [wið'in], *prep.* dans, en; à moins de (*pas plus de*); *within a pound or so*, à une livre près; *within reach of*, à portée de.—*adv.* en dedans, à l'intérieur; à la maison, chez soi.

without [wið'aut], *prep.* sans (*manquant de*).—*conj.* à moins que, sans que (*unless*).—**adv.* en dehors, au dehors.

withstand [wið'stænd], *v.t. irr.* (*conjug. like* STAND) résister à, combattre.

withy ['wiði], *a.* d'osier.—*n.* osier, *m.*

witless ['witlis], *a.* sans esprit; sot.

witness ['witnis], *n.* témoin; témoignage (*preuve*), *m.*—*v.t.* témoigner; être témoin de.—*v.i.* témoigner, porter témoignage.

witticism ['witisizm], *n.* bon mot, *m.*

wittily ['witili], *adv.* spirituellement, avec esprit.

wittiness ['witinis], *n.* esprit, caractère spirituel, *m.*

wittingly ['witiŋli], *adv.* sciemment, à dessein.

witty ['witi], *a.* spirituel; plaisant (*facétieux*).

wives [WIFE].

wizard ['wizəd], *n.* sorcier, magicien, *m.*

wizened ['wizənd], *a.* ratatiné, ridé.

wobble ['wɔbl], *v.i.* vaciller, ballotter.

wobbling ['wɔbliŋ], *a.* vacillant, branlant.—
n. vacillation, *f.*; dandinement, *m.*

wobbly ['wɔbli], *a.* branlant, vacillant.

woe [wou], *n.* (*fig.*) peine, douleur, *f.*; malheur, *m.*

woebegone ['woubigɔn], **woeful** ['wouful], *a.*
triste, malheureux, abattu.

woefully ['woufuli], *adv.* tristement.

wolf [wulf], *n.* (*pl.* **wolves** [wulvz]) loup, *m.*;
she-wolf, louve, *f.*

wolf cub ['wulfkʌb], *n.* louveteau, *m.*

wolf dog ['wulfdɔg], *n.* chien-loup, *m.*

wolfish ['wulfiʃ], *a.* de loup; (*fig.*) rapace.

wolves [WOLF].

woman ['wumən], *n.* (*pl.* **women** ['wimin])
femme, *f.*

woman hater ['wumənheitə], *n.* misogyne,
m.

womanhood ['wumənhud], *n.* état de femme,
m.

womankind ['wumənkaind], *n.* le sexe
féminin, *m.*; les femmes, *f.pl.*

womanly ['wumənli], *a.* de femme.

womanliness ['wumənlinis], *n.* fémininité, *f.*

womb [wu:m], *n.* (*Anat.*) matrice, *f.*; (*fig.*)
sein, *m.*, flancs, *m.pl.*

women [WOMAN].

wonder ['wʌndə], *n.* étonnement, *m.*, surprise; merveille (*spectacle etc.*), *f.*, miracle,
prodige, *m.*—*v.i.* s'étonner, être étonné; se
demander; *to wonder whether*, se demander si.

wonderful ['wʌndəful], *a.* étonnant, merveilleux.

wonderfully ['wʌndəfuli], *adv.* étonnamment, merveilleusement.

wonderment ['wʌndəmənt], *n.* étonnement,
m.

wondrous ['wʌndrəs], *a.* merveilleux.

wondrously ['wʌndrəsli], *adv.* merveilleusement.

wont [wount], *a.* *to be wont to*, avoir
l'habitude de.—*n.* coutume, habitude, *f.*

wonted ['wountid], *a.* accoutumé, habituel.

woo [wu:], *v.t.* faire la cour à; courtiser.

wood [wud], *n.* bois (*matériel ou forêt*), *m.*

woodbine ['wudbain], *n.* chèvrefeuille, *m.*

woodcock ['wudkɔk], *n.* bécasse, *f.*

woodcut ['wudkʌt], *n.* gravure sur bois, *f.*

wood-cutter ['wudkʌtə], *n.* bûcheron, *m.*

wooded ['wudid], *a.* boisé.

wooden ['wudn], *a.* de bois, en bois; (*fig.*)
gauche (*mouvement etc.*).

woodland ['wudlənd], *a.* des bois, sylvestre.
—*n.* pays boisé, bois, *m.*

woodman ['wudmən], *n.* (*pl.* **-men** [men])
garde forestier; bûcheron, *m.*

wood nymph ['wudnimf], *n.* nymphe des
bois, dryade, *f.*

woodpecker ['wudpekə], *n.* pic, *m.*; *green
woodpecker*, pivert, *m.*

wood pigeon ['wudpidʒin], *n.* pigeon ramier,
m.

wood pulp ['wudpʌlp], *n.* pâte de bois, *f.*

wood-winds ['wudwindz], *n.pl.* (*Mus.*) les
bois, *m.pl.*

woodwork ['wudwə:k], *n.* boiserie; menuiserie; charpente, *f.*

wood-worm ['wudwə:m], *n.* artison, *m.*

woody ['wudi], *a.* boisé; ligneux.

wood yard ['wudjɑ:d], *n.* chantier, *m.*

wooer ['wu:ə], *n.* amoureux, prétendant, *m.*

woof [wu:f], *n.* trame, *f.*; tissu (*texture*), *m.*

wooing ['wu:iŋ], *n.* cour, *f.*

wool [wul], *n.* laine, *f.*

woollen ['wulən], *a.* de laine, à laine.—*n.*(*pl.*)
tissus de laine, *m.pl.*, laines, *f.pl.*, lainages,
m.pl.; *woollen cloth*, drap, *m.*; *wool
dealer*, marchand de draps, *m.*; *woollen
goods*, (*fam.*) *woollies*, lainages, *m.pl.*

woolliness ['wulinis], *n.* nature laineuse; (*fig.*)
imprécision, *f.*

woolly ['wuli], *a.* laineux.

Woolsack ['wulsæk], *n.* sac de laine (*siège du
Lord Chancellor*), *m.*

word [wə:d], *n.* mot, *m.*; parole (*prononcée*),
f.; avis, *m.*, nouvelle (*communication*), *f.*; *by
word of mouth*, de vive voix; *in a word*,
en un mot; *not a word!* bouche close!—
v.t. exprimer; énoncer; rédiger (*télégramme*).

word-book ['wə:dbuk], *n.* vocabulaire,
lexique, *m.*

wordiness ['wə:dinis], *n.* prolixité, verbosité,
f.

wording ['wə:diŋ], *n.* expression, *f.*; énoncé
(*d'un problème*), *m.*

wordy ['wə:di], *a.* verbeux, diffus.

work [wə:k], *v.t.* travailler; façonner (*ouvrager*); se frayer (*un chemin*); payer (*son
passage*) en travaillant; broder (*coudre*); faire
aller, manœuvrer (*machine etc.*); exploiter
(*mine etc.*); *to work off*, user; *to work oneself up*, s'exciter; *to work out*, résoudre
(*problème*).—*v.i.* travailler; fonctionner,
marcher, aller, jouer; opérer, avoir de
l'effet (*agir*); *to work loose*, se desserrer.—
n. travail; ouvrage, *m.*, besogne (*tâche*);
(*fig.*) affaire; (*Lit.*) œuvre, *f.*; (*pl.*) mécanisme (*de moteur*), *m.*; manœuvres (*d'une
machine*), *f.pl.*; (*Ind.*) fabrique, usine, *f.*;
(*Fort.*) travaux, *m.pl.*; mouvement (*de
montre*), *m.*; *road works ahead*, attention,
travaux! *to be out of work*, chômer.

workable ['wə:kəbl], *a.* réalisable; exploitable
(*mine etc.*).

workaday ['wə:kədei], *a.* de tous les jours.

work-bench ['wə:kbentʃ], *n.* établi, *m.*

work-box ['wə:kbɔks], *n.* boîte à ouvrage, *f.*

worker ['wə:kə], *n.* travailleur; ouvrier;
employé, *m.*

workhouse ['wə:khaus], *n.* maison des
pauvres, *f.*; hospice, *m.*

working ['wə:kiŋ], *a.* qui travaille, ouvrier;
de travail (*vêtements*); *hard-working*, laborieux; *in working order*, en état de
fonctionnement; *working capital*, capital
d'exploitation, *m.*; *working man*, ouvrier,
m.—*n.* travail, *m.*; marche, *f.*; fonctionnement, jeu (*de machine*), *m.*; opération; exploitation (*de mine etc.*), *f.*

working class ['wə:kiŋklɑ:s], *n.* classe ou-
vrière, *f.*

working day ['wə:kiŋdei], *n.* jour ouvrable, *m.*

workman ['wə:kmən], *n.* (*pl.* **-men** [men])
ouvrier, artisan, *m.*

workmanlike ['wə:kmənlaik], *a.* bien fait,
bien travaillé.

workmanship ['wə:kmənʃip], *n.* ouvrage,
travail, *m.*

work-room ['wə:kru:m], **work-shop** ['wə:k
ʃɔp], *n.* atelier, *m.*

world [wə:ld], *n.* monde; l'univers; (*fig.*)
monde, *m.*, vie, *f.*; *all the world over*,

dans le monde entier; *a world of good*, un bien infini; *the first world war*, la première guerre mondiale.

worldliness ['wə:ldlinis], *n.* mondanité; frivolité, *f.*

worldly ['wə:ldli], *a.* mondain, du monde.

worldwide ['wə:ldwaid], *a.* universel, répandu partout.

worm [wə:m], *n.* ver, *m.*; chenille, larve, *f.*; filet (*de vis*), *m.*—*v.t.* miner; *to worm oneself into*, s'insinuer; se faufiler dans.

worm cast ['wə:mkɑ:st], *n.* déjection de ver (de terre), *f.*

worm-eaten ['wə:mi:tn], *a.* rongé des vers, vermoulu.

worm screw ['wə:mskru:], *n.* tire-bourre, *m.*

wormwood ['wə:mwud], *n.* armoise amère, *f.*; (*fig.*) fiel, *m.*

worried ['wʌrid], *a.* tourmenté, harassé, ennuyé.

worry ['wʌri], *n.* ennui, tracas, souci, *m.*—*v.t.* tourmenter, tracasser.—*v.i.* tracasser; *don't worry!* soyez tranquille!

worse [wə:s], *a.* pire; plus mauvais; plus malade, plus mal (*santé*).—*n.* pire; plus mauvais, *m.*—*adv.* plus mal, pis; *far worse*, bien pis, bien pire; *so much the worse*, tant pis.

worsen [wə:sn], *v.i.* empirer.

worsening ['wə:sniŋ], *n.* aggravation, *f.*

worship ['wə:ʃip], *n.* culte, *m.*, adoration, *f.*; honneur (*titre*), *m.*—*v.t.*, *v.i.* adorer.

worshipful ['wə:ʃipful], *a.* honorable.

worshipper ['wə:ʃipə], *n.* adorateur, *m.*

worst [wə:st], *a.* le plus mauvais, le pire.—*adv.* le pis, le plus mal.—*n.* le plus mauvais, le pire, le pis.—*v.t.* battre, vaincre, défaire.

worsted ['wustid], *a.* de laine peignée.—*n.* laine peignée, *f.*

worth [wə:θ], *a.* qui vaut, valant; qui mérite (*digne*); qui est riche de (*qui possède*); *to be worth doing*, valoir la peine de faire.—*n.* valeur, *f.*; prix, *m.*; *for all one's worth*, de toutes ses forces.

worthily ['wə:ðili], *adv.* dignement.

worthiness ['wə:ðinis], *n.* mérite, *m.*

worthless ['wə:θlis], *a.* sans valeur, qui ne vaut rien; *worthless fellow*, vaurien, *m.*

worth-while ['wə:θ'hwail], *a.* qui vaut la peine (*de*).

worthy ['wə:ði], *a.* digne, honorable; (*colloq.*) brave (*de*).—*n.* (*colloq.*) brave homme; homme illustre, *m.*

would [wud], *v.aux. past* and *cond.* [WILL]. *When used emphatically* **would** *is translated by* **vouloir**.

would-be ['wudbi:], *a.* prétendu, soi-disant.

wound (1) [waund], *past* and *p.p.* [WIND (2)].

wound (2) [wu:nd], *n.* blessure, plaie, *f.*—*v.t.* blesser.

wounded ['wu:ndid], *a.* blessé.

woven [wouvn], *a.* tissé.

wrack [ræk], *n.* varech, *m.*; ruine, *f.*, débris, *m.*

wraith [reiθ], *n.* revenant, *m.*

wrangle [ræŋgl], *n.* dispute, querelle, *f.*—*v.i.* se disputer, se quereller.

wrangling ['ræŋgliŋ], *n.* dispute, *f.*, chamailleries, *f.pl.*

wrap [ræp], *v.t.* enrouler, envelopper.—*n.* châle, peignoir, *m.*

wrapper ['ræpə], *n.* enveloppe; toile d'embal-

lage (*pour paquets*); bande (*pour journal*); couverture (*de livre*), *f.*

wrapping ['ræpiŋ], *n.* enveloppe, couverture, *f.*; *wrapping-paper*, papier d'emballage, *m.*

wrath [rɔ:θ], *n.* courroux, *m.*, colère, *f.*

wrathful ['rɔ:θful], *a.* courroucé.

wreak [ri:k], *v.t.* exécuter, satisfaire.

wreath [ri:θ], *n.* guirlande, *f.*, feston, *m.*; couronne (*d'épouse etc.*), *f.*

wreathe [ri:ð], *v.t.* entrelacer, tresser (*de*).—*v.i.* s'entrelacer, s'enrouler.

wreathed [ri:ðd], *a.* entrelacé.

wreck [rek], *n.* naufrage; navire naufragé, *m.*, épave; (*fig.*) ruine, *f.*—*v.t.* faire faire naufrage à; (*fig.*) ruiner.

wreckage ['rekidʒ], *n.* débris de naufrage, *m.*, épaves, *f.pl.*

wrecked [rekt], *a.* naufragé; ruiné.

wrecker ['rekə], *n.* pilleur d'épaves, naufrageur, *m.*; (*Motor.*) dépanneuse, *f.* [see **house-breaker; train**]

wren [ren], *n.* (*Orn.*) roitelet, *m.*

wrench [rentʃ], *n.* torsion, *f.*, arrachement, *m.*; entorse (*des muscles*); clef (*outil*), *f.*—*v.t.* arracher (*à* ou *de*); se fouler (*cheville etc.*).

wrest [rest], *v.t.* arracher (*à*).

wrestle [resl], *v.i.* lutter.

wrestler ['reslə], *n.* lutteur, *m.*

wrestling ['resliŋ], *n.* lutte, *f.*; catch, *m.*; *all-in wrestling*, lutte libre.

wretch [retʃ], *n.* malheureux, *m.*; misérable (*scélérat*), *m.*, *f.*; *poor wretch*, pauvre diable, *m.*

wretched ['retʃid], *a.* malheureux, misérable; vilain, triste; pitoyable, à faire pitié.

wretchedly ['retʃidli], *adv.* malheureusement, misérablement; d'une manière pitoyable.

wretchedness ['retʃidnis], *n.* misère, pauvreté, *f.*

wriggle [rigl], *v.i.* se tortiller, se remuer.

wriggling ['rigliŋ], *n.* tortillement, *m.*

wring [riŋ], *v.t. irr.* tordre; arracher (*à*); presser, serrer (*étreindre*).

wringer ['riŋə], *n.* essoreuse (*à linge*), *f.*

wringing ['riŋiŋ], *a.* *wringing wet*, trempé jusqu'aux os (*personne*); mouillé à tordre (*vêtement*).

wrinkle [riŋkl], *n.* ride (*à la figure etc.*), *f.*; pli, faux pli (*de vêtement*); (*slang*) tuyau (*renseignement*), *m.*—*v.t.* rider; plisser; *to wrinkle one's brow*, froncer les sourcils. —*v.i.* se rider.

wrinkled [riŋkld], *a.* ridé; (*Bot.*) plissé.

wrist [rist], *n.* poignet, *m.*

wristband ['ristbænd], *n.* poignet, *m.*

wrist watch ['ristwɔtʃ], *n.* montre-bracelet, *f.*

writ [rit], *n.* exploit, mandat, *m.*, ordonnance; (*Parl.*) lettre de convocation, *f.*

write [rait], *v.t.*, *v.i. irr.* écrire; *to write off*, (*Comm.*) passer au compte des profits et pertes.

write-off ['raitɔf], *n.* annulation; non-valeur (*personne*), *f.*

writer ['raitə], *n.* écrivain, *m.*

writhe [raið], *v.i.* se tordre (*de douleur*); se crisper.

writing ['raitiŋ], *n.* écriture (*calligraphie*), *f.*; écrit (*chose écrite*); (*fig.*) ouvrage, document, *m.*; inscription, *f.*; *in writing*, par écrit.

writing case ['raitiŋkeis], *n.* papeterie, *f.*

writing desk ['raitiŋdesk], *n.* pupitre, bureau, secrétaire, *m.*

writing paper ['raitiŋpeipə], *n.* papier à écrire, *m.*
writing table ['raitiŋteibl], *n.* table à écrire, *f.*
written [ritn], *a.* écrit, par écrit.
wrong [rɔŋ], *a.* faux, erroné, inexact (*pas vrai*); mal, mauvais; *to be wrong*, avoir tort (*personne*), n'être pas à l'heure, aller mal (*montre*); *what's wrong with you?* qu'avez-vous? *wrong number*, (*Teleph.*) mauvais numéro, *m.*; *wrong side*, envers, *m.*; *wrong side up*, sens dessus dessous.— *adv.* mal, à tort, à faux.—*n.* mal, *m.*, injustice, *f.*, tort; dommage, *m.*—*v.t.* faire du tort à, nuire à.
wrongdoer ['rɔŋduə], *n.* pervers, méchant, *m.*
wrongdoing ['rɔŋduiŋ], *n.* le mal, *m.*
wrongful ['rɔŋful], *a.* injuste.
wrongfully ['rɔŋfuli], *adv.* à tort, injustement.
wrongly ['rɔŋli], *adv.* mal, à tort; *rightly or wrongly*, à tort ou à raison.
wroth [rouθ], *a.* (*poet.*) en colère, irrité, courroucé.
wrought [rɔːt], *a.* travaillé; façonné; ouvré (*tissu*); *wrought iron*, fer forgé, *m.*
wry [rai], *a.* de travers, tordu, tors; *to pull a wry face*, faire la grimace.

X

X, x [eks]. vingt-quatrième lettre de l'alphabet; X, dix, *m.*
Xerxes ['zəːksiːz]. Xerxès, *m.*
Xmas ['krisməs]. (*abbr.* CHRISTMAS) Noël, *m.*
X-ray ['eksrei], *a.* radiographique; *X-ray photograph*, radiographie, *f.*—*n.* (*pl.*) rayons X, *m.pl.*—*v.t.* radiographier.
xylophone ['zailəfoun], *n.* xylophone; (*slang*) claquebois, *m.*

Y

Y, y [wai]. vingt-cinquième lettre de l'alphabet; (l')i grec, *m.*
yacht [jɔt], *n.* yacht, *m.*
yacht club ['jɔtklʌb], *n.* cercle nautique, *m.*
yachting ['jɔtiŋ], *n.* yachting, *m.*
yachtsman ['jɔtsmən], *n.* (*pl.* **-men** [men]) yachtman, *m.*
yak [jæk], *n.* (*Zool.*) ya(c)k, *m.*
yam [jæm], *n.* igname, *f.*
yank [jæŋk], *v.t.* (*fam.*) tirer brusquement.
Yankee ['jæŋki], *n.* Yankee, Américain, *m.*
yap [jæp], *v.i.* japper, aboyer.—*n.* jappement, *m.*
yard (1) [jaːd], *n.* cour, *f.*, préau, *m.*
yard (2) [jaːd], *n.* (*Naut.*) vergue, *f.*; (*Measure*) yard (*mètre 0,914383*), *m.*
yard-arm ['jaːdaːm], *n.* bout de vergue, *m.*
yarn [jaːn], *n.* fil, *m.*; (*Naut.*) fil de caret; récit, conte (*histoire*), *m.*

yawl [jɔːl], *n.* (*Naut.*) sloop, *m.*; (*Row.*) yole de mer, *f.*
yawn [jɔːn], *n.* bâillement, *m.*—*v.i.* bâiller.
yawning ['jɔːniŋ], *a.* qui bâille; (*fig.*) béant.
***ye** [jiː], *pron.pl.* vous.
yea [jei], *adv.* oui; vraiment, en vérité.—*n.* vote affirmatif, *m.*
year [jiə], *n.* an (*unité de temps*), *m.*; année (*particulière*), *f.*; *every year*, tous les ans; *four times a year*, quatre fois par an; *new year*, nouvel an; *next year*, l'an prochain.
year-book ['jiəbuk], *n.* annuaire, *m.*
yearling ['jiəliŋ], *a.* âgé d'un an.—*n.* poulain, *m.*, *ou* pouliche, *f.*, d'un an.
yearly ['jiəli], *a.* annuel.—*adv.* tous les ans.
yearn [jəːn], *v.i. to yearn after*, soupirer après; *to yearn to do something*, brûler de faire quelque chose.
yearning ['jəːniŋ], *n.* désir ardent, *m.*
yeast [jiːst], *n.* levure, *f.*
yell [jel], *n.* hurlement, *m.*—*v.i.* hurler, pousser des hurlements.
yelling ['jeliŋ], *n.* hurlements, *m.pl.*
yellow ['jelou], *a.* jaune; (*slang*) poltron.—*n.* jaune, *m.*—*v.t., v.i.* jaunir.
yellow-hammer ['jelouhæmə], *n.* (*Orn.*) bruant jaune, *m.*
yellowish ['jelouiʃ], *a.* jaunâtre.
yellowness ['jelounis], *n.* couleur jaune, *f.*
yelp [jelp], *v.i.* glapir, japper.
yelping ['jelpiŋ], *n.* glapissement, jappement, *m.*
Yemen ['jemən]. le Yémen, *m.*
Yemeni ['jeməni], *a.* yémenite.—*n.* Yémenite (*personne*), *m., f.*
yeoman ['joumən], *n.* (*pl.* **-men** [men]) fermier-propriétaire, *m.*
yeomanry ['joumənri], *n.* fermiers-propriétaires, *m.pl.*
yes [jes], *adv.* oui; si (*in reply to a negative*).
yes-man ['jesmæn], *n.* (*pl.* **men** [men]) (*pop.*) Béni-oui-oui, *m.*
yesterday ['jestəd(e)i], *adv.* and *n.* hier, *m.*; *the day before yesterday*, avant-hier; *yesterday evening*, hier soir.
yet [jet], *conj.* pourtant, cependant, tout de même.—*adv.* encore, déjà; *as yet*, jusqu'ici; *not yet*, pas encore.
yew [juː], *n.* (*Bot.*) if, *m.*
yield [jiːld], *v.t.* produire, rapporter; livrer; céder (*au vainqueur*); *to yield up*, rendre.—*v.i.* se rendre, céder (*à*); consentir (*à*).—*n.* rendement, produit, rapport, *m.*
yielding ['jiːldiŋ], *a.* complaisant, facile.—*n.* reddition; soumission, *f.*
yoke [jouk], *n.* joug; attelage, *m.*, paire; palanche (*pour seaux*), *f.*; (*Dress.*) empiècement, *m.*—*v.t.* atteler, accoupler.
yokel ['joukl], *n.* rustre, campagnard, *m.*
yolk [jouk], *n.* jaune (d'œuf), *m.*
yonder ['jondə], *adv.* là, là-bas.—*a. yonder castle*, ce château-là.
***yore** [jɔː], *adv.* autrefois, jadis.
you [juː], *pron.* vous; (*to a child, relative, pet etc.*) tu, te, toi; (*indef.*) on.
young [jʌŋ], *a.* jeune; novice, neuf, inexpérimenté (*non éprouvé*); (*fig.*) naissant; *young folks* or *young people*, jeunes gens, *m.pl.*; *young lady*, demoiselle, *f.*—*n.pl.* les jeunes, les jeunes gens; les petits, *m.pl.*; *with young*, pleine (*animal*).

younger ['jʌŋgə], *a.* plus jeune; cadet *(de deux frères etc.)*.
youngest ['jʌŋgist], *a.* le plus jeune.
youngish ['jʌŋiʃ], *a.* assez jeune.
youngster ['jʌŋstə], *n.* jeune homme; gamin, mioche, *m.*, gosse, *m.*, *f.*
your [jɔ:], *a.* votre, *(pl.)* vos; *(to a child, relative, pet etc.)* ton, ta, tes; *(indef.)* son, sa, ses.
yours [jɔ:z], *pron.* le vôtre, *m.*, la vôtre, *f.*, les vôtres, *pl.*; à vous *(your property)*; de vous *(by you)*; *(to a child, relative, pet etc.)* le tien, la tienne, les tiens, les tiennes; à toi *(your property)*; de toi *(by you)*.
yourself [jɔ:'self], *pron. (pl.* **yourselves** [jɔ:'selvz]) vous-même, toi-même; *(pl.)* vous-mêmes; *(reflexive)* vous, te.
youth [ju:θ], *n.* jeunesse, adolescence, *f.*; jeune homme, adolescent *(personne)*, *m.*; *(fig.)* jeunes gens, *m.pl.*
youthful ['ju:θful], *a.* jeune; de jeunesse.
youthfulness ['ju:θfulnis], *n.* jeunesse, *f.*
Yugoslav ['ju:go'slɑ:v], *a.* yougoslave.—*n.* Yougoslave *(personne)*, *m.*, *f.*
Yugoslavia [ju:go'slɑ:vjə]. la Yougoslavie, *f.*
***Yule** [ju:l], **Yule-tide** ['ju:ltaid], *n.* Noël, *m.*, fête de Noël, *f.*
Yule log ['ju:lləg], *n.* bûche de Noël, *f.*

Z

Z, z [zed, *(Am.)* zi:]. vingt-sixième lettre de l'alphabet, *m.*

Zambesi [zæm'bi:zi]. le Zambèze, *m.*
Zambia ['zæmbjə]. la Zambie, *f.*
zany ['zeini], *n.* zani, bouffon, *m.*
zeal [zi:l], *n.* zèle, *m.*
zealot ['zelət], *n.* zélateur, *m.*, fanatique, *m.*, *f.*
zealous ['zeləs], *a.* zélé, zélateur.
zealously ['zeləsli], *adv.* avec zèle.
zebra ['zi:brə], *n.* zèbre, *m.*; **zebra crossing** *(pedestrian crossing)*, passage clouté, *m.*
zenith ['zeniθ], *n.* zénith; *(fig.)* apogée, *m.*
zephyr ['zefə], *n.* zéphyr, zéphire, Zéphyre, *m.*
zero ['ziərou], *n.* zéro; *(fig.)* rien, *m.*; **zero hour**, l'heure H, *f.*
zest [zest], *n.* goût, *m.*, saveur, *f.*; zeste *(d'orange, de citron)*; *(fig.)* entrain, *m.*, verve, *f.*
Zeus [zju:s]. *(Myth.)* Zeus, *m.*
zigzag ['zigzæg], *a.* en zigzag.—*n.* zigzag, *m.* —*v.i.* aller en zigzag, zigzaguer.
zinc [ziŋk], *n.* zinc, *m.*—*v.t.* zinguer.
zinnia ['zinjə], *n.* *(Bot.)* zinnia, *m.*
Zion ['zaiən]. Sion, *m.*
zip [zip], *n.* sifflement *(de balle)*, *m.*; énergie, verve, *f.*—*v.t.* siffler; **zip fastener**, fermeture à glissière, *f.*
zither ['ziðə], *n.* cithare, *f.*
zodiac ['zoudiæk], *n.* zodiaque, *m.*
zone [zoun], *n.* zone, *f.*
zoo [zu:], *n.* jardin zoologique, *(fam.)* zoo, *m.*
zoological [zouə'lɔdʒikl], *a.* zoologique; **zoological gardens**, jardin zoologique, *m.*
zoologist [zou'ɔlədʒist], *n.* zoologiste, zoologue, *m.*, *f.*
zoology [zou'ɔlədʒi], *n.* zoologie, *f.*
zoom [zu:m], *n.* bourdonnement, ronflement, *m.*—*v.i.* vrombir.
Zulu ['zu:lu:], *a.* zoulou.—*n.* Zoulou, *m.*

French Verbs

1. All verbs not marked *irr.* in the French-English section of the Dictionary are either
   (a) regular, and conjugated like AIMER, FINIR or VENDRE according to their ending (see below) or
   (b) anomalous, and conjugated like the verb in that group to which the user is referred.
2. The Imperfect Indicative, Conditional, Imperative, and Imperfect Subjunctive are not given and may be assumed to be formed as follows:
   Imperfect Indicative: by substituting for the final *-ons* of 1st Person Plural, Present Indicative the endings *-ais, -ais, -ait, -ions, -iez, -aient* (except *être: j'étais*).
   Conditional: by substituting for the endings of the Future those of the Imperfect Indicative given above.
   Imperative: (a) 2nd Person Singular, 1st and 2nd Person Plural, by using these forms of

Infinitive	Participles	Present Indicative	Past Historic
REGULAR VERBS First Conjugation Infinitive in *-er*			
aim-*er*	aim-*ant* aim-*é*	aim-*e* aim-*es* aim-*e* aim-*ons* aim-*ez* aim-*ent*	aim-*ai* aim-*as* aim-*a* aim-*âmes* aim-*âtes* aim-*èrent*
Second Conjugation Infinitive in *-ir*			
fin-*ir*	fin-*issant* fin-*i*	fin-*is* fin-*is* fin-*it* fin-*issons* fin-*issez* fin-*issent*	fin-*is* fin-*is* fin-*it* fin-*îmes* fin-*îtes* fin-*irent*
Third Conjugation Infinitive in *-re*			
vend-*re*	vend-*ant* vend-*u*	vend-*s* vend-*s* vend vend-*ons* vend-*ez* vend-*ent*	vend-*is* vend-*is* vend-*it* vend-*îmes* vend-*îtes* vend-*irent*
ANOMALOUS VERBS			
amener	amenant amené	amène amènes amène amenons amenez amènent	amenai . . . amenâmes . . .
appeler	appelant appelé	appelle appelles appelle appelons appelez appellent	appelai . . . appelâmes . . .
assiéger	assiégeant assiégé	assiège assièges assiège assiégeons assiégez assiègent	assiégeai . . . assiégeâmes . . .

636

French Verbs

the Present Indicative without pronouns (-*er* verbs drop the final *s* of the 2nd Person Singular).

  (*b*) 3rd Person Singular and Plural by using these forms of the Present Subjunctive.

  Imperfect Subjunctive: from the 2nd Person Singular of the Past Historic by adding -*se*, -*ses*, -^*t*, -*sions*, -*siez*, -*sent*.
3. Exceptions to the above rules are indicated in footnotes.
4. Compound verbs (e.g. DEVENIR, REVENIR, etc.) are given only where they differ from the simple form (e.g. VENIR).
5. Defective verbs are marked † and all existing forms are given.

Future	Present Subjunctive	English
aimer-*ai*	aim-*e*	to like, to love
aimer-*as*	aim-*es*	
aimer-*a*	aim-*e*	
aimer-*ons*	aim-*ions*	
aimer-*ez*	aim-*iez*	
aimer-*ont*	aim-*ent*	
finir-*ai*	fini-*sse*	to finish
finir-*as*	fini-*sses*	
finir-*a*	fini-*sse*	
finir-*ons*	fini-*ssions*	
finir-*ez*	fini-*ssiez*	
finir-*ont*	fini-*ssent*	
vendr-*ai*	vend-*e*	to sell
vendr-*as*	vend-*es*	
vendr-*a*	vend-*e*	
vendr-*ons*	vend-*ions*	
vendr-*ez*	vend-*iez*	
vendr-*ont*	vend-*ent*	
amènerai...	amène	to bring
amènerons...	amènes	
	amène	
	amenions	
	ameniez	
	amènent	
appellerai...	appelle	to call
appellerons...	appelles	
	appelle	
	appelions	
	appeliez	
	appellent	
assiégerai...	assiège	to besiege
assiégerons...	assièges	
	assiège	
	assiégions	
	assiégiez	
	assiègent	

French Verbs

Infinitive	Participles	Present Indicative	Past Historic
battre	battant battu	bats bats bat battons battez battent	battis . . . battîmes . . .
céder	cédant cédé	cède cèdes cède cédons cédez cèdent	cédai . . . cédâmes . . .
commencer	commençant commencé	commence commences commence commençons commencez commencent	commençai commenças commença commençâmes commençâtes commencèrent
dépecer	dépeçant dépecé	dépèce dépèces dépèce dépeçons dépecez dépècent	dépeçai dépeças dépeça dépeçâmes dépeçâtes dépecèrent
employer[1]	employant employé	emploie emploies emploie employons employez emploient	employai . . . employâmes . . .
manger	mangeant mangé	mange manges mange mangeons mangez mangent	mangeai mangeas mangea mangeâmes mangeâtes mangèrent
payer[1]	(See footnote)		
rapiécer	rapiéçant rapiécé	rapièce rapièces rapièce rapiéçons rapiécez rapiècent	rapiéçai rapiéças rapiéça rapiéçâmes rapiéçâtes rapiécèrent
rompre	rompant rompu	romps romps rompt rompons rompez rompent	rompis . . . rompîmes . . .

IRREGULAR VERBS

† absoudre	absolvant absous, m., absoute, f.	absous absous absout absolvons absolvez absolvent	

[1] All verbs in -oyer and -uyer change y to i before a mute e.   With verbs in -ayer, y or i may

638

Future	Present Subjunctive	English
battrai . . . battrons . . .	batte . . . battions . . .	to beat
céderai . . . céderons . . .	cède cèdes cède cédions cédiez cèdent	to yield
commencerai . . . commencerons . . .	commence . . . commencions . . .	to begin
dépècerai . . . dépècerons . . .	dépèce dépèces dépèce dépecions dépeciez dépècent	to cut up
emploierai . . . emploierons . . .	emploie emploies emploie employions employiez emploient	to employ, to use
mangerai . . . mangerons . . .	mange . . . mangions . . .	to eat
		to pay (for)
rapiécerai . . . rapiécerons . . .	rapièce rapièces rapièce rapiécions rapiéciez rapiècent	to patch
romprai . . . romprons . . .	rompe . . . rompions . . .	to break
absoudrai . . . absoudrons . . .	absolve . . . absolvions . . .	to absolve

be used. With *grasseyer, y* is always used.

French Verbs

Infinitive	Participles	Present Indicative	Past Historic
† accroire	(used only in the infinitive in the phrase *'faire accroire'*, to make one
acquérir	acquérant acquis	acquiers acquiers acquiert acquérons acquérez acquièrent	acquis... acquîmes...
† advenir	advenant advenu	il advient	il advint
aller[1]	allant allé	vais vas va allons allez vont	allai... allâmes...
assaillir	assaillant assailli	assaille... assaillons...	assaillis... assaillîmes...
asseoir	asseyant *or* assoyant assis	assieds[2] assieds assied asseyons asseyez asseyent	assis... assîmes...
avoir[3]	ayant eu	ai as a avons avez ont	eus... eûmes...
boire	buvant bu	bois bois boit buvons buvez boivent	bus... bûmes...
bouillir	bouillant bouilli	bous bous bout bouillons bouillez bouillent	bouillis... bouillîmes...
† braire[4]	brayant brait	il brait ils braient	
† bruire[5]	bruissant bruit	il bruit ils bruissent	
† choir	chu	chois chois choit	chus... chûmes...
† clore	clos	clos clos clôt closent	

[1] 2nd pers. sing. Imperative: *va*.
[2] The forms in *-oi* (or *-eoi*) (same conjugation as *prévoir*) are accepted by the Académie Française but considered as familiar or even vulgar.

Future	Present Subjunctive	English
believe)		
acquerrai... acquerrons...	acquière acquières acquière acquérions acquériez acquièrent	to acquire
il adviendra	il advienne	to happen
irai... irons...	aille ailles aille allions alliez aillent	to go
assaillirai... assaillirons...	assaille... assaillions...	to assault
assiérai... or assoirai... assiérons... or assoirons...	asseye[2]... asseyions...	to set to seat
aurai... aurons...	aie aies ait ayons ayez aient	to have
boirai... boirons...	boive boives boive buvions buviez boivent	to drink
bouillirai... bouillirons...	bouille... bouillions...	to boil
il braira ils brairont		to bray
		to rustle
cherrai... or choirai... cherrons... or choirons...		to fall
clorai... clorons...	close... closions...	to close

[3] Imperative: *aie, ayons, ayez.*
[4] Imperfect Indicative: *il brayait, ils brayaient.*
[5] Imperfect Indicative: *il bruissait, ils bruissaient* or *il bruyait, ils bruyaient.*

French Verbs

Infinitive	Participles	Present Indicative	Past Historic
conclure	concluant conclu	conclus, -s, -t concluons...	conclus... conclûmes...
conduire	conduisant conduit	conduis, -s, -t conduisons...	conduisis... conduisîmes...
confire	confisant confit	confis, -s, -t confisons...	confis... confîmes...
connaître	connaissant connu	connais connais connaît connaissons connaissez connaissent	connus... connûmes...
coudre	cousant cousu	couds... cousons...	cousis... cousîmes...
courir	courant couru	cours, -s, -t courons...	courus... courûmes...
craindre	craignant craint	crains, -s, -t craignons...	craignis... craignîmes...
croire	croyant cru	crois crois croit croyons croyez croient	crus... crûmes...
croître	croissant [1] crû, *m.*, crue, *f.*,	croîs croîs croît croissons croissez croissent	crûs... crûmes...
cueillir	cueillant cueilli	cueille... cueillons...	cueillis... cueillîmes...
† déchoir[2]	déchu	déchois déchois déchoit déchoyons déchoyez déchoient	déchus... déchûmes...
devoir	devant dû, *m.*, due, *f.*, dus, *m.pl.*	dois dois doit devons devez doivent	dus... dûmes...
dire	disant dit	dis dis dit disons dites disent	dis... dîmes...
† échoir	échéant échu	il échoit ils échoient	il échut ils échurent

[1] The past part. of **accroître** is **accru**, and of **décroître**, **décru** (no circumflex on the *u* of the masculine sing.). [2] No Imperfect Indicative.

Future	Present Subjunctive	English
conclurai... conclurons...	conclue... concluions...	to conclude
conduirai... conduirons...	conduise... conduisions...	to lead to drive
confirai... confirons...	confise... confisions...	to preserve
connaîtrai... connaîtrons...	connaisse... connaissions...	to know
coudrai... coudrons...	couse... cousions...	to sew
courrai... courrons...	coure... courions...	to run
craindrai... craindrons...	craigne... craignions...	to fear
croirai... croirons...	croie croies croie croyions croyiez croient	to believe
croîtrai... croîtrons...	croisse... croissions...	to grow
cueillerai... cueillerons...	cueille... cueillions...	to gather
décherrai... décherrons...	déchoie déchoies déchoie déchoyions déchoyiez déchoient	to fall to lose
devrai... devrons...	doive doives doive devions deviez doivent	to owe to have to
dirai... dirons...	dise... disions...	to say
il échoira *or* écherra ils échoiront *or* écherront	il échoie *or* échée ils échéent	to fall due

French Verbs

Infinitive	Participles	Present Indicative	Past Historic
écrire	écrivant écrit	écris,-s,-t écrivons...	écrivis... écrivîmes...
envoyer	envoyant envoyé	envoie envoies envoie envoyons envoyez envoient	envoyai... envoyâmes...
être[1]	étant été	suis es est sommes êtes sont	fus... fûmes...
† faillir	faillant failli	faut[2]	faillis[3]... faillîmes...
faire	faisant fait	fais fais fait faisons faites font	fis... fîmes...
† falloir[4]	fallu	il faut	il fallut
† férir[5]	féru		
† forfaire (à)	forfait		
† frire	frit	fris fris frit	
fuir	fuyant fui	fuis fuis fuit fuyons fuyez fuient	fuis... fuîmes...
† gésir[6]	gisant	gît gisons gisez gisent	
haïr	haïssant haï	hais,-s,-t haïssons...	haïs... haïmes[7]...
lire	lisant lu	lis,-s,-t lisons...	lus... lûmes...
luire	luisant lui	luis,-s,-t luisons...	luis... luîmes...
maudire	conjugated like the regular verbs in -ir, e.g. finir, except for the past		
médire (de)	médisant médit	médis... médisons...	médis... médîmes...

[1] Imperfect Indic.: *j'étais*; Imperative: *sois, soyons, soyez*.
[2] Only in the phrase *le cœur me faut*.
[3] In current usage followed by an infinitive, *e.g. il faillit tomber*, he nearly fell.
[4] Imperfect Indic.: *il fallait*.

Future	Present Subjunctive	English
écrirai... écrirons...	écrive... écrivions...	to write
enverrai... enverrons...	envoie envoies envoie envoyions envoyiez envoient	to send
serai... serons...	sois sois soit soyons soyez soient	to be
faudrai *or* faillirai		to fail
ferai... ferons...	fasse... fassions...	to make, to do
il faudra	il faille	to be necessary
		to strike
		to be false (to)
frirai... frirons...		to fry
fuirai... fuirons...	fuie... fuyions...	to flee
		to lie
haïrai... haïrons...	haïsse... haïssions...	to hate
lirai... lirons...	lise... lisions...	to read
luirai... luirons...	luise... luisions...	to gleam
participle (*maudit*).		to curse
médirai... médirons...	médise... médisions...	to speak ill of

[5] The infinitive is used only in the phrase *sans coup férir*, without striking a blow. *Féru* is adjectival only (*féru d'amour*, lovesick).
[6] The Imperfect Indic., *je gisais*, etc., is used.
[7] The plural is written without a circumflex: *haïmes, haïtes.*

645

French Verbs

Infinitive	Participles	Present Indicative	Past Historic
mettre	mettant mis	mets,-s,-t mettons...	mis... mîmes...
moudre	moulant moulu	mouds mouds moud moulons moulez moulent	moulus... moulûmes...
mourir	mourant mort	meurs meurs meurt mourons mourez meurent	mourus... mourûmes...
mouvoir	mouvant [1]mû, *m.*, mue, *f.*, mus, *m.pl.*	meus meus meut mouvons mouvez meuvent	mus... mûmes...
naître	naissant né	nais nais naît naissons naissez naissent	naquis... naquîmes...
nuire (à)	nuisant nui	nuis,-s,-t nuisons...	nuisis... nuisîmes...
† oindre[2]	oint		
† ouïr[3]	oyant ouï		ouïs... ouïmes...
ouvrir	ouvrant ouvert	ouvre... ouvrons...	ouvris... ouvrîmes...
† paître	paissant	pais pais paît paissons paissez paissent	
plaire	plaisant plu	plais plais plaît plaisons plaisez plaisent	plus... plûmes...
† pleuvoir	pleuvant plu	il pleut	il plut
† poindre	poignant point	il point	
pourvoir	pourvoyant pourvu	pourvois,-s,-t pourvoyons,-yez,-ient	pourvus... pourvûmes...

[1] The past part. of *émouvoir* is *ému*, and of *promouvoir*, *promu* (no circumflex on the *u* of the masculine sing.).

Future	Present Subjunctive	English
mettrai... mettrons...	mette... mettions...	to put
moudrai... moudrons...	moule... moulions...	to grind
mourrai... mourrons...	meure meures meure mourions mouriez meurent	to die
mouvrai... mouvrons...	meuve meuves meuve mouvions mouviez meuvent	to move
naîtrai... naîtrons...	naisse... naissions...	to be born
nuirai... nuirons...	nuise... nuisions...	to harm
oindrai...		to anoint
ouïrai... ouïrons...		to hear
ouvrirai... ouvrirons...	ouvre... ouvrions...	to open
paîtrai... paîtrons...	paisse... paissions...	to graze
plairai... plairons...	plaise... plaisions...	to please
il pleuvra	il pleuve	to rain
il poindra ils poindront		to dawn to sting
pourvoirai... pourvoirons...	pourvoie... pourvoyions...	to provide

[2] Imperfect Indic.: *je oignais.*
[3] This verb is seldom used other than in the infinitive and in the compound tenses.

647

French Verbs

Infinitive	Participles	Present Indicative	Past Historic
pouvoir	pouvant pu	peux *or* puis peux peut pouvons pouvez peuvent	pus... pûmes...
prendre	prenant pris	prends prends prend prenons prenez prennent	pris... prîmes...
prévoir	prévoyant prévu	prévois,-s,-t prévoyons, -yez, -ient	prévis... prévîmes...
recevoir	recevant reçu	reçois reçois reçoit recevons recevez reçoivent	reçus... reçûmes...
résoudre	résolvant résolu *or* résous	résous résous résout résolvons résolvez résolvent	résolus... résolûmes...
rire	riant ri	ris,-s,-t rions...	ris... rîmes...
savoir[1]	sachant su	sais,-s,-t savons...	sus... sûmes...
sentir	sentant senti	sens,-s,-t sentons...	sentis... sentîmes...
† seoir	seyant	il sied ils siéent	
suffire	suffisant suffi	suffis,-s,-t suffisons...	suffis... suffîmes...
suivre	suivant suivi	suis,-s,-t suivons...	suivis... suivîmes...
surseoir[2]	sursoyant sursis	sursois,-s,-t sursoyons, -yez, -ient	sursis... sursîmes...
taire	conjug. like *plaire* except that there is no circumflex on the *i* of the 3rd		
tenir[3]	tenant tenu	tiens tiens tient tenons tenez tiennent	tins tins tint tînmes tîntes tinrent
† traire	trayant trait	trais,-s,-t trayons...	

[1] Imperative: *sache, sachons, sachez.*
[2] The Past Historic and the Imperfect Indicative are seldom used.

Future	Present Subjunctive	English
pourrai... pourrons...	puisse... puissions...	to be able
prendrai... prendrons...	prenne... prenions...	to take
prévoirai... prévoirons...	prévoie... prévoyions...	to foresee
recevrai... recevrons...	reçoive reçoives reçoive recevions receviez reçoivent	to receive
résoudrai... résoudrons...	résolve... résolvions...	to resolve
rirai... rirons...	rie... riions...	to laugh
saurai... saurons...	sache... sachions...	to know
sentirai... sentirons...	sente... sentions...	to feel to smell
il siéra ils siéront	il siée ils siéent	to become to suit
suffirai... suffirons...	suffise... suffisions...	to suffice
suivrai... suivrons...	suive... suivions...	to follow
surseoirai... surseoirons...	sursoie... sursoyions...	to delay to suspend
Pers. Sing. Pres. Indic.: *il tait*.		to keep silent about
tiendrai... tiendrons...	tienne tiennes tienne tenions teniez tiennent	to hold
trairai... trairons...	traie... trayions...	to milk

[3] Imperfect Subjunctive: *tinsse, -es, tînt, tinssions, -iez, -ent.*

French Verbs

Infinitive	Participles	Present Indicative	Past Historic
vaincre	vainquant vaincu	vaincs vaincs vainc vainquons vainquez vainquent	vainquis... vainquîmes...
valoir	valant valu	vaux, -x, -t valons...	valus... valûmes...
vêtir	vêtant vêtu	vêts, vêts, vêt vêtons...	vêtis... vêtîmes...
vivre	vivant vécu	vis,-s,-t vivons...	vécus... vécûmes...
voir	voyant vu	vois,-s,-t voyons, -yez, -ient	vis... vîmes...
vouloir[1]	voulant voulu	veux veux veut voulons voulez veulent	voulus... voulûmes...

[1] Imperative: *veuille, veuillons, veuillez.*

Future	Present Subjunctive	English
vaincrai... vaincrons...	vainque... vainquions...	to conquer
vaudrai... vaudrons...	[2]vaille... valions...	to be worth
vêtirai... vêtirons...	vête... vêtions...	to clothe
vivrai... vivrons...	vive... vivions...	to live
verrai... verrons...	voie... voyions...	to see
voudrai... voudrons...	veuille... voulions...	to be willing to want, to wish

[2] *prévaloir: prévale, prévalions.*

English Verbs

All verbs not marked *irr.* in the English-French section of the Dictionary come in one of the following categories:

(a) Regular verbs, conjugated like WORK or LIVE.

(b) Verbs ending in *-y* preceded by one or more consonants, e.g. DENY, REPLY, IMPLY, conjugated like CARRY (i.e. the *y* changes to *i* in the Past Tense and Past Participle).

(c) Verbs ending in a single consonant preceded by one or more vowels (but not a diphthong, e.g. WAIT, or a double vowel, e.g. SEEM), which are monosyllabic or in which the stress falls on the last syllable, conjugated like DROP and PREFER (i.e. the final consonant is doubled in the Past Tense and Past Participle).

N.B. Apart from those which are irregular, all verbs ending in *-l* preceded by one or more vowels (but not a diphthong, e.g. SAIL, or a double vowel, e.g. PEEL) may double the *l* in the Past and Past Participle even if the stress does not fall on the last syllable, e.g. IMPERIL, DIAL.

* = obsolete.   *A = obsolete, but still used adjectivally.   † = becoming obsolete.
†A = becoming obsolete, but still used adjectivally.

Infinitive	Past Tense	Past Participle	French
REGULAR VERBS (a)			
work	worked	worked	travailler
live	lived	lived	vivre
REGULAR VERBS (b)			
carry	carried	carried	porter
REGULAR VERBS (c)			
drop	dropped	dropped	laisser tomber
prefer	preferred	preferred	préférer
imperil	imperilled	imperilled	hasarder
dial	dialled	dialled	composer un numéro
IRREGULAR VERBS			
abide	abode	abode	demeurer
awake	awoke	awoke *or* awaked	éveiller
be *Pres. Indic.* am, art, is, are	was, were	been	être
bear	bore	borne *or* born[1]	porter
beat	beat	beaten	battre
beget	begot *begat	begotten	engendrer
begin	began	begun	commencer
bend	bent	bent	courber
bereave	bereaved *or* bereft	bereaved *or* bereft	priver (de)
beseech	besought	besought	supplier
bid	bade *or* bid	bidden *or* bid	ordonner

[1] *born* = né; *borne* = porté.

Infinitive	Past Tense	Past Participle	French
bind	bound	bound *A bounden[1]	lier
bite	bit	bitten	mordre
bleed	bled	bled	saigner
blow	blew	blown	souffler
break	broke	broken	casser
breed	bred	bred	élever
bring	brought	brought	apporter
build	built	built	construire
burn	burnt *or* burned	burnt *or* burned	brûler
burst	burst	burst	éclater
buy	bought	bought	acheter
Pres. Indic. can	could	——	pouvoir
cast	cast	cast	jeter
catch	caught	caught	attraper
choose	chose	chosen	choisir
cleave (*v.t.*)	cleft *clove	cleft *A cloven[2]	fendre
cling	clung	clung	s'attacher
come	came	come	venir
cost	cost	cost	coûter
creep	crept	crept	ramper
crow	crowed *or* †crew	crowed	chanter (coq)
cut	cut	cut	couper
deal	dealt	dealt	distribuer
dig	dug	dug	creuser
do	did	done	faire
draw	drew	drawn	tirer, dessiner
dream	dreamt *or* dreamed	dreamt *or* dreamed	rêver
drink	drank	drunk *A drunken[3]	boire
drive	drove	driven	conduire

[1] It is his *bounden* duty.   [2] *Cloven* hoof.   [3] A *drunken* brawl.

English Verbs

Infinitive	Past Tense	Past Participle	French
dwell	dwelt	dwelt	demeurer
eat	ate	eaten	manger
fall	fell	fallen	tomber
feed	fed	fed	nourrir
feel	felt	felt	sentir
fight	fought	fought	combattre
find	found	found	trouver
flee	fled	fled	fuir
fling	flung	flung	lancer
fly	flew	flown	voler
forbear	forbore	forborne	s'abstenir
forbid	forbade *or* forbad	forbidden	interdire
forget	forgot	forgotten	oublier
forsake	forsook	forsaken	abandonner
freeze	froze	frozen	geler
get	got	got *A gotten[1]	obtenir, devenir
gird	girded *or* girt	girded *or* girt	ceindre
give	gave	given	donner
go	went	gone	aller
grind	ground	ground	moudre
grow	grew	grown	croître, devenir
hang[2]	hung	hung	pendre
have *Pres. Indic.* have,*hast, has	had	had	avoir
hear	heard	heard	entendre
heave	heaved *or* hove	heaved *or* hove	soulever
hew	hewed	hewn *or* hewed	tailler
hide	hid	hidden	cacher
hit	hit	hit	frapper

[1] Ill-*gotten* gains; but in America *gotten* is often standard usage as an alternative Past Participle.
[2] To suspend. In the meaning 'to execute by hanging', the verb is regular.

654

Infinitive	Past Tense	Past Participle	French
hold	held	held	tenir
hurt	hurt	hurt	blesser
keep	kept	kept	garder
kneel	knelt	knelt	s'agenouiller
know	knew	known	savoir
lay	laid	laid	poser
lead	led	led	conduire
lean	leant *or* leaned	leant *or* leaned	pencher
leap	leapt *or* leaped	leapt *or* leaped	sauter
learn	learnt *or* learned	learnt *or* learned	apprendre
leave	left	left	laisser, quitter
lend	lent	lent	prêter
let	let	let	laisser
lie[1]	lay	lain	être couché
light	lit *or* lighted	lit *or* lighted	allumer
lose	lost	lost	perdre
make	made	made	faire
Pres. Indic. may	might	——	pouvoir (permission, probabilité)
mean	meant	meant	signifier
meet	met	met	rencontrer
mow	mowed	mowed *or* mown	faucher
pay	paid	paid	payer
put	put	put	mettre
quit	quitted *or* quit	quitted *or* quit	quitter
read	read	read	lire
rend	rent	rent	déchirer
rid	rid	rid	débarrasser
ride	rode	ridden	aller à cheval *etc.*
ring[2]	rang	rung	sonner

[1] To recline. In the meaning 'to be untruthful', the verb is regular.
[2] (Of a bell). In the meaning 'to put a ring round', the verb is regular.

English Verbs

Infinitive	Past Tense	Past Participle	French
rise	rose	risen	se lever
rive	rived	riven *or* rived	fendre
run	ran	run	courir
saw	sawed	sawn	scier
say	said	said	dire
see	saw	seen	voir
seek	sought	sought	chercher
sell	sold	sold	vendre
send	sent	sent	envoyer
set	set	set	placer
sew	sewed	sewn *or* sewed	coudre
shake	shook	shaken	secouer
Pres. Indic. shall[1]	should[1]	——	——
shear	sheared	shorn *or* sheared	tondre
shed	shed	shed	verser
shine	shone	shone	briller
shoe	shod	shod	chausser
shoot	shot	shot	tirer (au fusil)
show	showed	shown *or* showed	montrer
shrink	shrank	shrunk *A shrunken	rétrécir
shrive	shrove	shriven	se confesser
shut	shut	shut	fermer
sing	sang	sung	chanter
sink	sank	sunk *A sunken[2]	sombrer
sit	sat	sat	être assis
slay	slew	slain	tuer
sleep	slept	slept	dormir
slide	slid	slid	glisser
sling	slung	slung	lancer

[1] Used as auxiliaries only.   [2] *Sunken* cheeks.

Infinitive	Past Tense	Past Participle	French
slink	slunk	slunk	s'esquiver
slit	slit	slit	fendre
smell	smelt *or* smelled	smelt *or* smelled	sentir
smite	smote	smitten	frapper
sow	sowed	sown *or* sowed	semer
speak	spoke *spake	spoken	parler
speed	sped *or* speeded	sped *or* speeded	se hâter
spell	spelt *or* spelled	spelt *or* spelled	épeler
spend	spent	spent	dépenser
spill	spilt *or* spilled	spilt *or* spilled	verser
spin	spun	spun	filer
spit[1]	spat *or* spit	spat *or* spit	cracher
split	split	split	fendre
spoil	spoilt *or* spoiled	spoilt *or* spoiled	gâter
spread	spread	spread	s'étendre
spring	sprang	sprung	s'élancer
stand	stood	stood	être debout
stave	staved *or* stove	staved *or* stove	crever
steal	stole	stolen	voler
stick	stuck	stuck	coller
sting	stung	stung	piquer
stink	stank	stunk	puer
strew	strewed	strewed *or* strewn	répandre
stride	strode	stridden	marcher à grands pas
strike	struck	struck †A stricken[2]	frapper
string	strung	strung	ficeler
strive	strove	striven	s'efforcer
swear	swore	sworn	jurer
sweep	swept	swept	balayer

[1] To expectorate. In the meaning 'to put on a spit', the verb is regular.
[2] *Stricken* in years.

English Verbs

Infinitive	Past Tense	Past Participle	French
swell	swelled	swollen *or* swelled	enfler
swim	swam	swum	nager
swing	swung	swung	se balancer
take	took	taken	prendre
teach	taught	taught	enseigner
tear	tore	torn	déchirer
tell	told	told	dire
think	thought	thought	penser
thrive	thrived *or* throve	thrived *or* thriven	prospérer
throw	threw	thrown	jeter
thrust	thrust	thrust	lancer
tread	trod	trodden	fouler
wake	woke *or* waked	waked	éveiller
wear	wore	worn	porter (vêtements)
weave	wove	woven	tisser
weep	wept	wept	pleurer
wet	wetted *or* wet	wetted *or* wet	mouiller
will	would	——	vouloir
win	won	won	gagner
wind	wound	wound	enrouler
wring	wrung	wrung	tordre
write	wrote	written	écrire